SCOTT®

1990 Specialized Catalogue of United States Stamps

SIXTY-EIGHTH EDITION

CONFEDERATE STATES • CANAL ZONE • DANISH WEST INDIES
GUAM • HAWAII • UNITED NATIONS

UNITED STATES ADMINISTRATION:
Cuba • Puerto Rico • Philippines • Ryukyu Islands
Marshall Islands • Micronesia • Palau

Scott Publishing Co.
911 Vandemark Road, Sidney, Ohio 45365
A division of AMOS PRESS INC., publishers of *Linn's Stamp News*, *Coin World*, *Cars & Parts* magazine and *The Sidney Daily News*.

Table of Contents

Copyright Notice

Trademark Notice

Please Note

Effective as of 1978, designs of all United States stamps are copyrighted.

Scott Catalogue accepts all advertisements in good faith, but does not endorse or assume any responsibility for the contents of advertisements.

ISBN 0-89487-124-2 Soft cover
ISBN 0-89487-129-3 Hard cover
Library of Congress Card No. 2-3301

UNITED STATES
Commemorative Album Pages!

Your first investment will be a lasting investment with White Ace

When everything has to be perfect, choose a White Ace stamp album . . . just as generations of satisfied collectors have done.

Consider, for example, White Ace pages for U.S. commemoratives. Made of acid-free card stock, so they won't yellow or crease with use, they have colorful border illuminations to highlight your displays, and under each mounting frame is the story behind the stamp. Also, because the album is looseleaf style and published in sections, you have maximum flexibility when it comes to building your collection. What more can you expect? Annual supplements, of course; a large capacity binder with gold titling; matching border blank pages for covers and other items; and a dustcase that gives the ultimate in protection. If you're a typical philatelist, you seek top quality when purchasing stamps. If this desire for the best extends to your albums, then White Ace probably is the logical choice.

White Ace

Colorful . . .
Historical . . .
Sectional !

WHITE ACE COMMEMORATIVE ALBUM PAGE PRICES	
Commemorative Singles (1893-1939) . . .	$11.15
Commemorative Singles (1940-1949)	8.35
Commemorative Singles (1950-1970)	20.40
Commemorative Singles (1971-1979)	18.20
Commemorative Singles (1980-1986)	19.00
Commemorative Singles (1987-1988)	7.50
Gold-Stamped Deluxe Binder	11.75
Matching Binder Dustcase	7.95
Also available for blocks and plate blocks	

On Mail Shipments

Please Add $2.00 Packing Charge (Canada & Foreign by Weight)

WHITE ACE Albums never grow old... thanks to the extra-heavy rag card stock that lasts for a lifetime of collecting...thanks to the rounded page corners that prevent dog-earing... and thanks to the annual supplements published each year.

Your name, address and zip code on a postal card will bring you a complete price list of WHITE ACE Albums.

Available at Your Favorite Stamp Shop or Direct

THE WASHINGTON PRESS
PUBLISHERS
FLORHAM PARK, NEW JERSEY 07932

Scott Publishing Co.

911 VANDEMARK ROAD, SIDNEY, OHIO 45365 513-498-0802

SCOTT®

Welcome to our 1990 Specialized Catalogue:

Very quickly as you look through the pages of this volume, you will find that this truly is a new Catalogue built onto an old chassis...126 years old, to be sure. We have been listening to you since Scott Publishing Co. arrived at its home in Sidney, Ohio, and we are continuing to adjust our Catalogue presentation to meet your needs. This volume completes our 1990 series.

The 1990 edition of the Scott Catalogue cannot have the catalogue value of stamps within its pages compared to the values of the preceding year. Catalogue values of all stamps listed this year reflect *actual retail values* as we have found them in the marketplace.

Also, we have adjusted the grading level at which stamps are valued. Scott now values stamps at a grade of Fine-Very Fine, with an illustrated description of what we mean by that grade on the pages which follow.

The practice of purchasing stamps at a fraction of "Scott" no longer is valid. You now can expect to pay approximately the listed catalogue value when you purchase from dealer price lists, approval selections, or at stamp shows. Deep discounts will now be the exception rather than the rule.

If you purchase stamps at auction, you may need to adjust your bidding habits. Bidding at large discounts from catalogue value will decrease your chances of acquiring a lot. For best results, compare the catalogue values in this volume with recent auction realizations and place your own bids with that information in mind.

Bargains may still occur at auction sales, particularly when a specific lot is not in demand at the time of the sale. Also, when reviewing auction catalogues, be aware of the terms and conditions of that sale. Be certain of which stamp catalogue is being used as reference, and which catalogue values are being used in the text of the auction catalogue.

To determine the catalogue values used this year, we have consulted literally hundreds of dealer price lists, carefully reviewed the results of scores of public auctions, scoured the philatelic media for ads with prices, and listened to the advice of more outside experts than Scott has ever used in the past.

As an example, more than 450 dealers — known to produce price lists — were queried for a copy. In addition, more than 150 dealers, collectors and specialty societies accepted our invitation to provide more explicit information on stamps within their areas of expertise. Response has been tremendous, with the accompanying Acknowledgments section a testament. Other important information that we use comes from you the user of this catalogue. We receive hundreds of letters with questions which lead to corrections and amplifications within our pages. Our thanks go out to everyone who helps in that way.

You have given us direction in more areas than only that of catalogue values. The introduction to this catalogue is very different than in the past. A "mini-introduction" is designed to quickly acclimate everyone to what can be an awesome bulk of information. The pages which follow the "mini-introduction" are a completely revised approach to both our Catalogue and the basics of stamp collecting in general.

By the time you complete the introduction, you should not be surprised by terms and concepts you find in the individual country listings within the text of this volume.

For the first time, we note in the listings themselves where Scott begins to value unused stamps as never-hinged. If there is no note in a section, such as the Postal Card section, it means that the concept of "never-hinged" does not apply, or that we are valuing all unused items in that section as lightly hinged.

This Catalogue continues to evolve in response to what we hear you telling us. Some years the evolution process appears to be moving more rapidly than in others, but the process continues nevertheless. That evolution is much easier with all of the support we receive from those who use the Catalogue.

Sincerely,

Richard L. Sine

Richard L. Sine
Editorial Director

Index

The capital letters in parentheses and below "Revenues" are used with the catalogue numbers to indicate the different classifications.

Catalogue Information

Catalogue Value

The Scott Catalogue value is a retail price, what you could expect to pay for the stamp in a grade of Fine-Very Fine. The value listed is a reference which reflects recent actual dealer selling prices.

Dealer retail price lists, public auction results, published prices in advertising, and individual solicitation of retail prices from dealers, collectors, and specialty organizations have been used in establishing the values found in this catalogue.

Use this catalogue as a guide in your own buying and selling. The actual price you pay for a stamp may be higher or lower than the catalogue value because of one or more of the following: the amount of personal service a dealer offers, increased interest in the country or topic represented by the stamp or set, whether an item is a "loss leader," part of a special sale, or otherwise is being sold for a short period of time at a lower price, or if at a public auction you are able to obtain an item inexpensively because of little interest in the item at that time.

For unused stamps, more recent issues are valued as never-hinged, with the beginning point determined on a country-by-country basis. Notes to show the beginning points are prominently noted in the text.

Grade

A stamp's grade and condition are crucial to its value. Values quoted in this catalogue are for stamps graded at Fine-Very Fine and with no faults. The accompanying illustrations show an example of a Fine-Very Fine grade between the grades immediately below and above it: Fine and Very Fine.

FINE stamps have the design noticeably off-center on two sides. Imperforate stamps may have small margins and earlier issues may show the design touching one edge of the stamp. Used stamps may have heavier than usual cancellations.

FINE-VERY FINE stamps may be somewhat off-center on one side, or only slightly off-center on two sides. Imperforate stamps will have two margins at least normal size and the design will not touch the edge. *Early issues of a country may be printed in such a way that the design naturally is very close to the edges.* Used stamps will not have a cancellation that detracts from the design. This is the grade used to establish Scott Catalogue values.

VERY FINE stamps may be slightly off-center on one side, with the design well clear of the edge. Imperforate stamps will have three margins at least normal size. Used stamps will have light or otherwise neat cancellations.

Condition

The above definitions describe *grade,* which is centering and (for used stamps) cancellation. *Condition* refers to the soundness of the stamp, i.e., faults, repairs, and other factors influencing price.

Copies of a stamp which are of a lesser grade and/or condition trade at lower prices. Those of exceptional quality often command higher prices.

Factors that increase the value of a stamp include exceptionally wide margins, particularly fresh color, and the presence of selvage.

Factors other than faults that decrease the value of a stamp include no gum or regumming, hinge remnant, foreign object adhering to gum, natural inclusion, or a straight edge.

Faults include a missing piece, tear, clipped perforations, pin or other hole, surface scuff, thin spot, crease, toning, oxidation or other form of color changeling, short or pulled perforation, stains or such man-made changes as reperforation or the chemical removal or lightening of a cancellation.

Scott Publishing Co. recognizes that there is no formal, enforced grading scheme for postage stamps, and that the final price you pay for a stamp or obtain for a stamp you are selling will be determined by individual agreement at the time of the transaction.

Acknowledgments

Our appreciation and gratitude go to the following individuals and organizations who have assisted us in preparing information included in the 1990 Scott Catalogues. These individuals have generously shared their stamp knowledge with others through the medium of the Scott Catalogue.

Those who follow provided information that is in addition to the hundreds of dealer price lists and advertisements and scores of auction catalogues and realizations which were used in producing the Catalogue Values used herein. It is from those noted here that we have been able to obtain information on items not normally seen in published lists and advertisements. Support from these people of course goes beyond data leading to Catalogue Values, for they also are key to editorial changes.

Joseph F. Albert
Michael E. Aldrich
Simon Andrews
B.J. Ammel
Mike Armus
Joseph J. Atallah
Philip Bansner
M.S. Batchelor
Frederick Bean
Wallace R. Beardsley
Jules K. Beck
C.A. Beckwith
David Bein
Russ Bell
Ernest L. Bergman
Hank Bieniecki
Brian M. Bleckwenn
John R. Boker
Vernon E. Bressler
George Brett
Mike Bryne
Frank Buono
Roman Burkiewicz
Joseph Bush
Lawrence A. Bustillo
E.J. Chamberlin
Richard Chellevold
Henry Chlanda
Dr. Leonard Cohen
Ray L. Coughlin
Howard G. DeVoe
P.J. Drossos
Bob Dumaine
Donald W. East
Stephen I. Esrati
Fabio Famiglietti
Henry O. Feldman
Richard J. Frajola
Stephen I. Frater
Marvin Frey
Richard Friedberg
Earl H. Galitz
Raul Gandara
Frank Geiger
Peter Georgiadis
Richard B. Graham
Brian M. Green
Horacio E. Groio
Rudolf Hamar
Ray Hanser
Leo John Harris
Allan Hauck
John B. Head
Bruce Hecht
Robert R. Hegland
Dale S. Hendricks
Clifford O. Herrick
William Herzig
Rollin C. Huggins, Jr.
Jayson Hyun
Eric Jackson
Vincent E. Jay
Jack M. Jonza
Marjorie Kantor
H. Karen
Stanford M. Katz
Lewis S. Kaufman
Patricia Kaufmann
James Kerr
Herman Kerst
Thomas C. Kingsley
Robert E. Kitson
W. Kolakowski
Stanley Kronenberg
Warren Lauzon
Steve Levine
Rosario LoGuidice
Bob Lovell
Gary J. Lyon
David MacDonnel
Donald L. MacPeek
Nick Macris
Walter J. Mader
Sam Malamud
Nick Markov
Clyde E. Maxwell
Max Mayo
Mike McKillip
James T. McCusker
Timothy M. McRee
Herb Meisels
Hector Mena
Robert B. Meyersburg
Jack Molesworth
Richard H. Muller
J. Nalbandian
Victor Ostolaza
Souren V. Panirian
Frank E. Patterson
David G. Phillips
Stanley Piller
Daniel N. Pinchot
Gilbert N. Plass
Richard Pyznar
John Reznikoff
Patrick Riggs
Peter A. Robertson
Michael Rogers
P.J. Ronay
Richard H. Salz
Byron J. Sandfield
Jacques C. Schiff, Jr.
Richard Schwartz
Michael Shamilzadeh
William E. Shelton
J. Randall Shoemaker
Richard Simchak
Hubert C. Skinner
James W. Smith
Jay Smith
Sherwood Springer
Linda Stanfield
Joanna Taylor
Ernst Theimer
Scott Trepel
Gary A. Van Cott
Carlos Vieiro
W.H. Waggoner
Jerome S. Wagshal
Daniel C. Warren
Richard A. Washburn
Raymond H. Weill
William R. Weiss
Charles Yeager
Robert Zeigler

American Philatelic Society
P.O. Box 8000, State College, PA 16803

American Revenue Association
Bruce Miller, Suite 332, 701 S. First Ave., Arcadia, CA 91006

American Society of Netherlands Philately
Harold F. MacDonald, 2354 Roan Lane, Walnut Creek, CA 94596

Booklet Collectors Club
Larry Rosenblum, 1016 East El Camino Real, P.O. Box 107, Sunnyvale, CA 94087

Bureau Issues Association
William S. Dunn, 750 Jersey St., Denver, CO 80220

Canal Zone Study Group
Richard H. Salz, 60 27th Ave., San Francisco, CA 94121

China Stamp Society
Paul H. Gault, 140 W. 18th Ave., Columbus, OH 43210

Confederate Stamp Alliance
Brian Green, P.O. Box 1816, Kernersville, NC 27285

Costa Rica Collectors, Society of
T.C. Willoughby, 7600 Ridgemont Dr., Newburgh, IN 47630

Eire Philatelic Association
Robert C. Jones, 8 Beach St., Brockton, MA 02402

Estonian Philatelic Society
Rudolf Hamar, 243 34th St., New York, NY 10016

Ethiopian Philatelic Society
Miss Hugette Gagnon, P.O. Box F110-45, Blaine, WA 98230

Great Britain Collectors Club
Larry Rosenblum, 1016 East El Camino Real, P.O. Box 107, Sunnyvale, Ca 94087

Haiti Philatelic Society
Carroll L. Lloyd, 2117 Oak Lodge Road, Baltimore, MD 21228

Hellenic Philatelic Society of America
Nicholas Asimakopulos, MD, 541 Cedar Hill Ave., Wyckoff NJ 07481

International Philippine Philatelic Society
Mrs. E.C. Stanfield, P.O. Box 1936, Manila, PHILIPPINES

Korea Stamp Society
Harold L. Klein, P.O. Box 750, Lebanon, PA 17042

Latin American Philatelic Society
Piet Steen, P.O. Box 820, Hinton, AB, CANADA T0E1B0

Mexico-Elmhurst Philatelic Society International
Robert Jones, 2350 Bunker Hill Way, Costa Mesa, CA 92626

Nepal and Tibet Philatelic Study Group
Roger D. Skinner, 1020 Covington Road, Los Altos, CA 94022

Philatelic Foundation
21 E. 40th St., New York, NY 10016

Rhodesian Study Circle
William R. Wallace, P.O. Box 16381, San Francisco, CA 94116

Sarawak Specialists Society
C. Jackson Selsor, 2300 Front St., San Diego, CA 92102

Society for Hungarian Philately
P.O. Box 1162, Fairfield, CT 06432

St. Helena, Ascension & Tristan da Cunha Philatelic Society
R.V. Skavaril, 222 East Torrence Road, Columbus, OH 43214

The Spanish Main Society
Brian Moorhouse, P.O. Box 105, Peterborough, PE3 8TQ, ENGLAND

Ukrainian Philatelic/Numismatic Society
I. Kuzyck, P.O. Box 8363, Alexandria, VA 22360

Understanding the Listings

On the opposite page is an enlarged "typical" listing from this catalogue. Following are detailed explanations of each of the highlighted parts of the listing.

1 **Scott number** — Stamp collectors use Scott numbers to identify specific stamps when buying, selling, or trading stamps, and for ease in organizing their collections. Each stamp issued by a country has a unique number. Therefore, U.S. Scott 219 can only refer to a single stamp. Although the Scott Catalogue usually lists stamps in chronological order by date of issue, when a country issues a set of stamps over a period of time the stamps within that set are kept together without regard of date of issue. This follows the normal collecting approach of keeping stamps in their natural sets.

When a country is known to be issuing a set of stamps over a period of time, a group of consecutive catalogue numbers is reserved for the stamps in that set, as issued. If that group of numbers proves to be too few, capital-letter suffixes are added to numbers to create enough catalogue numbers to cover all items in the set. Scott uses a suffix letter, e.g., "A," "b," etc., only once. If there is a Scott 296B in a set, there will not be a Scott 296b also.

There are times when the block of numbers is too large for the set, leaving some numbers unused. Such gaps in the sequence also occur when the editors move an item elsewhere in the catalogue or remove it from the listings entirely. Scott does not attempt to account for every possible number, but rather it does attempt to assure that each stamp is assigned its own number.

Scott numbers designating regular postage normally are only numerals. Scott numbers for other types of stamps, e.g., air post, special delivery, and so on, will have a prefix of either a capital letter or a combination of numerals and capital letters.

2 **Illustration number** — used to identify each illustration. Where more than one stamp in a set uses the same illustration number, that number needs to be used with the description line (noted below) to be certain of the exact variety of the stamp within the set. Illustrations normally are 75, 100, or 150 percent of the original size of the stamp. An effort has been made to note all illustrations not at those percentages. Overprints are shown at 100 percent of the original, unless otherwise noted.

3 **Listing styles** — there are two principal types of catalogue listings: major and minor.

Majors may be distinguished by having as their catalogue number a numeral with or without a capital-letter suffix and with or without a prefix.

Minors have a small-letter suffix (or, only have the small letter itself shown if the listing is immediately beneath its major listing). These listings show a variety of the "normal," or major item. Examples include color variation or a different watermark used for that stamp only.

Examples of major numbers are 9X1, 16, 28A, 6LB1, C133A, 10N5, and TS1. Examples of minor numbers are 11a and C3a.

4 **Denomination** — normally the face value of the stamp, i.e., the cost of the stamp at the post office at the time of issue.

5 **Basic information on stamp or set** — introducing each stamp issue, this section normally includes the date of issue, method of printing, perforation, watermark, and sometimes some additional information. New information on method of printing, watermark or perforation measurement may appear when that information changes. Dates of issues are as precise as Scott is able to confirm, either year only; month and year; or month, day, and year.

In stamp sets issued over more than one date, the year or span of years will be in bold type above the first catalogue number. Individual stamps in the set will have a date-of-issue appear in italics. Stamps without a year listed appeared during the first year of the span. Dates are not always given for minor varieties.

6 **Color or other description** — this line provides information to solidify identification of the stamp. Historically, when stamps normally were printed in a single color, only the color appeared here. With modern printing techniques, which include multicolor presses which mix inks on the paper, earlier methods of color identification are no longer applicable. When space permits, a description of the stamp design will replace the terms "multi" or "multicolored." The color of the paper is noted in italic type when the paper used is not white.

7 **Date of issue** — As precisely as Scott is able to confirm, either year only; month and year; or month, day and year. In some cases, the earliest known use (eku) is given. All dates, especially where no official date of issue has been given, are subject to change as new information is obtained.

8 **Value unused** and **value used** — the catalogue values are based on stamps which are in a grade of Fine-Very Fine. Unused values refer to items which have not seen postal or other duty for which they were intended. For pre-1890 issue, unused stamps must have at least most of their original gum; for later issues, complete gum is expected. Stamps issued without gum are noted. Unused values are for never-hinged stamps beginning at the point immediately following a prominent notice in the actual listing. The same information also appears at the beginning of the country's information. See the section "Catalogue Values" for an explanation of the meaning of these values.

9 **Changes in basic set information** — bold or other type is used to show any change in the basic data between stamps within a set of stamps, e.g., perforation from one stamp to the next or a different paper or printing method or watermark.

10 **Other varieties** — these include additional shades, plate varieties, multiples, used on cover, plate number blocks, coil line pairs, coil plate number strips of three, ZIP blocks, etc.

On early issues, there may be a "Cancellation" section. Values in this section refer to single stamps off cover, unless otherwise noted. Values with a "+" are added to the basic used value. See "Basic Stamp Information" for more details on stamp and cancellation varieties.

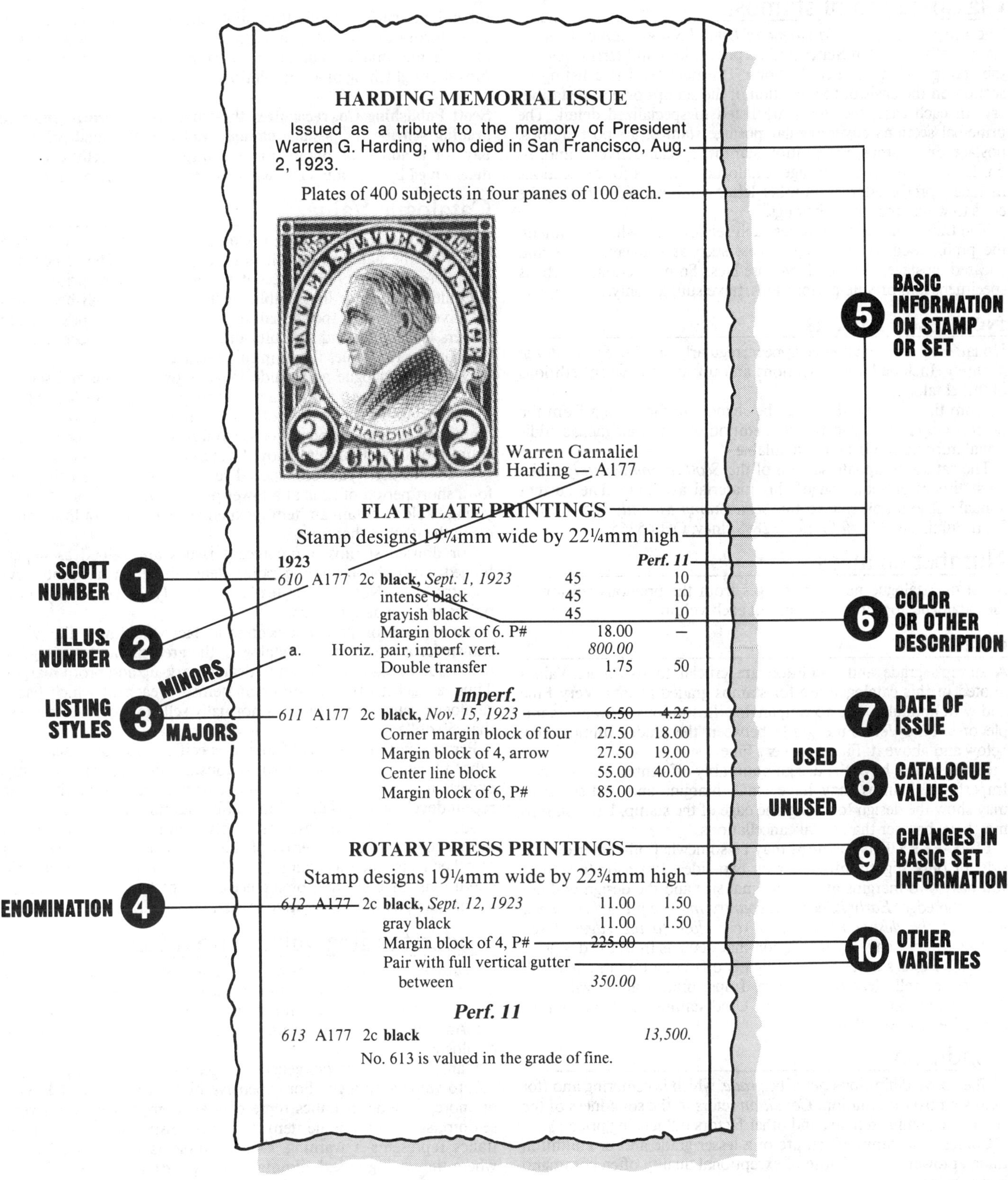

HARDING MEMORIAL ISSUE

Issued as a tribute to the memory of President Warren G. Harding, who died in San Francisco, Aug. 2, 1923.

Plates of 400 subjects in four panes of 100 each.

Warren Gamaliel Harding — A177

FLAT PLATE PRINTINGS

Stamp designs 19¼mm wide by 22¼mm high

1923					*Perf. 11*
610	A177	2c	**black,** *Sept. 1, 1923*	45	10
			intense black	45	10
			grayish black	45	10
			Margin block of 6. P#	18.00	—
a.			Horiz. pair, imperf. vert.	*800.00*	
			Double transfer	1.75	50

Imperf.

611	A177	2c	**black,** *Nov. 15, 1923*	6.50	4.25
			Corner margin block of four	27.50	18.00
			Margin block of 4, arrow	27.50	19.00
			Center line block	55.00	40.00
			Margin block of 6, P#	85.00	

ROTARY PRESS PRINTINGS

Stamp designs 19¼mm wide by 22¾mm high

612	A177	2c	**black,** *Sept. 12, 1923*	11.00	1.50
			gray black	11.00	1.50
			Margin block of 4, P#	225.00	
			Pair with full vertical gutter between	*350.00*	

Perf. 11

613	A177	2c	**black**		*13,500.*

No. 613 is valued in the grade of fine.

Special Notices

Classification of stamps

The Scott *Specialized Catalogue of United States Stamps* lists the stamps of the United States and its possessions and territories and the stamps of the United Nations. The next level is a listing by section on the basis of the function of the stamps or postal stationery. In each case, the items are listed in specialized detail. The principal sections cover regular postage stamps, air post stamps, postage due stamps, registration stamps, special delivery, and, so on. Except for regular postage, catalogue numbers for all sections include a prefix letter (or number-letter combination) denoting the class to which the stamp belongs.

The Index, on Page vii, notes each section and, where pertinent, the prefix used. Non-postage areas, such as souvenir cards and encased postage, do not have prefixes. Some sections, such as specimens and private perforations, have suffixes only.

New issue listings

Updates to this catalogue appear regularly in the *Scott Stamp Monthly*. Included are corrections and updates to current editions of this catalogue.

From time to time there will be changes in the listings from the *Scott Stamp Monthly* to the next edition of the catalogue, as additional information becomes available.

The catalogue update section of the *Scott Stamp Monthly* is the most timely presentation of this material available. The current annual subscription rate to the *Scott Stamp Monthly* is $18 from Scott Publishing Co., P.O. Box 828, Sidney, OH 45365.

Number changes

A list of catalogue number changes from the previous edition of the catalogue appears at the back of each volume.

Grade

A stamp's grade and condition are crucial to its value. Values quoted in this catalogue are for stamps graded at Fine-Very Fine and with no faults. The accompanying illustrations show an example of a Fine-Very Fine grade between the grades immediately below and above it: Fine and Very Fine.

FINE stamps have the design noticeably off-center on two sides. Imperforate stamps may have small margins and earlier issues may show the design touching one edge of the stamp. Used stamps may have heavier than usual cancellations.

FINE-VERY FINE stamps may be somewhat off-center on one side, or only slightly off-center on two sides. Imperforate stamps will have two margins at least normal size and the design will not touch the edge. *Early issues of a country may be printed in such a way that the design naturally is very close to the edges.* Used stamps will not have a cancellation that detracts from the design.

VERY FINE stamps may be slightly off-center on one side, with the design well clear of the edge. Imperforate stamps will have three margins at least normal size. Used stamps will have light or otherwise neat cancellations.

Condition

The above definitions describe *grade,* which is centering and (for used stamps) cancellation. *Condition* refers to the soundness of the stamp, i.e., faults, repairs, and other factors influencing price.

Copies of a stamp which are of a lesser grade and/or condition trade at lower prices. Those of exceptional quality often command higher prices.

Factors that increase the value of a stamp include exceptionally wide margins, particularly fresh color, and the presence of selvage.

Factors other than faults that decrease the value of a stamp include no gum or regumming, hinge remnant, foreign object adhering to gum, natural inclusion, or a straight edge.

Faults include a missing piece, tear, clipped perforation, pin or other hole, surface scuff, thin spot, crease, toning, oxidation or other form of color changeling, short or pulled perforation, stains or such man-made changes as reperforation or the chemical removal or lightening of a cancellation.

Scott Publishing Co. recognizes that there is no formal, enforced grading scheme for postage stamps, and that the final price you pay for a stamp or obtain for a stamp you are selling will be determined by individual agreement at the time of the transaction.

Catalogue Value

The Scott Catalogue value is a retail price, what you could expect to pay for the stamp in a grade of Fine-Very Fine. The value listed is a reference which reflects recent actual dealer selling prices.

Dealer retail price lists, public auction results, published prices in advertising, and individual solicitation of retail prices from dealers, collectors, and specialty organizations have been used in establishing the values found in this catalogue.

Use this catalogue as a guide in your own buying and selling. The actual price you pay for a stamp may be higher or lower than the catalogue value because of one or more of the following: the amount of personal service a dealer offers, increased interest in the country or topic represented by the stamp or set, whether an item is a "loss leader," part of a special sale, or otherwise is being sold for a short period of time at a lower price, or if at a public auction you are able to obtain an item inexpensively because of little interest in the item at that time.

For unused stamps, more recent issues are valued as never-hinged, with the beginning point determined on a country-by-country basis. Notes in the text prominently show the beginning points of these designations.

As a point of philatelic-economic fact, the lower the value shown for an item in this catalogue, the greater the percentage of that value which is attributed to dealer mark-up and profit margin. Thus, a packet of 1,000 different items — each of which has a catalogue value of five cents — normally sells for considerably less than 50 dollars!

Persons wishing to establish the specific value of a stamp or other philatelic item may wish to consult with recognized stamp experts (collectors or dealers) and review current information or recent developments which would affect stamp prices.

Scott Publishing Co. assumes no obligation to revise the values during the distribution period of this catalogue or to advise users of other facts, such as stamp availability, political and economic conditions, or collecting preferences, any of which may have an immediate positive or negative impact on values.

Understanding valuing notations

The *absence of a value* does not necessarily suggest that a stamp is scarce or rare. In the U.S. listings, a dash in the value column means that the stamp is known in a stated form or variety, but information is lacking or insufficient for purposes of establishing a catalogue value.

Stamp values in *italics* generally refer to items which are difficult to value accurately. For expensive items, e.g., value at $1,000 or more, a value in italics represents an item which trades very seldom, such as a unique item. For inexpensive items, a value in italics represents a warning. One example is a "blocked" issue where the issuing postal administration controlled one stamp in a set in an attempt to make the whole set more valuable. Another example is a single item with a very low face value which sells in the marketplace, at the time of issue, at an extreme multiple of face value. Some countries have released back issues of stamps in a canceled-to-order form, sometimes covering at much as 10 years.

The Scott Catalogue values for used stamps reflect canceled-to-order material when such are found to predominate in the marketplace for the issue involved. Frequently notes appear in the stamp listings to specify items which are valued as canceled-to-order or if there is a premium for postally used examples.

Another example of a warning to collectors is a stamp that used has a value considerably higher than the unused version. Here, the collector is cautioned to be certain the used version has a readable, contemporary cancellation.

The *minimum catalogue value* of a stamp is five cents, to cover a dealer's cost of purchase and preparation for resale. As noted, the sum of these values does not properly represent the "value" of a packet of unsorted or unmounted stamps sold in bulk. Such large collections, mixtures or packets generally consist of only the lower-valued stamps.

Values in the "unused" column are for stamps with original gum, if issued with gum, that have been hinged, unless there is a specific note in a listing after which unused stamps are valued as never-hinged. A similar note will appear at the beginning of the country's listings, noting exactly where the dividing point between hinged and never-hinged is for each section of the listings. Where a value for a used stamp is considerably higher than for the unused stamp, the value applies to a stamp showing a distinct contemporary cancellation.

Many countries sell canceled-to-order stamps at a marked reduction from face value. Countries which sell or have sold canceled-to-order stamps at *full* face value include Australia, Netherlands, France, and Switzerland. It is almost impossible to identify such stamps, if the gum has been removed, because official government canceling devices are used. Postally used copies on cover, of these items, are usually worth more than the canceled-to-order stamps with original gum.

Abbreviations

Scott Publishing Co. uses a consistent set of abbreviations throughout this catalogue and the *Standard Postage Stamp Catalogue* to conserve space while still providing necessary information. The first block shown here refers to color names only:

COLOR ABBREVIATIONS

amb	amber
anil	aniline
ap	apple
aqua	aquamarine
az	azure
bis	bister
bl	blue
bld	blood
blk	black
bril	brilliant
brn	brown
brnsh	brownish
brnz	bronze
brt	bright
brnt	burnt
car	carmine
cer	cerise
chlky	chalky
cham	chamois
chnt	chestnut
choc	chocolate
chr	chrome
cit	citron
cl	claret
cob	cobalt
cop	copper
crim	crimson
cr	cream
dk	dark
dl	dull
dp	deep
db	drab
emer	emerald
gldn	golden
grysh	grayish
grn	green
grnsh	greenish
hel	heliotrope
hn	henna
ind	indigo
int	intense
lav	lavender
lem	lemon
lil	lilac
lt	light
mag	magenta
man	manila
mar	maroon
mv	mauve
multi	multicolored
mlky	milky
myr	myrtle
ol	olive
olvn	olvine
org	orange
pck	peacock
pnksh	pinkish
Prus	Prussian
pur	purple
redsh	reddish
res	reseda
ros	rosine
ryl	royal
sal	salmon
saph	sapphire
scar	scarlet
sep	sepia
sien	sienna
sil	silver
sl	slate
stl	steel
turq	turquoise
ultra	ultramarine
ven	venetian
ver	vermilion
vio	violet
yel	yellow
yelsh	yellowish

When no color is given for an overprint or surcharge, black is the color used. Abbreviations for colors used for overprints and surcharges are: "(B)" or "(Bk)," black; "(Bl)," blue; "(R)," red; "(G)," green; etc.

Additional abbreviations used in the Scott Catalogue system are shown below:

Adm.	Administration, Admiral
AFL	American Federation of Labor
Anniv.	Anniversary
APU	Arab Postal Union
APS	American Philatelic Society
ASEAN	Association of South East Asian Nations
ASPCA	American Society for the Prevention of Cruelty to Animals
Assoc.	Association
b.	Born
BEP	Bureau of Engraving and Printing
Bicent.	Bicentennial
Bklt.	Booklet
Brit.	British
btwn.	Between
Bur.	Bureau
c. or ca.	Circa
CAR	Central African Republic
Cat.	Catalogue
Cent.	Centennial, century, centenary
CEPT	Conference Europeenne des Administrations des Postes et des Telecommunications
CIO	Congress of Industrial Organizations
Conf.	Conference
Cong.	Congress
Cpl.	Corporal
CTO	Canceled to order
d.	Died
Dbl.	Double
DDR	German Democratic Republic (East Germany)
EC	European Community
ECU	European currency unit
EEC	European Economic Community
EKU	Earliest known use
Engr.	Engraved
Exhib.	Exhibition
Expo.	Exposition
FAO	Food and Agricultural Organization of the United Nations
Fed.	Federation
FIP	Federation International de Philatelie

GB........ Great Britain
Gen. .... General
GPO ...... General post office

Horiz. ...... Horizontal

ICAO ..... International Civil Aviation Organization
ICY .... International Cooperation Year
ILO .... International Labor Organization
Imperf. ..... Imperforate
Impt. ...... Imprint
Intl. .... International
Invtd. ..... Inverted
IQSY...... International Quiet Sun Year
ITU ...... International Telecommunications Union
ITY .... International Tourism Year
IWY ...... International Women's Year
IYC .... International Year of the Child
IYD....... International Year of the Disabled

L .... Left
Lieut....... Lieutenant
Litho. ...... Lithographed
LL........ Lower left
LR........ Lower right

mm .... Millimeter
Ms. .... Manuscript

NASA ..... National Aeronautics and Space Administration
Natl. ...... National
NATO..... North Atlantic Treaty Organization
No. .... Number
NY .... New York
NYC ...... New York City

OAU ...... Organization of African Unity
OPEC ..... Organization of Petroleum Exporting Countries
Ovpt....... Overprint
Ovptd...... Overprinted

P# .... Plate number
Perf.. ...... Perforated, perforation
Phil.........Philatelic
Photo...... Photogravure
PO....... Post office
Pr. .... Pair
P.R......... Puerto Rico
PRC ...... People's Republic of China (Mainland China)
Prec. ...... Precancel, precanceled
Pres. ...... President

Rio .... Rio de Janeiro
ROC ...... Republic of China (Taiwan)

SEATO .... South East Asia Treaty Organization
Sgt. .... Sergeant
Soc........ Society
Souv....... Souvenir
SSR .... Soviet Socialist Republic
St. .... Saint, street
Surch. ..... Surcharge

Typo....... Typographed

UAE ...... United Arab Emirates
UAMPT ... Union of African and Malagasy Posts and Telecommunications
UL......... Upper left
UN .... United Nations
UNESCO .. United Nations Educational, Scientific and Cultural Organization
UNICEF... United Nations Children's Fund
Univ....... University
UNPA..... United Nations Postal Administration
Unwmkd. .. Unwatermarked
UPU ...... Universal Postal Union
UR .... Upper Right
US........ United States
USPO ..... United States Post Office Department
USPS...... United States Postal Service
USSR ..... Union of Soviet Socialist Republics

Vert. ...... Vertical
VP........ Vice president

WCY...... World Communications Year
WFUNA... World Federation of United Nations Associations
WHO ...... World Health Organization
Wmk. ...... Watermark
Wmkd. ..... Watermarked
WMO ..... World Meteorological Organization
WRY...... World Refugee Year
WWF ...... World Wildlife Fund
WWI .... World War I
WWII ..... World War II

YAR ...... Yemen Arab Republic
Yemen PDR Yemen People's Democratic Republic

Examination

Scott Publishing Co. will not pass upon the genuineness, grade or condition of stamps, because of the time and responsibility involved. Rather, there are several expertizing groups which undertake this work for both collectors and dealers. Neither can Scott Publishing Co. appraise or identify philatelic material. The Company cannot take responsibility for unsolicited stamps or covers.

Covers

Prices paid for stamps on original covers vary greatly according to condition, appearance, cancellation or postmark and usage. Values given in this volume are for the commonest form with stamps in fine-very fine condition "tied on" by the cancellation. A stamp is said to be "tied" to an envelope or card when the cancellation or postmark falls on both the stamp and envelope or card. Letters addressed to foreign countries showing unusual rates and transit markings normally are much in demand and often command large premiums.

Values are for covers bearing a single copy of the stamp referenced and used during the period when the stamp was on sale at post offices. If the postage rate was higher than the denomination of the stamp, then the stamp must represent the highest denomination possible to use in making up this rate. In this case the value is the on-cover value of the stamp plus the used values of the additional stamps. As a general rule, the stamp must be tied to the cover. Exceptions include some of the early local adhesives, for which canceling was not customary, as well as covers with two or more values on them.

Values for patriotic covers of the Civil War period (bearing pictorial designs of a patriotic nature) are for the commonest designs. More than 11,000 varieties of designs are known.

How to order from your dealer

It is not necessary to write the full description of a stamp as listed in this catalogue. All that you need is the name of the country, the Scott Catalogue number and whether the item is unused or used. For example, "U.S. Scott 833" is sufficient to identify the stamp of the United states listed as the 2-dollar value of a set of stamps issued between 1938-43. This stamp was issued September 29, 1938. It is yellow green and black in color, has a perforation of 11 x 10½, and is printed on paper without a watermark by a rotary press.

Cancellations

A complete treatment of this subject is impossible in a catalogue of this limited size. Only postal markings of meaning — those which were necessary to the proper function of the postal service — are recorded here, while those of value owing to their fanciness only are disregarded. The latter are the results of the whim of some postal official. Many of these odd designs, however, command high prices, based on their popularity, scarcity and clearness of impression.

Although there are many types of most of the cancellations listed, only one of each is illustrated. The values quoted are for the most common type of each.

Values for cancellation varieties are for stamp specimens off cover. If on cover, the distinctive cancellation must be on the stamp in order to merit catalogue valuation. Postmarks that denote origin or a service (as distinguished from canceling a stamp) merit catalogue valuation when on a cover apart from the stamp, provided the stamp is otherwise tied to the cover by a cancellation.

One type of "Paid" cancellation used in Boston, and shown in this introduction under "Postal Markings," is common and values given are for types other than this.

Postmasters General of the United States

1775 Benjamin Franklin, July 26.
1776 Richard Bache, Nov. 7.
1782 Ebenezer Hazard, Jan. 28.
1789 Samuel Osgood, Sept. 26.
1791 Timothy Pickering, Aug. 12.
1795 Joseph Habersham, Feb. 25.
1801 Gideon Granger, Nov. 28.
1814 Return J. Meigs, Jr., Apr. 11.
1823 John McLean, July 1.
1829 William T. Barry, Apr. 6.
1835 Amos Kendall, May 1.
1840 John M. Niles, May 26.
1841 Francis Granger, Mar. 8.
1841 Charles A. Wickliffe, Oct. 13.
1845 Cave Johnson, Mar. 7.
1849 Jacob Collamer, Mar. 8.
1850 Nathan K. Hall, July 23.
1852 Samuel D. Hubbard, Sept. 14.
1853 James Campbell, Mar. 8.
1857 Aaron V. Brown, Mar. 7.
1859 Joseph Holt, Mar. 14.
1861 Horatio King, Feb. 12.
1861 Montgomery Blair, Mar. 9.
1864 William Dennison, Oct. 1.
1866 Alexander W. Randall, July 25.
1869 John A. J. Creswell, Mar. 6.
1874 Jas. W. Marshall, July 7.
1874 Marshall Jewell, Sept. 1.
1876 James N. Tyner, July 13.
1877 David McK. Key, Mar. 13.
1880 Horace Maynard, Aug. 25.
1881 Thomas L. James, Mar. 8.
1882 Timothy O. Howe, Jan. 5.
1883 Walter Q. Gresham, Apr. 11.
1884 Frank Hatton, Oct. 14.
1885 Wm. F. Vilas, Mar. 7.
1888 Don M. Dickinson, Jan. 17.
1889 John Wanamaker, Mar. 6.
1893 Wilson S. Bissell, Mar. 7.
1895 William L. Wilson, Apr. 4.
1897 James A. Gary, Mar. 6.
1898 Charles Emory Smith, Apr. 22.
1902 Henry C. Payne, Jan. 15.
1904 Robert J. Wynne, Oct. 10.
1905 Geo. B. Cortelyou, Mar. 7.
1907 Geo. von L. Meyer, Mar. 4.
1909 Frank H. Hitchcock, Mar. 6.
1913 Albert S. Burleson, Mar. 5.
1921 Will H. Hays, Mar. 5.
1922 Hubert Work, Mar. 4.
1923 Harry S. New, Mar. 4.
1929 Walter F. Brown, Mar. 6.
1933 James A. Farley, Mar. 4.
1940 Frank C. Walker, Sept. 11.
1945 Robert E. Hannegan, July 1.
1947 Jesse M. Donaldson, Dec. 16.
1953 Arthur E. Summerfield, Jan. 21.
1961 J. Edward Day, Jan. 21.
1963 John A. Gronouski, Sept. 30.
1965 Lawrence F. O'Brien, Nov. 3.
1968 W. Marvin Watson, Apr. 26.
1969 Winton M. Blount, Jan. 22.

U.S. POSTAL SERVICE

1971 Elmer T. Klassen, Dec. 7.
1975 Benjamin Bailar, Feb. 15
1978 William F. Bolger, Mar. 1.
1985 Paul N. Carlin, Jan. 1.
1986 Albert V. Casey, Jan. 6.
1986 Preston R. Tisch, Aug. 17.
1988 Anthony M. Frank, Mar. 1.

Basic Stamp Information

A stamp collector's knowledge of the combined elements that make a given issue of a stamp unique determines his or her ability to identify stamps. These elements include paper, watermark, method of separation, printing, design and gum. On the following pages these important areas are described in detail.

The guide below will direct you to those philatelic terms which are not major headings in the following introductory material. The major headings are:

Plate	Paper	Luminescence	Terminology
Printing	Perforations	Postal Markings	

Guide to Subjects

Arrows	See Plate Markings
Bisect	See Terminology
Blocks	See Plate
Booklet Panes	See Plate
Booklets	See Plate
Booklets, A.E.F.	See Plate
Bureau Issues	See Terminology
Bureau Prints	See Terminology
Cancellations	See Postal Markings
Carrier Postmark	See Postal Markings
Center Line Blocks	See Plate
Coarse Perforation	See Perforations
Coils	See Plate
Coil Waste	See Plate
Color Trials	See Printing
Commemorative Stamps	See Terminology
Compound Perforation	See Perforations
Corner Blocks	See Plate
Cracked Plate	See Plate
Crystallization Cracks	See Plate
Curvature Cracks	See Plate
Cut Square	See Terminology
Diagonal Half	See Terminology (Bisect)
Die	See Plate
Double Impression	See Printing
Double Paper	See Paper
Double Perforation	See Perforations
Double Transfer	See Plate
Dry Printings	See note after Scott 1029
Electric Eye	See Perforations
Embossed Printing	See Printing
End Roller Grills	See Paper
Engraving	See Printing
Error	See Terminology
Essay	See Printing
Fine Perforation	See Perforations
First Day Cover	See Terminology
Flat Plate Printing	See Printing
Flat Press Printing	See Printing
Giori Press	See Printing
Gridiron Cancellation	See Postal Markings
Grills	See Paper
Gripper Cracks	See Plate
Guide Dots	See Plate
Guide Lines	See Plate Markings
Guide Line Blocks	See Plate
Gum Breaker Ridges	See Terminology
Gutter	See Plate Markings
Hidden Plate Number	See Plate
Horizontal Half	See Terminology (Bisect)
Imperforate	See Perforations
Imprint	See Plate Markings
Imprint Blocks	See Plate
India Paper	See Paper
Intaglio	See Printing
Inverted Center	See Printing
Joint Line Pair	See Plate
Laid Paper	See Paper
Line Engraved	See Printing
Line Pair	See Plate
Lithography	See Printing
Luminescent Coating	See Luminescence
Manila Paper	See Paper
Margin	See Plate Markings
Margin Blocks	See Plate
Multicolored Stamps	See Printing
New York City Foreign Mail Cancellations	See Postal Markings
Offset Printing	See Printing
Original Gum	See Terminology
Overprint	See Printing
Pair Imperf. Between	See Perforations
Pane	See Plate
Part Perforate	See Perforations
Paste-up	See Plate
Paste-up Pair	See Plate
Patent Cancellations	See Postal Markings
Pelure Paper	See Paper
Phosphor Tagged	See Luminescence
Plate Arrangement	See Plate
Plate Flaws	See Plate
Plate Markings	See Plate
Plate Numbers	See Plate
Postmarks	See Postal Markings
Precancels	See Postal Markings
Printed on Both Sides	See Printing
Proofs	See Printing
Railroad Postmarks	See Postal Markings
Receiving Mark	See Postal Markings
Recut	See Plate
Re-engraved	See Plate
Re-entry	See Plate
Registry Markings	See Plate Markings
Re-issues	See Printing
Relief	See Plate
Reprints	See Printing
Retouch	See Plate
Rosette Crack	See Printing
Rotary Press Printings	See Printing
Rotary Press Double Paper	See Paper
Rough Perforation	See Perforations
Rouletting	See Perforations
Se-Tenant	See Terminology
Sheet	See Plate
Shifted Transfer	See Plate
Ship Postmarks	See Postal Markings
Short Transfer	See Plate
Silk Paper	See Paper
Special Printings	See Printing
Split Grill	See Paper
Stars	See Plate
Stitch Watermark	See Paper
Strip	See Terminology
Surface Printing	See Printing
Supplementary Mail Cancellations	See Postal Markings
Surcharges	See Printing
Tete Beche	See Terminology
Tied On	See Postal Markings
Transfer	See Plate

Plate

Die

Transfer Roll

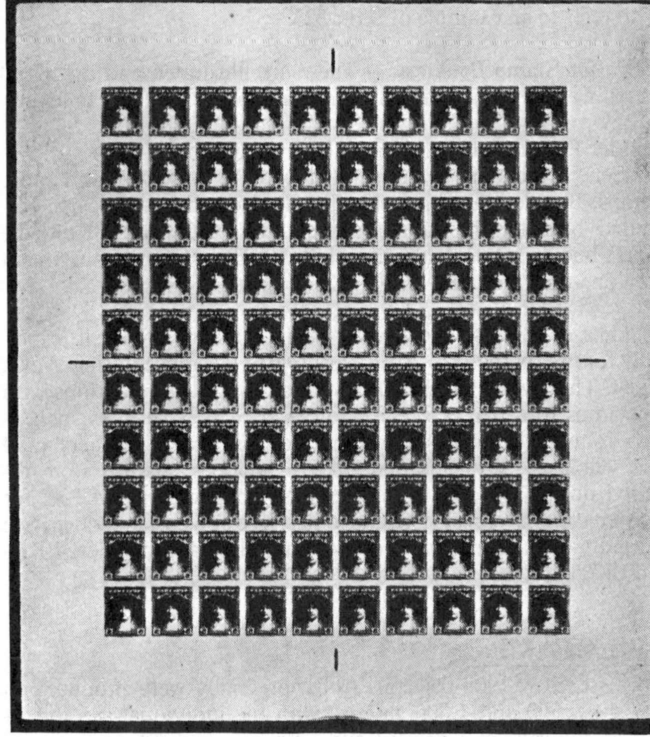
Plate

LINE ENGRAVING (Itaglio)

Die — Making the die is the initial operation in developing the intaglio plate. The die is a small flat piece of soft steel on which the subject (design) is recess-engraved in reverse. Dies are usually of a single-subject type, but dies exist with multiple subjects of the same design, or even different designs. After the engraving is completed, the die is hardened to withstand the stress of subsequent operations.

Transfer Roll — The next operation is making the transfer roll, which is the medium used to transfer the subject from the die to the plate. A blank roll of soft steel, mounted on a mandrel, is placed under the bearers of a transfer press. The hardened die is placed on the bed of the press and the face of the roll is brought to bear on the die. The bed is then rocked back and forth under increasing pressure until the soft steel of the roll is forced into every line of the die. The resulting impression on the roll is known as a "relief" or "relief transfer." Several reliefs usually are rocked in on each roll. After the required reliefs are completed, the roll is hardened.

Relief — A relief is the normal reproduction of the design on the die, in reverse. A defective relief, caused by a minute piece of foreign material lodging on the die, may occur during the rocking-in process, or from other causes. Imperfections in the steel of the transfer roll may also result in a breaking away of parts of the design. If the damaged relief is continued in use, it will transfer a repeating defect to the plate. Also, reliefs sometime are deliberately altered. "Broken relief" and "altered relief" are terms used to designate these changed conditions.

Plate — A flat piece of soft steel replaces the die on the bed of the transfer press and one of the reliefs on the transfer roll is brought to bear on this soft steel. The position of the plate is determined by position dots, which have been lightly marked on the plate in advance. After the position of the relief is determined, pressure is brought to bear and, by following the same method used in the making of the transfer roll, a transfer is entered. This transfer reproduces, in reverse, every detail of the design of the relief. As many transfers are entered on the plate as there are to be subjects printed at one time.

After the required transfers have been entered, the position dots, layouts and lines, scratches, etc., are burnished out. Also, any required guide lines, plate numbers, or other marginal markings are added. A proof impression is then taken and if certified (approved), the plate is machined for fitting to the press, hardened and sent to the plate vault until used.

Rotary press plates, after being certified, require additional machining. They are curved to fit the press cylinder and gripper slots are cut into the back of each plate to receive the grippers, which hold the plate securely to the press. The rotary press plate is not hardened until these additional processes are completed.

Transfer — An impression entered on the plate by the transfer roll. A relief transfer is made when entering the design of the die onto the transfer roll.

Double Transfer — The condition of a transfer on a plate that shows evidences of a duplication of all or a portion of the design. A double transfer usually is the result of the changing of the registration between the relief and the plate during the rolling of the original entry. Occasionally it is necessary to remove the original transfer from a plate and enter the relief a second time. When the finished re-transfer shows indications of the original transfer, because of incomplete erasure, the result also is known as a double transfer.

Triple Transfer — Similar to a double transfer, this situation shows evidences of a third entry or two duplications.

Re-entry — When executing a re-entry, the transfer roll is reapplied to the plate at some time after the latter has been put to press. Thus, worn-out designs may be resharpened by carefully re-entering the transfer roll. If the transfer roll is not carefully entered, the registration will not be true and a double transfer will result. With the protective qualities of chromium plating, it is no longer necessary to resharpen the plate. In fact, after a plate has been curved for the rotary press, it is impossible to make a re-entry.

Shifted Transfer (Shift) — In transferring, the metal displaced on the plate by the entry of the ridges, constituting the design on the transfer roll, is forced ahead of the roll as well as pressed out at the sides.

The amount of displaced metal increases with the depth of the entry. When the depth is increased evenly, the design will be uniformly entered. Most of the displaced metal is pressed ahead of the roll. If too much pressure is exerted on any pass (rocking), the impression on the previous partial entry may be floated (pushed) ahead of the roll and cause a duplication of the final design. The duplication appears as an increased width of frame lines or a doubling of the lines.

The ridges of the displaced metal are flattened out by the hammering or rolling back of the plate along the space occupied by the subject margins.

Short Transfer — Occasionally the transfer roll is not rocked its entire length in the entering of a transfer onto a plate, with the result that the finished transfer fails to show the complete design. This is known as a short transfer. Short transfers are known to have been made deliberately, as in the Type III of the 1-cent issue of 1851-60 (Scott 8, 21), or accidentally, as in the 10-cent 1847 (Scott 2).

Re-engraved — Either the die that has been used to make a plate or the plate itself may have its temper drawn (softened) and be recut. The resulting impressions for such re-engraved die or plate may differ very slightly from the original issue and are given the label "re-engraved."

Re-cut — A re-cut is the strengthening or altering of a line by use of an engraving tool on unhardened plates.

Retouching — A retouch is the strengthening or altering of a line by means of etching.

PLATE ARRANGEMENT

Arrangement - The first engraved plates used to produce U.S. postage stamps in 1847 contained 200 subjects. The number of subjects to a plate varied between 100 and 300 until the issue of 1890, when the 400-subject plate was first laid down. Since that time, this size of plate has been used for a majority of the regular postal issues (those other than commemoratives). Exceptions to this practice exist, particularly among the more recent issues, and are listed under the headings of the appropriate issues in the catalogue.

Sheet — In single-color printings, the complete impression from a plate is termed a sheet. A sheet of multicolored stamps (two or more colors) may come from a single impression of a plate, i.e., many Giori-type press printings from 1957, or from as many impressions from separate plates as there are inks used for the particular stamp. Combination process printings may use both methods of multicolor production: Giori-type intaglio with offset lithography or with photogravure.

The Huck multicolor press used plates of different format (40, 72 or 80 subjects). The sheet it produced had 200 subjects for normal-sized commemoratives or 400 subjects for regular-issue stamps, similar to the regular products of other presses.

See the note on the Combination Press following the listing for Scott 1703.

In casual usage, a "pane" often is referred to as a "sheet."

Pane — A pane is the part of the original sheet that is issued for sale at post offices. A pane may be the same as an entire sheet, where the plate is small, or it may be a half, quarter, or some other fraction of a sheet where the plate is large. The illustration shown later under the subtopic "Plate Markings" shows the layout of a 400-subject sheet from a flat plate, which for issuance would have been divided along the intersecting guide lines into four panes of 100.

Panes are classified into normal reading position according to their location on the printed sheet: U.L., upper left; U.R., upper right; L.L., lower left; and, L.R., lower right. Where only two panes appear on a sheet, they are designed "R" (right) and "L" (left) or "T" (top) and "B" (bottom), on the basis of the division of the sheet vertically or horizontally.

To fix the location of a particular stamp on any pane, the pane is held with the subjects in the normal position and a position number is given to each stamp starting with the first stamp in the upper left corner and proceeding horizontally to the right, then starting on the second row at the left and counting across to the right, and so on to the last stamp in the lower right corner.

In describing the location of a stamp on a sheet of stamp issued prior to 1894, the practice is to give the stamp position number first, then the pane position and finally the plate number, i.e., "1 R 22." Beginning with the 1894 issue and on all later issues the method used is to give the plate number first, then the position of the pane, and finally the position number of the stamp, i.e., "16807 L.L. 48" to identify an example of Scott 619 or "2138 L. 2" to refer to an example of Scott 323.

Plates for Stamp Booklets — These are illustrated and described preceding the listing of booklet panes and covers in this catalogue.

Booklet Panes — Panes especially printed and cut to be sold in booklets, which are a convenient way to purchase and store stamps. Booklet panes are straight-edged on three sides, but perforated between the stamps. Except for BK64 and BK65, the A.E.F. booklets, booklets were sold by the Post Office Department for a one-cent premium until 1962.

Booklets, A.E.F. — These were special booklets prepared principally for use by the U.S. Army Post Office in France during World War I. They were issued in 1-cent and 2-cent denominations with 30 stamps to a pane (10 x 3), bound at right or left. As soon as Gen. John J. Pershing's organization reached France, soldiers' mail was sent free by means of franked envelopes. Stamps were required during the war for the civilian personnel, as well as for registered mail, parcel post and other types of postal service. See the individual listings for Scott 498f and 499f and booklets BK64 and BK65.

COIL STAMPS

First issued in 1908-09, coils (rolls) originally were produced in two sizes, 500 and 1,000 stamps, with the individual stamps arranged endways or sideways and with and without perforations between.

Rolls of stamps for use in affixing or vending machines were first constructed by private companies and later by the Bureau of Engraving and Printing. Originally, it was customary for the Post Office Department to sell to the private vending companies and others imperforate sheets of stamps printed from the ordinary 400-subject flatplates. These sheets were then pasted together end-to-end or side-to-side by the purchaser and cut into rolls as desired, with the perforations being applied to suit the requirements of the individual machines. Such stamps with private perforations are listed in this catalogue under "Vending and Affixing Machine Perforations."

Later the Bureau produced coils by the same method, also in rolls of 500 and 1,000. These coils were arranged endways or sideways and were issued with or without perforation.

With the introduction of the Stickney rotary press, curved plates made for use on these presses were put into use at the Bureau of

Engraving and Printing, and the sale of imperforate sheets was discontinued. This move marked the end of the private perforations. Rotary press coils have been printed on a number of presses over the years and have been made in sizes of 100, 500, 1,000 and 3,000 stamps.

Paste-up — the junction of two flat-plate printings joined by pasting the edge of one sheet onto the edge of another sheet to make coils. A two-stamp example of this joining is a "paste-up pair."

Guide Line Pair — attached pair of flat-plate-printed coil stamps with printed line between. This line is identical with the guide line (See listing under "Plate Markings") found in sheets.

Joint Line — The edges of two curved plates do not meet exactly on the press and the small space between the plates takes ink and prints a line. A pair of rotary-press-printed stamps with such a line is called a "joint line pair."

Coil stamps printed on the Multicolor Huck Press do not consistently produce such lines. Occasionally accumulated ink will print partial lines in one or more colors. Stamps resulting from such situations are not listed in this Catalogue. The "B" and "C" presses do not print joint lines at all.

Splice — the junction of two rotary-press printings by butting the ends of the web (roll) of paper together and pasting a strip of perforated translucent paper on the back of the junction. The two-stamp specimen to show this situation is a "spliced pair."

Splices occur when a web breaks and is repaired or when one web is finished and another begins.

Plate Number — for stamps prior to Scott 1891:

On a rotary-press horizontal coil the top or bottom part of a plate number may show. On a vertical coil, the left or right part of a plate number may show. The number was entered on the plate to be cut off when the web was sliced into coils and is found only when the web was sliced off center. Every rotary press coil plate number was adjacent to a joint line, so both features could occur together in one strip.

For stamps from Scott 1891 onward:

The plate number is placed in the design area of the stamp, so it will not be trimmed off. Such items are normally collected unused with the stamp containing the plate number in the center of a strip of three or five stamps. They normally are collected used as singles. The line, if any, will be at the right of the plate-number stamp. On the Cottrell press, the number occurs every 24th stamp, on the "B" press every 52nd stamp, and on the "C" press every 48th stamp.

Unused plate number strips of three are valued in this catalogue.

Hidden Plate Number — A plate number may be found entire on a coil made from flat plates, but usually is hidden by a part of the next sheet which has been lapped over it.

Coil Waste — an occurrence brought about by stamps issued in perforated sheets from a printing intended for coils. These stamps came from short lengths of paper at the end of the coil run. Sometimes the salvaged sections were those which had been laid aside for mutilation because of some defect. Because the paper had been moistened during printing, it sometimes stretched slightly and provided added printing area. Sheets of 70, 100, and 170 are known. See Scott 538-541, 544-546, 578-579, and 594-596.

"T" — Letter which appears in the lower design area of Scott 2115b, which was printed on an experimental pre-phosphored paper. The stamp with the plate number is inscribed "T1."

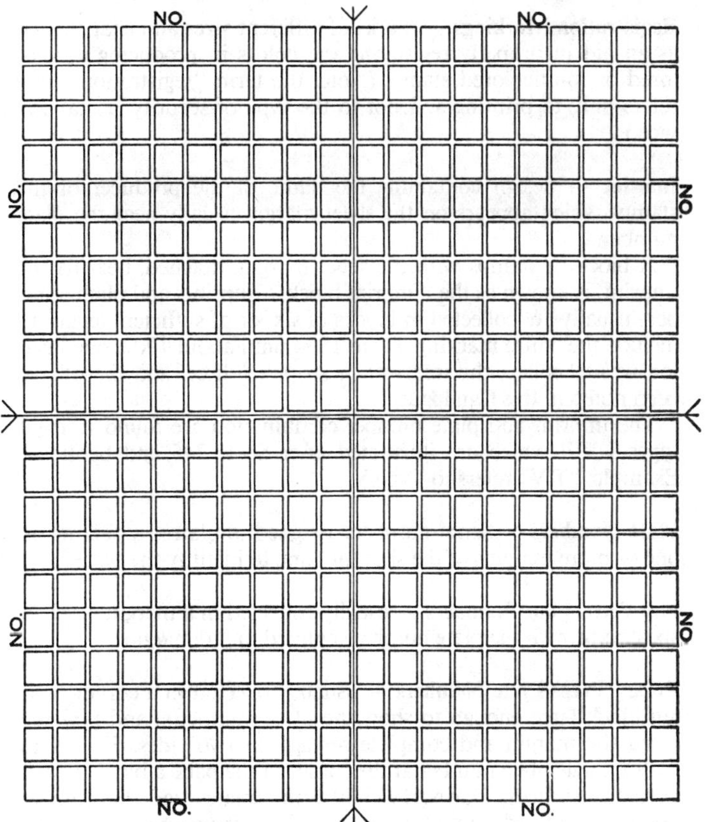

A typical 400-subject plate of 1922

Plate Markings — The illustration above shows a typical 400-subject plate of the 1922 issue with markings as found on this type of plate. Other layouts and markings are found further in the Catalogue text.

Guide Lines — Horizontal or vertical colored lines between the stamps, extending wholly or partially across the sheet. They serve as guides for the operators of perforating machines or to indicate the point of separation of the sheet into panes.

A block of stamps divided by any of the guide lines is known as a "line block" or "guide line block." The block of stamps from the exact center of the sheet, showing the crossed guide lines, is a "center line block."

Gutters — When guide lines are used to mark the division of the sheet into panes, the space between the stamps at the edge of the pane is no different than the space between any other stamps on the sheet. Some plates provide a wide space, or gutter, between the panes. These plates do not produce guide lines.

A pair of stamps with the wide space between is known as a "gutter pair"; and blocks with that situation are "gutter blocks." A block of stamps from the exact center of the sheet, showing the two wide spaces crossing, is a "center gutter block" or "cross gutter block."

Gutter pairs or gutter blocks must contain complete stamps on both sides of the gutter, intact including perforation teeth unless imperforate.

Arrows — arrow-shaped markings were used in the margins of stamp sheets, in place of guide lines, on the issues of 1870 through 1894. Since 1894, guide lines with arrows at both ends have been the standard practice on flat-plate printings.

A margin block of at least four stamps, showing the arrow centered at one edge, is known as a "margin block with arrow."

Registration Markings — marks of different sizes and shapes used as an aid in properly registering the colors in producing a bicolored or multicolored stamp. (Note: the term "registration" here refers only to printing and not to the type of security postal service.)

Imprint — design containing the name of the producer of the stamps which appears on the sheet margin usually near the plate number.

A block of stamps with the sheet margin attached, bearing the imprint, is known as the "imprint block." Imprints and plate numbers usually are collected in blocks of six, or of sufficient length to include the entire marking. From 1894 until about 1907, one fashion was to collect the imprints in strips of three, and these have been noted in this Catalogue.

The imprint and plate number combination are found in eight types I-VII, which are illustrated after Scott 245 and Scott E3. Example: "T V" refers to Type V.

Plate Numbers — Serial numbers assigned to plates, appearing on one or more margins of the sheet or pane to identify the plate.

Flat Press Plate Numbers — usually collected in a margin block of six stamps with the plate number centered in the margin.

Rotary Press Plate Numbers — usually collected in a corner margin block large enough to show the plate number(s) and position along the margin and complete selvage on two sides. For issues with a single plate number at the corner of the pane a block of four normally suffices. During 1933-39, some plates had the number opposite the third stamp (up or down) from the corner of the sheet and for these the number is customarily collected in a corner block of no less than eight stamps. Multicolored stamps may have more than one plate number in the margin and the "plate block" may then be expanded to suit the collector's desire.

The Catalogue listing for plate blocks includes enough stamps to accommodate all numbers on the plate. Plate block listings for setenant issues include all the designs as part of the block. When a continuous design is involved, such as Scott 1629-31, the complete design will be included in the plate number block. The entire pane constitutes the plate number block for issues such as the State Birds and Flowers (Scott 1953-2002).

Plate numbers take a further designation from the position on the sheet on which they appear, e.g. U.L. refers to upper left pane, etc.

See note following Scott 1703 for description of combination press markings.

Stars — used on the flat plates to indicate a change from the previous spacing of the stamps. They also were used as a check on the assignment of the printed sheets to a perforating machine of the proper setting. Stars appear on certain rotary plates used for printing stamps for coils, appearing adjacent to the plate joint line and above stamp No. 1 on the 170-subject plates, and to the left of stamp No. 141 on the 150-subject plates.

"A" — On flat plates: used on plates having uniform vertical spacing between rows of subjects, but wider than those with the star marking.

On rotary plates from Scott 1789 onward: denotes issues produced by private contractor and not the Bureau of Engraving and Printing.

"C.S." and "C" — plate is made of chrome steel.

"E.I." — abbreviation for Electrolytic Iron. The designation is for plates made by the electrolytic process.

"F" — used to indicate the plate is ready for hardening. This appears only on flat plates and general precedes the upper right plate number.

"Top" — marking on the top sheet margin of printings from both plates of some bicolored issues. This marking is used to check printings for "inverts." Beginning with the 6-cent bicolored airpost issue of 1938 (Scott C23), bicolored crosses also were used as an additional check.

"Coil Stamps" — appearing on the side sheet margins, designates plates used in the production of endwise coils.

"S 20," "S 30," "S 40" — marginal markings appearing on certain 150- and 170-subject rotary press plates to designate experimental variations in the depth and character of the frame line to overcome excess inking. "S 30" was adopted as the standard. Blocks showing these markings are listed as "Margin Block with S 20," etc., in this Catalogue.

Initials — used in sheet margins to identify individuals in the Bureau of Engraving and Printing who participated in the production or use of the plates.

Gutter Dashes — on the first 400-subject rotary plates, 3/16 inch horizontal dashes appear in the gutter between the 10th and 11th vertical rows of stamps. This arrangement was superseded by dashes 3/16-inch at the extreme ends of the vertical and horizontal gutters, and a 1/4-inch cross at the central gutter intersection. This latter arrangement continued until replaced by the scanning marks on the Electric Eye plates. See Electric Eye.

Margin — border outside the printed design or perforated area of a stamp, also known as selvage, or the similar border of a sheet of stamps. A block of stamps from the top, side or bottom of a sheet or pane to which is attached the selvage (margin) is known as a "margin block." A block of stamps from the corner of a sheet with full selvage attached to two adjoining sides is known as a "corner block."

NOTE — The descriptions and definitions above indicate that a certain number of stamps make up an arrow or plate number block. Any block of stamps, no matter now large or small, which had an arrow or plate number on its margin would be considered by that name. The usual practice is to collect flat-plate numbers in margin blocks of six and arrow blocks in margin blocks of four. Plate number blocks from rotary press printings generally are collected in blocks of 4 when the plate number appears beside the stamp at any of the four corners of the sheet. Particularly relative to bi-colored stamps, an arrow block is not separated from a plate number block. Thus, in those situations, the two individual types of blocks might form a block of eight or 10, as the situation dictates.

Printing

Methods Used — all four basic forms of printing have been used in producing U.S. stamps: engraved, photogravure, lithography, and typography.

Engraved (Recess or Intaglio) — process where ink is received and held in lines depressed below the surface of the plate. Initially, in printing from such plates damp paper was forced into the depressed lines and therefore picked up ink. Consequently, ink lines on the stamp are slightly raised. This also is noted from the back of the stamp, where depressions mark where ink is placed on the front.

When the ornamental work for a stamp is engraved by a machine, the process is called "engine turned" or lathe-work engraving. An example of such lathe-work background is the 3-cent stamp of 1861 (Scott Illustration No. A25).

Engraved stamps were printed only with flat plates until 1915, when rotary press printing was introduced. "Wet" and "dry" printings are explained in the note in the text of the Catalogue following Scott 1029. The Giori press, used to print some U.S. stamps from 1957 (see Scott 1094, 4-cent Flag issue), applied two or three different colored inks simultaneously.

The Huck Multicolor press, put into service at the Bureau of Engraving and Printing in 1968, was used first to produce the 1969 Christmas stamp (Scott 1363) and the 6-cent flag coil of 1969 (Scott 1338A). Developed by the Bureau's technical staff and the firm of graphic arts engineers whose name it bears, the Huck press printed, tagged with phosphor ink, gummed and perforated stamps in a continuous operation. Printing was accomplished in as many as nine colors. Fed by paper from a roll, the Huck Multicolor used many recess-engraved plates of smaller size than any used previously for U.S. stamp printing. Its product has certain characteristics which other U.S. stamps do not have. Post office panes of the 1969 Christmas stamp, for example, show seven or eight plate numbers in the margins. Joint lines appear after every two or four stamps. Other presses providing multiple plate numbers are the Andreotti, Champlain, Combination, Miller Offset, A Press, D Press, and more.

Photogravure — the design of a stamp to be printed by photogravure usually is photographed through an extremely fine screen, lined in minute quadrille. The screen breaks up the reproduction into tiny dots, which are etched onto the plate and the depressions formed hold the ink. Somewhat similar to engraved printing, the ink is lifted out of the lines by the paper, which is pressed against the plate. Unlike engraved printing, however, the ink does not appear to be raised relative to the surface of the paper.

For U.S. stamps, photogravure first appeared in 1967 with the Thomas Eakins issue (Scott 1335). The early photogravure stamps were printed by outside contractors until the Bureau obtained the multicolor Andreotti press in 1971. The earliest stamp printed on that press was the 8-cent Missouri Statehood issue of 1971 (Scott 1426).

Color control bars, dashes or dots are printed in the margin of one pane in each "Andreotti" sheet of 200, 160, or 128 stamps. These markings generally are collected in blocks of 20 or 16 (two full rows of one pane), which include the full complement of plate numbers, Mr. Zip and the Zip and Mail Early slogans.

Details on the Combination Press follow the listing for Scott 1703.

Lithography — this is the most common and least expensive process for printing stamps. In this method, the design is drawn by hand or transferred in greasy ink from an original engraving to the surface of a lithographic stone or metal plate. The stone or plate is wet with an acid fluid, which causes it to repel the printing ink except at the greasy lines of the design. A fine lithographic print closely resembles an engraving, but the lines are not raised on the face or depressed on the back. Thus, there usually is a more dull appearance to the lithograph than to the engraving.

Offset Printing or **Offset Lithography** — a modern development of the lithographic process. Anything that will print — type, woodcuts, photoengravings, plates engraved or etched in intaglio, halftone plates, linoleum blocks, lithographic stones or plates, photogravure plates, rubber stamps, etc. — may be used. Greasy ink is applied to the dampened plate or form and an impression made on a rubber blanket. Paper immediately is pressed against the blanket, which transfers the ink. Because of its greater flexibility, offset printing has largely displaced lithography.

Because the processes and results obtained are similar, stamps printed by either of these two methods normally are considered to be "lithographed."

The first application of lithographic printing for any U.S. items listed in this Catalogue was for Post Office seals, probably using stone printing bases. See also some Confederates States general issues. Offset lithography was used for the 1914 documentary revenues (Scott R195-R216). Postage stamps followed in 1918-20 (Scott 525-536) because of war-time shortages of ink, plates, and manpower relative to the regular intaglio production.

The next use of offset lithography for postage stamps was in 1964 with the Homemakers issue (Scott 1253), in combination with intaglio printing. Many similar issues followed, including the U.S. Bicentennial souvenir sheets of 1976 (Scott 1686-1689), all of which were produced by the combination of the two printing methods. The combination process serves best for soft backgrounds and tonal effects.

Typography — an exact reverse of engraved-plate printing, this process provides for the parts of the design which are to show in color to be left at the original level of the plate and the spaces between cut away. Ink is applied to the raised lines and the pressure of the printing forces these lines, more or less, into the paper. The process impresses the lines on the face of the stamp and slightly raises them on the back. Normally, a large number of electrotypes of the original are made and assembled into a plate with the requisite number of designs for printing a sheet of stamps. Stamps printed by this process show greater uniformity, and the stamps are less expensive to print than with intaglio printing.

The first U.S. postal usage of an item printed by lithography, or letterpress, under national authority was the 1846 "2" surcharge on the United States City Despatch Post 3-cent carrier stamp (Scott 6LB7). The next usage was the 1865 newspaper and periodical stamp issue, which for security reasons combined the techniques of machine engraving, colorless embossing and typography. This created an unusual first.

Most U.S. stamp typography consists of overprints, such as those for the Canal Zone, the Molly Pitcher and Hawaii Sesquicentennial stamps of 1928 (Scott 646-648), the Kansas-Nebraska control markings (Scott 658-679), Bureau-printed precancels, and "specimen" markings.

Embossed (relief) Printing — method in which the design is sunk in the metal of the die and the printing is done against a platen that is forced into the depression, thus forming the design on the paper in relief. Embossing may be done without ink (blind embossing), totally with ink, or a combination thereof. The U.S. stamped envelopes are an example of this form of printing.

ADDITIONAL TERMS

Multicolored Stamps — until 1957 when the Giori press was introduced, bicolored stamps were printed on a flat-bed press in two runs, one for each color (example: Norse-American Issue of 1925, Scott 620-621). In the flat-press bicolors, if the sheet were fed to the press on the second run in reversed position, the part printed in the second color would be upside down, producing an "invert" such as the famed Scott C3a.

With the Giori press and subsequent presses, stamps could be printed in more than one color at the same time.

Many bicolored and multicolored stamps show varying degrees of poor color registration (alignment). Such varieties are not listed in this Catalogue.

Bureau Prints (precancels) — stamps having cancellations applied before sale to persons or firms holding permits for their use. The cancellations were printed on the stamps by the Bureau of Engraving and Printing during the process of manufacture. The cancellations consist of the name of the city and state where the stamps are to be used, lines, or the class of mail.

"City type" precancels also have the cancellations applied before entering the mail stream, but the cancels not only differ in style, but also are performed locally.

Color Trials — printings in various colors, made to facilitate selection of color for the issued stamp.

Double Impression — a second impression of a stamp over the original impression.

This is not to be confused with a "double transfer," which is a plate imperfection and does not show a doubling of the entire design. A double impression shows every line clearly doubled. See also "Printed on Both Sides."

Essay — design submitted in stamp form, but not accepted for issuance in that form.

Inverted Center — bicolored or multicolored stamp with the center printed upside down relative to the remainder of the design. A stamp may be described as having an inverted center even if the center is printed first. See "Multicolored Stamps."

Flat Plate Printing — stamp printed on a flat-bed press, rather than on a rotary press. See "Plate."

Overprint — any word, inscription or device printed across the face of a stamp to alter its use or locality or otherwise to serve a special purpose. An example is U.S. Scott 646, the "Molly Pitcher" overprint, which is Scott 634 with a black overprinted inscription as a memorial to the Revolutionary War heroine. See "Surcharge."

Printed on Both Sides — Occasionally a sheet of stamps already printed will, through error, be turned over and passed through the press a second time, creating the rare "printed on both sides" variety. On one side the impression is almost always poor or incomplete. This often is confused with an "offset," which occurs when sheets of stamps are stacked while the ink is still wet.

The "printed on both sides" variety will show the design as a positive (all inscriptions reading correctly) and the offset shows a reverse impression. See "Double Impression."

Proofs — trial printings of a stamp made from the original die or the finished plate.

Reissues — An official printing of a stamp, or stamps, that had been discontinued. This term usually applies to fresh printings of such stamps, which can be distinguished in some way from those of the original issue.

While reissues normally are intended for regular usage, there are exceptions, such as those which were reissued during 1875 and sold for several years thereafter expressly for stamp collectors. See "Reprints," "Special Printings."

Reprints — impressions from the original plates, blocks or stones, from which the original stamps were printed. These reprints were taken after the original issues no longer was available at post offices and their postal use had been voided. See "Reissues," "Special Printings."

Reproductions — Stamps made from a new plate to imitate the original issue. See U.S. Scott 3-4. See "Souvenir Cards" section of this Catalogue.

Rotary Press Printings — stamps which have been printed on a rotary-type press from curved plates. Rotary press-printed stamps are longer or wider than stamps of the same design printed from flat plates. All rotary press printings through 1953, except coil waste (such as Scott 538), exist with horizontal "gum breaker ridges" varying from one to four per stamp. See: "Plate."

Special Printings — Stamps of current design reissued, such as those reissued during the Centennial Exposition of 1876 and several years thereafter. Examples are Scott 167-177 and 752-771. See: "Reissues" and "Reprints."

Surcharge — overprint which alters or restates the face value or denomination of the stamp to which it was applied. An example is Scott K1, where U.S. stamps were surcharged for used by U.S. Offices in China. Many surcharges are typeset. See: "Overprint" and "Typeset."

Typeset — made from movable type.

Typeset Stamps — printed from ordinary printer's type. Sometimes electrotype or stereotype plates are made, but because such stamps usually are printed only in small quantities for temporary use, movable type often is used for the purpose. This method of printing is apt to show broken type and lack of uniformity. See Hawaii Scott 1-4 and 12-26.

COMMON FLAWS

Cracked Plate — A term to describe stamps which show evidences that the plate from which they were printed was cracked.

Plate cracks have various causes, each which may result in a different formation and intensity of the crack. Cracks similar to the left-hand illustration are quite common in older issues and are largely due to the plate being too-quickly immersed in the cooling bath when being tempered. These cracks are known as crystallization cracks. A jagged line running generally in one direction and most often in the gutter between stamps is due to the stress of the steel during the rolling in or transferring process.

In curved (rotary) plates, there are two types of cracks. One is the bending or curving crack, which is quite marked and always runs in the direction in which the plate is curved.

The right-hand illustration shows the second type, the gripper crack. This type is caused by the cracking of the plate over the slots cut in the underside of the plate, which receive the "grippers" that fasten the plate to the press. These occur only on curved plates and are to be found in the row of stamps adjoining the plate joint. The appear on the printed impression as light irregularly colored lines, usually parallel to the plate joint line.

Rosette Crack — cluster of fine cracks radiating from a central point in irregular lines. These usually are caused by the plate receiving a blow.

Scratched Plate — caused by foreign matter scratching the plate, these usually are too minor to mention. See: "Gouge."

Gouge — exceptionally heavy and usually short scratches, these may be caused by a tool falling onto the plate.

Surface Stains — irregular surface marks resembling the outline of a point on a map. Experts differ on the cause. These are too minor to list.

Paper

Paper falls broadly into two types: wove and laid. The difference in the appearance is caused by the wire cloth upon which the pulp is first formed.

Paper also is distinguished as thick or thin, hard or soft, and by its color (such as bluish, yellowish, greenish, etc.).

Wove — where the wire cloth is of even and closely woven nature, producing a sheet of uniform texture throughout. This type shows no light or dark figures when held to the light.

Laid - where the wire cloth is formed of closely spaced parallel wires crossed at much wider intervals by cross wires. The resultant paper shows alternate light and dark lines. The distances between the widely spaced lines and the thickness of these lines may vary, but on any one piece of paper they will be the same.

Pelure — type of paper which is very thin and semi-transparent. It may be either wove or laid.

Bluish — The 1909 so-called "bluish" paper was made with 35 percent rag stock instead of all wood pulp. The bluish (actually grayish-blue) color goes through the paper, showing clearly on back and face. See the note with Scott 331.

Manila — a coarse paper formerly made of Manila hemp fiber. Since about 1890, so-called "manila" paper has been manufactured entirely from wood fiber. It is used for cheaper grades of envelopes and newspaper wrappers and normally is a natural light brown. Sometimes color is added, such as in the U.S. "amber manila" envelopes. It may be either wove or laid.

Silk — refers to two kinds of paper found by stamp collectors.

One type has one or more threads of silk embedded in the substance of the paper, extending across the stamp. In the catalogues, this type of paper usually is designated as "with silk threads."

The other type, used to print many U.S. revenue stamps, has short silk fibers strewn over it and impressed into it during manufacture. This is simply called "silk paper."

Ribbed — paper which shows fine parallel ridges on one or both sides of a stamp.

India — a soft, silky appearing wove paper, usually used for proof impressions.

Double Paper — as patented by Charles F. Steel, this style of paper consists of two layers, a thin surface paper and a thicker backing paper. Double paper was supposed to be an absolute safeguard against cleaning cancellations off stamps to permit reuse, for any attempt to remove the cancellation would result in the destruction of the upper layer. The Continental Bank Note Co. experimented with this paper in the course of printing Scott 156-165. See "Rotary Press Double Paper."

China Clay Paper — See note preceding Scott 331.

Fluorescent or **Bright Paper** — See: "Luminescence."

Rotary Press Double Paper — Rotary press printings occasionally are found on a double sheet of paper. The web (roll) of paper used on these press must be continuous. Therefore, any break in the web during the process of manufacture must be lapped and pasted. This overlapping portion, when printed upon, is known as a "double paper" variety. More recently, the lapped ends are joined with colored or transparent adhesive tape.

Such results of splicing normally are removed from the final printed material, although some slip through quality control efforts.

In one instance known, two splices have been made, thus leaving three thicknesses of paper. All rotary press stamps may exist on double paper.

Watermarks — Closely allied to the study of paper, watermarks normally are formed in the process of paper manufacture. Watermarks used on U.S. items consist of the letters "USPS" (found on postage stamps), "USPOD" (found on postal cards), the Seal of the United States (found on official seals), "USIR" (found on revenue items), and various monograms of letters, numbers, and so on, found on stamped envelopes.

The letters may be single- or double-lined and are formed from dies made of wire or cut from metal and soldered to the frame on which the pulp is caught or to a roll under which it is passed.The action of these dies is similar to the wires causing the prominent lines of laid paper, with the designs making thin places in the paper which show by more easily transmitting light.

The best method of detecting watermarks is to lay the stamp face down on a dark tray and immerse the stamp in a commercial brand of watermark fluid, which brings up the watermark in dark lines against a lighter background.

Note: This method of detecting watermarks may damage certain stamps printed with inks that run when immersed (such as U.S. Scott 1260 and 1832). It is advisable to first test a damaged stamp of the same type, if possible.

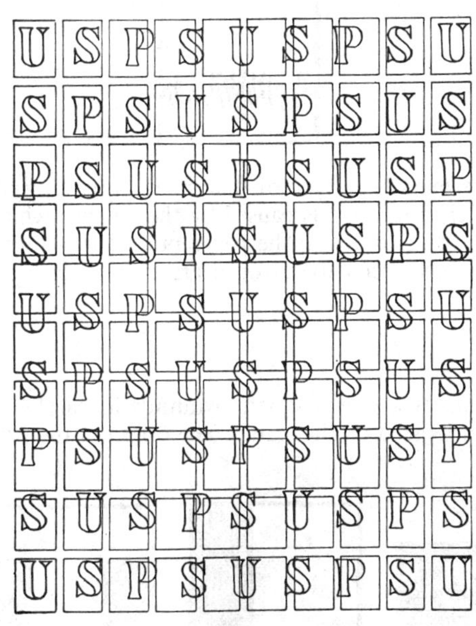

Wmk. 191

PERIOD OF USE

Postage: 1895-1910 Revenue: none

In the 1895-98 U.S. issues, the paper was fed through the press so that the watermark letter read horizontally on some impressions and vertically on other impressions.

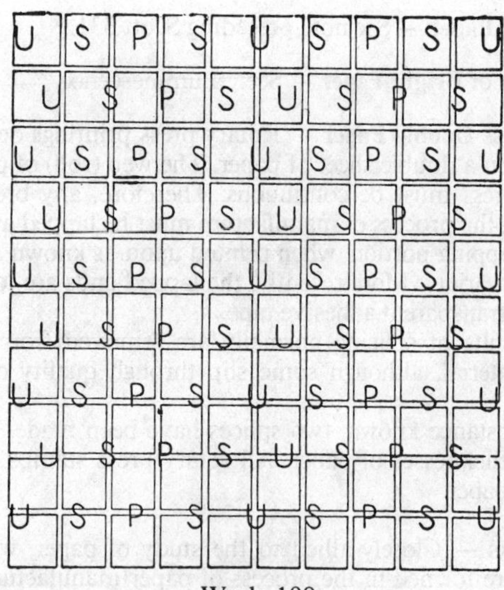

Wmk. 190
PERIOD OF USE
Postage: 1910-1916 Revenue: 1914

USIR
Wmk. 191R
PERIOD OF USE
Postage (unintentionally): 1895 (Scott 271a, 272a), 1951 (832b) Revenue: 1878-1958

Paper watermarked "USPOD" was used for postal cards from 1873 to 1875. For watermarks used on stamped envelopes, see Envelope Section in the text.

Watermarks may be found normal, reversed, inverted, inverted reversed and sideways, as seen from the back of the stamp.

Stitch Watermark — a type of watermark consisting of a row of short parallel lines. This is caused by the stitches which join the ends of the band on which the paper pulp is first formed. Stitch watermarks have been found on a great many issues, and may exist on all.

GRILLS

The grill consists of small square pyramids in parallel rows, impressed or embossed on the stamp. The object of the process is to break the fibers of the paper so that the ink from the cancellation would soak into the paper and make washing for reuse impossible. Grill impressions, when viewed from the face of the stamp, may be either "points up" or "points down." This process was used on U.S. Scott 79-101, 112-122 and 134-144 as well as some examples of 156-165 and 178-179.

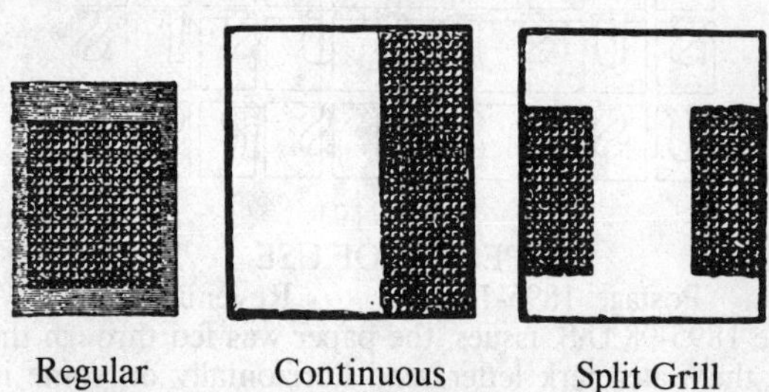

Regular Grill — Continuous Marginal Grill — Split Grill

Continuous Marginal Grill — includes continuous rows of grill points impressed by the untrimmed parts of the ends of the grill rollers, noted as "end roller grill" on the 1870 and 1873 issues, and those grills which came from a continuous band lengthwise of the roller.

Split Grill — situation on a stamp showing portions of two or more grills, caused by a sheet being fed under the grill roller off center.

Double (or Triple) Grill — stamp showing two or more separate grill impressions. This is not to be confused with a split grill, which shows two or four partial impressions from a single grill impression.

Rotary Grills — grilled appearance occasionally found on rotary press printings that was produced unintentionally by a knurled roller during the perforating process.

Similarly, grill-like impressions can be left on stamps dispensed from vending machines.

Perforations

The chief style of separation of stamps, and the one which today is used nearly universally, is produced by cutting away the paper between the stamps in a line of holes (usually round) and leaving little bridges of paper between the stamps. These little bridges are the "teeth" of the perforation and, of course, project from the stamp when it is torn from the pane.

As the gauge of the perforation often is the distinguishing difference among stamps, it is necessary to measure them and describe by a gauge number. The standard for this measurement is the number of such teeth within two centimeters. Thus, we say that a stamp is perforated 12 or 10½ to note that there are either 12 or 10½ teeth counted within two centimeters.

Perforation Gauge — tool for measuring perforation, as described above.

Fine Perforation — perforation with small holes and teeth close together.

Coarse Perforation — perforation with large holes and teeth far apart, frequently irregularly spaced.

Rough Perforation — holes not clean cut, but jagged.

Compound Perforation — normally where perforations at the top and bottom differ from the perforations at the sides of the stamp. In describing compound perforations, the gauge of the top is given first, then the sides.

Some stamps are found where one side will differ from the other three, and in this case the reading will be the top first, then the right side, then the bottom, then the left side.

Double Perforations — often found on early U.S. revenue stamps and occasionally on postage issues, double perforations are applied in error. They do not generally command a premium over catalogue values of properly perforated stamps and are not to be confused with a variety found on occasional rotary press printings where stamps adjacent to the center gutters will show the entire width of the gutter and a line of perforations on the far end of the gutter. These are caused by the sheet having been cut off center and are called "gutter snipes." They command a small premium.

Many double perforations were privately made to increase the value of the stamp, and are to be considered damaged stamps.

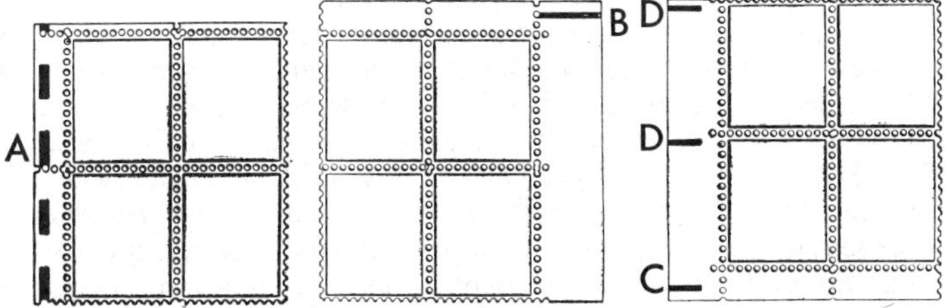

Electric Eye — an electronically controlled mechanical device acting as a guide in the operation of the perforating machine. Positive identification of stamps perforated by the electric eye process may be made by means of the distinctive marks in the gutters and margins of the full sheets on the printed web of paper. The original marks consisted of a series of heavy dashes dividing the vertical sheet gutter between the left and right panes (illustration A), together with a single line (margin line, illustration B), in the right sheet margin at the end of the horizontal sheet gutter between the upper and lower panes.

They first were used in 1933 on 400-subject plates for Scott 634, which was distributed to post offices in 1935 (used were plates 21149-50 and 21367-68). On these plates the plate numbers were placed opposite the ends of the third row of stamps from the top or bottom of the full sheet.

In later experiments, the margin line was broken into closely spaced thin vertical lines. Then it was again returned to its original form, but somewhat narrower.

In 1939, the Bureau of Engraving and Printing installed a new perforating machine which required a different layout to operate the centering mechanism. The vertical dashes remained the same, but the margin line was removed from the right sheet margin and a corresponding line ("gutter bar," illustration C) was placed in the left sheet margin at the end of the horizontal sheet gutter. Additional horizontal lines ("frame bars," illustration D) were added in the left sheet margin opposite the top frame line of the adjacent stamp design of all horizontal rows except the upper horizontal row of each left pane, where the frame bar is omitted. The plate numbers were moved back to their normal positions adjoining the corner stamps. Plates for the two types of machines could not be interchanged.

Later in 1939 a "convertible" plate was employed, consisting of a combination of the two previous layouts, the current one with the addition of a margin line (B) in its former position in the right sheet margin, thus making the perforation possible on either machine.

Originally laid out as 400-subject plates, electric eye plates were later used for 200-subject horizontal or vertical format (commemorative, special delivery and airpost issues), 280-subject (Famous Americans and those with similar formats) and 180- and 360-subject plates (booklet panes of definitives, airpost, postal savings and war savings issues).

In laying out the plates for the 400-subject and 200-subject horizontal format issues, the marks retained the same relative position to the stamp designs. This was changed, however, in entering the designs for the stamps of the 200-subject vertical format and 280-subject issues because the stamp designs were turned 90 degrees. That is, the designs were entered on the plates with the longer dimension horizontal. Although the electric eye marks were entered on the plates in the usual positions, on the printed sheets they appear as though shifted 90 degrees when the stamps are held in the customary upright position.

Thus, a "horizontal" mark on a 400-subject or 200-subject horizontal format sheet would become a "vertical" mark on a 200 subject vertical format or 280-subject sheet. This situation has caused confusion among collectors and dealers in determining a definite description of the various marks. The designation of the position of the plate numbers also has not been uniform for the "turned" designs.

To solve this confusion, the Bureau Issues Association adopted a standard terminology for all the marks appearing on the electric eye sheets. Dashes (A), Margin Line (B), Gutter Bar (C) and Frame Bars (D), whereby each type of mark may be identified readily without referring to its plate number position. The plate number designation of the panes will continue to be established by holding the pane of stamps with the designs in an upright position; the corner of the pane on which the plate number appears will determine the pane is upper left, upper right, lower left, or lower right.

Luminescence

Kinds of Luminescence — Fluorescence and phosphorescence, two different luminescent qualities, are found in U.S. postage stamps and postal stationery. While all luminescent stamps glow when exposed to short-wave ultraviolet (UV) light, only those with phosphorescent properties display brief afterglow when the UV light source is extinguished.

Fluorescent or **"Hi-Bright" Papers** — The Bureau of Engraving and Printing, at one point accepting paper for the printing of stamps without regard to fluorescent properties, unknowingly used a mix of paper with infinitely varying amounts of fluorescent optical brighteners added during the papermaking process. In March 1964, to preserve uniformity of product and as a safeguard for an emerging but still incomplete plan for nationwide use of luminescent stamps, BEP purchasing specifications were amended to limit the use of fluorescent paper brighteners. The amended specification permitted paper with some brightener content, but excluded brilliantly glowing papers known in the printing trade as "hi-bright."

Stamps printed on such papers emit a distinctive, intense whitish-violet glow when viewed with either long or short-wave UV. In following years, stamps were produced on papers with lower levels of fluorescence permitted by amended specifications.

Tagged Stamps — The Post Office Department (now the U.S. Postal Service) field-tested automated mail-handling equipment to face, cancel and sort mail at rates up to 30,000 pieces an hour, by sensing UV-light-activated afterglow from phosphorescent substances. For the first tests at Dayton, Ohio, started after August 1, 1963, the 8-cent carmine airpost stamp (Scott C64a) was overprinted (tagged) with a so-called "nearly-invisible"calcium silicate compound which phosphoresces orange-red when exposed to short-wave UV. A facer-canceler, with modifications that included a rapidly cycling on-off UV light, activated the phosphor-tagged airpost stamps and extracted envelopes bearing them from the regular flow of mail.

While the airpost extraction test was still in progress, the entire printing of the City Mail Delivery commemorative (Scott 1238) was ordered tagged with a yellow-green glowing zincorthosilicate compound intended for use with the automated recognition circuits to be tested with surface transported letter mail.

After the first-day ceremonies October 26, 1963, at Washington, D.C., it was learned the stamps had been tagged to publicize the innovative tests by coupling tagging with stamps memorializing "100 years of postal progress" and to provide the first national distribution of tagged stamps for collectors. Between October 28 and November 2, to broaden the scope of the test in the Dayton area, the 4-cent and 5-cent denominations of the regular issue then in use were issued with the same green glowing compound applied in an experimental tagging format (Scott 1036b, 1213b, 1213c, and 1229a).

By June 1964, testing had proven sufficiently effective for the Post Office Department to order all 8-cent airpost adhesive stamps phosphor-tagged for general distribution. By January 1966, all airpost stamps, regardless of denomination, were ordered tagged. Meanwhile, from 1963 through 1965, limited quantities of the Christmas issues were tagged for use in the continuing test in the Dayton area (Scott 1240a, 1254a-1257a, and 1276a).

On May 19, 1966, the use of phosphor-tagged stamps was expanded to the Cincinnati Postal Region, which then included offices in Ohio, Kentucky and Indiana. During the last half of 1966, primarily to meet postal needs of that region, phosphor tagged issues were authorized to include additional denominations of regular issues, some postal stationery, and about 12 percent of each commemorative issue starting with the National Park Service 5-cent issue (Scott 1314a) and continuing through the Mary Cassatt 5-cent commemorative (Scott 1322a). After January 1, 1967, most regular values through the 16-cent, all commemoratives, and additional items of postal stationery were ordered tagged.

Adhesive stamps precanceled by the Bureau of Engraving and Printing (Bureau precancels), however, were not tagged, with the exception of Scott 1394, 1596, 1608, and 1610. Because there was no need to cancel mail with these stamps and since precancel permit holders post such mail already faced, postal officials bypassed facer-canceler operations and avoided the cost of tagging.

Overall phosphorescent overprints, when newly issued, are practically invisible in ordinary light. After aging three to five years, the tagging discolors and becomes more easily visible. When viewed with UV light, there is little change in the hue of either orange-red or yellow-green emitted light. Even though observable discoloration exists, the presence or absence of tagging is best determined by examination with UV light.

Bar, or block, tagging, instead of the usual overall phosphorescent overprint, was used for some stamps beginning with the Andreotti-printed Mail Order Business commemorative (Scott 1468). These are much easier to identify than the overall overprint, often without need for a UV light.

Band tagging, a bar extending across two or more stamps, was first used with Scott 1489-1498.

Most of the luminescent issues of 1967-70 exist with the luminescent coating unintentionally omitted. This group includes Scott 1323-1338, 1339, 1342-1356, 1358, 1360, 1365-1370, and 1372-1374. Earlier omissions of luminescence are found with Scott 1238, 1278, 1281, 1298, and 1305.

In some postal stationery, such as Scott U551, UC40, UX48a, and UX55, the luminescent element is in the ink with which the stamp design is printed. The luminescent varieties of stamp envelopes Scott U550 and UC37 were made by adding a vertical phosphorescent bar or panel at left of the stamp. On Scott UC42, this "glow-bar" passes through the tri-globe design.

NOTE: Users of UV light should avoid prolonged exposure, which can burn the eyes. Sunglasses (particularly those that feature a "UV block") or prescription eyeglasses, tinted or plain, screen the rays and provide protection.

Postal Markings

Postal markings are those marks placed by postal employees of this and other countries on the stamp or cover or both. These marks may indicate the mailing place of a letter, date, rate, route, accounting between post offices, and so on.

In addition to the basis town designations, there are many varieties of supplemental markings. Among these are rate marks, route marks, obliterators, special dating markings usually found on advertised or dead letter covers, transportation markings (rail, steam, ship, airpost, etc.), and service markings (advertised, forwarded, missent, second delivery, mail route, too late, charged, paid box, due, returned for postage, soldier's letter, held for postage, short paid, unpaid, not paid, paid, free, dead letter office, etc.).

These markings originated, for material mailed in what is now the United States, in the Colonial period when manuscript postal markings were first introduced under the Ordinance of December 10, 1672, of New York, which established an inland postal system between the colonies. A "Post Payd" is found on the first letter ever sent under this system, on January 22, 1673. Manuscript postal markings continued in use right through the pre-stamp period and even can be found on some letters today.

Handstamp postal markings were introduced at New York in 1756, when a post office packet service was established between Falmouth, England, and New York. The marking merely was "NEW YORK" on two lines of type. The marking (see illustration), with each word of the city name on a separate line, is represented in presentations such as this as "NEW/YORK."

Similar markings were later introduced at other towns, such as ANNA/POLIS, by 1766; CHARLES/TOWN, by 1770; PHILA/DELPHIA, by 1766; HART/FORD, by 1766; while other offices received a singleline marking: BOSTON, by 1769; ALBANY, by 1773; PENSACOLA, by 1772; SAVANNA, by 1765, BALTIMORE, by 1772,and WMSBURG, by 1770.

Some of these early letters also bear a circular date stamp containing the month in abbreviated form, i.e., "IV" for June and "IY" for July, and the date in a 14-17 mm circle. Known from at least nine towns, these are called "Franklin marks" after Benjamin Franklin, then deputy postmaster general for the English crown. The marks also are known as "American Bishopmarks" to distinguish them from the Bishopmark used in England, which has a center line.

First U.S.Handstamp

Franklin Mark

During 1774-1775, an American provisional postal system was established in opposition to that of the English crown. Both manuscript and handstamp markings have been attributed to it. This system was taken over by Congress on July 26, 1775, and the same markings were continued in use. The earliest reported Congressional marks are a manuscript "Camb Au 8" and a blue-green straightline "NEW*YORK*AU*24." Postal markings are known throughout the Revolution, including English occupation markings. Most are manuscript.

In the post-war Confederation period, handstamped circular markings were introduced at Charleston, South Carolina, in 1778-1780, and later at New London, Connecticut. Straightlines and manuscripts continued to dominate until the use of oval markings became widespread about 1800, with circles becoming the predominant marking shortly thereafter.

Handstamp rate markings are known as early as the 1789 pennyweight markings of Albany. Such types of markings became more common in the 1830's and almost the standard by the "5" and "10"-cent rate period which began on July 1, 1845. This period also is when envelopes began to replace folded lettersheets. Before that date, envelopes were charged with an extra rate of postage. These "5," "10," and succeeding "3," "6," "5," and "10" rates of 1851-56 were common on domestic mail until prepayment became compulsory April 1, 1855, on all but drop or local letters domestically. The markings were common on foreign mail through about 1875.

Only 1.3 percent of all letters posted between 1847 and 1852 bore stamps. This proportion increased to 25 percent in 1852, 32 percent in 1853, 34 percent in 1854, 40 percent in 1855, and 64 percent in 1856. Stampless covers are commonplace, although there are some which are highly prized on the basis of their markings. Most are more common than stamped covers of the same period.

While the government began issuing handstamps as early as 1799 and obliterators in 1847, many postmasters were required, or at least permitted, to purchase their own canceling devices or to use pen strokes. Pen cancellations continued to be common in the smaller offices into the 1880's. Because of collector prejudice against pen-canceled stamps, many have ended up being "cleaned" (having the pen cancel removed). These are sold either as unused or with a different, faked cancellation to cover the evidence of cleaning. Ultraviolet light (long-wave) usually will reveal traces of the original pen marking.

From around 1850 until 1900, many postmasters used obliterators cut from wood or cork. Many bear fanciful designs, such as bees, bears, chickens, locks, eagles, Masonic symbols, flags, numerals and so on. Some of the designs symbolized the town of origin. These are not listed in this Catalogue, for they owe their origin to the whim of some individual rather than a requirement of the postal regulations. Many command high prices and are eagerly sought by collectors. This has led to extensive forgery of such markings so that collectors are advised to check them carefully.

Rapid machine cancellations were introduced at Boston in 1880-90 and later spread across the country. Each of the various canceling machine types had identifiable characteristics and collectors form collections based on type. One sub-specialty is that of flag cancellations. While handstamp flag designs are known earlier, the first machine flag cancellation was that of Boston in November-December 1894.

Specialists have noted that different canceling inks are used at different times, depending partly on the type of canceling device used. Rubber handstamps, prohibited in 1893 although used for parcel post and precanceling after that date, require a different type of ink from the boxwood or type-metal cancelers of the classic period, while a still different ink is used for the steel devices of the machine cancels.

Registry of letters was first authorized in this country in the Dutch colony of New Netherlands on overseas mail. Records of valuable letters were kept by postmasters throughout the stampless period while an "R" marking was introduced at Philadelphia in 1845 for "recorded" mail. Cincinnati also had such a "recorded" system. The first appearance of the word "registered" appears on mail in November 1847, in manuscript, and in handstamp in May 1850. The official registration for U.S. mail, however, did not begin in July 1, 1855.

In recent years, the handstamped and machine types of cancellations have been standardized by the Post Office Department and its successor and supplied to the various post offices.

Postmarks — markings to indicate the office of origin or manner of postal conveyance. In general terms, the postmark refers to the post office of origin, but sometimes there also are receiving postmarks of the post office of destination or of transit. Other post office markings include: advertised, forwarded, mail route, missent, paid, not paid, second delivery, too late, etc. Postmarks often serve to cancel postage stamps with or without additional obliterating cancels.

Cancellations — postal marking which makes further use of the postage stamps impossible. As used in the listings in this Catalogue, cancellations include both postmarks used as cancellations and obliterations intended primarily to cancel (or "kill") the stamp.

Carrier Postmarks — usually show the words "Carrier," "City Delivery," or "U.S.P.O. Dispatch." They were applied to letters to indicate the delivery of mail by U.S. Government carriers. These markings should not be confused with those of local posts or other private mail services which used postmarks of their own. Free delivery of city mail by carriers was begun on July 1, 1863.

Free — handstamp generally used on free, franked mail. The marking occasionally is seen on early adhesives of the United States used as a canceling device.

Railroad Postmarks — usually handstamps, the markings were used to postmark unpouched mail received by route agents of the Post Office Department traveling on trains on railway mail routes. The route name in an agent's postmark often was similar to the name of the railroad or included the terminals of the route. The earliest known use of the word "Railroad" as a postmark is 1838. Route agents gradually became R.P.O. clerks and some continued to use their handstamps after the route agent service ceased June 30, 1882. The railroad postmarks of the 1850 period and later usually carried the name of the railroad.

A sub-group of railroad postmarks is made up of those applied in the early days by railroad station agents, using the railroad's ticket dating handstamp as a postmark. Sometimes the station agent was also the postmaster.

In 1864, the Post Office Department equipped cars for the general distribution of mails between Chicago and Clinton, Iowa.

Modern railroad marks, such as "R.P.O." (Railway Post Office), indicate transportation by railroad cars on designated routes and distribution of mail in transit. "R.M.S." (Railway Mail Service) is a mark indicating transportation by railroad, and includes Railway Post office, Terminal Railway Post Office, Transfer Office, Closed Mail Service, Air Mail Field, and Highway Post Office.

Effective November 1, 1949, the Railway Mail Service was merged with others of like nature under the consolidated title Postal Transportation Service (PTS). The service was discontinued June 30, 1977.

The modern "railway marks" are quite common and are not the types referred to under cancellations as listed in the Catalogue.

Way Markings — Way letters are those received by a mail carrier on his way between post offices and delivered at the first post office he reached. The postmaster ascertained where the carrier received them and charged, in his postbills, the postage from those places to destination. He wrote "Way" against those charges in his bills and also wrote or stamped "Way" on each letter. If the letter was exempt from postage, it should have been marked "Free."

The term "mail carrier" above refers to any carrier under contract to carry U.S. mail: a stage line, a horseback rider, or a steamboat or railroad that did not have a route agent on board. Only unpouched mail (not previously placed in a post office) was eligible for a Way fee of one cent. The postmaster paid this fee to the carrier, if demanded, for the carrier's extra work of bringing the letter individually to the post office. For a limited time at certain post offices, the Way fee was added to the regular postage. This explains the use of a numeral with the "Way" marking.

Packet Markings — Packet markings listed in this Catalogue are those applied on a boat traveling on inland or coastal waterways. This group does not include mail to foreign countries that contains the words "British Packet." "American Packet," etc., or their abbreviations. These are U.S. foreign-mail exchange-office markings.

Listed packet markings are in two groups: 1) waterways route-agent markings which denote service exactly the same as that of the railroad route-agent markings, except that the route agent traveled on a boat instead of a train; 2) name-of-boat markings placed on the cover to advertise the boat or, as some believe, to expedite payment of Way and Steam fees at the post office where such letters entered the U.S. mails.

Occasionally waterways route-agent markings included the name of a boat, or "S.B.," "STEAMBOAT," "STEAM," or merely a route number. Such supplemental designations do not alter the character of the markings as those of a route-agent.

19th Century U.S. Express Mail Postmarks — In pre-stamp days these represented either an extra-fast mail service or mail under the care of an express-mail messenger who also carried out-of-mail express packages. The service was permitted as a practical means of competing with package express companies that also carried mail in competition with the U.S. Mail. Several of these early postmarks were later used by U.S. Mail route agents on the New York-Boston and New York-Albany runs, or by U.S. steamboat letter carriers on the coastal run between Boston and St. John, New Brunswick.

Steamboat or **Steam Markings** — Except for the circular markings "Maysville Ky. Steam" and "Terre Haute Stb." and the rectangular "Troy & New York Steam Boat," these markings contain only the word "STEAMBOAT" or "STEAM," with or without a rating numeral. They represent service the same as that of Way markings, except that the carrier was an inland or coastal steamer that had no contract to carry U.S. mails. Such boats, however, were required by law to carry to the nearest post office any mail given them at landings. The boat owner was paid a two-cent fee for each letter so delivered, except on Lake Erie where the fee was one cent. At some post offices, the Steamboat fee was added to regular postage. In 1861, the two-cent fee was again added to the postage, and in 1863 double postage was charged.

Ship Postmarks — postal markings indicating arrival on a private ship (one not under contract to carry mail). This marking was applied to letters delivered by such ships to the post office at their port of entry as required by law, for which they received a fee and the letters were taxed with a specified fee for the service in place of the ordinary open postage.

The use of U.S. postage stamps on ship letters is unusual, except for letters from Hawaii, because the U.S. inland postage on ship letters from a foreign point did not need to be prepaid. "U.S. SHIP" is a special marking applied to mail posted on naval vessels, especially during the Civil War period.

Steamship Postmarks — akin to Ship postmarks, but they appear to have been used mostly on mail from Caribbean or Pacific ports to New Orleans or Atlantic ports carried on steamships having a U.S. mail contract. An associated numeral usually designates the through rate from where the letter was received by the ship to its inland destination.

Receiving Mark — impression placed on the back of envelopes by the receiving post office to indicate the name of the office and date of arrival. It also is known as a "backstamp." Generally discontinued about 1913, the marking was employed for a time on air mail service until it was found the practice slowed the service. The markings now are used on registry and special delivery mail.

Miscellaneous Route Markings — wordings associated with the previously described markings include Bay Route, River Mail, Steamer, Mail Route, etc. Classification of the marking ordinarily is evident from the usage, or it can be identified from publications on postal markings.

U.S. Foreign-Mail Exchange-Office Markings — These served to meet the accounting requirements of the various mail treaties before the Universal Postal Union was established. The markings usually designate the exchange office or the carrier (British Packet, Bremen Packet, American Packet, etc.). Sometimes these markings are a restatement of the through rate, or a numeral designating the amount credited or debited to the foreign country as a means of allocating the respective parts of the total postage, according to conditions of route, method of transit, weight, etc.

Gridiron Cancellation — commonest types of cancellations on early U.S. stamps. The markings consist of circles enclosing parallel lines. There are, however, many varieties of grid cancellations.

Paid Markings — generally consist of the word "PAID," sometimes within a frame, indicating regular postage prepaid by the sender of a letter. They are found as separate handstamps, within town or city postmarks, and as a part of obliterating cancels. In each case, the "paid" marking may be used with or without an accompanying or combined rate numeral indication.

Precancels — stamps having the cancellation applied before the article is presented for mailing. The purpose is to reduce handling and speed up the mails. A permit is required for use by the public, except for special cases, such as the experiments using Scott 1384a, 1414a-1418a, or 1552 for Christmas mail. Normally the precanceling is done with devices not used for ordinary postal service. Most precancellations consist of the city and state names between two lines or bars.

Precancels are divided into two groups: locals and Bureaus. Locals are printed, usually from 100-subject plates, or handstamped, usually by means of a 10- or 25-subject device having a rubber, metal or vinyl surface at the town using the stamps. Most locals are made with devices furnished by the Postal Service, but a number have been made with devices created in the city using them. Early locals include the printed "PAID" or "paid" on Scott 7 and 9, "CUMBERLAND, ME." on Scott 24-26 and the Glen Allen, Virginia, stars.

Many styles of precancellation are known. More than 600,000 different precancels exist from more than 20,000 post offices in the United States.

The Bureaus, or Bureau Prints, are precancels printed by the Bureau of Engraving and Printing. They originated in 1916 when postal officials were seeking ways to reduce costs as well as increase the legibility of the overprint. The BEP was low bidder in three cities, which resulted in the "experimentals." These 16 denominations, including two postage dues, were issued for Augusta, Maine (one value); Springfield, Massachusetts (14 values); and New Orleans (six values) in quantities ranging from 4,000,000 down to 10,000. Electrotype plates mounted on a flat bed press were used to print the precancellations.

Regular production of Bureau Prints began on May 2, 1923, with Scott 581 precanceled "New York, N.Y." All regular Bureaus until 1954 were produced by the Stickney rotary press, whereby the stamps, immediately after printing, pass under the precanceling plates. Then the roll is gummed, perforated and cut into sheets or coils. Since 1954, a variety of printing methods have been used.

Tied On — when the cancellation (or postmark) extends from the stamp to the envelope.

Postal Markings, Cancellations Examples

Numerals
Values are for rating marks such as those illustrated. Later types of numerals in grids targets, etc., are common.

PAID ALL

PAID

The common Boston Paid cancellation
(Values are for types other than this)

STEAMBOAT

SHIP STEAM

Steamship

FREE

Steamboat
(Route agent marking)

ST. LOUIS, CAIRO AND NEW ORLEANS
RAILROAD LINE STEAMER
CHAMPION
LEAVES NEW ORLEANS FOR
CAIRO AND ST LOUIS.
MAR 25

Packet Boat
(Name-of-boat marking)

STEAMER
BAYOU BELLE.
CAPT. J.S. WALKER.

Packet Boat
(Name-of-boat marking)

Packet Boat
(Name-of-boat marking)

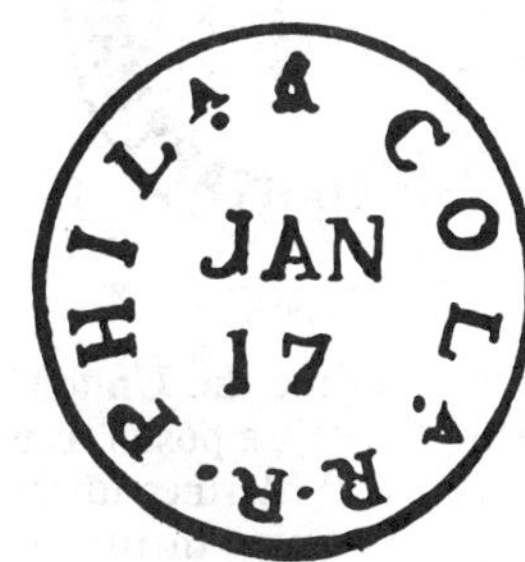

Railroad
(Route agent marking)

U.S. Express Mail
(Route agent marking)

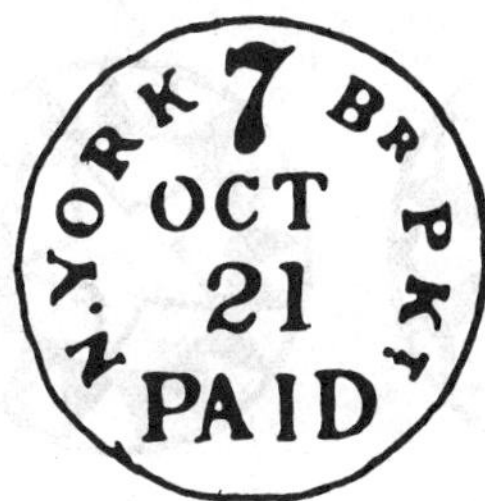

(In red on letter to Germany via Prussian Closed Mail, via British Packet. Credits 7 cent to Prussia.)

Express Company

Carrier

Army Field Post

Canadian

Town

Fort

Year dated

Vera Cruz, Mexico, 1914

U.S. Postmark used in China

Exposition Station.
Used while exposition is open. Many styles.

U.S. Postmark used in Japan

WORLD'S FAIR ST LOUIS 1903

Exposition advertising.
Used before exposition opens. Many styles.

New York City Foreign Mail — A group of design cancellations used between 1871 and 1877 in New York City on outgoing foreign mail only. This group of handstamps totals about 200 different fancy stars, geometric designs, wheels, conventionalized flowers, etc., the majority within a circle 26-29 mm in diameter.

Patent Defacing Cancellations — When adhesive stamps came into general use, the Post Office Department made constant efforts to find a type of cancellation which would make the re-use of the stamp impossible. Many patents were granted to inventors and some of the cancellations (killers) came into more or less general use. Some of them appear in combination with the town postmarks.

About 125 different types are known on the stamps issues up to about 1887. Their principal use and greatest variety occur on Scott 65, 147, 158, 183 and 184.

Patent cancellations generally fall into three groups:

1) Small pins or punches which pierce the paper or depress it sufficiently to break the fiber.

2) Sharp blades or other devices for cutting the paper.

3) Rotation of a portion of the canceler so that part of the paper is scraped away.

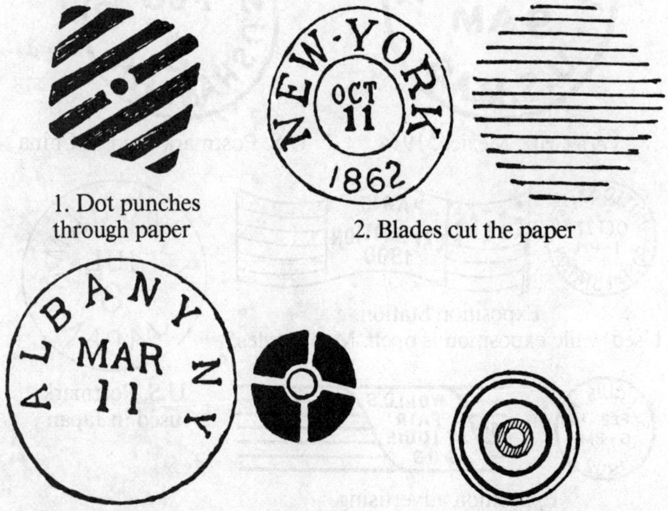

1. Dot punches through paper

2. Blades cut the paper

2. Small circle cuts the paper

3. Scraped in the shaded circle

Supplementary Mail — markings which designate the special post office service of dispatching mail after the regular mail closed. Two kinds of supplementary mail were available:

1. Foreign mail. For New York, the postmaster general established in 1853 a fee of double the regular rate. This paid to get the mail aboard ship after the regular mail closing and beforc sailing time. The service continued until 1939. Postmark Types A, D, E, F, and G were used.

2. Domestic mail. For Chicago, the extra fee entitled a letter to catch the last eastbound train. Postmark Types B and C were used. No foreign destination was implied.

Similar service with "Supplementary" in the postmark apparently available in Philadelphia and possibly elsewhere.

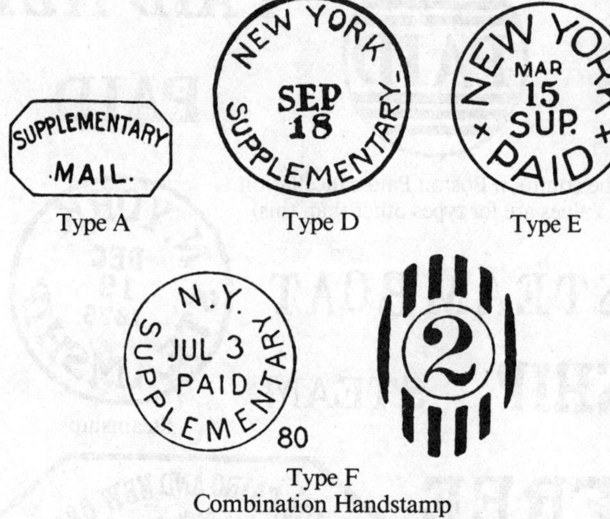

Type A

Type D

Type E

Type F

Combination Handstamp

(Also comes with numeral "1")

(Stamps with numeral cancel alone do not qualify for Supplementary Mail cancel premiums.)

Type G

(also with other numerals)

Type B

Type C

World War I Soldiers' Letters — At the time the United States declared war against Germany on April 6, 1917, a postal regulation existed which permitted soldiers, sailors and Marines to send letters without prepayment of postage by endorsing them "Soldier's letter" and having them countersigned by an officer. The single postage rate would then be collected from the recipient. Few of the enlisted men, however, took advantage of this privilege in sending letters while in the United States and practically all letters sent by soldiers from some 200 World War I military post offices (Fig. A) in the United States bear regular postage stamps.

Fig. A

Soon after the arrival of the first units of the American Expeditionary Force in France, this regulation was modified to include letters which, although not endorsed, bore the postmark of the United States Army Postal Service. The War Revenue Act of Congress of October 3, 1917, provided free postage for soldiers, sailors and marines assigned to duty overseas.

Therefore, letters from members of the A.E.F. sent before October 1917 without postage stamps were properly charged with postage due, while those sent after that time went through post free.

This provision for free postage did not ordinarily apply to civilians permitted to accompany the army, such as welfare workers, Post Office Department representatives, war correspondents and others. Neither did it apply to the registration fee on soldiers' letters nor to parcel post matter. It was necessary to pay such postage by means of postage stamps.

Fig. B Fig. C

The first U.S. Army post office (Fig. B), known as an A.P.O., was established at St. Nazaire, France, on July 10, 1917. The A.P.O.'s were at first operated by the Post Office Department, but in May 1918 the Military Express Service was established (Fig. C) and the army took over the operation. Later the name was changed to Postal Express Service (Fig D).

Fig. D Fig. E

Army post offices were given code numbers and were at first numbered from No. 1 (St. Nazaire) to No. 18 (Saumur). In December 1917, they were renumbered 701, 702, etc., and some 169 A.P.O.'s were established on the Western Front, including offices in Italy, Belgium, Netherlands, Luxembourg, and Germany after the Armistice. Most of the A.P.O.'s were located at fixed places, but "mobile" post offices were assigned to divisions, army corps and armies and were moved from place to place. Many A.P.O.'s had stations or branches, some of which used postmarks with different code numbers from those assigned to the main office.

Until July 1919, all A.E.F. mail was censored, and letters will be found with "company" censor marks (Fig. E) as well as "regimental" censor marks (Fig. F). Distinctive censor marks were used at the base censor's office in Paris (Fig. G).

Fig. F Fig. G

An interesting variety of subsidiary markings may be found on soldiers' letters: "ADDRESSEE RETURNED TO U.S.A.," "CANNOT BE FOUND," "DECEASED – VERIFIED," "NO RECORD," "SOLDIER'S MAIL," and "UNIT RETURNED TO U.S."

Many styles of stationery were used, mainly those furnished by welfare organizations. Only a few pictorial envelopes were used, but a considerable variety of patriotic and pictorial postcards may be found in addition to officially printed-form postcards.

Fig. H Fig. I

A postal agency was in operation in Siberia from 1918 to 1920 and distinctive postmarks (Fig. H) and censor marks were used there. A few American soldiers were sent to North Russia, and postmarks used there were those of the British Expeditionary Force's North Russia postal service (Fig. I).

World War I postmarks have been classified by collectors and the "American Classification System" prepared by the War Cover Club is in general use by collectors of these items.

World War II – Beginning in January 1941, U.S. post offices were established in Newfoundland, Bermuda and other naval bases acquired as a result of the exchange of destroyers with Great Britain. The names of the bases were at first included in the postmark. Later A.P.O. code numbers were adopted, in a similar manner to those used during World War I. Toward the middle of 1942, the A.P.O. numbers were cut out of the postmark so that nothing appears to indicate the A.P.O. at which a letter was mailed, although the already established practice was continued of the writer giving the A.P.O. number in the return address. Early in 1943, A.P.O. numbers were replaced in the postmarks at many military post offices.

More than 1,000 different A.P.O. numbers were used. At least 90 types of postmarks exist, of which 45 are handstamped and 40 machine struck.

The armed services, both at home and abroad, were given the franking privilege early in April 1942, the frank consisting of the written word "Free" in the upper right corner of the envelope.

A wide variety of censor marks was used, differing radically in design from those used in World War I.

Bureau Precancels

AUGUSTA
MAINE

NEW
ORLEANS
LA.

SPRINGFIELD
MASS.

Experimentals

PERU
IND.

LANSING
MICH.

SAINT LOUIS
MO.

New Orleans
La.

San Francisco
Calif.

PORTLAND
ME.

LAKEWOOD
N. J.

KANSAS
CITY
MO.

POUGHKEEPSIE
N. Y.

LONG ISLAND
CITY, N. Y.

CORPUS
CHRISTI
TEXAS

ATLANTA
GEORGIA

ATLANTA
GA.

PEORIA
IL

CINCINNATI
OH

Blk. Rt.
CAR-RT
SORT

Bulk Rate

Nonprofit
Org.

Nonprofit
Org.

PRESORTED
FIRST-CLASS

ZIP+4

Local Precancels

QUINCY
ILLINOIS

FITCHBURG
MASS.

LOS ANGELES
CALIF.

Fergus Falls
Minn.

COVINGTON
KY.

REDWOOD CITY
CALIF.

BELMONT
CALIF.

ELGIN
ILLINOIS

Electroplates

Ashland
Wis.

PALMYRA
N. Y.

Northhampton
MASS.

DES PLAINES
ILL.

RICHMOND
VA.

BROOKFIELD
ILLINOIS

PAONIA
COLO.

GOSHEN
IND

TOWER CITY
N. DAK.

NEW BRUNSWICK
N. J.

ORLANDO,
FLA.

RICHTON PARK
ILL.

MULINO,
OREG.

PINE HILL
N.Y.

FARRELL,
PA

SACRAMENTO
CA

Handstamps

Terminology

Scott Publishing Co. uses the following terms in its Catalogues, as appropriate. Definitions follow each term.

Imperforate — stamps without perforations, rouletting, or other form of separation.

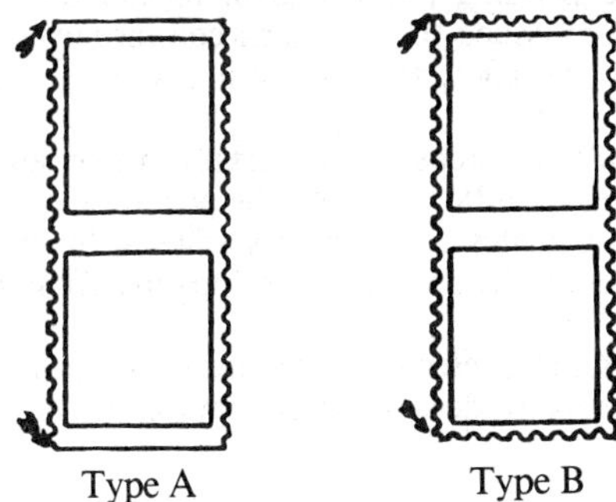

Type A Type B

Part-Perforate — Stamps with perforations on the two opposite sides, the other two sides remaining imperforate. See coils.

Vertical Pair, Imperforate Horizontally — (Type A illustratcd) in dicating that a pair of stamps is fully perforated vertically, but has no horizontal perforations.

Horizontal Pair, Imperforate Vertically — (Type A) indicating that a pair of stamps is fully perforated horizontally but has no vertical perforations.

Vertical Pair, Imperforate Between — (Type B illustrated) indicating that the vertical pair is fully perforated at the top, sides, and bottom, but has no perforations between the stamps.

Horizontal Pair, Imperforate Between — (Type B) indicating that the horizontal pair is fully perforated at the top, sides, and bottom, but has no perforations between the stamps.

Note: Of the above two types (A & B), Type A is the more common.

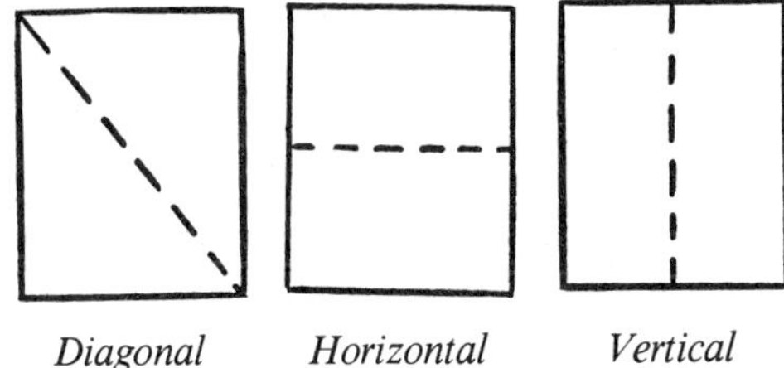

Diagonal *Horizontal* *Vertical*

Bisect — Stamps cut in half so that each portion prepaid postage. These items were used in emergencies where no stamps of the lower denomination were available. These may be diagonal, horizontal or vertical. Listings are for bisects on full covers. Those in piece or part of a cover sell for considerably less.

Block of Four, Imperforate Within — Examples exist of blocks of four stamps that are perforated on all four outside edges, but lack both horizontal and vertical perforations within the block. Scott 2096c, the Smokey the Bear commemorative, is an example of an accidental example of this phenomenon. Scott RS173j and RS174j are examples of a situation where internal perforations were omitted intentionally to create 4-cent "stamps" from four 1-cent stamps.

Rouletting — short consecutive cuts in the paper to facilitate separation of the stamps, made with a toothed wheel or disc.

Booklets — Many countries have issued stamps in booklets for the convenience of users. This idea is becoming increasingly popular today in many countries. Booklets have been issued in all sizes and forms, often with advertising on the covers, on the panes of stamps or on the interleaving.

The panes may be printed from special plates or made from regular sheets. All panes from booklets issued by the United States and many from those of other countries contain stamps which are imperforate on three sides, but perforated between. Any stamp-like unit in the pane, either printed or blank, which is not a postage stamp, is considered a *label* in the Catalogue listings.

Scott lists and values booklets in this volume. In the Standard Postage Stamp Catalogue, complete booklets are listed only in rare cases. See Grenada Scott 1055. Panes are not listed when they are fashioned from existing sheet stamps and, therefore, are not distinguishable from their sheet-stamp foreign counterparts.

Panes usually do not have a "used" value because there is little market activity in used panes, even though many exist used.

Cancellations — the marks or obliterations put on a stamp by the postal authorities to show that it has done service and is no longer valid for postage. If made with a pen, it is a "pen cancellation." When the location of the post office appears in the cancellation, it is a "town cancellation." When calling attention to a cause or celebration, it is a "slogan cancellation." Many other types and styles of cancellations exist, such as duplex, numerals, targets, etc.

Coil Stamps — stamps issued in rolls for use in dispensers, affixing and vending machines. Those of the United States, Canada, Sweden and some other countries are perforated horizontally or vertically only, with the outer edges imperforate. Coil stamps of some countries, such as Great Britain, are perforated on all four sides.

Commemorative Stamps — special issues which commemorate some anniversary or event or person. Usually such stamps are used for a limited period concurrently with the regular issue of stamps. Examples of commemorative issues are Scott 230-245, 620-621, 946, 1266, C68, and U218-U221.

Covers — envelopes, with or without adhesive postage stamps, which have passed through the mail and bear postal or other markings of philatelic interest. Before the introduction of envelopes in about 1840, people folded letters and wrote the address on the outside. Many people covered their letters with an extra sheet of paper on the outside for the address, producing the term "cover." Used air letter sheets and stamped envelopes also are considered covers. See postal cards.

Errors — stamps having some unintentional major deviation from the normal. Errors include, but are not limited to, mistakes in color, paper, or watermark; inverted centers or frames on multicolor printing; inverted or double surcharges or overprints; imperforates and part-perforates; and double impressions. A factually wrong or misspelled inscription, if it appears on all examples of a stamp, even if corrected later, is not classified as a philatelic error.

First Day Cover — A philatelic term to designate the use of a certain stamp (on cover) on the first day of sale at a place officially designated for such sale or so postmarked. Current U.S. stamps may have such a postal marking applied considerably after the actual issue date.

Gum Breaker Ridges — Colorless marks across the backs of some rotary press stamps, impressed during manufacture to prevent curling. Many varieties of "gum breaks" exist.

Original Gum — A stamp is described as "O.G." if it has the original gum as applied when printed. Some are issued without gum, such as Scott 730, 731, 735, 752, etc.; government reproductions, such as Scott 3 and 4; and official reprints.

Overprinted and Surcharged Stamps — Overprinting is a wording or design placed on stamps to alter the place of use (i.e., "Canal Zone" on U.S. stamps), to adapt them for a special purpose ("I.R. on 1-cent and 2-cent U.S. stamps of the 1898 regular issue for use as revenue stamps, Scott R153-R155) or for a special occasion (U.S. Scott 646-648).

Surcharge is an overprint which changes or restates the face value of the item.

Surcharges and overprints may be handstamped, typeset or, occasionally, lithographed or engraved. A few hand-written overprints and surcharges are known.

Postal Cards — cards that have postage printed on them. Ones without printed stamps are referred to as "postcards."

Precancels — stamps canceled before they are placed in the mail. Precanceling is done to expedite the handling of large mailings.

In the United States, precancellations generally identified the point of origin. That is, the city and state names or initials appeared, usually centered between parallel lines. More recently, bureau precancels retained the parallel lines, but the city and state designation was dropped. Recent coils have a "service inscription" to show the mail service paid for by the stamp. Because these stamps do not receive any further cancellation when used as intended, they are under the general precancel umbrella.

Such new items may not have parallel lines as part of the precancellation.

Precancels are listed in the Catalogue only if the precanceled stamp is different from the nonprecanceled version (untagged stamps such as Scott 1582a); or, if the stamp only exists precanceled (Scott 2265). Classical locals and experimental bureaus are also included as cancellations.

Proofs and Essays — Proofs are impressions taken from an approved die, plate or stone in which the design and color are the same as the stamp issued to the public. Trial color proofs are impressions taken from approved dies, plates or stones in varying colors. An essay is the impression of a design that differs in some way from the stamp as issued.

Provisionals — stamps issued on short notice and intended for temporary use pending the arrival of regular (definitive) issues. They usually are issued to meet such contingencies as changes in government or currency, shortage of necessary postage values, or military occupation.

In the 1840's, postmasters in certain American cities issued stamps that were valid only at specific post offices. Postmasters of the Confederate States also issued stamps with limited validity. Both of these examples are known as "postmaster's provisionals."

Se-Tenant — joined, referring to an unsevered pair, strip or block of stamps differing in design, denomination or overprint. See U.S. Scott 2158a.

Tete Beche — A pair of stamps in which one is upside down in relation to the other. Some of these are the result of intentional sheet arrangements, i.e. Morocco Scott B10-B11. Others occurred when one or more electrotypes accidentally were placed upside down on the plate. See Hawaii Scott 21a and 22a. Separation of the stamps, of course, destroys the tete beche variety.

Specimens — One of the regulations of the Universal Postal Union requires member nations to send samples of all stamps they put into service to the International Bureau in Switzerland. Member nations of the UPU receive these specimens as samples of what stamps are valid for postage. Many are overprinted, handstamped or initial-perforated "Specimen," "Canceled" or "Muestra." Some are marked with bars across the denominations (China-Taiwan), punched holes (Czechoslovakia) or back inscriptions (Mongolia).

Stamps distributed to government officials or for publicity purposes, and stamps submitted by private security printers for official approval also may receive such defacements.

These markings prevent postal use, and all such items generally are known as "specimens." There is a section in this volume devoted to this type of material.

Territorial and Statehood Dates

	Territorial Date	Statehood Date	
Alabama	Aug. 15, 1817	Dec. 14, 1819	Territory by Act of March 3, 1817, effective Aug. 15, 1817.
Alaska	Oct. 18, 1867	Jan. 3, 1959	A District from Oct. 18, 1867, until it became an Organized Territory Aug. 24, 1912.
Arizona	Feb. 24, 1863	Feb. 14, 1912	This region was sometimes called Arizona before 1863 though still in the Territory of New Mexico.
Arkansas	July 5, 1819*	June 15, 1836	The Territory was larger than the State. The left-over area to the west after statehood had post offices which continued for some years to use an Arkansas abbreviation in the postmarks though really in the "Indian Country."
California		Sept. 9, 1850	Ceded by Mexico by the Guadalupe-Hidalgo Treaty, concluded Feb. 2, 1848 and proclaimed July 4, 1848. From then until statehood, California had first a military government until Dec. 20, 1849 and then a local civil government. It never had a territorial form of government.
Colorado	Feb. 28, 1861	Aug. 1, 1876	
Dakota	March 2, 1861	Nov. 2, 1889	Became two states — North and South Dakota.
Deseret	March 5, 1849		March 5,1849 Brigham Young created the unofficial territory of Deseret. In spite of the fact that Utah Territory was created Sept. 9, 1850, Deseret continued to exist unofficially in what is now Utah for several years, at least as late as 1862.
Frankland or Franklin			This unofficial state was formed in Aug. 1784 in the northeast corner of what is now Tennessee, and the government existed until 1788. In reality it was part of North Carolina.
Florida	March 30, 1822	March 3, 1845	
Hawaii	Aug. 12, 1898	Aug. 21, 1959	The territorial date given is that of the formal transfer to the United States, with Sanford B. Dole as first Governor.
Idaho	March 3, 1863	July 3, 1890	
Illinois	March 2, 1809*	Dec. 3, 1818	
Indiana	July 5, 1800*	Dec. 11, 1816	There was a residue of Indiana Territory which continued to exist under that name from Dec. 11, 1816 until Dec. 3, 1818 when it was attached to Michigan Territory.
Indian Territory		Nov. 16, 1907	In the region first called the "Indian Country," established June 30, 1834. Never had a territorial form of government. Finally, with Oklahoma Territory, became the State of Oklahoma, Nov. 16, 1907.
Iowa	July 4, 1838	Dec. 28, 1846	
Jefferson	Oct. 24, 1859		An unofficial territory from Oct. 24, 1859 to Feb. 28, 1861. In reality it included parts of Kansas, Nebraska, Utah and New Mexico Territories, about 30% being in each of the first three and 10% in New Mexico. The settled portion was mostly in Kansas Territory until Jan. 29, 1861 when the State of Kansas was formed from the eastern part of Kansas Territory. From this date the heart of "Jefferson" was in unorganized territory until Feb. 28, 1861, when it became the Territory of Colorado.
Kansas	May 30, 1854	Jan. 29, 1861	
Kentucky		June 1, 1792	Never a territory. Was part of Virginia until statehood.
District of Louisiana	Oct. 1, 1804		An enormous region — all of the Louisiana Purchase except the Territory of Orleans. Created by Act of March 26, 1804, effective Oct. 1, 1804 and attached for administrative purposes to the Territory of Indiana.
Territory of Louisiana	July 4, 1805		By Act of March 3, 1805, effective July 4, 1805, the District of Louisiana became the Territory of Louisiana.
District of Maine		March 16, 1820	What is now the State of Maine was before statehood called the District of Maine and belonged to Massachusettes.

	Territorial Date	Statehood Date	
Michigan	July 1, 1805	Jan. 26, 1837	
Minnesota	March 3, 1849	May 11, 1858	
Mississippi	May 7, 1798	Dec. 10, 1817	Territory by Act of April 7, 1798, effective May 7, 1798.
Missouri	Dec. 7, 1812	Aug. 10, 1821	The State was much smaller than the Territory. The area to the west and northwest of the State, which had been in the Territory, was commonly known as the "Missouri Country" until May 30, 1854 and certain of the post offices in this area show a Missouri abbreviation in the postmark.
Montana	May 26, 1864	Nov. 8, 1889	
Nebraska	May 30, 1854	March 1, 1867	
Nevada	March 2, 1861	Oct. 31, 1864	
New Mexico	Dec. 13, 1850	Jan. 6, 1912	
North Dakota		Nov. 2, 1889	Had been part of the Territory of Dakota.
Northwest Territory	July 13, 1787		Ceased to exist March 1, 1803 when Ohio became a state. The date given is in dispute, Nov. 29, 1802 often being accepted.
Ohio		March 1, 1803	Had been part of Northwest Territory until statehood.
Oklahoma	May 2, 1890	Nov. 16, 1907	The State was formed from Oklahoma Territory and Indian Territory.
Oregon	Aug. 14, 1848	Feb. 14, 1859	
Orelans	Oct. 1, 1804		A Territory by Act of March 26, 1804, effective Oct. 1, 1804. Became with certain boundary changes, the State of Louisiana, April 30, 1812.
South Dakota		Nov. 2, 1889	Had been part of Dakota Territory.
Southwest Territory			Became the State of Tennessee, with minor boundary changes, June 1, 1796.
Tennessee		June 1, 1796	Had been Southwest Territory before statehood.
Texas		Dec. 29, 1845	Had been an independent Republic before statehood.
Utah	Sept. 9, 1850	Jan. 4, 1896	
Vermont		March 4, 1791	Until statehood, had been a region claimed by both New York and New Hampshire.
Washington	March 2, 1853	Nov. 11, 1889	
West Virginia		June 20, 1863	Had been part of Virginia until statehood.
Wisconsin	July 4, 1836	May 29, 1848	The State was smaller than the Territory, and the left-over area continued to be called the Territory of Wisconsin until March 3, 1849.
Wyoming	July 29, 1868	July 10, 1890	

* The dates followed by an asterisk are one day later than those generally accepted. The reason is that the Act states, with Arkansas for example, "from and after July 4." While it was undoubtedly the intention of Congress to create Arkansas as a Territory on July 4, the United States Supreme Court decided that "from and after July 4," for instance, meant "July 5."

Territorial and statehood data compiled by Dr. Carroll Chase and Richard McP. Cabeen.

Domestic Letter Rates

Effective Date	Prepaid	Collect
1845, July 1		
Reduction from 6¢ to 25¢ range on single-sheet letters		
Under 300 miles, per ½ oz.	5¢	5¢
Over 300 miles, per ½ oz.	10¢	10¢
Drop letters	2¢	
1847-1848		
East, to or from Havana (Cuba) per ½ oz.	12½c	12½c
East, to or from Chagres (Panama) per ½ oz.	20c	20c
East, to or from Panama, across Isthmus, per ½ oz.	30c	30c
To or from Astoria (Ore.) or Pacific Coast, per ½ oz.	40c	40c
Along Pacific Coast, per ½ oz.	12½c	12½c
1847, July 1		
Unsealed circulars		
1 oz. or less	3c	
1851, July 1		
Elimination of rates of 1847-1848 listed above		
Up to 3,000 miles, per ½ oz.	3c	5c
Over 3,000 miles, per ½ oz.	6c	10c
Drop letters	1c	
Unsealed circulars		
1 oz. or less up to 500 miles	1c	
Over 500 miles to 1,500 miles	2c	
Over 1,500 miles to 2,500 miles	3c	
Over 2,500 miles to 3,500 miles	4c	
Over 3,500 miles	5c	
1852, September 30		
Unsealed circulars		
3 oz. or less anywhere in U.S.	1c	
Each additional ounce	1c	
(Double charge if collect)		
1855, April 1		
Prepayment made compulsory		
Not over 3,000 miles, per ½ oz.	3c	
Over 3,000 miles, per ½ oz.	10c	
Drop letters	1c	
1863, July 1		
Distance differential eliminated		
All parts of United States, per ½ oz.	3c	

Effective Date	Prepaid
1883, October 1	
Letter rate reduced one-third	
All parts of United States, per ½ oz.	2c
1885, July 1	
Weight increased to 1 oz.	
All parts of United States, per 1 oz.	2c
1896, October 1	
Rural Free Delivery started	
1917, November 2	
War emergency	
All parts of United States, per 1 oz.	3c
1919, July 1	
Restoration of pre-war rate	
All parts of United States, per 1 oz.	2c
1932, July 6	
Rise due to depression	
All parts of United States, per 1 oz.	3c
1958, August 1	
All parts of United States, per 1 oz.	4c
1963, January 7	
All parts of United States, per 1 oz.	5c
1968, January 7	
All parts of United States, per 1 oz.	6c
1971, May 16	
All parts of United States, per 1 oz.	8c
1974, March 2	
All parts of United States, per 1 oz.	10c
1975, December 31	
All parts of United States, 1st oz.	13c
1978, May 29	
All parts of United States, 1st oz.	15c
1981, March 22	
All parts of United States, 1st oz.	18c
1981, November 1	
All parts of United States, 1st oz.	20c
1985, February 17	
All parts of United States, 1st oz.	22c
1988, April 3	
All parts of United States, 1st oz.	25c

Identifier of Definitive Issues — Arranged by Type Numbers

ISSUES OF 1847-75

A1 Benjamin Franklin

Reproduction

5c On the originals the left side of the white shirt frill touches the oval on a level with the top of the "F" of "Five". On the reproductions it touches the oval about on a level with the top of the figure "5".

A2 George Washington

Reproduction

Original

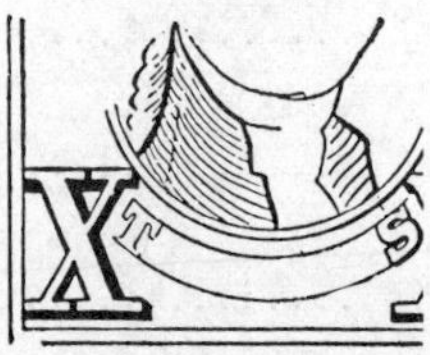
Reproduction

10c On the originals line of coat (A) points to "T" of TEN and (B) it points between "T" and "S" of CENTS.

On the reproductions line of coat (A) points to right tip of "X" and line of coat (B) points to center of "S."

On the reproductions the eyes have a sleepy look, the line of the mouth is straighter, and in the curl of the hair near the left cheek is a strong black dot, while the originals have only a faint one.

Imperforate and Unwatermarked

Design Number		Scott Number
A1	5c red brown	1
A1	5c dark brown	1a
A1	5c orange brown	1b
A1	5c red orange	1c
A1	5c blue (reproduction)	948a
A3	5c red brown (reproduction)	3
A2	10c black	2
A2	10c brown orange (reproduction)	948b
A4	10c black (reproduction)	4

ISSUE OF 1851-75

A5 Franklin

A5

Type I Has a curved line outside the labels with "U. S. Postage" and "One Cent". The scrolls below the lower label are turned under, forming little balls. The scrolls and outer line at top are complete.

A6

Type Ia Same as I at bottom but top ornaments and outer line at top are partly cut away.

Type Ib Same as I but balls below the bottom label are not so clear. The plume-like scrolls at bottom are not complete.

A7

Type II The little balls of the bottom scrolls and the bottoms of the lower plume ornaments are missing. The side ornaments are complete.

A8

Type III The top and bottom curved lines outside the labels are broken in the middle. The side ornaments are complete.

Type IIIa Similar to III with the outer line broken at top or bottom but not both. Type IIIa from Plate IV generally shows signs of plate erasure between the horizontal rows. Those from Plate IE show only a slight break in the line at top or bottom.

A9 Type IV

A20 Type V

Type IV Similar to II, but with the curved lines outside the labels recut at top or bottom or both.

The seven types listed account for most of the varieties of recutting.

Type V Similar to type III of 1851-56 but with side ornaments partly cut away.

A5	1c blue, type I, imperf.	5
A5	1c blue, type Ib, imperf.	5A
A5	1c blue, type I, perf. 15	18
A5	1c bright blue, perf. 12	40
A6	1c blue, type Ia, imperf.	6
A6	1c blue, type Ia, perf. 15	19
A7	1c blue, type II, imperf.	7
A7	1c blue, type II, perf. 15	20
A8	1c blue, type III, imperf.	8
A8	1c blue, type IIIa, imperf.	8A
A8	1c blue, type III, perf. 15	21
A8	1c blue, type IIIa, perf. 15	22
A9	1c blue, type IV, imperf.	9
A9	1c blue, type IV, perf. 15	23
A20	1c blue, type V, perf. 15	24
A20	1c blue, type V, perf. 15, laid paper	24b

A10 Washington, Type I

A10 Type I *There is an outer frame line at top and bottom.*

A21 Type II *The outer line has been removed at top and bottom.*

Type IIa The side frame lines extend only to the top and bottom of the stamp design. All type IIa stamps are from plates X and XI (each exists in 3 states), and these plates produced only type IIa. The side frame lines were recut individually for each stamp, thus being broken between the stamps vertically.

A11 Jefferson, Type I *There are projections on all four sides.*

A22 Type II *The projections at top and bottom are partly cut away. Several minor types could be made according to the extent of cutting of the projections.*

Nos. 40-47 are reprints produced by the Continental Bank Note Co. for the Centennial Exposition of 1876. The stamps are on white paper without gum, perf. 12. They were not good for postal use. They also exist imperforate.

A10 3c orange brown, type I, imperf. **10**
A10 3c dull red, type I, imperf. **11**
A10 3c claret, type I, imperf. **11a**
A10 3c rose, type I, perf. 15 .... **25**
A10 3c scarlet, perf. 12 .... **41**
A21 3c dull red, type II, perf. 15 .... **26**
A21 3c dull red, type IIa, perf. 15 .... **26a**
A11 5c red brown, type I, imperf. **12**
A11 5c brick red, type I, perf. 15 .... **27**
A11 5c red brown, type I, perf. 15 .... **28**
A11 5c Indian red, type I, perf. 15 .... **28A**
A11 5c brown, type I, perf. 15 .... **29**
A22 5c orange brown, type II, perf. 15 .... **30**
A22 5c brown, type II, perf. 15 .... **30A**
A22 5c orange brown, type II, perf. 12 .... **42**

A12 Washington, Type I

A16 Washington

A12 Type I *The shells at the lower corners are practically complete. The outer line below the label is very nearly complete. The outer lines are broken above the middle of the top label and the "X" in each upper corner.*

A13 Type II *The design is complete at the top. The outer line at the bottom is broken in the middle. The shells are partly cut away.*

A14 Type III *The outer lines are broken above the top label and the "X" numerals. The outer line at the bottom and the shells are partly cut away as in Type II.*

A15 Type IV *The outer lines have been recut at top or bottom or both.*

A23 Type V *The side ornaments are slightly cut away. Usually only one pearl remains at each end of the lower label but some copies show two or three pearls at the right side. At the bottom, the outer line is complete and the shells nearly so. The outer lines at top are complete except over the right "X".*

A12 10c green, type I, imperf. **13**
A12 10c green, type I, perf. 15 .... **31**
A12 10c blue green, perf. 12 .... **43**
A13 10c green, type II, imperf. **14**
A13 10c green, type II, perf. 15 .... **32**
A14 10c green, type III, imperf. **15**
A14 10c green, type III, perf. 15 .... **33**
A15 10c green, type IV, imperf. **16**
A15 10c green, type IV, perf. 15 .... **34**
A23 10c green, type V, perf. 15 .... **35**
A16 12c black, imperf. **17**
A16 12c black, plate I, perf. 15 .... **36**
A16 12c black, plate III **36b**
A16 12c greenish black, perf. 12 .... **44**

A17 Washington

A18 Franklin

A19 Washington

A17 24c gray lilac, perf. 15 .... **37**
A17 24c gray, perf. 15 .... **37a**
A17 24c red lilac, perf. 15 .... **37b**
A17 24c gray lilac, imperf. **37c**
A17 24c blackish violet, perf. 12 .... **45**
A18 30c orange, perf. 15 .... **38**
A18 30c orange, imperf. **38a**
A18 30c yellow orange, perf. 12 .... **46**
A19 90c blue, perf. 15 .... **39**
A19 90c blue, imperf. **39a**
A19 90c deep blue, perf. 12 .... **47**

ISSUES OF 1861-75

This series is divided into three groups known as "First Designs," "Second Designs" and "Grills." The first issue is printed on thin, semi-transparent paper; the paper used for the second and grilled issues is usually thicker and opaque.

A24a

A24 Franklin

A24 *A dash has been added under the tip of the ornament at right of the numeral in upper left corner.*

A24a 1c indigo, thin paper, perf. 12 .... **55**
A24 1c blue, perf. 12 .... **63**
A24 1c ultramarine, perf. 12 .... **63a**
A24 1c dark blue, perf. 12 .... **63b**
A24 1c blue, same, laid paper **63c**
A24 1c blue, grill 11x14 mm **85A**
A24 1c blue, grill 11x13 mm **86**
A24 1c dull blue, same **86a**
A24 1c blue, grill 9x13 mm **92**
A24 1c pale blue, same **92a**
A24 1c blue, no grill, hard white paper ... **102**

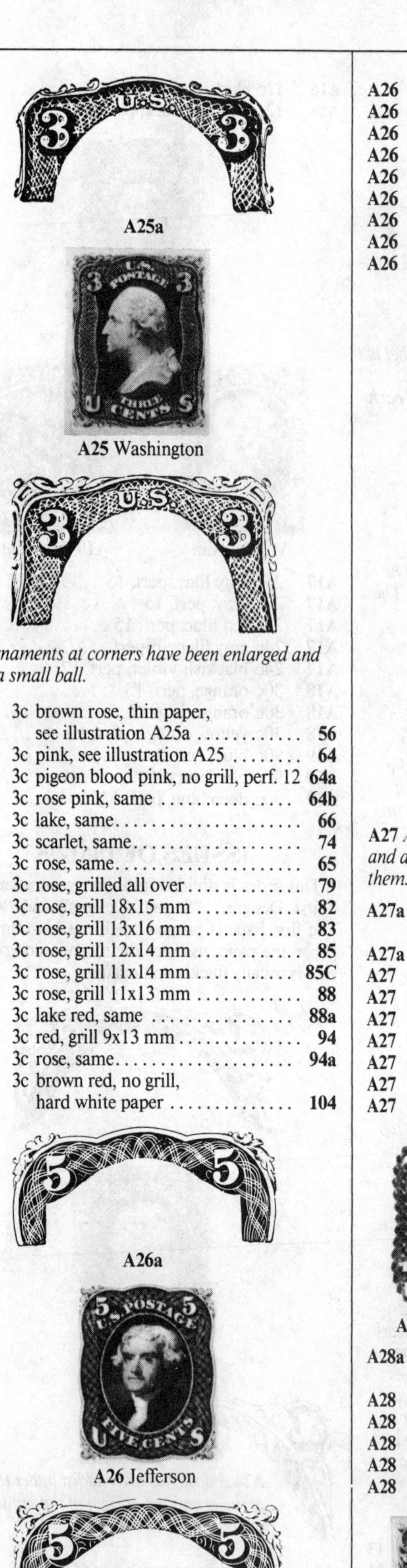

A25a

A25 Washington

A25 *Ornaments at corners have been enlarged and end in a small ball.*

A25a	3c brown rose, thin paper, see illustration A25a	**56**
A25	3c pink, see illustration A25	**64**
A25	3c pigeon blood pink, no grill, perf. 12	**64a**
A25	3c rose pink, same	**64b**
A25	3c lake, same	**66**
A25	3c scarlet, same	**74**
A25	3c rose, same	**65**
A25	3c rose, grilled all over	**79**
A25	3c rose, grill 18x15 mm	**82**
A25	3c rose, grill 13x16 mm	**83**
A25	3c rose, grill 12x14 mm	**85**
A25	3c rose, grill 11x14 mm	**85C**
A25	3c rose, grill 11x13 mm	**88**
A25	3c lake red, same	**88a**
A25	3c red, grill 9x13 mm	**94**
A25	3c rose, same	**94a**
A25	3c brown red, no grill, hard white paper	**104**

A26a

A26 Jefferson

A26 *A leaflet has been added to the foliated ornaments at each corner.*

A26a	5c brown, thin paper, see illustration A26a	**57**
A26	5c buff, see illustration A26	**67**
A26	5c brown yellow, no grill	**67a**
A26	5c olive yellow, no grill	**67b**
A26	5c red brown, no grill	**75**
A26	5c brown, no grill	**76**
A26	5c dark brown, no grill	**76a**
A26	5c brown, laid paper	**76b**
A26	5c brown, grilled all over	**80**
A26	5c dark brown, same	**80a**
A26	5c brown, grill 9x13 mm	**95**
A26	5c black brown, same	**95a**
A26	5c brown, no grill, hard white paper	**105**

A27a

A27 Washington

A27 *A heavy curved line has been cut below the stars and an outer line added to the ornaments above them.*

A27a	10c dark green, thin paper, see illustration A27a	**58**
A27a	Same used	**62B**
A27	10c yellow green, see illustration A27	**68**
A27	10c dark green, same	**68a**
A27	10c green, grill 11x14 mm	**85D**
A27	10c green, grill 11x13 mm	**89**
A27	10c yellow green, grill 9x13 mm	**96**
A27	10c dark green, same	**96a**
A27	10c green, no grill, hard white paper	**106**

A28a Washington

A28 Washington

A28a	12c black, thin paper, see illustration A28a	**59**
A28	12c black, see illustration A28	**69**
A28	12c black, grill 11x14 mm	**85E**
A28	12c black, grill 11x13 mm	**90**
A28	12c black, grill 9x13 mm	**97**
A28	12c black, hard white paper, no grill	**107**

A29 Washington

A30 Franklin

A29	24c dark violet, thin paper, no grill	**60**
A29	24c violet, same	**70c**
A29	24c grayish lilac, same	**70d**
A29	24c red lilac, no grill	**70**
A29	24c brown lilac, no grill	**70a**
A29	24c steel blue, no grill	**70b**
A29	24c lilac, no grill	**78**
A29	24c grayish lilac, no grill	**78a**
A29	24c gray, no grill	**78b**
A29	24c blackish violet, no grill	**78c**
A29	24c gray lilac, grill 9x13 mm	**99**
A29	24c deep violet, hard white paper, no grill	**109**
A30	30c red orange, thin paper, no grill	**61**
A30	30c orange, no grill	**71**
A30	30c orange, grilled all over	**81**
A30	30c orange, grill 9x13 mm	**100**
A30	30c brownish orange, hard white paper, no grill	**110**

A31a

A31 Washington

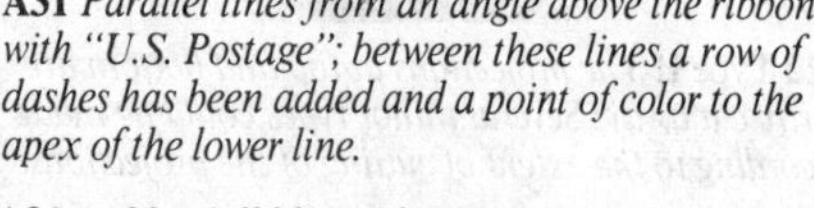

A31 *Parallel lines from an angle above the ribbon with "U.S. Postage"; between these lines a row of dashes has been added and a point of color to the apex of the lower line.*

A31a	90c dull blue, thin paper, see illustration A31a	**62**
A31a	90c dull blue, imperf., pair	**62a**
A31	90c blue, see illustration A31	**72**
A31	90c pale blue, same	**72a**
A31	90c dark blue, same	**72b**
A31	90c blue, grill 9x13 mm	**101**
A31	90c blue, hard white paper, no grill	**111**

ISSUES OF 1861-75

A32 Jackson

A33 Lincoln

Perf. 12, Unwmkd.

A32	2c black, no grill	**73**
A32	2c black, laid paper	**73d**
A32	2c black, grill 12x14 mm	**84**
A32	2c black, grill 11x14 mm	**85B**
A32	2c black, grill 11x13 mm	**87**
A32	2c black, grill 9x13 mm	**93**
A32	2c black, hard white paper, no grill	**103**
A33	15c black, no grill	**77**
A33	15c black, grill 11x14 mm	**85F**
A33	15c black, grill 11x13 mm	**91**
A33	15c black, grill 9x13 mm	**98**
A33	15c black, hard white paper, no grill	**108**

ISSUES OF 1869-80

A34 Franklin

A34	1c buff, grill 9½x9 mm	**112**
A34	1c buff, no grill	**112b**
A34	1c buff, no grill, hard white paper	**123**
A34	1c buff, no grill, soft porous paper	**133**
A34	1c brown orange, same without gum	**133a**

A35 Pony Express

A36 Baldwin 4-4-0 Locomotive, c. 1857

A35	2c brown, grill 9½x9 mm	**113**
A35	2c brown, no grill	**113b**
A35	2c brown, no grill, hard white paper	**124**
A36	3c ultramarine, grill 9½x9 mm	**114**
A36	3c ultramarine, no grill	**114a**
A36	3c blue, no grill, hard white paper	**125**

A37 Washington

A38 Shield and Eagle

A39 S. S. Adriatic

A37	6c ultramarine, grill 9½x9 mm	**115**
A37	6c blue, no grill, hard white paper	**126**
A38	10c yellow, grill 9½x9 mm	**116**
A38	10c yellow, no grill, hard white paper	**127**
A39	12c green, grill 9½x9 mm	**117**
A39	12c green, no grill, hard white paper	**128**

A40 Landing of Columbus

A40 Type I *Picture unframed*

A40a Type II *Picture framed*

Type III same as Type I but without the fringe of brown shading lines around central vignette.

A40	15c brown & blue, type I, grill 9½x9 mm	**118**
A40	15c brown & blue, type I, no grill	**118a**
A40	15c brown & blue, type III, no grill, hard white paper	**129**
A40a	15c brown & blue, type II, grill 9½x9 mm	**119**

A41 The Declaration of Independence

A42 Shield, Eagle and Flags

A43 Lincoln

A41	24c green & violet, grill 9½x9 mm	**120**
A41	24c green & violet, no grill	**120a**
A41	24c green & violet, no grill, hard white paper	**130**
A42	30c blue & carmine, grill 9½x9 mm	**121**
A42	30c blue & carmine, no grill	**121a**
A42	30c blue & carmine, no grill, hard white paper	**131**
A43	90c carmine & black, grill 9½x9 mm	**122**
A43	90c carmine & black, no grill	**122a**
A43	90c carmine & black, no grill, hard white paper	**132**

ISSUES OF 1870-88

The secret mark shown in the detail of A45a is seldom found on the actual stamps. Stamps Nos. 146 and 157 are best identified by color which is red brown for No. 146 and brown for No. 157.

Note I: Special printings of 1880-83 — All denominations of this series were printed on special order from the Post Office Department during the period the stamps were current. The paper being the same as used on the then current issue, the special printings are extremely difficult to identify. The 2c brown, 7c scarlet vermilion, 12c blackish purple and 24c dark violet are easily distinguished by the soft porous paper as these denominations were never previously printed on soft paper. The other denominations can be distinguished by shades only, those of the special printings being slightly deeper and richer than the regular issue. The special printings except No. 211B were issued without gum. The only certain way to identify them is by comparison with stamps previously established as special printings.

A44 Franklin

A44

A44a With secret mark *In the pearl at the left of the numeral "1" there is a small dash.*

A44b Re-engraved *The vertical lines in the upper part of the stamp have been so deepened that the background often appears to be solid. Lines of shading have been added to the upper arabesques.*

A44	1c ultramarine, with grill	**134**
A44	1c ultramarine, no grill	**145**
A44a	1c ultramarine, white wove paper	**156**
A44a	1c ultramarine, with grill	**156e**
A44a	1c ultramarine, hard white paper, without gum	**167**
A44a	1c dark ultra, soft porous paper	**182**
A44a	1c dark ultra, soft porous paper, without gum (See note I)	**192**
A44b	1c gray blue	**206**

A45 Jackson

A45

45a *Under the scroll at the left of "U.S." there is a small diagonal line.*

A45	2c red brown, with grill	**135**
A45	2c red brown, no grill	**146**
A45a	2c brown, white wove paper	**157**
A45a	2c brown, with grill	**157c**
A45a	2c dark brown, hard white paper, without gum	**168**
A45a	2c black brown, soft porous paper, without gum	**193**
A45a	2c vermilion, yellowish paper	**178**
A45a	2c vermilion, imperf.	**178a**
A45a	2c vermilion, with grill	**178c**
A45a	2c vermilion, soft porous paper	**183**
A45a	2c carmine vermilion, hard white paper, without gum	**180**
A45a	2c scarlet vermilion, soft porous paper (See note I)	**203**

A46 Washington

A46

A46a With secret mark *The under part of the tail of the left ribbon is heavily shaded.*

A46b Re-engraved *The shading at the sides of the central oval appears only about one half the previous width. A short horizontal dash has been cut about 1 mm. below the "TS" of "CENTS".*

A46	3c green, with grill	**136**
A46	3c green, no grill	**147**
A46	3c green, imperf., pair	**147c**
A46a	3c green, white wove paper	**158**
A46a	3c blue green, hard white paper, without gum	**169**
A46a	3c green, soft porous paper	**184**
A46a	3c green, same, imperf.	**184a**
A46a	3c blue green, soft porous paper, without gum (See note I)	**194**
A46b	3c blue green, re-engraved	**207**
A46b	3c vermilion	**214**

A47 Lincoln

A47

A47a With secret mark *The first four vertical lines of the shading in the lower part of the left ribbon have been strengthened.*

A47b Re-engraved. *6c on the original stamps four vertical lines can be counted from the edge of the panel to the outside of the stamp. On the re-engraved stamps there are but three lines in the same place.*

A47	6c carmine, with grill	**137**
A47	6c carmine, no grill	**148**
A47a	6c dull pink, no grill, white wove paper	**159**
A47a	6c dull pink, with grill	**159b**
A47a	6c dull rose, hard white paper, without gum	**170**
A47a	6c pink, soft porous paper	**186**
A47a	6c dull rose, soft porous paper, without gum (See note I)	**195**
A47b	6c rose, re-engraved	**208**
A47b	6c brown red	**208a**

A48 Edwin McMasters Stanton **A49** Thomas Jefferson

A48

A48a With secret mark *Two small semi-circles are drawn around the ends of the lines which outline the ball in the lower right hand corner.*

A49

A49a With secret mark *A small semi-circle in the scroll at the right end of the upper label.*

A49b Re-engraved *On the original stamps there are five vertical lines between the left side of the oval and the edge of the shield. There are only four lines on the re-engraved stamps. In the lower part of the re-engraved stamps the horizontal lines of the background have been strengthened.*

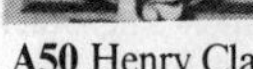

A50 Henry Clay **A50**

A50a With secret mark *The balls of the figure "2" are crescent shaped.*

A48	7c vermilion, with grill	**138**
A48	7c vermilion, no grill	**149**
A48a	7c orange verm., white wove paper	**160**
A48a	7c reddish verm., hard white paper, without gum	**171**
A48a	7c scarlet verm., soft porous paper, without gum	**196**
A49	10c brown, with grill	**139**
A49	10c brown, no grill	**150**
A49	10c brown, soft porous paper	**187**
A49a	10c brown, white wove paper	**161**
A49a	10c brown, with grill	**161c**
A49a	10c pale brown, hard white paper, without gum	**172**
A49a	10c brown, soft porous paper	**188**
A49a	10c deep brown, (See note I)	**197**
A49b	10c brown, re-engraved	**209**
A49b	10c black brown, re-engraved	**209b**
A50	12c dull violet, with grill	**140**
A50	12c dull violet, no grill	**151**
A50a	12c blackish violet, white wove paper.	**162**
A50a	12c blackish violet, with grill	**162a**
A50a	12c dark violet, hard white paper, without gum	**173**
A50a	12c blackish purple, soft porous paper, without gum	**198**

A51 Webster **A51**

A51a With secret mark *In the lower part of the triangle in the upper left corner two lines have been made heavier forming a "V". This mark can be found on some of the Continental and American (1879) printings, but not all stamps show it.*

A51	15c orange, with grill	**141**
A51	15c bright orange, no grill	**152**
A51a	15c yellow orange, white wove paper .	**163**
A51a	15c yellow orange, with grill	**163a**
A51a	15c bright orange, hard white paper, without gum	**174**
A51a	15c red orange, soft porous paper	**189**
A51a	15c orange, (See note I)	**199**

A52 General Winfield Scott

A53 Hamilton **A54** Perry

Secret marks were added to the dies of the 24c, 30c and 90c but new plates were not made from them. The various printings of these stamps can be distinguished only by the shades and paper.

A52	24c purple, with grill	**142**
A52	24c purple, no grill	**153**
A52	24c dull purple, hard white paper, without gum	**175**
A52	24c dark violet, soft porous paper, without gum	**200**
A53	30c black, with grill	**143**
A53	30c black, no grill	**154**
A53	30c full black, soft porous paper	**190**

A53	30c gray black, white wove paper, no grill	165
A53	30c greenish black, white wove paper	165a
A53	30c greenish black, with grill	165c
A53	30c greenish black, hard white paper, without gum	176
A53	30c greenish black, soft porous paper, without gum (See note I)	201
A53	30c orange brown	217
A54	90c carmine, with grill	144
A54	90c carmine, no grill	155
A54	90c carmine, soft porous paper	191
A54	90c rose carmine, white wove paper	166
A54	90c violet carmine, hard white paper, without gum	177
A54	90c dull carmine, soft porous paper, without gum (See note I)	202
A54	90c purple	218

ISSUES OF 1875-88

A55 Taylor

A56 Garfield

Perf. 12, Unwmkd.

A55	5c blue, yellowish wove paper, no grill	179
A55	5c blue, with grill	179c
A55	5c bright blue, hard, white wove paper, without gum	181
A55	5c blue, soft porous paper	185
A55	5c deep blue, soft porous paper, without gum (See note I)	204
A56	5c yellow brown	205
A56	5c gray brown, soft porous paper, without gum (See note I)	205C
A56	5c indigo	216

A57 Washington

A58 Jackson

A57	2c red brown	210
A57	2c pale red brown, soft porous paper, with gum (See note I)	211B
A57	2c green	213
A58	4c blue green	211
A58	4c deep blue green, soft porous paper, without gum (See note I)	211D
A58	4c carmine	215

A59 Franklin

A59	1c ultramarine	212

ISSUES OF 1890-93

A60 Franklin

A61 Washington

A62 Jackson

A63 Lincoln

A64 Grant

A65 Garfield

A66 William T. Sherman

A67 Daniel Webster

A68 Henry Clay

A69 Jefferson

A70 Perry

A60	1c dull blue	219
A61	2c lake	219D
A61	2c carmine	220
A62	3c purple	221
A63	4c dark brown	222
A64	5c chocolate	223
A65	6c brown red	224
A66	8c lilac	225
A67	10c green	226
A68	15c indigo	227
A69	30c black	228
A70	90c orange	229

ISSUES OF 1894 TO 1899

This series, the first to be printed by the Bureau of Engraving and Printing, closely resembles the 1890 series but is identified by the triangles which have been added to the upper corners of the designs.

The Catalogue divides this group into three separate series, the first of which was issued in 1894 and is unwatermarked. In 1895 the paper used was watermarked with the double line letters USPS (United States Postal Service). The stamps show one complete letter of the watermark or parts of two or more letters.

This watermark appears on all United States stamps issued from 1895 until 1910.

In 1898 the colors of some of the denominations were changed, which created the third series noted in the Catalogue.

Other than the watermark, or lack of it, there are three types of the corner triangles used on the 2 cent stamps and two variations of designs are noted on the 10 cent and $1 denomination. In the following list all of these variations are illustrated and described immediately preceding the denominations on which they appear.

Wmkd. USPS **(191) Horizontally**

or USPS **Vertically**

(Actual size of letter)

A87 Franklin

A88 Washington

A89 Jackson

A90 Lincoln

A91 Grant

A92 Garfield

A93 Sherman

A94 Webster

A95 Clay

A96 Jefferson

A97 Perry

A98 James Madison

A99 John Marshall

A87 1c ultramarine, unwmkd. **246**
A87 1c blue, unwmkd. **247**
A87 1c blue, wmkd. **264**
A87 1c deep green, wmkd. **279**
A87 1c on 1c yellow green, "CUBA" **Cuba 221**
A87 1c deep green, "GUAM" **Guam 1**
A87 1c yellow green, "PHILIPPINES" **Phil. 213**
A87 1c yellow green, "PORTO RICO" **P.R. 210**
A87 1c yellow green, "PUERTO RICO" **P.R. 215**

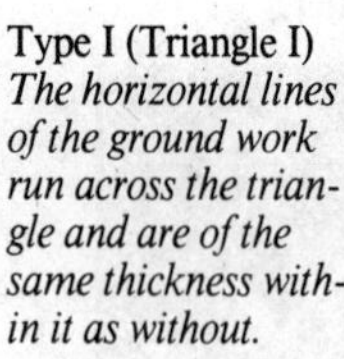
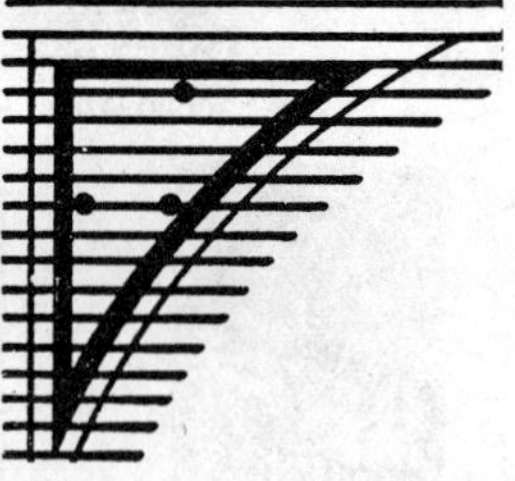

Type I (Triangle I) *The horizontal lines of the ground work run across the triangle and are of the same thickness within it as without.*

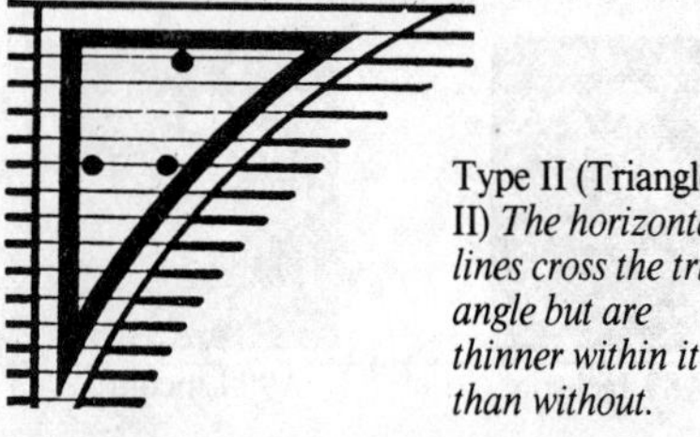

Type II (Triangle II) *The horizontal lines cross the triangle but are thinner within it than without.*

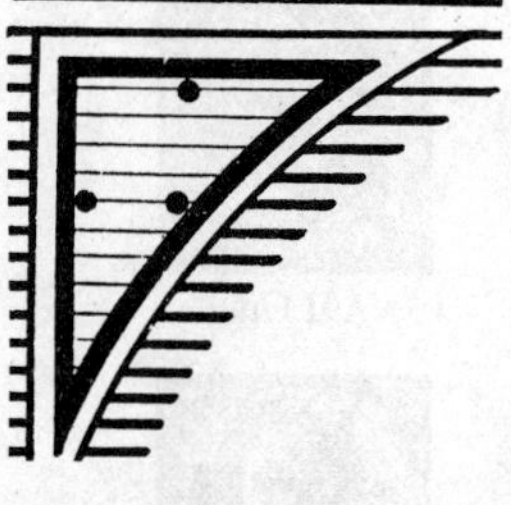

Type III (Triangle III) *The horizontal lines do not cross the double lines of the triangle. The lines within the triangle are thin, as in Type II. Two varieties of Type III are known, but the variations are minor.*

A88 2c pink, type I, unwmkd. **248**
A88 2c carmine lake, type I, unwmkd. **249**
A88 2c carmine, type I, unwmkd. **250**
A88 2c carmine, type I, wmkd. USPS **265**
A88 2c carmine, type II, unwmkd. **251**
A88 2c carmine, type II, wmkd. **266**
A88 2c carmine, type III, unwmkd. **252**
A88 2c carmine, type III, wmkd. **267**
A88 2c red, type III, wmkd. **279B**
A88 2c rose carmine, type III, wmkd. **279c**
A88 2c orange red, type III, wmkd. **279d**
A88 2c booklet pane of 6, wmkd., single stamps with 1 or 2 straight edges **279e**
A88 2c on 2c carmine, type III "CUBA" **Cuba 222**
A88 2½c on 2c red, type III, "CUBA" **Cuba 223**
A88 2c carmine, type III, "GUAM" **Guam 2**
A88 2c orange red, type III, "PHILIPPINES" **Phil. 214**
A88 2c carmine, type III, "PHILIPPINES" **Phil. 214a**
A88 Same, booklet pane of 6 **Phil. 214b**
A88 2c carmine, type III, "PORTO RICO" **P.R. 211**
A88 Same, "PUERTO RICO" **P.R. 216**
A89 3c purple, unwmkd. **253**
A89 3c purple, wmkd. **268**
A89 3c on 3c purple, "CUBA" **Cuba 224**
A89 3c purple, "GUAM" **Guam 3**
A89 3c purple "PHILIPPINES" **Phil. 215**
A90 4c dark brown, unwmkd. **254**
A90 4c dark brown, wmkd. **269**
A90 4c rose brown, wmkd. **280**
A90 4c lilac brown, wmkd. **280a**
A90 4c orange brown, wmkd. **280b**
A90 4c lilac brown, "GUAM" **Guam 4**
A90 4c orange brown, "PHILIPPINES" **Phil. 220**
A91 5c chocolate, unwmkd. **255**
A91 5c chocolate, wmkd. **270**
A91 5c dark blue, wmkd. **281**
A91 5c on 5c blue, "CUBA" **Cuba 225**
A91 5c blue, "GUAM" **Guam 5**
A91 5c blue, "PHILIPPINES" **Phil. 216**
A91 5c blue, "PORTO RICO" **P.R. 212**
A92 6c dull brown, unwmkd. **256**
A92 6c dull brown, wmkd. USPS **271**
A92 6c dull brown, wmkd. USIR **271a**
A92 6c lake, wmkd. USPS **282**
A92 6c purplish lake, wmkd. **282a**
A92 6c lake, "GUAM" **Guam 6**
A92 6c lake, "PHILIPPINES" **Phil. 221**
A93 8c violet brown, unwmkd. **257**
A93 8c violet brown, wmkd. USPS **272**
A93 8c violet brown, wmkd. USIR **272a**
A93 8c violet brown, "GUAM" **Guam 7**
A93 8c violet brown, "PHILIPPINES" **Phil. 222**
A93 8c violet brown, "PORTO RICO" **P.R. 213**

Type I *The tips of the foliate ornaments do not impinge on the white curved line below "ten cents."*

Type II *The tips of the ornaments break the curved line below the "e" of "ten" and the "t" of "cents."*

A94 10c dark green, unwmkd. **258**
A94 10c dark green, wmkd. **273**
A94 10c brown, type I, wmkd. **282C**
A94 10c orange brown, type II, wmkd. **283**
A94 10c on 10c brown, type I, "CUBA" **Cuba 226**
A94 Same, type II, "CUBA" **Cuba 226A**
A94 10c brown, type I, "GUAM" **Guam 8**
A94 10c brown, type II, "GUAM" **Guam 9**
A94 10c brown, type I, "PHILIPPINES" **Phil. 217**
A94 10c orange brown, type II, "PHILIPPINES" **Phil. 217A**
A94 10c brown, type I, "PORTO RICO" **P.R. 214**
A95 15c dark blue, unwmkd. **259**
A95 15c dark blue, wmkd. **274**
A95 15c olive green, wmkd. **284**
A95 15c olive green, "GUAM" **Guam 10**
A95 15c olive green, "PHILIPPINES" **Phil. 218**
A95 15c light olive green, "PHILIPPINES" **Phil. 218a**
A96 50c orange, unwmkd. **260**
A96 50c orange, wmkd. **275**
A96 50c orange, "GUAM" **Guam 11**
A96 50c orange, "PHILIPPINES" **Phil. 219**

A97 Type I *The circles enclosing "$1" are broken where they meet the curved line below "One Dollar."*

A97 Type II *The circles are complete.*

A97 $1 black, type I, unwmkd. **261**
A97 $1 black, type I, wmkd. **276**
A97 $1 black, type II, unwmkd. **261A**
A97 $1 black, type II, wmkd. **276A**
A97 $1 black, type I, "GUAM" **Guam 12**
A97 $1 black, type II, "GUAM" **Guam 13**
A97 $1 black, type I, "PHILIPPINES" **Phil. 223**
A98 $2 bright blue, unwmkd. **262**
A98 $2 bright blue, wmkd. **277**
A98 $2 dark blue, wmkd. **277a**
A98 $2 dark blue, "PHILIPPINES" **Phil. 224**
A99 $5 dark green, unwmkd. **263**
A99 $5 dark green, wmkd. **278**
A99 $5 dark green, "PHILIPPINES" **Phil. 225**

ISSUES OF 1902-17

A115 Franklin

A116 Washington

A117 Jackson

A118 Grant

A119 Lincoln

A120 Garfield

A121 Martha Washington

A122 Daniel Webster

A123 Benjamin Harrison

A124 Henry Clay

A125 Jefferson

A126 David G. Farragut

A127 Madison

A128 Marshall

Unless otherwise noted all stamps are Perf. 12 and Wmkd. (191)

Single stamps from booklet panes show 1 or 2 straight edges.

A115	1c blue green	**300**
A115	1c booklet pane of 6	**300b**
A115	1c blue green, imperf.	**314**
A115	1c blue green, perf. 12 horiz., pair	**316**
A115	1c blue green, perf. 12 vert., pair	**318**
A115	1c blue green, "CANAL ZONE PANAMA"	**C.Z. 4**
A115	1c blue green, "PHILIPPINES"	**Phil. 226**
A116	2c carmine	**301**
A116	2c booklet pane of 6	**301c**
A116	2c carmine, "PHILIPPINES"	**Phil. 227**
A116	2c carmine, same, booklet pane of 6	**Phil. 227a**
A117	3c bright violet	**302**
A117	3c bright violet, "PHILIPPINES"	**Phil. 228**
A118	4c brown	**303**
A118	4c brown, imperf.	**314A**
A118	4c brown, "PHILIPPINES"	**Phil. 229**
A118	4c orange brown, "PHILIPPINES"	**Phil. 229a**
A119	5c blue	**304**
A119	5c blue, imperf.	**315**
A119	5c blue, perf. 12 horiz. pair	**317**
A119	5c blue, "CANAL ZONE PANAMA"	**C.Z. 6**
A119	5c blue, "PHILIPPINES"	**Phil. 230**
A120	6c claret	**305**
A120	6c brownish lake, "PHILIPPINES"	**Phil. 321**
A121	8c violet black	**306**
A121	8c violet black, "CANAL ZONE PANAMA"	**C.Z. 7**
A121	8c violet black, "PHILIPPINES"	**Phil. 232**
A122	10c pale red brown	**307**
A122	10c pale red brown, "CANAL ZONE PANAMA"	**C.Z. 8**
A122	10c pale red brown, "PHILIPPINES"	**Phil. 233**
A122	10c red brown, "PHILIPPINES"	**Phil. 233a**
A123	13c purple black	**308**
A123	13c purple black, "PHILIPPINES"	**Phil. 234**
A124	15c olive green	**309**
A124	15c olive green, "PHILIPPINES"	**Phil. 235**
A125	50c orange	**310**
A125	50c orange, "PHILIPPINES"	**Phil. 236**
A126	$1 black	**311**
A126	$1 black, "PHILIPPINES"	**Phil. 237**
A127	$2 dark blue	**312**
A127	$2 dark blue, unwmkd., perf. 10	**479**
A127	$2 dark blue, "PHILIPPINES"	**Phil. 238**
A128	$5 dark green	**313**
A128	$5 light green, unwmkd., perf. 10	**480**
A128	$5 dark green, "PHILIPPINES"	**Phil. 239**

ISSUES OF 1903

A129 Washington

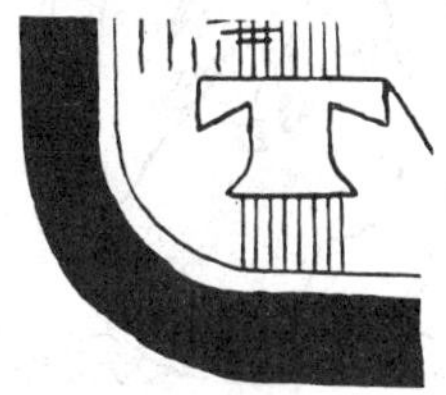

Die I

Die II

Specialists recognize over a hundred shades of this stamp in various hues of vermilion, red, carmine and lake. The Scott Catalogue lists only the most striking differences.

The Government coil stamp, No. 322 should not be confused with the scarlet vermilion coil of the International Vending Machine Co., which is perforated 12½ to 13.

A129	2c carmine, wmkd.	**319**
A129	2c lake, die I	**319a**
A129	2c carmine rose, die I	**319b**
A129	2c scarlet, die II	**319c**
A129	2c lake, die II	**319f**
A129	2c various shades, booklet pane of 6, die I	**319g**
A129	Same, die II	**319h**
A129	2c carmine, die II	**319i**
A129	2c carmine, imperf.	**320**
A129	2c lake, imperf.	**320a**
A129	2c scarlet, imperf.	**320b**
A129	2c carmine, perf. 12 horiz.	**321**
A129	2c carmine, perf. 12 vert.	**322**
A129	2c carmine, "CANAL ZONE PANAMA"	**C.Z. 5**
A129	2c scarlet, same	**C.Z. 5a**
A129	2c carmine, "PHILIPPINES"	**Phil. 240**
A129	2c carmine, same, booklet pane of 6	**Phil. 240a**

ISSUES OF 1908-09

This series introduces for the first time the single line watermark USPS. Only a small portion of several letters is often all that can be seen on a single stamp.

A138 Franklin

A139 Washington

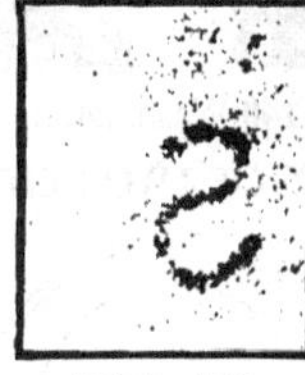

Wmk. 190

A138	1c green, perf. 12, double line wmk.	**331**
A138	1c green, perf. 12, single line wmk.	**374**
A138	1c green, perf. 12, bluish paper	**357**
A138	1c green, imperf., double line wmk.	**343**
A138	1c green, imperf., single line wmk.	**383**
A138	1c green, perf. 12 horiz., double line wmk.	**348**
A138	1c green, perf. 12 horiz., single line wmk.	**385**
A138	1c green, perf. 12 vert., double line wmk.	**352**
A138	1c green, perf. 12 vert., single line wmk.	**387**
A138	1c green, perf. 8½ horiz., single line wmk.	**390**
A138	1c green, perf. 8½ vert., single line wmk.	**392**
A139	2c carmine, perf. 12, double line wmk.	**332**
A139	2c carmine, perf. 12, single line wmk.	**375**
A139	2c carmine, perf. 12, bluish paper	**358**
A139	2c carmine, perf. 11, double line wmk.	**519**
A139	2c carmine, imperf., double line wmk.	**344**
A139	2c carmine, imperf., single line wmk.	**384**
A139	2c carmine, perf. 12 horiz., double line wmk.	**349**
A139	2c carmine, perf. 12 horiz., single line wmk.	**386**
A139	2c carmine, perf. 12 vert., double line wmk.	**353**
A139	2c carmine, perf. 12 vert., single line wmk.	**388**
A139	2c carmine, perf. 8½ horiz. single line wmk.	**391**
A139	2c carmine, perf. 8½ vert., single line wmk.	**393**

Single stamps from booklet panes show 1 or 2 straight edges.

A138	1c green, booklet pane of 6	**331a**
A138	1c green, booklet pane of 6	**374a**
A139	2c carmine, booklet pane of 6	**332a**
A139	2c carmine, booklet pane of 6	**375a**

ISSUES OF 1908-21

FLAT BED AND ROTARY PRESS STAMPS

The Rotary Press Stamps are printed from plates that are curved to fit around a cylinder. This curvature produces stamps that are slightly larger, either horizontally or vertically, than those printed from flat plates. Designs of stamps from flat plates measure about 18½-19 mm. wide by 22 mm. high. When the impressions are placed sidewise on the curved plates the designs are 19½-20 mm. wide; when they are placed vertically the designs are 22½ to 23 mm. high. A line of color (not a guide line) shows where the curved plates meet or join on the press.

Rotary Press Coil Stamps were printed from plates of 170 subjects for stamps coiled sidewise, and from plates of 150 subjects for stamps coiled endwise.

A140 Washington

TYPES OF TWO CENTS

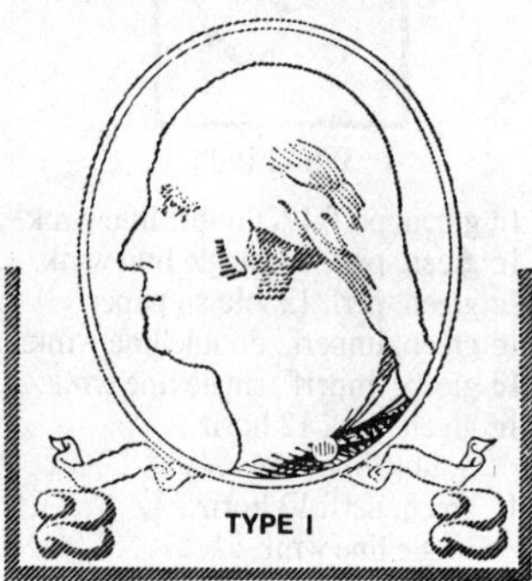

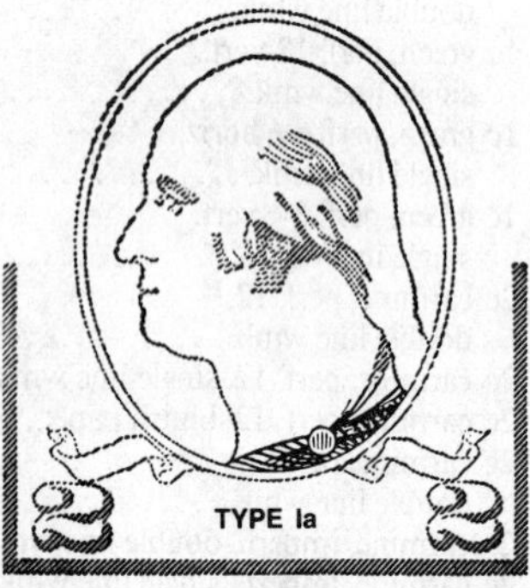

Type Ia *The design characteristics are similar to type I except that all of the lines of the design are stronger.*

The toga button, toga rope and rope shading lines are heavy.

The latter characteristics are those of type II, which, however, occur only on impressions from rotary plates.

Used only on flat plates 10208 and 10209.

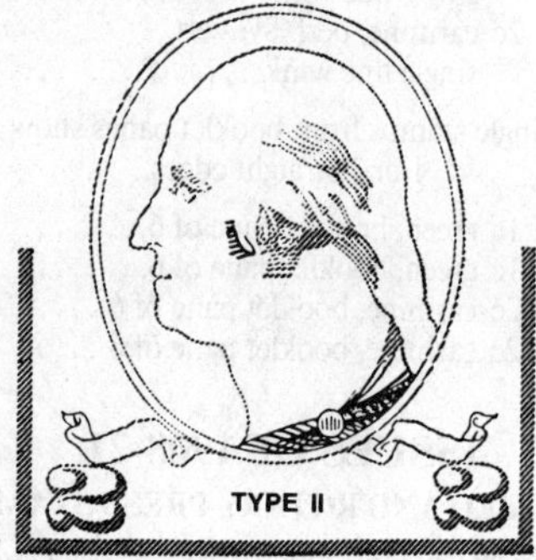

Type II *Shading lines in ribbons as on type I.*

The toga button, rope and rope shading lines are heavy.

The shading lines of the face at the lock of hair ends in a strong vertical curved line.

Used on rotary press printings only.

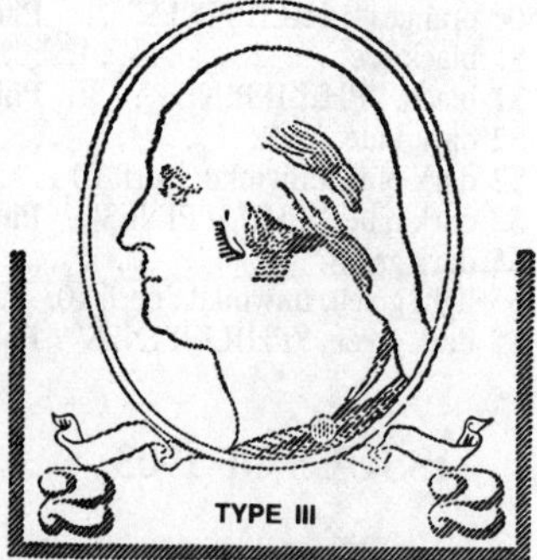

Type III *Two lines of shading in the curves of the ribbons.*

Other characteristics similar to type II.

Used on rotary press printings only.

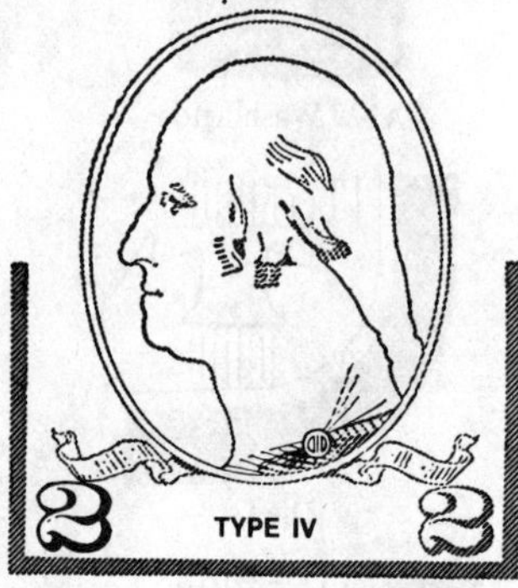

Type IV *Top line of the toga rope is broken.*

The shading lines in the toga button are so arranged that the curving of the first and last form "ΊID".

The line of color in the left "2" is very thin and usually broken. Used on offset printings only.

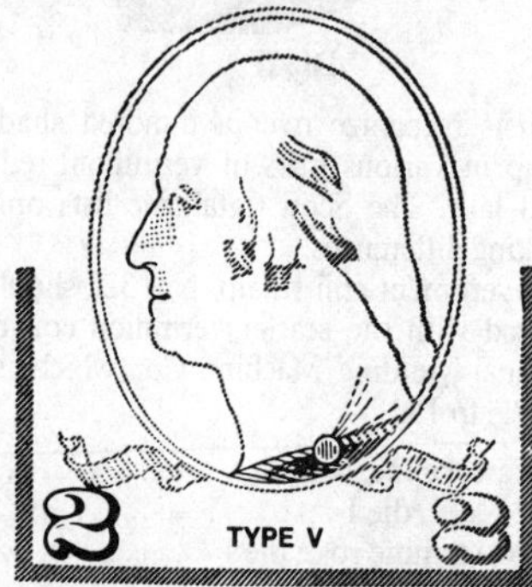

Type V *Top line of the toga is complete.*

There are five vertical shading lines in the toga button.

The line of color is the left "2" is very thin and usually broken.

The shading dots on the nose are as shown on the diagram.

Used on offset printings only.

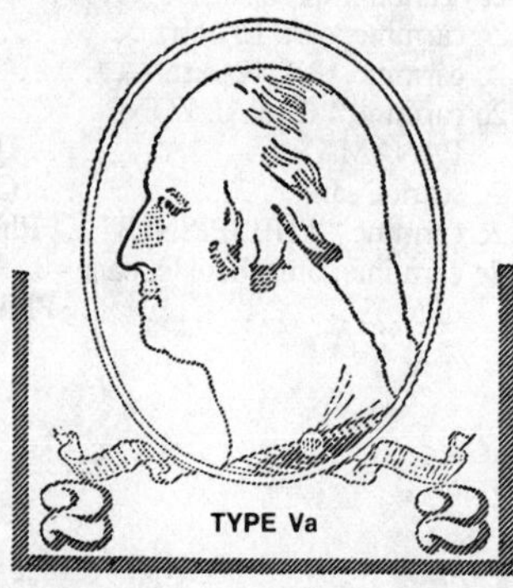

Type Va *Characteristics are the same as type V except in the shading dots of the nose. The third row of dots from the bottom has four dots instead of six. The overall height is ⅓ mm. shorter than type V.*

Used on offset printings only.

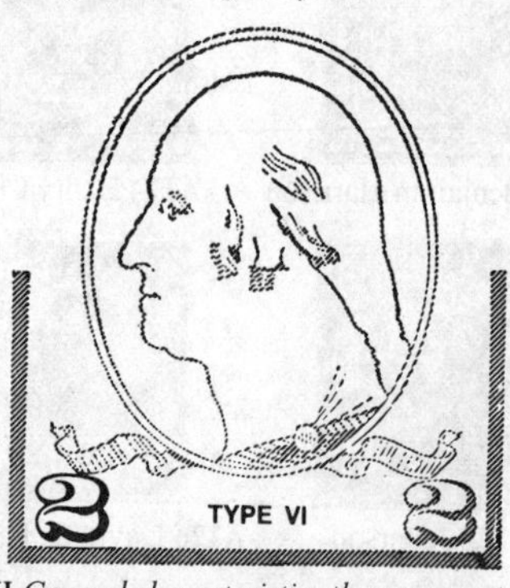

Type VI *General characteristics the same as type V except that the line of color in the left "2" is very heavy. Used on offset printings only.*

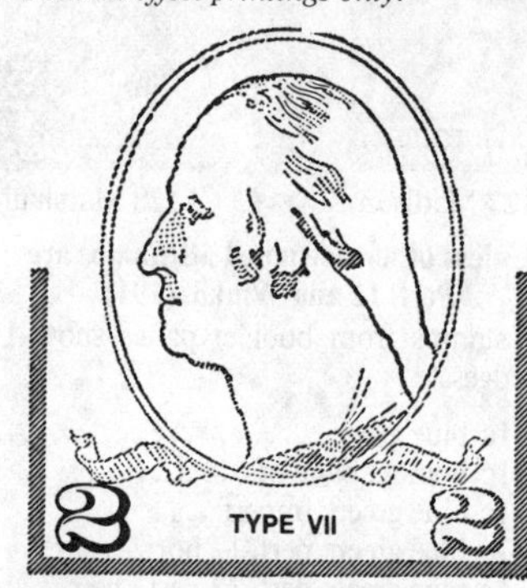

Type VII *The line of color in the left "2" is invariably continuous, clearly defined and heavier than in type V or Va but not as heavy as type VI.*

An additional vertical row of dots has been added to the upper lip.

Numerous additional dots have been added to the hair on top of the head.

Used on offset printings only.

1c A138 Portrait of Franklin, value in words.
1c A140 Portrait of Washington, value in numerals.
2c A139 Portrait of Washington, value in words.
2c A140 Portrait of Washington, value in numerals.

A140	1c green, perf. 12, single line wmk. . .	**405**
A140	1c green, same, booklet pane of 6 . .	**405b**
A140	1c green, perf. 11, flat plate, unwmkd.	**498**
A140	1c green, same, booklet pane of 6 . . .	**498e**
A140	1c green, same, booklet pane of 30 . .	**498f**
A140	1c green, perf. 11, rotary press measuring 19mm.x22½mm., unwmkd..	**544**
A140	1c green, same, measuring 19½ to 20mmx22mm	**545**
A140	1c gray green, perf. 11, offset, unwmkd..	**525**
A140	1c dark green, same	**525a**
A140	1c gray green, perf. 12½	**536**
A140	1c green, perf. 11x10.	**538**
A140	1c green, perf. 10x11.	**542**
A140	1c green, perf. 10, single line wmk. . .	**424**
A140	1c green, same, perf. 12x10	**424a**
A140	1c green, same, perf. 10x12	**424b**
A140	1c green, same, booklet pane of 6 . .	**424d**
A140	1c green, perf. 10, flat plate, unwmkd.	**462**
A140	1c green, same, booklet pane of 6 . .	**462a**
A140	1c green, perf. 10, rotary press, unwmkd..	**543**
A140	1c green, imperf., single line wmk. . .	**408**
A140	1c green, imperf., unwmkd.	**481**
A140	1c green, imperf., offset	**531**
A140	1c green, perf. 10 horiz., flat plate, single line wmk.	**441**
A140	1c green, same, rotary press	**448**

A140 1c green, perf. 10 horiz., rotary press, unwmkd.. 486

A140 1c green, perf. 10 vert., flat plate, single line wmk. 443

A140 1c green, same, rotary press 452

A140 1c green, perf. 10 vert., rotary press, unwmkd.. 490

A140 1c green, perf. 8½ horiz. single line wmk. 410

A140 1c green, perf. 8½ vert., same 412

A140 2c carmine, perf. 12, type I, single line wmk. 406

A140 2c carmine, same, booklet pane of 6 406a

A140 2c pale car. red, perf. 11, single line wmk., type I 461

A140 2c rose, perf. 11, flat plate, unwmkd., type I. 499

A140 2c rose, same, booklet pane of 6 499e

A140 2c rose, same, booklet pane of 30 499f

A140 2c deep rose, perf. 11, unwmkd., type Ia. 500

A140 2c carmine rose, perf. 11, rotary press, unwmkd., type III 546

A140 2c carmine, perf. 11, offset, unwmkd., type IV 526

A140 2c carmine, same, type V 527

A140 2c carmine, same, type Va 528

A140 2c carmine, same, type VI 528A

A140 2c carmine, same, type VII 528B

A140 2c carmine rose, perf. 11x10, type II. 539

A140 2c carmine rose, same, type III 540

A140 2c rose red, perf. 10, single line wmk., type I. 425

A140 2c rose red, perf. 10x12 425c

A140 2c rose red, perf. 12x10, single line wmk., type I 425d

A140 2c rose red, same, perf. 10, booklet pane of 6 425e

A140 2c carmine, perf. 10, unwmkd., type I 463

A140 2c carmine, same, booklet pane of 6 463a

A140 2c carmine, imperf., flat plate, single line wmk., type I 409

A140 2c carmine, imperf., rotary press, single line wmk., type I 459

A140 2c carmine, imperf., flat plate, unwmkd., type I. 482

A140 2c deep rose, same, type Ia 482A

A140 2c carmine rose, imperf., offset, unwmkd., type IV 532

A140 2c carmine rose, same, type V 533

A140 2c carmine, same, type Va 534

A140 2c carmine, same, type VI 534A

A140 2c carmine, same, type VII 534B

A140 2c carmine rose, perf. 10 horiz., flat plate, single line wmk., type I 442

A140 2c red, same, rotary press 449

A140 2c carmine, same, type III 450

A140 2c carmine, perf. 10 horiz., rotary press unwmkd., type II 487

A140 2c carmine, same, type III 488

A140 2c carmine, perf. 10 vert., flat plate, single line wmk., type I 444

A140 2c carmine rose, same, rotary press.. 453

A140 2c red, same, type II 454

A140 2c carmine, same, type III 455

A140 2c carmine, perf. 10 vert., rotary press, unwmkd., type II 491

A140 2c carmine, same, type III 492

A140 2c carmine, perf. 8½ horiz., type I 411

A140 2c carmine, perf. 8½ vert., type I 413

A140 3c deep violet, perf. 12, double line wmk., type I 333

A140 3c deep violet, perf. 12, single line wmk., type I 376

A140 3c deep violet, perf. 12, bluish paper, type I. 359

A140 3c light violet, perf. 11, unwmkd., type I. 501

A140 3c light violet, same, booklet pane of 6 501b

A140 3c dark violet, perf. 11, unwmkd., type II 502

A140 3c dark violet, same, booklet pane of 6 502b

A140 3c violet, perf. 11, offset, type III 529

A140 3c purple, same, type IV 530

A140 3c violet, perf. 11x10, type II 541

A140 3c deep violet, perf. 10, single line wmk., type I 426

A140 3c violet, perf. 10, unwmkd., type I.. 464

A140 3c deep violet, imperf., double line wmk., type I 345

A140 3c violet, imperf., unwmkd., type I.. 483

TYPES OF THREE CENTS

Type I *The top line of the toga rope is weak and the rope shading lines are thin. The 5th line from the left is missing. The line between the lips is thin.*

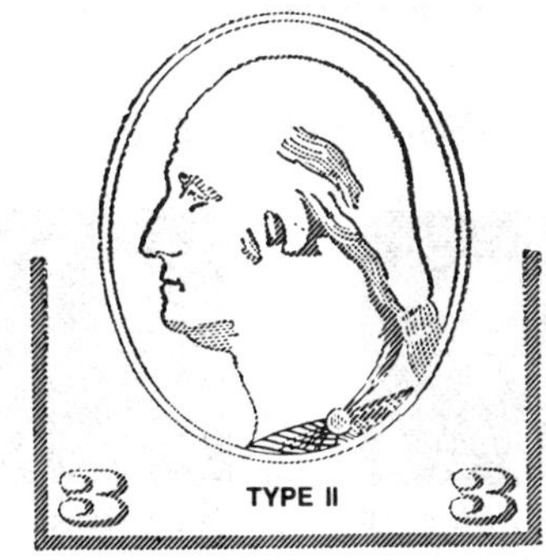

Type II *The top line of the toga rope is strong and the rope shading lines are heavy and complete.*

The line between the lips is heavy.

Used on both flat plate and rotary press printings.

Type III *The top line of the toga rope is strong but the 5th shading line is missing as in type I.*

Center shading line of the toga button consists of two dashes with a central dot.

The "P" and "O" of "POSTAGE" are separated by a line of color.

The frame line at the bottom of the vignette is complete.

Used on offset printings only.

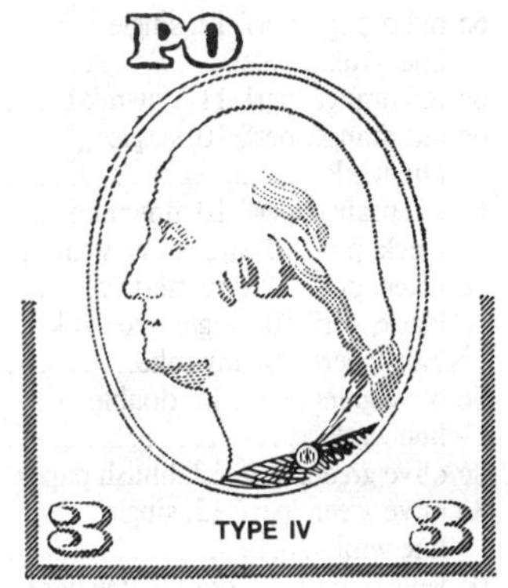

Type IV *The shading lines of the toga rope are complete.*

The second and fourth shading lines in the toga button are broken in the middle and the third line is continuous with a dot in the center.

The "P" and "O" of "POSTAGE" are joined.

The frame line at the bottom of the vignette is broken.

Used on offset printings only.

A140 3c violet, same, type II 484

A140 3c violet, imperf., offset, type IV 535

A140 3c deep violet, perf. 12 vert., single line wmk., type I 389

A140 3c violet, perf. 10 vert., flat plate, single line wmk., type I 445

A140 3c violet, perf. 10 vert., rotary press, single line wmk., type I 456

A140 3c violet, perf. 10 vert., rotary press, unwmkd., type I. 493

A140 3c violet, same, type II 494

A140 3c violet, perf. 10 horiz., type I 489

A140 3c deep violet, perf. 8½ vert., type I. 394

A140 4c orange brown, perf. 12, double line wmk. 334

A140 4c orange brown, perf. 12, bluish paper 360

A140 4c brown, perf. 12, single line wmk. 377

A140 4c brown, perf. 11, unwmkd. 503

A140 4c brown, perf. 10, single line wmk. 427

A140 4c orange brown, perf. 10, unwmkd. 465

A140 4c orange brown, imperf. 346

A140 4c orange brown, perf. 12 horiz. 350

A140 4c orange brown, perf. 12 vert. 354

A140 4c brown, perf. 10 vert., flat plate, single line wmk. 446

A140 4c brown, same, rotary press 457

A140 4c orange brown, perf. 10 vert., rotary press, unwmkd. 495

A140 4c brown, perf. 8½ vert., single line wmk. 395

A140 5c blue, perf. 12, double line wmk. 335

A140 5c blue, perf. 12 bluish paper 361

A140 5c blue, perf. 12, single line wmk. 378

A140 5c blue, perf. 11, unwmkd. 504

A140 5c rose (error), same 505

A140 5c carmine (error), perf. 10, unwmkd. 467

A140 5c blue, perf. 10, single line wmk. 428

A140 5c blue, perf. 12x10 428a

A140 5c blue, perf. 10, unwmkd. 466

A140 5c blue, imperf. 347

A140 5c carmine (error), imperf. 485

A140 5c blue, perf. 12 horiz. 351

A140 5c blue, perf. 12 vert. 355

A140 5c blue, perf. 10 vert., flat plate, single line wmk. 447

A140 5c blue, same, rotary press 458

A140 5c blue, perf. 10 vert., rotary press, unwmkd.. 496

A140 5c blue, perf. 8½ vert. 396

A140 6c red orange, perf. 12, double line wmk. 336

A140 6c red orange, perf. 12, bluish paper. 362

A140 6c red orange, perf. 12, single line wmk. 379
A140 6c red orange, perf. 11, unwmkd. 506
A140 6c red orange, perf. 10, single line wmk. 429
A140 6c red orange, perf. 10, unwmkd. 468
A140 7c black, perf. 12, single line wmk. .. 407
A140 7c black, perf. 11, unwmkd. 507
A140 7c black, perf. 10, single line wmk. .. 430
A140 7c black, perf. 10, unwmkd. 469
A140 8c olive green, perf. 12, double line wmk. 337
A140 8c olive green, perf. 12, bluish paper. 363
A140 8c olive green, perf. 12, single line wmk. 380
A140 10c yellow, perf. 12, double line wmk. 338
A140 10c yellow, perf. 12, bluish paper 364
A140 10c yellow, perf. 12, single line wmk. . 381
A140 10c yellow, perf. 12 vert. 356
A140 13c blue green, perf. 12, double line wmk. 339
A140 13c blue green, perf. 12, bluish paper . 365
A140 15c pale ultra, perf. 12, double line wmk. 340
A140 15c pale ultra, perf. 12, bluish paper .. 366
A140 15c pale ultra, perf. 12, single line wmk. 382
A140 50c violet. 341
A140 $1 violet brown 342

ISSUES OF 1912-19

A148

A149 Franklin

Designs of 8c to $1 denominations differ only in figures of value.

A148 8c pale olive green, perf. 12, single line wmk. 414
A148 8c olive bister, perf. 11, unwmkd. ... 508
A148 8c pale olive grn., perf. 10, single line wmk. 431
A148 8c olive green, perf. 10, unwmkd. 470
A148 9c salmon red, perf. 12, single line wmk. 415
A148 9c salmon red, perf. 11, unwmkd. ... 509
A148 9c salmon red, perf. 10, single line wmk. 432
A148 9c salmon red, perf. 10, unwmkd. 471
A148 10c orange yellow, perf. 12, single line wmk. 416
A148 10c orange yellow, perf. 11, unwmkd.. 510
A148 10c orange yellow, perf. 10, single line wmk. 433
A148 10c orange yellow, perf. 10, unwmkd.. 472
A148 10c orange yellow, perf. 10 vert., same 497
A148 11c light green, perf. 11, unwmkd. 511
A148 11c dark green, perf. 10, single line wmk. 434
A148 11c dark green, perf. 10, unwmkd. ... 473
A148 12c claret brown, perf. 12, single line wmk. 417
A148 12c claret brown, perf. 11, unwmkd... 512
A148 12c brown carmine, same 512a
A148 12c claret brown, perf. 10, single line wmk. 435
A148 12c copper red, same 435a
A148 12c claret brown, perf. 10, unwmkd... 474
A148 13c apple green, perf. 11, unwmkd. ... 513
A148 15c gray, perf. 12, single line wmk. ... 418
A148 15c gray, perf. 11, unwmkd. 514
A148 15c gray, perf. 10, single line wmk. ... 437
A148 15c gray, perf. 10, unwmkd. 475
A148 20c ultramarine, perf. 12, single line wmk. 419
A148 20c light ultra., perf. 11, unwmkd..... 515
A148 20c ultramarine, perf. 10, single line wmk. 438
A148 20c light ultra, perf. 10, unwmkd. 476
A148 30c orange red, perf. 12, single line wmk. 420
A148 30c orange red, perf. 11, unwmkd. ... 516
A148 30c orange red, perf. 10, single line wmk. 439
A148 30c orange red, perf. 10, unwmkd. .. 476A
A148 50c violet, perf. 12, single line wmk... 421
A148 50c violet, perf. 12, double line wmk. . 422
A148 50c red violet, perf. 11, unwmkd. 517
A148 50c violet, perf. 10, single line wmk... 440
A148 50c light violet, perf. 10, unwmkd. ... 477
A148 $1 violet brown, perf. 12, double line wmk. 423
A148 $1 violet brown, perf. 11, unwmkd... 518
A148 $1 deep brown, same 518b
A148 $1 violet black, perf. 10, double line wmk. 460
A148 $1 violet black, perf. 10, unwmkd... 478

ISSUES OF 1918-20

Perf. 11 Unwmkd.

A149 $2 org. red & blk. 523
A149 $2 car. & blk. 547
A149 $5 dp. grn. & blk. 524

ISSUES OF 1922-32

A154 Nathan Hale

A155 Franklin

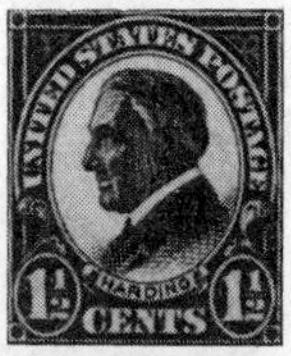

A156 Warren G. Harding

A157 Washington

A158 Lincoln

A159 Martha Washington

A160 Theodore Roosevelt

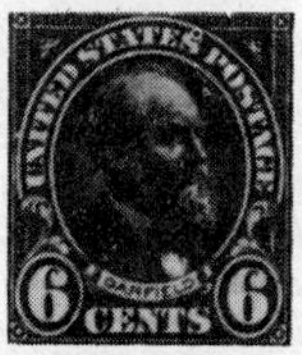

A161 Garfield

A162 McKinley

A163 Grant

A164 Jefferson

A165 Monroe

A166 Hayes

A167 Cleveland

A168 American Indian

A169 Statue of Liberty

A170 Golden Gate

A171 Niagara Falls

A172 Buffalo

A173 Arlington Amphitheater and Tomb of the Unknown Soldier

A174 Lincoln Memorial

A175 United States Capitol

A176 "America"

Unwmkd.

A154 ½c olive brown, perf. 11 551
A154 ½c olive brown, perf. 11x10½. 653
A154 ½c olive brown, "CANAL ZONE" C.Z. 70
A155 1c deep green, perf. 11, flat plate 552

Design	Description	No.
A155	1c deep green, booklet pane of 6	552a
A155	1c green, perf. 11, rotary press 19¾x2¼mm	594
A155	1c green, same, 19¼x22¾mm (used)	596
A155	1c green, perf. 11x10, rotary press	578
A155	1c green, perf. 10	581
A155	1c green, perf. 11x10½	632
A155	1c green, booklet pane of 6	632a
A155	1c green, overprt. Kans.	658
A155	1c green, overprt. Nebr.	669
A155	1c green, imperf.	575
A155	1c green, perf. 10 vert.	597
A155	1c yellow green, perf. 10 horiz.	604
A155	1c deep green, "CANAL ZONE" type A	C.Z. 71
A55	1c deep green, same, booklet pane of 6	C.Z. 71e
A155	1c green, "CANAL ZONE" type B	C.Z. 100
A156	1½c yellow brown, perf. 11	553
A156	1½c yellow brown, perf. 11x10½	633
A156	1½c brown, overpt. Kans.	659
A156	1½c brown, overprt. Nebr.	670
A156	1½c brown, perf. 10	582
A156	1½c brown, perf. 10 vert.	598
A156	1½c yellow brown, perf. 10 horiz.	605
A156	1½c yellow brown, imperf., flat plate	576
A156	1½c yellow brown, imperf., rotary press	631
A156	1½c yellow brown "CANAL ZONE"	C.Z. 72

No heavy hair lines at top center of head. Outline of left acanthus scroll generally faint at top and toward base at left side.

Type I

Three heavy hair lines at top center of head; two being outstanding in the white area. Outline of left acanthus scroll very strong and clearly defined at top (under left edge of lettered panel) and at lower curve (above and to left of numeral oval).

Type II

Design	Description	No.
A157	2c carmine, perf. 11, flat plate	554
A157	2c carmine, same, booklet pane of 6	554c
A157	2c carmine, perf. 11, rotary press	595
A157	2c carmine, perf. 11x10	579
A157	2c carmine, perf. 11x10½, type I	634
A157	2c carmine, perf. 11x10½, type II	634A
A157	2c carmine lake, same, type I	634b
A157	2c carmine lake, same, booklet pane of 6	634d
A157	2c carmine, overprt. Molly Pitcher	646
A157	2c carmine, overprt. Hawaii 1778-1928	647
A157	2c carmine, overprt. Kans.	660
A157	2c carmine, overprt. Nebr.	671
A157	2c carmine, perf. 10	583
A157	2c carmine, same, booklet pane of 6	583a
A157	2c carmine, imperf.	577
A157	2c carmine, perf. 10 vert., type I	599
A157	2c carmine, same, type II	599A
A157	2c carmine, perf. 10 horiz.	606
A157	2 carmine, "CANAL ZONE" type A	C.Z. 73
A157	2c carmine, same, booklet pane of 6	C.Z. 73a
A157	2c carmine, "CANAL ZONE" type B, perf. 11	C.Z. 84
A157	2c carmine, same, booklet pane of 6	C.Z. 84d
A157	2c carmine, "CANAL ZONE" type B, perf. 10	C.Z. 97
A157	2c carmine, same, booklet pane of 6	C.Z. 97b
A157	2c carmine, "CANAL ZONE" type B, perf. 11x10½	C.Z. 101
A157	2c carmine, same, booklet pane of 6	C.Z. 101a
A158	3c violet, perf. 11	555
A158	3c violet, perf. 11x10½	635
A158	3c bright violet, same	635a
A158	3c violet, overprt. Kans.	661
A158	3c violet, overprt. Nebr.	672
A158	3c violet, perf. 10	584
A158	3c violet, perf. 10 vert.	600
A158	3c violet, "CANAL ZONE" perf. 11	C.Z. 85
A158	3c violet, "CANAL ZONE" perf. 10	C.Z. 98
A158	3c violet, "CANAL ZONE" perf. 11x10½	C.Z. 102
A159	4c yellow brown, perf. 11	556
A159	4c yellow brown, perf. 11x10½	636
A159	4c yellow brown, overprt. Kans.	662
A159	4c yellow brown, overprt. Nebr.	673
A159	4c yellow brown, perf. 10	585
A159	4c yellow brown, perf. 10 vert.	601
A160	5c dark blue, perf. 11	557
A160	5c dark blue, perf. 11x10½	637
A160	5c dark blue, overprt. Hawaii 1778-1928	648
A160	5c deep blue, overprt. Kans.	663
A160	5c deep blue, overprt. Nebr.	674
A160	5c blue, perf. 10	586
A160	5c dark blue, perf. 10 vert.	602
A160	5c dark blue, "CANAL ZONE" type A, perf. 11	C.Z. 74
A160	5c dark blue, same, type B	C.Z. 86
A160	5c dark blue, same, perf. 11x10½	C.Z. 103
A161	6c red orange, perf. 11	558
A161	6c red orange, perf. 11x10½	638
A161	6c red orange, overprt. Kans.	664
A161	6c red orange, overprt. Nebr.	675
A161	6c red orange, perf. 10	587
A161	6c deep orange, perf. 10 vert.	723
A162	7c black, perf. 11	559
A162	7c black, perf. 11x10½	639
A162	7c black, overprt. Kans.	665
A162	7c black, overprt. Nebr.	676
A162	7c black, perf. 10	588
A163	8c olive green, perf. 11	560
A163	8c olive green, perf. 11x10½	640
A163	8c olive green, overprt. Kans.	666
A163	8c olive green, overprt. Nebr.	677
A163	8c olive green, perf. 10	589
A164	9c rose, perf. 11	561
A164	9c orange red, perf. 11x10½	641
A164	9c light rose, overprt. Kans.	667
A164	9c light rose, overprt. Nebr.	678
A164	9c rose, perf. 10	590
A165	10c orange, perf. 11	562
A165	10c orange, perf. 11x10½	642
A165	10c orange yellow, overprt. Kans.	668
A165	10c orange yellow, overprt. Nebr.	679
A165	10c orange, perf. 10	591
A165	10c orange, perf. 10 vert.	603
A165	10c orange, "CANAL ZONE" type A, perf. 11	C.Z. 75
A165	10c orange, same, type B	C.Z. 87
A165	10c orange, same, perf. 10	C.Z. 99
A165	10c orange, same, perf. 11x10½	C.Z. 104
A166	11c light blue, perf. 11	563
A166	11c light blue, perf. 11x10½	692
A167	12c brown violet, perf. 11	564
A167	12c brown violet, perf. 11x10½	693
A167	12c brown violet, "CANAL ZONE" type A	C.Z. 76
A167	12c brown violet, same, type B	C.Z. 88
A168	14c blue, perf. 11	565
A168	14c dark blue, perf. 11x10½	695
A168	14c dark blue, "CANAL ZONE" type A, perf. 11	C.Z. 77
A168	14c dark blue, same, type B	C.Z. 89
A168	14c dark blue, same, perf. 11x10½	C.Z. 116
A169	15c gray, perf. 11	566
A169	15c gray, perf. 11x10½	696
A169	15c gray, "CANAL ZONE"	C.Z. 90
A170	20c carmine rose, perf. 11	567
A170	20c carmine rose, perf. 10½x11	698
A170	20c carmine rose, "CANAL ZONE"	C.Z. 92
A171	25c yellow green, perf. 11	568
A171	25c blue green, perf. 10½x11	699
A172	30c olive brown, perf. 11	569
A172	30c brown, perf. 10½x11	700
A172	30c olive brown, "CANAL ZONE" type A	C.Z. 79
A172	30c olive brown, "CANAL ZONE" type B	C.Z. 93
A173	50c lilac, perf. 11	570
A173	50c lilac, perf. 10½x11	701
A173	50c lilac, "CANAL ZONE" type A	C.Z. 80
A173	50c lilac, "CANAL ZONE" type B	C.Z. 94
A174	$1 violet black, perf. 11	571
A174	$1 violet brown, "CANAL ZONE" type A	C.Z. 81
A174	$1 violet brown, "CANAL ZONE" type B	C.Z. 95
A175	$2 deep blue, perf. 11	572
A176	$5 car. & blue, perf. 11	573

REGULAR ISSUES OF 1925-26, 1930 and 1932

A186 Harrison **A187** Wilson

Design	Description	No.
A186	13c green, perf. 11	622
A186	13c yellow green, perf. 11x10½	694
A187	17c black, perf. 11	623
A187	17c black, perf. 10½x11	697
A187	17c black, "CANAL ZONE"	C.Z. 91

A203 Harding **A204** Taft

Design	Description	No.
A203	1½c brown, perf. 11x10½	684
A203	1½c brown, perf. 10 vert.	686

A204 4c brown, perf. 11x10½ **685**
A204 4c brown, perf. 10 vert. **687**

A226 Washington

A226 3c deep violet, perf. 11x10½ **720**
A226 3c deep violet, booklet pane of 6 ... **720b**
A226 3c deep violet, perf. 10 vert. **721**
A226 3c deep violet, perf. 10 horiz. **722**
A226 3c deep violet, "CANAL ZONE" .... **C.Z. 115**

PRESIDENTIAL ISSUE OF 1938

A275 Benjamin Franklin **A276** George Washington

A277 Martha Washington **A278** John Adams

A279 Thomas Jefferson **A280** James Madison

A281 The White House **A282** James Monroe

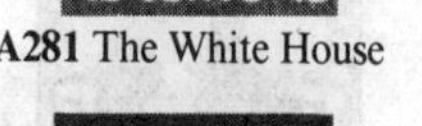

A283 John Quincy Adams **A284** Andrew Jackson

A285 Martin Van Buren **A286** William H. Harrison

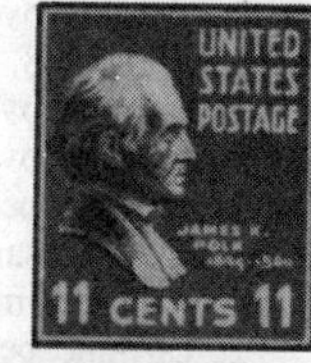

A287 John Tyler **A288** James K. Polk

A289 Zachary Taylor **A290** Millard Fillmore

A291 Franklin Pierce **A292** James Buchanan

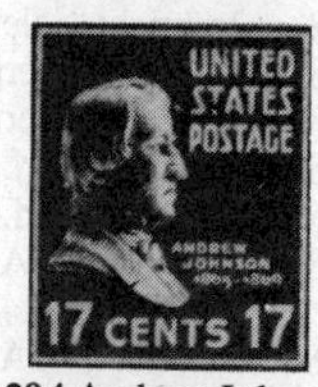

A293 Abraham Lincoln **A294** Andrew Johnson

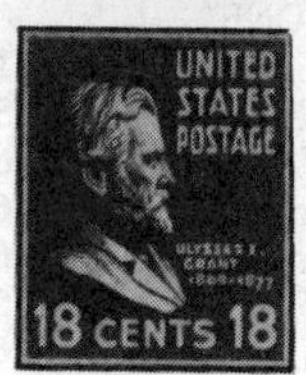

A295 Ulysses S. Grant **A296** Rutherford B. Hayes

A297 James A. Garfield **A298** Chester A. Arthur

A299 Grover Cleveland **A300** Benjamin Harrison

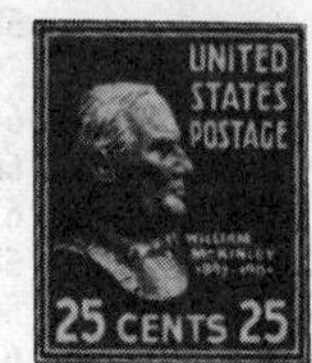

A301 William McKinley **A302** Theodore Roosevelt

A303 William Howard Taft **A304** Woodrow Wilson

A305 Warren G. Harding **A306** Calvin Coolidge

Rotary Press Printing
Unwmkd.

A275 ½c deep orange, perf. 11x10½....... **803**
A275 ½c red orange, "CANAL ZONE" **C.Z. 118**
A276 1c green, perf. 11x10½............ **804**
A276 1c green, booklet pane of 6.......... **804b**
A276 1c green, perf. 10 vert.............. **839**
A276 1c green, perf. 10 horiz. **848**
A277 1½c bister brown, perf. 11x10½....... **805**
A277 1½c bister brown, perf. 10 vert. **840**
A277 1½c bister brown, perf. 10 horiz. **849**
A277 1½c bister brown, "CANAL ZONE" .... **C.Z. 119**
A278 2c rose carmine, perf. 11x10½...... **806**
A278 2c booklet pane of 6 .... **806b**
A278 2c rose carmine, perf. 10 vert. **841**
A278 2c rose carmine, perf. 10 horiz. **850**
A279 3c deep violet, perf. 11x10½ **807**
A279 3c deep violet, booklet pane of 6... **807a**
A279 3c deep violet, perf. 10 vert......... **842**
A279 3c deep violet, perf. 10 horiz......... **851**
A280 4c red violet, perf. 11x10½......... **808**
A280 4c red violet, perf. 10 vert........... **843**
A281 4½c dark gray, perf. 11x10½........ **809**
A281 4½c dark gray, perf. 10 vert.......... **844**
A282 5c bright blue, perf. 11x10½........ **810**
A282 5c bright blue, perf. 10 vert......... **845**
A283 6c red orange, perf. 11x10½ **811**
A283 6c red orange, perf. 10 vert.......... **846**
A284 7c sepia, perf. 11x10½ **812**
A285 8c olive green, perf. 11x10½ **813**
A286 9c rose pink, perf. 11x10½ **814**
A287 10c brown red, perf. 11x10½ **815**
A287 10c brown red, perf. 10 vert. **847**
A288 11c ultramarine, perf. 11x10½........ **816**
A289 12c bright violet, perf. 11x10½ **817**
A290 13c blue green, perf. 11x10½ **818**
A291 14c blue, perf. 11x10½ **819**
A292 15c blue gray, perf. 11x10½ **820**
A293 16c black, perf. 11x10½ **821**
A294 17c rose red, perf. 11x10½ **822**
A295 18c brn. carmine, perf. 11x10½ **823**
A296 19c bright violet, perf. 11x10½ **824**
A297 20c bright blue green, perf. 11x10½. . **825**
A298 21c dull blue, perf. 11x10½ **826**
A299 22c vermilion, perf. 11x10½ **827**
A300 24c gray black, perf. 11x10½ **828**
A301 25c dp. red lilac, perf. 11x10½....... **829**
A302 30c deep ultra, perf. 11x10½ **830**
A303 50c lt. red violet, perf. 11x10½ **831**

Flat Plate Printing
Perf. 11

A304 $1 pur. & blk., unwmkd. **832**
A304 $1 pur. & blk., wmkd. USIR **832b**
A304 $1 red vio. & blk., thick white paper, smooth colorless gum **832c**
A305 $2 yel. grn. & blk. **833**
A306 $5 car. & blk.................... **834**

LIBERTY ISSUE 1954-73

A477 Benjamin Franklin

A478 George Washington

A478a Palace of the Governors, Santa Fe

A479 Mount Vernon

A480 Thomas Jefferson

A481 Bunker Hill Monument and Massachusetts Flag 1776

A482 Statue of Liberty

A483 Abraham Lincoln

A484 The Hermitage

A485 James Monroe

A486 Theodore Roosevelt

A487 Woodrow Wilson

A488 Statue of Liberty (Rotary and flat plate printing)

A489 Design slightly altered; see position of torch (Giorgi press printing)

A489a John J. Pershing

A490 The Alamo

A491 Independence Hall

A491a Statue of Liberty

A492 Benjamin Harrison

A493 John Jay

A494 Monticello

A495 Paul Revere

A496 Robert E. Lee

A497 John Marshall

A498 Susan B. Anthony

A499 Patrick Henry

A500 Alexander Hamilton

Unwmkd.

A477	½c red orange, perf. 11x10½	**1030**
A478	1c dark green, perf. 11x10½	**1031**
A478	1c dark green, perf. 10 vert.	**1054**
A478	1c dark green, imperf., pair	**1054b**
A478a	1¼c turquoise, perf. 10½x11	**1031A**
A478a	1¼c turquoise, perf. 10 horiz.	**1054A**
A479	1½c brown carmine, perf. 10½x11 ...	**1032**
A480	2c carmine rose, perf. 11x10½	**1033**
A480	2c carmine rose, perf. 10 vert.	**1055**
A480	2c carmine rose, same, tagged	**1055a**
A481	2½c gray blue, perf. 11x10½	**1034**
A481	2½c gray blue, perf. 10 vert.	**1056**
A482	3c deep violet, perf. 11x10½	**1035**
A482	3c deep violet, same, tagged......	**1035b**
A482	3c deep violet, booklet pane of 6 ..	**1035a**
A482	3c deep violet, perf. 10 vert.	**1057**
A482	3c deep violet, same, tagged......	**1057b**
A482	3c deep violet, imperf., pair	**1057a**
A482	3c deep violet, imperf., size: 24x28mm	**1075a**
A483	4c red violet, perf. 11x10½	**1036**
A483	4c red violet, same, tagged	**1036b**
A483	4c red violet, booklet pane of 6 ...	**1036a**
A483	4c red violet, perf. 10 vert.	**1058**
A483	4c red violet, imperf. pair	**1058a**
A484	4½c blue green, perf. 10½x11	**1037**
A484	4½c blue green, perf. 10 horiz.	**1059**
A485	5c deep blue, perf. 11x10½	**1038**
A486	6c carmine, same	**1039**
A487	7c rose carmine, same	**1040**
A488	8c dk. violet blue & carmine, perf. 11	**1041**
A488	8c dk. violet blue & carmine, imperf., size: 24x28mm	**1075b**
A489	8c dk. violet blue & car. rose, perf. 11	**1042**
A489a	8c brown, perf. 11x10½	**1042A**
A490	9c rose lilac, perf. 10½x11	**1043**
A491	10c rose lake, same	**1044**
A491	10c rose lake, same, tagged	**1044b**
A491a	11c carmine & dk. vio. blue, perf. 11	**1044A**
A491a	Same, tagged	**1044c**
A492	12c red, perf. 11x10½	**1045**
A492	12c red, same, tagged	**1045a**
A493	15c rose lake, same	**1046**
A493	15c rose lake, same, tagged	**1046a**
A494	20c ultramarine, perf. 10½x11	**1047**
A495	25c green, perf. 11x10½	**1048**
A495	25c green, perf. 10 vert.	**1059A**
A495	25c green, same, tagged	**1059b**
A496	30c black, perf. 11x10½	**1049**
A497	40c brown red, same	**1050**
A498	50c bright purple, same	**1051**
A499	$1 purple, same	**1052**
A500	$5 black, perf. 11	**1053**

ISSUE OF 1962-66

A646 Andrew Jackson

A650 George Washington

A646	1c green, perf. 11x10½, untagged...	**1209**
A646	1c green, same, tagged	**1209a**
A646	1c green, perf. 10 vert., untagged ...	**1225**
A646	1c green, same, tagged	**1225a**
A650	5c dk. bl. gray, perf. 11x10½, untagged	**1213**
A650	5c dk. bl. gray, same, tagged......	**1213b**
A650	5c dk. bl. gray, booklet pane of 5+ label, untagged	**1213a**
A650	5c dk. bl. gray, same, tagged.......	**1213c**
A650	5c dk. bl. gray, perf. 10 vert. untagged	**12129**
A650	5c dk. bl. gray, same, tagged......	**1229a**

PROMINENT AMERICANS ISSUE 1965-75

A710 Thomas Jefferson

A711 Albert Gallatin

A712 Frank Lloyd Wright and Guggenheim Museum, New York

A713 Francis Parkman

A714 Abraham Lincoln

A715 George Washington

A715a re-engraved

A716 Franklin D. Roosevelt

A727a Franklin D. Roosevelt (vertical coil)

A816 Benjamin Franklin and his signature

A717 Albert Einstein

A718 Andrew Jackson

A718a Henry Ford and 1909 Model I

A719 John F. Kennedy

A817a Fiorello H. LaGuardia and New York skyline

A720 Oliver Wendell Holmes

A818 Ernest (Ernie) Taylor Pyle

A818a Dr. Elizabeth Blackwell

A721 George C. Marshall

A818b Amadeo P. Giannini

A722 Frederick Douglass

A723 John Dewey

A724 Thomas Paine

A725 Lucy Stone

A726 Eugene O'Neill

A727 John Bassett Moore

Unwmkd.
Rotary Press Printing

A710 1c green, perf. 11x10½, tagged **1278**
A710 1c green, booklet pane of 8....... **1278a**
A710 1c green, booklet pane of 4+2 labels **1278b**
A710 1c green, perf. 11x10½, untagged... **1278c**
A710 1c green, perf. 10, vert., tagged **1299**
A710 1c green, untagged (Bureau precanceled)........ **1299a**
A711 1¼c light green, perf. 11x10½, untagged.................... **1279**
A712 2c dk. bl. gray, perf. 11x10½, tagged **1280**
A712 2c dk. bl. gray, booklet pane of 5+label................ **1280a**
A712 2c dk. bl. gray, perf. 11x10½, untagged (Bureau precanceled). **1280b**
A712 2c dk. bl. gray, booklet pane of 6... **1280c**
A713 3c violet, perf. 10½x11, tagged..... **1281**
A713 3c violet, same, untagged (Bureau precanceled)......... **1281a**
A713 3c violet, perf. 10 horiz., tagged.... **1297**
A713 3c violet, same, untagged (Bureau precanceled)......... **1297b**
A714 4c black, perf. 11x10½, untagged... **1282**
A714 4c black, same, tagged **1282a**
A714 4c black, perf. 10, vert., tagged **1303**
A714 4c black, same, untagged (Bureau precanceled)......... **1303a**
A715 5c blue, perf. 11x10½, untagged.... **1283**
A715 5c blue, same, tagged **1283a**
A715 5c blue, perf. 10 vert., tagged...... **1304**
A715 5c blue, same, untagged (Bureau precanceled)......... **1304a**
A715a 5c blue, perf. 11x10½, tagged..... **1283B**
A715a 5c blue, untagged (Bureau precanceled)......... **1283d**
A716 6c gray brown, perf. 10½x11, tagged **1284**
A716 6c gray brown, tagged.......... **1284a**
A716 6c gray brown, booklet pane of 8.. **1284b**
A716 6c gray brown, booklet pane of 5+label **1284c**
A716 6c gray brown, perf. 10 horiz., tagged **1298**
A727a 6c gray brown, perf. 10 vert., tagged **1305**
A727a 6c gray brown, untagged (Bureau precanceled)......... **1305b**
A816 7c bright blue, perf. 10½x11, tagged **1393D**
A816 7c bright blue, same, untagged (Bureau precanceled).......... **1393e**
A717 8c violet, perf. 11x10½, untagged .. **1285**
A717 8c violet, tagged **1285a**
A718 10c lilac, perf. 11x10½, tagged...... **1286**
A718 10c lilac, untagged (Bureau precanceled)............... **1286b**
A718a 12c black, perf. 10½x11, tagged.... **1286A**
A718a 12c black, untagged (Bureau precanceled)................ **1286c**
A719 13c brown, perf. 11x10½, tagged.... **1287**
A719 13c brown, untagged (Bureau precanceled)............... **1287a**
A817a 14c gray brown, perf. 11x10½ **1397**
A817a 14c gray brown, untagged (Bureau precanceled)............... **1397a**
A720 15c maroon, perf. 11x10½, tagged... **1288**
A720 15c maroon, untagged (Bureau precanceled)............... **1288a**
A720 15c dark rose claret, perf. 10 (bklt. panes only).......... **1288B**
A720 15c dark rose claret, booklet pane of 8.................. **1288c**
A818 16c brown, tagged.............. **1398**
A818 16c brown, untagged (Bureau precanceled)............... **1398a**
A818a 18c violet, perf. 11x10½........... **1399**
A721 20c deep olive, perf. 11x10½, untagged................... **1289**
A721 20c deep olive, tagged............ **1289a**
A818b 21c green, perf. 11x10½ **1400**
A722 25c rose lake, perf. 11x10½, untagged **1290**
A722 25c rose lake, tagged............ **1290a**
A723 30c red lilac, perf. 10½x11, untagged **1291**
A723 30c red lilac, tagged **1291a**
A724 40c blue black, perf. 11x10½, untagged.................... **1292**
A724 40c blue black, tagged........... **1292a**
A725 50c rose magenta, perf. 11x10½, untagged.................... **1293**
A725 50c rose magenta, tagged **1293a**

A726	$1 dull purple, perf. 11x10½, untagged	1294
A726	$1 dull purple, tagged	1294a
A726	$1 dull purple, perf. 10 vert., tagged	1305C
A727	$5 gray black, perf. 11x10½, untagged	1295
A727	$5 gray black, tagged	1295a

A815 Dwight D. Eisenhower

A815a

A815	6c dark blue gray, perf. 11x10½, tagged	1393
A815	6c dk. bl. gray, booklet pane of 8	1393a
A815	6c dk. bl. gray, booklet pane of 5+label	1393b
A815	6c dk. bl. gray, untagged (Bureau precanceled)	1393c
A815	6c dk. bl. gray, perf. 10, vert., tagged	1401
A815	6c dk. bl. gray, same, untagged (Bureau precanceled)	1401a
A815	8c deep claret, perf. 11x10½ (Booklet panes only)	1395
A815	8c deep claret, booklet pane of 8	1395a
A815	8c deep claret, booklet pane of 6	1395b
A815	8c deep claret, booklet pane of 4+2 labels	1395c
A815	8c deep claret, booklet pane of 7+label	1395d
A815	8c deep claret, perf. 10 vert., tagged	1402
A815	8c deep claret, same, untagged (Bureau precanceled)	1402b
A815a	8c blk., red & bl. gray, perf. 11	1394

FLAG ISSUE, 1968-71

A760 Flag and White House

A760	6c dark blue, red & green, perf. 11, size:19x22mm	1338
A760	6c dark blue, red & green, perf. 11x10½, size: 18¼x21mm.	1338D
A760	6c dark blue, red & green, perf. 10 vert., size: 18¼x21mm.	1338A
A760	8c multicolored, perf. 11x10½	1338F
A760	8c multicolored, perf. 10 vert.	1338G

REGULAR ISSUE 1970-76

A817 U.S. Postal Service Emblem

A923 50-Star and 13-Star Flags

A924 Jefferson Memorial and quotation from Declaration of Independence

A925 Mail Transport and "Zip Code"

A926 Liberty Bell

A817	8c multicolored, perf. 11x10½	1396
A923	10c red & blue, perf. 11x10½	1509
A923	10c red & blue, perf. 10 vert.	1519
A924	10c blue, perf. 11x10½	1510
A924	10c blue, same, untagged (Bureau precanceled)	1510a
A924	10c blue, booklet pane of 5+label	1510b
A924	10c blue, booklet pane of 8	1510c
A924	10c blue, booklet pane of 6	1510d
A924	10c blue, perf. 10 vert.	1520
A924	10c blue, same, untagged (Bureau precanceled)	1520a
A925	10c multicolored, perf. 11x10½	1511
A926	6.3c brick red, perf. 10 vert.	1518
A926	6.3c brick red, same, untagged (Bureau precanceled)	1518a

AMERICANA ISSUE 1975-81

A984 Inkwell and Quill

A985 Speaker's Stand

A987 Early Ballot Box

A988 Books, Bookmark, Eyeglasses

A994 Dome of Capitol

A995 Contemplation of Justice

A996 Early American Printing Press

A997 Torch Statue of Liberty

A998 Liberty Bell

A999 Eagle and Shield

A1001 Ft. McHenry Flag

A1002 Head Statue of Liberty

A1006 Old North Church

A1007 Ft. Nisqually

A1008 Sandy Hook Lighthouse

A1009 Morris Township School No. 2, Devil's Lake

A1001 Iron "Betty" Lamp Plymouth Colony, 17th-18th Centuries

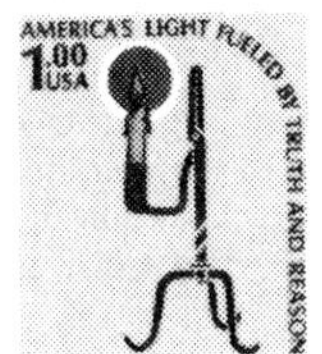

A1013 Rush Lamp and Candle Holder

A1013a Kerosene Table Lamp

A1014 Railroad Conductors Lantern, c. 1850

COIL STAMPS

A1014a Six-string guitar

A1199 Weaver violins

A1015 Saxhorns

A1016 Drum

A1017 Steinway Grand Piano, 1857

A984 1c dark blue, greenish, perf. 11x10½ **1581**
A984 1c dark blue, greenish, same, untagged (Bureau precanceled) **1581a**
A984 1c dark blue, greenish, perf. 10 vert. **1811**
A985 2c red brown, greenish, perf. 11x10½ **1582**
A985 2c red brown, greenish, same, untagged (Bureau precanceled) **1582a**
A987 3c olive, greenish, perf. 11x10½ ... **1584**
A987 3c olive, greenish, same, untagged (Bureau Precanceled) **1584a**
A988 4c rose magenta, cream, perf. 11x10½ **1585**
A988 4c rose magenta, cream, same, untagged (Bureau precanceled) **1585a**
A994 9c slate green, perf. 11x10½ (booklet panes only) **1590**
A994 9c slate green, perf. 10 (booklet panes only) **1590a**
A994 9c slate green, gray, perf. 11x10½.. **1591**
A994 9c slate green, gray, same, untagged (Bureau precanceled) **1591a**
A994 9c slate green, gray, perf. 10 vert... **1616**
A994 9c slate green, gray, same, untagged (Bureau precanceled) **1616a**
A995 10c violet, gray, perf. 10 vert....... **1617**
A995 10c violet, gray, perf. 11x10½...... **1592**
A995 10c violet, gray, same, untagged (Bureau precanceled) **1592a**
A996 11c orange, gray, perf. 11x10½ **1593**
A997 12c red brown, beige, perf. 10 vert. **1816**
A997 12c red brown, beige, same, untagged (Bureau precanceled) **1816a**
A998 13c brown, perf. 11x10½ **1595**
A998 13c brown, booklet pane of 6..... **1595a**
A998 13c brown, booklet pane of 7+label **1595b**
A998 13c brown, booklet pane of 8....... **1595c**
A998 13c brown, booklet pane of 5+label **1595d**
A998 13c brown, perf. 10 vert........... **1618**
A998 13c brown, same, untagged (Bureau precanceled) **1618a**
A999 13c multicolored, perf. 11x10½ **1596**
A1001 15c gray, dark blue & red, perf. 11.. **1597**
A1001 15c gray, dark blue & red, perf. 11x10½ (booklet panes only)... **1598**
A1001 15c gray, dark blue & red, booklet pane of 8 .... **1598a**
A1001 15c gray, dark blue & red, perf. 10 vert. **1618C**
A1002 16c blue, perf. 11x10½ **1599**
A1002 16c blue, perf. 10 vert. **1619**
A1006 24c red, blue, perf. 11x10½........ **1603**
A1007 28c brown, blue, perf. 11x10½..... **1604**
A1008 29c blue, blue, perf. 11x10½........ **1605**
A1009 30c green, perf. 11x10½ **1606**
A1011 50c black & orange, perf. 11........ **1608**
A1013 $1 brown, orange & yellow, tan, perf. 11 **1610**
A1013a $2 dark green & red, tan, perf. 11.. **1611**
A1014 $5 red brown, yellow & orange, tan, perf. 11................ **1612**
A1014a 3.1c brown, yellow, perf. 10 vert. ... **1613**
A1014a 3.1c brown, yellow, same, untagged (Bureau precanceled) **1613a**
A1199 3.5c purple, yellow, perf. 10 vert. ... **1813**
A1199 3.5c purple, yellow, same, untagged (Bureau precanceled) **1813a**
A1015 7.7c brown, bright yellow, perf. 10 vert. **1614**
A1015 7.7c brown, bright yellow, same, untagged (Bureau precanceled) .. **1614a**
A1016 7.9c carmine, yellow, perf. 10 vert.... **1615**
A1016 7.9c carmine, yellow, same, untagged (Bureau precanceled) **1615a**
A1017 8.4c dark blue, yellow, perf. 10 vert. **1615C**
A1017 8.4c dark blue, yellow, same, untagged (Bureau precanceled) **1615d**

FLAG ISSUE 1975-77

A1018 13-star Flag over Independence Hall

A1018a Flag over Capitol

A1018 13c dark blue & red, perf. 11x10½ **1622**
A1018 13c dark blue & red, perf. 10 vert. **1625**
A1018a 13c blue & red, perf. 11x10½ (booklet panes only) **1623**
A1018a 13c blue & red, booklet pane of 7 #1623 + 1 #1590 .... **1623a**
A1018a 13c blue & red, perf. 10 (booklet panes only)............... **1623b**
A1018a 13c blue & red, booklet pane of 7 #1623b + 1 #1590a **1623c**

REGULAR ISSUE 1978

A1123 Indian Head Penny, 1877

A1209 Dolley Madison

A1126 Red Masterpiece and Medallion Roses

A1123 13c brown & blue, green, bister, perf. 11 .... **1734**
A1126 15c multicolored, perf. 10 (booklet panes only)........... **1737**
A1126 15c multicolored, booklet pane of 8 **1737a**
A1209 15c red brown & sepia, perf. 11..... **1822**

REGULAR ISSUE 1978-85

A1124 "A" Eagle

A1207 "B" Eagle

A1332 "C" Eagle

A1333 "C" Eagle (Booklet)

A1496 "D" Eagle

A1497 "D" Eagle (Booklet)

A1124 (15c) orange, Perf. 11 .... **1735**
A1124 (15c) orange, perf. 11x10½ (booklet panes only)................. **1736**
A1124 (15c) orange, booklet pane of 8 ... **1736a**
A1124 (15c) orange, perf. 10 vert......... **1743**
A1207 (18c) violet, perf. 11x10½ **1818**
A1207 (18c) violet, perf. 10 (booklet panes only)...................... **1819**
A1207 (18c) violet, booklet pane of 8.... **1819a**
A1207 (18c) violet, perf. 10 vert.......... **1820**
A1332 (20c) brown, perf. 11x10½......... **1946**
A1332 (20c) brown, perf. 10 vert......... **1947**
A1333 (20c) brown, perf. 11x10½ (booklet panes only)................ **1948**
A1333 (20c) brown, booklet pane of 10 .. **1948a**
A1496 (22c) green, perf. 11 **2111**
A1496 (22c) green, perf. 10 vert.......... **2112**
A1497 (22c) green, perf. 11 (booklet panes only)...................... **2113**
A1497 (22c) green, booklet pane of 10 ... **2113a**

REGULAR ISSUE 1980

A1127 Virginia

A1128 Rhode Island

A1129 Massachusetts

A1130 Illinois

A1131 Texas

A1127	15c sepia, yellow, perf. 11	**1738**
A1128	15c sepia, yellow, perf. 11	**1739**
A1129	15c sepia, yellow, perf. 11	**1740**
A1130	15c sepia, yellow, perf. 11	**1741**
A1131	15c sepia, yellow, perf. 11	**1742**
A1131	15c sepia, yellow, booklet pane of 10	**1742a**

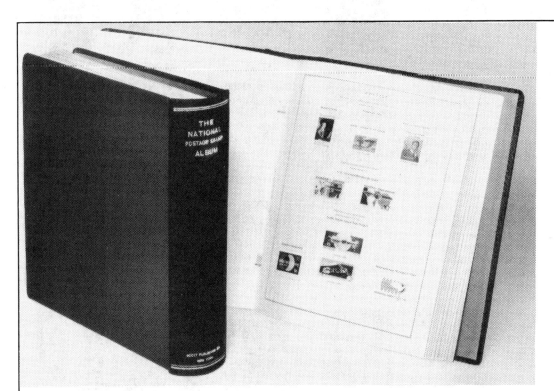

GREAT AMERICANS ISSUE
1980-89

A1231 A1551 A1232 A1552 A1233 A1553 A1234
A1554 A1235 A1555 A1236 A1237 A1238 A1239
A1240 A1559 A1241 A1242 A1243 A1560 A1561
A1244 A1562 A1245 A1246 A1247 A1248 A1249
A1563 A1250 A1565 A1566 A1567 A1251 A1252
A1253 A1254 A1255 A1571 A1256 A1574 A1575
A1577 A1577a A1578 A1579

A1231	1c black, Perf. 11	1844
A1551	1c brownish vermilion, perf. 11	2168
A1232	2c brown black, perf. 10½x11	1845
A1552	2c brt blue, perf. 11	2169
A1233	3c olive green, perf. 10½x11	1846
A1553	3c bright blue, perf. 11	2170
A1234	4c violet, perf. 10½x11	1847
A1554	4c blue violet, perf. 11	2171
A1235	5c henna brown, perf. 10½x11	1848
A1555	5c dark olive green, perf. 11	2172
A1236	6c orange vermilion, perf. 11	1849
A1237	7c bright carmine, perf. 10½x11	1850
A1238	8c olive black, perf. 10½x11	1851
A1239	9c dark green, perf. 10½x11	1852
A1240	10c Prussian blue, perf. 10½x11	1853
A1559	10c perf. 11	2176
A1241	11c dark blue, perf. 11	1854
A1242	13c light maroon, perf. 10½x11	1855
A1243	14c slate green, perf. 11	1856
A1560	14c crimson, perf. 11	2177
A1244	17c green, perf. 10½x11	1857
A1562	17c dull blue green, perf. 11	2179
A1245	18c dark blue, perf. 10½x11	1858
A1246	19c brown, perf. 10½x11	1859
A1247	20c claret, perf. 10½x11	1860
A1248	20c green, perf. 10½x11	1861
A1249	20c black, perf. 11	1862
A1563	21c	2180
A1250	22c dark chalky blue, perf. 11	1863
A1565	23c	2182
A1566	25c blue, perf. 11	2183
A1566	25c blue, booklet pane of 10	2183a
A1566	25c blue, perf. 10	2197

A1566 25c blue, booklet pane of 6 .... **2197a**
A1567 28c **2184**
A1251 30c olive gray, perf. 11 .... **1864**
A1252 35c gray, perf. 10½x11 .... **1865**
A1253 37c blue, perf. 10½x11 .... **1866**
A1254 39c rose lilac, perf. 11............ **1867**
A1255 40c dark green, perf. 11 .... **1868**
A1571 45c bright blue, perf. 11 .... **2188**
A1256 50c brown, perf. 11................ **1869**
A1574 56c scarlet, perf. 11............... **2191**
A1575 65c **2192**
A1577 $1 dk. plus green, perf. 11........ **2194**
A1577a $1 dark blue, perf. 11 .... **2194A**
A1578 $2 bright violet, perf. 11.......... **2195**
A1579 $5 copper red, perf. 11 .... **2196**

REGULAR ISSUE 1981

A1267 Bighorn **A1268** Puma

A1269 Harbor Seal **A1270** Bison

A1271 Brown bear **A1272** Polar bear

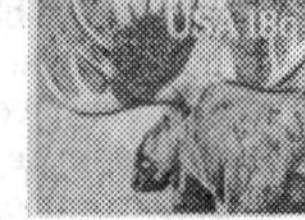

A1273 Elk (wapiti) **A1274** Moose

A1275 White-tailed deer **A1276** Pronghorn

From Booklet Panes

A1267 18c dark brown, perf. 11 .... **1880**
A1268 18c dark brown, perf. 11 .... **1881**
A1269 18c dark brown, perf. 11 .... **1882**
A1270 18c dark brown, perf. 11 .... **1883**
A1271 18c dark brown, perf. 11 .... **1884**
A1272 18c dark brown, perf. 11 .... **1885**
A1273 18c dark brown, perf. 11 .... **1886**
A1274 18c dark brown, perf. 11 .... **1887**
A1275 18c dark brown, perf. 11 .... **1888**
A1276 18c dark brown, perf. 11 .... **1889**
A1276 18c dark brown, booklet pane of 10 **1889a**

FLAG ISSUES 1981

A1277 **A1278**

A1279 Field of 1777 flag **A1280**

A1281 **A1498**

A1499 Of the People, By the People, For the People

A1277 18c multicolored, perf. 11 .... **1890**
A1278 18c multicolored, perf. 10 vert...... **1891**
A1279 6c multicolored, perf. 11 (booklet panes only).................. **1892**
A1280 18c multicolored, perf. 11 (booklet panes only).................. **1893**
A1280 18c multicolored, booklet pane of 8 **1893a**
A1281 20c black, dark blue & red, perf. 11.. **1894**

A1281 20c black, dark blue & red, perf. 11x10½ (booklet panes only) **1896**
A1281 20c black, dark blue & red, booklet pane of 6 .... **1896a**
A1281 20c black, dark blue & red, booklet pane of 8 .... **1896b**
A1498 22c blue, red & black, perf. 11 ...... **2114**
A1498 22c blue, red & black, perf. 10 vert. . **2115**
A1499 22c blue, red & black, perf. 10 horiz. (booklet panes only) **2116**
A1499 22c blue, red and black, booklet pane of 5 .... **2116a**

TRANSPORTATION ISSUE 1981-88

A1283 1c violet, perf. 10 vert. **1897**
A1284 2c black, perf. 10 vert. **1897A**
A1284a 3c dark green, perf. 10 vert. **1898**
A1506 3.4c dark bluish green, perf. 10 vert. **2123**
A1506 3.4c dark bluish green, same, untagged (Bureau precanceled) .. **2123a**
A1285 4c reddish brown, perf. 10 vert. **1898A**
A1285 4c reddish brown, same, untagged (Bureau precanceled) **1898b**
A1507 4.9c brown black, perf. 10 vert. .. **2124**
A1507 4.9c brown black, same, untagged (Bureau precanceled) **2124a**
A1286 5c gray green, perf. 10 vert. **1899**
A1287 5.2c carmine, perf. 10 vert. **1900**
A1287 5.2c carmine, same, untagged (Bureau precanceled) **1900a**
A1508 5.5c deep magenta, perf. 10 vert. . **2125**
A1508 5.5c deep magenta, same, untagged (Bureau precanceled) **2125a**
A1288 5.9c blue, perf. 10 vert. **1901**
A1288 5.9c blue, same, untagged (Bureau precanceled) **1901a**
A1509 6c red brown, perf. 10 vert. **2126**
A1509 6c red brown, same, untagged (Bureau precanceled) **2126a**
A1510 7.1c lake, perf. 10 vert. **2127**
A1510 7.1c lake, same, untagged (Bureau precanceled) **2127a**
A1288a 7.4c brown, perf. 10 vert. **1902**
A1288a 7.4c brown, same, untagged (Bureau precanceled) **1902a**
A1511 8.3c green, perf. 10 vert. **2128**
A1511 8.3c green, same, untagged (Bureau precanceled) **2128a**
A1512 8.5c dark Prussian green, perf. 10 vert. **2129**
A1512 8.5c dark Prussian green, same, untagged (Bureau precanceled) **2129a**
A1289 9.3c carmine rose, perf. 10 vert... **1903**
A1289 9.3c carmine rose, same, untagged (Bureau precanceled) **1903a**
A1513 10.1c slate blue, perf. 10 vert...... **2130**
A1513 10.1c slate blue, same, untagged (Bureau precanceled) **2130a**
A1290 10.9c purple, perf. 10 vert. **1904**
A1290 10.9c purple, same, untagged (Bureau precanceled) **1904a**
A1291 11c red, perf. 10 vert. **1905**
A1291 11c red, same, untagged (Bureau precanceled) **1905a**
A1514 11c dark green, perf. 10 vert. **2131**
A1515 12c dark blue, perf. 10 vert. **2132**
A1515 12c dark blue, same, untagged (Bureau precanceled) **2132a**
A1516 12.5c olive green, perf. 10 vert. ... **2133**
A1516 12.5c olive green, same, untagged (Bureau precanceled) **2133a**
A1517 14c sky blue, perf. 10 vert. **2134**
A1292 17c ultramarine, perf. 10 vert. ... **1906**
A1292 17c ultramarine, same, untagged (Bureau precanceled) **1906a**
A1518 17c sky blue, perf. 10 vert. **2135**
A1293 18c dark brown, perf. 10 vert. ... **1907**
A1294 20c vermilion, perf. 10 vert. **1908**
A1519 25c orange brown, perf. 10 vert. . **2136**

A1283  **A1284**  **A1284a**  **A1506**  **A1285**  **A1507**  **A1286**

A1287  **A1508**  **A1288**  **A1509**  **A1510**  **A1288a**  **A1511**

A1512  **A1289**  **A1513**  **A1290**  **A1291**  **A1514**  **A1515**

A1516  **A1517**  **A1292**  **A1518**  **A1293**  **A1294**  **A1519**

REGULAR ISSUE 1983-85

A1296 Eagle and Moon

A1505 Eagle and Half Moon

A1296 $9.35 multicolored, perf. 10 vert. (booklet panes only) **1909**
A1296 $9.35 multicolored, booklet pane of 3 .... **1909a**
A1505 $10.75 multicolored, perf. 10 vert. (booklet panes only) ... **2122**
A1505 $10.75 multicolored, booklet pane of 3 .... **2122a**

REGULAR ISSUE 1982-85

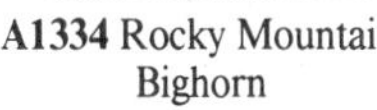

A1334 Rocky Mountain Bighorn

A1390 Consumer Education

A1334 20c dark blue, perf. 11 (bklt. panes only) **1949**
A1334 20c dark blue, booklet pane of 10 .. **1949a**
A1390 20c sky blue, perf. 10 vert. **2005**

A1500 Filled Dogwinkle

A1501 Reticulated Helmet

A1502 New England Neptune

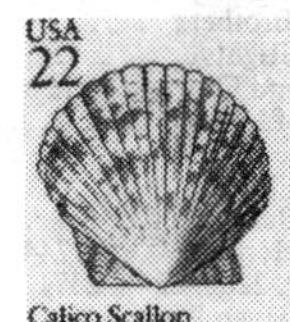

A1503 Calico Scallop

A1504 Lightning Whelk

From Booklet Pane

A1500 22c black & brown, perf. 10 .... **2117**
A1501 22c black & brown, perf. 10 .... **2118**
A1502 22c black & brown, perf. 10 .... **2119**
A1503 22c black & brown, perf. 10 .... **2120**
A1504 22c black & brown, perf. 10 .... **2121**
A1504 22c black & brown, booklet pane of 10 .... **2121a**

REGULAR ISSUE 1985-86

A1532 George Washington Washington Monument

A1533 Sealed Envelopes

A1532 18c multicolored, perf. 10 vert... **2149**
A1532 18c multicolored, same, untagged (Bureau precanceled) **2149a**
A1533 21.1c multicolored, perf. 10 vert... **2150**
A1533 21.1c multicolored, same, untagged (Bureau precanceled) **2150a**

A1588 Muskellunge

A1589 Atlantic Cod

A1590 Largemouth Bass

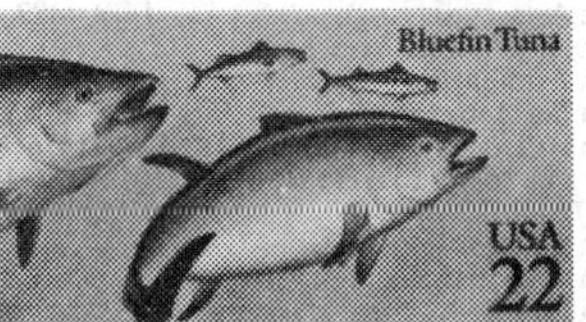

A1591 Bluefin Tuna

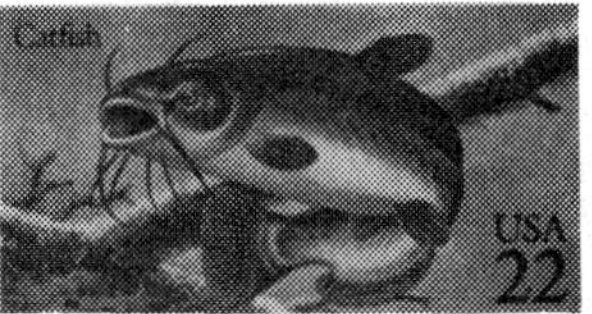

A1592 Catfish

From Booklet Pane

A1588 22c multicolored, perf. 10 horiz. **2205**
A1589 22c multicolored, perf. 10 horiz. **2206**
A1590 22c multicolored, perf. 10 horiz. **2207**
A1591 22c multicolored, perf. 10 horiz. **2208**
A1592 22c multicolored, perf. 10 horiz. **2209**
A1592 22c multicolored, booklet pane of 5 #2205-2209 .... **2209a**

Index of Regular and Airpost Issues

POSTMASTERS' PROVISIONALS

PROVISIONAL ISSUES BY POSTMASTERS.

The Act of Congress of March 3, 1845, effective July 1, 1845, established rates of postage as follows:

'For every single letter in manuscript or paper of any kind by or upon which information shall be asked or communicated in writing or by marks designs, conveyed in the mail, for any distance under 300 miles, five cents; and for any distance over 300 miles, ten cents; and for a double letter there shall be charged double these rates; and for a treble letter, treble these rates; and for a quadruple letter, quadruple these rates; and every letter or parcel not exceeding half an ounce in weight shall be deemed a single letter, and every additional weight of half an ounce, shall be charged with an additional single postage. All drop letters, or letters placed in any post office, not for transmission through the mail but for delivery only, shall be charged with postage at the rate of two cents each.'

Circulars were charged 2 cents, magazines and pamphlets 2½ cents; newspapers according to size.

Between the time of the Act of 1845, effecting uniform postage rates, and the Act of Congress of March 3, 1847, authorizing the postmaster-general to issue stamps, postmasters in various cities issued provisional stamps.

Before adhesive stamps were introduced, prepaid mail was marked 'Paid' either with pen and ink or handstamps of various designs. Unpaid mail occasionally was marked 'Due.' Most often, however, unpaid mail did not have a 'Due' marking, only the amount of postage to be collected from the recipient, e.g. '5,' '10,' '18¾,' etc. Thus, if a letter was not marked 'Paid,' it was assumed to be unpaid. These 'stampless covers' are found in numerous types and usually carry the town postmark.

New York Postmaster Robert H. Morris issued the first postmaster provisional in July 1845. Other postmasters soon followed. The provisionals served until superseded by the federal government's 5c and 10c stamps issued July 1, 1847.

Postmasters recognized the provisionals as indicating postage prepaid. On several provisionals, the signature of initials of the postmaster vouched for their legitimate use.

On July 12, 1845, Postmaster Morris sent examples of his new stamp to the postmasters of Boston, Philadelphia, Albany and Washington, asking that they be treated as unpaid until they reached the New York office. Starting in that year, the New York stamps were distributed to other offices. Postmaster General Cave Johnson reportedly authorized this practice with the understanding that these stamps were to be sold for letters directed to or passing through New York. This was an experiment to test the practicality of the use of adhesive postage stamps.

VALUES FOR ENVELOPES ARE FOR ENITRES

ALEXANDRIA, VA.

Daniel Bryan, Postmaster

A1

All known copies cut to shape.
Type I- 40 asterisks in circle.
Type II-39 asterisks in circle.

1846	**Typeset**		***Imperf.***
1X1 A1	5c **black,** *buff,* type I		*20,000.*
a.	5c black, *buff,* type II	*40,000.*	
	On cover (I or II)		*100,000.*
1X2 A1	5c **black,** *blue,* type I, on cover		—

CANCELLATIONS

Red circular town
Black "PAID"
Black ms. accounting number ("No. 45," "No. 70")

The few copies of Nos. 1X1 and 1X1a known on cover are generally not tied by postmark and some are uncanceled. The value for "on cover" is for a stamp obviously belonging on a cover which bears the proper circular dated town, boxed "5" and straight line "PAID" markings.

No. 1X2 is unique. It is canceled with a black straight line "PAID" marking which is repeated on the cover. The cover also bears a black circular "Alexandria Nov. 25" postmark.

ANNAPOLIS, MD.

Martin F. Revell, Postmaster
ENVELOPE

E1

1846	**Printed in upper right corner of envelope**	
2XU1 E1	5c **carmine red,** *white*	*45,000.*

No. 2XU1 exists in two sizes of envelope.

Envelopes and letter sheets are known showing the circular design and figure "2" handstamped in blue or red. They were used locally. Value, blue $2,500, red $3,500.

Letter sheets are known showing the circular design and figure "5" handstamped in blue or red. Value, blue $3,500, red $5,000.

Similar circular design in blue without numeral or "PAID" is known to have been used as a postmark.

BALTIMORE, MD.

James Madison Buchanan, Postmaster

Signature of Postmaster A1 — *James M. Buchanan* 5 Cents.

Printed from a plate of 12 (2x6) containing nine 5c stamps (Pos. 1-6, 8, 10, 12) and three 10c (Pos. 7, 9, 11).

1845	**Engr.**		***Imperf.***
3X1 A1	5c **black,** *white*		*4,000.*
	On cover		*6,000.*
	Vertical pair on cover		*25,000.*
3X2 A1	10c **black,** *white*		
	On cover		*40,000.*
3X3 A1	5c **black,** *bluish*	*25,000.*	*5,000.*
	On cover		*7,500.*
3X4 A1	10c **black,** *bluish*		*50,000.*
	On cover		—

Nos. 3X3-3X4 preceded Nos. 3X1-3X2 in use.

CANCELLATIONS.

Blue circular town	Blue "5" in oval
Blue straight line "PAID"	Blue "10" in oval
	Black pen

Values are for stamps canceled by either pen or handstamp.

ENVELOPES

James M. Buchanan.
PAID
5

E1

Three Separate Handstamps.

The "PAID" and "5" in oval were handstamped in blue or red, always both in the same color on the same entire. "James M. Buchanan" was handstamped in black, blue or red. The paper is manila, buff, white, salmon or grayish. Manila is by far the most frequently found 5c envelope. All 10c envelopes are rare, with manila or buff the more frequent. Of the 10c on salmon, only one example is known.

The general attractiveness of the envelope and the clarity of the handstamps primarily determine the value.

The color listed is that of the "PAID" and "5" in oval.

1845	**Various Papers**	**Handstamped**
3XU1 E1	5c **blue**	*3,000.*
3XU2 E1	5c **red**	*3,500.*
3XU3 E1	10c **blue**	*13,000.*
3XU4 E1	10c **red**	*13,500.*

CANCELLATIONS.

Blue circular town	Blue "5" in oval

The second "5" in oval on the unlisted "5 + 5" envelopes is believed not to be part of the basic prepaid marking, but envelopes bearing this marking merit a premium over the values for Nos. 3XU1-3XU2.

BOSCAWEN, N. H.

Worcester Webster, Postmaster

PAID
5
CENTS

A1

1846 (?)	Typeset	Imperf.
4X1 A1 5c **dull blue,** *yellowish,* on cover		*100,000.*

One copy known, uncanceled on cover with ms. postal markings.

BRATTLEBORO, VT.

Frederick N. Palmer, Postmaster

Initials of Postmaster — A1

Printed from plate of 10 (5x2) separately engraved subjects with imprint "Eng'd by Thos. Chubbuck, Bratto." below the middle stamp of the lower row (Pos. 8).

1846 *Imperf.*

Thick Softwove Paper Colored Through

5X1 A1 5c **black,** *buff*	—	*5,000.*
On cover		*12,500.*

CANCELLATIONS.

Red straight line "PAID"	Red pen

The red pen-marks are small and lightly applied. They may have been used to invalidate a sample sheet since each plate position is known so canceled.

LOCKPORT, N. Y.

Hezekiah W. Scovell, Postmaster

A1

"Lockport, N.Y." oval and "PAID" separately handstamped in red, "5" in black ms.

1846		Imperf.
6X1 A1 5c **red,** *buff,* on cover		*100,000.*

CANCELLATION

Black ms. "X"

One copy of No. 6X1 is known. Small fragments of two other copies adhering to one cover have been found.

MILLBURY, MASS.

Asa H. Waters, Postmaster

George Washington — A1

Printed from a woodcut, singly, on a hand press.

1846		Imperf.
7X1 A1 5c **black,** *bluish*	—	*17,500.*
On cover		*35,000.*

CANCELLATION

Red straight line "PAID"
Red circular "MILBURY, MS.", date in center

NEW HAVEN, CONN.

Edward A. Mitchell, Postmaster
ENVELOPES

E1

Impressed from a brass handstamp at upper right of envelope.

Signed in blue, black, magenta or red ms., as indicated in parenthesis.

1845	
8XU1 E1 5c **red,** *white* (Bl or M)	—
Cut square	*5,000.*
Cut to shape	*2,000.*
8XU2 E1 5c **red,** *light bluish* (Bk)	*35,000.*
8XU3 E1 5c **dull blue,** *buff* (Bl)	*25,000*
Cut to shape (Bk)	*6,500.*
8XU4 E1 5c **dull blue,** *white* (Bl)	*25,000.*

Values of Nos. 8XU1-8XU4 are a guide to value. They are based on auction realizations and take condition into consideration. All New Haven envelopes are of almost equal rarity. An entire of No. 8XU2 is the finest example known. The other envelopes and cut squares are valued according to condition as much as rarity.

Reprints

Twenty reprints in dull blue on white paper, signed by E. A. Mitchell in lilac rose ink, were made in 1871 for W. P. Brown and others. Thirty reprints in carmine on hard white paper, signed in dark blue or red, were made in 1874 for Cyrus B. Peets, Chief Clerk for Mitchell. Unsigned reprints were made for N. F. Seebeck and others about 1872.

Edward A. Mitchell, grandson of the Postmaster, in 1923 delivered reprints in lilac on soft white wove paper, dated "1923" in place of the signature.

In 1932, the New Haven Philatelic Society bought the original handstamp and gave it to the New Haven Colony Historical Society. To make the purchase possible (at the $1000 price) it was decided to print 260 stamps from the original handstamp. Of these, 130 were in red and 130 in dull blue, all on hard, white wove paper.

According to Carroll Alton Means' booklet on the New Haven Provisional Envelope, after this last reprinting the brass handstamp was so treated that further reprints cannot be made. The reprints were sold originally at $5 each. A facsimile signature of the postmaster, "E. A. Mitchell," (blue on the red reprints, black on the blue) was applied with a rubber handstamp. These 260 reprints are all numbered to correspond with the number of the booklet issued then.

NEW YORK, N.Y.

Robert H. Morris, Postmaster

George Washington — A1

Printed by Rawdon, Wright & Hatch from a plate of 40 (5x8). The die for Washingtons head on the contemporary bank notes was used for the vignette. It had a small flaw-a line extending from the corner of the mouth down the chin-which is quite visible on the paper money. This was corrected for the stamp.

The stamps were usually initialed "ACM" (Alonzo Castle Monson) in magenta ink as a control before being sold or passed through the mails. There are four or five styles of these initials. The most common is "ACM" without periods. The scarcest is "A.C.M.", believed written by Marcena Monson. The rare initials "RHM" (Robert H. Morris, the postmaster) and "MMJr" (Marcena Monson) are listed separately.

The stamps were printed on a variety of wove papers varying in thickness from pelure to thick, and in color from gray to bluish and blue. Some stamps appear to have a slight ribbing or mesh effect. A few also show letters of a double-line papermaker's watermark, a scarce variety. The blue paper is listed separately since it is the rarest and most distinctive. All used true blue copies carry "ACM" without periods; of the three unused copies, two lack initials.

Earliest known use: July 15, 1845.

1845	Engr.		Imperf.
9X1 A1 5c **black,** *bluish*		800.	325.
On cover			450.
On cover to foreign country			*1,500.*
Pair		2,000.	800.
Pair on cover			1,250.
Pair on cover to foreign country			*4,000.*
Strip of three			*3,500.*
Strip of four		*6,000.*	
Block of four			—
Double transfer at bottom (Pos. 2)		1,000.	425.
Double transfer at top (Pos. 7)		1,000.	425.
Bottom frame line double (Pos. 31)		1,000.	425.
Top frame line double (Pos. 36)		1,000.	425.
a. Blue paper		*6,000.*	*2,000.*
On cover, blue paper			*4,000.*
Pair, blue paper			*5,500.*
b. Signed "RHM"		*12,500.*	*2,500.*
c. Signed "MMJr", on cover			—
d. Without signature		1,450.	650.

Known used from Albany, Boston, Jersey City, N.J., New Hamburgh, N.Y., Philadelphia, Sing Sing, N.Y., Washington, D.C., and Hamilton, Canada, as well as by route agents on the Baltimore R.R. Covers originating in New Hamburgh are known only with No. 9X1b; some also bear the U.S. City Despatch Post carrier.

CANCELLATIONS.

Black pen	325.	Red "U.S." in octagon frame (Carrier)	+650.
Blue pen	325.	Red Baltimore R.R.	—
Magenta pen	+50.		
Red grid	+50.		
Red town	+100.		

Another plate of nine subjects (3x3) was made from the original die. Each subject differs slightly from the others, with Position 8 showing the white stock shaded by crossed diagonal lines. Prints were struck from this plate in black on deep blue and white papers, as well as in blue, green, scarlet and brown on white bond paper.

ENVELOPES

Postmaster Morris, according to a newspaper report of July 7, 1845, issued envelopes. The design was not stated and no example has been seen.

PROVIDENCE, R. I.

Welcome B. Sayles, Postmaster

A1

A2

Engraved on copper plate containing 12 stamps (3x4). Upper right corner stamp (Pos. 3) "TEN"; all others "FIVE". The stamps were engraved directly on the plate, each differing from the other. The "TEN" and Pos. 4, 5, 6, 9, 11 and 12 have no period after "CENTS".

Yellowish White Handmade Paper

1846, Aug. 24		Imperf.
10X1 A1 5c **gray black**	200.	*1,250.*
On cover, tied by postmark		*12,500.*
On cover, pen canceled		*4,000.*
Two on cover		—
Pair	425.	
Block of four	875.	
10X2 A2 10c **gray black**	1,000.	—
On cover, pen canceled		—
a. Se-tenant with 5c	*1,300.*	
Complete sheet	*3,850.*	

CANCELLATIONS.

Black pen check mark	Red straight line "PAID" (2 types)
Red circular town	Red "5"

All canceled copies of Nos. 10X1-10X2, whether or not bearing an additional handstamped cancellation, are obliterated with a black pen check mark. All genuine covers must bear the red straight line "PAID," the red circular town postmark, and the red numeral "5" or "10" rating mark.

Reprints were made in 1898. In general, each stamp bears one of the following letters on the back: B. O. G. E. R. T. D. U. R. B. I. N. However, some reprint sheets received no such printing on the reverse. All reprints are without gum. Value for 5c, $50; for 10c, $125; for sheet, $725.

United States New York, Providence and St. Louis Postmaster Provisionals can be mounted in Scott's National and Platinum Albums.

ST. LOUIS, MO.

John M. Wimer, Postmaster

Missouri Coat of Arms
A1 A2 A3

Printed from a copper plate of 6 (2x3) subjects separately engaved by J. M. Kershaw.

The plate in its first state, referred to as Plate I, comprised: three 5c stamps in the left vertical row and three 10c in the right vertical row. The stamps vary slightly in size, measuring from 17¾ to 18¼ by 22 to 22½mm.

Later a 20c denomination was believed necessary. So two of the 5c stamps, types I (pos. 1) and II (pos. 3) were changed to 20c by placing the plate face down on a hard surface and hammering on the back of the parts to be altered until the face was driven flush at those points. The new numerals were then engraved. Both 20c stamps show broken frame lines and the paw of the right bear on type II is missing. The 20c type II (pos. 3) also shows retouching in the dashes under "SAINT" and "LOUIS." The characteristics of types I and II of the 5c also serve to distinguish the two types of the 20c. This altered, second state of the plate is referred to as Plate II. It is the only state to contain the 20c.

The demand for the 20c apparently proved inadequate, and the plate was altered again. The "20" was erased and "5" engraved in its place, resulting in noticeable differences from the 5c stamps from Plate I. In type I (pos. 1) reengraved, the "5" is twice as far from the top frame line as in the original state, and the four dashes under "SAINT" and "LOUIS" have disappeared except for about half of the upper dash under each word. In type II (pos. 3) reengraved, the ornament in the flag of the "5" is a diamond instead of a triangle; the diamond in the bow is much longer than in the first state, and the ball of the "5," originally blank, contains a large dot. At right of the shading of the "5" is a short curved line which is evidently a remnant of the "0" of "20." Type III (pos. 5) of the 5c was slightly retouched. This second alteration of the plate is referred to as Plate III.

Type characteristics common to Plates I, II and III:

5 Cent. Type I (pos. 1). Haunches of both bears almost touch frame lines.

Type II (pos. 3). Bear at right almost touches frame line, but left bear is about ¼mm. from it.

Type III (pos. 5). Haunches of both bears about ½mm. from frame lines. Small spur on "S" of "POST."

10 Cent. Type I (pos. 2). Three dashes below "POST OFFICE."

Type II (pos. 4). Three pairs of dashes.

Type III (pos. 6). Pairs of dashes (with rows of dots between) at left and right. Dash in center with row of dots above it.

20 Cent. Type I. See 5c Type I.

Type II. See 5c Type II.

Wove Paper Colored Through

1845, Nov.-1846 ***Imperf.***

11X1	A1	5c	**black,** *greenish*	*5,000.*	*2,350.*
			On cover		*4,000.*
			Pair		*5,250.*
			Two on cover		*7,000.*
			Strip of three on cover		*10,000.*
11X2	A2	10c	**black,** *greenish*	*4,500.*	*2,000.*
			On cover		*3,000.*
			Pair on cover		*6,500.*
			Strip of three on cover		*9,500.*
11X3	A3	20c	**black,** *greenish*		—
			On cover		—

Three varieties of the 5c and three of the 10c were printed from Plate I. One variety of the 5c, three of the 10c, and two of the 20c were printed from Plate II.

1846

11X4	A1	5c	**black,** *gray lilac*	—	*3,500.*
			On cover		*5,000.*
11X5	A2	10c	**black,** *gray lilac*	*4,500.*	*1,750.*
			On cover		*2,750.*
			Pair		*5,000.*
			Strip of 3		*8,250.*
			Strip of three on cover		*13,500.*
			Pair (II & III) se-tenant with 5c (III)		*18,500.*
11X6	A3	20c	**black,** *gray lilac*		*10,000.*
			On cover		*13,500.*
			Pair on cover		*30,000.*
			Se-tenant with 10c		*27,500.*
			Strip of 3, 20c + 20c + 5c se-tenant		*40,000.*

One variety of the 5c, three of the 10c and two of the 20c. Printed from Plate II.

1846 **Pelure Paper**

11X7	A1	5c	**black,** *bluish*	—	*5,000.*
			On cover		*6,500.*
			Pair		—
			Two on cover		*12,500.*
11X8	A2	10c	**black,** *bluish*		*5,000.*
			On cover		*6,500.*
	a.		Impression of 5c on back		—

Three varieties of the 5c and three of the 10c. Printed from Plate III.

CANCELLATIONS, Nos. 11X1-11X8

Black pen
Ms. initials of postmaster (#11X2, type I)
Red circular town
Red straight line "PAID"
Red grid (#11X7)

Values for used off-cover stamps are for pen-canceled copies. Handstamp canceled copies sell for much more. Values for stamps on cover are pen cancels. Covers with the stamps tied by handstamp sell at considerable premiums depending upon the condition of the stamps and the general attractiveness of the cover. In general, covers with multiple frankings (unless separately valued) are valued at the "on cover" value of the highest item, plus the "off cover" value of the other stamps.

TUSCUMBIA, ALA.

ENVELOPE

E1

1858 **Handstamped at upper right of envelope**

12XU1	E1	3c	**dull red,** *buff*	*9,000.*

No. 12XU1 also exists with a 3c 1857 stamp affixed at upper right over the provisional handstamp, tied by black circular "TUSCUMBIA, ALA." town postmark. Value $2,000.

See Confederate States Nos. 84XU1-84XU3.

POSTAGE

GENERAL ISSUES

All issues from 1847 to 1894 are Unwatermarked.

Benjamin Franklin — A1

Double transfer of top frame line. — 80RI(A)

Double transfer of top and bottom frame lines — 90RI(B)

Double transfer of bottom frame line and lower part of left frame line — (C)

The Catalogue editors cannot undertake to appraise, identify or judge the genuineness or condition of stamps.

Double transfer of top, bottom and left frame lines, also numerals. — (D)

This issue was authorized by an Act of Congress, approved March 3, 1847, to take effect July 1, 1847, from which date the use of Postmasters' Stamps or any which were not authorized by the Postmaster General became illegal.

Earliest known use: 5c, July 7; 10c, July 2, 1847.

This issue was declared invalid as of July 1, 1851.

Produced by Rawdon, Wright, Hatch & Edson.
Plates of 200 subjects in two panes of 100 each.

1847, July 1 **Engr.** ***Imperf.***

Thin Bluish Wove Paper

1	A1	5c	**red brown**	4,000.	500.00
			pale brown	4,000.	500.00
			brown	4,000.	500.00
a.		5c	dark brown	4,000.	500.00
			grayish brown	4,000.	500.00
			blackish brown	4,000.	500.00
b.		5c	orange brown	4,500.	600.00
			brown orange	—	1,000.
c.		5c	red orange	*10,000.*	*1,850.*
			On cover		575.00
			Pair	9,000	1,100.
			Pair on cover		1,250.
			Strip of three	14,000.	2,150.
			Block of four	*30,000.*	25,000.
			Block of four on cover		—

	Dot in S in upper right corner	4,500.	550.00
(A)	Double transfer of top frame line (80RI)		600.00
(B)	Double transfer of top and bottom frame lines (90RI)		600.00
(C)	Double transfer of bottom frame line and lower part of left frame line		600.00
(D)	Double transfer of top, bottom and left frame lines, also numerals		1,000.

CANCELLATIONS.

Red	500.00	U. S. Express Mail	+100.00
Blue	+25.00	"Way"	+250.00
Black	+35.00	"Steamboat"	+350.00
Magenta	+200.00	"Steam"	+200.00
Orange	+200.00	"Steamship"	+300.00
Ultramarine	+175.00	Hotel	*+2000.*
Ultra., town	+300.00	Numeral	+50.00
Violet	+300.00	Canada	+1200.
Green	+750.00	Wheeling, Va., grid	—
"Paid"	+50.00	Pen	250.00
"Free"	+150.00		
Railroad	+200.00		

George Washington — A2

Double transfer in "X" at lower right — 1RI(A)

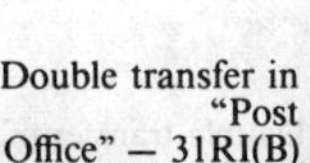

Double transfer in "Post Office" — 31RI(B)

Double transfer in "X" at lower right — 2RI(C)

Double transfer of left and bottom frame line. — 41RI(D)

2	A2	10c **black**	*17,500.*	1,400.
		gray black	*17,500.*	1,400.
		greenish black	—	1,400.
		On cover		1,500.
		On cover with 5c No. 1		*15,000.*
		Pair	*36,000.*	*3,000.*
		Pair on cover		*3,500.*
		Strip of three	—	*8,500.*
		Block of four	*100,000.*	*45,000.*
a.		Diagonal half used as 5 cents on cover		*10,000.*
b.		Vertical half used as 5 cents on cover		*15,000.*
c.		Horizontal half used as 5 cents on cover		—
		Short transfer at top	*17,500.*	1,400.
		Vertical line through second "F" of "OFFICE" (68RI)	—	1,600.
		With "Stick Pin" in tie (52LI)	—	1,600.
		With "harelip" (57LI)	—	1,600.
(A)		Double transfer in "X" at lower right (1RI)	—	1,600.
(B)		Double transfer in "Post Office" (31RI)	—	1,600.
(C)		Double transfer in "X" at lower right (2RI)		1,600.
(D)		Double transfer of left and bottom frame line (41RI)	—	1,600.

CANCELLATIONS.

Red	1,400.	U.S. Express Mail	+350.00
Blue	+50.00	"Way"	+400.00
Orange	+250.00	Numeral	+100.00
Black	+100.00	"Steam"	+350.00
Magenta	+300.00	"Steamship"	+450.00
Violet	+350.00	"Steamboat"	+650.00
Green	+1000.	"Steamer 10"	+1000.
Ultramarine	**+400.00**	**Canada**	**+1250.**
"Paid"	**+100.00**	**Panama**	—
"Free"	+300.00	Wheeling, Va., grid	+1500.
Railroad	+350.00	Pen	700.00

REPRODUCTIONS

Actually, official imitations made from new plates of 50 subjects made by the Bureau of Engraving and Printing by order of the Post Office Department for display at the Centennial Exposition of 1876. These were not valid for postal use.

Reproductions. The letters R. W. H. & E. at the bottom of each stamp are less distinct on the reproductions than on the originals.

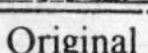

Original

Reproduction

5c. On the originals the left side of the white shirt frill touches the oval on a level with the top of the "F" of "Five". On the reproductions it touches the oval about on a level with the top of the figure "5".

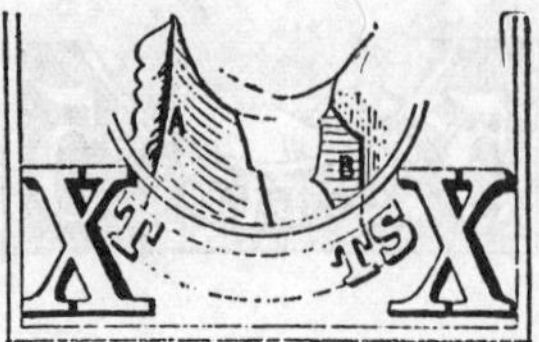

Original

Reproduction

10c. On the originals line of coat (A) points to "T" of TEN and (B) it points between "T" and "S" of CENTS.

On the reproductions line of coat (A) points to right tip of "X" and line of coat (B) points to center of "S."

On the reproductions the eyes have a sleepy look, the line of the mouth is straighter, and in the curl of the hair near the left cheek is a strong black dot, while the originals have only a faint one.

(See Nos. 948a and 948b for 1947 reproductions-5c blue and 10c brown orange in larger size.)

A3

A4

1875		**Bluish paper, without gum**	***Imperf.***
3	A3	5c **red brown** *(4779)*	850.00
		brown	850.00
		dark brown	850.00
		Pair	2,000.
		Block of four	**6,000.**
4	A4	10c **black** *(3883)*	1,000.
		gray black	1,000.
		Pair	2,250.
		Block of four	*7,500.*

Produced by Toppan, Carpenter, Casilear & Co.

Stamps of the 1847, 1851-57 series were printed from plates consisting of 200 subjects and the sheets were divided into panes of 100 each. In order that each stamp in the sheet could be identified easily in regard to its relative position it was devised that the stamps in each pane be numbered from one to one hundred, starting with the top horizontal row and numbering consecutively from left to right. Thus the first stamp at the upper left corner would be No. 1 and the last stamp at the bottom right corner, would be No. 100. The left and right panes are indicated by the letters "L" or "R". The number of the plate is last. As an example, the scarce type III, 1c 1851 being the 99th stamp in the right pane of Plate No. 2 is listed as (99 R 2),*i.e.* 99th stamp, right pane, Plate No. 2.

One plate of the one cent and several plates of the three cents were extensively recut after they had been in use. The original state of the plate is called "Early" and the recut state is termed "Late". Identification of "Early" state or "Late" state is explained by the addition of the letters "E" or "L" after the plate numbers. The sixth stamp of the right pane of Plate No. 1 from the "Early" state would be 6 R 1 E. The same plate position from the "Late" state would be 6 R 1 L.

The position of the stamp in the sheet is placed within parentheses, for example: (99 R 2).

The different values of this issue were intended primarily for the payment of specific rates, though any value might be used in making up a rate. The 1c was to pay the postage on newspapers, drop letters and circulars, and the one cent carrier fee in some cities from 1856. The 3c stamp represented the rate on ordinary letters and two of them made up the rate for distances over 3000 miles. The 5c was originally registration fee but the fee was usually paid in cash. Occasionally two of them were used to pay the rate over 3000 miles, after it was changed in April, 1855. Singles paid the "Shore to ship" rate to certain foreign countries and, from 1857, triples paid the 15c rate to France. Ten cents was the rate to California and points distant more than 3000 miles. The 12c was for quadruple the ordinary rate. The 24c represented the single letter rate to Great Britain. Thirty cents was the rate to Germany. The 90c was apparently

Know Your Options

The United States 1¢ Z Grill. *The rarest U.S. stamp, only 2 known. We acted as agents for purchase at auction, November, 1986, for $418,000.*

Buying or Selling, Explore Your Options With

The 2¢ Hawaii Missionary. *The most valuable Possessions issue. Andrew Levitt acted as auctioneer and President of Sotheby Parke Bernet Stamp Auction Co., 1980.*

Andrew Levitt, Philatelic Consultant

Levitt Offers You:

An unbiased client/consultant relationship.

$220,000,000 and 27 years experience buying, placing and appraising important properties.

Full market coverage from auctions to tax-free donations.

Professionalism, integrity and confidentiality.

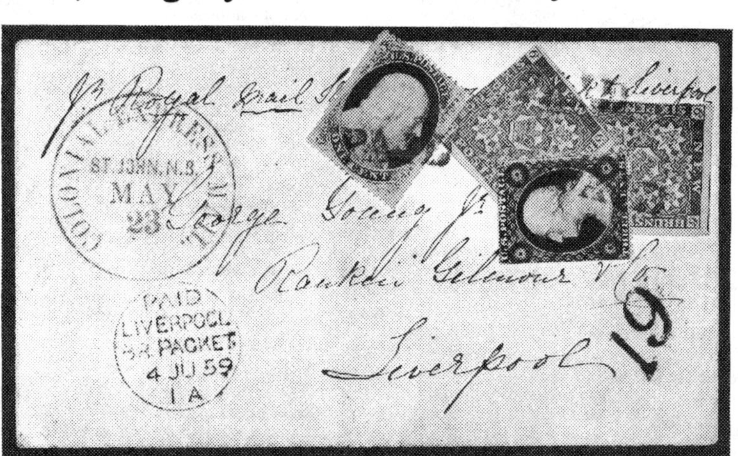

The most outstanding U.S. & New Brunswick Combination Cover in existence. Ex Seybold, Dale-Lichtenstein.

ANDREW LEVITT

PHILATELIC CONSULTANT

BOX 342 DANBURY, CT 06813 (203) 743-5291

Life Member APS, ASDA, Philatelic Foundation, Classics Society and Collectors Club of NY • Bank Letter of Credit Available

intended to facilitate the payment of large amounts of postage.

Act of Congress, March 3, 1851. "From and after June 30, 1851, there shall be charged the following rates: Every single letter not exceeding 3000 miles, prepaid postage, 3 cents; not prepaid, 5 cents; for any greater distance, double these rates. Every single letter or paper conveyed wholly or in part by sea, and to or from a foreign country over 2500 miles, 20 cents; under 2500 miles, 10 cents. Drop or local letters, 1 cent each. Letters uncalled for and advertised, to be charged 1 cent in addition to the regular postage."

Act of Congress, March 3, 1855. "For every single letter, in manuscript or paper of any kind, in writing, marks or signs, conveyed in the mail between places in the United States not exceeding 3000 miles, 3 cents; and for any greater distance, 10 cents. Drop or local letters, 1 cent."

Act of March 3, 1855, effective April 1, 1855, also said: "the foregoing rates to be prepaid on domestic letters." The Act also made the prepayment of postage on domestic letters compulsory.

The Act of March 3, 1855, effective July 1, 1855, authorized the Postmaster to establish a system for the registration of valuable letters, and to require prepayment of postage on such letters as well as registration fee of 5 cents. Stamps to prepay the registry fee were not required until June 1, 1867.

In Nos. 5-17 the 1c, 3c and 12c have very small margins between the stamps. The 5c and 10c have moderate size margins. The values of these stamps take the margin size into consideration.

Franklin — A5

ONE CENT. Issued July 1, 1851.

Type I. Has complete curved lines outside the labels with "U. S. Postage" and "One Cent". The scrolls below the lower label are turned under, forming little balls. The ornaments at top are substantially complete.

Type Ib. As I, but balls below bottom label are not so clear. Plume-like scrolls at bottom are incomplete.

1851-57 ***Imperf.***

No.	Description	Unused	Used
5	A5 1c **blue,** type I (7 R 1 E)	*200,000.*	*17,500.*
	On cover, single (7 R 1 E)		*25,000.*
	On cover, pair, one stamp (7 R 1 E)		—
	On cover strip of three, one stamp (7 R 1 E)		*47,500.*

CANCELLATIONS.

Blue	+500.00	Red town	—
Red grid	+1000.	Red "Paid"	—

No.	Description	Unused	Used
5A	A5 1c **blue,** type Ib, July 1, *1851* (Best examples, 6R, 8R, 1E)	*12,000.*	*4,250.*
	On cover		*5,000.*
	blue, type Ib (Less distinct 3R, 4R, 5R, 9R, Plate 1E)	*7,500.*	*2,500.*
	Pair	*16,000.*	*5,500.*
	On cover		*3,000.*
	Block of four, combination pair type Ib and pair type IIIa (8, 9-18, 19 R 1 E)		—

CANCELLATIONS.

Blue town	+100.00	Pen (6 or 8 R1E)	*2,750.*
Red Carrier	—	Pen (3, 4, 5 or 9 R1E)	*1,400.*

A6

Type Ia. Same as I at bottom but top ornaments and outer line at top are partly cut away.

No.	Description	Unused	Used
6	A6 1c **blue,** type Ia, *April 19, 1857*	*20,000.*	*6,500.*
	On cover		*7,000.*
	Pair	—	*13,500.*
	Vertical pair, combination types Ia and III	—	—
	Vertical pair, combination types Ia and IIIa	23,500.	—
	Block of 4, combination types Ia and IIIa	50,000.	
	"Curl on shoulder" (97 L 4)	*21,000.*	*7,000.*
	"Curl in C" (97 R 4)	*21,000.*	*7,000.*

Type Ia comes only from the bottom row of both panes of Plate 4. All type Ia stamps have the flaw below "U" of "U.S." But this flaw also appears on some stamps of types III and IIIa, Plate 4.

CANCELLATIONS.

		Black Carrier	+350.00
Blue	+100.00	Red Carrier	+350.00
		Pen	*3,500.*

A7

Type II. The little balls of the bottom scrolls and the bottoms of the lower plume ornaments are missing. The side ornaments are complete.

No.	Description	Unused	Used
7	A7 1c **blue,** type II, (Plates 1, 2); *July 1, 1851, Dec. 5, 1855*	450.00	85.00
	On cover		100.00
	Pair	950.00	185.00
	Strip of three	1,500.	285.00
	Pair, combination types II and IIIa (Plate 1E)	2,600	725.00
	Plate 3, *May, 1856*	—	325.00
	On cover (Plate 3)		500.00
	Pair (Plate 3)	—	750.00
	Plate 4, *April, 1857*	—	*500.00*
	On cover (Plate 4)		*600.00*
	Pair (Plate 4)	—	*1,100.*
	"Curl in hair" (3 R, 4 R 4)	—	*650.00*
	Block of four (Plate 1 E)	—	—
	Block of four (Plate 2)	2,100.	600.00
	Block of four (Plate 3)	—	—
	Block of four, combination, type II and type III and IIIa	—	
	Margin block of 8, Impt. & P# (Plate 2)	—	
	Double transfer (Plate 1E or 2)	500.00	100.00
	Double transfer (4 R 1L)	1,000.	250.00
	Double transfer (89 R 2)	550.00	110.00
	Double transfer (Plate 3)		350.00
	Double transfer (10 R 4)	—	*750.00*
	Double transfer, one inverted (71 L1E)	750.00	225.00
	Triple transfer, one inverted (91 L1E)	750.00	225.00
	Cracked Plate (2L, 12L, 13L, 23L and 33L, Plate 2)	650.00	200.00
	Perf. 12½, unofficial	—	*4,000.*

In addition to the cracked plates listed above (Plate 2) there exist a number of surface cracks coming from the rare Plate 3.

CANCELLATIONS.

		"Way"	+35.00
Blue	+2.50	Numeral	+15.00
Red	+5.00	Railroad	+50.00
Magenta	+20.00	"Steam"	+50.00
Ultramarine	+30.00	"Steamboat"	+70.00
Green	+225.00	Red Carrier	+15.00
1855 year date	+10.00	Black Carrier	+25.00
1856 year date	+5.00	U. S. Express Mail	+25.00
1857 year date	+2.50	Printed Precancellation "PAID"	— +325.00
1858 year date	—	Pen	45.00
"Paid"	+5.00		

A8

Type III. The top and bottom curved lines outside the labels are broken in the middle. The side ornaments are substantially complete.

The most desirable examples of type III are those showing the widest breaks in the top and bottom framelines.

The finest example is 99 R 2. All other stamps come from plate 4 and show the breaks in the lines less clearly defined. Some of these breaks, especially of the bottom line, are very small.

Type IIIa. Similar to III with the outer line broken at top or bottom but not both. The outside ornaments are substantially complete.

No.	Description	Unused	Used
8	A8 1c **blue,** type III (Plate 4) *April, 1857,* see below for 99 R 2	*5,500.*	1,500.
	On cover		1,850.
	Pair		3,100.
	Pair, combination types III and IIIa	—	—
	Strip of three		*5,500.*
	Block of four, combination types III and IIIa	—	—

CANCELLATIONS.

		Red Carrier	+150.00
Blue	+50.00	Black Carrier	+200.00
		Pen	700.00

Examples of type III with wide breaks in outer lines command higher prices than those with small breaks.

No.	Description	Unused	Used
(8)	A8 1c **blue,** type III (99 R 2)	*8,000.*	*2,750.*
	Pair, combination types III (99 R 2) and II	—	—
	Pair, combination types III (99 R 2) and IIIa	*10,500.*	—
	Block of 4, combination type III (99 R 2) and 3 of type II	*18,500.*	
	On cover (99 R 2)		*5,000.*

CANCELLATIONS.

		"Paid"	—
Blue	**+100.00**	**Red Carrier**	**+250.00**

No.	Description	Unused	Used
8A	A8 1c **blue,** type IIIa (Plate 1E)	2,000.	600.00
	On cover		750.00
	Pair	—	1,250.
	Double transfer, one inverted (81 L 1 E)	2,400.	775.00
	Plate 1 E (100 R)	—	—
	Plate 2 (100 R)	—	—
	Plate 4, *April, 1857*	2,100.	650.00
	On cover (Plate 4)		850.00
	Pair (Plate 4)	—	1,350.
	Vertical pair, combination types IIIa and II (Plate 4)	—	—
	Block of four (Plate 4)	—	*6,000.*

CANCELLATIONS.

		"Paid"	+75.00
Blue	+25.00	Black Carrier	+150.00
Red	+50.00	Red Carrier	+125.00
		Pen	300.00

Stamps of type IIIa with bottom line broken command higher prices than those with top line broken. See note after type III on width of break of outer lines.

A9

Type IV. Similar to II, but with the curved lines outside the labels recut at top or bottom or both.

No.	Description	Unused	Used
9	A9 1c **blue,** type IV, *June 8, 1852*	300.00	75.00
	On cover		95.00
	Pair	625.00	160.00
	Strip of three	975.00	265.00
	Block of four	1,500.	850.00
	Margin block of 8, Impt. & P# (Plate 1)	—	
a.	Printed on both sides, reverse inverted		—
	Double transfer	325.00	77.50
	Triple transfer, one inverted (71L1L, 81L1L and 91L1L)	450.00	125.00
	Cracked plate	450.00	125.00

Perf. 12½, unofficial	*3,000.*	

VARIETIES OF RECUTTING.

Stamps of this type were printed from Plate 1 after it had been recut in 1852. All but one stamp (4 R) were recut and all varieties of recutting are listed below:

Recut once at top and once at bottom, (113 on plate)	300.00	75.00
Recut once at top, (40 on plate)	310.00	77.50
Recut once at top and twice at bottom, (21 on plate)	320.00	80.00
Recut twice at bottom, (11 on plate)	325.00	85.00
Recut once at bottom, (8 on plate)	335.00	90.00
Recut once at bottom and twice at top, (4 on plate)	350.00	95.00
Recut twice at bottom and twice at top, (2 on plate)	400.00	125.00
Pair, combination, type II (4 R 1 L) and type IV	*1750.*	*700.00*

CANCELLATIONS.

		Railroad	+75.00
Blue	+2.50	"Steam"	+60.00
Red	+7.50	Numeral	+10.00
Ultramarine	+15.00	"Steamboat"	+75.00
Brown	+20.00	"Steamship"	+60.00
Green	+200.00	Red Carrier	+10.00
Violet	+50.00	Black Carrier	+25.00
1853 year date	+250.00	U. S. Express Mail	+60.00
1855 year date	+10.00	Express Company	—
1856 year date	+7.50	Packet boat	—
1857 year date	+10.00	Printed precancellation "PAID"	+450.00
"Paid"	+10.00	Printed precancellation "paid"	+450.00
"U. S. PAID"	+50.00	Pen	40.00
"Way"	+35.00		
"Free"	+50.00		

These 1c stamps were often cut apart carelessly, destroying part or all of the top and bottom lines. This makes it difficult to determine whether a stamp is type II or IV without plating the position. Such mutilated examples sell for much less.

Washington — A10

THREE CENTS. Issued July 1, 1851.
Type I. There is an outer frame line on all four sides.

10	A10 3c **orange brown,** type I	1,000.	40.00
	deep orange brown	1,000.	40.00
	copper brown	1,150.	60.00
	On cover		90.00
	Pair	2,100.	95.00
	Strip of three	3,200.	175.00
	Block of four	*8,500.*	—
a.	Printed on both sides		—
	Double transfer		55.00
	Triple transfer		200.00
	Gash on shoulder		45.00
	Dot in lower right diamond block (69 L 5 E)		80.00
	On part-India paper		250.00

VARIETIES OF RECUTTING.

All of these stamps were recut at least to the extent of four outer frame lines and usually much more. Some of the most prominent varieties are listed below (others are described in "The 3c Stamp of U.S. 1851-57 Issue," by Carroll Chase). Values for No. 10 are for copies with recut inner frame lines:

No inner frame lines	1,050.	42.50
Left inner line only recut		47.50
Right inner line only recut		42.50
1 line recut in upper left triangle	1,050.	42.50
2 lines recut in upper left triangle		47.50
3 lines recut in upper left triangle		65.00
5 lines recut in upper left triangle (47 L O)		200.00
1 line recut in lower left triangle		60.00
1 line recut in lower right triangle		55.00
2 lines recut in lower right triangle (57 L O)		175.00
2 lines recut in upper left triangle, 1 line recut in lower right triangle		—
1 line recut in upper right triangle		55.00
Upper part of top label and diamond block recut	1,050.	45.00
Top label and right diamond block joined		47.50
Top label, left diamond, block joined		50.00
Lower label and right diamond block joined		47.50
2 lines recut at top of upper right diamond block		52.50
1 line recut at bottom of lower left diamond block (34 R 2 E)		60.00

CANCELLATIONS.

		"Free"	+50.00
Blue	+2.00	Numeral	+15.00
Red	+5.00	Railroad	+50.00
Orange	+35.00	U. S. Express Mail	+20.00
Brown	+40.00	"Steam"	+35.00
Ultramarine	+25.00	"Steamship"	+60.00
Green	+175.00	"Steamboat"	+60.00
Violet	+85.00	Packet Boat	+300.00
1851 year date	*+350.00*	Blue Carrier (New Orleans)	+300.00
1852 year date	*+350.00*	Green Carrier (New Orleans)	+600.00
"Paid"	+5.00	Canadian	—
"Way"	+40.00	Territorial	+175.00
"Way" with numeral	+150.00	Pen	25.00

11	A10 3c **dull red** (1853-54-55), type I	130.00	7.00
	orange red (1855)	130.00	7.00
	rose red (1854-55)	130.00	7.00
	brownish carmine (1852 and 1856)	145.00	8.50
	claret (1857)	160.00	10.00
	deep claret (1857)	185.00	13.50
	On cover, dull red		9.00
	On cover, claret		200.00
	On propaganda cover		350.00
	Pair	270.00	15.00
	Strip of three	425.00	30.00
	Block of four	675.00	300.00
	Margin block of 8, Impt. & P#		—
c.	Vertical half used as 1c on cover		*6,000.*
d.	Diagonal half used as 1c on cover		*5,500.*
e.	Double impression		
	Double transfer in "Three Cents"	150.00	8.00
	Double transfer line through "Three Cents" and rosettes double (92 L 1 L)	225.00	35.00
	Triple transfer (92 L 2 L)	200.00	25.00
	Double transfer, "Gents" instead of "Cents" (66 R 2 L)	200.00	25.00
	Gash on shoulder	140.00	7.50
	Dot on lower right diamond block 69 L 5 L)	175.00	20.00
	Cracked plate (51L, 74L, 84L, 94L, 96L, and 9R, Plate 5 L)	*375.00*	60.00
	Worn plate	130.00	7.00
	Perf. 12½, unofficial		*1,500.*

VARIETIES OF RECUTTING.

All of these stamps were recut at least to the extent of three frame lines and usually much more. Some of the most prominent varieties are listed below (others are described in "The 3c Stamp of U.S. 1851-57 Issue," by Carroll Chase):

Recut inner frame lines	130.00	7.00
No inner frame lines	130.00	7.00
Right inner line only recut	140.00	7.25
1 line recut in upper left triangle	140.00	7.25
2 lines recut in upper left triangle	140.00	7.25
3 lines recut in upper left triangle	150.00	8.00
5 lines recut in upper left triangle	250.00	70.00
1 line recut in lower left triangle	160.00	8.00
1 line recut in lower right triangle	140.00	7.50
1 line recut in upper right triangle	200.00	10.00
Recut button on shoulder (10 R 2 L)	200.00	40.00
Lines on bust and bottom of medallion circle recut (47 R 6)	*300.00*	100.00
Upper part of top label and diamond block recut	140.00	7.25
Top label and right diamond block joined	140.00	7.25
Top label and left diamond block joined	150.00	9.50
Lower label and right diamond block joined	150.00	9.50
1 extra vertical line outside of left frame line (29L, 39L, 49L, 59L, 69L, 79L, Plate 3)	145.00	8.50
2 extra vertical lines outside of left frame line 89L, 99L, Plate 3)	180.00	20.00
1 extra vertical line outside of right frame line (58L, 68L, 78L, 88L, 98L, Plate 3)	155.00	10.00
No inner line and frame line close to design at right (9L, 19L, Plate 3)	165.00	12.50
No inner line and frame line close to design at left (70L, 80L, 90L, 100L, Plate 3)	150.00	10.00

CANCELLATIONS.

		"Free"	+25.00
Blue	+.25	Numeral	+7.50
Red	+1.00	Railroad	+20.00
Orange	+15.00	U. S. Express Mail	+5.00
Brown	+20.00	"Steam"	+15.00
Magenta	+15.00	"Ship"	+20.00
Ultramarine	+15.00	"New York Ship"	+35.00
Green	+75.00	"Steamboat"	+45.00
Violet	+30.00	"Steamship"	+45.00
Purple	+30.00	Packet boat	+120.00
Olive	+50.00	Express Company	+120.00
Yellow	*+300.00*	Black Carrier	+60.00
1852 year date	*+300.00*	Red Carrier (New York)	+50.00
1853 year date	+90.00	Green Carrier (New Orleans)	+350.00
1855 year date	+10.00	Blue Carrier (New Orleans)	+200.00
1858 year date	+.50	Canada	—
1859 year date	—	Territorial	+70.00
"Paid"	+1.00	Pen	3.00
"Way"	+10.00		
"Way" with numeral	+60.00		

Thomas Jefferson — A11

FIVE CENTS. Earliest known use Mar. 24, 1856.
Type I. Projections on all four sides.

12	A11 5c **red brown,** type I	*10,000.*	1,300.
	dark red brown	*10,000.*	1,300.
	single on cover to France		2,000.
	Pair	*21,000.*	2,750.
	Strip of three	*35,000.*	5,000.
	Block of four	*125,000.*	*45,000.*

CANCELLATIONS.

		"Paid"	+50.00
Red	+50.00	"Steamship"	+200.00
Magenta	+125.00	U. S. Express Mail	+150.00
Blue	+25.00	Express Company	+300.00
Green	+600.00	"Steamboat"	+250.00
1856 year date	+25.00	Railroad	+250.00
1857 year date	+25.00	Pen	600.00
1858 year date	—		

Washington — A12

TEN CENTS. Earliest known use May 12, 1855

Type I. The "shells" at the lower corners are practically complete. The outer line below the label is very nearly complete. The outer lines are broken above the middle of the top label and the "X" in each upper corner.

Types I, II, III and IV have complete ornaments at the sides of the stamps, and three pearls at each outer edge of the bottom panel.

Type I comes only from the bottom row of both panes of Plate 1.

13 A12 10c **green,** type I	9,000.	700.00
dark green	9,000.	700.00
yellowish green	9,000.	700.00
On cover		850.00
Pair	*19,000.*	1,550.
Strip of three		2,250.
Pair, combination types I & III	12,000.	1,250.
Pair, combination type I and type IV		3,000.
Vertical strip of three, combination types I, II, III		3,500.
Block of four, combination type I and type III	*27,500*	10,000.
Block of four, combination types I, III and IV		15,000.
Double transfer (100 R 1)	9,500.	775.00
"Curl" in left "X" (99 R 1)	9,500.	775.00

CANCELLATIONS.

		"Paid"	+50.00
Blue	+25.00	"Steamship"	+150.00
Red	+50.00	Railroad	+175.00
Magenta	+150.00	Territorial	+400.00
Orange	—	Numeral	+50.00
1855 year date	+25.00	U.S. Express Mail	—
1856 year date	+25.00	Pen	325.00
1857 year date	+25.00		

A13

Type II. The design is complete at the top. The outer line at the bottom is broken in the middle. The shells are partly cut away.

14 A13 10c **green,** type II	2,000.	275.00
dark green	2,000.	275.00
yellowish green	2,000.	275.00
On cover		350.00
Pair	4,100.	600.00
Strip of 3	—	—
Block of four	*9,750.*	*4,000.*
Pair, combination type II and type III	4,100.	600.00
Pair, combination type II and type IV	*15,000.*	*2,000.*
Vertical strip of three, combination types II, III and IV		—
Block of four, combination type II and type III	—	*2,750.*
Block of four, combination types II and IV		—
Block of four, combination types II, III, and IV		*10,000.*
Double transfer (31L, 51L, and 20R, Plate 1)	2,100.	325.00
"Curl" opposite "X" (10 R 1)	2,100.	350.00

CANCELLATIONS.

		"Paid"	+25.00
Blue	+10.00	"Way"	+50.00
Red	+25.00	"Free"	+75.00
Brown	+25.00	Railroad	+75.00
Ultramarine	+75.00	Steamship	+75.00
Magenta	+75.00	Steamboat	+100.00
Green	+200.00	Numeral	+50.00
1855 year date	—	Territorial	+150.00
1856 year date	+50.00	Express Company	+200.00
1857 year date	+10.00	U. S. Express Mail	+75.00
1858 year date	+10.00	Pen	150.00

A14

Type III. The outer lines are broken above the top label and the "X" numerals. The outer line at the bottom and the shells are partly cut away as in Type II.

15 A14 10c **green,** type III	2,000.	275.00
dark green	2,000.	275.00
yellowish green	2,000.	275.00
On cover		350.00
Pair	4,100.	600.00
Strip of 3	—	—
Pair, combination type III and type IV	*15,000.*	*2,000.*
Double transfer at top and at bottom		—
"Curl" on forehead (85 L 1)	2,100.	350.00
"Curl" to right of left "X" (87 R 1)	2,100.	350.00

CANCELLATIONS.

		"Paid"	+25.00
Blue	+10.00	Steamship	+75.00
Red	+25.00	U. S. Express Mail	+75.00
Magenta	+75.00	Express Company	+200.00
Brown	+25.00	Packet boat	—
Orange	+35.00	Canada (on cover)	+1000.
Green	+200.00	Territorial	+150.00
1855 year date	—	Railroad	+75.00
1856 year date	+50.00	Numeral	+50.00
1857 year date	+10.00	Pen	150.00
1858 year date	+10.00		

A15

Type IV. The outer lines have been recut at top or bottom or both.

16 A15 10c **green,** type IV	*11,500.*	1,500.
dark green	*11,500.*	1,500.
yellowish green	*11,500.*	1,500.
On cover		1,750.
Pair	—	3,500.
Block of four (54-55, 64-65L)		—

VARIETIES OF RECUTTING

Eight stamps on Plate 1 were recut. All are listed below.

Outer line recut at top (65L, 74L, 86L, and 3R, Plate 1)	*11,500.*	1,500.
Outer line recut at bottom (54L, 55L, 76L, Plate 1)	*12,000.*	1,550.
Outer line recut at top and bottom (64 L 1)	*13,000.*	1,650.

Positions 65 L 1 and 86 L 1 have both "X" ovals recut at top, as well as the outer line.

CANCELLATIONS.

		"Paid"	+100.00
Blue	+50.00	Steamship	+300.00
Red	+100.00	Territorial	+500.00
Brown	—	Express Company	+750.00
1857 year date	—	Numeral	+100.00
1859 year date	—	Pen	750.00

Types I, II, III and IV occur on the same sheet, so it is possible to obtain pairs and blocks showing combinations of types. For listings of type combinations in pairs and blocks, see Nos. 13-15.

Washington — A16

17 A16 12c **black,** *July 1, 1851*	2,000.	250.00
gray black	2,000.	250.00
intense black	2,000.	250.00
Single, on cover		1,300.
Single on cover with No. 11 to France		1,000.
Pair	4,100.	525.00
Pair, on cover to England		625.00
Block of four	*11,000.*	*2,750.*
a. Diagonal half used as 6c on cover		*3,500.*
Diagonal half used as 6c on "Via Nicaragua" cover		*6,500.*
b. Vertical half used as 6c on cover		*8,500.*
c. Printed on both sides		*3,500.*
Double transfer	2,100.	275.00
Triple transfer (5 R 1 & 49 R 1)	2,400.	325.00
Not recut in lower right corner	2,000.	275.00
Recut in lower left corner (43L, 53L, 63L, 73L and 100L, Plate 1)	2,200.	300.00
On part-India paper	—	600.00

CANCELLATIONS.

Red	+20.00	Steamship	+100.00
Blue	+5.00	Steamboat	+125.00
Brown	+20.00	Supplementary Mail Type A	+75.00
Magenta	+65.00	Railroad	+75.00
Orange	+40.00	"Honolulu" in red	+400.00
Green	+300.00	U. S. Express Mail	+125.00
"Paid"	+25.00	Pen	125.00
"Way"	+75.00		

SAME DESIGNS AS 1851-57 ISSUES
Printed by Toppan, Carpenter & Co.

Nos. 18-23, 25, 27-29, 31-34 and 38 have very small margins. The values take into account the margin size.

1857-61 ***Perf. 15***

18 A5 1c **blue,** type I (Plate 12), *Jan. 25, 1861*	800.00	375.00
On cover		475.00
On patriotic cover		1,000.
Pair	1,650.	800.00
Strip of three	2,600.	1,350.
Block of four	*4,750.*	
Pair, combination types I & II	1,400.	600.00
Pair, combination types I and IIIa	1,600.	650.00
Block of four, combination types I and II	3,000.	1,750.
Block of four, combination types I, II and IIIa	3,400.	2,250.
Double transfer	850.00	450.00
Cracked plate (91 R 12)		500.00

Plate 12 consists of types I and II. A few positions are type IIIa.

CANCELLATIONS.

		"Paid"	+25.00
Blue	+10.00	Black Carrier	+85.00
Red	+35.00	Red Carrier	+75.00
Violet	+100.00	Pen	200.00

19 A6 1c **blue,** type Ia (Plate 4), *July 26, 1857*	*10,000.*	*2,500.*
On cover		*3,250.*
Pair	*21,000.*	*5,500.*
Strip of three	*35,000.*	*8,500.*
Vertical pair, types Ia & III	*16,000.*	*4,000.*
Vertical pair, types Ia & IIIa	*12,500.*	*3,000.*
Block of four, combination, pair type Ia and types III or IIIa	—	—
"Curl on shoulder" (97 L 4)	*10,500.*	*2,500.*

Copies of this stamp exist with perforations not touching the design at any point. Such copies command very high prices.

Type Ia comes only from the bottom row of both panes of Plate 4. Examples called "Ashbrook type Ic" are sometimes offered as varieties of type Ia. Actually they are varieties of type IIIa (No. 22) except 91 R 4 and 96 R 4 which are varieties of type Ia.

CANCELLATIONS.

Red Carrier	+200.00	Pen	1,500.

20 A7 1c **blue,** type II (Plate 2) *July 25, 1857*	450.00	150.00
On cover		175.00
Pair	950.00	325.00
Strip of three	1,500.	500.00
Block of four	2,300.	1,250.

Double transfer (Plate 2)	500.00	170.00
Cracked plate (2L, 12L, 13L, 23L & 33L, Plate 2)	700.00	275.00
Double transfer (4 R 1 L)		450.00
Plate 4, *July 26, 1857*	—	*600.00*
On cover (Plate 4)		*700.00*
Pair (Plate 4)	—	*1,250.*
Strip of three (Plate 4)	—	—
Double transfer (10 R 4)		*750.00*
"Curl in hair" (3 R, 4 R 4)	—	*650.00*
Plate 11, *Jan. 12, 1861*	575.00	175.00
On cover (Plate 11)		200.00
On patriotic cover (Plate 11)		650.00
Pair (Plate 11)	1,200.	375.00
Strip of three (Plate 11)		—
Double transfer (Plate 11)	—	—
Plate 12, *Jan. 25, 1861*	450.00	150.00
On cover (Plate 12)		175.00
On patriotic cover (Plate 12)		450.00
Pair (Plate 12)	950.00	325.00
Strip of three (Plate 12)	1,500.	475.00
Block of four (Plate 12)	2,400.	*1,250.*

CANCELLATIONS.

		1863 year date	+200.00
Blue	+5.00	"Paid"	+15.00
Red	+20.00	Railroad	+60.00
Green	+200.00	"Way"	+75.00
1857 year date	+10.00	Steamboat	+75.00
1858 year date	+5.00	Red Carrier	+35.00
1861 year date	+5.00	Black Carrier	+50.00
"FREE"	—	Pen	65.00

21 A8 1c **blue,** type III (Plate 4), *July 26, 1857,* see below for 99 R 2 — 4,500. 1,400.

On cover		1,750.
Pair	9,250.	2,900.
Strip of three		4,400.
Block of four	—	
Pair, types III & IIIa	5,250.	1,750.
Vertical pair, types III & II	—	—
Block of 4, types III & IIIa	—	
Top & bottom lines broken (46 L 12)	—	—

CANCELLATIONS.

Blue	+25.00	"Paid"	+50.00
Red	+50.00	Black Carrier	+175.00
Green	+350.00	Red Carrier	+150.00
1858 year date	+25.00	Pen	750.00

(21) A8 1c **blue,** type III, (99 R 2), *July 26, 1857* — *6,000.*

On cover		*7,500.*
Pair, combination type III (99 R 2) and type II		—
Pair, combination types III (99 R 2) and IIIa		—
Strip of three, combination type III (99 R 2II) and types II and IIIa		—
Block of 12, combination one type III (99 R 2), others type II		—

22 A8 1c **blue,** type IIIa (Plate 4), *July 26, 1857* — 700.00 250.00

On cover		275.00
On patriotic cover		600.00
Pair	1,450.	525.00
Vertical pair, combination types IIIa and II (Plate 4)	—	*900.00*
Strip of three	2,400.	800.00
Block of four	*3,750.*	*3,750.*
Block of four, combination types IIIa and II (Plate 4)	—	—
Double transfer	750.00	275.00

b. Horizontal pair, imperf. between — *3,500.*

Plate 2 (100 R), *July 25, 1857*		—
Plate 11, *Jan. 12, 1861,* and Plate 12, *Jan. 25, 1861*	800.00	275.00
On cover		325.00
On patriotic cover		800.00
Pair	1,700.	575.00
Vertical pair, combination types IIIa and II (Plate 11)	1,700.	550.00
Strip of three	2,600.	850.00
Block of four	4,000.	
Block of four, combination types IIIa and II (Plate 11)	*4,250.*	*2,500.*
Double transfer	800.00	300.00
Triple transfer (Plate 11)	—	—
Bottom line broken (46 L 12)	—	—

One pair of No. 22b is reported. Beware of numerous pairs that have blind perforations. These are not to be confused with No. 22b.

CANCELLATIONS.

		1861 year date	—
Blue	+5.00	1863 year date	—
Red	+20.00	"Paid"	+25.00
Green	+225.00	Red Carrier	+35.00
1857 year date	—	Black Carrier	+50.00
1858 year date	—	Blue Carrier	+100.00
		Pen	125.00

23 A9 1c **blue,** type IV, *July 25, 1857* — 2,000. 300.00

On cover		450.00
Pair	4,100.	650.00
Strip of three	6,250.	1,050.
Block of four	—	*7,500.*
Double transfer	2,100.	325.00
Triple transfer, one inverted (71 L 1 L, 81 L 1 L and 91 L 1 L)	2,500.	425.00
Cracked plate	2,400.	400.00

VARIETIES OF RECUTTING

Recut once at top and once at bottom, (113 on plate)	2,000.	300.00
Recut once at top, (40 on plate)	2,050.	305.00
Recut once at top and twice at bottom, (21 on plate)	2,100.	310.00
Recut twice at bottom, (11 on plate)	2,150.	325.00
Recut once at bottom, (8 on plate)	2,200.	325.00
Recut once at bottom and twice at top, (4 on plate)	2,250.	335.00
Recut twice at top and twice at bottom, (2 on plate)	2.350.	350.00
Pair, combination, type II (4 R 1 L) and type IV		*1,200.*

CANCELLATIONS.

		Black Carrier	+60.00
Blue	+5.00	Railroad	+85.00
Red	+25.00	"Way"	+90.00
"Paid"	+25.00	Steamboat	+135.00
Red Carrier	+40.00	"Steam"	+100.00
		Pen	175.00

A20

Type V. Similar to type III of 1851-57 but with side ornaments partly cut away. Wide breaks in top and bottom framelines.

Type Va: Stamps from Plate 5 with almost complete ornaments at right side and no side scratches.

24 A20 1c **blue,** type V (Plates 7, 8, 9, 10) *1857* — 110.00 20.00

On cover		30.00
On patriotic cover		250.00
Pair	225.00	45.00
Strip of three	340.00	70.00
Block of four	450.00	275.00
Margin block of 8, Impt. & P#	*3,250.*	—
Double transfer at top (8R and 10R, Plate 8)	150.00	45.00
Double transfer at bottom (52 R 9)	185.00	50.00
Curl on shoulder, (57R, 58R, 59R, 98R, 99R, Plate 7)	150.00	35.00
With "Earring" below ear (10 L 9)	200.00	50.00
"Curl" over "C" of "Cent"	160.00	35.00
"Curl" over "E" of "Cent" (41R and 81R 8)	170.00	42.20
"Curl in hair," 23L VII; 39, 69L 8; 34, 74R 9	150.00	30.00
Horizontal dash in hair (24 L 7)	200.00	45.00
Horizontal dash in hair (36 L 8)	200.00	45.00
Long double "curl" in hair (52, 92R 8)	185.00	40.00

b. Laid paper — 450.00 200.00

Plate 5, *Jan. 2, 1858*	300.00	70.00
On cover (Plate 5)		110.00
Pair (Plate 5)	—	—
Strip of three (Plate 5)	—	—
Block of four (Plate V)	—	—
"Curl" in "O" of "ONE" (62 L 5)	—	—
"Curl" on shoulder (48 L 5)	—	—

Earliest known use; Nov. 17.

CANCELLATIONS.

		"Free"	+25.00
Blue	+1.00	Railroad	+50.00
Red	+5.00	Numeral	+7.50
Green	+150.00	Express Company	+90.00
Brown	+30.00	Steamboat	+55.00
Magenta	+35.00	"Steam"	+30.00
Ultramarine	+17.50	Steamship	+40.00
1857 year date	+70.00	Packet boat	—
1858 year date	+1.00	Supplementary Mail Types A, B, or C	+55.00
1859 year date	+1.00	"Way"	+30.00
1860 year date	+1.00	Red Carrier	+7.50

1861 year date	+1.00	Black Carrier	+12.50
1863 year date	+80.00	Blue Carrier	+50.00
Printed Precancellation "CUMBERLAND, ME." (on cover)	—	Brown Carrier	—
		"Old Stamps—Not Recognized"	+1000.
		Territorial	+80.00
"Paid"	+3.50	Pen	10.00

25 A10 3c **rose,** type I (no inner framelines), *Feb. 28, 1857* — 675.00 27.50

rose red	675.00	27.50
claret	725.00	32.50
dull red	675.00	27.50
On cover		32.50
On patriotic cover		275.00
Pair	1,400.	57.50
Strip of three	2,250.	95.00
Block of four	3,250.	3,500.

All type I stamps were printed from 7 of the plates used for the imperfs., so many varieties exist both imperf. and perf.

b. Vert. pair, imperf. horizontally — —

Gash on shoulder	700.00	30.00
Double transfer	725.00	40.00
Double transfer "Gents" instead of "Cents" (66 R 2 L)	—	250.00
Triple transfer (92 L 2 L)	—	300.00
Worn plate	675.00	27.50
Cracked plate	900.00	100.00

VARIETIES OF RECUTTING

Recut inner frame lines	750.00	40.00
Recut inner frame line only at right		45.00
1 extra vertical line outside of left frame line (29L, 39L, 49L, 59L, 69L, 79L, Plate 3)	—	50.00
2 extra vertical lines outside of left frame line (89L, 99L, Plate 3)	—	65.00
1 extra vertical line outside of right frame line (58L, 68L, 78L, 88L, 98L, Plate 3)	—	50.00
No inner line and frame line close to design at right (9L, 19L, Plate 3)	—	65.00
No inner line and frame line close to design at left (70L, 80L, 90L, 100L, Plate 3)	—	60.00
Lines on bust and bottom of medallion circle recut (47 R 6)	—	250.00
Recut button (10 R 2)		300.00

Other varieties of recutting are described in "The 3c Stamp of U.S. 1851-57 Issue," by Carroll Chase.

CANCELLATIONS.

		Steamship	+35.00
Blue	+1.00	Steamboat	+45.00
Red	+5.00	Packet Boat	+50.00
Orange	+20.00	Supplementary Mail Type A	+40.00
Brown	+15.00	U. S. Express Mail	+5.00
Ultramarine	+15.00	Express Company	+65.00
Green	+150.00	Black Carrier	+30.00
1857 year date	+1.00	"Old Stamps—Not Recognized"	+1000.
1858 year date	+1.00	Territorial	+35.00
1859 year date	+1.00	Printed precancellation "Cumberland, Me." (on cover)	—
"Paid"	+2.50	Pen	15.00
"Way"	+20.00		
Railroad	+25.00		
Numeral	+7.50		
"Steam"	+20.00		

A21

Type II. The outer frame line has been removed at top and bottom. The side frame lines were recut so as to be continuous from the top to the bottom of the plate.

Type IIa. The side frame lines extend only to the top and bottom of the stamp design. All Type IIa stamps are from plates 10 and 11 (each of which exists in three states), and these plates produced only Type IIa. The side frame lines were recut individually for each stamp, thus being broken between the stamp vertically.

26 A21 3c **dull red,** type II, *1857* — 45.00 2.75

red	45.00	2.75
rose	45.00	2.75
brownish carmine	50.00	3.00
claret	60.00	3.50
orange brown	—	—
On cover		3.50
On patriotic cover		75.00
On Confederate patriotic cover		1,200.
On Pony express cover		—

Pair	92.50	5.75
Strip of three	140.00	9.00
Block of four	200.00	50.00
Margin block of 8, Impt. & P#	—	
b. Horiz. pair, imperf. vertically	—	—
c. Vert. pair, imperf. horizontally		—
d. Horizontal pair, imperf. between		—
e. Double impression		—
Double transfer	65.00	10.00
Double transfer, rosettes double and line through "Postage"	—	60.00
Left frame line double	65.00	8.75
Right frame line double	65.00	8.75
Cracked plate	*425.00*	125.00
Damaged transfer above lower left rosette	50.00	3.25
Same, retouched	55.00	3.50
1 line recut in upper left triangle	—	16.50
5 lines recut in upper left triangle		60.00
Inner line recut at right	—	32.50
Worn plate	50.00	3.00

Frame line double varieties are separate and distinct for virtually the entire length of the stamp. Copies with partly split lines are worth considerably less.

Earliest known use: Sept. 15.

CANCELLATIONS.

Blue	+.10	"Steam"	+12.50
Red	+1.50	Steamer	—
Orange	+5.00	Steamboat	+22.50
Brown	+7.50	Steamship	+22.50
Ultramarine	+7.50	"Way"	+12.50
Violet	+15.00	Railroad	+15.00
Green	+50.00	U. S. Express Mail	+20.00
1857—1861 year date	+.25	Express Company	+65.00
Printed Circular Precan—cellation "Cumberland, Me." (on cover)	—	Packet boat	+65.00
"Paid"	+.25	Supplementary Mail Types A, B or C	+75.00
"Paid All"	+15.00	Black Carrier	+30.00
"Free"	+20.00	Red Carrier	+25.00
"Collect"	+40.00	"Southn. Letter Unpaid"	—
Numeral	+2.50	Territorial	+20.00
		"Old Stamps—Not Recognized"	+500.00

26a A21 3c **dull red,** type IIa, *July 11, 1857*	110.00	20.00
brownish carmine	110.00	20.00
rose	110.00	20.00
claret	120.00	22.50
On cover		30.00
On patriotic cover		175.00
Pair	225.00	42.50
Strip of three	350.00	70.00
Block of four	550.00	120.00
Double transfer	175.00	30.00
Double transfer of rosettes and lower part of stamp (91R 11 L)		75.00
Triple transfer	—	90.00
Damaged transfer above lower left rosette	120.00	21.00
Same, retouched	125.00	22.00
Inner line recut at right	—	40.00
Inner line recut at left	—	75.00
Left frame line double	—	45.00
Worn plate	110.00	20.00

CANCELLATIONS.

Blue	+2.50	"Collect"	+40.00
Red	+10.00	Numeral	+2.50
Orange	+15.00	"Steam"	+15.00
Brown	+12.50	Steamer	—
Ultramarine	+12.50	Steamboat	+25.00
Violet	+25.00	Steamship	+25.00
Green	+135.00	"Way"	+15.00
1857 year date	+2.50	Railroad	+17.50
1858 or 1859 year date	+1.50	U. S. Express Mail	+17.50
"Paid"	+2.50	Express Company	+65.00
"Paid All"	+15.00	Packet boat	+65.00
"Free"	+20.00	Black Carrier	+30.00
		Red Carrier	+20.00
		Territorial	+25.00
		Pen	10.00

27 A11 5c **brick red,** type I, *Oct. 6, 1858*	*8,500.*	800.00
On cover		1,250.
On patriotic cover		4,000.
Pair	*17,500.*	1,700.
Strip of three		2,750.
Block of four	—	*30,000.*

CANCELLATIONS.

Blue	+25.00	"Paid"	+25.00
Red	+50.00	Supplementary Mail Type A	+100.00
Ultramarine	+150.00	"Steamship"	+100.00
1859 year date	+25.00	Pen	450.00
1860 year date	+25.00		

28 A11 5c **red brown,** type I, *Aug. 23, 1857*	1,350.	250.00
pale red brown	1,350.	250.00
On cover		400.00
Pair	2,750.	550.00
Strip of three		850.00
Block of four	*15,000.*	*3,500.*
b. Bright red brown	1,850.	400.00

CANCELLATIONS.

Blue	+10.00	"Paid"	+35.00
Red	+25.00	Railroad	+75.00
1857 year date	+20.00	"Short Paid"	—
1858 year date	+10.00	Pen	120.00

28A A11 5c **Indian red,** type I, *Mar. 31, 1858*	*10,000.*	2,000.
On cover		2,600.
Pair		4,250.
Strip of three		7,000.
Block of four		—

CANCELLATIONS.

Red	+50.00	1858 year date	+50.00
		1859 year date	+25.00
		Pen	1,250.

29 A11 5c **brown,** type I, *July 4, 1859*	750.00	200.00
pale brown	750.00	200.00
deep brown	750.00	200.00
yellowish brown	750.00	200.00
On cover		300.00
Pair	1,550.	425.00
Strip of three	2,500.	650.00
Block of four	*15,000.*	*4,000.*

CANCELLATIONS.

Blue	+5.00	1859 year date	+5.00
Red	+15.00	1860 year date	+5.00
Brown	+20.00	"Paid"	+15.00
Magenta	+65.00	"Steam"	+75.00
Green	+250.00	Steamship	+85.00
		Numeral	+50.00
		Pen	95.00

Jefferson — A22

FIVE CENTS.

Type II. The projections at top and bottom are partly cut away. Several minor types could be made according to the extent of cutting of the projections.

30 A22 5c **orange brown,** Type II, *May 8, 1861*	750.00	900.00
deep orange brown	750.00	900.00
On cover		*1,750.*
On patriotic cover		*4,000.*
Pair	1,550.	2,250.
Strip of three	2,500.	—
Block of four	4,000.	—

CANCELLATIONS.

Blue	+25.00	Steamship	+110.00
Red	+50.00	Supp. Mail A	+150.00
Green	—	Railroad	—
"Paid"	+75.00	Pen	300.00

30A A22 5c **brown,** type II, *Mar. 4, 1860*	450.00	175.00
dark brown	450.00	175.00
yellowish brown	450.00	175.00
On cover		225.00
On patriotic cover		
Pair	925.00	360.00
Strip of three	1,450.	550.00
Block of four	2,400.	*2,500.*
b. Printed on both sides	*3,750.*	*3,000.*
Cracked plate		—

CANCELLATIONS.

Blue	+5.00	"Steamship"	+50.00
Red	+20.00	"Steam"	+40.00
		Express Company	+250.00
Magenta	+50.00	Railroad	—
Green	+250.00	Packet boat	—
"Paid"	+20.00	Pen	75.00
Supp. Mail, A	+50.00		

31 A12 10c **green,** type I, *July 27, 1857*	5,250.	525.00
dark green	5,250.	525.00
bluish green	5,250.	525.00
yellowish green	5,250.	525.00
On cover		800.00
On patriotic cover		2,500.
Pair	*11,000.*	1,100.
Pair combination, type I and type III	*7,250.*	750.00
Pair, combination, type I and type IV		—
Strip of three		—
Vertical strip of 3, combination, type I, type III, type II		—
Block of four, combination, type I and type III	*15,000.*	—
Block of four, combination, types I, III and IV		—
Double transfer (100 R 1)	5,750.	600.00
"Curl" in left "X" (99 R 1)	5,750.	600.00

Type I comes only from the bottom row of both panes of Plate 1.

CANCELLATIONS.

Blue	+10.00	Supplementary Mail Type A	—
Red	+25.00	"Steamship"	+100.00
Green	+225.00	Canadian	—
		Pen	250.00

Act of February 27, 1861. Ten cent rate of postage to be prepaid on letters conveyed in the mail from any point in the United States east of the Rocky Mountains to any State or Territory on the Pacific Coast and vice versa, for each half-ounce.

32 A13 10c **green,** type II, *July 27, 1857*	1,750.	185.00
dark green	1,750.	185.00
bluish green	1,750.	185.00
yellowish green	1,750.	185.00
On cover		225.00
On pony express cover		—
Pair	3,600.	400.00
Strip of 3		600.00
Block of four	*9,000.*	*3,500.*
Pair, combination, types II & III	3,750.	400.00
Pair, combination, types II & IV	*20,000.*	2,000.
Vertical strip of three, combination types II, III and IV		—
Block of four, combination, type II and type III	*8,000.*	*1,650.*
Block of four, combination types II and IV		—
Block of 4, types II, III, IV	*40,000.*	
Double transfer (31L, 51L and 20R, Plate 1)	1,850.	200.00
"Curl opposite left X" (10 R 1)		235.00

CANCELLATIONS.

Blue	+5.00	1857 year date	+5.00
Red	+20.00	Steamship	+50.00
Brown	+25.00	Packet boat	—
Green	+225.00	Railroad	—
		Express Company	—
"Paid"	+20.00	Pen	70.00

33 A14 10c **green,** type III, *July 27, 1857*	1,750.	185.00
dark green	1,750.	185.00
bluish green	1,750.	185.00
yellowish green	1,750.	185.00
On cover		225.00
Pair	3,600.	385.00
Strip of 3	—	—
Pair, combination ,types III & IV		2,100.
"Curl" on forehead (85 L 1)	—	235.00
"Curl in left X" (87 R 1)		235.00

CANCELLATIONS.

Blue	+5.00	"Paid"	+20.00
Red	+20.00	"Steam"	+45.00
Brown	+25.00	Steamboat	—
Ultramarine	+45.00	Steamship	+50.00
1857 year date	+5.00	Numeral	+15.00
		Packet boat	—
		Pen	75.00

34 A15 10c **green,** type IV, *July 27, 1857*	*17,500.*	1,750.
dark green	*17,500.*	1,750.
bluish green	*17,500.*	1,750.
yellowish green	*17,500.*	1,750.
On cover		2,250.
Pair		3,750.
Block of four (54-55, 64-65L)		—

VARIETIES OF RECUTTING

Eight stamps on Plate I were recut. All are listed below.

Outer line recut at top (65L, 74L, 86L and 3R, Plate 1)	*17,500.*	1,750.
Outer line recut at bottom (54L, 55L, 76L, Plate 1)	*18,000.*	1,800.
Outer line recut at top and bottom (64 L 1)	*18,500.*	1,850.

CANCELLATIONS.

Blue	+25.00	Steamship	+150.00
Red	+50.00	Packet boat	—
		Pen	750.00

Types I, II, III and IV occur on the same sheet, so it is possible to obtain pairs and blocks showing combinations of types. For listings of type combinations in pairs and blocks, see Nos. 31-33.

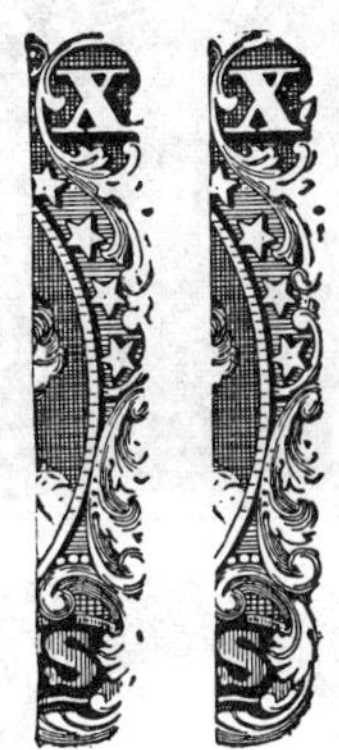

(Two typical examples) — A23

Type V. The side ornaments are slightly cut away. Usually only one pearl remains at each end of the lower label, but some copies show two or three pearls at the right side. At the bottom the outer line is complete and the shells nearly so. The outer lines at top are complete except over the right "X".

No.	Description	Unused	Used
35	A23 10c **green,** type V, (Plate 2), *May 9, 1859*	175.00	50.00
	dark green	175.00	50.00
	yellowish green	175.00	50.00
	On cover		60.00
	On patriotic cover		600.00
	On pony express cover		—
	Pair	360.00	105.00
	Block of four	730.00	500.00
	Margin block of 8, Impt. & P#	9,000.	
	Double transfer at bottom (47 R 2)	225.00	70.00
	Small "Curl" on forehead (37, 78L 2)	210.00	60.00
	Curl in "e" of "cents" (93 L 2)	225.00	70.00
	Curl in "t" of "cents" (73 R 2)	225.00	70.00

CANCELLATIONS.

		Steamship	+35.00
Red	+2.50	"Steam"	+30.00
Brown	+15.00	Numerals	+15.00
Blue	+1.50	Supplementary Mail Type A or C	+60.00
Orange	+15.00	Express Company	+135.00
Magenta	+40.00	"Southn Letter Unpaid"	—
Green	+125.00	Territorial	—
1859 year date	+5.00	Pen	30.00
"Paid"	+5.00		
Red carrier	—		
Railroad	+40.00		

TWELVE CENTS. Printed from two plates.
Plate I. Outer frame lines complete.
Plate III. Outer frame lines noticeably uneven or broken, sometimes partly missing. Imperforate stamps, Plate III, are from a trial printing.

No.	Description	Unused	Used
36	A16 12c **black** (Plate 1), *July 30, 1857*	325.00	75.00
	gray black	325.00	75.00
	Single on cover		450.00
	Single on cover with No. 26 to France		150.00
	Pair on cover to England		175.00
	Pair on patriotic cover		—
	Pair	700.00	155.00
	Block of four	1,750.	750.00
a.	Diagonal half used as 6c on cover		—
c.	Horizontal pair, imperf. between (I)		—
	Not recut in lower right corner	350.00	85.00
	Recut in lower left corner (43L, 53L, 63L, 73L and 100L)	375.00	80.00
	Double transfer	375.00	85.00
	Triple transfer	450.00	—

CANCELLATIONS.

Blue	+2.50	Supplementary Mail Type A	+60.00
		Express Company	—
Red	+7.50	Railroad	+60.00
Brown	+20.00	Numeral	+20.00
Magenta	+45.00	"Southn Letter Unpaid"	—
Green	+250.00	Pen	40.00
1857 year date	+20.00		
"Paid"	+10.00		

No.	Description	Unused	Used
36b	A16 12c **black** (Plate 3), *Dec. 3, 1859*	250.00	100.00
	intense black	250.00	100.00
	Single on cover		550.00
	Single on cover with No. 26 to France		175.00
	Pair on cover to England		250.00
	Pair	525.00	210.00
	Block of four	1,200.	1,100.
	Double frame line at right	275.00	110.00
	Double frame line at left	275.00	110.00
	Vertical line through rosette (95 R 3)	350.00	135.00

Washington — A17

No.	Description	Unused	Used
37	A17 24c **gray lilac,** *1860*	600.00	235.00
a.	24c gray	600.00	235.00
	On cover to England		750.00
	On patriotic cover		*3,500.*
	Pair	1,250.	525.00
	Block of four, gray lilac	*3,000.*	*5,000.*
	Margin block of 12, Impt. & P#	*30,000.*	
b.	24c red lilac	1,000.	
b.	Block of four, red lilac	6,000.	
c.	Imperforate	*2,500.*	
c.	Pair, imperforate	*6,000.*	

Earliest known use: July 8.

CANCELLATIONS.

		"Free"	+100.00
Blue	+10.00	Supplementary Mail Type A	+100.00
Red	+20.00	Railroad	+150.00
Magenta	+45.00	Packet Boat	+200.00
Violet	+75.00	Red Carrier	—
Green	+450.00	Numeral	+40.00
1860 year date	+15.00	"Southn Letter Unpaid"	+2500.
"Paid"	+25.00	Pen	120.00
"Paid All"	+50.00		

Franklin — A18

No.	Description	Unused	Used
38	A18 30c **orange,** *Aug. 8, 1860*	775.00	300.00
	yellow orange	775.00	300.00
	reddish orange	775.00	300.00
	On cover to France or Germany		*1,250.*
	On patriotic cover		*8,500.*
	Pair	1,600.	675.00
	Block of four	4,500.	*6,500.*
a.	Imperforate	*2,500.*	
a.	Pair, imperforate	*6,000.*	
	Double transfer (89 L 1 and 99 L 1)	875.00	350.00
	Recut at bottom (52 L 1)	925.00	400.00
	Cracked plate	—	—

CANCELLATIONS.

		"Free"	—
Blue	+10.00	Black town	+25.00
Red	+25.00	Supplementary Mail Type A	+75.00
Magenta	+60.00	Steamship	—
Violet	+75.00	Express Company	—
Green	+450.00	"Southn Letter Unpaid"	—
1860 year date	+25.00	Pen	175.00
"Paid"	+35.00		

The 30c was first printed in black. It was not perforated or gummed. It is listed in the Trial Color Proofs section.

Scott's editorial staff cannot undertake to identify, authenticate or appraise stamps and postal markings.

Washington — A19

No.	Description	Unused	Used
39	A19 90c **blue,** *1860*	1,250.	*3,500.*
	deep blue	1,250.	*3,500.*
	On cover		—
	Pair	2,650.	—
	Block of four	10,000.	—
a.	Imperforate	*2,500.*	
a.	Pair, imperforate	*6,000.*	
	Double transfer at bottom	1,400.	—
	Double transfer at top	1,400.	—
	Short transfer at bottom right and left (13 L 1 and 68 R 1)	1,350.	

Earliest known use: Sept. 11.

CANCELLATIONS.

		"Paid"	—
Blue	+100.00	Red Carrier	—
Red	+250.00	Pen	1000.
1861 year date	—		

Genuine cancellations on the 90c are rare.
Nos. 37b, 37c, 38a and 39a were probably not regularly issued but came from trial printings.

REPRINTS OF 1857-60 ISSUE

Issued for the Centennial Exposition of 1876. These were not valid postal use.
Produced by the Continental Bank Note Co.
White paper, without gum.
The 1, 3, 10 and 12c were printed from new plates of 100 subjects each differing from those used for the regular issue.

1875 *Perf. 12*

No.	Description	Unused
40	A5 1c **bright blue** *(3846)*	*500.00*
	Pair	*1,100.*
	Block of four	*2,500.*
	Cracked plate, pos. 91	*600.00*
	Double transfer, pos. 94	*600.00*
41	A10 3c **scarlet** *(479)*	*3,000.*
42	A22 5c **orange brown** *(878)*	*1,000.*
	Pair	*3,000.*
	Vertical margin strip of 4, Impt. & P#	*10,000.*
43	A12 10c **blue green** *(516)*	*2,000.*
	Pair	*6,000.*
44	A16 12c **greenish black** *(489)*	*2,250.*
	Pair	*5,500.*
45	A17 24c **blackish violet** *(479)*	*2,500.*
46	A18 30c **yellow orange** *(480)*	*2,500.*
47	A19 90c **deep blue** *(454)*	*3,500.*

Nos. 40 to 47 exist imperforate.
Numbers in parentheses are quantities issued.

Produced by the National Bank Note Co.

Franklin — A24a

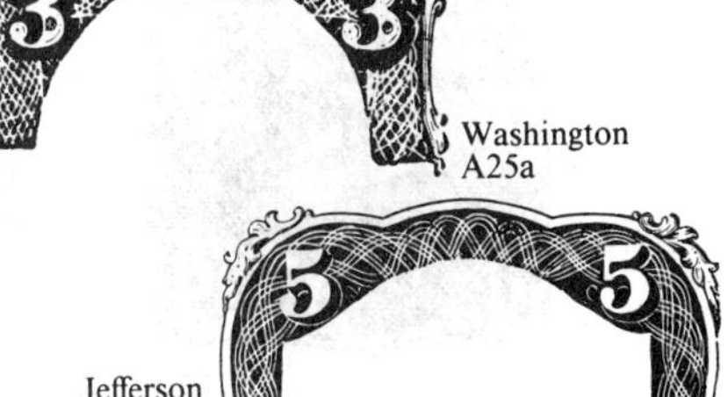

Washington A25a

Jefferson A26a

Washington
A27a

Washington — A28a

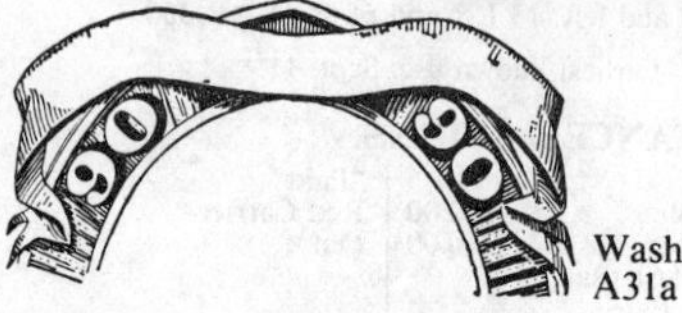

Washington
A31a

Plates of 200 subjects in two panes of 100 each.

The paper of Nos. 55-62 is thin and semitransparent. That of the following issues is thicker and more opaque, except Nos. 62B, 70c, and 70d.

Nos. 55-62 were not regularly issued.

1861 ***Perf. 12***

55	A24a	1c	**indigo**	*20,000.*
56	A25a	3c	**brown rose**	*500.00*
			Pair	*1,050.*
			Block of four	*2,200.*
			Margin of 8, Impt. & P#	*15,000.*
a.			Imperf., pair	*1,750.*
57	A26a	5c	**brown**	*14,000.*
58	A27a	10c	**dark green**	*6,000.*
59	A28a	12c	**black**	*40,000.*
60	A29	24c	**dark violet**	*6,500.*
			Block of four	—
61	A30	30c	**red orange**	*17,500.*
62	A31a	90c	**dull blue**	*22,500.*
a.			Imperf., pair	*5,500.*

1861

62B	A27a	10c	**dark green**, *Sept. 17, 1861*	*6,000.*	450.00
			dark yellow green	*6,000.*	450.00
			On cover		750.00
			On patriotic cover		2,000.
			Pair	*12,500.*	1,000.
			Block of four	*26,000.*	*5,000.*
			Double transfer 94 R 4	*6,500.*	525.00

CANCELLATIONS.

Red	+50.00	Steamship	+100.00
Blue	+25.00	Express Company	+200.00
"Paid"	+50.00	Supplementary Mail Type A	+125.00

No. 62B unused cannot be distinguished from No. 58, which does not exist used.

Designs modified (except 24c and 30c)

Franklin — A24

Washington — A25

Jefferson — A26

Washington — A27

Washington — A28

Washington — A29

Franklin — A30

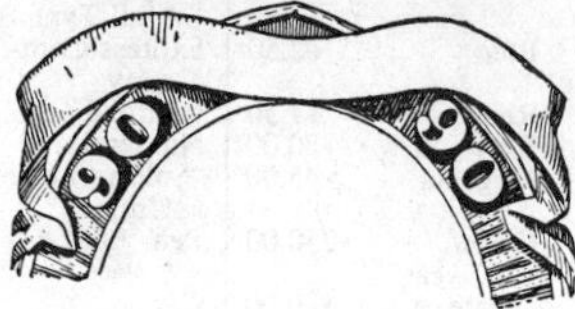

Washington — A31

1c. A dash has been added under the tip of the ornament at right of the numeral in upper left corner.

3c. Ornaments at corners have been enlarged and end in a small ball.

5c. A leaflet has been added to the foliated ornaments at each corner.

10c. A heavy curved line has been cut below the stars and an outer line added to the ornaments above them.

12c. Ovals and scrolls have been added to the corners.

90c. Parallel lines form an angle above the ribbon with "U. S. Postage"; between these lines a row of dashes has been added and a point of color to the apex of the lower line.

Patriotic Covers covering a wide range of historical interest were used during the Civil War period, in the North as well as the South, and are collected in State groups as well as generally. There are known to be over 11,000 varieties.

During the war, these stamps were used as small change until Postage Currency was issued.

The Act of Congress of March 3, 1863, effective July 1, 1863, created a rate of three cents for each half ounce, first class domestic mail. This Act was the first law which established uniform rate of postage regardless of the distance. This rate remained in effect for twenty years.

1861-62 ***Perf. 12***

63	A24 1c **blue,** *Aug. 17, 1861*	125.00	15.00
	pale blue	125.00	15.00
	bright blue	125.00	15.00
a.	1c ultramarine	225.00	40.00
b.	1c dark blue	175.00	25.00
	On cover (single)		20.00
	On prisoner's letter		—
	On patriotic cover		175.00
	Pair	265.00	32.00
	Block of four	525.00	125.00
	Margin block of 8, Impr. & P#	*2,400.*	
	Double transfer	—	22.50
	Dot in "U"	130.00	17.50
c.	Laid paper, horiz. or vert.	—	150.00
d.	Vertical pair, imperf. horiz.		—
e.	Printed on both sides	—	*2,500.*

CANCELLATIONS.

Blue	+1.00	Supp. Mail, A, B	+30.00
Red	+5.00	Steamship	+35.00
Magenta	+10.00	Steam	+30.00
Green	+90.00	Express Company	+85.00
Violet	+25.00	Red Carrier	+5.00
1861 year date	+7.50	Black Carrier	+10.00
1865 year date	+1.00	Railroad	+30.00
1866 year date	+1.00	Numeral	+10.00
"Free"	+20.00	"Steamboat"	+50.00
"Paid"	+2.50	Printed Precancel "CUMBERLAND, ME." (on cover)	—
"Paid All"	+15.00		

64	A25 3c **pink**	4,000.	300.00
	On cover (pink)		400.00
	On patriotic cover (pink)		650.00
	Block of four (pink)	*17,500.*	—
a.	3c pigeon blood pink	—	*1,350.*
	On cover (pigeon blood pink)		*2,250.*
	On patriotic cover (pig. bld. pink)		*3,500.*
b.	3c **rose pink**	260.00	45.00
	On cover (rose pink)		65.00
	On patriotic cover (rose pink)		150.00
	Block of four (rose pink)	1,300.	275.00

CANCELLATIONS. Nos. 64 & 64b

Blue No. 64	+10.00	Blue No. 64b	+5.00
"Paid" No. 64	+25.00	"Paid" No. 64b	+10.00
Red No. 64	+25.00	Red No. 64b	+10.00
"Ship" No. 64	+85.00	"Ship" No. 64b	+30.00
Green No. 64	+500.00	Green No. 64b	+150.00
"Free" No. 64	+125.00	"Free" No. 64b	+50.00
1861 date No. 64	—		
Railroad No. 64	+125.00	Railroad No. 64b	+50.00
Steamboat No. 64	+175.00	Steamboat No. 64b	+75.00
Supp. Mail, B No. 64	+150.00		

65	A25 3c **rose,** *1861*	65.00	1.00
	bright rose	65.00	1.00
	dull red	65.00	1.00
	rose red	65.00	1.00
	brown red	65.00	1.00
	pale brown red	65.00	1.00
	On cover		1.25
	On patriotic cover		30.00
	On prisoner's letter		150.00
	On pony express cover		—
	Pair	135.00	2.25
	Block of four	275.00	15.00
	Margin block of 8, Impt. & P#	*1,750.*	
b.	Laid paper, horiz. or vert.	*250.00*	35.00
c.	Imperf., pair	*450.00*	—
c.	Margin block of 8, Impt. & P#	—	
d.	Vertical pair, imperf. horiz.	*1,200.*	*750.00*
e.	Printed on both sides	*1,650.*	*1,000.*
f.	Double impression		*1,200.*
	Double transfer	80.00	2.50
	Cracked plate	—	—

CANCELLATIONS.

Blue	+10	"Collect"	+35.00
Ultramarine	+2.75	"Ship"	+15.00
Brown	+2.50	"U. S. Ship"	+35.00
Red	+2.50	"Steam"	+12.00
Violet	+4.50	Steamship	+15.00
Magenta	+4.50	Steamboat	+20.00
Green	+45.00	"Ship Letter"	+35.00
Olive	+12.00	Red Carrier	+15.00
Orange	+10.00	Blue Carrier	+25.00
1861 year date	+.50	Black Carrier	+20.00
1867 or 1868 year date	+.50	Numeral	+3.00
"Paid"	+35	Supplementary Mail Types A, B or C	+15.00
"Paid All"	+7.50	Express Company	+40.00
"Mails Suspended"	—	Army Field Post	+60.00
Railroad	+12.50	Packet Boat	+40.00
"Way"	+20.00	"Registered"	+30.00
"Free"	+20.00	"Postage Due"	+25.00
		"Advertised"	+15.00
		Territorial	+25.00
		St. Thomas	—
		China	—

66	A25 3c **lake**	*1,650.*	
	Pair	*3,400.*	
	Block of four	*7,000.*	
a.	Imperf., (pair)	*1,850.*	
a.	Margin block of 8, Impt. & P#	—	
	Double transfer	*1,900.*	

Nos. 66 and 66a were not regularly issued. John N. Luff recorded the plate number as 34.

67	A26 5c **buff,** *Aug. 19, 1861*	5,000.	400.00
a.	5c brown yellow	5,000.	400.00
b.	5c olive yellow	5,000.	400.00
	On cover		700.00
	On patriotic cover		3,500.
	Pair	10,500.	850.00
	Block of four	*50,000.*	9,000.

CANCELLATIONS.

Red	+25.00	"Paid"	+25.00
Blue	+10.00	Supplementary Mail Type A	+100.00
Magenta	+50.00	Express Company	+250.00
Green	—		
1861 year date	+10.00	Numeral	+50.00
		"Steamship"	+100.00

68	A27 10c **yellow green,** *Aug. 20, 1861*	250.00	30.00
	deep yellow green on thin paper	325.00	40.00
	green	250.00	30.00
a.	10c dark green	265.00	31.00
	blue green	265.00	32.50
	On cover		45.00
	On patriotic cover		350.00
	Pair	510.00	62.50
	Block of four	1,050.	250.00
	Margin block of 8, Impt. & P#	*5,000.*	
b.	Vertical pair, imperf. horiz.		*3,500.*
	Double transfer	300.00	40.00

CANCELLATIONS.

Blue	+1.00	"Free"	+25.00
Red	+2.50	Numeral	+7.50
Purple	+5.00	Red Carrier	+45.00
Magenta	+5.00	Railroad	+20.00
Brown	+2.50	Steamship	+15.00
Green	+110.00	"Steamboat"	+35.00
1865 year date	+3.50	Supplementary Mail Types A or D	+30.00
"Paid"	+2.50	Express Company	+70.00
"Collect"	+32.50	China	—
"Short Paid"	+50.00	Japan	+200.00
"P.D." in circle	+30.00	St. Thomas	—

69	A28 12c **black,** *Aug. 1861*	475.00	55.00
	gray black	475.00	55.00
	intense black	500.00	60.00
	On cover		85.00
	On patriotic cover		800.00
	Pair	975.00	115.00
	Block of four	2,250.	550.00
	Double transfer of top frame line	525.00	65.00
	Double transfer of bottom frame line	525.00	65.00
	Double transfer of top and bottom frame lines	550.00	70.00

Earliest known use: Aug. 20.

CANCELLATIONS.

Blue	+2.00	"Paid"	+5.00
Red	+5.00	"Registered"	+35.00
Purple	+10.00	Supplementary Mail Types A, B or C	+45.00
Magenta	+10.00	Express Company	+175.00
Green	+175.00	Railroad	+50.00
1861 year date	+5.00	Numeral	+15.00

70	A29 24c **red lilac,** *Jan. 7, 1862*	575.00	80.00
	On cover		125.00
	On patriotic cover		*3,000.*
	Pair	1,200.	165.00
	Block of four	3,750.	750.00
a.	24c brown lilac	475.00	67.50
a.	Block of four	3,000.	
b.	24c steel blue ('61)	3,750.	275.00
b.	On cover		800.00
b.	Block of four	*15,500.*	
c.	24c violet, *Aug. 20, 1861*	3,750.	550.00
d.	24c grayish lilac	1,250.	275.00
	Scratch under "A" of "Postage"		95.00

There are numerous shades of the 24c stamp in this and the following issue.

Color changelings, especially of No. 78, are frequently offered as No. 70b.

Nos. 70c and 70d are on a thinner, harder and more transparent paper than Nos. 70, 70a, 70b or the latter Nos. 78, 78a, 78b and 78c. No. 60 is distinguished by its distinctive dark color.

CANCELLATIONS. (No. 70)

Blue	+2.50	1865 year date	+5.00
Red	+5.00	"Paid"	+15.00
Magenta	+15.00	Supplementary Mail Types A or B	+75.00
Brown	+7.50	Express Company	+350.00
Green	+300.00		

71	A30 30c **orange,** *Aug. 20, 1861*	475.00	70.00
	deep orange	475.00	70.00
	On cover to France or Germany		300.00
	On patriotic cover		*3,500.*
	Pair	975.00	160.00
	Block of four	2,250.	900.00
a.	Printed on both sides		—

CANCELLATIONS.

Blue	+2.50	Railroad	—
Magenta	+15.00	Packet Boat	—
Brown	+10.00	"Steamship"	+75.00
Red	+15.00	Supplementary Mail Type A	+75.00
"Paid"	+15.00	Express Company	+350.00
"Paid All"	+35.00	Japan	—

72	A31 90c **blue,** *Aug., 1861*	1,300.	250.00
a.	90c pale blue	1,300.	250.00
b.	90c dark blue	1,400.	275.00
	dull blue	1,300.	250.00
	On cover		*13,500.*
	Pair	2,700.	550.00
	Block of four	*6,250.*	*2,500.*

Earliest known use: Nov. 27.

CANCELLATIONS.

Blue	+10.00	"Paid"	+25.00
Red	+25.00	"Registered"	+75.00
Green	+450.00	Express Company	+500.00
1865 year date	+35.00	Supplementary Mail Type A	+100.00

Nos. 65c, 68a, 69, 71 and 72 exist as imperforate sheet-margin singles with pen cancel. They were not regularly issued.

The 90c was distributed to several post offices in the last two weeks of August, 1861.

Owing to the Civil War, stamps and stamped envelopes in current use or available for postage in 1860, were demonetized by various post office orders, beginning in August, 1861, and extending to early January, 1862.

P. O. Department Bulletin.

"A reasonable time after hostilities began in 1861 was given for the return to the Department of all these (1851-56) stamps in the hands of postmasters, and as early as 1863 the Department issued an order declining to longer redeem them."

The Act of Congress, approved March 3, 1863, abolished carriers' fees and established a prepaid rate of two cents for drop letters, making necessary the 2-cent Jackson (No. 73).

Free City Delivery was authorized by the Act of Congress of March 3, 1863, effective in 49 cities with 449 carriers, beginning July 1, 1863.

Produced by the National Bank Note Co.
DESIGNS AS 1861 ISSUE

Andrew Jackson — A32

Earliest known use: 2c, July 6, 1863.

1861-66 ***Perf. 12***

73	A32 2c **black,** *July 1863*	110.00	22.50
	gray black	110.00	22.50
	intense black	120.00	27.50
	On cover		40.00
	On prisoner's letter		—
	On patriotic cover		1,000.
	Pair	235.00	50.00

Block of four 500.00 400.00
Margin block of 8, Impt. & P# *8,000.*
a. Half used as 1c on cover, diagonal, vert. or horiz. *1,250.*
d. Laid paper — —
e. Printed on both sides *4,000.*
Double transfer 125.00 25.00
Major double transfer of top left corner 250.00
Major overall double transfer ("Atherton shift") 6,000.
Triple transfer —
Short transfer 115.00 24.00
Cracked plate — —

CANCELLATIONS.

Blue	+1.00	"Paid"	+10.00
Brown	+5.00	Numeral	+15.00
Red	+7.50	Railroad	+85.00
Magenta	+12.50	"Steam"	+40.00
Ultramarine	+12.50	Steamship	+65.00
Orange	+10.00	"Steamboat"	+65.00
Green	+265.00	"Ship Letter"	—
1863 year date	+5.00	Black Carrier	+20.00
Printed Precancellation "Jefferson, Ohio"	—	Blue Carrier	+35.00
"PAID ALL"	+40.00	Supplementary Mail Types A or B	+60.00
		Express Company	+200.00
		"Short Paid"	+130.00
		China	—

74 A25 3c **scarlet** *4,500.*
Block of four *20,000.*
With 4 horiz. black pen strokes *1,850.*
a. Imperf., pair *3,750.*

Nos. 74 and 74a were not regularly issued. John N. Luff recorded the plate number as 19.

75 A26 5c **red brown,** *Jan. 2, 1862* 1,300. 225.00
dark red brown 1,300. 225.00
On cover 475.00
On patriotic cover *2,500.*
Pair 2,700. 475.00
Block of four — 3,000.
Double transfer 1,500. 250.00

CANCELLATIONS.

Blue	+10.00	"Paid"	+25.00
Red	+25.00	Supplementary Mail Type A	+50.00
Magenta	+50.00	Express Company	+300.00

76 A26 5c **brown,** *Feb. 3, 1863* 325.00 52.50
pale brown 325.00 52.50
On cover 120.00
On patriotic cover 800.00
Pair 675.00 110.00
Block of four 1,500. 450.00
a. 5c dark brown 375.00 65.00
a. Block of four 1,750. 500.00
Double transfer of top frame line 400.00 65.00
Double transfer of bottom frame line 400.00 65.00
Double transfer of top and bottom frame lines 425.00 70.00
b. Laid paper —

CANCELLATIONS.

Blue	+2.50	"Paid"	+15.00
Magenta	+5.00	"Short Paid"	+75.00
Red	+5.00	Supplementary Mail Type A or F	+55.00
Brown	+5.00	Express Company	+175.00
Green	+225.00	"Steamship"	+65.00
1865 year date	+10.00	Packet boat	—

Abraham Lincoln — A33

77 A33 15c **black,** *1866* 500.00 67.50
full black 500.00 67.50
On cover to France or Germany 150.00
Pair 1,050. 140.00
Block of four 14,000. —

Margin block of 8, Impt. & P# —
Double transfer 500.00 75.00
Cracked plate —

Earliest known use; April 14.

CANCELLATIONS.

Blue	+2.50	"Paid"	+15.00
Magenta	+10.00	"Short Paid"	+85.00
Red	+10.00	"Insufficiently Paid"	+150.00
Brown	+10.00	"Ship"	+50.00
Green	+250.00	Steamship	+50.00
Ultramarine	+25.00	Supplementary Mail Type A	+70.00

78 A29 24c **lilac,** *Feb. 20, 1863* 275.00 50.00
dark lilac 275.00 50.00
a. 24c grayish lilac 275.00 50.00
b. 24c gray 275.00 50.00
c. 24c blackish violet *10,000. 600.00*
On cover 125.00
Pair 600.00 110.00
Block of four 1,350. 450.00
d. Printed on both sides *3,500.*
Scratch under "A" of "Postage" 350.00 65.00

CANCELLATIONS.

Blue	+2.50	"Paid"	+12.50
Red	+7.50	Numeral	+17.50
Magenta	+10.00	Supplementary Mail Type A	+50.00
Green	+275.00	"Free"	+75.00

Nos. 73, 76-78 exist as imperforate sheet-margin singles, all with pen cancel except No. 76 which is uncanceled. They were not regularly issued.

SAME DESIGNS AS 1861-66 ISSUES
Printed by the National Bank Note Co.

Grill

Embossed with grills of various sizes.

A peculiarity of the United States issues from 1867 to 1870 is the grill or embossing. The object was to break the fibre of the paper so that the ink of the canceling stamp would soak in and make washing for a second using impossible. The exact date at which grilled stamps came into use is unsettled. Luff's "Postage Stamps of the United States" places the date as probably August 8, 1867. Some authorities believe that more than one size of grill probably existed on one of the grill rolls.

GRILL WITH POINTS UP

Grills A and C were made by a roller covered with ridges shaped like an inverted V. Pressing the ridges into the stamp paper forced the paper into the pyramidal pits between the ridges, causing irregular breaks in the paper. Grill B was made by a roller with raised bosses.

A. Grill Covering the Entire Stamp.

1867 ***Perf. 12***

79 A25 3c **rose** 1,750. 425.00
On cover 600.00
Pair 3,750. 1,000.
Block of four *10,000.* —
a. Imperf., pair *1,650.*
a. Block of four *3,750.*
a. Margin block of 8, Impt. & P# *10,000.*
b. Printed on both sides —

Earliest known use: Aug. 13, 1867.

CANCELLATIONS.

Blue	+25.00	Railroad	—

An essay which is often mistaken for No. 79 shows the points of the grill as small squares faintly impressed in the paper but not cutting through it. On the issued stamp the grill generally breaks through the paper. Copies without defects are rare.

No. 79a was not regularly issued.

80 A26 5c **brown** *40,000.* —
a. 5c dark brown *37,500.*
81 A30 30c **orange** *32,500.*

B. Grill about 18x15mm (22x18 points)

82 A25 3c **rose** *45,000.*

C. Grill about 13x16mm (16 to 17 by 18 to 21 points)

The grilled area on each of four C grills in the sheet may total about 18x15mm. when a normal C grill adjoins a fainter grill extending to the right or left edge of the stamp. This is caused by a partial erasure on the grill roller when it was changed to produce C grills instead of the all-over A grill. Do not mistake these for the B grill. Value, used $5,000; on cover $7,500.

83 A25 3c **rose** 1,750. 400.00
On cover 550.00
Pair 3,600. 850.00
Block of four *8,500.* —
a. Imperf., pair *1,650.*
Double grill 3,500. 1,500.
Grill with points down 3,000. 650.00

CANCELLATIONS.

Blue	+10.00		

No. 83a was not regularly issued.

A 1c blue (A24) with C grill points down exists unused. It was not issued. Experts consider it an essay.

GRILL WITH POINTS DOWN

The grills were produced by rollers with the surface covered, or partly covered, by pyramidal bosses. On the D, E and F grills the tips of the pyramids are vertical ridges. On the Z grill the ridges are horizontal.

D. Grill about 12x14mm (15 by 17 to 18 points)

84 A32 2c **black** 3,500. 1,000.
On cover 1,300.
Pair 7,250. 2,100.
Block of four *16,000.* —
Double transfer — —
Split grill 1,050.

CANCELLATIONS.

Red	+75.00	"Paid All"	+100.00

85 A25 3c **rose** 1,500. 450.00
On cover 550.00
Pair 3,250. 925.00
Block of four *8,500.* —
Double grill —
Split grill 500.00

CANCELLATIONS.

Blue	+10.00	"Paid"	+50.00
Green	+200.00		

Z. Grill about 11x14mm (13 to 14 by 18 points)

85A A24 1c **blue** —
85B A32 2c **black** 1,300. 350.00
On cover 550.00
Pair 2,700. 750.00
Block of four *8,000.* —
Double transfer 1,400. 375.00
Double grill —

CANCELLATIONS.

Blue	+10.00	Black Carrier	+75.00
Red	+50.00	"Paid All"	+75.00

85C A25 3c **rose** 4,000. 950.00
On cover 1,250.
Block of four *17,500.*
Double grill *5,000.*

CANCELLATIONS.

Green	+250.00	Red	+75.00
Blue	+25.00	"Paid"	+50.00

85D A27 10c **green** — *25,000.*
85E A28 12c **black** 1,650. 575.00
On cover 900.00
Strip of three —
Block of four — —
Double transfer of top frame line 625.00
85F A33 15c **black** —

E. Grill about 11x13mm (14 by 15 to 17 points)

86 A24 1c **blue** 800.00 250.00
a. 1c dull blue 800.00 250.00
On cover 325.00
Pair 1,650. 525.00
Block of four 3,500. 1,250.
Double grill — 375.00
Split grill 850.00 275.00

CANCELLATIONS.

Blue	+5.00	"Paid"	+20.00
Red	+25.00	Steamboat	+85.00
Green	+140.00	Red Carrier	+60.00

87 A32 2c **black** 350.00 70.00
intense black 375.00 75.00
gray black 350.00 70.00
On cover 100.00
Pair 725.00 145.00
Block of four 1,600. —
a. Half used as 1c on cover, diag. or vert. *2,000.*
Double grill 475.00 100.00
Triple grill —
Split grill 400.00 80.00
Grill with points up —
Double transfer 375.00 75.00

CANCELLATIONS.

Blue	+2.50	"Paid"	+10.00
Purple	+15.00	Steamship	+60.00
Brown	+10.00	Black Carrier	+35.00
Red	+15.00	"Paid All"	+20.00
Green	+175.00	"Short Paid"	+65.00
		Japan	—

88 A25 3c **rose** 250.00 10.00
pale rose 250.00 10.00
rose red 250.00 10.00
a. 3c lake red 300.00 12.50
On cover 13.50
Pair 510.00 21.00
Block of four 1,050. 110.00
Double grill 375.00 35.00
Triple grill —
Split grill 275.00 11.50

Very thin paper 265.00 11.00

CANCELLATIONS.

Blue	+.25	"Paid"	+3.00
Red	+3.00	"Way"	+20.00
Ultramarine	+3.00	Numeral	+2.00
Green	+80.00	Steamboat	+35.00
		Railroad	+25.00
		Express Company	+80.00

89 A27 10c **green** 1,300. 175.00
dark green 1,300. 175.00
blue green 1,300. 175.00
On cover 275.00
Pair 2,700. 360.00
Block of four *6,500. 1,500.*
Double grill 1,800. 300.00
Split grill 1,350. 190.00
Double transfer — 200.00
Very thin paper 1,350. 190.00

CANCELLATIONS.

Blue	+5.00	"Paid"	+15.00
Red	+20.00	Steamship	+50.00
		Japan	+225.00

90 A28 12c **black** 1,500. 190.00
gray black 1,500. 190.00
intense black 1,500. 190.00
On cover 325.00
Pair 3,100. 400.00
Block of four *7,250. 1,500.*
Double transfer of top frame line 1,600. 210.00
Double transfer of bottom frame line 1,600. 210.00
Double transfer of top and bottom frame lines 1,700. 235.00
Double grill 2,000. 400.00
Split grill 1,550. 210.00

CANCELLATIONS.

Blue	+5.00	Railroad	+60.00
Red	+20.00	"Paid"	+20.00
Green	+225.00		

91 A33 15c **black** 3,250. 450.00
gray black 3,250. 450.00
On cover 700.00
Pair 6,600. 950.00
Block of four *14,000. 3,500.*
Double grill — 700.00
Split grill — 500.00

CANCELLATIONS.

Blue	+10.00	"Paid"	+30.00
Red	+50.00	Supplementary Mail Type A	+100.00

F. Grill about 9x13mm
(11 to 12 by 15 to 17 points)

92 A24 1c **blue** 350.00 100.00
a. 1c pale blue 350.00 100.00
dark blue 350.00 100.00
On cover 130.00
Pair 725.00 210.00
Block of four 1,600. 550.00
Double transfer 375.00 120.00
Double grill — 200.00
Split grill 375.00 110.00
Very thin paper 365.00 105.00

CANCELLATIONS.

Blue	+2.50	"Paid"	+10.00
Red	+10.00	Red Carrier	+25.00
Green	+175.00	"Paid All"	+15.00

93 A32 2c **black** 135.00 25.00
gray black 135.00 25.00
On cover 35.00
Pair 275.00 52.50
Block of four 600.00 225.00
Margin block of 8, Impr. & P# —
a. Half used as 1c on cover, diagonal, vertical or horizontal *1,250.*
Double transfer 140.00 30.00
Double grill — 100.00
Split grill 140.00 30.00
Very thin paper 140.00 30.00

CANCELLATIONS.

Blue	+2.50	"Paid"	+5.00
Red	+7.50	"Paid All"	+15.00
Green	+200.00	Black Carrier	+20.00
Japan	—	Red Carrier	+30.00

94 A25 3c **red** 95.00 2.50
rose red 95.00 2.50
a. 3c rose 95.00 2.50
On cover 3.25
Pair 200.00 5.25
Block of four 425.00 45.00
Margin block of 8, Impt. & P# *2,500.*
b. Imperf., pair *650.00*
c. Vertical pair, imperf. horiz. *1,000.*
d. Printed on both sides *950.00*
Double transfer 110.00 4.00
Double grill 175.00 20.00
Triple grill — 100.00
End roller grill 200.00
Split grill 100.00 2.75
Quadruple split grill 225.00 75.00
Grill with points up —
Very thin paper 97.50 2.75

CANCELLATIONS.

Blue	+10	"Paid"	+2.25
Ultramarine	+3.00	"Paid All"	+12.50
Red	+3.50	"Free"	+20.00
Violet	+5.50	Railroad	+30.00
Green	+70.00	Steamboat	+40.00

Numeral	+3.00	Packet boat	+60.00
		Express Company	+50.00

95 A26 5c **brown** 900.00 225.00
a. 5c dark brown 950.00 250.00
On cover 350.00
Pair 1,850. 475.00
Block of four 3,900. 1,250.
Double transfer of top frame line — —
Double grill — —
Split grill 1,000. 250.00
Very thin paper 925.00 235.00

CANCELLATIONS.

Blue	+5.00	Green	+200.00
Magenta	+30.00	"Paid"	+25.00
Violet	+35.00	"Free"	+50.00
Red	+30.00	"Steamship"	+100.00

96 A27 10c **yellow green** 700.00 110.00
green 700.00 110.00
a. 10c dark green 700.00 110.00
blue green 700.00 110.00
On cover 150.00
Pair 1,450. 230.00
Block of four *3,500. 800.00*
Double transfer — —
Double grill — 200.00
Split grill 750.00 120.00
Quadruple split grill 350.00
Very thin paper 725.00 120.00

CANCELLATIONS.

Blue	+2.50	"Paid"	+10.00
Red	+15.00	"Free"	+50.00
Magenta	+20.00	Steamship	+75.00
Green	+175.00	Japan	+250.00
		China	—

97 A28 12c **black** 700.00 120.00
gray black 700.00 120.00
On cover 150.00
Pair 1,450. 250.00
Block of four *3,500. 1,200.*
Double transfer of top frame line 750.00 130.00
Double transfer of bottom frame line 750.00 130.00
Double transfer of top and bottom frame lines — 160.00
Double grill — 250.00
Triple grill *400.00*
Split grill 750.00 140.00
End roller grill —
Very thin paper 725.00 125.00

CANCELLATIONS.

Blue	+2.50	"Paid"	+15.00
Red	**+15.00**	**"Insufficiently** Prepaid"	+100.00
Magenta	+20.00	"Paid All"	+25.00
Brown	+15.00	Supplementary Mail Type A	+50.00
Green	+200.00		

98 A33 15c **black** 700.00 135.00
gray black 700.00 135.00
On cover 150.00
Pair 1,450. 300.00
Block of four *3,750. 1,200.*
Margin block of 8, Impt. & P# *25,000.*
Double transfer of upper right corner — —
Double grill — 250.00
Split grill 700.00 145.00
Quadruple split grill 1,400. 350.00
Very thin paper 700.00 140.00

CANCELLATIONS.

Blue	+2.50	"Paid"	+20.00
Magenta	+20.00	"Insufficiently Prepaid"	+135.00
Red	+15.00	"Insufficiently Paid"	+135.00
Green	+225.00	Japan	+300.00
Orange	+20.00	Supplementary Mail Type A	+60.00

99 A29 24c **gray lilac** 1,350. 475.00
gray 1,350. 475.00
On cover 800.00
Pair 2,800. 1,000.
Block of four *6,500. 4,000.*
Margin block of 8, Impt. & P# *30,000.*
Double grill 1,850. 750.00
Split grill 1,450. 500.00

CANCELLATIONS.

Blue	+10.00	Red	+50.00
		"Paid"	+50.00

100 A30 30c **orange** 1,500. 375.00
deep orange 1,500. 375.00
On cover 1,000.
Pair 3,100. 775.00
Block of four *7,500. 3,000.*
Double grill 2,000 700.00
Split grill 1,600. 425.00

CANCELLATIONS.

Blue	+10.00	"Paid"	+50.00
Red	+50.00	Supplementary Mail Type A	+100.00
Magenta	+75.00	Japan	+400.00

101 A31 90c **blue** 4,400. 950.00
dark blue 4,400. 950.00
On cover —
Pair 9,000. 1,950.
Block of four *20,000. 5,000.*
Double grill *6,500.*
Split grill 4,600. 1,000.

CANCELLATIONS.

Blue	+25.00	Japan	+600.00
Red	+50.00	"Paid"	+50.00

RE-ISSUE OF 1861-66 ISSUES

Issued for the Centennial Exposition of 1876.
Produced by the National Bank Note Co.
Without grill, hard white paper, with white crackly gum.
The 1, 2, 5, 10 and 12c were printed from new plates of 100 subjects each.

1875 ***Perf. 12***

102 A24 1c **blue** *(3195)* *500.00 800.00*
Block of four *3,500.* —
103 A32 2c **black** *(979)* *2,500. 4,000.*
Block of four *13,500.*
104 A25 3c **brown red** *(465)* *3,250. 4,250.*
Block of four *16,000.*
105 A26 5c **brown** *(672)* *1,800. 2,250.*
Block of four *10,000.*
106 A27 10c **green** *(451)* *2,100. 3,750.*
Block of four *12,500.*
107 A28 12c **black** *(389)* *3,000. 4,500.*
Block of four *15,000.*
108 A33 15c **black** *(397)* *3,000. 4,750.*
Block of four *15,000.*
109 A29 24c **deep violet** *(346)* *4,000. 6,000.*
Block of four *19,000.*
110 A30 30c **brownish orange** *(346)* *4,500. 7,000.*
Block of four *22,500.*
111 A31 90c **blue** *(317)* *5,750. 18,500.*

These stamps can be distinguished from the 1861-66 issue by the brighter colors, the sharper proof-like impressions and the paper which is very white instead of yellowish.
Numbers in parentheses are quantities issued.

Produced by the National Bank Note Co.
Plates for the 1c, 2c, 3c, 6c, 10c and 12c consisted of 300 subjects in two panes of 150 each. For the 15c, 24c, 30c and 90c plates of 100 subjects each.

NOTE. Stamps of the 1869 issue without grill cannot be guaranteed except when unused and with the original gum.

Franklin — A34

G. Grill measuring 9½x9mm
(12 by 11 to 11½ points)

1869 **Hard Wove Paper** ***Perf. 12***

112 A34 1c **buff,** *Mar. 27, 1869* 225.00 60.00
brown orange 225.00 60.00
dark brown orange 225.00 60.00
On cover, single 150.00
Pair 465.00 125.00
Block of four 1,000. 450.00
Margin block of 4, arrow 1,100.
Margin block of 10, Impt. & P# —
Double transfer — —
b. Without grill, original gum *750.00*
Double grill 450.00 150.00
Split grill 250.00 70.00
Double grill, one split —

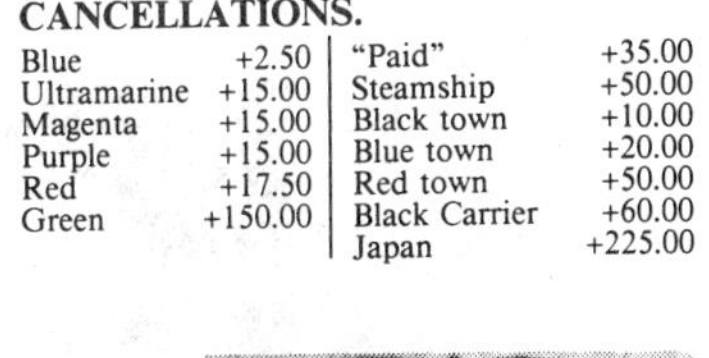

CANCELLATIONS.

Blue	+2.50	"Paid"	+35.00
Ultramarine	+15.00	Steamship	+50.00
Magenta	+15.00	Black town	+10.00
Purple	+15.00	Blue town	+20.00
Red	+17.50	Red town	+50.00
Green	+150.00	Black Carrier	+60.00
		Japan	+225.00

Post Horse and Rider — A35

113 A35 2c **brown,** *Mar. 27, 1869* 160.00 25.00
pale brown 160.00 25.00
dark brown 160.00 25.00
yellow brown 160.00 25.00

	Unused	Used
On cover, single		60.00
Pair	325.00	52.50
Block of four	725.00	275.00
Margin block of 4, arrow	775.00	
Margin block of 10, Impt. & P#	—	
b. Without grill, original gum	*600.00*	
c. Half used as 1c on cover, diagonal, vertical or horizontal		—
d. Printed on both sides		—
Double grill	—	125.00
Split grill	185.00	35.00
Quadruple split grill	—	200.00
Double transfer		30.00

CANCELLATIONS.

Blue	+1.00	Steamship	+50.00
Red	+15.00	Black town	+10.00
Orange	+15.00	Blue town	+20.00
Magenta	+12.50	Japan	+200.00
Purple	+12.50	Blue Carrier	+75.00
Ultramarine	+15.00	Black Carrier	+60.00
Green	+175.00	China	—
"Paid"	+15.00	Printed Pre-cancellation "Jefferson, Ohio"	—
"Paid All"	+25.00		

Locomotive — A36

114 A36 3c **ultramarine,** *Mar. 27, 1869*	135.00	5.50
pale ultramarine	135.00	5.50
dark ultramarine	135.00	5.50
blue	135.00	5.50
dark blue	135.00	5.50
On cover		12.00
Pair	275.00	11.50
Block of four	625.00	125.00
Margin block of 4, arrow	675.00	
Margin block of 10, Impt. & P#	*7,000.*	
a. Without grill, original gum	*600.00*	
b. Vertical one-third used as 1c on cover		—
c. Vertical two-thirds used as 2c on cover		—
d. Double impression		—
Double transfer	150.00	6.50
Double grill	275.00	45.00
Triple grill	—	100.00
Split grill	145.00	6.50
Quadruple split grill	325.00	60.00
Sextuple grill	*2,000.*	
End roller grill	—	—
Gray paper	—	—
Cracked plate	—	—

CANCELLATIONS.

Blue	+.25	"Paid"	+10.00
Ultramarine	+3.00	"Paid All"	+15.00
Magenta	+5.00	"Steamboat"	—
Purple	+5.00	"Steamship"	+40.00
Violet	+5.00	Ship	+35.00
Red	+7.00	Railroad	+30.00
Brown	+3.00	Packet Boat	+100.00
Green	+125.00	Black Carrier	+30.00
Orang	+7.00	Blue Carrier	+40.00
Black town	+2.50	Express Company	—
Blue town	+4.00	"Way"	—
Red town	+25.00	"Free"	+30.00
Numeral	+10.00	Alaska	—
		Japan	+150.00

Washington — A37

115 A37 6c **ultramarine,** *1869*	775.00	100.00
pale ultramarine	775.00	100.00
On cover		300.00
Pair	1,600.	210.00
Block of four	4,000.	1,000.
Margin block of 4, arrow	4,500.	
Double grill	—	300.00
Split grill	825.00	115.00
Quadruple split grill	—	400.00
Double transfer		115.00
b. Vertical half used as 3c on cover		—

Earliest known use: Apr. 26.

CANCELLATIONS.

Blue	+5.00	"Paid"	+15.00
Brown	+10.00	"Paid All"	+25.00
Magenta	+20.00	Black town	+20.00
Purple	+20.00	"Short Paid"	+75.00
Red	+30.00	Steamship	+35.00
Green	+225.00	Railroad	+35.00
		Japan	+175.00

Shield and Eagle — A38

116 A38 10c **yellow,** *Apr. 1, 1869*	850.00	95.00
yellowish orange	850.00	95.00
On cover		325.00
Pair	1,750.	200.00
Block of four	4,500.	1,150.
Margin block of 4, arrow	5,000.	
Double grill	—	275.00
Split grill	900.00	105.00
End roller grill	—	—

CANCELLATIONS.

Blue	+5.00	"Paid"	+15.00
Magenta	+20.00	"Paid All"	+30.00
		"Insufficiently Paid"	+50.00
Purple	+20.00	Supplementary Mail Type A	+150.00
Red	+30.00	Express Company	—
Ultramarine	+30.00	St. Thomas	—
Green	+225.00	Hawaii	—
Black town	+20.00	Japan	+200.00
Steamship	+45.00	China	—
Railroad	+45.00		

S.S. "Adriatic" — A39

117 A39 12c **green,** *Apr. 5, 1869*	750.00	90.00
bluish green	750.00	90.00
yellowish green	750.00	90.00
On cover		325.00
Pair	1,550.	190.00
Block of four	4,000.	850.00
Margin block of 4, arrow	4,500.	
Double grill	—	275.00
Split grill	800.00	100.00
End roller grill		—

CANCELLATIONS.

Blue	+5.00	"Paid"	+25.00
Magenta	+20.00	"Paid All"	+40.00
Purple	+20.00	"Too Late"	+100.00
		"Insufficiently Paid"	+125.00
Brown	+15.00	Black town	+20.00
Red	+30.00	Japan	+175.00
Green	+225.00		
Numeral	—		

Landing of Columbus — A40

118 A40 15c **brown & blue,** type I, Picture unframed, *Apr. 2, 1869*	1,750.	300.00
dark brown & blue	1,750.	300.00
On cover		1,000.
Pair	3,650.	625.00
Block of four	*12,000.*	*20,000.*
a. Without grill, original gum	*3,500.*	
Double grill	—	450.00
Split grill	1,900.	325.00

CANCELLATIONS.

Blue	+10.00	"Paid"	+50.00
		"Insufficiently Paid"	+150.00
Red	+40.00	Black town	+50.00
Brown	+25.00	Steamship	+100.00

A40a

119 A40a 15c **brown & blue,** type II, Picture framed	850.00	150.00
dark brown & blue	850.00	150.00
On cover		750.00
Pair	1,750.	325.00
Block of four	4,000.	3,500.
Margin block of 8, Impt. & P#	*20,000.*	
b. Center inverted	*145,000.*	*17,500.*
c. Center double, one inverted		
Double transfer	—	—
Double grill	1,750.	285.00
Split grill	1,000.	175.00

Earliest known use: May 23, 1869.

CANCELLATIONS.

Blue	+10.00	"Paid"	+20.00
Purple	+35.00	"Paid All"	+35.00
Magenta	+35.00	Black town	+30.00
Red	+35.00	"Steamship"	+60.00
Brown	+20.00	Supp. Mail, A, F	+40.00
Green	+250.00	Japan	+275.00

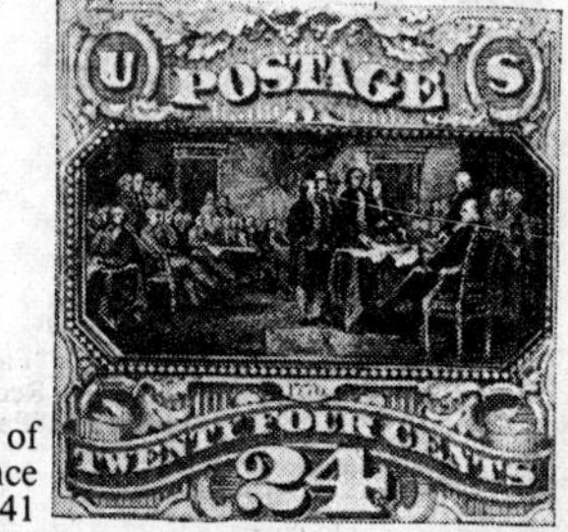

The Declaration of Independence A41

120 A41 24c **green & violet,** *Apr. 7, 1869*	2,500.	450.00
bluish green & violet	2,500.	450.00
On cover		*7,500.*
Pair	5,250.	950.00
Block of four	*14,000.*	*18,000.*
a. Without grill, original gum	*5,000.*	
b. Center inverted	*125,000.*	*16,500.*
b. On cover		—
b. Block of four		—
Double grill	—	1,000.
Split grill	2,750.	500.00

CANCELLATIONS.

		Red town	+150.00
Red	+75.00	"Paid All"	+100.00
Blue	+25.00	"Steamship"	+175.00
Black town	+50.00	Supp. Mail, A	+125.00

The Scott Catalogue value is a retail price, what you could expect to pay for the stamp in a grade of Fine-Very Fine. The value listed is a reference which reflects recent actual dealer selling price.

Shield, Eagle and Flags — A42

			Unused	Used
121	A42 30c	**blue & carmine,** *May 15, 1869*	2,250.	225.00
		blue & dark carmine	2,250.	225.00
		On cover		11,000.
		Pair	4,600.	475.00
		Block of four	*12,000.*	1,150.
a.		Without grill, original gum	*3,750.*	
a.		Block of four	*18,500.*	
b.		Flags inverted	*120,000.*	*45,000.*
		Double grill	—	500.00
		Split grill	2,400.	250.00
		Double paper (without grill), original gum	*2,750.*	

CANCELLATIONS.

		Black town	+35.00
Red	+50.00	Steamship	+75.00
Blue	+10.00	"Steam"	+60.00
Brown	+25.00	Supplementary Mail Type A	+75.00
Green	+400.00	Japan	+400.00
"Paid"	+50.00	China	—
"Paid All"	+75.00		

Lincoln — A43

			Unused	Used
122	A43 90c	**carmine & black**	7,000.	1,200.
		carmine rose & black	7,000.	1,200.
		On cover		—
		Pair	*16,000.*	3,000.
		Block of four	*65,000.*	*25,000.*
a.		Without grill, original gum	*13,500.*	
		Split grill	—	—

Earliest known use: May 10, 1869.

CANCELLATIONS.

		Red	+200.00
Blue	+100.00	Black town	+200.00

CANCELLATIONS

The common type of cancellation on the 1869 issue is the block or cork similar to illustrations above. Japanese cancellations seen on this issue (not illustrated) resulted from the sale of U. S. stamps in Japanese cities where post offices were maintained for mail going from Japan to the United States.

RE-ISSUE OF 1869 ISSUE

Issued for the Centennial Exposition of 1876.

Produced by the National Bank Note Co.

Without grill, hard white paper, with white crackly gum.

A new plate of 150 subjects was made for the 1c and for the frame of the 15c. The frame on the 15c is the same as type I but without the fringe of brown shading lines around central vignette.

1875 ***Perf. 12***

			Unused	Used
123	A34 1c	**buff** *(+8252)*	325.00	225.00
		Block of four	1,850.	
		On cover		2,500.
124	A35 2c	**brown** *(4755)*	375.00	325.00
		Block of four	2,500.	
125	A36 3c	**blue** *(1406)*	2,750.	10,000.

CANCELLATIONS.

Supplementary Mail Type F	—

Only one authenticated sound used copy of No. 125 is recorded. The used value is for an attractive example with minimal faults. Copies of No. 114 with faint or pressed-out grill are frequently offered as No. 125.

			Unused	Used
126	A37 6c	**blue** *(2226)*	850.00	550.00
		Block of four	*12,500.*	
127	A38 10c	**yellow** *(1947)*	1,400.	1,200.
		Block of four	*9,000.*	
128	A39 12c	**green** *(1584)*	1,500.	1,200.
		Block of four	*12,500.*	
129	A40 15c	**brown & blue,** Type III, *(1981)*	1,300.	550.00
		Block of four	*20,000.*	
a.		Imperf. horizontally, single	1,600.	—
130	A41 24c	**green & violet** *(2091)*	1,250.	550.00
131	A42 30c	**blue & carmine** *(1535)*	1,750.	1,000.
132	A43 90c	**carmine & black** *(1356)*	5,500.	*6,000.*
		Block of four	*32,500.*	

Numbers in parentheses are quantities issued.

\+ This quantity probably includes the 1880 Re-issue No. 133.

RE-ISSUE OF 1869 ISSUE

Produced by the American Bank Note Co.

Without grill, soft porous paper.

1880

			Unused	Used
133	A34 1c	**buff,** issued with gum	200.00	135.00
		Block of four, with gum	950.00	
a.		1c brown orange, issued without gum	175.00	120.00
a.		Block of four, without gum	800.00	
		Margin block of 10, Impt. & P#	*17,500.*	
		On cover		1,850.

Produced by the National Bank Note Company.

Plates of 200 subjects in two panes of 100 each.

Franklin — A44

Jackson — A45

Washington — A46

Lincoln — A47

Edwin M. Stanton — A48

United States Postage Stamps can be mounted in Scott's annually supplemented Platinum, National, Pony Express, Minuteman, U.S. Commemoratives Singles, U.S. Commemorative and Commemorative Air Plate Blocks, U.S. Blocks of Four and U.S. Regular and Regular Air Plate Blocks Album.

Jefferson — A49

Henry Clay — A50

Daniel Webster — A51

Two varieties of grill are known on this issue.

H. Grill about 10x12mm (11 to 13 by 14 to 16 points.) On all values 1c to 90c.

I. Grill about 8½x10mm (10 to 11 by 10 to 13 points.) On 1, 2, 3, 6 and 7c.

On the 1870-71 stamps the grill impressions are usually faint or incomplete. This is especially true of the H grill, which often shows only a few points.

Values for 1c-7c are for stamps showing well defined grills.

Killer cancellation of the oval grid type with letters or numeral centers was first used in 1876 Bank Note issues. By order of the Postmaster-General (July 23, 1860) it was prohibited to use the town mark as a canceling instrument, and a joined town and killer cancellation was developed.

Numeral cancellations-see "Postal Markings-Examples."

White Wove Paper, Thin to Medium Thick.

1870-71 ***Perf. 12***

134 A44 1c **ultramarine,** *April 1870*	500.00	57.50
pale ultramarine	500.00	57.50
dark ultramarine	500.00	57.50
On cover		80.00
Pair	1,050.	120.00
Block of four	2,200.	300.00
Double transfer	525.00	65.00
Double grill	—	120.00
Split grill	550.00	60.00
Quadruple split grill	—	200.00
End roller grill		300.00

CANCELLATIONS.

		"Paid"	+10.00
Blue	+2.50	"Paid All"	+20.00
Red	+10.00	"Steamship"	+45.00
Green	+100.00		

135 A45 2c **red brown,** *April 1870*	350.00	37.50
pale red brown	350.00	37.50
dark red brown	350.00	37.50
On cover		55.00
Pair	725.00	80.00
Block of four	1,500.	200.00
a. Diagonal half used as 1c on cover		—
Double grill	500.00	75.00
Split grill	375.00	45.00
Quadruple split grill	*1,100.*	120.00
End roller grill	*700.00*	*225.00*

CANCELLATIONS.

		"Paid"	+5.00
Blue	+1.00	"Paid All"	+10.00
Red	+5.00	Numeral	+5.00
Brown	+3.00	China	—
Green	+100.00		

136 A46 3c **green,** *April 12, 1870*	285.00	10.00
pale green	285.00	10.00
yellow green	285.00	10.00
deep green	285.00	10.00
On cover		15.00
Pair	585.00	21.00
Block of four	1,200.	75.00
Margin block of 10, Impt. & P#	*5,500.*	
Margin block of 12, Impt. & P#	*6,500.*	
Printed on both sides	—	
Double transfer	—	12.00
Double grill	450.00	40.00
Split grill	300.00	11.00
Quadruple split grill	—	75.00
End roller grill		150.00
Cracked plate	—	50.00
b. Imperf., pair	*1,200.*	
b. Margin block of 12, Impt. & P#	—	

CANCELLATIONS.

Blue	+.25	"Paid"	+2.50
Purple	+2.50	Railroad	+10.00
Magenta	+2.50	"Steamship"	+20.00
Red	+3.50	"Paid All"	+15.00
Orange	**+3.50**	**Numeral**	**+4.00**
Brown	**+1.50**	**"Free"**	**+25.00**
Green	**+45.00**		

137 A47 6c **carmine,** *April 1870*	1,650.	250.00
pale carmine	1,650.	250.00
carmine rose	1,650.	250.00
On cover		500.00
Pair	3,400.	525.00
Block of four	*7,250.*	
Double grill	—	450.00
Split grill	1,700.	275.00
Quadruple split grill	—	500.00
End roller grill	*2,750.*	*550.00*

CANCELLATIONS.

Blue	+5.00	"Paid"	+35.00
Red	+35.00		

138 A48 7c **vermilion,** *Mar. 1871*	1,100.	225.00
deep vermilion	1,100.	225.00
On cover		450.00
Pair	2,300.	475.00
Block of four	*4,750.*	—
Double grill		400.00
Split grill	1,150.	250.00
Quadruple split grill		450.00
End roller grill		*500.00*

CANCELLATIONS.

Blue	+5.00	Red	+35.00
Purple	+20.00	Green	+200.00
		"Paid"	+25.00

The 7c stamps, Nos. 138 and 149, were issued for a 7c rate of July 1, 1870, to Prussia, German States and Austria, including Hungary, via Hamburg (on the Hamburg-American Line steamers), or Bremen (on North German Lloyd ships), but issue was delayed by the Franco-Prussian War. The rate for this service was reduced to 6c in 1871. For several months there was no 7c rate, but late in 1871 the Prussian closed mail rate via England was reduced to 7c which revived an important use for the 7c stamps. The rate to Denmark direct via Baltic Lloyd ships, or via Bremen and Hamburg as above, was 7c from Jan. 1, 1872.

139 A49 10c **brown,** *April 1870*	1,450.	400.00
yellow brown	1,450.	400.00
dark brown	1,450.	400.00
On cover		700.00
Pair	3,000.	825.00
Block of four	*10,000.*	—
Double grill		750.00
Split grill	1,600.	450.00
End roller grill		*1,000.*

CANCELLATIONS.

Blue	+5.00	"Steamship"	+50.00
Red	+30.00	"Honolulu Paid All"	—

140 A50 12c **dull violet,** *April 18, 1870*	*12,000.*	1,500.
On cover		*4,500.*
Pair	*25,000.*	3,200.
Block of four	*55,000.*	
Split grill	—	1,600.
End roller grill		*4,500.*

CANCELLATIONS.

Blue	+50.00	"Paid all"	—
Red	+100.00		

141 A51 15c **orange,** *April 1870*	1,850.	700.00
bright orange	1,850.	700.00
deep orange	1,850.	700.00
On cover		1,350.
Pair	3,800.	1,500.
Block of four	*10,000.*	—
Double grill		—
Split grill	1,850.	750.00

CANCELLATIONS.

Blue	+10.00	Red	+75.00
Purple	+50.00	Green	+300.00

General Winfield Scott — A52

142 A52 24c **purple**	—	*9,500.*
On cover		—
Block of four		—
Split grill		—

CANCELLATIONS.

Red	+500.00

Alexander Hamilton — A53

143 A53 30c **black,** *April 1870*	4,500.	825.00
full black	4,500.	825.00
On cover		2,000.
Pair	9,250.	1,800.
Block of four	*20,000.*	
Double grill		—
End roller grill		*1,750.*

CANCELLATIONS.

Blue	+25.00
Red	+100.00

Commodore Oliver Hazard Perry — A54

144 A54 90c **carmine,** *April 12, 1870*	6,000.	750.00
dark carmine	6,000.	750.00
On cover		—
Pair	*12,500.*	1,600.
Block of four	*28,500.*	*4,000.*
Double grill		—
Split grill		800.00

CANCELLATIONS.

Blue	+25.00
Red	+75.00

Produced by the National Bank Note Co.
White Wove Paper, Thin to Medium Thick.
Issued (except 3c and 7c) in April, 1870.
Without Grill.

1870-71 *Perf. 12*

145 A44	1c **ultramarine**	165.00	6.50
	pale ultramarine	165.00	6.50
	dark ultramarine	165.00	6.50
	gray blue	165.00	6.50
	On cover		10.00
	Pair	340.00	14.00
	Block of four	700.00	50.00
	Double transfer	—	9.00
	Worn plate	165.00	6.50

CANCELLATIONS.

Blue	+ 25	"Paid"	+3.00
Ultramarine	+1.50	"Paid All"	+15.00
Magenta	+1.00	"Steamship"	+25.00
Purple	+1.00	Railroad	+20.00
Brown	+1.00	Numeral	+2.00
Red	+3.00		
Green	+55.00		

146 A45	2c **red brown**	57.50	4.50
	pale red brown	57.50	4.50
	dark red brown	57.50	4.50
	orange brown	60.00	4.75
	On cover		6.50
	Pair	120.00	9.25
	Block of four	250.00	30.00
a.	Half used as 1c on cover, diagonal or vertical		—
c.	Double impression	—	
	Double transfer	—	6.00

CANCELLATIONS.

Blue	+ 10	"Paid"	+2.00
Purple	+ 75	"Paid All"	+10.00
Red	+2.50	Numeral	+2.00
Green	+55.00	"Steamship"	+22.50
Brown	+1.00	Black Carrier	+12.50
		Japan	—
		China	—
		Curacao	—

147 A46	3c **green,** *Mar. 13, 1870*	120.00	50
	pale green	120.00	50
	dark green	120.00	50
	yellow green	125.00	55
	On cover		1.00
	Pair	250.00	1.05
	Block of four	525.00	9.00
	Margin block of 10, Impt. & P#	*1,850.*	
a.	Printed on both sides		*1,500.*
b.	Double impression		*1,000.*
	Double transfer	—	4.50
	Short transfer at bottom	130.00	75
	Cracked plate	—	25.00
	Worn plate	120.00	50
c.	Imperf., pair	*700.00*	
c.	Margin block of 10, Impt. & P#	—	

CANCELLATIONS.

Blue	+5	"Paid"	+2.00
Purple	+35	"Paid All"	+10.00
Magenta	+35	"Free"	+15.00
Brown	+1.50	Numeral	+2.00
Red	+2.50	Railroad	+10.00
Ultramarine	+2.00	Express Company	—
Green	+35.00	"Steamboat"	+20.00
		"Steamship"	+17.50
		Ship	+15.00
		Japan	+75.00

148 A47	6c **carmine**	225.00	12.00
	dark carmine	225.00	12.00
	rose	225.00	12.00
	brown carmine	225.00	12.00
	violet carmine	240.00	15.00
	On cover		30.00
	Pair	475.00	24.50
	Block of four	975.00	125.00
a.	Vertical half used as 3c on cover		—
b.	Double impression		*1,250.*
	Double transfer		—
	Double paper	—	—

CANCELLATIONS.

Blue	+ 25	"Paid"	+3.00
Purple	+1.00	"Steamship"	+25.00
Violet	+1.00	"Paid All"	+15.00
Ultramarine	+2.00	Numeral	—
Brown	+1.00	Supplementary Mail Type A or D	+25.00
Red	+3.00	China	—
Green	+90.00	Japan	+150.00

149 A48	7c **vermilion,** *Mar. 1871*	325.00	50.00
	deep vermilion	325.00	50.00
	On cover		125.00
	Pair	675.00	105.00
	Block of four	1,450.	*450.00*
	Cracked plate		—

CANCELLATIONS.

Blue	+2.50	Ultramarine	+12.50
Purple	+7.50	Red	+10.00
		Japan	+150.00

150 A49	10c **brown**	225.00	12.00
	dark brown	225.00	12.00
	yellow brown	225.00	12.00
	On cover		27.50
	Pair	475.00	25.00
	Block of four	1,000.	*125.00*
	Margin block of 10, Impt. & P#	—	
	Double transfer	—	47.50

CANCELLATIONS.

Blue	+.25	Brown	+3.00
Purple	+2.00	"Paid All"	+20.00
Magenta	+2.00	"Steamship"	+20.00
Ultramarine	+4.00	Supplementary Mail Type A or D	+25.00
Red	+4.00	Japan	+120.00
Green	+120.00	China	—
Orange	+4.00	St. Thomas	—

151 A50	12c **dull violet**	525.00	60.00
	violet	525.00	60.00
	dark violet	525.00	60.00
	On cover		350.00
	Pair	1,100.	125.00
	Block of four	*2,750.*	*600.00*

CANCELLATIONS.

Blue	+2.50	"Paid All"	+25.00
Magenta	+7.50	"Steamship"	+50.00
Red	+10.00	Supplementary Mail Type A or D	+40.00
Green	+150.00		

152 A51	15c **bright orange**	500.00	60.00
	deep orange	500.00	60.00
	On cover		225.00
	Pair	1,050.	125.00
	Block of four	2,200.	*550.00*

CANCELLATIONS.

Blue	+2.50	"Paid"	+12.50
Magenta	+7.50	"Steamship"	+40.00
Ultramarine	+10.00	Supplementary Mail Type A or F	+30.00
Red	+12.50	China	—

153 A52	24c **purple**	600.00	80.00
	bright purple	600.00	80.00
	On cover to India		*1,500.*
	Pair	1,250.	185.00
	Block of four	*4,500.*	*2,500.*
	Double paper	—	—

CANCELLATIONS.

Red	+10.00	"Paid"	+25.00
Blue	+2.50	Town	+15.00
Purple	+7.50	"Steamship"	—
China	—	Supplementary Mail Types A, D or F	+30.00

154 A53	30c **black**	1,000.	95.00
	full black	1,000.	95.00
	On cover		700.00
	Pair	2,100.	200.00
	Block of four	*7,000.*	

CANCELLATIONS.

Magenta	+15.00	"Steamship"	+55.00
Red	+25.00	Supplementary Mail Type A	+40.00
Brown	+15.00		
Blue	+2.50		

155 A54	90c **carmine**	1,350.	175.00
	dark carmine	1,350.	175.00
	On cover		—
	Pair	2,800.	375.00
	Block of four	*7,000.*	1,100.

CANCELLATIONS.

Blue	+5.00	Town	+20.00
Purple	+15.00	Supplementary Mail Type A or F	+40.00
Magenta	+15.00	Japan	—
Green	+275.00		
Red	+30.00		

Printed by the Continental Bank Note Co.
Plates of 200 subjects in two panes of 100 each.
Issued in July (?), 1873.

Designs of the 1870-71 Issue with secret marks on the values from 1c to 15c, as described and illustrated:

The object of secret marks was to provide a simple and positive proof that these stamps were produced by the Continental Bank Note Company and not by their predecessors.

Franklin A44a

1c. In the pearl at the left of the numeral "1" there is a small crescent.

Jackson — A45a

2c. Under the scroll at the left of "U. S." there is a small diagonal line. This mark seldom shows clearly. The stamp, No. 157, can be distinguished by its color.

Washington A46a

3c. The under part of the upper tail of the left ribbon is heavily shaded.

Lincoln — A47a

6c. The first four vertical lines of the shading in the lower part of the left ribbon have been strengthened.

Stanton A48a

7c. Two small semi-circles are drawn around the ends of the lines which outline the ball in the lower right hand corner.

Jefferson A49a

10c. There is a small semi-circle in the scroll at the right end of the upper label.

Clay — A50a

12c. The balls of the figure "2" are crescent shaped.

Webster A51a

15c. In the lower part of the triangle in the upper left corner two lines have been made heavier forming a "V". This mark can be found on some of the Continental and American (1879) printings, but not all stamps show it.

Secret marks were added to the dies of the 24c, 30c and 90c but new plates were not made from them. The various printings of the 30c and 90c can be distinguished only by the shades and paper.

J. Grill about 7x9½mm exists on all values except 90c. Grill was composed of truncated pyramids and was so strongly impressed that some points often broke through the paper.

White Wove Paper, Thin to Thick

1873 *Perf. 12*

156 A44a	1c **ultramarine**	55.00	1.75
	pale ultramarine	55.00	1.75
	dark ultramarine	60.00	1.75
	gray blue	55.00	1.75
	blue	55.00	1.75
	On cover		3.00
	Pair	115.00	3.75
	Block of four	235.00	20.00
	Margin block of 12, Impt. & P#	*2,500.*	
	Double transfer	65.00	4.00
	Double paper	*200.00*	—
	Ribbed paper	60.00	2.50
	Paper with silk fibers	—	15.00
e.	With grill	*1,200.*	
	Cracked plate		—
f.	Imperf., pair	—	*500.00*
	Paper cut with "cogwheel" punch	*275.00*	

CANCELLATIONS.

Blue	+10	Railroad	+12.00
Purple	+35	"Free"	+12.00
Magenta	+35	Black carrier	+15.00
Ultramarine	+1.00	Numeral	+2.50
Red	+3.50	Alaska	—
Orange	+3.50	Japan	—
Brown	+1.50	Printed "G." Precancellation (Glastonbury, Conn.)	+200.00

Green	+60.00	Printed Star Precancellation (Glen Allen, Va.)	+100.00
"Paid All"	+7.00		
"Paid"	+1.00		

157 A45a 2c **brown** 150.00 7.00
dark brown 150.00 7.00
dark reddish brown 150.00 7.00
yellowish brown 150.00 7.00
With secret mark 160.00 7.50
On cover 12.50
Pair 325.00 14.50
Block of four 700.00 70.00
Margin block of 12, Impt. & P# —
Margin block of 14, Impt. & P# —
Double paper 225.00 20.00
Ribbed paper 160.00 8.50
c. With grill *850.00 600.00*
d. Double impression —
e. Vertical half used as 1c on cover —
Double transfer — 9.50
Cracked plate —

CANCELLATIONS.

Blue	+ 25	"P. D." in circle	+15.00
Magenta	+1.00	Town	+2.00
Purple	+1.00	Numeral	+1.50
Red	+3.00	Black Carrier	+8.50
Orange	+3.50	"Steamship"	+15.00
Green	+60.00	Supplementary Mail Type F	+5.00
"Paid"	+2.50	China	—
"Insufficiently Paid"	—	Japan	+100.00
"Paid All"	+13.50	Printed Star Precancellation (Glen Allen, Va.)	—

158 A46a 3c **green** 45.00 15
bluish green 45.00 15
yellow green 45.00 15
dark yellow green 45.00 15
dark green 45.00 15
olive green 60.00 2.50
On cover 30
Pair 92.50 35
Block of four 225.00 7.50
Margin strip of 5, Impt. & P# 250.00
Margin strip of 6, Impt. & P# 325.00
Margin block of 10, Impt. & P# 1,300.
Margin block of 12, Impt. & P# *2,000.*
Margin block of 14, Impt. & P# *2,650.*
Double paper 75.00 5.00
Paper cut with "cogwheel" punch 150.00 150.00
Ribbed paper 50.00 1.00
Paper with silk fibers — 4.00
e. With grill *175.00*
End roller grill *400.00 300.00*
f. Imperf. with grill (pair) *650.00*
g. Imperf. without grill (pair) *750.00*
h. Horizontal pair, imperf. vert. —
i. Horizontal pair, imperf. between *1,300.*
j. Double impression *600.00*
k. Printed on both sides —
Cracked plate — 27.50
Double transfer — 4.00
Short transfer 2.25

CANCELLATIONS.

Blue	+2	Railroad	+7.00
Magenta	+20	"R. P. O."	+1.50
Purple	+20	"P. D." in circle	—
Ultramarine	+1.25	"Steamboat"	—
Red	+2.50	"Steamship"	—
Orange	+2.50	Supplementary Mail Type D	+11.00
Green	+25.00	Supplementary Mail Type F	+8.50
Town	+5	Express Company	—
"Paid"	+2.50	Black Carrier	+8.00
"Paid All"	+20.00	Red Carrier	+25.00
"Free"	+15.00	Japan	+65.00
Numeral	+1.00	Alaska	—
China	—		

159 A47a 6c **dull pink** 200.00 9.00
brown rose 200.00 9.00
On cover 35.00
Pair 425.00 18.50
Block of four 875.00 *85.00*
Margin block of 12, Impt. & P# *12,000.*
Double paper — —
Ribbed paper — 10.00
Paper with silk fibers — 25.00
b. With grill *650.00*
End roller grill *1,000.*

CANCELLATIONS.

Blue	+25	"Paid"	+7.00
Magenta	+1.50	"Paid All"	—
Purple	+1.50	Supplementary Mail Types D, E or F	+15.00
Ultramarine	+2.50	Japan	+100.00
Red	+6.50	China	—
Green	+80.00	Railroad	—
Numeral	+1.50	"R. P. O."	+2.00

160 A48a 7c **orange vermillion** 400.00 55.00
vermilion 400.00 55.00
On cover 150.00
Pair 825.00 115.00
Block of four 1,700.
Margin block of 12, Impt. & P# —
a. With grill *1,350.*
Double transfer of "7 cents" (1 R 22) — 150.00
Double transfer in lower left corner — 70.00
Double paper —
Ribbed paper — 70.00
Paper with silk fibers — 90.00

CANCELLATIONS.

Blue	+2.50	Purple	+10.00
Red	+7.50	Brown	+5.00
		"Paid"	+15.00

161 A49a 10c **brown** 225.00 10.00
dark brown 225.00 10.00
yellow brown 225.00 10.00
On cover 25.00
Pair 475.00 21.00
Block of four 975.00 *85.00*
Margin block of 10, Impt. & P# *6,500.*
Margin block of 12, Impt. & P# *7,500.*
Double paper 300.00
Ribbed paper — 15.00
Paper with silk fibers — 20.00
c. With grill *1,750.*
d. Horizontal pair, imperf. between *2,500.*
Double transfer — 25.00

CANCELLATIONS.

Blue	+50	"Paid"	+4.00
Purple	+1.50	"P. D." in circle	+20.00
Red	+4.00	"Steamship"	+15.00
Magenta	+1.50	Supplementary Mail Type E	+7.00
Orange	+4.00	Supplementary Mail Type F	+2.50
Brown	+1.50	Japan	+100.00
Green	+100.00	China	—
		Alaska	—

162 A50a 12c **blackish violet** 600.00 65.00
On cover 300.00
Pair 1,250. 135.00
Block of four *3,000. 600.00*
a. With grill *3,000.*
Ribbed paper — 70.00

CANCELLATIONS.

Blue	+2.50	Supplementary Mail Type D	+15.00
Ultramarine	+15.00	Japan	+200.00
Brown	+5.00		
Red	**+15.00**		

163 A51a 15c **yellow orange** 575.00 60.00
pale orange 575.00 60.00
reddish orange 575.00 60.00
On cover 250.00
Pair 1,200. 125.00
Block of four *2,700. 550.00*
Double paper —
Paper with silk fibers 650.00 80.00
Vertical ribbed paper 600.00 70.00
a. With grill *3,000.*

CANCELLATIONS.

Blue	+2.50	Supplementary Mail Type F	+10.00
Purple	+10.00	"Steamship"	—
Red	+15.00	Numeral	+7.50
		Puerto Rico	—
		China	—

It is generally accepted as fact that the Continental Bank Note Co. printed and delivered a quantity of 24c stamps. Normally they are impossible to distinguish from those printed by the National Bank Note Co.

The Philatelic Foundation has certified as genuine a 24c on horizontally ribbed paper. Specialists believe that only Continental used ribbed paper.

165 A53 30c **gray black** 650.00 60.00
greenish black 650.00 60.00
On cover *650.00*
Pair 1,350. 125.00
Block of four *3,250. 600.00*
Double transfer — 75.00
Double paper —
Ribbed paper 700.00 70.00
Paper with silk fibers — —
c. With grill *3,000.*

CANCELLATIONS.

Purple	+7.50	"Steamship"	—
Blue	+2.50	Supplementary Mail Type E	+10.00
Red	+15.00	Supplementary Mail Type F	+5.00
Brown	+7.50		
Magenta	+7.50		

166 A54 90c **rose carmine** 1,350. 185.00
pale rose carmine 1,350. 185.00
On cover *7,500.*
Pair 2,800. 385.00
Block of four *6,000. 1,750.*

CANCELLATIONS.

Blue	+10.00	Supplementary Mail Type F	+30.00
Purple	+15.00		
Red	+30.00		

SPECIAL PRINTING OF 1873 ISSUE

Produced by the Continental Bank Note Co.
Issued for the Centennial Exposition of 1876.

1875 *Perf. 12*

Hard, white wove paper, without gum.

167 A44a 1c **ultramarine** *8,000.*
168 A45a 2c **dark brown** *3,500.*
169 A46a 3c **blue green** *9,500.* —
On cover —
170 A47a 6c **dull rose** *8,500.*
171 A48a 7c **reddish vermilion** *2,250.*
172 A49a 10c **pale brown** *8,250.*
173 A50a 12c **dark violet** *2,750.*
Horizontal pair —
174 A51a 15c **bright orange** *8,250.*
175 A52 24c **dull purple** *1,850.* —
Horizontal pair —
176 A53 30c **greenish black** *7,500.*
177 A54 90c **violet carmine** *7,500.*

Although perforated, these stamps were usually cut apart with scissors. As a result, the perforations are often much mutilated and the design is frequently damaged.

These can be distinguished from the 1873 issue by the shades; also by the paper, which is very white instead of yellowish.

These and the subsequent issues listed under the heading of "Special Printings" are special printings of stamps then in current use which, together with the reprints and re-issues, were made for sale to collectors. They were available for postage.

REGULAR ISSUE

Printed by the Continental Bank Note Co.
Yellowish Wove Paper

1875 *Perf. 12*

178 A45a 2c **vermilion,** *June 1875* 160.00 5.00
On cover 10.00
Pair 325.00 10.50
Block of four 675.00 60.00
Margin block of 12, Impt. & P# —
Margin block of 14, Impt. & P# —
a. Imperf., pair 600.00
a. Margin block of 12, Impt. & P# —
b. Half used as 1c on cover —
Double transfer —
Double paper — —
Ribbed paper — —
c. With grill *250.00*
Paper with silk fibers 200.00 7.50

CANCELLATIONS.

Blue	+10	"Paid"	+8.00
Purple	**+25**	**"Steamship"**	—
Magenta	+25	Supplementary Mail Type F	+5.50
Red	+6.00	Black Carrier	+15.00
		Railroad	+12.50

Zachary Taylor — A55

179 A55 5c **blue,** *June 1875* 175.00 9.00
dark blue 175.00 9.00
bright blue 175.00 9.00
light blue 175.00 9.00
greenish blue 185.00 11.00
On cover 20.00
Pair 360.00 19.00
Block of four 750.00 100.00
Cracked plate — *100.00*
Double transfer — 15.00
Double paper *200.00*
Ribbed paper — —
c. With grill 325.00
End roller grill —
Paper with silk fibers — 15.00

CANCELLATIONS.

Blue	+25	Railroad	+17.50
Ultramarine	+3.00	"Steamship"	+12.50
Purple	+1.50	Ship	+12.50
Magenta	+1.50	Supplementary Mail Type E	+5.00
Red	+5.00	Supplementary Mail Type F	+2.00
Green	+70.00	China	—
Numeral	+5.00	Japan	+100.00
		Peru	—

The five cent rate to foreign countries in the Universal Postal Union began on July 1, 1875. No. 179 was issued for that purpose.

SPECIAL PRINTING OF 1875 ISSUE
Produced by the Continental Bank Note Co.
Issued for the Centennial Exposition of 1876.
Hard, White Wove Paper, without gum.

1875

180 A45a	2c **carmine vermilion**	*20,000.*	
181 A55	5c **bright blue**	*32,500.*	

Printed by the American Bank Note Company.

The Continental Bank Note Co. was consolidated with the American Bank Note Co. on February 4, 1879. The American Bank Note Company used many plates of the Continental Bank Note Company to print the ordinary postage, Departmental and Newspaper stamps. Therefore, stamps bearing the Continental Company's imprint were not always its product.

The A. B. N. Co. also used the 30c and 90c plates of the N. B. N. Co. Some of No. 190 and all of No. 217 were from. A. B. N. Co. plate 405.

Early printings of No. 188 were from Continental plates 302 and 303 which contained the normal secret mark of 1873. After those plates were re-entered by the A. B. N. Co. in 1880, pairs or multiple pieces contained combinations of normal, hairline or missing marks. The pairs or other multiples usually found contain at least one hairline mark which tended to disappear as the plate wore.

A. B. N. Co. plates 377 and 378 were made in 1881 from the National transfer roll of 1870. No. 187 from these plates has no secret mark.

SAME AS 1870-75 ISSUES
Soft Porous Paper

1879 *Perf. 12*

182 A44a	1c **dark ultramarine**	120.00	1.20
	blue	120.00	1.20
	gray blue	120.00	1.20
	On cover		1.75
	Pair	250.00	2.50
	Block of four	525.00	25.00
	Margin block of 10, Impt. & P#	*3,250.*	
	Double transfer	—	3.00

CANCELLATIONS.

Blue	+5	Green	+35.00
Magenta	+10	"Paid"	+4.00
Purple	+10	Supplementary Mail Type F	+10.00
Red	+7.00	Railroad	+12.50
Printed Star Precancellation (Glen Allen, Va.)	+75.00	Printed "G." Precancellation (Glastonbury, Conn.)	+100.00

183 A45a	2c **vermilion**	55.00	1.20
	orange vermilion	55.00	1.20
	On cover		1.75
	Pair	110.00	2.50
	Block of four	225.00	20.00
	Margin block of 10, Impt. & P#	1,250.	
	Margin block of 12, Impt. & P#	*1,700.*	
a.	Double impression	—	*500.00*
	Double transfer	—	—

CANCELLATIONS.

Blue	+10	Numeral	+4.00
Purple	+20	Railroad	+15.00
Magenta	+20	Supplementary Mail Type F	+8.00
Red	+6.00	China	—
"Paid"	+5.00	Printed Star Precancellation (Glen Allen, Va.)	—
"Paid All"	—		
"Ship"	—		

184 A46a	3c **green**	42.50	10
	light green	42.50	10
	dark green	42.50	10
	On cover		20
	Pair	85.00	20
	Block of four	175.00	6.00
	Margin block of 10, Impt. & P#	900.00	
	Margin block of 12, Impt. & P#	1,100.	
	Margin block of 14, Impt. & P#	1,400.	
a.	Imperf., pair	500.00	
b.	Double impression		—
	Double transfer	—	4.00
	Short transfer	—	5.00

CANCELLATIONS.

Blue	+2	Numeral	+2.00
Magenta	+15	Railroad	+12.50
Purple	+15	"Steamboat"	—
Violet	+15	Supplementary Mail Type F	+8.00
Brown	+1.00	Printed Star Precancellation (Glen Allen, Va.)	—
Red	+7.50	China	+60.00
Green	+25.00		
"Paid"	+3.00		
"Free"	+15.00		

185 A55	5c **blue**	225.00	7.50
	light blue	225.00	7.50
	bright blue	225.00	7.50
	dark blue	225.00	7.50
	On cover		17.50
	Pair	460.00	15.50
	Block of four	950.00	100.00
	Margin block of 12, Impt. & P#	*5,000.*	

CANCELLATIONS.

Blue	+25	Numeral	+2.00
Purple	+1.00	Supplementary Mail Type F	+1.50
Magenta	+1.00	"Steamship"	+35.00
Ultramarine	+3.50	China	+60.00
Red	+7.50	Peru	—
Railroad	+20.00	Panama	—

186 A47a	6c **pink**	450.00	12.00
	dull pink	450.00	12.00
	brown rose	450.00	12.00
	On cover		30.00
	Pair	925.00	24.50
	Block of four	1,900.	*300.00*

CANCELLATIONS.

Blue	+50	Supplementary Mail Type F	+4.00
Purple	+1.00	Railroad	+22.50
Magenta	+1.00	Numeral	+4.00
Red	+12.00	China	+70.00

187 A49	10c **brown,** without secret mark	750.00	14.00
	yellow brown	750.00	14.00
	On cover		35.00
	Pair	1,550.	29.00
	Block of four	*3,250.*	—
	Double transfer	—	30.00

CANCELLATIONS.

Blue	+50	"Paid"	+3.50
Magenta	+1.50	Supplementary Mail Type F	+3.00
Red	+10.00	China	+70.00

188 A49a	10c **brown,** with secret mark	475.00	15.00
	yellow brown	475.00	15.00
	black brown	525.00	22.50
	On cover		30.00
	Pair	975.00	31.00
	Block of four	2,000.	130.00
	Pair, one stamp No. 187	—	150.00
	Double transfer		30.00
	Cracked plate		—

CANCELLATIONS.

Blue	+50	Red	+10.00
Ultramarine	+3.00	Green	+70.00
Purple	+2.00	"Paid"	+7.50
Magenta	+2.00	Supp. Mail Type F	+5.00
		Numeral	+3.00
		Printed Star Precancellation (Glen Allen, Va.)	—

189 A51a	15c **red orange**	165.00	14.00
	orange	165.00	14.00
	yellow orange	165.00	14.00
	On cover		75.00
	Pair	340.00	29.00
	Block of four	700.00	100.00
	Margin block of 12, Impt. & P#	*6,000.*	

CANCELLATIONS.

		"Steamship"	+22.50
Blue	+1.00	Supplementary Mail Type F	+5.00
Purple	+3.00	Japan	+120.00
Magenta	+3.00	China	—
Ultramarine	+5.00		
Red	+12.00		

190 A53	30c **full black**	475.00	32.50
	greenish black	475.00	32.50
	On cover		400.00
	Pair	975.00	67.50
	Block of four	1,950.	225.00
	Margin block of 10, Impt. & P#	*8,250.*	

CANCELLATIONS.

		Supplementary Mail Type F	+6.00
Blue	+1.50	"Steamship"	+35.00
Purple	+3.00	Tahiti	—
Magenta	+3.00	Samoa	—
Red	+20.00		

191 A54	90c **carmine**	1,000.	150.00
	rose	1,000.	150.00
	carmine rose	1,000.	150.00
	On cover		*5,000.*
	Pair	2,050.	310.00
	Block of four	4,750.	750.00
b.	Imperf., pair	*3,250.*	

CANCELLATIONS.

		Red	+35.00
Blue	+10.00	Supplementary Mail Type F	+20.00
Purple	+20.00		

No. 191b, imperforate, was not regularly issued.

SPECIAL PRINTING OF 1879 ISSUE
Produced by the American Bank Note Co.

1880 *Perf. 12*

Soft porous paper, without gum

192 A44a	1c **dark ultramarine**	*10,000.*
193 A45a	2c **black brown**	*6,500.*
194 A46a	3c **blue green**	*15,000.*
195 A47a	6c **dull rose**	*10,500.*
196 A48a	7c **scarlet vermilion**	*2,250.*
197 A49a	10c **deep brown**	*10,000.*
198 A50a	12c **blackish purple**	*4,500.*
199 A51a	15c **orange**	*9,750.*
200 A52	24c **dark violet**	*3,000.*
201 A53	30c **greenish black**	*8,000.*
202 A54	90c **dull carmine**	*9,000.*
203 A45a	2c **scarlet vermilion**	*18,000.*
204 A55	5c **deep blue**	*32,500.*

No. 197 was printed from Continental plate 302 (or 303) after plate was re-entered, therefore stamp may show normal, hairline or missing secret mark.

The Post Office Department did not keep separate records of the 1875 and 1880 Special Printings of the 1873 and 1879 issues, but the total quantity sold of both is recorded. The 1880 Special Printing is much the rarer.

Number Issued of 1875 and 1880 Special Printings.

1c ultramarine & dark ultramarine *(388)*
2c dark brown & black brown *(416)*
2c carmine vermilion & scarlet vermilion *(917)*
3c blue green *(267)*
5c bright blue & deep blue *(317)*
6c dull rose *(185)*
7c reddish vermilion & scarlet vermilion *(473)*
10c pale brown & deep brown *(180)*
12c dark violet & blackish purple *(282)*
15c bright orange & orange *(169)*
24c dull purple & dark violet *(286)*
30c greenish black *(179)*
90c violet carmine & dull carmine *(170)*

REGULAR ISSUE
Printed by the American Bank Note Co.

James A. Garfield — A56

1882 *Perf. 12*

205 A56	5c **yellow brown,** *April 10, 1882*	120.00	4.00
	brown	120.00	4.00
	gray brown	120.00	4.00
	On cover		12.50
	Pair	245.00	8.25
	Block of four	500.00	65.00
	Margin strip of 5, Impt. & P#	700.00	
	Margin strip of 6, Impt. & P#	875.00	
	Margin block of 12, Impt. & P#	*3,750.*	

CANCELLATIONS.

Purple	+50	Supplementary Mail Type F	+2.50
Magenta	+50	Red Express Co.	—
Blue	+25	China	+125.00
Red	+7.00		
"Ship"	—	Samoa	+150.00
Numeral	+2.00	Puerto Rico	—

SPECIAL PRINTING
Printed by the American Bank Note Co.

1882 *Perf. 12*

Soft porous paper, without gum

205C A56	5c **gray brown**	*18,500.*	
	Block of four	—	

DESIGNS OF 1873 RE-ENGRAVED

A44b

1c. The vertical lines in the upper part of the stamp have been so deepened that the background often appears to be solid. Lines of shading have been added to the upper arabesques.

1881-82

206 A44b	1c **gray blue,** *August 1881*	32.50	40
	ultramarine	32.50	40
	dull blue	32.50	40
	slate blue	32.50	40
	On cover		75
	Pair	67.50	85
	Block of four	140.00	10.00
	Margin strip of 5, Impt. & P#	225.00	
	Margin strip of 6, Impt. & P#	275.00	
	Margin block of 10, Impt. & P#	1,000.	
	Margin block of 12, Impt. & P#	1,250.	
	Double transfer	47.50	4.00

Punched with eight small holes in a circle 175.00
Margin block of 10, Impt. & P# (8-hole punch) *3,750.*

CANCELLATIONS.

		"Paid"	+4.75
Purple	+10	"Paid All"	+12.00
Magenta	+10	Numeral	+3.50
Blue	+20	Supp. Mail Type F	+5.00
Red	+3.00	Railroad	+10.00
Green	+35.00	Printed Star Precancel (Glen Allen, Va.)	+55.00
Orange	+3.00	China	—

A46b

3c. The shading at the sides of the central oval appears only about one-half the previous width. A short horizontal dash has been cut about 1 mm. below the "TS" of "CENTS".

207 A46b 3c **blue green,** *July 16, 1881*	40.00	12
green	40.00	12
yellow green	40.00	12
On cover		35
Pair	82.50	25
Block of four	170.00	25.00
Margin strip of 5, Impt. & P#	275.00	
Margin block of 10, Impt. & P#	*1,250.*	
Double transfer	—	7.50
Cracked plate	—	
Punched with eight small holes in a circle	*200.00*	

CANCELLATIONS.

		Numeral	+2.50
Purple	+10	"Ship"	—
Magenta	+10	Railroad	+5.00
Blue	+25	Supplementary Mail Type F	+8.00
Brown	+1.50	Printed Star Precancellation (Glen Allen, Va.)	—
Red	+2.50		
"Paid"	+3.00		
"Paid All"	—		

Lincoln — A47b

6c. On the original stamps four vertical lines can be counted from the edge of the panel to the outside of the stamp. On the re-engraved stamps there are but three lines in the same place.

208 A47b 6c **rose,** *June, 1882*	225.00	45.00
dull rose	225.00	45.00
On cover (rose)		125.00
Pair (rose)	460.00	95.00
Block of four (rose)	950.00	300.00
a. 6c brown red	200.00	55.00
On cover (brown red)		175.00
Pair (brown red)	410.00	120.00
Block of four (brown red)	825.00	350.00
a. Margin strip of 6, Impt. & P#	*1,800.*	
a. Margin block of 10, Impt. & P#	—	
a. Margin block of 12, Impt. & P#	—	
Double transfer	275.00	60.00

CANCELLATIONS.

		Blue	+4.00
Magenta	+2.50	Red	+15.00
Purple	+2.50	Supp. Mail Type F	+10.00

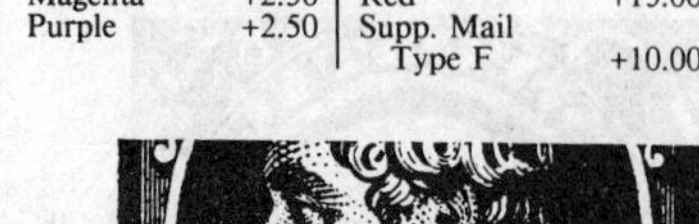

Jefferson A49b

10c. On the original stamps there are five vertical lines between the left side of the oval and the edge of the shield. There are only four lines on the re-engraved stamps. In the lower part of the latter, also, the horizontal lines of the background have been strengthened.

209 A49b 10c **brown,** *April, 1882*	75.00	2.50
yellow brown	75.00	2.50
orange brown	75.00	2.50
purple brown	85.00	2.75
olive brown	85.00	2.75
On cover		7.50
Pair	160.00	4.75
Block of four	325.00	22.50
Margin strip of 5, Impt. & P#	450.00	
Margin strip of 6, Impt. & P#	575.00	
Margin block of 10, Impt. & P#	*1,850.*	
Margin block of 12, Impt. & P#	*2,250.*	
b. 10c black brown	110.00	6.75
On cover		30.00
Pair	—	17.50
Block of four	—	—
c. Double impression		—

CANCELLATIONS.

		"Paid"	+2.50
Purple	+25	Supplementary Mail Type F	+3.00
Magenta	+25	Express Company	—
Blue	+75	Japan	+75.00
Red	+3.50	China	—
Green	+35.00	Samoa	—
Numeral	+2.00		

Printed by the American Bank Note Company.

Washington — A57

Nos. 210-211 were issued to meet the reduced first class rate of 2 cents for each half ounce, and the double rate, which Congress approved Mar. 3, 1883, effective Oct. 1, 1883.

1883 **Perf. 12**

210 A57 2c **red brown,** *Oct. 1, 1883*	32.50	8
dark red brown	32.50	8
orange brown	32.50	8
On cover		25
Pair	65.00	20
Block of four	140.00	9.00
Margin strip of 5, Impt. & P#	200.00	
Margin strip of 6, Impt. & P#	275.00	
Margin block of 10, Impt. & P#	*950.00*	
Margin block of 12, Impt. & P#	*1,200.*	
b. Imperf., pair	—	
Double transfer	35.00	1.25

CANCELLATIONS.

		Numeral	+2.50
Purple	+10	"Paid"	+3.00
Margenta	+10	Railroad	+5.00
Blue	+20	Express Company	—
Violet	+30	Supplementary Mail Type F	+5.00
Brown	+30	"Ship"	—
Red	+3.50	"Steamboat"	—
Green	+25.00	China	—

Jackson — A58

211 A58 4c **blue green,** *Oct. 1, 1883*	140.00	7.50
deep blue green	140.00	7.50
On cover		40.00
Pair	285.00	16.00
Block of four	575.00	65.00
Margin strip of 6, Impt. & P#	1,100.	
Margin block of 12, Impt. & P#	*4,000.*	
a. Imperf., pair	—	
Double transfer	—	—
Cracked plate	—	

CANCELLATIONS.

		Blue	+1.00
Purple	+1.00	Numeral	+2.00
Magenta	+1.00	Supp. Mail Type F	+5.00
Green	+35.00		

SPECIAL PRINTING
Printed by the American Bank Note Company.

1883 **Soft porous paper** **Perf. 12**

211B A57 2c **pale red brown,** with gum	750.00	—
Block of four	3,250.	
c. Horizontal pair, imperf. between	*2,250.*	
211D A58 4c **deep blue green,** without gum	*15,000.*	

The quantity issued of Nos. 211B and 211D is not definitely known, but 2,000 of each were delivered.

No. 211B is from a trial operation of a new steam-powered American Bank Note Company press.

REGULAR ISSUE
Printed by the American Bank Note Company.

Franklin — A59

1887 **Perf. 12**

212 A59 1c **ultramarine,** *June 1887*	60.00	65
bright ultramarine	60.00	65
On cover		1.50
Pair	125.00	1.35
Block of four	260.00	20.00
Margin strip of 5, Impt. & P#	350.00	
Margin strip of 6, Impt. & P#	425.00	
Margin block of 10, Impt. & P#	*1,200.*	
Margin block of 12, Impt. & P#	*1,500.*	
a. Imperf., pair	*750.00*	*325.00*
Double transfer		—

CANCELLATIONS.

		Numeral	+2.00
Purple	+10	Railroad	+10.00
Magenta	+10	Supplementary Mail Type F	+5.00
Blue	+10	China	—
Red	+5.50		

213 A57 2c **green,** *Sept. 10, 1887*	22.50	8
bright green	22.50	8
dark green	22.50	8
On cover		20
Pair	47.50	18
Block of four	100.00	7.50
Margin strip of 5, Impt. & P#	150.00	
Margin strip of 6, Impt. & P#	185.00	
Margin block of 10, Impt. & P#	*700.00*	
Margin block of 12, Impt. & P#	*850.00*	
a. Imperf., pair	*750.00*	*325.00*
b. Printed on both sides		—
Double transfer	—	3.00

CANCELLATIONS.

		Railroad	+12.00
Purple	+10	Numeral	+2.00
Magenta	+10	"Steam"	—
Blue	+90	"Steamboat"	—
Red	+5.00	Supp. Mail Type F	+7.50
Green	+25.00	China	—
"Paid"	+5.00	Japan	—

214 A46b 3c **vermilion,** *Oct. 3, 1887*	45.00	37.50
On cover (single)		85.00
Pair	92.50	80.00
Block of four	190.00	200.00
Margin strip of 5, Impt. & P#	275.00	
Margin strip of 6, Impt. & P#	325.00	
Margin block of 10, Impt. & P#	*1,100.*	
Margin block of 12, Impt. & P#	*1,300.*	

CANCELLATIONS.

		Blue	+10.00
Purple	+5.00	Supplementary Mail Type F	+15.00
Magenta	+5.00	Railroad	+30.00
Green	+150.00		

Printed by the American Bank Note Company.
SAME AS 1870-83 ISSUES

1888 **Perf. 12**

215 A58 4c **carmine,** *Nov. 1888*	140.00	11.00
rose carmine	140.00	11.00
pale rose	140.00	11.00
On cover		35.00
Pair	290.00	23.00
Block of four	600.00	75.00
Margin strip of 5, Impt. & P#	800.00	
Margin strip of 6, Impt. & P#	1,000.	
Margin block of 10, Impt. & P#	*3,500.*	
Margin block of 12, Impt. & P#	*4,250.*	

CANCELLATIONS.

		Magenta	+2.00

Blue	+1.00	Supplementary Mail Type F	+5.00
Red	+5.00		
Purple	+2.00		

216 A56 5c **indigo,** *Feb. 1888* 140.00 6.50
deep blue 140.00 6.50
On cover 25.00
Pair 290.00 13.50
Block of four 600.00 60.00
Margin strip of 5, Impt. & P# 800.00
Margin strip of 6, Impt. & P# 1,000.
Margin block of 10, Impt. & P# *3,500.*
Margin block of 12, Impt. & P# *4,250.*
b. Imperf., pair *1,000.*

CANCELLATIONS.

		Supplementary Mail Type F	+3.00
Purple	+1.00	China	+85.00
Magenta	+1.00	Japan	+85.00
Blue	+1.00	Puerto Rico	+75.00
Samoa	—		

217 A53 30c **orange brown,** *Jan. 1888* 325.00 75.00
deep orange brown 325.00 75.00
On cover *1,400.*
Pair 675.00 160.00
Block of four 1,500. 350.00
Margin strip of 5, Impt. & P# *2,100.*
Margin block of 10, Impt. & P# *6,750.*
Margin block of 12, Impt. & P# —
a. Imperf., pair *1,350.*

CANCELLATIONS.

		Supplementary Mail Type F	+10.00
Blue	+5.00	"Paid All"	+25.00
Magenta	+10.00	"Paid"	+15.00

218 A54 90c **purple,** *Feb. 1888* 700.00 130.00
bright purple 700.00 130.00
On cover *7,500*
Pair 1,450. 270.00
Block of four 3,000. 600.00
Margin strip of 5, Impt. & P# *4,250.*
Margin block of 10, Impt. & P# *22,500.*
Margin block of 12, Impt. & P# —
a. Imperf., pair —

CANCELLATIONS.

		Supplementary Mail Type F	+25.00
Blue	+10.00		
Purple	+15.00		

Nos. 216b, 217a and 218 were not regularly issued.

Printed by the American Bank Note Company. Plates for the 1c and 2c were of 400 subjects in four panes of 100 each. All other values were from plates of 200 subjects in two panes of 100 each.

Franklin — A60

Washington — A61

Jackson — A62

Lincoln — A63

Grant — A64

Garfield — A65

William T. Sherman — A66

Daniel Webster — A67

Henry Clay — A68

Jefferson — A69

Perry — A70

The lack of a value for a listed item does not necessarily indicate rarity.

1890-93 ***Perf. 12***

219 A60 1c **dull blue,** *Feb. 22, 1890* 18.50 10
deep blue 18.50 10
ultramarine 18.50 12
On cover 35
Block of four 75.00 3.50
Margin strip of 5, Impt. & P# 120.00
Margin strip of 6, Impt. & P# 145.00
Margin strip of 7, Impt. & P# 175.00
Margin block of 10, Impt. & P# 475.00
Margin block of 12, Impt. & P# 600.00
Margin block of 14, Impt. & P# 750.00
c. Imperf., pair 225.00
Double transfer — —

CANCELLATIONS.

Samoa	—	China	—

219D A61 2c **lake,** *Feb. 22, 1890* 150.00 45
On cover 1.25
Block of four 625.00 7.00
Margin strip of 5, Impt. & P# 750.00
Margin block of 10, Impt. & P# 2,750.
e. Imperf., pair 100.00
Double transfer — —

CANCELLATIONS.

Supplementary Mail Type F	3.00

220 A61 2c **carmine,** *1890* 15.00 5
dark carmine, rose or carmine rose 15.00 5
On cover 15
Block of four 60.00 1.50
Margin strip of 5, Impt. & P# 100.00
Margin strip of 6, Impt. & P# 125.00
Margin strip of 7, Impt. & P# 160.00
Margin block of 10, Impt. & P# 450.00
Margin block of 12, Impt. & P# 550.00
Margin block of 14, Impt. & P# 700.00
a. Cap on left "2" (Plates 235-236, 246-247-248) 35.00 1.00
Pair, cap on left, one normal — —
a. Margin block of 12, Impt. & P# *1,200.*
c. Cap on both "2's" (Plates 245, 246) 110.00 8.00
Pair, cap on left, cap on both — —
d. Imperf., pair 100.00
d. Imperf., pair, without gum 40.00
d. Margin block of 12, Impt. & P# —
Double transfer — 3.00

CANCELLATIONS.

Blue	+5	Supplementary Mail Types F or G	+3.00
Purple	+5	China	+20.00

221 A62 3c **purple,** *Feb. 22, 1890* 50.00 4.50

			bright purple	50.00	4.50
			dark purple	50.00	4.50
			On cover		12.50
			Block of four	210.00	30.00
			Margin strip of 5, Impt. & P#	325.00	
			Margin block of 10, Impt. & P#	1,750.	
a.			Imperf., pair	275.00	

CANCELLATIONS.

Samoa —

222	A63	4c	**dark brown,** *June 2, 1890*	50.00	1.50
			blackish brown	50.00	1.50
			On cover		12.50
			Block of four	210.00	13.50
			Margin strip of 5, Impt. & P#	325.00	
			Margin block of 10, Impt. & P#	1,850.	
a.			Imperf., pair	250.00	
			Double transfer	65.00	—

CANCELLATIONS.

China +40.00

223	A64	5c	**chocolate,** *June 2, 1890*	50.00	1.50
			yellow brown	50.00	1.50
			On cover		10.00
			Block of four	210.00	12.50
			Margin strip of 5, Impt. & P#	325.00	
			Margin block of 10, Impt. & P#	1,850.	
b.			Imperf., pair, yellow brown	275.00	
			Double transfer	65.00	1.75

CANCELLATIONS.

China +35.00
Samoa —
Supplementary Mail Types F or G +3.00

224	A65	6c	**brown red,** *Feb. 22, 1890*	55.00	15.00
			dark brown red	55.00	15.00
			On cover		30.00
			Block of four	230.00	70.00
			Margin strip of 5, Impt. & P#	375.00	
			Margin block of 10, Impt. & P#	1,850.	
a.			Imperf., pair	275.00	

CANCELLATIONS.

Supplementary Mail Type F +3.00

225	A66	8c	**lilac,** *Mar. 21, 1893*	40.00	8.50
			grayish lilac	40.00	8.50
			magenta	40.00	8.50
			On cover		25.00
			Block of four	165.00	50.00
			Margin strip of 5, Impt. & P#	275.00	
			Margin block of 10, Impt. & P#	1,300.	
a.			Imperf., pair	*1,250.*	

The 8c was issued because the registry fee was reduced from 10 to 8 cents effective Jan. 1, 1893.

226	A67	10c	**green,** *Feb. 22, 1890*	95.00	1.75
			bluish green	95.00	1.75
			dark green	95.00	1.75
			On cover		7.50
			Block of four	390.00	20.00
			Margin strip of 5, Impt. & P#	650.00	
			Margin block of 10, Impt. & P#	3,000.	
a.			Imperf., pair	400.00	
			Double transfer	—	—

CANCELLATIONS.

Samoa —
Supplementary Mail Types F or G +2.50

227	A68	15c	**indigo,** *Feb. 22, 1890*	135.00	15.00
			deep indigo	135.00	15.00
			On cover		60.00
			Block of four	550.00	75.00
			Margin strip of 5, Impt. & P#	900.00	
			Margin block of 10, Impt. & P#	*5,750.*	
a.			Imperf., pair	750.00	
			Double transfer	—	—
			Triple transfer		—

CANCELLATIONS.

Supplementary Mail Type F +3.00

228	A69	30c	**black,** *Feb. 22, 1890*	200.00	20.00
			gray black	200.00	20.00
			full black	200.00	20.00
			On cover		*600.00*
			Block of four	825.00	100.00
			Margin strip of 5, Impt. & P#	1,400.	
			Margin block of 10, Impt. & P#	*9,000.*	
a.			Imperf., pair	*1,350.*	
			Double transfer	—	—

CANCELLATIONS.

Supplementary Mail Type F +5.00

229	A70	90c	**orange,** *Feb. 22, 1890*	325.00	95.00
			yellow orange	325.00	95.00
			red orange	325.00	95.00
			On cover		*2,500.*
			Block of four	1,400.	425.00
			Margin strip of 5, Impt. & P#	2,350.	
			Margin block of 10, Impt. & P#	*18,500.*	
a.			Imperf., pair	*2,750.*	
			Short transfer at bottom	—	—

CANCELLATIONS.

Supp. Mail Type F or G +10.00

Imperforate stamps of this issue were not regularly issued. The imperforate 1c, 2c, 4c, 5c and 6c values exist in many trial colors. Value slightly less than for those in normal colors.

COLUMBIAN EXPOSITION ISSUE

Issued to commemorate the World's Columbian Exposition held at Chicago, Ill., from May 1, 1893 to October 30, 1893, which was to celebrate the 400th anniversary of the discovery of America by Christopher Columbus.

Columbus in Sight of Land — A71

Landing of Columbus — A72

"Santa Maria," Flagship of Columbus — A73

Fleet of Columbus — A74

Columbus Soliciting Aid from Queen Isabella — A75

Columbus Welcomed at Barcelona — A76

Columbus Restored to Favor — A77

Columbus Presenting Natives — A78

Columbus Announcing His Discovery — A79

Columbus at La Rábida — A80

Recall of Columbus — A81

Queen Isabella Pledging Her Jewels — A82

Columbus in Chains — A83

Columbus Describing His Third Voyage — A84

Queen Isabella and Columbus — A85

Columbus — A86

AMERICAN BANK NOTE COMPANY.

Type of imprint and plate number

Exposition Station Cancellation

Printed by the American Bank Note Company.
Plates of 200 subjects in two panes of 100 each (1c, 2c).
Plates of 100 subjects in two panes of 50 each (2c-$5).
Issued (except 8c) Jan. 2, 1893.

1893 *Perf. 12*

No.	Type		Description	Unused	Used
230	A71	1c	**deep blue**	17.50	25
			blue	17.50	25
			pale blue	17.50	25
			On cover		75
			On cover or card, Expo. sta. canc.		150.00
			Block of four	72.50	6.00
			Margin strip of 3, Impt. & P#	67.50	
			Margin strip of 4, Impt. & P#	97.50	
			Margin block of 6, Impt. & P#	275.00	
			Margin block of 8, Impt., letter & P#	425.00	
			Double transfer	24.00	50
			Cracked plate	80.00	

CANCELLATIONS.
| China — |

No.	Type		Description	Unused	Used
231	A72	2c	**brown violet**	16.00	6
			deep brown violet	16.00	6
			gray violet	16.00	6
			On cover		25
			On cover or card, Expo. sta. cancel		125.00
			Block of four	65.00	3.00
			Margin strip of 3, Impt. & P#	60.00	
			Margin strip of 4, Impt. & P#	90.00	
			Margin block of 6, Impt. & P#	225.00	
			Margin block of 8, Impt., letter & P#	375.00	
b.			Imperf., pair	1,200.	
			Double transfer	22.50	25
			Triple transfer	57.50	—
			Quadruple transfer	85.00	
			Third figure to left of Columbus shows broken hat	50.00	20
			Broken frame line	19.00	8
			Recut frame lines	19.00	—
			Cracked plate	80.00	—

CANCELLATIONS.
China — | Supp. Mail, G +3.50

No.	Type		Description	Unused	Used
232	A73	3c	**green**	38.50	12.50
			dull green	38.50	12.50
			dark green	38.50	12.50
			On cover		30.00
			On cover, Expo. station canc.		300.00
			Block of four	155.00	75.00
			Margin strip of 3, Impt. & P#	150.00	
			Margin strip of 4, Impt. & P#	225.00	
			Margin block of 6, Impt. & P#	500.00	
			Margin block of 8, Impt., letter & P#	800.00	
			Double transfer	57.50	—

CANCELLATIONS.
China — | Supp. Mail, F, G +7.50

No.	Type		Description	Unused	Used
233	A74	4c	**ultramarine**	55.00	5.00
			dull ultramarine	55.00	5.00
			deep ultramarine	55.00	5.00
			On cover		20.00
			On cover, Expo. station canc.		400.00
			Block of four	225.00	35.00
			Margin strip of 3, Impt. & P#	215.00	
			Margin strip of 4, Impt. & P#	325.00	—
			Margin block of 6, Impt. & P#	750.00	
			Margin block of 8, Impt., letter & P#	1,400.	
a.			**4c blue** (error)	*8,500.*	*3,250.*
a.			Block of four	*35,000.*	—
a.			Margin strip of 4, Impt., letter & P#	*42,500.*	
			Double transfer	87.50	—

CANCELLATIONS.
| Supp. Mail, G +3.00

No. 233a exists in two shades.

No.	Type		Description	Unused	Used
234	A75	5c	**chocolate**	62.50	6.00
			dark chocolate	62.50	6.00
			pale brown	62.50	6.00
			yellow brown	62.50	6.00
			On cover		20.00
			On cover, Expo. station canc.		400.00
			Block of four	325.00	45.00
			Margin strip of 3, Impt. & P#	320.00	
			Margin strip of 4, Impt. & P#	450.00	
			Margin block of 6, Impt. & P#	1,350.	
			Margin block of 8, Impt., letter & P#	2,500.	
			Double transfer	120.00	—

CANCELLATIONS.
China — | Supp. Mail, F +3.00

No.	Type		Description	Unused	Used
235	A76	6c	**purple**	55.00	16.50
			dull purple	55.00	16.50
a.			6c red violet	55.00	16.50
			On cover		45.00
			On cover, Expo. station canc.		450.00
			Block of four	225.00	85.00
			Margin strip of 3, Impt. & P#	215.00	
			Margin strip of 4, Impt. & P#	325.00	
			Margin block of 6, Impt. & P#	825.00	
			Margin block of 8, Impt., letter & P#	1,500.	
			Double transfer	80.00	25.00

CANCELLATIONS.
China — | Supp. Mail, F +5.00

No.	Type		Description	Unused	Used
236	A77	8c	**magenta**, *Mar. 1893*	45.00	7.00
			light magenta	45.00	7.00
			dark magenta	45.00	7.00
			On cover		20.00
			On cover, Expo. station canc.		450.00
			Block of four	185.00	40.00
			Margin strip of 3, Impt. & P#	170.00	
			Margin strip of 4, Impt. & P#	240.00	
			Margin block of 6, Impt. & P#	510.00	
			Margin block of 8, Impt., letter & P#	825.00	
			Double transfer	58.50	—

Earliest known use; Mar. 3.

CANCELLATIONS.
China — | Supp. Mail, F +4.50

No.	Type		Description	Unused	Used
237	A78	10c	**black brown**	90.00	5.00
			dark brown	90.00	5.00
			gray black	90.00	5.00
			On cover		30.00
			On cover, Expo. station canc.		500.00
			Block of four	375.00	40.00
			Margin strip of 3, Impt. & P#	360.00	
			Margin strip of 4, Impt. & P#	510.00	
			Margin block of 6, Impt. & P#	2,250.	
			Margin block of 8, Impt., letter & P#	3,400.	
			Double transfer	135.00	10.00
			Triple transfer	—	

Values quoted in this catalogue are for stamps graded at Fine-Very Fine and with no faults. An illustrated guide to grade is provided in introductory material, beginning on Page V.

CANCELLATIONS.

Supp. Mail Types F or G		+4.00

238	A79	15c	**dark green**	150.00	45.00
			green	150.00	45.00
			dull green	150.00	45.00
			On cover		200.00
			On cover, Expo. station canc.		900.00
			Block of four	650.00	300.00
			Margin strip of 3, Impt. & P#	650.00	
			Margin strip of 4, Impt. & P#	875.00	
			Margin block of 6, Impt. & P#	*3,600.*	
			Margin block of 8, Impt., letter & P#	*5,750.*	
			Double transfer	—	—

CANCELLATIONS.

China	+75.00	Supp. Mail, F or G	+10.00

239	A80	30c	**orange brown**	210.00	65.00
			bright orange brown	210.00	65.00
			On cover		375.00
			On cover, Expo. station canc.		*1,500.*
			Block of four	875.00	425.00
			Margin strip of 3, Impt. & P#	850.00	
			Margin strip of 4, Impt. & P#	1,200.	
			Margin block of 6, Impt. & P#	*5,400.*	
			Margin block of 8, Impt., letter & P#	*8,000.*	

CANCELLATIONS.

Supp. Mail Types F or G		+25.00

240	A81	50c	**slate blue**	300.00	110.00
			dull state blue	300.00	110.00
			On cover		600.00
			On cover, Expo. station canc.		*2,250.*
			Block of four	1,250.	650.00
			Margin strip of 3, Impt. & P#	1,200.	
			Margin strip of 4, Impt. & P#	1,725.	
			Margin block of 6, Impt. & P#	*8,200.*	
			Margin block of 8, Impt., letter & P#	*12,000.*	
			Double transfer	—	—
			Triple transfer	—	—

CANCELLATIONS.

Supp. Mail Types F or G		+30.00

241	A82	$1	**salmon**	1,050.	475.00
			dark salmon	1,050.	475.00
			On cover		*1,900.*
			On cover, Expo. station canc.		*4,500.*
			Block of four	4,500.	2,500.
			Margin strip of 3, Impt. & P#	4,250.	
			Margin strip of 4, Impt. & P#	5,900.	
			Margin block of 6, Impt. & P#	*18,000.*	
			Margin block of 8, Impt., letter & P#	*25,000.*	
			Double transfer	—	—

CANCELLATIONS.

Supp. Mail Types F or G		+50.00

242	A83	$2	**brown red**	1,150.	400.00
			deep brown red	1,150.	400.00
			On cover		*1,850.*
			On cover, Expo. station canc.		*4,500.*
			Block of four	5,100.	2,250.
			Margin strip of 3, Impt. & P#	4,850.	
			Margin strip of 4, Impt. & P#	6,500.	
			Margin block of 6, Impt. & P#	*20,000.*	
			Margin block of 8, Impt., letter & P#	*27,500.*	

CANCELLATIONS.

Supp. Mail Type G		+50.00

243	A84	$3	**yellow green**	1,950.	700.00
			pale yellow green	1,950.	700.00
a.		$3	olive green	1,950.	700.00
			On cover		*2,500.*
			On cover, Expo. station canc.		*6,250.*
			Block of four	*8,750.*	*5,500.*
			Margin strip of 3, Impt. & P#	*8,250.*	
			Margin strip of 4, Impt. & P#	*11,250.*	
			Margin block of 6, Impt. & P#	*34,000.*	
			Margin block of 8, Impt., letter & P#	*52,500.*	
244	A85	$4	**crimson lake**	2,750.	1,000.
a.		$4	rose carmine	2,750.	1,000.
			pale aniline rose	2,750.	1,000.
			On cover		*3,750.*
			On cover, Expo. station canc.		*8,500.*
			Block of four	*13,000.*	*7,000.*
			Margin strip of 3, Impt. & P#	*12,000.*	
			Margin strip of 4, Impt. & P#	*17,000.*	
			Margin block of 6, Impt. & P#	*72,500.*	
			Margin block of 8, Impt., letter & P#	*105,000.*	
245	A86	$5	**black**	3,000.	1,300.
			grayish black	3,000.	1,300.
			On cover		4,500.
			On cover, Expo. station canc.		*12,000.*
			Block of four	*13,500.*	9,000.
			Margin strip of 3, Impt. & P#	*13,000.*	
			Margin strip of 4, Impt. & P#	*18,500.*	
			Margin block of 6, Impt. & P#	*82,500.*	
			Margin block of 8, Impt., letter & P#	*125,000.*	

Nos. 230-245 exist imperforate; not issued.

BUREAU ISSUES

In the following listings of postal issues mostly printed by the Bureau of Engraving and Printing at Washington, D.C., the editors acknowledge with thanks the use of material prepared by the Catalogue Listing Committee of the Bureau Issues Association.

The Bureau-printed stamps until 1965 were engraved except the Offset Issues of 1918-19 (Nos. 525-536). Engraving and lithography were combined for the first time for the Homemakers 5c (no. 1253). The Bureau used photogravure first in 1971 on the Missouri 8c (No. 1426).

Stamps in this section which were not printed by the Bureau begin with Nos. 909-921 and are so noted.

"*On cover*" listings carry through No. 550. Beyond this point a few covers of special significance are listed. Many Bureau Issue stamps are undoubtly scarce properly used on cover. Most higher denominations exist almost exclusively on pieces of package wrapping and usually in combination with other values. Collector interest in covers is generally limited to fancy cancellations, attractive corner cards, use abroad and other special usages.

Plate number blocks are valued unused. Although many exist used, and are scarcer in that condition, they command only a fraction of the value of the unused examples because they are less sought after.

IMPRINTS AND PLATE NUMBERS

In listing the Bureau of Engraving & Printing Imprints, the editors have followed the classification of types adopted by the Bureau Issues Association. Types I, II, IV, V and VIII occur on postage issues and are illustrated below. Types III, VI and VII occur only on Special Delivery plates, so are illustrated with the listings of those stamps; other types are illustrated with the listings of the issues on which they occur.

1   76   170   488   715

Bureau, Engraving & Printing

Type I   II   IV   V   VIII

In listing Imprint block and strips, the editors have designated for each stamp the various types known to exist. If, however, the Catalogue listing sufficiently describes the Imprint, no type number is given. Thus a listing reading: "Imprint (Impt.) & P# & A" in the 1912-14 series would not be followed by a type number as the description is self-explanatory. Values are for the commonest types.

PLATE POSITIONS

At the suggestion of the Catalogue Listing Committe of the Bureau Issues Association, all plate positions of these issues are indicated by giving the plate number first, next the pane position, and finally the stamp position. For example: 20234 L.L. 58.

Franklin — A87

Washington — A88

Jackson — A89

Lincoln — A90

Grant — A91

Garfield — A92

Sherman — A93

Webster — A94

Clay — A95

Jefferson — A96

Perry — A97

James Madison — A98

John Marshall — A99

REGULAR ISSUE

Plates for the issues of 1894, 1895 and 1898 were of two sizes: 400 subjects for all 1c, 2c and 10c denominations; 200 subjects for all 6c, 8c, 15c, 50c, $1.00, $2.00 and $5.00, and both 400 and 200 subjects for the 3c, 4c and 5c denominations; all issued in panes of 100 each.

Dates of issue of the 1894, 1895 and 1898 denominations are taken from the Report of the Third Assistant Postmaster General, dated June 30, 1899.

1894 **Unwmk.** ***Perf. 12***

246 A87 1c **ultramarine,** *Oct. 1894* 15.00 2.00
bright ultramarine 15.00 2.00
dark ultramarine 15.00 2.00
On cover 10.00
Block of four 62.50 12.50
Margin strip of 3, Impt. & P#, T I 65.00
Margin block of 6, Impt. & P#, T I 200.00
Double transfer 20.00 3.00

CANCELLATIONS.

China —

247 A87 1c **blue** 37.50 85
bright blue 37.50 85
dark blue 37.50 85
On cover 15.00
Block of four 150.00 10.00
Margin strip of 3, Impt. & P#, T I or II 150.00
Margin block of 6, Impt. & P#, T I or II 400.00
Double transfer — 2.50

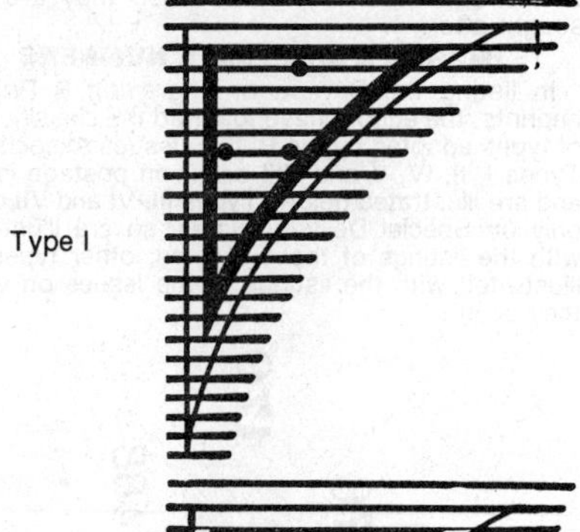
Type I

Type II

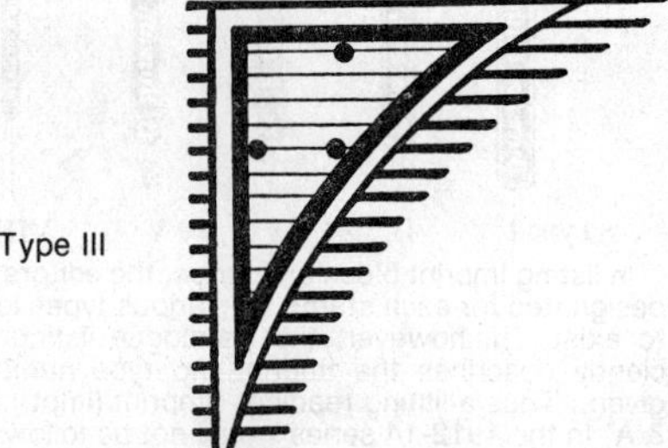
Type III

TWO CENTS.

Type I (Triangle I). The horizontal lines of the ground work run across the triangle and are of the same thickness within it as without.

Type II (Triangle II). The horizontal lines cross the triangle but are thinner within it than without.

Type III (Triangle III). The horizontal lines do not cross the double lines of the triangle. The lines within the triangle are thin, as in Type II. Two varieties of Type III are known but the variations are minor. For further information see the March, 1937 issue of the "Bureau Specialist."

248 A88 2c **pink,** type I, *Oct. 1894* 12.50 1.45
pale pink 12.50 1.45
On cover 10.00
Block of four 52.50 15.00
Margin strip of 3, Impt. & P#, T I or II 55.00
Margin block of 6, Impt. & P#, T I or II 145.00
a. Vert. pair, imperf. horiz. *2,000.*
Double transfer — —

249 A88 2c **carmine lake,** type I 85.00 95
dark carmine lake 85.00 95
On cover 7.50
Block of four 350.00 15.00
Margin strip of 3, Impt. & P#, T I or II 350.00
Margin block of 6, Impt. & P#, T I or II 850.00
Double transfer — 1.50

250 A88 2c **carmine,** type I 14.00 25
dark carmine 14.00 25
scarlet 14.00 25
On cover 1.50
Block of four 57.50 3.00
Margin strip of 3, Impt. & P#, T I or II 57.50
Margin block of 6, Impt. & P#, T I or II 200.00
a. Vert. pair, imperf. horiz. *1,500.*
b. Horizontal pair, imperf. between *1,500.*
Double transfer — 1.10

251 A88 2c **carmine,** type II 110.00 1.50
dark carmine 110.00 1.50
On cover 11.00
Block of four 450.00 22.50
Margin strip of 3, Impt. & P#, T II 450.00
Margin block of 6, Impt. & P#, T II 1,450.

252 A88 2c **carmine,** type III 70.00 2.00
pale carmine 70.00 2.00
On cover 11.00
Block of four 300.00 40.00
Margin strip of 3, Impt. & P#, T II or IV 300.00
Margin block of 6, Impt. & P#, T II or IV 950.00
a. Horiz. pair, imperf. vert. *1,350.*
b. Horiz. pair, imperf. between *1,500.*

253 A89 3c **purple,** *Sept. 1894* 55.00 4.25
dark purple 55.00 4.25
On cover 20.00
Block of four 235.00 40.00
Margin block of 4, arrow, R or L 250.00
Margin strip of 3, Impt. & P#, T I or II 225.00
Margin block of 6, Impt. & P#, T I or II 700.00
a. Imperf., pair 350.00
a. Block of four 750.00
a. Margin block of 6, Impt. & P# —

254 A90 4c **dark brown,** *Sept. 1894* 60.00 1.75
brown 60.00 1.75
On cover 15.00
Block of four 250.00 20.00
Margin block of 4, arrow, R or L 260.00
Margin strip of 3, Impt. & P#, T I or II 250.00
Margin block of 6, Impt. & P#, T I or II 850.00
a. Imperf., pair 350.00
a. Block of four 750.00
a. Margin block of 6, Impt. & P# —

CANCELLATIONS.

Supplementary Mail Type F +2.00

255 A91 5c **chocolate,** *Sept. 1894* 52.50 2.50
deep chocolate 52.50 2.50
yellow brown 52.50 2.50
On cover 15.00
Block of four 225.00 20.00
Margin block of 4, arrow, R or L 240.00
Margin strip of 3, Impt. & P#, T I, II or IV 225.00
Margin block of 6, Impt. & P#, T I, II or IV 575.00
b. Imperf., pair 350.00
b. Block of four 750.00
b. Margin block of 6, Impt. & P# —
c. Vert. pair, imperf. horiz. *900.00*
Worn plate, diagonal lines missing in oval background 57.50 3.00
Double transfer 67.50 3.00

CANCELLATIONS.

Supplementary Mail Type G +2.00
China —

256 A92 6c **dull brown,** *July 1894* 95.00 12.00
On cover 35.00
Block of four 400.00 80.00
Margin block of 4, arrow, R or L 420.00

Margin strip of 3, Impt. & P#, T I 400.00
Margin block of 6, Impt. & P#, T I 1,500.
a. Vert. pair, imperf. horiz. *850.00*
a. Margin block of 6, Impt. & P#, T I *10,000.*
257 A93 8c **violet brown,** *Mar. 1895* 80.00 8.00
bright violet brown 80.00 8.00
On cover 35.00
Block of four 325.00 65.00
Margin block of 4, arrow, R or L 340.00
Margin strip of 3, Impt. & P#, T I 325.00
Margin block of 6, Impt. & P#, T I 800.00
258 A94 10c **dark green,** *Sept. 1894* 115.00 5.00
green 115.00 5.00
dull green 115.00 5.00
On cover 27.50
Block of four 500.00 40.00
Margin strip of 3, Impt. & P#, T I 500.00
Margin block of 6, Impt. & P#, T I 1,600.
a. Imperf., pair 650.00
a. Block of four 1,400.
a. Margin block of 6, Impt. & P# —
Double transfer 150.00 6.00

CANCELLATIONS.

China — | Supp. Mail Types F or G +2.00

259 A95 15c **dark blue,** *Oct. 1894* 175.00 30.00
indigo 175.00 30.00
On cover 90.00
Block of four 750.00 250.00
Margin block of 4, arrow, R or L 800.00
Margin strip of 3, Impt. & P#, T I 800.00
Margin block of 6, Impt. & P#, T I 2,750.

CANCELLATIONS.

| China —

260 A96 50c **orange,** *Nov. 1894* 225.00 50.00
deep orange 225.00 50.00
On cover 750.00
Block of four 975.00 450.00
Margin block of 4, arrow, R or L 1,050.
Margin strip of 3, Impt. & P#, T I 975.00
Margin block of 6, Impt. & P#, T I 4,250.

CANCELLATIONS.

| Supp. Mail Types F or G —
| China —

Type I

Type II

ONE DOLLAR.
Type I. The circles enclosing "$1" are broken where they meet the curved line below "One Dollar".
Type II. The circles are complete.
The fifteen left vertical rows of impressions from plate 76 are Type I, the balance being Type II.

261 A97 $1 **black,** type I, *Nov. 1894* 550.00 160.00
grayish black 550.00 160.00
On cover 1,250.
Block of four 2,300. 1,100.
Margin block of 4, arrow, L 2,500.
Margin strip of 3, Impt. & P#, T II 2,300.
Margin block of 6, Impt. & P#, T II *11,000.*
261A A97 $1 **black,** type II, *Nov. 1894* 1,200. 325.00
On cover *3,250.*
Block of four 5,000. 2,750.
Margin block of 4, arrow, R 5,250.
Horizontal pair, types I and II 2,100. 650.00
Block of four, two each of types I and II 4,500. —
Margin strip of 3, Impt. & P#, T II, one stamp No. 261 4,000.
Margin block of 6, Impt. & P#, T II, two stamps No. 261 *18,500.*
262 A98 $2 **bright blue,** *Dec. 1894* 1,400. 400.00
dark blue 1,500. 425.00
On cover *3,500.*
Block of four 6,000. 2,750.
Margin block of 4, arrow, R or L 6,500.
Margin strip of 3, Impt. & P#, T II 6,250.
Margin block of 6, Impt. & P#, T II *26,000.*
263 A99 $5 **dark green,** *Dec. 1894* 2,250. 750.00
On cover *6,000.*
Block of four *10,000.* 5,500.

Margin block of 4, arrow, R or L *11,000.*
Margin strip of 3, Impt. & P#, TII *11,000.*

The Imperf. horizontally variety, No. 248a, and the imperforate varieties Nos. 253a, 254a, 255b and 258a were not regularly issued.

REGULAR ISSUE

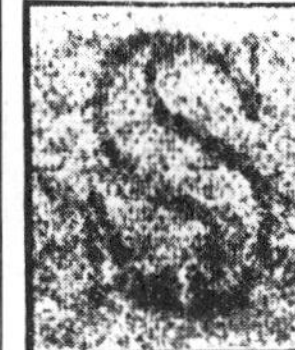

(Actual size of letter)

repeated in rows, thus

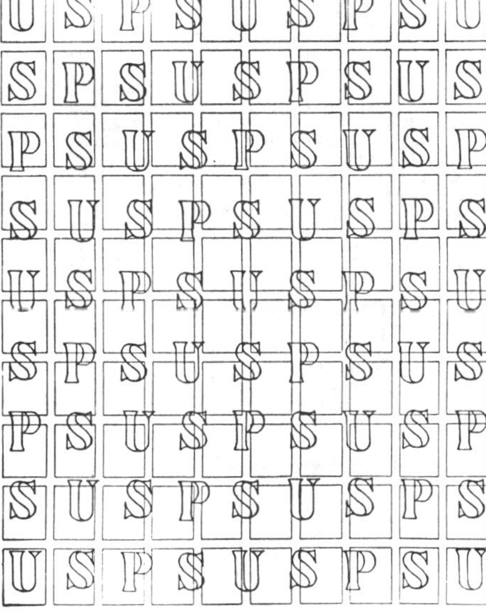

The letters stand for "U.S. Postage Stamp."
Plates for the 1895 issue were of two sizes:-
400 subjects for all 1c, 2c and 10c denominations; 200 subjects for all 4c, 5c, 6c, 8c, 15c, 50c, $1, $2 and $5; and both 400 and 200 subjects for the 3c denomination; all issued in panes of 100 each.
Printings from the 400 subject plates show the watermark reading horizontally, on the 200 subject printings the watermark reads vertically (with the tops and bottoms of the letters toward the vertical sides of the stamps.)

Wmk. 191 Horizontally or Vertically

1895 ***Perf. 12***

264 A87 1c **blue,** *Apr. 1895* 3.50 10
dark blue 3.50 10
pale blue 3.50 10
On cover 1.00
Block of four 14.50 2.00
Margin strip of 3, Impt. & P#, T I, II, IV or V 14.50
Margin block of 6, Impt. & P#, T I, II, IV or V 130.00
b. Horiz. pair, imperf. vert. —
c. Imperf., pair 325.00
c. Block of four, imperf. 700.00
Double transfer — 75

CANCELLATIONS.

China — | Philippines —
| Samoa —

265 A88 2c **carmine,** type I, *May 1895* 15.00 40
deep carmine 15.00 40
On cover 2.25
Block of four 65.00 6.00
Margin strip of 3, Impt. & P#, T II 65.00
Margin block of 6, Impt. & P#, T II 225.00
Double transfer 25.00 3.00
266 A88 2c **carmine,** type II 13.00 1.75
On cover 5.00
Block of four 54.00 18.50
Horizontal pair, types II and III 35.00 6.50
Margin strip of 3, Impt. & P#, T II or IV 55.00
Margin block of 6, Impt. & P#, T II or IV 200.00
267 A88 2c **carmine,** type III 3.00 5
deep carmine 3.00 5
On cover 20
Block of four 12.50 1.00

Margin strip of 3, Impt. & P#, T II, IV or V 11.50
Margin block of 6, Impt. & P#, T II, IV or V 90.00
a. Imperf., pair 300.00
a. Block of four, imperf. 650.00
Double transfer 10.00 1.00
Triple transfer —
Triangle at upper right without shading 17.50 5.00

CANCELLATIONS.

China — | Philippines —
Hawaii — | Samoa —

The three left vertical rows of impressions from plate 170 are Type II, the balance being Type III.

268 A89 3c **purple,** *Oct. 1895* 22.50 65
dark purple 22.50 65
On cover 7.00
Block of four 92.50 7.50
Margin block of 4, arrow, R or L 97.50
Margin strip of 3, Impt. & P#, T II or V 145.00
Margin block of 6, Impt. & P#, T II or IV 375.00
a. Imperf., pair 350.00
a. Block of four, imperf. 800.00
Double transfer 32.50 2.25

CANCELLATIONS.

Guam — | Philippines —
China — |

269 A90 4c **dark brown,** *June 1895* 24.00 75
dark yellow brown 24.00 75
On cover 9.00
Block of four 100.00 10.00
Margin block of 4, arrow, R or L 105.00
Margin strip of 3, Impt. & P#, T I, II, IV or V 105.00
Margin block of 6, Impt. & P#, T I, II, IV or V 400.00
a. Imperf., pair 350.00
a. Block of four, imperf. 800.00
Double transfer 25.00 2.25

CANCELLATIONS.

Philippines — | Samoa —
China — |

270 A91 5c **chocolate,** *June 11, 1895* 22.50 1.20
deep brown 22.50 1.20
chestnut 22.50 1.20
On cover 5.75
Block of four 105.00 10.00
Margin block of 4, arrow, R or L 115.00
Margin strip of 3, Impt. & P#, T I, II, IV or V 105.00
Margin block of 6, Impt. & P#, T I, II, IV or V 400.00
b. Imperf., pair 350.00
b. Block of four, imperf. 800.00
Double transfer 32.50 2.50
Worn plate, diagonal lines missing in oval background 25.00 1.60

CANCELLATIONS.

China — | Supp. Mail, G +2.50

271 A92 6c **dull brown,** *Aug. 1895* 42.50 2.50
claret brown 42.50 2.50
On cover 22.50
Block of four 175.00 25.00
Margin block of 4, arrow, R or L 185.00
Margin strip of 3, Impt. & P#, T I, IV or V 175.00
Margin block of 6, Impt. & P#, T I, IV or V 1,100.
Very thin paper 47.50 2.50
a. Wmkd. USIR *2,250.* 350.00
b. Imperf., pair 400.00
b. Block of four, imperf. 850.00

CANCELLATIONS.

| Philippines —

272 A93 8c **violet brown,** *July 1895* 30.00 65
dark violet brown 30.00 65
On cover 13.50
Block of four 125.00 7.50
Margin block of 4, arrow, R or L 130.00
Margin strip of 3, Impt. & P#, T I, IV or V 125.00
Margin block of 6, Impt. & P#, T I, IV or V 475.00
a. Wmkd. USIR 1,100. 110.00
a. Wmkd. USIR, P# strip of 3 *4,500.*
b. Imperf., pair 550.00
b. Block of four, imperf. 1,150.
Double transfer 45.00 2.00

CANCELLATIONS.

China — | Puerto Rico, 1898 —
Guam — | Samoa —
Philippines — | Supplementary Mail Type G +2.50

273 A94 10c **dark green,** *June 1895* 40.00 80
green 40.00 80
On cover 15.00
Block of four 165.00 10.00
Margin strip of 3, Impt. & P#, T I or IV 165.00

Margin block of 6, Impt. & P#, T I or IV 800.00
a. Imperf., pair 450.00
a. Block of four, imperf. 950.00
Double transfer 60.00 2.75

CANCELLATIONS.

China — | Philippines —
Cuba — | Supp. Mail Types F or G +2.00

274 A95 15c **dark blue,** *Sept. 1895* 110.00 5.55
indigo 110.00 5.50
On cover 50.00
Block of four 450.00 50.00
Margin block of 4, arrow, R or L 475.00
Margin strip of 3, Impt. & P#, T I or IV 450.00
Margin block of 6, Impt. & P#, T I or IV 2,100.
a. Imperf., pair 1,450.
a. Block of four, imperf. 3,000.

CANCELLATIONS.

China — | Supplementary Mail Type G +3.00
Philippines —

275 A96 50c **orange,** *Nov. 1895* 160.00 14.00
On cover 400.00
Block of four 650.00 100.00
Margin block of 4, arrow, R or L 675.00
Margin strip of 3, Impt. & P#, T I 650.00
Margin block of 6, Impt. & P#, T I 4,000.
a. 50c red orange 170.00 16.00
a. Block of four 700.00 120.00
b. Imperf., pair *1,600.*
b. Block of four, imperf. *3,350.*

CANCELLATIONS.

China — | Supp. Mail Types F or G +5.00

276 A97 $1 **black,** type I, *Aug. 1895* 375.00 45.00
greenish black 375.00 45.00
On cover 1,000.
Block of four 1,550. 350.00
Margin block of 4, arrow, L 1,700.
Margin strip of 3, Impt. & P#, T II 1,600.
Margin block of 6, Impt. & P#, T II *7,500.*
b. Imperf., pair *2,750.*
b. Block of four, imperf. *6,000.*

CANCELLATIONS.

| Philippines —

276A A97 $1 **black,** type II, *Aug. 1895* 825.00 92.50
greenish black 825.00 92.50
On cover 1,350.
Block of four 3,400. 650.00
Margin block of 4, arrow, R 3,500.
Horizontal pair, types I and II 1,500. 225.00
Block of four, two each of types I and II 3,100. 700.00
Margin strip of 3, Impt. & P#, T II, one stamp No. 276 3,100.
Margin block of 6, Impt. & P#, T II, two stamps No. 276 *15,000.*

CANCELLATIONS.

| China —

The fifteen left vertical rows of impressions from plate 76 are Type I, the balance being Type II.

277 A98 $2 **bright blue,** *Aug. 1895* 600.00 200.00
On cover *2,750.*
Block of four 2,500. 1,400.
Margin block of 4, arrow, R or L 2,600.
Margin strip of 3, Impt. & P#, T II 2,750.
Margin block of 6, Impt. & P#, T II *14,000.*
a. $2 dark blue 650.00 210.00
a. Block of four 2,700. 1,500.
b. Imperf., pair *3,500.*
b. Block of four, imperf. *7,500.*

CANCELLATIONS.

| Supplementary Mail Type G —

278 A99 $5 **dark green,** *Aug. 1895* 1,350. 275.00
On cover *5,000.*
Block of four 5,500. 2,250.
Margin block of 4, arrow, R or L 5,600.
Margin strip of 3, Impt. & P#, T II 5,750.
Margin block of 6, Impt. & P#, T II *50,000.*
a. Imperf., pair *6,000.*
a. Block of four, imperf. *13,000.*

The Imperf. vertically variety, No. 264b and the imperforate varieties of all the denominations in the 1895 issue were not regularly issued.

REGULAR ISSUE

Wmk. 191 Horizontally or Vertically

1898 ***Perf. 12***

Plates for the 1898 issue were of two sizes:-

400 subjects for the 1c and 2c denominations; 200 subjects for all 5c, 6c and 15c denominations; and both 400 and 200 for the 4c and 0c denominations; all issued in panes of 100 each.

Printings from the 400 subject plates show the watermark reading horizontally, on the 200 subject plate printings the watermark reads vertically.

In January, 1898, the color of the 1-cent stamp was changed to green and in March, 1898, that of the 5-cents to dark blue in order to conform to the colors assigned these values by the Universal Postal Union. These changes necessitated changing the colors of the 10c and 15c denominations in order to avoid confusion.

279 A87 1c **deep green,** *Jan. 1898* 6.00 6
green 6.00 6
yellow green 6.00 6
dark yellow green 6.00 6
On cover 35
Block of four 25.00 1.75
Strip of 3, Impt. & P#, T V 26.50 —
Block of 6, Impt. & P#, T V 110.00
Double transfer 9.00 75

CANCELLATIONS.

China — | Puerto Rico, 1898 —
Guam — | Philippines —

279B A88 2c **red,** type III 5.50 5
On cover 15
Block of four 22.50 75
Margin strip of 3, Impt. & P#, T V (red) 21.00
Margin block of 6, Impt. & P#, T V (red) 120.00
c. 2c rose carmine, type III 120.00 20.00
c. Block of four 425.00 —
c. Margin strip of 3, Impt. & P#, T V 425.00
c. Margin block of 6, Impt. & P#, T V 1,500.
d. 2c orange red, type III 6.50 9
d. Block of four 26.50 1.25
d. Margin strip of 3, Impt. & P#, T V 25.00
d. Margin block of 6, Impt. & P#, T V 120.00
e. Booklet pane of six 350.00 *200.00*
f. 2c deep red, type III 12.50 75
Double transfer 13.50 50

CANCELLATIONS.

Puerto Rico, 1898 — | Supplementary Mail Type G +4.00
Philippines, 1898 — | Cuba, 1898 —
Guam, 1899 or 1900 — | China —
| Samoa —

280 A90 4c **rose brown,** *Oct. 1898* 20.00 45
a. 4c lilac brown 20.00 45
brownish claret 20.00 45
b. 4c orange brown 20.00 45
On cover 9.50
Block of four 85.00 7.50
Margin block of 4, arrow, R or L 90.00
Margin strip of 3, Impt. & P#, T V 90.00
Margin block of 6, Impt. & P#, T V 400.00
Double transfer 25.00 1.10
Extra frame line at top (Plate 793 R 62) 32.50 3.50

CANCELLATIONS.

| Supplementary Mail Type G +3.00
| China —
| Philippines —

281 A91 5c **dark blue,** *Mar. 1898* 22.50 40
blue 22.50 40
bright blue 22.50 40
On cover 8.50
Block of four 92.50 5.00
Margin block of 4, arrow, R or L 97.50
Margin strip of 3, Impt. & P#, T V 95.00
Margin block of 6, Impt. & P#, T V 425.00
Double transfer 32.50 1.75
Worn plate diagonal lines missing in oval background 26.00 55

CANCELLATIONS.

Puerto Rico, 1898 — | Supplementary Mail Type G +4.00
| China —
| Cuba —
| Guam —
| Philippines —

282 A92 6c **lake,** *Dec. 1898* 35.00 1.40
claret 35.00 1.40
On cover 15.00
Block of four 145.00 20.00
Margin block of 4, arrow, R or L 160.00
Margin strip of 3, Impt. & P#, T V 150.00
Margin block of 6, Impt. & P#, T V 650.00
a. 6c purplish lake 37.50 1.65
a. Block of four 155.00 30.00
a. Margin block of 4, arrow 165.00
a. Margin strip of 3, Impt. & P#, T V 160.00
a. Margin block of 6, Impt. & P#, T V 750.00
Double transfer 42.50 2.50

CANCELLATIONS.

| Supplementary Mail Type G +4.00
| China —
| Philippines —

TEN CENTS.

Type I. The tips of the foliate ornaments do not impinge on the white curved line below "ten cents".

282C A94 10c **brown,** type I, *Nov. 1898* 100.00 1.20
dark brown 100.00 1.20
On cover 13.00
Block of four 410.00 20.00
Margin strip of 3, Impt. & P#, T IV or V 410.00
Margin block of 6, Impt. & P#, T IV or V 1,600.
Double transfer 125.00 3.00

CANCELLATIONS.

| Supplementary Mail Type G +2.50

Type II. The tips of the ornaments break the curved line below the "e" of "ten" and the "t" of "cents".

283 A94 10c **orange brown,** type II 60.00 1.00
brown 60.00 1.00
yellow brown 60.00 1.00
On cover 15.00
Block of four 245.00 15.00
Margin block of 4, arrow, R or L 255.00 —
Margin strip of 3, Impt. & P#, T V 245.00
Margin block of 6, Impt. & P#, T V 950.00
Pair, type I and type II *15,000. 850.00*

CANCELLATIONS.

Supp. Mail Type G +2.50 | China —
| Puerto Rico —

On the 400 subject plate 932, all the subjects are Type I except the following: U. L. 20; U. R. 11, 12, 13; L. L. 61, 71, 86, these seven being Type II.

284 A95 15c **olive green,** *Nov. 1898* 85.00 4.50
dark olive green 85.00 4.50
On cover 30.00
Block of four 345.00 35.00
Margin block of 4, arrow, R or L 355.00
Margin strip of 3, Impt. & P#, T IV 345.00
Margin block of 6, Impt. & P#, T IV 1,600.

CANCELLATIONS.

Supplementary Mail Types F or G +2.50 | China —
| Samoa —

TRANS-MISSISSIPPI EXPOSITION ISSUE

Trans-Mississippi Exposition held in Omaha, Nebraska, June 1 to November 1, 1898.

Jacques Marquette on the Mississippi — A100

The Catalogue editors cannot undertake to appraise, identify or judge the genuineness or condition of stamps.

Farming in the West – A101

Indian Hunting Buffalo – A102

John Charles Frémont on the Rocky Mountains – A103

Troops Guarding Wagon Train – A104

Hardships of Emigration – A105

Western Mining Prospector – A106

Western Cattle in Storm – A107

Mississippi River Bridge, St. Louis – A108

Exposition Station Cancellation

Condition is extremely important in evaluating Nos. 285-293. Values are for stamps free from faults and with the design well clear of the perforations. Stamps of superior quality command substantial premiums.

Plates of 100 (10x10) subjects, divided vertically into 2 panes of 50.

1898, June 17 **Wmk. 191** ***Perf. 12***

No.	Type	Denom.	Description	Unused	Used
285	A100	1c	**dark yellow green**	20.00	3.75
			yellow green	20.00	3.75
			green	20.00	3.75
			On cover		7.50
			On card, Expo. station canc.		200.00
			Block of four	82.50	25.00
			Margin block of 4, arrow, R or L	85.00	—
			Margin pair, Impt. & P#, T VIII	52.50	
			Margin strip of 3, Impt. & P#, T VIII	80.00	
			Margin block of 4, Impt. & P#, T VIII	175.00	
			Margin block of 6, Impt. & P#, T VIII	250.00	
			Double transfer	30.00	5.25

CANCELLATIONS.

Supplementary Mail, Types F or G	+1.50	China	—
		Philippines	—
		Puerto Rico, 1898	—

No.	Type	Denom.	Description	Unused	Used
286	A101	2c	**copper red**	17.50	1.00
			brown red	17.50	1.00
			light brown red	17.50	1.00
			On cover		2.00
			On cover, Expo. station canc.		175.00
			Block of four	72.50	9.00
			Margin block of 4, arrow, R or L	75.00	—
			Margin pair, Impt. & P#, T VIII	45.00	
			Margin strip of 3, Impt. & P#, T VIII	75.00	
			Margin block of 4, Impt. & P#, T VIII	150.00	
			Margin block of 6, Impt. & P#, T VIII	210.00	
			Double transfer	27.50	1.75
			Worn plate	20.00	1.25

CANCELLATIONS.

China	—	Puerto Rico, 1898	—
Hawaii	—	Philippines	—

No.	Type	Denom.	Description	Unused	Used
287	A102	4c	**orange**	100.00	16.00
			deep orange	100.00	16.00
			On cover		50.00
			On cover, Expo. station canc.		400.00
			Block of four	410.00	100.00
			Margin block of 4, arrow, R or L	425.00	—
			Margin pair, Impt. & P#, T VIII	235.00	
			Margin strip of 3, Impt. & P#, T VIII	375.00	
			Margin block of four, Impt. & P#, T VIII	750.00	
			Margin block of 6, Impt. & P#, T VIII	1,150.	

CANCELLATIONS.

Supplementary Mail Types F or G	+5.00	China	—
		Philippines	—

No.	Type	Denom.	Description	Unused	Used
288	A103	5c	**dull blue**	87.50	14.00
			bright blue	87.50	14.00
			On cover		45.00
			On cover, Expo. station canc.		400.00
			Block of four	375.00	90.00
			Margin block of 4, arrow, R or L	400.00	—
			Margin pair, Impt. & P#, T VIII	210.00	—
			Margin strip of 3, Impt. & P#, T VIII	310.00	
			Margin block of four, Impt. & P#, T VIII	650.00	
			Margin block of 6, Impt. & P#, T VIII	1,000.	

CANCELLATIONS.

Supplementary Mail Types F or G	+5.00	China	—
		Philippines	—
		Puerto Rico, 1898	—

No.	Type	Denom.	Description	Unused	Used
289	A104	8c	**violet brown**	125.00	30.00
			dark violet brown	125.00	30.00
			On cover		100.00
			On cover, Expo. station canc.		750.00
			Block of four	510.00	185.00
			Margin block of 4, arrow, R or L	525.00	—
			Margin pair, Impt. & P#, T VIII	290.00	
			Margin strip of 3, Impt. & P#, T VIII	465.00	
			Margin block of 4, Impt. & P#, T VIII	1,250.	
			Margin block of 6, Impt. & P#, T VIII	1,900.	
a.			Vert. pair, imperf. horiz.	*12,000.*	

CANCELLATIONS.

Philippines	—	Samoa	—

No.	Type	Denom.	Description	Unused	Used
290	A105	10c	**gray violet**	140.00	17.50
			blackish violet	140.00	17.50
			On cover		75.00
			On cover, Expo. station canc.		750.00
			Block of four	575.00	100.00
			Margin block of 4, arrow, R or L	600.00	—
			Margin pair, Impt. & P#, T VIII	325.00	
			Margin strip of 3, Impt. & P#, T VIII	500.00	
			Margin block of 4, Impt. & P#, T VIII	1,600.	
			Margin block of 6, Impt. & P#, T VIII	2,500.	

CANCELLATIONS.

China	—	Supplementary Mail Type G	+5.00
Philippines	—		

No.	Type	Denom.	Description	Unused	Used
291	A106	50c	**sage green**	500.00	150.00
			dark sage green	500.00	150.00
			On cover		1,200.
			Block of four	2,100.	950.00
			Margin block of 4, arrow, R or L	2,250.	—
			Margin pair, Impt. & P#, T VIII	1,200.	
			Margin strip of 3, Impt. & P#, T VIII	2,000.	
			Margin block of 4, Impt. & P#, T VIII	*9,500.*	
			Margin block of 6, Impt. & P#, T VIII	*14,000.*	

CANCELLATIONS.

Cuba	—	Supp. Mail Types F or G	+25.00
Philippines	—		

No.	Type	Denom.	Description	Unused	Used
292	A107	$1	**black**	1,325.	475.00
			On cover		4,000.
			Block of four	5,400.	3,500.
			Margin block of 4, arrow, R or L	5,600.	
			Margin pair, Impt. & P#, T VIII	3,200.	
			Margin strip of 3, Impt. & P#, T VIII	5,500.	
			Margin block of 4, Impt. & P#, T VIII	*30,000.*	
			Margin block of 6, Impt. & P#, T VIII	*40,000.*	

CANCELLATIONS.

Philippines	—

No.	Type	Denom.	Description	Unused	Used
293	A108	$2	**orange brown**	1,950.	725.00
			dark orange brown	1,950.	725.00
			On cover		*9,500.*
			Block of four	8,000.	*4,250.*
			Margin block of 4, arrow, R or L	8,500.	

Margin pair, Impt. & P#, T VII	4,750.	
Margin strip of 3, Impt. & P#, T VIII	*7,250.*	
Margin block of 4, Impt. & P#, T VII	*55,000.*	
Margin block of 6, Impt. & P#, T VIII	*80,000.*	

PAN-AMERICAN EXPOSITION ISSUE

Issued to commemorate the Pan-American Exposition held at Buffalo, N. Y., May 1 to Nov. 1, 1901. On sale May 1-Oct. 31, 1901.

Fast Lake Navigation (Steamship "City of Alpena") A109

Empire State Express A110

Electric Automobile in Washington A111

Bridge at Niagara Falls A112

Canal Locks at Sault Ste. Marie A113

Fast Ocean Navigation (Steamship "St. Paul") A114

Exposition Station Cancellation.

Note on condition and pricing above No. 285 also applies to Nos. 294-299.

Plates of 200 subjects in two panes of 100 each.

1901, May 1 Wmk. 191 *Perf. 12*

No.	Type	Denom.	Description	Unused	Used
294	A109	1c	**green & black**	13.50	2.50
			dark blue green & black	13.50	2.50
			On cover		4.00
			On cover or card, Expo. sta. canc.		90.00
			Block of four	55.00	20.00
			Margin block of 4, top arrow & markers	57.50	
			Margin block of 4, bottom arrow & markers & black P#	60.00	
			Margin strip of 3, Impt. & P#, T V	60.00	
			Margin block of 6, Impt. & P#, T V	210.00	
			Margin strip of 5, bottom two P#, T V Impt., arrow & markers	110.00	
			Margin block of 10, bottom, Impt., T V, two P#, arrow & markers	425.00	
a.			Center inverted	*8,000.*	*4,500.*
a.			Center inverted, on cover		*16,500.*
a.			Center inverted, block of 4	*35,000.*	
a.			Same, Margin strip of 3, Impt. & P#	*36,500.*	
			Double transfer	21.00	4.75
295	A110	2c	**carmine & black**	13.50	75
			carmine & gray black	13.50	75
			rose carmine & black	13.50	75
			scarlet & black	13.50	75
			On cover		1.25
			On cover or card, Expo. sta. canc.		75.00
			Block of four	55.00	6.00
			Margin block of 4, top arrow & markers	57.50	
			Margin block of 4, bottom arrow & markers and black P#	60.00	
			Margin strip of 3, Impt. & P#, T V	60.00	
			Margin block of 6, Impt. & P#, T V	210.00	
			Margin strip of 5, bottom, Impt., T V, two P#, arrow & markers	110.00	
			Margin block of 10, bottom, Impt., T V, two P#, arrow & markers	400.00	
a.			Center inverted	*35,000.*	*13,500.*
a.			Center inverted, block of 4	*150,000.*	
			Double transfer	21.00	2.00
296	A111	4c	**deep red brown & black**	70.00	12.50
			chocolate & black	70.00	12.50
			On cover		35.00
			On cover, Expo. station canc.		250.00
			Block of four	290.00	85.00
			Margin block of 4, top arrow & markers	300.00	
			Margin block of 4, bottom arrow & markers & black P#	310.00	
			Margin strip of 3, Impt. & P#, T V	290.00	
			Margin block of 6, Impt. & P#, T V	1,900.	
			Margin strip of 5, bottom Impt., T V two P#, arrow & markers	550.00	
			Margin block of 10, bottom, Impt., TV, two P#, arrow & markers	3,750.	
a.			Center inverted	*10,000.*	
a.			Center inverted, block of 4	*45,000.*	
a.			Same, Margin strip of 4, Impt. & P#	*52,500.*	

No. 296a was not regularly issued.
See No. 296a-S, "Specimen" Stamps.

No.	Type	Denom.	Description	Unused	Used
297	A112	5c	**ultramarine & black**	82.50	12.50
			dark ultramarine & black	82.50	12.50
			On cover		37.50
			On cover, Expo. station canc.		250.00
			Block of four	340.00	85.00
			Margin block of 4, top arrow & markers	350.00	
			Margin block of 4, bottom arrow & markers & black P#	360.00	
			Margin strip of 3, Impt. & P#, T V	340.00	
			Margin block of 6, Impt. & P#, T V	2,250.	
			Margin strip of 5, bottom Impt., T V two P#, arrow & markers	675.00	
			Margin block of 10, bottom Impt., T V, two P#, arrow & markers	4,100.	
298	A113	8c	**brown violet & black**	100.00	50.00
			purplish brown & black	100.00	50.00
			On cover		90.00
			On cover, Expo. station canc.		500.00
			Block of four	410.00	375.00
			Margin block of 4, top arrow & markers	420.00	
			Margin block of 4, bottom arrow & markers & black P#	430.00	
			Margin strip of 3, Impt. & P#, T V	410.00	
			Margin block of 6, Impt. & P#, T V	3,700.	
			Margin strip of 5, bottom Impt., T V, two P#, arrow & markers	775.00	
			Margin block of 10, bottom, Impt., T V, two P#, arrow & markers	6,250.	
299	A114	10c	**yellow brown & black**	150.00	22.50
			dark yellow brown & black	150.00	22.50
			On cover		100.00
			On cover, Expo. station canc.		650.00
			Block of four	625.00	175.00
			Margin block of 4, top arrow & markers	640.00	
			Margin block of 4, bottom arrow & markers & black P#	660.00	
			Margin strip of 3, Impt. & P#, T V	640.00	
			Margin block of 6, Impt. & P#, T V	5,750.	
			Margin strip of 5, bottom Impt., T V, two P#, arrow & markers	1,150.	
			Margin block of 10, bottom Impt., T V, two P#, arrow & markers	8,750.	

Franklin — A115

Washington — A116

Jackson — A117

Grant — A118

Lincoln — A119

Garfield — A120

Martha Washington — A121

Daniel Webster — A122

Benjamin Harrison — A123

Henry Clay — A124

Jefferson — A125

David G. Farragut — A126

Madison — A127

Marshall — A128

A particular stamp may be scarce, but if few collectors want it, its market value may remain relatively low.

REGULAR ISSUE

Plates of 400 subjects in four panes of 100 each for all values from 1c to 15c inclusive. Certain plates of 1c, 2c type A129, 3c and 5c show a round marker in margin opposite the horizontal guide line at right or left.

Plates of 200 subjects in two panes of 100 each for 15c, 50c, $1, $2 and $5.

1902-03 **Wmk. 191** ***Perf. 12***

Many stamps of this issue are known with blurred printing due to having been printed on dry paper.

No.	Type	Denom.	Description	Unused	Used
300	A115	1c	**blue green,** *Feb. 1903*	6.50	5
			green	6.50	5
			deep green	6.50	5
			gray green	6.50	5
			yellow green	6.50	6
			On cover		15
			Block of four	26.00	2.00
			Margin strip of 3, Impt. & P#, T V	26.00	
			Margin block of 6, Impt. & P#, T V	125.00	
b.			Booklet pane of six, *Mar. 6, 1907*	*400.00*	*250.00*
			Double transfer	10.00	1.00
			Worn plate	7.00	25
			Cracked plate	—	—
301	A116	2c	**carmine,** *Jan. 17, 1903*	7.50	5
			bright carmine	7.50	5
			deep carmine	7.50	5
			carmine rose	7.50	8
			On cover		15
			Block of four	30.00	2.00
			Margin strip of 3, Impt. & P#, T V	30.00	
			Margin block of 6, Impt. & P#, T V	125.00	
c.			Booklet pane of six, *Jan. 24, 1903*	*400.00*	*250.00*
			Double transfer	12.50	90
			Cracked plate	—	
302	A117	3c	**bright violet,** *Feb. 1903*	30.00	2.00
			violet	30.00	2.00
			deep violet	30.00	2.00
			On cover		9.00
			Block of four	125.00	17.50
			Margin strip of 3, Impt. & P#, T V	125.00	
			Margin block of 6, Impt. & P#, T V	535.00	
			Double transfer	52.50	3.00
			Cracked plate	—	
303	A118	4c	**brown,** *Feb. 1903*	30.00	60
			dark brown	30.00	60
			yellow brown	30.00	60
			orange brown	30.00	60
			red brown	30.00	60
			On cover		12.50
			Block of four	125.00	8.50
			Margin strip of 3, Impt. & P#, T V	125.00	
			Margin block of 6, Impt. & P#, T V	535.00	
			Double transfer	47.50	2.00
304	A119	5c	**blue,** *Jan. 1903*	35.00	65
			pale blue	35.00	65
			bright blue	35.00	65
			dark blue	35.00	65
			On cover		6.50
			Block of four	145.00	6.00
			Margin strip of 3, Impt. & P#, T V	145.00	
			Margin block of 6, Impt. & P#, T V	600.00	—
			Double transfer	57.50	2.50
			Cracked plate	—	—
305	A120	6c	**claret,** *Feb. 1903*	37.50	1.50
			deep claret	37.50	1.50
			brownish lake	45.00	1.50
			dull brownish lake	37.50	1.50
			On cover		12.50
			Block of four	155.00	20.00
			Margin strip of 3, Impt. & P#, T V	155.00	
			Margin block of 6, Impt. & P#, T V	625.00	
			Double transfer	57.50	2.00
306	A121	8c	**violet black,** *Dec. 1902*	25.00	1.25
			black	25.00	1.25
			slate black	25.00	1.25
			gray lilac	25.00	1.25
			lavender	32.50	1.50
			On cover		8.00
			Block of four	105.00	15.00
			Margin strip of 3, Impt. & P#, T V	105.00	
			Margin block of 6, Impt. & P#, T V	450.00	
			Double transfer	30.00	1.90
307	A122	10c	**pale red brown,** *Feb. 1903*	30.00	70
			red brown	30.00	70
			dark red brown	30.00	70
			On cover		7.00
			Block of four	125.00	6.00
			Margin strip of 3, Impt. & P#, T V	125.00	
			Margin block of 6, Impt. & P#, T V	700.00	
			Double transfer	60.00	9.00
308	A123	13c	**purple black,** *Nov. 18, 1902*	25.00	5.00
			brown violet	25.00	5.00
			On cover		35.00
			Block of four	105.00	40.00
			Margin strip of 3, Impt. & P#, T V	105.00	
			Margin block of 6, Impt. & P#, T V	425.00	
309	A124	15c	**olive green,** *May 27, 1903*	87.50	3.75
			dark olive green	87.50	3.75
			On cover		75.00
			Block of four	360.00	60.00
			Margin block of 4, arrow	375.00	
			Margin strip of 3, Impt. & P#, T V	360.00	
			Margin block of 6, Impt. & P#, T V	2,000.	
			Double transfer	135.00	7.50
310	A125	50c	**orange,** *Mar. 23, 1903*	250.00	17.50
			deep orange	250.00	17.50
			On cover		500.00
			Block of four	1,050.	135.00
			Margin block of 4, arrow	1,150.	
			Margin strip of 3, Impt. & P#, T V	1,050.	
			Margin block of 6, Impt. & P#, T V	4,500.	
311	A126	$1	**black,** *June 5, 1903*	450.00	35.00
			grayish black	450.00	35.00
			On cover		1,350.
			Block of four	1,900.	275.00
			Margin block of 4, arrow	2,000.	
			Margin strip of 3, Impt. & P#, T V	1,900.	
			Margin block of 6, Impt. & P#, T V	*10,000.*	
312	A127	$2	**dark blue,** *June 5, 1903*	600.00	125.00
			blue	600.00	125.00
			On cover		2,500.
			Block of four	2,500.	850.00
			Margin block of 4, arrow	2,700.	
			Margin strip of 3, Impt. & P#, T V	2,600.	
			Margin block of 6, Impt. & P#, T V	*17,500.*	
313	A128	$5	**dark green,** *June 5, 1903*	1,650.	450.00
			On cover		5,000.
			Block of four	7,000.	3,000.
			Margin block of 4, arrow	7,500.	
			Margin strip of 3, Impt. & P#, T V	7,500.	
			Margin block of 6, Impt. & P#, T V	*45,000.*	

For listings of designs A127 and A128 with Perf. 10 see Nos. 479 and 480.

1906-08 ***Imperf.***

No.	Description	Unused	Used
314 A115 1c	**blue green,** *Oct. 2, 1906*	16.00	13.00
	green	16.00	13.00
	deep green	16.00	13.00
	On cover		22.50
	Block of four	65.00	60.00
	Corner margin block of four	67.50	62.50
	Margin block of 4, arrow	70.00	65.00
	Margin block of 4, arrow & round marker	95.00	
	Center line block	135.00	82.50
	Margin block of 6, Impt. & P#	150.00	
	Double transfer	30.00	16.00
314A A118 4c	**brown,** *April 1908*	*18,500.*	*10,000.*
	On cover		*22,500.*
	Pair	*47,500.*	
	Guide line pair	—	

This stamp was issued imperforate but all copies were privately perforated with large oblong perforations at the sides. (Schermack type III).

No.	Description	Unused	Used
315 A119 5c	**blue,** *May 12, 1908*	375.00	150.00
	On cover		—
	Block of four	1,600.	750.00
	Corner margin block of 4	1,700.	
	Margin block of 4, arrow	1,750.	
	Margin block of 4, arrow & round marker	2,000.	
	Center line block	2,250.	
	Margin block of 6, Impt. & P#	3,500.	

Beware of copies of No. 304 with perforations removed.

COIL STAMPS

Warning! Imperforate stamps have been fraudulently perforated to resemble coil stamps and part-perforate varieties.

1908 ***Perf. 12 Horizontally***

No.	Description	Unused	Used
316 A115 1c	**blue green,** pair, *Feb. 18, 1908*	*50,000.*	—
	Guide line pair	*100,000.*	
317 A119 5c	**blue,** pair, *Feb. 24, 1908*	*6,000.*	—
	Guide line pair	*8,000.*	

Perf. 12 Vertically

No.	Description	Unused	Used
318 A115 1c	**blue green,** pair, *July 31, 1908*	*4,250.*	—
	Guide line pair	*6,250.*	
	Double transfer	—	—

Coil stamps for use in vending and affixing machines are perforated on two sides only, either horizontally or vertically. They were first issued in 1908, using perf. 12. This was changed to 8½ in 1910, and to 10 in 1914.

Imperforate sheets of certain denominations were sold to the vending machine companies which applied a variety of private perforations and separations. (See Vending and Affixing Machine Perforations section of this catalogue.)

Several values of the 1902 and later issues are found on an apparently coarse-ribbed paper. This is caused by worn blankets on the printing presses and is not a true paper variety.

Washington — A129

Plate of 400 subjects in four panes of 100 each.

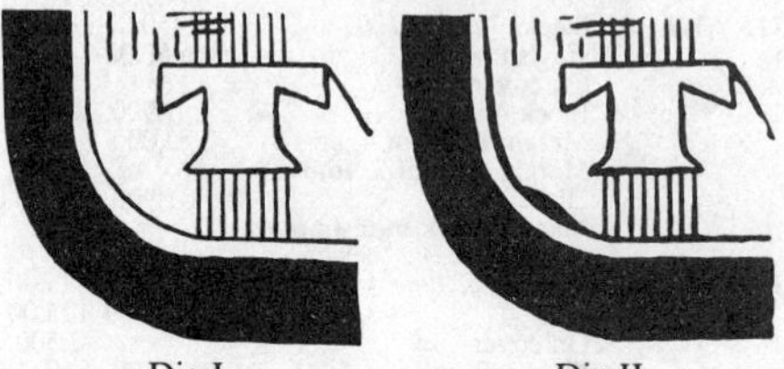

Die I Die II

1903 **Wmk. 191** ***Perf. 12***

No.	Description	Unused	Used
319 A129 2c	**carmine,** Die I, *Nov. 12, 1903*	4.00	5
	bright carmine	4.00	5
	carmine lake	4.00	5
	On cover		10
	Block of four	16.50	2.00
	Margin strip of 3, Impt. & P#, T V (carmine)	15.00	
	Margin block of 6, Impt. & P#, T V (carmine)	67.50	
a.	2c lake, Die I	—	—
	On cover		—
	Block of four (lake)	—	—
	Margin strip of 3, Impt. & P#, T V (lake)	—	
	Margin block of 6, Impt. & P#, T V (lake)	—	
b.	2c carmine rose, Die I	6.00	20
	On cover		50
	Block of four (carmine rose)	25.00	4.00
	Margin strip of 3, Impt. & P#, T V (carmine rose)	26.50	
	Margin block of 6, Impt. & P#, T V (carmine rose)	125.00	
c.	2c scarlet, Die I	4.00	6
	On cover		10
	Block of four (scarlet)	17.00	2.00
	Margin strip of 3, Impt. & P#, T V (scarlet)	16.00	
	Margin block of 6, Impt. & P#, T V (scarlet)	60.00	
d.	Vert. pair, imperf. horiz.	*1,750.*	
e.	Vertical pair, imperf. between	*950.00*	
	Vertical pair, rouletted between	*1,000.*	
f.	2c lake, Die II	4.50	10
	On cover		20
	Block of four	18.50	3.50
g.	Booklet pane of six, car., Die I	90.00	*20.00*
h.	Booklet pane of six, car., Die II	125.00	
i.	2c carmine, Die II	17.50	—
j.	2c carmine rose, Die II	—	
k.	2c scarlet, Die II	—	
m.	Booklet pane of six, lake (I)	—	
n.	Booklet pane of six, car. rose (I)	—	
p.	Booklet pane of six, scarlet (I)	90.00	
q.	Booklet pane of six, lake, (II)	125.00	
	Double transfer	10.00	2.00

During the use of this stamp, the Postmaster at San Francisco discovered in his stock sheets of No. 319, each of which had the horizontal perforations missing between the two top rows of stamps. To facilitate their separation, the imperf. rows were rouletted, and the stamps sold over the counter. So vertical pairs are found with regular perforations all around and rouletted between.

1906 ***Imperf.***

No.	Description	Unused	Used
320 A129 2c	**carmine,** *Oct. 2, 1906*	17.50	11.00
	On cover		20.00
	Block of four, carmine	70.00	50.00
	Corner margin block of four, carmine	72.50	
	Margin block of 4, arrow, carmine	75.00	—
	Center line block, carmine	145.00	—
	Margin block of 6, Impt. & P#, T V, carmine	200.00	—
a.	2c lake, Die II	50.00	35.00
	On cover		75.00
	Block of four, lake	200.00	160.00
	Corner margin block of four, lake	205.00	
	Margin block of 4, arrow, lake	215.00	
	Center line block, lake	425.00	
	Margin block of 6, Impt. & P#, T V, lake	625.00	
b.	2c scarlet	16.00	12.00
	On cover		20.00
	Block of four, scarlet	64.00	
	Corner margin block of four, scarlet	65.00	
	Margin block of 4, arrow, scarlet	67.50	—
	Center line block, scarlet	130.00	—
	Margin block of 6, Impt. & P#, T V, scarlet	175.00	
	Die II, scarlet	—	—
	Double transfer	24.00	15.00

COIL STAMPS

1908 ***Perf. 12 Horizontally***

No.	Description	Unused	Used
321 A129 2c	**carmine,** pair, *Feb. 18, 1908*	*60,000.*	—
	Guide line pair	—	
322 A129 2c	**carmine,** pair, *July 31, 1908*	*6,000.*	—
	Guide line pair	*8,000.*	
	Double transfer	—	

This Government Coil Stamp should not be confused with those of the International Vending Machine Co., which are perforated 12½ to 13.

LOUISIANA PURCHASE EXPOSITION ISSUE

St. Louis, Mo., Apr. 30-Dec. 1, 1904

Robert R. Livingston — A130

Thomas Jefferson — A131

James Monroe — A132

William McKinley — A133

Map of Louisiana Purchase — A134

Plates of 100 (10x10) subjects, divided vertically into 2 panes of 50.

Exposition Station Cancellation

1904, Apr. 30 **Wmk. 191** ***Perf. 12***

No.	Description	Unused	Used
323 A130 1c	**green**	17.50	2.75
	dark green	17.50	2.75
	On cover		5.00
	On card, Expo. station canc.		40.00
	Block of four	70.00	25.00
	Margin block of 4, arrow, R or L	75.00	—
	Margin pair, Impt. & P#, T V	50.00	
	Margin strip of 3, Impt. & P#, T V	77.50	
	Margin block of 4, Impt. & P#, T V	125.00	
	Margin block of 6, Impt. & P#, T V	200.00	
	Diagonal line through left "1" (2138 L 2)	35.00	10.00
	Double transfer	—	
324 A131 2c	**carmine**	15.00	90
	bright carmine	15.00	90
	On cover		2.00
	On cover, Expo. station canc.		60.00
	Block of four	60.00	12.50
	Margin block of 4, arrow, R or L	65.00	—
	Margin pair, Impt. & P#, T V	47.50	

			Margin strip of 3, Impt. & P#, T V	75.00	
			Margin block of 4, Impt. & P#, T V	135.00	
			Margin block of 6, Impt. & P#, T V	200.00	
a.			Vertical pair, imperf. horiz.	*6,000.*	
325	A132	3c	**violet**	60.00	22.50
			On cover		45.00
			On cover, Expo. station canc.		250.00
			Block of four	240.00	165.00
			Margin block of 4, arrow, R or L	260.00	—
			Margin pair, Impt. & P#, T V	160.00	
			Margin strip of 3, Impt. & P#, T V	240.00	
			Margin block of 4, Impt. & P#, T V	500.00	
			Margin block of 6, Impt. & P#, T V	750.00	
			Double transfer		—
326	A133	5c	**dark blue**	65.00	14.50
			On cover		40.00
			On cover, Expo. station canc.		300.00
			Block of four	260.00	120.00
			Margin block of 4, arrow, R or L	270.00	—
			Margin pair, Impt. & P#, T V	165.00	
			Margin strip of 3, Impt. & P#, T V	250.00	
			Margin block of 4, Impt. & P#, T V	550.00	
			Margin block of 6, Impt. & P#, T V	800.00	
327	A134	10c	**red brown**	115.00	20.00
			dark red brown	115.00	20.00
			On cover		80.00
			On cover, Expo. station canc.		450.00
			Block of four	460.00	165.00
			Margin block of 4, arrow, R or L	475.00	—
			Margin pair, Impt. & P#, T V	300.00	
			Margin strip of 3, Impt. & P#, T V	440.00	
			Margin block of 4, Impt. & P#, T V	1,000.	
			Margin block of 6, Impt. & P#, T V	1,600.	

JAMESTOWN EXPOSITION ISSUE

Hampton Roads, Va., Apr. 26 to Dec. 1, 1907

Captain John Smith
A135

Founding of Jamestown
A136

Pocahontas
A137

Plates of 200 subjects in two panes of 100 each.

—EXPOSITION STATION—
C

Exposition Station Cancellation

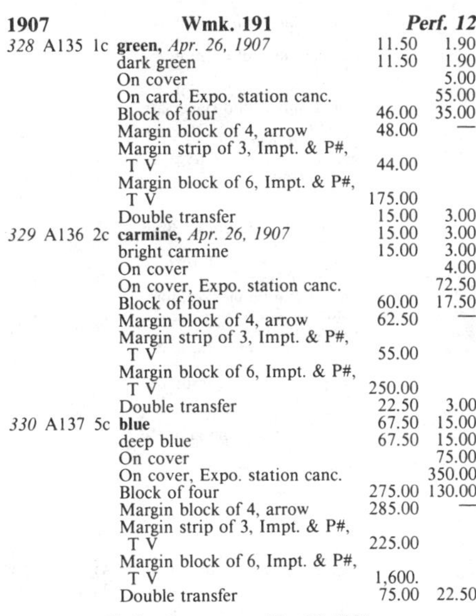

1907			**Wmk. 191**	***Perf. 12***	
328	A135	1c	**green,** *Apr. 26, 1907*	11.50	1.90
			dark green	11.50	1.90
			On cover		5.00
			On card, Expo. station canc.		55.00
			Block of four	46.00	35.00
			Margin block of 4, arrow	48.00	—
			Margin strip of 3, Impt. & P#, T V	44.00	
			Margin block of 6, Impt. & P#, T V	175.00	
			Double transfer	15.00	3.00
329	A136	2c	**carmine,** *Apr. 26, 1907*	15.00	3.00
			bright carmine	15.00	3.00
			On cover		4.00
			On cover, Expo. station canc.		72.50
			Block of four	60.00	17.50
			Margin block of 4, arrow	62.50	—
			Margin strip of 3, Impt. & P#, T V	55.00	
			Margin block of 6, Impt. & P#, T V	250.00	
			Double transfer	22.50	3.00
330	A137	5c	**blue**	67.50	15.00
			deep blue	67.50	15.00
			On cover		75.00
			On cover, Expo. station canc.		350.00
			Block of four	275.00	130.00
			Margin block of 4, arrow	285.00	—
			Margin strip of 3, Impt. & P#, T V	225.00	
			Margin block of 6, Impt. & P#, T V	1,600.	
			Double transfer	75.00	22.50

Earliest known use: May 10, 1907.

Values are for fine centered copies. Well centered copies sell for substantially more.

REGULAR ISSUE

Plates of 400 subjects in four panes of 100 each for all values 1c to 15c inclusive.

Plates of 200 subjects in two panes of 100 each for 50c and $1 denominations.

In 1909 the Bureau prepared certain plates with horizontal spacings of 3mm. between the outer six vertical rows and 2mm. between the others. This was done to try to counteract the effect of unequal shrinkage of the paper. *However, shrinkage did occur and intermediate spacings are frequently found.* The listings of 2mm. and 3mm. spacings are for exact measurements. Intermediate spacings sell for approximately the same as the cheaper of the two listed spacings. All such plates were marked with an open star added to the imprint and exist on the 1c, 2c, 3c, 4c, and 5c denominations only. A small solid star was added to the imprint and plate number for 1c plate No. 4980, 2c plate No. 4988 and for the 2c Lincoln. All other plates for this issue are spaced 2mm. throughout.

There are several types of some of the 2c and 3c stamps of this and succeeding issues. These types are described under the dates at which they first appeared. The differences between the types are usually minute and difficult to distinguish. Illustrations of Types I-VII of the 2c (A140) and Types I-IV of the 3c (A140) are reproduced by permission of H. L. Lindquist.

China Clay Paper. A small quantity of Nos. 331-340 was printed on paper containing a high mineral content (5-20%), instead of the specified 2%. The minerals, principally aluminum silicate, produced China clay paper. It is thick, hard and grayish, often darker than "bluish" paper.

Bureau, Engraving & Printing ✡ 4968

Imprint, plate number and open star

Bureau, Engraving & Printing ★ 4976

Imprint, plate number and small solid star

Bureau, Engraving & Printing A 5557

Imprint, plate number and "A"

(Above illustrations reduced in size)

A 5805 — "A" and number only

988 — Number only

The above illustrations are the several styles used on plates of issues from 1908 to date.

Franklin — A138

Washington — A139

			Wmk. 191 1908-09	***Perf. 12***	
331	A138	1c	**green,** *Dec. 1908*	4.50	5
			bright green	4.50	5
			dark green	4.50	5
			yellow green	4.50	5
			On cover		40
			Block of four (2mm spacing)	18.50	1.50
			Block of four (3mm spacing)	19.50	1.75
			Margin block of 6, Impt. & P#, T V	32.50	
			Margin block of 6, Impt. & P# & star	45.00	
			Margin block of 6, Impt. & P# & small solid star (plate 4980)	*750.00*	
a.			Booklet pane of six, *Dec. 2, 1908*	165.00	*35.00*
			Double transfer	6.75	60
			Cracked plate	—	—

No. 331 exists in horizontal pair, imperforate between, a variety resulting from booklet experiments. Not regularly issued.

332	A139	2c	**carmine,** *Nov. 1908*	4.25	5
			light carmine	4.25	5
			dark carmine	4.25	5
			On cover		10
			Block of four (2mm spacing)	17.50	75
			Block of four (3mm spacing)	19.00	85
			Margin block of 6, Impt. & P#, T V	45.00	
			Margin block of 6, Impt. & P# & star	42.50	
			Margin block of 6, Impt. & P# & small solid star (plate 4988)	*700.00*	
a.			Booklet pane of six	100.00	*35.00*
			Double transfer	9.00	90
			Double transfer, design of 1c (plate 5299)	*1,500.*	*1,250.*
			Rosette crack	—	
			Cracked plate	—	—

Washington — A140

TYPE I

THREE CENTS.

Type I. The top line of the toga rope is weak and the rope shading lines are thin. The 5th line from the left is missing. The line between the lips is thin. (For descriptions of 3c types II, III and IV, see notes and illustrations preceding Nos. 484, 529-530.)

Used on both flat plate and rotary press printings.

333 A140 3c **deep violet,** type I, *Dec. 1908* 20.00 1.75
violet 20.00 1.75
light violet 20.00 1.75
On cover 7.50
Block of four (2mm spacing) 82.50 16.00
Block of four (3mm spacing) 85.00 17.50
Margin block of 6, Impt. & P#, T V 200.00
Margin block of 6, Impt. & P# & star 220.00
Double transfer 25.00 4.25

334 A140 4c **orange brown,** *Dec. 1908* 23.50 55
brown 23.50 55
light brown 23.50 55
dark brown 23.50 55
On cover 6.00
Block of four (2mm spacing) 95.00 7.50
Block of four (3mm spacing) 100.00 8.50
Margin block of 6, Impt. & P#, T V 250.00
Margin block of 6, Impt. & P# & star 250.00
Double transfer 40.00 2.50

335 A140 5c **blue,** *Dec. 1908* 30.00 1.50
bright blue 30.00 1.50
dark blue 30.00 1.50
On cover 7.50
Block of four (2mm spacing) 125.00 12.00
Block of four (3mm spacing) 130.00 10.00
Margin block of 6, Impt. & P#, T V 345.00
Margin block of 6, Impt. & P# & star 400.00
Double transfer 32.50 2.75

336 A140 6c **red orange,** *Jan. 1909* 32.50 3.50
pale red orange 32.50 3.50
orange 32.50 3.50
On cover 20.00
Block of four 135.00 30.00
Margin block of 6, Impt. & P#, T V 550.00

337 A140 8c **olive green,** *Dec. 1908* 26.00 1.75
deep olive green 26.00 1.75
On cover 17.50
Block of four 110.00 15.00
Margin block of 6, Impt. & P#, T V 300.00
Double transfer 40.00 3.75

338 A140 10c **yellow,** *Jan. 1909* 42.50 1.00
On cover 10.00
Block of four 175.00 7.50
Margin block of 6, Impt. & P#, T V 650.00
Double transfer — —
Very thin paper —

339 A140 13c **blue green,** *Jan. 1909* 25.00 14.00
deep blue green 25.00 14.00
On cover 110.00
Block of four 105.00 120.00
Margin block of 6, Impt. & P#, T V 300.00
Line through "TAG" of "POSTAGE" (4948 L. R. 96) 47.50 *25.00*

340 A140 15c **pale ultramarine,** *Jan. 1909* 40.00 3.75
ultramarine 40.00 3.75
On cover 125.00
Block of four 165.00 40.00
Margin block of 6, Impt. & P#, T V 400.00

341 A140 50c **violet,** *Jan. 13, 1909* 175.00 10.00
dull violet 175.00 10.00
On cover *5,000.*
Block of four 725.00 85.00
Margin block of 4, arrow, right or left 800.00
Margin block of 6, Impt. & P#, T V *6,000.*

342 A140 $1 **violet brown,** *Jan. 29, 1909* 300.00 50.00
light violet brown 300.00 50.00
On cover *6,000.*
Block of four 1,250. 425.00
Margin block of 4, arrow, right or left 1,350. 450.00
Margin block of 6, Impt. & P#, T V *10,000.*
Double transfer — —

For listings of other perforated stamps of A138 A139 and A140 see
Nos. 357 to 366 Bluish paper
Nos. 374 to 382, 405 to 407 Single line wmk. Perf. 12
Nos. 424 to 430 Single line wmk. Perf. 10
Nos. 461 Single line wmk. Perf. 11
Nos. 462 to 469 unwmk. Perf. 10
Nos. 498 to 507 unwmk. Perf. 11
Nos. 519 Double line wmk. Perf. 11
Nos. 525 to 530 and 536 Offset printing
Nos. 538 to 546 Rotary press printing

Imperf

343 A138 1c **green,** *Dec. 1908* 4.50 2.75
dark green 4.50 2.75
yellowish green 4.50 2.75
On cover 7.50
Block of four (2mm or 3mm spacing) 18.00 12.00
Margin block of 4, arrow, 2mm or 3mm 20.00 12.50
Corner margin block of four, 2mm or 3mm 18.50 12.50
Center line block 30.00 16.00
Margin block of 6, Impt. & P#, T V 45.00 28.00
Margin block of 6, Impt. & P# & star 52.50 30.00
Margin block of 6, Impt. & P# & small solid star (plate 4980) *575.00*
Double transfer 11.00 5.50

344 A139 2c **carmine,** *Dec. 10, 1908* 6.50 2.00
light carmine 6.50 2.00
dark carmine 6.50 2.00
On cover 5.00
Block of four (2mm or 3mm spacing) 26.00 8.75
Margin block of 4, arrow, 2mm or 3mm 28.00 9.50
Corner margin block of four, 2mm or 3mm 26.00 9.50
Center line block 38.50 17.00
Margin block of 6, Impt. & P#, T V 85.00
Margin block of 6, Impt. & P# & star 77.50
Double transfer 12.00 3.50
Double transfer, design of 1c (plate 5299) *1,250.*

345 A140 3c **deep violet,** type I, *Mar. 3, 1909* 12.00 10.00
violet 12.00 10.00
On cover 30.00
Block of four 48.00 42.50
Corner margin block of four 52.50 45.00
Margin block of 4, arrow 57.50 45.00
Center line block 75.00 60.00
Margin block of 6, Impt. & P#, T V 180.00
Double transfer 21.00 15.00

346 A140 4c **orange brown,** *Feb. 25, 1909* 21.00 12.00
brown 21.00 12.00
On cover 75.00
Block of four (2mm or 3mm spacing) 160.00 65.00
Margin block of 4, arrow, 2mm or 3mm 95.00 67.50
Corner margin block of four 2mm or 3mm 87.50 67.50
Center line block 125.00 75.00
Margin block of 6, Impt. & P#, T V 210.00
Margin block of 6, Impt. & P# & star 240.00
Double transfer 40.00 22.50

347 A140 5c **blue,** *Feb. 25, 1909* 37.50 27.50
dark blue 37.50 27.50
On cover 100.00
Block of four 150.00 100.00
Corner margin block of four 155.00 110.00
Margin block of 4, arrow 165.00 125.00
Center line block 210.00 140.00
Margin block of 6, Impt. & P#, T V 350.00
Cracked plate —

For listings of other imperforate stamps of designs A138, A139 and A140 see
Nos. 383, 384, 408, 409 and 459 Single line wmk.
Nos. 481 to 485 unwmk.
Nos. 531 to 535 Offset printing

COIL STAMPS

1908-10 ***Perf. 12 Horizontally***

348 A138 1c **green,** *Dec. 29, 1908* 17.50 9.25
dark green 17.50 9.25
On cover 25.00
Pair 40.00 25.00
Guide line pair 125.00 85.00

349 A139 2c **carmine,** *Jan. 1909* 30.00 5.00
dark carmine 30.00 5.00
On cover 15.00
Pair 75.00 13.50
Guide line pair 200.00 40.00
Double transfer, design of 1c (plate 5299) — *1,750.*

350 A140 4c **orange brown,** *Aug. 15, 1910* 67.50 50.00
On cover 125.00
Pair 155.00 120.00
Guide line pair 500.00 275.00

351 A140 5c **blue,** *Jan. 1909* 75.00 67.50
dark blue 75.00 67.50
On cover 150.00
Pair 170.00 160.00
Guide line pair 500.00 350.00

1909 ***Perf. 12 Vertically***

352 A138 1c **green,** *Jan. 1909* 32.50 20.00
dark green 32.50 20.00
On cover 40.00
Pair (2mm spacing) 80.00 50.00
Pair (3mm spacing) 75.00 47.50
Guide line pair 200.00 85.00
Double transfer — —

353 A139 2c **carmine,** *Jan. 12, 1909* 30.00 5.00
dark carmine 30.00 5.00
On cover 20.00
Pair (2mm spacing) 75.00 15.00
Pair (3mm spacing) 70.00 12.50
Guide line pair 200.00 50.00

354 A140 4c **orange brown,** *Feb. 23, 1909* 87.50 37.50
On cover 85.00
Pair (2mm spacing) 210.00 95.00
Pair (3mm spacing) 200.00 90.00
Guide line pair 625.00 200.00

355 A140 5c **blue,** *Feb. 23, 1909* 95.00 55.00
On cover 125.00
Pair 225.00 120.00
Guide line pair 650.00 250.00

356 A140 10c **yellow,** *Jan. 7, 1909* 1,300. 400.00
On cover *10,000.*
Pair 3,250. 1,000.
Guide line pair 7,500. *3,500.*

These Government Coil Stamps, Nos. 352-355, should not be confused with those of the International Vending Machine Co., which are perf. 12½-13.

For listings of other coil stamps of designs A138 A139 and A140 see
Nos. 385 to 396, 410 to 413, 441 to 459 Single line wmk.
Nos. 486 to 496 unwmk.

BLUISH PAPER

This was made with 35 per cent rag stock instead of all wood pulp. The "bluish" color (actually grayish blue) goes through the paper showing clearly on the back as well as on the face.

1909 ***Perf. 12***

357 A138 1c **green,** *Feb. 16, 1909* 75.00 65.00
On cover 200.00
Block of four (2mm spacing) 310.00 400.00
Block of four (3mm spacing) *650.00*
Margin block of 6, Impt. & P#, T V 875.00
Margin block of 6, Impt. & P# & star *2,500.*

358 A139 2c **carmine,** *Feb. 16, 1909* 70.00 55.00
On cover 200.00
Block of four (2mm spacing) 290.00 325.00
Block of four (3mm spacing) 325.00
Margin block of 6, Impt. & P#, T V 850.00
Margin block of 6, Impt. & P# & star 1,350.
Double transfer —

359 A140 3c **deep violet,** type I 1,500. 1,250.
On cover *2,000.*
Block of four 6,250.
Margin block of 6, Impt. & P#, T V *15,000.*

360 A140 4c **orange brown** *17,500.*
Block of four *72,500.*
Margin strip of 3, Impt. & P#, T V *75,000.*

361 A140 5c **blue** 2,900. 3,000.
Block of four *12,000.* —
Margin block of 6, Impt. & P#, T V *30,000.*

362 A140 6c **red orange** 1,150. 750.00
On cover —
Block of four 4,750.
Margin block of 6, Impt. & P#, T V *13,000.*

363 A140 8c **olive green** *17,500.*
Block of four *72,500.*
Margin strip of 3, Impt. & P#, T V *75,000.*

364 A140 10c **yellow** 1,200. 800.00
On cover —
Block of four 5,000.
Margin block of 6, Impt. & P#, T V *13,500.*

365 A140 13c **blue green** 2,000. 1,100.
On cover 1,750.
Block of four 8,500. *5,500.*
Margin block of 6, Impt. & P#, T V *18,500.*

366 A140 15c **pale ultramarine** 900.00 600.00
On cover —
Block of four 3,800.
Margin block of 6, Impt. & P#, T V *10,000.*

LINCOLN MEMORIAL ISSUE

Issued to commemorate the 100th anniversary of the birth of Abraham Lincoln.

Lincoln — A141

Plates of 400 subjects in four panes of 100 each

1909 **Wmk. 191**

Perf. 12

367 A141 2c **carmine,** *Feb. 12, 1909* 4.25 1.40
bright carmine 4.25 1.40
On cover 3.50
Block of four (2mm spacing) 17.00 12.00
Block of four (3mm spacing) 17.00 11.50
Margin block of 6, Impt. & P# & small solid star 100.00
Double transfer 6.75 2.50

Imperf

368 A141 2c **carmine,** *Feb. 12, 1909* 19.50 15.00
On cover 30.00
Block of four (2mm or 3mm spacing) 80.00 70.00
Corner margin block of four 85.00
Margin block of 4, arrow 90.00 80.00

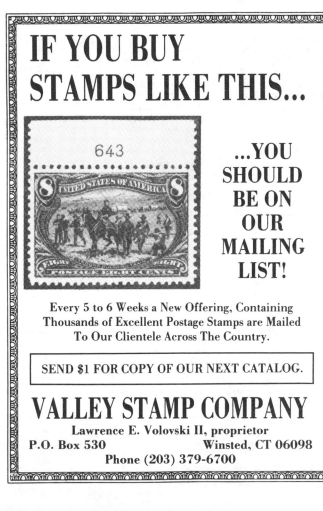

Center line block 125.00 90.00
Margin block of 6, Impt. & P# & small solid star 190.00
Double transfer 37.50 24.00

BLUISH PAPER

Perf. 12

369 A141 2c **carmine,** *Feb. 1909* 170.00 165.00
On cover 350.00
Block of four (2mm or 3mm spacing) 725.00 650.00
Margin block of 6, Impt. & P# & small solid star *3,250.*

ALASKA-YUKON-PACIFIC EXPOSITION ISSUE

Seattle, Wash., June 1-Oct. 16, 1909

William H. Seward A142

Plates of 280 subjects in four panes of 70 each

1909 **Wmk. 191** ***Perf. 12***

370 A142 2c **carmine,** *June 1, 1909* 7.00 1.10
bright carmine 7.00 1.10
On cover 4.00
On cover, Expo. station canc. 60.00
Block of four 30.00 11.00
Margin block of 6, Impt. & P#, T V 175.00
Double transfer (5249 U.L.8) 10.00 4.00

Imperf

371 A142 2c **carmine,** *June 1909* 27.50 19.00
On cover 40.00
On cover, Expo. station canc. 175.00
Block of four 120.00 80.00
Corner margin block of four 125.00
Margin block of 4, arrow 130.00 85.00
Center line block 175.00 95.00
Margin block of 6, Impt. & P#, T V 225.00
Double transfer 40.00 25.00

Earliest known use: June 13.

HUDSON-FULTON CELEBRATION ISSUE

Issued to commemorate the tercentenary of the discovery of the Hudson River and the centenary of Robert Fulton's steamship, the "Clermont."

Henry Hudson's "Half Moon" and Fulton's Steamship "Clermont" — A143

Plates of 240 subjects in four panes of 60 each

1909 **Wmk. 191** ***Perf. 12***

372 A143 2c **carmine,** *Sept. 25, 1909* 10.00 3.25
On cover 7.50
Block of four 42.50 20.00
Margin block of 6, Impt. & P#, T V 250.00
Double transfer (5393 and 5394) 14.00 4.25

Imperf

373 A143 2c **carmine,** *Sept. 25, 1909* 30.00 21.00
On cover 40.00
Block of four 120.00 87.50
Corner margin block of four 125.00
Margin block of 4, arrow 135.00 95.00
Center line block 210.00 105.00
Margin block of 6, Impt. & P#, T V 250.00
Double transfer (5393 and 5394) 42.50 25.00

REGULAR ISSUE
DESIGNS OF 1908-09 ISSUES

In this issue the Bureau used three groups of plates:

(1) The old standard plates with uniform 2mm spacing throughout (6c, 8c, 10c and 15c values);

(2) Those having an open star in the margin and showing spacings of 2mm and 3mm between stamps (for all values 1c to 10c); and

(3) A third set of plates with uniform spacing of approximately 2¾mm between all stamps. These plates have imprints showing

a. "Bureau of Engraving & Printing", "A" and number.

b. "A" and number only.

c. Number only.

(See above No. 331)

These were used for the 1c, 2c, 3c, 4c and 5c values.

On or about Nov. 1, 1910 the Bureau began using paper watermarked with single-lined letters:

(Actual size of letter)

repeated in rows, this way:

U S P S U S P S U
U S P S U S P S
U S P S U S P S U
U S P S U S P S
U S P S U S P S U
U S P S U S P S
U S P S U S P S U
U S P S U S P S
U S P S U S P S U

Plates of 400 subjects in four panes of 100 each

1910-11 **Wmk. 190** ***Perf. 12***

374 A138 1c **green,** *Nov. 23, 1910* 5.00 6
light green 5.00 6
dark green 5.00 6
On cover 10
Block of four (2mm. spacing) 21.00 3.00
Block of four (3mm. spacing) 20.50 2.75
Margin block of 6, Impt. & P#, & star 65.00
Margin block of 6, Impt. & P# & "A" 75.00 —
a. Booklet pane of six, *Oct. 7, 1910* 110.00 *30.00*
Double transfer 12.50 2.50
Cracked plate — —
Pane of sixty *925.00* —

Panes of 60 of No. 374 were regularly issued in Washington, D.C. during Sept. and Oct., 1912. They were made from the six outer vertical rows of imperforate "Star Plate" sheets that had been rejected for use in vending machines on account of the 3mm spacing. These panes have sheet margins on two adjoining sides and are imperforate along the other two sides. Both sheet margins show the plate number, imprint and star.

375 A139 2c **carmine,** *Nov. 23, 1910* 5.00 5
bright carmine 5.00 5
dark carmine 5.00 5
lake 100.00
On cover 10
Block of four (2mm spacing) 21.00 1.25
Block of four (3mm spacing) 20.00 1.00
Margin block of 6, Impt. & P# & star 70.00
Margin block of 6, Impt. & P# & "A" 80.00
a. Booklet pane of six, *Nov. 30, 1910* 95.00 *25.00*
Cracked plate — —
Double transfer 10.00 2.00
Double transfer, design of 1c (plate 5299) — *1,000.*

376 A140 3c **deep violet,** type I, *Jan. 16, 1911* 11.50 1.00
violet 11.50 1.00
lilac 13.00 1.10
On cover 7.50

Block of four (2mm spacing) 47.50 8.50
Block of four (3mm spacing) 45.00 8.00
Margin block of 6, Impt. & P# & star 100.00
Margin block of 6, P# only 115.00

377 A140 4c **brown,** *Jan. 20, 1911* 17.50 30
dark brown 17.50 30
orange brown 17.50 30
On cover 7.50
Block of four (2mm spacing) 72.50 3.25
Block of four (3mm spacing) 70.00 3.00
Margin block of 6, Impt. & P# & star 130.00
Margin block of 6, P# only 145.00
Double transfer — —

378 A140 5c **blue,** *Jan. 25, 1911* 17.50 30
light blue 17.50 30
dark blue 17.50 30
bright blue 17.50 30
On cover 5.00
Block of four (2mm spacing) 72.50 5.00
Block of four (3mm spacing) 70.00 4.00
Margin block of 6, Impt. & P#, T V 160.00
Margin block of 6, Impt. & P# & star 155.00
Margin block of 6, "A" & P# 190.00
Margin block of 6, P# only 190.00
Double transfer — —

379 A140 6c **red orange,** *Jan. 25, 1911* 24.00 40
light red orange 24.00 40
On cover 12.50
Block of four (2mm spacing) 97.50 8.50
Block of four (3mm spacing) 96..00 8.00
Margin block of 6, Impt. & P# T V 325.00
Margin block of 6, Impt. & P# & star 300.00

380 A140 8c **olive green,** *Feb. 8, 1911* 70.00 8.50
dark olive green 70.00 8.50
On cover 40.00
Block of four (2mm spacing) 290.00 60.00
Block of four (3mm spacing) 290.00 57.50
Margin block of 6, Impt. & P# T V 775.00
Margin block of 6, Impt. & P# & star *1,100.*

381 A140 10c **yellow,** *Jan. 24, 1911* 65.00 2.50
On cover 17.50
Block of four (2mm spacing) 270.00 25.00
Block of four (3mm spacing) 270.00 22.50
Margin block of 6, Impt. & P#, T V 775.00
Margin block of 6, Impt. & P# & star 750.00

382 A140 15c **pale ultramarine,** *Mar. 1, 1911* 175.00 11.50
On cover 100.00
Block of four 725.00 90.00
Margin block of 6, Impt. & P#, T V 1,750.

1911 ***Imperf.***

383 A138 1c **green,** *Jan. 3, 1911* 2.25 2.00
dark green 2.25 2.00
yellowish green 2.25 2.00
bright green 2.25 2.00
On cover 5.00
Block of four (2mm or 3mm spacing) 9.00 13.00
Corner margin block of four 10.00
Margin block of 4, arrow 10.50 13.50
Center line block 20.00 16.00
Margin block of 6, Impt. & P# & star 37.50
Margin block of 6, Impt. & P# & "A" 70.00 —
Double transfer 5.75 3.50

384 A139 2c **carmine,** *Jan. 3, 1911* 3.50 1.75
light carmine 3.50 1.75
dark carmine 30.00 12.50
On cover 2.50
Horizontal pair 10.00 5.25
Block of four (2mm or 3mm spacing) 21.00 10.50
Corner margin block of four 22.00
Margin block of 4, arrow 22.00 16.00
Center line block 45.00 26.00
Margin block of 6, Impt. & P# & star 115.00
Margin block of 6, Impt. & P# & "A" 145.00
Double transfer, design of 1c (plate 5299) *1,250.*
Double transfer 7.00 2.25
Cracked plate 17.50 —

COIL STAMPS

1910 ***Perf. 12 Horizontally***

385 A138 1c **green,** *Nov. 1, 1910* 15.00 7.00
dark green 15.00 7.00
On cover 30.00
Pair 37.50 16.50
Guide line pair 165.00 85.00

386 A139 2c **carmine,** *Nov. 1, 1910* 27.50 10.00
light carmine 27.50 10.00
On cover 35.00
Pair 92.50 40.00
Guide line pair 325.00 100.00

1910-11 ***Perf. 12 Vertically***

387 A138 1c **green,** *Nov. 1, 1910* 40.00 20.00
On cover 35.00
Pair (2mm spacing) 92.50 50.00
Pair (3mm spacing) 97.50 52.50
Guide line pair 200.00 120.00

388 A139 2c **carmine,** *Nov. 1, 1910* 400.00 75.00

On cover 250.00
Pair (2mm spacing) 1,200. 200.00
Pair (3mm spacing) 1,250. 225.00
Guide line pair 3,000. 850.00

Stamps sold as No. 388 frequently are privately perforated copies of 384, or copies of 375, with horizontal perforations removed.

389 A140 3c **deep vio.,** type I, *Jan. 24, 1911* *15,000.* 6,500.
On cover 14,000.
Pair *50,000.*

This is the rarest coil, only a small supply being used at Orangeburg, N.Y.
(See note above No. 316.)

1910 ***Perf. 8½ Horizontally***

390 A138 1c **green,** *Dec. 12, 1910* 3.00 3.00
dark green 3.00 3.00
On cover 6.00
Pair 7.00 7.00
Guide line pair 20.00 11.00
Double transfer — —
391 A139 2c **carmine,** *Dec. 23, 1910* 20.00 4.75
light carmine 20.00 4.75
On cover 20.00
Pair 50.00 15.00
Guide line pair 115.00 50.00

1910-13 ***Perf. 8½ Vertically***

392 A138 1c **green,** *Dec. 12, 1910* 12.00 12.00
dark green 12.00 12.00
On cover 40.00
Pair 30.00 32.50
Guide line pair 85.00 60.00
Double transfer — —
393 A139 2c **carmine,** *Dec. 16, 1910* 24.00 4.50
dark carmine 24.00 4.50
On cover 18.50
Pair 55.00 12.50
Guide line pair 140.00 25.00
394 A140 3c **deep violet,** type I, *Sept. 18, 1911* 32.50 27.50
violet 32.50 27.50
red violet 32.50 27.50
On cover 85.00
Pair (2mm spacing) 75.00 65.00
Pair (3mm spacing) 72.50 62.50
Guide line pair 210.00 110.00
395 A140 4c **brown,** *Apr. 15, 1912* 32.50 27.50
dark brown 32.50 27.50
On cover 85.00
Pair (2mm spacing) 75.00 65.00
Pair (3mm spacing) 72.50 62.50
Guide line pair 210.00 110.00
396 A140 5c **blue,** *Mar. 1913* 32.50 27.50
dark blue 32.50 27.50
On cover 85.00
Pair 72.50 65.00
Guide line pair 210.00 120.00

PANAMA-PACIFIC EXPOSITION ISSUE

San Francisco, Cal., Feb. 20-Dec. 4, 1915

Vasco Nunez de Balboa A144

Pedro Miguel Locks, Panama Canal A145

Golden Gate A146

Discovery of San Francisco Bay — A147

MODEL POST OFFICE
PANAMA PACIFIC
INTERNATIONAL
EXPOSITION

Exposition Station Cancellation.

Plates of 280 subjects in four panes of 70 each.

1913 **Wmk. 190** ***Perf. 12***

397 A144 1c **green,** *Jan. 1, 1913* 11.00 85
deep green 11.00 85
yellowish green 11.00 85
On cover 2.50
On card, Expo. station 1915 canc. *50.00*
Block of four 44.00 7.50
Margin block of 6, P# only 110.00
Double transfer 17.50 2.00
398 A145 2c **carmine,** *Jan. 1913* 12.50 28
deep carmine 12.50 28
lake 200.00
On cover 1.00
On cover, Expo. station 1915 canc. 65.00
Block of four 50.00 5.00
Margin block of 6, P# only 210.00
Double transfer 35.00 2.00

Earliest known use: Jan. 17.

399 A146 5c **blue,** *Jan. 1, 1913* 47.50 6.50
dark blue 47.50 6.50
On cover 25.00
On cover, Expo. station 1915 canc. 300.00
Block of four 200.00 55.00
Margin block of 6, P# only 1,500.
400 A147 10c **orange yellow,** *Jan. 1, 1913* 90.00 14.00
On cover 50.00
On cover, Expo. station 1915 canc. 400.00
Block of four 370.00 110.00
Margin block of 6, P# only 2,000.
400A A147 10c **orange,** *Aug. 1913* 160.00 10.50
On cover 60.00
On cover, Expo. station 1915 canc. 425.00
Block of four 650.00 85.00
Margin block of 6, P# only *7,750.*

1914-15 ***Perf. 10***

401 A144 1c **green,** *Dec. 1914* 16.00 4.00
dark green 16.00 4.00
On cover 15.00
On card, Expo. station 1915 canc. 120.00
Block of four 64.00 30.00
Margin block of 6, P# only 225.00
402 A145 2c **carmine,** *Jan. 1915* 52.50 1.00
deep carmine 52.50 1.00
red 52.50 1.00
On cover 5.00
On cover, Expo. station 1915 canc. 185.00
Block of four 210.00 13.50
Margin block of 6, P# only 1,150.
403 A146 5c **blue,** *Feb. 1915* 115.00 11.00
dark blue 115.00 11.00
On cover 50.00
On cover, Expo. station 1915 canc. 450.00
Block of four 470.00 75.00
Margin block of 6, P# only 3,250.
404 A147 10c **orange,** *July 1915* 775.00 42.50
On cover 135.00
On cover, Expo. station 1915 canc. 850.00
Block of four *3,250.* 325.00
Margin block of 6, P# only *10,000.*

An enhanced introduction to the Scott Catalogue begins on Page V. A thorough understanding of the material presented there will greatly aid your use of the catalogue itself.

REGULAR ISSUE

Washington — A140

1912-14 **Wmk. 190** ***Perf. 12***

The plates for this and later issues were the so-called "A" plates with uniform spacing of 2¾mm between stamps.

Plates of 400 subjects in four panes of 100 each for all values 1c to 50c inclusive.

Plates of 200 subjects in two panes of 100 each for $1 and some of the 50c (No. 422) denomination.

405 A140 1c **green,** *Feb. 1912* 3.50 6
light green 3.50 6
dark green 3.50 6
yellowish green 3.50 6
On cover 10
Block of four 14,00 1.00
Margin block of 6, Impt. & P# & "A" 67.50
Margin block of 6, "A" & P# 60.00
Margin block of 6, P# only 55.00
a. Vert. pair, imperf. horiz. *650.00* —
b. Booklet pane of six, *Feb. 8, 1912* 50.00 *7.50*
Cracked plate 12.00 —
Double transfer 5.75 —

TYPE I

TWO CENTS.

Type I. There is one shading line in the first curve of the ribbon above the left "2" and one in the second curve of the ribbon above the right "2".

The button of the toga has only a faint outline.

The top line of the toga rope, from the button to the front of the throat, is also very faint.

The shading lines of the face terminate in front of the ear with little or no joining, to form a lock of hair.

Used on both flat plate and rotary press printings.

406 A140 2c **carmine,** type I, *Feb. 1912* 3.25 5
bright carmine 3.25 5
dark carmine 3.25 5
lake 100.00 25.00
On cover 10
Block of four 13.00 75
Margin block of 6, Impt. & P# & "A" 85.00
Margin block of 6, "A" & P# 75.00
Margin block of 6, P# only 70.00
Margin block of 6, Electrolytic, (Pl. 6023) *200.00*
a. Booklet pane of six, *Feb. 8, 1912* 60.00 *17.50*
b. Double impression —
Double transfer 6.50 50
407 A140 7c **black,** *Apr. 1914* 60.00 8.00
grayish black 60.00 8.00
intense black 60.00 8.00
On cover 30.00
Block of four 250.00 45.00
Margin block of 6, P# only 900.00

1912 ***Imperf.***

408 A140 1c **green,** *Mar. 1912* 90 50
yellowish green 90 50
dark green 90 50
On cover 1.10
Block of four 3.60 2.50
Corner margin block of four 3.75 2.65
Margin block of 4, arrow 3.75 2.65
Center line block 6.75 6.50
Margin block of 6, Impt. & P# & "A", T, B or L 42.50
Margin block of 6, Impt. & P# & "A", at right *500.00*
Margin block of 6, "A" & P# 22.50
Margin block of 6, P# only 15.00
Double transfer 2.50 1.00
Cracked plate — —

409 A140 2c **carmine,** type I, *Feb. 1912* 1.00 50
deep carmine 1.00 50
scarlet 1.00 50
On cover 1.00
Block of four 4.00 2.75
Corner margin block of four 4.15
Margin block of 4, arrow 4.15 3.25
Center line block 7.75 7.00
Margin block of 6, Impt. & P# & "A" 45.00 10.00
Margin block of 6, "A" & P# 40.00
Margin block of 6, P# only 30.00
Cracked plate (Plates 7580, 7582) 15.00 —

In December, 1914, the Post Office at Kansas City, Missouri, had on hand a stock of imperforate sheets of 400 of stamps Nos. 408 and 409, formerly sold for use in vending machines, but not then in demand. In order to make them salable, they were rouletted with ordinary tracing wheels and were sold over the counter with official approval of the Post Office Department given January 5, 1915.

These stamps were sold until the supply was exhausted. Except for one full sheet of 400 of each value, all were cut into panes of 100 before being rouletted and sold. They are known as "Kansas City Roulettes".

COIL STAMPS

1912 ***Perf. 8½ Horizontally***

410 A140 1c **green,** *Mar. 1912* 4.00 2.50
dark green 4.00 2.50
On cover 7.50
Pair 9.00 5.75
Guide line pair 22.50 14.00
Double transfer — —
411 A140 2c **carmine,** type I, *Mar. 1912* 5.00 2.00
deep carmine 5.00 2.00
On cover 10.00
Pair 12.00 4.75
Guide line pair 27.00 14.00
Double transfer 7.00 3.25

Perf. 8½ Vertically

412 A140 1c **green,** *Mar. 18, 1912* 13.00 3.00
deep green 13.00 3.00
On cover 12.50
Pair 27.50 7.50
Guide line pair 60.00 20.00
413 A140 2c **carmine,** type I, *Mar. 1912* 22.00 60
dark carmine 22.00 60
On cover 7.50
Pair 47.50 4.00
Guide line pair 120.00 12.50
Double transfer 37.50 2.50

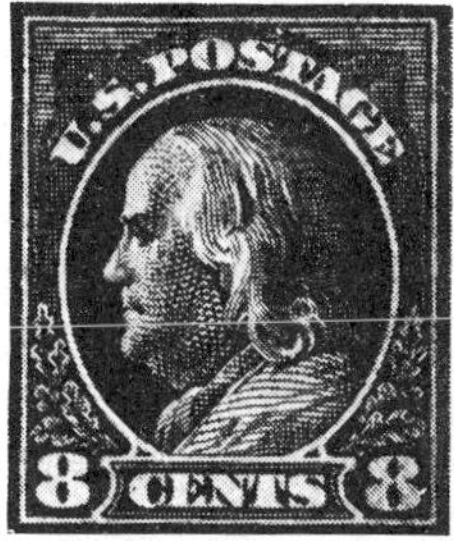
Franklin — A148

1912-14 **Wmk. 190** ***Perf. 12***

414 A148 8c **pale olive green,** *Feb. 1912* 25.00 85
olive green 25.00 85
On cover 15.00
Block of four 105.00 12.00
Margin block of 6, Impt. & P# & "A" 325.00
415 A148 9c **salmon red,** *Apr. 1914* 32.50 9.50
rose red 32.50 9.50
On cover 45.00
Block of four 135.00 75.00
Margin block of 6, P# only 500.00
416 A148 10c **orange yellow,** *Jan. 1912* 26.00 25
yellow 26.00 25
brown yellow *100.00* —
On cover 2.50
Block of four 107.50 1.75
Margin block of 6, Impt. & P# & "A" 365.00
Margin block of 6, "A" & P# 380.00
Double transfer — —
417 A148 12c **claret brown,** *Apr. 1914* 28.50 3.00
deep claret brown 28.50 3.00
On cover 22.50
Block of four 117.50 22.50
Margin block of 6, P# only 350.00
Double transfer 37.50 5.00
Triple transfer 52.50 6.75
418 A148 15c **gray,** *Feb. 1912* 47.50 2.00
dark gray 47.50 2.00
On cover 15.00
Block of four 200.00 20.00
Margin block of 6, Impt. & P# & "A" 475.00
Margin block of 6, "A" & P# 500.00
Margin block of 6, P# only 525.00
Double transfer — —
419 A148 20c **ultramarine,** *Apr. 1914* 110.00 9.00
dark ultramarine 110.00 9.00
On cover 150.00
Block of four 450.00 75.00
Margin block of 6, P# only 1,300.
420 A148 30c **orange red,** *Apr. 1914* 80.00 10.00
dark orange red 80.00 10.00
On cover 250.00
Block of four 330.00 75.00
Margin block of 6, P# only 1,150.
421 A148 50c **violet,** *Apr. 29, 1914* 300.00 10.00
bright violet 300.00 10.00
On cover *2,000.*
Block of four 1,250. 85.00
Margin block of 6, P# only 5,750.

No. 421 always has an offset of the frame lines on the back under the gum.

Nos. 422 does not have this offset.

1912 **Wmk. 191**

422 A148 50c **violet,** *Feb. 12, 1912* 160.00 9.50
On cover *2,000.*
Block of four 650.00 80.00
Margin block of 4, arrow, R or L 800.00
Margin block of 6, Impt. & P# & "A" 3,750.
423 A148 $1 **violet brown,** *Feb. 12, 1912* 360.00 40.00
On cover *7,000.*
Block of four 1,500. 300.00
Margin block of 4, arrow, R or L 1,600.
Margin block of 6, Impt. & P# & "A" *8,000.*
Double transfer (5782 L. 66) 400.00 45.00

During the United States occupation of Vera Cruz, Mexico, from April to November, 1914, letters sent from there show Provisional Postmarks.

For other listings of perforated stamps of design A148, see:
Nos. 431 to 440 Single line wmk. Perf. 10
Nos. 460 Double line wmk. Perf. 10
Nos. 470 to 478 unwmk. Perf. 10
Nos. 508 to 518 unwmk. Perf. 11

Plates of 400 subjects in four panes of 100 each.

1913-15 **Wmk. 190** ***Perf. 10***

424 A140 1c **green,** *Sept. 5, 1914* 1.60 6
bright green 1.60 6
deep green 1.60 6
yellowish green 1.60 6
On cover 10
Block of four 6.40 75
Margin block of 6, P# only 26.00
Block of ten with imprint "COIL STAMPS" and number (6581-82, 85, 89) 100.00
Cracked plate — —
Double transfer 4.25 60
Experimental bureau precancel, New Orleans —
a. Perf. 12x10 *600.00 500.00*
b. Perf. 10x12 250.00
c. Vert. pair, imperf. horiz. *425.00 250.00*
d. Booklet pane of six 3.50 *75*
e. Vert. pair, imperf. btwn. —

Most copies of No. 424b are precanceled Dayton, Ohio, to which the value applies.

Earliest known use of No. 424d is Dec. 1913.

425 A140 2c **rose red,** type I, *Sept. 5, 1914* 1.50 5
dark rose red 1.50 5
carmine rose 1.50 5
carmine 1.50 5
dark carmine 1.50 5
scarlet 1.50 5
red 1.50 5
On cover 10
Block of four 6.00 35
Margin block of 6, P# only 17.50
Block of ten with imprint "COIL STAMPS" and number (6566-73) 110.00
Cracked plate 9.00 —
Double transfer — —
c. Perf. 10x12 —
d. Perf. 12x10 *500.00*
e. Booklet pane of six, *Jan. 6, 1914* 12.50 *3.00*

The aniline inks used on some printings of Nos. 425, 426 and 435 caused a pink tinge to permeate the paper and appear on the back. These are called "pink backs."

426 A140 3c **deep violet,** type I, *Sept. 18, 1914* 8.50 90
violet 8.50 90
bright violet 8.50 90
reddish violet 8.50 90
On cover 3.00
Block of four 35.00 6.50
Margin block of 6, P# only 85.00
427 A140 4c **brown,** *Sept. 7, 1914* 22.00 28
dark brown 22.00 28
orange brown 22.00 28
yellowish brown 22.00 28
On cover 5.00
Block of four 92.50 3.75
Margin block of 6, P# only 250.00
Double transfer 37.50 1.75
428 A140 5c **blue,** *Sept. 14, 1914* 18.50 28
bright blue 18.50 28
dark blue 18.50 28
indigo blue 18.50 35
On cover 2.50
Block of four 77.50 2.50
Margin block of 6, P# only 185.00
a. Perf. 12x10 *1,000.*
429 A140 6c **red orange,** *Sept. 28, 1914* 29.00 90
deep red orange 29.00 90
pale red orange 29.00 90
On cover 8.50
Block of four (2mm. spacing) 125.00 11.00
Block of four (3mm. spacing) 120.00 10.00
Margin block of 6, Impt. & P# & star 235.00
Margin block of 6, P# only 275.00
430 A140 7c **black,** *Sept. 10, 1914* 55.00 2.50
gray black 55.00 2.50
intense black 55.00 2.50
On cover 35.00
Block of four 230.00 25.00
Margin block of 6, P# only 525.00
431 A148 8c **pale olive green,** *Sept. 26, 1914* 24.00 1.10
olive green 24.00 1.10
On cover 7.50
Block of four 100.00 10.00
Margin block of 6, Impt. & P# & "A" 260.00
Margin block of 6, "A" & P# 290.00
Double impression —
Double transfer — —
432 A148 9c **salmon red,** *Oct. 6, 1914* 32.50 5.00
dark salmon red 32.50 5.00
On cover 25.00
Block of four 135.00 40.00
Margin block of 6, P# only 360.00
433 A148 10c **orange yellow,** *Sept. 9, 1914* 30.00 18
golden yellow 30.00 18
On cover 7.50
Block of four 125.00 1.50
Margin block of 6, Impt. & P# & "A" 350.00
Margin block of 6, "A" & P# 350.00
Margin block of 6, P# only 350.00
434 A148 11c **dark green,** *Aug. 11, 1915* 13.50 5.50
bluish green 13.50 5.50
On cover 22.50
Block of four 55.00 32.50
Margin block of 6, P# only 125.00
435 A148 12c **claret brown,** *Sept. 10, 1914* 15.00 2.75
deep claret brown 15.00 2.75
On cover 17.50
Block of four 60.00 25.00
Margin block of 6, P# only 150.00
a. 12c copper red 16.00 2.75
a. On cover 17.50
a. Block of four 65.00 25.00
a. Margin block of 6, P# only 160.00
b. Vertical pair, imperf. between *650.00*
Double transfer 22.50 4.50
Triple transfer 27.50 5.25
437 A148 15c **gray,** *Sept. 16, 1914* 72.50 4.50
dark gray 72.50 4.50
On cover 50.00
Block of four 300.00 40.00
Margin block of 6, Impt. & P# & "A" 480.00
Margin block of 6, "A" & P# 500.00
Margin block of 6, P# only 480.00
438 A148 20c **ultramarine,** *Sept. 19, 1914* 140.00 2.50
dark ultramarine 140.00 2.50
On cover 150.00
Block of four 575.00 25.00
Margin block of 6, P# only 1,600.
439 A148 30c **orange red,** *Sept. 19, 1914* 190.00 10.00
dark orange red 190.00 10.00
On cover 250.00
Block of four 775.00 95.00
Margin block of 6, P# only 2,500.
440 A148 50c **violet,** *Dec. 10, 1915* 500.00 10.00
On cover *1,750.*
Block of four 2,100. 85.00
Margin block of 6, P# only 9,000.

COIL STAMPS

1914 ***Perf. 10 Horizontally***

441 A140 1c **green,** *Nov. 14, 1914* 55 80
deep green 55 80
On cover 2.00
Pair 1.50 2.00
Guide line pair 4.25 3.50
442 A140 2c **carmine,** type I, *July 22, 1914* 6.00 4.50
deep carmine 6.00 4.50
On cover 12.50
Pair 15.00 11.00
Guide line pair 35.00 35.00

1914 ***Perf. 10 Vertically***

443 A14 1c **green,** *May 29, 1914* 14.00 4.00
deep green 14.00 4.00
On cover 12.00
Pair 35.00 9.00
Guide line pair 72.50 30.00
444 A140 2c **carmine,** type I, *Apr. 25, 1914* 19.00 1.00
deep carmine 19.00 1.00
red 19.00 1.00
On cover 10.00
Pair 47.50 2.75
Guide line pair 110.00 9.50
445 A140 3c **violet,** type I, *Dec. 18, 1914* 160.00 75.00
deep violet 160.00 75.00
On cover 200.00
Pair 350.00 175.00
Guide line pair 800.00 600.00
446 A140 4c **brown,** *Oct. 2, 1914* 82.50 21.00
On cover 100.00
Pair 190.00 47.50
Guide line pair 410.00 275.00
447 A140 5c **blue,** *July 30, 1914* 27.50 17.50
On cover 50.00
Pair 65.00 44.00
Guide line pair 150.00 200.00

No. 443 represents stamps from coils. Part of a sheet of No. 424 is known which is perforated vertically and imperforate horizontally.

ROTARY PRESS STAMPS

The Rotary Press Stamps are printed from plates that are curved to fit around a cylinder. This curvature produces stamps that are slightly larger, either horizontally or vertically, than those printed from flat plates. Designs of stamps from flat plates measure about 18½-19mm wide by 22mm high.

When the impressions are placed sidewise on the curved plates the designs are 19½-20mm wide; when they are placed vertically the designs are 22½to 23mm high. A line of color (not a guide line) shows where the curved plates meet or join on the press.

Rotary Press Coil Stamps were printed from plates of 170 subjects for stamps coiled sidewise, and from plates of 150 subjects for stamps coiled endwise.

Double paper varieties of Rotary Press stamps are not listed in this catalogue. Collectors are referred to the note on "Rotary Press Double Paper" in the "Information for Collectors" in the front of the catalogue.

ROTARY PRESS COIL STAMPS

Stamp designs 18½-19mm wide by 22½mm high

448 A140 1c **green,** *Dec. 12, 1915* 4.25 2.25
light green 4.25 2.25
On cover 6.50
Pair 10.00 5.25
Joint line pair 25.00 17.50

6568 **COIL STAMPS**

Type of plate number and imprint used for the 12 special 1c and 2c plates designed for the production of coil stamps.

TYPE II

TWO CENTS.
Type II. Shading lines in ribbons as on type I.
The toga button, rope and rope shading lines are heavy.
The shading lines of the face at the lock of hair end in a strong vertical curved line.
Used on rotary press printings only.

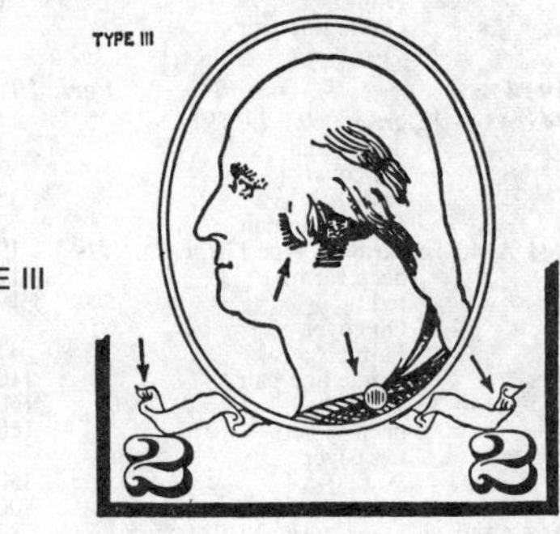

TYPE III

Type III. Two lines of shading in the curves of the ribbons.
Other characteristics similar to type II.
Used on rotary press printings only.

1915-16 ***Perf. 10 Horizontally***

449 A140 2c **red,** type I, *Dec. 5, 1915* 1,750. 190.00
carmine rose, type I — —
On cover, type I 600.00
Pair, type I 3,750. 400.00
Joint line pair, type I 8,500. 1,500.
450 A140 2c **carmine,** type III, *Feb. 1916* 7.00 2.25
carmine rose, type III 7.00 2.25
red, type III 7.00 2.25
On cover, type III 7.00
Pair, type III 15.00 6.00
Joint line pair, type III 35.00 15.00

1914-16 ***Perf. 10 Vertically***

Stamp designs 19½-20mm wide by 22mm high

452 A140 1c **green,** *Nov. 11, 1914* 7.00 1.40
On cover 3.00
Pair 16.00 3.25
Joint line pair 47.50 8.00
453 A140 2c **carmine rose,** type I, *July 3, 1914* 72.50 3.25
On cover, type I 10.00
Pair, type I 150.00 8.00
Joint line pair, type I 375.00 35.00
Cracked plate, type I — —
454 A140 2c **red,** type II, *June, 1915* 70.00 7.50
carmine, type II 70.00 7.50
On cover, type II 35.00
Pair, type II 150.00 20.00
Joint line pair, type II 350.00 90.00
455 A140 2c **carmine,** type III, *Dec. 1915* 6.50 75
carmine rose, type III 6.50 75
On cover, type III 2.00
Pair, type III 14.00 1.90
Joint line pair, type III 37.50 5.00

Fraudulently altered copies of Type III (Nos. 455, 488, 492 and 540) have had one line of shading scraped off to make them resemble Type II (Nos. 454, 487, 491 and 539).

456 A140 3c **violet,** type I, *Feb. 2, 1916* 190.00 75.00
deep violet 190.00 75.00
red violet 190.00 75.00
On cover 175.00
Pair 400.00 180.00
Joint line pair 825.00 400.00
457 A140 4c **brown,** *Feb. 18, 1916* 18.00 15.00
light brown 18.00 15.00
On cover 40.00
Pair 38.50 37.50
Joint line pair 100.00 75.00
Cracked plate 35.00 —
458 A140 5c **blue,** *Mar. 9, 1916* 22.50 15.00
On cover 40.00
Pair 50.00 37.50
Joint line pair 125.00 75.00
Double transfer — —

No. 457 was shipped to Annapolis, Md. in late 1915. At least two covers are known postmarked Nov. 5, 1915.

Horizontal Coil

1914 ***Imperf.***

459 A140 2c **carmine,** type I, *June 30, 1914* 375.00 *600.00*
On cover —
Pair 800.00 *1,350.*
Joint line pair 1,750. *3,250.*

Most line pairs of No. 459 are creased. Uncreased pairs command a premium.

FLAT PLATE PRINTINGS

1915 **Wmk. 191** ***Perf. 10***

460 A148 $1 **violet black,** *Feb. 8, 1915* 600.00 55.00
On cover —
Block of four 2,500. 425.00
Margin block of 4, arrow, R or L 2,600.
Margin block of 6, Impt. & P# & "A" *8,000.*
Double transfer (5782 L. 66) 650.00 60.00

1915 **Wmk. 190** ***Perf. 11***

461 A140 2c **pale car. red,** type I, *June 17, 1915* 75.00 50.00
On cover *850.00*
Block of four 310.00 375.00
Margin block of 6, P# only 725.00

Fraudulently perforated copies of No. 409 are offered as No. 461.

FLAT PLATE PRINTINGS

Plates of 400 subjects in four panes of 100 each for all values 1c to 50c inclusive.

Plates of 200 subjects in two panes of 100 each for $1, $2 and $5 denominations.

The Act of Oct. 3, 1917, effective Nov. 2, 1917, created a 3 cent rate. Local rate, 2 cents.

1916-17 **Unwmk.** ***Perf. 10***

462 A140 1c **green,** *Sept. 27, 1916* 5.00 15
light green 5.00 15
dark green 5.00 15
bluish green 5.00 15
On cover 40
Block of four 21.00 2.00
Margin block of 6, P# only 90.00
Experimental bureau precancel, New Orleans 10.00
Experimental bureau precancel, Springfield, Mass. 10.00
Experimental bureau precancel, Augusta, Me. 25.00
a. Booklet pane of six, *Oct. 15, 1916* 7.50 *1.00*
463 A140 2c **carmine,** type I, *Sept. 25, 1916* 3.25 10
dark carmine 3.25 10
rose red 3.25 10
On cover 15
Block of four 14.00 1.25
Margin block of 6, P# only 80.00
Experimental bureau precancel, New Orleans *500.00*
Experimental bureau precancel, Springfield, Mass. 20.00
a. Booklet pane of six, *Oct. 8, 1916* 70.00 *20.00*
Double transfer 5.75 75
464 A140 3c **violet,** type I, *Nov. 11, 1916* 47.50 8.00
deep violet 47.50 8.00
On cover 35.00
Block of four 195.00 60.00
Margin block of 6, P# only 800.00
Double transfer in "CENTS" 65.00 —
Experimental bureau precancel, New Orleans *1,000.*
Experimental bureau precancel, Springfield, Mass. 200.00
465 A140 4c **orange brown,** *Oct. 7, 1916* 27.50 1.00
deep brown 27.50 1.00
brown 27.50 1.00
On cover 10.00
Block of four 115.00 15.00
Margin block of 6, P# only 365.00
Double transfer — —
Experimental bureau precancel, Springfield, Mass. 150.00
466 A140 5c **blue,** *Oct. 17, 1916* 47.50 1.00
dark blue 47.50 1.00
On cover 12.50
Block of four 195.00 12.00
Margin block of 6, P# only 535.00
Experimental bureau precancel, Springfield, Mass. 150.00
467 A140 5c **carmine** (error in plate of 2c) 475.00 500.00
On cover *2,000.*
Block of 9, middle stamp the error 650.00 850.00
Block of 12, two middle stamps errors 1,100. 1,500.
Margin block of six 2c stamps (#463), P#7942 85.00

No. 467 is an error caused by using a 5c transfer roll in reentering three subjects: 7942 U. L. 74, 7942 U. L. 84, 7942 L. R. 18; the balance of the subjects on the plate being normal 2c entries. No. 467 imperf. is listed as No. 485.

468 A140 6c **red orange,** *Oct. 10, 1916* 60.00 5.00
On cover 35.00
Block of four 245.00 40.00
Margin block of 6, P# only 725.00
Double transfer — —
Experimental bureau precancel, New Orleans *2,000.*
Experimental bureau precancel, Springfield, Mass. 175.00
469 A140 7c **black,** *Oct. 10, 1916* 77.50 7.50
gray black 77.50 7.50
On cover 40.00
Block of four 315.00 70.00
Margin block of 6, P# only 850.00
Experimental bureau precancel, Springfield, Mass. 175.00
470 A148 8c **olive green,** *Nov. 13, 1916* 35.00 3.75
dark olive green 35.00 3.75
On cover 25.00
Block of four 145.00 35.00
Margin block of 6, Impt. & P# & "A" 335.00
Margin block of 6, "A" & P# 370.00
Experimental bureau precancel, Springfield, Mass. 165.00
471 A148 9c **salmon red,** *Nov. 16, 1916* 37.50 9.50
On cover 35.00
Block of four 155.00 65.00
Margin block of 6, P# only 425.00
Experimental bureau precancel, Springfield, Mass. 150.00
472 A148 10c **orange yellow,** *Oct. 17, 1916* 70.00 75
On cover 7.50
Block of four 300.00 7.50
Margin block of 6, P# only 800.00
Experimental bureau precancel, Springfield, Mass. 160.00
473 A148 11c **dark green,** *Nov. 16, 1916* 20.00 11.00
On cover 40.00
Block of four 85.00 85.00
Margin block of 6, P# only 200.00
Experimental bureau precancel, Springfield, Mass. *650.00*
474 A148 12c **claret brown,** *Oct. 10, 1916* 32.50 3.50
On cover 20.00
Block of four 135.00 25.00
Margin block of 6, P# only 365.00
Double transfer 40.00 5.25
Triple transfer 52.50 8.50
Experimental bureau precancel, Springfield, Mass. 200.00
475 A148 15c **gray,** *Nov. 16, 1916* 110.00 7.00
dark gray 110.00 7.00
On cover 80.00
Block of four 450.00 75.00
Margin block of 6, P# only 1,600.
Margin block of 6, Impt. & P# & "A" —
Experimental bureau precancel, Springfield, Mass. 150.00
476 A148 20c **light ultramarine,** *Dec. 5, 1916* 160.00 7.50
ultramarine 160.00 7.50
On cover 250.00
Block of four 650.00 75.00
Margin block of 6, P# only 2,250.
Experimental bureau precancel, Springfield, Mass. 125.00
476A A148 30c **orange red** — —

Block of four —
Margin block of 6, P# only —
477 A148 50c **light violet,** *Mar. 2, 1917* 900.00 40.00
On cover *2,250.*
Block of four 3,700. 375.00
Margin block of 6, P# only *40,000.*
478 A148 $1 **violet black,** *Dec. 22, 1916* 600.00 11.00
On cover *3,000.*
Block of four 2,500. 110.00
Margin block of 4, arrow, R or L 2,650.
Margin block of 6, Impt. & P# & "A" *13,000.*
Double transfer (5782 L. 66) 675.00 15.00

TYPES OF 1902-03 ISSUE

1917 **Unwmk.** ***Perf. 10***
479 A127 $2 **dark blue,** *Mar. 22, 1917* 325.00 30.00
On cover (other than first flight) *1,250.*
On flight cover *350.00*
On Zeppelin flight cover *750.00*
Block of four 1,300. 200.00
Margin block of 4, arrow, R or L 1,400.
Margin block of 6, P# only 4,000.
Double transfer —
480 A128 $5 **light green,** *Mar. 22, 1917* 250.00 32.50
On cover *1,250.*
Block of four 1,000. 210.00
Margin block of 4, arrow, R or L 1,100.
Margin block of 6, P# only 2,800.

1916-17 ***Imperf.***
481 A140 1c **green,** *Nov. 1916* 65 45
bluish green 65 45
deep green 65 45
On cover 1.25
Block of four 2.60 2.00
Corner margin block of four 2.80
Margin block of 4, arrow 3.00 2.50
Center line block 6.50
Margin block of 6, P# only 9.75
Margin block of 6, Electrolytic (Pl. 13376-13377) 250.00
Double transfer 2.50 1.25

During September, 1921, the Bureau of Engraving and Printing issued a 1c stamp printed from experimental electrolytic plates made in accordance with patent granted to George U. Rose. Tests at that time did not prove satisfactory and the method was discontinued. Four plates were made, viz., 13376, 13377, 13389 and 13390 from which stamps were issued. They are difficult to distinguish from the normal varieties. (See No. 498).

TYPE Ia

TWO CENTS.
Type Ia. The design characteristics are similar to type I except that all of the lines of the design are stronger.
The toga button, toga rope and rope and rope shading lines are heavy.
The latter characteristics are those of type II, which, however, occur only on impressions from rotary plates.
Used only on flat plates 10208 and 10209.

482 A140 2c **carmine,** type I, *Dec. 8, 1916* 1.00 1.00
deep carmine 1.00 1.00
carmine rose 1.00 1.00
deep rose 1.00 1.00
On cover 2.25
Block of four 4.00 4.00
Corner margin block of four 4.25 4.25
Margin block of 4, arrow 4.50 4.50
Center line block 6.50
Margin block of 6, P# only 20.00
Cracked plate — —
482A A140 2c **deep rose,** type Ia *6,000.*
On cover *12,500.*
Pair *70,000.*

The imperforate, type Ia, was issued but all known copies were privately perforated with large oblong perforations at the sides. (Schermack type III)
Earliest known use: Feb. 27, 1920.

The Demand, as well as supply, determines a stamp's market value. One is as important as the other.

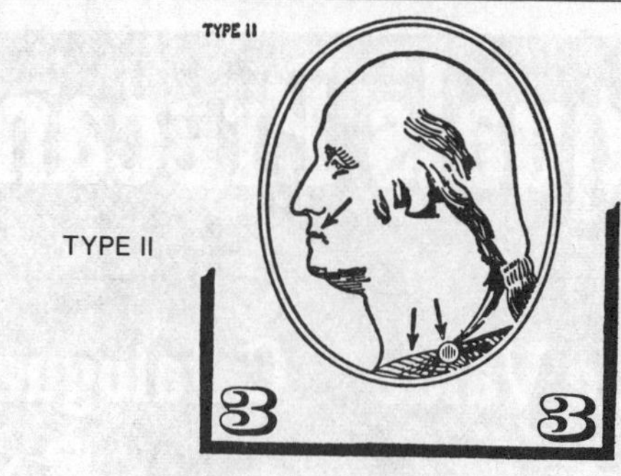

THREE CENTS.
Type II. The top line of the toga rope is strong and the rope shading lines are heavy and complete.
The line between the lips is heavy.
Used on both flat plate and rotary press printings.

483 A140 3c **violet,** type I, *Oct. 13, 1917* 9.50 6.50
light violet, type I 9.50 6.50
On cover, type I 15.00
Block of four, type I 38.00 24.50
Corner margin block of four, type I 40.00
Margin block of 4, arrow, type I 42.50
Center line block, type I 57.50
Margin block of 6, P# only, type I 110.00
Double transfer, type I 16.00 —
Triple transfer, type I —
484 A140 3c **violet,** type II 7.00 3.00
deep violet, type II 7.00 3.00
On cover, type II 10.00
Block of four, type II 28.00 13.50
Corner margin block of four, type I 29.00
Margin block of 4, arrow, type II 29.00
Center line block, type II 42.50
Margin block of 6, P# only, type II 87.50
Double transfer, type II 12.50 5.50
485 A140 5c **carmine** (error), *Mar. 1917* *13,000.*
Block of 9, middle stamp the error *15,000.*
Block of 12, two middle stamps errors *28,500.*
Margin block of six 2c stamps (#482), P#7942 200.00

(See note under No. 467.)

ROTARY PRESS COIL STAMPS

(See note over No. 448)

1916-19 ***Perf. 10 Horizontally***
Stamp designs 18 1/2-19mm wide by 22 1/2mm high
486 A140 1c **green,** *Jan. 1918* 60 20
yellowish green 60 20
On cover 35
Pair 1.30 45
Joint line pair 3.00 75
Cracked plate — —
Double transfer 2.25 1.50
487 A140 2c **carmine,** type II, *Nov. 15, 1916* 10.00 2.50
On cover, type II 10.00
Pair, type II 21.00 6.00
Joint line pair, type II 80.00 20.00
Cracked plate —

(See note after No. 455)

488 A140 2c **carmine,** type III, *1919* 1.75 1.35
carmine rose, type III 1.75 1.35
On cover, type II 3.00
Pair, type III 3.75 3.00
Joint line pair, type III 12.00 8.00
Cracked plate, type III 12.00 7.50
489 A140 3c **violet,** type I, *Oct. 10, 1917* 3.75 1.00
dull violet 3.75 1.00
bluish violet 3.75 1.00
On cover 2.00
Pair 8.00 2.50
Joint line pair 22.50 7.00

1916-22 ***Perf. 10 Vertically***
Stamp designs 19 1/2-20mm wide by 22mm high
490 A140 1c **green,** *Nov. 17, 1916* 40 15
yellowish green 40 15
On cover 25
Pair 95 35
Joint line pair 2.50 75
Double transfer — —
Cracked plate (horizontal) 7.50 —
Cracked plate (vertical) retouched 9.00 —
Rosette crack 11.00 —
491 A140 2c **carmine,** type II, *Nov. 17, 1916* 1,450. 300.00
On cover, type II 450.00
Pair, type II 3,100. 700.00
Joint line pair, type II 7,000. *3,000.*

(See note after No. 455)

492 A140 2c **carmine,** type III 5.75 15
carmine rose, type III 5.75 15
On cover, type III 25
Pair, type III 12.00 40
Joint line pair, type III 35.00 2.00
Double transfer, type III — —
Cracked plate — —
493 A140 3c **violet,** type I, *July 23, 1917* 13.50 1.75
reddish violet, type I 13.50 1.75
On cover, type I 6.00
Pair, type I 28.50 4.50
Joint line pair, type I 90.00 25.00
494 A140 3c **violet,** type II, *Feb. 4, 1918* 7.50 90
dull violet, type II 7.50 90
gray violet, type II 7.50 90
On cover, type II 1.00
Pair, type II 16.00 1.40
Joint line pair, type II 50.00 2.00
495 A140 4c **orange brown,** *Apr. 15, 1917* 8.00 3.00
On cover 7.50
Pair 17.00 7.00
Joint line pair 55.00 13.50
Cracked plate 25.00 5.00
496 A140 5c **blue,** *Jan. 15, 1919* 2.75 90
On cover 1.50
Pair 6.00 2.00
Joint line pair 20.00 6.00
497 A148 10c **orange yellow,** *Jan. 31, 1922* 16.00 7.00
On cover 15.00
Pair 34.00 18.50
Joint line pair 100.00 37.50

FLAT PLATE PRINTINGS

Plates of 400 subjects in four panes of 100 each.

TYPES OF 1913-15 ISSUE

1917-19 **Unwmk.** ***Perf. 11***
498 A140 1c **green,** *Mar. 1917* 30 5
light green 30 5
dark green 30 5
yellowish green 30 5
On cover 10
Block of four 1.20 25
Margin block of 6, P# only 13.00
Margin block of 6, Electrolytic (Pl. 13376-7, 13389-90) *see note after No. 481* *450.00*
a. Vertical pair, imperf. horiz. 175.00
b. Horizontal pair, imperf. between 75.00
c. Vertical pair, imperf. between *450.00* —
d. Double impression 150.00
e. Booklet pane of six, *Apr. 6, 1917* 3.00 *35*
f. Booklet pane of thirty *550.00*
g. Perf. 10 at top or bottom *500.00* —
Cracked plate (10656 U. L. and 10645 L. R.) 7.50 —
Double transfer 5.50 2.00
499 A140 2c **rose,** type I, *Mar. 1917* 35 5
dark rose, type I 35 5
carmine rose, type I 35 5
deep rose, type I 45 5
On cover, type I 10
Block of four, type I 1.40 20
Margin block of 6, P# only, type I 14.00
a. Vertical pair, imperf. horiz., type I 150.00
b. Horiz. pair, imperf. vert., type I 150.00 *100.00*
c. Vert. pair, imperf. btwn., type I *500.00* *225.00*
e. Booklet pane of six, type I, *Mar. 31, 1917* 2.00 *50*
f. Booklet pane of thirty, type I *10,000.*
g. Double impression, type I 125.00 —
Double impression, type I, 15 mm. wide —
Cracked plate, type I — —
Recut in hair, type I — —
Double transfer, type I 6.00 —
500 A140 2c **deep rose,** type Ia 200.00 85.00
On cover, type Ia 300.00
Block of four, type Ia 850.00 550.00
Margin block of 6, P# only, type Ia 1,650.
Margin block of 6, P#, two stamps type I (P# 10208 L.L) *5,000.*
Pair, types I and Ia (10208 L. L. 95 or 96) *1,000.*
501 A140 3c **light violet,** type I, *Mar. 1917* 8.00 10
violet, type I 8.00 10
dark violet, type I 8.00 10
reddish violet, type I 8.00 10
On cover, type I 15
Block of four, type I 32.00 1.60
Margin block of 6, P# only, type I 80.00
b. Bklt. pane of 6, type I, *Oct. 17, 1917* 65.00 *15.00*
c. Vert. pair, imper. horiz., type I 300.00
d. Double impression 150.00
Double transfer, type I 12.00
502 A140 3c **dark violet,** type II 11.00 15
violet, type II 11.00 15
On cover, type II 40
Block of four, type II 44.00 1.75
Margin block of 6, P# only, type II 120.00
b. Bklt. pane of 6, type II, *Feb. 25, 1918* 50.00 *10.00*
c. Vert. pair, imperf. horiz., type II 250.00 125.00
d. Double impression 125.00
e. Perf. 10 at top or bottom *425.00* —
503 A140 4c **brown,** *Mar. 1917* 7.50 12
dark brown 7.50 12
orange brown 7.50 12
yellow brown 7.50 12
On cover 2.00
Block of four 30.00 85
Margin block of 6, P# only 110.00
b. Double impression —
Double transfer 15.00 1.00
504 A140 5c **blue,** *Mar. 1917* 6.50 8
light blue 6.50 8
dark blue 6.50 8
On cover 20

No.	Design	Denom.	Description	Unused	Used
			Block of four	26.00	75
			Margin block of 6, P# only	110.00	
a.			Horizontal pair, imperf. between	*1,250.*	—
			Double transfer	10.00	—
505	A140	5c	**rose** (error)	350.00	400.00
			On cover		1,500.
			Block of 9, middle stamp the error	500.00	500.00
			Block of 12, two middle stamps errors	850.00	
			Margin block of six 2c stamps (#499), P# 7942	22.50	

(See note under No. 467.)

No.	Design	Denom.	Description	Unused	Used
506	A140	6c	**red orange,** *Mar. 1917*	9.50	20
			orange	9.50	20
			On cover		2.50
			Block of four	38.00	1.35
			Margin block of 6, P# only	135.00	
a.			Perf. 10 at top or bottom	*500.00*	*250.00*
			Double transfer	—	—
507	A140	7c	**black,** *Mar. 1917*	20.00	85
			gray black	20.00	85
			intense black	20.00	85
			On cover		7.50
			Block of four	82.50	8.50
			Margin block of 6, P# only	200.00	
			Double transfer	—	—
508	A148	8c	**olive bister,** *Mar. 1917*	8.50	40
			dark olive green	8.50	40
			olive green	8.50	40
			On cover		2.50
			Block of four	35.00	4.00
			Margin block of 6, Impt. & P# & "A"	145.00	
			Margin block of 6, "A" & P#	175.00	
			Margin block of 6, P# only	130.00	
b.			Vertical pair, imperf. between	—	—
c.			Perf. 10 at top or bottom		*500.00*
509	A148	9c	**salmon red,** *Mar. 1917*	11.00	1.40
			salmon	11.00	1.40
			On cover		12.50
			Block of four	45.00	14.00
			Margin block of 6, P# only	125.00	
			Double transfer	20.00	4.50
a.			Perf. 10 at top or bottom	—	*300.00*
510	A148	10c	**orange yellow,** *Mar. 1917*	12.50	10
			golden yellow	12.50	10
			On cover		2.00
			Block of four	52.50	75
			Margin block of 6, "A" & P#	220.00	
			Margin block of 6, P# only	160.00	
511	A148	11c	**light green,** *May 1917*	6.75	2.00
			green	6.75	2.00
			dark green	7.50	2.00
			On cover		8.00
			Block of four	28.00	17.50
			Margin block of 6, P# only	115.00	
			Double transfer	12.50	3.00
a.			Perf. 10 at top or bottom	*650.00*	*275.00*
512	A148	12c	**claret brown,** *May 1917*	6.50	30
a.			brown carmine	7.00	35
			On cover		4.00
			Block of four	27.00	3.00
			Margin block of 6, P# only	105.00	
			Double transfer	12.50	2.00
			Triple transfer	20.00	3.50
b.			Perf. 10 at top or bottom	—	*300.00*
513	A148	13c	**apple green,** *Jan. 10, 1919*	8.00	4.75
			pale apple green	8.00	4.75
			deep apple green	9.75	5.25
			On cover		17.50
			Block of four	33.00	35.00
			Margin block of 6, P# only	115.00	
514	A148	15c	**gray,** *May 1917*	30.00	80
			dark gray	30.00	80
			On cover		25.00
			Block of four	125.00	10.00
			Margin block of 6, P# only	425.00	
			Double transfer	—	—
515	A148	20c	**light ultramarine,** *May 1917*	37.50	16
			deep ultramarine	39.00	16
			gray blue	37.50	16
			On cover		75.00
			Block of four	155.00	2.00
			Margin block of 6, P# only	475.00	
b.			Vertical pair, imperf. between	*325.00*	
c.			Double impression	*400.00*	
			Double transfer	—	—
d.			Perf. 10 at top or bottom	*1,200.*	—
516	A148	30c	**orange red,** *May 1917*	30.00	55
			dark orange red	30.00	55
			On cover		150.00
			Block of four	125.00	6.00
			Margin block of 6, P# only	475.00	
			Double transfer	—	
a.			Perf. 10 at top or bottom	*850.00*	—
517	A148	50c	**red violet,** *May 1917*	60.00	40
			violet	72.50	40
			light violet	75.00	50
			On cover		400.00
			Block of four	300.00	3.00
			Margin block of 6, P# only	1,500.	
b.			Vertical pair, imperf. between	*1,750.*	*750.00*
			Double transfer	100.00	1.50
c.			Perf. 10 at top or bottom		*700.00*
518	A148	$1	**violet brown,** *May 1917*	45.00	1.10
			violet black	45.00	1.10
b.			deep brown	*750.00*	*250.00*
			On cover		450.00
			Block of four	190.00	8.00
			Margin block of 4, arrow right or left	200.00	
			Margin block of 6, Impt. & P# & "A"	1,200.	
			Double transfer (5782 L. 66)	60.00	1.50

TYPE OF 1908-09 ISSUE

1917 **Wmk. 191** ***Perf. 11***

This is the result of an old stock of No. 344 which was returned to the Bureau in 1917 and perforated with the then current gauge 11.

No.	Design	Denom.	Description	Unused	Used
519	A139	2c	**carmine,** *Oct. 10, 1917*	200.00	*400.00*
			On cover		2,500.
			Block of four	825.00	—
			Margin block of 6, T V, Impt. & P#	2,000.	—

Franklin — A149

Plates of 100 subjects.

1918, Aug. **Unwmk.** ***Perf. 11***

No.	Design	Denom.	Description	Unused	Used
523	A149	$2	**orange red & black**	675.00	250.00
			red orange & black	675.00	250.00
			On cover		2,000.
			Block of four	2,750.	1,100.
			Margin block of 4, arrow	2,850.	
			Center line block	2,950.	1,200.
			Margin block of 8, two P# & arrow	*14,000.*	
524	A149	$5	**deep green & black**	275.00	20.00
			On cover		*1,500.*
			Block of four	1,150.	110.00
			Margin block of 4, arrow	1,200.	115.00
			Center line block	1,300.	125.00
			Margin block of 8, two P# & arrow	*4,500.*	

For other listing of design A149 see No. 547.

OFFSET PRINTING

Plates of 400, 800 or 1600 subjects in panes of 100 each, as follows:

No. 525-400 and 1600 subjects
No. 526-400, 800 and 1600 subjects
No. 529-400 subjects only
No. 531-400 subjects only
No. 532-400, 800 and 1600 subjects
No. 535-400 subjects only
No. 536-400 and 1600 subjects

TYPES OF 1917-19 ISSUE

1918-20 **Unwmk.** ***Perf. 11.***

No.	Design	Denom.	Description	Unused	Used
525	A140	1c	**gray green,** *Dec. 1918*	1.15	35
			emerald	2.00	85
			On cover		1.25
			Block of four	4.75	2.75
			Margin block of 6, P# only	15.00	
a.			1c dark green	1.35	75
c.			Horizontal pair, imperf. between	60.00	
d.			Double impression	15.00	15.00
			"Flat nose"	—	

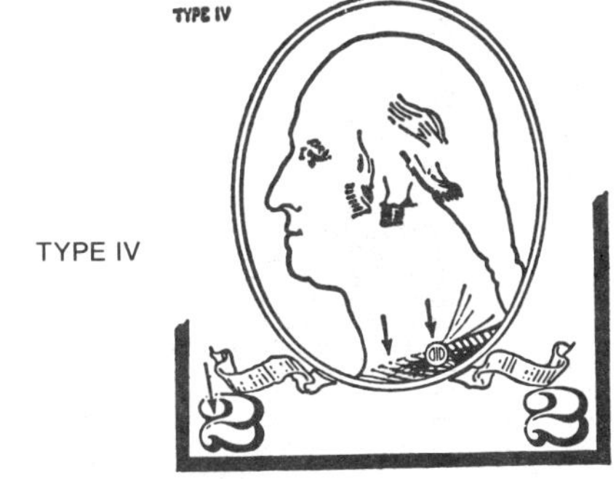

TYPE IV

TWO CENTS.
Type IV. Top line of the toga rope is broken.
The shading lines in the toga button are so arranged that the curving of the first and last form "D (reversed) ID".
The line of color in the left "2" is very thin and usually broken.
Used on offset printings only.

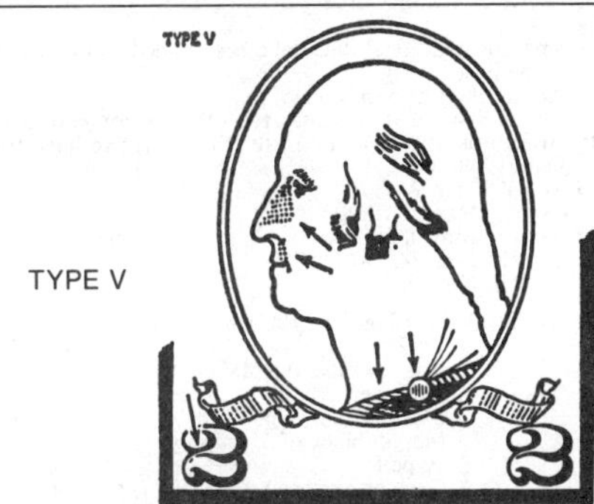

TYPE V

Type V. Top line of the toga is complete.
There are five vertical shading lines in the toga button.
The line of color in the left "2" is very thin and usually broken.
The shading dots on the nose are as shown on the diagram.
Used on offset printings only.

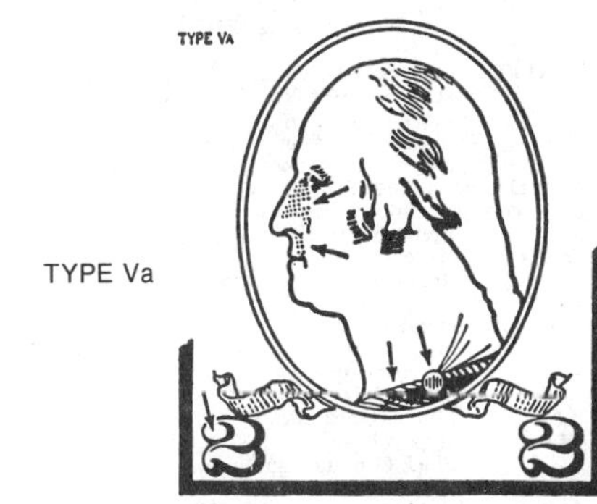

TYPE Va

Type Va. Characteristics are the same as type V except in the shading dots of the nose. The third row of dots from the bottom has four dots instead of six. The overall height is 1/3 mm. shorter than type V.
Used on offset printings only.

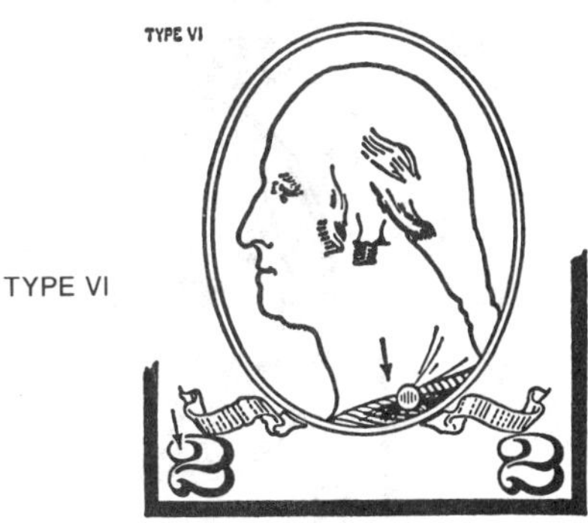

TYPE VI

Type VI. General characteristics the same as type V except that the line of color in the left "2" is very heavy.
Used on offset printings only.

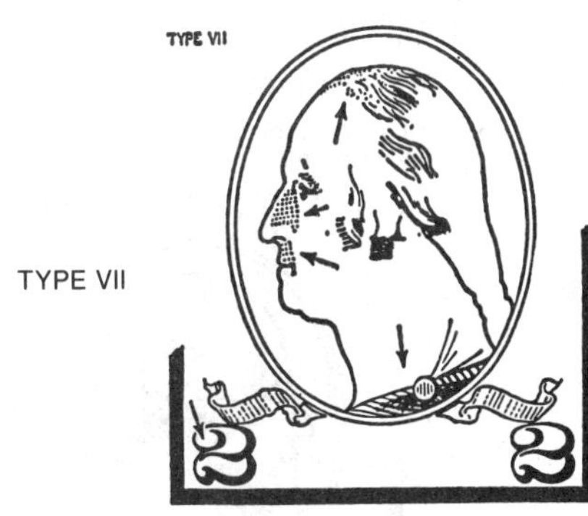

TYPE VII

Type VII. The line of color in the left "2" is invariably continuous, clearly defined and heavier than in type V or Va but not as heavy as type VI.
An additional vertical row of dots has been added to the upper lip.

Numerous additional dots have been added to the hair on top of the head.

Used on offset printings only.

Dates of issue of types after type IV are not known but official records show the first plate of each type to have been certified as follows:

Type IV, Mar. 6, 1920
Type V, Mar. 20, 1920
Type Va, May 4, 1920
Type VI, June 24, 1920
Type VII, Nov. 3, 1920

526 A140 2c **carmine,** type IV, *Mar. 15, 1920* 19.00 2.75
rose carmine, type IV 19.00 2.75
On cover, type IV 10.00
Block of four, type IV 77.50 18.00
Margin block of 6, P# only, type IV 160.00
Gash on forehead, type IV 26.00 4.50
Malformed "2" at left, type IV (10823 L. R. 93) 26.00 5.25

527 A140 2c **carmine,** type V 10.00 60
bright carmine, type V 10.00 60
rose carmine, type V 10.00 60
On cover 2.00
Block of four, type V 41.00 6.50
Block of 6, P# only, type V 85.00
a. Double impression, type V 45.00 10.00
b. Vert. pair, imperf. horiz., type V *600.00*
c. Horiz. pair, imperf. vert., type V —
Line through "2" & "EN", type V 18.50 4.50

528 A140 2c **carmine,** type Va 5.25 15
On cover, type Va 35
Block of four, type Va 21.00 2.00
Block of 6, P# only, type Va 42.50
Block of 6, monogram over P# 60.00
c. Double impression, type Va 25.00
g. Vert. pair, imperf. between —
Retouches in "P" of Postage type Va 8.00 —
Retouched on toga, type Va 16.50 —
Variety "CRNTS", type Va 14.50

528A A140 2c **carmine,** type VI 32.50 1.00
bright carmine, type VI 32.50 1.00
On cover, type VI 3.00
Block of four, type VI 130.00 5.00
Margin block of 6, P# only, type VI 235.00
Block of 6, monogram over P# 300.00
d. Double impression, type VI 100.00 —
f. Vert. pair, imperf. horiz., type VI —
h. Vert. pair, imperf. between —

528B A140 2c **carmine,** type VII 12.50 12
On cover, type VII 18
Block of four, type VII 52.50 1.10
Margin block of 6, P# only, type VII 100.00
e. Double impression, type VII 45.00
Retouched on cheek, type VII 22.50 —

TYPE III

THREE CENTS.

Type III. The top line of the toga rope is strong but the 5th shading line is missing as in type I.

Center shading line of the toga button consists of two dashes with a central dot.

The "P" and "O" of "POSTAGE" are separated by a line of color.

The frame line at the bottom of the vignette is complete.

Used on offset printings only.

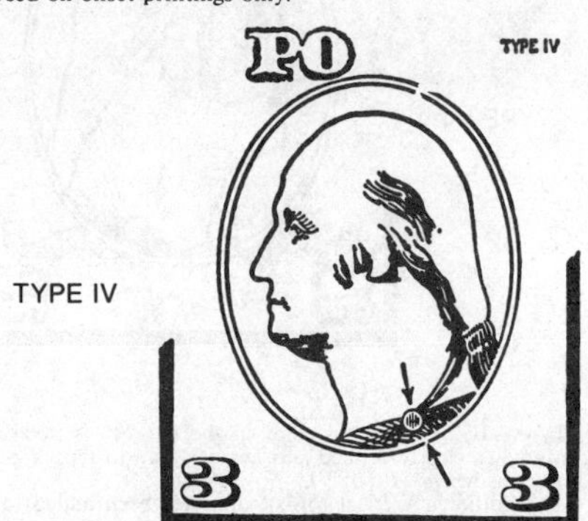

TYPE IV

Type IV. The shading lines of the toga rope are complete.

The second and fourth shading lines in the toga button are broken in the middle and the third line is continuous with a dot in the center.

The "P" and "O" of "POSTAGE" are joined.

The frame line at the bottom of the vignette is broken.

Used on offset printings only.

529 A140 3c **violet,** type III, *March 1918* 1.75 10
light violet, type III 1.75 10
dark violet, type III 1.75 10
On cover, type III 15
Block of four, type III 7.00 55
Margin block of 6, P# only, type III 40.00
a. Double impression, type III 20.00 —
b. Printed on both sides, type III *350.00*

530 A140 3c **purple,** type IV 50 6
light purple, type IV 50 6
deep purple, type IV 50 6
violet, type IV 50 10
On cover, type IV 10
Block of four, type IV 2.00 30
Margin block of 6, P# only, type IV 8.50
a. Double impression, type IV 12.50 6.00
b. Printed on both sides, type IV 150.00
"Blister" under "U.S.," type IV 2.00 —
Recut under "U.S.," type IV 2.00 —

Earliest known use, June 30, 1918.

1918-20 ***Imperf.***

Dates of issue of 2c types are not known, but official records show that the first plate of each type known to have been issued imperforate was certified as follows:

Type IV, Mar. 1920
Type V, May 4, 1920
Type Va, May 25, 1920
Type VI, July 26, 1920
Type VII, Dec. 2, 1920

531 A140 1c **green,** *Jan. 1919* 6.00 7.00
gray green 6.00 7.00
On cover 12.50
Block of four 24.00 30.00
Corner margin block of four 25.00
Margin block of 4, arrow 25.00 31.00
Center line block 45.00
Margin block of 6, P# only 60.00

532 A140 2c **carmine rose,** type IV 30.00 22.50
On cover, type IV 35.00
Block of four, type IV 120.00 95.00
Corner margin block of four, type IV 125.00
Margin block of 4, arrow, type IV 125.00
Center line block, type IV 145.00
Margin block of 6, P# only, type IV 225.00

533 A140 2c **carmine,** type V 150.00 55.00
On cover, type V 95.00
Block of four, type V 600.00 230.00
Corner margin block of 4, type V 650.00
Margin block of 4, arrow, type V 650.00
Center line block, type V 750.00 300.00
Margin block of 6, P# only, type V 1,300.

534 A140 2c **carmine,** type Va 8.50 6.00
carmine rose, type Va 8.50 6.00
On cover, type Va 13.50
Block of four, type Va 34.00 27.50
Corner margin block of four, type Va 35.00
Margin block of 4, arrow, type Va 35.00
Center line block, type Va 45.00
Margin block of 6, P# only, type Va 75.00
Block of 6, monogram over P# 150.00

534A A140 2c **carmine,** type VI 27.50 17.50
On cover, type VI 35.00
Block of four, type VI 110.00 80.00
Corner block of four, type VI 115.00
Block of 4, arrow, type VI 115.00
Center line block, type VI 135.00
Block of 6, P# only, type VI 250.00

534B A140 2c **carmine,** type VII 1,250. 425.00
On cover, type VII *1,000.*
Block of four, type VII 5,100. 1,800.
Corner margin block of four, type VII 5,150.
Margin block of 4, arrow, type VII 5,200.
Center line block, type VII 5,800.
Margin block of 6, P# only, type VII *10,000.*

Copies of the 2c type VII with Schermack III vending machine perforations, have been cut down at sides to simulate the rarer No. 534B imperforate.

535 A140 3c **violet,** type IV, *1918* 6.00 4.50
On cover 10.00
Block of four 24.00 27.50
Corner margin block of four 25.00
Margin block of 4, arrow 25.00
Center line block 30.00
Margin block of 6, P# only 50.00
a. Double impression 80.00 —

CANCELLATIONS.

Haiti —

1919 ***Perf. 12½***

536 A140 1c **gray green,** *Aug. 1919* 9.00 11.00
On cover 50.00
Block of four 37.50 50.00
Margin block of 6, P# only 120.00
a. Horiz. pair, imperf. vert. *500.00*

VICTORY ISSUE

Victory of the Allies in World War I

"Victory" and Flags of Allies — A150

Designed by Charles A. Huston

FLAT PLATE PRINTING

Plates of 400 subjects in four panes of 100 each

1919, Mar. 3 **Unwmk.** ***Perf. 11***

537 A150 3c **violet** 6.25 2.75
On cover 5.00
Block of four 25.00 11.00
Margin block of 6, P# only 85.00
a. deep red violet 250.00 30.00
On cover 150.00
Block of four 1,000. 135.00
Margin block of 6, P# only *2,250.*
b. light reddish violet 6.25 2.75
c. red violet 30.00 7.50
Double transfer — —

REGULAR ISSUE

ROTARY PRESS PRINTINGS

(See note over No. 448)

1919 **Unwmk.** ***Perf. 11x10***

Issued in sheets of 170 stamps (coil waste)

Stamp designs 19½-20mm wide by 22-22¼mm high

538 A140 1c **green,** *June 1919* 6.50 6.00
yellowish green 6.500 6.00
bluish green 6.50 6.00
On cover 20.00
Block of four 27.00 37.50
Margin block of 4, P# & "S 30" 65.00
Margin block of 4, P# only 72.50
Margin block of 4, star & P# 90.00
a. Vert. pair, imperf. horiz. 50.00 100.00
a. Margin block of 4, P# only 750.00
Double transfer 15.00 7.00

539 A140 2c **carmine rose,** type II 2,500. 750.00
On cover, type II —
Block of four, type II 10,100.
Margin block of 4, type II, P# & "S 20" *15,000.*

(See note after No. 455)

540 A140 2c **carmine rose,** type III, *June 14* 7.00 6.00
carmine 7.00 6.00
On cover, type III 22.50
Block of four, type III 28.00 37.50
Margin block of 4, type III, P# & "S 30" 70.00
Margin block of 4, type III, P# & "S 30" inverted 400.00
Margin block of 4, type III, P# only 75.00
Margin block of 4, type III, star & P# 95.00
a. Vert. pair, imperf. horiz., type III 50.00 100.00
a. Margin block of 4, type III P# only 500.00
a. Margin block of 4, type III, Star & P# 550.00
b. Horiz. pair, imperf. vert., type III *550.00*
Double transfer, type III 20.00 20.00

541 A140 3c **violet,** type II, *June 1919* 22.50 20.00
gray violet, type II 22.50 20.00
On cover 90.00
Block of four 92.50 145.00
Margin block of 4, P# only 265.00

1920, May 26 ***Perf. 10x11***

Plates of 400 subjects in four panes of 100 each.

Stamp design 19mm. wide by 22½ to 22¾mm. high.

542 A140 1c **green** 6.50 65
bluish green 6.50 65
On cover 5.00
Block of four 26.00 6.00
Vertical margin block of 6, P# opposite center horizontal row 100.00

1921, May ***Perf. 10***

Plates of 400 subjects in four panes of 100 each

Stamp design 19mm wide by 22½mm high

543 A140 1c **green** 35 6
deep green 35 6
On cover 10

	Block of four	1.40	25
	Vertical margin block of 6, P# opposite center horizontal row	26.00	
	Corner margin block of 4, P# only	11.50	
a.	Horizontal pair, imperf. between	*550.00*	
	Double transfer		—
	Triple transfer	—	—

1923 *Perf. 11*

Stamp design 19mm wide by 22½mm high

544 A140 1c	**green**	*7,500.*	*2,400.*
	On cover		*3,000.*

1921, May

Issued in sheets of 170 stamps (coil waste)

Stamp designs 19½-20mm wide by 22mm high

545 A140 1c	**green**	95.00	110.00
	yellowish green	95.00	110.00
	On cover		*2,000.*
	Block of four	390.00	550.00
	Margin block of 4, P# & "S 30"	700.00	
	Margin block of 4, P# only	750.00	
	Margin block of 4, star & P#	800.00	
546 A140 2c	**carmine rose,** type III	60.00	45.00
	deep carmine rose	60.00	45.00
	On cover		500.00
	Block of four	250.00	300.00
	Margin block of 4, P# & "S 30"	500.00	
	Margin block of 4, P# only	525.00	
	Margin block of 4, star & P#	550.00	
a.	Perf. 10 on left side	*350.00*	
	Recut in hair	85.00	60.00

FLAT PLATE PRINTING

Plates of 100 subjects

1920, Nov. 1 *Perf. 11*

547 A149 $2	**carmine & black**	225.00	25.00
	lake & black	225.00	25.00
	On cover (commercial)		1,000.
	On flown cover (philatelic)		250.00
	Block of four	925.00	125.00
	Margin block of 4, arrow	950.00	
	Center line block	1,150.	—
	Margin block of 8, two P#, & arrow	4,000.	

PILGRIM TERCENTENARY ISSUE

Issued to commemorate the tercentenary of the Landing of the Pilgrims at Plymouth, Mass.

The "Mayflower" A151

Landing of the Pilgrims A152

Signing of the Compact A153

Designed by Charles A. Huston

Plates of 280 subjects in four panes of 70 each

1920, Dec. 21 **Unwmk.** *Perf. 11*

548 A151 1c	**green**	3.25	1.65
	dark green	3.25	1.65
	On cover		3.00
	Block of four	13.00	10.00
	Margin block of 6, P# only	40.00	
	Double transfer	—	—

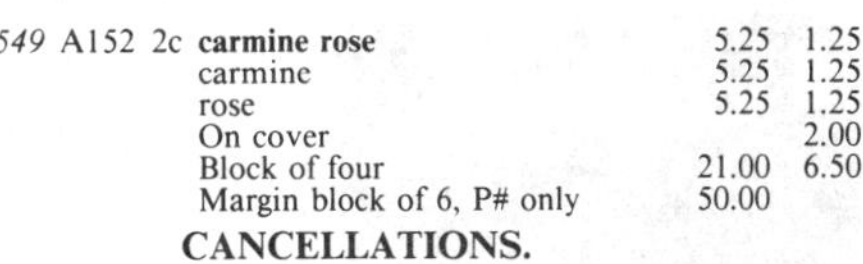

549 A152 2c	**carmine rose**	5.25	1.25
	carmine	5.25	1.25
	rose	5.25	1.25
	On cover		2.00
	Block of four	21.00	6.50
	Margin block of 6, P# only	50.00	

CANCELLATIONS.

| China — |

550 A153 5c	**deep blue**	32.50	10.00
	dark blue	32.50	10.00
	On cover		20.00
	Block of four	130.00	50.00
	Margin block of 6, P# only	400.00	

REGULAR ISSUE

Nathan Hale — A154

Franklin — A155

Warren G. Harding — A156

Washington — A157

Lincoln — A158

Martha Washington — A159

Theodore Roosevelt — A160

Garfield — A161

McKinley — A162

Grant — A163

Jefferson — A164

Monroe — A165

Hayes — A166

Cleveland — A167

American Indian — A168

Statue of Liberty — A169

Golden Gate — A170

Niagara Falls — A171

Buffalo — A172

Arlington Amphitheater A173

Lincoln Memorial — A174

United States Capitol — A175

Head of Freedom Statue, Capitol Dome — A176

Plates of 400 subjects in four panes of 100 each for all values 1c to 50c inclusive.

Plates of 200 subjects for $1 and $2. The sheets were cut along the horizontal guide line into two panes, upper and lower, of 100 subjects each.

Plates of 100 subjects for the $5 denomination, and sheets of 100 subjects were issued intact.

The Bureau of Engraving and Printing in 1925 in experimenting to overcome the loss due to uneven perforations, produced what is known as the "Star Plate". The vertical rows of designs on these plates are spaced 3 mm. apart in place of 2¾ mm. as on the regular plates. These plates were identified with a star added to the plate number.

Designed by Charles Aubrey Huston

FLAT PLATE PRINTINGS

1922-25 **Unwmk.** ***Perf. 11***

No.	Type	Denom.	Description	Unused	Used
551	A154	½c	**olive brown,** *Apr. 4, 1925*	9	8
			pale olive brown	9	8
			deep olive brown	9	8
			Block of four	36	40
			Margin block of 6, P# only	4.25	
			"Cap" on fraction bar (Pl. 17041)	45	15
552	A155	1c	**deep green,** *Jan. 17, 1923*	1.10	5
			green	1.10	5
			pale green	1.10	5
			Block of four	4.40	35
			Margin block of 6, P# only	17.50	
a.			Booklet pane of six, *Aug. 11, 1923*	4.50	*50*
			Double transfer	3.50	—
553	A156	1½c	**yellow brown,** *Mar. 19, 1925*	1.90	15
			pale yellow brown	1.90	15
			brown	1.90	15
			Block of four	7.60	1.00
			Margin block of 6, P# only	25.00	2.25
			Double transfer	—	—
554	A157	2c	**carmine,** *Jan. 15, 1923*	1.00	5
			light carmine	1.00	5
			Block of four	4.00	20
			Margin block of 6, P# only	17.50	
			Margin block of 6, P# & small 5 point star, top only	350.00	
			Margin block of 6, P# & large 5 point star, side only	57.50	
			Same, large 5-pt. star, top	425.00	
			Same, large 6-pt. star, top	575.00	
			Same, large 6-pt. star, side only (Pl. 17196)	700.00	
a.			Horiz. pair, imperf. vert	175.00	
b.			Vert. pair, imperf. horiz.	*500.00*	
c.			Booklet pane of six, *Feb. 10, 1923*	6.00	*1.00*
			Double transfer	2.25	60
d.			Perf. 10 at top or bottom		—
555	A158	3c	**violet,** *Feb. 12, 1923*	12.50	85
			deep violet	12.50	85
			dark violet	12.50	85
			red violet	12.50	85
			bright violet	12.50	85
			Block of four	50.00	5.25
			Margin block of 6, P# only	125.00	
556	A159	4c	**yellow brown,** *Jan. 15, 1923*	12.50	20
			brown	12.50	20
			Block of four	50.00	1.35
			Margin block of 6, P# only	125.00	
a.			Vert. pair, imperf. horiz.	—	
b.			Perf. 10 at top or bottom	*425.00*	—
			Double transfer	—	—
557	A160	5c	**dark blue,** *Oct. 27, 1922*	12.50	8
			deep blue	12.50	8
			Block of four	50.00	75
			Margin block of 6, P# only	150.00	
a.			Imperf., pair	*700.00*	
b.			Horiz. pair, imperf. vert.	—	
c.			Perf. 10 at top or bottom	—	*375.00*
			Double transfer (15571 U.L. 86)	—	
558	A161	6c	**red orange,** *Nov. 20, 1922*	24.00	75
			pale red orange	24.00	75
			Block of four	96.00	4.25
			Margin block of 6, P# only	325.00	
			Double transfer (Plate 14169 L. R. 60 and 70)	40.00	2.00
			Same, recut	40.00	2.00
559	A162	7c	**black,** *May 1, 1923*	5.75	45
			gray black	5.75	45
			Block of four	23.00	3.00
			Margin block of 6, P# only	50.00	
			Double transfer	—	—
560	A163	8c	**olive green,** *May 1, 1923*	35.00	35
			pale olive green	35.00	35
			Block of four	140.00	3.25
			Margin block of 6, P# only	400.00	
			Margin block of 6, P# & large 5 point star, side only	—	
			Double transfer	—	—
561	A164	9c	**rose,** *Jan. 15, 1923*	10.00	90
			pale rose	10.00	90
			Block of four	40.00	6.00
			Margin block of 6, P# only	115.00	
			Double transfer	—	—
562	A165	10c	**orange,** *Jan. 15, 1923*	14.00	10
			pale orange	14.00	10
			Block of four	56.00	50
			Margin block of 6, P# only	150.00	
a.			Vert. pair, imperf. horiz.	*500.00*	
b.			Imperf., pair	*650.00*	
c.			Perf. 10 at top or bottom		*600.00*
563	A166	11c	**light blue,** *Oct. 4, 1922*	1.10	25
			greenish blue	1.10	25
			light bluish green	1.10	25
			light yellow green	1.10	40
			Block of four	4.40	1.25
			Margin block of 6, P# only	22.50	
d.			Imperf., pair		—
564	A167	12c	**brown violet,** *Mar. 20, 1923*	4.50	8
			deep brown violet	4.50	8
			Block of four	18.00	80
			Margin block of 6, P# only	62.50	
			Margin block of 6, P# & large 5 point star, side only	100.00	
			Margin block of 6, P# & large 6 point star, side only	200.00	
a.			Horiz. pair, imperf. vert.	*650.00*	
b.			Imperf., pair	—	
			Double transfer, (14404 U.L. 73 & 74)	11.00	1.00
565	A168	14c	**blue,** *May 1, 1923*	3.25	65
			deep blue	3.25	65
			Block of four	13.00	3.75
			Margin block of 6, P# only	45.00	
			Double transfer	—	—

Horizontal pairs of No. 565 are known with spacings up to 3¾mm instead of 2mm between. These are from the 5th and 6th vertical rows of the upper right pane of Plate 14515 and also between stamps Nos. 3 and 4 of the same pane. A plate block of Pl. 14512 is known with 3mm spacing.

No.	Type	Denom.	Description	Unused	Used
566	A169	15c	**gray,** *Nov. 11, 1922*	17.50	6
			light gray	17.50	6

Block of four 70.00 40
Margin block of 6, P# only 225.00
Margin block of 6, P# & large 5 point star, side only 350.00
567 A170 20c **carmine rose,** *May 1, 1923* 17.50 6
deep carmine rose 17.50 6
Block of four 70.00 50
Margin block of 6, P# only 165.00
Margin block of 6, P# & large 5 point star, side only 400.00
a. Horiz. pair, imperf. vert. *750.00*
Double transfer (Pl. 18925) 37.50 1.50
568 A171 25c **yellow green,** *Nov. 11, 1922* 15.00 38
green 15.00 38
deep green 15.00 38
Block of four 60.00 2.25
Margin block of 6, P# only 175.00
b. Vert. pair, imperf. horiz. *850.00*
c. Perf. 10 at one side —
Double transfer — —
569 A172 30c **olive brown,** *Mar. 20, 1923* 27.50 30
Block of four 110.00 2.75
Margin block of 6, P# only 235.00
Double transfer (16065 U.R. 52) 37.50 1.50
570 A173 50c **lilac,** *Nov. 11, 1922* 50.00 12
dull lilac 50.00 12
Block of four 200.00 75
Margin block of 6, P# only 600.00
571 A174 $1 **violet black,** *Feb. 12, 1923* 37.50 35
violet brown 37.50 35
Block of four 150.00 2.00
Margin block of 4, arrow, top or bottom 160.00
Margin block of 6, P# only 425.00
Double transfers, Pl. 18642 L 30 and Pl. 18682 80.00 1.50
572 A175 $2 **deep blue,** *Mar. 20, 1923* 85.00 8.00
Block of four 340.00 45.00
Margin block of 4, arrow, top or bottom 350.00
Margin block of 6, P# only 1,000.
573 A176 $5 **carmine & blue,** *Mar. 20, 1923* 200.00 12.50
carmine lake & dark blue 200.00 12.50
Block of four 800.00 65.00
Margin block of 4, arrow 825.00
Center line block 875.00 *85.00*
Margin block of 8, two P# & arrow 3,250.

For other listings of perforated stamps of designs A154 to A176 see
Nos. 578 & 579, Perf. 11x10
Nos. 581 to 591, Perf. 10
Nos. 594 to 596, Perf. 11
Nos. 632 to 642, 653, 692 to 696, Perf. 11x10½
Nos. 697 to 701, Perf. 10½x11
This series also includes Nos. 622-623 (perf. 11).

1923-25 ***Imperf.***
575 A155 1c **green,** *Mar. 20, 1923* 6.00 2.75
deep green 6.00 2.75
Corner margin block of four 25.00
Margin block of 4, arrow 26.00
Center line block 30.00
Margin block of 6, P# only 70.00
576 A156 1½c **yellow brown,** *Apr. 4, 1925* 1.25 1.00
pale yellow brown 1.25 1.00
brown 1.25 1.00
Corner margin block of four 5.50
Margin block of 4, arrow 6.00
Center line block 10.00 *10.00*
Margin block of 6, P# only 17.00
Double transfer — —

The 1½c A156 Rotary press imperforate is listed as No. 631.

577 A157 2c **carmine** 1.40 1.25
light carmine 1.40 1.25
Block of four 5.60 5.25
Corner margin block of four 6.00
Margin block of 4, arrow 6.50
Center line block 11.00
Margin block of 6, P# only 25.00
Margin block of 6, P# & large 5 point star 60.00

ROTARY PRESS PRINTINGS
(See note over No. 448)
Issued in sheets of 70 or 100 stamps, coil waste
Stamp designs: 19¾x22¼mm

1923 ***Perf. 11x10***
578 A155 1c **green** 50.00 47.50
On cover 175.00
Margin block of 4, star & P# 450.00
579 A157 2c **carmine** 35.00 35.00
deep carmine 35.00 35.00
On cover 200.00
Margin block of 4, star & P# 275.00
Recut in eye, plate 14731 45.00 45.00

Plates of 400 subjects in four panes of 100 each
Stamp designs: 19x22½mm

1923-26 ***Perf. 10***
581 A155 1c **green,** *Apr. 21, 1923* 6.00 55
yellow green 6.00 55
pale green 6.00 55
Block of four 24.00 3.00
Margin block of 4, P# only 75.00
582 A156 1½c **brown,** *Mar. 19, 1925* 3.00 45
dark brown 3.00 45
Block of four 12.00 2.75
Margin block of 4, P# only 27.50
Pair with full horiz. gutter btwn. *135.00*
Pair with full vert. gutter btwn. *175.00*

No. 582 was available in full sheets of 400 subjects but was not regularly issued in that form.

583 A157 2c **carmine,** *Apr. 14, 1924* 1.40 5
deep carmine 1.40 5
Block of four 5.60 50
Margin block of 4, P# only 17.00
a. Booklet pane of six, *Aug. 27, 1926* 75.00 *25.00*
584 A158 3c **violet,** *Aug. 1, 1925* 17.50 1.75
Block of four 70.00 8.00
Margin block of 4, P# only 160.00
585 A159 4c **yellow brown,** *Mar. 1925* 11.00 40
deep yellow brown 11.00 40
Block of four 44.00 2.00
Margin block of 4, P# only 140.00
586 A160 5c **blue,** *Dec. 1924* 11.50 18
deep blue 11.50 18
Block of four 46.00 90
Margin block of 4, P# only 135.00
a. Horizontal pair, imperf. between — —
Double transfer — —
587 A161 6c **red orange,** *Mar. 1925* 4.50 25
pale red orange 4.50 25
Block of four 18.00 2.25
Margin block of 4, P# only 60.00
588 A162 7c **black,** *May 29, 1926* 7.00 4.25
Block of four 28.00 25.00
Margin block of 4, P# only 67.50
589 A163 8c **olive green,** *May 29, 1926* 17.50 2.75
pale olive green 17.50 2.75
Block of four 70.00 14.00
Margin block of 4, P# only 150.00
590 A164 9c **rose,** *May 29, 1926* 3.25 1.90
Block of four 13.00 11.00
Margin block of 4, P# only 30.00
591 A165 10c **orange,** *June 8, 1925* 45.00 15
Block of four 180.00 1.00
Margin block of 4, P# only 350.00

Bureau Precancels: 1c, 64 diff., 1½c, 76 diff., 2c, 58 diff., 3c, 41 diff., 4c, 36 diff., 5c, 38 diff., 6c, 36 diff., 7c, 18 diff., 8c, 18 diff., 9c, 13 diff., 10c, 39 diff.

Issued in sheets of 70 or 100 stamps, coil waste of Nos. 597, 599
Stamp designs approximately 19¾x22¼mm

1923 ***Perf. 11***
594 A155 1c **green** *10,000.* 3,500.
On cover *4,500.*
595 A157 2c **carmine** 150.00 225.00
deep carmine 150.00 225.00
On cover 450.00
Margin block of 4, star & P# 900.00
Recut in eye, plate 14731 —

Stamp design approximately 19¼x22¾mm
596 A155 1c **green** *15,000.*

Most copies of No. 596 carry the Bureau precancel "Kansas City, Mo."

COIL STAMPS, ROTARY PRESS

1923-29 ***Perf. 10 Vertically***
Stamp designs aproximately 19¾x22¼mm.
597 A155 1c **green,** *July 18, 1923* 20 6
yellow green 20 6
Pair 45 12
Joint line pair 1.65 25
Gripper cracks 2.25 1.00
Double transfer 2.25 1.00
598 A156 1½c **brown,** *Mar. 19, 1925* 40 10
deep brown 40 10
Pair 90 25
Joint line pair 2.85 50

TYPE I

TYPE II

TYPE I

TYPE II

TYPE I-No heavy hair lines at top center of head. Outline of left acanthus scroll generally faint at top and toward base at left side.

TYPE II-Three heavy hair lines at top center of head; two being outstanding in the white area. Outline of left acanthus scroll very strong and clearly defined at top (under left edge of lettered panel) and at lower curve (above and to left of numeral oval). This type appears only on Nos. 599A and 634A.

599 A157 2c **carmine,** type I, *Jan. 1923* 25 5
deep carmine, type I 25 5
Pair, type I 55 12
Joint line pair, type I 1.65 20
Double transfer, type I 1.65 1.00
Gripper cracks, type I 2.00 2.00
599A A157 2c **carmine,** type II, *Mar. 1929* 100.00 8.50
Pair, type II 210.00 20.00
Joint line pair, type II 550.00 60.00
Joint line pair, types I & II 625.00 120.00
600 A158 3c **violet,** *May 10, 1924* 4.25 8
deep violet 4.25 8
Pair 9.00 20
Joint line pair 18.50 85
Cracked plate —
601 A159 4c **yellow brown,** *Aug. 5, 1923* 2.50 30
brown 2.50 30
Pair 5.35 80
Joint line pair 17.50 2.00
602 A160 5c **dark blue,** *Mar. 5, 1924* 1.10 14
Pair 2.35 32
Joint line pair 7.250 60
603 A165 10c **orange,** *Dec. 1, 1924* 2.25 8
Pair 5.00 25
Joint line pair 17.50 1.00

The 6c design A161 coil stamp is listed as No. 723.

Bureau Precancels: 1c, 296 diff., 1½c, 188 diff., 2c, type I, 113 diff., 2c, type II, Boston, Detroit, 3c, 62 diff., 4c, 34 diff., 5c, 36 diff., 10c, 32 diff.

1923-25 ***Perf. 10 Horizontally***
Stamp designs 19¼-19½mm wide by 22-22½mm high
604 A155 1c **yellow green** 18 8
green, *July 19, 1924* 18 10
Pair 40 20
Joint line pair 2.15 35
605 A156 1½c **yellow brown,** *May 9, 1925* 18 15
brown 18 15
Pair 40 35
Joint line pair 1.65 50
606 A157 2c **carmine,** *Dec. 31, 1923* 18 12
Pair 40 25
Joint line pair 1.25 35
Cracked plate 4.50 2.00

HARDING MEMORIAL ISSUE.

Issued as a tribute to the memory of President Warren G. Harding, who died in San Francisco, Aug. 2, 1923.

Plates of 400 subjects in four panes of 100 each

Warren Gamaliel Harding — A177

FLAT PLATE PRINTINGS
Stamp designs 19¼mm wide by 22¼mm high

1923 ***Perf. 11***
610 A177 2c **black,** *Sept. 1, 1923* 45 10
intense black 45 10
grayish black 45 10
Margin block of 6, P# 18.00 —
a. Horiz. pair, imperf. vert. *800.00*
Double transfer 1.75 50

Imperf
611 A177 2c **black,** *Nov. 15, 1923* 6.50 4.25
Corner margin block of four 27.50 18.00
Margin block of 4, arrow 27.50 19.00
Center line block 55.00 40.00
Margin block of 6, P# 85.00 —

ROTARY PRESS PRINTINGS

Stamp designs 19¼mm wide by 22¾mm high

612 A177 2c	**black,** *Sept. 12, 1923*	11.00	1.50
	gray black	11.00	1.50
	Margin block of 4, P#	225.00	
	Pair with full vertical gutter between	*350.00*	

Perf. 11

613 A177 2c	**black**	*13,500.*	

No. 613 is valued in the grade of fine.

HUGUENOT-WALLOON TERCENTENARY ISSUE

300th anniversary of the settling of the Walloons, and in honor of the Huguenots.

Ship "Nieu Nederland" — A178

Walloons Landing at Fort Orange (Albany) — A179

Jan Ribault Monument at Mayport, Fla. — A180

Designed by Charles Aubrey Huston

FLAT PLATE PRINTINGS

Plates of 200 subjects in four panes of 50 each

1924, May 1 ***Perf. 11***

614 A178 1c	**dark green**	2.25	3.00
	green	2.25	3.00
	Margin block of 6, P#	30.00	—
	Double transfer	6.75	6.50
615 A179 2c	**carmine rose**	5.25	1.90
	dark carmine rose	5.25	1.90
	Margin block of 6, P#	60.00	—
	Double transfer	12.50	3.50
616 A180 5c	**dark blue**	26.00	11.00
	deep blue	26.00	11.00
	Margin block of 6, P#	300.00	—
	Added line at bottom of white circle around right numeral, so-called "broken circle" (15754 UR 2, 3, 4, 5)	45.00	14.00

LEXINGTON-CONCORD ISSUE

150th anniv. of the Battle of Lexington-Concord.

Washington at Cambridge — A181

"Birth of Liberty," by Henry Sandham — A182

The Minute Man, by Daniel Chester French — A183

Plates of 200 subjects in four panes of 50 each

1925, Apr. 4 ***Perf. 11***

617 A181 1c	**deep green**	2.50	2.25
	green	2.50	2.25
	Margin block of 6, P#	40.00	—
618 A182 2c	**carmine rose**	5.00	3.75
	pale carmine rose	5.00	3.75
	Margin block of 6, P#	67.50	—
619 A183 5c	**dark blue**	24.00	12.00
	blue	24.00	12.50
	Margin block of 6, P#	275.00	—
	Line over head (16807 L.L. 48)	50.00	18.50

NORSE-AMERICAN ISSUE

Arrival in New York, on Oct. 9, 1825, of the sloop "Restaurationen" with the first group of immigrants from Norway.

Sloop "Restaurationen" A184

Viking Ship — A185

Designed by Charles Aubrey Huston.

Plates of 100 subjects.

1925, May 18 ***Perf. 11***

620 A184 2c	**carmine & black**	3.50	2.75
	deep carmine & black	3.50	2.75
	Margin block of 4, arrow	17.00	
	Center line block	20.00	
	Margin block of 8, two P# & arrow	200.00	—
	Margin block of 8, carmine P# & arrow; black P# omitted	*2,750.*	—
621 A185 5c	**dark blue & black**	14.00	10.50
	Margin block of 4, arrow	57.50	
	Center line block	67.50	
	Margin block of 8, two P# & arrow	650.00	—

REGULAR ISSUE

Benjamin Harrison — A186

Woodrow Wilson — A187

Plates of 400 subjects in four panes of 100 each.

1925-26 ***Perf. 11***

622 A186 13c	**green,** *Jan. 11, 1926*	11.00	40
	light green	11.00	40
	Margin block of 6, P# only	150.00	—
	Margin block of 6, P# & large 5 point star	900.00	—
623 A187 17c	**black,** *Dec. 28, 1925*	15.00	20
	gray black	15.00	20
	Margin block of 6, P# only	165.00	—

SESQUICENTENNIAL EXPOSITION ISSUE

Issued in connection with the Sesquicentennial Exposition held at Philadelphia, Pa., from June 1 to Dec. 1, 1926, to commemorate the 150th anniversary of the Declaration of Independence.

Liberty Bell — A188

Designed by Charles Aubrey Huston.

Plates of 200 subjects in four panes of 50 each.

1926 ***Perf. 11***

627 A188 2c	**carmine rose,** *May 10, 1926*	2.25	35
	On cover, Expo. station canc.		3.50
	Margin block of 6, P#	35.00	—
	Double transfer	—	—

ERICSSON MEMORIAL ISSUE

Issued as a memorial to John Ericsson, builder of the "Monitor" and in connection with the unveiling of his statue by the Crown Prince of Sweden at Washington, D. C., May 29, 1926.

A little time given to the study of the arrangement of the Scott Catalogue can make it easier to use effectively.

Statue of John Ericsson — A189

Designed by Charles Aubrey Huston.

Plates of 200 subjects in four panes of 50 each.

1926 *Perf. 11*

628 A189 5c **gray lilac,** *May 29, 1926* 5.00 2.50
Margin block of 6, P# 75.00 —

BATTLE OF WHITE PLAINS ISSUE

Issued to commemorate the 150th anniversary of the Battle of White Plains, N. Y.

Alexander Hamilton's Battery — A190

Designed by Charles Aubrey Huston.

Plates of 400 subjects in four panes of 100 each.

1926 *Perf. 11*

629 A190 2c **carmine rose,** *Oct. 18, 1926* 1.50 1.25
Margin block of 6, P# 35.00 —
a. Vertical pair, imperf. between *1,250.*

INTERNATIONAL PHILATELIC EXHIBITION ISSUE
SOUVENIR SHEET

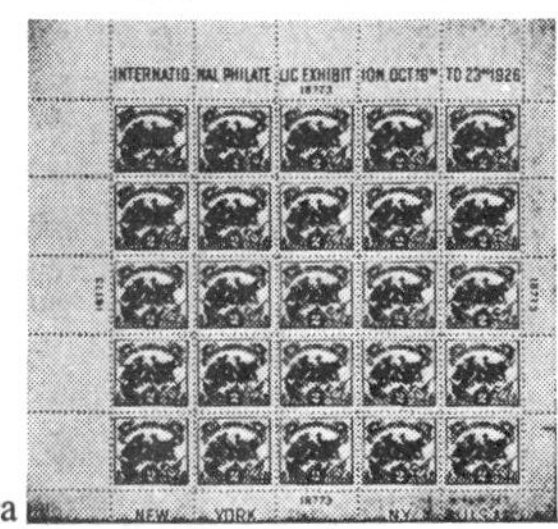

A190a

Plates of 100 subjects in four panes of 25 each, separated by one inch wide gutters with central guide lines.

1926, Oct. 18 *Perf. 11*

630 A190a 2c **carmine rose,** sheet of 25 350.00 300.00
Dot over first "S" of "States" 18774 LL9 or 18773 LL11, sheet 375.00 325.00

Issued in sheets measuring 158-160¼x136-146½mm containing 25 stamps with inscription "International Philatelic Exhibition, Oct. 16 to 23, 1926" in top margin.

REGULAR ISSUE
ROTARY PRESS PRINTINGS
(See note over No. 448.)

Plates of 400 subjects in four panes of 100 each
Stamp designs 18½-19mm wide by 22½mm high

1926 *Imperf.*

631 A156 1½c **yellow brown,** *Aug. 27, 1926* 1.40 1.40
light brown 1.40 1.40
Gutter block of four 6.25 6.25
Margin block with dash (left, right, top or bottom) 7.00 6.50
Center block with crossed gutters and dashes 15.00
Margin block of 4, P# 42.50 —
Without gum breaker ridges 2.00 —

1926-34 *Perf. 11x10½*

632 A155 1c **green,** *June 10, 1927* 12 5
yellow green 12 5
Margin block of 4, P# 1.65 —
a. Booklet pane of six, *Nov. 2, 1927* 4.50 *25*
b. Vertical pair, imperf. between 175.00 *100.00*
Pair with full vertical gutter btwn. 150.00 —
Cracked plate — —
633 A156 1½c **yellow brown,** *May 17, 1927* 1.25 8
deep brown 1.25 8
Block of four 5.00 75
Margin block of 4, P# 50.00 —
634 A157 2c **carmine,** type I, *Dec. 10, 1926* 10 5
Margin block of 4, type I, P# opposite corner stamp 1.00 —
Vertical margin block of 10, P# opposite third horizontal row from top or bottom (Experimental Electric Eye plates) 4.00 —
Margin block of 4, Electric Eye marking 45 25
Pair with full vertical gutter between 200.00
b. 2c carmine lake, type I 3.00 1.00
b. Margin block of 4, P# 30.00
c. Horizontal pair, type I, imperf. between *2,000.*
d. Booklet pane of six, type I, *Feb. 25, 1927* 1.75 *15*
Recut face, type I, 20234 LL58 —

No. 634, Type I, exists on a thin, tough experimental paper.

634A A157 2c **carmine,** type II, *Dec. 1928* 285.00 10.00
On cover 50.00
Margin block of 4, type II, P# 1,500. —
Pair with full horiz. gutter btwn. 1,000. —
Pair with full vert. gutter btwn. 1,000. —

No. 634A, Type II, was available in full sheet of 400 subjects but was not regularly issued in that form.

635 A158 3c **violet,** *Feb. 3, 1927* 35 5
Margin block of 4, P# 5.00 —
a. 3c bright violet, *Feb. 7, 1934* re-issue, Plates 21185 & 21186 25 5
a. Margin block of 4, P# 3.25 —
a. Gripper cracks 3.25 2.00
636 A159 4c **yellow brown,** *May 17, 1927* 1.75 8
Block of four 7.00 75
Margin block of 4, P# 60.00 —
Pair with full vert. gutter btwn. *200.00*
637 A160 5c **dark blue,** *Mar. 24, 1927* 1.65 5
Margin block of 4, P# 12.00 —
Pair with full vert. gutter btwn. *275.00*
Double transfer — —
638 A161 6c **red orange,** *July 27, 1927* 1.75 5
Margin block of 4, P# 12.00 —
Pair with full horiz. gutter btwn. —
Pair with full vert. gutter btwn. *200.00*
639 A162 7c **black,** *Mar. 24, 1927* 1.75 8
Margin block of 4, P# 21.00 —
a. Vertical pair, imperf. between 125.00 80.00
640 A163 8c **olive green,** *June 10, 1927* 1.75 5
olive bister 1.75 5
Margin block of 4, P# 12.00 —
641 A164 9c **orange red,** *1931* 1.75 5
salmon rose 1.75 5
rose, *May 17, 1927* 1.75 5
Margin block of 4, P# 12.00 —
Pair with full vert. gutter btwn. —
642 A165 10c **orange,** *Feb. 3, 1927* 2.75 5
Margin block of 4, P# 23.50 —
Double transfer — —

The 2c, 5c and 8c imperf. (dry print) are printer's waste. See No. 653.

Bureau Precancels: 1c, 292 diff., 1½c, 147 diff., 2c, type I, 99 diff., 2c, type II, 4 diff., 3c, 101 diff., 4c, 60 diff., 5c, 91 diff., 6c, 78 diff., 7c, 66 diff., 8c, 78 diff., 9c, 60 diff., 10c, 97 diff.

VERMONT SESQUICENTENNIAL ISSUE

Battle of Bennington, 150th anniv. and State independence.

Values for stamps vary greatly, depending upon centering, gum and condition.

Green Mountain Boy — A191

FLAT PLATE PRINTING

Plates of 400 subjects in four panes of 100 each.

1927 *Perf. 11*

643 A191 2c **carmine rose,** *Aug. 3, 1927* 1.00 75
Margin block of 6, P# 35.00 —

BURGOYNE CAMPAIGN ISSUE

Issued to commemorate the Battles of Bennington, Oriskany, Fort Stanwix and Saratoga.

Surrender of Gen. John Burgoyne — A192

Plates of 200 subjects in four panes of 50 each.

1927 *Perf. 11*

644 A192 2c **carmine rose,** *Aug. 3, 1927* 2.50 1.90
Margin block of 6, P# 35.00 —

VALLEY FORGE ISSUE

Issued to commemorate the 150th anniversary of Washington's encampment at Valley Forge, Pa.

Washington at Prayer — A193

Plates of 400 subjects in four panes of 100 each.

1928 *Perf. 11*

645 A193 2c **carmine rose,** *May 26, 1928* 70 35
Margin block of 6, P# 22.50 —

BATTLE OF MONMOUTH ISSUE

Issued to commemorate the 150th anniversary of the Battle of Monmouth, N.J., and a memorial to Molly Pitcher, the heroine of the battle.

No. 634 Overprinted **MOLLY PITCHER**

ROTARY PRESS PRINTING

1928 *Perf. 11x10½*

646 A157 2c **carmine,** *Oct. 20, 1928* 80 80
Margin block of 4, P# 25.00 —
Wide spacing, vert. pair 20.00 —

The normal space between a vertical pair of the overprints is 18mm, but pairs are known with the space measuring 28mm.

HAWAII SESQUICENTENNIAL ISSUE

Sesquicentennial Celebration of the discovery of the Hawaiian Islands.

Nos. 634 and 637 Overprinted **HAWAII 1778 - 1928**

ROTARY PRESS PRINTING

1928, Aug. 13				***Perf. 11x10½***	
647	A157	2c	**carmine**	3.00	3.25
			Margin block of 4, P#	90.00	—
			Wide spacing, vert. pair	75.00	
648	A160	5c	**dark blue**	10.00	10.00
			Margin block of 4, P#	225.00	—

Nos. 647-648 were sold at post offices in Hawaii and at the Postal Agency in Washington, D.C. They were valid throughout the nation.

Normally the overprints were placed 18mm apart vertically, but pairs exist with a space of 28mm between the overprints.

AERONAUTICS CONFERENCE ISSUE

Issued in commemoration of the International Civil Aeronautics Conference at Washington, D.C., Dec. 12 to 14, 1928, and of the twenty-fifth anniversary of the first airplane flight by the Wright Brothers, Dec. 17, 1903.

Wright Airplane — A194

Globe and Airplane — A195

FLAT PLATE PRINTING

Plates of 200 subjects in four panes of 50 each.

1928, Dec. 12				***Perf. 11***	
649	A194	2c	**carmine rose**	70	75
			Margin block of 6, P#	11.50	—
650	A195	5c	**blue**	4.50	3.00
			Margin block of 6, P#	50.00	—
			Plate flaw "prairie dog" (19658 L.L. 50)	27.50	12.50

GEORGE ROGERS CLARK ISSUE

Issued to commemorate the 150th anniversary of the surrender of Fort Sackville, the present site of Vincennes, Ind., to George Rogers Clark.

Surrender of Fort Sackville — A196

Plates of 100 subjects in two panes of 50 each.

1929				***Perf. 11***	
651	A196	2c	**carmine & black,** *Feb. 25, 1929*	45	35
			Margin block of 4, arrow (line only) right or left	1.90	
			Margin block of 6, two P# & "Top"	8.50	—
			Margin block of 10, red P# only	—	—
			Double transfer (19721 R. 14, 29 & 44)	4.00	2.00

REGULAR ISSUE

Type of 1922-26 Issue

ROTARY PRESS PRINTING

Plates of 400 subjects in four panes of 100 each.

1929				***Perf. 11x10½***	
653	A154	½c	**olive brown,** *May 25, 1929*	5	5
			Damaged plate, (19652 L.L. 72)	1.50	75
			Retouched plate, (19652 L.L. 72)	1.50	75
			Margin block of 4, P#	1.00	—
			Pair with full horiz. gutter btwn.	*150.00*	

Bureau Precancels: 99 diff.

ELECTRIC LIGHT'S GOLDEN JUBILEE ISSUE

Issued to commemorate the 50th anniversary of the invention of the first incandescent electric lamp by Thomas Alva Edison on October 21, 1879.

Edison's First Lamp — A197

Designed by Alvin R. Meissner.

FLAT PLATE PRINTING

Plates of 400 subjects in four panes of 100 each.

1929				***Perf. 11***	
654	A197	2c	**carmine rose,** *June 5, 1929*	50	50
			Margin block of 6, P#	25.00	—

ROTARY PRESS PRINTING

Perf. 11x10½

655	A197	2c	**carmine rose,** *June 11, 1929*	45	15
			Margin block of 4, P#	30.00	—

ROTARY PRESS COIL STAMP

656	A197	2c	**carmine rose,** *June 11, 1929*	9.50	1.25
			Pair	20.00	3.00
			Joint line pair	50.00	20.00

SULLIVAN EXPEDITION ISSUE

150th anniversary of the Sullivan Expedition in New York State during the Revolutionary War.

Major General John Sullivan — A198

PLAT PLATE PRINTING

Plates of 400 subjects in four panes of 100 each.

1929				***Perf. 11***	
657	A196	2c	**carmine rose,** *June 17, 1929*	60	50
			lake	30.00	—
			Margin block of 6, P#	24.00	—

REGULAR ISSUE

Nos. 632 to 642 Overprinted **Kans.**

Officially issued May 1, 1929.

Some values are known canceled as early as Apr. 15.

Special issue prepared by overprinting the abbreviations "Kans." and "Nebr." on stamps of the 1926-27 series. This special issue was authorized as a measure of preventing losses from post office burglaries. Approximately a year's supply was printed and issued to postmasters. The P.O. Dept. found it desirable to discontinue the State overprinted stamps after the initial supply was used.

ROTARY PRESS PRINTING

1929, May 1				***Perf. 11x10½***	
658	A155	1c	**green**	1.40	1.25
			Margin block of 4, P#	25.00	—
a.			Vertical pair, one without ovpt.	*300.00*	
			Wide spacing, pair	30.00	
659	A156	1½c	**brown**	1.90	1.75
			Margin block of 4, P#	35.00	—
a.			Vertical pair, one without ovpt.	*325.00*	
			Wide spacing, pair	65.00	
660	A157	2c	**carmine**	2.50	70
			Margin block of 4, P#	30.00	—
			Wide spacing, pair	50.00	
661	A158	3c	**violet**	11.00	9.00
			Margin block of 4, P#	115.00	—
a.			Vertical pair, one without ovpt.	*400.00*	
662	A159	4c	**yellow brown**	11.00	5.50
			Margin block of 4, P#	120.00	—
a.			Vertical pair, one without ovpt.	*400.00*	
663	A160	5c	**deep blue**	8.00	6.00
			Margin block of 4, P#	92.50	—
664	A161	6c	**red orange**	17.50	11.50
			Margin block of 4, P#	275.00	—
665	A162	7c	**black**	16.00	17.00
			Margin block of 4, P#	350.00	—
a.			Vertical pair, one without ovpt.	*400.00*	
666	A163	8c	**olive green**	55.00	45.00
			Margin block of 4, P#	525.00	—
667	A164	9c	**light rose**	8.00	7.00
			Margin block of 4, P#	110.00	—
668	A165	10c	**orange yellow**	14.00	7.50
			Margin block of 4, P#	200.00	—
			Pair with full horizontal gutter between		—

See notes following No. 679.

Overprinted **Nebr.**

May 1, 1929					
669	A155	1c	**green**	2.00	1.40
			Margin block of 4, P#	30.00	—
a.			Vertical pair, one without ovpt.	*275.00*	
			Wide spacing, pair	35.00	45.00
			No period after "Nebr." (19338, 19339 L.R. 26, 36)	—	
670	A156	1½c	**brown**	1.65	1.50
			Margin block of 4, P#	32.50	—
			Wide spacing, pair	32.50	
671	A157	2c	**carmine**	1.65	70
			Margin block of 4, P#	25.00	—
			Wide spacing, pair	50.00	
672	A158	3c	**violet**	7.00	6.50
			Margin block of 4, P#	87.50	—
a.			Vertical pair, one without ovpt.	*400.00*	
			Wide spacing, pair	75.00	
673	A159	4c	**yellow brown**	12.50	9.00
			Margin block of 4, P#	140.00	—
			Wide spacing, pair	110.00	
674	A160	5c	**deep blue**	10.00	9.00
			Margin block of 4, P#	150.00	—
675	A161	6c	**red orange**	24.00	14.00
			Margin block of 4, P#	300.00	—
676	A162	7c	**black**	13.00	11.00
			Margin block of 4, P#	180.00	—
677	A163	8c	**olive green**	17.00	15.00
			Margin block of 4, P#	275.00	—
			Wide spacing, pair	160.00	
678	A164	9c	**light rose**	22.50	17.00
			Margin block of 4, P#	350.00	—
a.			Vertical pair, one without ovpt.	*600.00*	
			Wide spacing, pair	150.00	
679	A165	10c	**orange yellow**	70.00	14.00
			Margin block of 4, P#	750.00	—

Nos. 658, 659, 660, 669, 670, 671, 672, 673, 677 and 678 are known with the overprints on vertical pairs spaced 32mm apart instead of the normal 22mm.

Important: Nos. 658-679 with original gum have either one horizontal gum breaker ridge per stamp or portions of two at the extreme top and bottom of the stamps, 21mm apart. Multiple complete gum breaker ridges indicate a fake overprint. Absence of the gum breaker ridge indicates either regumming or regumming and a fake overprint.

BATTLE OF FALLEN TIMBERS ISSUE

Issued as a memorial to Gen. Anthony Wayne and to commemorate the 135th anniversary of the Battle of Fallen Timbers, Ohio.

General Wayne Memorial — A199

FLAT PLATE PRINTING

Plates of 400 subjects in four panes of 100 each.

1929				***Perf. 11***	
680	A199	2c	**carmine rose,** *Sept. 14, 1929*	60	65
			deep carmine rose	60	65
			Margin block of 6, P#	21.00	—

OHIO RIVER CANALIZATION ISSUE

Issued to commemorate the completion of the Ohio River Canalization Project, between Cairo, Ill. and Pittsburgh, Pa.

Lock No. 5, Monongahela River — A200

Plates of 400 subjects in four panes of 100 each.

1929				***Perf. 11***	
681	A200	2c	**carmine rose,** *Oct. 19, 1929*	45	50
			Margin block of 6, P#	16.00	—

MASSACHUSETTS BAY COLONY ISSUE

Issued in commemoration of the 300th anniversary of the founding of the Massachusetts Bay Colony.

Massachusetts Bay Colony Seal — A201

Plates of 400 subjects in four panes of 100 each.

1930				***Perf. 11***	
682	A201	2c	**carmine rose,** *April 8, 1930*	40	38
			Margin block of 6, P#	20.00	—

CAROLINA-CHARLESTON ISSUE

Issued in commemoration of the 260th anniversary of the founding of the Province of Carolina and the 250th anniversary of the city of Charleston, S.C.

Gov. Joseph West and Chief Shadoo, a Kiawah — A202

Plates of 400 subjects in four panes of 100 each.

1930				***Perf. 11***	
683	A202	2c	**carmine rose,** *April 10, 1930*	85	85
			Margin block of 6, P#	35.00	—

The Scott Catalogue value is a retail price, what you could expect to pay for the stamp in a grade of Fine-Very Fine. The value listed is a reference which reflects recent actual dealer selling price.

REGULAR ISSUE

Harding — A203

Taft — A204

Type of 1922-26 Issue

ROTARY PRESS PRINTING

1930				***Perf. 11x10½***	
684	A203	1½c	**brown,** *Dec. 1, 1930*	18	5
			yellow brown	18	5
			Margin block of 4, P#	1.25	—
			Pair with full horiz. gutter btwn.	*175.00*	
			Pair with full vert. gutter btwn.	—	
685	A204	4c	**brown,** *June 4, 1930*	55	6
			deep brown	55	6
			Margin block of 4, P#	9.00	—
			Gouge on right "4" (20141 U.L. 24)	2.00	60
			Recut right "4" (20141 U.L. 24)	2.00	65
			Pair with full horiz. gutter btwn.	—	

Bureau Precancels: 1½c, 96 diff., 4c, 46 diff.

ROTARY PRESS COIL STAMPS

686	A203	1½c	**brown,** *Dec. 1, 1930*	1.25	7
			Pair	2.65	16
			Joint line pair	4.50	50
687	A204	4c	**brown,** *Sept. 18, 1930*	2.25	38
			Pair	4.75	85
			Joint line pair	8.50	1.75

Bureau Precancels: 1½c, 107 diff., 4c, 23 diff.

BRADDOCK'S FIELD ISSUE

Issued in commemoration of the 175th anniversary of the Battle of Braddock's Field, otherwise the Battle of Monongahela.

Statue of Colonel George Washington — A205

Designed by Alvin R. Meissner.

FLAT PLATE PRINTING

Plates of 400 subjects in four panes of 100 each.

1930				***Perf. 11***	
688	A205	2c	**carmine rose,** *July 9, 1930*	65	65
			Margin block of 6, P#	28.50	—

VON STEUBEN ISSUE

Issued in commemoration of the 200th anniversary of the birth of Baron Friedrich Wilhelm von Steuben (1730-1794) and his participation in the American Revolution.

General von Steuben — A206

FLAT PLATE PRINTING

Plates of 400 subjects in four panes of 100 each.

1930				***Perf. 11***	
689	A206	2c	**carmine rose,** *Sept. 17, 1930*	38	40
			Margin block of 6, P#	17.00	—
a.			Imperf., (pair)	*2,250.*	
a.			Margin block of 6, P#, imperf.	*10,000.*	

PULASKI ISSUE

Issued to commemorate the 150th anniversary (in 1929) of the death of Gen. Casimir Pulaski, Polish patriot and hero of the American Revolutionary War.

General Casimir Pulaski — A207

Plates of 400 subjects in four panes of 100 each.

1931				***Perf. 11***	
690	A207	2c	**carmine rose,** *Jan. 16, 1931*	16	10
			deep carmine rose	16	10
			Margin block of 6, P#	10.00	—

REGULAR ISSUE

TYPE OF 1922-26 ISSUES

ROTARY PRESS PRINTING

1931				***Perf. 11x10½***	
692	A166	11c	**light blue,** *Sept. 4, 1931*	1.65	10
			Margin block of 4, P#	10.50	—
			Retouched forehead (20617 L.L. 2, 3)	6.50	1.00
693	A167	12c	**brown violet,** *Aug. 25, 1931*	3.25	6
			violet brown	3.25	6
			Margin block of 4, P#	17.50	—
694	A186	13c	**yellow green,** *Sept. 4, 1931*	1.40	10
			light yellow green	1.40	10
			blue green	1.40	10
			Block of four	5.60	75
			Margin block of 4, P#	10.00	
			Pair with full vert. gutter btwn.	150.00	
695	A168	14c	**dark blue,** *Sept. 8, 1931*	2.00	22
			Margin block of 4, P#	12.50	—
696	A169	15c	**gray,** *Aug. 27, 1931*	5.75	6
			dark gray	5.75	6
			Margin block of 4, P#	30.00	—
			Perf. 10½x11		
697	A187	17c	**black,** *July 25, 1931*	3.25	14
			Margin block of 4, P#	16.50	—
698	A170	20c	**carmine rose,** *Sept. 8, 1931*	7.00	5
			Margin block of 4, P#	35.00	—
			Double transfer (20538 L.R. 26)	20.00	—
699	A171	25c	**blue green,** *July 25, 1931*	6.75	8
			Margin block of 4, P#	34.00	—
700	A172	30c	**brown,** *Sept. 8, 1931*	10.50	7
			Block of four	42.00	60
			Margin block of 4, P#	57.50	—
			Retouched in head (20552 U.L. 83)	22.50	85
			Cracked plate (20552 U.R. 30)	22.50	85
701	A173	50c	**lilac,** *Sept. 4, 1931*	30.00	7
			red lilac	30.00	7
			Block of four	120.00	50
			Margin block of 4, P#	170.00	—

Bureau Precancels: 11c, 33 diff., 12c, 33 diff., 13c, 28 diff., 14c, 27 diff., 15c, 33 diff., 17c, 29 diff., 20c, 37 diff., 25c, 29 diff., 30c, 31 diff., 50c, 28 diff.

RED CROSS ISSUE

Issued in commemoration of the fiftieth anniversary of the founding of the American Red Cross Society.

"The Greatest Mother" — A208

FLAT PLATE PRINTING

Plates of 200 subjects in two panes of 100 each.

1931				*Perf. 11*	
702	A208	2c	**black & red,** *May 21, 1931*	8	8
			Margin block of 4, arrow right or left	40	
			Margin block of 4, two P#	1.60	—
			Red cross omitted	—	
			Double transfer	1.25	50

The cross tends to shift, appearing in many slightly varied positions. The cross omitted variety is caused by a foldover of the paper.

YORKTOWN ISSUE

Issued in commemoration of the Sesquicentennial of the surrender of Cornwallis at Yorktown.

Rochambeau, Washington, de Grasse — A209

First Plate Layout - Border and vignette plates of 100 subjects in two panes of 50 subjects each. Plate numbers between 20461 and 20602.

Second Plate Layout - Border plates of 100 subjects in two panes of 50 each, separated by a 1 inch wide vertical gutter with central guide line and vignette plates of 50 subjects. Plate numbers between 20646 and 20671.

Issued in panes of 50 subjects.

1931				*Perf. 11*	
703	A209	2c	**carmine rose & black,** *Oct. 19, 1931*	24	20
			Margin block of 4, arrow marker, right or left	1.05	
			Center line block	1.15	
			Margin block of 4, two P#	2.25	—
			Margin block of 4, two P# & arrow & marker block	2.25	—
			Margin block of 6, two P# & "TOP", arrow & marker	3.00	—
			Margin block of 8, two P# & "TOP"	3.75	—
a.			2c lake & black	3.50	50
b.			2c dark lake & black	*300.00*	
b.			Margin block of 4, two P#	*1,750.*	
c.			Imperf., vertically, pair	*2,500.*	
			Double transfer	1.75	75

WASHINGTON BICENTENNIAL ISSUE

200th anniversary of the birth of George Washington. Various Portraits of George Washington.

By Charles Willson Peale, 1777 — A210

From Houdon Bust, 1785 — A211

By Charles Willson Peale, 1772 — A212

By Gilbert Stuart, 1796 — A213

By Charles Willson Peale, 1777 — A214

By Charles Peale Polk — A215

By Charles Willson Peale, 1795 — A216

By John Trumbull, 1792 — A217

By John Trumbull, 1780 — A218

By Charles B. J. F. Saint Memin, 1798 — A219

By W. Williams, 1794 — A220

By Gilbert Stuart, 1795 — A221

Broken Circle

ROTARY PRESS PRINTINGS

Plates of 400 subjects in four panes of 100 each

1932, Jan. 1				*Perf. 11x10½*	
704	A210	½c	**olive brown**	9	8
			Margin block of 4, P#	3.00	—
			Broken circle (20560 U.R. 8)	60	15
705	A211	1c	**green**	10	5
			Margin block of 4, P#	4.00	—
			Gripper cracks (20742 U.L. and U.R.)	2.50	1.50
706	A212	1½c	**brown**	32	8
			Margin block of 4, P#	13.00	—
707	A213	2c	**carmine rose**	10	5

Margin block of 4, P# 1.50 —
Pair with full vert. gutter between —
Gripper cracks (20752 L.R., 20755 L.L. & L.R., 20756 L.L., 20774 L.R., 20792 L.L. & L.R., 20796 L.L. & L.R.) 1.50 50

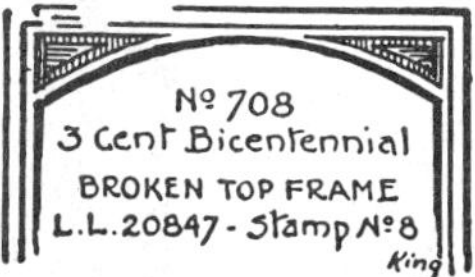

Double Transfer

708 A214 3c **deep violet** 40 6
Margin block of 4, P# 10.50 —
Double transfer 1.50 50
Broken top frame line (20847 L.L. 8) 3.50 75

Retouch in Eyes

709 A215 4c **light brown** 22 6
Margin block of 4, P# 4.25 —
Double transfer (20568 L.R. 60) 1.50 25
Retouch in eyes (20568 L.R. 89) 2.00 35
Broken bottom frame line (20568 L.R. 100) 1.50 50

Cracked Plate

710 A216 5c **blue** 1.40 10
Margin block of 4, P# 14.50 —
Cracked plate (20637 U.R. 80) 5.00 1.00
711 A217 6c **red orange** 2.75 6
Margin block of 4, P# 50.00 —

Double Transfer

712 A218 7c **black** 22 10
Margin block of 4, P# 4.25 —
Double transfer (20563 U.L. 1 or 20564 L.L. 91) 1.00 20
713 A219 8c **olive bister** 2.25 50
Margin block of 4, P# 50.00 —
Pair, gutter between —
714 A220 9c **pale red** 2.00 15
orange red 2.00 15
Margin block of 4, P# 30.00 —
715 A221 10c **orange yellow** 8.50 10
Margin block of 4, P# 95.00 —

OLYMPIC WINTER GAMES ISSUE

Issued in honor of the 3rd Olympic Winter Games, held at Lake Placid, N. Y., February 4-13, 1932.

Ski Jumper — A222

FLAT PLATE PRINTING

Plates of 400 subjects in four panes of 100 each.

1932 ***Perf. 11***

716 A222 2c **carmine rose,** *Jan. 25, 1932* 35 16
carmine 35 16
Margin block of 6, P# 10.00 —
Cracked plate (20823 UR 41, 42; UL 48, 49, 50) 5.00 1.65
Recut (20823 UR 61) 3.50 1.50
Colored "snowball" (20815 UR 64) 25.00 5.00

ARBOR DAY ISSUE

Issued in commemoration of the sixtieth anniversary of the first observance of Arbor Day in the state of Nebraska in April, 1872, and of the centenary of the birth of Julius Sterling Morton, who conceived the plan and the name "Arbor Day", while he was a member of the Nebraska State Board of Agriculture.

Boy and Girl Planting Tree — A223

ROTARY PRESS PRINTING

Plates of 400 subjects in four panes of 100 each.

1932 ***Perf. 11x10½***

717 A223 2c **carmine rose,** *April 22, 1932* 10 8
Margin block of 4, P# 6.50 —

OLYMPIC GAMES ISSUE

Issued in honor of the 10th Olympic Games, held at Los Angeles, Calif., July 30 to Aug. 14, 1932.

Runner at Starting Mark — A224

Myron's Discobolus — A225

Designed by Victor S. McCloskey, Jr.

ROTARY PRESS PRINTING

Plates of 400 subjects in four panes of 100 each.

1932, June 15 ***Perf. 11x10½***

718 A224 3c **violet** 1.10 8
deep violet 1.10 8
Margin block of 4, P# 9.50 —
Gripper cracks (20906 UL 1) 4.00 75
719 A225 5c **blue** 1.90 20
deep blue 1.90 20
Margin block of 4, P# 18.00 —
Gripper cracks (20868 UL & UR) 4.00 1.00

Washington, by Gilbert Stuart — A226

REGULAR ISSUE

ROTARY PRESS PRINTING

Plates of 400 subjects in four panes of 100 each.

1932 ***Perf. 11x10½***

720 A226 3c **deep violet,** *June 16, 1932* 12 5
light violet 12 5
Margin block of 4, P# 1.20 —
Pair with full vert. gutter btwn. *200.00*
Pair with full horiz. gutter btwn. *200.00*
b. Booklet pane of six, *July 25, 1932* 22.50 *5.00*
c. Vertical pair, imperf. between 225.00
Double transfer 1.00 30
Recut lines on nose 2.00 75
Gripper cracks 1.25 30

Bureau Precancels: 64 diff.

ROTARY PRESS COIL STAMPS

1932 ***Perf. 10 Vertically***

721 A226 3c **deep violet,** *June 24, 1932* 2.25 8
light violet 2.25 8
Pair 4.75 20
Joint line pair 8.25 75
Gripper cracks — —
Recut lines on nose — —
Recut lines around eyes — —

Perf. 10 Horizontally

722 A226 3c **deep violet,** *Oct. 12, 1932* 1.00 30
light violet 1.00 30
Pair 2.25 70
Joint line pair 5.00 1.75

Bureau Precancels: No. 721, 46 diff.

TYPE OF 1922-26 ISSUES

1932 ***Perf. 10 Vertically***

723 A161 6c **deep orange,** *Aug. 18, 1932* 7.50 25
Pair 16.00 60
Joint line pair 42.50 2.50

Bureau Precancels: 5 diff.

WILLIAM PENN ISSUE

Issued in commemoration of the 250th anniversary of the arrival in America of William Penn (1644-1718), English Quaker and founder of Pennsylvania.

William Penn — A227

FLAT PLATE PRINTING

Plates of 400 subjects in four panes of 100 each

1932 ***Perf. 11***

724 A227 3c **violet,** *Oct. 24, 1932* 22 15
Margin block of 6, P# 8.00 —
a. Vert. pair, imperf. horiz. —

DANIEL WEBSTER ISSUE

Issued in commemoration of the 150th anniversary of the birth of Daniel Webster (1782-1852), statesman.

Values for well-centered, early U.S. stamps will often exceed catalogue price.

Daniel Webster — A228

FLAT PLATE PRINTING

Plates of 400 subjects in four panes of 100 each.

1932 *Perf. 11*

725 A228 3c **violet,** *Oct. 24, 1932* 28 24
light violet 28 24
Margin block of 6, P# 16.50 —

GEORGIA BICENTENNIAL ISSUE

Issued in commemoration of the 200th anniversary of the founding of the Colony of Georgia and in honor of James Edward Oglethorpe, who landed from England, Feb. 12, 1733, and personally supervised the establishing of the colony.

Gen. James Edward Oglethorpe — A229

FLAT PLATE PRINTING

Plates of 400 subjects in four panes of 100 each.

1933 *Perf. 11.*

726 A229 3c **violet,** *Feb. 12, 1933* 20 18
Margin block of 6, P# 10.00 —
Margin block of 10, "CS" & P# 14.00
Bottom margin block of 20, no P# —

PEACE OF 1783 ISSUE

Issued to commemorate the 150th anniversary of the issuance by George Washington of the official order containing the Proclamation of Peace marking officially the ending of hostilities in the War for Independence.

Washington"s Headquarters at Newburgh, N.Y. — A230

ROTARY PRESS PRINTING

Plates of 400 subjects in four panes of 100 each

1933 *Perf. 10 ½x11*

727 A230 3c **violet,** *April 19, 1933* 9 8
Margin block of 4, P# 4.00 —
Block of 4, horizontal gutter between 75.00 —
Block of 4, vertical gutter between 85.00 —
Center block with crossed gutters and dashes —

No. 727 was available in full sheets of 400 subjects with gum, but was not regularly issued in that form.

CENTURY OF PROGRESS ISSUES

Issued to commemorate the "Century of Progress" International Exhibition at Chicago, which opened June 1, 1933, and the centenary of the incorporation of Chicago as a city.

Restoration of Fort Dearborn — A231

Federal Building — A232

ROTARY PRESS PRINTING

Plates of 400 subjects in four panes of 100 each.

1933, May 25 *Perf. 10 ½x11*

728 A231 1c **yellow green** 10 6
On cover, Expo. station canc. 50
Margin block of 4, P# 2.00 —
Block of 4, horizontal gutter between 100.00 —
Block of 4, vertical gutter between 100.00 —
Center block with crossed gutters and dashes —
Gripper cracks (21133 UR & LR) 2.00 —
729 A232 3c **violet** 18 5
On cover, Expo. station canc. 50
Margin block of 4, P# 2.00 —
Block of 4, horizontal gutter between 125.00 —
Block of 4, vertical gutter between 125.00 —
Center block with crossed gutters and dashes —

Nos. 728 and 729 were available in full sheets of 400 subjects with gum, but were not regularly issued in that form.

AMERICAN PHILATELIC SOCIETY ISSUE SOUVENIR SHEETS

A231a

A232a

FLAT PLATE PRINTING

Plates of 225 subjects in nine panes of 25 each.

1933 *Imperf.*

Without Gum

730 A231a 1c **deep yellow green,** sheet of 25, *Aug. 25* 24.00 24.00
a. Single stamp 65 35
731 A232a 3c **deep violet,** sheet of 25 22.50 22.50
a. Single stamp 50 35

Issued in sheets measuring 134x120mm containing twenty-five stamps, inscribed in the margins:

PRINTED BY THE TREASURY DEPARTMENT, BUREAU OF ENGRAVING AND PRINTING, - UNDER AUTHORITY OF JAMES A. FARLEY, POSTMASTER-GENERAL, AT CENTURY OF PROGRESS, - IN COMPLIMENT TO THE AMERICAN PHILATELIC SOCIETY FOR ITS CONVENTION AND EXHIBITION - CHICAGO, ILLINOIS, AUGUST, 1933. PLATE NO. 21145.

Also used were plates 21159 (1c), 21146 and 21160 (3c).

See Nos. 766-767.

NATIONAL RECOVERY ACT ISSUE

Issued to direct attention to and arouse the support of the Nation for the National Recovery Act.

Group of Workers — A233

ROTARY PRESS PRINTING

Plates of 400 subjects in four panes of 100 each.

1933 *Perf. 10 ½x11.*

732 A233 3c **violet,** *Aug. 15, 1933* 10 5
Margin block of 4, P# 1.50 —
Gripper cracks (21151 UL & UR, 21153 UR & LR) 1.50 —
Recut at right (21151 UR 47) 2.00

BYRD ANTARCTIC ISSUE

Issued in connection with the Byrd Antarctic Expedition of 1933 and for use on letters mailed through the Little America Post Office established at the Base Camp of the Expedition in the territory of the South Pole.

A Map of the World (on van der Grinten's Projection) — A234

Designed by Victor S. McCloskey, Jr.

FLAT PLATE PRINTING

Plates of 200 subjects in four panes of 50 each

1933 *Perf. 11*

733 A234 3c **dark blue,** *Oct. 9, 1933* 40 48
Margin block of 6, P# 15.00 —
Double transfer (21167 LR 2) 2.50 1.00

In addition to the postage charge of 3 cents, letters sent by the ships of the expedition to be canceled in Little America were subject to a service charge of 50 cents each.

See No. 753.

KOSCIUSZKO ISSUE

Issued to commemorate Gen. Tadeusz Kosciuszko (1746-1807), Polish soldier and statesman who served in the American Revolution, and to mark the 150th anniversary of the granting to him of American citizenship.

Statue of General Tadeusz Kosciuszko — A235

Designed by Victor S. McCloskey, Jr.

FLAT PLATE PRINTING
Plates of 400 subjects in four panes of 100 each

1933 ***Perf. 11***

734 A235 5c **blue,** *Oct. 13, 1933* 40 22
Margin block of 6, P# 27.50 —
a. Horiz. pair, imperf. vert. *1,750.*
Cracked plate —

NATIONAL STAMP EXHIBITION ISSUE
SOUVENIR SHEET

A235a

TYPE OF BYRD ISSUE
Plates of 150 subjects in 25 panes of six each.

1934 ***Imperf.***

Without Gum

735 A235a 3c **dark blue,** sheet of six, *Feb. 10* 15.00 12.50
a. Single stamp 2.00 2.00

Issued in sheets measuring 87x93mm containing six stamps, inscribed in the margins: "Printed by the Treasury Department, Bureau of Engraving and Printing, under authority of James A. Farley, Postmaster General, in the National Stamp Exhibition of 1934. New York, N. Y., February 10-18, 1934. Plate No. 21184." Plate No. 21187 was used for sheets printed at the Exhibition, but all these were destroyed.
See No. 768.

MARYLAND TERCENTENARY ISSUE

Issued to commemorate the 300th anniversary of the founding of Maryland.

"The Ark" and "The Dove" — A236

Designed by Alvin R. Meissner.

FLAT PLATE PRINTING
Plates of 400 subjects in four panes of 100 each.

1934 ***Perf. 11***

736 A236 3c **carmine rose,** *Mar. 23, 1934* 12 8
Margin block of 6, P# 7.50 —
Double transfer (21190 UL 1) — —

MOTHERS OF AMERICA ISSUE

Issued to commemorate Mother's Day.

Adaptation of Whistler's Portrait of his Mother — A237

Designed by Victor S. McCloskey, Jr.

Plates of 200 subjects in four panes of 50 each.
ROTARY PRESS PRINTING

1934 ***Perf. 11x10½***

737 A237 3c **deep violet,** *May 2, 1934* 9 6
Margin block of 4, P# 1.00 —

FLAT PLATE PRINTING
Perf. 11

738 A237 3c **deep violet,** *May 2, 1934* 12 10
Margin block of 6, P# 4.25 —

See No. 754.

WISCONSIN TERCENTENARY ISSUE

Issued to commemorate the 300th anniversary of the arrival of Jean Nicolet, French explorer, on the shores of Green Bay. According to historical records, Nicolet was the first white man to reach the territory now comprising the State of Wisconsin.

Nicolet's Landing — A238

Designed by Victor S. McCloskey, Jr.

FLAT PLATE PRINTING
Plates of 200 subjects in four panes of 50 each.

1934 ***Perf. 11***

739 A238 3c **deep violet,** *July 7, 1934* 12 10
violet 12 10
Margin block of 6, P# 3.00 —
a. Vert. pair, imperf. horiz. 250.00
b. Horiz. pair, imperf. vert. 325.00

See No. 755.

NATIONAL PARKS ISSUE

Issued to commemorate "National Parks Year".

El Capitan, Yosemite (California) — A239

View of Grand Canyon (Arizona) — A240

Mt. Rainier and Mirror Lake (Washington) — A241

Cliff Palace, Mesa Verde Park (Colorado) — A242

Old Faithful, Yellowstone (Wyoming) — A243

Crater Lake (Oregon) — A244

Great Head, Acadia Park (Maine) — A245

Great White Throne, Zion Park (Utah) — A246

Mt. Rockwell (Mt. Sinopah) and Two Medicine Lake, Glacier National Park (Montana) — A247

Great Smoky Mountains (North Carolina) — A248

FLAT PLATE PRINTING

Plates of 200 subjects in four panes of 50 each.

1934 **Unwmk.** ***Perf. 11***

740 A239 1c **green,** *July 16, 1934* 7 6
light green 7 6
Margin block of 6, P# 1.00 —
Recut 1.50 50
a. Vert. pair, imperf. horiz., with gum 450.00
741 A240 2c **red,** *July 24, 1934* 9 6
orange red 9 6
Margin block of 6, P# 1.25 —
a. Vert. pair, imperf., horiz., with gum 300.00
b. Horiz. pair, imperf. vert., with gum 300.00
Double transfer 1.25 —
742 A241 3c **deep violet,** *Aug. 3, 1934* 10 6
Margin block of 6, P# 1.75 —
Recut 1.50 —
a. Vert. pair, imperf. horiz., with gum 350.00
743 A242 4c **brown,** *Sept. 25, 1934* 35 32
light brown 35 32
Margin block of 6, P# 7.00 —
a. Vert. pair, imperf. horiz., with gum 500.00
744 A243 5c **blue,** *July 30, 1934* 60 55
light blue 60 55
Margin block of 6, P# 8.75 —
a. Horiz. pair, imperf. vert., with gum 400.00
745 A244 6c **dark blue,** *Sept. 5, 1934* 1.00 75
Margin block of 6, P# 15.00 —
746 A245 7c **black,** *Oct. 2, 1934* 55 65
Margin block of 6, P# 10.00 —
a. Horiz. pair, imperf. vert., with gum 450.00
Double transfer 3.00 1.25
747 A246 8c **sage green,** *Sept. 18, 1934* 1.40 1.65
Margin block of 6, P# 15.00 —
748 A247 9c **red orange,** *Aug. 27, 1934* 1.50 55
orange 1.50 55
Margin block of 6, P# 15.00 —
749 A248 10c **gray black,** *Oct. 8, 1934* 2.75 90
gray 2.75 90
Margin block of 6, P# 25.00 —

Imperforate varieties of the 2c and 5c exist as errors of the perforated Parks set, but are virtually impossible to distinguish from gummed copies from the imperforate sheets of 200. (See note above No. 752).

AMERICAN PHILATELIC SOCIETY ISSUE

SOUVENIR SHEET

A248a

Plates of 120 subjects in 20 panes of 6 stamps each.

1934 ***Imperf.***

750 A248a 3c **deep violet,** sheet of six, *Aug. 28* 25.00 22.50
a. Single stamp 3.00 2.75

Issued in sheets measuring 97x99mm containing six stamps, inscribed in the margins: PRINTED BY THE TREASURY DEPARTMENT, BUREAU OF ENGRAVING AND PRINTING, - UNDER AUTHORITY OF JAMES A. FARLEY, POSTMASTER GENERAL, - IN COMPLIMENT TO THE AMERICAN PHILATELIC SOCIETY FOR ITS CONVENTION AND EXHIBITION, - ATLANTIC CITY, NEW JERSEY, AUGUST, 1934. PLATE NO. 21303.

TRANS-MISSISSIPPI PHILATELIC EXPOSITION ISSUE

SOUVENIR SHEET

A248b

Plates of 120 subjects in 20 panes of 6 stamps each.

1934 ***Imperf.***

751 A248b 1c **green,** sheet of six, *Oct. 10* 10.00 10.00
a. Single stamp 1.25 1.50

Issued in sheets measuring 94x99mm. containing six stamps, inscribed in the margins: PRINTED BY THE TREASURY DEPARTMENT, BUREAU OF ENGRAVING AND PRINTING, - UNDER AUTHORITY OF JAMES A. FARLEY, POSTMASTER GENERAL, - IN COMPLIMENT TO THE TRANS-MISSISSIPPI PHILATELIC EXPOSITION AND CONVENTION, OMAHA, NEBRASKA, - OCTOBER, 1934. PLATE NO. 21341.

SPECIAL PRINTING

(Nos. 752 to 771 inclusive)

Issued March 15, 1935

"Issued for a limited time in full sheets as printed, and in blocks thereof, to meet the requirements of collectors and others who may be interested." - From Postal Bulletin No. 16614.

Issuance of the following 20 stamps in complete sheets resulted from the protest of collectors and others at the practice of presenting, to certain government officials, complete sheets of unsevered panes, imperforate (except Nos. 752 and 753) and generally ungummed.

Gutter or line pairs sell for half the price of gutter or line blocks of four.

Designs of Commemorative Issues

Without Gum

NOTE: In 1940 the P.O. Department offered to and did gum full sheets of Nos. 754 to 771 sent in by owners.

TYPE OF PEACE ISSUE

Issued in sheets of 400, consisting of four panes of 100 each, with vertical and horizontal gutters between and plate numbers at outside corners at sides.

ROTARY PRESS PRINTING

1935 **Unwmk.** ***Perf. 10½x11***

752 A230 3c **violet** 14 10
Horiz. gutter block of four 9.00 —
Vert. gutter block of four 15.00 —
Gutter block of four with dash (left or right) 10.00 —
Gutter block of four with dash (top or bottom) 15.00 —
Center block with crossed gutters and dashes 35.00 —
Margin block of 4, P# 11.00 —

TYPE OF BYRD ISSUE

Issued in sheets of 200, consisting of four panes of 50 each, with vertical and horizontal guide lines in gutters between panes, and plate numbers centered at top and bottom of each pane. This applies to Nos. 753-765 and 771.

FLAT PLATE PRINTING

753 A234 3c **dark blue** 40 40
Horiz. line block of four 3.50 —
Vert. line block of four 37.50 —
Margin block of 4, arrow & guide line (left or right) 3.75 —
Margin block of 4, arrow & guide-line (top or bottom) 40.00 —
Center line block 42.50 14.00
Margin block of 6, P# (Number at top or bottom) 15.00 —

No. 753 is similar to No. 733. Positive identification is by blocks or pairs showing guide line between stamps. These lines between stamps are found only on No. 753.

TYPE OF MOTHERS OF AMERICA ISSUE

Issued in sheets of 200

FLAT PLATE PRINTING

754 A237 3c **deep violet** 50 50
Horiz. or vert. line block of four 2.10 —
Margin block of 4, arrow & guideline (left, right, top or bottom) 2.25 —
Center line block 5.00 —
Margin block of 6, P# (Number at top or bottom) 16.50 —

TYPE OF WISCONSIN ISSUE

Issued in sheets of 200

FLAT PLATE PRINTING

755 A238 3c **deep violet** 50 50
Horiz. or vert. line block of four 2.10 —
Margin block of 4, arrow & guideline (left, right, top or bottom) 2.25 —
Center line block 5.00 —
Margin block of 6, P# (Number at top or bottom) 16.50 —

TYPES OF NATIONAL PARKS ISSUE

Issued in sheets of 200

FLAT PLATE PRINTING

756 A239 1c **green** 20 20
Horiz. or vert. line block of four 90 —
Margin block of 4, arrow & guideline (left, right, top or bottom) 1.00 —
Center line block 2.35 —
Margin block of 6, P# (Number at top or bottom) 3.65 —

See note above No. 766.

757 A240 2c **red** 22 22
Horiz. or vert. line block of four 95
Margin block of 4, arrow & guideline (left, right, top or bottom) 1.00 —
Center line block 2.75
Margin block of 6, P# (Number at top or bottom) 4.50
Double transfer —
758 A241 3c **deep violet** 45 40
Horiz. or vert. line block of four 1.95 —
Margin block of 4, arrow & guideline (left, right, top or bottom) 2.00 —
Center line block 4.00 —
Margin block of 6, P# (Number at top or bottom) 12.50 —
759 A242 4c **brown** 90 90
Horiz. or vert. line block of four 3.75 —
Margin block of 4, arrow & guideline (left, right, top or bottom) 4.00 —
Center line block 5.50 —
Margin block of 6, P# (Number at top or bottom) 16.50 —
760 A243 5c **blue** 1.40 1.25
Horiz. or vert. line block of four 6.50 —
Margin block of 4, arrow & guideline (left, right, top or bottom) 7.00 —
Center line block 11.00 —
Margin block of 6, P# (Number at top or bottom) 18.50 —
Double transfer —
761 A244 6c **dark blue** 2.25 2.00
Horiz. or vert. line block of four 9.25 —

Margin block of 4, arrow & guideline (left, right, top or bottom) 9.50 —
Center line block 14.50 —
Margin block of 6, P# (Number at top or bottom) 30.00 —

762 A245 7c **black** 1.40 1.25
Horiz. or vert. line block of four 6.00 —
Margin block of 4, arrow & guideline (left, right, top or bottom) 6.50 —
Center line block 10.00 —
Margin block of 6, P# (Number at top or bottom) 25.00 —
Double transfer —

763 A246 8c **sage green** 1.50 1.40
Horiz. or vert. line block of four 6.50 —
Margin block of 4, arrow & guideline (left, right, top or bottom) 7.00 —
Center line block 11.00 —
Margin block of 6, P# (Number at top or bottom) 30.00 —

764 A247 9c **red orange** 1.75 1.50
Horiz. or vert. line block of four 7.50 —
Margin block of 4, arrow & guideline (left, right, top or bottom) 8.00 —
Center line block12 21.00 —
Margin block of 6, P# (Number at top or bottom) 32.50 —

765 A248 10c **gray black** 3.50 3.00
Horiz. or vert. line block of four 14.50 —
Margin block of 4, arrow & guideline (left, right, top or bottom) 15.00 —
Center line block 21.50 —
Margin block of 6, P# (Number at top or bottom) 41.50 —

SOUVENIR SHEETS
TYPE OF CENTURY OF PROGRESS ISSUE

Issued in sheets of 9 panes of 25 stamps each, with vertical and horizontal gutters between panes. This applies to Nos. 766-770.

Note: Single items from these sheets are identical with other varieties, 766 and 730, 766a and 730a, 767 and 731, 767a and 731a, 768 and 735, 768a and 735a, 769 and 756, 770 and 758.

Positive identification is by blocks or pairs showing wide gutters between stamps. These wide gutters occur only on Nos. 766 to 770 and measure, horizontally, 13mm. on Nos. 766-767; 16mm. on No. 768, and 23mm. on Nos. 769-770.

FLAT PLATE PRINTING

766 A231a 1c **yellow green,** pane of 25 24.00 24.00
a. Single stamp 65 35
Block of four 2.60 1.50
Horiz. gutter block 8.50 —
Vert. gutter block 9.75 —
Block with crossed gutters 11.50
Block of 50 stamps (two panes) 57.50

767 A232a 3c **violet,** pane of 25 22.50 22.50
a. Single stamp 50 35
Horiz. gutter block 7.50 —
Vert. gutter block 8.75 —
Block with crossed gutters 11.50 —
Block of 50 stamps (two panes) 55.00

NATIONAL EXHIBITION ISSUE
TYPE OF BYRD ISSUE

Issued in sheets of 25 panes of 6 stamps each.

FLAT PLATE PRINTING

768 A235a 3c **dark blue,** pane of six 15.00 12.50
a. Single stamp 2.00 2.00
Horiz. gutter block 10.00 —
Vert. gutter block 11.00 —
Block of four with crossed gutters 12.50 —
Block of 12 stamps (two panes) 35.00

TYPES OF NATIONAL PARKS ISSUE

Issued in sheets of 20 panes of 6 stamps each.

FLAT PLATE PRINTING

769 A248b 1c **green,** pane of six 10.00 10.00
a. Single stamp 1.40 1.40
Horiz. or vert. gutter block 9.50 —
Block of four with crossed gutters 10.00 —
Block of 12 stamps (two panes) 21.00

770 A248a 3c **deep violet,** pane of six 25.00 22.50
a. Single stamp 3.00 2.75
Horiz. or vert. gutter block 20.00 —
Block of four with crossed gutters 21.50 —
Block of 12 stamps (two panes) 55.00

TYPE OF AIR POST SPECIAL DELIVERY

Issued in sheets of 200

FLAT PLATE PRINTING

771 APSD1 16c **dark blue** 2.00 2.00
Horiz. or vert. line block of four 8.75 8.75
Margin block of 4, arrow & guide line (left, right, top or bottom) 10.00 10.00
Center line block 36.50 —
Margin block of 6, P# (Number at top or bottom) 43.50 —

CONNECTICUT TERCENTENARY ISSUE

Issued in commemoration of the 300th anniversary of the settlement of Connecticut.

The Charter Oak — A249

ROTARY PRESS PRINTING

Plates of 200 subjects in four panes of 50 each.

1935 **Unwmk.** ***Perf. 11x10½***

772 A249 3c **violet,** *April 26, 1935* 10 6
rose violet 10 8
Margin block of 4, P# 1.40 —
Defect in cent sign (21395 UR 4) 1.00 25

CALIFORNIA PACIFIC EXPOSITION ISSUE

Issued in commemoration of the California Pacific Exposition at San Diego.

View of San Diego Exposition — A250

ROTARY PRESS PRINTING

Plates of 200 subjects in four panes of 50 each.

1935 **Unwmk.** ***Perf. 11x10½***

773 A250 3c **purple,** *May 29, 1935* 9 6
On cover, Expo. station canc. 50
Margin block of 4, P# 1.40 —
Pair with full vertical gutter between —

BOULDER DAM ISSUE

Dedication of Boulder Dam.

Boulder Dam (Hoover Dam) — A251

FLAT PLATE PRINTING

Plates of 200 subjects in four panes of 50 each.

1935 **Unwmk.** ***Perf. 11***

774 A251 3c **purple,** *Sept. 30, 1935* 9 6
deep purple 9 6
Margin block of 6, P# 1.85 —

MICHIGAN CENTENARY ISSUE

Advance celebration of Michigan Statehood centenary. Michigan was admitted to the Union Jan. 26, 1837.

Michigan State Seal — A252

Designed by Alvin R. Meissner.

ROTARY PRESS PRINTING

Plates of 200 subjects in four panes of 50 each.

1935 **Unwmk.** ***Perf. 11x10½***

775 A252 3c **purple,** *Nov. 1, 1935* 9 6
Margin block of 4, P# 1.40 —

TEXAS CENTENNIAL ISSUE

Issued in commemoration of the centennial of Texas independence.

Sam Houston, Stephen F. Austin and the Alamo — A253

Designed by Alvin R. Meissner.

ROTARY PRESS PRINTING

Plates of 200 subjects in four panes of 50 each.

1936 **Unwmk.** ***Perf. 11x10½***

776 A253 3c **purple,** *Mar. 2, 1936* 9 6
On cover, Expo. station canc. 50
Margin block of 4, P# 1.40 —

RHODE ISLAND TERCENTENARY ISSUE

Issued in commemoration of the 300th anniversary of the settlement of Rhode Island.

Statue of Roger Williams — A254

ROTARY PRESS PRINTING

Plates of 200 subjects in four panes of 50 each.

1936 **Unwmk.** ***Perf. 10½x11***

777 A254 3c **purple,** *May 4, 1936* 10 6
rose violet 10 6
Margin block of 4, P# 1.40 —
Pair with full gutter between *200.00*

THIRD INTERNATIONAL PHILATELIC EXHIBITION ISSUE

SOUVENIR SHEET

A254a

TYPES OF CONNECTICUT, CALIFORNIA, MICHIGAN AND TEXAS ISSUES

Plates of 120 subjects in thirty panes of 4 each.

FLAT PLATE PRINTING

1936, May 9	**Unwmk.**	***Imperf.***	
778 A254a	**violet,** sheet of four	1.75	1.75
a.	3c type A249	35	30
b.	3c type A250	35	30
c.	3c type A252	35	30
d.	3c type A253	35	30

Issued in sheets measuring 98x66mm. containing four stamps, inscribed in the margins: "Printed by the Treasury Department, Bureau of Engraving and Printing, under authority of James A. Farley, Postmaster General, in compliment to the third International Philatelic Exhibition of 1936. New York, N. Y., May 9-17, 1936. Plate No. 21557 (or 21558)."

ARKANSAS CENTENNIAL ISSUE

Issued in commemoration of the 100th anniversary of the State of Arkansas.

Arkansas Post, Old and New State Houses — A255

ROTARY PRESS PRINTING

Plates of 200 subjects in four panes of 50 each.

1936	**Unwmk.**	***Perf. 11x10½***	
782 A255 3c	**purple,** *June 15, 1936*	9	6
	Margin block of 4, P#	1.40	—

OREGON TERRITORY ISSUE

Issued in commemoration of the 100th anniversary of the opening of the Oregon Territory, 1836.

Map of Oregon Territory — A256

ROTARY PRESS PRINTING

Plates of 200 subjects in four panes of 50 each.

1936	**Unwmk.**	***Perf. 11x10½***	
783 A256 3c	**purple,** *July 14, 1936*	9	6
	Margin block of 4, P#	1.40	—
	Double transfer (21579 UL 3)	1.00	50

SUSAN B. ANTHONY ISSUE

Issued in honor of Susan Brownell Anthony (1820-1906), woman-suffrage advocate, on the 16th anniversary of the ratification of the 19th Amendment which grants American women the right to vote.

Susan B. Anthony — A257

ROTARY PRESS PRINTING

Plates of 400 subjects in four panes of 100 each.

1936	**Unwmk.**	***Perf. 11x10½***	
784 A257 3c	**dark violet,** *Aug. 26, 1936*	9	5
	Margin block of 4, P#	75	—
	Period missing after "B" (21590 LR 100)	75	25

ARMY ISSUE

Issued in honor of the United States Army.

Generals George Washington, Nathanael Greene and Mt. Vernon — A258

Maj. Gen. Andrew Jackson, Gen. Winfield Scott and the Hermitage — A259

Generals William T. Sherman, Ulysses S. Grant and Philip H. Sheridan — A260

Generals Robert E. Lee, "Stonewall" Jackson and Stratford Hall — A261

U. S. Military Academy, West Point — A262

ROTARY PRESS PRINTING

Plates of 200 subjects in four panes of 50 each.

1936-37	**Unwmk.**	***Perf. 11x10½***	
785 A258 1c	**green,** *Dec. 15, 1936*	8	6
	yellow green	8	6
	Margin block of 4, P#	85	—
	Pair with full vertical gutter between	—	
786 A259 2c	**carmine,** *Jan. 15, 1937*	8	6
	Margin block of 4, P#	85	—
787 A260 3c	**purple,** *Feb. 18, 1937*	12	6
	Margin block of 4, P#	1.10	—
788 A261 4c	**gray,** *Mar. 23, 1937*	30	12
	Margin block of 4, P#	8.00	—
789 A262 5c	**ultramarine,** *May 26, 1937*	60	12
	Margin block of 4, P#	8.50	—

NAVY ISSUE

Issued in honor of the United States Navy.

John Paul Jones and John Barry — A263

Stephen Decatur and Thomas MacDonough — A264

Admirals David G. Farragut and David D. Porter — A265

Values quoted in this catalogue are for stamps graded at Fine-Very Fine and with no faults. An illustrated guide to grade is provided in introductory material, beginning on Page V.

Admirals William T. Sampson, George Dewey and Winfield S. Schley — A266

Seal of U.S. Naval Academy and Naval Cadets — A267

ROTARY PRESS PRINTING

Plates of 200 subjects in four panes of 50 each.

1936-37			Unwmk.	Perf. 11x10½	
790	A263	1c	**green,** *Dec. 15, 1936*	8	6
			yellow green	8	6
			Margin block of 4, P#	85	—
791	A264	2c	**carmine,** *Jan. 15, 1937*	9	6
			Margin block of 4, P#	80	—
792	A265	3c	**purple,** *Feb. 18, 1937*	14	8
			Margin block of 4, P#	1.00	—
793	A266	4c	**gray,** *Mar. 23, 1937*	32	12
			Margin block of 4, P#	8.00	—
794	A267	5c	**ultramarine,** *May 26, 1937*	60	15
			Margin block of 4, P#	8.50	—
			Pair with full vert. gutter btwn.	—	

ORDINANCE OF 1787 SESQUICENTENNIAL ISSUE

Issued in commemoration of the 150th anniversary of the adoption of the Ordinance of 1787 and the creation of the Northwest Territory.

Manasseh Cutler, Rufus Putnam and Map of Northwest Territory — A268

ROTARY PRESS PRINTING

Plates of 200 subjects in four panes of 50 each.

1937			Unwmk.	Perf. 11x10½	
795	A268	3c	**red violet,** *July 13, 1937*	10	6
			Margin block of 4, P#	1.10	—

VIRGINIA DARE ISSUE

Issued to commemorate the 350th anniversary of the birth of Virginia Dare and the settlement at Roanoke Island. Virginia was the first child born in America of English parents (Aug. 18, 1587).

Virginia Dare and Parents A269

FLAT PLATE PRINTING

Plates of 192 subjects in four panes of 48 each, separated by 1¼ inch wide gutters with central guide lines.

1937			Unwmk.	Perf. 11	
796	A269	5c	**gray blue,** *Aug. 18, 1937*	20	18
			Margin block of 6, P#	7.00	—

SOCIETY OF PHILATELIC AMERICANS ISSUE

SOUVENIR SHEET

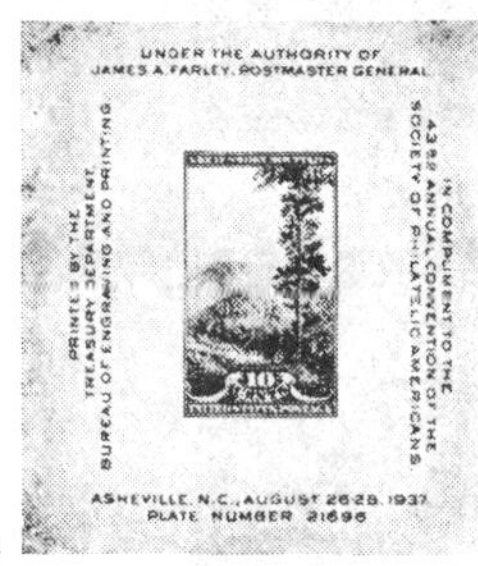

A269a

TYPE OF NATIONAL PARKS ISSUE

Plates of 36 subjects

FLAT PLATE PRINTING

1937			Unwmk.	Imperf.	
797	A269a	10c	**blue green,** *Aug. 26*	60	40

Issued in sheets measuring 67x78mm, inscribed in margins: "Printed by the Treasury Department, Bureau of Engraving and Printing - Under the Authority of James A. Farley, Postmaster General - In Compliment to the 43rd Annual Convention of the Society of Philatelic Americans - Asheville, N.C., August 26-28, 1937. Plate Number 21695 (6)."

CONSTITUTION SESQUICENTENNIAL ISSUE

Issued in commemoration of the 150th anniversary of the signing of the Constitution on September 17, 1787.

"Adoption of the Constitution" — A270

ROTARY PRESS PRINTING

Plates of 200 subjects in four panes of 50 each.

1937			Unwmk.	Perf. 11x10½	
798	A270	3c	**bright red violet,** *Sept. 17, 1937*	12	7
			Margin block of 4, P#	1.00	—

Prices paid for stamps on original covers vary greatly in accordance with condition, appearance, cancellation or postmark and usage.

TERRITORIAL ISSUES

Hawaii

Statue of Kamehameha I, Honolulu — A271

Alaska

Mt. McKinley — A272

Puerto Rico

La Fortaleza, San Juan — A273

Virgin Islands

Charlotte Amalie Harbor, St. Thomas — A274

ROTARY PRESS PRINTING

Plates of 200 subjects in panes of 50 each.

1937			Unwmk.	Perf. 10½x11	
799	A271	3c	**violet,** *Oct. 18, 1937*	10	7
			Margin block of 4, P#	1.25	—
			Perf. 11x10½		
800	A272	3c	**violet,** *Nov. 12, 1937*	10	7
			Margin block of 4, P#	1.25	—
			Pair with full gutter between	—	
801	A273	3c	**bright violet,** *Nov. 25, 1937*	10	7
			Margin block of 4, P#	1.25	—
802	A274	3c	**light violet,** *Dec. 15, 1937*	10	7
			Margin block of 4, P#	1.25	—
			Pair with full vertical gutter between	*275.00*	

PRESIDENTIAL ISSUE

Benjamin Franklin A275

George Washington A276

Martha Washington A277

John Adams A278

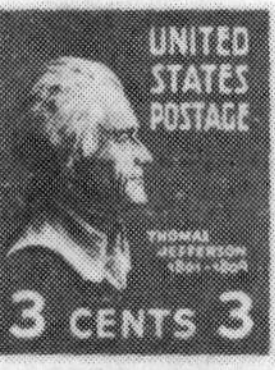

Thomas Jefferson — A279

James Madison — A280

The White House — A281

James Monroe — A282

John Quincy Adams — A283

Andrew Jackson — A284

Martin Van Buren — A285

William H. Harrison — A286

John Tyler — A287

James K. Polk — A288

The Catalogue editors cannot undertake to appraise, identify or judge the genuineness or condition of stamps.

Zachary Taylor — A289

Millard Fillmore — A290

Franklin Pierce A291

James Buchanan A292

Abraham Lincoln — A293

Andrew Johnson — A294

Ulysses S. Grant — A295

Rutherford B. Hayes — A296

James A. Garfield — A297

Chester A. Arthur — A298

Grover Cleveland A299

Benjamin Harrison A300

William McKinley A301

Theodore Roosevelt A302

William Howard Taft — A303

Woodrow Wilson — A304

Warren G. Harding — A305

Calvin Coolidge — A306

ROTARY PRESS PRINTING

Ordinary and Electric Eye Plates of 400 subjects in four panes of 100 each. (For details of Electric Eye Markings, see Information for Collectors in first part of this Catalogue.)

1938-43			**Unwmk.**	***Perf. 11x10½***	
803	A275	½c	**deep orange,** *May 19, 1938*	5	5
			Margin block of 4, P#	35	—
804	A276	1c	**green,** *Apr. 25, 1938*	5	5
			light green	5	5
			Margin block of 4, P#	35	—
b.			Booklet pane of six	1.50	*20*
			Pair with full vertical gutter between	*125.00*	—
805	A277	1½c	**bister brown,** *May 5, 1938*	6	5
			buff ('43)	6	5
			Margin block of 4, P#	30	—
b.			Horiz. pair, imperf. between	175.00	15.00
			Pair with full horizontal gutter between	*150.00*	
			Pair with full vertical gutter between	—	

Used pairs of No. 805b are Bureau precanceled St. Louis, Mo., and generally with gum.

806	A278	2c	**rose carmine,** *June 3, 1938*	7	5
			rose pink ('43)	7	5
			Margin block of 4, P# opposite corner stamp	35	—
			Vertical margin block of 10, P# opposite third horizontal row (Experimental Electric Eye plates)	4.00	
b.			Booklet pane of six	3.25	*50*
			Recut at top of head, Pl. 22156 U.L. 3	3.00	1.50
			Pair with full horiz. gutter btwn.	—	
			Pair with full vert. gutter btwn.	—	
807	A279	3c	**deep violet,** *June 16, 1938*	7	5
			Margin block of 4, P# opposite corner stamp	35	25
			Vertical margin block of 10, P# opposite third horizontal row (Experimental Electric Eye plates)	20.00	
a.			Booklet pane of six	6.50	*50*
b.			Horiz. pair, imperf. between	*650.00*	—
c.			Imperf., pair	*2,500.*	
			Pair with full vertical gutter between	*150.00*	
			Pair with full horizontal gutter between	*225.00*	
808	A280	4c	**red violet,** *July 1, 1938*	80	5
			rose violet ('43)	80	5
			Margin block of 4, P#	4.00	—
809	A281	4½c	**dark gray,** *July 11, 1938*	14	6
			gray ('43)	14	6
			Block of four	56	50
			Margin block of 4, P#	1.60	—
810	A282	5c	**bright blue,** *July 21, 1938*	22	5
			light blue	22	5
			Margin block of 4, P#	1.25	—
			Pair full vert. gutter btwn.	—	
811	A283	6c	**red orange,** *July 28, 1938*	25	5
			Margin block of 4, P#	1.75	—
812	A284	7c	**sepia,** *Aug. 4, 1938*	28	5
			violet brown	28	5
			Margin block of 4, P#	1.75	—
813	A285	8c	**olive green,** *Aug. 11, 1938*	30	5
			light olive green ('43)	30	5
			olive ('42)	30	5
			Margin block of 4, P#	1.75	—
814	A286	9c	**rose pink,** *Aug. 18, 1938*	38	5
			pink ('43)	38	5
			Margin block of 4, P#	1.90	—
			Pair with full vertical gutter between	—	
815	A287	10c	**brown red,** *Sept. 2, 1938*	28	5
			pale brown red ('43)	28	5
			Margin block of 4, P#	1.40	—
816	A288	11c	**ultramarine,** *Sept. 8, 1938*	65	8
			bright ultramarine	65	8
			Margin block of 4, P#	3.25	—
817	A289	12c	**bright violet,** *Sept. 14, 1938*	1.10	6
			Margin block of 4, P#	4.50	—
818	A290	13c	**blue green,** *Sept. 22, 1938*	1.25	8
			deep blue green	1.25	8
			Margin block of 4, P#	6.25	—
819	A291	14c	**blue,** *Oct. 6, 1938*	90	8
			Margin block of 4, P#	4.50	—
820	A292	15c	**blue gray,** *Oct. 13, 1938*	50	5
			Margin block of 4, P#	2.50	—
821	A293	16c	**black,** *Oct. 20, 1938*	90	25
			Margin block of 4, P#	4.50	—
822	A294	17c	**rose red,** *Oct. 27, 1938*	85	12
			deep rose red	85	12
			Block of four	3.40	75
			Margin block of 4, P#	4.25	—
823	A295	18c	**brown carmine,** *Nov. 3, 1938*	1.50	8

No.	Type	Denom.	Description	Unused	Used
			rose brown ('43)	1.50	8
			Block of four	6.00	75
			Margin block of 4, P#	7.50	—
824	A296	19c	**bright violet,** *Nov. 10, 1938*	1.25	35
			Margin block of 4, P#	6.25	—
825	A297	20c	**bright blue green,** *Nov. 10, 1938*	70	5
			deep blue green ('43)	70	5
			Margin block of 4, P#	3.50	—
826	A298	21c	**dull blue,** *Nov. 22, 1938*	1.50	10
			Block of four	6.00	1.25
			Margin block of 4, P#	7.50	—
827	A299	22c	**vermilion,** *Nov. 22, 1938*	1.25	40
			Margin block of 4, P#	9.50	—
828	A300	24c	**gray black,** *Dec. 2, 1938*	3.75	18
			Block of four	15.00	1.25
			Margin block of 4, P#	18.75	—
829	A301	25c	**deep red lilac,** *Dec. 2, 1938*	80	5
			rose lilac ('43)	80	5
			Margin block of 4, P#	4.00	—
			Pair with full vert. gutter btwn.	—	
830	A302	30c	**deep ultramarine,** *Dec. 8, 1938*	4.75	5
			blue	15.00	—
			deep blue	*75.00*	—
			Block of four	19.00	50
			Margin block of 4, P#	24.00	—
831	A303	50c	**light red violet,** *Dec. 8, 1938*	6.50	6
			Margin block of 4, P#	32.50	—

Bureau Precancels: ½c, 199 diff., 1c, 701 diff., 1½c, 404 diff., 2c, 161 diff., 3c, 87 diff., 4c, 30 diff., 4½c, 27 diff., 5c, 44 diff., 6c, 45 diff., 7c, 44 diff., 8c, 44 diff., 9c, 38 diff., 10c, 43 diff.

Also, 11c, 41 diff., 12c, 33 diff., 13c, 28 diff., 14c, 23 diff., 15c, 38 diff., 16c, 6 diff., 17c, 27 diff., 18c, 5 diff., 19c, 8 diff., 20c, 39 diff., 21c, 5 diff., 22c, 4 diff., 24c, 8 diff., 25c, 23 diff., 30c, 27 diff., 50c, 24 diff.

FLAT PLATE PRINTING

Plates of 100 subjects

1938-54 ***Perf. 11***

No.	Type	Denom.	Description	Unused	Used
832	A304	$1	**purple & black,** *Aug. 29, 1938*	8.25	10
			Margin block of 4, bottom or side arrow	34.00	—
			Top margin block of 4, 2P#	37.50	—
			Center line block	35.00	*4.00*
			Top margin block of 20, 2P#, arrow, 2 TOP, 2 registration markers and denomination	175.00	—
a.			Vert. pair, imperf. horiz.	*1,000.*	
b.			Watermarked USIR ('51)	350.00	90.00
b.			Margin block of 4, 2P#	1,850.	
c.			Red violet & black, *Aug. 31, 1954*	6.75	15
c.			Top or bottom margin block of 4, 2P#	34.00	—
d.			As "c", vert. pair, imperf. horiz.	*1,000.*	
e.			Vertical pair, imperf. between	*2,500.*	
f.			As "c", vert. pair, imperf. btwn.	6,000.	

No. 832c is dry printed from 400-subject flat plates on thick white paper with smooth, colorless gum.

No.	Type	Denom.	Description	Unused	Used
833	A305	$2	**yellow green & black,** *Sept. 29, 1938*	21.00	3.75
			green & black ('43)	21.00	3.75
			Margin block of 4, bottom or side arrow	85.00	—
			Top margin block of 4, 2 P#	110.00	—
			Center line block	87.50	35.00
			Top margin block of 20, 2 P#, arrow, 2 TOP, 2 registration markers and denominations	450.00	—
834	A306	$5	**car. & black,** *Nov. 17, 1938*	105.00	3.00
a.			$5 red brown & black	*1,000.*	*500.00*
			Margin block of four, bottom or side arrow	425.00	—
			Top margin block of 4, 2 P#	450.00	—
			Center line block	435.00	*25.00*
			Top margin block of 20, 2 P#, arrow, 2 TOP, 2 registration markers and denominations	2,200.	

Top plate number blocks of Nos. 832, 833 and 834 are found both with and without top arrow or registration markers.

CONSTITUTION RATIFICATION ISSUE

Issued in commemoration of the 150th anniversary of the ratification of the United States Constitution.

Old Courthouse, Williamsburg, Va. — A307

ROTARY PRESS PRINTING

Plates of 200 subjects in four panes of 50 each.

1938 **Unwmk.** ***Perf. 11x10½***

No.	Type	Denom.	Description	Unused	Used
835	A307	3c	**deep violet,** *June 21, 1938*	16	7
			Margin block of 4, P#	3.50	—

SWEDISH-FINNISH TERCENTENARY ISSUE

Issued in commemoration of the tercentenary of the founding of the Swedish and Finnish Settlement at Wilmington, Delaware.

"Landing of the First Swedish and Finnish Settlers in America," by Stanley M. Arthurs — A308

FLAT PLATE PRINTING

Plates of 192 subjects in four panes of 48 each, separated by 1¼ inch wide gutters with central guide lines.

1938 **Unwmk.** ***Perf. 11***

No.	Type	Denom.	Description	Unused	Used
836	A308	3c	**red violet,** *June 27, 1938*	12	8
			Margin block of 6, P#	2.75	—

NORTHWEST TERRITORY SESQUICENTENNIAL ISSUE

Issued in commemoration of the sesquicentennial of the settlement of the Northwest Territory.

"Colonization of the West," by Gutzon Borglum — A309

ROTARY PRESS PRINTING

Plates of 400 subjects in four panes of 100 each.

1938 **Unwmk.** ***Perf. 11x10½***

No.	Type	Denom.	Description	Unused	Used
837	A309	3c	**bright violet,** *July 15, 1938*	14	8
			rose violet	14	8
			Margin block of 4, P#	8.00	—

IOWA TERRITORY CENTENNIAL ISSUE

Issued in commemoration of the 100th anniversary of the establishment of Iowa Territory.

Old Capitol, Iowa City — A310

ROTARY PRESS PRINTING

Plates of 200 subjects in four panes of 50 each.

1938 **Unwmk.** ***Perf. 11x10½***

No.	Type	Denom.	Description	Unused	Used
838	A310	3c	**violet,** *Aug. 24, 1938*	14	8
			Margin block of 4, P#	4.50	—
			Pair with full vertical gutter between	—	

REGULAR ISSUE

ROTARY PRESS COIL STAMPS

Types of 1938

1939 **Unwmk.** ***Perf. 10 Vertically***

No.	Type	Denom.	Description	Unused	Used
839	A276	1c	**green,** *Jan. 20, 1939*	20	6
			light green	20	6
			Pair	40	14
			Joint line pair	90	25
840	A277	1½c	**bister brown,** *Jan. 20, 1939*	24	6
			buff	24	6
			Pair	48	12
			Joint line pair	95	25
841	A278	2c	**rose carmine,** *Jan. 20, 1939*	24	5
			Pair	48	10
			Joint line pair	1.25	15
842	A279	3c	**deep violet,** *Jan. 20, 1939*	42	5
			violet	42	5
			Pair	85	11
			Joint line pair	1.50	15
			Gripper cracks	—	
			Thin translucent paper	2.00	—
843	A280	4c	**red violet,** *Jan. 20, 1939*	6.75	35
			Pair	13.50	70
			Joint line pair	22.50	2.00
844	A281	4½c	**dark gray,** *Jan. 20, 1939*	42	35
			Pair	85	70
			Joint line pair	3.25	1.50
845	A282	5c	**bright blue,** *Jan. 20, 1939*	4.75	30
			Pair	9.50	60
			Joint line pair	20.00	1.50
846	A283	6c	**red orange,** *Jan. 20, 1939*	1.10	15
			Pair	2.20	30
			Joint line pair	7.00	80
847	A287	10c	**brown red,** *Jan. 20, 1939*	11.00	40
			Pair	22.00	80
			Joint line pair	35.00	2.75

Bureau Precancels: 1c, 269 diff., 1½c, 179 diff., 2c, 101 diff., 3c, 46 diff., 4c, 13 diff., 4½c, 3 diff., 5c, 6 diff., 6c, 8 diff., 10c, 4 diff.

Perf. 10 Horizontally

No.	Type	Denom.	Description	Unused	Used
848	A276	1c	**green,** *Jan. 27, 1939*	55	12
			Pair	1.10	25
			Joint line pair	2.00	50
849	A277	1½c	**bister brown,** *Jan. 27, 1939*	1.10	30
			Pair	2.20	60
			Joint line pair	3.00	1.10
850	A278	2c	**rose carmine,** *Jan. 27, 1939*	2.50	40
			Pair	5.00	80
			Joint line pair	6.00	1.40
851	A279	3c	**deep violet,** *Jan. 27, 1939*	2.25	35
			Pair	4.50	70
			Joint line pair	5.00	1.40

GOLDEN GATE INTERNATIONAL EXPOSITION ISSUE

Issued in commemoration of the Golden Gate International Exposition at San Francisco.

"Tower of the Sun" — A311

ROTARY PRESS PRINTING

Plates of 200 subjects in four panes of 50 each.

1939 **Unwmk.** ***Perf. 10½x11***

No.	Type	Denom.	Description	Unused	Used
852	A311	3c	**bright purple,** *Feb. 18, 1939*	10	6
			On cover, Expo. station canc.		5.50
			Margin block of 4, P#	1.40	—

NEW YORK WORLD'S FAIR ISSUE

Issued to commemorate the New York World's Fair.

Trylon and Perisphere — A312

ROTARY PRESS PRINTING

Plates of 200 subjects in four panes of 50 each.

1939 **Unwmk.** ***Perf. 10½x11***

No.	Type	Denom.	Description	Unused	Used
853	A312	3c	**deep purple,** *Apr. 1, 1939*	10	6
			On cover, Expo. station canc.		30
			Margin block of 4, P#	1.90	—

WASHINGTON INAUGURATION ISSUE

Issued in commemoration of the sesquicentennial of the inauguration of George Washington as First President.

Washington Taking Oath of Office, Federal Building, New York City — A313

FLAT PLATE PRINTING

Plates of 200 subjects in four panes of 50 each.

1939	**Unwmk.**	***Perf. 11***	
854 A313 3c **bright red violet,** *Apr. 30, 1939*		25	10
Margin block of 6, P#		3.00	—

BASEBALL CENTENNIAL ISSUE

Issued in commemoration of the centennial of Baseball.

Sandlot Baseball Game — A314

Designed by William A. Roach.

ROTARY PRESS PRINTING

Plates of 200 subjects in four panes of 50 each.

1939	**Unwmk.**	***Perf. 11x10½***	
855 A314 3c **violet,** *June 12, 1939*		32	8
Margin block of 4, P#		3.25	—

PANAMA CANAL ISSUE

25th anniversary of the opening of the Panama Canal.

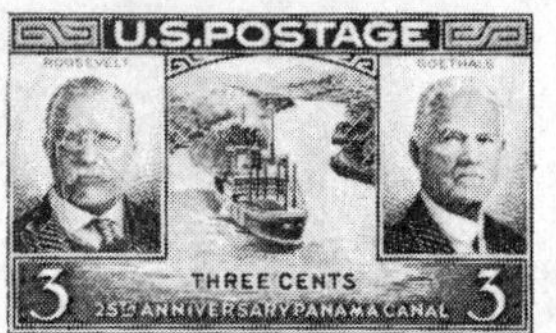

Theodore Roosevelt, Gen. George W. Goethals and Ship in Gaillard Cut — A315

Designed by William A. Roach.

FLAT PLATE PRINTING

Plates of 200 subjects in four panes of 50 each.

1939	**Unwmk.**	***Perf. 11***	
856 A315 3c **deep red violet,** *Aug. 15, 1939*		18	8
Margin block of 6, P#		3.00	—

PRINTING TERCENTENARY ISSUE

Issued in commemoration of the 300th anniversary of printing in Colonial America. The Stephen Daye press is in the Harvard University Museum.

Stephen Daye Press — A316

Designed by William K. Schrage.

ROTARY PRESS PRINTING

E.E. Plates of 200 subjects in four panes of 50 each.

1939	**Unwmk.**	***Perf. 10½x11***	
857 A316 3c **violet,** *Sept. 25, 1939*		9	8
Margin block of 4, P#		1.00	—

50th ANNIVERSARY OF STATEHOOD ISSUE

Issued in commemoration of the 50th anniversary of the admission to statehood of North Dakota, South Dakota, Montana and Washington.

Map of North and South Dakota, Montana and Washington A317

ROTARY PRESS PRINTING

E.E. Plates of 200 subjects in four panes of 50 each.

1939	**Unwmk.**	***Perf. 11x10½***	
858 A317 3c **rose violet,** *Nov. 2, 1939*		9	8
Margin block of 4, P#		1.25	—

FAMOUS AMERICANS ISSUES

ROTARY PRESS PRINTING

E.E. Plates of 280 subjects in four panes of 70 each.

AUTHORS

Issued in honor of famous American authors.

Washington Irving — A318

James Fenimore Cooper — A319

Ralph Waldo Emerson — A320

Louisa May Alcott — A321

Samuel L. Clemens (Mark Twain) — A322

1940	**Unwmk.**	***Perf. 10½x11***	
859 A318 1c **bright blue green,** *Jan. 29, 1940*		7	6
Margin block of 4, P#		90	—
860 A319 2c **rose carmine,** *Jan. 29, 1940*		8	8
Margin block of 4, P#		90	—
861 A320 3c **bright red violet,** *Feb. 5, 1940*		10	6
Block of four		40	40
Margin block of 4, P#		1.25	—
862 A321 5c **ultramarine,** *Feb. 5, 1940*		28	20
Margin block of 4, P#		8.00	—
863 A322 10c **dark brown,** *Feb. 13, 1940*		1.60	1.35
Margin block of 4, P#		35.00	—

POETS

Issued in honor of famous American poets

Henry Wadsworth Longfellow — A323

John Greenleaf Whittier — A324

James Russell Lowell — A325

Walt Whitman — A326

James Witcomb Riley — A327

864 A323 1c **bright blue green,** *Feb. 16, 1940*		10	8
Margin block of 4, P#		2.00	—
865 A324 2c **rose carmine,** *Feb. 16, 1940*		10	8
Margin block of 4, P#		2.00	—
866 A325 3c **bright red violet,** *Feb. 20, 1940*		14	6
Block of four		56	50
Margin block of 4, P#		2.50	—
867 A326 5c **ultramarine,** *Feb. 20, 1940*		32	18
Margin block of 4, P#		10.50	—
868 A327 10c **dark brown,** *Feb. 24, 1940*		1.75	1.40
Margin block of 4, P#		35.00	—

EDUCATORS

Issued in honor of famous American educators.

Horace Mann — A328

Mark Hopkins — A329

Charles W. Eliot — A330

Frances E. Willard — A331

Booker T. Washington — A332

869 A328 1c **bright blue green,** *Mar. 14, 1940*		12	8
Margin block of 4, P#		2.25	—
870 A329 2c **rose carmine,** *Mar. 14, 1940*		9	6
Margin block of 4, P#		1.00	—
871 A330 3c **bright red violet,** *Mar. 28, 1940*		15	6
Block of four		60	60
Margin block of 4, P#		2.00	—
872 A331 5c **ultramarine,** *Mar. 28, 1940*		38	25
Margin block of 4, P#		10.00	—
873 A332 10c **dark brown,** *Apr. 7, 1940*		1.25	1.25
Margin block of 4, P#		25.00	—

SCIENTISTS

Issued in honor of famous American scientists.

John James Audubon — A333

Dr. Crawford W. Long — A334

Values for cancellation varieties are for specimens off cover.

Luther Burbank — A335

Dr. Walter Reed — A336

Jane Addams — A337

874	A333	1c	**bright blue green,** *Apr. 8, 1940*	8	6
			Margin block of 4, P#	90	—
875	A334	2c	**rose carmine,** *Apr. 8, 1940*	8	6
			Margin block of 4, P#	75	—
876	A335	3c	**bright red violet,** *Apr. 17, 1940*	10	6
			Margin block of 4, P#	1.00	—
877	A336	5c	**ultramarine,** *Apr. 17, 1940*	25	25
			Block of four	1.00	2.00
			Margin block of 4, P#	7.00	—
878	A337	10c	**dark brown,** *Apr. 26, 1940*	1.05	95
			Margin block of 4, P#	20.00	—

COMPOSERS

Issued in honor of famous American composers.

Stephen Collins Foster — A338

John Philip Sousa — A339

Victor Herbert — A340

Edward A. MacDowell — A341

Ethelbert Nevin — A342

879	A338	1c	**bright blue green,** *May 3, 1940*	7	6
			Margin block of 4, P#	1.00	—
880	A339	2c	**rose carmine,** *May 3, 1940*	9	6
			Margin block of 4, P#	1.00	—
881	A340	3c	**bright red violet,** *May 13, 1940*	10	6
			Block of four	40	35
			Margin block of 4, P#	1.00	—
882	A341	5c	**ultramarine,** *May 13, 1940*	35	22
			Margin block of 4, P#	9.00	—
883	A342	10c	**dark brown,** *June 10, 1940*	3.75	1.35
			Margin block of 4, P#	32.50	—

ARTISTS

Issued in honor of famous American artists.

Gilbert Charles Stuart — A343

James A. McNeill Whistler — A344

Augustus Saint-Gaudens A345

Daniel Chester French A346

Frederic Remington — A347

884	A343	1c	**bright blue green,** *Sept. 5, 1940*	6	6
			Margin block of 4, P#	1.00	—
885	A344	2c	**rose carmine,** *Sept. 5, 1940*	8	6
			Margin block of 4, P#	1.00	—
886	A345	3c	**bright red violet,** *Sept. 16, 1940*	10	6
			Margin block of 4, P#	1.00	—
887	A346	5c	**ultramarine,** *Sept. 16, 1940*	45	22
			Margin block of 4, P#	8.00	—
888	A347	10c	**dark brown,** *Sept. 30, 1940*	1.65	1.40
			Margin block of 4, P#	30.00	—

INVENTORS

Issued in honor of famous American inventors.

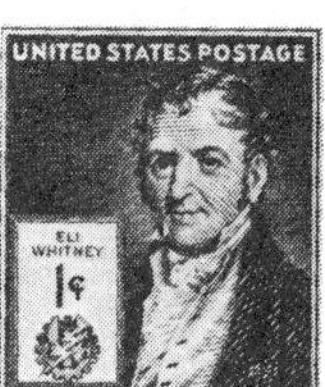

Eli Whitney — A348

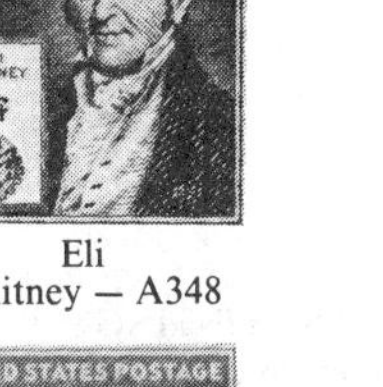

Samuel F. B. Morse — A349

Cyrus Hall McCormick A350

Elias Howe A351

Alexander Graham Bell — A352

889	A348	1c	**bright blue green,** *Oct. 7, 1940*	12	8
			Margin block of 4, P#	2.00	—
890	A349	2c	**rose carmine,** *Oct. 7, 1940*	12	6
			Margin block of 4, P#	1.10	—
891	A350	3c	**bright red violet,** *Oct. 14, 1940*	25	6
			Margin block of 4, P#	1.75	—
892	A351	5c	**ultramarine,** *Oct. 14, 1940*	1.00	32
			Margin block of 4, P#	14.00	—
893	A352	10c	**dark brown,** *Oct. 28, 1940*	11.00	2.25
			Margin block of 4, P#	70.00	—

PONY EXPRESS ISSUE

Issued in commemoration of the 80th anniversary of the Pony Express.

Pony Express Rider — A353

ROTARY PRESS PRINTING

E.E. Plates of 200 subjects in four panes of 50 each.

1940			**Unwmk.**	***Perf. 11x10½***	
894	A353	3c	**henna brown,** *Apr. 3, 1940*	22	10
			Margin block of 4, P#	3.00	—

PAN AMERICAN UNION ISSUE

Issued in commemoration of the 50th anniversary of the founding of the Pan American Union.

The Three Graces (Botticelli) — A354

ROTARY PRESS PRINTING

E.E. Plates of 200 subjects in four panes of 50 each.

1940			**Unwmk.**	***Perf. 10½x11***	
895	A354	3c	**light violet,** *Apr. 14, 1940*	18	12
			Margin block of 4, P#	2.75	—

IDAHO STATEHOOD ISSUE

Issued in commemoration of the 50th anniversary of admission of Idaho to statehood.

Idaho State Capitol — A355

ROTARY PRESS PRINTING

E.E. Plates of 200 subjects in four panes of 50 each.

1940			**Unwmk.**	***Perf. 11x10½***	
896	A355	3c	**bright violet,** *July 3, 1940*	14	8
			Margin block of 4, P#	1.75	—

WYOMING STATEHOOD ISSUE

Issued in commemoration of the 50th anniversary of admission of Wyoming to statehood.

Wyoming State Seal — A356

ROTARY PRESS PRINTING

E.E. Plates of 200 subjects in four panes of 50 each.

1940			**Unwmk.**	***Perf. 10½x11***	
897	A356	3c	**brown violet,** *July 10, 1940*	14	8
			Margin block of 4, P#	1.50	—

CORONADO EXPEDITION ISSUE

Issued in commemoration of the 400th anniversary of the Coronado Expedition.

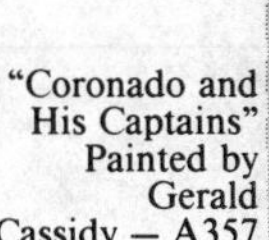

"Coronado and His Captains" Painted by Gerald Cassidy — A357

ROTARY PRESS PRINTING

E.E. Plates of 200 subjects in four panes of 50 each.

1940	**Unwmk.**	***Perf. 11x10½***	
898 A357 3c **violet,** *Sept. 7, 1940*		14	8
Margin block of 4, P#		1.50	—

NATIONAL DEFENSE ISSUE

Issued in connection with the National Defense Program.

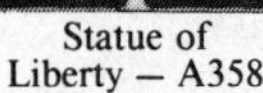

Statue of Liberty — A358

90-millimeter Anti-aircraft Gun — A359

Torch of Enlightenment — A360

ROTARY PRESS PRINTING

E.E. Plates of 400 subjects in four panes of 100

1940, Oct. 16	**Unwmk.**	***Perf. 11x10½***	
899 A358 1c **bright blue green**		5	5
Margin block of 4, P#		45	—
a. Vertical pair, imperf. between		500.00	—
b. Horizontal pair, imperf. between		40.00	—
Pair with full vert. gutter between		*200.00*	
Cracked plate (22684 UR 10)		3.00	
Gripper cracks		3.00	
900 A359 2c **rose carmine**		6	5
Margin block of 4, P#		50	—
a. Horizontal pair, imperf. between		45.00	—
Pair with full vert. gutter between		*275.00*	
901 A360 3c **bright violet**		9	5
Margin block of 4, P#		70	—
a. Horizontal pair, imperf. between		25.00	—
Pair with full vert. gutter between			—

Bureau Precancels: 1c, 316 diff., 2c, 25 diff., 3c, 22 diff.

THIRTEENTH AMENDMENT ISSUE

Issued to commemorate the 75th anniversary of the 13th Amendment to the Constitution abolishing slavery.

Emancipation Monument; Lincoln and Kneeling Slave, by Thomas Bell — A361

Designed by William A. Roach.

ROTARY PRESS PRINTING

E.E. Plates of 200 subjects in four panes of 50 each.

1940	**Unwmk.**	***Perf. 10½x11***	
902 A361 3c **deep violet,** *Oct. 20, 1940*		16	10
dark violet		16	10
Margin block of 4, P#		3.25	—

VERMONT STATEHOOD ISSUE

Issued in commemoration of the 150th anniversary of the admission of Vermont to statehood.

State Capitol, Montpelier A362

Designed by Alvin R. Meissner.

ROTARY PRESS PRINTING

E.E. Plates of 200 subjects in four panes of 50 each.

1941	**Unwmk.**	***Perf. 11x10½***	
903 A362 3c **light violet,** *Mar. 4, 1941*		14	8
Margin block of 4, P#		1.75	—

KENTUCKY STATEHOOD ISSUE

Issued in commemoration of the 150th anniversary of the admission of Kentucky to statehood.

Daniel Boone and Three Frontiersmen, from Mural by Gilbert White — A363

Designed by William A. Roach.

ROTARY PRESS PRINTING

E.E. Plates of 200 subjects in four panes of 50 each.

1942	**Unwmk.**	***Perf. 11x10½***	
904 A363 3c **violet,** *June 1, 1942*		10	9
Margin block of 4, P#		1.10	—

WIN THE WAR ISSUE

American Eagle — A364

ROTARY PRESS PRINTING

E.E. Plates of 400 subjects in four panes of 100 each.

1942	**Unwmk.**	***Perf. 11x10½***	
905 A364 3c **violet,** *July 4, 1942*		8	5
light violet		8	5
a. 3c purple		20.00	8.00
Margin block of 4, P#		40	—
Pair with full vert. or horiz. gutter between		*175.00*	

Bureau Precancels: 26 diff.

CHINESE RESISTANCE ISSUE

Issued to commemorate the Chinese people's five years of resistance to Japanese aggression.

Map of China, Abraham Lincoln and Sun Yat-sen, Founder of the Chinese Republic — A365

ROTARY PRESS PRINTING

E.E. Plates of 200 subjects in four panes of 50 each.

1942	**Unwmk.**	***Perf. 11x10½***	
906 A365 5c **bright blue,** *July 7, 1942*		18	16
Margin block of 4, P#		10.00	—

ALLIED NATIONS ISSUE

Allegory of Victory — A366

Designed by Leon Helguera.

ROTARY PRESS PRINTING

E.E. Plates of 400 subjects in four panes of 100 each.

1943	**Unwmk.**	***Perf. 11x10½***	
907 A366 2c **rose carmine,** *Jan. 14, 1943*		8	5
Margin block of 4, P#		40	—
Pair with full vert. or horiz. gutter between		*225.00*	

Bureau Precancels: 2 different.

FOUR FREEDOMS ISSUE

Liberty Holding the Torch of Freedom and Enlightenment — A367

Designed by Paul Manship.

ROTARY PRESS PRINTING

E.E. Plates of 400 subjects in four panes of 100 each.

1943	**Unwmk.**	***Perf. 11x10½***	
908 A367 1c **bright blue green,** *Feb. 12, 1943*		8	5
Margin block of 4, P#		50	—

Bureau Precancels: 20 diff.

OVERRUN COUNTRIES ISSUE

Printed by the American Bank Note Co.

FRAMES ENGRAVED, CENTERS OFFSET PRINTING

FLAT PLATE PRINTING

Plates of 200 subjects in four panes of 50 each.

Due to the failure of the printers to divulge detailed information as to printing processes used, the editors omit listings of irregularities, flaws, blemishes and "errors" which are numerous in this issue. These include shifted prints (not true double prints), etc. An exception is made for the widely recognized "KORPA" variety.

Flag of Poland — A368

1943-44	**Unwmk.**	***Perf. 12***	
909 A368 5c **blue violet, bright red & black,** *June 22, 1943*		18	12
Margin block of 4, Inscribed "Poland"		6.00	—
Top margin block of 6, with red & blue violet guide markings and "Poland"		6.50	—
Bottom margin block of 6, with red & black guide markings		1.30	—

Flag of Czechoslovakia A368a

910 A368a 5c **blue violet, blue, bright red & black,** *July 12, 1943*		18	9
Margin block of 4, inscribed "Czechoslovakia"		3.00	—
Top margin block of 6, with red & blue violet guide markings and "Czechoslovakia"		3.50	—

Flag of Norway — A368b

911 A368b 5c **blue violet, dark rose, deep blue & black,** *July 27, 1943* 14 7
Margin block of 4, inscribed "Norway" 1.50 —
Bottom margin block of 6 with dark rose & blue violet guide markings 1.00 —

Flag of Luxembourg A368c

912 A368c 5c **blue violet, dark rose, light blue & black,** *Aug. 10, 1943* 14 7
Margin block of 4, inscribed "Luxembourg" 1.25 —
Top margin block of 6 with light blue & blue violet guide markings & "Luxembourg" 1.75 —

Flag of Netherlands A368d

913 A368d 5c **blue violet, dark rose, blue & black,** *Aug. 24, 1943* 14 7
Margin block of 4, inscribed "Netherlands" 1.25 —
Bottom margin block of 6 with blue & blue violet guide markings 1.00 —

Flag of Belgium — A368e

914 A368e 5c **blue violet, dark rose, yellow & black,** *Sept. 14, 1943* 14 7
Margin block of 4, inscribed "Belgium" 1.25 —
Top margin block of 6, with yellow & blue violet guide markings and "Belgium" 1.75 —

Flag of France — A368f

915 A368f 5c **blue violet, deep blue, dark rose & black,** *Sept. 28, 1943* 14 7
Margin block of 4, inscribed "France" 1.25 —
Bottom margin block of 6 with dark rose & blue violet guide markings 1.00 —

Flag of Greece — A368g

916 A368g 5c **blue violet, pale blue & black,** *Oct. 12, 1943* 38 25
Margin block of 4, inscribed "Greece" 13.00 —
Top margin block of 6 with pale blue & blue violet guide markings & "Greece" 14.00 —

Flag of Yugoslavia A368h

917 A368h 5c **blue violet, blue, dark rose & black,** *Oct. 26, 1943* 28 15
Margin block of 4, inscribed "Yugoslavia" 7.00 —
Bottom margin block of 6 with dark rose & blue violet guide markings 2.00 —

Flag of Albania — A368i

918 A368i 5c **blue violet, dark red & black,** *Nov. 9, 1943* 18 15
Margin block of 4, inscribed "Albania" 7.50 —
Top margin block of 6, with dark red & blue violet guide markings & "Albania" 8.00 —

Flag of Austria — A368j

919 A368j 5c **blue violet, red & black,** *Nov. 23, 1943* 18 15
Margin block of 4, inscribed "Austria" 4.00 —
Bottom margin block of 6, with red & blue violet guide markings 1.40 —

Flag of Denmark — A368k

920 A368k 5c **blue violet, red & black,** *Dec. 7, 1943* 18 15
Margin block of 4, inscribed "Denmark" 6.00 —
Top margin block of 6, with red & blue violet guide markings & "Denmark" 6.50 —

See the "Information for Collectors" section at beginning of catalogue for illustrations of types of postmarks and precancels.

Flag of Korea — A368m

921 A368m 5c **blue violet, red, black & light blue,** *Nov. 2, 1944* 15 12
Margin block of 4, inscribed "Korea" 5.25 —
Top margin block of 6 with blue & black guide markings and "Korea" 5.75 —
"KORPA" plate flaw 17.50 12.50

TRANSCONTINENTAL RAILROAD ISSUE

Issued to commemorate the 75th anniversary of the completion of the first transcontinental railroad.

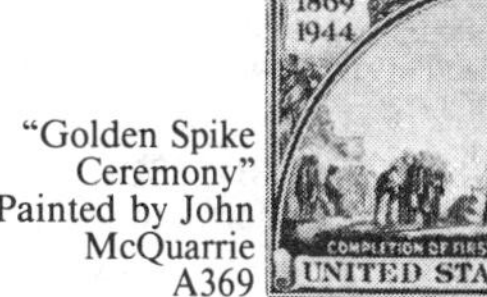

"Golden Spike Ceremony" Painted by John McQuarrie A369

ENGRAVED
ROTARY PRESS PRINTING
E.E. Plates of 200 subjects in four panes of 50 each.

1944 **Unwmk.** ***Perf. 11x10½***

922 A369 3c **violet,** *May 10, 1944* 15 5
Margin block of 4, P# 1.50 —

STEAMSHIP ISSUE

Issued to commemorate the 125th anniversary of the first steamship to cross the Atlantic Ocean.

"Savannah" A370

ROTARY PRESS PRINTING
E.E. Plates of 200 subjects in four panes of 50 each.

1944 **Unwmk.** ***Perf. 11x10½***

923 A370 3c **violet,** *May 22, 1944* 9 5
Margin block of 4, P# 1.50 —

TELEGRAPH ISSUE

Issued to commemorate the 100th anniversary of the first message transmitted by telegraph.

Telegraph Wires and Morse's First Transmitted Words "What Hath God Wrought" — A371

ROTARY PRESS PRINTING
E.E. Plates of 200 subjects in four panes of 50 each.

1944 **Unwmk.** ***Perf. 11x10½***

924 A371 3c **bright red violet,** *May 24, 1944* 8 5
Margin block of 4, P# 90 —

PHILLIPPINE ISSUE

Issued to commemorate the final resistance of the United States and Philippine defenders on Corregidor to the Japanese invaders in 1942.

Aerial View of Corregidor, Manila Bay — A372

ROTARY PRESS PRINTING

E.E. Plates of 200 subjects in four panes of 50 each.

1944 **Unwmk.** ***Perf. 11x10½***

925 A372 3c **deep violet,** *Sept. 27, 1944* 8 5
Margin block of 4, P# 1.00 —

MOTION PICTURE ISSUE

Issued to commemorate the 50th anniversary of motion pictures.

Motion Picture Showing for Armed Forces in South Pacific — A373

ROTARY PRESS PRINTING

E.E. Plates of 200 subjects in four panes of 50 each.

1944 **Unwmk.** ***Perf. 11x10½***

926 A373 3c **deep violet,** *Oct. 31, 1944* 8 5
Margin block of 4, P# 85 —

FLORIDA STATEHOOD ISSUE

Centenary of the admission of Florida to statehood.

State Seal, Gates of St. Augustine and Capitol at Tallahassee A374

ROTARY PRESS PRINTING

E.E. Plates of 200 subjects in four panes of 50 each.

1945 **Unwmk.** ***Perf. 11x10½***

927 A374 3c **bright red violet,** *Mar. 3, 1945* 8 5
Margin block of 4, P# 50 —

UNITED NATIONS CONFERENCE ISSUE

United Nations Conference, San Francisco, Calif.

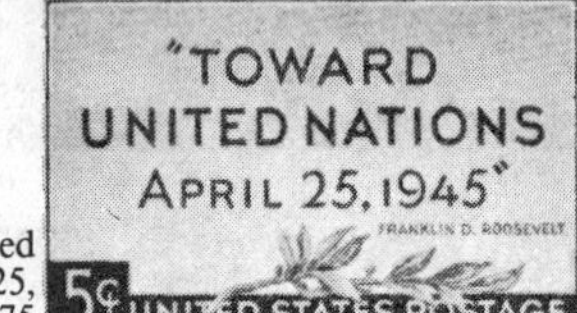

"Toward United Nations, April 25, 1945" — A375

ROTARY PRESS PRINTING

E.E. Plates of 200 subjects in four panes of 50 each.

1945 **Unwmk.** ***Perf. 11x10½***

928 A375 5c **ultramarine,** *Apr. 25, 1945* 9 5
Margin block of 4, P# 45 —

IWO JIMA (MARINES) ISSUE

Issued to commemorate the battle of Iwo Jima and to honor the achievements of the United States Marines.

Marines Raising American Flag on Mount Suribachi, Iwo Jima — A376

ROTARY PRESS PRINTING

E.E. Plates of 200 subjects in four panes of 50 each.

1945 **Unwmk.** ***Perf. 10½x11***

929 A376 3c **yellow green,** *July 11, 1945* 8 5
Margin block of 4, P# 40 —

FRANKLIN D. ROOSEVELT ISSUE

Issued in tribute to Franklin Delano Roosevelt (1882-1945).

Roosevelt and Hyde Park Residence — A377

Roosevelt and the "Little White House" at Warm Springs, Ga. — A378

Roosevelt and White House — A379

Roosevelt, Map of Western Hemisphere and Four Freedoms — A380

ROTARY PRESS PRINTING

E.E. Plates of 200 subjects in four panes of 50 each.

1945-46 **Unwmk.** ***Perf. 11x10½***

930 A377 1c **blue green,** *July 26, 1945* 5 5
Margin block of 4, P# 25 —
931 A378 2c **carmine rose,** *Aug. 24, 1945* 6 5
Margin block of 4, P# 30 —
932 A379 3c **purple,** *June 27, 1945* 6 5
Margin block of 4, P# 30 —
933 A380 5c **bright blue,** *Jan. 30, 1946* 9 5
Margin block of 4, P# 45 —

ARMY ISSUE

Issued to commemorate the achievements of the United States Army in World War II.

United States Troops Passing Arch of Triumph, Paris — A381

ROTARY PRESS PRINTING

E.E. Plates of 200 subjects in four panes of 50 each.

1945 **Unwmk.** ***Perf. 11x10½***

934 A381 3c **olive,** *Sept. 28, 1945* 6 5
Margin block of 4, P# 30 —

NAVY ISSUE

Issued to commemorate the achievements of the United States Navy in World War II.

United States Sailors — A382

ROTARY PRESS PRINTING

E.E. Plates of 200 subjects in four panes of 50 each.

1945 **Unwmk.** ***Perf. 11x10½***

935 A382 3c **blue,** *Oct. 27, 1945* 6 5
Margin block of 4, P# 30 —

COAST GUARD ISSUE

Issued to commemorate the achievements of the United States Coast Guard in World War II.

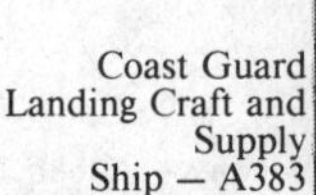

Coast Guard Landing Craft and Supply Ship — A383

ROTARY PRESS PRINTING

E.E. Plates of 200 subjects in four panes of 50 each.

1945 **Unwmk.** ***Perf. 11x10½***

936 A383 3c **bright blue green,** *Nov. 10, 1945* 6 5
Margin block of 4, P# 30 —

ALFRED E. SMITH ISSUE

Issued in honor of Alfred E. Smith, governor of New York.

Alfred E. Smith — A384

ROTARY PRESS PRINTING

E.E. Plates of 400 subjects in four panes of 100 each.

1945 **Unwmk.** ***Perf. 11x10½***

937 A384 3c **purple,** *Nov. 26, 1945* 6 5
Margin block of 4, P# 30 —
Pair with full vert. gutter btwn. — —

TEXAS STATEHOOD ISSUE

Issued to commemorate the 100th anniversary of the admission of Texas to statehood.

Flags of the United States and the State of Texas — A385

ROTARY PRESS PRINTING

E.E. Plates of 200 subjects in four panes of 50 each.

1945 **Unwmk.** ***Perf. 11x10½***

938 A385 3c **dark blue,** *Dec. 29, 1945* 6 5
Margin block of 4, P# 30 —

MERCHANT MARINE ISSUE

Issued to commemorate the achievements of the United States Merchant Marine in World War II.

Liberty Ship Unloading Cargo — A386

ROTARY PRESS PRINTING

E.E. Plates of 200 subjects in four panes of 50 each.

1946 **Unwmk.** ***Perf. 11x10½***

939 A386 3c **blue green,** *Feb. 26, 1946* 6 5
Margin block of 4, P# 30 —

VETERANS OF WORLD WAR II ISSUE

Issued to honor all veterans of World War II.

Honorable Discharge Emblem — A387

ROTARY PRESS PRINTING

E.E. Plates of 400 subjects in four panes of 100 each.

1946 **Unwmk.** ***Perf. 11x10½***

940 A387 3c **dark violet,** *May 9, 1946* 6 5
Margin block of 4, P# 30 —

TENNESSEE STATEHOOD ISSUE

Issued to commemorate the 150th anniversary of the admission of Tennessee to statehood.

Andrew Jackson, John Sevier and State Capitol, Nashville — A388

ROTARY PRESS PRINTING

E.E. Plates of 200 subjects in four panes of 50 each.

1946 **Unwmk.** ***Perf. 11x10½***

941 A388 3c **dark violet,** *June 1, 1946* 6 5
Margin block of 4, P# 30 —

IOWA STATEHOOD ISSUE

Centenary of the admission of Iowa to statehood.

Iowa State Flag and Map — A389

ROTARY PRESS PRINTING

E.E. Plates of 200 subjects in four panes of 50 each.

1946 **Unwmk.** ***Perf. 11x10½***

942 A389 3c **deep blue,** *Aug. 3, 1946* 6 5
Margin block of 4, P# 30 —

SMITHSONIAN INSTITUTION ISSUE

Issued to commemorate the 100th anniversary of the establishment of the Smithsonian Institution, Washington, D.C.

Smithsonian Institution A390

ROTARY PRESS PRINTING

E.E. Plates of 200 subjects in four panes of 50 each.

1946 **Unwmk.** ***Perf. 11x10½***

943 A390 3c **violet brown,** *Aug. 10, 1946* 6 5
Margin block of 4, P# 30 —

KEARNY EXPEDITION ISSUE

Issued to commemorate the 100th anniversary of the entry of General Stephen Watts Kearny into Santa Fe.

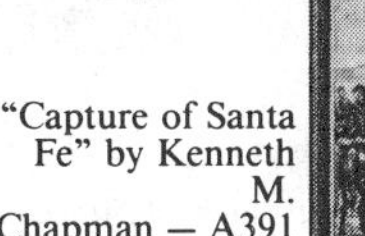

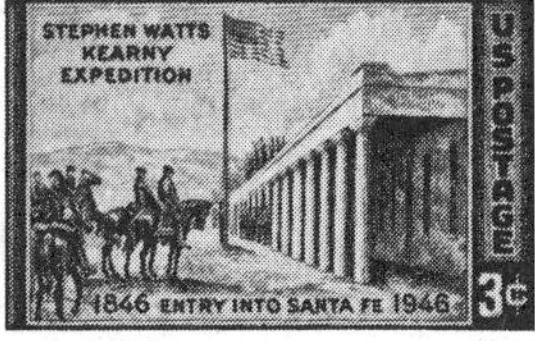

"Capture of Santa Fe" by Kenneth M. Chapman — A391

ROTARY PRESS PRINTING

E.E. Plates of 200 subjects in four panes of 50 each.

1946 **Unwmk.** ***Perf. 11x10½***

944 A391 3c **brown violet,** *Oct. 16, 1946* 6 5
Margin block of 4, P# 30 —

THOMAS A. EDISON ISSUE

Centenary of the birth of Thomas Alva Edison (1847-1931), inventor.

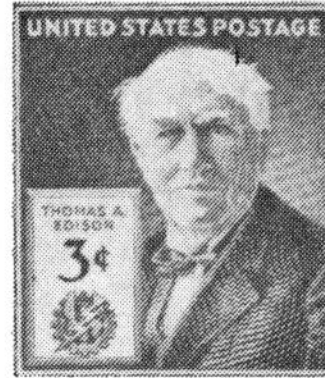

Thomas A. Edison — A392

ROTARY PRESS PRINTING

E.E. Plates of 280 subjects in four panes of 70 each.

1947 **Unwmk.** ***Perf. 10½x11***

945 A392 3c **bright red violet,** *Feb. 11, 1947* 6 5
Margin block of 4, P# 30 —

JOSEPH PULITZER ISSUE

Centenary of the birth of Joseph Pulitzer (1847-1911), journalist.

Joseph Pulitzer and Statue of Liberty — A393

Designed by Victor S. McCloskey, Jr.

ROTARY PRESS PRINTING

E.E. Plates of 200 subjects in four panes of 50 each.

1947 **Unwmk.** ***Perf. 11x10½***

946 A393 3c **purple,** *Apr. 10, 1947* 6 5
Margin block of 4, P# 30 —

POSTAGE STAMP CENTENARY ISSUE

Issued to commemorate the centenary of the first postage stamps issued by the United States Government

Washington and Franklin, Early and Modern Mail-carrying Vehicles — A394

Designed by Leon Helguera.

ROTARY PRESS PRINTING

E.E. Plates of 200 subjects in four panes of 50 each.

1947 **Unwmk.** ***Perf. 11x10½***

947 A394 3c **deep blue,** *May 17, 1947* 6 5
Margin block of 4, P# 30 —

CENTENARY INTERNATIONAL PHILATELIC EXHIBITION ISSUE

SOUVENIR SHEET

A395

FLAT PLATE PRINTING

Plates of 30 subjects

1947 **Unwmk.** ***Imperf.***

948 A395 **Sheet of two,** *May 19, 1947* 55 45
a. 5c blue, type A1 15 15
b. 10c brown orange, type A2 20 20

Sheet inscribed below stamps: "100th Anniversary United States Postage Stamps" and in the margins:
"PRINTED BY THE TREASURY DEPARTMENT, BUREAU OF ENGRAVING AND PRINTING. - UNDER AUTHORITY OF ROBERT E. HANNEGAN, POSTMASTER GENERAL. - IN COMPLIMENT TO THE CENTENARY INTERNATIONAL PHILATELIC EXHIBITION. - NEW YORK, N.Y., MAY 17-25, 1947."
Sheet size varies: 96-98x66-68mm.

DOCTORS ISSUE

Issued to honor the physicians of America.

"The Doctor" by Sir Luke Fildes — A396

Designed by Charles R. Chickering.

ROTARY PRESS PRINTING

E.E. Plates of 200 subjects in four panes of 50 each.

1947 **Unwmk.** ***Perf. 11x10½***

949 A396 3c **brown violet,** *June 9, 1947* 6 5
Margin block of 4, P# 30 —

UTAH ISSUE

Issued to commemorate the centenary of the settlement of Utah.

Pioneers Entering the Valley of Great Salt Lake — A397

Designed by Charles R. Chickering.

ROTARY PRESS PRINTING

E.E. Plates of 200 subjects in four panes of 50 each.

1947 **Unwmk.** ***Perf. 11x10½***

950 A397 3c **dark violet,** *July 24, 1947* 6 5
Margin block of 4, P# 30 —

U.S. FRIGATE CONSTITUTION ISSUE

Issued to commemorate the 150th anniversary of the launching of the U.S. frigate Constitution ("Old Ironsides").

Naval Architect's Drawing of Frigate Constitution A398

Designed by Andrew H. Hepburn.

ROTARY PRESS PRINTING

E.E. Plates of 200 subjects in four panes of 50 each.

1947 **Unwmk.** ***Perf. 11x10½***

951 A398 3c **blue green,** *Oct. 21, 1947* 6 5
Margin block of 4, P# 30 —

EVERGLADES NATIONAL PARK ISSUE

Issued to commemorate the dedication of the Everglades National Park, Florida, December 6, 1947.

See table of Territorial and Statehood Dates at beginning of catalogue. See catalogue index.

Great White Heron and Map of Florida — A399

Designed by Robert I. Miller, Jr.

ROTARY PRESS PRINTING
E.E. Plates of 200 subjects in four panes of 50 each.

1947 **Unwmk.** ***Perf. 10½x11***
952 A399 3c **bright green,** *Dec. 5, 1947* 6 5
Margin block of 4, P# 30 —

GEORGE WASHINGTON CARVER ISSUE

Issued to commemorate the fifth anniversary of the death of Dr. George Washington Carver, (1864-1943), botanist.

Dr. George Washington Carver — A400

ROTARY PRESS PRINTING
E.E. Plates of 280 subjects in four panes of 70 each.

1948 **Unwmk.** ***Perf. 10½x11***
953 A400 3c **bright red violet,** *Jan. 5, 1948* 6 5
Margin block of 4, P# 30 —

CALIFORNIA GOLD CENTENNIAL ISSUE

Centenary of the discovery of gold in California.

Sutter's Mill, Coloma, California — A401

Designed by Charles R. Chickering.

ROTARY PRESS PRINTING
E.E. Plates of 200 subjects in four panes of 50 each.

1948 **Unwmk.** ***Perf. 11x10½***
954 A401 3c **dark violet,** *Jan. 24, 1948* 6 5
Margin block of 4, P# 30 —

MISSISSIPPI TERRITORY ISSUE

Issued to commemorate the 150th anniversary of the establishment of the Mississippi Territory.

Map, Seal of Mississippi Territory and Gov. Winthrop Sargent — A402

Designed by William K. Schrage.

ROTARY PRESS PRINTING
E.E. Plates of 200 subjects in four panes of 50 each.

1948 **Unwmk.** ***Perf. 11x10½***
955 A402 3c **brown violet,** *Apr. 7, 1948* 6 5
Margin block of 4, P# 30 —

FOUR CHAPLAINS ISSUE

Issued in honor of George L. Fox, Clark V. Poling, John P. Washington and Alexander D. Goode, the four chaplains who sacrificed their lives in the sinking of the S.S. Dorchester, February 3, 1943.

Four Chaplains and Sinking S.S. Dorchester A403

Designed by Charles R. Chickering.

ROTARY PRESS PRINTING
E.E. Plates of 200 subjects in four panes of 50 each.

1948 **Unwmk.** ***Perf. 11x10½***
956 A403 3c **gray black,** *May 28, 1948* 6 5
Margin block of 4, P# 30 —

WISCONSIN CENTENNIAL ISSUE

Issued to commemorate the centenary of the admission of Wisconsin to statehood.

Map on Scroll and State Capitol — A404

Designed by Victor S. McCloskey, Jr.

ROTARY PRESS PRINTING
E.E. Plates of 200 subjects in four panes of 50 each.

1948 **Unwmk.** ***Perf. 11x10½***
957 A404 3c **dark violet,** *May 29, 1948* 6 5
Margin block of 4, P# 30 —

SWEDISH PIONEER ISSUE

Issued to commemorate the centenary of the coming of the Swedish pioneers to the Middle West.

Swedish Pioneer with Covered Wagon Moving Westward — A405

Designed by Charles R. Chickering.

ROTARY PRESS PRINTING
E.E. Plates of 200 subjects in four panes of 50 each.

1948 **Unwmk.** ***Perf. 11x10½***
958 A405 5c **deep blue,** *June 4, 1948* 9 5
Margin block of 4, P# 45 —

PROGRESS OF WOMEN ISSUE

Issued to commemorate a century of progress of American Women.

Elizabeth Stanton, Carrie Chapman Catt and Lucretia Mott — A406

Designed by Victor S. McCloskey, Jr.

ROTARY PRESS PRINTING
E.E. Plates of 200 subjects in four panes of 50 each.

1948 **Unwmk.** ***Perf. 11x10½***
959 A406 3c **dark violet,** *July 19, 1948* 6 5
Margin block of 4, P# 30 —

WILLIAM ALLEN WHITE ISSUE

Issued to honor William Allen White, (1868-1944), writer and journalist.

William Allen White — A407

ROTARY PRESS PRINTING
E.E. Plates of 280 subjects in four panes of 70 each.

1948 **Unwmk.** ***Perf. 10½x11***
960 A407 3c **bright red violet,** *July 31, 1948* 6 6
Margin block of 4, P# 30 —

UNITED STATES-CANADA FRIENDSHIP ISSUE

Issued to commemorate a century of friendship between the United States and Canada.

Niagara Railway Suspension Bridge — A408

Designed by Leon Helguera, modeled by V. S. McCloskey, Jr.

ROTARY PRESS PRINTING
E.E. Plates of 200 subjects in four panes of 50 each.

1948 **Unwmk.** ***Perf. 11x10½***
961 A408 3c **blue,** *Aug. 2, 1948* 6 5
Margin block of 4, P# 30 —

FRANCIS SCOTT KEY ISSUE

Issued to honor Francis Scott Key (1779-1843), Maryland lawyer and author of "The Star-Spangled Banner" (1813).

Francis Scott Key and American Flags of 1814 and 1948 — A409

Designed by Victor S. McCloskey, Jr.

ROTARY PRESS PRINTING
E.E. Plates of 200 subjects in four panes of 50 each.

1948 **Unwmk.** ***Perf. 11x10½***
962 A409 3c **rose pink,** *Aug. 9, 1948* 6 5
Margin block of 4, P# 30 —

SALUTE TO YOUTH ISSUE

Issued to honor the Youth of America and to publicize "Youth Month," September, 1948.

Girl and Boy Carrying Books — A410

ROTARY PRESS PRINTING
E.E. Plates of 200 subjects in four panes of 50 each.

1948 **Unwmk.** ***Perf. 11x10½***
963 A410 3c **deep blue,** *Aug. 11, 1948* 6 6
Margin block of 4, P# 30 —

OREGON TERRITORY ISSUE

Issued to commemorate the centenary of the establishment of Oregon Territory.

John McLoughlin, Jason Lee and Wagon on Oregon Trail — A411

ROTARY PRESS PRINTING

E.E. Plates of 200 subjects in four panes of 50 each.

1948	**Unwmk.**	***Perf. 11x10½***	
964 A411 3c **brown red,** *Aug. 14, 1948*		6	5
Margin block of 4, P#		30	—

HARLAN F. STONE ISSUE

Issued to honor Harlan Fiske Stone (1872-1946) of New York, associate justice of the Supreme Court, 1925-1941, and chief justice, 1941-1946.

Chief Justice Harlan F. Stone — A412

ROTARY PRESS PRINTING

E.E. Plates of 280 subjects in four panes of 70 each.

1948	**Unwmk.**	***Perf. 10½x11***	
965 A412 3c **bright violet,** *Aug. 25, 1948*		9	8
Margin block of 4, P#		60	—

PALOMAR MOUNTAIN OBSERVATORY ISSUE

Issued to commemorate the dedication of the Palomar Mountain Observatory, August 30, 1948.

Observatory, Palomar Mountain, California — A413

Designed by Victor S. McCloskey, Jr.

ROTARY PRESS PRINTING

E.E. Plates of 280 subjects in four panes of 70 each.

1948	**Unwmk.**	***Perf. 10½x11***	
966 A413 3c **blue,** *Aug. 30 1948*		9	5
Margin block of 4, P#		1.10	—
a. Vert. pair, imperf. btwn.		*550.00*	

CLARA BARTON ISSUE

Issued to honor Clara Barton (1821-1912), who founded the American Red Cross in 1882.

Clara Barton and Cross — A414

Designed by Charles R. Chickering.

ROTARY PRESS PRINTING

E.E. Plates of 200 subjects in four panes of 50 each.

1948	**Unwmk.**	***Perf. 11x10½***	
967 A414 3c **rose pink,** *Sept. 7, 1948*		6	5
Margin block of 4, P#		30	—

POULTRY INDUSTRY CENTENNIAL ISSUE

Issued to commemorate the centenary of the establishment of the American Poultry Industry.

Light Brahma Rooster — A415

Designed by Charles R. Chickering.

ROTARY PRESS PRINTING

E.E. Plates of 200 subjects in four panes of 50 each.

1948	**Unwmk.**	***Perf. 11x10½***	
968 A415 3c **sepia,** *Sept. 9, 1948*		6	5
Margin block of 4, P#		35	—

GOLD STAR MOTHERS ISSUE

Issued to honor the mothers of deceased members of the United States armed forces.

Star and Palm Frond — A416

Designed by Charles R. Chickering.

ROTARY PRESS PRINTING

E.E. Plates of 200 subjects in four panes of 50 each.

1948	**Unwmk.**	***Perf. 10½x11***	
969 A416 3c **orange yellow,** *Sept. 21, 1948*		6	5
Margin block of 4, P#		35	—

FORT KEARNY ISSUE

Centenary of the establishment of Fort Kearny, Neb.

Fort Kearny and Pioneer Group — A417

ROTARY PRESS PRINTING

E.E. Plates of 200 subjects in four panes of 50 each.

1948	**Unwmk.**	***Perf. 11x10½***	
970 A417 3c **violet,** *Sept. 22, 1948*		6	5
Margin block of 4, P#		35	—

VOLUNTEER FIREMEN ISSUE

Issued to commemorate the 300th anniversary of the organization of the first volunteer firemen in America by Peter Stuyvesant.

Peter Stuyvesant, Early and Modern Fire Engines — A418

ROTARY PRESS PRINTING

E.E. Plates of 200 subjects in four panes of 50 each.

1948	**Unwmk.**	***Perf. 11x10½***	
971 A418 3c **bright rose carmine,** *Oct. 4, 1948*		6	5
Margin block of 4, P#		35	—

INDIAN CENTENNIAL ISSUE

Issued to commemorate the centenary of the arrival in Indian Territory, later Oklahoma, of the Five Civilized Indian Tribes: Cherokee, Chickasaw, Choctaw, Muscogee and Seminole.

Map of Indian Territory and Seals of Five Tribes — A419

ROTARY PRESS PRINTING

E.E. Plates of 200 subjects in four panes of 50 each.

1948	**Unwmk.**	***Perf. 11x10½***	
972 A419 3c **dark brown,** *Oct. 15, 1948*		6	5
Margin block of 4, P#		35	—

ROUGH RIDERS ISSUE

Issued to commemorate the 50th anniversary of the organization of the Rough Riders of the Spanish-American War.

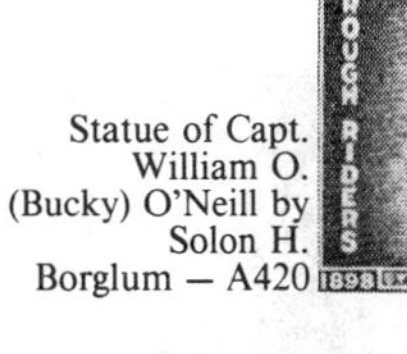

Statue of Capt. William O. (Bucky) O'Neill by Solon H. Borglum — A420

Designed by Victor S. McCloskey, Jr.

ROTARY PRESS PRINTING

E.E. Plates of 200 subjects in four panes of 50 each.

1948	**Unwmk.**	***Perf. 11x10½***	
973 A420 3c **violet brown,** *Oct. 27, 1948*		6	5
Margin block of 4, P#		35	—

JULIETTE LOW ISSUE

Issued to honor Juliette Gordon Low (1860-1927), founder of the Girl Scouts of America. Mrs. Low organized the first troop of Girl Guides in 1912 at Savannah. The name was changed to Girl Scouts in 1913 and headquarters moved to New York.

Juliette Gordon Low and Girl Scout Emblem — A421

Designed by William K. Schrage.

ROTARY PRESS PRINTING

E.E. Plates of 200 subjects in four panes of 50 each.

1948	**Unwmk.**	***Perf. 11x10½***	
974 A421 3c **blue green,** *Oct. 29, 1948*		6	5
Margin block of 4, P#		35	—

WILL ROGERS ISSUE

Issued to honor Will Rogers, (1879-1935), humorist and political commentator.

Will Rogers — A422

ROTARY PRESS PRINTING

E.E. Plates of 280 subjects in four panes of 70 each.

1948	**Unwmk.**	***Perf. 10½x11***	
975 A422 3c **bright red violet,** *Nov. 4, 1948*		6	5
Margin block of 4, P#		40	—

FORT BLISS CENTENNIAL ISSUE

Issued to commemorate the centenary of the establishment of Fort Bliss at El Paso, Texas.

Fort Bliss and Rocket Firing — A423

Designed by Charles R. Chickering.

ROTARY PRESS PRINTING

E.E. Plates of 280 subjects in four panes of 70 each.

1948 **Unwmk.** ***Perf. 10½x11***

976 A423 3c **henna brown,** *Nov. 5, 1948* 9 5
Margin block of 4, P# 1.25 —

MOINA MICHAEL ISSUE

Issued to honor Moina Michael (1870-1944), educator who originated (1918) the Flanders Field Poppy Day idea as a memorial to the war dead.

Moina Michael and Poppy Plant — A424

ROTARY PRESS PRINTING

E.E. Plates of 200 subjects in four panes of 50 each.

1948 **Unwmk.** ***Perf. 11x10½***

977 A424 3c **rose pink,** *Nov. 9, 1948* 6 5
Margin block of 4, P# 35 —

GETTYSBURG ADDRESS ISSUE

Issued to commemorate the 85th anniversary of Abraham Lincoln's address at Gettysburg, Pennsylvania.

Abraham Lincoln and Quotation from Gettysburg Address — A425

Designed by Charles R. Chickering.

ROTARY PRESS PRINTING

E.E. Plates of 200 subjects in four panes of 50 each.

1948 **Unwmk.** ***Perf. 11x10½***

978 A425 3c **bright blue,** *Nov. 19, 1948* 6 5
Margin block of 4, P# 35 —

AMERICAN TURNERS ISSUE

Issued to commemorate the centenary of the formation of the American Turners Society.

Torch and Emblem of American Turners — A426

Designed by Alvin R. Meissner.

ROTARY PRESS PRINTING

E.E. Plates of 200 subjects in four panes of 50 each.

1948 **Unwmk.** ***Perf. 10½x11***

979 A426 3c **carmine,** *Nov. 20, 1948* 6 5
Margin block of 4, P# 35 —

JOEL CHANDLER HARRIS ISSUE

Issued to commemorate the centenary of the birth of Joel Chandler Harris (1848-1908), Georgia writer, creator of "Uncle Remus" and newspaperman.

Joel Chandler Harris — A427

ROTARY PRESS PRINTING

E.E. Plates of 280 subjects in four panes of 70 each.

1948 **Unwmk.** ***Perf. 10½x11***

980 A427 3c **bright red violet,** *Dec. 9, 1948* 6 5
Margin block of 4, P# 50 —

MINNESOTA TERRITORY ISSUE

Issued to commemorate the centenary of the establishment of Minnesota Territory.

Pioneer and Red River Oxcart — A428

ROTARY PRESS PRINTING

E.E. Plates of 200 subjects in four panes of 50 each.

1949 **Unwmk.** ***Perf. 11x10½***

981 A428 3c **blue green,** *Mar. 3, 1949* 6 5
Margin block of 4, P# 30 —

WASHINGTON AND LEE UNIVERSITY ISSUE

Bicentenary of Washington and Lee University.

George Washington, Robert E. Lee and University Building, Lexington, Va. — A429

ROTARY PRESS PRINTING

E.E. Plates of 200 subjects in four panes of 50 each.

1949 **Unwmk.** ***Perf. 11x10½***

982 A429 3c **ultramarine,** *Apr. 12, 1949* 6 5
Margin block of 4, P# 30 —

PUERTO RICO ELECTION ISSUE

Issued to commemorate the first gubernatorial election in the Territory of Puerto Rico, Nov. 2, 1948.

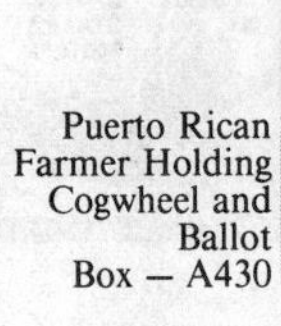
Puerto Rican Farmer Holding Cogwheel and Ballot Box — A430

ROTARY PRESS PRINTING

E.E. Plates of 200 subjects in four panes of 50 each.

1949 **Unwmk.** ***Perf. 11x10½***

983 A430 3c **green,** *Apr. 27, 1949* 6 5
Margin block of 4, P# 30 —

ANNAPOLIS TERCENTENARY ISSUE

Issued to commemorate the 300th anniversary of the founding of Annapolis, Maryland.

James Stoddert's 1718 Map of Regions about Annapolis, Redrawn — A431

ROTARY PRESS PRINTING

E.E. Plates of 200 subjects in four panes of 50 each.

1949 **Unwmk.** ***Perf. 11x10½***

984 A431 3c **aquamarine,** *May 23, 1949* 6 5
Margin block of 4, P# 30 —

G.A.R. ISSUE

Issued to commemorate the final encampment of the Grand Army of the Republic, Indianapolis, August 28 to September 1, 1949.

Union Soldier and G.A.R. Veteran of 1949 — A432

Designed by Charles R. Chickering.

ROTARY PRESS PRINTING

E.E. Plates of 200 subjects in four panes of 50 each.

1949 **Unwmk.** ***Perf. 11x10½***

985 A432 3c **bright rose carmine,** *Aug. 29, 1949* 6 5
Margin block of 4, P# 30 —

EDGAR ALLAN POE ISSUE

Issued to commemorate the centenary of the death of Edgar Allan Poe (1809-1849), Boston-born poet, story writer and editor.

Edgar Allan Poe — A433

ROTARY PRESS PRINTING

E.E. Plates of 280 subjects in four panes of 70 each.

1949 **Unwmk.** ***Perf. 10½x11***

986 A433 3c **bright red violet,** *Oct. 7, 1949* 6 5
Margin block of 4, P# 45 —
Thin outer frame line at top, inner line missing (24143 LL 42) 6.00

AMERICAN BANKERS ASSOCIATION ISSUE

Issued to commemorate the 75th anniversary of the formation of the American Bankers Association.

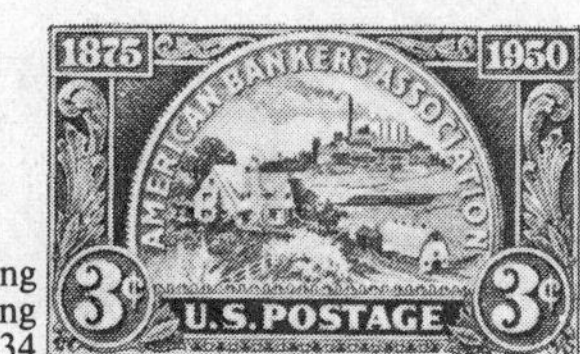

Coin, Symbolizing Fields of Banking Service — A434

Designed by Charles R. Chickering.

ROTARY PRESS PRINTING

E.E. Plates of 200 subjects in four panes of 50 each.

1950 **Unwmk.** ***Perf. 11x10½***

987 A434 3c **yellow green,** *Jan. 3, 1950* 6 5
Margin block of 4, P# 30 —

SAMUEL GOMPERS ISSUE

Issued to commemorate the centenary of the birth of Samuel Gompers (1850-1924), British-born American labor leader.

Samuel Gompers — A435

ROTARY PRESS PRINTING

E.E. Plates of 280 subjects in four panes of 70 each.

1950 **Unwmk.** ***Perf. 10½x11***

988 A435 3c **bright red violet,** *Jan. 27, 1950* 6 5
Margin block of 4, P# 30 —

NATIONAL CAPITAL SESQUICENTENNIAL ISSUE

Issued to commemorate the 150th anniversary of the establishment of the National Capital, Washington, D.C.

Statue of Freedom on Capitol Dome — A436

Executive Mansion — A437

Supreme Court Building — A438

United States Capitol — A439

ROTARY PRESS PRINTING

E.E. Plates of 200 subjects in four panes of 50 each.

1950 **Unwmk.** ***Perf. 10½x11, 11x10½***

989 A436 3c **bright blue,** *Apr. 20, 1950* 6 5
Margin block of 4, P# 30 —
990 A437 3c **deep green,** *June 12, 1950* 6 5
Margin block of 4, P# 35 —
991 A438 3c **light violet,** *Aug. 2, 1950* 6 5
Margin block of 4, P# 30 —
992 A439 3c **bright red violet,** *Nov. 22, 1950* 6 5
Margin block of 4, P# 30 —
Gripper cracks (24285 UL 11) 1.00 50

RAILROAD ENGINEERS ISSUE

Issued to honor the Railroad Engineers of America. Stamp portrays John Luther (Casey) Jones (1864-1900), locomotive engineer killed in train wreck near Vaughn, Miss.

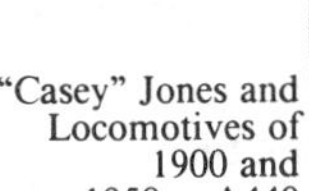

"Casey" Jones and Locomotives of 1900 and 1950 — A440

ROTARY PRESS PRINTING

E.E. Plates of 200 subjects in four panes of 50 each.

1950 **Unwmk.** ***Perf. 11x10½***

993 A440 3c **violet brown,** *April 29, 1950* 6 5
Margin block of 4, P# 30 —

KANSAS CITY, MISSOURI, CENTENARY ISSUE

Issued to commemorate the centenary of the incorporation of Kansas City, Missouri.

Kansas City Skyline, 1950 and Westport Landing, 1850 — A441

ROTARY PRESS PRINTING

E.E. Plates of 200 subjects in four panes of 50 each.

1950 **Unwmk.** ***Perf. 11x10½***

994 A441 3c **violet,** *June 3, 1950* 6 5
Margin block of 4, P# 30 —

BOY SCOUTS ISSUE

Issued to honor the Boy Scouts of America on the occasion of the second National Jamboree, Valley Forge, Pa.

Three Boys, Statue of Liberty and Scout Badge — A442

ROTARY PRESS PRINTING

E.E. Plates of 200 subjects in four panes of 50 each.

1950 **Unwmk.** ***Perf. 11x10½***

995 A442 3c **sepia,** *June 30, 1950* 6 6
Margin block of 4, P# 35 —

INDIANA TERRITORY ISSUE

Issued to commemorate the 150th anniversary of the establishment of Indiana Territory.

Gov. William Henry Harrison and First Indiana Capitol, Vincennes — A443

ROTARY PRESS PRINTING

E.E. Plates of 200 subjects in four panes of 50 each.

1950 **Unwmk.** ***Perf. 11x10½***

996 A443 3c **bright blue,** *July 4, 1950* 6 5
Margin block of 4, P# 30 —

CALIFORNIA STATEHOOD ISSUE

Issued to commemorate the centenary of the admission of California to statehood.

Gold Miner, Pioneers and S.S. Oregon — A444

ROTARY PRESS PRINTING

E.E. Plates of 200 subjects in four panes of 50 each.

1950 **Unwmk.** ***Perf. 11x10½***

997 A444 3c **yellow orange,** *Sept. 9, 1950* 6 5
Margin block of 4, P# 30 —

UNITED CONFEDERATE VETERANS FINAL REUNION ISSUE

Issued to commemorate the final reunion of the United Confederate Veterans, Norfolk, Virginia, May 30, 1951.

Confederate Soldier and United Confederate Veteran — A445

ROTARY PRESS PRINTING

E.E. Plates of 200 subjects in four panes of 50 each.

1951 **Unwmk.** ***Perf. 11x10½***

998 A445 3c **gray,** *May 30, 1951* 6 5
Margin block of 4, P# 30 —

NEVADA CENTENNIAL ISSUE

Issued to commemorate the centenary of the settlement of Nevada.

Carson Valley, c. 1851 — A446

Designed by Charles R. Chickering.

ROTARY PRESS PRINTING

E.E. Plates of 200 subjects in four panes of 50 each.

1951 **Unwmk.** ***Perf. 11x10½***

999 A446 3c **light olive green,** *July 14, 1951* 6 5
Margin block of 4, P# 30 —

LANDING OF CADILLAC ISSUE

Issued to commemorate the 250th anniversary of the landing of Antoine de la Mothe Cadillac at Detroit.

Detroit Skyline and Cadillac Landing — A447

ROTARY PRESS PRINTING

E.E. Plates of 200 subjects in four panes of 50 each.

1951 **Unwmk.** ***Perf. 11x10½***

1000 A447 3c **blue,** *July 24, 1951* 6 5
Margin block of 4, P# 30 —

COLORADO STATEHOOD ISSUE

Issued to commemorate the 75th anniversary of the admission of Colorado to statehood.

Colorado Capitol, Mount of the Holy Cross, Columbine and Bronco Buster by Proctor — A448

ROTARY PRESS PRINTING

E.E. Plates of 200 subjects in four panes of 50 each.

1951 **Unwmk.** ***Perf. 11x10½***

1001 A448 3c **blue violet,** *Aug. 1, 1951* 6 5
Margin block of 4, P# 30 —

AMERICAN CHEMICAL SOCIETY ISSUE

Issued to commemorate the 75th anniversary of the formation of the American Chemical Society.

A.C.S. Emblem and Symbols of Chemistry — A449

ROTARY PRESS PRINTING

E.E. Plates of 200 subjects in four panes of 50 each.

1951 **Unwmk.** ***Perf. 11x10½***

1002 A449 3c **violet brown,** *Sept. 4, 1951* 6 5
Margin block of 4, P# 30 —

BATTLE OF BROOKLYN ISSUE

Issued to commemorate the 175th anniversary of the Battle of Brooklyn.

Gen. George Washington Evacuating Army; Fulton Ferry House at Right — A450

ROTARY PRESS PRINTING

E.E. Plates of 200 subjects in four panes of 50 each.

1951 **Unwmk.** ***Perf. 11x10½***

1003 A450 3c **violet,** *Dec. 10, 1951* 7 5
Margin block of 4, P# 30 —

BETSY ROSS ISSUE

Issued to commemorate the 200th anniversary of the birth of Betsy Ross, maker of the first American flag.

Betsy Ross Showing Flag to Gen. George Washington, Robert Morris and George Ross — A451

ROTARY PRESS PRINTING

E.E. Plates of 200 subjects in four panes of 50 each.

1952 **Unwmk.** ***Perf. 11x10½***

1004 A451 3c **carmine rose,** *Jan. 2, 1952* 7 5
Margin block of 4, P# 35 —

4-H CLUB ISSUE

Issue to honor the 4-H Club movement.

Farm, Club Emblem, Boy and Girl — A452

ROTARY PRESS PRINTING

E.E. Plates of 200 subjects in four panes of 50 each.

1952 **Unwmk.** ***Perf. 11x10½***

1005 A452 3c **blue green,** *Jan. 15, 1952* 6 5
Margin block of 4, P# 30 —

B. & O. RAILROAD ISSUE

Issued to commemorate the 125th anniversary of the granting of a charter to the Baltimore and Ohio Railroad Company by the Maryland Legislature.

Charter and Three Stages of Rail Transportation A453

ROTARY PRESS PRINTING

E.E. Plates of 200 subjects in four panes of 50 each.

1952 **Unwmk.** ***Perf. 11x10½***

1006 A453 3c **bright blue,** *Feb. 28, 1952* 7 5
Margin block of 4, P# 35 —

A. A. A. ISSUE.

Issued to commemorate the 50th anniversary of the formation of the American Automobile Association.

School Girls and Safety Patrolman Automobiles of 1902 and 1952 — A454

ROTARY PRESS PRINTING

E.E. Plates of 200 subjects in four panes of 50 each.

1952 **Unwmk.** ***Perf. 11x10½***

1007 A454 3c **deep blue,** *Mar. 4, 1952* 6 5
Margin block of 4, P# 30 —

NATO ISSUE

Issued to commemorate the third anniversary of the signing of the North Atlantic Treaty.

Torch of Liberty and Globe — A455

ROTARY PRESS PRINTING

E.E. Plates of 400 subjects in four panes of 100 each.

1952 **Unwmk.** ***Perf. 11x10½***

1008 A455 3c **deep violet,** *Apr. 4, 1952* 6 5
Margin block of 4, P# 30 —

GRAND COULEE DAM ISSUE

Issued to commemorate 50 years of Federal cooperation in developing the resources of rivers and streams in the West.

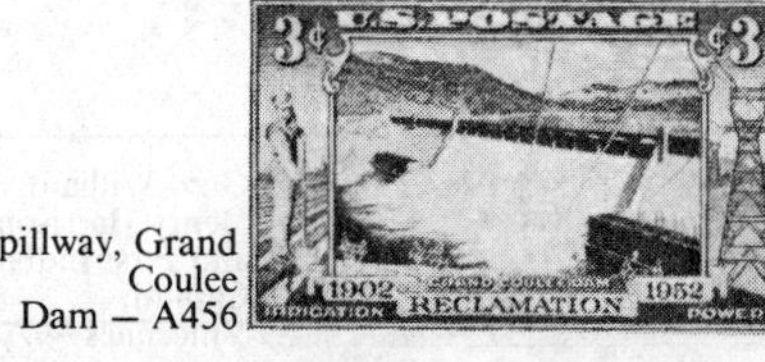
Spillway, Grand Coulee Dam — A456

ROTARY PRESS PRINTING

E.E. Plates of 200 subjects in four panes of 50 each.

1952 **Unwmk.** ***Perf. 11x10½***

1009 A456 3c **blue green,** *May 15, 1952* 6 5
Margin block of 4, P# 30 —

LAFAYETTE ISSUE

Issued to commemorate the 175th anniversary of the arrival of Marquis de Lafayette in America.

Marquis de Lafayette, Flags, Cannon and Landing Party — A457

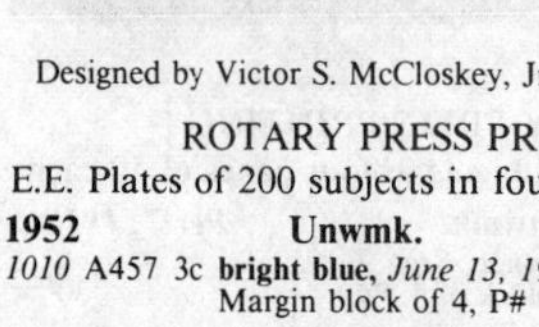

Designed by Victor S. McCloskey, Jr.

ROTARY PRESS PRINTING

E.E. Plates of 200 subjects in four panes of 50 each.

1952 **Unwmk.** ***Perf. 11x10½***

1010 A457 3c **bright blue,** *June 13, 1952* 6 5
Margin block of 4, P# 30 —

MT. RUSHMORE MEMORIAL ISSUE

Issued to commemorate the 25th anniversary of the dedication of the Mt. Rushmore National Memorial in the Black Hills of South Dakota.

Sculptured Heads on Mt. Rushmore — A458

Designed by William K. Schrage.

ROTARY PRESS PRINTING

E.E. Plates of 200 subjects in four panes of 50 each.

1952 **Unwmk.** ***Perf. 10½x11***

1011 A458 3c **blue green,** *Aug. 11, 1952* 6 5
Margin block of 4, P# 35 —

ENGINEERING CENTENNIAL ISSUE

Issued to commemorate the centenary of the founding of the American Society of Civil Engineers.

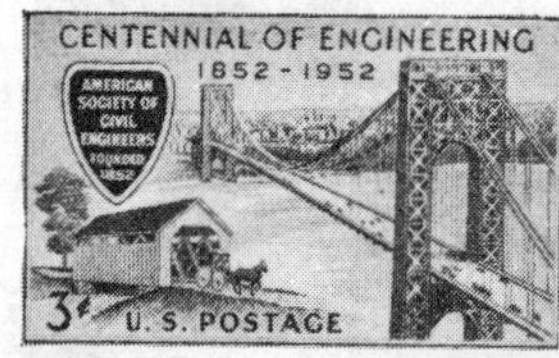
George Washington Bridge and Covered Bridge of 1850's — A459

ROTARY PRESS PRINTING

E.E. Plates of 200 subjects in four panes of 50 each.

1952 **Unwmk.** ***Perf. 11x10½***

1012 A459 3c **violet blue,** *Sept. 6, 1952* 6 5
Margin block of 4, P# 30 —

SERVICE WOMEN ISSUE

Issued to honor the women in the United States Armed Services.

Women of the Marine Corps, Army, Navy and Air Force — A460

ROTARY PRESS PRINTING

E.E. Plates of 200 subjects in four panes of 50 each.

1952 **Unwmk.** ***Perf. 11x10½***

1013 A460 3c **deep blue,** *Sept. 11, 1952* 6 5
Margin block of 4, P# 30 —

GUTENBERG BIBLE ISSUE

Issued to commemorate the 500th anniversary of the printing of the first book, the Holy Bible, from movable type, by Johann Gutenberg.

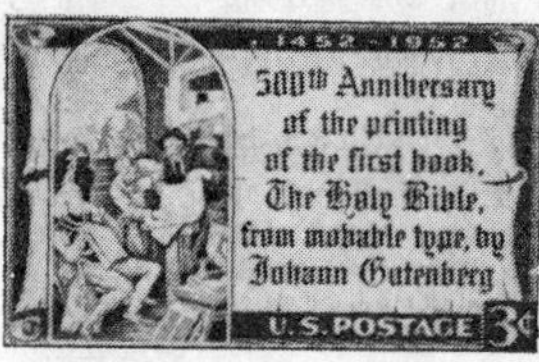
Gutenberg Showing Proof to the Elector of Mainz — A461

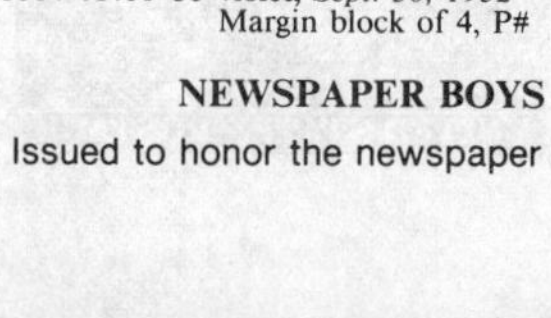

ROTARY PRESS PRINTING

E.E. Plates of 200 subjects in four panes of 50 each.

1952 **Unwmk.** ***Perf. 11x10½***

1014 A461 3c **violet,** *Sept. 30, 1952* 6 5
Margin block of 4, P# 30 —

NEWSPAPER BOYS ISSUE

Issued to honor the newspaper boys of America.

Newspaper Boy, Torch and Group of Homes — A462

ROTARY PRESS PRINTING
E.E. Plates of 200 subjects in four panes of 50 each.

1952 **Unwmk.** ***Perf. 11x10½***
1015 A462 3c **violet,** *Oct. 4, 1952* 6 5
Margin block of 4, P# 30 —

RED CROSS ISSUE

Issued to honor the International Red Cross.

Globe, Sun and Cross — A463

ROTARY PRESS PRINTING
Cross Typographed
E.E. Plates of 200 subjects in four panes of 50 each.

1952 **Unwmk.** ***Perf. 11x10½***
1016 A463 3c **deep blue & carmine,** *Nov. 21, 1952* 6 5
Margin block of 4, P# 30 —

NATIONAL GUARD ISSUE

Issued to honor the National Guard of the United States.

National Guardsman, Amphibious Landing and Disaster Service — A464

ROTARY PRESS PRINTING
E.E. Plates of 200 subjects in four panes of 50 each.

1953 **Unwmk.** ***Perf. 11x10½***
1017 A464 3c **bright blue,** *Feb. 23, 1953* 6 5
Margin block of 4, P# 35 —

OHIO STATEHOOD ISSUE

Sesquicentennial of Ohio statehood.

Ohio Map, State Seal, Buckeye Leaf — A465

ROTARY PRESS PRINTING
E.E. Plates of 280 subjects in four panes of 70 each.

1953 **Unwmk.** ***Perf. 11x10½***
1018 A465 3c **chocolate,** *Mar. 2, 1953* 6 5
Margin block of 4, P# 35 —

WASHINGTON TERRITORY ISSUE

Issued to commemorate the centenary of the organization of Washington Territory.

Medallion, Pioneers and Washington Scene — A466

ROTARY PRESS PRINTING
E.E. Plates of 200 subjects in four panes of 50 each.

1953 **Unwmk.** ***Perf. 11x10½***
1019 A466 3c **green,** *Mar. 2, 1953* 6 5
Margin block of 4, P# 30 —

LOUISIANA PURCHASE ISSUE

Issued to commemorate the 150th anniversary of the Louisiana Purchase, 1803.

James Monroe, Robert R. Livingston and Marquis Francois de Barbé-Marbois A467

ROTARY PRESS PRINTING
E.E. Plates of 200 subjects in four panes of 50 each.

1953 **Unwmk.** ***Perf. 11x10½***
1020 A467 3c **violet brown,** *April 30, 1953* 6 5
Margin block of 4, P# 30 —

OPENING OF JAPAN CENTENNIAL ISSUE

Issued to commemorate the centenary of Commodore Matthew Calbraith Perry's negotiations with Japan, which opened her doors to foreign trade.

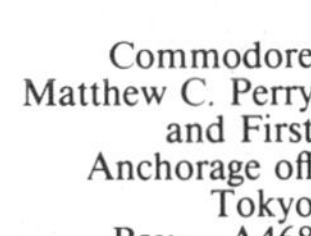

Commodore Matthew C. Perry and First Anchorage off Tokyo Bay — A468

ROTARY PRESS PRINTING
E.E. Plates of 200 subjects in four panes of 50 each.

1953 **Unwmk.** ***Perf. 11x10½***
1021 A468 5c **green,** *July 14, 1953* 9 5
Margin block of 4, P# 90 —

AMERICAN BAR ASSOCIATION ISSUE

Issued to commemorate the 75th anniversary of the formation of the American Bar Association.

Section of Frieze, Supreme Court Room — A469

ROTARY PRESS PRINTING
E.E. Plates of 200 subjects in four panes of 50 each.

1953 **Unwmk.** ***Perf. 11x10½***
1022 A469 3c **rose violet,** *Aug. 24, 1953* 6 5
Margin block of 4, P# 30 —

SAGAMORE HILL ISSUE

Issued to commemorate the opening of Sagamore Hill, Theodore Roosevelt's home, as a national shrine.

Home of Theodore Roosevelt — A470

ROTARY PRESS PRINTING
E.E. Plates of 200 subjects in four panes of 50 each.

1953 **Unwmk.** ***Perf. 11x10½***
1023 A470 3c **yellow green,** *Sept. 14, 1953* 6 5
Margin block of 4, P# 30 —

FUTURE FARMERS ISSUE

Issued to commemorate the 25th anniversary of the organization of Future Farmers of America.

Agricultural Scene and Future Farmer — A471

ROTARY PRESS PRINTING
E.E. Plates of 200 subjects in four panes of 50 each.

1953 **Unwmk.** ***Perf. 11x10½***
1024 A471 3c **deep blue,** *Oct. 13, 1953* 6 5
Margin block of 4, P# 30 —

TRUCKING INDUSTRY ISSUE

Issued to commemorate the 50th anniversary of the Trucking Industry in the United States.

Truck, Farm and Distant City — A472

ROTARY PRESS PRINTING
E.E. Plates of 200 subjects in four panes of 50 each.

1953 **Unwmk.** ***Perf. 11x10½***
1025 A472 3c **violet,** *Oct. 27, 1953* 6 5
Margin block of 4, P# 30 —

GENERAL PATTON ISSUE

Issued to honor Gen. George S. Patton, Jr. (1885-1945), and the armored forces of the United States Army.

Gen. George S. Patton, Jr., and Tanks in Action — A473

ROTARY PRESS PRINTING
E.E. Plates of 200 subjects in four panes of 50 each.

1953 **Unwmk.** ***Perf. 11x10½***
1026 A473 3c **blue violet,** *Nov. 11, 1953* 7 5
Margin block of 4, P# 40 —

NEW YORK CITY ISSUE

Issued to commemorate the 300th anniversary of the founding of New York City.

Dutch Ship in New Amsterdam Harbor — A474

ROTARY PRESS PRINTING
E.E. Plates of 200 subjects in four panes of 50 each.

1953 **Unwmk.** ***Perf. 11x10½***
1027 A474 3c **bright red violet,** *Nov. 20, 1953* 6 5
Margin block of 4, P# 35 —

GADSDEN PURCHASE ISSUE

Issued to commemorate the centenary of James Gadsden's purchase of territory from Mexico to adjust the U.S.-Mexico boundary.

Map and Pioneer Group — A475

ROTARY PRESS PRINTING

E.E. Plates of 200 subjects in four panes of 50 each.

1953	**Unwmk.**	***Perf. 11x10½***		
1028 A475 3c	**copper brown,** *Dec. 30, 1953*		6	5
	Margin block of 4, P#		30	—

COLUMBIA UNIVERSITY ISSUE

Issued to commemorate the 200th anniversary of the founding of Columbia University.

Low Memorial Library — A476

ROTARY PRESS PRINTING

E.E. Plates of 200 subjects in four panes of 50 each.

1954	**Unwmk.**	***Perf. 11x10½***		
1029 A476 3c	**blue,** *Jan. 4, 1954*		6	5
	Margin block of 4, P#		30	—

Wet and Dry Printings

In 1953 the Bureau of Engraving and Printing began experiments in printing on "dry" paper (moisture content 5-10 per cent). In previous "wet" printings the paper had a moisture content of 15-35 per cent.

The new process required a thicker, stiffer paper, special types of inks and greater pressure to force the paper into the recessed plates. The "dry" printings show whiter paper, a higher sheen on the surface, feel thicker and stiffer, and the designs stand out more clearly than on the "wet" printings.

Nos. 832c and 1041 (flat plate) were the first "dry" printings to be issued of flat-plate, regular-issue stamps. No. 1063 was the first rotary press stamp to be produced entirely by "dry" printing.

Stamps printed by both the "wet" and "dry" process are Nos. 1030, 1031, 1035, 1035a, 1036, 1039, 1049, 1050-1052, 1054, 1055, 1057, 1058, C34-C36, C39, C39a, J78, J80-J84, QE1-QE3, RF26. The "wet" printed 4c coil, No. 1058, exists only Bureau precanceled.

All postage stamps have been printed by the "dry" process since the late 1950's.

LIBERTY ISSUE

Benjamin Franklin A477

George Washington A478

Palace of the Governors, Santa Fe — A478a

Mount Vernon — A479

Thomas Jefferson — A480

Bunker Hill Monument and Massachusetts Flag, 1776 — A481

Abraham Lincoln — A483

James Monroe A485

Woodrow Wilson — A487

Statue of Liberty A489

The Alamo, San Antonio — A490

Statue of Liberty A491a

Statue of Liberty — A482

The Hermitage, Home of Andrew Jackson, near Nashville — A484

Theodore Roosevelt A486

Statue of Liberty — A488

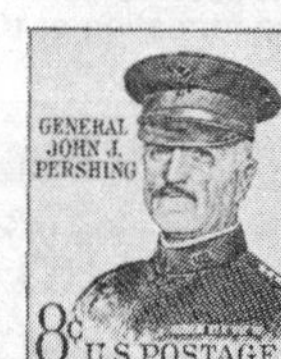

John J. Pershing A489a

Independence Hall — A491

Benjamin Harrison A492

John Jay — A493

Monticello, Home of Thomas Jefferson, near Charlottesville, Va. — A494

Paul Revere — A495

Robert E. Lee — A496

John Marshall A497

Susan B. Anthony A498

Patrick Henry A499

Alexander Hamilton A500

ROTARY PRESS PRINTING

E.E. Plates of 400 subjects in four panes of 100

1954-68			**Unwmk.**	***Perf. 11x10½***	
1030	A477	½c	**red orange,** *Oct. 20, 1955*	5	5
a.			Dry printing	5	5
			Margin block of 4, P#	25	—
1031	A478	1c	**dark green**	5	5
			Margin block of 4, P#	25	—
			Pair with full vert. or horiz. gutter between	*150.00*	
b.			Wet printing, *Aug. 26, 1954*	8	5
			Perf. 10½x11		
1031A	A478a	1¼c	**turquoise,** *June 17, 1960*	5	5
			Margin block of 4, P#	45	—
1032	A479	1½c	**brown carmine,** *Feb. 22, 1956*	7	5
			Margin block of 4, P#	2.00	—
			Perf. 11x10½		
1033	A480	2c	**carmine rose,** *Sept. 15, 1954*	5	5
			Margin block of 4, P#	25	—
			Pair with full vert. or horiz. gutter between	—	
1034	A481	2½c	**gray blue,** *June 17, 1959*	6	5
			Margin block of 4, P#	50	—
1035	A482	3c	**deep violet**	6	5
			Margin block of 4, P#	30	—
			Pair with full vert. or horiz. gutter between	*150.00*	
a.			Booklet pane of 6, *June 30, 1954*	3.00	*50*
b.			Tagged, *July 6, 1966*	25	20
b.			Margin block of 4, P#	5.00	—
c.			Imperf., pair	*1,500.*	
d.			Horiz. pair, imperf. between	*800.00*	
e.			Wet printing, *June 24, 1954*	12	5
f.			As "a," dry printing	4.00	*60*
1036	A483	4c	**red violet**	7	5
			Margin block of 4, P#	35	—
			Pair with full vert. or horiz. gutter between	—	
a.			Booklet pane of 6, *July 31, 1958*	2.25	*50*
b.			Tagged, *Nov. 2, 1963*	48	16
b.			Margin block of 4, P#	7.00	—
c.			Wet printing, *Nov. 19, 1954*	8	10
			Perf. 10½x11		
1037	A484	4½c	**blue green,** *Mar. 16, 1959*	8	8
			Margin block of 4, P#	50	—
			Perf. 11x10½		
1038	A485	5c	**deep blue,** *Dec. 2, 1954*	10	5
			Margin block of 4, P#	50	—
			Pair with full vert. gutter btwn.	*200.00*	

United States postage and air mail first day covers are listed and valued in a separate section of the catalogue. See catalogue index.

No.	Type	Description	Unused	Used
1039	A486	6c **carmine**	25	5
		Margin block of 4, P#	1.25	—
a.		Wet printing, *Nov. 18, 1955*	42	6
1040	A487	7c **rose carmine,** *Jan. 10, 1956*	20	5
		Margin block of 4, P#	1.00	—

FLAT PLATE OR ROTARY PRESS PRINTING

Plates of 400 subjects in four panes of 100 each

Perf. 11

No.	Type	Description	Unused	Used
1041	A488	8c **dark violet blue & carmine,** *Apr. 9, 1954*	24	6
		Margin block of 4, 2 P# (flat plate)	2.50	—
		Margin block of 4, 2 P# (rotary)	2.50	—
		Corner margin block of 4, blue P# only		—
		Corner margin block of 4, red P# only		—
a.		Carmine dbl. impression	*750.00*	

FLAT PRINTING PLATES
Frame: 24912-13-14-15, 24926, 24929-30, 24932-33.
Vignette: 24916-17-18-19-20, 24935-36-37, 24939.
ROTARY PRINTING PLATES
Frame: 24923-24, 24928, 24940, 24942.
Vignette: 24927, 24938.

GIORI PRESS PRINTING

Plates of 400 subjects in four panes of 100 each

Redrawn design

Perf. 11

No.	Type	Description	Unused	Used
1042	A489	8c **dark violet blue & carmine rose,** *Mar. 22, 1958*	25	5
		Margin block of 4, P#	1.25	—

ROTARY PRESS PRINTING

E.E. Plates of 400 subjects in four panes of 100 each.

Perf. 11x10½

No.	Type	Description	Unused	Used
1042A	A489a	8c **brown,** *Nov. 17, 1961*	22	5
		Margin block of 4, P#	1.10	—

Perf. 10½x11

No.	Type	Description	Unused	Used
1043	A490	9c **rose lilac,** *June 14, 1956*	28	5
		Margin block of 4, P#	1.40	—
1044	A491	10c **rose lake,** *July 4, 1956*	22	5
		Margin block of 4, P#	1.10	—
b.		Tagged, *July 6, 1966*	1.20	1.00
b.		Margin block of 4, P#	7.50	—

GIORI PRESS PRINTING

Plates of 400 subjects in four panes of 100 each.

Perf. 11

No.	Type	Description	Unused	Used
1044A	A491a	11c **carmine & dark violet blue,** *June 15, 1961*	30	6
		Margin block of 4, P#	1.50	—
c.		Tagged, *Jan. 11, 1967*	2.00	1.60
c.		Margin block of 4, P#	9.00	—

ROTARY PRESS PRINTING

E.E. Plates of 400 subjects in four panes of 100 each.

Perf. 11x10½

No.	Type	Description	Unused	Used
1045	A492	12c **red,** *June 6, 1959*	32	5
		Margin block of 4, P#	1.60	—
a.		Tagged, *1968*	55	15
a.		Margin block of 4, P#	3.00	—
1046	A493	15c **rose lake,** *Dec. 12, 1958*	95	5
		Margin block of 4, P#	5.00	—
a.		Tagged, *July 6, 1966*	80	22
a.		Margin block of 4, P#	5.00	—

Perf. 10½x11

No.	Type	Description	Unused	Used
1047	A494	20c **ultramarine,** *Apr. 13, 1956*	50	5
		Margin block of 4, P#	2.50	—

Perf. 11x10½

No.	Type	Description	Unused	Used
1048	A495	25c **green,** *Apr. 18, 1958*	1.50	5
		Margin block of 4, P#	7.50	—
1049	A496	30c **black**	1.20	8
		Margin block of 4, P#	6.00	—
a.		Wet printing, *Sept. 21, 1955*	1.75	12
1050	A497	40c **brown red**	1.90	10
		Margin block of 4, P#	9.50	—
a.		Wet printing, *Sept. 24, 1955*	2.50	25
1051	A498	50c **bright purple**	1.75	5
		Margin block of 4, P#	8.75	—
		Cracked plate (25231 UL 1)	—	—
a.		Wet printing, *Aug. 25, 1955*	2.50	8
1052	A499	$1 **purple**	5.75	6
		Margin block of 4, P#	25.00	—
a.		Wet printing, *Oct. 7, 1955*	6.50	10

FLAT PLATE PRINTING

Plates of 400 subjects in four panes of 100 each.

Perf. 11

No.	Type	Description	Unused	Used
1053	A500	$5 **black,** *Mar. 19, 1956*	75.00	6.75
		Margin block of 4, P#	325.00	—

Bureau Precancels: ½c, 37 diff., 1c, 113 diff., 1¼c, 142 diff., 1½c, 45 diff., 2c, 86 diff., 2½c, 123 diff., 3c, 106 diff., 4c, 95 diff., 4½c, 23 diff., 5c, 20 diff., 6c, 23 diff., 7c, 16 diff.

Also, No. 1041, 11 diff., No. 1042, 12 diff., No. 1042A, 16 diff., 9c, 15 diff., 10c, 16 diff., 11c, New York, 12c, 6 diff., 15c, 12 diff., 20c, 20 diff., 25c, 11 diff., 30c, 17 diff., 40c, 10 diff., 50c, 19 diff., $1, 5 diff.

ROTARY PRESS COIL STAMPS

1954-73 Unwmk. *Perf. 10 Vertically*

No.	Type	Description	Unused	Used
1054	A478	1c **dark green**	18	12
		Pair	36	24
		Joint line pair	75	35
b.		Imperf., pair	*2,000.*	—
c.		Wet printing, *Oct. 8, 1954*	35	16

Perf. 10 Horizontally

No.	Type	Description	Unused	Used
1054A	A478a	1¼c **turquoise,** *June 17, 1960*	18	12
		Pair	36	24
		Joint line pair	2.25	1.00

Perf. 10 Vertically

No.	Type	Description	Unused	Used
1055	A480	2c **carmine rose**	8	5
		Pair	16	10
		Joint line pair	45	20
a.		Tagged, *May 6, 1968*	5	5
a.		Dull finish gum	12	
b.		Imperf., pair (Bureau precanceled, Riverdale, MD)		*325.00*
c.		As "a," imperf. pair	*350.00*	
d.		Wet printing, *Oct. 22, 1954*	16	6
1056	A481	2½c **gray blue,** *Sept. 9, 1959*	38	25
		Pair	76	50
		Joint line pair	4.00	1.20
1057	A482	3c **deep violet**	10	5
		Pair	20	10
		Joint line pair	55	20
		Gripper cracks	—	—
a.		Imperf., pair	*750.00*	—
a.		Imperf., joint line pair	*1,000.*	—
b.		Tagged, *Oct. 1966*	50	25
c.		Wet printing, *July 20, 1954*	24	6

No. 1057a measures about 19½x22mm.; No. 1035c, about 18¾x22½mm.

No.	Type	Description	Unused	Used
1058	A483	4c **red violet,** *July 31, 1958*	12	5
		Pair	24	10
		Joint line pair	60	20
a.		Imperf. (pair)	90.00	*70.00*
a.		Imperf., joint line pair	200.00	
b.		Wet printing (Bureau precanceled)		50

Perf. 10 Horizontally

No.	Type	Description	Unused	Used
1059	A484	4½c **blue green,** *May 1, 1959*	1.75	1.20
		Pair	3.50	2.40
		Joint line pair	13.00	3.00

Perf. 10 Vertically

No.	Type	Description	Unused	Used
1059A	A495	25c **green,** *Feb. 25, 1965*	50	30
		Pair	1.00	60
		Joint line pair	1.75	1.20
b.		Tagged, *April 3, 1973*	55	20
b.		Dull finish gum	55	
		Pair	1.10	40
		Joint line pair	1.75	1.00
c.		Imperf., pair	*45.00*	

Value for No. 1059c is for fine centering.

Bureau Precancels: 1c, 118 diff., 1¼c, 105 diff., 2c, 191 diff., 2½c, 94 diff., 3c, 142 diff., 4c, 83 diff., 4½c, 23 diff.

NEBRASKA TERRITORY ISSUE

Issued to commemorate the centenary of the establishment of the Nebraska Territory.

"The Sower," Mitchell Pass and Scotts Bluff — A507

ROTARY PRESS PRINTING

E.E. Plates of 200 subjects in four panes of 50 each.

1954 Unwmk. *Perf. 11x10½*

No.	Type	Description	Unused	Used
1060	A507	3c **violet,** *May 7, 1954*	6	5
		Margin block of 4, P#	30	—

KANSAS TERRITORY ISSUE

Issued to commemorate the centenary of the establishment of the Kansas Territory

Wheat Field and Pioneer Wagon Train — A508

ROTARY PRESS PRINTING

E.E. Plates of 200 subjects in four panes of 50 each.

1954 Unwmk. *Perf. 11x10½*

No.	Type	Description	Unused	Used
1061	A508	3c **brown orange,** *May 31, 1954*	6	5
		Margin block of 4, P#	30	—

GEORGE EASTMAN ISSUE

Issued to commemorate the birth centenary of George Eastman (1854-1932), inventor of photographic dry plates, flexible film and the Kodak camera; Rochester, N.Y., industrialist.

George Eastman — A509

ROTARY PRESS PRINTING

E.E. Plates of 280 subjects in four panes of 70 each.

1954 Unwmk. *Perf. 10½x11*

No.	Type	Description	Unused	Used
1062	A509	3c **violet brown,** *July 12, 1954*	6	5
		Margin block of 4, P#	35	—

LEWIS AND CLARK EXPEDITION

Issued to commemorate the 150th anniversary of the Lewis and Clark expedition.

Meriwether Lewis, William Clark and Sacagawea Landing on Missouri Riverbank A510

ROTARY PRESS PRINTING

E.E. Plates of 200 subjects in four panes of 50 each.

1954 Unwmk. *Perf. 11x10½*

No.	Type	Description	Unused	Used
1063	A510	3c **violet brown,** *July 28, 1954*	6	5
		Margin block of 4, P#	35	—

PENNSYLVANIA ACADEMY OF THE FINE ARTS ISSUE

Issued to commemorate the 150th anniversary of the founding of the Pennsylvania Academy of the Fine Arts, Philadelphia.

Charles Willson Peale in his Museum, Self-portrait — A511

ROTARY PRESS PRINTING

E.E. Plates of 200 subjects in four panes of 50 each.

1955 Unwmk. *Perf. 10½x11*

No.	Type	Description	Unused	Used
1064	A511	3c **rose brown,** *Jan. 15, 1955*	6	5
		Margin block of 4, P#	30	—

LAND GRANT COLLEGES ISSUE

Issued to commemorate the centenary of the founding of Michigan State College and Pennsylvania State University, first of the land grant institutions.

Open Book and Symbols of Subjects Taught — A512

ROTARY PRESS PRINTING

E.E. Plates of 200 subjects in four panes of 50 each.

1955 Unwmk. *Perf. 11x10½*

No.	Type	Description	Unused	Used
1065	A512	3c **green,** *Feb. 12, 1955*	6	5
		Margin block, P#	30	—

ROTARY INTERNATIONAL ISSUE

Issued to commemorate the 50th anniversary of the founding of Rotary International.

Torch, Globe and Rotary Emblem — A513

ROTARY PRESS PRINTING

E.E. Plates of 200 subjects in four panes of 50 each.

1955 **Unwmk.** ***Perf. 11x10½***

1066 A513 8c **deep blue,** *Feb. 23, 1955* 15 5
Margin block of 4, P# 90 —

ARMED FORCES RESERVE ISSUE

Issued to honor the Armed Forces Reserve.

Marine, Coast Guard, Army, Navy and Air Force Personnel A514

ROTARY PRESS PRINTING

E.E. Plates of 200 subjects in four panes of 50 each.

1955 **Unwmk.** ***Perf. 11x10½***

1067 A514 3c **purple,** *May 21, 1955* 6 5
Margin block of 4, P# 30 —

NEW HAMPSHIRE ISSUE

Issued to honor New Hampshire on the occasion of the sesquicentennial of the discovery of the "Old Man of the Mountains."

Great Stone Face — A515

ROTARY PRESS PRINTING

E.E. Plates of 200 subjects in four panes of 50 each.

1955 **Unwmk.** ***Perf. 10½x11***

1068 A515 3c **green,** *June 21, 1955* 7 5
Margin block of 4, P# 35 —

SOO LOCKS ISSUE

Centenary of the opening of the Soo Locks.

Map of Great Lakes and Two Steamers — A516

ROTARY PRESS PRINTING

E.E. Plates of 200 subjects in four panes of 50 each.

1955 **Unwmk.** ***Perf. 11x10½***

1069 A516 3c **blue,** *June 28, 1955* 6 5
Margin block of 4, P# 30 —

ATOMS FOR PEACE ISSUE

Issued to promote an Atoms for Peace policy.

Atomic Energy Encircling the Hemispheres A517

Designed by George R. Cox.

ROTARY PRESS PRINTING

E.E. Plates of 200 subjects in four panes of 50 each.

1955 **Unwmk.** ***Perf. 11x10½***

1070 A517 3c **deep blue,** *July 28, 1955* 8 5
Margin block of 4, P# 40 —

FORT TICONDEROGA ISSUE

Issued to commemorate the bicentenary of Fort Ticonderoga, New York.

Map of the Fort, Ethan Allen and Artillery — A518

Designed by Enrico Arno.

ROTARY PRESS PRINTING

E.E. Plates of 200 subjects in four panes of 50 each.

1955 **Unwmk.** ***Perf. 11x10½***

1071 A518 3c **light brown,** *Sept. 18, 1955* 6 5
Margin block of 4, P# 40 —

ANDREW W. MELLON ISSUE

Issued to commemorate the centenary of the birth of Andrew W. Mellon (1855-1937), U.S. Secretary of the Treasury (1921-32), financier and art collector.

Andrew W. Mellon — A519

Designed by Victor S. McCloskey, Jr.

ROTARY PRESS PRINTING

E.E. Plates of 280 subjects in four panes of 70 each.

1955 **Unwmk.** ***Perf. 10½x11***

1072 A519 3c **rose carmine,** *Dec. 20, 1955* 6 5
Margin block of 4, P# 30 —

BENJAMIN FRANKLIN ISSUE

Issued to commemorate the 250th anniversary of the birth of Benjamin Franklin.

"Franklin Taking Electricity from the Sky," by Benjamin West — A520

Designed by Charles R. Chickering.

ROTARY PRESS PRINTING

E.E. Plates of 200 subjects in four panes of 50 each.

1956 **Unwmk.** ***Perf. 10½x11***

1073 A520 3c **bright carmine,** *Jan. 17, 1956* 6 5
Margin block of 4, P# 30 —

BOOKER T. WASHINGTON ISSUE

Issued to commemorate the centenary of the birth of Booker T. Washington (1856-1915), black educator, founder and head of Tuskegee Institute in Alabama.

Log Cabin — A521

Designed by Charles R. Chickering.

ROTARY PRESS PRINTING

E.E. Plates of 200 subjects in four panes of 50 each.

1956 **Unwmk.** ***Perf. 11x10½***

1074 A521 3c **deep blue,** *April 5, 1956* 6 5
Margin block of 4, P# 30 —

FIFTH INTERNATIONAL PHILATELIC EXHIBITION ISSUES

Issued to commemorate the Fifth International Philatelic Exhibition (FIPEX), New York City, April 28-May 6, 1956.

SOUVENIR SHEET

A522

FLAT PLATE PRINTING

Plates of 24 subjects

1956 **Unwmk.** ***Imperf.***

1075 A522 **Sheet of two,** *Apr. 28, 1956* 2.25 2.00
a. A482 3c deep violet 90 80
b. A488 8c dark violet blue & carmine 1.25 1.00

No. 1075 measures 108x73mm. Nos. 1075a and 1075b measure 24x28mm. Below the stamps appears the signature of Arthur E. Summerfield, Postmaster, General of the United States. Marginal inscription reads: "In compliment to 5th International Philatelic Exhibition, 1956. New York, N.Y. Apr. 28-May 6."

Inscriptions printed in dark violet blue; scrolls and stars in carmine.

New York Coliseum and Columbus Monument A523

Designed by William K. Schrage.

ROTARY PRESS PRINTING

E.E. Plates of 200 subjects in four panes of 50 each.

1956 **Unwmk.** ***Perf. 11x10½***

1076 A523 3c **deep violet,** *April 30, 1956* 6 5
Margin block of 4, P# 30 —

WILDLIFE CONSERVATION ISSUE

Issued to emphasize the importance of Wildlife Conservation in America.

Wild Turkey — A524

Pronghorn Antelope — A525

King Salmon — A526

Designed by Robert W. (Bob) Hines.

ROTARY PRESS PRINTING

E.E. Plates of 200 subjects in four panes of 50 each.

1956 **Unwmk.** ***Perf. 11x10½***

1077	A524	3c **rose lake,** *May 5, 1956*	6	5
		Margin block of 4, P#	35	—
1078	A525	3c **brown,** *June 22, 1956*	6	5
		Margin block of 4, P#	35	—
1079	A526	3c **blue green,** *Nov. 9, 1956*	6	5
		Margin block of 4, P#	35	—

PURE FOOD AND DRUG LAWS ISSUE

Issued to commemorate the 50th anniversary of the passage of the Pure Food and Drug Laws.

Harvey Washington Wiley — A527

Designed by Robert L. Miller

ROTARY PRESS PRINTING

E.E. Plates of 200 subjects in four panes of 50 each.

1956 **Unwmk.** ***Perf. 10½x11***

1080	A527	3c **dark blue green,** *June 27, 1956*	6	5
		Margin block of 4, P#	30	—

WHEATLAND ISSUE

Pres. Buchanan's Home, Lancaster, Pa. — A528

ROTARY PRESS PRINTING

E.E. Plates of 200 subjects in four panes of 50 each.

1956 **Unwmk.** ***Perf. 11x10½***

1081	A528	3c **black brown,** *Aug. 5, 1956*	6	5
		Margin block of 4, P#	30	—

LABOR DAY ISSUE

Issued to commemorate Labor Day.

Mosaic, AFL-CIO Headquarters — A529

Designed by Victor S. McCloskey, Jr.

ROTARY PRESS PRINTING

E.E. Plates of 200 subjects in four panes of 50 each.

1956 **Unwmk.** ***Perf. 10½x11***

1082	A529	3c **deep blue,** *Sept. 3, 1956*	6	5
		Margin block of 4, P#	30	—

NASSAU HALL ISSUE

Issued to commemorate the 200th anniversary of Nassau Hall, Princeton University.

Nassau Hall, Princeton, N.J. — A530

ROTARY PRESS PRINTING

E.E. Plates of 200 subjects in four panes of 50 each.

1956, Sept. 22 **Unwmk.** ***Perf. 11x10½***

1083	A530	3c **black,** *orange*	6	5
		Margin block of 4, P#	30	—

DEVILS TOWER ISSUE

Issued to commemorate the 50th anniversary of the Federal law providing for protection of American natural antiquities. Devils Tower National Monument, Wyoming, is an outstanding example.

Devils Tower — A531

Designed by Charles R. Chickering.

ROTARY PRESS PRINTING

E.E. Plates of 200 subjects in four panes of 50 each.

1956 **Unwmk.** ***Perf. 10½x11***

1084	A531	3c **violet,** *Sept. 24, 1956*	6	5
		Margin block of 4, P#	30	—
		Pair with full horiz. gutter btwn.	—	

CHILDREN'S ISSUE

Issued to promote friendship among the children of the world.

Children of the World — A532

Designed by Ronald Dias.

ROTARY PRESS PRINTING

E.E. Plates of 200 subjects in four panes of 50 each.

1956 **Unwmk.** ***Perf. 11x10½***

1085	A532	3c **dark blue,** *Dec. 15, 1956*	6	5
		Margin block of 4, P#	30	—

ALEXANDER HAMILTON ISSUE

Issued to commemorate the 200th anniversary of the birth of Alexander Hamilton (1755-1804).

Alexander Hamilton and Federal Hall — A533

Designed by William K. Schrage.

ROTARY PRESS PRINTING

E.E. Plates of 200 subjects in four panes of 50 each.

1957 **Unwmk.** ***Perf. 11x10½***

1086	A533	3c **rose red,** *Jan. 11, 1957*	6	5
		Margin block of 4, P#	30	—

POLIO ISSUE

Issued to honor "those who helped fight polio," and on the occasion of the 20th anniversary of the National Foundation for Infantile Paralysis and the March of Dimes.

Allegory — A534

Designed by Charles R. Chickering.

ROTARY PRESS PRINTING

E.E. Plates of 200 subjects in four panes of 50 each.

1957 **Unwmk.** ***Perf. 10½x11***

1087	A534	3c **red lilac,** *Jan. 15, 1957*	6	5
		Margin block of 4, P#	30	—

COAST AND GEODETIC SURVEY ISSUE

Issued to commemorate the 150th anniversary of the establishment of the Coast and Geodetic Survey.

Flag of Coast and Geodetic Survey and Ships at Sea — A535

Designed by Harold E. MacEwen.

ROTARY PRESS PRINTING

E.E. Plates of 200 subjects in four panes of 50 each.

1957 **Unwmk.** ***Perf. 11x10½***

1088	A535	3c **dark blue,** *Feb. 11, 1957*	6	5
		Margin block of 4, P#	30	—

ARCHITECTS ISSUE

Issued to commemorate the centenary of the American Institute of Architects.

Corinthian Capital and Mushroom Type Head and Shaft — A536

Designed by Robert J. Schultz.

ROTARY PRESS PRINTING

E.E. Plates of 200 subjects in four panes of 50 each.

1957 **Unwmk.** ***Perf. 11x10½***

1089 A536 3c **red lilac,** *Feb. 23, 1957* 6 5
Margin block of 4, P# 30 —

STEEL INDUSTRY ISSUE

Issued to commemorate the centenary of the steel industry in America.

American Eagle and Pouring Ladle — A537

Designed by Anthony Petruccelli.

ROTARY PRESS PRINTING

E.E. Plates of 200 subjects in four panes of 50 each.

1957 **Unwmk.** ***Perf. 10½x11***

1090 A537 3c **bright ultramarine,** *May 22, 1957* 6 5
Margin block of 4, P# 30 —

INTERNATIONAL NAVAL REVIEW ISSUE

Issued to commemorate the International Naval Review and the Jamestown Festival.

Aircraft Carrier and Jamestown Festival Emblem — A538

Designed by Richard A. Genders.

ROTARY PRESS PRINTING

E.E. Plates of 200 subjects in four panes of 50 each.

1957 **Unwmk.** ***Perf. 11x10½***

1091 A538 3c **blue green,** *June 10, 1957* 6 5
Margin block of 4, P# 30 —

OKLAHOMA STATEHOOD ISSUE

Issued to commemorate the 50th anniversary of the admission of Oklahoma to Statehood.

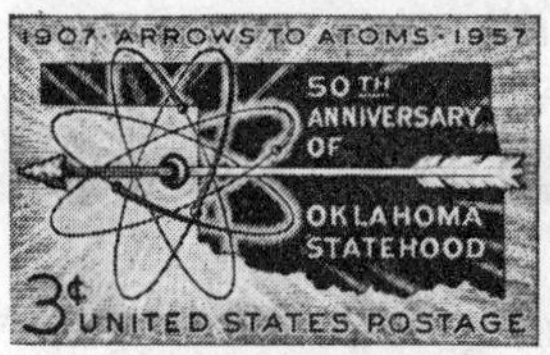

Map of Oklahoma, Arrow and Atom Diagram — A539

Designed by William K. Schrage.

ROTARY PRESS PRINTING

E.E. Plates of 200 subjects in four panes of 50 each.

1957 **Unwmk.** ***Perf. 11x10½***

1092 A539 3c **dark blue,** *June 14, 1957* 6 5
Margin block of 4, P# 35 —

SCHOOL TEACHERS ISSUE

Issued to honor the school teachers of America.

Teacher and Pupils — A540

ROTARY PRESS PRINTING

E.E. Plates of 200 subjects in four panes of 50 each.

1957 **Unwmk.** ***Perf. 11x10½***

1093 A540 3c **rose lake,** *July 1, 1957* 6 5
Margin block of 4, P# 30 —

FLAG ISSUE

"Old Glory" (48 Stars) — A541

Designed by Victor S. McCloskey, Jr.

GIORI PRESS PRINTING

Plates of 200 subjects in four panes of 50 each.

1957 **Unwmk.** ***Perf. 11***

1094 A541 4c **dark blue & deep carmine,** *July 4, 1957* 7 5
Margin block of 4, P# 35 —

SHIPBUILDING ISSUE

Issued to commemorate the 350th anniversary of shipbuilding in America.

"Virginia of Sagadahock" and Seal of Maine — A542

Designed by Ervine Metzel, Mrs. William Zorach, A. M. Main, Jr., and George F. Cary II.

ROTARY PRESS PRINTING

E.E. Plates of 280 subjects in four panes of 70 each.

1957 **Unwmk.** ***Perf. 10½x11***

1095 A542 3c **deep violet,** *Aug. 15, 1957* 6 5
Margin block of 4, P# 30 —

CHAMPION OF LIBERTY ISSUE

Issued to honor Ramon Magsaysay (1907-1957), President of the Philippines.

Ramon Magsaysay — A543

Designed by Arnold Copeland, Ervine Metzl and William H. Buckley.

GIORI PRESS PRINTING

Plates of 192 subjects in four panes of 48 each.

1957 **Unwmk.** ***Perf. 11***

1096 A543 8c **carmine, ultramarine & ocher,** *Aug. 31, 1957* 15 8
Margin block of 4, two P# 75 —
Margin block of 4, ultra. P# omitted —

LAFAYETTE BICENTENARY ISSUE

Issued to commemorate the bicentenary of the birth of the Marquis de Lafayette (1757-1834).

Marquis de Lafayette — A544

Designed by Ervine Metzl.

ROTARY PRESS PRINTING

E.E. Plates of 200 subjects in four panes of 50 each.

1957 **Unwmk.** ***Perf. 10½x11***

1097 A544 3c **rose lake,** *Sept. 6, 1957* 6 5
Margin block of 4, P# 30 —

WILDLIFE CONSERVATION ISSUE

Issued to emphasize the importance of Wildlife Conservation in America.

Whooping Cranes — A545

Designed by Bob Hines and C.R. Chickering.

GIORI PRESS PRINTING

Plates of 200 subjects in four panes of 50 each.

1957 **Unwmk.** ***Perf. 11***

1098 A545 3c **blue, ocher & green,** *Nov. 22, 1957* 6 5
Margin block of 4, P# 35 —

RELIGIOUS FREEDOM ISSUE

Issued to commemorate the 300th anniversary of the Flushing Remonstrance.

Bible, Hat and Quill Pen — A546

Designed by Robert Geissmann.

ROTARY PRESS PRINTING

E.E. Plates of 200 subjects in four panes of 50 each.

1957 **Unwmk.** ***Perf. 10½x11***

1099 A546 3c **black,** *Dec. 27, 1957* 6 5
Margin block of 4, P# 30 —

GARDENING HORTICULTURE ISSUE

Issued to honor the garden clubs of America and in connection with the centenary of the birth of Liberty Hyde Bailey, horticulturist.

Stamp booklets and booklet panes are listed and valued in a separate section of the catalogue. See catalogue index.

"Bountiful Earth" — A547

Designed by Denver Gillen.

ROTARY PRESS PRINTING

E.E. Plates of 200 subjects in four panes of 50 each.

1958 **Unwmk.** ***Perf. 10½x11***

1100 A547 3c **green,** *March 15, 1958* 6 5
Margin block of 4, P# 30 —

BRUSSELS EXHIBITION ISSUE

Issued in honor of the opening of the Universal and International Exhibition at Brussels, April 17.

U.S. Pavilion at Brussels — A551

Designed by Bradbury Thompson.

ROTARY PRESS PRINTING

E.E. Plates of 200 subjects in four panes of 50 each.

1958 **Unwmk.** ***Perf. 11x10½***

1104 A551 3c **deep claret,** *April 17, 1958* 6 5
Margin block of 4, P# 30 —

JAMES MONROE ISSUE

Issued to commemorate the bicentenary of the birth of James Monroe (1758-1831), fifth President of the United States.

James Monroe — A552

Designed by Frank P. Conley.

ROTARY PRESS PRINTING

E.E. Plates of 280 subjects in four panes of 70 each.

1958 **Unwmk.** ***Perf. 11x10½***

1105 A552 3c **purple,** *April 28, 1958* 6 5
Margin block of 4, P# 30 —

MINNESOTA STATEHOOD ISSUE

Issued to commemorate the centenary of Minnesota's admission to statehood.

Minnesota Lakes and Pines — A553

Designed by Homer Hill.

ROTARY PRESS PRINTING

E.E. Plates of 200 subjects in four panes of 50 each.

1958 **Unwmk.** ***Perf. 11x10½***

1106 A553 3c **green,** *May 11, 1958* 6 5
Margin block of 4, P# 30 —

GEOPHYSICAL YEAR ISSUE

Issued to commemorate the International Geophysical Year, 1957-58.

Solar Disc and Hands from Michelangelo's "Creation of Adam" — A554

Designed by Ervine Metzl.

GIORI PRESS PRINTING

Plates of 200 subjects in four panes of 50 each.

1958 ***Perf. 11***

1107 A554 3c **black & red orange,** *May 31, 1958* 6 5
Margin block of 4, P# 35 —

GUNSTON HALL ISSUE

Issued for the bicentenary of Gunston Hall and to honor George Mason, author of the Constitution of Virginia and the Virginia Bill of Rights.

Gunston Hall, Virginia — A555

Designed by Rene Clarke.

ROTARY PRESS PRINTING

E.E. Plates of 200 subjects in four panes of 50 each.

1958 **Unwmk.** ***Perf. 11x10½***

1108 A555 3c **light green,** *June 12, 1958* 6 5
Margin block of 4, P# 30 —

MACKINAC BRIDGE ISSUE

Issued to commemorate the dedication of Mackinac Bridge, Michigan.

Mackinac Bridge — A556

Designed by Arnold J. Copeland.

ROTARY PRESS PRINTING

E.E. Plates of 200 subjects in four panes of 50 each.

1958 **Unwmk.** ***Perf. 10½x11***

1109 A556 3c **bright greenish blue,** *June 25, 1958* 6 5
Margin block of 4, P# 30 —

CHAMPION OF LIBERTY ISSUE

Issued in honor of Simon Bolívar, South American freedom fighter.

Simon Bolívar — A557

ROTARY PRESS PRINTING

E.E. Plates of 280 subjects in four panes of 70 each.

1958 **Unwmk.** ***Perf. 10½x11***

1110 A557 4c **olive bister,** *July 24, 1958* 7 5
Margin block of 4, P# 35 —

GIORI PRESS PRINTING

Plates of 288 subjects in four panes of 72 each.

1111 A557 8c **carmine, ultramarine & ocher,** *July 24, 1958* 15 8
Margin block of 4, two P# 1.50 —
Corner block of 4, ocher P# only —

ATLANTIC CABLE CENTENNIAL ISSUE

Issued to commemorate the centenary of the Atlantic Cable, linking the Eastern and Western hemispheres.

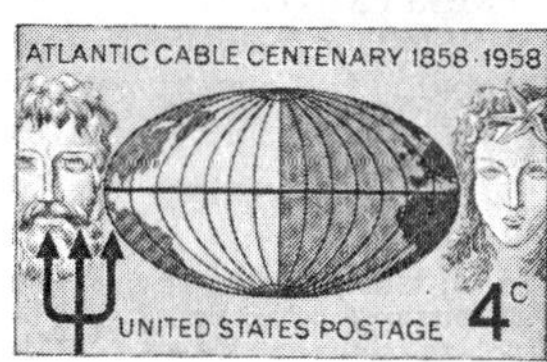

Neptune, Globe and Mermaid — A558

Designed by George Giusti.

ROTARY PRESS PRINTING

E.E. Plates of 200 subjects in four panes of 50 each.

1958 **Unwmk.** ***Perf. 11x10½***

1112 A558 4c **reddish purple,** *Aug. 15, 1958* 8 5
Margin block of 4, P# 40 —

LINCOLN SESQUICENTENNIAL ISSUE

Issued to commemorate the sesquicentennial of the birth of Abraham Lincoln. No. 1114 also commemorates the centenary of the founding of Cooper Union, New York City. No. 1115 marks the centenary of the Lincoln-Douglas Debates.

Lincoln by George Healy — A559

Lincoln by Gutzon Borglum — A560

Lincoln and Stephen A. Douglas Debating, from Painting by Joseph Boggs Beale — A561

Daniel Chester French Statue of Lincoln as Drawn by Fritz Busse — A562

Designed by Ervine Metzl.

ROTARY PRESS PRINTING

E.E. Plates of 200 subjects in four panes of 50 each.

1958-59 **Unwmk.** ***Perf. 10½x11***

1113 A559 1c **green,** *Feb. 12, 1959* 5 5
Margin block of 4, P# 25 —
1114 A560 3c **purple,** *Feb. 27, 1959* 6 6
Margin block of 4, P# 30 —

Perf. 11x10½

1115 A561 4c **sepia,** *Aug. 27, 1958* 8 5
Margin block, P# 40 —
1116 A562 4c **dark blue,** *May 30, 1959* 8 5
Margin block of 4, P# 40 —

CHAMPION OF LIBERTY ISSUE

Issued in honor of Lajos Kossuth, Hungarian freedom fighter.

Lajos Kossuth — A563

ROTARY PRESS PRINTING

E.E. Plates of 280 subjects in four panes of 70 each.

1958 **Unwmk.** ***Perf. 10½x11***

1117 A563 4c **green,** *Sept. 19, 1958* 8 5
Margin block of 4, P# 40 —

GIORI PRESS PRINTING

Plates of 288 subjects in four panes of 72 each.

1118 A563 8c **carmine, ultramarine & ocher,** *Sept. 19, 1958* 16 12
Margin block of 4, two P# 1.25 —

FREEDOM OF PRESS ISSUE

Issued in honor of Journalism and freedom of the press in connection with the 50th anniversary of the first School of Journalism at the University of Missouri.

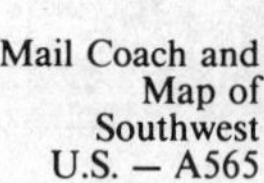

Early Press and Hand Holding Quill — A564

Designed by Lester Beall and Charles Goslin.

ROTARY PRESS PRINTING

E.E. Plates of 200 subjects in four panes of 50 each.

1958 **Unwmk.** ***Perf. 10½x11***

1119 A564 4c **black,** *Sept. 22, 1958* 8 5
Margin block of 4, P# 40 —

OVERLAND MAIL ISSUE

Issued to commemorate the centenary of Overland Mail Service.

Mail Coach and Map of Southwest U.S. — A565

Designed by William H. Buckley.

ROTARY PRESS PRINTING

E.E. Plates of 200 subjects in four panes of 50 each.

1958 **Unwmk.** ***Perf. 11x10½***

1120 A565 4c **crimson rose,** *Oct. 10, 1958* 8 5
Margin block of 4, P# 40 —

NOAH WEBSTER ISSUE

Issued to commemorate the bicentenary of the birth of Noah Webster (1758-1843), lexicographer and author.

Noah Webster — A566

Designed by Charles R. Chickering.

ROTARY PRESS PRINTING

E.E. Plates of 280 subjects in four panes of 70 each.

1958 **Unwmk.** ***Perf. 10½x11***

1121 A566 4c **dark carmine rose,** *Oct. 16, 1958* 8 5
Margin block of 4, P# 40 —

FOREST CONSERVATION ISSUE

Issued to publicize forest conservation and the protection of natural resources and to honor Theodore Roosevelt, a leading forest conservationist, on the centenary of his birth.

Forest Scene — A567

Designed by Rudolph Wendelin.

GIORI PRESS PRINTING

Plates of 200 subjects in four panes of 50 each.

1958 **Unwmk.** ***Perf. 11***

1122 A567 4c **green, yellow & brown,** *Oct. 27, 1958* 8 5
Margin block of 4, P# 40 —

FORT DUQUESNE ISSUE

Issued to commemorate the bicentennial of Fort Duquesne (Fort Pitt) at future site of Pittsburgh.

British Capture of Fort Duquesne, 1758; Brig. Gen. John Forbes on Litter, Colonel Washington Mounted — A568

Designed by William H. Buckley and Douglas Gorsline.

ROTARY PRESS PRINTING

E.E. Plates of 200 subjects in four panes of 50 each.

1958 **Unwmk.** ***Perf. 11x10½***

1123 A568 4c **blue,** *Nov. 25, 1958* 8 5
Margin block of 4, P# 40 —

OREGON STATEHOOD ISSUE

Issued to commemorate the centenary of Oregon's admission to Statehood.

Covered Wagon and Mt. Hood — A569

Designed by Robert Hallock.

ROTARY PRESS PRINTING

E.E. Plates of 200 subjects in four panes of 50 each.

1959 **Unwmk.** ***Perf. 11x10½***

1124 A569 4c **blue green,** *Feb. 14, 1959* 8 5
Margin block of 4, P# 40 —

CHAMPION OF LIBERTY ISSUE

Issued to honor José de San Martin, South American soldier and statesman.

U.S. Proofs are listed and valued in a separate section of the catalogue. See catalogue index.

José de San Martin — A570

ROTARY PRESS PRINTING

E.E. Plates of 280 subjects in four panes of 70 each.

1959, Feb. 25 **Unwmk.** ***Perf. 10½x11***

1125 A570 4c **blue** 8 5
Margin block of 4, P# 40 —
a. Horiz. pair, imperf. between *1,250.*

GIORI PRESS PRINTING

Plates of 288 subjects in four panes of 72 each.

1126 A570 8c **carmine, ultramarine & ocher** 16 8
Margin block of 4, P# 80 —

NATO ISSUE

Issued to commemorate the 10th anniversary of the North Atlantic Treaty Organization.

NATO Emblem — A571

Designed by Stevan Dohanos.

ROTARY PRESS PRINTING

E.E. Plates of 280 subjects in four panes of 70 each.

1959 **Unwmk.** ***Perf. 10½x11***

1127 A571 4c **blue,** *April 1, 1959* 8 5
Margin block of 4, P# 40 —

ARCTIC EXPLORATIONS ISSUE

Issued to commemorate the conquest of the Arctic by land by Rear Admiral Robert Edwin Peary in 1909 and by sea by the submarine "Nautilus" in 1958.

North Pole, Dog Sled and "Nautilus" A572

Designed by George Samerjan.

ROTARY PRESS PRINTING

E.E. Plates of 200 subjects in four panes of 50 each.

1959, Apr. 6 **Unwmk.** ***Perf. 11x10½***

1128 A572 4c **bright greenish blue** 8 5
Margin block of 4, P# 40 —

WORLD PEACE THROUGH WORLD TRADE ISSUE

Issued in conjunction with the 17th Congress of the International Chamber of Commerce, Washington, D.C., April 19-25.

Globe and Laurel — A573

Designed by Robert Baker.

ROTARY PRESS PRINTING

E.E. Plates of 200 subjects in four panes of 50 each.

1959 **Unwmk.** ***Perf. 11x10½***

1129 A573 8c **rose lake,** *Apr. 20, 1959* 15 12
Margin block of 4, P# 75 —

SILVER CENTENNIAL ISSUE

Issued to commemorate the centenary of the discovery of silver at the Comstock Lode, Nevada.

Henry Comstock at Mount Davidson Site — A574

Designed by Robert L. Miller and W.K. Schrage.

ROTARY PRESS PRINTING
E.E. Plates of 200 subjects in four panes of 50 each.

1959 **Unwmk.** ***Perf. 11x10½***
1130 A574 4c **black,** *June 8, 1959* 8 5
Margin block of 4, P# 40 —

ST. LAWRENCE SEAWAY ISSUE

Issued to commemorate the opening of the St. Lawrence Seaway.

Great Lakes, Maple Leaf and Eagle Emblems — A575

GIORI PRESS PRINTING
Plates of 200 subjects in four panes of 50 each.

1959 **Unwmk.** ***Perf. 11***
1131 A575 4c **red & dark blue,** *June 26, 1959* 8 5
Margin block of 4, P# 40 —
Pair with full horiz. gutter btwn. —

49-STAR FLAG ISSUE

U.S. Flag, 1959 — A576

Designed by Stevan Dohanos.

GIORI PRESS PRINTING
Plates of 200 subjects in four panes of 50 each.

1959 **Unwmk.** ***Perf. 11***
1132 A576 4c **ocher, dark blue & deep carmine,** *July 4, 1959* 8 5
Margin block of 4, P# 40 —

SOIL CONSERVATION ISSUE

Issued as a tribute to farmers and ranchers who use soil and water conservation measures.

Modern Farm — A577

Designed by Walter Hortens.

GIORI PRESS PRINTING
Plates of 200 subjects in four panes of 50 each.

1959 **Unwmk.** ***Perf. 11***
1133 A577 4c **blue, green & ocher,** *Aug. 26, 1959* 8 5
Margin block of 4, P# 40 —

PETROLEUM INDUSTRY ISSUE

Issued to commemorate the centenary of the completion of the nation's first oil well at Titusville, Pa.

Oil Derrick — A578

Designed by Robert Foster.

ROTARY PRESS PRINTING
E.E. Plates of 200 subjects in four panes of 50 each.

1959 **Unwmk.** ***Perf. 10½x11***
1134 A578 4c **brown,** *Aug. 27, 1959* 8 5
Margin block of 4, P# 40 —

DENTAL HEALTH ISSUE

Issued to publicize Dental Health and for the centenary of the American Dental Association.

Children — A579

Designed by Charles Henry Carter.

ROTARY PRESS PRINTING
E.E. Plates of 200 subjects in four panes of 50 each.

1959 **Unwmk.** ***Perf. 11x10½***
1135 A579 4c **green,** *Sept. 14, 1959* 8 5
Margin block of 4, P# 40 —

CHAMPION OF LIBERTY ISSUE

Issued to honor Ernst Reuter, Mayor of Berlin, 1948-53.

Ernst Reuter — A580

ROTARY PRESS PRINTING
E.E. Plates of 280 subjects in four panes of 70 each.

1959, Sept. 29 **Unwmk.** ***Perf. 10½x11***
1136 A580 4c **gray** 8 5
Margin block of 4, P# 40 —

GIORI PRESS PRINTING
Plates of 288 subjects in four panes of 72 each.

1137 A580 8c **carmine, ultramarine & ocher** 16 8
Margin block of 4, P# 80 —

DR. EPHRAIM McDOWELL ISSUE

Issued to honor Dr. Ephraim McDowell (1771-1830) on the 150th anniversary of the first successful ovarian operation in the United States, performed at Danville, Ky., 1809.

Dr. Ephraim McDowell — A581

Designed by Charles R. Chickering.

ROTARY PRESS PRINTING
E.E. Plates of 280 subjects in four panes of 70 each.

1959 **Unwmk.** ***Perf. 10½x11***
1138 A581 4c **rose lake,** *Dec. 3, 1959* 8 5
Margin block of 4, P# 40 —
a. Vert. pair, imperf. btwn. *600.00*
b. Vert. pair, imperf. horiz. *500.00*

AMERICAN CREDO ISSUE

Issued to re-emphasize the ideals upon which America was founded and to honor those great Americans who wrote or uttered the credos.

Quotation from Washington's Farewell Address, 1796 — A582

Benjamin Franklin Quotation A583

Thomas Jefferson Quotation A584

Francis Scott Key Quotation A585

Abraham Lincoln Quotation A586

Patrick Henry Quotation A587

Designed by Frank Conley.

GIORI PRESS PRINTING
Plates of 200 subjects in four panes of 50 each.

1960-61 **Unwmk.** ***Perf. 11***
1139 A582 4c **dark violet blue, & carmine,** *Jan. 20, 1960* 8 5
Margin block of 4, P# 40 —
1140 A583 4c **olive bister & green,** *Mar. 31, 1960* 8 5
Margin block of 4, P# 40 —
1141 A584 4c **gray & vermilion,** *May 18, 1960* 9 5
Margin block of 4, P# 45 —
1142 A585 4c **carmine & dark blue,** *Sept. 14, 1960* 10 5
Margin block of 4, P# 45 —
1143 A586 4c **magenta & green,** *Nov. 19, 1960* 10 5
Margin block of 4, P# 50 —
Pair with full horiz. gutter between —
1144 A587 4c **green & brown,** *Jan. 11, 1961* 12 5
Margin block of 4, P# 60 —

BOY SCOUT JUBILEE ISSUE

Issued to commemorate the 50th anniversary of the Boy Scouts of America.

Boy Scout Giving Scout Sign — A588

Designed by Norman Rockwell.

GIORI PRESS PRINTING
Plates of 200 subjects in four panes of 50 each.

1960 **Unwmk.** ***Perf. 11***
1145 A588 4c **red, dark blue & dark bister,** *Feb. 8, 1960* 8 5
Margin block of 4, P# 40 —

OLYMPIC WINTER GAMES ISSUE

Issued to commemorate the opening of the 8th Olympic Winter Games, Squaw Valley, Feb. 18-29, 1960.

Olympic Rings and Snowflake — A589

Designed by Ervine Metzl.

ROTARY PRESS PRINTING
E.E. Plates of 200 subjects in four panes of 50 each.

1960 **Unwmk.** ***Perf. 10½x11***
1146 A589 4c **dull blue,** *Feb. 18, 1960* 8 5
Margin block of 4, P# 40 —

CHAMPION OF LIBERTY ISSUE

Issued to honor Thomas G. Masaryk, founder and president of Czechoslovakia (1918-35), on the 110th anniversary of his birth.

Thomas G. Masaryk — A590

ROTARY PRESS PRINTING
E.E. Plates of 280 subjects in four panes of 70 each.

1960 **Unwmk.** ***Perf. 10½x11***
1147 A590 4c **blue,** *March 7, 1960* 8 5
Margin block of 4, P# 40 —
a. Vert. pair, imperf. between *1,600.*

GIORI PRESS PRINTING
Plates of 288 subjects in four panes of 72 each.

1148 A590 8c **carmine, ultramarine & ocher,** *March 7, 1960* 16 8
Margin block of 4, P# 1.10 —
a. Horiz. pair, imperf. between —

WORLD REFUGEE YEAR ISSUE

Issued to publicize World Refugee Year, July 1, 1959-June 30, 1960.

Family Walking Toward New Life — A591

Designed by Ervine Metzl.

ROTARY PRESS PRINTING
E.E. Plates of 200 subjects in four panes of 50 each.

1960 **Unwmk.** ***Perf. 11x10½***
1149 A591 4c **gray black,** *Apr. 7, 1960* 8 5
Margin block of 4, P# 40 —

WATER CONSERVATION ISSUE

Issued to stress the importance of water conservation and to commemorate the 7th Watershed Congress, Washington, D.C.

Water: From Watershed to Consumer A592

Designed by Elmo White.

GIORI PRESS PRINTING
Plates of 200 subjects in four panes of 50 each.

1960 **Unwmk.** ***Perf. 11***
1150 A592 4c **dark blue, brown orange & green,** *Apr. 18, 1960* 8 5
Margin block of 4, P# 40 —

SEATO ISSUE

Issued to honor the South-East Asia Treaty Organization and to publicize the SEATO Conference, Washington, D.C., May 31-June 3.

SEATO Emblem — A593

Designed by John Maass.

ROTARY PRESS PRINTING
E.E. plates of 280 subjects in four panes of 70 each.

1960 **Unwmk.** ***Perf. 10½x11***
1151 A593 4c **blue,** *May 31, 1960* 8 5
Margin block of 4, P# 40 —
a. Vertical pair, imperf. between *175.00*

AMERICAN WOMAN ISSUE

Issued to pay tribute to American women and their accomplishments in civic affairs, education, arts and industry.

Mother and Daughter — A594

Designed by Robert Sivard.

ROTARY PRESS PRINTING
E.E. Plates of 200 subjects in four panes of 50 each.

1960 **Unwmk.** ***Perf. 11x10½***
1152 A594 4c **deep violet,** *June 2, 1960* 8 5
Margin block of 4, P# 40 —

An enhanced introduction to the Scott Catalogue begins on Page V. A thorough understanding of the material presented there will greatly aid your use of the catalogue itself.

50-STAR FLAG ISSUE

U.S. Flag, 1960 — A595

Designed by Stevan Dohanos.

GIORI PRESS PRINTING
Plates of 200 subjects in four panes of 50 each.

1960 **Unwmk.** ***Perf. 11***
1153 A595 4c **dark blue & red,** *July 4, 1960* 8 5
Margin block of 4, P# 40 —

PONY EXPRESS CENTENNIAL ISSUE

Issued to commemorate the centenary of the Pony Express.

Pony Express Rider — A596

Designed by Harold von Schmidt.

ROTARY PRESS PRINTING
E.E. Plates of 200 subjects in four panes of 50 each.

1960 **Unwmk.** ***Perf. 11x10½***
1154 A596 4c **sepia,** *July 19, 1960* 8 5
Margin block of 4, P# 40 —

EMPLOY THE HANDICAPPED ISSUE

Issued to promote the employment of the physically handicapped and to publicize the Eighth World Congress of the International Society for the Welfare of Cripples, New York City.

Man in Wheelchair Operating Drill Press — A597

Designed by Carl Bobertz.

ROTARY PRESS PRINTING
E.E. Plates of 200 subjects in four panes of 50 each.

1960 **Unwmk.** ***Perf. 10½x11***
1155 A597 4c **dark blue,** *Aug. 28, 1960* 8 5
Margin block of 4, P# 40 —

WORLD FORESTRY CONGRESS ISSUE

Issued to commemorate the Fifth World Forestry Congress, Seattle, Washington, Aug. 29-Sept. 10.

World Forestry Congress Seal — A598

ROTARY PRESS PRINTING

E.E. Plates of 200 subjects in four panes of 50 each.

1960, Aug. 29 **Unwmk.** ***Perf. 10½x11***

1156 A598 4c **green** 8 5
Margin block of 4, P# 40 —

MEXICAN INDEPENDENCE ISSUE

Issued to commemorate the 150th anniversary of Mexican Independence.

Independence Bell — A599

Designed by Leon Helguera and Charles R. Chickering.

GIORI PRESS PRINTING

Plates of 200 subjects in four panes of 50 each.

1960 **Unwmk.** ***Perf. 11***

1157 A599 4c **green & rose red,** *Sept. 16, 1960* 8 5
Margin block of 4, P# 40 —

U.S.-JAPAN TREATY ISSUE

Issued to commemorate the centenary of the United States-Japan Treaty of Amity and Commerce.

Washington Monument and Cherry Blossoms — A600

Designed by Gyo Fujikawa.

GIORI PRESS PRINTING

Plates of 200 subjects in four panes of 50 each.

1960, Sept. 28 **Unwmk.** ***Perf. 11***

1158 A600 4c **blue & pink** 8 5
Margin block of 4, P# 40 —

CHAMPION OF LIBERTY ISSUE

Issued to honor Ignacy Jan Paderewski, Polish statesman and musician.

Ignacy Jan Paderewski — A601

ROTARY PRESS PRINTING

E.E. Plates of 280 subjects in four panes of 70 each.

1960, Oct. 8 **Unwmk.** ***Perf. 10½x11***

1159 A601 4c **blue** 8 5
Margin block of 4, P# 40 —

GIORI PRESS PRINTING

Plates of 288 subjects in four panes of 72 each.

1160 A601 8c **carmine, ultramarine & ocher** 16 8
Margin block of 4, P# 1.10 —

SENATOR TAFT MEMORIAL ISSUE

Issued in memory of Senator Robert A. Taft (1889-1953) of Ohio.

Robert A. Taft — A602

Designed by William K. Schrage.

ROTARY PRESS PRINTING

E.E. Plates of 280 subjects in four panes of 70 each.

1960 **Unwmk.** ***Perf. 10½x11***

1161 A602 4c **dull violet,** *Oct. 10, 1960* 8 5
Margin block of 4, P# 40 —

WHEELS OF FREEDOM ISSUE

Issued to honor the automotive industry and in connection with the National Automobile Show, Detroit, Oct. 15-23.

Globe and Steering Wheel with Tractor, Car and Truck — A603

Designed by Arnold J. Copeland.

ROTARY PRESS PRINTING

E.E. Plates of 200 subjects in four panes of 50 each.

1960 **Unwmk.** ***Perf. 11x10½***

1162 A603 4c **dark blue,** *Oct. 15, 1960* 8 5
Margin block of 4, P# 40 —

BOYS' CLUBS OF AMERICA ISSUE

Issued to commemorate the centenary of the Boys' Clubs of America movement.

Profile of Boy — A604

Designed by Charles T. Coiner.

GIORI PRESS PRINTING

Plates of 200 subjects in four panes of 50 each.

1960 **Unwmk.** ***Perf. 11***

1163 A604 4c **indigo, slate & rose red,** *Oct. 18, 1960* 8 5
Margin block of 4, P# 40 —

FIRST AUTOMATED POST OFFICE IN THE U.S.A. ISSUE

Issued to publicize the opening of the first automated post office in the United States at Providence, R.I.

Architect's Sketch of New Post Office, Providence, R.I. — A605

Designed by Arnold J. Copeland and Victor S. McCloskey, Jr.

GIORI PRESS PRINTING

Plates of 200 subjects in four panes of 50 each.

1960 **Unwmk.** ***Perf. 11***

1164 A605 4c **dark blue & carmine,** *Oct. 20, 1960* 8 5
Margin block of 4, P# 40 —

CHAMPION OF LIBERTY ISSUE

Issued to honor Baron Karl Gustaf Emil Mannerheim (1867-1951), Marshal and President of Finland.

Baron Gustaf Mannerheim — A606

ROTARY PRESS PRINTING

E.E. Plates of 280 subjects in four panes of 70 each.

1960, Oct. 26 **Unwmk.** ***Perf. 10½x11***

1165 A606 4c **blue** 8 5
Margin block of 4, P# 40 —

GIORI PRESS PRINTING

Plates of 288 subjects in four panes of 72 each.

1166 A606 8c **carmine, ultramarine & ocher** 16 8
Margin block of 4, P# 80 —

CAMP FIRE GIRLS ISSUE

Issued to commemorate the 50th anniversary of the Camp Fire Girls' movement and in connection with the Golden Jubilee Convention celebration of the Camp Fire Girls.

Camp Fire Girls Emblem — A607

Designed by H. Edward Oliver.

GIORI PRESS PRINTING

Plates of 200 subjects in four panes of 50 each.

1960, Nov. 1 **Unwmk.** ***Perf. 11***

1167 A607 4c **dark blue & bright red** 8 5
Margin block of 4, P# 40 —

CHAMPION OF LIBERTY ISSUE

Issued to honor Giuseppe Garibaldi (1807-1882), Italian patriot and freedom fighter.

Giuseppe Garibaldi — A608

ROTARY PRESS PRINTING

E.E. Plates of 280 subjects in four panes of 70 each.

1960, Nov. 2 **Unwmk.** ***Perf. 10½x11***

1168 A608 4c **green** 8 5
Margin block of 4, P# 40 —

GIORI PRESS PRINTING

Plates of 288 subjects in four panes of 72 each.

1169 A608 8c **carmine, ultramarine & ocher** 16 8
Margin block of 4, P# 80 —

SENATOR GEORGE MEMORIAL ISSUE

Issued in memory of Senator Walter F. George (1878-1957) of Georgia.

Walter F. George — A609

Designed by William K. Schrage.

ROTARY PRESS PRINTING

E.E. Plates of 280 subjects in four panes of 70 each.

1960 **Unwmk.** ***Perf. 10½x11***

1170 A609 4c **dull violet,** *Nov. 5, 1960* 8 5
Margin block of 4, P# 40 —

ANDREW CARNEGIE ISSUE

Issued to honor Andrew Carnegie (1835-1919), industrialist and philanthropist.

Andrew Carnegie — A610

Designed by Charles R. Chickering.

ROTARY PRESS PRINTING

E.E. Plates of 280 subjects in four panes of 70 each.

1960 **Unwmk.** ***Perf. 10½x11***

1171 A610 4c **deep claret,** *Nov. 25, 1960* 8 5
Margin block of 4, P# 40 —

JOHN FOSTER DULLES MEMORIAL ISSUE

Issued in memory of John Foster Dulles (1888-1959), Secretary of State (1953-1959).

John Foster Dulles — A611

Designed by William K. Schrage.

ROTARY PRESS PRINTING

E.E. Plates of 280 subjects in four panes of 70 each.

1960 **Unwmk.** ***Perf. 10½x11***

1172 A611 4c **dull violet,** *Dec. 6, 1960* 8 5
Margin block of 4, P# 40 —

ECHO I - COMMUNICATIONS FOR PEACE ISSUE

Issued to commemorate the world's first communications satellite, Echo I, placed in orbit by the National Aeronautics and Space Administration, Aug. 12, 1960.

Radio Waves Connecting Echo I and Earth — A612

Designed by Ervine Metzl.

ROTARY PRESS PRINTING

E.E. Plates of 200 subjects in four panes of 50 each.

1960, Dec. 15 **Unwmk.** ***Perf. 11x10½***

1173 A612 4c **deep violet,** *Dec. 15, 1960* 25 8
Margin block of 4, P# 1.25 —

CHAMPION OF LIBERTY ISSUE

Issued to honor Mohandas K. Gandhi, leader in India's struggle for independence.

Mahatma Gandhi — A613

ROTARY PRESS PRINTING

E.E. Plates of 280 subjects in four panes of 70 each.

1961, Jan. 26 **Unwmk.** ***Perf. 10½x11***

1174 A613 4c **red orange** 8 5
Margin block of 4, P# 40 —

GIORI PRESS PRINTING

Plates of 288 subjects in four panes of 72 each.

1175 A613 8c **carmine, ultramarine & ocher** 16 8
Margin block of 4, P# 1.25 —

RANGE CONSERVATION ISSUE

Issued to stress the importance of range conservation and to commemorate the meeting of the American Society of Range Management, Washington, D.C. "The Trail Boss" from a drawing by Charles M. Russell is the Society's emblem.

The Trail Boss and Modern Range — A614

Designed by Rudolph Wendelin.

GIORI PRESS PRINTING

Plates of 200 subjects in four panes of 50 each.

1961, Feb. 2 **Unwmk.** ***Perf. 11***

1176 A614 4c **blue, slate & brown orange** 8 5
Margin block of 4, P# 40 —

HORACE GREELEY ISSUE

Issued to honor Horace Greeley (1811-1872), publisher and editor.

Horace Greeley — A615

Designed by Charles R. Chickering.

ROTARY PRESS PRINTING

E.E. Plates of 280 subjects in four panes of 70 each.

1961 **Unwmk.** ***Perf. 10½x11***

1177 A615 4c **dull violet,** *Feb. 3, 1961* 8 5
Margin block of 4, P# 40 —

CIVIL WAR CENTENNIAL ISSUE

Issued to commemorate the centenaries of the firing on Fort Sumter (No. 1178), the Battle of Shiloh (No. 1179), the Battle of Gettysburg (No. 1180), the Battle of the Wilderness (No. 1181) and the surrender at Appomattox (No. 1182).

Sea Coast Gun of 1861 — A616

Rifleman at Battle of Shiloh, 1862 — A617

Blue and Gray at Gettysburg, 1863 — A618

Battle of the Wilderness, 1864 — A619

Appomattox, 1865 — A620

Designed by Charles R. Chickering (Sumter), Noel Sickles (Shiloh), Roy Gjertson (Gettysburg), B. Harold Christenson (Wilderness), Leonard Fellman (Appomattox).

ROTARY PRESS PRINTING

E.E. Plates of 200 subjects in four panes of 50 each.

1961-65 **Unwmk.** ***Perf. 11x10½***

1178 A616 4c **light green,** *Apr. 12, 1961* 12 5
Margin block of 4, P# 60 —
1179 A617 4c **black,** *peach blossom, Apr. 7, 1962* 10 5
Margin block of 4, P# 50 —

GIORI PRESS PRINTING

Plates of 200 subjects in four panes of 50 each.

1180 A618 5c **gray & blue,** *July 1, 1963* 10 5
Margin block of 4, P# 50 —
1181 A619 5c **dark red & black,** *May 5, 1964* 10 5
Margin block of 4, P# 50 —
Margin block of 4, Mr. Zip and "Use Zip Code" 45 —
1182 A620 5c **Prus. blue & black,** *Apr. 9, 1965* 12 5
Margin block of 4, P# 90 —
Margin block of 4, Mr. Zip and "Use Zip Code" 60 —
a. Horiz. pair, imperf. vert. —

KANSAS STATEHOOD ISSUE

Issued to commemorate the centenary of the admission of Kansas to statehood.

Sunflower, Pioneer Couple and Stockade — A621

GIORI PRESS PRINTING
Plates of 200 subjects in four panes of 50 each.

1961 **Unwmk.** ***Perf. 11***
1183 A621 4c **brown, dark red & green,** *yellow, May 10, 1961* 8 5
Margin block of 4, P# 40 —

SENATOR NORRIS ISSUE

Issued to commemorate the centenary of the birth of Senator George W. Norris (1861-1944), of Nebraska.

Senator George W. Norris and Norris Dam — A622

Designed by C. R. Chickering.

ROTARY PRESS PRINTING
E.E. Plates of 200 subjects in four panes of 50 each.

1961 **Unwmk.** ***Perf. 11x10½***
1184 A622 4c **blue green,** *July 11, 1961* 8 5
Margin block of 4, P# 40 —

NAVAL AVIATION ISSUE

Issued to commemorate the 50th anniversary of Naval Aviation.

Navy's First Plane (Curtiss A-1 of 1911) and Naval Air Wings — A623

Designed by John Maass.

ROTARY PRESS PRINTING
E.E. Plates of 200 subjects in four panes of 50 each.

1961 **Unwmk.** ***Perf. 11x10½***
1185 A623 4c **blue,** *Aug. 20, 1961* 8 5
Margin block of 4, P# 40 —
Pair with full vertical gutter between *150.00*

WORKMEN'S COMPENSATION ISSUE

Issued to commemorate the 50th anniversary of the first successful Workmen's Compensation Law, enacted by the Wisconsin legislature.

Scales of Justice, Factory, Worker and Family — A624

Designed by Norman Todhunter.

ROTARY PRESS PRINTING
E.E. Plates of 200 subjects in four panes of 50 each.

1961 **Unwmk.** ***Perf. 10½x11***
1186 A624 4c **ultramarine,** *grayish, Sept. 4, 1961* 8 5
Margin block of 4, P# 40 —
Margin block of 4, P# inverted 60 —

FREDERIC REMINGTON ISSUE

Issued to commemorate the centenary of the birth of Frederic Remington (1861-1909), artist of the West. The design is from an oil painting, Amon Carter Museum of Western Art, Fort Worth, Texas.

"The Smoke Signal" — A625

Designed by Charles R. Chickering.

GIORI PRESS PRINTING
Panes of 200 subjects in four panes of 50 each.

1961 **Unwmk.** ***Perf. 11***
1187 A625 4c **multicolored,** *Oct. 4, 1961* 8 5
Margin block of 4, P# 40 —

REPUBLIC OF CHINA ISSUE

Issued to commemorate the 50th anniversary of the Republic of China.

Sun Yat-sen — A626

ROTARY PRESS PRINTING
E.E. Plates of 200 subjects in four panes of 50 each.

1961 **Unwmk.** ***Perf. 10½x11***
1188 A626 4c **blue,** *Oct. 10, 1961* 8 5
Margin block of 4, P# 40 —

NAISMITH - BASKETBALL ISSUE

Issued in honor of basketball and to commemorate the centenary of the birth of James A. Naismith (1861-1939), Canada-born director of physical education, who invented the game in 1891 at Y.M.C.A. College, Springfield, Mass.

Basketball — A627

Designed by Charles R. Chickering.

ROTARY PRESS PRINTING
E.E. Plates of 200 subjects in four panes of 50 each.

1961 **Unwmk.** ***Perf. 10½x11***
1189 A627 4c **brown,** *Nov. 6, 1961* 8 5
Margin block of 4, P# 40 —

NURSING ISSUE

Issued to honor the nursing profession.

Student Nurse Lighting Candle — A628

Designed by Alfred Charles Parker.

GIORI PRESS PRINTING
Plates of 200 subjects in four panes of 50 each.

1961, Dec. 28 **Unwmk.** ***Perf. 11***
1190 A628 4c **blue, green, orange & black** 8 5
Margin block of 4, two P# 40 —

NEW MEXICO STATEHOOD ISSUE

Issued to commemorate the 50th anniversary of New Mexico's admission to statehood.

Shiprock — A629

Designed by Robert J. Jones.

GIORI PRESS PRINTING
Plates of 200 subjects in four panes of 50 each.

1962, Jan. 6 **Unwmk.** ***Perf. 11***
1191 A629 4c **lt. blue, maroon & bister** 8 5
Margin block of 4, P# 40 —

ARIZONA STATEHOOD ISSUE

Issued to commemorate the 50th anniversary of the admission of Arizona to statehood.

Giant Saguaro Cactus — A630

Designed by Jimmie E. Ihms and James M. Chemi.

GIORI PRESS PRINTING
Plates of 200 subjects in four panes of 50 each.

1962, Feb. 14 **Unwmk.** ***Perf. 11***
1192 A630 4c **carmine, violet blue & green** 8 5
Margin block of 4, P# 40 —

PROJECT MERCURY ISSUE

Issued to commemorate the first orbital flight of a U.S. astronaut, Feb. 20, 1962. The flight was made by Lt. Col. John H. Glenn, Jr.

"Friendship 7" Capsule and Globe — A631

GIORI PRESS PRINTING

Plates of 200 subjects in four panes of 50 each.

1962 **Unwmk.** *Perf. 11*

1193 A631 4c **dark blue & yellow,** *Feb. 20, 1962* 8 5
Margin block of 4, P# 40 —

Imperfs. are printers waste.

MALARIA ERADICATION ISSUE

Issued for the World Health Organization's drive to eradicate malaria.

Great Seal of U.S. and W.H.O. Symbol — A632

Designed by Charles R. Chickering.

GIORI PRESS PRINTING

Plates of 200 subjects in four panes of 50 each.

1962 **Unwmk.** *Perf. 11*

1194 A632 4c **blue & bister,** *March 30, 1962* 8 5
Margin block of 4, P# 40 —

CHARLES EVANS HUGHES ISSUE

Issued to commemorate the centenary of the birth of Charles Evans Hughes (1862-1948), Governor of New York, Chief Justice of the U.S.

Charles Evans Hughes — A633

Designed by Charles R. Chickering.

ROTARY PRESS PRINTING

E.E. Plates of 200 subjects in four panes of 50 each.

1962 **Unwmk.** *Perf. 10½x11*

1195 A633 4c **black,** *buff, Apr. 11, 1962* 8 5
Margin block of 4, P# 40 —

SEATTLE WORLD'S FAIR ISSUE

Issued to publicize the "Century 21" International Exposition, Seattle, Wash., Apr. 21-Oct. 21.

"Space Needle" and Monorail — A634

Designed by John Maass.

GIORI PRESS PRINTING

Plates of 200 subjects in four panes of 50 each.

1962 **Unwmk.** *Perf. 11*

1196 A634 4c **red & dark blue,** *Apr. 25, 1962* 8 5
Margin block of 4, P# 40 —

LOUISIANA STATEHOOD ISSUE

Issued to commemorate the sesquicentennial of Louisiana statehood.

Riverboat on the Mississippi A635

Designed by Norman Todhunter.

GIORI PRESS PRINTING

Plates of 200 subjects in four panes of 50 each.

1962 **Unwmk.** *Perf. 11*

1197 A635 4c **blue, dark slate green & red,** *Apr. 30, 1962* 8 5
Margin block of 4, P# 40 —

HOMESTEAD ACT ISSUE

Issued to commemorate the centenary of the Homestead Act.

Sod Hut and Settlers — A636

Designed by Charles R. Chickering.

ROTARY PRESS PRINTING

E.E. Plates of 200 subjects in four panes of 50 each.

1962 **Unwmk.** *Perf. 11x10½*

1198 A636 4c **slate,** *May 20, 1962* 8 5
Margin block of 4, P# 40 —

GIRL SCOUTS ISSUE

Issued to commemorate the 50th anniversary of the Girl Scouts of America.

Senior Girl Scout and Flag — A637

Designed by Ward Brackett.

ROTARY PRESS PRINTING

E.E. Plates of 200 subjects in four panes of 50 each.

1962 **Unwmk.** *Perf. 11x10½*

1199 A637 4c **rose red,** *July 24, 1962* 8 5
Margin block of 4, P# 40 —
Pair with full vertical gutter between 250.00

SENATOR BRIEN McMAHON ISSUE

Issued to honor Sen. Brien McMahon (1903-1952) of Connecticut for his role in opening the way to peaceful uses of atomic energy through the Atomic Energy Act establishing the Atomic Energy Commission.

Brien McMahon and Atomic Symbol — A638

Designed by V. S. McCloskey, Jr.

ROTARY PRESS PRINTING

E.E. Plates of 200 subjects in four panes of 50 each.

1962 **Unwmk.** *Perf. 11x10½*

1200 A638 4c **purple,** *July 28, 1962* 8 5
Margin block of 4, P# 40 —

APPRENTICESHIP ISSUE

Issued to publicize the National Apprenticeship Program and to commemorate the 25th anniversary of the National Apprenticeship Act.

Machinist Handing Micrometer to Apprentice A639

Designed by Robert Geissmann.

ROTARY PRESS PRINTING

E.E. Plates of 200 subjects in four panes of 50 each.

1962 **Unwmk.** *Perf. 11x10½*

1201 A639 4c **black,** *yellow bister, Aug. 31, 1962* 8 5
Margin block of 4, P# 40 —

SAM RAYBURN ISSUE

Issued to honor Sam Rayburn (1882-1961), Speaker of the House of Representatives.

Sam Rayburn and Capitol — A640

Designed by Robert L. Miller.

GIORI PRESS PRINTING

Plates of 200 subjects in four panes of 50 each.

1962, Sept. 16 **Unwmk.** *Perf. 11*

1202 A640 4c **dark blue & red brown** 8 5
Margin block of 4, P# 40 —

DAG HAMMARSKJOLD ISSUE

Issued to honor Dag Hammarskjold, Secretary General of the United Nations, 1953-61.

U.N. Headquarters and Dag Hammarskjold A641

Designed by Herbert M. Sanborn.

GIORI PRESS PRINTING

Plates of 200 subjects in four panes of 50 each.

1962 **Unwmk.** *Perf. 11*

1203 A641 4c **black, brown & yellow,** *Oct. 23, 1962* 8 5
Margin block of 4, two P# 40 —

Hammarskjold Special Printing

No. 1204 was issued following discovery of No. 1203 with yellow background inverted.

GIORI PRESS PRINTING

Plates of 200 subjects in four panes of 50 each.

1962 **Unwmk.** *Perf. 11*

1204 A641 4c **black, brown & yellow** (yellow inverted), *Nov. 16, 1962* 9 6
Margin block of 4, two P#, yellow # inverted 1.25 —

The inverted yellow impression is shifted to the right in relation to the black and brown impression. Stamps of first vertical row of UL and LL panes show no yellow at left side for a space of 11-11½mm in from the perforations. Stamps of first vertical row of UR and LR panes show vertical no-yellow strip 9¾mm wide, covering UN Building. On all others, the vertical no-yellow strip is 3½mm wide, and touches UN Building.

CHRISTMAS ISSUE

Wreath and Candles — A642

Designed by Jim Crawford.

GIORI PRESS PRINTING
Plates of 400 subjects in four panes of 100 each. Panes of 90 and 100 exist without plate numbers due to provisional use of smaller paper.

1962 **Unwmk.** ***Perf. 11***
1205 A642 4c **green & red,** *Nov. 1, 1962* 8 5
Margin block of 4, P# 40 —

HIGHER EDUCATION ISSUE

Issued to publicize higher education's role in American cultural and industrial development in connection with the centenary celebrations of the signing of the law creating land-grant colleges and universities.

Map of U.S. and Lamp — A643

Designed by Henry K. Bencsath.

GIORI PRESS PRINTING
Plates of 200 subjects in panes of 50 each.

1962 **Unwmk.** ***Perf. 11***
1206 A643 4c **blue green & black,** *Nov. 14, 1962* 8 5
Margin block of 4, two P# 40 —

WINSLOW HOMER ISSUE

Issued to honor Winslow Homer (1836-1910), painter, showing his oil, "Breezing Up," which hangs in the National Gallery, Washington, D.C.

"Breezing Up" — A644

Designed by Victor S. McCloskey, Jr.

GIORI PRESS PRINTING
Plates of 200 subjects in four panes of 50 each.

1962 **Unwmk.** ***Perf. 11***
1207 A644 4c **multicolored,** *Dec. 15, 1962* 8 5
Margin block of 4, P# 50 —
a. Horiz. pair, imperf. between —

FLAG ISSUE

Flag over White House — A645

Designed by Robert J. Jones.

GIORI PRESS PRINTING
Plates of 400 subjects in four panes of 100 each.

1963-66 **Unwmk.** ***Perf. 11***
1208 A645 5c **blue & red,** *Jan. 9, 1963* 10 5
Margin block of 4, P# 50 —
a. Tagged, *Aug. 25, 1966* 16 5
a. Margin block of 4, P# 80 —
b. Horiz. pair, imperf. between, tagged *1,250.*
Pair with full horiz. gutter between —

REGULAR ISSUE

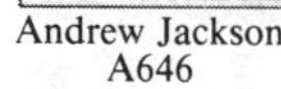

Andrew Jackson
A646

George Washington
A650

Designed by William K. Schrage.

ROTARY PRESS PRINTING
E.E. Plates of 400 subjects in four panes of 100 each.

1962-66 **Unwmk.** ***Perf. 11x10½***
1209 A646 1c **green,** *March 22, 1963* 5 5
Margin block of 4, P# 25 —
a. Tagged, *July 6, 1966* 6 5
a. Margin block of 4, P# 30 —
Pair with full vert. gutter btwn. —
1213 A650 5c **dark blue gray,** *Nov. 23, 1962* 12 5
Margin block of 4, P# 60 —
a. Booklet pane of 5 + label 2.25 *75*
b. Tagged, *Oct. 28, 1963* 50 22
b. Margin block of 4, P# 3.00 —
c. As "a," tagged, *Oct. 28, 1963* 1.25 *50*
Pair with full vert. or horiz. gutter btwn. —

Bureau Precancels: 1c, 10 diff., 5c, 18 diff.

COIL STAMPS (Rotary Press)

1962-66 ***Perf. 10 Vertically***
1225 A646 1c **green,** *May 31, 1963* 15 5
Pair 30 10
Joint line pair 2.25 12
a. Tagged, *July 6, 1966* 12 5
1229 A650 5c **dark blue gray,** *Nov. 23, 1962* 1.25 5
Pair 2.50 10
Joint line pair 4.00 15
a. Tagged, *Oct. 28, 1963* 1.00 6
b. Imperf., pair *300.00*

Bureau Precancels: 1c, 5 diff., 5c, 14 diff.

See Luminescence note in "Information for Collectors" at front of book.

CAROLINA CHARTER ISSUE

Issued to commemorate the tercentenary of the Carolina Charter granting to eight Englishmen lands extending coast-to-coast roughly along the present border of Virginia to the north and Florida to the south. Original charter on display at Raleigh.

First Page of Carolina Charter — A662

Designed by Robert L. Miller.

GIORI PRESS PRINTING
Plates of 200 subjects in four panes of 50 each.

1963 **Unwmk.** ***Perf. 11***
1230 A662 5c **dk. car. & brown,** *Apr. 6, 1963* 10 5
Margin block of 4, P# 50 —

FOOD FOR PEACE-FREEDOM FROM HUNGER ISSUE

Issued for the American "Food for Peace" program and the "Freedom from Hunger" campaign of the U.N. Food and Agriculture Organization.

Wheat — A663

Designed by Stevan Dohanos.

GIORI PRESS PRINTING
Plates of 200 subjects in four panes of 50 each.

1963 **Unwmk.** ***Perf. 11***
1231 A663 5c **green, buff & red,** *June 4, 1963* 10 5
Margin block of 4, P# 50 —

WEST VIRGINIA STATEHOOD ISSUE

Issued to commemorate the centenary of the admission of West Virginia to statehood.

Map of West Virginia and State Capitol — A664

Designed by Dr. Dwight Mutchler.

GIORI PRESS PRINTING
Plates of 200 subjects in four panes of 50 each.

1963 **Unwmk.** ***Perf. 11***
1232 A664 5c **green, red & black,** *June 20, 1963* 10 5
Margin block of 4, P# 50 —

EMANCIPATION PROCLAMATION ISSUE

Issued to commemorate the centenary of President Lincoln's Emancipation Proclamation freeing about 3,000,000 slaves in 10 southern states.

Severed Chain — A665

Designed by Georg Olden.

GIORI PRESS PRINTING
Plates of 200 subjects in four panes of 50 each.

1963, Aug. 16 **Unwmk.** ***Perf. 11***
1233 A665 5c **dark blue, black & red** 10 5
Margin block of 4, P# 50 —

ALLIANCE FOR PROGRESS ISSUE

Issued to commemorate the second anniversary of the Alliance for Progress, which aims to stimulate economic growth and raise living standards in Latin America.

Alliance Emblem — A666

Designed by William K. Schrage.

GIORI PRESS PRINTING
Plates of 200 subjects in four panes of 50 each.

1963 **Unwmk.** ***Perf. 11***
1234 A666 5c **ultramarine & green,** *Aug. 17, 1963* 10 5
Margin block of 4, P# 50 —

CORDELL HULL ISSUE

Issued to honor Cordell Hull (1871-1955), Secretary of State (1933-44).

The Catalogue editors cannot undertake to appraise, identify or judge the genuineness or condition of stamps.

Cordell Hull — A667

Designed by Robert J. Jones.

ROTARY PRESS PRINTING

E.E. Plates of 200 subjects in four panes of 50 each.

1963 **Unwmk.** ***Perf. 10½x11***

1235 A667 5c **blue green,** *Oct. 5, 1963* 10 5
Margin block of 4, P# 50 —

ELEANOR ROOSEVELT ISSUE

Issued to honor Mrs. Franklin D. Roosevelt (1884-1962).

Eleanor Roosevelt — A668

Designed by Robert L. Miller.

ROTARY PRESS PRINTING

E.E. Plates of 200 subjects in four panes of 50 each.

1963, Oct. 11 **Unwmk.** ***Perf. 11x10½***

1236 A668 5c **bright purple** 10 5
Margin block of 4, P# 50 —

SCIENCE ISSUE

Issued to honor the sciences and in connection with the centenary of the National Academy of Science.

"The Universe" A669

Designed by Antonio Frasconi.

GIORI PRESS PRINTING

Plates of 200 subjects in four panes of 50 each.

1963 **Unwmk.** ***Perf. 11***

1237 A669 5c **Prussian blue & black,** *Oct. 14, 1963* 10 5
Margin block of 4, P# 50 —

CITY MAIL DELIVERY ISSUE

Issued to commemorate the centenary of free city mail delivery.

Letter Carrier, 1863 — A670

Designed by Norman Rockwell.

GIORI PRESS PRINTING

Plates of 200 subjects in four panes of 50 each.

1963 **Unwmk.** **Tagged** ***Perf. 11***

1238 A670 5c **gray, dk, blue & red,** *Oct. 26, 1963* 10 5
Margin block of 4, P# 50 —

RED CROSS CENTENARY ISSUE

Issued to commemorate the centenary of the International Red Cross.

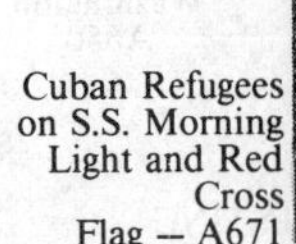

Cuban Refugees on S.S. Morning Light and Red Cross Flag — A671

Designed by Victor S. McCloskey, Jr.

GIORI PRESS PRINTING

Plates of 200 subjects in four panes of 50 each.

1963 **Unwmk.** ***Perf. 11***

1239 A671 5c **bluish black & red,** *Oct. 29, 1963* 10 5
Margin block of 4, P# 50 —

CHRISTMAS ISSUE

National Christmas Tree and White House — A672

Designed by Lily Spandorf; modified by Norman Todhunter.

GIORI PRESS PRINTING

Plates of 400 subjects in four panes of 100 each.

1963 **Unwmk.** ***Perf. 11***

1240 A672 5c **dk. blue, bluish black & red,** *Nov. 1, 1963* 10 5
Margin block of 4, P# 50 —
a. Tagged, *Nov. 2, 1963* 65 25
a. Margin block of 4, P# 5.00 —
Pair with full horiz. gutter between —

JOHN JAMES AUDUBON ISSUE

Issued to honor John James Audubon (1785-1851), ornithologist and artist. The birds pictured are actually Collie's magpie jays.

"Columbia Jays" by Audubon — A673

Designed by Robert L. Miller.

GIORI PRESS PRINTING

Plates of 200 subjects in four panes of 50 each.

1963 **Unwmk.** ***Perf. 11***

1241 A673 5c **dark blue & multicolored,** *Dec. 7, 1963* 10 5
Margin block of 4, P# 50 —

SAM HOUSTON ISSUE

Issued to commemorate the centenary of the death of Sam Houston (1793-1863), soldier, president of Texas, U.S. senator.

Sam Houston — A674

Designed by Tom Lea.

ROTARY PRESS PRINTING

E.E. Plates of 200 subjects in four panes of 50 each.

1964 **Unwmk.** ***Perf. 10½x11***

1242 A674 5c **black,** *Jan. 10, 1964* 10 5
Margin block of 4, P# 50 —
Margin block of 4, Mr. Zip and "Use Zip Code" 45 —

CHARLES M. RUSSELL ISSUE

Issued to commemorate the centenary of the birth of Charles M. Russell (1864-1926), painter. The design is from a painting, Thomas Gilcrease Institute of American History and Art, Tulsa, Okla.

"Jerked Down" — A675

Designed by William K. Schrage.

GIORI PRESS PRINTING

Plates of 200 subjects in four panes of 50 each.

1964 **Unwmk.** ***Perf. 11***

1243 A675 5c **multicolored,** *March 19, 1964* 10 5
Margin block of 4, P# 50 —
Margin block of 4, Mr. Zip and "Use Zip Code" 45 —

NEW YORK WORLD'S FAIR ISSUE

Issued to publicize the New York World's Fair, 1964-65.

Mall with Unisphere and "Rocket Thrower" by Donald De Lue — A676

Designed by Robert J. Jones.

ROTARY PRESS PRINTING

E.E. Plates of 200 subjects in four panes of 50 each.

1964 **Unwmk.** ***Perf. 11x10½***

1244 A676 5c **blue green,** *Apr. 22, 1964* 10 5
On cover, Expo. station canc. 15
Margin block of 4, P# 50 —
Margin block of 4, Mr. Zip and "Use Zip Code" 45 —

JOHN MUIR ISSUE

Issued to honor John Muir (1838-1914), naturalist and conservationist.

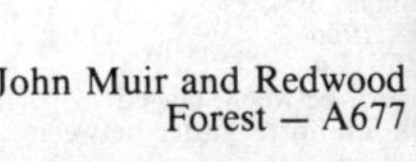

John Muir and Redwood Forest — A677

Designed by Rudolph Wendelin.

GIORI PRESS PRINTING

Plates of 200 subjects in four panes of 50 each.

1964 **Unwmk.** ***Perf. 11***

1245 A677 5c **brown, green, yel. grn. & olive,** *Apr. 29, 1964* 10 5
Margin block of 4, P# 50 —

KENNEDY MEMORIAL ISSUE

Issued in memory of President John Fitzgerald Kennedy, (1917-1963).

John F. Kennedy and Eternal Flame — A678

Designed by Raymond Loewy/William Snaith, Inc. photograph by William S. Murphy.

ROTARY PRESS PRINTING

E.E. Plates of 200 subjects in four panes of 50 each.

1964 ***Perf. 11x10½***

1246 A678 5c **blue gray,** *May 29, 1964* 10 5
Margin block of 4, P# 50 —

NEW JERSEY TERCENTENARY ISSUE

Issued to commemorate the 300th anniversary of English colonization of New Jersey. The design is from a mural by Howard Pyle in the Essex County Courthouse, Newark, N.J.

Philip Carteret Landing at Elizabethtown, and Map of New Jersey — A679

Designed by Douglas Allen.

ROTARY PRESS PRINTING

E.E. Plates of 200 subjects in four panes of 50 each.

1964 **Unwmk.** ***Perf. 10½x11***

1247 A679 5c **brt. ultramarine,** *June 15, 1964* 10 5
Margin block of 4, P# 50 —
Margin block of 4, Mr. Zip and "Use Zip Code" 45 —

NEVADA STATEHOOD ISSUE

Issued to commemorate the centenary of the admission of Nevada to statehood.

Virginia City and Map of Nevada — A680

Designed by William K. Schrage.

GIORI PRESS PRINTING

Plates of 200 subjects in four panes of 50 each.

1964 ***Perf. 11***

1248 A680 5c **red, yellow & blue,** *July 22, 1964* 10 5
Margin block of 4, P# 50 —
Margin block of 4, Mr. Zip and "Use Zip Code" 45 —

REGISTER AND VOTE ISSUE

Issued to publicize the campaign to draw more voters to the polls.

Flag — A681

Designed by Victor S. McCloskey, Jr.

GIORI PRESS PRINTING

Plates of 200 subjects in four panes of 50 each.

1964 **Unwmk.** ***Perf. 11***

1249 A681 5c **dk. blue & red,** *Aug. 1, 1964* 10 5
Margin block of 4, P# 50 —
Margin block of 4, Mr. Zip and "Use Zip Code" 45 —

SHAKESPEARE ISSUE

Issued to commemorate the 400th anniversary of the birth of William Shakespeare (1564-1616).

William Shakespeare — A682

Designed by Douglas Gorsline.

ROTARY PRESS PRINTING

E.E. Plates of 200 subjects in four panes of 50 each.

1964 **Unwmk.** ***Perf. 10½x11***

1250 A682 5c **black brown,** *tan, Aug. 14, 1964* 10 5
Margin block of 4, P# 50 —
Margin block of 4, Mr. Zip and "Use Zip Code" 45 —

DOCTORS MAYO ISSUE

Issued to honor Dr. William James Mayo (1861-1939) and his brother, Dr. Charles Horace Mayo (1865-1939), surgeons who founded the Mayo Foundation for Medical Education and Research in affiliation with the University of Minnesota at Rochester, Minn. Heads on stamp are from a sculpture by James Earle Fraser.

Drs. William and Charles Mayo — A683

ROTARY PRESS PRINTING

E.E. Plates of 200 subjects in four panes of 50 each.

1964 **Unwmk.** ***Perf. 10½x11***

1251 A683 5c **green,** *Sept. 11, 1964* 10 5
Margin block of 4, P# 50 —
Margin block of 4, Mr. Zip and "Use Zip Code" 45 —

AMERICAN MUSIC ISSUE

Issued in tribute to American Music on the 50th anniversary of the founding of the American Society of Composers, Authors and Publishers (ASCAP).

Lute, Horn, Laurel, Oak and Music Score — A684

Designed by Bradbury Thompson.

GIORI PRESS PRINTING

Plates of 200 subjects in four panes of 50 each.

1964 **Unwmk.** ***Perf. 11***

Gray Paper with Blue Threads

1252 A684 5c **red, black & blue,** *Oct. 15, 1964* 10 5
Margin block of 4, P# 50 —
Margin block of 4, Mr. Zip and "Use Zip Code" 45 —
a. Blue omitted *1,500.*

HOMEMAKERS ISSUE

Issued to honor American women as homemakers and to commemorate the 50th anniversary of the passage of the Smith-Lever Act. By providing economic experts under an extension service of the U.S. Department of Agriculture, this legislation helped to improve homelife.

Farm Scene Sampler — A685

Designed by Norman Todhunter.

Plates of 200 subjects in four panes of 50 each.

Engraved (Giori Press); Background Lithographed

1964 **Unwmk.** ***Perf. 11***

1253 A685 5c **multicolored,** *Oct. 26, 1964* 10 5
Margin block of 4, P# 50 —
Margin block of 4, Mr. Zip and "Use Zip Code" 45 —

CHRISTMAS ISSUE

Holly — A686

Mistletoe — A687

Poinsettia A688

Sprig of Conifer A689

Designed by Thomas F. Naegele.

GIORI PRESS PRINTING

Plates of 400 subjects in four panes of 100 each.

Panes contain 25 subjects each of Nos. 1254-1257

1964 **Unwmk.** ***Perf. 11***

1254 A686 5c **green, carmine & black,** *Nov. 9* 35 5
Margin block of 4, P# adjoining #1254 1.75 —
Margin block of 4, Mr. Zip and "Use Zip Code" adjoining #1254 1.50 —
a. Tagged, *Nov. 10* 75 25
1255 A687 5c **carmine, green & black,** *Nov. 9* 35 5
Margin block of 4, P# adjoining #1255 1.75 —
Margin block of 4, Mr. Zip and "Use Zip Code" adjoining #1255 1.50 —
a. Tagged, *Nov. 10* 75 25
1256 A688 5c **carmine, green & black,** *Nov. 9* 35 5
Margin block of 4, P# adjoining #1256 1.75 —

Margin block of 4, Mr. Zip and "Use Zip Code" adjoining #1256 1.50 —
a. Tagged, *Nov. 10* 75 25
1257 A689 5c **black, green & carmine,** *Nov. 9* 35 5
Margin block of 4, P# adjoining #1257 1.75 —
Margin block of 4, Mr. Zip and "Use Zip Code" adjoining #1257 1.50 —
a. Tagged, *Nov. 10* 75 25
a. Margin block of 4, P# 5.00 —
b. Block of four, #1254-1257 1.25 1.00
c. Block of four, tagged 3.25 2.00

VERRAZANO-NARROWS BRIDGE ISSUE

Issued to commemorate the opening of the Verrazano-Narrows Bridge connecting Staten Island and Brooklyn.

Verrazano-Narrows Bridge and Map of New York Bay — A690

ROTARY PRESS PRINTING
E.E. Plates of 200 subjects in four panes of 50 each.

1964 **Unwmk.** ***Perf. 10½x11***
1258 A690 5c **blue green,** *Nov. 21* 10 5
Margin block of 4, P# 40 —
Margin block of 4, Mr. Zip and "Use Zip Code" 45 —

FINE ARTS ISSUE

Abstract Design by Stuart Davis — A691

GIORI PRESS PRINTING
Plates of 200 subjects in four panes of 50 each.

1964 **Unwmk.** ***Perf. 11***
1259 A691 5c **ultra., black & dull red,** *Dec. 2* 10 5
Margin block of 4, two P# 50 —
Margin block of 4, Mr. Zip and "Use Zip Code" 45 —

AMATEUR RADIO ISSUE

Issued to honor the radio amateurs on the 50th anniversary of the American Radio Relay League.

Radio Waves and Dial — A692

Designed by Emil J. Willett.

ROTARY PRESS PRINTING
E.E. Plates of 200 subjects in four panes of 50 each.

1964 **Unwmk.** ***Perf. 10½x11***
1260 A692 5c **red lilac,** *Dec. 15* 10 5
Margin block of 4, P# 50 —
Margin block of 4, Mr. Zip and "Use Zip Code" 45 —

BATTLE OF NEW ORLEANS ISSUE

Issued to commemorate the sesquicentennial of the Battle of New Orleans, Chalmette Plantation, Jan. 8-18, 1815, which established 150 years of peace and friendship between the United States and Great Britain.

General Andrew Jackson and Sesquicentennial Medal — A693

Designed by Robert J. Jones.

GIORI PRESS PRINTING
Plates of 200 subjects in four panes of 50 each.

1965 **Unwmk.** ***Perf. 11***
1261 A693 5c **dp. carmine, violet blue & gray,** *Jan. 8* 10 5
Margin block of 4, P# 50 —
Margin block of 4, Mr. Zip and "Use Zip Code" 45 —

PHYSICAL FITNESS-SOKOL ISSUE

Issued to publicize the importance of physical fitness and to commemorate the centenary of the founding of the Sokol (athletic) organization in America.

Discus Thrower — A694

Designed by Norman Todhunter.

GIORI PRESS PRINTING
Plates of 200 subjects in four panes of 50 each.

1965 **Unwmk.** ***Perf. 11***
1262 A694 5c **maroon & black,** *Feb. 15* 10 5
Margin block of 4, P# 50 —
Margin block of 4, Mr. Zip and "Use Zip Code" 45 —

CRUSADE AGAINST CANCER ISSUE

Issued to publicize the "Crusade Against Cancer" and to stress the importance of early diagnosis.

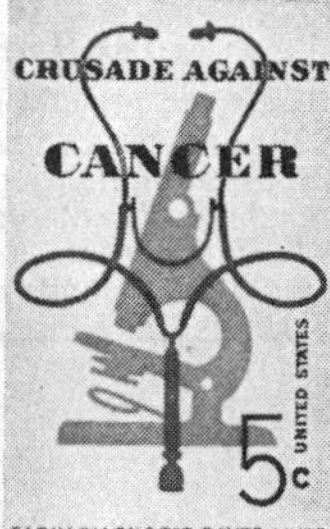

Microscope and Stethoscope — A695

Designed by Stevan Dohanos.

GIORI PRESS PRINTING
Plates of 200 subjects in four panes of 50 each.

1965 **Unwmk.** ***Perf. 11***
1263 A695 5c **black, purple & red orange,** *Apr. 1* 10 5
Margin block of 4, two P# 50 —
Margin block of 4, Mr. Zip and "Use Zip Code" 45 —

CHURCHILL MEMORIAL ISSUE

Issued in memory of Sir Winston Spencer Churchill (1874-1965), British statesman and World War II leader.

Winston Churchill — A696

Designed by Richard Hurd.

ROTARY PRESS PRINTING
E.E. Plates of 200 subjects in four panes of 50 each.

1965 **Unwmk.** ***Perf. 10½x11***
1264 A696 5c **black,** *May 13* 10 5
Margin block of 4, P# 50 —
Margin block of 4, Mr. Zip and "Use Zip Code" 45 —

MAGNA CARTA ISSUE

Issued to commemorate the 750th anniversary of the Magna Carta, the basis of English and American common law.

Procession of Barons and King John's Crown — A697

Designed by Brook Temple.

GIORI PRESS PRINTING
Plates of 200 subjects in four panes of 50 each.

1965 **Unwmk.** ***Perf. 11***
1265 A697 5c **black, yellow ocher & red lilac,** *June 15* 10 5
Margin block of 4, two P# 50 —
Margin block of 4, Mr. Zip and "Use Zip Code" 45 —
Corner block of 4, black P# omitted —

INTERNATIONAL COOPERATION YEAR ISSUE

Issued for the International Cooperation Year, 1965, and to commemorate the 20th anniversary of the United Nations.

International Cooperation Year Emblem — A698

Designed by Herbert M. Sanborn and Olav S. Mathiesen.

GIORI PRESS PRINTING
Plates of 200 subjects in four panes of 50 each.

1965 **Unwmk.** ***Perf. 11***
1266 A698 5c **dull blue & black,** *June 26* 10 5
Margin block of 4, P# 50 —
Margin block of 4, Mr. Zip and "Use Zip Code" 45 —

SALVATION ARMY ISSUE

Issued to commemorate the centenary of the founding of the Salvation Army by William Booth in London.

The Scott Catalogue value is a retail price, what you could expect to pay for the stamp in a grade of Fine-Very Fine. The value listed is a reference which reflects recent actual dealer selling price.

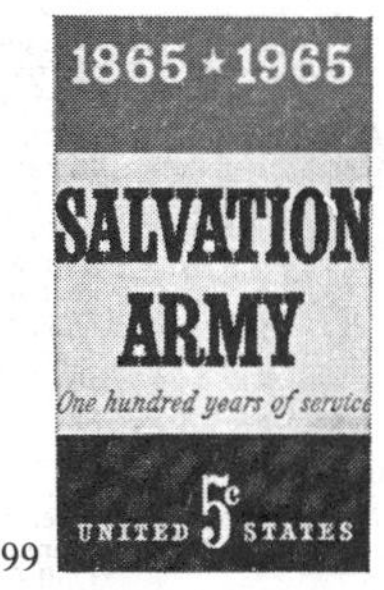

A699

Designed by Sam Marsh.

GIORI PRESS PRINTING

Plates of 200 subjects in four panes of 50 each.

1965 **Unwmk.** ***Perf. 11***

1267 A699 5c **red, black & dark blue,** *July 2* 10 5
Margin block of 4, P# 50 —
Margin block of 4, Mr. Zip and "Use Zip Code" 45 —

DANTE ISSUE

Issued to commemorate the 700th anniversary of the birth of Dante Alighieri (1265-1321), Italian poet.

Dante after a 16th Century Painting — A700

Designed by Douglas Gorsline.

ROTARY PRESS PRINTING

E.E. Plates of 200 subjects in four panes of 50 each.

1965 **Unwmk.** ***Perf. 10½x11***

1268 A700 5c **maroon,** *July 17* 10 5
Margin block of 4, P# 50 —
Margin block of 4, Mr. Zip and "Use Zip Code" 45 —

HERBERT HOOVER ISSUE

Issued in memory of President Herbert Clark Hoover, (1874-1964).

Herbert Hoover — A701

Designed by Norman Todhunter; photograph by Fabian Bachrach, Sr.

ROTARY PRESS PRINTING

E.E. Plates of 200 subjects in four panes of 50 each.

1965 **Unwmk.** ***Perf. 10½x11***

1269 A701 5c **rose red,** *Aug. 10* 10 5
Margin block of 4, P# 50 —
Margin block of 4, Mr. Zip and "Use Zip Code" 45 —

ROBERT FULTON ISSUE

Issued to commemorate the 200th anniversary of the birth of Robert Fulton (1765-1815), inventor of the first commercial steamship.

Robert Fulton and the Clermont — A702

Designed by John Maass; bust by Jean Antoine Houdon.

GIORI PRESS PRINTING

Plates of 200 subjects in four panes of 50 each.

1965 **Unwmk.** ***Perf. 11***

1270 A702 5c **black & blue,** *Aug. 19* 10 5
Margin block of 4, P# 50 —
Margin block of 4, Mr. Zip and "Use Zip Code" 45 —

FLORIDA SETTLEMENT ISSUE

Issued to commemorate the 400th anniversary of the settlement of Florida, and the first permanent European settlement in the continental United States, St. Augustine, Fla. Similar stamp issued by Spain, No. 1312.

Spanish Explorer, Royal Flag of Spain and Ships — A703

Designed by Brook Temple.

GIORI PRESS PRINTING

Plates of 200 subjects with four panes of 50 each.

1965 **Unwmk.** ***Perf. 11***

1271 A703 5c **red, yellow & black,** *Aug. 28* 10 5
Margin block of 4, three P# 50 —
Margin block of 4, Mr. Zip and "Use Zip Code" 45 —
a. Yellow omitted *700.00*

TRAFFIC SAFETY ISSUE

Issued to publicize traffic safety and the prevention of traffic accidents.

Traffic Signal — A704

Designed by Richard F. Hurd.

GIORI PRESS PRINTING

Plates of 200 subjects in four panes of 50 each.

1965 **Unwmk.** ***Perf. 11***

1272 A704 5c **emerald, black & red,** *Sept. 3* 10 5
Margin block of 4, two P# 50 —
Margin block of 4, Mr. Zip and "Use Zip Code" 45 —

JOHN SINGLETON COPLEY ISSUE

Issued to honor John Singleton Copley (1738-1815), painter. The portrait of the artist's daughter is from the oil painting "The Copley Family," which hangs in the National Gallery of Art, Washington, D.C.

Souvenir cards are listed and valued in a separate section of the catalogue. See catalogue index.

Elizabeth Clarke Copley — A705

Designed by John Carter Brown.

GIORI PRESS PRINTING

Plates of 200 subjects in four panes of 50 each.

1965 **Unwmk.** ***Perf. 11***

1273 A705 5c **black, brown & olive,** *Sept. 17* 10 5
Margin block of 4, P# 50 —
Margin block of 4, Mr. Zip and "Use Zip Code" 45 —

INTERNATIONAL TELECOMMUNICATION UNION ISSUE

Issued to commemorate the centenary of the International Telecommunication Union.

Galt Projection World Map and Radio Sine Wave — A706

Designed by Thomas F. Naegele.

GIORI PRESS PRINTING

Plates of 200 subjects with four panes of 50 each.

1965 **Unwmk.** ***Perf. 11***

1274 A706 11c **black, carmine & bister,** *Oct. 6* 32 16
Margin block of 4, 2 P# 6.00 —
Margin block of 4, Mr. Zip and "Use Zip Code" 2.50 —

ADLAI STEVENSON ISSUE

Issued in memory of Adlai Ewing Stevenson (1900-65), governor of Illinois, U.S. ambassador to the U.N.

Adlai E. Stevenson — A707

Designed by George Samerjan; photograph by Philippe Halsman.

LITHOGRAPHED, ENGRAVED (Giori)

Plates of 200 subjects in four panes of 50 each.

1965 **Unwmk.** ***Perf. 11***

1275 A707 5c **pale blue, black, carmine & violet blue,** *Oct. 23* 10 5
Margin block of 4, P# 50 —

CHRISTMAS ISSUE

Angel with Trumpet, 1840 Weather Vane — A708

Designed by Robert Jones after a watercolor by Lucille Gloria Chabot of the 1840 weather vane from the People's Methodist Church, Newburyport, Mass.

GIORI PRESS PRINTING

Plates of 400 subjects in four panes of 100 each.

1965 **Unwmk.** ***Perf. 11***

No.	Type	Description	Unused	Used
1276	A708	5c **carmine, dark olive green & bister,** *Nov. 2*	10	5
		Margin block of 4, P#	50	—
		Margin block of 4, Mr. Zip and "Use Zip Code"	45	—
		Pair with full vert. gutter btwn.	—	
a.		Tagged, *Nov. 15*	75	15
a.		Margin block of 4, P#	7.50	—

PROMINENT AMERICANS ISSUE

Thomas Jefferson A710

Albert Gallatin A711

Frank Lloyd Wright and Guggenheim Museum, New York – A712

Francis Parkman – A713

LINCOLN
4c
UNITED STATES
Abraham Lincoln A714

George Washington A715

WASHINGTON 5c
UNITED STATES
George Washington (redrawn) A715a

Franklin D. Roosevelt A716

Albert Einstein – A717

Andrew Jackson – A718

Henry Ford and 1909 Model T – A718a

John F. Kennedy – A719

Oliver Wendell Holmes A720

STATESMAN SOLDIER
GEORGE C. MARSHALL
20c
UNITED STATES
George Catlett Marshall A721

Frederick Douglass – A722

John Dewey – A723

Thomas Paine – A724

Lucy Stone – A725

Eugene O'Neill – A726

John Bassett Moore – A727

Designers: 1c, Robert Geissmann, after portrait by Rembrandt Peale. 1¼c, Robert Gallatin. 2c, Patricia Amarantides; photograph by Blackstone-Shelburne. 3c, Bill Hyde. 4c, Bill Hyde; photograph by Mathew Brady. 5c, Bill Hyde, after portrait by Rembrandt Peale. 5c, No. 1283B, Redrawn by Stevan Dohanos. 6c, 30c, Richard L. Clark. 8c, Frank Sebastiano; photograph by Philippe Halsman. 10c, Lester Beall. 12c, Norman Todhunter. 13c, Stevan Dohanos; photograph by Jacques Lowe. 15c, Richard F. Hurd. 20c, Robert Geissmann. 25c, Walter DuBois Richards. 40c, Robert Geissmann, after portrait by John Wesley Jarvis. 50c, Mark English. $1, Norman Todhunter. $5, Tom Laufer.

ROTARY PRESS PRINTING

E.E. Plates of 400 subjects in four panes of 100

1965-78 **Unwmk.** ***Perf. 11x10½, 10½x11***

Types of 15c:

I. Necktie barely touches coat at bottom; crosshatching of tie strong and complete. Flag of "5" is true horizontal. Crosshatching of "15" is colorless when visible.

II. Necktie does not touch coat at bottom; LL to UR crosshatching lines strong, UL to LR lines very faint. Flag of "5" slants down slightly at right. Crosshatching of "15" is colored and visible when magnified.

A third type, used only for No. 1288B, is smaller in overall size and "15¢" is ¾mm. closer to head.

No.	Type	Description	Unused	Used
1278	A710	1c **green,** tagged, *Jan. 12, 1968*	5	5
		Margin block of 4, P#	25	—
		Margin block of 4, "Use Zip Codes"	20	—
		Margin block of 6, "Mail Early in the Day"	32	—
a.		Booklet pane of 8, *Jan. 12, 1968*	1.00	*25*
b.		Bklt. pane of 4+2 labels, *May 10, 1971*	75	*20*
c.		Untagged (Bureau precanceled)		7
1279	A711	1¼c **light green,** *Jan. 30, 1967*	8	5
		Margin block of 4, P#	12.00	—
1280	A712	2c **dark blue gray,** tagged, *June 8, 1966*	5	5
		Margin block of 4, P#	25	—
		Margin block of 4, "Use Zip Codes"	20	—
		Margin block of 6, "Mail Early in the Day"	32	—
a.		Bklt. pane of 5+ label, *Jan. 8, 1968*	1.20	*40*
b.		Untagged (Bureau precanceled)		10
c.		Bklt. pane of 6, *May 7, 1971*	1.00	*35*
		Pair with full vert. gutter btwn.	—	
1281	A713	3c **violet,** tagged, *Sept. 16, 1967*	6	5
		Margin block of 4, P#	30	—
		Margin block of 4, "Use Zip Codes"	1.20	—
		Margin block of 6, "Mail Early in the Day"	1.40	—
a.		Untagged (Bureau precanceled)		12
1282	A714	4c **black,** *Nov. 19, 1965*	8	5
		Margin block of 4, P#	40	—
a.		Tagged, *Dec. 1, 1965*	8	5
a.		Margin block of 4, P#	50	—
		Pair with full horiz. gutter between	—	
1283	A715	5c **blue,** *Feb. 22, 1966*	10	5
		Margin block of 4, P#	50	—
		Pair with full vert. gutter btwn.	—	
a.		Tagged, *Feb. 23, 1966*	10	5
a.		Margin block of 4, P#	60	—
1283B	A715a	5c **blue,** tagged, *Nov. 17, 1967*	10	5
		Margin block of 4, P#	50	—
		Dull finish gum	20	
d.		Untagged (Bureau precanceled)		15

No. 1283B is redrawn; highlights, shadows softened.

No.	Type	Description	Unused	Used
1284	A716	6c **gray brown,** *Jan. 29, 1966*	12	5
		Margin block of 4, P#	60	—
		Margin block of 4, "Use Zip Codes" (Bureau precanceled)		3.50
		Margin block of 6, "Mail Early in the Day" (Bureau precanceled)		4.25
		Pair with full horiz. gutter btwn.	*150.00*	
		Pair with full vert. gutter btwn.	*150.00*	
a.		Tagged, *Dec. 29, 1966*	15	5
a.		Margin block of 4, P#	80	—
a.		Margin block of 4, "Use Zip Codes"	65	—
a.		Margin block of 6, "Mail Early in the Day"	90	—
b.		Booklet pane of 8, *Dec. 28, 1967*	1.50	*50*
c.		Bklt. pane of 5+ label, *Jan. 9, 1968*	1.25	*50*

For untagged stamps, "Use Zip Codes" and "Mail Early in the Day" marginal markings are found only on panes with Bureau precancels.

No.	Type	Description	Unused	Used
1285	A717	8c **violet,** *March 14, 1966*	20	5
		Margin block of 4, P#	1.00	—
a.		Tagged, *July 6, 1966*	16	5
a.		Margin block of 4, P#	90	—
a.		Margin block of 4, "Use Zip Codes"	75	—
a.		Margin block of 6, "Mail Early in the Day"	1.10	—
1286	A718	10c **lilac,** tagged, *March 15, 1967*	20	5
		Margin block of 4, P#	1.00	
		Margin block of 4, "Use Zip Codes"	85	—
		Margin block of 6, "Mail Early in the Day"	1.20	—
b.		Untagged (Bureau precanceled)		20
1286A	718a	12c **black,** tagged, *July 30, 1968*	28	5
		Margin block of 4, P#	1.40	
		Margin block of 4, "Use Zip Code"	1.15	—
		Margin block of 6, "Mail Early in the Day"	1.70	—
c.		Untagged (Bureau precanceled)		25
1287	A719	13c **brown,** tagged, *May 29, 1967*	24	5
		Margin block of 4, P#	1.20	—
a.		Untagged (Bureau precanceled)		25
1288	A720	15c **maroon,** type I, tagged, *Mar. 8, 1968*	30	6
		Margin block of 4, P#	1.50	—
		Margin block of 4, "Use Zip Codes"	1.45	—
		Margin block of 6, "Mail Early in the Day"	1.85	—
a.		Untagged (Bureau precanceled)		30
d.		Type II	30	6
		Pair with full vert. gutter between	—	
1288B	A720	15c **dark rose claret,** tagged, perf. 10 (from blkt. pane)	30	5
c.		Booklet pane of 8, *June 14, 1978*	2.40	*1.25*

No. 1288B issued in booklets only. All stamps have one or two straight edges. Plates made from redrawn die.

No.	Type	Description	Unused	Used
1289	A721	20c **deep olive,** *Oct. 24, 1967*	42	6
		Margin block of 4, P#	2.10	—
		Margin block of 4, "Use Zip Codes"	1.75	—
		Margin block of 6, "Mail Early in the Day"	2.55	—
a.		Tagged, *Apr. 3, 1973*	40	6
a.		Margin block of 4, P#	2.00	—
a.		Dull finish gum	40	
1290	A722	25c **rose lake,** *Feb. 14, 1967*	55	5
		Margin block of 4, P#	2.75	—
		Margin block of 4, "Use Zip Codes"	2.25	—
		Margin block of 6, "Mail Early in the Day"	3.35	—
a.		Tagged, *Apr. 3, 1973*	50	5
a.		Margin block of 4, P#	2.50	—
a.		Dull finish gum	55	
1291	A723	30c **red lilac,** *Oct. 21, 1968*	65	8
		Margin block of 4, P#	3.25	—
		Margin block of 4, "Use Zip Codes"	2.65	—
		Margin block of 6, "Mail Early in the Day"	4.00	—
a.		Tagged, *Apr. 3, 1973*	60	6
a.		Margin block of 4, P#	3.00	—
1292	A724	40c **blue black,** *Jan. 29, 1968*	85	10
		Margin block of 4, P#	4.25	—
		Margin block of 4, "Use Zip Codes"	3.50	—

Margin block of 6, "Mail Early in the Day" 5.15 —
a. Tagged, *Apr. 3, 1973* 80 8
a. Margin block of 4, P# 4.00 —
a. Dull finish gum 1.00
1293 A725 50c **rose magenta,** *Aug. 13, 1968* 1.00 5
Margin block of 4, P# 5.00 —
Margin block of 4, "Use Zip Codes" 4.10 —
Margin block of 6, "Mail Early in the Day" 6.15 —
Pair with full vert. gutter btwn. —
a. Tagged, *Apr. 3, 1973* 1.00 5
a. Margin block of 4, P# 5.00 —
1294 A726 $1 **dull purple,** *Oct. 16, 1967* 2.50 8
Margin block of 4, P# 12.50 —
Margin block of 4, "Use Zip Codes" 10.50 —
Margin block of 6, "Mail Early in the Day" 15.00 —
a. Tagged, *Apr. 3, 1973* 2.00 8
a. Margin block of 4, P# 10.00 —
1295 A727 $5 **gray black,** *Dec. 3, 1966* 12.50 2.00
Margin block of 4, P# 62.50 —
a. Tagged, *Apr. 3, 1973* 10.00 2.00
a. Margin block of 4, P# 50.00 —

Bureau Precancels: 1c, 19 diff., 1 1/4c, 2c, 41 diff., 3c, 11 diff., 4c, 49 diff., No. 1283, 7 diff., No. 1283B, 29 diff., 6c, 35 diff., 8c, 18 diff., 10c, 12 diff., 12c, 3 diff., 13c, 3 diff., No. 1288, 4 diff., 20c, 14 diff., 25c, 9 diff., 30c, 14 diff., 40c, 7 diff., 50c, 14 diff., $1, 8 diff.

See Luminescence note in "Information for Collectors" at front of book.

COIL STAMPS

1967-75 Tagged *Perf. 10 Horizontally*

1297 A713 3c **violet,** *Nov. 4, 1975* 8 5
Pair 16 10
Joint line pair 45 8
Dull finish gum 1.00
a. Imperf., pair *30.00*
a. Imperf., joint line pair *50.00*
b. Untagged (Bureau precanceled) 12
c. As "b," imperf. pair 10.00

No. 1297c is precanceled "Nonprofit Org. / CAR RT SORT."

1298 A716 6c **gray brown,** *Dec. 28, 1967* 15 5
Pair 30 12
Joint line pair 1.25 25
a. Imperf., pair *2,250.*

Bureau Precancels: 3c, 8 diff.

Franklin D. Roosevelt — A727a

Revised Design by Robert J. Jones and Howard C. Mildner.

COIL STAMPS

1966-78 Tagged *Perf. 10 Vertically*

1299 A710 1c **green,** *Jan. 12, 1968* 7 5
Pair 14 10
Joint line pair 20 18
a. Untagged (Bureau precanceled) 7
b. Imperf., pair *40.00* —
b. Imperf., joint line pair *65.00*
1303 A714 4c **black,** *May 28, 1966* 14 5
Pair 28 10
Joint line pair 75 20
a. Untagged (Bureau precanceled) 15
b. Imperf., pair *500.00*
b. Imperf., joint line pair *750.00*
1304 A715 5c **blue,** *Sept. 8, 1966* 12 5
Pair 24 10
Joint line pair 40 20
a. Untagged (Bureau precanceled) 15
b. Imperf., pair *250.00*
b. Imperf., joint line pair *375.00*
e. As "a," imperf., pair 300.00

No. 1304e is precanceled Mount Pleasant, IA. Also exists from Chicago, IL.

1304C A715a 5c **blue,** *1981* 12 5
Pair 24 10
Joint line pair 60 —
d. Imperf., pair —
1305 A727a 6c **gray brown,** *Feb. 28, 1968* 15 5
Pair 30 10
Joint line pair 55 18
a. Imperf., pair *75.00*
a. Imperf., joint line pair *120.00*
b. Untagged (Bureau precanceled) 20
1305E A720 15c **rose claret,** type I, *June 14, 1978* 25 5
Pair 50 10
Joint line pair 1.25 30
Dull finish gum 60
f. Untagged (Bureau precanceled, Chicago, IL) 30
g. Imperf., pair *30.00*
Imperf., joint line pair —
h. Pair, imperf. between *200.00*
i. Type II 25 5
i. Type II, dull finish gum 35
j. Type II, dull finish gum, Imperf., pair —
As "j," joint line pair —
1305C A726 $1 **dull purple,** *Jan. 12, 1973* 1.75 20
Pair 3.50 40
Joint line pair 5.00 70
Dull finish gum 2.00
d. Imperf., pair *2,000.*
Imperf., joint line pair —

Bureau Precancels: 1c, 5 diff., 4c, 35 diff., No. 1304, 45 diff., 6c, 30 diff.

MIGRATORY BIRD TREATY ISSUE

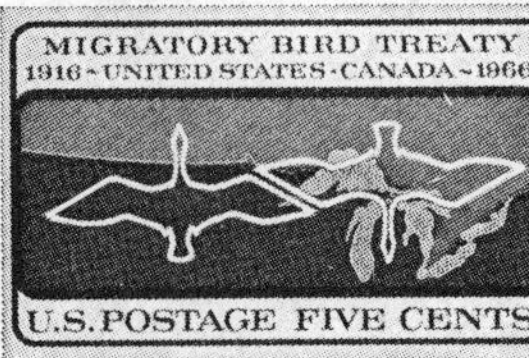

Migratory Birds over Canada-U.S. Border — A728

Designed by Burt E. Pringle.

GIORI PRESS PRINTING

Plates of 200 subjects in four panes of 50 each.

1966 Unwmk. *Perf. 11*

1306 A728 5c **black, crimson & dark blue,** *March 16* 10 5
Margin block of 4, two P# 50 —
Margin block of 4, Mr. Zip and "Use Zip Code" 45 —

HUMANE TREATMENT OF ANIMALS ISSUE

Issued to promote humane treatment of all animals and to commemorate the centenary of the American Society for the Prevention of Cruelty to Animals.

Mongrel — A729

Designed by Norman Todhunter.

LITHOGRAPHED, ENGRAVED (Giori)

Plates of 200 subjects in four panes of 50 each.

1966 Unwmk. *Perf. 11*

1307 A729 5c **orange brown & black,** *Apr. 9* 10 5
Margin block of 4, P# 50 —
Margin block of 4, Mr. Zip and "Use Zip Code" 45 —

INDIANA STATEHOOD ISSUE

Issued to commemorate the sesquicentennial of Indiana statehood.

Sesquicentennial Seal; Map of Indiana with 19 Stars and old Capitol at Corydon — A730

CIRCUS

5c

UNITED STATES

Clown — A731

Designed by Paul A. Wehr.

GIORI PRESS PRINTING

Plates of 200 subjects in four panes of 50 each.

1966 Unwmk. *Perf. 11*

1308 A730 5c **ocher, brown & violet blue,** *Apr. 16* 10 5
Margin block of 4, two P# 50 —
Margin block of 4, Mr. Zip and "Use Zip Code" 45 —

AMERICAN CIRCUS ISSUE

Issued to honor the American Circus on the centenary of the birth of John Ringling.

Designed by Edward Klauck.

GIORI PRESS PRINTING

Plates of 200 subjects in four panes of 50 each.

1966 Unwmk. *Perf. 11*

1309 A731 5c **multicolored,** *May 2* 10 5
Margin block of 4, two P# 50 —
Margin block of 4, Mr. Zip and "Use Zip Code" 45 —

SIXTH INTERNATIONAL PHILATELIC EXHIBITION ISSUES

Issued to commemorate the Sixth International Philatelic Exhibition (SIPEX), Washington, D.C., May 21-30.

Stamped Cover — A732

Designed by Thomas F. Naegele.

LITHOGRAPHED, ENGRAVED (Giori)

Plates of 200 subjects in four panes of 50 each.

1966 *Perf. 11*

1310 A732 5c **multicolored,** *May 21* 10 5
Margin block of 4, P# 50 —
Margin block of 4, Mr. Zip and "Use Zip Code" 45 —

SOUVENIR SHEET

Designed by Brook Temple.

LITHOGRAPHED, ENGRAVED (Giori)

Plates of 24 subjects

1966 *Imperf.*

1311 A732 5c **multicolored,** *May 23* 15 12

No. 1311 measures 108x74mm. Below the stamp appears a line drawing of the Capitol and Washington Monument. Marginal inscriptions and drawing are green.

BILL OF RIGHTS ISSUE

Issued to commemorate the 175th anniversary of the Bill of Rights.

"Freedom" Checking "Tyranny" — A734

Designed by Herbert L. Block (Herblock).

GIORI PRESS PRINTING

Plates of 200 subjects in four panes of 50 each.

1966 Unwmk. *Perf. 11*

1312 A734 5c **carmine, dark & light blue,** *July 1* 10 5
Margin block of 4, two P# 50 —
Margin block of 4, Mr. Zip and "Use Zip Code" 45 —

POLISH MILLENNIUM ISSUE

Issued to commemorate the thousandth anniversary of the adoption of Christianity in Poland.

Polish Eagle and Cross — A735

Designed by Edmund D. Lewandowski.

ROTARY PRESS PRINTING

E.E. Plates of 200 subjects in four panes of 50 each.

1966 **Unwmk.** ***Perf. 10 1/2x11***

1313 A735 5c **red,** *July 30* 10 5
Margin block of 4, P# 50 —
Margin block of 4, Mr. Zip and "Use Zip Code" 45 —

NATIONAL PARK SERVICE ISSUE

Issued to commemorate the 50th anniversary of the National Park Service of the Interior Department. The design "Parkscape U.S.A." identifies National Park Service facilities.

National Park Service Emblem — A736

Designed by Thomas H. Geismar.

LITHOGRAPHED, ENGRAVED (Giori)

Plates of 200 subjects in four panes of 50 each.

1966 ***Perf. 11***

1314 A736 5c **yellow, black & green,** *Aug. 25* 10 5
Margin block of 4, P# 50 —
Margin block of 4, Mr. Zip and "Use Zip Code" 45 —
a. Tagged, *Aug. 26.* 32 15
a. Margin block of 4, P# 2.00 —

MARINE CORPS RESERVE ISSUE

Issued to commemorate the 50th anniversary of the founding of the U.S. Marine Corps Reserve.

Combat Marine, 1966; Frogman; World War II Flier; World War I "Devil Dog" and Marine, 1775 — A737

Designed by Stella Grafakos.

LITHOGRAPHED, ENGRAVED (Giori)

Plates of 200 subjects in four panes of 50 each.

1966 ***Perf. 11***

1315 A737 5c **black, bister, red & ultra.,** *Aug. 29* 10 5
Margin block of 4, P# 50 —
Margin block of 4, Mr. Zip and "Use Zip Code" 45 —
a. Tagged, *Aug. 29* 30 15
a. Margin block of 4, P# 2.00 —
b. Black & bister (engraved) missing —

GENERAL FEDERATION OF WOMEN'S CLUBS ISSUE

Issued to honor 75 years of service by the General Federation of Women's Clubs.

Women of 1890 and 1966 — A738

Designed by Charles Henry Carter.

GIORI PRESS PRINTING

Plates of 200 subjects in four panes of 50 each.

1966 ***Perf. 11***

1316 A738 5c **black, pink & blue,** *Sept. 12* 10 5
Margin block of 4, 2 P# 50 —
Margin block of 4, Mr. Zip and "Use Zip Code" 45 —
a. Tagged, *Sept. 13* 30 15
a. Margin block of 4, 2 P# 2.00 —

AMERICAN FOLKLORE ISSUE

Johnny Appleseed

Issued to honor Johnny Appleseed (John Chapman 1774-1845), who wandered over 100,000 square miles planting apple trees, and who gave away and sold seedlings to Midwest pioneers.

Johnny Appleseed — A739

Designed by Robert Bode.

GIORI PRESS PRINTING

Plates of 200 subjects in four panes of 50 each.

1966 ***Perf. 11***

1317 A739 5c **green, red & black,** *Sept. 24* 10 5
Margin block of 4, 2 P# 50 —
Margin block of 4, Mr. Zip and "Use Zip Code" 45 —
a. Tagged, *Sept. 26* 30 15
a. Margin block of 4, 2 P# 2.00 —

BEAUTIFICATION OF AMERICA ISSUE

Issued to publicize President Johnson's "Plant for a more beautiful America" campaign.

Jefferson Memorial, Tidal Basin and Cherry Blossoms — A740

Designed by Miss Gyo Fujikawa

GIORI PRESS PRINTING

Plates of 200 subjects in four panes of 50 each.

1966 **Unwmk.** ***Perf. 11***

1318 A740 5c **emerald, pink & black,** *Oct. 5* 10 5
Margin block of 4, two P# 50 —
Margin block of 4, Mr. Zip and "Use Zip Code" 45 —
a. Tagged, *Oct. 5* 30 15
a. Margin block of 4, 2 P# 1.50 —

GREAT RIVER ROAD ISSUE

Issued to publicize the 5,600-mile Great River Road connecting New Orleans with Kenora, Ontario, and following the Mississippi most of the way.

See the "Information for Collectors" section at beginning of catalogue for information on printing methods and varieties.

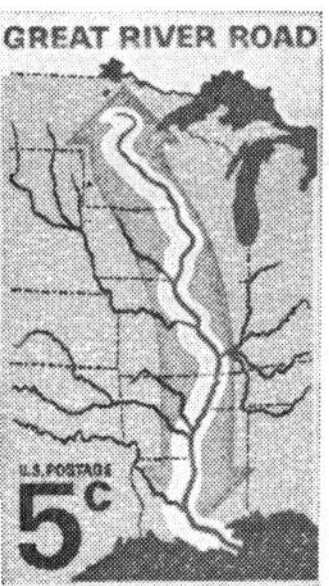

Map of Central United States with Great River Road — A741

Designed by Herbert Bayer.

LITHOGRAPHED, ENGRAVED (Giori)

Plates of 200 subjects in four panes of 50 each.

1966

1319 A741 5c **vermilion, yellow, blue & green,** *Oct. 21* 10 5
Margin block of 4, P# 50 —
Margin block of 4, Mr. Zip and "Use Zip Code" 45 —
a. Tagged, *Oct. 22* 30 15
a. Margin block of 4, P# 2.00 —

SAVINGS BOND-SERVICEMEN ISSUE

Issued to commemorate the 25th anniversary of U.S. Savings Bonds, and to honor American servicemen.

Statue of Liberty and "Old Glory" — A742

Designed by Steven Dohanos, photo by Bob Noble.

LITHOGRAPHED, ENGRAVED (Giori)

Plates of 200 subjects in four panes of 50 each.

1966 **Unwmk.** ***Perf. 11***

1320 A742 5c **red, dark blue, light blue & black,** *Oct. 26* 10 5
Margin block of 4, P# 50 —
Margin block of 4, Mr. Zip and "Use Zip Code" 45 —
a. Tagged, *Oct. 27* 30 15
a. Margin block of 4, P# 2.00 —
b. Red, dark blue & black omitted *3,500.*

CHRISTMAS ISSUE

Madonna and Child, by Hans Memling — A743

Modeled by Howard C. Mildner after "Madonna and Child with Angels," by the Flemish artist Hans Memling (c.1430-1494), Mellon Collection, National Gallery of Art, Washington, D.C.

LITHOGRAPHED, ENGRAVED (Giori)

Plates of 400 subjects in four panes of 100 each.

1966 **Unwmk.** ***Perf. 11***

1321 A743 5c **multicolored,** *Nov. 1* 10 5
Margin block of 4, P# 50 —
Margin block of 4, Mr. Zip and "Use Zip Code" 45 —
a. Tagged, *Nov. 2* 25 10
a. Margin block of 4, P# 1.90 —

MARY CASSATT ISSUE

Issued to honor Mary Cassatt (1844-1926), painter. The original painting "The Boating Party" is in the National Gallery of Art, Washington, D.C.

"The Boating Party" — A744

Designed by Robert J. Jones.

GIORI PRESS PRINTING

Plates of 200 subjects in four panes of 50 each.

1966 **Unwmk.** ***Perf. 11***

1322 A744 5c **multicolored,** *Nov. 17* 12 5
- Margin block of 4, 2 P# 60 —
- Margin block of 4, Mr. Zip and "Use Zip Code" 52 —

a. Tagged, *Nov. 17* 30 15
a. Margin block of 4, 2 P# 1.90 —

NATIONAL GRANGE ISSUE

Issued to commemorate the centenary of the founding of the National Grange, American farmers' organization.

Grange Poster, 1870 — A745

Designed by Lee Pavao.

GIORI PRESS PRINTING

Plates of 200 subjects in four panes of 50 each.

1967 **Unwmk.** **Tagged** ***Perf. 11***

1323 A745 5c **orange, yellow, brown, green & black,** *April 17* 10 5
- Margin block of 4, 2 P# 50 —
- Margin block of 4, Mr. Zip and "Use Zip Code" 45 —

CANADA CENTENARY ISSUE

Issued to commemorate the centenary of Canada's emergence as a nation.

Canadian Landscape — A746

Designed by Ivan Chermayeff.

GIORI PRESS PRINTING

Plates of 200 subjects in four panes of 50 each.

1967 **Unwmk.** **Tagged** ***Perf. 11***

1324 A746 5c **lt. blue, dp. green, ultra., olive & black,** *May 25* 10 5
- Margin block of 4, 2 P# 50 —
- Margin block of 4, Mr. Zip and "Use Zip Code" 45 —

ERIE CANAL ISSUE

Issued to commemorate the 150th anniversary of the Erie Canal ground-breaking ceremony at Rome, N.Y. The canal links Lake Erie and New York City.

Stern of Early Canal Boat — A747

Designed by George Samerjan.

LITHOGRAPHED, ENGRAVED (Giori)

Plates of 200 subjects in four panes of 50 each.

1967 **Tagged** ***Perf. 11***

1325 A747 5c **ultra., greenish blue, black & crimson,** *July 4* 10 5
- Margin block of 4, P# 50 —
- Margin block of 4, Mr. Zip and "Use Zip Code" 45 —

"SEARCH FOR PEACE" - LIONS ISSUE

Issued to publicize the search for peace. "Search for Peace" was the theme of an essay contest for young men and women sponsored by Lions International on its 50th anniversary.

Peace Dove — A748

Designed by Bradbury Thompson.

GIORI PRESS PRINTING

Plates of 200 subjects in four panes of 50 each.

1967 **Tagged** ***Perf. 11***

Gray Paper with Blue Threads

1326 A748 5c **blue, red & black,** *July 5* 10 5
- Margin block of 4, P# 50 —
- Margin block of 4, Mr. Zip and "Use Zip Code" 45 —

HENRY DAVID THOREAU ISSUE

Issued to commemorate the 150th anniversary of the birth of Henry David Thoreau (1817-1862), writer.

Henry David Thoreau — A749

Designed by Leonard Baskin.

GIORI PRESS PRINTING

Plates of 200 subjects in four panes of 50 each.

1967 **Tagged** ***Perf. 11***

1327 A749 5c **carmine, black & blue green,** *July 12* 10 5
- Margin block of 4, P# 50 —
- Margin block of 4, Mr. Zip and "Use Zip Code" 45 —

NEBRASKA STATEHOOD ISSUE

Issued to commemorate the centenary of the admission of Nebraska to Statehood.

Hereford Steer and Ear of Corn — A750

Designed by Julian K. Billings.

LITHOGRAPHED, ENGRAVED (Giori)

Plates of 200 subjects in four panes of 50 each.

1967 **Tagged** ***Perf. 11***

1328 A750 5c **dark red brown, lemon & yellow,** *July 29* 10 5
- Margin block of 4, P# 50 —
- Margin block of 4, Mr. Zip and "Use Zip Code" 45 —

VOICE OF AMERICA ISSUE

Issued to commemorate the 25th anniversary of the radio branch of the United States Information Agency (USIA).

Radio Transmission Tower and Waves — A751

Designed by Georg Olden.

LITHOGRAPHED, ENGRAVED (Giori)

Plates of 200 subjects in four panes of 50 each.

1967 **Tagged** ***Perf. 11***

1329 A751 5c **red, blue, black & carmine,** *Aug. 1* 10 5
- Margin block of 4, P# 50 —
- Margin block of 4, Mr. Zip and "Use Zip Code" 45 —

AMERICAN FOLKLORE ISSUE

Issued to honor Davy Crockett (1786-1836), frontiersman, hunter, and congressman from Tennessee who died at the Alamo.

Davy Crockett and Scrub Pine — A752

Designed by Robert Bode.

LITHOGRAPHED, ENGRAVED (Giori)

Plates of 200 subjects in four panes of 50 each.

1967 **Tagged** ***Perf. 11***

1330 A752 5c **green, black, & yellow,** *Aug. 17* 10 5
- Margin block of 4, P# 50 —
- Margin block of 4, Mr. Zip and "Use Zip Code" 45 —

a. Vertical pair, imperf. between —

A foldover on a pane of No. 1330 resulted in one example each of: green (engr.) omitted; black and green (engr,) omitted; yellow and green (litho.) omitted. Part of the colors appear on the back of the selvage and some stamps.

ACCOMPLISHMENTS IN SPACE ISSUE

Issued to commemorate United States' accomplishments in space. Nos. 1331-1332 are printed se-tenant in horizontal rows of 5 in panes of 50. In the upper and lower left panes the astronaut stamp is first, third and fifth, the spaceship second and fourth. This arrangement is reversed in the upper and lower right panes.

Space-Walking Astronaut — A753

Gemini 4 Capsule — A754

Designed by Paul Calle.

LITHOGRAPHED, ENGRAVED (Giori)
Plates of 200 subjects in four panes of 50 each.

1967 **Tagged** ***Perf. 11***
1331 A753 5c **multicolored,** *Sept. 29* 65 15
a. Pair, #1331-1332 1.40 1.25
Block of four, 2 #1331 + 2 #1332 3.00 3.00
Margin block of 4, P# adjoining #1331 3.50 —
Margin block of 4, Mr. Zip and "Use Zip Code" adjoining #1331 3.25 —
1332 A754 5c **multicolored,** *Sept. 29* 65 15
Margin block of 4, P# adjoining #1332 3.50 —
Margin block of 4, Mr. Zip and "Use Zip Code" adjoining #1332 3.25 —
Red stripes of flag on capsule omitted (29322, 29325 UL 19) *200.00*

URBAN PLANNING ISSUE

Issued to publicize the importance of Urban Planning in connection with the International Conference of the American Institute of Planners, Washington, D.C., Oct. 1-6.

View of Model City — A755

Designed by Francis Ferguson.

LITHOGRAPHED, ENGRAVED (Giori)
Plates of 200 subjects in four panes of 50 each.

1967 **Tagged** ***Perf. 11***
1333 A755 5c **dark blue, light blue & black,** *Oct. 2* 10 5
Margin block of 4, P# 50 —
Margin block of 4, Mr. Zip and "Use Zip Code" 45 —

FINNISH INDEPENDENCE ISSUE

Issued to commemorate the 50th anniversary of Finland's independence.

Finnish Coat of Arms — A756

Designed by Bradbury Thompson.

ENGRAVED (Giori)
Plates of 200 subjects in four panes of 50 each.

1967 **Tagged** ***Perf. 11***
1334 A756 5c **blue,** *Oct. 6* 10 5
Margin block of 4, P# 50 —
Margin block of 4, Mr. Zip and "Use Zip Code" 45 —

THOMAS EAKINS ISSUE

Issued to honor Thomas Eakins (1844-1916), painter and sculptor. The original painting is in the National Gallery of Art, Washington, D.C.

"The Biglin Brothers Racing" (Sculling on Schuylkill River, Philadelphia) A757

Printed by Photogravure & Color Co., Moonachie, N.J.

PHOTOGRAVURE
Plates of 200 subjects in four panes of 50 each.

1967 **Tagged** ***Perf. 12***
1335 A757 5c **gold & multicolored,** *Nov. 2* 10 5
Margin block of 4, 6 P# 50 —

Plate number blocks from upper left or lower left panes show clipped corner of margin.

CHRISTMAS ISSUE

Madonna and Child, by Hans Memling — A758

LITHOGRAPHED, ENGRAVED (Giori)
Plates of 200 subjects in four panes of 50 each.

1967 **Tagged** ***Perf. 11***
1336 A758 5c **multicolored,** *Nov. 6* 10 5
Margin block of 4, P# 45 —
Margin block of 4, Mr. Zip and "Use Zip Code" 42 —

See note on painting above No. 1321.

MISSISSIPPI STATEHOOD ISSUE

Issued to commemorate the 150th anniversary of Mississippi statehood.

Magnolia — A759

Designed by Andrew Bucci.

GIORI PRESS PRINTING
Plates of 200 subjects in four panes of 50 each.

1967 **Unwmk.** ***Perf. 11***
Tagged
1337 A759 5c **brt. greenish blue, green & red brown,** *Dec. 11* 10 5
Margin block of 4, 2 P# 50 —
Margin block of 4, Mr. Zip and "Use Zip Code" 45 —

FLAG ISSUE

Flag and White House — A760

Designed by Stevan Dohanos.

GIORI PRESS PRINTING
Plates of 400 subjects in four panes of 100 each.

1968 **Tagged** ***Perf. 11***
Size: 19x22mm
1338 A760 6c **dark blue, red & green,** *Jan. 24* 10 5
Margin block of 4, P# 45 —
Margin block of 4, "Use Zip Code" 42 —
Margin block of 6, "Mail Early in the Day" 65 —
k. Vert. pair, imperf. btwn. *400.00*

Vertical pairs have been offered as imperf. horizontally. Some have had the gum washed off to remove blind perfs.

MULTICOLOR HUCK PRESS
Panes of 100 (10x10) each

1970-71 **Tagged** ***Perf. 11x10½***
Size: 18¼x21mm
1338D A760 6c **dark blue, red & green,** *Aug. 7, 1970* 12 5
Margin block of 20+ 2.60 —
e. Horiz. pair, imperf. between *150.00*
1338F A760 8c **dk. blue, red & slate green,** *May 10, 1971* 16 5
Margin block of 20+ 3.50 —
i. Imperf., vert. pair *60.00*
j. Horiz. pair, imperf. between *50.00*

\+ Margin blocks of 20 come in four versions: (1) 2 P#, 3 ME, 3 zip; (2) 3 P#, 2 ME, 2 zip; (3) 2 P#, 3 ME, 2 zip; (4) 3 P#, 2 ME, 3 zip.

COIL STAMPS
MULTICOLOR HUCK PRESS

1969-71 **Tagged** ***Perf. 10 Vertically***
Size: 18¼x21mm.
1338A A760 6c **dk. blue, red & green,** *May 30, 1969* 14 5
Pair 28 10
b. Imperf., pair *500.00*
1338G A760 8c **dk. blue, red & slate green,** *May 10, 1971* 18 5
Pair 36 10
h. Imperf., pair *50.00*

ILLINOIS STATEHOOD ISSUE

Issued to commemorate the 150th anniversary of Illinois statehood.

Farm Buildings and Fields of Ripening Grain — A761

Designed by George Barford.

LITHOGRAPHED, ENGRAVED (Giori)
Plates of 200 subjects in four panes of 50 each.

1968 **Tagged** ***Perf. 11***
1339 A761 6c **dk. blue, blue, red & ocher,** *Feb. 12* 12 5
Margin block of 4, P# 55 —
Margin block of 4, Mr. Zip and "Use Zip Code" 50 —

HEMISFAIR '68 ISSUE

Issued to publicize the HemisFair '68 exhibition at San Antonio, Texas, Apr. 6-Oct. 6, commemorating the 250th anniversary of San Antonio.

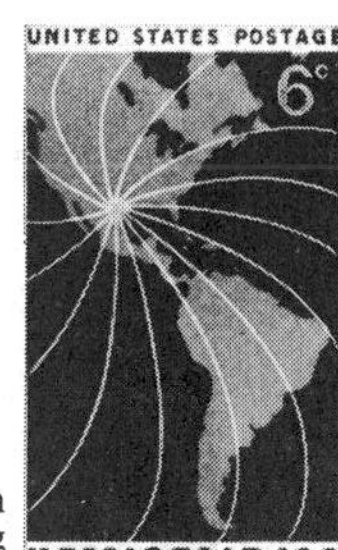

Map of North and South America and Lines Converging on San Antonio — A762

Designed by Louis Macouillard.

LITHOGRAPHED, ENGRAVED (Giori)
Plates of 200 subjects in four panes of 50 each.

1968 **Tagged** ***Perf. 11***
1340 A762 6c **blue, rose red & white,** *Mar. 30* 12 5
Margin block of 4, P# 55 —
Margin block of 4, Mr. Zip and "Use Zip Code" 50 —
Margin block of 6, "Mail Early in the Day" 75 —
a. White omitted *1,350.*

AIRLIFT ISSUE

Issued to pay for airlift of parcels from and to U.S. ports to servicemen overseas and in Alaska, Hawaii and Puerto Rico. Valid for all regular postage. On Apr. 26, 1969, the Post Office Department ruled that henceforth No. 1341 "may be used toward paying the postage or fees for special services on *airmail* articles."

Eagle Holding Pennant – A763

Designed by Steven Dohanos after a late 19th century wood carrying, part of the Index of American Design, National Gallery of Art.

LITHOGRAPHED, ENGRAVED (Giori)
Plates of 200 subjects in four panes of 50 each.

1968 **Unwmk.** ***Perf. 11***

1341 A763 $1 **sepia, dk. blue, ocher & brown red,** *Apr. 4* 2.75 1.25
Margin block of 4, P# 14.00 —
Margin block of 4, Mr. Zip and "Use Zip Code" 11.50 —
Margin block of 6, "Mail Early in the Day" 17.00 —
Pair with full horiz. gutter btwn. —

"SUPPORT OUR YOUTH" - ELKS ISSUE

Issued to publicize the Support Our Youth program, and to honor the Benevolent and Protective Order of Elks, which extended its youth service program in observance of its centennial year.

Girls and Boys – A764

Designed by Edward Vebell.

LITHOGRAPHED, ENGRAVED (Giori)
Plates of 200 subjects in four panes of 50 each.

1968 **Tagged** ***Perf. 11***

1342 A764 6c **ultramarine & orange red,** *May 1* 12 5
Margin block of 4, P# 55 —
Margin block of 4, Mr. Zip and "Use Zip Code" 50 —
Margin block of 6, "Mail Early in the Day" 75 —

LAW AND ORDER ISSUE

Issued to publicize the policeman as protector and friend and to encourage respect for law and order.

Policeman and Boy – A765

Designed by Ward Brackett.

GIORI PRESS PRINTING
Plates of 200 subjects in four panes of 50 each

1968 **Tagged** ***Perf. 11***

1343 A765 6c **blue & black,** *May 17* 12 5
Margin block of 4, P# 55 —
Margin block of 4, Mr. Zip and "Use Zip Code" 50 —
Margin block of 6, "Mail Early in the Day" 75 —

REGISTER AND VOTE ISSUE

Issued to publicize the campaign to draw more voters to the polls. The weather vane is from an old house in the Russian Hill section of San Francisco, Cal.

Eagle Weather Vane – A766

Designed by Norman Todhunter and Bill Hyde; photograph by M. Halberstadt.

LITHOGRAPHED, ENGRAVED (Giori)
Plates of 200 subjects in four panes of 50 each.

1968 **Unwmk.** ***Perf. 11***
Tagged

1344 A766 6c **black, yellow & orange,** *June 27* 12 5
Margin block of 4, P# 55 —
Margin block of 4, Mr. Zip and "Use Zip Code" 50 —
Margin block of 6, "Mail Early in the Day" 75 —

HISTORIC FLAG SERIES

Issued to show flags carried by American colonists and by citizens of the new United States. Nos. 1345-1354 are printed se-tenant in vertical rows of 10 in panes of 50. The flag sequence on the 2 upper panes is as listed. On the 2 lower panes the sequence is reversed with the Navy Jack in the first row and the Fort Moultrie flag in the 10th.

Ft. Moultrie, 1776 – A767

Ft. McHenry, 1795-1818 A768

Washington's Cruisers, 1775 – A769

Bennington, 1777 – A770

Rhode Island, 1775 – A771

First Stars and Stripes, 1777 – A772

Bunker Hill, 1775 – A773

Grand Union, 1776 – A774

Philadelphia Light Horse, 1775 – A775

First Navy Jack, 1775 – A776

ENGR. (Giori) (#1345-1348, 1350);
ENGR. & LITHO. (#1349, 1351-1354)
Plates of 200 subjects in four panes of 50 each.

1968, July 4 **Unwmk.** **Tagged** ***Perf. 11***

1345 A767 6c **dark blue** 70 25
1346 A768 6c **dark blue & red** 35 25
1347 A769 6c **dark blue & olive green** 30 25
1348 A770 6c **dark blue & red** 30 25
1349 A771 6c **dark blue, yellow & red** 30 25
1350 A772 6c **dark blue & red** 00 25
1351 A773 6c **dark blue, olive green & red** 00 25
1352 A774 6c **dark blue & red** 00 25
1353 A775 6c **dark blue, yellow & red** 30 25
1354 A776 6c **dark blue, red & yellow** 30 25
a. Strip of ten (#1345-#1354) 3.25 3.00
Margin block of 20, P#, inscriptions (#1345-1354) 6.75 —

WALT DISNEY ISSUE

Issued in memory of Walt Disney (1901-1966), cartoonist, film producer and creator of Mickey Mouse.

Walt Disney and Children of the World – A777

Designed by C. Robert Moore; portrait by Paul E. Wenzel. Printed by Achrovure Division of Union-Camp Corp., Englewood, N.J.

PHOTOGRAVURE

Plates of 400 subjects in eight panes of 50 each.

1968 **Tagged** **Unwmk.** ***Perf. 12***

1355 A777 6c **multicolored,** *Sept. 11* 15 5
Margin block of 4, 5P# 75 —
Margin block of 4, 5P# and 5 dashes 75 —
Margin block of 4, Mr. Zip and "Use Zip Code" 65 —
Margin block of 6, "Mail Early in the Day" 95 —
a. Ocher omitted ("Walt Disney," "6c," etc.) *750.00* —
b. Vert. pair, imperf. horiz. *725.00*
c. Imperf., pair *800.00*
d. Black omitted *2,250.*
e. Horiz. pair, imperf. between *3,250.*
f. Blue omitted *1,750.*

FATHER MARQUETTE ISSUE

Issued to honor Father Jacques Marquette (1637-1675), French Jesuit missionary, who together with Louis Jolliet explored the Mississippi River and its tributaries.

Father Marquette and Louis Jolliet Exploring the Mississippi A778

Designed by Stanley W. Galli.

GIORI PRESS PRINTING

Plates of 200 subjects in four panes of 50 each.

1968 **Tagged** ***Perf. 11***

1356 A778 6c **black, apple green & orange brown,** *Sept. 20* 12 5
Margin block of 4, P# 55 —
Margin block of 4, Mr. Zip and "Use Zip Code" 50 —
Margin block of 6, "Mail Early in the Day" 75 —

AMERICAN FOLKLORE ISSUE

Issued to honor Daniel Boone (1734-1820), frontiersman and trapper.

Pennsylvania Rifle, Powder Horn, Tomahawk Pipe and Knife — A779

Designed by Louis Macouillard.

LITHOGRAPHED, ENGRAVED (Giori)

Plates of 200 subjects in four panes of 50 each.

1968 **Tagged** ***Perf. 11***

1357 A779 6c **yellow, deep yellow, maroon & black,** *Sept. 26* 12 5
Margin block of 4, P# 55 —
Margin block of 4, Mr. Zip and "Use Zip Code" 50 —
Margin block of 6, "Mail Early in the Day" 75 —

ARKANSAS RIVER NAVIGATION ISSUE

Issued to commemorate the opening of the Arkansas River to commercial navigation.

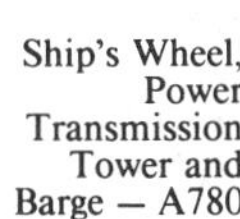

Ship's Wheel, Power Transmission Tower and Barge — A780

Designed by Dean Ellis.

LITHOGRAPHED, ENGRAVED (Giori)

Plates of 200 subjects in four panes of 50 each.

1968, Oct. 1 **Tagged** ***Perf. 11***

1358 A780 6c **bright blue, dark blue & black** 12 5
Margin block of 4, P# 55 —
Margin block of 4, Mr. Zip and "Use Zip Code" 50 —
Margin block of 6, "Mail Early in the Day" 75 —

LEIF ERIKSON ISSUE

Issued in memory of Leif Erikson, 11th century Norse explorer, called the first European to set foot on the American continent, at a place he called Vinland. The Leif Erikson statue by the American sculptor A. Stirling Calder is in Reykjavik, Iceland.

Leif Erikson by A. Stirling Calder — A781

Designed by Kurt Weiner.

LITHOGRAPHED & ENGRAVED

Plates of 200 subjects in four panes of 50 each.

1968, Oct. 9 **Tagged** ***Perf. 11***

1359 A781 6c **light gray brown & black brown** 12 5
Margin block of 4, P# 55 —
Margin block of 4, Mr. Zip and "Use Zip Code" 50 —
Margin block of 6, "Mail Early in the Day" 75 —

The luminescent element is in the light gray brown ink of the background. The engraved parts were printed on a rotary currency press.

CHEROKEE STRIP ISSUE

Issued to commemorate the 75th anniversary of the opening of the Cherokee Strip to settlers, Sept. 16, 1893.

Racing for Homesteads in Cherokee Strip, 1893 — A782

Designed by Norman Todhunter.

ROTARY PRESS PRINTING

E.E. Plates of 200 subjects in four panes of 50 each.

1968 **Tagged** ***Perf. 11x10½***

1360 A782 6c **brown,** *Oct. 15* 12 5
Margin block of 4, P# 55 —
Margin block of 4, Mr. Zip and "Use Zip Code" 50 —
Margin block of 6, "Mail Early in the Day" 75 —

JOHN TRUMBULL ISSUE

Issued to honor John Trumbull (1756-1843), painter. The stamp design shows Lt. Thomas Grosvenor and his attendant Peter Salem. The original painting hangs at Yale University, New Haven, Connecticut.

Detail from "The Battle of Bunker's Hill" — A783

Modeled by Robert J. Jones.

LITHOGRAPHED, ENGRAVED (Giori)

Plates of 200 subjects in four panes of 50 each.

1968 **Tagged** **Unwmk.** ***Perf. 11***

1361 A783 6c **multicolored,** *Oct. 18* 12 5
Margin block of 4, P# 60 —
Margin block of 4, Mr. Zip and "Use Zip Code" 50 —
Margin block of 6, "Mail Early in the Day" 75 —

WATERFOWL CONSERVATION ISSUE

Issued to publicize waterfowl conservation.

Wood Ducks — A784

Designed by Stanley W. Galli.

LITHOGRAPHED, ENGRAVED (Giori)

Plates of 200 subjects in four panes of 50 each.

1968 **Tagged** ***Perf. 11***

1362 A784 6c **black & multicolored,** *Oct. 24* 14 5
Margin block of 4, P# 70 —
Margin block of 4, Mr. Zip and "Use Zip Code" 60 —
Margin block of 6, "Mail Early in the Day" 85 —
a. Vertical pair, imperf. between *700.00*
b. Red & dark blue omitted *2,000.*

CHRISTMAS ISSUE

"The Annunciation" by the 15th century Flemish painter Jan van Eyck is in the National Gallery of Art, Washington, D.C.

Angel Gabriel, from "The Annunciation" by Jan van Eyck — A785

Designed by Robert J. Jones.

ENGRAVED (Multicolor Huck)

Panes of 50 (10x5)

1968 **Tagged** ***Perf. 11***

1363 A785 6c **multicolored,** *Nov. 1* 14 5
Margin block of 10, 7P# and 3 "Mail Early" 2.25 —
Margin block of 10, 8P# and 2 "Mail Early" 2.25 —
a. Untagged, *Nov. 2* 20 5
a. Margin block of 10, 7P# and 3 "Mail Early" 2.25 —
a. Margin block of 10, 8P# and 2 "Mail Early" 2.25 —
b. Imperf., pair (tagged) *350.00*
c. Light yellow omitted *150.00*
d. Imperf. pair, untagged *400.00*

AMERICAN INDIAN ISSUE

Issued to honor the American Indian and to commemorate the opening of the National Portrait Gallery, Washington, D.C. Chief Joseph (Indian name, Thunder Traveling over the Mountains), a leader of the Nez Perce, was born in eastern Oregon agout 1840 and died at the Colesville Reservation in Washington State in 1904.

Chief Joseph, by Cyrenius Hall – A786

Designed by Robert J. Jones; lettering by Crimilda Pontes.

LITHOGRAPHED, ENGRAVED (Giori)
Plates of 200 subjects in four panes of 50 each.

1968 **Tagged** ***Perf. 11***

1364 A786 6c **black & multicolored,** *Nov. 4* 14 5
Margin block of 4, P# 70 —
Margin block of 4, Mr. Zip and "Use Zip Code" 60 —
Margin block of 6, "Mail Early in the Day" 85 —

BEAUTIFICATION OF AMERICA ISSUE

Issued to publicize the Natural Beauty Campaign for more beautiful cities, parks, highways and streets. Nos. 1365-1368 are printed in blocks of four in panes of 50. In the upper and lower left panes Nos. 1365 and 1367 appear in first, third and fifth place, Nos. 1366 and 1368 in second and fourth place. This arrangement is reversed in the upper and lower right panes.

Capitol, Azaleas and Tulips – A787

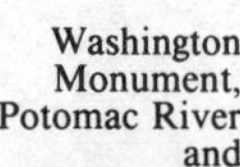

Washington Monument, Potomac River and Daffodils – A788

Poppies and Lupines along Highway – A789

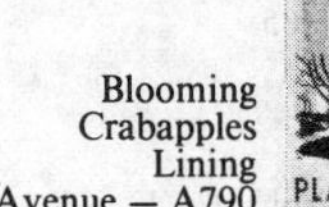

Blooming Crabapples Lining Avenue – A790

Designed by Walter DuBois Richards.

LITHOGRAPHED, ENGRAVED (Giori)
Plates of 200 subjects in four panes of 50 each.

1969, Jan. 16 **Tagged** ***Perf. 11***

1365 A787 6c **multicolored** 42 12
Margin block of 4, P# adjoining #1365 2.25 —
Margin block of 4, Mr. Zip and "Use Zip Code" adjoining #1365 1.80 —
Margin block of 6, "Mail Early in the Day" adjoining #1365 2.60 —

1366 A788 6c **multicolored** 42 12

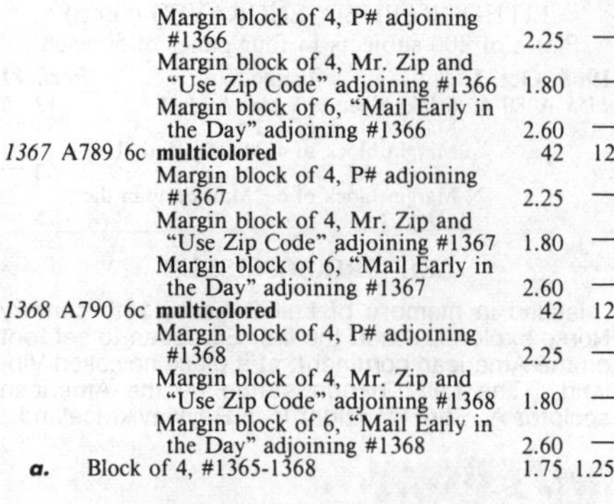

Margin block of 4, P# adjoining #1366 2.25 —
Margin block of 4, Mr. Zip and "Use Zip Code" adjoining #1366 1.80 —
Margin block of 6, "Mail Early in the Day" adjoining #1366 2.60 —

1367 A789 6c **multicolored** 42 12
Margin block of 4, P# adjoining #1367 2.25 —
Margin block of 4, Mr. Zip and "Use Zip Code" adjoining #1367 1.80 —
Margin block of 6, "Mail Early in the Day" adjoining #1367 2.60 —

1368 A790 6c **multicolored** 42 12
Margin block of 4, P# adjoining #1368 2.25 —
Margin block of 4, Mr. Zip and "Use Zip Code" adjoining #1368 1.80 —
Margin block of 6, "Mail Early in the Day" adjoining #1368 2.60 —
a. Block of 4, #1365-1368 1.75 1.25

AMERICAN LEGION ISSUE

Issued to commemorate the 50th anniversary of the American Legion.

Eagle from Great Seal – A791

Designed by Robert Hallock.

LITHOGRAPHED, ENGRAVED (Giori)
Plates of 200 subjects in four panes of 50 each.

1969 **Tagged** ***Perf. 11***

1369 A791 6c **red, blue & black,** *Mar. 15* 12 5
Margin block of 4, P# 55 —
Margin block of 4, Mr. Zip and "Use Zip Code" 50 —
Margin block of 6, "Mail Early in the Day" 75 —

AMERICAN FOLKLORE ISSUE

Issued to honor Grandma Moses (Anna Mary Robertson Moses, 1860-1961), primitive painter of American life.

July Fourth, by Grandma Moses – A792

Designed by Robert J. Jones.

LITHOGRAPHED, ENGRAVED (Giori)
Plates of 200 subjects in four panes of 50 each.

1969 **Tagged** ***Perf. 11***

1370 A792 6c **multicolored,** *May 1* 12 5
Margin block of 4, P# 55 —
Margin block of 4, Mr. Zip and "Use Zip Code" 50 —
Margin block of 6, "Mail Early in the Day" 75 —
a. Horizontal pair, imperf. between *300.00*
b. Black ("6c U.S. Postage") & Prus. blue ("Grandma Moses") omitted (engraved) *950.00*

APOLLO 8 ISSUE

Issued to commemorate the Apollo 8 mission, which first put men into orbit around the moon, Dec. 21-27, 1968. The astronauts were: Col. Frank Borman, Capt. James Lovell and Maj. William Anders.

Moon Surface and Earth – A793

Designed by Leonard E. Buckley after a photograph by the Apollo 8 astronauts.

GIORI PRESS PRINTING
Plates of 200 subjects in four panes of 50 each.

1969 **Tagged** ***Perf. 11***

1371 A793 6c **black, blue & ocher,** *May 5* 14 6
Margin block of 4, P# 65 —
Margin block of 4, Mr. Zip and "Use Zip Code" 60 —
Margin block of 6, "Mail Early in the Day" 85 —

W.C. HANDY ISSUE

Issued to honor W.C. Handy (1873-1958), jazz musician and composer.

William Christopher Handy – A794

Designed by Bernice Kochan.

LITHOGRAPHED, ENGRAVED (Giori)
Plates of 200 subjects in four panes of 50 each.

1969 **Tagged** ***Perf. 11***

1372 A794 6c **violet, dp. lilac & blue,** *May 17* 12 5
Margin block of 4, P# 55 —
Margin block of 4, Mr. Zip and "Use Zip Code" 50 —
Margin block of 6, "Mail Early in the Day" 75 —

CALIFORNIA SETTLEMENT ISSUE

Issued to commemorate the 200th anniversary of the settlement of California.

Carmel Mission Belfry – A795

Designed by Leonard Buckley and Howard C. Mildner.

LITHOGRAPHED, ENGRAVED (Giori)
Plates of 200 subjects in four panes of 50 each.

1969 **Tagged** ***Perf. 11***

1373 A795 6c **orange, red, black & light blue,** *July 16* 12 5
Margin block of 4, P# 55 —
Margin block of 4, Mr. Zip and "Use Zip Code" 50 —
Margin block of 6, "Mail Early in the Day" 75 —

JOHN WESLEY POWELL ISSUE

Issued to honor John Wesley Powell (1834-1902), geologist who explored the Green and Colorado Rivers 1869-1875, and ethnologist.

Major Powell Exploring Colorado River, 1869 — A796

Designed by Rudolph Wendelin.

LITHOGRAPHED, ENGRAVED (Giori)
Plates of 200 subjects in four panes of 50 each.

1969 **Tagged** ***Perf. 11***

1374 A796 6c **black, ocher & light blue,** *Aug. 1* 12 5
- Margin block of 4, P# 55 —
- Margin block of 4, Mr. Zip and "Use Zip Code" 50 —
- Margin block of 6, "Mail Early in the Day" 75 —

ALABAMA STATEHOOD ISSUE

Issued to commemorate the 150th anniversary of Alabama statehood.

Camellia and Yellow-shafted Flicker — A797

Designed by Bernice Kochan

LITHOGRAPHED, ENGRAVED (Giori)
Plates of 200 subjects in four panes of 50 each.

1969 **Tagged** ***Perf. 11***

1375 A797 6c **magenta, rose red, yellow, dark green & brown,** *Aug. 2* 12 5
- Margin block of 4, P# 55 —
- Margin block of 4, Mr. Zip and "Use Zip Code" 50 —
- Margin block of 6, "Mail Early in the Day" 75 —

BOTANICAL CONGRESS ISSUE

Issued to publicize the 11th International Botanical Congress, Seattle, Wash., Aug. 24-Sept. 2. Nos. 1376-1379 are printed in blocks of four in panes of 50. In upper and lower left panes Nos. 1376 and 1378 appear in first, third and fifth place; Nos. 1377 and 1379 in second and fourth place. This arrangement is reversed in upper and lower right panes.

Douglas Fir (Northwest) A798

Lady's-slipper (Northeast) A799

Ocotillo (Southwest) A800

Franklinia (Southeast) A801

Designed by Stanley Galli.

LITHOGRAPHED, ENGRAVED (Giori)
Plates of 200 subjects in four panes of 50 each.

1969, Aug. 23 **Tagged** ***Perf. 11***

1376 A798 6c **multicolored** 80 15
- Margin block of 4, P# adjoining #1376 3.50 —
- Margin block of 4, Mr. Zip and "Use Zip Code" adjoining #1376 3.30 —
- Margin block of 6, "Mail Early in the Day" adjoining #1376 5.00 —

1377 A799 6c **multicolored** 80 15
- Margin block of 4, P# adjoining #1377 3.50 —
- Margin block of 4, Mr. Zip and "Use Zip Code" adjoining #1377 3.30 —
- Margin block of 6, "Mail Early in the Day" adjoining #1377 5.00 —

1378 A800 6c **multicolored** 80 15
- Margin block of 4, P# adjoining #1378 3.50 —
- Margin block of 4, Mr. Zip and "Use Zip Code" adjoining #1378 3.30 —
- Margin block of 6, "Mail Early in the Day" adjoining #1378 5.00 —

1379 A801 6c **multicolored** 80 15
- Margin block of 4, P# adjoining #1379 3.50 —
- Margin block of 4, Mr. Zip and "Use Zip Code" adjoining #1379 3.30 —
- Margin block of 6, "Mail Early in the Day" adjoining #1379 5.00 —

a. Block of four, #1376-1379 3.25 3.00

DARTMOUTH COLLEGE CASE ISSUE

Issued to commemorate the 150th anniversary of the Dartmouth College Case, which Daniel Webster argued before the Supreme Court, reasserting the sanctity of contracts.

Daniel Webster and Dartmouth Hall — A802

Designed by John R. Scotford, Jr.

ROTARY PRESS PRINTING
E.E. Plates of 200 subjects in four panes of 50 each.

1969 **Tagged** ***Perf. 10 1/2x11***

1380 A802 6c **green,** *Sept. 22* 12 5
- Margin block of 4, P# 55 —
- Margin block of 4, Mr. Zip and "Use Zip Code" 50 —
- Margin block of 6, "Mail Early in the Day" 75 —

PROFESSIONAL BASEBALL ISSUE

Issued to commemorate the centenary of professional baseball.

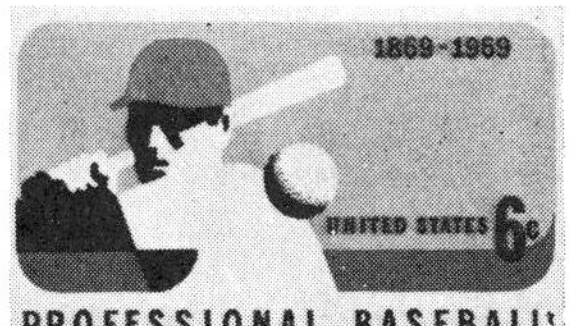

Batter — A803

Designed by Alex Ross.

LITHOGRAPHED, ENGRAVED (Giori)
Plates of 200 subjects in four panes of 50 each.

1969 **Tagged** ***Perf. 11***

1381 A803 6c **yel., red, blk. & grn.,** *Sept. 24* 22 5
- Margin block of 4, P# 95 —
- Margin block of 4, Mr. Zip and "Use Zip Code" 90 —
- Margin block of 6, "Mail Early in the Day" 1.40 —

a. Black omitted ("1869-1969, United States, 6c, Professional Baseball") *1,250.*

INTERCOLLEGIATE FOOTBALL ISSUE

Issued to commemorate the centenary of intercollegiate football.

Football Player and Coach — A804

Designed by Robert Peak.

LITHOGRAPHED, ENGRAVED (Giori)
Plates of 200 subjects in four panes of 50 each.

1969 **Tagged** ***Perf. 11***

1382 A804 6c **red & green,** *Sept. 26* 15 5
- Margin block of 4, P# 70 —
- Margin block of 4, Mr. Zip and "Use Zip Code" 65 —
- Margin block of 6, "Mail Early in the Day" 95 —

The engraved parts were printed on a rotary currency press.

DWIGHT D. EISENHOWER ISSUE

Issued in memory of Gen. Dwight David Eisenhower, 34th President (1890-1969).

Dwight D. Eisenhower — A805

Designed by Robert J. Jones; photograph by Bernie Noble.

GIORI PRESS PRINTING
Plates of 128 subjects in 4 panes of 32 each.

1969 **Tagged** ***Perf. 11***

1383 A805 6c **blue, black & red,** *Oct. 14* 12 5
- Margin block of 4, P# 55 —
- Margin block of 4, Mr. Zip and "Use Zip Code" 50 —
- Margin block of 6, "Mail Early in the Day" 75 —

CHRISTMAS ISSUE

The painting, painted about 1870 by an unknown primitive artist, is the property of the N.Y. State Historical Association, Cooperstown, N.Y.

Winter Sunday in Norway, Maine — A806

Designed by Stevan Dohanos.

ENGRAVED (Multicolor Huck)
Panes of 50 (5x10)

1969	Tagged	*Perf. 11x10½*	
1384 A806 6c **dark green & multi.**, *Nov. 3*		12	5
Margin block of 10, 5P#, 2-3 zip, 2-3 Mail Early		1.40	—
Precancel		30	6
b. Imperf., pair		*1,500.*	
c. Light green omitted		25.00	
d. Lt. grn., red & yel omitted		*1,200.*	—
e. Yellow omitted		—	

The precancel value applies to the least expensive of experimental precancels printed in four cities with the names between lines 4½mm apart: in black or green, "ATLANTA, GA" and in green only "BALTIMORE, MD", "MEMPHIS, TN" and "NEW HAVEN, CT". They were sold freely to the public and could be used on any class of mail at all post offices during the experimental program and thereafter.

HOPE FOR CRIPPLED ISSUE

Issued to encourage the rehabilitation of crippled children and adults and to honor the National Society for Crippled Children and Adults (Easter Seal Society) on its 50th anniversary.

Cured Child — A807

Designed by Mark English.

LITHOGRAPHED, ENGRAVED (Giori)
Plates of 200 subjects in four panes of 50 each.

1969	Tagged	*Perf. 11*	
1385 A807 6c **multicolored**, *Nov. 20*		12	5
Margin block of 4, P#		55	—
Margin block of 4, Mr. Zip and "Use Zip Code"		50	—
Margin block of 6, "Mail Early in the Day"		75	—

WILLIAM M. HARNETT ISSUE

Issued to honor William M. Harnett (1848-1892), painter. The painting hangs in the Museum of Fine Arts, Boston.

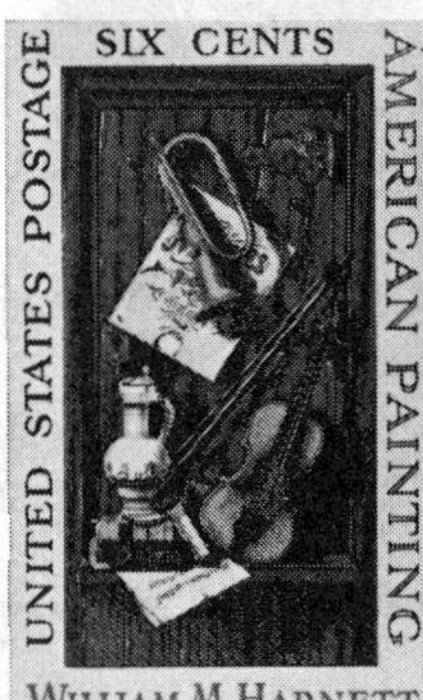

"Old Models" — A808

Designed by Robert J. Jones.

LITHOGRAPHED, ENGRAVED (Giori)
Plates of 128 subjects in 4 panes of 32 each.

1969	Tagged	*Perf. 11*	
1386 A808 6c **multicolored**, *Dec. 3*		12	5
Margin block of 4, P#		55	—
Margin block of 4, Mr. Zip and "Use Zip Code"		50	—
Margin block of 6, "Mail Early in the Day"		75	—

NATURAL HISTORY ISSUE

Issued in connection with the 1969-1970 celebration of the centenary of the American Museum of Natural History in New York City. Nos. 1387-1390 are printed in blocks of four in panes of 32. Nos. 1387-1388 alternate in first row, Nos. 1389-1390 in second row. This arrangement is repeated throughout the pane.

American Bald Eagle — A809

African Elephant Herd A810

Tlingit Chief in Haida Ceremonial Canoe — A811

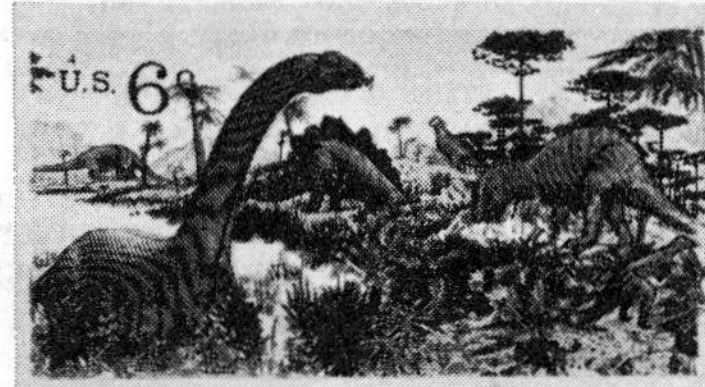

Brontosaurus, Stegosaurus and Allosaurus from Jurassic Period — A812

Designers: No. 1387 (eagle), Walter Richards; No. 1388 (elephants), Dean Ellis; No. 1389 (Haida canoe), Paul Rabut; No. 1390 (Age of Reptiles) detail from mural by Rudolph Zallinger in Yale's Peabody Museum, adapted by Robert J. Jones.

LITHOGRAPHED, ENGRAVED (Giori)
Plates of 128 subjects in 4 panes of 32 each (4x8).

1970, May 6	Tagged	*Perf. 11*	
1387 A809 6c **multicolored**		12	9
Margin block of 4, P# adjoining #1387		65	—
Margin block of 4, Mr. Zip and "Use Zip Code" adjoining #1387		55	—
Margin block of 6, "Mail Early in the Day" adjoining #1387		75	—
1388 A810 6c **multicolored**		12	9
Margin block of 4, P# adjoining #1388		65	—
Margin block of 4, Mr. Zip and "Use Zip Code" adjoining #1388		55	—
Margin block of 6, "Mail Early in the Day" adjoining #1388		75	—
1389 A811 6c **multicolored**		12	9
Margin block of 4, P# adjoining #1389		65	—
Margin block of 4, Mr. Zip and "Use Zip Code" adjoining #1389		55	—
Margin block of 6, "Mail Early in the Day" adjoining #1389		75	—
1390 A812 6c **multicolored**		12	9
Margin block of 4, P# adjoining #1390		65	—
Margin block of 4, Mr. Zip and "Use Zip Code" adjoining #1390		55	—
Margin block of 6, "Mail Early in the Day" adjoining #1390		75	—
a. Block of four (#1387-1390)		50	50

MAINE STATEHOOD ISSUE

Issued to commemorate the sesquicentennial of Maine Statehood. The painting by Edward Hopper (1882-1967) hangs in the Metropolitan Museum of Art, New York City.

The Lighthouse at Two Lights, Maine, by Edward Hopper — A813

Designed by Stevan Dohanos.

LITHOGRAPHED, ENGRAVED (Giori)
Plates of 200 subjects in four panes of 50 each.

1970	Tagged	*Perf. 11*	
1391 A813 6c **black & multicolored**, *July 9*		12	5
Margin block of 4, P#		55	—
Margin block of 4, Mr. Zip and "Use Zip Code"		50	—
Margin block of 6, "Mail Early in the Day"		75	—

WILDLIFE CONSERVATION ISSUE

Issued to emphasize the importance of wildlife conservation in America.

American Buffalo — A814

Designed by Robert Lougheed.

ROTARY PRESS PRINTING
E.E. Plates of 200 subjects in four panes of 50 each.

1970	Tagged	*Perf. 11x10½*	
1392 A814 6c **black**, *light brown, July 20*		12	5
Margin block of 4, P#		55	—
Margin block of 4, Mr. Zip and "Use Zip Code"		50	—
Margin block of 6, "Mail Early in the Day"		75	—

REGULAR ISSUE
Dwight David Eisenhower

Dot between "R" and "U" — A815

No Dot between "R" and "U" — A815a

Benjamin Franklin — A816

U.S. Postal Service Emblem — A817

Fiorello H. LaGuardia A817a

Ernest Taylor Pyle A818

See the "Information for Collectors" section at beginning of catalogue for an explanation of paper types, watermarks and grills.

Dr. Elizabeth Blackwell
A818a

Amadeo P. Giannini
A818b

Designers: Nos. 1393-1395, 1401-1402, Robert Geissman; photograph by George Tames. 7c, Bill Hyde. No. 1396, Raymond Loewy/William Smith, Inc. 14c, Robert Geissman; photograph by George Fayer. 16c, Robert Geissman; photograph by Alfred Eisenstadt. 18c, Robert Geissman; painting by Joseph Kozlowski. 21c, Robert Geissman.

ROTARY PRESS PRINTING

E.E. Plates of 400 subjects in four panes of 100 each.

1970-74 **Tagged** ***Perf. 11x10½***

1393 A815 6c **dark blue gray,** *Aug. 6, 1970* 12 5
- Margin block of 4, P# 55 —
- Margin block of 4, "Use Zip Codes" 50 —
- Margin block of 6, "Mail Early in the Day" 75 —
- Dull finish gum 12
- *a.* Booklet pane of 8 1.10 *50*
- *b.* Booklet pane of 5 + label 1.10 *35*
- *c.* Untagged (Bureau precanceled) 12

Perf. 10½x11

1393D A816 7c **bright blue,** *Oct. 20, 1972* 14 5
- Margin block of 4, P# 65 —
- Margin block of 4, "Use Zip Codes" 60 —
- Margin block of 6, "Mail Early in the Day" 85 —
- Dull finish gum 14
- *e.* Untagged (Bureau precanceled) 14

GIORI PRESS PRINTING

Plates of 400 subjects in four panes of 100 each.

1394 A815a 8c **black, red & blue gray,** *May 10, 1971* 16 5
- Margin block of 4, P# 70 —
- Margin block of 4, "Use Zip Codes" 65 —
- Margin block of 6, "Mail Early in the Day" 1.00 —
- Pair with full vert. gutter btwn. —

ROTARY PRESS PRINTING

1395 A815 8c **deep claret,** (from blkt. pane) 16 5
- *a.* Booklet pane of 8, *May 10, 1971* 1.80 *1.25*
- *b.* Booklet pane of 6, *May 10, 1971* 1.25 *75*
- *c.* Booklet pane of 4 + 2 labels, *Jan. 28, 1972* 1.40 *50*
- *d.* Booklet pane of 7 + label, *Jan. 28, 1972* 1.60 *1.00*

No. 1395 was issued only in booklets. All stamps have one or two straight edges.

PHOTOGRAVURE (Andreotti)

Plates of 400 subjects in four panes of 100 each.

1396 A817 8c **multicolored,** *July 1, 1971* 15 5
- Margin block of 12, 6P# 2.00
- Margin block of 20, 6P#, "Mail Early in the Day," "Use Zip Codes" and rectangular color contents (UL pane) 3.25
- Margin block of 4, "Use Zip Codes" 65 —
- Margin block of 4, "Mail Early in the Day" 65 —

ROTARY PRESS PRINTING

E.E. Plates of 400 subjects in four panes of 100 each.

1397 A817a 14c **gray brown,** *Apr. 24, 1972* 25 5
- Margin block of 4, P# 1.15 —
- Margin block of 4, "Use Zip Codes" 1.05 —
- Margin block of 6, "Mail Early in the Day" 1.60 —
- *a.* Untagged (Bureau precanceled) 25

1398 A818 16c **brown,** *May 7, 1971* 30 5
- Margin block of 4, P# 1.40 —
- Margin block of 4, "Use Zip Codes" 1.25 —
- Margin block of 6, "Mail Early in the Day" 1.90 —
- *a.* Untagged (Bureau precanceled) 35

1399 A818a 18c **violet,** *Jan. 23, 1974* 32 6
- Margin block of 4, P# 1.40 —
- Margin block of 4, "Use Zip Codes" 1.30 —
- Margin block of 6, "Mail Early in the Day" 2.00 —

1400 A818b 21c **green,** *June 27, 1973* 35 6
- Margin block of 4, P# 1.60 —
- Margin block of 4, "Use Zip Codes" 1.50 —
- Margin block of 6, "Mail Early in the Day" 2.25 —

Bureau Precancels: 6c, 6 diff., 7c, 13 diff., No. 1394, 24 diff., 14c, 3 diff., 16c, 9 diff.

COIL STAMPS
ROTARY PRESS PRINTING

1970-71 **Tagged** ***Perf. 10 Vert.***

1401 A815 6c **dark blue gray,** *Aug. 6, 1970* 14 5
- Pair 28 10
- Joint line pair 50 15
- Dull finish gum 14
- *a.* Untagged (Bureau precanceled) 14
- *b.* Imperf., pair *1,000.*

1402 A815 8c **deep claret,** *May 10, 1971* 15 5
- Pair 30 10
- Joint line pair 45 20
- *a.* Imperf., pair 50.00
- *a.* Joint line pair 75.00
- *b.* Untagged (Bureau precanceled) 15
- *c.* Pair, imperf. between —

Bureau Precancels: 6c, 4 diff., 8c, 34 diff.

EDGAR LEE MASTERS ISSUE

Issued to honor Edgar Lee Masters (1869-1950), poet.

Edgar Lee Masters — A819

Designed by Fred Otnes.

LITHOGRAPHED, ENGRAVED (Giori)

E.E. Plates of 200 subjects in four panes of 50 each.

1970 **Tagged** ***Perf. 11***

1405 A819 6c **black & olive bister,** *Aug. 22* 12 5
- Margin block of 4, P# 55 —
- Margin block of 4, Mr. Zip and "Use Zip Code" 50 —
- Margin block of 6, "Mail Early in the Day" 75 —

WOMAN SUFFRAGE ISSUE

Issued to commemorate the 50th anniversary of the 19th Amendment, which gave the vote to women.

Suffragettes, 1920, and Woman Voter, 1970 — A820

Designed by Ward Brackett.

GIORI PRESS PRINTING

Plates of 200 subjects in four panes of 50 each.

1970 **Tagged** ***Perf. 11***

1406 A820 6c **blue,** *Aug. 26* 12 5
- Margin block of 4, P# 55 —
- Margin block of 4, Mr. Zip and "Use Zip Code" 50 —
- Margin block of 6, "Mail Early in the Day" 75 —

SOUTH CAROLINA ISSUE

Issued to commemorate the 300th anniversary of the founding of Charles Town (Charleston), the first permanent settlement of South Carolina. Against a background of pine wood the line drawings of the design represent the economic and historic development of South Carolina: the spire of St. Phillip's Church, Capitol, state flag, a ship, 17th century man and woman, a Fort Sumter cannon, barrels, cotton, tobacco and yellow jasmine.

Symbols of South Carolina — A821

Designed by George Samerjan.

LITHOGRAPHED, ENGRAVED (Giori)

Plates of 200 subjects in four panes of 50 each.

1970 **Tagged** ***Perf. 11***

1407 A821 6c **bister, black & red,** *Sept. 12* 12 5
- Margin block of 4, P# 55 —
- Margin block of 4, Mr. Zip and "Use Zip Code" 50 —
- Margin block of 6, "Mail Early in the Day" 75 —

STONE MOUNTAIN MEMORIAL ISSUE

Issued to commemorate the dedication of the Stone Mountain Confederate Memorial, Georgia, May 9, 1970.

Robert E. Lee, Jefferson Davis and "Stonewall" Jackson — A822

Designed by Robert Hallock.

GIORI PRESS PRINTING

Plates of 200 subjects in four panes of 50 each.

1970 **Tagged** ***Perf. 11***

1408 A822 6c **gray,** *Sept. 19* 12 5
- Margin block of 4, P# 55 —
- Margin block of 4, Mr. Zip and "Use Zip Code" 50 —
- Margin block of 6, "Mail Early in the Day" 75 —

FORT SNELLING ISSUE

Issued to commemorate the 150th anniversary of Fort Snelling, Minnesota, which was an important outpost for the opening of the Northwest.

Fort Snelling, Keelboat and Tepees — A823

Designed by David K. Stone.

LITHOGRAPHED, ENGRAVED (Giori)

Plates of 200 in four panes of 50 each.

1970 **Tagged** ***Perf. 11***

1409 A823 6c **yellow & multicolored,** *Oct. 17* 12 5
- Margin block of 4, P# 55 —
- Margin block of 4, Mr. Zip and "Use Zip Code" 50 —
- Margin block of 6, "Mail Early in the Day" 75 —

ANTI-POLLUTION ISSUE

Issued to focus attention on the problems of pollution.

Nos. 1410-1413 are printed in blocks of four in panes of 50. In upper and lower left panes Nos. 1410 and 1412 appear in first, third and fifth place; Nos. 1411 and 1413 in second and fourth place. This arrangement is reversed in upper and lower right panes.

Globe and Wheat — A824

Globe and City — A825

Globe and Bluegill — A826

Globe and Seagull — A827

Designed by Arnold Copeland and Walter DuBois Richards. Printed by Bureau of Engraving and Printing at Guilford Gravure, Inc., Guilford, Conn.

PHOTOGRAVURE

Plates of 200 subjects in four panes of 50 each.

1970, Oct. 28 **Tagged** ***Perf. 11x10½***

1410 A824 6c **multicolored** 22 13
Margin block of 10, 5 P# adjoining #1410, 1412 2.50
Margin block of 4, Mr. Zip and "Use Zip Code" adjoining #1410 1.05 —
Margin block of 6, "Mail Early in the Day" adjoining #1410 1.50 —
1411 A825 6c **multicolored** 22 13
Margin block of 10, 5 P# adjoining #1411, 1413 2.50
Margin block of 4, Mr. Zip and "Use Zip Code" adjoining #1411 1.05 —
Margin block of 6, "Mail Early in the Day" adjoining #1411 1.50 —
1412 A826 6c **multicolored** 22 13
Margin block of 4, Mr. Zip and "Use Zip Code" adjoining #1412 1.05 —
Margin block of 6, "Mail Early in the Day" adjoining #1412 1.50 —
1413 A827 6c **multicolored** 22 13
Margin block of 4, Mr. Zip and "Use Zip Code" adjoining #1413 1.05 —
Margin block of 6, "Mail Early in the Day" adjoining #1413 1.50 —
a. Block of four, #1410-1413 1.00 1.00

CHRISTMAS ISSUE

Nos. 1415-1418 are printed in blocks of four in panes of 50. In upper and lower left panes Nos. 1415 and 1417 appear in first, third and fifth place; Nos. 1416 and 1418 in second and fourth place. This arrangement is reversed in upper and lower right panes.

Nativity, by Lorenzo Lotto — A828

Tin and Cast-iron Locomotive A829

Toy Horse on Wheels — A830

Mechanical Tricycle — A831

Doll Carriage — A832

Designers: No. 1414, Howard C. Mildner, from a painting by Lorenzo Lotto (1480-1556) in the National Gallery of Art, Washington, D.C. Nos. 1415-1418, Stevan Dohanos, from a drawing (locomotive) by Charles Hemming and from "Golden Age of Toys" by Fondin and Remise.

Printed by Guilford Gravure, Inc., Guilford, Conn.

PHOTOGRAVURE

Plates of 200 subjects in four panes of 50 each.

1970, Nov. 5 **Tagged** ***Perf. 10½x11***

1414 A828 6c **multicolored** 12 5
Margin block of 8, 4 P# 1.15
Margin block of 4, Mr. Zip and "Use Zip Code" 50 —
Margin block of 6, "Mail Early in the Day" 75 —
a. Precanceled 12 8
b. Black omitted *1,000.*
c. As "a," blue omitted *1,600.*

Perf. 11x10½

1415 A829 6c **multicolored** 40 10
Margin block of 8, 4 P# adjoining #1415, 1417 3.75
Margin block of 4, Mr. Zip and "Use Zip Code" adjoining #1415 1.80 —
Margin block of 6, "Mail Early in the Day" adjoining #1415 2.65 —
a. Precanceled 85 15
b. Black omitted —
1416 A830 6c **multicolored** 40 10
Margin block of 8, 4 P# adjoining #1416, 1418 3.75
Margin block of 4, Mr. Zip and "Use Zip Code" adjoining #1416 1.80 —
Margin block of 6, "Mail Early in the Day" adjoining #1416 2.65 —
a. Precanceled 85 15
b. Black omitted —
c. Imperf., pair (#1416, 1418) —
1417 A831 6c **multicolored** 40 10
Margin block of 4, Mr. Zip and "Use Zip Code" adjoining #1417 1.80 —
Margin block of 6, "Mail Early in the Day" adjoining #1417 2.65 —
a. Precanceled 85 15
b. Black omitted —
1418 A832 6c **multicolored** 40 10
Margin block of 4, Mr. Zip and "Use Zip Code" adjoining #1418 1.80 —
Margin block of 6, "Mail Early in the Day" adjoining #1418 2.65 —
a. Precanceled 85 15
b. Block of four, #1415-1418 1.75 1.75
c. As "b," precanceled 3.50 3.50
d. Black omitted —

The precanceled stamps, Nos. 1414a-1418a, were furnished to 68 cities. The plates include two straight (No. 1414a) or two wavy (Nos. 1415a-1418a) black lines that make up the precancellation. Unused values are for copies with gum and used values are for copies with an additional cancellation or without gum.

UNITED NATIONS ISSUE

Issued to commemorate the 25th anniversary of the United Nations.

"U.N." and U.N. Emblem — A833

Designed by Arnold Copeland.

LITHOGRAPHED, ENGRAVED (Giori)

Plates of 200 subjects in four panes of 50 each.

1970 **Tagged** ***Perf. 11***

1419 A833 6c **black, verm. & ultra.**, *Nov. 20* 12 5
Margin block of 4, P# 55 —
Margin block of 4, Mr. Zip and "Use Zip Code" 50 —
Margin block of 6, "Mail Early in the Day" 75 —
Pair with full horiz. gutter btwn. —

LANDING OF THE PILGRIMS ISSUE

Issued to commemorate the 350th anniversary of the landing of the Mayflower.

Mayflower and Pilgrims — A834

Designed by Mark English.

LITHOGRAPHED, ENGRAVED (Giori)

Plates of 200 subjects in four panes of 50 each.

1970 **Tagged** ***Perf. 11***

1420 A834 6c **blk., org., yel., magenta, bl. & brn.**, *Nov. 21* 12 5
Margin block of 4, P# 55 —
Margin block of 4, Mr. Zip and "Use Zip Code" 50 —
Margin block of 6, "Mail Early in the Day" 75 —
a. Orange & yellow omitted *1,250.*

DISABLED AMERICAN VETERANS AND SERVICEMEN ISSUE

No. 1421 commemorates the 50th anniversary of the Disabled Veterans of America Organization; No. 1422 honors the contribution of servicemen, particularly those who were prisoners of war, missing or killed in action. Nos. 1421-1422 are printed se-tenant in horizontal rows of 10 in panes of 50, four panes to a sheet.

Disabled American Veterans Emblem — A835

A836

Designed by Stevan Dohanos.

LITHOGRAPHED, ENGRAVED (Giori)

Plates of 200 subjects in four panes of 50 each.

1970, Nov. 24 **Tagged** ***Perf. 11***

1421 A835 6c **dk. blue, red & multicolored** 12 6
a. Pair, #1421-1422 25 25
Margin block of 4, P# No. adjoining #1421 1.00 —
Margin block of 4, Mr. Zip and "Use Zip Code" adjoining #1421 55 —
Margin block of 6, "Mail Early in the Day" adjoining #1421 80 —

ENGRAVED

1422 A836 6c **dark blue, black & red** 12 6
Margin block of 4, P# adjoining #1422 1.00 —
Margin block of 4, Mr. Zip and "Use Zip Code" adjoining #1422 55 —
Margin block of 6, "Mail Early in the Day" adjoining #1422 80 —

AMERICAN WOOL INDUSTRY ISSUE

Issued to commemorate the 450th anniversary of the introduction of sheep to the North American continent and the beginning of the American wool industry.

Ewe and Lamb — A837

Designed by Dean Ellis.

LITHOGRAPHED, ENGRAVED (Giori)
Plates of 200 subjects in four panes of 50 each.

1971 **Tagged** ***Perf. 11***

1423 A837 6c **multicolored,** *Jan. 19* 12 5
Margin block of 4, P# 55 —
Margin block of 4, Mr. Zip and "Use Zip Code" 50 —
Margin block of 6, "Mail Early in the Day" 75 —

GEN. DOUGLAS MacARTHUR ISSUE

Issued in honor of Gen. Douglas MacArthur (1880-1964), Chief of Staff, Supreme Commander for the Allied Powers in the Pacific Area during World War II and Supreme Commander in Japan after the war.

Gen. Douglas MacArthur — A838

Designed by Paul Calle; Wide World photograph.

GIORI PRESS PRINTING
Plates of 200 subjects in four panes of 50 each.

1971 **Tagged** ***Perf. 11***

1424 A838 6c **black, red & dark blue,** *Jan. 26* 12 5
Margin block of 4, P# 55 —
Margin block of 4, Mr. Zip and "Use Zip Code" 50 —
Margin block of 6, "Mail Early in the Day" 75 —

BLOOD DONOR ISSUE

Salute to blood donors and spur to increased participation in the blood donor program.

"Giving Blood Saves Lives" — A839

Designed by Howard Munce.

LITHOGRAPHED, ENGRAVED (Giori)
Plates of 200 subjects in four panes of 50 each.

1971 **Tagged** ***Perf. 11***

1425 A839 6c **blue, scarlet & indigo,** *Mar. 12* 12 5
Margin block of 4, P# 55 —
Margin block of 4, Mr. Zip and "Use Zip Code" 50 —
Margin block of 6, "Mail Early in the Day" 75 —

MISSOURI SESQUICENTENNIAL ISSUE

Sesquicentennial of Missouri's admission to the Union. The stamp design shows a Pawnee facing a hunter-trapper and a group of settlers. It is from a mural by Thomas Hart Benton in the Harry S. Truman Library, Independence, Mo.

"Independence and the Opening of the West," Detail, by Thomas Hart Benton — A840

Designed by Bradbury Thompson.

PHOTOGRAVURE (Andreotti)
Plates of 200 subjects in four panes of 50 each.

1971 **Tagged** ***Perf. 11x10½***

1426 A840 8c **multicolored,** *May 8* 15 5
Margin block of 12, 6P# 2.00 —
Margin block of 4, Mr. Zip and "Use Zip Code" 65 —
Margin block of 4, "Mail Early in the Day" 65 —

See note on Andreotti printings and their color control markings in Information for Collectors under Printing, Photogravure.

WILDLIFE CONSERVATION ISSUE

Nos. 1427-1430 are printed in blocks of 4 in panes of 32. Nos. 1427-1428 alternate in first row, Nos. 1429-1430 in second row. This arrangement repeated throughout pane.

Trout A841

Alligator A842

Polar Bear and Cubs A843

California Condor — A844

Designed by Stanley W. Galli.

LITHOGRAPHED, ENGRAVED (Giori)
Plates of 128 subjects in 4 panes of 32 each (4x8).

1971, June 12 **Tagged** ***Perf. 11***

1427 A841 8c **multicolored** 16 8
Margin block of 4, P# adjoining #1427 75 —
Margin block of 4, Mr. Zip and "Use Zip Code" adjoining #1427 70 —
Margin block of 6, "Mail Early in the Day" adjoining #1427 1.00 —
1428 A842 8c **multicolored** 16 8
Margin block of 4, P# adjoining #1428 75 —
Margin block of 4, Mr. Zip and "Use Zip Code" adjoining #1428 70 —
Margin block of 6, "Mail Early in the Day" adjoining #1428 1.00 —
1429 A843 8c **multicolored** 16 8
Margin block of 4, P# adjoining #1429 75 —
Margin block of 4, Mr. Zip and "Use Zip Code" adjoining #1429 70 —
Margin block of 6, "Mail Early in the Day" adjoining #1429 1.00 —
1430 A844 8c **multicolored** 16 8
Margin block of 4, P# adjoining #1430 75 —
Margin block of 4, Mr. Zip and "Use Zip Code" adjoining #1430 70 —
Margin block of 6, "Mail Early in the Day" adjoining #1430 1.00 —
a. Block of four, #1427-1430 65 65
b. As "a", light green & dark green omitted from #1427-1428 *3,000.*
c. As "a", red omitted from #1427 1429-1430 —

ANTARCTIC TREATY ISSUE

Map of Antarctica A845

Designed by Howard Koslow; adapted from emblem on official documents of Consultative Meetings.

GIORI PRESS PRINTING
Plates of 200 subjects in four panes of 50 each.

1971 **Tagged** ***Perf. 11***

1431 A845 8c **red & dark blue,** *June 23* 15 5
Margin block of 4, P# 70 —
Margin block of 4, Mr. Zip and "Use Zip Code" 65 —
Margin block of 6, "Mail Early in the Day" 95 —

AMERICAN REVOLUTION BICENTENNIAL

Bicentennial of the American Revolution.

Bicentennial Commission Emblem — A846

Designed by Chermayeff & Geismar.

LITHOGRAPHED, ENGRAVED (Giori)
Plates of 200 subjects in four panes of 50 each.

1971 **Tagged** ***Perf. 11***

1432 A846 8c **gray, red, blue & black,** *July 4* 16 5
Margin block of 4, P# 80 —
Margin block of 4, Mr. Zip and "Use Zip Code" 65 —
Margin block of 6, "Mail Early in the Day" 1.00 —
a. Gray & black omitted *700.00*
b. Gray ("U.S. Postage 8c") omitted *1,250.*

JOHN SLOAN ISSUE

Issued to honor John Sloan (1871-1951), painter. The painting hangs in the Phillips Gallery, Washington, D.C.

The Wake of the Ferry — A847

Designed by Bradbury Thompson.

LITHOGRAPHED, ENGRAVED (Giori)

Plates of 200 subjects in four panes of 50 each.

1971	Tagged		*Perf. 11*	
1433	A847 8c	**multicolored,** *Aug. 2*	15	5
		Margin block of 4, P#	70	—
		Margin block of 4, Mr. Zip and "Use Zip Code"	65	—
		Margin block of 6, "Mail Early in the Day"	95	—

SPACE ACHIEVEMENT DECADE ISSUE

Issued to commemorate a decade of space achievements and the Apollo 15 moon exploration mission, July 26-Aug. 7. Nos. 1434-1435 are printed se-tenant in horizontal rows of 5 in panes of 50. In the upper and lower left panes the earth and sun stamp is first, third and fifth, the rover second and fourth. This arrangement is reversed in the upper and lower right panes.

Earth, Sun and Landing Craft on Moon — A848

Lunar Rover and Astronauts A849

Designed by Robert McCall.

LITHOGRAPHED, ENGRAVED (Giori)

Plates of 200 subjects in four panes of 50 each.

1971, Aug. 2	Tagged		*Perf. 11*	
1434	A848 8c	**black, blue, gray, yellow & red**	15	10
a.		Pair, #1434-1435	30	25
		Block of 4, P# adjoining #1434	70	—
		Margin block of 4, Mr. Zip and "Use Zip Code" adjoining #1434	65	—
		Margin block of 6, "Mail Early in the Day" adjoining #1434	95	—
b.		As "a," blue & red (litho.) omitted	*1,250.*	
1435	A849 8c	**black, blue, gray, yellow & red**	15	10
		Margin block of 4, P# adjoining #1435	70	—
		Margin block of 4, Mr. Zip and "Use Zip Code" adjoining #1435	65	—
		Margin block of 6, "Mail Early in the Day" adjoining #1435	95	—

EMILY DICKINSON ISSUE

Issued to honor Emily Elizabeth Dickinson (1830-1886), poet.

Emily Dickinson — A850

Designed by Bernard Fuchs after a photograph.

LITHOGRAPHED, ENGRAVED (Giori)

Plates of 200 subjects in four panes of 50 each.

1971, Aug. 28	Tagged		*Perf. 11*	
1436	A850 8c	**multicolored,** *greenish*	15	5
		Margin block of 4, P#	70	—
		Margin block of 4, Mr. Zip and "Use Zip Code"	65	—
		Margin block of 6, "Mail Early in the Day"	95	—
a.		Black & olive (engr.) omitted	*1,100.*	
b.		Pale rose omitted	—	

SAN JUAN ISSUE

Issued for the 450th anniversary of San Juan, Puerto Rico.

Sentry Box, Morro Castle, San Juan — A851

Designed as a woodcut by Walter Brooks.

LITHOGRAPHED, ENGRAVED (Giori)

Plates of 200 subjects in four panes of 50 each.

1971, Sept. 12	Tagged		*Perf. 11*	
1437	A851 8c	**pale brown, black, yellow & dark brown**	15	5
		Margin block of 4, P#	70	—
		Margin block of 4, Mr. Zip and "Use Zip Code"	65	—
		Margin block of 6, "Mail Early in the Day"	95	—

PREVENT DRUG ABUSE ISSUE

Drug Abuse Prevention Week, Oct. 3-9.

Young Woman Drug Addict — A852

Designed by Miggs Burroughs.

PHOTOGRAVURE (Andreotti)

Plates of 200 subjects in four panes of 50 each.

1971, Oct. 4	Tagged		*Perf. 10½x11*	
1438	A852 8c	**blue, deep blue & black**	15	5
		Margin block of 6, 3P#	1.00	—
		Margin block of 4, "Use Zip Code"	65	—
		Margin block of 6, "Mail Early in the Day"	95	—

CARE ISSUE

25th anniversary of CARE, a U.S.-Canadian Cooperative for American Relief everywhere.

Hands Reaching for CARE — A853

Designed by Soren Noring

PHOTOGRAVURE (Andreotti)

Plates of 200 subjects in four panes of 50 each.

1971, Oct. 27	Tagged		*Perf. 10½x11*	
1439	A853 8c	**blue, blk., vio. & red lilac**	12	5
		Margin block of 8, 4P#	1.25	—
		Margin block of 4, Mr. Zi2 and "Use Zip Code"	65	—
		Margin block of 6, "Mail Early in the Day"	95	—
a.		Black omitted	—	

HISTORIC PRESERVATION ISSUE

Nos. 1440-1443 are printed in blocks of 4 in panes of 32. Nos. 1440-1441 alternate in first row, Nos. 1442-1443 in second row. This arrangement is repeated throughout the pane.

Decatur House, Washington, D.C. — A854

Whaling Ship Charles W. Morgan, Mystic, Conn. A855

Cable Car, San Francisco — A856

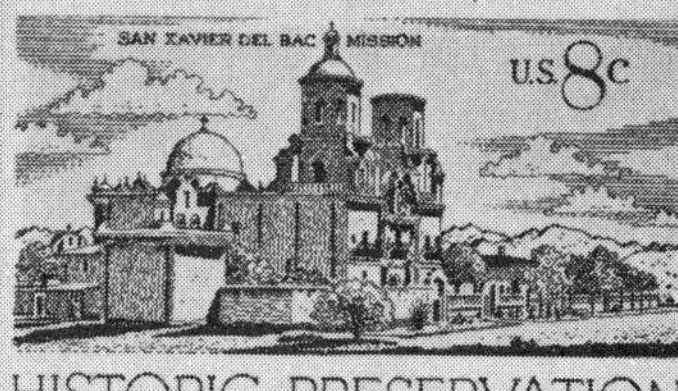

San Xavier del Bac Mission, Tucson, Ariz. A857

Designed by Melbourne Brindle.

LITHOGRAPHED, ENGRAVED (Giori)

1971, Oct. 29	Tagged		*Perf. 11*	
1440	A854 8c	**black brown & ocher,** *buff*	16	12
		Margin block of 4, P# adjoining #1440	75	—
		Margin block of 4, Mr. Zip and "Use Zip Code" adjoining #1440	70	—
		Margin block of 6, "Mail Early in the Day" adjoining #1440	1.00	—
1441	A855 8c	**black brown & ocher,** *buff*	16	12
		Margin block of 4, P# adjoining #1441	75	—
		Margin block of 4, Mr. Zip and "Use Zip Code" adjoining #1441	70	—
		Margin block of 6, "Mail Early in the Day" adjoining #1441	1.00	—
1442	A856 8c	**black brown & ocher,** *buff*	16	12
		Margin block of 4, P# adjoining #1442	75	—
		Margin block of 4, Mr. Zip and "Use Zip Code" adjoining #1442	70	—
		Margin block of 6, "Mail Early in the Day" adjoining #1442	1.00	—
1443	A857 8c	**black brown & ocher,** *buff*	16	12
		Margin block of 4, P# adjoining #1443	75	—
		Margin block of 4, Mr. Zip and "Use Zip Code" adjoining #1443	70	—
		Margin block of 6, "Mail Early in the Day" adjoining #1443	1.00	—
a.		Block of four (#1440-1443)	65	65
b.		As "a," black brown omitted	*2,800.*	
c.		As "a," ocher omitted	—	

Values quoted in this catalogue are for stamps graded at Fine-Very Fine and with no faults. An illustrated guide to grade is provided in introductory material, beginning on Page V.

CHRISTMAS ISSUE

Adoration of the Shepherds, by Giorgione — A858

"Partridge in a Pear Tree" — A859

Designers: No. 1444, Bradbury Thompson, using a painting by Giorgione in the National Gallery of Art, Washington, D.C. No. 1445, Jamie Wyeth.

PHOTOGRAVURE (Andreotti)

Plates of 200 subjects in four panes of 50 each.

1971, Nov. 10 **Tagged** ***Perf. 10½x11***

1444 A858 8c **gold & multicolored** 15 5
Margin block of 12, 6P# 2.00 —
Margin block of 4, Mr. Zip and "Use Zip Code" 65 —
Margin block of 4, "Mail Early in the Day" 65 —
a. Gold omitted *525.00*
1445 A859 8c **dark green, red & multicolored** 15 5
Margin block of 12, 6P# 2.00
Margin block of 4, Mr. Zip and "Use Zip Code" 65 —
Margin block of 4, "Mail Early in the Day" 65 —

SIDNEY LANIER ISSUE

Issued to honor Sidney Lanier (1842-1881), poet, musician, lawyer and educator.

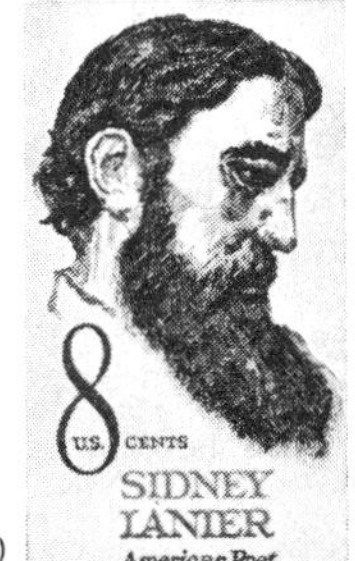

Sidney Lanier — A860

Designed by William A. Smith.

GIORI PRESS PRINTING

Plates of 200 subjects in four panes of 50 each.

1972, Feb. 3 **Tagged** ***Perf. 11***

1446 A860 8c **black, brown & light blue** 15 5
Margin block of 4, P# 70 —
Margin block of 4, Mr. Zip and "Use Zip Code" 65 —
Margin block of 6, "Mail Early in the Day" 95 —

PEACE CORPS ISSUE

Issued to honor the Peace Corps.

Peace Corps Poster, by David Battle — A861

Designed by Bradbury Thompson.

PHOTOGRAVURE (Andreotti)

Plates of 200 subjects in four panes of 50 each.

1972, Feb. 11 **Tagged** ***Perf. 10½x11***

1447 A861 8c **dk. blue, lt. blue & red** 12 5
Margin block of 6, 3 P# 1.00 —
Margin block of 4, Mr. Zip and "Use Zip Code" 65 —
Margin block of 6, "Mail Early in the Day" 95 —

NATIONAL PARKS CENTENNIAL ISSUE

Centenary of Yellowstone National Park, the first National Park, and of the entire National Park System. The four 2c stamps were issued for Cape Hatteras, N.C., National Seashore; 6c for Wolf Trap Farm, Vienna, Va.; 8c for Yellowstone National Park, Wyo., and 15c for Mt. McKinley National Park, Alaska. See No. C84.

A862 A863

A864 A865

Cape Hatteras National Seashore

Wolf Trap Farm, Va. — A866

Old Faithful, Yellowstone — A867

Mt. McKinley, Alaska — A868

Designers: 2c, Walter D. Richards; 6c, Howard Koslow; 8c, Robert Handville; 15c, James Barkley.

LITHOGRAPHED, ENGRAVED (Giori)

Plates of 400 subjects in 4 panes of 100 each

Panes contain 25 subjects each of Nos. 1448-1451

1972 **Tagged** ***Perf. 11***

1448 A862 2c **black & multi.**, *Apr. 5* 5 5
Margin block of 4, P# adjoining #1448 45 —
Margin block of 4, "Use Zip Codes" adjoining #1448 22 —
Margin block of 8, "Mail Early in the Day" adjoining #1448 45 —
1449 A863 2c **black & multi.**, *Apr. 5* 5 5
Margin block of 4, P# adjoining #1449 45 —
Margin block of 4, "Use Zip Codes" adjoining #1449 22 —
Margin block of 8, "Mail Early in the Day" adjoining #1449 45 —
1450 A864 2c **black & multi.**, *Apr. 5* 5 5
Margin block of 4, P# adjoining #1450 45 —
Margin block of 4, "Use Zip Codes" adjoining #1450 22 —
Margin block of 8, "Mail Early in the Day" adjoining #1450 45 —
1451 A865 2c **black & multi.**, *Apr. 5* 5 5
Margin block of 4, P# adjoining #1451 45 —
Margin block of 4, "Use Zip Codes" adjoining #1451 22 —
Margin block of 8, "Mail Early in the Day" adjoining #1451 45 —
a. Block of four (#1448-1451) 20 20
b. As "a," black (litho.) omitted *2,000.*

Plates of 200 subjects in four panes of 50 each

1452 A866 6c **black & multicolored,** *June 26* 12 8
Margin block of 4, P# 55 —
Margin block of 4, Mr. Zip and "Use Zip Code" 50 —
Margin block of 6, "Mail Early in the Day" 75 —

Plates of 128 subjects in four panes of 32 (8x4)

1453 A867 8c **blk., blue, brn. & multi.,** *Mar. 1* 15 5
Margin block of 4, P# 70 —
Margin block of 4, Mr. Zip and "Use Zip Code" 65 —
Margin block of 6, "Mail Early in the Day" 95 —

Plates of 200 subjects in four panes of 50 each

1454 A868 15c **black & multi.,** *July 28* 30 22
Margin block of 4, P# 1.30 —
Margin block of 4, Mr. Zip 1.25 —
Margin block of 6, Mail Early 1.90 —

FAMILY PLANNING ISSUE

Family — A869

LITHOGRAPHED, ENGRAVED (Giori)

Plates of 200 subjects in four panes of 50 each.

1972, Mar. 18 **Tagged** ***Perf. 11***

1455 A869 8c **black & multicolored** 15 5
Margin block of 4, P# 70 —
Margin block of 4, Mr. Zip and "Use Zip Code" 65 —
Margin block of 6, "Mail Early in the Day" 95 —
a. Yellow omitted —

AMERICAN BICENTENNIAL ISSUE

Colonial American Craftsmen

Nos. 1456-1459 are printed in blocks of four in panes of 50. In upper and lower left panes Nos. 1456 and 1458 appear in first, third and fifth place; Nos. 1457 and 1459 in second and fourth place. This arrangement is reversed in upper and lower right panes.

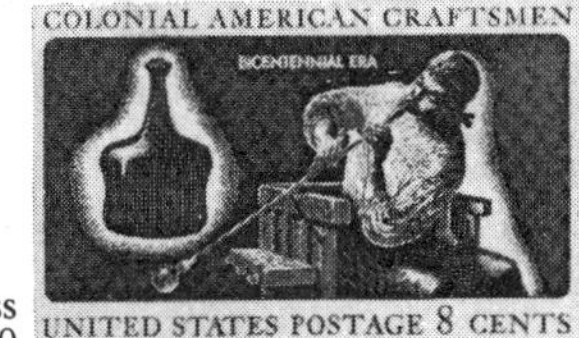

Glass Blower — A870

Silversmith A871

Wigmaker
A872

Hatter — A873

Designed by Leonard Everett Fisher.

ENGRAVED

E.E. Plates of 200 subjects in four panes of 50 each.

1972, July 4 **Tagged** ***Perf. 11x10½***

1456 A870 8c **deep brown**, *dull yellow* 16 8
Margin block of 4, P# adjoining #1456 75 —
Margin block of 4, Mr. Zip and "Use Zip Code" adjoining #1456 70 —
Margin block of 6, Bicentennial emblem adjoining #1456 1.00 —

1457 A871 8c **deep brown**, *dull yellow* 16 8
Margin block of 4, P# adjoining #1457 75 —
Margin block of 4, Mr. Zip and "Use Zip Code" adjoining #1457 70 —
Margin block of 6, Bicentennial emblem adjoining #1457 1.00 —

1458 A872 8c **deep brown**, *dull yellow* 16 8
Margin block of 4, P# adjoining #1458 75 —
Margin block of 4, Mr. Zip and "Use Zip Code" adjoining #1458 70 —
Margin block of 6, Bicentennial emblem adjoining #1458 1.00 —

1459 A873 8c **deep brown**, *dull yellow* 16 8
Margin block of 4, P# adjoining #1459 75 —
Margin block of 4, Mr. Zip and "Use Zip Code" adjoining #1459 70 —
Margin block of 6, Bicentennial emblem adjoining #1459 1.00 —

a. Block of 4, #1456-1459 65 65

Margin blocks of 6 include Bicentennial Commission emblem and inscription: USA BICENTENNIAL / HONORS COLONIAL / AMERICAN CRAFTSMEN.

OLYMPIC GAMES ISSUE

11th Winter Olympic Games, Sapporo, Japan, Feb. 3-13 and 20th Summer Olympic Games, Munich, Germany, Aug. 26-Sept. 11. See No. C85.

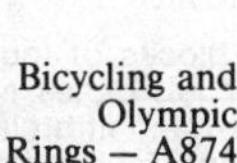

Bicycling and Olympic Rings — A874

Bobsledding and Olympic Rings — A875

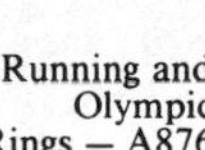

Running and Olympic Rings — A876

Designed by Lance Wyman.

PHOTOGRAVURE (Andreotti)

Plates of 200 subjects in four panes of 50 each.

1972, Aug. 17 **Tagged** ***Perf. 11x10½***

1460 A874 6c **black, blue, red, emerald & yellow** 12 8
Margin block of 10, 5P# 1.25 —
Margin block of 4, Mr. Zip and "Use Zip Code" 50 —
Margin block of 6, "Mail Early in the Day" 75 —
Plate flaw (broken red ring) (33313 UL 43) 7.50

1461 A875 8c **black, blue, red, emerald & yellow** 15 5
Margin block of 10, 5# 1.60 —
Margin block of 4, Mr. Zip and "Use Zip Code" 65 —
Margin block of 6, "Mail Early in the Day" 95 —

1462 A876 15c **black, blue, red, emerald & yel.** 28 18
Margin block of 10, 5P# 3.00 —
Margin block of 4, Mr. Zip and "Use Zip Code" 1.15 —
Margin block of 6, "Mail Early in the Day" 1.70 —

PARENT TEACHER ASSN. ISSUE

75th anniversary of the Parent Teacher Association.

Blackboard — A877

Designed by Arthur S. Congdon III.

PHOTOGRAVURE (Andreotti)

Plates of 200 subjects in four panes of 50 each.

1972, Sept. 15 **Tagged** ***Perf. 11x10½***

1463 A877 8c **yellow & black** 15 5
Margin block of 4, 2 P# 70 —
Margin block of 4, yel. P# reversed 75 —
Margin block of 4, Mr. Zip and "Use Zip Code" 65 —
Margin block of 6, "Mail Early in the Day" 95 —

WILDLIFE CONSERVATION ISSUE

Nos. 1464-1467 are printed in blocks of 4 in panes of 32. Nos. 1464-1465 alternate in first row, Nos. 1468-1469 in second row. This arrangement repeated throughout pane.

Fur Seals A878

Cardinal A879

Brown Pelican A880

See the "Information for Collectors" section at beginning of catalogue for an explanation of perforation types, imperforates and coils.

Bighorn Sheep A881

Designed by Stanley W. Galli.

LITHOGRAPHED, ENGRAVED (Giori)

Plates of 128 subjects in 4 panes of 32 (4x8).

1972, Sept. 20 **Tagged** ***Perf. 11***

1464 A878 8c **multicolored** 16 8
Margin block of 4, P# adjoining #1464 75 —
Margin block of 4, Mr. Zip and "Use Zip Code" adjoining #1464 70 —
Margin block of 6, "Mail Early in the Day" adjoining #1464 1.00 —

1465 A879 8c **multicolored** 16 8
Margin block of 4, P# adjoining #1465 75 —
Margin block of 4, Mr. Zip and "Use Zip Code" adjoining #1465 70 —
Margin block of 6, "Mail Early in the Day" adjoining #1465 1.00 —

1466 A880 8c **multicolored** 16 8
Margin block of 4, P# adjoining #1466 75 —
Margin block of 4, Mr. Zip and "Use Zip Code" adjoining #1466 70 —
Margin block of 6, "Mail Early in the Day" adjoining #1466 1.00 —

1467 A881 8c **multicolored** 16 8
Margin block of 4, P# adjoining #1467 75 —
Margin block of 4, Mr. Zip and "Use Zip Code" adjoining #1467 70 —
Margin block of 6, "Mail Early in the Day" adjoining #1467 1.00 —

a. Block of four (#1464-1467) 65 65
b. As "a," brown omitted *3,500.*
c. As "a," green & blue omitted —

MAIL ORDER BUSINESS ISSUE

Centenary of mail order business, originated by Aaron Montgomery Ward, Chicago. Design based on Headsville, W.Va., post office in Smithsonian Institution, Washington, D.C.

Rural Post Office Store — A882

Designed by Robert Lambdin.

PHOTOGRAVURE (Andreotti)

Plates of 200 subjects in four panes of 50 each.

1972, Sept, 27 **Tagged** ***Perf. 11x10½***

1468 A882 8c **multicolored** 15 5
Margin block of 12, 6 P# 1.90 —
Margin block of 4, Mr. Zip and "Use Zip Code" 65 —
Margin block of 4, "Mail Early in the Day" 65 —

The tagging on No. 1468 consists of a vertical bar of phosphor 10 mm. wide.

OSTEOPATHIC MEDICINE ISSUE

75th anniversary of the American Osteopathic Association, founded by Dr. Andrew T. Still (1828-1917), who developed the principles of osteopathy in 1874.

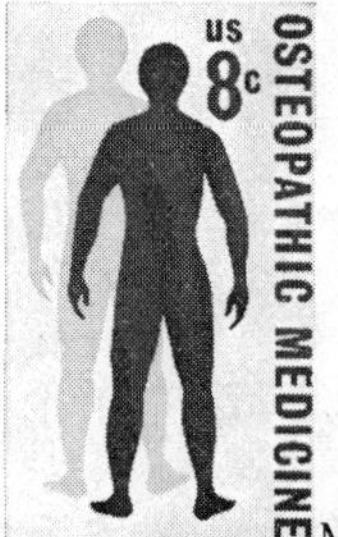

Man's Quest for Health — A883

Designed by V. Jack Ruther.

PHOTOGRAVURE (Andreotti)
Plates of 200 subjects in four panes of 50 each.

1972, Oct. 9 **Tagged** ***Perf. 10½x11***

1469 A883 8c **multicolored** 15 5
Margin block of 6, 3 P# 1.00 —
Margin block of 4, Mr. Zip and "Use Zip Code" 65 —
Margin block of 6, "Mail Early in the Day" 95 —

AMERICAN FOLKLORE ISSUE
Tom Sawyer

Tom Sawyer, by Norman Rockwell — A884

Designed by Bradbury Thompson.

LITHOGRAPHED, ENGRAVED (Giori)
Plates of 200 subjects in four panes of 50 each.

1972, Oct. 13 **Tagged** ***Perf. 11***

1470 A884 8c **black, red, yellow, tan, blue & rose red** 15 5
Margin block of 4, P# 70 —
Margin block of 4, Mr. Zip and "Use Zip Code" 65 —
Margin block of 6, "Mail Early in the Day" 95 —
a. Horiz. pair, imperf. between *2,500.*
b. Red & black (engr.) omitted *1,250.*
c. Yellow & tan (litho.) omitted *1,500.*

CHRISTMAS ISSUE

Angels from "Mary, Queen of Heaven" — A885

Santa Claus — A886

Designers: No. 1471, Bradbury Thompson, using detail from a painting by the Master of the St. Lucy legend, in the National Gallery of Art, Washington, D.C. No. 1472, Stevan Dohanos.

PHOTOGRAVURE (Andreotti)
Plates of 200 subjects in four panes of 50 each.

1972, Nov. 9 **Tagged** ***Perf. 10½x11***

1471 A885 8c **multicolored** 15 5
Margin block of 12, 6 P# 1.90 —
Margin block of 4, Mr. Zip and "Use Zip Code" 65 —
Margin block of 4, "Mail Early in the Day" 65 —
a. Pink omitted *400.00*
b. Black omitted —

1472 A886 8c **multicolored** 15 5
Margin block of 12, 6 P# 1.90 —
Margin block of 4, Mr. Zip and "Use Zip Code" 65 —
Margin block of 4, "Mail Early in the Day" 65 —

PHARMACY ISSUE

Honoring American druggists in connection with the 120th anniversary of the American Pharmaceutical Association.

Mortar and Pestle, Bowl of Hygeia, 19th Century Medicine Bottles — A887

Designed by Ken Davies.

LITHOGRAPHED, ENGRAVED (Giori)
Plates of 200 subjects in four panes of 50 each.

1972, Nov. 10 **Tagged** ***Perf. 11***

1473 A887 8c **black & multicolored** 15 5
Margin block of 4, P# 70 —
Margin block of 4, Mr. Zip and "Use Zip Code" 65 —
Margin block of 6, "Mail Early in the Day" 95 —
a. Blue & orange omitted *1,150.*
b. Blue omitted —

STAMP COLLECTING ISSUE

Issued to publicize stamp collecting.

U.S. No. 1 under Magnifying Glass — A888

Designed by Frank E. Livia.

LITHOGRAPHED, ENGRAVED (Giori)
Plates of 160 subjects in four panes of 40 each.

1972, Nov. 17 **Tagged** ***Perf. 11***

1474 A888 8c **multicolored** 15 5
Margin block of 4, P# 70 —
Margin block of 4, Mr. Zip and "Use Zip Code" 65 —
Margin block of 6, "Mail Early in the Day" 95 —
a. Black (litho.) omitted *950.00*

LOVE ISSUE

"Love," by Robert Indiana — A889

Designed by Robert Indiana.

PHOTOGRAVURE (Andreotti)
Plates of 200 subjects in four panes of 50 each.

1973, Jan. 26 **Tagged** ***Perf. 11x10½***

1475 A889 8c **red, emerald & violet blue** 15 5
Margin block of 6, 3 P# 1.00 —
Margin block of 4, Mr. Zip and "Use Zip Code" 65 —
Margin block of 6, "Mail Early in the Day" 95 —

AMERICAN BICENTENNIAL ISSUE
Communications in Colonial Times

Printer and Patriots Examining Pamphlet — A890

Posting a Broadside A891

Postrider — A892

Drummer A893

Designed by William A. Smith.

GIORI PRESS PRINTING
Plates of 200 subjects in four panes of 50 each.

1973 **Tagged** ***Perf. 11***

1476 A890 8c **ultra., greenish blk. & red,** *Feb. 16* 15 5
Margin block of 4, P# 70 —
Margin block of 4, Mr. Zip and "Use Zip Code" 65 —
Margin block of 6, "Mail Early in the Day" 95 —

1477 A891 8c **black, vermilion & ultra.,** *Apr. 13* 15 5
Margin block of 4, P# 70 —
Margin block of 4, Mr. Zip and "Use Zip Code" 65 —
Margin block of 6, "Mail Early in the Day" 95 —
Margin block of 6, Bicentennial emblem and "USA Bicentennial Era" 95 —
Pair with full horiz. gutter btwn. —

LITHOGRAPHED, ENGRAVED (Giori)

1478 A892 8c **blue, black, red & green,** *June 22* 15 5
Margin block of 4, P# 70 —
Margin block of 4, Mr. Zip and "Use Zip Code" 65 —
Margin block of 6, "Mail Early in the Day" 95 —
Margin block of 6, Bicentennial emblem and "USA Bicentennial Era" 95 —

1479 A893 8c **blue, black, yellow & red,** *Sept. 28* 15 5
Margin block of 4, P# 70 —
Margin block of 4, Mr. Zip and "Use Zip Code" 65 —
Margin block of 6, "Mail Early in the Day" 95 —
Margin block of 6, Bicentennial emblem and "USA Bicentennial Era" 95 —

AMERICAN BICENTENNIAL ISSUE
Boston Tea Party

Nos. 1480-1483 are printed in blocks of four in panes of 50. In upper and lower left panes Nos. 1480 and 1482 appear in first, third and fifth place, Nos. 1481 and 1483 appear in second and fourth place. This arrangement is reversed in upper and lower right panes.

British Merchantman A894

British Three-master A895

Boats and Ship's Hull — A896

Boat and Dock – A897

Designed by William A. Smith.

LITHOGRAPHED, ENGRAVED (Giori)
Plates of 200 subjects in four panes of 50 each.

1973, July 4 **Tagged** ***Perf. 11***

1480 A894 8c **black & multicolored** 15 10
Margin block of 4, P# adjoining #1480 70 —
Margin block of 4, Mr. Zip and "Use Zip Code" adjoining #1480 65 —
Margin block of 6, "Mail Early in the Day" adjoining #1480 95 —
Margin block of 6, Bicentennial emblem and "USA Bicentennial Era" 95 —

1481 A895 8c **black & multicolored** 15 10
Margin block of 4, P# adjoining #1481 70 —
Margin block of 4, Mr. Zip and "Use Zip Code" adjoining #1481 65 —
Margin block of 6, "Mail Early in the Day" adjoining #1481 95 —
Margin block of 6, Bicentennial emblem and "USA Bicentennial Era" adjoining #1481 95 —

1482 A896 8c **black & multicolored** 15 10
Margin block of 4, P# adjoining #1482 70 —
Margin block of 4, Mr. Zip and "Use Zip Code" adjoining #1482 65 —
Margin block of 6, "Mail Early in the Day" adjoining #1482 95 —
Margin block of 6, Bicentennial emblem and "USA Bicentennial Era" adjoining #1482 95 —

1483 A897 8c **black & multicolored** 15 10
Margin block of 4, P# adjoining #1483 70 —
Margin block of 4, Mr. Zip and "Use Zip Code" adjoining #1483 65 —
Margin block of 6, "Mail Early in the Day" adjoining #1483 95 —
Margin block of 6, Bicentennial emblem and "USA Bicentennial Era" adjoining #1483 95 —

a. Block of 4, #1480-1483 60 45
b. As "a," black (engraved) omitted *2,000.*
c. As "a," black (litho.) omitted *1,700.*

AMERICAN ARTS ISSUE

George Gershwin (1899-1937), composer (No. 1484); Robinson Jeffers (1887-1962), poet (No. 1485); Henry Ossawa Tanner (1859-1937), black painter (No. 1486); Willa Cather (1873-1947), novelist (No. 1487).

Gershwin, Sportin' Life, Porgy and Bess – A898

Robinson Jeffers, Man and Children of Carmel with Burro – A899

Henry Ossawa Tanner, Palette and Rainbow – A900

Willa Cather, Pioneer Family and Covered Wagon – A901

Designed by Mark English.

PHOTOGRAVURE (Andreotti)
Plates of 160 subjects in four panes of 40 each.

1973 **Tagged** ***Perf. 11***

1484 A898 8c **dp. green & multi.**, *Feb. 28* 15 5
Margin block of 12, 6 P# 1.85 —
Margin block of 4, Mr. Zip, "Use Zip Code" and "Mail Early in the Day" 65 —
Margin block of 16, 6 P#, Mr. Zip and slogans 2.50 —
a. Vertical pair, imperf. horiz *300.00*

1485 A899 8c **Prussian blue & multi.**, *Aug. 13* 15 5
Margin block of 12, 6 P# 1.85 —
Margin block of 4, Mr. Zip, "Use Zip Code" "Mail Early in the Day" 65 —
Margin block of 16, 6 P#, Mr. Zip and slogans 2.50 —
a. Vertical pair, imperf. horiz. *350.00*

1486 A900 8c **yellow brown & multi.**, *Sept. 10* 15 5
Margin block of 12, 6 P# 1.85 —
Margin block of 4, Mr. Zip, "Use Zip Code" "Mail Early in the Day" 65 —
Margin block of 16, 6 P#, Mr. Zip and slogans 2.50 —

1487 A901 8c **deep brown & multi.**, *Sept. 20* 15 5
Margin block of 12, 6 P# 1.85 —
Margin block of 4, Mr. Zip, "Use Zip Code" "Mail Early in the Day" 65 —
Margin block of 16, 6 P#, Mr. Zip and slogans 2.50 —
a. Vertical pair, imperf. horiz. *350.00*

COPERNICUS ISSUE

500th anniversary of the birth of Nicolaus Copernicus (1473-1543), Polish astronomer.

Nicolaus Copernicus – A902

Designed by Alvin Eisenman after 18th century engraving.

LITHOGRAPHED, ENGRAVED (Giori)
Plates of 200 subjects in four panes of 50 each.

1973, Apr. 23 **Tagged** ***Perf. 11***

1488 A902 8c **black & orange** 15 5
Margin block of 4, P# 70 —
Margin block of 4, Mr. Zip and "Use Zip Code" 65 —
Margin block of 6, "Mail Early in the Day" 95 —
a. Orange omitted *1,100.*
b. Black (engraved) omitted *1,750.*

The orange can be chemically removed.

POSTAL SERVICE EMPLOYEES ISSUE

A tribute to U.S. Postal Service employees. Nos. 1489-1498 are printed se-tenant in horizontal rows of 10. Emerald inscription on back, printed beneath gum in water-soluble ink, includes Postal Service emblem, "People Serving You" and a statement, differing for each of the 10 stamps, about some aspect of postal service.

Each stamp in top or bottom row has a tab with blue inscription enumerating various jobs in postal service.

Stamp Counter – A903

Mail Collection – A904

Letter Facing on Conveyor Belt – A905

Parcel Post Sorting – A906

Mail Canceling – A907

Manual Letter Routing – A908

Electronic Letter Routing – A909

Loading Mail on Truck – A910

Mailman – A911

Rural Mail Delivery – A912

Designed by Edward Vebell.

PHOTOGRAVURE (Andreotti)
Plates of 200 subjects in four panes of 50 each.

1973, Apr. 30 **Tagged** ***Perf. 10½x11***

1489 A903 8c **multicolored** 15 10
1490 A904 8c **multicolored** 15 10
1491 A905 8c **multicolored** 15 10

1492 A906 8c **multicolored** 15 10
1493 A907 8c **multicolored** 15 10
1494 A908 8c **multicolored** 15 10
1495 A909 8c **multicolored** 15 10
1496 A910 8c **multicolored** 15 10
1497 A911 8c **multicolored** 15 10
1498 A912 8c **multicolored** 15 10
Margin block of 20, 5 P# and 10 tabs 3.10 —
a. Strip of 10 (#1489-1498) 1.50 1.00

The tagging on Nos. 1489-1498 consists of a ½-inch horizontal band of phosphor.

HARRY S TRUMAN ISSUE

Harry S Truman, 33rd President, (1884-1972) — A913

Designed by Bradbury Thompson; photograph by Leo Stern.

GIORI PRESS PRINTING
Plates of 128 subjects in four panes of 32 each.

1973, May 8 **Tagged** ***Perf. 11***
1499 A913 8c **carmine rose, black & blue** 15 5
Margin block of 4, P# 65 —

ELECTRONICS PROGRESS ISSUE

See No. C86.

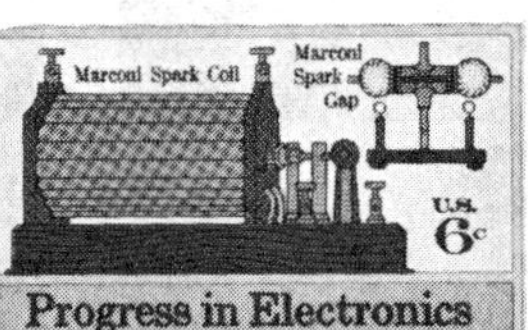

Marconi's Spark Coil and Spark Gap — A914

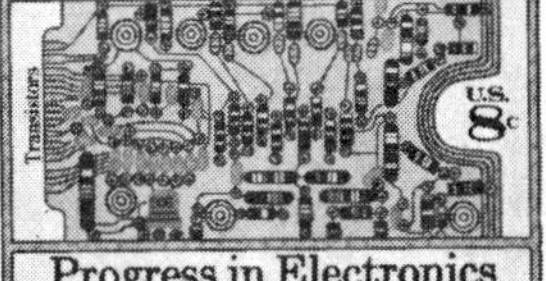

Transistors and Printed Circuit Board — A915

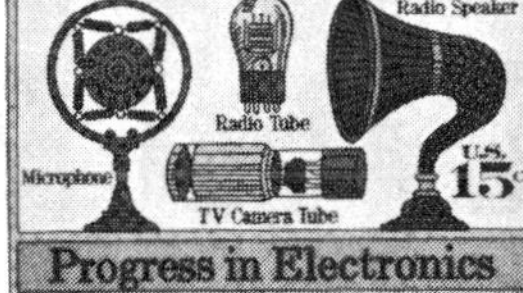

Microphone, Speaker, Vacuum Tube and TV Camera Tube — A916

Designed by Walter and Naiad Einsel.

LITHOGRAPHED, ENGRAVED (Giori)
Plates of 200 subjects in four panes of 50 each.

1973, July 10 **Tagged** ***Perf. 11***
1500 A914 6c **lilac & multicolored** 12 10
Margin block of 4, P# 55 —
Margin block of 4, Mr. Zip and "Use Zip Code" 50 —
Margin block of 6, "Mail Early in the Day" 70 —
1501 A915 8c **tan & multicolored** 15 5
Margin block of 4, P# 70 —
Margin block of 4, Mr. Zip and "Use Zip Code" 65 —
Margin block of 6, "Mail Early in the Day" 95 —
a. Black (inscriptions & "U.S. 8c") omitted *750.00*
b. Tan (background) & lilac omitted *1,600.*
1502 A916 15c **gray green & multicolored** 28 15
Margin block of 4, P# 1.20 —
Margin block of 4, Mr. Zip and "Use Zip Code" 1.15 —
Margin block of 6, "Mail Early in the Day" 1.70 —
a. Black (inscriptions & "U.S. 15c") omitted *1,750.*

LYNDON B. JOHNSON ISSUE

Lyndon B. Johnson, 36th President (1908-1973) — A917

Designed by Bradbury Thompson, portrait by Elizabeth Shoumatoff.

PHOTOGRAVURE (Andreotti)
Plates of 128 subjects in four panes of 32 each.

1973, Aug. 27 ***Perf. 11***
1503 A917 8c **black & multicolored,** *Aug. 27* 15 5
Margin block of 12, 6 P# 1.85 —
a. Horiz. pair, imperf. vert. *375.00*

RURAL AMERICA ISSUE

Centenary of the introduction of Aberdeen Angus cattle into the United States (No. 1504); of the Chautauqua Institution (No. 1505); and of the introduction of hard winter wheat into Kansas by Mennonite immigrants (No. 1506).

Angus and Longhorn Cattle — A918

Chautauqua Tent and Buggies — A919

Wheat Fields and Train — A920

No. 1504 modeled by Frank Waslick after painting by F. C. "Frank" Murphy. Nos. 1505-1506 designed by John Falter.

LITHOGRAPHED, ENGRAVED (Giori)
Plates of 200 subjects in four panes of 50 each.

1973-74 **Tagged** ***Perf. 11***
1504 A918 8c **multicolored,** *Oct. 5, 1973* 15 5
Margin block of 4, P# 70 —
Margin block of 4, Mr. Zip and "Use Zip Code" 65 —
Margin block of 6, "Mail Early in the Day" 95 —
a. Green & red brown omitted *550.00*
1505 A919 10c **multicolored,** *Aug. 6, 1974* 18 5
Margin block of 4, P# 80 —
Margin block of 4, Mr. Zip and "Use Zip Code" 75 —
Margin block of 6, "Mail Early in the Day" 1.10 —
1506 A920 10c **multicolored,** *Aug. 16, 1974* 18 5
Margin block of 4, P# 80 —
Margin block of 4, Mr. Zip and "Use Zip Code" 75 —
Margin block of 6, "Mail Early in the Day" 1.10 —
a. Black and blue (engr.) omitted *600.00*

CHRISTMAS ISSUE

Small Cowper Madonna, by Raphael — A921

Christmas Tree in Needlepoint — A922

Designers: No. 1507, Bradbury Thompson, using a painting in the National Gallery of Art, Washington, D.C. No. 1508, Dolli Tingle.

PHOTOGRAVURE (Andreotti)
Plates of 200 subjects in four panes of 50 each.

1973, Nov. 7 **Tagged** ***Perf. 10½x11***
1507 A921 8c **multicolored** 15 5
Margin block of 12, 6 P# 1.85 —
Margin block of 4, Mr. Zip and "Use Zip Code" 65 —
Margin block of 4, "Mail Early in the Day" 65 —
Pair with full vert. gutter btwn. —
1508 A922 8c **multicolored** 15 5
Margin block of 12, 6 P# 1.85 —
Margin block of 4, Mr. Zip and "Use Zip Code" 65 —
Margin block of 4, "Mail Early in the Day" 65 —
a. Vertical pair, imperf. between *550.00*
Pair with full horiz. gutter btwn. —

The tagging on Nos. 1507-1508 consists of a 20x12mm horizontal bar of phosphor.

50-Star and 13-Star Flags A923

Jefferson Memorial and Signature A924

Mail Transport A925

Liberty Bell A926

Designers: No. 1509, Ren Wicks. No. 1510, Dean Ellis. No. 1511, Randall McDougall. 6.3c, Frank Lionetti.

MULTICOLOR HUCK PRESS
Panes of 100 (10x10)

1973-74 **Tagged** ***Perf. 11x10½***
1509 A923 10c **red & blue,** *Dec. 8, 1973* 18 5
Margin block of 20, 4-6 P#, 2-3 "Mail Early" and 2-3 "Use Zip Code" 3.75 —
a. Horizontal pair, imperf. between *60.00*
b. Blue omitted *200.00*
c. Imperf., vert. pair *850.00*

ROTARY PRESS PRINTING

E.E. Plates of 400 subjects in four panes of 100 each.

1510 A924 10c **blue,** *Dec. 14, 1973* 18 5
Margin block of 4, P# 80 —
Margin block of 4, "Use Zip Codes" 75 —
Margin block of 6, "Mail Early in the Day" 1.10 —
a. Untagged (Bureau precanceled) 18
b. Booklet pane of 5 + label 1.50 *30*
c. Booklet pane of 8 1.65 *30*

d. Booklet pane of 6, *Aug. 5, 1974* 4.25 *30*
e. Vert. pair, imperf. horiz. *250.00*
f. Vert. pair, imperf. between —

Bureau Precancels: 10 different.

PHOTOGRAVURE (Andreotti)

Plates of 400 subjects in four panes of 100 each.

1511 A925 10c **multicolored,** *Jan. 4, 1974* 18 5
Margin block of 8, 4 P# 1.50 —
Margin block of 4, "Use Zip Codes" 75 —
Margin block of 6, "Mail Early in the Day" 1.10 —
a. Yellow omitted *50.00*
Pair with full horiz. gutter btwn. —

COIL STAMPS
ROTARY PRESS PRINTING

1973-74 Tagged *Perf. 10 Vert.*

1518 A926 6.3c **brick red,** *Oct. 1, 1974* 12 7
Pair 25 14
Joint line pair 65 —
a. Untagged (Bureau precanceled) 14
b. Imperf., pair *250.00*
c. As "a," imperf., pair *125.00*
c. Joint line pair —

A total of 129 different Bureau precancels were used by 117 cities.

No. 1518c is precanceled Washington, DC. Also exists from Columbus, Ohio and Garden City, N.Y. Values higher.

MULTICOLOR HUCK PRESS

1519 A923 10c **red & blue,** *Dec. 8, 1973* 22 5
Pair 44 10
a. Imperf., pair *30.00*

ROTARY PRESS PRINTING

1520 A924 10c **blue,** *Dec. 14, 1973* 18 5
Pair 36 10
Joint line pair 55 —
a. Untagged (Bureau precanceled) 25
b. Imperf., pair *40.00*

Bureau Precancels: No. 1520, 14 diff.

VETERANS OF FOREIGN WARS ISSUE

75th anniversary of Veterans of Spanish-American and Other Foreign Wars.

Emblem and Initials of Veterans of Foreign Wars — A928

Designed by Robert Hallock.

GIORI PRESS PRINTING

Plates of 200 subjects in 4 plates of 50 each.

1974, Mar. 11 Tagged *Perf. 11*

1525 A928 10c **red & dark blue** 18 5
Margin block of 4, P# 80 —
Margin block of 4, Mr. Zip and "Use Zip Code" 75 —
Margin block of 6, "Mail Early in the Day" 1.10 —

ROBERT FROST ISSUE

Centenary of the birth of Robert Frost (1873-1963), poet.

Robert Frost — A929

Designed by Paul Calle; photograph by David Rhinelander.

ROTARY PRESS PRINTING

E.E. Plates of 200 subjects in four panes of 50 each.

1974, Mar. 26 Tagged *Perf. 10½x11*

1526 A929 10c **black** 18 5
Margin block of 4, P# 80 —
Margin block of 4, Mr. Zip and "Use Zip Code" 75 —
Margin block of 6, "Mail Early in the Day" 1.10 —

EXPO '74 WORLD'S FAIR ISSUE

EXPO '74 World's Fair "Preserve the Environment," Spokane, Wash., May 4-Nov. 4.

"Cosmic Jumper" and "Smiling Sage" — A930

Designed by Peter Max.

PHOTOGRAVURE (Andreotti)

Plates of 160 subjects in four panes of 40 each.

1974, Apr. 18 Tagged *Perf. 11*

1527 A930 10c **multicolored** 18 5
Margin block of 12, 6 P# 2.20 —
Margin block of 4, Mr. Zip, "Use Zip Code" and "Mail Early in the Day" 75 —
Margin block of 16, 6 P#, Mr. Zip and slogans 3.00 —

HORSE RACING ISSUE

Centenary of the Kentucky Derby, Churchill Downs.

Horses Rounding Turn — A931

Designed by Henry Koehler.

PHOTOGRAVURE (Andreotti)

Plates of 200 subjects in four panes of 50 each.

1974, May 4 Tagged *Perf. 11x10½*

1528 A931 10c **yellow & multicolored** 18 5
Margin block of 12, 6 P# 2.20 —
Margin block of 4, Mr. Zip and "Use Zip Code" 75 —
Margin block of 4, "Mail Early in the Day" 75 —
a. Blue ("Horse Racing") omitted *1,300.*
b. Red ("U.S. postage 10 cents") omitted —

SKYLAB ISSUE

First anniversary of the launching of Skylab I, honoring all who participated in the Skylab project.

Skylab — A932

Designed by Robert T. McCall.

LITHOGRAPHED, ENGRAVED (Giori)

Plates of 200 subjects in four panes of 50 each.

1974, May 14 Tagged *Perf. 11*

1529 A932 10c **multicolored** 18 5
Margin block of 4, P# 80 —
Margin block of 4, Mr. Zip and "Use Zip Code" 75 —
Margin block of 6, "Mail Early in the Day" 1.10 —
a. Vert. pair, imperf. between —

UNIVERSAL POSTAL UNION ISSUE

Centenary of Universal Postal Union. Nos. 1530-1537 are arranged in blocks of 8 (4x2), four blocks of a pane (8x4). In the first row Nos. 1530-1537 are in sequence as listed. In the second row Nos. 1534-1537 are followed by Nos. 1530-1533. Every row of 8 and every horizontal block of 8 contains all 8 designs. All four panes have this arrangement. The letter writing designs are from famous works of art; some are details. The quotation on every second stamp, "Letters mingle souls," is from a letter by poet John Donne.

Michelangelo, from "School of Athens," by Raphael, 1509 — A933

"Five Feminine Virtues," by Hokusai, c. 1811 — A934

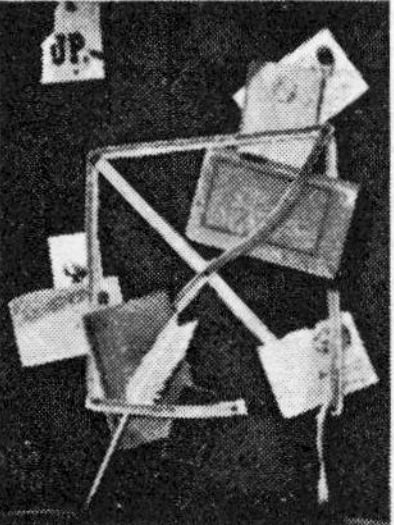

"Old Scraps," by John Fredrick Peto, 1894 — A935

"The Lovely Reader," by Jean Etienne Liotard, 1746 — A936

"Lady Writing Letter," by Gerard Terborch, 1654 — A937

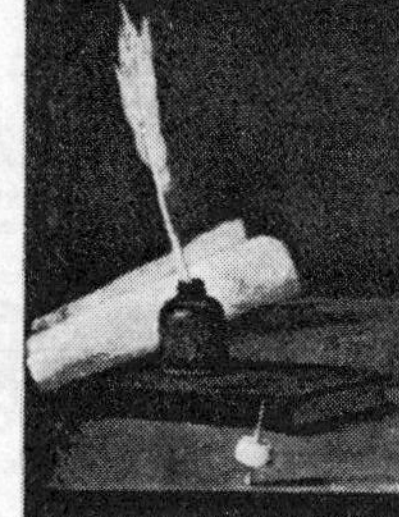

Inkwell and Quill, from "Boy with a Top," by Jean-Baptiste Simeon Chardin, 1738 — A938

An enhanced introduction to the Scott Catalogue begins on Page V. A thorough understanding of the material presented there will greatly aid your use of the catalogue itself.

Mrs. John Douglas, by Thomas Gainsborough, 1784 — A939

Don Antonio Noriega, by Francisco de Goya, 1801 — A940

Designed by Bradbury Thompson.

PHOTOGRAVURE (Andreotti)

Plates of 128 subjects in four panes of 32 each.

1974, June 6 **Tagged** ***Perf. 11***

1530 A933 10c **multicolored** 20 15
1531 A934 10c **multicolored** 20 15
1532 A935 10c **multicolored** 20 15
1533 A936 10c **multicolored** 20 15
1534 A937 10c **multicolored** 20 15
1535 A938 10c **multicolored** 20 15
1536 A939 10c **multicolored** 20 15
1537 A940 10c **multicolored** 20 15
a. Block or strip of 8 (#1530-1537) 1.60 1.50
b. As "a," (block), imperf. vert. *6,000.*
Margin block of 16, 5 P# adjoining #1530-1534, "Mail Early in the Day" adjoining #1535 and Mr. Zip and "Use Zip Code" adjoining #1537 3.50 —
Margin block of 16, 5 P# adjoining #1533-1537, "Mail Early in the Day" adjoining #1532 and Mr. Zip and "Use Zip Code" adjoining #1530 3.50 —
Margin block of 16, 5 P# adjoining #1534-1537, 1530, "Mail Early in the Day" adjoining #1531 and Mr. Zip and "Use Zip Code" adjoining #1533 3.50 —
Margin block of 16, 5 P# adjoining #1537, 1530-1533, "Mail Early in the Day" adjoining #1536 and Mr. Zip and "Use Zip Code" adjoining #1534 3.50 —
Margin block of 10, 5 P# as above; no slogans 2.25 —

MINERAL HERITAGE ISSUE

Panes contain 12 blocks of 4 (3x4). The sequence of stamps in first horizontal row is Nos. 1538-1541, 1538-1539. In second row Nos. 1540-1541 are followed by Nos. 1538-1541. All four panes have this arrangement.

Petrified Wood A941

Tourmaline A942

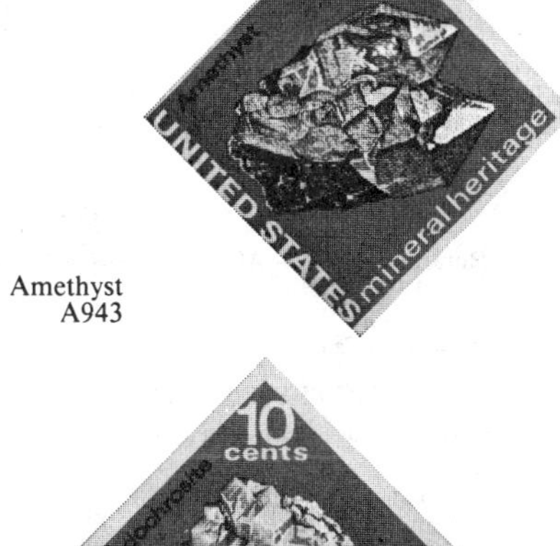

Amethyst A943

Rhodochrosite — A944

Designed by Leonard F. Buckley.

LITHOGRAPHED, ENGRAVED (Giori)

Plates of 192 subjects in four panes of 48 (6x8).

1974, June 13 **Tagged** ***Perf. 11***

1538 A941 10c **blue & multicolored** 18 10
Margin block of 4, P# adjoining #1538 85 —
Margin block of 4, Mr. Zip and "Use Zip Code" adjoining #1538 80 —
Margin block of 6, "Mail Early in the Day" adjoining #1538 1.10 —
a. Light blue & yellow omitted —
1539 A942 10c **blue & multicolored** 18 10
Margin block of 4, P# adjoining #1539 85 —
Margin block of 4, Mr. Zip and "Use Zip Code" adjoining #1539 80 —
Margin block of 6, "Mail Early in the Day" adjoining #1539 1.10
a. Light blue omitted —
b. Black & purple omitted —
1540 A943 10c **blue & multicolored** 18 10
Margin block of 4, P# adjoining #1540 85 —
Margin block of 4, Mr. Zip and "Use Zip Code" adjoining #1540 80 —
Margin block of 6, "Mail Early in the Day" adjoining #1540 1.10 —
a. Light blue & yellow omitted —
1541 A944 10c **blue & multicolored** 18 10
Margin block of 4, P# adjoining #1541 85 —
Margin block of 4, Mr. Zip and "Use Zip Code" adjoining #1541 80 —
Margin block of 6, "Mail Early in the Day" adjoining #1541 1.10 —
a. Block or strip of 4, #1538-1541 75 75
b. As "a," lt. blue & yellow omitted *1,900.* —
c. Light blue omitted —
d. Black & red omitted —

KENTUCKY SETTLEMENT ISSUE

Bicentenary of Fort Harrod, first settlement in Kentucky.

Covered Wagons at Fort Harrod — A945

Designed by David K. Stone.

LITHOGRAPHED, ENGRAVED (Giori)

Plates of 200 subjects in four panes of 50 each.

1974, June 15 **Tagged** ***Perf. 11***

1542 A945 10c **green & multicolored** 18 5
Margin block of 4, P# 80 —
Margin block of 4, Mr. Zip and "Use Zip Code" 75 —
Margin block of 6, "Mail Early in the Day" 1.10 —
a. Dull black (litho.) omitted *1,250.*
b. Green (engr. & litho.), black (engr. & litho.) & blue omitted *3,000.*

After the lithographed red and yellow colors were printed a piece of paper fell on one pane, which was then printed and perforated. The removal of the piece of paper results in four stamps with some printing missing. One stamp has the green (engr.) completely omitted, another the green (engr,) and black (litho.) completely omitted.

AMERICAN REVOLUTION BICENTENNIAL ISSUE

First Continental Congress

Nos. 1543-1546 are printed in blocks of four in panes of 50. Nos. 1543-1544 alternate in first row, Nos. 1545-1546 in second row. This arrangement is repeated throughout the pane.

Carpenters' Hall, Philadelphia A946

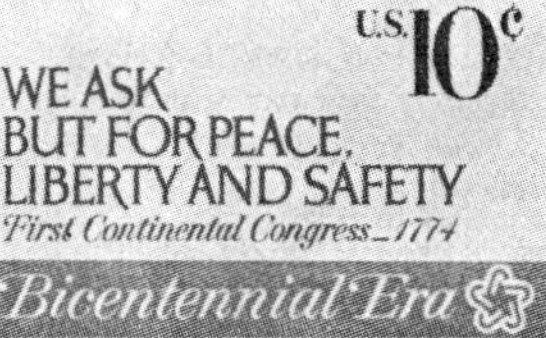

"We ask but for peace . . ." A947

"Deriving their just powers . . ." A948

Independence Hall — A949

Designed by Frank P. Conley

GIORI PRESS PRINTING

Plates of 200 subjects in four panes of 50 each.

1974, July 4 **Tagged** ***Perf. 11***

1543 A946 10c **dark blue & red** 18 10
Margin block of 4, P# adjoining #1543 85 —
Margin block of 4, Mr. Zip and "Use Zip Code" adjoining #1543 80 —
Margin block of 6, "Mail Early in the Day" adjoining #1543 1.10 —
Margin block of 6, Bicentennial Emblem and "USA Bicentennial Era" adjoining #1543 1.10 —

1544 A947 10c **gray, dark blue & red** 18 10
Margin block of 4, P# adjoining #1544 85 —
Margin block of 4, Mr. Zip and "Use Zip Code" adjoining #1544 80 —
Margin block of 6, "Mail Early in the Day" adjoining #1544 1.10 —
Margin block of 6, Bicentennial Emblem and "USA Bicentennial Era" adjoining #1544 1.10 —

1545 A948 10c **gray, dark blue & red** 18 10
Margin block of 4, P# adjoining #1545 85 —
Margin block of 4, Mr. Zip and "Use Zip Code" adjoining #1545 80 —
Margin block of 6, "Mail Early in the Day" adjoining #1545 1.10 —
Margin block of 6, Bicentennial Emblem and "USA Bicentennial Era" adjoining #1545 1.10 —

1546 A949 10c **red & dark blue** 18 10
Margin block of 4, P# adjoining #1546 85 —
Margin block of 4, Mr. Zip and "Use Zip Code" adjoining #1546 80 —
Margin block of 6, "Mail Early in the Day" adjoining #1546 1.10 —
Margin block of 6, Bicentennial Emblem and "USA Bicentennial Era" adjoining #1546 1.10 —
a. Block of four, #1543-1546 75 75

ENERGY CONSERVATION ISSUE

Publicizing the importance of conserving all forms of energy.

Molecules and Drops of Gasoline and Oil — A950

Designed by Robert W. Bode.

LITHOGRAPHED, ENGRAVED (Giori)

Plates of 200 subjects in four panes of 50 each.

1974, Sept. 23 **Tagged** ***Perf. 11***

1547 A950 10c **multicolored** 18 5
Margin block of 4, P# 80 —
Margin block of 4, Mr. Zip and "Use Zip Code" 75 —
Margin block of 6, "Mail Early in the Day" 1.10 —
a. Blue & orange omitted *800.00*
b. Orange & green omitted *850.00*
c. Green omitted *800.00*

AMERICAN FOLKLORE ISSUE

Legend of Sleepy Hollow

The Headless Horseman in pursuit of Ichabod Crane from "Legend of Sleepy Hollow," by Washington Irving.

Headless Horseman and Ichabod — A951

Designed by Leonard Everett Fisher.

LITHOGRAPHED, ENGRAVED (Giori)

Plates of 200 subjects in four panes of 50 each.

1974, Oct. 12 **Tagged** ***Perf. 11***

1548 A951 10c **dk. bl., blk., org. & yel.** 18 5
Margin block of 4, P# 80 —
Margin block of 4, Mr. Zip and "Use Zip Code" 75 —
Margin block of 6, "Mail Early in the Day" 1.10 —

RETARDED CHILDREN ISSUE

Retarded Children Can Be Helped, theme of annual convention of the National Association of Retarded Citizens.

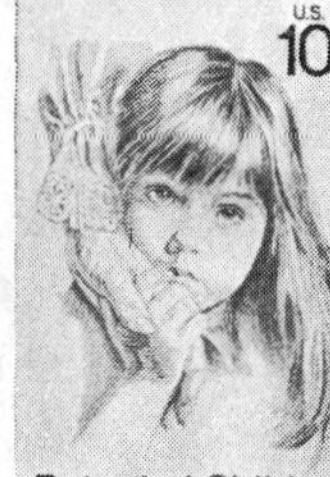

Retarded Child — A952

Designed by Paul Calle.

GIORI PRESS PRINTING

Plates of 200 subjects in four panes of 50 each.

1974, Oct. 12 **Tagged** ***Perf. 11***

1549 A952 10c **brown red & dark brown** 18 5
Margin block of 4, P# 80 —
Margin block of 4, Mr. Zip and "Use Zip Code" 75 —
Margin block of 6, "Mail Early in the Day" 1.10 —

CHRISTMAS ISSUE

Angel — A953

"The Road-Winter," by Currier and Ives — A954

Dove Weather Vane atop Mount Vernon — A955

Designers: No. 1550, Bradbury Thompson, using detail from the Perussis altarpiece painted by anonymous French artist, 1480, in Metropolitan Museum of Art, New York City. No. 1551, Stevan Dohanos, using Currier and Ives print from drawing by Otto Knirsch. No. 1552, Don Hedin and Robert Geissman.

PHOTOGRAVURE (Andreotti)

Plates of 200 subjects in four panes of 50 each.

1974, Oct. 23 **Tagged** ***Perf. 10½x11***

1550 A953 10c **multicolored** 18 5
Margin block of 10, 5 P# 1.85 —
Margin block of 4, Mr. Zip and "Use Zip Code" 75 —
Margin block of 6, "Mail Early in the Day" 1.10 —

Perf. 11x10½

1551 A954 10c **multicolored** 18 5
Margin block of 12, P# 2.20 —
Margin block of 4, Mr. Zip and "Use Zip Code" 75 —
Margin block of 4, "Mail Early in the Day" 75 —

Imperf., Paper Backing Rouletted

1974, Nov. 15 **Untagged**

Self-adhesive; Inscribed "Precanceled"

1552 A955 10c **multicolored** 18 8
Margin block of 20, 6 P# and 5 slogans 3.70
Margin block of 12, 6 P# and 5 different slogans 2.25

Unused value of No. 1552 is for copy on rouletted paper backing as issued. Used value is for copy on piece, with or without postmark. Most copies are becoming discolored, probably from the adhesive. The Catalogue value is for discolored copies.

Die cutting includes crossed slashes through dove, applied to prevent removal and re-use of the stamp. The stamp will separate into layers if soaked.

Two different machines were used to roulette the sheet.

AMERICAN ARTS ISSUE

Benjamin West (1738-1820), painter (No. 1553); Paul Laurence Dunbar (1872-1906), poet (No. 1554); David (Lewelyn) Wark Griffith (1875-1948), motion picture producer (No. 1555).

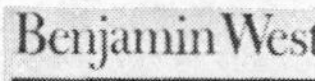

Self-portrait — A956

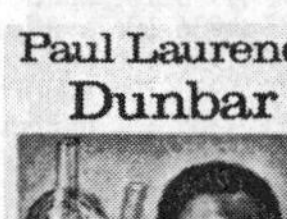

A957

A958

Designed by Bradbury Thompson (No. 1553); Walter D. Richards (No. 1554); Fred Otnes (No. 1555).

PHOTOGRAVURE (Andreotti)

Plates of 200 subjects in four panes of 50 each.

1975 **Tagged** ***Perf. 10½x11***

1553 A956 10c **multicolored,** *Feb. 10* 18 5
Margin block of 10, 5 P# 1.85 —
Margin block of 4, Mr. Zip and "Use Zip Code" 75 —
Margin block of 6, "Mail Early in the Day" 1.10 —

Perf. 11

1554 A957 10c **multicolored,** *May 1* 18 5
Margin block of 10, 5 P# 1.85 —
Margin block of 4, Mr. Zip and "Use Zip Code" 75 —
Margin block of 6, "Mail Early in the Day" 1.10 —
a. Imperf., pair *1,100.*

LITHOGRAPHED, ENGRAVED (Giori)

Perf. 11

1555 A958 10c **brown & multicolored,** *May 27* 18 5
Margin block of 4, P# 80 —
Margin block of 4, Mr. Zip and "Use Zip Code" 75 —
Margin block of 6, "Mail Early in the Day" 1.10 —
a. Brown (engraved) omitted *900.00*

SPACE ISSUES

U.S. space accomplishments with unmanned craft. Pioneer 10 passed with 81,000 miles of Jupiter, Dec. 10, 1973. Mariner 10 explored Venus and Mercury in 1974 and Mercury again in 1975.

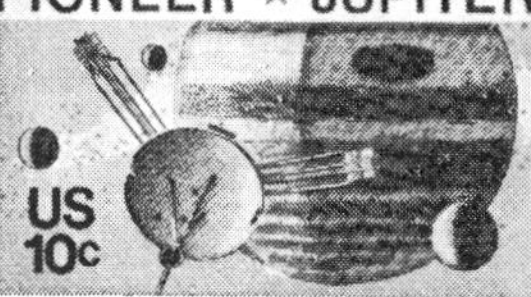

Pioneer 10 Passing Jupiter — A959

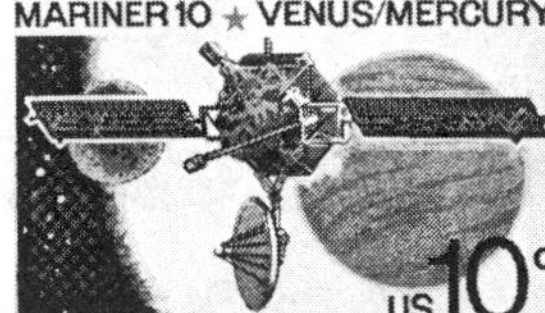

Mariner 10, Venus and Mercury — A960

Designed by Robert McCall (No. 1556); Roy Gjertson (No. 1557).

LITHOGRAPHED, ENGRAVED (Giori)
Plates of 200 subjects in four panes of 50 each.

1975 **Tagged** ***Perf. 11***

1556 A959 10c **violet blue, yellow & red,** *Feb. 28* 18 5
Margin block of 4, P# 80 —
Margin block of 4, Mr. Zip and "Use Zip Code" 75 —
Margin block of 6, "Mail Early in the Day" 1.10 —
a. Red & yellow (litho.) omitted *1,450.*
b. Blue omitted *1,100.*
1557 A960 10c **black, red, ultra. & bister,** *Apr. 4* 18 5
Margin block of 4, P# 80 —
Margin block of 4, Mr. Zip and "Use Zip Code" 75 —
Margin block of 6, "Mail Early in the Day" 1.10 —
a. Red omitted *600.00*
b. Ultra. & bister omitted *1,900.*

COLLECTIVE BARGAINING ISSUE

Collective Bargaining law, enacted 1935, in Wagner Act.

"Labor and Management" A961

Designed by Robert Hallock.

PHOTOGRAVURE (Andreotti)
Plates of 200 subjects in four panes of 50 each.

1975, Mar. 13 **Tagged** ***Perf. 11***

1558 A961 10c **multicolored** 18 5
Margin block of 8, 4 P# 1.60 —
Margin block of 4, Mr. Zip and "Use Zip Code" 75 —
Margin block of 6, "Mail Early in the Day" 1.10 —

Imperforates exist from printer's waste.

AMERICAN BICENTENNIAL ISSUE
Contributors to the Cause

Sybil Ludington, age 16, rallied militia, Apr. 26, 1777; Salem Poor, black freeman, fought in Battle of Bunker Hill; Haym Salomon, Jewish immigrant, raised money to finance Revolutionary War; Peter Francisco, Portuguese-French immigrant, joined Continental Army at 15. Emerald inscription on back, printed beneath gum in water-soluble ink, gives thumbnail sketch of portrayed contributor.

Sybil Ludington A962

Salem Poor — A963

Haym Salomon — A964

Peter Francisco — A965

Designed by Neil Boyle.

PHOTOGRAVURE (Andreotti)
Plates of 200 subjects in four panes of 50 each.

1975, Mar. 25 **Tagged** ***Perf. 11x10½***

1559 A962 8c **multicolored** 16 13
Margin block of 10, 5 P# 1.65 —
Margin block of 4, Mr. Zip and "Use Zip Code" 65 —
Margin block of 6, "Mail Early in the Day" 1.00 —
a. Back inscriptions omitted *200.00*
1560 A963 10c **multicolored** 18 5
Margin block of 10, 5 P# 1.85 —
Margin block of 4, Mr. Zip and "Use Zip Code" 75 —
Margin block of 6, "Mail Early in the Day" 1.10 —
a. Back inscription omitted *325.00*
1561 A964 10c **multicolored** 18 5
Margin block of 10, 5 P# 1.85 —
Margin block of 4, Mr. Zip and "Use Zip Code" 75 —
Margin block of 6, "Mail Early in the Day" 1.10 —
a. Back inscription omitted *300.00*
b. Red omitted *275.00*
1562 A965 18c **multicolored** 35 20
Margin block of 10, 5 P# 3.60 —
Margin block of 4, Mr. Zip and "Use Zip Code" 1.45 —
Margin block of 6, "Mail Early in the Day" 2.15 —

Lexington-Concord Battle

Bicentenary of the Battle of Lexington and Concord.

"Birth of Liberty," by Henry Sandham — A966

Designed by Bradbury Thompson.

PHOTOGRAVURE (Andreotti)
Plates of 160 subjects in four panes of 40 each.

1975, Apr. 19 **Tagged** ***Perf. 11***

1563 A966 10c **multicolored** 18 5
Margin block of 12, 6 P# 2.20 —
Margin block of 4, Mr. Zip, "Use Zip Code" and "Mail Early in the Day" 75 —
Margin block of 16, 6 P#, Mr. Zip and slogans 3.00 —
a. Vert. pair, imperf. horiz. *450.00*

Bunker Hill Battle

Bicentenary of the Battle of Bunker Hill.

See the "Information for Collectors" section at beginning of catalogue for information on electric eye markings, luminescene and tagging.

Battle of Bunker Hill, by John Trumbull — A967

Designed by Bradbury Thompson.

PHOTOGRAVURE (Andreotti)
Plates of 160 subjects in four panes of 40 each.

1975, June 17 **Tagged** ***Perf. 11***

1564 A967 10c **multicolored** 18 5
Margin block of 12, 6 P# 2.20 —
Margin block of 4, Mr. Zip, "Use Zip Code" and "Mail Early in the Day" 75 —
Margin block of 16, 6 P#, Mr. Zip and slogans 3.00 —

Military Uniforms

Bicentenary of U.S. Military Services. Nos. 1565-1568 are printed in blocks of four in panes of 50. Nos. 1565-1566 alternate in one row, Nos. 1567-1568 in next row.

Soldier with Flintlock Musket, Uniform Button — A968

Sailor with Grappling Hook, First Navy Jack, 1775 — A969

Marine with Musket, Fullrigged Ship — A970

Militaman with Musket and Powder Horn — A971

Designed by Edward Vebell.

PHOTOGRAVURE (Andreotti)
Plates of 200 subjects in four panes of 50 each.

1975, July 4 **Tagged** ***Perf. 11***

1565 A968 10c **multicolored** 18 8
Margin block of 12, 6 P# adjoining Nos. 1565-1566 2.30 —
Margin block of 20, 6 P# adjoining Nos. 1565-1566, Mr. Zip and slogans 4.00 —
Margin block of 4, Mr. Zip and "Use Zip Code" adjoining No. 1565 80 —
Margin block of 4, "Mail Early in the Day" adjoining No. 1565 80 —
1566 A969 10c **multicolored** 18 8
Margin block of 4, Mr. Zip and "Use Zip Code" adjoining No. 1566 80 —
Margin block of 4, "Mail Early in the Day" adjoining No. 1566 80 —
1567 A970 10c **multicolored** 18 8
Margin block of 12, 6 P# adjoining Nos. 1567-1568 2.30 —
Margin block of 20, 6 P# adjoining Nos. 1567-1568, Mr. Zip and slogans 4.00 —

Margin block of 4, Mr. Zip and "Use Zip Code" adjoining No. 1567 — 80 —
Margin block of 4, "Mail Early in the Day" adjoining No. 1567 — 80 —

1568 A971 10c **multicolored** — 18 8
Margin block of 4, Mr. Zip and "Use Zip Code" adjoining No. 1568 — 80 —
Margin block of 4, "Mail Early in the Day" adjoining No. 1568 — 80 —
a. Block of 4, #1565-1568 — 75 75

APOLLO SOYUZ SPACE ISSUE

Apollo Soyuz space test project, Russo-American cooperation, launched July 15; link-up, July 17. Nos. 1569-1570 are printed se-tenant in horizontal rows of 3 in panes of 24. In the first row of the pane No. 1569 is in first and third space, No. 1570 is second space; in the second row No. 1570 is in first and third space, No. 1569 in second space, etc.

Participating U.S. and U.S.S.R. crews: Thomas P. Stafford, Donald K. Slayton, Vance D. Brand, Aleksei A. Leonov, Valery N. Kubasov.

See Russia Nos. 4339-4340.

Apollo and Soyuz after Link-up, and Earth — A972

Spacecraft before Link-up, Earth and Project Emblem — A973

Designed by Robert McCall (No. 1569) and Anatoly M. Aksamit of USSR (No. 1570).

PHOTOGRAVURE (Andreotti)
Plates of 96 subjects in four panes of 24 each.

1975, July 15 **Tagged** ***Perf. 11***

1569 A972 10c **multicolored** — 18 10
a. Pair, #1569-1570 — 36 25
Margin block of 12, 6 P# — 2.20 —
Margin block of 4, Mr. Zip, "Use Zip Code" adjoining No. 1569; "Mail Early in the Day" adjoining No. 1570 — 75 —
Margin block of 16, 6 P#, Mr. Zip "Use Zip Code" adjoining No. 1569, "Mail Early in the Day" adjoining No. 1570 — 3.00 —
b. As "a," vert. pair imperf. horiz. — *900.00*
Pair with full horiz. gutter btwn. — —

1570 A973 10c **multicolored** — 18 10
Margin block of 4, Mr. Zip, "Use Zip Code" adjoining No. 1570; "Mail Early in the Day" adjoining No. 1569 — 75 —
Margin block of 16, 6 P#, Mr. Zip, "Use Zip Code" adjoining No. 1570, "Mail Early in the Day" adjoining No. 1569 — 3.00 —

INTERNATIONAL WOMEN'S YEAR ISSUE

International Women's Year 1975.

Worldwide Equality for Women — A974

Designed by Miriam Schottland.

PHOTOGRAVURE (Andreotti)
Plates of 200 subjects in four panes of 50 each.

1975, Aug. 26 **Tagged** ***Perf. 11x10½***

1571 A974 10c **blue, orange & dark blue** — 18 5
Margin block of 6, 3 P# — 1.15 —
Margin block of 4, Mr. Zip and "Use Zip Code" — 75 —
Margin block of 6, "Mail Early in the Day" — 1.10 —

U.S. POSTAL SERVICE BICENTENNIAL ISSUE

Nos. 1572-1575 are printed in blocks of four in panes of 50. Nos. 1572-1573 alternate in first row, Nos. 1574-1575 in second row. This arrangement is repeated throughout the pane.

Stagecoach and Trailer Truck — A975

Old and New Locomotives A976

Early Mail Plane and Jet — A977

Satellite for Transmission of Mailgrams A978

Designed by James L. Womer.

PHOTOGRAVURE (Andreotti)
Plates of 200 subjects in four panes of 50 each.

1975, Sept. 3 **Tagged** ***Perf. 11x10½***

1572 A975 10c **multicolored** — 18 8
Margin block of 12, 6 P# adjoining Nos. 1572, 1574 — 2.30 —
Margin block of 20, 6 P# adjoining Nos. 1572, 1574, Mr. Zip and slogans — 4.00 —
Margin block of 4, Mr. Zip and "Use Zip Code" adjoining No. 1572 — 80 —
Margin block of 4, "Mail Early in the Day" adjoining No. 1572 — 80 —

1573 A976 10c **multicolored** — 18 8
Margin block of 12, 6 P# adjoining Nos. 1573, 1575 — 2.30 —
Margin block of 20, 6 P# adjoining Nos. 1573, 1575, Mr. Zip and slogans — 4.00 —
Margin block of 4, Mr. Zip and "Use Zip Code" adjoining No. 1573 — 80 —
Margin block of 4, "Mail Early in the Day" adjoining No. 1573 — 80 —

1574 A977 10c **multicolored** — 18 8
Margin block of 4, Mr. Zip and "Use Zip Code" adjoining No. 1574 — 80 —
Margin block of 4, "Mail Early in the Day" adjoining No. 1574 — 80 —

1575 A978 10c **multicolored** — 18 8
Margin block of 4, Mr. Zip and "Use Zip Code" adjoining No. 1575 — 80 —
Margin block of 4, "Mail Early in the Day" adjoining No. 1575 — 80 —
a. Block of 4, #1572-1575 — 75 75
b. As "a," red "10c" omitted — —

WORLD PEACE THROUGH LAW ISSUE

A prelude to 7th World Law Conference of the World Peace Through Law Center at Washington, D.C., Oct. 12-17.

Law Book, Gavel, Olive Branch and Globe — A979

Designed by Melbourne Brindle.

GIORI PRESS PRINTING
Plates of 200 subjects in four panes of 50 each.

1975, Sept. 29 **Tagged** ***Perf. 11***

1576 A979 10c **green, Prussian blue & rose brown** — 18 5
Margin block of 4, P# — 80 —
Margin block of 4, Mr. Zip and "Use Zip Code" — 75 —
Margin block of 6, "Mail Early in the Day" — 1.10 —

BANKING AND COMMERCE ISSUE

Banking and commerce in the U.S., and for the Centennial Convention of the American Bankers Association.

Engine Turning, Indian Head Penny, Morgan-type Silver Dollar — A980

Seated Liberty Quarter, $20 Gold Double Eagle and Engine Turning — A981

LITHOGRAPHED, ENGRAVED (Giori)
Plates of 160 subjects in four panes of 40 each.

1975, Oct. 6 ***Perf. 11***

1577 A980 10c **multicolored** — 18 8
a. Pair, #1577-1578 — 36 20
b. Brown & blue (litho) omitted — *1,250.*
Margin block of 4, P# adjoining #1577 — 80 —
Margin block of 4, Mr. Zip and "Use Zip Code" adjoining #1577 — 75 —
Margin block of 6, "Mail Early in the Day" adjoining #1577 — 1.10 —

1578 A981 10c **multicolored** — 18 8
Margin block of 4, P# adjoining #1578 — 80 —
Margin block of 4, Mr. Zip and "Use Zip Code" adjoining #1578 — 75 —
Margin block of 6, "Mail Early in the Day" adjoining #1578 — 1.10 —

CHRISTMAS ISSUE

Madonna and Child, by Domenico Ghirlandaio A982

Christmas Card, by Louis Prang, 1878 A983

Designed by Steven Dohanos.

PHOTOGRAVURE (Andreotti)
Plates of 200 subjects in four panes of 50 each.

1975, Oct. 14 **Tagged** ***Perf. 11***
1579 A982 (10c) **multicolored** 18 5
Margin block of 12, 6 P# 2.20 —
Margin block of 4, Mr. Zip and "Use Zip Code" 75 —
Margin block of 4, "Mail Early in the Day" 75 —
a. Imperf., pair *100.00*
Plate flaw ("d" damaged) (36741-36746 LL 47) 5.00 —
1580 A983 (10c) **multicolored,** perf. 11.2 18 5
Margin block of 12, 6 P# 2.20 —
Margin block of 4, Mr. Zip and "Use Zip Code" 75 —
Margin block of 4, "Mail Early in the Day" 75 —
Perf. 10.9 25 5
a. Imperf., pair *105.00*
b. Perf. 10½x11 60 5
b. Margin block of 12, 6 P# 7.25 —

AMERICANA ISSUE

Inkwell and Quill — A984

Speaker's Stand — A985

Early Ballot Box A987

Books, Bookmark, Eyeglasses A988

Dome of Capitol — A994

Contemplation of Justice, by J. E. Fraser — A995

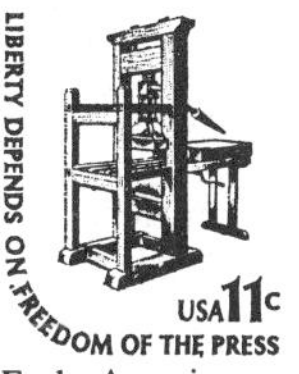

Early American Printing Press — A996

Torch, Statue of Liberty — A997

Liberty Bell — A998

Eagle and Shield — A999

Fort McHenry Flag (15 Stars) — A1001

Head, Statue of Liberty — A1002

Old North Church, Boston — A1006

Fort Nisqually, Wash. — A1007

Sandy Hook Lighthouse, N.J. — A1008

Morris Township School No. 2, Devils Lake — A1009

Iron "Betty" Lamp, Plymouth Colony, 17th-18th Centuries A1011

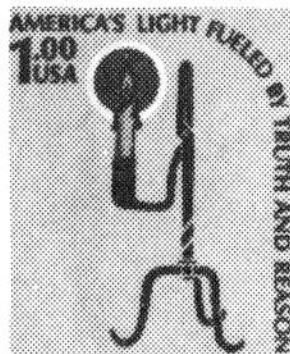

Rush Lamp and Candle Holder A1013

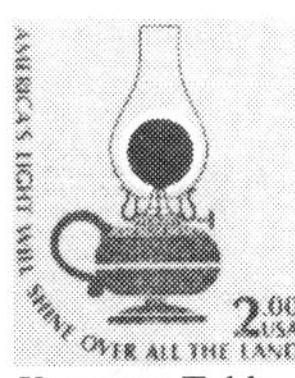

Kerosene Table Lamp — A1013a

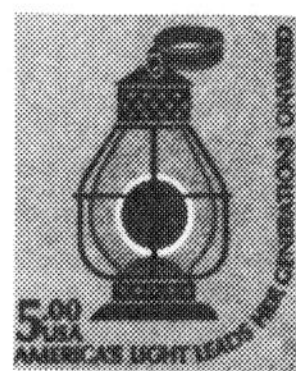

Railroad Conductor's Lantern, c. 1850 — A1014

ROTARY PRESS PRINTING
E.E. Plates of 400 subjects in four panes of 100 each.

1975-81 **Tagged** ***Perf. 11x10½***
Size: 18½x22½mm
1581 A984 1c **dark blue,** *greenish, Dec. 8, 1977* 5 5
Margin block of 4, P# 25 —
Margin block of 4, "Use Zip Code" 22 —
Margin block of 6, "Mail Early in the Day" 32 —
Dull finish gum 8
Pair with full vert. gutter btwn. —
a. Untagged (Bureau precanceled) 5
1582 A985 2c **red brown,** *greenish, Dec. 8, 1977* 5 5
Margin block of 4, P# 25 —
Margin block of 4, "Use Zip Code" 22 —
Margin block of 6, "Mail Early in the Day" 32 —
Dull finish gum 9
a. Untagged (Bureau precanceled) 6
b. Cream paper, dull finish gum, *1981* 5 5
1584 A987 3c **olive,** *greenish, Dec. 8, 1977* 6 5
Margin block of 4, P# 28 —
Margin block of 4, "Use Zip Code" 25 —
Margin block of 6, "Mail Early in the Day" 38 —
Dull finish gum 8
Pair with full horiz. gutter btwn. —
a. Untagged (Bureau precanceled) 6
1585 A988 4c **rose magenta,** *cream, Dec. 8, 1977* 8 5
Margin block of 4, P# 38 —
Margin block of 4, "Use Zip Code" 35 —
Margin block of 6, "Mail Early in the Day" 50 —

Dull finish gum 14
a. Untagged (Bureau precanceled) 8

Size: 17½x20½mm
1590 A994 9c **slate green** (from bklt. pane), *Mar. 11, 1977* 45 20
a. Perf. 10 (from bklt. pane) 17.00 10.00

Size: 18½x22½mm
1591 A994 9c **slate green,** *gray, Nov. 24, 1975* 16 5
Margin block of 4, P# 70 —
Margin block of 4, "Use Zip Code" 65 —
Margin block of 6, "Mail Early in the Day" 1.00 —
Dull finish gum 1.00
a. Untagged (Bureau precanceled) 18
1592 A995 10c **violet,** *gray, Nov. 17, 1977* 18 5
Margin block of 4, P# 90 —
Margin block of 4, "Use Zip Code" 75 —
Margin block of 6, "Mail Early in the Day" 1.10 —
Dull finish gum 24
a. Untagged (Bureau precanceled, Chicago, IL) 25
1593 A996 11c **orange,** *gray, Nov. 13, 1975* 20 5
Margin block of 4, P# 90 —
Margin block of 4, "Use Zip Code" 85 —
Margin block of 6, "Mail Early in the Day" 1.25 —
Pair with full horiz. gutter btwn. —
1594 A997 12c **red brown,** *beige, Apr. 8, 1981* 22 5
P# block of 4 1.25 —
Zip block of 4 90 —
Mail Early block of 6 1.35 —
1595 A998 13c **brown** (from bklt. pane), *Oct. 31, 1975* 26 5
a. Booklet pane of 6 1.90 *50*
b. Booklet pane of 7 + label 2.00 *50*
c. Booklet pane of 8 2.25 *50*
d. Booklet pane of 5 + label, *Apr. 2, 1976* 1.30 *50*
e. Vert. pair, imperf. btwn. —

PHOTOGRAVURE (Andreotti)
Plates of 400 subjects in four panes of 100 each.
1596 A999 13c **multicolored,** *Dec. 1, 1975* 26 5
Margin block of 12, 6 P# 3.25 —
Margin block of 20, 6 P# and slogans 5.50 —
Margin block of 4, "Use Zip Code" 1.05 —
Margin block of 4, "Mail Early in the Day" 1.05 —
a. Imperf., pair *45.00* —
b. Yellow omitted *175.00*
Line perforated — —
Pair with full horiz. gutter btwn. —

No. 1596 perforation measures close to 11¼. The entire sheet is perforated at one time so the perforations meet perfectly at the corners of the stamp. The line perforations do not line up perfectly and are perf. 11.

ENGRAVED (Combination Press)
Plates of 460 subjects (20x23) in panes of 100 (10x10)
1597 A1001 15c **gray, dark blue & red,** *June 30, 1978* 28 5
Margin block of 6, P# 1.75 —
Margin block of 20, 1 or 2 P# 6.00 —
a. Imperf., vert. pair *17.50*
b. Gray omitted —

Plate number appears 3 times on each plate of 23 rows. With no separating gutters, each pane has only left or right sheet margin. Plate numbers appear on both margins; there are no slogans. Margin blocks of 20 have one or two plate numbers.

ENGRAVED
1598 A1001 15c **gray, dark blue & red** (from bklt. pane), *June 30, 1978* 30 5
a. Booklet pane of 8 3.50 *60*
1599 A1002 16c **blue,** *Mar. 31, 1978* 34 5
Margin block of 4, P# 1.90 —
Margin block of 4, "Use Correct Zip Code" 1.40 —
Margin block of 4, copyright 1.40 —
1603 A1006 24c **red,** *blue, Nov. 14, 1975* 45 9
Margin block of 4, P# 1.90 —
Margin block of 4, "Use Zip Code" 1.85 —
Margin block of 6, "Mail Early in the Day" 2.75 —
1604 A1007 28c **brown,** *blue, Aug. 11, 1978* 55 8
Margin block of 4, P# 2.30 —
Margin block of 4, "Use Correct Zip Code" 2.25 —
Margin block of 4, copyright 2.25 —
Dull finish gum 1.50
1605 A1008 29c **blue,** *light blue, Apr. 14, 1978* 55 8
Margin block of 4, P# 2.60 —
Margin block of 4, "Use Correct Zip Code" 2.25 —
Margin block of 4, copyright 2.25 —
Dull finish gum 3.00
1606 A1009 30c **green,** *blue, Aug. 27, 1979* 55 8
Margin block of 4, P# 2.30 —
Margin block of 4, "Use Correct Zip Code" 2.30 —
Margin block of 4, "United States Postal Service 1979" 2.25 —

Perf. 11

LITHOGRAPHED AND ENGRAVED

1608	A1011	50c **tan, black & orange,** *Sept. 11, 1979*	95	15
		Margin block of 4, P#	4.00	—
		Margin block of 4, "Use Correct Zip Code"	3.90	—
		Margin block of 4, "United States Postal Service 1979"	3.90	—
a.		Black omitted	—	
1610	A1013	$1 **tan, brown, orange & yellow,** *July 2, 1979*	1.75	20
		Margin block of 4, P#	7.50	—
		Margin block of 4, "Use Correct Zip Code"	7.25	—
		Margin block of 4, "United States Postal Service 1979"	7.25	—
a.		Brown (engraved) omitted	*400.00*	
b.		Tan, orange & yellow omitted	*425.00*	
c.		Brown inverted	—	
1611	A1013a	$2 **tan, dark green, orange & yellow,** *Nov. 16, 1978*	3.75	45
		Margin block of 4, P#	15.50	—
		Margin block of 4, "Use Correct Zip Code"	15.25	—
		Margin block of 4, "United States Postal Service 1978"	15.25	—
1612	A1014	$5 **tan, red brown, yellow & orange,** *Aug. 23, 1979*	9.00	1.50
		Margin block of 4, P#	37.50	—
		Margin block of 4, "Use Correct Zip Code"	36.50	—
		Margin block of 4, "United States Postal Service 1979"	36.50	—

Nos. 1590, 1590a, 1595, 1598, 1623 and 1623b were issued only in booklets. All stamps have one or two straight edges.

Bureau Precancels: 1c, 3 diff., 2c, Chicago, Greensboro, NC, 3c, 6 diff., 4c, Chicago, lines only, No. 1591, 4 diff., No. 1596, 5 diff., 50c, lines only, $1, lines only.

Six-string Guitar A1014a

Saxhorns A1015

Drum — A1016

Steinway Grand Piano, 1857 — A1017

Designers: 3.1c, George Mercer. 7.7c, Susan Robb. 7.9c, Bernard Glassman. 10c, Walter Brooks. 15c, V. Jack Ruther.

COIL STAMPS

1975-79 *Perf. 10 Vertically*

1613	A1014a	3.1c **brown,** *yellow, Oct. 25, 1979*	14	5
		Pair	28	10
		Joint line pair	1.50	—
a.		Untagged (Bureau precanceled, lines only)		40
b.		Imperf., pair	*1,000.*	
1614	A1015	7.7c **brown,** *bright yellow, Nov. 20, 1976*	18	8
		Pair	36	16
		Joint line pair	1.00	—
a.		Untagged (Bureau precanceled)		35
b.		As "a," imperf., pair		*1,100.*

A total of 159 different Bureau precancels were used by 153 cities.

No. 1614b is precanceled Washington, DC. Also exists from Marion, OH.

1615	A1016	7.9c **carmine,** *yellow, Apr. 23, 1976*	15	8
		Pair	30	16
		Joint line pair	65	—
		Dull finish gum	32	
a.		Untagged (Bureau precanceled)		16
b.		Imperf., pair	*700.00*	

A total of 108 different Bureau precancels were used by 107 cities.

1615C	A1017	8.4c **dark blue,** *yellow, July 13, 1978*	22	8
		Pair	44	16
		Joint line pair	3.25	30
d.		Untagged (Bureau precanceled)		16
e.		As "d," pair, imperf. between		60.00
f.		As "d," imperf., pair		25.00

A total of 145 different Bureau precancels were used by 144 cities.

No. 1615e is precanceled with lines only. No. 1615f is precanceled Newark, NJ. Also exists from Brownstown, Ind., Oklahoma City, Okla. and with lines only.

1616	A994	9c **slate green,** *gray, Mar. 5, 1976*	20	5
		Pair	40	10
		Joint line pair	90	—
a.		Imperf., pair	*110.00*	
b.		Untagged (Bureau precanceled)		28
c.		As "b," imperf., pair		*190.00*

No. 1616c is precanceled Pleasantville, NY.

1617	A995	10c **violet,** *gray, Nov. 4, 1977*	24	5
		Pair	48	10
		Joint line pair	1.10	—
		Dull finish gum	20	
a.		Untagged (Bureau precanceled)		25
b.		Imperf., pair	*60.00*	
1618	A998	13c **brown,** *Nov. 25, 1975*	25	5
		Pair	50	10
		Joint line pair	60	—
		Dull finish gum	30	
a.		Untagged (Bureau precanceled)		38
b.		Imperf., pair	25.00	
g.		Pair, imperf. between	—	
1618C	A1001	15c **gray, dark blue & red,** *June 30, 1978*	40	5
		Pair	80	10
d.		Imperf., pair	20.00	
e.		Pair, imperf. between	200.00	
f.		gray omitted	*40.00*	
1619	A1002	16c **ultramarine,** *Mar. 31, 1978*	32	5
		Pair	65	10
		Joint line pair	1.50	—
		Huck press printing	50	10
		Huck press, pair	1.00	25

No. 1619 was printed on two different presses. Huck press printings have white background without bluish tinge, are a fraction of a millimeter smaller and have block instead of overall tagging. Cottrell press printings show a joint line.

Nos. 1615a, 1615d, 1616b, 1617a, 1618a, issued aslo with dull finish gum.

Bureau Precancels: 9c, 6 diff., 10c, 3 diff., 13c, 11 diff.

See Nos. 1811, 1813, 1816.

13-Star Flag over Independence Hall A1018

Flag over Capitol A1018a

Designers: No. 1622, Melbourne Brindle. No. 1623, Esther Porter.

Panes of 100 (10x10) each.

1975-81 *Perf. 11x10½*

1622	A1018	13c **dark blue & red,** *Nov. 15, 1975*	24	5
		Margin block of 20, 2-3 P#, 2-3 Zip, 2-3 Mail Early	5.75	—
a.		Horiz. pair, imperf. between	55.00	
b.		Imperf., pair	—	
c.		Perf. 11, *1981*	52	5
c.		Margin block of 20, 1-2 P#, 1-2 Zip	*50.00*	—
c.		Margin block of 6, P#	*15.00*	—
d.		As "c," vert. pair, imperf.	—	

No. 1622 was printed on the Multicolored Huck Press. Plate markings are at top or bottom of pane. See note after No. 1338F for marginal markings.

No. 1622c was printed on the Combination Press. Plate markings are at sides of pane. See note after No. 1703.

No. 1622 has overall tagging and nearly vertical multiple gum ridges. No. 1622c has block tagging and flat gum.

Engr.

1623	A1018a	13c **blue & red** (from bklt. pane), *Mar. 11, 1977*	24	5
a.		Booklet pane of 8 (1 #1590 + 7 #1623)	2.50	*60*
b.		Perf. 10 (from bklt. pane)	1.10	1.00
c.		Booklet pane of 8, perf. 10 (1 #1590a + 7 #1623b)	30.00	—
d.		Se-tenant pair, #1590 & #1623	75	—
e.		Se-tenant pair, #1590a & #1623b	19.00	

COIL STAMP

1975, Nov. 15 *Perf. 10 Vertically*

1625	A1018	13c **dark blue & red**	30	5
		Pair	60	10
a.		Imperf., pair	20.00	

AMERICAN BICENTENNIAL ISSUE

The Spirit of '76

Designed after painting by Archibald M. Willard in Abbot Hall, Marblehead, Massachusetts. Nos. 1629-1631 printed se-tenant in panes of 50 (10x5). Left panes contain 3 No. 1631a and one No. 1629; right panes contain one No. 1631 and 3 No. 1631a.

Drummer Boy A1019

Old Drummer A1020

Fifer — A1021

Designed by Vincent E. Hoffman.

PHOTOGRAVURE (Andreotti)

Plates of 200 subjects in four panes of 50 each.

1976, Jan. 1 **Tagged** *Perf. 11*

1629	A1019	13c **blue violet & multi.**	25	8
1630	A1020	13c **blue violet & multi.**	25	8
1631	A1021	13c **blue violet & multi.**	25	8
a.		Strip of 3, #1629-1631	75	60
b.		As "a," imperf.	*1,500.*	
c.		Imperf., vert. pair, #1631	*1,000.*	
		Margin block of 12, 5 P#	3.10	—
		Margin block of 20, 5 P# and slogans	5.25	—

INTERPHIL ISSUE

Interphil 76 International Philatelic Exhibition, Philadelphia, Pa., May 29-June 6.

"Interphil 76" — A1022

Designed by Terrence W. McCaffrey.

LITHOGRAPHED, ENGRAVED (Giori)

Plates of 200 subjects of four panes of 50 each.

1976, Jan. 17 **Tagged** *Perf. 11*

1632	A1022	13c **dark blue, red & ultra.**	24	5
		Margin block of 4, P#	1.05	—
		Margin block of 4, Mr. Zip and "Use Zip Code"	1.00	—
		Margin block of 6, "Mail Early in the Day"	1.50	—

Scott's editorial staff cannot undertake to identify, authenticate or appraise stamps and postal markings.

Designed by Walt Reed.

PHOTOGRAVURE (Andreotti)
Plates of 200 subjects in four panes of 50 each.

1976, Feb. 23	**Tagged**	***Perf. 11***
1633 A1023 13c *Delaware*		24 20
1634 A1024 13c *Pennsylvania*		24 20
1635 A1025 13c *New Jersey*		24 20
1636 A1026 13c *Georgia*		24 20
1637 A1027 13c *Connecticut*		24 20
1638 A1028 13c *Massachusetts*		24 20
1639 A1029 13c *Maryland*		24 20
1640 A1030 13c *South Carolina*		24 20
1641 A1031 13c *New Hampshire*		24 20
1642 A1032 13c *Virginia*		24 20
1643 A1033 13c *New York*		24 20
1644 A1034 13c *North Carolina*		24 20
1645 A1035 13c *Rhode Island*		24 20
1646 A1036 13c *Vermont*		24 20
1647 A1037 13c *Kentucky*		24 20
1648 A1038 13c *Tennessee*		24 20
1649 A1039 13c *Ohio*		24 20
1650 A1040 13c *Louisiana*		24 20
1651 A1041 13c *Indiana*		24 20
1652 A1042 13c *Mississippi*		24 20
1653 A1043 13c *Illinois*		24 20
1654 A1044 13c *Alabama*		24 20
1655 A1045 13c *Maine*		24 20
1656 A1046 13c *Missouri*		24 20
1657 A1047 13c *Arkansas*		24 20
1658 A1048 13c *Michigan*		24 20
1659 A1049 13c *Florida*		24 20
1660 A1050 13c *Texas*		24 20
1661 A1051 13c *Iowa*		24 20
1662 A1052 13c *Wisconsin*		24 20
1663 A1053 13c *California*		24 20
1664 A1054 13c *Minnesota*		24 20
1665 A1055 13c *Oregon*		24 20
1666 A1056 13c *Kansas*		24 20
1667 A1057 13c *West Virginia*		24 20
1668 A1058 13c *Nevada*		24 20
1669 A1059 13c *Nebraska*		24 20
1670 A1060 13c *Colorado*		24 20
1671 A1061 13c *North Dakota*		24 20
1672 A1062 13c *South Dakota*		24 20
1673 A1063 13c *Montana*		24 20
1674 A1064 13c *Washington*		24 20
1675 A1065 13c *Idaho*		24 20
1676 A1066 13c *Wyoming*		24 20
1677 A1067 13c *Utah*		24 20
1678 A1068 13c *Oklahoma*		24 20
1679 A1069 13c *New Mexico*		24 20
1680 A1070 13c *Arizona*		24 20
1681 A1071 13c *Alaska*		24 20
1682 A1072 13c *Hawaii*		24 20
a. Pane of 50		12.00 —
Pane of 50, 6 P# adjoining Nos. 1633, 1638, 1643, 1648, 1653, 1658; "Mail Early in the Day" adjoining No. 1663, Mr. Zip and "Use Zip Code" adjoining No. 1678		12.00
Pane of 50, 6 P# adjoining Nos. 1637, 1642, 1647, 1652, 1657, 1662; "Mail Early in the Day" adjoining No. 1667, Mr. Zip and "Use Zip Code" adjoining No. 1682		12.00
Pane of 50, 6 P# adjoining Nos. 1653, 1658, 1663, 1668, 1673, 1678 "Mail Early in the Day" adjoining No. 1648, Mr. Zip and "Use Zip Code" adjoining No. 1633		12.00
Pane of 50, 6 P# adjoining Nos. 1657, 1662, 1667, 1672, 1677, 1682; "Mail Early in the Day" adjoining No. 1652, Mr. Zip and "Use Zip Code" adjoining No. 1637		12.00

TELEPHONE CENTENNIAL ISSUE

Centenary of first telephone call by Alexander Graham Bell, March 10, 1876.

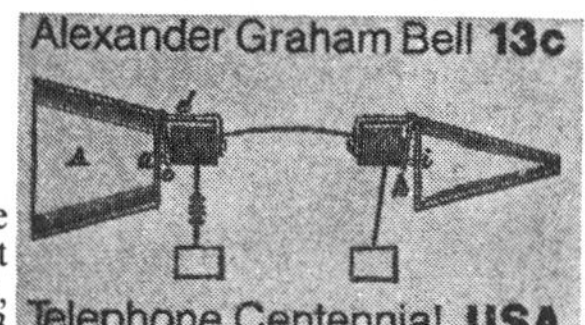

Bell's Telephone Patent Application, 1876 — A1073

Designed by George Tscherny.

ENGRAVED (Giori)
Plates of 200 subjects in four panes of 50 each.

1976, Mar. 10	**Tagged**	***Perf. 11***
1683 A1073 13c **black, purple & red,** *tan*		24 5
Margin block of 4, P#		1.05 —
Margin block of 4, Mr. Zip and "Use Zip Code"		1.00 —
Margin block of 6, "Mail Early in the Day"		1.50 —

COMMERCIAL AVIATION ISSUE

50th anniversary of first contract airmail flights: Dearborn, Mich. to Cleveland, Ohio, Feb. 15, 1926; and Pasco, Wash. to Elko, Nev., Apr. 6, 1926.

Ford-Pullman Monoplane and Laird Swallow Biplane — A1074

Designed by Robert E. Cunningham.

PHOTOGRAVURE (Andreotti)
Plates of 200 subjects in four panes of 50 each

1976, Mar. 19	**Tagged**	***Perf. 11***
1684 A1074 13c **blue & multicolored**		24 5
Margin block of 10, 5 P#		2.50 —
Margin block of 4, Mr. Zip and "Use Zip Code"		1.00 —
Margin block of 6, "Mail Early in the Day"		1.50 —

CHEMISTRY ISSUE

Honoring American chemists, in conjunction with the centenary of the American Chemical Society.

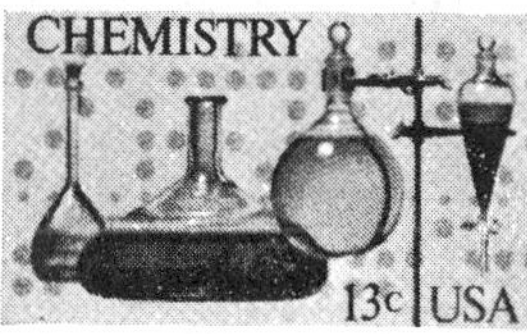

Various Flasks, Separatory Funnel, Computer Tape — A1075

Designed by Ken Davies.

PHOTOGRAVURE (Andreotti)
Plates of 200 subjects in four panes of 50 each.

1976, Apr. 6	**Tagged**	***Perf. 11***
1685 A1075 13c **multicolored**		24 5
Margin block of 12, 6 P#		3.00 —
Margin block of 4, Mr. Zip and "Use Zip Code"		1.00 —
Margin block of 4, "Mail Early in the Day"		1.00 —
Pair with full vert. gutter btwn.		—

AMERICAN BICENTENNIAL ISSUES
SOUVENIR SHEETS

Designs, from Left to Right, No. 1686: a. Two British officers. b. Gen. Benjamin Lincoln. c. George Washington. d. John Trumbull, Col. Cobb, von Steuben, Lafayette, Thomas Nelson. e. Alexander Hamilton, John Laurens, Walter Stewart (all vert.).

No. 1687: a. John Adams, Roger Sherman, Robert R. Livingston. b. Jefferson, Franklin. c. Thomas Nelson, Jr., Francis Lewis, John Witherspoon, Samuel Huntington. d. John Hancock, Charles Thomson, e. George Read, John Dickinson, Edward Rutledge (a, d, vert., b, c, e, horiz.).

No. 1688: a. Boatsman. b. Washington. c. Flag bearer. d. Men in boat. e. Men on shore (a, d, horiz., b, c, e, vert.).

No. 1689: a. Two officers. b. Washington. c. Officer, black horse. d. Officer, white horse. e. Three soldiers (a, c, e, horiz., b, d, vert.).

Surrender of Cornwallis at Yorktown, by John Trumbull — A1076

Declaration of Independence, by John Trumbull — A1077

Washington Crossing the Delaware, by Emmanuel Leutze / Eastman Johnson — A1078

Washington Reviewing Army at Valley Forge, by William T. Trego — A1079

Designed by Vincent E. Hoffman.

LITHOGRAPHED
Plates of 30 subjects in six panes of 5 each.

1976, May 29	**Tagged**	***Perf. 11***
1686 A1076 13c, sheet of 5		3.25 —
a. 13c multicolored		45 40
b. 13c multicolored		45 40
c. 13c multicolored		45 40
d. 13c multicolored		45 40
e. 13c multicolored		45 40
f. "USA/13c" omitted on "b," "c" & "d," imperf.		— —
g. "USA/13c" omitted on "a" & "e"		— —
h. Imperf., untagged		—
i. "USA/13c" omitted on "b," "c" & "d"		—
j. "USA/13c" double on "b"		—
k. "USA/13c" omitted on "c" & "d"		—
l. "USA/13c" omitted on "e"		—
m. "USA/13c" omitted, imperf. untagged		—
1687 A1077 18c, sheet of 5		4.25 —
a. 18c multicolored		55 55
b. 18c multicolored		55 55
c. 18c multicolored		55 55
d. 18c multicolored		55 55
e. 18c multicolored		55 55
f. Design & marginal inscriptions omitted		—
g. "USA/18c" omitted on "a" & "c"		—
h. "USA/18c" omitted on "b," "d" & "e"		—
i. "USA/18c" omitted on "d"		—
j. Black omitted in design		—
k. "USA/18c" omitted, imperf., untagged		—
m. "USA/18c" omitted on "b" & "e"		—
1688 A1078 24c, sheet of 5		5.25 —
a. 24c multicolored		70 70
b. 24c multicolored		70 70
c. 24c multicolored		70 70

d.	24c multicolored	70	70
e.	24c multicolored	70	70
f.	"USA/24c" omitted, imperf.	—	
g.	"USA/24c" omitted on "d" & "e"	—	—
h.	Design & marginal inscriptions omitted	—	
i.	"USA/24c" omitted on "a," "b" & "c"	—	—
j.	Imperf., untagged	—	
k.	"USA/24c" of "d" & "e" inverted	—	
1689	A1079 31c, sheet of 5	6.25	—
a.	31c multicolored	85	85
b.	31c multicolored	85	85
c.	31c multicolored	85	85
d.	31c multicolored	85	85
e.	31c multicolored	85	85
f.	"USA/31c" omitted, imperf.	—	
g.	"USA/31c" omitted on "a" & "c"	—	
h.	"USA/31c" omitted on "b," "d" & "e"	—	—
i.	"USA/31c" omitted on "e"	—	
j.	Black omitted in design	—	
k.	Imperf., untagged		—
l.	"USA/31c" omitted on "b" & "d"	—	
m.	"USA/31c" omitted on "a," "b" & "e"	—	
n.	As "m," imperf., untagged	—	
p.	As "h," imperf., untagged		—

Issued in connection with Interphil 76 International Philatelic Exhibition, Philadelphia, Pa., May 29-June 6. Size of sheets: 153x204mm; size of stamps: 25x39½mm, 39½x25mm.

Nos. 1688-1689 exist with inverted perforations.

Benjamin Franklin

American Bicentennial; Benjamin Franklin (1706-1790), deputy postmaster general for the colonies (1753-1774) and statesman. Design based on marble bust by anonymous Italian sculptor after terra cotta bust by Jean Jacques Caffieri, 1777. Map published by R. Sayer and J. Bennett in London. See Canada No. 691.

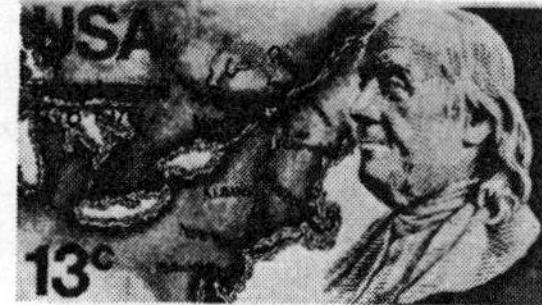

Franklin and Map of North America, 1776 — A1080

Designed by Bernard Reilander (Canada).

LITHOGRAPHED, ENGRAVED (Giori)

Plates of 200 subjects in four panes of 50 each.

1976, June 1 **Tagged** ***Perf. 11***

1690	A1080 13c **ultramarine & multicolored**	20	5
	Margin block of 4, P#	90	—
	Margin block of 4, Mr. Zip and "Use Zip Code"	85	—
	Margin block of 6, "Mail Early in the Day"	1.25	—
a.	Light blue omitted	*575.00*	

Declaration of Independence

Designed after painting in the Rotunda of the Capitol, Washington, D.C. Nos. 1691-1694 printed se-tenant in sheets of 50 (10x5). Left panes contain 10 No. 1694a and 5 each of Nos. 1691-1692; right panes contain 5 each of Nos. 1693-1694 and 10 No. 1694a.

A1081

A1082

AMERICAN BICENTENNIAL ISSUE

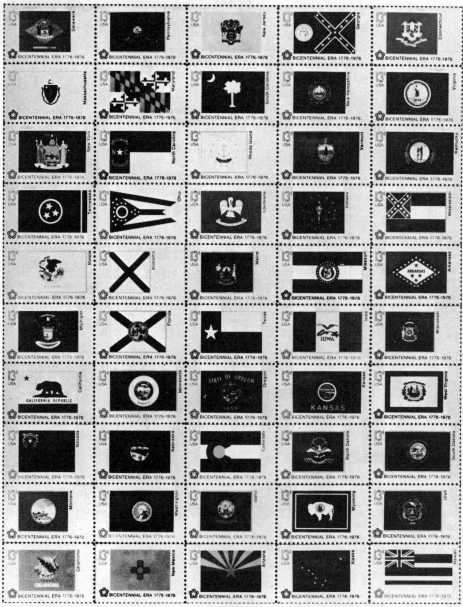

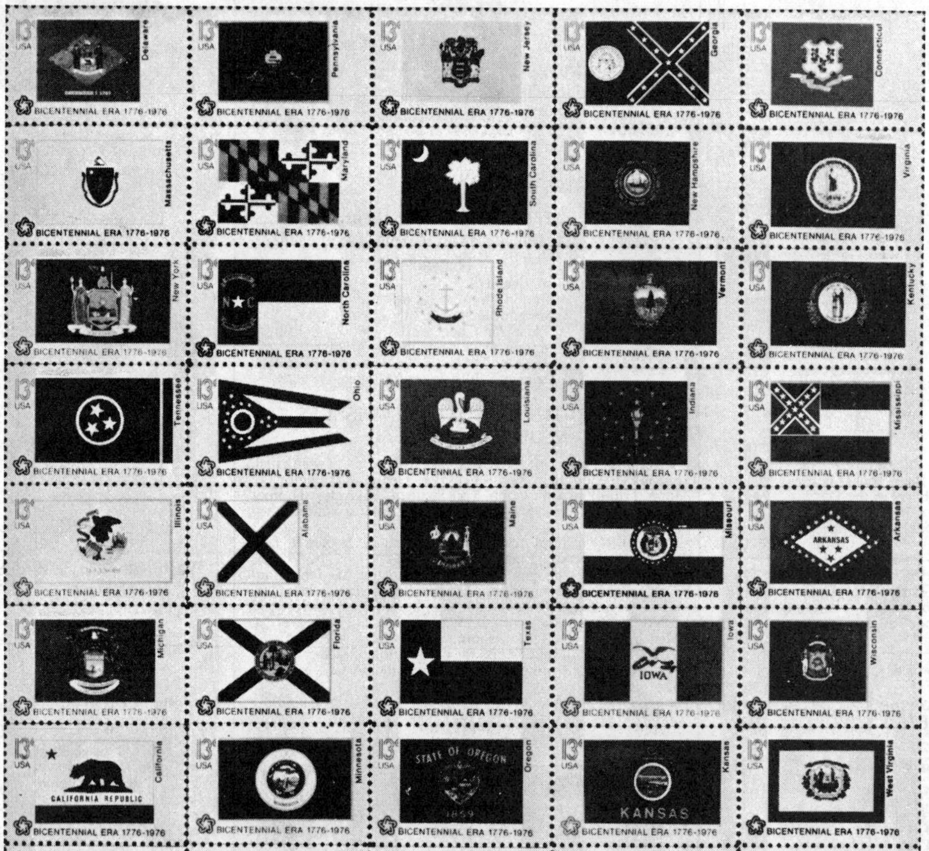

State Flags
A1023-A1072

A1083

Declaration of Independence, by John Trumbull — A1084

Designed by Vincent E. Hoffman.

PHOTOGRAVURE (Andreotti)
Plates of 200 subjects in four panes of 50 each.

1976, July 4 **Tagged** ***Perf. 11***

1691 A1081 13c **blue & multicolored** 22 8
Margin block of 20, 5 P# adjoining Nos. 1691-1694 & 1691, "Mail Early in the Day" adjoining No. 1693, Mr. Zip and "Use Zip Code" adjoining No. 1692 4.75 —
Margin block of 16, 5 P# as above, "Mail Early in the Day" 3.85 —
1692 A1082 13c **blue & multicolored** 22 8
Margin block of 8, "Mail Early in the Day" adjoining No. 1692 2.00 —
Margin block of 4, Mr. Zip and "Use Zip Code" adjoining No. 1692 90 —
1693 A1083 13c **blue & multicolored** 22 8
Margin block of 8, "Mail Early in the Day" adjoining No. 1693 2.00 —
Margin block of 4, Mr. Zip and "Use Zip Code" adjoining No. 1693 90 —
1694 A1084 13c **blue & multicolored** 22 8
Margin block of 20, 5 P# adjoining Nos. 1691-1694 & 1694, "Mail Early in the Day" adjoining No. 1692, Mr. Zip and "Use Zip Code" adjoining No. 1693 4.75 —
Margin block of 16, 5 P# as above, "Mail Early in the Day" 3.85 —
a. Strip of 4, #1691-1694 95 75

OLYMPIC GAMES ISSUE

12th Winter Olympic Games, Innsbruck, Austria, Feb. 4-15, and 21st Summer Olympic Games, Montreal, Canada, July 17-Aug. 1. Nos. 1695-1698 are printed in blocks of four in panes of 50. Nos. 1695-1696 alternate in one row, Nos. 1697-1698 in other row.

Diving — A1085

Skiing — A1086

Running — A1087

Skating — A1088

Designed by Donald Moss.

PHOTOGRAVURE (Andreotti)
Plates of 200 subjects in four panes of 50 each.

1976, July 16 **Tagged** ***Perf. 11***

1695 A1085 13c **multicolored** 28 8
Margin block of 12, 6 P# adjoining Nos. 1695-1696 3.50 —
Margin block of 20, 6 P# adjoining Nos. 1695-1696, Mr. Zip and slogans 6.00 —
Margin block of 4, Mr. Zip and "Use Zip Code" adjoining No. 1695 1.20 —
Margin block of 4, "Mail Early in the Day" adjoining No. 1695 1.20 —
1696 A1086 13c **multicolored** 28 8
Margin block of 4, Mr. Zip and "Use Zip Code" adjoining No. 1696 1.20 —
Margin block of 4, "Mail Early in the Day" adjoining No. 1696 1.20 —
1697 A1087 13c **multicolored** 28 8
Margin block of 12, 6 P# adjoining Nos. 1697-1698 3.50 —
Margin block of 20, 6 P# adjoining Nos. 1697-1698, Mr. Zip and slogans 6.00 —
Margin block of 4, Mr. Zip and "Use Zip Code" adjoining No. 1697 1.20 —
Margin block of 4, "Mail Early in the Day" adjoining No. 1697 1.20 —
1698 A1088 13c **multicolored** 28 8
Margin block of 4, Mr. Zip and "Use Zip Code" adjoining No. 1698 1.20 —
Margin block of 4, "Mail Early in the Day" adjoining No. 1698 1.20 —
a. Block of 4, #1695-1698 1.15 1.00
b. As "a," imperf. *900.00*

CLARA MAASS ISSUE

Clara Louise Maass (1876-1901), volunteer in fight against yellow fever, birth centenary.

Clara Maass and Newark German Hospital Pin — A1089

Designed by Paul Calle.

PHOTOGRAVURE (Andreotti)
Plates of 160 subjects in four panes of 40 each.

1976, Aug. 18 **Tagged** ***Perf. 11***

1699 A1089 13c **multicolored** 26 6
Margin block of 12, 6 P# 3.40 —
Margin block of 4, Mr. Zip, "Use Zip Code" and "Mail Early in the Day" 1.20 —
Margin block of 16, 6 P#, Mr. Zip and slogans 4.60 —
a. Horiz. pair, imperf. vert. *525.00*

ADOLPH S. OCHS ISSUE

Adolph S. Ochs (1858-1935), publisher of the New York Times, 1896-1935.

Adolph S. Ochs — A1090

Designed by Bradbury Thompson; photograph by S. J. Woolf.

GIORI PRESS PRINTING
Plates of 128 subjects in four panes of 32 (8x4).

1976, Sept. 18 **Tagged** ***Perf. 11***

1700 A1090 13c **black & gray** 24 5
Margin block of 4, P# 1.05 —
Margin block of 4, Mr. Zip and "Use Zip Code" 1.00 —
Margin block of 6, "Mail Early in the Day" 1.50 —

CHRISTMAS ISSUE

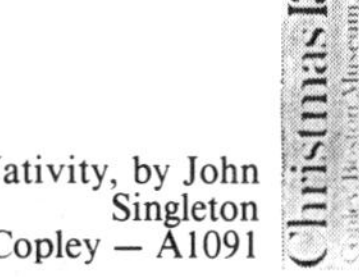

Nativity, by John Singleton Copley — A1091

"Winter Pastime," by Nathaniel Currier — A1092

Designers: No. 1701, Bradbury Thompson after 1776 painting in Museum of Fine Arts, Boston. No. 1702, Stevan Dohanos after 1855 lithograph in Museum of the City of New York.

PHOTOGRAVURE (Andreotti)
Plates of 200 subjects in four panes of 50 each.

1976, Oct. 27 **Tagged, Overall** ***Perf. 11***

1701 A1091 13c **multicolored** 24 5
Margin block of 12, 6 P# 3.00 —
Margin block of 4, Mr. Zip and "Use Zip Code" 1.00 —
Margin block of 4, "Mail Early in the Day" 1.00 —
a. Imperf., pair *95.00*
1702 A1092 13c **multicolored** 24 5
Margin block of 10, 5 P# 2.50 —
Margin block of 4, Mr. Zip and "Use Zip Code" 1.00 —
Margin block of 6, "Mail Early in the Day" 1.50 —
a. Imperf., pair *120.00*

Plates of 230 (10x23) subjects in panes of 50 (5x10)
Tagged, Block

1703 A1092 13c **multicolored** 24 5
Margin block of 20 5-8 P# 5.00 —
a. Imperf., pair *120.00*
b. Vert. pair, imperf. btwn. —

No. 1702 has overall tagging. Lettering at base is black and usually ½mm. below design. As a rule, no "snowflaking" in sky or pond. Pane of 50 has margins on 4 sides with slogans. Plate Nos. 37465-37478.

No. 1703 has block tagging the size of printed area. Lettering at base is gray black and usually ¾mm. below design. "Snowflaking" generally in sky and pond. Plate Nos. 37617-37621 or 37634-37638.

COMBINATION PRESS

Cylindrical plates consist of 23 rows of subjects, 10 across for commemoratives (230 subjects), 20 across for definitives (460 subjects), with margins on the two outer edges only. Guillotining through the perforations creates individual panes of 50 or 100 with one margin.

Failure of the guillotine to separate through the perforations resulted in straight edges on some stamps. Perforating teeth along the center column and the tenth rows were removed for issues released on or after May 31, 1984 (the 10c Richard Russell, for definitives; the 20c Horace Moses, for commemoratives), creating panes with straight edged stamps on three sides.

Three sets of plate numbers, copyright notices (starting with No. 1787), and zip insignia (starting with No. 1927) are arranged identically on the left and right sides of the plate so that each pane has at least one of each marking. The markings adjacent to any particular row are repeated either seven or eight rows away on the cylinder.

Fifteen combinations of the three marginal markings and blank rows are possible on panes.

AMERICAN BICENTENNIAL ISSUE
Washington at Princeton

Washington's Victory over Lord Cornwallis at Princeton, N.J., bicentenary.

Washington, Nassau Hall, Hessian Prisoners and 13-star Flag, by Charles Willson Peale — A1093

Designed by Bradbury Thompson.

PHOTOGRAVURE (Andreotti)

Plates of 160 subjects in four panes of 40 each.

1977, Jan. 3	**Tagged**	***Perf. 11***	
1704 A1093 13c	**multicolored**	24	5
	Margin block of 10, 5 P#	2.50	—
	Margin block of 4, Mr. Zip and "Use Zip Code", "Mail Early in the Day"	1.00	—
a.	Horiz. pair, imperf. vert.	*450.00*	

SOUND RECORDING ISSUE

Centenary of the invention of the phonograph by Thomas Alva Edison and development of sophisticated recording industry.

Tin Foil Phonograph A1094

Designed by Walter and Naiad Einsel.

LITHOGRAPHED, ENGRAVED (Giori)

Plates of 200 subjects in four panes of 50 each.

1977, March 23	**Tagged**	***Perf. 11***	
1705 A1094 13c	**black & multicolored**	24	5
	Margin block of 4, P#	1.05	—
	Margin block of 4, Mr. Zip and "Use Zip Code"	1.00	—
	Margin block of 6, "Mail Early in the Day"	1.50	—

AMERICAN FOLK ART ISSUE

Pueblo Pottery

Pueblo art, 1880-1920, from Museums in New Mexico, Arizona and Colorado.

Nos. 1706-1709 are printed in blocks and strips of four in panes of 40. In the first row Nos. 1706-1709 are in sequence as listed. In the second row Nos. 1708-1709 are followed by Nos. 1706-1709, 1708-1709.

Zia Pot — A1095

San Ildefonso: Denver Art Museum
Pueblo Art USA 13c

San Ildefonso Pot — A1096

Hopi Pot — A1097

Acoma: School of American Research
Pueblo Art USA 13c

Acoma Pot — A1098

Designed by Ford Ruthling.

PHOTOGRAVURE (Andreotti)

Plates of 160 subjects in four panes of 40 each.

1977, Apr. 13	**Tagged**	***Perf. 11***	
1706 A1095 13c	**multicolored**	24	8
	Margin block of 10, 5 P#	2.50	—
	Margin block of 16, 5 P#; Mr. Zip and slogans adjoining Nos. 1706-1707	4.00	—
	Margin block of 6, Mr. Zip and "Use Zip Code" "Mail Early in the Day" adjoining Nos. 1706-1707	1.50	—
1707 A1096 13c	**multicolored**	24	8
1708 A1097 13c	**multicolored**	24	8
	Margin block of 16, 5 P#; Mr. Zip and slogans adjoining Nos. 1708-1709	4.00	—
	Margin block of 6, Mr. Zip and "Use Zip Code" "Mail Early in the Day" adjoining Nos. 1708-1709	1.50	—
1709 A1098 13c	**multicolored**	24	8
a.	Block or strip of 4, #1706-1709	1.00	80
b.	As "a", imperf. vert.	*2,500.*	

LINDBERGH FLIGHT ISSUE

Charles A. Lindbergh's solo transatlantic flight from New York to Paris, 50th anniversary.

Spirit of St. Louis — A1099

Designed by Robert E. Cunningham.

PHOTOGRAVURE (Andreotti)

Plates of 200 subjects in four panes of 50 each.

1977, May 20	**Tagged**	***Perf. 11***	
1710 A1099 13c	**multicolored**	24	5
	Margin block of 12, 6 P#	3.00	—
	Margin block of 4, Mr. Zip and "Use Zip Code"	1.00	—
	Margin block of 4, "Mail Early in the Day"	1.00	—
a.	Imperf., pair	*1,500.*	

COLORADO STATEHOOD ISSUE

Issued to honor Colorado as the "Centennial State." It achieved statehood in 1876.

The lack of a value for a listed item does not necessarily indicate rarity.

Columbine and Rocky Mountains — A1100

Designed by V. Jack Ruther.

PHOTOGRAVURE (Andreotti)

Plates of 200 subjects in four panes of 50 each.

1977, May 21	**Tagged**	***Perf. 11***	
1711 A1100 13c	**multicolored**	24	5
	Margin block of 12, 6 P#	3.00	—
	Margin block of 4, Mr. Zip and "Use Zip Code"	1.00	—
	Margin block of 4, "Mail Early in the Day"	1.00	—
	Perf. 11.2	35	25
a.	Horiz. pair, imperf. btwn.	—	
b.	Horiz. pair, imperf. vert.	—	

Perforations do not run through the sheet margin on about 10 percent of the sheets of No. 1711.

BUTTERFLY ISSUE

Nos. 1712-1715 are printed in blocks of 4, in panes of 50. Nos. 1712-1713 alternate in first row, Nos. 1714-1715 in second row. This arrangement is repeated throughout the pane. Butterflies represent different geographic U.S. areas.

Swallowtail A1101

Checkerspot A1102

Dogface — A1103

Orange-Tip A1104

Designed by Stanley Galli.

PHOTOGRAVURE (Andreotti)

Plates of 200 subjects in four panes of 50 each.

1977, June 6	**Tagged**	***Perf. 11***	
1712 A1101 13c	**tan & multicolored**	24	8
	Margin block of 12, 6 P# adjoining Nos. 1712, 1714	3.10	—
	Margin block of 20, 6 P# adjoining Nos. 1712, 1714, Mr. Zip and slogans	5.25	—
	Margin block of 4, Mr. Zip and "Use Zip Code" adjoining No. 1712	1.05	—
	Margin block of 4, "Mail Early in the Day" adjoining No. 1712	1.05	—
1713 A1102 13c	**tan & multicolored**	24	8

Margin block of 12, 6 P# adjoining Nos. 1713, 1715 3.10 —
Margin block of 20, 6 P# adjoining Nos. 1713, 1715 5.25 —
Margin block of 4, Mr. Zip and "Use Zip Code" adjoining No. 1713 1.05 —
Margin block of 4, "Mail Early in the Day" adjoining No. 1713 1.05 —

1714 A1103 13c **tan & multicolored** 24 8
Margin block of 4, Mr. Zip and "Use Zip Code" adjoining No. 1714 1.05 —
Margin block of 4, "Mail Early in the Day" adjoining No. 1714 1.05 —

1715 A1104 13c **tan & multicolored** 24 8
Margin block of 4, Mr. Zip and "Use Zip Code" adjoining No. 1715 1.05 —
Margin block of 4, "Mail Early in the Day" adjoining No. 1715 1.05 —

a. Block of 4, #1712-1715 1.00 80
b. As a, imperf. horiz. —

AMERICAN BICENTENNIAL ISSUES
Marquis de Lafayette

200th anniversary of Lafayette's Landing on the coast of South Carolina, north of Charleston.

Lafayette

Marquis de Lafayette — A1105 US Bicentennial 13c

Designed by Bradbury Thompson.

GIORI PRESS PRINTING
Plates of 160 subjects in four panes of 40 each.

1977, June 13 **Tagged** ***Perf. 11***

1716 A1105 13c **blue, black & red** 24 5
Margin block of 4, P# 1.05 —
Margin block of 4, Mr. Zip and "Use Zip Code" 1.05 —
Margin block of 6, "Mail Early in the Day" 1.50 —

Skilled Hands for Independence

Nos. 1717-1720 are printed se-tenant in blocks of four, in panes of 50. Nos. 1717-1718 alternate in first row, Nos. 1719-1720 in second row. This arrangement is repeated throughout the pane.

Seamstress A1106

Blacksmith A1107

Wheelwright A1108

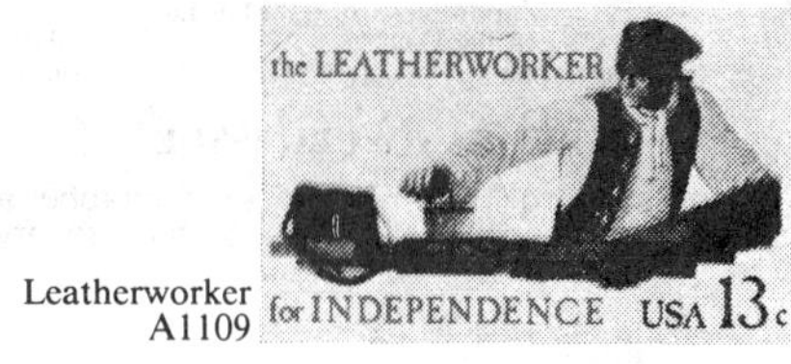

Leatherworker A1109

Designed by Leonard Everett Fisher.

PHOTOGRAVURE (Andreotti)
Plates of 200 subjects in four panes of 50 each.

1977, July 4 **Tagged** ***Perf. 11***

1717 A1106 13c **multicolored** 24 8
Margin block of 12, 6 P# adjoining Nos. 1717, 1719 3.10 —
Margin block of 20, 6 P# adjoining Nos. 1717, 1719, Mr. Zip and slogans 5.25 —
Margin block of 4, Mr. Zip and "Use Zip Code" adjoining No. 1717 1.05 —
Margin block of 4, "Mail Early in the Day" adjoining No. 1717 1.05 —

1718 A1107 13c **multicolored** 24 8
Margin block of 12, 6 P# adjoining Nos. 1718, 1720 3.10 —
Margin block of 20, 6 P# adjoining Nos. 1718, 1720 5.25 —
Margin block of 4, Mr. Zip and "Use Zip Code" adjoining No. 1718 1.05 —
Margin block of 4, "Mail Early in the Day" adjoining No. 1718 1.05 —

1719 A1108 13c **multicolored** 24 8
Margin block of 4, Mr. Zip and "Use Zip Code" adjoining No. 1719 1.05 —
Margin block of 4, "Mail Early in the Day" adjoining No. 1719 1.05 —

1720 A1109 13c **multicolored** 24 8
Margin block of 4, Mr. Zip and "Use Zip Code" adjoining No. 1720 1.05 —
Margin block of 4, "Mail Early in the Day" adjoining No. 1720 1.05 —

a. Block of 4, #1717-1720 1.00 80

PEACE BRIDGE ISSUE

50th anniversary of the Peace Bridge, connecting Buffalo (Fort Porter), N.Y. and Fort Erie, Ontario.

Peace Bridge and Dove — A1110

Designed by Bernard Brussel-Smith (wood-cut).

ENGRAVED
Plates of 200 subjects in four panes of 50 each.

1977, Aug. 4 **Tagged** ***Perf. 11x10½***

1721 A1110 13c **blue** 24 5
Margin block of 4, P# 1.05 —
Margin block of 4, Mr. Zip and "Use Zip Code" 1.00 —
Margin block of 6, "Mail Early in the Day" 1.50 —

AMERICAN BICENTENNIAL ISSUE
Battle of Oriskany

200th anniversary of the Battle of Oriskany, American Militia led by Brig. Gen. Nicholas Herkimer (1728-1777).

Herkimer at Oriskany, by Frederick Yohn — A1111

Designed by Bradbury Thompson after painting in Utica, N.Y. Public Library.

PHOTOGRAVURE (Andreotti)
Plates of 160 subjects in four panes of 40 each.

1977, Aug. 6 **Tagged** ***Perf. 11***

1722 A1111 13c **multicolored** 24 5
Margin block of 10, 5 P# 2.50 —
Margin block of 6, Mr. Zip and "Use Zip Code" and "Mail Early in the Day" 1.50 —

ENERGY ISSUE

Conservation and development of nations energy resources. Nos. 1723-1724 printed se-tenant vertically.

"Conservation" A1112

"Development" A1113

Designed by Terrance W. McCaffrey.

PHOTOGRAVURE (Andreotti)
Plates of 160 subjects in four panes of 40 each.

1977, Oct. 20 **Tagged** ***Perf. 11***

1723 A1112 13c **multicolored** 24 8
a. Pair, #1723-1724 48 40
Margin block of 12, 6 P# 3.00 —
Margin block of 4, Mr. Zip, "Use Zip Code" and "Mail Early in the Day" 1.00 —

1724 A1113 13c **multicolored** 24 8

ALTA CALIFORNIA ISSUE

Founding of El Pueblo de San José de Guadalupe, first civil settlement in Alta California, 200th anniversary.

Farm Houses — A1114

Designed by Earl Thollander.

LITHOGRAPHED, ENGRAVED (Giori)
Plates of 200 subjects in four panes of 50 each.

1977, Sept. 9 **Tagged** ***Perf. 11***

1725 A1114 13c **black & multicolored** 24 5
Margin block of 4, P# 1.05 —
Margin block of 4, Mr. Zip and "Use Zip Code" 1.05 —
Margin block of 6, "Mail Early in the Day" 1.50 —

AMERICAN BICENTENNIAL ISSUE
Articles of Confederation

200th anniversary of drafting the Articles of Confederation, York Town, Pa.

Members of Continental Congress in Conference A1115

Designed by David Blossom.

ENGRAVED (Giori)

Plates of 200 subjects in four panes of 50 each.

1977, Sept. 30 **Tagged** ***Perf. 11***

1726 A1115 13c **red & brown,** *cream* 24 5
Margin block of 4, P# 1.05 —
Margin block of 4, Mr. Zip and "Use Zip Code" 1.00 —
Margin block of 6, "Mail Early in the Day" 1.50 —

TALKING PICTURES ISSUE

50th anniversary of talking pictures.

Movie Projector and Phonograph A1116

Designed by Walter Einsel.

LITHOGRAPHED, ENGRAVED (Giori)

Plates of 200 subjects in four panes of 50 each.

1977, Oct. 6 **Tagged** ***Perf. 11***

1727 A1116 13c **multicolored** 24 5
Margin block of 4, P# 1.05 —
Margin block of 4, Mr. Zip and "Use Zip Code" 1.00 —
Margin block of 6, "Mail Early in the Day" 1.50 —

AMERICAN BICENTENNIAL ISSUE
Surrender at Saratoga

200th anniversary of Gen. John Burgoyne's surrender at Saratoga.

Surrender of Burgoyne, by John Trumbull A1117

Designed by Bradbury Thompson.

PHOTOGRAVURE (Andreotti)

Plates of 160 subjects in four panes of 40 each.

1977, Oct. 7 **Tagged** ***Perf. 11***

1728 A1117 13c **multicolored** 24 5
Margin block of 10, 5 P# 2.50 —
Margin block of 6, Mr. Zip, "Use Zip Code" and "Mail Early in the Day" 1.50 —

CHRISTMAS ISSUE

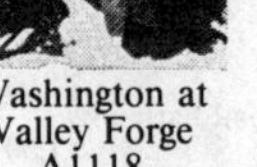

Washington at Valley Forge A1118

Rural Mailbox A1119

Designers: No. 1729, Stevan Dohanos, after painting by J. C. Leyendecker. No. 1730, Dolli Tingle.

PHOTOGRAVURE (Combination Press)

Plates of 460 subjects (20x23) in panes of 100 (10x10).

1977, Oct. 21 **Tagged** ***Perf. 11***

1729 A1118 13c **multicolored** 24 5
Margin block of 20, 5-8 P# 5.75 —
a. Imperf., pair *70.00*

See Combination Press note after No. 1703.

PHOTOGRAVURE (Andreotti)

Plates of 400 subjects in 4 panes of 100 each.

1730 A1119 13c **multicolored** 24 5
Margin block of 10, 5 P# 2.50 —
Margin block of 4, Mr. Zip and "Use Zip Code" 1.00 —
Margin block of 6, "Mail Early in the Day" 1.50 —
a. Imperf., pair *250.00*

CARL SANDBURG ISSUE

Carl Sandburg (1878-1967), poet, biographer and collector of American folk songs, birth centenary.

Carl Sandburg, by William A. Smith, 1952 — A1120

Designed by William A. Smith.

GIORI PRESS PRINTING

Plates of 200 subjects in four panes of 50 each.

1978, Jan. 6 **Tagged** ***Perf. 11***

1731 A1120 13c **black & brown** 24 5
Margin block of 4, P# 1.05 —
Margin block of 4, Mr. Zip 1.00 —
Margin block of 4, copyright 1.00 —

CAPTAIN COOK ISSUE

Capt. James Cook, 200th anniversary of his arrival in Hawaii, at Waimea, Kauai, Jan. 20, 1778, and of his anchorage in Cook Inlet, near Anchorage, Alaska, June 1, 1778. Nos. 1732-1733 printed in panes of 50, containing 25 each of Nos. 1732-1733 including 5 No. 1732a.

Capt. Cook, by Nathaniel Dance — A1121

"Resolution" and "Discovery," by John Webber — A1122

GIORI PRESS PRINTING

Plates of 200 subjects in four panes of 50 each.

1978, Jan. 20 **Tagged** ***Perf. 11***

1732 A1121 13c **dark blue** 24 8
a. Pair, #1732-1733 50 30
b. As "a," imperf. between —
Margin block of 4, P# 1.10 —
Margin block of 4, Mr. Zip 1.05 —
Margin block of 4, copyright 1.05 —
Margin block of 20, 10 each, #1732-1733, P# adjoining #1732, and slogans 5.25 —

1733 A1122 13c **green** 24 8
a. Vert. pair, imperf. horiz. —
Margin block of 4, P# 1.10 —
Margin block of 4, Mr. Zip 1.05 —
Margin block of 4, copyright 1.05 —
Margin block of 20, 10 each #1732-1733, P# adjoining #1733, and slogans 5.25 —

> The Scott Catalogue value is a retail price, what you could expect to pay for the stamp in a grade of Fine-Very Fine. The value listed is a reference which reflects recent actual dealer selling price.

Indian Head Penny, 1877 A1123

Eagle A1124

Red Masterpiece and Medallion Roses — A1126

ENGRAVED (Giori)

Plates of 600 subjects in four panes of 150 each.

1978 **Tagged** ***Perf. 11***

1734 A1123 13c **brown & blue green,** *bister, Jan. 11, 1978* 24 8
Margin block of 4, P# 1.50 —
Margin block of 4, "Use Correct Zip Code" 1.00 —
Margin block of 4, copyright 1.00 —
Pair with full horiz. gutter btwn. —
a. Horiz. pair, imperf. vert. *325.00*

PHOTOGRAVURE (Andreotti)

Plates of 400 subjects in four panes of 100 each.

1735 A1124 (15c) **orange,** *May 22, 1978* 24 5
Margin block of 4, P# 1.05 —
Margin block of 4, "Use Zip Code" 1.00 —
Margin block of 6, "Mail Early in the Day" 1.50 —
Perf. 11.2 24 5
a. Imperf., vert. pair *65.00*
b. Vert. pair, imperf. horiz. *300.00*

ENGRAVED

1736 A1124 (15c) **orange** (from booklet pane) 25 5
a. Booklet pane of 8, *May 22, 1978* 2.40 *60*

Perf. 10

1737 A1126 15c **multicolored** (from booklet pane) 25 6
a. Booklet pane of 8, *July 11, 1978* 2.50 *60*
b. As "a", imperf. —

Nos. 1736, 1737 issued in booklets only. All stamps have one or two straight edges.

A1127

A1128

A1130

A1131

A1129

Designed by Ronald Sharpe.

ENGRAVED

1980, Feb. 7 **Tagged** ***Perf. 11***

1738 A1127 15c **sepia,** *yellow* 30 5
1739 A1128 15c **sepia,** *yellow* 30 5
1740 A1129 15c **sepia,** *yellow* 30 5
1741 A1130 15c **sepia,** *yellow* 30 5
1742 A1131 15c **sepia,** *yellow* 30 5
a. Booklet pane of 10, 2 each #1738-1742 3.60 *60*

Nos. 1738-1742 issued in booklets only. All stamps have one or two straight edges.

COIL STAMP

1978, May 22 *Perf. 10 Vert.*

1743 A1124 (15c) **orange** 25 5
Pair 50 —
Joint line pair 65 —
a. Imperf. pair *110.00*

BLACK HERITAGE ISSUE
Harriet Tubman

Harriet Tubman (1820-1913), born a slave, helped more than 300 slaves escape to freedom.

Harriet Tubman and Cart Carrying Slaves — A1133

Designed by Jerry Pinkney after photograph.

PHOTOGRAVURE (Andreotti)
Plates of 200 subjects in four panes of 50 each.

1978, Feb. 1 **Tagged** *Perf. 10½x11*

1744 A1133 13c **multicolored** 24 5
Margin block of 12, 6 P# 3.00 —
Margin block of 4, Mr. Zip 1.00 —
Margin block of 4, copyright 1.00 —

AMERICAN FOLK ART ISSUE
Quilts

Nos. 1745-1748 are printed in blocks of four. Nos. 1745-1746 alternate in first row, Nos. 1747-1748 in second.

Basket Design

A1134

A1135

A1136

A1137

Designed by Christopher Pullman after 1875 quilt made in New York City.

PHOTOGRAVURE (Andreotti)
Plates of 192 subjects in four panes of 48 (6x8).

1978, Mar. 8 *Perf. 11*

1745 A1134 13c **multicolored** 24 8
Margin block of 12, 6 P#, adjoining Nos. 1745, 1747 3.10 —
Margin block of 16, 6 P# adjoining Nos. 1745, 1747, Mr. Zip and copyright 4.25 —
Margin block of 4, Mr. Zip adjoining No. 1745, copyright No. 1747 1.05 —
Margin block of 4, Mr. Zip adjoining No. 1747, copyright No. 1745 1.05 —
1746 A1135 13c **multicolored** 24 8
Margin block of 12, 6 P#, adjoining Nos. 1746, 1748 3.10 —
Margin block of 16, 6 P# adjoining Nos. 1746, 1748, Mr. Zip and copyright 4.25 —
Margin block of 4, Mr. Zip adjoining No. 1746, copyright No. 1748 1.05 —
Margin block of 4, Mr. Zip adjoining No. 1748, copyright No. 1746 1.05 —
1747 A1136 13c **multicolored** 24 8
1748 A1137 13c **multicolored** 24 8
a. Block of 4, #1745-1748 1.00 75

AMERICAN DANCE ISSUE

Nos. 1749-1752 printed se-tenant in blocks of four. Nos. 1749-1750 alternate in first row, Nos. 1751-1752 in second.

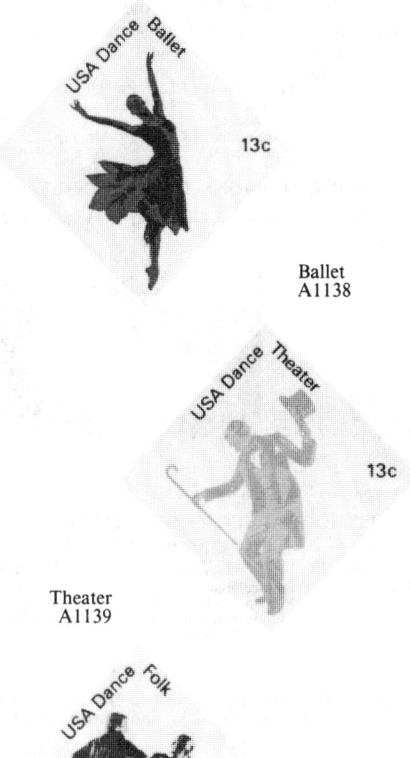

Ballet
A1138

Theater
A1139

Folk Dance
A1140

Values quoted in this catalogue are for stamps graded at Fine-Very Fine and with no faults. An illustrated guide to grade is provided in introductory material, beginning on Page V.

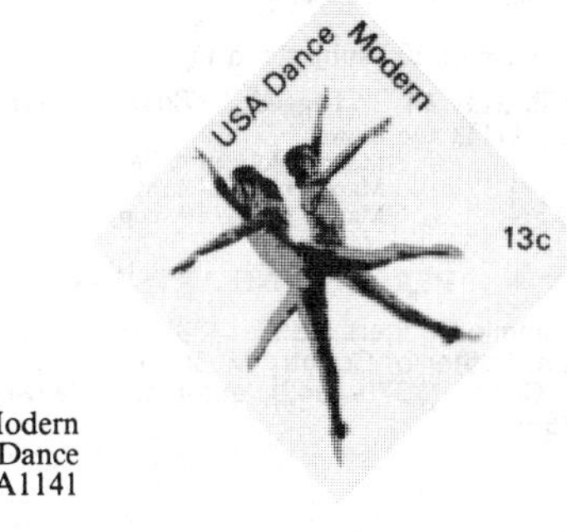

Modern Dance
A1141

Designed by John Hill.

PHOTOGRAVURE (Andreotti)
Plates of 192 subjects in four panes of 48 (6x8).

1978, Apr. 26 *Perf. 11*

1749 A1138 13c **multicolored** 24 8
Margin block of 12, 6 P#, adjoining Nos. 1749, 1751 3.10 —
Margin block of 16, 6 P#, adjoining Nos. 1749, 1751, Mr. Zip and copyright 4.25 —
Margin block of 4, Mr. Zip adjoining No. 1749, copyright No. 1751 1.05 —
Margin block of 4, Mr. Zip adjoining No. 1751, copyright No. 1749 1.05 —
1750 A1139 13c **multicolored** 24 8
Margin block of 12, 6 P#, adjoining Nos. 1750, 1752 3.10 —
Margin block of 16, 6 P# adjoining Nos. 1750, 1752, Mr. Zip and copyright 4.25 —
Margin block of 4, Mr. Zip adjoining No. 1750, copyright No. 1752 1.05 —
Margin block of 4, Mr. Zip adjoining No. 1752, copyright No. 1750 1.05 —
1751 A1140 13c **multicolored** 24 8
1752 A1141 13c **multicolored** 24 8
a. Block of 4, #1749-1752 1.00 75

AMERICAN BICENTENNIAL ISSUE
French Alliance

Bicentenary of French Alliance, signed in Paris, Feb. 6, 1778 and ratified by Continental Congress, May 4, 1778.

King Louis XVI and Benjamin Franklin, by Charles Gabriel Sauvage — A1142

Designed by Bradbury Thompson after 1785 porcelain sculpture in Du Pont Winterthur Museum, Delaware.

GIORI PRESS PRINTING
Plates of 160 subjects in four panes of 40 each.

1978, May 4 **Tagged** *Perf. 11*

1753 A1142 13c **blue, black & red** 24 5
Margin block of 4, P# 1.05 —
Margin block of 4, Mr. Zip 1.00 —
Margin block of 4, copyright 1.00 —

EARLY CANCER DETECTION ISSUE

George Papanicolaou, M.D. (1883-1962), cytologist and developer of Pap Test, early cancer detection in women.

Dr. Papanicolaou and Microscope — A1143

Designed by Paul Calle.

Plates of 200 subjects in four panes of 50 each.

1978, May 18	**Tagged**	**Engr.**	***Perf. 10½x11***	
1754 A1143 13c **brown**			24	5
Margin block of 4, P#			1.05	—
Margin block of 4, Mr. Zip			1.00	—
Margin block of 4, copyright			1.00	—

PERFORMING ARTS ISSUE

Jimmie Rodgers (1897-1933), the "Singing Brakeman, Father of Country Music" (No. 1755); George M. Cohan (1878-1942), actor and playwright (No. 1756).

Jimmie Rodgers with Guitar and Brakeman's Cap, Locomotive A1144

George M. Cohan, "Yankee Doodle Dandy" and Stars A1145

Designed by Jim Sharpe.

PHOTOGRAVURE (Andreotti)

Plates of 200 subjects in four panes of 50 each.

1978	**Tagged**	***Perf. 11***	
1755 A1144 13c **multicolored,** *May 24*		24	5
Margin block of 12, 6 P#		3.00	—
Margin block of 4, Mr. Zip		1.00	—
Margin block of 4, copyright		1.00	—
1756 A1145 15c **multicolored,** *July 3*		28	5
Margin block of 12, 6 P#		3.50	—
Margin block of 4, Mr. Zip		1.15	—
Margin block of 4, copyright		1.15	—

CAPEX ISSUE

CAPEX '78, Canadian International Philatelic Exhibition, Toronto, Ont., June 9-18. No. 1757 has black inscriptions on green panel: "Canadian International Exhibition, Toronto" and in French and English "This tribute features wildlife that share the Canadian-United States Border." Signature of Postmaster General William F. Bolger. Size: 108x74mm.

Wildlife from Canadian-United States Border — A1146

Designed by Stanley Galli.

LITHOGRAPHED, ENGRAVED (Giori)

Plates of 24 subjects in four panes of 6 each.

1978, June 10	**Tagged**	***Perf. 11***	
1757 A1146 Block of 8, **multicolored**		1.65	1.65
a. 13c *Cardinal*		20	10
b. 13c *Mallard*		20	10
c. 13c *Canada goose*		20	10
d. 13c *Blue jay*		20	10
e. 13c *Moose*		20	10
f. 13c *Chipmunk*		20	10
g. 13c *Red fox*		20	10
h. 13c *Raccoon*		20	10
i. Yel., grn., red, brn., bl., blk. (litho) omitted		—	
Margin block of 8, P#		1.90	
Margin block of 8, Mr. Zip and copyright		1.70	
Pane of 6 (No. 1757), P#, Mr. Zip and copyright		10.50	—

At least one pane of No. 1757 is known with shifted perforations creating rows of No. 1757a-1757d and 1757e-1757h that are imperforate vertically.

PHOTOGRAPHY ISSUE

Photography's contribution to communications and understanding.

Camera, Lens, Color Filters, Adapter Ring, Studio Light Bulb and Album — A1147

Designed by Ben Somoroff.

PHOTOGRAVURE (Andreotti)

Plates of 160 subjects in four panes of 40 each.

1978, June 26	**Tagged**	***Perf. 11***	
1758 A1147 15c **multicolored**		26	5
Margin block of 12, 6 P#		3.25	—
Margin block of 4, Mr. Zip and copyright		1.05	—
Margin block of 16, 6 P#, Mr. Zip and copyright		4.40	—

VIKING MISSIONS TO MARS ISSUE

Second anniversary of landing of Viking 1 on Mars.

Viking 1 Lander Scooping up Soil on Mars — A1148

Designed by Robert McCall.

LITHOGRAPHED, ENGRAVED (Giori)

Plates of 200 subjects in four panes of 50 each.

1978, July 20	**Tagged**	***Perf. 11***	
1759 A1148 15c **multicolored**		28	5
Margin block of 4, P#		1.20	—
Margin block of 4, Mr. Zip		1.15	—
Margin block of 4, copyright		1.15	—

AMERICAN OWLS ISSUE

Nos. 1760-1763 are printed in blocks of four. Nos. 1760-1761 alternate in one horizontal row. Nos. 1762-1763 in the next.

Great Gray Owl — A1149

Saw-whet Owl — A1150

Barred Owl — A1151

Great Horned Owl — A1152

Designed by Frank J. Waslick.

LITHOGRAPHED, ENGRAVED (Giori)

Plates of 200 subjects in four panes of 50 each.

1978, Aug. 26	**Tagged**	***Perf. 11***	
1760 A1149 15c **multicolored**		28	8
Margin block of 4, P# adjoining #1760		1.25	—
Margin block of 4, Mr. Zip adjoining #1760		1.20	—
Margin block of 4, copyright adjoining #1760		1.20	—
1761 A1150 15c **multicolored**		28	8
Margin block of 4, P# adjoining #1761		1.25	—
Margin block of 4, Mr. Zip adjoining #1761		1.20	—
Margin block of 4, copyright adjoining #1761		1.20	—
1762 A1151 15c **multicolored**		28	8
Margin block of 4, P# adjoining #1762		1.25	—
Margin block of 4, Mr. Zip adjoining #1762		1.20	—
Margin block of 4, copyright adjoining #1762		1.20	—
1763 A1152 15c **multicolored**		28	8
Margin block of 4, P# adjoining #1763		1.25	—
Margin block of 4, Mr. Zip adjoining #1763		1.20	—
Margin block of 4, copyright adjoining #1763		1.20	—
a. Block of four, #1760-1763		1.15	85

AMERICAN TRESS ISSUE

Nos. 1764-1767 are printed se-tenant in blocks of four. Nos. 1764-1765 alternate in first row, Nos. 1766-1767 in second.

Giant Sequoia — A1153

White Pine — A1154

White Oak — A1155

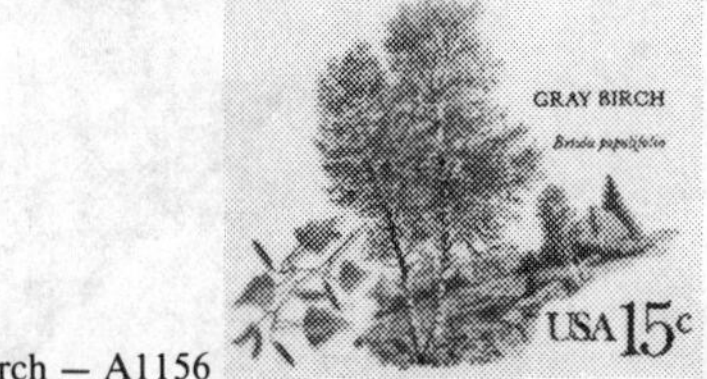

Gray Birch — A1156

Designed by Walter D. Richards.

PHOTOGRAVURE (Andreotti)
Plates of 160 subjects in four panes of 40 each.

1978, Oct. 9 **Tagged** ***Perf. 11***

1764 A1153 15c **multicolored** 28 8
Margin block of 12, 6 P# adjoining #1764, 1766 3.50 —
Margin block of 16, 6 P# adjoining #1764, 1766, Mr. Zip and copyright 4.75 —
Margin block of 4, Mr. Zip adjoining #1764, copyright #1766 1.20 —
Margin block of 4, Mr. Zip adjoining #1766, copyright #1764 1.20 —
1765 A1154 15c **multicolored** 28 8
Margin block of 12, 6 P# adjoining #1765, 1767 3.50 —
Margin block of 16, 6 P# adjoining #1765, 1767, Mr. Zip and copyright 4.75 —
Margin block of 4, Mr. Zip adjoining #1765, copyright #1767 1.20 —
Margin block of 4, Mr. Zip adjoining #1767, copyright #1765 1.20 —
1766 A1155 15c **multicolored** 28 8
1767 A1156 15c **multicolored** 28 8
a. Block of 4, #1764-1767 1.15 85
b. As "a," imperf. horiz. —

CHRISTMAS ISSUE

Madonna and Child with Cherubim, by Andrea della Robbia — A1157

Child on Hobby Horse and Christmas Trees — A1158

Designed by Bradbury Thompson (No. 1768) after terra cotta sculpture in National Gallery, Washington, D.C., and by Dolli Tingle (No. 1769).

PHOTOGRAVURE (Andreotti)
Plates of 400 subjects in four panes of 100 each.

1978, Oct. 18 ***Perf. 11***

1768 A1157 15c **blue & multicolored** 28 5
Margin block of 12, 6 P# 3.50 —
Margin block of 4, "Use Correct Zip Code" 1.15 —
Margin block of 4, copyright 1.15 —
a. Imperf., pair *100.00*
1769 A1158 15c **red & multicolored** 28 5
Margin block of 12, 6 P# 3.50 —
Margin block of 4, "Use Correct Zip Code" 1.15 —
Margin block of 4, copyright 1.15 —
a. Imperf., pair *100.00*
b. Vert. pair, imperf. horiz. —
Pair with full horiz. gutter btwn. —

ROBERT F. KENNEDY ISSUE

Robert F. Kennedy — A1159

Designed by Bradbury Thompson after photograph by Stanley Tretick.

ENGRAVED
Plates of 192 subjects in four panes of 48 (8x6).

1979, Jan. 12 **Tagged** ***Perf. 11***

1770 A1159 15c **blue** 28 5
Margin block of 4, P# 1.20 —
Margin block of 4, Mr. Zip 1.15 —
Margin block of 4, copyright 1.15 —

BLACK HERITAGE ISSUE
Martin Luther King, Jr.

Dr. Martin Luther King, Jr. (1929-1968), Civil Rights leader.

Martin Luther King, Jr. and Civil Rights Marchers — A1160

Designed by Jerry Pinkney.

PHOTOGRAVURE (Andreotti)
Plates of 200 subjects in four panes of 50 each.

1979, Jan. 13 **Tagged** ***Perf. 11***

1771 A1160 15c **multicolored** 28 5
Margin block of 12, 6 P# 3.50 —
Margin block of 4, Mr. Zip 1.15 —
Margin block of 4, copyright 1.15 —
a. Imperf. pair —

INTERNATIONAL YEAR OF THE CHILD ISSUE

Children of Different Races — A1161

Designed by Paul Calle.

ENGRAVED
Plates of 200 subjects in four panes of 50 each.

1979, Feb. 15 **Tagged** ***Perf. 11***

1772 A1161 15c **orange red** 28 5
Margin block of 4, P# 1.20 —
Margin block of 4, Mr. Zip 1.15 —
Margin block of 4, copyright 1.15 —

JOHN STEINBECK ISSUE

John Steinbeck (1902-1968), Novelist — A1162

Designed by Bradbury Thompson after photograph by Philippe Halsman.

ENGRAVED
Plates of 200 subjects in four panes of 50 each.

1979, Feb. 27 **Tagged** ***Perf. 10½x11***

1773 A1162 15c **dark blue** 28 5
Margin block of 4, P# 1.20 —
Margin block of 4, Mr. Zip 1.15 —
Margin block of 4, copyright 1.15 —

ALBERT EINSTEIN ISSUE

Albert Einstein (1879-1955), Theoretical Physicist. — A1163

Designed by Bradbury Thompson after photograph by Hermann Landshoff.

ENGRAVED
Plates of 200 subjects in four panes of 50 each.

1979, Mar. 4 **Tagged** ***Perf. 10½x11***

1774 A1163 15c **chocolate** 28 5
Margin block of 4, P# 1.20 —
Margin block of 4, Mr. Zip 1.15 —
Margin block of 4, copyright 1.15 —
Pair, horiz. gutter btwn. —

AMERICAN FOLK ART ISSUE
Pennsylvania Toleware, c. 1800

Coffeepot — A1164

Tea Caddy — A1165

Sugar Bowl — A1166

Coffeepot — A1167

Designed by Bradbury Thompson.

PHOTOGRAVURE (Andreotti)
Plates of 160 subjects in four panes of 40 each.

1979, Apr. 19 **Tagged** ***Perf. 11***

1775 A1164 15c **multicolored** 28 8
Margin block of 10, 5 P# 2.90 —
Margin block of 16, 5 P#; Mr. Zip and copyright adjoining Nos. 1775-1776 4.75 —
Margin block of 6, Mr. Zip and copyright adjoining Nos. 1775-1776 1.75 —
1776 A1165 15c **multicolored** 28 8
1777 A1166 15c **multicolored** 28 8
Margin block of 16, 5 P#; Mr. Zip and copyright adjoining Nos. 1777-1778 4.75 —
Margin block of 6, Mr. Zip and copyright adjoining Nos. 1777-1778 1.75 —
1778 A1167 15c **multicolored** 28 8
a. Block of 4, #1775-1778 1.15 85
b. As "a," imperf. horiz. —

AMERICAN ARCHITECTURE ISSUE

Nos. 1779-1782 printed se-tenant in blocks of four. Nos. 1779-1780 alternate in first row, Nos. 1781-1782 in second.

Virginia Rotunda, by Thomas Jefferson — A1168

Latrobe 1764-1820 Baltimore Cathedral
Architecture USA 15c

Baltimore Cathedral, by Benjamin Latrobe — A1169

The Catalogue editors cannot undertake to appraise, identify or judge the genuineness or condition of stamps.

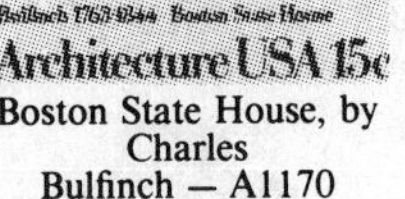

Boston State House, by Charles Bulfinch — A1170

Philadelphia Exchange, by William Strickland — A1171

Designed by Walter D. Richards.

ENGRAVED (Giori)

Plates of 192 subjects in four panes of 48 (6x8).

1979, June 4 **Tagged** ***Perf. 11***

1779 A1168 15c **black & brick red** 28 8
Margin block of 4, P# adjoining #1779 1.25 —
Margin block of 4, Mr. Zip adjoining #1779 1.20 —
Margin block of 4, copyright adjoining #1779 1.20 —

1780 A1169 15c **black & brick red** 28 8
Margin block of 4, P# adjoining #1780 1.25 —
Margin block of 4, Mr. Zip adjoining #1780 1.20 —
Margin block of 4, copyright adjoining #1780 1.20 —

1781 A1170 15c **black & brick red** 28 8
Margin block of 4, P# adjoining #1781 1.25 —
Margin block of 4, Mr. Zip adjoining #1781 1.20 —
Margin block of 4, copyright adjoining #1781 1.20 —

1782 A1171 15c **black & brick red** 28 8
Margin block of 4, P# adjoining #1782 1.25 —
Margin block of 4, Mr. Zip adjoining #1782 1.20 —
Margin block of 4, copyright adjoining #1782 1.20 —
a. Block of 4, #1779-1782 1.15 85

ENDANGERED FLORA ISSUE

Nos. 1783-1786 are printed in blocks of four. Nos. 1783-1784 alternate in one horizontal row. Nos. 1785-1786 in the next.

Persistent Trillium A1172

Hawaiian Wild Broadbean A1173

Contra Costa Wallflower A1174

Antioch Dunes Evening Primrose A1175

Designed by Frank J. Waslick.

PHOTOGRAVURE (Andreotti)

Plates of 200 subjects in four panes of 50 each.

1979, June 7 **Tagged** ***Perf. 11***

1783 A1172 15c **multicolored** 28 8
Margin block of 12, 6 P# adjoining Nos. 1783-1784 3.50 —

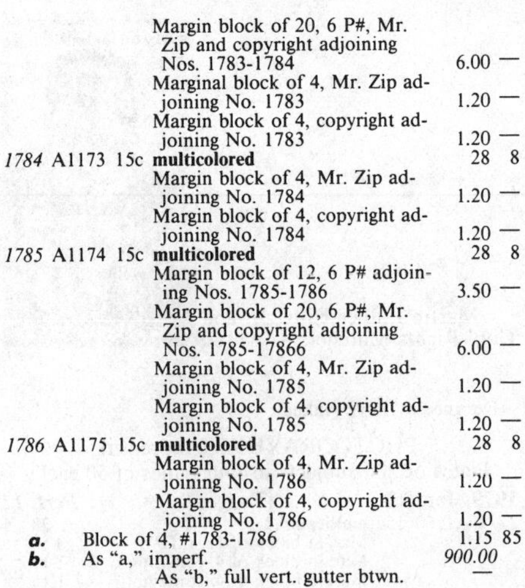

Margin block of 20, 6 P#, Mr. Zip and copyright adjoining Nos. 1783-1784 6.00 —
Marginal block of 4, Mr. Zip adjoining No. 1783 1.20 —
Margin block of 4, copyright adjoining No. 1783 1.20 —

1784 A1173 15c **multicolored** 28 8
Margin block of 4, Mr. Zip adjoining No. 1784 1.20 —
Margin block of 4, copyright adjoining No. 1784 1.20 —

1785 A1174 15c **multicolored** 28 8
Margin block of 12, 6 P# adjoining Nos. 1785-1786 3.50 —
Margin block of 20, 6 P#, Mr. Zip and copyright adjoining Nos. 1785-17866 6.00 —
Margin block of 4, Mr. Zip adjoining No. 1785 1.20 —
Margin block of 4, copyright adjoining No. 1785 1.20 —

1786 A1175 15c **multicolored** 28 8
Margin block of 4, Mr. Zip adjoining No. 1786 1.20 —
Margin block of 4, copyright adjoining No. 1786 1.20 —
a. Block of 4, #1783-1786 1.15 85
b. As "a," imperf. *900.00*
As "b," full vert. gutter btwn. —

SEEING EYE DOGS ISSUE

First guide dog program in the United States, 50th anniversary.

German Shepherd Leading Man — A1176

Designed by Joseph Csatari.

PHOTOGRAVURE (Combination Press)

Plates of 230 (10x23) subjects in panes of 50 (10x5).

1979, June 15 **Tagged** ***Perf. 11***

1787 A1176 15c **multicolored** 28 5
Margin block of 20, 5-8 P#, 1-2 copyright 5.75 —
a. Imperf. pair *500.00*

See Combination Press note after No. 1703.

Child Holding Winner's Medal — A1177

I have not yet begun to fight
John Paul Jones
US Bicentennial 15c

John Paul Jones, by Charles Willson Peale — A1178

SPECIAL OLYMPICS ISSUE

Special Olympics for special children, Brockport, N.Y., Aug. 8-13.

Designed by Jeff Cornell.

PHOTOGRAVURE (Andreotti)

Plates of 200 subjects in four panes of 50 each.

1979, Aug. 9 **Tagged** ***Perf. 11***

1788 A1177 15c **multicolored** 28 5
Margin block of 10, 5 P# 2.90 —
Margin block of 4, Mr. Zip 1.20 —
Margin block of 4, copyright 1.20 —

JOHN PAUL JONES ISSUE

John Paul Jones (1747-1792), Naval Commander, American Revolution.

Designed by Bradbury Thompson after painting in Independence National Historical Park, Philadelphia.

Printed by American Bank Note Co. and J. W. Fergusson and Sons.

PHOTOGRAVURE (Champlain)

Plates of 200 subjects in four panes of 50 each.

1979, Sept. 23 **Tagged** ***Perf. 11x12***

1789 A1178 15c **multicolored** 28 5
P# block of 10, 5 P# 2.90 —
Zip block of 4 1.20 —
Copyright block of 4 1.20 —
a. Perf. 11 30 6
a. P# block of 10, 5 P# 3.10 —
b. Perf. 12 —
c. Vert. pair, imperf. horiz. *200.00*
d. As "a," vert. pair, imperf. horiz. *150.00*

Numerous varieties of printer's waste exist. These include imperforates, perforated or imperforate gutter pairs or blocks and missing colors.

OLYMPIC GAMES ISSUE

22nd Summer Olympic Games, Moscow, July 19-Aug. 3, 1980. Nos. 1791-1794 printed se-tenant. Nos. 1791-1792 alternate in one horizontal row, Nos. 1793-1794 in next.

Decathlon, Javelin — A1179

Running — A1180

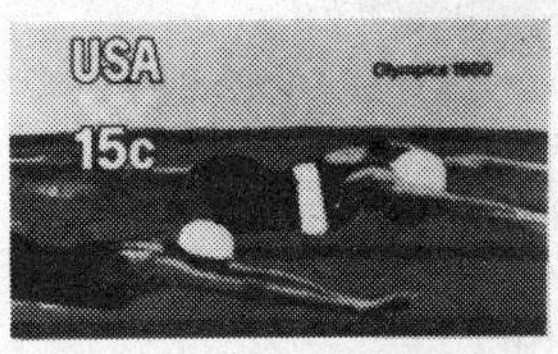

Swimming, Women's A1181

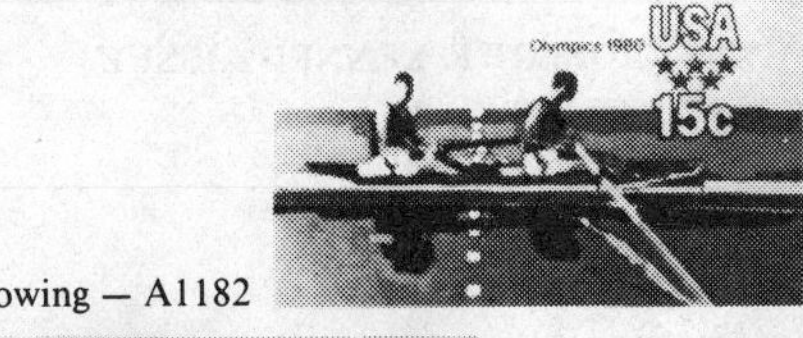

Rowing — A1182

Equestrian A1183

Designed by Robert M. Cunningham.

PHOTOGRAVURE

Plates of 200 subjects in four panes of 50 each.

1979, Sept. 5 **Tagged** ***Perf. 11***

1790 A1179 10c **multicolored** 20 22
P# block of 12, 6 P# 2.50 —
Zip block of 4 85 —
Copyright block of 4 85 —

1979, Sept. 28

1791 A1180 15c **multicolored** 28 8
P# block of 12, 6 P# adjoining Nos. 1791, 1793 3.50 —
Zip block of 4 1.20 —
Copyright block of 4 1.20 —
P# block of 20, 6 P#, zip, copyright adjoining Nos. 1791, 1793 6.00 —

1792 A1181 15c **multicolored** 28 8

P# block of 12, 6 P# adjoining Nos. 1792, 1794 — 3.50 —
Zip block of 4 — 1.20 —
Copyright block of 4 — 1.20 —
P# block of 20, 6 P#, zip, copyright adjoining Nos. 1792, 1794 — 6.00 —

1793 A1182 15c **multicolored** — 28 8
Zip block of 4 — 1.20 —
Copyright block of 4 — 1.20 —

1794 A1183 15c **multicolored** — 28 8
Zip block of 4 — 1.20 —
Copyright block of 4 — 1.20 —
a. Block of 4, #1791-1794 — 1.15 85
b. As "a," imperf. — *1,850.*

OLYMPIC GAMES ISSUE

13th Winter Olympic Games, Lake Placid, N. Y., Feb. 12-24. Nos. 1795-1798 printed se-tenant. Nos. 1795-1796 alternate in one horizontal row, Nos. 1797-1798 in next.

Speed Skating — A1184

Downhill Skiing — A1185

Ski Jump — A1186

Hockey Goaltender A1187

Designed by Robert M. Cunningham

Plates of 200 subject in four panes of 50 each.
PHOTOGRAVURE

1980, Feb. 1 **Tagged** ***Perf. 11x10½***

1795 A1184 15c **multicolored** — 32 8
a. Perf. 11 — 1.05 —
1796 A1185 15c **multicolored** — 32 8
a. Perf. 11 — 1.05 —
1797 A1186 15c **multicolored** — 32 8
a. Perf. 11 — 1.05 —
1798 A1187 15c **multicolored** — 32 8
P# block of 12, 6 P# — 4.00 —
Zip block of 4 — 1.35 —
Copyright block of 4 — 1.35 —
P# block of 20, 6 P#, zip and copyright — 6.75 —
a. Perf. 11 — 1.05 —
a. P# block of 12, 6 P# — 13.00 —
a. P# block of 20, 6 P#, zip and copyright — 22.00 —
b. Block of 4, #1795-1798 — 1.30 85
c. Block of 4, #1795a-1798a — 4.25 —

CHRISTMAS ISSUE

Virgin and Child by Gerard David A1188

Santa Claus, Christmas Tree Ornament A1189

Designed by Bradbury Thompson (No. 1799) after painting in National Gallery of Art, Washington, D.C. and by Eskil Ohlsson (No. 1800).

PHOTOGRAVURE (Andreotti)
Plates of 400 subjects in four panes of 100 each.

1979, Oct. 18 **Tagged** ***Perf. 11***

1799 A1188 15c **multicolored** — 28 5
P# block of 12, 6 P# — 3.40 —
Zip block of 4 — 1.15 —
Copyright block of 4 — 1.15 —
P# block of 20, 6 P#, zip, copyright — 5.75 —
a. Imperf. pair — *100.00*
b. Vert. pair, imperf. horiz. — *1,000.*
c. Vert. pair, imperf. between

1800 A1189 15c **multicolored** — 28 5
P# block of 12, 6 P# — 3.40 —
Zip block of 4 — 1.15 —
Copyright block of 4 — 1.15 —
P# block of 20, 6 P#, zip, copyright — 5.75 —
a. Green & yellow omitted — *750.00*
b. Green, yellow & tan omitted — *800.00*

PERFORMING ARTS ISSUE

Will Rogers (1879-1935), actor and humorist.

Will Rogers — A1190

Designed by Jim Sharpe.

Plates of 200 subjects in four panes of 50 each.
PHOTOGRAVURE (Andreotti)

1979, Nov. 4 **Tagged** ***Perf. 11***

1801 A1190 15c **multicolored** — 28 5
P# block of 12, 6 P# — 3.40 —
Zip block of 4 — 1.15 —
Copyright block of 4 — 1.15 —
P# block of 20, 6 P#, zip, copyright — 5.75 —
a. Imperf. pair — *275.00*

VIETNAM VETERANS ISSUE

A tribute to veterans of the Vietnam War.

Ribbon for Vietnam Service Medal — A1191

Designed by Stevan Dohanos.

PHOTOGRAVURE (Andreotti)
Plates of 200 subjects in four panes of 50 each.

1979, Nov. 11 **Tagged** ***Perf. 11***

1802 A1191 15c **multicolored** — 28 5
P# block of 10, 5 P# — 2.90 —
Zip block of 4 — 1.15 —
Copyright block of 4 — 1.15 —

PERFORMING ARTS ISSUE

W.C. Fields (1800-1946), actor and comedian.

W.C. Fields — A1192

Designed by Jim Sharpe.

Plates of 200 subjects in four panes of 50 each.
PHOTOGRAVURE

1980, Jan. 29 **Tagged** ***Perf. 11***

1803 A1192 15c **multicolored** — 28 5
P# block of 12, 6 P# — 3.40 —
Zip block of 4 — 1.15 —
Copyright block of 4 — 1.15 —
P# block of 20, 6 P#, zip, copyright — 5.75 —

BLACK HERITAGE ISSUE

Benjamin Banneker (1731-1806), astronomer and mathematician.

Benjamin Banneker — A1193

Designed by Jerry Pinkney.
Printed by American Bank Note Co. and J. W. Fergusson and Sons.

Plates of 200 subjects in four panes of 50 each.
PHOTOGRAVURE

1980, Feb. 15 **Tagged** ***Perf. 11***

1804 A1193 15c **multicolored** — 28 5
P# block of 12, 6 P# — 3.40 —
Zip block of 4 — 1.15 —
Copyright block of 4 — 1.15 —
Plate block of 20, 6 P#, zip, copyright — 5.75 —
a. Horiz. pair, imperf. vert. — —

Imperfs, including gutter pairs and blocks, exist from printer's waste.

NATIONAL LETTER WRITING WEEK ISSUE

National Letter Writing Week, Feb. 24-Mar. 1. Nos. 1805-1810 are printed vertically se-tenant.

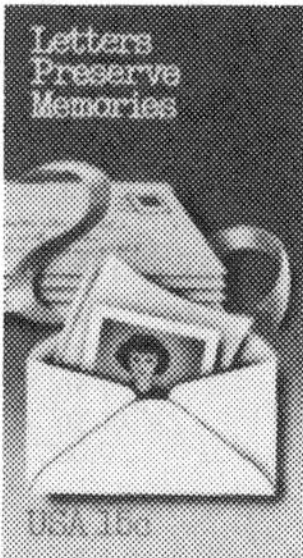

Letters Preserve Memories — A1194

P.S. Write Soon — A1195

Letters Lift Spirits — A1196

Letters Shape Opinions — A1197

Designed by Randall McDougall.

Plates of 240 subjects in four panes of 60 (10x6) each.
PHOTOGRAVURE

1980, Feb. 25 **Tagged** ***Perf. 11***

1805 A1194 15c **multicolored** — 28 8
P# block of 36, 6 P# adjoining #1805 — 10.50 —

Zip block of 12, adjoining #1805 — 3.50 —
Copyright block of 12, adjoining #1805 — 3.50 —
1806 A1195 15c **purple & multi** 28 8
1807 A1196 15c **multicolored** 28 8
1808 A1195 15c **green & multi** 28 8
1809 A1197 15c **multicolored** 28 8
1810 A1195 15c **red & multi** 28 8
P# block of 36, 6 P# adjoining #1810 — 10.50 —
Zip block of 12, adjoining #1810 — 3.50 —
Copyright block of 12, adjoining #1810 — 3.50 —
a. Vertical strip of 6, #1805-1810 1.70 1.25

AMERICANA TYPE

Weaver Violins — A1199

Designer: 3.5c, George Mercer.

COIL STAMPS

1980-81 **Engr.** ***Perf. 10 Vertically***
1811 A984 1c **dark blue,** *greenish, Mar. 6, 1980* 5 5
Pair 10 10
Joint line pair 30 30
Dull finish gum 5
a. Imperf., pair *220.00*
1813 A1199 3.5c **purple,** *yellow, June 23, 1980* 8 5
Pair 16 10
Joint line pair 90 —
a. Untagged (Bureau precanceled, lines only) 10
b. Imperf., pair *275.00*
1816 A997 12c **red brown,** *beige, Apr. 8, 1981* 24 5
Pair 48 10
Joint line pair 1.25 —
a. Untagged (Bureau precanceled, lines only) 25
b. Imperf., pair *200.00*

Eagle — A1207

PHOTOGRAVURE

Plates of 400 subjects in four panes of 100 each.

1981, Mar. 15 **Tagged** ***Perf. 11x10½***
1818 A1207 (18c) **violet** 32 5
P# block of 4 1.50 —
Zip block of 4 1.30 —
Mail Early block of 6 2.00 —

ENGRAVED

1819 A1207 (18c) **violet** (from booklet pane) 38 5
a. Booklet pane of 8 4.50 *1.50*

COIL STAMP

1820 A1207 (18c) **violet** 40 5
Pair 80 10
Joint line pair 1.60 —
a. Imperf., pair *110.00*

Frances Perkins
A1208

Dolley
Madison
A1209

FRANCES PERKINS ISSUE

Frances Perkins (1882-1965), Secretary of Labor, 1933-1945 (first woman cabinet member).

Designed by F.R. Petrie.

ENGRAVED

Plates of 200 subjects in four panes of 50 each.

1980, Apr. 10 **Tagged** ***Perf. 10½x11***
1821 A1208 15c **Prussian blue** 28 5
P# block of 4 1.20 —
Zip block of 4 1.15 —
Copyright block of 4 1.15 —

DOLLEY MADISON ISSUE

Dolley Madison (1768-1849), First Lady, 1809-1817.

Designed by Esther Porter.

ENGRAVED

Plates of 600 subjects in four panes of 150 each.

1980, May 20 **Tagged** ***Perf. 11***
1822 A1209 15c **red brown & sepia** 28 5
P# block of 4 1.40 —
Zip block of 4 1.15 —
Copyright block of 4 1.15 —

Emily
Bissell — A1210

Helen Keller and
Anne
Sullivan — A1211

EMILY BISSELL ISSUE

Emily Bissell (1861-1948), social worker; introduced Christmas seals in United States.

Designed by Stevan Dohanos.

ENGRAVED

Plates of 200 subjects in four panes of 50 each.

1980, May 31 **Tagged** ***Perf. 11***
1823 A1210 15c **black & red** 28 5
P# block of 4 1.20 —
Zip block of 4 1.15 —
Copyright block of 4 1.15 —
a. Vert. pair, imperf. horiz. *325.00*

HELEN KELLER ISSUE

Helen Keller (1880-1968), blind and deaf writer and lecturer taught by Anne Sullivan (1867-1936).

Designed by Paul Calle.

LITHOGRAPHED AND ENGRAVED

Plates of 200 subjects in four panes of 50 each.

1980, June 27 **Tagged** ***Perf. 11***
1824 A1121 15c **multicolored** 28 5
P# block of 4 1.20 —
Zip block of 4 1.15 —
Copyright block of 4 1.15 —

Veterans
Administration
Emblem — A1212

Gen. Bernardo de
Galvez — A1213

VETERANS ADMINISTRATION ISSUE

Veterans Administration, 50th anniversary.

Designed by Malcolm Grear.
Printed by American Bank Note Co. and J. W. Fergusson and Sons.

PHOTOGRAVURE

Plates of 200 subjects in four panes of 50 each.

1980, July 21 **Tagged** ***Perf. 11***
1825 A1212 15c **carmine & violet blue** 28 5
P# block of 4, 2 P# 1.20 —
Zip block of 4 1.15 —
Copyright block of 4 1.15 —
a. Horiz. pair, imperf. vert. *500.00*

BERNARDO DE GALVEZ ISSUE

Gen. Bernardo de Galvez (1746-1786), helped defeat British in Battle of Mobile, 1780.

Designed by Roy H. Andersen.

LITHOGRAPHED & ENGRAVED

Plates of 200 subjects in four panes of 50 each.

1980, July 23 **Tagged** ***Perf. 11***
1826 A1213 15c **multicolored** 28 5
P# block of 4 1.20 —
Zip block of 4 1.15 —
Copyright block of 4 1.15 —
a. Red, brown & blue (engr.) omitted —
b. Blue, brown, red (engr.) & yellow (litho.) omitted —

CORAL REEFS ISSUE

Nos. 1827-1830 are printed in blocks of four. Nos. 1827-1828 alternate in one horizontal row. Nos. 1829-1830 in the next.

Brain Coral,
Beaugregory
Fish — A1214

Elkhorn Coral,
Porkfish — A1215

Chalice Coral,
Moorish
Idol — A1216

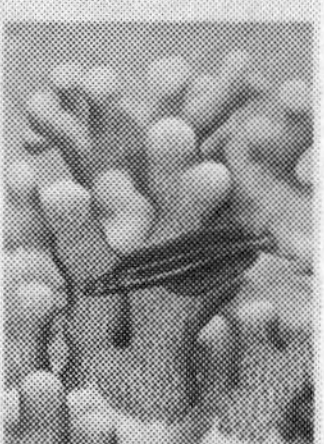

Finger Coral,
Sabertooth
Blenny — A1217

Designed by Chuck Ripper.

PHOTOGRAVURE

Plates of 200 subjects in four panes of 50 each.

1980, Aug. 26 **Tagged** ***Perf. 11***
1827 A1214 15c **multi** 30 8
P# block of 12, 6 P# adjoining #1827, 1828 3.65 —
Zip block of 4, adjoining #1827 1.25 —
Copyright block of 4, adjoining #1827 1.25 —
1828 A1215 15c **multi** 30 8
Zip block of 4, adjoining #1828 1.25 —
Copyright block of 4, adjoining #1828 1.25 —
1829 A1216 15c **multi** 30 8
P# block of 12, 6 P# adjoining #1829, 1830 3.65 —
Zip block of 4, adjoining #1829 1.25 —
Copyright block of 4, adjoining #1829 1.25 —
1830 A1217 15c **multi** 30 8
Zip block of 4, adjoining #1830 1.25 —
Copyright block of 4, adjoining #1830 1.25 —
a. Block of 4, #1827-1830 1.20 85
b. As "a," imperf. *1,500.*
c. As "a," imperf. btwn., vert —
d. As "a," imperf. vert. —

American Bald Eagle — A1218

Edith Wharton — A1219

ORGANIZED LABOR ISSUE

Designed by Peter Cocci.

PHOTOGRAVURE
Plates of 200 subjects in four panes of 50 each.

1980, Sept. 1	Tagged	Perf. 11	
1831 A1218 15c **multi**		28	5
	P# block of 12, 6 P#	3.50	—
	Zip block of 4	1.15	—
	Copyright block of 4	1.15	—
a. Imperf., pair		*450.00*	

EDITH WHARTON ISSUE

Edith Wharton (1862-1937), novelist.

Designed by Bradbury Thompson after 1905 photograph.

ENGRAVED
Plates of 200 subjects in four panes of 50 each.

1980, Sept. 5	Tagged	Perf. 10½x11	
1832 A1219 15c **purple**		28	5
	P# block of 4	1.20	—
	Zip block of 4	1.15	—
	Copyright block of 4	1.15	—

EDUCATION ISSUE

"Homage to the Square: Glow" by Josef Albers — A1220

Designed by Bradbury Thompson
Printed by American Bank Note Co. and J. W. Fergusson and Sons.

PHOTOGRAVURE
Plates of 200 subjects in four panes of 50 each.

1980, Sept. 12	Tagged	Perf. 11	
1833 A1220 15c **multi**		28	5
	P# block of 6, 3 P#	1.70	—
	Zip block of 4	1.15	—
	Copyright block of 4	1.15	—
a. Horiz. pair, imperf. vert.		*300.00*	

AMERICAN FOLK ART ISSUE

Pacific Northwest Indian Masks

Heiltsuk, Bella Bella Tribe — A1221

Chilkat Tlingit Tribe — A1222

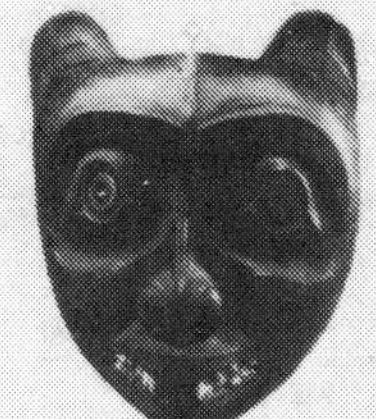

Tlingit Tribe — A1223

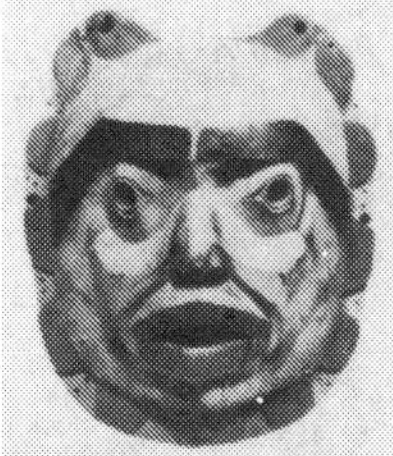

Bella Coola Tribe — A1224

Designed by Bradbury Thompson after photographs.

PHOTOGRAVURE
Plates of 160 subjects in four panes of 40 each.

1980, Sept. 25	Tagged	Perf. 11	
1834 A1221 15c **multi**		30	8
1835 A1222 15c **multi**		30	8
1836 A1223 15c **multi**		30	8
1837 A1224 15c **multi**		30	8
	P# block of 10, 5 P#	3.10	—
	Zip, copyright block of 6	1.85	—
a. Block of 4, #1834-1837		1.20	85

AMERICAN ARCHITECTURE ISSUE

Smithsonian A1225

Trinity Church — A1226

Penn Academy A1227

Lyndhurst A1228

Designed by Walter D. Richards.

ENGRAVED (Giori)
Plates of 160 subjects in four panes of 40 each.

1980, Oct. 9	Tagged	Perf. 11	
1838 A1225 15c **black & red**		30	8
1839 A1226 15c **black & red**		30	8
1840 A1227 15c **black & red**		30	8
1841 A1228 15c **black & red**		30	8
	P# block of 4	1.30	—
	Zip block of 4	1.25	—
	Copyright block of 4	1.25	—
a. Block of 4, #1838-1841		1.20	85

CHRISTMAS ISSUE

Madonna and Child — A1229

Wreath and Toys — A1230

Designed by Esther Porter (No. 1842) after Epiphany Window, Washington Cathedral, and by Bob Timberlake (No. 1843).

PHOTOGRAVURE
Plate of 200 subjects in four panes of 50 each.

1980, Oct. 31	Tagged	Perf. 11	
1842 A1229 15c **multi**		28	5
	P# block of 12, 6 P#	3.40	—
	Zip block of 4	1.15	—
	Copyright block of 4	1.15	—
a. Imperf., pair		*100.00*	
	Pair with full vert. gutter btwn.	—	

PHOTOGRAVURE (Combination Press)
Plates of 230 subjects (10x23) in panes of 50 (10x5).

1843 A1230 15c **multi**		28	5
	P# block of 20, 5-8 P#, 1-2 copyright	5.75	—
	Copyright block of 4	1.15	—
a. Imperf., pair		*100.00*	

See Combination Press note after No. 1703.

GREAT AMERICANS ISSUE

A1231

A1232

A1233

A1234

A1235

A1236

A1237

A1238

A1239

A1240

A1241 A1242
A1243 A1244
A1245 A1246
A1247 A1248
A1249 A1250
A1251 A1252
A1253 A1254
A1255 A1256

Designers: 1c, Bernie Fuchs. 2c, Burt Silverman, 3c, 17c, 40c, Ward Brackett. 4c, 7c, 10c, 18c, 30c, Richard Sparks. 6c, No. 1862, Dennis Lyall. 8c, Arthur Lidov. 9c, 11c, Robert Alexander Anderson. 13c, Brad Holland. 14c, Bradbury Thompson. 19c, 39c, Roy H. Andersen. No. 1860, Jim Sharpe. No. 1861, 22c, 50c, 37c, Christopher Calle. 35c, Nathan Jones.

ENGRAVED

Perf. 10½x11, Perf. 11 (1c, 6c-11c, 14c, No. 1862, 22c, 30c, 39c, 40c, 50c)

1980-85 **Tagged**

1844 A1231 1c **black,** *Sept. 23, 1983* 5 5
P# block of 6, P# 35 —
P# block of 20, 1-2 P 1-2 copyright 1.00 —
Perf. 11.2 5 5
a. Imperf., pair *300.00*
b. Vert. pair, imperf. between —
1845 A1232 2c **brn blk,** *Nov. 18, 1982* 5 5
P# block of 4 25 —
Zip block of 4 20 —
Copyright block of 4 20 —
1846 A1233 3c **olive green,** *July 13, 1983* 6 5
P# block of 4 30 —
Zip block of 4 25 —
Copyright block of 4 25 —
1847 A1234 4c **violet,** *June 3, 1983* 7 5
P# block of 4 32 —
Zip block of 4 30 —
Copyright block of 4 30 —
1848 A1235 5c **henna brown,** *June 25, 1983* 9 5
P# block of 4 40 —
Zip block of 4 38 —
Copyright block of 4 38 —
1849 A1236 6c **orange vermilion,** *Sept. 19, 1985* 12 5
P# block of 6, P# 75 —
P# block of 20, 1-2 P 1-2 zip, 1-2 copyright 2.50 —
a. Vert. pair, imperf. horiz. —
1850 A1237 7c **bright carmine,** *Jan. 25, 1985* 12 5
P# block of 6, P# 75 —
P# block of 20, 1-2 P 1-2 zip, 1-2 copyright 2.60 —
1851 A1238 8c **olive black,** *July 25, 1985* 14 5
P# block of 4 70 —
Zip block of 4 60 —
Copyright block of 4 60 —
1852 A1239 9c **dark green,** *June 7, 1985* 16 5
P# block of 6, P# 1.00 —
P# block of 20, 1-2 P 1-2 zip, 1-2 copyright 3.25 —
1853 A1240 10c **Prus. blue,** *May 31, 1984* 18 5
P# block of 6, P# 1.10 —
P# block of 20, 1-2 P 1-2 copyright, 1-2 zip 4.00 —
a. Vert. pair, imperf. between —

Completely imperforate and untagged stamps are from printer's waste.

1854 A1241 11c **dark blue,** *Feb. 12, 1985* 20 5
P# block of 4 95 —
Zip block of 4 85 —
Copyright block of 4 85 —
1855 A1242 13c **lt. maroon,** *Jan. 15, 1982* 24 5
P# block of 4 1.35 —
Zip block of 4 1.00 —
Copyright block of 4 1.00 —
1856 A1243 14c **slate green,** *Mar. 21, 1985* 25 5
P# block of 6, P# 1.55 —
P# block of 20, 1-2 P 1-2 zip, 1-2 copyright 5.10 —
a. Vert. pair, imperf. horiz. *175.00*
b. Horiz. pair, imperf. btwn. 12.50
c. Vert. pair, imperf. btwn. *1,500.*
1857 A1244 17c **green,** *May 28, 1981* 32 5
P# block of 4 1.40 —
Zip block of 4 1.30 —
Copyright block of 4 1.30 —
1858 A1245 18c **dark blue,** *May 7, 1981* 32 5
P# block of 4 2.00 —
Zip block of 4 1.30 —
Copyright block of 4 1.30 —
1859 A1246 19c **brown,** *Dec. 27, 1980* 35 7
P# block of 4 2.00 —
Zip block of 4 1.45 —
Copyright block of 4 1.45 —
1860 A1247 20c **claret,** *Jan. 12, 1982* 40 5
P# block of 4 2.50 —
Zip block of 4 1.65 —
Copyright block of 4 1.65 —
1861 A1248 20c **green,** *June 10, 1983* 38 5
P# block of 4 2.50 —
Zip block of 4 1.55 —
Copyright block of 4 1.55 —
1862 A1249 20c **black,** *Jan. 26, 1984* 38 5
P# block of 6, P# 2.40 —
P# block of 20, 1-2 P 1-2 copyright, 1-2 zip 9.25 —
Perf. 11.2 38 5
Corner P# block of 4, perf. 11.2 1.60 —
1863 A1250 22c **dark chalky blue,** *Apr. 23, 1985* 40 5
P# block of 6, P# 2.50 —
P# block of 20, 1-2 P 1-2 zip, 1-2 copyright 8.50 —
Perf. 11.2 40 5
Corner P# block of 4, perf. 11.2 2.75 —
a. Vert. pair, imperf. horiz. —
b. Vert. pair, imperf. btwn. —
1864 A1251 30c **olive gray,** *Sept. 2, 1984* 55 8
P# block of 6, P# 3.50 —
P# block of 20, 1-2 P 1-2 copyright, 1-2 zip 11.00 —
Perf. 11.2 55 8
Corner P# block of 4, perf. 11.2 2.25 —
1865 A1252 35c **gray,** *June 3, 1981* 65 8
P# block of 4 2.75 —
Zip block of 4 2.65 —
Copyright block of 4 2.65 —
1866 A1253 37c **blue,** *Jan. 26, 1982* 70 5
P# block of 4 2.90 —
Zip block of 4 2.85 —
Copyright block of 4 2.85 —
1867 A1254 39c **rose lilac,** *May 20, 1985* 70 8
P# block of 6, P# 4.25 —
P# block of 20, 1-2 P 1-2 zip, 1-2 copyright 14.50 —
Perf. 11.2 70 8
Corner P# block of 4, perf. 11.2 3.25 —
a. Vert. pair, imperf. horiz. *700.00*
b. Vert. pair, imperf. between *1,100.*
1868 A1255 40c **dark green,** *Feb. 24, 1984* 75 10
P# block of 6, P# 4.60 —
P# block of 20, 1-2 P 1-2 copyright, 1-2 zip 15.50 —
Perf. 11.2 75 10
Corner P# block of 4, perf. 11.2 3.10 —
1869 A1256 50c **brown,** *Feb. 22, 1985* 90 10
P# block of 4 4.50 —
Zip block of 4 3.65 —
Copyright block of 4 3.65 —
Perf. 11.2 90 10
P# block of 4 4.50 —

A1261

A1262

EVERETT DIRKSEN (1896-1969)

Senate minority leader, 1960-1969.

Designed by Ron Adair

ENGRAVED

Plates of 200 subjects in four panes of 50 each.

1981, Jan. 4 **Tagged** ***Perf. 11***

1874 A1261 15c **gray** 28 5
P# block of 4 1.20 —
Zip block of 4 1.15 —
Copyright block of 4 1.15 —

BLACK HERITAGE

Whitney Moore Young, Jr. (1921-1971), civil rights leader.

Designed by Jerry Pinkney.

PHOTOGRAVURE

Plates of 200 subjects in four panes of 50 each.

1981, Jan. 30 **Tagged** ***Perf. 11***

1875 A1262 15c **multi** 28 5
P# block of 4 1.25 —
Zip block of 4 1.15 —
Copyright block of 4 1.15 —

FLOWER ISSUE

Rose — A1263

Camellia — A1264

An enhanced introduction to the Scott Catalogue begins on Page V. A thorough understanding of the material presented there will greatly aid your use of the catalogue itself.

Dahlia — A1265

Lily — A1266

Designed by Lowell Nesbitt.

PHOTOGRAVURE

Plates of 192 subjects in four panes of 48 (8x6).

1981, Apr. 23 **Tagged** ***Perf. 11***

1876	A1263	18c	**multicolored**	35	8
1877	A1264	18c	**multicolored**	35	8
1878	A1265	18c	**multicolored**	35	8
1879	A1266	18c	**multicolored**	35	8
			P# block of 4	1.50	—
			Zip block of 4	1.45	—
			Copyright block of 4	1.45	—
a.			Block of 4, #1876-1879	1.40	85

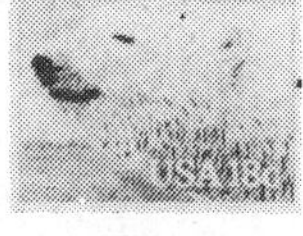

A1267-A1276

Designs from photographs by Jim Brandenburg.

ENGRAVED

1981, May 14 **Tagged** ***Perf. 11***

Dark brown

1880	A1267	18c	Bighorn	32	5
1881	A1268	18c	Puma	32	5
1882	A1269	18c	Harbor seal	32	5
1883	A1270	18c	Bison	32	5
1884	A1271	18c	Brown bear	32	5
1885	A1272	18c	Polar bear	32	5
1886	A1273	18c	Elk (wapiti)	32	5
1887	A1274	18c	Moose	32	5
1888	A1275	18c	White-tailed deer	32	5
1889	A1276	18c	Pronghorn	32	5
a.			Booklet pane of 10	8.00	—

Nos. 1880-1889 issued in booklet only. All stamps have one or two straight edges.

FLAG AND ANTHEM ISSUE

A1277

A1278

A1279

A1280

Designed by Peter Cocci.

ENGRAVED

Plates of 460 subjects (20x23) in panes of 100 (10x10).

1981, Apr. 24 **Tagged** ***Perf. 11***

1890	A1277	18c	**multi**	32	5
			P# block of 6, P#	2.00	—
			P# block of 20, 1-2 P#	9.00	—
a.			Imperf., pair	100.00	

See Combination Press note after No. 1703.

Coil Stamp

Perf. 10 Vert.

1891	A1278	18c	**multi**	36	5
			Pair	72	10
			P# strip of 3, P# 5	5.50	
			P# strip of 3, P# 1	130.00	
			P# strip of 3, P# 2	27.50	
			P# strip of 3, P# 3	350.00	
			P# strip of 3, P# 4	8.00	
			P# strip of 3, P# 6	—	
			P# strip of 3, P# 7	20.00	
a.			Imperf., pair	20.00	

Booklet Stamps

Perf. 11

1892	A1279	6c	**multi**	55	10
1893	A1280	18c	**multi**	32	5
a.			Booklet pane of 8 (2 #1892, 6 #1893)	3.20	—
b.			As "a," vert. imperf. btwn.	*85.00*	
c.			Se-tenant pair, #1892 & #1893	90	

FLAG OVER SUPREME COURT ISSUE

A1281

Designed by Dean Ellis

ENGRAVED

Plates of 460 subjects (20x23) in panes of 100 (10x10)

1981, Dec. 17 **Tagged** ***Perf. 11***

1894	A1281	20c	**blk., dk. blue & red**	35	5
			P# block of 6, P#	2.25	—
			P# block of 20, 1-2 P#	7.25	—
			Dull finish gum, perf. 11.2	35	10
a.			Vert. pair, imperf.	25.00	
b.			Vert. pair, imperf. horiz.	*650.00*	
c.			Dark blue omitted	*250.00*	
d.			Black omitted	*400.00*	

Coil Stamp

Perf. 10 Vert.

1895	A1281	20c	**blk., dk. blue & red**	35	5
			Pair	70	10
			P# strip of 3, P# 9, 13, 14	4.50	
			P# strip of 3, P# 1, 2, 8	8.50	
			P# strip of 3, P# 3, 12	5.75	
			P# strip of 3, P# 4	55.00	
			P# strip of 3, P# 5	5.00	
			P# strip of 3, P# 6	45.00	
			P# strip of 3, P# 10	6.50	
			P# strip of 3, P# 11	10.50	
a.			Imperf., pair	6.00	
b.			Black omitted	*65.00*	
c.			Blue omitted	—	
d.			Pair, imperf. btwn.	—	
e.			Untagged (Bureau precanceled, line only)		48
			P# strip of 3, P# 14		9.25

BOOKLET STAMP

Perf. 11x10½

1896	A1281	20c	**blk., dk. blue & red**	35	5
a.			Booklet pane of 6	2.60	—
b.			Booklet pane of 10, *June 1, 1982*	4.00	—

Booklets containing two panes of ten were issued Nov. 17, 1983.

TRANSPORTATION ISSUE

A1283

A1284

A1284a

A1285

A1286

A1287

A1288

A1288a

A1289

A1290

A1291

A1292

A1293

A1294

Designers: 1c, 2c, 5.9c, 10.9c, 18c, David Stone. 3c, 5c, 5.2c, Walter Brooks. 4c, 7.4c, 9.3c, 11c, 20c, Jim Schleyer. 17c Chuck Jaquays.

COIL STAMPS

ENGRAVED

1981-84 **Tagged** ***Perf. 10 Vert.***

1897	A1283	1c	**violet,** *Aug. 19, 1983*	5	5
			Pair	10	10
			P# strip of 3, line, P# 1, 2, 5, 6	50	

P# strip of 3, line, P# 3, 4 60
b. Imperf., pair *650.00*
1897A A1284 2c **black,** *May 20, 1982* 10 5
Pair 20 10
P# strip of 3, line, P# 3, 4, 8 55
P# strip of 3, line, P# 2, 6 85
P# strip of 3, line, P# 10 65
e. Imperf., pair *70.00*
1898 A1284a 3c **dark green,** *Mar. 25, 1983* 9 5
Pair 18 10
P# strip of 3, line, P# 1, 2 85
P# strip of 3, line, P# 3, 4 1.10
1898A A1285 4c **reddish brown,** *Aug. 19, 1982* 9 5
Pair 18 10
P# strip of 3, line, P# 3, 4 1.50
P# strip of 3, line, P# 1, 2, 5, 6 2.00
b. Untagged (Bureau precanceled) 9
P# strip of 3, line, P# 3-6 2.25
c. As "b," imperf. pair *700.00*
1899 A1286 5c **gray green,** *Oct. 10, 1983* 12 5
Pair 24 10
P# strip of 3, line, P# 1-4 1.50
a. Imperf., pair —
1900 A1287 5.2c **carmine,** *Mar. 21, 1983* 12 5
Pair 24 10
P# strip of 3, line, P# 1, 2 11.00
P# strip of 3, line, P# 3, 5 110.00
a. Untagged (Bureau precanceled) 12
P# strip of 3, line, P# 1-3, 5 9.50
P# strip of 3, line, P# 4, 6 11.00
1901 A1288 5.9c **blue,** *Feb. 17, 1982* 18 5
Pair 36 10
P# strip of 3, line, P# 3, 4 11.00
a. Untagged (Bureau Precanceled, lines only) 18
P# strip of 3, line, P# 3, 4 15.00
P# strip of 3, line, P# 5, 6 67.50
b. As "a,", imperf. pair *300.00*
1902 A1288a 7.4c **brown,** *Apr. 7, 1984* 18 8
Pair 36 16
P# strip of 3, P# 2 9.50
a. Untagged (Bureau precanceled) 20
P# strip of 3, P# 2 3.00
1903 A1289 9.3c **carmine rose,** *Dec. 15* 22 8
Pair 44 16
P# strip of 3, line, P# 1, 2 9.50
P# strip of 3, line, P# 3, 4 21.00
P# strip of 3, line, P# 5, 6 190.00
a. Untagged (Bureau precanceled, lines only) 22
P# strip of 3, line, P# 5, 6 4.25
P# strip of 3, line, P# 1 17.50
P# strip of 3, line. P# 2 15.00
P# strip of 3, line, P# 3, 4 22.00
P# strip of 3, line, P# 8 100.00
b. As "a," imperf. pair *125.00*
1904 A1290 10.9c **purple,** *Mar. 26, 1982* 24 5
Pair 48 10
P# strip of 3, line, P# 1, 2 21.00
a. Untagged (Bureau precanceled, lines only) 24
P# strip of 3, line, P# 1, 2 20.00
P# strip of 3, line, P# 3, 4 350.00
b. As "a," imperf. pair *200.00*
1905 A1291 11c **red,** *Feb. 3, 1984* 24 8
Pair 48 16
P# strip of 3, P# 1 4.00
a. Untagged (Bureau precanceled, lines only) 24
P# strip of 3, P# 1 3.25
1906 A1292 17c **ultramarine,** *June 25* 32 5
Pair 65 10
P# strip of 3, line, P# 1-5 3.00
P# strip of 3, line, P# 6 18.00
P# strip of 3, line, P# 7 6.50
a. Untagged (Bureau precanceled, Presorted First Class) 35
P# strip of 3, line, P# 3-5 4.25
P# strip of 3, line, P# 1, 2 12.00
P# strip of 3, line, P# 6 7.75
P# strip of 3, line, P# 7 8.75

Three different precancel styles exist: "PRESORTED" measuring 11.3mm, 12.8mm and 13.4mm.

b. Imperf., pair *200.00*
c. As "a," imperf. pair *500.00*

1907 A1293 18c **dark brown,** *May 18* 34 5
Pair 70 10
P# strip of 3, line, P# 2, 5, 6, 8-10 4.00
P# strip of 3, line, P# 1 70.00
P# strip of 3, line, P# 3, 4 40.00
P# strip of 3, line, P# 7 35.00
P# strip of 3, line, P# 11 9.50
P# strip of 3, line, P# 12 8.00
P# strip of 3, line P# 13, 14 6.75
P# strip of 3, line, P# 15-18 4.50
a. Imperf., pair *125.00*
1908 A1294 20c **vermilion,** *Dec. 10* 32 5
Pair 65 10
P# strip of 3, line, P# 5, 9, 10 3.50
P# strip of 3, line, P# 1 47.50
P# strip of 3, line, P# 2 200.00
P# strip of 3, line, P# 3, 4, 6, 15, 16 4.25
P# strip of 3, line, P# 7, 8 72.50
P# strip of 3, line, P# 11 42.50
P# strip of 3, line, P# 12, 14 8.25
P# strip of 3, line, P# 13 4.75
a. Imperf., pair *120.00*

See Nos. 2225-2228.

Eagle and Moon
A1296

Booklet Stamp
PHOTOGRAVURE

1983, Aug. 12 ***Perf. 10 Vert.***
1909 A1296 $9.35 **multi** 26.00 12.00
a. Booklet pane of 3 80.00 —

AMERICAN RED CROSS CENTENNIAL

A1297

Designed by Joseph Csatari.

PHOTOGRAVURE
Plates of 200 subjects in four panes of 50.

1981, May 1 **Tagged** ***Perf. 10½x11***
1910 A1297 18c **multi** 32 5
P# block of 4 1.35 —
Zip block of 4 1.30 —
Copyright block of 4 1.30 —

United States Transportation coils can be mounted in Scott's annually supplemented Plate Number Coils, U.S. Comprehensive Plate Number Coils Albums and Comprehensive Plate Number Coil Singles Albums.

SAVINGS & LOAN SESQUICENTENNIAL

A1298

Designed by Don Hedin.

PHOTOGRAVURE
Plates of 200 subjects in four panes of 50.

1981, May 8 **Tagged** ***Perf. 11***
1911 A1298 18c **multi** 32 5
P# block of 4 1.40 —
Zip block of 4 1.30 —
Copyright block of 4 1.30 —

SPACE ACHIEVEMENT ISSUE

A1299

A1300

Benefiting Mankind
USA 18c
A1301

A1302

Probing the Planets
USA 18c
A1303

A1304

A1305

A1306

Designs: A1299, Moon walk. A1300-A1301, A1304-A1305, Columbia space shuttle. A1302, Skylab. A1303, Pioneer II. A1306, Telescope. Se-tenant in blocks of 8.
Designed by Robert McCall

PHOTOGRAVURE
Plates of 192 subjects in four panes of 48 each.

1981, May 21	Tagged	Perf. 11	
1912 A1299 18c **multi**		32	10
1913 A1300 18c **multi**		32	10
1914 A1301 18c **multi**		32	10
1915 A1302 18c **multi**		32	10
1916 A1303 18c **multi**		32	10
1917 A1304 18c **multi**		32	10
1918 A1305 18c **multi**		32	10
1919 A1306 18c **multi**		32	10
P# block of 8, 6 P#		3.00	—
Zip, copyright block of 8		2.80	—
a. Block of 8, #1912-1919		2.75	2.25
b. As "a," imperf.			

PROFESSIONAL MANAGEMENT ISSUE

Joseph Wharton (Founder of Wharton School of Business) — A1307

Professional management education centenary.
Designed by Rudolph de Harak.

PHOTOGRAVURE
Plates of 200 subject in four panes of 50 each.

1981, June 18	Tagged	Perf. 11	
1920 A1307 18c **blue & black**		32	5
P# block of 4, 2 P#		1.40	—
Zip block of 4		1.30	—
Copyright block of 4		1.30	—

PRESERVATION OF WILDLIFE HABITATS ISSUE

Great Blue Heron — A1308

Badger — A1309

Save Mountain Habitats
Grizzly Bear — A1310

Save Woodland Habitats
Ruffed Grouse — A1311

Designed by Chuck Ripper

PHOTOGRAVURE
Plates of 200 subjects in four panes of 50 each.

1981, June 26	Tagged	Perf. 11	
1921 A1308 18c **multi**		35	8
1922 A1309 18c **multi**		35	8
1923 A1310 18c **multi**		35	8
1924 A1311 18c **multi**		35	8
P# block of 4, 5 P#		1.50	—
Zip block of 4		1.45	
Copyright block of 4		1.45	—
a. Block of 4, #1921-1924		1.40	1.00

INTERNATIONAL YEAR OF THE DISABLED ISSUE

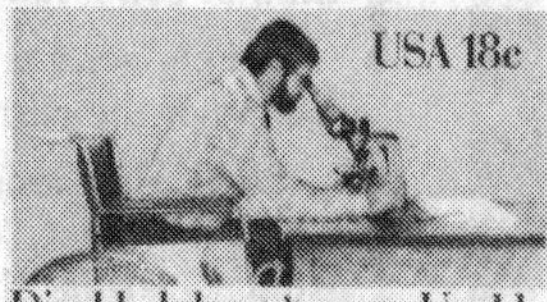

Man Using Microscope A1312

Designed by Martha Perske

PHOTOGRAVURE
Plates of 200 subjects in four panes of 50 each.

1981, June 29	Tagged	Perf. 11	
1925 A1312 18c **multi**		32	5
P# block of 4, 6 P#		1.40	—
Zip block of 4		1.30	—
Copyright block of 4		1.30	—
a. Vert. pair, imperf. horiz.		*2,000.*	

EDNA ST. VINCENT MILLAY ISSUE

A1313

Designed by Glenora Case Richards

LITHOGRAPHED AND ENGRAVED
Plates of 200 subjects in four panes of 50 each.

1981, July 10	Tagged	Perf. 11	
1926 A1313 18c **multi**		32	5
P# block of 4, 7 P#		1.40	—
Zip block of 4		1.30	—
Copyright block of 4		1.30	—
a. Black (engr., inscriptions) omitted		*600.00*	

ALCOHOLISM

A1314

Designed by John Boyd

ENGRAVED
Plates of 230 (10x23) subjects in panes of 50 (5x10)

1981, Aug. 19	Tagged	Perf. 11	
1927 A1314 18c **blue & black**		42	5
P# block of 6, P#		13.50	—
P# block of 20, 1-2 P#, 1-2 copyright, 1-2 Zip		45.00	—
a. Imperf., pair		*300.00*	

See Combination Press note after No. 1703.

AMERICAN ARCHITECTURE

New York University Library by Stanford White — A1315

Biltmore House By Richard Morris Hunt — A1316

Palace of the Arts by Bernard Maybeck A1317

National Farmer's Bank by Louis Sullivan A1318

Designed by Walter D. Richards

ENGRAVED
Plates of 160 subjects in four panes of 40 each.

1981, Aug. 28	Tagged	Perf. 11	
1928 A1315 18c **black & red**		42	8
1929 A1316 18c **black & red**		42	8
1930 A1317 18c **black & red**		42	8
1931 A1318 18c **black & red**		42	8
P# block of 4		1.85	—
Zip block of 4		1.80	—
Copyright block of 4		1.80	—
a. Block of 4, #1928-1931		1.75	1.00

SPORTS PERSONALITIES

Mildred Didrikson Zaharias — A1319

Robert Tyre Jones — A1320

Designed by Richard Gangel

ENGRAVED

Plates of 200 subjects in four panes of 50.

1981, Sept. 22 **Tagged** ***Perf. 10½x11***

1932	A1319	18c	**purple**	32	5
			P# block of 4	1.75	—
			Zip block of 4	1.30	—
			Copyright block of 4	1.30	—
1933	A1320	18c	**green**	32	5
			P# block of 4	1.50	—
			Zip block of 4	1.30	—
			Copyright block of 4	1.30	—

Coming Through the Rye — A1321

Designed by Paul Calle

LITHOGRAPHED AND ENGRAVED

Plates of 200 in four panes of 50.

1981, Oct. 9 **Tagged** ***Perf. 11***

1934	A1321	18c	**gray, olive green & brown**	32	5
			P# block of 4, 3 P#	1.50	—
			Zip block of 4	1.30	—
			Copyright block of 4	1.30	—
a.			Vert. pair, imperf. btwn.	*250.00*	
b.			Brown omitted	*500.00*	

JAMES HOBAN

Irish-American Architect of the White House — A1322

Designed by Ron Mercer and Walter D. Richards

PHOTOGRAVURE

Plates of 200 in four panes of 50.

1981, Oct. 13 **Tagged** ***Perf. 11***

1935	A1322	18c	**multi**	32	15
			P# block of 4, 6 P#	1.60	—
			Zip block of 4	1.30	—
			Copyright block of 4	1.30	—
1936	A1322	20c	**multi**	35	5
			P# block of 4, 6 P#	1.65	—
			Zip block of 4	1.45	—
			Copyright block of 4	1.45	—

AMERICAN BICENTENNIAL

Battle of Yorktown A1323

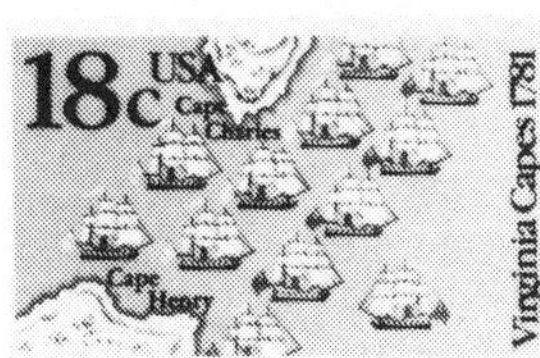

Battle of the Virginia Capes — A1324

Designed by Cal Sacks

LITHOGRAPHED AND ENGRAVED

Plates of 200 in four panes of 50.

1981, Oct. 16 **Tagged** ***Perf. 11***

1937	A1323	18c	**multicolored**	35	6
1938	A1324	18c	**multicolored**	35	6
			P# block of 4, 7 P#	1.60	—
			Zip block of 4	1.45	—
			Copyright block of 4	1.45	—
a.			Pair, #1937-1938	70	15
b.			As "a," black (engr., inscriptions) omitted	*600.00*	

CHRISTMAS

Madonna and Child, Botticelli A1325

Felt Bear on Sleigh A1326

Designed by Bradbury Thompson (No. 1939) and by Naiad Einsel (No. 1940)

PHOTOGRAVURE

Plates of 400 in four panes of 100 (No. 1939)

Plates of 200 in four panes of 50 (No. 1940)

1981, Oct. 28 **Tagged** ***Perf. 11***

1939	A1325	(20c)	**multi**	38	5
			P# block of 4, 6 P#	1.60	—
			Zip block of 4	1.55	—
			Copyright block of 4	1.55	—
a.			Imperf. pair	*115.00*	
1940	A1326	(20c)	**multi**	38	5
			P# block of 4, 5 P#	1.60	—
			Zip block of 4	1.55	—
			Copyright block of 4	1.55	—
a.			Imperf. pair	*225.00*	
b.			Vert. pair, horiz. imperf.	—	

JOHN HANSON

First President of the Continental Congress — A1327

Designed by Ron Adair

PHOTOGRAVURE

Plates of 200 in panes of 50

1981, Nov. 5 **Tagged** ***Perf. 11***

1941	A1327	20c	**multicolored**	38	5
			P# block of 4, 5 P#	1.60	—
			Zip block of 4	1.55	—
			Copyright block of 4	1.55	—

DESERT PLANTS

Barrel Cactus — A1328

Agave A1329

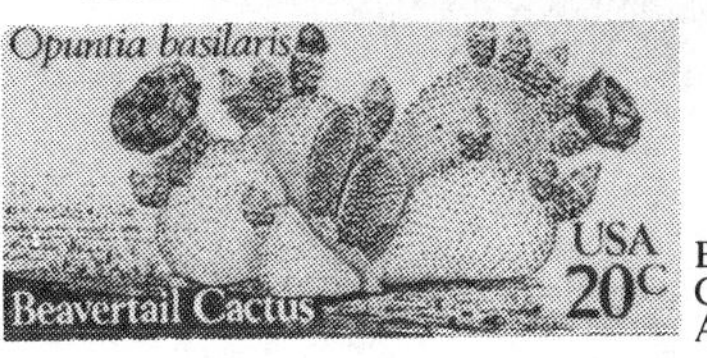

Beavertail Cactus A1330

Saguaro — A1331

Designed by Frank J. Waslick.

LITHOGRAPHED AND ENGRAVED

Plates of 160 in four panes of 40

1981 Dec. 11 **Tagged** ***Perf. 11***

1942	A1328	20c	**multi**	35	6
1943	A1329	20c	**multi**	35	6
1944	A1330	20c	**multi**	35	6
1945	A1331	20c	**multi**	35	6
			P# block of 4, 7 P#	1.60	—
			Zip block of 4	1.55	—
			Copyright block of 4	1.55	—
a.			Block of 4, #1942-1945	1.50	85

A1332

A1333

Designed by Bradbury Thompson.

PHOTOGRAVURE

Plates of 400 in panes of 100.

1981, Oct. 11 **Tagged** ***Perf. 11x10½***

1946	A1332	(20c)	**brown**	38	5
			P# block of 4	1.85	—
			Zip block of 4	1.55	—
			Copyright block of 4	1.55	—

COIL STAMP

Perf. 10 Vert.

1947	A1332	(20c)	**brown**	65	5
			Pair	1.30	10
			Joint line pair	1.50	—
a.			Imperf. pair	—	

BOOKLET STAMPS

Perf. 11x10½

1948	A1333	(20c)	**brown**	38	5
a.			Booklet pane of 10	4.50	—

Rocky Mountain Bighorn — A1334

ENGRAVED

1982, Jan. 8 **Tagged** ***Perf. 11***

1949	A1334	20c	**dark blue** (from bklt. pane)	42	5
a.			Booklet pane of 10	4.50	—
b.			As "a," imperf. between	*85.00*	

A1335

Designed by Clarence Holbert.

ENGRAVED

Plates of 192 in four panes of 48

1982, Jan. 30 **Tagged** ***Perf. 11***

1950	A1335	20c	**blue**	38	5
			P# block of 4	1.60	—
			Zip block of 4	1.55	—
			Copyright block of 4	1.55	—

LOVE ISSUE

A1336

Designed by Mary Faulconer.

PHOTOGRAVURE

Plates of 200 in four panes of 50.

1982, Feb. 1 **Tagged** ***Perf. 11x10½***

1951	A1336	20c	**multicolored**	38	5
			P# block of 4, 5 P#	1.60	—
			Zip block of 4	1.55	—
			Copyright block of 4	1.55	—
a.			Perf. 11	48	5
a.			P# block of 4, 5 P#	2.00	—
b.			Imperf. pair	*250.00*	
c.			Blue omitted	*150.00*	

GEORGE WASHINGTON

A1337

Designed by Mark English.

PHOTOGRAVURE

Plates of 200 in four panes of 50.

1982, Feb. 22 **Tagged** ***Perf. 11***

1952	A1337	20c	**multicolored**	38	5
			P# block of 4, 6 P#	1.60	—
			Zip block of 4	1.55	—
			Copyright block of 4	1.55	—

STATE BIRDS AND FLOWERS ISSUE

State Birds and Flowers
A1338-A1387

Designed by Arthur and Alan Singer.

PHOTOGRAVURE (Andreotti)

Plates of 200 subjects in four panes of 50 each.

1982, Apr. 14 **Tagged** ***Perf. 10½x11***

1953	A1338	20c	*Alabama*	40	25
1954	A1339	20c	*Alaska*	40	25
1955	A1340	20c	*Arizona*	40	25
1956	A1341	20c	*Arkansas*	40	25
1957	A1342	20c	*California*	40	25
1958	A1343	20c	*Colorado*	40	25
1959	A1344	20c	*Connecticut*	40	25
1960	A1345	20c	*Delaware*	40	25
1961	A1346	20c	*Florida*	40	25
1962	A1347	20c	*Georgia*	40	25
1963	A1348	20c	*Hawaii*	40	25
1964	A1349	20c	*Idaho*	40	25
1965	A1350	20c	*Illinois*	40	25
1966	A1351	20c	*Indiana*	40	25
1967	A1352	20c	*Iowa*	40	25
1968	A1353	20c	*Kansas*	40	25
1969	A1354	20c	*Kentucky*	40	25
1970	A1355	20c	*Louisiana*	40	25
1971	A1356	20c	*Maine*	40	25
1972	A1357	20c	*Maryland*	40	25
1973	A1358	20c	*Massachusetts*	40	25
1974	A1359	20c	*Michigan*	40	25
1975	A1360	20c	*Minnesota*	40	25
1976	A1360	20c	*Mississippi*	40	25
1977	A1361	20c	*Missouri*	40	25
1978	A1362	20c	*Montana*	40	25
1979	A1363	20c	*Nebraska*	40	25
1980	A1364	20c	*Nevada*	40	25
1981	A1364	20c	*New Hampshire*	40	25
1982	A1365	20c	*New Jersey*	40	25
1983	A1366	20c	*New Mexico*	40	25
1984	A1369	20c	*New York*	40	25
1985	A1370	20c	*North Carolina*	40	25
1986	A1371	20c	*North Dakota*	40	25
1987	A1372	20c	*Ohio*	40	25
1988	A1373	20c	*Oklahoma*	40	25
1989	A1374	20c	*Oregon*	40	25
1990	A1375	20c	*Pennsylvania*	40	25
1991	A1376	20c	*Rhode Island*	40	25
1992	A1377	20c	*South Carolina*	40	25
1993	A1378	20c	*South Dakota*	40	25
1994	A1379	20c	*Tennessee*	40	25
1995	A1380	20c	*Texas*	40	25
1996	A1381	20c	*Utah*	40	25
1997	A1382	20c	*Vermont*	40	25
1998	A1383	20c	*Virginia*	40	25
1999	A1384	20c	*Washington*	40	25
2000	A1385	20c	*West Virginia*	40	25
2001	A1386	20c	*Wisconsin*	40	25
2002	A1387	20c	*Wyoming*	40	25
a.			1953a-2002a, any single, perf. 11	45	30
b.			Pane of 50, perf. 10½x11	20.00	—
c.			Pane of 50, perf. 11	22.50	—
d.			Pane of 50, imperf.	—	

US-NETHERLANDS

200th Anniv. of Diplomatic Recognition by The Netherlands
A1388

Designed by Heleen Tigler Wybrandi-Raue.

PHOTOGRAVURE

Plates of 230 (10x23) subjects in panes of 50 (5x10).

1982, Apr. 20 **Tagged** ***Perf. 11***

2003	A1388	20c	**verm., brt. blue & gray blk.**	38	5
			P# block of 6, P#	3.50	—
			P# block of 20, 1-2 P#, 1-2 copyright, 1-2 zip	11.50	—
a.			Imperf. pair	*450.00*	

See Combination Press note after No. 1703.

LIBRARY OF CONGRESS

A1389

Designed by Bradbury Thompson.

ENGRAVED

Plates of 200 subjects in four panes of 50.

1982, Apr. 21 **Tagged** ***Perf. 11***

2004	A1389	20c	**red & black**	38	5
			P# block of 4	1.60	—
			Zip block of 4	1.55	—
			Copyright block of 4	1.55	—

A1390

Designed by John Boyd.

ENGRAVED
Coil Stamp

1982, Apr. 27 Tagged *Perf. 10 Vert.*

2005 A1390 20c **sky blue** 50 5
Pair 1.00 10
P# strip of 3, line, P# 1-4 40.00
a. Imperf. pair *110.00*

KNOXVILLE WORLD'S FAIR

A1391

A1392

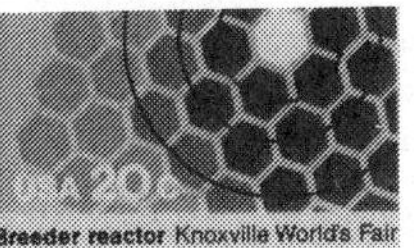

A1393

A1394

Designed by Charles Harper.

PHOTOGRAVURE
Plates of 200 in four panes of 50.

1982, Apr. 29 Tagged *Perf. 11*

2006 A1391 20c **multi** 38 8
2007 A1392 20c **multi** 38 8
2008 A1393 20c **multi** 38 8
2009 A1394 20c **multi** 38 8
P# block of 4, 5 P# 1.65 —
Zip block of 4 1.60 —
Copyright block of 4 1.60 —
a. Block of 4, #2006-2009 1.55 85

AMERICAN AUTHOR, 1832-1899

A1395

Designed by Robert Hallock.

ENGRAVED
Plates of 200 in four panes of 50.

1982, Apr. 30 Tagged *Perf. 11*

2010 A1395 20c **red & black,** *tan* 38 5
P# block of 4 1.60 —
Zip block of 4 1.55 —
Copyright block of 4 1.55 —

AGING TOGETHER

A1396

Designed by Paul Calle.

ENGRAVED
Plates of 200 in four panes of 50.

1982, May 21 Tagged *Perf. 11*

2011 A1396 20c **brown** 38 5
P# block of 4 1.60 —
Zip block of 4 1.55 —
Copyright block of 4 1.55 —

John, Lionel and Ethel Barrymore — A1397

A1398

PERFORMING ARTS

Designed by Jim Sharpe.

PHOTOGRAVURE
Plates of 200 in four panes of 50.

1982, June 8 Tagged *Perf. 11*

2012 A1397 20c **multicolored** 38 5
P# block of 4, 6 P# 1.60 —
Zip block of 4 1.55 —
Copyright block of 4 1.55 —

WOMENS RIGHTS

Designed by Glenora Richards.

PHOTOGRAVURE
Plate of 200 in four panes of 50.

1982, June 10 Tagged *Perf. 11*

2013 A1398 20c **multicolored** 38 5
P# block of 4, 6 P# 1.60 —
Zip block of 4 1.55 —
Copyright block of 4 1.55 —

Dunseith, ND-Boissevain, Manitoba A1399

Designed by Gyo Fujikawa.

LITHOGRAPHED AND ENGRAVED
Plate of 200 in four panes of 50.

1982, June 30 Tagged *Perf. 11*

2014 A1399 20c **multicolored** 38 5
P# block of 4, 5 P# 1.60 —
Zip block of 4 1.55 —
Copyright block of 4 1.55 —
a. Black, green & brown (engr.) omitted *350.00*

A1400

A1401

AMERICA'S LIBRARIES

Designed by Bradbury Thompson.

ENGRAVED
Plate of 200 subjects in four panes of 50.

1982, July 13 Tagged *Perf. 11*

2015 A1400 20c **red & black** 38 5
P# block of 4 1.60 —
Zip block of 4 1.55 —
Copyright block of 4 1.55 —
a. Vert. pair, imperf. horiz. *350.00*

JACKIE ROBINSON

Designed by Jerry Pinkney.

PHOTOGRAVURE
Plate of 200 subjects in four panes of 50.

1982, Aug. 2 Tagged *Perf. 10½x11*

2016 A1401 20c **multicolored** 38 5
P# block of 4, 5 P# 1.65 —
Zip block of 4 1.55 —
Copyright block of 4 1.55 —

TOURO SYNAGOGUE

Oldest Existing Synagogue Building in the U.S. — A1402

Designed by Donald Moss and Bradbury Thompson.

PHOTOGRAVURE AND ENGRAVED
Plates of 230 (10x23) subjects in panes of 50 (5x10).

1982, Aug. 22 Tagged *Perf. 11*

2017 A1402 20c **multi** 38 5
P# block of 20, 6-12, #, 1-2 copyright, 1-2 zip 11.50 —
a. Imperf. pair *850.00*

See Combination Press note after No. 1703.

WOLF TRAP FARM PARK

A1403

Designed by Richard Schlecht.

PHOTOGRAVURE
Plates of 200 in four panes of 50.

1982, Sept. 1 Tagged *Perf. 11*

2018 A1403 20c **multi** 38 5
P# block of 4, 5 P# 1.60 —
Zip block of 4 1.55 —
Copyright block of 4 1.55 —

A1404

A1405

A1406

A1407

Designed by Walter D. Richards.

ENGRAVED
Plates of 160 subjects in four panes of 40.

1982, Sept. 30		**Tagged**	***Perf. 11***	
2019	A1404 20c	**black & brown**	38	8
2020	A1405 20c	**black & brown**	38	8
2021	A1406 20c	**black & brown**	38	8
2022	A1407 20c	**black & brown**	38	8
		P# block of 4	1.65	—
		Zip block of 4	1.60	—
		Copyright block of 4	1.60	—
a.		Block of 4, #2019-2022	1.55	1.00

FRANCIS OF ASSISI

A1408

Designed by Ned Seidler.
Printed by American Bank Note Co. and J.W. Fergusson and Sons.

Plates of 200 subjects in four panes of 50 each.
PHOTOGRAVURE

1982, Oct. 7		**Tagged**	***Perf. 11***	
2023	A1408 20c	**multi**	38	5
		P# block of 4, 6 P#	1.60	—
		Zip block of 4	1.55	—
		Copyright block of 4	1.55	—

PONCE DE LEON

A1409

Designed by Richard Schlecht.

PHOTOGRAVURE (Combination press)
Plates of 230 subjects (10x23) in panes of 50 (5x10).

1982, Oct. 12		**Tagged**	***Perf. 11***	
2024	A1409 20c	**multi**	38	5
		P# block of 6, 5P#	3.25	—
		P# block of 20, 5 or 10 P#, 1-2 zip, 1-2 copyright	11.50	—
a.		Imperf., pair	*800.00*	

See Combination Press note after No. 1703.

CHRISTMAS

A1410

A1411

A1412

A1413

A1414

A1415

PHOTOGRAVURE
Plates of 200 subjects in four panes of 50

Designed by Chuck Ripper.

1982, Nov. 3			**Tagged**	
2025	A1410 13c	**multi**	24	5
		P# block of 4	1.05	
		Zip block of 4	1.00	
		Copyright block of 4	1.00	
a.		Imperf., pair	*500.00*	

PHOTOGRAVURE (Combination Press)
Plates of 230 subjects (10x23) in panes of 50 (5x10).

Designed by Bradbury Thompson.

1982, Oct. 28			**Tagged**	
2026	A1411 20c	**multi**	38	5
		P# block of 20, 5 or 10 P#, 1-2 copyright, 1-2 zip	11.00	—
a.		Imperf. pair	*175.00*	
b.		Horiz. pair, imperf. vert.	—	
c.		Vert. pair, imperf. horiz.	—	

See Combination Press note after No. 1703.

PHOTOGRAVURE
Plates of 200 in four panes of 50.

Designed by Dolli Tingle.

1982, Oct. 28				
2027	A1412 20c	**multi**	45	5
2028	A1413 20c	**multi**	45	5
2029	A1414 20c	**multi**	45	5
2030	A1415 20c	**multi**	45	5
		P# block of 4, 4 P#	2.00	
		Zip block of 4	1.90	
		Copyright block of 4	1.90	
a.		Block of 4, #2027-2030	1.85	1.00
b.		As "a," imperf.	—	
c.		As "a," imperf. horiz.	—	

SCIENCE & INDUSTRY

Science & Industry USA 20c
A1416

Designed by Saul Bass.

LITHOGRAPHED AND ENGRAVED
Plates of 200 in four panes of 50.

1983, Jan. 19		**Tagged**	***Perf. 11***	
2031	A1416 20c	**multi**	38	5
		P# block of 4, 4P#	1.60	—
		Zip block of 4	1.55	—
		Copyright block of 4	1.55	—
a.		Black (engr.) omitted	*1,250.*	

BALLOONS

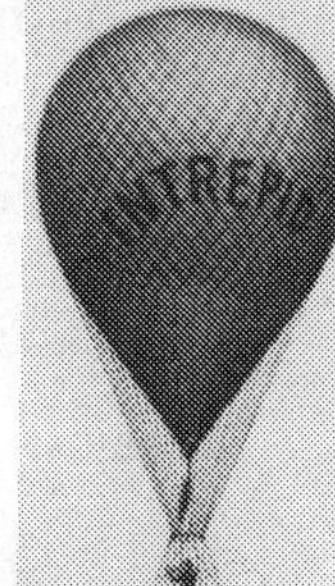

Intrepid — A1417

A1418

A1419

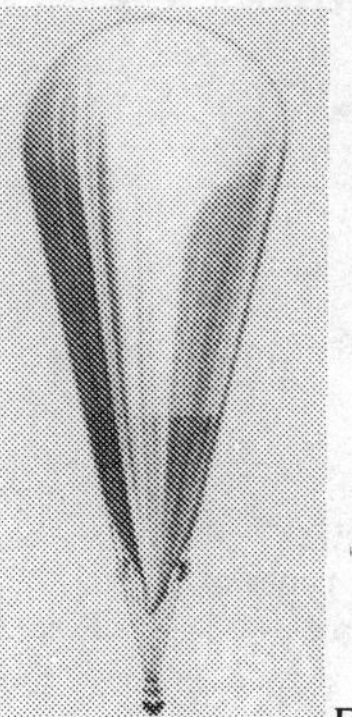
Explorer II — A1420

Designed by David Meltzer.

PHOTOGRAVURE
Plates of 160 in four panes of 40.

1983, Mar. 31 **Tagged** ***Perf. 11***

2032	A1417	20c	**multi**	38	8
2033	A1418	20c	**multi**	38	8
2034	A1419	20c	**multi**	38	8
2035	A1420	20c	**multi**	38	8
			P# block of 4, 5P#	1.65	—
			Zip block of 4	1.60	—
			Copyright block of 4	1.60	—
a.			Block of 4, #2032-2035	1.55	1.00
b.			As "a," imperf.	—	

US-SWEDEN

Benjamin Franklin — A1421

Designed by Czeslaw Slania, court engraver of Sweden.

ENGRAVED
Plates of 200 in four panes of 50.

1983, Mar. 24 **Tagged** ***Perf. 11***

2036	A1421	20c	**blue, blk & red brn**	38	5
			P# block of 4	1.60	—
			Zip block of 4	1.55	—
			Copyright block of 4	1.55	—

CCC, 50th ANNIV.

A1422

Designed by David K. Stone.

PHOTOGRAVURE
Plates of 200 in four panes of 50.

1983, Apr. 5 **Tagged** ***Perf. 11***

2037	A1422	20c	**multi**	38	5
			P# block of 4, 6P#	1.60	—
			Zip block of 4	1.55	—
			Copyright block of 4	1.55	—
a.			Imperf., pair	*2,250.*	

JOSEPH PRIESTLEY

Discoverer of Oxygen — A1423

Designed by Dennis Lyall.
Printed by American Bank Note Company and J.W. Ferguson And Sons.

PHOTOGRAVURE
Plates of 200 in four panes of 50.

1983, Apr. 13 **Tagged** ***Perf. 11***

2038	A1423	20c	**multi**	38	5
			P# block of 4, 6P#	1.60	—
			Zip block of 4	1.55	—
			Copyright block of 4	1.55	—

VOLUNTARISM

A1424

Designed by Paul Calle.

ENGRAVED (Combination Press)
Plates of 230 (10x23) subjects in panes of 50 (5x10).

1983, Apr. 20 **Tagged** ***Perf. 11***

2039	A1424	20c	**red & black**	38	5
			P# block of 6, P#	3.00	—
			P# block of 20, 1-2 P#, 1-2 copyright, 1-2 zip	11.00	—
a.			Imperf., pair	*1,000.*	

See Combination Press note after No. 1703.

US-GERMANY

A1425

Designed by Richard Schlecht.

ENGRAVED
Plates of 200 in four panes of 50.

1983, Apr. 29 **Tagged** ***Perf. 11***

2040	A1425	20c	**brown**	38	5
			P# block of 4	1.60	—
			Zip block of 4	1.55	—
			Copyright block of 4	1.55	—

BROOKLYN BRIDGE

A1426

Designed by Howard Koslow.

ENGRAVED
Plates of 200 in four panes of 50.

1983, May 5 **Tagged** ***Perf. 11***

2041	A1426	20c	**blue**	38	5
			P# block of 4	1.60	—
			Zip block of 4	1.55	—
			Copyright block of 4	1.55	—

TVA

Norris Hydroelectric Dam — A1427

Designed by Howard Koslow.

PHOTOGRAVURE AND ENGRAVED
(Combination Press)
Plates of 230 in panes of 50

1983, May 18 **Tagged** ***Perf. 11***

2042	A1427	20c	**multi**	38	5
			P# block of 20, 5-10 P#, 1-2 copyright, 1-2 zip	11.50	—

Runners, Electrocardiograph Tracing — A1428

Designed by Donald Moss.

PHOTOGRAVURE (Combination Press)
Plates of 230 in panes of 50.

1983, May 14 **Tagged** ***Perf. 11***

2043	A1428	20c	**multi**	38	5
			P# block of 6, 4 P#	3.00	—
			P# block of 20, 4-8 P#, 1-2 copyright, 1-2 zip	11.00	—

SCOTT JOPLIN (1868-1917)
Black Heritage

A1429

Designed by Jerry Pinkney.

PHOTOGRAVURE
Plates of 200 in four panes of 50.

1983, June 9 **Tagged** ***Perf. 11***

2044	A1429	20c	**multi**	38	5
			P# block of 4, 6P#	1.60	—
			Zip block of 4	1.55	—
			Copyright block of 4	1.55	—
a.			Imperf. pair	*500.00*	

MEDAL OF HONOR

A1430

Designed by Dennis J. Hom.

LITHOGRAPHED AND ENGRAVED
Plates of 160 in four panes of 40.

1983, June 7 **Tagged** ***Perf. 11***

2045	A1430	20c	**multi**	38	5
			P# block of 4, 5P#	1.65	—
			Zip block of 4	1.55	—
			Copyright block of 4	1.55	—
a.			Red omitted	*325.00*	

A1431

A1432

GEORGE HERMAN RUTH (1895-1948)

Designed by Richard Gangel.

ENGRAVED
Plates of 200 in four panes of 50.

1983, July 6 **Tagged** ***Perf. 10½x11***

2046	A1431	20c	**blue**	40	5
			P# block of 4	1.75	—
			Zip block of 4	1.65	—
			Copyright block of 4	1.65	—

NATHANIEL HAWTHORNE (1804-1864)

Designed by Bradbury Thompson after 1851 painting by Cephus Giovanni Thompson.

PHOTOGRAVURE
Plates of 200 in four panes of 50.

1983, July 8 **Tagged** ***Perf. 11***

2047	A1432	20c	**multi**	38	5
			P# block of 4, 4P#	1.60	—
			Zip block of 4	1.55	—
			Copyright block of 4	1.55	—

LOS ANGELES OLYMPICS

July 28-August 12, 1984

A1433

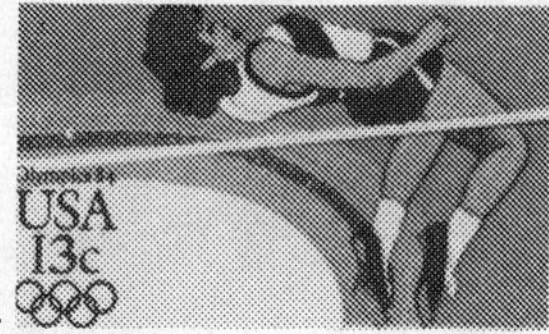

A1434

A1435

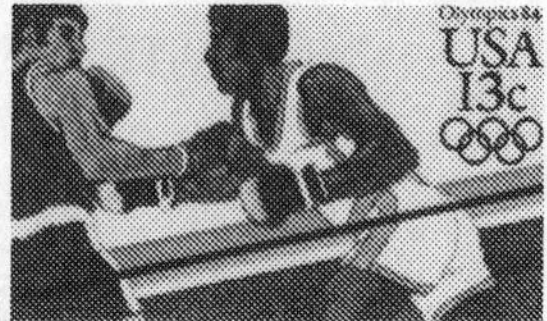

A1436

Designed by Bob Peake.

PHOTOGRAVURE

Plates of 200 in four panes of 50.

1983, July 28	**Tagged**			***Perf. 11***	
2048	A1433	13c	**multi**	28	5
2049	A1434	13c	**multi**	28	5
2050	A1435	13c	**multi**	28	5
2051	A1436	13c	**multi**	28	5
			P# block of 4, 4P#	1.30	—
			Zip block of 4	1.25	—
			Copyright block of 4	1.25	—
a.			Block of 4, #2048-2051	1.20	80

SIGNING OF TREATY OF PARIS

John Adams, B. Franklin, John Jay, David Hartley — A1437

Designed by David Blossom based on unfinished painting by Benjamin West in Winterthur Museum.

PHOTOGRAVURE

Plates of 160 in four panes of 40.

1983, Sept. 2	**Tagged**			***Perf. 11***	
2052	A1437	20c	**multi**	38	5
			P# block of 4, 4P#	1.60	—
			Zip block of 4	1.55	—
			Copyright block of 4	1.55	—

CIVIL SERVICE

A1438

Designed by MDB Communications, Inc.

PHOTOGRAVURE AND ENGRAVED

Plates of 230 in four panes of 50.

1983, Sept. 9	**Tagged**			***Perf. 11***	
2053	A1438	20c	**buff, blue & red**	38	5
			P# block of 6, P#	3.00	—
			P# block of 20, 1-2P#, 1-2 Zip, 1-2 Copyright	11.00	—

METROPOLITAN OPERA

Original State Arch and Current 5-arch Entrance A1439

Designed by Ken Davies.

LITHOGRAPHED AND ENGRAVED

Plates of 200 in four panes of 50.

1983, Sept. 14	**Tagged**			***Perf. 11***	
2054	A1439	20c	**yel & maroon**	38	5
			P# block of 4	1.65	—
			Zip block of 4	1.55	—
			Copyright block of 4	1.55	—

AMERICAN INVENTORS

Charles Steinmetz and Curve on Graph — A1440

Edwin Armstrong and Frequency Modulator A1441

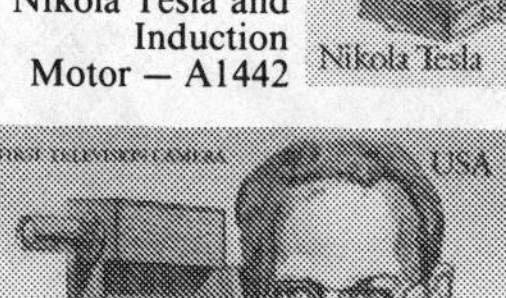

Nikola Tesla and Induction Motor — A1442

Philo T. Farnsworth and First Television Camera — A1443

Designed by Dennis Lyall.

LITHOGRAPHED AND ENGRAVED

Plates of 200 in four panes of 50.

1983, Sept. 21	**Tagged**			***Perf. 11***	
2055	A1440	20c	**multi**	38	8
2056	A1441	20c	**multi**	38	8
2057	A1442	20c	**multi**	38	8
2058	A1443	20c	**multi**	38	8
			P# block of 4, 2 P#	1.65	—
			Zip block of 4	1.65	—
			Copyright block of 4	1.65	—
a.			Block of 4, #2055-2058	1.55	1.00
b.			As "a," black omitted	*500.00*	

STREET CARS

A1444

A1445

A1446

USA20c
St. Charles streetcar, New Orleans, La., 1923

A1447

Designed by Richard Leech.

PHOTOGRAVURE AND ENGRAVED

Plates of 200 in four panes of 50.

1983, Oct. 8	**Tagged**			***Perf. 11***	
2059	A1444	20c	**multi**	38	8
2060	A1445	20c	**multi**	38	8
2061	A1446	20c	**multi**	38	8
2062	A1447	20c	**multi**	38	8
			P# block of 4, 5#	1.65	—
			Zip block of 4	1.60	—
			Copyright block of 4	1.60	—
a.			Block of 4, #2059-2062	1.55	1.00
b.			As "a," black omitted	*525.00*	

CHRISTMAS

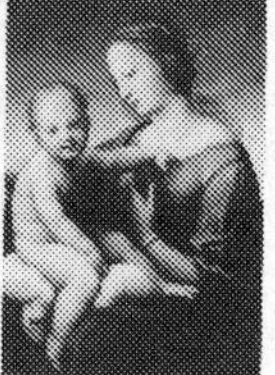

Niccolini-Cowper Madonna, by Raphael A1448

Santa Claus A1449

Designed by Bradbury Thompson (No. 2063), and John Berkey (No. 2064).

PHOTOGRAVURE

Plates of 200 in four panes of 50 (No. 2063), Plates of 230 in panes of 50 (Combination Press, No. 2064)

1983, Oct. 28	**Tagged**			***Perf. 11***	
2063	A1448	20c	**multi**	38	5
			P# block of 4, 5#	1.65	—
			Zip block of 4	1.55	—
			Copyright block of 4	1.55	—
2064	A1449	20c	**multi**	38	5
			P# block of 6, 5 P#	3.00	—
			P# block of 20, 5-10 P#, 1-2 copyright, 1-2 zip	11.50	—
a.			Imperf. pair	*150.00*	

See Combination Press note after No. 1703.

A particular stamp may be scarce, but if few collectors want it, its market value may remain relatively low.

German Religious Leader, Founder of Lutheran Church (1483-1546)
A1450

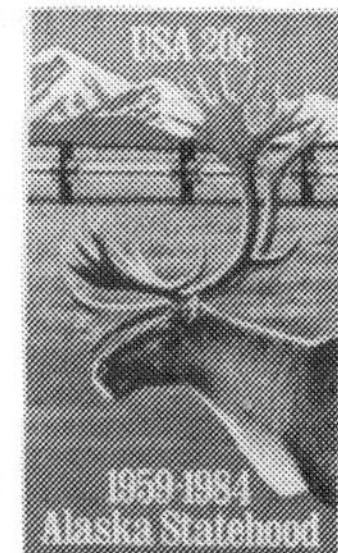

Caribou and Alaska Pipeline
A1451

MARTIN LUTHER

Designed by Bradbury Thompson.
Printed by American Bank Note Company.

PHOTOGRAVURE
Plates of 200 in four panes of 50.

1983, Nov. 11	**Tagged**	***Perf. 11***	
2065 A1450 20c **multi**		38	5
	P# block of 4, 5#	1.60	—
	Zip block of 4	1.55	—
	Copyright block of 4	1.55	—

25th ANNIVERSARY OF ALASKA STATEHOOD

Designed by Bill Bond.
Printed by American Bank Note Company and J.W. Fergus-son And Sons.

PHOTOGRAVURE
Plates of 200 in four panes of 50.

1984, Jan. 3	**Tagged**	***Perf. 11***	
2066 A1451 20c **multi**		38	5
	P# block of 4, 5#	1.65	—
	Zip block of 4	1.55	—
	Copyright block of 4	1.55	—

14th WINTER OLYMPIC GAMES, SARAJEVO, JUGOSLAVIA, FEB. 8-19

Ice Dancing — A1452

Alpine Skiing — A1453

Nordic Skiing — A1454

Hockey — A1455

Designed by Bob Peak.

PHOTOGRAVURE
Plates of 200 in four panes of 50.

1984, Jan. 6	**Tagged**	***Perf. 10½x11***	
2067 A1452 20c **multi**		42	8
2068 A1453 20c **multi**		42	8
2069 A1454 20c **multi**		42	8
2070 A1455 20c **multi**		42	8
	P# block of 4, 4#	1.95	—
	Zip block of 4	1.75	—
	Copyright block of 4	1.75	—
a. Block of 4, #2067-2070		1.70	1.00

Pillar, Dollar Sign — A1456

A1457

FEDERAL DEPOSIT INSURANCE CORPORATION, 50TH ANNIV.

Designed by Michael David Brown.

PHOTOGRAVURE
Plates of 200 in four panes of 50
(1 pane each #2071, 2074, 2075 and 2081)

1984, Jan. 12	**Tagged**	***Perf. 11***	
2071 A1456 20c **multi**		38	5
	P# block of 4, 6#, UL only	1.60	—
	Zip block of 4	1.55	—
	Copyright block of 4	1.55	—

LOVE

Designed by Bradbury Thompson.

PHOTOGRAVURE AND ENGRAVED
(Combination Press)
Plates of 230 in four panes of 50.

1984, Jan. 31	**Tagged**	***Perf. 11 x 10½***	
2072 A1457 20c **multi**		42	5
	P# block of 20, 6-12#, 1-2 copy-right, 1-2 zip	11.50	—
a. Horiz. pair, imperf. vert.		*225.00*	

See Combination Press note after No. 1703.

Carter G. Woodson (1875-1950), Black Historian — A1458

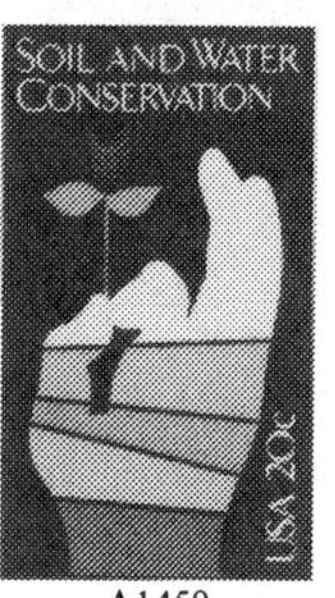

A1459

BLACK HERITAGE

Designed by Jerry Pinkney.
Printed by American Bank Note Company.

PHOTOGRAVURE
Plates of 200 in four panes of 50.

1984, Feb. 1	**Tagged**	***Perf. 11***	
2073 A1458 20c **multi**		38	5
	P# block of 4, 6#	1.60	—
	Zip block of 4	1.55	—
	Copyright block of 4	1.55	—
a. Horiz. pair, imperf. vert.		—	

SOIL & WATER CONSERVATION

Designed by Michael David Brown.

See No. 2071 for printing information.

1984, Feb. 6	**Tagged**	***Perf. 11***	
2074 A1459 20c **multi**		38	5
	P# block of 4, 6#, UR only	1.75	—
	Zip block of 4	1.55	—
	Copyright block of 4	1.55	—

50TH ANNIVERSARY OF CREDIT UNION ACT

Dollar Sign, Coin — A1460

Designed by Michael David Brown.

See No. 2071 for printing information.

1984, Feb. 10	**Tagged**	***Perf. 11***	
2075 A1460 20c **multi**		38	5
	P# block of 4, 6#, LR only	1.60	—
	Zip block of 4	1.55	—
	Copyright block of 4	1.55	—

ORCHIDS

Wild Pink — A1461

Yellow Lady's-slipper — A1462

Spreading Pogonia — A1463

Pacific Calypso — A1464

Designed by Manabu Saito.

PHOTOGRAVURE
Plates of 192 in four panes of 48.

1984, Mar. 5	**Tagged**	***Perf. 11***	
2076 A1461 20c **multi**		38	8
2077 A1462 20c **multi**		38	8
2078 A1463 20c **multi**		38	8
2079 A1464 20c **multi**		38	8
	P# block of 4, 5#	1.65	—
	Zip block of 4	1.60	—
	Copyright block of 4	1.60	—
a. Block of 4, #2076-2079		1.55	1.00

25th ANNIVERSARY OF HAWAII STATEHOOD

Eastern Polynesian Canoe, Golden Plover, Mauna Loa Volcano — A1465

Designed by Herb Kane.
Printed by American Bank Note Company.

PHOTOGRAVURE
Plates of 200 in four panes of 50.

1984, Mar. 12	**Tagged**	***Perf. 11***	
2080 A1465 20c **multi**		38	5
	P# block of 4, 5#	1.60	—
	Zip block of 4	1.55	—
	Copyright block of 4	1.55	—

50TH ANNIVERSARY, NATIONAL ARCHIVES

Abraham Lincoln, George Washington — A1466

Designed by Michael David Brown.

See No. 2071 for printing information.

1984, Apr. 16	Tagged	Perf. 11	
2081 A1466 20c **multi**		38	5
P# block of 4, 6#, LL only		1.60	—
Zip block of 4		1.55	—
Copyright block of 4		1.55	—

LOS ANGELES SUMMER OLYMPICS

July 28-August 12

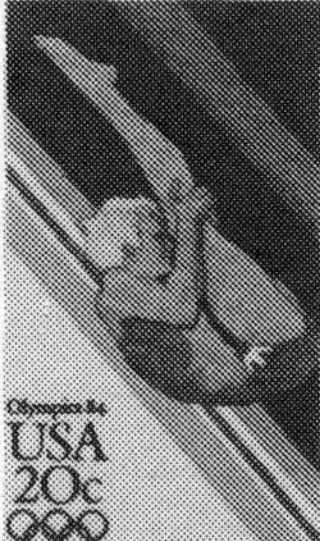

Diving — A1467

Long Jump — A1468

Wrestling — A1469

Kayak — A1470

Designed by Bob Peak.

PHOTOGRAVURE

Plates of 200 in four panes of 50.

1984, May 4	Tagged	Perf. 11	
2082 A1467 20c **multi**		40	8
2083 A1468 20c **multi**		40	8
2084 A1469 20c **multi**		40	8
2085 A1470 20c **multi**		40	8
P# block of 4, 4#		1.80	—
Zip block of 4		1.70	—
Copyright block of 4		1.70	—
a. Block of 4, #2082-2085		1.65	1.00

LOUISIANA WORLD EXPOSITION

New Orleans, May 12-Nov. 11

Bayou Wildlife — A1471

Designed by Chuck Ripper.

PHOTOGRAVURE

Plates of 160 in four panes of 40.

1984, May 11	Tagged	Perf. 11	
2086 A1471 20c **multi**		38	5
P# block of 4, 5#		1.60	—
Zip block of 4		1.55	—
Copyright block of 4		1.55	—

HEALTH RESEARCH

Lab Equipment A1472

Designed by Tyler Smith.
Printed by American Bank Note Company.

PHOTOGRAVURE

Plates of 200 in four panes of 50.

1984, May 17	Tagged	Perf. 11	
2087 A1472 20c **multi**		38	5
P# block of 4, 5#		1.60	—
Zip block of 4		1.55	—
Copyright block of 4		1.55	—

Actor Douglas Fairbanks (1883-1939) — A1473

A1474

PERFORMING ARTS

Designed by Jim Sharpe.

PHOTOGRAVURE AND ENGRAVED

(Combination Press)

Plates of 230 in panes of 50.

1984, May 23	Tagged	Perf. 11	
2088 A1473 20c **multi**		38	5
P# block of 20, 5-10#, 1-2 copyright, 1-2 zip		11.50	—

See Combination Press note after No. 1703.

JIM THORPE, 1888-1953

Designed by Richard Gangel.

ENGRAVED

Plates of 200 in four panes of 50.

1984, May 24	Tagged	Perf. 11	
2089 A1474 20c **dark brown**		38	5
P# block of 4		1.75	—
Zip block of 4		1.55	—
Copyright block of 4		1.55	—

The Scott Catalogue value is a retail price, what you could expect to pay for the stamp in a grade of Fine-Very Fine. The value listed is a reference which reflects recent actual dealer selling price.

PERFORMING ARTS

John McCormack (1884-1945), Operatic Tenor — A1475

Designed by Jim Sharpe (U.S.) and Ron Mercer (Ireland).

PHOTOGRAVURE

Plates of 200 in four panes of 50.

1984, June 6	Tagged	Perf. 11	
2090 A1475 20c **multi**		38	5
P# block of 4, 5#		1.75	—
Zip block of 4		1.55	—
Copyright block of 4		1.55	—

See Ireland No. 594.

25TH ANNIVERSARY OF ST. LAWRENCE SEAWAY

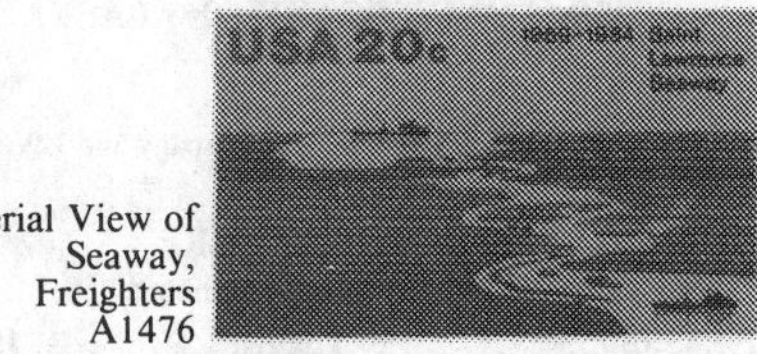

Aerial View of Seaway, Freighters A1476

Designed by Ernst Barenscher (Canada).
Printed by American Bank Note Company.

PHOTOGRAVURE

Plates of 200 in four panes of 50.

1984, June 26	Tagged	Perf. 11	
2091 A1476 20c **multi**		38	5
P# block of 4, 4#		1.60	—
Zip block of 4		1.55	—
Copyright block of 4		1.55	—

50TH ANNIVERSARY OF WATERFOWL PRESERVATION ACT

"Mallards Dropping In" by Jay N. Darling — A1477

Design adapted from Darling's work (No. RW1) by Donald M. McDowell.

ENGRAVED

Plates of 200 in four panes of 50.

1984, July 2	Tagged	Perf. 11	
2092 A1477 20c **multi**		38	5
P# block of 4		1.60	—
Zip block of 4		1.55	—
Copyright block of 4		1.55	—
a. Horiz. pair, imperf. vert.		*500.00*	

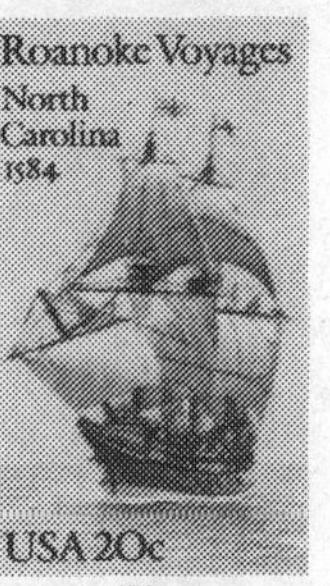

The Elizabeth — A1478

A1479

ROANOKE VOYAGES

Designed by Charles Lundgren.
Printed by American Bank Note Company.

PHOTOGRAVURE
Plates of 200 in four panes of 50.

1984, July 13	**Tagged**	*Perf. 11*	
2093 A1478 20c **multi**		38	5
	P# block of 4, 5#	1.60	—
	Zip block of 4	1.55	—
	Copyright block of 4	1.55	—
	Pair with full horiz. gutter btwn.	—	

HERMAN MELVILLE (1819-1891), AUTHOR

Designed by Bradbury Thompson.

ENGRAVED
Plates of 200 in four panes of 50.

1984, Aug. 1	**Tagged**	*Perf. 11*	
2094 A1479 20c **sage green**		38	5
	P# block of 4	1.60	—
	Zip block of 4	1.55	—
	Copyright block of 4	1.55	—

Founder of Junior Achievement
A1480

Smokey the Bear
A1481

HORACE MOSES (1862-1947)

Designed by Dennis Lyall.

PHOTOGRAVURE AND ENGRAVED
(Combination Press)
Plates of 200 in panes of 50.

1984, Aug. 6	**Tagged**	*Perf. 11*	
2095 A1480 20c **orange & dark brown**		38	5
	P# block of 6, P#	3.00	—
	P# block of 20, 1-2#, 1-2 copyright, 1-2 zip	11.00	—

See Combination Press note after No. 1703.

SMOKEY THE BEAR

Designed by Rudolph Wendelin.

LITHOGRAPHED AND ENGRAVED
Plates of 200 in panes of 50.

1984, Aug. 13	**Tagged**	*Perf. 11*	
2096 A1481 20c **multi**		38	5
	P# block of 4, 5#	1.75	—
	Zip block of 4	1.55	—
	Copyright block of 4	1.55	—
a.	Horiz. pair, imperf. btwn.	*400.00*	
b.	Vert. pair, imperf. btwn.	*275.00*	
c.	Block of 4, imperf. btwn. vert. and horiz.	*3,500.*	

ROBERTO CLEMENTE (1934-1972)

Clemente Wearing Pittsburgh Pirates Cap, Puerto Rican Flag — A1482

Designed by Juan Lopez-Bonilla.

PHOTOGRAVURE
Plates of 200 in panes of 50.

1984, Aug. 17	**Tagged**	*Perf. 11*	
2097 A1482 20c **multi**		40	5
	P# block of 4, 6#	1.75	—
	Zip block of 4	1.65	—
	Copyright block of 4	1.65	—
a.	Horiz. pair, imperf. vert.	—	

DOGS

Beagle and Boston Terrier — A1483

Chesapeake Bay Retriever and Cocker Spaniel — A1484

Alaskan Malamute and Collie — A1485

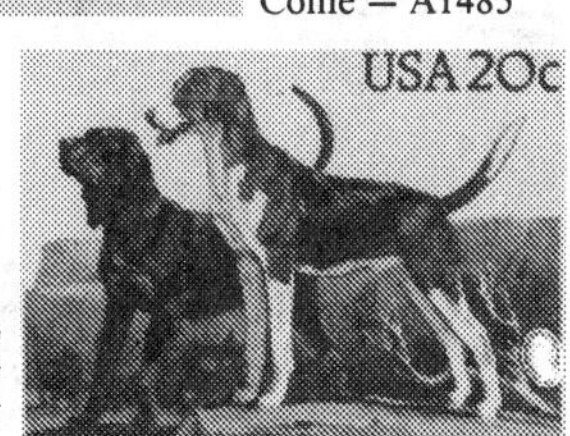

Black and Tan Coonhound and American Foxhound
A1486

Designed by Roy Andersen.

PHOTOGRAVURE
Plates of 160 in panes of 40.

1984, Sept. 7	**Tagged**	*Perf. 11*	
2098 A1483 20c **multi**		38	8
2099 A1484 20c **multi**		38	8
2100 A1485 20c **multi**		38	8
2101 A1486 20c **multi**		38	8
	P# block of 4, 4#	1.65	—
	Zip block of 4	1.60	—
	Copyright block of 4	1.60	—
a.	Block of 4, #2098-2101	1.55	1.00

CRIME PREVENTION

McGruff, the Crime Dog — A1487

Designed by Randall McDougall.
Printed by American Bank Note Company.

PHOTOGRAVURE
Plates of 200 in panes of 50.

1984, Sept. 26	**Tagged**	*Perf. 11*	
2102 A1487 20c **multi**		38	5
	P# block of 4, 4#	1.70	—
	Zip block of 4	1.55	—
	Copyright block of 4	1.55	—

HISPANIC AMERICANS

A1488

Designed by Robert McCall.

PHOTOGRAVURE
Plates of 160 in four panes of 40.

1984, Oct. 31	**Tagged**	*Perf. 11*	
2103 A1488 20c **multi**		38	5
	P# block of 4, 5 #	1.60	—
	Zip block of 4	1.55	—
	Copyright block of 4	1.55	—
a.	Vert. pair, imperf. horiz.	—	

FAMILY UNITY

Stick Figures — A1489

Designed by Molly LaRue.

PHOTOGRAVURE AND ENGRAVED
(Combination Press)
Plates of 230 in panes of 50.

1984, Oct. 1	**Tagged**	*Perf. 11*	
2104 A1489 20c **multi**		38	5
	P# block of 20, 3-6#, 1-2 copyright, 1-2 zip	12.00	—
a.	Horiz. pair, imperf. vert.	*550.00*	

See Combination Press note after No. 1703.

ELEANOR ROOSEVELT (1884-1962)

A1490

Designed by Bradbury Thompson.

ENGRAVED
Plates of 192 in panes of 48.

1984, Oct. 11	**Tagged**	*Perf. 11*	
2105 A1490 20c **deep blue**		38	5
	P# block of 4	1.60	—
	Zip block of 4	1.55	—
	Copyright block of 4	1.55	—

NATION OF READERS

Abraham Lincoln Reading to Son, Tad — A1491

Designed adapted from Matthew Brady daguerrotype by Bradbury Thompson.

ENGRAVED

Plates of 200 in panes of 50.

1984, Oct. 16	**Tagged**	***Perf. 11***	
2106 A1491 20c	**brown & maroon**	38	5
	P# block of 4	1.60	—
	Zip block of 4	1.55	—
	Copyright block of 4	1.55	—

CHRISTMAS

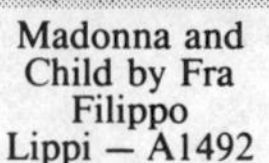

Madonna and Child by Fra Filippo Lippi — A1492

Santa Claus — A1493

Designed by Bradbury Thompson (No. 2107) and Danny La Boccetta (No. 2108).

PHOTOGRAVURE

Plates of 200 in panes of 50.

1984, Oct. 30	**Tagged**	***Perf. 11***	
2107 A1492 20c	**multi**	40	5
	P# block of 4, 5 #	1.70	—
	Zip block of 4	1.65	—
	Copyright block of 4	1.65	—
2108 A1493 20c	**multi**	40	5
	P# block of 4, 5 #	1.70	—
	Zip block of 4	1.65	—
	Copyright block of 4	1.65	—
a.	Horiz. pair, imperf. vert.	—	

VIETNAM VETERANS' MEMORIAL

Memorial and Visitors — A1494

Designed by Paul Calle.

ENGRAVED

Plates of 160 in panes of 40.

1984, Nov. 10	**Tagged**	***Perf. 10½***	
2109 A1494 20c	**multi**	38	5
	P# block of 4	1.60	—
	Zip block of 4	1.55	—
	Copyright block of 4	1.55	—

PERFORMING ARTS

Jerome Kern (1885-1945), Composer — A1495

Designed by Jim Sharpe.
Printed by the American Bank Note Company.

PHOTOGRAVURE

Plates of 200 in four panes of 50.

1985, Jan. 23	**Tagged**	***Perf. 11***	
2110 A1495 22c	**multi**	38	5
	P# block of 4, 5 #	1.75	—
	Zip block of 4	1.55	—
	Copyright block of 4	1.55	—

A1496

A1497

Designed by Bradbury Thompson.

PHOTOGRAVURE

Plates of 460 (20x23) in panes of 100.

1985, Feb. 1	**Tagged**	***Perf. 11***	
2111 A1496 (22c)	**green**	60	5
	P# block of 6, P#	4.50	—
	P# block of 20, 1-2 #, 1-2 Zip, 1-2 Copyright	15.00	—
a.	Vert. pair, imperf.	*50.00*	
b.	Vert. pair, imperf. horiz.	—	

COIL STAMP

Perf. 10 Vert.

2112 A1496 (22c)	**green**	60	5
	Pair	1.20	10
	P# strip of 3, P# 1, 2	5.25	
a.	Imperf., pair	45.00	

BOOKLET STAMP

Perf. 11

2113 A1497 (22c)	**green**	60	5
a.	Booklet pane of 10	6.50	—

A1498

Flag Over Capitol Dome A1499

Designed by Frank Waslick.

ENGRAVED

Plates of 400 subjects in panes of 100.

1985, Mar. 29	**Tagged**	***Perf. 11***	
2114 A1498 22c	**blue, red & black**	40	5
	P# block of 4	1.80	—
	Zip block of 4	1.65	—
	Copyright block of 4	1.65	—
	Pair with full horizontal gutter	—	

COIL STAMP

Perf. 10 Vert.

2115 A1498 22c	**blue, red & black**	40	5
	Pair	80	10
	P# strip of 3, P# 2, 4, 5, 8, 10, 12, 18, 21	3.50	
	P# strip of 3, P# 1, 7, 14	12.00	
	P# strip of 3, P# 3	14.00	
	P# strip of 3, P# 6	5.50	
	P# strip of 3, P# 11, 13, 17, 20	12.50	
	P# strip of 3, P# 15, 16, 19, 22	4.25	
a.	Imperf. pair	17.50	
b.	Inscribed "T" at bottom, *May 23, 1987*	48	8
b.	P# strip of 3, P# T1	2.50	

Copies of No. 2115 exist with the field of stars printed in black instead of blue, according to the Bureau of Engraving and Printing.

BOOKLET STAMP

Perf. 10 Horiz.

2116 A1499 22c	**blue, red & black**	44	5
a.	Booklet pane of 5	2.20	—

BOOKLET STAMPS

Frilled Dogwinkle A1500

Reticulated Helmet A1501

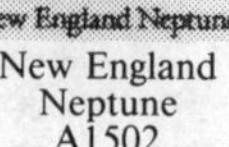

New England Neptune A1502

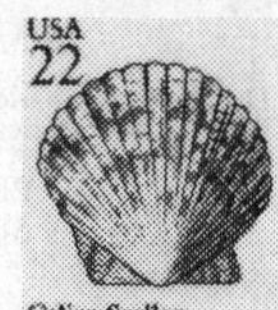

Calico Scallop A1503

Lightning Whelk — A1504

Designed by Pete Cocci.

ENGRAVED

1985, Apr. 4	**Tagged**	***Perf. 10***	
2117 A1500 22c	**black & brown**	40	5
2118 A1501 22c	**black & multi**	40	5
2119 A1502 22c	**black & brown**	40	5
2120 A1503 22c	**black & violet**	40	5
2121 A1504 22c	**black & multi**	40	5
a.	Booklet pane of 10	4.25	—
b.	As "a," violet omitted on both Nos. 2120	—	
c.	As "a," vert. imperf. between	—	
d.	As "a," imperf.		—
e.	Strip of 5, Nos. 2117-2121	2.20	—

Eagle and Half Moon A1505

Designed by Young & Rubicam.

PHOTOGRAVURE

1985, Apr. 29	**Tagged**	***Perf. 10 Vert.***	
2122 A1505 $10.75	**multicolored**	20.00	—
a.	Booklet pane of 3	62.50	—

TRANSPORTATION ISSUE

A1506

A1507

A1508

A1509

A1510

A1511

A1512

A1513

A1514

A1515

A1516

A1517

A1518

A1519

Designers: 3.4c, 17c, Lou Nolan. 4.9c, 8.5c, 14c, 25c, William H. Bond. 5.5c, David K. Stone. 6c, 8.3c, 10.1c, 12.5c. James Schleyer. 7.1c, 11c, 12c, Ken Dallison.

COIL STAMPS
ENGRAVED

1985-87 **Tagged** ***Perf. 10 Vert.***

Number	Description	Unused	Used
2123 A1506 3.4c	**dark bluish green,** *June 8*	7	5
	Pair	14	10
	P# strip of 3, line, P# 1, 2	1.25	
a.	Untagged (Bureau precancel)		15
	P# strip of 3, line, P# 1, 2		1.40
2124 A1507 4.9c	**brown black,** *June 21*	9	5
	Pair	18	10
	P# strip of 3, line, P# 3, 4	1.25	
a.	Untagged (Bureau precancel)		16
	P# strip of 3, line, P# 1-6		1.30
2125 A1508 5.5c	**deep magenta,** *Nov. 1, 1986*	10	5
	Pair	20	10
	P# strip of 3, P# 1	1.25	
a.	Untagged (Bureau precancel)		11
	P# strip of 3, P# 1, 2		1.50
2126 A1509 6c	**red brown,** *May 6*	12	5
	Pair	24	10
	P# strip of 3, P# 1	1.40	
a.	Untagged (Bureau precancel)		12
	P# strip of 3, P# 1		1.90
	P# strip of 3, P# 2		3.75
b.	As "a", imperf. pair		—
2127 A1510 7.1c	**lake,** *Feb. 6, 1987*	15	5
	Pair	30	10
	P# strip of 3, P# 1	1.75	
a.	Untagged (Bureau precancel "Nonprofit Org." in black)		15
	P# strip of 3, P# 1		2.00
a.	Untagged (Bureau precancel "Nonprofit 5-Digit Zip + 3" in black)		15
	P# strip of 3, P# 1		1.75
2128 A1511 8.3c	**green,** *June 21*	18	5
	Pair	36	10
	P# strip of 3, line, P# 1, 2	1.75	
a.	Untagged (Bureau precancel)		18
	P# strip of 3, line, P# 1, 2		1.50
	P# strip of 3, line, P# 3, 4		3.75
2129 A1512 8.5c	**dark Prussian green,** *Jan. 24, 1987*	16	5
	Pair	32	10
	P# strip of 3, P# 1	2.50	
a.	Untagged (Bureau precancel)		16
	P# strip of 3, P# 1, 2		2.75
2130 A1513 10.1c	**slate blue,** *Apr. 18*	22	5
	Pair	44	10
	P# strip of 3, P# 1	2.50	
a.	Untagged (Bureau precancel "Bulk Rate" and lines in black)		22
a.	P# strip of 3, P# 1, 2		3.00
a.	Untagged (Bureau precancel "Bulk Rate Carrier Route Sort" in red)		22
a.	P# strip of 3, P# 2, 3		3.02
b.	As "a", black precancel, imperf. pair		*175.00*
2131 A1514 11c	**dark green,** *June 11*	22	5
	Pair	44	10
	P# strip of 3, line, P# 1-4	2.00	
2132 A1515 12c	**dark blue,** *Apr. 2*	24	5
	Pair	48	10
	P# strip of 3, line, P# 1, 2	2.25	
a.	Untagged (Bureau precancel)		24
	P# strip of 3, line, P# 1, 2		2.50
	P# strip of 3, no line, P# 1		3.25
2133 A1516 12.5c	**olive green,** *Apr. 18*	25	5
	Pair	50	10
	P# strip of 3, P# 1	3.00	
	P# strip of 3, P# 2	4.25	
a.	Untagged (Bureau precancel)		25
	P# strip of 3, P# 1, 2		3.00
b.	As "a", imperf. pair		60.00
2134 A1517 14c	**sky blue,** *Mar. 23*	28	5
	Pair	56	10
	P# strip of 3, line, P# 1-4	2.00	
	P# strip of 3, no line, P# 2	2.50	
a.	Imperf., pair	100.00	
2135 A1518 17c	**sky blue,** *Aug. 20, 1986*	30	5
	Pair	60	10
	P# strip of 3, P# 2	3.00	
a.	Imperf., pair	—	
2136 A1519 25c	**orange brown,** *Nov. 22, 1986*	45	5
	Pair	90	10
	P# strip of 3, P# 2, 4	4.25	
	P# strip of 3, P# 1	4.50	
	P# strip of 3, P# 3, 5	5.00	
a.	Imperf., pair	15.00	
b.	Pair, imperf. between	—	

Precancellations on Nos. 2125a, 2127a do not have lines. Precancellation on No. 2129a is in red. See No. 2231.

BLACK HERITAGE

Mary McLeod Bethune (1875-1955), Educator — A1520

Designed by Jerry Pinkney from a photograph.
Printed by American Bank Note Company.

PHOTOGRAVURE
Plates of 200 in four panes of 50.

1985, Mar. 5 **Tagged** ***Perf. 11***

Number	Description	Unused	Used
2137 A1520 22c	**multi**	40	5
	P# block of 4, 6 #	1.70	—
	Zip block of 4	1.65	—
	Copyright block of 4	1.65	—

AMERICAN FOLK ART ISSUE
Duck Decoys

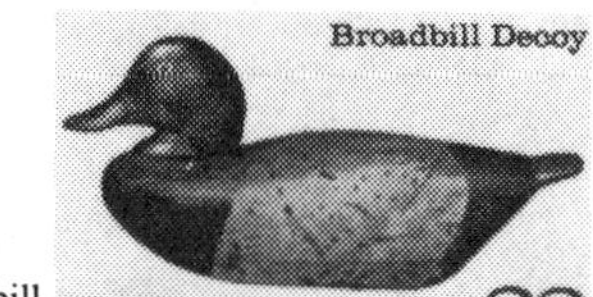

Broadbill A1521

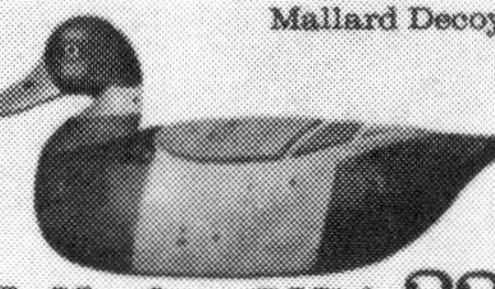

Mallard — A1522

Canvasback A1523

Redhead A1524

Designed by Stevan Dohanos.
Printed by American Bank Note Company

PHOTOGRAVURE
Plates of 200 in four panes of 50.

1985, Mar. 22 **Tagged** ***Perf. 11***

Number	Description	Unused	Used
2138 A1521 22c	**multi**	42	8
2139 A1522 22c	**multi**	42	8
2140 A1523 22c	**multi**	42	8
2141 A1524 22c	**multi**	42	8
	P# block of 4, 5 #	1.80	—
	Zip block of 4	1.75	—
	Copyright block of 4	1.75	—
a.	Block of 4, #2138-2141	1.70	1.00

WINTER SPECIAL OLYMPICS

Ice Skater, Emblem, Skier — A1525

Designed by Jeff Carnell.

PHOTOGRAVURE
Plates of 160 in four panes of 40.

1985, Mar. 25 **Tagged** ***Perf. 11***

Number	Description	Unused	Used
2142 A1525 22c	**multi**	40	5
	P# block of 4, 6 #	1.70	—
	Zip block of 4	1.65	—
	Copyright block of 4	1.65	—
a.	Vert. pair, imperf. horiz.	*850.00*	

LOVE

A1526

Designed by Corita Kent.

PHOTOGRAVURE
Plates of 200 in four panes of 50.

1985, Apr. 17 **Tagged** ***Perf. 11***

Number	Description	Unused	Used
2143 A1526 22c	**multi**	40	5
	P# block of 4, 6 #	1.70	—
	Zip block of 4	1.65	—
	Copyright block of 4	1.65	—
a.	Imperf., pair		—

RURAL ELECTRIFICATION ADMINISTRATION

REA Power Lines, Farmland A1527

Designed by Howard Koslow.

PHOTOGRAVURE & ENGRAVED (Combination Press)
Plates of 200 in four panes of 50.

1985, May 11 **Tagged** ***Perf. 11***

Number	Description	Unused	Used
2144 A1527 22c	**multi**	40	5
	P# block of 20, 5-10 P#, 1-2 Zip, 1-2 Copyright	14.00	—

See Combination Press note after No. 1703.

AMERIPEX '86

U.S. No. 134 — A1528

Designed by Richard D. Sheaff

LITHOGRAPHED & ENGRAVED
Plates of 192 in four panes of 48

1985, May 25 **Tagged** ***Perf. 11***

2145	A1528	22c	**multi**	40	5
			P# block of 4, 3 #	1.70	—
			Zip block of 4	1.65	—
			Copyright block of 4	1.65	—
a.			Red, black & blue (engr.) omitted	*275.00*	

Abigail Adams (1744-1818) — A1529

Designed by Bart Forbes.

PHOTOGRAVURE
Plates of 200 in four panes of 50.

1985, June 14 **Tagged** ***Perf. 11***

2146	A1529	22c	**multi**	40	5
			P# block of 4, 4 #	1.80	—
			Zip block of 4	1.65	—
			Copyright block of 4	1.65	—
a.			Imperf., pair	*400.00*	

FREDERIC AUGUSTE BARTHOLDI (1834-1904)

Architect and Sculptor, Statue of Liberty — A1530

Designed by Howard Paine from paintings by Jose Frappa and James Dean.

LITHOGRAPHED & ENGRAVED
Plates of 200 in four panes of 50.

1985, July 18 **Tagged** ***Perf. 11***

2147	A1530	22c	**multi**	40	5
			P# block of 4, 5 #	1.80	—
			Zip block of 4	1.65	—
			Copyright block of 4	1.65	—

COIL STAMPS

George Washington, Washington Monument A1532

Sealed Envelopes A1533

Designed by Thomas Szumowski (#2149) based on a portrait by Gilbert Stuart, and Richard Sheaff (#2150).

PHOTOGRAVURE

1985 ***Perf. 10 Vertically***

2149	A1532	18c	**multi,** *Nov. 6*	32	8
			Pair	65	16
			P# strip of 3, P# 1112, 3333	2.75	
a.			Untagged (Bureau Precancel)		35
			P# strip of 3, P# 33333		3.00
			P# strip of 3, P# 11121, 43444		4.75
b.			Imperf., pair	*1,250.*	
c.			As "a," imperf. pair		900.00
2150	A1533	21.1c	**multi,** *Oct. 22*	40	8
			Pair	80	16
			P# strip of 3, P# 111111	—	
			P# strip of 3, P# 111121	3.25	
a.			Untagged (Bureau Precancel)		38
			P# strip of 3, P# 111111, 111121		4.00

Precancellations on Nos. 2149a ("PRESORTED FIRST-CLASS") and 2150a ("ZIP+4") do not have lines.
No. 2149a was also issued with dull finish gum.

KOREAN WAR VETERANS

American Troops Marching A1535

Designed by Dick Sheaff from a photograph by David D. Duncan.

ENGRAVED
Plates of 200 in four panes of 50.

1985, July 26 **Tagged** ***Perf. 11***

2152	A1535	22c	**gray green & rose red**	40	5
			P# block of 4	1.70	—
			Zip block of 4	1.65	—
			Copyright block of 4	1.65	—

SOCIAL SECURITY ACT, 50th ANNIV.

Men, Women, Children, Corinthian Columns — A1536

Designed by Robert Brangwynne.
Printed by American Bank Note Company

PHOTOGRAVURE
Plates of 200 in four panes of 50.

1985, Aug. 14 **Tagged** ***Perf. 11***

2153	A1536	22c	**deep & light blue**	40	5
			P# block of 4, 2 #	1.70	—
			Zip block of 4	1.65	—
			Copyright block of 4	1.65	—

WORLD WAR I VETERANS

The Battle of Marne, France — A1537

Designed by Dick Sheaff from Harvey Dunn's charcoal drawing.

ENGRAVED
Plates of 200 in four panes of 50.

1985, Aug. 26 **Tagged** ***Perf. 11***

2154	A1537	22c	**gray green & rose red**	40	5
			P# block of 4	1.70	—
			Zip block of 4	1.65	—
			Copyright block of 4	1.65	—

The Demand, as well as supply, determines a stamp's market value. One is as important as the other.

HORSES

Quarter Horse — A1538

Morgan — A1539

Saddlebred A1540

USA 22
Appaloosa

Appaloosa A1541

Designed by Roy Andersen.

PHOTOGRAVURE
Plates of 160 in four panes of 40.

1985, Sept. 25 **Tagged** ***Perf. 11***

2155	A1538	22c	**multi**	40	8
2156	A1539	22c	**multi**	40	8
2157	A1540	22c	**multi**	40	8
2158	A1541	22c	**multi**	40	8
			P# block of 4, 5#	1.90	—
			Zip block of 4	1.70	—
			Copyright block of 4	1.70	—
a.			Block of 4, #2155-2158	1.65	1.00

PUBLIC EDUCATION IN AMERICA

Quill Pen, Apple, Spectacles, Penmanship Quiz — A1542

Designed by Uldis Purins.
Printed by American Bank Note Company

PHOTOGRAVURE
Plates of 200 in four panes of 50.

1985, Oct. 1 **Tagged** ***Perf. 11***

2159	A1542	22c	**multi**	40	5
			P# block of 4, 5 #	1.70	—
			Zip block of 4	1.65	—
			Copyright block of 4	1.65	—

INTERNATIONAL YOUTH YEAR

YMCA Youth Camping, Cent. — A1543

Boy Scouts, 75th Anniv. — A1544

Big Brothers / Big Sisters Federation, 40th Anniv. — A1545

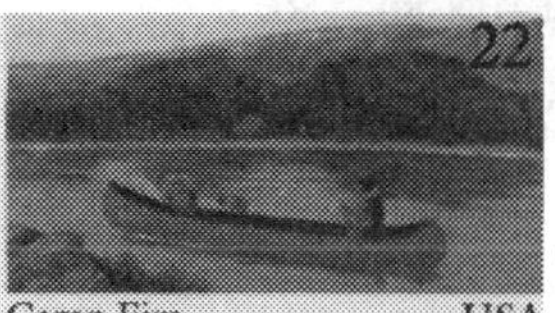

Camp Fire Inc., 75th Anniv. — A1546

Designed by Dennis Luzak.
Printed by American Bank Note Company

PHOTOGRAVURE
Plates of 200 in four panes of 50.

1985, Oct. 7			**Tagged**	***Perf. 11***	
2160	A1543	22c	**multi**	42	8
2161	A1544	22c	**multi**	42	8
2162	A1545	22c	**multi**	42	8
2163	A1546	22c	**multi**	42	8
			P# block of 4, 5 #	2.00	—
			Zip block of 4	1.75	—
			Copyright block of 4	1.75	—
a.			Block of 4, #2160-2163	1.70	1.00

HELP END HUNGER

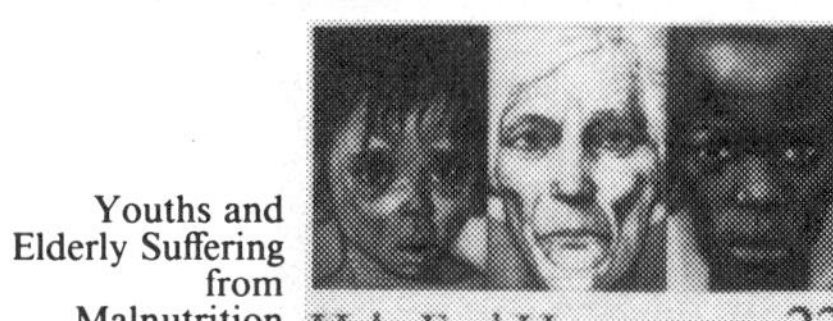

Youths and Elderly Suffering from Malnutrition A1547

Designed by Jerry Pinkney.
Printed by the American Bank Note Company.

PHOTOGRAVURE
Plates of 200 in four panes of 50.

1985, Oct. 15			**Tagged**	***Perf. 11***	
2164	A1547	22c	**multi**	40	5
			P# block of 4, 5 #	1.70	—
			Zip block of 4	1.65	—
			Copyright block of 4	1.65	—

CHRISTMAS

Genoa Madonna, Enameled Terra-Cotta by Luca Della Robbia (1400-1482) — A1548

Poinsettia Plants — A1549

Designed by Bradbury Thompson (No. 2165) and James Dean (No. 2166).

PHOTOGRAVURE
Plates of 200 in panes of 50.

1985, Oct. 30			**Tagged**	***Perf. 11***	
2165	A1548	22c	**multi**	40	5
			P# block of 4, 4 #	1.70	—
			Zip block of 4	1.65	—
			Copyright block of 4	1.65	—
a.			Imperf., pair	*130.00*	
2166	A1549	22c	**multi**	40	5
			P# block of 4, 5 #	1.70	—
			Zip block of 4	1.65	—
			Copyright block of 4	1.65	—
a.			Imperf., pair	*150.00*	

ARKANSAS STATEHOOD SESQUICENTENARY

Old State House, Little Rock — A1550

Designed by Roger Carlisle.
Printed by the American Bank Note Company

PHOTOGRAVURE
Plates of 200 in four panes of 50.

1986, Jan. 3			**Tagged**	***Perf. 11***	
2167	A1550	22c	**multi**	40	5
			P# block of 4, 6#	1.70	—
			Zip block of 4	1.65	—
			Copyright block of 4	1.65	—
a.			Vert. pair, imperf. horiz.	—	

GREAT AMERICANS ISSUE

A1551

A1552

A1553

Father Flanagan USA 4

A1554

A1555

A1559

A1560

A1561

A1562

A1563

A1565

A1566

A1567

A1571

A1574

A1575

A1577

A1577a

A1578

A1579

Designers: 1c, 2c, Ron Adair. 3c, 4c, 5c, 17c, 65c, Christopher Calle. 10c, 28c, 56c, Robert Anderson. 14c, Ward Brackett. 15c, Jack Rosenthal. 21c, Susan Sanford. 23c, Dennis Lyall. 25c, Richard Sparks. 45c, No. 2194A, Bradbury Thompson. No. 2194, $2, Tom Broad. $5, Arthur Lidov.

ENGRAVED

1986-89			**Tagged**	***Perf. 11***	
2168	A1551	1c	**brownish vermilion,** *June 30*	5	5
			P# block of 4	25	—
			Zip block of 4	22	—
			Copyright block of 4	22	—
2169	A1552	2c	**bright blue,** *Feb. 28, 1987*	5	5
			P# block of 4	25	—
			Zip block of 4	22	—
			Copyright block of 4	22	—
2170	A1553	3c	**bright blue,** *Sept. 15*	5	5
			P# block of 4	25	—
			Zip block of 4	22	—
			Copyright block of 4	22	—
2171	A1554	4c	**blue violet,** *July 14*	7	5
			P# block of 4	35	—
			Zip block of 4	30	—
			Copyright block of 4	30	—
2172	A1555	5c	**dark olive green,** *Feb. 27*	9	5
			P# block of 4	40	—
			Zip block of 4	38	—
			Copyright block of 4	38	—
2176	A1559	10c	**lake,** *Aug. 15, 1987*	18	5
			P# block of 4	85	—
			Zip block of 4	75	—
			Copyright block of 4	75	—
2177	A1560	14c	**crimson,** *Feb. 12, 1987*	25	5
			P# block of 4	1.10	—
			Zip block of 4	1.05	—
			Copyright block of 4	1.05	—
2178	A1561	15c	**claret,** *June 6, 1988*	28	5

			P# block of 4	1.20	—
			Zip block of 4	1.15	—
			Copyright block of 4	1.15	—
2179	A1562	17c	**dull blue green,** *June 18*	30	6
			P# block of 4	1.45	—
			Zip block of 4	1.25	—
			Copyright block of 4	1.25	—
2180	A1563	21c	**blue violet,** *Oct. 21, 1988*	38	5
			P# block of 4	1.65	—
			Zip block of 4	1.55	—
			Copyright block of 4	1.55	—
2182	A1565	23c	**purple,** *Nov. 4, 1988*	42	5
			P# block of 4	1.75	—
			Zip block of 4	1.70	—
			Copyright block of 4	1.70	—
2183	A1566	25c	**blue,** *Jan. 11*	45	6
			P# block of 4	2.00	—
			Zip block of 4	1.85	—
			Copyright block of 4	1.85	—
a.			Booklet pane of 10, *May 3, 1988*	4.75	—

See Nos. 2197, 2197a.

2184	A1567	28c	*Sept. 14, 1989*	56	8
			P# block of 4	2.80	—
			Zip block of 4	2.50	—
			Copyright block of 4	2.50	—
2188	A1571	45c	**bright blue,** *June 17, 1988*	80	6
			P# block of 4	3.50	—
			Zip block of 4	3.25	—
			Copyright block of 4	3.25	—
2191	A1574	56c	**scarlet,** *Sept. 3*	1.00	8
			P# block of 4	4.25	—
			Zip block of 4	4.10	—
			Copyright block of 4	4.10	—
2192	A1575	65c	**dark blue,** *Nov. 5, 1988*	1.20	18
			P# block of 4	5.00	—
			Zip block of 4	4.90	—
			Copyright block of 4	4.90	—
2194	A1577	$1	**dark Prussian green,** *Sept. 23*	1.75	50
			P# block of 4	7.25	—
			Zip block of 4	7.10	
			Copyright block of 4	7.10	
2194A	A1577a	$1	**deep blue,** *June 7, 1989*	1.75	50
			P# block of 4	7.25	—
			Zip block of 4	7.10	
			Copyright block of 4	7.10	
2195	A1578	$2	**bright violet,** *Mar. 19*	3.50	50
			P# block of 4	15.00	—
			Zip block of 4	14.50	—
			Copyright block of 4	14.50	—

Plates of 320 in sixteen panes of 20 (5x4).
The first and fifth rows of horizontal perforations extend into the side selvage.
Copyright information appears in the center of the top or bottom selvage.

2196	A1579	$5	**copper red,** *Aug. 25, 1987*	7.75	1.00
			P# block of 4	32.50	—

Booklet Stamp

Perf. 10 on 2 or 3 sides

2197	A1566	25c	**blue,** *May 3, 1988*	45	5
a.			Bklt. pane of 6	3.00	—

This is an expanding set. Numbers will change if necessary.

UNITED STATES - SWEDEN STAMP COLLECTING

Handstamped Cover, Philatelic Memorabilia A1581

Boy Examining Stamp Collection — A1582

No. 836 Under Magnifying Glass, Sweden Nos. 268, 271 — A1583

1986 Presidents Miniature Sheet — A1584

Designed by Richard Sheaff and Eva Jern (No. 2200).

BOOKLET STAMPS
LITHOGRAPHED & ENGRAVED
Perf. 10 Vert. on 1 or 2 Sides

1986, Jan. 23 **Tagged**

2198	A1581	22c	**multi**	40	5
2199	A1582	22c	**multi**	40	5
2200	A1583	22c	**multi**	40	5
2201	A1584	22c	**multi**	40	5
a.			Bklt. pane of 4, #2198-2201	2.00	—
b.			As "a," black omitted on Nos. 2198, 2201	50.00	
c.			As "a," blue (litho.) omitted on Nos. 2198-2200		—
d.			As "a," buff (litho.) omitted		—

LOVE ISSUE

A1585

Designed by Saul Mandel.

Plates of 200 in four panes of 50.
PHOTOGRAVURE

1986, Jan. 30 **Tagged** ***Perf. 11***

2202	A1585	22c	**multi**	40	5
			P# block of 4, 5#	1.70	—
			Zip block of 4	1.65	—
			Copyright block of 4	1.65	—

BLACK HERITAGE ISSUE

Sojourner Truth (c. 1797-1883), Human Rights Activist — A1586

Designed by Jerry Pinkney.
Printed by American Bank Note Co.

Plates of 200 in four panes of 50
PHOTOGRAVURE

1986, Feb. 4 **Tagged** ***Perf. 11***

2203	A1586	22c	**multi**	40	5
			P# block of 4, 6#	1.70	—
			Zip block of 4	1.65	—
			Copyright block of 4	1.65	—

REPUBLIC OF TEXAS, 150th Anniv.

Texas State Flag and Silver Spur — A1587

Designed by Don Adair.
Printed by the American Bank Note Co.

Plates of 200 in four panes of 50.
PHOTOGRAVURE

1986, Mar. 2 **Tagged** ***Perf. 11***

2204	A1587	22c	**dark blue, dark red & grayish black**	40	5
			P# block of 4, 3 #	1.70	—
			Zip block of 4	1.65	—
			Copyright block of 4	1.65	—
a.			Horiz. pair, imperf. vert.	*950.00*	

FISH

Muskellunge A1588

Atlantic Cod — A1589

Largemouth Bass — A1590

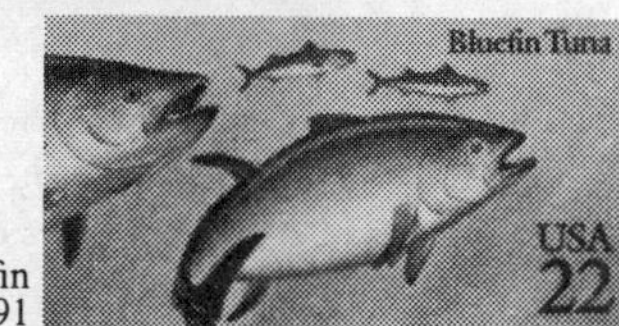

Bluefin Tuna — A1591

Catfish A1592

Designed by Chuck Ripper.

BOOKLET STAMPS
PHOTOGRAVURE

1986, Mar. 21 **Tagged** ***Perf. 10 Horiz.***

2205	A1588	22c	**multi**	40	5
2206	A1589	22c	**multi**	40	5
2207	A1590	22c	**multi**	40	5
2208	A1591	22c	**multi**	40	5
2209	A1592	22c	**multi**	40	5
a.			Bklt. pane of 5, #2205-2209	2.75	—

PUBLIC HOSPITALS

A1593

Designed by Uldis Purins.
Printed by the American Bank Note Co.

PHOTOGRAVURE

Plates of 200 in four panes of 50.

1986, Apr. 11 **Tagged** ***Perf. 11***

2210 A1593 22c **multi**		40	5
	P# block of 4, 5#	1.70	—
	Zip block of 4	1.65	—
	Copyright block of 4	1.65	—
a.	ert. pair, imperf. horiz.	*425.00*	
b.	Horiz. pair, imperf. vert.	—	

PERFORMING ARTS

Edward Kennedy "Duke" Ellington (1899-1974), Jazz Composer — A1594

Designed by Jim Sharpe.
Printed by the American Bank Note Co.

PHOTOGRAVURE

Plates of 200 in four panes of 50.

1986, Apr. 29 **Tagged** ***Perf. 11***

2211 A1594 22c **multi**		40	5
	P# block of 4, 6#	1.70	—
	Zip block of 4	1.65	—
	Copyright block of 4	1.65	—
a.	Vert. pair, imperf. horiz.	—	

AMERIPEX '86 ISSUE

Miniature Sheets

35 Presidents — A1599a

A1599b

Presidents of
the United States: III
AMERIPEX 86
International
Stamp Show
Chicago, Illinois
May 22-June 1, 1986

A1599c

A1599d

Designs: No. 2216: a, George Washington. b, John Adams. c, Thomas Jefferson. d, James Madison. e, James Monroe. f, John Quincy Adams. g, Andrew Jackson. h, Martin Van Buren. i, William H. Harrison.

No. 2217: a, John Tyler. b, James Knox Polk. c, Zachary Taylor. d, Millard Fillmore. e, Franklin Pierce. f, James Buchanan. g, Abraham Lincoln. h, Andrew Johnson. i, Ulysses S. Grant.

No. 2218: a, Rutherford B. Hayes. b, James A. Garfield. c, Chester A. Arthur. d, Grover Cleveland. e, Benjamin Harrison. f, William McKinley. g, Theodore Roosevelt. h, William H. Taft. i, Woodrow Wilson.

No. 2219: a, Warren G. Harding. b, Calvin Coolidge. c, Herbert Hoover. d, Franklin Delano Roosevelt. e, White House. f, Harry S. Truman. g, Dwight D. Eisenhower. h, John F. Kennedy. i, Lyndon B. Johnson.

Designed by Jerry Dadds

LITHOGRAPHED & ENGRAVED

1986, May 22		**Tagged**	***Perf. 11***	
2216	A1599a	**Sheet of 9**	3.50	—
a.-i.		22c, any single	38	20
j.		Blue (engr.) omitted		—
k.		Black inscription omitted		—
2217	A1599b	**Sheet of 9**	3.50	—
a-i.		22c, any single	38	20
2218	A1599c	**Sheet of 9**	3.50	—
a.-i.		22c, any single	38	20
j.		Brown (engr.) omitted		—
k.		Black inscription omitted		—
2219	A1599d	**Sheet of 9**	3.50	—
a.-i.		22c, any single	38	20

Issued in conjunction with AMERIPEX '86 Intl. Philatelic Exhibition, Chicago, IL May 22-June 1. Sheet size: 120x207mm (sheet size varied).

ARCTIC EXPLORERS

Elisha Kent Kane — A1600

Adolphus W. Greely — A1601

Vilhjalmur Stefansson A1602

Robert E. Peary, Matthew Henson — A1603

Designed by Dennis Lyall.
Printed by the American Bank Note Company

PHOTOGRAVURE
Plates of 200 in four panes of 50.

1986, May 28			**Tagged**	***Perf. 11***	
2220	A1600	22c	**multi**	45	8
2221	A1601	22c	**multi**	45	8
2222	A1602	22c	**multi**	45	8
2223	A1603	22c	**multi**	45	8
			P# block of 4, 5#	2.25	—
			Zip block of 4	1.90	—
			Copyright block of 4	1.90	—
a.			Block of 4, #2220-2223	1.85	1.00
b.			As "a," black (engr.) omitted		—

STATUE OF LIBERTY, CENT.

A1604

Designed by Howard Paine.

ENGRAVED
Plates of 200 in four panes of 50.

1986, July 4			**Tagged**	***Perf. 11***	
2224	A1604	22c	**scar & dk bl**	40	5
			P# block of 4, 2#	1.80	—
			Zip block of 4	1.65	—
			Copyright block of 4	1.65	—

TRANSPORTATION ISSUE

A1604a

A1604b

Designers: 1c, 2c, David Stone.

COIL STAMPS
ENGRAVED

1986-87			**Tagged**	***Perf. 10 Vert.***	
2225	A1604a	1c	**violet,** *Nov. 26*	5	5
			Pair	10	10
			P# strip of 3, P# 1, 2	70	—
2226	A1604b	2c	**black,** *Mar. 6, 1987*	5	5
			Pair	10	10
			P# strip of 3, P# 1	75	
			REDUCED SIZE		
2228	A1285	4c	**reddish brown,** *Aug.*	8	5
			Pair	16	10
			P# strip of 3, P#1	1.10	
			UNTAGGED		
2231	A1511	8.3c	**green** (Bureau precancel), *Aug. 29*		16
			Pair		32
			P# strip of 3, P# 1, 2		2.75

Earliest known usage of No. 2228: Aug. 15, 1986.

On No. 2228 "Stagecoach 1890s" is 17mm long; on No. 1898A, 19½mm long.

On No. 2231 "Ambulance 1860s" is 18mm long; on No. 2128, 18½mm long.

Joint lines do not appear on Nos. 2225-2231.

This is an expanding set. Numbers will change if necessary.

NAVAJO ART

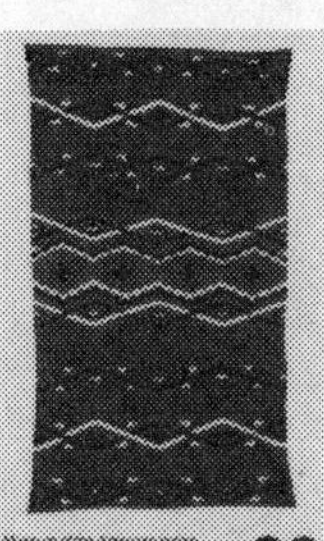

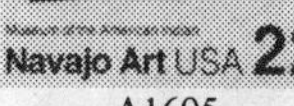

A1605

A1606

A1607

A1608

Designed by Derry Noyes.

LITHOGRAPHED & ENGRAVED
Plates of 200 in four panes of 50.

1986, Sept. 4			**Tagged**	***Perf. 11***	
2235	A1605	22c	**multi**	40	8
2236	A1606	22c	**multi**	40	8
2237	A1607	22c	**multi**	40	8
2238	A1608	22c	**multi**	40	8
			P# block of 4, 5#	1.90	—
			Zip block of 4	1.70	—
			Copyright block of 4	1.70	—
a.			Block of 4, #2235-2238	1.65	1.00
b.			As "a," black (engr.) omitted	*475.00*	

LITERARY ARTS

T.S. Eliot (1888-1965), Poet — A1609

Designed by Bradbury Thompson.

ENGRAVED
Plates of 200 in four panes of 50.

1986, Sept. 26			**Tagged**	***Perf. 11***	
2239	A1609	22c	**copper red**	40	5
			P# block of 4	1.90	—
			Zip block of 4	1.65	—
			Copyright block of 4	1.65	—

AMERICAN FOLK ART ISSUE
Woodcarved Figurines

A1610

A1611

A1612

A1613

Designed by Bradbury Thompson.
Printed by the American Bank Note Company

PHOTOGRAVURE
Plates of 200 in four panes of 50.

1986, Oct. 1			**Tagged**	***Perf. 11***	
2240	A1610	22c	**multi**	40	8
2241	A1611	22c	**multi**	40	8
2242	A1612	22c	**multi**	40	8
2243	A1613	22c	**multi**	40	8
			P# block of 4, 5#	1.90	—
			Zip block of 4	1.70	—
			Copyright block of 4	1.70	—
a.			Block of 4, #2240-2243	1.65	1.00
b.			As "a," imperf. vert.		—

CHRISTMAS

Madonna, National Gallery, by Perugino (c. 1450-1513) A1614

Village Scene A1615

Designed by Dolli Tingle (No. 2244) and Bradbury Thompson (No. 2245).

PHOTOGRAVURE
Plates of 200 in four panes of 50.

1986, Oct. 24 **Tagged** ***Perf. 11***

2244 A1614 22c	**multi**	40	5
	P# block of 4, 6#	1.90	—
	Zip block of 4	1.65	—
	Copyright block of 4	1.65	—
2245 A1615 22c	**multi**	40	5
	P# block of 4, 5#	1.90	—
	Zip block of 4	1.65	—
	Copyright block of 4	1.65	—

MICHIGAN STATEHOOD SESQUICENTENARY

White Pine — A1616

Designed by Robert Wilbert.

PHOTOGRAVURE
Plates of 200 in four panes of 50.

1987, Jan. 26 **Tagged** ***Perf. 11***

2246 A1616 22c	**multi**	40	5
	P# block of 4, 4#	1.90	—
	Zip block of 4	1.65	—
	Copyright block of 4	1.65	—
	Pair with full vert. gutter between		—

PAN AMERICAN GAMES, INDIANAPOLIS, AUG. 7-25

Runner in Full Stride — A1617

Designed by Lon Busch.

PHOTOGRAVURE
Plates of 200 in four panes of 50.

1987, Jan. 29 **Tagged** ***Perf. 11***

2247 A1617 22c	**multi**	40	5
	P# block of 4, 5#	1.90	—
	Zip block of 4	1.65	—
	Copyright block of 4	1.65	—
a.	Silver omitted		—

LOVE ISSUE

A1618

Designed by John Alcorn.

PHOTOGRAVURE
Panes of 100

1987, Jan. 30 **Tagged** ***Perf. 11½x11***

2248 A1618 22c	**multi**	40	5
	P# block of 4, 5#	1.90	—
	Zip block of 4	1.65	—
	Copyright block of 4	1.65	—
	Pair with full horiz. gutter between		—

United States Transportation coils can be mounted in Scott's annually supplemented Plate Number Coils, U.S. Comprehensive Plate Number Coils Albums and Comprehensive Plate Number Coil Singles Albums.

BLACK HERITAGE

Jean Baptiste Pointe du Sable (c. 1750-1818), Pioneer Trader, Founder of Chicago — A1619

Designed by Thomas Blackshear.

PHOTOGRAVURE
Plates of 200 in four panes of 50.

1987, Feb. 20 **Tagged** ***Perf. 11***

2249 A1619 22c	**multi**	40	5
	P# block of 4, 5#	1.90	—
	Zip block of 4	1.65	—
	Copyright block of 4	1.65	—

PERFORMING ARTS

Enrico Caruso (1873-1921), Opera Tenor — A1620

Designed by Jim Sharpe.
Printed by American Bank Note Co.

PHOTOGRAVURE
Plates of 200 in four panes of 50.

1987, Feb. 27 **Tagged** ***Perf. 11***

2250 A1620 22c	**multi**	40	5
	P# block of 4, 4#	1.90	—
	Zip block of 4	1.65	—
	Copyright block of 4	1.65	—
a.	Black (engr.) omitted		—

GIRL SCOUTS, 75TH ANNIVERSARY

Fourteen Achievement Badges — A1621

Designed by Richard D. Sheaff.

LITHOGRAPHED & ENGRAVED
Plates of 200 in four panes of 50.

1987, Mar. 12 **Tagged** ***Perf. 11***

2251 A1621 22c	**multi**	40	5
	P# block of 4, 6#	1.90	—
	Zip block of 4	1.65	—
	Copyright block of 4	1.65	—

TRANSPORTATION ISSUE

A1622

A1623

A1624

A1625

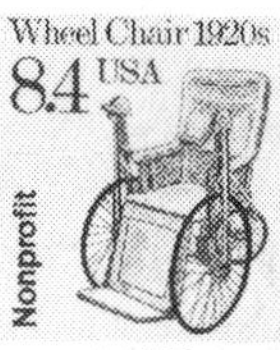

A1626

A1627

A1628

A1629

A1630

A1631

A1632

A1633

A1634

A1635

A1636

Designers: 3c, 7.6c, 13.2c, 15c, Richard Schlect. 5c, 5.3c 16.7c, Lou Nolan. 8.4c, 20.5c, 24.1c, Christopher Calle. 10c, William H. Bond. 13c, Joe Brockert. 17.5c, Tom Broad. 20c, Dan Romano. 21c, David Stone.

COIL STAMPS
ENGRAVED

1987-88 ***Perf. 10 Vert.***

Tagged, Untagged (5.3c, 7.6c, 8.4c, 13c, 13.2c, 16.7c, 20.5c, 21c, 24.1c)

2252 A1622	3c	**claret**, *Feb. 29, 1988*	6	5
		Pair	12	10
		P# strip of 3, P# 1	80	
2253 A1623	5c	**black**, *Sept. 25*	9	5
		Pair	18	10
		P# strip of 3, P# 1	1.25	
2254 A1624	5.3c	**black** (Bureau precancel), *Sept. 16, 1988*		10
		Pair		20
		P# strip of 3, P# 1		1.65

"Nonprofit Carrier Route Sort" is in scarlet.

2255 A1625	7.6c	**brown** (Bureau precancel), *Aug. 30, 1988*		14
		Pair		28
		P# strip of 3, P# 1, 2		1.90

"Nonprofit" is in scarlet.

2256 A1626 8.4c **deep claret** (Bureau precancel), *Aug. 12, 1988* 15
Pair 30
P# strip of 3, P# 1, 2 2.50

"Nonprofit" is in red.

2257 A1627 10c **sky blue,** *Apr. 11* 18 5
pair 36 10
P# strip of 3, P# 1 1.40
2258 A1628 13c **black** (Bureau precancel), *Oct. 29, 1988* 22
Pair 45
P# strip of 3, P# 1 3.00

"Presorted First-Class" is in red.

2259 A1629 13.2c **slate green** (Bureau precancel), *July 19, 1988* 22
Pair 45
P# strip of 3, P# 1 3.00
a. Imperf., pair *350.00*

"Bulk Rate" is in red.

2260 A1630 15c **violet,** *July 12, 1988* 24 5
Pair 48 10
P# strip of 3, P# 1 2.75
2261 A1631 16.7c **rose** (Bureau precancel), *July 7, 1988* 28
Pair 56
P# strip of 3, P# 1 3.50
a. Imperf., pair —

"Bulk Rate " is in black.

2262 A1632 17.5c **dark vio,** *Sept. 25* 30 5
Pair 60 10
P# strip of 3, P# 1 3.25
a. Untagged (Bureau Precancel) 30
P# strip of 3, P# 1 3.50
b. Imperf., pair —
2263 A1633 20c **blue violet,** *Oct. 28, 1988* 35 5
Pair 70 10
P# strip of 3, P# 1, 2 3.50
2264 A1634 20.5c **rose** (Bureau precancel), *Sept. 28, 1988* 38
Pair 76
P# strip of 3, P# 1 3.50

"ZIP + 4 Presort" is in black.

2265 A1635 21c **olive green** (Bureau precancel), *Aug. 16, 1988* 38
Pair 76
P# strip of 3, P# 1, 2 3.50
a. Imperf., pair — 325.00

"Presorted First-Class" is in red.

2266 A1636 24.1c **deep ultra** (Bureau precancel), *Oct. 26, 1988* 42
Pair 85
P# strip of 3, P# 1 4.50

5.3c, 7.6c, 8.4c, 13.2c, 16.7c, 20.5c, 21c and 24.1c only available precanceled.

SPECIAL OCCASIONS

A1637

A1638

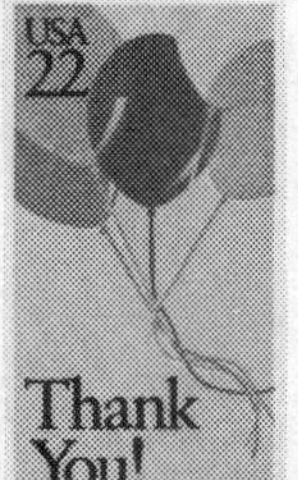

A1639

A1640

A1641

A1642

A1643

A1644

Designed by Oren Sherman.

BOOKLET STAMPS
PHOTOGRAVURE

1987, Apr. 20 Tagged ***Perf. 10 on 1, 2 or 3 Sides***
2267 A1637 22c **multi** 40 5
2268 A1638 22c **multi** 40 5
2269 A1639 22c **multi** 40 5
2270 A1640 22c **multi** 40 5
2271 A1641 22c **multi** 40 5
2272 A1642 22c **multi** 40 5
2273 A1643 22c **multi** 40 5
2274 A1644 22c **multi** 40 5
a. Bklt. pane of 10 (#2268-2271, 2273-2274, 2 of each #2267, 2272) 4.25 —

UNITED WAY CENTENARY

Six Profiles — A1645

Designed by Jerry Pinkney.

LITHOGRAPHED & ENGRAVED
Plates of 200 in four panes of 50.

1987, Apr. 28 Tagged ***Perf. 11***
2275 A1645 22c **multi** 40 5
P# block of 4, 6# 1.90 —
Zip block of 4 1.65 —
Copyright block of 4 1.65 —

A1646

A1647

A1648

A1649

Pheasant
A1649a

Owl
A1649c

Honeybee
A1649d

25 USA
Grosbeak
A1649b

A little time given to the study of the arrangement of the Scott Catalogue can make it easier to use effectively.

Designs: Nos. 2276, 2278, 2280, Peter Cocci. Nos. 2277, 2279, 2282, Robert McCall. Nos. 2281, 2283-2285, Chuck Ripper.

PHOTOGRAVURE (Nos. 2276-2279), Panes of 100

1987-88 Tagged ***Perf. 11***
2276 A1646 22c **multi,** *May 9* 40 5
P# block of 4, 4# 1.90
Zip block of 4 1.65
Copyright block of 4 1.65
a. Booklet pane of 20, *Nov. 30* 8.50 —
2277 A1647 (25c) **multi,** *Mar. 22, 1988* 45 5
P# block of 4, 4# 1.90
Zip block of 4 1.85
Copyright block of 4 1.85
2278 A1648 25c **multi,** *May 6, 1988* 45 5
P# block of 4, 4# 1.90
Zip block of 4 1.85
Copyright block of 4 1.85
Pair with full vert. gutter between —

COIL STAMPS
Perf. 10 Vert.

2279 A1647 (25c) **multi,** *Mar. 22, 1988* 45 5
Pair 90 10
P# strip of 3, P# 1111, 1222 3.50
P# strip of 3, P# 1211 5.75
P# strip of 3, P# 2222 4.75
a. Imperf., pair —

ENGRAVED

2280 A1649 25c **multi,** *May 20, 1988* 45 5
Pair 90 10
P# strip of 3, P# 1-5, 7-9 4.00
Pre-phosphorized paper 45 5
P# strip of 3, P# 6 3.50
a. Imperf., pair —

LITHOGRAPHED AND ENGRAVED

2281 A1649d 25c **multi,** *Sept. 2, 1988* 45 5
Pair 90 10
P# strip of 3, P# 1, 2 4.00
a. Imperf., pair —
b. Black (engr.) omitted —

BOOKLET STAMPS

Printed by American Bank Note Co. (#2283)

PHOTOGRAVURE
Perf. 10, 11 (#2283)

2282 A1647 (25c) **multi,** *Mar. 22, 1988* 45 5
a. Bklt. pane of 10 4.75
2283 A1649a 25c **multi,** *Apr. 29, 1988* 45 5
a. Bklt. pane of 10 4.75
b. 25c multicolored, red removed 45 5
c. As "b," bklt. pane of 10 4.75

Imperf. and part perf. pairs and panes exist from printers waste.

2284 A1649b 25c **multi,** *May 28, 1988* 45 5
2285 A1649c 25c **multi,** *May 28, 1988* 45 5
b. Bklt. pane of 10, 5 each Nos. 2284-2285 4.75
d. Se-tenant pair, Nos. 2284-2285 90 —
2285A A1648 25c **multi,** *July 5, 1988* 45 5
c. Bklt. pane of 6 2.75

Fauna and Flora
A1650-A1699

Designed by Chuck Ripper.

PHOTOGRAVURE
Plates of 200 in four panes of 50.

1987, June 13			**Tagged**	*Perf. 11*	
2286	A1650	22c	Barn swallow	40	15
2287	A1651	22c	Monarch butterily	40	15
2288	A1652	22c	Bighorn sheep	40	15
2289	A1653	22c	Broad-tailed hummingbird	40	15
2290	A1654	22c	Cottontail	40	15
2291	A1655	22c	Osprey	40	15
2292	A1656	22c	Mountain lion	40	15
2293	A1657	22c	Luna moth	40	15
2294	A1658	22c	Mule deer	40	15
2295	A1659	22c	Gray squirrel	40	15
2296	A1660	22c	Armadillo	40	15
2297	A1661	22c	Eastern chipmunk	40	15
2298	A1662	22c	Moose	40	15
2299	A1663	22c	Black bear	40	15
2300	A1664	22c	Tiger swallowtail	40	15
2301	A1665	22c	Bobwhite	40	15
2302	A1666	22c	Ringtail	40	15
2303	A1667	22c	Red-winged blackbird	40	15
2304	A1668	22c	American lobster	40	15
2305	A1669	22c	Black-tailed jack rabbit	40	15
2306	A1670	22c	Scarlet tanager	40	15
2307	A1671	22c	Woodchuck	40	15
2308	A1672	22c	Roseate spoonbill	40	15
2309	A1673	22c	Bald eagle	40	15
2310	A1674	22c	Alaskan brown bear	40	15
2311	A1675	22c	Iiwi	40	15
2312	A1676	22c	Badger	40	15
2313	A1677	22c	Pronghorn	40	15
2314	A1678	22c	River otter	40	15
2315	A1679	22c	Ladybug	40	15
2316	A1680	22c	Beaver	40	15
2317	A1681	22c	White-tailed deer	40	15
2318	A1682	22c	Blue jay	40	15
2319	A1683	22c	Pika	40	15
2320	A1684	22c	Bison	40	15
2321	A1685	22c	Snowy egret	40	15
2322	A1686	22c	Gray wolf	40	15
2323	A1687	22c	Mountain goat	40	15
2324	A1688	22c	Deer mouse	40	15
2325	A1689	22c	Black-tailed prairie dog	40	15
2326	A1690	22c	Box turtle	40	15
2327	A1691	22c	Wolverine	40	15
2328	A1692	22c	American elk	40	15
2329	A1693	22c	California sea lion	40	15
2330	A1694	22c	Mockingbird	40	15
2331	A1695	22c	Raccoon	40	15
2332	A1696	22c	Bobcat	40	15
2333	A1697	22c	Black-footed ferret	40	15
2334	A1698	22c	Canada goose	40	15
2335	A1699	22c	Red fox	40	15
a.			Pane of 50, #2286-2335	20.00	

RATIFICATION OF THE CONSTITUTION BICENTENNIAL
13 States

A1700

A1701

A1702

A1703

A1704

A1705

A1706

A1707

A1708

A1709

A1710

A1711

Designers: Nos. 2336-2337, Richard D. Sheaff. No. 2338, Jim Lamb. No. 2339, Greg Harlin. No. 2340, Christopher Calle, No. 2342, Stephen Hustuedt. Nos. 2343, 2347, Bob Timberlake. No. 2344, Thomas Szumowski. No. 2345, Pierre Mion. No. 2346, Bradbury Thompson.

Printed by the Bureau of Engraving or the American Bank Note Co. (Nos. 2343-2344, 2347).

LITHOGRAPHED & ENGRAVED, PHOTOGRAVURE (Nos. 2337, 2339, 2343-2344, 2347), ENGRAVED (No. 2341).

Plates of 200 in four panes of 50.

1987-89		**Tagged**	***Perf. 11***	
2336	A1700 22c	**multi,** *July 4*	40	5
		P# block of 4, 5#	1.70	—
		Zip block of 4	1.65	—
		Copyright block of 4	1.65	—
2337	A1701 22c	**multi,** *Aug. 26*	40	5
		P# block of 4, 5#	1.70	—
		Zip block of 4	1.65	—
		Copyright block of 4	1.65	—
2338	A1702 22c	**multi,** *Sept. 11*	40	5
		P# block of 4, 5#	1.70	—
		Zip block of 4	1.65	—
		Copyright block of 4	1.65	—
2339	A1703 22c	**multi,** *Jan. 6, 1988*	40	5
		P# block of 4, 5#	1.70	—
		Zip block of 4	1.65	—
		Copyright block of 4	1.65	—
2340	A1704 22c	**multi,** *Jan. 9, 1988*	40	5
		P# block of 4, 4#	1.70	—
		Zip block of 4	1.65	—
		Copyright block of 4	1.65	—
2341	A1705 22c	**dark blue & dark red,** *Feb. 6, 1988*	40	5
		P# block of 4, 1#	1.70	—
		Zip block of 4	1.65	—
		Copyright block of 4	1.65	—
2342	A1706 22c	**multi,** *Feb. 15, 1988*	40	5
		P# block of 4, 6#	1.70	—
		Zip block of 4	1.65	—
		Copyright block of 4	1.65	—
2343	A1707 25c	**multi,** *May 23, 1988*	45	5
		P# block of 4, 5#	1.90	—
		Zip block of 4	1.85	—
		Copyright block of 4	1.85	—
2344	A1708 25c	**multi,** *June 21, 1988*	45	5
		P# block of 4, 4#	1.90	—
		Zip block of 4	1.85	—
		Copyright block of 4	1.85	—
2345	A1709 25c	**multi,** *June 25, 1988*	45	5
		P# block of 4, 5#	1.90	—
		Zip block of 4	1.85	—
		Copyright block of 4	1.85	—
2346	A1710 25c	**multi,** *July 26, 1988*	45	5
		P# block of 4, 5#	1.90	—
		Zip block of 4	1.85	—
		Copyright block of 4	1.85	—
2347	A1711 25c	**multi,** *Aug. 22, 1989*	50	5
		P# block of 4, 5#	2.50	—
		Zip block of 4	2.00	—
		Copyright block of 4	2.00	—

US-MOROCCO DIPLOMATIC RELATIONS BICENTENNIAL

Arabesque, Dar Batha Palace Door, Fez — A1713

Designed by Howard Paine.

LITHOGRAPHED & ENGRAVED

Plates of 200 in four panes of 50.

1987, July 17		**Tagged**	***Perf. 11***	
2349	A1713 22c	**scarlet & black**	40	5
		P# block of 4, 2#	1.70	—
		Zip block of 4	1.65	—
		Copyright block of 4	1.65	—
a.		Black (engr.) omitted	*450.00*	

LITERARY ARTS

William Cuthbert Faulkner (1897-1962), Novelist — A1714

Designed by Bradbury Thompson.

ENGRAVED

Plates of 200 in four panes of 50

1987, Aug. 3		**Tagged**	***Perf. 11***	
2350	A1714 22c	**bright green**	40	5
		P# block of 4	1.70	—
		Zip block of 4	1.65	—
		Copyright block of 4	1.65	—

FOLK ART ISSUE
Lacemaking

A1715

A1716

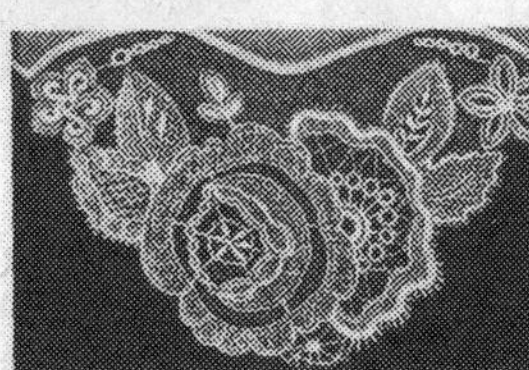

A1717

A1718

Designed by Libby Thiel.

LITHOGRAPHED & ENGRAVED

Plates of 160 in four panes of 40.

1987, Aug. 14		**Tagged**	***Perf. 11***	
2351	A1715 22c	**ultra & white**	40	8
2352	A1716 22c	**ultra & white**	40	8
2353	A1717 22c	**ultra & white**	40	8
2354	A1718 22c	**ultra & white**	40	8
		P# block of 4, 4#	1.75	—
		Zip block of 4	1.70	—
		Copyright block of 4	1.70	—
a.		Block of 4, #2351-2354	1.65	1.00
b.		As "a," white omitted	*1,750.*	

DRAFTING OF THE CONSTITUTION BICENTENNIAL
Excerpts from the Preamble

The Bicentennial of the Constitution of the United States of America 1787-1987 USA 22

A1719

We the people of the United States, in order to form a more perfect Union... Preamble, U.S. Constitution USA 22

A1720

Establish justice, insure domestic tranquility, provide for the common defense, promote the general welfare... Preamble, U.S. Constitution USA 22

A1721

And secure the blessings of liberty to ourselves and our posterity... Preamble, U.S. Constitution USA 22

A1722

Do ordain and establish this Constitution for the United States of America. Preamble, U.S. Constitution USA 22

A1723

Designed by Bradbury Thompson.

BOOKLET STAMPS
PHOTOGRAVURE

1987, Aug. 28		**Tagged**	***Perf. 10 Horiz.***	
2355	A1719 22c	**multi**	40	8
2356	A1720 22c	**multi**	40	8
2357	A1721 22c	**multi**	40	8
2358	A1722 22c	**multi**	40	8
2359	A1723 22c	**multi**	40	8
a.		Bklt. pane of 5, #2355-2359	2.10	

SIGNING OF THE CONSTITUTION

A1724

Designed by Howard Koslow.

LITHOGRAPHED & ENGRAVED

Plates of 200 in four panes of 50.

1987, Sept. 17		**Tagged**	***Perf. 11***	
2360	A1724 22c	**multi**	40	5
		P# block of 4, 5#	1.70	—
		Zip block of 4	1.65	—
		Copyright block of 4	1.65	—

CERTIFIED PUBLIC ACCOUNTING

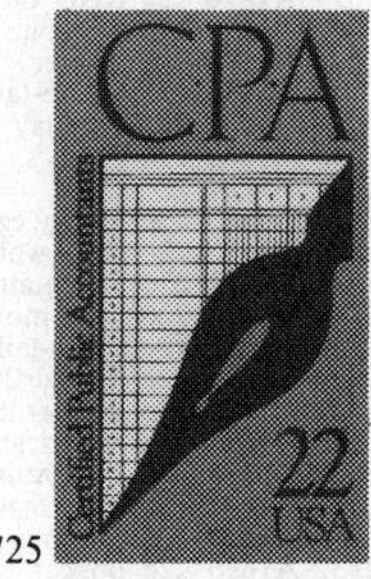

A1725

Designed by Lou Nolan.

LITHOGRAPHED & ENGRAVED

Plates of 200 in four panes of 50.

1987, Sept. 21		**Tagged**	***Perf. 11***	
2361	A1725 22c	**multi**	40	5
		P# block of 4, 4#	1.70	—
		Zip block of 4	1.65	—
		Copyright block of 4	1.65	—
a.		Black (engr.) omitted	—	

LOCOMOTIVES

Stourbridge Lion, 1829 A1726

Best Friend of Charleston, 1830 A1727

John Bull, 1831 A1728

Brother Jonathan, 1832 A1729

Gowan & Marx, 1839 A1730

Designed by Richard Leech.

BOOKLET STAMPS
LITHOGRAPHED & ENGRAVED

1987, Oct. 1 **Tagged** ***Perf. 10 Horiz.***

2362 A1726 22c **multi**		40	8
2363 A1727 22c **multi**		40	8
2364 A1728 22c **multi**		40	8
2365 A1729 22c **multi**		40	8
2366 A1730 22c **multi**		40	8
a.	Bklt. pane of 5, #2362-2366	2.10	

CHRISTMAS

Moroni Madonna A1731

Christmas Ornaments A1732

Designed by Bradbury Thompson (No. 2367) and Jim Dean (No. 2368).

PHOTOGRAVURE
Plates of 200 in four panes of 50.

1987, Oct. 23 **Tagged** ***Perf. 11***

2367 A1731 22c **multi**		40	5
	P# block of 4, 6#	1.70	—
	Zip block of 4	1.65	—
	Copyright block of 4	1.65	—
2368 A1732 22c **multi**		40	5
	P# block of 4, #	1.70	—
	Zip block of 4	1.65	—
	Copyright block of 4	1.65	—
	Pair with full vert. gutter between		—

1988 WINTER OLYMPICS, CALGARY

Skiing — A1733

Designed by Bart Forbes.
Printed by the American Bank Note Company

PHOTOGRAVURE
Plates of 200 in four panes of 50.

1988, Jan. 10 **Tagged** ***Perf. 11***

2369 A1733 22c **multi**		40	5
	P# block of 4, 4#	1.70	—
	Zip block of 4	1.65	—
	Copyright block of 4	1.65	—

AUSTRALIA BICENTENNIAL

Caricature of an Australian Koala and an American Bald Eagle — A1734

Designed by Roland Harvey.

PHOTOGRAVURE
Plates of 160 in four panes of 40.

1988, Jan. 26 **Tagged**

2370 A1734 22c **multi**		40	5
	P# block of 4, 5	1.70	—
	Zip block of 4	1.65	—
	Copyright block of 4	1.65	—

See Australia No. 1052.

BLACK HERITAGE

James Weldon Johnson (1871-1938), Author and Lyricist — A1735

Designed by Thomas Blackshear.
Printed by the American Bank Note Co.

PHOTOGRAVURE
Plates of 200 in four panes of 50.

1988, Feb. 2 **Tagged**

2371 A1735 22c **multi**		40	5
	P# block of 4, 5#	1.70	—
	Zip block of 4	1.65	—
	Copyright block of 4	1.65	—

CATS

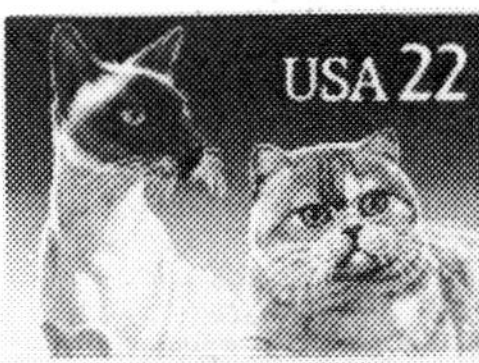

Siamese and Exotic Shorthair A1736

Abyssinian and Himalayan A1737

Maine Coon and Burmese A1738

American Shorthair and Persian — A1739

Designed by John Dawson.
Printed by the American Bank Note Co.

PHOTOGRAVURE
Plates of 160 in four panes of 40.

1988, Feb. 5 **Tagged**

2372 A1736 22c **multi**		40	8
2373 A1737 22c **multi**		40	8
2374 A1738 22c **multi**		40	8
2375 A1739 22c **multi**		40	8
	P# block of 4, 5#	1.75	—
	Zip block of 4	1.70	—
	Copyright block of 4	1.70	—
a.	Block of 4, # 2372-2375	1.65	1.00

AMERICAN SPORTS

Knute Rockne (1883-1931), Notre Dame Football Coach — A1740

Designed by Peter Cocci and Thomas Hipschen.

LITHOGRAPHED & ENGRAVED
Plates of 200 in four panes of 50.

1988, Mar. 9 **Tagged**

2376 A1740 22c **multi**		40	5
	P# block of 4, 7#	1.70	—
	Zip block of 4	1.65	—
	Copyright block of 4	1.65	—

Francis Ouimet (1893-1967), 1st Amateur Golfer to Win the U.S. Open Championship — A1741

Designed by M. Gregory Rudd.
Printed by the American Bank Note Co.

PHOTOGRAVURE
Plates of 200 in four panes of 50.

1988, June 13		Tagged	
2377 A1741 25c **multi**		45	5
	P# block of 4, 5#	1.90	—
	Zip block of 4	1.85	—
	Copyright block of 4	1.85	—

LOVE ISSUE
Roses

A1742

A1743

Designed by Richard Sheaff.

PHOTOGRAVURE
Plates of 400 in four panes of 100 (25c) and plates of 200 in four panes of 50 (45c).

1988		Tagged	
2378 A1742 25c **multi,** *July 4*		45	5
	P# block of 4, 5#	1.90	—
	Zip block of 4	1.85	—
	Copyright block of 4	1.85	—
2379 A1743 45c **multi,** *Aug. 8*		65	20
	P# block of 4, 4#	3.00	—
	Zip block of 4	2.65	—
	Copyright block of 4	2.65	—

1988 SUMMER OLYMPICS, SEOUL

Gymnastic Rings — A1744

Desinged by Bart Forbes.

PHOTOGRAVURE
Plates of 200 in four panes of 50

1988, Aug. 19		Tagged	
2380 A1744 25c **multi**		45	5
	P# block of 4, 5#	1.90	—
	Zip block of 4	1.85	—
	Copyright block of 4	1.85	—

CLASSIC AUTOMOBILES

1928 Locomobile A1745

1929 Pierce-Arrow A1746

1931 Cord — A1747

1932 Packard A1748

1935 Duesenberg A1749

Designed by Ken Dallison.

LITHOGRAPHED & ENGRAVED
BOOKLET STAMPS

1988, Aug. 25	Tagged	*Perf. 10 Horiz.*	
2381 A1745 25c **multi**		45	8
2382 A1746 25c **multi**		45	8
2383 A1747 25c **multi**		45	8
2384 A1748 25c **multi**		45	8
2385 A1749 25c **multi**		45	8
a. Bklt. pane of 5, Nos. 2381-2385		2.30	—

ANTARCTIC EXPLORERS

Nathaniel Palmer (1799-1877) A1750

Lt. Charles Wilkes (1798-1877) A1751

Richard E. Byrd (1888-1957) A1752

Lincoln Ellsworth (1880-1951) A1753

Designed by Dennis Lyall.
Printed by the American Bank Note Co.

PHOTOGRAVURE
Plates of 160 in four panes of 40.

1988, Sept. 14	Tagged	*Perf. 11*	
2386 A1750 25c **multi**		45	8
2387 A1751 25c **multi**		45	8
2388 A1752 25c **multi**		45	8
2389 A1753 25c **multi**		45	8
	P# block of 4, 6#	2.00	—
	Zip block of 4	1.90	—
	Copyright block of 4	1.90	—
a. Block of 4, Nos. 2386-2389		1.85	1.25

United States Postage Stamps can be mounted in Scott's annually supplemented Platinum, National, Pony Express, Minuteman, U.S. Commemorative Singles, U.S. Commemorative and Commemorative Air Plate Blocks, U.S. Blocks of Four and U.S. Regular and Regular Air Plate Blocks Album.

FOLK ART ISSUE
Carousel Animals

Deer — A1754

Horse — A1755

Camel — A1756

Goat — A1757

Designed by Paul Calle.

LITHOGRAPHED & ENGRAVED
Plates of 200 in four panes of 50.

1988, Oct. 1	Tagged	*Perf. 11*	
2390 A1754 25c **multi**		45	8
2391 A1755 25c **multi**		45	8
2392 A1756 25c **multi**		45	8
2393 A1757 25c **multi**		45	8
	P# block of 4, 6#	2.00	—
	Zip block of 4	1.90	—
	Copyright block of 4	1.90	—
a. Block of 4, Nos. 2390-2393		1.85	1.25

Eagle and Moon A1758

Designed by Ned Seidler.

LITHOGRAPHED & ENGRAVED
Panes of 20

1988, Oct. 4	Tagged	*Perf. 11*	
2394 A1758 $8.75 **multicolored**		17.50	—
	P# block of 4, 6#	87.50	—

SPECIAL OCCASIONS

Happy Birthday A1759

Best Wishes A1760

Thinking of You — A1761

Love You — A1762

Designed by Harry Zelenko
Printed by the American Bank Note Co.

BOOKLET STAMPS
PHOTOGRAVURE

1988, Oct. 22 **Tagged** ***Perf. 11***

2395 A1759 25c **multi** 45 5
2396 A1760 25c **multi** 45 5
a. Bklt. pane of 6, 3 #2395 + 2396 with gutter between 2.75 —
2397 A1761 25c **multi** 45 5
2398 A1762 25c **multi** 45 5
a. Bklt. pane of 6, 3 #2397 + 2398 with gutter between 2.75 —

CHRISTMAS

Madonna and Child, by Botticelli A1763

One-horse Open Sleigh and Village Scene A1764

Designed by Bradbury Thompson (No. 2399) and Joan Landis (No. 2400).

LITHOGRAPHED & ENGRAVED (No. 2399),
PHOTOGRAVURE (No. 2400)
Plates of 300 in 6 Panes of 50

1988, Oct 20 **Tagged** ***Perf. 11½***

2399 A1763 25c **multi** 45 5
P# block of 4, # 1.90 —
Zip, copyright block of 4 2.25 —
a. Gold omitted *75.00*
2400 A1764 25c **multi** 45 5
P# block of 4, # 1.90 —
Zip, copyright block of 4 2.25 —
Pair with full vert. gutter btwn. —

MONTANA CENTENARY

C.M. Russell and Friends, by Charles M. Russell (1865-1926) A1765

Designed by Bradbury Thompson

LITHOGRAPHED & ENGRAVED
Plates of 200 in four panes of 50.

1989, Jan. 15 **Tagged** ***Perf. 11***

2401 A1765 25c **multicolored** 50 5
P# block of 4, 5# 2.50 —
Zip block of 4 2.25 —
Copyright block of 4 2.25 —

Values for stamps vary greatly, depending upon centering, gum and condition.

BLACK HERITAGE

Asa Philip Randolph (1889-1979), Labor and Civil Rights Leader — A1766

Designed by Thomas Blackshear.

PHOTOGRAVURE
Plates of 200 in four panes of 50.

1989, Feb. 3 **Tagged**

2402 A1766 25c **multicolored** 50 5
P# block of 4, 5# 2.50 —
Zip block of 4 2.25 —
Copyright block of 4 2.25 —

NORTH DAKOTA CENTENARY

Grain Elevator on the Prairie — A1767

Designed by Wendell Minor. Printed by the American Bank Note Co.

PHOTOGRAVURE
Plates of 200 in four panes of 50.

1989, Feb. 21 **Tagged**

2403 A1767 25c **multicolored** 50 5
P# block of 4 2.50 —
Zip block of 4 2.25 —
Copyright block of 4 2.25 —

WASHINGTON CENTENARY

Mt. Rainier — A1768

Designed by Howard Rogers. Printed by the American Bank Note Co.

PHOTOGRAVURE
Plates of 200 in four panes of 50.

1989, Feb. 22 **Tagged**

2404 A1768 25c **multicolored** 50 5
P# block of 4, 4# 2.50 —
Zip block of 4 2.25 —
Copyright block of 4 2.25 —

STEAMBOATS

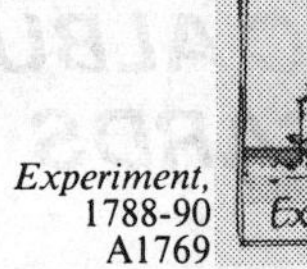

Experiment, 1788-90 A1769

Phoenix, 1809 — A1770

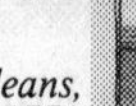

New Orleans, 1812 — A1771

Washington, 1816 — A1772

Walk in the Water, 1818 — A1773

Designed by Richard Schlecht.

LITHOGRAPHED & ENGRAVED
BOOKLET STAMPS
Perf. 10 Horiz. on 1 or 2 Sides

1989, Mar. 3 **Tagged**

2405 A1769 25c **multicolored** 50 8
2406 A1770 25c **multicolored** 50 8
2407 A1771 25c **multicolored** 50 8
2408 A1772 25c **multicolored** 50 8
2409 A1773 25c **multicolored** 50 8
a. Bklt. pane of 5, Nos. 2405-2409 2.50 —

WORLD STAMP EXPO '89

Nov. 17-Dec. 3. Washington, D.C.

No. 122 — A1774

Designed by Richard D. Sheaff.

LITHOGRAPHED & ENGRAVED
Plates of 200 in four panes of 50.

1989, Mar. 16 **Tagged** ***Perf. 11***

2410 A1774 25c **grayish brn, blk & car rose** 50 5
P# block of 4, 4# 2.50 —
Zip block of 4 2.25 —
Copyright block of 4 2.25 —

PERFORMING ARTS

Arturo Toscanini (1867-1957), Conductor — A1775

Designed by Jim Sharpe. Printed by the American Bank Note Co.

PHOTOGRAVURE
Plates of 200 in four panes of 50.

1989, Mar. 25 **Tagged** ***Perf. 11***

2411 A1775 25c **multicolored** 50 5
P# block of 4, 5# 2.50 —
Zip block of 4 2.25 —
Copyright block of 4 2.25 —

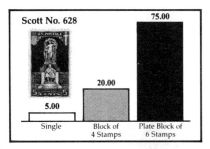

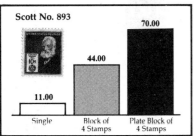

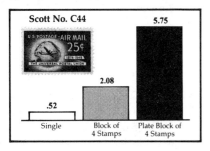

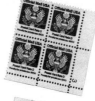

CONSTITUTION BICENTENNIAL SERIES

House of Representatives A1776

Senate A1777

Executive Branch — A1778

Designed by Howard Koslow.

LITHOGRAPHED & ENGRAVED
Plates of 200 in four panes of 50.

1989			**Tagged**		*Perf. 11*
2412	A1776	25c	**multi,** *Apr. 4*	50	5
			P# block of 4, 4#	2.50	—
			Zip block of 4	2.25	—
			Copyright block of 4	2.25	—
2413	A1777	25c	**multi,** *Apr. 6*	50	5
			P# block of 4, 4#	2.50	—
			Zip block of 4	2.25	—
			Copyright block of 4	2.25	—
2414	A1778	25c	**multi,** *Apr. 16*	50	5
			P# block of 4, 4#	2.50	—
			Zip block of 4	2.25	—
			Copyright block of 4	2.25	—

SOUTH DAKOTA CENTENARY

Pasque Flowers, Pioneer Woman and Sod House on Grasslands A1780

Designed by Marian Henjum. Printed by the American Bank Note Co.

PHOTOGRAVURE
Plates of 200 in four panes of 50.

1989, May 3			**Tagged**		*Perf. 11*
2416	A1780	25c	**multi**	50	5
			P# block of 4, 4#	2.50	—
			Zip block of 4	2.25	—
			Copyright block of 4	2.25	—

AMERICAN SPORTS

Henry Louis "Lou" Gehrig (1903-1941), New York Yankee Baseball Player — A1781

Designed by Bart Forbes. Printed by the American Bank Note Co.

1989, June 10			**Tagged**		*Perf. 11*
2417	A1781	25c	**multicolored**	50	5
			P# block of 4, 6#	2.50	—
			Zip block of 4	2.25	—
			Copyright block of 4	2.25	—

LITERARY ARTS

Ernest Miller Hemingway (1899-1961), Nobel Prize winner for Literature in 1954 — A1782

Designed by M. Gregory Rudd. Printed by the American Bank Note Co.

PHOTOGRAVURE
Plates of 200 in four panes of 50.

1989, July 17			**Tagged**		*Perf. 11*
2418	A1782	25c	**multicolored**	50	5
			P# block of 4, 5#	2.50	—
			Zip block of 4	2.25	—
			Copyright block of 4	2.25	—

MOON LANDING, 20TH ANNIVERSARY

Raising of the Flag on the Lunar Surface, July 20, 1969 — A1783

Designed by Christopher Calle.

LITHOGRAPHED & ENGRAVED
Panes of 20

1989, July 20			**Tagged**		*Perf. 11x11½*
2419	A1783	$2.40	**multicolored**	4.80	2.40
			P# block of 4, 6#	24.00	—

LETTER CARRIERS

A1784

Designed by Jack Davis. Printed by the American Bank Note Co.

PHOTOGRAVURE
Plates of 160 in four panes of 40.

1989, Aug. 20			**Tagged**		*Perf. 11*
2420	A1784	25c	**multicolored**	50	5
			P# block of 4, 5#	2.50	—
			Zip block of 4	2.25	—
			Copyright block of 4	2.25	—

DRAFTING OF THE BILL OF RIGHTS

A1785

Designed by Lou Nolan.

LITHOGRAPHED & ENGRAVED
Plates of 200 in four panes of 50.

1989, Sept. 25			**Tagged**		*Perf.*
2421	A1785	25c	**multicolored**	50	5
			P# block of 4	2.50	—
			Zip block of 4	2.25	—
			Copyright block of 4	2.25	—

DINOSAURS

Tyrannosaurus Rex — A1786

Pteranodon A1787

Stegosaurus A1788

Brontosaurus A1789

Designed by John Gurche.

1989, Oct. 1			**Tagged**		*Perf.*
2422	A1786	25c	**multicolored**	50	8
2423	A1787	25c	**multicolored**	50	8
2424	A1788	25c	**multicolored**	50	8
2425	A1789	25c	**multicolored**	50	8
a.			Block of 4, Nos. 2422-2425	2.00	—
			P# block of 4	2.50	—
			Zip block of 4	2.25	—
			Copyright block of 4	2.25	—

The correct scientific name for Brontosaurus is Apatosaurus.

CHRISTMAS

Madonna and Child, by Caracci — A1791

Sleigh Full of Presents — A1792

1989, Oct. 19 *Perf.*

No.	Type	Value	Description	Unused	Used
2427	A1791	25c	**multicolored**	50	5
			P# block of 4	2.50	—
			Zip block of 4	2.25	—
			Copyright block of 4	2.25	—
2428	A1792	25c	**multicolored**	50	5
			P# block of 4	2.50	—
			Zip block of 4	2.25	—
			Copyright block of 4	2.25	—

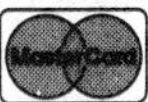

AIR POST STAMPS

Air mail in the U. S. postal system developed in three stages: pioneer period (with many unofficial or semi-official flights before 1918), government flights and contract air mail (C.A.M.). Contract air mail began on February 15, 1926. All C.A.M. contracts were canceled on February 19, 1934, and air mail was carried by Army planes for six months. After that the contract plan was resumed.

Curtiss Jenny — AP1

No. C3 first used on airplane mail service between Washington, Philadelphia and New York, on May 15, 1918, but was valid for ordinary postage. The rate of postage was 24 cents per ounce, which included immediate individual delivery.

Rate of postage was reduced to 16 cents for the first ounce and 6 cents for each additional ounce, which included 10 cents for immediate individual delivery, on July 15, 1918, by Postmaster General's order of June 26, 1918. No. C2 was first used for air mail in the tri-city service on July 15.

Rate of postage was reduced on December 15, 1918, by Postmaster General's order of November 30, 1918, to 6 cents per ounce. No. C1 was first used for air mail (same three-way service) on Dec. 16.

FLAT PLATE PRINTINGS
Plates of 100 subjects.

1918 **Unwmk.** **Engr.** ***Perf. 11***

No.	Type	Value	Description	Unused	Used
C1	AP1	6c	**orange,** *Dec. 10*	70.00	30.00
			pale orange	70.00	30.00
			On cover		45.00
			First flight cover, *Dec. 16*		2,750.
			Margin block of 4, arrow top or left	300.00	135.00
			Center line block	325.00	140.00
			Margin block of 6, arrow & P#	850.00	—
			Double transfer (#9155-14)	100.00	45.00
C2	AP1	16c	**green,** *July 11*	100.00	32.50
			dark green	100.00	32.50
			On cover		50.00
			First flight cover, *July 15*		800.00
			Margin block of 4, arrow top or left	425.00	140.00
			Center line block	450.00	150.00
			Margin block of 6, arrow & P#	1,500.	—
C3	AP1	24c	**carmine rose & blue,** *May 13*	100.00	35.00
			dark carmine rose & blue	100.00	35.00
			On cover		55.00
			First flight cover, *May 15*		750.00
			Margin block of 4, arrow top or left	425.00	150.00
			Margin block of 4, arrow bottom	450.00	160.00
			Margin block of 4, arrow right	500.00	200.00
			Center line block	475.00	175.00
			Margin block of 4, red P# only	500.00	—
			Margin block of 12, two P#, arrow & two "TOP"	1,800.	—

	Margin block of 12, two P#, arrow & blue "TOP" only	*7,000.*
a.	Center inverted	*135,000.*
a.	Same, in block of four	*550,000.*
a.	Same, center line block	*575,000.*
a.	Same, margin block of 4, blue P#	*600,000.*

Airplane Radiator and Wooden Propeller — AP2

Air Service Emblem — AP3

DeHavilland Biplane — AP4

Nos. C4 to C6 were issued primarily for use in the new night-flying air mail service between New York and San Francisco, but valid for all purposes. Three zones were established; the first from New York to Chicago, the second from Chicago to Cheyenne, and the third from Cheyenne to San Francisco, and the rate of postage was 8 cents an ounce for each zone. Service was inaugurated on July 1, 1924.

These stamps were placed on sale at the Philatelic Agency at Washington on the dates indicated in the listings but were not issued to postmasters at that time.

Plates of 400 subjects in four panes of 100 each.

1923			**Unwmk.**	***Perf. 11***	
C4	AP2	8c	**dark green,** *Aug. 15*	25.00	11.00
			deep green	25.00	11.00
			On cover		20.00
			Margin block of 6, P#	275.00	—
			Double transfer	42.50	20.00
C5	AP3	16c	**dark blue,** *Aug. 17*	95.00	80.00
			On cover		42.50
			Margin block of 6, P#	2,150.	—
			Double transfer	125.00	45.00
C6	AP4	24c	**carmine,** *Aug. 21*	100.00	25.00
			On cover		35.00
			Margin block of 6, P#	2,600.	—
			Double transfer (Pl. 14841)	125.00	32.50

Map of United States and Two Mail Planes AP5

The Act of Congress of February 2, 1925, created a rate of 10 cents per ounce for distances to 1000 miles, 15 cents per ounce for 1500 miles and 20 cents for more than 1500 miles on contract air mail routes.

Plates of 200 subjects in four panes of 50 each.

1926-27			**Unwmk.**	***Perf. 11***	
C7	AP5	10c	**dark blue,** *Feb. 13, 1926*	2.25	25
			light blue	2.25	25
			Margin block of 6, P#	35.00	—
			Double transfer (18246 UL 11)	5.00	1.00
C8	AP5	15c	**olive brown,** *Sept. 18, 1926*	2.50	1.65
			light brown	2.50	1.65
			Margin block of 6, P#	40.00	—
C9	AP5	20c	**yellow green,** *Jan. 25, 1927*	8.00	1.25
			green	8.00	1.25
			Margin block of 6, P#	95.00	—

Lindbergh's Plane "Spirit of St. Louis" and Flight Route — AP6

A tribute to Col. Charles A. Lindbergh, who made the first non-stop (and solo) flight from New York to Paris, May 20-21, 1927.

Plates of 200 subjects in four panes of 50 each.

1927			**Unwmk.**	***Perf. 11***	
C10	AP6	10c	**dark blue,** *June 18*	6.00	1.50
			Margin block of 6, P#	130.00	—
a.			Bklt. pane of 3, *May 26, 1928*	110.00	*60.00*
			Double transfer	11.00	2.50

First day covers of No. C10a and other airmail booklet panes are listed in the Booklet Panes section of this catalogue.

Beacon on Rocky Mountains AP7

Issued to meet the new rate, effective August 1, of 5 cents per ounce.

Plates of 100 subjects in two panes of 50

1928			**Unwmk.**	***Perf. 11***	
C11	AP7	5c	**carmine and blue,** *July 25*	3.00	25
			On cover, first day of 5c airmail rate, *Aug. 1*		3.00
			Margin block of 4, arrow, (line) right or left	15.00	3.00
			Margin block of 8, two P# only	175.00	—
			Margin block of 6, two P# & red "TOP"	45.00	—
			Margin block of 6, two P# & blue "TOP"	45.00	—
			Margin block of 6, two P# & double "TOP"	100.00	—
a.			Vert. pair, imperf. btwn.	*5,500.*	
			Recut frame line at left	6.00	1.00
			Double transfer	—	—

Winged Globe AP8

Plates of 200 subjects in four panes of 50 each.

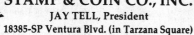

1930 Unwmk. *Perf. 11*

Stamp design: 46½x19mm.

C12 AP8 5c **violet,** *Feb. 10*	8.00	22
Margin block of 6, P#	140.00	—
a. Horiz. pair, imperf. btwn.	*4,500.*	
Double transfer (Pl. 20189)	15.00	1.00

See Nos. C16-C17, C19.

GRAF ZEPPELIN ISSUE

Zeppelin Over Atlantic Ocean AP9

Zeppelin Between Continents — AP10

Zeppelin Passing Globe AP11

Issued for use on mail carried on the first Europe-Pan-America round trip flight of the Graf Zeppelin in May, 1930. They were withdrawn from sale June 30, 1930.

Plates of 200 subjects in four panes of 50 each.

1930, Apr. 19 Unwmk. *Perf. 11*

C13 AP9 65c **green**	250.00	200.00
On cover or card		250.00
Block of four	1,025.	900.00
Margin block of 6, P#	2,250.	—
C14 AP10 $1.30 **brown**	700.00	450.00
On cover		500.00
Block of four	2,850.	1,900.
Margin block of 6, P#	5,750.	—
C15 AP11 $2.60 **blue**	1,050.	600.00
On cover		650.00
Block of four	4,300.	2,500.
Margin block of 6, P#	8,500.	—

ROTARY PRESS PRINTING

Plates of 200 subjects in four panes of 50 each.

1931-32 Unwmk. *Perf. 10½x11*

Stamp design: 47½x19mm

C16 AP8 5c **violet,** *Aug. 19, 1931*	4.75	30
Block of four	19.00	1.65
Margin block of 4, P#	75.00	—

Issued to conform with new air mail rate of 8 cents per ounce which became effective July 6, 1932.

C17 AP8 8c **olive bister,** *Sept. 26, 1932*	1.90	20
Block of four	7.60	1.10
Margin block of 4, P#	30.00	—

CENTURY OF PROGRESS ISSUE

"Graf Zeppelin," Federal Building at Chicago Exposition and Hangar at Friedrichshafen — AP12

Issued in connection with the flight of the airship "Graf Zeppelin" in October, 1933, to Miami, Akron and Chicago and from the last city to Europe.

FLAT PLATE PRINTING

Plates of 200 subjects in four panes of 50 each.

1933 Unwmk. *Perf. 11*

C18 AP12 50c **green,** *Oct. 2*	90.00	75.00
On cover		85.00
Block of four	360.00	310.00
Margin block of 6, P#	800.00	—

Type of 1930 Issue.

ROTARY PRESS PRINTING.

Issued to conform with new air mail rate of 6 cents per ounce which became effective July 1, 1934.

Plates of 200 subjects in four panes of 50 each.

1934 Unwmk. *Perf. 10½x11*

C19 AP8 6c **dull orange,** *June 30*	2.25	12
On cover, first day of 6c airmail rate, *July 1*		10.00
Block of four	9.00	70
Margin block of 4, P#	27.50	—
Pair with full vert. gutter btwn.	*425.00*	

TRANSPACIFIC ISSUES

"China Clipper" over Pacific — AP13

Issued to pay postage on mail transported by the Transpacific air mail service, inaugurated Nov. 22, 1935.

FLAT PLATE PRINTING

Plates of 200 subjects in four panes of 50 each.

1935 Unwmk. *Perf. 11*

C20 AP13 25c **blue,** *Nov. 22*	1.10	75
Margin block of 6, P#	22.50	—

"China Clipper" over Pacific — AP14

Issued primarily for use on the Transpacific service to China, but valid for all air mail purposes.

FLAT PLATE PRINTING

Plates of 200 subjects in four panes of 50 each.

1937			**Unwmk.**	***Perf. 11.***	
C21	AP14	20c	**green,** *Feb. 15*	8.00	1.25
			dark green	8.00	1.25
			Block of four	32.00	7.00
			Margin block of 6, P#	120.00	—
C22	AP14	50c	**carmine,** *Feb. 15*	7.75	3.25
			Block of four	31.00	14.00
			Margin block of 6, P#	130.00	—

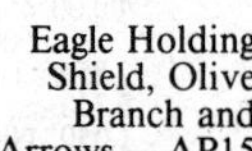

Eagle Holding Shield, Olive Branch and Arrows — AP15

FLAT PLATE PRINTING

Frame plates of 100 subjects in two panes of 50 each separated by a 1 ½-inch wide vertical gutter with central guide line, and vignette plates of 50 subjects. Some plates were made of iron, then chromed; several of these carry an additional imprint, "E.I." (Electrolytic Iron).

1938			**Unwmk.**	***Perf. 11***	
C23	AP15	6c	**dark blue & carmine,** *May 14*	40	6
			Margin block of 4, bottom or side arrow	1.75	55
			Margin block of 4, 2 P#	8.50	—
			Center line block	2.25	95
			Top margin block of 10, with two P#, arrow, two "TOP" and two registration markers	13.50	
a.			Vert. pair, imperf. horiz.	275.00	
b.			Horiz. pair, imperf. vert.	*8,500.*	
c.			ultramarine & carmine	150.00	

Top plate number blocks of No. C23 are found both with and without top arrow.

TRANSATLANTIC ISSUE

Winged Globe AP16

Inauguration of Transatlantic air mail service.

FLAT PLATE PRINTING

Plates of 200 subjects in four panes of 50 each.

1939			**Unwmk.**	***Perf. 11***	
C24	AP16	30c	**dull blue,** *May 16*	7.50	1.25
			Margin block of 6, P#	175.00	—

Twin-Motored Transport Plane — AP17

ROTARY PRESS PRINTING

E. E. Plates of 200 subjects in four panes of 50 each.

1941-44			**Unwmk.**	***Perf. 11x10 ½***	
C25	AP17	6c	**carmine,** *June 25, 1941*	12	5
			Margin block of 4, P#	80	—
			Pair with full vertical gutter between	225.00	
a.			Booklet pane of three, *March, 18, 1943*	4.25	*1.00*
b.			Horiz. pair, imperf. between	*2,000.*	
C26	AP17	8c	**olive green,** *Mar. 21, 1944*	16	5
			Margin block of 4, P#	1.40	—
			Pair with full horiz. gutter btwn.	325.00	
C27	AP17	10c	**violet,** *Aug. 15, 1941*	1.10	20
			Margin block of 4, P#	9.00	—
C28	AP17	15c	**brown carmine,** *Aug. 19, 1941*	2.25	35
			Margin block of 4, P#	12.00	—
C29	AP17	20c	**bright green,** *Aug. 27, 1941*	1.65	30
			Margin block of 4, P#	11.00	—
C30	AP17	30c	**blue,** *Sept. 25, 1941*	2.00	30
			Margin block of 4, P#	12.00	—
C31	AP17	50c	**orange,** *Oct. 29, 1941*	10.00	3.75
			Margin block of 4, P#	70.00	—

DC-4 Skymaster AP18

ROTARY PRESS PRINTING

E. E. Plates of 200 subjects in four panes of 50 each.

1946			**Unwmk.**	***Perf. 11x10 ½.***	
C32	AP18	5c	**carmine,** *Sept. 25*	10	5
			Margin block of 4, P#	50	—

DC-4 Skymaster — AP19

ROTARY PRESS PRINTING

E. E. Plates of 400 subjects in four panes of 100 each.

1947			**Unwmk.**	***Perf. 10 ½x11***	
C33	AP19	5c	**carmine,** *March 26*	10	5
			Margin block of 4, P#	50	—

Pan American Union Building, Washington, D.C., and Martin 2-0-2 — AP20

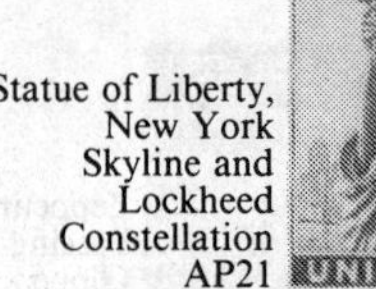

Statue of Liberty, New York Skyline and Lockheed Constellation AP21

San Francisco-Oakland Bay Bridge and Boeing B377 Stratocruiser — AP22

Designed by Victor S. McCloskey, Jr., Leon Helguera and William K. Schrage.

ROTARY PRESS PRINTING

E. E. Plates of 200 subjects in four panes of 50 each.

1947			**Unwmk.**	***Perf. 11x10 ½***	
C34	AP20	10c	**black,** *Aug. 30*	20	6
			Margin block of 4, P#	1.25	—
a.			Dry printing	38	6
C35	AP21	15c	**bright blue green,** *Aug. 20*	30	5
			blue green	30	5
			Margin block of 4, P#	1.50	—
			Pair with full horiz. gutter btwn.	*400.00*	
a.			Horiz. pair, imperf. between	*1,500.*	
b.			Dry printing	55	5
C36	AP22	25c	**blue,** *July 30*	75	12
			Margin block of 4, P#	3.75	—
a.			Dry printing	1.00	12

See note on wet and dry printings following No. 1029.

ROTARY PRESS COIL STAMP

Type of 1947

1948			**Unwmk.**	***Perf. 10 Horizontally***	
C37	AP19	5c	**carmine,** *Jan. 15*	80	75
			Pair	1.60	1.65
			Joint line pair	7.50	3.00

NEW YORK CITY ISSUE

Map of Five Boroughs, Circular Band and Planes — AP23

Issued to commemorate the 50th anniversary of the consolidation of the five boroughs of New York City.

ROTARY PRESS PRINTING

E. E. Plates of 400 subjects in four panes of 100 each.

1948			**Unwmk.**	***Perf. 11x10 ½***	
C38	AP23	5c	**bright carmine,** *July 31*	10	10
			Margin block of 4, P#	6.50	—

Type of 1947
ROTARY PRESS PRINTING
E. E. Plates of 400 subjects in four panes of 100 each.

1949	**Unwmk.**	***Perf. 10½x11***	
C39 AP19 6c **carmine,** *Jan. 18*		12	5
Margin block of 4, P#		60	—
a. Booklet pane of 6, *Nov. 18*		9.50	*4.00*
b. 6c carmine, dry printing		50	6
c. as "a," dry printing		15.00	—

See note on wet and dry printings following No. 1029.

ALEXANDRIA BICENTENNIAL ISSUE

Home of John Carlyle, Alexandria Seal and Gadsby's Tavern — AP24

Issued to commemorate the 200th anniversary of the founding of Alexandria, Virginia.
ROTARY PRESS PRINTING
E. E. Plates of 200 subjects in four panes of 50 each.

1949	**Unwmk.**	***Perf. 11x10½***	
C40 AP24 6c **carmine,** *May 11*		12	10
Margin block of 4, P#		60	—

ROTARY PRESS COIL STAMP
Type of 1947

1949	**Unwmk.**	***Perf. 10 Horizontally***	
C41 AP19 6c **carmine,** *Aug. 25*		2.75	5
Pair		5.50	15
Joint line pair		13.00	1.35

UNIVERSAL POSTAL UNION ISSUE

Post Office Department Building — AP25

Globe and Doves Carrying Messages — AP26

Boeing Stratocruiser and Globe — AP27

Issued to commemorate the 75th anniversary of the formation of the Universal Postal Union.
ROTARY PRESS PRINTING
E. E. Plates of 200 subjects in four panes of 50 each.

1949	**Unwmk.**	***Perf. 11x10½***	
C42 AP25 10c **violet,** *Nov. 18*		22	18
Margin block of 4, P#		1.50	—
C43 AP26 15c **ultramarine,** *Oct. 7*		30	25
Margin block of 4, P#		1.50	—
C44 AP27 25c **rose carmine,** *Nov. 30*		52	42
Margin block of 4, P#		5.75	—

WRIGHT BROTHERS ISSUE

Wilbur and Orville Wright and their Plane, 1903 — AP28

Issued to commemorate the 46th anniversary of the first successful flight in a motor-powered airplane, made Dec. 17, 1903, at Kill Devil Hill near Kitty Hawk, N.C., by Wilbur Wright (1867-1912) and his brother Orville (1871-1948) of Dayton, O. The plane flew 852 feet in 59 seconds.

ROTARY PRESS PRINTING
E. E. Plates of 200 subjects in four panes of 50 each.

1949	**Unwmk.**	***Perf. 11x10½***	
C45 AP28 6c **magenta,** *Dec. 17*		12	10
Margin block of 4, P#		65	—

Diamond Head, Honolulu, Hawaii — AP29

ROTARY PRESS PRINTING
E. E. Plates of 200 subjects in four panes of 50 each.

1952, Mar. 26	**Unwmk.**	***Perf. 11x10½***	
C46 AP29 80c **bright red violet**		6.50	1.50
Margin block of 4, P#		30.00	—

POWERED FLIGHT ISSUE

First Plane and Modern Plane — AP30

Issued to commemorate the 50th anniversary of powered flight.
ROTARY PRESS PRINTING
E. E. Plates of 200 subjects in four panes of 50 each.

1953	**Unwmk.**	***Perf. 11x10½***	
C47 AP30 6c **carmine,** *May 29*		12	10
Margin block of 4, P#		50	—

Eagle in Flight — AP31

Issued primarily for use on domestic post cards.
ROTARY PRESS PRINTING
E. E. Plates of 400 subjects in four panes of 100 each.

1954	**Unwmk.**	***Perf. 11x10½***	
C48 AP31 4c **bright blue,** *Sept. 3*		8	8
Margin block of 4, P#		2.00	—

AIR FORCE ISSUE

B-52 Stratofortress and F-104 Starfighters AP32

Designed by Alexander Nagy, Jr.

Issued to commemorate the 50th anniversary of the U. S. Air Force.
ROTARY PRESS PRINTING
E. E. Plates of 200 subjects in four panes of 50 each.

1957	**Unwmk.**	***Perf. 11x10½***	
C49 AP32 6c **blue,** *Aug. 1*		12	10
Margin block of 4, P#		75	—

Type of 1954
Issued primarily for use on domestic post cards.

1958	**Unwmk.**	***Perf. 11x10½***	
C50 AP31 5c **red,** *July 31*		14	12
Margin block of 4, P#		2.00	—

Silhouette of Jet Airliner — AP33

Designed by William H. Buckley and Sam Marsh.

ROTARY PRESS PRINTING

E. E. Plates of 400 subjects in four panes of 100 each.

1958	Unwmk.	Perf. 10½x11		
C51	AP33 7c **blue,** *July 31*		14	5
	Margin block of 4, P#		60	—
a.	Booklet pane of 6		11.00	*6.00*

ROTARY PRESS COIL STAMP

C52	AP33 7c **blue,** *July 31*	2.00	10
	Pair	4.00	40
	Joint line pair	13.00	1.25

ALASKA STATEHOOD ISSUE

Big Dipper, North Star and Map of Alaska — AP34

Designed by Richard C. Lockwood.

Issued to commemorate Alaska's admission to statehood

ROTARY PRESS PRINTING

E. E. Plates of 200 subjects in four panes of 50 each.

1959	Unwmk.	Perf. 11x10½	
C53	AP34 7c **dark blue,** *Jan. 3*	14	9
	Margin block of 4, P#	75	—

BALLOON JUPITER ISSUE

Balloon and Crowd — AP35

Designed by Austin Briggs.

Issued to commemorate the centenary of the carrying of mail by the balloon Jupiter from Lafayette to Crawfordsville, Ind.

GIORI PRESS PRINTING

Plates of 200 subjects in four panes of 50 each.

1959	Unwmk.	Perf. 11	
C54	AP35 7c **dark blue & red,** *Aug. 17*	14	9
	Margin block of 4, P#	75	—

HAWAII STATEHOOD ISSUE

Alii Warrior, Map of Hawaii and Star of Statehood AP36

Designed by Joseph Feher.

Issued to commemorate Hawaii's admission to statehood.

ROTARY PRESS PRINTING

E. E. Plates of 200 subjects in four panes of 50 each.

1959	Unwmk.	Perf. 11 x 10½	
C55	AP36 7c **rose red,** *Aug. 21*	14	9
	Margin block of 4, P#	75	—

PAN AMERICAN GAMES ISSUE

Runner Holding Torch — AP37

Designed by Suren Ermoyan.

Issued to commemorate the 3rd Pan American Games at Chicago, Aug. 27-Sept. 7, 1959.

GIORI PRESS PRINTING

Plates of 200 subjects in four panes of 50 each.

1959	Unwmk.	Perf. 11	
C56	AP37 10c **violet blue & bright red,** *Aug. 27*	24	24
	Margin block of 4, P#	1.75	—

Liberty Bell — AP38

Statue of Liberty — AP39

Abraham Lincoln — AP40

GIORI PRESS PRINTING

Plates of 200 subjects in four panes of 50 each.

1959-66	Unwmk.	Perf. 11	
C57	AP38 10c **black & green,** *June 10, 1960*	1.40	70
	Margin block of 4, P#	7.25	—
C58	AP39 15c **black & orange,** *Nov. 20, 1959*	35	6
	Margin block of 4, P#	1.50	—
C59	AP40 25c **black & maroon,** *Apr. 22, 1960*	48	6
	Margin block of 4, P#	2.00	—
a.	Tagged, *Dec. 29, 1966*	50	20

See Luminescence data in Information for Collectors section.

Type of 1958

ROTARY PRESS PRINTING

E. E. Plates of 400 subjects in four panes of 100 each.

1960	Unwmk.	Perf. 10½x11	
C60	AP33 7c **carmine,** *Aug. 12*	14	5
	Margin block of 4, P#	60	—
	Pair with full horiz. gutter btwn.	—	
a.	Booklet pane of 6, *Aug. 19*	13.00	*6.00*

Type of 1958

ROTARY PRESS COIL STAMP

1960	Unwmk.	Perf. 10 Horizontally	
C61	AP33 7c **carmine,** *Oct. 22*	4.25	25
	Pair	8.50	55
	Joint line pair	32.50	3.25

Type of 1959-60 and

Statue of Liberty — AP41

GIORI PRESS PRINTING

Plates of 200 subjects in four panes of 50 each.

1961-67	Unwmk.	Perf. 11	
C62	AP38 13c **black & red,** *June 28, 1961*	35	8
	Margin block of 4, P#	1.50	—
a.	Tagged, *Feb. 15, 1967*	70	50
C63	AP41 15c **black & orange,** *Jan. 13, 1961*	28	8
	Margin block of 4, P#	1.20	—
a.	Tagged, *Jan. 11, 1967*	32	15
b.	As "a," horiz. pair, imperf. vert.	*15,000.*	

Jet Airliner over Capitol — AP42

Designed by Henry K. Bencsath.

ROTARY PRESS PRINTING

E.E. Plates of 400 subjects in four panes of 100 each.

1962-65	Unwmk.	Perf. 10½x11	
C64	AP42 8c **carmine,** *Dec. 5, 1962*	14	5
	Margin block of 4, P#	60	—
a.	Tagged, *Aug. 1, 1963*	18	5
a.	Pair with full horiz. gutter between	—	
b.	Booklet pane of 5 + label	6.50	*1.25*
c.	As "b", tagged, *1964*	1.90	*50*

Nos. C64a and C64c were made by overprinting Nos. C64 and C64b with phosphorescent ink. No. C64a was first issued at Dayton, O., for experiments in high speed mail sorting. The tagging is visible in ultraviolet light.

COIL STAMP; ROTARY PRESS

C65	AP42 8c **carmine,** *Dec. 5, 1962*	28	8
	Pair	70	20
	Joint line pair	3.75	35
a.	Tagged, *Jan. 14, 1965*	40	10

MONTGOMERY BLAIR ISSUE

Montgomery Blair — AP43

Designed by Robert J. Jones

Issued to honor Montgomery Blair (1813-1883), Postmaster General (1861-64), who called the first International Postal Conference, Paris, 1863, forerunner of the U.P.U.

GIORI PRESS PRINTING

Plates of 200 subjects in four panes of 50 each.

1963	Unwmk.	Perf. 11	
C66	AP43 15c **dull red, dk. brn. & bl.,** *May 3*	52	50
	Margin block of 4, P#	3.00	—

Bald Eagle — AP44

Designed by V. S. McCloskey, Jr.

Issued primarily for use on domestic post cards.
ROTARY PRESS PRINTING
E.E. Plates of 400 subjects in four panes of 100 each.

1963-67 **Unwmk.** ***Perf. 11x10½***
C67 AP44 6c **red,** *July 12, 1963* 12 10
Margin block of 4, P# 1.80 —
a. Tagged, *Feb. 15, 1967* 2.75 50

AMELIA EARHART ISSUE

Amelia Earhart and Lockheed Electra — AP45

Designed by Robert J. Jones.

Issued to honor Amelia Earhart (1898-1937), first woman to fly across the Atlantic.

GIORI PRESS PRINTING
Plates of 200 subjects in four panes of 50 each.

1963 **Unwmk.** ***Perf. 11***
C68 AP45 8c **carmine & maroon,** *July 24* 20 12
Margin block of 4, P# 1.25 —

ROBERT H. GODDARD ISSUE

Robert H. Goddard, Atlas Rocket and Launching tower, Cape Kennedy — AP46

Designed by Robert J. Jones.

Issued to honor Dr. Robert H. Goddard (1882-1945), physicist and pioneer rocket researcher.

GIORI PRESS PRINTING
Plates of 200 subjects in four panes of 50 each.

1964 **Tagged** ***Perf. 11***
C69 AP46 8c **blue, red & bister,** *Oct. 5* 48 12
Margin block of 4, P# 2.00 —
Margin block of 4, Mr. Zip and "Use Zip Code" 1.95 —

Luminescence
Air Post stamps issued after mid-1964 are tagged.

ALASKA PURCHASE ISSUE

Tlingit Totem, Southern Alaska — AP47

Designed by Willard R. Cox

Issued to commemorate the centenary of the Alaska Purchase. The totem pole shown is in the Alaska State Museum, Juneau.

GIORI PRESS PRINTING
Plates of 200 subjects in four panes of 50 each.

1967 **Unwmk.** ***Perf. 11***
C70 AP47 8c **brown,** *March 30* 24 14
Margin block of 4, P# 1.50 —
Margin block of 4, Mr. Zip and "Use Zip Code" 1.00 —

"Columbia Jays" by John James Audubon — AP48

Fifty-Star Runway — AP49

GIORI PRESS PRINTING
Designed by Robert J. Jones.

Plates of 200 subjects in four panes of 50 each.

1967 ***Perf. 11***
C71 AP48 20c **multicolored,** *Apr. 26* 70 9
Margin block of 4, P# 3.25 —
Margin block of 4, Mr. Zip and "Use Zip Code" 2.90 —

See note over No. 1241.

ROTARY PRESS PRINTING
Designed by Jaan Born.

E. E. Plates of 400 subjects in four panes of 100 each.

1968 **Unwmk.** ***Perf. 11x10½***
C72 AP49 10c **carmine,** *Jan. 5* 22 5
Margin block of 4, P# 1.05 —
Margin block of 4, "Use Zip Codes" 90 —
Margin block of 6, "Mail Early in the Day" 1.35 —
b. Booklet pane of 8 3.00 *75*
c. Booklet pane of 5 + label, *Jan. 6* 3.50 *75*

ROTARY PRESS COIL STAMP
C73 AP49 10c **carmine,** *Jan. 5* 32 5
Pair 70 10
Joint line pair 1.70 20
a. Imperf., pair *600.00*

$1 Air Lift
This stamp, listed as No. 1341, was issued Apr. 4, 1968, to pay for airlift of parcels to and from U.S. ports to servicemen overseas and in Alaska, Hawaii and Puerto Rico. It was "also valid for paying regular rates for other types of mail," the Post Office Department announced to the public in a philatelic release dated Mar. 10, 1968. The stamp is inscribed "U.S. Postage" and is untagged.

On Apr. 26, 1969, the P.O.D. stated in its Postal Manual (for postal employees) that this stamp "may be used toward paying the postage or fees for special services on *airmail* articles." On Jan. 1, 1970, the Department told postal employees through its Postal Bulletin that this $1 stamp "can only be used to pay the airlift fee or toward payment of postage or fees on *airmail* articles."

Some collectors prefer to consider No. 1341 an airmail stamp.

50th ANNIVERSARY OF AIR MAIL ISSUE

Curtiss Jenny — AP50

Designed by Hordur Karlsson.

Issued to commemorate the 50th anniversary of regularly scheduled air mail service.

LITHOGRAPHED, ENGRAVED (GIORI)
Plates of 200 subjects in four panes of 50 each.

1968 ***Perf. 11***
C74 AP50 10c **blue, black & red,** *May 15* 20 12
Margin block of 4, P# 2.50 —
Margin block of 4, Mr. Zip and "Use Zip Code" 85 —
Margin block of 6, "Mail Early in the Day" 1.25 —
a. Red (tail stripe) omitted —

"USA" and Jet — AP51

Designed by John Larrecq.

LITHOGRAPHED, ENGRAVED (GIORI)
Plates of 200 subjects in four panes of 50 each.

1968 ***Perf. 11***
C75 AP51 20c **red, blue & black,** *Nov. 22* 48 6
Margin block of 4, P# 2.25 —
Margin block of 4, Mr. Zip and "Use Zip Code" 2.00 —
Margin block of 6, "Mail Early in the Day" 3.00 —

MOON LANDING ISSUE

First Man on the Moon AP52

Designed by Paul Calle.

Man's first landing on the moon July 20, 1969, by U.S. astronauts Neil A. Armstrong and Col. Edwin E. Aldrin, Jr., with Lieut. Col. Michael Collins piloting Apollo 11.

LITHOGRAPHED, ENGRAVED (GIORI)
Plates of 128 subjects in four panes of 32 each.

1969 ***Perf. 11***
C76 AP52 10c **yellow, black, lt. blue, ultra., rose red & carmine,** *Sept. 9* 18 10
Margin block of 4, P# 85 —
Margin block of 4, Mr. Zip and "Use Zip Code" 75 —
Margin block of 6, "Mail Early in the Day" 1.10 —
a. Rose red (litho.) omitted *500.00* —

On No. C76a, the lithographed rose red is missing from the entire vignette-the dots on top of the yellow areas as well as the flag shoulder patch.

Silhouette of Delta Wing Plane — AP53

Silhouette of Jet Airliner — AP54

Winged Airmail Envelope — AP55

Statue of Liberty — AP56

Designed by George Vander Sluis (9c, 11c), Nelson Gruppo (13c) and Robert J. Jones (17c).

ROTARY PRESS PRINTING

E. E. Plates of 400 subjects in four panes of 100 each.

1971-73 *Perf. 10½x11*

C77 AP53 9c **red,** *May 15, 1971* 16 12
Margin block of 4, P# 70 —
Margin block of 4, "Use Zip Codes" 65 —
Margin block of 6, "Mail Early in the Day" 1.00 —

No. C77 issued primarily for use on domestic post cards.

C78 AP54 11c **carmine,** *May 7, 1971* 20 5
Margin block of 4, P# 90 —
Margin block of 4, "Use Zip Codes" 85 —
Margin block of 6, "Mail Early in the Day" 1.25 —
Pair with full vert. gutter btwn. —
a. Booklet pane of 4+2 labels 1.10 *40*
b. Untagged (Bureau precanceled) 30
C79 AP55 13c **carmine,** *Nov. 16, 1973* 22 10
Margin block of 4, P# 1.95 —
Margin block of 4, "Use Zip Codes" 90 —
Margin block of 6, "Mail Early in the Day" 1.35 —
a. Booklet pane of 5 + label, *Dec. 27, 1973* 1.35 *28*
b. Untagged (Bureau precanceled) 30

No. C78b Bureau precanceled "WASHINGTON D.C." (or "DC"), No. C79b "WASHINGTON DC" only; both for use of Congressmen, but available to any permit holder.

GIORI PRESS PRINTING

Panes of 200 subjects in four panes of 50 each.

C80 AP56 17c **bluish black, red, & dark green,** *July 13, 1971* 35 10
Margin block of 4, P# 1.50 —
Margin block of 4, Mr. Zip and "Use Zip Code" 1.45 —
Margin block of 6, "Mail Early in the day" 2.15 —

"USA" & Jet Type of 1968

LITHOGRAPHED, ENGRAVED (GIORI)

Plates of 200 subjects in four panes of 50 each.

C81 AP51 21c **red, blue & black,** *May 21, 1971* 38 10
Margin block of 4, P# 1.60 —
Margin block of 4, Mr. Zip and "Use Zip Code" 1.55 —
Margin block of 6, "Mail Early in the Day" 2.30 —

COIL STAMPS
ROTARY PRESS PRINTING

1971-73 *Perf. 10 Vertically*

C82 AP54 11c **carmine,** *May 7, 1971* 22 6
Pair 45 24
Joint line pair 80 32
a. Imperf., pair *200.00*
a. Joint line pair *300.00*
C83 AP55 13c **carmine,** *Dec. 27, 1973* 26 8
Pair 52 25
Joint line pair 1.00 —
a. Imperf., pair 90.00
a. Joint line pair 125.00

NATIONAL PARKS CENTENNIAL ISSUE

City of Refuge, Hawaii

Kii Statue and Temple — AP57

Designed by Paul Rabut.

Issued to commemorate the centenary of national parks. This 11c honors the City of Refuge National Historical Park, established in 1961 at Honaunau, island of Hawaii.

LITHOGRAPHED, ENGRAVED (GIORI)

Plates of 200 subjects in four panes of 50 each.

1972 *Perf. 11*

C84 AP57 11c **orange & multicolored,** *May 3* 20 15
Margin block of 4, P# 90 —
Margin block of 4, Mr. Zip and "Use Zip Code" 85 —
Margin block of 6, "Mail Early in the Day" 1.25 —
a. Blue & green (litho.) omitted *1,750.*

OLYMPIC GAMES ISSUE

Skiing and Olympic Rings — AP58

Designed by Lance Wyman.

Issued to commemorate the 11th Winter Olympic Games, Sapporo, Japan, Feb. 3-13, and the 20th Summer Olympic Games, Munich, Germany, Aug. 26-Sept. 11.

PHOTOGRAVURE (Andreotti)

Plates of 200 subjects in four panes of 50 each.

1972 *Perf. 11x10½*

C85 AP58 11c **black, blue, red, emerald & yellow,** *Aug. 17* 20 15
Margin block of 10, 5 P# 2.10 —
Margin block of 4, "Use Zip Code" 85 —
Margin block of 6, "Mail Early in the Day" 1.25 —

ELECTRONICS PROGRESS ISSUE

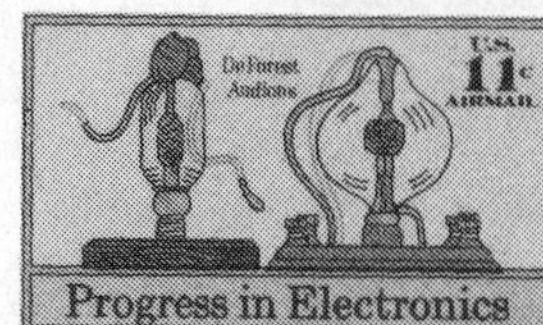

De Forest Audions — AP59

Designed by Walter and Naiad Einsel.

LITHOGRAPHED, ENGRAVED (GIORI)

Plates of 200 subjects in four panes of 50 each.

1973 *Perf. 11*

C86 AP59 11c **vermilion, lilac, pale lilac, olive, brown, deep carmine & black,** *July 10* 20 15
Margin block of 4, P# 90 —
Margin block of 4, Mr. Zip and "Use Zip Code" 85 —
Margin block of 6, "Mail Early in the Day" 1.25 —
a. Vermilion & olive (litho.) omitted *2,000.*

Statue of Liberty — AP60

Mt. Rushmore National Memorial AP61

Designed by Robert (Gene) Shehorn.

GIORI PRESS PRINTING

Panes of 200 subjects in four panes of 50 each.

1974 *Perf. 11*

C87 AP60 18c **carmine, black & ultramarine,** *Jan. 11* 32 25
Margin block of 4, 2 P# 1.40 —
Margin block of 4, Mr. Zip and "Use Zip Code" 1.30 —
Margin block of 6, "Mail Early in the Day" 1.95 —
C88 AP61 26c **ultramarine, black & carmine,** *Jan. 2* 38 14
Margin block of 4, P# 1.85 —
Margin block of 4, Mr. Zip and "Use Zip Code" 1.55 —
Margin block of 6, "Mail Early in the Day" 2.30 —

Values for well-centered, early U.S. stamps will often exceed catalogue price.

Plane and Globes — AP62

Plane, Globes and Flags — AP63

Designed by David G. Foote.

GIORI PRESS PRINTING

Panes of 200 subjects in four panes of 50 each.

1976, Jan. 2 *Perf. 11*

C89 AP62 25c **red, blue & black** 45 14
Margin block of 4, P# 1.90 —
Margin block of 4, Mr. Zip and "Use Zip Code" 1.85 —
Margin block of 6, "Mail Early in the Day" 2.75 —
C90 AP63 31c **red, blue & black** 55 10
Margin block of 4, P# 2.30 —
Margin block of 4, Mr. Zip and "Use Zip Code" 2.25 —
Margin block of 6, "Mail Early in the Day" 3.35 —

WRIGHT BROTHERS ISSUE

Orville and Wilbur Wright, and Flyer A — AP64

Wright Brothers, Flyer A and Shed — AP65

Designed by Ken Dallison.
75th anniversary of first powered flight, Kill Devil Hill, N.C., Dec. 17, 1903. Nos. C91-C92 printed se-tenant vertically.

LITHOGRAPHED, ENGRAVED (GIORI)

Plates of 400 subjects in four panes of 100 each.

1978, Sept. 23 *Perf. 11*

C91 AP64 31c **ultra. & multicolored** 65 15
C92 AP65 31c **ultra. & multicolored** 65 15
a. Pair, #C91-C92 1.30 85
Margin block of 4, P# 3.25 —
Margin block of 4, "Use Correct Zip Code" 2.65 —
Margin block of 4, copyright 2.65 —
b. As "a," ultra. & black (engr.) omitted *1,500.*
c. As "a," black (engr.) omitted —
d. As "a," black, yellow, magenta, blue & brown (litho.) omitted —

OCTAVE CHANUTE ISSUE

Chanute and Biplane Hang-glider AP66

Biplane Hang-glider and Chanute AP67

Designed by Ken Dallison.
Octave Chanute (1832-1910), civil engineer and aviation pioneer. Nos. C93-C94 printed se-tenant vertically.

LITHOGRAPHED, ENGRAVED (GIORI)

Plates of 400 subjects in four panes of 100 each.

1979, Mar. 29 **Tagged** *Perf. 11*

C93 AP66 21c **blue & multicolored** 85 32
C94 AP67 21c **blue & multicolored** 85 32
a. Pair, #C93-C94 1.70 95

	Margin block of 4, P#	3.50	—
	Margin block of 4, Mr. Zip	3.45	—
	Margin block of 4, copyright	3.45	—
b.	As "a," ultra & black (engr.) omitted	*3,500.*	

WILEY POST ISSUE

Wiley Post and "Winnie Mae" — AP68

NR-105-W, Post in Pressurized Suit, Portrait — AP69

Designed by Ken Dallison.

Wiley Post (1899-1935), first man to fly around the world alone and high-altitude flying pioneer. Nos. C95-C96 printed se-tenant vertically.

LITHOGRAPHED, ENGRAVED (GIORI)

Plates of 400 subjects in four panes of 100 each.

1979, Nov. 20	**Tagged**	***Perf. 11***	
C95 AP68 25c **blue & multicolored**		1.10	35
C96 AP69 25c **blue & multicolored**		1.10	35
a. Pair, #C95-C96		2.25	95
Margin block of 4, P#		9.00	—
Margin block of 4, Mr. Zip		4.60	—
Margin block of 4, copyright		4.60	—

OLYMPIC GAMES ISSUE

High Jump — AP70

Designed by Robert M. Cunningham.

PHOTOGRAVURE

22nd Olympic Games, Moscow, July 19-Aug. 3, 1980.

Plates of 200 subjects in four panes of 50 each.

1979, Nov. 1	**Tagged**	***Perf. 11***	
C97 AP70 31c **multi**		60	30
P# block of 12, 6 P#		8.50	—
Zip block of 4		2.50	—
Copyright block of 4		2.50	—

PHILIP MAZZEI (1730-1816)

Italian-born Political Writer — AP71

Designed by Sante Graziani

PHOTOGRAVURE

Plates of 200 subjects in four panes of 50 each.

1980, Oct. 13	**Tagged**	***Perf. 11***	
C98 AP71 40c **multi**		70	15
P# block of 12, 6 P#		8.75	—
Zip block of 4		2.85	—
Copyright block of 4		2.85	—
a. Perf. 10½x11, *1982*		1.00	—
b. Imperf., pair		*2,250.*	

United States Air Mail stamps can be mounted in Scott's annually supplemented Platinum, National, Pony Express, Minuteman, U.S. Commemorative and Commemorative Air Mail Plate Blocks, U.S. Blocks of Four and U.S. Regular and Regular Air Plate Blocks.

BLANCHE STUART SCOTT (1886-1970)

First Woman Pilot — AP72

Designed by Paul Calle.

PHOTOGRAVURE

Plates of 200 subjects in four panes of 50.

1980, Dec. 30	**Tagged**	***Perf. 11***	
C99 AP72 28c **multi**		55	15
P# block of 12, 6 P#		6.75	—
Zip block of 4		2.25	—
Copyright block of 4		2.25	—

GLENN CURTISS (1878-1930)

Aviation Pioneer and Aircraft Designer — AP73

Designed by Ken Dallison.

PHOTOGRAVURE

Plates of 200 subjects in four panes of 50.

1980, Dec. 30	**Tagged**	***Perf. 11***	
C100 AP73 35c **multi**		60	15
P# block of 12, 6 P#		7.75	—
Zip block of 4		2.50	—
Copyright block of 4		2.50	—

SUMMER OLYMPICS 1984

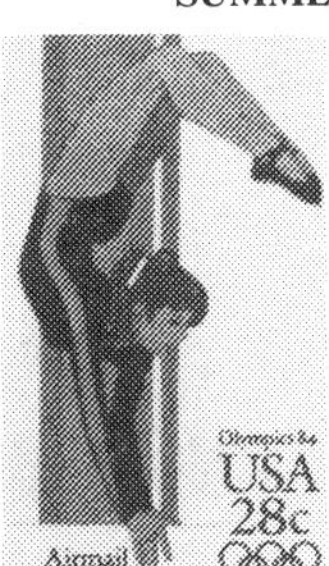

Women's Gymnastics AP74

Hurdles AP75

Women's Basketball — AP76

Soccer — AP77

Shot Put — AP78

Men's Gymnastics AP79

Women's Swimming AP80

Weight Lifting — AP81

Women's Fencing — AP82

Cycling — AP83

Women's Volleyball — AP84

Pole Vaulting — AP85

Designed by Robert Peak.

23rd Olympic Games, Los Angeles, July 28-Aug. 12, 1984.

PHOTOGRAVURE

Plates of 200 subjects in four panes of 50.

1983, June 17	**Tagged**	***Perf. 11***	
C101 AP74 28c **multi**		56	28
C102 AP75 28c **multi**		56	28
C103 AP76 28c **multi**		56	28
C104 AP77 28c **multi**		56	28
P# block of 4, 4 P#		3.25	—
Zip block of 4		2.60	—
Copyright block of 4		2.60	—
a. Block of 4, #C101-C104		2.50	1.75
b. As "a," imperf. vert.		—	

1983, Apr. 8	**Tagged**	***Perf. 11***	
C105 AP78 40c **multi**		80	40
a. Perf. 11x10½		90	45
C106 AP79 40c **multi**		80	40
a. Perf. 11x10½		90	45
C107 AP80 40c **multi**		80	40
a. Perf. 11x10½		90	45
C108 AP81 40c **multi**		80	40
P# block of 4, 4 P#		4.25	—
Zip block of 4		3.30	—
Copyright block of 4		3.30	—
a. Block of 4, #C105-C108		3.25	2.00
b. As "a," imperf.		—	
c. Perf. 11x10½		90	45
c. P# block of 4, 4 P#		6.00	—
d. As "a," perf. 11x10½		4.00	—

1983, Nov. 4	**Tagged**	***Perf. 11***	
C109 AP82 35c **multi**		70	35
C110 AP83 35c **multi**		70	35
C111 AP84 35c **multi**		70	35

C112 AP85 35c **multi**		70	35
	P# block of 4, 4#	4.00	—
	Zip block of 4	3.00	—
	Copyright block of 4	3.00	—
a.	Block of 4, #C109-C112	2.90	1.85

AVIATION PIONEERS

Alfred V. Verville (1890-1970), Inventor, Verville-Sperry R-3 Army Racer — AP86

Lawrence Sperry (1892-1931), Aircraft Designer, and Father Elmer (1860-1930), Designer and Pilot, 1st Seaplane — AP87

Designed by Ken Dallison (No. C113) and Howard Koslow (No. C114)

PHOTOGRAVURE

Plates of 200 in four panes of 50 (2 panes each, No. C113 and No. C114)

Plates of 200 in four panes of 50 (No. C114

1985, Feb. 13 **Tagged** ***Perf. 11***

C113 AP86 33c **multi**		60	20
	P# block of 4, 5 #, UL, LR	2.75	—
	Zip block of 4	2.50	—
	Copyright block of 4	2.50	—
a.	Imperf., pair	*900.00*	
C114 AP87 39c **multi**		70	20
	P# block of 4, 5 #, UR, LL	3.00	—
	P# block of 4, 4 #	3.00	—
	Zip block of 4	2.90	—
	Copyright block of 4	2.90	—
a.	Imperf., pair	—	

TRANSPACIFIC AIRMAIL

50th Anniversary

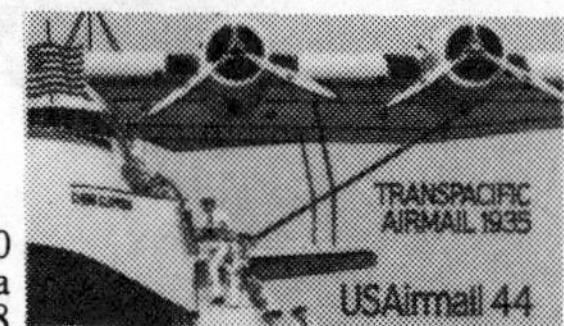

Martin M-130 China Clipper — AP88

Designed by Chuck Hodgson.

PHOTOGRAVURE

Plates of 200 in four panes of 50

1985, Feb. 15 **Tagged** ***Perf. 11***

C115 AP88 44c **multi**		80	20
	P# block of 4, 5 #	3.30	—
	Zip block of 4	3.25	—
	Copyright block of 4	3.25	—
a.	Imperf., pair	*1,000.*	

FR. JUNIPERO SERRA (1713-1784)

California Missionary

Outline Map of Southern California, Portrait, San Gabriel Mission — AP89

Designed by Richard Schlecht from a Spanish stamp.

PHOTOGRAVURE

Plates of 200 in four panes of 50

1985, Aug. 22 **Tagged** ***Perf. 11***

C116 AP89 44c **multi**		1.00	20
	P# block of 4	5.25	—
	Zip block of 4	4.10	—
	Copyright block of 4	4.10	—
a.	Imperf., pair	—	

SETTLING OF NEW SWEDEN, 350th ANNIV.

Settler, Two Indians, Map of New Sweden, Swedish Ships "Kalmar Nyckel" and "Fogel Grip" — AP90

Designed by Goran Osterland based on an 18th century illustration from a Swedish book about the Colonies.

LITHOGRAPHED AND ENGRAVED

Plates of 200 in four panes of 50

1988, Mar. 29 **Tagged** ***Perf. 11***

C117 AP90 44c **multi**		88	20
	P# block of 4, 5#	5.25	—
	Zip block of 4	3.60	—
	Copyright block of 4	3.60	—

SAMUEL P. LANGLEY (1834-1906)

Langley and Unmanned Aerodrome No. 5 — AP91

Designed by Ken Dallison.

LITHOGRAPHED AND ENGRAVED

Plates of 200 in four panes of 50

1988, May 14 **Tagged** ***Perf. 11***

C118 AP91 45c **multi**		90	20
	P# block of 4, 7#	3.75	—
	Zip block of 4	3.65	—
	Copyright block of 4	3.65	—

IGOR SIKORSKY (1889-1972)

Sikorsky and 1939 VS300 Helicopter AP92

Designed by Ren Wicks.

PHOTOGRAVURE AND ENGRAVED

Plates of 200 in four panes of 50

1988, June 23 **Tagged** ***Perf. 11***

C119 AP92 36c **multi**		72	20
	P# block of 4, 6#	3.10	—
	Zip block of 4	3.00	—
	Copyright block of 4	3.00	—

FRENCH REVOLUTION BICENTENNIAL

Liberty, Equality and Fraternity — AP93

Designed by Richard Sheaff.

LITHOGRAPHED AND ENGRAVED

Plates of 120 in four panes of 30

1989, July 14 **Tagged** ***Perf. 11½x11***

C120 AP93 45c **multicolored**		90	22
	P# block of 4, 4#	4.50	—
	Zip block of 4	4.05	—
	Copyright block of 4	4.05	—

AMERICA ISSUE

Southeast Carved Figure, 700-1430 A.D. — AP94

Designed by Lon Busch. Printed by American Bank Note Co.

PHOTOGRAVURE

Plates of 200 in four panes of 50

1989, Oct. 12 ***Perf.***

C121 AP94 45c **multicolored**		90	22
	P# block of 4	4.50	—
	Zip block of 4	4.05	—
	Copyright block of 4	4.05	—

AIR POST SPECIAL DELIVERY STAMPS

Great Seal of United States — APSD1

No. CE1 was issued for the prepayment of the air postage and the special delivery fee in one stamp. First day sale was at the American Air Mail Society Convention.

FLAT PLATE PRINTING
Plates of 200 subjects in four panes of 50 each.

1934, Aug. 30 **Unwmk.** ***Perf. 11***

CE1	APSD1 16c	**dark blue**	65	85
		blue	65	85
		First day cover, Chicago *(40,171)*		25.00
		First day cover, Washington, D.C., *Aug. 31*		15.00
		Margin block of 6, P#	16.00	—

For imperforate variety see No. 771.

Type of 1934

Frame plates of 100 subjects in two panes of 50 each separated by a 1 ½ inch wide vertical gutter with central guide line, and vignette plates of 50 subjects.

The "seal" design for No. CE2 was from a new engraving, slightly smaller than that used for No. CE1.

Top plate number blocks of No. CE2 are found both with and without top arrow.

Issued in panes of 50 each.

1936, Feb. 10

CE2	APSD1 16c	**red & blue**	40	25
		First day cover Washington, D.C. *(72,981)*		17.50
		Margin block of 4, two P#	8.50	—
		Margin block of 4, two P#, blue dotted registration marker	65.00	
		Same, arrow, red registration marker	50.00	
		Margin block of 4, bottom or side arrow	2.00	1.75
		Center line block	2.25	2.75
		Margin block of 10, two P#, two "TOP" and two registration markers	15.00	6.00
a.		Horiz. pair, imperf. vert.	*3,750.*	

Quantities issued: No. CE1, 9,215,750. No. CE2, 72,517,850.

AIR POST SEMI-OFFICIAL

Buffalo Balloon

This stamp was privately issued by John F. B. Lillard, a Nashville reporter. It was used on covers carried on a balloon ascension of June 18, 1877, which began at Nashville and landed at Gallatin, Tenn., and possibly on other flights. The balloon was owned and piloted by Samuel Archer King. The stamp was reported to have been engraved by (Mrs.?) J. H. Snively and printed in strips from a single die. Lillard wrote that 300 were printed and 23 used.

Buffalo Balloon — CS1

1877, June 18 **Typo.** ***Imperf.***

CL1	CS1 5c	**deep blue**	*6,000.*	
		On cover with 3c #158		—
		On cover with 1c, #156 & 2c #178		—
a.		Tête bêche pair, vertical	*13,000.*	

A black proof exists of No. CL1.

R.F. OVERPRINTS

Authorized as a control mark by the United States Fleet Post Office during 1944-45 for the accommodation of and exclusive use by French naval personnel on airmail correspondence to the United States and Canada. All "R.F." (Republique Francaise) mail had to be posted at the North African naval bases and had to bear the return address, rank and/or serial number of a French officer or seaman. It also had to be reviewed by a censor.

All "R.F." overprints were handstamped by the French naval authorities after the stamps were affixed for mailing. The stamps had to be canceled by a special French naval cancellation. The status of unused copies seems questionable; they are alleged to have been handstamped at a later date.

Several types of "R.F." overprints other than those illustrated are known, but their validity is doubtful.

United States No. C25 Handstamped in Black

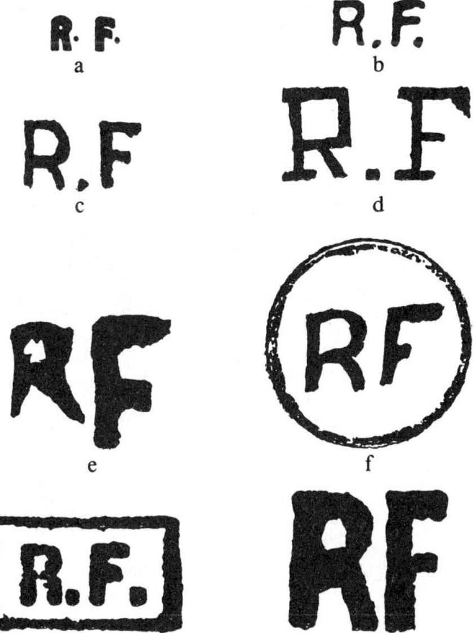

RF
i

R. F.
j

1944-45 **Unwmk.** ***Perf. 11x10 ½***

CM1	AP17 (a)	6c carmine, on cover	200.00
CM2	AP17 (b)	6c carmine, on cover	275.00
CM3	AP17 (c)	6c carmine, on cover	350.00
CM4	AP17 (d)	6c carmine, on cover	250.00
CM5	AP17 (e)	6c carmine, on cover	500.00
CM6	AP17 (f)	6c carmine, on cover	275.00
CM7	AP17 (g)	6c carmine, on cover	475.00
CM8	AP17 (h)	6c carmine, on cover	500.00
CM9	AP17 (i)	6c carmine, on cover	500.00
CM10	AP17 (j)	6c carmine, on cover	—

Counterfeits of several types exist.

No. 907 is known with type "c" overprint; No. C19 with type "e" or "h"; No. C25a (single) with type "c", and No. C26 with type "b" or "f." Type "i" exists in several variations.

STAMPED ENVELOPES
No. UC5 Handstamped in Black

1944-45

UCM1	AP17 (a)	6c carmine, entire	300.00
UCM1	AP17 (b)	6c carmine, entire	400.00
UCM1	AP17 (d)	6c carmine, entire	450.00
UCM1	AP17 (f)	6c carmine, entire	450.00
UCM1	AP17 (h)	6c carmine, entire	500.00

SPECIAL DELIVERY

Special Delivery service was instituted by the Act of Congress of March 3, 1885, and put into operation on October 1, 1885. The Act limited the service to free delivery offices and such others as served places with a population of 400 or more, and its privileges where thus operative in but 555 post offices. The Act of August 4, 1886, made the stamps and service available at all post offices and upon any article of mailable matter. To consume the supply of stamps of the first issue, Scott E3 was withheld until September 6, 1888.

A Special Delivery stamp, when affixed to any stamped letter or article of mailable matter, secures later delivery during daytime and evening as most post offices, so that the item will not have to wait until the next day for delivery.

Messenger Running — SD1

ENGRAVED

Printed by the American Bank Note Co.

Plates of 100 subjects in two panes of 50 each

1885, Oct. 1 **Unwmk.** ***Perf. 12***

E1 SD1 10c	**blue**	175.00	20.00
	deep blue	175.00	20.00
	On cover		40.00
	First day cover		*8,000.*
	Margin block of 8, Impt. & P# 495 or 496	*12,000.*	
	Margin strip of 4, same	1,100.	
	Double transfer at top	225.00	40.00

Messenger Running — SD2

1888, Sept. 6

E2 SD2 10c	**blue**	175.00	5.00
	deep blue	175.00	5.00
	On cover		25.00
	Margin block of 8, Impt. & P# 73 or 552	*12,000.*	
	Margin strip of 4, same	1,100.	

Earliest known use: Dec. 18, 1888.

See note above No. E3.

COLUMBIAN EXPOSITION ISSUE

Though not issued expressly for the Exposition, No. E3 is considered to be part of that issue. It was released in orange because No. E2 was easily confused with the 1c Columbian, No. 230.

From Jan. 24, 1893, until Jan. 5, 1894, the special delivery stamp was printed in orange; the issue in that color continued until May 19, 1894, when the stock on hand was exhausted. The stamp in blue was not issued from Jan. 24, 1893 to May 19, 1894. However, on Jan. 5, 1894, printing of the stamp in blue was resumed. Presumably it was reissued from May 19, 1894 until the appearance of No. E4 on Oct. 10, 1894. The emissions of the blue stamp of this design before Jan. 24, 1893 and after Jan. 5, 1894 are indistinguishable.

1893, Jan. 24

E3 SD2 10c	**orange**	110.00	11.00
	deep orange	110.00	11.00
	On cover		45.00
	Margin block of 8, Impt. & P# 73 or 552	*7,250.*	
	Margin strip of 4, same	800.00	

Earliest known use: Feb. 11, 1893.

United States Special Delivery stamps can be mounted in Scott's Platinum, National, Minuteman and Pony Express Albums.

Messenger Running — SD3

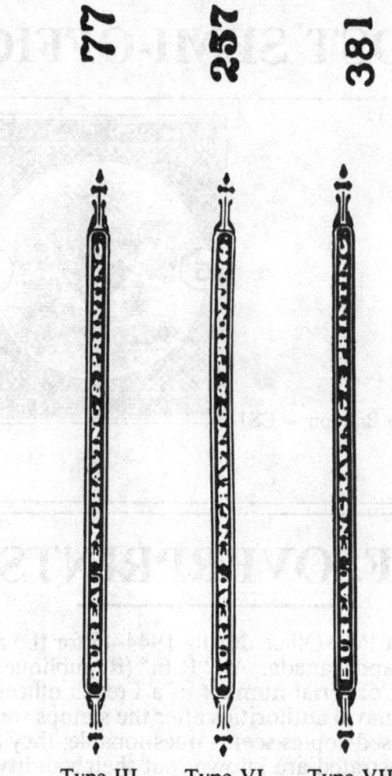

Type III Type VI Type VII

Printed by the Bureau of Engraving and Printing.

1894, Oct. 10

Line under "TEN CENTS"

E4 SD3 10c	**blue**	450.00	12.50
	dark blue	450.00	12.50
	bright blue	450.00	12.50
	On cover		80.00
	Block of four	1,850.	
	Margin block of 4, arrow	1,900.	
	Margin block of 6, T III Impt. & P# 77	*14,500.*	
	Margin strip of 3, same	2,100.	
a.	Imperf., pair	*5,500.*	
	Double transfer	—	—

Earliest known use: Nov. 21, 1894.

1895, Aug. 16 **Wmk. 191**

E5 SD3 10c	**blue**	85.00	1.50
	dark blue	85.00	1.50
	deep blue	85.00	1.50
	On cover		13.50
	Margin block of 4, arrow	375.00	
	Margin block of 6, T III, VI or VII Impt. & P#	*4,500.*	
	Margin strip of 3, same	400,00	
a.	Imperf., pair	*4,500.*	
b.	Printed on both sides	*1,250.*	
	Double transfer	—	15.00
	Line of color through "POSTAL DELIVERY", from bottom row of Plates 1257-1260	125.00	9.00
	Dots in curved frame above messenger (Pl. 882)	110.00	6.00

No. E5a was not regularly issued.

Earliest known use: Oct. 3, 1895.

Messenger on Bicycle — SD4

1902, Dec. 9

E6 SD4 10c	**ultramarine**	52.50	1.50
	dark ultramarine	52.50	1.50
	pale ultramarine	52.50	1.50
	blue	52.50	1.50
	On cover		7.50
	P# block of 6, "09"	*2,750.*	
	Margin block of 4, arrow	225.00	
	Margin block of 6, T VII Impt. & P#	*3,000.*	
	Margin strip of 3, same	200.00	
	Double transfer	—	—
	Damaged transfer under "N" of "CENTS"	85.00	3.00

Earliest known use: Jan. 22, 1903.

No. E6 was re-issued in 1909 from new plates 5240, 5243-5245. After a few months use the Bureau added "09" to these plate numbers. The stamp can be identified only by plate number.

Helmet of Mercury SD5

Plates of 280 subjects in four panes of 70 each

1908, Dec. 12

E7 SD5 10c	**green**	57.50	21.00
	dark green	57.50	21.00
	yellowish green	57.50	21.00
	On cover		60.00
	Margin block of 6, T V Impt. & P#	925.00	—
	Margin strip of 3, same	225.00	
	Double transfer	80.00	27.50

Earliest known use: Dec. 14, 1908.

Plates of 200 subjects in four panes of 50 each

1911, Jan. **Wmk. 190** ***Perf. 12***

E8 SD4 10c	**ultramarine**	55.00	2.25
	pale ultramarine	55.00	2.25
	dark ultramarine	55.00	2.25
b.	10c violet blue	55.00	2.25
	On cover		13.50
	Margin block of 6, T VII Impt. & P#	*2,750.*	
	Margin block of 6, P# only	*2,500.*	
	Top frame line missing (Pl. 5514)	72.50	3.25

Earliest known use: Jan. 14, 1911.

1914, Sept. ***Perf. 10***

E9 SD4 10c	**ultramarine**	110.00	2.50
	pale ultramarine	110.00	2.50
	blue	110.00	2.50
	On cover		22.50
	Margin block of 6, T VII Impt. & P#	*5,000.*	—

Margin block of 6, P# only	*4,250.*	—
Margin block of 8, T VII Impt. & P# (side)		—

Earliest known use: Oct. 26, 1914.

1916, Oct. 19 **Unwmk.** ***Perf. 10***

E10 SD4 10c **pale ultramarine**	200.00	12.50
ultramarine	200.00	12.50
blue	200.00	12.50
On cover		50.00
Margin block of 6, T VII Impt. & P# 5520	6,250.	—
Margin block of 6, P# only	5,750.	—

Earliest known use: Nov. 4, 1916.

1917, May 2 **Unwmk.** ***Perf. 11***

E11 SD4 10c **ultramarine**	10.00	20
pale ultramarine	10.00	20
dark ultramarine	10.00	20
a. 10c gray violet	10.00	20
c. 10c blue	20.00	50
On cover		3.00
Margin block of 6, T VII Impt. & P#	850.00	—
Margin block of 6, P# only	200.00	—
Margin block of 8, T VII Impt. & P# (side)		—
d. Perf. 10 at left		—

Earliest known use: June 12, 1917.

The aniline ink used on some printings of No. E11 permeated the paper causing a pink tinge to appear on the back. Such stamps are called "pink backs."

Motorcycle Delivery — SD6

FLAT PLATE PRINTING

1922, July 12 **Unwmk.** ***Perf. 11***

E12 SD6 10c **gray violet**	18.00	15
a. 10c deep ultramarine	25.00	20
On cover		1.00
First day cover		400.00
Margin block of 6, P# only	275.00	—
Double transfer	35.00	1.00

Post Office Truck — SD7

Issued to facilitate special delivery service for parcel post.

1925 **Unwmk.** ***Perf. 11***

E13 SD6 15c **deep orange,** *Apr. 11, 1925*	15.00	40
On cover		10.00
First day cover		225.00
Margin block of 6, P# only	150.00	—
Double transfer	20.00	1.00
E14 SD7 20c **black,** *Apr. 25, 1925*	1.90	85
On cover		1.50
First day cover		90.00
Margin block of 6, P# only	25.00	

Motorcycle Type of 1922
ROTARY PRESS PRINTING

1927, Nov. 29 **Unwmk.** ***Perf. 11x10½***

E15 SD6 10c **gray violet**	60	5
a. 10c red lilc	60	5
b. 10c gray lilac	60	5
violet	60	5
On cover		25
First day cover		90.00
Margin block of 4, P# only	4.00	—
c. Horizontal pair, imperf. between	275.00	
Gouged plate		—
Cracked plate 19280 LR	35.00	

The design of No. E15 measures 36½x21¾mm. Design of stamps from the flat plates measures 36x21½mm.

Motorcycle Type of 1922
ROTARY PRESS PRINTING

1931, Aug. 13 **Unwmk.** ***Perf. 11x10½***

E16 SD6 15c **orange**	70	8
On cover		25
First day cover, Washington, D.C.		125.00
First day cover, Easton, Pa., *Aug. 6, 1931*		1,000.
Margin block of 4, P# only	3.50	—

Design of No. E16 measures 36¾x22¼mm.
Design of No. E13 measures 36½x22½mm.

Motorcycle Type of 1922
ROTARY PRESS PRINTING
E. E. Plates of 200 subjects in four panes of 50 each.

1944, Oct. 30 **Unwmk.** ***Perf. 11x10½***

E17 SD6 13c **blue**	60	6
First day cover		12.00
Margin block of 4, P#	3.00	—
E18 SD6 17c **orange yellow**	2.75	1.25
First day cover		12.00
First day cover, Nos. E17 & E18		30.00
Margin block of 4, P#	22.50	—

Truck Type of 1925
ROTARY PRESS PRINTING
E. E. Plates of 200 subjects in four panes of 50 each

1951, Nov. 30 **Unwmk.** ***Perf. 11x10½***

E19 SD7 20c **black**	1.20	12
First day cover		5.00
Margin block of 4, P#	5.00	—

Design of No. E19 measures 36¼x22mm.
Design of No. E14 measures 35½x21½mm.

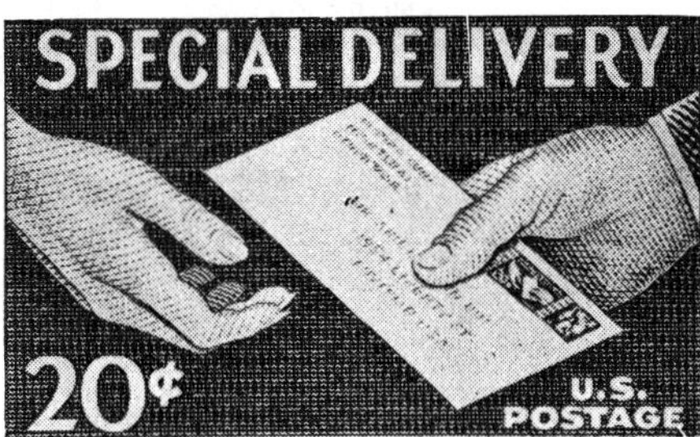

Special Delivery Letter, Hand to Hand — SD8

ROTARY PRESS PRINTING
E. E. Plates of 200 subjects in four panes of 50 each

1954, Oct. 13 **Unwmk.** ***Perf. 11x10½***

E20 SD8 20c **deep blue**	38	8
light blue	—	—
First day cover, Boston *(194,043)*		3.00
Margin block of 4, P#	1.90	—

1957, Sept. 3

E21 SD8 30c **lake**	48	5
First Day cover, Indianapolis *(111,451)*		2.25
Margin block of 4, P#	2.40	—

Arrows — SD9

Designed by Norman Yves.

GIORI PRESS PRINTING
Plates of 200 subjects in four panes of 50 each

1969, Nov. 21 **Unwmk.** ***Perf. 11***

E22 SD9 45c **carmine & violet blue**	90	12
First day cover, New York, N.Y.		3.50
Margin block of 4, P#	5.50	—
Margin block of 4, Mr. Zip and "Use Zip Code"	3.75	—
Margin block of 6, "Mail Early in the Day"	5.50	—

1971, May 10 ***Perf. 11***

E23 SD9 60c **violet blue & carmine**	85	10
First day cover, Phoenix, Ariz. *(129,562)*		3.50
Margin block of 4, P#	4.25	—
Margin block of 4, Mr. Zip and "Use Zip Code"	3.50	—
Margin block of 6, "Mail Early in the Day"	5.20	—

CERTIFIED MAIL

Certified Mail service was started on June 6, 1955, for use on first class mail for which no indemnity value is claimed, but for which proof of mailing land proof of delivery are available at less cost than registered mail. The mailer receives one receipt and the addressee signs another when the postman delivers the letter. The second receipt is kept on file at the post office for six months. The Certified Mail charge, originally 15 cents, is in addition to regular postage, whether surface mail, air mail, or special delivery.

Letter Carrier — CM1

ROTARY PRESS PRINTING
E. E. Plates of 200 subjects in four panes of 50

1955, June 6 **Unwmk.** ***Perf. 10½x11***

FA1 CM1 15c **red**		28	20
First day cover			3.25
Margin block of 4, P#		4.00	—

United States Certified Mail stamp can be mounted in Scott's Platinum, National and Minuteman Albums.

REGISTRATION

The Registry System for U.S. mail went into effect July 1, 1855, the fee being 5 cents. On June 30, 1863, the fee was increased to 20 cents.
On January 1, 1869, the fee was reduced to 15 cents and on January 1, 1874, to 8 cents. On July 1, 1875, the fee was increased to 10 cents. On January 1, 1893 the fee was again reduced to 8 cents and again it was increased to 10 cents on November 1, 1909.
Early registered covers with various stamps, rates and postal markings are of particular interest to collectors.
Registry stamps (10c ultramarine) were issued on December 1, 1911, to prepay registry fees (not postage), but ordinary stamps were valid for registry fees then as now. These special stamps were abolished May 28, 1913, by order of the Postmaster General, who permitted their use until supplies on hand were exhausted.

Eagle — RS1

ENGRAVED

1911, Dec. 11 **Wmk. 190** ***Perf. 12***

F1 RS1 10c **ultramarine**	55.00	2.25
pale ultramarine	55.00	2.25
On cover		40.00
First day cover		*8,000.*
Block of four	225.00	*75.00*
block of 6, Impt., P# & "A"	*1,350.*	—

United States Registration stamp can be mounted in Scott's Platinum, National and Minuteman Albums.

POSTAGE DUE

For affixing, by a postal clerk, to any piece of mailable matter, to denote the amount to be collected from the addressee because of insufficient prepayment of postage.
Prior to July 1879, whenever a letter was unpaid, or insufficiently prepaid, the amount of postage due was written by hand or handstamped on the envelope, and the deficiency collected by the carrier. No vouchers were given for money thus collected.
Postage Due Stamps were authorized by the Act of Congress, approved March 3, 1879, effective July 1, 1879.

Printed by the American Bank Note Co.
Plates of 200 subjects in two panes of 100 each.

Figure of Value in Oval — D1

1879 **Unwmk.** **Engr.** ***Perf. 12***

J1 D1 1c **brown**	30.00	5.00
pale brown	30.00	5.00
deep brown	30.00	5.00
Block of four	125.00	25.00
J2 D1 2c **brown**	200.00	4.00
pale brown	200.00	4.00
Block of four	825.00	—
J3 D1 3c **brown**	25.00	2.50
pale brown	25.00	2.50
deep brown	25.00	2.50
yellowish brown	27.50	3.50
Block of four	105.00	11.00
J4 D1 5c **brown**	300.00	25.00
pale brown	300.00	25.00
deep brown	300.00	25.00
Block of four	1,250.	—
J5 D1 10c **brown,** *Sept. 19*	350.00	12.50
pale brown	350.00	12.50
deep brown	350.00	12.50
Block of four	1,500.	
a. Imperf., pair	*1,600.*	
J6 D1 30c **brown,** *Sept. 19*	175.00	25.00
pale brown	175.00	25.00
Block of four	725.00	—
J7 D1 50c **brown,** *Sept. 19*	225.00	30.00
pale brown	225.00	30.00
Block of four	925.00	—

Special Printing

1879 **Unwmk.** ***Perf. 12***

Soft porous paper

Printed by the American Bank Note Co.

J8 D1 1c deep brown *(4,420)*	*5,750.*
J9 D1 2c deep brown *(1,361)*	*3,750.*
J10 D1 3c deep brown *(436)*	*3,500.*
J11 D1 5c deep brown *(249)*	*3,000.*
J12 D1 10c deep brown *(174)*	*1,850.*
J13 D1 30c deep brown *(179)*	*1,850.*
J14 D1 50c deep brown *(179)*	*2,000.*

1884 **Unwmk.** ***Perf. 12***

J15 D1 1c **red brown**	30.00	2.50
pale red brown	30.00	2.50
deep red brown	30.00	2.50
Block of four	125.00	12.00
J16 D1 2c **red brown**	37.50	2.50
pale red brown	37.50	2.50
deep red brown	37.50	2.50
Block of four	160.00	12.00
J17 D1 3c **red brown**	500.00	100.00
deep red brown	500.00	100.00
Block of four	2,100.	—
J18 D1 5c **red brown**	250.00	12.50
pale red brown	250.00	12.50
deep red brown	250.00	12.50
Block of four	1100.	—

No.	Description	Unused	Used
J19 D1 10c	**red brown**	225.00	7.00
	deep red brown	225.00	7.00
	Block of four	925.00	—
J20 D1 30c	**red brown**	110.00	22.50
	deep red brown	110.00	22.50
	Block of four	450.00	110.00
J21 D1 50c	**red brown**	1000.	125.00
	Block of four	4,250.	—

1891 Unwmk. *Perf. 12*

No.	Description	Unused	Used
J22 D1 1c	**bright claret**	12.50	50
	light claret	12.50	50
	dark claret	12.50	50
	Block of four	52.50	2.25
a.	Imperf., pair	450.00	
J23 D1 2c	**bright claret**	15.00	45
	light claret	15.00	45
	dark claret	15.00	45
	Block of four	62.50	2.25
a.	Imperf., pair	450.00	
J24 D1 3c	**bright claret**	32.50	4.00
	dark claret	32.50	4.00
	Block of four	135.00	17.50
a.	Imperf., pair	450.00	
J25 D1 5c	**bright claret**	35.00	4.00
	light claret	35.00	4.00
	dark claret	35.00	4.00
	Block of four	145.00	17.50
a.	Imperf., pair	450.00	
J26 D1 10c	**bright claret**	70.00	10.00
	light claret	70.00	10.00
	Block of four	300.00	45.00
a.	Imperf., pair	450.00	
J27 D1 30c	**bright claret**	250.00	85.00
	Block of four	1050.	—
a.	Imperf., pair	525.00	
J28 D1 50c	**bright claret**	275.00	85.00
	dark claret	275.00	85.00
	Block of four	1,200.	—
a.	Imperf., pair	525.00	

The imperforate varieties, Nos. J22a-J28a, were not regularly issued.

Printed by the Bureau of Engraving and Printing.

D2

1894 Unwmk. *Perf. 12*

No.	Description	Unused	Used
J29 D2 1c	**vermilion**	575.00	100.00
	pale vermilion	575.00	100.00
	Block of four	2,400.	425.00
	Margin block of 6, Impt. & P#	5,250.	
J30 D2 2c	**vermilion**	250.00	50.00
	deep vermilion	250.00	50.00
	Block of four	1,050.	
	Margin block of 6, Impt. & P#	2,400.	

1894-95

No.	Description	Unused	Used
J31 D2 1c	**deep claret,** *Aug. 14, 1894*	20.00	3.00
	claret	20.00	3.00
	lake	20.00	3.00
	Block of four	82.50	13.00
	Margin block of 6, Impt. & P#	375.00	
a.	Imperf., pair	225.00	
a.	Block of four	500.00	
b.	Vertical pair, imperf. horiz.	—	
J32 D2 2c	**deep claret,** *July 20, 1894*	17.50	1.75
	claret	17.50	1.75
	lake	17.50	1.75
	Block of four	72.50	8.00
	Margin block of 6, Impt. & P#	325.00	
J33 D2 3c	**deep claret,** *Apr. 27, 1895*	75.00	20.00
	lake	75.00	20.00
	Block of four	325.00	—
	Margin block of 6, Impt. & P#	850.00	
J34 D2 5c	**deep claret,** *Apr. 27, 1895*	100.00	22.50
	claret	100.00	22.50
	Block of four	450.00	—
	Margin block of 6, Impt. & P#	950.00	
J35 D2 10c	**deep claret,** *Sept. 24, 1894*	100.00	17.50
	Block of four	450.00	—
	Margin block of 6, Impt. & P#	950.00	
J36 D2 30c	**deep claret,** *Apr. 27, 1895*	225.00	50.00
	claret	225.00	50.00
	Block of four	950.00	—
a.	30c carmine	225.00	50.00
a.	Block of four (carmine)	950.00	—
b.	30c pale rose	210.00	45.00
b.	Block of four (pale rose)	850.00	—
	Margin block of 6, Impt. & P#	2,100.	
J37 D2 50c	**deep claret,** *Apr. 27, 1895*	500.00	150.00
	Block of four	2,250.	—
a.	50c pale rose	450.00	135.00
a.	Block of four (pale rose)	1,750.	—
	Margin block of 6, Impt. & P#	5,000.	

Shades are numerous in the 1894 and later issues.

Wmk. 191 Horizontally or Vertically

1895-97 *Perf. 12*

No.	Description	Unused	Used
J38 D2 1c	**deep claret,** *Aug. 29, 1895*	5.00	30
	claret	5.00	30
	carmine	5.00	30
	lake	5.00	30
	Block of four	21.00	1.40
	Margin block of 6, Impt. & P#	190.00	
J39 D2 2c	**deep claret,** *Sept. 14, 1895*	5.00	20
	claret	5.00	20
	carmine	5.00	20
	lake	5.00	20
	Block of four	21.00	1.00
	Margin block of 6, Impt. & P#	190.00	
	Double transfer	—	—

In October, 1895, the Postmaster at Jefferson, Iowa, surcharged a few 2 cent stamps with the words "Due 1 cent" in black on each side, subsequently dividing the stamps vertically and using each half as a 1 cent stamp. Twenty of these were used.

No.	Description	Unused	Used
J40 D2 3c	**deep claret,** *Oct. 30, 1895*	35.00	1.00
	claret	35.00	1.00
	rose red	35.00	1.00
	carmine	35.00	1.00
	Block of four	150.00	4.50
	Margin block of 6, Impt. & P#	425.00	
J41 D2 5c	**deep claret,** *Oct. 15, 1895*	37.50	1.00
	claret	37.50	1.00
	carmine rose	37.50	1.00
	Block of four	160.00	4.50
	Margin block of 6, Impt. & P#	450.00	
J42 D2 10c	**deep claret,** *Sept. 14, 1895*	40.00	2.00
	claret	40.00	2.00
	carmine	40.00	2.00
	lake	40.00	2.00
	Block of four	170.00	8.50
	Margin block of 6, Impt. & P#	550.00	
J43 D2 30c	**deep claret,** *Aug. 21, 1897*	300.00	25.00
	claret	300.00	25.00
	Block of four	1,250.	—
	Margin block of 6, Impt. & P#	3,750.	
J44 D2 50c	**deep claret,** *Mar. 17, 1896*	190.00	20.00
	claret	190.00	20.00
	Block of four	775.00	90.00
	Margin block of 6, Impt. & P#	2,250.	

1910-12 Wmk. 190 *Perf. 12*

No.	Description	Unused	Used
J45 D2 1c	**deep claret,** *Aug. 30, 1910*	20.00	2.00
a.	1c rose carmine	17.50	1.75
	Block of four (2 or 3mm spacing)	82.50	9.00
	Margin block of 6, Impt. & P# & star	400.00	
J46 D2 2c	**deep claret,** *Nov. 25, 1910*	20.00	15
	lake	20.00	15
a.	2c rose carmine	17.50	15
	Block of four (2 or 3mm spacing)	82.50	75
	Margin block of 6, Impt. & P# & star	350.00	—
	Margin block of 6, P# only	375.00	
	Double transfer	—	—
J47 D2 3c	**deep claret,** *Aug. 31, 1910*	350.00	17.50
	lake	350.00	17.50
	Block of four (2 or 3mm spacing)	1,450.	70.00
	Margin block of 6, Impt. & P# & star	3,850.	
J48 D2 5c	**deep claret,** *Aug. 31, 1910*	60.00	3.50
a.	5c rose carmine	—	—
	Block of four (2 or 3mm spacing)	250.00	15.00
	Margin block of 6, Impt. & P# & star	600.00	
J49 D2 10c	**deep claret,** *Aug. 31, 1910*	75.00	7.50
a.	10c rose carmine	—	—
	Block of four (2 or 3mm spacing)	310.00	32.50
	Margin block of 6, Impt. & P# & star	1,150.	
J50 D2 50c	**deep claret,** *Sept. 23, 1912*	600.00	75.00
	Block of four (2 or 3mm spacing)	2,500.	
	Margin block of 6, Impt. & P# & star	7,500.	

1914 *Perf. 10*

No.	Description	Unused	Used
J52 D2 1c	**carmine lake**	40.00	7.50
	deep carmine lake	40.00	7.50
a.	1c dull rose	40.00	7.50
	Block of four (2 or 3mm spacing)	165.00	32.00
	Margin block of 6, Impt. & P# & star	550.00	—
J53 D2 2c	**carmine lake**	32.50	20
a.	2c dull rose	32.50	20
b.	2c vermilion	32.50	20
	Block of four	135.00	1.00
	Margin block of 6, P# only	350.00	—
J54 D2 3c	**carmine lake**	425.00	20.00
a.	3c dull rose	425.00	20.00
	Block of four (2 or 3mm spacing)	1,800.	—
	Margin block of 6, Impt. & P# & star	4,500.	—
J55 D2 5c	**carmine lake**	25.00	1.50
a.	5c dull rose	25.00	1.50
	carmine rose	25.00	1.50
	deep claret	—	—
	Block of four (2 or 3mm spacing)	105.00	7.00
	Margin block of 6, Impt. & P# & star	285.00	—
J56 D2 10c	**carmine lake**	40.00	1.00
a.	10c dull rose	40.00	1.00
	carmine rose	40.00	1.00
	Block of four (2 or 3mm spacing)	165.00	4.75
	Margin block of 6, Impt. & P# & star	600.00	—
J57 D2 30c	**carmine lake**	140.00	12.00
	Block of four (2 or 3mm spacing)	575.00	50.00
	Margin block of 6, Impt. & P# & star	2,100.	—
J58 D2 50c	**carmine lake**	*5,500.*	375.00
	Block of four (2 or 3mm spacing)	*23,000.*	1,600.
	Margin block of 6, Impt. & P# & star	*40,000.*	

1916 Unwmk. *Perf. 10*

No.	Description	Unused	Used
J59 D2 1c	**rose**	1,100.	175.00
	Block of four (2 or 3mm spacing)	4,500.	750.00
	Margin block of 6, Impt. & P# & star	8,750.	
	Experimental bureau precancel, New Orleans		*125.00*
J60 D2 2c	**rose**	85.00	10.00
	Block of four	350.00	—
	Margin block of 6, P# only	800.00	—
	Experimental bureau precancel, New Orleans		12.50

1917 Unwmk. *Perf. 11*

No.	Description	Unused	Used
J61 D2 1c	**carmine rose**	1.75	8
	dull rose	1.75	8
a.	1c rose red	1.75	15
b.	1c deep claret	1.75	8
	claret brown	1.75	8
	Block of four (2 or 3mm spacing)	7.25	35
	Margin block of 6, Impt. & P# & star	85.00	—
	Margin block of 6, P# only	40.00	—
J62 D2 2c	**carmine rose**	1.50	5
a.	2c rose red	1.50	5
b.	2c deep claret	1.50	5
	claret brown	1.50	5
	Block of four	6.25	20
	Margin block of 6, P# only	35.00	—
	Double transfer	—	—
J63 D2 3c	**carmine rose**	8.50	8
a.	3c rose red	8.50	7
b.	3c deep claret	8.50	25

United States Postage Due stamps can be mounted in Scott's Platinum, National and Minuteman Albums.

		claret brown	8.50	25
		Block of four (2 or 3mm spacing)	35.00	30
		Margin block of 6, Impt. & P# & star	100.00	—
		Margin block of 6, P# only	85.00	—
J64	D2 5c	**carmine**	8.50	8
		carmine rose	8.50	8
a.		5c rose red	8.50	8
b.		5c deep claret	8.50	5
		claret brown	8.50	10
		Block of four (2 or 3mm spacing)	35.00	32
		Margin block of 6, Impt. & P# & star	100.00	—
		Margin block of 6, P# only	85.00	—
J65	D2 10c	**carmine rose**	12.50	20
a.		10c rose red	12.50	6
b.		10c deep claret	12.50	6
		claret brown	12.50	6
		Block of four (2 or 3mm spacing)	52.50	85
		Margin block of 6, Impt. & P# & star	125.00	—
		Margin block of 6, P# only	135.00	—
		Double transfer	—	—
J66	D2 30c	**carmine rose**	55.00	40
a.		30c deep claret	55.00	40
		claret brown	55.00	40
		Block of four (2 or 3mm spacing)	225.00	1.75
		Margin block of 6, Impt. & P# & star	525.00	—
		Margin block of 6, P# only	550.00	—
J67	D2 50c	**carmine rose**	75.00	12
a.		50c rose red	75.00	12
b.		50c deep claret	75.00	15
		claret brown	75.00	15
		Block of four (2 or 3mm spacing)	325.00	50
		Margin block of 6, Impt. & P# & star	750.00	—
		Margin block of 6, P# only	800.00	—

1925

J68	D2 ½c	**dull red,** *Apr. 13, 1925*	65	6
		Block of four	2.60	24
		Margin block of 6, P# only	11.00	—

D3

D4

1930 **Unwmk.** ***Perf. 11***

Design measures 19x22mm

J69	D3 ½c	**carmine**	3.00	1.00
		Margin block of 6, P#	35.00	—
J70	D3 1c	**carmine**	2.50	15
		Margin block of 6, P#	27.50	—
J71	D3 2c	**carmine**	3.00	15
		Margin block of 6, P#	40.00	—
J72	D3 3c	**carmine**	15.00	1.00
		Margin block of 6, P#	250.00	—
J73	D3 5c	**carmine**	14.00	1.50
		Margin block of 6, P#	225.00	—
J74	D3 10c	**carmine**	30.00	50
		Margin block of 6, P#	425.00	—
J75	D3 30c	**carmine**	85.00	1.00
		Margin block of 6, P#	1,000.	—
J76	D3 50c	**carmine**	100.00	30
		Margin block of 6, P#	1,250.	—

Design measures 22x19mm

J77	D4 $1	**carmine**	25.00	6
a.		$1 scarlet	20.00	6
		Margin block of 6, P#	275.00	—
J78	D4 $5	**carmine**	30.00	12
a.		$5 scarlet	25.00	12
b.		as "a," wet printing	27.50	12
		Margin block of 6, P#	375.00	—

See note on Wet and Dry Printings following No. 1029.

Type of 1930-31 Issue
Rotary Press Printing
Ordinary and Electric Eye Plates
Design measures 19x22½mm

1931 **Unwmk.** ***Perf. 11x10½***

J79	D3 ½c	**dull carmine**	75	8
a.		½c scarlet	75	8
		Margin block of 4, P#	22.50	—
J80	D3 1c	**dull carmine**	15	5
a.		1c scarlet	15	5
b.		as "a," wet printing	18	5
		Margin block of 4, P#	1.50	—
		Pair with full vertical gutter between	—	
J81	D3 2c	**dull carmine**	15	5
a.		2c scarlet	15	5
b.		as "a," wet printing	18	5
		Margin block of 4, P#	1.50	—
J82	D3 3c	**dull carmine**	25	5
a.		3c scarlet	25	5
b.		as "a," wet printing	28	5
		Margin block of 4, P#	2.00	—
J83	D3 5c	**dull carmine**	35	5
a.		5c scarlet	35	5
b.		as "a," wet printing	45	5
		Margin block of 4, P#	2.50	—
J84	D3 10c	**dull carmine**	1.10	5
a.		10c scarlet	1.10	5
b.		as "a," wet printing	1.25	5
		Margin block of 4, P#	6.00	—
J85	D3 30c	**dull carmine**	8.50	8
a.		30c scarlet	8.50	8
		Margin block of 4, P#	35.00	—
J86	D3 50c	**dull carmine**	9.50	6
a.		50c scarlet	9.50	6
		Margin block of 4, P#	50.00	—

Design measures 22½x19mm

1956 ***Perf. 10½x11***

J87	D4 $1	**scarlet**	40.00	20
		Margin block of 4, P#	300.00	—

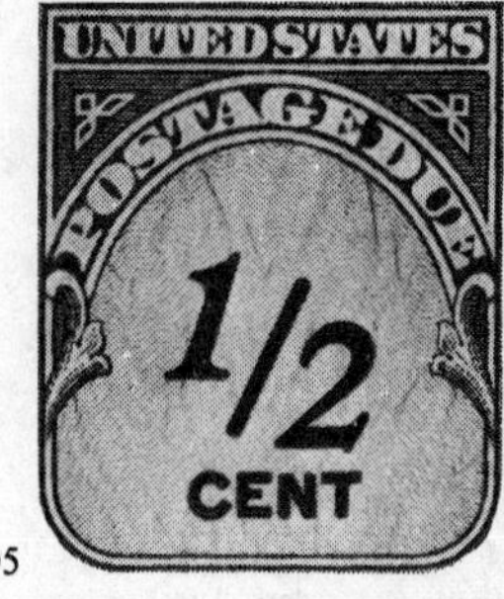

D5

Rotary Press Printing
Denominations added in black by rubber plates in an operation similar to precanceling.

1959, June 19 **Unwmk.** ***Perf. 11x10½***

Denomination in Black

J88	D5 ½c	**carmine rose**	1.25	85
		Margin block of 4, P#	165.00	—
J89	D5 1c	**carmine rose**	5	5
		Margin block of 4, P#	35	—
a.		"1 CENT" omitted	*400.00*	
b.		Pair, one without "1 CENT"	—	
J90	D5 2c	**carmine rose**	6	5
		Margin block of 4, P#	45	—
J91	D5 3c	**carmine rose**	7	5
		Margin block of 4, P#	50	—
a.		Pair, one without "3 CENTS"	—	
J92	D5 4c	**carmine rose**	8	5
		Margin block of 4, P#	60	—
J93	D5 5c	**carmine rose**	10	5
		Margin block of 4, P#	65	—
a.		Pair, one without "5 CENTS"	—	
J94	D5 6c	**carmine rose**	12	5
		Margin block of 4, P#	70	—
a.		Pair, one without "6 CENTS"	—	
		Pair with full vert. gutter between	—	
J95	D5 7c	**carmine rose**	14	6
		Margin block of 4, P#	80	—
J96	D5 8c	**carmine rose**	16	5
		Margin block of 4, P#	90	—
a.		Pair, one without "8 CENTS"	—	
J97	D5 10c	**carmine rose**	20	5
		Margin block of 4, P#	1.00	—
J98	D5 30c	**carmine rose**	55	5
		Margin block of 4, P#	2.75	—
J99	D5 50c	**carmine rose**	90	5
		Margin block of 4, P#	4.50	—

Straight Numeral Outlined in Black

J100	D5 $1	**carmine rose**	1.50	5
		Margin block of 4, P#	7.50	—
J101	D5 $5	**carmine rose**	8.00	15
		Margin block of 4, P#	40.00	—

The 2c, 4c, 7c and 8c exist in vertical pairs with numerals widely spaced. This spacing was intended to accommodate the gutter, but sometimes fell within the pane.

Rotary Press Printing

1978-85 ***Perf. 11x10½***

Denomination in Black

J102	D5 11c	**carmine rose,** *Jan. 2, 1978*	35	5
		Margin block of 4, P#	2.00	—
J103	D5 13c	**carmine rose,** *Jan. 2, 1978*	30	5
		Margin block of 4, P#	2.00	—
J104	D5 17c	**carmine rose,** *June 10, 1985*	40	5
		Margin block of 4, P#	15.00	—

OFFICES IN CHINA

Postage stamps of the 1917-19 U.S. series (then current) were issued to the U.S. Postal Agency, Shanghai, China, surcharged (as illustrated) at double the original value of the stamps. The surcharges on the 1919 issue are in black, except on the 7-cent and $1 which are surcharged in red ink.

These stamps were intended for sale at Shanghai at their surcharged value in local currency, valid for prepayment on mail despatched from the United States Postal Agency at Shanghai to addresses in the United States.

Stamps were first issued May 24, 1919, and were placed on sale at Shanghai on July 1, 1919. These stamps were not issued to postmasters in the United States. The Shanghai post office, according to the U.S.P.O. Bulletin was closed in December 1922. After the closing of the Shanghai office, the stamps were on sale at the Philatelic Agency in Washington, D.C. for a short time.

The postmarks of the China office included "U.S. Postal Agency Shanghai China" and "U.S.Pos. Service Shanghai China".

U. S. POSTAL AGENCY IN CHINA

United States Stamps Nos. 498 to 518 Surcharged

SHANGHAI
2¢
CHINA

1919 **Unwmk.** ***Perf. 11***

K1	A140 2c	on 1c **green**	20.00	22.50
		Block of four	82.50	100.00
		Margin block of six, P#	275.00	—
K2	A140 4c	on 2c **rose,** type I	20.00	22.50
		Block of four	82.50	100.00
		Margin block of six, P#	275.00	—
K3	A140 6c	on 3c **violet, type II**	37.50	50.00
		Block of four	155.00	235.00
		Margin block of six, P#	450.00	—
K4	A140 8c	on 4c **brown**	45.00	50.00
		Block of four	185.00	235.00
		Margin block of six, P#	550.00	—
K5	A140 10c	on 5c **blue**	50.00	57.50
		Block of four	210.00	250.00
		Margin block of six, P#	525.00	—
K6	A140 12c	on 6c **red orange**	60.00	72.50
		Block of four	250.00	325.00
		Margin block of six, P#	700.00	—
K7	A140 14c	on 7c **black**	65.00	80.00
		Block of four	270.00	375.00
		Margin block of six, P#	800.00	—
K8	A148 16c	on 8c **olive bister**	50.00	55.00
a.		16c on 8c olive green	45.00	47.50
		Block of four	210.00	275.00
		Margin block of six, P#	600.00	—
K9	A148 18c	on 9c **salmon red**	50.00	60.00

Block of four 210.00 300.00
Margin block of six, P# 650.00
K10 A148 20c on 10c **orange yellow** 45.00 52.50
Block of four 190.00 250.00
Margin block of six, P# 600.00
K11 A148 24c on 12c **brown carmine** 52.50 62.50
a. 24c on 12c claret brown 67.50 77.50
Block of four (brown carmine) 220.00 300.00
Margin block of six, P# 800.00
K12 A148 30c on 15c **gray** 65.00 80.00
Block of four 270.00 375.00
Margin block of six, P# 1,000.
K13 A148 40c on 20c **deep ultramarine** 100.00 125.00
Block of four 425.00 600.00
Margin block of six, P# 1,300.
K14 A148 60c on 30c **orange red** 90.00 110.00
Block of four 375.00 525.00
Margin block of six, P# 1,000.

K15 A148 $1 on 50c **light violet** 600.00 500.00
Block of four 2,500. 2,250.
Margin block of six, P# *10,000.*
K16 A148 $2 on $1 **violet brown** 425.00 425.00
Block of four 1,750. 2,000.
Margin block of four, arrow, right or left 1,850.
Margin block of six, P# *7,500.*
a. Double surcharge *2,500. 2,250.*

United States Stamps Nos. 498 and 528B Locally Surcharged

SHANGHAI
2 Cts.
CHINA

1922, July 3
K17 A140 2c on 1c **green** 90.00 75.00
Block of four 365.00 350.00
Margin block of six, P# 725.00
K18 A140 4c on 2c **carmine,** type VII 80.00 70.00
Block of four 325.00 350.00
Margin block of six, P# 675.00
"SHANGHAI" omitted —
"CHINA" only —

OFFICIAL

Official stamps were authorized by Act of Congress, approved March 3, 1873, abolishing the franking privilege. Stamps of special design for each government department to prepay postage on official matter were issued July 1, 1873. These stamps were supplanted on May 1, 1879, by penalty envelopes and on July 5, 1884, were declared obsolete. Postal Savings official stamps were used 1910-1914. The current Official Stamps series began in 1983.

DESIGNS. Official stamps of the 1870's have name of department at top. Large numerals form the central design of the Post Office Department stamps. Those for the other departments picture the same busts used in the regular postage issue: 1c Franklin, 2c Jackson, 3c Washington, 6c Lincoln, 7c Stanton, 10c Jefferson, 12c Clay, 15c Webster, 24c Scott, 30c Hamilton, 90c Perry, $2, $5, $10 and $20 Seward.

Designs of the various denominations are not identical, but resemble those illustrated.

PLATES. Plates of 200 subjects in two panes of 100 were used for Post Office Department 1c, 3c, 6c: Treasury Department 1c, 2c, 3c, and War Department 2c, 3c. Plates of 10 subjects were used for State Department $2, $5, $10 and $20. Plates of 100 subjects were used for all other Official stamps.

CANCELLATIONS. Odd or Town cancellations on Departmental stamps are relatively much scarcer than those appearing on the general issues of the same period. Town cancellations, especially on the 1873 issue, are scarce. The "Kicking Mule" cancellation is found used on stamps of the War Department and has also been seen on some stamps of the other Departments. Black is usual.

GRADE and CONDITION. Stamps from Scott O1-O126 are valued in the grade of fine-very fine. If unused, they will have at least most of their original gum. Scott O127 to date will have full original gum and be never-hinged. Examples that are fresh, well centered and (if unused) have full original gum sell at much higher prices.

Practically all official stamps of the 1870's exist imperforate, but little is known of their history.

SPECIAL PRINTING. In 1875 a Special printing of the Official stamps was made along with those of the regular issues. These stamps were overprinted "SPECIMEN". They are listed in the "Specimen" Stamps section.

Printed by the Continental Bank Note Co.
Thin Hard Paper
AGRICULTURE

Franklin — O1

1873 Engr. Unwmk. *Perf. 12*

O1 O1 1c **yellow** 65.00 35.00
golden yellow 67.50 37.50
olive yellow 70.00 40.00
On cover —
Block of four 300.00
Ribbed paper 75.00 40.00

CANCELLATIONS.
Magenta +7.50 | Town +7.50
Purple +7.50
Blue +5.00

O2 O1 2c **yellow** 45.00 15.00
golden yellow 47.50 16.00
olive yellow 52.50 17.50
On cover *1,100.*
Block of four 200.00
Ribbed paper 55.00 20.00

CANCELLATIONS.
Blue + 3.00 | Town +5.00
Red +15.00
Magenta + 5.00

O3 O1 3c **yellow** 40.00 3.50
golden yellow 42.50 4.00
olive yellow 45.00 4.50
On cover *600.00*
Block of four 185.00 —
Ribbed paper 50.00 6.00
Double transfer — —

CANCELLATIONS.
Blue + .50 | Town + 4.00
Purple + 1.00 | "Paid" +27.50
Magenta + 1.00 | Railroad +75.00
Violet + 1.00 | Numeral +35.00
Red + 12.00
Green +125.00

O4 O1 6c **yellow** 50.00 12.50
golden yellow 52.50 13.50
olive yellow 55.00 15.00
On cover *700.00*
Pair on cover —
Block of four 225.00

CANCELLATIONS.
Blue +3.00 | Town +7.00
Magenta +4.00 | Express Company —
Violet +4.00

O5 O1 10c **yellow** 110.00 47.50
golden yellow 115.00 50.00
olive yellow 125.00 52.00
On cover —
Block of four 500.00

CANCELLATIONS.
Purple +5.00 | Town +15.00
Blue +5.00

O6 O1 12c **yellow** 140.00 75.00
golden yellow 170.00 80.00
olive yellow 180.00 90.00
On cover —
Block of four 700.00

CANCELLATIONS.
Purple +10.00 | Town +20.00
Blue +10.00

O7 O1 15c **yellow** 110.00 50.00
golden yellow 115.00 52.50
olive yellow 120.00 57.50
Block of four 500.00 —

CANCELLATIONS.
| Purple +10.00

O8 O1 24c **yellow** 125.00 55.00
golden yellow 140.00 60.00
Block of four 550.00

CANCELLATIONS.
| Purple +10.00

O9 O1 30c **yellow** 165.00 85.00
golden yellow 175.00 90.00
oliven yellow 185.00 100.00
Block of four 725.00

CANCELLATIONS.
| Red +35.00

EXECUTIVE

Franklin — O2

1873

O10 O2 1c **carmine** 250.00 85.00
deep carmine 250.00 85.00
On cover *1,300.*
Block of four *5,000.*

CANCELLATIONS.
Purple +10.00 | Town +30.00
Blue +10.00
Red +50.00

O11 O2 2c **carmine** 165.00 55.00
deep carmine 165.00 55.00
On cover *1,500.*
Block of four *1,500.*
Double transfer — —

CANCELLATIONS.
Blue +10.00 | Red +50.00

O12 O2 3c **carmine** 190.00 50.00
a. 3c violet rose 165.00 50.00
On cover *700.00*
Block of four *950.00*

CANCELLATIONS.
Blue +10.00 | Town +25.00
Purple +10.00

O13 O2 6c **carmine** 350.00 160.00
pale carmine 350.00 160.00
deep carmine 350.00 160.00
On cover *2,000.*
Block of four *2,250.*

CANCELLATIONS.
Purple +15.00 | Town +50.00

O14 O2 10c **carmine** 275.00 150.00

pale carmine 275.00 150.00
deep carmine 275.00 150.00
On cover —
Block of four *2,250.*

CANCELLATIONS.
Blue +15.00 | Purple +15.00

INTERIOR

Franklin — O3

1873

O15 O3 1c **vermilion** 15.00 3.50
dull vermilion 15.00 3.50
bright vermilion 15.00 3.50
On cover 125.00
Block of four 65.00 —
Ribbed paper 18.50 4.50

CANCELLATIONS.
Purple + 1.00 | Town +3.00
Blue + 1.00
Red +12.50
Ultramarine + 8.00

O16 O3 2c **vermilion** 15.00 2.00
dull vermilion 15.00 2.00
bright vermilion 15.00 2.00
On cover 60.00
Block of four 60.00 12.50

CANCELLATIONS.
Purple + .75 | Town +2.00
Blue + .75
Red + 6.00

O17 O3 3c **vermilion** 25.00 2.00
dull vermilion 25.00 2.00
bright vermilion 25.00 2.00
On cover 40.00
Block of four 105.00 —
Ribbed paper 30.00 4.00

CANCELLATIONS.
Purple + 1.00 | Town + 2.00
Blue + 1.00 | Express Company +75.00
Red +15.00 | "Paid" +20.00
Green +65.00 | Fort —

O18 O3 6c **vermilion** 17.50 2.00
dull vermilion 17.50 2.00
bright vermilion 17.50 2.00
scarlet vermilion 17.50 3.00
On cover 85.00
Block of four 75.00 —

CANCELLATIONS.
Purple + 1.00 | Town +2.00
Blue + 1.00 | Express Company —
Red +15.00 | Railroad —
| Fort —

O19 O3 10c **vermilion** 16.00 4.00
dull vermilion 16.00 4.00
bright vermilion 16.00 4.00
On cover 225.00
Block of four 70.00 —

CANCELLATIONS.
Purple + 1.00 | Town +4.00
Blue + 1.00 | Fort —

O20 O3 12c **vermilion** 27.50 3.00
bright vermilion 27.50 3.00
On cover 275.00
Block of four 120.00 —

CANCELLATIONS.
Purple + 1.00 | Town +4.00
Magenta + 1.00 | Fort —
Blue + 1.00
Red +15.00

O21 O3 15c **vermilion** 40.00 6.00
bright vermilion 40.00 6.00
On cover *450.00*
Block of four 170.00 —
Double transfer 60.00 17.50

CANCELLATIONS.
Blue +1.50 | Town +5.00
Purple +1.50

O22 O3 24c **vermilion** 30.00 5.00
dull vermilion 30.00 5.00
bright vermilion 30.00 5.00
On cover *500.00*
Block of four 135.00 —

CANCELLATIONS.
Purple + 1.50 | Town +5.00

Blue + 1.50
Red +15.00

O23 O3 30c **vermilion** 40.00 6.00
bright vermilion 40.00 6.00
On cover —
Block of four 170.00 —

CANCELLATIONS.
Purple + 2.00 | Town +5.00
Blue + 2.00
Red +15.00

O24 O3 90c **vermilion** 90.00 10.00
bright vermilion 90.00 10.00
On cover —
Block of four 400.00 120.00
Double transfer —

CANCELLATIONS.
Purple +4.00 | Town +7.50
Blue +4.00

JUSTICE

Franklin — O4

1873

O25 O4 1c **purple** 40.00 20.00
dark purple 40.00 20.00
On cover *600.00*
Block of four 185.00 —

CANCELLATIONS.
Violet + 3.00 | Town + 7.50
Blue + 3.00
Red +20.00

O26 O4 2c **purple** 65.00 20.00
light purple 65.00 20.00
On cover —
Block of four 280.00

CANCELLATIONS.
Violet + 4.00 | Town +10.00
Blue + 4.00
Red +20.00

O27 O4 3c **purple** 65.00 6.00
dark purple 65.00 6.00
bluish purple 65.00 6.00
On cover *400.00*
Block of four 280.00 —
Double transfer —

CANCELLATIONS.
Purple + 2.00 | Town +5.00
Magenta + 2.00
Blue + 2.00
Red + 12.00
Green +100.00

O28 O4 6c **purple** 60.00 8.50
light purple 60.00 8.50
bluish purple 60.00 8.50
On cover *500.00*
Block of four 260.00 —

CANCELLATIONS.
Violet + 2.00 | Town +7.50
Purple + 2.00
Blue + 2.00
Red +15.00

O29 O4 10c **purple** 70.00 20.00
bluish purple 70.00 20.00
On cover *1,200.*
Block of four 325.00 —
Double transfer —

CANCELLATIONS.
Violet +4.00 | Town +10.00
Blue +4.00

O30 O4 12c **purple** 50.00 12.50
dark purple 50.00 12.50
On cover *800.00*
Block of four 225.00 —

CANCELLATIONS.
Purple +2.00 | Town +7.50
Blue +2.00

O31 O4 15c **purple** 110.00 45.00
On cover *900.00*
Block of four *575.00*
Double transfer — —

CANCELLATIONS.
Blue +5.00 | Town +10.00
Purple +5.00

O32 O4 24c **purple** 300.00 120.00
On cover *1,100.*
Block of four —

CANCELLATIONS.
Violet + 10.00 | Town +30.00
Purple + 10.00
Blue + 10.00
Red + 35.00

O33 O4 30c **purple** 275.00 67.50
On cover —
Block of four *1,400.*
Double transfer at top — —

CANCELLATIONS.
Blue + 10.00 | Town +30.00
Purple + 10.00
Red + 35.00

O34 O4 90c **purple** 400.00 160.00
dark purple 400.00 160.00
Block of four —

CANCELLATIONS.
Blue +25.00 | Violet +25.00

NAVY

Franklin — O5

1873

O35 O5 1c **ultramarine** 35.00 7.00
dark ultramarine 35.00 7.00
a. 1c dull blue 42.50 8.50
On cover *600.00*
Block of four 150.00

CANCELLATIONS.
Violet + 2.00 | Town + 7.50
Blue + 2.00 | Steamship +100.00
Red +20.00

O36 O5 2c **ultramarine** 25.00 6.00
dark ultramarine 25.00 6.00
a. 2c dull blue 32.50 7.50
gray blue 27.50 7.50
On cover *200.00*
Block of four 100.00 —
Double transfer —

The 2c deep green, both perforated and imperforate, is a trial color proof.

CANCELLATIONS.
Purple + 1.50 | Town +10.00
Violet + 1.50 | Steamship +85.00
Blue + 1.50
Red +15.00
Green +75.00

O37 O5 3c **ultramarine** 27.50 4.00
pale ultramarine 27.50 4.00
dark ultramarine 27.50 4.00
a. 3c dull blue 32.50 5.50
On cover *150.00*
Block of four 120.00 —
Double transfer —

CANCELLATIONS.
Violet + 1.50 | Town + 5.00
Blue + 1.50 | Blue town +15.00
Red +15.00 | Steamship +50.00

O38 O5 6c **ultramarine** 25.00 4.00
bright ultramarine 25.00 4.00
a. 6c dull blue 32.50 5.00
On cover *225.00*
Block of four 110.00 —
Vertical line through "N" of "Navy" (Pos. 2 & 6, plate 53) 57.50 10.00
Double transfer — —

CANCELLATIONS.
Violet + 1.50 | Town + 5.00
Purple + 1.50 | Steamship +65.00
Blue + 1.50
Red +17.50
Green +75.00

O39 O5 7c **ultramarine** 170.00 55.00
dark ultramarine 170.00 55.00
a. 7c dull blue 190.00 70.00
On cover —
Block of four 750.00
Double transfer — —

CANCELLATIONS.
Blue +10.00 | Town +15.00
Violet +10.00
Magenta +10.00
Red +40.00

O40 O5 10c **ultramarine** 35.00 11.00
dark ultramarine 35.00 11.00
a. 10c dull blue 40.00 13.00

On cover — *1,350.*
Block of four 150.00
Cracked plate 70.00 —
Ribbed paper 45.00 15.00

CANCELLATIONS.
Violet + 2.00 | Town +10.00
Blue + 2.00 | Steamship +85.00
Brown +20.00
Purple + 2.00
Red +25.00

O41 O5 12c **ultramarine** 45.00 7.00
pale ultramarine 45.00 7.00
dark ultramarine 45.00 7.00
On cover *1,500.*
Block of four 200.00
Double transfer of left side 90.00 —

CANCELLATIONS.
Purple + 2.50 | Town +10.00
Magenta + 2.50 | Supplementary Mail +80.00
Blue + 2.50 | Steamship +100.00
Red +25.00

O42 O5 15c **ultramarine** 75.00 18.00
dark ultramarine 75.00 18.00
Block of four 400.00

CANCELLATIONS.
Blue + 2.50 | Town +20.00
Red +35.00

O43 O5 24c **ultramarine** 75.00 20.00
dark ultramarine 75.00 20.00
a. 24c dull blue 85.00 —
Block of four 400.00

CANCELLATIONS.
Magenta + 5.00 | Town + 20.00
Blue + 5.00 | Steamship +100.00
Green +150.00

O44 O5 30c **ultramarine** 65.00 10.00
dark ultramarine 65.00 10.00
Block of four 325.00
Double transfer 95.00 20.00

CANCELLATIONS.
Blue + 4.00 | Town + 10.00
Red +30.00 | Supplementary Mail +125.00
Purple + 4.00
Violet + 4.00

O45 O5 90c **ultramarine** 300.00 57.50
Block of four 1,400.
a. Double impression *2,000.*

CANCELLATIONS.
Purple +15.00 | Town +25.00

POST OFFICE

Numeral of Value — O6

Stamps of the Post Office Department are often on paper with a gray surface. This is due to insufficient wiping of the excess ink off plates during printing.

1873

O47 O6 1c **black** 7.25 3.00
gray black 7.25 3.00
On cover 50.00
Block of four 32.50 —

CANCELLATIONS.
Purple + 1.00 | Town +3.50
Magenta + 1.00
Blue + 1.00
Red +12.50

O48 O6 2c **black** 7.00 2.50
gray black 7.00 2.50
On cover 50.00
Block of four 32.50 —
a. Double impression 300.00

CANCELLATIONS.
Magenta + 1.00 | Town +3.50
Purple + 1.00 | Blue town +7.50
Blue + 1.00
Red +12.50

O49 O6 3c **black** 2.50 55
gray black 2.50 55
On cover 25.00
Block of four 11.50 5.00
Cracked plate — —
Double transfer at bottom — —
Double paper — —
Vertical ribbed paper — —

CANCELLATIONS.
Purple + .75 | Town +1.50
Magenta + .75 | Railroad +25.00
Violet + .75 | "Paid" +12.00
Blue + .75
Ultramarine + 1.50
Red +10.00
Green +60.00

O50 O6 6c **black** 8.00 1.40
gray black 8.00 1.40
On cover 75.00
Block of four 35.00 —
a. Diagonal half used as 3c on cover *2,750.*
Vertical ribbed paper — 7.50

CANCELLATIONS.
Purple + .75 | Town + 2.50
Magenta + .75 | "Paid" +15.00
Blue + .75
Red +12.00

O51 O6 10c **black** 40.00 14.50
gray black 40.00 14.50
On cover *400.00*
Block of four 180.00 —

CANCELLATIONS.
Purple +3.50 | Red +15.00
Magenta +3.50 | Town +10.00
Blue +3.50

O52 O6 12c **black** 22.50 3.50
gray black 22.50 3.50
On cover 425.00
Block of four 100.00 —

CANCELLATIONS.
Purple + 1.00 | Town +4.00
Magenta + 1.00
Blue + 1.00
Red + 12.50

O53 O6 15c **black** 25.00 5.00
gray black 25.00 5.00
On cover *1,000.*
Block of four 110.00 —
a. Imperf., pair *600.00*
Double transfer 32.50 *12.00*

CANCELLATIONS.
Purple +1.50 | Town +7.50
Magenta +1.50
Blue +1.50

O54 O6 24c **black** 32.50 6.00
gray black 32.50 6.00
On cover *600.00*
Block of four 140.00 —
Double paper — —

CANCELLATIONS.
Purple + 1.50 | Town +7.50
Blue + 1.50
Red +20.00

O55 O6 30c **black** 32.50 5.50
gray black 32.50 5.50
On cover *800.00*
Block of four 140.00 —

CANCELLATIONS.
Purple + 1.50 | Town +12.50
Blue + 1.50
Red +20.00
Magenta + 1.50

O56 O6 90c **black** 47.50 7.50
gray black 47.50 7.50
Block of four 210.00 —
Double transfer — —
Double paper — —

CANCELLATIONS.
Purple +1.50 | Town +6.50
Magenta +1.50
Blue +1.50

STATE

Franklin — O7

1873

O57 O7 1c **dark green** 42.50 12.50
dark yellow green 42.50 12.50
light green 42.50 12.50
On cover —
Block of four 225.00

CANCELLATIONS.
Violet +2.00 | Town +7.50
Purple +2.00
Blue +2.00
Red +17.50

O58 O7 2c **dark green** 85.00 20.00
dark yellow green 85.00 20.00
yellow green — —
On cover *650.00*
Block of four —
Double transfer — —

CANCELLATIONS.
Purple + 5.00 | Town +10.00
Blue + 5.00 | Blue town +20.00
Red +30.00
Green +75.00

O59 O7 3c **bright green** 35.00 9.00
yellow green 35.00 9.00
dark green 35.00 9.00
On cover 450.00
First day cover, *July 1, 1873* —
Block of four 165.00 —
Double paper — —

CANCELLATIONS.
Purple + 1.50 | Town + 6.50
Blue + 1.50 | Blue town +10.00
Red +10.00

O60 O7 6c **bright green** 32.50 9.00
dark green 32.50 9.00
yellow green 32.50 9.00
On cover *550.00*
Block of four 140.00
Double transfer — —

CANCELLATIONS.
Purple + 2.00 | Town +7.50
Red +10.00

O61 O7 7c **dark green** 60.00 15.00
dark yellow green 60.00 15.00
On cover *1,000.*
Block of four 425.00
Ribbed paper 75.00 19.00

CANCELLATIONS.
Purple + 2.00 | Town +10.00
Blue + 2.00
Red +25.00

O62 O7 10c **dark green** 50.00 13.50
bright green 50.00 14.50
yellow green — —
On cover *1,200.*
Block of four *325.00*

CANCELLATIONS.
Purple + 2.50 | Town + 5.00
Magenta + 2.50 | Blue town +10.00
Blue + 2.50 | Numeral +15.00
Red +25.00

O63 O7 12c **dark green** 75.00 25.00
dark yellow green — —
On cover *1,400.*
Block of four 400.00

CANCELLATIONS.
Purple +5.00 | Town +15.00
Blue +5.00
Red +30.00

O64 O7 15c **dark green** 70.00 18.00
dark yellow green 70.00 18.00
On cover —
Block of four 350.00

CANCELLATIONS.
Purple + 2.50 | Town +15.00
Blue + 2.50
Red +20.00

O65 O7 24c **dark green** 175.00 55.00
dark yellow green 175.00 55.00
On cover *1,750.*
Block of four *850.00* —

CANCELLATIONS.
Purple +15.00 | Town +25.00
Blue +15.00
Red +65.00

O66 O7 30c **dark green** 160.00 40.00
dark yellow green 160.00 40.00
On cover —
Block of four — —

CANCELLATIONS.
Purple + 5.00 | Town +20.00
Blue + 5.00 | Blue town +30.00
Red +35.00

O67 O7 90c **dark green** 300.00 90.00
dark yellow green —
On cover —
Block of four —

CANCELLATIONS.
Purple +15.00 | Town +40.00
Blue +15.00
Red +75.00

The Catalogue editors cannot undertake to appraise, identify or judge the genuineness or condition of stamps.

William H. Seward — O8

O68 O8 $2 **green & black** 550.00 225.00
yellow green & black 550.00 225.00
On cover —
Block of four *17,000.*

CANCELLATIONS.

Blue	+ 25.00	Town	+ 75.00
Red	+125.00	Blue town	+150.00
Purple	+ 25.00	Manuscript	*100.00*

O69 O8 $5 **green & black** 4,250. 1,600.
dark green & black 4,250. 1,600.
yellow green & black 4,250. 1,600.
Block of four *20,000.*

CANCELLATIONS.

Blue	+250.00	Manuscript	*800.00*

O70 O8 $10 **green & black** 3,000. 1,000.
dark green & black 3,000. 1,000.
yellow green & black 3,000. 1,000.
Block of four *14,000.*

CANCELLATIONS.

Blue	+200.00	Manuscript	*600.00*

O71 O8 $20 **green & black** 2,250. 800.00
dark green & black 2,250. 800.00
yellow green & black 2,250. 800.00
Block of four *12,500.*
Block of four, ms. cancel *4,000.*

CANCELLATIONS.

Blue	+200.00	Manuscript	*400.00*

The design of Nos. O68 to O71 measures 25½x39½mm.

TREASURY

Franklin — O9

1873

O72 O9 1c **brown** 17.50 1.75
dark brown 17.50 1.75
yellow brown 17.50 1.75
On cover 85.00
Block of four 75.00 —
Double transfer 25.00 3.50

CANCELLATIONS.

Purple	+ 1.00	Town	+2.00
Magenta	+ 1.00	Blue town	+4.00
Blue	+ 1.00		
Red	+10.00		

O73 O9 2c **brown** 20.00 1.75
dark brown 20.00 1.75
yellow brown 20.00 1.75
On cover 75.00
Block of four 90.00 —
Double transfer — 5.00
Cracked plate 35.00 —

CANCELLATIONS.

Purple	+ 1.00	Town	+2.00
Magenta	+ 1.00	Blue town	+4.00
Blue	+ 1.00		
Red	+10.00		

O74 O9 3c **brown** 12.50 75
dark brown 12.50 75
yellow brown 12.50 75
On cover 30.00
First day cover, *July 1, 1873* —
Block of four 55.00 —
Double paper —
Shaded circle outside of right frame line — —

CANCELLATIONS.

Purple	+ .50	Town	+ 1.00
Magenta	+ .50	Railroad	+20.00
Blue	+ .50	"Paid"	+10.00
Ultramarine	+2.00		
Red	+3.50		

O75 O9 6c **brown** 17.50 1.50
dark brown 17.50 1.50
yellow brown 17.50 1.50
On cover 115.00
Block of four 80.00 —
Worn plate 18.50 2.50
Double transfer — —

CANCELLATIONS.

Purple	+ .50	Town	+1.50
Magenta	+ .50		
Blue	+ .50		
Ultramarine	+ 1.50		
Red	+ 5.00		
Green	+20.00		

O76 O9 7c **brown** 42.50 8.50
dark brown 42.50 8.50
yellow brown 42.50 8.50
On cover 750.00
Block of four 185.00

CANCELLATIONS.

Purple	+ 2.00	Town	+ 7.50
Blue	+ 2.00	Blue town	+12.50
Green	+60.00		

O77 O9 10c **brown** 42.50 3.00
dark brown 42.50 3.00
yellow brown 42.50 3.00
On cover 375.00
Block of four 185.00 —
Double paper —
Double transfer —

CANCELLATIONS.

Purple	+ 1.00	Town	+4.00
Magenta	+ 1.00	Blue town	+8.50
Blue	+ 1.00		
Ultramarine	+ 4.00		
Red	+12.00		

O78 O9 12c **brown** 42.50 1.75
dark brown 42.50 1.75
yellow brown 42.50 1.75
On cover 500.00
Block of four 185.00 —

CANCELLATIONS.

Purple	+ .50	Town	+2.50
Blue	+ .50		
Red	+10.00		
Green	+35.00		

O79 O9 15c **brown** 37.50 2.50
yellow brown 37.50 2.50
On cover 850.00
Block of four 160.00 —

CANCELLATIONS.

Blue	+ 1.00	Town	+ 2.50
Purple	+ 1.00	Blue town	+ 7.50
Red	+10.00	Numeral	+15.00

O80 O9 24c **brown** 185.00 35.00
dark brown 185.00 35.00
yellow brown 185.00 35.00
Block of four 800.00
Double transfer at top —

CANCELLATIONS.

Blue	+5.00	Town	+15.00
Magenta	+5.00	Blue town	+25.00

O81 O9 30c **brown** 62.50 3.00
dark brown 62.50 3.00
yellow brown 62.50 3.00
On cover *1,000.*
Block of four 270.00 —
Short transfer at top right — —

CANCELLATIONS.

Blue	+ 1.00	Black town	+3.50
Red	+12.00	Blue town	+7.50
Purple	+ 1.00		

O82 O9 90c **brown** 67.50 3.00
dark brown 67.50 3.00
yellow brown 67.50 3.00
Block of four 300.00 45.00
Double paper — —

CANCELLATIONS.

Purple	+1.00	Town	+3.50
Magenta	+1.00	Blue town	+7.50
Blue	+1.00		
Brown	+7.50		

WAR

Franklin — O10

1873

O83 O10 1c **rose** 60.00 3.25
rose red 60.00 3.25
On cover 125.00
Pair on cover 125.00
Block of four 260.00

CANCELLATIONS.

Purple	+ 1.00	Town	+ 3.50
Blue	+ 1.00	Fort	+50.00
Red	+15.00	Numeral	+12.50
		"Paid"	—

O84 O10 2c **rose** 55.00 4.50
rose red 55.00 4.50
On cover 70.00
Block of four 235.00 —
Ribbed paper 67.50 7.50

CANCELLATIONS.

Purple	+ 1.50	Town	+ 4.00
Magenta	+ 1.50	Fort	+50.00
Blue	+ 1.50		
Red	+15.00		

O85 O10 3c **rose** 50.00 1.00
rose red 50.00 1.00
On cover 40.00
Block of four 220.00 —

CANCELLATIONS.

Blue	+ 1.00	Town	+ 1.50
Purple	+ 1.00	Fort	+40.00
Magenta	+ 1.00	"Paid"	+12.00
Green	+35.00		

O86 O10 6c **rose** 200.00 2.00
pale rose 200.00 2.00
On cover 60.00
Block of four 950.00 —

CANCELLATIONS.

Purple	+ 1.50	Town	+ 3.50
Blue	+ 1.50	Blue town	+ 6.50
Red	+15.00	Fort	+40.00

O87 O10 7c **rose** 52.50 27.50
pale rose 52.50 27.50
rose red 52.50 27.50
On cover —
Block of four 220.00 —

CANCELLATIONS.

Purple	+2.50	Town	+7.50
Blue	+3.50		

O88 O10 10c **rose** 19.00 4.00
rose red 19.00 4.00
On cover —
Block of four 82.50 —
Cracked plate —

CANCELLATIONS.

Purple	+1.00	Town	+ 3.50
Blue	+1.00	Fort	+40.00

O89 O10 12c **rose** 52.50 2.00
On cover 300.00
Block of four 220.00
Ribbed paper 67.50 3.50

CANCELLATIONS.

Purple	+ 1.00	Town	+ 3.00
Magenta	+ 1.00	Fort	+35.00
Blue	+ 1.00		
Red	+10.00		

O90 O10 15c **rose** 12.50 2.50
pale rose 12.50 2.50
rose red 12.50 2.50
On cover 325.00
Block of four 55.00 20.00
Ribbed paper 17.50 4.50

CANCELLATIONS.

Purple	+ 1.00	Town	+ 2.50
Blue	+ 1.00	Fort	+30.00
Red	+10.00	Express Company	—

O91 O10 24c **rose** 12.50 3.00
pale rose 12.50 3.00
rose red 12.50 3.00
On cover —
Block of four 55.00 —

CANCELLATIONS.

Purple	+1.00	Town	+2.50
Blue	+1.00	Fort	+3.50

O92 O10 30c **rose** 17.50 2.50
rose red 17.50 2.50

On cover —
Block of four 72.50 25.00
Ribbed paper 22.50 5.00

CANCELLATIONS.
Purple +1.00 | Town + 2.50
Magenta +1.00 | Fort +35.00
Blue +1.00

O93 O10 90c **rose** 40.00 10.00
rose red 40.00 10.00
On cover *1,000.*
Block of four 170.00 —

CANCELLATIONS.
Purple +2.00 | Town + 7.50
Magenta +2.00 | Fort +90.00
Blue +2.00

Printed by the American Bank Note Co.

1879 **Soft Porous Paper**

AGRICULTURE

O94 O1 1c **yellow** (issued without gum) 1,400.
Block of four 6,000.
O95 O1 3c **yellow** 175.00 32.50
On cover —
Block of four 775.00

CANCELLATIONS.
Purple +5.00 | Town +17.50
Blue +5.00

INTERIOR

O96 O3 1c **vermilion** 125.00 65.00
pale vermilion 125.00 65.00
Block of four 550.00 —

CANCELLATIONS.
Blue +5.00 | Town +15.00

O97 O3 2c **vermilion** 2.50 1.00
pale vermilion 2.50 1.00
scarlet vermilion 2.50 1.00
On cover 35.00
Block of four 12.00 —

CANCELLATIONS.
Purple + .50 | Town + 1.50
Blue + .50 | Blue town + 3.00
Red +5.00 | Fort +25.00

O98 O3 3c **vermilion** 2.00 60
pale vermilion 2.00 60
On cover 30.00
Block of four 9.00 —

CANCELLATIONS.
Purple + .50 | Town +1.50
Blue + .50 | Blue town +3.00
Red +5.00 | Numeral +5.00

O99 O3 6c **vermilion** 3.00 1.50
pale vermilion 3.00 1.50
scarlet vermilion 3.00 1.50
On cover 200.00
Block of four 14.00 —

CANCELLATIONS.
Purple + .50 | Town +1.50
Blue + .50
Red +5.00

O100 O3 10c **vermilion** 32.50 17.50
pale vermilion 32.50 17.50
On cover *350.00*
Block of four 135.00

CANCELLATIONS.
Purple +5.00 | Town +10.00
Blue +5.00

O101 O3 12c **vermilion** 65.00 30.00
pale vermilion 65.00 30.00
On cover *550.00*
Block of four 275.00
O102 O3 15c **vermilion** 150.00 50.00
Block of four 625.00
On cover —
Double transfer 200.00 —

CANCELLATIONS.
| Purple +5.00

O103 O3 24c **vermilion** 1,200.
Block of four 5,000.

JUSTICE

1879
O106 O4 3c **bluish purple** 50.00 17.50
deep bluish purple 50.00 17.50
On cover 550.00
Block of four 220.00

CANCELLATIONS.
| Blue +5.00

O107 O4 6c **bluish purple** 110.00 60.00
Block of four 475.00

CANCELLATIONS.
Blue +10.00 | Town +20.00

POST OFFICE

O108 O6 3c **black** 7.50 1.75
gray black 7.50 1.75
On cover 40.00
Block of four 32.50 10.00

CANCELLATIONS.
Blue + 1.00 | Town + 2.00
Purple + 1.00 | "Paid" +12.00
Violet + 1.00
Magenta + 1.00
Green +40.00

TREASURY

O109 O9 3c **brown** 27.50 2.50
yellow brown 27.50 2.50
On cover 110.00
Block of four 120.00 —

CANCELLATIONS.
Purple +1.50 | Town +2.00
Blue +1.50 | Numeral +7.50

O110 O9 6c **brown** 50.00 13.50
yellow brown 50.00 13.50
dark brown 50.00 13.50
On cover 300.00
Block of four 210.00 —

CANCELLATIONS.
Purple +6.00
Magenta +6.00
Blue +6.00

O111 O9 10c **brown** 65.00 13.50
yellow brown 65.00 13.50
dark brown 65.00 13.50
On cover *900.00*
Block of four 275.00 —

CANCELLATIONS.
Purple +2.50 | Town +7.50
Blue +2.50

O112 O9 30c **brown** 750.00 100.00
Block of four 3,500.

CANCELLATIONS.
Blue +25.00 | Town +50.00

O113 O9 90c **brown** 775.00 100.00
dark brown 775.00 100.00
Block of four 3,750.

CANCELLATIONS.
Purple +25.00 | Town +75.00
Blue +25.00

WAR

1879
O114 O10 1c **rose red** 2.00 1.50
rose 2.00 1.50
dull rose red 2.00 1.50
brown rose 2.00 1.50
On cover 50.00
Block of four 9.00 8.00

CANCELLATIONS.
Purple +.50 | Town + 1.00
Blue +.50 | Fort +25.00

O115 O10 2c **rose red** 3.00 1.50
dark rose red 3.00 1.50
dull vermilion 3.00 1.75
On cover 40.00
Pair on cover —
Block of four 13.00 8.00

CANCELLATIONS.
Blue + .50 | Town + 2.00
Purple + .50 | Fort +25.00
Magenta + .50
Green +35.00

O116 O10 3c **rose red** 3.00 75
dull rose red 3.00 75
On cover 35.00
Pair on cover 40.00
Block of four 13.00 4.50
a. Imperf., pair *800.00*
b. Double impression 500.00
Double transfer 6.00 4.00

CANCELLATIONS.
Purple + .50 | Town + 1.00
Violet + .50 | Fort +25.00
Blue + .50
Red +5.00

O117 O10 6c **rose red** 2.50 70
dull rose red 2.50 70
dull vermilion — —
On cover 50.00
Block of four 10.50 6.00

CANCELLATIONS.
Purple +.50 | Town + 1.00
Blue +.50 | Fort +25.00
| Numeral + 7.50

O118 O10 10c **rose red** 20.00 7.50
dull rose red 20.00 7.50
On cover —
Block of four 85.00

CANCELLATIONS.
| Town + 5.00
| Fort +45.00

O119 O10 12c **rose red** 15.00 3.00
dull rose red 15.00 3.00
brown rose 15.00 3.00
On cover —
Block of four 62.50 20.00

CANCELLATIONS.
Purple + 1.00 | Town + 2.50
Violet + 1.00 | Fort +40.00
Red +10.00

O120 O10 30c **rose red** 47.50 25.00
dull rose red 47.50 25.00
On cover —
Block of four 200.00 —

CANCELLATIONS.
| Town +10.00
| Fort +80.00

POSTAL SAVINGS MAIL

The Act of Congress, approved June 25, 1910, establishing postal savings depositories, provided: "Sec. 2. That the Postmaster General is hereby directed to prepare and issue special stamps of the necessary denominations for use, in lieu of penalty or franked envelopes, in the transmittal of free mail resulting from the administration of this act."

The use of postal savings official stamps was discontinued by the Act of Congress, approved September 23, 1914. The unused stamps in the hands of postmasters were returned and destroyed.

O11

1910-11 **Engr.** **Wmk. 191**
O121 O11 2c **black,** *Dec. 22, 1910* 9.00 1.10
On cover 10.00
Block of four (2mm spacing) 40.00 6.00
Block of four (3mm spacing) 38.50 5.00
Margin block of 6, Impt. & P# & Star 225.00
Double transfer 12.50 2.00
O122 O11 50c **dark green,** *Feb. 1, 1911* 110.00 25.00
On cover 150.00
Block of four (2mm spacing) 465.00 150.00
Block of four (3mm spacing) 450.00 150.00
Margin block of 4, arrow 475.00
Margin block of 6, Impt. & P# & Star 2,200.
O123 O11 $1 **ultramarine,** *Feb. 1, 1911* 100.00 7.00
On cover 85.00
Block of four (2mm spacing) 425.00 40.00
Block of four (3mm spacing) 410.00 40.00
Margin block of 4, arrow 450.00
Margin block of 6, Impt. & P# & Star 2,000. 350.00

Wmk. 190

O124 O11 1c **dark violet,** *March 27, 1911* 5.50 1.00
On cover 10.00
Block of four (2mm spacing) 24.00 4.50
Block of four (3mm spacing) 23.50 4.25
Margin block of 6, Impt. & P# & Star 120.00
O125 O11 2c **black** 30.00 3.50
On cover 17.50
Block of four (2mm spacing) 125.00 17.50
Block of four (3mm spacing) 122.50 17.50
Margin block of 6, Impt. & P# & Star 550.00
Double transfer 35.00 4.50
O126 O11 10c **carmine,** *Feb. 1, 1911* 10.00 1.00
On cover 10.00
Block of four (2mm spacing) 37.50 5.50
Block of four (3mm spacing) 36.00 5.00
Margin block of 6, Impt. & P# & Star 250.00
Double transfer 15.00 2.50

OFFICIAL MAIL

O12

Designed by Bradbury Thompson

ENGRAVED

1983, Jan. 12-1985 ***Perf. 11x10½, 11 (14c)***
O127 O12 1c **red, blue & blk** 5 10
FDC, Washington, DC 75
P# block of 4, UL or UR 25
O128 O12 4c **red, blue & blk** 8 15
FDC, Washington, DC 75
P# block of 4, LR only 40
O129 O12 13c **red, blue & blk** 26 40
FDC, Washington, DC 60
P# block of 4, UR only 1.30
O129A O12 14c **red, blue & blk,** *May 15, 1985* 28 50
FDC, Washington, DC 65
O130 O12 17c **red, blue & blk** 34 50
FDC, Washington, DC 75
P# block of 4, LL only 1.70
O132 O12 $1 **red, blue & blk** 1.75 2.00
FDC, Washington, DC 2.25
P# block of 4, UL only 8.75

O133	O12 $5	**red, blue & blk**	9.00	9.00
		FDC, Washington, DC		12.50
		P# block of 4, LL only	45.00	

No. O129A does not have a "c" after the "14."

Coil Stamps
Perf. 10 Vert.

O135	O12 20c	**red, blue & blk**	2.00	40
		FDC, Washington, DC		75
		Pair	4.00	—
		P# strip of 3, P# 1	20.00	
a.		Imperf., pair	—	
O136	O12 22c	**red, blue & blk,** *May 15, 1985*	44	—
		FDC, Washington, DC		80
		Pair	90	

Inscribed: Postal Card Rate D

1985, Feb. 4 ***Perf. 11***

O138	O12 (14c)	**red, blue & blk**	3.50	—
		FDC, Washington, DC		65
		P# block of 4, LR only	30.00	—

Frame line completely around the design — O13

Insribed: No. O139, Domestic Letter Rate D. No. O140, Domestic Mail E.

Coil Stamps

1985-88 Litho., Engr. (#O139) ***Perf. 10 Vert.***

O138A	O13 15c	**red, blue & blk,** *June 11, 1988*	30	—
		FDC, Corpus Christi, TX		65
		Pair	60	
O138B	O13 20c	**red, blue & blk,** *May 19, 1988*	40	—
		FDC, Washington		75

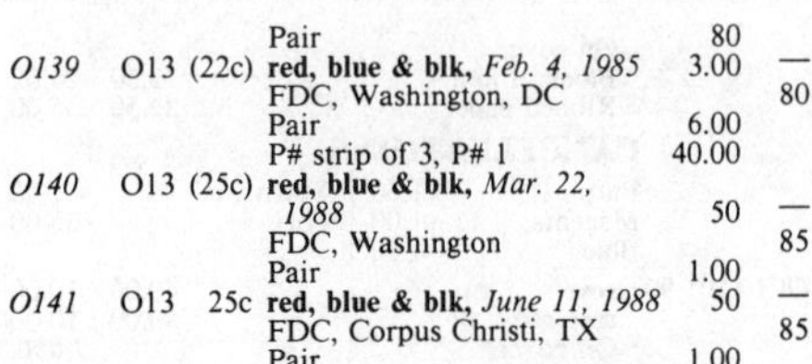

		Pair	80	
O139	O13 (22c)	**red, blue & blk,** *Feb. 4, 1985*	3.00	—
		FDC, Washington, DC		80
		Pair	6.00	
		P# strip of 3, P# 1	40.00	
O140	O13 (25c)	**red, blue & blk,** *Mar. 22, 1988*	50	—
		FDC, Washington		85
		Pair	1.00	
O141	O13 25c	**red, blue & blk,** *June 11, 1988*	50	—
		FDC, Corpus Christi, TX		85
		Pair	1.00	

First day cancellations was applied to 137,721 covers bearing Nos. O138A and O141.

Plates of 400 in four panes of 100

1989, July 5 Litho. ***Perf. 11***

O143	O13 1c	**red, blue & black**	5	—
		FDC, Washington, DC		40

NEWSPAPER

First issued in September 1865 for prepayment of postage on bulk shipments of newspapers and periodicals. From 1875 on, the stamps were affixed to memorandums of mailing, canceled and retained by the post office. Discontinued on July 1, 1898.

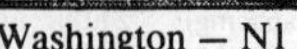

Washington — N1

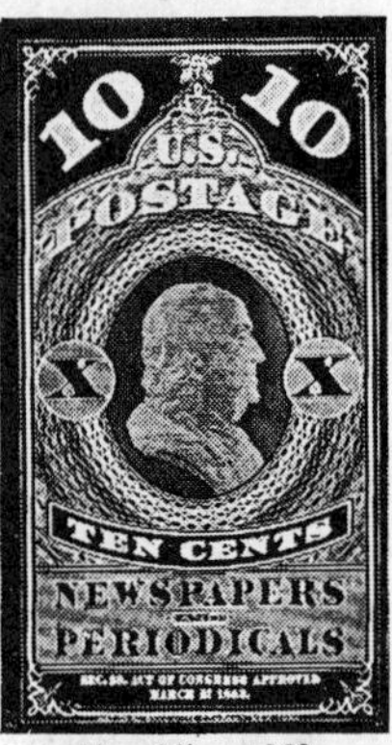

Franklin — N2

Lincoln — N3

(Illustrations N1, N2 and N3 are half the size of the stamps.)

Printed by the National Bank Note Co.
Plates of 20 subjects in two panes of 10 each.

Typographed and Embossed

1865 Unwmk. ***Perf. 12***

Thin hard paper, without gum

Size of design: 51x95mm

Colored Border

PR1	N1 5c	**dark blue**	150.00	—
a.		5c light blue	165.00	—
		blue	140.00	—
		Block of four	700.00	—
PR2	N2 10c	**blue green**	70.00	—
a.		10c green	70.00	—
		Block of four	350.00	—
b.		Pelure paper	75.00	—
PR3	N3 25c	**orange red**	70.00	—
a.		25c carmine red	70.00	—
		Block of four	350.00	—
b.		Pelure paper	75.00	—

White Border

Yellowish paper

PR4	N1 5c	**light blue**	35.00	30.00
		blue	35.00	30.00
a.		5c dark blue	25.00	30.00
		Block of four	220.00	
b.		Pelure paper	40.00	—

REPRINTS OF 1865 ISSUE

Printed by the Continental Bank Note Co.

1875 ***Perf. 12***

Hard white paper, without gum

5c White Border, 10c and 25c Colored Border

PR5	N1 5c	**dull blue** (6395)	60.00
		dark blue	60.00
		Block of four	300.00
a.		Printed on both sides	—
PR6	N2 10c	**dark bluish green** (8515)	37.50
		deep green	37.50
		Block of four	160.00
a.		Printed on both sides	*1,500.*
PR7	N3 25c	**dark carmine** (7434)	65.00
		dark carmine red	65.00
		Block of four	285.00

Printed by the American Bank Note Co.
Soft porous paper
White Border

1880

PR8	N1 5c	**dark blue**	110.00
		Block of four	450.00

The Continental Bank Note Co. made another special printing from new plates, which did not have the colored border. These exist imperforate and perforated, but they were not regularly issued.

Statue of Freedom on Capitol Dome, by Thomas Crawford — N4

"Justice" — N5

Ceres — N6

Values for cancellation varieties are for specimens off cover.

"Victory" — N7

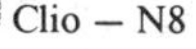
Clio — N8

Minerva — N9

Vesta — N10

"Peace" — N11

"Commerce" N12

Hebe — N13

Indian Maiden — N14

Printed by the Continental Bank Note Co.
Plates of 100 subjects in two panes of 50 each
Size of design: 24x35mm

1875, Jan. 1 **Engr.** ***Perf. 12***

Thin hard paper

No.	Design	Denom.	Color	Unused	Used
PR9	N4	2c	**black**	12.50	11.00
			gray black	12.50	11.00
			greenish black	12.50	11.00
			Block of four	57.50	65.00
PR10	N4	3c	**black**	16.00	14.50
			gray black	16.00	14.50
			Block of four	70.00	65.00
PR11	N4	4c	**black**	14.00	12.50
			gray black	14.00	12.50
			greenish black	14.00	12.50
			Block of four	60.00	
PR12	N4	6c	**black**	18.00	17.00
			gray black	18.00	17.00
			greenish black	18.00	17.00
			Block of four	80.00	
PR13	N4	8c	**black**	25.00	22.50
			gray black	25.00	22.50
			greenish black	25.00	22.50
PR14	N4	9c	**black**	55.00	50.00
			gray black	55.00	50.00
			Double transfer at top	65.00	60.00
PR15	N4	10c	**black**	25.00	20.00
			gray black	25.00	20.00
			greenish black	25.00	20.00
			Block of four	120.00	
PR16	N5	12c	**rose**	55.00	40.00
			pale rose	55.00	40.00
PR17	N5	24c	**rose**	67.50	45.00
			pale rose	67.50	45.00
PR18	N5	36c	**rose**	72.50	50.00
			pale rose	72.50	50.00
PR19	N5	48c	**rose**	135.00	85.00
			pale rose	135.00	85.00
PR20	N5	60c	**rose**	65.00	45.00
			pale rose	65.00	45.00
PR21	N5	72c	**rose**	165.00	110.00
			pale rose	165.00	110.00
PR22	N5	84c	**rose**	250.00	135.00
			pale rose	250.00	135.00
PR23	N5	96c	**rose**	135.00	100.00
			pale rose	135.00	100.00
PR24	N6	$1.92	**dark brown**	185.00	125.00
PR25	N7	$3	**vermilion**	240.00	135.00
PR26	N8	$6	**ultramarine**	400.00	
			dull ultramarine	400.00	165.00
PR27	N9	$9	**yellow**	525.00	225.00
PR28	N10	$12	**blue green**	650.00	300.00
PR29	N11	$24	**dark gray violet**	650.00	325.00
PR30	N12	$36	**brown rose**	675.00	375.00
PR31	N13	$48	**red brown**	875.00	500.00
PR32	N14	$60	**violet**	875.00	425.00

Special Printing of 1875 Issue
Hard white paper, without gum

1875 ***Perf. 12***

No.	Design	Denom.	Color	Unused
PR33	N4	2c	**gray black** *(19,514+)*	70.00
			Horizontally ribbed paper	70.00
PR34	N4	3c	**gray black** *(6952)*	75.00
			Block of four	—
			Horizontally ribbed paper	85.00
PR35	N4	4c	**gray black** *(4451)*	90.00
			Block of four	450.00
PR36	N4	6c	**gray black** *(2348)*	125.00
PR37	N4	8c	**gray black** *(1930)*	140.00
PR38	N4	9c	**gray black** *(1795)*	165.00
PR39	N4	10c	**gray black** *(1499)*	200.00
			Horizontally ribbed paper	220.00
PR40	N5	12c	**pale rose** *(1313)*	225.00
PR41	N5	24c	**pale rose** *(411)*	300.00
PR42	N5	36c	**pale rose** *(330)*	425.00
PR43	N5	48c	**pale rose** *(268)*	475.00
PR44	N5	60c	**pale rose** *(222)*	550.00
PR45	N5	72c	**pale rose** *(174)*	700.00
PR46	N5	84c	**pale rose** *(164)*	725.00
PR47	N5	96c	**pale rose** *(141)*	875.00
PR48	N6	$1.92	**dark brown** *(41)*	*2,750.*
PR49	N7	$3	**vermilion** *(20)*	*5,750.*
PR50	N8	$6	**ultramarine** *(14)*	*6,750.*
PR51	N9	$9	**yellow** *(4)*	*13,500.*
PR52	N10	$12	**blue green** *(5)*	*12,500.*
PR53	N11	$24	**dark gray violet** *(2)*	—
PR54	N12	$36	**brown rose** *(2)*	—
PR55	N13	$48	**red brown** *(1)*	—
PR56	N14	$60	**violet** *(1)*	—

All values of this issue, Nos. PR33 to PR56, exist imperforate but were not regularly issued.

Numbers in parenthesis are quantities issued.

\+ This quantity may include the 1883 Re-issue.

Printed by the American Bank Note Co.
Soft porous paper

1879 **Unwmk.** ***Perf. 12***

No.	Design	Denom.	Color	Unused	Used
PR57	N4	2c	**black**	6.00	4.50
			gray black	6.00	4.50
			greenish black	6.00	4.50
			Block of four	27.50	
			Imperf., pair	—	
			Double transfer at top	8.50	8.50
			Cracked plate	—	—
PR58	N4	3c	**black**	7.50	5.00
			gray black	7.50	5.00
			intense black	7.50	5.00
			Block of four	35.00	
			Imperf., pair	—	
			Double transfer at top	9.00	9.00
PR59	N4	4c	**black**	7.50	5.00
			gray black	7.50	5.00
			intense black	7.50	5.00

No.	Design	Denom.	Color / Variety	Unused	Used
			greenish black	7.50	5.00
			Block of four	35.00	
			Imperf., pair	—	
			Double transfer at top	9.00	9.00
PR60	N4	6c	**black**	15.00	11.00
			gray black	15.00	11.00
			intense black	15.00	11.00
			greenish black	15.00	11.00
			Block of four	65.00	
			Imperf., pair	—	
			Double transfer at top	17.50	17.50
PR61	N4	8c	**black**	15.00	11.00
			gray black	15.00	11.00
			greenish black	15.00	11.00
			Block of four	65.00	
			Imperf., pair	—	
			Double transfer at top	17.50	15.00
PR62	N4	10c	**black**	15.00	11.00
			gray black	15.00	11.00
			greenish black	15.00	11.00
			Block of four	65.00	
			Imperf., pair	—	
			Double transfer at top	17.50	
PR63	N5	12c	**red**	45.00	25.00
			Block of four	200.00	
PR64	N5	24c	**red**	45.00	22.50
			Block of four	200.00	
PR65	N5	36c	**red**	150.00	95.00
			Block of four	650.00	
PR66	N5	48c	**red**	115.00	60.00
PR67	N5	60c	**red**	85.00	60.00
			Block of four	350.00	
	a.		Imperf., pair	*600.00*	
PR68	N5	72c	**red**	185.00	115.00
PR69	N5	84c	**red**	140.00	85.00
			Block of four	—	
PR70	N5	96c	**red**	100.00	60.00
			Block of four	450.00	
PR71	N6	$1.92	**pale brown**	80.00	55.00
			brown	80.00	55.00
			Block of four	375.00	
			Cracked plate	125.00	
			Imperf., pair	—	
PR72	N7	$3	**red vermilion**	80.00	55.00
			Block of four	375.00	
			Imperf., pair	—	
PR73	N8	$6	**blue**	140.00	90.00
			ultramarine	140.00	90.00
			Imperf., pair	—	
PR74	N9	$9	**orange**	95.00	60.00
			Imperf., pair	—	
PR75	N10	$12	**yellow green**	140.00	85.00
			Imperf., pair	—	
PR76	N11	$24	**dark violet**	185.00	110.00
			Imperf., pair	—	
PR77	N12	$36	**Indian red**	225.00	135.00
			Imperf., pair	—	
PR78	N13	$48	**yellow brown**	300.00	165.00
			Imperf., pair	—	
PR79	N14	$60	**purple**	325.00	165.00
			bright purple	325.00	165.00
			Imperf., pair	—	

Imperforate stamps of this issue, except No. PR67a, were not regularly issued.

Special Printing of 1879 Issue

1883

No.	Design	Denom.	Color / Variety	Unused	Used
PR80	N4	2c	**intense black**	175.00	
			Block of four	700.00	

Printed by the American Bank Note Co.

1885, July 1 **Unwmk.** ***Perf. 12***

No.	Design	Denom.	Color / Variety	Unused	Used
PR81	N4	1c	**black**	8.50	5.00
			gray black	8.50	5.00
			intense black	8.50	5.00
			Block of four	40.00	
			Imperf., pair	—	
			Double transfer at top	11.00	8.50
PR82	N5	12c	**carmine**	27.50	12.50
			deep carmine	27.50	12.50
			rose carmine	27.50	12.50
			Block of four	120.00	
			Imperf., pair	—	
PR83	N5	24c	**carmine**	30.00	15.00
			deep carmine	30.00	15.00
			rose carmine	30.00	15.00
			Block of four	130.00	
			Imperf., pair	—	
PR84	N5	36c	**carmine**	42.50	17.50
			deep carmine	42.50	17.50
			rose carmine	42.50	17.50
			Block of four	180.00	
			Imperf., pair	—	
PR85	N5	48c	**carmine**	60.00	30.00
			deep carmine	60.00	30.00
			Block of four	250.00	
			Imperf., pair	—	
PR86	N5	60c	**carmine**	85.00	40.00
			deep carmine	85.00	40.00
			Block of four	375.00	
			Imperf., pair	—	
PR87	N5	72c	**carmine**	95.00	45.00
			deep carmine	95.00	45.00
			rose carmine	95.00	45.00
			Block of four	425.00	
			Imperf., pair	—	
PR88	N5	84c	**carmine**	200.00	110.00
			rose carmine	200.00	110.00
			Block of four	825.00	
			Imperf., pair	—	
PR89	N5	96c	**carmine**	140.00	85.00
			rose carmine	140.00	85.00
			Block of four	600.00	
			Imperf., pair	—	

Imperforate stamps of the 1885 issue were not regularly issued.

Printed by the Bureau of Engraving and Printing

1894 **Unwmk.** ***Perf. 12***

Soft wove paper

No.	Design	Denom.	Color / Variety	Unused	Used
PR90	N4	1c	**intense black**	42.50	
			Block of four	185.00	
			Double transfer at top	52.50	
PR91	N4	2c	**intense black**	42.50	
			Block of four	185.00	
			Double transfer at top	52.50	
PR92	N4	4c	**intense black**	60.00	
			Block of four	275.00	
PP93	N4	6c	**intense black**	850.00	
			Block of four	—	
PR94	N4	10c	**intense black**	110.00	
			Block of four	500.00	
PR95	N5	12c	**pink**	450.00	—
			Block of four	2,000.	
PR96	N5	24c	**pink**	400.00	
			Block of four	1,750.	
PR97	N5	36c	**pink**	*2,750.*	
			Block of four	—	
PR98	N5	60c	**pink**	*2,750.*	—
			Block of four	—	
PR99	N5	96c	**pink**	*4,000.*	
PR100	N7	$3	**scarlet**	*5,500.*	
			Block of four	—	
PR101	N8	$6	**pale blue**	*6,250.*	*3,000.*

Statue of Freedom on Capitol Dome, by Thomas Crawford — N15

"Justice" — N16

"Victory" N17

Clio — N18

Vesta — N19

"Peace" — N20

Values quoted in this catalogue are for stamps graded at Fine-Very Fine and with no faults. An illustrated guide to grade is provided in introductory material, beginning on Page V.

"Commerce"
N21

Indian Maiden
N22

The Scott Catalogue value is a retail price, what you could expect to pay for the stamp in a grade of Fine-Very Fine. The value listed is a reference which reflects recent actual dealer selling price.

1895, Feb. 1 Unwmk. *Perf. 12*
Size of designs: 1c-50c, 21x34mm. $2-$100, 24x35mm.

PR102	N15	1c	**black**	25.00	7.50
			Block of four	105.00	32.50
PR103	N15	2c	**black**	25.00	7.50
			gray black	25.00	7.50
			Block of four	110.00	—
			Double transfer at top	32.50	—
PR104	N15	5c	**black**	35.00	12.50
			gray black	35.00	12.50
			Block of four	150.00	
PR105	N15	10c	**black**	75.00	32.50
			Block of four	325.00	
PR106	N16	25c	**carmine**	100.00	35.00
			Block of four	425.00	
PR107	N16	50c	**carmine**	235.00	95.00
			Block of four	970.00	
PR108	N17	$2	**scarlet**	275.00	65.00
PR109	N18	$5	**ultramarine**	375.00	150.00
PR110	N19	$10	**green**	350.00	165.00
PR111	N20	$20	**slate**	675.00	300.00
PR112	N21	$50	**dull rose**	700.00	300.00
PR113	N22	$100	**purple**	775.00	350.00

1895-97 Wmk. 191 *Perf. 12*

PR114	N15	1c	**black,** *Jan. 11, 1896*	3.50	3.00
			gray black	3.50	3.00
			Block of four	15.00	—
PR115	N15	2c	**black,** *Nov. 21, 1895*	4.00	3.50
			gray black	4.00	3.50
			Block of four	17.50	—
PR116	N15	5c	**black,** *Feb. 12, 1896*	6.00	5.00
			gray black	6.00	5.00
			Block of four	25.00	—
PR117	N15	10c	**black,** *Sept. 13, 1895*	4.00	3.50
			gray black	4.00	3.50
			Block of four	18.00	—
PR118	N16	25c	**carmine,** *Oct. 11, 1895*	8.00	8.00
			lilac rose	8.00	8.00
			Block of four	35.00	—
PR119	N16	50c	**carmine,** *Sept. 19, 1895*	10.00	12.50
			rose carmine	10.00	12.50
			lilac rose	10.00	12.50
			Block of four	45.00	—
PR120	N17	$2	**scarlet,** *Jan. 23, 1897*	12.00	15.00
			scarlet vermilion	12.00	15.00
			Block of four	55.00	—
PR121	N18	$5	**dark blue,** *Jan. 16, 1896*	20.00	25.00
	a.		$5 light blue	100.00	45.00
			Block of four	85.00	
PR122	N19	$10	**green,** *Mar. 5, 1896*	18.00	25.00
			Block of four	75.00	—
PR123	N20	$20	**slate,** *Jan. 27, 1896*	20.00	27.50
			Block of four	82.50	—
PR124	N21	$50	**dull rose,** *July 31, 1897*	25.00	30.00
			Block of four	105.00	
PR125	N22	$100	**purple,** *Jan. 23, 1896*	30.00	37.50
			Block of four	130.00	

Nos. PR102-PR125 were printed from plates with guide lines and arrows both vertical and horizontal.

In 1899 the Government sold 26,989 sets of these stamps, but, as the stock of high values was not sufficient to make up the required number, an additional printing was made of the $5, $10, $20, $50 and $100. These are virtually indistinguishable from earlier printings.

The use of newspaper and periodical stamps was discontinued on July 1, 1898.

POSTAL NOTE

Postal notes were issued in amounts up to $10 to supplement the regular money order service. Postal note stamps were affixed and canceled by the clerk to make up fractions of a dollar. They were discontinued March 31, 1951.

MO1

ROTARY PRESS PRINTING

1945, Feb. 1 Unwmk. *Perf. 11x10½*

PN1	MO1	1c	**black** (155950-51)	10	5
PN2	MO1	2c	**black** (156003-04)	15	5
PN3	MO1	3c	**black** (156062-63)	20	5
PN4	MO1	4c	**black** (156942-43)	25	5
PN5	MO1	5c	**black** (156261-62)	35	5
PN6	MO1	6c	**black** (156064-65)	40	5
PN7	MO1	7c	**black** (156075-76)	50	5
PN8	MO1	8c	**black** (156077-78)	65	5
PN9	MO1	9c	**black** (156251-52)	70	5
PN10	MO1	10c	**black** (156274-75)	85	5
PN11	MO1	20c	**black** (156276-77)	1.65	5
PN12	MO1	30c	**black** (156303-04)	2.25	5
PN13	MO1	40c	**black** (156283-84)	2.75	6
PN14	MO1	50c	**black** (156322-23)	3.25	5
PN15	MO1	60c	**black** (156324-25)	4.50	5
PN16	MO1	70c	**black** (156344-45)	5.00	5
PN17	MO1	80c	**black** (156326-27)	6.00	8
PN18	MO1	90c	**black** (156352-53)	6.50	8

Blocks of four and plate number blocks of four are valued at 4 and 15 times the unused single value.

Postal note stamps exist on postal note cards with first day cancellation.

Numbers in parenthesis are plate Nos.

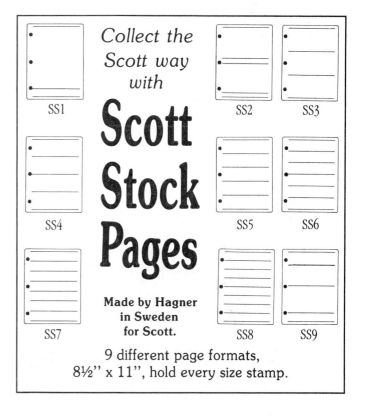

PARCEL POST

The Act of Congress approved August 24, 1912, created postage rates on fourth-class mail weighing 4 ounces or less at 1 cent per ounce or fraction. On mail over 4 ounces, the rate was by the pound. These rates were to be prepaid by distinctive postage stamps. Under this provision, the Post Office Department prepared 12 parcel post and 5 parcel post due stamps, usable only on parcel post packages starting January 1, 1913.

With the approval of the Interstate Commerce Commission, the Postmaster General directed, in Order No. 7241 dated June 26, 1913, and effective July 1, 1913, that regular postage stamps should be valid on parcels. Parcel post stamps then became usable as regular stamps.

Parcel post and parcel post due stamps remained on sale, but no further printings were made. Remainders, consisting of 3,510,345 of the 75c, were destroyed in September 1921.

The 20c was the first postage stamp of any country to show an airplane.

Post Office Clerk — PP1

City Carrier — PP2

Railway Postal Clerk — PP3

Rural Carrier — PP4

Mail Train and Mail Bag on Rack — PP5

Steamship "Kronprinz Wilhelm" and Mail Tender, New York — PP6

Automobile Service — PP7

Airplane Carrying Mail — PP8

United States Parcel Post stamps can be mounted in Scott's Platinum, National and Minuteman Albums.

Manufacturing (Steel Plant, South Chicago) — PP9

Dairying — PP10

Harvesting — PP11

Fruit Growing (Florida Orange Grove) — PP12

6161 TEN

Plate number and imprint consisting of value in words.

Marginal imprints, consisting of value in words, were added to the plates on January 27, 1913.

Plates of 180 subjects in four panes of 45 each.

1913 Wmk. 190 Engr. *Perf. 12*

No.	Design	Denom.	Description	Unused	Used
Q1	PP1	1c	**carmine rose** *(209,691,094)*	2.75	90
			carmine	2.75	90
			First day cover, *July 1, 1913*		*1,500.*
			On cover, 1913-25		5.00
			Block of four	11.50	5.00
			Margin block of 4, Impt. & P#	30.00	
			Margin block of 6, Impt. & P#	85.00	
			Margin block of 6, P# only	95.00	
			Double transfer	5.00	3.00
Q2	PP2	2c	**carmine rose** *(206,417,253)*	3.25	70
			carmine	3.25	70
			lake	—	
			First day cover, *July 1, 1913*		*1,500.*
			On cover, 1913-25		5.00
			Block of four	13.50	3.50
			Margin block of 4, Impt. & P#	35.00	
			Margin block of 6, Impt. & P#	95.00	
			Margin block of 6, P# only	115.00	
			Double transfer	—	—
Q3	PP3	3c	**carmine,** *Apr. 5, 1913 (29,027,433)*	6.50	5.00
			deep carmine	6.50	5.00
			First day cover, *July 1, 1913*		*3,000.*
			On cover, 1913-25		17.50
			Block of four	26.00	25.00
			Margin block of 4, Impt. & P#	65.00	
			Margin block of 6, Impt. & P#	185.00	
			Margin block of 6, P# only	175.00	
			Margin block of 8, Impt. & P# (side)	225.00	
			Retouched at lower right corner (No. 6257 LL 7)	15.00	12.50
			Double transfer (No. 6257 LL 6)	15.00	12.50
Q4	PP4	4c	**carmine rose** *(76,743,813)*	17.50	2.00
			carmine	17.50	2.00
			First day cover, *July 1, 1913*		*3,000.*
			On cover, 1913-25		60.00
			Block of four	72.50	
			Margin block of 4, Impt. & P#	250.00	
			Margin block of 6, Impt. & P#	775.00	
			Margin block of 6, P# only	750.00	
			Double transfer	—	—
Q5	PP5	5c	**carmine rose** *(108,153,993)*	13.50	1.25
			carmine	13.50	1.25
			First day cover, *July 1, 1913*		*3,000.*
			On cover, 1913-25		40.00
			Block of four	57.50	10.00
			Margin block of 4, Impt. & P#	250.00	
			Margin block of 6, Impt. & P#	775.00	
			Margin block of 6, P# only	750.00	
			Double transfer	25.00	5.00
Q6	PP6	10c	**carmine rose** *(56,896,653)*	25.00	1.75
			carmine	25.00	1.75
			On cover, 1913-25		50.00
			Block of four	105.00	20.00
			Margin block of 4, Impt. & P#	300.00	
			Margin block of 6, Impt. & P#	1,000.	
			Margin block of 6, P# only	950.00	
			Double transfer	—	—
Q7	PP7	15c	**carmine rose** *(21,147,033)*	40.00	9.00
			carmine	40.00	9.00
			First day cover, *July 1, 1913*		—
			On cover, 1913-25		350.00
			Block of four	165.00	60.00
			Margin block of 4, Impt. & P#	500.00	
			Margin block of 6, Impt. & P#	2,100.	
			Margin block of 8, Impt. & P#	2,650.	
			Margin block of 6, P# only	2,000.	
Q8	PP8	20c	**carmine rose** *(17,142,393)*	90.00	17.50
			carmine	90.00	17.50
			On cover, 1913-25		750.00
			Block of four	375.00	100.00
			Margin block of 4, Impt. & P#	1,050.	
			Margin block of 6, Impt. & P#	5,750.	
			Margin block of 8, Impt. & P# (side)	6,250.	
			Margin block of 6, P# only	5,750.	
Q9	PP9	25c	**carmine rose** *(21,940,653)*	40.00	4.50
			carmine	40.00	4.50
			On cover, 1913-25		300.00
			Block of four	165.00	35.00
			Margin block of 6, Impt. & P#	2,500.	
			Margin block of 8, Impt. & P# (side)	3,000.	
			Margin block of 6, P# only	2,350.	
Q10	PP10	50c	**carmine rose,** *Mar. 15, 1913 (2,117,793)*	175.00	35.00
			carmine	175.00	35.00
			On cover, 1913-25		—
			Block of four	710.00	200.00
			Margin block of 4, Impt. & P#	1,500.	
			Margin block of 6, Impt. & P#	13,500.	
Q11	PP11	75c	**carmine rose** *(2,772,615)*	55.00	30.00
			carmine	55.00	30.00
			On cover, 1913-25		—
			Block of four	225.00	140.00
			Margin block of 6, Impt. & P#	3,000.	
			Margin block of 8, Impt. & P# (side)	3,500.	
			Margin block of 6, P# only	2,900.	
Q12	PP12	$1	**carmine rose,** *Jan. 3, 1913 (1,053,273)*	300.00	20.00
			carmine	300.00	20.00
			On cover, 1913-25		1,100.
			Block of four	1,650.	100.00
			Margin block of 6, Impt. & P#	16,000.	
			Margin block of 8, Impt. & P# (side)	17,500.	
			Margin block of 6, P# only	16,000.	

The 1, 2, 4 and 5c are known in parcel post usage postmarked Jan. 1, 1913.

P.P. POSTAGE DUE

Parcel Post Due stamps were prepared in conformity with the Act of Congress, approved August 24, 1912, at the same time the Parcel Post stamps were issued. See note preceding Scott Q1. Parcel Post Due stamps were allowed to be used as regular postage due stamps from July 1, 1913.

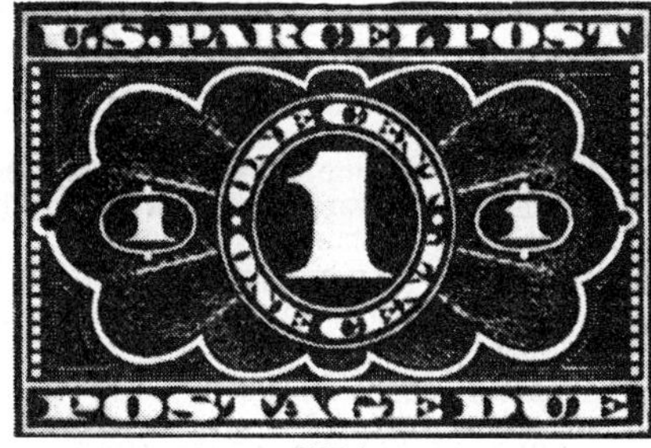

PPD1

Plates of 180 subjects in four panes of 45

1912 **Wmk. 190** **Engr.** ***Perf. 12***

No.	Design	Description	Unused	Used
JQ1	PPD1	1c **dark green,** *Nov. 27, 1912 (7,322,400)*	5.00	3.00
		yellowish green	5.00	3.00
		On cover, 1913-25		150.00
		Block of four	21.00	20.00
		Margin block of 6, P#	550.00	
JQ2	PPD1	2c **dark green,** *Dec. 9, 1912 (3,132,000)*	40.00	15.00
		yellowish green	40.00	15.00
		On cover, 1913-25		200.00
		Block of four	165.00	85.00
		Margin block of 6, P#	4,000.	
JQ3	PPD1	5c **dark green,** *Nov. 27, 1912 (5,840,100)*	6.00	3.50
		yellowish green	6.00	3.50
		On cover, 1913-25		185.00
		Block of four	25.00	20.00
		Margin block of 6, P#	675.00	
JQ4	PPD1	10c **dark green,** *Dec. 12, 1912 (2,124,540)*	110.00	35.00
		yellowish green	110.00	35.00
		On cover, 1913-25		650.00
		Block of four	450.00	200.00
		Margin block of 6, P#	10,000.	
JQ5	PPD1	25c **dark green,** *Dec. 16, 1912 (2,117,700)*	50.00	3.50
		yellowish green	50.00	3.50
		On cover, 1913-25		—
		Block of four	210.00	20.00
		Margin block of 6, P#	4,500.	

United States Parcel Post Postage Due stamps can be mounted in Scott's Platinum, National and Minuteman Albums.

SPECIAL HANDLING

The Postal Service Act, approved February 28, 1925, provided for a special handling stamp of the 25 cent denomination for use on fourth-class mail matter, which would secure for such mail matter the expeditious handling accorded to mail matter of the first class.

PP13

FLAT PLATE PRINTING

Plates of 200 subjects in four panes of 50

1925-55 **Unwmk.** ***Perf. 11***

No.	Design	Description	Unused	Used
QE1	PP13	10c **yellow green,** *1955*	1.25	90
		Block of four	5.00	5.00
		Margin block of 6, P# only	25.00	
a.		Wet printing, *June 25, 1928*	2.50	90
		First day cover		45.00
QE2	PP13	15c **yellow green,** *1955*	1.40	90
		Block of four	5.60	5.00
		Margin block of 6, P# only	35.00	
a.		Wet printing, *June 25, 1928*	2.50	90
		First day cover		45.00
QE3	PP13	20c **yellow green,** *1955*	2.25	1.75
		Block of four	9.00	9.00
		Margin block of 6, P# only	40.00	
a.		Wet printing, *June 25, 1928*	3.00	1.75
		First day cover		45.00
		First day cover, Nos. QE1-QE3		350.00
QE4	PP13	25c **yellow green,** *1929*	15.00	7.50
		Block of four	60.00	35.00
		Margin block of 6, P# only	240.00	
a.		25c deep green, *Apr. 11, 1925*	25.00	4.50
a.		First day cover		225.00
a.		Block of four	100.00	25.00
a.		Margin block of 6, P# only	325.00	
		"A" and "T" of "States" joined at top (Pl. 17103)	40.00	20.00
		"A" and "T" of "States" and "T" and "A" of "Postage" joined at top (Pl. 17103)	40.00	40.00

See note on Wet and Dry Printings following No. 1029.

POSTAL INSURANCE

Postal insurance labels were issued to pay insurance on parcels for loss or damage. The label comes in a booklet of one which also carries instructions for use and a receipt form for use if there is a claim. The booklets were sold by vending machine.

PPI1

1965, Aug. **Typo.** ***Rouletted 9 at Top***

No.	Design	Description	Unused	Used
QI1	PPI1	(10c) **dark red**	135.00	—

No. QI1 paid insurance up to $10. It was sold at the Canoga Park, Calif., automatic post office which opened Aug. 19, 1965. The "V" stands for "Vended."

PPI2

1966, Mar. 26 **Litho.** ***Perf. 11 at Top***

No.	Design	Description	Unused	Used
QI2	PPI2	(20c) **red**	2.00	—

No. QI2 paid insurance up to $15. The rate increased from 20c to 25c on Apr. 18, 1976, and to 40c on July 18, 1976.

No 25c labels were printed. Existing copies of No. QI2 had 5c stamps added and the value on the cover was changed to 25c, usually by hand. Twenty-cent stamps were added to make the 40c rate since new labels were not issued until 1978.

POSTMARK OF

MAILING OFFICE

FEE PAID THROUGH
VENDING MACHINE

PPI3

1978-81 **Litho.** ***Perf. 11 at Top***

No.	Design	Description	Unused	Used
QI3	PPI3	(40c) **black**	2.00	—
QI4	PPI3	(50c) **green**	1.25	—

The rate increased to 50c on May 29, 1978.

No.	Design	Description	Unused	Used
QI5	PPI3	(45c) **red,** *1981*	1.00	—

An enhanced introduction to the Scott Catalogue begins on Page V. A thorough understanding of the material presented there will greatly aid your use of the catalogue itself.

FIRST DAY COVERS

All envelopes or cards are postmarked Washington, D.C., unless otherwise stated.

Values are for covers bearing single stamps. Blocks of 4 on first day covers usually sell for about 1 ½ the value for singles; Plate Number blocks of 4 at about 3 times; Plate Number blocks of 6 at about 4 times; coil line pairs at about 3 times.

Dates given are those on which the stamps were first *officially* placed on sale. Instances are known of stamps being sold in advance, contrary to regulations.

Numbers in parentheses are quantities canceled on first day.

Listings since 1922 are all exclusively for covers canceled at cities officially designated by the Post Office Department or Postal Service. Some tagged varieties are exceptions.

Airmail first day covers are listed in the Air Post section of this catalogue. Booklet pane first day covers are listed in the Booklet Panes section.

Printed cachets on covers before No. 772 sell at a substantial premium. Values for covers from No. 772 and C20 onward are for those with the most common cachets and addressed. Unaddressed covers command a premium. Those without cachets sell at a substantial discount.

1851-57

5A 1c **blue, type Ib,** *July 1, 1851,* Boston, Mass. 18,500.
7 1c **blue, type II,** *July 1, 1851, any city* 13,000.
same on printed circular 2,500.
10 3c **orange brown,** *July 1, 1851, any city* 7,500.

1883

210 2c **red brown,** *Oct. 1, 1883, any city* 2,000.
211 4c **blue green,** *Oct. 1, 1883, any city* 8,500.
210 to 211 on one cover 10,000.

1890

219D 2c **lake,** *Feb. 22, 1890, any city* 14,500.

1893

COLUMBIAN EXPOSITION ISSUE

230 1c **deep blue,** *Jan. 2, 1893, any city* 3,500.
231 2c **brown violet,** *Jan. 2, 1893, any city* 2,600.
232 3c **green,** *Jan. 2, 1893, any city* 6,000.
233 4c **ultramarine,** *Jan. 2, 1893, any city* 6,000.
234 5c **chocolate,** *Jan. 2, 1893, any city* 6,250.
235 6c **purple,** *Jan. 2, 1893, any city* 6,750.
237 10c **black brown,** *Jan. 2, 1893, any city* 7,500.
242 $2 **brown red,** *Jan. 2, 1893, any city* 18,000.

Jan. 1, 1893, postmarks are known on the Columbian issue. As that day was a Sunday, specialists recognize both Jan. 1 and 2 as "first day."

1898

TRANS-MISSISSIPPI EXPOSITION ISSUE

285 1c **green,** *June 17, 1898, any city* 4,500.
286 2c **copper red,** *June 17, 1898, any city* 4,000.
288 5c **dull blue,** *June 17, 1898, any city* 5,000.
289 8c **violet brown,** *June 17, 1898, any city* 7,500.
285 to 290, all six on one cover, June 17, 1898, any city 13,000.
291 50c **sage green,** *June 17, 1898, any city* 9,000.
292 $1 **black,** *June 17, 1898, any city* 12,500.

1901

PAN AMERICAN EXPOSITION ISSUE

294 1c **green & black,** *May 1, 1901, any city* 3,750.
295 2c **carmine & black,** *May 1, 1901, any city* 3,250.
296 4c **deep red brown & black,** *May 1, 1901* 4,250.
297 5c **ultra. & blk.,** *May 1, 1901, any city* 4,500.
294 to 299, Complete set of six on one cover *May 1, 1901, any city* 10,000.

1903

301 2c **carmine,** *Jan. 17, 1903, any city* 2,750.

1904

LOUISIANA PURCHASE EXPOSITION ISSUE

323 1c **green,** *Apr. 30, 1904, any city* 3,000.
324 2c **carmine,** *Apr. 30, 1904, any city* 2,750.
325 3c **violet,** *Apr. 30, 1904, any city* 3,750.
326 5c **dark blue,** *Apr. 30, 1904, any city* 5,500.
327 10c **red brown,** *Apr. 30, 1904, any city* 8,500.
323 to 327, all five on one cover, *Apr. 30, 1904, any city* 12,500.

1907

JAMESTOWN EXPOSITION ISSUE

328 1c **green,** *Apr. 26, 1907, any city* 3,750.
329 2c **carmine,** *Apr. 26, 1907, any city* 5,500.

1909

LINCOLN ISSUE

367 2c **carmine,** *Feb. 12, 1909, any city* 350.00

Imperf

368 2c **carmine,** *Feb. 12, 1909, any city* 7,000.

1909

ALASKA-YUKON ISSUE

370 2c **carmine,** *June 1, 1909, any city* 1,800.
On Expo-related picture postcard, *June 1, 1909* 2,000.

1909

HUDSON-FULTON ISSUE

372 2c **carmine,** *Sept. 25, 1909, any city* 800.00
On Expo-related picture postcard, *Sept. 25, 1909* 1,000.

Imperf

373 2c **carmine,** *Sept. 25, 1909, any city* 2,000.

1913

PANAMA-PACIFIC ISSUE

397 1c **green,** *Jan. 1, 1913, any city* 3,750.
399 5c **blue,** *Jan. 1, 1913* 4,000.
400 10c **orange yellow,** *Jan. 1, 1913* —
397, 399 & 400, all 3 on one cover, San Francisco 5,000.

1916-22

COIL STAMP

497 10c **orange yellow,** *Jan. 31, 1922, any city* 2,000.

1918-20

OFFSET PRINTING

526 2c **carmine,** type IV, *Mar. 15, 1920* 800.00

1919

VICTORY ISSUE

537 3c **violet,** *Mar. 3, 1919, any city* 750.00

1920 ***Perf. 10x11***

REGULAR ISSUE

542 1c **green,** *May 26, 1920* 950.00

1920

PILGRIM TERCENTENARY ISSUE

548 1c **green,** *Dec. 21, 1920, any city* 800.00
549 2c **carmine rose,** *Dec. 21, 1920, any city* 650.00
Plymouth, Mass. 900.00
548 to 550, Complete set of three on one cover, *Dec. 21, 1920, any city* 2,500.
Washington, D.C. 3,000.

1922-26 ***Perf. 11***

551 ½c **Hale,** *Apr. 4, 1925,* (Block of 4) 15.00
New Haven, Conn. 17.50
552 1c **Franklin,** *Jan. 17, 1923* 20.00
Philadelphia, Pa. 50.00
553 1½c **Harding,** *Mar. 19, 1925* 25.00
554 2c **Washington,** *Jan. 15, 1923* 35.00
555 3c **Lincoln,** *Feb. 12, 1923* 30.00
Hodgenville, Ky. 250.00
556 4c **Martha Washington,** *Jan. 15, 1923* 50.00
557 5c **Roosevelt,** *Oct. 27, 1922* 125.00
New York, N.Y. 200.00
Oyster Bay, N.Y. 500.00
558 6c **Garfield,** *Nov. 20, 1922* 200.00
559 7c **McKinley,** *May 1, 1923* 80.00
Niles, O. 175.00
560 8c **Grant,** *May 1, 1923* 90.00
561 9c **Jefferson,** *Jan. 15, 1923* 90.00
562 10c **Monroe,** *Jan. 15, 1923* 140.00
563 11c **Hayes,** *Oct. 4, 1922* 550.00
Fremont, O. 1,200.
564 12c **Cleveland,** *Mar. 20, 1923* 150.00
Boston, Mass. (Philatelic Exhibition) 150.00
Caldwell, N.J. 175.00
565 14c **Indian,** *May 1, 1923* 325.00
Muskogee, Okla. 1,000.
566 15c **Statue of Liberty,** *Nov. 11, 1922* 400.00
567 20c **Golden Gate,** *May 1, 1923* 400.00
San Francisco, Cal. 1,200.
568 25c **Niagara Falls,** *Nov. 11, 1922* 625.00
569 30c **Bison,** *Mar. 20, 1923* 750.00
570 50c **Arlington,** *Nov. 11, 1922* 900.00
571 $1 **Lincoln Memorial,** *Feb. 12, 1923* 5,500.
Springfield, Ill. 5,500.
572 $2 **U.S. Capitol,** *Mar. 20, 1923* 10,000.
573 $5 **America,** *Mar. 20, 1923* 14,000.

Imperf

576 1½c **Harding,** *Apr. 4, 1925* 45.00

Perf. 10

581 1c **Franklin,** *Oct. 17, 1923,* not precanceled 2,000.
582 1½c **Harding,** *Mar. 19, 1925* 40.00
584 3c **Lincoln,** *Aug. 1, 1925* 47.50
585 4c **Martha Washington,** *Apr. 4, 1925* 47.50
586 5c **Roosevelt,** *Apr. 4, 1925* 50.00
587 6c **Garfield,** *Apr. 4, 1925* 60.00
588 7c **McKinley,** *May 29, 1926* 62.50
589 8c **Grant,** *May 29, 1926* 65.00
590 9c **Jefferson,** *May 29, 1926* 65.00
591 10c **Monroe,** *June 8, 1925* 85.00

ROTARY PRESS COIL STAMPS

Perf. 10 Vertically

597 1c **Franklin,** *July 18, 1923* 550.00
598 1½c **Harding,** *Mar. 19, 1925* 50.00
599 2c **Washington,** *Jan. 15, 1923* 850.00
600 3c **Lincoln,** *May 10, 1924* 60.00
602 5c **Roosevelt,** *Mar. 5, 1924* 82.50
603 10c **Monroe,** *Dec. 1, 1924* 100.00

Perf. 10 Horizontally

604 1c **Franklin,** *July 19, 1924* 90.00
605 1½c **Harding,** *May 9, 1925* 70.00
606 2c **Washington,** *Dec. 31, 1923* 100.00

1923

610 2c **Harding,** *Sept. 1, 1923* (Perf. 11) 30.00
Marion, O. 20.00
611 2c **Harding,** *Nov. 15, 1923* (Imperf.) 90.00
612 2c **Harding,** *Sept. 12, 1923* (Perf. 10) 100.00

1924 ***Perf. 11***

614 1c **Huguenot-Walloon,** *May 1, 1924* 25.00
Albany, N.Y 25.00
Allentown, Pa. 25.00
Charleston, S.C. 25.00
Jacksonville, Fla. 25.00
Lancaster, Pa. 25.00
Mayport, Fla. 25.00
New Rochelle, N.Y. 25.00
New York, N.Y. 25.00
Philadelphia, Pa. 25.00
Reading, Pa. 25.00
615 2c **Huguenot-Walloon,** *May 1, 1924* 27.50
Albany, N.Y. 27.50
Allentown, Pa. 27.50
Charleston, S.C. 27.50
Jacksonville, Fla. 27.50
Lancaster, Pa. 27.50
Mayport, Fla. 27.50
New Rochelle, N.Y. 27.50
New York, N.Y. 27.50
Philadelphia, Pa. 27.50
Reading, Pa. 27.50
616 5c **Huguenot-Walloon,** *May 1, 1924* 45.00
Albany, N.Y. 45.00
Allentown, Pa. 45.00
Charleston, S.C. 45.00
Jacksonville, Fla. 45.00
Lancaster, Pa. 45.00
Mayport, Fla. 45.00
New Rochelle, N.Y. 45.00
New York, N.Y. 45.00
Philadelphia, Pa. 45.00
Reading, Pa. 45.00
614 to 616, set of three on one cover, *any city* 125.00

1925

617 1c **Lexington-Concord,** *Apr. 4, 1925* 25.00
Boston, Mass. 25.00
Cambridge, Mass. 25.00
Concord, Mass. 25.00
Concord Junction, Mass. 27.50
Lexington, Mass. 27.50
618 2c **Lexington-Concord,** *Apr. 4, 1925* 27.50
Boston, Mass. 27.50
Cambridge, Mass. 27.50
Concord, Mass 27.50
Concord Junction, Mass. 27.50
Lexington, Mass. 40.00
619 5c **Lexington-Concord,** *Apr. 4, 1925* 60.00
Boston, Mass. 60.00
Combridge, Mass. 60.00
Concord, Mass. 60.00
Concord Junction, Mass. 60.00
Lexington, Mass. 60.00
617 to 619, set of three on one cover, Concord Junction, Mass., or Lexington, Mass. 140.00
Set of three on one cover, any other city 110.00

1925

620 2c **Norse-American,** *May 18, 1925* 20.00
Algona, Iowa 20.00
Benson, Minn. 20.00
Decorah, Iowa 20.00
Minneapolis, Minn. 20.00

		Northfield, Minn.	20.00
		St. Paul, Minn.	20.00
621	5c	**Norse-American,** *May 18, 1925*	30.00
		Algona, Iowa	30.00
		Benson, Minn.	30.00
		Decorah, Iowa	30.00
		Minneapolis, Minn.	30.00
		Northfield, Minn.	30.00
		St. Paul, Minn.	30.00
		620 and 621, set of two on one cover, *any city*	50.00

1925-26

622	13c	**Harrison,** *Jan. 11, 1926*	20.00
		Indianapolis, Ind.	30.00
		North Bend, Ohio *(500)*	175.00
623	17c	**Wilson,** *Dec. 28, 1925*	25.00
		New York, N.Y.	25.00
		Princeton, N.J.	25.00
		Staunton, Va.	25.00

1926

627	2c	**Sesquicentennial,** *May 10, 1926*	10.00
		Boston, Mass.	10.00
		Philadelphia, Pa.	10.00
628	5c	**Ericsson,** *May 29, 1926*	22.50
		Chicago, Ill.	22.50
		Minneapolis, Minn.	22.50
		New York, N.Y.	22.50
629	2c	**White Plains,** New York, N.Y., *Oct. 18, 1926*	6.25
		New York, N.Y., Inter-Philatelic Exhibition Agency cancellation	6.25
		White Plains, N.Y.	6.25
		Washington, D.C., *Oct. 28, 1926*	3.50
630		Sheet of 25, *Oct. 18, 1926*	1,400.
		Sheet of 25, *Oct. 28, 1926*	800.00

1926-34 ***Imperf.***

631	1½c	**Harding,** *Aug. 27, 1926*	30.00

Perf. 11x10½

632	1c	**Franklin,** *June 10, 1927*	45.00
633	1½c	**Harding,** *May 17, 1927*	45.00
634	2c	**Washington,** *Dec. 10, 1926*	47.50
635	3c	**Lincoln,** *Feb. 3, 1927*	47.50
635a	3c	**bright violet,** *Feb. 7, 1934*	25.00
636	4c	**Martha Washington,** *May 17, 1927*	50.00
637	5c	**Roosevelt,** *Mar. 24, 1927*	50.00
638	6c	**Garfield,** *July 27, 1927*	57.50
639	7c	**McKinley,** *Mar. 24, 1927*	57.50
640	8c	**Grant,** *June 10, 1927*	62.50
641	9c	**Jefferson,** *May 17, 1927*	72.50
642	10c	**Monroe,** *Feb. 3, 1927*	90.00

1927 ***Perf. 11***

643	2c	**Vermont,** *Aug. 3, 1927*	5.00
		Bennington, Vt.	5.00
644	2c	**Burgoyne,** *Aug. 3, 1927*	12.50
		Albany, N.Y.	12.50
		Rome, N.Y.	12.50
		Syracuse, N.Y.	12.50
		Utica, N.Y.	12.50

1928

645	2c	**Valley Forge,** *May 26, 1928*	4.00
		Cleveland, O.	60.00
		Lancaster, Pa.	4.00
		Norristown, Pa.	4.00
		Philadelphia, Pa.	4.00
		Valley Forge, Pa.	4.00
		West Chester, Pa.	4.00
		Cleveland, Midwestern Philatelic Sta. cancellation	4.00

Perf. 11x10½

646	2c	**Molly Pitcher,** *Oct. 20, 1928*	20.00
		Freehold, N.J.	20.00
		Red Bank, N.J.	20.00

1928 ***Perf. 11x10½***

647	2c	**Hawaii,** *Aug. 13, 1928*	15.00
		Honolulu, Hawaii	17.50
648	5c	**Hawaii,** *Aug. 13, 1928*	22.50
		Honolulu, Hawaii	25.00
		647 and 648, set of two on one cover	40.00

Perf. 11

649	2c	**Aero Conf.,** *Dec. 12, 1928*	7.00
650	5c	**Aero Conf.,** *Dec. 12, 1928*	10.00
		649 and 650, set of two on one cover	15.00

1929

651	2c	**Clark,** Vincennes, Indiana, *Feb. 25, 1929*	6.00
		Washington, *Feb. 26, 1929,* first day of sale by Philatelic Agency	3.00

Perf. 11x10½

653	½c	**olive brown,** *May 25, 1929* (Block of four)	25.00

Perf. 11

654	2c	**Electric Light,** Menlo Park, N.J., *June 5, 1929*	8.00
		Washington, *June 6, 1929,* first day of sale by Philatelic Agency	4.00

Perf. 11x10½

655	2c	**Electric Light,** *June 11, 1929*	80.00

Perf. 10 Vertically

656	2c	**Electric Light,** *June 11, 1929*	90.00

Perf. 11

657	2c	**Sullivan,** Auburn, N.Y., *June 17, 1929*	4.00
		Binghamton, N.Y.	4.00
		Canajoharie, N.Y.	4.00
		Canandaigua, N.Y.	4.00
		Elmira, N.Y.	4.00
		Geneva, N.Y.	4.00
		Geneseo, N.Y.	4.00
		Horseheads, N.Y.	4.00
		Owego, N.Y.	4.00
		Penn Yan, N.Y	4.00
		Perry, N.Y.	4.00
		Seneca Falls, N.Y.	4.00
		Waterloo, N.Y.	4.00
		Watkins Glen, N.Y.	4.00
		Waverly, N.Y.	4.00
		Washington, D.C., *June 18, 1929*	2.00

1929

KANSAS AND NEBRASKA

658	1c	**Kansas,** *May 1, 1929*	27.50
		Newton, Kan., *Apr. 15, 1929*	200.00
659	1½c	**Kansas,** *May 1, 1929*	27.50
		Colby, Kan., *Apr. 16, 1929*	—
660	2c	**Kansas,** *May 1, 1929*	27.50
		Colby, Kan., *Apr. 16, 1929*	—
661	3c	**Kansas,** *May 1, 1929*	30.00
		Colby, Kan., *Apr. 16, 1929*	—
662	4c	**Kansas,** *May 1, 1929*	32.50
		Colby, Kan., *Apr. 16, 1929*	—
663	5c	**Kansas,** *May 1, 1929*	35.00
		Colby, Kan., *Apr. 16, 1929*	—
664	6c	**Kansas,** *May 1, 1929*	42.50
		Newton, Kan., *Apr. 15, 1929*	350.00
665	7c	**Kansas,** *May 1, 1929*	42.50
		Colby, Kan., *Apr. 16, 1929*	—
666	8c	**Kansas,** *May 1, 1929*	80.00
		Newton, Kan., *Apr. 15, 1929*	350.00
667	9c	**Kansas,** *May 1, 1929*	72.50
		Colby, Kan., *Apr. 16, 1929*	—
668	10c	**Kansas,** *May 1, 1929*	85.00
		Colby, Kan., *Apr. 16, 1929*	—
		658 to 668, set of eleven on one cover, Washington, D.C., *May 1, 1929*	850.00
669	1c	**Nebraska,** *May 1, 1929*	27.50
		Beatrice, Neb., *Apr. 15, 1929*	—
670	1½c	**Nebraska,** *May 1, 1929*	25.00
		Hartington, Neb., *Apr. 15, 1929*	160.00
671	2c	**Nebraska,** *May 1, 1929*	25.00
		Auburn, Neb., *Apr. 15, 1929*	—
		Beatrice, Neb., *Apr. 15, 1929*	—
		Hartington, Neb., *Apr. 15, 1929*	160.00
672	3c	**Nebraska,** *May 1, 1929*	32.50
		Beatrice, Neb., *Apr. 15, 1929*	160.00
		Hartington, Neb., *Apr. 15, 1929*	160.00
673	4c	**Nebraska,** *May 1, 1929*	37.50
		Beatrice, Neb., *Apr. 15, 1929*	160.00
		Hartington, Neb., *Apr. 15, 1929*	160.00
674	5c	**Nebraska,** *May 1, 1929*	37.50
		Beatrice, Neb., *Apr. 15, 1929*	160.00
		Hartington, Neb., *Apr. 15, 1929*	160.00
675	6c	**Nebraska,** *May 1, 1929*	55.00
		Ravenna, Neb., *Apr. 17, 1929*	—
		Wahoo, Neb., *Apr. 17, 1929*	—
676	7c	**Nebraska,** *May 1, 1929*	57.50
		Auburn, Neb., *Apr. 17, 1929*	—
677	8c	**Nebraska,** *May 1, 1929*	60.00
		Humbolt, Neb., *Apr. 17, 1929*	—
		Pawnee City, Neb., *Apr. 17, 1929*	—
678	9c	**Nebraska,** *May 1, 1929*	62.50
		Cambridge, Neb., *Apr. 17, 1929*	—
679	10c	**Nebraska,** *May 1, 1929*	70.00
		Tecumseh, Neb., *Apr. 18, 1929*	—
		669 to 679, set of eleven on one cover, Washington, D.C., *May 1, 1929*	850.00

Perf. 11

680	2c	**Fallen Timbers,** Erie, Pa., *Sept. 14, 1929*	3.50
		Maumee, O.	3.50
		Perrysburg, O.	3.50
		Toledo, O.	3.50
		Waterville, O.	3.50
		Washington, D.C., *Sept. 16, 1929*	2.00
681	2c	**Ohio River,** Cairo, Ill., *Oct. 19, 1929*	3.50
		Cincinnati, O.	3.50
		Evansville, Ind.	3.50
		Homestead, Pa.	3.50
		Louisville, Ky.	3.50
		Pittsburgh, Pa.	3.50
		Wheeling, W. Va.	3.50
		Washington, D.C., *Oct. 21, 1929*	2.00

1930

682	2c	**Massachusetts Bay Colony,** Boston, Mass. *Apr. 8, 1930 (60,000)*	3.50
		Salem, Mass.	3.50
		Washington, D.C., *Apr. 11, 1930*	2.00
683	2c	**Carolina-Charleston,** Charleston, S.C. *Apr. 10, 1930*	3.50
		Washington, D.C., *Apr. 11, 1930*	2.00

Perf. 11x10½

684	1½c	**Harding,** Marion, O., *Dec. 1, 1930*	4.50
		Washington, D.C., *Dec. 2, 1930*	2.50
685	4c	**Taft,** Cincinnati, O., *June 4, 1930*	6.00
		Washington, D.C., *June 5, 1930*	3.00

Perf. 10 Vertically

686	1½c	**Harding,** Marion, Ohio, *Dec. 1, 1930*	5.00
		Washington, D.C., *Dec. 2, 1930*	3.00
687	4c	**Taft,** *Sept. 18, 1930*	20.00

Perf. 11

688 2c **Braddock,** Braddock, Pa., *July 9, 1930* 4.00
Washington, D.C., *July 10, 1930* 2.00
689 2c **Von Steuben,** New York, N.Y., *Sept. 17, 1930* 4.00
Washington, D.C., *Sept. 18, 1930* 2.00

1931

690 2c **Pulaski,** Brooklyn, N.Y., *Jan. 16, 1931* 4.00
Buffalo, N.Y. 4.00
Chicago, Ill. 4.00
Cleveland, O. 4.00
Detroit, Mich. 4.00
Gary, Ind. 4.00
Milwaukee, Wis. 4.00
New York, N.Y. 4.00
Pittsburgh, Pa. 4.00
Savannah, Ga. 4.00
South Bend, Ind. 4.00
Toledo, O. 4.00
Washington, D.C., *Jan. 17, 1931* 2.00

1931 *Perf. 11x10 1/2*

692 11c **Hayes,** *Sept. 4, 1931* 90.00
693 12c **Cleveland,** *Aug. 25, 1931* 90.00
694 13c **Harrison,** *Sept. 4, 1931* 90.00
695 14c **Indian,** *Sept. 8, 1931* 90.00
696 15c **Liberty,** *Aug. 27, 1931* 110.00

Perf. 10 1/2x11

697 17c **Wilson,** *July 25, 1931,* Brooklyn, N.Y. *1,000.*
Washington, D.C., *July 27* 275.00
698 20c **Golden Gate,** *Sept. 8, 1931* 300.00
699 25c **Niagara Falls,** *July 25, 1931,* Brooklyn, N.Y. *1,000.*
Washington, D.C., *July 27* 300.00
697, 699 on one cover *1,200.*
700 30c **Bison,** *Sept. 8, 1931* 300.00
701 50c **Arlington,** *Sept. 8, 1931* 375.00

1931

702 2c **Red Cross,** *May 21, 1931* 3.00
Dansville, N.Y. 3.00
703 2c **Yorktown,** *Oct. 19, 1931,* Wethersfield, Conn. 3.50
Yorktown, Va. 3.50
Washington, D.C., *Oct. 20* 2.00

1932

WASHINGTON BICENTENNIAL ISSUE

704 1/2c *Jan. 1, 1932* 4.00
705 1c *Jan. 1, 1932* 4.00
706 1 1/2c *Jan. 1, 1932* 4.00
707 2c *Jan. 1, 1932* 4.00
708 3c *Jan. 1, 1932* 4.00
709 4c *Jan. 1, 1932* 4.00
710 5c *Jan. 1, 1932* 4.00
711 6c *Jan. 1, 1932* 4.00
712 7c *Jan. 1, 1932* 4.00
713 8c *Jan. 1, 1932* 4.50
714 9c *Jan. 1, 1932* 4.50
715 10c *Jan. 1, 1932* 4.50
704 to 715, Complete set of twelve on one cover, Washington, D.C., *Jan. 1, 1932* 60.00

1932

716 2c **Olympic Winter Games,** *Jan. 25, 1932,* Lake Placid, N.Y. 6.00
Washington, D.C., *Jan. 26* 1.50
717 2c **Arbor Day,** *Apr. 22, 1933,* Nebraska City, Neb. 4.00
Washington, D.C., *Apr. 23* 1.50
Adams, N.Y., *Apr. 23* 6.50
718 3c **Olympic Summer Games,** *June 15, 1932,* Los Angeles, Cal. 6.00
Washington, D.C., *June 16* 2.75
719 5c **Olympic Summer Games,** *June 15, 1932,* Los Angeles, Cal. 8.00
Washington, D.C., *June 16* 2.75
718, 719 on one cover, Los Angeles, Cal. 10.00
718, 719 on one cover, Washington, D.C. 4.50
720 3c **Washington,** *June 16, 1932* 7.50
721 3c **Washington Coil,** Sideways, *June 24, 1932* 15.00
722 3c **Washington Coil,** Endways, *Oct. 12, 1932* 15.00
723 6c **Garfield Coil,** Sideways, *Aug. 18, 1932,* Los Angeles, Cal. 15.00
Washington, D.C., *Aug. 19* 4.00
724 3c **William Penn,** *Oct. 24, 1932,* New Castle, Del. 3.25
Chester, Pa. 3.25
Philadelphia, Pa. 3.25
Washington, D.C., *Oct. 25* 1.25
725 3c **Daniel Webster,** *Oct. 24, 1932,* Franklin, N.H. 3.25
Exeter, N.H. 3.25
Hanover, N.H. 3.25
Washington, D.C., *Oct. 25* 1.25

1933

726 3c **Gen. Oglethorpe,** *Feb. 12, 1933,* Savannah, Ga., *(200,000)* 3.25
Washington, D.C., *Feb. 13* 1.25
727 3c **Peace Proclamation,** *Apr. 19, 1933,* Newburgh, N.Y. *(349,571)* 3.50
Washington, D.C., *Apr. 20* 1.20
728 1c **Century of Progress,** *May 25, 1933,* Chicago, Ill. 3.00
Washington, D.C., *May 26* 1.00
729 3c **Century of Progress,** *May 25, 1933,* Chicago, Ill. 3.00
Washington, D.C., *May 26* 1.00
728, 729 on one cover 5.00

Covers mailed May 25, bearing Nos. 728 and 729 total 232,251.

730 1c **American Philatelic Society,** sheet of 25, *Aug. 25, 1933,* Chicago, Ill. 100.00
730a 1c **A.P.S.,** single, imperf., *Aug. 25, 1933,* Chicago, Ill. 3.25
Washington, D.C., *Aug. 28* 1.25
731 3c **American Philatelic Society,** sheet of 25, *Aug. 25, 1933,* Chicago, Ill. 100.00
731a 3c **A.P.S.,** single, imperf., *Aug. 25, 1933,* Chicago, Ill. 3.25
Washington, D.C., *Aug. 28* 1.25
730a, 731a on one cover 5.50

Covers mailed Aug. 25 bearing Nos. 730, 730a, 731, 731a total 65,218.

732 3c **National Recovery Administration,** *Aug. 15, 1933,* Washington, D.C. *(65,000)* 3.25
Nira, Iowa, *Aug. 17* 2.50
733 3c **Byrd Antarctic,** *Oct. 9, 1933* 5.00
734 5c **Kosciuszko,** *Oct. 13, 1933,* Boston, Mass. *(23,025)* 4.50
Buffalo, N.Y. *(14,981)* 5.50
Chicago, Ill, *(26,306)* 4.50
Detroit, Mich. *(17,792)* 5.25
Pittsburgh, Pa. *(6,282)* 32.50
Kosciusko, Miss. *(27,093)* 5.25
St. Louis, Mo. *(17,872)* 5.25
Washington, D.C., *Oct. 14* 1.60

1934

735 3c **National Exhibition,** sheet of 6, Byrd imperf., *Feb. 10, 1934,* New York, N.Y. 40.00
Washington, D.C., *Feb. 19* 27.50
735a 3c **National Exhibition,** single, imperf., New York, N.Y., *Feb. 10, 1934 (450,715)* 5.00
Washington, D.C., *Feb. 19* 2.75
736 3c **Maryland Tercentenary,** *Mar. 23, 1934* St. Mary's City, Md. *(148,785)* 1.60
Washington, D.C., *Mar. 24* .60

Perf. 11x10 1/2

738 3c **Mothers of America,** *May 2, 1934, any city* 1.60

Perf. 11

738 3c **Mothers of America,** *May 2, 1934, any city* 1.60
737, 738 on one cover 4.00

Covers mailed at Washington, May 2 bearing Nos. 737 and 738 total 183,359.

739 3c **Wisconsin,** *July 7, 1934,* Green Bay, Wisc. *(130,000)* 1.60
Washington, D.C., *July 9* .75
740 1c **Parks, Yosemite,** *July 16, 1934* 2.25
Yosemite, Cal., *(60,000)* 2.75
741 2c **Parks, Grand Canyon,** *July 24, 1934* 2.25
Grand Canyon, Ariz., *(75,000)* 2.75
742 3c **Parks, Mt. Rainier,** *Aug. 3, 1934* 2.50
Longmire, Wash., *(64,500)* 3.00
743 4c **Parks, Mesa Verde,** *Sept. 25, 1934* 2.25
Mesa Verde, Colo., *(51,882)* 2.50
744 5c **Parks, Yellowstone,** *July 30, 1934* 2.25
Yellowstone, Wyo., *(87,000)* 2.50
745 6c **Parks, Crater Lake,** *Sept. 5, 1934* 3.00
Crater Lake, Ore., *(45,282)* 3.25
746 7c **Parks, Arcadia,** *Oct. 2, 1934* 3.00
Bar Harbor, Maine *(51,312)* 3.25
747 8c **Parks, Zion,** *Sept. 18, 1934* 3.25
Zion, Utah, *(43,650)* 3.75
748 9c **Parks, Glacier Park,** *Aug. 27, 1934* 3.50
Glacier Park, Mont., *(52,626)* 3.75
749 10c **Parks, Smoky Mountains,** *Oct. 8, 1934* 6.00
Sevierville, Tenn., *(39,000)* 7.50

Imperf

750 3c **American Philatelic Society,** sheet of 6, *Aug. 28, 1934,* Atlantic City, N.J. 40.00
750a 3c **A.P.S.,** single, *Aug. 28, 1934,* Atlantic City, N.J. *(40,000)* 3.25
Washington, D.C., *Sept. 4* 2.00
751 1c **Trans-Mississippi Philatelic Expo.,** sheet of 6, *Oct. 10, 1934,* Omaha, Neb. 35.00
751a 1c **Trans-Miss. Phil. Expo.,** single, Omaha. Neb., *Oct. 10, 1934 (125,000)* 3.25
Washington, D.C., Oct. 15 2.00

1935

SPECIAL PRINTING

Nos. 752 to 771 issued Mar. 15, 1935

752 3c **Peace Commemoration** 5.00
753 3c **Byrd** 6.00
754 3c **Mothers of America** 6.00
755 3c **Wisconsin Tercentenary** 6.00
756 1c **Parks, Yosemite** 6.00
757 2c **Parks, Grand Canyon** 6.00
758 3c **Parks, Mount Rainier** 6.00
759 4c **Parks, Mesa Verde** 6.50
760 5c **Parks, Yellowstone** 6.50
761 6c **Parks, Crater Lake** 6.50
762 7c **Parks, Acadia** 6.50
763 8c **Parks, Zion** 7.50
764 9c **Parks, Glacier Park** 7.50
765 10c **Parks, Smoky Mountains** 7.50
766a 1c **Century of Progress** 5.50
Pane of 25 *250.00*
767a 3c **Century of Progress** 5.50
Pane of 25 *250.00*
768a 3c **Byrd** 6.50
Pane of 6 *250.00*
769a 1c **Parks, Yosemite** 4.00
Pane of 6 *250.00*
770a 3c **Parks, Mount Rainier** 5.00
Pane of 6 *250.00*
771 15c **Airmail Special Delivery** 12.50
772 3c **Connecticut Tercentenary,** *Apr. 26, 1935,* Hartford, Conn. *(217,800)* 8.00
Washington, D.C., *Apr. 27* 1.25
773 3c **California Exposition,** *May 29, 1935,* San Diego, Cal. *(214,042)* 8.00
Washington, D.C., *May 31* 1.25
774 3c **Boulder Dam,** *Sept. 30, 1935,* Boulder City, Nev. *(166,180)* 10.00
Washington, D.C., *Oct. 1* 2.00
775 3c **Michigan Centenary,** *Nov. 1, 1935,* Lansing, Mich. *(176,962)* 8.00
Washington, D.C., *Nov. 2* 1.25

1936

776 3c **Texas Centennial,** *Mar. 2, 1936,* Gonzales, Texas *(319,150)* 12.50
Washington, D.C., *Mar. 3* 1.25
777 3c **Rhode Island Tercentenary,** *May 4, 1936,* Providence, R.I. *(245,400)* 8.00
Washington, D.C., *May 5* 1.25
778 **TIPEX** souvenir sheet, *May 9, 1936 (297,194) New York, N.Y.* (TIPEX cancellation) 13.00
Washington, D.C., *May 11* 3.50
782 3c **Arkansas Centennial,** *June 15, 1936,* Little Rock, Ark. *(376,693)* 8.00
Washington, D.C, *June 16* 1.00
783 3c **Oregon Territory Centennial,** *July 14, 1936,* Astoria, Ore. *(91,110)* 8.50
Daniel, Wyo., *(67,013)* 8.50
Lewiston, Ida., *(86,100)* 8.00
Missoula, Mont., *(59,883)* 8.50
Walla Walla, Wash., *(106,150)* 8.00
Washington, D.C., *July 15* 1.25
784 3c **Susan Anthony,** *Aug. 26, 1936 (178,500)* 5.00

1936-37

No.	Description	Price
785	1c **Army,** *Dec. 15, 1936*	5.00
786	2c **Army,** *Jan. 15, 1937*	5.00
787	3c **Army,** *Feb. 18, 1937*	5.00
788	4c **Army,** *Mar. 23, 1937*	5.50
789	5c **Army,** *May 26, 1937,* West Point, N.Y., *(160,000)*	5.50
	Washington, D.C., *May 27*	1.25
790	1c **Navy,** *Dec. 15, 1936*	5.00
791	2c **Navy,** *Jan. 15, 1937*	5.00
792	3c **Navy,** *Feb. 18, 1937*	5.00
793	4c **Navy,** *Mar. 23, 1937*	5.50
794	5c **Navy,** *May 26, 1937,* Annapolis, Md., *(202,806)*	1.25
	Washington, D.C., *May 27*	1.25

Covers for both Nos. 785 and 790 total 390, 749; Nos. 786 and 791 total 292,570; Nos. 787 and 792 total 320,888; Nos. 788 and 793 total 331,000.

1937

No.	Description	Price
795	3c **Ordinance of 1787,** *July 13, 1937* Marietta, Ohio *(130,531)*	6.00
	New York, N.Y. *(125,134)*	6.00
	Washington, D.C., *July 14*	1.20
796	5c **Virginia Dare,** *Aug. 18, 1937,* Manteo, N.C. *(226,730)*	7.00
797	10c **Souvenir Sheet,** *Aug. 26, 1937,* Asheville, N.C. *(164,215)*	6.00
798	3c **Constitution,** *Sept. 17, 1937,* Philadelphia, Pa. *(281,478)*	6.50
799	3c **Hawaii,** *Oct. 18, 1937,* Honolulu, Hawaii *(320,334)*	7.00
800	3c **Alaska,** *Nov. 12, 1937,* Juneau, Alaska *(230,370)*	7.00
801	3c **Puerto Rico,** *Nov. 25, 1937,* San Juan, P.R. *(244,054)*	7.00
802	3c **Virgin Islands,** *Dec. 15, 1937,* Charlotte Amalie, V.I. *(225,469)*	7.00

1938

PRESIDENTIAL ISSUE

No.	Description	Price
803	½c *May 19, 1938,* Philadelphia, Pa. *(224,901)*	1.50
804	1c *Apr. 25, 1938 (124,037)*	2.25
805	1½c *May 5, 1938 (128,339)*	2.25
806	2c *June 3, 1938 (127,806)*	2.25
807	3c *June 16, 1938 (118,097)*	2.25
808	4c *July 1, 1938 (118,765)*	2.25
809	4½c *July 11, 1938 (115,820)*	2.75
810	5c *July 21, 1938 (98,282)*	2.50
811	6c *July 28, 1938 (97,428)*	2.50
812	7c *Aug. 4, 1938 (98,414)*	2.75
813	8c *Aug. 11, 1938 (94,857)*	2.75
814	9c *Aug. 18, 1938 (91,229)*	3.00
815	10c *Sept. 2, 1938 (83,707)*	3.00
816	11c *Sept. 8, 1938 (63,966)*	3.00
817	12c *Sept. 14, 1938 (62,935)*	3.25
818	13c *Sept. 22, 1938 (58,965)*	3.25
819	14c *Oct. 6, 1938 (49,819)*	3.50
820	15c *Oct. 13, 1938 (52,209)*	3.50
821	16c *Oct. 20, 1938 (59,566)*	3.75
822	17c *Oct. 27, 1938 (55,024)*	4.00
823	18c *Nov. 3, 1938 (53,124)*	4.50
824	19c *Nov. 10, 1938 (54,124)*	4.50
825	20c *Nov. 10, 1938 (51,971)*	4.75
821	21c *Nov. 22, 1938 (44,367)*	5.25
827	22c *Nov. 22, 1938 (44,358)*	5.50
828	24c *Dec. 2, 1938 (46,592)*	5.50
829	25c *Dec. 2, 1938 (45,691)*	6.75
830	30c *Dec. 8, 1938 (43,528)*	10.00
831	50c *Dec. 8, 1938 (41,984)*	15.00
832	$1 *Aug. 29, 1938 (24,618)*	40.00
832c	$1 *Aug. 31, 1954 (20,202)*	25.00
833	$2 *Sept. 29, 1938 (19,895)*	80.00
834	$5 *Nov. 17, 1938 (15,615)*	140.00

1938

No.	Description	Price
835	3c **Constitution,** *June 21, 1938,* Philadelphia, Pa. (232,873)	6.50
836	3c **Swedes and Finns,** *June 27, 1938,* Wilmington, Del. (225,617)	6.00
837	3c **Northwest Sesqui.,** *July 15, 1938,* Marietta, Ohio (180,170)	6.00
838	3c **Iowa,** *Aug. 24, 1938,* Des Moines, Iowa *(209,860)*	6.00

1939

COIL STAMPS

Perf. 10 Vertically

No.	Description	Price
839	1c Strip of 3, *Jan. 20, 1939*	7.00
840	1½c Pair, *Jan. 20, 1939*	7.00
841	2c Pair, *Jan. 20, 1939*	7.00
842	3c *Jan. 20, 1939*	7.00
843	4c *Jan. 20, 1939*	7.00
844	4½c *Jan. 20, 1939*	7.00
845	5c *Jan. 20, 1939*	7.00
846	6c *Jan. 20, 1939*	10.00
847	10c *Jan. 20, 1939*	15.00
	839 to 847, set of 9 on one cover, *Jan. 20, 1939*	60.00

Perf. 10 Horizontally

No.	Description	Price
848	1c Strip of 3, *Jan. 27, 1939*	7.00
849	1½c Pair, *Jan. 27, 1939*	7.00
850	2c Pair, *Jan. 27, 1939*	7.00
851	3c *Jan. 27, 1939*	7.00
	848 to 851, set of 4 on one cover, *Jan. 27, 1939*	30.00

1939

No.	Description	Price
852	3c **Golden Gate Expo,** *Feb. 18, 1939,* San Francisco, Cal. *(352,165)*	6.00
853	3c **N.Y. World's Fair,** *Apr. 1, 1939,* New York, N.Y. *(585,565)*	8.00
854	3c **Washington Inauguration,** *Apr. 30, 1939,* New York, N.Y. *(395,644)*	6.00
855	3c **Baseball Centennial,** *June 12, 1939,* Cooperstown, N.Y. *(398,199)*	30.00
856	3c **Panama Canal,** *Aug. 15, 1939,* U.S.S. Charleston, Canal Zone (230,974)	5.00
857	3c **Printing Tercentenary,** *Sept. 25, 1939,* New York, N.Y. *(295,270)*	5.00
858	3c **50th Statehood Anniversary,** Bismarck, N.D. *Nov. 2, 1939 (142,106)*	5.00
	Pierre, S.D., *Nov. 2, 1939 (150,429)*	5.00
	Helena, Mont., *Nov. 8, 1939 (130,273)*	5.00
	Olympia, Wash., *Nov. 11, 1939 (150,429)*	5.00

1940

FAMOUS AMERICANS

No.	Description	Price
859	1c **Washington Irving,** *Jan. 29,* Tarrytown, N.Y. *(170,969)*	1.50
860	2c **James Fenimore Cooper,** *Jan. 29,* Cooperstown, N.Y. *(154,836)*	1.50
861	3c **Ralph Waldo Emerson,** *Feb. 5,* Boston, Mass. *(185,148)*	1.50
862	5c **Louisa May Alcott,** *Feb. 5,* Concord, Mass. *(134,325)*	2.25
863	10c **Samuel L. Clemens,** *Feb. 13,* Hannibal, Mo. *(150,492)*	3.75
864	1c **Henry W. Longfellow,** *Feb. 16,* Portland, Me. *(160,508)*	1.50
865	2c **John Greenleaf Whittier,** *Feb. 16,* Haverhill, Mass. *(148,423)*	1.50
866	3c **James Russell Lowell,** *Feb. 20,* Cambridge, Mass. *(148,735)*	1.50
867	5c **Walt Whitman,** *Feb. 20,* Camden, N.J. *(134,185)*	4.00
868	10c **James Whitcomb Riley,** *Feb. 24,* Greenfield, Ind. *(131,760)*	6.00
869	1c **Horace Mann,** *Mar. 14,* Boston, Mass. *(186,854)*	1.50
870	2c **Mark Hopkins,** *Mar. 14,* Williamstown, Mass. *(140,286)*	1.50
871	3c **Charles W. Eliot,** *Mar. 28,* Cambridge, Mass. (155,708)	1.50
872	5c **Frances E. Willard,** *Mar. 28,* Evanston, Ill. *(140,483)*	4.00
873	10c **Booker T. Washington,** *Apr. 7,* Tuskegee Institute, Ala. *(163,507)*	6.00
874	1c **John James Audubon,** *Apr. 8,* St. Francisville, La. *(144,123)*	1.50
875	2c **Dr. Crawford W. Long,** *Apr. 8,* Jefferson, Ga. *(158,128)*	1.50
876	3c **Luther Burbank,** *Apr. 17,* Santa Rosa, Cal. *(147,033)*	2.00
877	5c **Dr. Walter Reed,** *Apr. 17,* Washington, D.C. *(154,464)*	2.50
878	10c **Jane Addams,** *Apr. 26,* Chicago, Ill. *(132,375)*	5.00
879	1c **Stephen Collins Foster,** *May 3,* Bardstown, Ky. *(183,461)*	1.50
880	2c **John Philip Sousa,** *May 3,* Washington, D.C. *(131,422)*	1.50
881	3c **Victor Herbert,** *May 13,* New York, N.Y. *(168,200)*	1.50
882	5c **Edward A. MacDowell,** *May 13,* Peterborough, N.H. *(135,155)*	2.50
883	10c **Ethelbert Nevin,** *June 10,* Pittsburgh, Pa. *(121,951)*	5.00
884	1c **Gilbert Charles Stuart,** *Sept. 5,* Narragansett, R.I. *(131,965)*	1.50
885	2c **James A. McNeill Whistler,** *Sept. 5,* Lowell, Mass. *(130,962)*	1.50
886	3c **Augustus Saint-Gaudens,** *Sept. 16,* New York, N.Y. *(138,200)*	1.50
887	5c **Daniel Chester French,** *Sept. 16,* Stockbridge, Mass. *(124,608)*	1.75
888	10c **Frederic Remington,** *Sept. 30,* Canton, N.Y. *(116,219)*	5.00
889	1c **Eli Whitney,** *Oct. 7,* Savannah, Ga. *(140,868)*	1.50
890	2c **Samuel F.B. Morse,** *Oct. 7,* New York, N.Y. *(135,388)*	1.50
891	3c **Cyrus Hall McCormick,** *Oct. 14,* Lexington, Va. *(137,415)*	1.50
892	5c **Elias Howe,** *Oct. 14,* Spencer, Mass. *(126,334)*	3.00
893	10c **Alexander Graham Bell,** *Oct. 28,* Boston, Mass. *(125,372)*	7.50

1940

No.	Description	Price
894	3c **Pony Express,** *Apr. 3, 1940,* St. Joseph, Mo. *(194,589)*	6.00
	Sacramento, Cal. *(160,849)*	6.00
895	3c **Pan American Union,** *Apr. 14, 1940 (182,401)*	4.50
896	3c **Idaho Statehood,** *July 3, 1940,* Boise, Idaho *(156,429)*	4.50
897	3c **Wyoming Statehood,** *July 10, 1940* Cheyenne, Wyo. *(156,709)*	4.50
898	3c **Coronado Expedition,** *Sept. 7, 1940,* Albuquerque, N.M. *(161,012)*	4.50
899	1c **Defense,** *Oct. 16, 1940*	4.25
900	2c **Defense,** *Oct. 16, 1940*	4.25
901	3c **Defense,** *Oct. 16, 1940*	4.25
	899 to 901 on one cover *(450,083)*	10.00
902	3c **Thirteenth Amendment,** *Oct. 20, 1940,* World's Fair, N.Y. *(156,146)*	5.00

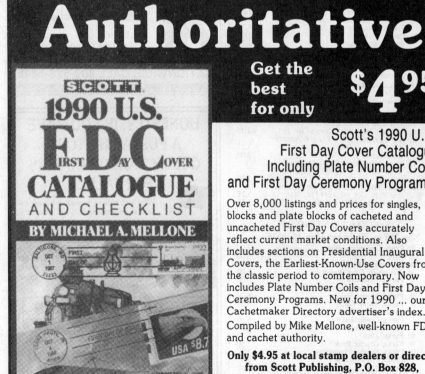

1941

No.		Description	Price
903	3c	**Vermont Statehood,** *Mar. 4, 1941,* Montpelier, Vt. *(182,423)*	6.00

1942

No.		Description	Price
904	3c	**Kentucky Statehood,** *June 1, 1942,* Frankfort, Ky. *(155,730)*	4.00
905	3c	**"Win the War",** *July 4, 1942 (191,168)*	3.75
906	5c	**Chinese Resistance,** *July 7, 1942,* Denver, Colo. *(168,746)*	6.00

1943-44

No.		Description	Price
907	2c	**United Nations,** *Jan. 14, 1943 (178,865)*	3.50
908	1c	**Four Freedoms,** *Feb. 12, 1943 (193,800)*	3.50
909	5c	**Poland,** *June 22, 1943,* Chicago, Ill. *(88,170)*	5.00
		Washington, D.C. *(136,002)*	4.00
910	5c	**Czechoslovakia,** *July 12, 1943 (145,112)*	4.00
911	5c	**Norway,** *July 27, 1943 (130,054)*	4.00
912	5c	**Luxemborg,** *Aug. 10, 1943 (166,367)*	4.00
913	5c	**Netherlands,** *Aug. 24, 1943 (148,763)*	4.00
914	5c	**Belgium,** *Sept. 14, 1943 (154,220)*	4.00
915	5c	**France,** *Sept. 28, 1943 (163,478)*	4.00
916	5c	**Greece,** *Oct. 12, 1943 (166,553)*	4.00
917	5c	**Yugoslavia,** *Oct. 26, 1943 (161,835)*	4.00
918	5c	**Albania,** *Nov. 9, 1943 (162,275)*	4.00
919	5c	**Austria,** *Nov. 23, 1943 (172,285)*	4.00
920	5c	**Denmark,** *Dec. 7, 1943 (173,784)*	4.00
921	5c	**Korea,** *Nov. 2, 1944 (192,860)*	4.00

1944

No.		Description	Price
922	3c	**Railroad,** *May 10, 1944,* Ogden, Utah *(151,324)*	5.00
		Omaha, Neb. (171,000)	5.00
		San Francisco, Cal. (125,000)	5.00
923	3c	**Steamship,** *May 22, 1944,* Kings Point, N.Y. *(152,324)*	4.00
		Savannah, Ga. *(181,472)*	4.00
924	3c	**Telegraph,** *May 24, 1944,* Washington, D.C. *(141,907)*	3.50
		Baltimore, Md. *(136,480)*	3.50
925	3c	**Philippines,** *Sept. 27, 1944 (214,865)*	3.50
926	3c	**Motion Picture,** *Oct. 31, 1944,* Hollywood, Cal. *(190,660)*	3.50
		New York, N.Y. *(176,473)*	3.50

1945

No.		Description	Price
927	3c	**Florida,** *Mar. 3, 1945,* Tallahassee, Fla. *(228,435)*	3.50
928	5c	**United Nations Conference,** *Apr. 25, 1945,* San Francisco, Cal. *(417,450)*	3.50
929	3c	**Iwo Jima,** *July 11, 1945 (391,650)*	6.00

1945-46

No.		Description	Price
930	1c	**Roosevelt,** *July 26, 1945,* Hyde Park, N.Y. *(390,219)*	2.50
931	2c	**Roosevelt,** *Aug. 24, 1945,* Warm Springs, Ga. *(426,142)*	2.50
932	3c	**Roosevelt,** *June 27, 1945 (391,650)*	2.50
933	5c	**Roosevelt,** *Jan. 30, 1946 (466,766)*	3.00
934	3c	**Army,** *Sept. 28, 1945 (392,300)*	4.00
935	3c	**Navy,** *Oct. 27, 1945,* Annapolis, Md. *(460,352)*	4.00
936	3c	**Coast Guard,** *Nov. 10, 1945* New York, N.Y. *(405,280)*	4.00
937	3c	**Alfred E. Smith,** *Nov. 26, 1945* New York, N.Y. *(424,950)*	2.50
938	3c	**Texas,** *Dec. 29, 1945,* Austin, Tex. *(397,860)*	4.00

1946

No.		Description	Price
939	3c	**Merchant Marine,** *Feb. 26, 1946 (432,141)*	4.00
940	3c	**Veterans of WWII,** *May 9, 1946 (492,786)*	1.50
941	3c	**Tennessee,** *June 1, 1946,* Nashville, Tenn. *(463,512)*	1.50
942	3c	**Iowa,** *Aug. 3, 1946,* Iowa City, Iowa *(517,505)*	1.50
943	3c	**Smithsonian,** *Aug. 10, 1946 (402,448)*	1.50
944	3c	**Kearny Expedition,** *Oct. 16, 1946,* Santa Fe, N.M. *(384,300)*	1.50

1947

No.		Description	Price
945	3c	**Thomas A. Edison,** *Feb. 11, 1947,* Milan, Ohio *(632,473)*	1.50
946	3c	**Joseph Pulitzer,** *Apr. 10, 1947,* New York, N.Y. *(580,870)*	1.50
947	3c	**Stamp Centenary,** *May 17, 1947,* New York, N.Y. *(712,873)*	1.50
948	5c	and 10c **Centenary Exhibition Sheet,** *May 19, 1947,* New York, N.Y. *(502,175)*	2.00
949	3c	**Doctors,** *June 9, 1947,* Atlantic City, N.J. *(508,016)*	1.00
950	3c	**Utah,** *July 24, 1947,* Salt Lake City, Utah *(456,416)*	1.00
951	3c	**"Constitution",** *Oct. 21, 1947,* Boston, Mass. *(683,416)*	1.00
952	3c	**Everglades Park,** *Dec. 5, 1947,* Florida City, Fla. *(466,647)*	1.00

1948

No.		Description	Price
953	3c	**Carver,** *Jan. 5, 1948,* Tuskegee Institute, Ala. *(402,179)*	1.00
954	3c	**California Gold,** *Jan. 24, 1948,* Coloma, Calif. *(526,154)*	1.00
955	3c	**Mississippi Territory,** *Apr. 7, 1948,* Natchez, Miss. *(434,804)*	1.00
956	3c	**Four Chaplains,** *May 28, 1948,* Washington, D.C. *(459,070)*	1.00
957	3c	**Wisconsin Centennial,** *May 29, 1948,* Madison, Wis. *(470,280)*	1.00
958	5c	**Swedish Pioneers,** *June 4, 1948* Chicago, Ill. (364,318)	1.00
959	3c	**Women's Progress,** *July 19, 1948,* Seneca Falls, N.Y. *(401,923)*	1.00
960	3c	**William Allen White,** *July 31, 1948,* Emporia, Kans. *(385,648)*	1.00
961	3c	**U.S.-Canada Friendship,** *Aug. 2, 1948,* Niagara Falls, N.Y. *(406,467)*	1.00
962	3c	**Francis Scott Key,** *Aug. 2, 1948,* Frederick, Md. *(505,930)*	1.00
963	3c	**Salute to Youth,** *Aug. 11, 1948,* Washington, D.C. *(347,070)*	1.00
964	3c	**Oregon Territory Establishment,** *Aug. 14, 1948,* Oregon City, Ore. *(365,898)*	1.00
965	3c	**Harlan Fiske Stone,** *Aug. 25, 1948,* Chesterfield, N.H. *(362,170)*	1.00
966	3c	**Palomar Observatory,** *Aug. 30, 1948,* Palomar Mountain, Calif. *(401,365)*	1.00
967	3c	**Clara Barton,** *Sept. 7, 1948,* Oxford, Mass. *(362,000)*	90
968	3c	**Poultry Industry,** *Sept. 9, 1948,* New Haven, Conn. *(475,000)*	90
969	3c	**Gold Star Mothers,** *Sept. 21, 1948,* Washington, D.C. *(386,064)*	1.00
970	3c	**Fort Kearny,** *Sept. 22, 1948,* Minden, Neb. *(429,633)*	1.00
971	3c	**Volunteer Firemen,** *Oct. 4, 1948,* Dover, Del. *(399,630)*	2.00
972	3c	**Indian Centennial,** *Oct. 15, 1948,* Muskogee, Okla. *(459,528)*	90
973	3c	**Rough Riders,** *Oct. 27, 1948,* Prescott, Ariz. *(399,198)*	90
974	3c	**Juliette Low,** *Oct. 29, 1948,* Savannah, Ga. *(476,573)*	90
975	3c	**Will Rogers,** *Nov. 4, 1948,* Claremore, Okla. *(450,350)*	90
976	3c	**Fort Bliss,** *Nov. 5, 1948,* El Paso, Tex. *(421,000)*	90
977	3c	**Moina Michael,** *Nov. 9, 1948,* Athens, Ga. *(374,090)*	90
978	3c	**Gettysburg Address,** *Nov. 19, 1948,* Gettysburg, Pa. *(511,990)*	90
979	3c	**American Turners Society,** *Nov. 20, 1948,* Cincinnati, Ohio *(434,090)*	90
980	3c	**Joel Chandler Harris,** *Dec. 9, 1948,* Eatonton, Ga. *(426,199)*	90

1949

No.		Description	Price
981	3c	**Minnesota Territory,** *May 3, 1949,* St. Paul, Minn. *(458,750)*	90
982	3c	**Washington and Lee University,** *Apr. 12, 1949,* Lexington, Va. *(447,910)*	90
983	3c	**Puerto Rico Election,** *Apr. 27, 1949,* San Juan, P.R. *(390,416)*	90
984	3c	**Annapolis, Md.,** *May 23, 1949,* Annapolis, Md. *(441,802)*	90
985	3c	**G.A.R.,** *Aug. 29, 1949,* Indianapolis, Ind. *(471,696)*	90
986	3c	**Edgar Allan Poe,** *Oct. 7, 1949,* Richmond, Va. *(371,020)*	90

1950

No.		Description	Price
987	3c	**American Bankers Assoc.,** *Jan. 3, 1950,* Saratoga Springs, N.Y. *(388,622)*	1.00
988	3c	**Samuel Gompers,** *Jan. 27, 1950,* Washington, D.C. *(332,023)*	1.00
989	3c	**National Capital Sesquicentennial (Freedom),** *Apr. 20, 1950,* Washington, D.C. *(371,743)*	1.00
990	3c	**National Capital Sesquicentennial (Executive),** *June 12, 1950,* Washington, D.C. *(376,789)*	1.00
991	3c	**National Capital Sesquicentennial (Judicial),** *Aug. 2, 1950,* Washington, D.C. *(324,007)*	1.00
992	3c	**National Capital Sesquicentennial, (Legislative),** *Nov. 22, 1950,* Washington, D.C. *(352,215)*	1.00
993	3c	**Railroad Engineers,** *Apr. 29, 1950,* Jackson, Tenn. *(420,830)*	1.00
994	3c	**Kansas City Centenary,** *June 3, 1950,* Kansas City, Mo. *(405,390)*	1.00
995	3c	**Boy Scouts,** *June 30, 1950,* Valley Forge, Pa. *(622,972)*	2.00
996	3c	**Indiana Territory Sesquicentennial,** *July 4, 1950,* Vincennes, Ind. *(359,643)*	1.00
997	3c	**California Statehood,** *Sept. 9, 1950,* Sacramento, Cal. *(391,919)*	1.00

1951

No.		Description	Price
998	3c	**United Confederate Veterans,** *May 30, 1951,* Norfolk, Va. *(374,235)*	1.00
999	3c	**Nevada Centennial,** *July 14, 1951,* Genoa, Nev. *(336,890)*	1.00
1000	3c	**Landing of Cadillac,** *July 24, 1951,* Detroit, Mich. *(323,094)*	1.00
1001	3c	**Colorado Statehood,** *Aug. 1, 1951,* Minturn, Colo. *(311,568)*	1.00
1002	3c	**American Chemical Society,** *Sept. 4, 1951,* New York, N.Y. *(436,419)*	1.00
1003	3c	**Battle of Brooklyn,** *Dec. 10, 1951,* Brooklyn, N.Y. *(420,000)*	1.00

1952

No.		Description	Price
1004	3c	**Betsy Ross,** *Jan. 2, 1952,* Philadelphia, Pa. *(314,312)*	1.00
1005	3c	**4-H Club,** *Jan. 15, 1952,* Springfield, Ohio *(383,290)*	1.00
1006	3c	**B. & O. Railroad,** *Feb. 28, 1952,* Baltimore, Md. *(441,600)*	1.25
1007	3c	**American Automobile Association,** *Mar. 4, 1952,* Chicago, Ill. *(520,123)*	85
1008	3c	**NATO,** *Apr. 4, 1952,* Washington, D.C. *(313,518)*	85
1009	3c	**Grand Coulee Dam,** *May 15, 1952,* Grand Coulee, Wash. *(341,680)*	85
1010	3c	**Lafayette,** *June 13, 1952,* Georgetown, S.C. *(349,102)*	85
1011	3c	**Mt. Rushmore Memorial,** *Aug. 11, 1952,* Keystone, S.D. *(337,027)*	85
1012	3c	**Civil Engineers,** *Sept. 6, 1952,* Chicago, Ill. *(318,483)*	85
1013	3c	**Service Women,** *Sept. 11, 1952,* Washington, D.C. *(308,062)*	85
1014	3c	**Gutenberg Bible,** *Sept. 30, 1952,* Washington, D.C. *(387,078)*	85
1015	3c	**Newspaper Boys,** *Oct. 4, 1952,* Philadelphia, Pa. *(626,000)*	85
1016	3c	**Red Cross,** *Nov. 21, 1952,* New York, N.Y. *(439,252)*	85

1953

No.		Description	Price
1017	3c	**National Guard,** *Feb. 23, 1953,* Washington, D.C. *(387,618)*	85
1018	3c	**Ohio Sesquicentennial,** *Mar. 2, 1953,* Chillicothe, Ohio *(407,983)*	85
1019	3c	**Washington Territory,** *Mar. 2, 1953,* Olympia, Wash. *(344,047)*	85
1020	3c	**Louisiana Purchase,** *Apr. 30, 1953,* St. Louis, Mo *(425,600)*	85
1021	5c	**Opening of Japan,** *July 14, 1953,* Washington, D.C. *(320,541)*	85
1022	3c	**American Bar Association,** *Aug. 24, 1953,* Boston, Mass. *(410,036)*	85
1023	3c	**Sagamore Hill,** *Sept. 14, 1953,* Oyster Bay, N.Y. *(379,750)*	90
1024	3c	**Future Farmers,** *Oct. 13, 1953,* Kansas City, Mo. *(424,193)*	85
1025	3c	**Trucking Industry,** *Oct. 27, 1953,* Los Angeles, Calif. *(875,021)*	85
1026	3c	**Gen. G.S. Patton, Jr.,** *Nov. 11, 1953,* Fort Knox, Ky. *(342,600)*	85
1027	3c	**New York City,** *Nov. 20, 1953,* New York, N.Y. *(387,914)*	85
1028	3c	**Gadsden Purchase,** *Dec. 30, 1953,* Tucson, Ariz. *(363,250)*	85

1954

No.		Description	Price
1029	3c	**Columbia University,** *Jan. 4, 1954,* New York, N.Y. *(550,745)*	85

1954-67

LIBERTY ISSUE

No.		Description	Price
1030	½c	*Oct. 20, 1955,* Washington, D.C. *(223,122)*Block of four	85
1031	1c	*Aug. 26, 1954,* Chicago, Ill. *(272,581)*	85
1031A	1¼c	*June 17, 1960,* Santa Fe, N.M. (total for #1031A, 1054A and combination covers, *501,848)*	85
		1031A and 1054A on one cover	1.50
1031	1½c	*Feb. 22, 1956,* Mount Vernon, Va. *(270,109)*	60
1033	2c	*Sept. 15, 1954,* San Francisco, Cal. *(307,300)*	60
1034	2½c	*June 17, 1959,* Boston, Mass. *(315,060)*	60
1035	3c	*June 24, 1954,* Albany, N.Y. *(340,001)*	60
1035b	3c	Tagged, *July 6, 1966*	15.00
1036	4c	*Nov. 19, 1954,* New York, N.Y. *(374,064)*	60
1036b	4c	Tagged, *Nov. 2, 1963,* Washington, D.C.	50.00

No. 1036b was supposed to have been issued at Dayton Nov. 2, but a mix-up delayed its issuance there until Nov. 4. About 510 Covers received the Nov. 2 cancellation.

No.		Description	Price
1037	4½c	*Mar. 16, 1959,* Hermitage, Tenn. *(320,000)*	60
1038	5c	*Dec. 2, 1954,* Fredericksburg, Va. *(255,650)*	60
1039	6c	*Nov. 18, 1955,* New York, N.Y. *(257,551)*	65
1040	7c	*Jan. 10, 1956,* Staunton, Va. *(200,111)*	70
1041	8c	*Apr. 9, 1954,* Washington, D.C. *(340,077)*	80
1042	8c	(Giori press), *Mar. 22, 1958,* Cleveland, O. *(223,899)*	60
1042A	8c	**Pershing,** *Nov. 17, 1961,* New York, N.Y. *(321,031)*	60
1043	9c	*June 14, 1956,* San Antonio, Texas *(207,086)*	1.50
1044	10c	*July 4, 1956,* Philadelphia, Pa., *(220,930)*	90
1044b	10c	Tagged, *July 6, 1966*	15.00
1044A	11c	*June 15, 1961,* Washington, D.C. *(238,905)*	90
1044c	11c	Tagged, *Jan. 11, 1967*	22.50
1045	12c	*June 6, 1959,* Oxford, O. *(225,869)*	90
1045a	12c	Tagged, *May 6, 1968*	25.00
1046	15c	*Dec. 12, 1958,* Washington, D.C. *(205,680)*	1.00
1046a	15c	Tagged, *July 6, 1966*	20.00
1047	20c	*Apr. 13, 1956,* Charlottesville, Va. *(147,860)*	1.20
1048	25c	*Apr. 18, 1958,* Boston, Mass. *(196,530)*	1.30
1049	30c	*Sept. 21, 1955,* Norfolk, Va. *(120,166)*	1.50
1050	40c	*Sept. 24, 1955,* Richmond, Va. *(113,972)*	1.75
1051	50c	*Aug. 25, 1955,* Louisville, Ky. *(110,220)*	6.00
1052	$1	*Oct. 7, 1955,* Joplin, Mo. *(80,191)*	10.00
1053	$5	*Mar. 19, 1956,* Paterson, N.J. *(34,272)*	50.00

1954-65

COIL STAMPS

1054 1c *Oct. 8, 1954,* Baltimore, Md. *(196,318)*Strip of three 75
1054A 1¼c *June 17, 1960,* Santa Fe, N.M. (total for #1054A, 1031A and combination covers, *501,848)* 1.00
1055 2c *Oct. 22, 1954,* St. Louis, Mo. *(162,050)*Pair 75
1055a 2c Tagged, *May 6, 1968* pair 11.00
1056 2½c *Sept. 9, 1959,* Los Angeles, Calif. *(198,680)* 1.20
1057 3c *July 20, 1954,* Washington, D.C. *(137,139)* 75
1058 4c *July 31, 1958,* Mandan, N.D. *(184,079)* 75
1059 4½c *May 1, 1959,* Denver, Colo. *(202,454)* 1.75
1059A 25c *Feb. 25, 1965,* Wheaton, Md. *(184,954)* 1.20
1059b 25c Tagged, *Apr. 3, 1973,* New York, N.Y. 14.00

1954

1060 3c **Nebraska Territory,** *May 7, 1954,* Nebraska City, Neb. *(401,015)* 75
1061 3c **Kansas Territory,** *May 31, 1954,* Fort Leavenworth, Kans. *(349,145)* 75
1062 3c **George Eastman,** *July 12, 1954,* Rochester, N.Y. *(630,448)* 75
1063 3c **Lewis & Clark Expedition,** *July 28, 1954,* Sioux City, Iowa *(371,557)* 75

1955

1064 3c **Pennsylvania Academy of the Fine Arts,** *Jan. 15, 1955,* Philadelphia, Pa. *(307,040)* 75
1065 3c **Land Grant Colleges,** *Feb. 12, 1955,* East Lansing, Mich. *(419,241)* 75
1066 8c **Rotary International,** *Feb. 23, 1955,* Chicago, Ill. *(350,625)* 1.10
1067 3c **Armed Forces Reserve,** *May 21, 1955,* Washington, D.C. *(300,436)* 75
1068 3c **New Hampshire,** *June 21, 1955,* Franconia, N.H. *(330,630)* 75
1069 3c **Soo Locks,** *June 28, 1955,* Sault Sainte Marie, Mich. *(316,616)* 75
1070 3c **Atoms for Peace,** *July 28, 1955,* Washington, D.C. *(351,940)* 75
1071 3c **Fort Ticonderoga,** *Sept. 18, 1955,* Fort Ticonderoga, N.Y. *(342,946)* 75
1072 3c **Andrew W. Mellon,** *Dec. 20, 1955,* Washington, D.C. *(278,897)* 75

1956

1073 3c **Benjamin Franklin,** *Jan. 17, 1956,* Philadelphia, Pa. *(351,260)* 75
1074 3c **Booker T. Washington,** *Apr. 5, 1956,* Booker T. Washington Birthplace, Va. *(272,659)* 75
1075 11c **FIPEX Souvenir Sheet,** *Apr. 28, 1956,* New York, N.Y. *(429,327)* 5.00
1076 3c **FIPEX,** *Apr. 30, 1956,* New York, N.Y. *(526,090)* 75
1077 3c **Wildlife (Turkey),** *May 5, 1956,* Fond du Lac, Wis. *(292,121)* 1.10
1078 3c **Wildlife (Antelope),** *June 22, 1956,* Gunnison, Colo. *(294,731)* 1.10
1079 3c **Wildlife (Salmon),** *Nov. 9, 1956,* Seattle, Wash. *(346,800)* 1.10
1080 3c **Pure Food and Drug Laws,** *June 27, 1956,* Washington, D.C. *(411,761)* 80
1081 3c **Wheatland,** *Aug. 5, 1956,* Lancaster, Pa. *(340,142)* 80
1082 3c **Labor Day,** *Sept. 3, 1956,* Camden, N.J. *(338,450)* 80
1083 3c **Nassau Hall,** *Sept. 22, 1956,* Princeton, N.J. *(350,756)* 80
1084 3c **Devils Tower,** *Sept. 24, 1956,* Devils Tower, Wyo. *(285,090)* 80
1085 3c **Children,** *Dec. 15, 1956,* Washington, D.C. *(305,125)* 80

1957

1086 3c **Alexander Hamilton,** *Jan. 11, 1957,* New York, N.Y. *(305,117)* 80
1087 3c **Polio,** *Jan. 15, 1957,* Washington, D.C. *(307,630)* 80
1088 3c **Coast & Geodetic Survey,** *Feb. 11, 1957,* Seattle, Wash. *(309,931)* 80
1089 3c **Architects,** *Feb. 23, 1957,* New York, N.Y. *(368,840)* 80
1090 3c **Steel Industry,** *May 22, 1957,* New York, N.Y. *(473,284)* 80
1091 3c **Naval Review,** *June 10, 1957,* U.S.S. Saratoga, Norfolk, Va. *(365,933)* 80
1092 3c **Oklahoma Statehood,** *June 14, 1957,* Oklahoma City, Okla. *(327,172)* 80
1093 3c **School Teachers,** *July 1, 1957,* Philadelphia, Pa. *(357,986)* 80
(Spelling error) Philadelpia 5.00
1094 4c **Flag,** *July 4, 1957,* Washington, D.C. *(523,879)* 80
1095 3c **Shipbuilding,** *Aug. 15, 1957,* Bath, Maine *(347,432)* 80
1096 8c **Ramon Magsaysay,** *Aug. 31, 1957,* Washington, D.C. *(334,558)* 80
1097 3c **Lafayette Bicentenary,** *Sept. 6, 1957,* Easton, Pa. *(260,421)* 80
Fayetteville, N.C. *(230,000)* 80
Louisville, Ky. *(207,856)* 80
1098 3c **Wildlife** (Whooping Cranes), *Nov. 22, 1957,* New York, N.Y. *(342,970)* 1.00
New Orleans, La. *(154,327)* 1.00
Corpus Christi, Tex. *(280,990)* 1.00
1099 3c **Religious Freedom,** *Dec. 27, 1957,* Flushing, N.Y. *(357,770)* 80

1958

1100 3c **Gardening-Horticulture,** *Mar. 15, 1958,* Ithaca, N.Y. *(451,292)* 80
1104 3c **Brussels Exhibition,** *Apr. 17, 1958,* Detroit, Mich. *(428,073)* 80
1105 3c **James Monroe,** *Apr. 28, 1958,* Montross, Va. *(326,988)* 80
1106 3c **Minnesota Statehood,** *May 11, 1958,* Saint Paul, Minn. *(475,552)* 80
1107 3c **International Geophysical Year,** *May 31, 1958,* Chicago, Ill. *(397,000)* 80
1108 3c **Gunston Hall,** *June 12, 1958,* Lorton, Va. *(349,801)* 80
1109 3c **Mackinac Bridge,** *June 25, 1958,* Mackinac Bridge, Mich. *(445,605)* 80
1110 4c **Simon Bolivar,** *July 24, 1958,* Washington, D.C. 80
1111 8c **Simon Bolivar,** *July 24, 1958* Washington, D.C. 80
1110 and 1111, set of two on one cover 2.00

First day cancellation was applied to 708, 777 covers bearing No. 1110, No. 1111, or both.

1112 4c **Atlantic Cable,** *Aug. 15, 1958,* New York, N.Y. *(365,072)* 80

1958-59

1113 1c **Lincoln Sesquicentennial,** *Feb. 12, 1959,* Hodgenville, Ky. *(379,862)* 80
1114 3c **Lincoln Sesquicentennial,** *Feb. 12, 1959,* New York, N.Y. *(437,737)* 80
1115 4c **Lincoln-Douglas Debates,** *Aug. 27, 1958,* Freeport, Ill. *(373,063)* 80
1116 4c **Lincoln Sesquicentennial,** *May, 30, 1959,* Washington, D.C. *(894,887)* 80

1958

1117 4c **Lajos Kossuth,** *Sept. 19, 1958,* Washington, D.C. 80
1118 8c **Lajos Kossuth,** *Sept. 19, 1958,* Washington, D.C. 80
1117 and 1118, set of two on one cover 2.00

First day cancellation was applied to 722, 188 covers bearing No. 1117, No. 1118, or both.

1119 4c **Freedom of Press,** *Sept. 22, 1958,* Columbia, Mo. *(411,752)* 80
1120 4c **Overland Mail,** *Oct. 10, 1958,* San Francisco, Cal. *(352,760)* 80
1121 4c **Noah Webster,** *Oct. 16, 1958,* West Hartford, Conn. *(364,608)* 80
1122 4c **Forest Conservation,** *Oct. 27, 1958,* Tucson, Ariz. *(405,959)* 80
1123 4c **Fort Duquesne,** *Nov. 25, 1958,* Pittsburgh, Pa. *(421,764)* 80

1959

1124 4c **Oregon Statehood,** *Feb. 14, 1959,* Astoria, Ore. *(452,764)* 80
1125 4c **San Martin,** *Feb. 25, 1959,* Washington, D.C. 80
1126 8c **San Martin,** *Feb. 25, 1959,* Washington, D.C. 80
1125 and 1126, set of two on one cover 2.00

First day cancellation was applied to 910, 208 covers bearing No. 1125, No. 1126, or both.

1127 4c **NATO,** *Apr., 1, 1959,* Washington, D.C. *(361,040)* 80
1128 4c **Arctic Exploration,** *Apr. 6, 1959,* Cresson, Pa. *(397,770)* 80
1129 8c **World Trade,** *Apr. 20, 1959,* Washington, D.C. *(503,618)* 80
1130 4c **Silver Centennial,** *June 8, 1959,* Virginia City, Nev. *(337,233)* 80
1131 4c **St. Lawrence Seaway,** *June 26, 1959,* Massena, N.Y. *(543,211)* 80
1132 4c **Flag** (49 stars), *July 4, 1959,* Auburn, N.Y. *(523,773)* 80
1133 4c **Soil Conservation,** *Aug. 26, 1959,* Rapid City, S.D. *(400,613)* 80
1134 4c **Petroleum Industry,** *Aug. 27, 1959,* Titusville, Pa. *(801,859)* 80
1135 4c **Dental Health,** *Sept. 14, 1959,* New York, N.Y. *(649,813)* 80
1136 4c **Reuter,** *Sept. 29, 1959,* Washington, D.C. 80
1137 8c **Reuter,** *Sept. 29, 1959,* Washington, D.C. 80
1136 and 1137, set of two on one cover 2.00

First day cancellation was applied to 1,207,933 covers bearing No. 1136, No. 1137, or both.

1138 4c **Dr. Ephraim McDowell,** *Dec. 3, 1959,* Danville, Ky. *(344,603)* 80

1960-61

1139 4c **Washington "Credo,"** *Jan. 20, 1960,* Mount Vernon, Va. *(438,335)* 90
1140 4c **Franklin "Credo"** *March 31,1960,* Philadelphia, Pa. *(497,913)* 90
1141 4c **Jefferson "Credo,"** *May 18, 1960,* Charlottesville, Va. *(454,903)* 90
1142 4c **Francis Scott Key "Credo,"** *Sept. 14, 1960,* Baltimore, Md. *(501,129)* 90
1143 4c **Lincoln "Credo,"** *Nov. 19, 1960,* New York, N.Y. *(467,780)* 90
1144 4c **Patrick Henry "Credo,"** *Jan. 11, 1961,* Richmond, Va. *(415,252)* 90
1145 4c **Boy Scouts,** *Feb. 8, 1960,* Washington, D.C. *(1,419,955)* 1.10
1146 4c **Olympic Winter Games,** *Feb. 18, 1960,* Olympic Valley, Calif, *(516,456)* 80
1147 4c **Masaryk,** *Mar. 7, 1960,* Washington, D.C. 80
1148 8c **Masaryk,** *Mar. 7, 1960,* Washington, D.C. 80
1147 and 1148, set of two on one cover 2.00

First day cancellation was applied to 1,710,726 covers bearing No. 1147, No. 1148, or both.

1149 4c **World Refugee Year,** *Apr. 7, 1960,* Washington, D.C. *(413,298)* 80
1150 4c **Water Conservation,** *Apr. 18, 1960,* Washington, D.C. *(648,988)* 80
1151 4c **SEATO,***May 31, 1960,* Washington, D.C. *(514,926)* 80
1152 4c **American Woman,** *June 2, 1960,* Washington, D.C. *(830,385)* 80
1153 4c **50-Star Flag,** *July 4, 1960,* Honolulu, Hawaii *(820,900)* 80
1154 4c **Pony Express Centennial,** *July 19, 1960,* Sacramento, Calif, *(520,223)* 80
1155 4c **Employ the Handicapped,** *Aug. 28, 1960,* New York, N.Y. *(439,638)* 80
1156 4c **World Forestry Congress,** *Aug. 29, 1960,* Seattle, Wash. *(350,848)* 80
1157 4c **Mexican Independence,** *Sept. 16, 1960,* Los Angeles, Calif, *(360,297)* 80
1158 4c **U.S.-Japan Treaty,** *Sept. 28, 1960,* Washington, D.C. *(545,150)* 80
1159 4c **Paderewski,** *Oct. 8, 1960,* Washington, D.C. 80
1160 8c **Paderewski,** *Oct. 8, 1960,* Washington, D.C. 80
1159 and 1160 on one cover 2.00

First day cancellation was applied to 1,057,438 covers bearing No. 1159, No. 1160, or both.

1161 4c **Robert A. Taft,** *Oct. 10, 1960,* Cincinnati, Ohio *(312,116)* 80
1162 4c **Wheels of Freedom,** *Oct. 15, 1960,* Detroit, Mich. *(380,551)* 80
1163 4c **Boys' Clubs,** *Oct. 18, 1960,* New York, N.Y. *(435,009)* 80
1164 4c **Automated P.O.,** *Oct. 20, 1960,* Providence, R.I. *(458,237)* 80
1165 4c **Mannerheim,** *Oct. 26, 1960,* Washington, D.C. 80
1166 8c **Mannerheim,** *Oct. 26, 1960,* Washington, D.C. 80
1165 and 1166 on one cover 2.00

First day cancellation was applied to 1,168,770 covers bearing No. 1165, No. 1166, or both.

1167 4c **Camp Fire Girls,** *Nov. 1, 1960,* New York, N.Y. *(324,944)* 80
1168 4c **Garibaldi,** *Nov. 2, 1960,* Washington, D.C. 80
1169 8c **Garibaldi,** *Nov. 2, 1960,* Washington, D.C. 80
1168 and 1169 on one cover 2.00

First day cancellation was applied to 1,001,490 covers bearing No. 1168, No. 1169, or both.

1170 4c **Senator George,** *Nov. 5, 1960,* New York, N.Y. *(318,180)* 80
1171 4c **Andrew Carnegie,** *Nov. 25, 1960,* New York, N.Y. *(318,180)* 80
1172 4c **John Foster Dulles,** *Dec. 6, 1960,* Washington, D.C. *(400,055)* 80
1173 4c **Echo I,** *Dec. 15, 1960,* Washington, D.C. *(583,747)* 2.00

1961-65

1174 4c **Gandhi,** *Jan. 26, 1961,* Washington, D.C. 80
1175 8c **Gandhi,** *Jan. 26, 1961,* Washington, D.C. 80
1174 and 1175 on one cover 2.00

First day cancellation was applied to 1,013,515 covers bearing No. 1174, No. 1175, or both.

1176 4c **Range Conservation,** *Feb. 2, 1961,* Salt Lake City, Utah *(357,101)* 75
1177 4c **Horace Greeley,** *Feb. 3, 1961,* Chappaqua, N.Y. *(359,205)* 75
1178 4c **Fort Sumter,** *Apr. 12, 1961,* Charleston, S.C. *(602,599)* 1.25
1179 4c **Battle of Shiloh,** *Apr. 7, 1962,* Shiloh, Tenn. *(526,062)* 1.25
1180 5c **Battle of Gettysburg,** *July 1, 1963,* Gettysburg, Pa. *(600,205)* 1.25
1181 5c **Battle of Wilderness,** *May 5, 1964,* Fredericksburg, Va. *(450,904)* 1.25
1182 5c **Appomattox,** *Apr. 9, 1965,* Appomattox, Va. *(653,121)* 1.25
1183 4c **Kansas Statehood,** *May 10, 1961,* Council Grove, Kansas *(480,561)* 75
1184 4c **Senator Norris,** *July 11, 1961,* Washington, D.C. *(482,875)* 75
1185 4c **Naval Aviation,** *Aug. 20, 1961,* San Diego, Calif. *(416,391)* 90
1186 4c **Workmen's Compensation,** *Sept. 4, 1961,* Milwaukee, Wis, *(410,236)* 75
1187 4c **Frederic Remington,** *Oct. 4, 1961,* Washington, D.C. *(723,443)* 75
1188 4c **China Republic,** *Oct. 10, 1961,* Washington, D.C. *(463,900)* 75
1189 4c **Naismith-Basketball,** *Nov. 6, 1961,* Springfield, Mass. *(479,917)* 1.50
1190 4c **Nursing,** *Dec. 28, 1961,* Washington, D.C. *(964,005)* 75

1962

1191 4c **New Mexico Statehood,** *Jan. 6, 1962,* Sante Fe, N.M. *(365,330)* 75

1192 4c **Arizona Statehood,** *Feb. 14, 1962,* Phoenix, Ariz. *(508,216)* 75

1193 4c **Project Mercury,** *Feb. 20, 1962,* Cape Canaveral, Fla. *(3,000,000)* 2.00
Any city 5.00

1194 4c **Malaria Eradication,** *Mar. 30, 1962,* Washington, D.C. *(554,175)* 75

1195 4c **Charles Evans Hughes,** *Apr. 11, 1962,* Washington, D.C. *(544,424)* 75

1196 4c **Seattle World's Fair,** *Apr. 25, 1962,* Seattle, Wash. *(771,856)* 75

1197 4c **Louisiana Statehood,** *Apr. 30, 1962,* New Orleans, La. *(436,681)* 75

1198 4c **Homestead Act,** *May 20, 1962,* Beatrice, Nebr. *(487,450)* 75

1199 4c **Girl Scouts,** *July 24, 1962,* Burlington, Vt. *(634,347)* 1.00

1200 4c **Brien McMahon,** *July 28, 1962,* Norwalk, Conn. *(384,419)* 75

1201 4c **Apprenticeship,** *Aug. 31, 1962,* Washington, D.C. *(1,003,548)* 75

1202 4c **Sam Rayburn,** *Sept. 16, 1962,* Bonham, Texas *(401,042)* 75

1203 4c **Dag Hammarskjold,** *Oct. 23, 1962,* New York, N.Y. *(500,683)* 75

1204 4c **Hammarskjold,** yellow inverted, *Nov. 16, 1962,* Washington, D.C. (about *75,000)* 6.00

1205 4c **Christmas,** *Nov. 1, 1962,* Pittsburgh, Pa. *(491,312)* 75

1206 4c **Higher Education,** *Nov. 14, 1962,* Washington, D.C. *(627,347)* 75

1207 4c **Winslow Homer,** *Dec. 15, 1962,* Gloucester, Mass. *(498,866)* 75

1963-66

1208 5c **Flag,** *Jan. 9, 1963,* Washington, D.C. *(696,185)* 75

1208a 5c Tagged, *Aug. 25, 1966* 11.50

1962-66

REGULAR ISSUE

1209 1c **Jackson,** *Mar. 22, 1963,* New York, N.Y. *(392,363)* 75

1209a 1c Tagged, *July 6, 1966,* Washington, D.C. 5.75

1213 5c **Washington,** *Nov. 23, 1962* New York, N.Y. *(360,531)* 75

1213b 5c Tagged, *Oct. 28, 1963* Dayton, Ohio, (about *15,000)* 5.75

1225 1c Coil, *May 31, 1963,* Chicago, Ill. *(238,952)* 75

1225a 1c Coil, tagged, *July 6, 1966,* Washington, D.C., Pair 5.75

1229 5c Coil, *Nov. 23, 1962,* New York, N.Y. *(184,627)* 75

1229a 5c Coil, tagged, *Oct. 28, 1963,* Dayton, Ohio, (about *2,000)* 20.00

1963

1230 5c **Carolina Charter,** *Apr. 6, 1963,* Edenton, N.C. *(426,200)* 75

1231 5c **Food for Peace,** *June 4, 1963,* Washington, D.C. *(624,342)* 75

1232 5c **West Virginia Statehood,** *June 20, 1963,* Wheeling, W. Va. *(413,389)* 75

1233 5c **Emancipation Proclamation,** *Aug. 16, 1963,* Chicago, Ill, *(494,886)* 75

1234 5c **Alliance for Progress,** *Aug. 17, 1963,* Washington, D.C. *(528,095)* 75

1235 5c **Cordell Hull,** *Oct. 5, 1963* Carthage, Tenn. *(391,631)* 75

1236 5c **Eleanor Roosevelt,** *Oct. 11, 1963,* Washington, D.C. *(860,155)* 75

1237 5c **Science,** *Oct. 14, 1963,* Washington, D.C. *(504,503)* 75

1238 5c **City Mail Delivery,** *Oct. 26, 1963,* Washington, D.C. *(544,806)* 75

1239 5c **Red Cross,** *Oct. 29, 1963,* Washington, D.C. *(557,678)* 75

1240 5c **Christmas,** *Nov. 1, 1963,* Santa Claus, Ind. *(458,619)* 75

1240a 5c **Christmas,** tagged, *Nov. 2, 1963,* Washington, D.C. (about *500)* 60.00

Note below No. 1036b also applies to No. 1240a.

1241 5c **Audubon,** *Dec. 7, 1963,* Henderson, Ky. *(518,855)* 75

1964

1242 5c **Sam Houston,** *Jan. 10, 1964,* Houston, Tex. *(487,986)* 75

1243 5c **Charles Russell,** *Mar. 19, 1964,* Great Falls, Mont. *(658,745)* 75

1244 5c **N.Y. World's Fair,** *Apr. 22, 1964,* World's Fair, N.Y. *(1,656,346)* 75

1245 5c **John Muir,** *Apr. 29, 1964,* Martinez, Calif. *(446,925)* 75

1246 5c **John F. Kennedy,** *May 29, 1964,* Boston, Mass. *(2,003,096)* 75
Any city 75

1247 5c **New Jersey Tercentenary,** *June 15, 1964,* Elizabeth, N.J. *(526,879)* 75

1248 5c **Nevada Statehood,** *July 22, 1964,* Carson City, Nev. *(584,973)* 75

1249 5c **Register & Vote,** *Aug. 1, 1964,* Washington, D.C. *(533,439)* 75

1250 5c **Shakespeare,** *Aug. 14, 1964,* Stratford, Conn. *(524,053)* 75

1251 5c **Drs. Mayo,** *Sept. 11, 1964,* Rochester, Minn. *(674,846)* 75

1252 5c **American Music,** *Oct. 15, 1964,* New York, N.Y. *(466,107)* 75

1253 5c **Homemakers,** *Oct. 26, 1964,* Honolulu, Hawaii *(435,392)* 75

1254 5c **Christmas (holly),** *Nov. 9, 1964,*Bethlehem, Pa. 75

1254a 5c Tagged, *Nov. 10, 1964,* Dayton, O. 12.50

1255 5c **Christmas (mistletoe),** *Nov. 9, 1964,*Bethlehem, Pa. 75

1255a 5c Tagged, *Nov. 10, 1964,* Dayton, O. 12.50

1256 5c **Christmas (poinsettia),** *Nov. 9, 1964,*Bethlehem, Pa. 75

1256a 5c Tagged, *Nov. 10, 1964,* Dayton, O. 12.50

1257 5c **Christmas (conifer),** *Nov. 9, 1964,*Bethlehem, Pa. 75

1257a 5c Tagged, *Nov. 10, 1964,* Dayton, O. 12.50
1257b 3.00
1257c 57.50

First day cancellation was applied to 794,900 covers bearing Nos. 1254 to 1257 in singles or block and (at Dayton) to about 2,700 covers bearing Nos. 1254a to 1257a in singles or multiples.

1258 5c **Verrazano-Narrows Bridge,** *Nov. 21, 1964,* Staten Island, N.Y. *(619,780)* 75

1259 5c **Fine Arts,** *Dec. 2, 1964,* Washington, D.C. *(558,046)* 75

1260 5c **Amateur Radio,** *Dec. 15, 1964,* Anchorage, Alaska *(452,255)* 75

1965

1261 5c **Battle of New Orleans,** *Jan. 8,* New Orleans, La. *(466,029)* 75

1262 5c **Physical Fitness-Sokol,** *Feb. 15,* Washington, D.C. *(864,848)* 75

1263 5c **Cancer Crusade,** *Apr. 1,* Washington, D.C. *(744,485)* 75

1264 5c **Churchill,** *May 13,* Fulton, Mo. *(773,580)* 75

1265 5c **Magna Carta,** *June 15,* Jamestown, Va. *(479,065)* 75

1266 5c **Intl. Cooperation Year,** *June 26,* San Francisco, Cal. *(402,925)* 75

1267 5c **Salvation Army,** *July 2,* New York, N.Y. *(634,228)* 75

1268 5c **Dante,** *July 17,* San Francisco, Cal. *(424,893)* 75

1269 5c **Herbet Hoover,** *Aug. 10,* West Branch, Iowa *(698,182)* 75

1270 5c **Robert Fulton,** *Aug. 19,* Clermont, N.Y. *(550,330)* 75

1271 5c **Florida Settlement,** *Aug. 28,* St. Augustine, Fla. *(465,000)* 75

1272 5c **Traffic Safety,** *Sept. 3,* Baltimore, Md. *(527,075)* 75

1273 5c **Copley,** *Sept. 17,* Washington, D.C. *(613,484)* 75

1274 11c **Intl. Telecommunication Union,** *Oct. 6,* Washington, D.C. *(332,818)* 75

1275 5c **Adlai Stevenson,** *Oct. 23,* Bloomington, Ill. *(755,656)* 75

1276 5c **Christmas,** *Nov. 2,* Silver Bell, Ariz. *(705,039)* 75

1276a 5c Tagged, *Nov. 15,* Washington, D.C. (about *300)* 42.50

1965-78

PROMINENT AMERICANS ISSUE

1278 1c *Jan. 12, 1968,* Jeffersonville, Ind. 60

First day cancellation was applied to 655,680 covers bearing Nos. 1278, 1278a or 1299.

1279 1¼c *Jan. 30, 1967,* Gallatin, Mo. *(439,010)* 60

1280 2c *June 8, 1966,* Spring Green, Wis. *(460,427)* 60

1281 3c *Sept. 16, 1967,* Boston, Mass. *(518,355)* 60

1282 4c *Nov. 19, 1965,* New York, N.Y. *(445,629)* 60

1282a 4c Tagged, *Dec. 1, 1965,* Dayton, O. (about *2,000)* 20.00
Washington, D.C. *(1,200)* 32.50

1283 5c *Feb. 22, 1966,* Washington, D.C. *(525,372)* 60

1283a 5c Tagged, *Feb. 23, 1966,* Washington, D.C. (about *900)* 22.50
Dayton, Ohio (about *200)* 57.50

1283B 5c Redrawn, *Nov. 17, 1967,* New York, N.Y. *(328,983)* 50

1284 6c *Jan. 29, 1966,* Hyde Park, N.Y. *(448,631)* 50

1284a 6c Tagged, *Dec. 29, 1966,* Washington, D.C. 20.00

1285 8c *Mar. 14, 1966,* Princeton, N.J. *(366,803)* 50

1285a 8c Tagged, *July 6, 1966* 14.00

1286 10c *Mar. 15, 1967,* Hermitage, Tenn. *(255,945)* 60

1286A 12c *July 30, 1968,* Greenfield Village, Mich. *(342,850)* 50

1287 13c *May 29, 1967,* Brookline, Mass. *(391,195)* 65

1288 15c *Mar. 8, 1968,* Washington, D.C. *(322,970)* 60

1288B 15c *June 14, 1978,* Boston, Mass. 65

First day cancellation was applied to 387,119 covers bearing Nos. 1288B or 1305E.

1289 20c *Oct. 24, 1967,* Lexington, Va. *(221,206)* 80

1289a 20c Tagged, *Apr. 3, 1973,* New York, N.Y. 12.50

1290 25c *Feb. 14, 1967,* Washington, D.C. *(213,730)* 1.00

1290a 25c Tagged, *Apr. 3, 1973,* New York, N.Y. 14.00

1291 30c *Oct. 21, 1968,* Burlington, Vt. *(162,790)* 1.20

1291a 30c Tagged, *Apr. 3, 1973,* New York, N.Y. 14.00

1292 40c *Jan. 29, 1968,* Philadelphia, Pa. *(157,947)* 1.60

1292a 40c Tagged, *Apr. 3, 1973,* New York, N.Y. 15.00

1293 50c *Aug. 13, 1968,* Dorchester, Mass. *(140,410)* 3.25

1293a 50c Tagged, *Apr. 3, 1973,* New York, N.Y. 20.00

1294 $1 *Oct. 16, 1967,* New London, Conn. *(103,102)* 7.50

1294a $1 Tagged, *Apr. 3,* New York, N.Y. 22.50

1295 $5 *Dec. 3, 1966,* Smyrna, Del. *(41,130)* 50.00

1295a $5 Tagged, *Apr. 3, 1973,* New York, N.Y. 65.00

First day cancellation was applied to 17,533 covers bearing one or more of Nos. 1059b, 1289a, 1290a, 1291a, 1292a, 1293a, 1294a and 1295a.

1297 3c *Nov. 4, 1975,* Pendleton, Ore. *(166,798)* 75

1298 6c Perf. 10 Horiz., *Dec. 28, 1967,* Washington, D.C. 75

First day cancellation was applied to 312,330 covers bearing Nos. 1298 and 1284b.

1299 1c *Jan. 12, 1968,* Jeffersonville, Ind. 75

1303 4c *May 28, 1966,* Springfield, Ill. *(322,563)* 75

1304 5c *Sept. 8, 1966,* Cincinnati, O. *(245,400)* 75

1305 6c Perf. 10 vert., *Feb. 28, 1968,* Washington, D.C. *(317,199)* 75

1305E 15c *June 14, 1978,* Boston, Mass. 75

1305C $1 *Jan. 12, 1973,* Hempstead, N.Y. *(121,217)* 5.00

1966

1306 5c **Migratory Bird Treaty,** *Mar. 16, 1966,* Pittsburgh, Pa. *(555,485)* 75

1307 5c **Humane Treatment of Animals,** *Apr. 9, 1966,* New York, N.Y. *(524,420)* 75

1308 5c **Indiana Statehood,** *Apr. 16, 1966,* Corydon, Ind. *(575,557)* 75

1309 5c **Circus,** *May 2, 1966,* Delavan, Wis. *(754,076)* 75

1310 5c **SIPEX,** *May 21, 1966,* Washington, D.C. *(637,802)* 75

1311 5c **SIPEX, Souvenir Sheet,** *May 23, 1966,* Washington, D.C. *(700,882)* 75

1312 5c **Bill of Rights,** *July 1, 1966,* Miami Beach, Fla. *(562,920)* 75

1313 5c **Polish Millennium,** *July 30, 1966,* Washington, D.C. *(715,603)* 75

1314 5c **National Park Service,** *Aug. 25, 1966,* Yellowstone National Park, Wyo. (528,170 75

1314a 5c **Tagged,** *Aug. 26, 1966* 20.00

1315 5c **Marine Corps Reserve,** *Aug. 29, 1966* Washington, D.C. *(585,923)* 75

1315a 5c **Tagged,** *Aug. 29, 1966,* Washington, D.C. 20.00

1316 5c **Gen. Fed. of Women's Clubs,** *Sept. 12, 1966,* New York, N.Y. *(383,334)* 75

1316a 5c Tagged, *Sept. 13, 1966* 22.50

1317 5c **Johnny Appleseed,** *Sept. 24, 1966,* Leominster, Mass. *(794,610)* 75

1317a 5c Tagged, *Sept. 26, 1966* 22.50

1318 5c **Beautification of America,** *Oct. 5, 1966,*Washington, D.C. *(564,440)* 75

1318a 5c Tagged, *Oct. 5, 1966,* Washington, D.C. 20.00

1319 5c **Great River Road,** *Oct. 21, 1966,* Baton Rouge, La. *(330,933)* 75

1319a 5c Tagged, *Oct. 22, 1966* 22.50

1320 5c **Savings Bond-Servicemen,** *Oct. 26, 1966,* Sioux City, Iowa *(444,421)* 75

1320a 5c Tagged, *Oct. 27, 1966* 22.50

1321 5c **Christmas,** *Nov. 1, 1966,* Christmas, Mich. *(537,650)* 75

1321a 5c Tagged, *Nov. 2, 1966* 9.50

1322 5c **Mary Cassatt,** *Nov. 17, 1966,* Washington, D.C. *(593,389)* 75

1322a 5c Tagged, *Nov. 17, 1966,* Washington, D.C. 20.00

1967

1323 5c **National Grange,** *Apr. 17, 1967,* Washington, D.C. *(603,460)* 75

1324 5c **Canada Centenary,** *May 25, 1967,* Montreal, Canada *(711,795)* 75

1325 5c **Erie Canal,** *July 4, 1967,* Rome, N.Y. *(784,611)* 75

1326 5c **Search for Peace-Lions,** *July 5, 1967,* Chicago, Ill. *(393,197)* 75

1327 5c **Thoreau,** *July 12, 1967,* Concord, Mass. *(696,789)* 75

1328 5c **Nebraska Statehood,** *July 29, 1967,* Lincoln, Nebr. *(1,146,957)* 75

1329 5c **Voice of America,** *Aug. 1, 1967,* Washington, D.C. *(455,190)* 75

1330 5c **Davy Crockett,** *Aug. 17, 1967,* San Antonio, Tex. *(462,291)* 75

1331a 5c **Space Accomplishments,** *Sept. 29, 1967,* Kennedy Space Center, Fla. *(667,267)* 8.00
1331 or 1332 3.00

1333 5c **Urban Planning,** *Oct. 2, 1967,* Washington, D.C. *(389,009)* 75

1334 5c **Finland Independence,** *Oct. 6, 1967,* Finland, Minn. *(408,532)* 75

1335 5c **Thomas Eakins,** *Nov. 2, 1967,* Washington, D.C. *(648,054)* 75

1336 5c **Christmas,** *Nov. 6, 1967,* Bethlehem, Ga. *(462,118)* 75

1337 5c **Mississippi Statehood,** *Dec. 11, 1967,* Natchez, Miss. *(379,612)* 75

1968-71

1338 6c **Flag** (Giori), *Jan. 24, 1968,* Washington, D.C. *(412,120)* 75

1338A 6c **Flag coil,** *May 30, 1969,* Chicago, Ill. *(248,434)* 75

1338D 6c **Flag** (Huck) *Aug. 7, 1970,* Washington, D.C. *(365,280)* 75

1338F 8c **Flag,** *May 10, 1971,* Washington, D.C. 75

1338G 8c **Flag coil,** *May 10, 1971,* Washington, D.C.

First day cancellation (May 10) was applied to 235,543 covers bearing either No. 1338F or 1338G.

1339 6c **Illinois Statehood,** *Feb. 12, 1968,* Shawneetown, Ill. *(761,640)* 75

1340 6c **HemisFair'68,** *Mar. 30, 1968,* San Antonio, Tex. *(469,909)* 75

1341 $1 **Airlift,** *Apr. 4, 1968,* Seattle, Wash. *(105,088)* 6.50

1342 6c **Youth-Elks,** *May 1, 1968,* Chicago, Ill. *(354,711)* 75

1343 6c **Law and Order,** *May 17, 1968,* Washington, D.C. *(407,081)* 75

1344 6c **Register and Vote,** *June 27, 1968,* Washington, D.C. *(355,685)* 75

1354a 6c **Historic Flag series of 10,** *July 4, 1968,* Pittsburgh, Pa. 12.00
1345-1354, any single 3.00

First day cancellation was applied to 2,924,962 covers bearing one or more of Nos. 1345 to 1354.

1355 6c **Disney,** *Sept. 11, 1968,* Marceline, Mo. *(499,505)* 1.00

1356 6c **Marquette,** *Sept. 20, 1968,* Sault Ste. Marie, Mich. *(379,710)* 75

1357 6c **Daniel Boone,** *Sept. 26, 1968,* Frankfort, Ky. *(333,440)* 75

1358 6c **Arkansas River,** *Oct. 1, 1968,* Little Rock, Ark. *(358,025)* 75

1359 6c **Leif Erikson,** *Oct. 9, 1968,* Seattle, Wash. *(376,565)* 75

1360 6c **Cherokee Strip,** *Oct. 15, 1968,* Ponca, Okla. *(339,330)* 75

1361 6c **John Trumbull,** *Oct. 18, 1968,* New Haven, Conn. *(378,285)* 75

1362 6c **Waterfowl Conservation,** *Oct. 24, 1968,* Cleveland, Ohio, *(349,719)* 75

1363 6c **Christmas,tagged,** *Nov. 1, 1968,* Washington, D.C. *(739,055)* 75

1363a 6c Untagged, *Nov. 2, 1968,* Washington, D.C. 6.50

1364 6c **American Indian,** *Nov. 4, 1968,* Washington, D.C. *(415,964)* 75

1969

1368a 6c **Beautification of America,** *Jan. 16, 1969,* Washington, D.C. 4.00
1365-1368, any single 1.50

First day cancellation was applied to 1,094,184 covers bearing one or more of Nos. 1365 to 1368.

1369 6c **American Legion,** *Mar. 15, 1959,* Washington, D.C. *(632,035)* 75

1370 6c **Grandma Moses,** *May 1, 1969,* Washington, D.C. *(367,880)* 75

1371 6c **Apollo 8,** *May 5, 1969,* Houston, Texas *(908,634)* 2.50

1372 6c **W.C. Handy,** *May 17, 1969,* Memphis, Tenn. *(398,216)* 75

1373 6c **California Bicentenary,** *July 16, 1969,* San Diego, Calif, *(530,210)* 75

1374 6c **J.W. Powell,** *Aug. 1, 1969,* Page, Ariz. *(434,433)* 75

1375 6c **Alabama Statehood,** *Aug. 2, 1969,* Huntsville, Ala. *(485,801)* 75

1379a 6c **Botanical Congress,** *Aug. 23, 1969,* Seattle, Wash. 5.00
1376-1379, any single 1.50

First day cancellation was applied to 737,935 covers bearing one or more of Nos. 1376 to 1379.

1380 6c **Dartmouth Case,** *Sept. 22, 1969,* Hanover N.H. *(416,327)* 75

1381 6c **Professional Baseball,** *Sept. 24, 1969,* Cincinnati, Ohio *(414,942)* 1.50

1382 6c **Intercollegiate Football,** *Sept. 26, 1969,* New Brunswick, N.J. *(414,860)* 1.50

1383 6c **Dwight D. Eisenhower,** *Oct. 14, 1969,*Abilene, Kans. *(1,009,560)* 75

1384 6c **Christmas,** *Nov. 3, 1969,* Christmas, Fla. *(555,500)* 75

1385 6c **Hope for Crippled,** *Nov. 20, 1969,* Columbus, Ohio *(342,676)* 75

1386 6c **William M. Harnett,** *Dec. 3, 1969,* Boston, Mass. *(408,860)* 75

1970-74

1390a 6c **National History,** *May 6, 1970,* New York, N.Y. 4.00
1387-1390, any single 1.50

First day cancellation was applied to 834,260 covers bearing one or more of Nos. 1387 to 1390.

1391 6c **Maine Statehood,** *July 9, 1970,* Portland, Maine, *(472,165)* 75

1392 6c **Wildlife Conservation,** *July 20, 1970,* Custer, S.D. *(309,418)* 90

1393 6c **Eisenhower,** *Aug. 6, 1970,* Washington, D.C. 75

First day cancellations were applied to 823,540 covers bearing one or more of Nos. 1393 and 1401.

1393D 7c **Franklin,** *Oct. 20, 1972,* Philadelphia, Pa. *(309,276)* 75

1394 8c **Eisenhower** (multi), *May 10, 1971,* Washington, D.C. 75

1395 8c **Eisenhower** (claret), *May 10, 1971,* Washington, D.C. 75

First day cancellations were applied to 813,947 covers bearing one or more of Nos. 1394, 1395 and 1402.

1396 8c **Postal Service Emblem,** *July 1, 1971, any city (est. 16,300,000)* 75

1397 14c **Fiorello H. LaGuardia,** *Apr. 24, 1972,* New York, N.Y. *(180,114)* 85

1398 16c **Ernie Pyle,** *May 7, 1971,* Washington, D.C. *(444,410)* 75

1399 18c **Elizabeth Blackwell,** *Jan. 23, 1974,* Geneva, N.Y. *(217,938)* 1.00

1400 21c **Amadeo Giannini,** *June 27, 1973,* San Mateo, Calif. *(282,520)* 1.00

1401 6c **Eisenhower coil,** *Aug. 6, 1970,* Washington, D.C. 75

1402 8c **Eisenhower coil,** *May 10, 1971,* Washington, D.C. 75

1405 6c **Edgar Lee Masters,** *Aug. 22, 1970,* Petersburg Ill. *(372,804)* 75

1406 6c **Woman Suffrage,** *Aug. 26, 1970,* Adams, Mass. *(508,142)* 75

1407 6c **South Carolina Anniv.** *Sept. 12, 1970,* Charleston, S.C. *(533,000)* 75

1408 6c **Stone Mt. Memorial,** *Sept. 19, 1970,* Stone Mountain, Ga. *(558,546)* 75

1409 6c **Fort Snelling,** *Oct. 17, 1970,* Fort Snelling, Minn. *(497,611)* 75

1413a 6c **Anti-Pollution,** *Oct. 28, 1970,* San Clemente, Calif. 4.00
1410-1413, any single 1.25

First day cancellation was applied to 1,033, 147 covers bearing one or more of Nos. 1410 to 1413.

1414 6c **Christmas,** *Nov. 5, 1970,* Washington, D.C. 1.40

1415 6c **Christmas,** *Nov. 5, 1970,* Washington, D.C. 1.40

1416 6c **Christmas,** *Nov. 5, 1970,* Washington, D.C. 1.40

1417 6c **Christmas,** *Nov. 5, 1970,* Washington, D.C. 1.40

1418 6c **Christmas,** *Nov. 5, 1970,* Washington, D.C. 1.40
1414 to 1418 on one cover 3.50

First day cancellation was applied to 2,014,450 covers bearing one or more of Nos. 1414 to 1418 or 1414a to 1418a.

1419 6c **United Nations,** *Nov. 20, 1970,* New York, N.Y. *(474,070)* 75

1420 6c **Pilgrims' Landing,** *Nov. 21, 1970,* Plymouth, Mass. *(629,850)* 75

1421 6c **Disabled Veterans,** *Nov. 24, 1970,*Cincinnati, Ohio, or Montgomery, Ala. 75

1422 6c **U.S. Servicemen,** *Nov. 24, 1970,* Cincinnati, Ohio, or Montgomery, Ala. 75
1421a 1.20

First day cancellation was applied to 476,610 covers at Cincinnati and 336,417 at Montgomery, each cover bearing one or both of Nos. 1421 to 1422.

1971

1423 6c **Wool Industry,** *Jan. 19, 1971,* Las Vegas, Nev. *(379,911)* 75

1424 6c **MacArthur,** *Jan. 26, 1971,* Norfolk, Va. *(720,035)* 75

1425 6c **Blood Donor,** *Mar. 12, 1971,* New York, N.Y. (644,497) 75

1426 8c **Missouri Sesquicentennial,** *May 8, 1971,* Independence, Mo. *(551,000)* 75

1430a 8c **Wildlife Conservation,** *June 12, 1971,* Avery Island, La. 3.00
1427-1430, any single 1.25

First day cancellation was applied to 679,483 covers bearing one or more of Nos. 1427 to 1430.

1431 8c **Antarctic Treaty,** *June 23, 1971,* Washington D.C. *(419,200)* 75

1432 8c **American Revolution Bicentennial,** *July 4, 1971,* Washington, D.C. *(434,930)* 75

1433 8c **John Sloan,** *Aug. 2, 1971,* Lock Haven, Pa. *(482,265)* 75

1434a 8c **Space Achievement Decade,** *Aug. 2, 1971,* Kennedy Space Center, Fla. *(1,403,644)* 1.75
Houston, Texas *(811,560)* 2.00
Huntsville, Ala. *(524,000)* 2.25

1436 8c **Emily Dickinson,** *Aug. 28, 1971,* Amherst, Mass. *(498,180)* 75

1437 8c **San Juan,** *Sept. 12, 1971,* San Juan, P.R. *(501,668)* 75

1438 8c **Drug Abuse,** *Oct. 4, 1971,* Dallas, Texas *(425,330)* 75

1439 8c **CARE,** *Oct. 27, 1971,* New York, N.Y. *(402,121)* 75

1443a 8c **Historic Preservation,** *Oct. 29, 1971,* San Diego, Calif. 3.00
1440-1443, any single 1.25

First day cancellation was applied to 783,242 covers bearing one or more of Nos. 1440 to 1443.

1444 8c **Christmas,** *Nov. 10, 1971,* Washington, D.C. 75

1445 8c **Christmas,** *Nov. 10, 1971,* Washington, D.C. 75
1444 to 1445 on one cover 1.20

First day cancellation was applied to 348,038 covers with No. 1444 (Nativity) and 580,062 with No. 1445 (partridge).

1972

1446 8c **Sidney Lanier,** *Feb. 3, 1972,* Macon Ga. *(394,800)* 75

1447 8c **Peace Corps,** *Feb. 11, 1972,* Washington, D.C. *(453,660)* 75

1451a 2c **National Parks Centennial,** *Apr. 5, 1972,* Hatteras, N.C., block of 4 *(505,697)* 1.25

1452 6c **National Parks,** *June 26, 1972,* Vienna, Va. *(403,396)* 75

1453 8c **National Parks,** *Mar. 1, 1972* Yellowstone National Park, Wyo. 75
Washington, D.C. *(847,500)* 75

1454 15c **National Parks,** *July 28, 1972,* Mt. McKinley National Park, Alaska *(491,456)* 75

1455 8c **Family Planning,** *Mar. 18, 1972,* New York, N.Y. *(691,385)* 75

1459a 8c **Colonial Craftsmen** (Rev. Bicentennial), *July 4, 1972,* Williamsburg, Va. *(1,914,976)* 2.50
1456-1459, any single 1.00

1460 6c **Olympics,** *Aug. 17, 1972,* Washington, D.C. 75

1461 8c **Winter Olympics,** *Aug. 17, 1972,* Washington, D.C. 85

1462 15c **Olympics,** *Aug. 17, 1972,* Washington, D.C. 1.00
1460 to 1462 and C85 on one cover 2.75

First day cancellation was applied to 971,536 covers bearing one or more of Nos. 1460 to 1462 and C85.

1463 8c **P.T.A.,** *Sept. 15, 1972,* San Francisco, Cal. *(523,454)* 75

1467a 8c **Wildlife,** *Sept. 20, 1972,* Warm Springs, Ore. 3.00
1463-1467, any single 1.50

First day cancellation was applied to 733,778 covers bearing one or more of Nos. 1464 to 1467.

1468 8c **Mail Order,** *Sept. 27, 1972,* Chicago, Ill. *(759,666)* 75

1469 8c **Osteopathy,** *Oct. 9, 1972,* Miami, Fla. *(607,160)* 75

1470 8c **Tom Sawyer,** *Oct. 13, 1972,* Hannibal, Mo. *(459,013)* 75

1471 8c **Christmas,** *Nov. 9, 1972,* Washington, D.C. 75

1472 8c **Christmas,** *Nov. 9, 1972,* Washington, D.C. 75
1471 and 1472 on one cover 1.00

First day cancellation was applied to 713,821 covers bearing one or more of Nos. 1471 to 1472.

1473 8c **Pharmacy,** *Nov. 10, 1972,* Cincinnati, Ohio *(804,320)* 75

1474 8c **Stamp Collecting,** *Nov. 17, 1972,* New York, N.Y. *(434,680)* 75

1973

1475 8c **Love,** *Jan. 26, 1973,* Philadelphia, Pa. *(422,492)* 75

1476 8c **Pamphleteer** (Rev. Bicentennial), *Feb. 16, 1973,* Portland, Ore. *(431,784)* 75

1477 8c **Broadside** (Rev. Bicentennial), *Apr. 13, 1973,* Atlantic City, N.J. *(423,437)* 75

1478 8c **Post Rider** (Rev. Bicentennial), *June 22, 1973,* Rochester, N.Y. *(586,850)* 75

1479 8c **Drummer** (Rev. Bicentennial), *Sept. 28, 1973,* New Orleans, La. *(522,427)* 75

1483a 8c **Boston Tea Party** (Rev. Bicentennial), *July 4, 1973,* Boston, Mass. 3.00
1480-1483, any single 1.50

First day cancellation was applied to 897,870 covers bearing one or more of Nos. 1480 to 1483.

1484 8c **George Gershwin,** *Feb. 28, 1973,* Beverly Hills, Calif. *(448,814)* 75

1485 8c **Robinson Jeffers,** *Aug. 13, 1973,* Carmel, Calif. *(394,261)* 75

1486 8c **Henry O. Tanner,** *Sept. 10, 1973,* Pittsburgh, Pa. *(424,065)* 75

1487 8c **Willa Cather,** *Sept. 20, 1973,* Red Cloud, Nebr. *(435,784)* 75

1488 8c **Nicolaus Copernicus,** *Apr. 23, 1973,* Washington, D.C. *(734,190)* 75

1498a 8c **Postal People,** *Apr. 30, 1973, any city* 5.00
1489-1498, any single 1.00

First day cancellation was applied at Boston to 1,205,212 covers bearing one or more of Nos. 1489 to 1498. Cancellations at other cities unrecorded.

1499 8c **Harry S Truman,** *May 8, 1973,* Independence, Mo. *(938,636)* 75

1500 6c **Electronics,** *July 10, 1973,* New York, N.Y. 75

1501 8c **Electronics,** *July 10, 1973,* New York, N.Y. 75

1502 15c **Electronics,** *July 10, 1973,* New York, N.Y. 80
1500 to 1502 and C86 on one cover 3.00

First day cancellation was applied to 1,197,700 covers bearing one or more of Nos. 1500 to 1502 and C86.

1503 8c **Lyndon B. Johnson,** *Aug. 27, 1973,* Austin, Texas *(701,490)* 75

1973-74

1504 8c **Angus Cattle,** *Oct. 5, 1973,* St. Joseph, Mo. *(521,427)* 75
1505 10c **Chautauqua,** *Aug. 6, 1974,* Chautauqua, N.Y. *(411,105)* 75
1506 10c **Wheat,** *Aug. 16, 1974,* Hillsboro, Kans. *(468,280)* 75
1507 8c **Christmas,** *Nov. 7, 1973,* Washington, D.C. 75
1508 8c **Christmas,** *Nov. 7, 1973,* Washington, D.C. 75
1507 and 1508 on one cover 1.00

First day cancellation was applied to 807,468 covers bearing one or both of Nos. 1507 to 1508.

1509 10c **Crossed Flags,** *Dec. 8, 1973,* San Francisco, Calif. 75

First day cancellation was applied to 341,528 covers bearing one or more of Nos. 1509 and 1519.

1510 10c **Jefferson Memorial,** *Dec. 14, 1973,* Washington, D.C. 75

First day cancellation was applied to 686,300 covers bearing one or more of Nos. 1510, 1510b, 1510c, 1520.

1511 10c **Zip Code,** *Jan. 4, 1974,* Washington, D.C. *(335,220)* 75
1518 6.3c **Bell Coil,** *Oct. 1, 1974,* Washington, D.C. *(221,141)* 75
1519 10c **Crossed Flags coil,** *Dec. 8, 1973,* San Francisco, Calif. 75
1520 10c **Jefferson Memorial coil,** *Dec. 14, 1973,* Washington, D.C. 75

1974

1525 10c **Veterans of Foreign Wars,** *Mar. 11, 1974,* Washington, D.C. *(543,598)* 75
1526 10c **Robert Frost,** *Mar. 26, 1974,* Derry, N.H. *(500,425)* 75
1527 10c **EXPO '74,** *Apr. 18, 1974,* Spokane, Wash. *(565,548)* 75
1528 10c **Horse Racing,** *May 4, 1974,* Louisville, Ky. *(623,983)* 75
1529 10c **Skylab,** *May 14, 1974,* Houston, Tex. *(972,326)* 1.25
1537a 10c **UPU Centenary,** *June 6, 1974,* Washington, D.C. 3.00
1530-1537, any single 1.00

First day cancellation was applied to 1,374,765 covers bearing one or more of Nos. 1530 to 1537.

1541a 10c **Mineral Heritage,** *June 13, 1974,* Lincoln, Neb. 2.50
1538-1541, any single 1.10

First day cancellation was applied to 865,368 covers bearing one or more of Nos. 1538 to 1541.

1542 10c **Kentucky Settlement,** *June 15, 1974,* Harrodsburg, Ky. *(478,239)* 75
1546a 10c **Continental Congress** (Rev. Bicentennial), *July 4, 1974,* Philadelphia 2.75
1543-1546, any single 90

First day cancellation was applied to 2,124,957 covers bearing one or more of Nos. 1543 to 1546.

1547 10c **Energy Conservation,** *Sept. 23, 1974,* Detroit, Mich. *(587,210)* 75
1548 10c **Sleepy Hollow,** *Oct. 10, 1974,* North Tarrytown, N.Y. *(514,836)* 75
1549 10c **Retarded Children,** *Oct. 12, 1974,* Arlington Tex. *(412,882)* 75
1550 10c **Christmas,** *Oct. 23, 1974,* New York, N.Y. *(634,990)* 75
1551 10c **Christmas,** *Oct. 23, 1974,* New York, N.Y. *(634,990)* 75
1550 and 1551 on one cover 1.10
1552 10c **Christmas,** *Nov. 15, 1974,* New York, N.Y. *(477,410)* 75

1975

1553 10c **Benjamin West,** *Feb. 10, 1975,* Swarthmore, Pa. *(465,017)* 75
1554 10c **Paul L. Dunbar,** *May 1, 1975,* Dayton, Ohio *(397,347)* 75
1555 10c **D.W. Griffith,** *May 27, 1975,* Beverly Hills, Calif. *(424,167)* 75
1556 10c **Pioneer-Jupiter,** *Feb. 28, 1975,* Mountain View, Calif. *(594,896)* 1.25
1557 10c **Mariner 10,** *Apr. 4, 1975,* Pasadena, Calif. *(563,636)* 1.25
1558 10c **Collective Bargaining,** *Mar. 13, 1975,* Washington, D.C. *(412,329)* 75
1559 8c **Sybil Ludington** (Rev. Bicentennial), *Mar. 25, 1975,* Carmel, N.Y. *(394,550)* 75
1560 10c **Salem Poor** (Rev. Bicentennial, *Mar. 25, 1975,* Cambridge, Mass. *(415,565)* 75
1561 10c **Haym Salomon** (Rev. Bicentennial), *Mar. 25, 1975,* Chicago, Ill. *(442,630)* 75
1562 18c **Peter Francisco** (Rev. Bicentennial), *Mar. 25, 1975,* Greensboro, N.C. *(415,000)* 75
1563 10c **Lexington-Concord** (Rev. Bicentennial), *Apr. 19, 1975,* Lexington, Mass., or Concord, Mass, *(975,020)* 75
1564 10c **Bunker Hill** (Rev. Bicentennial), *June 17, 1975,* Charlestown, Mass. *(557,130)* 75
1568a 10c **Military Services** (Rev. Bicentennial), *July 4, 1975,* Washington, D.C. 2.40
1565-1568, any single 90

First day cancellation was applied to 1,134,831 covers bearing one or more of Nos. 1565 to 1568.

1569a 10c **Apollo-Soyuz,** *July 15, 1975,* Kennedy Space Center, Fla. *(1,427,046)* 3.00
1569-1570, any single 1.25
1571 10c **International Women's Year,** *Aug. 26, 1975,* Seneca Falls, N.Y. *(476,769)* 75
1575a 10c **Postal Service Bicentenary,** *Sept. 3, 1975,* Philadelphia, Pa. 2.40
1572-1575, any single 75

First day cancellation was applied to *(969,999)* covers bearing one or more of Nos. 1572 to 1575.

1576 10c **World Peace through Law,** *Sept. 29, 1975,* Washington, D.C. *(386,736)* 75
1577a 10c **Banking-Commerce,** *Oct. 6, 1975,* New York, N.Y. *(555,580)* 1.00
1577-1578, any single 75
1579 10c **Christmas,** *Oct. 14, 1975,* Washington 75
1580 10c **Christmas,** *Oct. 14, 1975,* Washington 75
1579 and 1580 on one cover 1.10

First day cancellation was applied to 730,079 covers bearing one or more of Nos. 1579 to 1580.

1975-79

AMERICANA ISSUE

1581 1c *Dec. 8, 1977,* St. Louis, Mo. 60
1582 2c *Dec. 8, 1977,* St. Louis, Mo. 60
1584 3c *Dec. 8, 1977,* St. Louis, Mo. 60
1585 4c *Dec. 8, 1977,* St. Louis, Mo. 60

First day cancellation was applied to 530,033 covers bearing one or more of Nos. 1581 to 1582, 1584 to 1585.

1590 9c *Mar. 11, 1977,* New York, N.Y. 1.00
1591 9c *Nov. 24, 1975,* Washington, D.C. *(190,117)* 60
1592 10c *Nov. 17, 1977,* New York, N.Y. *(359,050)* 60
1593 11c *Nov. 13, 1975,* Philadelphia, Pa. *(217,755)* 60
1594 12c *Apr. 8, 1981,* Dallas, TX 60

First day cancellation was applied to 280,930 covers bearing Nos. 1594 or 1816.

1595 13c *Oct. 31, 1975,* Cleveland, Ohio *(256,734)* 60
1596 13c *Dec. 1, 1975,* Juneau, Alaska *(418,272)* 60
1597 15c *June 30, 1978,* Baltimore, Md. 65
1598 15c *June 30, 1978,* Baltimore, Md. 65

First day cancellation was applied to 315,359 covers bearing Nos. 1597, 1598, or 1618C.

1599 16c *Mar. 31, 1978,* New York, N.Y. 65
1603 24c *Nov. 14, 1975,* Boston, Mass. *(208,973)* 75
1604 28c *Aug. 11, 1978,* Tacoma, Wash. *(159,639)* 1.20
1605 29c *Apr. 14, 1978,* Atlantic City, N.J. *(193,476)* 1.10
1606 30c *Aug. 27, 1979,* Devils Lake, N.D. *(186,882)* 1.10
1608 50c *Sept. 11, 1979,* San Juan, P.R. *(159,540)* 1.50
1610 $1 *July 2, 1979,* San Francisco, Calif. *(255,575)* 3.00
1611 $2 *Nov. 16, 1978,* New York, N.Y. *(173,596)* 5.00
1612 $5 *Aug. 23, 1989,* Boston, Mass. *(129,192)* 12.50

COIL STAMPS

1613 3.1c *Oct. 25, 1979,* Shreveport, La. *(230,403)* 60
1614 7.7c *Nov. 20, 1976,* New York, N.Y. *(285,290)* 60
1615 7.9c *Apr. 23, 1976,* Miami, Fla. *(193,270)* 60
1615C 8.4c *July 13, 1978,* Interlochen, Mich. *(200,392)* 60
1616 9c *Mar. 5, 1976,* Milwaukee, Wis. *(128,171)* 60
1617 10c *Nov. 4, 1977,* Tampa, Fla. *(184,954)* 60
1618 13c **Liberty Bell,** *Nov. 25, 1975,* Allentown, Pa. *(320,387)* 65
1618C 15c *June 30, 1978,* Boston, Mass. 65
1619 16c *Mar. 31, 1978,* New York, N.Y. 60

First day cancellation was applied to 376,338 covers bearing one or more of Nos. 1599 or 1619.

1975

1622 13c **13-Star Flag,** *Nov. 15, 1975,* Philadelphia, Pa. 65
1623 13c *Mar. 11, 1977,* New York, N.Y. *(242,208)* 1.00
1625 13c **13-Star Flag coil,** *Nov. 15, 1975,* Philadelphia, PA 65

First day cancellation was applied to 362,959 covers bearing Nos. 1622 or 1625.

1976

1631a 13c **Spirit of '76,** *Jan. 1, 1976,* Pasadena, CA 1.75
1629-1631, any single 65

First day cancellation was applied to 1,013,067 covers bearing one or more of Nos. 1629 to 1631.

1632 13c **Interphil '76,** *Jan. 17, 1976,* Philadelphia, Pa. *(519,902)* 65
1682a 13c **State Flags,** *Feb. 23, 1976,* Washington, D.C. 27.50
1633-1682, any single 1.00
1683 13c **Telephone,** *Mar. 10, 1976,* Boston, Mass. *(662,515)* 65
1684 13c **Commercial Aviation,** *Mar. 19, 1976,* Chicago Ill. *(631,555)* 65
1685 13c **Chemistry,** *Apr. 6, 1976,* New York, N.Y. *(557,600)* 65
1686 13c **Bicentennial Souvenir Sheet of 5, Surrender of Cornwallis,** *May 29, 1976,* Philadelphia, Pa. 6.00
1687 18c **Bicentennial Souvenir Sheet of 5, Declaration of Independence,** *May 29, 1976,* Philadelphia, Pa. 7.50
1688 24c **Bicentennial Souvenir Sheet of 5, Declaration of Independence,** *May 29, 1976,* Philadelphia, Pa. 8.50
1689 31c **Bicentennial Souvenir Sheet of 5, Washington at Valley Forge,** *May 29, 1976,* Philadelphia, Pa. 9.50

First day cancellation was applied to 879,890 covers bearing one of Nos. 1686 to 1689.

1690 13c **Franklin,** *June 1, 1976,* Philadelphia, Pa. *(588,740)* 65
1694a 13c **Declaration of Independence,** *July 4, 1976,* Philadelphia, Pa. 2.00
1691-1694, any single 65

First day cancellation was applied to 2,093,880 covers bearing one or more of Nos. 1691 to 1694.

1698a 13c **Olympic Games,** *July 16, 1976,* Lake Placid, N.Y. *(1,140,189)* 2.00
1695-1698, any single 75
1699 13c **Clara Maass,** *Aug. 18, 1976,* Belleville, N.J. *(646,506)* 75
1700 13c **Adolph S. Ochs,** *Sept. 18, 1976,* New York, N.Y. *(582,580)* 75
1701 13c **Christmas,** *Oct. 27, 1976,* Boston, Mass. (540,050) 65
1702 13c **Christmas,** *Oct. 27, 1976,* Boston, Mass. (181,410) 65
1703 13c **Christmas,** *Oct. 27, 1976,* Boston, Mass. (330,450) 65
1701 and 1702 or 1703 on one cover 1.20

1977

1704 13c **Washington at Princeton,** *Jan. 3, 1977,* Princeton, N.J. *(695,335)* 65
1705 13c **Sound Recording,** *Mar. 23, 1977,* Washington, D.C. *(632,216)* 65
1709a 13c **Pueblo Art,** *Apr. 13, 1977,* Santa Fe, N.M. *(1,194,554)* 2.00
1706-1709, any single 75
1710 13c **Lindbergh Flight,** *May 20, 1977,* Roosevelt Sta., N.Y. *(3,985,989)* 75
1711 13c **Colorado Statehood,** *May 21, 1977,* Denver, Colo. *(510,880)* 65
1715a 13c **Butterflies,** *June 6, 1977,* Indianapolis, Ind. *(1,218,278)* 2.00
1712-1715, any single 75
1716 13c **Lafayette's Landing,** *June 13, 1977,* Charleston, S.C. *(514,506)* 65
1720a 13c **Skilled Hands,** *July 4, 1977,* Cincinnati, Ohio *(1,263,568)* 1.75
1717-1720, any single 65
1721 13c **Peace Bridge,** *Aug. 4, 1977,* Buffalo, N.Y. *(512,995)* 65
1722 13c **Battle of Oriskany,** *Aug. 6, 1977,* Utica, N.Y. *(605,906)* 65
1723a 13c **Energy Conservation,** *Oct. 20, 1977,* Washington, D.C. *(410,299)* 1.00
1723-1724, any single 65
1725 13c **Alta California,** *Sept. 9, 1977,* San Jose, Calif. *(709,457)* 65
1726 13c **Articles of Confederation,** *Sept. 30, 1977,* York, Pa. *(605,455)* 65
1727 13c **Talking Pictures,** *Oct. 6, 1977,* Hollywood, Calif. *(570,195)* 75
1728 13c **Surrender at Saratoga,** *Oct. 7, 1977,* Schuylerville, N.Y. *(557,529)* 65
1729 13c **Christmas (Valley Forge),** *Oct. 21, 1977,* Valley Forge, Pa. *(583,139)* 65
1730 13c **Christmas (mailbox),** *Oct. 21, 1977,* Omaha, Nebr. *(675,786)* 65

1978

1731 13c **Carl Sandburg,** *Jan. 6,* Galesburg, Ill. *(493,826)* 65
1732a 13c **Captain Cook,** *Jan. 20,* Honolulu, Hawaii, or Anchorage, Alaska 1.50
1732-1733, any single 75

First day cancellation was applied to 823,855 covers at Honolulu, and 672,804 at Anchorage, each cover bearing one or both of Nos. 1732 to 1733.

1734 13c **Indian Head Penny,** *Jan. 11,* Kansas City, Mo. *(512,426)* 1.00

1978-80

REGULAR ISSUE

1735 (15c) **"A" Eagle,** *May 22,* Memphis, Tenn. 65
1736 (15c) **"A" Eagle,** *May 22,* Memphis, Tenn. 65
1737 15c **Roses,** *July 11,* Shreveport, La. *(445,003)* 65
1738 15c **Windmills,** *Feb. 7, 1980,* Lubbock, TX 65
1739 15c **Windmills,** *Feb. 7, 1980,* Lubbock, TX 65
1740 15c **Windmills,** *Feb. 7, 1980,* Lubbock, TX 65
1741 15c **Windmills,** *Feb. 7, 1980,* Lubbock, TX 65

1742 15c **Windmills,** *Feb. 7, 1980,* Lubbock, TX 65

1743 15c **"A" Eagle coil,** *May 22,* Memphis, Tenn. 65

First day cancellation was applied to 689,049 covers bearing Nos. 1735, 1736 or 1743. First day cancellation was applied to 708,411 covers bearing one or more of Nos. 1738-1742.

1978

1744 13c **Harriet Tubman,** *Feb. 1,* Washington, D.C. *(493,495)* 1.00

1748a 13c **American Quilts,** *Mar. 8,* Charleston, W.Va. 2.00
1745-1748, any single 75

First day cancellation was applied to 1,081,827 covers bearing one or more of Nos. 1745 to 1748.

1752a 13c **American Dance,** *Apr. 26,* New York, N.Y. *(1,626,493)* 1.75
1749-1752, any single 75

1753 13c **French Alliance,** *May 4,* York, Pa. *(705,240)* 65

1754 13c **Papanicolaou,** *May 18,* Washington, D.C. *(535,584)* 65

1755 13c **Jimmie Rodgers,** *May 24,* Meridian, Miss. *(599,287)* 65

1756 15c **George M. Cohan,** *July 3,* Providence, R.I. *(740,750)* 65

1757 **CAPEX** souv. sheet, *June 10,* Toronto, Canada *(1,994,067)* 2.75

1758 15c **Photography,** *June 26,* Las Vegas, Nev. *(684,987)* 65

1759 15c **Viking Missions,** *July 20,* Hampton, Va. *(805,051)* 1.10

1763a 15c **American Owls,** *Aug. 26,* Fairbanks, Alas. *(1,690,474)* 2.00
1760-1763, any single 75

1767a 15c **American Trees,** *Oct. 9,* Hot Springs National Park, Ark. *(1,139,100)* 2.00
1764-1767, any single 75

1768 15c **Christmas (Madonna),** *Oct. 18,* Washington, D.C. *(553,064)* 65

1769 15c **Christmas (Hobby Horse),** *Oct. 18,* Holly, Mich. *(603,008)* 65

1979-80

1770 15c **Robert Kennedy,** *Jan. 12,* Washington, D.C. *(624,582)* 65

1771 15c **Martin L. King,** *Jan. 13,* Atlanta, Ga. *(726,149)* 65

1772 15c **Year of Child,** *Feb. 15,* Philadelphia, Pa. *(716,782)* 65

1773 15c **John Steinbeck,** *Feb. 27,* Salinas, Calif. *(709,073)* 65

1774 15c **Albert Einstein,** *Mar. 4,* Princeton, N.J. *(641,423)* 65

1778a 15c **Toleware,** *Apr. 19,* Lancaster, Pa. *(1,581,962)* 2.00
1775-1778, any single 75

1782a 15c **American Architecture,** *June 4,* Kansas City, Mo. *(1,219,258)* 2.00
1779-1782, any single 75

1786a 15c **Endangered Flora,** *June 7,* Milwaukee, Wis. *(1,436,268)* 2.00
1783-1786, any single 75

1787 15c **Guide Dogs,** *June 15,* Morristown, N.J. *(588,826)* 65

1788 15c **Special Olympics,** *Aug. 9,* Brockport, N.Y. *(651,344)* 65

1789 15c **John Paul Jones,** *Sept. 23,* Annapolis, Md. *(587,018)* 65

1790 10c **Olympic Javelin,** *Sept. 5,* Olympia, Wash. *(305,122)* 1.00

1794a 15c **Olympics 1980,** *Sept. 28,* Los Angeles, Calif. *(1,561,366)* 2.00
1791-1794, any single 75

1798b 15c **Winter Olympics,** *Feb. 1, 1980,* Lake Placid, N.Y. *(1,166,302)* 2.00
1795-1798, any single 75

1799 15c **Christmas (Madonna),** *Oct. 18,* Washington, D.C. *(686,990)* 65

1800 15c **Christmas (Santa Claus),** *Oct. 18,* North Pole, Alaska *(511,829)* 65

1801 15c **Will Rogers,** *Nov. 4,* Claremore, Okla. *(1,643,151)* 65

1802 15c **Viet Nam Veterans,** *Nov. 11,* Washington, D.C. *(445,934)* 1.25

1980

1803 15c **W.C. Fields,** *Jan. 29,* Beverly Hills, CA *(633,303)* 65

1804 15c **Benjamin Banneker,** *Feb. 15,* Annapolis, MD *(647,126)* 65

1810a 15c **Letter Writing,** *Feb. 25,* Washington, DC *(1,083,360)* 2.50
1805-1810, any single 65

1980-81

DEFINITIVES

1811 1c **Quill Pen,** coil, *Mar. 6, 1980,* New York, NY *(262,921)* 60

1813 3.5c **Violins,** coil, *June 23, 1980,* Williamsburg, PA 60

FD cancel was applied to 716,988 covers bearing Nos. 1813 or U590.

1816 12c **Torch,** coil, *Apr. 8, 1981,* Dallas, TX 60

1818 (18c) **"B" Eagle,** *Mar. 15, 1981,* San Francisco, CA 75

FD cancel was applied to 511,688 covers bearing Nos. 1818 to 1820, U592 or UX88.

1819 (18c) **"B" Eagle,** bklt. single, *Mar. 15, 1981,* San Francisco, CA 75

1820 (18c) **"B" Eagle,** coil, *Mar. 15, 1981,* San Francisco, CA 75

1980

1821 15c **Frances Perkins,** *Apr. 10,* Washington, DC *(678,966)* 65

1822 15c **Dolley Madison,** *May 20,* Washington, DC *(331,048)* 65

1823 15c **Emily Bissell,** *May 31,* Wilmington, DE *(649,509)* 65

1824 15c **Helen Keller, Anne Sullivan,** *June 27,* Tuscumbia, AL *(713,061)* 80

1825 15c **Veterans Administration,** *July 21,* Washington, DC *(634,101)* 65

1826 15c **Bernardo de Galvez,** *July 23,* New Orleans, LA *(658,061)* 65

1830a 15c **Coral Reefs,** *Aug. 26,* Charlotte Amalie, VI *(1,195,126)* 2.00
1827-1830, any single 85

1831 15c **Organized Labor,** *Sept. 1,* Washington, DC *(759,973)* 65

1832 15c **Edith Wharton,** *Sept. 5,* New Haven, CT *(633,917)* 65

1833 15c **Education,** *Sept. 12,* Washington, DC *(672,592)* 65

1837a 15c **Indian Masks,** *Sept. 25,* Spokane, WA *(2,195,136)* 2.00
1834-1837, any single 75

1841a 15c **Architecture,** *Oct. 9,* New York, NY *(2,164,721)* 2.00
1837-1841, any single 75

1842 15c **Christmas (Madonna),** *Oct. 31,* Washington, DC *(718,614)* 65

1843 15c **Christmas (Toys),** *Oct. 31,* Christmas, MI *(755,108)* 65

1980-85

GREAT AMERICANS ISSUE

1844 1c **Dorothea Dix,** *Sept. 23, 1983,* Hampden, ME *(164,140)* 60

1845 2c **Igor Stravinsky,** *Nov. 18, 1982,* New York, NY *(501,719)* 60

1846 3c **Henry Clay,** *July 13, 1983,* Washington, DC *(204,320)* 60

1847 4c **Carl Schurz,** *June 3, 1983,* Watertown, WI *(165,010)* 60

1848 5c **Pearl Buck,** *June 23, 1983,* Hillsboro, WV *(231,852)* 60

1849 6c **Walter Lippman,** *Sept. 19, 1985,* Minneapolis, MN *(371,990)* 60

1850 7c **Abraham Baldwin,** *Jan. 25, 1985,* Athens, GA *(402,285)* 60

1851 8c **Henry Knox,** *July 25, 1985,* Thomaston, ME *(315,937)* 60

1852 9c **Sylvanus Thayer,** *June 7, 1985,* Braintree, MA *(345,649)* 60

1853 10c **Richard Russell,** *May 31, 1984,* Winder, GA *(183,581)* 65

1854 11c **Alden Partridge,** *Feb. 12, 1985,* Northfield, VT *(442,311)* 65

1855 13c **Crazy Horse,** *Jan. 15, 1982,* Crazy Horse, SD 65

1856 14c **Sinclair Lewis,** *Mar. 21, 1985,* Sauk Centre, MN *(308,612)* 65

1857 17c **Rachel Carson,** *May 28, 1981,* Springdale, PA *(273,686)* 75

1858 18c **George Mason,** *May 7, 1981,* Gunston Hall, VA *(461,937)* 75

1859 19c **Sequoyah,** *Dec. 27, 1980,* Tahlequah, OK *(241,325)* 80

1860 20c **Ralph Bunche,** *Jan. 12, 1982,* New York, NY 75

1861 20c **Thomas Gallaudet,** *June 10, 1983,* West Hartford, CT *(261,336)* 75

1862 20c **Harry S Truman,** *Jan. 26, 1984,* Washington, DC *(267,631)* 75

1863 22c **John J. Audubon,** *Apr. 23, 1985,* New York, NY *(516,249)* 80

1864 30c **Frank Laubach,** *Sept. 2, 1984,* Benton, PA *(118,974)* 85

1865 35c **Charles Drew,** *June 3, 1981,* Washington, DC *(383,882)* 1.00

1866 37c **Robert Millikan,** *Jan. 26, 1982,* Pasadena, CA 1.00

1867 39c **Grenville Clark,** *Mar. 20, 1985,* Hanover, NH *(297,797)* 1.00

1868 40c **Lillian Gilbreth,** *Feb. 24, 1984,* Montclair, NJ *(110,588)* 1.00

1869 50c **Chester W. Nimitz,** *Feb. 22, 1985,* Fredericksburg, TX *(376,166)* 1.25

1981

1874 15c **Everett Dirksen,** *Jan. 4,* Pekin, IL *(665,755)* 65

1875 15c **Whitney M. Young,** *Jan. 30,* New York, NY *(963,870)* 65

1879a 15c **Flowers,** *Apr. 23,* Fort Valley, GA *(1,966,599)* 2.50
1876-1879, any single 75

DEFINITIVES

1880 18c **Animals,** *May 14,* Boise, ID 75

1881 18c **Animals,** *May 14,* Boise, ID 75

1882 18c **Animals,** *May 14,* Boise, ID 75

1883 18c **Animals,** *May 14,* Boise, ID 75

1884 18c **Animals,** *May 14,* Boise, ID 75

1885 18c **Animals,** *May 14,* Boise, ID 75

1886 18c **Animals,** *May 14,* Boise, ID 75

1887 18c **Animals,** *May 14,* Boise, ID 75

1888 18c **Animals,** *May 14,* Boise, ID 75

1889 18c **Animals,** *May 14,* Boise, ID 75

1890 18c **Flag-Anthem (grain),** *Apr. 24,* Portland, ME 75

1891 18c **Flag-Anthem (sea),** *Apr. 24,* Portland, ME 75

1892 6c **Star Circle,** *Apr. 24,* Portland, ME 75

1893 18c **Flag-Anthem (mountain),** *Apr. 24,* Portland, ME 75

FDC cancel was applied to 691,526 covers bearing Nos. 1890 to 1893 & 1893a.

1894 20c **Flag-Court,** *Dec. 17,* Washington, DC 75

1895 20c **Flag-Court,** coil, *Dec. 17,* Washington, DC 75

1896 20c **Flag-Court,** perf. 11x10½, *Dec. 17,* Washington, DC *(185,543)* 75

First day cancellations were applied to 598,169 covers bearing one or more of Nos. 1894 to 1896.

1981-84

TRANSPORTATION ISSUE

1897 1c **Omnibus,** *Aug. 19, 1983,* Arlington, VA *(109,463)* 60

1897A 2c **Locomotive,** *May 20, 1982,* Chicago, IL *(290,020)* 60

1898 3c **Handcar,** *Mar. 25, 1983,* Rochester, NY *(77,900)* 60

1898A 4c **Stagecoach,** *Aug. 19, 1982,* Milwaukee, WI *(152,940)* 60

1899 5c **Motorcycle,** *Oct. 10, 1983,* San Francisco, CA *(188,240)* 60

1900 5.2c **Sleigh,** *Mar. 21, 1983,* Memphis, TN *(141,979)* 60

1901 5.9c **Bicycle,** *Feb. 17, 1982,* Wheeling, WV *(814,419)* 60

1902 7.4c **Baby Buggy,** *Apr. 7, 1984,* San Diego, CA 65

1903 9.3c **Mail Wagon,** *Dec. 15, 1981,* Shreveport, LA *(199,645)* 65

1904 10.9c **Hansom,** *May 26, 1982,* Chattanooga, TN 65

1905 11c **Railroad Caboose,** *Feb. 3, 1984,* Chicago, IL *(172,753)* 65

1906 17c **Electric Auto,** *June 25, 1982,* Greenfield Village, MI *(239,458)* 75

1907 18c **Surrey,** *May 18, 1981,* Notch, MO *(207,801)* 75

1908 20c **Fire Pumper,** *Dec. 10, 1981,* Alexandria, VA *(304,668)* 65

1909 $9.35 **Eagle,** *Aug. 12, 1983,* Kennedy Space Center, FL *(77,858)* 45.00

1981

1910 18c **Red Cross,** *May 1,* Washington, DC *(874,972)* 75

1911 18c **Savings & Loan,** *May 8,* Chicago, IL *(740,910)* 75

1919a 18c **Space Achievement,** *May 21,* Kennedy Space Center, FL *(7,027,549)* 4.00
1912-1919, any single 75

1920 18c **Professional Management,** *June 18,* Philadelphia, PA *(713,096)* 75

1924a 18c **Wildlife Habitats,** *June 26,* Reno, NV *(2,327,609)* 2.50
1921-1924, any single 75

1925 18c **Year of Disabled,** *June 29,* Milford, MI *(714,244)* 75

1926 18c **Edna St. V. Millay,** *July 10,* Austerlitz, NY *(725,978)* 75

1927 18c **Alcoholism,** *Aug. 19,* Washington, DC *(874,972)* 75

1931a 18c **Architecture,** *Aug. 28,* New York, NY *(1,998,208)* 2.00
1928-1931, any single 75

1932 18c **Babe Zaharias,** *Sept. 22,* Pinehurst, NC 75

1933 18c **Bobby Jones,** *Sept. 22,* Pinehurst, NC 75

First day cancel was applied to 1,231,543 covers bearing No. 1932 or 1933.

1934 18c **Frederic Remington,** *Oct. 9,* Oklahoma City, OK *(1,367,099)* 75

1935 18c **James Hoban,** *Oct. 13,* Washington, DC 75

1936 20c **James Hoban,** *Oct. 13,* Washington, DC 75

FD cancel was applied to 635,012 covers bearing No. 1935 or 1936.

1938a 18c **Yorktown-Va. Capes Battle,** *Oct. 16,* Yorktown, VA *(1,098,278)* 1.00
1937-1938, any single 75

1939 (20c) **Christmas (Madonna),** *Oct. 28,* Chicago, IL *(481,395)* 75

1940 (20c) **Christmas (Teddy Bear),** *Oct. 28,* Christmas Valley, OR *(517,898)* 75

1941 20c **John Hanson,** *Nov. 5,* Frederick, MD *(605,616)* 75

1945a 20c **Desert Plants,** *Dec. 11,* Tucson, AZ *(1,770,187)* 2.50
1942-1945, any single 75

REGULAR ISSUE

1946 (20c) **"C" Eagle,** *Oct. 11,* Memphis, TN 75

1947 (20c) **"C" Eagle,** coil, *Oct. 11,* Memphis, TN 75

1948 (20c) **"C" Eagle,** bklt. single, *Oct. 11,* Memphis, TN 75

First day cancellations were applied to 304,404 covers bearing Nos. 1946 to 1948.

1982

1949 20c **Bighorn,** *Jan. 8,* Bighorn, MT

1950 20c **F.D. Roosevelt,** *Jan. 30,* Hyde Park, NY 75

1951 20c **Love,** *Feb. 1,* Boston, MA *(325,727)* 75
1952 20c **Washington,** *Feb. 22,* Mt. Vernon, VA 75
2002b 20c **Birds-Flowers,** *Apr. 14,* Washington, DC, or State Capital —
1953-2002, any single 1.00
2003 20c **U.S.-Netherlands,** *Apr. 20,* Washington, DC 75
2004 20c **Library of Congress,** *Apr. 21,* Washington, DC 75
2005 20c **Consumer Education,** *Apr. 27,* Washington, DC 75
2009a 20c **Knoxville Fair,** *Apr. 29,* Knoxville, TN 2.50
2006-2009, any single 75
2010 20c **Horatio Alger,** *Apr. 30,* Willow Grove, PA 75
2011 20c **Aging,** *May 21,* Sun City, AZ *(510,677)* 75
2012 20c **Barrymores,** *June 8,* New York, NY 75
2013 20c **Dr. Mary Walker,** *June 10,* Oswego, NY 75
2014 20c **Peace Garden,** *June 30,* Dunseith, ND 75
2015 20c **America's Libraries,** *July 13,* Philadelphia, PA 75
2016 20c **Jackie Robinson,** *Aug. 2,* Cooperstown, NY 75
2017 20c **Touro Synagogue,** *Aug. 22,* Newport, RI *(517,264)* 85
2018 20c **Wolf Trap Farm Park,** *Sept. 1,* Vienna, VA *(704,361)* 75
2022a 20c **Architecture,** *Sept. 30,* Washington, DC *(1,552,567)* 2.50
2019-2022, any single 75
2023 20c **St. Francis,** *Oct. 7,* San Francisco, CA *(530,275)* 75
2024 20c **Ponce de Leon,** *Oct. 12,* San Juan, PR *(530,275)* 75
2025 13c **Puppy, Kitten,** *Nov. 3,* Danvers, MA *(239,219)* 75
2026 20c **Christmas (Madonna),** *Oct. 28,* Washington, DC *(462,982)* 75
2030a 20c **Christmas (Children),** *Oct. 28,* Snow, OK *(676,950)* 2.50
2027-2030, any single 75

1983
2031 20c **Science & Industry,** *Jan. 19,* Chicago, IL *(526,693)* 75
2035a 20c **Balloons,** *Mar. 31,* Albuquerque, NM or Wash., DC *(989,305)* 2.50
2032-2035, any single 75
2036 20c **U.S.-Sweden,** *Mar. 24,* Philadelphia, PA *(526,373)* 75
2037 20c **Civilian Conservation Corps.,** *Apr. 5,* Luray, VA *(483,824)* 75
2038 20c **Joseph Priestley,** *Apr. 13,* Northumberland, PA *(673,266)* 75
2039 20c **Voluntarism,** *Apr. 20,* Washington, DC *(574,708)* 75
2040 20c **U.S.-Germany,** *Apr. 29,* Germantown, PA *(611,109)* 75
2041 20c **Brooklyn Bridge,** *May 17,* Brooklyn, NY *(815,085)* 75
2042 20c **TVA,** *May 18,* Knoxville, TN *(837,588)* 75
2043 20c **Physical Fitness,** *May 14,* Houston, TX *(501,336)* 75
2044 20c **Scott Joplin,** *June 9,* Sedalia, MO *(472,667)* 75
2045 20c **Medal of Honor,** *June 7,* Washington, DC *(1,623,995)* 75
2046 20c **Babe Ruth,** *July 6,* Chicago, IL *(1,277,907)* 75
2047 20c **Nathaniel Hawthorne,** *July 8,* Salem, MA *(442,793)* 75
2051a 13c **Summer Olympics,** *July 28,* South Bend, IN *(909,332)* 2.50
2048-2051, any single 75
2052 20c **Treaty of Paris,** *Sept. 2,* Washington, DC *(651,208)* 75
2053 20c **Civil Service,** *Sept. 9,* Washington, DC *(422,206)* 75
2054 20c **Metropolitan Opera,** *Sept. 14,* New York, NY *(807,609)* 75
2058a 20c **American Inventors,** *Sept. 21,* Washington, D.C. *(1,006,516)* 2.50
2055-2058, any single 75
2062a 20c **Streetcars,** *Oct. 8,* Kennebunkport, ME*(1,116,909)* 2.50
2059-2062, any single 75
2063 20c **Christmas (Madonna),** *Oct. 28,* Washington, DC *(361,874)* 75
2064 20c **Christmas (Santa),** *Oct. 28,* Santa Claus, IN *(388,749)* 75
2065 20c **Martin Luther,** *Nov. 11,* Washington, DC *(463,777)* 75

1984
2066 20c **Alaska Statehood,** *Jan. 3,* Fairbanks, AK *(816,591)* 75
2070a 20c **Winter Olympics,** *Jan. 6,* Lake Placid, NY *(1,245,807)* 2.50
2067-2070, any single 75
2071 20c **Federal Deposit Ins. Corp.,** *Jan. 12,* Washington, DC *(536,329)* 75
2072 20c **Love,** *Jan. 31,* Washington, DC *(327,727)* 75
2073 20c **Carter Woodson,** *Feb. 1,* Washington, DC *(387,583)* 75
2074 20c **Soil & Water Conservation,** *Feb. 6,* Denver, CO *(426,101)* 75
2075 20c **Credit Union Act,** *Feb. 10,* Salem, MA *(523,583)* 75
2079a 20c **Orchids,** *Mar. 5,* Miami, FL*(1,063,237)* 2.50
2076-2079, any single 75
2080 20c **Hawaii Statehood,** *Mar. 12,* Honolulu, HI *(546,930)* 75
2081 20c **National Archives,** *Apr. 16,* Washington, DC *(414,415)* 75
2085a 20c **Olympics 1984,** *May 4,* Los Angeles, CA *(1,172,313)* 2.50
2082-2085, any single 75
2086 20c **Louisiana Exposition,** *May 11,* New Orleans, LA *(467,408)* 75
2087 20c **Health Research,** *May, 17,* New York, NY *(845,007)* 75
2088 20c **Douglas Fairbanks,** *May 23,* Denver CO *(547,134)* 75
2089 20c **Jim Thorpe,** *May 24,* Shawnee, OK *(568,544)* 75
2090 20c **John McCormack,** *June 6,* Boston, MA *(464,117)* 75
2091 20c **St. Lawrence Seaway,** *June 26,* Massena, NY *(550,173)* 75
2092 20c **Waterfowl Preservation Act,** *July 2,* Des Moines, IA *(549,388)* 75
2093 20c **Roanoke Voyages,** *July 13,* Manteo, NC *(443,725)* 75
2094 20c **Herman Melville,** *Aug. 1,* New Bedford, MA *(378,293)* 75
2095 20c **Horace A. Moses,** *Aug. 6,* Bloomington, IN *(459,386)* 75
2096 20c **Smokey the Bear,** *Aug. 13,* Capitan, NM *(506,833)* 75
2097 20c **Roberto Clemente,** *Aug. 17,* Carolina, PR *(547,387)* 75
2101a 20c **Dogs,** *Sept. 7,* New York, NY *(1,157,373)* 2.50
2098-2101, any single 75
2102 20c **Crime Prevention,** *Sept. 26,* Washington, DC *(427,564)* 75
2103 20c **Hispanic Americans,** *Oct. 31,* Washington, DC *(416,796)* 75
2104 20c **Family Unity,** *Oct. 1,* Shaker Heights, OH *(400,659)* 75
2105 20c **Eleanor Roosevelt,** *Oct. 11,* Hyde Park, NY *(479,919)* 75
2106 20c **Nation of Readers,** *Oct. 16,* Washington, DC *(437,559)* 75
2107 20c **Christmas (Madonna),** *Oct. 30,* Washington, DC *(386,385)* 75
2108 20c **Christmas (Santa),** *Oct. 30,* Jamaica, NY *(430,843)* 75
2109 20c **Vietnam Veterans' Memorial,** *Nov. 10,* Washington, DC *(434,489)* 75

1985
2110 22c **Jerome Kern,** *Jan. 23,* New York, NY (503,855) 80

REGULAR ISSUE
2111 (22c) **"D" Eagle,** *Feb. 1,* Los Angeles, CA 80
2112 (22c) **"D" Eagle, coil,** *Feb. 1,* Los Angeles, CA 80
2113 (22c) **"D" Eagle, bklt. single,** *Feb. 1,* Los Angeles, CA 80

First Day cancel was applied to 513,027 covers bearing Nos. 2111 to 2113.

DEFINITIVES
2114 22c **Flag over Capitol Dome,** *Mar. 29,* Washington, DC 80
2115 22c **Flag Over Capitol Dome,** coil, *Mar. 29,* Washington, DC 80

First Day Cancel was applied to 268,161 covers bearing Nos. 2114 to 2115.

2116 22c **Flag Over Capitol Dome,** bklt. single, *Mar. 29,* Waubeka, WI *(234,318)* 80
2117 22c **Seashells,** *Apr. 4,* Boston, MA *(426,290)* 80
2118 22c **Seashells,** *Apr. 4,* Boston, MA *(426,290)* 80
2119 22c **Seashells,** *Apr. 4,* Boston, MA *(426,290)* 80
2120 22c **Seashells,** *Apr. 4,* Boston, MA *(426,290)* 80
2121 22c **Seashells,** *Apr. 4,* Boston, MA *(426,290)* 80
2122 $10.75 **Eagle and Half Moon,** *Apr. 29,* San Francisco, CA *(93,154)* 35.00

1985-87

TRANSPORTATION ISSUE
2123 3.4c **School Bus,** *June 8, 1985* Arlington, VA *(131,480)* 70
2124 4.9c **Buckboard,** *June 21, 1985,* Reno, NV 70
2125 5.5c **Star Route Truck,** *Nov. 1, 1986,* Fort Worth, TX *(136,021)* 70
2126 6c **Tricycle,** *May 6, 1985,* Childs, MD *(151,494)* 70
2127 7.1c **Tractor,** *Feb. 6, 1987,* Sarasota, FL *(167,555)* 70
2127a 7.1c **Tractor,** Zip+4 precancel, untagged, *May 26, 1989,* Rosemont, IL 70
2128 8.3c **Ambulance,** *June 21, 1986,* Reno, NV 70

First day cancel was applied to 338,765 covers bearing Nos. 2124 and 2128.

2129 8.5c **Tow Truck,** *Jan. 24, 1987,* Tucson, AZ *(224,285)* 70
2130 10.1c **Oil Wagon,** *Apr. 18, 1985,* Oil Center, NM 75
2130a 10.1c "Bulk Rate Carrier Route Sort" precancel, *June 27, 1988* Washington, DC *(136,428)* 75
2131 11c **Stutz Bearcat,** *June 11, 1985,* Baton Rouge, LA *(135,037)* 75
2132 12c **Stanley Steamer,** *Apr. 2, 1985,* Kingfield, ME *(173,998)* 75
2133 12.5c **Pushcart,** *Apr. 18, 1985,* Oil Center, NM 75

First day cancel was applied to 319,953 covers bearing Nos. 2130 and 2133.

2134 14c **Ice Boat,** *Mar. 23, 1985,* Rochester, NY *(324,710)* 80
2135 17c **Dog Sled,** *Aug. 20, 1986,* Anchorage, AK 80
2136 25c **Bread Wagon,** *Nov. 22, 1986,* Virginia Beach, VA *(151,950)* 85

1985
2137 22c **Mary McLeod Bethune,** *Mar. 5,* Washington, DC *(413,244)* 80
2141a 22c **Duck Decoys,** *Mar. 22,* Shelburne, VT *(932,249)* 2.75
2138-2141, any single 80
2142 22c **Winter Special Olympics,** *Mar. 25,* Park City, UT *(253,074)* 80
2143 22c **Love,** *Apr. 17,* Hollywood, CA *(283,072)* 80
2144 22c **Rural Electrification Administration,** *May 11,* Madison, SD *(472,895)* 80
2145 22c **AMERIPEX '86,** *May 25,* Rosemont, IL *(457,038)* 80
2146 22c **Abigail Adams,** *June 14,* Quincy, MA *(491,026)* 80
2147 22c **Frederic Auguste Bartholdi,** *July 18,* New York, NY *(594,896)* 80
2149 18c **George Washington, Washington Monument,** *Nov. 6,* Washington, DC *(376,238)* 80
2150 21.1c **Envelopes,** *Oct. 22,* Washington, DC *(119,941)* 80
2152 22c **Korean War Veterans,** *July 26,* Washington, DC *(391,754)* 80
2153 22c **Social Security Act,** *Aug. 14,* Baltimore, MD *(265,143)* 80
2154 22c **World War I Veterans,** *Aug. 26,* Milwaukee, WI 80
2158a 22c **Horses,** *Sept. 25,* Lexington, KY *(1,135,368)* 2.75
2155-2158, any single 80
2159 22c **Public Education in America,** *Oct. 1,* Boston, MA *(356,030)* 80
2163a 22c **International Youth Year,** *Oct. 7,* Chicago, IL *(1,202,541)* 2.75
2160-2163, any single 80
2164 22c **Help End Hunger,** *Oct. 15,* Washington, DC *(299,485)* 80
2165 22c **Christmas (Madonna & Child),** *Oct. 30,* Detroit, MI 80
2166 22c **Christmas (Poinsettia),** *Oct. 30,* Nazareth, MI *(524,929)* 80

1986
2167 22c **Arkansas Statehood,** *Jan. 3,* Little Rock, AR *(364,729)* 80

1986-88

GREAT AMERICANS ISSUE
2168 1c **Margaret Mitchell,** *June 30, 1986,* Atlanta, GA *(316,764)* 80
2169 2c **Mary Lyon,** *Feb. 28, 1987,* South Hadley, MA *(349,831)* 80
2170 3c **Dr. Paul Dudley White,** *Sept. 15, 1986,* Washington, DC 80
2171 4c **Father Flanagan,** *July 14, 1986,* Boys Town, NE *(367,883)* 80
2172 5c **Hugo Black,** *Feb. 27, 1986,* Washington, DC *(303,012)* 80
2176 10c **Red Cloud,** *Aug. 15, 1987,* Red Cloud, NE *(300,472)* 80
2177 14c **Julia Ward Howe,** *Feb. 12, 1987,* Boston, MA *(454,829)* 80
2178 15c **Buffalo Bill Cody,** *June 6, 1988* Cody, WY *(356,395)* 75
2179 17c **Belva Ann Lockwood,** *June 18, 1986,* Middleport, NY *(249,215)* 80
2180 21c **Chester Carlson,** *Oct. 21, 1988,* Rochester, NY *(288,073)* 80
2182 23c **Mary Cassatt,** *Nov. 4, 1988,* Philadelphia, PA *(322,537)* 80
2183 25c **Jack London,** *Jan. 11, 1986,* Glen Ellen, CA *(358,686)* 85
2188 45c **Harvey Cushing,** *June 17, 1988,* Cleveland, OH *(135,140)* 1.05
2191 56c **John Harvard,** *Sept. 3, 1986,* Boston, MA 1.25
2192 65c **Hap Arnold,** *Nov. 5, 1988,* Gladwyne, PA *(129,829)* 1.50
2194 $1 **Dr. Bernard Revel,** *Sept. 23, 1986,* New York, NY 2.00
2194A $1 **Johns Hopkins,** *June 7, 1989,* Baltimore, MD 2.00
2195 $2 **William Jennings Bryan,** *Mar. 19, 1986,* Salem, IL *(123,430)* 4.00
2196 $5 **Bret Harte,** *Aug. 25, 1987,* Twain Harte, CA *(111,431)* 12.50
2197 25c **Jack London,** bklt. single, *May 3, 1988,* San Francisco, CA 85

First day cancel was applied to 94,655 covers bearing Nos. 2183a, 2197, or 2197a.

1986
2198 22c **Stamp Collecting,** *Jan. 23,* State College, PA *(675,924)* 80
2199 22c **Stamp Collecting,** *Jan. 23,* State College, PA *(675,924)* 80
2200 22c **Stamp Collecting,** *Jan. 23,* State College, PA *(675,924)* 80

2201 22c **Stamp Collecting,** *Jan. 23,* State College, PA *(675,924)* 80
2202 22c **Love,** *Jan. 30,* New York, NY 80
2203 22c **Sojourner Truth,** *Feb. 4,* New Paltz, NY *(342,985)* 80
2204 22c **Republic of Texas,** *Mar. 2,* San Antonio, TX *(380,450)* 80
2205 22c **Fish,** *Mar. 21,* Seattle, WA 80
2206 22c **Fish,** *Mar. 21,* Seattle, WA 80
2207 22c **Fish,** *Mar. 21,* Seattle, WA 80
2208 22c **Fish,** *Mar. 21,* Seattle, WA 80
2209 22c **Fish,** *Mar. 21,* Seattle, WA 80

First day cancellation was applied to 988,184 covers bearing one or more of Nos. 2205-2209.

2210 22c **Public Hospitals,** *Apr. 11,* New York, NY *(403,665)* 80
2211 22c **Duke Ellington,** *Apr. 29,* New York, NY *(397,894)* 80
2216 22c **Presidents Souvenir Sheet of 9,** *May 22,* Chicago, IL 4.00
2217 22c **Presidents Souvenir Sheet of 9,** *May 22,* Chicago, IL 4.00
2218 22c **Presidents Souvenir Sheet of 9,** *May 22,* Chicago, IL 4.00
2219 22c **Presidents Souvenir Sheet of 9,** *May 22,* Chicago, IL 4.00
2216a to 2219i, any single 80

First day cancellation was applied to 9,009,599 covers bearing one or more of Nos. 2216-2219, 2216a-2219i.

2223a 22c **Polar Explorers,** *May 28,* North Pole, AK *(760,999)* 2.25
2220-2223, any single 80
2224 22c **Statue of Liberty,** *July 4,* New York, NY *(1,540,308)* 80

1986-87

TRANSPORTATION ISSUE

2225 1c **Omnibus,** *Nov. 26, 1986,* Washington, DC *(57,845)* 70
2226 2c **Locomotive,** *Mar. 6, 1987,* Milwaukee, WI *(169,484)* 70

1986

2238a 22c **Navajo Art,** *Sept. 4,* Window Rock, AZ *(1,102,520)* 2.25
2235-2238, any single 80
2239 22c **T.S. Eliot,** *Sept. 26,* St. Louis, MO *(304,764)* 80
2243a 22c **Woodcarved Figurines,** *Oct. 1,* Washington, DC *(629,399)* 2.25
2240-2243, any single 80
2244 22c **Christmas (Madonna),** *Oct. 24,* Washington, DC *(467,999)* 80
2245 22c **Christmas (Winter Village),** *Oct. 24,* Snow Hill, MD *(504,851)* 80

1987

2246 22c **Michigan Statehood Sesquicent.,** *Jan. 26,* Lansing, MI *(379,117)* 80
2247 22c **Pan American Games,** *Jan. 29,* Indianapolis, IN *(344,731)* 80
2248 22c **Love,** *Jan. 30,* San Francisco, CA *(333,329)* 80
2249 22c **Pointe du Sable,** *Feb. 20,* Chicago, IL *(313,054)* 80
2250 22c **Enrico Caruso,** *Feb. 27,* New York, NY *(389,834)* 80
2251 22c **Girl Scouts of America,** *Mar. 12,* Washington, DC *(556,391)* 80

1987-88

TRANSPORTATION ISSUE

2252 3c **Conestoga Wagon,** *Feb. 29, 1988,* Conestoga, PA *(155,203)* 65
2253 5c **Milk Wagon,** *Sept. 25, 1987,* Indianapolis, IN 70

First day cancel was applied to 162,571 covers bearing Nos. 2253 and 2262.

2254 5.3c **Elevator,** *Sept. 16, 1988,* New York, NY *(142,705)* 70
2255 7.6c **Carretta,** *Aug. 30, 1988,* San Jose, CA *(140,024)* 70
2256 8.4c **Wheelchair,** *Aug. 12, 1988,* Tucson, AZ *(136,337)* 70
2257 10c **Canal Boat,** *Apr. 11, 1987,* Buffalo, NY *(171,952)* 75
2258 13c **Police Patrol Wagon,** *Oct. 29, 1988,* Anaheim, CA *(132,928)* 75
2259 13.2c **Railway Coal Car,** *July 19, 1988,* Pittsburgh, PA *(123,965)* 75
2260 15c **Tugboat,** *July 12, 1988,* Long Beach, CA *(134,926)* 75
2261 16.7c **Popcorn Wagon,** *July 7, 1988,* Chicago, IL *(117,908)* 75
2262 17.5c **Marmon Wasp,** *Sept. 25, 1987,* Indianapolis, IN 80
2263 20c **Cable Car,** *Oct. 28, 1988,* San Francisco, CA *(150,068)* 80
2264 20.5c **Fire Engine,** *Sept. 28, 1988,* San Angelo, TX *(123,043)* 80
2265 21.5c **Railway Mail Car,** *Aug. 16, 1988,* Santa Fe, NM *(124,430)* 80
2266 24.1c **Tandem Bicycle,** *Oct. 26, 1988,* Redmond, WA *(138,593)* 80

1987

2267 22c **Special Occasions,** *Apr. 20,* Atlanta, GA 80
2268 22c **Special Occasions,** *Apr. 20,* Atlanta, GA 80
2269 22c **Special Occasions,** *Apr. 20,* Atlanta, GA 80
2270 22c **Special Occasions,** *Apr. 20,* Atlanta, GA 80
2271 22c **Special Occasions,** *Apr. 20,* Atlanta, GA 80
2272 22c **Special Occasions,** *Apr. 20,* Atlanta, GA 80
2273 22c **Special Occasions,** *Apr. 20,* Atlanta, GA 80
2274 22c **Special Occasions,** *Apr. 20,* Atlanta, GA 80

First day cancellation was applied to 1,588,129 covers bearing one or more of Nos. 2267-2274.

2275 22c **United Way,** *Apr. 28,* Washington, DC *(556,391)* 80

1987-88

2276 22c **Flag and Fireworks,** *May 9, 1987* Denver, CO *(398,855)* 80
2277 (25c) **"E" Earth,** *Mar. 22, 1988,* Washington, DC 85
2278 25c **Flag and Clouds,** *May 6, 1988,* Boxborough, MA *(131,265)* 85
2279 (25c) **"E" Earth,** coil, *Mar. 22, 1988,* Washington, DC 85
2280 25c **Flag over Yosemite,** *May 20, 1988,* Yosemite, CA *(144,339)* 85
Prephosphored paper, *Feb. 14, 1989,* Yosemite, CA 85
2281 25c **Honey Bee,** *Sept. 2, 1988,* Omaha, NE *(122,853)* 85
2282 (25c) **"E" Earth,** bklt. single, *Mar. 22, 1988,* Washington, DC 85

First day cancel was applied to 363,639 covers bearing one or more of Nos. 2277, 2279 and 2282.

2283 25c **Pheasant,** *Apr. 29, 1988,* Rapid City, SD *(167,053)* 85
2284 25c **Grosbeak,** *May 28, 1988,* Arlington, VA 85
2285 25c **Owl,** *May 28, 1988,* Arlington, VA 85

First day cancel was applied to 272,359 covers bearing one or more of Nos. 2284 and 2285.

2285A 25c **Flag and Clouds,** bklt. single, *July 5, 1988,* Washington, DC *(117,303)* 85
2335a 22c **American Wildlife,** *June 13, 1987* Toronto, Canada —
2286-2335, any single 80

1987-89

RATIFICATION OF THE CONSTITUTION

2336 22c **Delaware,** *July 4, 1987,* Dover, DE *(505,770)* 80
2337 22c **Pennsylvania,** *Aug. 26, 1987,* Harrisburg, PA *(367,184)* 80
2338 22c **New Jersey,** *Sept. 11, 1987,* Trenton, NJ *(432,899)* 80
2339 22c **Georgia,** *Jan. 6, 1988,* Atlanta, GA *(467,804)* 80
2340 22c **Connecticut,** *Jan. 9, 1988,* Hartford, CT *(379,706)* 80
2341 22c **Massachusetts,** *Feb. 6, 1988,* Boston, MA *(412,616)* 80
2342 22c **Maryland,** *Feb. 15, 1988,* Annapolis, MD *(376,403)* 80
2343 25c **South Carolina,** *May 23, 1988,* Columbia, SC *(322,938)* 85
2344 25c **New Hampshire,** *June 21, 1988,* Concord, NH *(374,402)* 85
2345 25c **Virginia,** *June 25, 1988,* Williamsburg, VA *(474,079)* 85
2346 25c **New York,** *July 26, 1988,* Albany, NY *(385,793)* 85
2347 25c **North Carolina,** *Aug. 22, 1989,* Fayetteville, NC 85

1987

2349 22c **U.S.-Morocco Diplomatic Relations Bicent.,** *July 17,* Washington, DC *(372,814)* 80
2350 22c **William Faulkner,** *Aug. 3,* Oxford, MS *(480,024)* 80
2354a 22c **Lacemaking,** *Aug. 14,* Ypsilanti, MI 2.75
2351-2354, any single 80
2355 22c **Drafting of Constitution Bicent.,** *Aug. 28,* Washington, DC 80
2356 22c **Drafting of Constitution Bicent.,** *Aug. 28,* Washington, DC 80
2357 22c **Drafting of Constitution Bicent.,** *Aug. 28,* Washington, DC 80
2358 22c **Drafting of Constitution Bicent.,** *Aug. 28,* Washington, DC 80
2359 22c **Drafting of Constitution Bicent.,** *Aug. 28,* Washington, DC 80

First day cancellation was applied to 1,008,799 covers bearing one or more of Nos. 2355-2359.

2360 22c **Signing of Constitution Bicent.,** *Sept. 17,* Philadelphia, PA *(719,975)* 80
2361 22c **Certified Public Accounting,** *Sept. 21,* New York, NY *(362,099)* 80
2362 22c **Locomotives,** *Oct. 1,* Baltimore, MD 80
2363 22c **Locomotives,** *Oct. 1,* Baltimore, MD 80
2364 22c **Locomotives,** *Oct. 1,* Baltimore, MD 80
2365 22c **Locomotives,** *Oct. 1,* Baltimore, MD 80
2366 22c **Locomotives,** *Oct. 1,* Baltimore, MD 80

First day cancellation was applied to 976,694 covers bearing one or more of Nos. 2362-2366.

2367 22c **Christmas (Madonna),** *Oct. 23,* Washington, DC *(320,406)* 80
2368 22c **Christmas (Ornaments),** *Oct. 23,* Holiday-Anaheim, CA *(375,858)* 80

1988

2369 22c **Winter Olympics, Calgary,** *Jan. 10,* Anchorage, AK *(395,198)* 80
2370 22c **Australia Bicentennial,** *Jan. 26,* Washington, DC *(523,465)* 80
2371 22c **James Weldon Johnson,** *Feb. 2,* Nashville, TN *(465,282)* 80
2375a 22c **Cats,** *Feb. 5,* New York, NY *(872,734)* 2.75
2372-2375, any single 80
2376 22c **Knute Rockne,** *Mar. 9,* Notre Dame, IN *(404,311)* 80
2377 25c **Francis Ouimet,** *June 13,* Brookline, MA *(383,168)* 85
2378 25c **Love,** *July 4,* Pasadena, CA *(399,038)* 85
2379 45c **Love,** *Aug. 8,* Shreveport, LA *(121,808)* 1.05
2380 25c **Summer Olympics, Seoul,** *Aug. 19,* Colorado Springs, CO *(402,616)* 85
2381 25c **Classic Automobiles,** *Aug. 25,* Detroit, MI 85
2382 25c **Classic Automobiles,** *Aug. 25,* Detroit, MI 85
2383 25c **Classic Automobiles,** *Aug. 25,* Detroit, MI 85
2384 25c **Classic Automobiles,** *Aug. 25,* Detroit, MI 85
2385 25c **Classic Automobiles,** *Aug. 25,* Detroit, MI 85

First day cancel was applied to 875,801 covers bearing one or more of Nos. 2281-2285.

2389a 25c **Antartic Explorers,** *Sept. 14,* Washington, DC *(720,537)* 3.00
2383-2389, any single 85
2393a 25c **Carousel Animals,** *Oct. 1,* Sandusky, OH *(856,380)* 3.00
2390-2393, any single 85
2394 $8.75 **Express Mail,** *Oct. 6,* Terre Haute, IN *(66,558)* 25.00
2395 25c **Special Occasions,** *Oct. 22,* King of Prussia, PA 85
2396 25c **Special Occasions,** *Oct. 22,* King of Prussia, PA 85
2397 25c **Special Occasions,** *Oct. 22,* King of Prussia, PA 85
2398 25c **Special Occasions,** *Oct. 22,* King of Prussia, PA 85

First day cancel was applied to 126,767 covers bearing one or more of Nos. 2395-2398.

2399 25c **Christmas (Madonna),** *Oct. 20,* Washington, DC *(247,291)* 85
2400 25c **Christmas (Contemporary),** *Oct. 20,* Berlin, NH *(412,213)* 85

1989

2401 25c **Montana,** *Jan. 15,* Helena, MT 85
2402 25c **A. Philip Randolph,** *Feb. 3,* New York, NY 85
2403 25c **North Dakota,** *Feb. 21,* Bismarck, ND 85
2404 25c **Washington Statehood,** *Feb. 22,* Olympia, WA 85
2405 25c **Steamboats,** *Mar. 3,* New Orleans, LA 85
2406 25c **Steamboats,** *Mar. 3,* New Orleans, LA 85
2407 25c **Steamboats,** *Mar. 3,* New Orleans, LA 85
2408 25c **Steamboats,** *Mar. 3,* New Orleans, LA 85
2409 25c **Steamboats,** *Mar. 3,* New Orleans, LA 85
2410 25c **World Stamp Expo,** *Mar. 16,* New York, NY 85
2411 25c **Arturo Toscanini,** *Mar. 25,* New York, NY 85

1989

BRANCHES OF GOVERNMENT

2412 25c **House of Representatives,** *Apr. 4,* Washington, DC 85
2413 25c **Senate,** *Apr. 6,* Washington, DC 85
2414 25c **Executive Branch,** *Apr. 30,* Mount Vernon, VA 85

1989

2416 25c **South Dakota,** *May 3,* Pierre, SD 85
2417 25c **Lou Gehrig,** *June 10,* Cooperstown, NY 85
2418 25c **Ernest Hemingway,** *July 17,* Key West, FL 85
2419 $2.40 **Moon Landing,** *July 20,* Washington, DC 85
2420 25c **Letter Carriers,** *Aug. 30,* Milwaukee, WI 85
2421 25c **Bill of Rights,** *Sept. 25,* Philadelphia, PA 85
2425a 25c **Dinosaurs,** *Oct. 1,* Orlando, FL 3.00
2422-2425, any single 85

See the "Information for Collectors" section at beginning of catalogue for illustrations of types of postmarks and precancels.

Values quoted in this catalogue are for stamps graded at Fine-Very Fine and with no faults. An illustrated guide to grade is provided in introductory material, beginning on Page V.

AIR POST FIRST DAY COVERS

See first day cover pages for postage issues for introductory notes.

1918

C1 6c **orange,** *Dec. 10* 17,500.
C2 16c **green,** *July 11* 22,500.
C3 24c **carmine rose & blue,** *May 13* 27,500.

1923

C4 8c **dark green,** *Aug. 15* 300.00
C5 16c **dark blue,** *Aug. 17* 500.00
C6 24c **carmine,** *Aug. 21* 600.00

1926-27

C7 10c **dark blue,** *Feb. 13, 1926,*
Chicago, Ill. 55.00
Detroit, Mich. 65.00
Cleveland, Ohio 65.00
Dearborn, Mich. 125.00
125.00
C8 15c **olive brown,** *Sept. 18, 1926,* 75.00
C9 20c **yellow green,** *Jan. 25, 1927,* 100.00
New York, N.Y. 125.00
C10 10c **dark blue,** *June 18, 1927,* 20.00
St. Louis, Mo. 20.00
Little Falls, Minn. 30.00
Detroit, Mich. 30.00

1928-30

C11 5c **carmine & blue,** *July 25, 1928,* pair 50.00
C12 5c **violet,** *Feb. 10, 1930* 10.00
C13 65c **green,** *Apr. 19, 1930* 1,500.
C14 $1.30 **brown,** *Apr. 19, 1930* 1,100.
C15 $2.60 **blue,** *Apr. 19, 1930* 1,300.
C13 to C15 on one cover 15,000.

1931-33

C16 5c **violet,** *Aug. 19, 1931* 175.00
C17 8c **olive bister,** *Sept. 26, 1932* 15.00
C18 50c **green,** *Oct. 2, 1933,* New York, N.Y. *(3,500)* 200.00
Akron, Ohio, *Oct. 4* 350.00
Washington, D.C., *Oct. 5* 300.00
Miami, Fla., *Oct. 6* 150.00
Chicago, Ill., *Oct. 7* 275.00

1934-37

C19 6c **dull orange,** *June 30, 1934,* Baltimore, Md. 175.00
New York, N.Y. 750.00
C20 25c **blue,** *Nov. 22, 1935 (10,910)* 20.00
San Francisco, Cal. *(15,000)* 17.50
C21 20c **green,** *Feb. 15, 1937* 20.00
C22 50c **carmine,** *Feb. 15, 1937* 20.00
C21 to C22 on one cover 37.50

First day covers of Nos. C21 and C22 total 40,000.

1938-39

C23 6c **dark blue & carmine,** *May 14, 1938,* Dayton, Ohio *(116,443)* 15.00
St. Petersburg, Fla. *(95,121)* 15.00
Washington, D.C., *May 15* 3.50
C24 30c **dull blue,** *May 16, 1939,* New York, N.Y. *(68,634)* 45.00

1941-44

C25 6c **carmine,** *June 25, 1941 (99,986)* 2.25
C26 8c **olive green,** *Mar. 21, 1944 (147,484)* 3.75
C27 10c **violet,** *Aug. 15, 1941,* Atlantic City, N.J. *(87,712)* 8.00
C28 15c **brown carmine,** *Aug. 19, 1941,* Baltimore, Md. *(74,000)* 10.00
C29 20c **bright green,** *Aug. 27, 1941,* Philadelphia, Pa. *(66,225)* 12.00
C30 30c **blue,** *Sept. 25, 1941,* Kansas City, Mo. *(57,175)* 20.00
C31 50c **orange,** *Oct. 29, 1941,* St. Louis, Mo. *(54,580)* 40.00

1946-48

C32 5c **carmine,** *Sept. 25, 1946* 2.00

First day covers of both Nos. C32 and UC14 (5c stamped envelope) total 396,669.

C33 5c **carmine,** *Mar. 26, 1947 (342,634)* 2.00
C34 10c **black,** *Aug. 30, 1947 (265,773)* 2.00
C35 15c **bright blue green,** *Aug. 20, 1947,* New York, N.Y. *(230,338)* 2.75
C36 25c **blue,** *July 30, 1947,* San Francisco, Cal. *(201,762)* 3.75
C37 5c **carmine, coil,** *Jan. 15, 1948 (192,084)* 2.00
C38 5c **New York City,** *July 31, 1948,* New York, N.Y. *(371,265)* 1.75

1949

C39 6c **carmine,** *Jan. 18 (266,790)* 1.50
C40 6c **Alexandria Bicentennial,** *May 11,* Alexandria, Va. *(386,717)* 1.25
C41 6c **carmine coil,** *Aug. 25 (240,386)* 1.25
C42 10c **U.P.U.,** *Nov. 18,* New Orleans, La. *(270,000)* 1.75
C43 15c **U.P.U.,** *Oct. 7,* Chicago, Ill. *(246,833)* 2.25
C44 25c **U.P.U.,** *Nov. 30,* Seattle, Wash. *(220,215)* 3.00
C45 6c **Wright Brothers,** *Dec. 17,* Kitty Hawk, N.C. *(378,585)* 3.50

1952-59

C46 80c **Hawaii,** *Mar. 26, 1952,* Honolulu, Hawaii, *(89,864)* 17.50
C47 6c **Powered Flight,** *May 29, 1953,* Dayton, Ohio *(359,050)* 1.50
C48 4c **bright blue,** *Sept. 3, 1954,* Philadelphia, Pa. *(295,720)* 75
C49 6c **Air Force,** *Aug. 1, 1957 (356,683)* 1.75
C50 5c **red,** *July 31, 1958,* Colorado Springs, Colo. *(207,954)* 80
C51 7c **blue,** *July 31, 1958,* Philadelphia, Pa. *(204,401)* 75
C52 7c **blue coil,** *July 31, 1958,* Miami, Fla. *(181,603)* 90
C53 7c **Alaska Statehood,** *Jan. 3, 1959,* Juneau, Alaska *(489,752)* 75
C54 7c **Balloon Jupiter,** *Aug. 17, 1959,* Lafayette, Ind.*(383,556)* 1.10
C55 7c **Hawaii Statehood,** *Aug. 21, 1959,* Honolulu, Hawaii *(533,464)* 1.00
C56 10c **Pan American Games,** *Aug. 27, 1959,* Chicago, Ill. *(302,306)* 90

1959-66

C57 10c **Liberty Bell,** *June 10, 1960,* Miami, Fla. *(246,509)* 1.25
C58 15c **Statue of Liberty,** *Nov. 20, 1959,* New York, N.Y. *(259,412)* 1.25
C59 25c **Abraham Lincoln,** *Apr. 22, 1960,* San Francisco, Cal. *(211,235)* 1.75
C59a 25c **Tagged,** *Dec. 29, 1966 (about 3,000)* 12.50
C60 7c **carmine,** *Aug. 12, 1960,* Arlington, Va. *(247,190)* 75
C61 7c **carmine coil,** *Oct. 22, 1960,* Atlantic City, N.J. *(197,995)* 1.00

1961-67

C62 13c **Liberty Bell,** *June 28, 1961,* New York, N.Y. *(316,166)* 80
C62a 13c **Tagged,** *Feb. 15, 1967* 10.00
C63 15c **Redrawn Statue of Liberty,** *Jan. 13, 1961,* Buffalo, N.Y. *(192,976)* 1.00
C63a 15c **Tagged,** *Jan. 11, 1967* 12.00
C64 8c **carmine,** *Dec. 5, 1962 (288,355)* 75
C64a 8c **Tagged,** *Aug. 1, 1963,* Dayton, Ohio *(262,720)* 75
C65 8c **carmine coil,** *Dec. 5, 1962 (220,173)* 80
C65a 8c **Tagged,** *Jan. 14, 1965,* New Orleans, La. —

1963-69

C66 15c **Montgomery Blair,** *May 3, 1963,* Silver Spring, Md. *(260,031)* 1.10
C67 6c **Bald Eagle,** *July 12, 1963,* Boston, Mass. *(268,265)* 75
C67a 6c **Tagged,** *Feb. 15, 1967* 12.50
C68 8c **Amelia Earhart,** *July 24, 1963,* Atchison, Kan. *(437,996)* 1.75
C69 8c **Robert H. Goddard,** *Oct. 5, 1964,* Roswell, N.M. *(421,020)* 1.75
C70 8c **Alaska Purchase,** *Mar. 30, 1967,* Sitka, Alaska *(554,784)* 75
C71 20c **Audubon,** *Apr. 26, 1967,* Audubon (Station of N.Y.C.), N.Y. *(227,930)* 2.00
C72 10c **carmine,** *Jan. 5, 1968,* San Francisco, Cal. 75
C73 10c **carmine coil,** *Jan. 5, 1968,* San Francisco, Cal. 75
C74 10c **Air Mail Service,** *May 15, 1968 (521,084)* 1.50
C75 20c **USA and Jet,** *Nov. 22, 1968,* New York, N.Y. *(276,244)* 1.10
C76 10c **Moon Landing,** *Sept. 9, 1969 (8,743,070)* 3.50

1971-73

C77 9c **red,** *May 15, 1971,* Kitty Hawk, N.C. 75

First day cancellation was applied to 379,442 covers of Nos. C77 and UXC10.

C78 11c **carmine,** *May 7, 1971,* Spokane, Wash. 75
C79 13c **carmine,** *Nov. 16, 1973,* New York, N.Y. *(282,550)* 75

First day cancellation was applied to 464,750 covers of Nos. C78, C78a and C82, and to 204,756 covers of Nos. C79a and C83.

C80 17c **Statue of Liberty,** *July 13, 1971,* Lakehurst, N.J. *(172,269)* 75
C81 21c **USA and Jet,** *May 21, 1971 (293,140)* 75
C82 11c **carmine coil,** *May 7, 1971,* Spokane, Wash. 75
C83 13c **carmine coil,** *Dec. 27, 1973,* Chicago, Ill. 50
C84 11c **National Parks Centennial,** *May 3, 1972,* Honaunau, Hawaii *(364,816)* 75
C85 11c **Olympics,** *Aug. 17, 1972* 75

First day cancellation was applied to 971,536 covers of Nos. 1460 to 1462 and C85.

C86 11c **Electronics,** *July 10, 1973,* New York, N.Y. 75

First day cancellation was applied to 1,197,700 covers of Nos. 1500 to 1502 and C86.

1974-79

C87 18c **Statue of Liberty,** *Jan. 11, 1974,* Hempstead, N.Y. *(216,902)* 75
C88 26c **Mt. Rushmore,** *Jan. 2, 1974,* Rapid City, S.D. *(210,470)* 85
C89 25c **Plane and Globes,** *Jan. 2, 1976,* Honolulu, Hawaii 85
C90 31c **Plane, Globes and Flag,** *Jan. 2, 1976,* Honolulu, Hawaii 85
C92a 31c **Wright Brothers,** *Sept. 23, 1978,* Dayton, Ohio 2.30
C91 or C92 2.00
C94a 21c **Octave Chanute,** *Mar. 29, 1979,* Chanute, Kan. 2.00
C93 or C94 1.00

First day cancellation was applied to 459,235 covers bearing Nos. C93, C94 or pair.

C96a 25c **Wiley Post,** *Nov. 20, 1979,* Oklahoma City, Okla. 2.00
C95 or C96 1.00
C97 31c **Olympics,** *Nov. 1, 1979,* Colorado Springs, CO 1.15

1980

C98 40c **Philip Mazzei,** *Oct. 13* 1.35
C99 28c **Blanche Stuart Scott,** *Dec. 30,* Hammondsport, NY *(238,502)* 1.10
C100 35c **Glenn Curtiss,** *Dec. 30,* Hammondsport, NY *(208,502)* 1.25

1983

C104a 28c **Olympics,** *June 17,* San Antonio, TX *(901,028)* 3.75
C101-C104, any single 1.10
C108a 40c **Olympics,** *Apr. 8,* Los Angeles, CA *(1,001,657)* 5.00
C105-C108, any single 1.35
C112a 35c **Olympics,** *Nov. 4,* Colorado Springs, CO*(897,729)* 4.50
C109-C112, any single 1.25

1985

C113 33c **Alfred V. Verville,** *Feb. 13,* Garden City, NY 1.25
C114 39c **Lawrence & Elmer Sperry,** *Feb. 13,* Garden City, NY 1.35

First day cancel was applied to 429,290 covers bearing Nos. C113 and C114.

C115 44c **Transpacific Air Mail,** *Feb. 15,* San Francisco, CA *(269,229)* 1.35

A total of 269,229 first day cancels were applied for Nos. C115 and UXC22.

C116 44c **Junipero Serra,** *Aug. 22,* San Diego, CA *(254,977)* 1.35

1988

C117 44c **Settling of New Sweden,** *Mar. 29,* Wilmington, DE *(213,445)* 1.35
C118 45c **Samuel P. Langley,** *May 14,* San Diego, CA 1.40
C119 36c **Igor Sikorsky,** *June 23,* Stratford, CT *(162,986)* 1.30

1989

C120 45c **French Revolution,** *July 14* 1.40
C121 45c **Southeast Carved Figure,** *Oct. 12,* San Juan, PR 1.40

BOOKLETS: PANES & COVERS

Most booklet panes issued before 1962 consist of a vertical block of 6 stamps perforated vertically through the center. The panes are perforated horizontally on all but the bottom edge. The two sides and bottom are straight edged. Exceptions for panes issued before 1962 are the 1917 American Expeditionary Forces panes (30 stamps); Lindbergh and 6¢ 1943 air mails (3), and the Savings Stamps (10). Since 1962, panes have been issued with 3 to 10 stamps and various configurations. They have included one or more labels and two or more stamps se-tenant.

Flat plate booklet panes, with the exceptions noted above, were made from specially designed plates of 180 or 360 subjects. They are collected in plate positions. There are nine collectible positions on the 180-subject plate and 12 on the 360-subject plate.

Rotary booklet panes issued from 1926 to May 1978 (except for Nos. 1623a and 1623c) were made from specially designed plates of 180, 320, 360, and 400 subjects. They also are collected in plate positions. There are five collectible positions on the 360-subject plates which were printed before electric eye plates came into use, and 20 collectible positions on the Type II "new design" 360-subject rotary plates. There are 21 collectible positions in the rotary air mail 180-subject plate as well as the Type IV "modified design" 360-subject plate. There are 16 collectible positions on the 320-subject plates and 20 on the 400 subject plates. There are five collectible positions on Defense and War Savings 300-subject plates.

The generally accepted methods of designating pane positions as illustrated and explained hereafter are those suggested by George H. Beans in the May 1913 issue of "Everybody's Philatelist" and by B. H. Mosher in his monograph "Discovering U.S. Rotary Pane Varieties 1926-78". Some collectors take all varieties possible, but the majority collect unused (A) panes and plate number (D) panes from flat plate issues, and plain panes and panes with electric eye bars and electric eye dashes where available from rotary plates.

Starting in 1977, BEP made two major changes in booklet production. Printing of panes was gradually moved from rotary plates to sleeves for modern high speed presses. Also, booklet production was transferred to Goebel booklet-forming machines. These changes virtually eliminated collectible pane positions. Also, because of the requirements of the Goebel machine, the subject size of printing plates or sleeves varied widely. For these reasons, plate layouts are not shown for each issue. The plate layout for No. 1288c and the sleeve layout for No. 1623a are shown as typical. The subject size of the plates or sleeves will be given with each issue.

The following panes, issued after March 11, 1977, were printed from rotary plates and assembled into booklets on the Goebel machine: Nos. 1288c, 1736a, 1742a, 1819a, 1889a, and most printings of No. 1949a. All other issues from March 11, 1977 on were printed from sleeves. Except for No. 1736a; one pane in 12 of the plate issues may have a plate join line along either long side of the pane, creating three collectible positions: no join line, join line top (or right), and join line bottom (or left).

All panes printed for booklet assembly on the Goebel machine contain two register marks in the tab: a cross register mark 1.5mm wide which runs across the tab and a length register mark (LRM), 1.5x5mm, usually placed vertically above the right hand (or top) stamp on the pane. Nos. 1623a and 1623c were regularly issued with the LRM over either stamp. Some copies of No. 1893a were issued with the LRM over the left stamp.

Starting with No. 1889a (except for 1948a), plate numbers (1 to 5 digits) were placed in the tab, normally over the left stamp. On Nos. 1889a and 1893a, the plate numbers are 3mm high. On all subsequent issues, the numbers are 1mm high. On booklets containing Nos. 1889a and 1949a, the plate number is only on the top pane, the second pane in each case not having a number. All subsequent multi-pane booklets have the plate number on each pane.

Panes in all booklets assembled on the Goebel machine will be folded at least once.

Booklet panes with tabs attached by adhesive instead of staples are valued on the basis of the tab intact. Minor damage on the back of the tab due to removal from the booklet does not affect the value.

Dr. William R. Bush, Robert E. Kitson, Richard F. Larkin, Dr. Robert Marks, Bruce H. Mosher, the Bureau Issues Association, and the Booklet Collectors Club helped the editors extensively in compiling the listings and preparing the illustrations of booklets, covers and plate layouts.

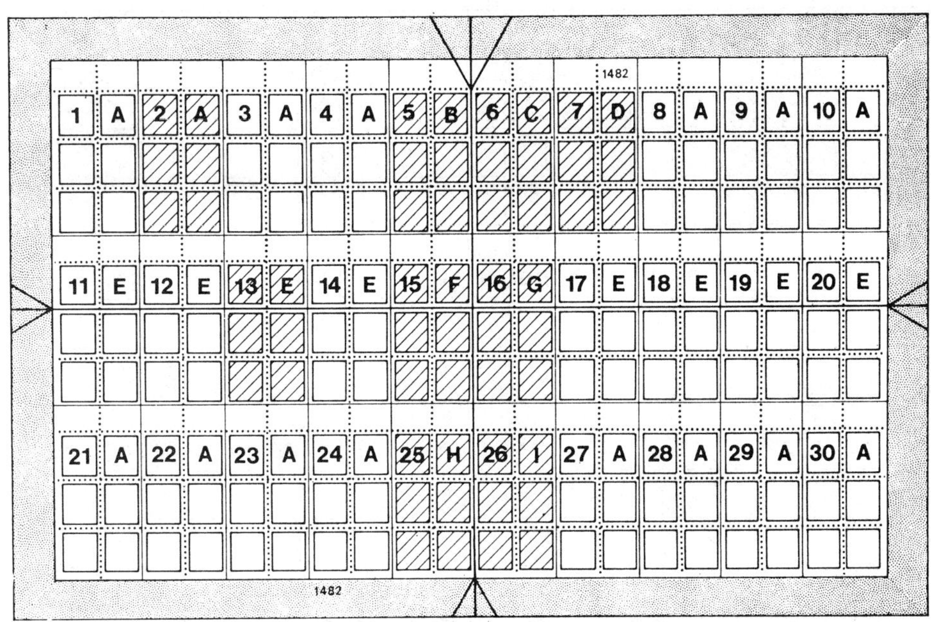

The 180-Subject Plate — 9 Collectible Positions

Beginning at upper left and reading from left to right, the panes are designated from 1 to 30. All positions not otherwise identifiable are designated by the letter A: Pane 1A, 2A, 3A, 4A, etc.

The identifiable positions are as follows:

A The ordinary booklet pane without distinguishing features. Occurs in Position 1, 2, 3, 4, 8, 9, 10, 21, 22, 23, 24, 27, 28, 29, 30.
B Split arrow and guide line at right. Occurs in Position 5 only.
C Split arrow and guide line at left. Occurs in Position 6 only.
D Plate number pane. Occurs in Position 7 only.
E Guide line pane showing horizontal guide line between stamps 1-2 and 3-4 of the pane. Occurs in Positions 11, 12, 13, 14, 17, 18, 19, and 20.
F Guide line through pane and at right. Occurs in Position 15 only.
G Guide line through pane and at left. Occurs in Position 16 only.
H Guide line at right. Occurs in Position 25 only.
I Guide line at left. Occurs in Position 26 only.

Only positions B, F and H or C, G and I may be obtained from the same sheet, depending on whether the knife which separated the panes fell to right or left of the line.

Side arrows, bottom arrows, or bottom plate numbers are seldom found because the margin of the sheets is usually cut off, as are the sides and bottom of each pane.

In the illustrations, the dotted lines represent the rows of perforations, the unbroken lines represents the knife cut.

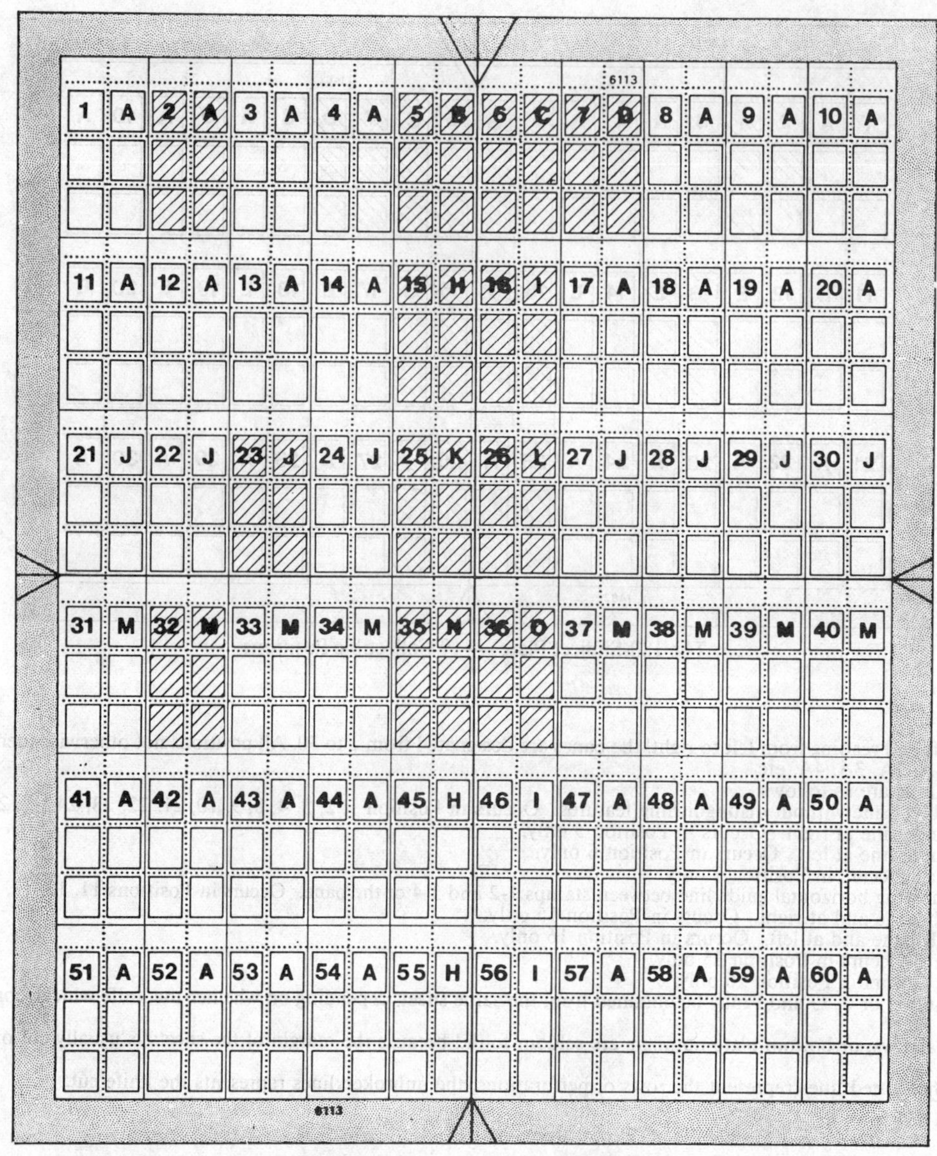

The 360-Subject Plate — 12 Collectible Positions

As with the 180-Subject Sheets, the position of the various panes is indicated by numbers beginning in the upper left corner with the No. 1 and reading from left to right to No. 60.

The identifiable positions are as follows:

A The ordinary booklet pane without distinguishing features. Occurs in Positions 1, 2, 3, 4, 8, 9, 10, 11, 12, 13, 14, 17, 18, 19, 20, 41, 42, 43, 44, 47, 48, 49, 50, 51, 52, 53, 54, 57, 58, 59, and 60.
B Split arrow and guide line at right. Occurs in Position 5 only.
C Split arrow and guide line at left. Occurs in Position 6 only.
D Plate number pane. Occurs in Position 7 only.
E, F, G Do not occur in the 360-Subject Plate.
H Guide line at right. Occurs in Positions 15, 45, and 55.
I Guide line at left. Occurs in Positions 16, 46, and 56.
J Guide line at bottom. Occurs in Positions 21, 22, 23, 24, 27, 28, 29 and 30.
K Guide line at right and bottom. Occurs in Position 25 only.
L Guide line at left and bottom. Occurs in Position 26 only.
M Guide line at top. Occurs in Positions 31, 32, 33, 34, 37, 38, 39 and 40.
N Guide line at top and right. Occurs in Position 35 only.
O Guide line at top and left. Occurs in Position 36 only.

Only one each of Positions B or C, K, L, N or O; four positions of H or I, and eight or nine positions of J or M may be obtained from each 360 subject sheet, depending on whether the knife fell to the right or left, top or bottom of the guide lines.

Because the horizontal guide line appears so close to the bottom row of stamps on panes Nos. 21 to 30, Positions M, N, and O occur with great deal less frequency than Positions J, K and L.

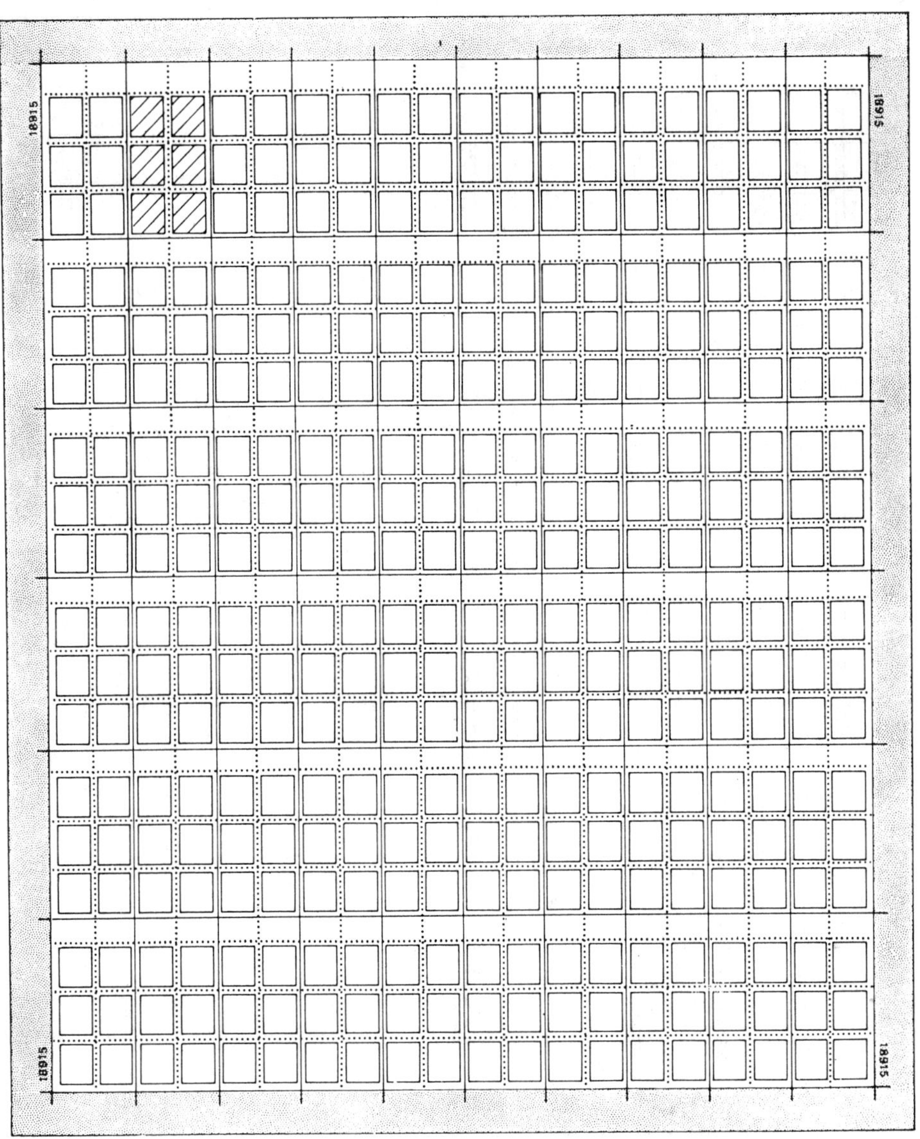

The 360-Subject Rotary Press Plate (before Electric Eye) Position A only

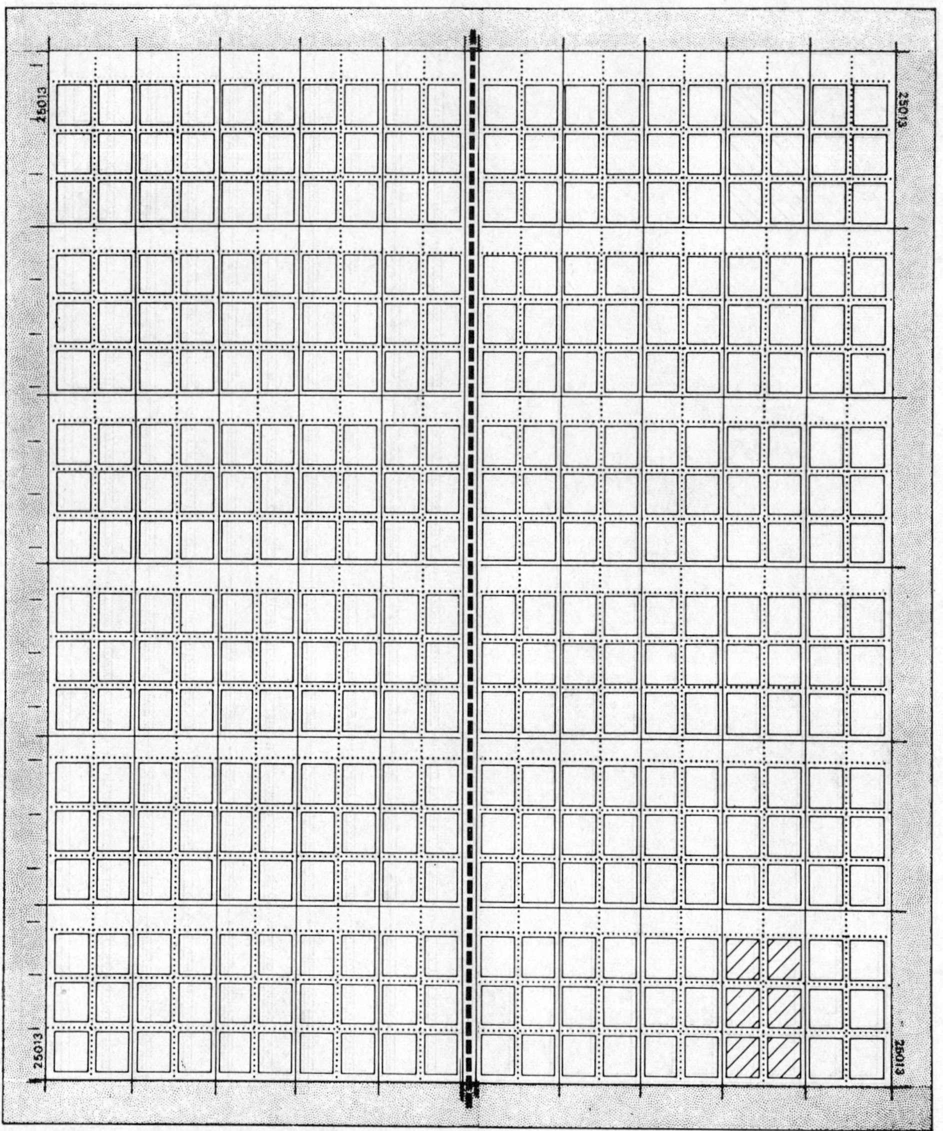

The 360-Subject Rotary Press Plate — Electric Eye
A modified design was put into use in 1956. The new plates have 20 frame bars instead of 17.

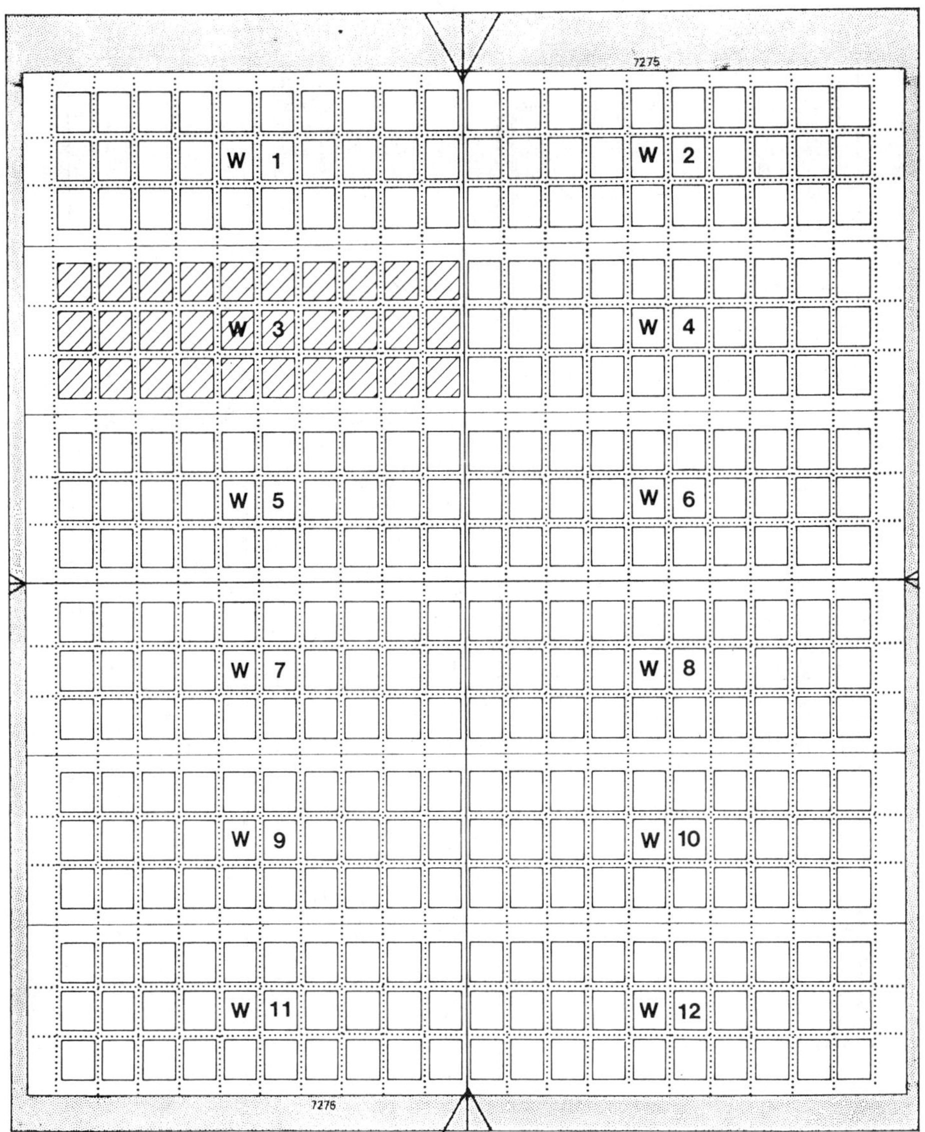

The A.E.F. Plate — 360-Subject Flat Plate — 10 Collectible Positions

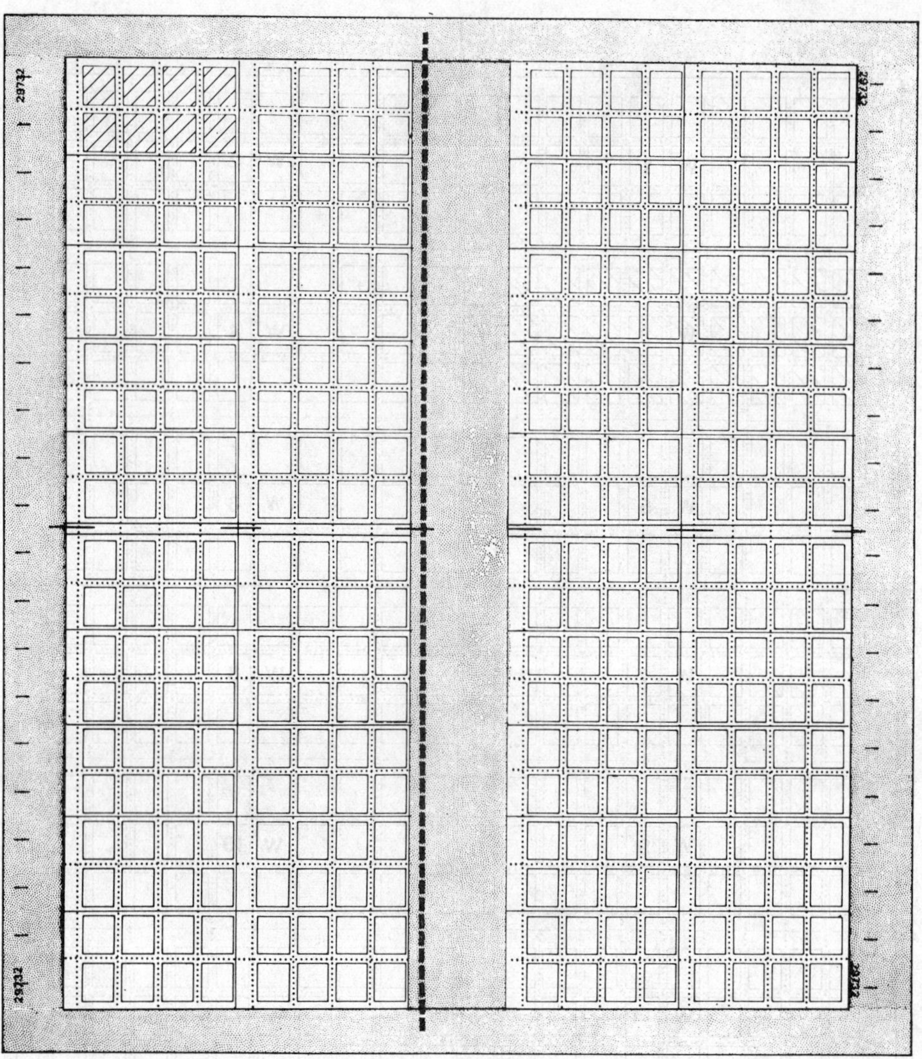

The 320-Subject Plate

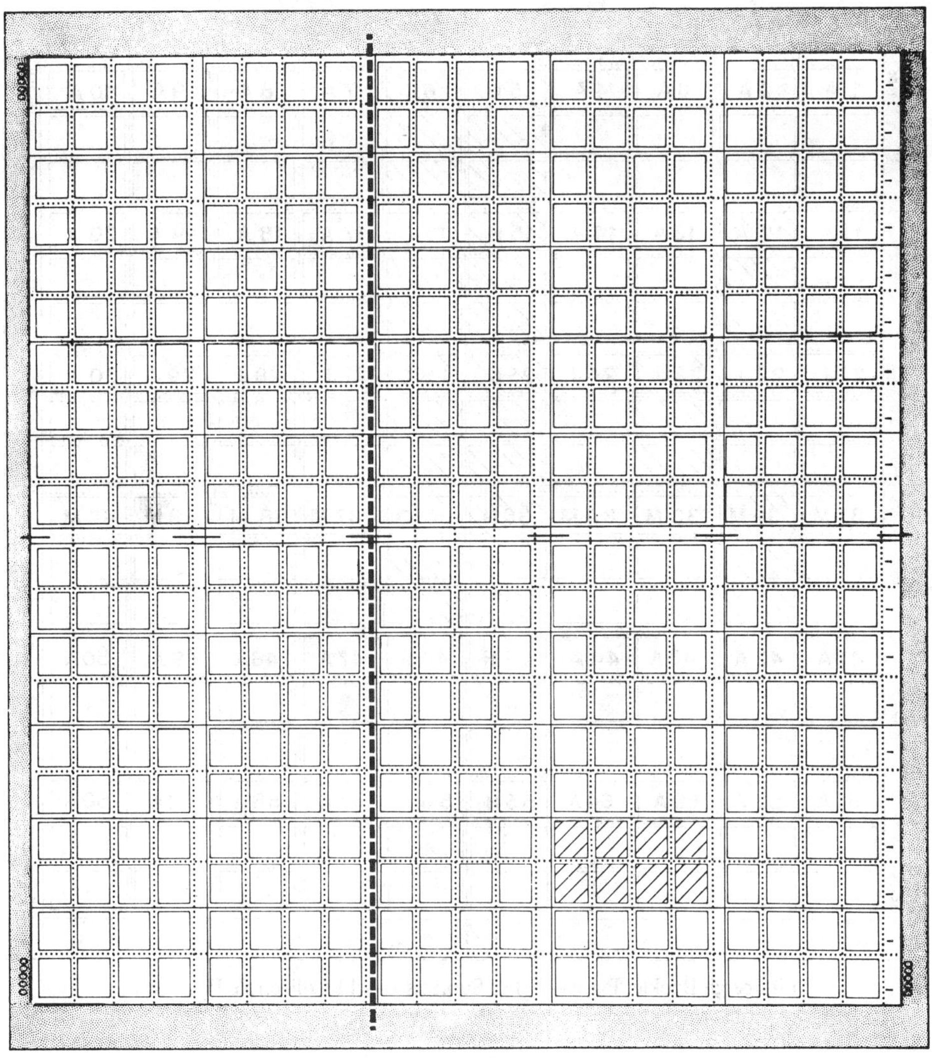

The 400-Subject Plate — The 300-Subject Plate with double labels has the same layout

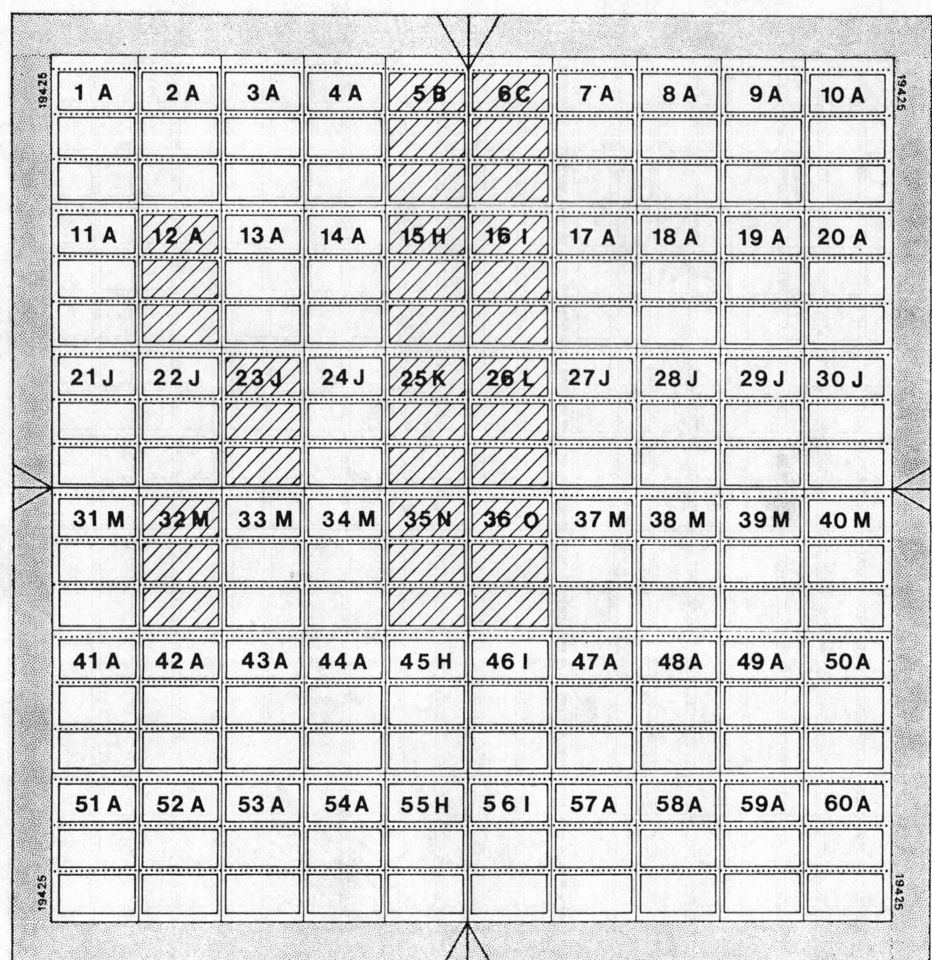

Lindbergh Booklet Plate — 180 Subjects — 11 Collectible Positions

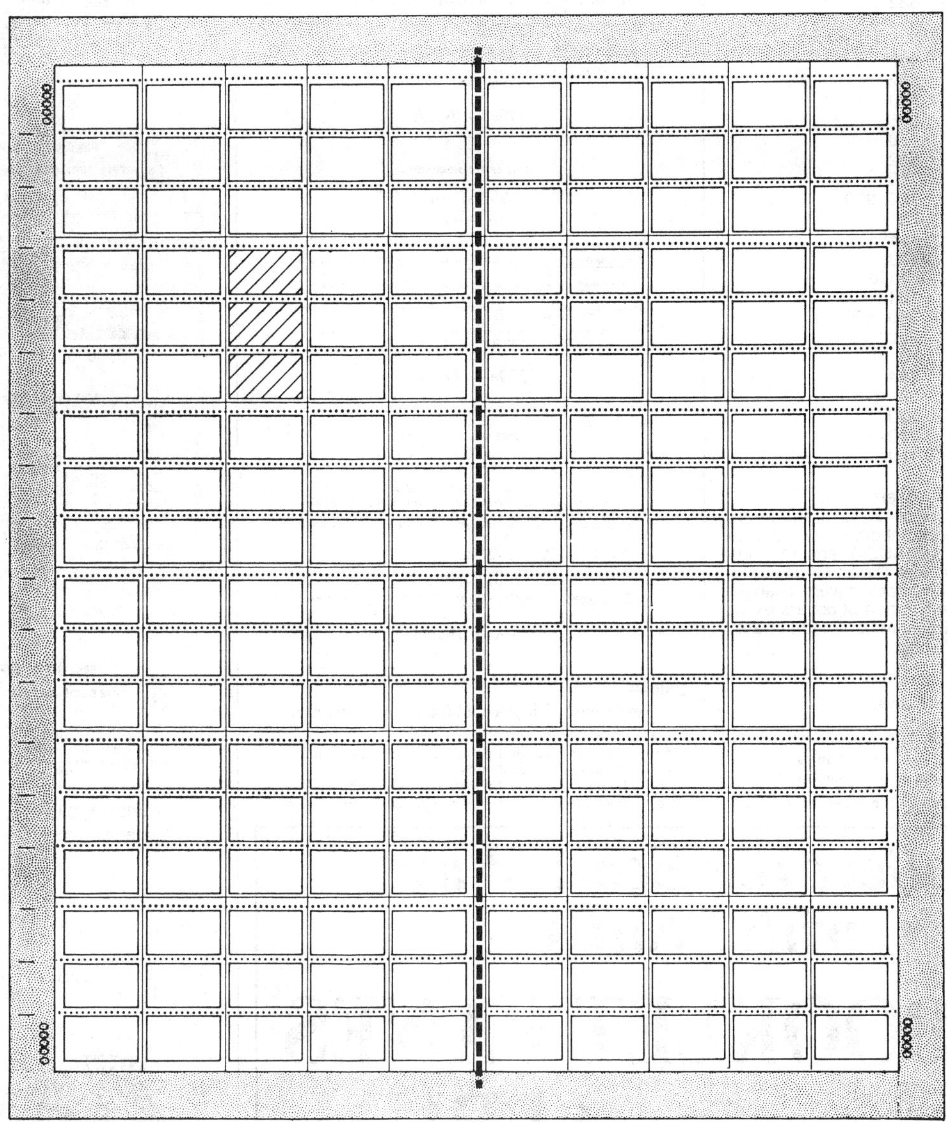

Airmail 180-Subject Rotary Press Plate — Electric Eye

Values are for complete panes with selvage, and for panes of six unless otherwise stated.

Plate Sizes:

1288c	288
1598a	832
1623a, 1623c	832
1736a	400
1737a	832
1742a	480
1819a	288
1889a	480
1893a	832
1896a	780
1896b	780, 960
1909a	78
1948a	1040
1949a	480, 1040
2113a	1040
2116a	390, 480
2121a	960
2122a	78
2197a	864
2201a	96
2209a	120
2282a	480
2285b	480

Booklet Covers

Front covers of booklets of postage and airmail issues are illustrated and numbered. Included are the Booklet Cover number (BC2A); and the catalogue numbers of the Booklet Panes (300b, 331a). The text of the inside /and back covers changes. When more than one combination of covers exists, the number of possible booklets is noted in parenthesis after the booklet listing.

1900

Text only cover

25c	booklet contains 2 panes of six 2c stamps.
49c	booklet contains 4 panes of six 2c stamps.
97c	booklet contains 8 panes of six 2c stamps.

Booklets sold for 1c more than the face value of the stamps.

POST OFFICE DEPARTMENT.
THIS BOOK CONTAINS 12 TWO-CENT STAMPS.
Price, 25 cents.
DOMESTIC POSTAGE RATES.
(Apply to mail matter sent to Puerto Rico, Guam, Philippines, Canada, and Mexico.)
First-class. Letters and sealed matter: 2 cts. for each ounce or fraction.
Second-class. Newspapers and periodicals: 1 ct. for each four ounces or fraction.
Third-class. Miscellaneous printed matter: 1 ct. for each two ounces or fraction.
Fourth-class. All matter not included in first three classes: 1 ct. for each ounce or fraction.

279e — BC1A

POST OFFICE DEPARTMENT.
THIS BOOK CONTAINS 24 TWO-CENT STAMPS.
Price, 49 cents.
DOMESTIC POSTAGE RATES.
(Apply to mail matter sent to Puerto Rico, Guam, Philippines, Canada, and Mexico.)
First-class. Letters and sealed matter: 2 cts. for each ounce or fraction.
Second-class. Newspapers and periodicals: 1 ct. for each four ounces or fraction.
Third-class. Miscellaneous printed matter: 1 ct. for each two ounces or fraction.
Fourth-class. All matter not included in first three classes: 1 ct. for each ounce or fraction.

279e — BC1B

POST OFFICE DEPARTMENT.
THIS BOOK CONTAINS 48 TWO-CENT STAMPS.
Price, 97 cents.
DOMESTIC POSTAGE RATES.
(Apply to mail matter sent to Porto Rico, Guam, Philippines, Canada, and Mexico.)
First-class. Letters and sealed matter: 2 cts. for each ounce or fraction.
Second-class. Newspapers and periodicals: 1 ct. for each four ounces or fraction.
Third-class. Miscellaneous printed matter: 1 ct. for each two ounces or fraction.
Fourth-class. All matter not included in first three classes: 1 ct. for each ounce or fraction.

279e — BC1C

1900-08

Text cover with price added in upper corners

25c	booklets contain 4 panes of six 1c stamps or 2 panes of six 2c stamps.
49c	booklet contains 4 panes of six 2c stamps.
97c	booklet contains 8 panes of six 2c stamps.

25c. POST OFFICE DEPARTMENT, U. S. A. 25c.
—THIS BOOK CONTAINS 24 ONE-CENT STAMPS—
PRICE, 25 CENTS.
DOMESTIC POSTAGE RATES.
(Apply to Guam, Hawaii, Philippines, Porto Rico, Tutuila, Canal Zone, and to Canada, Cuba, Mexico, and the Republic of Panama.)
First-class. Letters and sealed matter: 2 cts. for each ounce or fraction. Postal cards and post cards 1 ct. each.
Second-class. Newspapers and periodicals: 1 ct. for each four ounces or fraction.
Third-class. Miscellaneous printed matter: 1 ct. for each two ounces or fraction.
Fourth-class. All matter not included in first three classes: 1 ct. for each ounce or fraction.
Special-delivery. A special-delivery stamp, in addition to postage, secures immediate delivery within the carrier-delivery limit of city free delivery and within one mile of any other United States post office.

300b, 331a — BC2A

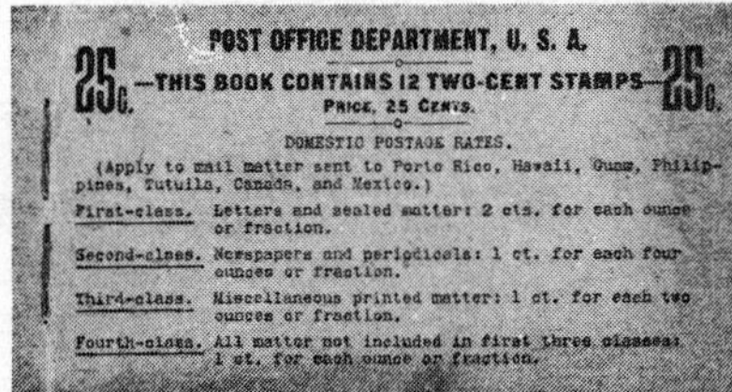
25c. POST OFFICE DEPARTMENT, U. S. A. 25c.
—THIS BOOK CONTAINS 12 TWO-CENT STAMPS—
PRICE, 25 CENTS.
DOMESTIC POSTAGE RATES.
(Apply to mail matter sent to Porto Rico, Hawaii, Guam, Philippines, Tutuila, Canada, and Mexico.)
First-class. Letters and sealed matter: 2 cts. for each ounce or fraction.
Second-class. Newspapers and periodicals: 1 ct. for each four ounces or fraction.
Third-class. Miscellaneous printed matter: 1 ct. for each two ounces or fraction.
Fourth-class. All matter not included in first three classes: 1 ct. for each ounce or fraction.

279e, 301c, 319, 332a — BC2B

49c. POST OFFICE DEPARTMENT, U. S. A. 49c.
—THIS BOOK CONTAINS 24 TWO-CENT STAMPS—
PRICE, 49 CENTS.
DOMESTIC POSTAGE RATES.
(Apply to Guam, Hawaii, Philippines, Porto Rico, Tutuila, Canal Zone, and to Canada, Cuba, Mexico, and the Republic of Panama.)
First-class. Letters and sealed matter: 2 cts. for each ounce or fraction. Postal cards and post cards, 1 ct. each.
Second-class. Newspapers and periodicals: 1 ct. for each four ounces or fraction.
Third-class. Miscellaneous printed matter: 1 ct. for each two ounces or fraction.
Fourth-class. All matter not included in first three classes: 1 ct. for each ounce or fraction.
Special-delivery. A special-delivery stamp, in addition to postage, secures immediate delivery within the carrier-delivery limit of city free delivery and within one mile of any other United States post office.

279e, 301c, 319, 332a — BC2C

97c. POST OFFICE DEPARTMENT, U. S. A. 97c.
—THIS BOOK CONTAINS 48 TWO-CENT STAMPS—
PRICE, 97 CENTS.
DOMESTIC POSTAGE RATES.
(Apply to mail matter sent to Porto Rico, Hawaii, Guam, Philippines, Tutuila, Canada, and Mexico.)
First-class. Letters and sealed matter: 2 cts. for each ounce or fraction.
Second-class. Newspapers and periodicals: 1 ct. for each four ounces or fraction.
Third-class. Miscellaneous printed matter: 1 ct. for each two ounces or fraction.
Fourth-class. All matter not included in first three classes: 1 ct. for each ounce or fraction.

279e, 301c, 319, 332a — BC2D

1908-12 **Postrider**

25c	booklet contains 2 panes of six 2c stamps.
49c	booklet contains 4 panes of six 2c stamps.
97c	booklet contains 8 panes of six 2c stamps.

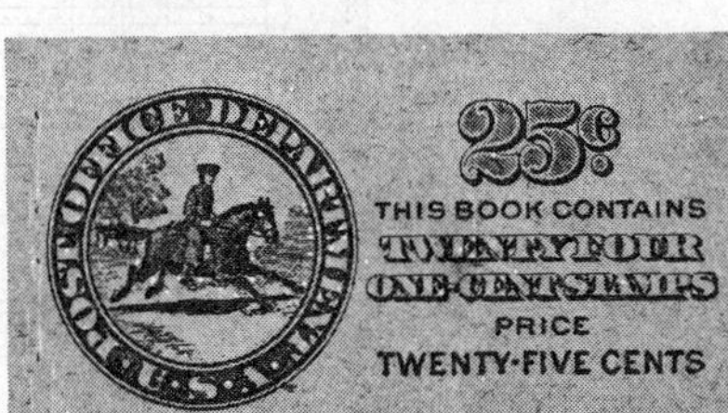

331a, 374a, 405b — BC3A

332a, 375a, 406a — BC3B

332a, 375a, 406a — BC3C

332a, 375a, 406a — BC3D

1912-39 **Washington P.O.**

Price of booklet in large numerals behind contents information

25c booklet contains 4 panes of six 1c stamps.
73c booklet contains 4 panes of six 1c stamps and 4 panes of six 2c stamps.
97c booklet contains 16 panes of six 1c stamps.

405b, 424d, 462a, 498e — BC4A

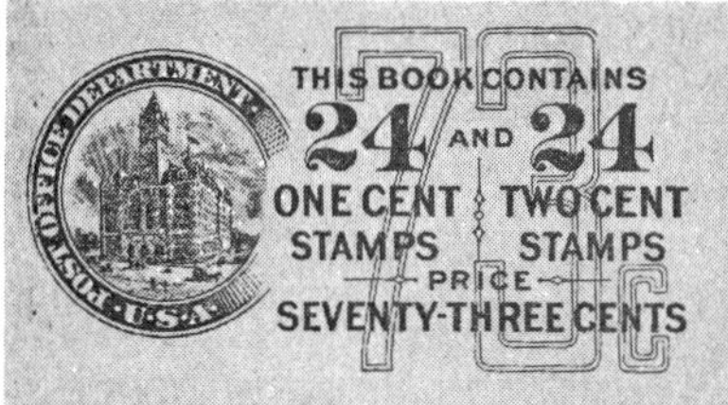

405b, 424d, 462a, 498e, 552a, 632a — BC4B

405b, 424d, 462a, 498e, 552a, 632a, 804b — BC4C

1912-39 **Small Postrider**

Large background numerals

25c booklets contain 4 panes of six 1c stamps or 2 panes of six 2c stamps.
49c booklet contains 4 panes of six 2c stamps.
73c booklet contains 4 panes of six 1c stamps and 2 panes of six 2c stamps.
97c booklets contain 16 panes of six 1c stamps or 8 panes of six 2c stamps.

See table of Territorial and Statehood Dates at beginning of catalogue. See catalogue index.

632a, 804b — BC5A

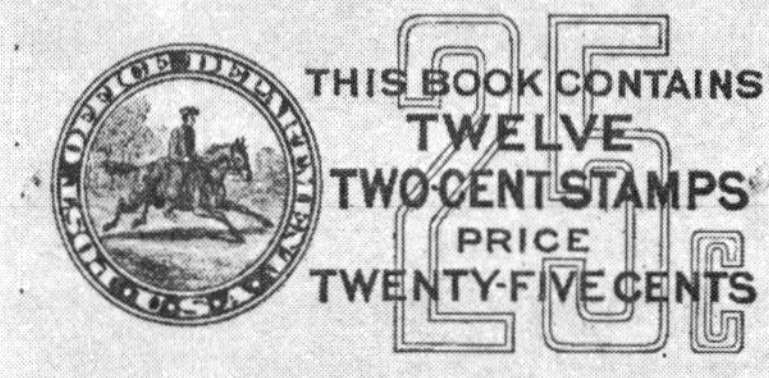

406a, 425e, 463a, 499e, 554c, 583a, 634d, 806b — BC5B

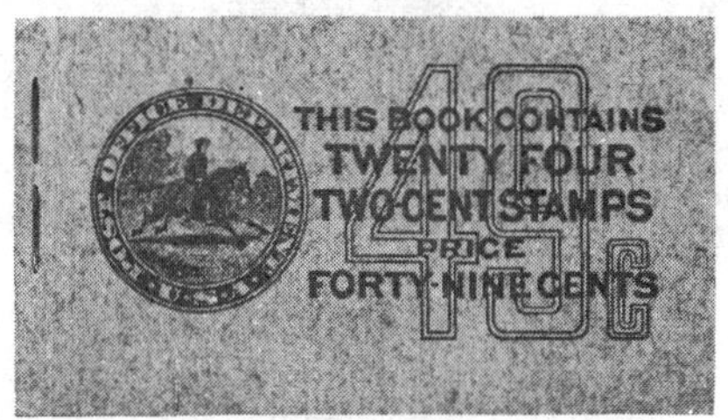

406a, 425e, 463a, 499e, 554c, 583a, 634d, 806b — BC5C

632a, 804b — BC5D

632a, 804b — BC5E

406a, 425e, 463a, 499e, 634d 806b — BC5F

1917-27 **Oval designs**

25c booklet contains 4 panes of six 1c stamps.
37c booklet contains 2 panes of six 3c stamps.
97c booklet contains 8 panes of six 2c stamps.

498e, 552a — BC6A

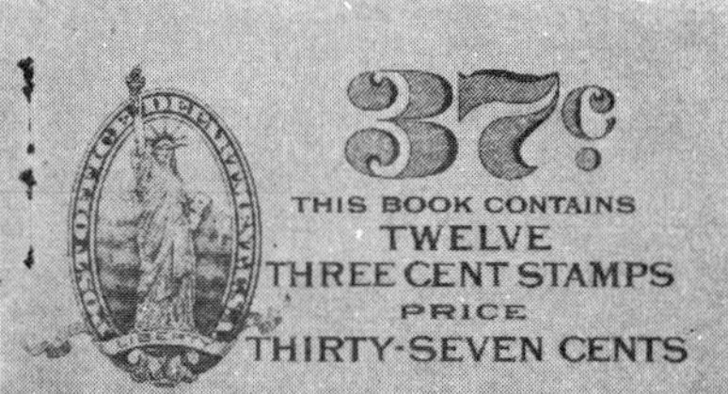

501b, 502b — BC6B

499e, 554c, 583a, 634d — BC6C

1918 **A.E.F.**

$3 booklet contains 10 panes of thirty 1c stamps.
$6 booklet contains 10 panes of thirty 2c stamps.

Booklets sold for face value.

498f
BC7A

300
1 CENT POSTAGE STAMPS
$3.

499f
BC7B

1928 **Postrider and Wings**

61c booklet contains 2 panes of three 10c stamps.

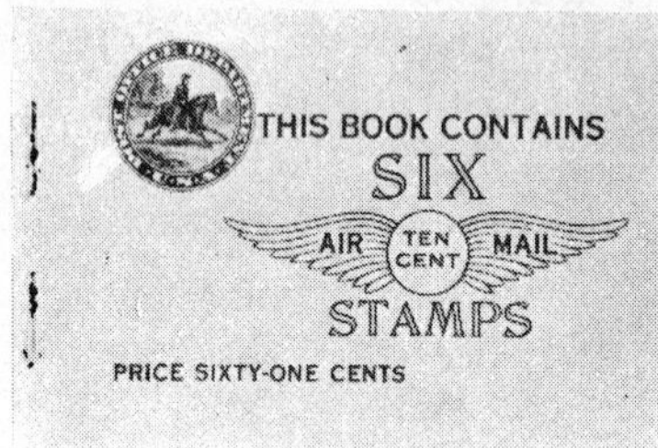

C10a – BC8

Large background numerals

1932-54 **Post Office Seal**

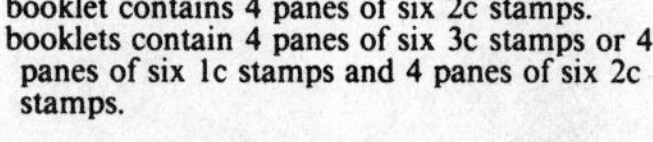

25c booklet contains 2 panes of six 2c stamps.
37c booklet contains 2 panes of six 3c stamps.
49c booklet contains 4 panes of six 2c stamps.
73c booklets contain 4 panes of six 3c stamps or 4 panes of six 1c stamps and 4 panes of six 2c stamps.

806b – BC9A

720b, 807a, 1035a – BC9B

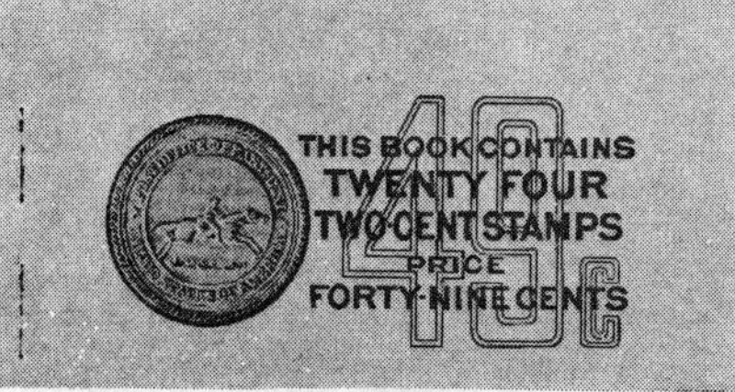

806b – BC9C

720b, 807a, 1035a – BC9D

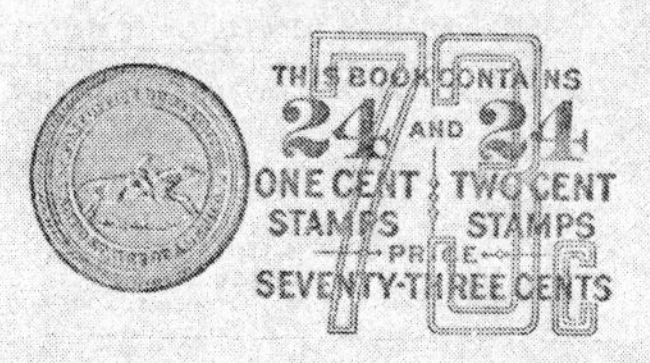

804b – BC9E

United States Booklet Panes can be mounted in Scott's U.S. Booklet Panes Album.

1958

97c booklet contains 4 panes of six 4c stamps.

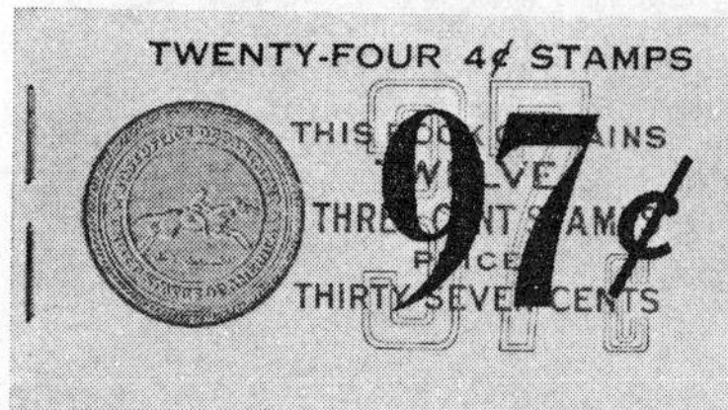

1036a – BC9F

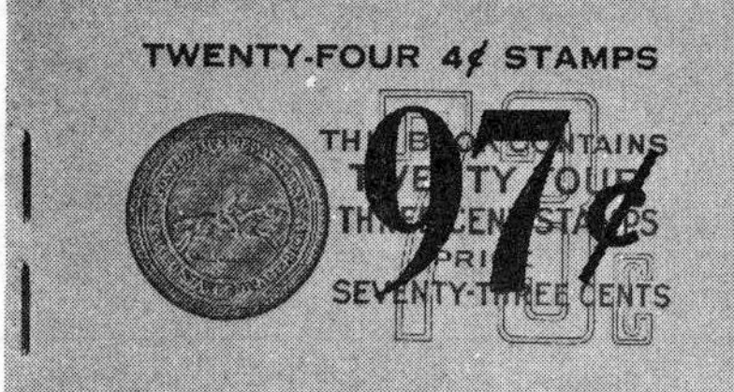

1036a – BC9G

1036a – BC9H

Large background numerals

1943 **Postrider and Wings**

37c booklet contains 2 panes of three 6c stamps.
73c booklet contains 4 panes of three 6c stamps.

C25a – BC10A

C25a – BC10B

1949-63 **U.S. Airmail Wings**

The 73c and 85c booklets were the last sold for 1c over face value.

73c booklet contains 2 panes of six 6c stamps.
85c booklet contains 2 panes of six 7c stamps.
80c booklet contains 2 panes of five 8c stamps.
$2 booklet contains 5 panes of five 8c stamps.

C39a – BC11A

C51a — BC11B

C51a, C60a — BC11C

C64b, C64c — BC11D

C64b — BC11E

1962-63 **Small Postrider**

$1 booklet contains 4 panes of five 5c stamps.

1213a — BC12A

1963-64 **Mr. Zip**

$1 booklet contains 4 panes of five 5c stamps.
$2 booklet contains 5 panes of five 8c stamps.

1213a, 1213c — BC13A

C64b, C64c — BC13B

1967-68

$2 booklet contains 4 panes of eight 6c stamps and 1 pane of eight 1c stamps.
$4 booklet contains 5 panes of eight 10c stamps.

1284b — BC14A

C72b — BC14B

1968-71

$1 booklets contain 2 panes of five 10c stamps or 2 panes of six 8c stamps and 1 pane of four 1c stamps; 3 panes of five 6c stamps and 1 pane of five 2c stamps or 2 panes of four 11c stamps and 1 pane of six 2c stamps.

C72c — BC15A

1395b — BC15B

1284c, 1393b — BC15C

C78a — BC15D

1970-71 **Eisenhower**

$2 booklet contains 4 panes of eight 6c stamps and 1 pane of eight 1c stamps.
$1.92 booklet contains 3 panes of eight 8c stamps.

1393a — BC16A

1395a — BC16B

1972-74 **Postal Service Emblem**

$2 booklet contains 3 panes of seven 8c stamps and 1 pane of four 8c stamps.
$1 booklet contains 2 panes of five 10c stamps.
$4 booklet contains 5 panes of eight 10c stamps.
$1.25 booklet contains 1 pane of five 13c stamps and 1 pane of six 10c stamps.

1395d — BC17A

An enhanced introduction to the Scott Catalogue begins on Page V. A thorough understanding of the material presented there will greatly aid your use of the catalogue itself.

1510b — BC17B

1510c — BC17C

1510d — BC17D

1973

$1.30 booklet contains 2 panes of five 13c stamps.

C79a — BC18

1975-76

90c booklet contains 1 pane of six 13c stamps and 1 pane of six 2c stamps.
$1.30 booklet contains 2 panes of five 13c stamps.
$2.99 booklet contains 2 panes of eight 13c stamps and 1 pane of seven 13c stamps.

1595a, 1595d — BC19A

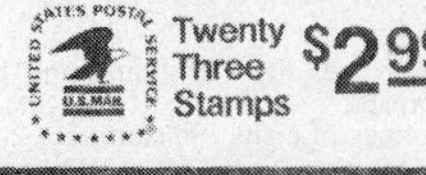

1595c — BC19B

1977-78

$1 booklet contains 1 pane of one 9c stamp and seven 13c stamps.
$1.20 booklet contains 1 pane of eight 15c stamps.
$2.40 booklet contains 2 panes of eight 15c stamps.
$3.60 booklet contains 3 panes of eight 15c stamps.

1623a — BC20

1598a — BC21

1738a — BC22

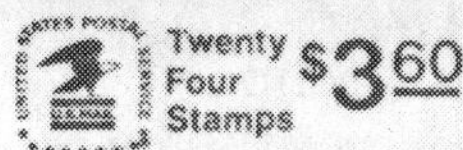

1288c — BC23

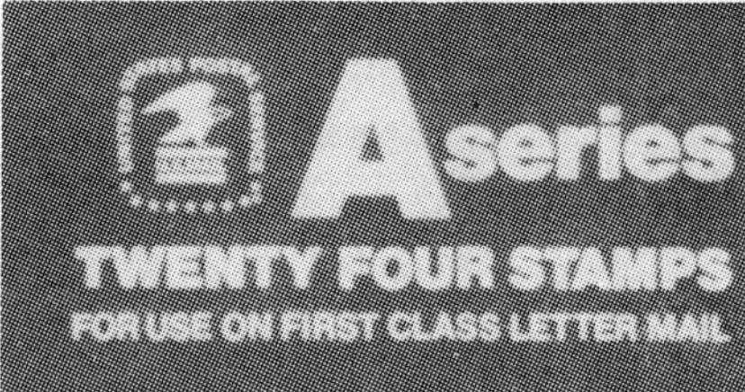

1736c — BC24

1980

$3 booklet contains 2 panes of ten 15c stamps.

1742a — BC25

1981-82

$4.32 booklet contains 3 panes of eight B stamps.
$4 booklet contains 2 panes of ten C stamps.
$4.40 booklet contains 2 panes of ten D stamps.

1819a, 1948a, 2113a — BC26

1981

$1.20 booklet contains 1 pane of two 6c and six 18c stamps.
$3.60 booklet contains 2 panes of ten 18c stamps.

1893a — BC27

1889a — BC28

1982

$1.20 booklet contains 2 panes of six 20c stamps.
$2 booklet contains 1 pane of ten 20c stamps.
$4 booklet contains 2 panes of ten 20c stamps.

1896a — BC29

1896b — BC29B

1949a — BC30

1983

$28.05 booklet contains 1 pane of three $9.35 stamps.
$32.25 booklet contains 1 pane of three $10.75 stamps.

1909a, 2121a — BC31

1985

$1.10 booklet contains one pane of five 22c stamps.
$2.20 booklet contains two panes of five 22c stamps.
$4.40 booklet contains two panes of ten 22c stamps.

2116a — BC32

2121a — BC33A

2121a — BC33B

Many different seashell configurations are possible on BC33A. Seven adjacent covers are necessary to show all 25 shells.

2116a — BC33C

1986

$1.76 booklet contains 2 panes of four 22c stamps.
$2.20 booklet contains 2 panes of five 22c stamps.

2201a — BC34

2209a — BC35

1987

$2.20 booklet contains 1 pane of ten 22c stamps.

FOR 22 CENTS, YOU CAN ADD ONE OF THESE GREETINGS TO A LETTER TO ANYONE IN THE UNITED STATES, CANADA OR MEXICO.
Get Well!
Thank You!
Best Wishes!
Keep in Touch!
Love You, Dad!
Happy Birthday!
Congratulations!
Love You, Mother!
10 TWENTY-TWO CENT U.S. POSTAGE STAMPS 2.20

2274a — BC36

1987

$4.40 booklet contains four panes of five 22c stamps.

We the People
$4.40
Twenty 22-cent stamps
USA

2359a — BC37

1987

$4.40 booklet contains four panes of five 22c stamps.

STEAM LOCOMOTIVES
TWENTY U.S. 22 CENT STAMPS
$4.40

2366a — BC38

1987

$4.40 booklet contains one pane of twenty 22c stamps.

2276a — BC39

1988

$5 booklet contains two panes of ten E stamps.

TWENTY U.S. STAMPS
Meets First-Class Letter Mail Rate
E SERIES
DOMESTIC MAIL ONLY

2282a — BC40

1988

$5 booklet contains two panes of ten 25c stamps.

2283a — BC41

1988

$1.50 booklet contains one pane of six 25c stamps.
$3 booklet contains two panes of six 25c stamps.
$5 booklet contains two panes of ten 25c stamps.

Jack London
Great American Series
TWELVE
twenty-five cent
STAMPS
$3.00

2197a — BC43

1988

$5 booklet contains two panes of ten 25c stamps.

2285b — BC45

1988

$3 booklet contains two panes of six 25c stamps.

2285c — BC46

1988

$5 booklet contains four panes of five 25c stamps.

2385a — BC47

1988

$3 booklet contains two panes of six 25c stamps.

Twelve 25cent
Special Occasion
Stamps
$3
Happy Birthday
Best Wishes
Thinking of you
Love you

2396a, 2398a — BC48

United States postage and air mail first day covers are listed and valued in a separate section of the catalogue. See catalogue index.

2409a — BC49

1989

$5 booklet contains four panes of five 25c stamps.

BOOKLET PANES

Washington — A88

Wmk. 191 Horizontally or Vertically

1900 *Perf. 12*

279e	A88	2c orange red, *April 16*	350.00	*200.00*
		2c red	350.00	*200.00*
		With plate number (D)	750.00	

180- and 360-Subject Plates. All plate positions exist, except J, K, and L, due to the horizontal guide line being placed too far below stamps to appear on the upper panes.

Booklets

BK1	BC1A	25c black, *cream*	—
BK2	BC1A	25c black, *buff*	—
BK3	BC1B	49c green, *cream*	—
BK4	BC1B	49c black, *buff*	—
BK5	BC1C	97c red, *cream*	—
BK6	BC1C	97c black, *gray*	—
BK7	BC2B	25c black, *cream* (3)	—
BK8	BC2C	49c black, *buff* (3)	—
BK9	BC2D	97c black, *gray* (3)	—

BK1-BK6 and one type each of BK7-BK9 exist with specimen overprints handstamped on cover and individual stamps.

All covers of BK7-BK9 exist with "Philippines" overprint in 50mm or 48mm.

Franklin — A115

Washington — A116

1903-07 **Wmk. 191 Vertically**

300b	A115	1c blue green, *Mar. 6, 1907*	*400.00*	*250.00*
		With plate number (D)	*1,000.*	

180-Subject Plates only. All plate positions exist.

Booklet

BK10	BC2A	25c black, *green* (6)	—

301c	A116	2c carmine, *Jan. 24, 1903*	*400.00*	*250.00*
		With plate number (D)	*1,100.*	

180-Subject Plates only. All plate positions exist.

Booklets

BK11	BC2B	25c black, *cream*	—
BK12	BC2C	49c black, *buff*	—
BK13	BC2D	97c black, *gray*	—

Washington — A129

1903 **Wmk. 191 Vertically**

319g	A129	2c carmine, Die I, *Dec. 3, 1903*	90.00	*20.00*
319m	A129	2c lake (I)	—	
319n	A129	2c carmine rose (I)	—	
319p	A129	2c scarlet (I)	90.00	
319h	A129	2c carmine, Die II	125.00	
319q	A129	2c lake (II)	125.00	
		With plate number, Die I (D)	225.00	
		With plate number, Die II (D)	325.00	
		Wmk. horizontal	150.00	*30.00*

180-Subject Plates only. All plate positions exist.

Booklet

BK14	BC2B	25c black, *cream* (11)	—
BK15	BC2C	49c black, *buff* (11)	—
BK16	BC2C	49c black, *pink*	—
BK17	BC2D	97c black, *gray* (11)	—

Franklin — A138

Washington — A139

1908 **Wmk. 191 Vertically**

331a	A138	1c green, *Dec. 2, 1908*	165.00	*35.00*
		With plate number (D)	250.00	

180- and 360-Subject Plates. All plate positions exist.

Booklets

BK18	BC2A	25c black, *green* (3)	—
BK19	BC3A	25c black, *green*	—

332a	A139	2c carmine, *Nov. 16, 1908*	100.00	*35.00*
		With plate number (D)	190.00	

180- and 360-Subject Plates. All plate positions exist.

Booklets

BK20	BC2B	25c black, *cream* (2)	—
BK21	BC2C	49c black, *buff* (2)	—
BK22	BC2C	49c black, *pink*	—
BK23	BC2D	97c black, *gray* (3)	—
BK24	BC3B	25c black, *cream*	—
BK25	BC3C	49c black, *pink*	—
BK26	BC3D	97c black, *gray*	—

1910 **Wmk. 190 Vertically** *Perf. 12*

374a	A138	1c green, *Oct. 7, 1910*	110.00	*30.00*
		With plate number (D)	190.00	

360-Subject Plates only. All plate positions exist.

Booklet

BK27	BC3A	25c black, *green* (2)	—

375a	A139	2c carmine, *Nov. 30, 1910*	95.00	*25.00*
		With plate number (D)	170.00	

360-Subject Plates only. All plate positions exist.

Booklets

BK28	BC3B	25c black, *cream* (2)	—
BK29	BC3C	49c black, *pink* (2)	—
BK30	BC3D	97c black, *gray* (2)	—

Washington — A140

1912 **Wmk. 190 Vertically**

405b	A140	1c green, *Feb. 8, 1912*	50.00	*7.50*
		With plate number (D)	100.00	

360-Subject Plates only. All plate positions exist.

Ordinary Booklets

BK31	BC3A	25c black, *green* (2)	—
BK32	BC4A	25c green, *green* (3)	—
BK33	BC4C	97c green, *lavender*	—

Combination Booklet

BK34	BC4B	73c red, 4 #405b (1c) + 4 #406a (2c)	—

406a	A140	2c carmine, *Feb. 8, 1912*	70.00	*17.50*
		With plate number (D)	10.00	

360-Subject Plates only. All plate positions exist.

Ordinary Booklets

BK35	BC3B	25c black, *cream* (2)	—
BK36	BC3C	49c black, *pink* (2)	—
BK37	BC3D	97c black, *gray* (2)	—
BK38	BC5B	25c red, *buff* (3)	—
BK39	BC5C	49c red, *pink* (3)	—
BK40	BC5F	97c red, *blue,* (3)	—

Combination Booklet

See No. BK34.

1914 **Wmk. 190 Vertically** ***Perf. 10***

424d	A140	1c green	3.50	*75*
		Double transfer, Plate 6363	—	—
		With plate number (D)	12.00	
		Cracked plate	—	
		Imperf.	—	

360-Subject Plates only. All plate positions exist.

Ordinary Booklets

BK41	BC4A	25c green, *green* (3)	25.00
BK42	BC4C	97c green, *lavender* (2)	75.00

Combination Booklet

BK43	BC4B	73c red, 4 #424d (1c) + 4 #425e (2c) (3)	225.00

425e	A140	2c carmine, *Jan. 6, 1914*	12.50	*3.00*
		With plate number (D)	35.00	

360-Subject Plates only. All plate positions exist.

Ordinary Booklets

BK44	BC5B	25c red, *buff* (3)	—
BK45	BC5C	49c red, *pink* (3)	—
BK46	BC5F	97c red, *blue* (3)	—

Combination Booklet

See No. BK43.

1916 **Unwmk.** ***Perf. 10***

462a	A140	1c green, *Oct. 15, 1916*	7.50	*1.00*
		Cracked plate at right	65.00	—
		Cracked plate at left	65.00	
		With plate number (D)	25.00	

360-Subject Plates only. All plate positions exist.

Ordinary Booklets

BK47	BC4A	25c green, *green*	—
BK48	BC4C	97c green, *lavender*	—

Combination Booklets

BK49	BC4B	73c red, 4 #462a (1c) + 4 #463a (2c) (2)	—

463a	A140	2c carmine, *Oct. 8, 1916*	70.00	*20.00*
		With plate number (D)	150.00	

360-Subject Plates only. All plate positions exist.

Ordinary Booklets

BK50	BC5B	25c red, *buff*	—
BK51	BC5C	49c red, *pink*	—
BK52	BC5F	97c red, *blue*	—

Combination Booklets

See No. BK49.

1917-18 **Unwmk.** ***Perf. 11***

498e	A140	1c green, *Apr. 6, 1917*	1.75	*35*
		Double transfer	—	—
		With plate number (D)	5.00	*60*

360-Subject Plates only. All plate positions exist.

Ordinary Booklets

BK53	BC4A	25c green, *green* (2)	20.00
BK54	BC4C	97c green, *lavender* (4)	35.00
BK55	BC6A	25c green, *green* (5)	—

Combination Booklets

BK56	BC4B	73c red, 4 #498e (1c) + 4 #499e (2c) (4)	40.00
BK57	BC4B	73c red, 4 #498e (1c) + 4 #554c (2c) (3)	65.00

499e	A140	2c rose, type I, *Mar. 31, 1917*	3.50	*50*
		With plate number (D)	5.00	*90*

360-Subject Plates only. All plate positions exist.

Ordinary Booklets

BK58	BC5B	25c red, *buff* (5)	18.00
BK59	BC5C	49c red, *pink* (4)	—
BK60	BC5F	97c red, *blue* (3)	—
BK61	BC6C	97c red, *blue* (2)	—

Combination Booklets

See No. BK56.

501b	A140	3c violet, type I, *Oct. 17, 1917*	65.00	*15.00*
		With plate number (D)	100.00	

360-Subject Plates only. All plate positions exist.

Booklet

BK62	BC6B	37c violet, *sage*	—

502b	A140	3c violet, type II, *Mar. 1918*	50.00	*10.00*
		With plate number (D)	70.00	

360-Subject Plates only. All plate positions exist.

Booklet

BK63	BC6B	37c violet, *sage*	125.00

Washington — A140

A.E.F. Panes of 30

498f	A140	1c green (pane of 30) *Sept. 1917*	*600.00*

Booklet

BK64	BC7A	$3 black, *green*	—

499f	A140	2c rose, (pane of 30) type I, *Sept. 1917*	*10,000.*

Booklet

BK65	BC7B	$6 black, *pink*	

No copies of No. BK65 are known. The number and description is provided only for specialist reference.

Nos. 498f and 499f were for use of the American Expeditionary Force in France.

They were printed from the ordinary 360-Subject Plates, the sheet being cut into 12 leaves of 30 stamps each in place of 60 leaves of 6 stamps each, and, of course, the lines of perforations changed accordingly.

The same system as used for designating plate positions on the ordinary booklet panes is used for designating the war booklet, only each war booklet pane is composed of 5 ordinary panes. Thus, No. 1 was booklet pane would be composed of positions 1, 2, 3, 4, and 5 of an ordinary pane.

The following varieties are noted, the figures in parentheses indicating the number of ordinary booklet panes:

W 1 (1 to 5) Split arrow and guide line at right.
W 2 (6 to 10) Split arrow and guide line at left. Plate number over fourth stamp.
W 3 (11 to 15) Guide line at right.
W 4 (16 to 20) Guide line at left.
W 5 (21 to 25) Guide line at right and at bottom. Arrow at lower left.
W 6 (26 to 30) Guide line at left and at bottom. Arrow at lower right.
W 7 (31 to 35) Guide line at right and top. Arrow at upper left.
W 8 (36 to 40) Guide line at left and top. Arrow at upper right.
W 9 (41 to 45) Guide line at right.
W10 (46 to 50) Guide line at left.
W11 (51 to 55) Guide line at right. Arrow at lower right. Initials.
W12 (56 to 60) Guide line at left. Arrow at lower left. Initials.

The A. E. F. booklet panes were bound at side margins which accounts or side arrows being found. More often than not, the positions are not found on the sheets as when knifing them apart, very little attention was paid to the location of the margins. Positions W3 and W4 cannot be distinguished from W9 and W10.

Franklin — A155

Washington — A157

1923 **Unwmk.** ***Perf. 11***

552a	A155	1c deep green, *Aug. 1923*	4.50	*50*
		With plate number (D)	10.00	

360-Subject Plates only. All plate positions exist.

Ordinary Booklets

BK66	BC6A	25c green, *green* (2)	35.00
BK67	BC4C	97c green, *lavender* (3)	—

Combination Booklet

BK68	BC4B	73c white, *red*, 4 #552a (1c) + 4 #554c (2c) (3)	—

554c	A157	2c carmine	6.00	*1.00*
		With plate number (D)	13.00	

360-Subject Plates only. All plate positions exist.

Ordinary Booklets

BK69	BC5B	25c red, *buff* (3)	—
BK70	BC5C	49c red, *pink* (3)	—
BK71	BC6C	97c red, *blue* (3)	—

Combination Booklets

See Nos. BK57 and BK68.

ROTARY PRESS PRINTINGS

The rotary press booklet panes were printed from specially prepared plates of 360-subjects in arrangement as before, but without the guide lines and the plate numbers are at the sides instead of at the top as on the flat plates. The only varieties possible are the ordinary pane (A) and Partial plate numbers appearing at the right or left of the upper or lower stamps of a booklet pane when the trimming of the sheets is off center. The note applies to Nos. 583a, 632a, 634d, 720b, 804b, 806b and 807a, before Electric Eyes.

1926 ***Perf. 10***

583a	A157	2c carmine, *Aug. 1926*	75.00	*25.00*
		First day cover		*1,500.*

Ordinary Booklets

BK72	BC5B	25c red, *buff* (3)	—
BK73	BC5C	49c red, *pink*	—
BK74	BC6C	97c red, *blue*	—

1927 ***Perf. 11x10½***

632a	A155	1c green, *Nov. 2, 1927*	4.50	*25*
		First day cover		*3,000.*

Ordinary Booklets

BK75	BC5A	25c green, *green* (3)	35.00
BK76	BC4C	97c green, *lavender*	—
BK77	BC5E	97c green, *lavender*	—

Combination Booklets

BK78	BC4B	73c red, 4 #632a (1c) + 4 #634d (2c)	—
BK79	BC5D	73c red, 4 #632a (1c) + 4 #634d (2c) (2)	50.00

634d	A157	2c carmine, type I, *Feb. 25, 1927*	1.75	*15*

Ordinary Booklets

BK80	BC5B	25c red, *buff* (2)	6.00
BK81	BC5C	49c red, *pink* (2)	9.00
BK82	BC5F	97c red, *blue* (3)	30.00
BK83	BC6C	97c red, *blue*	—

Combination Booklets

See Nos. BK78 and BK79.

Washington — A226

1932

720b	A226	3c deep violet, *July 25, 1932*	22.50	*5.00*
		First day cover		100.00

Ordinary Booklets

BK84	BC9B	37c violet, *buff* (2)	95.00
BK85	BC9D	73c violet, *pink* (2)	250.00

Washington — A276

Adams — A278

Jefferson — A279

In 1942 plates were changed to the Type II "new design" and the E. E. marks may appear at the right or left margins of panes of Nos. 804b, 806b and 807a. Panes printed from E. E. plates have 2½mm vertical gutter; those from pre-E. E. plates have 3mm vertical gutter.

1939-42 ***Perf. 11x10½***

804b	A276	1c green (3mm vert. gutter), *Jan. 27, 1939*	2.75	*30*
		First day cover		15.00

Ordinary Booklets

BK86	BC5A	25c green, *green*	—
BK87	BC5E	97c green, *lavender*	—
BK88	BC4C	97c green, *lavender*	—

Combination Booklet

BK89	BC5D	73c red, 4 #804b (1c) + 4 #806b (2c)	120.00

804b	A276	1c green (2½mm vert. gutter), *Apr. 14, 1942*	1.50	*20*

Ordinary Booklets

BK90	BC5A	25c green, *green*	—
BK91	BC5E	97c green, *lavender*	—

Combination Booklets

BK92	BC5D	73c red, 4 #804b (1c) + 4 #806b (2c)	25.00
BK93	BC9E	73c red, 4 #804b (1c) + 4 #806b (2c)	25.00

806b	A278	2c rose carmine (3mm vert. gutter), *Jan. 27, 1939*	5.00	*85*
		First day cover		15.00

Ordinary Booklets

BK94	BC5F	97c red, *blue*	—

Combination Booklets

See No. BK89.

806b	A278	2c rose carmine, (2½mm vert. gutter), *Apr. 25, 1942*	3.25	*50*

Ordinary Booklets

BK95	BC5F	97c red, *blue*	—
BK96	BC5B	25c red, *buff*	16.00
BK97	BC9A	25c red, *buff*	—
BK98	BC5C	49c red, *pink*	—
BK99	BC9C	49c red, *pink*	—

Combination Booklets

See Nos. BK92 and BK93.

807a	A279	3c deep violet (3mm vert. gutter), *Jan. 27, 1939*	10.00	*1.50*
		First day cover		20.00

Booklets

BK100	BC9B	37c violet, *buff*	—
BK101	BC9D	73c violet, *pink*	—

807a	A279	3c deep violet, (2½mm vert. gutter), *Mar. 6, 1942*	6.50	*50*
		With full vert. gutter (6mm.) btwn.	—	

Booklets

BK102	BC9B	37c violet, *buff* (3)	18.00
BK103	BC9D	73c violet, *pink* (3)	40.00

Statue of Liberty — A482

Lincoln — A483

1954-58 *Perf. 11x10½*

No.	Type	Description	Unused	Used
1035a	A482	3c deep violet, *June 30, 1954*	3.00	*50*
		First day cover		5.00
1035f		Dry printing	4.00	*60*

Booklets

No.	Cover	Description	Value
BK104	BC9B	37c violet, *buff*	12.00
BK105	BC9D	73c violet, *pink*	17.00

No.	Type	Description	Unused	Used
1036a	A483	4c red violet, *July 31, 1958*	2.25	*50*
		First day cover, Wheeling, W. Va. *(135,825)*		4.00
		Imperf. horizontally	—	

Booklets

No.	Cover	Description	Value
BK106	BC9F	97c on 37c violet, *buff*	50.00
BK107	BC9G	97c on 73c violet, *pink*	30.00
BK108	BC9H	97c blue, *yellow*	40.00
BK109	BC9H	97c blue, *pink* (3)	15.00

Washington (Slogan 1) — A650

Stamp booklets and booklet panes are listed and valued in a separate section of the catalogue. See catalogue index.

(Slogan 2)

(Slogan 3)

1962-64 *Perf. 11x10½*

Plate of 300 stamps, 60 labels

No.	Type	Description	Unused	Used
1213a	A650	5c dark blue gray, pane of 5+label, slogan 1, *Nov. 23, 1962*	5.50	*2.00*
		First day cover, New York, N. Y. *(111,452)*		4.00
		With slogan 2, *1963*	11.00	*3.50*
		With slogan 3, *1964*	2.25	*75*
		Imperf. vertically	—	

Booklets

No.	Cover	Description	Value
BK110	BC12A	$1 blue, slogan 1	27.50
BK111	BC12A	$1 blue, slogan 2	125.00
BK112	BC13A	$1 blue, slogan 2	65.00
BK113	BC13A	$1 blue, slogan 3 (4)	9.50

No.	Type	Description	Unused	Used
1213c	A650	As No. 1213a, tagged, slogan 2, *Oct. 28, 1963*	55.00	*7.50*
		First day cover, Dayton, O.		100.00
		Washington, D.C. *(750)*		115.00
		With slogan 3, *1964*	1.25	*50*

Booklets

No.	Cover	Description	Value
BK114	BC13A	$1 blue, slogan 2	275.00
BK115	BC13A	$1 blue, slogan 3 (4)	5.50

Jefferson — A710

Wright — A712

(Slogan 4)

(Slogan 5)

1967-78 **Tagged** *Perf. 11x10½*

No.	Type	Description	Unused	Used
1278a	A710	1c green, pane of 8, *Jan. 12, 1968*	1.00	*25*
		First day cover, Jeffersonville, Ind.		2.50
		Dull finish gum	2.00	

Combination Booklets

See Nos. BK116, BK117B, BK118 and BK119.

No.	Type	Description	Unused	Used
1278b	A710	1c green, pane of 4+2 labels, slogans 5 & 4, *May 10, 1971*	75	*20*
		First day cover, Washington, D.C.		12.50

Combination Booklet

See No. BK122.

No.	Type	Description	Unused	Used
1280a	A712	2c dark blue gray, pane of 5+label, slogan 4, *Jan. 8, 1968*	1.20	*40*
		First day cover, Buffalo, N.Y. *(147,244)*		4.00
		With slogan 5	1.20	*40*

Combination Booklets

See Nos. BK117 and BK120.

No.	Type	Description	Unused	Used
1280c	A712	2c dark blue gray, pane of 6, *May 7, 1971*	1.00	*35*
		First day cover, Spokane, Wash.		15.00
		Dull finish gum	1.00	

Combination Booklets

See Nos. BK127 and BKC22.

The 1c and 6c panes of 8, Nos. 1278a and 1284b, were printed from 320-subject plates and from 400-subject plates, both with electric eye markings. The 2c and 6c panes of 5 stamps plus label, Nos. 1280a and 1284c, were printed from 360-subject plates.

An experimental moisture-resistant gum was used on 1,000,000 panes of No. 1278a and 4,000,000 of No. 1393a released in March, 1971. This dull finish gum shows no breaker ridges. The booklets lack interleaving. This gum was also used for Nos. 1395c, 1395d, 1288c and all panes from No. 1510b on unless noted.

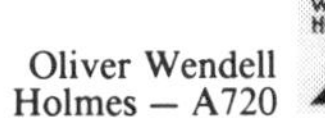

Oliver Wendell Holmes — A720

Roosevelt — A716

1284b	A716	6c gray brown, pane of 8, *Dec. 28, 1967*	1.50	*50*
		First day cover, Washington, D.C.		3.00

Combination Booklet

BK116	BC14A	$2 brown, 4 #1284b (6c)+1 #1278a(1c)(2)	7.75

1284c	A716	6c gray brown, pane of 5+label, slogan 4, *Jan. 9, 1968*	1.25	*50*
		First day cover, Washington, D.C.		100.00
		With slogan 5	1.25	*50*

Combination Booklet

BK117	BC15C	$1 brown, 3 #1284c (6c) + 1 #1280a (2c) (2)	6.00

No. BK117 contains panes with slogan 4, slogan 5 or combinations of 4 and 5.

Perf. 10

1288c	A720	15c dark rose claret, pane of 8, *June 14, 1978*	2.40	*1.25*
		First day cover, Boston, Mass.		3.00
1288e		As "c," vert. imperf. btwn.	—	

Booklet

BK117A	BC23	$3.60 red & light blue	7.75

Eisenhower — A815

Plate of 400 subjects for No. 1393a. Plate of 300 stamps and 60 labels for No. 1393b.

1970 **Tagged** ***Perf. 11x10½***

1393a	A815	6c dark gray, pane of 8, *Aug. 6*	1.10	*50*
		First day cover, Washington, D.C.		3.00
		Dull finish gum	1.50	

Combination Booklets

BK117B	BC14A	$2 blue, 4 #1393a (6c) + 1 #1278a (1c)	8.00
BK118	BC16A	$2 blue, 4 #1393a (6c) + 1 #1278a (1c)	6.00
BK119	BC16A	$2 blue, dull finish gum, 4 #1393a (6c) + 1 #1278a (1c) (2)	8.50

1393b	A815	6c dark blue gray, pane of 5+label, slogan 4, *Aug. 6*	1.10	*35*
		With slogan 5	1.10	*35*
		First day cover, Washington, D.C. (either slogan)		1.50

Combination Booklet

BK120	BC15C	$1 blue, 3 #1393b (6c) + 1 #1280a (2c)	4.75

No. BK120 contains panes with slogan 4, slogan 5 or combinations of 4 and 5.

U.S. Proofs are listed and valued in a separate section of the catalogue. See catalogue index.

Stamps in this book have been gummed with a matte finish adhesive which permits the elimination of the separation tissues.

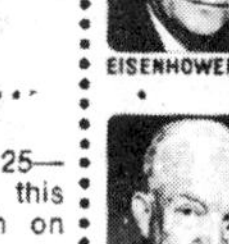

This book contains 25—8¢ stamps — four on this pane and seven each on three additional panes. Selling price $2.00.

Slogans 6 and 7

Eisenhower — A815a

1971-72 **Tagged** ***Perf. 11x10½***

1395a	A815a	8c deep claret, pane of 8, *May 10, 1971*	1.80	*1.25*
		First day cover, Washington, D.C.		3.00

Booklet

BK121	BC16B	$1.92 claret (2)	5.50

1395b	A815a	8c deep claret, pane of 6, *May 10, 1971*	1.25	*75*
		First day cover, Washington, D.C.		3.00

Combination Booklet

BK122	BC15B	$1 claret, 2 #1395b (8c) + 1 #1278b (1c) (2)	4.00

Dull Finish Gum

1395c	A815a	8c deep claret, pane of 4+2 labels, slogans 6 and 7, *Jan. 28, 1972*	1.40	*50*
		First day cover, Casa Grande, Ariz.		2.25
1395d	A815	8c deep claret, pane of 7+label, slogan 4, *Jan. 28, 1972*	1.60	*1.00*
		With slogan 5	1.60	*1.00*
		First day cover, Casa Grande, Ariz.		2.00

The first day cancellation was applied to 181,601 covers bearing Nos. 1395c or 1395d.

Combination Booklet

BK123	BC17A	$2 claret, *yellow*, 3 #1395d + 1 #1395c	6.50

Plate of 400 subjects for No. 1395a. Plate of 360 subjects for No. 1395b. Plate of 300 subjects (200 stamps and 100 double-size labels) for No. 1395c. Plate of 400 subjects (350 stamps and 50 labels) for No. 1395d.

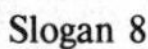

Slogan 8

Jefferson Memorial — A924

1973-74		**Tagged**	**Perf. 11x10½**	
1510b	A924	10c blue, pane of 5+label, slogan 8, *Dec. 14, 1973*	1.50	*30*
		First day cover, Washington, D.C.		2.25

Booklet

BK124	BC17B	$1 red & blue	3.25

1510c	A924	10c blue, pane of 8, *Dec. 14, 1973*	1.65	*30*
		First day cover, Washington, D.C.		2.50

Booklet

BK125	BC17C	$4 red & blue	8.50

1510d	A924	10c blue, pane of 6, *Aug. 5, 1974*	4.25	*30*
		First day cover, Oakland, Calif.		3.00

Combination Booklet

BK126	BC17D	$1.25 red & blue, 1 #1510d (10c) + 1 #C79a (13c)	5.75

Slogan 9

Liberty Bell — A998

1975-78		**Tagged**	**Perf. 11x10½**	
1595a	A998	13c brown, pane of 6, *Oct. 31, 1975*	1.90	*50*
		First day cover, Cleveland, Ohio		2.00

Combination Booklet

BK127	BC19A	90c red & blue, 1 #1595a (13c) + 1 #1280c (2c) (2)	3.00

1595b	A998	13c brown, pane of 7+label, slogan 8, *Oct. 31, 1975*	2.00	*50*
		First day cover, Cleveland, Ohio		2.75
1595c	A998	13c brown, pane of 8, *Oct. 31, 1975*	2.25	*50*
		First day cover, Cleveland, Ohio		2.50

Combination Booklet

BK128	BC19B	$2.99 red & blue, 2 #1595c (13c) + 1 #1595b (13c) (2)	6.75

1595d	A998	13c brown, pane of 5+label, slogan 9, *Apr. 2, 1976*	1.30	*50*
		First day cover, Liberty, Mo.		2.25

Booklet

BK129	BC19A	$1.30 red & blue	3.00

A994-A1018a

Fort McHenry Flag (15 Stars) — A1001

1977-78		**Tagged**	**Perf. 11x10½**	
1598a	A1001	15c gray, dark blue & red, pane of 8, *June 30, 1978*	3.50	*60*
		First day cover, Baltimore, Md.		2.50

Booklet

BK130	BC21	$1.20 red & light blue	3.50

1623a	A1018a	Pane of 8 (1 #1590 + 7 #1623), *Mar. 11, 1977*	2.50	*60*
		First day cover, New York, N.Y.		25.00

Booklet

BK131	BC20	$1 red & light blue (3)	2.75

Perf. 10

1623c	A1018a	Pane of 8 (1 #1590a + 7 #1623b), *Mar. 11, 1977*	30.00	—
		First day cover, New York, N.Y.		12.50

First day cancellation was applied to 242,208 covers bearing Nos. 1623a or 1623c.

Booklet

BK132	BC20	$1 red & light blue (2)	35.00

Eagle — A1124

1978 **Tagged** ***Perf. 11x10½***

1736a	A1124		A orange, pane of 8, *May 22, 1978*	2.40	*60*
			First day cover, Memphis, Tenn.		2.50
			Booklet		
BK133	BC24	$3.60	deep orange	7.50	

Red Masterpiece and Medallion Roses — A1126

1737a	A1126	15c	multicolored, pane of 8, *July 11, 1978*	2.50	*60*
			First day cover, Shreveport, La.		2.50
1737b			As "a," imperf.	—	
			Booklet		
BK134	BC22	$2.40	rose red & yellow green	5.25	

Windmills — A1127-A1131

1980 **Tagged** ***Perf. 11***

1742a	A1131	15c	sepia, *yellow,* pane of 10, *Feb. 7*	3.60	*60*
			First day cover, Lubbock, TX		3.50
			Booklet		
BK135	BC25	$3	light blue & dark blue, *blue*	7.50	

A1207

A1267-A1276

A1279-A1280

1981

1819a	A1207		B violet, pane of 8, *Mar. 15*	4.50	*1.50*
			First day cover, San Francisco, CA		3.00
			Booklet		
BK136	BC26	$4.32	dull violet	14.00	
1889a	A1267-A1276	18c	dark brown, pane of 10, *May 14*	8.00	—
			First day cover, Boise, ID		5.00
			Booklet		
BK137	BC28	$3.60	gray & olive	16.50	
1893a	A1279-A1280		Pane of 8 (2 #1892, 6 #1893), *Apr. 24*	3.20	—
			First day cover, Portland, ME		2.50
1893b			As "a," vert. imperf. btwn.	*85.00*	
			Booklet		
BK138	BC27	$1.20	blue & red	3.25	

A1281

1896a	A1281	20c	black, dark blue & red, pane of 6, *Dec. 17, 1981*	2.60	—
			First day cover, Washington, D.C.		6.00
			Booklet		
BK139	BC29	$1.20	blue & red (2)	2.75	
1896b	A1281	20c	black, dark blue & red, pane of 10, *June 1, 1982*	4.25	—
			First day cover, Washington, D.C.		*10.00*
			Scored perforation	4.25	—
			Booklets		
BK140	BC29	$2	blue & red (4)	4.50	
BK140A	BC29B	$4	blue & red	8.25	

A1296

1983

1909a	A1296	$9.35	multi, pane of 3, *Aug. 12, 1983*	80.00	—
			First day cover, Kennedy Space Center, FL		*100.00*
			Booklet		
BK140B	BC31	28.05	blue & red	82.50	

The Catalogue editors cannot undertake to appraise, identify or judge the genuineness or condition of stamps.

A1333

1981

1948a	A1333	C brown, pane of 10, *Oct. 11, 1981*	4.50	—
		First day cover, Memphis, TN		*3.50*

Booklet

BK141	BC26	$4 brown, *blue*	9.25

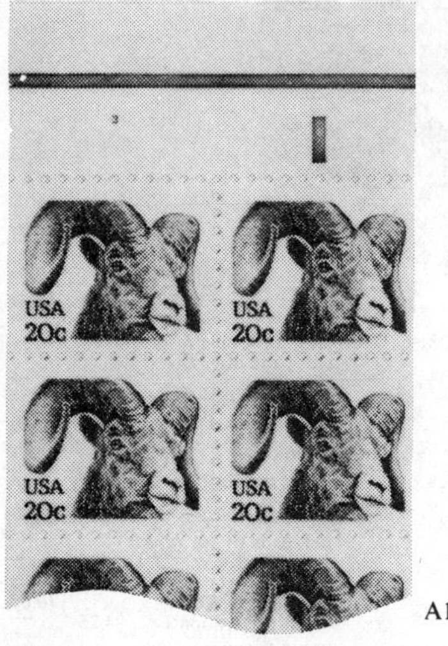

A1334

1982

1949a	A1334	20c dark blue, pane of 10, *Jan. 8, 1982*	4.50	—
		First day cover, Bighorn, MI		*6.00*
1949b		As "a," vert. imperf. btwn.	*85.00*	

Booklet

BK142	BC30	$4 blue, *yellow green*	9.25

A1497

1985 ***Perf. 11***

2113a	A1497	D green, pane of 10 *Feb. 1, 1985*	6.50	—
		First day cover, Los Angeles, CA		*7.50*

Booklet

BK143	BC26	$4.40 green	13.50

A1499

2116a	A1499	22c blue, red & black, pane of 5, *Mar. 29, 1985*	2.50	—
		First day cover, Waubeka, WI		3.50

Booklets

BK144	BC33C	$1.10 blue & red	2.75
BK145	BC32	$2.20 blue & red	5.25

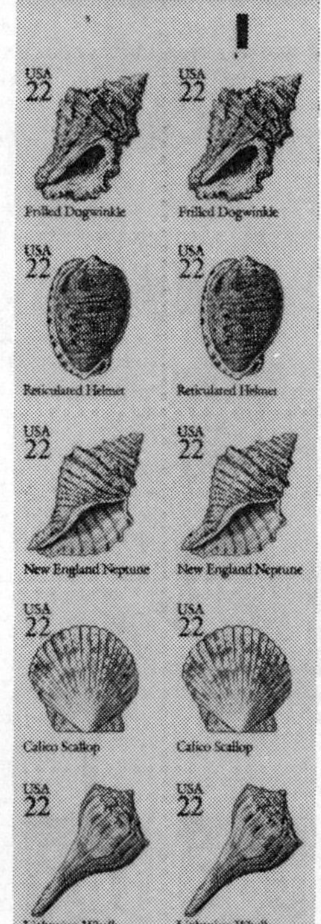

A1500-A1504

2121a	A1500-A1504	22c multicolored, pane of 10, *Apr. 4, 1985*	4.25	—
		First day cover, Boston, MA		*7.50*
2121b		As "a," violet omitted	—	
2121c		As "a," vert. imperf. between	—	
2121d		As "a," imperf.		—

Booklets

BK146	BC33A	$4.40 multi	8.75
BK147	BC33B	$4.40 multi	8.75

A1505

2122a	A1505	10.75 multicolored, pane of 3, *Apr. 29, 1985*	62.50	—
		First day cover, San Francisco, CA		*85.00*

Booklet

BK148	BC31	32.25 multicolored	65.00

A1566

1988 ***Perf. 11***

2183a	A1566	25c blue, pane of 10, *May 3, 1988*	4.75	—
		First day cover, San Francisco, CA		6.00

Booklet

BK148A	BC43	$5 multicolored	10.00

2197a	A1566	25c blue, pane of 6, *May 3, 1988*	3.00	—
		First day cover, San Francisco, CA		4.00

Booklets

BK148B	BC43	$1.50 blue & brown	3.25
BK148C	BC43	$3 brown & blue	6.50

A1581-A1584

1986

2201a	A1581-A1584	22c multicolored, pane of 4, *Jan. 23, 1986*	2.00	—
		First day cover, State College, PA		3.00
2201b		As "a," black omitted on Nos. 2198, 2201	50.00	

2201c		As "a," blue (litho.) omitted on Nos. 2198-2200		—
2201d		As "a," buff (litho.) omitted		—

Booklet

BK149	BC34	$1.76 purple & black	4.25	

A1588-A1592

2209a	A1588-A1592	22c multicolored, pane of 5, *Mar. 21, 1986*	2.75	—
		First day cover, Seattle, WA		2.50

Booklet

BK150	BC35	$2.20 blue green and red	6.00	

The Scott Catalogue value is a retail price, what you could expect to pay for the stamp in a grade of Fine-Very Fine. The value listed is a reference which reflects recent actual dealer selling price.

A1637-A1644

1987

2274a	A1637-A1644	22c multicolored, pane of 10, *Apr. 20, 1987*	4.25	—
		First day cover, Atlanta, GA		5.00

Booklet

BK151	BC36	$2.20 blue & red	4.50	

A1646

2276a	A1646	22c multicolored, pane of 20, *Nov. 30, 1987*	8.50	—
		First day cover, Washington, DC		12.00

Booklet

BK151A	BC39	$4.40 multicolored	8.75	

A1647

1988

2282a	A1647	E multicolored, pane of 10, *Mar. 22, 1988*	4.75	—
		First day cover, Washington, DC		6.00

Booklet

BK151B	BC40	$5 blue	10.00	

A1649a

2283a	A1649a	25c multicolored, pane of 10, *Apr. 29, 1988*	4.75	—
		First day cover, Rapid City, SD		6.00

Booklet

BK151C	BC41	$5 multicolored	10.00	

A1649b-A1649c

2285b	A1649b-A1649c	25c multicolored, pane of 10, *May 28, 1988*	4.75	—
		First day cover, Arlington, VA		6.00

Booklet

BK151D	BC45	$5 red & black	10.00

A1648

2285c	A1648	25c multicolored, pane of 6, *July 5, 1988*	2.75	—
		First day cover, Washington, DC		4.00

Booklet

BK151E	BC46	$3 blue & red	5.75

A1719-A1723

2359a	A1719-A1723	22c multicolored, pane of 5, *Aug. 28, 1987*	2.10	—
		First day cover, Washington, DC		3.00

Booklet

BK152	BC37	$4.40 red & blue	8.75

A1726-A1730

2366a	A1726-A1730	22c multicolored, pane of 5, *Oct. 1, 1987*	2.10	—
		First day cover, Baltimore, MD		3.00

Booklet

BK153	BC38	$4.40 black & yellow	8.75

A1745-A1749

1988

2385a	A1745-A1749	25c multicolored, pane of 5, *Aug. 25, 1988*	2.30	—
		First day cover, Detroit, MI		3.00

Booklet

BK154	BC47	$5 black & red	9.50

A1759-A1760

A1761-A1762

2396a	A1759-A1760	25c multicolored, pane of 6, *Oct. 22, 1988*	2.75	—
		First day cover, King of Prussia, PA		4.00
2398a	A1761-A1762	25c multicolored, pane of 6, *Oct. 22, 1988*	2.75	—
		First day cover, King of Prussia, PA		4.00

Combination Booklet

BK155	BC48	$3 multicolored, 1 #2396a, 1 #2398a	5.75

A1769-A1773

1989

2409a	A1769-A1773	25c multicolored, pane of 5, *Mar. 3, 1989*	2.50	—

		First day cover, New Orleans, LA		4.00

Booklet

BK156	BC49	$5 blue & black	10.50	—

AIR POST STAMPS

Spirit of St. Louis — AP6

FLAT PLATE PRINTING

1928 *Perf. 11*

C10a	AP6	10c dark blue, *May 26*	110.00	*60.00*
		First day cover, Washington, D.C.		825.00
		First day cover, Cleveland Midwestern Philatelic Sta. cancel		800.00
		First day cover, Nos. C10a & 645, Washington, D.C		1,000.
		Tab at bottom	—	

No. C10a was printed from specially designed 180-subject plates arranged exactly as a 360-subject plate-each pane of three occupying the relative position of a pane of six in a 360-subject plate. Plate numbers appear at the sides, therefore Position D does not exist except partially on panes which have been trimmed off center All other plate positions common to a 360-subject plate are known.

Booklet

BKC1	BC8	61c blue	275.00

AP17

ROTARY PRESS PRINTINGS

1943

C25a	AP17	6c carmine, *Mar. 18, 1943*	4.25	*1.00*
		First day cover, Washington, D.C.		25.00

180-Subject Plates Electric Eye Convertible.

Booklets

BKC2	BC10A	37c red	14.00
BKC3	BC10B	37c red	30.00

AP19

1949 *Perf. 10½x11*

C39a	AP19	6c carmine, *Nov. 18, 1949*	9.50	*4.00*
		First day cover, New York, N.Y.		9.00
C39c		Dry printing	15.00	—

Booklet

BKC4	BC11A	73c red (3)	26.00

AP33

1958

C51a	AP33	7c blue, *July 31, 1958*	11.00	*6.00*
		First day cover, San Antonio, Tex. *(119,769)*		9.50

Booklets

BKC5	BC11B	85c on 73c red	35.00
BKC6	BC11C	85c blue	35.00

1960

C60a	AP33	7c carmine, *Aug. 19, 1960*	13.00	*6.00*
		First day cover, St. Louis, Mo. *(143,363)*		9.50

Booklets

BKC7	BC11C	85c blue	45.00
BKC8	BC11C	85c red	45.00

AP42

1962-64

C64b	AP42	8c carmine, pane of 5+label, slogan 1, *Dec. 5, 1962*	6.50	*1.25*
		First day cover, Washington, D.C. *(146,835)*		2.00
		With slogan 2, *1963*	21.00	*5.00*
		With slogan 3, *1964*	10.00	*1.25*

Booklets

BKC9	BC11D	80c black, *pink*, slogan 1	17.00
BKC10	BC11E	$2 red, *pink*, slogan 1	40.00
BKC11	BC11D	80c black, *pink*, slogan 3 (2)	35.00
BKC12	BC11E	$2 red, *pink*, slogan 2	175.00
BKC13	BC13B	$2 red, *pink*, slogan 2	160.00
BKC14	BC13B	$2 red, slogan 3	
BKC15	BC13B	$2 red, *pink*, slogan 3	85.00

C64c	AP42	As No.C64b, tagged, slogan 3, *1964*	1.90	*50*

Plate of 360 subjects (300 stamps, 60 labels).

Booklets

BKC16	BC11D	80c black (2)	25.00
BKC17	BC11D	80c black, *pink*	18.00
BKC18	BC13B	$2 red, *pink*	65.00
BKC19	BC13B	$2 red (3)	13.00

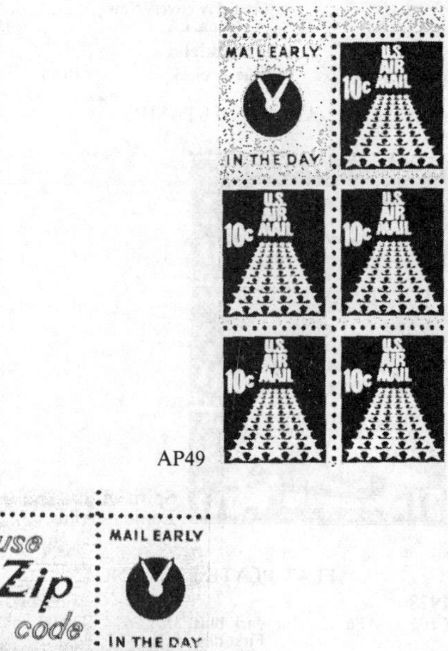

AP49

AP54

AP55

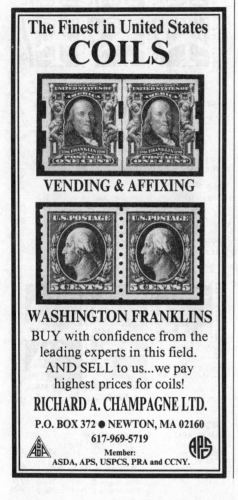

1968-73		**Tagged**	***Perf. 11x10½***	
C72b	AP49	10c carmine, pane of 8, *Jan. 5, 1968*	3.00	*75*
		First day cover, San Francisco, Cal.		2.50
		Booklet		
BKC20	BC14B	$4 red (2)	14.00	
C72c	AP49	10c carmine, pane of 5+label, slogan 4, *Jan. 6, 1968*	3.50	*75*
		First day cover, Washington, D.C.		115.00
		With slogan 5	3.50	*75*
		First day cover, Washington, D.C.		115.00
		Booklet		
BKC21	BC15A	$1 red (2)	7.75	
C78a	AP54	11c carmine, pane of 4+2 labels, slogans 5 & 4, *May 7, 1971*	1.10	*40*
		First day cover, Spokane, Wash.		1.75
		Combination Booklet		
BKC22	BC15D	$1 red, 2 #C78a (11c) + 1 œ1280c (2c) (2)	3.50	
C79a	AP55	13c carmine, pane of 5+label, slogan 8, *Dec. 27, 1973*	1.35	*70*
		First day cover, Chicago, Ill.		1.75
		Booklet		
BKC23	BC18	$1.30 blue & red	2.75	
		Combination Booklet		

See No. BK126.

No. C72b, the 8-stamp pane, was printed from 320-subject plate and from 400-subject plate; No. C72c, C78a and C79a from 360-subject plates.

VENDING AND AFFIXING MACHINE PERFORATIONS

Imperforate sheets of 400 were first issued in 1906 on the request of several markers of vending and affixing machines. The machine manufacturers made coils from the imperforate sheets and applied various perforations to suit the particular needs of their machines. These privately applied perforations were used for many years and form a chapter of postal history.

Unused values are for pairs, used values for singles. 'On cover' values are for single stamps used commercially in the proper period when known that way. Several, primarily the Alaska-Yukon and Hudson-Fulton commemoratives, are known only on covers from stamp collectors and stamp dealers. Virtually all are rare and highly prized by specialists.

The 2mm and 3mm spacings refer only to the 1908-11 issues. Values for intermediate spacings would roughly correspond to the lower-valued of the two listed spacings. Guide line pairs of 1906-11 issues have 2mm spacing except the Alaska-Yukon and Hudson-Fulton issues, have 3mm spacing. Scott 408-611 have 3mm spacing, except Scott 577, which has both 2¾ and 3mm spacing. (All spacing measurements are approximate.)

Spacing on paste-up pairs is not a factor in valuing them. Because they were joined together by hand, many different spacings can occur, from less than 2mm to more than 3 mm.

Many varieties are suspected or known to have been perforated for philatelic purposes and not actually used in machines. These are indicated by as asterisk before the number. Several of these privately applied perforation varieties exist in blocks, which were not produced in the regular course of business. They are generally valued as a multiple of the coil pairs contains, with a slight premium for plate numbers attached.

Counterfeits are prevalent, especially of items having a basic imperf. variety valued far lower than the vending machine coil.

The Vending and Affixing Machine Perforations Committee of the Bureau Issues Association and William R. Weiss, Jr., compiled these listings.

THE BRINKERHOFF COMPANY

Sedalia, Mo.
Manufacturers of Vending Machines.

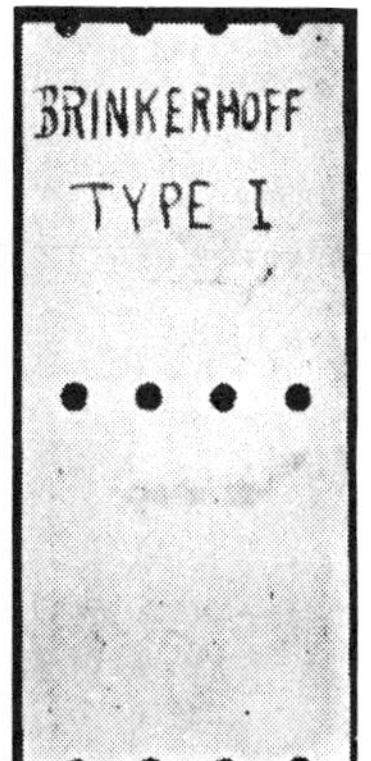

Perforations Type I

Stamps were cut into strips and joined before being perforated.

On Issue of 1906-08

			Unused Pair	Used Single
314	1c	blue green	110.00	25.00
		Guide line or pasteup pair	140.00	
320	2c	carmine	120.00	25.00
		Guide line or pasteup pair	170.00	
*320a	2c	lake	80.00	20.00
		Guide line or pasteup pair	170.00	
		On Issue of 1908-09		
*343	1c	green	60.00	16.00
		Guide line or pasteup pair	85.00	
*344	2c	carmine	70.00	16.00
		On cover		200.00
		Guide line or pasteup pair	100.00	
*345	3c	deep violet	100.00	
		Guide line or pasteup pair	120.00	
*346	4c	orange brown	100.00	50.00
		Guide line or pasteup pair	150.00	
*347	5c	blue	105.00	50.00
		Guide line or pasteup pair	175.00	
		On Lincoln Issue of 1909		
*368	2c	carmine, coiled endwise	70.00	50.00
		Guide line or pasteup pair	100.00	
		On Alaska-Yukon Issue of 1909		
*371	2c	carmine, coiled sideways	200.00	—
		Guide line or pasteup pair	—	
		On Issue of 1911		
*383	1c	Green	170.00	
		Guide line or pasteup pair	250.00	
		On Issue of 1912		
*408	1c	green	25.00	12.00
		On cover		250.00
		Guide line or pasteup pair	45.00	
*409	2c	carmine	25.00	12.00
		Guide line or pasteup pair	45.00	

Type IIa. One knife cut.

Type IIb. Two knife cuts.

Perforations Type II, 2 Holes

The Type II items listed below are without knife cuts and did not pass through the vending machine. Types IIa and IIb (illustrated above) have knife cuts separating the stamps applied by the vending machine.

	Type			Unused Pair	Used Single
			On Issue of 1906-08		
314	*II	1c	blue green	70.00	10.00
			Guide line or pasteup pair	90.00	
	IIa	1c	blue green	60.00	10.00
			Guide line or pasteup pair	75.00	
	*IIb	1c	blue green	260.00	—
			Guide line or pasteup pair	—	
320	*II	2c	carmine	150.00	40.00
			Guide line or pasteup pair	—	
	IIa	2c	carmine	30.00	10.00
			On cover		450.00
			Guide line or pasteup pair	100.00	
320a	*II	2c	lake	150.00	40.00
			Guide line or pasteup pair	200.00	
	IIa	2c	lake	40.00	10.00
			On cover		500.00
			Guide line or pasteup pair	90.00	
	*IIb	2c	lake	150.00	45.00
			Guide line or pasteup pair	—	
			On Issue of 1908-09		
343	*II	1c	green	45.00	
			Guide line or pasteup pair	65.00	
	IIa	1c	green	15.00	3.00
			Guide line or pasteup pair	20.00	
	IIb	1c	green	25.00	
			Guide line or pasteup pair	40.00	
344	*II	2c	carmine	50.00	
			On cover, pair		550.00
			Guide line or pasteup pair	90.00	
	IIa	2c	carmine	14.00	3.00
			Guide line or pasteup pair	20.00	
			On cover		450.00
	IIb	2c	carmine	30.00	6.00
			Guide line or pasteup pair	40.00	
345	*II	3c	deep violet	65.00	10.00
			Guide line or pasteup pair	175.00	
	*IIa	3c	deep violet	70.00	10.00
			Guide line or pasteup pair	110.00	
	*IIb	3c	deep violet	200.00	
			Guide line or pasteup pair	—	
346	*II	4c	orange brown	105.00	
			Guide line or pasteup pair	175.00	
	*IIa	4c	orange brown	90.00	30.00
			On cover		800.00
			Guide line or pasteup pair	120.00	
	*IIb	4c	orange brown	130.00	30.00
			Guide line or pasteup pair	150.00	
347	*II	5c	blue	140.00	
			Guide line or pasteup pair	170.00	
	*IIa	5c	blue	90.00	40.00
			On cover		800.00
			Guide line or pasteup pair	—	
	*IIb	5c	blue	120.00	
			Guide line or pasteup pair	200.00	
			On Lincoln Issue of 1909		
368	*II	2c	carmine	65.00	
			Guide line or pasteup pair	90.00	
	IIa	2c	carmine	60.00	12.00
			On cover		1,000.
			Guide line or pasteup pair	175.00	
	IIb	2c	carmine	150.00	20.00
			Guide line or pasteup pair	200.00	
			On Alaska-Yukon Issue of 1909		
371	*II	2c	carmine, coiled sideways	120.00	
			On cover, pair		—
			Guide line or pasteup pair	160.00	
	II	2c	carmine, coiled endwise	225.00	
			Guide line or pasteup pair	250.00	
	IIa	2c	carmine, coiled sideways	130.00	25.00
			On cover		625.00
			Guide line or pasteup pair	140.00	
			On Hudson-Fulton Issue of 1909		
373	*II	2c	carmine, coiled sidewise	185.00	
			Guide line or pasteup pair	325.00	
			On Issue of 1911		
383	*II	1c	green	30.00	
			Guide line or pasteup pair	45.00	
	IIa	1c	green	40.00	8.00
			Guide line or pasteup pair	60.00	
	IIb	1c	green	50.00	30.00
			Guide line or pasteup pair	75.00	
384	*II	2c	carmine	30.00	
			Guide line or pasteup pair	45.00	
	IIa	2c	carmine	100.00	
			Guide line or pasteup pair	150.00	
	IIb	2c	carmine	50.00	8.00
			Guide line or pasteup pair	150.00	
			On Issue of 1912		
408	*II	1c	green	50.00	—
			On cover		200.00
			Guide line or pasteup pair	65.00	
	*IIa	1c	green	80.00	
			Guide line or pasteup pair	90.00	
	IIb	1c	green	20.00	5.00
			Guide line or pasteup pair	40.00	
409	*II	2c	carmine	60.00	
			Guide line or pasteup pair	120.00	
	*IIa	2c	carmine	100.00	—
			On cover		575.00
			Guide line or pasteup pair	150.00	
	IIb	2c	carmine	25.00	5.00
			Guide line or pasteup pair	40.00	

THE FARWELL COMPANY

Chicago, Ill.

A wholesale dry goods firm using Schermack (Mailometer) affixing machines. In 1911 the Farwell Company began to make and perforate their own coils. These were sometimes wrongly called "Chambers" perforations.

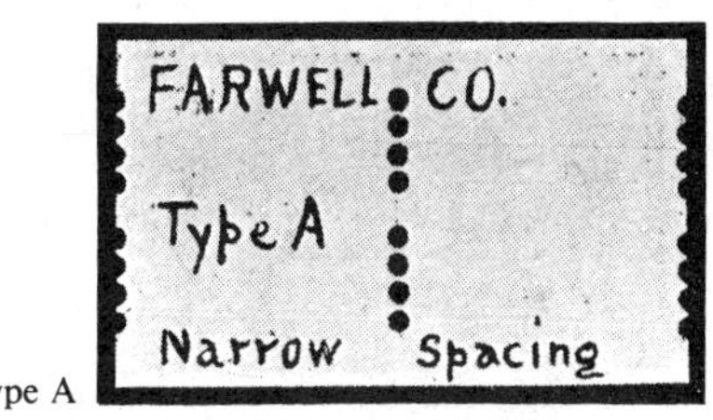

Type A

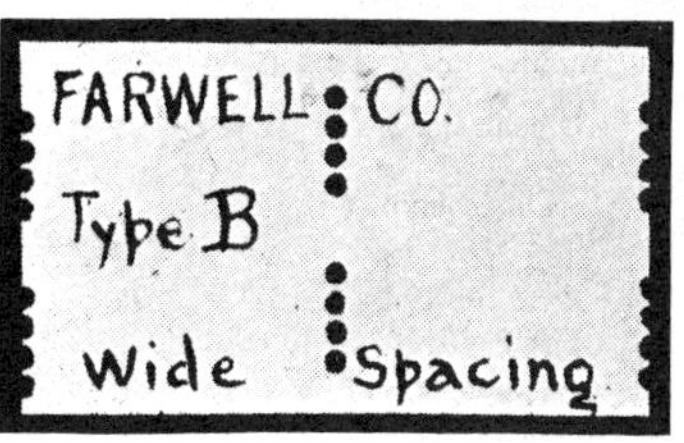

Type B

Stamps were perforated in sheets, then cut into strips and coiled. Blocks exist. The following listings are grouped according to the number of holes, further divided into two types of spacing, narrow and wide. The type symbols (3A2) indicate 3 holes over 2 holes with narrow, type A, spacing between groups. Types A and B occurred in different rows on the same sheet. Left margin or pasteup stamps sometimes show different perforation type on the two sides.

Group I, no spacing

On Issue of 1911

				Unused Pair Spacing 2mm	Unused Pair Spacing 3mm	Used Single
384		2c	carmine, 7 holes	500.00	500.00	200.00
			On cover			1,250.
			Guide line or pasteup pair	—		
384		2c	carmine, 6 holes	600.00	600.00	

Group 2, two and three holes

On Issue of 1911

	Type			2mm	3mm	Used Single
383	2B3	1c	green	225.00	350.00	150.00
			Guide line or pasteup pair	500.00		
	3A2	1c	green	225.00	350.00	
			Guide line or pasteup pair	350.00		
384	2A3	2c	carmine	225.00	350.00	150.00
			On cover			950.00
			Guide line or pasteup pair	—		
	2B3	2c	carmine	250.00	350.00	175.00
			On cover			—
			Guide line or pasteup pair	—		
	3A2	2c	carmine	250.00	250.00	160.00
			On cover			950.00
			Guide line or pasteup pair	350.00		
	3B2	2c	carmine	250.00	250.00	180.00
			Guide line or pasteup pair	350.00		
			Group 3, three and four holes			
			On Issue of 1911			
383	3B4	1c	green	—	—	175.00
			Guide line or pasteup pair	—		
	4B3	1c	green	200.00	200.00	175.00
384	3B4	2c	carmine	200.00	200.00	175.00
			On cover			—
			Guide line or pasteup pair	300.00		
	4B3	2c	carmine	275.00	275.00	100.00
			On cover			650.00
			Guide line or pasteup pair	—		
	4A3	2c	Carmine			—

	Type					
			Group 4, four and four holes			
			On Issue of 1908-09			
343	*A	1c	green	125.00		
	*B	1c	green	120.00		
344	*A	2c	carmine	125.00	125.00	
			Guide line or pasteup pair	—		
	*B	2c	carmine	120.00	120.00	
			Guide line or pasteup pair	—		
			On Lincoln Issue of 1909			
368	*A	2c	carmine	300.00	300.00	
			Guide line or pasteup pair	—		
	*B	2c	carmine	300.00	300.00	
			Guide line or pasteup pair	—		
			On Issue of 1911			
383	A	1c	green	45.00	40.00	25.00
			Guide line or pasteup pair	75.00		
	B	1c	green	45.00	40.00	—
			Guide line or pasteup pair	75.00		
384	A	2c	carmine	50.00	45.00	10.00
			Guide line or pasteup pair	75.00		
	B	2c	carmine	50.00	45.00	10.00
			On cover			225.00
			Guide line or pasteup pair	75.00		
			On Issue of 1912			
408	A	1c	green		20.00	2.00
			On cover			60.00
			Guide line or pasteup pair		30.00	
	B	1c	green		20.00	2.00
			On cover			60.00
			Guide line or pasteup pair		30.00	
409	A	2c	carmine		15.00	2.00
			On cover			60.00
			Guide line or pasteup pair		30.00	
	B	2c	carmine		15.00	2.00
			On cover			60.00
			Guide line or pasteup pair		30.00	
			On Issue of 1916-17			
482	A	2c	carmine		100.00	35.00
	B	2c	carmine		120.00	35.00
			On cover			200.00
			Group 5, four and five holes			
			On Issue of 1911			
383	4A5	1c	green	150.00	125.00	—
			Guide line or pasteup pair	180.00		
384	4A5	2c	carmine	120.00	120.00	—
			Guide line or pasteup pair	140.00		
			On Issue of 1912			
408	4A5	1c	green		250.00	
			Guide line or pasteup pair		350.00	
	*5A4	1c	green		250.00	
			Guide line or pasteup pair		350.00	
409	*4A5	2c	carmine		250.00	—
			Guide line or pasteup pair		350.00	
	*5A4	2c	carmine		250.00	
			Guide line or pasteup pair		350.00	

INTERNATIONAL VENDING MACHINE CO.

Baltimore, Md.

Similar to the Government Coil stamp No. 322, but perforated 12½ to 13.

On Issue of 1906

320b	2c	scarlet	1,100.
		On Issue of 1908-09	
343	1c	green	1,000.
344	2c	carmine	1,000.
345	3c	deep violet	1,000.
346	4c	orange brown	—
347	5c	blue	—

THE MAILOMETER COMPANY

Detroit, Mich.

Formerly the Schermack Mailing Machine Co., then Mail-om-eter Co., and later the Mail-O-Meter Co. Their round-hole perforations were developed in an attempt to get the Bureau of Engraving and Printing to adopt a larger perforation for coil stamps.

Souvenir cards are listed and valued in a separate section of the catalogue. See catalogue index.

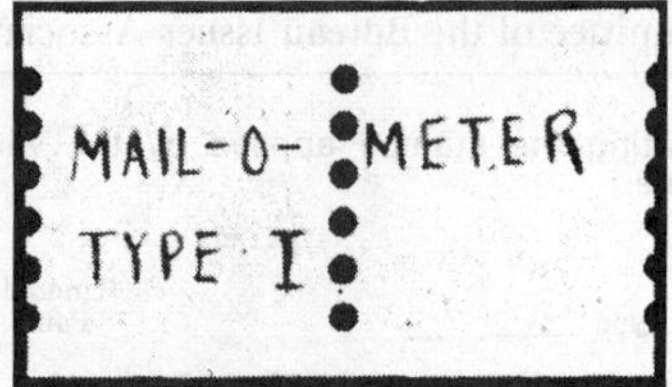

Perforations Type I

Used experimentally in Detroit and Chicago in August, 1909. Later used regularly in the St. Louis branch.

On Issue of 1906-08

			Unused Pair Spacing 2mm	3mm	Used Single
*320	2c	carmine	150.00		
*320a	2c	lake	130.00		
		Guide line or pasteup pair	150.00		
*320b	2c	scarlet	150.00		
		On Issue of 1908-09			
343	1c	green	30.00	35.00	20.00
		On cover			175.00
		Guide line or pasteup pair	45.00		
344	2c	carmine	30.00	35.00	4.00
		On cover, St. Louis			80.00
		On cover, Detroit or Chicago			250.00
		Guide line or pasteup pair	45.00		
		With perforated control mark, single	75.00		75.00
		Same, on cover			225.00
345	3c	deep violet	40.00		15.00
		Guide line or pasteup pair	60.00		
346	4c	orange brown	75.00	65.00	30.00
		Guide line or pasteup pair	100.00		
347	5c	blue	100.00		30.00
		Guide line or pasteup pair	125.00		
		On Lincoln Issue of 1909			
*368	2c	carmine	120.00	95.00	75.00
		Guide line or pasteup pair	150.00		
		On Alaska-Yukon Issue of 1909			
*371	2c	carmine		100.00	75.00
		Guide line or pasteup pair		125.00	
		On Hudson-Fulton Issue of 1909			
*373	2c	carmine		150.00	65.00
		Guide line or pasteup pair		175.00	
		On Issue of 1911			
383	1c	green	25.00	20.00	3.00
		Guide line or pasteup pair	30.00		
384	2c	carmine	35.00	30.00	4.00
		On cover			65.00
		Guide line or pasteup pair	45.00		
		On Issue of 1912			
*408	1c	green		20.00	4.00
		Guide line or pasteup pair		25.00	
*409	2c	carmine		20.00	4.00
		Guide line or pasteup pair		25.00	

Perforations Type II

Used experimentally in Detroit from 1909 to 1911.

On Issue of 1906-08

*320	2c	carmine	140.00		
		Guide line or pasteup pair	—		
*320b	2c	scarlet	210.00		
		Guide line or pasteup pair	—		
		On Issue of 1908-09			
343	1c	green	25.00	25.00	10.00
		Guide line or pasteup pair	30.00		
344	2c	carmine	30.00	30.00	10.00
		On cover			500.00
		Guide line or pasteup pair	40.00		
*345	3c	deep violet	110.00		40.00
		Guide line or pasteup pair	—		
*346	4c	orange brown	180.00	180.00	
		Guide line or pasteup pair	200.00		
*347	5c	blue	350.00		
		Guide line or pasteup pair	—		
		On Lincoln Issue of 1909			
*368	2c	carmine	150.00	140.00	
		Guide line or pasteup pair	170.00		
		On Alaska-Yukon Issue of 1909			
*371	2c	carmine		140.00	
		Guide line or pasteup pair		170.00	
		On Hudson-Fulton Issue of 1909			
*373	2c	carmine		160.00	
		Guide line or pasteup pair		180.00	
		On Issue of 1911			
383	1c	green	70.00	70.00	20.00
		Guide line or pasteup pair	100.00		
384	2c	carmine	100.00	85.00	35.00
		On cover			500.00
		Guide line or pasteup pair	—		

Perforations Type III

Used experimentally in Detroit in 1910.

On Issue of 1906-08

*320	2c	carmine	135.00		
		Guide line or pasteup pair	—		
*320b	2c	scarlet	185.00		
		Guide line or pasteup pair	—		
		On Issue of 1908-09			
343	1c	green	45.00	35.00	
		Guide line or pasteup pair	55.00		
344	2c	carmine	60.00	50.00	
		Guide line or pasteup pair	70.00		
*345	3c	deep violet	90.00		
		Guide line or pasteup pair	130.00		
*346	4c	orange brown	130.00	120.00	
		Guide line or pasteup pair	175.00		
*347	5c	blue	400.00		
		Guide line or pasteup pair	500.00		
		On Lincoln Issue of 1909			
*368	2c	carmine	180.00	150.00	50.00
		Guide line or pasteup pair	350.00		
		On Alaska-Yukon Issue of 1909			
*371	2c	carmine		220.00	
		Guide line or pasteup pair		350.00	
		On Hudson-Fulton Issue of 1909			
*373	2c	carmine		220.00	
		Guide line or pasteup pair		350.00	

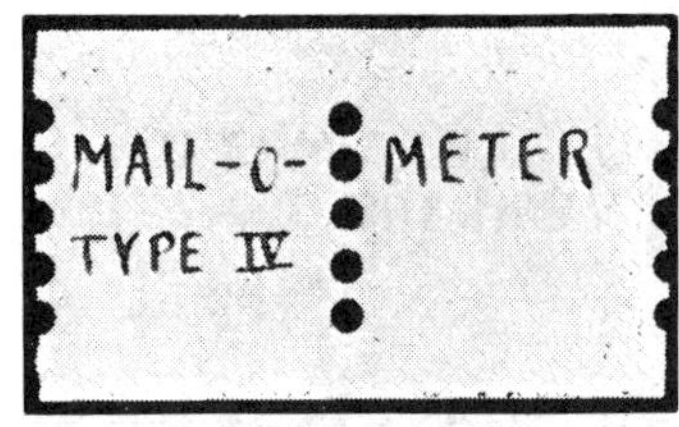

Perforations Type IV

Used in St. Louis branch office. Blocks exist but were not regularly produced or issued.

On Issue of 1906-08

No.			2mm.	3mm.	Used Single
*320	2c	carmine	120.00		50.00
		Guide line or pasteup pair	350.00		
*320b	2c	scarlet	100.00		40.00
		Guide line or pasteup pair	—		

On Issue of 1908-09

No.			2mm.	3mm.	Used Single
343	1c	green	40.00	35.00	8.00
		Guide line or pasteup pair	50.00		
344	2c	carmine	50.00	40.00	8.00
		Guide line or pasteup pair	65.00		
345	3c	deep violet	75.00		
		Guide line or pasteup pair	130.00		
346	4c	orange brown	120.00	110.00	
		Guide line or pasteup pair	150.00		
347	5c	blue	150.00		40.00
		Guide line or pasteup pair	190.00		

On Lincoln Issue of 1909

No.			2mm.	3mm.	Used Single
*368	2c	carmine	85.00	75.00	20.00
		Guide line or pasteup pair	120.00		

On Alaska-Yukon Issue of 1909

No.			2mm.	3mm.	Used Single
*371	2c	carmine		250.00	
		Guide line or pasteup pair		350.00	

On Hudson-Fulton Issue of 1909

No.			2mm.	3mm.	Used Single
*373	2c	carmine		250.00	
		Guide line or pasteup pair		350.00	

On Issue of 1911

No.			2mm.	3mm.	Used Single
383	1c	green	10.00	8.00	2.00
		On cover			85.00
		Guide line or pasteup pair	12.50		
384	2c	carmine	20.00	18.00	1.00
		On cover			60.00
		Guide line or pasteup pair	25.00		

On Issue of 1912

No.			2mm.	3mm.	Used Single
408	1c	green		6.00	1.00
		On cover			15.00
		Guide line or pasteup pair		8.00	
409	2c	carmine		7.00	50
		On cover			15.00
		Guide line or pasteup pair		10.00	

On Issue of 1916-17

No.			2mm.	3mm.	Used Single
482	2c	carmine		80.00	40.00
		On cover			275.00
		Guide line or pasteup pair		110.00	
483	3c	violet, type I		85.00	40.00
		On cover			275.00
		Pasteup pair		110.00	

THE SCHERMACK COMPANY

Detroit, Mich.

These perforations were developed by the Schermack Mailing Machine Co. before it became the Mailometer Co. The Type III perforation was used in Mailometer affixing machines from 1909 through 1927.

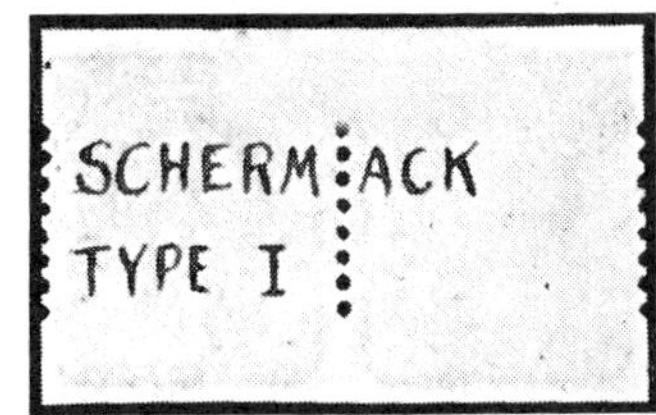

Perforations Type I. Eight Holes.

Perforated in sheets, then cut into strips and coiled.

On Issue of 1906-08

No.			Unused Pair Spacing 2mm.	3mm.	Used Single
314	1c	blue green	100.00		50.00
		Guide line or pasteup pair	125.00		
		*Seven holes	400.00		
		Guide line or pasteup pair	—		
		*Six holes	300.00		
		Guide line or pasteup pair	375.00		
320	2c	carmine	100.00		30.00
		On cover			2,000.
		Guide line or pasteup pair	120.00		
		Seven holes	300.00		—
		On cover			2,000.
		Guide line or pasteup pair	375.00		
		*Six holes	300.00		
		Guide line or pasteup pair	—		
*320a	2c	lake	150.00		65.00
		Guide line or pasteup pair	—		
		*Seven holes	225.00		
		Guide line or pasteup pair	400.00		
		*Six holes	200.00		
		Guide line or pasteup pair	—		
*315	5c	blue	2,000.		

On Issue of 1908-09

No.			2mm.	3mm.	Used Single
*343	1c	green	100.00	—	50.00
		Guide line or pasteup pair	—		
*344	2c	carmine	200.00	—	
		Guide line or pasteup pair	—		
*345	3c	deep violet	250.00		
		Guide line or pasteup pair	—		
*346	4c	orange brown	300.00	—	
		Guide line or pasteup pair	—		
*347	5c	blue	300.00		
		Guide line or pasteup pair	—		

On Lincoln Issue of 1909

No.			2mm.	3mm.	Used Single
*368	2c	carmine	120.00	110.00	50.00
		Guide line or pasteup pair	140.00		
		*Seven holes	375.00		
		Guide line or pasteup pair	—		
		*Six holes	375.00		
		Guide line or pasteup pair	—		

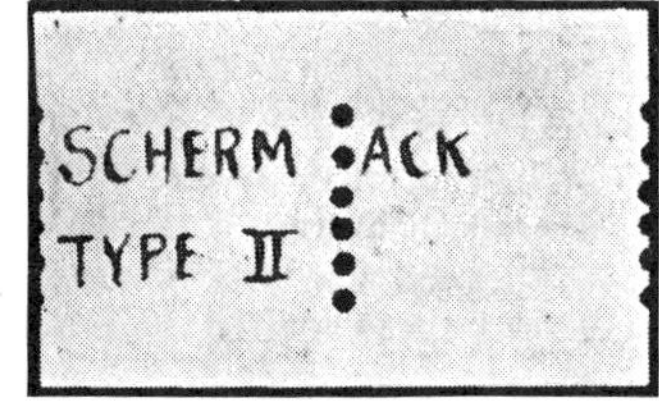

Perforations Type II

Cut into strips and joined before being perforated.

On Issue of 1906-08

No.			2mm.	3mm.	Used Single
314	1c	blue green	100.00		50.00
		Guide line or pasteup pair	150.00		
320	2c	carmine	60.00		35.00
		Guide line or pasteup pair	75.00		
*320a	2c	lake	120.00		65.00
		Guide line or pasteup pair	180.00		
*315	5c	blue	2,000.		550.00
		Guide line or pasteup pair	—		

On Issue of 1908-09

No.			2mm.	3mm.	Used Single
*343	1c	green	200.00	200.00	
		Guide line or pasteup pair	230.00		
*344	2c	carmine	200.00	200.00	
		Guide line or pasteup pair	230.00		
*345	3c	deep violet	200.00		
		Guide line or pasteup pair	230.00		
*346	4c	orange brown	250.00	—	
		Guide line or pasteup pair	280.00		
*347	5c	blue	270.00		
		Guide line or pasteup pair	300.00		

On Lincoln Issue of 1909

No.			2mm.	3mm.	Used Single
*368	2c	carmine	95.00	90.00	40.00
		Guide line or pasteup pair	115.00		

On Issue of 1912

No.			2mm.	3mm.	Used Single
*383	1c	green	—	—	
		Guide line or pasteup pair	—		
*384	2c	carmine	—	—	
		Guide line or pasteup pair	—		

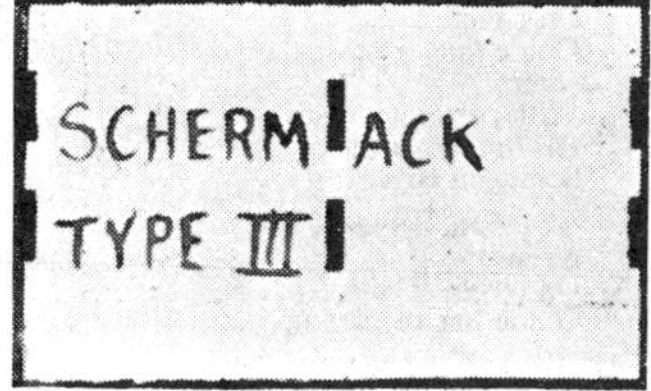

Perforations Type III

Blocks exist but were not regularly produced or issued.

On Issue of 1906-08

No.			Unused Pair Spacing 2mm	3mm	Used Single
314	1c	blue green	10.00		2.00
		On cover			100.00
		Guide line or pasteup pair	15.00		
320	2c	carmine	15.00		5.00
		On cover			75.00
		Guide line or pasteup pair	20.00		
320a	2c	lake	20.00		2.50
		On cover			75.00
		Guide line or pasteup pair	25.00		
*320b	2c	scarlet	20.00		5.00
		Guide line or pasteup pair	25.00		
314A	4c	brown	47,500.		10,000.
		On cover			22,500.
		Guide line pair	—		
*315	5c	blue	1,500.		
		Guide line or pasteup pair	—		

On Issue of 1908-09

No.			2mm	3mm	Used Single
343	1c	green	5.00	6.00	1.00
		On cover			25.00
		Guide line or pasteup pair	6.00		
		With perforated control mark, single	20.00		15.00
		Same, on cover			150.00
344	2c	carmine	5.00	6.00	1.00
		On cover			25.00
		Guide line or pasteup pair	6.00		
		With perforated control mark, single	20.00		15.00
		Same, on cover			150.00
345	3c	deep violet	20.00	140.00	5.00
		Guide line or pasteup pair	25.00		
346	4c	orange brown	30.00	20.00	5.00
		On cover			225.00
		With perforated control mark, single	—		—
		Guide line or pasteup pair	40.00		
347	5c	blue	50.00		15.00
		Guide line or pasteup pair	60.00		

On Lincoln Issue of 1909

No.			2mm	3mm	Used Single
368	2c	carmine	50.00	45.00	10.00
		On cover			200.00
		Guide line or pasteup pair	65.00		

On Alaska-Yukon Issue of 1909

No.			2mm	3mm	Used Single
*371	2c	carmine		70.00	
		Guide line or pasteup pair		85.00	

On Hudson-Fulton Issue of 1909

No.			2mm	3mm	Used Single
*373	2c	carmine		70.00	
		Guide line or pasteup pair		85.00	

On Issue of 1911

No.			2mm	3mm	Used Single
383	1c	green	4.00	3.00	1.00
		On cover			17.50
		Guide line or pasteup pair	8.00		
		With perforated control mark, single	20.00		15.00
		Same, on cover			150.00
384	2c	carmine	9.00	7.00	1.00
		On cover			17.50
		Guide line or pasteup pair	11.00		
		With perforated control mark, single	20.00		15.00
		Same, on cover			150.00

On Issue of 1912

No.			2mm	3mm	Used Single
408	1c	green		2.00	50

			Unused Pair Spacing 2mm	3mm	Used Single
		On cover			15.00
		Guide line or pasteup pair		3.00	
		With perforated control mark, single	*50.00*		*35.00*
		Same, on cover			*200.00*
409	2c	carmine		2.00	40
		On cover			15.00
		Guide line or pasteup pair		3.00	
		With perforated control mark, single	*50.00*		*35.00*
		Same, on cover			*200.00*
		On Issue of 1916-17			
481	1c	green		3.00	30
		On cover			15.00
		Guide line or pasteup pair		4.00	
482	2c	carmine, type I		4.00	50
		On cover			15.00
		Guide line or pasteup pair		5.00	
482A	2c	carmine, type Ia			*6,000.*
		On cover			*12,500.*
483	3c	violet, type I		10.00	2.50
		On cover			55.00
		Guide line or pasteup pair		15.00	
484	3c	violet, type II		15.00	4.00
		On cover			75.00
		Guide line or pasteup pair		20.00	
		On Issue of 1918-20			
531	1c	green		10.00	4.00
		On cover			65.00
		Guide line or pasteup pair		15.00	
532	2c	carmine, type IV		30.00	3.00
		On cover			75.00
		Guide line or pasteup pair		35.00	
533	2c	carmine, type V		*250.00*	*30.00*
		On cover			*200.00*
		Guide line or pasteup pair		*450.00*	
534	2c	carmine, type Va		15.00	2.00
		On cover			75.00
		Guide line or pasteup pair		20.00	
534A	2c	carmine, type VI		35.00	4.00
		On cover			75.00
		Guide line or pasteup pair		45.00	
534B	2c	carmine, type VII		600.00	100.00
		On cover			*300.00*
		Guide line or pasteup pair		*1,000.*	
535	3c	violet, type IV		12.50	3.00
		On cover			50.00
		Guide line or pasteup pair		15.00	
		On Issue of 1923-26			
575	1c	green		*150.00*	6.00
		Unused single		20.00	
		On cover			200.00
		Guide line or pasteup pair		*200.00*	
		Precanceled		4.00	1.00
576	1½c	yellow brown		20.00	2.00
		Guide line or pasteup pair		30.00	
		Precanceled		4.00	1.00
577	2c	carmine	25.00	20.00	1.00
		On cover			20.00
		Guide line or pasteup pair	35.00	30.00	
		On Harding Issue of 1923			
611	2c	black		65.00	15.00
		On cover			*75.00*
		Guide line or pasteup pair		100.00	

See the "Information for Collectors" section at beginning of catalogue for information on printing methods and varieties.

U. S. AUTOMATIC VENDING COMPANY

New York, N.Y.

Separations Type I

Cut into strips and joined before being perforated.

On Issue of 1906-08
Coiled Endwise

			Unused Pair	Used Single
314	1c	blue green	50.00	10.00
		On cover		*500.00*
		Guide line or pasteup pair	60.00	
320	2c	carmine	45.00	8.00
		Guide line or pasteup pair	55.00	
**320a*	2c	lake	100.00	9.00
		Guide line or pasteup pair	200.00	
320b	2c	scarlet	60.00	7.00
		On cover		*500.00*
		Guide line or pasteup pair	100.00	
315	5c	blue	1,150.	—
		On cover		
		Guide line or pasteup pair	1,350.	
		On Issue of 1908-09 **Coiled Endwise**		
343	1c	green	10.00	1.50
		On cover		75.00
		Guide line or pasteup pair	20.00	
344	2c	carmine	8.00	1.50
		On cover		75.00
		Guide line or pasteup pair	10.00	
**345*	3c	deep violet	30.00	8.00
		On cover		*300.00*
		Guide line or pasteup pair	50.00	
**346*	4c	orange brown	45.00	9.00
		Guide line or pasteup pair	100.00	
347	5c	blue	85.00	30.00
		On cover		*500.00*
		Guide line or pasteup pair	110.00	
		On Lincoln Issue of 1909		
368	2c	carmine, coiled endwise	35.00	7.00
		On cover		350.00
		Guide line or pasteup pair	75.00	
		On Alaska-Yukon Issue of 1909		
**371*	2c	carmine, coiled sideways	70.00	10.00
		On cover		*500.00*
		Guide line or pasteup pair	100.00	
		Type Ia, No T. and B. margins	80.00	15.00
		Type Ia, Guide line or pasteup pair	110.00	
		On Issue of 1911		
383	1c	green	6.00	2.50
		On cover		30.00
		Guide line or pasteup pair	9.00	
**384*	2c	carmine	20.00	4.50
		Guide line or pasteup pair	30.00	
		On Issue of 1912		
**408*	1c	green	10.00	2.00
		Guide line or pasteup pair	14.00	
**409*	2c	carmine	12.00	4.00
		Guide line pair	17.50	

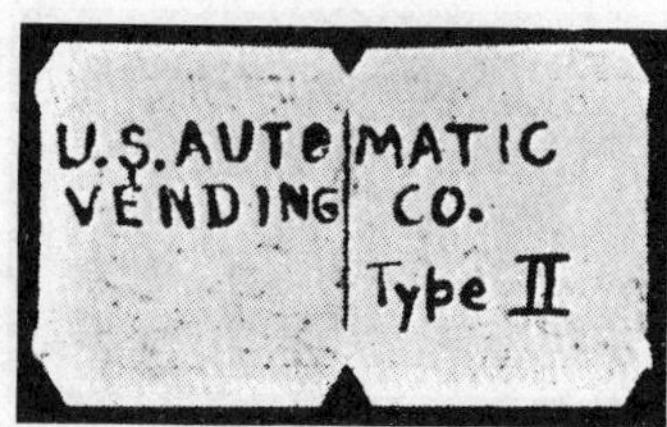

Separations Type II

Similar to Type I but with notches farther apart and a longer slit. Cut into strips and joined before being perforated.

Coiled Sideways

			Unused Pair Spacing 2mm	3mm	Used Single
		On Issue of 1906-08			
**314*	1c	blue green	45.00		8.00
		On cover			*350.00*
		Guide line or pasteup pair	55.00		
**320*	2c	carmine	80.00		
		Guide line or pasteup pair	—		
**320b*	2c	scarlet	55.00		5.00
		Guide line or pasteup pair	65.00		
**315*	5c	blue	1,200.		
		Guide line or pasteup pair	1,500.		
		On Issue of 1908-09			
343	1c	green	10.00		3.00
		On cover			—
		Guide line or pasteup pair	12.50		
344	2c	carmine	12.50		
		Guide line or pasteup pair	14.50		
**345*	3c	deep violet	55.00	—	
		Guide line or pasteup pair	70.00		
**346*	4c	orange brown	75.00	65.00	
		Guide line or pasteup pair	85.00		
**347*	5c	blue	150.00		
		Guide line or pasteup pair	180.00		
		On Lincoln Issue of 1909			
368	2c	carmine	90.00	80.00	20.00
		Guide line or pasteup pair	130.00		
		On Alaska-Yukon Issue of 1909			
**371*	2c	carmine		60.00	—
		On cover			
		Guide line or pasteup pair		75.00	
		On Hudson-Fulton Issue of 1909			
**373*	2c	carmine		65.00	*15.00*
		On cover			*250.00*
		Guide line or pasteup pair		85.00	
		Without slit		65.00	
		Without slit, Guide line or pasteup pair		85.00	
		On Issue of 1911			
383	1c	green	15.00	12.00	
		Guide line or pasteup pair	20.00		
384	2c	carmine	20.00	15.00	
		Guide line or pasteup pair	25.00		
		On Issue of 1912			
408	1c	green		10.00	2.00
		Guide line or pasteup pair		15.00	
409	2c	carmine		15.00	4.00
		Guide line pair		20.00	

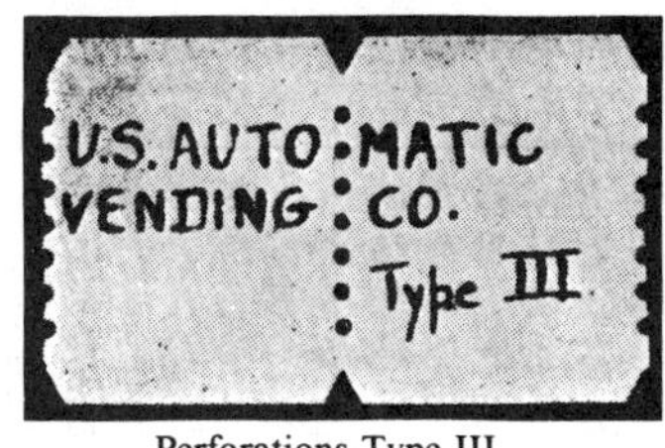

Perforations Type III

Cut into strips and joined before being perforated.

On Issue of 1906-08

*314	1c	blue green	50.00		10.00
		Guide line or pasteup pair	60.00		
*320	2c	carmine	70.00		
		Guide line or pasteup pair	—		
*320b	2c	scarlet	60.00		10.00
		Guide line or pasteup pair	75.00		
*315	5c	blue	1,000.		
		Guide line or pasteup pair	—		

On Issue of 1908-09

343	1c	green	25.00	23.00	5.00
		Guide line or pasteup pair	35.00		
344	2c	carmine	25.00		5.00
		Guide line or pasteup pair	35.00		
*345	3c	deep violet	100.00		
		Guide line or pasteup pair	120.00		
*346	4c	orange brown	100.00	100.00	12.00
		Guide line or pasteup pair	120.00		
*347	5c	blue	120.00		
		Guide line or pasteup pair	150.00		
		Experimental perf. 12	*850.00*		

On Lincoln Issue of 1909

*368	2c	carmine	65.00	55.00	16.00
		Guide line pair	95.00		

On Alaska-Yukon Issue of 1909

*371	2c	carmine		60.00	16.00
		Guide line or pasteup pair		85.00	

On Hudson-Fulton Issue of 1909

*373	2c	carmine		60.00	16.00
		Guide line or pasteup pair		100.00	

On Issue of 1911

383	1c	green	14.00	12.00	2.50
		Guide line or pasteup pair	18.00		
384	2c	carmine	16.00	14.00	2.50
		Guide line or pasteup pair	20.00		

On Issue of 1912

408	1c	green		8.00	
		Guide line or pasteup pair		10.00	
409	2c	carmine		12.00	
		Guide line or pasteup pair		16.00	

On 1914 Rotary Press Coil

459	2c	carmine		*9,000.*	*5,000.*

This firm also produced coil strips of manila paper, folded so as to form small "pockets", each "pocket" containing one 1c stamp and two 2c stamps, usually imperforate but occasionally with either government or U.S.A.V. private perforations. The manila "pockets" were perforated type II, coiled sideways. They fit U.S.A.V. ticket vending machines. Multiples exist.

Values are for "pockets" with known combinations of stamps, listed by basic Scott Number. Other combinations exist, but are not listed due to the fact that the stamps may have been added at a later date.

Pocket Type 1 (1908)

("Patents Pending" on front and green advertising on reverse)

314 + 320	2,500.
314 + 320b	2,500.

Pocket Type 2 (1909)

("Patents Applied For" Handstamped in greenish blue)

343 + 371	450.00
343 + 372	450.00
343 (USAV Type I) + 371	450.00
343 + 375	450.00

Pocket Type 3 (1909)

("Patents Pending" printed in red)

343 + 372	300.00
343 + 373	300.00
343 + 375	300.00
383 + 406	300.00

Pocket Type 4 (1909)

(No printing on front, serial number on back)

343 + 344	225.00
343 + 368	225.00
343 + 371	225.00
383 + 344	225.00
383 (USAV Type II) + 344	225.00
383 + 384	225.00
383 + 406	225.00

IMPERFORATE COILS

The imperforate coil stamps were made from imperforate sheets of the regular issues, and were issued in coils of 500 or 1,000. The numbers assigned below are those of the regular imperforate stamps to which "S" or "E" has been added to indicate that the stamps are coiled horizontally (side by side), or vertically (end to end). These coil stamps are virtually indistinguishable from the corresponding imperforate stamps, although they can be authenticated, particularly when in strips of four or longer. Many genuine imperforate coil stamps bear authenticating signatures of contemporary experts.

FLAT PLATE PRINTING

1908 Wmk. 191 *Imperf.*

314E	A115	1c	**blue green,** pair	250.00	—
			Strip of 4	650.00	—
			Guide line pair	—	
			Guide line strip of 4	—	
314S	A115	1c	**blue green,** pair	—	—
			Strip of 4	—	—
			Guide line pair	—	
			Guide line strip of 4	—	
320E	A129	2c	**carmine,** pair	—	
			Strip of 4	—	—
			Guide line pair	—	
			Guide line strip of 4	—	
320S	A129	2c	**carmine,** pair	—	—
			Strip of 4	—	—
			Guide line pair	—	
			Guide line strip of 4	—	

1908-10 *Imperf.*

343E	A138	1c	**green,** pair	22.00	8.50
			Strip of 4	50.00	—
			Guide line pair	30.00	—
			Guide line strip of 4	65.00	
343S	A138	1c	**green,** pair	42.50	—
			Strip of 4	105.00	—
			Guide line pair	70.00	—
			Guide line strip of 4	—	
344E	A139	2c	**carmine,** pair	27.50	20.00
			Strip of 4	65.00	—
			Guide line pair	40.00	—
			Guide line strip of 4	75.00	
			Double transfer, design of 1c	*1,250.*	
344S	A139	2c	**carmine,** pair (2mm spacing)	27.50	20.00
			Strip of 4	—	
			Guide line pair	—	
			Guide line strip of 4	—	
			Pair (3mm spacing)	30.00	—
			Strip of 4	—	
			Guide line pair	45.00	—
			Guide line strip of 4	—	
346E	A140	4c	**orange brown,** pair	110.00	
			Strip of 4	250.00	—
			Guide line pair	135.00	75.00
			Guide line strip of 4	—	
347E	A140	5c	**blue,** pair	150.00	—
			Strip of 4	325.00	—
			Guide line pair	185.00	—
			Guide line strip of 4	375.00	

1909 *Imperf.*

368E	A141	2c	**carmine,** *Lincoln,* pair	85.00	—
			Strip of 4	200.00	—
			Guide line pair	150.00	—
			Guide line strip of 4	325.00	—
368S	A141	2c	**carmine,** *Lincoln,* pair	150.00	—
			Strip of 4	—	
			Guide line pair	—	
			Guide line strip of 4	—	

1910 Wmk. 190 *Imperf.*

383E	A138	1c	**green,** pair	11.00	—
			Strip of 4	25.00	—
			Guide line pair	15.00	—
			Guide line strip of 4	50.00	—
			Double transfer	—	—
383S	A138	1c	**green,** pair (2mm spacing)	12.00	—
			Strip of 4	26.00	—
			Guide line pair	—	—
			Guide line strip of 4	—	—
			Pair (3mm spacing)	12.00	—
			Strip of 4	26.00	—
			Guide line pair	15.00	—
			Guide line strip of 4	—	—
384E	A139	2c	**carmine,** pair	12.50	—
			Strip of 4	27.50	—
			Guide line pair	17.50	—
			Guide line strip of 4	32.50	—
			Double transfer, design of 1c	*1,000.*	—
384S	A139	2c	**carmine,** pair (2mm spacing)	25.00	—
			Strip of 4	60.00	
			Guide line pair	—	—
			Guide line strip of 4	—	—
			Pair (3mm spacing)	22.50	—
			Strip of 4	55.00	—
			Guide line pair	30.00	—
			Guide line strip of 4	—	—

1912 Wmk. 190 *Imperf.*

408E	A140	1c	**green,** pair	3.50	
			Strip of 4	7.75	
			Guide line pair	5.50	
			Guide line strip of 4	10.00	
408S	A140	1c	**green,** pair	3.75	
			Strip of 4	—	
			Guide line pair	—	
			Guide line strip of 4	—	
409E	A140	2c	**carmine,** pair	3.75	
			Strip of 4	8.25	
			Guide line pair	6.00	
			Guide line strip of 4	10.50	
409S	A140	2c	**carmine,** pair	5.00	
			Strip of 4	—	
			Guide line pair	—	
			Guide line strip of 4	—	
			Double transfer	—	

Values quoted in this catalogue are for stamps graded at Fine-Very Fine and with no faults. An illustrated guide to grade is provided in introductory material, beginning on Page V.

COMMEMORATIVE

QUANTITIES ISSUED

Cat. No.		Quantity
230		449,195,550
231		1,464,588,750
232		11,501,250
233		19,181,550
234		35,248,250
235		4,707,550
236		10,656,550
237		16,516,950
238		1,576,950
239		617,250
240		243,750
241		55,050
242		45,550
243		27,650
244		26,350
245		27,350
285		70,993,400
286		159,720,800
287		4,924,500
288		7,694,180
289		2,927,200
290		4,629,760
291		530,400
292		56,900
293		56,200
294		91,401,500
295		209,759,700
296		5,737,100
297		7,201,300
298		4,921,700
299		5,043,700
323		79,779,200
324		192,732,400
325		4,542,600
326		6,926,700
327		4,011,200
328		77,728,794
329		149,497,994
330		7,980,594
367		148,387,191
368		1,273,900
369		637,000
370		152,887,311
371		525,400
372		72,634,631
373		216,480
397 & 401		334,796,926
398 & 402		503,713,086
399 & 403		29,088,726
400 & 404		16,968,365
537		99,585,200
548		137,978,207
549		196,037,327
550		11,321,607
610		1,459,487,085
611		770,000
612		99,950,300
614		51,378,023
615		77,753,423
616		5,659,023
617		15,615,000
618		26,596,600
619		5,348,800
620		9,104,983
621		1,900,983
627		307,731,900
628		20,280,500
629		40,639,485
630	(sheet of 25)	107,398
643		39,974,900
644		25,628,450
645		101,330,328
646		9,779,896
647		5,519,897
648		1,459,897
649		51,342,273
650		10,319,700
651		16,684,674
654		31,679,200
655		210,119,474
656		133,530,000
657		51,451,880
658		13,390,000
659		8,240,000
660		87,410,000
661		2,540,000
662		2,290,000
663		2,700,000
664		1,450,000
665		1,320,000
666		1,530,000
667		1,130,000
668		2,860,000
669		8,220,000
670		8,990,000
671		73,220,000
672		2,110,000
673		1,600,000
674		1,860,000
675		980,000
676		850,000
677		1,480,000
678		530,000
679		1,890,000
680		29,338,274
681		32,680,900
682		74,000,774
683		25,215,574
688		25,609,470

Cat. No.		Quantity
689		66,487,000
690		96,559,400
702		99,074,600
703		25,006,400
704		87,969,700
705		1,265,555,100
706		304,926,800
707		4,222,198,300
708		456,198,500
709		151,201,300
710		170,565,100
711		111,739,400
712		83,257,400
713		96,506,100
714		75,709,200
715		147,216,000
716		51,102,800
717		100,869,300
718		168,885,300
719		52,376,100
724		49,949,000
725		49,538,500
726		61,719,200
727		73,382,400
728		348,266,800
729		480,239,300
730	(sheet of 25)	456,704
730a		11,417,600
731	(sheet of 25)	441,172
731a		11,029,300
732		1,978,707,300
733		5,735,944
734		45,137,700
735	(sheet of six)	811,404
735a		4,868,424
736		46,258,300
737		193,239,100
738		15,432,200
739		64,525,400
740		84,896,350
741		74,400,200
742		95,089,000
743		19,178,650
744		30,980,100
745		16,923,350
746		15,988,250
747		15,288,700
748		17,472,600
749		18,874,300
750	(sheet of six)	511,391
750a		3,068,346
751	(sheet of six)	793,551
751a		4,761,306
752		3,274,556
753		2,040,760
754		2,389,288
755		2,294,948
756		3,217,636
757		2,746,640
758		2,168,088
759		1,822,684
760		1,724,576
761		1,647,696
762		1,682,948
763		1,638,644
764		1,625,224
765		1,644,900
766	(pane of 25)	98,712
766a		2,467,800
767	(pane of 25)	85,914
767a		2,147,850
768	(pane of six)	267,200
768a		1,603,200
769	(pane of six)	279,960
769a		1,679,760
770	(pane of six)	215,920
770a		1,295,520
771		1,370,560
772		70,726,800
773		100,839,600
774		73,610,650
775		75,823,900
776		124,324,500
777		67,127,650
778	(sheet of four)	2,809,039
778a		2,809,039
778b		2,809,039
778c		2,809,039
778d		2,809,039
782		72,992,650
783		74,407,450
784		269,522,200
785		105,196,150
786		93,848,500
787		87,741,150
788		35,794,150
789		36,839,250
790		104,773,450
791		92,054,550
792		93,291,650
793		34,552,950
794		36,819,050
795		84,825,250
796		25,040,400
797		5,277,445
798		99,882,300
799		78,454,450
800		77,004,200
801		81,292,450
802		76,474,550
835		73,043,650

Cat. No.	Quantity
836	58,564,368
837	65,939,500
838	47,064,300
852	114,439,600
853	101,699,550
854	72,764,550
855	81,269,600
856	67,813,350
857	71,394,750
858	66,835,000
859	56,348,320
860	53,177,110
861	53,260,270
862	22,104,950
863	13,201,270
864	51,603,580
865	52,100,510
866	51,666,580
867	22,207,780
868	11,835,530
869	52,471,160
870	52,366,440
871	51,636,270
872	20,729,030
873	14,125,580
874	59,409,000
875	57,888,600
876	58,273,180
877	23,779,000
878	15,112,580
879	57,322,790
880	58,281,580
881	56,398,790
882	21,147,000
883	13,328,000
884	54,389,510
885	53,636,580
886	55,313,230
887	21,720,580
888	13,600,580
889	47,599,580
890	53,766,510
891	54,193,580
892	20,264,580
893	13,726,580
894	46,497,400
895	47,700,000
896	50,618,150
897	50,034,400
898	60,943,700
902	44,389,550
903	54,574,550
904	63,558,400
906	21,272,800
907	1,671,564,200
908	1,227,334,200
909	19,999,646
910	19,999,646
911	19,999,646
912	19,999,646
913	19,999,646
914	19,999,646
915	19,999,646
916	14,999,646
917	14,999,646
918	14,999,646
919	14,999,646
920	14,999,646
921	14,999,646
922	61,303,000
923	61,001,450
924	60,605,000
925	50,129,350
926	53,479,400
927	61,617,350
928	75,500,000
929	137,321,000
930	128,140,000
931	67,255,000
932	133,870,000
933	76,455,400
934	128,357,750
935	138,863,000
936	111,616,700
937	308,587,700
938	170,640,000
939	135,927,000
940	260,339,100
941	132,274,500
942	132,430,000
943	139,209,500
944	114,684,450
945	156,540,510
946	120,452,600
947	127,104,300
948	10,299,600
949	132,902,000
950	131,968,000
951	131,488,000
952	122,362,000
953	121,548,000
954	131,109,500
955	122,650,500
956	121,953,500
957	115,250,000
958	64,198,500
959	117,642,500
960	77,649,600
961	113,474,500
962	120,868,500
963	77,800,500

Cat. No.	Quantity
964	52,214,000
965	53,958,100
966	61,120,010
967	57,823,000
968	52,975,000
969	77,149,000
970	58,332,000
971	56,228,000
972	57,832,000
973	53,875,000
974	63,834,000
975	67,162,200
976	64,561,000
977	64,079,500
978	63,388,000
979	62,285,000
980	57,492,610
981	99,190,000
982	104,790,000
983	108,805,000
984	107,340,000
985	117,020,000
986	122,633,000
987	130,960,000
988	128,478,000
989	132,090,000
990	130,050,000
991	131,350,000
992	129,980,000
993	122,315,000
994	122,170,000
995	131,635,000
996	121,860,000
997	121,120,000
998	119,120,000
999	112,125,000
1000	114,140,000
1001	114,490,000
1002	117,200,000
1003	116,130,000
1004	116,175,000
1005	115,945,000
1006	112,540,000
1007	117,415,000
1008	2,899,580,000
1009	114,540,000
1010	113,135,000
1011	116,255,000
1012	113,860,000
1013	124,260,000
1014	115,735,000
1015	115,430,000
1016	136,220,000
1017	114,894,600
1018	118,706,000
1019	114,190,000
1020	113,990,000
1021	89,289,600
1022	114,865,000
1023	115,780,000
1024	115,244,600
1025	123,709,600
1026	114,789,600
1027	115,759,600
1028	116,134,600
1029	118,540,000
1060	115,810,000
1061	113,603,700
1062	128,002,000
1063	116,078,150
1064	116,139,800
1065	120,484,800
1066	53,854,750
1067	176,075,000
1068	125,944,400
1069	122,284,600
1070	133,638,850
1071	118,664,600
1072	112,434,000
1073	129,384,550
1074	121,184,600
1075	2,900,731
1076	119,784,200
1077	123,159,400
1078	123,138,800
1079	109,275,000
1080	112,932,200
1081	125,475,000
1082	117,855,000
1083	122,100,000
1084	118,180,000
1085	100,975,000
1086	115,299,450
1087	186,949,627
1088	115,235,000
1089	106,647,500
1090	112,010,000
1091	118,470,000
1092	102,230,000
1093	102,410,000
1094	84,054,400
1095	126,266,000
1096	39,489,600
1097	122,990,000
1098	174,372,800
1099	114,365,000
1100	122,765,200
1104	113,660,200
1105	120,196,580
1106	120,805,200
1107	125,815,200
1108	108,415,200
1109	107,195,200
1110	115,745,280
1111	39,743,640
1112	114,570,200
1113	120,400,200

Cat. No.	Quantity
1114	91,160,200
1115	114,860,200
1116	126,500,000
1117	120,561,280
1118	44,064,576
1119	118,390,200
1120	125,770,200
1121	114,114,280
1122	156,600,200
1123	124,200,200
1124	120,740,200
1125	133,623,280
1126	45,569,088
1127	122,493,280
1128	131,260,200
1129	47,125,200
1130	123,105,000
1131	126,105,050
1132	209,170,000
1133	120,835,000
1134	115,715,000
1135	118,445,000
1136	111,685,000
1137	43,099,200
1138	115,444,000
1139	126,470,000
1140	124,560,000
1141	115,455,000
1142	122,060,000
1143	120,540,000
1144	113,075,000
1145	139,325,000
1146	124,445,000
1147	113,792,000
1148	44,215,200
1149	113,195,000
1150	121,805,000
1151	115,353,000
1152	111,080,000
1153	153,025,000
1154	119,665,000
1155	117,855,000
1156	118,185,000
1157	112,260,000
1158	125,010,000
1159	119,798,000
1160	42,696,000
1161	106,610,000
1162	109,695,000
1163	123,690,000
1164	123,970,000
1165	124,796,000
1166	42,076,800
1167	116,210,000
1168	126,252,000
1169	42,746,400
1170	124,117,000
1171	119,840,000
1172	117,187,000
1173	124,390,000
1174	112,966,000
1175	41,644,200
1176	110,850,000
1177	98,616,000
1178	101,125,000
1179	124,865,000
1180	79,905,000
1181	125,410,000
1182	112,845,000
1183	106,210,000
1184	110,810,000
1185	116,995,000
1186	121,015,000
1187	111,600,000
1188	110,620,000
1189	109,110,000
1190	145,350,000
1191	112,870,000
1192	121,820,000
1193	289,240,000
1194	120,155,000
1195	124,595,000
1196	147,310,000
1197	118,690,000
1198	122,730,000
1199	126,515,000
1200	130,960,000
1201	120,055,000
1202	120,715,000
1203	121,440,000
1204	40,270,000
1205	861,970,000
1206	120,035,000
1207	117,870,000
1230	129,945,000
1231	135,620,000
1232	137,540,000
1233	132,435,000
1234	135,520,000
1235	131,420,000
1236	133,170,000
1237	130,195,000
1238	128,450,000
1239	118,665,000
1240	1,291,250,000
1241	175,175,000
1242	125,995,000
1243	128,025,000
1244	145,700,000
1245	120,310,000
1246	511,750,000
1247	123,845,000
1248	122,825,000
1249	453,090,000
1250	123,245,000
1251	123,355,000
1252	126,970,000

Cat. No.	Quantity
1253	121,250,000
1254—1257	1,407,760,000
1258	120,005,000
1259	125,800,000
1260	122,230,000
1261	115,695,000
1262	115,095,000
1263	119,560,000
1264	125,180,000
1265	120,135,000
1266	115,405,000
1267	115,855,000
1268	115,340,000
1269	114,840,000
1270	116,140,000
1271	116,900,000
1272	114,085,000
1273	114,880,000
1274	26,995,000
1275	128,495,000
1276	1,139,930,000
1306	116,835,000
1307	117,470,000
1308	123,770,000
1309	131,270,000
1310	122,285,000
1311	14,680,000
1312	114,160,000
1313	128,475,000
1314	119,535,000
1315	125,110,000
1316	114,853,200
1317	124,290,000
1318	128,460,000
1319	127,585,000
1320	115,875,000
1321	1,173,547,420
1322	114,015,000
1323	121,105,000
1324	132,045,000
1325	118,780,000
1326	121,985,000
1327	111,850,000
1328	117,225,000
1329	111,515,000
1330	114,270,000
1331—1332	120,865,000
1333	110,675,000
1334	110,670,000
1335	113,825,000
1336	1,208,700,000
1337	113,330,000
1339	141,350,000
1340	144,345,000
1342	147,120,000
1343	130,125,000
1344	158,700,000
1345—1354	228,040,000
1355	153,015,000
1356	132,560,000
1357	130,385,000
1358	132,265,000
1359	128,710,000
1360	124,775,000
1361	128,295,000
1362	142,245,000
1363	1,410,580,000
1364	125,100,000
1365—1368	192,570,000
1369	148,770,000
1370	139,475,000
1371	187,165,000
1372	125,555,000
1373	144,425,000
1374	135,875,000
1375	151,110,000
1376—1379	159,195,000
1380	129,540,000
1381	130,925,000
1382	139,055,000
1383	150,611,200
1384	1,709,795,000
1385	127,545,000
1386	145,788,800
1387—1390	201,794,200
1391	171,850,000
1392	142,205,000
1405	137,660,000
1406	135,125,000
1407	135,895,000
1408	132,675,000
1409	134,795,000
1410—1413	161,600,000
1414—1414a	683,730,000
1415—1418, 1415a—1418a	489,255,000
1419	127,610,000
1420	129,785,000
1421—1422	134,380,000
1423	136,305,000
1424	134,840,000
1425	130,975,000
1426	161,235,000
1427—1430	175,679,600
1431	138,700,000
1432	138,165,000
1433	152,125,000
1434—1435	176,295,000
1436	142,845,000
1437	148,755,000
1438	139,080,000
1439	130,755,000
1440—1443	170,208,000
1444	1,074,350,000
1445	979,540,000
1446	137,355,000
1447	150,400,000

Cat. No.	Quantity
1448—1451	172,730,000
1452	104,090,000
1453	164,096,000
1454	53,920,000
1455	153,025,000
1456—1459	201,890,000
1460	67,335,000
1461	179,675,000
1462	46,340,000
1463	180,155,000
1464—1467	198,364,800
1468	185,490,000
1469	162,335,000
1470	162,789,950
1471	1,003,475,000
1472	1,017,025,000
1473	165,895,000
1474	166,508,000
1475	320,055,000
1476	166,005,000
1477	163,050,000
1478	159,005,000
1479	147,295,000
1480—1483	196,275,000
1484	139,152,000
1485	128,048,000
1486	146,008,000
1487	139,608,000
1488	159,475,000
1489—1498	486,020,000
1499	157,052,800
1500	53,005,000
1501	159,775,000
1502	39,005,000
1503	152,624,000
1504	145,840,000
1505	151,335,000
1506	141,085,000
1507	885,160,000
1508	939,835,000
1525	143,930,000
1526	145,235,000
1527	135,052,000
1528	156,750,000
1529	164,670,000
1530—1537	190,156,800
1538—1541	167,212,800
1542	156,265,000
1543—1546	195,585,000
1547	148,850,000
1548	157,270,000
1549	150,245,000
1550	835,180,000
1551	882,520,000
1552	213,155,000
1553	156,995,000
1554	146,365,000
1555	148,805,000
1556	173,685,000
1557	158,600,000
1558	153,355,000
1559	63,205,000
1560	157,865,000
1561	166,810,000
1562	44,825,000
1563	144,028,000
1564	139,928,000
1565—1568	179,855,000
1569—1570	161,863,200
1571	145,640,000
1572—1575	168,655,000
1576	146,615,000
1577—1578	146,196,000
1579	739,430,000
1580	878,690,000
1629—1631	219,455,000
1632	157,825,000
1633—1682	436,005,000
1683	159,915,000
1684	156,960,000
1685	158,470,000
1686	1,990,000
1687	1,983,000
1688	1,953,000
1689	1,903,000
1690	164,890,000
1691—1694	208,035,000
1695—1698	185,715,000
1699	130,592,000
1700	158,332,800
1701	809,955,000
1702—1703	963,370,000
1704	150,328,000
1705	176,830,000
1706—1709	195,976,000
1710	208,820,000
1711	192,250,000
1712—1715	219,830,000
1716	159,852,000
1717—1720	188,310,000
1721	163,625,000
1722	156,296,000
1723—1724	158,676,000
1725	154,495,000
1726	168,050,000
1727	156,810,000
1728	153,736,000
1729	882,260,000
1730	921,530,000
1731	156,560,000
1732—1733	202,155,000
1744	156,525,000
1745—1748	165,182,400
1749—1752	157,598,400
1753	102,856,000
1754	152,270,000
1755	94,600,000

Cat. No.	Quantity
1756	151,570,000
1757	15,170,400
1758	161,228,000
1759	158,880,000
1760—1763	186,550,000
1764—1767	168,136,000
1768	963,120,000
1769	916,800,000
1770	159,297,600
1771	166,435,000
1772	162,535,000
1773	155,000,000
1774	157,310,000
1775—1778	174,096,000
1779—1782	164,793,600
1783—1786	163,055,000
1787	161,860,000
1788	165,775,000
1789	160,000,000
1790	67,195,000
1791—1794	186,905,000
1795—1798	208,295,000
1799	873,710,000
1800	931,880,000
1801	161,290,000
1802	172,740,000
1803	168,995,000
1804	160,000,000
1805—1810	232,134,000
1821	163,510,000
1822	256,620,000
1823	95,695,000
1824	153,975,000
1825	160,000,000
1826	103,850,000
1827—1830	204,715,000
1831	166,545,000
1832	163,310,000
1833	160,000,000
1834—1837	152,404,000
1838—1841	152,420,000
1842	692,500,000
1843	718,715,000
1874	160,155,000
1875	159,505,000
1876—1879	210,633,000
1910	165,175,000
1911	107,240,000
1912—1919	337,819,000
1920	99,420,000
1921—1924	178,930,000
1925	100,265,000
1926	99,615,000
1927	97,535,000
1928—1931	167,308,000
1932	101,625,000
1922	99,170,000
1934	101,155,000
1935	101,200,000
1936	167,360,000
1937—1938	162,420,000
1939	597,720,000
1940	792,600,000
1941	167,130,000
1942—1945	191,560,000
1950	163,939,200
1952	180,700,000
1953—2002	666,950,000
2003	109,245,000
2004	112,535,000
2006—2009	124,640,000
2010	107,605,000
2011	173,160,000
2012	107,285,000
2013	109,040,000
2014	183,270,000
2015	169,495,000
2016	164,235,000
2017	110,130,000
2018	110,995,000
2019—2022	165,340,000
2023	174,180,000
2024	110,261,000
2026	703,295,000
2027—2030	788,880,000
2031	118,555,000
2032—2035	226,128,000
2036	118,225,000
2037	114,290,000
2038	165,000,000
2039	120,430,000
2040	117,025,000
2041	181,700,000
2042	114,250,000
2043	111,775,000
2044	115,200,000
2045	108,820,000
2046	184,950,000
2047	110,925,000
2048—2051	395,424,000
2052	104,340,000
2053	114,725,000
2054	112,525,000
2055—2058	193,055,000
2059—2062	207,725,000
2063	715,975,000
2064	848,525,000
2065	165,000,000
2066	120,000,000
2067—2070	319,675,000
2071	103,975,000
2072	554,675,000
2073	120,000,000
2074	106,975,000
2075	107,325,000
2076—2079	306,912,000
2080	120,000,000

Cat. No.	Quantity
2081	108,000,000
2082—2085	313,350,000
2086	130,320,000
2087	120,000,000
2088	117,050,000
2089	115,725,000
2090	116,600,000
2091	120,000,000
2092	123,575,000
2093	120,000,000
2094	117,125,000
2095	117,225,000
2096	95,525,000
2097	119,125,000
2098—2101	216,260,000
2102	120,000,000
2103	108,140,000
2104	117,625,000
2105	112,896,000
2106	116,500,000
2107	751,300,000
2108	786,225,000
2109	105,300,000
2110	124,500,000
2137	120,000,000
2138—2141	300,000,000
2142	120,580,000
2143	729,700,000
2144	124,750,000
2145	203,496,000
2146	126,325,000
2147	130,000,000
2152	119,975,000
2153	120,000,000
2154	119,975,000
2155—2158	147,940,000
2159	120,000,000
2160—2163	130,000,000
2164	120,000,000
2165	759,200,000
2166	757,600,000
2198—2201	67,996,800
2202	947,450,000
2203	130,000,000
2204	136,500,000
2205—2209	219,990,000
2210	130,000,000
2211	130,000,000
2216	5,825,050
2217	5,825,050
2218	5,825,050
2219	5,825,050
2220—2223	130,000,000
2224	220,725,000
2235—2238	240,525,000
2239	131,700,000
2240—2243	240,000,000
2244	690,100,000
2245	882,150,000

AIRPOST STAMPS

Cat. No.	Quantity
C1	3,395,854
C2	3,793,887
C3	2,134,888
C4	6,414,576
C5	5,309,275
C6	5,285,775
C7	42,092,800
C8	15,597,307
C9	17,616,350
C10	20,379,179
C11	106,887,675
C12	97,641,200
C13	93,536
C14	72,428
C15	61,296
C16	57,340,050
C17	76,648,803
C18	324,070
C19	302,205,100
C20	10,205,400
C21	12,794,600
C22	9,285,300
C23	349,946,500
C24	19,768,150
C25	4,746,527,700
C26	1,744,878,650
C27	67,117,400
C28	78,434,800
C29	42,359,850
C30	59,880,850
C31	11,160,600
C32	864,753,100
C33	971,903,700
C34	207,976,550
C35	756,186,350
C36	132,956,100
C37	33,244,500
C38	38,449,100
C39	5,070,095,200
C40	75,085,000
C41	260,307,500
C42	21,061,300
C43	36,613,100
C44	16,217,100
C45	80,405,000
C46	18,876,800
C47	78,415,000
C48	50,483,977
C49	63,185,000

Cat. No.	Quantity
C50	72,480,000
C51	1,326,960,000
C52	157,035,000
C53	90,055,200
C54	79,290,000
C55	84,815,000
C56	38,770,000
C57	39,960,000
C58	98,160,000
C59	
C60	1,289,460,000
C61	87,140,000
C62	
C63	
C64	
C65	
C66	42,245,000
C67	
C68	63,890,000
C69	62,255,000
C70	55,710,000
C71	+50,000,000
C72	
C73	
C74	+60,000,000
C75	
C76	152,364,800
C77	
C78	
C79	
C80	
C81	
C82	
C83	
C84	78,210,000
C85	96,240,000
C86	58,705,000
C87	
C88	
C89	
C90	
C91—C92	
C93—C94	
C95—C96	
C97	

+ Quantity ordered printed.

CARRIERS'

The term "Carriers' Stamps" is applied to certain stamps of the United States used to defray delivery to a post office on letters going to another post office, and for collection and delivery in the same city (local letters handled only by the carrier department). A less common usage was for collection fee to the addressee at the post office ("drop letters"). During the period when these were in use, the ordinary postage fee defrayed the carriage of mail matter from post office to post office only.

In many of the larger cities the private ("Local") posts delivered mail to the post office or to an addressee in the city direct for a fee of 1 or 2 cents (seldom more), and adhesive stamps were often employed to indicate payment. In some cases mail was delivered by private posts from the post office to the addressee as well. (See introduction to "Local Stamps" section.)

In 1851 the Federal Government, under the acts of 1825 and 1836, began to deliver letters in many cities and so issued Carriers' stamps for local delivery service. This Act of Congress of March 3, 1851, effective July 1, 1851 (succeeding Act of 1836), provided for the collecting and delivering of letters to the post office by carriers, "for which not exceeding 1 or 2 cents shall be charged."

Carriers' stamps were issued under the authority of, or derived from, the postmaster general. The "Official Issues" (Nos. L01-L02) were general issues of which No. L02 was valid for postage at face value, and No. L01 at the value set upon sale, in any post office. They were issued under the direct authority of the postmaster general. The "Semi-official Issues" were valid in the city in which they were issued either directly by or sanctioned by the local postmaster under authority derived from the postmaster general.

These "Official" and "Semi-official" Carriers' stamps prepaid the fees of official letter carriers who were appointed by the postmaster general and were under heavy bond to the United States for the faithful performance of their duties. Some of the letter carriers received fixed salaries from the government. Others were paid from the fees received for the delivery and collection of letters carried by them. After discontinuance of carrier fees on June 30, 1863, all carriers of the United States Post Office were government employees, paid by salary at a yearly rate.

Some Carriers' stamps are often found on cover with the regular government stamps and have the official post office cancellation applied to them as well. Only Williams' City Post in Cincinnati used its own cancellation, which is sometimes found on No. L02. Honour's City Express and the other Charleston, S.C., Carrier stamps almost always have the stamp uncanceled or canceled with pen, or less frequently pencil.

Values for Carriers' stamps on cover are for covers having the stamp tied by a handstamped cancellation.

Carriers' stamps, either uncanceled or pen-canceled, **on covers to which they apparently belong** deserve **a premium of at least 25 percent** over the values for the respective uncanceled or canceled off-cover stamps.

Stamps are listed "On cover" **only** when they are known to exist tied by a handstamped cancellation.

All Carriers' stamps are imperforate and on wove paper, either white or colored through, unless otherwise stated.

Counterfeits exist of many Carriers' stamps.

OFFICIAL ISSUES

Franklin Carrier

Franklin — OC1

Engraved and printed by Toppan, Carpenter, Casilear & Co. Plate of 200 subjects divided into two panes of 100 each, one left, one right

1851, Sept. **Unwmk.** ***Imperf.***

LO1	OC1 (1c) **dull blue** (shades), *rose*	*1,500.*	*2,000.*
	On cover		*5,000.*
	Cracked plate	*2,000.*	—
	Double transfer	—	—
	Pair	*3,500.*	*5,000.*
	Strip of three	*6,250.*	*9,500.*

CANCELLATIONS.

Philadelphia		New Orleans	
Red star	*2,000.*	Blue grid	—
Blue town	—	Black grid	—
New York		Green grid	—
Red town	—		

Of the entire issue of 310,000 stamps, 250,000 were sent to New York, 50,000 to New Orleans, 10,000 to Philadelphia. However, the quantity sent to each city is not indicative of proportionate use. More appear to have been used in Philadelphia than in the other two cities. The use in all three cities was notably limited.

Eagle Carrier

Eagle — OC2

Engraved and printed by Toppan, Carpenter, Casilear & Co. Plate of 200 subjects divided into two panes of 100 each, one upper, one lower

1851, Nov. 17 **Unwmk.** ***Imperf.***

LO2	OC2 1c **blue** (shades)	20.00	20.00
	On cover, used alone		125.00
	On cover with block of 3, 1c #9		*1,500.*
	On cover with 3c #11		150.00
	On cover with 3c #26		*1,500.*
	On cover with strip of 3, 3c #26		*400.00*
	On 3c envelope #U2, #U9 or U10		*175.00*
	Pair	42.50	
	Block of four	90.00	
	Double transfer	—	—

CANCELLATIONS.

Red star	20.00	Red town	—
Philadelphia	+20.00	Kensington, Pa. (red)	—
Cincinnati	+100.00	Washington, D.C.	+200.00
Black grid	+5.00	Blue squared target	—
Red grid	—	Red squared target	+100.00
Black town	+5.00	Railroad	—
Blue town	+50.00	Black carrier (Type C32)	—
		Red carrier (Type C32)	—

Used principally in Philadelphia, Cincinnati, Washington, D.C., and Kensington, Pa. One cover bearing a strip of 3 is known used from Andalusia, Pa.

GOVERNMENT REPRINTS

Made for the Centennial Exposition of 1876.
Printed by the Continental Bank Note Co.
First reprinting-10,000 copies, on April 2, 1875.
Second reprinting-10,000 copies, on Dec. 22, 1875.

The first reprinting of the Franklin stamp was on the rose paper of the original, obtained from Toppan, Carpenter, Casilear & Co. The second was on slightly thicker, softer paper of paler tint. The Franklin reprints are in dark blue instead of the dull or deep blue of the originals. First and second reprints and originals all differ under ultraviolet light.

Reprints of the Eagle stamp are on the same hard white paper used for reprints and special printings of the postage issue, and on a coarse wove paper. Originals are on yellowish paper with brown gum.

Franklin Reprints

1875 ***Imperf.***

LO3	OC1 (1c) **blue,** *rose*	40.00
	Block of four	175.00
	Cracked plate	60.00

SPECIAL PRINTING

Perf. 12

LO4	OC1 (1c) **blue**	*2,500.*
	Pair	*8,500.*

Eagle Reprints

Imperf.

LO5	OC2 1c **blue**	20.00
	Block of four	90.00

SPECIAL PRINTING

Perf. 12

LO6	OC2	1c **blue**	175.00	
		Block of four	750.00	

Nos. LO3-LO6 were issued without gum.

SEMI-OFFICIAL ISSUES

All are imperforate.

Baltimore, Md.

C1

1850-55 Typo. Settings of 10 (2x5) varieties

1LB1	C1	1c **red** (shades), *bluish*	100.00	60.00
		On cover		*250.00*
1LB2	C1	1c **blue** (shades), *bluish*	125.00	90.00
		On cover		*300.00*
a.		Bluish laid paper	—	—
1LB3	C1	1c **blue** (shades)	75.00	50.00
		On cover		*250.00*
		Block of four	*750.00*	
a.		Laid paper	150.00	100.00
		On cover		*300.00*
1LB4	C1	1c **green**	—	600.00
		On cover		*1,750.*
		Pair		
1LB5	C1	1c **red**	350.00	275.00
		On cover		*550.00*
		On cover with 3c #11		*900.00*

CANCELLATIONS. Nos. 1LB1-1LB5

Black grid	—	Blue town	—
Blue grid	—	Black numeral	—
Black cross	—	Blue numeral	—
Black town	—	Black pen	—

C2

1856 Typo.

1LB6	C2	1c **blue** (shades)	90.00	60.00
		On cover with 3c #26		350.00
1LB7	C2	1c **red** (shades)	65.00	40.00
		On cover		350.00
		On cover with 3c #26		450.00
		Block of four	*600.00*	

C3

Plate of 10 (2x5); 10 Varieties

The sheet consisted of at least four panes of 10 placed horizontally, the two center panes tete beche. This makes possible five horizontal tete beche gutter pairs.

1857 Typo.

1LB8	C3	1c **black** (shades)	25.00	20.00
		On cover		*150.00*
		On cover with 3c #26		175.00
		On 3c envelope #U10		*200.00*
		Block of four	125.00	
a.		"SENT", Pos. 7	35.00	25.00
b.		Short rays, Pos. 2	35.00	25.00
		Tete beche gutter pair	*400.00*	

CANCELLATIONS.

Black pen (or pencil)	20.00	Black town	22.50
Blue town	22.50	Black Steamship	

1LB9	C3	1c **red** (shades)	40.00	30.00
		On cover		100.00
		On cover with 3c #26		150.00
		On 3c envelope #U9		200.00
		On 3c envelope #U10		200.00
a.		"SENT", Pos. 7	50.00	40.00
b.		Short rays, Pos. 2	50.00	40.00

CANCELLATIONS. Nos. 1LB6-1LB7, 1LB9:

Black town	—	Blue numeral	—
Blue town	—	Black pen	—

Boston, Mass.

C6

Several Varieties

1849-50 Pelure Paper Typeset

3LB1	C6	1c **blue**	120.00	75.00
		On cover		200.00
		On cover with 5c #1		*1,200.*

CANCELLATIONS.

Red town	—	Black ornate double oval	—
Red grid	—		

C7

Typeset

Several Varieties

Wove Paper Colored Through

3LB2	C7	1c **blue** (shades), *grayish*	135.00	65.00
		On cover		175.00
		On cover with 3c #10		300.00
		On cover with 3c #11		250.00
3LB3	C7	1c **blue** (shades), *bluish*	125.00	65.00
		On cover		200.00
		On cover with 3c #11		225.00
		On 3c envelope #U9		275.00

CANCELLATIONS. Nos. 3LB2-3LB3:

Black small fancy circle	—	Red small fancy circle	—
Black diamond grid	—	Red diamond grid	—
Red town	—	Black railroad	—
Black grid	—	Black hollow star	—
Black PAID	—	Black pencil	—
Black crayon	—	Red crayon	—

Charleston, S. C.

John H. Honour was appointed a letter carrier at Charleston, in 1849, and engaged his brother-in-law, E. J. Kingman, to assist him. They separated in 1851, dividing the carrier business of the city between them. At the same time Kingman was appointed a letter carrier. In March, 1858, Kingman retired, being replaced by Joseph G. Martin. In the summer of 1858, John F. Steinmeyer, Jr., was added to the carrier force. When Honour retired in 1860, John C. Beckman was appointed in his place.

Each of these carriers had stamps prepared. These stamps were sold by the carriers. The Federal Government apparently encouraged their use.

Honour's City Express

C8

1849 Typo. Wove Paper Colored Through

4LB1	C8	2c **black**, *brown rose*	*1,300.*	*1,300.*
		Cut to shape		*600.00*
4LB2	C8	2c **black**, *yellow*		*1,300.*
		On cover with 10c #2		*7,000.*

CANCELLATIONS. Nos. 4LB1-4LB2:

Red grid	—	Red town	—

C10

1854 Wove Paper Typeset

4LB3	C10	2c **black**		*650.00*
		On cover with 3c #11		*1,650.*

CANCELLATIONS.

Black "PAID"	—	Black pen	*650.00*

C11

Several Varieties

1849-50 Wove Paper Colored Through Typeset

4LB5	C11	2c **black**, *bluish*, pelure	*400.00*	*300.00*
		On cover with pair 5c #1b		*3,500.*
		On cover with 3c #11		*750.00*
4LB7	C11	2c **black**, *yellow*	*400.00*	*400.00*
		On cover		*1,500.*

CANCELLATIONS. Nos. 4LB5, 4LB7:

Red town	—
Black pen	—
Red crayon	—

The varieties of type C11 on bluish wove (thicker) paper and pink, pelure paper are not believed genuine.

C13

C14

C15

Several varieties of each type

1851-58 Wove Paper Colored Through Typeset

4LB8	C13	2c **black**, *bluish*	175.00	100.00
		On cover		*250.00*
		On cover with 3c #10		850.00
		On cover with 3c #11		*850.00*
		On cover with 3c #26		*850.00*
		Horiz. pair		*1,000.*
a.		Period after "PAID"	350.00	150.00
		On cover		375.00
b.		"Cens"		*700.00*
c.		"Conours" and "Bents"		*2,000.*
4LB9	C13	2c **black**, *bluish*, pelure	*375.00*	*425.00*
4LB11	C14	(2c) **black**, *bluish*	—	*250.00*
		On cover with 3c #11		*2,500.*
4LB12	C14	(2c) **black**, *bluish*, pelure	—	*250.00*
4LB13	C15	(2c) **black**, *bluish* ('58)	250.00	125.00
		On cover with 3c #26		*1,750.*
a.		Comma after "PAID"	300.00	
b.		No period after "Post"	300.00	

A 2c of type C13 exists on pink pelure paper. It is believed not to have been issued by the post, but to have been created later and perhaps accidentally.

CANCELLATIONS. Nos. 4LB8-4LB13

Black town	—	Black pen	—
Blue town	—	Black pencil	—
Red town	—	Red crayon	—

Kingman's City Post

C16

C17

Several varieties of each

1851(?)-58(?) Typeset

Wove Paper Colored Through

4LB14	C16	2c **black**, *bluish*	*450.00*	*450.00*
		On cover with 3c #11		*1,500.*
		On cover with 3c #26		*2,500.*
4LB15	C17	2c **black**, *bluish*	*500.00*	*500.00*
		On cover		—
		Vertical pair		*1,400.*
		Vertical strip of three	*2,200.*	

CANCELLATIONS. Nos. 4LB14-4LB15

Black town	—	Black pen	—

Martin's City Post

C18

Several varieties

1858 Wove Paper Colored Through Typeset

4LB16	C18	2c **black**, *bluish*	*2,750.*	

Beckman's City Post

Same as C19, but inscribed "Beckmann's City Post."

1860

4LB17	C19	2c **black**, on cover		—

No. 4LB17 is unique. It is on cover with 3c No. 26, both tied by black circle townmark: "CHARLESTON, S.C. JUN 18, 1860".

Steinmeyer's City Post

C19

C20

Several varieties of Type C19
Type C20 printed from plate of 10 (2x5) varieties

1859 Wove Paper Colored Through Typeset

4LB18	C19	2c	**black,** *bluish*	*2,500*	
4LB19	C20	2c	**black,** *bluish*	*1,500*	—
4LB20	C20	2c	**black,** *pink*	*100.00*	—
			Block of four	*450.00*	
			Sheet of ten	*1,250.*	
4LB21	C20	2c	**black,** *yellow*	85.00	
			Block of four	400.00	
			Sheet of ten	*1,500.*	

Cancellation on Nos. 4LB19-4LB21: Black pen.

Cincinnati, Ohio

Williams' City Post

Organized by C. C. Williams, who was appointed and commissioned by the Postmaster General.

C20a

1854 Wove Paper Litho.

9LB1	C20a	2c	**brown**	*500.00*	*500.00*
			On cover		*1,000.*
			On cover with 1c #9		*3,500.*
			Pair	*1,500.*	

CANCELLATIONS.

Red squared target —
Black pen —
Blue company circle —

Cleveland, Ohio

Bishop's City Post.

Organized by Henry S. Bishop, "Penny Postman" who was appointed and commissioned by the Postmaster General.

C20b

C20c

1854 Wove Paper Litho.

10LB1	C20b		**blue**	*400.00*	*400.00*
			On cover		*1,500.*

Vertically Laid Paper

10LB2	C20c	2c	**black,** *bluish*	*400.00*	*400.00*
			On cover		*1,250.*
			Pair		*1,750.*

CANCELLATIONS. #10LB1-10LB2

Red town —
Red boxed numeral —
Black pencil —
Black pen —

Louisville, Ky.

Carrier Service was first established by the Louisville Post Office about 1854, with one carrier. David B. Wharton, appointed a carrier in 1856, issued an adhesive stamp in 1857, but as he was soon thereafter replaced in the service, it is not believed that any of these stamps were used. Brown & McGill, carriers who succeeded Wharton, issued stamps in April, 1858.

Wharton's U.S.P.O. Despatch

C21

Sheet of 50 subjects in two panes of 25 (5x5) each, one upper, one lower

1857 Lithographed by Robyn & Co.

5LB1	C21	(2c)	**black,** *bluish green*	*35.00*
			Block of four	*150.00*
			Pane of 25	*950.00*
			Sheet of 50	*2,500.*

Brown & McGill's U. S. P. O. Despatch

C22

1858 Litho. by Hart & Maypother

5LB2	C22	(2c)	**black,** *blue* (shades)	100.00	150.00
			On cover with 3c #26		*1,350.*
			Block of four	650.00	
5LB3	C22	(2c)	black	*600.00*	*1,750.*

CANCELLATIONS. #5LB2-5LB3

Blue town —
Black pencil —

New York, N. Y.

UNITED STATES CITY DESPATCH POST

By an order made on August 1, 1842, the Postmaster General established a carrier service in New York known as the "United States City Despatch Post". Local delivery service had been authorized by the Act of Congress of July 2, 1836.

Greig's City Despatch Post was sold to the U. S. P. O. Department and on August 16, 1842, began operation as the "United States City Despatch Post" under the superintendence of Alexander M. Greig who was appointed a U. S. letter carrier for that purpose.

The Greig circular introducing this service stated that letter boxes had been placed throughout the city, that letters might be sent prepaid or collect, and that registry service was available for an extra 3 cents.

The City Despatch Post stamps were accepted for the service of the United States City Despatch Post. The stamps thus used bear the cancellation of the New York Post Office, usually "U.S." in an octagon:

Occasionally they bear a circle with the date and the words "U.S. CITY DESPATCH POST" or infrequently a New York town postmark.

No. 6LB3 was the first stamp issued by authority of the U.S.P.O. Department. The 3c denomination included 1 cent in lieu of drop letter postage until June 30, 1845, and the maximum legal carrier fee of 2 cents. Service was discontinued late in November, 1846.

C23

Engraved and printed by Rawdon, Wright & Hatch.

Plate of 42 (6x7) subjects
Wove Paper Colored Through

1842

6LB1	C23	3c	**black,** *grayish*	*750.00*
			On cover	*7,500.*

CANCELLATIONS.

Red circle "U.S." City Despatch —
Red "U.S." in octagon —
Red town —

Used copies which do not bear the official cancellation of the New York Post Office and unused copies are classed as Local stamps. See No. 40L1.

C24

Plate of 100 subjects

1842-45 Engraved by Rawdon, Wright & Hatch
Wove Paper (unsurfaced) Colored Through

6LB2	C24	3c	**black,** *rosy buff*	*550.00*	
6LB3	C24	3c	**black,** *light blue*	*300.00*	200.00
			On cover		500.00
			Pair	*700.00*	
6LB4	C24	3c	**black,** *green*	*2,000.*	

Some authorities consider No. 6LB2 to be an essay, and No. 6LB4 a color changeling.

Glazed Paper, Surface Colored

6LB5	C24	3c	**black,** *darkblue* (shades)	100.00	75.00
			On cover		350.00
			Pair	—	300.00
			Strip of three	—	500.00
			Block of four	*2,000.*	
a.			Double impression		*500.00*
			Ribbed paper	—	—
			Double transfer		—
6LB6	C24	3c	**black,** *bluish green*	125.00	75.00
			On cover		350.00
			Five on cover		*2,500.*
			Pair		250.00
			Strip of three		—
			Strip of four		—
			Strip of five		—
a.			Double impression		*550.00*
			Ribbed paper		—
			Double transfer		—

CANCELLATIONS.

Red curved PAID —
Red "U.S. City Despatch Post" —
Red "U.S." in octagon —
Red New York —
Red double line circle "U.S. City Despatch Post" —

No. 6LB6 has been noted on cover with the 5c New York signed "R.H.M.", No. 9X1b.

C25

1846

No. 6LB6 Surcharged in Red

6LB7	C25	2c on 3c	**black,** *bluish green,* on cover	*5,000.*

The existance of No. 6LB7 has been questioned.

The City Dispatch 2c red formerly listed as No. 6LB8 is now listed under Local Stamps as No. 160L1.

U.S. MAIL

C27

Issued by the Postmaster at New York, N.Y.

1849 Wove Paper, Colored Through Typo.

6LB9	C27	1c	**black,** *rose*	50.00	25.00
			On cover		*125.00*
			On cover with 5c #1		*2,000.*
			Pair	—	
			Block of four	—	

1849-50

Glazed Surface Paper

6LB10	C27	1c	**black,** *yellow*	45.00	25.00
			On cover		*100.00*
			On cover with 5c #1		*1,500.*
			Pair	—	
			Block of four	—	
6LB11	C27	1c	**black,** *buff*	40.00	25.00
			On cover		*100.00*

On cover with 5c #1 — 1,500.
a. Pair, one stamp sideways — 1,000.

CANCELLATIONS. #6LB9-6LB11

Red town	—	Red "N.Y. U.S. CITY MAIL" in circle	—
Red grid	—	Black pen	—
Red "PAID"	—	Black pencil	—
Black numeral in circle	—		

Philadelphia, Pa.

C28

Several Varieties
Thick Wove Paper Colored Through

1849-50			**Typeset**	
7LB1	C28	1c **black,** *rose* (with "L P")	175.00	
		On cover		500.00
7LB2	C28	1c **black,** *rose* (with "S")	*500.00*	
7LB3	C28	1c **black,** *rose* (with "H")	175.00	
		On cover		*400.00*
7LB4	C28	1c **black,** *rose* (with "L S")	175.00	
7LB5	C28	1c **black,** *rose* (with "J J")	*2,000.*	

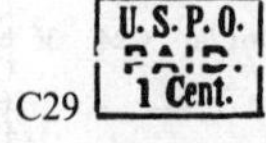

C29

Several Varieties

7LB6	C29	1c **black,** *rose*	150.00	125.00
		On cover		*400.00*
7LB7	C29	1c **black,** *blue,* glazed	*600.00*	
7LB8	C29	1c **black,** *vermilion,* glazed	*600.00*	
7LB9	C29	1c **black,** *yellow,* glazed	*1,350.*	

Cancellations on Nos. 7LB1-7LB9: Normally these stamps were left uncanceled on the letter, but occasionally were accidentally tied by the Philadelphia town postmark which was normally struck in blue ink.

A 1c black on buff (unglazed) of type C29 is believed to be a color changeling.

C30

Settings of 25 (5x5) varieties (Five basic types)

1850-52			**Litho.**	
7LB11	C30	1c **gold,** *black,* glazed	60.00	55.00
		On cover		*200.00*
		On cover with 5c #1		*1,500.*
		On cover with 3c #10		*800.00*

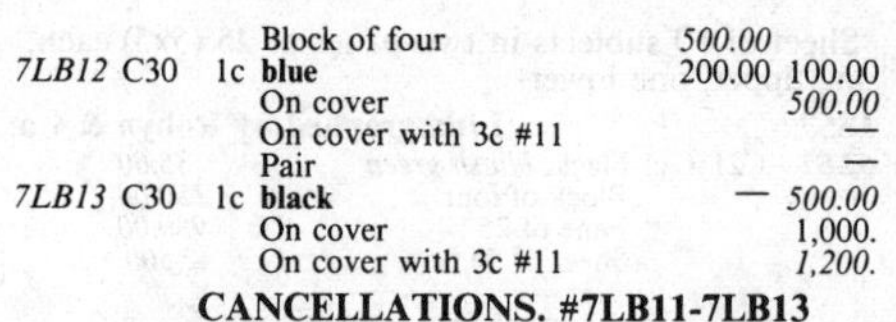

		Block of four	*500.00*	
7LB12	C30	1c **blue**	200.00	100.00
		On cover		*500.00*
		On cover with 3c #11		—
		Pair		—
7LB13	C30	1c **black**	—	*500.00*
		On cover		1,000.
		On cover with 3c #11		*1,200.*

CANCELLATIONS. #7LB11-7LB13

Red star —

C31

Handstamped

7LB14 C31 1c **blue,** *buff* 1,000.

No. 7LB14 was handstamped on coarse dark buff paper on which rectangles in the approximate size of the type C31 handstamp had been ruled in pencil. The stamps so produced were later cut out and show traces of the adjoining handstamp markings as well as parts of the penciled rectangle.

1855(?)				
7LB16	C31	1c **black**		*1,650.*
		On cover with strip of 3, 1c #9		—

C32

1856(?)			**Handstamped**	
7LB18	C32	1c **black**	*1,200.*	*1,300.*
		On cover (cut diamond-shaped) with pair 1c #7 and single 1c #9		*2,750.*
		On cover with strip of 3, 1c #9		—
		On cover with 3c #11		*2,750.*

CANCELLATIONS. #7LB16, 7LB18

Black circled grid	—	Black town	—

Nos. 7LB16 and 7LB18 were handstamped on the sheet margins of U.S. 1851 1c stamps, cut out and used as adhesives. The paper therefore has some surface bluing, and some stamps show parts of the plate imprint. Values are for stamps cut square unless otherwise mentioned.

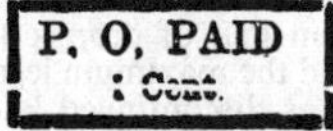

P. O. PAID,
One Cent.

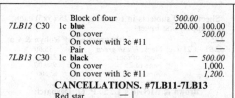

The authenticity of stamps of these designs, typeset and on thin wove paper, is in doubt. Those seen are uncanceled, either off cover or affixed to stampless covers of the early 1850's.

ENVELOPES

Handstamps of types C31 and C32 were also used to make stamped envelopes and letter sheets or circulars. These same types were also used as postmarks or cancellations in the same period. A handstamp similar to C32, but with "U.S.P. DESPATCH" in serif capitals, is believed to have been used only as a postmark.

Type C31 exists struck in blue or red, type C32 in blue, black or red. When found on cover, on various papers, struck alone, they are probably postmarks and not prepaid stamped envelopes. As such, these entire covers, depending upon the clarity of the handstamp and the general attractiveness of the letter are valued between $100 and $200.

When found on envelopes with the Carrier stamp canceled by a handstamp (such as type C31 struck in blue on a buff envelope canceled by the red solid star cancellation) they can be regarded as probably having been sold as prepaid envelopes. Value approximately $600.

St. Louis, Mo.

C36

C37

1849		**White Wove Paper Two Types**	**Litho.**	
8LB1	C36	2c **black**	*2,000.*	*2,750.*

CANCELLATIONS.

Black town —

1857			**Litho.**	
8LB2	C37	2c **blue**		*2,500.*
		On cover		—

CANCELLATIONS.

Black boxed "1ct"	—
Black pen	—

LOCAL

This listing of Local stamps includes stamps issued by Local Posts (city delivery), Independent Mail Routes and Services, Express Companies and other private posts which competed with, or supplemented, official services.

The Independent Mail Routes began using stamps early in 1844 and were put out of business by an Act of March, 1845, which became effective July 1, 1845. By this Act, the Government reduced the zones to two, reduced the rates to 5c and 10c and applied them to weight instead of the number of sheets of paper which composed a letter.

Most of the Local Posts still in business were forced to discontinue service by an Act of 1861, except Boyd's and Hussey's which were able to continue about 20 years longer because of the particular nature of their business. Other posts appeared illegally and sporadically after 1861 and were quickly suppressed.

City posts generally charged 1c to deliver a letter to the Post Office (usually the letter bore a government stamp as well) and 2c for intracity delivery (such letters naturally bore only local stamps). These usages are not catalogued separately because the value of a cover is determined as much by its attractiveness as its franking, rarity being the basic criterion.

Only a few Local Posts used special handstamps for canceling. The stamps frequently were left uncanceled, were canceled by pen, or less often by pencil. **Values for stamps on cover are for covers having the stamp tied by a handstamped cancellation, either private or governmental.** Local stamps, either uncanceled or pen canceled, **on covers to which they apparently belong** deserve **a premium of at least 25 percent** over the values for the respective uncanceled or canceled off-cover stamp.

The absence of any specific cancellation listed indicates that no company handstamp is known so used, and that the canceling, if any, was done by pen, pencil or government handstamp.

Stamps are listed "on cover" **only** when they are known to exist tied by private or governmental handstamp. Local stamps used on letters directed out of town (and consequently bearing government stamps) sometimes, because of their position, are tied together with the government stamp by the cancellation used to cancel the latter.

Values for envelopes are for entires unless specifically mentioned where entires are unknown.

All Local stamps are imperforate and on wove paper, either white or colored through, unless otherwise stated.

Counterfeits exist of many Local stamps, but most of these are crude reproductions and would deceive only the novice.

Adams & Co.'s Express, California

This post started in September, 1849, operating only on the Pacific Coast.

D. H. Haskell, Manager

L1 L2

Nos. 1L2-1L5 Printed in Sheets of 40 (8x5).

1854			**Litho.**	
1L1	L1	25c **black,** *blue*	175.00	—
		On cover		—
1L2	L2	25c **black** (initials in black)	50.00	—
		Block of four	225.00	
a.		Initials in red		—
b.		Without initials		—

Cancellation (1L1-1L2): Black Express Co.

Nos. 1L1-1L2 were the earliest adhesive franks issued west of the Mississippi River.

Glazed Surface Cardboard

1L3	L2	25c **black,** *pink*	20.00	
		Block of four	90.00	
		Retouched flaw above LR "25"	100.00	

No. 1L3 was probably never placed in use as a postage stamp.

L3

Overprinted in red "Over our California lines only"

1L4	L3	25c **black**	200.00	—

L4 L5

1L5	L4	25c **black** (black surcharge)	300.00	—
1L6	L5	25c **black**	300.00	
		Pair	*750.00*	

NEWSPAPER STAMP

L6

1LP1	L6	**black,** *claret*	350.00	450.00

Cancellation: Blue company oval.

ENVELOPES

L6a L6b

Typo.

1LU1	L6a	25c **blue** (cut square)		—
1LU2	L6b	25c **black** (on U.S. #U9)	250.00	*400.00*
1LU3	L6b	50c **black** (on U.S. #U9)	250.00	*400.00*
1LU4	L6b	50c **black,** *buff*	—	—

No. 1LU2 exists cut out and apparently used as an adhesive.

Cancellation: Blue company oval.

Adams' City Express Post, New York, N.Y.

L7 L8

1850-51				**Typo.**
2L2	L7	2c **black,** *buff*	250.00	250.00
2L3	L8	1c **black,** *gray*	300.00	300.00
2L4	L8	2c **black,** *gray*	275.00	275.00

Nos. 2L3-2L4 were reprinted in black and in blue on white wove paper. Some students claim that the 1c and 2c in blue exist as originals.

Allen's City Dispatch, Chicago, Ill.

Established by Edwin Allen for intracity delivery of letters and circulars. The price of the stamps is believed to have been determined on a quantity basis. Uncanceled and canceled remainders were sold to collectors after suppression of the post.

L9

1882 **Typo.** ***Perf. 10.***

Sheet of 100

3L1	L9	**pink**	3.00	8.00
		On cover		225.00
3L2	L9	**black**	7.00	—
		On cover		200.00
a.		Horizontal pair, imperf. between		—
3L3	L9	**red,** *yellow*	50	2.00
		On cover		200.00
a.		Imperf., pair	—	
b.		Horizontal pair, imperf. between	—	
3L4	L9	**purple**	50.00	

Cancellations: Violet company oval. Violet "eagle."

American Express Co., New York, N.Y.

Believed by some researchers to have been established by Smith & Dobson in 1856, and short-lived.

L10

Typeset

Glazed Surface Paper

4L1	L10	2c **black,** *green*	—

American Letter Mail Co.

Lysander Spooner established this independent mail line operating to and from New York, Philadelphia and Boston.

L12

1844				**Engr.**

Sheet of 20 (5x4)

5L1	L12	5c **black,** thin paper (2nd printing)	4.00	15.00
		Thick paper (1st printing)	15.00	25.00
		On cover		85.00
		Pair on cover		—
		Block of four, thin paper	20.00	
		Sheet of 20, thin paper	100.00	

No. 5L1 has been extensively reprinted in several colors.

Cancellations: Red dotted star (2 types). Red "PAID".

L13

Engr.

5L2	L13	**black,** *gray*	45.00	45.00
		On cover		150.00
		Pair on cover		250.00
		Block of four	*250.00*	
5L3	L13	**blue,** *gray*	225.00	225.00
		On cover		300.00

Cancellations: Red "PAID". Red company oval.

A. W. Auner's Despatch Post, Philadelphia, Pa.

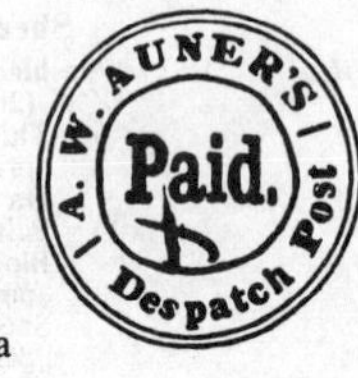
L13a

1851 **Typeset**

Cut to shape

154L1	L13a	**black,** *grayish*	*1,000.*	*1,000.*

Baker's City Express Post, Cincinnati, Ohio

L14

1849

6L1	L14	2c **black,** *pink*	800.00	

Barnard's Cariboo Express, British Columbia

The adhesives were used on British Columbia mail and the post did not operate in the United States, so the formerly listed PAID and COLLECT types are omitted. This company had an arrangement with Wells, Fargo & Co. to exchange mail at San Francisco.

Barnard's City Letter Express, Boston, Mass.

Established by Moses Barnard

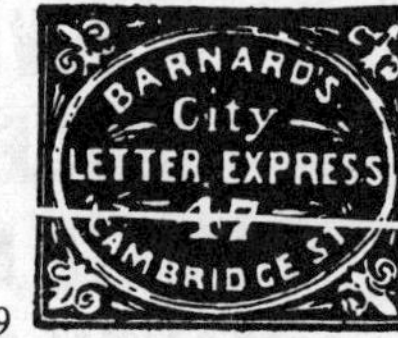
L19

1845

7L1	L19	**black,** *yellow,* glazed paper	*350.00*	*350.00*
7L2	L19	**red**	*800.00*	

Barr's Penny Dispatch, Lancaster, Pa.

Established by Elias Barr.

L20

1855 **Typeset**

Five varieties of each

8L1	L20	**red**	250.00	250.00
		On cover		*2,500.*
8L2	L20	**black,** *green*	45.00	—
		Pair	100.00	

Bayonne City Dispatch, Bayonne City, N.J.

Organized April 1, 1883, to carry mail, with three daily deliveries. Stamps sold at 80 cents per 100.

L21

1883 **Electrotyped**

Sheet of 10

9L1	L21	1c	**black**	125.00	125.00
			On cover		350.00

Cancellation: Purple concentric circles.

ENVELOPE

1883, May 15 **Handstamped**

9LU1	L21	1c	**purple,** *amber*	100.00	500.00

Bentley's Dispatch, New York, N.Y.

Established by H. W. Bentley, who acquired Cornwell's Madison Square Post Office, operating until 1856, when the business was sold to Lockwood. Bentley's postmark was double circle handstamp.

L22

BENTLEY'S
Despatch,
MADISON SQ.

L22a

1856(?) **Glazed Surface Paper**

10L1	L22	**gold**	*1,500.*	*1,500.*
10L2	L22a	**gold**		*1,500.*

Cancellation: Black "PAID."

Berford & Co.'s Express, New York, N.Y.

Organized by Richard G. Berford and Loring L. Lombard.

Carried letters, newspapers and packages by steamer to Panama and points on the West Coast, North and South America. Agencies in West Indies, West Coast of South America, Panama, Hawaii, etc.

L23

1851

11L1	L23	3c	**black**	*500.00*	*500.00*
			On cover		—
11L2	L23	6c	**green**	*500.00*	*500.00*
			On cover		*750.00*
11L3	L23	10c	**violet**	*500.00*	*500.00*
			On cover		—
			Pair	*1,250.*	
			Horiz. tete beche pair	*1,500.*	
11L4	L23	25c	**red**	*500.00*	*500.00*
			On cover		—

Values of cut to shape copies are about half of those quoted.

Cancellation: Red "B & Co. Paid" (sometimes impressed without ink). Dangerous counterfeits exist of Nos. 11L1-11L4.

Bicycle Mail Route, California.

During the American Railway Union strike, Arthur C. Banta, Fresno agent for Victor bicycles, established this post to carry mail from Fresno to San Francisco and return, employing messengers on bicycles. The first trip was made from Fresno on July 6, 1894. Service was discontinued on July 18 when the strike ended. In all, 380 letters were carried. Stamps were used on covers with U.S. Government adhesive stamps and on stamped envelopes.

(Illustration reduced size) — L24

Printed from single die. Sheet of six.
Error of spelling "SAN FRANSISCO"

1894 **Typo.** ***Rouletted 10***

12L1	L24	25c	**green**	60.00	85.00
			On cover		1,250.

(Illustration reduced size) — L25

Retouched die. Spelling error corrected.

12L2	L25	25c	**green**	20.00	40.00
			On cover		1,400.
			Block of 4	85.00	
			Pane of 6	165.00	
a.			"Horiz." pair, imperf. "vert"	65.00	

ENVELOPES

12LU1	L25	25c	**brown,** on 2c No. U311	85.00	*1,350.*
12LU2	L25	25c	**brown,** on 2c No. U312	85.00	*1,350.*

Cancellation: Two black parallel bars 2mm apart.
Stamps and envelopes were reprinted from the defaced die.

Bigelow's Express, Boston, Mass.

Authorities consider items of this design to be express company labels rather than stamps.

Bishop's City Post, Cleveland, Ohio
See Carriers' Stamps, Nos. 10LB1-12LB2.

Blizzard Mail

Organized March, 1888, to carry mail to New York City during the interruption of U.S. mail by the Blizzard of 1888. Used March 12-16.

L27

1888, Mar. 12 **Quadrille Paper** **Typo.**

163L1	L27	5c **black**	300.00	

D.O. Blood & Co., Philadelphia, Pa.
I. Philadelphia Despatch Post

Operated by Robertson & Co., predecessor of D.O. Blood & Co.

L28

L29

Initialed "R & Co."

1843 **Handstamped**

Cut to Shape

No.	Design	Description	Unused	Used
15L1	L28	3c **red,** *bluish*	*750.00*	
		On cover	*3,250.*	
15L2	L28	3c **black**	*750.00*	
		On cover	—	

Cancellations on Nos. 15L1-15L2: Red "3". Red pattern of segments.

Without shading in background.
Initialed "R & Co"

1843 **Litho.**

No.	Design	Description	Unused	Used
15L3	L29	(3c) **black,** *grayish*		225.00
		On cover		600.00
a.		Double impression		—

Cancellation on No. 15L3: Red "3"

The design shows a messenger stepping over the Merchants' Exchange Building, which then housed the Government Post Office, implying that the private post gave faster service.

II. D.O. Blood & Co.

Formed by Daniel Otis Blood and Walter H. Blood in 1845. Successor to Philadelphia Despatch Post which issued Nos. 15L1-15L3.

L30

Initialed "Dob & Cos" or "D.O.B. & Co."

1845

Shading in background

No.	Design	Description	Unused	Used
15L4	L30	(3c) **black,** *grayish*		125.00
		On cover		600.00

L31

L32

1845

No.	Design	Description	Unused	Used
15L5	L31	(2c) **black**	75.00	100.00
		On cover		*450.00*
		Block of four	*350.00*	

1846

No.	Design	Description	Unused	Used
15L6	L32	(2c) **black**	—	125.00
		On cover		*500.00*

Cancellations on Nos. 15L4-15L6: Black dot pattern. Black cross. Red "PAID".

Dangerous counterfeits exist of Nos. 15L3-15L6.

L33

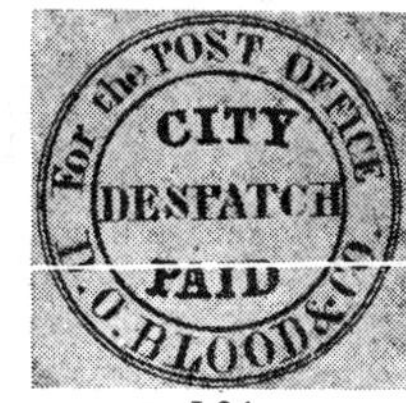

L34

L35

1846-47

No.	Design	Description	Unused	Used
15L7	L33	(1c) **black**	85.00	60.00
		On cover		300.00
15L8	L34	(1c) **black**	60.00	40.00
		On cover		275.00
15L9	L35	(1c) **black**	40.00	30.00
		On cover		275.00
		Block of four		—

Values for Nos. 15L7-15L9 cut to shape are half of those quoted.

"On cover" listings of Nos. 15L7-15L9 are for stamps tied by government town postmarks, either Philadelphia, or rarely Baltimore.

L36

L37

1848

No.	Design	Description	Unused	Used
15L10	L36	**black & blue**	85.00	85.00
		On cover		*250.00*
15L11	L37	**black,** *pale green*	—	50.00
		On cover		*150.00*

Cancellation: Black grid.

L38

L39

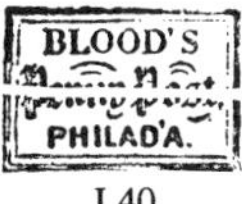

L40

L41

1848-54

No.	Design	Description	Unused	Used
15L12	L38	(1c) **gold,** *black,* glazed	*40.00*	25.00
		On cover		*100.00*
15L13	L39	1c **bronze,** *black,* glazed ('50)	7.50	6.00
		On cover		*75.00*
		On cover, acid tied		25.00
		Block of four	50.00	
15L14	L40	(1c) **bronze,** *lilac* ('54)	3.50	2.50
		On cover		*75.00*
		On cover, acid tied		25.00
		Block of four	35.00	
a.		Laid paper	—	—
15L15	L40	(1c) **blue & pink,** *bluish* ('53)	9.00	6.00
		On cover		*85.00*
		On cover, acid tied		40.00
		Block of four	60.00	
a.		Laid paper	—	—
15L16	L40	(1c) **bronze,** *black,* glazed ('54)	12.00	9.00
		On cover		*90.00*
		On cover, acid tied		40.00
15L17	L41	(1c) **bronze,** *black,* glazed	15.00	8.00
		On cover		*90.00*
		On cover, acid tied		40.00

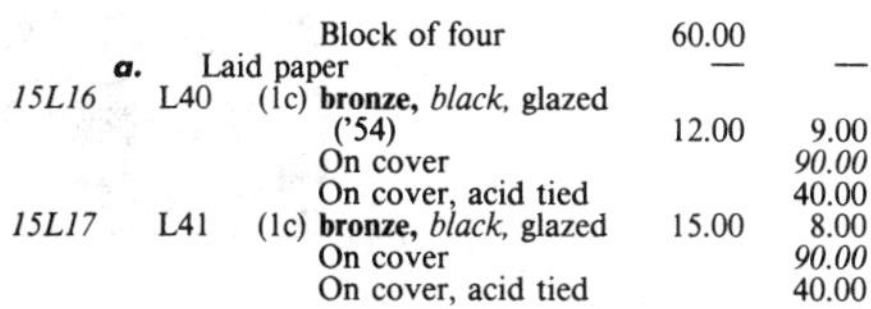

Cancellations: Black grid (No. 15L12, 15L17). Nos. 15L13-15L16 were almost always canceled with an acid which discolored both stamp and cover.

"On cover" values for Nos. 15L13-15L17 are minimum quotations for stamps tied by government postmarks to stampless covers or covers bearing contemporary government stamps, usually the 3c denomination. Covers with less usual frankings such as 5c or 10c 1847, or 1c or 10c 1851-57, merit substantial premiums.

III. Blood's Penny Post

Blood's Penny Post was acquired by the general manager, Charles Kochersperger, in 1855, when Daniel O. Blood died.

Henry Clay — L42

1855 **Engr. by Draper, Welsh & Co.**

No.	Design	Description	Unused	Used
15L18	L42	(1c) **black**	10.00	5.00
		On cover		75.00
		Block of four	60.00	

Cancellations: Black circular "Blood's Penny Post". Black "1" in frame. Red "1" in frame.

ENVELOPES

L43

L44

1850-60 **Embossed**

No.	Design	Description	Unused	Used
15LU1	L43	**red,** *white*	30.00	50.00
a.		pink, *white*		50.00
b.		Impressed on U.S. Env. #U9		200.00
15LU2	L43	**red,** *buff*	—	65.00
15LU3	L44	**red,** *white*	30.00	45.00
15LU4	L44	**red,** *buff*	30,00	45.00

L45

No.	Design	Description	Unused	Used
15LU5	L45	**red,** *white*	20.00	50.00
		Used with 3c No. 11		125.00
a.		Impressed on U.S. Env. #U7		175.00
b.		Impressed on U.S. Env. #U9		175.00
c.		Impressed on U.S. Env. #U1		250.00
d.		Impressed on U.S. Env. #U3		—
e.		Impressed on U.S. Env. #U2		200.00
15LU6	L45	**red,** *amber*	20.00	30.00
15LU6A	L45	**red,** *buff*		65.00
		Used with 10c No. 2		—
b.		red, *brown*		—

Laid Paper

No.	Design	Description	Unused	Used
15LU7	L45	**red,** *white*	20.00	60.00
15LU8	L45	**red,** *amber*	20.00	60.00
		Used with 3c No. 25		125.00
15LU9	L45	**red,** *buff*	20.00	60.00
15LU10	L45	**red,** *blue*	*200.00*	*200.00*

Nos. 15LU1-15LU9 exist in several envelope sizes.

Cancellations: Black grid (Nos. 15LU1-15LU4). Black company circle (2 sizes and types). When on government envelope, the Blood stamp was often left uncanceled.

Bouton's Post, New York, N.Y.
I. Franklin City Despatch Post

Organized by John R. Bouton

L46

1847		**Glazed Surface Paper**		**Typo.**
16L1	L46	(2c) **black,** *green*	500.00	
a.		"Bouton" in blk. ms. vert. at side	500.00	

II. Bouton's Manhattan Express

Acquired from William V. Barr

L47

1847				**Typo.**
17L1	L47	2c **black,** *pink*	350.00	
		Cut to shape	80.00	

III. Bouton's City Dispatch Post

(Sold to Swart's in 1849.)

Corner Leaves — L48

Corner Dots — L49

Design: Zachary Taylor

1848				**Litho.**
18L1	L48	2c **black**	—	150.00
		On cover		600.00
18L2	L49	2c **black,** *gray blue*	125.00	100.00
		On cover		550.00

Cancellations on Nos. 18L1-18L2: Red "PAID BOUTON".

Boyce's City Express Post, New York, N.Y.

L50

Center background has 17 parallel lines

1852		**Glazed Surface Paper**		**Typo.**
19L1	L50	2c **black,** *green*	350.00	300.00
		On cover		*1,250.*

Boyd's City Express, New York, N.Y.

Boyd's City Express, as a post, was established by John T. Boyd, on June 17, 1844. In 1860 the post was briefly operated by John T. Boyd, Jr., under whose management No. 20L15 was issued. For about six months in 1860 the post was suspended. It was then sold to William and Mary Blackham who resumed operation on Dec. 24, 1860. The Blackham issues began with No. 20L16. Boyd's had arrangements to handle local delivery mail for Pomeroy, Letter Express, Brooklyn City Express Post, Staten Island Express Post and possibly others.

L51 (Type I)

Types I to VI, IX and X have a rectangular frame of fine lines surrounding the design.

1844		**Glazed Surface Paper**		**Litho.**
20L1	L51	2c **black,** *green,* type I		200.00
		On cover		*600.00*

Cancellation: Red "FREE".

L52 (Type II)

1844		**Plain background. Map on globe.**		
20L2	L52	2c **black,** *yellow green,* type II		75.00
		On cover		*150.00*

Cancellation: Red "FREE".

L53 (Type III)

1845		**Plain background. Only globe shaded.**		
20L3	L53	2c **black,** *bluish green,* type III	—	95.00
		On cover		*150.00*

Cancellation: Red "FREE".

L54 (Type IV)

1845

Inner oval frame of two thin lines. Netted background, showing but faintly on late impressions.

20L4	L54	2c **black,** *green,* type IV	10.00	10.00
		On cover		75.00
		On cover with 5c #1		1,000.
		Double transfer		30.00
		Diagonal half used as 1c on cover		—

Cancellations: Red "FREE". Black grid.

1847				
20L5	L54	2c **gold,** *cream,* type IV	60.00	

Types IV to IX (except No. 20L23) were also obtainable die cut. An extra charge was made for such stamps. In general, genuine Boyd die-cuts sell for 75% of rectangular cut copies. Stamps hand cut to shape are worth much less.

L55 (Type V)

1848

No period after "CENTS". Inner oval frame has heavy inner line.

20L7	L55	2c **black,** *green,* type V (glazed)	5.00	8.00
		On cover		75.00
		Block of four	25.00	
a.		2c **black,** *yellow green,* type V		8.00
		On cover		85.00

Cancellation: Black grid.

No. 20L7a is on unglazed surface-colored paper.

L56 (Type VI)

Period after "CENTS." Inner frame as in type V.

1852				**Litho.**
20L8	L56	2c **black,** *green,* type VI	15.00	20.00
		On cover		*100.00*
		Vert. strip of 3 on cover		*300.00*
20L9	L56	2c **gold,** type VI	8.00	20.00
		On cover		*100.00*
		Block of four	35.00	

Cancellations on Nos. 20L8-20L9: Black cork. Black "PAID J.T.B."

No. 20L8 was reprinted in 1862 on unglazed paper, and about 1880 on glazed paper without rectangular frame.

L57 (Type VII)

1854

Period after "CENTS." Inner oval frame has heavy outer line. Eagle's tail pointed. Upper part of "2" open, with heavy downstroke at left shorter than one at right. "2C" closer than "T2".

20L10	L57	2c **black,** *green,* type VII	20.00	15.00
		On cover		100.00

Cancellation: Black "PAID J.T.B."

L58 (Type VIII)

1856		**Unglazed Paper Colored Through**		**Typo.**

Outer oval frame of three lines, outermost heavy. Solid background.

20L11	L58	2c **black,** *olive green,* type VIII	*20.00*	15.00
		On cover		*100.00*
1857				
20L12	L58	2c **brick red,** *white,* type VIII	17.50	17.50
		On cover		*100.00*
20L13	L58	2c **dull orange,** *white,* type VIII	22.50	22.50
		On cover		*110.00*

Cancellation on Nos. 20L11-20L13: Black "PAID J.T.B.'

Nos. 20L11-20L13 were reprinted in the 1880s for sale to collectors. They were printed from a new small plate of 25 on lighter weight paper and in colors of ink and paper lighter than the originals.

L59 (Type IX)

1857		**Glazed Surface Paper**		**Litho.**

Similar to type VII, but eagle's tail square. Upper part of "2" closed (in well printed specimens) forming a symmetrical "o" with downstrokes equal. "T2" closer than "2C".

20L14	L59	2c **black,** *green,* type IX	6.00	5.00
		On cover		100.00
		Pair on cover		—
		Block of four	30.00	
a.		Serrate perf.		—

The serrate perf. is probably of private origin.

No. 20L15 was made by altering the stone of type IX, and many traces of the "S" of "CENTS" remain.

1860

20L15	L59	1c **black,** *green,* type IX	1.00	15.00
		On cover		*100.00*
		Block of four	5.00	
a.		"CENTS" instead of "CENT"	—	—

Cancellation on Nos. 20L14-20L15: Black "PAID J.T.B."

(Type X) — L60

Center dots before "POST" and after "CENTS".

1860

20L16	L60	2c **black,** *red,* type X	5.00	7.00
		On cover		100.00
		Block of four	25.00	
a.		Tete beche pair	25.00	
20L17	L60	1c **black,** *lilac,* type X	5.00	7.00
		On cover		125.00
		Block of four	25.00	
a.		"CENTS" instead of "CENT"	15.00	20.00
		Two on cover (No. 20L17a)		—
b.		Tete beche pair	35.00	
c.		"1" inverted		—
20L18	L60	1c **black,** *blue gray,* type X	5.00	10.00
		On cover		125.00
		Block of four	25.00	
a.		"CENTS" instead of "CENT"	15.00	20.00
a.		On cover		200.00
b.		Tete beche pair	35.00	

Cancellations on Nos. 20L16-20L18: Black company oval. Black company circle. Black "PAID" in circle.

1861

20L19	L60	2c **gold,** type X	60.00	
		Block of four	—	
a.		Tete beche pair	—	
20L20	L60	2c **gold,** *green,* type X	15.00	
		Block of four	65.00	
a.		Tete beche pair	50.00	
20L21	L60	2c **gold,** *dark blue,* type X	5.00	
		On cover		*100.00*
		Block of four	22.50	
a.		Tete beche pair	25.00	
20L22	L60	2c **gold,** *crimson,* type X	12.00	
		Block of four	50.00	
a.		Tete beche pair	40.00	

1863 **Typo.**

20L23	L58	2c **black,** *red,* type VIII	5.00	10.00
		On cover		100.00
		Block of four	25.00	
a.		Tete beche pair	35.00	

Cancellations: Black company. Black "PAID" in circle.

No. 20L23 was reprinted from a new stone on paper of normal color. See note after No. 20L13.

a

(Type XI) — L61

No period or center dots.

1867 **Typo.**

20L24	L61	1c **black,** *lilac,* type XI	6.00	12.00
		On cover		*100.00*
		Block of four	30.00	
20L25	L61	1c **black,** *blue,* type XI	4.00	10.00
		On cover		*100.00*
		Block of four	20.00	

Cancellation on Nos. 20L24-20L25: Black company.

Boyd's City Dispatch

(Change in Name)

See the "Information for Collectors" section at beginning of catalogue for an explanation of paper types, watermarks and grills.

L62

1874 **Glazed Surface Paper** **Litho.**

20L26	L62	2c **light blue**	15.00	12.00
		On cover		100.00
		Block of four	70.00	

The 2c black on wove paper, type L62, is a cut-out from the Bank Notices envelope, No. 20LU45.

Surface Colored Paper

20L28	L62	2c **black,** *red*	*50.00*	
20L29	L62	2c **blue,** *red*	*50.00*	

The adhesives of type L62 were made from the third state of the envelope die.

Nos. 20L28 and 20L29 are color trials, possibly used postally.

L63

L64

1876 **Litho.**

20L30	L63	2c **lilac,** *roseate*		—

Laid Paper

20L31	L63	2c **lilac,** *roseate*		—

Perf. 12½

20L32	L63	2c **lilac,** *roseate*	10.00	15.00
		On cover		*150.00*
a.		2c lilac, *grayish*	10.00	15.00

Laid Paper

20L33	L63	2c **lilac,** *roseate*		10.00
a.		2c lilac, *grayish*		12.00

Glazed Surface Paper

20L34	L63	2c **brown,** *yellow*	15.00	15.00
a.		Imperf. horizontally	—	

1877 **Laid Paper** ***Perf. 11, 12, 12½***

20L35	L64	(1c) **violet,** *lilac*	10.00	10.00
		On cover		*150.00*
a.		(1c) red lilac, *lilac*	10.00	10.00
b.		(1c) gray lilac, *lilac*	8.00	8.00
c.		Vert. pair, imperf. horiz.	*100.00*	
20L36	L64	(1c) **gray,** *roseate*	10.00	10.00
		On cover		*150.00*
a.		(1c) gray, *grayish*		10.00

Boyd's Dispatch

(Change in Name)

Mercury Series-Type I — L65

Printed in sheets of 100.
Inner frame line at bottom broken below foot of Mercury.
Printed by C.O. Jones.

1878 **Litho.** **Wove Paper** ***Imperf.***

20L37	L65	**black,** *pink*	*50.00*	*50.00*

Surface Colored Wove Paper

20L38	L65	**black,** *orange red*	*110.00*	*110.00*
20L39	L65	**black,** *crimson*	*110.00*	*110.00*

Laid Paper

20L40	L65	**black,** *salmon*	*150.00*	
20L41	L65	**black,** *lemon*	*150.00*	*150.00*
20L42	L65	**black,** *lilac pink*	*150.00*	

Nos. 20L37-20L42 are color trials, some of which may have been used postally.

Surface Colored Paper

Perf. 12

20L43	L65	**black,** *crimson*	20.00	20.00
		On cover		*100.00*
20L43A	L65	**black,** *orange red*	50.00	—

Wove Paper

Perf. 11, 11½, 12, 12½ and Compound

20L44	L65	**black,** *pink*	1.00	1.00
		On cover		*75.00*
a.		Horizontal pair, imperf. between	—	—

1879 ***Perf. 11, 11½, 12***

20L45	L65	**black,** *blue*	5.00	5.00
		On cover		85.00
20L46	L65	**blue,** *blue*	12.00	15.00
		On cover		*125.00*

1880 ***Perf. 11, 12, 13½***

20L47	L65	**black,** *lavender*	3.00	3.00
		On cover		*100.00*
20L48	L65	**blue,** *lavender*	—	—

1881 **Laid Paper** ***Perf. 12, 12½, 14***

20L49	L65	**black,** *pink*	—	
20L50	L65	**black,** *lilac pink*	4.00	4.00
		On cover		*100.00*

Mercury Series-Type II — L65a

No break in frame, the great toe raised, other toes touching line.
Printed by J. Gibson

1881 **Wove Paper** ***Perf. 12, 16 & Compound.***

20L51	L65a	**black,** *blue*	7.50	7.50
20L52	L65a	**black,** *pink*	—	—
		On cover		100.00

Laid Paper

20L53	L65a	**black,** *pink*	3.00	3.00
		On cover		100.00
20L54	L65a	**black,** *lilac pink*	4.00	4.00
		On cover		100.00

Mercury Series-Type III — L65b

No break in frame, the great toe touching.
Printed by the "Evening Post"

Perf. 10, 11½, 12, 16 & Compound.

1882 **Wove Paper**

20L55	L65b	**black,** *blue*	3.00	3.00
		On cover		100.00
20L56	L65b	**black,** *pink*	35	2.00
		On cover		100.00
		Block of 4	1.75	

Cancellation on Nos. 20L37-20L56: Purple company.

Boyd's City Post

ENVELOPES

L66

Imprinted in upper right corner.
Used envelopes show Boyd's handstamps.

1864 **Laid Paper** **Embossed**

20LU1	L66	**red**	40.00	
20LU2	L66	**red,** *amber*	35.00	
20LU3	L66	**red,** *yellow*	—	—

20LU4	L66	**blue**	60.00	—
20LU5	L66	**blue,** *amber*	50.00	
20LU6	L66	**blue,** *yellow*	—	—

Several shades of red and blue.

20LU7	L66	**deep blue,** *orange*	—	*350.00*

Reprinted on pieces of white, fawn and oriental buff papers, vertically, horizontally or diagonally laid.

Wove Paper

20LU8	L66	**red,** *cream*	65.00	
20LU9	L66	**red,** *orange*	—	*150.00*
20LU10	L66	**blue,** *cream*	65.00	*150.00*
20LU11	L66	**blue,** *orange*	—	
20LU11A	L66	**blue,** *amber*	—	1,250.

Boyd's City Dispatch

L67 (A)

L67 (B)

A. First state of die. Lines and letters sharp and clear. Trefoils at sides pointed and blotchy, middle leaf at right long and thick at end.

B. Second state. Lines and letters thick and rough. Lobes of trefoils rounded and definitely outlined. Stamp impressed normally in upper right corner of envelope; in second state rarely in upper left.

1867 **Laid Paper** **Typo.**

20LU12	L67	2c **red** (A) (B)	25.00	40.00
20LU13	L67	2c **red,** *amber* (B)	25.00	12.00
20LU14	L67	2c **red,** *cream* (B)	25.00	40.00
20LU15	L67	2c **red,** *yellow* (A) (B)	25.00	50.00
20LU16	L67	2c **red,** *orange* (B)	30.00	50.00

Wove Paper

20LU17	L67	2c **red** (A) (B)	25.00	—
20LU18	L67	2c **red,** *cream* (A) (B)	25.00	40.00
20LU19	L67	2c **red,** *yellow* (A)	25.00	40.00
20LU20	L67	2c **red,** *orange* (A)	30.00	50.00
20LU21	L67	2c **red,** *blue* (A) (B)	50.00	75.00

Design as Type L62

First state of die, showing traces of old address.

1874

Laid Paper

20LU22	L62	2c **red,** *amber*		—
20LU23	L62	2c **red,** *cream*	30.00	30.00

Wove Paper

20LU24	L62	2c **red,** *amber*		—
20LU25	L62	2c **red,** *yellow*		30.00

Second state of die, no traces of address.

1875

Laid Paper

20LU26	L62	2c **red,** *amber*		—
20LU27	L62	2c **red,** *cream*	30.00	30.00

Wove Paper

20LU28	L62	2c **red,** *amber*		—

L68

L69

1877

Laid Paper

20LU29	L68	2c **red,** *amber*		90.00

Stamp usually impressed in upper left corner of envelope.

1878

Laid Paper

20LU30	L69	(1c) **red,** *amber*	25.00	45.00

Wove Paper

20LU31	L69	(1c) **red,** *cream*		—
20LU32	L69	(1c) **red,** *yellow*		—

Boyd's Dispatch

L70

Mercury Series-Type IV — L71

Shading omitted in banner. No period after "Dispatch." Short line extends to left from great toe.

1878

Laid Paper

20LU33	L70	**black**	25.00	60.00
20LU34	L70	**black,** *amber*		45.00
20LU35	L70	**black,** *cream*	30.00	60.00
20LU36	L70	**red**		30.00
20LU37	L70	**red,** *amber*	20.00	25.00
20LU38	L70	**red,** *cream*	20.00	45.00
20LU39	L70	**red,** *yellow green*		—
20LU40	L70	**red,** *orange*		80.00
20LU41	L70	**red,** *fawn*		—

Wove Paper

20LU42	L70	**red**	15.00	

Mercury Series-Type V

Colorless crosshatching lines in frame work

1878

Laid Paper

20LU43	L71	**red**		—
20LU44	L71	**red,** *cream*	6.00	20.00

BANK NOTICES

IMPORTERS' AND TRADERS' NATIONAL BANK

1874

Thin to Thick White Wove Paper

Incomplete Year Date on Card

20LU45	L62	2c **black**	40.00

1875-83

Complete Year Date on Card

20LU46	L62	2c **black**	40.00
20LU47	L63	2c **black** ('76-'77)	40.00
20LU48	L69	2c **black** ('78)	40.00
20LU49	L70	2c **black** ('79)	40.00
20LU50	L70	2c **black** ('80)	40.00
20LU51	L71	2c **black** ('81)	—
20LU52	L71	2c **black** ('82)	—
20LU53	L71	2c **black** ('83)	—

NATIONAL PARK BANK

1880

20LU54	L71	**black,** 120x65mm	—

The Bank Notices are in the class of postal cards. No postmarks or cancellations were used on Bank Notices.

Bradway's Despatch, Millville, N.J.

Operated by Isaac Bradway

L72

1857 **Typo.**

21L1	L72	**gold,** *lilac*	*750.00*	*750.00*

Brady & Co., New York, N.Y.

Operated by Abner S. Brady at 97 Duane St. Successor to Clark & Co.

L73

1857 **Typo.**

22L1	L73	1c **red,** *yellow*	175.00	150.00
		On cover		1,000.

Cancellations: Blue boxed "PAID". Blue company oval. *Reprints exist.*

Brady & Co.s Penny Post, Chicago, Ill.

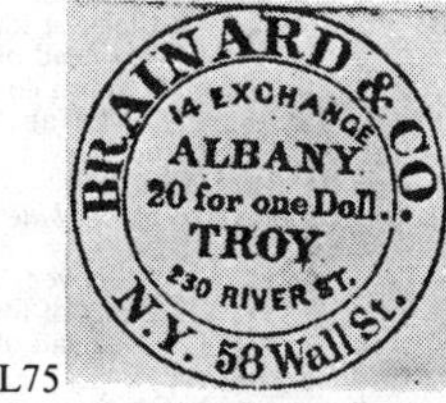

L74

1860(?) **Litho.**

23L1	L74	1c **violet**	*100.00*

The authenticity of this stamp has not been fully established.

Brainard & Co.

Established by Charles H. Brainard in 1844, operating between New York, Albany and Troy, Exchanged mail with Hale & Co. by whom Brainard had been employed.

L75

1844 **Typo.**

24L1	L75	**black**	*100.00*	*125.00*
24L2	L75	**blue**	*150.00*	*175.00*
		On Cover		350.00

Nos. 21L1-24L2 cut to shape are one half of values quoted.

Brigg's Despatch, Philadelphia, Pa.

Established by George W. Briggs

L76

L77

1847

25L1	L76	(2c) **black,** *yellow buff*	*500.00*
25L2	L76	(2c) **black,** *blue,* cut to shape	*1,000.*

1848

25L4	L77	(2c) **gold,** *yellow,* glazed		*400.00*
25L5	L77	(2c) **gold,** *black,* glazed		*400.00*
25L6	L77	(2c) **gold,** *pink*	—	

Handstamps formerly illustrated as types L78 and L79 are included in the section "Local Handstamped Covers" at the end of the Local Stamp listings. They were used as postmarks and there is no evidence that any prepaid handstamped envelopes or letter sheets were ever sold.

Broadway Post Office, New York, N.Y.

Started by James C. Harriott in 1848. Sold to Dunham & Lockwood in 1855.

L80

1849(?) **Typo.**

26L1	L80	(1c) **gold,** *black,* glazed	300.00	250.00
		Cut to shape		150.00
		On cover		—
		Pair on cover		*2,500.*

1851(?)

No.	Design	Description	Unused	Used
26L2	L80	(1c) **black**	45.00	60.00
		On cover		750.00
		On cover with 3c #11		*1,250.*
		Pair on cover		*2,000.*
		Block of four	300.00	

Cancellation: Black oval "Broadway City Express Post-Office 2 Cts".

Bronson & Forbes' City Express Post, Chicago, Ill.

Operated by W.H. Bronson and G.F. Forbes.

L81

1855 **Typo.**

No.	Design	Description	Unused	Used
27L1	L81	**black,** *green*	100.00	110.00
		On cover		*2,500.*
27L2	L81	**black,** *lilac*		*750.00*

Cancellation: Black circle "Bronson & Forbes' City Express Post" (2 types).

Brooklyn City Express Post, Brooklyn, N.Y.

According to the foremost students of local stamps, when this concern was organized its main asset was the business of Kidder's City Express Post, of which Isaac C. Snedeker was the proprietor.

L82

1855-64 **Glazed Surface Paper** **Typo.**

No.	Design	Description	Unused	Used
28L1	L82	1c **black,** *blue* (shades)	15.00	30.00
		On cover		*175.00*
a.		Tete beche pair	50.00	
28L2	L82	1c **black,** *green*	15.00	30.00
		On cover		*175.00*
a.		Tete beche pair	50.00	

L83

No. 28L5 has frame (dividing) lines around design.

No.	Design	Description	Unused	Used
28L3	L83	2c **black,** *crimson*	—	40.00
		On cover		130.00
28L4	L83	2c **black,** *pink*	15.00	30.00
		On cover		*200.00*
		Block of four	75.00	
a.		Tete beche pair	50.00	
28L5	L83	2c **black,** *dark blue*	40.00	30.00
		On cover		*175.00*
		Block of four	*225.00*	
28L6	L83	2c **black,** *orange*	—	—
		On cover		—
a.		Tete beche pair	150.00	
		Unsurfaced Paper Colored Through		
28L7	L83	2c **black,** *pink*	*100.00*	

Cancellation: Black ring.

Reprints exist of Nos. 28L1-28L4, 28L6.

Browne & Co.'s City Post Office, Cincinnati, Ohio

Operated by John W.S. Browne

L84

L85

1852-55 **Litho.**

No.	Design	Description	Unused	Used
29L1	L84	1c **black** (Brown & Co.)	85.00	50.00
		On cover		*850.00*
		On cover with 3c #11		*1,500.*
		Pair	*350.00*	
29L2	L85	2c **black** (Browne & Co.)	120.00	100.00
		On cover		*1,000.*
		On cover with 3c #11		*1,500.*
		Pair	*500.00*	

Cancellations: Black, blue or red circle "City Post*". Red, bright blue or dull blue circle "Browne & Co. City Post Paid".

Browne's Easton Despatch, Easton, Pa.

Established by William J. Browne

L87

L88

1857 **Glazed Surface Paper** **Typeset**

No.	Design	Description	Unused	Used
30L1	L87	2c **black,** *red*	—	*500.00*
30L2	L88	2c **black,** *red*	—	*600.00*

George Washington — L89

Wove Paper **Engr.**

No.	Design	Description	Unused	Used
30L3	L89	2c **black**	150.00	*350.00*
		Pair	*375.00*	
		Block of four	*1,000.*	

Cancellation on No. 30L3: Black oval "Browne's Despatch Easton Pa."

Brown's City Post, New York, N.Y.

Established by stamp dealer William P. Brown for philatelic purposes.

L86

1876 **Glazed Surface Paper** **Typo.**

No.	Design	Description	Unused	Used
31L1	L86	1c **black,** *bright red*	45.00	60.00
		On cover		*400.00*
31L2	L86	1c **black,** *yellow*	45.00	60.00
		On cover		*400.00*
31L3	L86	1c **black,** *green*	45.00	60.00
		On cover		400.00
31L4	L86	1c **black,** *violet*	45.00	60.00
		On cover		*400.00*
31L5	L86	1c **black,** *vermilion*	45.00	60.00
		On cover		*400.00*

Cancellation: Black circle "Brown's Despatch Paid".

Bury's City Post, New York, N.Y.

L90

L91

1857 **Embossed without color**

No.	Design	Description	Unused	Used
32L1	L90	1c *blue*		*1,250.*
		Handstamped		
32L2	L91	**black,** *blue*		*200.00*

Bush's Brooklyn City Express, Brooklyn, N.Y.

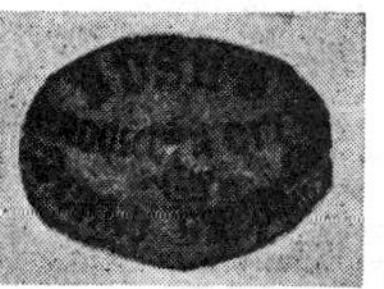

L91a

1848(?) **Cut to shape** **Handstamped**

No.	Design	Description	Unused	Used
157L1	L91a	2c **red,** *green,* glazed		*1,500.*

See Bush handstamp in Local Handstamped Covers section.

California City Letter Express Co., San Francisco, Calif.

Organized by J.W. Hoag, proprietor of the Contra-Costa Express, for local delivery. Known also as the California Letter Express Co.

L92

L93

1862-66 **Typeset**

No.	Design	Description	Unused	Used
33L1	L92	10c **red**	—	*750.00*
33L2	L92	10c **blue**	—	*1,000.*
33L3	L92	10c **green**	—	—
33L4	L93	10c **red**	—	—
33L5	L93	10c **blue**	—	—
33L6	L93	10c **green**	*1,000.*	*750.00*
33L7	L93	10c **red** (no side ornaments, "Hoogs & Madison's" in one line)		*1,000.*
33L8	L93	10c **blue** (Same as #33L7)		*1,000.*

California Penny Post Co.

Established in 1855 by J. P. Goodwin and partners. At first confined its operations to San Francisco, Sacramento, Stockton and Marysville, but branches were soon established at Benicia, Coloma, Nevada, Grass Valley and Mokelumne Hill. Operation was principally that of a city delivery post, as it transported mail to the General Post Office and received mail for local delivery. Most of the business of this post was done by means of prepaid envelopes

L94

L95

1855 **Litho.**

34L1 L94 2c **blue** 200.00 250.00
On cover *1,500.*
Block of four *900.00*
34L1A L95 3c **blue** *600.00*
34L2 L95 5c **blue** 60.00 125.00
On cover *1,000.*
Block of four 300.00
34L3 L95 10c **blue** 225.00 —
On cover *3,000.*

Cancellation: Blue circle "Penny Post Co."

L96

34L4 L96 5c **blue** 300.00 325.00
On cover *2,000.*
Strip of three 1,000.

ENVELOPES

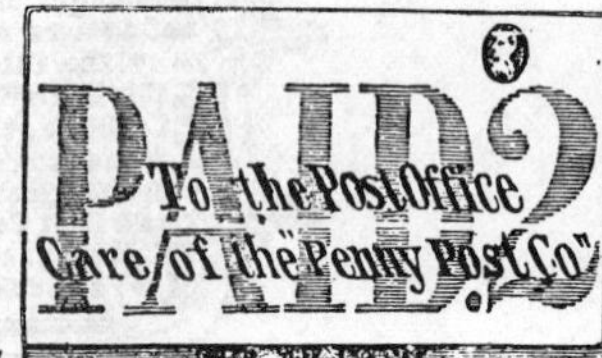

L97

(Illustration reduced size.)

1855-59

34LU1 L97 2c **black, *white*** 150.00 *750.00*
a. Impressed on 3c U.S. env. No. U10 200.00 *750.00*
34LU2 L97 5c **blue, *blue*** 120.00 —
34LU3 L97 5c **black, *buff*** 120.00 —
a. Impressed on 3c U.S. env. No. U10 *750.00*
34LU4 L97 7c **black, *buff*** 120.00 —

L98

34LU6 L98 7c **vermilion** on 3c U.S. env. No. U9 90.00 500.00
34LU7 L98 7c **vermilion** on 3c U.S. env. No. U10 90.00 600.00

PENNY-POSTAGE PAID, 5.

L98A

34LU8 L98A 5c **black, *white*** 100.00 400.00
34LU9 L98A 5c **black, *buff*** 100.00 400.00
a. Impressed on 3c U.S. env. No. U10 600.00
34LU10 L98A 7c **black, *white*** 100.00 400.00
a. Impressed on 3c U.S. env. No U10 *750.00*
34LU11 L98A 7c **black, *buff*** 400.00
a. Impressed on 3c U.S. env. No U10 1,000.
34LU11C L98A **black,** *buff,* "Collect Penny Postage" (no denomination) 750.00

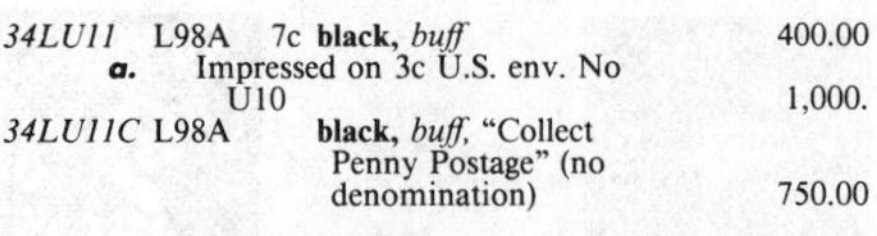

L98B

34LU11B L98B 7c **black** on 3c U.S. env. No. U10 850.00
34LU12 L98B 7c **black** on 3c U.S. env. No. U9 600.00

OCEAN PENNY POSTAGE.
PAID 5.

L98C

34LU13 L98C 5c **black, *buff*** *750.00*

L98D

34LU13A L98D 5c **black, *buff*** —
34LU14 L98D 7c **black, *buff*** 100.00 *2,500.*
34LU15 L98D 7c **black** on 3c U.S. env. No. U9 125.00 *2,500.*

The non-government envelopes of types L97, L98A, L98C and L98D bear either 1c No. 9 or 3c No. 11 adhesives. These adhesives are normally canceled with the government postmark of the town of original mailing. Values are for covers of this kind. The U.S. adhesives are seldom canceled with the Penny Post cancellation. When they are, the cover sells for more.

Carnes' City Letter Express, San Francisco, Calif.

Established by George A. Carnes, former P.O. clerk.

L99

L100

1864 **Typo.**

35L1 L99 (5c) **rose** 30.00 50.00
On cover *1,500.*

Cancellations: Black dots. Blue dots. Blue "Paid". Blue oval "Wm. A. Frey".

Overprinted "X" in Blue

35L2 L99 10c **rose** 40.00

Litho.

35L3 L100 5c **bronze** 15.00
a. Tete beche pair 40.00
35L4 L100 5c **gold** 15.00
a. Tete beche pair 40.00
35L5 L100 5c **silver** 15.00
a. Tete beche pair 40.00
35L6 L100 5c **black** 15.00
a. Tete beche pair 40.00
35L7 L100 5c **blue** 15.00
a. Tete beche pair 40.00
35L8 L100 5c **red** 15.00
a. Tete beche pair 40.00

Printed in panes of 15 (3x5), the last two horizontal rows being tete beche.

G. Carter's Despatch, Philadelphia, Pa.

Operated by George Carter

L101

1849-51

36L1 L101 2c **black** — 50.00
On cover *150.00*
a. Ribbed paper — 75.00

No. 36L1 exists on paper with a blue, green, red or maroon wash. The origin and status are unclear.

Cancellation: Black circle "Carter's Despatch".

ENVELOPE

L102

36LU1 L102 **blue, *buff*** *500.00*
Cut to shape *150.00*
On cover with 3c No. 10 *2,500.*
On cover with 3c No. 11 *750.00*

Cheever & Towle, Boston, Mass.

Sold to George H. Barker in 1851

L104

1849(?)

37L1 L104 2c **blue** *200.00* *200.00*
On cover *750.00*

Cancellation: Red oval "Towle's City Despatch Post 7 State Street".

Chicago Penny Post, Chicago, Ill.

L105

1862 **Typo.**

38L1 L105 (1c) **orange brown** 185.00 350.00
On cover *3,000.*

Cancellation: Black circle "Chicago Penny Post A. E. Cooke Sup't".

Cincinnati City Delivery, Cincinnati, Ohio

Operated by J. Staley, who also conducted the St. Louis City Delivery Co. He established the Cincinnati post in January, 1883. The government suppressed both posts after a few weeks. Of the 25,000 Cincinnati City Delivery stamps printed, about 5,000 were sold for postal use. The remainders, both canceled and uncanceled, were sold to collectors.

L106

1883 **Typo.** ***Perf. 11***

39L1	L106	(1c) **carmine**	2.00	*20.00*
a.		Imperf., pair	—	—

Cancellation: Purple target.

City Despatch Post, New York, N.Y.

The City Despatch Post was started Feb. 1, 1842, by Alexander M. Greig. Greig's Post extended to 23rd St. Its operations were explained in a circular which throws light on the operations of all Local Posts:

New York City Despatch Post, Principal Office, 46 William Street.

"The necessity of a medium of communication by letter from one part of the city to another being universally admitted, and the Penny Post, lately existing having been relinquished, the opportunity has been embraced to reorganize it under an entirely new proprietory and management, and upon a much more comprehensive basis, by which Despatch, Punctuality and Security-those essential elements of success-may at once be attained, and the inconvenience now experienced be entirely removed."

"*** Branch Offices-Letter boxes are placed throughout every part of the city in conspicuous places; and all letters deposited therein not exceeding two ounces in weight, will be punctually delivered three times a day *** at three cents each."

"*** Post-Paid Letters.-Letters which the writers desire to send free, must have a free stamp affixed to them. An ornamental stamp has been prepared for this purpose *** 36 cents per dozen or 2 dolls. 50c per hundred. ***"

"No money must be put in boxes. All letters intended to be sent forward to the General Post Office for the inland mails must have a free stamp affixed to them."

"Unpaid Letters.-Letters not having a free stamp will be charged three cents, payable by the party to whom they are addressed, on delivery."

"Registry and Despatch.-A Registry will be kept for letters which it may be wished to place under special charge. Free stamps must be affixed for such letters for the ordinary postage, and three cents additional be paid (or an additional fee stamp be affixed), for the Registration."

The City Despatch Post ceased to operate as a private carrier on August 15, 1842. It was replaced by the "United States City Despatch Post" which began operation on August 16, 1842, as a Government carrier.

No. 40L1 was issued by Alexander M. Greig; No. 40L2 and possibly No. 40L3 by Abraham Mead; Nos. 40L4-40L8 probably by Charles Cole.

L106a

Cancellation

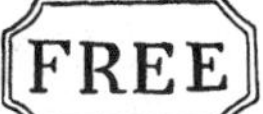

Plate of 42 (6x7) subjects

The City Despatch Post was started Feb. 1, 1842, by Alexander M. Greig. Greig's Post extended to 23rd St. Its operations were explained in a circular which throws light on the operations of all Local Posts: This was the first adhesive stamp used in the United States. This stamp was also used as a carrier stamp. See No. 6LB1.

Engraved by Rawdon, Wright & Hatch

1842, Feb. 1

40L1	L106a	3c	**black,** *grayish*	350.00	250.00
			On cover		700.00
			First day cover		10,000.
			Pair	750.00	
			Block of four	1,600.	

Cancellations: Red framed "FREE" (see illustration above). Red circle "City Despatch Post" (2 types).

1847

Glazed Surface Paper

40L2	L106a	2c	**black,** *green*	*100.00*	60.00
			On cover		150.00
40L3	L106a	2c	**black,***pink*		*600.00*
			On cover		*1,750.*

Cancellations: Red framed "FREE". Black framed "FREE". Red circle "City Despatch Post".

Die reprints of No. 40L1 were made in 1892 on various colored papers.

L107

Similar to L106a with "CC" at sides.

1847-50

40L4	L107	2c	**black,** *green*	350.00	90.00
			On cover		225.00
a.			"C" at right inverted		200.00
b.			"C" at left sideways		200.00
c.			"C" at right only		—
40L5	L107	2c	**black,** *grayish*		165.00
			On cover		650.00
a.			"C" at right inverted		250.00
b.			"C" at left sideways		250.00
c.			"C" in ms. between "Two" and "Cents"		200.00
40L6	L107	2c	**black,** *vermilion*	450.00	175.00
			On cover		500.00
a.			"C" at right inverted		250.00
b.			"C" at left sideways		250.00
40L7	L107	2c	**black,** *yellow*		*1,000.*
40L8	L107	2c	**black,** *buff*		*650.00*
a.			"C" at right inverted		*750.00*
b.			"C" at left sideways		*750.00*

Cancellations: Red framed "FREE". Black framed "FREE". Black "PAID". Red "PAID". Red circle company. Black grid of 4 short parallel bars.

City Dispatch, New York, N.Y.

L107a

1846 **Typo.**

160L1	L107a	2c	**red**	*800.00*	*750.00*
			On cover		*1,750.*
			Pair	2,000.	

Cancellation: Red "PAID".

City Dispatch, Philadelphia, Pa.

Justice — L108

1860 **Thick to Thin Wove Paper** **Litho.**

41L1	L108	1c	**black**	5.00	20.00
			On cover		*350.00*
			Block of four	25.00	

Cancellations: Black circle "Penny Post Philada." Black circled grid of X's.

City Dispatch, St. Louis, Mo.

L109

Initials in black ms.

1851 **Litho.**

42L1	L109	2c	**black,** *blue*	*1,750.*

City Dispatch Post Office, New Orleans, La.

Stamps sold at 5c each, or 30 for $1.

L110

1847 **Glazed Surface Paper** **Typeset**

43L1	L110	(5c)	**black,** *green*	*1,000.*	
			On cover		—
43L2	L110	(5c)	**black,** *pink*	*1,000.*	
			On cover		—

City Express Post, Philadelphia, Pa.

L111

L112

184-(?) **Typeset**

44L1	L111	2c	**black**	*1,000.*
44L2	L112	(2c)	**black,** *pink*	*500.00*
44L3	L112	(2c)	**red,** *yellow*	*3,000.*

City Letter Express Mail, Newark, N.J.

Began business under the management of Augustus Peck at a time when there was no free city delivery in Newark.

L113

1856 **Litho.**

45L1	L113	1c	**red**	*125.00*	*200.00*
			Cut to shape		65.00
			On cover		*500.00*
45L2	L113	2c	**red** (on cover)		—

On No. 45L2, the inscription reads "City Letter/Express/City Delivery" in three lines across the top.

City Mail Co., New York, N.Y.

There is evidence that Overton & Co. owned this post.

L114

1845

46L1	L114	(2c)	**black,** *grayish*	*1,500.*	*1,000.*
			On cover		*1,500.*

Cancellation: Red "PAID".

City One Cent Dispatch, Baltimore, Md.

L115

1851
47L1 L115 1c **black,** *pink* (on cover) —

Clark & Co., New York, N.Y.

(See Brady & Co.)

L116

1857 **Typo.**
48L1 L116 1c **red,** *yellow* 150.00 150.00
On cover 750.00

Cancellation: Blue boxed "PAID".

Clark & Hall, St. Louis, Mo.

Established by William J. Clark and Charles F. Hall.

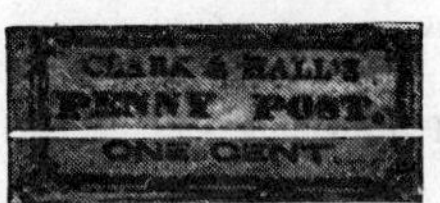

L117

Several varieties

1851 **Typeset**
49L1 L117 1c **black,** *pink* 750.00

Clarke's Circular Express, New York, N.Y.

Established by Marion M. Clarke

George Washington — L118

Impression handstamped through inked ribbon.
Cut squares from envelopes or wrappers.

1865-68(?)
50LU1 L118 **blue,** wove paper 350.00
a. diagonally laid paper —
50LU2 L118 **black,** diag. laid paper 350.00

Cancellation: Blue dated company circle.

Clinton's Penny Post, Philadelphia, Pa.

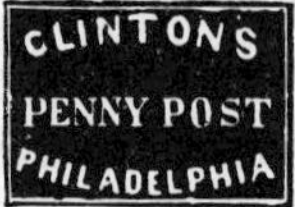

L118a

Typo.
161L1 L188a (1c) **black** —

Cook's Dispatch, Baltimore, Md.

Established by Isaac Cook

L119

1853
51L1 L119 (1c) **green,** *white* 500.00
On cover 3,000.

Cancellation: Red straight-line "I cook"

Cornwell's Madison Square Post Office, New York, N.Y.

Established by Daniel H. Cornwell. Sold to H.W. Bentley.

L120

1856 **Typo.**
52L1 L120 (1c) **red,** *blue* 75.00 —
52L2 L120 (1c) **red** 100.00 100.00
On cover 1,000.
Pair 250.00

Cancellation: Black oval "Cornwall's Madison Square Post Office". Covers also bear black boxed "Paid Swarts".

Cressman & Co.'s Penny Post, Philadelphia, Pa.

L121

1856

Glazed Surface Paper

53L1 L121 (1c) **gold,** *black* — 125.00
Pair 400.00
53L2 L121 (1c) **gold,** *lilac* 1,750.
On cover 3,750.

Cancellation: Acid. (See D.O. Blood & Co. Nos. 15L13-15L16.)

Crosby's City Post, New York, N.Y.

Established by Oliver H. Crosby. Stamps printed by J.W. Scott & Co.

L123

1870 **Typo.**

Printed in sheets 25 (5x5), imprint at left.

54L1 L123 2c **carmine** (shades) 1.00 25.00
On cover 250.00
Sheet of 25 30.00

Cancellation: Black oval "Crosby's City Post".

Cummings' City Post, New York, N.Y.

Established by A. H. Cummings.

L124

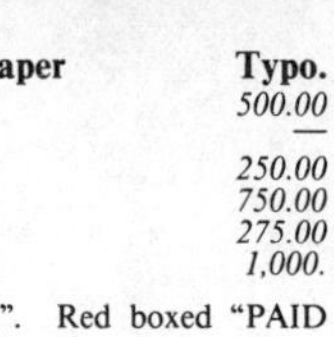

1844 **Glazed Surface Paper** **Typo.**
55L1 L124 2c **black,** *rose* 500.00
On cover —
55L2 L124 2c **black,** *green* 250.00
On cover 750.00
55L3 L124 2c **black,** *yellow* 275.00
On cover 1,000.

Cancellations: Red boxed "FREE". Red boxed "PAID AHC". Black cork (3 types).

L125

55L4 L125 2c **black,** *green* 750.00 750.00
55L5 L125 2c **black,** *olive* 750.00 750.00

L126

55L7 L126 2c **black,** *vermilion* 2,000.
On cover 3,500.

As L124, but "Cummings" erased on cliche

55L8 L124 2c **black,** *vermilion* 5,000.

Cutting's Despatch Post, Buffalo, N.Y.

Established by Thomas S. Cutting

L127

Cut to shape

1847

Glazed Surface Paper

56L1 L127 2c **black,** *vermilion* 2,500.

Davis's Penny Post, Baltimore, Md.

Established by William D. Davis and brother.

L128

1856 **Typeset**

Several varieties

57L1 L128 (1c) **black,** *lilac* 400.00
On cover 1,500.

Cancellation: Red company circle.

Deming's Penny Post, Frankford, Pa.

Established by Sidney Deming

L129

1854 **Litho.**
58L1 L129 (1c) **black,** *grayish* 750.00 750.00

Douglas' City Despatch, New York, N.Y.

Established by George H. Douglas

L130

L131

Printed in sheets of 25

1879 **Typo.** ***Perf. 11***

59L1	L130	(1c) **pink**	4.00	5.00
		On cover		150.00
59L2	L130	(2c) **blue**	4.00	5.00
a.		Imperf.	10.00	—
b.		Printed on both sides		—
59L3	L131	1c **vermilion**	3.50	8.00
		On cover		*100.00*
a.		Imperf.	40	—
59L4	L131	1c **orange**	5.00	8.00
59L5	L131	1c **blue**	8.00	10.00
		On cover		*100.00*
a		Imperf.	40	—
59L6	L131	1c **slate blue**	10.00	12.50
a.		Imperf.	75	—

Imperforates are believed to be remainders sold by the printer.

Dupuy & Schenck, New York, N.Y.

Established by Henry J. Dupuy and Jacob H. Schenck, formerly carriers for City Despatch Post and U. S. City Despatch Post.

Beehive — L132

1846-48 **Engr.**

60L1	L132	(1c) **black,** glazed paper	125.00	125.00
60L2	L132	(1c) **black,** *gray*	85.00	75.00
		On cover		*500.00*

Cancellation: Red "PAID".

Eagle City Post, Philadelphia, Pa.

Established by W. Stait, an employee of Adams' Express Co.

L133

Black "WS" manuscript control

1847 **Pelure Paper** **Typeset**

61L1	L133	(2c) **black,** *grayish*	*1,500.*	
		Cut to shape		*500.00*

L134

L135

Two types: 39 and 46 points around circle

1848 **Litho.**

61L2	L134	(2c) **black**	50.00	65.00
		On cover		*350.00*
		Block of four	225.00	
a.		Tete beche pair		175.00

Paper varies in thickness.

1850

61L3	L135	(1c) **red,** *bluish*	75.00	75.00
		On cover		*200.00*
61L4	L135	(1c) **blue,** *bluish*	65.00	65.00
		On cover		*200.00*
		Block of four	*450.00*	

Cancellations on Nos. 61L2-61L4: Red "PAID" in large box. Red circular "Stait's at Adams Express."

East River Post Office, New York, N. Y.

Established by Jacob D. Clark and Henry Wilson in 1850, and sold to Sigmund Adler in 1852.

L136

L137

1852 **Typo.**

62L1	L136	(1c) **black,** *rose* (on cover)		—

1852-54 **Litho.**

62L3	L137	(1c) **black,** *green,* glazed	*200.00*	—

L138

1855

62L4	L138	(1c) **black,** *green,* glazed	100.00	125.00
		On cover		*750.00*
		Pair	*300.00*	

Eighth Avenue Post Office. New York, N. Y.

L139

1852 **Typo.**

63L1	L139	**red**	*2,500.*	

Empire City Dispatch, New York, N. Y.

Established by J. Bevan & Son and almost immediately suppressed by the Government.

L140

1881 **Typo.** **Laid Paper** ***Perf. 12***

64L1	L140	**black,** *green*	1.00	
		Block of four	5.00	
a.		Imperf.	—	
b.		Horiz. or vert. pair, imperf. between	35.00	

Essex Letter Express, New York, N. Y.

L141

1856 **Glazed Surface Paper** **Typo.**

65L1	L141	2c **black,** *red*	*250.00*	

Some authorities doubt that No. 65L1 was placed in use.

Faunce's Penny Post, Atlantic City, N. J.

Established in 1884 by Ancil Faunce to provide local delivery of letters to and from the post office. Discontinued in 1887.

L141a

1885 **Die cut**

152L1	L141a	(1c) **black,** *red*	150.00	200.00
		On cover		*900.00*

Jabez Fearey & Co.'s Mustang Express, Newark, N.J.

Established by Jabez Fearey, Local Agent of the Pacific & Atlantic Telegraph Co.

L142

1870 **Glazed Surface Paper** **Typeset**

66L1	L142	**black,** *red*	*125.00*	

Some authorities consider this item to be an express company label rather than a stamp.

Fiske & Rice

Fiske

Authorities consider items of this design to be express company labels rather than stamps.

Floyd's Penny Post, Chicago, Ill.

Established by John R. Floyd early in 1860, operated by him until June 20, 1861, then continued by Charles W. Mappa.

John R. Floyd — L144

1860 **Typo.**

68L1	L144	(1c) **blue** (shades)	—	65.00
		On cover		*2,500.*
		Pair		200.00
68L2	L144	(1c) **brown**	—	90.00
		On cover		*4,250.*
68L3	L144	(1c) **green**	—	100.00
		On cover		*4,250.*
		On cover with U.S. #11		*3,000.*

Cancellations: Black circle "Floyd's Penny Post Chicago". Black circle "Floyd's Penny Post" and sunburst. Black or blue oval "Floyd's Penny Post Chicago".

Franklin City Despatch Post, N.Y.

(See Bouton's Manhattan Express.)

Frazer & Co., Cincinnati, Ohio.

Established by Hiram Frazer. Stamps used while he was a Cincinnati letter carrier.

L145

Cut to shape

1845

Glazed Surface Paper

69L1	L145	2c **black,** *green*		*750.00*
		On cover		*1,250.*

L146

1845-51 **Wove Paper** **Litho.**

69L2	L146	2c **black,** *pink*	—	200.00
69L3	L146	2c **black,** *green*	200.00	200.00
69L4	L146	2c **black,** *yellow*	200.00	200.00
69L5	L146	2c **black,** *grayish*	200.00	200.00

Some stamps of type L146 show manual erasure of "& Co."

L147

1848-51

69L6	L147	2c **black,** *rose*	*600.00*	
69L7	L147	2c **black,** *blue* (shades)	*600.00*	*600.00*
69L8	L147	2c **black,** *yellow*	*1,000.*	

Freeman & Co.'s Express, New York, N. Y.

L147a

1855 (?) **Litho.**

164L1	L145a (25c)**blue**	*500.00*	

Friend's Boarding School, Barnesville, Ohio.

(Barclay W. Stratton, Supt.)

On Nov. 6, 1877 the school committee decided to charge the students one cent for each letter carried to or from the post office, one and a half miles away. Adhesive labels were prepared and sold for one cent each. Their sale and use continued until 1884.

L147b

Several varieties and sizes of frame

1877 **Typo.**

151L1	L147b (1c) **black**		75.00	—
		On cover		*150.00*

No. 151L1 was usually affixed to the back of the envelope and left uncanceled.

Gahagan & Howe City Express, San Francisco, Calif.

Established by Dennis Gahagan and C. E. B. Howe, as successors to John C. Robinson, proprietor of the San Francisco Letter Express. Sold in 1865 to William E. Loomis, who later purchased the G. A. Carnes business. Loomis used the adhesive stamps and handstamps of these posts, changing the Carnes stamp by erasing his name.

L148

L149

1849-70 **Typeset**

70L1	L148	5c **light blue**	75.00	85.00
70L2	L149	(5c) **blue**	75.00	85.00
a.		Tete beche pair	200.00	

Sheets of No. 70L2 contain five vertical rows of four, the first two rows being reversed against the others, making horizontal tete beche pairs with wide margins between. The pairs were not evenly locked up in the form.

L150

70L3	L150	(5c) **black**	25.00	20.00
		Pair		45.00
		Strip of three		75.00

Overprinted "X" in Blue

70L4	L150	10c **black**	85.00	

Cancellations: Blue or black oval "Gahagan & Howe". Blue or black oval "San Francisco Letter Express" and horseman (Robinson). Blue or black oval "PAID" (Loomis).

Glen Haven Daily Mail, Glen Haven, N.Y.

Glen Haven was located at the head of Skaneateles Lake, Cayuga County, N.Y., until 1910 when the City of Syracuse, having purchased the land for reservoir purposes, razed all the buildings.

Glen Haven, by 1848, had become a famous Water Cure resort, with many sanitariums conducted there. The hamlet had a large summer colony interested in dress reform under the leadership of Amelia Jenks Bloomer; also antislavery, and other reform movements.

A local post was established by the hotel and sanitarium managements for their guests' convenience to deliver mail to the U.S. post offices at Homer or Scott, N.Y. The local stamps were occasionally pen canceled. They are known tied to cover with the Homer or Scott town postmark when the local stamp was placed adjacent to the government stamp and received the cancellation accidentally. The local stamps are only known used in conjunction with government stamps.

L151

L152

1854-58 **Typeset**

Several varieties of each

71L1	L151	1c **black,** *dark green*	300.00	
a.		"Gien" instead of "Glen"	*500.00*	

Glazed Surface Paper

71L2	L152	1c **black,** *green*	*400.00*	*400.00*
		On cover		*1,500.*

Links at corners — L153

Varying ornaments at corners — L153a

Several varieties of each

Glazed Surface Paper

71L3	L153	1c **black,** *green*	125.00	125.00
		On cover		*2,000.*
		Pair	500.00	
71L4	L153a	1c **black,** *green*	200.00	200.00
		On cover		*850.00*

Gordon's City Express, New York, N. Y.

Established by Samuel B. Gordon

L154

1848-52 **Typo.** **Surface Colored Paper**

72L1	L154	2c **black,** *vermilion*	*750.00*	*750.00*
		On cover		*1,000.*
72L2	L154	2c **black,** *green*	75.00	75.00
		On cover		400.00

Glazed Surface Paper

72L3	L154	2c **black,** *green*	85.00	85.00
		On cover		450.00

Cancellation: Small black or red "PAID".

Grafflin's Baltimore Despatch, Baltimore, Md.

Established by Joseph Grafflin

L155

1856 **Litho.**

73L1	L155	1c **black**	85.00	125.00
		On cover		*400.00*
		Block of four	*600.00*	

Originals show traces of a fine horizontal line through tops of most of the letters in "BALTIMORE".

Guy's City Despatch, Philadelphia, Pa.

Established by F. A. Guy, who employed 8 carriers

L156

Sheets of 25 (5x5)

1879 **Typo.** ***Perf. 11, 12, 12½***

74L1	L156 (1c) **pink**		12.00	12.00
		On cover		300.00
a.	Imperf., pair			—
74L2	L156 (1c) **blue**		15.00	20.00
		On cover		300.00
a.	Imperf., pair			—
b.	Ultramarine		20.00	25.00

When Guy's City Despatch was suppressed, the remainders were sold to a New York stamp dealer.

Hackney & Bolte Penny Post, Atlantic City, N. J.

Established in 1886 by Evan Hackney and Charles Bolte to provide delivery of mail to and from the post office. Discontinued in 1887.

L156a

Die cut

153L1	L156a (1c) **black,** *red*		150.00	200.00
		On cover		*900.00*
		On cover with 2c No. 210		*1,000.*

Hale & Co.

Established by James W. Hale at New York, N.Y., to carry mail to points in New England, New York State, Philadelphia and Baltimore. Stamps sold at 6 cents each or "20 for $1.00."

L157

1844 Wove Paper (several thicknesses) Typo.

75L1	L157	(6c) **light blue** (shades)	40.00	25.00
		Cut to shape		15.00
		On cover		150.00
		Cut to shape on cover		50.00
		Strip of 3 on cover		250.00
75L2	L157	(6c) **red,** *bluish*	100.00	85.00
		Cut to shape		40.00
		On cover		400.00
		Cut to shape on cover		100.00
		Pair on cover		—

Same Handstamped in Black or Red, "City Despatch Office, 23 State St."

75L3	L157	(6c) **red,** *bluish* (Bk), cut to shape	*400.00*	
		Pair, partly cut to shape	*1,000.*	
75L4	L157	(6c) **blue** (R), cut to shape	*400.00*	

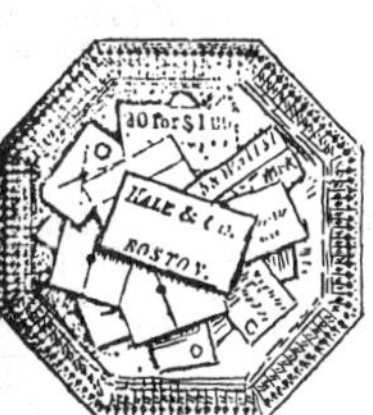
L158

Same as Type L157 but street address omitted

75L5	L158	(6c) **blue** (shades)	15.00	10.00
		Cut to shape		5.00
		On cover		150.00
		Cut to shape on cover		40.00
		Pair on cover		175.00
		Block of four	*75.00*	
		Sheet of 20 (5x4)	*450.00*	

Cancellations on Nos. 75L1-75L5: Large red "PAID". Red, black or blue oval "Hale & Co." (several types and cities). Small red ornamental framed box (several types). Red negative monogram "WE".

Hall & Mills' Despatch Post, New York, N.Y.

Established by Gustavus A. Mills and A. C. Hall.

L159

Several Varieties

1847 Glazed Surface Paper Typeset

76L1	L159	(2c) **black,** *green*	*250.00*	*250.00*
		On cover		*500.00*
		On cover with 5c #1		*2,000.*

T.A. Hampton City Despatch, Philadelphia, Pa.

L159a

L159b

Several Varieties of L159a

1847 Cut to shape Typeset

77L1	L159a	(2c) **black**	*350.00*	*350.00*
		On cover		*900.00*
77L2	L159b	**black**		*800.00*

A handstamp similar to type L159b with denomination "2cts" or "3c" instead of "PAID." in center has been used as a postmark.

Hanford's Pony Express, New York, N.Y.

Established by John W. Hanford.

L160

1845 Glazed Surface Paper Typo.

78L1	L160	2c **black,** *orange yellow* (shades)	65.00	85.00
		Cut to shape		35.00
		On cover		*600.00*

Cancellation: Small red "PAID".

The handstamp in black or red formerly listed as Nos. 78LU1-78LU6 is illustrated in the Local Handstamped Covers section. It was used as a postmark and there is no evidence that any prepaid handstamped envelopes or lettersheets were ever sold.

George S. Harris City Despatch Post, Philadelphia, Pa.

L160a

L160b

1847 (?) Typeset

79L1	L160a	(2c) **black**	*500.00*
79L2	L160b	**black**	*750.00*

Hartford, Conn. Mail Route

L161

Plate of 12 (6x2) varieties

1844 Glazed Surface Paper Engr.

80L1	L161	(5c) **black,** *yellow*	250.00	150.00
		Pair		400.00
		On cover		*1,000.*
80L3	L161	**black,** *pink*	300.00	300.00

Chemically affected copies of No. 80L1 appear as buff, and of No. 80L3 as salmon.

Cancellations are usually initials or words ("S", "W", "South", etc.) in black ms. This may indicate destination or routing.

Hill's Post, Boston, Mass.

Established by Oliver B. Hill

L162

1849 Typo.

81L1	L162	1c **black,** *rose*	*750.00*

A. M. Hinkley's Express Co., New York, N.Y.

Organized by Abraham M. Hinkley, Hiram Dixon and Hiram M. Dixon, in 1855, and business transferred to the Metropolitan Errand & Carrier Express Co. in same year.

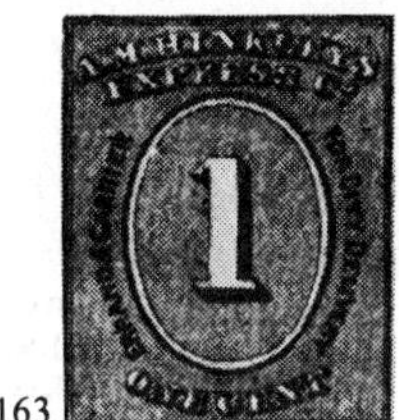
L163

Sheets of 64 (8x8)

1855 Litho.

82L1	L163	1c **red,** *bluish*	*250.00*

It is doubtful that No. 82L1 was ever placed in use.

Reprints exist on white paper somewhat thicker than the originals.

Homan's Empire Express, New York, N.Y.

Established by Richard S. Homan

L164

Several varieties

1852 Typeset

83L1	L164	**black,** *yellow*	*400.00*	*400.00*
a.		"1" for "I" in "PAID"	*500.00*	

Hopedale Penny Post, Milford, Mass.

Hopedale was a large farm community southwest of Milford, Mass. The community meeting of Feb. 2, 1849, voted to arrange for regular transportation of mail to the nearest post office, which was at Milford, a mile and a half distant, at a charge of 1c a letter. A complete history of this community may be found in "The Hopedale Community," published in 1897.

Hopedale Penny Post

Rayed asterisks in corners — L165

Hopedale Penny Post

Plain asterisks in corners — L166

Several varieties of Types L165-L166

1849 Glazed Surface Paper Typeset

84L1	L165	(1c) **black,** *pink*	*400.00*	*400.00*
84L2	L166	(1c) **black,** *pink*	*400.00*	*400.00*

Types L165 and L166 probably were printed together in a single small plate.

L167

Wove Paper Typo.

84L3	L167	(1c) **black,** *yellow*	*400.00*	*400.00*
		On cover		*1,250.*
84L4	L167	(1c) **black,** *pink*	*450.00*	*450.00*
		Pair	*1,100.*	

J. A. Howell's City Despatch, Philadelphia, Pa.

L167a

184 ? Typo.

165L1	L167a	**black**	—

Hoyt's Letter Express, Rochester, N.Y.

David Hoyt, agent at Rochester for the express company of Livingston, Wells & Pomeroy, operated a letter and package express by boats on the Genesee Canal between Dansville, N.Y., and Rochester, where connection was also made with Pomeroy's Letter Express.

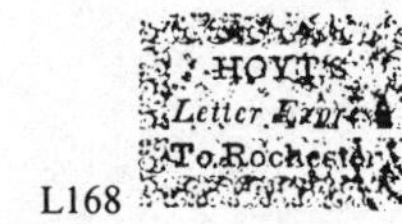

L168

Several varieties

1844 Glazed Surface Paper Typeset

85L1	L168 (5c) **black**, *vermilion*		300.00	300.00
a.	"Lettcr" instead of "Letter"			450.00

Humboldt Express, Nevada

A branch of Langton's Pioneer Express, connecting with the main line of Pioneer Express at Carson City, Nevada, and making tri-weekly trips to adjacent points.

L169

1863 Litho.

86L1	L169	25c **brown**		250.00	300.00
		Pair			700.00
		On cover (U.S. Envelopes Nos. U34 or U35)			*50,000.*

Cancellations: Blue oval "Langton's Pioneer Express Unionville". Red "Langton & Co."

Hussey's Post, New York City, N.Y.

Established by George Hussey.
Reprints available for postage are so described.

L170

L171

1854 Litho.

87L1	L170	(1c) **blue**			50.00
		On cover			*250.00*

1856

87L2	L171	(1c) **black**		150.00	50.00
		On cover			*300.00*
87L3	L171	(1c) **red**			35.00
		On cover			*275.00*

Cancellation on Nos. 87L1-87L3: Black "FREE".

L172

L173

1858

87L4	L172	1c **brown red**		17.50	25.00
		On cover			*150.00*
		Pair			*400.00*
87L5	L172	1c **black**		*50.00*	—
		On cover			

Cancellation on Nos. 87L4-87L5: Black circle "1ct PAID HUSSEY 50 Wm. ST", date in center.

1858

87L6	L173	(1c) **black**		2.00	—
		On cover			—
87L7	L173	(1c) **rose red**		2.00	—
		On cover			—
87L8	L173	(1c) **red**		8.00	—
		On cover			—

Type L173 was printed in sheets of 46: 5 horizontal rows of 8, one row of 6 sideways at botton. Type L173 saw little, if any, commercial use and was probably issued mainly for collectors. Covers exist, many with apparently contemporary corner cards. On cover stamps bear a black HUSSEY'S POST handstamp, but most if not all of Nos. 87L6-87L8 were canceled after the post ceased to operate.

L174

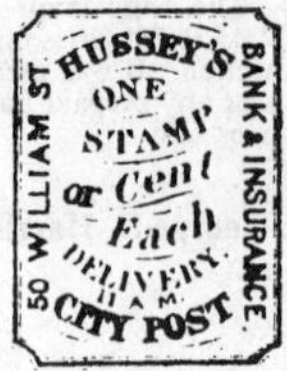

L175

1858 Typo.

87L9	L174	(1c) **blue**		2.00	

1859 Litho.

87L10	L175	1c **rose red**		10.00	20.00
		On cover			*200.00*

No. 87L10 in orange red is not known to have been placed in use.

Cancellations: Black "FREE". Black company circle "1 CT PAID HUSSEY 50 WM ST.", no date in center (smaller than cancel on Nos. 87L4-87L5).

87L11	L175	1c **lake**			—
87L12	L175	1c **black**			—

L176

L177

1862

87L13	L176	1c **black**		15.00	
87L14	L176	1c **blue**		7.00	10.00
		On cover			*125.00*
87L15	L176	1c **green**		8.00	
		On cover			*125.00*
87L16	L176	1c **red**		15.00	
87L17	L176	1c **red brown**		15.00	
87L18	L176	1c **brown**		15.00	
87L19	L176	1c **lake**		17.50	
87L20	L176	1c **purple**		12.00	
87L21	L176	1c **yellow**		12.00	

Similar to L174 but has condensed "50" and shows a short flourish line over the "I" of "DELIVERY".

1862

87L22	L177	(1c) **blue**		70	—
		On cover			—

L178

Similar to L171, but no dots in corners — L179

1863

87L23	L178	(1c) **blue**		5.00	
87L24	L179	(1c) **black**		2.00	
87L25	L179	(1c) **red**		5.00	

See No. 87L52.

Scott's editorial staff cannot undertake to identify, authenticate or appraise stamps and postal markings.

L180

HUSSEY'S BANK & INSURANCE Special MESSAGE POST 50 WILLIAM ST. CLOSES AT 11 AM 1 CENT DELIVERY 18 63

L182

87L26	L180	1c **brown red**		4.00	—
		Block of four		20.00	
		On cover			*125.00*

A so-called "reprint" of No. 87L26, made for J. W. Scott, has a colored flaw extending diagonally upward from the "I" in "CITY."

Reprints of types L173, L174, L178, L179 and L180 were made in 1875-76 on thicker paper in approximately normal colors and were available for postage.

1863

Dated 1863

87L27	L182	1c **blue**		8.00	10.00
		On cover			*125.00*
87L28	L182	1c **green**		12.00	—
		On cover			—
87L29	L182	1c **yellow**		15.00	—
		On cover			—
87L30	L182	1c **brown**		10.00	
87L31	L182	1c **red brown**		10.00	
87L32	L182	1c **red**		10.00	
87L33	L182	1c **black**		20.00	
87L34	L182	1c **violet**		20.00	
87L35	L182	2c **brown**		10.00	12.00
		On cover			*125.00*

The 2c blue dated 1863 exists only as a counterfeit.

1865

Dated 1865

87L38	L182	2c **blue**		12.00	12.00
		On cover			*225.00*

1867

Dated 1867

87L39	L182	2c **blue**		22.50	20.00
		On cover			*225.00*

1868

Dated 1868

87L40	L182	2c **blue**		20.00	17.50
		On cover			*225.00*

1869

Dated 1870

87L41	L182	2c **blue**		22.50	20.00
		On cover			*225.00*

1871

Dated 1871

87L42	L182	2c **blue**		25.00	22.50
		On cover			*225.00*

L183

L184

1872

Wove Paper

87L43	L183	**black**		3.00	5.00
		On cover			125.00
87L44	L183	**red lilac**		6.00	—
		On cover			*125.00*
87L45	L183	**blue**		5.00	—
87L46	L183	**green**		6.00	—
		On cover			*125.00*

Sheets contain four panes of 28 each. Double periods after "A.M." on two stamps in two panes, and on four stamps in the other two panes.

Covers show postmark reading: "HUSSEY'S SPECIAL-MESSENGER EXPRESS-PAID-54 PINE ST."

1872

Thick Laid paper

87L47	L184	**black**		5.00	8.00
		Block of four		22.50	
		On cover			—
87L48	L184	**yellow**		9.00	10.00
87L49	L184	**red brown**		7.00	—

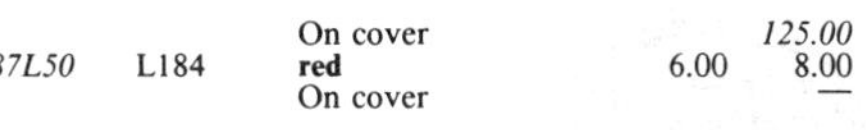

		On cover		*125.00*
87L50	L184	**red**	6.00	8.00
		On cover		—

L185

1873

Thin Wove Paper

87L51	L185	2c **black**	10.00	10.00
		On cover		*100.00*

A reprint of No. 87L51, believed to have been made for J. W. Scott, shows a 4mm break in the bottom frameline under "54."

Type of 1863

1875

Thick Wove Paper

87L52	L179	(1c) **blue**	—

L186

L186 in imitation of L180, but no corner dots, "S" for "$", etc.

1875

87L53	L186	1c **black**	1.00

Some authorities believe Nos. 87L52-87L53 are imitations made from new stones. Attributed to J. W. Scott.

"Copyright 1877" – L188

L188a

1877

Thick Wove Paper

87L55	L188	**black**	*75.00*	—
		On cover		*500.00*

Error of design, used provisionally. Stamp was never copyrighted. Printed singly.

87L56	L188a	**black**	50.00	

Thin Wove Paper

87L57	L188a	**blue**	10.00	
87L58	L188a	**rose**	6.00	
		On cover		—

Perf. 12½

87L59	L188a	**blue**	2.00	5.00
a.		Imperf. horizontally, pair	—	
		On cover		*125.00*
87L60	L188a	**rose**	2.00	5.00
		On cover		*125.00*

L189

L190

L191

L189-"TRADE MARK" small.
L190-"TRADE MARK" medium.
L191-"TRADE MARK" larger, touching "s" of "Easson".

1878 Wove Paper *Perf. 11, 11½, 11x12, 12*

87L61	L189	**blue**	5.00	—
		On cover		*125.00*
87L62	L189	**carmine**	8.50	—
		On cover		*100.00*
87L63	L189	**black**	50.00	

Nos. 87L61-87L63 exist imperforate.

Perf. 11, 12, 12½, 14, 16 and Compound

87L64	L190	**blue**	2.00	5.00
		On cover		*100.00*
87L65	L190	**red**	2.00	5.00
		On cover		*75.00*
87L66	L190	**black**	—	

Nos. 87L64-87L66 imperf. are reprints.

1879 ***Perf. 11, 12, and Compound***

87L67	L191	**blue**	2.00	5.00
		On cover		*100.00*
87L69	L191	**black**	—	

1880 ***Imperf.***

87L70	L191	**blue**	—	
		On cover		225.00
87L71	L191	**red**	—	
87L72	L191	**black**	—	

The authenticity of Nos. 87L69-87L72 has not been fully established.

L192

Two types of L192: I. Imprint "N. F. Seebeck, 97 Wall St. N. Y." is in lower tablet below "R Easson, etc." II. Imprint in margin below stamp.

1880 Glazed Surface Wove Paper *Perf. 12*

87L73	L192	**brown,** type I	5.00	8.00
a.		brown, type II	5.00	8.00
b.		Horiz. pair, imperf. between	20.00	
c.		Imperf., pair	20.00	
		On cover		150.00
		Block of four, type I	—	
87L74	L192	**ultramarine,** type I	7.00	8.00
a.		Imperf., pair	—	
b.		deep blue, type II	20.00	
87L75	L192	**red, type II**	*1.00*	—
		On cover		*100.00*
		Block of four	5.00	

1882 ***Perf. 16, 12x16***

87L76	L192	**brown,** type I	6.00	10.00
		On cover		—
87L77	L192	**ultramarine,** type I	6.00	10.00
		On cover		*100.00*

Cancellations: Violet 3-ring target. Violet ornamental "T".

Imperf. impressions of Type I in various colors, on horizontally laid paper, ungummed, are color trials.

SPECIAL DELIVERY STAMPS

L181

Typographed; Numerals Inserted Separately

1863 Glazed Surface Paper

87LE1	L181	5c **black,** *red*	1.50	7.50
		On cover		*250.00*
87LE2	L181	10c **gold,** *green*	1.50	8.50
		On cover		*250.00*
87LE3	L181	15c **gold,** *black*	1.50	10.00
		On cover		*300.00*
87LE4	L181	20c **black**	1.50	10.00
		On cover		*300.00*
87LE5	L181	25c **gold,** *blue*	1.50	8.50
		On cover		*300.00*
87LE6	L181	30c **gold,** *red*		—
87LE7	L181	50c **black,** *green*		—

Nos. 87LE1-87LE7 on cover show Hussey handstamp cancellations in various types.

Nos. 87LE4 and 87LE5 are on unglazed paper, the latter surface colored. Ten minor varieties of each value, except the 30c and 50c, which have the figures in manuscript. Printed in two panes of 10, certain values exist in horizontal cross-gutter tete beche pairs.

Originals of the 5c to 20c have large figures of value. The 25c has condensed figures with decimal point. Reprints exist with both large and condensed figures. Reprints of the 25c also exist with serifs on large figures.

Most of the Hussey adhesives are known on cover, tied with Hussey Express postmarks. Many of these were canceled after the post ceased to operate as a mail carrier. "On cover" values are for original stamps used while the post was operating.

WRAPPERS

L192a

1856 Handstamped Inscribed: "82 Broadway"

87LUP1	L192	**black**	—	175.00

1858 Inscribed: "50 William St. Basement"

87LUP2	L192a	**black,** *manila*	—	175.00
87LUP3	L192a	**black**	—	175.00

Jefferson Market P. O., New York, N. Y.

Established by Godfrey Schmidt

L193

1850 Glazed Surface Paper Litho.

88L1	L193	(2c) **black,** *pink*	*600.00*	*450.00*
88L2	L193	(2c) **black,** *blue*	—	*500.00*
		On cover		*1,250.*

Jenkins' Camden Dispatch, Camden, N. J.

Established by Samuel H. Jenkins and continued by William H. Jenkins.

George Washington – L194

L195

1853 Litho.

89L1	L194	**black** (fine impression)	80.00	80.00
		On cover		*700.00*
		Block of four	*400.00*	
89L2	L194	**black,** *yellow* (coarse impression)		*350.00*

Typeset

89L3	L195	1c **black,** *bluish*	—	—

Type L194 printed on envelopes at upper left is considered a corner card.

Some authorities believe No. 89L3 is bogus.

Johnson & Co.'s City Despatch Post, Baltimore, Md.

Operated by Ezekiel C. Johnson, letter carrier

L196

1848			Typeset
90L1	L196	2c **black**, *lavender*	*2,000.*

Jones' City Express, Brooklyn, N. Y.

George Washington — L197

1845		Glazed Surface Paper		Engr.
91L1	L197	2c **black**, *pink*	350.00	350.00
		On cover		850.00

Cancellation: Red oval "Boyd's City Express Post".

Kellogg's Penny Post & City Despatch, Cleveland, Ohio

L198

1853			Typo.
92L1	L198	(1c) **vermilion**	*400.00*
		On cover	*600.00*

Cancellation: Black grid.

Kidder's City Express Post, Brooklyn, N.Y.

In 1847, Henry A. Kidder took over the post of Walton & Co., and with the brothers Isaac C. Snedeker and George H. Snedeker increased its scope. In 1851, the business was sold to the Snedekers. It was operated under the old name until 1853 when the Brooklyn City Express Post was founded.

L199

Stamps bear black manuscript "I S" control in two styles.

1847		Glazed Surface Paper		Typo.
93L1	L199	2c **black**, *pale blue*	275.00	250.00
		On cover		450.00
		Block of four	1,400.	

Cancellation: Red "PAID".

Reprinted on green paper.

Kurtz Union Despatch Post, New York, N. Y.

L200

Typeset; "T" in Black Ms.

1853		Glazed Surface Paper	
94L1	L200	2c **black**, *green*	*3,500.*

Langton & Co.

(See Humboldt Express.)

Ledger Dispatch, Brooklyn, N.Y.

Established by Edwin Pidgeon. Stamps reported to have been sold at 80 cents per 100. Suppressed after a few months.

L201

1882		Typo.		*Rouletted 12 in color*
95L1	L201	**rose** (shades)	65.00	—
		Block of four	350.00	

Letter Express

Established by Henry Wells. Carried mail for points in Western New York, Chicago, Detroit and Duluth.

L202

L203

1844		Glazed Surface Paper		Typo.
96L1	L202	5c **black**, *pink*	100.00	75.00
		Pair	250.00	200.00
		Block of four	*750.00*	
96L2	L202	5c **black**, *green*	—	75.00
		Pair		200.00
96L3	L203	10c **pink**	150.00	100.00
		Pair		*300.00*
	a.	Bisect on cover		*750.00*

No. 96L3a was sold as a horizontal or vertical bisect. It is known used singly for 5c (rare), or as two bisects for 10c (extremely rate). Stamps are known almost exclusively tied with black ms. "X" covering the cut, and can be authenticated by experts.

L204

96L4	L204	10c **black**, *scarlet*	—	350.00

Cancellations: Red large partly boxed "PAID". Red boxed "Boyd's City Express Post".

Locomotive Express Post

L205

1847 (?)			Handstamped
97L1	L205	**black**	—

Wm. E. Loomis Letter Express, San Francisco, Calif.

William E. Loomis established this post as the successor to the Gahagan & Howe City Express, which he bought in 1865. He continued to use the Gahagan & Howe stamps unchanged. Later Loomis bought Carnes' City Letter Express. He altered the Carnes stamp by erasing "CARNES" from the plate and adding the address below the oval: "S.E. cor. Sans'e & Wash'n."

L206

1868				Typo.
98L1	L206	(5c) **rose**	45.00	*125.00*

McGreely's Express, Alaska

Established in 1898 by S. C. Marcuse to carry letters and packages by motorboat between Dyea and Skagway, Alaska.

L208

1898		Typo.	*Perf. 14*
155L1	L208	25c **blue**	12.00
		Block of four	60.00

The status of No. 155L1 is questioned.

McIntire's City Express Post, New York, N. Y.

Established by William H. McIntire

Mercury — L207

1859				Litho.
99L1	L207	2c **pink**	10.00	30.00
		Block of four	60.00	
		On cover		*300.00*
	a.	Period after CENTS omitted	—	

Cancellation: Black oval "McIntire's City Express Post Paid".

McMillan's City Dispatch Post, Chicago, Ill.

L208a

1855			Typeset
100L1	L208a	**black**, *rose*	*5,000.*

Magic Letter Express, Richmond, Va.

Established by Evans, Porter & Co.

L209

1865				Typo.
101L1	L209	2c **black**, *brown*		*1,200.*
101L2	L209	5c **black**, *brown*	—	—

Mason's New Orleans City Express, New Orleans, La.

J. Mason, proprietor

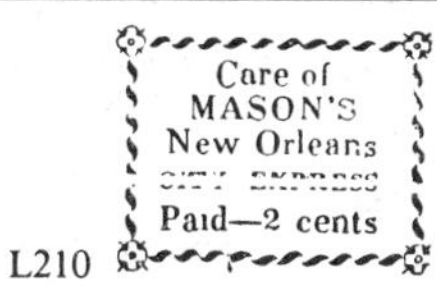

L210

1850-57			Typeset	
102L1	L210	½c **black,** *blue* (value changed to "1" in black ms.)		*750.00*
		On cover		*2,000.*
102L2	L210	2c **black,** *yellow*	—	*250.00*
		On cover		*1,250.*

Cancellations: Red grid. Small red circle "Mason's City Express".

Mearis' City Despatch Post, Baltimore, Md.

Established by Malcom W. Mearis

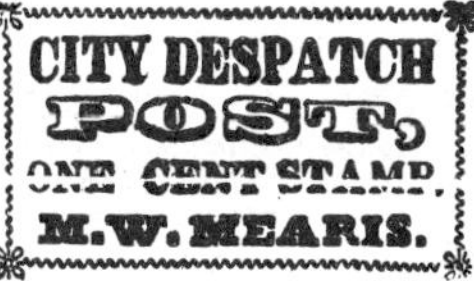

L211

L212

Black ms. initials "M W M" control on all stamps

1846				Typeset
103L1	L211	1c **black,** *gray*	*300.00*	*300.00*
		On cover		*750.00*
103L2	L212	1c **black,** *gray*	*400.00*	
103L3	L212	2c **black,** *gray*	*400.00*	
a.		Horiz. pair, Nos. 103L2-103L3 se-tenant	*1,500.*	

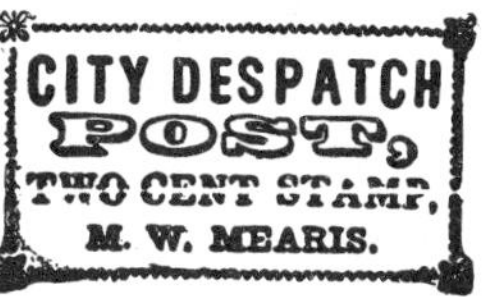

L213

103L4	L213	1c **black,** *gray*	*400.00*
103L5	L213	2c **black,** *gray*	*400.00*
a.		Horiz. pair, Nos. 103L4-103L5 se-tenant	*1,500.*

L214

103L6	L214	1c **black,** *gray*	*500.00*

Corner ornaments of Nos. 103L1-103L6 differ on each stamp. All varieties probably contained in one plate.

Menant & Co.'s Express, New Orleans, La.

L215

1853 (?)			Typo.
104L1	L215	2c **dark red**	*750.00*

Mercantile Library Association, New York, N. Y.

Stamps paid for special delivery service of books ordered from the library, and of forms especially provided to subscribers. The forms bore a government stamp on the outside, a library stamp inside.

L216

1870-75				Litho.
105L1	L216	5c **black,** *maroon*	60.00	60.00
105L2	L216	5c **black,** *yellow*	85.00	85.00
105L3	L216	5c **blue**	85.00	85.00
		Pair		200.00
105L5	L216	6c **black,** *maroon*	200.00	
105L6	L216	10c **black,** *yellow*	125.00	150.00

No. 105L5 is slightly larger than the 5c and 10c stamps.

The stamps "on cover" are affixed to cutouts from order blanks showing order number, title of book desired, and subscriber's name and address. When canceled, the stamps and order blanks show a dull blue double-lined oval inscribed "MERCANTILE LIBRARY ASSOCIATION" and date in center. The stamps are really more a form of receipt for a prepaid parcel delivery service than postage stamps.

POSTAL CARD

Printed on U. S. Postal Card, First Issue

105LU1	L216	10c **yellow**	*500.00*

Messenkope's Union Square Post Office, New York, N. Y.

Established by Charles F. Messenkope in 1849 and sold to Joseph E. Dunham in 1850.

L217

1849		Glazed Surface Paper		Litho.
106L1	L217	(1c) **black,** *green*	70.00	70.00
		On cover		*250.00*
		Two on cover (2c rate)		*350.00*
		On cover with 5c #1		*1,200.*
106L2	L217	(2c) **black,** *pink*	*400.00*	*350.00*
		On cover		*500.00*

Some examples of No. 106L1 are found with "MESSENKOPES" crossed through in black ms. in an apparent attempt (by Dunham ?) to obliterate it.

Cancellations: Red "PAID". Red oval "DUNHAMS UNION SQUARE POST OFFICE". Red grid of dots.

Metropolitan Errand and Carrier Express Co., New York, N. Y.

Organized Aug. 1, 1855, by Abraham M. Hinkley, Hiram Dixon, and others

L218

Printed in sheets of 100 (10x10), each stamp separated by thin ruled lines.

1855		Thin to Medium Wove Paper		Engr.
107L1	L218	1c **red orange** (shades)	10.00	15.00
		Cut to shape	2.50	3.50
		Pair	30.00	
		Block of four	*75.00*	
		On cover		250.00
107L2	L218	5c **red orange**	85.00	
		Cut to shape	30.00	
107L3	L218	10c **red orange**	85.00	
		Cut to shape	30.00	
107L4	L218	20c **red orange**	125.00	
		Cut to shape	40.00	

Cancellations: Black, blue or green boxed "PAID".

Nos. 107L1-107L4 have been extensively reprinted in brown and in blue on paper much thicker than the originals.

ENVELOPE

L219

Embossed
Wide Diagonally Laid Paper

107LU1	L219	2c **red,** *amber*	*65.00*

No. 107LU1 has been reprinted on amber wove, diagonally laid or horizontally laid paper with narrow lines. The embossing is sharper than on the original.

Metropolitan Post Office, New York, N. Y.

Established by Lemuel Williams who later took William H. Laws as a partner.

L220

L221

L222

Nos. 108L1-108L5 were issued die cut, and only exist thus.

1852-53		Glazed Surface Paper		Embossed
108L1	L220	(2c) **red** (L. Williams)	*350.00*	*350.00*
		On cover		*500.00*
108L2	L221	(2c) **red** (address and name erased)	*400.00*	*400.00*
108L3	L222	(2c) **red**	*100.00*	*75.00*
		On cover		*1,000.*
108L3A	L222	(2c) **blue**	*350.00*	*350.00*
		On cover		*2,500.*

L223

Wove Paper

108L4	L223	1c **red**	60.00	70.00
		On cover		225.00
108L5	L223	1c **blue**	60.00	70.00
		On cover		200.00

Cancellations: Black circle "METROPOLITAN P. O." Black boxed "PAID W. H. LAWS."

G. A. Mills' Despatch Post, New York, N. Y.

Established by Gustavus A. Mills at 6 Wall St., succeeding Hall & Mills.

L224

Several varieties

1847		Glazed Surface Paper		Typeset
109L1	L224	(2c) **black,** *green*	*200.00*	*200.00*
		On cover		*500.00*

Moody's Penny Dispatch, Chicago, Ill.

Robert J. Moody, proprietor

L225

Several varieties

1856		Glazed Surface Paper		Typeset
110L1	L225	(1c) **black**, *red*, "CHICA-GO" 8mm	*200.00*	*250.00*
		Vert. strip of 3 showing 3 varieties:period, colon, comma after "Dispatch"	*1,500.*	
		On cover		*4,500.*
a.		"CHICAGO" 12½mm		*200.00*

Cancellations: Black or blue circle "Moody's Despatch".

New York City Express Post, New York, N.Y.

L226

Several varieties

1847		Glazed Surface Paper		Engr.
111L1	L226	2c **black**, *green*	*250.00*	*150.00*
		Cut to shape	*75.00*	*60.00*
		On cover		*600.00*
		Cut to shape on cover		*125.00*
		Wove Paper		
111L2	L226	2c **orange**	*500.00*	*500.00*
		On cover		*1,000.*

One Cent Despatch, Baltimore, Md., Washington, D.C.

Established by J.H. Wiley to deliver mail in Washington, Georgetown and Baltimore. Made as many as five deliveries daily at 1 cent if prepaid, or 2 cents payable on delivery.

L227

Two types: I. Courier's letter points to "O" of "ONE." II. Letter points to "N" of "ONE."

1856		Washington, D.C.		Litho.
		Inscribed at bottom "Washington City"		
112L1	L227	1c **violet**	*125.00*	85.00
		On cover		*900.00*
		Horiz. pair, Types I & II se-tenant		*600.00*
		Baltimore, Maryland		
		No name at bottom		
112L2	L227	1c **red**	125.00	100.00
		On cover		*750.00*

Cancellation on Nos. 112L1-112L2: Black circle "City Despatch".

Overton & Co.

Carried mail principally between New York and Boston; also to Albany. Stamps sold for 6c each, 20 for $1.

L229

1844				
113L1	L229	(6c) **black**, *greenish*	*200.00*	*150.00*
		On cover		*350.00*
		Pair		*400.00*
		"FREE" printed below design		*250.00*
		On cover		*4,000.*

Cancellation: Black "PAID".

Penny Express Co.

Little information is available on this post, but a sheet is known carrying the ms. initials of Henry Reed of the Holladay staff. The post was part of the Holladay Overland Mail and Express Co. system.

In 1866 in the West the "short-bit" or 10 cents was the smallest currency generally used. The word "penny" is believed to refer to the "half-bit" or 5 cents (nickel)

L230

Printed in sheets of 32 (8x4)

1866				Litho.
114L1	L230	5c **black**	100.00	
a.		Initialed "HR", black ms.		—
		As "a," block of four		—
114L2	L230	5c **blue**	5.00	
		Block of four	21.00	
114L3	L230	5c **red**	5.00	
		Block of four	21.00	

Nos. 114L1-114L3 lack gum and probably were never placed in use.

Philadelphia Despatch Post, Philadelphia, Pa.

See D.O. Blood & Co.

Pinkney's Express Post, New York, N.Y.

L231

1851		Glazed Surface Paper		Typo.
115L1	L231	2c **black**, *green*	*1,000.*	
		Cut to shape	*600.00*	

Pips Daily Mail, Brooklyn, N.Y.

L232

1862 (?)				Litho.
116L1	L232	1c **black**	85.00	
116L2	L232	1c **black**, *buff*	65.00	—
116L3	L232	1c **black**, *yellow*	80.00	
116L4	L232	1c **black**, *dark blue*	80.00	
116L5	L232	1c **black**, *rose*	80.00	
		Block of four	—	

Pomeroy's Letter Express.

Established in 1844 by George E. Pomeroy. Carried mail principally to points in New York State. Connected with Letter Express for Western points.

L233

Engraved by John E. Gavit, Albany, N. Y. (Seen as "GAVIT" in bottom part of stamp). Sheets of 40 (8x5).

1844				
		Surface Colored Wove Paper		
117L1	L233	5c **black**, *yellow*	3.00	15.00
		On cover		*125.00*
		Pair		*100.00*
		Pair on cover		*300.00*
117L2	L233	**black**, *yellow* (value incomplete)		100.00
		On cover		200.00
		Thin Bond Paper		
117L3	L233	5c **blue**	1.50	25.00
		On cover		100.00
		Pair on cover		*300.00*
117L4	L233	5c **black**	1.50	25.00
		On cover		*125.00*
		Strip of four on cover		*500.00*
117L5	L233	5c **red**	1.50	35.00
		On cover		125.00
		Strip of three on cover		600.00
117L6	L233	5c **lake**	*100.00*	*100.00*
		On cover		—
		Pair on cover		—
117L7	L233	5c **orange**	5.00	—

Cancellations: Large red partly boxed "PAID" (Nos. 117L1, 117L6). Red "Cd" (Nos. 117L1-117L2, 117L4); stamps are considered "tied to cover" by this "Cd" when the impression shows through the letter paper.

All stamps except No. 117L2 have "20 for $1" in tablet at the bottom. On No. 117L2 the value is incomplete.

Remainders (reprints?) of Nos. 117L1, 117L3, 117L4 and 117L5 are plentiful in unused condition, including multiples and sheets. A 5c black on yellow paper colored through and a 5c brown were prepared for use but never issued. No. 117L2 was never reprinted.

P. O. Paid, Philadelphia, Pa.

See note in Carriers' Stamps Section.

Price's City Express, New York, N. Y.

L235

L236

1857-58		Glazed Surface Paper		Litho.
119L1	L235	2c **black**, *vermilion*		100.00
		On cover		*750.00*
119L2	L235	2c **black**, *green*		85.00
		Cut to shape		40.00
1858				
		Sheets of 108 (12x9)		
119L3	L236	2c **black**, *green*	5.00	*55.00*
		On cover		—
		Block of four	25.00	

Cancellation on No. 119L3: Black oval "Price's City Express".

Price's Eighth Avenue Post Office, New York, N. Y.

Established by James Price at 350 Eighth Avenue, in 1854, and sold to Russell in the same year.

L237

1854				Litho.
120L1	L237	(2c) **red**, *bluish*	*200.00*	

Priest's Despatch, Philadelphia, Pa.

Established by Solomon Priest

L238

L239

1851		Glazed Surface Paper		Typo.
121L1	L238	(2c) **silver,** *vermilion*	*300.00*	*300.00*
121L2	L238	(2c) **gold,** *dark blue*	*500.00*	

Wove Paper

121L2A	L238	(2c) **bronze,** *bluish*	*250.00*	*250.00*
121L3	L238	(2c) **black,** *yellow*	150.00	
121L4	L238	(2c) **black,** *rose*	150.00	
121L5	L238	(2c) **black,** *blue*	150.00	
121L6	L239	(2c) **black,** *yellow*	150.00	
121L7	L239	(2c) **black,** *blue*	150.00	
121L8	L239	(2c) **black,** *rose*	150.00	
121L9	L239	(2c) **black,** *emerald*	250.00	

Prince's Letter Dispatch, Portland, Maine.

Established by J. H. Prince of Portland. Mail carried nightly by messenger travelling by steamer to Boston. Stamp engraved by Lowell of Lowell & Brett, Boston, his name appearing in the design below the steamship.

L240

Printed in sheets of 40 (5x8)

1861				Litho.
122L1	L240	**black**	5.00	*50.00*
		On cover		*750.00*
		Block of four	25.00	
		Sheet of forty	275.00	

Private Post Office, San Francisco, Calif.
ENVELOPES

L241

(Illustration reduced size.)

Impressed on U. S. Envelopes, 1863-64 Issue

1864				Typo.
123LU1	L241	15c **blue,** *orange* (on U. S. No. U56)		*350.00*
123LU2	L241	15c **blue,** *buff* (on U. S. No. U54)		*350.00*
a.		15c blue, *buff* (on U. S. No. U58)	*150.00*	
b.		15c blue, *buff* (on U. S. No. U59)	*150.00*	
123LU3	L241	25c **blue,** *buff* (on U. S. No. U54)	*350.00*	

Providence Despatch, Providence, R.I.

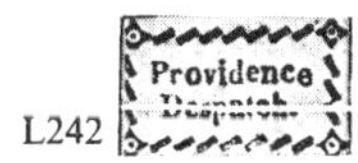

L242

1849				Typeset
124L1	L242	**black**	*2,000.*	

Public Letter Office, San Francisco, Calif.
ENVELOPES

L243

(Illustration reduced size.)

Impressed on U. S. Envelopes, 1863-64 Issue

1864				Typeset
125LU1	L243	**black**	*200.00*	
125LU2	L243	**blue**	*200.00*	
125LU3	L243	15c **blue**	*250.00*	
125LU4	L243	25c **blue**	*250.00*	

Reed's City Despatch Post, San Francisco, Calif.

Pioneer San Francisco private post. Also serving Adams & Co. for city delivery.

L244

1853-54		Glazed Surface Paper		Litho.
126L1	L244	**black,** *green,* on cover		—
126L2	L244	**black,** *blue*	*3,000.*	

Cancellation: Blue double-circle "Adams & Co. San Francisco".

Ricketts & Hall, Baltimore, Md.

Successors to Cook's Dispatch

L244a

1857		Cut to shape		Typo.
127L1	L244a	1c **red,** *bluish*	*750.00*	*1,500.*

Robison & Co., Brooklyn, N. Y.

L245

1855-56				Typo.
128L1	L245	1c **black,** *blue*	*300.00*	*300.00*
		On cover		*4,000.*

Cancellation: Blue "PAID".

Roche's City Dispatch, Wilmington, Del.

L246

1850		Glazed Surface Paper		Typo.
129L1	L246	(2c) **black,** *green*	*750.00*	
		Cut to shape	*400.00*	
		On cover		*1,250.*

A black negative handstamp similar to type L246 served solely as a postmark and no evidence exists that any prepaid handstamped envelopes or lettersheets were ever sold.

Rogers' Penny Post, Newark, N.J.

Established by Alfred H. Rogers, bookseller, at 194 Broad St., Newark, N.J.

L246a

Cut to shape

1856		Glazed Surface Paper		Handstamped
162L1	L246a	(1c) **black,** *green*	—	

See Rogers' handstamp in Local Handstamp Covers section.

Russell 8th Ave. Post Office, New York, N. Y.

(See Price's Eighth Avenue Post Office.)

L247

1854-58				Wood Engraving
130L1	L247	(2c) **blue,** *rose*	*150.00*	*125.00*
		On cover		*400.00*
130L2	L247	(2c) **black,** *yellow*	*175.00*	*150.00*
		On cover		*400.00*
130L3	L247	(2c) **red,** *bluish*	*250.00*	*200.00*
		On cover		*500.00*
130L4	L247	(2c) **blue green,** *green*		—

St. Louis City Delivery Company, St. Louis, Mo.

(See Cincinnati City Delivery)

L249

1883		Typo.		*Perf. 12*
131L1	L249	(1c) **red**	1.50	2.50
		Block of four	8.50	
		On cover		*200.00*
a.		Imperf., pair	—	

Cancellation: Purple target.

Smith & Stephens' City Delivery, St. Louis, Mo.

L284

Typeset

158L1	L284	1c **black,** *pale rose*		—

Spaulding's Penny Post, Buffalo, N. Y.

L283

L283a

1848-49				
156L1	L283	2c **vermilion**	*1,250.*	
156L2	L283a	2c **carmine**	*2,000.*	

Spence & Brown Express Post, Philadelphia, Pa.

L285

L286

(Illustrations reduced size)

1847 (?)				Typeset
159L1	L285	2c **black,** *bluish*	*900.00*	*900.00*

1848				Litho.
159L2	L286	(2c) **black**	*800.00*	*800.00*

Squier & Co. City Letter Dispatch, St. Louis, Mo.

(Jordan & Co.)

This post began to operate as a local carrier on July 6, 1859 and was discontinued in the early part of 1860. Squier & Co. used imperforate stamps; their successors (Jordan & Co.) about Jan. 1 1860, used the roulettes.

L248

1859 Litho. *Imperf.*

No.	Type	Description	Unused	Used
132L1	L248	1c **green**	—	*75.00*
		On cover		*500.00*

1860 *Rouletted 19*

No.	Type	Description	Unused	Used
132L2	L248	1c **rose brown**	*75.00*	*75.00*
		On cover		*400.00*
132L3	L248	1c **brownish purple**	*75.00*	*75.00*
		On cover		*400.00*
132L4	L248	1c **green**	*75.00*	*75.00*
		On cover		*400.00*

Cancellation: Black circle "Jordan's Penny Post Saint Louis".

Staten Island Express Post, Staten Island, N. Y.

Established by Hagadorn & Co., with office at Stapleton, Staten Island. Connected with Boyd for delivery in New York City.

L250

1849 Typo.

No.	Type	Description	Unused	Used
133L1	L250	3c **vermilion**	*350.00*	*300.00*
133L2	L250	6c **vermilion**	—	*1,250.*

Stringer & Morton's City Despatch, Baltimore, Md.

According to an advertisement in the Baltimore newspapers, dated October 19, 1850, this post aimed to emulate the successful posts of other cities, and divided the city into six districts, with a carrier in each district. Stamps were made available throughout the city.

L251

1850 Glazed Surface Paper

No.	Type	Description	Unused	Used
134L1	L251	(1c) **gold,** *black*	*150.00*	—
		On cover		*750.00*

Cancellation: Black circle "Baltimore City Despatch & Express Paid".

Sullivan's Dispatch Post, Cincinnati, Ohio

L252

1853 Glazed Surface Paper Litho.

No.	Type	Description	Unused	Used
135L1	L252	(2c) **black,** *green*	*1,500.*	

Wove Paper

No.	Type	Description	Unused	Used
135L2	L252	(2c) **bluish black**	*1,500.*	
135L3	L252	(2c) **green**	—	*1,200.*

Nos. 135L1-135L2 are either die cut octagonally or cut round. They do not exist cut square.

Swarts' City Dispatch Post, New York, N. Y.

Established by Aaron Swarts, at Chatham Square, in 1847, becoming one of the largest local posts in the city.

The postmarks of Swarts' Post Office are often found on stampless covers, as this post carried large quantities of mail without using adhesive stamps.

Zachary Taylor
L253

George Washington
L254

1849-53 Glazed Surface Paper Litho.

No.	Type	Description	Unused	Used
136L1	L253	(2c) **black,** *light green*	—	100.00
		On cover		250.00
136L2	L253	(2c) **black,** *dark green*	—	75.00
		On cover		250.00

Wove Paper

No.	Type	Description	Unused	Used
136L3	L253	(2c) **pink**	—	20.00
		On cover		150.00
136L4	L253	(2c) **red** (shades)	20.00	15.00
		On cover		150.00
136L5	L253	(2c) **pink,** *blue*		35.00
		On cover		250.00
136L6	L253	(2c) **red,** *blue*		35.00
		On cover		200.00
136L7	L253	(2c) **black,** *blue gray*	100.00	85.00
		On cover		250.00
136L8	L253	(2c) **blue**		90.00
		On cover		350.00
136L9	L254	(1c) **red**	—	20.00
		On cover		250.00
136L10	L254	(1c) **pink**	—	15.00
		On cover		200.00
136L11	L254	(1c) **red,** *bluish*	—	25.00
		On cover		200.00
136L12	L254	(1c) **pink,** *bluish*	—	35.00
		On cover		200.00

Bouton's Stamp with Red ms. "Swarts" at Top

No.	Type	Description	Unused	Used
136L13	L49	2c **black,** *gray blue*	*250.00*	*250.00*
		On cover		*500.00*

L255

Printed in sheets of 25 (5x5). Five minor varieties, the stamps in each vertical row being identical.

No.	Type	Description	Unused	Used
136L14	L255	1c **blue**	—	40.00
		On cover		200.00
a.		Thin paper	5.00	
		As "a," block of four	25.00	
136L15	L255	1c **red**	—	50.00
		On cover		250.00
136L16	L255	1c **red,** *bluish*	—	75.00
		On cover		*350.00*
136L17	L255	1c **black,** on cover		*1250.00*

Nos. 136L3-136L4, 136L9-136L10, 136L14-136L15 have been reprinted.

Cancellations: Red boxed "PAID" (mostly on Nos. 136L1-136L8, 136L13). Black boxed "PAID SWARTS" (mostly on Nos. 136L9-136L12). Black oval "Swarts Post Office Chatham Square" (Nos. 136L9-136L12). Black oval "Swarts B Post Chatham Square". Black grids (5-bar rectangle, 6-bar circle, solid star, hollow star, star in circle, etc). Other handstamp postmarks of the post have been found as cancellations. Government town postmarks exist on almost all Swarts stamps.

Teese & Co. Penny Post, Philadelphia, Pa.

L256

Printed in sheet of 200 divided into two panes of 100. Each pane includes setting of 20, repeated 5 times. Vertical or horizontal tete beche pairs appear twice in each setting. Twenty varieties.

1852 Wove Paper Litho.

No.	Type	Description	Unused	Used
137L1	L256	(1c) **blue,** *bluish*	7.50	35.00
		On cover		*400.00*
		Block of four	35.00	
a.		Tete beche pair	45.00	

Telegraph Despatch P. O., Philadelphia, Pa.

L257

1848

No.	Type	Description	Unused	Used
138L1	L257	1c **black,** *yellowish*		*600.00*
138L2	L257	2c **black,** *yellowish*		*2,000.*

The 2c differs in design, including the address, "Office No. 6 Sth 8 St" at bottom.

Third Avenue Post Office, New York, N. Y.

Established by S. Rotheneim, a former carrier for Boyd's City Express. All stamps were cut to shape by hand before being sold and exist only in that form.

L258

1855 Glazed Surface Paper Handstamped

No.	Type	Description	Unused	Used
139L1	L258	2c **black,** *green*	*250.00*	*250.00*
		On cover		*700.00*
139L1A	L258	2c **blue,** *green*	*400.00*	
139L2	L258	2c **black,** *maroon*	*400.00*	

Unsurfaced Paper colored through

No.	Type	Description	Unused	Used
139L3	L258	2c **black,** *yellow*	*200.00*	
139L4	L258	2c **black,** *blue*	*450.00*	
139L5	L258	2c **black,** *brown*	*450.00*	
139L6	L258	2c **black,** *buff*	*250.00*	
139L7	L258	2c **black,** *pink*	*450.00*	
139L8	L258	2c **black,** *green*	*400.00*	*400.00*

Cancellation on No. 139L1: Black "PAID".

Union Post, New York, N. Y.

L259

1846 Thick Glazed Surface Paper Handstamped

No.	Type	Description	Unused	Used
140L3	L259	**blue,** *green* ("UNOIN")	*3,000.*	
140L4	L259	**red,** *blue* ("UNION")	*2,000.*	
		On cover		—

Type L259 was used also as a postmark, usually struck in blue.

Union Square Post Office, New York, N. Y.

Established by Joseph E. Dunham about 1850. In 1851 Dunham acquired Messenkope's Union Square Post Office, operating the combined posts until 1854 or 1855. The business was sold in 1855 to Phineas C. Godfrey.

L259a

L260

1852 Typo.

No.	Type	Description	Unused	Used
141L1	L259a	1c **black,** *dark green*	6.00	20.00
		On cover		350.00
141L2	L259a	1c **black,** *light apple green*	30.00	40.00
		On cover		300.00
141L3	L260	2c **black,** *rose*	2.25	
		Block of four	10.00	

Walton & Co.'s City Express, Brooklyn, N. Y.

Operated by Wellington Walton

L261

1846		Glazed Surface Paper		Litho.
142L1	L261	2c **black,** *pink*	*400.00*	*300.00*
		On cover		*700.00*

Cancellations: Black "PAID / W. W." Black oblong quad (ties stamp "through" to cover).

Wells, Fargo and Co.

Wells, Fargo & Company entered the Western field about July 1, 1852, to engage in business on the Pacific Coast, and soon began to acquire other express businesses, eventually becoming the most important express company in its territory.

The Central Overland, California and Pikes Peak Express Company, inaugurated in 1860, was the pioneer Pony Express system and was developed to bring about quicker communication between the extreme portions of the United States. Via water the time was 28 to 30 days, with two monthly sailings, and by the overland route the time was 28 days. In 1860 the pioneer Pony Express carried letters only, reducing the time for the 2,100 miles (St. Joseph to San Francisco) to about 12 days. The postage rate was originally $5 the half-ounce.

About April 1, 1861, Wells, Fargo & Company became agents for the Central Overland, California and Pikes Peak Express Company and issued $2 red and $4 green stamps.

The rates were cut in half about July 1, 1861, and new stamps were issued: the $1 red, $2 green and $4 black, and the $1 garter design.

The revival of the Pony Express in 1862, known as the "Virginia City Pony" resulted in the appearance of the "cents" values, first rate.

Advertisement in the Placerville newspaper, Aug. 7, 1862: "Wells, Fargo & Co.'s Pony Express. On and after Monday, the 11th inst., we will run a Pony Express Daily between Sacramento and Virginia City, carrying letters and exchange papers, through from San Francisco in 24 hours, Sacramento in 15 hours and Placerville in 10 hours. Rates: All letters to be enclosed in our franks, and TEN CENTS PREPAID, in addition, for each letter weighing half an ounce or less, and ten cents for each additional half-ounce."

Wells, Fargo & Company used various handstamps to indicate mail transit. These are illustrated and described in the handbook, "Wells, Fargo & Co.'s Handstamps and Franks" by V. M. Berthold, published by Scott Stamp & Coin Co., Ltd. (out of print). The history of the Pony Express, a study of the stamps and reprints, and a survey of existing covers are covered in "The Pony Express," by M. C. Nathan and Winthrop S. Boggs, published by the Collectors Club, 22 E. 35th., New York, N.Y. 10016.

Wells Fargo stamps of types L262-L264 were lithographed by Britton & Rey, San Francisco.

L262

Printed in sheets of 40 (8x5), two panes of 20 (4x5) each.

1861		(April to July 1)		Litho.
143L1	L262	$2 **red**	100.00	250.00
		On U. S. envelope No. U10		—
		On U. S. envelope No. U16		—
		On U. S. envelope No. U17		*6,000.*
		On U. S. envelope No. U18		*6,000.*
		On U. S. envelope No. U32 (patriotic cover)		*13,000.*
		On U. S. envelope No. U33		*6,000.*
		On U. S. envelope No. U65		—
143L2	L262	$4 **green**	200.00	400.00
		Block of four	—	
		On U. S. envelope No. U33		—

1861		(July 1 to Nov.)		
143L3	L262	$1 **red**	60.00	135.00
		Block of four	325.00	
		On U. S. envelope No. U11		—
		On U. S. envelope No. U15		*4,500.*
		On U. S. envelope No. U17		*4,500.*
		On U. S. envelope No. U32		*6,000.*
		On U. S. envelope No. U33		*6,000.*
		On U. S. envelope No. U35		*4,500.*
		On U. S. envelope No. U40		*6,000.*
		On U. S. envelope No. U41		*5,000.*
143L4	L262	$2 **green**	150.00	250.00
		Block of four	900.00	
		On U. S. envelope No. U41		*11,000.*
143L5	L262	$4 **black**	125.00	500.00
		Block of four	—	
		On cover		—

Cancellations: Blue, black or magenta express company.

Nos. 143L1-143L5 and 143L7-143L9 were reprinted in 1897. The reprints are retouched. Shades vary from originals. Originals and reprints are fully described in "The Pony Express," by M. C. Nathan and W. S. Boggs (Collectors Club).

L263

Printed in sheets of 16 (4x4)

1861		Thin Wove Paper		
143L6	L263	$1 **blue**	325.00	600.00
		On 10c U.S. envelope No. U40		*17,500.*

No. 143L6 apparently used only from east to west.

Most counterfeits have a horizontal line bisecting the shield. Some genuine stamps have a similar line drawn in with blue ink.

L264

Printed in sheets of 40 (8x5), four panes of 10, each pane 2x5.

1862-64				
143L7	L264	10c **brown** (shades)	30.00	75.00
		Pair	75.00	*350.00*
		Block of four	250.00	
		On U.S. envelope No. U26		*5,000.*
		On U.S. envelope No. U34		*4,500.*
		On U.S. envelope No. U35		*3,500.*
		On cover with 3c #65		—
143L8	L264	25c **blue**	50.00	75.00
		Pair	125.00	
		Block of four	350.00	
		On plain cover		*2,250.*
		On U.S. envelope No. U10		—
		On U.S. envelope No. U34		*3,500.*
		On U.S. envelope No. U35		*4,000.*
143L9	L264	25c **red**	20.00	40.00
		Pair	60.00	
		Block of four	150.00	
		On U.S. envelope No. U9		—
		On U.S. envelope No. U10		*4,000.*
		On U.S. envelope No. U34		*4,000.*
		On U.S. envelope No. U35		*4,000.*
		Pair on U.S. envelope No. U35		*9,000.*

Cancellations on Nos. 143L7-143L9: Blue or black express company. Black town.

NEWSPAPER STAMPS

L265

L266

L267

L268

L269

L270

1861-70				
143LP1	L265	**black**	250.00	300.00
143LP2	L266	**blue**	350.00	
143LP3	L267	**blue**	10.00	
a.		Thin paper	20.00	
143LP4	L268	**blue**	25.00	
		Rouletted 10		
143LP5	L267	**blue**	15.00	25.00
		On wrapper		—
		Block of four	75.00	
a.		Thin paper	—	
143LP6	L268	**blue**	15.00	
a.		Tete beche	100.00	

Type L267 was printed in sheets of 50 (5x10).

1883-88			*Perf. 11, 12, 12½*	
143LP7	L268	**blue**	7.50	
143LP8	L269	**blue**	12.50	17.50
143LP9	L270	**blue**	2.00	2.50
		On wrapper		—
a.		Vertical pair, imperf. between	60.00	
b.		Horiz. pair, imperf. vert.	—	
		Double transfer	—	

FOR PUBLISHERS' USE

L271

1876				Typo.
143LP10	L271	**blue**	6.00	*15.00*
		Block of four	30.00	
		On wrapper		*850.00*

Cancellation: Blue company

ENVELOPES

1862				
143LU1	L264	10c **red**	—	*1,250.*
143LU2	L264	10c **blue**	—	*750.00*
143LU3	L264	25c **red**	350.00	

On "Gould & Curry" overall advertising envelope		350.00	

Westervelt's Post, Chester, N. Y.

Operated by Charles H. Westervelt. Rate was 1 cent for letters and 2 cents for packages carried to the post office. Local and government postage required prepayment.

L273

Several varieties

1863 (?)			**Typeset**	
144L1	L273	(1c) **black,** *buff*	20.00	—
		On cover		500.00
144L2	L273	**black,** *lavender*	25.00	—
		On cover		—

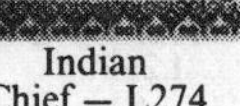

Indian Chief — L274

General U. S. Grant — L275

Six varieties

1864 (?)			**Typeset**	
144L9	L274	(1c) **red,** *pink*	20.00	—
		On cover		500.00

Six varieties

1865			**Typo.**	
144L29	L275	2c **black,** *yellow*	20.00	—
144L30	L275	2c **black,** *gray green*	25.00	—
144L40	L275	2c **red,** *pink*	25.00	—

All of the Westervelt stamps are believed to have a philatelic flavor, although it is possible that Nos. 144L1-144L2 were originally issued primarily for postal purposes. It is possible that Nos. 144L9, 144L29-144L30 and 144L40 were used in the regular course of business, particularly No. 144L9.

However,the large number of varieties on various colors of paper, which exist both as originals as well as contemporary and near-contemporary reprints, are believed to have been produced solely for sale to collectors. Type L275 was certainly issued primarily for sale to collectors. Many of the unlisted colors in all three types exist only as reprints. Forgeries of all three types also exist.

L276

ENVELOPES

Impressed at top left

1865			**Typo.**	
144LU1	L276	**red,** *white*	—	
144LU2	L276	**red brown,** *orange*	—	200.00
144LU3	L276	**black,** *bluish*	—	
144LU4	L276	**black,** *buff*	—	
144LU5	L276	**black,** *white*	—	

It is possible that Nos. 114LU1-144LU5 were corner cards and had no franking value.

Westtown, Westtown, Pa.

The Westtown School at Westtown, Pa., is the oldest of the secondary schools in America, managed by the Society of Friends. It was established in 1799. In 1853 the school authorities decided that all outgoing letters carried by stage should pay a fee of 2 cents. Prepaid stamps were placed on sale at the school. Stamps were usually affixed to the reverse of the letter sheets or envelopes.

At first, letters were usually mailed at West Chester, Pa. After March 4, 1859, letters were sent from Street Road Post Office, located at the railroad station. Later this became the Westtown Post Office. The larger stamp was the first used. The smaller stamp came into use about 1867.

L277

L277a

Several types of each, with and without hyphen

1853-67(?)			**Litho.**	
145L1	L277	(2c) **gold**	30.00	—
145L2	L277a	(2c) **gold**	12.50	30.00
		On cover		110.00
		Block of four	500.00	
a.		Tete beche pair	100.00	

No. 145L1 in red brown is a color changeling.

Whittelsey's Express, Chicago, Ill.

Operated by Edmund A. and Samuel M. Whittelsey

George Washington — L278

1857			**Typo.**	
146L1	L278	2c **red**	600.00	1.000.
		Block of four	—	

Cancellation: Blue oval "Whittelsey's Express".

Williams' City Post, Cincinnati, Ohio.
See Carriers' Stamps, No. 9LB1.

Wood & Co. City Despatch, Baltimore, Md.

Operated by W. Wood

L280

1856			**Typeset**
148L1	L280	(1c) **black,** *yellow*	750.00

W. Wyman, Boston, Mass.

Established to carry mail between Boston and New York

L281

1844			**Litho.**	
149L1	L281	5c **black**	—	150.00
		On cover		750.00

No. 149L1 may have been sold singly at 6 cents each.

Zieber's One Cent Dispatch, Pittsburgh, Pa.

L282

1851			**Typeset**
150L1	L282	1c **black,** *gray blue*	3,000.

Cancellation: Acid

For Local 151L1 see under **Friend's Boarding School.**

For Local 152L1 see under **Faunce's Penny Post.**

For Local 153L1 see under **Hackney & Bolte Penny Post.**

For Local 154L1 see under **A. W. Auner's Despatch Post.**

For Local 155L1 see under **McGreely's Express.**

For Local 156L1-2 see under **Spaulding's Penny Post.**

For Local 157L1 see under **Bush's Brooklyn City Express.**

For Local 158L1 see under **Smith & Stephens City Delivery.**

For Local 159L1-2 see under **Spence & Brown Express Post.**

For Local 160L1 see under **City Dispatch, New York City.**

For Local 161L1 see under **Clinton's Penny Post.**

For Local 162L1 see under **Rogers' Penny Post.**

For Local 163L1 see under **Blizzard Mail.**

For Local 164L1 see under **Freeman & Co.'s Express, New York City.**

For Local 165L1 see under **J. A. Howell's City Despatch**

LOCAL HANDSTAMPED COVERS

In 1836-1860 when private companies carried mail, many of them used handstamps on the covers they carried. Examples of these handstamps are shown on this and following pages.

Accessory Transit Co. of Nicaragua

Blue or Black

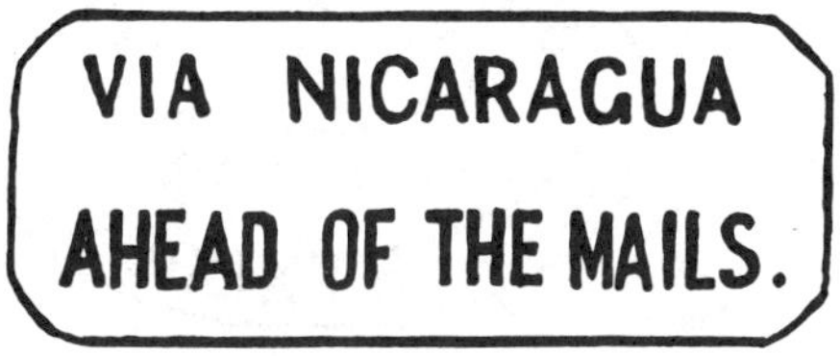

VIA NICARAGUA
AHEAD OF THE MAILS.

Red, Black or Blue

A sub-variety shows "Leland" below "MAILS" in lower right corner.

Red or Blue

1853

Barker's City Post, Boston, Mass.

Black

1855-59

Also known with "10" instead of "34" Court Square.

E. N. Barry's Despatch Post, New York City, N.Y.

Black

1852

Bates & Co., New Bedford, Mass.
(Agent for Hale & Co. at New Bedford)

Red

1845

Branch Post Office, New York City, N. Y.
(Swarts' Chatham Square Post Office)

Red

1847

Brigg's Despatch, Philadelphia, Pa.

Black

1848

Bush's Brooklyn City Express, Brooklyn, N. Y.

Red

1848

Cover shows red PAID.

Central Post Office, New York, N.Y.

Black

1856

Cover shows black PAID.

City Despatch Post, New York City, N. Y.
(Used by Mead, successor to United States City Despatch Post.)

Black

1848

City Dispatch Post, Baltimore, Md.

Red

1846-47

City Despatch & Express, Baltimore, Md.

Black

1850

Cole's City Despatch P. O., New York City, N. Y.
(Used by Cole with some of the City Despatch Post stamps.)

Black or Red

1848-50

Dunhams Post Office, New York City, N. Y.
(See Union Square Post Office).

Red

1850-52

Gay, Kinsley & Co., Boston, Mass.
(A package express)

Red

Hanford's Pony Express Post, New York, N.Y.

Black or Red

1845-51

Hartford Penny Post, Hartford, Conn.

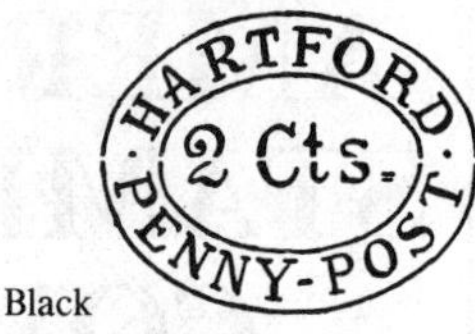

Black

1852-61

Hudson Street Post Office, New York City, N. Y.

Red

1850

Cover shows red PAID.

Jones & Russell's Pikes Peak Express Co., Denver, Colo.

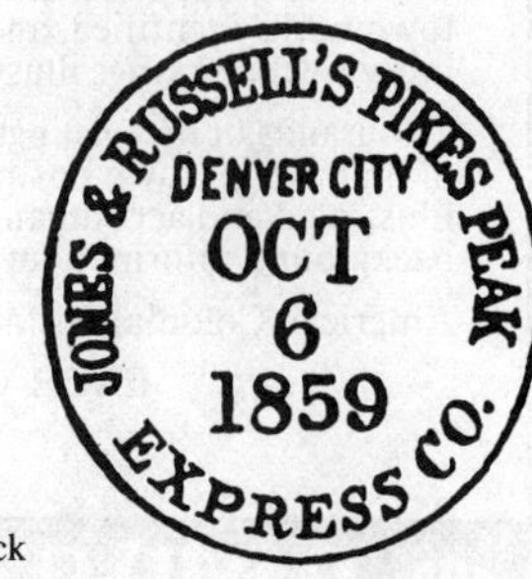

Black

1859-60

Kenyon's Letter Office, 91 Wall St., New York City

Red

1846-60

Letter Express, San Francisco, Cal.
(See Gahagan & Howe, San Francisco, Cal.)

Blue

1865-66

Libbey & Co.'s City Post, Boston, Mass.

LIBBEY & CO'S
CITY POST.
10 COURT SQUARE

Black or Red

1852

Cover has 3c 1851 postmarked Boston, Mass.

Manhattan Express, New York City, N. Y.
(W. V. Barr. See also Bouton's Manhattan Express.)

Red

1847

New York Penny Post,
New York City, N. Y.

Black or Red

1840-41

Also known with hour indicated.

Noisy Carriers, San Francisco, Cal.

Blue or Green

Blue

By Mail Steamer FROM NOISY CARRIER'S

Black or Red

FROM NOISY CARRIERS. MAIL. 77 LONG WHARF S.F. CAL.

Black, Blue or Green

NOISY CARRIER'S MAIL, SAN FRANCISCO.

Black

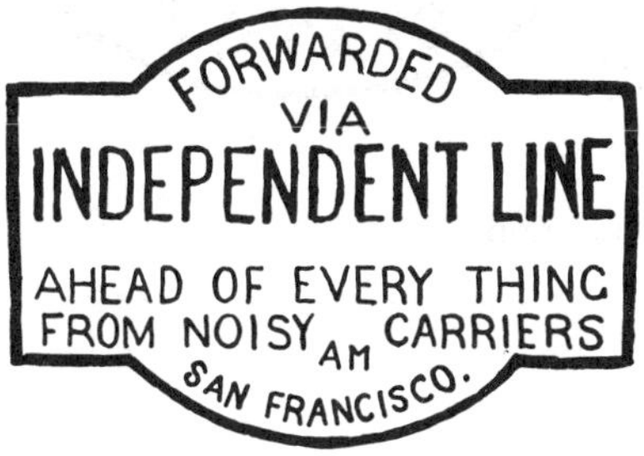

FORWARDED VIA INDEPENDENT LINE AHEAD OF EVERY THING FROM NOISY AM CARRIERS SAN FRANCISCO.

Black or Blue

1853-56

Northern Liberties News Rooms, Philadelphia, Pa.

Black

Black

1836

Press printed.

Two types.

The lack of a value for a listed item does not necessarily indicate rarity.

Overton & Co.'s City Mail, New York City, N. Y.

Red

1844-5

Pony Express

Blue or Red

1860

Blue (Enlarged)

1861

Black or Carmine

1860-61

1853-56

from St. Joseph, Mo.

Black or Green

Denver City, K. T. Black
Leavenworth City, K. T. Black
San Francisco, Cal. Blue

Black or Green

1860-61

Red

Blue or Red
Blue

1860

Rogers' Penny Post, Newark, N. J.

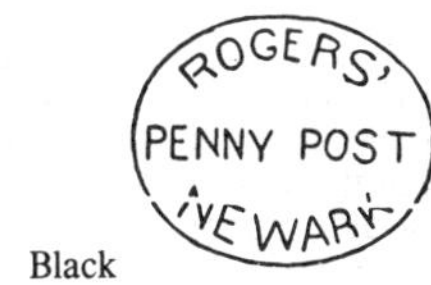

Black

1856

Spark's Post Office, New York City, N. Y.

Red, Green, Blue or Black

1848

Spaulding's Penny Post, Buffalo, N. Y.

Black

1848

Spence & Brown Express Post, Philadelphia, Pa.

Black

1848

Stait's Despatch Post, Philadelphia, Pa. (Eagle City Post)

Red or Black

1850-51

Red

1850-55

Stone's City Post, New York City, N. Y.

Red

1858-59

J. W. Sullivan's Newspaper Office, San Francisco, Cal.

Black or Red

1854-55

Towle & Co. Letter Delivery, Boston, Mass.

Red

1847

Towle's City Dispatch Post, Boston, Mass.

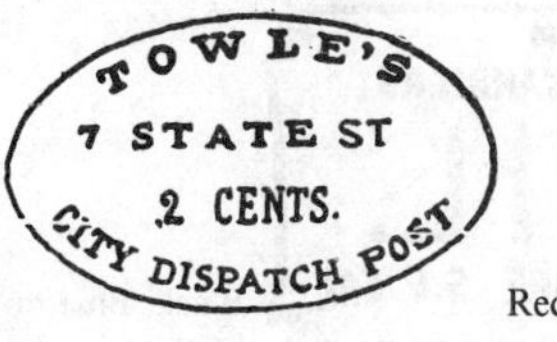

Red

1849

Towle's City Post, Boston, Mass.

(Also 10 Court Sq.) Red

1849-50

Cover shows PAID.

TELEGRAPH

These stamps were issued by the individual companies for use on their own telegrams, and can usually be divided into three classes: Free franking privileges issued to various railroad, newspaper and express company officials, etc., whose companies were large users of the lines; those issued at part cost to the lesser officials of the same type companies; and those bearing values which were usually sold to the general public. Some of the companies on occasions granted the franking privilege to stockholders and minor State (not Federal) officials. Most Telegraph Stamps were issued in booklet form and will be found with one or more straight edges.

American Rapid Telegraph Company

Organized Feb. 21, 1879, in New York State. Its wires extended as far north as Boston, Mass., and west to Cleveland, Ohio. It was amalgamated with the Bankers and Merchants Telegraph Co., but when that company was unable to pay the fixed charges, the properties of the American Rapid Telegraph Company were sold on Mar. 11, 1891, to a purchasing committee comprised of James W. Converse and others. This purchasing committee deeded the property and franchise of the American Rapid Telegraph Company to the Western Union Telegraph Company on June 25, 1894. Issued three types of stamps: Telegram, Collect and Duplicate. Telegram stamps were issued in sheets of 100 and were used to prepay messages which could be dropped in convenient boxes for collection. Collect and duplicate stamps were issued in alternate rows on the same sheet of 100 subjects. Collect stamps were attached to telegrams sent collect, the receiver of which paid the amount shown by the stamps, while the Duplicate stamps were retained by the Company as vouchers. Remainders with punched cancellations were bought up by a New York dealer.

T1

"Prepaid Telegram" Stamps

Engraved and Printed by the American Bank Note Co.

1881 *Perf. 12*

				Unused	*Used*	*Punched*
1T1	T1	1c	black	6.50	3.75	10
			Block of four	30.00		1.00
1T2	T1	3c	orange	22.50	17.50	1.00
			Block of four			10.00
1T3	T1	5c	bister brown	1.40	40	8
			Block of four	6.25		40
		a.	5c brown	1.40	75	10
			Block of four	6.25		1.00
1T4	T1	10c	purple	9.00	4.75	10
			Block of four	40.00		1.00
1T5	T1	15c	green	2.50	90	10
			Block of four	14.00		1.00
1T6	T1	20c	red	2.50	85	8
			Block of four			80

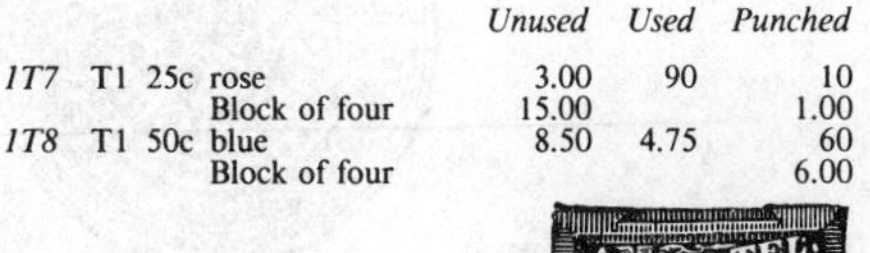

				Unused	*Used*	*Punched*
1T7	T1	25c	rose	3.00	90	10
			Block of four	15.00		1.00
1T8	T1	50c	blue	8.50	4.75	60
			Block of four			6.00

T2

"Collect" Stamps

1T9	T2	1c	brown	3.50	2.75	10
1T10	T2	5c	blue	1.75	90	10
1T11	T2	15c	red brown	1.40	85	25
1T12	T2	20c	olive green	1.25	85	10

T3

"Office Coupon" Stamps

				Unused	Used	Punched
1T13	T3	1c	brown	5.50	2.00	10
a.			Pair, se-tenant with "Collect"			1.50
			Block of four, same as "a"			3.25
1T14	T3	5c	blue	4.50	2.00	10
a.			Pair, se-tenant with "Collect"	17.50		2.25
			Block of four, same as "a"	37.50		5.00
1T15	T3	15c	red brown	8.50	2.50	20
a.			Pair, se-tenant with "Collect"	17.50		2.50
			Block of four, same as "a"	37.50		5.50
1T16	T3	20c	olive green	8.50	3.00	10
a.			Pair, se-tenant with "Collect"			2.75
			Block of four, same as "a"			6.00

Atlantic Telegraph Company

Organized 1884 at Portland, Maine. Its lines extended from Portland, Me., to Boston, Mass., and terminated in the office of the Baltimore and Ohio Telegraph Company at Boston. Later bought out by the Baltimore and Ohio Telegraph Co. Stamps issued by the Atlantic Telegraph Company could also be used for messages destined to any point on the Baltimore and Ohio system. Stamps were printed in panes of six and a full book sold for $10. Remainders of these stamps, without control numbers, were purchased by a Boston dealer and put on the market about 1932.

T4

1888 *Perf. 13*

				Unused	Used	Remainders (no control numbers)
2T1	T4	1c	green	3.50	—	2.00
			Pane of six	—		14.00
2T2	T4	5c	blue	3.50	—	2.00
			Pane of six	—		14.00
a.			Imperf. vert., pair	—		
b.			Imperf. horiz., pair	20.00	—	
2T3	T4	10c	purple brown	3.50	—	2.00
			Pane of six	—		14.00
a.			Horiz. pair, imperf. between	30.00		
2T4	T4	25c	carmine	3.50	—	2.25
			Pane of six			16.00

Baltimore & Ohio Telegraph Companies

"The Baltimore & Ohio Telegraph Co. of the State of New York" was incorporated May 17, 1882. Organization took place under similar charter in 26 other states. It absorbed the National Telegraph Co. and several others. Extended generally along the lines of the Baltimore & Ohio Railroad, but acquired interests in other states. Company absorbed in 1887 by the Western Union Telegraph Co. Stamps were issued in booklet form and sold for $5 and $10, containing all denominations.

T5

T6

Engraved by the American Bank Note Co.

1885 *Perf. 12*

				Unused	Used
3T1	T5	1c	vermilion	25.00	10.00
			Pane of six	160.00	
3T2	T5	5c	blue	25.00	20.00
3T3	T5	10c	red brown	12.00	8.00
			Pane of six	75.00	
3T4	T5	25c	orange	25.00	12.00
3T5	T6		brown	1.00	
			Pane of four	6.00	

1886

				Unused	Used
3T6	T6		black	1.00	
			Pane of four	6.00	

Imprint of Kendall Bank Note Co.
Thin Paper

1886 *Perf. 14*

				Unused	Used
3T7	T5	1c	green	5.00	50
a.			Thick paper	7.00	85
b.			Imperf., pair	70.00	
3T8	T5	5c	blue	3.00	75
a.			Thick paper	5.00	75
b.			Imperf, pair		55.00
3T9	T5	10c	brown	5.00	60
a.			Thick paper	8.25	85
3T10	T5	25c	deep orange	17.50	75
a.			Thick paper	21.50	1.00

Used copies of Nos. 3T7-3T20 normally have heavy grid cancellations. Lightly canceled copies command a premium.

Litho. by A. Hoen & Co.

1886 **Imprint of firm** *Perf. 12*

				Unused	Used
3T11	T5	1c	green	2.50	35
			Pane of six	22.50	—
3T12	T5	5c	blue	6.50	35
			Pane of six	50.00	—
a.			Imperf., pair	85.00	
3T13	T5	10c	dark brown	6.25	60
			Pane of six	45.00	—
a.			Vertical pair, imperf. between		55.00

Wmk. "A HOEN AND CO. BALTIMORE" in double lined capitals in sheet
Perf. 12

				Unused	Used
3T14	T5	1c	green	9.00	1.10
			Pane of six	57.50	—
3T15	T5	5c	blue	15.00	1.10
			Pane of six	100.00	—
a.			Imperf., pair	52.50	—
3T16	T5	10c	dark brown	10.00	1.00
			Pane of six	72.50	—

Lithographed by Forbes Co., Boston

1887 **Imprint of firm** *Perf. 12½*

				Unused	Used
3T17	T5	1c	green	25.00	1.00
3T18	T5	5c	blue	27.50	1.50
3T19	T5	10c	brown	19.00	1.50
3T20	T5	25c	yellow	25.00	1.00
a.			25c orange	21.00	1.00

Baltimore & Ohio-Connecticut River Telegraph Companies

The Connecticut River Telegraph Co. ran from New Haven to Hartford. An agreement was entered wherein the Baltimore &, Ohio System had mutual use of their lines. This agreement terminated when the Baltimore & Ohio System was absorbed by the Western Union. The Connecticut River Telegraph Company then joined the United Lines. In 1885 stamps (black on yellow) were issued and sold in booklets for $10. In 1887 the Connecticut River Telegraph Co. had extended its lines to New Boston, Mass., and new books of stamps (black on blue) were issued for use on this extension. Remainders were canceled with bars and sold to a New York dealer.

T7

1885 *Perf. 11*

				Unused	Used	Remainders (Bar canc.)
4T1	T7	1c	black, *yellow*	3.00	7.50	30
			Pane of ten	35.00		4.00
a.			Imperf., pair	40.00		
b.			Imperf. horizontally, pair			—
4T2	T7	5c	black, *yellow*	3.00	7.50	25
			Pane of ten	35.00		3.00
a.			Horizontal pair, imperf. between			—
b.			Vertical pair, imperf. between			35.00
c.			Imperf., pair			35.00
4T3	T7	1c	black, *blue*	7.00	—	2.00
			Pane of ten	80.00		22.50
4T4	T7	5c	black, *blue*	6.00	—	2.00
			Pane of ten	65.00		22.50

California State Telegraph Company

Incorporated June 17, 1854 as the California Telegraph Company and constructed a line from Nevada through Grass Valley to Auburn. Extended to run from San Francisco to Marysville via San Jose and Stockton. Later absorbed Northern Telegraph Co. and thus extended to Eureka. It was incorporated as the California State Telegraph Company on April 6, 1861. At the time of its lease to the Western Union on May 16, 1867 the California State consisted of the following companies which had been previously absorbed: Alta California Telegraph Co., Atlantic and Pacific States Telegraph Co., National Telegraph Co., Northern California Telegraph Co., Overland Telegraph Co., Placerville and Humboldt Telegraph Co., Tuolumne Telegraph Co. Stamps were issued in booklets, six to a pane. Remainders of Nos. 5T1 and 5T4, without frank numbers are known.

T8

1870 *Perf. 13½*

			Unused	Used
5T1	T8	black & blue	85.00	—
		Pane of six	550.00	
a.		Without number	75.00	

T9

T10

1870 *Perf. 12, 13*

5T2	T9	black & red, without number	145.00	145.00

1871 **Dated "1871"**

5T3	T9	black & red, without number	275.00	
	a.	Imperf., pair	—	—
5T4	T10	black & salmon, blue number	140.00	—
		Pane of six	—	
	a.	Without number	125.00	

1872

5T5	T10	green & red, red number (No year date)	100.00	—
		Pane of six	—	

1873 **Dated "1873"**

5T6	T10	red & salmon, blue number	140.00	140.00

1874 **Dated "1874"**

5T7	T10	blue & salmon, black number	85.00	—
		Pane of six	—	

1875 **Dated "1875"**

5T8	T10	brown & green, black number	110.00	—
		Pane of six	—	

City & Suburban Telegraph Company (New York City and Suburban Printing Telegraph Company)

Organized 1855. Extended only through New York City and Brooklyn. Sold out to the American Telegraph Co. Stamps were sold to the public for prepayment of messages, which could be dropped in convenient boxes for collection. Stamps were issued in sheets of 60 having a face value of $1. These were arranged in six vertical rows of ten, the horizontal rows having the following denominations: 2c, 1c, 1c, 1c, 2c, 3c.

Counterfeits are known both in black and blue, mostly on pelure or hard white paper. Originals are on soft wove paper, somewhat yellowish. Scalloped edge is more sharply etched on the counterfeits.

T11

Typo. ***Imperf.***

6T1	T11	1c	black	130.00	110.00
			Pair	—	
			Block of four	—	
6T2	T11	2c	black	200.00	150.00
			Pair	—	
			Pair, 2c + 1c	375.00	
6T3	T11	3c	black	325.00	225.00
			Pair	—	
			Strip of three, 1c, 2c and 3c	1100.	

Colusa, Lake & Mendocino Telegraph Company

Was organized in California early in 1873. First known as the Princeton, Colusa and Grand Island Telegraph Co. In May, 1873 they completed their line from Princeton through Colusa, at which point it was connected with the Western Union office, to Grand Island. On Feb. 10, 1875 it was incorporated as the Colusa, Lake & Mendocino Telegraph Co. Its lines were extended into the counties of Colusa, Lake, Mendocino and Napa. Eventually reached a length of 260 miles. Went out of business in 1892. Stamps were issued for prepayment of messages and were sold in books. When sold they were stamped "P.L.W." (the superintendent's initials) in blue. The 5c value was printed 10 to a pane, being two horizontal rows of five. Of the 10c and 25c nothing definite is known about the settings.

T11a

1876 ***Perf. 12***

7T1	T11a	5c	black	190.00	—
			Block of four	850.00	
			Pane of ten	2,000.	
			Without "P.L.W."	250.00	
7T2	T11a	10c	black	*9,000.*	—
7T3	T11a	25c	red	*9,000.*	—

Commercial Union Telegraph Company

Incorporated in New York State on March 31, 1886. Its lines ran from Albany through Troy to Berlin, N.Y., thence to North Adams, Mass. The lines of this Company, which was controlled by the Postal Telegraph Company, were later extended throughout Northern New York and the States of Massachusetts, Vermont, New Hampshire and Maine. Stamps issued in panes of four.

T12

T13

T14

1891 **Lithographed by A. C. Goodwin** ***Perf. 12***

8T1	T12	25c	yellow	12.50	—
			Pane of four	55.00	
8T2	T13	25c	green	10.00	—
			Pane of four	45.00	
		a.	Horiz. pair, imperf. vertically	40.00	
8T3	T14		lilac rose	30.00	—

Mutual Union Telegraph Company

Incorporated October 4, 1880. Extended over 22 states. Absorbed about 1883 by the Western Union Telegraph Co. Franks issued for use of stockholders, in books, four to a pane.

T15

Engr. by Van Campen Engraving Co., New York
1882-83 ***Perf. 14***

9T1	T15		blue	20.00	20.00
			Pane of four	90.00	
		a.	Vert. pair, imperf. horizontally	60.00	—
		b.	Imperf., pair	60.00	
9T2	T15		carmine	20.00	—
			Pane of four	90.00	

North American Telegraph Company

Incorporated October 15, 1885 to run from Chicago to Minneapolis, later being extended into North and South Dakota. Absorbed 1n 1929 by the Postal System.

Apparently these stamps were not canceled when used. Issued in panes of four.

T15a

1899-1907 ***Perf. 12***

10T1	T15a	violet (1899)	55.00
		Pane of four	210.00
10T2	T15a	green (1901)	70.00
10T3	T15a	dark brown (1902)	110.00
10T4	T15a	blue (1903)	70.00
10T5	T15a	violet (1904)	65.00
		Pane of four	275.00
	a.	Imperf. vertically (pair)	225.00
10T6	T15a	red brown (1905)	55.00
10T7	T15a	rose (1906)	65.00
10T8	T15a	green (1907)	350.00

Nos. 10T1 to 10T8 are known imperforate.

Northern Mutual Telegraph Company

Incorporated in New York State as the Northern Mutual Telegraph and Telephone Company on June 20, 1882. Its line, which consisted of a single wire, extended from Syracuse to Ogdensburg via Oswego, Watertown and Clayton, a distance of 170 miles. It was sold to the Bankers and Merchants Telegraph Company in 1883. Stamps were in use for a few days only in April, 1883. Issued in panes of 35 having a face value of $5. Seven horizontal rows of five covering all denominations as follows: 2 rows of 25c, 1 of 20c, 2 of 10c, 2 of 5c. The remainders and plates were purchased by a New York dealer in 1887.

T16

1883 ***Perf. 14***

11T1	T16	5c	yellow brown	4.50	—
			Block of four	20.00	
11T2	T16	10c	yellow brown	4.50	—
			Block of four	20.00	
11T3	T16	20c	yellow brown	12.50	—
			Horizontal pair	27.50	
11T4	T16	25c	yellow brown	4.50	—
			Block of four	20.00	
			Pane of 35	275.00	

The first reprints are lighter in color than the originals, perf. 14 and the gum is yellowish instead of white. The pane makeup differs in the reprints. The second reprints are darker than the original, perf. 12. Value 75c each.

Northern New York Telegraph Company

Organized about 1892. Extended from Malone, N. Y. to Massena, N.Y. Re-incorporated as the New York Union Telegraph Co. on April 2, 1896.

T16a

Typo. by Charles H. Smith, Brushton, N.Y.
1894-95 ***Rouletted***

12T1	T16a		green (overprinted in red "Frank 1894")	45.00
			Pane of six	275.00
		a.	Imperf. pair	50.00
12T2	T16a		red (overprinted in black "Frank 1895")	200.00
			Pane of six	1,300.
		a.	Imperf. pair	50.00
12T3	T16a	1c	yellow (overprinted in black "One")	80.00
			Pane of 6	500.00
		a.	Imperf. pair	50.00

12T4 T16a 10c blue (overprinted in red "10") 125.00
Pane of six 800.00
a. Imperf. pair 50.00

Some specialists believe that Nos. 12T1-12T4 were not issued and probably are essays.

Pacific Mutual Telegraph Company

Incorporated in Missouri on June 21, 1883. Operated between St. Louis and Kansas City, Mo., during the years 1884 and 1885. It had 15 offices, 425 miles of poles and 850 miles of wire. The controlling interests were held by the Bankers and Merchants Telegraph Company. The name was changed on Sept. 10, 1910 to Postal Telegraph-Cable Company of Missouri. Stamps were issued in booklets having a face value of $10 and containing 131 stamps as follows: 50-1c, 20-5c, 45-10c, 16-25c. They are not known used.

T17

1883 *Perf. 12*

13T1 T17 1c black 22.50
13T2 T17 1c slate 35
Block of four 1.50
a. 1c gray 35
Block of four 1.50
13T3 T17 5c black, *buff* 40
Block of four 1.75
13T4 T17 10c black, *green* 35
Block of four 1.75
a. Horizontal pair, imperf. between —
13T5 T17 25c black, *salmon buff* 30
Block of four 1.50

Pacific Postal Telegraph-Cable Company

The Pacific Postal Telegraph-Cable Company was the Pacific Coast Department of the Postal Telegraph-Cable Company, and was organized in 1886. Its first wire ran from San Francisco to New Westminster, B.C., where it touched the lines of the Canadian Pacific Railway Company, then the only connection between the Eastern and Western Postal systems. Later the Postal's own wires spanned the continent and the two companies were united.

Stamps issued in booklet form in vertical panes of five.

T16b

14T1 T16b 10c brown 30.00 25.00
Pane of five 150.00
14T2 T16b 15c black 20.00 15.00
Pane of five 105.00
14T3 T16b 25c rose red 30.00 25.00
Pane of five 160.00
14T4 T16b 40c green 25.00 20.00
Pane of five 135.00
14T5 T16b 50c blue 30.00 25.00
Pane of five 160.00

These stamps were issued with three sizes of frank numbers; large closely spaced, small closely spaced and small widely spaced figures.

They also exist without frank numbers.

Postal Telegraph Company

Organized in New York in 1881. Reorganized in 1891 as the Postal Telegraph-Cable Co. The Postal Telegraph Co stamps of 1885 were issued in sheets of 100. Some years after the reorganization a New York dealer purchased the remainders which were canceled with a purple star. The Postal Telegraph-Cable Co. issued frank stamps in booklets, usually four stamps to a pane. This company was merged with the Western Union Telegraph Company in 1943.

T18

T19

T20

T21

Engraved by Hamilton Bank Note Co.

1885 *Perf. 14*

	Unused	Used	Remainders (Purple Star)
15T1 T18 10c green	1.75	—	25
Block of four	8.00		1.25
a. Horizontal pair, imperf. between			20.00
b. 10c deep green	1.75	—	25
Block of four	8.00		1.25
15T2 T19 15c orange red	2.50	—	60
Block of four	12.00	—	3.00
a. Horizontal pair, imperf. between	25.00		
15T3 T20 25c blue	1.00	4.00	15
Block of four	5.00		75
a. Horizontal pair, imperf. between	30.00		
15T4 T21 50c brown	1.50	—	60
Block of four	7.00		3.00

The 25c in ultramarine and the 50c in black were printed and perforated 16 but are not known to have been issued. Value about $5 each.

T22

T22a

Typographed by Moss Engraving Co.

1892-1920 *Perf. 14*

Signature of A.B. Chandler

15T5 T22 blue gray (1892) 15.00
a. Imperf., pair 50.00

Perf. 13 to 14½ and Compound

15T6 T22 gray lilac (1892) 15.00
15T7 T22 red (1893) 12.00 10.00
Pane of four 50.00
15T8 T22 red brown (1893) 4.00 3.00

Perf. 12

15T9 T22 violet brown (1894) 6.00
15T10 T22 gray green (1894) 4.00
a. Imperf., pair 20.00
15T11 T22 blue (1895) 20.00
15T12 T22 rose (1895) 125.00
15T13 T22a slate green (1896) 5.00
Pane of four 17.50
15T14 T22a brown (1896) 100.00

Nos. 15T11 and 15T12 are from a new die resembling T22 but without shading under "Postal Telegraph Co."

Signature of Albert B. Chandler

15T15 T22a lilac brown (1897) 1.50
Pane of four 6.50
15T16 T22a orange (1897) 80.00

Typographed by Knapp & Co.

15T17 T22a pale blue (1898) 1.25
Pane of four 5.50
15T18 T22a rose (1898) 100.00

Typographed by Moss Engraving Co.

Perf. 12

15T19 T22a orange brown (1899) 1.25
Pane of four 5.50

Perf. 11

15T20 T22a blue (1900) 3.00 3.00
a. "I" "Complimentary" omitted 40 80
Pane of four 2.50

The variety 15T20a represents a different die with many variations in the design.

Perf. 14

15T21 T22a sea green (1901) 40 40
Pane of four 1.75
a. Horiz. pair, imperf. between —

Signature of John W. Mackay

15T22 T22a chocolate (1902) 50 60
Pane of four 2.50

Signature of Clarence H. Mackay

15T23 T22a blue (1903) 2.50 2.50
Pane of four

Perf. 12

15T24 T22a blue, *blue* (1904) 2.00 2.00
Pane of four 9.00
15T25 T22a blue, *yellow* (1905) 4.50
Pane of four 20.00
15T26 T22a blue, *light blue* (1906) 3.00
Pane of four 13.00
a. Horiz. pair, imperf. vertically —

T22b

T22c

15T27 T22b black, *yellow* (laid paper) (1907) 25.00
Pane of four 105.00
15T28 T22b blue, *pink* (laid paper) (1907) 17.50
Pane of four 75.00

"One Telegram of 10 Words"

15T29 T22c blue (1908) 25.00
Pane of four 105.00
15T30 T22c yellow (1908) 100.00
Pane of four 350.00
15T31 T22c black (1908) 22.50
Pane of four 95.00
15T32 T22c brown (1909) 20.00
Pane of four 85.00
a. Date reads "1908" 165.00
15T33 T22c olive green (1909) 12.50
Pane of four 55.00
15T34 T22c dark blue (1910) 17.50
15T35 T22c dark brown (1910) 15.00
15T36 T22c violet (1911) 140.00
15T37 T22c blue (1912) 160.00
15T38 T22c violet (1913) 160.00

Perf. 14

15T39 T22c violet (not dated) (1914) 45.00
a. Red violet 45.00
Pane of four 200.00

"One Telegram"

Perf. 12

15T40 T22c blue, (1908) 30.00
Pane of four 125.00
15T41 T22c lilac (1909) 15.00
Pane of four 60.00
15T42 T22c black, *yellow* (laid paper) (1910) 85.00
15T43 T22c violet (1910) 10.00
a. Red violet 10.00
Pane of four —
Pane of eight 90.00
15T44 T22c dark blue, (1911) 25.00
Pane of four 100.00
15T45 T22c light violet, (1912) 20.00
Pane of four 85.00

Perf. 14

15T46 T22c dark blue (1913) 50.00
Pane of eight 600.00
a. Imperf. vertically, pair 100.00
b. Perf. 12 40.00
15T47 T22c dark blue, (not dated) (1914) 20
Pane of four 1.50
Pane of eight 2.50

In panes of four the stamps are 4½mm apart horizontally, panes of eight 5½mm. There are two types of design T22c, one with and one without spurs on colored curved lines above

An enhanced introduction to the Scott Catalogue begins on Page V. A thorough understanding of the material presented there will greatly aid your use of the catalogue itself.

"O" of "Postal" and below "M" of "Company". Both types are known of 15T47.

Nos. 15T39 and 15T47 handstamped with date in double line numerals, all four numerals complete on each stamp.

15T47A	T22c	violet	(1916)	365.00
15T48	T22c	dark blue	(1917)	650.00
15T49	T22c	dark blue	(1918)	775.00
15T49A	T22c	dark blue	(1919)	70.00
15T49B	T22c	dark blue	(1920)	60.00

No. 15T49B is handstamped "1920" in small single line numerals.

T22d

1907 *Perf. 12*

15T50	T22d 1c	dark brown		20.00	20.00
		Pane of four		85.00	
15T51	T22d 2c	dull violet		20.00	20.00
		Pane of four		85.00	
15T52	T22d 5c	green		20.00	20.00
		Pane of four		85.00	
15T53	T22d 25c	light red		20.00	20.00
		Pane of four		85.00	

T22e

1931 *Perf. 14*

15T54	T22e 25c	gray blue (1931)	25	
		Pane of six	1.50	

1932

Stamp of 1931 overprinted "1932" and control number in red.

15T55	T22e 25c	gray blue	30.00
		Pane of six	200.00

Many varieties between Nos. 15T5 and 15T55 are known without frank numbers.

OFFICIAL

1900 **Inscribed "Supts."** *Perf. 11, 12*

15TO1	T22c	black, *magenta*	1.00	1.00

For Use of Railroad Superintendents

Perf. 12

"C. G. W." (Chicago, Great Western Railroad) at top

15TO2	T22c	carmine	(1908)	30.00
		Pane of four		120.00
15TO3	T22c	carmine	(1909)	50.00
15TO4	T22c	carmine	(1910)	70.00
15TO5	T22c	carmine	(1911)	45.00
15TO6	T22c	carmine	(1912)	50.00

Perf. 14

15TO7	T22c	carmine	(1913)	85.00
	a.	Perf. 12		—
15TO8	T22c	dull red (not dated)	(1914)	25
		Pane of eight		2.50

Perf. 12

"E. P." (El Paso and Northeastern Railroad) at top

15TO9	T22c	orange	(1908)	90.00

"I. C." (Illinois Central Railroad) at top

15TO10	T22c	green	(1908)	27.50
		Pane of four		125.00
15TO11	T22c	yellow green	(1909)	10.00
		Pane of four		—
		Pane of eight		75.00
15TO12	T22c	dark green	(1910)	55.00
15TO13	T22c	dark green	(1911)	45.00
		Pane of four		185.00
		Pane of eight		375.00
15TO14	T22c	dark green	(1912)	85.00
15TO15	T22c	dark green	(1913)	140.00

Perf. 14

15TO16	T22c	dark green (not dated)	(1914)	2.00
		Pane of four		9.00
		Pane of eight		17.50
	a.	Green (spurs)		1.25
		Pane of four		6.00
	b.	Line under "PRESIDENT" (no spurs)		20
		Pane of eight		2.00

(See note after No. 15T47.)
Both types of design T22c are known of 15TO16.

Perf. 12

"O. D." (Old Dominion Steamship Co.) at top

15TO17	T22c	violet	(1908)	275.00

"P. R." (Pennsylvania Railroad) at top

15TO18	T22c	orange brown	(1908)	10.00
		Pane of four		42.50
		Pane of eight		90.00
15TO19	T22c	orange brown	(1909)	25.00
		Pane of four		110.00
		Pane of eight		225.00
15TO20	T22c	orange brown	(1910)	15.00
		Pane of four		65.00
		Pane of eight		125.00
15TO21	T22c	orange brown	(1911)	60.00
15TO22	T22c	orange brown	(1912)	50.00

Perf. 14

15TO23	T22c	orange brown	(1913)	17.50
		Pane of eight		145.00
	a.	Perf. 12		85.00

"P. R. R." (Pennsylvania Rail Road) at top

15TO24	T22c	orange (not dated)	(1914)	20.00
		Pane of eight		175.00

Perf. 12

"S. W." (El Paso Southwestern Railroad) at top

15TO25	T22c	yellow	(1909)	110.00
15TO26	T22c	yellow	(1910)	325.00
15TO27	T22c	yellow	(1911)	100.00
15TO28	T22c	yellow	(1912)	110.00
		Pane of four		500.00

Nos. 15TO1 to 15TO17 and 15TO25 to 15TO28 are without frank numbers.

TO1

1942 **Litho.** **Unwmk.**

15TO29	TO1 5c	pink	6.00	3.00
		Pane of eight	50.00	
15TO30	TO1 25c	pale blue	7.00	4.00
		Pane of eight	57.50	

The stamps were issued in booklets to all Postal Telegraph employees in the Armed Forces for use in the United States. They were discontinued Oct. 8, 1943. Used copies normally bear manuscript cancellations.

Western Union Telegraph Company

Organized by consolidation in 1856. Now extends throughout the United States. Frank stamps have been issued regularly since 1871 in booklet form. The large size, early issues, were in panes of four, 1871-1913; the medium size, later issues, were in panes of six, 1914-32; and the recent small size issues are in panes of nine, 1933 to 1946.

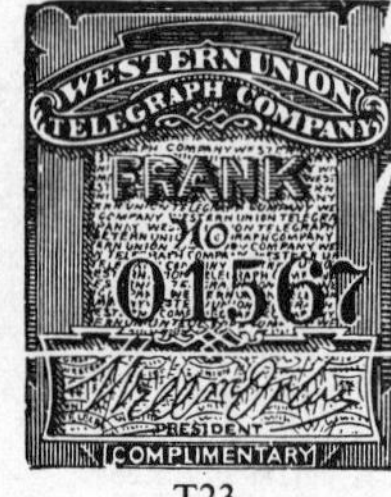

T23

T24

Engraved by the National Bank Note Co.

1871-94 *Perf. 12*

Signature of William Orton

16T1	T23	green (not dated)	(1871)	20.00
16T2	T23	red (not dated)	(1872)	20.00
		Pane of four		85.00
16T3	T23	blue (not dated)	(1873)	20.00
		Pane of four		85.00
16T4	T23	brown (not dated)	(1874)	20.00
		Pane of four		85.00
16T5	T24	deep green	(1875)	20.00
16T6	T24	red	(1876)	17.50
		Pane of four		75.00
16T7	T24	violet	(1877)	20.00
16T8	T24	gray brown	(1878)	22.50

Signature of Norvin Green

16T9	T24	blue	(1879)	22.50	
		Pane of four		100.00	

Engraved by the American Bank Note Co.

16T10	T24	lilac rose	(1880)	15.00	
		Pane of four		65.00	
16T11	T24	green	(1881)	12.00	
		Pane of four		50.00	
16T12	T24	blue	(1882)	7.50	
		Pane of four		35.00	
16T13	T24	yellow brown	(1883)	15.00	
		Pane of four		65.00	
16T14	T24	gray violet	(1884)	40	30
		Pane of four		2.00	
16T15	T24	green	(1885)	2.00	1.25
		Pane of four		10.00	
16T16	T24	brown violet	(1886)	2.25	
		Pane of four		11.00	
16T17	T24	red brown	(1887)	4.00	
		Pane of four		20.00	
16T18	T24	blue	(1888)	2.00	
		Pane of four		10.00	
16T19	T24	olive green	(1889)	1.25	80
		Pane of four		5.00	
16T20	T24	purple	(1890)	60	40
		Pane of four		3.00	
16T21	T24	brown	(1891)	80	
		Pane of four		4.00	
16T22	T24	vermilion	(1892)	1.25	
		Pane of four		6.00	
16T23	T24	blue	(1893)	60	25
		Pane of four		3.00	

Signature of Thos. T. Eckert

16T24	T24	green	(1894)	50	40
		Pane of four		2.50	

T25

Engraved by the International Bank Note Co.

1895-1913 *Perf. 14*

16T25	T25	dark brown	(1895)	50	35
		pane of four		2.50	
16T26	T25	violet	(1896)	50	35
		Pane of four		2.50	
16T27	T25	rose red	(1897)	50	40
		Pane of four		2.50	
16T28	T25	yellow green	(1898)	50	40
		Pane of four		2.50	
	a.	Vert. pair, imperf. between		—	
16T29	T25	olive green	(1899)	40	40
		Pane of four		2.00	
16T30	T25	red violet, perf. 13	(1900)	50	45
		Pane of four		2.25	
16T31	T25	brown, perf. 13	(1901)	40	
		Pane of four		2.00	
16T32	T25	blue	(1902)	5.00	
		Pane of four		25.00	

Signature of R.C. Clowry

16T33	T25	blue	(1902)	5.00	
		Pane of four		25.00	
16T34	T25	green	(1903)	50	40
		Pane of four		2.25	
16T35	T25	red violet	(1904)	50	
		Pane of four		2.25	
16T36	T25	carmine rose	(1905)	40	30
		Pane of four		1.75	
16T37	T25	blue	(1906)	40	30
		Pane of four		2.00	
	a.	Vertical pair, imperf., between		30.00	
16T38	T25	orange brown	(1907)	40	30
		Pane of four		2.00	
16T39	T25	violet	(1908)	75	40
		Pane of four		4.00	
16T40	T25	olive green	(1909)	1.00	
		Pane of four		5.00	

Perf. 12

16T41	T25	buff	(1910)	50	40
		Pane of four		2.25	

Engraved by the American Bank Note Co.

Signature of Theo. N. Vail

16T42	T24	green	(1911)	11.00
		Pane of four		55.00
16T43	T24	violet	(1912)	7.00
		Pane of four		32.50

Imprint of Kihn Brothers Bank Note Company

Perf. ***14***

No.	Type	Denom.	Description	Year	Unused	Used
16T44	T24		brown	(1913)	10.00	
			Pane of four		50.00	
		a.	Vert. pair, imperf. between		35.00	
		b.	Horiz. pair, imperf. between		40.00	

T26

T27

Engraved by the E.A. Wright Bank Note Co.

1914-15 **Signature of Theo. N. Vail** *Perf.* ***12***

No.	Type	Denom.	Description	Year	Unused	Used
16T45	T26	5c	brown	(1914)	1.00	
			Pane of six		7.00	
		a.	Vert. pair, imperf. between		—	
		b.	Horiz. pair, imperf. between		—	
16T46	T26	25c	slate	(1914)	4.00	4.00
			Pane of six		25.00	

Signature of Newcomb Carlton

No.	Type	Denom.	Description	Year	Unused	Used
16T47	T26	5c	orange	(1915)	1.25	
			Pane of six		8.00	
			orange yellow		5.00	
16T48	T26	25c	olive green	(1915)	4.00	
			Pane of six		25.00	
		a.	Vert. pair, imperf. horizontally		45.00	

Engraved by the American Bank Note Co.

1916-32

No.	Type	Denom.	Description	Year	Unused	Used
16T49	T27	5c	light blue	(1916)	1.50	
			Pane of six		10.00	
16T50	T27	25c	carmine lake	(1916)	1.50	
			Pane of six		10.00	

Engraved by the Security Bank Note Co.

Perf. ***11***

No.	Type	Denom.	Description	Year	Unused	Used
16T51	T27	5c	yellow brown	(1917)	1.00	
			Pane of six		6.50	
16T52	T27	25c	deep green	(1917)	2.75	
			Pane of six		18.00	
16T53	T27	5c	olive green	(1918)	60	
			Pane of six		4.00	
16T54	T27	25c	dark violet	(1918)	1.75	
			Pane of six		11.00	
16T55	T27	5c	brown	(1919)	1.25	
			Pane of six		8.00	
16T56	T27	25c	blue	(1919)	3.00	
			Pane of six		20.00	

Engraved by the E.A. Wright Bank Note Co.

Perf. ***12***

No.	Type	Denom.	Description	Year	Unused	Used
16T57	T27	5c	dark green	(1920)	50	
			Pane of six		3.25	
		a.	Vert. pair, imperf between		—	
16T58	T27	25c	olive green	(1920)	60	
			Pane of six		4.00	

Engraved by the Security Bank Note Co.

No.	Type	Denom.	Description	Year	Unused	Used
16T59	T27	5c	carmine rose	(1921)	40	
			Pane of six		2.75	
16T60	T27	25c	deep blue	(1921)	1.00	
			Pane of six		6.50	
16T61	T27	5c	yellow brown	(1922)	40	
			Pane of six		2.75	
		a.	Horizontal pair, imperf. between		12.00	
16T62	T27	25c	claret	(1922)	1.25	
			Pane of six		8.50	
16T63	T27	5c	olive green	(1923)	50	
			Pane of six		3.25	
16T64	T27	25c	dull violet	(1923)	1.00	
			Pane of six		7.00	
16T65	T27	5c	brown	(1924)	1.25	
			Pane of six		8.00	
16T66	T27	25c	ultramarine	(1924)	3.00	
			Pane of six		20.00	
16T67	T27	5c	olive green	(1925)	40	
			Pane of six		2.75	
16T68	T27	25c	carmine rose	(1925)	75	
			Pane of six		5.00	
16T69	T27	5c	blue	(1926)	50	
			Pane of six		3.50	
16T70	T27	25c	light brown	(1926)	1.25	
			Pane of six		8.00	
16T71	T27	5c	carmine	(1927)	60	
			Pane of six		4.00	
16T72	T27	25c	green	(1927)	4.50	
			Pane of six		30.00	

Engraved by the E. A. Wright Bank Note Co.

Without Imprint

No.	Type	Denom.	Description	Year	Unused	Used
16T73	T27	5c	yellow brown	(1928)	35	
			Pane of six		2.25	
16T74	T27	25c	dark blue	(1928)	75	
			Pane of six		5.00	

Engraved by the Security Bank Note Co.

Without Imprint

No.	Type	Denom.	Description	Year	Unused	Used
16T75	T27	5c	dark green	(1929)	25	25
			Pane of six		1.50	
16T76	T27	25c	red violet	(1929)	75	50
			Pane of six		5.00	
16T77	T27	5c	olive green	(1930)	20	15
			Pane of six		1.25	
16T78	T27	25c	carmine	(1930)	20	12
			Pane of six		1.40	
		a.	Imperf. vertically (pair)		35.00	
16T79	T27	5c	brown	(1931)	15	10
			Pane of six		1.00	
16T80	T27	25c	blue	(1931)	15	10
			Pane of six		1.00	
16T81	T27	5c	green	(1932)	15	10
			Pane of six		1.00	
16T82	T27	25c	rose carmine	(1932)	15	10
			Pane of six		1.00	

T28

Perf. 14x12½ Lithographed by Oberly & Newell Co.

1933-40

Without Imprint

No.	Type	Denom.	Description	Year	Unused	Used
16T83	T28	5c	pale brown	(1933)	25	
			Pane of nine		2.50	
16T84	T28	25c	green	(1933)	25	
			Pane of nine		2.50	

Lithographed by Security Bank Note Co.

Without Imprint

Perf. ***12, 12½***

Signature of R. B. White

No.	Type	Denom.	Description	Year	Unused	Used
16T85	T28	5c	lake	(1934)	15	
			Pane of nine		1.50	
16T86	T28	25c	dark blue	(1934)	15	
			Pane of nine		1.75	
16T87	T28	5c	yellow brown	(1935)	12	
			Pane of nine		1.50	
16T88	T28	25c	lake	(1935)	15	
			Pane of nine		1.50	
16T89	T28	25c	blue	(1936)	20	15
			Pane of nine		2.00	
16T90	T28	25c	apple green	(1936)	15	10
			Pane of nine		1.50	
16T91	T28	5c	bister brown	(1937)	20	
			Pane of nine		2.00	
16T92	T28	25c	carmine rose	(1937)	20	
			Pane of nine		2.00	
16T93	T28	5c	green	(1938)	20	15
			Pane of nine		2.00	
16T94	T28	25c	blue	(1938)	25	15
			Pane of nine		2.50	
16T95	T28	5c	dull vermilion	(1939)	60	
			Pane of nine		6.00	
		a.	Horiz. pair, imperf. between		—	
16T96	T28	25c	bright violet	(1939)	50	
			Pane of nine		5.00	
16T97	T28	5c	light blue	(1940)	40	
			Pane of nine		4.00	
16T98	T28	25c	bright green	(1940)	40	
			Pane of nine		4.00	

Samuel F. B. Morse — T29

Plates of 90 stamps.

Stamp designed by Nathaniel Yontiff.

Unlike the frank stamps, Nos. 16T99 to 16T103 were sold to the public in booklet form for use in prepayment of telegraph services.

Engraved by Security Bank Note Co. of Philadelphia

1940 **Unwmk.** *Perf.* ***12, 12½x12, 12x12½***

No.	Type	Denom.	Description	Unused	Used
16T99	T29	1c	yellow green	1.00	
			Pane of five	6.00	
		a.	Imperf. pair	—	
16T100	T29	2c	chestnut	1.75	1.00
			Pane of five	12.00	
		a.	Imperf. pair	—	
16T101	T29	5c	deep blue	3.00	
			Pane of five	18.00	
		a.	Vert. pair, imperf. btwn.	65.00	
		b.	Iperf. pair	—	
16T102	T29	10c	orange	3.50	
			Pane of five	20.00	
		a.	Imperf. pair	—	
16T103	T29	25c	bright carmine	4.00	
			Pane of five	25.00	
		a.	Imperf. pair	—	

Type of 1933-40

1941 **Litho.** *Perf.* ***12½***

Without Imprint

Signature of R.B. White

No.	Type	Denom.	Description	Unused
16T104	T28	5c	dull rose lilac	25
			Pane of nine	2.50
16T105	T28	25c	vermilion	25
			Pane of nine	2.50

1942 **Signature of A.N. Williams**

No.	Type	Denom.	Description	Unused
16T106	T28	5c	brown	30
			Pane of nine	3.00
16T107	T28	25c	ultramarine	30
			Pane of nine	3.00

1943

No.	Type	Denom.	Description	Unused
16T108	T28	5c	salmon	30
			Pane of nine	3.00
16T109	T28	25c	red violet	25
			Pane of nine	2.50

1944

No.	Type	Denom.	Description	Unused
16T110	T28	5c	light green	30
			Pane of nine	3.00
16T111	T28	25c	buff	25
			Pane of nine	2.50

1945

No.	Type	Denom.	Description	Unused
16T112	T28	5c	light blue	35
			Pane of nine	3.50
		a.	Pair, imperf. between	—
16T113	T28	25c	light green	35
			Pane of nine	3.50

1946

No.	Type	Denom.	Description	Unused
16T114	T28	5c	light bister brown	1.00
			Pane of nine	10.00
16T115	T28	25c	rose pink	1.00
			Pane of nine	10.00

Many of the stamps between 16T1 and 16T98 and 16T104 to 16T115 are known without frank numbers. Several of them are also known with more than one color used in the frank number and with handstamped and manuscript numbers. The numbers are also found in combination with various letters: O, A, B, C, D, etc.

Western Union discontinued the use of Telegraph stamps with the 1946 issue.

United States Telegraph-Cable-Radio Carriers

Booklets issued to accredited representatives to the World Telecommunications Conferences, Atlantic City, New Jersey, 1947. Valid for messages to points outside the United States. Issued by All America Cables & Radio, Inc., The Commercial Cable Company, Globe Wireless, Limited, Mackay Radio and Telegraph Company, Inc., R C A Communications, Inc., Tropical Radio Telegraph Company and The Western Union Telegraph Company.

TX1

1947 **Litho.** **Unwmk.** *Perf.* ***12½***

No.	Type	Denom.	Description	Unused
17T1	TX1	5c	olive bister	5.00
			Pane of nine	50.00
			Pane of 8+1 No. 17T2	375.00
17T2	TX1	10c	olive bister	275.00
17T3	TX1	50c	olive bister	7.00
			Pane of nine	75.00

UNLISTED ISSUES

Several telegraph or wireless companies other than those listed above have issued stamps or franks, but as evidence of actual use is lacking, they are not listed. Among these are:

American District Telegraph Co.
American Telegraph Typewriter Co.
Continental Telegraph Co.
Marconi Wireless Telegraph Co.
Telepost Co.
Tropical Radio Telegraph Co.
United Fruit Co. Wireless Service.
United Wireless Telegraph Co.

SANITARY FAIR

The United States Sanitary Commission was authorized by the Secretary of War on June 9, 1861, and approved by President Lincoln on June 13, 1861. It was a committee of inquiry, advice and aid dealing with the health and general comfort of Union troops, supported by public contributions.

Many Sanitary Fairs were held to raise funds for the Commission, and eight issued stamps. The first took place in 1863 at Chicago, where no stamp was issued. Some Sanitary Fairs advertised on envelopes.

Sanitary Fair stamps occupy a position midway between United States semi-official carrier stamps and the private local posts. Although Sanitary Fair stamps were not valid for U.S. postal service, they were prepared for, sold and used at the fair post offices, usually with the approval and participation of the local postmaster.

The Commission undertook to forward soldiers' unpaid and postage due letters. These letters were handstamped "Forwarded by the U.S. Sanitary Commission."

Details about the Sanitary Fair stamps may be found in the following publications:
American Journal of Philately, Jan. 1889, by J. W. Scott
The Collector's Journal, Aug-Sept. 1909, by C. E. Severn
Scott's Monthly Journal, Jan. 1927 (reprint, Apr. 1973), by Elliott Perry
Stamps, April 24th, 1937, by Harry M. Konwiser
Pat Paragraphs, July, 1939, by Elliott Perry
Covers, Aug. 1952, by George B. Wray
The listings were compiled originally by H. M. Konwiser and Dorsey F. Wheless.

Albany, New York
Army Relief Bazaar

SF1

Pane of 12 (Narrow Spacing), or Sheet of 25 (Wide Spacing)

1864, Feb. 22-Mar. 30 Litho. *Imperf.*
Thin White Paper

WV1	SF1 10c	rose	45.00	
		Block of four	190.00	
		Pane of 12	*750.00*	
		Sheet of 25	*1,250.*	
		Used on cover (tied "Albany")		*925.00*
WV2	SF1 10c	black	190.00	
		Block of five	*1,250.*	

Imitations are typographed in red, blue, black or green on a thin white or ordinary white paper, also on colored papers and are:

(a) Eagle with topknot, printed in sheets of 30 (6x5).
(b) Eagle without shading around it.
(c) Eagle with shading around it, but with a period instead of a circle in "C" of "Cents", and "Ten Cents" is smaller.

Boston, Mass.
National Sailors' Fair

SF2

1864, Nov. 9-22 Litho.
Die Cut

WV3	SF2 10c	green	150.00

Brooklyn, N. Y.
Brooklyn Sanitary Fair

SF3

1864, Feb. 22-Mar. 8 Litho. *Imperf.*

WV4	SF3	green	350.00	—
		Block of four	1,500.	
		Block of six	2,250.	
		On cover, Fair postmark on envelope		*1,250.*
WV5	SF	black	—	
		On cover, Fair postmark on envelope		*1,750.*

Imitations: *(a)* Typographed and shows "Sanitary" with a heavy cross bar to "T" and second "A" with a long left leg. *(b)* Is a rough typograph print without shading in letters of "Fair".

SF4

SF5

1863, Dec. Typeset *Imperf.*

WV6	SF4 5c	black, *rosy buff*	375.00
WV7	SF5 10c	green	500.00
	a.	Tete beche pair	*1,500.*

New York, N. Y.
Metropolitan Fair

SF6

1864, Apr. 4-27 Engr. *Imperf.*
Thin White Paper

WV8	SF6 10c	blue	35.00
		Sheet of four	185.00
WV9	SF6 10c	red	375.00
		Pair	*900.00*
WV10	SF6 10c	black	*750.00*

Engraved and printed by John E. Gavit of Albany, N.Y. from a steel plate composed of four stamps, 2x2. Can be plated by the positions of scrolls and dots around "Ten Cents".

Philadelphia, Pa.
Great Central Fair

SF7

1864, June 7-28 Engr. *Perf. 12*
Printed by Butler & Carpenter, Philadelphia
Sheets of 126 (14x9)

WV11	SF7 10c	blue	15.00	110.00
		Block of four	67.50	
		On cover tied with Fair postmark		*900.00*
		On cover with 3c #65, Fair and Philadelphia postmarks		*1500.00*
WV12	SF7 20c	green	7.50	90.00
		Block of four	32.50	
		Block of 12	135.00	
		On cover tied with Fair postmark		*800.00*
WV13	SF7 30c	black	16.50	75.00
		Block of four	75.00	
		On cover tied with Fair postmark		*750.00*

Imprint "Engraved by Butler & Carpenter, Philadelphia" on right margin adjoining three stamps.

Used examples of Nos. WV11-WV13 have Fair cancellation.

Imitation of No. WV13 comes typographed in blue or green on thick paper.

White and amber envelopes were sold by the fair inscribed "Great Central Fair for the Sanitary Commission," showing picture of wounded soldier, doctors and ambulance marked "U. S. Sanitary Commission." Same design and inscription are known on U.S. envelope No. U46.

Springfield, Mass.
Soldiers' Fair

SF8

1864, Dec. 19-24 Typo. *Imperf.*

WV14	SF8 10c	lilac	75.00	
		Horizontal strip of four	350.00	
		On unaddressed cover, Fair postmark on envelope		250.00

Design by Thomas Chubbuck, engraver of the postmaster provisional stamp of Brattleboro, Vt.

Imitations: (a) Without designer's name in lower right corner, in lilac on laid paper. *(b)* With designer's name, but roughly typographed, in lilac on white wove paper. Originals show 5 buttons on uniform.

Stamford, Conn.
Soldiers' Fair

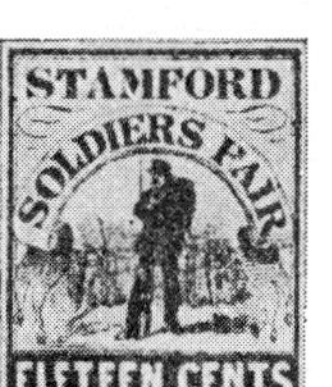

SF9

Sheets of 8

1864, July 27-29

WV15 SF9 15c pale brown	450.00	475.00

Originals have tassels at ends of ribbon inscribed "SOLDIERS FAIR."

Imitations have leaning "s" in "CENTS" and come in lilac, brown, green, also black on white paper, green on pinkish paper and other colors.

PROOFS

New York Metropolitan Fair

1864

		Plate on India Mounted on Card
WV10P	10c black	225.00

Philadelphia Great Central Fair

1864

		LARGE DIE	Card	PLATE Wove Imperf.	Wove, Perf.
WV11P	10c blue		40.00		
	Block of four		200.00		
WV11TC to WV13TC	10c 30c greenish black, setenant vert., glazed paper	450.00			
WV12P	20c green		45.00		
	Block of four		200.00		
WV12TC	20c carmine				35.00
	Block of four				175.00
WV12TC	20c vermilion, India on card	275.00			
WV12TC	20c vermilion			22.50	35.00
	Block of four			115.00	175.00
WV12TC	20c orange			22.50	
	Block of four			115.00	
WV12TC	20c brown orange, opaque paper			22.50	
	Block of four			115.00	
WV12TC	20c red brown				35.00
	Block of four				175.00
WV12TC	20c black brown			25.00	
	Block of four			125.00	
WV12TC	20c olive			22.50	
	Block of four			100.00	
WV12TC	20c yellow green			22.50	
	Block of four			125.00	
WV12TC	20c light green				35.00
	Block of four				175.00
WV12TC	20c blue, India on card	275.00			
WV12TC	20c bright blue			22.50	35.00
	Block of four			125.00	175.00
WV12TC	20c lt. ultramarine			22.50	
	Block of four			125.00	
WV12TC	20c purple			22.50	
	Block of four			125.00	
WV12TC	20c claret			35.00	
	Block of four			200.00	
WV12TC	20c brown black				35.00
	Block of four				175.00
WV12TC	20c greenish black, glazed paper	225.00			
WV12TC	20c gray black, opaque paper			22.50	
	Block of four			125.00	
WV12TC	20c gray black				35.00
	Block of four				175.00
WV12TC	20c black, experimental double paper			25.00	
	Block of four			140.00	
WV13P	30c black		22.50		
	Block of four		125.00		

Reprints (1903?) exist of WV11TC and WV13TC, se-tenant vertically, large die on glazed white, pink or yellow card and small die on India paper (mounted se-tenant) in carmine, red carmine, vermilion, orange, brown, yellow brown, olive, yellow green, blue green, gray blue, ultramarine, light violet, violet, claret and gray black. There also exist large die essay reprints on India paper, green bond paper and glazed cardboard without denomination or with 20c. The 20c value has an added line below the center shield.

STAMPED ENVELOPES AND WRAPPERS

STAMPED ENVELOPES were first issued on July 1, 1853. They have always been made by private contractors, after public bidding, usually at four-year intervals. They have always been sold to the public at postage value plus cost of manufacture. They have appeared in many sizes and shapes, made of a variety of papers, with a number of modifications.

George F. Nesbitt & Co. made the government envelopes during the 1853-70 period. The Nesbitt seal or crest on the tip of the top flap was officially ordered discontinued July 7, 1853.

Watermarks in envelope paper, illustrated in this introduction, have been mandatory since their first appearance in 1853. One important exception started in 1919 and lasted until the manila newspaper wrappers were discontinued in October 1934. The envelope contractor, due to inability to obtain watermarked Manila paper, was permitted to buy unwatermarked stock in the open market, a procedure that accounts for the wide range of shades and weights in this paper, including glazed and unglazed brown (kraft) paper. Also, Scott U615 (1989) also is not watermarked. A diagonally laid paper has been used for some envelopes beginning with Scott U571.

A few stamped envelopes, in addition to the Manila items noted above, have been found without watermarks or with unauthorized watermarks. Such unusual watermarks or lack of watermarks are errors, bidders' samples or "specimen" envelopes, and most of them are quite rare.

Watermarks usually have been changed with every four-year contract, and thus serve to identify the envelope contractor, and since 1911, the manufacturer of the paper.

Envelope paper watermarks can be seen by spreading the envelope open and holding it against the light.

COLORS IN ENVELOPE PAPER.

Stamped envelopes usually have been supplied in several colors and qualities of paper, some of which blend into each other and require study for identification. The following are the principal colors and their approximate years of use for stamped envelopes and wrappers:

Amber: 1870-1920 and 1929-1943; in two qualities; a pale yellow color; its intentional use in the Nesbitt series is doubtful.

Amber-Manila: 1886-98; same as Manila-amber.

Blue: 1874-1943; usually in two qualities; light and dark shades.

Buff: 1853-70; called cream, 1870-78; and oriental buff, 1886-1920; varies widely in shades.

Canary: 1873-78; another designation given to lemon.

Cream: 1870-78; see buff; second quality in 1c and 2c envelopes.

Fawn: 1874-86; very dark buff, almost light chocolate.

Lemon: 1873-78; Post Office official envelopes only, same as canary.

Manila: 1861-1934; second quality envelopes 1886-1928, and most wrappers; light and dark shades 1920-34; also kraft colored paper in later years.

Manila-Amber: 1886-98; amber shade of Manila quality.

Orange: 1861-83; second and third qualities only.

Oriental Buff: 1886-1920; see buff.

White: 1853-date; two qualities 1915-date; three qualities 1915-25; many shades including ivory, light gray, and bluish; far more common than any other color of paper. Envelopes that have no paper color giver are white.

Laid paper was used almost exclusively from 1853 to 1915, but there were a few exceptions, mostly in the Manila papers. Wove paper has been the rule since 1915.

EMBOSSING AND PRINTING DIES.

Stamped envelopes have always been embossed, with the colorless areas slightly raised above the colored (or printed) flat background. While this process was not made mandatory in the original act, custom and tradition have firmly established this policy. It is an unusual procedure, seldom seen in other printed matter. Embossed impressions without color and those where lines are raised are not unusual. The method of making envelope embossings has few counterparts in the typographic industries, and hence is not well understood, even by stamp collectors.

Three types of dies are used, closely inter-related in their derivation, MASTER dies, HUB dies and WORKING (or PRINTING) dies. These types and the ways in which they are made, have undergone many changes with the years, and some of the earlier techniques are unrecorded and rather vague. No attempt will be made to describe other than the present day-methods. As an aid to clarity, the design illustrated herewith is the interlocked monogram "US," within a single circular border. Dies with curved faces for rotary printing are used extensively, as well as with straight faces for flat printing; only the latter will be described, since the basic principles are the same for both.

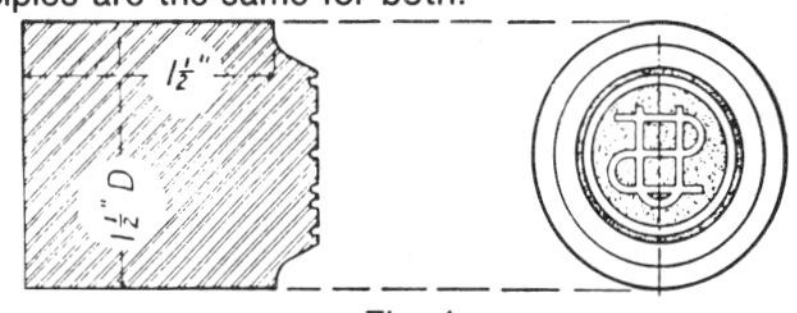

Fig. 1

Master Die for Envelope Stamps

Colorless Lines are Recessed Below the Printing Surface.

It Reads Backward.

The MASTER die (Fig. 1) is engraved on the squared end of a small soft steel cylinder, before hardening. The lines that are to remain colorless are cut or engraved into the face of this die, leaving the flat area of the face to carry the printing ink. The monogram is reversed, reading backward, as with any printing type or plate Instead of engraving, a master die may be made by transfer under heavy pressure, usually for some modification in design, in which case it is called a sub-master or supplementary-master die. Sub-master dies are sometimes made without figures of value, when the balance of the design is as desired, and only the figures of value engraved by hand. Various other combinations of transfer and engraving are known, always resulting in a reversed design, with recessed lines and figures, from which proofs can be pulled, and which accurately represents the printing surface that is desired in the eventual working die. The soft steel of a master die, after engraving and transferring is completed, is hardened by heat treatments before it can be used for making hubs.

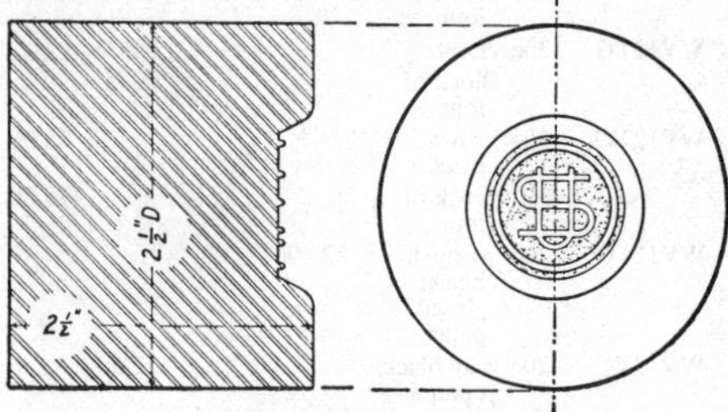

Fig. 2

Hub Die for Envelope Stamps
Colorless Lines Protrude above the Surface.
The Monogram Reads Forward.

The HUB die (Fig. 2), also called HOB die, is made from soft steel by transfer under pressure from the hardened master or sub-master die, which serves as a matrix or pattern. Since it is a transfer from the master die, the colorless lines protrude from the surface and it reads forward. This transfer impression of the hub die is made in a depression at the end of a sturdy cylinder, as it is subject to extremely hard service in making many working dies.

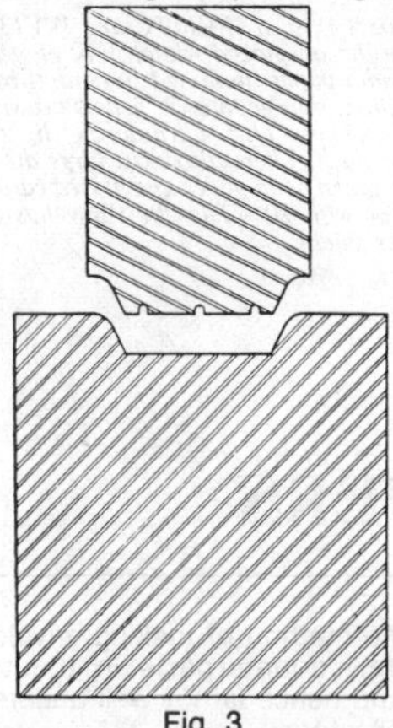

Fig. 3

Pressure Transfer from Master Die to Hub Die
Above, Hardened Steel Master Die with Recessed Monogram.
Below, Soft Steel Hub Die Blank.

Fig. 3 shows the relative position of the hardened steel master die as it enters the depression in the soft steel hub die blank. Some surplus metal may be squeezed out as the master die is forced into the hub blank, and require removal, leading to possible minor differences between the hub and master dies. At the completion of the pressure transfer the engraver may need to touch up the protruding surfaces to eliminate imperfections, to make letters and figures more symmetrical, and to improve the facial lines of the bust.

A hub die may be made by normal transfer, as above, the figures of value then ground off, and thus be ready for use in making a sub-master die without figures of value, and in which the figures of value may be engraved or punched. Since a hub die may be used to make a hundred or more working dies, it must be exceedingly sturdy and withstand terrific punishment without damage. Duplicate hub dies are frequently made from master dies, as stand-bys or reserves. After completion, hub dies are hardened. Hub dies cannot be engraved, nor can proof impressions be taken from them.

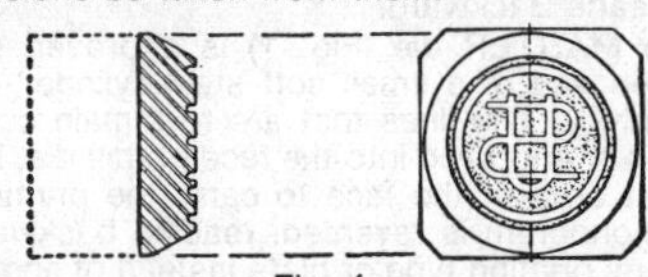

Fig. 4

Working or Printing Die for Envelope Stamps
An exact Replica of the Master Die, except for size and shape of shank, which is designed for Printers lock-up.
It Reads Backward.

The WORKING, or PRINTING, die (Fig. 4) is like the type or plate that printers use, and may be thin to clamp to a base block, or type-high with square sides to lock in a printer's form. Its face reads backward, i.e., in reverse, and it is an exact replica of the master die as well as an exact matrix of the hub die.

Fig. 5

Pressure Transfer from Hub to Working Die
Above, Soft Steel Blank for Working Die.
Below, Hardened Steel Hub Die with Protruding Lines.

The process of pressure transfer is shown in Fig. 5. where the soft steel blank of the working die is entering the depression on the top end of the hardened hub die, In fact the pressure transfer of working dies from hub dies closely resembles that of minting coins, and many of these envelope stamp dies are made at the United States Mint in Philadelphia.

In some cases even working dies may be made without figures of value, and the figures of value individually engraved thereon. This is known to be the case in Die B of the 6c orange airmail stamped envelope die, where the size and position of the "6" has eleven variations.

There are some known instances, as in the case of the 4c and 5c envelopes dies of 1903 and 1907, where the engraved master dies were used as printing dies, since the anticipated demand did not justify the expense of making hub dies.

While working envelope dies are heat treated to the hardest temper known, they do wear down eventually to a point where impressions deteriorate and are unsatisfactory, due to shallow recesses or to broken areas, and such dies are destroyed. In many cases these printing dies can be reworked, or deepened, by annealing the steel, touching up the lines or busts by hand engraving to restore the letters or renew the facial contour lines, and then rehardened for subsequent use. This recutting is the principal cause for minor die varieties in envelope stamps. When working dies are no longer useful, they are mutilated and eventually melted down into scrap metal.

The average "life" (in number of good impressions obtained) of a hardened steel working die, as used in envelope printing and embossing machines is around 30,000,000 on flat bed presses, and 43,000,000 on rotary presses. The present production of stamped envelopes is approximately 2,000,000,000 annually, indicating that 60 to 75 working dies are worn out each year, and require replacement with new dies or a reworking of old dies. Some 200 to 250 working dies are in constant use, since most envelope printing presses are set up for a special size, type or value, and few can be operated continuously at maximum capacity.

Master and hub dies of obsolete envelope issues are kept in the vaults of the Bureau of Engraving and printing in Washington, as are the original dies of adhesive stamps, revenue paper, government securities and paper currency.

PRINTING ENVELOPE STAMPS.

Embossed envelope stamps are not printed against a rigid flat platen, as is the normal printed page, but against a somewhat flexible or resilient platen or make-ready (Fig. 6). This resilient platen is hard enough to produce a clear full impression from the ink on the face of the working die, and soft enough to push the paper into the uninked recesses that correspond to the engraved lines cut into the master die. The normal result is raised lines or embossments without ink or color, standing out in relief against an inked or colored background. The method differs from the usual embossing technique, where rigid dies are used on both sides of the paper, as in notarial seals. The use of the resilient platen in envelope embossing permits far higher operating speeds than can be obtained with rigid embossing dies, without the need of such accurate register between the printing surface and the platen.

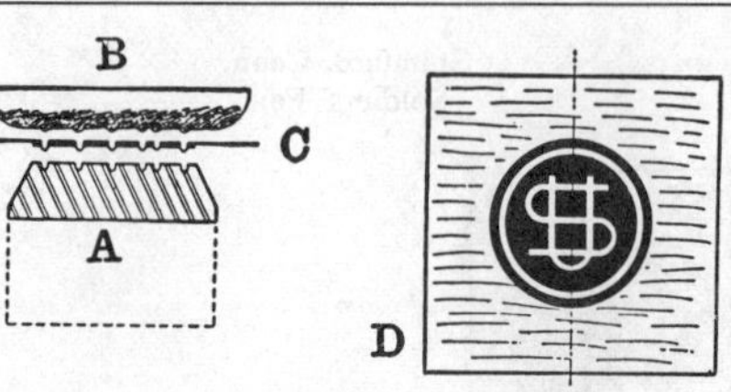

Fig. 6

Printing Process for embossed
A. Working Die, Carrying ink on its surface.
B. Resilient Platen, or Make-ready, Pushing Paper into uninked recesses, so that lines of Embossed Monogram receive no color.
C. Paper of Envelope Blank, after Printing and Embossing. Heavy line shows deposit of ink on surface of paper, but Embossed Lines are not inked.
D. Front view of Embossed impression.

When these recessed lines in a working die become filled with ink or other foreign material, the paper is not pushed in, the plugged area receives ink, and the corresponding colorless line does not appear on the stamp. This accounts for missing letters, lines or figures, and is a printing error, not a die variety.

An ALBINO impression is where two or more envelope blanks are fed into the printing press. The one adjacent to the printing die receives the color and the embossing, while the others are embossed only. Albinos are printing errors and are worth more than normal, inked impressions. Albinos of earlier issues, canceled while current, are scarce.

Before January 1, 1965, stamped envelopes were printed by two processes: (1.) The rotary, with curved dies, on Huckins and Harris presses. (2.) The flat process, with straight dies, as illustrated, on the O'Connell-type press, which is a redesigned Hartford press. The flat bed presses include a gumming and folding attachment, while the rotary presses, running at higher speeds, require separate folding machines.

Different master dies in every denomination are required for Huckins, Harris and flat bed presses. This difference gives rise to most of the major die varieties in envelope stamps.

Web-fed equipment which converts paper from a roll into finished envelopes in a continuous operation has produced envelopes starting with Nos.

U547 and UC37. Albino impressions do not occur on envelopes produced by web-fed equipment.

Some authorities claim that Scott U37, U48, U49, U110, U124, U125, U130, U133A, U137A, U137B, U137C, W138, U145, U162, U178A, U185, U220, U285, U286, U298, U299, UO3, UO32, UO38, UO45 and UO45A (with plus sign + before number), were not regularly issued and are not known to have been used.

Wrappers are listed with envelopes of corresponding design, and are numbered with the prefix "W" instead of "U."

VALUES

Values for cut squares and most unused entires are for a grade of very fine. Very fine cut squares will have the design well centered within moderately large margins. Precanceled cut squares must include the entire precancellation. Values for unused entires are for those without printed or manuscript address. Values for letter sheets are for folded entires. Unfolded copies sell for more. A "full corner" includes back and side flaps and commands a premium.

A plus sign (+) before a Catalogue number indicates that the item was not regularly issued and is not known used.

ENVELOPE WATERMARKS

Watermark Illustrations 5, 6, 17 and 18 are condensed. Watermark 4 was used only on Officials. Watermarks 9 and 10 are found on Specimens and Errors. Watermarks 17-18 were the last laid paper watermarks; watermarks 19-21 the first wove paper watermarks.

1-(1853-70)

2-(1870-78)

3-(1876)

4-(1877-82)

5-(1878-82)

6-(1882-86)

7-(1886-90)

8-(1890-94)

9-(1886-87)

10-(1886-99)

11-(1893)

12-(1894-98)

13-(1899-1902)

14-(1903-07)

15-(1907-11)

15A-(1907-11)

16-(1911-15)

17-(1911-15)

18-(1911-15)

19-(1915-19)

20-(1915-19)

21-(1915-19)

22-(1919-20)

23-(1919-20)

24-(1921-24)

25-(1921-24)

26-(1925-28)

27-(1925-28)

28-(1929-32)

28A-(1929-32)

29-(1929-32)

30-(1929-32)

30A-(1929-32)

31-(1933-36)

32-(1933-36)

33-(1933-36)

35-(1937-40)

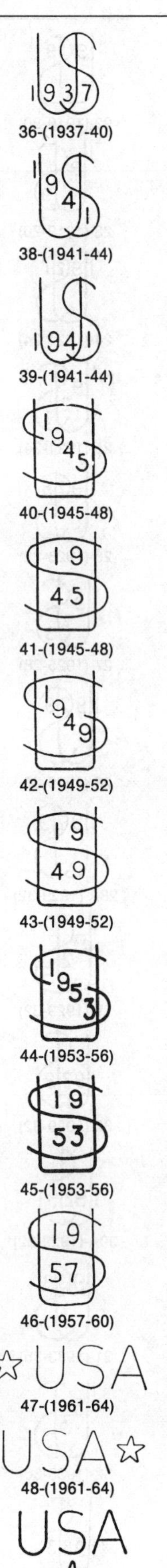

50-(1965-68)

Letter Sheet (1886-94)

Washington — U1

Die 1 - "THREE" in short label with curved ends; 13mm wide at top. (12 varieties.)

U2

Die 2 - "THREE" in short label with straight ends; 15½mm wide at top. (Three varieties.)

U3

Die 3 - "THREE" in short label with octagon ends. (Two varieties.)

U4

Die 4 - "THREE" in wide label with straight ends; 20 mm. wide at top.

U5

Die 5 - "THREE" in medium wide label with curved ends; 14½mm wide at top (10 varieties). A sub-variety shows curved lines at either end of label omitted; both T's have longer cross stroke; R is smaller (20 varieties).

U6

Four varieties.

U7

Die 1 - "TEN" in short label; 15½mm wide at top.

U8

Die 2 - "TEN" in wide label; 20mm wide at top.

Printed by George F. Nesbitt & Co., New York, N.Y.

1853-55

On Diagonally Laid Paper (Early printings of Nos. U1, U3 on Horizontally Laid Paper)

No.	Type	Denom.	Description	Unused	Used
U1	U1	3c	**red,** die 1	225.00	17.50
			Entire	1,100.	25.00
U2	U1	3c	**red,** die 1, *buff*	80.00	7.50
			Entire	700.00	15.00
U3	U2	3c	**red,** die 2	750.00	37.50
			Entire	2,750.	55.00
U4	U2	3c	**red,** die 2, *buff*	225.00	15.00
			Entire	1,400.	25.00
U5	U3	3c	**red,** die 3 ('54)	3,500.	425.00
			Entire	*10,000.*	550.00
U6	U3	3c	**red,** die 3, *buff* ('54)	150.00	30.00
			Entire	900.00	62.50
U7	U4	3c	**red,** die 4	600.00	100.00
			Entire	*5,000.*	100.00
U8	U4	3c	**red,** die 4, *buff*	1,250.	100.00
			Entire	4,500.	140.00
U9	U5	3c	**red,** die 5 ('54)	18.00	1.75
			Entire	60.00	5.00
U10	U5	3c	**red,** die 5, *buff* ('54)	12.00	1.25
			Entire	50.00	3.00
U11	U6	6c	**red**	150.00	67.50
			Entire	225.00	110.00
U12	U6	6c	**red,** *buff*	100.00	60.00
			Entire	200.00	160.00
U13	U6	6c	**green**	200.00	100.00
			Entire	300.00	150.00
U14	U6	6c	**green,** *buff*	200.00	90.00
			Entire	325.00	150.00
U15	U7	10c	**green,** die 1 ('55)	150.00	65.00
			Entire	275.00	100.00
U16	U7	10c	**green,** die 1, *buff* ('55)	65.00	50.00
			Entire	190.00	80.00
	a.	10c	pale green, die 1, *buff*	65.00	50.00
			Entire	190.00	85.00
U17	U8	10c	**green,** die 2 ('55)	200.00	110.00
			Entire	350.00	150.00
	a.	10c	pale green, die 2	175.00	110.00
			Entire	225.00	125.00
U18	U8	10c	**green,** die 2, *buff* ('55)	100.00	60.00
			Entire	165.00	75.00
	a.	10c	pale green, die 2, *buff*	100.00	60.00
			Entire	165.00	80.00

Nos. U9, U10, U11, U12, U13, U14, U17, and U18 have been reprinted on white and buff paper, vertically laid, and are not known entire. The originals are on diagonally laid paper. Value, set of 8 reprints, $125.

Franklin — U9

Die 1 - Period after "POSTAGE." (Eleven varieties.)

Franklin — U10

Die 2 - Bust touches inner frame-line at front and back.

Franklin — U11

Die 3 - No period after "POSTAGE." (Two varieties.)

Washington U12

Nine varieties of type U12.

Envelopes are on diagonally laid paper.
Wrappers on vertically or horizontally laid paper.

Wrappers of the 1 cent denomination were authorized by an Act of Congress, February 27, 1861, and were issued in October, 1861. These were suspended in 1863, and their use resumed in June, 1864.

1860-61

No.	Type	Denom.	Description	Unused	Used
U19	U9	1c	**blue,** die 1, *buff*	27.50	12.00
			Entire	55.00	25.00
W20	U9	1c	**blue,** die 1, *buff*	60.00	50.00
			Entire	100.00	65.00
W21	U9	1c	**blue,** die 1, *manila* ('61)	42.50	42.50
			Entire	80.00	80.00
W22	U9	1c	**blue,** die 1, *orange* ('61)	1.500.	
			Entire	2,250.	
U23	U10	1c	**blue,** die 2, *orange*	450.00	450.00
			Entire	500.00	500.00
U24	U11	1c	**blue,** die 3, *buff*	225.00	100.00
			Entire	350.00	175.00
W25	U11	1c	**blue,** die 3, *manila* ('61)	1,500.	1,150.
			Entire	*8,000.*	*2,750.*
U26	U12	3c	**red**	25.00	12.00
			Entire	35.00	20.00
U27	U12	3c	**red,** *buff*	18.00	11.00
			Entire	27.50	17.50
U28	U12 + U9	3c + 1c	**red & blue**	400.00	275.00
			Entire	550.00	400.00
U29	U12 + U9	3c + 1c	**red & blue,** *buff*	300.00	250.00
			Entire	500.00	475.00
U30	U12	6c	**red**	2,500.	1,500.
			Entire	3,000.	
U31	U12	6c	**red,** *buff*	1,750.	1,000.
			Entire	3,000.	*3,750.*
U32	U12	10c	**green**	1,000.	300.00
			Entire	9,000.	375.00
U33	U12	10c	**green,** *buff*	900.00	275.00
			Entire	2,500.	400.00

Nos. U26, U27, U30 to U33 have been reprinted on the same papers as the reprints of the 1853-55 issue, and are not known entire. Value, set of 6 reprints, $160.

Washington U13

17 varieties for Nos. U34-U35; 2 varieties for No. U36.

Washington U14

Washington — U15

Washington — U16

Envelopes are on diagonally laid paper.

U36 comes on vertically or horizontally laid paper. It appeared in August, 1861, and was withdrawn in 1864. Total issue 211,800.

1861

No.	Type	Denom.	Description	Unused	Used
U34	U13	3c	**pink**	17.50	5.00
			Entire	40.00	10.00
U35	U13	3c	**pink,** *buff*	15.00	5.00
			Entire	40.00	10.00

No.	Type	Description	Unused	Used
U36	U13	3c **pink,** *blue* (Letter Sheet)	75.00	50.00
		Entire	200.00	85.00
+*U37*	U13	3c **pink,** *orange*	*2,500.*	
		Entire	*4,000.*	
U38	U14	6c **pink**	100.00	90.00
		Entire	150.00	150.00
U39	U14	6c **pink,** *buff*	65.00	65.00
		Entire	110.00	150.00
U40	U15	10c **yellow green**	30.00	27.50
		Entire	60.00	42.50
a.		10c blue green	30.00	30.00
		Entire	60.00	37.50
U41	U15	10c **yellow green,** *buff*	27.50	22.50
		Entire	60.00	37.50
a.		10c blue green, *buff*	25.00	25.00
		Entire	40.00	40.00
U42	U16	12c **red & brown,** *buff*	200.00	165.00
		Entire	450.00	*600.00*
a.		12c lake & brown, *buff*	*900.00*	
U43	U16	20c **red & blue,** *buff*	185.00	165.00
		Entire	500.00	*750.00*
U44	U16	24c **red & green,** *buff*	200.00	165.00
		Entire	650.00	*750.00*
a.		24c lake & green, *salmon*	210.00	175.00
		Entire	550.00	*950.00*
U45	U16	40c **black & red,** *buff*	300.00	300.00
		Entire	800.00	*1,250.*

Nos. U38 and U39 have been reprinted on the same papers as the reprints of the 1853-55 issue, and are not known entire. Value, set of 2 reprints, $30.

Jackson — U17

Die 1 - "U.S. POSTAGE" above. Downstroke and tail of "2" unite near the point (seven varieties.)

Jackson — U18

Die 2 - "U.S. POSTAGE" above. The downstroke and tail of the "2" touch but do not merge.

Jackson U19

Die 3 - "U.S. POST" above. Stamp 24-25mm wide. (Sixteen varieties.)

Jackson U20

Die 4 - "U.S. POST" above. Stamp 25½-26¼mm wide. (Twenty-five varieties.)

Envelopes are on diagonally laid paper.
Wrappers on vertically or horizontally laid paper.

1863-64

No.	Type	Description	Unused	Used
U46	U17	2c **black,** die 1, *buff*	30.00	15.00
		Entire	55.00	30.00
W47	U17	2c **black,** die 1, *dark manila*	42.50	35.00
		Entire	65.00	55.00
+*U48*	U18	2c **black,** die 2, *buff*	1,750.	
		Entire	*3,500.*	
+*U49*	U18	2c **black,** die 2, *orange*	1,050.	
		Entire	2,250.	
U50	U19	2c **black,** die 3, *buff* ('64)	9.00	8.00
		Entire	25.00	14.00
W51	U19	2c **black,** die 3, *buff* ('64)	170.00	170.00
		Entire	275.00	250.00
U52	U19	2c **black,** die 3, *orange* ('64)	11.00	7.00
		Entire	22.50	10.00
W53	U19	2c **black,** die 3, *dark manila* ('64)	30.00	20.00
		Entire	110.00	60.00
U54	U20	2c **black,** die 4, *buff* ('64)	11.00	9.00
		Entire	22.50	12.00
W55	U20	2c **black,** die 4, *buff* ('64)	75.00	50.00
		Entire	125.00	95.00
U56	U20	2c **black,** die 4, *orange* ('64)	10.00	7.00
		Entire	16.00	10.00
W57	U20	2c **black,** die 4, *light manila* ('64)	11.50	10.00
		Entire	24.00	21.50

Washington U21

79 varieties for Nos. U58-U61; 2 varieties for Nos. U63-U65

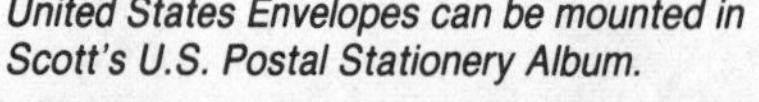

Washington — U22

1864-65

No.	Type	Description	Unused	Used
U58	U21	3c **pink**	6.00	1.50
		Entire	9.00	3.00
U59	U21	3c **pink,** *buff*	4.50	1.00
		Entire	9.50	2.25
U60	U21	3c **brown** ('65)	40.00	22.50
		Entire	80.00	80.00
U61	U21	3c **brown,** *buff* ('65)	40.00	22.50
		Entire	80.00	60.00
U62	U21	6c **pink**	50.00	27.50
		Entire	85.00	50.00
U63	U21	6c **pink,** *buff*	32.50	22.50
		Entire	85.00	50.00
U64	U21	6c **purple** ('65)	40.00	22.50
		Entire	70.00	50.00
U65	U21	6c **purple,** *buff* ('65)	35.00	20.00
		Entire	57.50	50.00
U66	U22	9c **lemon,** *buff* ('65)	350.00	250.00
		Entire	575.00	450.00
U67	U22	9c **orange,** *buff* ('65)	90.00	85.00
		Entire	200.00	250.00
a.		9c orange yellow, *buff*	100.00	95.00
		Entire	175.00	275.00
U68	U22	12c **brown,** *buff* ('65)	350.00	225.00
		Entire	575.00	900.00
U69	U22	12c **red brown,** *buff* ('65)	90.00	60.00
		Entire	140.00	200.00
U70	U22	18c **red,** *buff* ('65)	90.00	90.00
		Entire	225.00	*750.00*
U71	U22	24c **blue,** *buff* ('65)	90.00	85.00
		Entire	225.00	750.00
U72	U22	30c **green,** *buff* ('65)	60.00	60.00
		Entire	190.00	*750.00*
a.		30c yellow green, *buff*	60.00	75.00
		Entire	190.00	*850.00*
U73	U22	40c **rose,** *buff* ('65)	70.00	*250.00*
		Entire	275.00	*1,250.*

Printed by George H. Reay, Brooklyn, N. Y.
The engravings in this issue are finely executed.

Franklin U23

Bust points to the end of the "N" of "ONE".

Jackson
U24

Bust narrow at back. Small, thick figures of value.

Washington — U25

Queue projects below bust.

Lincoln
U26

Neck very long at the back.

Stanton
U27

Bust pointed at the back; figures "7" are normal.

Jefferson
U28

Queue forms straight line with the bust.

Clay
U29

Ear partly concealed by hair, mouth large, chin prominent.

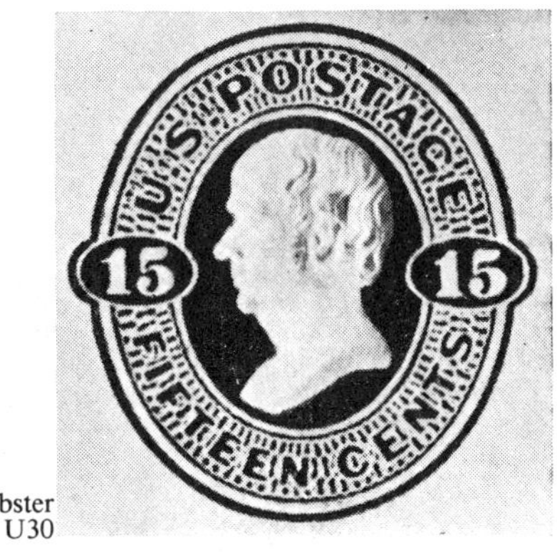

Webster
U30

Has side whiskers.

Scott
U31

Straggling locks of hair at top of head; ornaments around the inner oval end in squares.

Hamilton
U32

Back of bust very narrow, chin almost straight; labels containing figures of value are exactly parallel.

Perry
U33

Front of bust very narrow and pointed; inner lines of shields project very slightly beyond the oval.

1870-71

U74	U23	1c **blue**	30.00	25.00
		Entire	55.00	30.00
a.		1c ultramarine	60.00	30.00
		Entire	85.00	50.00
U75	U23	1c **blue,** *amber*	30.00	25.00
		Entire	55.00	25.00
a.		1c ultramarine, *amber*	50.00	30.00
		Entire	65.00	50.00
U76	U23	1c **blue,** *orange*	13.00	10.00
		Entire	26.00	18.00
W77	U23	1c **blue,** *manila*	40.00	30.00
		Entire	70.00	55.00
U78	U24	2c **brown**	35.00	14.00
		Entire	55.00	16.00
U79	U24	2c **brown,** *amber*	15.00	7.50
		Entire	30.00	15.00
U80	U24	2c **brown,** *orange*	8.00	5.00
		Entire	12.50	6.50
W81	U24	2c **brown,** *manila*	22.50	17.50
		Entire	45.00	35.00
U82	U25	3c **green**	6.00	75
		Entire	11.00	2.25
U83	U25	3c **green,** *amber*	4.50	1.75
		Entire	11.00	2.50
U84	U25	3c **green,** *cream*	7.50	3.00
		Entire	15.00	4.00
U85	U26	6c **dark red**	16.00	12.50
		Entire	27.50	17.50
a.		6c vermilion	14.00	14.00
		Entire	27.50	16.00
U86	U26	6c **dark red,** *amber*	21.00	14.00
		Entire	40.00	16.00
a.		6c vermilion, *amber*	21.00	14.00
		Entire	40.00	16.00
U87	U26	6c **dark red,** *cream*	25.00	14.00
		Entire	45.00	20.00
a.		6c vermilion, *cream*	25.00	14.00
		Entire	40.00	20.00
U88	U27	7c **vermilion,** *amber* ('71)	40.00	*200.00*
		Entire	55.00	*600.00*
U89	U28	10c **olive black**	350.00	350.00
		Entire	450.00	*800.00*
U90	U28	10c **olive black,** *amber*	350.00	350.00
		Entire	450.00	*800.00*
U91	U28	10c **brown**	50.00	75.00
		Entire	75.00	75.00
U92	U28	10c **brown,** *amber*	70.00	50.00
		Entire	90.00	70.00
a.		10c dark brown, *amber*	70.00	60.00
		Entire	90.00	75.00
U93	U29	12c **plum**	115.00	70.00
		Entire	240.00	*350.00*
U94	U29	12c **plum,** *amber*	110.00	100.00
		Entire	225.00	*500.00*
U95	U29	12c **plum,** *cream*	225.00	225.00
		Entire	375.00	
U96	U30	15c **red orange**	60.00	75.00

			Entire	165.00	
a.		15c orange		60.00	
			Entire	165.00	
U97	U30	15c	**red orange,** *amber*	165.00	200.00
			Entire	400.00	
a.		15c orange, *amber*		165.00	
			Entire	400.00	
U98	U30	15c	**red orange,** *cream*	250.00	250.00
			Entire	350.00	
a.		15c orange, *cream*		250.00	
			Entire	350.00	
U99	U31	24c	**purple**	125.00	90.00
			Entire	175.00	
U100	U31	24c	**purple,** *amber*	180.00	300.00
			Entire	390.00	
U101	U31	24c	**purple,** *cream*	180.00	300.00
			Entire	390.00	
U102	U32	30c	**black**	75.00	100.00
			Entire	315.00	
U103	U32	30c	**black,** *amber*	180.00	250.00
			Entire	575.00	
U104	U32	30c	**black,** *cream*	225.00	400.00
			Entire	450.00	
U105	U33	90c	**carmine**	140.00	225.00
			Entire	200.00	
U106	U33	90c	**carmine,** *amber*	300.00	400.00
			Entire	850.00	
U107	U33	90c	**carmine,** *cream*	350.00	500.00
			Entire	900.00	

Printed by Plimpton Manufacturing Co.

U34

Die 1 - Bust forms an angle at the back near the frame. Lettering poorly executed. Distinct circle in "O" of "Postage".

U35

Die 2 - Lower part of bust points to the end of the "E" in "ONE". Head inclined downward.

U36

Die 1 - Bust narrow at back. Thin numerals. Head of "P" narrow. Bust broad at front, ending in sharp corners.

U37

Die 2 - Bust broad. Figures of value in long ovals.

U38

Die 3 - Similar to die 2 but the figure "2" at the left touches the oval.

U39

Die 4 - Similar to die 2 but the "O" of "TWO" has the center netted instead of plain and the "G" of "POSTAGE" and the "C" of "CENTS" have diagonal crossline.

U40

Die 5 - Bust broad: numerals in ovals short and thick.

U41

Die 6 - Similar to die 5 but the ovals containing the numerals are much heavier. A diagonal line runs from the upper part of the "U" to the white frame-line.

U42

Die 7 - Similar to die 5 but the middle stroke of "N" in "CENTS" is as thin as the vertical strokes.

U43

Die 8 - Bottom of bust cut almost semi-circularly.

U44

Die 1 - Thin lettering, long thin figures of value.

U45

Die 2 - Thick lettering, well-formed figures of value, queue does not project below bust.

U46

Die 3 - Top of head egg-shaped; knot of queue well marked and projects triangularly.

Taylor
U47

Die 1 - Figures of value with thick, curved tops.

Die 2 - Figures of value with long, thin tops.

U48

Neck short at back.

U49

Figures of value turned up at the ends.

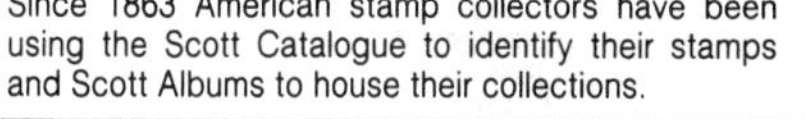
Since 1863 American stamp collectors have been using the Scott Catalogue to identify their stamps and Scott Albums to house their collections.

U50

Die 1 - Very large head.

U51

Die 2 - Knot of queue stands out prominently.

U52

Ear prominent, chin receding.

U53

No side whiskers, forelock projects above head.

U54

Hair does not project; ornaments around the inner oval end in points.

U55

Back of bust rather broad, chin slopes considerably; labels containing figures of value are not exactly parallel.

U56

Front of bust sloping; inner lines of shields project considerably into the inner oval.

1874-86

U108	U34	1c **dark blue,** die 1	90.00	40.00
		Entire	110.00	75.00
a.		light blue, die 1		
U109	U34	1c **dark blue,** die 1, *amber*	100.00	65.00
		Entire	140.00	80.00
+U110	U34	1c **dark blue,** die 1, *cream*	700.00	
U111	U34	1c **dark blue,** die 1, *orange*	17.50	15.00
		Entire	27.50	20.00
a.		1c light blue, die 1, *orange*	20.00	10.00
		Entire	21.00	15.00
W112	U34	1c **dark blue,** die 1, *manila*	40.00	30.00
		Entire	65.00	60.00
U113	U35	1c **light blue,** die 2	1.25	75
		Entire	2.00	1.00
a.		1c dark blue, die 2	7.00	5.00
		Entire	16.00	10.00
U114	U35	1c **light blue,** die 2, *amber*	3.75	3.00
		Entire	5.00	3.00
a.		1c dark blue, die 2, *amber*	14.00	10.00
		Entire	22.50	10.00
U115	U35	1c **blue,** die 2, *cream*	3.75	4.00
		Entire	6.00	3.00
a.		1c dark blue, die 2, *cream*	17.00	5.00
		Entire	24.00	15.00
U116	U35	1c **light blue,** die 2, *orange*	50	40
		Entire	60	40
a.		1c dark blue, die 2, *orange*	1.75	1.00
		Entire	7.00	5.00
U117	U35	1c **light blue,** die 2, *blue* ('80)	5.00	4.00
		Entire	7.00	5.00
U118	U35	1c **light blue,** die 2, *fawn* ('79)	5.00	4.00
		Entire	6.00	5.00
U119	U35	1c **light blue,** die 2, *manila* ('86)	5.00	3.00
		Entire	6.00	5.00
W120	U35	1c **light blue,** die 2, *manila*	1.25	1.00
		Entire	2.00	1.50
a.		1c dark blue, die 2, *manila*	4.00	2.50
		Entire	8.00	5.00
U121	U35	1c **light blue,** die 2, *amber manila* ('86)	10.00	9.00
		Entire	13.00	10.00
U122	U36	2c **brown,** die 1	85.00	40.00
		Entire	100.00	80.00
U123	U36	2c **brown,** die 1, *amber*	50.00	40.00
		Entire	75.00	65.00
+U124	U36	2c **brown,** die 1, *cream*	600.00	
+U125	U36	2c **brown,** die 1, *orange*	*7,000.*	
		Entire	*13,500.*	
W126	U36	2c **brown,** die 1, *manila*	90.00	40.00
		Entire	100.00	60.00
W127	U36	2c **vermilion,** die 1, *manila*	1,250.	300.00
		Entire	1,750.	
U128	U37	2c **brown,** die 2	40.00	25.00
		Entire	80.00	70.00
U129	U37	2c **brown,** die 1, *amber*	65.00	35.00
		Entire	80.00	40.00
+U130	U37	2c **brown,** die 2, *cream*	*18,500.*	
W131	U37	2c **brown,** die 2, *manila*	14.00	14.00
		Entire	20.00	20.00
U132	U38	2c **brown,** die 3	60.00	25.00
		Entire	80.00	70.00
U133	U38	2c **brown,** die 3, *amber*	200.00	60.00
		Entire	225.00	100.00
+U133A	U38	2c **brown,** die 3, *cream*	—	
U134	U39	2c **brown,** die 4	700.00	125.00
		Entire	800.00	150.00
U135	U39	2c **brown,** die 4, *amber*	425.00	125.00
		Entire	600.00	150.00
U136	U39	2c **brown,** die 4, *orange*	30.00	30.00
		Entire	60.00	40.00
W137	U39	2c **brown,** die 4, *manila*	55.00	30.00
		Entire	65.00	40.00
+U137A	U39	2c **vermilion,** die 4	*17,500.*	
+U137B	U39	2c **vermilion,** die 4, *amber*	*17,500.*	
		Entire	—	
+U137C	U39	2c **vermilion,** die 4, *orange*	*17,500.*	
+W138	U39	2c **vermilion,** die 4, *manila*	*6,500.*	
U139	U40	2c **brown,** die 5 ('75)	40.00	35.00
		Entire	50.00	40.00
U140	U40	2c **brown,** die 5, *amber* ('75)	70.00	60.00
		Entire	90.00	60.00
W141	U40	2c **brown,** die 5, *manila* ('75)	35.00	25.00
		Entire	40.00	35.00
U142	U40	2c **vermilion,** die 5 ('75)	5.00	2.25
		Entire	6.00	2.75
a.		2c pink, die 5	8.50	6.00
		Entire	14.00	7.50
U143	U40	2c **vermilion,** die 5, *amber* ('75)	5.00	2.25
		Entire	6.00	4.00
U144	U40	2c **vermilion,** die 5, *cream* ('75)	10.00	5.00
		Entire	13.00	5.00
+U145	U40	2c **vermilion,** die 5, *orange* ('75)	*8,000.*	
		Entire	*11,500.*	
U146	U40	2c **vermilion,** die 5, *blue* ('80)	125.00	32.50
		Entire	200.00	150.00
U147	U40	2c **vermilion,** die 5, *fawn* ('75)	6.00	4.00
		Entire	11.00	6.00
W148	U40	2c **vermilion,** die 5, *manila* ('75)	3.00	3.00
		Entire	6.00	5.00
U149	U41	2c **vermilion,** die 6 ('78)	40.00	25.00
		Entire	60.00	35.00
a.		2c pink, die 6	40.00	25.00
		Entire	60.00	30.00
U150	U41	2c **vermilion,** die 6, *amber* ('78)	20.00	14.00
		Entire	30.00	16.00
U151	U41	2c **vermilion,** die 6, *blue* ('80)	8.00	7.00
		Entire	1000	9.00
a.		2c pink, die 6, *blue*	8.00	7.00
		Entire	11.00	7.50
U152	U41	2c **vermilion,** die 6, *fawn* ('78)	8.75	3.50
		Entire	11.50	9.00
U153	U42	2c **vermilion,** die 7 ('76)	45.00	20.00
		Entire	70.00	27.50
U154	U42	2c **vermilion,** die 7, *amber* ('76)	300.00	80.00
		Entire	375.00	110.00
W155	U42	2c **vermilion,** die 7, *manila* ('76)	16.00	8.00
		Entire	40.00	10.00
U156	U43	2c **vermillion,** die 8 ('81)	525.00	125.00
		Entire	550.00	300.00
U157	U43	2c **vermilion,** die 8, *amber* ('81)	*14,000.*	*14,000.*
		Entire	*45,000.*	
W158	U43	2c **vermilion,** die 8, *manila* ('81)	75.00	60.00
		Entire	140.00	100.00
U159	U44	3c **green,** die 1	20.00	5.00
		Entire	32.50	10.00
U160	U44	3c **green,** die 1, *amber*	24.00	9.00
		Entire	40.00	12.00
U161	U44	3c **green,** die 1, *cream*	35.00	10.00
		Entire	45.00	15.00
+U162	U44	3c **green,** die 1, *blue*	—	
U163	U45	3c **green,** die 2	1.00	25
		Entire	2.00	75
U164	U45	3c **green,** die 2, *amber*	1.25	50
		Entire	2.25	1.00
U165	U45	3c **green,** die 2, *cream*	5.50	5.00
		Entire	9.00	6.00
U166	U45	3c **green,** die 2, *blue*	6.00	4.00
		Entire	10.00	7.00
U167	U45	3c **green,** die 2, *fawn* ('75)	4.00	2.50
		Entire	7.00	3.00
U168	U46	3c **green,** die 3 ('81)	500.00	40.00
		Entire	*1,900.*	75.00
U169	U46	3c **green,** die 3, *amber*	200.00	100.00
		Entire	300.00	125.00
U170	U46	3c **green,** die 3, *blue* ('81)	*7,000.*	*1,750.*
		Entire	*15,000.*	*4,000.*
U171	U46	3c **green,** die 3, *fawn* ('81)	*24,000.*	*1,500.*
		Entire		*12,500.*
U172	U47	5c **blue,** die 1 ('75)	7.50	7.00
		Entire	9.75	8.00
U173	U47	5c **blue,** die 1, *amber* ('75)	8.75	7.50
		Entire	10.50	6.00
U174	U47	5c **blue,** die 1, *cream* ('75)	90.00	45.00
		Entire	125.00	85.00
U175	U47	5c **blue,** die 1, *blue* ('75)	14.00	14.00
		Entire	18.00	17.00
U176	U47	5c **blue,** die 1, *fawn* ('75)	110.00	60.00
		Entire	190.00	
U177	U47	5c **blue,** die 2 ('75)	5.25	5.25
		Entire	9.50	11.00
U178	U47	5c **blue,** die 2, *amber* ('75)	6.00	5.75
		Entire	11.00	12.00
+U178A	U47	5c **blue,** die 2, *cream* ('76)	1,750.	
		Entire	*4,500.*	
U179	U47	5c **blue,** die 2, *blue* ('75)	11.00	7.00
		Entire	15.00	12.00
U180	U47	5c **blue,** die 2, *fawn* ('75)	80.00	50.00
		Entire	110.00	90.00
U181	U48	6c **red**	5.00	5.00
		Entire	9.00	7.00
a.		6c vermilion	4.75	4.75
		Entire	9.50	7.00
U182	U48	6c **red,** *amber*	5.00	5.00
		Entire	15.00	10.00
a.		6c vermilion, *amber*	8.00	5.00
		Entire	14.00	10.00
U183	U48	6c **red,** *cream*	16.00	10.00
		Entire	20.00	18.00
a.		6c vermilion, *cream*	16.00	10.00
		Entire	20.00	18.00
U184	U48	6c **red,** *fawn* ('75)	17.50	10.00
		Entire	25.00	16.00
+U185	U49	7c **vermilion**	*1,400.*	
U186	U49	7c **vermilion,** *amber*	90.00	65.00
		Entire	125.00	
U187	U50	10c **brown,** die 1	30.00	17.50
		Entire	50.00	
U188	U50	10c **brown,** die 1, *amber*	60.00	25.00
		Entire	90.00	
U189	U51	10c **chocolate,** die 2 ('75)	4.50	3.00
		Entire	8.00	7.00
a.		10c bister brown, die 2	5.50	3.50
		Entire	9.00	8.00
b.		10c yellow ocher	1,100.	
		Entire	1,400.	
U190	U51	10c **chocolate,** die 2, *amber* ('75)	6.00	5.50
		Entire	8.00	7.00
a.		10c bister brown, die 2, *amber*	6.00	5.50
		Entire	8.75	8.75
b.		10c yellow ocher	1,100.	
		Entire	1,400.	
U191	U51	10c **brown,** die 2, *oriental buff* ('86)	7.75	6.50
		Entire	9.25	7.00
U192	U51	10c **brown,** die 2, *blue* ('86)	9.00	6.50
		Entire	10.00	7.00
a.		10c gray black, die 2, *blue*	9.00	6.50
		Entire	10.00	7.00
b.		10c red brown, die 2, *blue*	9.00	6.50
		Entire	10.00	7.00
U193	U51	10c **brown,** die 2, *manila* ('86)	9.50	7.50
		Entire	12.00	12.00
a.		10c red brown, die 2, *manila*	9.50	7.50
		Entire	12.00	12.00
U194	U51	10c **brown,** die 2, *amber manila* ('86)	11.00	6.00
		Entire	13.00	12.00
a.		10c red brown, die 2, *amber manila*	11.00	6.25
		Entire	16.00	15.00
U195	U52	12c **plum**	175.00	90.00
		Entire	190.00	
U196	U52	12c **plum,** *amber*	165.00	165.00
		Entire	275.00	
U197	U52	12c **plum,** *cream*	200.00	175.00
		Entire	850.00	
U198	U53	15c **orange**	35.00	30.00
		Entire	85.00	45.00
U199	U53	15c **orange,** *amber*	125.00	100.00
		Entire	200.00	
U200	U53	15c **orange,** *cream*	400.00	400.00
		Entire	1,000.	
U201	U54	24c **purple**	175.00	125.00
		Entire	250.00	
U202	U54	24c **purple,** *amber*	175.00	125.00
		Entire	250.00	
U203	U54	24c **purple,** *cream*	175.00	125.00
		Entire	825.00	
U204	U55	30c **black**	60.00	30.00
		Entire	75.00	75.00
U205	U55	30c **black,** *amber*	65.00	60.00
		Entire	125.00	*250.00*
U206	U55	30c **black,** *cream* ('75)	475.00	450.00
		Entire	850.00	
U207	U55	30c **black,** *oriental buff* ('81)	100.00	85.00
		Entire	140.00	
U208	U55	30c **black,** *blue* ('81)	100.00	85.00
		Entire	125.00	
U209	U55	30c **black,** *manila* ('81)	90.00	85.00
		Entire	125.00	

U210	U55	30c	**black,** *amber manila* ('86)	125.00	85.00
			Entire	140.00	
U211	U56	90c	**carmine** ('75)	125.00	85.00
			Entire	140.00	100.00
U212	U56	90c	**carmine,** *amber* ('75)	175.00	225.00
			Entire	265.00	
U213	U56	90c	**carmine,** *cream* ('75)	1,400.	
			Entire	2,250.	
U214	U56	90c	**carmine,** *oriental buff* ('86)	200.00	275.00
			Entire	275.00	
U215	U56	90c	**carmine,** *blue* ('86)	175.00	250.00
			Entire	275.00	
U216	U56	90c	**carmine,** *manila* ('86)	125.00	250.00
			Entire	225.00	
U217	U56	90c	**carmine,** *amber manila* ('86)	125.00	200.00
			Entire	225.00	

Note: No. U206 has watermark #2; No. U207 watermark #6 or #7. No U213 has watermark #2; No. U214 watermark #7. These envelopes cannot be positively identified except by the watermark.

U57

Single line under "POSTAGE".

U58

Double line under "POSTAGE".

1876

Printed by Plimpton Manufacturing Co.

U218	U57	3c	**red**	60.00	25.00
			Entire	70.00	40.00
U219	U57	3c	**green**	45.00	16.00
			Entire	60.00	30.00
U220	U58	3c	**red**	*20,000.*	
			Entire	*27,500.*	
U221	U58	3c	**green**	60.00	17.50
			Entire	80.00	45.00

Garfield
U59

1882-86

Printed by Plimpton Manufacturing Co. and Morgan Envelope Co.

U222	U59	5c	**brown**	3.25	2.00
			Entire	6.00	5.00
U223	U59	5c	**brown,** *amber*	3.75	2.25
			Entire	7.00	6.00
U224	U59	5c	**brown,** *oriental buff* ('86)	100.00	75.00
			Entire	125.00	
U225	U59	5c	**brown,** *blue*	50.00	37.50
			Entire	85.00	40.00
U226	U59	5c	**brown,** *fawn*	225.00	
			Entire	300.00	

Washington — U60

1883, October

U227	U60	2c	**red**	3.25	1.50
			Entire	6.00	1.75
	a.		2c brown (error), entire	*2,000.*	
U228	U60	2c	**red,** *amber*	4.00	1.75
			Entire	7.00	3.00
U229	U60	2c	**red,** *blue*	5.75	4.00
			Entire	7.75	5.00
U230	U60	2c	**red,** *fawn*	4.25	2.50
			Entire	8.00	3.00

Washington — U61

Wavy lines fine and clear.

1883, November

Four Wavy Lines in Oval

U231	U61	2c	**red**	2.50	1.25
			Entire	6.00	1.50
U232	U61	2c	**red,** *amber*	2.50	1.50
			Entire	6.00	2.75
U233	U61	2c	**red,** *blue*	6.00	4.00
			Entire	10.00	4.50
U234	U61	2c	**red,** *fawn*	4.00	2.50
			Entire	6.00	3.00
W235	U61	2c	**red,** *manila*	17.50	3.50
			Entire	11.50	6.00

U62

Retouched die. Wavy lines thick and blurred.

1884, June

U236	U62	2c	**red**	5.00	3.00
			Entire	8.00	4.00
U237	U62	2c	**red,** *amber*	8.50	7.00
			Entire	13.00	6.50
U238	U62	2c	**red,** *blue*	12.50	7.00
			Entire	19.00	7.00
U239	U62	2c	**red,** *fawn*	9.00	6.50
			Entire	12.00	7.50

U63

3½ links over left "2".

U240	U63	2c	**red**	40.00	30.00
			Entire	67.50	45.00
U241	U63	2c	**red,** *amber*	625.00	300.00
			Entire	1,000.	600.00
U242	U63	2c	**red,** *fawn*		*6,250.*
			Entire		—

U64

2 links below right "2".

U243	U64	2c	**red**	60.00	40.00
			Entire	90.00	70.00
U244	U64	2c	**red,** *amber*	125.00	70.00
			Entire	165.00	100.00
U245	U64	2c	**red,** *blue*	275.00	110.00
			Entire	450.00	150.00
U246	U64	2c	**red,** *fawn*	275.00	110.00
			Entire	350.00	225.00

U65

Round "O" in "TWO".

U247	U65	2c	**red**	900.00	250.00
			Entire	1,350.	600.00
U248	U65	2c	**red,** *amber*	1,750.	675.00
			Entire	2,750.	900.00
U249	U65	2c	**red,** *fawn*	500.00	300.00
			Entire	825.00	375.00

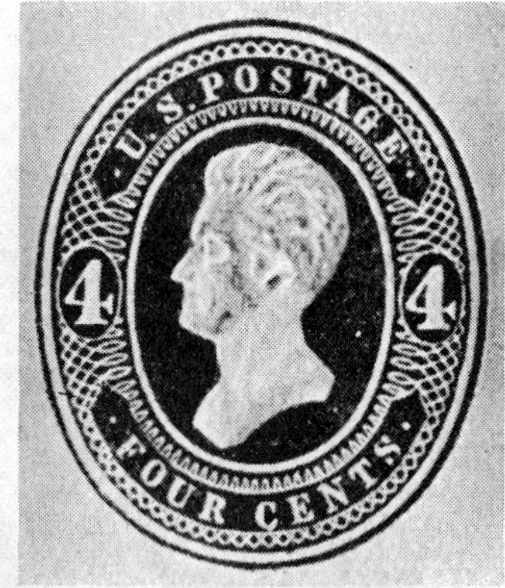

Jackson, Die 1 — U66

Die 1 - Numeral at left is 2¾mm wide.

Die 2 - Numeral at left is 3¼mm wide

1883-86

U250	U66	4c	**green,** die 1	2.50	2.50
			Entire	4.75	4.75
U251	U66	4c	**green,** die 1, *amber*	3.50	2.50
			Entire	5.00	4.00
U252	U66	4c	**green,** die 1, *oriental buff* ('86)	6.00	6.00
			Entire	9.00	6.00
U253	U66	4c	**green,** die 1, *blue* ('86)	6.00	5.00
			Entire	9.00	6.00
U254	U66	4c	**green,** die 1, *manila* ('86)	7.00	5.00
			Entire	10.00	10.00
U255	U66	4c	**green,** die 1, *amber manila* ('86)	17.50	9.00
			Entire	25.00	12.00
U256	U66	4c	**green,** die 2	4.00	3.00
			Entire	10.00	5.00
U257	U66	4c	**green,** die 2, *amber*	8.00	5.00
			Entire	13.00	8.00
U258	U66	4c	**green,** die 2, *manila* ('86)	7.00	5.00
			Entire	11.00	9.00
U259	U66	4c	**green,** die 2, *amber manila* ('86)	7.50	5.00
			Entire	11.00	8.00

1884, May

U260	U61	2c	**brown**	11.00	4.00
			Entire	14.00	7.50
U261	U61	2c	**brown,** *amber*	10.00	5.00
			Entire	12.00	5.75
U262	U61	2c	**brown,** *blue*	10.50	8.00
			Entire	14.00	12.00
U263	U61	2c	**brown,** *fawn*	9.00	7.50
			Entire	12.00	12.00
W264	U61	2c	**brown,** *manila*	10.50	8.00
			Entire	17.00	12.00

1884, June

Retouched Die

U265	U62	2c	**brown**	11.00	4.00
			Entire	16.00	8.00
U266	U62	2c	**brown,** *amber*	50.00	37.50
			Entire	62.50	57.50
U267	U62	2c	**brown,** *blue*	9.00	5.00
			Entire	12.00	7.50
U268	U62	2c	**brown,** *fawn*	9.00	8.00
			Entire	13.00	12.00
W269	U62	2c	**brown,** *manila*	17.50	12.00
			Entire	27.50	14.00

2 Links Below Right "2"

U270	U64	2c	**brown**	75.00	40.00
			Entire	100.00	80.00
U271	U64	2c	**brown,** *amber*	200.00	100.00
			Entire	300.00	175.00
U272	U64	2c	**brown,** *fawn*	*2,400.*	1,100.
			Entire	*4,000.*	2,250.

Round "O" in "Two"

U273	U65	2c	**brown**	125.00	65.00
			Entire	140.00	85.00
U274	U65	2c	**brown,** *amber*	140.00	65.00
			Entire	160.00	75.00
U275	U65	2c	**brown,** *blue*		*5,000.*
U276	U65	2c	**brown,** *fawn*	675.00	450.00
			Entire	950.00	600.00

Washington — U67

Die 1 - Extremity of bust below the queue forms a point.

U68

Die 2 - Extremity of bust is rounded. Similar to U61. Two wavy lines in oval.

1884-86

U277	U67	2c	**brown,** die 1	35	15
			Entire	70	25
a.		2c	brown lake, die 1	17.50	12.00
			Entire	20.00	14.00
U278	U67	2c	**brown,** die 1, *amber*	60	40
			Entire	1.20	50
a.		2c	brown lake, die 1, *amber*	35.00	12.00
			Entire	40.00	14.00
U279	U67	2c	**brown,** die 1, *oriental buff* ('86)	2.50	1.50
			Entire	3.75	2.25
U280	U67	2c	**brown,** die 1, *blue*	2.00	1.25
			Entire	2.75	1.50
U281	U67	2c	**brown,** die 1, *fawn*	2.50	1.50
			Entire	3.25	1.50
U282	U67	2c	**brown,** die 1, *manila* ('86)	8.50	3.00
			Entire	11.50	3.00
W283	U67	2c	**brown,** die 1, *manila*	4.75	4.50
			Entire	6.75	5.00
U284	U67	2c	**brown,** die 1, *amber manila* ('86)	5.00	5.00
			Entire	8.50	5.00
U285	U67	2c	**red,** die 1	600.00	
			Entire	800.00	
U286	U67	2c	**red,** die 1, *blue*	250.00	
			Entire	325.00	
W287	U67	2c	**red,** die 1, *manila*	100.00	
			Entire	140.00	
U288	U68	2c	**brown,** die 2	175.00	35.00
			Entire	450.00	75.00
U289	U68	2c	**brown,** die 2, *amber*	11.00	10.00
			Entire	15.00	12.00
U290	U68	2c	**brown,** die 2, *blue*	750.00	150.00
			Entire	850.00	190.00
U291	U68	2c	**brown,** die 2, *fawn*	20.00	16.00
			Entire	27.50	19.00
W292	U68	2c	**brown,** die 2, *manila*	21.00	16.00
			Entire	27.50	19.00

Gen. U.S. Grant — US1

1886

Printed by American Bank Note Co.

Issued August 18, 1886. Withdrawn June 30, 1894.

Letter Sheet, 160x271mm. Stamp in upper right corner.

Creamy White Paper.

U293	US1	2c	**green,** entire	22.50	8.50

Perforation varieties:

83 perforations at top	22.50	8.50
41 perforations at top	22.50	8.50
33 perforations at top	40.00	10.50

All with 41 perforations at top.

Inscribed: Series 1	22.50	8.50
Inscribed: Series 2	22.50	8.50
Inscribed: Series 3	22.50	8.50
Inscribed: Series 4	22.50	8.50
Inscribed: Series 5	22.50	8.50
Inscribed: Series 6	22.50	8.50
Inscribed: Series 7	22.50	8.50

Franklin U69

The Scott Catalogue value is a retail price, what you could expect to pay for the stamp in a grade of Fine-Very Fine. The value listed is a reference which reflects recent actual dealer selling price.

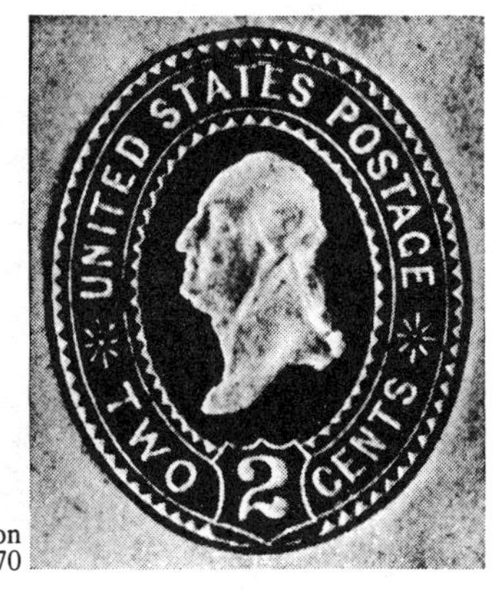

Washington
U70

Die 1 - Bust points between third and fourth notches of inner oval "G" of "POSTAGE" has no bar.

U71

Die 2 - Bust points between second and third notches of inner oval; "G" of "POSTAGE" has a bar; ear is indicated by one heavy line; one vertical line at corner of mouth.

U72

Die 3 - Frame same as die 2; upper part of head more rounded; ear indicated by two curved lines with two locks of hair in front; two vertical lines at corner of mouth.

Jackson
U73

Grant — U74

Die 1 - There is a space between the beard and the collar of the coat. A button is on the collar.

U75

Die 2 - The collar touches the beard and there is no button.

1887-94

Printed by Plimpton Manufacturing Co. and Morgan Envelope Co., Hartford, Conn.; James Purcell, Holyoke, Mass.

U294	U69	1c	**blue**	50	20
			Entire	75	30
U295	U69	1c	**dark blue** ('94)	6.50	2.50
			Entire	9.50	5.50
U296	U69	1c	**blue,** *amber*	2.50	1.25
			Entire	4.00	2.50
U297	U69	1c	**dark blue,** *amber* ('94)	40.00	22.50
			Entire	50.00	25.00
+U298	U69	1c	**blue,** *oriental buff*	*2,500.*	
			Entire	*4,500.*	
+U299	U69	1c	**blue,** *blue*	*3,250.*	
			Entire	*4,750.*	
U300	U69	1c	**blue,** *manila*	60	25
			Entire	95	40
W301	U69	1c	**blue,** *manila*	40	25
			Entire	75	40
U302	U69	1c	**dark blue,** *manila* ('94)	20.00	9.00
			Entire	27.50	15.00
W303	U69	1c	**dark blue,** *manila* ('94)	12.00	10.00
			Entire	22.50	15.00
U304	U69	1c	**blue,** *amber manila*	4.00	2.75
			Entire	6.00	3.50
U305	U70	2c	**green,** die 1	8.00	7.00
			Entire	17.50	10.00
U306	U70	2c	**green,** die 1, *amber*	20.00	12.00
			Entire	25.00	12.00
U307	U70	2c	**green,** die 1, *oriental buff*	65.00	30.00
			Entire	90.00	40.00
U308	U70	2c	**green,** die 1, *blue*	*3,000.*	750.00
			Entire		*4,000.*
U309	U70	2c	**green,** die 1, *manila*	2,000.	500.00
			Entire	*6,000.*	700.00
U310	U70	2c	**green,** die 1, *amber manila*	1,650.	600.00
			Entire	*5,500.*	*2,500.*
U311	U71	2c	**green,** die 2	25	10
			Entire	50	20
U312	U71	2c	**green,** die 2, *amber*	35	10
			Entire	55	25
U313	U71	2c	**green,** die 2, *oriental buff*	50	20
			Entire	85	35
U314	U71	2c	**green,** die 2, *blue*	50	20
			Entire	90	30
U315	U71	2c	**green,** die 2, *manila*	1.40	45
			Entire	1.90	1.00
W316	U71	2c	**green,** die 2, *manila*	2.50	2.00
			Entire	6.00	5.00
U317	U71	2c	**green,** die 2, *amber manila*	1.75	1.50
			Entire	4.00	2.00
U318	U72	2c	**green,** die 3	100.00	12.50
			Entire	140.00	35.00
U319	U72	2c	**green,** die 3, *amber*	140.00	20.00
			Entire	160.00	35.00
U320	U72	2c	**green,** die 3, *oriental buff*	150.00	40.00
			Entire	190.00	60.00
U321	U72	2c	**green,** die 3, *blue*	165.00	55.00
			Entire	200.00	60.00
U322	U72	2c	**green,** die 3, *manila*	150.00	75.00
			Entire	190.00	100.00
U323	U72	2c	**green,** die 3, *amber manila*	350.00	90.00
			Entire	400.00	125.00
U324	U73	4c	**carmine**	1.40	1.10
			Entire	3.00	1.40
	a.		4c lake	1.65	1.25
			Entire	4.00	3.00
	b.		4c scarlet ('94)	1.75	1.25
			Entire	4.00	3.00
U325	U73	4c	**carmine,** *amber*	2.00	1.75
			Entire	4.00	2.50
	a.		4c lake, *amber*	2.50	2.00
			Entire	4.50	3.00
	b.		4c scarlet, *amber* ('94)	2.25	2.50
			Entire	5.00	3.50
U326	U73	4c	**carmine,** *oriental buff*	5.00	2.50
			Entire	8.00	3.50
	a.		4c lake, *oriental buff*	6.00	3.00
			Entire	9.00	5.00
U327	U73	4c	**carmine,** *blue*	4.00	3.50
			Entire	5.50	5.00
	a.		4c lake, *blue*	4.00	3.50
			Entire	8.00	4.00
U328	U73	4c	**carmine,** *manila*	5.75	5.00
			Entire	7.50	6.50
	a.		4c lake, *manila*	6.50	5.50
			Entire	8.50	7.00
	b.		4c pink, *manila*	6.75	4.00
			Entire	8.50	7.50
U329	U73	4c	**carmine,** *amber manila*	4.00	2.50
			Entire	7.00	3.50
	a.		4c lake, *amber manila*	4.50	3.00
			Entire	7.50	4.50
	b.		4c pink, *amber manila*	5.00	3.50
			Entire	8.00	6.00
U330	U74	5c	**blue,** die 1	3.00	2.50
			Entire	5.00	9.25
U331	U74	5c	**blue,** die 1, *amber*	3.00	1.75
			Entire	6.00	12.00
U332	U74	5c	**blue,** die 1, *oriental buff*	3.25	3.00
			Entire	8.25	13.00
U333	U74	5c	**blue,** die 1, *blue*	5.00	4.00
			Entire	9.00	11.00
U334	U75	5c	**blue,** die 2 ('94)	9.00	4.50
			Entire	12.50	13.00
U335	U75	5c	**blue,** die 2, *amber* ('94)	9.00	5.00
			Entire	14.00	15.00
U336	U55	30c	**red brown**	35.00	40.00
			Entire	45.00	*200.00*
	a.		30c yellow brown	45.00	45.00
			Entire	55.00	*300.00*
	b.		30c chocolate	45.00	50.00
			Entire	55.00	*300.00*
U337	U55	30c	**red brown,** *amber*	40.00	60.00
			Entire	50.00	*300.00*
	a.		30c yellow brown, *amber*	45.00	45.00
			Entire	65.00	*300.00*
	b.		30c chocolate, *amber*	45.00	45.00
			Entire	65.00	*300.00*
U338	U55	30c	**red brown,** *oriental buff*	35.00	45.00
			Entire	45.00	*300.00*
	a.		30c yellow brown, *oriental buff*	35.00	45.00
			Entire	45.00	*300.00*
U339	U55	30c	**red brown,** *blue*	35.00	40.00
			Entire	40.00	*300.00*
	a.		30c yellow brown, *blue*	35.00	45.00
			Entire	40.00	*300.00*
U340	U55	30c	**red brown,** *manila*	40.00	40.00
			Entire	45.00	*250.00*
	a.		30c brown, *manila*	40.00	35.00
			Entire	50.00	*250.00*
U341	U55	30c	**red brown,** *amber manila*	45.00	30.00
			Entire	50.00	*250.00*
	a.		30c yellow brown, *amber manila*	45.00	30.00
			Entire	50.00	*250.00*
U342	U56	90c	**purple**	55.00	70.00
			Entire	70.00	*400.00*
U343	U56	90c	**purple,** *amber*	70.00	70.00
			Entire	90.00	*400.00*
U344	U56	90c	**purple,** *oriental buff*	70.00	75.00
			Entire	90.00	*400.00*
U345	U56	90c	**purple,** *blue*	70.00	80.00
			Entire	100.00	*400.00*
U346	U56	90c	**purple,** *manila*	70.00	80.00
			Entire	100.00	*400.00*
U347	U56	90c	**purple,** *amber manila*	75.00	80.00
			Entire	110.00	*400.00*

Columbus and Liberty — U76

Four dies were used for the 1c, 2c and 5c:
1. Meridian behind Columbus' head. Period after "CENTS".
2. No meridian. With period.
3. With meridian. No period.
4. No meridian. No period.

1893

U348	U76	1c **deep blue**	2.00	1.00
		Entire	2.50	1.25
U349	U76	2c **violet**	1.75	50
		Entire	2.00	60
a.		2c dark slate (error)	*1,100.*	
		Entire	—	
U350	U76	5c **chocolate**	8.00	7.50
		Entire	13.00	10.00
a.		5c slate brown (error)	650.00	650.00
		Entire	725.00	1,000.
U351	U76	10c **slate brown**	40.00	30.00
		Entire	60.00	45.00

Franklin
U77

Washington
U78

Die 1 - Bust points to first notch of inner oval and is only slightly concave below.

U79

Die 2 - Bust points to middle of second notch of inner oval and is quite hollow below. Queue has ribbon around it.

U80

Die 3 - Same as die 2, but hair flowing. No ribbon on queue.

Lincoln
U81

Die 1 - Bust pointed but not draped.

U82

Die 2 - Bust broad and draped.

U83

Die 3 - Head larger, inner oval has no notches.

Grant
U84

Similar to design of 1887-95 but smaller.

1899

U352	U77	1c **green**	50	20
		Entire	90	50
U353	U77	1c **green,** *amber*	4.00	1.50
		Entire	6.50	2.50
U354	U77	1c **green,** *oriental buff*	9.00	2.50
		Entire	11.50	3.50
U355	U77	1c **green,** *blue*	8.00	6.00
		Entire	9.50	*15.00*
U356	U77	1c **green,** *manila*	1.75	90
		Entire	5.00	1.75
W357	U77	1c **green,** *manila*	1.75	90
		Entire	7.00	2.50
U358	U78	2c **carmine,** die 1	2.00	90
		Entire	6.75	2.50
U359	U78	2c **carmine,** die 1, *amber*	15.00	10.00
		Entire	20.00	12.00
U360	U78	2c **carmine,** die 1, *oriental buff*	13.00	8.00
		Entire	22.50	9.00
U361	U78	2c **carmine,** die 1, *blue*	52.50	25.00
		Entire	60.00	25.00
U362	U79	2c **carmine,** die 2	25	20
		Entire	50	30
a.		2c dark lake, die 2	30.00	35.00
		Entire	35.00	40.00
U363	U79	2c **carmine,** die 2, *amber*	90	15
		Entire	2.25	60
U364	U79	2c **carmine,** die 2, *oriental buff*	90	15
		Entire	2.25	60
U365	U79	2c **carmine,** die 2, *blue*	1.10	50
		Entire	3.00	1.65
W366	U79	2c **carmine,** die 2, *manila*	4.50	2.50
		Entire	9.50	5.00
U367	U80	2c **carmine,** die 3	4.00	1.75
		Entire	7.50	6.00
U368	U80	2c **carmine,** die 3, *amber*	7.50	5.25
		Entire	12.00	9.00
U369	U80	2c **carmine,** die 3, *oriental buff*	20.00	12.50
		Entire	26.00	18.00
U370	U80	2c **carmine,** die 3, *blue*	10.00	7.00
		Entire	20.00	8.50
U371	U81	4c **brown,** die 1	14.00	11.00
		Entire	22.50	14.00
U372	U81	4c **brown,** die 1, *amber*	15.00	11.00
		Entire	27.50	22.50
U373	U82	4c **brown,** die 2	*4,000.*	375.00
		Entire	*4,500.*	
U374	U83	4c **brown,** die 3	8.00	6.00
		Entire	16.00	10.00
U375	U83	4c **brown,** die 3, *amber*	37.50	12.50
		Entire	42.50	15.00
W376	U83	4c **brown,** die 3, *manila*	14.00	7.50
		Entire	18.00	9.50
U377	U84	5c **blue**	8.75	8.50
		Entire	12.50	10.00
U378	U84	5c **blue,** *amber*	12.50	9.50
		Entire	17.00	13.00

Franklin — U85

Washington U86

One short and two long vertical lines at the right of "CENTS".

Grant U87

Lincoln — U88

1903

Printed by Hartford Manufacturing Co., Hartford, Conn.

U379	U85	1c	**green**	50	10
			Entire	75	30
U380	U85	1c	**green,** *amber*	10.00	2.00
			Entire	15.00	2.50
U381	U85	1c	**green,** *oriental buff*	10.00	1.90
			Entire	14.00	2.50
U382	U85	1c	**green,** *blue*	11.00	2.00
			Entire	2.50	2.50
U383	U85	1c	**green,** *manila*	3.50	1.00
			Entire	3.00	1.25
W384	U85	1c	**green,** *manila*	1.00	40
			Entire	1.40	75
U385	U86	2c	**carmine**	30	15
			Entire	50	35
			Pink	1.50	1.00
U386	U86	2c	**carmine,** *amber*	1.50	20
			Entire	3.00	80
			Pink, *amber*	3.00	1.50
U387	U86	2c	**carmine,** *oriental buff*	1.50	30
			Entire	2.00	35
			Pink, *oriental buff*	2.25	1.25
U388	U86	2c	**carmine,** *blue*	1.25	50
			Entire	3.00	60
			Pink, *blue*	3.00	1.75
W389	U86	2c	**carmine,** *manila*	14.00	7.00
			Entire	16.00	8.00
U390	U87	4c	**chocolate**	17.00	10.00
			Entire	20.00	12.50
U391	U87	4c	**chocolate,** *amber*	16.00	10.00
			Entire	20.00	12.00
W392	U87	4c	**chocolate,** *manila*	16.00	11.50
			Entire	20.00	13.00
U393	U88	5c	**blue**	16.00	9.00
			Entire	20.00	15.00
U394	U88	5c	**blue,** *amber*	16.00	10.00
			Entire	20.00	18.00

U89

Re-cut die - The three lines at the right of "CENTS" and at the left of "TWO" are usually all short; the lettering is heavier and the ends of the ribbons slightly changed.

1904

Re-cut Die

U395	U89	2c	**carmine**	40	15
			Entire	80	45
			Pink	5.00	2.50
U396	U89	2c	**carmine,** *amber*	6.50	50
			Entire	9.00	1.25
			Pink, *amber*	8.50	2.50
U397	U89	2c	**carmine,** *oriental buff*	5.00	1.25
			Entire	6.50	1.50
			Pink, *oriental buff*	6.50	2.50
U398	U89	2c	**carmine,** *blue*	3.00	90
			Entire	4.00	1.25
			Pink, *amber*	5.00	2.50
W399	U89	2c	**carmine,** *manila*	10.50	6.50
			Entire	17.00	6.00
			Pink, *manila*	15.00	7.00

Franklin U90

U90 Die 1

U90 Die 2

U90 Die 3

U90 Die 4

Die 1. Wide "D" in "UNITED".
Die 2. Narrow "D" in "UNITED".
Die 3. Wide "S-S" in "STATES" (1910).
Die 4. Sharp angle at back of bust, "N" and "E" of "ONE" are parallel (1912).

1907-16

Printed by Mercantile Corp. and Middle West Supply Co., Dayton, Ohio.

U400	U90	1c	**green,** die 1	25	10
			Entire	35	30
	a.		Die 2	75	15
			Entire	1.00	25
	b.		Die 3	75	25
			Entire	1.00	45
	c.		Die 4	65	20
			Entire	75	25
U401	U90	1c	**green,** *amber,* die 1	70	40
			Entire	1.00	60
	a.		Die 2	85	50
			Entire	1.25	70
	b.		Die 3	90	60
			Entire	1.50	80
	c.		Die 4	80	45
			Entire	1.10	60
U402	U90	1c	**green,** *oriental buff,* die 1	3.00	1.00
			Entire	4.00	1.75
	a.		Die 2	3.00	1.00
			Entire	4.00	1.75
	b.		Die 3	4.50	1.50
			Entire	5.50	1.75
	c.		Die 4	3.75	1.25
			Entire	4.25	1.75
U403	U90	1c	**green,** *blue,* die 1	4.00	1.50
			Entire	5.00	2.25
	a.		Die 2	4.00	1.50
			Entire	5.00	2.00
	b.		Die 3	4.00	1.50
			Entire	4.50	2.25
	c.		Die 4	3.50	1.25
			Entire	5.25	2.00
U404	U90	1c	**green,** *manila,* die 1	2.75	1.75
			Entire	3.75	2.75
	a.		Die 3	3.50	2.50
			Entire	5.50	4.00
W405	U90	1c	**green,** *manila,* die 1	40	25
			Entire	50	30
	a.		Die 2	35.00	25.00
			Entire	40.00	30.00
	b.		Die 3	5.00	3.00
			Entire	8.50	5.50
	c.		Die 4	30.00	25.00
			Entire	35.00	30.00

Washington — U91

U91 Die 1

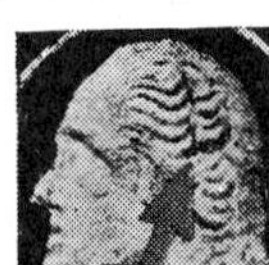

U91 Die 2

U91 Die 3

U91 Die 4

U91 Die 5

U91 Die 6

U91 Die 7 U91 Die 8

Die 1. Oval "O" in "TWO" and "C" in "CENTS". front of bust broad.
Die 2. Similar to 1 but hair re-cut in two distinct locks at top of head.
Die 3. Round "O" in "TWO" and "C" in "CENTS", coarse lettering.
Die 4. Similar to 3 but lettering fine and clear, hair lines clearly embossed. Inner oval thin and clear.
Die 5. All "S's" wide (1910).
Die 6. Similar to 1 but front of bust narrow (1913).
Die 7. Similar to 6 but upper corner of front of bust cut away (1916).
Die 8. Similar to 7 but lower stroke of "S" in "CENTS" is a straight line. Hair as in Die 2 (1916).

U406	U91 2c **brown red,** die 1	70	15
	Entire	1.40	30
a.	Die 2	25.00	6.25
	Entire	35.00	19.00
b.	Die 3	35	32
	Entire	50	38
U407	U91 2c **brown red,** *amber,* die 1	5.00	2.50
	Entire	6.25	6.00
a.	Die 2	100.00	45.00
	Entire	125.00	70.00
b.	Die 3	2.75	1.00
	Entire	4.00	90
U408	U91 2c **brown red,** *oriental buff,* die 1	6.50	1.50
	Entire	9.00	3.50
a.	Die 2	125.00	55.00
	Entire	140.00	90.00
b.	Die 3	6.00	2.50
	Entire	9.00	5.00
U409	U91 2c **brown red,** *blue,* die 1	3.50	1.75
	Entire	5.00	3.50
a.	Die 2	125.00	100.00
	Entire	160.00	125.00
b.	Die 3	3.50	1.50
	Entire	5.00	3.00
W410	U91 2c **brown red,** *manila,* die 1	40.00	30.00
	Entire	50.00	37.50
U411	U91 2c **carmine,** die 1	20	15
	Entire	50	35
a.	Die 2	30	8
	Entire	75	35
b.	Die 3	45	30
	Entire	90	50
c.	Die 4	20	15
	Entire	60	25
d.	Die 5	38	20
	Entire	75	50
e.	Die 6	20	8
	Entire	65	25
f.	Die 7	12.50	11.00
	Entire	15.00	13.00
g.	Die 8	13.00	11.00
	Entire	17.50	13.00
h.	2c carmine, die 1, with added impression of 1c green (#U400), die 1, entire	250.00	
i.	2c carmine, die 1, with added impression of 4c black (#U416a), entire	200.00	
U412	U91 2c **carmine,** *amber,* die 1	20	10
	Entire	80	16
a.	Die 2	25	10
	Entire	50	15
b.	Die 3	1.25	30
	Entire	1.65	65
c.	Die 4	20	15
	Entire	50	35
d.	Die 5	50	32
	Entire	80	50
e.	Die 6	20	10
	Entire	60	20
f.	Die 7	11.00	8.00
	Entire	13.00	11.00
U413	U91 2c **carmine,** *oriental buff,* die 1	40	20
	Entire	50	25
a.	Die 2	50	55
	Entire	75	45
b.	Die 3	6.00	3.00
	Entire	10.00	5.50
c.	Die 4	10	10
	Entire	35	15
d.	Die 5	45	25
	Entire	1.00	50
e.	Die 6	42	25
	Entire	1.00	50
f.	Die 7	35.00	17.50
	Entire	45.00	25.00
g.	Die 8	11.00	8.50
	Entire	16.00	11.00
U414	U91 2c **carmine,** *blue,* die 1	40	10
	Entire	90	16
a.	Die 2	40	30
	Entire	75	45
b.	Die 3	65	42
	Entire	1.40	65
c.	Die 4	18	8
	Entire	42	15
d.	Die 5	65	35
	Entire	1.25	45
e.	Die 6	42	15
	Entire	1.10	30
f.	Die 7	12.50	7.50
	Entire	17.00	14.00
g.	Die 8	12.50	7.50
	Entire	16.00	14.00
W415	U91 2c **carmine,** *manila,* die 1	4.00	2.00
	Entire	6.50	4.75
a.	Die 2	4.00	1.10
	Entire	6.50	1.75
b.	Die 5	4.00	1.10
	Entire	6.50	2.50
c.	Die 7	40.00	35.00
	Entire	50.00	42.50

U90 4c Die 1

U90 4c Die 2

4c-Die 1. "F" close to (1mm) left "4".
4c-Die 2. "F" far from (1¾mm) left "4".

U416	U90 4c **black,** die 2	3.00	1.00
	Entire	7.50	2.00
a.	Die 1	3.50	3.00
	Entire	8.00	5.00
U417	U90 4c **black,** *amber,* die 2	5.00	2.50
	Entire	9.00	4.00
a.	Die 1	5.00	2.50
	Entire	9.00	4.00

U91 5c Die 1

U91 5c Die 2

5c-Die 1. Tall "F" in "FIVE".
5c-Die 2. Short "F" in "FIVE".

U418	U91 5c **blue,** die 2	6.00	2.25
	Entire	10.00	5.00
a.	Die 1	6.00	2.25
	Entire	10.00	5.00
b.	5c blue, *buff,* die 2 (error)	*800.00*	
c.	5c blue, *blue,* die 2 (error)	*800.00*	
d.	5c blue, *blue,* die 1 (error)	*900.00*	
	Entire	*1,400.*	
U419	U91 5c **blue,** *amber,* die 2	12.00	11.00
	Entire	15.00	13.00
a.	Die 1	12.00	11.00
	Entire	20.00	13.00

On July 1, 1915 the use of laid paper was discontinued and wove paper was substituted. Nos. U400 to W405 and U411 to U419 exist on both papers: U406 to W410 come on laid only. Nos. U429 and U430 exist on laid paper.

Franklin U92

Die 1

Die 2

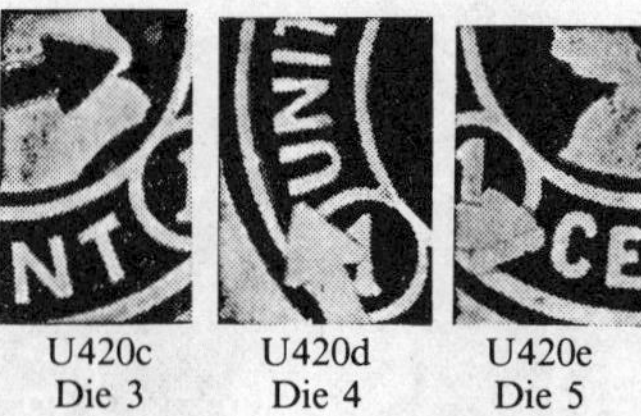
U420c Die 3 U420d Die 4 U420e Die 5

(The 1c and 4c dies are the same except for figures of value.)
Die 1. UNITED nearer inner circle than outer circle.
Die 2. Large U; large NT closely spaced.
Die 3. Knob of hair at back of neck. Large NT widely spaced.
Die 4. UNITED nearer outer circle than inner circle.
Die 5. Narrow oval C, (also O and G).
Some of the engraved dies of this series represent printing methods now obsolete, others are still in service. Some are best distinguished in the entire envelope. Many electrotypes were used.

Printed by Middle West Supply Co. and International Envelope Corp., Dayton, Ohio.

1916-32

U420	U92 1c **green,** die 1	6	5
	Entire	20	10
a.	Die 2	70.00	55.00
	Entire, size 8	90.00	70.00
b.	Die 3	8	5
	Entire	25	10
c.	Die 4	12	10
	Entire	30	15
d.	Die 5	12	10
	Entire	50	25
U421	U92 1c **green,** *amber,* die 1	35	30
	Entire	45	35
a.	Die 2	300.00	175.00
	Entire, size 8	450.00	200.00
b.	Die 3	1.25	60
	Entire	1.65	95
c.	Die 4	1.25	50
	Entire	1.65	1.25
d.	Die 5	1.00	40
	Entire	1.25	80
U422	U92 1c **green,** *oriental buff,* die 1	1.50	90
	Entire	1.90	1.40
a.	Die 4	2.75	1.25
	Entire	4.75	2.75
U423	U92 1c **green,** *blue,* die 1	40	8
	Entire	55	15
a.	Die 3	75	45
	Entire	1.00	70
b.	Die 4	1.25	50
	Entire	1.75	80
c.	Die 5	65	30
	Entire	1.00	50
U424	U92 1c **green,** *manila,* (unglazed) die 1	6.00	4.00
	Entire	7.50	5.00
W425	U92 1c **green,** *manila,* (unglazed) die 1	12	6
	Entire	15	8
a.	Die 3	140.00	125.00
	Entire	165.00	140.00
U426	U92 1c **green,** (glazed) *brown* ('20), die 1	25.00	16.00
	Entire	35.00	20.00
W427	U92 1c **green,** (glazed) *brown* ('20), die 1	65.00	
	Entire	75.00	
U428	U92 1c **green,** (unglazed) *brown* ('20), die 1	7.50	7.50
	Entire	10.00	9.00

All manila envelopes of circular dies are unwatermarked. Manila paper, including that of Nos. U424 and W425, exists in many shades.

Washington — U93

Die 1

Die 2

Die 3

Die 4

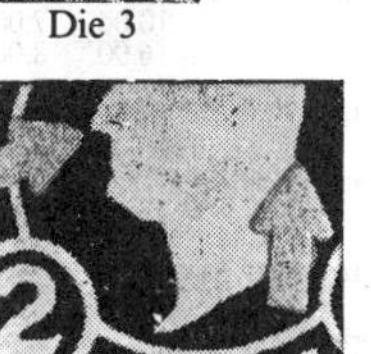
Die 5

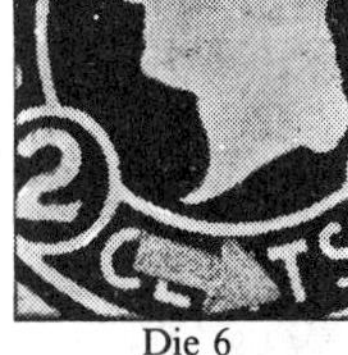
Die 6

Die 7

Die 8

Die 9

(The 1½c, 2c, 3c, 5c, and 6c dies are the same except for figures of value.)

Die 1. Letters broad. Numerals vertical. Large head (9¼ mm.) from tip of nose to back of neck. E closer to inner circle than N of cents.

Die 2. Similar to 1; but U far from left circle.

Die 3. Similar to 2; but all inner circles very thin (Rejected die).

Die 4. Similar to 1; but C very close to left circle.

Die 5. Small head (8¾ mm.) from tip of nose to back of neck. T and S of CENTS close at bottom.

Die 6. Similar to 5; but T and S of CENTS far apart at bottom. Left numeral slopes to right.

Die 7. Large head. Both numerals slope to right. Clean cut lettering. All letters T have short to strokes.

Die 8. Similar to 7; but all letters T have long top strokes.

Die 9. Narrow oval C (also O and G).

No.	Design	Description	Unused	Used
U429	U93	2c **carmine,** die 1	5	5
		Entire	20	5
a.		Die 2	9.00	6.00
		Entire	15.00	9.00
b.		Die 3	30.00	25.00
		Entire	40.00	30.00
c.		Die 4	9.00	7.50
		Entire	12.00	10.00
d.		Die 5	30	15
		Entire	50	35
e.		Die 6	30	15
		Entire	65	35
f.		Die 7	30	15
		Entire	65	35
g.		Die 8	25	10
		Entire	50	35
h.		Die 9	15	6
		Entire	55	35
i.		2c green, die 1 (error), entire	*4,250.*	
j.		carmine, die 1, with added impression of 1c green (#U420), die 1, entire	550.00	
k.		2c carmine, die 1, with added impression of 4c black (#U416a), entire	550.00	
l.		2c carmine, die 1, with added impression of 1c green (#U400), die 1, entire	450.00	
U430	U93	2c **carmine,** *amber,* die 1	12	6
		Entire	30	10
a.		Die 2	9.25	7.50
		Entire	15.00	10.00
b.		Die 4	20.00	10.00
		Entire	25.00	13.00
c.		Die 5	35	25
		Entire	90	60
d.		Die 6	80	15
		Entire	1.25	40
e.		Die 7	60	20
		Entire	90	35
f.		Die 8	52	20
		Entire	80	35
g.		Die 9	35	8
		Entire	65	35
U431	U93	2c **carmine,** *oriental buff,* die 1	1.75	45
		Entire	3.00	1.00
a.		Die 2	100.00	40.00
		Entire	125.00	70.00
b.		Die 4	30.00	30.00
		Entire	40.00	40.00
c.		Die 5	2.75	1.40
		Entire	5.00	1.75
d.		Die 6	3.50	1.50
		Entire	6.00	1.90
e.		Die 7	3.00	1.25
		Entire	4.00	1.65
U432	U93	2c **carmine,** *blue,* die 1	10	5
		Entire	40	20
b.		Die 2	25.00	20.00
		Entire	30.00	30.00
c.		Die 3	100.00	90.00
		Entire	140.00	110.00
d.		Die 4	25.00	25.00
		Entire	30.00	27.50
e.		Die 5	45	10
		Entire	1.00	30
f.		Die 6	30	16
		Entire	1.25	45
g.		Die 7	45	15
		Entire	1.25	45
h.		Die 8	52	20
		Entire	90	30
i.		Die 9	45	20
		Entire	2.50	50
U432A	U93	2c **car,** *manila,* die 1, entire	—	
W433	U93	2c **carmine,** *manila,* die 1	20	15
		Entire	25	20
W434	U93	2c **carmine,** (glazed) *brown* ('20), die 1	80.00	60.00
		Entire	100.00	70.00
W435	U93	2c **carmine,** (unglazed) *brown* ('20), die 1	80.00	60.00
		Entire	100.00	70.00
U436	U93	3c **dark violet,** die 1	50	15
		Entire	65	20
a.		3c purple ('32), die 1	25	15
		Entire	60	20
b.		3c dark violet, die 5	1.25	10
		Entire	2.00	30
c.		3c dark violet, die 6	1.50	25
		Entire	2.25	35
d.		3c dark violet, die 7	1.40	10
		Entire	2.00	30
e.		3c purple ('32), die 7	40	10
		Entire	1.25	20
f.		3c purple ('32), die 9	10	5
		Entire	35	10
g.		3c carmine (error), die 1	27.50	27.50
		Entire	32.50	32.50
h.		3c carmine (error), die 5	27.50	27.50
		Entire	32.50	32.50
i.		3c dark violet, die 1, with added impression of 1c green (#U420), die 1, entire	550.00	
j.		3c dark violet, die 1, with added impression of 2c carmine (#U429), die 1, entire	650.00	—
U437	U93	3c **dark violet,** *amber,* die 1	2.25	1.00
		Entire	5.00	2.00
a.		3c purple ('32), die 1	15	5
		Entire	45	25
b.		3c dark violet, die 5	3.00	1.50
		Entire	8.00	3.00
c.		3c dark violet, die 6	6.00	1.40
		Entire	7.50	3.00
d.		3c dark violet, die 7	3.75	1.00
		Entire	5.00	2.00
e.		3c purple ('32), die 7	60	10
		Entire	1.00	50
f.		3c purple ('32), die 9	50	10
		Entire	1.00	25
g.		3c carmine (error), die 5	350.00	250.00
		Entire	400.00	300.00
h.		3c black (error), die 1	165.00	—
		Entire	200.00	—
U438	U93	3c **dark violet,** *oriental buff,* die 1	20.00	1.50
		Entire	25.00	2.00
a.		Die 5	20.00	1.00
		Entire	25.00	1.10
b.		Die 6	25.00	1.65
		Entire	35.00	2.50
c.		Die 7	35.00	3.50
		Entire	40.00	7.75
U439	U93	3c **dark violet,** *blue,* die 1	6.00	1.40
		Entire	9.00	6.00
a.		3c purple ('32), die 1	18	5
		Entire	65	10
b.		3c dark violet, die 5	6.50	2.50
		Entire	8.25	3.50
c.		3c dark violet, die 6	6.00	3.50
		Entire	9.00	4.00
d.		3c dark violet, die 7	8.50	3.00
		Entire	12.50	6.50
e.		3c purple ('32), die 7	50	20
		Entire	1.00	30
f.		3c purple ('32), die 9	50	10
		Entire	1.00	40
g.		3c carmine (error), die 5	325.00	325.00
		Entire	400.00	400.00
U440	U92	4c **black,** die 1	1.00	50
		Entire	2.00	1.65
a.		4c black with added impression of 2c carmine (#U429), die 1, entire	250.00	
U441	U92	4c **black,** *amber,* die 1	2.50	75
		Entire	4.00	1.90
U442	U92	4c **black,** *blue,* ('21), die 1	2.50	75
		Entire	4.50	1.65
U443	U93	5c **blue,** die 1	2.75	90
		Entire	5.00	2.75
U444	U93	5c **blue,** *amber,* die 1	3.00	1.40
		Entire	4.50	3.00
U445	U93	5c **blue,** *blue,* ('21), die 1	3.50	1.00
		Entire	7.00	3.50

The provisional 2c surcharges of 1920-21 were made at central post offices with canceling machines using slugs provided by the Post Office Department.

Double or triple surcharge listings of 1920-25 are for specimens with surcharge directly or partly upon the stamp.

Type 1

1920-21

Surcharged on 1874-1920 Envelopes indicated by Numbers in Parentheses

Surcharged in Black

No.	Design	Description	Unused	Used
U446	U93	2c on 3c **dark violet,** (U436, die 1)	10.00	9.50
		Entire	12.50	11.00
a.		Die 5	10.00	9.50
		Entire	12.50	11.00

Surcharged

Type 2

Rose Surcharge

No.	Design	Description	Unused	Used
U447	U93	2c on 3c **dark violet** (U436, die 1)	6.00	5.50
		Entire	7.50	7.00
b.		Die 6	6.00	5.50
		Entire	8.50	8.00

Black Surcharge

No.	Design	Description	Unused	Used
U447A	U93	2c on 2c **carmine** (U429)	*1,750.*	
U447C	U93	2c on 2c **carmine,** *amber* (U430)	—	
U448	U93	2c on 3c **dark violet** (U436)	2.00	1.75
		Entire	2.50	2.00
U449	U93	2c on 3c **dark violet,** *amber* (U437)	5.00	5.00
		Entire	6.00	6.00
U450	U93	2c on 3c **dark violet,** *oriental buff* (U438)	14.00	14.00
		Entire	18.00	18.00
U451	U93	2c on 3c **dark violet,** *blue* (U439)	10.00	10.00
		Entire	11.50	10.50

Type 2 exists in three city sub-types.

Surcharged

Type 3

Bars 2mm apart

No.	Design	Description	Unused	Used
U451A	U90	2c on 1c **green** (U400, die 1)	1,650.	
U452	U92	2c on 1c **green** (U420)	850.00	
		Entire	950.00	
a.		Double surcharge, type 3	1,000.	
U453	U91	2c on 2c **carmine** (U411, die 1)	850.00	
		Entire	950.00	
a.		Die 4	850.00	
		Entire	950.00	
U453B	U91	2c on 2c **carmine,** *blue* (U414e, die 6)	700.00	
		Entire	750.00	
U453C	U91	2c on 2c **carmine,** *oriental buff* (U413e, die 6)	700.00	650.00
		Entire	800.00	
d.		Die 1	700.00	
		Entire	800.00	
U454	U93	2c on 2c **carmine** (U429)	90.00	
		Entire	110.00	
U455	U93	2c on 2c **carmine,** *amber* (U430, die 1)	950.00	
		Entire	1,000.	
U456	U93	2c on 2c **carmine,** *oriental buff* (U431)	175.00	
		Entire	225.00	
a.		Double surcharge, type 3	250.00	
U457	U93	2c on 2c **carmine,** *blue* (U432)	200.00	
		Entire	250.00	
U458	U93	2c on 3c **dark violet** (U436)	45	35
		Entire	60	45
a.		Double surcharge	13.00	7.50
b.		Triple surcharge	30.00	
c.		Double surcharge, one in magenta	65.00	
d.		Double surcharge, types 2 & 3	95.00	

U459 U93 2c on 3c **dark violet,** *amber* (U437) 2.50 1.00
Entire 3.75 1.75
a. Double surcharge, type 3 17.50
b. Double surcharge, types 2 & 3 75.00
U460 U93 2c on 3c **dark violet,** *oriental buff* (U438) 2.50 1.00
Entire 3.25 1.40
a. Double surcharge 12.50
b. Triple surcharge 25.00
U461 U93 2c on 3c **dark violet,** *blue* (U439) 4.00 1.00
Entire 5.50 1.50
a. Double surcharge 15.00
U462 U87 2c on 4c **chocolate** (U390) 350.00 175.00
Entire 400.00 200.00
U463 U93 2c on 4c **chocolate,** *amber* (U391) 325.00 100.00
Entire 375.00 200.00
U463A U90 2c on 4c **black** (U416) 750.00 425.00
Entire 850.00
U464 U93 2c on 5c **blue** (U443) 875.00
Entire 1,000.

Type 3 exists in 11 city sub-types.

Type 4

Same as Type 3, but bars 1 ½mm apart.

U465 U92 2c on 1c **green** (U420) 850.00
Entire 1,000.
U466 U91 2c on 2c **carmine** (U411e, die 6) *3,000.*
Entire *3,500.*
U466A U93 2c on 2c **carmine** (U429) 225.00
Entire 275.00
c. Die 5 400.00
U466B U93 2c on 2c **carmine,** *amber* (U430, die 1) 1,750.
Entire 2,000.
U467 U45 2c on 3c **green,** die 2 (U163) 250.00
Entire 300.00
U468 U93 2c on 3c **dark violet** (U436) 60 35
Entire 80 50
a. Double surcharge 15.00
b. Triple surcharge 20.00
c. Inverted surcharge 70.00
d. Double surcharge, types 2 & 4 75.00
e. 2c on 3c carmine (error), (U436h) 400.00
Entire 450.00
U469 U93 2c on 3c **dark violet,** *amber* (U437) 3.00 1.90
Entire 4.00 2.50
a. Double surcharge, types 2 & 4 60.00
U470 U93 2c on 3c **dark violet,** *oriental buff* (U438) 4.25 2.50
Entire 6.00 4.00
a. Double surcharge, type 4 17.50
b. Double surcharge, types 2 & 4 55.00
U471 U93 2c on 3c **dark violet,** *blue* (U439) 4.00 1.25
Entire 8.00 3.00
a. Double surcharge, type 4 17.50
b. Double surcharge, types 2 & 4 110.00
U472 U87 2c on 4c **chocolate** (U390) 9.50 8.00
Entire 22.50 14.00
a. Double surcharge 35.00
U473 U93 2c on 4c **chocolate,** *amber* (U391) 13.00 9.00
Entire 17.50 12.50

Type 4 exists in 30 city sub-types.

1 CENT

Double Surcharge, Type 4 and 1 c as above.

U474 U93 2c on 1c on 3c **dark violet** (U436) 225.00
Entire 250.00
U475 U93 2c on 1c on 3c **dark violet,** *amber* (U437, die 1) 225.00
Entire 250.00

Type 5

U476 U93 2c on 3c **dark violet,** *amber* (U437, die 1) 100.00
Entire 125.00
a. Double surcharge —

Surcharged

Type 6

U477 U93 2c on 3c **dark violet** (U436) 100.00
Entire 125.00
U478 U93 2c on 3c **dark violet,** *amber* (U437, die 1) 175.00
Entire 200.00

Handstamped Surcharged in Black or Violet

Type 7

U479 U93 2c on 3c **dark violet** (Bk) (U436) 300.00
Entire 350.00
U480 U93 2c on 3c **dark violet** (V) (U436d) 1,100.
Entire 1,250.

1925

Type of 1916-32 Issue

U481 U93 1½c **brown,** die 1 *(Washington)* 10 6
Entire 50 10
a. Die 8 15 10
Entire 75 15
b. 1½c purple, die 1 (error) ('34) 85.00
Entire 100.00
U482 U93 1½c **brown,** die 1, *amber* 90 20
Entire 1.40 45
a. Die 8 1.00 40
Entire 1.50 75
U483 U93 1½c **brown,** die 1, *blue* 1.50 75
Entire 1.75 1.10
a. Die 8 1.65 90
Entire 2.00 1.25
U484 U93 1½c **brown,** die 1, *manila* 6.00 3.00
Entire 11.00 6.00
W485 U93 1½c **brown,** die 1, *manila* 75 10
Entire 1.00 40
a. With added impression of #W433 110.00 —

The manufacture of newspaper wrappers was discontinued in 1934.

New rates on printed matter effective Apr. 15, 1925, resulted in revaluing some of the current envelopes.

Under the caption "Revaluation of Surplus Stocks of the 1 cent envelopes", W. Irving Glover, Third Assistant Postmaster-General, distributed through the Postal Bulletin a notice to postmasters authorizing the surcharging of envelopes under stipulated conditions.

Surcharging was permitted "at certain offices where the excessive quantities of 1 cent stamped envelopes remained in stock on April 15, 1925."

Envelopes were revalued by means of post office canceling machines equipped with special dies designed to imprint "1½" in the center of the embossed stamp and four vertical bars over the original numerals "1" in the lower corners.

Postmasters were notified that the revaluing dies would be available for use only in the International and "Universal" Model G machines and that the overprinting of surplus envelopes would be restricted to post offices having such canceling equipment available.

Envelopes of Preceding Issues Surcharged

Type 8

1925

On Envelopes of 1887

U486 U71 1½c on 2c **green** (U311) 600.00
Entire 475.00
U487 U71 1½c on 2c **green,** *amber* (U312) 700.00
Entire 800.00

On Envelopes of 1899

U488 U77 1½c on 1c **green** (U352) 550.00
Entire 650.00
U489 U77 1½c on 1c **green,** *amber* (U353) 80.00 75.00
Entire 110.00 100.00

On Envelopes of 1907-16

U490 U90 1½c on 1c **green** (U400, die 1) 3.50 3.50
Entire 5.00 5.00
a. Die 2 11.00 9.00
Entire 13.00 12.00
b. Die 4 6.00 2.50
Entire 8.00 4.00
U491 U90 1½c on 1c **green,** *amber* (U401, die 1) 7.50 2.50
Entire 11.00 6.00
a. Die 2 65.00 65.00
Entire 70.00 70.00
b. Die 4 4.00 2.25
Entire 7.00 4.50
U492 U90 1½c on 1c **green,** *oriental buff* (U402a, die 2) 190.00 85.00
Entire 200.00 100.00
a. Die 4 190.00 85.00
Entire 200.00 100.00
U493 U90 1½c on 1c **green,** *blue* (U403c, die 4) 85.00 65.00
Entire 100.00 75.00
a. Die 2 85.00 65.00
Entire 100.00 75.00
U494 U90 1½c on 1c **green,** *manila* (U404, die 1) 210.00 90.00
Entire 250.00 110.00

On Envelopes of 1916-20

U495 U92 1½c on 1c **green** (U420, die 1) 25 15
Entire 50 25
a. Die 3 1.25 60
b. Die 4 1.65 75
c. Double surcharge 4.00 1.90
U496 U92 1½c on 1c **green,** *amber* (U421) 14.00 14.00
Entire 19.00 17.00
U497 U92 1½c on 1c **green,** *oriental buff* (U422, die 1) 2.75 1.90
Entire 4.50 2.25
U498 U92 1½c on 1c **green,** *blue* (U423) 90 75
Entire 1.75 1.00
U499 U92 1½c on 1c **green,** *manila* (U424, die 1) 10.00 7.00
Entire 16.00 8.00
U500 U92 1½c on 1c **green,** *brown* (unglazed) (U428, die 1) 55.00 35.00
Entire 60.00 40.00
U501 U92 1½c on 1c **green,** *brown* (glazed) (U426, die 1) 55.00 30.00
Entire 60.00 32.50
U502 U93 1½c on 2c **carmine** (U429, die 1) 250.00 —
Entire 300.00 —
U503 U93 1½c on 2c **carmine,** *oriental buff* (U431c, die 5) 275.00 —
Entire 300.00 —
a. Double surcharge —
U504 U93 1½c on 2c **carmine,** *blue* (U432f, die 6) 250.00 —
Entire 300.00 —

On Envelopes of 1925

U505 U93 1½c on 1½c **brown** (U481, die 1) 400.00
Entire 500.00
a. Die 8 475.00
Entire 550.00
U506 U93 1½c on 1½c **brown,** *blue* (U483a, die 8) 350.00
Entire 400.00

The paper of No. U500 is not glazed and appears to be the same as that used for the wrappers of 1920.

Type 8 exists in 20 city sub-types.

Surcharged

Type 9

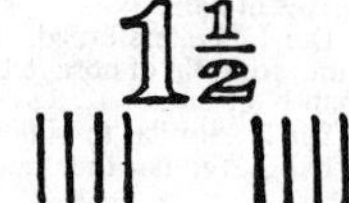

Black Surcharge

On Envelope of 1887

U507 U69 1½c on 1c **blue** (U294) 1,100.
Entire 1,250.

On Envelope of 1899

U508 U77 1½c on 1c **green,** *amber* (U353) 50.00
Entire 60.00

On Envelope of 1903

U508A U85 1½c on 1c **green** (U379) 1,250.
Entire 1,500.
U509 U85 1½c on 1c **green,** *amber* (U380) 10.00 10.00
Entire 22.50 12.00
a. Double surcharge 25.00
Entire 30.00
U509B U69 1½c on 1c **green,** *oriental buff* (U381) 50.00 45.00
Entire 65.00 50.50

On Envelopes of 1907-16

U510 U90 1½c on 1c **green** (U400, die 1) 1.75 1.25
Entire 3.25 1.50
a. Double surcharge 7.50
b. Die 2 5.75 4.00
Entire 8.25 6.00
c. Die 3 16.00 8.00
Entire 22.50 11.00
d. Die 4 3.00 1.25
Entire 6.00 2.00
U511 U90 1½c on 1c **green,** *amber* (U401, die 1) 175.00 90.00
Entire 200.00 100.00
U512 U90 1½c on 1c **green,** *oriental buff* (U402, die 1) 5.50 4.00
Entire 9.00 6.50
a. Die 4 17.00 14.00
Entire 22.50 17.00
U513 U90 1½c on 1c **green,** *blue* (U403, die 1) 4.50 2.50
Entire 6.75 4.25
a. Die 4 4.50 4.00
Entire 6.50 5.00
U514 U90 1½c on 1c **green,** *manila* (U404, die 1) 17.50 10.00
Entire 30.00 25.00
a. Die 3 45.00 42.50
Entire 52.50 52.50

On Envelopes of 1916-20

U515	U92	1½c on 1c **green** (U420)	30	15
		Entire	55	25
a.		Double surcharge	6.00	
b.		Inverted surcharge	8.50	
c.		Triple surcharge	10.00	
U516	U92	1½c on 1c **green,** *amber* (U421)	40.00	30.00
		Entire	50.00	40.00
U517	U92	1½c on 1c **green,** *oriental buff* (U422)	4.00	1.25
		Entire	5.00	1.50
U518	U92	1½c on 1c **green,** *blue* (U423)	4.00	1.25
		Entire	5.00	1.50
a.		Double surcharge	9.00	
U519	U92	1½c on 1c **green,** *manila* (U424, die 1)	12.50	11.00
		Entire	20.00	14.00
a.		Double surcharge	25.00	
U520	U93	1½c on 2c **carmine** (U429)	175.00	—
		Entire	200.00	—

Magenta Surcharge

U521	U92	1½c on 1c **green** (U420)	4.00	3.50
		Entire	4.50	4.75
a.		Double surcharge	25.00	

Sesquicentennial Exposition Issue

Issued to commemorate the 150th anniversary of the Declaration of Independence.

Liberty Bell — U94

Die 1. The center bar of "E" of "postage" is shorter than top bar.
Die 2. The center bar of "E" of "postage" is of same length as top bar.

1926, July 27

U522	U94	2c **carmine,** die 1	1.50	50
		Entire	2.25	95
		Entire, 1st day cancel, Washington, D.C.		22.50
		Entire, 1st day cancel, Philadelphia		20.00
a.		Die 2	8.50	6.00
		Entire	12.00	9.50

Washington Bicentennial Issue.

200th anniversary of the birth of George Washington.

Mount Vernon — U95

2c Die 1. "S" of "Postage" normal.
2c Die 2. "S" of "Postage" raised.

1932

U523	U95	1c **olive green,** *Jan. 1*	1.75	1.00
		Entire	2.75	2.50
		Entire, 1st day cancel		10.00
U524	U95	1½c **chocolate,** *Jan. 1*	3.50	1.50
		Entire	4.00	2.00
		Entire, 1st day cancel		10.00
U525	U95	2c **carmine,** die 1, *Jan. 1*	40	5
		Entire	60	10
		Entire, 1st day cancel		8.00
a.		2c carmine, die 2	90.00	15.00
		Entire	125.00	55.00
b.		2c carmine, die 1, *blue* (error) entire	10,000.	
U526	U95	3c **violet,** *June 16*	4.00	35
		Entire	5.00	40
		Entire, 1st day cancel		18.00
U527	U95	4c **black,** *Jan. 1*	25.00	15.00
		Entire	32.50	21.00
		Entire, 1st day cancel		30.00
U528	U95	5c **dark blue,** *Jan. 1*	5.00	3.25
		Entire	6.50	4.75
		Entire, 1st day cancel		18.00

1932, Aug. 18

Type of 1916-32 Issue

U529	U93	6c **orange,** die 7	5.00	2.75
		Entire	7.50	4.50
		Entire, 1st day cancel		20.00
U530	U93	6c **orange,** die 7, *amber*	11.00	8.00
		Entire	14.00	10.00
		Entire, 1st day cancel		20.00
U531	U93	6c **orange,** die 7, *blue*	11.00	8.00
		Entire	14.00	10.00
		Entire, 1st day cancel		20.00

Franklin U96

Washington U97

Die 1

Die 2

Die 3

Die 1. Short (3½mm) and thick "1" in thick circle.
Die 2. Tall (4½mm) and thin "1" in thin circle; upper and lower bars of E in ONE long and 1mm from circle
Die 3. As in Die 2, but E normal and 1½mm from circle.

Printed by International Envelope Corp.

1950

U532	U96	1c **green,** die 1, *Nov. 16, 1950*	5.00	1.75
		Entire	7.50	2.25
		Entire, 1st day cancel		1.00
a.		Die 2	6.00	3.00
		Entire	8.00	3.75
b.		Die 3	6.00	3.00
		Entire	8.00	3.75
b.		Precanceled		60
		Entire, precanceled		90

Die 1

Die 2

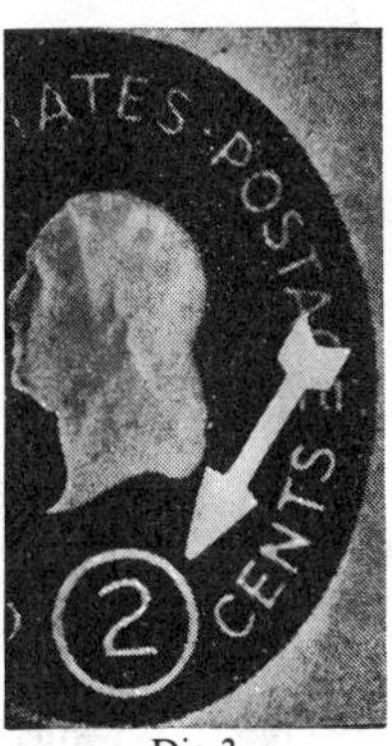

Die 3

Die 4

Die 1. Thick "2" in thick circle; toe of "2" is acute right angle.
Die 2. Thin "2" in thin circle; toe of "2" is almost right angle; line through left stand of "N" in UNITED and stand of "E" in POSTAGE goes considerably below tip of chin; "N" of UNITED is tall; "O" of TWO is high.
Die 3. Figure "2" as in Die 2. Short UN in UNITED thin crossbar in A of STATES.
Die 4. Tall UN in UNITED; thick crossbar in A of STATES; otherwise like Die 3.

U533	U97	2c **carmine,** die 3	65	8
		Entire	1.10	10
a.		Die 1, *Nov. 17, 1950*	75	25
		Entire	1.25	40
		Entire, 1st day cancel		1.65
b.		Die 2	1.30	80
		Entire	1.70	85
c.		Die 4	1.20	50
		Entire	1.40	60

Die 1

Die 2

Die 3

Die 4

Die 5

Die 1. Thick and tall (4½mm) "3" in thick circle; long top bars and short stems in T's of STATES.
Thin and tall (4½mm) "3" in medium circle; short top bars and long stems in T's of STATES
Die 3. Thin and short (4mm) "3" in thin circle; lettering wider than Dies 1 and 2; line from left stand of N to stand of E is distinctly below tip of chin.
Die 4. Figure and letters as in Die 3. Line hits tip of chin; short N in UNITED and thin crossbar in A of STATES.
Die 5. Figure, letter and chin line as in Die 4; but tall N in UNITED and thick crossbar in A of STATES.

U534	U97	3c **dark violet,** die 4	35	10
		Entire	40	15
a.		Die 1, *Nov. 18, 1950*	1.25	30
		Entire	1.75	80
		Entire, 1st day cancel		1.00
b.		Die 2, *Nov. 19, 1950*	75	25
		Entire	1.25	30
c.		Die 3	50	25
		Entire	95	35
d.		Die 5	50	30
		Entire	75	35

Washington — U98

1952

U535 U98	1½c **brown**		4.50	3.50
	Entire		5.50	4.25
	Precanceled			50
	Entire, precanceled			1.10

Die 1

Die 2

Die 3

Die 1. Head high in oval (2mm below T of STATES). Circle near (1mm) bottom of colored oval.

Die 2. Head low in oval (3mm). Circle 1½mm from edge of oval. Right leg of A in POSTAGE shorter than left. Short leg on P.

Die 3. Head centered in oval (2½mm). Circle as in Die 2. Legs of A of POSTAGE about equal. Long leg on P.

1958

U536 U96	4c **red violet,** die 1, *July 31*		75	10
	Entire		90	12
	Entire, 1st day cancel, Montpelier, Vt. *(163,746)*			75
a.	Die 2		1.00	10
	Entire		1.25	12
b.	Die 3		1.00	10
	Entire		1.25	12

Nos. U429, U429f, U429h, U533, U533a-U533c Surcharged in Red at Left of Stamp

b

1958

U537 U93	2c + 2c **carmine,** die 1		3.00	1.50
	Entire		3.50	—
a.	Die 7		10.00	7.00
	Entire		12.50	—
b.	Die 9		5.00	4.00
	Entire		6.50	—
U538 U97	2c + 2c **carmine,** die 1		75	18
	Entire		90	25
a.	Die 2		1.00	—
	Entire		1.20	—
b.	Die 3		80	15
	Entire		1.00	20
c.	Die 4		80	—
	Entire		1.00	—

A particular stamp may be scarce, but if few collectors want it, its market value may remain relatively low.

Nos. U436a, U436e-U436f, U534, U534b-U534d Surcharged in Green at Left of Stamp

a

U539 U93	3c + 1c **purple,** die 1		14.00	11.50
	Entire		16.00	—
a.	Die 7		12.00	10.00
	Entire		14.00	—
b.	Die 9		30.00	17.50
	Entire		35.00	—
U540 U97	3c + 1c **dark violet,** die 3		50	10
	Entire		60	12
a.	Die 2		—	—
	Entire		*1,000.*	—
b.	Die 4		75	10
	Entire		85	15
c.	Die 5		75	10
	Entire		85	15

Benjamin Franklin U99

George Washington U100

Die 1

Die 2

Dies of 1¼c

Die 1. The "4" is 3mm high. Upper leaf in left cluster is 2mm from "U."

Die 2. The "4" is 3½mm high. Leaf clusters are larger. Upper leaf at left is 1mm from "U".

1960

U541 U99	1¼c **turquoise,** die 1, *June 25, 1960*		70	50
	Entire		80	55
	Entire, 1st day cancel, Birmingham, Ala. *(211,500)*			75
	Precanceled			5
	Entire, precanceled			10
a.	Die 2, precanceled			2.00
	Entire, precanceled			2.25
U542 U100	2½c **dull blue,** *May 28, 1960*		80	50
	Entire		90	60
	Entire, 1st day cancel, Chicago, Ill. *(196,977)*			75
	Precanceled			10
	Entire, precanceled			12

Pony Express Centennial Issue

Pony Express Rider — U101

White Outside, Blue Inside.

1960

U543 U101	4c **brown,** *July 19, 1960*		60	30
	Entire		75	40
	Entire, 1st day cancel, St. Joseph, Mo. *(407,160)*			75

Abraham Lincoln — U102

Die 1

Die 2

Die 3

Die 1. Center bar of E of POSTAGE is above the middle. Center bar of E of STATES slants slightly upward. Nose sharper, more pointed. No offset ink specks inside envelope on back of die impression.

Die 2. Center bar of E of POSTAGE in middle. P of POSTAGE has short stem. Ink specks on back of die impression.

Die 3. FI of FIVE closer than Die 1 or 2. Second T of STATES seems taller than ES. Ink specks on back of die impression.

1962

U544 U102	5c **dark blue,** die 2, *Nov. 19, 1962*		80	20
	Entire		90	25
	Entire, 1st day cancel, Springfield, Ill. *(163,258)*			75
a.	Die 1		85	25
	Entire		95	30
b.	Die 3		90	30
	Entire		1.00	35
c.	Die 2 with albino 4c impression, entire		50.00	—
d.	Die 3 with albino 4c impression, entire		70.00	—

No. U536 Surcharged in Green at left of Stamp

a

Two types of surcharge:

Type I. "U.S. POSTAGE" 18½mm high. Serifs on cross of T both diagonal. Two lines of shading in C of CENT.

Type II. "U.S. POSTAGE" 17½mm high. Right serif on cross of T is vertical. Three shading lines in C.

1962

U545 U96	4c + 1c **red vio.,** die 1, type I, *Nov. 1962*		1.30	50
	Entire		1.50	60
a.	Type II		1.30	50
	Entire		1.50	60

New York World's Fair Issue

Issued to publicize the New York World's Fair, 1964-65.

Globe with Satellite Orbit — U103

1964

U546	U103	5c **maroon,** *Apr. 22, 1964*	60	40
		Entire	75	50
		Entire, 1st day cancel World's Fair N.Y. *(466,422)*		75

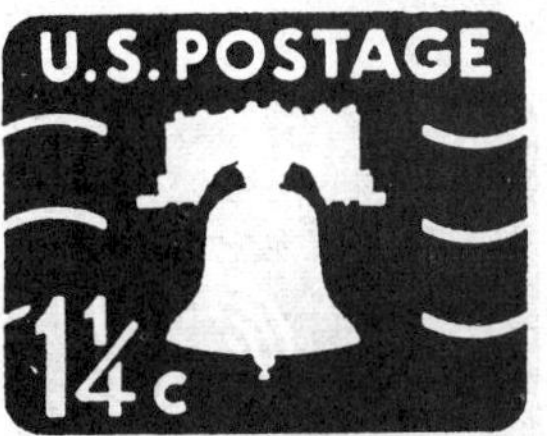

Liberty Bell — U104

Old Ironsides — U105

Eagle — U106

Head of Statue of Liberty — U107

Printed by the United States Envelope Company, Williamsburg, Pa. Designed (6c) by Howard C. Mildner and (others) by Robert J. Jones.

1965-69

U547	U104	1 1/4c **brown,** *Jan. 6, 1965*		15
		Entire	90	35
		Entire, 1st day cancel, Washington, D.C.		75
U548	U104	1 4/10c **brown,** *Mar. 26, 1968*		10
		Entire	1.00	25
		Entire, 1st day cancel, Springfield, Mass. *(134,832)*		75
U548A	U104	1 6/10c **orange,** *June 16, 1969*		10
		Entire	85	18
		Entire, 1st day cancel, Washington, D.C.		75
U549	U105	4c **bright blue,** *Jan. 6, 1965*	75	10
		Entire	95	15
		Entire, 1st day cancel, Washington, D.C.		75
U550	U106	5c **bright purple,** *Jan. 5, 1965*	75	5
		Entire	85	8
		Entire, 1st day cancel, Williamsburg, Pa. *(246,496)*		75
a.		Tagged, *Aug. 15, 1967*	1.00	5
		Entire	1.25	20
		Entire, tagged, 1st day cancel		3.50

Tagged

U551	U107	6c **light green,** *Jan. 4, 1968*	70	5
		Entire	80	8
		Entire, 1st day cancel, New York, N.Y. *(184,784)*		1.00

No. U550a has a 9x29mm panel at left of stamp that glows yellow green under ultraviolet light.
First day covers of the 1 1/4c and 4c total 451,960.

Nos. U549-U550 Surcharged Types "b" and "a" in Red or Green at Left of Stamp

1968, Feb. 5

U552	U105	4c + 2c **bright blue** (R)	3.75	2.00
		Entire	4.00	2.50
		Entire, 1st day cancel		4.50
U553	U106	5c + 1c **bright purple** (G)	3.50	2.25
		Entire	4.00	2.75
a.		Tagged	3.50	2.50
		Entire	4.00	3.00
		Entire, 1st day cancel		4.50

Tagged

Envelopes from No. U554 onward are tagged, with the tagging element in the ink unless otherwise noted.

Herman Melville Issue

Issued to honor Herman Melville (1819-1891), writer, and the whaling industry.

Moby Dick — U108

1970, Mar. 7

U554	U108	6c **blue**	50	15
		Entire	60	25
		Entire, 1st day cancel, New Bedford, Mass. *(433,777)*		75

Youth Conference Issue

Issued to publicize the White House Conference on Youth, Estes Park, Colo., Apr. 18-22.

Conference Emblem Symbolic of Man's Expectant Soul and of Universal Brotherhood U109

Printed by United States Envelope Company, Williamsburg, Pa. Designed by Chermayeff and Geismar Associates.

1971, Feb. 24

U555	U109	6c **light blue**	75	15
		Entire	85	40
		Entire, 1st day cancel, Washington, D.C. *(264,559)*		75

Liberty Bell Type of 1965 and U110

Eagle — U110

Printed by the United States Envelope Co., Williamsburg, Pa. Designed (8c) by Bradbury Thompson.

1971

U556	U104	1 7/10c **deep lilac,** untagged, *May 10*		8
		Entire	30	10
		Entire, 1st day cancel, Baltimore, Md. *(150,767)*		75
U557	U110	8c **ultramarine,** *May 6*	40	5
		Entire	50	8
		Entire, 1st day cancel, Williamsburg, Pa. *(193,000)*		75

Nos. U551 and U555 Surcharged in Green at Left of Stamp

c

1971, May 16

U561	U107	6c + (2c) **light green**	1.00	30
		Entire	1.10	45
		Entire, 1st day cancel, Washington, D.C.		4.00
U562	U109	6c + (2c) **light blue**	2.50	1.00
		Entire	2.75	1.25
		Entire, 1st day cancel, Washington, D.C.		4.50

Bowling Issue

Issued as a salute to bowling and in connection with the 7th World Tournament of the International Bowling Federation, Milwaukee, Wis.

Bowling Ball and Pin — U111

Designed by George Giusti.

1971, Aug. 21

U563	U111	8c **rose red**	50	15
		Entire	65	18
		Entire, 1st day cancel, Milwaukee, Wis. *(281,242)*		75

Aging Conference Issue

White House Conference on Aging, Washington, D.C., Nov. 28-Dec. 2, 1971.

Conference Symbol — U112

Designed by Thomas H. Geismar.

1971, Nov. 15

U564	U112	8c **light blue**	50	15
		Entire	65	18
		Entire, 1st day cancel, Washington, D.C. *(125,000)*		75

International Transportation Exhibition Issue

U.S. International Transportation Exhibition, Dulles International Airport, Washington, D.C., May 27-June 4.

Transportation Exhibition Emblem — U113

(Size of actual stamp: 64x70mm)

Emblem designed by Toshihiki Sakow.

1972, May 2

U565 U113	8c	**ultramarine & rose red**	50	5
		Entire	75	15
		Entire, 1st day cancel, Washington, D.C.		75

No. U557 Surcharged Type "b" in Ultramarine at Left of Stamp

1973, Dec. 1

U566 U110	8c + 2c	**brt. ultramarine**	40	5
		Entire	50	10
		Entire, 1st day cancel, Washington, D.C.		75

Liberty Bell – U114

1973, Dec. 5

U567 U114	10c	**emerald**	40	5
		Entire	50	8
		Entire, 1st day cancel, Philadelphia, Pa. *(142,141)*		75

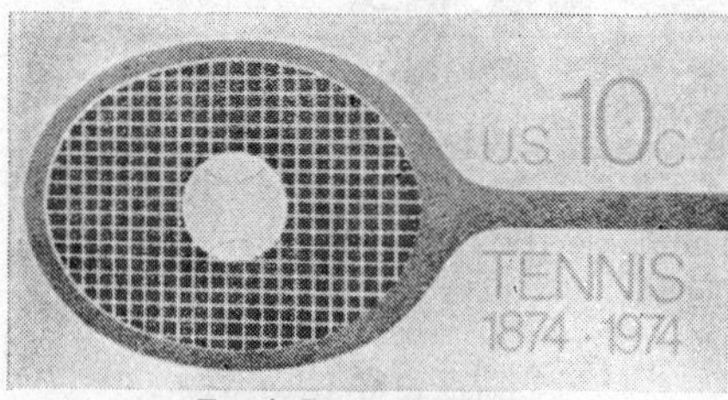

"Volunteer Yourself" – U115

Designed by Norman Ives.

1974, Aug. 23

Untagged

U568 U115	1 8/10c	**blue green**		8
		Entire	30	12
		Entire, 1st day cancel, Cincinnati, Ohio		75

Tennis Centenary Issue

Centenary of tennis in the United States.

Tennis Racquet – U116

Designed by Donald Moss.

1974, Aug. 31

U569 U116	10c	**yellow, brt. blue & light green**	24	15
		Entire	35	20
		Entire, 1st day cancel, Forest Hills, N.Y. *(245,000)*		75

Bicentennial Era Issue

10c USA

The Seafaring Tradition - Compass Rose – U118

The American Homemaker - Quilt Pattern U119

The American Farmer - Sheaf of Wheat U120

The American Doctor - Mortar U121

The American Craftsman - Tools, c. 1750 – U122

Designs (in brown on left side of envelope): 10c, Norwegian sloop Restaurationen. No. U572, Spinning wheel. No. U573, Plow. No. U574, Colonial era medical instruments and bottle. No. U575, Shaker rocking chair.

Designed by Arthur Congdon.

1975-76 **Embossed**

Diagonally Laid Paper

U571 U118	10c	**brown & blue,** *light brown, Oct. 13, 1975*	30	15
		Entire	40	20
		Entire, 1st day cancel, Minneapolis, Minn. *(255,304)*		75
a.		Brown ("10c/USA") omitted, entire	110.00	
U572 U119	13c	**brown & blue green,** *light brown, Feb. 2, 1976*	35	15
		Entire	50	20
		Entire, 1st day cancel, Biloxi, Miss. *(196,647)*		75
a.		Brown ("13c/USA") omitted, entire	110.00	
U573 U120	13c	**brown & bright green,** *light brown, Mar. 15, 1976*	35	15
		Entire	50	20
		Entire, 1st day cancel, New Orleans, La. *(214,563)*		75
a.		Brown ("13c/USA") omitted, entire	—	
U574 U121	13c	**brn. & org.,** *light brown, June 30, 1976*	35	15
		Entire	50	20
		Entire, 1st day cancel, Dallas, Texas		75
U575 U122	13c	**brn. & car.,** *lt. brown, Aug. 6, 1976*	35	13
		Entire	50	15
		Entire, 1st day cancel, Hancock, Mass.		75
a.		Brown ("13c/USA") omitted, entire	—	

Liberty Tree, Boston, 1646 – U123

Designed by Leonard Everett Fisher.

1975, Nov. 8 **Embossed**

U576 U123	13c	**orange brown**	30	13
		Entire	40	15
		Entire, 1st day cancel, Memphis, Tenn. *(226,824)*		75

Star and Pinwheel – U124

U125

U126

Eagle – U127

Uncle Sam – U128

Designers: 2c, Rudolph de Harak. 2.1c, Norman Ives. 2.7c, Ann Sforza Clementino. 15c, George Mercer.

1976-78 **Embossed**

U577 U124	2c	**red,** untagged, *Sept. 10, 1976*		5
		Entire	30	
		Entire, 1st day cancel, Hempstead, N.Y. *(81,388)*		70
U578 U125	2.1c	**green,** untagged, *June 3, 1977*		5
		Entire	30	10
		Entire, 1st day cancel, Houston, Tex. *(120,280)*		70
U579 U126	2.7c	**green,** untagged, *July 5, 1978*		5
		Entire	35	15
		Entire, 1st day cancel, Raleigh, N.C. *(92,687)*		75
U580 U127	(15c)	**orange,** *May 22, 1978*	35	15
		Entire	48	18
		Entire, 1st day cancel, Memphis, Tenn.		75
U581 U128	15c	**red,** *June 3, 1978*	35	15
		Entire	48	18
		Entire, 1st day cancel, Williamsburg, Pa. *(176,000)*		75

Bicentennial Issue

Centennial Envelope, 1876 — U129

1976, Oct. 15 **Embossed**

U582 U129 13c **emerald** 35 13
Entire 45 15
Entire, 1st day cancel, Los Angeles, Cal. *(277,222)* 75

Golf Issue

Golf Club in Motion and Golf Ball — U130

Designed by Guy Salvato.

1977, Apr. 7 **Photogravure and Embossed**

U583 U130 13c **black, blue & yellow green** 40 13
Entire 60 10
Entire, 1st day cancel, Augusta, Ga. *(252,000)* 75
a. Black omitted, entire —
b. Black & blue omitted, entire —

Energy Issue

Conservation and development of national resources.

"Conservation" U131

"Development" U132

Designed by Terrance W. McCaffrey.

1977, Oct. 20 **Embossed**

U584 U131 13c **black, red & yellow** 40 13
Entire 50 15
Entire, 1st day cancel, Ridley Park, Pa 75
a. Red & yellow omitted, entire —
b. Yellow omitted, entire —
c. Black omitted, entire —
d. Black & red omitted, entire —
U585 U132 13c **black, red & yellow** 40 13
Entire 50 15
Entire, 1st day cancel, Ridley Park, Pa. 75

First day cancellation a applied to 353,515 of Nos. U584 and U585.

Nos. U584-U585 have a luminescent panel at left of stamp which glows green under ultraviolet light.

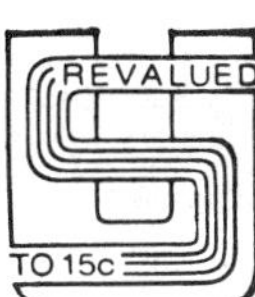

Olive Branch and Star — U133

Designed by George Mercer.

1978, July 28 **Embossed**

Black Surcharge

U586 U133 15c on 16c **blue** 35 15
Entire 48 18
Entire, 1st day cancel, Williamsburg, Pa. *(193,153)* 75
a. Surcharge omitted, entire — —
b. Surch. on No. U581, entire — —

Auto Racing Issue

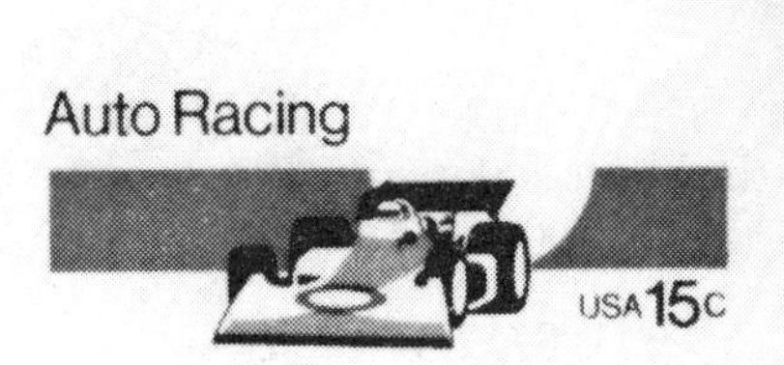

Indianapolis 500 Racing Car — U134

Designed by Robert Peak.

1978, Sept. 2 **Embossed**

U587 U134 15c **red, blue & black** 35 15
Entire 48 18
Entire, 1st day cancel, Ontario, Cal. *(209,147)* 75
a. Black omitted, entire 200.00
b. Black & blue omitted, entire —
c. Red omitted, entire —
d. Red & blue omitted, entire —

No. U576 Surcharged Like No. U586

1978, Nov. 28 **Embossed**

U588 U123 15c on 13c **orange brown** 35 15
Entire 48 18
Entire, 1st day cancel, Williamsburg, Pa. *(137,500)* 75

U135

Weaver Violins — U136

U137

Eagle — U138

U139

Eagle — U140

1979, May 18 **Untagged** **Embossed**

U589 U135 3.1c **ultramarine,** untagged 5
Entire 12 5
Entire, 1st day cancel, Denver, Colo. *(117,575)* 75

1980, June 23 **Untagged** **Embossed**

U590 U136 3.5c **purple,** untagged 8
Entire 30 15
Entire, 1st day cancel, Williamsburg, Pa. 65

1982, Feb. 17 **Untagged** **Embossed**

U591 U137 5.9c **brown,** untagged 8
Entire 30 10
Entire, 1st day cancel, Wheeling, WV 70

1981, Mar. 15 **Embossed**

U592 U138 (18c) **violet** 45 18
Entire 55 22
Entire, 1st day cancel, Memphis, TN *(179,171)* 75

1981, Apr. 2 **Embossed**

U593 U139 18c **dark blue** 45 18
Entire 55 22
Entire, 1st day cancel, Star City, IN *(160,439)* 75

1981, Oct. 11 **Embossed**

U594 U140 (20c) **brown** 45 10
Entire 55 15
Entire, 1st day cancel, Memphis, TN *(304,404)* 2.00

Veterinary Medicine Issue

Seal of Veterinarians U141

Design at left side of envelope shows 5 animals and bird in brown, "Veterinary Medicine" in gray.

Designed by Guy Salvato.

1979, July 24 **Embossed**

U595 U141 15c **brown & gray** 35 15
Entire 48 18
Entire, 1st day cancel, Seattle, WA *(209,658)* 75

Olympic Games Issue

22nd Olympic Games, Moscow, July 19-Aug. 3, 1980.

U142

Design (multicolored on left side of envelope) shows two soccer players with ball.
Designed by Robert M. Cunningham.

1979, Dec. 10 — **Embossed**

U596 U142 15c **red, green & black** 60 15
Entire 65 18
Entire, 1st day cancel, East Rutherford, NJ *(179,336)* 75
a. Red & grn omitted, untagged 200.00
b. Black omitted, untagged 200.00
c. Black & green omitted 200.00
d. Red omitted, untagged —

Highwheeler Bicycle — U143

Design (blue on left side of envelope) shows racing bicycle.
Designed by Robert Hallock.

1980, May 16 — **Embossed**

U597 U143 15c **blue & rose claret** 40 15
Entire 55 15
Entire, 1st day cancel, Baltimore, MD *(173,978)* 75
a. Blue ("15c USA") omitted —

Yacht — U144 AMERICA'S CUP

Designed by Cal Sachs.

1980, Sept. 15 — **Embossed**

U598 U144 15c **blue & red** 40 15
Entire 55 18
Entire, 1st day cancel, Newport, RI *(192,220)* 75

Italian Honeybee and Orange Blossoms U145

Bee and petals colorless embossed.
Designed by Jerry Pinkney.

1980, Oct. 10 — **Photogravure and Embossed**

U599 U145 15c **brown, green & yel.** 35 15
Entire 48 18
Entire, 1st day cancel, Pairs, IL *(202,050)* 75
a. Brown ("USA 15c") omitted —

Hand and Braille U146

Hand and braille colorless embossed.
Designed by John Boyd.

1981, Aug. 13 — **Embossed**

U600 U146 18c **blue & red** 45 18
Entire 55 22
Entire, 1st day cancel, Arlington, VA *(175,966)* 75

Capital Dome — U147

1981, Nov. 13 — **Embossed**

U601 U147 20c **deep magenta** 45 10
Entire 55 15
Entire, first day cancel, Los Angeles, CA 75

The Great Seal of the United States
1782-1982
USA 20c

U148

Designed by Bradbury Thompson.

1982, June 15 — **Embossed**

U602 U148 20c **dark blue, black & magenta** 45 10
Entire 55 15
Entire, first day cancel, Washington, DC *(163,905)* 75
a. Dark blue omitted, entire —

U149

Designed by John Boyd.

1982, Aug. 6 — **Embossed**

U603 U149 20c **purple & black** 45 10
Entire 55 10
Entire, first day cancel, Washington, DC *(110,679)* 75

U150

1983, Mar. 21 — **Embossed**

U604 U150 5.2c **orange** 10
Entire 20 15
Entire, first day cancel, Memphis, TN 75

U151

1983, Aug. 3 — **Embossed**

U605 U151 20c **red, blue & black** 45 10
Entire 55 15
Entire, first day cancel, Portland, OR 75
a. Red omitted —
b. Blue omitted —
c. Red & black omitted —
d. Blue & black omitted —

Small Business USA 20c U152

Designed by Peter Spier and Pat Taylor.
Design shows storefronts at lower left. Stamp and design continue on back of envelope.

1984, May 7

U606 U152 20c **multi** 50 10
Entire 55 15
Entire, first day cancel, Washington, DC 75

U153

Designed by Bradbury Thompson.

1985, Feb. 1 — **Embossed**

U607 U153 (22c) **deep green** 55 12
Entire 65 18
Entire, first day cancel, Washington, DC 90

Bison — U154

Designed by George Mercer.

1985, Feb. 25 — **Embossed**

U608 U154 22c **violet brown** 55 10
Entire 65 15
Entire, first day cancel, Washington, DC 75
a. Untagged, 3 precancel lines 15
Entire 60 20

Original printings of No. U608 were printed with luminescent ink. later printings have a luminescent vertical bar to the left of the stamp.

Frigate U.S.S. Constitution — U155

Designed by Cal Sacks.

1985, May 3				Embossed	
U609	U155	6c	**green blue**		5
			Entire	22	6
			Entire, first day cancel, Washington, DC		60

The Mayflower — U156

Designed by Robert Brangwynne.

1986, Dec. 4			Embossed		Precanceled
U610	U156	8.5c	**black & gray**		10
			Entire	28	14
			Entire, first day cancel, Plymouth, MA *(105,164)*		75

Stars U157

Designed by Joe Brockert.

1988, Mar. 26				Typo. & Embossed	
U611	U157	25c	**dark red & deep blue**	50	25
			Entire	60	30
			Entire, first day cancel, Star, MS *(29,393)*		75
a.			Dark red ("25") omitted	—	—

US Frigate Constellation — U158

Designed by Jerry Dadds.

1988, Apr. 12			Typo. & Embossed		Precanceled
U612	U158	8.4c	**black & bright blue**		10
			Entire	28	14
			Entire, first day cancel, Baltimore, MD *(41,420)*		75

Values quoted in this catalogue are for stamps graded at Fine-Very Fine and with no faults. An illustrated guide to grade is provided in introductory material, beginning on Page V.

Snowflake — U159

Designed by Randall McDougall. "Holiday Greetings!" inscribed in lower left.

1988, Sept. 8				Typo.	
U613	U159	25c	**dark red & green**	55	25
			Entire	65	30
			Entire, first day cancel, Snowflake, AZ		75

Stars U160

Designed by Joe Brockert. "Philatelic Mail" and asterisks in dark red below vignette; continuous across envelope face and partly on reverse.

1989, Mar. 10				Typo.	
U614	U160	25c	**dark red & deep blue**	50	25
			Entire	60	30
			Entire, first day cancel, Cleveland, OH		75

Stars U161

Designed by Joe Brockert.

1989, July 10			Typo.		Unwmk.
U615	U161	25c	**dark red & deep blue**	50	25
			Entire	60	30
			Entire, first day cancel, Washington, DC		75

Lined with a blue design to provide security for enclosures.

AIR POST STAMPED ENVELOPES AND AIR LETTER SHEETS

All envelopes have carmine and blue borders, unless noted. There are seven types of borders:

Carmine Diamond in Upper Right Corner.

a. Diamonds measure 9 to 10mm paralled to edge of envelope and 11 to 12mm along oblique side (with top flap open). Sizes 5 and 13 only.

b. Like "a" except diamonds measure 7 to 8mm along oblique side (with top flap open). Sizes 5 and 13 only.

c. Diamonds measure 11 to 12mm parallel to edge of envelope. Size 8 only.

Blue Diamond in Upper Right Corner.

d. Lower points of top row of diamonds point to left. Size 8 only.

e. Lower points of top row of diamonds point to right. Size 8 only.

Diamonds Omitted in Upper Right Corner (1965 Onward)

f. Blue diamond above at left of stamp.

g. Red diamond above at left of stamp.

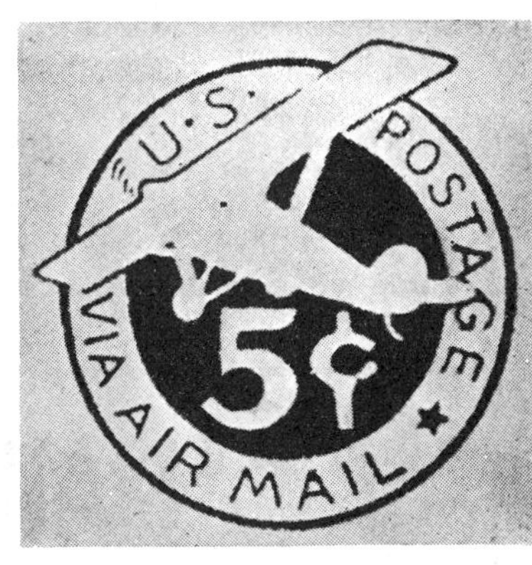

UC1

Die 1 (5c) - Vertical rudder is not semi-circular but slopes down to the left. The tail of the plane projects into the G of POSTAGE. Border types a, b, c, d and e.

UC2

Die 2 (5c and 8c): Vertical rudder is semi-circular. The tail of the plane touches but does not project into the G of POSTAGE. Border types b, d, and e for the 5c; b and d for the 8c.

Die 2 (6c): Same as UC2 except three types of numeral.

2a. The numeral "6" is 6½mm wide.

2b. The numeral "6" is 6mm wide.

2c. The numeral "6" is 5½mm wide.

Eleven working dies were used in printing the 6c. On each, the numeral "6" was engraved by hand, producing several variations in position, size and thickness.

Nos. UC1 and UC2 occur with varying size blue blobs, caused by a shallow printing die. They are not constant.

Border types b and d for dies 2a and 2b; also without border (June 1944 to Sept. 1945) for dies 2a, 2b and 2c.

Die 3 (6c): Vertical rudder leans forward. S closer to O than to T of POSTAGE. E of POSTAGE has short center bar. Border types b and d, also without border.

No. UC1 with 1933 and 1937 watermarks and No. UC2 with 1929 and 1933 watermarks were issued in Puerto Rico.

No. UC1 in blue black, with 1925 watermark #26 and border type a, is a proof.

1929-44					
UC1	UC1	5c	**blue,** die 1, *Jan. 12, 1929*	3.00	1.75
			Entire, border a or b	4.25	2.25
			Entire, border c, d or e	8.00	5.75
			First day cancel, border a, entire		40.00
			1933 wmk. #33, border d, entire	*700.00*	*700.00*
			1933 wmk. #33, border b, entire	—	—
			1937 wmk. #36, border d, entire	—	*950.00*
			1937 wmk. #36, border b, entire	—	—
			Bicolored border omitted, entire	600.00	
UC2	UC2	5c	**blue,** die 2	12.50	5.00
			Entire, border b	15.00	6.50
			Entire, border e	21.00	12.50
			1929 wmk. #28, border d, entire	—	*1,500.*
			1933 wmk. #33, border b, entire	*600.00*	—
			1933 wmk. #33, border d, entire	300.00	—
UC3	UC2	6c	**orange,** die 2a, *July 1, 1934*	1.25	25
			Entire, bicolored border	1.50	50
			Entire, without border	1.75	1.25
			Entire, 1st day cancel		14.00
a.			6c orange, die 2a, with added impression of 3c purple (#U436a), entire without border	*3,000.*	
UC4	UC2	6c	**orange,** die 2b ('42)	2.50	1.25
			Entire, bicolored border, 1941 wmk. #39	50.00	12.50
			Entire, without border	4.00	2.00
UC5	UC2	6c	**orange,** die 2c ('44)	75	30
			Entire, without border	1.00	40
UC6	UC2	6c	**orange,** die 3 ('42)	1.00	35
			Entire, bicolored border	1.50	75

Entire, without border 2.50 90
Entire, carmine of border omitted *1,000.*
Double impression, entire 350.00
a. 6c orange, *blue,* die 3 (error) Entire, without border *3,500. 2,250.*
UC7 UC2 8c **olive green,** die 2, *Sept. 26, 1932* 12.50 3.50
Entire, bicolored border 16.00 6.00
Entire, 1st day cancel 11.00

Surcharged in black on envelopes indicated by number in parenthesis

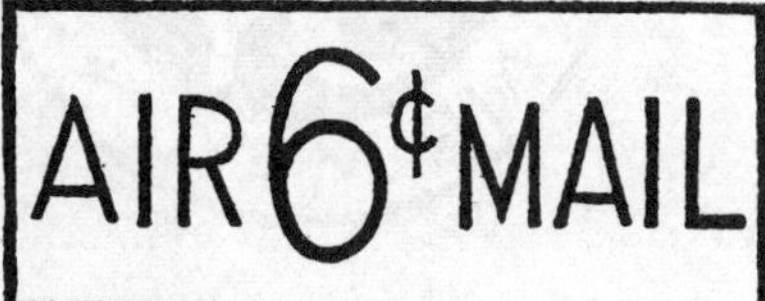

1945
UC8 U93 6c on 2c **carmine** (U429) 1.25 65
Entire 1.65 1.00
a. 6c on 1c green (error) (U420) *1,750.*
Entire *2,500.*
b. 6c on 3c purple (error) (U436a) *1,750.*
Entire *2,500.*
c. 6c on 3c purple (error), *amber* (U437a) *3,000.*
Entire *3,500.*
d. 6c on 3c violet (error) (U526) *3,000.*
Entire *3,500.*
UC9 U95 6c on 2c **carmine** (U525) 75.00 40.00
Entire 100.00 50.00

Ten surcharge varieties are found on Nos. UC8-UC9.

Surcharged in Black on 6c Air Post Envelopes without borders

REVALUED
5¢
P.O. DEPT.

1946
UC10 UC2 5c on 6c **orange,** die 2a 2.75 1.50
Entire 3.50 2.50
a. Double surcharge 60.00
UC11 UC2 5c on 6c **orange,** die 2b 9.00 5.00
Entire 9.50 6.25
UC12 UC2 5c on 6c **orange,** die 2c 75 50
Entire 1.25 60
a. Double surcharge 60.00 20.00
UC13 UC2 5c on 6c **orange,** die 3 80 60
Entire 95 75
a. Double surcharge 60.00

The 6c borderless envelopes and the revalued envelopes were issued primarily for use to and from members of the armed forces. The 5c rate came into effect Oct. 1, 1946.
Ten surcharge varieties are found on Nos. UC10-UC13.

DC-4 Skymaster — UC3

Envelopes with borders types b and d.
Die 1. The end of the wing at the right is a smooth curve. The juncture of the front end of the plane and the engine forms an acute angle. The first T of STATES and the E's of UNITED STATES lean to the left.
Die 2. The end of the wing at the right is a straight line. The juncture of the front end of the plane and the engine is wide open. The first T of STATES and the E's of UNITED STATES lean to the right.

1946
UC14 UC3 5c **carmine,** die 1, *Sept. 25, 1946* 75 20
Entire, bicolored border 1.10 40
Entire, 1st day cancel 2.00
Entire, bicolored border omitted —
UC15 UC3 5c **carmine,** die 2 85 25
Entire, bicolored border 1.10 40

No. UC14, printed on flat bed press, measures 21½mm high. No. UC15, printed on rotary press, measures 22mm high.

DC-4 Skymaster UC4

1947-55 Typographed, Without Embossing Letter Sheets for Foreign Postage
UC16 UC4 10c **bright red,** *pale blue,* "Air Letter" on face, 2-line inscription on back, entire 7.50 6.00
Entire, 1st day cancel, *Apr. 29, 1947* 2.50
Die cutting reversed, entire 110.00
UC16a UC4 10c **bright red,** *pale blue, Sept. 1951,* "Air Letter" on face, 4-line inscription on back, entire 14.00 12.00
Die cutting reversed, entire 275.00
b. 10c chocolate, *pale blue,* entire 400.00
UC16c UC4 10c **bright red,** *pale blue, Nov. 1953,* "Air Letter" and "Aerogramme" on face, 4-line inscription on back, entire 47.50 10.00
Die cutting reversed, entire —
UC16d UC4 10c **bright red,** *pale blue, 1955,* "Air Letter" and "Aerogramme" on face, 3-line inscription on back, entire 8.00 8.00
Die cutting reversed, entire 60.00
Dark blue (inscriptions & border diamonds) omitted —

Printed on protective tinted paper containing colorless inscription,
UNITED STATES FOREIGN AIR MAIL multiple, repeated in parallel vertical or horizontal lines.

Postage Stamp Centenary Issue

Issued to commemorate the centenary of the first postage stamps issued by the United States Government.

Washington and Franklin, Early and Modern Mail-carrying Methods — UC5

Two dies: Rotary, design measures 22¼mm high; and flat bed press, design 21¾mm high.

1947, May 21 For Domestic Postage Embossed
UC17 UC5 5c **carmine** (rotary) 40 25
Entire, bicolored border b 50 30
Entire, 1st day cancel 1.25
a. Flat plate printing 50 30
a. Entire 60 40

Type of 1946

Type I: 6's lean to right.
Type II: 6's upright.

1950
UC18 UC3 6c **carmine,** type I, *Sept. 22, 1950* 25 8
Entire, bicolored border 50 15
Entire, 1st day cancel 75
a. Type II 75 25
Entire 1.00 30

Several other types differ slightly from the two listed.

Nos. UC14, UC15, UC18 Surcharged in Red at Left of Stamp

REVALUED

P. O. DEPT.

1951
UC19 UC3 6c on 5c **carmine,** die 1 85 50
Entire 1.25 75
UC20 UC3 6c on 5c **carmine,** die 2 80 50
Entire 1.15 70
a. 6c on 6c carmine (error) entire *1,500.*
b. Double surcharge *250.00* —

Nos. UC14 and UC15 Surcharged in Red at Left of Stamp

REVALUED

P.O. DEPT.

1952
UC21 UC3 6c on 5c **carmine,** die 1 26.00 15.00
Entire 32.50 18.00
UC22 UC3 6c on 5c **carmine,** die 2, *Aug. 29, 1952* 3.50 2.50
Entire 5.00 4.25
a. Double surcharge 75.00

Same Surcharge in Red on No. UC17
UC23 UC5 6c on 5c **carmine**
Entire 1,100.

The 6c on 4c black (No. U440) is believed to be a favor printing.

Fifth International Philatelic Exhibition Issue

FIPEX, the Fifth International Philatelic Exhibition, New York, N.Y., Apr. 28-May 6, 1956.

Eagle in Flight — UC6

1956, May 2
UC25 UC6 6c **red** 75 50
Entire 1.00 80
Entire, 1st day cancel, New York, N.Y. *(363,239)* 1.25

Two types exist, differing slightly in the clouds at top.

Skymaster Type of 1946

1958, July 31
UC26 UC3 7c **blue** 65 50
Entire 1.00 1.00
Entire, 1st day cancel, Dayton, O. *(143,428)* 1.50

Nos. UC3-UC5, UC18 and UC25 Surcharged in Green at Left of Stamp

1958
UC27 UC2 6c + 1c **orange,** die 2a 200.00 215.00
Entire, without border 250.00 250.00
UC28 UC2 6c + 1c **orange,** die 2b 60.00 75.00
Entire, without border 75.00 110.00
UC29 UC2 6c + 1c **orange,** die 2c 35.00 50.00
Entire 40.00 75.00
UC30 UC3 6c + 1c **carmine,** type I 1.00 50
Entire 1.25 65
a. Type II 1.00 50
Entire 1.25 65
UC31 UC6 6c + 1c **red** 1.00 50
Entire 1.40 85

Jet Airliner — UC7

Letter Sheet for Foreign Postage

Type I: Back inscription in 3 lines.
Type II: Back inscription in 2 lines

1958-59 **Typographed, Without Embossing**

UC32 UC7 10c **blue & red,** *blue,* II, *May, 1959,* entire 6.00 5.00
b. Red omitted, II, entire —
c. Blue omitted, II, entire *850.00*
UC32a UC7 10c **blue & red,** *blue,* I, *Sept. 12, 1958,* entire 10.00 5.00
Entire, 1st day cancel, St. Louis, Mo. *(92,400)* 2.50
Die cutting reversed, entire 75.00

Silhouette of Jet Airliner — UC8

1958, Nov. 21 **Embossed**

UC33 UC8 7c **blue** 60 12
Entire 70 15
Entire, 1st day cancel, New York, N.Y. *(208,980)* 75

1960, Aug. 18

UC34 UC8 7c **carmine** 60 12
Entire 70 15
Entire, 1st day cancel, Portland, Ore. *(196,851)* 75

Jet Airliner and Globe — UC9

Letter Sheet for Foreign Postage

1961, June 16 **Typographed, Without Embossing**

UC35 UC9 11c **red & blue,** *blue,* entire 2.25 1.50
Entire, 1st day cancel, Johnstown, Pa. *(163,460)* 1.00
a. Red omitted, entire *850.00*
b. Blue omitted, entire *850.00*
Die cutting reversed, entire 35.00

Jet Airliner — UC10

1962, Nov. 17 **Embossed**

UC36 UC10 8c **red** 50 8
Entire 80 15
Entire, 1st day cancel, Chantilly, Va. *(194,810)* 75

Jet Airliner UC11

1965-67

UC37 UC11 8c **red,** *Jan. 7* 35 6
Entire, border "f" 50 10
Entire, border "g" *18.00*
Entire, 1st day cancel, Chicago, Ill. *(226,178)* 60
a. Tagged, *Aug. 15, 1967* 1.25 30
Entire 1.75 75
Tagged, 1st day cancel 3.50

No. UC37a has a ⅜x1-inch panel at left of stamp that glows orange red under ultraviolet light.

Pres. John F. Kennedy and Jet Plane — UC12

Letter Sheets for Foreign Postage

1965, May 29 **Typographed, Without Embossing**

UC38 UC12 11c **red & dark blue,** *blue,* entire 3.25 1.00
Entire, 1st day cancel, Boston, Mass. *(337,422)* 75
Die cutting reversed, entire 40.00

1967, May 29

UC39 UC12 13c **red & dark blue,** *blue,* entire 3.00 75
Entire, 1st day cancel, Chicago, Ill. *(211,387)* 75
a. Red omitted *500.00*
b. Dark blue omitted *500.00*
Die cutting reversed, entire —

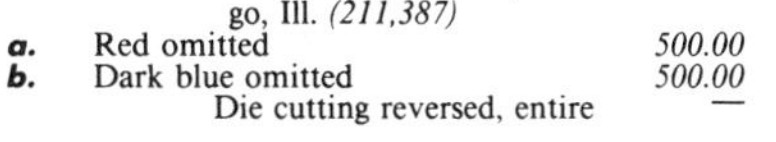

Jet Liner UC13

Designed by Robert J. Jones.

1968, Jan. 8 **Tagged** **Embossed**

UC40 UC13 10c **red** 50 6
Entire 80 15
Entire, 1st day cancel, Chicago, Ill. *(157,553)* 75

No. UC37 Surcharged in Red at Left of Stamp

1968, Feb. 5

UC41 UC11 8c + 2c **red** 65 15
Entire 90 40
Entire, 1st day cancel, Washington, D.C. 4.50

Human Rights Year Issue

Issued for International Human Rights Year, and to commemorate the 20th anniversary of the United Nations' Declaration of Human Rights.

Globes and Flock of Birds — UC14

Printed by Acrovure Division of Union-Camp Corporation, Englewood, N.J. Designed by Antonio Frasconi.

Letter Sheet for Foreign Postage

1968, Dec. 3 **Tagged** **Photo.**

UC42 UC14 13c **gray, brown, orange & black,** *blue,* entire 7.50 2.00
Entire, 1st day cancel, Washington, D.C. *(145,898)* 1.00
a. Orange omitted —
b. Brown omitted —
c. Black omitted —

No. UC42 has a luminescent panel ⅜x1 inch on the right globe. The panel glows orange red under ultraviolet light.

Jet Plane — UC15

Printed by United States Envelope Co., Williamsburg, Pa. Designed by Robert Geissmann.

1971, May 6 **Embossed (Plane)**

Center Circle Luminescent

UC43 UC15 11c **red & blue** 50 10
Entire 60 13
Entire, 1st day cancel, Williamsburg, Pa. *(187,000)* 75

Birds in Flight — UC16

Printed by Bureau of Engraving and Printing. Designed by Soren Noring.

Letter Sheet for Foreign Postage

1971 **Tagged** **Photo.**

UC44 UC16 15c **gray, red, white & blue,** *blue,* entire, *May 28* 1.50 90
Entire, 1st day cancel, Chicago, Ill. *(130,669)* 75
Die cutting reversed, entire 30.00
a. "AEROGRAMME" added to inscription, entire, *Dec. 13* 1.50 90
Entire, 1st day cancel, Philadelphia, Pa. 75
Die cutting reversed, entire 30.00

Folding instructions (2 steps) in capitals on No. C44; (4 steps) in upper and lower case on No. UC44a.

On Nos. UC44-UC44a the white rhomboid background of "USA postage 15c" is luminescent. No. UC44 is inscribed: "VIA AIR MAIL-PAR AVION". "postage 15c" is in gray. See No. UC46.

No. UC40 Surcharged in Green at Left of Stamp

1971, June 28 **Embossed**

UC45 UC13 10c + (1c) **red** 1.50 20
Entire 1.90 25
Entire, 1st day cancel, Washington, D.C. 4.50

HOT AIR BALLOONING CHAMPIONSHIPS ISSUE

Hot Air Ballooning World Championships, Albuquerque, N.M., Feb. 10-17, 1973.

"usa" Type of 1971

Design: Three balloons and cloud at left in address section; no birds beside stamp. Inscribed "INTERNATIONAL HOT AIR BALLOONING." "postage 15c" in blue.
Printed by Bureau of Engraving and Printing. Designed by Soren Noring (vignette) and Esther Porter (balloons).

Letter Sheet for Foreign Postage

1973, Feb. 10 **Tagged** **Photo.**

UC46 UC16 15c **red, white & blue,** *blue,* entire 75 40
Entire, 1st day cancel, Albuquerque, N.M. *(210,000)* 70

Folding instructions as on No. UC44a. See notes after No. UC44.

Bird in Flight — UC17

1973, Dec. 1 **Luminescent Ink**

UC47 UC17 13c **rose red** 28 10
Entire 40 13
Entire, 1st day cancel, Memphis, Tenn. *(132,658)* 55

"usa" — UC18

Printed by the Bureau of Engraving and Printing. Designed by Bill Hyde.

Letter Sheet for Foreign Postage.

1974, Jan. 4 **Tagged** **Photo.**

UC48 UC18 18c **red & blue,** *blue,* entire 90 30
Entire, 1st day cancel, Atlanta, Ga. *(119,615)* 75
a. Red omitted, entire —
Die cutting reversed, entire —

25TH ANNIVERSARY OF NATO ISSUE

"USA" — UC19

Design: "NATO" and NATO emblem at left in address section.
Printed by Bureau of Engraving and Printing. Designed by Soren Noring.

Letter Sheet for Foreign Postage

1974, Apr. 4 **Tagged** **Photo.**

UC49 UC19 18c **red & blue,** *blue,* entire 90 25
Entire, 1st day cancel, Washington, D.C. 75

"USA" — UC20

Printed by Bureau of Engraving and Printing. Designed by Robert Geissmann.

Letter Sheet for Foreign Postage

1976, Jan. 16 **Tagged** **Photo.**

UC50 UC20 22c **red & blue,** *blue,* entire 90 25
Entire, 1st day cancel, Tempe, Ariz. *(118,303)* 90
Die cutting reversed, entire 25.00

"USA" — UC21

Printed by Bureau of Engraving and Printing. Designed by Soren Noring.

Letter Sheet for Foreign Postage

1978, Nov. 3 **Tagged** **Photo.**

UC51 UC21 22c **blue,** *blue,* entire 70 25
Entire, 1st day cancel, St. Petersburg, Fla. *(86,099)* 75
Die cutting reversed, entire 25.00

22nd OLYMPIC GAMES, MOSCOW, JULY 19-AUG. 3, 1980.

UC22

Design (multicolored in bottom left corner) shows discus thrower.
Printed by Bureau of Engraving and Printing. Designed by Robert M. Cunningham.

Letter Sheet for Foreign Postage

1979, Dec. 5 **Tagged** **Photo.**

UC52 UC22 22c **red, black & green,** *bluish,* entire 1.50 22
Entire, 1st day cancel, Bay Shore, N.Y. 90

"USA" — UC23

Design (brown): lower left, Statue of Liberty. Inscribed "Tour the United States." Folding area shows tourist attractions.
Printed by Bureau of Engraving and Printing.
Designed by Frank J. Waslick.

Letter Sheet for Foreign Postage

1980, Dec. 29 **Tagged** **Photo.**

UC53 UC23 30c **blue, red & brn.,** *blue,* entire 60 30
Entire, 1st day cancel, San Francisco, CA 1.00
Die cutting reversed, entire 22.50
a. Red ("30") omitted —
a. Die cutting reversed, entire —

1981, Sept. 21 **Tagged** **Photo.**

UC54 UC23 30c **yel., mag., blue & black,** *blue,* entire 60 30
First day cancel, Honolulu, HI 1.00
Die cutting reversed, entire 20.00

UC24

Design: "Made in USA . . . world's best buys!" on flap, ship, tractor in lower left. Reverse folding area shows chemicals, jet silhouette, wheat, typewriter and computer tape disks. Printed by Bureau of Engraving and Printing.
Designed by Frank J. Waslick.

Letter Sheet for Foreign Postage

1982, Sept. 16 **Tagged** **Photo.**

UC55 UC24 30c **multi.,** *blue,* entire 60 30
First day cancel, Seattle, WA 1.00

WORLD COMMUNICATIONS YEAR

World Map Showing Locations of Satellite Tracking Stations — UC25

Design: Reverse folding area shows satellite, tracking station.
Printed by Bureau of Engraving and Printing.
Designed by Esther Porter.

Letter Sheet for Foreign Postage

1983, Jan. 7 **Tagged** **Photo.**

UC56 UC25 30c **multi,** *blue,* entire 60 30
First day cancel, Anaheim, CA 1.10
Die cutting reversed, entire 27.50

1984 OLYMPICS

UC26

Design: Woman equestrian at lower left with montage of competitive events on reverse folding area.
Printed by the Bureau of Engraving & Printing.
Designed by Bob Peak.

Letter Sheet for Foreign Postage

1983, Oct. 14 **Tagged** **Photo.**

UC57 UC26 30c **multi,** *blue,* entire 60 30
First day cancel, Los Angeles, CA 1.10

WEATHER SATELLITES, 25TH ANNIV.

Landsat Infrared and Thermal Mapping Bands — UC27

Design: Landsat orbiting the earth at lower left with three Landsat photographs on reverse folding area. Inscribed: "Landsat views the Earth."
Printed by the Bureau of Engraving & Printing.

Designed by Esther Porter.

Letter Sheet for Foreign Postage

1985, Feb. 14			**Tagged**	**Photo.**	
UC58	UC27	36c	**multi,** *blue*, entire	72	36
			First day cancel, Goddard Flight Center, MD		1.35
			Die cutting reversed, entire	30.00	

NATIONAL TOURISM WEEK

Urban Skyline — UC28

Design: Inscribed "Celebrate America" at lower left and "Travel. . . the perfect freedom" on folding area. Skier, Indian chief, cowboy, jazz trumpeter and pilgrims on reverse folding area.

Printed by the Bureau of Engraving & Printing.

Designed by Dennis Luzak.

Letter Sheet for Foreign Postage

1985, May 21			**Tagged**	**Photo.**	
UC59	UC28	36c	**multi,** *blue*, entire	72	36
			First day cancel, Washington, DC		1.35
a.			Black omitted	—	
			Die cutting reversed, entire	25.00	

MARK TWAIN AND HALLEY'S COMET

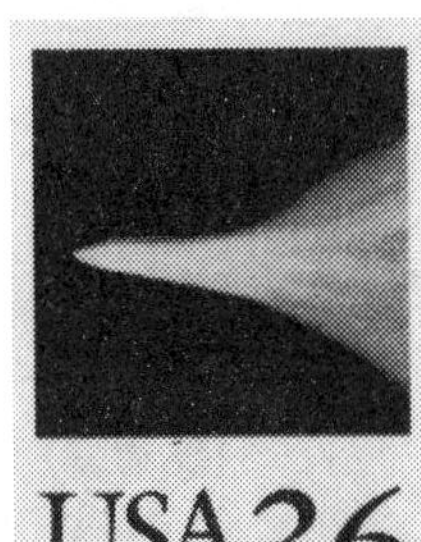

Comet Tail Viewed from Space — UC29

Design: Portrait of Twain at lower left and inscribed "I came in with Halley's Comet in 1835. It is coming again next year, and I expect to go out with it. It will be the greatest disappointment of my life if I don't go out with Halley's Comet." "1835 . Mark Twain . 1910 . Halley's Comet . 1985" and Twain, Huckleberry Finn, steamboat and comet on reverse folding areas.

Printed by the Bureau of Engraving & Printing.

Designed by Dennis Luzak.

Letter Sheet for Foreign Postage

1985, Dec. 4			**Tagged**	**Photo.**	
UC60	UC29	36c	**multi,** entire	72	36
			First day cancel, Washington, DC		1.35
			Die cutting reversed, entire	25.00	

UC30

Printed by the Bureau of Engraving & Printing.

Letter Sheet for Foreign Postage

1988, May 9			**Litho.**	**Tagged**	
UC61	UC30	39c	**multi,** entire	78	39
			First day cancel, Miami, FL *(27,446)*		1.55

OFFICIAL ENVELOPES

By the Act of Congress, January 31, 1873, the franking privilege of officials was abolished as of July 1, 1873 and the Postmaster General was authorized to prepare official envelopes. At the same time official stamps were prepared for all Departments. Department envelopes became obsolete July 5, 1884. After that, government offices began to use franked envelopes of varied design. These indicate no denomination and lie beyond the scope of this Catalogue.

Post Office Department

UO1

Numeral 9mm high.

UO2

Numeral 9mm high

UO3

Numeral 9½mm high.

Printed by George H. Reay, Brooklyn, N.Y.

1873					
UO1	UO1	2c	**black,** *lemon*	10.00	6.00
			Entire	13.00	9.50
UO2	UO2	3c	**black,** *lemon*	5.00	3.50
			Entire	9.00	7.00
+UO3	UO2	3c	**black**	*6,500.*	
			Entire	*15,000.*	
UO4	UO3	6c	**black,** *lemon*	12.50	7.75
			Entire	14.00	12.50

UO4

Numeral 9¼mm high.

UO5

Numeral 9¼mm high.

UO6

Numeral 10½mm high.

Printed by Plimpton Manufacturing Co., Hartford, Conn.

1874-79					
UO5	UO4	2c	**black,** *lemon*	3.50	3.00
			Entire	6.00	4.00
UO6	UO4	2c	**black**	45.00	32.50
			Entire	37.50	32.50
UO7	UO5	3c	**black,** *lemon*	2.50	65
			Entire	3.00	1.10
UO8	UO5	3c	**black**	800.00	800.00
			Entire	900.00	
UO9	UO5	3c	**black,** *amber*	40.00	25.00
			Entire	50.00	27.50
UO10	UO5	3c	**black,** *blue*	*15,000.*	
			Entire	*18,000.*	
UO11	UO5	3c	**blue,** *blue* ('75)	*14,000.*	
			Entire	*16,000.*	
UO12	UO6	6c	**black,** *lemon*	3.50	2.00
			Entire	6.00	6.00
UO13	UO6	6c	**black**	550.00	
			Entire	725.00	

Fakes exist of Nos. UO3, UO8 and UO13.

Postal Service

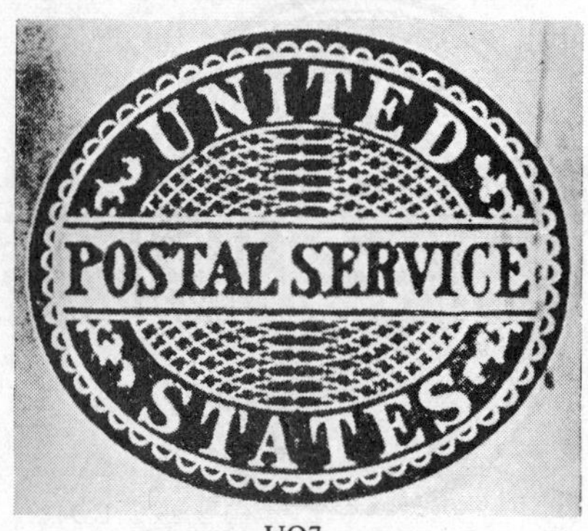

UO7

1877

UO14	UO7	**black**	3.50	3.00
		Entire	5.00	4.00
UO15	UO7	**black,** *amber*	25.00	17.50
		Entire	85.00	26.00
UO16	UO7	**blue,** *amber*	30.00	19.00
		Entire	80.00	30.00
UO17	UO7	**blue,** *blue*	5.00	5.00
		Entire	7.50	6.50

War Department

Franklin
UO8

Bust points to the end of "N" of "ONE".

Jackson
UO9

Bust narrow at the back.

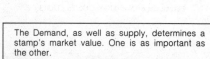

The Demand, as well as supply, determines a stamp's market value. One is as important as the other.

Washington
UO10

Queue projects below the bust.

Lincoln
UO11

Neck very long at the back.

Jefferson
UO12

Queue forms straight line with bust.

Clay
UO13

Ear partly concealed by hair, mouth large, chin prominent.

Webster
UO14

Has side whiskers.

Scott
UO15

Hamilton
UO16

Back of bust very narrow; chin almost straight; the labels containing the letters "U S" are exactly parallel.

Printed by George H. Reay.

1873

UO18	UO8	1c	**dark red**	550.00	250.00
			Entire	700.00	325.00
UO19	UO9	2c	**dark red**	600.00	300.00
			Entire	700.00	
UO20	UO10	3c	**dark red**	50.00	35.00
			Entire	65.00	40.00
UO21	UO10	3c	**dark red,** *amber*	*10,000.*	
			Entire	*15,000.*	
UO22	UO10	3c	**dark red,** *cream*	400.00	175.00
			Entire	500.00	200.00
UO23	UO11	6c	**dark red**	175.00	65.00
			Entire	200.00	—
UO24	UO11	6c	**dark red,** *cream*	1,500.	350.00
			Entire	2,500.	*1,250.*
UO25	UO12	10c	**dark red**	2,500.	275.00
			Entire	*4,500.*	550.00
UO26	UO13	12c	**dark red**	10.00	40.00
			Entire	135.00	—
UO27	UO14	15c	**dark red**	110.00	45.00
			Entire	135.00	—
UO28	UO15	24c	**dark red**	125.00	35.00
			Entire	165.00	—
UO29	UO16	30c	**dark red**	350.00	100.00
			Entire	400.00	150.00

1873

UO30	UO8	1c	**vermilion**	150.00	
			Entire	250.00	
WO31	UO8	1c	**vermilion,** *manila*	8.00	3.00
			Entire	12.50	6.00
+*UO32*	UO9	2c	**vermilion**	225.00	
			Entire	*4,500.*	
WO33	UO9	2c	**vermilion,** *manila*	175.00	
			Entire	250.00	

UO34	UO10	3c	**vermilion**	75.00	37.50
			Entire	140.00	—
UO35	UO10	3c	**vermilion,** *amber*	85.00	
			Entire	240.00	
UO36	UO10	3c	**vermilion,** *cream*	12.00	4.00
			Entire	30.00	13.00
UO37	UO11	6c	**vermilion,** *manila*	80.00	
			Entire	100.00	
+UO38	UO11	6c	**vermilion,** *cream*	350.00	
			Entire	*6,500.*	
UO39	UO12	10c	**vermilion**	200.00	
			Entire	350.00	
UO40	UO13	12c	**vermilion**	125.00	
			Entire	190.00	
UO41	UO14	15c	**vermilion**	200.00	
			Entire	2,250.	
UO42	UO15	24c	**vermilion**	350.00	
			Entire	375.00	
UO43	UO16	30c	**vermilion**	400.00	
			Entire	525.00	

UO17

Bottom serif on "S" is thick and short; bust at bottom below hair forms a sharp point.

UO18

Bottom serif on "S" is thick and short; front part of bust is rounded.

UO19

Bottom serif on "S" is short; queue does not project below bust.

UO20

Neck very short at the back.

UO21

Knot of queue stands out prominently.

UO22

Ear prominent, chin receding.

UO23

Has no side whiskers; forelock projects above head.

UO24

Back of bust rather broad; chin slopes considerably; the label containing letters "U S" are not exactly parallel.

Printed by Plimpton Manufacturing Co.

1875

UO44	UO17	1c	**red**	100.00	85.00
			Entire	110.00	—
+UO45	UO17	1c	**red,** *amber*	700.00	
+UO45A	UO17	1c	**red,** *orange*	*17,500.*	
WO46	UO17	1c	**red,** *manila*	2.50	90
			Entire	5.50	2.50
UO47	UO18	2c	**red**	85.00	
			Entire	100.00	
UO48	UO18	2c	**red,** *amber*	25.00	7.50
			Entire	30.00	20.00
UO49	UO18	2c	**red,** *orange*	35.00	12.50
			Entire	40.00	25.00
WO50	UO18	2c	**red,** *manila*	67.50	50.00
			Entire	90.00	—
UO51	UO19	3c	**red**	9.00	6.00
			Entire	10.50	9.50
UO52	UO19	3c	**red,** *amber*	10.00	6.00
			Entire	12.50	9.50
UO53	UO19	3c	**red,** *cream*	5.00	2.50
			Entire	6.50	4.00
UO54	UO19	3c	**red,** *blue*	2.50	2.00
			Ent	3.50	3.50
UO55	UO19	3c	**red,** *fawn*	4.00	75
			Entire	5.50	1.50
UO56	UO20	6c	**red**	30.00	22.50
			Entire	70.00	—
UO57	UO20	6c	**red,** *amber*	67.50	25.00
			Entire	75.00	—
UO58	UO20	6c	**red,** *cream*	175.00	70.00
			Entire	200.00	
UO59	UO21	10c	**red**	125.00	85.00
			Entire	140.00	—
UO60	UO21	10c	**red,** *amber*	1,100.	
			Entire	1,250.	
UO61	UO22	12c	**red**	35.00	35.00
			Entire	90.00	—
UO62	UO22	12c	**red,** *amber*	650.00	
			Entire	700.00	
UO63	UO22	12c	**red,** *cream*	550.00	
			Entire	700.00	
UO64	UO23	15c	**red**	150.00	110.00
			Entire	190.00	—
UO65	UO23	15c	**red,** *amber*	675.00	
			Entire	725.00	
UO66	UO23	15c	**red,** *cream*	600.00	
			Entire	650.00	
UO67	UO24	30c	**red**	150.00	110.00
			Entire	165.00	—
UO68	UO24	30c	**red,** *amber*	950.00	
			Entire	1,050.	
UO69	UO24	30c	**red,** *cream*	900.00	
			Entire	1,000.	

POSTAL SAVINGS ENVELOPES

Issued under the Act of Congress, approved June 25, 1910, in lieu of penalty or franked envelopes. Unused remainders, after October 5, 1914, were overprinted with the Penalty Clause. Regular stamped envelopes, redeemed by the Government, were also overprinted for official use.

UO25

1911

UO70 UO25	1c **green**		60.00	10.00
	Entire		75.00	35.00
UO71 UO25	1c **green,** *oriental buff*		165.00	50.00
	Entire		200.00	65.00
UO72 UO25	2c **carmine**		7.50	2.00
	Entire		10.00	7.00
a.	2c carmine, *manila* (error)		*1,500.*	—
	Entire		*2,250.*	

OFFICIAL MAIL

UO26

1983, Jan. 12 **Embossed**

UO73 UO26 20c **blue,** entire		60	—
First day cancel, Washington, DC			75

UO27

1985, Feb. 26 **Embossed**

UO74 UO27 22c **blue,** entire		60	—
First day cancel, Washington, DC			80

UO28

1987, Mar. 2 **Typo.**

UO75 UO28 22c **blue,** entire		60	—
First day cancel, Washington, DC			80

Used exclusively to mail U.S. Savings Bonds.

UO29

1988, Mar. 22 **Typo.**

UO76 UO29 (25c) **black & blue,** entire		65	—
First day cancel, Washington, DC			85

Used exclusively to mail U.S. Savings Bonds.

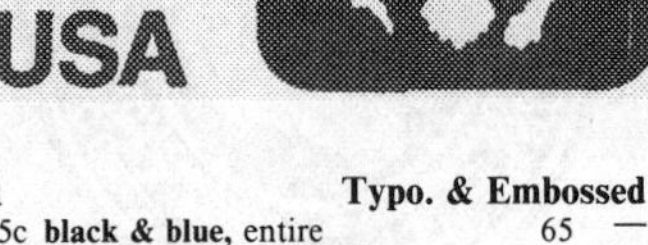

UO30

1988, Apr. 11 **Typo. & Embossed**

UO77 UO30 25c **black & blue,** entire		65	—
First day cancel, Washington, DC			85

UO31

1988, Apr. 11 **Typo.**

UO78 UO31 25c **black & blue,** entire		60	—
First day cancel, Washington, DC *(12,017)*			85

Used exclusively to mail U.S. Savings Bonds.

OFFICIAL WRAPPERS

Included in listings of Official Envelopes with prefix letters WO instead of UO.

POSTAL CARDS

Values are for unused cards as sold by the Post Office, without printed or written address or message, and used cards with Post Office cancellation, when current. Used cards for international rates are for proper usage. Those used domestically sell for less.

The "Preprinted" valuees are for unused cards with printed or written address or message. Used value applies after 1952.

Starting with No. UX21, all postal cards have been printed by the Government Printing Office.

Nos. UX1-UX48 are typographed; others are lithographed (offset) unless otherwise stated.

Numerous printing varieties exist. Varieties of surcharged cards include (a) inverted surcharge at lower left, (b) double surcharge, one inverted at lower left, (c) surcharge in other abnormal positions, including back of card. Such surcharge varieties command a premium.

Colored cancellations sell for more than black in some instances.

All values are for entire cards.

Since 1875 it has been possible to purchase some postal cards in sheets for multiple printing, hence pairs, strips and blocks are available. The sheets have been cut up so that cards exist with stamp inverted, in center of card, two on one card, in another corner, etc. These are only curiosities and of minimal value.

Liberty — PC1

Size: 130x76mm

Wmk. Large "U S P O D" in Monogram, (90x60mm)

1873

UX1 PC1 1c **brown,** *buff, May 13*	275.00	20.00
Preprinted	50.00	
First day cancel, Boston, New York or Washington		*2,250.*

A card is known canceled May 12th in Springfield, Mass.

Wmk. Small "U S P O D" in Monogram, (53x36mm)

UX3 PC1 1c **brown,** *buff, July 6*	50.00	2.25
Preprinted	15.00	
a. Without watermark		—

The watermarks on Nos. UX1, UX3 and UX4 are found in normal position, inverted, reversed, and inverted and reversed. They are often dim, especially on No. UX4.

No. UX3a is not known unused. Cards offered as such are either unwatermarked proofs, or have partial or vague watermarks. See No. UX65.

Liberty PC2

Inscribed: "WRITE THE ADDRESS . . ."

1875 Wmk. Small "U S P O D" in Monogram

UX4 PC2 1c **black,** *buff, Sept. 28*	1,500.	200.00
Preprinted	525.00	

Unwmk.

UX5 PC2 1c **black,** *buff, Sept. 30*	45.00	40
Preprinted	5.00	

For other postal card of type PC2 see No. UX7.

A little time given to the study of the arrangement of the Scott Catalogue can make it easier to use effectively.

Liberty — PC3

1879, Dec. 1

UX6 PC3 2c **blue,** *buff*	19.00	17.50
Preprinted	8.50	
a. 2c dark blue, *buff*	25.00	19.00
Preprinted	10.00	

See Nos. UX13 and UX16.

Design of PC2, Inscribed "NOTHING BUT THE ADDRESS."

1881, Oct. 17 (?)

UX7 PC2 1c **black,** *buff*	45.00	35
Preprinted	4.50	
a. 23 teeth below "ONE CENT"	500.00	30.00
Preprinted	165.00	
b. Printed on both sides	*575.00*	*400.00*

Jefferson — PC4

1885, Aug. 24

UX8 PC4 1c **brown,** *buff*	35.00	1.25
Preprinted	7.50	
a. 1c orange brown, *buff*	35.00	1.25
Preprinted	7.50	
b. 1c red brown, *buff*	35.00	1.25
Preprinted	7.50	
c. 1c chocolate, *buff*	60.00	6.00
Preprinted	15.00	
d. Double impression		—
e. Double impression, one inverted	*525.00*	
f. Printed on both sides	*550.00*	

PC5

Head of Jefferson facing right, centered on card.

1886, Dec 1

UX9 PC5 1c **black,** *buff*	9.00	55
Preprinted	1.10	
a. 1c black, *dark buff*	16.50	1.10
Preprinted	4.50	
b. Double impression	*450.00*	
c. Double impression, one inverted	*925.00*	

Grant — PC6

1891, Dec. 16 Size: 155x95mm

UX10 PC61 1c **black,** *buff*	27.50	1.40
Preprinted	5.50	
a. Double impression, one inverted	*600.00*	
b. Double impression	*600.00*	

Two types exist of No. UX10.

Size: 117x75mm

UX11 PC6 1c **blue,** *grayish white*	10.00	1.75
Preprinted	1.75	
b. Double impression, one inverted	185.00	

Cards printed in black instead of blue are invariably proofs.

PC7

Head of Jefferson facing left.
Small wreath and name below.
Size: 140x89mm

1894, Jan. 2

UX12 PC7 1c **black,** *buff*	30.00	40
Preprinted	1.75	
a. Double impression	*250.00*	

1897, Jan. 25 Design of PC3

Size: 140x89mm

UX13 PC3 2c **blue,** *cream*	125.00	75.00
Preprinted	70.00	

PC8

Head same as PC7. Large wreath and name below.

1897, Dec. 1

Size: 139x82mm

UX14 PC8 1c **black,** *buff*	22.50	25
Preprinted	2.25	
a. Double impression, one inverted	—	*700.00*
Preprinted	*650.00*	
b. Printed both sides	—	—
Preprinted	—	
c. Double impression	*350.00*	—
Preprinted	—	

John Adams PC9

1898

Size: 126x74mm

UX15 PC9 1c **black,** *buff, Mar. 31*	30.00	15.00
Preprinted	9.00	

Design same as PC3, without frame around card.

Size: 140x82mm

UX16 PC3 2c black, *buff*	9.00	9.00
Preprinted	5.00	

McKinley — PC10

1902

UX17 PC10 1c **black,** *buff*	*4,500.*	*2,000.*
Preprinted	*2,750.*	

Earliest known use: May 27, 1902.

McKinley PC11

1902

UX18 PC11 1c **black,** *buff*	9.00	30
Preprinted	1.50	

Earliest known use: July 14, 1902.
Two types exist of Nos. UX18-UX20.

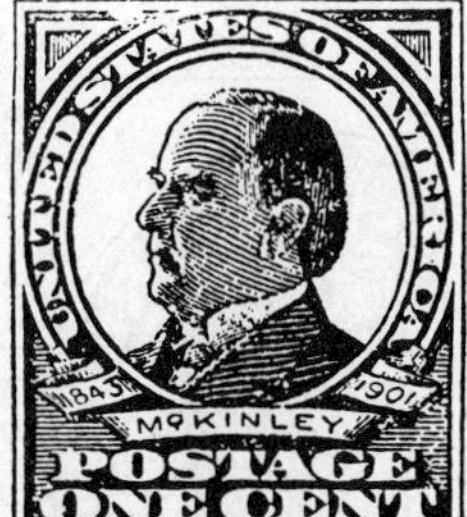

McKinley — PC12

1907

UX19 PC12 1c **black,** *buff*	30.00	50
Preprinted	1.75	

Earliest known use: June 28, 1907.

Same design, correspondence space at left

1908, Jan. 2

UX20 PC12 1c **black,** *buff*	45.00	5.00
Preprinted	7.50	

PC13

McKinley, background shaded.

1910

UX21 PC13 1c **blue,** *bluish*	90.00	6.50
Preprinted	17.50	
a. 1c bronze blue, *bluish*	165.00	12.50
Preprinted	30.00	
b. Double impression	300.00	
Preprinted	—	
c. Triple impression	350.00	
d. Double impression, one inverted	450.00	
e. Four arcs above and below "IS" of inscription to left of stamp impression are pointed	*800.00*	*450.00*
Preprinted	*450.00*	

A No. UX21 card exists with Philippines No. UX11 printed on the back.

PC14

Same design, white background.

1910, Apr. 13

UX22 PC14 1c **blue,** *bluish*	12.50	25
Preprinted	1.50	
a. Double impression	200.00	
b. Triple impression	225.00	
c. Triple impression, one inverted		

See No. UX24.

PC15

Head of Lincoln, solid background.

1911, Jan. 21

Size: 127x76mm

UX23 PC15 1c **red,** *cream*	6.00	5.50
Preprinted	3.00	
a. Triple impression	500.00	

For other postal card of type PC15 see No. UX26.

Design same as PC14

1911, Aug. 10 **Size: 140x82mm**

UX24 PC14 1c **red,** *cream*	8.25	25
Preprinted	1.40	
a. Double impression	*225.00*	
b. Triple impression	*275.00*	

Grant — PC16

1911, Oct. 27

UX25 PC16 2c **red,** *cream*	1.25	8.50
Preprinted	65	
a. Double impression	—	

For other postal card of type PC16 see No. UX36.

1913, July 29

Size: 127x76mm

UX26 PC15 1c **green,** *cream*	7.00	6.00
Preprinted	2.25	

Jefferson — PC17

Die I-End of queue small, sloping sharply downward to right.

Die II (re-cut)-End of queue large and rounded.

1914-16

Size: 140x82mm

UX27	PC17 1c **green,** *buff,* die I, *June 4*	25	10
	Preprinted	20	
a.	green, *cream*	3.50	60
	Preprinted	1.25	
b.	Double impression	125.00	

On gray, rough surfaced card

UX27C	PC17 1c **green,** die I, *1916*	*1,750.*	
	Preprinted	—	
UX27D	PC17 1c **dark green,** die II, *Dec. 22, 1916*	*1,750.*	120.00
	Preprinted	225.00	

Lincoln — PC19

1917, Mar. 14 **Size: 127x76mm**

UX28	PC19 1c **green,** *cream*	60	30
	Preprinted	30	
a.	1c green, *dark buff*	1.50	60
	Preprinted	50	
b.	Double impression		—
	Preprinted	—	

No. UX28 was printed also on light buff and canary.

Jefferson — PC20

Die I. Rough, coarse impression. End of queue slopes sharply downward to right. Left basal ends of "2" form sharp points.

Size: 140x82mm

Die II. Clear fine lines in hair. Left basal ends of "2" form balls.

1917-18

UX29	PC20 2c **red,** *buff,* die I, *Oct. 22*	35.00	1.50
	Preprinted	5.50	
a.	2c lake, *cream,* die I	45.00	2.50
	Preprinted	9.00	
c.	2c vermilion, *buff,* die I	275.00	60.00
	Preprinted	70.00	
UX30	PC20 2c **red,** *cream,* die II, *Jan. 23, 1918*	19.00	1.50
	Preprinted	3.50	

2c Postal Cards of 1917-18 Revalued

Surcharged in one line by canceling machine at Washington, DC

1920, Apr.

UX31	PC20 1c on 2c **red,** *cream,* die II	*3,250.*	*3,250.*
	Preprinted	*2,500.*	

Surcharged in two lines by canceling machine (46 Types)

UX32	PC20 1c on 2c **red,** *buff,* die I	40.00	10.00
	Preprinted	12.50	
a.	1c on 2c vermilion, *buff*	*95.00*	60.00
b.	Double surcharge	—	*82.50*
UX33	PC20 1c on 2c **red,** *cream,* die II	6.50	1.40
	Preprinted	1.75	
a.	Inverted surcharge	55.00	
b.	Double surcharge	45.00	35.00
	Preprinted	35.00	
c.	Double surcharge, one inverted, preprinted	325.00	
d.	Triple surcharge	350.00	

Values for surcharge varieties of Nos. UX32 and UX33 are for cards having the surcharges *on the stamp.* Copies having the surcharge inverted in the lower left corner, either alone or in combination with a normal surcharge, exist in many of the 46 types.

Surcharged in Two Lines by Press Printing

1920

UX34	PC20 1c on 2c **red,** *buff,* die I	400.00	45.00
	Preprinted	100.00	
a.	Double surcharge	550.00	
UX35	PC20 1c 2c **red,** *cream,* die II	190.00	30.00
	Preprinted	50.00	

Surcharges were prepared from (a) special dies fitting International and Universal post office canceling machines (Nos. UX31-UX33), and (b) printing press dies (Nos. UX34-UX35). There are 38 canceling machine types on Die I, and 44 on Die II. There are two printing press types of each die.

UX36	PC16 1c on 2c **red,** *cream* (#UX25)	3,500.	

Unused copies of No. UX36 (New York surcharge) were probably made by favor. Used copies of No. UX36 (Los Angeles surcharge) are unquestionably authentic. Surcharges on other numbers exist, but their validity is doubtful.

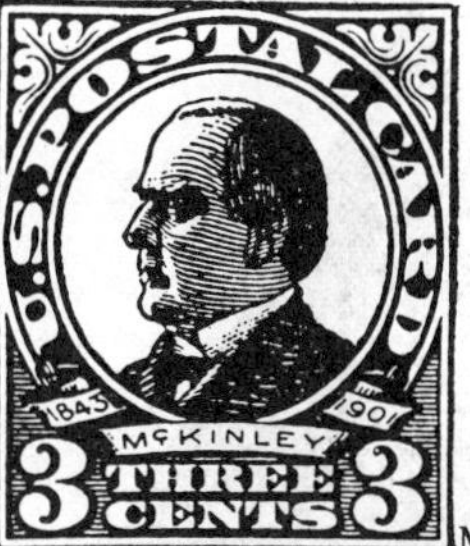

McKinley — PC21

1926, Feb. 1

For International Use

UX37	PC21 3c **red,** *buff*	3.50	*9.00*
	Preprinted	1.75	
	First day cancel, Washington, DC		200.00
a.	3c red, *yellow*	4.00	*11.00*
	Preprinted	1.75	

Franklin — PC22

1951, Nov. 16

UX38	PC22 2c **carmine rose,** *buff*	30	25
	Preprinted	25	
	First day cancel		1.00
a.	Double impression	200.00	

Nos. UX27 and UX28 Surcharged by Canceling Machine at Left of Stamp in Light Green

REVALUED
2¢
P. O. DEPT.

1952

UX39	PC17 2c on 1c **green,** *buff, Jan. 1*	50	25
	Preprinted	25	
	First day cancel, any city		12.00
a.	Surcharged vertically, reading down	6.50	8.50
	Preprinted	3.00	
b.	Double surcharge	17.50	20.00
UX40	PC19 2c on 1c **green,** *cream, Mar. 22*	60	30
	Preprinted	40	
	First day cancel, Washington, D.C.		*100.00*
a.	Surcharged vertically, reading down	7.50	5.00
	Preprinted	4.00	

Nos. UX27 and UX28 with Similar Surcharge Typographed at Left of Stamp in Dark Green.

1952

UX41	PC17 2c on 1c **green,** *buff*	3.50	1.50
	Preprinted	1.75	
a.	Inverted surcharge at lower left	90.00	125.00
	Preprinted	50.00	
UX42	PC19 2c on 1c **green,** *cream*	5.00	2.00
	Preprinted	3.00	
a.	Surcharged on back	80.00	

Type of 1917

1952, July 31 **Size: 127x76mm**

UX43	PC19 2c **carmine,** *buff*	25	20
	Preprinted	15	
	First day cancel		75

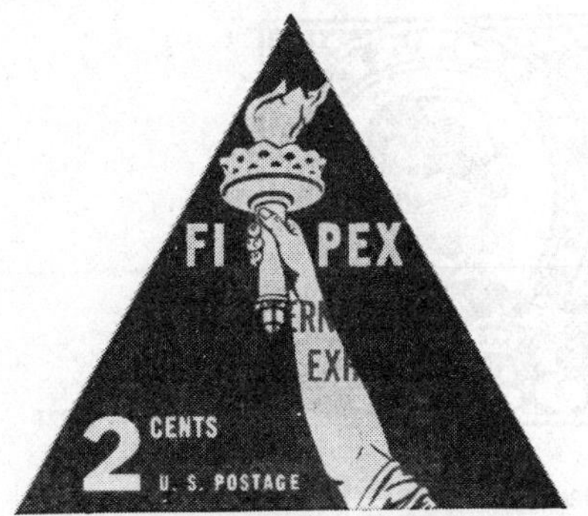

Torch and Arm of Statue of Liberty – PC23

Issued to commemorate the Fifth International Philatelic Exhibition (FIPEX), New York City, Apr. 28-May 6, 1956.

1956, May 4

UX44 PC23 2c **deep carmine & dark violet blue,** *buff*	25	20
First day cancel, New York, NY *(537,474)*		75
a. 2c lilac rose & dark violet blue, *buff*	1.50	50
b. Dark violet blue omitted	450.00	225.00
c. Double impression of dark violet blue	16.00	10.00

Statue of Liberty
PC24 PC25

For International Use

1956, Nov. 16

UX45 PC24 4c **deep red & ultramarine,** *buff*	1.25	*30.00*
First day cancel, New York, NY *(129,841)*		75

Issued at the American Stamp Dealers' Association National Postage Stamp Show, New York, NY, Nov. 16-18.

1958, Aug. 1

UX46 PC25 3c **purple,** *buff*	40	20
First day cancel, Philadelphia *(180,610)*		75
a. "N GOD WE TRUST"	12.50	25.00
b. Double impression	*325.00*	
c. Precanceled with 3 printed purple lines, *1961*	3.50	2.50

Issued at the convention and exhibition of the American First Day Cover Society, Philadelphia, Pa.

On No. UX46c, the precanceling lines are incorporated with the design. The earliest known postmark on this experimental card is Sept. 15, 1961.

No. UX38 Surcharged by Canceling Machine at Left of Stamp in Black

ONE CENT
ADDITIONAL
PAID

1958

UX47 PC221 2c + 1c **carmine rose,** *buff*	160.00	250.00

The surcharge was applied to 750,000 cards for the use of the General Electric Co., Owensboro, Ky. A variety of the surcharge shows the D of PAID beneath the N of ADDITIONAL. All known examples of No. UX47 have a printed advertisement on the back and a small punch hole near lower left corner.

No. UX47 exists with inverted surcharge at lower left.

Lincoln – PC26

1962, Nov. 19

Precanceled with 3 printed red violet lines

UX48 PC26 4c **red violet**	25	20
First day cancel, Springfield, IL *(162,939)*		75
a. Tagged, *June 25, 1966*	50	20
First day cancel, Bellevue, OH		—

No. UX48a was printed with luminescent ink. See note on Luminescence in "Information for Collectors."

Map of Continental United States – PC27

Designed by Suren H. Ermoyan

For International Use

1963, Aug. 30

UX49 PC27 7c **blue & red**	2.00	*25.00*
First day cancel, New York, NY		75
a. Blue omitted		—

First day cancellation was applied to 270,464 of Nos. UX49 and UY19. See Nos. UX54, UX59.

Flags and Map of U.S. – PC28

175th anniv. of the U.S. Customs Service.

Designed by Gerald N. Kurtz

1964, Feb. 22

Precanceled with 3 printed blue lines

UX50 PC28 4c **red & blue**	40	50
First day cancel, Washington, DC *(313,275)*		75
a. Blue omitted	450.00	
b. Red omitted		—

Americans "Moving Forward" (Street Scene) – PC29

Issued to publicize the need to strengthen the US Social Security system. Released in connection with the 15th conf. of the Intl. Social Security Association at Washington, DC.

Designed by Gerald N. Kurtz

1964, Sept. 26

Precanceled with a blue and 2 red printed lines

UX51 PC29 4c **dull blue & red**	40	20
First day cancel, Washington, D.C. *(293,650)*		75
a. Red omitted		—
b. Blue omitted	550.00	

Coast Guard Flag – PC30

175th anniv. of the U.S. Coast Guard.

Designed by Muriel R. Chamberlain

1965, Aug. 4 Precanceled with 3 printed red lines

UX52 PC30 4c **blue & red**	30	20
First day cancel, Newburyport, Mass. *(338,225)*		1.00
a. Blue omitted		—

Crowd and Census Bureau Punch Card – PC31

Designed by Emilio Grossi

1965, Oct. 21

Precanceled with 3 bright blue printed lines

UX53 PC31 4c **bright blue & black**	30	20
First day cancel, Philadelphia, Pa. *(275,100)*		1.00

Map Type of 1963

For International Use

1967, Dec. 4

UX54 PC27 8c **blue & red**	2.00	*20.00*
First day cancel, Washington, DC		50

First day cancellation was applied to 268,077 of Nos. UX54 and UY20.

Lincoln – PC33

Designed by Robert J. Jones

Luminescent Ink

1968, Jan. 4

Precanceled with 3 printed green lines

UX55 PC33 5c **emerald**	25	15
First day cancel, Hodgenville, Ky.		1.00
a. Double impression	—	

First day cancellation was applied to 274,000 of Nos. UX55 and UY21.

Woman Marine, 1968, and Marines of Earlier Wars – PC34

25th anniv. of the Women Marines.

Designed by Muriel R. Chamberlain

1968, July 26

UX56 PC34 5c **rose red & green**	35	20
First day cancel, San Francisco, Cal. *(203,714)*		75

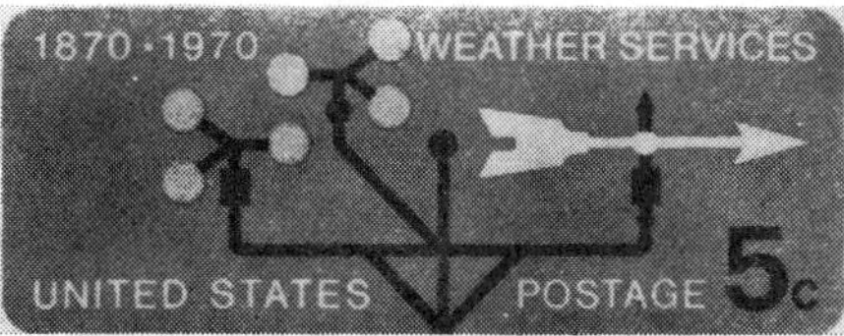

Weather Vane – PC35

Issued to commemorate the centenary of the Army's Signal Service, the Weather Services (Weather Bureau).

Designed by Robert Geissmann

1970, Sept. 1 **Tagged**

UX57 PC35 5c **blue, yellow, red & black**	30	15
First day cancel, Fort Myer, Va. *(285,800)*		75
a. Yellow & black omitted	700.00	
b. Blue omitted	650.00	
c. Black omitted	600.00	

Paul Revere – PC36

Issued to honor Paul Revere, Revolutionary War patriot.

Designed by Howard C. Mildner after statue near Old North Church, Boston

Luminescent Ink

1971, May 15

Precanceled with 3 printed brown lines.

UX58 PC36 6c **brown**	25	20
First day cancel, Boston, Mass.		75
a. Double impression	300.00	

First day cancellation was applied to 340,000 of Nos. UX58 and UY22.

Map Type of 1963

For International Use

1971, June 10 **Tagged**

UX59 PC27 10c **blue & red**	2.00	*25.00*
First day cancel, New York, NY		75

First day cancellation was applied to 297,000 of Nos. UX59 and UXC11.

New York Hospital, New York City – PC37

Issued as a tribute to America's hospitals in connection with the 200th anniversary of New York Hospital.

Designed by Dean Ellis

1971 **Tagged**

UX60 PC37 6c **blue & multi**	25	20
First day cancel, New York, NY *(218,200)*		75
a. Blue & yellow omitted	700.00	

U.S.F. Constellation – PC38

Monument Valley PC39

Gloucester, Mass. PC40

Tourism Year of the Americas.

Designed by Melbourne Brindle

1972, June 29 **Tagged**

Size: 152½x108½mm

UX61 PC38 6c **black,** *buff (Yosemite, Mt. Rushmore, Niagara Falls, Williamsburg on back)*	30	50
First day cancel, any city		40
a. Address side blank	*300.00*	
UX62 PC39 6c **black,** *buff (Monterey, Redwoods, Gloucester, U.S.F. Constellation on back)*	30	50
First day cancel, any city		
UX63 PC40 6c **black,** *buff (Rodeo, Mississippi Riverboat, Grand Canyon, Monument Valley on back)*	30	50
First day cancel, any city		40

Nos. UX61-UX63, UXC12-UXC13 went on sale throughout the United States. They were sold as souvenirs without postal validity at Belgica Philatelic Exhibition in Brussels and were displayed at the American Embassies in Paris and Rome. This is reflected in the first day cancel.

Nos. UX61-UX63 have a luminescent panel at left of stamp which glows green under ultraviolet light.

Varieties of the pictorial back printing include: black omitted (UX62), black and pale salmon omitted (UX63), and back inverted in relation to address side (UX63).

John Hanson – PC41

Designed by Thomas Kronen after statue by Richard Edwin Brooks in Maryland Capitol

1972, Sept. 1 **Luminescent Ink**

Precanceled with 3 printed blue lines.

UX64 PC41 6c **blue**	25	15
First day cancel, Baltimore, MD		75

Liberty Type of 1873

Centenary of first U.S. postal card.

1973, Sept. 1

UX65 PC1 6c **magenta**	25	15
First day cancel, Washington, D.C. *(289,950)*		75

Samuel Adams – PC42

Designed by Howard C. Mildner

1973, Dec. 16 **Luminescent Ink**

Precanceled with 3 printed orange lines

UX66 PC42 8c **orange**	25	15
First day cancel, Boston, Mass. *(147,522)*		75

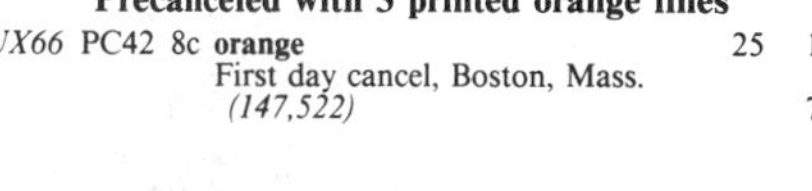
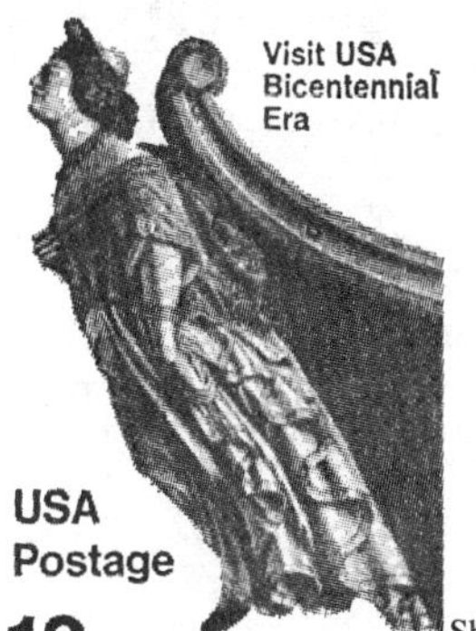

Ship's Figurehead, 1883 – PC43

Design is after a watercolor by Elizabeth Moutal of the oak figurehead by John Rogerson from the barque Edinburgh

1974, Jan. 4 **Tagged**

For International Use

UX67 PC43 12c **multicolored** 35 *15.00*
First day cancel, Miami, Fla.
(138,500) 75

No. UX67 has a luminescent panel at left of stamp which glows green under ultraviolet light.

Charles Thomson — PC44

John Witherspoon — PC45

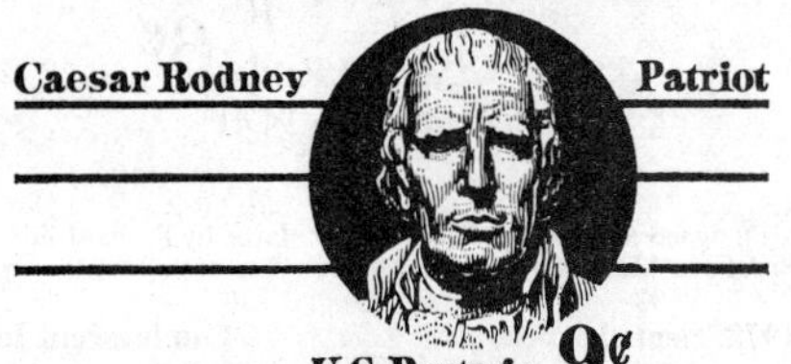

Caesar Rodney — PC46

Designed by Howard C. Mildner

Luminescent Ink

1975-76

Precanceled with 3 printed emerald lines

UX68 PC44 7c **emerald,** *Sept. 14, 1975* 25 10
First day cancel, Bryn Mawr, Pa. 75

Precanceled with 3 printed brown lines

UX69 PC45 9c **yellow brown,** *Nov. 10, 1975* 25 10
First day cancel, Princeton, N.J. 75

Precanceled with 3 printed blue lines

UX70 PC46 9c **blue,** *July 1, 1976* 25 10
First day cancel, Dover, Del. 75
a. Double impression —

First day cancellation applied to 231,919 of Nos. UX68 and UY25; 254,239 of Nos. UX69 and UY26; 304,061 of Nos. UX70 and UY27.

Federal Court House, Galveston, Texas — PC47

The Court House, completed in 1861, is on the National Register of Historic Places.

Designed by Donald Moss

1977, July 20 **Tagged**

UX71 PC47 9c **multicolored** 25 16
First day cancel, Galveston, Tex.
(245,535) 75

Nathan Hale — PC48

Designed by Howard C. Mildner

Luminescent Ink

1977, Oct. 14

Precanceled with 3 printed green lines

UX72 PC48 9c **green** 25 10
First day cancel, Coventry, Conn. 75

First day cancellation applied to 304,592 of Nos. UX72 and UY28.

Cincinnati Music Hall — PC49

Centenary of Cincinnati Music Hall, Cincinnati, Ohio.

Designed by Clinton Orlemann

1978, May 12 **Tagged**

UX73 PC49 10c **multicolored** 25 16
First day cancel, Cincinnati, O.
(300,000) 75

John Hancock — PC50

Designed by Howard Behrens

Luminescent Ink

1978

Precanceled with 3 printed brown orange lines.

UX74 PC50 (10c) **brown orange,** *May 19* 25 10
First day cancel, Quincy, Mass.
(299,623) 75

Inscribed "U.S. Postage 10¢"

UX75 PC50 10c **brown orange,** *June 20* 25 10
First day cancel, Quincy, Mass.
(187,120) 75

Coast Guard Cutter Eagle — PC51

Designed by Carl G. Evers

For International Use

1978, Aug. 4 **Tagged**

UX76 PC51 14c **multicolored** 45 *8.00*
First day cancel, Seattle, Wash.
(196,400) 75

Molly Pitcher Firing Cannon at Monmouth — PC52

Bicentennial of Battle of Monmouth, June 28, 1778, and to honor Molly Pitcher (Mary Ludwig Hays).

Designed by David Blossom

1978, Sept. 8 **Tagged** **Litho.**

UX77 PC52 10c **multicolored** 25 16
First day cancel, Freehold, N.J.
(180,280) 75

Clark and his Frontiersmen Approaching Fort Sackville — PC53

Bicentenary of capture of Fort Sackville from the British by George Rogers Clark.

Designed by David Blossom

1979, Feb. 23 **Tagged** **Litho.**

UX78 PC53 10c **multicolored** 25 16
First day cancel, Vincennes, Ind. 75

Gen. Casimir Pulaski — PC54

Bicentenary of the death of Gen. Casimir Pulaski (1748-1779), Polish nobleman who served in American Revolutionary Army.

1979, Oct. 11 **Tagged** **Litho.**

UX79 PC54 10c **multicolored** 25 16
First day cancel, Savannah. GA
(210,000) 75

Olympic Games Issue

Sprinter PC55

22nd Olympic Games, Moscow, July 19-Aug. 3, 1980.

Designed by Robert M. Cunningham

1979, Dept. 17 **Tagged** **Litho.**
UX80 PC55 10c **multicolored** 50 25
First day cancel, Eugene, Ore. 75

Iolani Palace, Honolulu PC56

1979, Oct. 1 **Tagged** **Litho.**
UX81 PC56 10c **multicolored** 25 16
First day cancel, Honolulu, HI *(242,804)* 75

Women's Figure Skating PC57

13th Winter Olympic Games, Lake Placid, N.Y., Feb. 12-24.

Designed by Robert M. Cunningham

For International Use

1980, Jan. 15 **Tagged** **Litho.**
UX82 PC57 14c **multicolored** 50 *1.00*
First day cancel, Atlanta, GA *(160,977)* 75

Salt Lake Temple, Salt Lake City — PC58

1980, Apr. 5 **Tagged** **Litho.**
UX83 PC58 10c **multicolored** 22 15
First day cancel, Salt Lake City, UT *(325,260)* 75

Rochambeau's Fleet — PC59

Count Jean-Baptiste de Rochambeau's landing at Newport, R.I. (American Revolution) bicentenary.

Designed by David Blossom

1980, July 11 **Tagged** **Litho.**
UX84 PC59 10c **multicolored** 22 15
First day cancel, Newport, R.I. *(180,567)* 75
a. Front normal, black & yellow on back —

Whig Infantrymen — PC60

Bicentenary of the Battle of Kings Mountain (American Revolution).

Designed by David Blossom

1980, Oct. 7 **Tagged** **Litho.**
UX85 PC60 10c **multicolored** 22 15
First day cancel, Kings Mountain, NC *(136,130)* 75

Golden Hinde — PC61

300th anniv. of Sir Francis Drake's circumnavigation (1578-1580).

Designed by Charles J. Lundgren

For International Use

1980, Nov. 21
UX86 PC61 19c **multicolored** 60 *5.00*
First day cancel, San Rafael, CA *(290,547)* 75

Cols. Washington and Tarleton — PC62

Bicentenary of the Battle of Cowpens (American Revolution).

Designed by David Blossom

1981, Jan. 17
UX87 PC62 10c **multicolored** 22 15
First day cancel, Cowpens, SC *(160,000)* 75

Eagle — PC63

Luminescent Ink

1981, Mar. 15
Precanceled with 3 printed violet lines
UX88 PC63 (12c) **violet** 28 18
First day cancel, Memphis, TN 75

See No. 1818, FDC section.

Isaiah Thomas — PC64

Designed by Chet Jezierski

1981, May 5 **Precanceled with 3 printed lines**
UX89 PC64 12c **light blue** 28 12
First day cancel, Worchester, MA *(185,610)* 75

PC65

Bicentenary of the Battle at Eutaw Springs (American Revolution)

Designed by David Blossom

1981, Sept. 8 **Litho.**
UX90 PC65 12c **multicolored** 28 18
First day cancel, Eutaw Springs, SC *(115,755)* 75
a. Red & yellow omitted —

PC66

Designed by David Blossom

1981, Sept. 23
UX91 PC66 12c **multicolored** 28 18
First day cancel, Saint Louis, MO 75

Robert Morris — PC67

1981

Precanceled with 3 printed lines

UX92 PC67 (13c) **buff**, *Oct. 11* 30 20
First day cancel, Memphis, TN 55

See No. 1946, FDC section.

Inscribed: U.S. Postage 13¢

UX93 PC67 13c **buff**, *Nov. 10* 30 12
First day cancel, Philadelphia, PA 55

General Francis Marion (1732?-1795) — PC68

Designed by David Blossom

1982, Apr. 3 **Litho.**

UX94 PC68 13c **multicolored** 30 20
First day cancel, Marion, SC *(141,162)* 55

Rene Robert Cavelier, Sieur de la Salle (1643-1687) — PC69

Designed by David Blossom

1982, Apr. 7 **Litho.**

UX95 PC69 13c **multicolored** 30 20
First day cancel, New Orleans, LA 55

PC70

Designed by Melbourne Brindle

1982, June 18 **Litho.**

UX96 PC70 13c brown, red & cream, *buff* 30 20
First day cancel, Philadelphia, PA — 55
a. Brown & cream omitted —

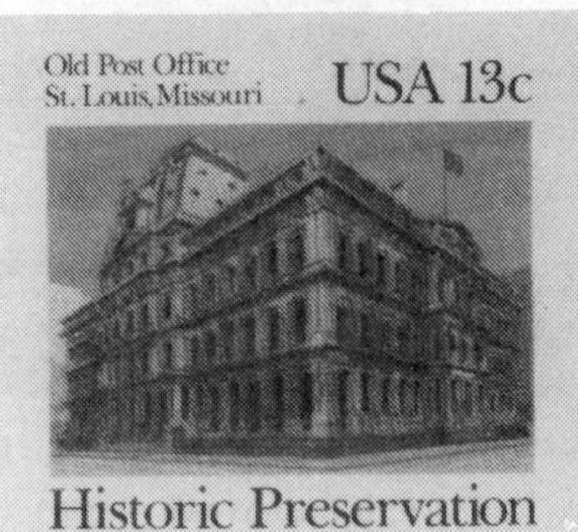

PC71

Designed by Clint Orlemann

1982, Oct. 14 **Litho.**

UX97 PC71 13c **multicolored** 30 20
First day cancel, St. Louis, MO 55

Gen. Oglethorpe Meeting Chief Tomo-Chi-Chi of the Yamacraw — PC72

Designed by David Blossom

1983, Feb. 12 **Litho.**

UX98 PC72 13c **multicolored** 30 20
First day cancel, Savannah, GA 55

PC73

Designed by Walter Brooks

1983, Apr. 19 **Litho.**

UX99 PC73 13c **multicolored** 30 20
First day cancel, Washington, DC *(125,056)* 55

Olympics 84, Yachting — PC74

Designed by Bob Peak

1983, Aug. 5 **Litho.**

UX100 PC74 13c **multicolored** 30 20
First day cancel, Long Beach, CA 55
a. Black, yellow & red omitted

The Ark and the Dove — PC75

Designed by David Blossom

1984, Mar. 25 **Litho.**

UX101 PC75 13c **multicolored** 30 20
First day cancel, St. Clement's Island, MD 55

Runner Carrying Olympic Torch — PC76

Designed by Robert Peak

1984, Apr. 30 **Litho.**

UX102 PC76 13c **multicolored** 30 20
First day cancel, Los Angeles, CA 55
a. Black & yellow inverted —

Father Baraga and Indian Guide in Canoe — PC77

Designed by David Blossom

1984, June 29 **Litho.**

UX103 PC77 13c **multicolored** 30 20
First day cancel, Marquette, MI 55

Dominguez Adobe at Rancho San Pedro — PC78

Designed by Earl Thollander

1984, Sept. 16 **Litho.**

UX104 PC78 13c **multicolored** 30 20
First day cancel, Compton, CA 55
a. Black & blue omitted —

Charles Carroll (1737-1832) — PC79

Designed by Richard Sparks

1985

Precanceled with 3 printed lines

UX105 PC79 (14c) **pale green,** *Feb. 1* 28 18
First day cancel, New Carrollton, MD 58

Inscribed: USA 14

UX106 PC79 14c **pale green,** *Mar. 6* 28 14
First day cancel, Annapolis, MD 58

Clipper Flying Cloud — PC80

Designed by Richard Schlecht

For International Use

1985, Feb. 27 **Litho.**

UX107 PC80 25c **multicolored** 70 *5.00*
First day cancel, Salem, MA 95

No. UX107 was sold by the USPS at CUP-PEX 87, Perth, Western Australia, with a cachet honoring CUP-PEX 87 and the America's Cup race.

George Wythe (1726-1806) — PC81

Designed by Chet Jezierski from a portrait by John Fergusson

1985, June 20

Precanceled with 3 printed lines

UX108 PC81 14c **bright apple green** 28 14
First day cancel, Williamsburg, VA 58

Arrival of Thomas Hooker and Hartford Congregation — PC82

Settlement of Connecticut, 350th Anniv.

Designed by David Blossom

1986, Apr. 18 **Litho.**

UX109 PC82 14c **multicolored** 28 18
First day cancel, Hartford, CT 58

Stamp Collecting — PC83

Designed by Ray Ameijide

1986, May 23 **Litho.**

UX110 PC83 14c **multicolored** 28 18
First day cancel, Chicago, IL 58

No. UX110 was sold by the USPS at "najubria 86" with a show cachet.

Francis Vigo (1747-1836) — PC84

Designed by David Blossom

1986, May 24 **Litho.**

UX111 PC84 14c **multicolored** 28 18
First day cancel, Vincennes, IN 58

Roger Williams (1603-1683), Clergyman, Landing at Providence — PC85

Settling of Rhode Island, 350th Anniv.

Designed by David Blossom

1986, June 26 **Litho.**

UX112 PC85 14c **multicolored** 28 18
First day cancel, Providence, RI 58

Miners, Shake Rag Street Housing — PC86

Wisconsin Territory Sesquicentennial.

Designed by David Blossom

1986, July 3 **Litho.**

UX113 PC86 14c **multicolored** 28 18
First day cancel, Mineral Point, WI 58

The First Muster, by Don Troiani — PC87

Designed by Bradbury Thompson

1986, Dec. 12 **Litho.**

UX114 PC87 14c **multicolored** 28 18
First day cancel, Boston, MA *(72,316)* 58

PC88

The self-scouring steel plow invented by blacksmith John Deere in 1837 pictured at lower left.

Designed by William H. Bond

1987, May 22 **Litho.**

UX115 PC88 14c **multicolored** 28 18
First day cancel, Moline, IL *(160,009)* 58

Convening of the Constitutional Convention, 1787 — PC89

George Mason, Gouverneur Morris, James Madison, Alexander Hamilton and Charles C. Pinckney are listed in the lower left corner of the card.

Designed by David K. Stone

1987, May 25 **Litho.**
UX116 PC89 14c **multicolored** 28 18
First day cancel, Philadelphia, PA *(138,207)* 58

Stars and Stripes — PC90

Designed by Steven Dohanos

1987, June 14 **Litho.**
UX117 PC90 14c **black, blue & red** 28 14
First day cancel, Baltimore, MD 58

No. UX117 was sold by the USPS at Cologne, Germany, with a cachet for Philatelia'87.

Take Pride in America — PC91

Designed by Lou Nolan

1987, Sept. 22 **Litho.**
UX118 PC91 14c **multicolored** 28 18
First day cancel, Jackson, WY *(47,281)* 58

Timberline Lodge, 50th Anniversary — PC92

Designed by Walter DuBois Richards

1987, Sept. 28 **Litho.**
UX119 PC92 14c **multicolored** 28 18
First day cancel, Timberline, OR *(63,595)* 58

Bison and Prairie — PC93

Designed by Bart Forbes

1988, Mar. 28 **Litho.**
UX120 PC93 15c **multicolored** 30 15
First day cancel, Buffalo, WY *(52,075)* 60
a. Black omitted —
b. Printed on both sides —
c. Front normal, blue & black on back —

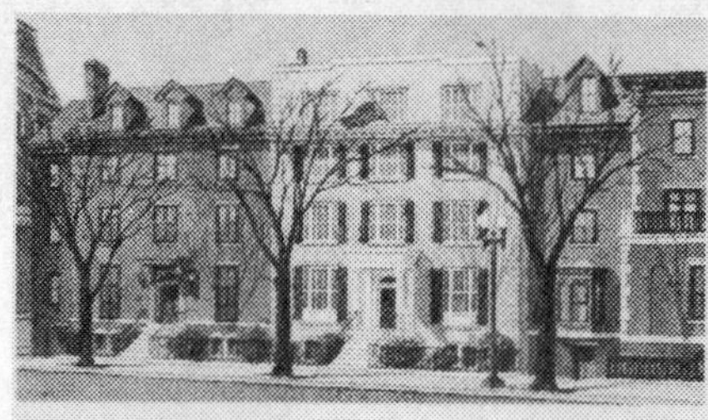

Blair House — PC94

Designed by Pierre Mion

1988, May 4 **Litho.**
UX121 PC94 15c **multicolored** 30 15
First day cancel, Washington, DC *(52,188)* 60

Yorkshire, Squarerigged Packet — PC95

Inscribed: Yorkshire, Black Ball Line, Packet Ship, circa 1850 at lower left.

Designed by Richard Schlect

For International Use

1988, June 29 **Litho.**
UX122 PC95 28c **multicolored** 60 *1.00*
First day cancel, Mystic, CT *(46,505)* 1.00

Harvesting Corn Fields — PC96

Iowa Territory Sesquicentennial.

Designed by Greg Hargreaves

1988, July 2 **Litho.**
UX123 PC96 15c **multicolored** 30 15
First day cancel, Burlington, IA *(45,565)* 60

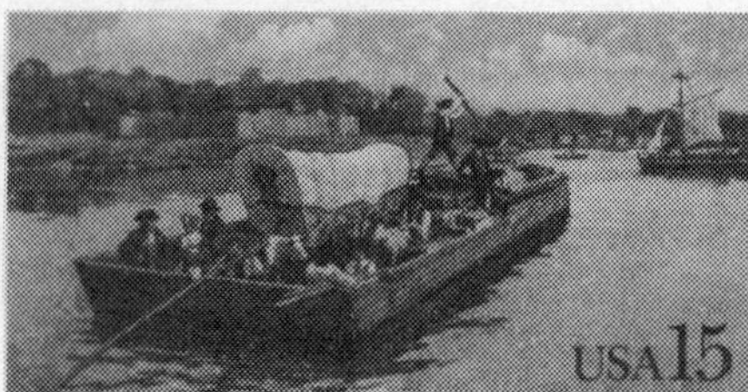

Flatboat Ferry Transporting Settlers Down the Ohio River — PC97

Bicentenary of the settlement of Ohio, the Northwest Territory. Design at lower left shows map of the eastern United States with Northwest Territory highlighted.

Designed by James M. Gurney and Susan Sanford

1988, July 15 **Litho.**
UX124 PC97 15c **multicolored** 30 15
First day cancel, Marietta, OH *(28,778)* 60

Hearst Castle — PC98

Designed by Robert Reynolds

1988, Sept. 20 **Litho.**
UX125 PC98 15c **multicolored** 30 15
First day cancel, San Simeon, CA *(84,786)* 60

Pressman, New Yorker Reading Newspaper, 1787 — PC99

Designed by Roy Andersen

1988, Oct. 27 **Litho.**
UX126 PC99 15c **multicolored** 30 15
First day cancel, New York, NY *(37,661)* 60

Red-tailed Hawk and Sonora Desert at Sunset — PC100

Designed by Bart Forbes

1989, Jan. 13 **Litho.**
UX127 PC100 15c **multicolored** 30 15
First day cancel, Tucson, AZ 60

Healy Hall, Georgetown University — PC101

Designed by John Morrell. Inscription at lower left: "Healy Hall / Georgetown / Washington, DC / HISTORIC PRESERVATION."

1989, Jan. 23 **Litho.**

UX128 PC101 15c **multicolored** 30 15
First day cancel, Washington, DC 60

Great Blue Heron, Marsh — PC102

Designed by Bart Forbes

1989, Mar. 17 **Litho.**

UX129 PC102 15c **multicolored** 30 15
First day cancel, Waycross, GA 60

Settling of Oklahoma — PC103

Designed by Bradbury Thompson

1989, Apr. 22 **Litho.**

UX130 PC103 15c **multicolored** 30 15
First day cancel, Guthrie, OK 60

Canada Geese and Mountains — PC104

Designed by Bart Forbes

1989, May 5 **Litho.**

UX131 PC104 21c **multicolored** 42 21
First day cancel, Denver, CO 85

Seashore — PC105

Designed by Bart Forbes

1989, June 17 **Litho.**

UX132 PC105 15c **multicolored** 30 15
First day cancel, Cape Hatteras, NC 60

Deer Beside Woodland Waterfall — PC106

1989, Aug. 26 **Litho.**

UX133 PC106 15c **multi** 30 15
First day cancel, Cherokee, NC 60

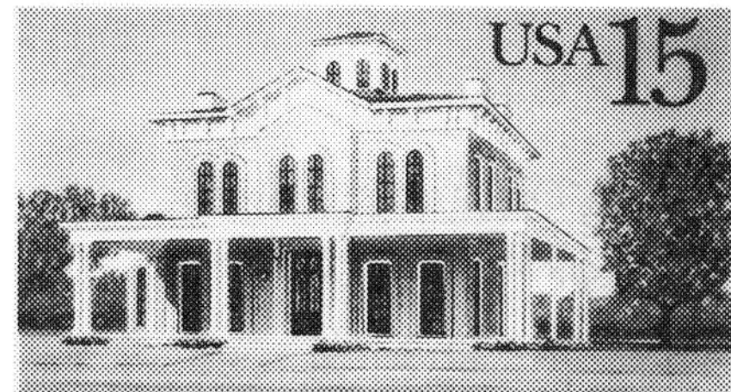

Hull House, Chicago — PC107

Designed by Michael Hagel

1989, Sept. 18 **Litho.**

UX134 PC107 15c **multicolored** 30 15
First day cancel, Chicago, IL 60

PAID REPLY POSTAL CARDS

These are sold to the public as two unsevered cards, one for message and one for reply. These are listed first as unsevered cards and then as severed cards. Values are for

Unused cards (both unsevered and severed) without printed or written address or message.

Unsevered cards sell for a premium if never folded.

Used unsevered cards, Message Card with Post Office cancellation and Reply Card uncanceled (from 1968 value is for a single used severed card); and used severed cards with cancellation when current.

Used values for International Paid Reply Cards are for proper usage. Those domestically used sell for less than the unused value.

"Preprinted," unused cards (both unsevered and severed) with printed or written address or message. Used value applies after 1952.

First day cancel values are for cards without cachets.

PM1

PR1

Head of Grant, card framed.

1892, Oct. 25 **Size: 140x89mm**

UY1	PM1+PR1 1c +1c black, *buff*, unsevered	35.00	7.50
	Preprinted	15.00	
a.	Message card printed on both sides, reply card blank	250.00	
b.	Message card blank, reply card printed on both sides	300.00	
c.	Cards joined at bottom	175.00	75.00
	Preprinted	75.00	
m.	PM1 Message card detached	6.00	1.25
	Preprinted	3.00	
r.	PR1 Reply card detached	6.00	1.25
	Preprinted	3.00	

For other postal cards of types PM1 and PR1 see No. UY3.

PM2

Liberty — PR2

1893, Mar. 1 **For International Use**

UY2	PM2+PR2 2c +2c blue, *grayish white*, unsevered	17.50	*20.00*
	Preprinted	12.50	
a.	2c+2c dark blue, *grayish white*, unsevered	12.50	*20.00*
	Preprinted	12.50	
b.	Message card printed on both sides, reply card blank	300.00	
c.	Message card blank, reply card printed on both sides	—	
d.	Message card normal, reply card blank	300.00	
m.	PM2 Message card detached	5.00	*6.00*
	Preprinted	2.50	
r.	PR2 Reply card detached	5.00	*6.00*
	Preprinted	2.50	

For other postal cards of types PM2 and PR2 see No. UY11.

Design same as PM1 and PR1, without frame around card

1898, Sept.

Size: 140x82mm

UY3	PM1+PR1 1c +1c black, *buff*, unsevered	60.00	12.50
	Preprinted	12.50	
a.	Message card normal, reply card blank	250.00	
b.	Message card printed on both sides, reply card blank	250.00	
c.	Message card blank, reply card printed on both sides	250.00	
d.	Message card without "Detach annexed card/for answer"	250.00	150.00
	Preprinted	—	
e.	Message card blank, reply card normal	250.00	
m.	PM1 Message card detached	12.50	2.50
	Preprinted	6.00	
r.	PR1 Reply card detached	12.50	2.50
	Preprinted	6.00	

PM3

PR3

1904, Mar, 31

UY4	PM3+PR3 1c +1c black, *buff*, unsevered	45.00	2.75
	Preprinted	9.00	
a.	Message card normal, reply card blank	275.00	
b.	Message card printed on both sides, reply card blank	—	
c.	Message card blank, reply card normal	275.00	
d.	Message card blank, reply card printed on both sides	—	175.00
	Preprinted	200.00	
m.	PM3 Message card detached	9.00	1.00
	Preprinted	4.00	
r.	PR3 Reply card detached	9.00	1.00
	Preprinted	4.00	

PM4

PR4

Double frame line around instructions

1910, Sept. 14

UY5	PM4+PR4 1c +1c blue, *bluish*, unsevered	140.00	20.00
	Preprinted	40.00	
a.	Message card normal, reply card blank	200.00	
m.	PM4 Message card detached	10.00	3.00
	Preprinted	6.00	
r.	PR4 Reply card detached	10.00	3.00
	Preprinted	6.00	

1911, Oct. 27

UY6	PM4+PR4 1c +1c green, *cream*, unsevered	140.00	22.50
	Preprinted	60.00	
a.	Message card normal, reply card blank	—	
m.	PM4 Message card detached	22.50	5.00
	Preprinted	12.50	
r.	PR4 Reply card detached	22.50	5.00
	Preprinted	12.50	

Single frame line around instructions

1915, Sept. 18

UY7	PM4+PR4 1c +1c green, *cream*, unsevered	1.00	50
	Preprinted	50	
a.	1c+1c dark green, *buff*, unsevered	1.00	50
	Preprinted	50	
m.	PM4 Message card detached	25	20
	Preprinted	15	
r.	PR4 Reply card detached	25	20
	Preprinted	15	

PM5

PR5

1918, Aug. 2

UY8	PM5+PR5 2c +2c red, *buff*, unsevered	75.00	40.00
	Preprinted	30.00	
m.	PM5 Message card detached	20.00	7.50
	Preprinted	10.00	
r.	PR5 Reply card detached	20.00	7.50
	Preprinted	10.00	

Same Surcharged

Fifteen canceling machine types

1920, Apr.

UY9	PM5+PR5 1c on 2c+1c on 2c **red**, *buff*, unsevered	17.50	10.00
	Preprinted	10.00	
a.	Message card normal, reply card no surcharge	85.00	—
	Preprinted	—	
b.	Message card normal, reply card double surcharge	75.00	—
	Preprinted	—	
c.	Message card double surcharge, reply card normal	75.00	—
	Preprinted	—	
d.	Message card no surcharge, reply card normal	75.00	—
	Preprinted	—	
e.	Message card no surcharge, reply card double surcharge	75.00	
m.	PM5 Message card detached	5.00	3.00
	Preprinted	3.00	
r.	PR5 Reply card detached	5.00	3.00
	Preprinted	3.00	

One press printed type

UY10	PM5+PR5 1c on 2c+1c on 2c **red**, *buff*, unsevered	300.00	175.00
	Preprinted	150.00	
a.	Message card no surcharge, reply card normal	—	
	Preprinted	—	
m.	PM5 Message card detached	90.00	40.00
	Preprinted	40.00	
r.	PR5 Reply card detached	90.00	40.00
	Preprinted	40.00	

Designs same as PM2 and PR2

1924, Mar. 18 **For International Use**

Size: 139x89mm

UY11	PM2+PR2 2c +2c **red**, *cream*, unsevered	1.75	*30.00*
	Preprinted	1.50	
m.	PM2 Message card detached	50	*10.00*
	Preprinted	40	
r.	PR2 Reply card detached	50	*10.00*
	Preprinted	40	

PM6

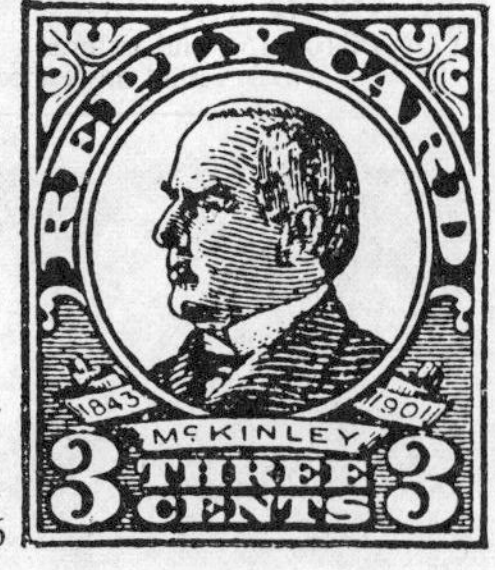

PR6

For International Use

1926, Feb. 1

UY12	PM6+PR6 3c +3c **red**, *buff*, unsevered	9.00	*25.00*
	Preprinted	5.00	
a.	3c +3c **red**, *yellow*, unsevered	10.00	*17.50*
	Preprinted	6.00	
	First day cancel		—
m.	PM6 Message card detached	3.00	*6.00*
	Preprinted	1.50	
r.	PR6 Reply card detached	3.00	*6.00*
	Preprinted	1.50	

Type of 1910

Single frame line around instructions

1951, Dec. 29

UY13	PM4+PR4 2c +2c **carmine**, *buff*, unsevered	1.00	50
	Preprinted	50	
	First day cancel, Washington, D.C.		1.25
m.	PM4 Message card detached	35	20

Preprinted 25
r. PR4 Reply card detached 35 20
Preprinted 25

No. UY7a Surcharged Below Stamp in Green by Canceling Machine

REVALUED 2¢ P. O. DEPT.

1952, Jan. 1

UY14 PM4+PR4 2c on 1c+2c on 1c **green,** *buff,* unsevered 1.00 50
Preprinted 50
a. Surcharge vertical at left of stamps 7.00 6.00
Preprinted 6.00
b. Surcharge horizontal at left of stamps 14.00 12.50
Preprinted 8.50
c. Inverted surcharge horizontal at left of stamps 140.00 90.00
Preprinted 75.00
d. Message card normal, reply card no surcharge 35.00 40.00
Preprinted —
e. Message card normal, reply card double surcharge 40.00 25.00
Preprinted —
f. Message card no surcharge, reply card normal 35.00 40.00
Preprinted —
g. Message card double surcharge, reply card normal 40.00 25.00
Preprinted —
h. Both cards, dbl. surch. 50.00 35.00
Preprinted —
m. PM4 Message card detached 40 25
Preprinted 30
r. PR4 Reply card detached 40 25
Preprinted 30

No. UY7a with Similar Surcharge (horizontal) Typographed at Left of Stamp in Dark Green

1952

UY15 PM4+PR4 2c on 1c+2c on 1c **green,** *buff,* unsevered 100.00 45.00
Preprinted 35.00
a. Surcharge on message card only 140.00
m. PM4 Message card detached 17.50 10.00
Preprinted 9.00
r. PR4 Reply card detached 17.50 10.00
Preprinted 9.00

On No. UY15a, the surcharge also appears on blank side of card.

Liberty Type of Postal Card, 1956
For International Use

1956, Nov. 16

UY16 PC24 4c +4c **carmine & dark violet blue,** *buff,* unsevered 1.00 *42.50*
First day cancel, New York, N. Y. *(127,874)* 75
a. Message card printed on both halves 125.00 —
b. Reply card printed on both halves 125.00 —
m. Message card detached 40 *30.00*
r. Reply card detached 40 *25.00*

See note after UX45.

Liberty Type of Postal Card, 1956

1958, July 31

UY17 PC25 3c +3c **purple,** *buff,* unsevered 3.00 60
First day cancel, Boise, Idaho *(136,768)* 75
a. One card blank 125.00 —

Both halves of No. UY17 are identical, inscribed as No. UX46, "This side of card is for address."

Lincoln Type of Postal Card, 1962

1962, Nov. 19
Precanceled with 3 printed red violet lines

UY18 PC26 4c +4c **red violet,** unsevered 4.00 75
First day cancel, Springfield, Ill. *(107,746)* 75
a. Tagged, *Mar. 7, 1967* 6.00 3.00
a. First day cancel, Dayton, OH 30.00

Both halves of No. UY18 are identical, inscribed as No. UX48, "This side of card is for address."
No. UY18a was printed with luminescent ink.

Map Type of Postal Card, 1963

1963, Aug. 30 **For International Use**

UY19 PC27 7c +7c **blue & red,** unsevered 2.00 *30.00*
First day cancel, New York 75
a. Message card normal, reply card blank 125.00 100.00
b. Message card blank, reply card normal 125.00 —
c. Additional message card on back of reply card —
m. Message card detached 75 *20.00*
r. Reply card detached 75 *17.50*

Message card inscribed "Postal Card With Paid Reply" in English and French. Reply card inscribed "Reply Postal Card Carte Postale Reponse".

Map Type of Postal Card, 1963

1967, Dec. 4
For International Use

UY20 PC27 8c +8c **blue & red,** unsevered 2.00 *25.00*
First day cancel, Washington, D.C. 75
m. Message card detached 75 *20.00*
r. Reply card detached 75 *17.50*

Message card inscribed "Postal Card With Paid Reply" in English and French. Reply card inscribed "Reply Postal Card Carte Postale Response."

Lincoln Type of Postal Card, 1968

1968, Jan. 4
Tagged

UY21 PC33 5c +5c **emerald,** unsevered 1.00 40
First day cancel, Hodgenville, Ky. 75

Paul Revere Type of Postal Card, 1971
Luminescent Ink

1971, May 15
Precanceled with 3 printed brown lines.

UY22 PC36 6c +6c **brown,** unsevered 75 25
First day cancel, Boston, Mass. 75

John Hanson Type of Postal Card, 1972
Luminescent Ink

1972, Sept. 1
Precanceled with 3 printed blue lines.

UY23 PC41 6c +6c **blue,** unsevered 75 25
First day cancel, Baltimore, Md. 75

Samuel Adams Type of Postal Card, 1973
Luminescent Ink

1973, Dec. 16
Precanceled with 3 printed orange lines

UY24 PC42 8c +8c **orange,** unsevered 75 25
First day cancel, Boston, Mass. *(105,369)* 75

Thomson, Witherspoon, Rodney, Hale & Hancock Types of Postal Cards, 1975-78
Luminescent Ink

1975-78
Precanceled with 3 printed emerald lines

UY25 PC44 7c +7c **emerald,** unsevered, *Sept. 14, 1975* 75 40
First day cancel, Bryn Mawr, Pa. 75

Precanceled with 3 printed yellow brown lines

UY26 PC45 9c +9c **yellow brown,** unsevered, *Nov. 10, 1975* 75 25
First day cancel, Princeton, N.J. 75

Precanceled with 3 printed blue lines

UY27 PC46 9c +9c **blue,** unsevered, *July 1, 1976* 75 30
First day cancel, Dover, Del. 75

Precanceled with 3 printed green lines

UY28 PC48 9c +9c **green,** unsevered, *Oct. 14, 1977* 75 25
First day cancel, Coventry, Conn. 75

Inscribed "U.S. Domestic Rate"
Precanceled with 3 printed brown orange lines

UY29 PC50 (10c +10c) **brown orange,** unsevered, *May 19, 1978* 12.00 4.50
First day cancel, Quincy, Mass. 1.75

Precanceled with 3 printed brown orange lines

UY30 PC50 10c +10c **brown orange,** unsevered, *June 20, 1978* 75 25
First day cancel, Quincy, Mass. 75
a. One card "Domestic Rate," other "Postage 10¢" —

Eagle Type of 1981
Inscribed "U. S. Domestic Rate"
Luminescent Ink

1981, Mar. 15
Precanceled with 3 printed violet lines

UY31 PC63 (12c +12) **violet,** unsevered 75 25
First day cancel, Memphis, TN 1.00

Isaiah Thomas Type
Luminescent Ink

1981, May 5
Precanceled with 3 printed lines

UY32 PC64 12c +12c **light blue,** unsevered 75 15
First day cancel, Worcester, MA 1.00
a. Small die on one side 3.00 2.00

Morris Type of 1981
Inscribed "U.S. Domestic Rate"

1981
Precanceled with 3 printed lines

UY33 PC67 (13c +13c) **buff,** *Oct. 11,* unsevered 1.25 25
First day cancel, Memphis, TN 75

Inscribed "U.S. Postage 13¢"

UY34 PC67 13c +13c **buff,** *Nov. 10,* unsevered 75 15
First day cancel, Philadelphia, PA 85

Charles Carroll Type of 1985
Inscribed: U.S. Domestic Rate

1985
Precanceled with 3 printed lines

UY35 PC79 (14c +14c) **pale green,** *Feb. 1,* unsevered 1.00 25
First day cancel, New Carrollton, MD 90

Inscribed: USA

UY36 PC79 14c +14c **pale green,** *Mar. 6,* unsevered 75 18
First day cancel, Annapolis, MD 90

George Wythe Type of 1985

1985, June 20
Precanceled with 3 printed lines

UY37 PC81 14c +14c **bright apple green,** unsevered 75 18
First day cancel, Williamsburg, VA 90

Flag Type of 1987

1987, Sept. 1

UY38 PC90 14c +14c **black, blue & red,** unsevered 75 18
First day cancel, Baltimore, MD *(22,314)* 90

America the Beautiful Type

1988, July 11

UY39 PC93 15c +15c **multicolored,** unsevered 75 20
First day cancel, Buffalo, WY *(24,338)* 90

AIR POST POSTAL CARDS

Eagle in Flight — APC1

1949, Jan.10 **Typo.**

UXC1 APC1 4c **orange,** *buff* 40 35
Preprinted 30
First day cancel, Washington, D.C. *(236,620)* 75

Type of Air Post Stamp, 1954

1958, July 31

UXC2 AP31 5c **red,** *buff* 1.50 75
First day cancel, Wichita, Kans. *(156,474)* 75

Type of 1958 Redrawn

1960, June 18 **Lithographed (Offset)**

UXC3 AP31 5c **red,** *buff,* bicolored border 6.00 2.00
First day cancel, Minneapolis, Minn. *(228,500)* 2.75

Size of stamp of No. UXC3: 18½x21mm; on No. UXC2: 19x22mm. White cloud around eagle enlarged and finer detail of design on No. UXC3. Inscription "AIR MAIL-POSTAL CARD" has been omitted and blue and red border added on No. UXC3.

Bald Eagle — APC2

1963, Feb. 15 Precanceled with 3 printed red lines

UXC4 APC2 6c **red**, bicolored border 40 20
First day cancel, Maitland, Fla. *(216,203)* 75

Emblem of Commerce Department's Travel Service — APC3

Issued at the Sixth International Philatelic Exhibition (SIPEX), Washington, D.C., May 21-30.

1966, May 27 For International Use

UXC5 APC3 11c **blue & red** 50 *12.50*
First day cancel, Washington, D.C. *(272,813)* 75

Four photographs at left on address side show: Mt. Rainier, New York skyline, Indian on horseback and Miami Beach. The card has blue and red border.
See Nos. UXC8, UXC11.

Virgin Islands and Territorial Flag — APC4

50th anniv. of the purchase of the Virgin Islands.

Designed by Burt Pringle

1967, Mar. 31 Litho.

UXC6 APC4 6c **multicolored** 40 25
First day cancel, Charlotte Amalie, V. I. *(346,906)* 75
a. Red & yellow omitted —

Borah Peak, Lost River Range, Idaho, and Scout Emblem — APC5

Issued to commemorate the 12th Boy Scout World Jamboree, Farragut State Park, Idaho, Aug. 1-9.

Designed by Stevan Dohanos

1967, Aug. 4 Litho.

UXC7 APC5 6c **blue, yellow, black & red** 40 20
First day cancel, Farragut State Park, ID *(471,585)* 75
a. Blue omitted —
b. Blue & black omitted —
c. Red & yellow omitted

Travel Service Type of 1966

Issued in connection with the American Air Mail Society Convention, Detroit, Mich.

1967, Sept. 8 For International Use

UXC8 APC3 13c **blue & red** 1.25 *8.00*
First day cancel, Detroit, Mich. *(178,189)* 75

Stylized Eagle — APC6

Designed by Muriel R. Chamberlain

1968, Mar. 1 Precanceled with 3 printed red lines

UXC9 APC6 8c **blue & red** 60 35
First day cancel, New York, N.Y. *(179,923)* 75
a. Tagged, *Mar. 19, 1969* 1.75 2.50
Tagged, first day cancel 10.00

1971, May 15 Tagged

Precanceled with 3 printed blue lines

UXC10 APC6 9c **red & blue** 50 30
First day cancel, Kitty Hawk, N.C. 75

Travel Service Type of 1966

1971, June 10 Tagged

For International Use

UXC11 APC3 15c **blue & red** 1.50 *12.50*
First day cancel, New York, N.Y. 75

Grand Canyon APC7

Niagara Falls APC8

Tourism Year of the Americas 1972.

Designed by Melbourne Brindle

1972, June 29 Tagged Litho.

Size: 152½x108½mm

UXC12 APC7 9c **black**, *buff* (Statue of Liberty, Hawaii, Alaska, San Francisco on back) 45 1.00
First day cancel, any city 75

For International Use

UXC13 APC8 15c **black**, *buff* (Mt. Vernon, Washington, D.C., Lincoln, Liberty Bell on back) 55 *15.00*
First day cancel, any city 75
a. Address side blank 400.00

See note after No. UX63. Nos. UXC12-UXC13 have a luminescent panel at left of stamp which glows orange under ultraviolet light.

Stylized Eagle — APC9

Eagle Weather Vane — APC10

Designed by David G. Foote (11c) & Stevan Dohanos (18c)

1974, Jan. 4 Tagged Litho.

UXC14 APC9 11c **ultramarine & red** 70 40
First day cancel, State College, Pa. *(160,500)* 75

For International Use

UXC15 APC10 18c **multicolored** 85 *7.00*
First day cancel, Miami, Fla. *(132,114)* 75

All following issues are for international use

Angel Gabriel Weather Vane — APC11

Designed by Stevan Dohanos

1975, Dec. 17 Tagged Litho.

UXC16 APC11 21c **multicolored** 80 *7.50*
First day cancel, Kitty Hawk, N.C. 75
a. Blue & red omitted —

Nos. UXC14-UXC16 have a luminescent panel at left of stamp which glows orange under ultraviolet light.

Curtiss (JN4H) Jenny — APC12

Designed by Keith Ferris

1978, Sept. 16 Tagged Litho.

UXC17 APC12 21c **multicolored** 75 *6.00*
First day cancel, San Diego, Cal. *(174,886)* 75

No. UXC17 has luminescent panel at left of stamp which glows green under ultraviolet light.

Gymnast
APC13

22nd Olympic Games, Moscow, July 19-Aug. 3, 1980.

Designed by Robert M. Cunningham

1979, Dec. 1 **Tagged** **Litho.**

UXC18 APC13 21c **multicolored** 75 *10.00*
First day cancel, Fort Worth, Tex. 75

Pangborn, Herndon and Miss Veedol — APC14

First non-stop transpacific flight by Clyde Pangborn and Hugh Herndon, Jr., 50th anniv.

Designed by Ken Dallison

1981, Jan. 2 **Tagged** **Litho.**

UXC19 APC14 28c **multicolored** 85 *1.00*
First day cancel, Wenatchee, WA 75

Gliders
APC15

Designed by Robert E. Cunningham

1982, Mar. 5 **Tagged** **Litho.**

UXC20 APC15 28c **magenta, yellow, blue & black** 85 *1.00*
First day cancel, Houston, TX *(106,932)* 75

Speedskater — APC16

Designed by Robert Peak

1983, Dec. 29 **Litho.**

UXC21 APC16 28c **multicolored** 75 *1.00*
First day cancel, Milwaukee, WI 75

Martin M-130 China Clipper Seaplane — APC17

Designed by Chuck Hodgson

1985, Feb. 15 **Litho.**

UXC22 APC17 33c **multicolored** 90 *1.00*
First day cancel, San Francisco, CA 75

Chicago Skyline — APC18

AMERIPEX '86, Chicago, May 22-June 1.

Designed by Ray Ameijide

1986, Feb. 1 **Tagged** **Litho.**

UXC23 APC18 33c **multicolored** 66 *1.00*
First day cancel, Chicago, IL 75

No. UXC23 was sold at Sudposta '87 by the U.S.P.S. with a show cachet.

DC-3 — APC19

Designed by Chuck Hodgson

1988, May 14 **Litho.** **Tagged**

UXC24 APC19 36c **multicolored** 72 *1.00*
First day cancel, San Diego, CA 90

No. UXC24 was sold at SYDPEX '88 by the USPS with a cachet for Australia's bicentennial and SYDPEX '88.

First day cancellations applied to 167,575 of Nos. UXC24 and C118.

OFFICIAL POSTAL CARDS

PO1

1913, July

Size: 126x76mm

UZ1 PO1 1c **black** 325.00 150.00

All No. UZ1 cards have printed address and printed form on message side.

PO2

1983-85

UZ2 PO2 13c **blue,** *Jan. 12* 40 —
First day cancel, Washington, DC 75

UZ3 PO2 14c **blue,** *Feb. 26, 1985* 45 —
First day cancel, Washington, DC 80

PO3

Designed by Bradbury Thompson

1988, June 10 **Litho.**

UZ4 PO3 15c 30 —
First day cancel, Washington, DC *(133,498)* 85

REVENUE

The Commissioner of Internal Revenue advertised for bids for revenue stamps in August, 1862, and the contract was awarded to Butler & Carpenter of Philadelphia.

Nos. R1-R102 were used to pay taxes on documents and proprietary articles including playing cards. Until December 25, 1862, the law stated that a stamp could be used only for payment of the tax upon the particular instrument or article specified on its face. After that date, stamps, except the Proprietary, could be used indiscriminately.

Most stamps of the first issue appeared in the latter part of 1862 or early in 1863. The 5c and 10c Proprietary were issued in the fall of 1864, and the 6c Proprietary on April 13, 1871.

Plate numbers and imprints are usually found at the bottom of the plate on all denominations except 25c and $1 to $3.50. On these it is nearly always at the left of the plate. The imprint reads "Engraved by Butler & Carpenter, Philadelphia" or "Jos. R. Carpenter".

Plates were of various sizes: 1c and 2c, 210 subjects (14x15); 3c to 20c, 170 subjects (17x10); 25c to 30c, 102 subjects (17x6); 50c to 70c, 85 subjects (17x5); $1 to $1.90, 90 subjects (15x6); $2 to $10, 73 subjects (12x6); $15 to $50, 54 subjects (9x6); $200, 8 subjects (2x4). No. R132, one subject.

The paper varies, the first employed being thin, hard and brittle until September, 1869, from which time it acquired a softer texture and varied from medium to very thick. Early printings of some revenue stamps occur on paper which appears to have laid lines. Some are found on experimental silk paper, first employed about August, 1870.

In the first issue, canceling usually was done with pen and ink and all values quoted are for stamps canceled in that way. Handstamped cancellations as a rule sell for more than pen. Printed cancellations are scarce and command much higher prices. Herringbone, punched or other types of cancellation which break the surface of the paper adversely affect prices.

Some of the stamps were in use eight years and were printed several times. Many color variations occurred, particularly if unstable pigments were used and the color was intended to be purple or violet, such as the 4c Proprietary, 30c and $2.50 stamps. Before 1868 dull colors predominate on these and the early red stamps. In later printings of the 4c Proprietary, 30c and $2.50 stamps, red predominates in the mixture and on the dollar values of red is brighter. The early $1.90 stamp is dull purple, imperforate or perforated. In a later printing, perforated only, the purple is darker.

Where a stamp is known in a given form or variety but insufficient information is available on which to base a value, its existence is indicated by a dash.

Part perforate stamps are understood to be imperforate horizontally unless otherwise stated.

Part perforate stamps with an asterisk (*) exist imperforate horizontally or vertically.

Part perforate PAIRS should be imperforate between the stamps as well as imperforate at opposite ends. See illustration **Type A** under "Information For Collectors-Perforations."

All imperforate or part perforate stamps listed are known in pairs or larger multiples. Certain unlisted varieties of this nature exist as singles and specialists believe them genuine.

Values are for fine-very fine specimens. Imperforates and part-perforate singles in very fine or better condition and with large margins usually command substantial premiums.

Documentary revenue stamps were no longer required after December 31, 1967.

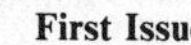

First Issue

George Washington
R1 R2

1862-71 **Engr.** ***Imperf. or Perf. 12***

				a. Imperf.	b. Part Perf.	Perforated Old Paper	d. Silk Paper
R1	R1	1c	**Express, red**	50.00	30.00*	1.00	67.50
			Pair	130.00	80.00	2.50	
			Block of four	400.00	425.00	10.00	
			Double transfer			—	
			Short transfer, No. 156	—	—	75.00	
R2	R1	1c	**Playing Cards, red**	800.00	400.00	100.00	
			Pair	*1,700.*	950.00	225.00	
			Block of four	—		675.00	
			Cracked plate			—	
R3	R1	1c	**Proprietary, red**	500.00	100.00	35	9.00
			Pair	*1,750.*	325.00	75	
			Block of four		800.00	2.00	
R4	R1	1c	**Telegraph, red**	275.00		8.00	
			Pair	700.00		20.00	
			Block of four			70.00	

Double transfer (T5)

				a. Imperf.	b. Part Perf.	Perforated Old Paper	d. Silk Paper
R5	R2	2c	**Bank Check, blue**	75	90*	6	
			Pair	15.00	4.00	25	

				a. Imperf.	b. Part Perf.	Perforated c. Old Paper	d. Silk Paper
			Block of four	75.00	40.00	1.50	
			Double transfer (T5)	55.00	60.00	45.00	
			Cracked plate		—	—	
			Double impression			—	
			e. Vertical pair, imperf. between			—	
R6	R2	2c	**Bank Check, orange**		75.00*	5	175.00
			Pair		—	20	
			Block of four			1.00	
			Double transfer (T5)			100.00	
			Vertical half used as 1c			—	
			e. 2c orange, *green*			325.00	

Double transfer (T7)

				a. Imperf.	b. Part Perf.	Perforated c. Old Paper	d. Silk Paper
R7	R2	2c	**Certificate, blue**	10.00		21.00	
			Pair	30.00		50.00	
			Block of four	125.00		150.00	
			Double transfer (T7)	160.00		175.00	
			Cracked plate			30.00	
R8	R2	2c	**Certificate, orange**			20.00	
			Pair			125.00	
			Block of four			—	
			Double transfer (T7)			275.00	
R9	R2	2c	**Express, blue**	10.00	12.00*	25	
			Pair	30.00	30.00	90	
			Block of four	90.00	125.00	3.00	
			Double transfer	60.00		17.50	
			Cracked plate			—	
R10	R2	2c	**Express, orange**			6.00	30.00
			Pair			14.00	
			Block of four			35.00	
			Double transfer			21.00	
R11	R2	2c	**Playing Cards, blue**		115.00	3.00	
			Pair		400.00	10.00	
			Block of four			40.00	
			Cracked plate			—	
R12	R2	2c	**Playing Cards, orange**			25.00	
			Pair			—	

Double transfer (T13)

Double transfer (T13a)

				a. Imperf.	b. Part Perf.	c. Old Paper	d. Silk Paper
R13	R2	2c	**Proprietary, blue**		100.00	35	17.50
			Pair		240.00	80	
			Block of four		750.00	5.00	
			Double transfer (T13)			70.00	
			Complete double transfer (T13a)			100.00	
			Cracked plate			25.00	
			Horizontal half used as 1c			—	
			e. 2c ultramarine			150.00	
			Pair			325.00	
			Block of four			875.00	
			Double transfer			—	
R14	R2	2c	**Proprietary, orange**			30.00	
			Pair			—	
			Block of four			—	
			Double transfer (T13)			110.00	
			Complete double transfer (T13a)			350.00	

Double transfer (T15)

Double transfer (T15a)

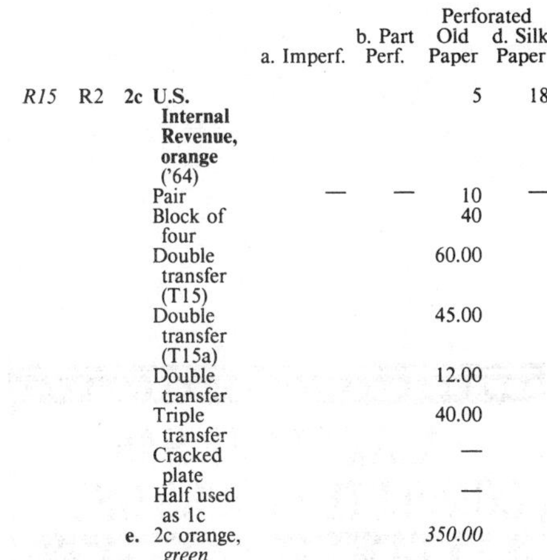

				a. Imperf.	b. Part Perf.	Perforated c. Old Paper	d. Silk Paper
R15	R2	2c	**U.S. Internal Revenue, orange** ('64)			5	18
			Pair	—	—	10	—
			Block of four			40	
			Double transfer (T15)			60.00	
			Double transfer (T15a)			45.00	
			Double transfer			12.00	
			Triple transfer			40.00	
			Cracked plate			—	
			Half used as 1c			—	
			e. 2c orange, *green*			*350.00*	

R3

				a. Imperf.	b. Part Perf.	c. Old Paper	d. Silk Paper
R16	R3	3c	**Foreign Exchange, green**		150.00	2.50	21.00
			Pair		—	5.75	
			Block of four			45.00	
			Double transfer			—	
R17	R3	3c	**Playing Cards, green** ('63)	*7,000.*		100.00	
			Pair	*17,000.*		275.00	
			Block of four			*700.00*	

No.	Design	Denom.	Description	a. Imperf.	b. Part Perf.	c. Old Paper	d. Silk Paper
R18	R3	3c	**Proprietary, green**		190.00	1.75	17.50
			Pair		*450.00*	4.50	—
			Block of four		—	15.00	
			Double transfer			8.00	
			Double impression			—	
		e.	Printed on both sides			—	
R19	R3	3c	**Telegraph, green**	45.00	16.00	2.25	
			Pair	160.00	35.00	6.00	
			Block of four	600.00	150.00	50.00	
R20	R3	4c	**Inland Exchange, brown ('63)**			1.50	20.00
			Pair			4.50	
			Block of four			20.00	
			Double transfer at top			4.00	
R21	R3	4c	**Playing Cards, slate ('63)**			350.00	
			Pair			*875.00*	
			Block of four			*2,000.*	
R22	R3	4c	**Proprietary, purple**		200.00	2.50	35.00
			Pair		450.00	6.00	
			Block of four		—	25.00	
			Double transfer at top			7.50	
			Double transfer at bottom			11.00	

There are shade and color variations of Nos. R21-R22. See foreword of Revenue Stamps section.

No.	Design	Denom.	Description	a. Imperf.	b. Part Perf.	Perforated Old Paper	d. Silk Paper
R23	R3	5c	**Agreement, red**			20	1.00
			Pair			40	2.50
			Block of four			1.25	12.50
			Double transfer in numerals			25.00	
R24	R3	5c	**Certificate, red**	2.00	8.00	10	30
			Pair	25.00	60.00	20	90
			Block of four	125.00	200.00	60	6.00
			Double transfer in upper label			10.00	
			Double transfer throughout			70.00	
			Triple transfer (No. 121)			35.00	
			Impression of No. R3 on back			—	
R25	R3	5c	**Express, red**	3.50	4.00*	25	
			Pair	12.00	40.00	60	
			Block of four	70.00	100.00	2.00	
			Double transfer			5.00	
R26	R3	5c	**Foreign Exchange, red**		—	25	100.00
			Pair		—	75	
			Block of four			10.00	
			Double transfer at top			—	
			Double transfer at bottom			—	
R27	R3	5c	**Inland Exchange, red**	3.50	3.00	10	9.00
			Pair	20.00	15.00	20	
			Block of four	50.00	50.00	1.25	
			Dbl. transfer at top	60.00	40.00	25.00	
			Cracked plate	60.00	60.00	30.00	
R28	R3	5c	**Playing Cards, red ('63)**			12.00	
			Pair			26.00	
			Block of four			60.00	

No.	Design	Denom.	Description	a. Imperf.	b. Part Perf.	Perforated Old Paper	d. Silk Paper
			Double impression			250.00	
R29	R3	5c	**Proprietary, red ('64)**			16.00	47.50
			Pair			40.00	
			Block of four			120.00	
R30	R3	6c	**Inland Exchange, orange ('63)**			90	30.00
			Pair			10.00	
			Block of four			60.00	
R31	R3	6c	**Proprietary, orange ('71)**			*1,250.*	

Nearly all copies of No. R31 are faulty and poorly centered. The Catalogue value is for a fine centered copy with minor faults which do not detract from its appearance.

No.	Design	Denom.	Description	a. Imperf.	b. Part Perf.	Perforated Old Paper	d. Silk Paper
R32	R3	10c	**Bill of Lading, blue**	40.00	150.00	85	
			Pair	125.00	500.00	2.00	
			Block of four	325.00		7.00	
			Double transfer (Nos. 33 & 143)			—	
			Half used as 5c			*200.00*	
R33	R3	10c	**Certificate, blue**	90.00	100.00	20	3.00
			Pair	225.00	250.00	45	
			Block of four	*1,000.*	—	1.50	
			Double transfer			7.00	
			Cracked plate			15.00	
			Half used as 5c			*200.00*	
R34	R3	10c	**Contract, blue**		100.00	20	2.00
			Pair		275.00	50	5.00
			Block of four		—	2.00	50.00
			Complete double transfer			70.00	
			Vertical half used as 5c			*200.00*	
		e.	10c ultramarine		250.00		
		f.	10c ultramarine			50	
			Pair			1.25	
			Block of four			15.00	
R35	R3	10c	**Foreign Exchange, blue**			3.00	
			Pair			7.00	
			Block of four			35.00	
		e.	10c ultramarine			6.50	
			Pair			15.00	
			Block of four			35.00	
R36	R3	10c	**Inland Exchange, blue**	90.00	3.00*	15	18.00
			Pair	250.00	10.00	35	—
			Block of four	*750.00*	50.00	1.50	—
			Half used as 5c			*200.00*	
R37	R3	10c	**Power of Attorney, blue**	300.00	17.00	25	
			Pair	650.00	65.00	60	
			Block of four	*1,800.*	200.00	3.50	
			Half used as 5c			*100.00*	
R38	R3	10c	**Proprietary, blue ('64)**			13.00	
			Pair			30.00	
			Block of four			75.00	
R39	R3	15c	**Foreign Exchange, brown ('63)**			12.00	
			Pair			45.00	
			Block of four			225.00	
			Double impression			*500.00*	
R40	R3	15c	**Inland Exchange, brown**	25.00	10.00	1.00	
			Pair	95.00	30.00	2.25	

No.	Design	Denom.	Description	a. Imperf.	b. Part Perf.	Perforated: Old Paper	d. Silk Paper
			Block of four	325.00	150.00	8.00	
			Double transfer			5.00	
			Cracked plate	40.00		—	
			Double impression		—	*550.00*	
R41	R3	20c	**Foreign Exchange, red**	40.00		30.00	
			Pair	125.00		70.00	
			Block of four	500.00		200.00	
R42	R3	20c	**Inland Exchange, red**	12.00	16.00	30	—
			Pair	50.00	45.00	70	
			Block of four	160.00	150.00	12.50	
			Half used as 10c			*200.00*	
R43	R4	25c	**Bond, red**	80.00	5.00	1.75	
			Pair	500.00	35.00	4.50	
			Block of four		200.00	40.00	
R44	R4	25c	**Certificate, red**	5.00	5.00*	10	2.50
			Pair	35.00	30.00	20	—
			Block of four	300.00	150.00	2.50	—
			Double transfer, top or bottom			2.00	
			Triple transfer			—	
		e.	Printed on both sides			—	
		f.	Impression of No. R48 on back			—	
R45	R4	25c	**Entry of Goods, red**	15.00	30.00*	40	10.00
			Pair	55.00	—	35.00	
			Block of four	300.00		50.00	
			Top frame line double	60.00	75.00	10.00	
R46	R4	25c	**Insurance, red**	8.00	9.00	20	4.00
			Pair	35.00	20.00	50	10.00
			Block of four	*500.00*	175.00	5.00	
			Double impression			—	
			Cracked plate			15.00	
R47	R4	25c	**Life Insurance, red**	30.00	100.00	5.00	
			Pair	90.00	525.00	50.00	
			Block of four	—		—	
R48	R4	25c	**Power of Attorney, red**	5.00	15.00	25	
			Pair	40.00	55.00	60	
			Block of four	300.00	200.00	6.00	
			Double transfer			1.00	
			Bottom frame line double			5.00	
R49	R4	25c	**Protest, red**	20.00	140.00	6.00	
			Pair	80.00	350.00	25.00	
			Block of four	350.00		100.00	
R50	R4	25c	**Warehouse Receipt, red**	35.00	125.00	21.00	
			Pair	100.00	350.00	65.00	
			Block of four	*750.00*		200.00	
R51	R4	30c	**Foreign Exchange, lilac**	60.00	400.00	35.00	
			Pair	250.00	1,000.	150.00	
			Block of four	—		—	
			Double transfer			70.00	
			Top frame line double			—	
R52	R4	30c	**Inland Exchange, lilac**	40.00	40.00	2.25	
			Pair	155.00	150.00	25.00	
			Block of four	—	—	100.00	
			Double transfer			—	

There are shade and color variations of Nos. R51-R52. See foreword of "Revenues" section.

No.	Design	Denom.	Description	a. Imperf.	b. Part Perf.	Perforated: Old Paper	d. Silk Paper
R53	R4	40c	**Inland Exchange, brown**	425.00	3.50	2.25	
			Pair	—	15.00	5.50	
			Block of four		150.00	100.00	
			Double transfer		35.00	30.00	
R54	R5	50c	**Conveyance, blue**	10.00	1.00	10	2.75
			Pair	50.00	30.00	25	6.00
			Block of four	250.00	100.00	2.50	
			Double transfer			6.00	
			Cracked plate			15.00	

R4

R5

No.	Type	Denom.	Description	a. Imperf.	b. Part Perf.	c. Old Paper	d. Silk Paper
		e.	50c ultramarine			20	
			Pair			1.00	
			Block of four			10.00	
		f.	50c ultramarine			—	
R55	R5	**50c**	**Entry of Goods, blue**		10.00	20	15.00
			Pair		60.00	50	45.00
			Block of four		—	20.00	
			Double transfer			5.00	
			Cracked plate			20.00	
R56	R5	**50c**	**Foreign Exchange, blue**	35.00	30.00	4.50	
			Pair	85.00	80.00	30.00	
			Block of four			100.00	
			Double impression			—	
			Double transfer at left			10.00	
			Half used as 25c			*200.00*	
R57	R5	**50c**	**Lease, blue**	20.00	50.00	6.50	
			Pair	80.00	130.00	100.00	
			Block of four	*650.00*	400.00	225.00	

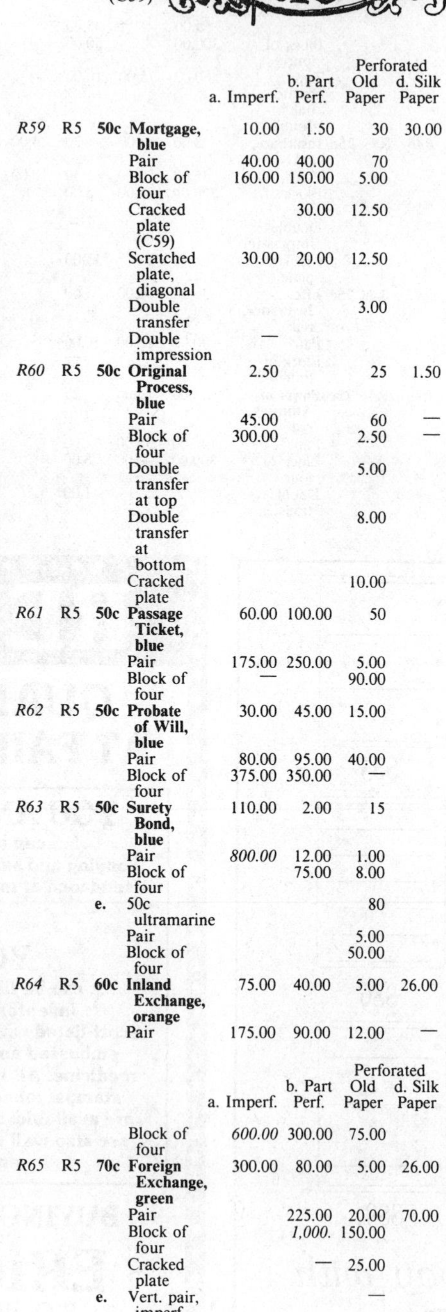

No.	Type	Denom.	Description	a. Imperf.	b. Part Perf.	c. Old Paper	d. Silk Paper
R58	R5	**50c**	**Life Insurance, blue**	25.00	50.00	60	
			Pair	80.00		5.00	
			Block of four	400.00		30.00	
			Double transfer	25.00		10.00	
			Double impression			—	

Cracked Plate (C59)

No.	Type	Denom.	Description	a. Imperf.	b. Part Perf.	Perforated c. Old Paper	d. Silk Paper
R59	R5	**50c**	**Mortgage, blue**	10.00	1.50	30	30.00
			Pair	40.00	40.00	70	
			Block of four	160.00	150.00	5.00	
			Cracked plate (C59)		30.00	12.50	
			Scratched plate, diagonal	30.00	20.00	12.50	
			Double transfer			3.00	
			Double impression	—			
R60	R5	**50c**	**Original Process, blue**	2.50		25	1.50
			Pair	45.00		60	—
			Block of four	300.00		2.50	—
			Double transfer at top			5.00	
			Double transfer at bottom			8.00	
			Cracked plate			10.00	
R61	R5	**50c**	**Passage Ticket, blue**	60.00	100.00	50	
			Pair	175.00	250.00	5.00	
			Block of four		—	90.00	
R62	R5	**50c**	**Probate of Will, blue**	30.00	45.00	15.00	
			Pair	80.00	95.00	40.00	
			Block of four	375.00	350.00	—	
R63	R5	**50c**	**Surety Bond, blue**	110.00	2.00	15	
			Pair	*800.00*	12.00	1.00	
			Block of four		75.00	8.00	
		e.	50c ultramarine			80	
			Pair			5.00	
			Block of four			50.00	
R64	R5	**60c**	**Inland Exchange, orange**	75.00	40.00	5.00	26.00
			Pair	175.00	90.00	12.00	—

No.	Type	Denom.	Description	a. Imperf.	b. Part Perf.	Perforated c. Old Paper	d. Silk Paper
			Block of four	*600.00*	300.00	75.00	
R65	R5	**70c**	**Foreign Exchange, green**	300.00	80.00	5.00	26.00
			Pair		225.00	20.00	70.00
			Block of four		*1,000.*	150.00	
			Cracked plate		—	25.00	
		e.	Vert. pair, imperf. between			—	

R6

R7

No.	Type	Denom.	Description	a. Imperf.	b. Part Perf.	c. Old Paper	d. Silk Paper
R66	R6	**$1**	**Conveyance, red**	10.00	275.00	2.00	35.00
			Pair	40.00	*1,250.*	6.00	
			Block of four	250.00		20.00	
			Double transfer	25.00		6.00	
			Right frame line double	70.00		15.00	
			Top frame line double			12.00	
R67	R6	**$1**	**Entry of Goods, red**	25.00		1.25	27.50
			Pair	80.00		4.00	
			Block of four	275.00		40.00	
R68	R6	**$1**	**Foreign Exchange, red**	45.00		50	16.00
			Pair	120.00		1.25	
			Block of four	—		9.00	
			Double transfer			4.50	
			Left frame line double	125.00		17.50	
			Diagonal half used as 50c				*200.00*
R69	R6	**$1**	**Inland Exchange, red**	10.00	225.00*	35	2.00
			Pair	45.00	*1,500.*	1.50	6.50
			Block of four	425.00	—	8.00	20.00
			Double transfer at bottom			3.50	
			Double transfer of top shields	50.00		20.00	
R70	R6	**$1**	**Lease, red**	30.00		1.50	
			Pair	80.00		5.00	
			Block of four	350.00		40.00	
			Double transfer at bottom	40.00		7.50	
			Cracked plate			25.00	
R71	R6	**$1**	**Life Insurance, red**	140.00		4.50	—
			Pair	300.00		12.00	
			Block of four	*650.00*		45.00	
			Right frame line double	250.00		17.50	

No.	Type	Denom.	Description	a. Imperf.	b. Part Perf.	Perforated Old Paper	d. Silk Paper
R72	R6	**$1**	**Manifest, red**	50.00		21.00	
			Pair	120.00		50.00	
			Block of four	275.00		120.00	
R73	R6	**$1**	**Mortgage, red**	15.00		100.00	
			Pair	50.00		225.00	
			Block of four	250.00		500.00	
			Double transfer at left	—		150.00	
			Bottom frame line double	60.00		250.00	
R74	R6	**$1**	**Passage Ticket, red**	150.00		125.00	
			Pair	325.00		275.00	
			Block of four	700.00		700.00	
R75	R6	**$1**	**Power of Attorney, red**	60.00		1.50	
			Pair	140.00		4.00	
			Block of four	325.00		18.00	
			Double transfer			7.50	
			Recut			10.00	
R76	R6	**$1**	**Probate of Will, red**	55.00		27.50	
			Pair	140.00		75.00	
			Block of four	*550.00*		200.00	
			Right frame line double	125.00		60.00	
R77	R7	**$1.30**	**Foreign Exchange, orange** ('63)	*2,000.*		45.00	
			Pair			125.00	
			Block of four			—	

Double transfer (T78)

No.	Type	Denom.	Description	a. Imperf.	b. Part Perf.	Perforated Old Paper	d. Silk Paper
R78	R7	**$1.50**	**Inland Exchange, blue**	20.00		2.75	
			Pair	80.00		40.00	
			Block of four	250.00		225.00	
			Double transfer (T78)			4.00	
R79	R7	**$1.60**	**Foreign Exchange, green** ('63)	600.00		85.00	
			Pair	*3,000.*		—	
R80	R7	**$1.90**	**Foreign Exchange, purple** ('63)	*1,900.*		60.00	125.00
			Pair	—		130.00	
			Block of four			350.00	

There are many shade and color variations of No. R80. See foreword of "Revenues" section.

R8

No.	Type	Denom.	Description	a. Imperf.	b. Part Perf.	Perforated Old Paper	d. Silk Paper
R81	R8	**$2**	**Conveyance, red**	85.00	700.00	1.50	15.00
			Pair	200.00	—	5.00	
			Block of four	600.00		35.00	
			Cracked plate			—	
			Half used as $1			—	
R82	R8	**$2**	**Mortgage, red**	75.00		2.50	35.00
			Pair	180.00		6.00	
			Block of four	450.00		35.00	
			Double transfer			10.00	
			Half used as $1			—	
R83	R8	**$2**	**Probate of Will, red** ('63)	*2,100.*		45.00	
			Pair	*4,400.*		100.00	
			Block of four			225.00	
			Double transfer			60.00	
R84	R8	**$2.50**	**Inland Exchange, purple** ('63)	850.00		3.00	12.50
			Pair	—		8.00	35.00
			Block of four			75.00	350.00
			Double impression			—	

There are many shade and color variations of Nos. R84 and R84d. See foreword of "Revenues" section.

No.	Type	Denom.	Description	a. Imperf.	b. Part Perf.	Perforated Old Paper	d. Silk Paper
R85	R8	**$3**	**Charter Party, green**	90.00		3.00	42.50
			Pair	260.00		40.00	95.00
			Block of four	—		150.00	
			Double transfer at top			—	
			Double transfer at bottom			9.00	
			Half used as $1.50			—	
		e.	Printed on both sides			*2,000.*	
		g.	Impression of No. RS208 on back			*4,000.*	
R86	R8	**$3**	**Manifest, green**	85.00		20.00	
			Pair	210.00		50.00	
			Block of four	*1,000.*		150.00	
			Double transfer			30.00	
R87	R8	**$3.50**	**Inland Exchange, blue** ('63)	900.00		37.50	
			Pair	*2,500.*		120.00	
			Block of four			350.00	

R9

R10

No.	Type	Denom.	Description	a. Imperf.	b. Part Perf.	Perforated Old Paper	d. Silk Paper
R88	R9	**$5**	**Charter Party, red**	225.00		4.50	37.50
			Pair	500.00		50.00	
			Block of four	—		150.00	
			Right frame line double	375.00		50.00	
			Top frame line double	350.00		50.00	
R89	R9	**$5**	**Conveyance, red**	30.00		3.50	27.50
			Pair	95.00		10.00	
			Block of four	*500.00*		25.00	
R90	R9	**$5**	**Manifest, red**	90.00		70.00	
			Pair	225.00		200.00	
			Block of four	*1,000.*		500.00	
			Left frame line double	135.00		135.00	
R91	R9	**$5**	**Mortgage, red**	80.00		14.00	
			Pair	400.00		60.00	
			Block of four	—		—	
R92	R9	**$5**	**Probate of Will, red**	375.00		16.00	
			Pair	800.00		70.00	
			Block of four	*1,750.*		300.00	
R93	R9	**$10**	**Charter Party, green**	400.00		20.00	
			Pair	*1,000.*		60.00	
			Block of four	—		300.00	
			Double transfer			60.00	
R94	R9	**$10**	**Conveyance, green**	70.00		50.00	
			Pair	160.00		120.00	
			Block of four	400.00		600.00	
			Double transfer at top	100.00		80.00	
			Right frame line double	135.00			
R95	R9	**$10**	**Mortgage, green**	300.00		20.00	
			Pair	700.00		80.00	
			Block of four	—		—	
			Top frame line double	300.00		40.00	
R96	R9	**$10**	**Probate of Will, green**	900.00		20.00	
			Pair	—		60.00	
			Block of four			250.00	
			Double transfer at top			45.00	
R97	R10	**$15**	**Mortgage, blue**	900.00		100.00	
			Pair	2,100.		275.00	
			Block of four	4,500.		2,500.	

				a. Imperf.	b. Part Perf.	Perforated Old Paper	d. Silk Paper
		e.	$15 ultra marine			165.00	
			Pair			400.00	
			Block of four			—	
			Milky blue			150.00	
R98	R10	**$20**	**Conveyance, orange**	50.00		30.00	50.00
			Pair	130.00		75.00	130.00
			Block of four	300.00		225.00	
R99	R10	**$20**	**Probate of Will, orange**	900.00		850.00	
			Pair	1,900.		1,750.	
			Block of four	4,250.		3,750.	
R100	R10	**$25**	**Mortgage, red** ('63)	750.00		80.00	125.00
			Pair	1,600.		190.00	
			Block of four	—		*900.00*	
		e.	Horiz. pair, imperf. between			*1,100.*	
R101	R10	**$50**	**U.S. Internal Revenue, green** ('63)	150.00		65.00	
			Pair	325.00		190.00	
			Block of four	800.00		450.00	
			Cracked plate			—	

R11

				a. Imperf.	b. Part Perf.	Perforated Old Paper	d. Silk Paper
R102	R11	**$200**	**U.S. Internal Revenue, green & red** ('64)	1,000.		550.00	
			Pair	2,250.		1,200.	
			Block of four	5,500.		2,750.	

DOCUMENTARY STAMPS
Second Issue

After release of the First Issue revenue stamps, the Bureau of Internal Revenue received many reports of fraudulent cleaning and re-use. The Bureau ordered a Second Issue with new designs and colors, using a patented "chameleon" paper which is usually violet or pinkish, with silk fibers.

While designs are different from those of the first issue, stamp sizes and make up of the plates are the same as for corresponding denominations.

George Washington

R12 R12a

Engraved and printed by Jos. R. Carpenter, Philadelphia.

Various Frames and Numeral Arrangements

1871 ***Perf. 12***

				Single	Pair	Block of Four
R103	R12	1c	blue & black	25.00	60.00	150.00
		a.	Inverted center	*1,300.*		
R104	R12	2c	blue & black	1.00	3.00	15.00
		a.	Inverted center	*4,000.*		
R105	R12a	3c	blue & black	12.00	27.50	60.00
R106	R12a	4c	blue & black	45.00	110.00	
			Horiz. or vert. half used as 2c	—		
R107	R12a	5c	blue & black	1.00	2.50	10.00
		a.	Inverted center	*1,850.*		
R108	R12a	6c	blue & black	65.00	150.00	450.00
R109	R12a	10c	blue & black	75	2.00	6.00
			Double impression of medallion	—		
			Half used as 5c	—		
		a.	Inverted center	*1,500.*		
R110	R12a	15c	blue & black	20.00	42.50	95.00
R111	R12a	20c	blue & black	4.00	9.00	35.00
		a.	Inverted center	*7,500.*		

R13

R13a

				Single	Pair	Block of Four
R112	R13	25c	blue & black	50	1.50	7.50
			Double transfer, position 57	15.00		
		a.	Inverted center	*9,500.*		
		b.	Sewing machine perf.	90.00	250.00	750.00
		c.	Perf. 8	250.00		
R113	R13	30c	blue & black	45.00	100.00	275.00
R114	R13	40c	blue & black	27.50	90.00	
R115	R13a	50c	blue & black	50	1.25	6.50
			Double transfer	15.00		
		a.	Sewing machine perf.	75.00	200.00	*1,200.*
		b.	Inverted center	650.00	*1,800.*	
			Inverted center, punch cancellation	200.00	500.00	
R116	R13a	60c	blue & black	60.00	160.00	
			Double transfer, design of 70c	125.00		
R117	R13a	70c	blue & black	25.00	80.00	
		a.	Inverted center	*3,000.*		

R13b

R13c

				Single	Pair	Block of Four
R118	R13b	$1	blue & black	2.50	6.00	20.00
		a.	Inverted center	*4,250.*		
			Inverted center, punch cancellation	*750.00*		
R119	R13b	$1.30	blue & black	225.00	500.00	
R120	R13b	$1.50	blue & black	10.00	30.00	—
		a.	Sewing machine perf.	350.00	—	
R121	R13b	$1.60	blue & black	325.00	750.00	
R122	R13b	$1.90	blue & black	125.00	300.00	—
R123	R13c	$2	blue & black	10.00	25.00	100.00
			Double transfer	15.00		
R124	R13c	$2.50	blue & black	18.00	45.00	525.00
R125	R13c	$3	blue & black	30.00	80.00	—
			Double transfer	—		
R126	R13c	$3.50	blue & black	110.00	250.00	

R13d

R13e

				Single	Pair	Block of Four
R127	R13d	$5	blue & black	15.00	40.00	150.00
		a.	Inverted center	*2,150.*		
			Inverted center, punch cancel	*600.00*		
R128	R13d	$10	blue & black	80.00	225.00	—
R129	R13e	$20	blue & black	275.00	650.00	—
R130	R13e	$25	blue & black	275.00	650.00	—
R131	R13e	$50	blue & black	325.00	700.00	—

R13f

				Single	Pair	Block of Four
R132	R13f	$200	blue, black & red	*4,750.*		

R13g

				Single
R133	R13g	$500	blk., green & red	*12,500.*

Inverted Centers: Fraudulently produced inverted centers exist, some excellently made.

Third Issue

Confusion resulting from the fact that all denominations of the Second Issue were uniform in color, caused the ordering of a new printing with values in distinctive colors.
Plates used were those of the preceding issue.

Engraved and printed by Jos. R. Carpenter, Philadelphia.
Various Frames and Numeral Arrangements.
Violet "Chameleon" Paper with Silk Fibers.

1871-72 *Perf. 12*

				Single	Pair	Block of Four
R134	R12	1c	claret & black ('72)	20.00	50.00	175.00
R135	R12	2c	orange & black	5	12	1.00
			Double transfer	—		
			Double impression of frame	—		
			Frame printed on both sides	*1,000.*		
			Double impression of head	*150.00*		
	a.		2c vermilion & black (error)	*375.00*		
	b.		Inverted center	350.00	*1,000.*	—
R136	R12a	4c	brown & black ('72)	27.50	70.00	
R137	R12a	5c	orange & black	20	40	1.00
	a.		Inverted center	*3,000.*		
R138	R12a	6c	orange & black ('72)	30.00	70.00	150.00
R139	R12a	15c	brown & black ('72)	7.50	20.00	110.00
	a.		Inverted center	*8,000.*		
R140	R13	30c	orange & black ('72)	11.00	30.00	—
			Double transfer	—		
	a.		Inverted center	*1,100.*		
R141	R13	40c	brown & black ('72)	20.00	55.00	125.00
R142	R13	60c	orange & black ('72)	45.00	100.00	225.00
			Double transfer, design of 70c	100.00		
R143	R13	70c	green & black ('72)	30.00	75.00	—
R144	R13b	$1	green & black ('72)	1.10	3.00	25.00
	a.		Inverted center	*6,000.*		
R145	R13c	$2	vermilion & black ('72)	18.00	40.00	140.00
			Double transfer	25.00		
R146	R13c	$2.50	claret & black ('72)	30.00	70.00	175.00
	a.		Inverted center	*12,500.*		
R147	R13c	$3	green & black ('72)	30.00	80.00	250.00
			Double transfer	—		
R148	R13d	$5	vermilion & black ('72)	17.50	45.00	125.00
R149	R13d	$10	green & black ('72)	60.00	150.00	700.00
R150	R13e	$20	orange & black ('72)	375.00	800.00	—
	a.		$20 vermilion & black (error)	525.00		

(See note on Inverted Centers after No. R133.)

1874 *Perf. 12*

				Single	Pair	Block of Four
R151	R12	2c	orange & black, *green*	6	12	60
	a.		Inverted center	325.00		

Liberty — R14

1875-78

				Silk Paper a. Perf.	Wmkd. USIR 191R b. Perf.	c. Rouletted 6
R152	R14	2c	blue, *blue*	6	6	32.50
			Pair	75	75	150.00
			Block of four	*2.50*	*2.50*	
			Double transfer	5.00	5.00	
	d.		Vert. pair, imperf. horiz.	100.00		
	e.		Imperf., pair		*250.00*	

The watermarked paper came into use in 1878.

Postage Stamps of 1895-98 Overprinted:

I. R. (a) I. R. (b)

Overprint "a" exists in two or possibly more settings, with upright rectangular periods, as illustrated, or with square periods, taller thicker letters and a slight upturn to the right leg of the "R.". The latter are from the right row of the plate. Overprint "b" has 4 stamps with small period in each sheet of 100.

1898 **Wmk. 191** *Perf. 12*

				Unused	Used
R153	A87	1c	green, red overprint *(a)*	1.25	1.25
			Block of four	7.50	7.50
			Margin strip of 3, Impt. & P #	17.50	
			Margin block of 6, Impt. & P #	50.00	
R154	A87	1c	green, red overprint *(b)*	12	10
			Block of four	50	45
			Margin strip of 3, Impt. & P #	9.00	
			Margin block of 6, Impt. & P #	40.00	
	a.		Overprint inverted	10.00	7.50
	a.		Block of four	50.00	—
	a.		Margin strip of 3, Impt. & P #	55.00	
	a.		Margin block of 6, Impt. & P #	140.00	
	b.		Overprint on back instead of face, inverted	—	
	c.		Pair, one without overprint	—	
R155	A88	2c	carmine, blue overprint *(b)*	15	6
			Block of four	65	30
			Margin strip of 3, Impt. & P #	8.50	
			Margin block of 6, Impt. & P #	30.00	
	a.		Overprint inverted	1.25	1.00
	a.		Block of four	6.00	5.00
	b.		Pair, one without overprint	*400.00*	
	c.		Overprint on back instead of face, inverted	*400.00*	

Handstamped Type "b" in Magenta

R156	*A93*	*8c*	*violet brown*	*2,000.*
R157	*A94*	*10c*	*dark green*	*2,250.*
R158	*A95*	*15c*	*dark blue*	*2,750.*

Nos. R156-R158 were emergency provisionals, privately prepared, not officially issued.

Privately Prepared Provisionals

No. 285 Overprinted in Red **I. R. L. H. C.**

1898 **Wmk. 191** *Perf. 12*

R158A	A100	1c	dark yellow green	—	*3,500.*

Same Overprinted "I.R./P.I.D. & Son" in Red

R158B	A100	1c	dark yellow green	—	*6,000.*

Nos. R158A-R158B were overprinted with federal government permission by the Purvis Printing Co. upon order of Capt. L. H. Chapman of the Chapman Steamboat Line. Both the Chapman Line and P. I. Daprix & Son operated freight-carrying steamboats on the Erie Canal. The Chapman Line touched at Syracuse, Utica, Little Falls and Fort Plain; the Daprix boat ran between Utica and Rome. Overprintings of 250 of each stamp were made.

Dr. Kilmer & Co. provisional overprints are listed under "Private Die Medicine Stamps," Nos. RS307-RS315.

Newspaper Stamp No. PR121 Surcharged in Red: **INT. REV. $5. DOCUMENTARY.**

1898 *Perf. 12*

				Unused	Used
R159	N18	$5	dark blue, surcharge reading down	150.00	125.00
			Block of four	650.00	550.00
			Margin strip of 3, Impt. & P #	—	
	a.		"OCUMENTARY"	300.00	200.00
R160	N18	$5	dark blue, surcharge reading up	80.00	55.00
			Block of four	350.00	—
			Margin strip of 3, Impt. & P #	—	
	a.		"OCUMENTARY"	300.00	200.00

Battleship – R15

There are two styles of rouletting for the proprietary and documentary stamps of the 1898 issue, an ordinary rouletting 5½ and one by which small rectangles of the paper are cut out, usually called hyphen-hole perforation 7. Several stamps are known with an apparent roulette 14 caused by slippage of a hyphen-hole 7 rouletting wheel.

1898 **Wmk. 191R** ***Rouletted 5½, 7***

				Rouletted 5½ Unused	Used	p. Hyphen Hole Perf. 7 Unused	Used
R161	R15	½c	orange	1.50	5.00		
			Block of four	7.00	35.00		
R162	R15	½c	dark gray	15	10		
			Block of four	75	50		
			Double transfer		—		
		a.	Vert. pair, imperf. horiz.	40.00			
R163	R15	1c	pale blue	8	5	25	15
			Block of four	40	25	2.50	1.25
			Double transfer	—			
		a.	Vert. pair, imperf. horiz.	7.50			
R164	R15	2c	carmine rose	10	5	30	10
			Block of four	45	25	2.50	50
			Double transfer	1.00	25		
		a.	Vert. pair, imperf. horiz.	30.00			
		b.	Imperf., pair	125.00			
		c.	Horiz. pair, imperf. vert.	—			
R165	R15	3c	dark blue	70	12	3.00	30
			Block of four	3.50	75	15.00	1.50
			Double transfer				
R166	R15	4c	pale rose	25	10	60	25
			Block of four	1.25	50	3.00	1.50
		a.	Vert. pair, imperf. horiz.	75.00			
R167	R15	5c	lilac	15	6	40	15
			Block of four	75	30	2.00	1.00
		a.	Pair, imperf. horiz. or vert.	125.00	75.00		
R168	R15	10c	dark brown	20	6	40	15
			Block of four	1.00	30	2.00	75
		a.	Vert. pair, imperf. horiz.	20.00	20.00		
		b.	Horiz. pair, imperf. vert.	—			
R169	R15	25c	purple brown	20	10	50	20
			Block of four	1.00	50	2.50	1.00
			Double transfer	—			
R170	R15	40c	blue lilac	42.50	2.00	60.00	12.50
			Block of four	200.00	50.00	265.00	100.00
			Cut cancellation		15		
R171	R15	50c	slate violet	3.75	12	4.50	20
			Block of four	17.50	2.00	25.00	2.00
		a.	Imperf., pair	*300.00*			
		b.	Horiz. pair, imperf. between			—	
R172	R15	80c	bister	17.50	25	50.00	20.00
			Block of four	80.00	30.00	225.00	100.00
			Cut cancellation		8		

Numerous double transfers exist on this issue.

Commerce – R16

				Rouletted 5½ Unused	Used	p. Hyphen Hole Perf. 7 Unused	Used
R173	R16	$1	dark green	3.50	10	—	50
			Block of four	—	50		2.50
		a.	Vert. pair, imperf. horiz.	—			
		b.	Horiz. pair, imperf. vert.	—	250.00		
R174	R16	$3	dark brown	6.50	20	—	1.25
			Block of four	—	1.25		6.00
			Cut cancellation		12		25
		a.	Horiz. pair, imperf. vert.		325.00		

Rouletted 5½

				Unused	Used
R175	R16	$5	orange red	—	1.00
			Block of four	—	6.00
			Cut cancellation		18
R176	R16	$10	black	35.00	2.50
			Block of four		12.00
			Cut cancellation		50
		a.	Horiz. pair, imperf. vert.		—
R177	R16	$30	red	110.00	70.00
			Block of four		325.00
			Cut cancellation		35.00
R178	R16	$50	gray brown	45.00	3.50
			Block of four		15.00
			Cut cancellation		2.00

John Marshall – R17

Alexander Hamilton – R18

James Madison – R19

Various Portraits in Various Frames, Each Inscribed "Series of 1898."

1899 **Without Gum** ***Imperf.***

				Unused	Used
R179	R17	$100	yellow brown & black	60.00	27.50
			Vertical strip of four	—	125.00
			Cut cancellation		16.00
			Vertical strip of four, cut canc.	—	45.00
R180	R18	$500	carmine lake & black	—	400.00
			Vertical strip of four	—	1,700.
			Cut cancellation		200.00
			Vertical strip of four, cut canc		900.00
R181	R19	$1000	green & black	475.00	300.00
			Vertical strip of four		1,300.
			Cut cancellation		90.00
			Vertical strip of four, cut canc.		400.00

1900 ***Hyphen-hole perf. 7***

Allegorical Figure of Commerce

				Unused	Used
R182	R16	$1	carmine	6.00	50
			Block of four	—	2.25
			Cut cancellation		10
			Block of four, cut canc.		50
R183	R16	$3	lake (fugitive ink)	60.00	40.00
			Block of four	—	200.00
			Cut cancellation		7.00
			Block of four, cut canc.		30.00

Surcharged in Black with Open Numerals of Value

				Unused	Used
R184	R16	$1	gray	3.75	12
			Block of four	—	55
			Cut cancellation		6
			Block of four, cut canc.		30
		a.	Horiz. pair, imperf. vert		—
		b.	Surcharge omitted	125.00	
			Surcharge omitted, cut canc.		80.00
R185	R16	$2	gray	3.00	12
			Block of four	14.00	50
			Cut cancellation		6
			Block of four, cut canc.		30
R186	R16	$3	gray	30.00	11.00
			Block of four	—	50.00
			Cut cancellation		2.00
			Block of four, cut canc.		9.00
R187	R16	$5	gray	15.00	4.50
			Block of four	—	20.00
			Cut cancellation		25
			Block of four, cut canc.		1.25
R188	R16	$10	gray	35.00	10.00
			Block of four		45.00
			Cut cancellation		3.00
			Block of four, cut canc.		14.00
R189	R16	$50	gray	500.00	350.00
			Block of four		1,500.
			Cut cancellation		70.00
			Block of four, cut canc.		300.00

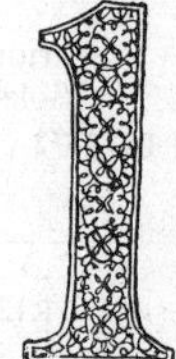
Surcharged in Black with Ornamental Numerals of Value

1902

Warning: If Nos. R190-R194 are soaked, the center part of the surcharged numeral may wash off. Before the surcharging, a square of soluble varnish was applied to the middle of some stamps.

				Unused	Used
R190	R16	$1	green	7.00	2.25
			Block of four	—	10.00
			Cut cancellation		20
			Block of four, cut canc.		85
		a.	Inverted surcharge		*150.00*
R191	R16	$2	green	6.50	1.00
			Block of four	—	5.00
			Cut cancellation		20
			Block of four, cut canc.		1.00
		a.	Surcharged as No. R185	75.00	75.00
		b.	Surcharged as No. R185, in violet	—	—
		c.	Double surcharge	*100.00*	
R192	R16	$5	green	40.00	15.00
			Block of four	—	65.00
			Cut cancellation		3.00
			Block of four, cut canc.		3.00
		a.	Surcharge omitted	40.00	
		b.	Pair, one without surcharge	*300.00*	
R193	R16	$10	green	225.00	125.00
			Block of four		550.00
			Cut cancellation		25.00
			Block of four, cut canc.		110.00
R194	R16	$50	green	900.00	700.00
			Block of four		—
			Cut cancellation		225.00
			Block of four, cut canc.		950.00

R20

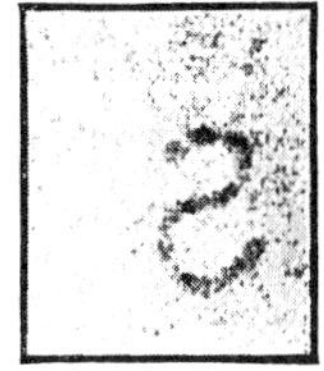
Wmk. 190

Inscribed "Series of 1914"

1914 Wmk. 190 Offset Printing *Perf. 10*

R195	R20	½c	rose	4.25	2.50
			Block of four	19.00	11.00
R196	R20	1c	rose	1.25	12
			Block of four	5.50	50
			Creased transfer, left side		—
R197	R20	2c	rose	1.25	10
			Block of four	5.50	45
			Double impression	—	
R198	R20	3c	rose	27.50	20.00
			Block of four	125.00	90.00
R199	R20	4c	rose	6.50	1.00
			Block of four	30.00	4.50
			Recut U. L. corner	—	
R200	R20	5c	rose	2.50	12
			Block of four	11.00	75
R201	R20	10c	rose	2.25	8
			Block of four	10.00	35
R202	R20	25c	rose	12.50	40
			Block of four	55.00	1.75
R203	R20	40c	rose	7.50	50
			Block of four	35.00	2.25
R204	R20	50c	rose	3.50	10
			Block of four	16.00	45
R205	R20	80c	rose	40.00	6.00
			Block of four	175.00	26.00
			Wmk. 191R		
R206	R20	½c	rose	1.25	45
			Block of four	5.50	2.00
R207	R20	1c	rose	12	5
			Block of four	55	18
			Double impression	—	—
R208	R20	2c	rose	15	5
			Block of four	65	20
R209	R20	3c	rose	1.25	20
			Block of four	5.50	85
R210	R20	4c	rose	2.25	30
			Block of four	10.00	1.35
R211	R20	5c	rose	1.25	.10
			Block of four	5.50	45
R212	R20	10c	rose	40	6
			Block of four	1.75	30
R213	R20	25c	rose	3.50	60
			Block of four	16.00	2.75
R214	R20	40c	rose	35.00	7.00
			Block of four	150.00	30.00
			Cut cancellation		45
R215	R20	50	rose	7.50	12
			Block of four	32.50	45
R216	R20	80c	rose	40.00	7.50
			Block of four	175.00	35.00
			Cut cancellation		1.00

Liberty — R21

Inscribed "Series 1914"

Engr.

R217	R21	$1	green	12.50	15
			Block of four	—	75
			Cut cancellation		5
			Block of four, cut canc.		25
a.			$1 yellow green	—	12
R218	R21	$2	carmine	25.00	20
			Block of four	—	1.00
			Cut cancellation		6
			Block of four, cut canc.		25
R219	R21	$3	purple	35.00	1.25
			Block of four	—	6.00
			Cut cancellation		20
			Block of four, cut canc.		1.00
R220	R21	$5	blue	30.00	2.00
			Block of four	135.00	9.00
			Cut cancellation		50
			Block of four, cut canc.		2.50
R221	R21	$10	orange	65.00	4.50
			Block of four	—	20.00
			Cut cancellation		75
			Block of four, cut canc.		3.50
R222	R21	$30	vermilion	110.00	10.00
			Block of four	—	45.00
			Cut cancellation		2.00
			Block of four, cut canc.		10.00
R223	R21	$50	violet	800.00	600.00
			Block of four		—
			Cut cancellation		250.00

Portrait Types of 1899 Inscribed "Series of 1915" (#R224), or "Series of 1914"

1914-15 Without Gum *Perf. 12*

R224	R19	$60	brown *(Lincoln)*	—	100.00
			Cut cancellation		45.00
			Vertical strip of four, cut canc.		200.00
R225	R17	$100	green *(Washington)*	—	40.00
			Cut cancellation		15.00
			Vertical strip of four, cut canc.		65.00
R226	R18	$500	blue *(Hamilton)*	—	450.00
			Cut cancellation		200.00
			Vertical strip of four, cut canc.		850.00
R227	R19	$1000	orange *(Madison)*	—	450.00
			Cut cancellation		200.00
			Vert. strip of 4, cut cancel		850.00

The stamps of types R17, R18 and R19 in this and subsequent issues are issued in vertical strips of four which are imperforate at the top, bottom and right side; therefore, single copies are always imperforate on one or two sides.

R22

1917 Offset Printing Wmk. 191R *Perf. 11*
Size: 21x18mm

Two types of design R22 are known.

Type I - With dot in centers of periods before and after "CENTS".

Type II - Without such dots.

First printings were done by commercial companies, later printings by the Bureau of Engraving and Printing.

R228	R22	1c	carmine rose	12	8
			Block of four	55	40
			Double impression	7.00	4.00
R229	R22	2c	carmine rose	8	5
			Block of four	40	25
			Double impression	7.50	5.00
R230	R22	3c	carmine rose	25	15
			Block of four	1.10	70
			Double impression	—	—
R231	R22	4c	carmine rose	12	5
			Block of four	60	25
			Double impression	—	—
R232	R22	5c	carmine rose	15	5
			Block of four	70	25
R233	R22	8c	carmine rose	1.50	12
			Block of four	7.00	55
R234	R22	10c	carmine rose	15	5
			Block of four	75	25
			Double impression		5.00
R235	R22	20c	carmine rose	30	5
			Block of four	1.40	25
			Double impression		—
R236	R22	25c	carmine rose	60	5
			Block of four	2.60	25
			Double impression	—	—
R237	R22	40c	carmine rose	1.00	8
			Block of four	—	35
			Double impression	8.00	5.00
R238	R22	50c	carmine rose	1.25	5
			Block of four	5.25	25
			Double impression	—	—
R239	R22	80c	carmine rose	3.00	8
			Block of four	13.00	35
			Double impression	40.00	—

Liberty Type of 1914 without "Series 1914"

1917-33 **Engr.**

Size: 18½x27½mm.

R240	R21	$1	yellow green	3.75	5
			Block of four	—	25
a.			$1 green	4.50	5
R241	R21	$2	rose	8.50	8
			Block of four	—	35
R242	R21	$3	violet	20.00	40
			Block of four		1.75
			Cut cancellation		8
R243	R21	$4	yellow brown ('33)	12.50	1.00
			Block of four	—	4.50
			Cut cancellation		12
			Block of four, cut canc.		50
R244	R21	$5	dark blue	9.00	15
			Block of four		75
			Cut cancellation		6
R245	R21	$10	orange	17.50	50
			Block of four	—	3.00
			Cut cancellation		12
			Block of four, cut canc.		60

Portrait Types of 1899 without "Series of" and Date

1917 **Without Gum** ***Perf. 12***

R246	R17	$30	deep orange, green numerals *(Grant)*	25.00	2.00
			Vertical strip of four		—
			Cut cancellation		55
			Vertical strip of four, cut canc.		3.00
a.			Imperf., pair		—
b.			Numerals in blue	—	1.75
			Numerals in blue, cut canc.		90
R247	R19	$60	brown *(Lincoln)*	35.00	7.00
			Vertical strip of four		—
			Cut cancellation		80
			Vertical strip of four cut canc.		5.00
R248	R17	$100	green *(Washington)*	20.00	75
			Vertical strip of four		—
			Cut cancellation		35
			Vertical strip of four, cut canc.		1.90
R249	R18	$500	blue, red numerals *(Hamilton)*	—	30.00
			Vertical strip of four		—
			Cut cancellation		7.00
			Vertical strip of four, cut canc.		45.00
			Double transfer	—	50.00
a.			Numerals in orange	—	70.00
R250	R19	$1000	orange *(Madison)*	80.00	11.00
			Vertical strip of four		—
			Cut cancellation		4.00
			Vertical strip of four, cut canc.		17.50
a.			Imperf., pair		—

See note after No. R227.

1928-29 **Offset Printing** ***Perf. 10***

R251	R22	1c	carmine rose	2.00	1.10
			Block of four	9.00	5.00
R252	R22	2c	carmine rose	60	20
			Block of four	3.00	1.00
R253	R22	4c	carmine rose	5.50	3.75
			Block of four	25.00	17.50
R254	R22	5c	carmine rose	1.10	35
			Block of four	5.00	1.75
R255	R22	10c	carmine rose	1.75	1.00
			Block of four	8.00	4.50
R256	R22	20c	carmine rose	5.50	4.50
			Block of four	25.00	20.00
			Double impression		—

Engr.

R257	R21	$1	green	55.00	25.00
			Block of four	—	—
			Cut cancellation		5.00
R258	R21	$2	rose	15.00	2.00
			Block of four	—	10.00
R259	R21	$10	orange	82.50	35.00
			Block of four	—	—
			Cut cancellation		20.00

1929 **Offset Printing** ***Perf. 11x10***

R260	R22	2c	carmine rose ('30)	2.75	2.25
			Block of four	12.00	10.00
			Double impression		—
R261	R22	5c	carmine rose ('30)	2.00	1.75
			Block of four	10.00	8.00
R262	R22	10c	carmine rose	7.50	6.50
			Block of four	35.00	30.00
R263	R22	20c	carmine rose	15.00	7.75
			Block of four	70.00	40.00

Types of 1917-33 Overprinted in Black

SERIES 1940

1940 **Wmk. 191R** **Offset Printing** ***Perf. 11***

				Unused	Used (uncut)	Used (cut canc.)	Used (perf. initials)
R264	R22	1c	rose pink	1.90	1.40	35	20
R265	R22	2c	rose pink	1.90	1.40	40	30
R266	R22	3c	rose pink	5.50	3.25	70	50
R267	R22	4c	rose pink	2.25	38	12	8
R268	R22	5c	rose pink	2.75	65	25	15
R269	R22	8c	rose pink	14.00	12.00	3.00	2.00
R270	R22	10c	rose pink	1.10	28	8	5
R271	R22	20c	rose pink	1.65	32	10	5
R272	R22	25c	rose pink	3.00	45	10	6
R273	R22	40c	rose pink	3.25	45	8	5
R274	R22	50c	rose pink	3.75	32	8	5
R275	R22	80c	rose pink	5.50	55	20	10

Engr.

R276	R21	$1	green	14.00	38	10	8
R277	R21	$2	rose	14.00	65	10	8
R278	R21	$3	violet	17.00	13.00	2.25	1.25
R279	R21	$4	yellow brown	37.50	19.00	3.00	1.25
R280	R21	$5	dark blue	22.50	5.50	50	15
R281	R21	$10	orange	50.00	17.00	1.25	35

Types of 1917 Handstamped in Green "Series 1940".

1940 **Wmk. 191R** ***Perf. 12***

Without Gum

R282	R17	$30	vermilion	425.00	325.00	
R283	R19	$60	brown	600.00	450.00	
a.			As #R285a		—	
R284	R17	$100	green	900.00	725.00	
R285	R18	$500	blue	1,200.	1,000.	800.00
			Double transfer	1,250.		
a.			With black 2 line handstamp in larger type	*1,600.*	*1,200.*	
			Double transfer	—		
b.			Blue handstamp; double transfer	—		
R286	R19	$1000	orange	650.00	375.00	250.00

Alexander Hamilton — R23

Levi Woodbury — R24

Thomas Corwin — R25

Overprinted in Black SERIES 1940

Various Portraits

1940 **Engr.** **Wmk. 191R** ***Perf. 11***

Plates of 400 subjects, issued in panes of 100

Size: 19x22mm

The "sensitive ink" varieties are in a bluish-purple overprint showing minute flecks of gold.

				Unused	Used (uncut)	Used (cut canc.)	Used (perf. initials)
R288	R23	1c	carmine	3.00	2.25	1.25	65
			Sensitive ink	10.00	—		
R289	R23	2c	carmine *(Oliver Wolcott, Jr.)*	3.25	2.25	1.25	80
			Sensitive ink	10.00	—		
R290	R23	3c	carmine *(Samuel Dexter)*	12.50	5.50	3.25	2.25
			Sensitive ink	25.00	—		
R291	R23	4c	carmine *(Albert Gallatin)*	27.50	20.00	4.50	3.75
R292	R23	5c	carmine *(G.W. Campbell)*	2.75	60	25	18
R293	R23	8c	carmine *(Alexander Dallas)*	37.50	32.50	17.50	12.00
R294	R23	10c	carmine *(William H. Crawford)*	2.00	30	12	10
R295	R23	20c	carmine *(Richard Rush)*	2.75	2.00	1.00	75
R296	R23	25c	carmine *(S.D. Ingham)*	2.00	20	12	10
R297	R23	40c	carmine *(Louis McLane)*	25.00	12.00	4.00	2.25
R298	R23	50c	carmine *(Wm. J. Duane)*	3.00	20	6	5
R299	R23	80c	carmine *(Roger B. Taney)*	50.00	45.00	22.50	16.50

Plates of 200 subjects, issued in panes of 50

Size: 21½x36¼mm

				Unused	Used (uncut)	Used (cut canc.)	Used (perf. initials)
R300	R24	$1	carmine	—	15	6	5
			Sensitive ink	40.00	—		
R301	R24	$2	carmine *(Thomas Ewing)*	—	25	8	6
			Sensitive ink	55.00	—		
R302	R24	$3	carmine *(Walter Forward)*	—	50.00	10.00	7.00
			Sensitive ink	120.00	—		
R303	R24	$4	carmine *(J.C. Spencer)*	—	20.00	5.00	1.50
R304	R24	$5	carmine *(G.M. Bibb)*	—	80	30	20
R305	R24	$10	carmine *(R.J. Walker)*	—	3.00	70	25
R305A	R24	$20	carmine *(Wm.M. Meredith)*	600.00	550.00	325.00	225.00
b.			Imperf. pair	750.00			

(Overprint: "SERIES 1940")

Various Frames and Portraits

Plates of 16 subjects, issued in strips of 4

Without Gum

Size: 28½x42mm

R306	R25	$30	carmine	82.50	37.50	15.00	10.00
R306A	R25	$50	carmine *(James Guthrie)*	—	800.00	650.00	—
R307	R25	$60	carmine *(Howell Cobb)*	—	40.00	25.00	15.00
a.			Vert. pair, imperf. between		—		
R308	R25	$100	carmine *(P.F. Thomas)*	—	50.00	17.50	9.00
R309	R25	$500	carmine *(J.A. Dix)*	—	550.00	300.00	160.00
R310	R25	$1000	carmine *(S.P. Chase)*	—	300.00	125.00	85.00

The $30 to $1,000 denominations in this and following similar issues, and the $2,500, $5,000 and $10,000 stamps of 1952-58 have straight edges on one or two sides. They were issued without gum through No. R723.

Nos. R288-R310 Overprinted Instead: SERIES 1941

1941 **Wmk. 191R** ***Perf. 11***

Size: 19x22mm

R311	R23	1c	carmine	2.00	1.75	70	60
R312	R23	2c	carmine	2.50	1.75	40	35
R313	R23	3c	carmine	6.50	3.00	1.25	85
R314	R23	4c	carmine	4.00	75	30	12
R315	R23	5c	carmine	75	15	8	6
R316	R23	8c	carmine	12.00	4.50	3.00	2.50
R317	R23	10c	carmine	1.00	20	10	8
R318	R23	20c	carmine	2.25	40	20	15
R319	R23	25c	carmine	1.25	10	5	5
R320	R23	40c	carmine	7.00	2.00	1.00	60

R321	R23	50c	carmine	2.00	10	5	5
R322	R23	80c	carmine	32.50	6.00	2.25	1.65

Size: 21½x36¼mm

R323	R24	$1	carmine	5.00	10	6	5
R324	R24	$2	carmine	6.00	12	5	5
R325	R24	$3	carmine	10.00	1.75	35	30
R326	R24	$4	carmine	16.00	12.00	85	70
R327	R24	$5	carmine	25.00	30	10	8
R328	R24	$10	carmine	30.00	2.00	25	20
R329	R24	$20	carmine	100.00	80.00	30.00	20.00

Perf. 12

Without Gum

Size: 28½x42mm

R330	R25	$30	carmine	—	19.00	9.00	6.00
R331	R25	$50	carmine	110.00	87.50	50.00	25.00
R332	R25	$60	carmine	—	42.50	7.50	5.00
R333	R25	$100	carmine	—	16.00	4.00	2.75
R334	R25	$500	carmine	—	160.00	90.00	45.00
R335	R25	$1000	carmine	—	100.00	30.00	20.00

Nos. R288-R310 Overprinted Instead: SERIES 1942

1942 **Wmk. 191R** ***Perf. 11***

Size: 19x22mm

R336	R23	1c	carmine	30	25	10	8
R337	R23	2c	carmine	35	25	10	8
R338	R23	3c	carmine	50	35	22	15
R339	R23	4c	carmine	80	40	25	20
R340	R23	5c	carmine	35	10	6	5
R341	R23	8c	carmine	3.50	2.25	1.00	1.00
R342	R23	10c	carmine	70	10	6	5
R343	R23	20c	carmine	75	30	15	15
R344	R23	25c	carmine	1.40	15	5	5
R345	R23	40c	carmine	3.50	75	50	30
R346	R23	50c	carmine	2.25	10	5	5
R347	R23	80c	carmine	9.00	6.00	2.50	1.75

Size: 21½x36¼mm

R348	R24	$1	carmine	4.50	10	5	5
R349	R24	$2	carmine	5.50	10	5	5
R350	R24	$3	carmine	9.00	1.50	25	20
R351	R24	$4	carmine	11.00	3.25	30	25
R352	R24	$5	carmine	18.00	65	7	5
R353	R24	$10	carmine	30.00	1.75	10	8
R354	R24	$20	carmine	50.00	25.00	14.00	10.00

Perf. 12

Without Gum

Size: 28½x42mm

R355	R25	$30	carmine	—	18.00	6.00	5.00
R356	R25	$50	carmine	150.00	110.00	70.00	50.00
R357	R25	$60	carmine	160.00	135.00	65.00	50.00
R358	R25	$100	carmine	—	50.00	25.00	16.00
R359	R25	$500	carmine	—	150.00	100.00	45.00
R360	R25	$1000	carmine	—	100.00	50.00	40.00

Nos. R288-R310 Overprinted Instead: SERIES 1943

1943 **Wmk. 191R** ***Perf. 11***

Size: 19x22mm

R361	R23	1c	carmine	50	32	12	10
R362	R23	2c	carmine	40	20	8	6
R363	R23	3c	carmine	1.75	1.50	50	30
R364	R23	4c	carmine	90	85	30	25
R365	R23	5c	carmine	35	20	8	5
R366	R23	8c	carmine	3.00	2.50	1.50	1.00
R367	R23	10c	carmine	40	15	7	6
R368	R23	20c	carmine	1.25	40	25	20
R369	R23	25c	carmine	1.00	20	8	6
R370	R23	40c	carmine	4.00	1.50	1.00	60
R371	R23	50c	carmine	1.10	10	5	5
R372	R23	80c	carmine	7.00	4.50	1.10	90

Size: 21½x36¼mm

R373	R24	$1	carmine	3.75	8	5	5
R374	R24	$2	carmine	5.50	10	6	5
R375	R24	$3	carmine	9.00	1.75	30	10
R376	R24	$4	carmine	11.00	2.50	40	30
R377	R24	$5	carmine	16.00	40	8	6
R378	R24	$10	carmine	25.00	2.00	50	35
R379	R24	$20	carmine	45.00	10.00	3.50	2.25

Perf. 12

Without Gum

Size: 28½x42mm

R380	R25	$30	carmine	—	15.00	4.00	3.00
R381	R25	$50	carmine	—	22.00	8.00	5.00
R382	R25	$60	carmine	—	47.50	11.00	6.00
R383	R25	$100	carmine	—	10.00	5.50	3.50
R384	R25	$500	carmine	—	110.00	75.00	60.00
R385	R25	$1000	carmine	—	140.00	45.00	37.50

Nos. R288-R310 Overprinted Instead: **Series 1944**

1944 **Wmk. 191R** ***Perf. 11***

Size: 19x22mm

R386	R23	1c	carmine	25	20	12	10
R387	R23	2c	carmine	25	20	8	8
R388	R23	3c	carmine	32	20	10	8
R389	R23	4c	carmine	52	50	12	10
R390	R23	5c	carmine	30	10	6	5
R391	R23	8c	carmine	1.25	75	45	40
R392	R23	10c	carmine	40	6	5	5
R393	R23	20c	carmine	65	20	15	12
R394	R23	25c	carmine	1.10	10	6	5
R395	R23	40c	carmine	2.25	45	25	20
R396	R23	50c	carmine	2.25	10	5	5
R397	R23	80c	carmine	7.00	3.50	1.00	80

Size: 21½x36¼mm

R398	R24	$1	carmine	3.75	8	5	5
R399	R24	$2	carmine	5.00	10	7	5
R400	R24	$3	carmine	7.50	1.50	45	10
R401	R24	$4	carmine	12.00	8.00	1.00	90
R402	R24	$5	carmine	12.00	25	10	7
R403	R24	$10	carmine	25.00	90	25	10
R404	R24	$20	carmine	45.00	12.50	3.00	2.00

Perf. 12

Without Gum

Size: 28½x42mm

R405	R25	$30	carmine	50.00	20.00	5.00	4.75
R406	R25	$50	carmine	20.00	10.00	4.00	3.75
R407	R25	$60	carmine	90.00	35.00	8.00	6.75
R408	R25	$100	carmine	—	8.00	4.00	3.00
R409	R25	$500	carmine	—	450.00	325.00	250.00
R410	R25	$1000	carmine	—	125.00	50.00	40.00

Nos. R288-R310 Overprinted Instead: **Series 1945**

1945 **Wmk. 191R** ***Perf. 11***

Size: 19x22mm

R411	R23	1c	carmine	20	12	8	5
R412	R23	2c	carmine	15	10	8	6
R413	R23	3c	carmine	40	30	15	10
R414	R23	4c	carmine	25	15	10	8
R415	R23	5c	carmine	25	6	5	5
R416	R23	8c	carmine	3.00	1.25	60	30
R417	R23	10c	carmine	60	10	5	5
R418	R23	20c	carmine	3.50	75	40	15
R419	R23	25c	carmine	90	15	6	5
R420	R23	40c	carmine	3.75	85	40	35
R421	R23	50c	carmine	2.00	10	6	5
R422	R23	80c	carmine	11.00	6.00	3.00	1.75

Size: 21½x36¼mm

R423	R24	$1	carmine	3.75	10	6	6
R424	R24	$2	carmine	5.00	15	8	6
R425	R24	$3	carmine	7.50	2.25	80	60
R426	R24	$4	carmine	11.00	2.50	50	30
R427	R24	$5	carmine	12.00	30	15	10
R428	R24	$10	carmine	25.00	1.10	25	18
R429	R24	$20	carmine	40.00	8.00	3.00	2.50

Perf. 12

Without Gum

Size: 28½x42mm

R430	R25	$30	carmine	—	20.00	5.25	4.25
R431	R25	$50	carmine	—	25.00	15.00	6.75
R432	R25	$60	carmine	75.00	32.50	11.50	9.00
R433	R25	$100	carmine	—	11.50	7.75	5.25
R434	R25	$500	carmine	150.00	135.00	67.50	50.00
R435	R25	$1000	carmine	100.00	82.50	25.00	17.50

Nos. R288-R310 Overprinted Instead: **Series 1946**

1946 **Wmk. 191R** ***Perf. 11***

Size: 19x22mm

R436	R23	1c	carmine	18	12	5	5
R437	R23	2c	carmine	22	20	6	5
R438	R23	3c	carmine	25	15	10	8
R439	R23	4c	carmine	35	30	8	6
R440	R23	5c	carmine	30	8	6	5
R441	R23	8c	carmine	90	75	25	10
R442	R23	10c	carmine	60	8	6	5
R443	R23	20c	carmine	1.00	40	12	6
R444	R23	25c	carmine	1.10	15	8	6
R445	R23	40c	carmine	1.25	70	30	15
R446	R23	50c	carmine	2.00	10	6	5
R447	R23	80c	carmine	5.50	3.25	60	45

Size: 21½x36¼mm

R448	R24	$1	carmine	3.75	15	8	5
R449	R24	$2	carmine	5.50	20	10	8
R450	R24	$3	carmine	8.00	4.50	85	35
R451	R24	$4	carmine	10.00	8.00	2.00	1.00
R452	R24	$5	carmine	11.00	40	15	10
R453	R24	$10	carmine	22.00	1.25	30	18
R454	R24	$20	carmine	40.00	7.50	2.00	1.50

Without Gum ***Perf. 12***

Size: 28½x42mm

				Unused	Used (uncut)	Used (cut canc.)	Used (perf. initials)
R455	R25	$30	carmine	40.00	10.00	4.00	2.50
R456	R25	$50	carmine	20.00	8.00	4.00	2.50
R457	R25	$60	carmine	40.00	16.00	12.00	6.00
R458	R25	$100	carmine	—	8.00	3.00	3.00
R459	R25	$500	carmine	—	75.00	35.00	22.50
R460	R25	$1000	carmine	—	85.00	27.50	18.00

Nos. R288-R310 Overprinted Instead: **Series 1947**

1947 **Wmk. 191R** ***Perf. 11***

Size: 19x22mm

R461	R23	1c	carmine	48	25	8	5
R462	R23	2c	carmine	38	25	8	5
R463	R23	3c	carmine	40	25	15	5
R464	R23	4c	carmine	48	35	12	5
R465	R23	5c	carmine	30	15	5	5
R466	R23	8c	carmine	75	35	20	10
R467	R23	10c	carmine	70	15	8	5
R468	R23	20c	carmine	1.00	35	15	5
R469	R23	25c	carmine	1.50	35	12	8
R470	R23	40c	carmine	2.25	60	20	10
R471	R23	50c	carmine	2.00	15	8	5
R472	R23	80c	carmine	4.00	3.50	60	20

Size: 21½x36¼mm

R473	R24	$1	carmine	3.75	20	6	6
R474	R24	$2	carmine	5.00	20	10	8
R475	R24	$3	carmine	6.75	4.00	1.00	60
R476	R24	$4	carmine	8.00	3.50	40	30
R477	R24	$5	carmine	11.00	40	12	10
R478	R24	$10	carmine	25.00	2.00	60	20
R479	R24	$20	carmine	40.00	7.50	1.00	70

Perf. 12

Without Gum

Size: 28½x42mm

R480	R25	$30	carmine	60.00	17.50	4.00	2.00
R481	R25	$50	carmine	30.00	12.00	4.00	2.50
R482	R25	$60	carmine	—	27.50	14.00	6.00
R483	R25	$100	carmine	30.00	10.00	4.00	2.00
R484	R25	$500	carmine	—	125.00	50.00	35.00

No.	Type	Denom.	Color	Unused	Used (uncut)	Used (cut canc.)	Used (perf. initials)
R485	R25	$1000	carmine	—	70.00	35.00	22.50

Nos. R288-R310 Overprinted Instead: Series 1948

1948 Wmk. 191R *Perf. 11*

Size: 19x22mm

No.	Type	Denom.	Color	Unused	Used (uncut)	Used (cut canc.)	Used (perf. initials)
R486	R23	1c	carmine	18	12	8	6
R487	R23	2c	carmine	28	15	8	6
R488	R23	3c	carmine	38	25	12	10
R489	R23	4c	carmine	32	25	10	8
R490	R23	5c	carmine	32	10	6	5
R491	R23	8c	carmine	55	30	18	12
R492	R23	10c	carmine	55	10	6	5
R493	R23	20c	carmine	1.10	30	12	8
R494	R23	25c	carmine	1.00	15	8	6
R495	R23	40c	carmine	3.00	1.00	30	20
R496	R23	50c	carmine	1.75	12	6	5
R497	R23	80c	carmine	4.50	3.50	1.50	50
			Size: 21½x36¼mm				
R498	R24	$1	carmine	3.75	20	8	6
R499	R24	$2	carmine	5.00	15	8	6
R500	R24	$3	carmine	7.00	2.00	40	25
R501	R24	$4	carmine	10.00	2.50	75	40
R502	R24	$5	carmine	11.00	50	20	10
R503	R24	$10	carmine	20.00	1.00	25	15
		a.	Pair, one dated "1946"		—		
R504	R24	$20	carmine	40.00	7.50	3.00	1.25

Perf. 12

Without Gum

Size: 28½x42mm

No.	Type	Denom.	Color	Unused	Used (uncut)	Used (cut canc.)	Used (perf. initials)
R505	R25	$30	carmine	40.00	15.00	5.00	2.50
R506	R25	$50	carmine	40.00	12.50	6.00	2.50
		a.	Vert. pair, imperf. btwn.	—			
R507	R25	$60	carmine	50.00	17.50	9.00	5.00
		a.	Vert. pair, imperf. btwn.	—			
R508	R25	$100	carmine	—	10.00	4.00	2.50
		a.	Vert. pair, imperf. btwn.	350.00			
R509	R25	$500	carmine	125.00	90.00	45.00	27.50
R510	R25	$1000	carmine	80.00	50.00	27.50	18.00

Nos. R288-R310 Overprinted Instead: Series 1949

1949 Wmk. 191R Size: 19x22mm *Perf. 11*

No.	Type	Denom.	Color	Unused	Used (uncut)	Used (cut canc.)	Used (perf. initials)
R511	R23	1c	carmine	12	10	6	6
R512	R23	2c	carmine	20	15	8	6
R513	R23	3c	carmine	24	15	10	8
R514	R23	4c	carmine	30	25	10	8
R515	R23	5c	carmine	38	15	10	8
R516	R23	8c	carmine	55	30	20	18
R517	R23	10c	carmine	35	20	12	10
R518	R23	20c	carmine	75	40	30	25
R519	R23	25c	carmine	1.00	45	25	20
R520	R23	40c	carmine	2.25	1.25	40	30
R521	R23	50c	carmine	2.00	25	6	5
R522	R23	80c	carmine	4.25	3.00	1.50	75
			Size: 21½x36¼mm				
R523	R24	$1	carmine	3.75	30	12	10
R524	R24	$2	carmine	4.50	1.25	40	25
R525	R24	$3	carmine	8.25	5.00	2.00	1.00
R526	R24	$4	carmine	7.50	4.75	2.75	1.50
R527	R24	$5	carmine	10.00	1.75	60	40
R528	R24	$10	carmine	20.00	2.50	1.00	85
R529	R24	$20	carmine	40.00	6.00	2.00	1.00

Perf. 12

Without Gum

Size: 28½x42mm

No.	Type	Denom.	Color	Unused	Used (uncut)	Used (cut canc.)	Used (perf. initials)
R530	R25	$30	carmine	50.00	22.50	5.00	3.00
R531	R25	$50	carmine	—	35.00	10.00	6.00
R532	R25	$60	carmine	—	35.00	18.00	7.00
R533	R25	$100	carmine	—	15.00	3.00	2.50
R534	R25	$500	carmine	—	165.00	90.00	47.50
R535	R25	$1000	carmine	—	100.00	35.00	20.00

Nos. R288-R310 Overprinted Instead: Series 1950

1950 Wmk. 191R *Perf. 11*

Size: 19x22mm

No.	Type	Denom.	Color	Unused	Used (uncut)	Used (cut canc.)	Used (perf. initials)
R536	R23	1c	carmine	18	6	5	5
R537	R23	2c	carmine	20	10	5	5
R538	R23	3c	carmine	20	15	6	5
R539	R23	4c	carmine	22	20	10	8
R540	R23	5c	carmine	28	12	8	6
R541	R23	8c	carmine	50	30	20	12
R542	R23	10c	carmine	60	15	10	8
R543	R23	20c	carmine	75	35	25	12
R544	R23	25c	carmine	1.10	35	25	20
R545	R23	40c	carmine	2.50	1.25	40	25
R546	R23	50c	carmine	3.00	20	8	5
R547	R23	80c	carmine	4.00	3.50	85	50
			Size: 21½x36¼mm				
R548	R24	$1	carmine	3.50	20	12	8
R549	R24	$2	carmine	4.00	2.00	35	15
R550	R24	$3	carmine	5.50	3.00	1.25	75
R551	R24	$4	carmine	8.00	4.00	2.50	1.25
R552	R24	$5	carmine	10.00	75	30	18
R553	R24	$10	carmine	20.00	6.50	80	50
R554	R24	$20	carmine	47.50	7.00	2.50	1.50

Perf. 12

Without Gum

Size: 28½x42mm

No.	Type	Denom.	Color	Unused	Used (uncut)	Used (cut canc.)	Used (perf. initials)
R555	R25	$30	carmine	—	35.00	10.00	8.00
R556	R25	$50	carmine	—	14.00	6.75	4.50
		a.	Vert. pair, imperf. horiz.		—		
R557	R25	$60	carmine	—	45.00	14.00	6.00
R558	R25	$100	carmine	—	17.50	5.00	3.00
R559	R25	$500	carmine	—	100.00	47.50	30.00
R560	R25	$1000	carmine	—	70.00	25.00	18.00

Nos. R288-R310 Overprinted Instead: Series 1951

1951 Wmk. 191R *Perf. 11*

Size: 19x22mm

No.	Type	Denom.	Color	Unused	Used (uncut)	Used (cut canc.)	Used (perf. initials)
R561	R23	1c	carmine	12	10	6	5
R562	R23	2c	carmine	20	10	5	5
R563	R23	3c	carmine	18	15	8	6
R564	R23	4c	carmine	22	15	8	6
R565	R23	5c	carmine	30	15	8	6
R566	R23	8c	carmine	80	30	20	15
R567	R23	10c	carmine	55	15	10	8
R568	R23	20c	carmine	1.00	35	25	15
R569	R23	25c	carmine	1.00	35	25	15
R570	R23	40c	carmine	2.00	90	40	25
R571	R23	50c	carmine	2.00	30	10	6
R572	R23	80c	carmine	2.75	2.25	1.50	70

Size: 21½x36¼mm

No.	Type	Denom.	Color	Unused	Used (uncut)	Used (cut canc.)	Used (perf. initials)
R573	R24	$1	carmine	3.50	20	15	10
R574	R24	$2	carmine	4.00	25	18	12
R575	R24	$3	carmine	7.00	3.50	1.75	1.00
R576	R24	$4	carmine	9.00	4.50	2.50	1.25
R577	R24	$5	carmine	9.00	40	30	20
R578	R24	$10	carmine	20.00	2.25	1.00	75
R579	R24	$20	carmine	40.00	6.50	3.00	3.50

Perf. 12

Without Gum

Size: 28½x42mm

No.	Type	Denom.	Color	Unused	Used (uncut)	Used (cut canc.)	Used (perf. initials)
R580	R25	$30	carmine	—	10.00	5.00	3.50
		a.	Imperf., pair		750.00		
R581	R25	$50	carmine	—	12.50	6.00	4.00
R582	R25	$60	carmine	—	35.00		12.50
R583	R25	$100	carmine	—	12.50	6.75	5.00
R584	R25	$500	carmine	125.00	82.50	45.00	22.50
R585	R25	$1000	carmine	—	90.00	35.00	27.50

Documentary Stamps and Types of 1940 Overprinted in Black

Series 1952

Designs: 55c, $1.10, $1.65, $2.20, $2.75, $3.30, L. J. Gage; $2500, William Windom; $5000, C. J. Folger; $10,000, W. Q. Gresham.

1952 Wmk. 191R *Perf. 11*

Size: 19x22mm

No.	Type	Denom.	Color	Unused	Used (uncut)	Used (cut canc.)	Used (perf. initials)
R586	R23	1c	carmine	18	6	5	5
R587	R23	2c	carmine	32	10	5	5
R588	R23	3c	carmine	18	15	6	5
R589	R23	4c	carmine	22	15	8	6
R590	R23	5c	carmine	22	10	6	5
R591	R23	8c	carmine	45	30	12	8
R592	R23	10c	carmine	38	15	8	6
R593	R23	20c	carmine	85	35	20	18
R594	R23	25c	carmine	1.00	40	25	20
R595	R23	40c	carmine	1.90	80	50	40
R596	R23	50c	carmine	2.25	20	8	6
R597	R23	55c	carmine	10.00	5.00	1.25	1.00
R598	R23	80c	carmine	4.50	2.25	75	65
			Size: 21½x36¼mm				
R599	R24	$1	carmine	3.00	1.50		35
R600	R24	$1.10	carmine	20.00	14.00		
R601	R24	$1.65	carmine	75.00	40.00		
R602	R24	$2	carmine	5.00	40		10
R603	R24	$2.20	carmine	55.00	45.00		
R604	R24	$2.75	carmine	75.00	40.00		
R605	R24	$3	carmine	11.50	3.50	1.50	1.25
		a.	Horiz. pair, imperf. btwn.	—			
R606	R24	$3.30	carmine	55.00	40.00		
R607	R24	$4	carmine	10.00	3.50	2.00	1.50
R608	R24	$5	carmine	10.00	1.25	40	35
R609	R24	$10	carmine	22.00	1.25	40	35
R610	R24	$20	carmine	35.00	8.00	2.75	2.25

Perf. 12

Without Gum

Size: 28½x42mm

No.	Type	Denom.	Color	Unused	Used (uncut)	Used (cut canc.)	Used (perf. initials)
R611	R25	$30	carmine	—	16.00	5.00	4.00
R612	R25	$50	carmine	—	12.00	5.00	4.00
R613	R25	$60	carmine	—	35.00	10.00	8.00
R614	R25	$100	carmine	—	8.00	3.00	2.00
R615	R25	$500	carmine	—	90.00	57.50	30.00
R616	R25	$1000	carmine	—	30.00	15.00	10.00
R617	R25	$2500	carmine	—	140.00	125.00	90.00
R618	R25	$5000	carmine	—	850.00	650.00	550.00
R619	R25	$10,000	carmine	—	475.00	350.00	250.00

Documentary Stamps and Types of 1940 Overprinted in Black

Series 1953

1953 Wmk. 191R *Perf. 11*

Size: 19x22mm

No.	Type	Denom.	Color	Unused	Used (uncut)	Used (cut canc.)	Used (perf. initials)
R620	R23	1c	carmine	15	10	5	5
R621	R23	2c	carmine	15	10	5	5
R622	R23	3c	carmine	15	10	6	5

R623	R23	4c	carmine	20	10	8	5
R624	R23	5c	carmine	18	10	6	5
R625	R23	8c	carmine	45	20	15	12
R626	R23	10c	carmine	40	18	6	5
R627	R23	20c	carmine	55	40	20	15
R628	R23	25c	carmine	75	50	25	20
R629	R23	40c	carmine	1.50	75	40	30
R630	R23	50c	carmine	1.65	15	6	5
R631	R23	55c	carmine	2.75	1.50		
	a.		Horiz. pair, imperf. vert.	*275.00*			
R632	R23	80c	carmine	2.75	1.65	1.40	1.10

Size: 21½x36¼mm

R633	R24	$1	carmine	2.75	25	12	10
R634	R24	$1.10	carmine	4.00	2.50	2.00	1.50
	a.		Horiz. pair, imperf. vert.	300.00			
	b.		Imperf. pair	*450.00*			
R635	R24	$1.65	carmine	5.00	4.00		
R636	R24	$2	carmine	4.50	50	25	20
R637	R24	$2.20	carmine	7.25	5.00	2.50	2.00
R638	R24	$2.75	carmine	8.00	6.00	3.50	
R639	R24	$3	carmine	6.00	3.00	1.50	1.25
R640	R24	$3.30	carmine	14.00	7.00		
R641	R24	$4	carmine	11.00	6.50	1.75	1.50
R642	R24	$5	carmine	11.50	75	40	30
R643	R24	$10	carmine	20.00	1.75	1.00	85
R644	R24	$20	carmine	40.00	15.00	3.00	2.00

Perf. 12

Without Gum

Size: 28½x42mm

R645	R25	$30	carmine	—	12.00	5.00	4.00
R646	R25	$50	carmine	—	20.00	5.00	4.00
R647	R25	$60	carmine	—	57.50		
R648	R25	$100	carmine	35.00	12.00	5.00	3.50
R649	R25	$500	carmine	—	115.00	35.00	22.50
R650	R25	$1000	carmine	100.00	57.50	22.50	15.00
R651	R25	$2500	carmine	400.00	375.00	275.00	225.00
R652	R25	$5000	carmine	—	850.00	750.00	600.00
R653	R25	$10,000	carmine	—	*600.00*	500.00	150.00

Types of 1940
Without Overprint

1954 **Wmk. 191R** ***Perf. 11***

Size: 19x22mm

R654	R23	1c	carmine	6	5	5	5
	a.		Horiz. pair, imperf. vert.	—			
R655	R23	2c	carmine	8	6	5	5
R656	R23	3c	carmine	12	10	5	5
R657	R23	4c	carmine	12	10	5	5
R658	R23	5c	carmine	13	8	5	5
R659	R23	8c	carmine	25	20	12	10
R660	R23	10c	carmine	25	15	6	5
R661	R23	20c	carmine	50	35	15	12
R662	R23	25c	carmine	60	40	18	15
R663	R23	40c	carmine	1.25	60	40	35
R664	R23	50c	carmine	1.65	15	10	8
	a.		Horiz. pair, imperf. vert.	200.00			
R665	R23	55c	carmine	1.25	1.10		
R666	R23	80c	carmine	2.25	1.65	1.00	80

Size: 21½x36¼mm

R667	R24	$1	carmine	1.65	28	10	8
R668	R24	$1.10	carmine	3.25	2.35		
R669	R24	$1.65	carmine	100.00	75.00		
R670	R24	$2	carmine	1.75	45	25	20
R671	R24	$2.20	carmine	4.50	3.75		
R672	R24	$2.75	carmine	100.00	75.00		
R673	R24	$3	carmine	3.00	2.00	1.00	75
R674	R24	$3.30	carmine	6.50	5.00		
R675	R24	$4	carmine	4.50	3.50	2.00	1.50
R676	R24	$5	carmine	10.00	50	30	20
R677	R24	$10	carmine	19.00	1.50	80	70
R678	R24	$20	carmine	40.00	6.00	3.00	1.50

Documentary Stamps and Type of 1940 Overprinted in Black

Series 1954

1954 **Wmk. 191R** ***Perf. 12***

Without Gum

Size: 28½x42mm

R679	R25	$30	carmine	—	12.00	4.00	3.00
R680	R25	$50	carmine	—	15.00	9.00	4.50
R681	R25	$60	carmine	—	20.00	12.50	9.00
R682	R25	$100	carmine	—	7.00	4.75	4.00
R683	R25	$500	carmine	—	60.00	22.50	18.00
R684	R25	$1000	carmine	—	47.50	18.00	14.00
R685	R25	$2500	carmine	—	140.00	70.00	45.00
R686	R25	$5000	carmine	—	500.00	325.00	250.00
R687	R25	$10,000	carmine	—	400.00	110.00	125.00

Documentary Stamps and Type of 1940 Overprinted in Black

Series 1955

1955 **Wmk. 191R** ***Perf. 12***

Without Gum

Sizes: 28½x42mm

R688	R25	$30	carmine	—	11.50	5.75	
R689	R25	$50	carmine	—	13.50	9.00	6.25
R690	R25	$60	carmine	—	24.00	5.00	4.00
R691	R25	$100	carmine	—	7.00	5.00	3.50
R692	R25	$500	carmine	—	105.00	30.00	20.00
R693	R25	$1000	carmine	—	35.00	17.50	12.50
R694	R25	$2500	carmine	—	110.00	60.00	40.00
R695	R25	$5000	carmine	—	550.00	350.00	225.00
R696	R25	$10,000	carmine	—	375.00	150.00	80.00

Documentary Stamps and Type of 1940 Overprinted in Black "Series 1956"

1956 **Wmk. 191R** **Without Gum** ***Perf. 12***

Size: 28½x42mm

				Unused	Used (uncut)	Used (cut canc.)	Used (perf. initials)
R697	R25	$30	carmine	—	13.50	9.00	4.50
R698	R25	$50	carmine	—	17.00	10.00	4.50
R699	R25	$60	carmine	—	32.50	7.00	4.50
R700	R25	$100	carmine	—	10.00	5.00	4.00
R701	R25	$500	carmine	—	75.00	25.00	15.00
R702	R25	$1000	carmine	—	50.00	15.00	9.00
R703	R25	$2500	carmine	—	250.00	30.00	70.00
R704	R25	$5000	carmine	—	975.00	700.00	600.00
R705	R25	$10,000	carmine	—	350.00	150.00	100.00

Documentary Stamps and Type of 1940 Overprinted in Black "Series 1957"

1957 **Wmk. 191R** ***Perf. 12***

Without Gum

Size: 28½x42mm

R706	R25	$30	carmine	—	27.50	10.00	5.00
R707	R25	$50	carmine	—	24.00	7.00	4.00
R708	R25	$60	carmine	—	100.00		40.00
R709	R25	$100	carmine	—	12.50	8.00	4.00
R710	R25	$500	carmine	175.00	85.00	50.00	30.00
R711	R25	$1000	carmine	—	80.00	30.00	
R712	R25	$2500	carmine	—	525.00	375.00	165.00
R713	R25	$5000	carmine	—	550.00	375.00	110.00
R714	R25	$10,000	carmine	—	375.00	150.00	100.00

Documentary Stamps and Type of 1940 Overprinted in Black "Series 1958"

1958 **Wmk. 191R** ***Perf. 12***

Without Gum

Size: 28½x42mm

R715	R25	$30	carmine	—	20.00	15.00	
R716	R25	$50	carmine	—	20.00	14.00	6.00
R717	R25	$60	carmine	—	25.00		10.00
R718	R25	$100	carmine	—	10.00	5.00	
R719	R25	$500	carmine	100.00	55.00		18.00
R720	R25	$1000	carmine	—	67.50	30.00	
R721	R25	$2500	carmine	—	600.00	375.00	275.00
R722	R25	$5000	carmine	—	1,350.	1,100.	1,000.
R723	R25	$10,000	carmine	—	650.00	550.00	300.00

Documentary Stamps and Type of 1940 Without Overprint

1958 **Wmk. 191R** ***Perf. 12***

With Gum

Size: 28½x42mm

R724	R25	$30	car	35.00	7.00	5.75	4.75
	a.		Vert. pair, imperf. horiz.	—			
R725	R25	$50	car	37.50	7.00	3.75	3.00
	a.		Vert. pair, imperf. horiz.	—			
R726	R25	$60	carmine	—	20.00	10.00	
R727	R25	$100	car	17.50	4.75	3.00	2.25
R728	R25	$500	car	80.00	25.00	10.00	7.50
R729	R25	$1000	car	50.00	20.00	10.00	7.50
	a.		Vert. pair, imperf. horiz.	—			
R730	R25	$2500	carmine	—	140.00	85.00	
R731	R25	$5000	carmine	—	150.00	85.00	60.00
R732	R25	$10,000	carmine	—	125.00	50.00	25.00

Internal Revenue Building, Washington, D.C. — R26

Centenary of the Internal Revenue Service.

Giori Press Printing

1962, July 2 **Unwmk.** ***Perf. 11***

R733	R26	10c	vio. bl. & brt. grn.	1.10	35	10	8
			Margin block of 4, P#	15.00			

1963

"Established 1862" Removed

R734	R26	10c	vio. bl. & brt. grn.	4.00	10	5	5
			Margin block of 4, P	35.00			

Documentary revenue stamps were no longer required after Dec. 31, 1967.

PROPRIETARY STAMPS

Stamps for use on proprietary articles were included in the first general issue of 1862-71. They are R3, R13, R14, R18, R22, R29, R31 and R38.

Several varieties of "violet" paper were used in printing Nos. RB1-RB10. One is grayish with a slight greenish tinge, called "intermediate" paper by specialists. It should not be confused with the "green" paper, which is truly green.

All values prior to 1898 are for used copies. Printed cancellations on proprietary stamps command sizable premiums.

George Washington
RB1 RB1a

Engraved and printed by Jos. R. Carpenter, Philadelphia.

1871-74 ***Perf. 12***

				a. Violet Paper (1871)	b. Green Paper (1874)
RB1	RB1	1c	green & black	4.00	6.00
			Pair	9.00	14.00
			Block of four	20.00	35.00
	c.		Imperf.	100.00	
			Imperf. pair	250.00	
			Imperf. block of four	600.00	
	d.		Inverted center	*2,500.*	
RB2	RB1	2c	green & black	4.50	13.00
			Pair	10.00	30.00
			Block of four	22.50	65.00
			Double transfer	—	
	c.		Inverted center	*40,000.*	*9,500.*

				a. Violet Paper (1871)	b. Green Paper (1874)
			Vert. half used as 1c		—
RB3	RB1a	3c	green & black	12.00	35.00
			Pair	30.00	80.00
			Block of four	60.00	175.00
			Double transfer	—	
		c.	Sewing machine perf.	125.00	
		d.	Inverted center	*15,000.*	
RB4	RB1a	4c	green & black	7.00	12.50
			Pair	18.00	30.00
			Block of four	40.00	70.00
			Double transfer	—	
		c.	Inverted center	*16,500.*	
			Vert. half used as 2c		—
RB5	RB1a	5c	green & black	90.00	95.00
			Pair	225.00	225.00
			Block of four	500.00	500.00
		c.	Inverted center	*40,000.*	
RB6	RB1a	6c	green & black	27.50	70.00
			Pair	65.00	150.00
			Block of four	150.00	400.00
			Double transfer	—	
RB7	RB1a	10c	green & black ('73)	125.00	35.00
			Pair	300.00	75.00
			Block of four	—	175.00
			Double transfer	—	

(See note on Inverted Centers after No. R133.)

RB1b

				a. Violet Paper	b. Green Paper (1874)
RB8	RB1b	50c	green & black ('73)	550.00	875.00
			Pair	*1,300.*	
RB9	RB1b	$1	green & black ('73)	*1,200.*	*3,000.*
			Pair	—	

Values for stamps vary greatly, depending upon centering, gum and condition.

An enhanced introduction to the Scott Catalogue begins on Page V. A thorough understanding of the material presented there will greatly aid your use of the catalogue itself.

RB1c

				a. Violet Paper
RB10	RB1c	$5	green & black ('73)	*2,500.*
			Pair	*5,500.*

When the Carpenter contract expired Aug. 31, 1875, the proprietary stamps remaining unissued were delivered to the Bureau of Internal Revenue. Until the taxes expired, June 30, 1883, the B.I.R. issued 34,315 of the 50c, 6,585 of the $1 and 2,109 of the $5, Nos. RB8-RB10. No. RB19, the 10c blue, replaced No. RB7b, the 10c on green paper, after 336,000 copies were issued, exhausting the supply in 1881.

George Washington
RB2 RB2a

Engraved and printed by the National Bank Note Co.

1875-81

				Silk Paper a. Perf.	Wmkd. USIR 191R b. Perf.	c. Rouletted 6
RB11	RB2	1c	green	1.50	35	30.00
			Pair	3.00	1.00	65.00
			Block of four	8.00	2.50	150.00
		d.	Vertical pair, imperf. between		*250.00*	
RB12	RB2	2c	brown	2.00	1.25	45.00
			Pair	5.00	3.00	100.00
			Block of four	10.00	7.00	250.00
RB13	RB2a	3c	orange	9.00	2.25	45.00
			Pair	20.00	5.00	100.00
			Block of four	45.00	12.00	225.00
		d.	Horizontal pair, imperf. between			—
RB14	RB2a	4c	red brown	4.50	4.00	
			Pair	10.00	9.00	
			Block of four	22.00	20.00	
RB15	RB2a	4c	red		3.50	50.00
			Pair		8.00	110.00
			Block of four		20.00	
RB16	RB2a	5c	black	80.00	70.00	*800.00*
			Pair	170.00	150.00	—
			Block of four	375.00	325.00	—
RB17	RB2a	6c	violet blue	20.00	13.00	125.00
			Pair	45.00	30.00	275.00
			Block of four	100.00	65.00	
RB18	RB2a	6c	violet		20.00	150.00
			Pair		45.00	325.00
			Block of four		100.00	
RB19	RB2a	10c	blue ('81)		175.00	
			Pair		375.00	
			Block of four		800.00	

No. RB19 was produced by the Bureau of Engraving and Printing after taking over the stamp printing contract in 1880.

Battleship — RB3

Inscribed "Series of 1898." and "Proprietary."

1898 Wmk. 191R Engr. *Rouletted 5½, 7*

See note on rouletting preceding No. R161.

				Rouletted 5½ Unused	Rouletted 5½ Used	p. Hyphen Hole Perf. 7 Unused	p. Hyphen Hole Perf. 7 Used
RB20	RB3	⅛c	yellow green	6	6	12	10
			Block of four	25	25	55	50
			Double transfer	—			
		a.	Vert. pair, imperf. horiz.	—			
RB21	RB3	¼c	brown	6	6	12	10
		a.	¼c red brown	6	6		
		b.	¼c yellow brown	6	6	12	10
		c.	¼c orange brown	6	6	12	10
		d.	¼c bister	6	6		
			Block of four	25	25	55	50
			Double transfer	—	—		
		e.	Vert. pair, imperf. horiz.	—	—		
		f.	Printed on both sides	—			
RB22	RB3	⅜c	deep orange	12	8	25	15
			Block of four	60	32	1.25	—
		a.	Horiz. pair, imperf. vert.	9.00			
		b.	Vert. pair, imperf. horiz.	—			
RB23	RB3	⅝c	deep ultramarine	12	10	25	15
			Block of four	60	40	1.25	75
			Double transfer	1.50			
		a.	Vert. pair, imperf. horiz.	50.00			
		b.	Horiz. pair, imperf. vert.	*200.00*			
RB24	RB3	1c	dark green	30	15	12.00	7.00
			Block of four	1.50	75	—	—
		a.	Vert. pair, imperf. horiz.	—			
RB25	RB3	1¼c	violet	10	8	20	12
			Block of four	45	35	90	90
		a.	1¼c brown violet	12	10	20	12

				Rouletted 5 1/2 Unused	Rouletted 5 1/2 Used	p. Hyphen Hole Perf. 7 Unused	p. Hyphen Hole Perf. 7 Used
			b. Vertical pair, imperf. between	—			
RB26	RB3	1 7/8c	dull blue	2.00	65	7.50	—
			Block of four	10.00	—	50.00	—
			Double transfer	—			
RB27	RB3	2c	violet brown	35	18	75	25
			Block of four	1.75	—	4.00	—
			Double transfer		—		
			a. Horiz. pair, imperf. vert.	25.00			
RB28	RB3	2 1/2c	lake	40	12	50	20
			Block of four	2.00	60	—	—
			a. Vert. pair, imperf. horiz.	30.00			
RB29	RB3	3 3/4c	olive gray	5.00	2.50	10.00	5.00
			Block of four	25.00	—	55.00	25.00
RB30	RB3	4c	purple	2.00	75	—	—
			Block of four	10.00	3.75	—	—
			Double transfer	—			
RB31	RB3	5c	brown orange	2.00	75	10.00	6.00
			Block of four	10.00	4.00	—	—
			a. Vert. pair, imperf. horiz.	—	*225.00*		
			b. Horiz. pair, imperf. vert.	—			

See note after No. RS315 regarding St. Louis Provisional Labels of 1898.

RB4

Inscribed "Series of 1914"

1914 Wmk. 190 Offset Printing *Perf. 10*

				Unused	Used
RB32	RB4	1/8c	black	20	15
			Block of four	1.00	75
RB33	RB4	1/4c	black	1.25	1.00
			Block of four	6.00	
RB34	RB4	3/8c	black	20	15
			Block of four	90	75
RB35	RB4	5/8c	black	2.50	1.75
			Block of four	11.00	
RB36	RB4	1 1/4c	black	1.75	80
			Block of four	8.00	
RB37	RB4	1 7/8c	black	25.00	15.00
			Block of four	110.00	
RB38	RB4	2 1/2c	black	3.50	2.50
			Block of four	16.00	11.00
RB39	RB4	3 1/8c	black	70.00	50.00
			Block of four	300.00	
RB40	RB4	3 3/4c	black	25.00	19.00
			Block of four	110.00	
RB41	RB4	4c	black	45.00	24.00
			Block of four	200.00	
RB42	RB4	4 3/8c	black	*900.00*	—
			Block of four	—	
RB43	RB4	5c	black	90.00	65.00
			Block of four	375.00	
			Wmk. 191R		
RB44	RB4	1/8c	black	15	10
			Block of four	75	45
RB45	RB4	1/4c	black	15	10
			Block of four	75	45
			Double impression	12.50	
RB46	RB4	3/8c	black	60	30
			Block of four	3.00	1.50
RB47	RB4	1/2c	black	3.00	2.75
			Block of four	12.50	
RB48	RB4	5/8c	black	15	10
			Block of four	70	45
RB49	RB4	1c	black	4.25	4.00
			Block of four	17.50	14.00
RB50	RB4	1 1/4c	black	35	25
			Block of four	1.50	1.10
RB51	RB4	1 1/2c	black	3.00	2.25
			Block of four	14.00	10.00
RB52	RB4	1 7/8c	black	1.00	60
			Block of four	4.50	2.25
RB53	RB4	2c	black	5.00	4.00
			Block of four	22.50	
RB54	RB4	2 1/2c	black	1.25	1.00
			Block of four	5.50	4.50
RB55	RB4	3c	black	3.50	2.75
			Block of four	15.00	
RB56	RB4	3 1/8c	black	4.50	3.00
			Block of four	20.00	
RB57	RB4	3 3/4c	black	9.00	7.50
			Block of four	37.50	
RB58	RB4	4c	black	30	20
			Block of four	1.50	1.00
			Double impression	—	
RB59	RB4	4 3/8c	black	11.00	7.50
			Block of four	45.00	
RB60	RB4	5c	black	2.75	2.50
			Block of four	12.50	
RB61	RB4	6c	black	45.00	37.50
			Block of four	210.00	
RB62	RB4	8c	black	13.50	11.00
			Block of four	60.00	
RB63	RB4	10c	black	9.00	7.00
			Block of four	40.00	
RB64	RB4	20c	black	17.50	15.00
			Block of four	80.00	

RB5

1919 Offset Printing *Perf. 11*

				Unused	Used
RB65	RB5	1c	dark blue	10	8
			Block of four	50	40
			Double impression	17.50	—
RB66	RB5	2c	dark blue	12	8
			Block of four	55	40
			Double impression	—	
RB67	RB5	3c	dark blue	1.00	60
			Block of four	4.50	2.75
			Double impression	—	
RB68	RB5	4c	dark blue	1.00	50
			Block of four	4.50	
RB69	RB5	5c	dark blue	1.25	60
			Block of four	5.50	2.75
RB70	RB5	8c	dark blue	11.00	9.00
			Block of four	46.00	
RB71	RB5	10c	dark blue	2.25	1.75
			Block of four	10.00	7.50
RB72	RB5	20c	dark blue	4.00	3.00
			Block of four	17.50	
RB73	RB5	40c	dark blue	22.50	8.00
			Block of four	95.00	

FUTURE DELIVERY STAMPS

Issued to facilitate the collection of a tax upon each sale, agreement of sale or agreement to sell any products or merchandise at any exchange or board of trade, or other similar place for future delivery.

Documentary Stamps of 1917 Overprinted in Black or Red

FUTURE

Type I

DELIVERY

1918-34 Wmk. 191R Offset Printing *Perf. 11*
Overprint Horizontal (Lines 8mm apart)

				Unused	Used
RC1	R22	2c	carmine rose	1.25	10
			Block of four	6.00	50
RC2	R22	3c	carmine rose ('34)	25.00	22.50
			Cut cancellation		12.50
RC3	R22	4c	carmine rose	1.25	10
			Block of four	6.00	50
			Double impression of stamp		10.00
RC3A	R22	5c	carmine rose ('33)	—	3.00
			Block of four	—	15.00
RC4	R22	10c	carmine rose	2.50	15
			Block of four	11.00	75
		a.	Double overprint	—	5.00
		b.	"FUTURE" omitted	—	
		c.	"DELIVERY FUTURE"		35.00
RC5	R22	20c	carmine rose	2.75	10
			Block of four	12.00	50
		a.	Double overprint		20.00
RC6	R22	25c	carmine rose	10.00	40
			Block of four	42.50	1.75
			Cut cancellation		6
			Block of four, cut canc.		25
RC7	R22	40c	carmine rose	10.00	75
			Block of four	45.00	3.50
			Cut cancellation		6
			Block of four, cut canc.		25
RC8	R22	50c	carmine rose	3.00	12
			Block of four	14.00	55
		a.	"DELIVERY" omitted	—	
RC9	R22	80c	carmine rose	20.00	7.50
			Block of four	85.00	35.00
			Cut cancellation		1.00
			Block of four, cut canc.		4.50
		a.	Double overprint		25.00
		a.	Cut cancellation		6.00

Engr.

Overprint Vertical, Reading Up (Lines 2mm apart)

				Unused	Used
RC10	R21	$1	green (R)	—	25
			Block of four	—	1.25
			Cut cancellation		5
		a.	Overprint reading down		*275.00*
		b.	Black overprint		—
			Black ovpt., cut canc.		125.00
RC11	R21	$2	rose	—	25
			Block of four	—	1.25
			Cut cancellation		5
RC12	R21	$3	violet (R)	—	1.25
			Block of four	—	6.00
			Cut cancellation		12
			Block of four, cut canc.		50
		a.	Overprint reading down	—	50.00
RC13	R21	$5	dark blue (R)	—	35
			Block of four	—	1.50
			Cut cancellation		8
			Block of four, cut canc.		35
RC14	R21	$10	orange	—	60
			Block of four	—	3.00
			Cut cancellation		15
			Block of four, cut canc.		75
		a.	"DELIVERY FUTURE"		—
RC15	R21	$20	olive bister	—	3.75
			Block of four		17.50
			Cut cancellation		50
			Block of four, cut canc.		2.25

Overprint Horizontal (Lines 11 2/3mm apart)
Perf. 12
Without Gum

				Unused	Used
RC16	R17	$30	vermilion, green numerals	—	3.00
			Vertical strip of four		—
			Cut cancellation		1.25
			Vertical strip of four, cut canc.		6.00
		a.	Numerals in blue	55.00	3.00
			Cut cancellation		1.50
		b.	Imperf., blue numerals		—
RC17	R19	$50	olive green *(Cleveland)*	—	1.00
			Vertical strip of four		—
			Cut cancellation		40
			Vertical strip of four, cut canc.		1.75
		a.	$50 olive bister	—	1.00
			Cut cancellation		40
RC18	R19	$60	brown	—	2.00
			Vertical strip of four		—
			Cut cancellation		75
			Vertical strip of four, cut cance.		3.50
		a.	Vert. pair, imperf. horiz.		*400.00*
RC19	R17	$100	yellow green ('34)	55.00	22.50
			Vertical strip of four	—	
			Cut cancellation		6.75
			Vertical strip of four, cut canc.		30.00
RC20	R18	$500	blue, red numerals (R)	50.00	10.00
			Vertical strip of four		—
			Cut cancellation		4.50
			Vertical strip of four, cut canc.		20.00
			Double transfer		15.00
		a.	Numerals in orange	—	65.00
		a.	Cut cancellation		11.00
		a.	Double transfer		125.00
RC21	R19	$1000	orange	—	4.00
			Vertical strip of four		20.00
			Cut cancellation		1.50
			Vertical strip of four, cut canc.		7.50
		a.	Vert. pair, imperf. horiz.		*500.00*

See note after No. R227.

1923-24 Offset Printing *Perf. 11*
Overprint Horizontal (Lines 2mm apart)

				Unused	Used
RC22	R22	1c	carmine rose	75	15
			Block of four	3.50	70
RC23	R22	80c	carmine rose	—	1.75
			Block of four	—	8.00
			Cut cancellation		25
			Block of four, cut canc.		1.10

Documentary Stamps of 1917 Overprinted

FUTURE

Type II

DELIVERY

1925-34 Engr.

				Unused	Used
RC25	R21	$1	green (R)	8.00	60
			Block of four	—	2.75
			Cut cancellation		6

No.	Type	Value	Description	Unused	Used
			Block of four, cut canc.		30
RC26	R21	$10	orange (Bk) ('34)	—	12.00
			Cut cancellation		7.00

Overprint Type I

1928-29 Offset Printing *Perf. 10*

No.	Type	Value	Description	Unused	Used
RC27	R22	10c	carmine rose		*1,000.*
RC28	R22	20c	carmine rose		*1,000.*

STOCK TRANSFER STAMPS

Issued to facilitate the collection of a tax on all sales or agreements to sell, or memoranda of sales or delivery of, or transfers of legal title to shares or certificates of stock.

STOCK

Documentary Stamps of 1917 Overprinted in Black or Red

TRANSFER

1918-22 Offset Printing Wmk. 191R *Perf. 11*

Overprint Horizontal (Lines 8mm apart)

No.	Type	Value	Description	Unused	Used
RD1	R22	1c	carmine rose	30	10
			Block of four	1.50	45
		a.	Double overprint	—	—
RD2	R22	2c	carmine rose	15	5
			Block of four	—	20
		a.	Double overprint	—	5.00
		a.	Cut cancellation		2.50
			Double impression of stamp		—
RD3	R22	4c	carmine rose	12	5
			Block of four	50	20
		a.	Double overprint	—	4.00
		a.	Cut cancellation		2.00
		b.	"STOCK" omitted		10.00
		d.	Ovpt. lines 10mm. apart	—	
			Double impression of stamp		6.00
RD4	R22	5c	carmine rose	20	5
			Block of four	90	25
RD5	R22	10c	carmine rose	12	5
			Block of four	—	25
		a.	Double overprint	—	5.00
		a.	Cut cancellation		2.50
		b.	"STOCK" omitted		—
			Double impression of stamp		—
RD6	R22	20c	carmine rose	20	5
			Block of four	95	25
		a.	Double overprint		6.00
		b.	"STOCK" double		—
			Double impression of stamp		6.00
RD7	R22	25c	carmine rose	75	10
			Block of four	—	50
			Cut cancellation		5
RD8	R22	40c	carmine rose ('22)	65	6
			Block of four	—	30
RD9	R22	50c	carmine rose	25	5
			Block of four	70	25
		a.	Double overprint		
			Double impression of stamp		—
RD10	R22	80c	carmine rose	90	25
			Block of four	—	1.25
			Cut cancellation		5

Engr.

Overprint Vertical, Reading Up (Lines 2mm apart)

No.	Type	Value	Description	Unused	Used
RD11	R21	$1	green (R)	30.00	7.75
			Block of four	—	
			Cut cancellation		45
			Block of four, cut canc.		2.25
		a.	Overprint reading down	—	11.00
		a.	Cut cancellation		4.00
RD12	R21	$1	green (Bk)	1.50	5
			Block of four	—	25
		a.	Pair, one without overprint	—	
		b.	Overprinted on back instead of face, inverted	—	
		c.	Overprint reading down	—	6.00
		d.	$1 yellow green	—	6
RD13	R21	$2	rose	1.50	5
			Block of four	—	25
		a.	Overprint reading down		10.00
		a.	Cut cancellation		1.50
		b.	Vert. pair, imperf. horiz.	*500.00*	
		c.	"TRANSFER STOCK"		—
RD14	R21	$3	violet (R)	5.50	1.00
			Block of four	—	
			Cut cancellation		20
			Block of four, cut canc.		1.00
RD15	R21	$4	yellow brown	4.00	5
			Block of four	—	25
			Cut cancellation		5
RD16	R21	$5	dark blue (R)	2.25	5
			Block of four	—	25
			Cut cancellation		5
			Block of four, cut canc.		15
		a.	Overprint reading down	—	1.00
		a.	Cut cancellation		15
RD17	R21	$10	orange	3.50	12
			Block of four	19.00	75
			Cut cancellation		5
			Block of four, cut canc.		20
		a.	"TRANSFER STOCK"		—
		b.	"TRANSFER" omitted		—
RD18	R21	$20	olive bister ('21)	30.00	15.00
			Block of four	125.00	75.00
			Cut cancellation		3.00
			Block of four, cut canc.		15.00

Overprint Horizontal (Lines 11½mm apart)

1918 Without Gum *Perf. 12*

No.	Type	Value	Description	Unused	Used
RD19	R17	$30	vermilion, green numerals	12.50	4.00
			Vertical strip of four		17.50
			Cut cancellation		1.00
			Vertical strip of four, cut canc.		6.00
		a.	Numerals in blue		50.00
RD20	R19	$50	olive green *(Cleveland)*	75.00	50.00
			Vertical strip of four		225.00
			Cut cancellation		17.00
			Vertical strip of four, cut canc.		75.00
RD21	R19	$60	brown	50.00	16.00
			Vertical strip of four		70.00
			Cut cancellation		8.50
			Vertical strip of four, cut canc.		37.50
RD22	R17	$100	green	15.00	5.00
			Vertical strip of four		22.50
			Cut cancellation		2.00
			Vertical strip of four, cut canc.		9.00
RD23	R18	$500	blue (R)	—	100.00
			Vertical strip of four		—
			Cut cancellation		60.00
			Vertical strip of four, cut canc.		265.00
			Double transfer		125.00
		a.	Numerals in orange		125.00
RD24	R19	$1000	orange	—	65.00
			Vertical strip of four		275.00
			Cut cancellation		22.50
			Vertical strip of four, cut canc.		100.00

See note after No. R227.

1928 Offset Printing *Perf. 10*

Overprint Horizontal (Lines 8mm apart)

No.	Type	Value	Description	Unused	Used
RD25	R22	2c	carmine rose	50	5
			Block of four	2.25	25
RD26	R22	4c	carmine rose	45	5
			Block of four	2.00	25
RD27	R22	10c	carmine rose	50	6
			Block of four	2.25	25
		a.	Inverted overprint		*1,000.*
RD28	R22	20c	carmine rose	60	6
			Block of four	2.50	25
			Double impression of stamp		—
RD29	R22	50c	carmine rose	1.25	10
			Block of four	6.00	45

Engr.

Overprint Vertical, Reading Up (Lines 2mm apart)

No.	Type	Value	Description	Unused	Used
RD30	R21	$1	green	2.00	5
			Block of four	—	25
		a.	$1 yellow green	—	—
RD31	R21	$2	carmine rose	2.00	5
			Block of four	—	25
		a.	Pair, one without overprint	*150.00*	
RD32	R21	$10	orange	8.00	15
			Block of four	—	75
			Cut cancellation		5
			Perf. 11 at top or bottom		—

STOCK

Overprinted Horizontally in Black

TRANSFER

1920 Offset Printing *Perf. 11*

No.	Type	Value	Description	Unused	Used
RD33	R22	2c	carmine rose	3.00	50
			Block of four	13.00	2.25
RD34	R22	10c	carmine rose	50	5
			Block of four	2.25	20
		a.	"TRANSFER STOCK"		40.00
RD35	R22	20c	carmine rose	60	5
			Block of four	2.75	25
		a.	Pair, one without overprint	*175.00*	—
		b.	"TRANSFER STOCK"		75.00
		c.	"TRANSFER" omitted		65.00
RD36	R22	50c	carmine rose	1.25	8
			Block of four	5.25	35

Engr.

No.	Type	Value	Description	Unused	Used
RD37	R21	$1	green	12.50	6.50
			Block of four	—	22.50
			Cut cancellation		25
			Block of four, cut canc.		65
RD38	R21	$2	rose	10.00	6.00
			Block of four	45.00	27.50
			Cut cancellation		25
			Block of four, cut canc.		1.10

Offset Printing

Perf. 10

No.	Type	Value	Description	Unused	Used
RD39	R22	2c	carmine rose	2.75	35
			Block of four	12.00	1.65
			Double impression of stamp	—	
RD40	R22	10c	carmine rose	90	10
			Block of four	4.00	50
RD41	R22	20c	carmine rose	1.25	6
			Block of four	6.00	25

SERIES 1940

Documentary Stamps of 1917-33 Overprinted in Black

STOCK TRANSFER

1940 Offset Printing Wmk. 191R *Perf. 11*

No.	Type	Value	Color	Unused	Used (uncut)	Used (cut canc.)	Used (perf. initials)
RD42	R22	1c	rose pink	1.75	45	20	15
		a.	"Series 1940" inverted	—	225.00	100.00	
RD43	R22	2c	rose pink	1.10	50	8	6
RD45	R22	4c	rose pink	1.10	10	5	5
RD46	R22	5c	rose pink	1.25	10	5	5
RD48	R22	10c	rose pink	1.75	10	5	5
RD49	R22	20c	rose pink	5.00	15	5	5
RD50	R22	25c	rose pink	5.00	35	12	10
RD51	R22	40c	rose pink	2.50	60	15	10
RD52	R22	50c	rose pink	3.50	15	6	5
RD53	R22	80c	rose pink	45.00	25.00	7.50	5.50

Engr.

No.	Type	Value	Color	Unused	Used (uncut)	Used (cut canc.)	Used (perf. initials)
RD54	R21	$1	green	9.00	25	8	5
RD55	R21	$2	rose	9.00	25	8	6
RD56	R21	$3	violet	—	3.00	8	6
RD57	R21	$4	yellow brown	10.00	38	5	5
RD58	R21	$5	dark blue	12.00	42	12	5
RD59	R21	$10	orange	30.00	3.50	50	40
RD60	R21	$20	olive bister	55.00	22.50	6.75	5.50

Nos. RD19-RD24 Handstamped in Blue "Series 1940"

1940 Wmk. 191R *Perf. 12*

Without Gum

No.	Type	Value	Color			
RD61	R17	$30	vermilion	350.00	175.00	125.00
RD62	R19	$50	olive green	500.00	100.00	100.00
		a.	Double overprint			*325.00*
RD63	R19	$60	brown	475.00	125.00	100.00
RD64	R17	$100	green	400.00	100.00	60.00
RD65	R18	$500	blue	1,250.	900.00	375.00
RD66	R19	$1000	orange	1,750.	1,500.	1,250.

Alexander Hamilton — ST1

Levi Woodbury — ST2

Overprinted in Black **SERIES 1940**

Various Portraits

1940 **Engr.** **Wmk. 191R** ***Perf. 11***

Size: 19x22mm

RD67	ST1	1c	bright green	4.75	1.75	50	30
RD68	ST1	2c	bright green *(Oliver Wolcott, Jr.)*	2.00	75	12	10
RD70	ST1	4c	bright green *(Albert Gallatin)*	4.50	2.25	50	25
RD71	ST1	5c	bright green *(G. W. Campbell)*	3.00	1.00	15	8
		a.	Without overprint			—	
RD73	ST1	10c	bright green *(William H. Crawford)*	4.00	90	20	8
RD74	ST1	20c	bright green *(Richard Rush)*	4.00	75	15	10
RD75	ST1	25c	bright green *(S. D. Ingham)*	15.00	4.50	60	35
RD76	ST1	40c	bright green *(Louis McLane)*	30.00	21.00	1.75	85
RD77	ST1	50c	bright green *(Wm. J. Duane)*	4.00	90	30	25
RD78	ST1	80c	bright green *(R. B. Taney)*	40.00	25.00	12.00	2.50

Size: 21½x36¼mm

RD79	ST2	$1	bright green	7.00	1.25	35	25
		a.	Without overprint				*150.00*
RD80	ST2	$2	bright green *(Thomas Ewing)*	8.50	3.50	35	25
RD81	ST2	$3	bright green *(Walter Forward)*	16.00	5.00	50	8
RD82	ST2	$4	bright green *(J. C. Spencer)*	—	100.00	50.00	40.00
RD83	ST2	$5	bright green *(G. M. Bibb)*	16.00	7.00	30	20
RD84	ST2	$10	bright green *(R. J. Walker)*	—	20.00	75	90
RD85	ST2	$20	bright green *(Wm. M. Meredith)*	—	22.50	4.50	2.50

Nos. RD67-RD85 exist imperforate, without overprint.

Thomas Corwin — ST3

Overprinted "SERIES 1940"
Various Frames and Portraits
Without Gum
Size: 28½x42mm

RD86	ST3	$30	bright green	—	87.50	40.00	22.50
RD87	ST3	$50	bright green *(James Guthrie)*	—	125.00	45.00	37.50
RD88	ST3	$60	bright green *(Howell Cobb)*	—	165.00	45.00	40.00
RD89	ST3	$100	bright green *(P. F. Thomas)*	—	125.00	55.00	35.00
RD90	ST3	$500	bright green *(J. A. Dix)*	—	375.00	300.00	
RD91	ST3	$1000	bright green *(S. P. Chase)*	—	275.00	250.00	225.00

Nos. RD67-RD91 Overprint Instead: **SERIES 1941**

1941 **Wmk. 191R** ***Perf. 11***

Size: 19x22mm

RD92	ST1	1c	bright green	50	25	15	10
RD93	ST1	2c	bright green	25	8	6	5
RD95	ST1	4c	bright green	25	6	5	5
RD96	ST1	5c	bright green	25	6	5	5
RD98	ST1	10c	bright green	35	6	5	5
RD99	ST1	20c	bright green	80	6	5	5
RD100	ST1	25c	bright green	1.00	20	8	6
RD101	ST1	40c	bright green	1.10	25	8	6
RD102	ST1	50c	bright green	2.25	15	5	5
RD103	ST1	80c	bright green	9.00	3.75	25	12

Size: 21½x36¼mm

RD104	ST2	$1	bright green	5.00	10	5	5
RD105	ST2	$2	bright green	6.00	15	8	5
RD106	ST2	$3	bright green	8.00	1.00	30	5
RD107	ST2	$4	bright green	15.00	4.50	25	15
RD108	ST2	$5	bright green	18.00	40	10	6
RD109	ST2	$10	bright green	35.00	2.50	70	15
RD110	ST2	$20	bright green	—	32.50	7.50	1.65

Perf. 12
Without Gum
Size: 28½x42mm

RD111	ST3	$30	bright green	85.00	80.00	16.00	9.00
RD112	ST3	$50	bright green	—	85.00	18.00	13.00
RD113	ST3	$60	bright green	160.00	100.00		
RD114	ST3	$100	bright green	—	55.00	18.00	8.00
RD115	ST3	$500	bright green	—	325.00		150.00
RD116	ST3	$1000	bright green	—	275.00		165.00

Nos. RD67-RD91 Overprint Instead: **SERIES 1942**

1942 **Wmk. 191R** ***Perf. 11***

Size: 19x22mm

RD117	ST1	1c	bright green	35	15	10	7
RD118	ST1	2c	bright green	20	15	6	5
RD119	ST1	4c	bright green	2.25	70	50	40
RD120	ST1	5c	bright green	30	10	5	5
		a.	Overprint inverted (Cut cancel.)			*225.00*	
RD121	ST1	10c	bright green	75	10	5	5
RD122	ST1	20c	bright green	1.10	10	6	5
RD123	ST1	25c	bright green	1.25	10	6	5
RD124	ST1	40c	bright green	2.25	25	10	8
RD125	ST1	50c	bright green	3.00	10	5	5
RD126	ST1	80c	bright green	7.00	3.50	1.00	20

Size: 21½x36¼mm

RD127	ST2	$1	bright green	5.50	10	5	5
RD128	ST2	$2	bright green	8.50	15	8	6
RD129	ST2	$3	bright green	11.00	55	10	6
RD130	ST2	$4	bright green	17.50	11.00	35	18
RD131	ST2	$5	bright green	13.00	25	10	5
		a.	Double ovpt.				—
RD132	ST2	$10	bright green	27.50	4.50	65	20
RD133	ST2	$20	bright green	55.00	21.00	3.25	1.00

Perf. 12
Without Gum
Size: 28½x42mm

RD134	ST3	$30	bright green	—	35.00	12.00	6.00
RD135	ST3	$50	bright green	—	65.00	16.00	6.00
RD136	ST3	$60	bright green	—	85.00		35.00
RD137	ST3	$100	bright green	—	67.50	22.50	10.00
RD138	ST3	$500	bright green	—	—		
RD139	ST3	$1000	bright green	—	250.00	150.00	

Nos. RD67-RD91 Overprint Instead: **SERIES 1943**

1943 **Wmk. 191R** ***Perf. 11***

Size: 19x22mm

RD140	ST1	1c	bright green	30	20	15	10
RD141	ST1	2c	bright green	40	20	6	5
RD142	ST1	4c	bright green	1.10	10	8	5
RD143	ST1	5c	bright green	40	10	6	5
RD144	ST1	10c	bright green	45	10	5	5
RD145	ST1	20c	bright green	1.00	10	6	5
RD146	ST1	25c	bright green	2.25	25	12	8
RD147	ST1	40c	bright green	2.25	25	10	8
RD148	ST1	50c	bright green	2.25	10	5	5
RD149	ST1	80c	bright green	6.00	2.50	1.25	75

Size: 21½x36¼mm

RD150	ST2	$1	bright green	5.25	10	6	5
RD151	ST2	$2	bright green	6.00	20	10	5
RD152	ST2	$3	bright green	7.50	75	10	5
RD153	ST2	$4	bright green	16.00	10.00	35	15
RD154	ST2	$5	bright green	26.00	35	20	6
RD155	ST2	$10	bright green	27.50	3.00	75	8
RD156	ST2	$20	bright green	45.00	22.50	10.00	2.75

Perf. 12
Without Gum
Size: 28½x42mm

RD157	ST3	$30	bright green	175.00	90.00	20.00	17.50
RD158	ST3	$50	bright green	—	90.00	20.00	12.00
RD158	ST3	$60	bright green	—	110.00	60.00	40.00
RD160	ST3	$100	bright green	—	45.00	15.00	10.00
RD161	ST3	$500	bright green	—	175.00	90.00	
RD162	ST3	$1000	bright green	—	165.00	125.00	90.00

Nos. RD67-RD91 Overprint Instead: **Series 1944**

1944 **Wmk. 191R** ***Perf. 11***

Size: 19x22mm

RD163	ST1	1c	bright green	50	40	15	12
RD164	ST1	2c	bright green	35	15	10	8
RD165	ST1	4c	bright green	50	20	15	12
RD166	ST1	3c	bright green	40	10	5	5
RD167	ST1	10c	bright green	40	10	6	5
RD168	ST1	20c	bright green	60	15	10	8
RD169	ST1	25c	bright green	1.25	30	16	10
RD170	ST1	40c	bright green	4.50	3.75	2.00	1.25
RD171	ST1	50c	bright green	2.50	15	10	6
RD172	ST1	80c	bright green	4.00	3.00	1.90	1.25

Size: 21½x36¼mm

RD173	ST2	$1	bright green	3.50	30	10	8

RD174	ST2	$2	bright green	—	35	15	8
RD175	ST2	$3	bright green	9.00	75	25	8
RD176	ST2	$4	bright green	13.00	3.50	18	10
RD177	ST2	$5	bright green	11.00	60	30	15
RD178	ST2	$10	bright green	25.00	3.00	45	20
RD179	ST2	$20	bright green	50.00	5.50	3.00	1.50

Perf. 12
Without Gum
Size: 28½x42mm

RD180	ST3	$30	bright green	50.00	42.50	11.00	9.00
RD181	ST3	$50	bright green	50.00	35.00	11.00	8.00
RD182	ST3	$60	bright green	125.00	75.00		40.00
RD183	ST3	$100	bright green	—	40.00	15.00	9.00
RD184	ST3	$500	bright green	—	300.00	225.00	175.00
RD185	ST3	$1000	bright green	—		175.00	150.00
RD185A	ST3	$2500	bright green *(William Windom)*	—	—		
RD185B	ST3	$5000	bright green *(C.J. Folger)*	—	—		
RD185C	ST3	$10,000	bright green *(W.Q. Gresham)*	—	—	*800.00*	

Nos. RD67-RD91 Overprint Instead: **Series 1945**

1945 **Wmk. 191R** ***Perf. 11***
Size: 19x22mm

RD186	ST1	1c	bright green	12	10	6	5
RD187	ST1	2c	bright green	20	15	8	6
RD188	ST1	4c	bright green	15	10	6	5
RD189	ST1	5c	bright green	18	10	5	5
RD190	ST1	10c	bright green	40	30	10	8
RD191	ST1	20c	bright green	60	25	20	12
RD192	ST1	25c	bright green	1.00	35	25	20
RD193	ST1	40c	bright green	1.65	20	12	8
RD194	ST1	50c	bright green	1.75	20	8	6
RD195	ST1	80c	bright green	2.75	2.00	70	65

Size: 21½x36¼mm

RD196	ST2	$1	bright green	6.00	20	8	6
RD197	ST2	$2	bright green	8.50	25	10	8
RD198	ST2	$3	bright green	12.00	50	12	10
RD199	ST2	$4	bright green	12.00	1.25	45	40
RD200	ST2	$5	bright green	10.00	30	15	8
RD201	ST2	$10	bright green	20.00	3.75	75	60
RD202	ST2	$20	bright green	35.00	4.25	1.00	85

Perf. 12
Without Gum
Size: 28½x42mm

RD203	ST3	$30	bright green	60.00	35.00	17.50	17.00
RD204	ST3	$50	bright green	40.00	13.00	4.00	3.75
RD205	ST3	$60	bright green	100.00	70.00	22.50	15.00
RD206	ST3	$100	bright green	—	20.00	12.00	8.00
RD207	ST3	$500	bright green	—	200.00	135.00	115.00
RD208	ST3	$1000	bright green	—	225.00		140.00
RD208A	ST3	$2500	bright green	—	—		
RD208B	ST3	$5000	bright green	—	—		
RD208C	ST3	$10,000	bright green	—		*800.00*	

The Catalogue editors cannot undertake to appraise, identify or judge the genuineness or condition of stamps.

Stock Transfer Stamps and Type of 1940 Overprinted in Black

Series 1946

1946 **Wmk. 191R** ***Perf. 11***
Size: 19x22mm

RD209	ST1	1c	bright green	15	10	6	5
		a.	Pair, one dated "1945"	*375.00*			
RD210	ST1	2c	bright green	20	10	5	5
RD211	ST1	4c	bright green	15	10	6	5
RD212	ST1	5c	bright green	30	10	5	5
RD213	ST1	10c	bright green	40	10	5	5
RD214	ST1	20c	bright green	90	15	10	8
RD215	ST1	25c	bright green	85	20	10	8
RD216	ST1	40c	bright green	1.50	40	15	12
RD217	ST1	50c	bright green	1.75	20	12	10
RD218	ST1	80c	bright green	3.75	3.00	1.75	1.00

Size: 21½x36¼mm

RD219	ST2	$1	bright green	3.00	30	8	6
RD220	ST2	$2	bright green	4.00	30	15	12
RD221	ST2	$3	bright green	7.00	75	30	18
RD222	ST2	$4	bright green	7.50	3.00	1.75	85
RD223	ST2	$5	bright green	11.00	65	20	18
RD224	ST2	$10	bright green	22.50	1.25	60	15
RD225	ST2	$20	bright green	35.00	21.00	9.00	5.00

Perf. 12
Without Gum
Size: 28½x42mm

RD226	ST3	$30	bright green	45.00	25.00	15.00	14.00
RD227	ST3	$50	bright green	45.00	25.00	10.00	9.00
RD228	ST3	$60	bright green	100.00	60.00	27.50	10.00
RD229	ST3	$100	bright green	60.00	30.00	10.00	10.00
RD230	ST3	$500	bright green	—	125.00		65.00
RD231	ST3	$1000	bright green	—	110.00		75.00
RD232	ST3	$2500	bright green	—	—		
RD233	ST3	$5000	bright green	—	—		
RD234	ST3	$10,000	bright green	—	—	*800.00*	

Stock Transfer Stamps and Type of 1940 Overprinted in Black

Series 1947

1947 **Wmk. 191R** ***Perf. 11***
Size: 19x22mm

RD235	ST1	1c	bright green	50	40	8	6
RD236	ST1	2c	bright green	40	25	8	8
RD237	ST1	4c	bright green	30	25	6	5
RD238	ST1	5c	bright green	25	20	5	5
RD239	ST1	10c	bright green	40	25	6	5
RD240	ST1	20c	bright green	60	30	15	12
RD241	ST1	25c	bright green	90	35	18	15
RD242	ST1	40c	bright green	1.25	45	25	18
RD243	ST1	50c	bright green	1.65	15	5	5
RD244	ST1	80c	bright green	7.50	5.50	3.25	3.00

Size: 21½x36¼mm

RD245	ST2	$1	bright green	3.00	35	15	12
RD246	ST2	$2	bright green	5.00	50	15	12
RD247	ST2	$3	bright green	7.00	90	35	30
RD248	ST2	$4	bright green	15.00	4.50	85	70
RD249	ST2	$5	bright green	10.00	90	30	20
RD250	ST2	$10	bright green	17.50	3.00	1.90	1.10
RD251	ST2	$20	bright green	35.00	17.50		4.50

Perf. 12
Without Gum
Size: 28½x42mm

RD252	ST3	$30	bright green	50.00	27.50	7.00	6.50
RD253	ST3	$50	bright green	100.00	70.00	20.00	12.50
RD254	ST3	$60	bright green	100.00	85.00	30.00	27.50
RD255	ST3	$100	bright green	—	21.00	10.00	11.50
RD256	ST3	$500	bright green	—	200.00	90.00	67.50
RD257	ST3	$1000	bright green	—	75.00	42.50	25.00
RD258	ST3	$2500	bright green	—		*350.00*	
RD259	ST3	$5000	bright green	—		*350.00*	
RD260	ST3	$10,000	bright green	—		65.00	
		a.	Horiz. pair, imperf. vert.			—	

Nos. RD67-RD91 Overprint Instead: **Series 1948**

1948 **Wmk. 191R** ***Perf. 11***
Size: 19x22mm

RD261	ST1	1c	bright green	15	15	6	5
RD262	ST1	2c	bright green	15	15	6	5
RD263	ST1	4c	bright green	25	20	12	8
RD264	ST1	5c	bright green	20	15	6	5
RD265	ST1	10c	bright green	25	15	6	5
RD266	ST1	20c	bright green	65	25	10	8
RD267	ST1	25c	bright green	75	30	15	12
RD268	ST1	40c	bright green	1.10	40	25	20
RD269	ST1	50c	bright green	2.00	20	8	8
RD270	ST1	80c	bright green	6.00	5.00	1.90	1.65

Size: 21½x36¼mm

RD271	ST2	$1	bright green	3.50	30	12	10
RD272	ST2	$2	bright green	6.00	40	15	15
RD273	ST2	$3	bright green	7.00	2.50	1.40	1.00
RD274	ST2	$4	bright green	8.00	6.00	2.00	1.75
RD275	ST2	$5	bright green	12.00	1.25	25	20
RD276	ST2	$10	bright green	18.00	3.00	75	60
RD277	ST2	$20	bright green	35.00	12.00	4.50	

Perf. 12
Without Gum
Size: 28½x42mm

RD278	ST3	$30	bright green	50.00	32.50	18.00	10.00
RD279	ST3	$50	bright green	40.00	32.50	9.00	6.00
RD280	ST3	$60	bright green	75.00	65.00	22.50	15.00
RD281	ST3	$100	bright green	—	14.00	6.00	4.00
RD282	ST3	$500	bright green	—	150.00	85.00	40.00
RD283	ST3	$1000	bright green	—	85.00	30.00	25.00
RD284	ST3	$2500	bright green	275.00	250.00	117500	
RD285	ST3	$5000	bright green	—	250.00	175.00	
RD286	ST3	$10,000	bright green	—		60.00	

Nos. RD67-RD91 Overprint Instead: **Series 1949**

1949 **Wmk. 191R** ***Perf. 11***
Size: 19x22mm

RD287	ST1	1c	bright green	25	20	6	5
RD288	ST1	2c	bright green	25	20	5	5
RD289	ST1	4c	bright green	30	25	6	5
RD290	ST1	5c	bright green	30	25	6	5
RD291	ST1	10c	bright green	50	25	5	5

RD292	ST1	20c	bright green	1.00	30	10	8
RD293	ST1	25c	bright green	1.25	50	12	10
RD294	ST1	40c	bright green	2.50	90	20	15
RD295	ST1	50c	bright green	2.50	25	6	5
RD296	ST1	80c	bright green	5.00	3.50	2.50	2.25

Size: 21½x36¼mm

RD297	ST2	$1	bright green	3.50	40	10	8
RD298	ST2	$2	bright green	6.00	60	18	15
RD299	ST2	$3	bright green	10.00	3.50	1.10	90
RD300	ST2	$4	bright green	12.00	6.00	2.00	1.50
RD301	ST2	$5	bright green	17.50	1.75	25	20
RD302	ST2	$10	bright green	25.00	3.00	1.25	1.00
RD303	ST2	$20	bright green	50.00	12.00	5.00	4.00

Perf. 12

Without Gum

Size: 28½x42mm

RD304	ST3	$30	bright green	—	35.00	12.00	
RD305	ST3	$50	bright green	—	45.00	14.00	9.00
RD306	ST3	$60	bright green	125.00	90.00	32.50	
RD307	ST3	$100	bright green	—	45.00	20.00	14.00
RD308	ST3	$500	bright green	—	135.00	55.00	40.00
RD309	ST3	$1000	bright green	—	70.00	40.00	27.50
RD310	ST3	$2500	bright green	—		*400.00*	
RD311	ST3	$5000	bright green	—		*375.00*	275.00
RD312	ST3	$10,000	bright green	—		30.00	
	a.		Pair, one without overprint			—	

Nos. RD67-RD91 Overprint Instead: **Series 1950**

1950 **Wmk. 191R** ***Perf. 11***

Size: 19x22mm

RD313	ST1	1c	bright green	25	20	5	5
RD314	ST1	2c	bright green	25	20	5	5
RD315	ST1	4c	bright green	25	20	6	5
RD316	ST1	5c	bright green	30	15	5	5
RD317	ST1	10c	bright green	1.00	20	5	5
RD318	ST1	20c	bright green	1.25	30	6	5
RD319	ST1	25c	bright green	2.25	40	12	10
RD320	ST1	40c	bright green	2.50	60	20	18
RD321	ST1	50c	bright green	4.00	30	6	5
RD322	ST1	80c	bright green	3.50	3.50	2.00	1.10

Size: 21½x36¼mm

RD323	ST2	$1	bright green	4.00	35	8	6
RD324	ST2	$2	bright green	7.50	50	12	10
RD325	ST2	$3	bright green	11.00	2.75	60	50
RD326	ST2	$4	bright green	12.50	6.50	2.25	1.75
RD327	ST2	$5	bright green	16.00	1.25	20	18
RD328	ST2	$10	bright green	30.00	4.00	85	75
RD329	ST2	$20	bright green	40.00	14.00		4.00

Perf. 12

Without Gum

Size: 28½x42mm

RD330	ST3	$30	bright green	60.00	35.00	22.50	14.00
RD331	ST3	$50	bright green	70.00	55.00		22.50
RD332	ST3	$60	bright green	—	75.00	40.00	
RD333	ST3	$100	bright green	—	30.00	20.00	10.00
RD334	ST3	$500	bright green	—	110.00		75.00
RD335	ST3	$1000	bright green	—	70.00	27.50	22.50
RD336	ST3	$2500	bright green	—		500.00	
RD337	ST3	$5000	bright green	—	375.00	275.00	
RD338	ST3	$10,000	bright green	—		60.00	

Nos. RD67-RD91 Overprint Instead: **Series 1951**

1951 **Wmk. 191R** ***Perf. 11***

Size: 19x22mm

RD339	ST1	1c	bright green	30	25	5	5
RD340	ST1	2c	bright green	30	25	5	5
RD341	ST1	4c	bright green	40	30	5	5
RD342	ST1	5c	bright green	40	25	5	5
RD343	ST1	10c	bright green	50	25	5	5
RD344	ST1	20c	bright green	1.25	50	12	10
RD345	ST1	25c	bright green	1.75	50	15	12
RD346	ST1	40c	bright green	3.00	2.75	50	40
RD347	ST1	50c	bright green	3.00	50	8	6
RD348	ST1	80c	bright green	4.50	3.50	2.00	2.00

Size: 21½x36¼mm

RD349	ST2	$1	bright green	6.00	50	6	5
RD350	ST2	$2	bright green	7.00	75	18	12
RD351	ST2	$3	bright green	11.00	5.50		
RD352	ST2	$4	bright green	13.00	7.50		1.50
RD353	ST2	$5	bright green	18.00	2.00	25	20
RD354	ST2	$10	bright green	30.00	7.50	2.00	1.50
RD355	ST2	$20	bright green	45.00	12.50	6.00	4.50

Perf. 12

Without Gum

Size: 28½x42mm

RD356	ST3	$30	bright green	—	27.50		14.00
RD357	ST3	$50	bright green	—	32.50		13.00
RD358	ST3	$60	bright green	—	*200.00*		85.00
RD359	ST3	$100	bright green	—	37.50	18.00	
RD360	ST3	$500	bright green	—	90.00		60.00
RD361	ST3	$1000	bright green	—	50.00		40.00
RD362	ST3	$2500	bright green	—	*565.00*	225.00	175.00
RD363	ST3	$5000	bright green	—	*575.00*	250.00	
RD364	ST3	$10,000	bright green	—	100.00	65.00	

Nos. RD67-RD91 Overprint Instead: **Series 1952**

1952 **Wmk. 191R** ***Perf. 11***

Size: 19x22mm

RD365	ST1	1c	bright green	20.00	10.00	2.00	1.25
RD366	ST1	10c	bright green	15.00	7.50	1.00	90
RD367	ST1	20c	bright green	350.00	—		
RD368	ST1	25c	bright green	475.00	—		
RD369	ST1	40c	bright green	40.00	15.00	6.00	3.00

Size: 21½x36¼mm

RD370	ST2	$4	bright green	750.00	350.00
RD371	ST2	$10	bright green	1,500.	—
RD372	ST2	$20	bright green	2,000.	—

Stock Transfer Stamps were discontinued in 1952.

CORDIALS, WINES, Etc.

RE1

Inscribed "Series of 1914"

Size: 19½x22¼mm

1914 **Wmk. 190** **Offset Printing** ***Perf. 10***

RE1	RE1	¼c	green	40	30
RE2	RE1	½c	green	30	20
RE3	RE1	1c	green	35	25
RE4	RE1	1½c	green	1.75	75
RE5	RE1	2c	green	3.00	2.00
RE6	RE1	3c	green	1.50	55
RE7	RE1	4c	green	1.75	1.25
RE8	RE1	5c	green	55	30
RE9	RE1	6c	green	3.50	1.75
RE10	RE1	8c	green	2.25	75
RE11	RE1	10c	green	2.25	2.00
RE12	RE1	20c	green	2.00	90
RE13	RE1	24c	green	7.50	4.50
RE14	RE1	40c	green	1.75	50

RE1a

Without Gum ***Imperf.***

Size: 47x40mm

RE15	RE1a	$2	green	2.75	20
	a.		Double impression		90.00

1914 **Wmk. 191R** ***Perf. 10***

RE16	RE1	¼c	green	2.50	2.25
RE17	RE1	½c	green	1.25	1.00
RE18	RE1	1c	green	25	8
RE19	RE1	1½c	green	30.00	25.00
RE20	RE1	2c	green	10	8
RE21	RE1	3c	green	1.50	1.25
RE22	RE1	4c	green	75	60
RE23	RE1	5c	green	7.00	6.00
RE24	RE1	6c	green	50	25
RE25	RE1	8c	green	80	30
RE26	RE1	10c	green	35	12
RE27	RE1	20c	green	55	25
RE28	RE1	24c	green	7.00	55
RE29	RE1	40c	green	15.00	8.50

Imperf

Without Gum

RE30	RE1a	$2	green	15.00	2.00

Perf. 11

RE31	RE1	2c	green	40.00	36.00

WINE STAMPS

RE2

Inscribed: "Series of 1916"

1916 **Wmk. 191R** **Offset Printing** ***Rouletted 3½***

Without Gum

Plates of 100 subjects

Size: Approximately 40x47mm

RE32	RE2	1c	green	35	30
RE33	RE2	3c	green	3.50	3.00
RE34	RE2	4c	green	30	25
RE35	RE2	6c	green	1.00	75
RE36	RE2	7½c	green	6.00	3.50
RE37	RE2	10c	green	1.00	40
RE38	RE2	12c	green	1.75	1.65
RE39	RE2	15c	green	1.75	1.50
RE40	RE2	18c	green	24.00	21.00
RE41	RE2	20c	green	30	25
RE42	RE2	24c	green	2.75	2.00
RE43	RE2	30c	green	3.00	2.25
RE44	RE2	36c	green	13.50	10.00
RE45	RE2	50c	green	60	40

RE46	RE2	60c	green	2.75	2.00
RE47	RE2	72c	green	30.00	27.50
RE48	RE2	80c	green	75	55
RE49	RE2	$1.20	green	6.00	4.25
RE50	RE2	$1.44	green	5.00	2.50
RE51	RE2	$1.60	green	20.00	15.00
RE52	RE2	$2	green	1.25	1.25

For rouletted 7 see Nos. RE60-RE83, RE102-RE107.

RE3

Engr.
Plates of 50 subjects

RE53	RE3	$4	green	75	18
RE54	RE3	$4.80	green	2.75	2.50
RE55	RE3	$9.60	green	90	25

Nos. RE32 to RE55 exist in many shades. Size variations of 1c to $2 are believed due to offset printing. These designs in light green or green, rouletted 7, were issued in 1933-40. See Nos. RE60-RE83, RE102-RE107.

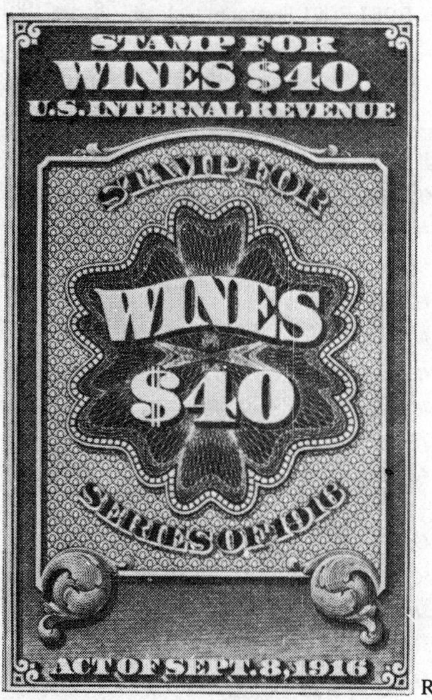

RE4

Size: Approximately 51x81mm
Plates of 6 subjects

RE56	RE4	$20	green	75.00	35.00
RE57	RE4	$40	green	150.00	45.00
RE58	RE4	$50	green	35.00	30.00
RE59	RE4	$100	green	200.00	125.00

Stamps of design RE4 have an adjoining tablet at right for affixing additional stamps. See Nos. RE107A-RE107D.

Same designs as Issue of 1916

1933 Wmk. 191R Offset Printing *Rouletted 7*

RE60	RE2	1c	light green	2.50	25
RE61	RE2	3c	light green	6.00	1.75
RE62	RE2	4c	light green	75	15
RE63	RE2	6c	light green	9.00	4.50
RE64	RE2	7½c	light green	1.50	25
RE65	RE2	10c	light green	1.25	10
RE66	RE2	12c	light green	4.50	90
RE67	RE2	15c	light green	2.00	10
RE69	RE2	20c	light green	2.25	5
		a.	Double impression		—
RE70	RE2	24c	light green	2.25	5
		a.	Double impression		—
RE71	RE2	30c	light green	2.25	10
RE72	RE2	36c	light green	6.50	45
RE73	RE2	50c	light green	3.75	25
RE74	RE2	60c	light green	4.00	10
RE75	RE2	72c	light green	7.50	30
RE76	RE2	80c	light green	7.00	10
RE77	RE2	$1.20	light green	7.50	1.25
RE78	RE2	$1.44	light green	6.00	3.50
RE79	RE2	$1.60	light green	175.00	75.00
RE80	RE2	$2	light green	27.50	3.00

Engr.

RE81	RE3	$4	light green	20.00	6.00
RE82	RE3	$4.80	light green	22.50	13.00
RE83	RE3	$9.60	light green	95.00	65.00

RE5

1934-40 Offset Printing Wmk. 191R *Rouletted 7*

Inscribed: "Series of 1934"

Size: Approximately 28x25mm

Plates of 200 and 224 subjects

Issued With and Without Gum

RE83A	RE5	1/5c	green ('40)	70	20
RE84	RE5	1/2c	green	55	25
RE85	RE5	1c	green	65	15
RE86	RE5	1 1/4c	green	1.00	75
RE87	RE5	1 1/2c	green	6.00	3.75
RE88	RE5	2c	green	1.65	50
RE89	RE5	2 1/2c	green	1.65	50
RE90	RE5	3c	green	5.00	4.00
RE91	RE5	4c	green	1.50	15
RE92	RE5	5c	green	55	10
RE93	RE5	6c	green	1.75	50
RE94	RE5	7 1/2c	green	1.25	15
RE95	RE5	10c	green	35	6
RE96	RE5	12c	green	1.25	10
RE96A	RE5	14 2/5c	green ('40)	80.00	3.00
RE97	RE5	15c	green	75	10
RE98	RE5	18c	green	1.40	12
RE99	RE5	20c	green	1.25	6
RE100	RE5	24c	green	1.40	10
RE101	RE5	30c	green	1.25	8

Size: Approximately 39x45mm

Plates of 100 subjects

Issued Without Gum

RE102	RE2	40c	green	1.50	25
RE102A	RE2	43 1/5c	green ('40)	8.00	2.00
RE103	RE2	48c	green	8.00	1.25
RE104	RE2	$1	green	13.00	10.00
RE105	RE2	$1.50	green	22.50	13.00
			Perforated initials		5.50

Engr.

Size: Approximately 39x46mm

Plates of 50 subjects.

RE106	RE3	$2.50	green	27.50	15.00
			Perforated initials		8.75
RE107	RE3	$5	green	22.50	6.25
			Perforated initials		2.50

Stamps of types RE5 and RE2 overprinted "Rectified Spirits / Puerto Rico" are listed under Puerto Rico.

Inscribed: "Series of 1916"

Size: Approximately 51x81mm

Plates of 6 subjects

1934 ***Perf. 11 1/2 at left***

RE107A	RE4	$20	yellow green	1,300.
RE107B	RE4	$40	yellow green	2,000.

Perf. 12 1/2 at left

RE107C	RE4	$50	yellow green	650.00
RE107D	RE4	$100	yellow green	300.00

The serial numbers of Nos. RE107A-RE107D are much thinner than on Nos. RE56-RE59.

RE6

Offset Printing

Size: 28x25mm

Inscribed "Series of 1941"

1942 Wmk. 191R *Rouletted 7*

RE108	RE6	1/5c	green & black	65	35
RE109	RE6	1/4c	green & black	1.50	75
RE110	RE6	1/2c	green & black	1.75	90
		a.	Imperf. vertically (pair)	90.00	
RE111	RE6	1c	green & black	90	60
RE112	RE6	2c	green & black	2.75	2.50
RE113	RE6	3c	green & black	3.50	2.00
RE114	RE6	3 1/2c	green & black		*2,500.*
RE115	RE6	3 3/4c	green & black	4.50	2.00
RE116	RE6	4c	green & black	2.00	1.25
RE117	RE6	5c	green & black	1.90	1.25
RE118	RE6	6c	green & black	1.90	1.25
RE119	RE6	7c	green & black	2.75	1.50
RE120	RE6	7 1/2c	green & black	3.50	2.00
RE121	RE6	8c	green & black	3.50	1.50
RE122	RE6	9c	green & black	4.75	2.75
RE123	RE6	10c	green & black	3.75	90
RE124	RE6	11 1/4c	green & black	4.00	2.50
RE125	RE6	12c	green & black	5.50	3.50
RE126	RE6	14c	green & black	15.00	8.00
RE127	RE6	15c	green & black	4.00	1.50
		a.	Imperf. vert., pair		—
RE128	RE6	16c	green & black	5.50	3.00
RE129	RE6	19 1/5c	green & black	100.00	4.00
RE130	RE6	20c	green & black	4.75	1.00
RE131	RE6	24c	green & black	3.25	10
RE132	RE6	28c	green & black	*1,200.*	550.00
RE133	RE6	30c	green & black	90	10
RE134	RE6	32c	green & black	50.00	3.25
RE135	RE6	36c	green & black	2.00	10
RE136	RE6	40c	green & black	1.50	15
RE137	RE6	45c	green & black	3.00	20
RE138	RE6	48c	green & black	7.00	2.25
RE139	RE6	50c	green & black	8.00	4.00
RE140	RE6	60c	green & black	2.75	15
RE141	RE6	72c	green & black	7.00	75
RE142	RE6	80c	green & black	25.00	3.50
RE143	RE6	84c	green & black	—	27.50
RE144	RE6	90c	green & black	10.00	15
RE145	RE6	96c	green & black	10.00	15

See Nos. RE182D-RE194.

Denomination Spelled Out in Two Lines — RE7

1942 Size: 39x45 1/2mm Engr.

RE146	RE7	$1.20	yellow green & black	3.75	10
RE147	RE7	$1.44	yellow green & black	1.50	6
RE148	RE7	$1.50	yellow green & black	90.00	50.00
RE149	RE7	$1.60	yellow green & black	7.50	1.00
RE150	RE7	$1.68	yellow green & black	60.00	40.00
RE151	RE7	$1.80	yellow green & black	3.00	8
		a.	Vertical pair, one without denomination	—	
RE152	RE7	$1.92	yellow green & black	42.50	32.50
RE153	RE7	$2.40	yellow green & black	7.75	60
RE154	RE7	$3	yellow green & black	52.50	27.50
RE155	RE7	$3.36	yellow green & black	—	25.00
RE156	RE7	$3.60	yellow green & black	—	5.25
RE157	RE7	$4	yellow green & black	14.00	4.00
RE158	RE7	$4.80	yellow green & black	—	3.00
RE159	RE7	$5	yellow green & black	11.00	8.00
RE160	RE7	$7.20	yellow green & black	17.50	50
RE161	RE7	$10	yellow green & black	125.00	60.00
RE162	RE7	$20	yellow green & black	110.00	70.00
RE163	RE7	$50	yellow green & black	110.00	55.00
			Perforated initials		18.00
RE164	RE7	$100	yellow green & black	250.00	30.00
			Perforated initials		27.50
RE165	RE7	$200	yellow green & black	100.00	20.00
			Perforated initials		8.50
RE165B	RE7	$400	yellow green & black	—	*1,400.*
RE166	RE7	$500	yellow green & black	—	140.00
			Perforated initials		27.50
RE167	RE7	$600	yellow green & black	—	125.00
RE168	RE7	$900	yellow green & black		*1,500.*
			Perforated initials		750.00
RE169	RE7	$1000	yellow green & black		180.00
RE170	RE7	$2000	yellow green & black		700.00
RE171	RE7	$3000	yellow green & black		160.00
RE172	RE7	$4000	yellow green & black		600.00

Denomination Repeated, Spelled Out in One Line

1949

RE173	RE7	$1	yellow green & black	3.25	1.50
RE174	RE7	$2	yellow green & black	5.00	1.75
RE175	RE7	$4	yellow green & black	475.00	275.00
RE176	RE7	$5	yellow green & black		70.00
RE177	RE7	$6	yellow green & black		400.00
RE178	RE7	$7	yellow green & black		45.00
RE179	RE7	$8	yellow green & black	400.00	250.00
RE180	RE7	$10	yellow green & black	7.50	5.00
			Perforated initials		2.00
RE181	RE7	$20	yellow green & black	20.00	3.75
			Perforated initials		1.75
RE182	RE7	$30	yellow green & black	600.00	550.00

Other denominations of engraved stamps, type RE7, that were printed and delivered to the Internal Revenue Service were: $7.14, $9, $12, $40, $60, $70, $80, $300, $700 and $800. None are reported in collectors' hands.

Types of 1942-49

1951-54 Size: 28x25mm Offset Printing

RE182D	RE6	1 7/10c	green & black		*4,000.*
RE183	RE6	3 2/5c	green & black	50.00	27.50

RE184	RE6	8½c	green & black	27.50	19.00
RE185	RE6	13⅗c	green & black	70.00	50.00
RE186	RE6	17c	green & black	16.00	15.00
RE187	RE6	20⅖c	green & black	70.00	35.00
RE188	RE6	33½c	green & black	70.00	47.50
RE189	RE6	38¼c	green & black	80.00	70.00
RE190	RE6	40⅘c	green & black	3.75	65
RE191	RE6	51c	green & black	3.75	75
RE192	RE6	67c	green & black	12.50	4.00
RE193	RE6	68c	green & black	3.75	65
RE194	RE6	80⅖c	green & black	100.00	70.00

Engr.

Size: 39x45½mm

Denomination Spelled Out in Two Lines in Small Letters

Two types of $1.60⅘:

I. The "4" slants sharply. Loop of "5" almost closes to form oval. Each numeral 2mm, high.

II. The "4" is less slanted. Loop of "5" more open and nearly circular. Each numeral 2½mm high.

RE195	RE7	$1.50¾	yellow green & black	50.00	32.50
RE196	RE7	$1.60⅘	yellow green & black (I)	4.25	35
	a.		"DOLLAR"	40.00	14.00
	b.		As "a," horiz. pair, one without denomination	*500.00*	
	c.		Type II	350.00	100.00
RE197	RE7	$1.88 3/10	yellow green & black	100.00	50.00

Denomination Spelled Out in Two Lines in Slightly Larger Letters Same as Nos. RE146-RE172

RE198	RE7	$1.60⅘	yellow green & black (II)	30.00	5.00
	a.		First line larger letters, second line small letters	—	825.00
	b.		Type I ('53)	65.00	20.00
RE199	RE7	$2.01	yellow green & black	3.50	35
RE200	RE7	$2.68	yellow green & black	3.50	35
RE201	RE7	$4.08	yellow green & black	50.00	25.00
RE202	RE7	$5.76	yellow green & black	200.00	85.00
RE203	RE7	$8.16	yellow green & black	15.00	4.00
RE204	RE7	$9.60	yellow green & black		*2,500.*

Other denominations that were printed out not delivered to the Internal Revenue Service were: 6 7/10c, 10⅕c and $90. None are reported in collectors' hands.

Wine stamps were discontinued on Dec. 31, 1954.

PLAYING CARD STAMPS

Stamps for use on packs of playing cards were included in the first general issue of 1862-71. They are Nos. R2, R11, R12, R17, R21 and R28.

The tax on playing cards was repealed effective June 22, 1965.

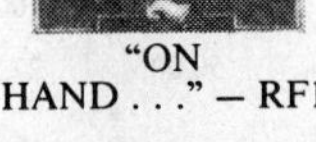

"ON HAND . . ." – RF1

"ACT OF . . ." – RF2

1894 Engr. Unwmk. *Rouletted 5½*

RF1	RF1	2c	lake	50	30
	a.		Horizontal pair, imperf. between	*150.00*	—
	b.		Horiz. pair, imperf. vert.	—	
RF2	RF2	2c	ultramarine	4.50	2.50
	a.		2c blue	—	3.50
	b.		Imperf., pair	125.00	
	c.		Imperf horizontally	100.00	100.00
	d.		Rouletted 12½	50.00	50.00
	e.		Imperf. horizontally, rouletted 12½ vertically, pair	80.00	80.00

Wmk. 191R

1896-99 Wmk. 191R *Rouletted 5½, 7*

RF3	RF2	2c	blue	4.00	50
	a.		2c ultramarine ('99)	5.50	1.25
	b.		Imperf., pair	65.00	

1902 *Perf. 12*

RF4	RF2	2c	deep blue	27.50

No. RF4 is known with cancellation date "1899" but that is due to the use of an old canceling plate. The stamp was first used in 1902.

Stamp of 1899 Surcharged in Rose

ACT OF 1917
7
CENTS

1917 Wmk. 191R *Rouletted 7*

RF5	RF2	7c	on 2c ultramarine	*750.00*	600.00
	a.		Inverted surcharge		—

The surcharge on No. RF5 was handstamped at the Internal Revenue Office in New York City. Handstamps were used at other Internal Revenue Offices as well.

The surcharges on Nos. RF6 to RF13 inclusive, and No. RF15 were applied by the manufacturers, together with their initials, dates, etc., thus forming a combination of surcharge and precancellation. The surcharge on No. RF16 was made by the Bureau of Engraving and Printing. After it appeared the use of the combinations was continued but only as cancellations.

Surcharged in Black

17

1917

RF6	RF2	(7c)	on 2c blue	37.50
	a.		Inverted surcharge	37.50

The "17" indicated that the 7 cent tax had been paid according to the Act of 1917.

Surcharged in Black

7

RF7	RF2	7c	on 2c blue	275.00
	a.		Inverted surcharge	275.00

Surcharged Vertically in Red or Violet

7 CTS.

RF8	RF2	7c	on 2c blue	475.00
	a.		Double surcharge	550.00

Surcharged Vertically, Reading Up in Black, Violet or Red

7 CENTS

RF9	RF2	7c	on 2c blue	8.00
	a.		Double surcharge	45.00
	b.		Numeral omitted	30.00
	c.		Surcharge reading down	10.00
	d.		As "c", numeral omitted	30.00
	e.		As "c", double surcharge	110.00
	f.		Double surcharge, one inverted	110.00
	g.		Surcharge and "A.D." in violet	150.00
	h.		Surcharge and "A.D." in red, "U.S.P.C." in black	300.00
	i.		Surcharge and "A.D." in red reading up, "U.S.P.C." in black reading down	*400.00*

"A.D." stands for Andrew Dougherty, the name of a playing card company. "U.S.P.C." stands for United States Playing Card Co.

On Nos. RF9g-RF9i, surcharge and company initials were applied simultaneously.

Surcharged in Carmine

7c

RF10	RF2	7c	on 2c blue	55.00
	a.		Inverted surcharge	25.00
	b.		Double surcharge	175.00
	c.		Double surcharge, inverted	135.00
	d.		Triple surcharge	—

RF3

1918 Size: 21x40mm. *Imperf.*

RF11	RF3	blue	37.50	27.50
		Block of four	165.00	125.00

Private Roulette 14

RF12	RF3	blue		140.00

		a.	Rouletted 13 in red	600.00	
		b.	Rouletted 6½	150.00	
		c.	Perf. 12 horiz., imperf. vert.	90.00	
		d.	Perf. 12 on 4 sides	—	

Nos. RF11 and RF12 served as 7c stamps when used before April 1, 1919, and as 8c stamps when used after that date.

Surcharged like No. RF9 in Violet, Red or Black

Private Roulette 9½

RF13	RF3	7c	blue	32.50	
		a.	Inverted surcharge	30.00	
		b.	Double surcharge	160.00	
		c.	Double surcharge, inverted	160.00	

Stamp of 1899 Surcharged in Magenta or Rose

REVENUE ACT OF 1918 8 CENTS

1919 ***Rouletted 7***

RF14	RF2	8c	on 2c ultramarine	70.00	
		a.	Double surcharge	125.00	
		b.	Inverted surcharge	125.00	

The surcharge on No. RF14 was handstamped at the Internal Revenue Office in New York City.

Surcharged in Carmine 8 (inverted)

RF15	RF2	8c	on 2c blue (inverted surcharge)	325.00	
		a.	Double surcharge, inverted	*425.00*	

No. RF15 is surcharged only with large "8c" inverted, and overprinted with date and initials. No. RF16 is often found with additional impression of large "8c," as on No. RF15, but in this usage the large "8c" is a cancellation.

Surcharged in Carmine 8 Cts.

RF16	RF2	8c	on 2c blue	30.00	75
		a.	Inverted surcharge		

See note after No. RF5.

RF4

1922 **Size: 19x22mm** ***Rouletted 7***

RF17	RF4	(8c)	blue	11.00	1.25
			Block of four	—	—

Surcharged in Carmine, Blue or Black 8c

RF18	RF4	8c	blue	32.50	
		a.	Inverted surcharge	27.50	

RF5

1924 ***Rouletted 7***

RF19	RF5	10c	blue	7.50	40
			Block of four	32.50	

ROTARY PRESS COIL STAMP

1926 ***Perf. 10 Vertically***

RF20	RF5	10c	blue		25

No. RF20 exists only precanceled. **Bureau precancels:** 11 different.

FLAT PLATE PRINTING

1927 ***Perf. 11***

RF21	RF5	10c	blue	10.00	5.00
			Block of four	45.00	

1929 ***Perf. 10***

RF22	RF5	10c	blue	7.00	4.00
			Block of four	—	—

RF6

ROTARY PRESS COIL STAMP

1929 ***Perf. 10 Horizontally***

RF23	RF6	10c	light blue		15

No. RF23 exists only precanceled. **Bureau precancels:** 16 different.

FLAT PLATE PRINTING

1930 ***Perf. 10***

RF24	RF6	10c	blue	8.50	1.25
			Block of four	40.00	10.00
		a.	Horiz. pair, imperf. vert.	150.00	

1931 ***Perf. 11***

RF25	RF6	10c	blue	7.00	1.25
			Block of four	—	—

RF7

ROTARY PRESS COIL STAMP

1940 ***Perf. 10 Vertically***

RF26	RF7		blue, wet printing	—	40
			Dry printing	—	40

See note after No. 1029.

Bureau precancels: 11 different.

RF8

ROTARY PRESS COIL STAMP

1940 **Wmk. 191R** ***Perf. 10 Horizontally***

RF27	RF8		blue		15

Bureau precancels: 10 different.

FLAT PLATE PRINTING

RF28	RF8		blue	5.00	75
			Block of four	—	—

ROTARY PRESS PRINTING.

RF29	RF8		blue	125.00	75.00
		a.	Imperforate (P.C. Co.)		150.00

PLAYING CARD STAMPS FOR THE VIRGIN ISLANDS

These stamps were overprinted by the Bureau of Engraving and Printing. Shipments of 10,000 each of Nos. RFV1-RFV3 were sent to the Virgin Islands on June 17, 1920, Jan. 16, 1926, and Mar. 5, 1934, respectively.

U. S. Playing Card Stamp No. RF3 Overprinted in Carmine

VIRGIN ISLANDS 4 CTS.

1920 **Engr.** **Wmk. 191R** ***Rouletted 7***

RFV1	RF2	4c	on 2c blue		150.00

U. S. Playing Card Stamp No. RF17 Overprinted in Carmine

VIRGIN ISLANDS 4 cts.

1926 ***Rouletted 7***

RFV2	RF4	4c	blue		37.50

RF2 was surcharged in ten styles for use in collecting a tobacco tax.

Same Overprint on U.S. Type RF4

1934 ***Perf. 11***

RFV3	RF4	4c	light blue		90.00

The above stamp with perforation 11 was not issued in the United States without the overprint.

SILVER TAX STAMPS

The Silver Purchase Act of 1934 imposed a 50 per cent tax on the net profit realized on a transfer of silver bullion. The tax was paid by affixing stamps to the transfer memorandum. Congress authorized the Silver Tax stamps on Feb. 20, 1934. They were discontinued on June 4, 1963.

Documentary Stamps of 1917 Overprinted

SILVER TAX

1934 **Offset Printing** **Wmk. 191R** ***Perf. 11***

RG1	R22	1c	carmine rose	90	75
RG2	R22	2c	carmine rose	85	35
		a.	Double impression of stamp	—	
RG3	R22	3c	carmine rose	1.00	45
RG4	R22	4c	carmine rose	1.75	1.25
RG5	R22	5c	carmine rose	2.50	1.25
RG6	R22	8c	carmine rose	3.50	2.50
RG7	R22	10c	carmine rose	3.50	1.75
RG8	R22	20c	carmine rose	5.00	2.75
RG9	R22	25c	carmine rose	5.25	3.25
RG10	R22	40c	carmine rose	5.75	4.25
RG11	R22	50c	carmine rose	6.00	5.00
		a.	Double impression of stamp	30.00	
RG12	R22	80c	carmine rose	9.00	6.00

Engr.

RG13	R21	$1	green	10.00	7.50
RG14	R21	$2	rose	13.00	11.00
RG15	R21	$3	violet	27.50	21.00
RG16	R21	$4	yellow brown	20.00	14.00
RG17	R21	$5	dark blue	25.00	13.00
RG18	R21	$10	orange	40.00	13.00

Perf. 12

Without Gum

RG19	R17	$30	vermilion	—	40.00
			Cut cancellation		17.50
RG20	R19	$60	brown	—	65.00

			Vertical strip of four		275.00
			Cut cancellation		25.00
RG21	R17	$100	green	90.00	30.00
			Vertical strip of four		125.00
RG22	R18	$500	blue	250.00	200.00
			Vertical strip of four		
			Cut cancellation		95.00
RG23	R19	$1000	orange	—	100.00
			Cut cancellation		60.00

See note after No. R227.

Same Overprint, spacing 11mm between words "SILVER TAX"
Without Gum

1936 *Perf. 12*

RG26	R17	$100	green	110.00	50.00
			Vertical strip of four		
RG27	R19	$1000	orange		425.00

Documentary Stamps of 1917 Handstamped "SILVER TAX" in Violet, Large Block Letters, in Two Lines

1939 **Wmk. 191R** **Offset Printing** *Perf. 11*

RG28	R22	3c	rose pink	—
RG30	R22	10c	rose pink	—
RG32	R22	80c	rose pink	—

Other handstamps exist on various values. One has letters 4mm. high, 2mm. wide with "SILVER" and "TAX" applied in separate operations. Another has "Silver Tax" in two lines in a box.

Engr.

Overprint Typewritten in Black

Perf. 11

RG35	R21	$3	violet	—
RG36	R21	$5	dark blue	—

Typewritten overprints also exist on 2c, 3c, 20c, 50c and in red on $5.

SERIES 1940

Type of Documentary Stamps 1917, Overprinted in Black **SILVER TAX**

1940 **Offset Printing** *Perf. 11*

RG37	R22	1c	rose pink	11.00	—
RG38	R22	2c	rose pink	11.00	—
RG39	R22	3c	rose pink	11.00	—
RG40	R22	4c	rose pink	12.50	—
RG41	R22	5c	rose pink	7.50	—
RG42	R22	8c	rose pink	12.50	—
RG43	R22	10c	rose pink	11.00	—
RG44	R22	20c	rose pink	12.50	—
RG45	R22	25c	rose pink	11.00	—
RG46	R22	40c	rose pink	20.00	—
RG47	R22	50c	rose pink	20.00	—
RG48	R22	80c	rose pink	20.00	—

Engr.

RG49	R21	$1	green	45.00	—
RG50	R21	$2	rose	70.00	—
RG51	R21	$3	violet	100.00	—
RG52	R21	$4	yellow brown	225.00	—
RG53	R21	$5	dark blue	250.00	—
RG54	R21	$10	orange	325.00	—

Nos. RG19-RG20, RG26 Handstamped in Blue "Series 1940"

1940 **Without Gum** *Perf. 12*

RG55	R17	$30	vermilion	—	*1,250.*
RG56	R19	$60	brown	—	*1,900.*
RG57	R17	$100	green	—	*1,500.*

Values for well-centered, early U.S. stamps will often exceed catalogue price.

Alexander Hamilton
RG1

Levi Woodbury
RG2

Thomas Corwin — RG3

Overprinted in Black **SERIES 1941**

1941 **Wmk. 191R** **Engr.** *Perf. 11*

Size: 19x22mm

RG58	RG1	1c	gray	1.50	—
RG59	RG1	2c	gray *(Oliver Wolcott, Jr.)*	1.50	—
RG60	RG1	3c	gray *(Samuel Dexter)*	1.75	—
RG61	RG1	4c	gray *(Albert Gallatin)*	2.50	—
RG62	RG1	5c	gray *(G.W. Campbell)*	2.50	—
RG63	RG1	8c	gray *(A.J. Dallas)*	3.50	—
RG64	RG1	10c	gray *(Wm. H. Crawford)*	3.75	—
RG65	RG1	20c	gray *(Richard Rush)*	4.75	—
RG66	RG1	25c	gray *(S.D. Ingham)*	7.00	—
RG67	RG1	40c	gray *(Louis McLane)*	12.50	—
RG68	RG1	50c	gray *(Wm. J. Duane)*	15.00	—
RG69	RG1	80c	gray *(Roger B. Taney)*	25.00	20.00

Size: 21½x36¼mm

RG70	RG2	$1	gray	25.00	—
RG71	RG2	$2	gray *(Thomas Ewing)*	80.00	35.00
RG72	RG2	$3	gray *(Walter Forward)*	60.00	40.00
RG73	RG2	$4	gray *(J.C. Spencer)*	80.00	—
RG74	RG2	$5	gray *(G.M. Bibb)*	80.00	50.00
RG75	RG2	$10	gray *(R.J. Walker)*	115.00	60.00
RG76	RG2	$20	gray *(Wm. M. Meredith)*	200.00	—

Perf. 12

Without Gum

Size: 28½x42mm

RG77	RG3	$30	gray	125.00	60.00
			Cut cancellation		45.00
RG78	RG3	$50	gray *(James Guthrie)*	—	—
RG79	RG3	$60	gray *(Howell Cobb)*	600.00	110.00
			Cut cancellation		75.00
RG80	RG3	$100	gray *(P.F. Thomas)*	—	190.00
			Vertical strip of four		—
			Cut cancellation		75.00
RG81	RG3	$500	gray *(J.A. Dix)*	—	—
RG82	RG3	$1000	gray *(S.P. Chase)*	—	700.00
			Cut cancellation		350.00

Nos. RG58-RG82 Overprinted Instead: **SERIES 1942**

1942 **Wmk. 191R** *Perf. 11*

Size: 19x22mm

RG83	RG1	1c	gray	1.00	—
RG84	RG1	2c	gray	1.00	—
RG85	RG1	3c	gray	1.00	—
RG86	RG1	4c	gray	1.00	—
RG87	RG1	5c	gray	1.00	—
RG88	RG1	8c	gray	1.50	—
RG89	RG1	10c	gray	3.00	—
RG90	RG1	20c	gray	4.50	—
RG91	RG1	25c	gray	8.254	—
RG92	RG1	40c	gray	10.00	—
RG93	RG1	50c	gray	10.00	—
RG94	RG1	80c	gray	30.00	—

Size: 21½x36¼mm

RG95	RG2	$1	gray	30.00	
		a.	Overprint "SERIES 5942"	275.00	
RG96	RG2	$2	gray	30.00	—
		a.	Overprint "SERIES 5942"	250.00	
RG97	RG2	$3	gray	55.00	—
		a.	Overprint "SERIES 5942"	—	
RG98	RG2	$4	gray	55.00	—
		a.	Overprint "SERIES 5942"	—	
RG99	RG2	$5	gray	60.00	—
		a.	Overprint "SERIES 5942"	250.00	
RG100	RG2	$10	gray	140.00	—
RG101	RG2	$20	gray	250.00	—
		a.	Overprint "SERIES 5942"	—	

Perf. 12

Without Gum

Size: 28½x42mm

RG102	RG3	$30	gray	350.00	325.00
RG103	RG3	$50	gray	350.00	325.00
RG104	RG3	$60	gray	—	325.00
			Cut cancellation		275.00
RG105	RG3	$100	gray	—	250.00
			Cut cancellation		200.00
RG106	RG3	$500	gray	—	—
RG107	RG3	$1000	gray	—	—
			Cut cancellation		—

Silver Purchase Stamps of 1941 without Overprint

1944 **Wmk. 191R** *Perf. 11*

Size: 19x22mm

RG108	RG1	1c	gray	40	15
RG109	RG1	2c	gray	50	—
RG110	RG1	3c	gray	60	—
RG111	RG1	4c	gray	90	—
RG112	RG1	5c	gray	1.25	—
RG113	RG1	8c	gray	1.75	—
RG114	RG1	10c	gray	1.75	—
RG115	RG1	20c	gray	3.75	—
RG116	RG1	25c	gray	4.25	—
RG117	RG1	40c	gray	7.00	—
RG118	RG1	50c	gray	7.00	—
RG119	RG1	80c	gray	10.00	—

Size: 21½x36¼mm

RG120	RG2	$1	gray	17.50	8.00
RG121	RG2	$2	gray	30.00	21.50
RG122	RG2	$3	gray	35.00	12.50
RG123	RG2	$4	gray	45.00	35.00
RG124	RG2	$5	gray	45.00	17.50
RG125	RG2	$10	gray	60.00	30.00
			Cut cancellation		12.50
RG126	RG2	$20	gray	225.00	—

Perf. 12

Without Gum

Size: 28½x42mm

RG127	RG3	$30	gray	110.00	85.00
			Vertical strip of four		—
			Cut cancellation		50.00
RG128	RG3	$50	gray	375.00	325.00
			Vertical strip of four		—
			Cut cancellation		225.00
RG129	RG3	$60	gray	—	125.00
			Cut cancellation		75.00
RG130	RG3	$100	gray	—	30.00

			Vertical strip of four		—
			Cut cancel-lation		15.00
RG131	RG3	$500	gray	—	250.00
			Cut cancel-lation		175.00
RG132	RG3	$1000	gray	—	150.00
			Vertical strip of four		—
			Cut cancel-lation		75.00

CIGARETTE TUBES STAMPS

These stamps were for a tax on the hollow tubes of cigarette paper, each with a thin cardboard mouthpiece attached. They were sold in packages so buyers could add loose tobacco to make cigarettes.

Documentary Stamp of 1917 Overprinted **CIGTTE. TUBES**

1919 Offset Printing Wmk. 191R *Perf. 11*

RH1	R22	1c	carmine rose	50	25
			Block of four	2.25	
		a.	Without period	10.00	6.00

1929 *Perf. 10*

RH2	R22	1c	carmine rose	17.50	6.00

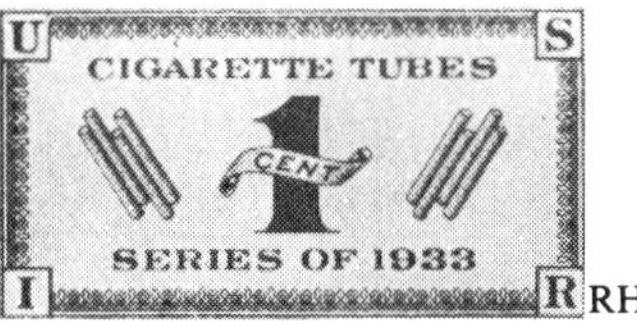

RH1

1933 Wmk. 191R *Perf. 11*

RH3	RH1	1c	rose	1.50	50
			Block of four	7.50	
RH4	RH1	2c	rose	3.00	1.25

POTATO TAX STAMPS

These stamps were required under the Agricultural Adjustment Act of Dec. 1, 1935. Their use ended Jan. 6, 1936, when this act was declared unconstitutional. Potato growers were given allotments and for excess had to pay ¾ cent a pound.

Young Woman — RI1

Engr. Unwmk. *Perf. 11*

RI1	RI1	¾c	carmine rose	25
RI2	RI1	1½c	black brown	40
RI3	RI1	2¼c	yellow green	40
RI4	RI1	3c	light violet	50
RI5	RI1	3¾c	olive bister	50
RI6	RI1	7½c	orange brown	1.25
RI7	RI1	11¼c	deep orange	1.50
RI8	RI1	18¾c	violet brown	4.00
RI9	RI1	37½c	red orange	3.50
RI10	RI1	75c	blue	4.00
RI11	RI1	93¾c	rose lake	6.00
RI12	RI1	$1.12½	green	11.00
RI13	RI1	$1.50	yellow brown	10.00

TOBACCO SALE TAX STAMPS

These stamps were required to pay the tax on the sale of tobacco in excess of quotas set by the Secretary of Agriculture. The tax was 25 per cent of the price for which the excess tobacco was sold. It was intended to affect tobacco harvested after June 28, 1934 and sold before May 1, 1936. The tax was stopped when the Agricultural Adjustment Act was declared unconstitutional by the Supreme Court on Dec. 1, 1935.

Values for unused stamps are for copies with original gum.

Stamps and Types of 1917 Documentary Issue Overprinted **TOBACCO SALE TAX**

1934 Offset Printing Wmk. 191R *Perf. 11*

RJ1	R22	1c	carmine rose	30	15
RJ2	R22	2c	carmine rose	35	20
RJ3	R22	5c	carmine rose	1.20	40
RJ4	R22	10c	carmine rose	1.50	40
		a.	Inverted overprint	9.00	6.50
RJ5	R22	25c	carmine rose	4.00	1.50
RJ6	R22	50c	carmine rose	4.00	1.50
			Engr.		
RJ7	R21	$1	green	7.00	1.60
RJ8	R21	$2	rose	12.50	1.75
RJ9	R21	$5	dark blue	15.00	4.00
RJ10	R21	$10	orange	25.00	10.00
RJ11	R21	$20	olive bister	60.00	12.00

On No. RJ11 the overprint is vertical, reading up.

NARCOTIC TAX STAMPS

The Revenue Act of 1918 imposed a tax of 1 cent per ounce or fraction thereof on opium, coca leaves and their derivatives. The tax was paid by affixing Narcotic stamps to the drug containers. The tax lasted from Feb. 25, 1919, through Apr. 30, 1971.

Members of the American Revenue Association compiled the listings in this section.

Documentary Stamps of 1914 Handstamped "NARCOTIC" in Magenta, Blue or Black

1919 Wmk. 191R Offset Printing *Perf. 10*

RJA1	R20	1c	rose	60.00	45.00

The overprint was applied by District Collectors of Internal Revenue. It is always in capital letters and exists in various type faces and sizes, including: 21½x2½mm, serif; 21x2¼mm, sans-serif boldface; 15½x2½mm, sans-serif; 13x2mm, sans-serif.

The ½c, 2c, 3c, 4c, 5c, 10c, 25c and 50c with similar handstamp in serif capitals measuring about 20x2¼mm are bogus.

Documentary Stamps of 1917 Handstamped "NARCOTIC" "Narcotic", "NARCOTICS" or "ACT/NARCOTIC/1918" in Magenta, Black, Blue, Violet or Red

1919 Wmk. 191R Offset Printing *Perf. 11*

RJA9	R22	1c	carmine rose	1.75	1.00
RJA10	R22	2c	carmine rose	4.50	3.00
RJA11	R22	3c	carmine rose	17.50	14.00
RJA12	R22	4c	carmine rose	7.50	5.50
RJA13	R22	5c	carmine rose	11.00	10.00
RJA14	R22	8c	carmine rose	9.00	12.00
RJA15	R22	10c	carmine rose	35.00	7.50
RJA16	R22	20c	carmine rose	40.00	35.00
RJA17	R22	25c	carmine rose	30.00	25.00
RJA18	R22	40c	carmine rose	70.00	60.00
RJA19	R22	50c	carmine rose	15.00	15.00
RJA20	R22	80c	carmine rose	85.00	60.00
			Engr.		
RJA21	R21	$1	green	40.00	30.00
RJA22	R21	$2	rose		—
RJA23	R21	$3	violet		—
RJA24	R21	$5	dark blue		—
RJA25	R21	$10	orange		—

The overprints were applied by District Collectors of Internal Revenue. They are known in at least 20 type faces and sizes of which the majority read "NARCOTIC" in capital letters. Two are in upper and lower case letters. Experts have identified 14 by city. The 3-line handstamp was used in Seattle; "NARCOTICS" in Philadelphia. Most handstamps are not found on all denominations.

No. R228 Overprinted in Black: "NARCOTIC / E.L. CO. / 3-19-19"

1919 Wmk. 191R *Perf. 11*
"NARCOTIC" 14½mm wide

RJA26	R22	1c	carmine rose		350.00

Overprinted by Eli Lilly Co., Indianapolis, for that firm's use.

No. R228 Overprinted in Black: "J W & B / NARCOTIC"

1919 Wmk. 191R *Perf. 11*
"NARCOTIC" 14½mm wide

RJA27	R22	1c	carmine rose		250.00

Overprinted by John Wyeth & Brother, Philadelphia, for that firm's use.

Nos. R228, R231-R232 Handstamped in Blue: "P-W-R-Co. / NARCOTIC"

1919 Wmk. 191R *Perf. 11*

RJA28	R22	1c	carmine rose		225.00
RJA28A	R22	4c	carmine rose		—
RJA29	R22	5c	carmine rose		—

The handstamp was applied by the Powers-Weightmann-Rosengarten Co., Philadelphia, for that firm's use.

Proprietary Stamps of 1919 Handstamped "NARCOTIC" in Blue

1919 Wmk. 191R Offset Printing *Perf. 11*

RJA30	RB5	1c	dark blue	—	—
RJA31	RB5	2c	dark blue	—	
RJA32	RB5	4c	dark blue	—	

No. RB65 is known with "Narcotic" applied in red ms.

Documentary Stamps of 1917 Overprinted in Black, "Narcotic" 17½mm wide **NARCOTIC**

1919 Wmk. 191R Offset Printing *Perf. 11*

RJA33	R22	1c	carmine rose *(6,900,000)*	75	50
RJA34	R22	2c	carmine rose *(3,650,000)*	1.50	1.00
RJA35	R22	3c	carmine rose *(388,400)*	25.00	15.00
RJA36	R22	4c	carmine rose *(2,400,000)*	5.00	3.50
RJA37	R22	5c	carmine rose *(2,400,000)*	12.00	10.00
RJA38	R22	8c	carmine rose *(1,200,000)*	17.50	13.00
RJA39	R22	10c	carmine rose *(3,400,000)*	3.00	2.50
RJA40	R22	25c	carmine rose *(700,000)*	17.50	13.00

Overprint Reading Up

Engr.

RJA41	R21	$1	green *(270,000)*	25.00	12.00

The overprint of Nos. RJA33-RJA41 has been counterfeited. In the genuine the C's are not slanted.

NT1

Imperf., Rouletted

1919-70 Offset Printing Wmk. 191R

				a. Imperf.	b. Rouletted 7
RJA42	NT1	1c	violet	3.50	10
		d.	1c purple		6.00

NT2

RJA43	NT2	1c	violet	50	15
		d.	1c purple	3.00	3.00
RJA44	NT2	2c	violet	1.00	40
		d.	2c purple		5.00
RJA45	NT2	3c	violet ('64)	—	80.00

NT3 NT4

				a. Imperf.	b. Rouletted 7
RJA46	NT3	1c	violet	2.00	65
		d.	1c purple		5.50
RJA47	NT3	2c	violet	1.50	50
		d.	2c purple		8.00
RJA48	NT3	3c	violet	450.00	
RJA49	NT3	4c	violet ('42)	—	7.50
		d.	4c purple		30.00
RJA50	NT3	5c	violet	40.00	3.25
		d.	5c purple		12.50
RJA51	NT3	6c	violet		65
		d.	6c purple		9.00
RJA52	NT3	8c	violet	55.00	3.00
		d.	8c purple		25.00
RJA53	NT3	9c	violet ('53)	65.00	6.50
RJA54	NT3	10c	violet	30.00	50
		d.	10c purple		7.00
RJA55	NT3	16c	violet	50.00	2.50
		d.	16c purple		14.00
RJA56	NT3	18c	violet ('61)	80.00	5.00
RJA57	NT3	19c	violet ('61)	110.00	15.00
RJA58	NT3	20c	violet	275.00	110.00

Nos. RJA47-RJA58 have "CENTS" below the value.

				a. Imperf.	b. Roul. 7	c. Roul. 3½
RJA59	NT4	1c	violet	45.00	10.00	4.00
RJA60	NT4	2c	violet		20.00	
RJA61	NT4	3c	violet	40.00	18.50	
RJA62	NT4	5c	violet		25.00	
RJA63	NT4	6c	violet	60.00	20.00	
RJA64	NT4	8c	violet		45.00	
RJA65	NT4	9c	violet ('61)	12.50	10.00	
RJA66	NT4	10c	violet	11.00	15.00	
RJA67	NT4	16c	violet	15.00	10.00	
RJA68	NT4	18c	violet ('61)	325.00	375.00	
RJA69	NT4	19c	violet	10.00	110.00	
RJA70	NT4	20c	violet	325.00	140.00	
RJA71	NT4	25c	violet	—	20.00	4.00
RJA72	NT4	40c	violet	350.00		65.00
RJA73	NT4	$1	green		1.25	
RJA74	NT4	$1.28	green	25.00	10.00	
RJA75	NT4	$4	green, unwmkd. ('70)	*750.00*		

On Nos. RJA60-RJA75 the value tablet is solid.

Many of Nos. RJA59a-RJA74a (imperfs.) exist unwatermarked.

NT5

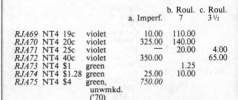

Denomination added in black by rubber plate in an operation similar to precanceling.

1963 Engr. Unwmk. *Imperf.*

RJA76	NT5	1c	violet	50.00

Denomination on Stamp Plate

1964 Offset Printing *Imperf.*

RJA77	NT5	1c	violet	5.00

The Scott Catalogue value is a retail price, what you could expect to pay for the stamp in a grade of Fine-Very Fine. The value listed is a reference which reflects recent actual dealer selling price.

CONSULAR SERVICE FEE

Act of Congress, April 5, 1906, effective June 1, 1906, provided that every consular officer should be provided with special adhesive stamps printed in denominations determined by the Department of State.

Every document for which a fee was prescribed had to have attached a stamp or stamps representing the amount collected, and such stamps were used to show payment of these prescribed fees.

These stamps were usually affixed close to the signature, or at the lower left corner of the document. If no document was issued, the stamp or stamps were attached to a receipt for the amount of the fee and canceled either with pen and ink or rubber stamp showing the date of cancellation and bearing the initials of the canceling officer or name of the Consular Office. These stamps were not sold to the public uncanceled. Their use was discontinued Sept. 30, 1955.

CS1

1906 Unwmk. Engr. *Perf. 12*

RK1	CS1	25c	dark green	27.50
RK2	CS1	50c	carmine	37.50
RK3	CS1	$1	dark violet	5.00
RK4	CS1	$2	brown	4.00
RK5	CS1	$2.50	dark blue	1.00
RK6	CS1	$5	brown red	12.50
		a.	Horizontal half used as $2.50	—
RK7	CS1	$10	orange	37.50

Perf. 10

RK8	CS1	25c	dark green	27.50
RK9	CS1	50c	carmine	30.00
RK10	CS1	$1	dark violet	175.00
RK11	CS1	$2	brown	45.00
		a.	Diagonal half used as $1	—
RK12	CS1	$2.50	dark blue	12.50
RK13	CS1	$5	brown red	50.00

Perf. 11

RK14	CS1	25c	dark green	35.00
RK15	CS1	50c	carmine	50.00
RK16	CS1	$1	dark violet	1.75
		a.	Diagonal half used as 50c	—
RK17	CS1	$2	brown	1.75
RK18	CS1	$2.50	dark blue	50
RK19	CS1	$5	brown red	3.00
		a.	Diagonal half used as $2.50	30.00
RK20	CS1	$9	gray	10.00
RK21	CS1	$10	orange	17.50
		a.	Diagonal half used as $5	50.00

For $2 black of type CS1, see No. RN-Y1 in Revenue Stamped Paper section.

CS2

1924 *Perf. 11*

RK22	CS2	$1	violet	40.00
RK23	CS2	$2	brown	42.50
RK24	CS2	$2.50	blue	8.50
RK25	CS2	$5	brown red	30.00
RK26	CS2	$9	gray	140.00

CS3

1925-52 *Perf. 10*

RK27	CS3	$1	violet	12.50
RK28	CS3	$2	brown	32.50
RK29	CS3	$2.50	ultramarine	1.00
RK30	CS3	$5	carmine	9.00
RK31	CS3	$9	gray	25.00

Perf. 11

RK32	CS3	25c	green ('37)	32.50
RK33	CS3	50c	orange ('34)	30.00

RK34	CS3	$1	violet	2.50
	a.		Diagonal half used as 50c	—
RK35	CS3	$2	brown	2.50
RK36	CS3	$2.50	blue	30
	a.		$2.50 ultramarine	25
RK37	CS3	$5	carmine	3.00
RK38	CS3	$9	gray	10.00
RK39	CS3	$10	blue gray ('37)	50.00
RK40	CS3	$20	violet ('52)	60.00

CUSTOMS FEE

New York Custom House

Issued to indicate the collection of miscellaneous customs fees. Use was discontinued on February 28, 1918. The stamps were not utilized in the collection of customs duties.

Silas Wright
CF1

Size: 48x34mm

1887 **Engr.** ***Rouletted 5½***

RL1	CF1	20c	dull rose	50
	a.		20c red, perf. 10	—
	b.		Vertical half used as 10c	—
	c.		20c red, rouletted 7	*110.00*
RL2	CF1	30c	orange	1.25
RL3	CF1	40c	green	2.25
RL4	CF1	50c	dark blue	4.50
RL5	CF1	60c	red violet	1.25
RL6	CF1	70c	brown violet	25.00
RL7	CF1	80c	brown	55.00
RL8	CF1	90c	black	75.00

Each of these eight stamps has its own distinctive background.

EMBOSSED REVENUE STAMPED PAPER

Some of the American colonies of Great Britain used embossed stamps in raising revenue, as Britain had done from 1694. The British government also imposed stamp taxes on the colonies, and in the early 19th century the U.S. government and some of the states enacted similar taxes.

Under one statue or another, these stamps were required on such documents as promissory notes, bills of exchange, insurance policies, bills of lading, bonds, protests, powers of attorney, stock certificates, letters patent, writs, conveyances, leases, mortgages, charter parties, commissions and liquor licenses.

A few of these stamps were printed, but most were colorless impressions resembling a notary public's seal.

The scant literature of these stamps includes E.B. Sterling's revenue catalogue of 1888, *New Discovery from British Archives on the 1765 Tax Stamps for America,* edited by Adolph Koeppel and published in 1962 by the American Revenue Association, and *First Federal Issue 1798-1801 U.S. Embossed Revenue Stamped Paper* by W.V. Coombs, published in 1979 by the American Philatelic Society.

Values are for stamps of clear impression on entire documents in good condition. Parts of documents, cut squares or poor impressions sell for much less. Values represent actual sales wherever possible. A dash in the value column indicates that few copies are known or information for valuing is inadequate.

Colin MacR. Makepeace originally compiled the listings in this section.

INCLUDING COLONIAL EMBOSSED REVENUES

I. COLONIAL ISSUES

A. MASSACHUSETTS

Act of January 8, 1755

In effect May 1, 1755-April 30, 1757

EP1

RM1

Prices paid for stamps on original covers vary greatly in accordance with condition, appearance, cancellation or postmark and usage.

EP2 EP3 EP4

Typo.

RM1	EP1	½p	red	2,000.

Embossed

RM2	EP2	2p	450.00
RM3	EP3	3p	110.00
RM4	EP4	4p	500.00

A second die of EP2 with no fin on the under side of the codfish has been seen. There were at least two dies of the ½p.

B. NEW YORK

Act of December 1, 1756

In effect January 1, 1757-December 31, 1760

EP9

Typo.

RM9	EP9	½p	red	2,500.

Embossed

RM10	EP9	1p	450.00
RM11	EP9	2p	200.00
RM12	EP9	3p	400.00
RM13	EP9	4p	300.00

II. BRITISH REVENUES FOR USE IN AMERICA

Act of March 22, 1765

In effect November 1, 1765-May 1, 1766.

A. ALMANAC STAMPS

EP15

Engr.

RM15 EP15 2p red		
RM16 EP15 4p red		—
RM17 EP15 8p red		

Proofs of all of these stamps printed in the issued color are known. Full size facsimile reproductions in the color of the originals were made about 1876 of the proof sheets of the 8p stamp, Plates 1 and 2, Dies 1 to 50 inclusive.

B. PAMPHLETS AND NEWSPAPER STAMPS

EP18

Engr.

RM18 EP18 ½p red	1,750.
RM19 EP18 1p red	—
RM20 EP18 2p red	

Proofs of all of these stamps printed in the issued color are known. Full size facsimile reproductions in the color of the originals were made about 1876 of the proof sheets of the 1p stamp, Plates 3 and 4, Dies 51 to 100 inclusive.

C. GENERAL ISSUE

EP24 EP25 EP26 EP27 EP28 EP29 EP30 EP31

EP33 EP34 EP35

Embossed

RM24 EP24 3p		1,250.
RM25 EP25 4p		3,000.
RM26 EP26 6p		2,000.
RM27 EP27 1sh		1,000.
RM28 EP28 1sh 6p		1,250.
RM29 EP29 2sh		3,000.
RM30 EP30 2sh 3p		2,250.
RM31 EP31 2sh 6p		800.00
a.	Not on document	500.00
RM33 EP33 4sh		2,500.
RM34 EP34 5sh		2,500.
RM35 EP35 10sh		3,250.

Proofs exist of similar 1sh, 1sh6p and 2sh6p stamps inscribed "AMERICA CONT.& c."

Various Similar Designs

RM36 £1	
RM37 £2	—
RM38 £3	—
RM39 £4	
RM40 £6	—
RM41 £10	—

The £1 to £10 denominations probably exist only as proofs.

D. PLAYING CARDS STAMP

Type similar to EP29, with Arms of George III Encircled by Garter.

RM42 1sh	—

All of these were embossed without color and most of them were embossed directly on the document except the 2sh 6p which was general embossed on a rectangular piece of bluish or brownish stiff paper or cardboard only slightly larger than the stamp which was attached to the document by a small piece of metal. Three dies exist of the 3p; two of the 4p, 6p, 1sh, 1sh 6p, 2sh and 2sh 3p.

All of these stamps have the word "America" somewhere in the design and this is the feature which distinguishes them from the other British revenues. The stamps of the general issue are occasionally found with a design of a British revenue stamp struck over the American design, as a number of them were afterwards re-struck and used elsewhere as British revenues.

These stamps are sometimes called the "Teaparty" or "Tax on Tea" stamps. This, however, is a misnomer, as the act under which these stamps were issued laid no tax on tea. The tax on tea was levied by an act passed two years later, and the duties imposed by that act were not collected by stamps.

It must be remembered that these stamps were issued under an act applicable to all of the British colonies in America which included many which are not now part of the United States. Copies have been seen which were used in Quebec, Nova Scotia and in the West Indies. So great was the popular clamor against taxation by a body in which the colonists had no representation that ships bringing the stamps from England were not allowed to land them in some of the colonies, the stamps were destroyed in others, and in practically all of those which are now a part of the United States the "Stamp Masters" who were to administer the act were forced to resign and to take oath that they would never carry out the duties of the offices. Notwithstanding the very general feeling about these stamps there is evidence that a very small number of them were actually used on ships' documents for one vessel clearing from New York and for a very small number of vessels clearing from the Savannah River. Florida was at this time under British authority and the only known copies of these stamps used in what is now the United States, a 4p (#RM25), a 1sh (#RM27), and two copies of the 5sh (#RM34) were used there.

III. ISSUES OF THE UNITED STATES

A. FIRST FEDERAL ISSUE

Act of July 6, 1797

In effect July 1, 1798-February 28, 1801

RM45

RM46

The distinguishing feature of the stamps of this issue is the name of a state in the design. These stamps were issued by the Federal Government, however, and not by the states. The design, with the exception of the name of the state, was the same for each denomination; but different denominations had the shield and the eagle in different positions. The design of only one denomination of these stamps is illustrated.

In addition to the eagle and shield design on the values from four cents to ten dollars there are two other stamps for each state, similar in design to one another, one of which is illustrated. All of these stamps are embossed without color.

Values are for clearly impressed examples.

RM45	4c	Connecticut	22.50
RM46	10c	Connecticut	22.50
RM47	20c	Connecticut	175.00
RM48	25c	Connecticut	27.50
RM49	30c	Connecticut	—
RM50	50c	Connecticut	135.00
RM51	75c	Connecticut	—
RM52	$1	Connecticut	850.00
RM54	$4	Connecticut	—
RM58	4c	Delaware	100.00
RM59	10c	Delaware	150.00
RM60	20c	Delaware	250.00
RM61	25c	Delaware	150.00
RM62	30c	Delaware	—
RM63	50c	Delaware	300.00
RM64	75c	Delaware	—
RM65	$1	Delaware	—
RM71	4c	Georgia	150.00
RM72	10c	Georgia	55.00
RM73	20c	Georgia	—
RM74	25c	Georgia	70.00
RM75	30c	Georgia	—
RM76	50c	Georgia	130.00
RM77	75c	Georgia	—
RM78	$1	Georgia	—
RM84	4c	Kentucky	15.00
RM85	10c	Kentucky	15.00
RM86	20c	Kentucky	150.00
RM87	25c	Kentucky	15.00
RM88	30c	Kentucky	475.00
RM89	50c	Kentucky	100.00
RM90	75c	Kentucky	75.00
RM91	$1	Kentucky	—
RM97	4c	Maryland	35.00
RM98	10c	Maryland	12.50
RM99	20c	Maryland	200.00
RM100	25c	Maryland	12.50
RM101	30c	Maryland	350.00
RM102	50c	Maryland	27.50
RM103	75c	Maryland	27.50
RM104	$1	Maryland	400.00
RM106	$4	Maryland	—
RM110	4c	Massachusetts	8.00
RM111	10c	Massachusetts	8.00
RM112	20c	Massachusetts	80.00
RM113	25c	Massachusetts	8.00
RM114	30c	Massachusetts	—
RM115	50c	Massachusetts	50.00
RM116	75c	Massachusetts	175.00
RM117	$1	Massachusetts	100.00
RM123	4c	New Hampshire	25.00
RM124	10c	New Hampshire	25.00
RM125	20c	New Hampshire	75.00
RM126	25c	New Hampshire	32.50
RM127	30c	New Hampshire	200.00
RM128	50c	New Hampshire	110.00
RM129	75c	New Hampshire	100.00
RM130	$1	New Hampshire	450.00
RM136	4c	New Jersey	275.00
RM137	10c	New Jersey	150.00
RM138	20c	New Jersey	—
RM139	25c	New Jersey	100.00
RM140	30c	New Jersey	450.00
RM141	50c	New Jersey	250.00
RM142	75c	New Jersey	—
RM143	$1	New Jersey	—
RM147	$10	New Jersey	—
RM149	4c	New York	25.00
RM150	10c	New York	15.00
RM151	20c	New York	25.00
RM152	25c	New York	10.00
RM153	30c	New York	18.00
RM154	50c	New York	22.50
RM155	75c	New York	55.00
RM156	$1	New York	110.00
RM157	$2	New York	—
RM159	$5	New York	—
RM160	$10	New York	—
RM162	4c	North Carolina	27.50
RM163	10c	North Carolina	22.50
RM164	20c	North Carolina	325.00

RM165	25c	North Carolina	40.00
RM166	30c	North Carolina	—
RM167	50c	North Carolina	110.00
RM168	75c	North Carolina	150.00
RM169	$1	North Carolina	300.00
RM175	4c	Pennsylvania	30.00
RM176	10c	Pennsylvania	17.50
RM177	20c	Pennsylvania	22.50
RM178	25c	Pennsylvania	17.50
RM179	30c	Pennsylvania	20.00
RM180	50c	Pennsylvania	17.50
RM181	75c	Pennsylvania	17.50
RM182	$1	Pennsylvania	70.00
RM187		Pennsylvania, "Ten cents per centum"	—
RM188	4c	Rhode Island	30.00
RM189	10c	Rhode Island	25.00
RM190	20c	Rhode Island	90.00
RM191	25c	Rhode Island	45.00
RM192	30c	Rhode Island	225.00
RM193	50c	Rhode Island	100.00
RM194	75c	Rhode Island	325.00
RM195	$1	Rhode Island	165.00
RM201	4c	South Carolina	50.00
RM202	10c	South Carolina	40.00
RM203	20c	South Carolina	—
RM204	25c	South Carolina	90.00
RM205	30c	South Carolina	—
RM206	50c	South Carolina	100.00
RM207	75	South Carolina	450.00
RM208	$1	South Carolina	—
RM211	$5	South Carolina	—
RM214	4c	Tennessee	175.00
RM215	10c	Tennessee	75.00
RM216	20c	Tennessee	—
RM217	25c	Tennessee	200.00
RM218	30c	Tennessee	—
RM219	50c	Tennessee	500.00
RM220	75c	Tennessee	—
RM221	$1	Tennessee	—
RM227	4c	Vermont	50.00
RM228	10c	Vermont	25.00
RM229	20c	Vermont	175.00
RM230	25c	Vermont	40.00
RM231	30c	Vermont	135.00
RM232	50c	Vermont	110.00
RM233	75c	Vermont	375.00
RM234	$1	Vermont	750.00
RM238	$10	Vermont	—
RM240	4c	Virginia	17.50
RM241	10c	Virginia	15.00
RM242	20c	Virginia	65.00
RM243	25c	Virginia	17.50
RM244	30c	Virginia	300.00
RM245	50c	Virginia	25.00
RM246	75c	Virginia	25.00
RM247	$1	Virginia	—

The Act calls for a $2, $4, $5 and $10 stamp for each state, only the listed ones have been seen.

The Act also calls for a "Ten cents per centum" and a "Six mills per dollar" stamp for each state, none of which has been seen except No. RM187.

A press and a set of dies, one die for each denomination, were prepared and sent to each state where it was the duty of the Supervisors of the Revenue to stamp all documents presented to them upon payment of the proper tax. The Supervisors were also to have on hand for sale blank paper stamped with the different rates of duty to be sold to the public upon which the purchaser would later write or print the proper type of instrument corresponding with the value of the stamp impressed thereon. So far as is now known there was no distinctive watermark for the paper sold by the government. The Vermont set of dies is in the Vermont Historical Society at Montpelier.

B. SECOND FEDERAL ISSUE

Act of April 23, 1800

In effect March 1, 1801-June 30, 1802

RM260

RM261

	(a)Government watermark in italics; laid paper	(b)Government watermark in Roman; wove paper	(c)No Government watermark
RM260 4c	15.00	15.00	50.00
RM261 10c	15.00	15.00	50.00
RM262 20c	55.00	50.00	85.00
RM263 25c	15.00	15.00	17.50
RM264 30c	37.50	55.00	500.00
RM265 50c	55.00	45.00	85.00
RM266 75c	30.00	40.00	100.00
RM267 $1	100.00	120.00	90.00
RM269 $4			500.00
RM271 $10		500.00	

The distinguishing feature of the stamps of this issue is the counter stamp, the left stamp shown in the illustration which usually appears on a document below the other stamp. In the right stamp the design of the eagle and the shield are similar to their design in the same denomination of the First Federal Issue but the name of the state is omitted and the denomination appears below instead of above the eagle and the shield. All of these stamps were embossed without color.

All the paper which was furnished by the government contained the watermark vertically along the edge of the sheet, "GEN STAMP OFFICE", either in Roman capitals on wove paper or in italic capitals on laid paper. The wove paper also had in the center of each half sheet either the watermark "W. Y. & Co." or "Delaware". William Young & Co. who owned the Delaware Mills made the government paper. The laid paper omitted the watermark "Delaware". The two stamps were separately impressed. The design of the eagle and shield differed in each value.

All the stamping was done in Washington, the right stamp being put on in the General Stamp Office and the left one or counter stamp in the office of the Commissioner of the Revenue as a check on the stamping done in the General Stamp Office. The "Com. Rev. C. S." in the design of the counter stamp stands for "Commissioner of the Revenue, Counter Stamp."

The Second Federal issue was intended to include $2 and $5 stamps, but these denominations have not been seen.

C. THIRD FEDERAL ISSUE

Act of August 2, 1813

In effect January 1, 1814-December 31, 1817

RM275

		a.Watermark	b.Unwmkd.
RM275	5c	10.00	15.00
RM276	10c	10.00	10.00
RM277	25c	10.00	10.00
RM278	50c	10.00	10.00
RM279	75c	13.00	17.50
RM280	$1	13.00	27.50
RM281	$1.50	13.00	32.50
RM282	$2	27.50	27.50
RM283	$2.50	27.50	55.00
RM284	$3.50	65.00	45.00
RM285	$4		110.00
RM286	$5	37.50	50.00

The distinguishing features of the stamps of this issue are the absence of the name of a state in the design and the absence of the counter stamp. Different values show different positions of the eagle.

All stamps of this issue were embossed without color at Washington. The paper with the watermark "Stamp U. S." was sold by the government. Unwatermarked paper may be either wove or laid.

IV. ISSUES BY VARIOUS STATES

A. DELAWARE

Act of June 19, 1973

In effect October 1, 1793-February 7, 1794

EP50

EP51

EP53

RM291	EP50	5c	900.00
RM292	EP51	20c	1,250.
RM294	EP53	50c	—

In some cases a reddish ink was used in impressing the stamp and in other cases the impressions are colorless.

Besides the denominations listed, 3c, 33c, and $1 stamps were called for by the taxing act. Stamps of these denominations have not been seen.

B. VIRGINIA

Act of February 20, 1813

In effect May 1, 1813-April 30, 1815

Act of December 21, 1814

In effect May 1, 1815-February 27, 1816

EP60 EP61

			a. Die cut	b. On Document
RM305	EP61	4c	17.50	—
RM306	EP60	6c	17.50	
RM307	EP61	10c		—
RM308	EP60	12c	17.50	—
RM309	EP61	20c	—	—
RM310	EP61	25c	17.50	200.00
RM311	EP61	37c	17.50	
RM312	EP61	45c	—	—
RM313	EP61	50c	17.50	—
RM314	EP61	70c	—	
RM315	EP61	75c	17.50	—
RM316	EP61	95c	—	—
RM317	EP61	100c	—	
RM318	EP61	120c		—
RM319	EP61	125c	17.50	
RM323	EP60	175c	17.50	
RM325	EP61	200c	17.50	—

All of these stamps are colorless impressions and with some exceptions as noted below those issued the 1813 Act cannot be distinguished from those issued under the 1814 Act. The 10c, 20c, 45c, 70c, 95c, 120c, 145c, 150c, 170c and 190c denominations were issued only under the 1813 Act and the 6c, 12c, and 37c denominations were issued only under the 1814 Act. The other denominations were common to both Acts.

No. RM311, the 37c denomination, has the large lettering of EP60 but the 37 is to the left and the XXXVII to the right as in EP61. The design of the dogwood branch and berries is similar but not identical in all values.

When the tax on the document exceeded "two hundred cents", two or more stamps were impressed or attached to the document. For instance a document has been seen with Nos. RM312 and RM325 both impressed on it to make up the $2.45 rate, and another with Nos. RM315 and RM325.

Since both the Virginia and the Third Federal Acts to some extent taxed the same kind of document, and since during the period from an. 1, 1814, to Feb. 27, 1816, both Acts were in effect in Virginia, some instruments have both Virginia and Third Federal stamps on them.

The circular die cut Virginia stamps about 29mm in diameter were cut out of previously stamped paper which after the Act was repealed, was presented for redemption at the office of the Auditor of Public Accounts. They were threaded on fine twine and until recently preserved in his office as required by law. Watermarked die cut Virginia stamps are all cut out of Third Federal watermarked paper.

Besides the denominations listed, 145c, 150c, and 170c stamps were called for by the 1813 Act, and a 195c by both the 1813 and 1814 Acts. Stamps of these four denominations have not been seen.

C. MARYLAND

1. Act of February 11, 1818
In effect May 1, 1818-March 7, 1819

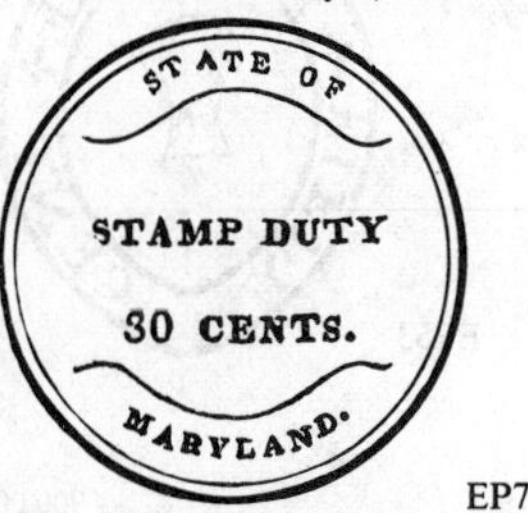

EP70

RM362	EP70	30c red (printed), unused	200.00
		Sheet of 4, unused	900.00

The Act called for six other denominations, none of which has been seen. The Act imposing this tax was held unconstitutional by the United States Supreme Court in the case of McCulloch vs. Maryland.

2. Act of March 10, 1845
In effect May 10, 1845-March 10, 1856

EP71

RM370	EP71	10c	8.00
RM371	EP71	15c	6.00
RM372	EP71	25c	6.00
RM373	EP71	50c	6.00
RM374	EP71	75c	6.00
RM375	EP71	$1	6.00
RM376	EP71	$1.50	12.00
RM377	EP71	$2	15.00
RM378	EP71	$2.50	15.00
RM379	EP71	$3.50	35.00
RM380	EP71	$4	60.00
RM381	EP71	$5.50	35.00
RM382	EP71	$6	35.00

Nos. RM370-RM382 are embossed without color with a similar design for each value. They vary in size from 20mm in diameter for the 10c to 33mm for the $6.

V. FEDERAL LICENSES TO SELL LIQUOR, ETC.

1. Act of June 5, 1794
In effect September 1, 1794-June 30, 1802

EP80

RM400	EP80	$5	350.00

Provisionals are in existence using the second issue Connecticut Supervisors' stamp with the words "Five Dollars" written or printed over it or the second issue of the New Hampshire Supervisors' stamp without the words "Five Dollars".

2. Act of August 2, 1813
In effect January 1, 1814-December 31, 1817

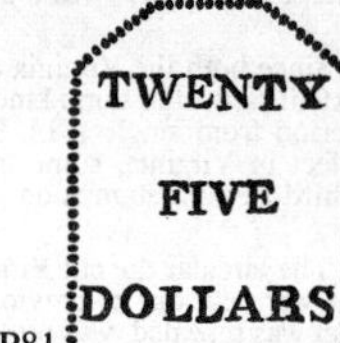

EP81

RM451	EP81	$10	400.00
RM452	EP81	$12	325.00
RM453	EP81	$15	275.00
RM454	EP81	$18	300.00
RM455	EP81	$20	300.00
RM456	EP81	$22.50	325.00
RM457	EP81	$25	275.00
RM458	EP81	$30	—
RM459	EP81	$37.50	350.00

The Act of December 23, 1814, increased the basic rates of $10, $12, $15, $20 and $25 by 50 per cent, effective February 1, 1815. This increase applied to the unexpired portions of the year so far as licenses then in effect were concerned and these licenses were required to be brought in and to have the payment of the additional tax endorsed on them.

VI. FEDERAL LICENSES TO WORK A STILL

Act of July 24, 1813
In effect January 1, 1814-December 31, 1817

(Embossed)
EP82

4½
CENTS
PER
GALLON.

(Printed)
EP83

		a. Embossed	b. Printed
RM466	4½c		900.00
RM468	9c	575.00	400.00
RM471	18c	—	—
RM480	52c	375.00	
RM488	$1.08	375.00	

The statute under which these were issued provided for additional rates of 2½c, 5c, 10c, 16c, 21c, 25c, 26c, 32c, 35c, 36c, 42c, 50c, 54c, 60c, 64c, 70c, 84c, $1.04, $1.05, $1.20, $1.35, $1.40, $2.10, $2.16 and $2.70 per gallon of the capacity of the still. Stamps of these denominations have not been seen.

VII. SUPERVISORS' AND CUSTOM HOUSE SEALS

1. Supervisors' Seals Act of March 3, 1791.
In effect July 1, 1792-March 2, 1799.

EP90

		Check Letter	State	
RM501	EP90	"B"	South Carolina	50.00
RM503	EP90	"D"	Virginia	—
RM506	EP90	"G"	Pennsylvania	75.00
RM508	EP90	"I"	New York	22.50
RM509	EP90	"K"	Connecticut	30.00
RM510	EP90	"L"	Rhode Island	90.00
RM511	EP90	"M"	Massachusetts	22.50
RM512	EP90	"N"	New Hampshire	—
RM514	EP90	"P"	Kentucky	—

2. Supervisors' Seals Act of March 2, 1799
In effect from March 2, 1799

EP91

RM552	EP91	North Carolina	—
RM553	EP91	Virginia	—
RM554	EP91	Maryland	75.00
RM556	EP91	Pennsylvania	—
RM558	EP91	New York	22.50
RM559	EP91	Connecticut	30.00
RM560	EP91	Rhode Island	35.00
RM561	EP91	Massachusetts	25.00
RM562	EP91	New Hampshire	90.00

3. Custom House Seals

EP92

RM575	EP92	Custom House, Philadelphia	60.00

Although no value is expressed in the Supervisors' and Custom House seals, and they do not evidence the payment of a tax in the same way that the other stamps do, some collectors of stamped paper include them in their collections if they are on instruments evidencing the payment of a tax. They were all embossed without color and, as to Supervisors' seals issued under the Act of 1791, the only difference in design is that at the left of the eagle there was a different check letter for each state. Custom House seals used in the other cities are in existence, but, in view of the doubtful status of Custom House seals as revenue stamps, it is not proposed to list them.

REVENUE STAMPED PAPER

These stamps were printed in various denominations and designs on checks, drafts, receipts, insurance policies, bonds, stock certificates, etc. They were authorized by Act of Congress of July 1, 1862, effective October 1, 1862, and were used until July 1, 1882, except for the Spanish-American War series of 1898.

Most of these stamps were lithographed; some were engraved. They were printed by private firms under supervision of government representatives from stones or dies loaned by the Bureau of Internal Revenue. Types A-F were printed by, or the stones originated with, the American Phototype Co., New York (1865-75); type G, American Graphic Co., New York (1875); types H-L, Joseph R. Carpenter, Philadelphia (1869-75); types M-N, Bureau of Engraving and Printing (1874); type O, St. Louis Lithograph Co., St. Louis.

Samples of these stamps were produced with special dies for types B-G and P. For each sample die a section of the design was removed and replaced by the word "Sample." Types G and P-W exist with a redemption clause added by typography or rubber stamp.

Multiples or single impressions on various plain papers are usually considered proofs or printers' waste.

For further information see "Handbook for United States Revenue Stamped Paper," published (1979) by the American Revenue Association.

Illustration size varies, with actual size quoted for each type.

Values for types A-O are for clear impressions on plain entire checks and receipts. Attractive documents with vignettes sell for more. Values for types P-W are for stamps on documents with attractive engravings, usually stock certificates, bonds and insurance policies. Examples on plain documents and cut squares sell for less.

Type A

Size: 22x25mm

No.	Type	Denom.	Description	Unused	Used
RN—A1	A	2c	black	75.00	65.00
			a. Printed on both sides		30.00
RN—A2	A	2c	orange		100.00
RN—A8	A	2c	purple (shades)		900.00
RN—A9	A	2c	green		675.00

Same Type with 1 Entire and 53 to 57 Partial Impressions in Vertical Format ("Tapeworm")

No.	Type	Denom.	Description	Full Document	Strip with Bank Names
RN—A10	A	2c	orange, 56 partial impressions	775.00	150.00
		a.	53 partial impressions	1,000.	250.00
		b.	54 partial impressions	1,250.	
		d.	57 partial impressions	1,250.	
			Cut square, stamp only		50.00

No. RN-A10 was used by the Mechanics' National Bank of New York on a bank specie clerk's statement. It was designed so that the full stamp or one of the repeated bottom segments fell on each line opposite the name of a bank.

Eagle Type B

Size: 31x48mm

No.	Type	Denom.	Description	Unused	Used
RN—B1	B	2c	orange	3.00	1.00
			yellow orange	3.00	1.00
			deep orange	3.00	1.00
		a.	Printed on both sides	—	20.00
		b.	Double impression	350.00	
		c.	Printed on back		—
		d.	With 10 centimes blue French handstamp, right	300.00	
RN—B2	B	2c	black	65.00	30.00
			slate	75.00	35.00
RN—B3	B	2c	blue	75.00	20.00
			light blue	75.00	12.50
RN—B4	B	2c	brown	—	40.00
RN—B5	B	2c	bronze	65.00	25.00
RN—B6	B	2c	green (shades)	75.00	20.00
RN—B7	B	2c	yellow	6.00	2.50
RN—B10	B	2c	red	75.00	20.00
			pale red	75.00	15.00
RN—B11	B	2c	purple	85.00	65.00
RN—B13	B	2c	violet (shades)	100.00	35.00
		a.	2c violet brown	100.00	65.00

"Good only for checks and drafts payable at sight." in Rectangular Tablet at Base

No.	Type	Denom.	Description	Unused	Used
RN—B16	B	2c	orange	40.00	7.50
			a. With 2c org. red Nevada	325.00	250.00

"Good only for checks and drafts payable at sight." in Octagonal Tablet at Base

No.	Type	Denom.	Description	Unused	Used
RN—B17	B	2c	orange	40.00	10.00
		a.	Tablet inverted		650.00
		b.	With 2c org. red Nevada	85.00	35.00
		c.	With 2c green Nevada	100.00	35.00
		d.	With 2c dull vio. Nevada		—

"Good when issued for the payment of money." in Octagonal Tablet at Base

No.	Type	Denom.	Description	Unused	Used
RN—B20	B	2c	orange	60.00	5.00
		a.	Printed on both sides	30.00	6.00
		b.	As "a," one stamp inverted		—

"Good when issued for the payment of money" in two lines at base in orange

No.	Type	Denom.	Description	Unused	Used
RN—B23	B	2c	orange		600.00

"Good when the amount does not exceed $100." in Octagonal Tablet at Base

No.	Type	Denom.	Description	Unused	Used
RN—B24	B	2c	orange	175.00	60.00

Washington-Type C

Size: 108x49mm

No.	Type	Denom.	Description	Unused	Used
RN—C1	C	2c	orange	5.00	2.00
			red orange	5.00	2.00
			yellow orange	5.00	2.00
			salmon	6.00	2.50
			brown orange	6.00	2.50
		a.	"Good when used . . ." vert. at left black		—
RN—C2	C	2c	brown	30.00	10.00
		a.	2c buff	30.00	10.00
RN—C5	C	2c	pale red	50.00	20.00
			red	50.00	22.50
		a.	2c pink		17.50
RN—C6	C	2c	yellow	7.50	3.00
RN—C8	C	2c	green	—	

"Good only for Sight Draft" in two lines in color of stamp

No.	Type	Denom.	Description	Unused	Used
RN—C9	C	2c	orange, legend at lower right	75.00	40.00
RN—C11	C	2c	brown, legend at lower left	75.00	55.00
RN—C13	C	2c	orange, legend at lower left	40.00	15.00

"Good only for Receipt for Money Paid" in two lines in color of stamp

No.	Type	Denom.	Description	Unused	Used
RN—C15	C	2c	orange, legend at lower right		—
RN—C16	C	2c	orange, legend at lower left		225.00

"Good when issued for the payment of money" in one line at base in color of stamp.

No.	Type	Denom.	Description	Unused	Used
RN—C17	C	2c	orange (shades)		340.00

"Good when issued for the/Payment of Money" in two tablets at lower left and right.

No.	Type	Denom.	Description	Unused	Used
RN—C19	C	2c	orange		340.00
		a.	Printed on both sides		32.50

"Good/only for Bank/Check" in 3-part Band

No.	Type	Denom.	Description	Unused	Used
RN—C21	C	2c	orange	50.00	10.00
			yellow		20.00
		a.	Inverted		575.00
		b.	With 2c red org. Nevada	70.00	30.00
		c.	Printed on back		—
RN—C22	C	2c	brown	—	22.50
		a.	Printed on back		125.00
RN—C23	C	2c	red		650.00

"Good when the amount does not exceed $100" in tablet at lower right.

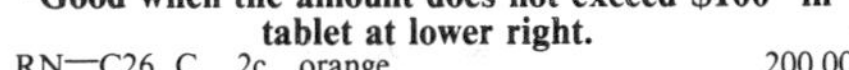

No.	Type	Denom.	Description	Unused	Used
RN—C26	C	2c	orange		200.00

Franklin Type D

Size: 80x43mm

No.	Type	Denom.	Description	Unused	Used
RN—D1	D	2c	orange (shades)	2.00	60
		a.	Double impression		—
		b.	Printed on back	—	400.00
		c.	Inverted		375.00
RN—D2	D	2c	yellow	10.00	4.00
RN—D3	D	2c	brown	7.50	3.00
			light brown	7.50	3.00
		a.	2c buff	7.50	3.00
RN—D5	D	2c	red		—

"Good only for/Bank Check" in panels within circles at left and right

No.	Type	Denom.	Description	Unused	Used
RN—D7	D	2c	orange	20.00	7.50
		a.	Printed on back		—

"Good only for/Bank Check" in two lines at lower right in color of stamp

No.	Type	Denom.	Description	Unused	Used
RN—D8	D	2c	orange		350.00

Values for cancellation varieties are for specimens off cover.

"Good only for Sight Draft" in two lines at lower left in color of stamp

RN—D9	D	2c	orange	150.00	50.00

Franklin Type E

Size: 28x50mm

RN—E4	E	2c	orange	5.00	3.00
		a.	Double impression		350.00
			Broken die, lower R or L	40.00	20.00

"Good only for sight draft" in two lines at base in orange

RN—E5	E	2c	orange	70.00	20.00

"Good only for/Bank Check" in colorless letters in two lines above and below portrait

RN—E7	E	2c	orange	55.00	17.50

Franklin Type F

Size: 56x34mm

RN—F1	F	2c	orange	8.00	3.00
RN—F2	F	2c	yellow	10.00	5.00
		a.	Inverted		—

Liberty Type G

Size: 80x48mm

RN—G1	G	2c	orange	1.25	25
		a.	Printed on back	50.00	35.00
RN—G2	G	2c	yellow	10.00	10.00

Imprint: "Graphic Co., New York" at left and right in minute type

RN—G3	G	2c	orange	100.00	85.00

Eagle Type H

Size: 32x50mm

RN—H3	H	2c	orange	7.50	2.00
		a.	Inverted		—
		b.	Double impression		400.00
		c.	"Good when used . . ." added in 2 lines at base, black		400.00
		d.	As "c," legend added in 1 line upward at left, black		—
		e.	As "c," legend added in 1 line horiz., black		500.00
		f.	"Good for bank check . . ." added in black		125.00

"Good for check or sight draft only" at left and right in color of stamp

RN—H5	H	2c	orange	800.00	

Type I

Design R2 of 1862-72 adhesive revenues

Size: 20x23mm

"BANK CHECK"

RN—I1	R2	2c	orange		160.00

"U.S. INTER. REV."

RN—I2	R2	2c	orange	750.00	300.00

Washington Type J

Size: 105x40mm

Background of medallion crosshatched, filling oval except for bust

RN—J4	J	2c	orange	10.00	4.00
			pale orange	10.00	4.00
			deep orange	20.00	7.50
		a.	Double impression		—
		b.	"Good only for . . ." added vert. at left in red org.		575.00
RN—J5	J	2c	red	35.00	12.00

"Good for check or sight draft only" curved, below

RN—J9	J	2c	red		750.00

Background shaded below bust and at left.

RN—J11	J	2c	orange	50.00	15.00

See the "Information for Collectors" section at beginning of catalogue for illustrations of types of postmarks and precancels.

Washington Type K

Size: 84x33mm

RN—K4	K	2c	gray	35.00	10.00
			pale gray	35.00	10.00
RN—K5	K	2c	brown	165.00	110.00
RN—K6	K	2c	orange	15.00	7.50
RN—K8	K	2c	red		300.00
RN—K11	K	2c	olive	175.00	150.00
			pale olive		125.00

Washington Type L

Size: 50x33mm

RN—L1	L	2c	blue (shades)	200.00	150.00
RN—L3	L	2c	gray	25.00	10.00
			pale gray	25.00	10.00
RN—L4	L	2c	green	350.00	250.00
			light green	350.00	250.00
RN—L5	L	2c	orange	12.50	5.00
RN—L6	L	2c	olive		55.00
			gray olive		30.00
RN—L10	L	2c	red	15.00	5.00
		a.	2c violet red	15.00	5.00
RN—L13	L	2c	brown	—	150.00

Washington Type M

Size: 68x37mm

RN—M1	M	2c	yellow	40.00	10.00
RN—M2	M	2c	orange	32.00	10.00
		a.	Printed on back, inverted.		—
RN—M3	M	2c	green		250.00
RN—M4	M	2c	gray		600.00

Eagle, Numeral and Monitor Type N

Size: 107x48mm

RN—N3	N	2c	orange	55.00	12.00
		a.	Printed on back	165.00	110.00
		b.	Inverted		—
RN—N4	N	2c	light brown		150.00

Liberty Type O

Size: 75x35mm

RN—O2	O	2c	orange	1,000.	1,250.

Values for type P-W are for stamps on documents with attractive engravings, usually stock certificates, bonds and insurance policies. Examples on plain documents and cut squares sell for less.

Type P
Frame as Type B, Lincoln in center
Size: 32x49mm

				Unused (full document)	Used (full document)	Cut Square
RN—P2	P	5c	brown		300.00	50.00
RN—P4	P	5c	yellow		40.00	6.00
RN—P5	P	5c	orange	40.00	35.00	4.00
RN—P6	P	5c	red (shades)	—	175.00	30.00

The 5c green, type P, only exists in combination with a 25c green or 50c green. See Nos. RN-T2, RN-V1

Madison Type Q

Size: 28x56mm

				Unused	Used	Cut Square
RN—Q1	Q	5c	orange	140.00	100.00	15.00
			brownish orange	140.00	100.00	
RN—Q2	Q	5c	brown			450.00

Type R
Frame as Type B, Lincoln in center
Size: 32x49mm

				Unused	Used	Cut Square
RN—R2	R	10c	red	—	675.00	100.00
RN—R3	R	10c	orange		500.00	50.00

"Good when the premium does not exceed $10" in tablet at base

				Unused	Used	Cut Square
RN—R6	R	10c	orange	—	375.00	50.00

Motto Without Tablet

				Unused	Used	Cut Square
RN—R7	R	10c	orange			500.00

Washington Type S

"Good when the premium does not exceed $10" in tablet at base

Size: 33x54mm

				Unused (full doc.)	Used (full doc.)	Cut Square
RN—S1	S	10c	orange no motto or tablet		3,500.	
RN—S2	S	10c	orange		3,750.	300.00

Eagle Type T

Size: 33x40mm

				Unused	Used	Cut Square
RN—T1	T	25c	black	—		—
RN—T2	T	25c	green		750.00	
RN—T3	T	25c	red	150.00	75.00	7.50
RN—T4	T	25c	orange	125.00	60.00	6.00
			light orange	125.00	60.00	6.00
			brown orange		70.00	7.50

RN-T2 includes a 5c green, type P, and a 25c green, type T, obliterating an RN-V4.

"Good when the premium does not exceed $50" in tablet at base

				Unused	Used	Cut Square
RN—T6	T	25c	orange	450.00	350.00	50.00
RN—T7	T	25c	org., motto without tablet			400.00

"Good when the amount insured shall not exceed $1000" in tablet at base

				Unused	Used	Cut Square
RN—T8	T	25c	deep orange	600.00	550.00	75.00

Values quoted in this catalogue are for stamps graded at Fine-Very Fine and with no faults. An illustrated guide to grade is provided in introductory material, beginning on Page V.

Franklin Type U

Size: 126x65mm

				Unused	Used	Cut Square
RN—U1	U	25c	orange	35.00	25.00	4.00
RN—U2	U	25c	brown	45.00	30.00	5.00

"Good when the premium does not exceed $50" in tablet at lower right

				Unused (full document)	Used (full document)	Cut Square
RN—U3	U	25c	orange			400.00

Tablet at lower left

				Unused	Used	Cut Square
RN—U4	U	25c	yellow	550.00	500.00	75.00
RN—U5	U	25c	red	600.00		250.00
RN—U6	U	25c	orange	500.00	450.00	60.00

Tablet at base

				Unused	Used	Cut Square
RN—U7	U	25c	brown		550.00	175.00
RN—U9	U	25c	orange		600.00	200.00

Type V
As Type T, Lincoln in center
Size: 32x41mm

				Unused	Used	Cut Square
RN—V1	V	50c	green		135.00	40.00
RN—V2	V	50c	brown	—	400.00	50.00
RN—V4	V	50c	orange	125.00	75.00	10.00
			deep orange	125.00	75.00	10.00
RN—V5	V	50c	red	700.00		200.00

RN-V1 includes a 50c green, type V, and a 5c green, type P, obliterating an RN-W2.

"Good when the amount insured shall not exceed $5000" in tablet at base

				Unused	Used	Cut Square
RN—V6	V	50c	orange	450.00	350.00	60.00
RN—V9	V	50c	red		—	550.00

Motto Without Tablet

				Unused	Used	Cut Square
RN—V10	V	50c	orange			400.00

Washington Type W

Size: 34x73mm

				Unused (full document)	Used (full document)	Cut Square
RN—W2	W	$1	orange (shades)	125.00	65.00	10.00
RN—W4	W	$1	light brown	175.00	150.00	30.00

SPANISH-AMERICAN WAR SERIES

Many of these stamps were used for parlor car tax and often were torn in two or more parts.

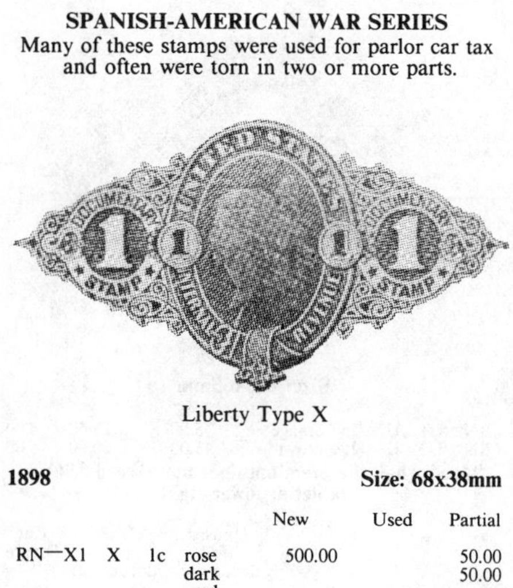

Liberty Type X

1898 **Size: 68x38mm**

				New	Used	Partial
RN—X1	X	1c	rose	500.00		50.00
			dark red			50.00
RN—X4	X	1c	orange	120.00		
		a.	On pullman ticket	350.00		20.00
		b.	As "a," printed on back			50.00
RN—X5	X	1c	green	50.00	30.00	
		a.	On parlor car ticket	50.00	15.00	
		b.	On pullman ticket	500.00		15.00
RN—X6	X	2c	yellow	5.00	2.00	
			pale olive		*1,000.*	
RN—X7	X	2c	orange	75	25	
			pale orange	75	25	
		a.	Printed on back only	125.00	100.00	
		c.	Printed on front and back	—	—	
		d.	Vertical		85.00	
		e.	Double impression		—	
		f.	On pullman ticket	500.00	200.00	
		g.	Inverted		—	

No. RN-X1 exists only as a four-part unused pullman ticket or as a used half of a two-part ticket. Nos. RN-X4a and RN-X5b exist as unused two-part tickets and as used half portions. No. RN-X7f exists as an unused four-part ticket and as a used two-piece portion with nearly complete stamp design.

CONSULAR FEE

Type of Consular Fee Stamps

1906 (?)

RN—Y1 CS1 $2 black —

PRIVATE DIE PROPRIETARY

The extraordinary demands of the Civil War upon the Federal Treasury resulted in Congress devising and passing the Revenue Act of 1862. The Government provided revenue stamps to be affixed to boxes or packages of matches, and to proprietary medicines, perfumery, playing cards -- as well as to documents, etc.

But manufacturers were permitted, at their expense, to have dies engraved and plates made for their exclusive use. Many were only too willing to do this because a discount or premium of from 5% to 10% was allowed on orders from the dies which often made it possible for them to undersell their competitors and too, the considerable advertising value of the stamps could not be overlooked. These are now known as Private Die Proprietary stamps.

The face value of the stamp used on matches was determined by the number, i.e., 1c for each 100 matches or fraction thereof. Medicines and perfumery were taxed at the rate of 1c for each 25 cents of the retail value or fraction thereof up to $1 and 2c for each 50 cents or fraction above that amount. Playing cards were first taxed at the same rate but subsequently the tax was 5c for a deck of 52 cards and 10c for a greater number of cards or double decks.

The stamp tax was repealed on March 3, 1883, effective July 1, 1883.

The various papers were:

a. **Old paper, 1862-71. First Issue. Hard and brittle varying from thick to thin.**
b. **Silk paper, 1871-77. Second Issue. Soft and porous with threads of silk, mostly red, blue and black, up to ¼inch in length.**
c. **Pink paper, 1877-78. Third Issue. Soft paper colored pink ranging from pale to deep shades.**
d. **Watermarked paper, 1878-83. Fourth Issue. Soft porous paper showing part of "USIR".**
e. **Experimental silk paper. Medium smooth paper, containing minute fragments of silk threads either blue alone or blue and red (infrequent), widely scattered, sometimes but a single fiber on a stamp.**

Early printings of some private die revenue stamps are on paper which appears to have laid lines.

These stamps were usually torn in opening the box or container. Values quoted are for specimens which are somewhat faulty but reasonably attractive, with the faults usually not readily apparent on the face. Sound specimens at a grade of fine-very fine can sell for 50% to 300% more. Examples of outstanding specimens of stamps in this section with a lower catalogue value can bring up to 10 times catalogue value.

PRIVATE DIE MATCH STAMPS

Arnold & Co. – RO14

Thos. Allen – RO5

Wm. Bond & Co. – RO32/RO33

1864 ***Perf. 12***

A

			a. Old Paper	b. Silk Paper	c. Pink Paper	d. Wmkd. USIR 191R
RO1	1c	blue, Akron Match Co.	120.00			
RO2	1c	orange, Alexander's Matches	8.00	60.00		
RO3	1c	blue, Alexander's Matches		1,250.		
RO4	1c	blue, Allen's, J. J., Sons				2.00
RO5	1c	green, Allen, Thos.	70.00			
RO6	1c	blue, Allen & Powers		3.50	15.00	3.00
RO7	1c	blue, Alligator Match Co.				15.00
RO8	1c	blue, Alligator Match Co. (Rouletted)				65.00
RO9	1c	black, American Fusee Co.		2.50	4.50	2.50
RO10	1c	black, American Match Co.	75.00	15.00		
RO11	3c	black, American Match Co.	325.00	90.00		
	e.	Experimental silk paper	425.00			
	f.	Double transfer		135.00		
RO12	1c	black, American Match Co. (Eagle)	40.00			
RO13	3c	green, American Match Co. (Rock Island)	1,500.			
RO14	1c	black, Arnold & Co.		25.00		

B

			a. Old Paper	b. Silk Paper	c. Pink Paper	d. Wmkd. USIR 191R
RO15	1c	green, Bagley & Dunham				15.00
RO16	1c	blue, Barber, Geo. & O. C.	50.00			
RO17	1c	blue, Barber Match Co.	15.00	50	9.00	50
	u.	1c ultra	150.00			
	e.	Experimental silk paper	45.00			
		Double transfer		—		—
RO18	1c	blue, Barber Match Co. (Rouletted)				1,000.
RO19	3c	black, Barber Match Co.	125.00	75.00		
	e.	Experimental silk paper	*200.00*			
RO20	1c	blue, Barber & Peckham	30.00			
RO21	3c	black, Barber & Peckham	150.00			
RO22	1c	blue, Bauer & Beudel	55.00	90.00		
	u.	1c ultra	80.00			

			a. Old Paper	b. Silk Paper	c. Pink Paper	d. Wmkd. USIR 191R
RO23	1c	orange, A. B. & S. (A. Beecher & Son)	5.00	40.00		
	e.	Experimental silk paper	40.00			
RO24	1c	brown, Bendel, B. & Co.		2.25		275.00
RO25	12c	brown, Bendel, B. & Co.		110.00		
RO26	1c	brown, Bendel, H.		4.00	1.50	50
RO27	12c	brown, Bendel, H.		350.00		

Nos. RO26-RO27 are RO24-RO25 altered to read "H. Bendel doing business as B. Bendel & Co."

			a. Old Paper	b. Silk Paper	c. Pink Paper	d. Wmkd. USIR 191R
RO28	1c	blue, Bentz, H. & M.	20.00			
RO29	1c	black, Bent & Lea	25.00			
	e.	Experimental silk paper	15.00			
		Double transfer at left	—			
RO30	1c	green, B. J. & Co. (Barber, Jones & Co.)		50.00		
RO31	1c	black, Bock, Schneider & Co.		6.00		
RO32	4c	black, Bond, Wm. & Co.		175.00		
RO33	4c	green, Bond, Wm. & Co.		90.00	100.00	10.00

Charles Busch — RO47

W.D. Curtis — RO68

Eichele & Co. — RO78

Excelsior Match — RO83

Gardner, Beer & Co. — RO86

Charles S. Hale — RO106

			a. Old Paper	b. Silk Paper	c. Pink Paper	d. Wmkd. USIR 191R
RO34	1c	lilac, Bousfield & Poole	80.00			
RO35	1c	black, Bousfield & Poole	10.00	3.00		
	e.	Experimental silk paper	30.00			
		Double transfer	—			
RO36	3c	lilac, Bousfield & Poole	1,500.			
RO37	3c	black, Bousfield & Poole	120.00	80.00		
	e.	Experimental silk paper	200.00			

			a. Old Paper	b. Silk Paper	c. Pink Paper	d. Wmkd. USIR 191R
RO38	1c	black, Boutell & Maynard		80.00		
RO39	1c	green, Bowers & Dunham				150.00
RO40	1c	blue, Bowers & Dunham				50.00
RO41	1c	lake, B. & N. (Brocket & Newton) die I		25.00		
RO42	1c	lake, B. & N. (Brocket & Newton) die II		4.50		

The initials "B. & N." measure 5¼mm across the top in Die I, and 4¾mm in Die II.

			a. Old Paper	b. Silk Paper	c. Pink Paper	d. Wmkd. USIR 191R
RO43	1c	black, Brown & Durling	800.00			
RO44	1c	green, Brown & Durling	50.00			
RO45	1c	black, Buck, L. W. & Co.	600.00			
	e.	Experimental silk paper	400.00			
RO46	1c	black, Burhans, D. & Co.	100.00	1,000.		
	e.	Experimental silk paper	350.00			
RO47	1c	black, Busch, Charles				15.00
RO48	1c	black, Byam, Carlton & Co., (41x75mm) (Two heads to left) (Imperf.)	1,300.			
RO49	1c	black, Byam, Carlton & Co., (19x23mm)	20.00	3.00		40
	e.	Experimental silk paper	40.00			
	i.	Imperf. horizontally (pair)				150.00
		Double transfer				—
RO50	1c	black, Byam, Carlton & Co., 2 heads to left, buff wrapper, 131x99mm	1,200.			
RO51	1c	black, Byam, Carlton & Co., 2 heads to left, buff wrapper, 131x89mm	150.00			
RO52	1c	black, Byam, Carlton & Co., 1 head to right, white wrapper, 94x54mm	55.00			
RO53	1c	black, Byam, Carlton & Co., 1 head to right, buff wrapper, 94x54mm	125.00			
RO54	1c	black, Byam, Carlton & Co., 2 heads to right, buff wrapper, 81x50mm	5.00			
		h. Right block reading up	20.00			
RO55	1c	black, Byam, Carlton & Co., 1 head to left, white wrapper, 94x56mm	17.50			
RO56	1c	black, Byam, Carlton & Co., 2 heads to left, buff wrapper, 95x57mm	2.25			

C

			a. Old Paper	b. Silk Paper	c. Pink Paper	d. Wmkd. USIR 191R
RO57	1c	green, Cannon Match Co.			15.00	
RO58	1c	lake, Cardinal Match Co.				6.00
RO59	1c	lake, C., F.E. (Frank E. Clark)	50.00	50.00		
	e.	Experimental silk paper	50.00			
RO60	3c	black, Chicago Match Co.	150.00			
RO61	1c	green, Clark, Henry A.		50.00		
RO62	1c	green, Clark, James L.		60	15.00	60
		Double transfer				—
RO63	1c	green, Clark, James L. (Rouletted)				275.00
RO64	1c	lake, Clark Match Co.		5.00		
RO65	1c	black, Cramer & Kemp	22.50			
RO66	1c	blue, Cramer & Kemp	55.00	3.00		
	e.	Experimental silk paper	125.00			
	u.	1c ultra	150.00			
RO67	1c	black, Crown Match Co		15.00		
RO68	1c	green, Curtis, W.D.	100.00	75.00		
	e.	Experimental silk paper	110.00			

D

			a. Old Paper	b. Silk Paper	c. Pink Paper	d. Wmkd. USIR 191R
RO69	1c	black, Davis, G.W.H.		35.00		
RO70	1c	carmine, Davis, G.W.H.				30.00
RO71	1c	blue, Doolittle, W.E.	225.00			
RO72	1c	green, Dunham, E.P.				50.00

E

			a. Old Paper	b. Silk Paper	c. Pink Paper	d. Wmkd. USIR 191R
RO73	1c	black, Eaton, James	25.00	85	7.00	85
	e.	Experimental silk paper	75.00			
RO74	1c	black, Eaton, James (Rouletted)				35.00
RO75	1c	carmine, Eddy, E.B., die I				9.00
RO75A	1c	carmine, Eddy, E.B., die II				25.00

Die II shows eagle strongly recut; ribbon across bottom is narrower; color is deeper.

			a. Old Paper	b. Silk Paper	c. Pink Paper	d. Wmkd. USIR 191R
RO76	1c	black, Eichele, Aug.	45.00			
RO77	1c	blue, Eichele, P., & Co.	45.00	4.50		
	u.	1c ultra	210.00			
	e.	Experimental silk paper	70.00			
RO78	1c	blue, Eichele & Co.		2.00	10.00	1.50
RO79	1c	blue, Eichele & Co. (Rouletted)				125.00
RO80	1c	blue, Eisenhart, J.W.		27.50	60.00	17.50
RO81	1c	black, Excelsior M. Co., Watertown		65.00		
RO82	1c	black, Excelsior M. Co., Syracuse		4.00	8.50	4.00
RO83	1c	blue, Excelsior Match, Baltimore	35.00	70.00		
	u.	1c ultra	200.00			

F

			a. Old Paper	b. Silk Paper	c. Pink Paper	d. Wmkd. USIR 191R
RO84	1c	black, Farr, G., & Co.	50.00			
RO85	1c	brown, Frank, L.		40.00		

G

			a. Old Paper	b. Silk Paper	c. Pink Paper	d. Wmkd. USIR 191R
RO86	1c	black, Gardner, Beer & Co.			90.00	
RO87	1c	black, Gates, Wm. die I	4.00	2.50		
RO88	1c	black, Gates, Wm. die 2	25.00	2.50		
		Double transfer		—		
	e.	Experimental silk paper	55.00			

The shirt collar is colorless in Die 1, and shaded in Die 2. Other differences exist.

			a. Old Paper	b. Silk Paper	c. Pink Paper	d. Wmkd. USIR 191R
RO89	3c	black, Gates, Wm.	45.00	35.00		
	e.	Experimental silk paper	125.00			
		Double transfer		75.00		

No.			a. Old Paper	b. Silk Paper	c. Pink Paper	d. Wmkd. USIR 191R
RO90	6c	black, Gates, Wm.	75.00			
RO91	3c	black, Gates, Wm. (three 1c stamps)		80.00		
RO92	1c	black, Gates, Wm., Sons		15.00	4.00	50
RO93	1c	black, Gates, Wm., Sons (Rouletted)				850.00
RO94	3c	black, Gates, Wm., Sons (three 1c stamps)		75.00	110.00	60.00
RO95	1c	green, Goldback, A. & Co.		25.00		
RO96	1c	green, Goldback, A.		50.00	*2,000.*	
RO97	1c	black, Gorman, T. & Bro.	200.00			
		Double transfer	—			
RO98	1c	green, Gorman, T. & Bro.	20.00	15.00		
		Double transfer	—			
RO99	1c	green, Gorman, Thomas		2.75	15.00	35.00
RO100	1c	green, Greenleaf & Co.	50.00	50.00		
RO101	3c	carmine, Greenleaf & Co.	75.00	110.00		
RO102	5c	orange, Greenleaf & Co.	110.00	900.00		
RO103	1c	black, Griggs & Goodwill		20.00		
RO104	1c	green, Griggs & Goodwill		8.50		
		Double transfer		—		
RO105	1c	black, Griggs & Scott	5.00	25.00		
	e.	Experimental silk paper	35.00			

H

No.			a.	b.	c.	d.
RO106	1c	green, Hale, Charles S.			100.00	
RO107	1c	blue, Henning & Bonhack	85.00			
RO108	1c	red, Henry, W.E. & Co.				20.00
RO109	1c	black, Henry, W.E. & Co.				6.00
RO110	1c	green, Hotchkiss, J.G.		4.00	30.00	6.00
RO111	1c	lake, Howard, B. & H.D.	65.00			
RO112	1c	blue, Howard, B. & H.D.	6.00			
	u.	1c ultra	125.00			
RO113	1c	black, Hunt, L.G.	125.00	600.00		
	e.	Experimental silk paper	100.00			
RO114	1c	lake, Hutchinson, D.F., Jr.				8.00

I

No.			a.	b.	c.	d.
RO115	1c	blue, Ives Matches	3.50	3.50		
	u.	1c ultra	90.00			
		Double transfer	—			
RO116	1c	blue, Ives, P.T.		2.50	15.00	2.50
RO117	1c	blue, Ives, P.T. (Rouletted)				200.00
RO118	8c	blue, Ives, P.T.	80.00			
	u.	8c ultra	500.00			
RO119	1c	green, Ives & Judd		8.00	30.00	65.00
RO120	1c	green, Ives & Judd Match Co.				65.00
		Double transfer				200.00

K

No.			a.	b.	c.	d.
RO121	1c	green, Kirby & Sons		30.00		
RO122	1c	black, Kyle, W.S.	10.00	6.00		
		Double transfer	—			

L

No.			a. Old Paper	b. Silk Paper	c. Pink Paper	d. Wmkd. USIR 191R
RO123	1c	black, Lacour's Matches	10.00	35.00		
	e.	Experimental silk paper	50.00			
RO124	1c	green, Leeds, Robinson & Co.				45.00
RO125	1c	blue, Leigh, H.				4.50
RO126	1c	black, Leigh & Palmer		20.00	45.00	30.00
RO127	1c	blue, Loehr, John		15.00		
RO128	1c	blue, Loehr, Joseph		1.50	8.00	1.75

M

No.			a.	b.	c.	d.
RO129	1c	black, Macklin, J.J. & Co. (Rouletted)	3,500.			
RO130	1c	blue, Mansfield, F. & Co.		2.50	5.00	6.50
RO131	1c	blue, Maryland M. Co.		70.00		2,500.
RO132	1c	blue, Matches, (head Franklin)	2.25	2.00		
	u.	1c ultra	*150.00*			
		Double transfer	90.00			
	e.	Experimental silk paper	50.00			
RO133	1c	black, Messinger, A.		1.00	8.00	1.00

N

No.			a.	b.	c.	d.
RO134	1c	blue, National M. Co.				50.00
RO135	1c	lake, Newton, F.P.		1.00	4.50	1.00
RO136	1c	blue, N.Y. Match Co. (Shield)	150.00	4.00		
RO137	1c	vermilion, N.Y. Match Co. (Eagle)	45.00	*3,000.*		
	e.	Experimental silk paper	110.00			
RO138	1c	green, N.Y. Match Co., 22x60mm	25.00	4.00		
	e.	Experimental silk paper	35.00			
RO139	5c	blue, N.Y. Match Co., Size 22x60mm		1,100.		
RO140	4c	green, N. & C. (Newbauer & Co.)		2.50	85.00	2.50

National Union Match Co. items are bogus.

O

No.			a.	b.	c.	d.
RO141	1c	blue, Orono Match Co.	20.00	20.00		
	u.	1c ultra	225.00			

P

No.			a.	b.	c.	d.
RO142	1c	green, Park City Match Co.	30.00	30.00		
	e.	Experimental silk paper	90.00			
RO143	3c	orange, Park City Match Co.	30.00			
RO144	1c	blue, Penn Match Co.				25.00
RO145	1c	green, Pierce Match Co.	1,000.			
RO146	1c	black, P.M. Co. (Portland M. Co.)	20.00			
RO147	1c	black, Portland M. Co. (wrapper)	55.00			

Value of No. RO147 applies to commonest date (Dec. 1866); all others are much rarer.

No.			a.	b.	c.	d.
RO148	1c	blue, Powell, V.R.	2.50	6.00		
	u.	1c ultra	175.00			
	e.	Experimental silk paper	40.00			
		Double transfer	—			

Ives & Judd Match Co. – RO120

Leeds, Robinson & Co. – RO124

"Matches" RO132

V.R. Powell RO148

Standard Match Co. – RO170

Washington Match Co. – RO181

No.			a.	b.	c.	d.
RO149	1c	black, Powell, V.R. (buff wrapper) uncut	*2,000.*			
RO150	1c	black, Powell, V. R. (buff wrapper) cut to shape	650.00			
RO151	1c	black, Powell, V. R. (white wrapper) cut to shape	1,150.			

R

No.			a.	b.	c.	d.
RO152	1c	black, Reading M. Co.				5.00
RO153	1c	black, Reed & Thompson				4.50
RO154	1c	red, Richardson, D. M.	80.00			
RO155	1c	black, Richardson, D. M.	2.50	1.50		
	e.	Experimental silk paper	25.00			
		Double transfer		30.00		
RO156	3c	vermilion, Richardson, D.M.	90.00			
RO157	3c	blue, Richardson, D. M.	3.50	2.00		
	e.	Experimental silk paper	35.00			
RO158	1c	black, Richardson Match Co.		75	3.50	75
RO159	3c	blue, Richardson Match Co.		55.00		
RO160	1c	blue, Roeber, H. & W.	6.00	1.50		
	u.	1c ultra	90.00			
		Double transfer	175.00			
RO161	1c	blue, Roeber, Wm.		1.25	4.00	1.25
RO162	1c	blue, Roeber, Wm. (Rouletted)				80.00
RO163	1c	black, Russell, E. T.	3.00	9.00		
	e.	Experimental silk paper	30.00			
RO164	1c	lake, R. C. & W. (Ryder, Crouse & Welch)				40.00

S

San Francisco Match Co. — RO165

RO165	12c	blue, San Francisco Match Co.		350.00		
RO166	1c	vermilion, Schmitt & Schmittdiel		2.00	40.00	2.00
RO167	3c	blue, Schmitt & Schmittdiel		30.00		
RO168	1c	blue, Smith, E. K.		8.00	30.00	12.00
RO169	1c	blue, Smith, E. K. (Rouletted)				1,250.
RO170	1c	black, Standard Match Co.				22.50
RO171	1c	black, Stanton, H.	8.00	3.50	12.50	5.00
e.		Experimental silk paper	40.00			
RO172	1c	black, Star Match	3.00	10	25	10
e.		Experimental silk paper	15.00			
		Double transfer		—		17.50
RO173	1c	blue, Swift & Courtney	1.25	1.25		
u.		1c ultra	35.00			
e.		Experimental silk paper	10.00			
		Double transfer		—		
RO174	1c	blue, Swift & Courtney & Beecher Co.		40	1.50	40
		Double transfer				—
RO175	1c	black, S. C. B. C. (Flag)				60.00

T

RO176	1c	blue, Trenton M. Co.				4.00
RO177	1c	green, T., E. R. (E. R. Tyler)	8.00	2.75		
e.		Experimental silk paper	30.00			
		Double transfer		—		

U

RO178	1c	green, Underwood, Alex. & Co.	45.00	110.00		
e.		Experimental silk paper	125.00			
RO179	1c	black, Union Match Co.				40.00
RO180	1c	black, U. S. M. Co. (Universal Safety M. Co.)	1.50	17.50		
e.		Experimental silk paper	25.00			

W

RO181	1c	black, Washington Match Co.		30.00		
RO182	1c	black, Wilmington Parlor Match Co.	60.00	2,500.		
e.		Experimental silk paper	55.00			
RO183	1c	black, Wise & Co.	800.00			

Z

RO184	1c	black, Zaiss, F. & Co.		75	2.00	1.00
RO185	1c	green, Zisemann, Griesheim & Co.	550.00			
RO186	1c	blue, Zisemann, Griesheim & Co.	90.00	15.00		
u.		1c ultra	175.00			

PRIVATE DIE CANNED FRUIT STAMP

T. Kensett & Co. — RP1

1867 ***Perf. 12***

RP1	1c	green, Kensett, T. & Co.	650.00

PRIVATE DIE MEDICINE STAMPS

Anglo-American Drug Co. — RS1

1862 ***Perf. 12***

			a. Old Paper	b. Silk Paper	c. Pink Paper	d. Wmkd. USIR 191R
A						
RS1	1c	black, Anglo—American Drug Co.				45.00
RS2	1c	brown carmine, Ayer J. C. & Co. (imperf.)	*2,000.*			
RS3	1c	green, Ayer, J. C. & Co. (imperf.)	*2,000.*			
RS4	1c	black, Ayer, J. C. & Co. (imperf.)	45.00	45.00	725.00	35.00
r.		Die II)	250.00			
		Double transfer		—		
RS5	1c	blue, Ayer, J. C. & Co. (imperf.)	*2,000.*			
RS6	1c	orange Ayer, J. C. & Co. (imperf.)	*2,000.*			
RS7	1c	gray lilac, Ayer, J.C. & Co. (imperf.)	2,000.			
RS8	4c	red, Ayer, J.C. & Co. (die cut)	2,000.			
RS9	4c	blue, Ayer, J.C. & Co. (die cut)	3.00	3.00		3.00
u.		4c ultra (die cut)	250.00			
RS10	4c	blue, Ayer, J.C. & Co. (imperf.)	350.00	325.00		375.00
RS11	4c	purple, Ayer, J.C. & Co. (die cut)	*2,500.*			
RS12	4c	green, Ayer, J.C. & Co. (die cut)	*1,750.*			
RS13	4c	vermilion, Ayer, J.C. & Co. (die cut)	*2,000.*			

The 4c in black was printed and sent to Ayer & Co. It may exist but has not been seen by collectors.

			a. Old Paper	b. Silk Paper	c. Pink Paper	d. Wmkd. USIR 191R
B						
RS14	4c	green, Barham, P.C. Co., wmkd. lozenges				60.00
RS15	1c	vermilion, Barnes, D.S.	100.00			
RS16	2c	vermilion, Barnes, D.S.	60.00			
RS17	4c	vermilion, Barnes, D.S.	250.00			
RS18	1c	black, Barnes, D.S.	17.50			
RS19	2c	black, Barnes, D.S.	50.00			
RS20	4c	black, Barnes, D.S.	50.00			
RS21	1c	black, Barnes, Demas	15.00			
RS22	2c	black, Barnes, Demas	40.00			
RS23	4c	black, Barnes, Demas	15.00			
RS24	1c	black, Barnes & Co., Demas	9.00	300.00		
RS25	2c	black, Barnes, Demas & Co.	5.00	250.00		
e.		Experimental silk paper	40.00			
RS26	4c	black, Barnes, Demas & Co.	5.00			
RS27	4c	black, Barr, T.H. & Co.	7.50			
		Double transfer	85.00			
RS28	2c	green, Barry's Tricopherous	9.00	10.00		
RS29	2c	green, Barry's Proprietary		2.25	95.00	3.00
		Double transfer		—		
RS30	1c	lake, Bennett, D.M.	5.00			
e.		Experimental silk paper	45.00			
RS31	1c	green, Blow, W.T.	200.00	55.00	275.00	50.00
e.		Experimental silk paper	300.00			
RS32	1c	black, Brandreth, (perf.)	250.00	300.00		
RS33	1c	black, Brandreth, (imperf.)	2.00	1.50		
e.		Experimental silk paper	12.50			
RS34	1c	black, Brandreth, Allcock's (41x50mm, imperf.)		100.00		
RS35	1c	black, Brandreth, Allcock's (24x30mm, imperf.)		85	3.00	85
p.		Perf.				—
RS36	1c	blue, Brown, C.F.	150.00	45.00		60.00
RS37	2c	black, Brown, Fred Co. (imperf.) die I, "E" of "Fred" incomplete	85.00	35.00	800.00	35.00
e.		Experimental silk paper	150.00			
RS38	2c	black, Brown, Fred Co. (imperf.) die II, "E" of "Fred" normal		40.00		

Die II shows recutting in the "E" of "Fred" and "Genuine".

			a. Old Paper	b. Silk Paper	c. Pink Paper	d. Wmkd. USIR 191R
RS39	1c	black, Brown, John I. & Son	6.00	20.00		4.00
RS40	2c	green, Brown, John I. & Son	7.00	7.00	150.00	175.00
e.		Experimental silk paper	40.00			
		Double transfer	—			
RS41	4c	brown, Brown, John I. & Son	150.00	70.00		800.00
RS42	1c	black, Bull, John	100.00	10.00	275.00	8.50
e.		Experimental silk paper	150.00			
RS43	4c	blue, Bull, John	150.00	8.00	175.00	6.00
u.		4c ultra	350.00			
e.		Experimental silk paper	200.00			
RS44	1c	black, Burdsal, J.S. & Co., wrapper white paper		40.00		25.00

			a. Old Paper	b. Silk Paper	c. Pink Paper	d. Wmkd. USIR 191R
RS45	1c	black, Burdsal, J.S. & Co., wrapper orange paper		*650.00*		300.00
RS46	4c	black, Burnett, Joseph & Co.	65.00	5.00	165.00	5.00

C

			a.	b.	c.	d.
RS47	4c	black, Campion, J.W. & Co. (imperf.)		300.00		250.00
	p.	Pair, perf. horiz.				1,000.
RS48	4c	black, Campion, J.W. & Co. (die cut)		120.00	175.00	70.00
RS49	4c	green, Cannon & Co. (imperf.)		75.00	165.00	55.00
RS50	1c	vermilion, Centaur Co.			40.00	5.00
RS51	2c	black, Centaur Co.			10.00	1.00
RS52	4c	black, Centaur Co.				40.00
RS53	1c	black, Chase, A.W., Son & Co.		60.00		1,500.
RS54	2c	black, Chase, A.W., Son & Co.		65.00		
RS55	4c	black, Chase, A.W., Son & Co.		95.00		
RS56	3c	blue, Clarke, Wm. E.				70.00
RS57	6c	black, Clarke, Wm. E.				60.00
RS58	4c	black, Clark, R.C. & C.S. (A.B.C.)		9.00		15.00
RS59	1c	black, Collins Bros.	12.00	150.00		
RS60	1c	black, Comstock, W.H.				2.00
RS61	4c	blue, Cook & Bernheimer				75.00
RS62	1c	black, Crittenton, Chas. N.		4.00		
RS63	1c	blue, Crittenton, Chas. N.			10.00	3.50
RS64	2c	black, Crittenton, Chas. N.		50.00	25.00	3.00
RS65	4c	black, Crook, Oliver & Co.	55.00	10.00		
	e.	Experimental silk paper	10.00			
RS66	1c	black, Curtis, Jeremiah, & Son, die I, small numerals	55.00			
RS67	1c	black, Curtis, Jeremiah, & Son, die II, large numerals				80.00
RS68	2c	black, Curtis, Jeremiah, & Son	8.00	8.00	80.00	150.00
		Double transfer		—		
RS69	1c	black, Curtis & Brown	3.50	2.50		
RS70	2c	black, Curtis & Brown		75.00		
RS71	1c	black, Curtis & Brown Mfg. Co.			100.00	2.50
RS72	2c	black, Curtis & Brown Mfg. Co.		1,000.		450.00

D

			a.	b.	c.	d.
RS73	2c	green, Dalley's Horse Salve	60.00	60.00		60.00
RS74	1c	black, Dalley's Pain Ext.	5.00	5.00		6.00
	h.	Error, $100 instead of $1.00	250.00			7.50
RS75	1c	blue, Davis, Perry & Son	5.00	2.00	175.00	2.00
	u.	1c ultra	80.00			
	e.	Experimental silk paper	50.00			
RS76	2c	brown red, Davis, Perry & Son	110.00			

Barry's Tricopherous RS28

Dr. C.F. Brown RS36

Wm. E. Clarke — RS56

Herrick's Pills & Plasters — RS118

Holman Liver Pad Co. — RS126

			a.	b.	c.	d.
RS77	2c	black, Davis, Perry & Son	50.00			
RS78	2c	dull purple, Davis, Perry & Son		4.50		
RS78A	2c	slate, Davis, Perry & Son		8.00		2.50
RS79	2c	dull red, Davis, Perry & Son		50.00		
RS80	2c	brown, Davis, Perry & Son		—		
RS81	4c	brown, Davis, Perry & Son	7.00	2.00		1.50
RS82	2c	black, Drake, P. H. & Co.	850.00			
RS83	4c	black, Drake, P. H. & Co.	25.00	45.00		
	e.	Experimental silk paper	85.00			

F

			a.	b.	c.	d.
RS84	1c	lake, Fahnestock, B. A. (imperf.)	100.00	85.00		
RS85	4c	black, Father Mathew T. M. Co.				3.50
RS86	1c	green, Flanders, A. H. (perf.)		10.00		9.00
RS87	1c	green, Flanders, A. H. (part perf.)	20.00	1.25	25.00	1.25
RS88	1c	black, Fleming Bros. (Vermifuge) (imperf.)	8.50	15.00		30.00
	e.	Experimental silk paper	50.00			
RS89	1c	black, Fleming Bros. (L. Pills) (imperf.)	1,500.			
RS90	1c	blue, Fleming Bros. (L. Pills) (imperf.)	2.50	2.50		2.00
	u.	1c ultra	150.00			
		Double transfer		45.00		45.00
RS91	4c	black, Fowle, Seth W. & Son.	10.00	2.00		3.00
	i.	Vertical pair, imperf. between				—

G

			a.	b.	c.	d.
RS92	3c	black, Green, G. G.				2.25
	h.	Tete beche pair				250.00
RS93	3c	black, Green, G. G. (rouletted)				100.00

H

			a.	b.	c.	d.
RS94	4c	black, Hall & Co. Reuben P.	15.00	14.00		16.00
RS95	1c	green, Hall & Ruckel	60	60	17.50	75
	e.	Experimental silk paper	10.00			
RS96	3c	black, Hall & Ruckel	1.25	1.25	45.00	1.50
RS97	1c	black, Harter, Dr. & Co.	15.00	10.00		
	e.	Experimental silk paper	60.00			
RS98	1c	black, Harter, Dr.		85	8.00	85
		Double impression		—		
RS99	4c	black, Hartman, S. B. & Co.	175.00	40.00	175.00	800.00
RS100	6c	black, Hartman, S. B. & Co.	200.00	150.00		
RS101	1c	black, Hazeltine, E. T.				10.00
RS102	2c	blue, Hazeltine, E. T.		22.50		
RS103	4c	black, Hazeltine, E. T.	250.00	15.00		12.00
	e.	Experimental silk paper	275.00			
	i.	Imperf., pair	800.00			
RS104	3c	black, H., E (Edward Heaton)				30.00
RS105	3c	brown, H., E. (Edward Heaton)				9.00
RS106	2c	blue, Helmbold	65	175.00		
		Double transfer	—			
RS107	3c	green, Helmbold	30.00	25.00		
RS108	4c	black, Helmbold	3.00	100.00		
		Double transfer	—			
RS109	6c	black, Helmbold	2.00	2.50		
	e.	Experimental silk	20.00			
RS110	2c	blue, Helmbold, A. L.		85.00	100.00	85.00
RS111	4c	black, Helmbold, A.L.		20.00	100.00	6.00
RS112	2c	violet, Henry, John F.	150.00			
RS113	4c	bistre, Henry, John F.	400.00			
RS114	1c	black, Henry, John F.	40.00	40	3.50	40
	e.	Experimental silk paper	75.00			
RS115	2c	blue, Henry, John F.	27.50	4.00	90.00	4.00
	u.	2c ultra	—			
RS116	4c	red, Henry, John F.	125.00	60	10.00	60
	e.	Experimental silk paper	35.00			
RS117	1c	black, Herrick's Pills	60.00	25.00	60.00	25.00
	e.	Experimental silk paper	110.00			
RS118	1c	red, Herrick's Pills & Plasters	1.00	2.50	50.00	1.25
	e.	Experimental silk paper		—		
RS119	1c	black, Hetherington, J. E.				10.00
RS120	2c	black, Hetherington, J. E.				250.00
RS121	3c	black, Hetherington, J. E.				15.00
	i.	Imperf.				200.00
RS122	2c	black, Hiscox & Co.				10.00
RS123	4c	black, Hiscox & Co.		75.00	150.00	950.00
RS124	1c	blue, Holloway's Pills, (perf.)	6.50			
RS125	1c	blue, Holloway's Pills, (imperf.)	200.00			
RS126	1c	green, Holman Liver Pad Co.				15.00
RS127	4c	green, Holman Liver Pad Co.				6.00
RS128	2c	blue, Home Bitters Co.				125.00
		Double transfer				—
RS129	3c	green, Home Bitters Co.		80.00	100.00	65.00
RS130	4c	green, Home Bitters Co.		150.00		175.00
RS131	4c	black, Hop Bitters Co.				5.00

No.	Denom.	Description				
RS132	4c	black, Hostetter & Smith (imperf.)	50.00	30.00	65.00	20.00
		Double transfer	—	—	—	—
RS133	6c	black, Hostetter & Smith (imperf.)	70.00			
	e.	Experimental silk paper	175.00			
RS134	4c	black, Howe, S. D. (Duponco's Pills)	75.00	150.00		

No. RS134 in red or green were never used.

No.	Denom.	Description				
RS137	4c	blue, Howe, S. D. (Arabian Milk)		4.00		110.00
RS138	1c	black, Hull, C. E. & Co.	90.00	3.00	25.00	4.00
RS139	2c	violet, Husband, T. J. (imperf.)	425.00			
RS140	2c	vermilion, Husband, T. J. (imperf.)	7.50	4.00		5.00
RS141	4c	green, Hutchings & Hillyer (imperf.)	15.00	17.50		
	e.	Experimental silk paper	80.00			

I

No.	Denom.	Description				
RS142	1c	black, Ingham, H. A. & Co.				45.00

J

No.	Denom.	Description				
RS143	4c	green, Jackson, J. A. & Co.	500.00	150.00		
RS144	1c	blue, Jayne, D. & Son (imperf.)		900.00		325.00
	p.	Perf.	800.00			—
RS145	2c	black, Jayne, D. & Son (imperf.)	*1,750.*	1,200.		750.00
	p.	Perf.	*2,250.*			—
RS146	4c	green, Jayne, D. & Son (imperf.)	*1,750.*	900.00	850.00	300.00
	p.	Perf.	*2,250.*			—
RS147	1c	blue, Jayne, D. & Son (die cut)	2.00	4.00	150.00	3.00
	p.	Perf. and die cut	55.00			
		On horizontally laid paper	—			
RS148	2c	black, Jayne, D. & Son (die cut)	3.50	4.00	65.00	4.50
	e.	Experimental silk paper	35.00			
	p.	Perf. and die cut	20.00			
		Double transfer	55.00	55.00	100.00	55.00
RS149	4c	green, Jayne, D. & Son (die cut)	3.00	3.00	65.00	3.00
	e.	Experimental silk paper	50.00			
	p.	Perf. and die cut	35.00			
		On vertically laid paper	—			
		Double transfer		—		
RS150	1c	vermilion, Johnson, I. S. & Co.		40	8.50	40
		Double transfer		17.50		17.50
RS151	1c	black, Johnston, Holloway & Co.		2.00		2.50
RS152	2c	green, Johnston, Holloway & Co.		1.25		1.25

K

No.	Denom.	Description				
RS153	4c	black, Kelly, J.B. & Co. (imperf.)	1,500.			
	e.	Experimental silk paper	1,250.			
RS154	4c	blue, Kendall, B. J. & Co.				20.00
RS155	2c	green, Kennedy, Dr.	35.00	2.50	22.50	2.50
		Double transfer				
RS156	6c	black, Kennedy, Dr.		4.00	50.00	4.00
RS157	2c	black, Kennedy & Co.		2.50	67.50	2.50
RS158	1c	green, Kennedy, (K & Co.)				3.50
RS159	4c	blue, Kerr, Jas. C.	*3,000.*	135.00		100.00
RS160	6c	black, Kerr, Jas. C.	300.00			

L

No.	Denom.	Description				
RS161	4c	black, Lawrence & Martin				20.00
RS162	1c	blue, Lee & Osgood	6.00	7.50		8.00
RS163	4c	blue, Lippman, J. & Bro.	1,000.	1,250.		
	e.	Experimental silk paper	1,250.			
RS164	1c	black, Littlefield, Alvah	75	75		15.00
	e.	Experimental silk paper	20.00			
		Double transfer	35.00			
RS165	4c	green, Littlefield, Alvah	500.00	120.00		
RS166	1c	black, Low, Prof.		1.50	10.00	1.50
		Double transfer		—	50.00	40.00
RS167	1c	black, Lyon Mfg. Co.		10.00	150.00	12.00
RS168	2c	black, Lyon Mfg. Co.		4.50	100.00	4.50
	i.	Vertical pair, imperf. between				500.00

M

No.	Denom.	Description				
RS169	4c	black, McCullough, J.		75.00		75.00
RS170	1c	black, McLean, J.H.	2.00	75	10.00	75
	e.	Experimental silk paper	40.00			
	i.	Imperf. horizontally		—		
		Double transfer		—	—	35.00
RS171	1c	violet, Manhattan Med. Co.				20.00
	u.	1c purple				30.00
RS172	2c	black, Manhattan Med. Co.		20.00	27.50	10.00
RS173	1c	blue, Mansfield & Higbee		12.00		
	i.	Pair, imperf. between		100.00		
	j.	Block of four, imperf. between		120.00		
RS174	1c	blue, Mansfield, S. & Co.		22.50	125.00	10.00
	i.	Pair, imperf. between		90.00	250.00	150.00
	j.	Block of four, imperf. between		110.00	300.00	150.00

Nos. RS173-RS174 are perf. on 4 sides. The i. and j. varieties served as 2c or 4c stamps. Straightedged copies from severed pairs or blocks are worth much less.

No.	Denom.	Description				
RS175	2c	blue, Marsden, T.W.	2,500.			
RS176	4c	black, Marsden, T.W.	225.00			
RS177	2c	black, Mercado & Seully (imperf.)	2,000.			
RS178	1c	black, Merchant's Gargling Oil	175.00	15.00	250.00	17.50
	e.	Experimental silk paper	*275.00*			
RS179	2c	green, Merchant's Gargling Oil	135.00	17.50	250.00	20.00
	e.	Experimental silk paper	250.00			
		Double transfer, over design of RO11		—		2,000.
RS180	3c	black, Mette & Kanne				175.00
RS181	4c	black, Mishler Herb Bitters Co.				80.00
	p.	Imperf. at ends				80.00
RS182	4c	black, Moody Michel & Co. (imperf.)		125.00		
RS183	1c	vermilion, Moore, C. C.				3.50
RS184	2c	black, Moore C.C.		50.00	2,000.	22.50
RS185	1c	black, Morehead's Mag. Plaster	17.50			
RS186	4c	black, Morehead's Neurodyne	825.00			

N

No.	Denom.	Description				
RS187	4c	black, New York Pharmacal Assn.		8.50	25.00	4.00

P

No.	Denom.	Description				
RS188	6c	black, Perl, Dr. M. & Co. (cut to shape)	1,100.			
RS189	1c	green, Pierce, R.V.		10.00	110.00	20.00
RS190	2c	black, Pierce, R.V.	20.00	3.00	22.50	3.50
	e.	Experimental silk paper	60.00			
		Double transfer		—		
RS191	4c	black, Pieters, Bennett & Co.	300.00	1,000.		
	e.	Experimental silk paper	350.00			
RS192	6c	black, Pieters, Bennett & Co.	850.00			
	i.	Imperf.	—			

R

No.	Denom.	Description				
RS193	2c	black, Radway & Co.	2.50	2.50	8.00	3.00
	e.	Experimental silk paper	40.00			
		Double transfer		65.00	125.00	—
RS194	1c	blue, Ransom, D. & Co.	2.00	1.75		
	e.	Experimental silk paper	40.00			
		Double transfer		—		
RS195	2c	black, Ransom, D. & Co.	12.50	14.00		
	e.	Experimental silk paper	55.00			
RS196	1c	blue, Ransom, D., Son & Co.		2.50	10.00	1.50
		Double transfer		—		
RS197	2c	black, Ransom, D., Son & Co.		8.00	50.00	7.00
RS198	1c	black, Redding's Russia Salve		4.50		4.50
		Double transfer		75.00		
RS199	2c	blue, Ring's Veg. Ambrosia (imperf.)		1,500.		
	p.	Perf.		1,250.		
RS200	4c	black, Ring's Veg. Ambrosia (imperf.)	1,100.	1,000.		
RS201	2c	blue, Ring's Veg. Ambrosia (die cut)		15.00		
RS202	4c	black, Ring's Veg. Ambrosia (die cut)	10.00	10.00		15.00
	e.	Experimental silk paper	55.00			
RS203	4c	black, Ring's Veg. Ambrosia (perf.)		1,000.		1,100.
	k.	Perf. and die cut				—
	p.	Part perf.		1,000.		—
RS204	2c	black, Rose, J.B. & Co.		2.50	20.00	*2,500.*
		Double transfer		40.00	—	
RS205	4c	black, Rose, J.B. & Co.		95.00		
		Double transfer		—		
RS206	2c	green, Rumford Chemical Works				2.25
RS207	2c	green, Rumford Chemical Works (imperf.)				17.50

New York Pharmacal Association – RS187

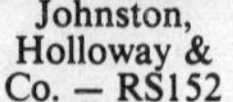

Johnston, Holloway & Co. – RS152

S. Mansfield & Co. – RS174

Merchant's Gargling Oil – RS178

J.B. Rose & Co. RS205

Redding's Russia Salve RS198

Seabury & Johnson – RS216

			a. Old Paper	b. Silk Paper	c. Pink Paper	d. Wmkd. USIR 191R
		S				
RS208	1c	green, Sands, A.B. & D.	9.00	9.00		
	e.	Experimental silk paper	50.00			
RS209	2c	green, Sands, M.P. J. & H.M.		12.00	85.00	10.00
RS210	4c	black, Scheetz's Bitter Cordial (perf.)		250.00		
RS211	4c	black, Scheetz's Bitter Cordial (imperf.)		1,250.		
RS212	1c	green, Schenck's Mandrake Pills (imperf.)	3.50	6.00.	100.00	3.00
	e.	Experimental silk paper	—			
		Double transfer		30.00		—
RS213	6c	black, Schenck's Pulmonic Syrup (imperf.)	3.00	3.00	85.00	95.00
	e.	Experimental silk paper	50.00			
	p.	Perforated	—			
		Double transfer		55.00		—

			a. Old Paper	b. Silk Paper	c. Pink Paper	d. Wmkd. USIR 191R
RS214	4c	black, Schenck, J.H. & Son				5.00
RS215	1c	lake, Schwartz, J.E. & Co. (imperf.)		70.00	225.00	55.00
RS216	1c	black, Seabury & Johnson				45.00
RS217	1c	black, Seabury & Johnson ("porous" obliterated by pen)				2.00
	h.	Printed obliteration				1.50
RS218	1c	lake, Seabury & Johnson				1,250.
RS219	4c	blue, Sigesmond, S. Brown				75.00
RS220	1c	black, Scovill, A.L. & Co.	75	1.25		
	e.	Experimental silk paper	15.00			
	r.	Printed on both sides		*750.00*		
		Double transfer	—			
RS221	4c	green, Scovill, A.L. & Co.	1.50	2.50		
	e.	Experimental silk paper	12.00			
RS222	8c	black, Seelye, D.H. & Co. (imperf.)	8.50			
RS223	1c	black, Simmons, M.A., Iuka, Miss.		60.00		2,000.
RS224	1c	black, Simmons, M.A., St. Louis, Mo.				85.00
RS225	4c	black, Smith, S.N. & Co.		27.50		22.50
RS226	1c	blue, Soule, E.L. & Co., New York (wrapper)	45.00			
RS227	1c	blue, Soule, E.L. & Co. Syracuse (wrapper)	50.00	20.00		
	u.	1c ultra	200.00			
RS228	1c	brown, Stevens, H.R.				12.00
RS229	2c	chocolate, Stevens, H.R.				3.50
RS230	6c	black, Stevens, H.R.			80.00	2.50
RS231	6c	orange, Swaim, Jas. (die cut), manuscript signature	*1,500.*			
RS232	8c	orange, Swaim, Jas. (imperf.)	850.00			
	h.	Manuscript signature	800.00	—		
RS233	8c	orange, Swaim, Jas. (die cut)	225.00			
	h.	Manuscript signature	700.00	—		
RS234	8c	orange, Swaim, Wm. (imperf.)	2,000.	1,750.		950.00
	k.	Without signature	450.00	450.00		
RS235	8c	orange, Swaim, Wm. (die cut)	500.00	150.00		140.00
	k.	Signature inverted		1,150.		
	i.	Manuscript signature		—		
RS236	4c	black, Swett, G.W. (die cut)	9.00			
RS237	4c	green, Swett, G.W. (perf.)		180.00		700.00
RS238	4c	green, Swett, G.W. (perf. and die cut)		225.00		1,000.

John L. Thompson RS242

H.H. Warner & Co. RS254

J.H. Zeilin & Co. – RS277

			a. Old Paper	b. Silk Paper	c. Pink Paper	d. Wmkd. USIR 191R
		T				
RS239	2c	vermilion, Tallcot, Geo				8.00
RS240	4c	black, Tallcot, Geo		50.00	*1,500.*	15.00
RS241	4c	red, Tarrant & Co.		1.50	60.00	1.50
RS242	1c	black, Thompson, John L.	2.25	2.50		2.25
	e.	Experimental silk paper	50.00			
		Double transfer	—			
		U				
RS243	4c	black, U.S. Prop. Med. Co.	45.00	75.00		
	e.	Experimental silk paper	75.00			
RS244	6c	black, U.S. Prop. Med. Co.	600.00			
RS245	1c	black, U.S. Prop. Med. Co. white wrapper	13.00	13.00		
	e.	Experimental silk paper	*450.00*			
RS246	1c	black, U.S. Prop. Med. Co. yellow wrapper	60.00	135.00		
RS247	1c	black, U.S. Prop. Med. Co. orange wrapper	135.00	800.00		
RS248	1c	black, U.S. Prop. Med. Co. orange red wrapper	500.00	*1,250.*		
		V				
RS249	4c	blk., Van Duzer, S.R.	27.50	20.00		125.00
RS250	6c	black, Van Duzer, S.R.				45.00
RS251	1c	black, Vogeler, A. & Co.		50		50
RS252	1c	vermilion, Vogeler, Meyer & Co.			2.50	25
		W				
RS253	4c	black, Walker, J.	25.00	12.50		12.50
	e.	Experimental silk paper	60.00			
		Double transfer		—		
RS254	1c	brown, W., H.H. & Co. (H.H. Warner & Co.)				4.00
RS255	6c	brown, W., H.H. & Co. (H.H. Warner & Co.) (19x26mm)				55.00
RS256	2c	brown, W., H.H. & Co. (H.H. Warner & Co.) (88x11mm)				22.50

			a. Old Paper	b. Silk Paper	c. Pink Paper	d. Wmkd. USIR 191R
RS257	4c	brown, W., H.H. & Co. (H.H. Warner & Co.) (95x18mm)				30.00
RS258	6c	brown, same				3.50
		Double transfer				45.00
RS259	1c	black, Weeks & Potter		4.50		1.50
RS260	2c	black, Weeks & Potter		90.00		
RS261	4c	black, Weeks & Potter		17.50	20.00	5.00
RS262	2c	red, Weeks & Potter			25.00	5.00
RS263	4c	black, Wells, Richardson & Co.				17.50
RS264	4c	black, West India Mfg. Co., die I		225.00	180.00	300.00
RS264A	4c	black, West India Mfg. Co., die II				225.00

Die II shows evidence of retouching, particularly in the central disk.

			a. Old Paper	b. Silk Paper	c. Pink Paper	d. Wmkd. USIR 191R
RS265	1c	green, Wilder, Edward (imperf.)	650.00	150.00		200.00
RS266	1c	green, Wilder, Edward (die cut)	40.00	30.00		17.50
	e.	Experimental silk paper	135.00			
RS266A	4c	vermilion, Wilder, Edward (imperf.)				
	e.	Experimental silk paper	—			
RS267	4c	vermilion, Wilder, Edward (die cut)	100.00	300.00		
	e.	Experimental silk paper	100.00			
RS268	4c	lake, Wilder, Edward (imperf.)		150.00		500.00
RS269	4c	lake, Wilder, Edward (die cut)	400.00	6.00		6.00
RS270	12c	blue, Wilson, E.A.		50.00		250.00
RS271	4c	black, Wilson, Thos. E.	*2,750.*			
RS272	1c	green, World Dispen. Med. Assn.				17.50
RS273	2c	black, World Dispen. Med. Assn.				2.50
RS274	1c	green, Wright's Indian Veg. Pills	1.25	1.25	20.00	1.25
	e.	Experimental silk paper	30.00			
		Double transfer				—

Z

			a. Old Paper	b. Silk Paper	c. Pink Paper	d. Wmkd. USIR 191R
RS275	2c	red, Zeilin, J.H. & Co. (perf.)		400.00		
RS276	2c	green, Zeilin, J.H. & Co. (perf.)		30.00		
RS277	2c	green, Zeilin, J.H. & Co. (imperf.)	200.00	3.50	100.00	2.00

1898-1900

See rouletting note preceding No. R161.

			Rouletted 5½ Unused	Rouletted 5½ Used	Hyphen Hole Perf. 7 Unused	Hyphen Hole Perf. 7 Used
RS278	2½c	carmine, Antikamnia Co.			1.75	1.75
RS279	4c	black, Branca Bros.	6.00	6.00	5.00	5.00
RS280	¼c	carmine, Emerson Drug Co.			3.50	75
RS281	⅝c	green, Emerson Drug Co.			3.50	1.00
RS282	1¼c	violet brown, Emerson Drug Co.			4.00	2.50
RS283	2½c	brown orange, Emerson Drug Co.			4.00	2.50
RS284	1¼c	black, Fletcher, C.H.	25	25	20	20
RS285	2½c	black, Hostetter Co. (imperf.)	40	40		
RS286	⅝c	carmine, Johnson & Johnson	10	10	10	10
RS287	⅝c	green, Lanman & Kemp	6.00	2.00	8.00	2.00
RS288	1¼c	brown, Lanman & Kemp	10.00	6.00	10.00	6.00
RS289	1⅞c	blue, Lanman & Kemp	10.00	3.00	12.00	3.00
RS290	⅛c	dark blue, Lee, J. Ellwood, Co.			1.75	1.75
RS291	⅝c	carmine, Lee, J. Ellwood, Co.			75	75
RS292	1¼c	dark green, Lee, J. Ellwood, Co.			1.50	1.50
RS293	2½c	orange, Lee, J. Ellwood, Co.			1.75	1.75
RS294	5c	chocolate, Lee. J. Ellwood, Co.			1.75	1.75
RS295	⅝c	black, Marchand, Chas.	4.00	4.00	5.00	5.00
RS296	1¼c	black, Marchand, Chas.	1.00	1.00	1.00	1.00
RS297	1⅞c	black, Marchand, Chas.	1.50	1.50	2.00	2.00
RS298	2½c	black, Marchand, Chas.	75	75	1.00	1.00
RS299	3⅛c	black, Marchand, Chas.	5.00	5.00	5.00	5.00
RS300	4⅜c	black, Marchand, Chas.	12.00	12.00	12.00	12.00
RS301	7½c	black, Marchand, Chas.	8.00	8.00	8.00	8.00
RS302	2½c	carmine, Od Chemical Co.				75
RS303	⅝c	blue, Piso Co.	15	15	15	15
RS304	⅝c	blue, Radway & Co.	60	60	60	60
RS305	3⅛c	brown, Warner's Safe Cure Co.	60	60	60	60
RS306	1¼c	pink, Williams Medicine Co., Dr.			1.25	1.25

Dr. Kilmer & Co., Provisionals.

Postage Stamps of 1895-98, Nos. 279, 279B and 268, Precancel Overprinted in Black:

Dr. K. & Co.
I. R.
7-5–'98.
a

Dr. K. & Co.
I. R.
Binghamton, N. Y.
7-11-'98
b

Dr. K. & Co.
I. R.
Binghamton, N. Y.
7-7-'98
c

1898 **Wmk. 191** ***Perf. 12***

Overprint "a," Large "I.R." Dated July 5, 1898

RS307	A87	1c	deep green	70.00
RS308	A88	2c	red	47.50
RS309	A89	3c	purple	50.00

Overprint "b," Small "I.R.," "Dr. K. & Co." with Serifs Dated July 6, 7, 9, 11 to 14, 1898

RS310	A87	1c	deep green	47.50
RS311	A88	2c	red	30.00
RS312	A89	3c	purple	42.50

Overprint "c," Small "I.R.," "Dr. K. & Co." without Serifs Dated July 7, 9, 11 to 14, 1898

RS313	A87	1c	deep green	60.00
RS314	A88	2c	red	25.00
RS315	A89	3c	purple	30.00

Many varieties, including inverts, of the Kilmer overprints exist. For the complete listing see "The Case of Dr. Kilmer," by Morton Dean Joyce.

St. Louis Provisional Labels, 1898

Ten proprietary drug companies of St. Louis prepared and used labels to denote payment of July 1, 1898, Proprietary Revenue tax because the government issue of "Battleship" stamps (Nos. RB20-RB31) was not available on the effective date. An illustrated descriptive list of these labels, compiled by Morton Dean Joyce, appeared in the December, 1970, issue of Scott's Monthly Journal.

PRIVATE DIE PERFUMERY STAMPS

Corning & Tappan — RT4

C.B. Woodworth & Son — RT20

R. & G.A. Wright — RT23

1864 ***Perf. 12***

			a. Old Paper	b. Silk Paper	c. Pink Paper	d. Wmkd. USIR 191R
RT1	2c	blue, Bazin, X. (die cut)	450.00			

This stamp was never placed in use.

			a. Old Paper	b. Silk Paper	c. Pink Paper	d. Wmkd. USIR 191R
RT2	1c	black, Corning & Tappan (imperf.)				700.00
	h.	Die cut, 19mm diameter				85.00
	k.	Die cut, 21mm diameter				95.00
RT3	1c	black, Corning & Tappan, (perf.)				250.00
RT4	1c	blue, Corning & Tappan, (perf.)				1.50
RT5	2c	vermilion, Fetridge & Co. (cut to shape)	100.00			
RT6	1c	black, Hoyt, E. W. & Co. (imperf.)		1,750.	1,000.	100.00
RT7	1c	black, Hoyt, E. W. & Co. (die cut)		20.00	20.00	8.00
RT8	2c	black, Hoyt, E. W. & Co. (imperf.)				275.00
RT9	2c	black, Hoyt, E. W. & Co. (die cut)				60.00
RT10	4c	black, Hoyt, E. W. & Co. (imperf.)		1,150.	250.00	725.00
RT11	4c	black, Hoyt, E. W. & Co. (die cut)		65.00	50.00	50.00
RT12	1c	vermilion, Kidder & Laird				6.00
RT13	2c	vermilion, Kidder & Laird				8.00
RT14	3c	black, Laird, Geo. W. (imperf.)		400.00	600.00	475.00
		Double transfer		600.00	800.00	
	p.	perf.	1,000.	—		
		As "p," double transfer	—			
RT15	3c	black, Laird, Geo. W. (die cut)	1,000.	70.00	500.00	75.00

			a. Old Paper	b. Silk Paper	c. Pink Paper	d. Wmkd. USIR 191R
	p.	Perf. and die cut	1,000.			
		Double transfer		—	800.00	
RT16	1c	black, Lanman & Kemp		3.50	150.00	3.50
		Double transfer		—		
RT17	2c	brown, Lanman & Kemp		22.50		6.00
RT18	3c	green, Lanman & Kemp		3.50		7.00
RT19	1c	vermilion, Tetlow's Perfumery				1.50
RT20	1c	green, Woodworth, C. B. & Son		4.00	12.00	4.00
		Double transfer		—	—	—
RT21	2c	blue, Woodworth, C. B. & Son		110.00	900.00	6.00
RT22	1c	blue, Wright, R. & G. A.	4.00	4.00		45.00
	e.	Experimental silk paper	30.00			
RT23	2c	black, Wright, R. & G. A.	8.50	15.00		140.00
RT24	3c	lake, Wright, R. & G. A.	22.50	80.00		175.00
RT25	4c	grn. Wright, R. & G. A.	60.00	80.00		165.00
RT26	1c	green, Young, Ladd & Coffin (imperf.)		65.00	65.00	60.00
RT27	1c	green, Young, Ladd & Coffin (perf.)		15.00	12.50	10.00
RT28	2c	blue, Young, Ladd & Coffin (imperf.)		90.00	75.00	45.00
RT29	2c	blue, Young, Ladd & Coffin (perf.)		50.00	60.00	10.00
RT30	3c	vermilion, Young, Ladd & Coffin (imperf.)		80.00	90.00	50.00
RT31	3c	vermilion, Young, Ladd & Coffin (perf.)		25.00	3.50	1.50
RT32	4c	brown, Young, Ladd & Coffin (imperf.)			90.00	40.00
RT33	4c	brown, Young, Ladd & Coffin (perf.)		30.00	9.00	3.00

PRIVATE DIE PLAYING CARD STAMPS

Eagle Card Co. — RU7

Victor E. Mauger & Petrie — RU13

Russell, Morgan & Co. — RU16

1864

			a. Old Paper	b. Silk Paper	c. Pink Paper	d. Wmkd. USIR 191R
RU1	5c	brown, Caterson Brotz & Co.				2,500.

This stamp was never placed in use.

			a. Old Paper	b. Silk Paper	c. Pink Paper	d. Wmkd. USIR 191R
RU2	2c	orange, Dougherty, A	50.00			
RU3	4c	black, Dougherty, A.	30.00			
RU4	5c	blue, Dougherty, A. (20x26mm)	35	35	7.50	
	u.	5c ultra	90.00			
		Double transfer		—		
RU5	5c	blue, Dougherty, A. (18x23mm)				50
RU6	10c	blue, Dougherty, A	30.00			
RU7	5c	black, Eagle Card Co.				65.00
RU8	5c	black, Goodall, Chas.	140.00	1.50		
	e.	Experimental silk paper	250.00			
RU9	5c	black, Hart, Samuel & Co.	4.00	4.00		
RU10	2c	blue, Lawrence & Cohen	50.00			
RU11	5c	green, Lawrence & Cohen	3.00	2.00		
	e.	Experimental silk paper	45.00			
RU12	5c	black, Levy, John J.	15.00	20.00		
	e.	Experimental silk paper	60.00			
RU13	5c	blue, Mauger, Victor E., & Petrie		1.00	1.00	30
RU14	5c	black, N. Y. Consolidated Card Co.		2.00	10.00	2.00
RU15	5c	black, Paper Fabrique Co.		3.50	12.00	4.00
RU16	5c	black, Russell, Morgan & Co.				6.00

MOTOR VEHICLE USE REVENUE

When affixed to a motor vehicle, permitted use of that vehicle for a stated period.

RV1

OFFSET PRINTING

1942 Wmk. 191R With Gum on Back *Perf. 11*

RV1	RV1	$2.09	light green *(February)*	1.25	40

With Gum on Face

Inscriptions on Back

RV2	RV1	$1.67	light green *(March)*	12.50	7.00
RV3	RV1	$1.25	light green *(April)*	11.00	6.00
RV4	RV1	84c	light green *(May)*	12.50	6.00
RV5	RV1	42c	light green *(June)*	11.00	6.00

With Gum and Control Number on Face

1942 Inscriptions on Back

RV6	RV1	$5	rose red *(July)*	2.50	75
RV7	RV1	$4.59	rose red *(August)*	20.00	10.00
RV8	RV1	$4.17	rose red *(September)*	25.00	10.00
RV9	RV1	$3.75	rose red *(October)*	22.50	10.00
RV10	RV1	$3.34	rose red *(November)*	21.00	10.00
RV11	RV1	$2.92	rose red *(December)*	20.00	—

1943

RV12	RV1	$2.50	rose red *(January)*	25.00	8.00
RV13	RV1	$2.09	rose red *(February)*	18.00	6.00
RV14	RV1	$1.67	rose red *(March)*	15.00	—
RV15	RV1	$1.25	rose red *(April)*	15.00	6.00
RV16	RV1	84c	rose red *(May)*	15.00	6.00
RV17	RV1	42c	rose red *(June)*	12.50	—
RV18	RV1	$5	yellow *(July)*	3.00	75
RV19	RV1	$4.59	yellow *(August)*	25.00	10.00
RV20	RV1	$4.17	yellow *(September)*	37.50	10.00
RV21	RV1	$3.75	yellow *(October)*	35.00	10.00
RV22	RV1	$3.34	yellow *(November)*	40.00	10.00
RV23	RV1	$2.92	yellow *(December)*	50.00	10.00

1944

RV24	RV1	$2.50	yellow *(January)*	50.00	12.50
RV25	RV1	$2.09	yellow *(February)*	32.50	8.00
RV26	RV1	$1.67	yellow *(March)*	25.00	8.00
RV27	RV1	$1.25	yellow *(April)*	25.00	6.00
RV28	RV1	84c	yellow *(May)*	20.00	—
RV29	RV1	42c	yellow *(June)*	20.00	—

Gum on Face

Control Number and Inscriptions on Back

RV30	RV1	$5	violet *(July)*	2.50	50
RV31	RV1	$4.59	violet *(August)*	40.00	12.50
RV32	RV1	$4.17	violet *(September)*	30.00	12.50
RV33	RV1	$3.75	violet *(October)*	30.00	10.00
RV34	RV1	$3.34	violet *(November)*	20.00	8.00
RV35	RV1	$2.92	violet *(December)*	22.50	8.00

1945

RV36	RV1	$2.50	violet *(January)*	22.50	7.00
RV37	RV1	$2.09	violet *(February)*	20.00	6.00
RV38	RV1	$1.67	violet *(March)*	17.50	6.00
RV39	RV1	$1.25	violet *(April)*	17.50	5.00
RV40	RV1	84c	violet *(May)*	15.00	4.00
RV41	RV1	42c	violet *(June)*	12.50	4.00

Daniel Manning RV2

Gum on Face
Control Number and Inscriptions on Back

1945 Wmk. 191R Offset Printing ***Perf. 11***

RV42	RV2	$5	bright blue green & yellow green *(July)*	2.50	50
RV43	RV2	$4.59	bright blue green & yellow green *(August)*	30.00	—
RV44	RV2	$4.17	bright blue green & yellow green *(Sept.)*	30.00	—
RV45	RV2	$3.75	bright blue green & yellow green *(October)*	25.00	—
RV46	RV2	$3.34	bright blue green & yellow green *(November)*	20.00	—
RV47	RV2	$2.92	bright blue green & yellow green *(December)*	17.50	—

1946

RV48	RV2	$2.50	bright blue green & yellow green *(January)*	20.00	—
RV49	RV2	$2.09	bright blue green & yellow green *(February)*	20.00	—
RV50	RV2	$1.67	bright blue green & yellow green *(March)*	15.00	—
RV51	RV2	$1.25	bright blue green & yellow green *(April)*	12.00	—
RV52	RV2	84c	bright blue green & yellow green *(May)*	12.00	—
RV53	RV2	42c	bright blue green & yellow green *(June)*	8.00	—

BOATING

Required on applications for the certificate of number for motorboats of more than 10 horsepower, starting April 1, 1960. The pictorial upper part of the $3 stamp was attached to the temporary certificate and kept by the boat owner. The lower part (stub), showing number only, was affixed to the application and sent by the post office to the U.S. Coast Guard, which issues permanent certificates. The $3 fee was for three years. The $1 stamp covered charges for reissue of a lost or destroyed certificate of number.

Outboard and Inboard Motorboats — B1

Offset Printing, Number Typographed

1960 Unwmk. ***Rouletted***

RVB1	B1	$1	rose red, black number	20.00	
			Margin block of 4, P#	90.00	
RVB2	B1	$3	blue, red number	35.00	25.00
			Margin block of 4, P#	150.00	

HUNTING PERMIT

Authorized by an Act of Congress, approved March 16, 1934, to license hunters. Receipts go to maintain waterfowl life in the United States. Sales to collectors were made legal June 15, 1935. The 1934 issue was designed by J.N. Darling, 1935 by Frank W. Benson, 1936 by Richard E. Bishop, 1937 by J.D. Knap, 1938 by Roland Clark, 1939 by Lynn Bogue Hunt, 1940 by Francis L. Jaques, 1941 by E.R. Kalmbach, 1942 by A. Lassell Ripley, 1943 by Walter E. Bohl, 1944 and 1950 by Walter A. Weber, 1945 by Owen J. Bromme, 1946 by Robert W. Hines, 1947 by Jack Murray, 1948, 1951, 1959, 1969, and 1971 by Maynard Reece, 1949 by 'Roge' E. Preuss, 1952 by John H. Dick, 1953 by Clayton B. Seagears, 1954 by Harvey D. Sandstrom, 1955, 1964 and 1966 by Stanley Searns, 1956, 1963 and 1970 by Edward J. Bierly, 1957 by Jackson Miles Abbott, 1958 and 1967 by Leslie C. Kouba, 1960 by John A. Ruthven, 1961-1962 by Edward A. Morris, 1965 by Ron Jenkins, 1968 by C.G. Pritchard, 1972 by Arthur M. Cook, 1973 by Lee LeBlanc, 1975 by James L. Fisher, 1976 by Alderson Magee, 1977 by Martin R. Murk, 1978 by Albert Earl Gilbert, 1979 by Kenneth L. Michaelsen, 1980 by Richard W. Plasschaert, 1981 by John S. Wilson, 1982 by David A. Maass, 1983 by Phil Scholer, 1984 by William C. Morris, 1985 by Gerald Mobely, 1986 by Burton E. Moore, Jr., 1987 by Arthur G. Anderson, 1988 by Daniel Smith, and 1989 by Neal R. Anderson.

Used value is for stamp with signature. Plate number blocks of six have margins on two sides.

Department of Agriculture

Mallards Alighting — HP1

Issued in panes of 28 subjects.

Engraved: Flat Plate Printing

1934 **Unwmk.** ***Perf. 11***

Inscribed "Void after June 30, 1935"

RW1	HP1	$1 **blue**	400.00	85.00
		P# block of 6	6,000.	
	a.	Imperf., pair	*4,000.*	
	b.	Vert. pair, imperf. horiz.	—	

1935 **Inscribed "Void after June 30, 1936"**

RW2	$1 **rose lake** *(Canvasbacks Taking to Flight)*	400.00	100.00
	P# block of 6	7,000.	

1936 **Inscribed "Void after June 30, 1937"**

RW3	$1 **brown black** *(Canada Geese in Flight)*	200.00	50.00
	P# block of 6	2,500.	

1937 **Inscribed "Void after June 30, 1938"**

RW4	$1 **light green** *(Scaup Ducks Taking to Flight)*	160.00	27.50
	P# block of 6	1,750.	

1938 **Inscribed "Void after June 30, 1939"**

RW5	$1 **light violet** *(Pintail Drake and Hen Alighting)*	160.00	35.00
	P# block of 6	1,800.	

Department of the Interior

Green-winged Teal — HP2

1939 **Inscribed "Void after June 30, 1940"**

RW6	HP2	$1 **chocolate**	115.00	15.00
		P# block of 6	1,200.	

1940 **Inscribed "Void after June 30, 1941"**

RW7	$1 **sepia** *(Black Mallards)*	110.00	15.00
	P# block of 6	1,100.	

1941 **Inscribed "Void after June 30, 1942"**

RW8	$1 **brown carmine** *(Family of Ruddy Ducks)*	110.00	15.00
	P# block of 6	1,000.	

1942 **Inscribed "Void after June 30, 1943"**

RW9	$1 **violet brown** *(Baldpates)*	110.00	14.00
	P# block of 6	1,000.	

1943 **Inscribed "Void After June 30, 1944"**

RW10	$1 **deep rose** *(Wood Ducks)*	47.50	15.00
	P# block of 6	425.00	

1944 **Inscribed "Void after June 30, 1945"**

RW11	$1 **red orange** *(White-fronted Geese)*	40.00	14.00
	P# block of 6	400.00	

1945 **Inscribed "Void after June 30, 1946"**

RW12	$1 **black** *(Shoveller Ducks in Flight)*	35.00	10.00
	P# block of 6	225.00	

1946 **Inscribed "Void after June 30, 1947"**

RW13	$1 **red brown** *(Redhead Ducks)*	32.50	9.00
	P# block of 6	225.00	

1947 **Inscribed "Void after June 30, 1948"**

RW14	$1 **black** *(Snow Geese)*	35.00	9.00
	P# block of 6	225.00	

1948 **Inscribed "Void after June 30, 1949"**

RW15	$1 **bright blue** *(Buffleheads in Flight)*	32.50	9.00
	P# block of 6	225.00	

Goldeneye Ducks — HP3

1949 **Inscribed "Void after June 30, 1950"**

RW16	HP3	$2 **bright green**	37.50	8.00
		P# block of 6	225.00	

1950 **Inscribed "Void after June 30, 1951"**

RW17	$2 **violet** *(Trumpeter Swans in Flight)*	45.00	7.00
	P# block of 6	325.00	

1951 **Inscribed "Void after June 30, 1952"**

RW18	$2 **gray black** *(Gadwall Ducks)*	45.00	5.00
	P# block of 6	325.00	

1952 **Inscribed "Void after June 30, 1953"**

RW19	$2 **deep ultramarine** *(Harlequin Ducks)*	45.00	5.00
	P# block of 6	325.00	

1953 **Inscribed "Void after June 30, 1954"**

RW20	$2 **dark rose brown** *(Blue-winged Teal)*	45.00	5.00
	P# block of 6	325.00	

1954 **Inscribed "Void after June 30, 1955"**

RW21	$2 **black** *(Ring-necked Ducks)*	45.00	4.75
	P# block of 6	325.00	

1955 **Inscribed "Void after June 30, 1956"**

RW22	$2 **dark blue** *(Blue Geese)*	45.00	4.75
	P# block of 6	325.00	

1956 **Inscribed: "Void after June 30, 1957"**

RW23	$2 **black** *(American Merganser)*	45.00	4.75
	P# block of 6	325.00	

1957 **Inscribed: "Void after June 30, 1958"**

RW24	$2 **emerald** *(American Eider)*	45.00	4.75
	P# block of 6	325.00	

1958 **Inscribed: "Void after June 30, 1959"**

RW25	$2 **black** *(Canada Geese)*	45.00	4.75
	P# block of 6	325.00	

Labrador Retriever Carrying Mallard Drake — HP4

Giori Press Printing

Issued in panes of 30 subjects

1959 **Inscribed: "Void after June 30, 1960"**

RW26	HP4	$3 **blue, ocher & black**	60.00	4.75
		P# block of 4	285.00	

Redhead Ducks — HP5

1960 **Inscribed: "Void after June 30, 1961"**

RW27	HP5	$3 red brown, dark blue & bister	60.00	4.00
		P# block of 4	285.00	

1961 **Inscribed: "Void after June 30, 1962"**

RW28	$3 *Mallard Hen and Ducklings*	60.00	4.00
	P# block of 4	285.00	

Pintail Drakes Coming in for Landing — HP6

1962 **Inscribed: "Void after June 30, 1963"**

RW29	HP6	$3 dark blue, dark red brown & black	70.00	5.50
		P# block of 4	350.00	

1963 **Inscribed: "Void after June 30, 1964"**

RW30	$3 *Pair of Brant Landing*	65.00	5.50
	P# block of 4	350.00	

1964 **Inscribed: "Void after June 30, 1965"**

RW31	$3 *Hawaiian Nene Geese*	65.00	5.50
	P# block of 6	2,250.	

1965 **Inscribed: "Void after June 30, 1966"**

RW32	$3 *Three Canvasback Drakes*	65.00	5.50
	P# block of 4	325.00	

Whistling Swans — HP7

1966 **Inscribed: "Void after June 30, 1967"**

RW33	HP7	$3 multicolored	65.00	5.00
		P# block of 4	300.00	

1967 **Inscribed "Void after June 30, 1968"**

RW34	$3 *Old Squaw Ducks*	65.00	5.00
	P# block of 4	300.00	

1968 **Inscribed: "Void after June 30, 1969"**

RW35	$3 *Hooded Mergansers*	40.00	5.50
	P# block of 4	200.00	

White-winged Scoters — HP8 MIGRATORY BIRD HUNTING STAMP

1969 **Inscribed: "Void after June 30, 1970"**

RW36	HP8	$3 multicolored	40.00	4.50
		P# block of 4	200.00	

1970 **Engraved & Lithographed**
Inscribed: "Void after June 30, 1971"

RW37	$3 *Ross's Geese*	40.00	4.00
	P# block of 4	200.00	

1971 **Inscribed: "Void after June 30, 1972"**

RW38	$3 *Three Cinnamon Teal*	27.50	3.75
	P# block of 4	140.00	

1972 **Inscribed: "Void after June 30, 1973"**

RW39	$5 *Emperor Geese*	17.00	3.75
	P# block of 4	75.00	

1973 **Inscribed: "Void after June 30, 1974"**

RW40	$5 *Steller's Eiders*	17.00	3.75
	P# block of 4	80.00	

1974 **Inscribed: "Void after June 30, 1975"**

RW41	$5 *Wood Ducks*	14.00	3.75
	P# block of 4	62.50	

1975 **Inscribed: "Void after June 30, 1976"**

RW42	$5 *Canvasback Decoy, 3 Flying Canvasbacks*	12.00	3.75
	P# block of 4	52.50	

1976 **Inscribed "Void after June 30, 1977"** **Engr.**

RW43	$5 *Family of Canada Geese*	9.50	3.75
	P# block of 4	50.00	

1977 **Litho. & Engr.**
Inscribed: "Void after June 30, 1978"

RW44	$5 *Pair of Ross's Geese*	9.50	3.75
	P# block of 4	50.00	

Hooded Merganser Drake — HP9

1978 **Inscribed: "Void after June 30, 1979"**

RW45	HP9	$5 multicolored	9.50	3.75
		P# block of 4	50.00	

1979 **Inscribed: "Void after June 30, 1980"**

RW46	$7.50 *Green-winged Teal*	13.00	4.00
	P# block of 4	75.00	

1980 **Inscribed: "Void after June 30, 1981"**

RW47	$7.50 *Mallards*	13.00	4.00
	P# block of 4	75.00	

1981 **Inscribed: "Void after June 30, 1982"**

RW48	$7.50 *Ruddy Ducks*	13.00	4.00
	P# block of 4	75.00	

1982 **Inscribed: "Void after June 30, 1983"**

RW49	$7.50 *Canvasbacks*	12.00	4.00
	P# block of 4	55.00	

1983 **Inscribed: "Void after June 30, 1984"**

RW50	$7.50 *Pintails*	12.00	4.00
	P# block of 4	55.00	

1984 **Inscribed: "Void after June 30, 1985"**

RW51	$7.50 *Wigeons*	12.00	4.00
	P# block of 4	55.00	

After No. RW51 became void, uncut sheets of 120 (4 panes of 30 separated by gutters) were overprinted in the margins and auctioned.

1985 **Inscribed: "Void after June 30, 1986"**

RW52	$7.50 *Cinnamon teal*	12.00	4.00
	P# block of 4	55.00	

1986 **Inscribed: "Void after June 30, 1987"**

RW53	$7.50 *Fulvous whistling duck*	12.00	4.00
	P# block of 4	55.00	
a.	Black omitted	—	

1987 **Perf. 11½x11**
Inscribed: "Void after June 30, 1988"

RW54	$10 *Redheads*	14.00	4.00
	P# block of 4	65.00	

1988 **Inscribed: "Void after June 30, 1989"**

RW55	$10 *Snow Goose*	14.00	4.00
	P# block of 4	65.00	

1989, June 30
Inscribed: "Void after June 30, 1990"

RW56	$12.50 *Lesser Scaup*	25.00	3.50
	P# block of 4	125.00	—

Gray inscription on back of Nos. RW13-RW34: "It is unlawful to hunt waterfowl unless you sign your name in ink on the face of this stamp". Additional wording on Nos. RW26-RW27: "Duck stamp dollars buy wetlands to perpetuate waterfowl," and on Nos. RW28-RW34: "Duck stamp dollars buy wetlands for waterfowl." Back inscription on Nos. RW35-RW36 reads: "Buy duck stamps/Save wetlands /Send in all bird bands/Sign your duck stamps."

Back inscription of Nos. RW37-RW53 repeats 4-line message of Nos. RW35-RW36 and also includes in two added lines the "It is unlawful . . ." warning. Nos. RW54-RW56 repeat the messages of Nos. RW37-RW53, and have as the first line, "Take pride in America."

No. RW21 and following issues are printed on dry, pregummed paper and the back inscription is printed on top of the gum.

QUANTITIES ISSUED

RW1	635,001
RW2	448,204
RW3	603,623
RW4	783,039
RW5	1,002,715
RW6	1,111,561
RW7	1,260,810
RW8	1,439,967
RW9	1,383,629
RW10	1,169,352
RW11	1,487,029
RW12	1,725,505
RW13	2,016,841
RW14	1,722,677
RW15	2,127,603
RW16	1,954,734
RW17	1,903,644
RW18	2,167,767
RW19	2,296,628
RW20	2,268,446
RW21	2,184,550
RW22	2,369,940
RW23	2,332,014
RW24	2,355,190
RW25	2,176,425
RW26	1,626,115
RW27	1,725,634
RW28	1,344,236
RW29	1,147,212
RW30	1,448,191
RW31	1,573,155
RW32	1,558,197
RW33	1,805,341
RW34	1,934,697
RW35	1,837,139
RW36	2,072,108
RW37	2,420,244
RW38	2,441,664
RW39	2,179,628
RW40	2,113,594
RW41	2,190,268
RW42	2,218,589
RW43	2,248,394
RW44	2,180,625
RW45	2,196,758
RW46	2,209,572
RW47	2,103,021
RW48	1,907,114
RW49	1,926,253
RW50	1,867,998
RW51	1,913,509

United States Hunting Permit stamps can be mounted in Scott's Platinum, National, Pony Express, Minuteman, U.S. Federal and State Duck Stamps and U.S. Federal Duck Plate Block Albums.

DISTILLED SPIRITS

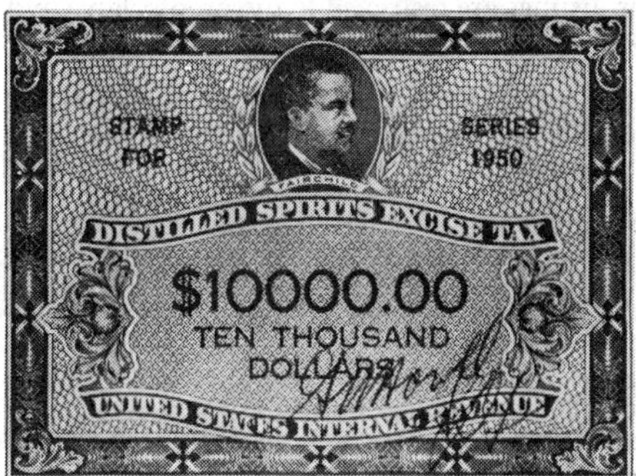

Charles S. Fairchild, Secretary of Treasury 1887-89 — DS1

Actual size: 89½x63½mm

1950 Wmk. 191R Offset Printing *Rouletted 7*
Inscribed "STAMP FOR SERIES 1950"

				Used	Punched Cancel
RX1	DS1	1c	yellow green & black	25.00	20.00
RX2	DS1	3c	yellow green & black	90.00	80.00
RX3	DS1	5c	yellow green & black	25.00	20.00
RX4	DS1	10c	yellow green & black	20.00	15.00
RX5	DS1	25c	yellow green & black	9.00	7.00
RX6	DS1	50c	yellow green & black	9.00	7.00
RX7	DS1	$1	yellow green & black	2.00	1.25
RX8	DS1	$3	yellow green & black	20.00	15.00
RX9	DS1	$5	yellow green & black	7.00	5.00
RX10	DS1	$10	yellow green & black	2.50	1.50
RX11	DS1	$25	yellow green & black	12.50	9.00
RX12	DS1	$50	yellow green & black	9.00	6.00
RX13	DS1	$100	yellow green & black	4.00	2.50
RX14	DS1	$300	yellow green & black	30.00	25.00
RX15	DS1	$500	yellow green & black	20.00	15.00
RX16	DS1	$1,000	yellow green & black	9.00	7.50
RX17	DS1	$1,500	yellow green & black	50.00	37.50
RX18	DS1	$2,000	yellow green & black	4.50	3.25
RX19	DS1	$3,000	yellow green & black	25.00	20.00
RX20	DS1	$5,000	yellow green & black	25.00	20.00
RX21	DS1	$10,000	yellow green & black	35.00	25.00
RX22	DS1	$20,000	yellow green & black	40.00	35.00
RX23	DS1	$30,000	yellow green & black	70.00	50.00
RX24	DS1	$40,000	yellow green & black	800.00	575.00
RX25	DS1	$50,000	yellow green & black	85.00	60.00

1952
Inscription "STAMP FOR SERIES 1950" omitted

				Used	Punched Cancel
RX28	DS1	5c	yellow green & black		40.00
RX29	DS1	10c	yellow green & black	—	4.00
RX30	DS1	25c	yellow green & black		17.50
RX31	DS1	50c	yellow green & black		15.00
RX32	DS1	$1	yellow green & black	20.00	1.25
RX33	DS1	$3	yellow green & black	35.00	22.50
RX34	DS1	$5	yellow green & black	40.00	27.50
RX35	DS1	$10	yellow green & black		1.50
RX36	DS1	$25	yellow green & black	25.00	10.00
RX37	DS1	$50	yellow green & black		30.00
RX38	DS1	$100	yellow green & black	20.00	2.50
RX39	DS1	$300	yellow green & black		7.00
RX40	DS1	$500	yellow green & black		35.00
RX41	DS1	$1,000	yellow green & black	—	6.00
RX43	DS1	$2,000	yellow green & black		60.00
RX44	DS1	$3,000	yellow green & black	—	700.00
RX45	DS1	$5,000	yellow green & black		45.00
RX46	DS1	$10,000	yellow green & black		80.00

Seven other denominations with "Stamp for Series 1950" omitted were prepared but are not known to have been put into use: 1c, 3c, $1,500, $20,000, $30,000, $40,000 and $50,000.

Copies listed as used have staple holes.

Distilled Spirits Excise Tax stamps were discontinued in 1959.

FIREARMS TRANSFER TAX

Documentary Stamp of 1917 Overprinted Vertically in Black. Reading Up

NATIONAL FIREARMS ACT

1934 Engr. Wmk. 191R *Perf. 11*
Without Gum

RY1	R21	$1 green	300.00	300.00

Eagle, Shield and Stars from U.S. Seal
RY1 (Type I) RY2

Two types of $200:
I. Serial number with serifs, not preceded by zeros. Tips of 6 lines project into left margin.
II. Gothic serial number preceded by zeros. Five line tips in left margin.

1934-74 Wmk. 191R Size: 28x42mm
Without Gum

RY2	RY1	$200 dull blue & red, type II, #3001-up, unwmkd. ('74)	225.00	100.00
a.		$200 dark blue & red, type I, #1-1500	1,350.	—
b.		$200 dull blue & red, type II, #1501-3000 ('50)	550.00	—

Issued in vertical strips of 4 which are imperforate at top, bottom and right side.

1938 Size: 28x33½mm *Perf. 11*

RY3	RY2	$1 green	75.00	—

1960, July 1 Size: 29x34mm *Perf. 11*

RY4	RY2	$5 red	10.00	—

No. RY4 was issued in sheets of 50 (10x5) with straight edge on four sides of sheet.

The watermark is hard to see on many copies of Nos. RY2-RY4.

RECTIFICATION TAX

RT1

Actual size: 89½x64mm

1946 Offset Printing Wmk. 191R *Rouletted 7*

				Unused	Used	Punched Cancel
RZ1	RT1	1c	blue & black	7.00	3.00	1.50
RZ2	RT1	3c	blue & black	25.00	8.00	7.50
RZ3	RT1	5c	blue & black	15.00	2.50	1.25
RZ4	RT1	10c	blue & black	15.00	2.50	1.25
RZ5	RT1	25c	blue & black	15.00	3.00	2.00
RZ6	RT1	50c	blue & black	20.00	5.00	3.00
RZ7	RT1	$1	blue & black	20.00	4.00	2.00
RZ8	RT1	$3	blue & black	—	18.00	9.00
RZ9	RT1	$5	blue & black	30.00	10.00	6.00
RZ10	RT1	$10	blue & black	25.00	3.00	1.00
RZ11	RT1	$25	blue & black	—	9.00	4.00
RZ12	RT1	$50	blue & black	—	6.50	3.00
RZ13	RT1	$100	blue & black	—	9.00	3.50
RZ14	RT1	$300	blue & black	—	10.00	7.50
RZ15	RT1	$500	blue & black	—	10.00	7.00
RZ16	RT1	$1000	blue & black	—	15.00	12.50
RZ17	RT1	$1500	blue & black	—	40.00	30.00
RZ18	RT1	$2000	blue & black	—	75.00	55.00

Copies listed as used have staple holes.

See table of Territorial and Statehood Dates at beginning of catalogue. See catalogue index.

DIE AND PLATE PROOFS

PROOFS are known in many styles other than those noted in this section. For the present, however, listings are restricted to die proofs, large and small, and plate proofs on India paper and card. The listing of normal color proofs includes several that differ somewhat from the colors of the issued stamps.

Large Die Proofs are so termed because of the relatively large piece of paper on which they are printed which is about the size of the die block, 40 mm. by 50 mm. or larger. The margins of this group of proofs usually are from 15 to 20 mm. in width though abnormal examples prevent the acceptance of these measurements as a complete means of identification.

These proofs were prepared in most cases by the original contracting companies and often show the imprint thereof and letters and numbers of identification. They are listed under "DIE-Large (1)." The India paper on which these proofs are printed is of an uneven texture and in some respects resembles hand-made paper. These large die proofs were mounted on cards though many are found removed from the card. Large Die Proofs autographed by the engraver or officially approved are worth much more.

Values for die proofs of the bicolored 1869 issue are for examples which are completely printed. Occasionally the vignette has been cut out and affixed to an impression of the border.

Die Proofs of all United States stamps of later issues exist. Only those known outside of government ownership are listed.

Small Die Proofs are so called because of the small piece of paper on which they are printed. Proofs of stamps issued prior to 1904, are reprints, and not in all cases from the same dies as the large die proofs. The margins are small, seldom being more than from 3 to 5mm. in width. These 302 small die proofs are from sets prepared for 85 ("Roosevelt presentation") albums in 1904 by the Bureau of Engraving and Printing but bear no imprint to this effect. The white wove paper on which they are printed is of a fibrous nature. These are listed under "DIE-Small (2)."

A special printing of 413 different small die proofs was made in 1915 for the Panama-Pacific Exposition. These have small margins (2 1/2 to 3 mm.) and are on soft yellowish wove paper. They are extremely scarce as only 3 to 5 of each are known and a few, such as the 1861 5c buff, exist only in this special printing. They are listed under "DIE-Small (2a)."

Plate Proofs are, quite obviously, impressions taken from finished plates and differ from the stamps themselves chiefly in their excellence of impression and the paper on which they are printed. Some of the colors vary.

Hybrids are plate proofs of all issues before 1894 which have been cut to shape, mounted and pressed on large cards to resemble large die proofs. These sell for somewhat less than the corresponding large die proofs.

India Paper is a thin, soft, opaque paper which wrinkles when wet. It varies in thickness and shows particles of bamboo.

Card is a plain, clear white card of good quality, which is found in varying thicknesses for different printings. Plate proofs on card were made in five printings in 1879-93. Quantities range from 500 to 2,500 of the card proofs listed between Scott 3P and 245P.

Margin blocks with full imprint and plate number are indicated by the abbreviation "P # blk. of -."

Numbers have been assigned to all proofs consisting of the number of the regular stamp with the suffix letter "P" to denote Proof.

Proofs in other than accepted or approved colors exist in a large variety of shades, colors and papers produced at various times by various people for many different reasons. The field is large. The task of listing has been begun under "Trial Colors" following the regular proofs.

Values are for items in very fine condition.

The editors are indebted to the Essay-Proof Society, through co-operation of its catalogue advisory committee, for help in preparing this section. Most "Panama-Pacific" small die proofs are toned. Values are for moderately toned examples.

NORMAL COLORS

1845

New York

			DIE (1) Large	DIE (2) Small	(2a)	PLATE (3) India	PLATE (4) Card
9X1P	5c	black on India paper	500.	300.		250.	
a.		With scar on neck		275.			
b.		Dot in "P" of "POST" and scar on neck	375.	275.			
c.		As "b" on Bond	375.	275.			225.
d.		As "b" on glazed paper	375.				

The above listed Large Die varieties have an additional impression of the portrait medallion. Plate proofs from the sheet of 9 also exist on white and bluish bond paper. Value $125.

Providence, R.I.

			Large	Small	(2a)	India	Card
10X1P	5c	black					325.
10X2P	10c	black					425.
		Sheet of 12					4,000.

General Issues

1847

			Large	Small	(2a)	India	Card
1P	5c	red brown on India paper	950.	750.		500.	
a.		White bond paper	950.	750.			
b.		Colored bond paper	950.				
c.		White laid paper	950.	750.			
d.		Bluish laid paper	950.	750.			
e.		Yellowish wove paper	950.				
f.		Bluish wove paper	950.				
g.		White wove paper	950.				
h.		Card		750.			
i.		Glazed paper	950.				
2P	10c	black on India paper	950.	750.		750.	
a.		White bond paper	950.	750.			
b.		Colored bond paper	950.				
c.		White laid paper	950.				
d.		Bluish laid paper	950.				
e.		Yellowish wove paper	950.				
g.		White wove paper	950.				
h.		Card		750.			
i.		Glazed paper	950.				

Original die proofs are generally found cut to stamp size.

Plate proofs overprinted "Specimen" sell for about half the above figures.

Reproductions of 1847 Issue

Actually, official imitations made about 1875 from new dies and plates by order of the Post Office Department.

			Large	Small	(2a)	India	Card
3P	5c	red brown	900.	400.	1,500.	160.	110.
		Block of four				750.	500.
a.		On bond paper		650.			
4P	10c	black	900.	400.	1,500.	160.	110.
		Block of four				750.	500.
a.		On bond paper		650.			

1851-60

			Large	Small	(2a)	India	Card
5P	1c	blue, type I	5,000.				
11P	3c	red, type I	5,000.				
		brush obliteration				600.	
		Block of four				3,000.	
12P	5c	brown, type I	5,000.		1,650.		
13P	10c	green, type I	5,000.				
17P	12c	black	5,000.				
24P	1c	blue, type V (pl. 9)				900.	
		Pair				2,300.	
26P	3c	red, type II (pl. 20)				900.	
30P	5c	brown, type II				900.	
35P	10c	green, type V				700.	
36P	12c	black, plate III (broken frame lines)				700.	
		Block of four				2,700.	
37P	24c	lilac	2,200.			525.	
		Pair				1,400.	
38P	30c	orange	2,200.	550.		525.	
		Pair				1,400.	
39P	90c	blue	2,200.	550.		775.	
		Pair				1,650.	

Plate proofs of 24P to 39P are from the original plates. They may be distinguished from the 40P to 47P by the type in the case of the 1c, 3c, 10c and 12c, and by the color in the case of the 5c, 24c, 30c and 90c.

The 3c plate proofs (No. 11) are on proof paper and nearly all known copies have a vertical brush stroke obliteration.

Reprints of 1857-60 Issue

			Large	Small	(2a)	India	Card
40P	1c	bright blue, type I (new plate)	400.	425.	1,500.	65.	45.
		Block of four				325.	225.
41P	3c	scarlet, type I (new plate)	400.	425.	1,500.	65.	45.
		Block of four				325.	225.
42P	5c	orange brown type II (plate II)	400.	425.		65.	45.
		Block of four				325.	225.
		P# blk. of 8				850.	—
43P	10c	blue green, type I (new plate)	400.	425.	1,500.	65.	45.
		Block of four				325.	225.
44P	12c	greenish black (new plate, frame line complete)	400.	425.	1,500.	95.	45.
		Block of four				475.	225.
45P	24c	blksh vio (pl. I)	400.	425.	1,500.	65.	45.
		Block of four				325.	225.
		P# blk. of 8				850.	
46P	30c	yel org (pl. I)	400.	425.	1,500.	65.	45.
		Block of four				325.	225.
		P# blk. of 8				975.	—
47P	90c	deep blue (pl. I)	400.	425.	1,500.	95.	65.
		Block of four				475.	325.
		P# blk. of 8				975.	925.

Nos. 40P-47P, large die, exist only as hybrids.

FIRST DESIGNS

1861

			Large	Small	(2a)	India	Card
55P	1c	indigo	1,350.	350.		200.	
		Block of four				1,000.	
56P	3c	red	1,350.	350.	1,750.	125.	
		Block of four				725.	
57P	5c	brown		350.	1,750.	125.	
		Block of four				725.	
		P# blk. of 12				3,000.	
58P	10c	dark green		350.		125.	
		Block of four				725.	
59P	12c	black	1,350.	500.	1,750.	250.	
		Block of four				1,250.	
60P	24c	violet	900.	400.	1,750.	125.	
		Block of four				725.	
61P	30c	red orange	1,750.	400.	1,750.	250.	
		Block of four				1,300.	
62P	90c	blue	1,350.	400.	1,750.	250.	
		Block of four				1,300.	

SECOND DESIGNS (Regular Issue)

1861

			Large	Small	(2a)	India	Card
63P	1c	blue	700.	275.	1,600.	45.	30.
		Block of four				200.	225.
		P# blk. of 8				1,100.	—
		Indigo			1,600.		
64P	3c	pink	3,500.	—			
65P	3c	rose	1,000.	—	1,600.	87.50	80.
		Block of four				525.	
		P# blk. of 8				1,350.	
a.		3c dull red				87.50	
66P	3c	lake		325.	1,600.	95.	
		Block of four				550.	
		P# blk. of 8				1,400.	
67P	5c	buff			1,600.		
76P	5c	brown	700.	250.	1,600.	40.	25.
		Block of four				200.	110.
		P# blk. of 8				775.	—
68P	10c	green	650.	250.	1,600.	60.	25.
		Block of four				275.	110.
		P# blk. of 8				875.	—
69P	12c	black	700.	250.	1,600.	60.	25.
		Block of four				275.	110.
		P# blk. of 8				875.	—
70P	24c	red lilac			2,100.		225.
78P	24c	lilac		250.	2,100.	75.	62.50
		Block of four				375.	300.
		P# blk. of 8				1,100.	—
71P	30c	orange	500.	300.	1,600.	45.	25.
		Block of four				225.	125.
		P# blk. of 8				1,000.	—
72P	90c	blue	500.	300.	1,600.	45.	25.
		Block of four				225.	125.
		P# blk. of 8				1,000.	—

1861-66

No.	Denom.	Description	Large (1)	Small (2)	(2a)	India (3)	Card (4)
73P	2c	black, die I	3,000.			100.	
		Block of four				500.	
		P# blk. of 8				1,500.	—
	a.	Die II	2,500.	1,500.	5,000.	90.	72.50
	a.	Block of four				450.	400.
	a.	P # blk. of 8				1,350.	—
74P	3c	scarlet	2,250.	450.	1,600.	82.50	100.
		Block of four				425.	450.
		P# blk. of 8					—
77P	15c	black	1,250.	550.	2,500.	45.	32.50
		Block of four				225.	150.
		P# blk. of 8				875.	—

The listed plate proofs of the 1c (63P), 5c (76P), 10c (68P) and 12c (69P) are from the 100 subject re-issue plates of 1875. The 2c Die II has a small dot on the left cheek.

1869

No.	Denom.	Description	Large (1)	Small (2)	(2a)	India (3)	Card (4)
112P	1c	buff	1,400.	650.	1,800.	50.	55.
		Block of four				225.	250.
		P# blk. of 10				750.	
113P	2c	brown	1,400.		1,800.	35.	37.50
		Block of four				150.	165.
		P# blk. of 10				600.	—
114P	3c	ultra.	1,750.	650.	1,800.	40.	42.50
		Block of four				165.	190.
		P# blk. of 10				800.	—
115P	6c	ultra.	1,500.	650.	1,800.	40.	45.
		Block of four				165.	235.
		P# blk. of 10				800.	—
116P	10c	yellow	1,500.	650.	1,800.	40.	45.
		Block of four				165.	235.
		P# blk. of 10				800.	—
117P	12c	green	1,500.	650.	1,800.	42.50	50.
		Block of four				190.	265.
		P# blk. of 10				875.	—
119P	15c	brown & blue (type II)	850.	700.	1,800.	110.	
		Block of four				550.	
		P# blk. of 8				1,450.	
129P	15c	Reissue (type III)	850.	700.	1,800.	225.	62.50
		Block of four				1,050.	340.
		P# blk. of 8				3,000.	—
	a.	Center inverted *(100)*					3,250.
	a.	Block of four					14,000.
	a.	P# blk. of 8					37,500.
120P	24c	green & violet	850.	700.	1,800.	125.	110.
		Block of four				550.	550.
		P# blk. of 8				1,450.	—
	a.	Center inverted *(100)*					3,250.
	a.	Block of four					14,000.
	a.	P# blk. of 8					37,500.
121P	30c	bl. & carmine	1,400.	700.	1,800.	125.	135.
		Block of four				550.	750.
		P# blk. of 8				1,450.	—
	a.	Flags inverted *(100)*					3,250.
	a.	Block of four					14,000.
	a.	P# blk. of 8					37,500.
122P	90c	carmine & black	850.	700.	1,800.	165.	135.
		Block of four				750.	750.
		P# blk. of 8				1,750.	—
	a.	Center inverted *(100)*					3,250.
	a.	Block of four					14,000.
	a.	P# blk. of 8					37,500.

Large die proofs of Nos. 119, 129, 120 and 122 exist only as hybrids.

1880

No.	Denom.	Description	Large (1)	Small (2)	(2a)	India (3)	Card (4)
133P	1c	dark buff	1,400.			70.	
		Block of four				350.	
		P# blk. of 10				1,100.	

1870-71 — National Bank Note Co.

No.	Denom.	Description	Large (1)	Small (2)	(2a)	India (3)	Card (4)
145P	1c	ultra	450.	250.	900.	16.50	
		Block of four				70.	
		P# blk. of 12				385.	
146P	2c	red brown	450.			16.50	
		Block of four				70.	
		P# blk. of 12				385.	
147P	3c	green	500.			20.	
		Block of four				82.50	
		P# blk. of 12				400.	
148P	6c	carmine	600.			35.	
		Block of four				150.	
		P# blk. of 12				650.	
149P	7c	vermilion	375.			15.	
		Block of four				67.50	
		P# blk. of 12				360.	
150P	10c	brown	500.			37.50	
		Block of four				165.	
		P# blk. of 12				750.	
151P	12c	violet	400.			16.50	
		Block of four				70.	
		P# blk. of 12				385.	
152P	15c	orange	450.			30.	
		Block of four				135.	
		P# blk. of 12				550.	
153P	24c	purple	450.			30.	
		Block of four				135.	
		P# blk. of 12				550.	
154P	30c	black	450.			37.50	
		Block of four				165.	
		P# blk. of 12				750.	
155P	90c	carmine	450.			45.	
		Block of four				195.	
		P# blk. of 12				800.	

Secret Marks on 24, 30 and 90c Dies of the Bank Note Issues

National 24c - Rays of lower star normal.

Continental 24c - Rays of lower star strengthened.

National 30c - Lower line does not join point of shield.

Continental and American 30c - Lower line joins point of shield and bottom line of shield thicker.

National 90c - Rays of star in upper right normal.

Continental and American 90c - Rays of star in upper right strengthened.

1873 — Continental Bank Note Co.

No.	Denom.	Description	DIE (1) Large	(2) Small	(2a)	PLATE (3) India	(4) Card
156P	1c	ultra.	750.			55.	95.
		Block of four				250.	
		P# blk. of 14				1,150.	
157P	2c	brown	600.	265.	900.	35.	16.50
		Block of four				165.	82.50
		P# blk. of 12				650.	—
158P	3c	green	600.	265.	900.	55.	110.
		Block of four				250.	
		P# blk. of 14				1,150.	
159P	6c	pink	1,000.	300.	900.	110.	150.
		Block of four				525.	
		P# blk. of 12				2,000.	
160P	7c	orange vermilion	450.	265.	900.	35.	11.
		Block of four				165.	55.
		P# blk. of 14				825.	—
161P	10c	brown	750.	285.	900.	60.	150.
		Block of four				300.	
		P# blk. of 14				1,300.	
162P	12c	blackish violet	400.	265.	900.	38.50	16.50
		Block of four				190.	77.50
		P# blk. of 14				975.	—
163P	15c	yellow orange	650.	265.	900.	65.	19.
		Block of four				250.	100.
		P# blk. of 12				1,000.	—
164P	24c	violet	650.	265.	900.	50.	27.50
		Block of four				225.	125.
		P# blk. of 12				975.	
165P	30c	gray black	650.	265.	900.	37.50	16.50
		Block of four				190.	75.
		P# blk. of 12				825.	
166P	90c	rose carmine	650.	265.	900.	55.	38.50
		Block of four				250.	175.
		P# blk. of 12				1,000.	

Die proofs of the 24c, 30c and 90c show secret marks, as illustrated, but as plates of these denominations were not made from these dies, plate proofs can be identified only by color.

No.	Denom.	Description	DIE (1) Large	(2) Small	(2a)	PLATE (3) India	(4) Card
182P	1c	gray blue	850.			60.	
		Block of four				275.	
		P# blk. of 12				1,000.	
183P	2c	vermilion	500.	275.	900.	25.	11.
		Block of four				110.	60.
		P# blk. of 12				450.	—
185P	5c	blue	600.	275.	900.	55.	19.
		Block of four				250.	90.
		P# blk. of 12				1,000.	—

1881-82 — American Bank Note Co.

No.	Denom.	Description	DIE (1) Large	(2) Small	(2a)	PLATE (3) India	(4) Card
205P	5c	yellow brown	350.	275.	900.	36.	14.
		Block of four				160.	68.50
		P# blk. of 12				600.	—
206P	1c	blue	550.	275.	900.	36.	16.50
		Block of four				160.	75.
		P# blk. of 12				600.	—
207P	3c	blue green	550.	275.	900.	36.	16.50
		Block of four				160.	75.
		P# blk. of 12				600.	—
208P	6c	rose	1,100.	275.	900.	87.50	44.
		Block of four				425.	190.
		P# blk. of 12				—	—
	a.	6c brown red			900.		50.
209P	10c	brown	1,100.	275.	900.	38.50	22.
		Block of four				165.	95.
		P# blk. of 12				650.	—

1883

No.	Denom.	Description	DIE (1) Large	(2) Small	(2a)	PLATE (3) India	(4) Card
210P	2c	red brown	550.	275.	900.	32.50	19.
		Block of four				145.	82.50
		P# blk. of 12				600.	—
211P	4c	green	550.	275.	900.	38.50	25.
		Block of four				165.	110.
		P# blk. of 12				750.	—

1887-88

No.	Denom.	Description	DIE (1) Large	(2) Small	(2a)	PLATE (3) India	(4) Card
212P	1c	ultra.	950.	275.	900.	95.	1,000.
		Block of four				450.	—
		P# blk. of 12				1,800.	
213P	2c	green	600.	275.	900.	36.	19.
		Block of four				160.	82.50
		P# blk. of 12				625.	—
214P	3c	vermilion	650.	275.	900.	38.50	25.
		Block of four				165.	110.
		P# blk. of 12				—	—

Nos. 207P-1 & 214P-1 inscribed: "Worked over by new company, June 29th, 1881."

No.	Denom.	Description	DIE (1) Large	(2) Small	(2a)	PLATE (3) India	(4) Card
215P	4c	carmine	900.	275.	900.	95.	38.50
		Block of four				475.	165.
		P# blk. of 12					—
216P	5c	indigo	900.	275.	900.	60.	25.
		Block of four				300.	110.
		P# blk. of 12					—
217P	30c	org. brown	1,000.	275.	900.	60.	25.
		Block of four				300.	110.
		P# blk. of 10					—
218P	90c	purple	1,000.	275.	900.	87.50	38.50
		Block of four				400.	165.
		P# blk. of 10					

1890-93

No.	Denom.	Description	DIE (1) Large	(2) Small	(2a)	PLATE (3) India	(4) Card
219P	1c	ultra.	300.	275.	550.	25.	36.
		Block of four				110.	160.
		P# blk. of 12				500.	650.
219DP	2c	lake	800.	275.	550.	82.50	165.
		Block of four				385.	700.
		P# blk. of 12				1,650.	3,250.
220P	2c	carmine	700.	275.		225.	150.
		Block of four				1,000.	650.
		P# blk. of 12				3,850.	2,500.
221P	3c	purple	300.	275.	550.	36.	22.
		Block of four				160.	95.
		P# blk. of 12				650.	600.
222P	4c	dark brown	300.	275.	550.	36.	22.
		Block of four				160.	95.
		P# blk. of 12				650.	600.
223P	5c	chocolate	300.	275.	550.	32.50	19.
		Block of four				135.	82.50
		P# blk. of 12				600.	625.
224P	6c	brown red	300.	275.	550.	32.50	19.
		Block of four				135.	82.50
		P# blk. of 12				600.	775.
225P	8c	lilac	850.	275.	550.	55.	110.
		Block of four				250.	500.
		P# blk. of 12				1,100.	2,000.
226P	10c	green	300.	275.	550.	38.50	38.50
		Block of four				165.	165.
		P# blk. of 12				700.	750.
227P	15c	indigo	400.	275.	550.	45.	38.50
		Block of four				190.	165.
		P# blk. of 12				825.	875.
228P	30c	black	400.	275.	550.	45.	45.
		Block of four				190.	190.
		P# blk. of 12				825.	875.
229P	90c	orange	400.	275.	550.	60.	50.
		Block of four				275.	225.
		P# blk. of 12				1,100.	1,150.

COLUMBIAN ISSUE

1893

No.	Denom.	Description	DIE (1) Large	(2) Small	(2a)	PLATE (3) India	(4) Card
230P	1c	blue	800.	450.	1,200.	40.	22.50
		Block of four				175.	110.
		P# blk. of 8				450.	340.
231P	2c	violet	800.	450.	1,200.	250.	82.50
		Block of four				1,100.	350.
		P# blk. of 8				2,500.	1,000.
232P	3c	green	800.	450.	1,200.	55.	50.
		Block of four				250.	225.
		P# blk. of 8				650.	550.
233P	4c	ultra.	800.	450.	1,200.	55.	50.
		Block of four				250.	225.
		P# blk. of 8				650.	550.

233aP	4c	blue (error) on thin card	2,750.				
234P	5c	chocolate	800.	450.	1,200.	55.	50.
		Block of four				250.	225.
		P# blk. of 8				650.	550.
235P	6c	purple	800.	450.	1,200.	60.	50.
		Block of four				275.	220.
		P# blk. of 8				825.	550.
236P	8c	magenta	800.	450.	1,200.	60.	110.
		Block of four				275.	525.
		P# blk. of 8				825.	1,350.
237P	10c	black brown	800.	450.	1,200.	60.	50.
		Block of four				275.	220.
		P# blk. of 8				825.	550.
238P	15c	dark green	800.	450.	1,200.	60.	60.
		Block of four				275.	275.
		P# blk. of 8				825.	1,500.
239P	30c	orange brown	800.	450.	1,200.	82.50	70.
		Block of four				375.	325.
		P# blk. of 8				1,250.	1,250.
240P	50c	slate blue	800.	450.	1,200.	125.	82.50
		Block of four				550.	385.
		P# blk. of 8				1,500.	1,200.
241P	$1	salmon	1,000.	550.	1,200.	150.	125.
		Block of four				700.	525.
		P# blk. of 8				1,900.	
242P	$2	brown red	1,000.	550.	1,200.	165.	135.
		Block of four				685.	600.
		P# blk. of 8				2,000.	1,600.
243P	$3	yellow green	1,000.	550.	1,200.	200.	165.
		Block of four				975.	725.
		P# blk of 8				2,750.	2,000.
244P	$4	crimson lake	1,000.	550.	1,200.	250.	190.
		Block of four				1,100.	875.
		P# blk. of 8				3,000.	2,650.
245P	$5	black	1,000.	550.	1,200.	300.	250.
		Block of four				1,250.	1,100.
		P# blk. of 8				3,500.	3,200.

This set also exists as Large Die proofs, not die sunk, but printed directly on thin card. Set value $4,725. 1c through 50c, $225 each; $1 through $5, $450 each. Nos. 234P1, 234P2 differ from issued stamp.

Bureau of Engraving and Printing

1894

246P	1c	ultra	450.				
247P	1c	blue	250.	250.	725.		100.
		Block of four					450.
		P# blk. of 6					800.
250P	2c	car (triangle I)	250.	250.			100.
		Block of four					475.
		P# blk. of 6					900.
251P	2c	car (triangle II)	250.	—			
252P	2c	car (triangle III)	400.		725.	275.	
		Block of four				1,200.	
253P	3c	purple (triangle I)	400.				
253P	3c	pur (triangle II)	325.	250.	725.		
254P	4c	dark brown	250.	250.	725.		
255P	5c	chocolate	250.	250.	725.		
256P	6c	brown					235.
		Block of four					1,000.
		P# blk. of 6					1,850.
257P	8c	violet brown	275.	250.	725.		
258P	10c	green	275.	250.	725.		
259P	15c	dark blue	300.	250.	725.		
260P	50c	orange	450.	210.	725.		
261AP	$1	black	475.	350.	725.		
262P	$2	dark blue	475.	350.			400.
		Block of four					1,700.
		P# blk. of 6					2,700.
263P	$5	dark green	650.	375.	725.		435.
		Block of four					1,800.
		P# blk. of 6					2,850.

258P to 263P (small die) are from the type II die.

1898-99

279P	1c	green	700.	375.	725.
279BP	2c	orange red			725.
280P	4c	rose brown	700.		725.
281P	5c	blue	700.	375.	725.
282P	6c	lake	700.		725.
283P	10c	orange brown (type II)	800.	375.	725.
283aP	10c	brown (type II)	800.		
284P	15c	olive green (type II)	800.	375.	725.

TRANS-MISSISSIPPI ISSUE

1898

285P	1c	green	1,000.	650.	1,000.	
286P	2c	copper red	1,000.	650.	1,000.	900.
287P	4c	orange	1,000.	650.	1,000.	
288P	5c	dull blue	1,000.	650.	1,000.	
289P	8c	violet brown	1,000.	650.	1,000.	
290P	10c	gray violet	1,000.	650.	1,000.	
291P	50c	sage green	1,000.	650.	1,000.	
292P	$1	black	1,100.	650.	1,000.	
293P	$2	orange brown	1,100.	650.	1,000.	1,850.
		Block of four				7,750.

PAN-AMERICAN ISSUE

1901

294P	1c	green & black	575.	575.	900.
295P	2c	carmine & black	575.	575.	900.
296P	4c	chocolate & black	575.	575.	900.
297P	5c	ultra & black	575.	575.	900.
298P	8c	brown violet & black	575.	575.	900.
299P	10c	yellow brown & black	575.	575.	900.

1902-03

300P	1c	green	750.	300.	750.
301P	2c	carmine	750.	300.	750.
302P	3c	purple	750.	300.	750.
303P	4c	orange brown	750.	300.	750.
304P	5c	blue	750.	300.	750.
305P	6c	lake	750.	300.	750.
306P	8c	violet black	750.	300.	750.
307P	10c	orange brown	750.	300.	750.
308P	13c	deep violet brown	750.	300.	750.
309P	15c	olive green	750.	300.	750.
310P	50c	orange	750.	300.	750.
311P	$1	black	750.	300.	750.
312P	$2	blue	750.	300.	750.
313P	$5	green	850.	375.	800.

1903

319P	2c	carmine, Die I	950.		900.
319iP	2c	carmine, Die II	950.	700.	

LOUISIANA PURCHASE ISSUE

1904

323P	1c	green	1,400.	750.	1,000.
324P	2c	carmine	1,400.	750.	1,000.
325P	3c	violet	1,400.	750.	1,000.
326P	5c	dark blue	1,400.	750.	1,000.
327P	10c	brown	1,400.	750.	1,000.

JAMESTOWN EXPOSITION ISSUE

1907

328P	1c	green	1,300.	900.	1,100.
329P	2c	carmine	1,300.	900.	1,100.
330P	5c	blue	1,300.	900.	1,100.

1908-09

331P	1c	green	1,050.	725.	800.
332P	2c	carmine	1,050.	725.	800.
333P	3c	deep violet	1,050.	725.	800.
334P	4c	brown	1,050.	725.	800.
335P	5c	blue	1,050.	725.	800.
336P	6c	red orange	1,050.	725.	800.
337P	8c	olive green	1,050.	725.	800.
338P	10c	yellow	1,050.	725.	800.
339P	13c	blue green	1,050.	725.	800.
340P	15c	pale ultramarine	1,050.	725.	800.
341P	50c	violet	1,050.	725.	800.
342P	$1	violet black	1,050.	725.	800.

LINCOLN MEMORIAL ISSUE

1909

367P	2c	carmine	1,100.	900.	1,250.

ALASKA-YUKON ISSUE

1909

370P	2c	carmine	1,100.	900.	1,250.

HUDSON-FULTON ISSUE

1909

372P	2c	carmine	1,100.	900.	1,250.

PANAMA-PACIFIC ISSUE

1912-13

397P	1c	green	1,250.	1,100.	1,100.
398P	2c	carmine	1,250.	1,100.	1,100.
399P	5c	blue	1,250.	1,100.	1,100.
400P	10c	org. yellow	1,250.	1,100.	1,100.
400AP	10c	orange	1,350.	1,100.	1,200.
398AP	2c	carmine *(Inscribed "Gatun Locks")*	*5,000.*	—	

Plates were made of this design and a large supply of stamps printed. It was discovered that the view shown did not in fact represent the Gatun Locks, but those of San Pedro Miguel. The stamps and plates were destroyed and the die altered to read Panama Canal. Only four impressions of the original die exist.

1912-19

			DIE (1) Large	(2) Small	(2a)
405P	1c	green	825.	650.	950.
406P	2c	carmine	825.	650.	950.
407P	7c	black	825.	650.	950.
414P	8c	olive green	825.	650.	950.
415P	9c	salmon red	825.	650.	950.
416P	10c	orange yellow	825.	650.	950.
434P	11c	dark green	950.		
417P	12c	claret brown	825.	650.	950.
513P	13c	apple green	950.		
418P	15c	gray	825.	650.	950.
419P	20c	ultramarine	825.	650.	950.
420P	30c	orange red	825.	650.	950.
421P	50c	violet	825.	650.	950.
423P	$1	violet black	825.	650.	950.

1918-20

524P	$5	deep green & black	1,500.
547P	$2	carmine & black	1,500.

VICTORY ISSUE

1919

537P	3c	violet	1,100.	850.

PILGRIM ISSUE

1920

548P	1c	green	1,250.	1,000.
549P	2c	carmine rose	1,250.	1,000.
550P	5c	deep blue	1,250.	1,000.

1922-26

			LARGE DIE (1) India	(1a) White Wove	PLATE (3) White Wove	(4) Card
551P	½c	olive brown	800.		—	—
552P	1c	deep green	800.	500.	—	
553P	1½c	yellow brown	800.		—	
554P	2c	carmine	800.	500.	—	
555P	3c	violet	800.	500.	—	
556P	4c	yellow brown	800.	500.	—	
557P	5c	dark blue	800.	500.	—	
558P	6c	red orange	800.	500.	—	
559P	7c	black	800.	500.	—	
560P	8c	olive green	800.	500.	—	
561P	9c	rose	800.	500.	—	
562P	10c	orange	800.	500.	—	
563P	11c	light blue	1,200.	500.	—	
564P	12c	brown violet	750.	500.	—	
622P	13c	green	1,000.	500.	—	
565P	14c	dark blue	750.	500.	—	
566P	15c	gray	1,000.	500.	—	
623P	17c	black	800.		—	
567P	20c	carmine rose	800.	500.	—	
568P	25c	deep green	800.	500.	—	
569P	30c	olive brown	800.	500.	—	
570P	50c	lilac	800.	500.	—	
571P	$1	violet brown	800.	500.	—	
572P	$2	deep blue	1,100.	500.	—	
573P	$5	carmine & dark blue	1,100.			

			SMALL DIE (2) India
572P	$2	deep blue	—

No. 573P1 exists only as a hybrid.

1923-26

		LARGE DIE (1) India	(1a) White Wove	SMALL DIE (2) White or Yellowish Wove
611P	Harding, 2c black	1000.	700.	700.
614P	Huguenot Walloon, 1c dark green	650.	600.	600.
615P	Huguenot Walloon, 2c carmine rose	650.	600.	600.
616P	Huguenot Walloon, 5c dark blue	650.	600.	600.
617P	Lexington Concord, 1c deep green	650.	600.	600.
618P	Lexington Concord, 2c carmine rose	650.	600.	600.
619P	Lexington Concord, 5c dark blue	650.	600.	600.
620P	Norse American, 2c car. & blk.	750.	750.	750.
621P	Norse American, 5c dk. bl. & blk.	750.	750.	750.
627P	Sesquicentennial, 2c carmine rose	700.	650.	750.
628P	Ericsson, 5c gray lilac	700.	650.	750.
629P	White Plains, 2c carmine rose	700.	650.	750.

1927-29

643P	Vermont, 2c carmine rose	700.	650.	750.
644P	Burgoyne, 2c carmine rose	700.	650.	750.
645P	Valley Forge, 2c carmine rose	700.	650.	750.
649P	Aeronautics, 2c carmine rose	1,250.	900.	900.
650P	Aeronautics, 5c blue	1,250.	900.	900.
651P	Clark, 2c carmine & black	800.	700.	650.
654P	Edison, 2c carmine rose	800.	700.	650.
657P	Sullivan, 2c carmine rose	750.	700.	650.
680P	Fallen Timbers, 2c carmine rose	750.	700.	650.
681P	Ohio River Canalization, 2c carmine rose	750.	700.	650.

1930-31

682P	Massachusetts Bay, 2c carmine rose	750.	700.	650.
683P	Carolina Charleston, 2c carmine rose	750.	700.	650.
684P	1½c brown	650.		
685P	4c brown	650.		
688P	Braddock's Field, 2c carmine rose	750.	700.	650.
689P	von Steuben, 2c carmine rose	750.	700.	650.
690P	Pulaski, 2c carmine rose	750.	700.	650.
702P	Red Cross, 2c black & red		700.	650.
703P	Yorktown, 2c carmine rose & black	1,000.	700.	650.

1932

No.	Description	Die (1) Large	Die (2) Small	Plate
704P	Bicentennial, ½c olive brown	850.	800.	750.
705P	Bicentennial, 1c green	850.	800.	750.
706P	Bicentennial, 1½c brown	850.	800.	750.
707P	Bicentennial, 2c carmine rose	850.	800.	750.
708P	Bicentennial, 3c deep violet	850.	800.	750.
709P	Bicentennial, 4c light brown	850.	800.	750.
710P	Bicentennial, 5c blue	850.	800.	750.
711P	Bicentennial, 6c red orange	850.	800.	750.
712P	Bicentennial, 7c black	850.	800.	750.
713P	Bicentennial, 8c olive bister	850.	800.	750.
714P	Bicentennial, 9c pale red	850.	800.	750.
715P	Bicentennial, 10c org. yellow	850.	800.	750.
716P	Winter Games, 2c carmine rose	1,000.	850.	800.
717P	Arbor Day, 2c carmine rose	800.	800.	700.
718P	Olympic Games, 3c violet	1,100.	850.	800.
719P	Olympic Games, 5c blue	1,100.	850.	800.
720P	3c deep violet	700.		
724P	Penn, 3c violet	700.	650.	650.
725P	Webster, 3c violet	700.	650.	650.

1933-34

No.	Description	Die (1) Large	Die (2) Small	Plate
726P	Georgia, 3c violet	700.	650.	650.
727P	Peace, 3c violet	700.	650.	650.
728P	Century of Progress, 1c yellow green	700.	650.	650.
729P	Century of Progress, 3c violet	700.	650.	650.
732P	N.R.A., 3c violet		650.	650.
733P	Byrd Antarctic, 3c dark blue		650.	650.
734P	Kosciuszko, 5c blue		650.	650.
736P	Maryland, 3c carmine rose		650.	650.
737P	Mothers Day, 3c deep violet	800.	650.	650.
739P	Wisconsin, 3c deep violet		650.	650.
740P	Parks, 1c green			650.
741P	Parks, 2c red			650.
742P	Parks, 3c violet			650.
743P	Parks, 4c brown			650.
744P	Parks, 5c blue			650.
745P	Parks, 6c dark blue			650.
746P	Parks, 7c black			650.
747P	Parks, 8c sage green			650.
748P	Parks, 9c red orange	800.		650.
749P	Parks, 10c gray black			650.

1935-37

No.	Description	Die (1) Large	Die (2) Small	Plate
772P	Conn., 3c violet			650.
773P	San Diego, 3c purple			650.
774P	Boulder Dam, 3c purple			650.
775P	Michigan, 3c purple			650.
776P	Texas, 3c purple			650.
777P	Rhode Is., 3c purple			650.
782P	Arkansas, 3c pur.	800.		650.
783P	Oregon, 3c purple	—	600.	650.
784P	Anthony, 3c violet			650.
785P	Army, 1c green			650.
786P	Army, 2c carmine			650.
787P	Army, 3c purple	800.		650.
788P	Army, 4c gray			650.
789P	Army, 5c ultramarine		800.	650.
790P	Navy, 1c green			650.
791P	Navy, 2c car.	800.		650.
792P	Navy, 3c purple			650.
793P	Navy, 4c gray			650.
794P	Navy, 5c ultramarine			650.
795P	Ordinance, 3c red violet			650.
796P	Virginia Dare, 5c gray blue	800.		650.
797P	S.P.A. Sheet, 10c blue green			650.
798P	Constitution, 3c red violet	800.		650.
799P	Hawaii, 3c violet			650.
800P	Alaska, 3c violet			650.
801P	Puerto Rico, 3c bright violet	800.		650.
802P	Virgin Is., 3c light violet	—		650.

PRESIDENTIAL ISSUE

1938

No.	Description	Die (1) Large	Die (2) Small	Plate
803P	½c deep orange	1,000.		650.
804P	1c green			650.
805P	1½c bister brown			650.
806P	2c rose carmine			650.
807P	3c deep violet			650.
808P	4c red violet			650.
809P	4½c dark gray			650.
810P	5c bright blue	1,000.		650.
811P	6c red orange			650.
812P	7c sepia			650.
813P	8c olive green			650.
814P	9c olive green			650.
815P	10c brown red			650.
816P	11c ultramarine			650.
817P	12c bright violet	1,000.		650.
818P	13c blue green			650.
819P	14c blue			650.
820P	15c blue gray			650.
821P	16c black	1,000.		650.
822P	17c rose red			650.
823P	18c brown carmine			650.
824P	19c bright violet			650.
825P	20c bright blue green			650.
826P	21c dull blue			650.
827P	22c vermilion			650.
828P	24c gray black			650.
829P	25c deep red lilac			650.
830P	30c deep ultramarine			650.
831P	50c light red violet			650.
832P	$1 purple & black			650.
833P	$2 yellow green & black			800.
834P	$5 carmine & black			800.

1938

No.	Description	Die (1) Large	Die (2) Small	Plate
835P	Constitution, 3c deep violet			600.
836P	Delaware, 3c red violet			600.
837P	N.W. Territory, 3c bright violet			600.
838P	Iowa, 3c violet	850.		600.

1939

No.	Description	Die (1) Large	Die (2) Small	Plate
852P	Golden Gate, 3c bright purple			600.
853P	World's Fair, 3c deep purple			600.
854P	Inauguration, 3c bright red violet	850.		600.
855P	Baseball, 3c violet			600.
856P	Panama Canal, 3c deep red violet			600.
857P	Printing, 3c violet			600.
858P	Statehood, 3c rose violet			600.

FAMOUS AMERICANS ISSUE

1940

No.	Description	Die (1) Large	Die (2) Small	Plate
859P	Authors, 1c bright blue green			800.
860P	Authors, 2c rose carmine			800.
861P	Authors, 3c bright red violet			800.
862P	Authors, 5c ultramarine	850.		800.
863P	Authors, 10c dark brown			800.
864P	Poets, 1c bright blue green			800.
865P	Poets, 2c rose carmine			800.
866P	Poets, 3c bright red violet			800.
867P	Poets, 5c ultramarine			800.
868P	Poets, 10c dark brown			800.
869P	Educators, 1c bright blue green			800.
870P	Educators, 2c rose carmine			800.
871P	Educators, 3c bright red violet			800.
872P	Educators, 5c ultramarine			800.
873P	Educators, 10c dark brown			800.
874P	Scientists, 1c bright blue green			800.
875P	Scientists, 2c rose carmine	900.		800.
876P	Scientists, 3c bright red violet			800.
877P	Scientists, 5c ultramarine			800.
878P	Scientists, 10c dark brown			800.
879P	Composers, 1c bright blue green			800.
880P	Composers, 2c rose carmine			800.
881P	Composers, 3c bright red violet			800.
882P	Composers, 5c ultramarine	900.		800.
883P	Composers, 10c dark brown			800.
884P	Artists, 1c bright blue green			800.
885P	Artists, 2c rose carmine			800.
886P	Artists, 3c bright red violet			800.
887P	Artists, 5c ultramarine			800.
888P	Artists, 10c dark brown			800.
889P	Inventors, 1c bright blue green			800.
890P	Inventors, 2c rose carmine			800.
891P	Inventors, 3c bright red violet	900.		800.
892P	Inventors, 5c ultramarine			800.
893P	Inventors, 10c dark brown			800.

1940

No.	Description	Die (1) Large	Die (2) Small	Plate
894P	Pony Express, 3c henna brown			500.
895P	Pan American, 3c light violet			500.
896P	Idaho, 3c bright violet			500.
897P	Wyoming, 3c brown violet			500.
898P	Coronado, 3c violet			500.
899P	Defense, 1c bright blue green	600.		500.
900P	Defense, 2c rose carmine			500.
901P	Defense, 3c bright violet			500.
902P	Emancipation, 3c deep violet	600.		500.

1941-44

No.	Description	Die (1) Large	Die (2) Small	Plate
903P	Vermont, 3c light violet			500.
904P	Kentucky, 3c violet			500.
905P	Win the War, 3c violet			500.
906P	China, 5c bright blue			500.
907P	Allied Nations, 2c rose carmine			500.
908P	Four Freedoms, 1c bright blue green	600.		500.
922P	Railroad, 3c violet	600.		500.
923P	Steamship, 3c violet			500.
924P	Telegraph, 3c bright red violet	600.		500.
925P	Corregidor, 3c deep violet			500.
926P	Motion Picture, 3c deep violet	600.		500.

1945-46

No.	Description	Die (1) Large	Die (2) Small	Plate
927P	Florida, 3c bright red violet			500.
928P	United Nations, 5c ultramarine			500.
929P	Iwo Jima, 3c yellow green			500.
930P	Roosevelt, 1c blue green			500.
931P	Roosevelt, 2c carmine rose	600.		500.
932P	Roosevelt, 3c purple			500.
934P	Army, 3c olive	600.		500.
935P	Navy, 3c blue	600.		500.
941P	Tennessee	600.		
942P	Iowa	600.		
944P	Kearny	600.		

1947-50

No.	Description	Die (1) Large	Die (2) Small	Plate
945P	Edison	600.		
946P	Pulitzer	600.		
949P	Doctors	600.		
951P	Constitution	600.		
958P	Wisconsin	600.		
959P	Women	600.		
962P	Key	600.		
965P	Stone	600.		
973P	Rough Riders	600.		
981P	Minnesota Terr., 3c blue green	600.	—	
983P	Puerto Rico	600.		
991P	Supreme Court	600.		
992P	Capitol	600.		

1951-53

No.	Description	Die (1) Large	Die (2) Small	Plate
1000P	Cadillac	600.		
1001P	Colorado	600.		
1002P	Chemical, 3c violet brown	600.		
1003P	Brooklyn	600.		
1004P	Betsy Ross	600.		
1005P	4H Clubs	600.		
1007P	A.A.A., 3c deep blue	600.	—	
1009P	Grand Coulee Dam, 3c blue green	600.		
1011P	Mt. Rushmore, 3c blue green	600.	—	
1017P	National Guard 3c bright blue	600.		
1018P	Ohio Statehood, 3c chocolate		—	
1019P	Washington	600.		
1020P	Louisiana	600.		
1021P	Japan	600.		
1022P	American Bar	600.		
1026P	Gen. Patton, 3c blue violet	600.	—	

1954

No.	Description	Die (1) Large	Die (2) Small	Plate
1029P	Columbia	600.		

LIBERTY ISSUE

No.	Description	Die (1) Large	Die (2) Small	Plate
1031P	Washington	600.		
1032P	Mount Vernon	600.		
1033P	Jefferson		—	
1036P	Lincoln	600.		
1038P	Monroe	600.		
1039P	Roosevelt		—	
1047P	Monticello	600.		
1050P	Marshall	600.		
1051P	Anthony	600.		
1052P	Henry	600.		

1954-57

No.	Description	Die (1) Large	Die (2) Small	Plate
1053P	Hamilton	600.		
1060P	Nebraska	600.		
1062P	Eastman	600.		
1063P	Lewis & Clark	600.		
1068P	New Hampshire	600.		
1073P	Franklin	600.		
1074P	Washington	600.		
1076P	FIPEX, 3c deep violet	600.	—	
1077P	Turkey	600.		
1078P	Antelope	600.		
1079P	Salmon	600.		
1081P	Wheatland	600.		
1082P	Labor Day	600.		
1083P	Nassau Hall	600.		
1085P	Children	600.		
1086P	Hamilton, 3c rose red	600.	—	
1087P	Polio	600.		
1090P	Steel	600.		

AIR POST

1918

No.	Denomination	Color	DIE (1) Large	DIE (2) Small
C1P	6c	orange	9,500.	
C2P	16c	green	8,000.	
C3P	24c	carmine rose & blue	9,500.	

1923

No.	Denomination	Color	DIE (1) Large	DIE (2) Small
C4P	8c	dark green	5,500.	
C5P	16c	dark blue	5,500.	
C6P	24c	carmine	5,500.	

1926-27

No.	Denomination	Color	DIE (1) Large	DIE (2) Small
C7P	10c	dark blue	4,000.	
C8P	15c	olive brown	4,000.	—
C9P	20c	yellow green	4,000.	

LINDBERGH ISSUE

1927

C10P	10c	dark blue	4,000.	4,000.

1930

C11P	5c	car. & blue	4,250.	
C12P	5c	violet	3,300.	

ZEPPELIN ISSUE

1930

C13P	65c	green	9,250.	8,250.
	a.	on wove	9,250.	
C14P	$1.30	brown	9,500.	8,500.
	a.	on wove	9,500.	
C15P	$2.60	blue	9,500.	8,500.
	a.	on wove	9,500.	

1932

C17P	8c	olive bister	2,750.	

CENTURY OF PROGRESS ISSUE

1933

C18P	50c	green	5,750.	5,750.

1935-39

C20P	25c	blue on wove		2,750.
C21P	20c	green on wove		2,750.
C22P	50c	carmine on wove		2,750.
C23P	6c	dark blue & carm. on wove		2,750.
C24P	30c	dull blue	3,500.	2,750.

1941-53

C25P	6c	carmine on wove		2,750.
C26P	8c	olive green on wove		2,750.
C27P	10c	violet on wove		2,750.
C28P	15c	brown carmine on wove		2,750.
C29P	20c	brt. grn. on wove		2,750.
C30P	30c	blue on wove		2,750.
C31P	50c	orange on wove		2,750.
C46P	80c	brt. red violet	1,650.	
C47P	6c	carmine	1,650.	
C48P	4c	brt. blue	—	

AIR POST SPECIAL DELIVERY

1934

CE1P	16c	dk. blue on wove		2,600.
CE2P	16c	red & blue on wove		2,600.

SPECIAL DELIVERY

1885

			DIE (1) Large	DIE (2) Small	(2a)	PLATE (3) India	PLATE (4) Card
E1P	10c	blue	500.	250.	1,000.	32.50	27.50
		Block of four				150.	125.
		P# blk. of 8					—

1888

			(1)	(2)	(2a)	(3)	(4)
E2P	10c	blue	750.	250.	1,000.	32.50	27.50
		Block of four				150.	125.
		P# blk. of 8				385.	—

1893

			(1)	(2)	(2a)	(3)	(4)
E3P	10c	orange	1,100.	300.	1,100.	60.	65.
		Block of four				260.	290.
		P# blk. of 8					825.

1894

			(1)	(2)	(2a)
E4P	10c	blue	400.	250.	1,100.

1902

			(1)	(2)	(2a)
E6P	10c	ultra.	900.	250.	1,000.

1908

			(1)	(2)	(2a)
E7P	10c	green	1,750.	1,000.	1,100.

1922

			LARGE DIE (1) India	LARGE DIE (1a) White Wove
E12P	10c	deep ultra.	1,250.	1,100.

1925-54

E13P	15c	deep orange	1,250.	
E14P	20c	black	1,250.	
E20P	20c	deep blue	1,000.	

REGISTRATION

1911

			DIE (1) Large	DIE (2) Small	(2a)	PLATE (3) India	PLATE (4) Card
F1P	10c	ultra	2,500.	1,000.	1,100.		

POSTAGE DUE

1879

			(1)	(2)	(2a)	(3)	(4)
J1P	1c	brown	115.	100.	400.	19.	8.25
		Block of four				95.	55.
		P# blk. of 12				400.	
J2P	2c	brown	115.	100.	400.	18.	8.25
		block of four				82.50	55.
		P# blk. of 12				400.	
		2c dark brown	—				
J3P	3c	brown	115.	100.	400.	18.	8.25
		block of four				82.50	55.
		P# blk. of 12				400.	
		3c dark brown	—	—			
J4P	5c	brown	115.	100.	400.	18.	8.25
		block of four				82.50	55.
		P# blk. of 12				400.	
		5c dark brown	—				
J5P	10c	brown	115.	100.	400.		8.25
		10c dark brown	—			27.50	
		block of four				135.	55.
		P# blk. of 12				650.	
J6P	30c	brown	115.	100.	400.		8.25
		30c dark brown	—			27.50	
		block of four				135.	55.
		P# blk. of 12				650.	
J7P	50c	brown	115.	100.	400.		8.25
		50c dark brown	—			27.50	
		block of four				135.	55.
		P# blk. of 12				650.	

1887

			(1)	(2)	(2a)	(3)	(4)
J15P	1c	red brown			400.		11.
		Block of four					
		P# blk. of 12					
J16P	2c	red brown			400.		11.
		Block of four					
		P# blk. of 12					
J17P	3c	red brown			400.		16.50
		Block of four					
		P# blk. of 12					
J18P	5c	red brown			400.		11.
		Block of four					
		P# blk. of 12					
J19P	10c	red brown			400.	16.50	22.
		Block of four				82.50	
		P# blk. of 12				325.	
J20P	30c	red brown			400.	16.50	14.
		Block of four				82.50	
		P# blk. of 12				325.	
J21P	50c	red brown			400.	40.	22.
		Block of four				190.	
		P# blk. of 12				825.	

1891-93

			(1)	(2)	(2a)	(3)	(4)
J22P	1c	bright claret	140.	125.	400.	11.	14.
		Block of four				60.	67.50
		P# blk. of 12					—
J23P	2c	bright claret	140.	125.	400.	11.	14.
		Block of four				60.	67.50
		P# blk. of 12					—
J24P	3c	bright claret	140.	125.	400.	11.	14.
		Block of four				60.	67.50
		P# blk. of 12					—
J25P	5c	bright claret	140.	125.	400.	11.	14.
		Block of four				60.	67.50
		P# blk. of 12					—
J26P	10c	bright claret	140.	125.	400.	11.	14.
		Block of four				60.	67.50
		P# blk. of 12					—
J27P	30c	bright claret	140.	125.	400.	25.	14.
		Block of four				125.	67.50
		P# blk. of 12					—
J28P	50c	bright claret	140.	125.	400.	16.50	14.
		Block of four				77.50	67.50
		P# blk. of 12					—

1894

			(1)	(2)	(2a)	(3)	(4)
J31P	1c	claret	165.	120.	350.		
J32P	2c	claret	165.	120.	350.		67.50
		Block of four					350.
		P# blk. of 6					650.
J33P	3c	claret	165.	120.	350.		
J34P	5c	claret	165.	120.	350.		
J35P	10c	claret	165.	120.	350.		
J36P	30c	claret	165.	120.	350.		
J37P	50c	claret	165.	120.	350.		

1930-31

J69P	½c	deep carmine	450.
J70P	1c	deep carmine	450.
J71P	2c	deep carmine	450.
J72P	3c	deep carmine	450.
J73P	5c	deep carmine	450.
J74P	10c	deep carmine	450.
J75P	30c	deep carmine	450.
J76P	50c	deep carmine	450.
J77P	$1	deep carmine	450.
J78P	$5	deep carmine	450.

PARCEL POST POSTAGE DUE

1912

			DIE (1) Large	DIE (2) Small	(2a)	PLATE (3) India	PLATE (4) Card
JQ1P	1c	dark green	600.	500.	700.		
JQ2P	2c	dark green	600.	500.	700.		
JQ3P	5c	dark green	600.	500.	700.		
JQ4P	10c	dark green	600.	500.	700.		
JQ5P	25c	dark green	600.	500.	700.		

CARRIERS

1851

			(1)	(2)	(2a)	(3)	(4)
LO1P	1c	bl. *(Franklin)*	700.	200.	700.	32.60	16.50
		Block of four				165.	80.
		Cracked plate				—	—
LO2P	1c	blue *(Eagle)*	700.	200.	700.	32.50	16.50
		Block of four				165.	80.
		P # blk. of 8				675.	

Nos. LO1P (1) and LO2P (1) exist only as hybrids.

OFFICIAL

AGRICULTURE

1873

			(1)	(2)	(2a)	(3)	(4)
O1P	1c	yellow	80.	55.	275.	5.	3.75
		Block of four				25.	30.
		P# blk. of 12					—
O2P	2c	yellow	80.	55.	275.	5.	3.75
		Block of four				25.	30.
		P# blk. of 10					—
O3P	3c	yellow	80.	55.	275.	5.	3.75
		Block of four				25.	30.
		P# blk. of 12					—
O4P	6c	yellow	80.	55.	275.	5.	3.75
		Block of four				25.	30.
		P# blk. of 12					—
O5P	10c	yellow	80.	55.	275.	5.	3.75
		Block of four				25.	30.
		P# blk. of 12					—
O6P	12c	yellow	80.	55.	275.	5.	3.75
		Block of four				25.	30.
		P# blk. of 12					—
O7P	15c	yellow	80.	55.	275.	5.	3.75
		Block of four				25.	30.
		P# blk. of 12					—
O8P	24c	yellow	80.	55.	275.	5.	3.75
		Block of four				25.	30.
		P# blk. of 12					—
O9P	30c	yellow	80.	55.	275.	5.	3.75
		Block of four				25.	30.
		P# blk. of 12					—

EXECUTIVE

			(1)	(2)	(2a)	(3)	(4)
O10P	1c	carmine	100.	70.	275.	7.75	5.50
		Block of four				35.	30.
		P# blk. of 14					—
O11P	2c	carmine	100.	70.	275.	7.75	5.50
		Block of four				35.	30.
		P# blk. of 12					—
O12P	3c	carmine	100.	70.	275.	7.75	5.50
		Block of four				35.	30.
		P# blk. of 12					—
O13P	6c	carmine	100.	70.	275.	13.50	8.25
		Block of four				67.50	45.
		P# blk. of 10					—
O14P	10c	carmine	100.	70.	275.	11.	5.50
		Block of four				55.	30.
		P# blk. of 12					—

INTERIOR

			(1)	(2)	(2a)	(3)	(4)
O15P	1c	vermilion	80.	55.	275.	5.	3.75
		Block of four				35.	30.
		P# blk. of 12					—
O16P	2c	vermilion	80.	55.	275.	5.	3.75
		Block of four				35.	30.
		P# blk. of 10					—
O17P	3c	vermilion	80.	55.	275.	5.	3.75
		Block of four				35.	30.
		P# blk. of 10					—
O18P	6c	vermilion	80.	55.	275.	9.50	8.25
		Block of four				45.	40.
		P# blk. of 12					—
O19P	10c	vermilion	80.	55.	275.	5.	3.75
		Block of four				35.	30.
		P# blk. of 12					—
O20P	12c	vermilion	80.	55.	275.	5.	3.75
		Block of four				35.	30.
		P# blk. of 10					—
O21P	15c	vermilion	80.	55.	275.	5.	3.75
		Block of four				35.	30.
		P# blk. of 12					—
O22P	24c	vermilion	80.	55.	275.	5.	3.75
		Block of four				35.	30.
		P# blk. of 12					—
O23P	30c	vermilion	80.	55.	275.	5.	3.75
		Block of four				35.	30.
		P# blk. of 12					—
O24P	90c	vermilion	80.	55.	275.	6.	5.
		Block of four				50.	45.
		P# blk. of 12					—

JUSTICE

			(1)	(2)	(2a)	(3)	(4)
O25P	1c	purple	80.	55.	275.	5.	3.75
		Block of four				30.	30.
		P# blk. of 12					—
O26P	2c	purple	80.	55.	275.	5.	3.75
		Block of four				30.	30.
		P# blk. of 12					—
O27P	3c	purple	80.	55.	275.	5.	3.75
		Block of four				30.	30.
		P# blk. of 12					—
O28P	6c	purple	80.	55.	275.	5.	3.75
		Block of four				30.	30.
		P# blk. of 12					—
O29P	10c	purple	80.	55.	275.	5.	3.75
		Block of four				30.	30.
		P# blk. of 10					—
O30P	12c	purple	80.	55.	275.	5.	3.75
		Block of four				30.	30.
		P# blk. of 12					—
O31P	15c	purple	80.	55.	275.	5.	3.75
		Block of four				30.	30.
		P# blk. of 10					—
O32P	24c	purple	80.	55.	275.	6.50	5.

No.	Description	(1)	(2)	(2a)	(3)	(4)
	Block of four				45.	35.
	P# blk. of 12					—
O33P 30c	purple	80.	55.	275.	6.50	5.
	Block of four				45.	35.
	P# blk. of 12					—
O34P 90c	purple	80.	55.	275.	8.25	5.
	Block of four				50.	35.
	P# blk. of 10					—

NAVY

No.	Description	(1)	(2)	(2a)	(3)	(4)
O35P 1c	ultramarine	80.	55.	275.	5.50	3.75
	Block of four				30.	30.
	P# blk. of 12					—
O36P 2c	ultramarine	80.	55.	275.	5.50	3.75
	Block of four				30.	30.
	P# blk. of 12					—
O37P 3c	ultramarine	80.	55.	275.	5.50	3.75
	Block of four				30.	30.
	P# blk. of 10					—
O38P 6c	ultramarine	80.	55.	275.	13.50	10.
	Block of four				67.50	50.
	P# blk. of 10					—
O39P 7c	ultramarine	80.	55.	275.	6.50	6.50
	Block of four				40.	40.
	P# blk. of 10					—
O40P 10c	ultramarine	80.	55.	275.	5.50	3.75
	Block of four				30.	30.
	P# blk. of 12					—
O41P 12c	ultramarine	80.	55.	275.	5.50	3.75
	Block of four				30.	30.
	P# blk. of 12					—
O42P 15c	ultramarine	80.	55.	275.	5.50	3.75
	Block of four				30.	30.
	P# blk. of 12					—
O43P 24c	ultramarine	80.	55.	275.	6.50	3.75
	Block of four				40.	30.
	P# blk. of 12					—
O44P 30c	ultramarine	80.	55.	275.	11.	5.50
	Block of four				57.50	40.
	P# blk. of 12					—
O45P 90c	ultramarine	80.	55.	275.	7.	5.50
	Block of four				45.	40.
	P# blk. of 12					—

POST OFFICE

No.	Description	(1)	(2)	(2a)	(3)	(4)
O47P 1c	black	80.	55.	275.	4.50	3.75
	Block of four				30.	30.
	P# blk. of 10					—
O48P 2c	black	80.	55.	275.	4.50	3.75
	Block of four				30.	30.
	P# blk. of 14					—
O49P 3c	black	80.	55.	275.	4.50	3.75
	Block of four				30.	30.
	P# blk. of 12					—
O50P 6c	black	80.	55.	275.	4.50	3.75
	Block of four				30.	30.
	P# blk. of 12					—
O51P 10c	black	80.	55.	275.	5.50	5.50
	Block of four				35.	35.
	P# blk. of 12					—
O52P 12c	black	80.	55.	275.	4.50	4.50
	Block of four				30.	30.
	P# blk. of 12					—
O53P 15c	black	80.	55.	275.	4.50	5.50
	Block of four				30.	35.
	P# blk. of 12					—
O54P 24c	black	80.	55.	275.	4.50	3.75
	Block of four				30.	30.
	P# blk. of 12					—
O55P 30c	black	80.	55.	275.	4.50	3.75
	Block of four				30.	30.
	P# blk. of 12					—
O56P 90c	black	80.	55.	275.	4.50	3.75
	Block of four				30.	30.
	P# blk. of 12					—

STATE

No.	Description	(1)	(2)	(2a)	(3)	(4)
O57P 1c	green	80.	55.	275.	5.50	5.
	Block of four				37.50	32.50
	P# blk. of 12					—
O58P 2c	green	80.	55.	275.	5.50	5.
	Block of four				37.50	32.50
	P# blk. of 10					—
O59P 3c	green	80.	55.	275.	5.50	5.
	Block of four				37.50	32.50
	P# blk. of 10					—
O60P 6c	green	80.	55.	275.	16.50	11.
	Block of four				82.50	62.50
	P# blk. of 12					—
O61P 7c	green	80.	55.	275.	5.50	5.
	Block of four				37.50	32.50
	P# blk. of 12					—
O62P 10c	green	80.	55.	275.	5.50	5.
	Block of four				37.50	32.50
	P# blk. of 12					—
O63P 12c	green	80.	55.	275.	5.50	5.
	Block of four				37.50	32.50
	P# blk. of 10					—
O64P 15c	green	80.	55.	275.	5.50	5.
	Block of four				37.50	32.50
	P# blk. of 12					—
O65P 24c	green	80.	55.	275.	11.	5.
	Block of four				55.	30.
	P# blk. of 12					—
O66P 30c	green	80.	55.	275.	11.	7.
	Block of four				55.	42.50
	P# blk. of 12					—
O67P 90c	green	80.	55.	275.	11.	7.
	Block of four				55.	42.50
	P# blk. of 12					—
O68P $2	green & black	150.	125.	300.	50.	30.
	Block of four				220.	150.
	Sheet of ten				650.	
a.	Invtd. center					750.
O69P $5	green & black	150.	125.	300.	50.	30.
	Block of four				220.	150.
	Sheet of ten				650.	
a.	Invtd. center					750.
O70P $10	green & black	150.	125.	350.	50.	30.
	Block of four				220.	—
	Sheet of ten				650.	
O71P $20	green & black	150.	125.	350.	50.	30.
	Block of four				220.	150.
	Sheet of ten				650.	
a.	Invtd. center					750.

O68P to O71P Large Dies exist as hybrids only.

TREASURY

No.	Description	(1)	(2)	(2a)	(3)	(4)
O72P 1c	brown	80.	55.	275.	4.50	3.75
	Block of four				30.	30.
	P# blk. of 12					—
O73P 2c	brown	80.	55.	275.	4.50	3.75
	Block of four				30.	30.
	P# blk. of 12					—
O74P 3c	brown	80.	55.	275.	4.50	3.75
	Block of four				30.	30.
	P# blk. of 14					—
O75P 6c	brown	80.	55.	275.	12.50	12.50
	Block of four				62.50	62.50
	P# blk. of 12					—
O76P 7c	brown	80.	55.	275.	4.50	3.75
	Block of four				30.	30.
	P# blk. of 12					—
O77P 10c	brown	80.	55.	275.	4.50	3.75
	Block of four				30.	30.
	P# blk. of 12					—
O78P 12c	brown	80.	55.	275.	4.50	3.75
	Block of four				30.	30.
	P# blk. of 12					—
O79P 15c	brown	80.	55.	275.	4.50	3.75
	Block of four				30.	53.
	P# blk. of 12					—
O80P 24c	brown	80.	55.	275.	11.	8.25
	Block of four				55.	44.
	P# blk. of 12					—
O81P 30c	brown	80.	55.	275.	11.	8.25
	Block of four				55.	44.
	P# blk. of 12					—
O82P 90c	brown	80.	55.	275.	6.50	3.75
	Block of four				45.	30.
	P# blk. of 12					—

WAR

No.	Description	(1)	(2)	(2a)	(3)	(4)
O83P 1c	rose	80.	55.	275.	8.25	3.75
	Block of four				40.	30.
	P# blk. of 12					—
O84P 2c	rose	80.	55.	275.	8.25	3.75
	Block of four				40.	30.
O85P 3c	rose	80.	55.	275.	8.25	3.75
	Block of four				40.	30.
O86P 6c	rose	80.	55.	275.	8.25	3.75
	Block of four				40.	30.
	P# blk. of 12					—
O87P 7c	rose	80.	55.	275.	8.25	3.75
	Block of four				40.	30.
	P# blk. of 10					—
O88P 10c	rose	80.	55.	275.	8.25	3.75
	Block of four				40.	30.
	P# blk. of 10					—
O89P 12c	rose	80.	55.	275.	8.25	3.75
	Block of four				40.	30.
	P# blk. of 12					—
O90P 15c	rose	80.	55.	275.	8.25	3.75
	Block of four				40.	30.
	P# blk. of 12					—
O91P 24c	rose	80.	55.	275.	8.25	3.75
	Block of four				40.	30.
	P# blk. of 10					—
O92P 30c	rose	80.	55.	275.	8.25	10.
	Block of four				40.	55.
	P# blk. of 10					—
O93P 90c	rose	80.	55.	275.	8.25	3.75
	Block of four				40.	30.
	P# blk. of 12					—

O83-O93 exist in a plum snade.

POSTAL SAVINGS MAIL

1911

O124P 1c	dark violet	385.	275.	750.
O121P 2c	black	385.	275.	750.
O126P 10c	carmine	385.	275.	750.
O122P 50c	dark green	385.	275.	750.
O123P $1	ultramarine	385.	275.	750.

POSTAL SAVINGS

1911

PS1P 10c	orange	1,000.	500.
PS4P 10c	deep blue		500.

POST OFFICE SEALS

1872

No.	Description	(1)	(2)	(3)	(4)
OX1P	green	275.	165.	60.	36.
	Block of four			275.	
a.	Wove paper	100.			
b.	Glazed paper	190.			

1877

No.	Description	(1)	(2)	(3)	(4)
OX3P	brown			18.	
	Block of four			80.	

1879

No.	Description	(1)	(2)	(3)	(4)
OX4P	brown	2,500.	110.	15.	
	Block of four			65.	

1888-94

No.	Color	DIE (2) Small
OX6bP	chocolate	140.

1901-03

No.	Color	DIE (2) Small
OX10P	yellow brown	100.
OX10aP	gray brown	100.
OX10bP	red brown	100.
OX10cP	dark brown	100.
OX10dP	orange brown	100.

NEWSPAPERS

1865

No.	Description	DIE (1) Large	DIE (2) Small	(2a)	PLATE (3) Wove Paper	PLATE (4) Card
PR2P 10c	green	275.	125.		36.50	45.
	Block of four				180.	225.
	P# blk. of 6					—
PR3P 25c	orange red	275.	125.		40.	45.
	Block of four				200.	225.
	P# blk. of 6					—
PR4P 5c	blue	275.	125.		36.50	45.
	Block of four				180.	225.
	P# blk. of 6					—

1875

No.	Description	(1)	(2)	(2a)	(3)	(4)
PR5P 5c	dark blue			750.		24.
PR6P 10c	deep green			750.		27.50
PR7P 25c	dark carmine red			750.		27.50
PR9P 2c	black	80.	40.	250.	5.50	3.25
	Block of four				25.	19.
	P# blk. of 8					—
PR10P 3c	black	80.	40.	250.	5.50	3.25
	Block of four				25.	19.
	P# blk. of 8					—
PR11P 4c	black	80.	40.	250.	5.50	3.25
	Block of four				25.	19.
	P# blk. of 8					—
PR12P 6c	black	80.	40.	250.	5.50	3.25
	Block of four				25.	19.
	P# blk. of 8					—
PR13P 8c	black	80.	40.	250.	5.50	3.25
	Block of four				25.	19.
	P# blk. of 8					—
PR14P 9c	black	80.	40.	250.	5.50	3.25
	Block of four				25.	19.
	P# blk. of 8					—
PR15P 10c	black	80.	40.	250.	5.50	3.25
	Block of four				25.	19.
	P# blk. of 8					—
PR16P 12c	rose	80.	40.	250.	5.50	4.50
	Block of four				25.	25.
	P# blk. of 8					—
PR17P 24c	rose	80.	40.	250.	5.50	4.50
	Block of four				25.	25.
	P# blk. of 8					—
PR18P 36c	rose	80.	40.	250.	5.50	4.50
	Block of four				25.	25.
	P# blk. of 8					—
PR19P 48c	rose	80.	40.	250.	5.50	4.50
	Block of four				25.	25.
	P# blk. of 8					—
PR20P 60c	rose	80.	40.	250.	5.50	4.50
	Block of four				25.	25.
	P# blk. of 8					—
PR21P 72c	rose	80.	40.	250.	5.50	4.50
	Block of four				25.	25.
	P# blk. of 8					—
PR22P 84c	rose	80.	40.	250.	5.50	4.50
	Block of four				25.	25.
	P# blk. of 8					—
PR23P 96c	rose	80.	40.	250.	5.50	4.50
	Block of four				25.	25.
	P# blk. of 8					—
PR24P $1.92	dark brown	80.	40.	250.	7.75	5.50
	Block of four				38.50	30.
	P# blk. of 8					—
PR25P $3	ver	80.	40.	250.	7.75	5.50
	Block of four				38.50	30.
	P# blk. of 8					—
PR26P $6	ultra	80.	40.	250.	7.75	5.50
	Block of four				38.50	30.
	P# blk. of 8					—
PR27P $9	yellow	80.	40.	250.	7.75	5.50
	Block of four				38.50	30.
	P# blk. of 8					—
PR28P $12	blue green	80.	40.	250.	8.75	5.50
	Block of four				44.	30.
	P# blk. of 8					—
PR29P $24	dark gray violet	80.	40.	250.	10.	6.50
	Block of four				50.	42.50
	P# blk. of 8					—
PR30P $36	brown rose	80.	40.	250.	11.	6.50
	Block of four				55.	42.50
	P# blk. of 8					—
PR31P $48	red brown	80.	40.	250.	14.	6.50
	Block of four				67.50	42.50
	P# blk. of 8					—
PR32P $60	violet	80.	40.	250.	16.50	8.25
	Block of four				82.50	45.
	P# blk. of 8					—

1879

No.	Description	(1)	(2)	(2a)	(3)	(4)
PR57P 2c	deep black	80.			6.50	3.25
	Block of four				32.50	19.
PR58P 3c	deep black	80.			6.50	3.25
	Block of four				32.50	19.
PR59P 4c	deep black	90.			6.50	3.25

No.	Denom.	Description	(1) Large	(2) Small	(2a)	(3) India	(4) Card
		Block of four				32.50	19.
PR60P	6c	deep black	90.			6.50	3.25
		Block of four				32.50	19.
PR61P	8c	deep black	90.			6.50	3.25
		Block of four				32.50	19.
PR62P	10c	deep black	90.			6.50	3.25
		Block of four				32.50	19.
PR63P	12c	red	90.			6.50	4.50
		Block of four				32.50	27.50
PR64P	24c	red	90.			6.50	4.50
		Block of four				32.50	27.50
PR65P	36c	red	90.			6.50	4.50
		Block of four				32.50	27.50
PR66P	48c	red	90.			6.50	4.50
		Block of four				32.50	27.50
PR67P	60c	red	90.			6.50	4.50
		Block of four				32.50	27.50
PR68P	72c	red	90.			6.50	4.50
		Block of four				32.50	27.50
PR69P	84c	red	90.			6.50	4.50
		Block of four				32.50	27.50
PR70P	96c	red	90.			6.50	4.50
		Block of four				32.50	27.50
PR71P	$1.92	pale brown	90.			7.75	6.
		Block of four				38.50	36.
PR72P	$3	red verm.	90.			7.75	6.
		Block of four				38.50	36.
PR73P	$6	blue	90.			7.75	6.
		Block of four				38.50	36.
PR74P	$9	orange	90.			7.75	6.
		Block of four				38.50	36.
PR75P	$12	yel. green	90.			7.75	6.
		Block of four				38.50	36.
PR76P	$24	dark violet	90.			10.	6.
		Block of four				50.	36.
PR77P	$36	Indian red	90.			10.50	6.
		Block of four				55.	36.
PR78P	$48	yel. brown	90.			14.	6.
		Block of four				68.50	36.
PR79P	$60	purple	90.			14.	6.
		Block of four				68.50	36.

1885

No.	Denom.	Description	(1) Large	(2) Small	(2a)	(3) India	(4) Card
PR81P	1c	black	100.	60.	250.	8.75	6.
		Block of four				38.50	30.
		P # blk. of 8					150.
PR82P	12c	carmine		80.	250.	14.	6.
		Block of four				66.	
PR83P	24c	carmine		80.	250.	14.	6.
		Block of four				66.	
PR84P	36c	carmine		80.	250.	14.	6.
		Block of four				66.	
PR85P	48c	carmine		80.	250.	14.	6.
		Block of four				66.	
PR86P	60c	carmine		80.	250.	14.	6.
		Block of four				66.	
PR87P	72c	carmine		80.	250.	14.	6.
		Block of four				66.	
PR88P	84c	carmine		80.	250.	14.	6.
		Block of four				66.	
PR89P	96c	carmine		80.	250.	14.	6.
		Block of four				66.	

1895

PR102P	1c	blk	125.	100.	275.
PR103P	2c	blk	125.	100.	275.
PR104P	5c	blk	125.	100.	275.
PR105P	10c	blk	125.	100.	275.
PR106P	25c	carm	125.	100.	275.
PR107P	50c	carm	125.	100.	275.
PR108P	$2	scar	125.	100.	275.
PR109P	$5	bl	125.	100.	275.
PR110P	$10	grn	125.	100.	275.
PR111P	$20	sl	125.	100.	275.
PR112P	$50	carm	125.	100.	275.
PR113P	$100	pur	125.	100.	275.

POSTAL SAVINGS

1940

PS7P	10c	deep ultra. on wove	1,200.
PS8P	25c	dk. car. rose on wove	1,200.
PS9P	50c	dk. bl. green on wove	1,200.
PS10P	$1	gray black on wove	1,200.

1941

PS11P	10c	rose red on wove	1,000.
PS12P	25c	blue green on wove	1,000.
PS13P	50c	ultramarine on wove	1,000.
PS14P	$1	gray black on wove	1,000.
PS15P	$5	sepia on wove	1,000.

PARCEL POST

1912-13

			DIE ON INDIA			PLATE	
			(1) Large	(2) Small	(2a)	(3) India	(4) Card
Q1P	1c	carmine rose	900.	700.	900.		
Q2P	2c	carmine rose	900.	700.	900.		
Q3P	3c	carmine rose	900.	700.	900.		
Q4P	4c	carmine rose	900.	700.	900.		
Q5P	5c	carmine rose	900.	700.	900.		
Q6P	10c	carmine rose	900.	700.	900.		
Q7P	15c	carmine rose	900.	700.	900.		
Q8P	20c	carmine rose	900.	700.	900.		
Q9P	25c	carmine rose	900.	700.	900.		
Q10	50c	carmine rose	900.	700.	900.		
Q11P	75c	carmine rose	900.	700.	900.		
Q12P	$1	carmine rose	900.	700.	900.		

SPECIAL HANDLING

1925-28

QE1P	10c	yellow grn.	900.
QE2P	15c	yellow grn.	900.
QE3P	20c	yellow grn.	900.
QE4aP	25c	deep green	900.

REVENUE PROOFS

NORMAL COLORS

1862-68 by Butler & Carpenter, Philadelphia.

1868-75 by Joseph R. Carpenter, Philadelphia.

In the following listings the so-called small die proofs on India paper may be, in fact probably are, plate proofs. The editors shall consider them die proofs, however, until they see them in pairs or blocks. Many revenue proofs on India are mounted on card.

FIRST ISSUE

1862-71

			DIE ON INDIA		PLATE	
			(1) Large	(2) Small	(3) India	(4) Card
R1P	1c	Express, red			110.	105.
		Block of four				450.
R2P	1c	Playing Cards, red	600.		95.	105.
		Block of four			400.	450.
R3P	1c	Proprietary, red			200.	67.50
		Block of four				300.
R4P	1c	Telegraph, red				40.
		Block of four				165.
R5P	2c	Bank Check, blue		525.		42.
		Block of four				185.
R6P	2c	Bank Check, orange			95.	
		Block of four			400.	
R7P	2c	Certificate, blue				40.
		Block of four				170.
R8P	2c	Certificate, orange			110.	
		Block of four			450.	
R9P	2c	Express, blue				40.
		Block of four				170.
R10P	2c	Express, orange	600.		95.	
		Pair			400.	
R11P	2c	Playing Cards, blue				55.
		Block of four				240.
R13P	2c	Proprietary, blue		400.		40.
		Block of four				170.
R15P	2c	U.S.I.R., orange			475.	
R16P	3c	Foreign Exchange, green	600.		275.	55.
		Block of four				240.
R17P	3c	Playing Cards, green		400.		150.
		Block of four				650.
R18P	3c	Proprietary, green			95.	40.
		Block of four			400.	170.
R19P	3c	Telegraph, green	600.		335.	40.
		Block of four				170.
R20P	4c	Inland Exchange, brown			300.	40.
		Block of four				170.
R21P	4c	Playing Cards, violet		400.		135.
		Block of four				600.
R22P	4c	Proprietary, violet	600.		170.	90.
		Block of four			750.	400.
R23P	5c	Agreement, red				50.
		Block of four				240.
R24P	5c	Certificate, red			135.	170.
		Block of four			550.	
R25P	5c	Express, red		250.		47.50
		Block of four				220.
R26P	5c	Foreign Exchange, red				300.
R27P	5c	Inland Exchange, red		250.		40.
		Block of four				185.
R28P	5c	Playing Cards, red		—	160.	300.
		Block of four			600.	
R30P	6c	Inland Exchange, orange			87.50	50.
		Block of four			375.	220.
R32P	10c	Bill of Lading, blue				50.
		Block of four				220.
R33P	10c	Certificate, blue			200.	50.
		Block of four				220.
R34P	10c	Contract, blue				50.
		Block of four				220.
R35P	10c	Foreign Exchange, blue				50.

			DIE ON INDIA		PLATE	
			(1) Large	(2) Small	(3) India	(4) Card
		Block of four				220.
R36P	10c	Inland Exchange, blue				50.
		Block of four				220.
R37P	10c	Power of Attorney, blue				50.
		Block of four				220.
R38P	10c	Proprietary, blue			110.	
		Block of four			450.	
R39P	15c	Foreign Exchange, brown			140.	325.
		Block of four			585.	
R40P	15c	Inland Exchange, brown			185.	50.
		Block of four				220.
R41P	20c	Foreign Exchange, red	600.		135.	150.
		Block of four			550.	625.
R42P	20c	Inland Exchange, red	600.	250.	235.	50.
		Block of four				220.
R43P	25c	Bond, red				250.
		Block of four				—
R44P	25c	Certificate, red				50.
		Block of four				220.
R45P	25c	Entry of Goods, red				300.
R46P	25c	Insurance, red			97.50	50.
		Block of four			400.	220.
R47P	25c	Life Insurance, red				50.
		Block of four				220.
R48P	25c	Power of Attorney, red				50.
		Block of four				220.
R49P	25c	Protest, red				50.
		Block of four				220.
R50P	25c	Warehouse Receipt, red				50.
		Block of four				220.
R51P	30c	Foreign Exchange, lilac			170.	150.
		Block of four			700.	675.
R52P	30c	Inland Exchange, lilac			95.	80.
		Block of four			400.	350.
R53P	40c	Inland Exchange, brown			135.	95.
		Block of four				400.
R54P	50c	Conveyance, blue		250.		45.
		Block of four				400.
R55P	50c	Entry of Goods, blue			95.	60.
		Block of four			400.	265.
R56P	50c	Foreign Exchange, blue			95.	60.
		Block of four			400.	265.
R57P	50c	Lease, blue			95.	55.
		Block of four			400.	235.
R58P	50c	Life Insurance, blue			95.	55.
		Block of four			400.	235.
R59P	50c	Mortgage, blue				135.
		Block of four				565.
R60P	50c	Original Process, blue			95.	55.
		Block of four			400.	235.
R61P	50c	Passage Ticket, blue				80.
		Block of four				350.
R62P	50c	Probate of Will, blue			95.	80.
		Block of four			400.	350.
R63P	50c	Surety Bond, blue				80.
		Block of four				350.
R64P	60c	Inland Exchange, orange			80.	60.
		Block of four				265.
R65P	70c	Foreign Exchange, green			185.	85.
		Block of four				350.
R66P	$1	Conveyance, red				67.50
		Block of four				425.
R67P	$1	Entry of Goods, red	500.			67.50
		Block of four				285.
R68P	$1	Foreign Exchange red				55.
		Block of four				235.
R69P	$1	Inland Exchange, red				80.
		Block of four				350.
R70P	$1	Lease, red				500.
R71P	$1	Life Insurance, red				55.
		Block of four				235.
R72P	$1	Manifest, red			87.50	55.

No.	Denom.		Die on India (1) Large	(2) Small	Plate (3) India	(4) Card
		Block of four			—	235.
R73P	$1	Mortgage, red				80.
		Block of four				350.
R74P	$1	Passage Ticket, red				500.
		Block of four				2,100.
R75P	$1	Power of Attorney, red				140.
		Block of four				600.
R76P	$1	Probate of Will, red				55.
		Block of four				235.
R77P	$1.30	Foreign Exchange, orange			200.	150.
		Block of four			835.	635.
R78P	$1.50	Inland Exchange, blue			165.	67.50
		Block of four			700.	285.
R79P	$1.60	Foreign Exchange green			200.	150.
		Block of four				635.
R80P	$1.90	Foreign Exchange, violet			200.	150.
		Block of four			875.	635.
R81P	$2	Conveyance, red			185.	55.
		Block of four				235.
R82P	$2	Mortgage, red			185.	55.
		Block of four			—	235.
R83P	$2	Probate of Will, red				165.
		Block of four				—
R84P	$2.50	Inland Exchange, violet			265.	235.
		Block of four				—
R85P	$3	Charter Party, green			185.	95.
		Block of four			775.	400.
R86P	$3	Manifest, green		350.	265.	95.
		Block of four				400.
R87P	$3.50	Inland Exchange, blue			265.	150.
		Block of four				635.
R88P	$5	Charter Party, red			105.	80.
		Block of four			435.	335.
R89P	$5	Conveyance, red			400.	80.
		Block of four				335.
R90P	$5	Manifest, red		300.		80.
		Block of four				335.
R91P	$5	Mortgage, red			600.	80.
		Block of four				335.
R92P	$5	Probate of Will, red		300.		80.
		Block of four				335.
R93P	$10	Charter Party, green			185.	80.
		Block of four				335.
R94P	$10	Conveyance, green				80.
		Block of four				335.
R95P	$10	Mortgage, green				80.
		Block of four				335.
R96P	$10	Probate of Will, green		300.		110.
		Block of four				450.
R97P	$15	Mortgage, dark blue		—		165.
		Block of four				735.
R97eP	$15	Mortgage, ultramarine		—		325.
		Block of four				—
	$15	Mortgage, milky blue			265.	
R98P	$20	Conveyance, orange			325.	150.
		Block of four			1,350.	635.
R99P	$20	Probate of Will, orange				335.
		Block of four				—
R100P	$25	Mortgage, red			265.	200.
		Block of four				835.
R101P	$50	U.S.I.R., green			335.	350.
		Block of four				1,475.
R102P	$200	U.S.I.R., green & red			1,300.	

SECOND ISSUE

1871-72

No.	Denom.		Die on India (1) Large	(2) Small	Plate (3) India	(4) Card
R105P	3c	blue & black			18.50	13.50
		Block of four			80.	60.
R109P	10c	blue & black			18.50	13.50
		Block of four			80.	60.
R111P	20c	blue & black			18.	13.50
		Block of four			80.	60.
R112P	25c	blue & black			18.50	13.50
		Block of four			80.	60.
R115P	50c	blue & black			44.	13.50
		Block of four			200.	60.
R119P	$1.30	blue & black			44.	33.50
		Block of four			200.	150.
R120P	$1.50	blue & black			23.50	20.
		Block of four			105.	87.50
R121P	$1.60	blue & black			53.50	53.50
		Block of four			235.	235.
R122P	$1.90	blue & black			44.	33.50
		Block of four			200.	150.
R126P	$3.50	blue & black			800.	90.
		Block of four			350.	385.
R130P	$25	blue & black			140.	105.
		Block of four			600.	465.
R131P	$50	blue & black			150.	135.
		Block of four			675.	600.
R132P	$200	blue, red & black	3,500.	2,750.	2,500.	
R133P	$500	green, red & black	3,500.	2,750.		
	$5000	green, orange & black	6,500.			
	$5000	light green, yellow & black	6,500.			
	$5000	blue, red & black	8,500.			
	$5000	light green, scarlet & black	8,500.			

The $5000 revenue stamp was approved but never issued.

The "small die proofs" formerly listed under Nos. R103P-R131P are plate proofs from the sheets listed under "Trial Color Proofs."

THIRD ISSUE

1871-72

No.	Denom.		Plate (3) India	(4) Card
R134P	1c	claret & black		15.
		Block of four		67.50
R135P	2c	orange & black	16.	15.
		Block of four	70.	67.50
R136P	4c	brown & black	18.50	15.
		Block of four	80.	67.50
R137P	5c	orange & black	18.50	15.
		Block of four	80.	67.50
R138P	6c	orange & black	18.50	15.
		Block of four	80.	67.50
R139P	15c	brown & black	18.50	15.
		Block of four	80.	67.50
R140P	30c	orange & black	23.50	18.50
		Block of four	100.	80.
R141P	40c	brown & black	23.50	18.50
		Block of four	100.	80.
R142P	60c	orange & black	63.50	53.50
		Block of four	265.	235.
	a.	Center inverted		300.
		Same, block of four		1,350.
		Double transfer, design of 70c		1,300.
R143P	70c	green & black	43.50	37.50
		Block of four	190.	165.
R144P	$1	green & black	37.50	37.50
		Block of four	165.	165.
R145P	$2	vermilion & black	80.	105.
		Block of four	335.	450.
R146P	$2.50	claret & black	46.50	37.50
		Block of four	200.	165.
R147P	$3	green & black	63.50	67.50
		Block of four	265.	285.
R148P	$5	vermilion & black	63.50	53.50
		Block of four	265.	235.
R149P	$10	green & black	80.	53.50
		Block of four	335.	235.
R150P	$20	orange & black	115.	150.
		Block of four	500.	635.

The "small die proofs" formerly listed under Nos. R134P-R150P are plate proofs from the sheets listed under "Trial Color Proofs."

1875 National Bank Note Co., New York City

No.	Denom.		Die on India (1) Large	(2) Small	Plate (3) India
R152P	2c	blue *(Liberty)*	450.		110.
		Block of four			475.

DOCUMENTARY

1898

No.	Denom.		Die on India (1) Large	(2) Small	Plate (3) India
R173P	$1	dark green	475.		
R176P	$10	black	575.		

1899

No.	Denom.		Die on India (1) Large	(2) Small	Plate (3) India
R180P	$500	carmine lake & black	1,200.		

1914

No.	Denom.		Die on India (1) Large	(2) Small	Plate (3) India
R197P	2c	rose		—	

1914-15

No.	Denom.		Die on India (1) Large	(2) Small	Plate (3) India
R226P	$500	blue	675.		

1952

No.	Denom.		Die on India (1) Large	(2) Small	Plate (3) India
R597P	55c	carmine	675.		

PROPRIETARY

1871-75 Joseph R. Carpenter, Philadelphia

No.	Denom.		Die on India (2) Small	Plate (3) India	(4) Card	(5) Bond
RB1P	1c	green & black		—	12.	12.
		Block of four			52.50	52.50
RB2P	2c	green & black		175.	12.	
		Block of four			52.50	
RB3P	3c	green & black		22.50	12.	
		Block of four		100.	52.50	
RB4P	4c	green & black		22.50	12.	
		Block of four		100.	52.50	
RB5P	5c	green & black		22.50	12.	
		Block of four		100.	52.50	
RB6P	6c	green & black		22.50	12.	
		Block of four		100.	52.50	
RB7P	10c	green & black		22.50	12.	
		Block of four		100.	52.50	
RB8P	50c	green & black	600.		725.	
RB9P	$1	green & black	700.			
RB10P	$5	green & black	850.		1,000.	

The "small die proofs" formerly listed under Nos. RB1P-RB7P are from the composite plate proofs listed under "Trial Color Proofs."

National Bank Note Co., New York City

1875-83

No.	Denom.		Die on India (1) Large	(2) Small	Plate (3) India	(4) Card
RB11P	1c	green	600.		47.50	—
		Block of four			200.	
RB12P	2c	brown	600.		47.50	—
		Pair			100.	
RB13P	3c	orange	600.		50.	—
		Pair			110.	—
		Block of four				—
RB14P	4c	red brown	600.		47.50	—
		Pair			100.	—
		Block of four				—
RB15P	4c	red	600.			
RB16P	5c	black	600.		50.	—
		Pair			110.	—
		Block of four				—
RB17P	6c	violet blue	600.		47.50	
		Pair			100.	
RB18P	6c	blue	600.		135.	
		Pair			285.	
RB19P	10c	blue	600.			

No. RB19P was produced by the Bureau of Engraving and Printing.

PLAYING CARDS

1896 Bureau of Engraving & Printing

No.	Denom.		Die on India (1) Large
RF2P	2c	ultramarine	145.
	a.	2c blue	145.

HUNTING PERMIT

No.	Year	Denom.		Die (Wove) (1) Large	(2) Small
RW1P	1934	$1	blue	—	2,750.
RW2P	1935	$1	rose lake		2,750.
RW3P	1936	$1	brown black		2,750.
RW4P	1937	$1	light green	—	2,750.
RW5P	1938	$1	light violet		2,750.
RW6P	1939	$1	chocolate		2,750.
RW7P	1940	$1	sepia		2,750.
RW8P	1941	$1	brown carmine		2,750.
RW9P	1942	$1	violet brown		2,750.
RW10P	1943	$1	deep rose		2,750.
RW11P	1944	$1	red orange		2,750.
RW12P	1945	$1	black	3,850.	2,750.
RW13P	1946	$1	red brown	3,850.	
RW14P	1947	$1	black	3,850.	
RW15P	1948	$1	bright blue	3,850.	
RW19P	1952	$2	deep ultra.	3,850.	

	DIE (Wove) (1) Large	(2) Small
RW23P 1956 $2 black		—

TELEGRAPH

AMERICAN RAPID TELEGRAPH CO.

1881

	DIE (2) Small	PLATE (3) India
1T1P 1c black	77.50	32.50
Pair		67.50

	DIE (2) Small	PLATE (3) India
1T2P 3c orange		32.50
Pair		67.50
1T3P 5c bister brown	77.50	32.50
Pair		67.50
1T4P 10c purple		32.50
Pair		67.50
1T5P 15c green	77.50	32.50
Pair		67.50
1T6P 20c red	77.50	32.50
Pair		67.50
1T7P 25c rose	77.50	32.50
Pair		67.50
1T8P 50c blue		32.50
Pair		67.50

"Collect"

	DIE (1) Large	(2) Small	PLATE (3) India
1T9P 1c brown			32.50
Pair, setenant with 1T13P			67.50
Same, block of four			145.
1T10P 5c blue			32.50
Pair, setenant with 1T14P			67.50
Same, block of four			145.
1T11P 15c red brown			32.50
Pair, setenant with 1T15P			67.50
Same, block of four			145.
1T12P 20c olive green			32.50
Pair, setenant with 1T16P			67.50
Same, block of four			145.

Office Coupon

	DIE (1) Large	(2) Small	PLATE (3) India
1T13P 1c brown			32.50
1T14P 5c blue			32.50
1T15P 15c red brown			32.50
1T16P 20c olive green			32.50

BALTIMORE & OHIO TELEGRAPH CO.

1885

	DIE (1) Large	(2) Small	PLATE (3) India
3T1P 1c vermilion			32.50
Pair			67.50
3T2P 5c blue			32.50
Pair			67.50
3T3P 10c red brown			32.50
Pair			67.50
3T4P 25c orange			32.50
Pair			67.50

1886

	DIE (1) Large	(2) Small	PLATE (3) India
3T6P black			32.50
Pair			67.50
3T7P 1c green			32.50
3T8P 5c blue			32.50
3T9P 10c brown			32.50
3T10P 25c orange			32.50

POSTAL TELEGRAPH CO.

1885

	DIE (1) Large	(2) Small	PLATE (3) India
15T1P 10c green		55.	32.50
15T2P 15c orange red			32.50
15T3P 25c blue	65.		32.50
15T4P 50c brown		65.	32.50

WESTERN UNION TELEGRAPH CO.

	DIE (1) Large	(2) Small	PLATE (3) India
16T1P (1871) green			16.50
Pair			35.
16T2P (1872) red			16.50
Pair			35.
16T3P (1873) blue			16.50
Pair			35.
16T4P (1874) brown			16.50
Pair			35.
16T5P (1875) deep green			16.50
16T6P (1876) red			16.50
16T7P (1877) violet			—
16T8P (1878) gray brown			20.
16T9P (1879) blue			14.
16T10P (1880) lilac rose			16.
16T11P (1881) green			16.
16T12P (1882) blue			20.
16T13P (1883) yellow brown			16.
16T14P (1884) gray violet			20.
16T15P (1885) green			20.
16T16P (1886) brown violet			13.
Pair			27.50
16T17P (1887) red brown			13.
Pair			27.50
16T18P (1888) blue			13.
Pair			27.50
16T19P (1889) olive green			16.
16T22P (1892) vermilion			16.
16T30P (1900) red violet			27.50
16T44P (1913) brown	—	—	—

TRIAL COLOR PROOFS

Values are for items in very fine condition. The listings of trial color proofs include several that are similar to the colors of the issues stamps.

New York

All on India paper unless otherwise stated.

Original Die

1845

	DIE (1) Lg.	(2) Sm.	PLATE (5) Bond
9X1TC 5c dull dark violet		250.	
9X1TC 5c brown violet		250.	
9X1TC 5c deep rose violet		250.	
9X1TC 5c deep blue		250.	175.
9X1TC 5c dark green		250.	175.
9X1TC 5c orange yellow		250.	
9X1TC 5c brown		250.	175.
9X1TC 5c scarlet			175.
With "Scar" on Neck			
9X1TC 5c dull blue		175.	
9X1TC 5c vermilion		175.	
With "Scar" and dot in "P" of "POST"			
9X1TC 5c sapphire	450.		
9X1TC 5c dull gray blue		300.	
9X1TC 5c deep blue on Bond		250.	
9X1TC 5c deep ultramarine on thin glazed card	450.		
9X1TC 5c deep green	450.	300.	
9X1TC 5c deep green on Bond		250.	
9X1TC 5c dull dark green		300.	
9X1TC 5c org. verm.	450.		
9X1TC 5c orange vermilion on thin glazed card	450.		
9X1TC 5c dark red org.	450.		
9X1TC 5c dull brown red on Bond		250.	
9X1TC 5c dark brown red		300.	
9X1TC 5c dull dark brown		300.	
9X1TC 5c dull dark brown on Bond		250.	
9X1TC 5c sepia	450.		
9X1TC 5c brown black on thin glazed card	450.		

The above listed Large Die varieties, except those on thin glazed card, have an additional impression of the portrait medallion. Plate proofs are from the small sheet of 9.

Providence, R. I.

1846

	Plate on Card
10X1TC 5c gray blue	275.
10X1TC 5c green	275.
10X1TC 5c brown carmine	275.
10X1TC 5c brown	275.
10X2TC 10c gray blue	400.
10X2TC 10c green	400.
10X2TC 10c brown carmine	400.
10X2TC 10c brown	400.
Sheet of 12, any color	3,750.

General Issues

1847

	DIE LARGE In dia	Bond	Wove	Thin Glazed Card	SMALL In dia	Bond
1TC 5c vio	900.					
1TC 5c dull bl.	900.					
1TC 5c deep blue		800.	800.		625.	
1TC 5c deep ultra.				800.		
1TC 5c bl green	900.				625.	
1TC 5c dull blue green		800.				
1TC 5c dull grn.	900.					600.
1TC 5c dk grn.	900.					
1TC 5c yellow green					625.	
1TC 5c org yel	900.	800.	800.		625.	
1TC 5c deep yellow			800.			
1TC 5c org vermilion	900.	800.	800.			
1TC 5c scar vermilion	900.	800.		800.		
1TC 5c rose lake	900.					625.
1TC 5c black brown				800.		
1TC 5c dull rose lake						625.
1TC 5c brn red	900.					
1TC 5c blk	900.	800.		800.	675.	
2TC 10c vio	900.					
2TC 10c dull blue						
2TC 10c dp blue	900.	800.	800.	800.	675.	
2TC 10c dull gray blue						625.
2TC 10c blue green		800.				
2TC 10c dull blue green		800.				
2TC 10c dull green		800.				
2TC 10c dk grn	900.					
2TC 10c yel grn					675.	
2TC 10c dull yel			800.			
2TC 10c org yel	900.		800.			
2TC 10c org vermilion	900.	800.	800.		675.	
2TC 10c scar verm				800.		
2TC 10c gld brown	900.	800.		800.		
2TC 10c lt brn	900.					
2TC 10c dk brn	900.	800.				
2TC 10c red brown					675.	
2TC 10c dull red					675.	
2TC 10c rose lake	900.					
2TC 10c dull rose lake						625.

	DIE LARGE				DIE SMALL	
	In dia	Bond	Wove	Thin Glazed Card	In dia	Bond
2TC 10c blk brn				800.		
2TC 10c yel grn on blue pelure paper	900.					

	DIE (1) Lg.	(2) Sm.	PLATE (3) India	(4) Card
1TC 5c orange			600.	
1TC 5c black			600.	
2TC 10c orange			600.	
2TC 10c deep brown			600.	

1875

	DIE (1) Lg.	(2) Sm.	PLATE (3) India	(4) Card
3TC 5c dull rose lake				550.
3TC 5c black	900.			
3TC 5c green	900.			
4TC 10c green	900.		750.	

1856-60

	DIE (1) Lg.	(2) Sm.	PLATE (3) India	(5) Wove Paper
11TC 3c black				1,500.
12TC 5c pale brown				300.
12TC 5c rose brown				300.
12TC 5c dp. red brown				1,500.
12TC 5c dark olive bister				300.
12TC 5c olive brown				300.
12TC 5c olive green				300.
12TC 5c deep orange				300.
12TC 5c black	—			*4,500.*
13TC 10c black	2,650.			—
37TC 24c claret brown				600.
37TC 24c red brown				600.
37TC 24c orange				600.
37TC 24c deep yellow				600.
37TC 24c yellow				600.
37TC 24c deep blue				600.
37TC 24c black				600.
37TC 24c violet black				600.
38TC 30c black	2,350.		1,400.	600.
Block of four			9,000.	
39TC 90c rose lake				625.
39TC 90c henna brown				625.
39TC 90c orange red				625.
39TC 90c brown orange	2,350.			625.
39TC 90c sepia				625.
39TC 90c dark green				625.
39TC 90c dark violet brown				625.
39TC 90c black	2,350.	1,250.		675.

1875

	DIE (1) Lg.	(2) Sm.	PLATE (3) India	(5) Wove Paper
40TC 1c orange vermilion				400.
40TC 1c orange				400.
40TC 1c yellow orange				400.
40TC 1c orange brown				400.
40TC 1c dark brown				400.
40TC 1c dull violet				400.
40TC 1c violet				400.
40TC 1c red violet				400.
40TC 1c gray				400.
41TC 3c red			—	

1861

	PLATE (5) Wove Paper, Imperf.	(6) Wove Paper, Perf.
63TC 1c rose	30.	33.
63TC 1c deep orange red	30.	33.
63TC 1c deep red orange	30.	
63TC 1c dark orange		33.
63TC 1c yellow orange	30.	
63TC 1c orange brown	30.	33.
63TC 1c dark brown	30.	
63TC 1c yellow green		33.
63TC 1c green	30.	
63TC 1c blue green	30.	33.
63TC 1c gray lilac	30.	33.
63TC 1c gray black	30.	33.
63TC 1c slate black	30.	
63TC 1c blue	30.	
63TC 1c light blue	30.	

There are many trial color impressions of the issues of 1861 to 1883 made for experimentation with various patent papers, grills, etc. Some are fully perforated, gummed and with grill.

1861

	DIE (1) Lg.	(2) Sm.	PLATE (3) India	(4) Card
55TC 1c ultramarine	2,250.		400.	
56TC 3c black	2,000.			
56TC 3c black on regular paper				400.
56TC 3c scarlet	2,000.		300.	
56TC 3c pink	2,850.			
56TC 3c orange red	2,000.			
56TC 3c dk. org. red	2,000.			
57TC 5c black	1,750.			
57TC 5c light brown			300.	
57TC 5c dark brown			300.	
58TC 10c black	1,750.			
58TC 10c green			300.	
58TC 10c light green			300.	
59TC 12c scarlet	1,750.			
60TC 24c scarlet	1,750.			
60TC 24c green	1,750.			
60TC 24c orange	1,750.			
60TC 24c red brown	1,750.			
60TC 24c orange brown	1,750.			
60TC 24c orange yellow	1,750.			
60TC 24c rose red	1,750.			
60TC 24c gray	1,750.			
60TC 24c steel blue	2,250.			
60TC 24c blue	1,750.			
61TC 30c black	1,750.			
61TC 30c green	1,750.			
61TC 30c dull gray blue	1,750.			
61TC 30c violet brown	1,750.			
61TC 30c scarlet	1,750.			
61TC 30c dull rose	1,750.			
62TC 90c black	1,750.			
62TC 90c blue green on regular paper				275.

1861-62

	DIE (1) Lg.	(2) Sm.	PLATE (3) India	(4) Card
63TC 1c black		600.		
63TC 1c red		600.		
63TC 1c brown		600.		
65TC 3c black	1,400.			
65TC 3c blk. on glazed	1,400.			
65TC 3c blue green	1,400.			
65TC 3c orange	1,400.			
65TC 3c brown	1,400.			
65TC 3c dark blue	1,400.			
65TC 3c ocher	1,400.			
65TC 3c green	1,400.			
65TC 3c dull red	1,400.			
65TC 3c slate	1,400.			
65TC 3c red brown	1,400.			
65TC 3c deep pink	1,400.			
65TC 3c rose pink	1,400.			
65TC 3c dark rose	1,400.			
68TC 10c orange	1,400.			
68TC 10c red brown	1,400.			
68TC 10c dull pink	1,400.			
68TC 10c scarlet	1,400.			
68TC 10c black	1,400.	550.		
69TC 12c scarlet verm.	1,400.			
69TC 12c brown	1,400.			
69TC 12c red brown	1,400.			
69TC 12c green	1,400.			
69TC 12c orange yellow	1,400.			
69TC 12c black		550.		
71TC 30c rose	1,400.			
71TC 30c black		600.		
72TC 90c black	1,400.	600.		
72TC 90c ultramarine	1,400.			
72TC 90c bluish gray	1,400.			
72TC 90c violet gray	1,400.			
72TC 90c red brown	1,400.			
72TC 90c orange	1,400.			
72TC 90c yellow orange	1,400.			
72TC 90c scarlet	1,400.			
72TC 90c green	1,400.			

1863

	DIE (1) Lg.	(2) Sm.	PLATE (3) India	(4) Card
73TC 2c light blue			335.	
73TC 2c dull chalky bl.	4,500.			
73TC 2c green	4,500.		335.	
73TC 2c olive green			335.	
73TC 2c dull yellow	4,500.			
73TC 2c dark orange	4,500.			
73TC 2c vermilion			335.	
73TC 2c scarlet	4,500.		335.	
73TC 2c dull red			335.	
73TC 2c dull rose	4,500.		335.	
73TC 2c brown	4,500.			
73TC 2c gray black			335.	
73TC 2c ultramarine	4,500.			
76TC 5c black	1,500.	—		
76TC 5c orange yellow	1,550.			
76TC 5c dark orange	1,500.			
76TC 5c green	1,500.			
76TC 5c ultramarine	1,500.			
76TC 5c gray	1,500.			
76TC 5c rose brown	—			
78TC 24c black		550.		

1866

	DIE (1) Lg.	(2) Sm.	PLATE (3) India	(4) Card
77TC 15c deep blue	1,900.		335.	
Block of four			1,650.	
77TC 15c dark red	1,900.			
77TC 15c orange red	1,900.			
77TC 15c dark orange	1,900.			
77TC 15c yellow orange	1,900.			
77TC 15c yellow				
77TC 15c sepia				
77TC 15c orange brown	1,900.			
77TC 15c red brown	1,900.			
77TC 15c blue green	1,900.			
77TC 15c dusky blue	1,900.			
77TC 15c gray black	1,900.			

1869

	DIE (1) Lg.	(2) Sm.	PLATE (3) India	(4) Card
112TC 1c black	2,250.			
113TC 2c black	2,250.			
114TC 3c black	2,250.			
115TC 6c deep dull blue	2,250.			
115TC 6c black	2,250.			
116TC 10c black	2,250.			
116TC 10c dull dk. violet	2,250.			
116TC 10c deep green	2,250.			
116TC 10c dull dk. orange	2,250.			
116TC 10c dull rose	2,250.			
116TC 10c copper red	2,250.			
116TC 10c chocolate	2,250.			
116TC 10c dk. Pruss. bl.	2,250.			
117TC 12c black	2,250.			
118TC 15c dull dk. violet	2,250.			
118TC 15c deep blue	2,250.			
118TC 15c dull red brown	2,250.			
118TC 15c black	2,250.			
118TC 15c dark blue gray	2,250.			
120TC 24c black	2,250.			
121TC 30c deep blue & deep green	2,250.			
121TC 30c dp. brn. & blue	2,250.			
121TC 30c golden brown & carmine lake	2,250.			
121TC 30c carmine lake & dull violet	2,250.			
121TC 30c carmine lake & green	2,250.			
121TC 30c carmine lake & brown	2,250.			
121TC 30c carmine lake & black	2,250.			
121TC 30c dull orange red & dp. green	2,250.			
121TC 30c deep ocher & golden brown	2,250.			
121TC 30c dull violet & golden brown	2,250.			
121TC 30c blk. & dp. green	2,250.			
122TC 90c brn. & dp. grn.	2,250.			
122TC 90c green & black				1,500.

1870-71

	DIE (1) Lg.	(2) Sm.	PLATE (3) India	(4) Card
145TC 1c yellow orange	800.			
145TC 1c red brown	800.			
145TC 1c red violet	800.			
145TC 1c green	800.			
146TC 2c black	800.			
147TC 3c brown			200.	
147TC 3c dark brown			200.	
147TC 3c dark red			200.	
147TC 3c light ultramarine			200.	
147TC 3c violet brown			200.	
147TC 3c bister			200.	
147TC 3c dull red violet			200.	
147TC 3c orange			200.	
148TC 6c deep magenta	800.			
148TC 6c ultramarine	800.			
148TC 6c carmine	800.			
148TC 6c maroon	800.			
149TC 7c black	800.			
150TC 10c blue	800.			
150TC 10c dull pale blue	800.			
150TC 10c ultramarine	800.			
150TC 10c blue green	800.			
150TC 10c carmine	800.			
150TC 10c bister	800.			
150TC 10c dull red	800.			
150TC 10c red orange	800.			
150TC 10c yellow brown	800.			
150TC 10c brown orange	800.			
151TC 12c orange	800.			
151TC 12c orange brown	800.			
151TC 12c brown red	800.			
151TC 12c dull red	800.			
151TC 12c carmine	800.			
151TC 12c blue	800.			
151TC 12c light blue	800.			
151TC 12c ultramarine	800.			
151TC 12c green	800.			
153TC 24c dark brown	800.			
155TC 90c carmine	800.			
155TC 90c ultramarine	800.			
155TC 90c black	800.			

1873

	DIE (1) Lg.	(2) Sm.	PLATE (3) India	(4) Card
156TC 1c black			15.	
Block of four			65.	
156TC 1c scarlet	—			
157TC 2c black			15.	
Block of four			65.	
157TC 2c dull blue	800.			
158TC 3c black			12.	
Block of four			55.	
159TC 6c black		250.	30.	
Block of four			150.	
159TC 6c deep green		225.		
159TC 6c deep brown		225.		
159TC 6c dull red		225.		
159TC 6c dull gray blue		225.		
160TC 7c black		250.	75.	
Block of four			325.	
160TC 7c deep green		225.		
160TC 7c deep brown		225.		
160TC 7c dull gray blue		225.		
160TC 7c dull red		225.		
161TC 10c black		250.		
161TC 10c deep green		225.		
161TC 10c deep brown		225.		
161TC 10c dull gray blue		225.		
161TC 10c dull red		225.		
162TC 12c black		250.		
162TC 12c deep green		225.		
162TC 12c dull gray blue		225.		
162TC 12c deep brown		225.		
162TC 12c dull red		225.		
163TC 15c black		250.		
163TC 15c deep green		225.		
163TC 15c dull gray blue		225.		
163TC 15c deep brown		225.		

			(1)	(2)	(3)	(4)
163TC	15c	dull red		225.		
164TC	24c	black		250.		
164TC	24c	deep green		225.		
164TC	24c	dull gray blue		225.		
164TC	24c	deep brown		225.		
164TC	24c	dull red		225.		
165TC	30c	black		250.		
165TC	30c	deep green		225.		
165TC	30c	dull gray blue		225.		
165TC	30c	deep brown		225.		
165TC	30c	dull red		225.		
166TC	90c	black		250.		
166TC	90c	deep green		225.		
166TC	90c	dull gray blue		225.		
166TC	90c	deep brown		225.		
166TC	90c	dull red		225.		

1875

			(1)	(2)	(3)	(4)
179TC	5c	black	850.	250.	25.	
		Block of four			125.	
179TC	5c	deep green		225.		
179TC	5c	dull gray blue		225.		
179TC	5c	deep brown		225.		
179TC	5c	dull red		225.		
179TC	5c	scarlet	1,000.			

Small die proofs of 1873-75 issues are "Goodall" prints.

1881-82

			(1)	(2)	(3)	(4)
206TC	1c	deep green	900.	200.		
206TC	1c	black	900.		125.	
206TC	1c	ultramarine	900.			
206TC	1c	dk. yel. green	900.			

1882-87

			LARGE DIE (1) India	(2) Card	PLATE (3) India	(4) Card
212TC	1c	indigo	800.			
212TC	1c	carmine	800.			
212TC	1c	green	800.	700.		
212TC	1c	deep green	800.	700.		
212TC	1c	copper brown	800.	700.		
212TC	1c	chestnut brown	800.			
210TC	2c	brown red	800.	700.		
210TC	2c	dp. dull orange	800.			
210TC	2c	chestnut brown	800.	700.		
210TC	2c	violet rose	800.	700.		
210TC	2c	indigo	800.	700.		
210TC	2c	black	800.			
210TC	2c	pale ultramarine	800.			
210TC	2c	olive green	800.	700.		
210TC	2c	olive brown		700.		
210TC	2c	lake				140.
210TC	2c	rose lake				140.
210TC	2c	dark carmine				140.
210TC	2c	deep red				140.
214TC	3c	green	750.	700.		
214TC	3c	dark brown	750.	700.		
214TC	3c	chestnut brown	750.	700.		
214TC	3c	dull red brown	750.	700.		

All of 214TC above bear inscription "Worked over by new company, June 29th, 1881."

			(1)	(2)	(3)	(4)
211TC	4c	green	900.	700.		
211TC	4c	chestnut brown	900.	700.		
211TC	4c	orange brown	900.	700.		
211TC	4c	pale ultra.	900.	700.		
211TC	4c	dark brown	900.			
211TC	4c	black	900.	700.		
205TC	5c	chestnut brown	900.			
205TC	5c	dp. dull orange	900.			
205TC	5c	pale ultra.	900.			
205TC	5c	deep green	900.			
205TC	5c	green	900.		200.	
205TC	5c	carmine	900.	700.		
205TC	5c	carmine lake	900.		225.	
205TC	5c	blue black	900.			
205TC	5c	black on glazed	900.			
208TC	6c	dp. dull orange	900.	700.		
208TC	6c	indigo	900.			
208TC	6c	org. vermilion	900.	700.		
208TC	6c	dark violet	900.	700.		
208TC	6c	chestnut brown	900.	700.		
208TC	6c	carmine	900.			
209TC	10c	carmine	900.	700.		
209TC	10c	orange brown	900.	700.		
209TC	10c	dp. dull orange	900.	700.		
209TC	10c	chestnut brown	900.	700.		
209TC	10c	indigo	900.	700.		
209TC	10c	pale ultra.	900.	700.		
209TC	10c	black (glazed)	900.			
189TC	15c	org. vermilion	900.	700.		
189TC	15c	orange brown	900.	700.		
189TC	15c	chestnut brown	900.	700.		
189TC	15c	dark brown	900.	700.		
189TC	15c	deep green	900.	700.		
189TC	15c	black	900.	700.		
190TC	30c	black	900.			
190TC	30c	org. vermilion	900.	700.		
190TC	30c	dark brown	900.	700.		
190TC	30c	deep green	900.	700.		
190TC	30c	dull red brown	900.	700.		
190TC	30c	green	900.	700.		
191TC	90c	carmine	900.	700.		
191TC	90c	dark brown	900.	700.		
191TC	90c	dp. dull orange	900.	700.		
191TC	90c	indigo	900.	700.		
191TC	90c	dull red brown	900.	700.		
191TC	90c	black	900.	700.		

1890-93

			DIE (1) India	(2) Card	PLATE (3) India	(4) Card
219TC	1c	green	550.			
219TC	1c	dull violet	550.			
220TC	2c	dull violet	550.			
220TC	2c	blue green	550.			
220TC	2c	slate black	550.			
222TC	4c	org. brn. on wove				—
222TC	4c	yel. brn. on wove				—
222TC	4c	green	550.			
223TC	5c	bl. on glossy wove	550.			
223TC	5c	dark brown on glossy wove	550.			
223TC	5c	bister on wove				—
223TC	5c	sepia on wove				—
223TC	5c	blk. brn. on wove				—
224TC	6c	deep orange red	550.			
224TC	6c	org. red on wove				120.
224TC	6c	vio. blk. on wove				120.
224TC	6c	yellow on wove				120.
224TC	6c	olive grn. on wove				120.
224TC	6c	purple on wove				120.
224TC	6c	red org. on wove				120.
224TC	6c	brown on wove				120.
224TC	6c	red brn. on wove				120.
224TC	6c	org. brn. on wove				120.
224TC	6c	blk. brn. on wove				120.
224TC	6c	slate grn. on wove				120.
224TC	6c	brn. olive on wove				120.
225TC	8c	dark violet red		550.		
225TC	8c	metallic green		550.		
225TC	8c	salmon		550.		
225TC	8c	orange brown		550.		
225TC	8c	light green		550.		
225TC	8c	blue		550.		
225TC	8c	steel blue		550.		

1893

			(1)	(2)	(3)	(4)
231TC	2c	sepia	850.	850.		
231TC	2c	orange brown		850.		
231TC	2c	deep orange		850.		
231TC	2c	light brown		850.		
231TC	2c	blue green		850.		
231TC	2c	bright rose red		850.		
231TC	2c	rose violet		850.		
232TC	3c	sepia		850.		
232TC	3c	blackish green		850.	800.	
232TC	3c	black		850.		
233TC	4c	sepia		850.		
233TC	4c	deep orange		850.		
233TC	4c	light brown		850.		
233TC	4c	blue green		850.		
233TC	4c	rose red		850.		
233TC	4c	rose violet		850.		
234TC	5c	black	850.			
234TC	5c	dark violet	850.	850.		
234TC	5c	rose violet	850.	850.		
234TC	5c	red violet	850.			
234TC	5c	brown violet	850.			
234TC	5c	deep blue	850.			
234TC	5c	deep ultra.	850.			
234TC	5c	green	850.			
234TC	5c	deep green	850.			
234TC	5c	blue green		850.		
234TC	5c	dk. olive green	850.			
234TC	5c	deep orange	850.			
234TC	5c	orange red	850.			
234TC	5c	orange brown	850.	850.		
234TC	5c	bright rose red	850.			
234TC	5c	claret	850.			
234TC	5c	brown rose	850.			
234TC	5c	dull rose brown		850.		
234TC	5c	sepia	850.	850.		

The 5c trial color proofs differ from the issued stamp.

			(1)	(2)	(3)	(4)
237TC	10c	bright rose red	1,000.			
237TC	10c	claret	1,000.			
239TC	30c	sepia		1,000.		
239TC	30c	black				350.
240TC	50c	sepia		1,000.		
242TC	$2	blackish brown			1,000.	

1894

			DIE (1) Lg.	(2) Sm.	PLATE (3) India	(4) Card
255TC	5c	black	900.			
257TC	8c	black	900.			
258TC	10c	olive	900.			
259TC	15c	red violet	900.			
259TC	15c	dark red orange	1,000.			
261ATC	$1	lake	1,000.			
262TC	$2	black	1,000.			
262TC	$2	dull violet	1,000.			
262TC	$2	violet	1,000.			
262TC	$2	turquoise blue	1,000.			
262TC	$2	orange brown	1,000.			
262TC	$2	olive green	1,000.			
262TC	$2	sepia	1,000.			
262TC	$2	greenish black	1,000.			
263TC	$5	black	1,000.			
263TC	$5	dark yellow	1,000.			
263TC	$5	orange brown	1,000.			
263TC	$5	olive green	1,000.			
263TC	$5	dull violet	1,000.			
263TC	$5	sepia	1,000.			
263TC	$5	brown red	1,000.			

1898

			(1)	(2)	(3)	(4)
283TC	10c	orange	1,000.			
283TC	10c	sepia	1,000.			

1898

			(1)	(2)	(3)	(4)
286TC	2c	purple				1,200.
286TC	2c	black				1,200.
286TC	2c	blue				1,200.
286TC	2c	brown				1,200.
286TC	2c	deep carmine rose				1,200.
290TC	10c	black	1,200.	1,000.		
291TC	50c	black	1,200.	1,000.		
293TC	$2	black	5,000.			

1903

			(1)	(2)	(3)	(4)
319TC	2c	black, Die I	900.			

1907

			(1)	(2)	(3)	(4)
330TC	5c	ultramarine	1,600.			
330TC	5c	black	1,700.			

1908

			(1)	(2)	(3)	(4)
332TC	2c	dull violet	450.			
332TC	2c	light ultra.	450.			
332TC	2c	bright ultra.	450.			
332TC	2c	light green	450.			
332TC	2c	dark olive green	450.			
332TC	2c	golden yellow	450.			
332TC	2c	dull orange	450.			
332TC	2c	rose carmine	450.			
332TC	2c	ultramarine	450.			
332TC	2c	ultra. on buff	450.			
332TC	2c	ultra. on green	450.			
332TC	2c	green on pink	450.			
332TC	2c	green on rose	450.			
332TC	2c	dk. green on grn	450.			

1909

			(1)	(2)	(3)	(4)
342TC	$1	carmine lake	1,200.	1,100.		
342TC	$1	pink	1,200.	1,100.		

1912-13

			(1)	(2)	(3)	(4)
400TC	10c	brown red	1,350.	1,100.		

1918

			(1)	(2)	(3)	(4)
524TC	$5	carmine & blk.	1,350.			

1919

			(1)	(2)	(3)	(4)
513TC	13c	violet	550.			
513TC	13c	lilac	550.			
513TC	13c	violet brown	550.			
513TC	13c	light ultra.	550.			
513TC	13c	ultramarine	550.			
513TC	13c	deep ultra.	550.			
513TC	13c	green	550.			
513TC	13c	dark green	550.			
513TC	13c	olive green	550.			
513TC	13c	orange yellow	550.			
513TC	13c	orange	550.			
513TC	13c	red orange	550.			
513TC	13c	ocher	550.			
513TC	13c	salmon red	550.			
513TC	13c	brown carmine	550.			
513TC	13c	claret brown	550.			
513TC	13c	brown	550.			
513TC	13c	black brown	550.			
513TC	13c	gray	550.			
513TC	13c	black	550.			

1920

			(1)	(2)	(3)	(4)
547TC	$2	green & black	1,300.			

1922-25

			(1)	(2)	(3)	(4)
554TC	2c	black (bond paper)		500.		
561TC	9c	red orange	900.			
563TC	11c	deep green	900.			
565TC	14c	dark brown	900.			
566TC	15c	black	900.			

1923

			(1)	(2)	(3)	(4)
611TC	2c	Harding, green	1,000.			

1926

			(1)	(2)	(3)	(4)
622TC	13c	black	1,000.			
628TC	5c	Ericsson, dull dusky blue	1,000.			
628TC		gray blue		1,000.		

1932

			(1)	(2)	(3)	(4)
718TC	3c	Olympic, car.	1,000.			
720TC	3c	black (bond paper)		750.		

1935

			(1)	(2)	(3)	(4)
773TC	3c	San Diego, org. red (yel. glazed card)	1,000.			

1936-43

			(1)	(2)	(3)	(4)
785TC	1c	Army, black (bond paper)		750.		
788TC	4c	Army, dk. brn.	900.			
789TC	5c	Army, blue	900.			
793TC	4c	Navy, dk. brn.	900.			
798TC	3c	Constitution, blk. (bond paper)		750.		
799TC	3c	Hawaii, black (bond paper)		750.		
800TC	3c	Alaska, black (bond paper)		750.		
800TC		(India paper)				
801TC	3c	Puerto Rico, blk (bond paper)	800.	750.		
801TC		(India paper)	800.			

802TC 3c	Virgin Islands, black (bond paper)		750.
815TC 10c	sepia	800.	
836TC 3c	Swedes & Finns, purple	800.	
837TC 3c	Northwest Terr., dark purple	800.	
854TC 3c	Inauguration, purple	800.	
862TC 5c	Authors, dull bl.	800.	
866TC 3c	Poets, dark blue violet	800.	
963TC 3c	Youth, violet	650.	
964TC 3c	Oregon, dull violet	650.	
968TC 3c	Poultry, red brown	650.	

1923-47

Air Post

		DIE (1) Lg.	(2) Sm.	PLATE (3) India	(4) Card
C5TC	16c dark green	5,000.			
C8TC	15c orange	4,500.			
C32TC	5c blue	4,500.			
C35TC	15c brown violet	4,500.			

1934

Air Post Special Delivery

CE1TC	16c black	4,000.	

1885-1902

Special Delivery

E1TC	10c black	1,000.	
E1TC	10c dark brown	1,000.	
E1TC	10c org. yellow (wove paper)		1,100.
E2TC	10c black	900.	
E2TC	10c green	900.	
E2TC	10c olive yellow		600.
E6TC	10c orange	1,000.	
E6TC	10c black	1,000.	
E6TC	10c rose red	1,500.	

1922-25

E12TC	10c black	1,100.	

1911

Registration

F1TC	10c black (glazed card)	900.	

Carriers

LO1TC	deep green	200.	
	Block of four	950.	
	a. orange (wove paper)		350.
LO2TC	deep green	200.	
	Block of four	950.	
	a. orange (wove paper)		350.

1879

Postage Due

		DIE (1) Lg.	(2) Sm.	PLATE (3) India	(4) Card
J1TC 1c	black	250.			25.
J1TC 1c	gray black	250.			
J1TC 1c	ultramarine	250.			
J1TC 1c	blue	250.			
J1TC 1c	blue green	250.			
J1TC 1c	orange	250.	80.		
J1TC 1c	red orange	250.			
J1TC 1c	olive bister	250.			
J2TC 2c	black	250.			
J2TC 2c	gray black	250.			
J2TC 2c	ultramarine	250.			
J2TC 2c	blue	250.			
J2TC 2c	blue green	250.			
J2TC 2c	orange	250.	80.		
J2TC 2c	red orange	250.			
J2TC 2c	sepia	250.			
J3TC 3c	black	250.			
J3TC 3c	gray black		80.		
J3TC 3c	ultramarine	250.			
J3TC 3c	blue	250.			
J3TC 3c	blue green	250.			
J3TC 3c	orange	250.	80.		
J3TC 3c	red orange	250.			
J3TC 3c	light brown	250.			
J4TC 5c	black	250.			
J4TC 5c	gray black	250.			
J4TC 5c	ultramarine	250.			
J4TC 5c	blue	250.			
J4TC 5c	blue green	250.			
J4TC 5c	orange	250.	80.		
J4TC 5c	red orange	250.			
J5TC 10c	black	250.			
J5TC 10c	gray black	250.			
J5TC 10c	blue	250.			
J5TC 10c	olive yellow	250.			
J5TC 10c	blue green	250.			
J5TC 10c	orange	250.	80.		
J5TC 10c	red orange	250.			
J5TC 10c	olive bister	250.			
J5TC 10c	sepia	250.			
J5TC 10c	gray	250.			
J6TC 30c	black	250.			
J6TC 30c	gray black	250.			
J6TC 30c	blue	250.			
J6TC 30c	olive yellow		80.		
J6TC 30c	blue green	250.			
J6TC 30c	orange	250.	80.		
J6TC 30c	red orange	250.			
J6TC 30c	olive bister	250.			
J6TC 30c	sepia		80.		
J7TC 50c	black	250.			
J7TC 50c	gray black	250.			
J7TC 50c	blue	250.	80.		
J7TC 50c	olive yellow		80.		
J7TC 50c	blue green	250.			
J7TC 50c	orange	250.	80.		
J7TC 50c	red orange	250.			
J7TC 50c	olive bister	250.			
J7TC 50c	sepia	250.			
J7TC 50c	gray	250.			

Official

		DIE (1) Lg.	(2) Sm.	PLATE (3) India	(4) Card
Agriculture					
O1TC 1c	black	190.		65.	
O2TC 2c	black	190.		65.	
O3TC 3c	black	190.			
O3TC 3c	deep green	190.			
O4TC 6c	black	190.		125.	
O5TC 10c	black	190.			
O6TC 12c	black	190.		65.	
O9TC 30c	black	190.			
Executive					
O11TC 2c	black	190.		65.	
O11TC 2c	deep brown	190.			
O11TC 2c	brown carmine				75.
O12TC 3c	black	190.		65.	
O12TC 3c	deep green	190.			
O13TC 6c	black			80.	
O14TC 10c	black			80.	
Interior					
O16TC 2c	black	190.			
O16TC 2c	deep brown	190.			
O17TC 3c	black	190.		80.	
O17TC 3c	deep green	190.			
Justice					
O27TC 3c	black	190.		80.	
O27TC 3c	deep green	190.			
O27TC 3c	bister yellow			80.	
O27TC 3c	dull orange			80.	
O27TC 3c	black violet			80.	
Navy					
O35TC 1c	black			80.	
O36TC 2c	black	190.			
O36TC 2c	deep brown	190.			
O36TC 2c	dp. green on wove paper, perf.				250.
O36TC 2c	dp. green on wove paper, imperf.				250.
O37TC 3c	black	190.		80.	
O37TC 3c	deep green	190.			
Post Office					
O48TC 2c	deep brown	190.			
O49TC 3c	deep green	190.			
O50TC 6c	deep brown	190.			
O50TC 6c	brown carmine	190.			
State					
O57TC 1c	black	190.			
O57TC 1c	lt. ultramarine	190.			
O58TC 2c	black	190.			
O58TC 2c	deep brown	190.			
O59TC 3c	black	190.			
O67TC 90c	black	190.			
O68TC $2	violet & black	1,000.			
O68TC $2	brown red & black	1,000.			
O68TC $2	orange red & slate blue	1,000.			
Treasury					
O72TC 1c	black	190.			
O72TC 1c	lt. ultramarine	190.			
O73TC 2c	black	190.			
O74TC 3c	black	190.			
O74TC 3c	deep green	190.			
O75TC 6c	black	190.			
O77TC 10c	black	190.			
O78TC 12c	black	190.			
O79TC 15c	black	190.			
O82TC 90c	black	190.			
War					
O83TC 1c	black	190.		80.	
O83TC 1c	lt. ultramarine	190.			
O84TC 2c	black	190.		80.	75.
O84TC 2c	deep brown	190.			
O85TC 3c	black	190.			
O85TC 3c	deep green	190.			
O86TC 6c	black			80.	
O89TC 12c	black			80.	

1910

Postal Savings Mail

O121TC 2c	lake	300.	

The so-called "Goodall" set of Small Die proofs on India Paper in five colors

		(a) Black	(b) Deep green	(c) Dull gray blue	(d) Deep brown	(e) Dull red
Agriculture						
O1TC	1c	150.	140.	140.	140.	140.
O2TC	2c	150.	140.	140.	140.	140.
O3TC	3c	150.	140.	140.	140.	140.
O4TC	6c	150.	140.	140.	140.	140.
O5TC	10c	150.	140.	140.	140.	140.
O6TC	12c	150.	140.	140.	140.	140.
O7TC	15c	150.	140.	140.	140.	140.
O8TC	24c	150.	140.	140.	140.	140.
O9TC	30c	150.	140.	140.	140.	140.
Executive						
O10TC	1c	150.	140.	140.	140.	140.
O11TC	2c	150.	140.	140.	140.	140.
O12TC	3c	150.	140.	140.	140.	140.
O13TC	6c	150.	140.	140.	140.	140.
O14TC	10c	150.	140.	140.	140.	140.
Interior						
O15TC	1c	150.	140.	140.	140.	140.
O16TC	2c	150.	140.	140.	140.	140.
O17TC	3c	150.	140.	140.	140.	140.
O18TC	6c	150.	140.	140.	140.	140.
O19TC	10c	150.	140.	140.	140.	140.
O20TC	12c	150.	140.	140.	140.	140.
O21TC	15c	150.	140.	140.	140.	140.
O22TC	24c	150.	140.	140.	140.	140.
O23TC	30c	150.	140.	140.	140.	140.
O24TC	90c	150.	140.	140.	140.	140.
Justice						
O25TC	1c	150.	140.	140.	140.	140.
O26TC	2c	150.	140.	140.	140.	140.
O27TC	3c	150.	140.	140.	140.	140.
O28TC	6c	150.	140.	140.	140.	140.
O29TC	10c	150.	140.	140.	140.	140.
O30TC	12c	150.	140.	140.	140.	140.
O31TC	15c	150.	140.	140.	140.	140.
O32TC	24c	150.	140.	140.	140.	140.
O33TC	30c	150.	140.	140.	140.	140.
O34TC	90c	150.	140.	140.	140.	140.
Navy						
O35TC	1c	150.	140.	140.	140.	140.
O36TC	2c	150.	140.	140.	140.	140.
O37TC	3c	150.	140.	140.	140.	140.
O38TC	6c	150.	140.	140.	140.	140.
O39TC	7c	150.	140.	140.	140.	140.
O40TC	10c	150.	140.	140.	140.	140.
O41TC	12c	150.	140.	140.	140.	140.
O42TC	15c	150.	140.	140.	140.	140.
O43TC	24c	150.	140.	140.	140.	140.
O44TC	30c	150.	140.	140.	140.	140.
O45TC	90c	150.	140.	140.	140.	140.
Post Office						
O47TC	1c	150.	140.	140.	140.	140.
O48TC	2c	150.	140.	140.	140.	140.
O49TC	3c	150.	140.	140.	140.	140.
O50TC	6c	150.	140.	140.	140.	140.
O51TC	10c	150.	140.	140.	140.	140.
O52TC	12c	150.	140.	140.	140.	140.
O53TC	15c	150.	140.	140.	140.	140.
O54TC	24c	150.	140.	140.	140.	140.
O55TC	30c	150.	140.	140.	140.	140.
O56TC	90c	150.	140.	140.	140.	140.
State						
O57TC	1c	150.	140.	140.	140.	140.
O58TC	2c	150.	140.	140.	140.	140.
O59TC	3c	150.	140.	140.	140.	140.
O60TC	6c	150.	140.	140.	140.	140.
O61TC	7c	150.	140.	140.	140.	140.
O62TC	10c	150.	140.	140.	140.	140.
O63TC	12c	150.	140.	140.	140.	140.
O64TC	15c	150.	140.	140.	140.	140.
O65TC	24c	150.	140.	140.	140.	140.
O66TC	30c	150.	140.	140.	140.	140.
O67TC	90c	150.	140.	140.	140.	140.

O68TC $2	scarlet frame, green center	900.
O68TC $2	scarlet frame, black center	900.
O68TC $2	scarlet frame, blue center	900.
O68TC $2	green frame, brown center	900.
O68TC $2	brown frame, green center	900.
O68TC $2	brown frame, black center	900.

		(a) Black	(b) Deep green	(c) Dull gray blue	(d) Deep brown	(e) Dull red
Treasury						
O72TC	1c	150.	140.	140.	140.	140.
O73TC	2c	150.	140.	140.	140.	140.
O74TC	3c	150.	140.	140.	140.	140.
O75TC	6c	150.	140.	140.	140.	140.
O76TC	7c	150.	140.	140.	140.	140.
O77TC	10c	150.	140.	140.	140.	140.
O78TC	12c	150.	140.	140.	140.	140.
O79TC	15c	150.	140.	140.	140.	140.
O80TC	24c	150.	140.	140.	140.	140.
O81TC	30c	150.	140.	140.	140.	140.
O82TC	90c	150.	140.	140.	140.	140.
War						
O83TC	1c	150.	140.	140.	140.	140.
O84TC	2c	150.	140.	140.	140.	140.
O85TC	3c	150.	140.	140.	140.	140.
O86TC	6c	150.	140.	140.	140.	140.
O87TC	7c	150.	140.	140.	140.	140.
O88TC	10c	150.	140.	140.	140.	140.
O89TC	12c	150.	140.	140.	140.	140.
O90TC	15c	150.	140.	140.	140.	140.
O91TC	24c	150.	140.	140.	140.	140.
O92TC	30c	150.	140.	140.	140.	140.
O93TC	90c	150.	140.	140.	140.	140.

Official Seals

1872

OX1TC	ultramarine	Die on India	250.
OX1TC	blue	Die on card, colored border	350.
OX1TC	deep blue	Die on card, colored border	350.
OX1TC	deep green	Die on card, colored border	350.

OX1TC	chocolate	Die on glossy bond	250.
OX1TC	chocolate	Die on card, colored border	350.
OX1TC	carmine	Die on India	250.
OX1TC	brown	Die on India	250.
OX1TC	red violet	Die on India	—

1877

OX3TC	blue	Die on India	150.
OX3TC	green	Die on India	150.
OX3TC	green	Plate on bond	150.
OX3TC	orange	Die on India	150.
OX3TC	red orange	Die on India	150.
OX3TC	black	Die on India	150.

Newspapers

1865

			(2) Sm. Die	(5) Thick cream wove paper
PR2TC	10c	black		70.
PR2TC	10c	lake		70.
PR2TC	10c	blue green		70.
PR2TC	10c	blue		70.
PR3TC	25c	black		70.
PR3TC	25c	lake		70.
PR3TC	25c	blue green		70.
PR3TC	25c	blue		70.
PR3TC	25c	ocher	200.	
PR3TC	25c	brick red	200.	
PR4TC	5c	black		70.
PR4TC	5c	lake		70.
PR4TC	5c	blue green		70.
PR4TC	5c	blue		70.

1875

			(1) Die on India	(3) Plate on India
PR9TC	2c	dark carmine		35.
PR9TC	2c	brown rose		35.
PR9TC	2c	scarlet		35.
PR9TC	2c	orange brown	110.	35.
PR9TC	2c	black brown	110.	
PR9TC	2c	sepia		35.
PR9TC	2c	orange yellow		35.
PR9TC	2c	dull orange		35.
PR9TC	2c	green		35.
PR9TC	2c	blue green	110.	
PR9TC	2c	light ultramarine		35.
PR9TC	2c	light blue		35.
PR9TC	2c	dark violet		35.
PR9TC	2c	violet black		35.
PR10TC	3c	rose lake	110.	
PR16TC	12c	dark carmine		35.
PR16TC	12c	brown rose	110.	35.
PR16TC	12c	scarlet	110.	35.
PR16TC	12c	orange brown		35.
PR16TC	12c	sepia	110.	35.
PR16TC	12c	orange yellow		35.
PR16TC	12c	dull orange		35.
PR16TC	12c	green	110.	35.
PR16TC	12c	light ultramarine	110.	35.
PR16TC	12c	light blue		35.
PR16TC	12c	dark violet	110.	35.
PR16TC	12c	violet black	110.	35.
PR16TC	12c	black	110.	35.
PR17TC	24c	sepia		
PR17TC	24c	green	110.	
PR17TC	24c	black	110.	35.
PR18TC	36c	black	110.	35.
PR18TC	36c	sepia	110.	
PR18TC	36c	green	110.	
PR19TC	48c	black	110.	35.
PR19TC	48c	sepia	110.	
PR19TC	48c	green	110.	
PR20TC	60c	black	110.	35.
PR21TC	72c	black	110.	35.
PR22TC	84c	black	110.	35.
PR23TC	96c	black		35.
PR24TC	$1.92	dark carmine		35.
PR24TC	$1.92	brown rose		35.
PR24TC	$1.92	scarlet		35.
PR24TC	$1.92	orange brown	110.	35.
PR24TC	$1.92	sepia		35.
PR24TC	$1.92	orange yellow		35.
PR24TC	$1.92	dull orange		35.
PR24TC	$1.92	green	110.	35.
PR24TC	$1.92	light ultramarine		35.
PR24TC	$1.92	dark violet		35.
PR24TC	$1.92	violet black		35.
PR24TC	$1.92	black		35.
PR25TC	$3	dark carmine	110.	35.
PR25TC	$3	brown rose		35.
PR25TC	$3	scarlet		35.
PR25TC	$3	orange brown		35.
PR25TC	$3	sepia		35.
PR25TC	$3	orange yellow	110.	35.
PR25TC	$3	dull orange	110.	35.
PR25TC	$3	green	110.	35.
PR25TC	$3	light ultramarine	110.	35.
PR25TC	$3	light blue		35.
PR25TC	$3	dark violet	110.	35.
PR25TC	$3	violet black	110.	35.
PR25TC	$3	black	110.	35.
PR26TC	$6	dark carmine	110.	35.
PR26TC	$6	brown rose	110.	35.
PR26TC	$6	scarlet	110.	35.
PR26TC	$6	orange brown		35.
PR26TC	$6	dark brown		35.
PR26TC	$6	sepia	110.	35.
PR26TC	$6	orange yellow	110.	35.
PR26TC	$6	dull orange	110.	35.
PR26TC	$6	green	110.	35.

			(1) Die on India	(3) Plate on India
PR26TC	$6	light ultramarine		35.
PR26TC	$6	light blue	110.	35.
PR26TC	$6	dark violet	110.	35.
PR26TC	$6	violet black	110.	35.
PR26TC	$6	black	110.	35.
PR27TC	$9	dark carmine	110.	35.
PR27TC	$9	brown rose	110.	35.
PR27TC	$9	scarlet	110.	35.
PR27TC	$9	orange brown		35.
PR27TC	$9	sepia	110.	35.
PR27TC	$9	orange yellow	110.	35.
PR27TC	$9	dull orange	110.	35.
PR27TC	$9	green	110.	35.
PR27TC	$9	light ultramarine	110.	35.
PR27TC	$9	light blue		35.
PR27TC	$9	dark violet	110.	35.
PR27TC	$9	violet black	110.	35.
PR27TC	$9	black	110.	35.
PR28TC	$12	black	110.	
PR28TC	$12	sepia	110.	
PR28TC	$12	orange brown	110.	
PR29TC	$24	black	110.	35.
PR29TC	$24	black brown	110.	
PR29TC	$24	orange brown	110.	
PR29TC	$24	green	110.	
PR30TC	$36	dark carmine	110.	
PR30TC	$36	black	110.	35.
PR30TC	$36	black brown	110.	
PR30TC	$36	orange brown	110.	
PR30TC	$36	sepia	110.	
PR30TC	$36	violet	110.	
PR30TC	$36	green	110.	
PR31TC	$48	violet brown	110.	35.
PR31TC	$48	black	110.	35.
PR31TC	$48	sepia	110.	
PR31TC	$48	green	110.	
PR32TC	$60	dark carmine	110.	40.
PR32TC	$60	scarlet	110.	40.
PR32TC	$60	sepia	110.	40.
PR32TC	$60	green	110.	40.
PR32TC	$60	light ultramarine	110.	40.
PR32TC	$60	black	110.	40.
PR32TC	$60	violet black	110.	
PR32TC	$60	orange brown	110.	
PR32TC	$60	orange yellow	110.	
PR32TC	$60	dull orange	110.	
PR32TC	$60	brown rose	110.	

1885

PR18TC	1c	salmon	110.	
PR18TC	1c	scarlet		120.
PR18TC	1c	dark brown		120.
PR18TC	1c	violet brown		120.
PR18TC	1c	dull orange		120.
PR18TC	1c	green		120.
PR18TC	1c	light blue		120.

1894

PR106TC	25c	deep carmine	150.
PR106TC	25c	dark carmine	150.
PR107TC	50c	black	150.
PR108TC	$2	deep scarlet	150.
PR108TC	$2	dark scarlet	150.
PR109TC	$5	light ultramarine	150.
PR109TC	$5	dark ultramarine	150.
PR110TC	$10	black	150.
PR112TC	$50	black	150.
PR112TC	$50	deep rose	150.
PR112TC	$50	dark rose	150.
PR113TC	$100	black	150.

The so-called "Goodall" set of Small Die proofs on India Paper in five colors

		(a) Black	(b) Deep green	(c) Dull gray blue	(d) Deep brown	(e) Dull red
PR9TC	2c	150.	125.	125.	125.	125.
PR10TC	3c	150.	125.	125.	125.	125.
PR11TC	4c	150.	125.	125.	125.	125.
PR12TC	6c	150.	125.	125.	125.	125.
PR13TC	8c	150.	125.	125.	125.	125.
PR14TC	9c	150.	125.	125.	125.	125.
PR15TC	10c	150.	125.	125.	125.	125.
PR16TC	12c	150.	125.	125.	125.	125.
PR17TC	24c	150.	125.	125.	125.	125.
PR18TC	36c	150.	125.	125.	125.	125.
PR19TC	48c	150.	125.	125.	125.	125.
PR20TC	60c	150.	125.	125.	125.	125.
PR21TC	72c	150.	125.	125.	125.	125.
PR22TC	84c	150.	125.	125.	125.	125.
PR23TC	96c	150.	125.	125.	125.	125.
PR24TC	$1.92	150.	125.	125.	125.	125.
PR25TC	$3	150.	125.	125.	125.	125.
PR26TC	$6	150.	125.	125.	125.	125.
PR27TC	$9	150.	125.	125.	125.	125.
PR28TC	$12	150.	125.	125.	125.	125.
PR29TC	$24	150.	125.	125.	125.	125.
PR30TC	$36	150.	125.	125.	125.	125.
PR31TC	$48	150.	125.	125.	125.	125.
PR32TC	$60	150.	125.	125.	125.	125.

1925

Special Handling

QE4TC	25c	apple green	700.
QE4TC	25c	olive green	700.
QE4TC	25c	light blue green	700.
QE4TC	25c	dark blue	700.
QE4TC	25c	orange yellow	700.
QE4TC	25c	orange	700.
QE4TC	25c	dull rose	700.
QE4TC	25c	carmine lake	700.
QE4TC	25c	brown	700.
QE4TC	25c	gray brown	700.
QE4TC	25c	dark violet brown	700.
QE4TC	25c	gray black	700.
QE4TC	25c	black	700.

THE "ATLANTA" SET OF PLATE PROOFS

A set in five colors on thin card reprinted in 1881 for display at
the International Cotton Exhibition in Atlanta, Ga.

1847 Designs (Reproductions)

		Black	Scarlet	Brown	Green	Blue
3TC	5c	300.	300.	300.	300.	300.
4TC	10c	300.	300.	300.	300.	300.

1851-60 Designs

		Black	Scarlet	Brown	Green	Blue
40TC	1c	150.	135.	135.	135.	135.
41TC	3c	150.	135.	135.	135.	135.
42TC	5c	150.	135.	135.	135.	135.
43TC	10c	150.	135.	135.	135.	135.
44TC	12c	150.	135.	135.	135.	135.
45TC	24c	150.	135.	135.	135.	135.
46TC	30c	150.	135.	135.	135.	135.
47TC	90c	150.	135.	135.	135.	135.

1861-66 Designs

		Black	Scarlet	Brown	Green	Blue
102TC	1c	125.	115.	115.	115.	115.
103TC	2c	200.	200.	200.	200.	200.
104TC	3c	125.	115.	115.	115.	115.
105TC	5c	125.	115.	115.	115.	115.
106TC	10c	125.	115.	115.	115.	115.
107TC	12c	125.	115.	115.	115.	115.
108TC	15c	125.	115.	115.	115.	115.
109TC	24c	125.	115.	115.	115.	115.
110TC	30c	125.	115.	115.	115.	115.
111TC	90c	125.	115.	115.	115.	115.

1869 Designs

		Black	Scarlet	Brown	Green	Blue
123TC	1c	200.	175.	175.	175.	175.
124TC	2c	200.	175.	175.	175.	175.
125TC	3c	200.	175.	175.	175.	175.
126TC	6c	200.	175.	175.	175.	175.
127TC	10c	200.	175.	175.	175.	175.
128TC	12c	200.	175.	175.	175.	175.

129TC	15c	black frame, scarlet center	450.
129TC	15c	black frame, green center	450.
129TC	15c	scarlet frame, black center	450.
129TC	15c	scarlet frame, blue center	450.
129TC	15c	brown frame, black center	450.
129TC	15c	brown frame, green center	450.
129TC	15c	brown frame, blue center	450.
129TC	15c	green frame, black center	450.
129TC	15c	green frame, blue center	450.
129TC	15c	blue frame, black center	450.
129TC	15c	blue frame, brown center	450.
129TC	15c	blue frame, green center	450.
130TC	24c	black frame, scarlet center	450.
130TC	24c	black frame, green center	450.
130TC	24c	black frame, blue center	450.
130TC	24c	scarlet frame, black center	450.
130TC	24c	scarlet frame, blue center	450.
130TC	24c	brown frame, black center	450.
130TC	24c	brown frame, blue center	450.
130TC	24c	green frame, black center	450.
130TC	24c	green frame, brown center	450.
130TC	24c	green frame, blue center	450.
130TC	24c	blue frame, brown center	450.
130TC	24c	blue frame, green center	450.
131TC	30c	black frame, scarlet center	450.
131TC	30c	black frame, green center	450.
131TC	30c	black frame, blue center	450.
131TC	30c	scarlet frame, black center	450.
131TC	30c	scarlet frame, green center	450.
131TC	30c	scarlet frame, blue center	450.
131TC	30c	brown frame, black center	450.
131TC	30c	brown frame, scarlet center	450.
131TC	30c	brown frame, blue center	450.
131TC	30c	green frame, black center	450.
131TC	30c	green frame, brown center	450.
131TC	30c	blue frame, scarlet center	450.
131TC	30c	blue frame, brown center	450.
131TC	30c	blue frame, green center	450.
132TC	90c	black frame, scarlet center	500.
132TC	90c	black frame, brown center	500.
132TC	90c	black frame, green center	500.
132TC	90c	scarlet frame, blue center	500.
132TC	90c	brown frame, black center	500.
132TC	90c	brown frame, blue center	500.
132TC	90c	green frame, brown center	500.
132TC	90c	green frame, blue center	500.
132TC	90c	blue frame, brown center	500.
132TC	90c	blue frame, green center	500.

1873-75 Designs

		Black	Scarlet	Brown	Green	Blue
156TC	1c	60.	55.	55.	55.	55.
157TC	2c	60.	55.	55.	55.	55.
158TC	3c	65.	60.	60.	60.	60.
159TC	6c	65.	60.	60.	60.	60.
160TC	7c	60.	55.	55.	55.	55.
161TC	10c	60.	55.	55.	55.	55.
162TC	12c	60.	55.	55.	55.	55.
163TC	15c	60.	55.	55.	55.	55.
164TC	24c	60.	55.	55.	55.	55.
165TC	30c	65.	60.	60.	60.	60.
166TC	90c	60.	55.	55.	55.	55.
179TC	5c	75.	70.	70.	70.	70.

		Black	Scarlet	Brown	Green	Blue
Postage Due						
J1TC	1c	60.	55.	55.	55.	55.
J2TC	2c	60.	55.	55.	55.	55.
J3TC	3c	60.	55.	55.	55.	55.
J4TC	5c	60.	55.	55.	55.	55.
J5TC	10c	60.	55.	55.	55.	55.
J6TC	30c	60.	55.	55.	55.	55.
J7TC	50c	60.	55.	55.	55.	55.
Carriers						
LO1TC	1c Franklin	100.	90.	90.	90.	90.
LO2TC	1c Eagle	100.	90.	90.	90.	90.
Agriculture						
O1TC	1c	45.	40.	40.	40.	40.
O2TC	2c	45.	40.	40.	40.	40.
O3TC	3c	45.	40.	40.	40.	40.
O4TC	6c	55.	50.	50.	50.	50.
O5TC	10c	45.	40.	40.	40.	40.
O6TC	12c	45.	40.	40.	40.	40.
O7TC	15c	45.	40.	40.	40.	40.
O8TC	24c	45.	40.	40.	40.	40.
O9TC	30c	45.	40.	40.	40.	40.
Executive						
O10TC	1c	45.	40.	40.	40.	40.
O11TC	2c	45.	40.	40.	40.	40.
O12TC	3c	45.	40.	40.	40.	40.
O13TC	6c	55.	50.	50.	50.	50.
O14TC	10c	45.	40.	40.	40.	40.
Interior						
O15TC	1c	45.	40.	40.	40.	40.
O16TC	2c	45.	40.	40.	40.	40.
O17TC	3c	45.	40.	40.	40.	40.
O18TC	6c	55.	50.	50.	50.	50.
O19TC	10c	45.	40.	40.	40.	40.
O20TC	12c	45.	40.	40.	40.	40.
O21TC	15c	45.	40.	40.	40.	40.
O22TC	24c	45.	40.	40.	40.	40.
O23TC	30c	60.	55.	55.	55.	55.
O24TC	90c	45.	40.	40.	40.	40.
Justice						
O25TC	1c	45.	40.	40.	40.	40.
O26TC	2c	45.	40.	40.	40.	40.
O27TC	3c	45.	40.	40.	40.	40.
O28TC	6c	55.	50.	50.	50.	50.
O29TC	10c	45.	40.	40.	40.	40.
O30TC	12c	45.	40.	40.	40.	40.
O31TC	15c	45.	40.	40.	40.	40.
O32TC	24c	45.	40.	40.	40.	40.
O33TC	30c	60.	55.	55.	55.	55.
O34TC	90c	45.	40.	40.	40.	40.
Navy						
O35TC	1c	45.	40.	40.	40.	40.
O36TC	2c	45.	40.	40.	40.	40.
O37TC	3c	45.	40.	40.	40.	40.
O38TC	6c	55.	50.	50.	50.	50.
O39TC	7c	45.	40.	40.	40.	40.
O40TC	10c	45.	40.	40.	40.	40.
O41TC	12c	45.	40.	40.	40.	40.
O42TC	15c	45.	40.	40.	40.	40.
O43TC	24c	45.	40.	40.	40.	40.
O44TC	30c	60.	55.	55.	55.	55.
O45TC	90c	45.	40.	40.	40.	40.
Post Office						
O48TC	2c	45.	40.	40.	40.	40.
O49TC	3c	45.	40.	40.	40.	40.
O50TC	6c	45.	40.	40.	40.	40.
O51TC	10c	45.	40.	40.	40.	40.
O52TC	12c	45.	40.	40.	40.	40.
O53TC	15c	45.	40.	40.	40.	40.
O54TC	24c	45.	40.	40.	40.	40.
O55TC	30c	45.	40.	40.	40.	40.
O56TC	90c	45.	40.	40.	40.	40.
State						
O57TC	1c	45.	40.	40.	40.	40.
O58TC	2c	45.	40.	40.	40.	40.
O59TC	3c	45.	40.	40.	40.	40.
O60TC	6c	55.	50.	50.	50.	50.
O61TC	7c	45.	40.	40.	40.	40.
O62TC	10c	45.	40.	40.	40.	40.
O63TC	12c	45.	40.	40.	40.	40.
O64TC	15c	45.	40.	40.	40.	40.
O65TC	24c	45.	40.	40.	40.	40.
O66TC	30c	60.	55.	55.	55.	55.
O67TC	90c	45.	40.	40.	40.	40.

O68TC	$2	scarlet frame, black center	850.
O68TC	$2	scarlet frame, blue center	850.
O68TC	$2	brown frame, black center	850.
O68TC	$2	brown frame, blue center	850.
O68TC	$2	green frame, brown center	850.
O68TC	$2	blue frame, brown center	850.
O68TC	$2	blue frame, green center	850.
O69TC	$5	scarlet frame, black center	850.
O69TC	$5	scarlet frame, blue center	850.
O69TC	$5	brown frame, black center	850.
O69TC	$5	brown frame, blue center	850.
O69TC	$5	green frame, brown center	850.
O69TC	$5	blue frame, brown center	850.
O69TC	$5	blue frame, green center	850.
O70TC	$10	scarlet frame, black center	850.
O70TC	$10	scarlet frame, blue center	850.
O70TC	$10	brown frame, black center	850.
O70TC	$10	brown frame, blue center	850.
O70TC	$10	green frame, brown center	850.
O70TC	$10	blue frame, brown center	850.
O70TC	$10	blue frame, green center	850.
O71TC	$20	scarlet frame, black center	850.
O71TC	$20	scarlet frame, blue center	850.
O71TC	$20	brown frame, black center	850.
O71TC	$20	brown frame, blue center	850.
O71TC	$20	green frame, brown center	850.
O71TC	$20	blue frame, brown center	850.
O71TC	$20	blue frame, green center	850.

		Black	Scarlet	Brown	Green	Blue
Treasury						
O72TC	1c	45.	40.	40.	40.	40.
O73TC	2c	45.	40.	40.	40.	40.
O74TC	3c	45.	40.	40.	40.	40.
O75TC	6c	55.	50.	50.	50.	50.
O76TC	7c	45.	40.	40.	40.	40.
O77TC	10c	45.	40.	40.	40.	40.
O78TC	12c	45.	40.	40.	40.	40.
O79TC	15c	45.	40.	40.	40.	40.
O80TC	24c	45.	40.	40.	40.	40.
O81TC	30c	60.	55.	55.	55.	55.
O82TC	90c	45.	40.	40.	40.	40.
War						
O83TC	1c	45.	40.	40.	40.	40.
O84TC	2c	45.	40.	40.	40.	40.
O85TC	3c	45.	40.	40.	40.	40.
O86TC	6c	55.	50.	50.	50.	50.
O87TC	7c	45.	40.	40.	40.	40.
O88TC	10c	45.	40.	40.	40.	40.
O89TC	12c	45.	40.	40.	40.	40.
O90TC	15c	45.	40.	40.	40.	40.
O91TC	24c	45.	40.	40.	40.	40.
O92TC	30c	60.	55.	55.	55.	55.
O93TC	90c	45.	40.	40.	40.	40.
Newspapers						
PR9TC	2c	45.	30.	30.	30.	30.
PR10TC	3c	45.	30.	30.	30.	30.
PR11TC	4c	45.	30.	30.	30.	30.
PR12TC	6c	45.	30.	30.	30.	30.
PR13TC	8c	45.	30.	30.	30.	30.
PR14TC	9c	45.	30.	30.	30.	30.
PR15TC	10c	45.	30.	30.	30.	30.
PR16TC	12c	45.	30.	30.	30.	30.
PR17TC	24c	45.	30.	30.	30.	30.
PR18TC	36c	45.	30.	30.	30.	30.
PR19TC	48c	45.	30.	30.	30.	30.
PR20TC	60c	45.	30.	30.	30.	30.
PR21TC	72c	45.	30.	30.	30.	30.
PR22TC	84c	45.	30.	30.	30.	30.
PR23TC	96c	45.	30.	30.	30.	30.
PR24TC	$ 1.92	45.	30.	30.	30.	30.
PR25TC	$ 3	45.	30.	30.	30.	30.
PR26TC	$ 6	45.	30.	30.	30.	30.
PR27TC	$ 9	45.	30.	30.	30.	30.
PR28TC	$12	45.	30.	30.	30.	30.
PR29TC	$24	45.	30.	30.	30.	30.
PR30TC	$36	45.	30.	30.	30.	30.
PR31TC	$48	45.	30.	30.	30.	30.
PR32TC	$60	45.	30.	30.	30.	30.

REVENUES

Several lists of revenue proofs in trial colors have been published, but the accuracy of some of them is questionable. The following listings are limited to items seen by the editors. The list is not complete.

1862-71 FIRST ISSUE

R3TC	1c	Proprietary, black	Plate on India	80.
R3TC	1c	Proprietary, carmine	Plate on Card	110.
R3TC	1c	Proprietary, dull red	Plate on Bond	110.
R3TC	1c	Proprietary, dull yel.	Plate on Bond	110.
R3TC	1c	Proprietary, vio. rose	Plate on Bond	110.
R3TC	1c	Proprietary, deep blue	Plate on Bond	110.
R3TC	1c	Proprietary, red on blue	Plate on Bond	110.
R3TC	1c	Proprietary, blue, perf. & gum	Plate on Bond	110.
R7TC	2c	Certificate, ultra.	Plate on Card	65.
R11TC	2c	Playing Cards, black	Die on India	400.
R13TC	2c	Proprietary, black	Plate on India	75.
R15TC	2c	U.S.I.R., violet rose	Plate on Bond	110.
R15TC	2c	U.S.I.R., light green	Plate on Bond	110.
R15TC	2c	U.S.I.R., pale blue	Plate on Bond	110.
R15TC	2c	U.S.I.R., black	Plate on India	110.
R16TC	3c	Foreign Exchange, green on blue	Plate on Bond	110.
R16TC	3c	Foreign Exchange, blue	Plate on Goldbeater's Skin	110.
R18TC	3c	Proprietary, black	Die on India	300.
R21TC	4c	Playing Cards, black	Die (?) on India	300.
R22TC	4c	Proprietary, black	Plate on India	110.
R22TC	4c	Proprietary, black	Die on India	350.
R22TC	4c	Proprietary, red lilac	Plate on Card	110.
R24TC	5c	Certificate, carmine	Plate on India	110.
R26TC	5c	Foreign Exchange, orange	Plate on India	110.
R28TC	5c	Playing Cards, black	Die (?) on India	300.
R30TC	6c	Inland Exchange, black	Die on India	350.
R31TC	6c	Proprietary, black	Die on India	—
R32TC	10c	Bill of Lading, greenish blue	Die on India	350.
R35TC	10c	Foreign Exchange, black	Die (?) on India	350.
R37TC	10c	Power of Attorney, greenish blue	Die on India	350.
R38TC	10c	Proprietary, black	Die on India	350.
R43TC	25c	Bond, carmine	Plate on Card	90.
R46TC	25c	Insurance, dull red	Plate on Bond	150.
R46TC	25c	Insurance, dull red	Plate on Goldbeater's Skin	210.
R46TC	25c	Insurance, vermilion	Plate on Goldbeater's Skin	210.
R46TC	25c	Insurance, vermilion	Plate on Bond	170.
R46TC	25c	Insurance, blue	Plate on Bond	170.
R46TC	25c	Insurance, blue	Plate on Goldbeater's Skin	215.
R46TC	25c	Insurance, dark blue	Plate on Bond	155.
R46TC	25c	Insurance, dark blue	Plate on Goldbeater's Skin	215.
R46TC	25c	Insurance, green	Plate on Goldbeater's Skin	215.
R51TC	30c	Foreign Exchange, violet	Plate on India	130.
R51TC	30c	violet gray	Plate on India	130.
R51TC	30c	black	Plate on India	155.
R51TC	30c	red	Plate on India	155.
R52TC	30c	Inland Exchange, deep red lilac	Plate on India	155.
R55TC	50c	Entry of Goods, orange	Plate on Bond	275.
R55TC	50c	green	Plate on Bond	275.
R55TC	50c	red	Plate on Bond	340.
R58TC	50c	Life Insurance, ultramarine	Plate on India	85.
R60TC	50c	Original Process, black	Die (?) on India	280.
R64TC	60c	Inland Exchange, green	Die (?) on India	—
R65TC	70c	Foreign Exchange, orange	Die (?) on India	—
R65TC	70c	Foreign Exchange, black	Die (?) on India	285.
R66TC	$1	Conveyance, carmine	Plate on India	85.
R67TC	$1	Entry of Goods, carmine	Plate on India	60.
R68TC	$1	Foreign Exchange, carmine	Plate on India	60.
R69TC	$1	Inland Exchange, carmine	Plate on India	60.
R70TC	$1	Lease, carmine	Plate on India	130.
R71TC	$1	Life Insurance, carmine	Plate on India	75.
R72TC	$1	Manifest, carmine	Plate on India	80.
R73TC	$1	Mortgage, carmine	Plate on India	85.
R74TC	$1	Passage Ticket, carmine	Plate on India	120.
R75TC	$1	Power of Attorney, carmine	Plate on India	120.
R76TC	$1	Probate of Will, carmine	Plate on India	60.
R78TC	$1.50	Inland Exchange, black	Die on India	475.
R80TC	$1.90	Foreign Exchange, black	Plate on India	155.
R81TC	$2	Conveyance, carmine	Plate on Card	85.
R82TC	$2	Mortgage, carmine	Plate on Card	85.
R84TC	$2.50	Inland Exchange, black	Die (?) on India	120.
R87TC	$3.50	Inland Exchange, black	Die on India	400.
R88TC	$5	Charter Party, carmine	Plate on India	85.
R89TC	$5	Conveyance, carmine	Plate on India	90.
R91TC	$5	Mortgage, carmine	Plate on India	90.
R95TC	$10	Mortgage, yel. green	Plate on India	—
R98TC	$20	Conveyance, red orange	Plate on Card	120.
R98TC	$20	red orange	Plate on India	220.
R99TC	$20	Probate of Will, red orange	Plate on Card	275.
R99TC	$20	black	Plate on Card	275.
R101TC	$50	U.S.I.R., orange	Plate on Bond	275.
R101TC	$50	U.S.I.R., deep blue	Plate on Bond	275.
R102TC	$200	U.S.I.R., black & red	Plate on India	1,400.
R102TC	$200	gray brown & red	Plate on India	1,400.
R102TC	$200	green & brown red	Plate on India	1,400.

SECOND ISSUE

R104TC	2c	pale blue & black	Plate on Bond	60.
R132TC	$200	green, red & black	Die on India	2,500.
R132TC	$200	orange	Die on India	2,500.
R132TC	$200	blue	Die on India	2,500.
R132TC	$200	green	Die on India	2,500.
R133TC	$500	green, yel. & black	Die on India	2,500.
R133TC	$500	black	Plate on Card	3,250.
R133TC	$500	yellow & black	Plate on Card	2,500.
R133TC	$500	red, green & black	Plate on Bond	3,000.
R133TC	$500	blue, scarlet & black	Plate on Bond	2,500.

THIRD ISSUE

R134TC	1c	brown & black	Plate on Card	60.

1875 National Bank Note Co., New York City

R152TC	2c	(Liberty), green	Die on India	600.
R152TC	2c	(Liberty), brown	Die on India	600.
R152TC	2c	(Liberty), black	Die on India	600.

1898

R161TC	½c	green	Lg. die on India	750.
R163TC	1c	green	Lg. die on India	750.
R163TC	1c	black	Lg. die on India	750.
R165TC	3c	green	Sm. die on India	650.
R169TC	25c	green	Lg. die on India	650.
R170TC	40c	black	Lg. die on India	650.
R172TC	80c	green	Lg. die on India	650.

1898

R174TC	$3	black	Die on India	650.
R176TC	$10	green	Die on India	650.

1899

R179TC	$100	dark green & black	Die on India	850.
R181TC	$1000	dark blue & black	Die on India	850.

1914

R195TC	½c	black	Small die on Wove	—
R196TC	1c	blue green	Small die on Wove	—
R198TC	3c	ultramarine	Small die on Wove	—
R199TC	4c	brown	Small die on Wove	—
R200TC	5c	blue	Small die on Wove	—
R201TC	10c	yellow	Small die on Wove	—
R202TC	25c	dull violet	Small die on Wove	—
R203TC	40c	blue green	Small die on Wove	—
R204TC	50c	red brown	Small die on Wove	—
R205TC	80c	orange	Small die on Wove	—

Proprietary

1871-75

RB1TC	1c	blue & black	Plate on Bond	70.
RB1TC	1c	scarlet & black	Plate on Bond	70.
RB1TC	1c	orange & black	Plate on Bond	70.
RB1TC	1c	orange & ultramarine	Plate on Granite Bond	60.
RB3TC	3c	blue & black, with gum	Plate on Bond	60.
RB3TC	3c	blue & black	Plate on Gray Bond	60.
RB8TC	50c	green & brown	Die on India	675.
RB8TC	50c	green & purple	Die on India	675.
RB8TC	50c	green & brown red	Die on India	675.
RB8TC	50c	green & violet	Die on India	675.
RB8TC	50c	green & dk. carmine	Die on India	675.
RB8TC	50c	ultramarine & red	Die on India	675.
RB9TC	$1	green & brown	Die on India	675.
RB9TC	$1	green & purple	Die on India	675.
RB9TC	$1	green & violet brown	Die on India	675.
RB9TC	$1	green & brown red	Die on India	675.
RB9TC	$1	green & violet	Die on India	675.
RB9TC	$1	green & dk. carmine	Die on India	675.

1875-83

RB11TC	1c	brown	Die on India	500.
RB11TC	1c	black	Die on India	500.
RB12TC	2c	green	Die on India	500.
RB12TC	2c	black	Die on India	500.
RB12TC	2c	brown	Die on India	500.
RB13TC	3c	brown	Die on India	500.
RB13TC	3c	green	Die on India	500.
RB13TC	3c	black	Plate on India	150.
RB14TC	4c	dark brown	Die on India	450.
RB14TC	4c	green	Die on India	450.
RB14TC	4c	black	Die on India	450.
RB14TC	4c	black	Plate on India	150.
RB16TC	5c	green	Die on India	450.
RB17TC	6c	green	Plate on India	150.
RB17TC	6c	black	Die on India	450.
RB17TC	6c	black	Plate on India	150.
RB17TC	6c	violet brown	Die on India	550.
RB19TC	10c	black	Die on India	550.

SECOND, THIRD AND PROPRIETARY ISSUES

Stamps Nos. R103 to R131, R134 to R150 and RB1 to RB7.

A special composite plate was made and impressions taken in various colors and shades. Although all varieties in all colors must have been made, only those seen by the editors are listed.

PLATE PROOFS ON INDIA PAPER CENTERS IN BLACK

1871-75

R103TC 1c

- a. dark purple 60.
- b. dull purple 60.
- d. brown 60.
- e. black brown 60.
- g. light blue 60.
- h. dark blue 70.
- i. ultramarine 70.
- k. yellow green 70.
- n. green 65.
- o. dark green 65.
- p. blue green 65.
- q. light orange 65.
- r. dark orange 65.
- s. deep orange 65.
- t. scarlet 65.
- u. carmine 65.
- x. dark brown red 65.
- y. dark brown orange, goldbeater's skin 90.

R104TC 2c

- a. dark purple 60.
- b. dull purple 60.
- d. brown 60.
- e. black brown 60.
- g. light blue 60.
- h. dark blue 70.
- i. ultramarine 70.
- k. yellow green 70.
- l. dark yellow green 70.
- n. green 65.
- o. dark green 65.
- p. blue green 65.
- q. light orange 65.
- r. dark orange 65.
- s. deep orange 65.
- t. scarlet 65.
- u. carmine 65.
- x. dark brown red 65.
- y. dark brown orange, goldbeater's skin 90.

R105TC 3c

- a. dark purple 60.
- b. dull purple 60.
- d. brown 60.
- e. black brown 60.
- g. light blue 60.
- h. dark blue 70.
- i. ultramarine 70.
- k. yellow green 70.
- n. green 65.
- o. dark green 65.
- p. blue green 65.
- q. light orange 65.
- r. dark orange 65.
- s. deep orange 65.
- t. scarlet 65.
- u. carmine 65.
- x. dark brown red 65.
- y. dark brown orange, goldbeater's skin 90.

R106TC 4c

- a. dark purple 60.
- b. dull purple 60.
- d. brown 60.
- e. black brown 60.
- f. orange brown 65.
- g. light blue 60.
- h. dark blue 70.
- i. ultramarine 70.
- k. yellow green 70.
- n. green 65.
- o. dark green 65.
- p. blue green 65.
- q. light orange 65.
- r. dark orange 65.
- s. deep orange 65.
- t. scarlet 65.
- u. carmine 65.
- x. dark brown red 65.
- y. dark brown orange, goldbeater's skin 90.

R107TC 5c

- a. dark purple 60.
- b. dull purple 60.
- d. brown 60.
- e. black brown 60.
- f. orange brown 65.
- g. light blue 60.
- h. dark blue 70.
- i. ultramarine 70.
- k. yellow green 70.
- n. green 65.
- o. dark green 65.
- p. blue green 65.
- q. light orange 65.
- r. dark orange 65.
- s. deep orange 65.
- t. scarlet 65.
- u. carmine 65.
- v. dark carmine 65.
- w. purplish carmine 65.
- x. dark brown red 65.
- y. dark brown orange, goldbeater's skin 90.

R108TC 6c

- a. dark purple 60.
- b. dull purple 60.
- d. brown 60.
- e. black brown 60.
- f. orange brown 65.
- g. light blue 60.
- h. dark blue 70.
- i. ultramarine 70.
- k. yellow green 70.
- n. green 65.
- o. dark green 65.
- p. blue green 65.
- q. light orange 65.
- r. dark orange 65.
- s. deep orange 65.
- t. scarlet 65.
- u. carmine 65.
- v. dark carmine 65.
- w. purplish carmine 65.
- x. dark brown red 65.
- y. dark brown orange, goldbeater's skin

R109TC 10c

- a. dark purple 60.
- b. dull purple 60.
- d. brown 60.
- e. black brown 60.
- g. light blue 60.
- h. dark blue 70.
- i. ultramarine 70.
- k. yellow green 70.
- n. green 65.
- o. dark green 65.
- p. blue green 65.
- q. light orange 65.
- r. dark orange 65.
- s. deep orange 65.
- t. scarlet 65.
- u. carmine 65.
- x. dark brown red 65.

R110TC 15c

- a. dark purple 60.
- b. dull purple 60.
- d. brown 60.
- e. black brown 60.
- f. orange brown 65.
- g. light blue 60.
- h. dark blue 70.
- i. ultramarine 70.
- k. yellow green 70.
- n. green 65.
- o. dark green 65.
- p. blue green 65.
- q. light orange 65.
- r. dark orange 65.
- s. deep orange 65.
- t. scarlet 65.
- u. carmine 65.
- w. purplish carmine 65.
- x. dark brown red 65.

R111TC 20c

- a. dark purple 60.
- b. dull purple 60.
- d. brown 60.
- e. black brown 60.
- g. light blue 60.
- h. dark blue 70.
- i. ultramarine 70.
- k. yellow green 70.
- n. green 65.
- o. dark green 65.
- p. blue green 65.
- q. light orange 65.
- r. dark orange 65.
- s. deep orange 65.
- t. scarlet 65.
- u. carmine 65.
- w. purplish carmine 65.
- x. dark brown red 65.
- y. dark brown orange, goldbeater's skin 90.

R112TC 25c

- a. dark purple 60.
- b. dull purple 60.
- d. brown 60.
- e. black brown 60.
- g. light blue 60.
- h. dark blue 70.
- i. ultramarine 70.
- k. yellow green 70.
- l. dark yellow green 70.
- n. green 65.
- o. dark green 65.
- p. blue green 65.
- q. light orange 65.
- r. dark orange 65.
- s. deep orange 65.
- t. scarlet 65.
- u. carmine 65.
- x. dark brown red 65.
- y. dark brown orange, goldbeater's skin 90.

R113TC 30c

- a. dark purple 60.
- b. dull purple 60.
- d. brown 60.
- e. black brown 60.
- g. light blue 60.
- h. dark blue 70.
- i. ultramarine 70.
- k. yellow green 70.
- n. green 65.
- o. dark green 65.

No.	Color	Price
	p. blue green	65.
	q. light orange	65.
	r. dark orange	65.
	s. deep orange	65.
	t. scarlet	65.
	u. carmine	65.
	v. dark carmine	65.
	w. purplish carmine	65.
	x. dark brown red	65.
	y. dark brown orange, goldbeater's skin	90.
R114TC 40c		
	a. dark purple	60.
	b. dull purple	60.
	d. brown	60.
	e. black brown	60.
	f. orange brown	65.
	g. light blue	60.
	h. dark blue	70.
	i. ultramarine	70.
	k. yellow green	70.
	n. green	65.
	o. dark green	65.
	p. blue green	65.
	q. light orange	65.
	r. dark orange	65.
	s. deep orange	65.
	t. scarlet	65.
	u. carmine	65.
	x. dark brown red	65.
R115TC 50c		
	a. dark purple	60.
	b. dull purple	60.
	d. brown	60.
	e. black brown	60.
	g. light blue	60.
	h. dark blue	70.
	i. ultramarine	70.
	k. yellow green	70.
	n. green	65.
	o. dark green	65.
	p. blue green	65.
	q. light orange	65.
	r. dark orange	65.
	s. deep orange	65.
	t. scarlet	65.
	u. carmine	65.
	x. dark brown red	65.
R116TC 60c		
	a. dark purple	60.
	b. dull purple	60.
	d. brown	60.
	e. black brown	60.
	g. light blue	60.
	h. dark blue	70.
	i. ultramarine	70.
	k. yellow green	70.
	n. green	65.
	o. dark green	65.
	p. blue green	65.
	q. light orange	65.
	r. dark orange	65.
	s. deep orange	65.
	t. scarlet	65.
	u. carmine	65.
	v. dark carmine	65.
	x. dark brown red	65.
	y. dark brown orange, goldbeater's skin	90.
R117TC 70c		
	a. dark purple	60.
	b. dull purple	60.
	d. brown	60.
	e. black brown	60.
	g. light blue	60.
	h. dark blue	70.
	i. ultramarine	70.
	k. yellow green	70.
	n. green	65.
	o. dark green	65.
	p. blue green	65.
	q. light orange	65.
	r. dark orange	65.
	s. deep orange	65.
	t. scarlet	65.
	u. carmine	65.
	x. dark brown red	65.
R118TC $1		
	a. dark purple	70.
	b. dull purple	70.
	d. brown	70.
	e. black brown	70.
	g. light blue	80.
	h. dark blue	82.50
	i. ultramarine	82.50
	k. yellow green	77.50
	n. green	72.50
	o. dark green	72.50
	p. blue green	72.50
	q. light orange	72.50
	r. dark orange	72.50
	s. deep orange	72.50
	t. scarlet	77.50
	u. carmine	77.50
	w. purplish carmine	77.50
	x. dark brown red	77.50
	y. dark brown orange, goldbeater's skin	90.
R119TC $1.30		
	a. dark purple	70.
	b. dull purple	70.
	d. brown	70.
	e. black brown	70.
	g. light blue	80.
	h. dark blue	82.50
	i. ultramarine	82.50
	j. bright yellow green, on card	72.50
	k. yellow green	77.50
	n. green	72.50
	o. dark green	72.50
	p. blue green	72.50
	q. light orange	72.50
	r. dark orange	72.50
	s. deep orange	72.50
	t. scarlet	77.50
	u. carmine	77.50
	x. dark brown red	77.50
R120TC $1.50		
	a. dark purple	70.
	b. dull purple	70.
	d. brown	70.
	e. black brown	70.
	g. light blue	80.
	h. dark blue	82.50
	i. ultramarine	82.50
	j. bright yellow green, on card	72.50
	k. yellow green	77.50
	n. green	72.50
	o. dark green	72.50
	p. blue green	72.50
	q. light orange	72.50
	r. dark orange	72.50
	s. deep orange	72.50
	t. scarlet	77.50
	u. carmine	77.50
	x. dark brown red	77.50
R121TC $1.60		
	a. dark purple	70.
	b. dull purple	70.
	d. brown	70.
	e. black brown	70.
	g. light blue	80.
	h. dark blue	82.50
	i. ultramarine	82.50
	k. yellow green	77.50
	n. green	72.50
	o. dark green	72.50
	p. blue green	72.50
	q. light orange	72.50
	r. dark orange	72.50
	s. deep orange	72.50
	t. scarlet	77.50
	u. carmine	77.50
	x. dark brown red	77.50
R122TC $1.90		
	a. dark purple	70.
	b. dull purple	70.
	d. brown	70.
	e. black brown	70.
	g. light blue	80.
	h. dark blue	82.50
	i. ultramarine	82.50
	j. bright yellow green, on card	72.50
	k. yellow green	77.50
	n. green	72.50
	o. dark green	72.50
	p. blue green	72.50
	q. light orange	72.50
	r. dark orange	72.50
	s. deep orange	72.50
	t. scarlet	77.50
	u. carmine	77.50
	x. dark brown red	77.50
R123TC $2		
	a. dark purple	70.
	b. dull purple	70.
	d. brown	70.
	e. black brown	70.
	g. light blue	80.
	h. dark blue	82.50
	i. ultramarine	82.50
	j. bright yellow green, on card	72.50
	k. yellow green	77.50
	n. green	72.50
	o. dark green	72.50
	p. blue green	72.50
	q. light orange	72.50
	r. dark orange	72.50
	s. deep orange	72.50
	t. scarlet	77.50
	u. carmine	77.50
	w. purplish carmine	77.50
	x. dark brown red	77.50
	y. dark brown orange, goldbeater's skin	100.
R124TC $2.50		
	a. dark purple	70.
	b. dull purple	70.
	d. brown	70.
	e. black brown	70.
	g. light blue	80.
	h. dark blue	82.50
	i. ultramarine	82.50
	k. yellow green	77.50
	n. green	72.50
	o. dark green	72.50
	p. blue green	72.50
	q. light orange	72.50
	r. dark orange	72.50
	s. deep orange	72.50
	t. scarlet	77.50
	u. carmine	77.50
	v. dark carmine	77.50
	x. dark brown red	77.50
R125TC $3		
	a. dark purple	70.
	b. dull purple	70.
	d. brown	70.
	e. black brown	70.
	g. light blue	80.
	h. dark blue	82.50
	i. ultramarine	82.50
	j. bright yellow green, on card	72.50
	k. yellow green	77.50
	n. green	72.50
	o. dark green	72.50
	p. blue green	72.50
	q. light orange	72.50
	r. dark orange	72.50
	s. deep orange	72.50
	t. scarlet	77.50
	u. carmine	77.50
	x. dark brown red	77.50
R126TC $3.50		
	a. dark purple	70.
	b. dull purple	70.
	c. red purple	75.
	d. brown	70.
	e. black brown	70.
	g. light blue	80.
	h. dark blue	82.50
	i. ultramarine	82.50
	k. yellow green	77.50
	n. green	72.50
	o. dark green	72.50
	p. blue green	72.50
	q. light orange	72.50
	r. dark orange	72.50
	s. deep orange	72.50
	t. scarlet	87.50
	u. carmine	77.50
	x. dark brown red	77.50
R127TC $5		
	a. dark purple	70.
	b. dull purple	70.
	d. brown	70.
	e. black brown	70.
	g. light blue	80.
	h. dark blue	82.50
	i. ultramarine	82.50
	k. yellow green	77.50
	n. green	72.50
	o. dark green	72.50
	p. blue green	72.50
	q. light orange	72.50
	r. dark orange	72.50
	s. deep orange	72.50
	t. scarlet	72.50
	u. carmine	72.50
	w. purplish carmine	72.50
	x. dark brown red	77.50
	y. dark brown orange, goldbeater's skin	100.
R128TC $10		
	a. dark purple	70.
	b. dull purple	70.
	d. brown	70.
	e. black brown	70.
	g. light blue	80.
	h. dark blue	82.50
	i. ultramarine	82.50
	j. bright yellow green, on card	72.50
	k. yellow green	75.
	n. green	72.50
	o. dark green	72.50
	p. blue green	72.50
	q. light orange	72.50
	r. dark orange	72.50
	s. deep orange	72.50
	t. scarlet	72.50
	u. carmine	77.50
	x. dark brown red	77.50
R129TC $20		
	a. dark purple	95.
	b. dull purple	95.
	d. brown	95.
	e. black brown	95.
	g. light blue	87.50
	h. dark blue	87.50
	i. ultramarine	87.50
	k. yellow green	85.
	m. emerald green	85.
	n. green	72.50
	o. dark green	72.50
	p. blue green	72.50
	q. light orange	72.50
	r. dark orange	85.
	s. deep orange	85.
	t. scarlet	87.50
	u. carmine	77.50
	v. dark carmine	87.50
	x. dark brown red	77.50
R130TC $25		
	a. dark purple	100.
	b. dull purple	100.
	d. brown	100.
	e. black brown	100.
	g. light blue	90.
	h. dark blue	87.50
	i. ultramarine	87.50
	k. yellow green	85.
	m. emerald green	85.
	n. green	72.50
	o. dark green	72.50
	p. blue green	72.50
	q. light orange	72.50
	r. dark orange	85.
	s. deep orange	85.
	t. scarlet	87.50
	u. carmine	77.50
	w. purplish carmine	87.50
	x. dark brown red	300.
	y. dark brown orange, goldbeater's skin	100.
R131TC $50		
	a. dark purple	95.
	b. dull purple	95.
	d. brown	95.
	e. black brown	95.
	g. light blue	87.50
	h. dark blue	87.50
	i. ultramarine	87.50
	j. bright yellow green, on card	85.
	k. yellow green	85.
	m. emerald green	85.
	n. green	72.50
	o. dark green	72.50

		Color	Price
		p. blue green	72.50
		q. light orange	72.50
		r. dark orange	85.
		s. deep orange	85.
		t. scarlet	87.50
		u. carmine	77.50
		x. dark brown red	77.50
RB1TC	1c		
		a. dark purple	67.50
		b. dull purple	67.50
		d. brown	65.
		e. black brown	65.
		g. light blue	75.
		h. dark blue	75.
		i. ultramarine	75.
		k. yellow green	70.
		l. dark yellow green	70.
		n. green	65.
		o. dark green	65.
		p. blue green	65.
		q. light orange	65.
		r. dark orange	65.
		s. deep orange	65.
		t. scarlet	65.
		u. carmine	65.
		x. dark brown red	65.
RB2TC	2c		
		a. dark purple	67.50
		b. dull purple	67.50
		d. brown	65.
		e. black brown	65.
		g. light blue	70.
		h. dark blue	70.
		i. ultramarine	70.
		j. bright yellow green, on card	70.
		k. yellow green	70.
		n. green	65.
		o. dark green	65.
		p. blue green	65.
		q. light orange	65.
		r. dark orange	65.
		s. deep orange	65.
		t. scarlet	65.
		u. carmine	65.
		x. dark brown red	65.
RB3TC	3c		
		a. dark purple	67.50
		b. dull purple	67.50
		d. brown	65.
		e. black brown	65.
		g. light blue	70.
		h. dark blue	70.
		i. ultramarine	70.
		k. yellow green	70.
		l. dark yellow green	70.
		n. green	65.
		o. dark green	65.
		p. blue green	65.
		q. light orange	65.
		r. dark orange	65.
		s. deep orange	65.
		t. scarlet	65.
		u. carmine	65.
		x. dark brown red	65.
RB4TC	4c		
		a. dark purple	67.50
		b. dull purple	67.50
		d. brown	65.
		e. black brown	65.
		g. light blue	70.
		h. dark blue	70.
		i. ultramarine	70.
		k. yellow green	70.
		n. green	65.
		o. dark green	65.
		p. blue green	65.
		q. light orange	65.
		r. dark orange	65.
		s. deep orange	65.
		t. scarlet	65.
		u. carmine	65.
		x. dark brown red	65.
RB5TC	5c		
		a. dark purple	67.50
		b. dull purple	67.50
		d. brown	65.
		e. black brown	65.
		g. light blue	70.
		h. dark blue	70.
		i. ultramarine	70.
		j. bright yellow green, on card	70.
		k. yellow green	70.
		l. dark yellow green	70.
		n. green	65.
		o. dark green	65.
		p. blue green	65.
		q. light orange	65.
		r. dark orange	65.
		s. deep orange	65.
		t. scarlet	65.
		u. carmine	65.
		x. dark brown red	65.
RB6TC	6c		
		a. dark purple	67.50
		b. dull purple	67.50
		d. brown	65.
		e. black brown	65.
		g. light blue	70.
		h. dark blue	70.
		i. ultramarine	70.
		k. yellow green	70.
		l. dark yellow green	70.
		n. green	65.
		o. dark green	65.
		p. blue green	65.
		q. light orange	65.
		r. dark orange	65.
		s. deep orange	65.
		t. scarlet	65.
		u. carmine	65.
		x. dark brown red	65.
RB7TC	10c		
		a. dark purple	67.50
		b. dull purple	67.50
		d. brown	65.
		e. black brown	65.
		g. light blue	70.
		h. dark blue	70.
		i. ultramarine	70.
		k. yellow green	70.
		l. dark yellow green	70.
		n. green	65.
		o. dark green	65.
		p. blue green	65.
		q. light orange	65.
		r. dark orange	65.
		s. deep orange	65.
		t. scarlet	65.
		u. carmine	65.
		x. dark brown red	65.

1898

RB21TC	¼c	green	Large die on India	500.
RB22TC	⅜c	green	Large die on India	500.
RB26TC	1⅞c	green	Large die on India	500.
RB26TC	1⅞c	black	Large die on India	500.
RB27TC	2c	green	Small die on India	350.
RB31TC	5c	green	Small die on India	350.

1918-29

Stock Transfer

RD20TC	$50	black	Die on India	400.
RD20TC	$50	blue	Die on India	400.

1894

Playing Cards

RF1TC	2c	black (On hand)	Die on India	400.
RF2TC	2c	lake (Act of)	Die on India	400.

Telegraph

American Rapid Telegraph Co.

			DIE (2) Small	PLATE (3) India	PLATE (4) Card
1T1TC	1c	green	55.		
1T1TC	1c	brown	55.		
1T1TC	1c	red	55.		
1T1TC	1c	blue	55.		
1T1TC	1c	bluish green	55.		
1T3TC	5c	green	55.		
1T3TC	5c	black	55.		
1T3TC	5c	red	55.		
1T3TC	5c	blue	55.		
1T3TC	5c	bluish green	55.		
1T5TC	15c	red	55.		
1T5TC	15c	black	55.		
1T5TC	15c	brown	55.		
1T5TC	15c	bluish green	55.		
1T6TC	20c	green	55.		
1T6TC	20c	black	55.		
1T6TC	20c	brown	55.		
1T6TC	20c	blue	55.		
1T6TC	20c	bluish green	55.		

Collect

			DIE (1) Large	DIE (2) Small	PLATE (3) India	PLATE (4) Card
1T10TC	5c	red		55.		
1T10TC	5c	black		55.		
1T10TC	5c	brown		55.		
1T10TC	5c	green		55.		
1T10TC	5c	bluish green		55.		
1T11TC	15c	red		55.		
1T11TC	15c	black		55.		
1T11TC	15c	brown		55.		
1T11TC	15c	green		55.		
1T11TC	15c	blue		55.		
1T11TC	15c	bluish green		55.		

Office Coupon

			DIE (1) Large	DIE (2) Small	PLATE (3) India	PLATE (4) Card
1T14TC	5c	red		55.		
1T14TC	5c	black		55.		
1T14TC	5c	brown		55.		
1T14TC	5c	green		55.		
1T14TC	5c	bluish green		55.		
1T15TC	15c	red		55.		
1T15TC	15c	black		55.		
1T15TC	15c	brown		55.		
1T15TC	15c	green		55.		
1T15TC	15c	blue		55.		
1T15TC	15c	bluish green		55.		

Baltimore & Ohio Telegraph Co.

			DIE (1) Large	DIE (2) Small	PLATE (3) India	PLATE (4) Card
3T2TC	5c	dark olive		65.		
3T4TC	25c	dark olive		65.		

Postal Telegraph Co.

			DIE (1) Large	DIE (2) Small	PLATE (3) India	PLATE (4) Card
15T1TC	10c	brown red		65.		
15T1TC	10c	red	65.			
15T1TC	10c	blue	65.			
15T1TC	10c	black	65.			
15T1TC	10c	orange			65.	
15T2TC	15c	black	65.		55.	
15T2TC	15c	red	65.	55.		
15T2TC	15c	blue	65.	55.		
15T2TC	25c	brown red		65.		
15T3TC	25c	black	65.			
15T3TC	25c	red	65.			
15T3TC	25c	ultramarine			40.	
15T3TC	25c	brown		65.	40.	
15T4TC	50c	dull blue		65.		
15T4TC	50c	black	65.		40.	
15T4TC	50c	red	65.			
15T4TC	50c	blue	65.			
15T6TC		red brown			40.	

Western Union Telegraph Co.

		DIE (1) Large	DIE (2) Small	PLATE (3) India	PLATE (4) Card
16T1TC	lilac (1871)			20.	20.
	Pair			45.	45.
16T1TC	orange			20.	20.
	Pair			45.	45.
16T1TC	black			20.	20.
	Pair			45.	45.
16T1TC	violet brown				20.
	Pair				45.
16T1TC	light olive				20.
	Pair				45.
16T1TC	brown				20.
	Pair				45.
16T1TC	orange brown				20.
	Pair				45.
16T1TC	blue green				20.
	Pair				45.
16T6TC	violet blue (1876)			20.	20.
16T7TC	orange yellow (1877)				20.
	Pair				45.
16T7TC	dark brown				20.
	Pair				45.
16T7TC	black				20.
	Pane of four				—
16T8TC	dark brown (1878)				—
16T9TC	blue (1879)				—
16T10TC	violet brown (1880)				—
16T10TC	rose				—
16T22TC	black (1892)				—

SPECIMEN

These are regular stamps overprinted "Specimen." Each number has a suffix letter "S" to denote "specimen." The Scott number is that of the stamp as shown in the regular listings and the second letter "A," etc., indicates the type of overprint. Values are for items of a grade of fine-very fine, with at least part original gum.

Specimen — Type A; 12mm long

Specimen. — Type B; 15mm long

Specimen. — Type C; 30mm long

SPECIMEN — Type D; Capital Letters

Specimen. — Type E; Initial Capital

Specimen. — Type F; 22mm long

SPECIMEN — Type G; 14mm long

SPECIMEN — Type H; 16mm long

Specimen — Type I; 20mm long

REGULAR ISSUES

Overprinted in Black Specimen

Type A. Overprint 12mm long

1851-56

7S	A	1c blue, Type II	*1,000.*
11S	A	3c dull red, Type I	*2,000.*

1857-60

21S	A	1c blue, Type III	*1,500.*
24S	A	1c blue, Type V	*1,000.*
26S	A	3c dull red, Type II	*1,000.*
30S	A	5c orange brown, Type II	*1,000.*
35S	A	10c green, Type V	*1,100.*
36bS	A	12c black	*1,000.*
37S	A	24c lilac	*1,000.*
38S	A	30c orange	*1,000.*
26S	F	3c dull red, Type II	*1,500.*
26S	I	3c dull red, Type II	*1,500.*

1861

63S	A	1c blue	750.00
65S	A	3c rose	750.00
68S	A	10c dark green	750.00
70S	A	24c red lilac	750.00
72S	A	90c blue	750.00
73S	A	2c black	*1,000.*
76S	A	5c brown	750.00

Specimen.

1861-66 **Type B. Overprint 15mm long**
Black, except as noted

63S	B	1c blue *(1300)*	120.00
		Without period	—
65S	B	3c rose *(1500)*	120.00
68S	B	10c dark green *(1600)*	120.00
69S	B	12c black (Orange) *(1300)*	120.00
71S	B	30c orange *(1400)*	120.00
72S	B	90c blue *(1394)*	120.00
73S	B	2c black (Vermilion) *(1306)*	275.00
		Without period	—
76S	B	5c brown *(1306)*	120.00
77S	B	15c black (Vermilion) *(1208)*	200.00
78S	B	24c lilac *(1300)*	120.00

1867-68

86S	A	1c blue	*1,000.*
85E—S	A	12c black	*1,000.*
93S	A	2c black	*1,100.*
94S	A	3c rose	*1,000.*
95S	A	5c brown	*1,100.*
98S	A	15c black	*1,000.*
100S	A	30c orange	*1,000.*

1869

112S	A	1c buff	*1,250.*
113S	A	2c brown	*1,250.*
115S	A	6c ultramarine	*1,250.*
116S	A	10c yellow	*1,250.*
117S	A	12c green	*1,250.*
119S	A	15c brown & blue	*1,500.*
120S	A	24c green & violet	*1,500.*
		a. Without grill	—
121S	A	30c blue & carmine	*1,500.*
		a. Without grill	—
122S	A	90c carmine & black	*2,000.*
		a. Without grill	—
125S	B	3c blue	—
126S	B	6c blue	—

1870-71

145S	A	1c ultramarine	*600.00*
146S	A	2c red brown	*600.00*
147S	A	3c green	*600.00*
148S	A	6c carmine	*600.00*
149S	A	7c vermilion	*600.00*
150S	A	10c brown	*600.00*
151S	A	12c dull violet	*600.00*
152S	A	15c bright orange	*600.00*
155S	A	90c carmine	*600.00*
147S	B	3c green	*750.00*
155S	B	90c carmine (Blue)	*750.00*

1873

159S	B	6c dull pink	*700.00*
160S	B	7c orange vermilion (Blue)	*700.00*
162S	B	12c blackish violet (Blue)	—

Overprinted in Red SPECIMEN.

1879

Type D

189S	D	15c red orange	80.00
190S	D	30c full black	80.00
191S	D	90c carmine	80.00
		a. Overprint in black brown	80.00

1881-82

205S	D	5c yellow brown	80.00
206S	D	1c gray blue	80.00
207S	D	3c blue green	80.00
208S	D	6c brown red	80.00
209S	D	10c brown	80.00

1883

210S	D	2c red brown	100.00
211S	D	4c blue green	100.00

Handstamped in Dull Purple Specimen.

1890-93

Type E

219S	E	1c dull blue	100.00
220S	E	2c carmine	100.00
221S	E	3c purple	100.00
222S	E	4c dark brown	100.00
223S	E	5c chocolate	100.00
224S	E	6c dull red	100.00
225S	E	8c lilac	100.00
226S	E	10c green	100.00
227S	E	15c blue	100.00
228S	E	30c black	100.00
229S	E	90c orange	135.00

COLUMBIAN ISSUE

1893

230S	E	1c deep blue	400.00
		Double overprint	—
231S	E	2c violet	400.00
232S	E	3c green	400.00
233S	E	4c ultramarine	400.00
234S	E	5c chocolate	400.00
235S	E	6c purple	400.00
236S	E	8c magenta	400.00
237S	E	10c black brown	400.00
238S	E	15c dark green	400.00
239S	E	30c orange brown	400.00
240S	E	50c slate blue	400.00
241S	E	$1 salmon	500.00
242S	E	$2 brown red	500.00
243S	E	$3 yellow green	550.00
244S	E	$4 crimson lake	575.00
245S	E	$5 black	675.00

Overprinted in Magenta Specimen.

Type F

230S	F	1c deep blue	550.00
232S	F	3c green	550.00
233S	F	4c ultramarine	550.00
234S	F	5c chocolate	550.00
235S	F	6c purple	550.00
237S	F	10c black brown	550.00
243S	F	$3 yellow green	700.00

Overprinted Type H in Black or Red

231S	H	2c violet (Bk)	625.00
233S	H	4c ultramarine (R)	625.00
234S	H	5c chocolate (R)	625.00

Overprinted Type I in Black or Red

231S	I	2c violet (R)	625.00
232S	I	3c green (R)	625.00
233S	I	4c ultramarine (R)	625.00
234S	I	5c chocolate (Bk)	625.00
235S	I	6c purple (R)	625.00
236S	I	8c magenta (Bk)	625.00
237S	I	10c black brown (R)	625.00
238S	I	15c dark green (R)	625.00
239S	I	30c orange brown (Bk)	625.00
240S	I	50c slate blue (R)	625.00

1895

Type E

264S	E	1c blue	90.00
267S	E	2c carmine	90.00
268S	E	3c purple	90.00
269S	E	4c dark brown	100.00
270S	E	5c chocolate	90.00
271S	E	6c dull brown	90.00
272S	E	8c violet brown	90.00
273S	E	10c dark green	90.00
274S	E	15c dark blue	90.00
275S	E	50c orange	90.00
276S	E	$1 black, Type I	325.00
277S	E	$2 dark blue	300.00
278S	E	$5 dark green	400.00

1898-99

279S	E	1c deep green	90.00
279B—S	E	2c orange red	90.00
		a. Booklet pane of 6	525.00
280S	E	4c rose brown	160.00
281S	E	5c dark blue	80.00
282S	E	6c lake	80.00
282C—S	E	10c brown, Type I	80.00
283S	E	10c brown, Type II	
284S	E	15c olive green	80.00

TRANS-MISSISSIPPI ISSUE

1898

285S	E	1c dark yellow green	250.00
286S	E	2c copper red	250.00
287S	E	4c orange	250.00
288S	E	5c dull blue	250.00
289S	E	8c violet brown	250.00
290S	E	10c gray violet	250.00
291S	E	50c sage green	300.00
292S	E	$1 black	450.00
293S	E	$2 orange brown	625.00

PAN-AMERICAN ISSUE

1901

294S	E	1c green & black	235.00
295S	E	2c carmine	235.00
296S	E	4c chocolate & black	235.00
		a. Center inverted	4,500.
297S	E	5c ultramarine & black	235.00
298S	E	8c brown violet & black	235.00
299S	E	10c yellow brown & black	235.00

1902

300S	E	1c blue green	90.00
301S	E	2c carmine	90.00
302S	E	3c bright violet	90.00
303S	E	4c brown	90.00
304S	E	5c blue	90.00
305S	E	6c claret	90.00
306S	E	8c violet black	90.00
307S	E	10c pale red brown	90.00
308S	E	13c purple black	90.00
309S	E	15c olive green	90.00
310S	E	50c orange	90.00
311S	E	$1 black	200.00
312S	E	$2 dark blue	300.00
313S	E	$5 dark green	400.00

1903

319S	E	2c carmine	110.00

LOUISIANA PURCHASE ISSUE

1904

323S	E	1c green	350.00
324S	E	2c carmine	350.00
325S	E	3c violet	350.00
326S	E	5c dark blue	350.00
327S	E	10c red brown	350.00

SPECIAL DELIVERY STAMPS

Overprinted in Red SPECIMEN.

1885

Type D

E1S	D	10c blue	110.00

Handstamped in Dull Purple **Specimen.**

1888

Type E

E2S	E	10c blue	110.00

1893

E3S	E	10c orange	150.00

1894

E4S	E	10c blue	225.00

1895

E5S	E	10c blue	150.00

1902

E6S	E	10c ultramarine	150.00

POSTAGE DUE STAMPS

Overprinted in Red **SPECIMEN·**

1879

Type D.

J1S	D	1c brown	250.00
J2S	D	2c brown	250.00
J3S	D	3c brown	250.00
J4S	D	5c brown	250.00

1884

J15S	D	1c red brown	45.00
J16S	D	2c red brown	45.00
J17S	D	3c red brown	45.00
J18S	D	5c red brown	45.00
J19S	D	10c red brown	45.00
J20S	D	30c red brown	45.00
J21S	D	50c red brown	45.00

Overprinted in Dull Purple **Specimen.**

1895

Type E

J38S	E	1c deep claret	85.00
J39S	E	2c deep claret	85.00
J40S	E	3c deep claret	85.00
J41S	E	5c deep claret	85.00
J42S	E	10c deep claret	85.00
J43S	E	30c deep claret	85.00
J44S	E	50c deep claret	85.00

OFFICIAL STAMPS

Special printings of Official stamps were made in 1875 at the time the other Reprints, Re-issues and Special Printings were printed. They are ungummed.

Although perforated, these stamps were sometimes (but not always) cut apart with scissors. As a result the perforations may be mutilated and the design damaged.

Number issued indicated in brackets.

All values exist imperforate.

Overprinted in Block Letters **SPECIMEN**

Type D

1875 **Thin, hard white paper** *Perf. 12*

AGRICULTURE

Carmine Overprint

O1S	D	1c yellow (15,234)	5.00
		a. "Sepcimen" error	475.00
		b. Small dotted "i" in "Specimen"	165.00
		c. Ribbed paper	15.00
O2S	D	2c yellow (4,192)	11.00
		a. "Sepcimen" error	525.00
O3S	D	3c yellow (389)	45.00
		a. "Sepcimen" error	1,900.
O4S	D	6c yellow (373)	80.00
		a. "Sepcimen" error	—
O5S	D	10c yellow (390)	80.00
		a. "Sepcimen" error	1,900.
O6S	D	12c yellow (379)	75.00
		a. "Sepcimen" error	1,900.
O7S	D	15c yellow (370)	75.00
		a. "Sepcimen" error	1,900.
O8S	D	24c yellow (352)	75.00
		a. "Sepcimen" error	1,900.
O9S	D	30c yellow (354)	75.00
		a. "Sepcimen" error	1,900.

EXECUTIVE

Blue Overprint

O10S	D	1c carmine (14,652)	7.00
		a. Small dotted "i" in "Specimen"	175.00
		b. Ribbed paper	13.50
O11S	D	2c carmine (7,430)	10.00
O12S	D	3c carmine (3,735)	15.00
O13S	D	6c carmine (3,485)	15.00
O14S	D	10c carmine (3,461)	15.00

INTERIOR

Blue Overprint

O15S	D	1c vermilion (7,194)	9.50
O16S	D	2c vermilion (1,263)	15.00
		a. "Sepcimen" error	1,150.
O17S	D	3c vermilion (88)	325.00
O18S	D	6c vermilion (83)	300.00
O19S	D	10c vermilion (82)	300.00
O20S	D	12c vermilion (75)	325.00
O21S	D	15c vermilion (78)	325.00
O22S	D	24c vermilion (77)	325.00
O23S	D	30c vermilion (75)	325.00
O24S	D	90c vermilion (77)	325.00

JUSTICE

Blue Overprint

O25S	D	1c purple (19,729)	8.00
		a. "Sepcimen" error	450.00
		b. Small dotted "i" in "Specimen"	150.00
		c. Ribbed paper	10.00
O26S	D	2c purple (3,395)	10.00
		a. "Sepcimen" error	750.00
O27S	D	3c purple (178)	140.00
		a. "Sepcimen" error	2,450.
O28S	D	6c purple (163)	140.00
O29S	D	10c purple (163)	135.00
O30S	D	12c purple (154)	135.00
		a. "Sepcimen" error	2,450.
O31S	D	15c purple (157)	160.00
		a. "Sepcimen" error	2,450.
O32S	D	24c purple (150)	175.00
		a. "Sepcimen" error	2,450.
O33S	D	30c purple (150)	175.00
		a. "Sepcimen" error	2,450.
O34S	D	90c purple (152)	175.00

NAVY

Carmine Overprint

O35S	D	1c ultramarine (9,182)	8.25
		a. "Sepcimen" error	375.00
		b. Broken "i" in "Specimen"	165.00
O36S	D	2c ultramarine (1,748)	13.00
		a. "Sepcimen" error	475.00
		b. Broken "i" in "Specimen"	575.00
O37S	D	3c ultramarine (126)	175.00
O38S	D	6c ultramarine (116)	200.00
O39S	D	7c ultramarine (501)	80.00
		a. "Sepcimen" error	1,200.
O40S	D	10c ultramarine (112)	200.00
		a. "Sepcimen" error	2,400.
O41S	D	12c ultramarine (107)	185.00
		a. "Sepcimen" error	2,400.
O42S	D	15c ultramarine (107)	185.00
		a. "Sepcimen" error	2,400.
O43S	D	24c ultramarine (106)	180.00
		a. "Sepcimen" error	2,400.
O44S	D	30c ultramarine (104)	180.00
		a. "Sepcimen" error	2,400.
O45S	D	90c ultramarine (102)	180.00

POST OFFICE

Carmine Overprint

O47S	D	1c black (6,015)	9.00
		a. "Sepcimen" error	450.00
		b. Inverted overprint	375.00
O48S	D	2c black (590)	32.00
		a. "Sepcimen" error	1,200.
O49S	D	3c black (91)	240.00
		a. "Sepcimen" error	2,400.
O50S	D	6c black (87)	240.00
O51S	D	10c black (177)	165.00
		a. "Sepcimen" error	2,000.
O52S	D	12c black (93)	240.00
O53S	D	15c black (82)	260.00
		a. "Sepcimen" error	2,400.
O54S	D	24c black (84)	240.00
		a. "Sepcimen" error	2,400.
O55S	D	30c black (81)	250.00
O56S	D	90c black (82)	250.00
		a. "Sepcimen" error	2,400.

STATE.

Carmine Overprint.

O57S	D	1c bluish green (21,672)	8.00
		a. "Sepcimen" error	275.00
		b. Small dotted "i" in "Specimen"	225.00
		c. Ribbed paper	10.00
O58S	D	2c bluish green (5,145)	11.00
		a. "Sepcimen" error	375.00
O59S	D	3c bluish green (793)	23.00
		a. "Sepcimen" error	1,200.
O60S	D	6c bluish green (467)	55.00
		a. "Sepcimen" error	1,300.
O61S	D	7c bluish green (791)	23.00
		a. "Sepcimen" error	1,200.
O62S	D	10c bluish green (346)	100.00
O63S	D	12c bluish green (280)	110.00
		a. "Sepcimen" error	2,000.
O64S	D	15c bluish green (257)	110.00
O65S	D	24c bluish green (253)	110.00
		a. "Sepcimen" error	2,000.
O66S	D	30c bluish green (249)	110.00
		a. "Sepcimen" error	2,000.
O67S	D	90c bluish green (245)	110.00
		a. "Sepcimen" error	2,000.
O68S	D	$2 green & black (32)	2,000.
O69S	D	$5 green & black (12)	3,750.
O70S	D	$10 green & black (8)	4,450.
O71S	D	$20 green & black (7)	4,750.

TREASURY

Blue Overprint

O72S	D	1c dark brown (2,185)	12.00
O73S	D	2c dark brown (309)	75.00
O74S	D	3c dark brown (84)	240.00
O75S	D	6c dark brown (85)	275.00
O76S	D	7c dark brown (198)	155.00
O77S	D	10c dark brown (82)	240.00
O78S	D	12c dark brown (75)	250.00
O79S	D	15c dark brown (75)	250.00
O80S	D	24c dark brown (99)	240.00
O81S	D	30c dark brown (74)	360.00
		Short transfer at top right	—
O82S	D	90c dark brown (72)	360.00

WAR

Blue Overprint

O83S	D	1c deep rose (4,610)	10.00
		a. "Sepcimen" error	375.00
O84S	D	2c deep rose (1,618)	15.00
		a. "Sepcimen" error	675.00
O85S	D	3c deep rose (118)	200.00
		a. "Sepcimen" error	2,000.
O86S	D	6c deep rose (111)	240.00
		a. "Sepcimen" error	2,000.
O87S	D	7c deep rose (539)	40.00
		a. "Sepcimen" error	1,000.
O88S	D	10c deep rose (119)	190.00
		a. "Sepcimen" error	2,000.
O89S	D	12c deep rose (105)	240.00
		a. "Sepcimen" error	2,000.
O90S	D	15c deep rose (105)	240.00
		a. "Sepcimen" error	2,000.
O91S	D	24c deep rose (106)	240.00
		a. "Sepcimen" error	2,000.
O92S	D	30c deep rose (104)	240.00
		a. "Sepcimen" error	2,000.
O93S	D	90c deep rose (106)	240.00
		a. "Sepcimen" error	2,000.

SOFT POROUS PAPER

EXECUTIVE

Blue Overprint

O10xS	D	1c violet rose	25.00
		Broken "i" in "Specimen"	200.00

NAVY

Carmine Overprint

O35xS	D	1c gray blue	30.00
		deep blue	35.00
		Broken "i" in "Specimen"	200.00
		a. Double overprint	550.00

STATE

O57xS	D	1c yellow green	110.00

The total number issued of the 1c Executive, 1c Navy, 1c State Departments possibly includes the soft paper "Specimen" printings.

SAVINGS STAMPS

Overprinted Vertically Reading Down in Red **SPECIMEN**

1911

PS4S	10c deep blue	—

1917-18 **Handstamped "SPECIMEN" in Violet**

WS1S	25c deep green	—
WS2S	$5 deep green	—

NEWSPAPER STAMPS

Overprinted in Red **Specimen.**

1865-75

Type C. Overprint 30mm long

PR5S	C	5c dark blue	150.00
		a. Triple overprint	260.00
PR2S	C	10c blue green	165.00
RP3S	C	25c carmine red	175.00

Handstamped in Black **Specimen**

1875

Type A

PR9S	A	2c black	225.00
PR11S	A	4c black	225.00
PR12S	A	6c black	225.00
PR16S	A	12c rose	225.00

Overprinted in Black, except as noted **Specimen.**

1875

Type B. Overprint 15mm long

PR9S	B	2c black	45.00
PR10S	B	3c black	45.00
PR11S	B	4c black	45.00
PR12S	B	6c black	45.00
PR13S	B	8c black	45.00
PR14S	B	9c black	45.00
		a. Overprint in blue	—
PR15S	B	10c black	45.00
PR16S	B	12c rose	45.00
PR17S	B	24c rose	45.00
PR18S	B	36c rose	45.00
PR19S	B	48c rose	45.00
		a. Overprint in blue	62.50
PR20S	B	60c rose	45.00
PR21S	B	72c rose	45.00
		a. Overprint in blue	62.50
PR22S	B	84c rose	45.00
		a. Overprint in blue	—
PR23S	B	96c rose	45.00
		a. Overprint in blue	—
PR24S	B	$1.92 dark brown	45.00
PR25S	B	$3 vermilion	45.00
		a. Overprint in blue	62.50
PR26S	B	$6 ultramarine	45.00
		a. Overprint in blue	250.00
PR27S	B	$9 yellow	45.00
		a. Overprint in blue	250.00
PR28S	B	$12 dark green	45.00
		a. Overprint in blue	250.00
PR29S	B	$24 dark gray violet	45.00
		a. Overprint in blue	60.00
PR30S	B	$36 brown rose	62.00
PR31S	B	$48 red brown	62.00
PR32S	B	$60 violet	62.00

Overprinted in Red SPECIMEN.

1875

Type D

PR14S	D	9c black	30.00

1879

PR57S	D	2c black	25.00
PR58S	D	3c black	25.00
PR59S	D	4c black	25.00
PR60S	D	6c black	25.00
PR61S	D	8c black	25.00
PR62S	D	10c black	25.00
		a. Double overprint	250.00
PR63S	D	12c red	25.00
PR64S	D	24c red	25.00
PR65S	D	36c red	25.00
PR66S	D	48c red	25.00
PR67S	D	60c red	25.00
PR68S	D	72c red	25.00
PR69S	D	84c red	25.00
PR70S	D	96c red	25.00
PR71S	D	$1.92 pale brown	25.00
PR72S	D	$3 red vermilion	25.00
PR73S	D	$6 blue	25.00
PR74S	D	$9 orange	25.00
PR75S	D	$12 yellow green	25.00
PR76S	D	$24 dark violet	25.00
PR77S	D	$36 Indian red	25.00
PR78S	D	$48 yellow brown	25.00
PR79S	D	$60 purple	25.00

1885

PR81S	D	1c black	25.00

Handstamped in Dull Purple Specimen.

1879

Type E

PR57S	E	2c black	22.50
PR58S	E	3c black	22.50
PR59S	E	4c black	22.50
PR60S	E	6c black	22.50
PR61S	E	8c black	22.50
PR62S	E	10c black	22.50
PR63S	E	12c red	22.50
PR64S	E	24c red	22.50
PR65S	E	36c red	22.50
PR66S	E	48c red	22.50
PR67S	E	60c red	22.50
PR68S	E	72c red	22.50
PR69S	E	84c red	22.50
PR70S	E	96c red	22.50
PR71S	E	$1.92 pale brown	22.50
PR72S	E	$3 red vermilion	22.50
PR73S	E	$6 blue	22.50
PR74S	E	$9 orange	22.50
PR75S	E	$12 yellow green	22.50
PR76S	E	$24 dark violet	22.50
PR77S	E	$36 Indian red	22.50
PR78S	E	$48 yellow brown	22.50
PR79S	E	$60 purple	22.50

1885

PR81S	E	1c black	22.50

1895 **Wmk. 191**

PR114S	E	1c black	35.00
PR115S	E	2c black	35.00
PR116S	E	5c black	35.00
PR117S	E	10c black	35.00
PR118S	E	25c carmine	35.00
PR119S	E	50c carmine	35.00
PR120S	E	$2 scarlet	35.00
PR121S	E	$5 dark blue	35.00
PR122S	E	$10 green	42.50
PR123S	E	$20 slate	42.50
PR124S	E	$50 dull rose	42.50
PR125S	E	$100 purple	42.50

REVENUE STAMPS

SPECIMEN

Type G

1862

Overprint 14mm long

R5S	G	2c Bank Check, blue (Red)	375.00
R15S	A	2c U. S. I. R., orange	—

SPECIMEN

Type H

Overprint 16mm long

R23S	H	5c Agreement, red (Black)	375.00
R34S	H	10c Contract, blue (Red)	375.00
R35eS	H	10c Foreign Exchange, ultramarine (Red)	375.00
R36S	H	10c Inland Exchange, blue (Red)	375.00
R46S	H	25c Insurance, red (Black)	375.00
R52S	H	30c Inland Exchange, lilac (Red)	375.00
R53S	H	40c Inland Exchange, brown (Red)	375.00
R68S	H	$1 Foreign Exchange, red (Black)	375.00

Specimen

Type I

1898 **Overprint 20mm long**

R153S	I	1c green (Red)	475.00

1875

RB11S	H	1c green (Red)	300.00

PRIVATE MATCH STAMP

Overprinted with Type G in Red SPECIMEN

RO133dS	G	1c black, A.Messinger	*500.00*

VARIOUS OVERPRINTS

Overprinted with control numbers in carmine 7890

1861 **Type J**

63S	J	A24	1c pale blue (overprint 9012)	200.00
65S	J	A25	3c brown red (overprint 7890)	200.00
68S	J	A27	10c green (overprint 5678)	200.00
69S	J	A28	12c gray black (overprint 4567)	200.00
71S	J	A30	30c orange (overprint 2345)	200.00
72S	J	A31	90c pale blue (overprint 1234)	200.00
			a. Pair, one without overprint	—

1861-66

73S	J	A32	2c black (overprint 8901)	275.00
76S	J	A26	5c brown (overprint 6789)	200.00
77S	J	A33	15c black (overprint 235)	250.00
78S	J	A29	24c gray lilac (overprint 3456)	200.00

Special Printings Overprinted in Red or Blue SAMPLE.

1889

Type K

212S	K	A59	1c ultramarine (red)	75.00
210S	K	A57	2c red brown (blue)	75.00
210S	K	A57	2c lake (blue)	75.00
210S	K	A57	2c rose lake (blue)	75.00
210S	K	A57	2c scarlet (blue)	75.00
214S	K	A46b	3c vermilion (blue)	75.00
211S	K	A58	4c blue green (red)	75.00
205S	K	A56	5c yellow brown (red)	75.00
208S	K	A47b	6c brown red (blue)	75.00
209S	K	A49b	10c brown (red)	75.00
			Without overprint	80.00
189S	K	A51a	15c orange (blue)	75.00
190S	K	A53	30c full black (red)	75.00
191S	K	A54	90c carmine (blue)	75.00

Special Printings Overprinted in Red or Blue SAMPLE A.

Type L

212S	L	A59	1c ultramarine (red)	75.00
210S	L	A57	2c rose lake (blue)	75.00
214S	L	A46b	3c purple (red)	75.00
211S	L	A58	4c dark brown (red)	75.00
205S	L	A56	5c gray brown (blue)	75.00
208S	L	A47b	6c vermilion (blue)	75.00
209S	L	A49b	10c green (red)	75.00
			Without overprint	100.00
189S	L	A51a	15c blue (red)	75.00
			Without overprint	100.00
190S	L	A53	30c full black (red)	75.00
191S	L	A54	90c orange (blue)	75.00

Overprinted with Type K together with "A" in Black manuscript

191S	M	A54	90c carmine (blue)	140.00
209S	M	A49b	10c brown (red)	140.00
211S	M	A58	4c blue green (red)	140.00

"SAMPLE A" in manuscript (red or black)

216S	N	A56	5c indigo	160.00

Regular Issues Overprinted in Blue or Red UNIVERSAL POSTAL CONGRESS

1897 **Type O**

125 sets were distributed to delegates to the Universal Postal Congress held in Washington, D. C., May 5 to June 15, 1897.

264S	O	A87	1c blue	135.00
267S	O	A88	2c carmine	135.00
268S	O	A89	3c purple	135.00
269S	O	A90	4c dark brown	135.00
270S	O	A91	5c chestnut	135.00
271S	O	A92	6c claret brown	135.00
272S	O	A93	8c violet brown	135.00
273S	O	A94	10c dark green	135.00
274S	O	A95	15c dark blue	135.00
275S	O	A96	50c red orange	135.00
276S	O	A97	$1 black, Type I	500.00
276A—S	O	A97	$1 black, Type II	450.00
277S	O	A98	$2 dark blue	325.00
278S	O	A99	$5 dark green	500.00

SPECIAL DELIVERY

E5S	O	SD3	10c blue (R)	250.00

POSTAGE DUE

J38S	O	D2	1c deep claret	125.00
J39S	O	D2	2c deep claret	125.00
J40S	O	D2	3c deep claret	125.00
J41S	O	D2	5c deep claret	125.00
J42S	O	D2	10c deep claret	125.00
J43S	O	D2	30c deep claret	125.00
J44S	O	D2	50c deep claret	125.00

NEWSPAPERS

PR114S	O	N15	1c black	85.00
PR115S	O	N15	2c black	85.00
PR116S	O	N15	5c black	85.00
PR117S	O	N15	10c black	85.00
PR118S	O	N16	25c carmine	85.00
PR119S	O	N16	50c carmine	85.00
PR120S	O	N17	$2 scarlet	85.00
PR121S	O	N18	$5 dark blue	85.00
PR122S	O	N19	$10 green	85.00
PR123S	O	N20	$20 slate	85.00
PR124S	O	N21	$50 dull rose	85.00
PR125S	O	N22	$100 purple	85.00

ENVELOPES

Overprinted UNIVERSAL POSTAL CONGRESS

Type P

U294S	P	1c blue	100.00
U296S	P	1c blue, *amber*	100.00
U300S	P	1c blue, *manila*	100.00
W301S	P	1c blue, *manila*	100.00
U304S	P	1c blue, *amber manila*	100.00
U311S	P	2c green, Die 2	100.00
U312S	P	2c green, Die 2, *amber*	100.00
U313S	P	2c green, Die 2, *oriental buff*	100.00
U314S	P	2c green, Die 2, *blue*	100.00
U315S	P	2c green, Die 2, *manila*	100.00
W316S	P	2c green, Die 2, *manila*	100.00
U317S	P	2c green, Die 2, *amber manila*	100.00
U324S	P	4c carmine	100.00
U325S	P	4c carmine, *amber*	120.00
U330S	P	5c blue, Die 1	110.00
U331S	P	5c blue, Die 1, *amber*	110.00

Two settings of type P overprint are found.

POSTAL CARDS

Overprinted UNIVERSAL POSTAL CONGRESS.

Type Q

UX12S	Q	1c black, *buff*	400.00
UX13S	Q	2c blue, *cream*	400.00

PAID REPLY POSTAL CARDS

Overprinted with Type Q

UY1S	Q	1c black, *buff*	400.00
UY2S	Q	2c blue, *grayish white*	400.00

As Nos. UY1S-UY2S were made by overprinting unsevered reply cards, values are for unsevered cards.

SOUVENIR CARDS

These cards were issued as souvenirs of the philatelic gatherings at which they were distributed by the United States Postal Service, its predecessor the United States Post Office Department, or the Bureau of Engraving and Printing. They were not valid for postage.

Most of the cards bear reproductions of United States stamps with the design enlarged or altered by removal of denomination, country name and "Postage" or "Air Mail." The cards are not perforated.

A forerunner of the souvenir cards is the 1938 Philatelic Truck souvenir sheet which the Post Office Department issued and distributed in various cities visited by the Philatelic Truck. It shows the White House, printed in blue on white paper. Issued with and without gum. Value, with gum, $85; without gum, $15.

1954

1 Postage Stamp Design Exhibition, National Philatelic Museum, Mar. 13, 1954, Philadelphia. Card of 4. Monochrome views of Washington, D.C. Inscribed: "Souvenir sheet designed, engraved and printed by members, Bureau, Engraving and Printing. Reissued by popular request". *1,500.*

1960

2 Barcelona, 1st International Philatelic Congress, Mar. 26—Apr. 5, 1960. Enlarged vignette, Landing of Columbus from No. 231. Printed in black. (P.O.D.) 275.00

1966

3 SIPEX, 6th International Philatelic Exhibition, May 21—30, 1966, Washington, D.C. Card of 3. Multicolored views of Washington, D.C. Inscribed: "Sixth International Phialtelic Exhibition / Washington, D.C. / Designed, Engraved, and Printed by Union Members of Bureau of Engraving and Printing". 160.00

1968

4 EFIMEX, International Philatelic Exhibition, Nov. 1—9, 1968, Mexico City. No. 292 enlarged to 58x37½mm. Card inscribed in Spanish. (P.O.D.) 2.25

1969

5 SANDIPEX, San Diego Philatelic Exhibition, July 16—20, 1969, San Diego, Cal. Card of 3. Multicolored views of Washington, D.C. Inscribed: "Sandipex—San Diego 200th Anniversary—1769—1969". (B.E.P.) 52.50

6 A.S.D.A. National Postage Stamp Show, Nov. 21—23, 1969, New York. Card of 4. No. E4 reengraved. Denomination and "United States" removed. (B.E.P.) 24.00

1970

7 INTERPEX, Mar. 13—15, 1970, New York. Card of 4. Nos. 1027, 1035, C35 and C38 reengraved. Denomination, etc. removed. (B.E.P.) 52.50

8 COMPEX, Combined Philatelic Exhibition of Chicagoland, May 29—31, 1970, Chicago. Card of 4 No. C18 reengraved. Denomination, etc. removed. (B.E.P.) 13.00

9 PHILYMPIA, London International Stamp Exhibition, Sept. 18—26 1970. Card of 3, Nos. 548—550 enlarged 1½ times. (P.O.D.) 2.50

10 HAPEX, American Philatelic Society Convention, Nov. 5—8, 1970, Honolulu, Hawaii. Card of 3, Nos. 799, C46 and C55 reengraved. Denomination, etc. removed. (B.E.P.) 13.00

1971

11 INTERPEX, Mar. 12—14, 1971, New York. Card of 4 No. 1193 reengraved. Denomination removed. Background tint includes enlargements of Nos. 1331—1332, 1371 and C76. (B.E.P.) 2.25

12 WESTPEX, Western Philatelic Exhibition, Apr. 23—25, 1971, San Francisco. Card of 4, Nos. 740, 852, 966 and 997. Denomination, etc. removed. (B.E.P.) 2.25

13 NAPEX 71, National Philatelic Exhibition, May 21—23, 1971, Washington, D.C. Card of 3, Nos. 990, 991, 992. Denomination, etc. removed. (B.E.P.) 3.00

14 TEXANEX 71, Texas Philatelic Association and American Philatelic Society conventions, Aug. 26—29, 1971, San Antonio, Tex. Card of 3, Nos. 938, 1043 and 1242. Denomination, etc. removed. (B.E.P.) 3.25

15 EXFILIMA 71, 3rd Inter—American Philatelic Exhibition, Nov. 6—14, 1971, Lima, Peru. Card of 3. Nos. 1111 and 1126 with denomination, etc. removed. Reproduction of Peru No. 360. Card inscribed in Spanish. (U.S.P.S.) 1.65

16 A.S.D.A. National Postage Stamp Show, Nov. 19—21, 1971, New York. Card of 3, Nos. C13—C15. Denomination, etc. removed. (B.E.P.) 2.50

17 ANPHILEX '71, Anniversary Philatelic Exhibition, Nov. 26—Dec. 1, 1971, New York. Card of 2, Nos. 1—2. Denomination, etc. removed. (B.E.P.) 1.40

1972

18 INTERPEX, Mar. 17—19, 1972, New York. Card of 4 No. 1173. Denomination, etc. removed. Background tint includes enlargements of Nos. 976, 1434—1435 and C69. (B.E.P.) 1.10

19 NOPEX, Apr. 6—9, 1972, New Orleans. Card of 4 No. 1020. Denomination, etc. removed. Background tint includes enlargements of Nos. 323—327. (B.E.P.) 1.50

20 BELGICA 72, Brussels International Philatelic Exhibition, June 24—July 9, 1972, Brussels, Belgium. Card of 3. No. 914 enlarged to 56x34mm. Nos. 1026 and 1104 with denomination, etc. removed. Card inscribed in Flemish and French. (U.S.P.S.) 1.25

21 Olympia Philatelic Munchen 72, Aug. 18—Sept. 10, 1972, Munich, Germany. Card of 4, Nos. 1460—1462 and C85 enlarged to 54x32mm. Card inscribed in German. (U.S.P.S.) 1.50

22 EXFILBRA 72, 4th Inter—American Philatelic Exhibition, Aug. 26—Sept. 2, 1972, Rio de Janeiro, Brazil. Card of 3. No. C14 enlarged to 69½x28½mm. and reproductions of Brazil Nos. C18—C19. Card inscribed in Portuguese. (U.S.P.S.) 1.65

23 National Philatelic Forum VI, Aug. 28—30, 1972, Washington, D.C. Card of 4 No. 1396 enlarged to 26x31mm. (U.S.P.S.) 1.65

24 SEPAD '72, Oct. 20—22, 1972, Philadelphia. Card of 4 No. 1044 reengraved, denomination, etc. removed. (B.E.P.) 1.65

25 A.S.D.A. National Postage Stamp Show, Nov. 17—19, 1972, New York. Card of 4, Nos. 883, 863, 868 and 888. Denomination, etc. removed. (B.E.P.) 1.25

26 STAMP EXPO, Nov. 24—26, 1972, San Francisco. Card of 4 No. C36 re—engraved with denomination, etc. removed. (B.E.P.) 2.00

1973

27 INTERPEX, Mar. 9—11, 1973, New York. Card of 4 No. 976. Denomination, etc. removed. (B.E.P.) 1.75

28 IBRA 73 International Philatelic Exhibition, Munich, May 11—20, 1973. No. C13 enlarged to 70x29mm. (U.S.P.S.) 2.00

29 COMPEX 73, May 25—27, 1973, Chicago. Card of 4 No. 245. Denomination, etc. removed. (B.E.P.) 1.90

30 APEX 73, International Airmail Exhibition, Manchester, England, July 4—7, 1973. Card of 3. No. C3a enlarged to 34x29mm., enlarged reproductions of Newfoundland No. C4 and Honduras No. C12. (U.S.P.S.) 2.25

31 POLSKA 73, World Philatelic Exhibition, Poznan, Poland, Aug. 19—Sept. 2, 1973. Card of 3. No. 1488 enlarged to 32x55mm., enlarged reproductions of Poland Nos. 1944—1945. Card inscribed in Polish. (U.S.P.S.) 2.25

32 NAPEX 73, Sept. 14—16, 1973, Washington, D.C. Card of 4 No. C3. Denomination, etc. removed. Background tint includes montage of enlarged reproductions of C4—C6. (B.E.P.) 1.90

33 A.S.D.A. National Postage Stamp Show, Nov. 16—18, 1973, New York. Card of 4 No. 908 reengraved. Denomination, etc. removed. Foreground includes enlarged reproductions of Nos. 1139—1144. (B.E.P.) 1.75

34 STAMP EXPO NORTH, Dec. 7—9, 1973, San Francisco. Card of 4 No. C20. Denomination, etc. removed. (B.E.P.) 2.25

A card of 10, Nos. 1489-1498, was distributed to postal employees. Not available to public. Size: about 14x11 inches.

1974

35 National Hobby Industry Trade Show, Feb. 3—6, 1974, Chicago. Card of 4; block of Nos. 1456—1459 reduced to 61x39mm. Enlarged reproductions of silversmith (from No. 1457) and glassmaker (from No. 1456). (U.S.P.S.) 3.00

36 MILCOPEX 1974, Mar. 8—10, 1974, Milwaukee. Card of 4 No. C43. Denomination, etc. removed. (B.E.P.) 2.75

37 INTERNABA 1974, June 6, 1974, Basel, Switzerland. Card of 8, strip of Nos. 1530—1537 reduced to 175x35mm. Card inscribed in German, French, and Italian. (U.S.P.S.) 2.75

38 STOCKHOLMIA 74, International Philatelic Exhibition, September 21—29, 1974, Stockholm, Sweden. Card of 3 No. 836 enlarged to 34x35mm., enlarged reproductions of Sweden Nos. 300 and 767. Card inscribed in Swedish. (U.S.P.S.) 3.25

39 EXFILMEX 74, Interamerican Philatelic Exposition, Oct. 26—Nov. 3, 1974, Mexico City. Card of 2. No. 1157 enlarged to 39x61 mm. Enlarged reproduction of Mexico No. 910. Card inscribed in Spanish. (U.S.P.S.) 2.75

1975

40 ESPANA 75, World Stamp Exhibition, Apr. 4—13, Madrid. Card of 3 No. 233 enlarged to 52x34 mm., No. 1271 and Spain No. 1312 reduced to 16x27mm. Card inscribed in Spanish. (U.S.P.S.) 2.00

41 NAPEX 75, May 9—11, 1975, Washington, D.C. Card of 4 No. 708. Denomination, etc. removed. (B.E.P.) 7.25

42 ARPHILA 75, June 6—16, 1975, Paris. Card of 3. Designs of No. 1187 enlarged to 32x55 mm., No. 1207 enlarged to 55x32 mm. Reproduction of France No. 1117. Card inscribed in French. (U.S.P.S.) 2.50

43 International Women's Year, 1975. Card of 3 Nos. 872, 878, and 959. Denomination, etc. removed. Reproduction of 1886 dollar bill. (B.E.P.) 20.00

44 A.S.D.A. National Postage Stamp Show, Nov. 21—23, 1975. Bicentennial series. Card of 4 No. 1003 reengraved. Denomination, etc. removed. Bicentennial insignia, Trumbull's Washington with his words, ". . . and maintain the liberty which we have derived from our ancestors". (B.E.P.) 32.50

1976

45 WERABA 76, Third International Space Stamp Exhibition, April 1—4, 1976, Zurich, Switzerland. Card of 2, Nos. 1434 and 1435 se—tenant enlarged to 114x32 mm. Quotation "Man is his own star . . .". (U.S.P.S.) 3.50

46 INTERPHIL 76, Seventh International Philatelic Exhibition, May 29—June 6, 1976. Philadelphia, Pa. Bicentennial series. Card of 4 No. 120. Denominations, etc. removed. Bicentennial insignia. Bust of Jefferson with words ". . . that all men are created equal." Reading of the Declaration of Independence. (B.E.P.) 6.75

An Interphil '76 card issued by the American Revolution Bicentennial Administration was bound into the Interphil program. It shows an altered No. 1044 in black brown, the Bicentennial emblem and a view of Independence Hall. Printed by B.E.P.

48 Bicentennial Exposition on Science and Technology, May 30—Sept. 6, 1976, Kennedy Space Center, Fla. No. C76 enlarged to 75x41mm. (U.S.P.S.) 3.50
49 STAMP EXPO 76, June 11—13, 1976, Los Angeles, Calif. Bicentennial series. Card of 4, Nos. 1351, 1352, 1345 and 1348 se—tenant vertically. Denominations, etc. removed. (B.E.P.) 7.50
50 Colorado Statehood Centennial, August 1, 1976. Card of 3, Nos. 743 and 288 denominations, etc. removed and No. 1670 (Colorado state flag) enlarged. (U.S.P.S.) 3.25
51 HAFNIA 76, International Stamp Exhibition, Copenhagen, Denmark, August 20—29, 1976. Card of 2. No. 5 and Denmark No. 2 enlarged. Card inscribed in Danish and English. (U.S.P.S.) 3.25
52 ITALIA 76, International Philatelic Exhibition, Oct. 14—24, Milan, Italy. Card of 3. No. 1168 and Italy Nos. 578 and 601. Card inscribed in Italian. (U.S.P.S.) 3.25
53 NORDPOSTA 76, North German Stamp Exhibition, Oct. 30—31, Hamburg, Germany. Card of 3. No. 689 and Germany Nos. B366 and B417. Card inscribed in German. (U.S.P.S.) 3.50

1977

54 MILCOPEX, Milwaukee Philatelic Society, Mar. 4—6, Milwaukee. Card of 2, Nos. 733 and 1128. (B.E.P.) 2.50
55 ROMPEX 77, Rocky Mountain Philatelic Exhibition, May 20—22, Denver. Card of 4. No. 1001. (B.E.P.) 2.75
56 AMPHILEX 77, International Philatelic Exhibition, May 26—June 5, Amsterdam, Netherlands. Card of 3. No. 1027 and Netherlands Nos. 41 and 294. Card inscribed in Dutch. (U.S.P.S.) 3.50
57 SAN MARINO 77, International Philatelic Exhibition, San Marino, Aug. 28—Sept. 4. Card of 3. Nos. 1—2 and San Marino No. 1. Card inscribed in Italian. (U.S.P.S.) 3.25
58 PURIPEX 77, Silver Anniversary Philatelic Exhibit, Sept. 2—5, San Juan, Puerto Rico. Card of 4 No. 801. (B.E.P.) 2.50
59 A.S.D.A. National Postage Stamp Show, Nov. 15—20, New York. Card of 4 No. C45. (B.E.P.) 3.75

1978

60 ROCPEX 78, International Philatelic Exhibition, Mar. 20—29, Taipei, Taiwan. Card of 6. Nos. 1706—1709 and China Nos. 1812 and 1816. Card inscribed in Chinese. (U.S.P.S.) 4.25
61 NAPOSTA '78 Philatelic Exhibition, May 20—25, Frankfurt, Germany. Card of 3. Nos. 555, 563 and Germany No. 1216. Card inscribed in German. (U.S.P.S.) 3.25
62 CENJEX 78, Federated Stamp Clubs of New Jersey, 30th annual exhibition, June 23—25, Freehold, N.J. Card of 9. Nos. 646, 680, 689, 1086, 1716 and 4 No. 785. (B.E.P.) 3.75

1979

63 BRASILIANA 79, International Philatelic Exhibition, Sept. 15—23, Rio de Janeiro. Card of 3. Nos. C91—C92 and Brazil No. 1295. Card inscribed in Portuguese. (U.S.P.S.) 5.50
64 JAPEX 79, International Philatelic Exhibition, Nov. 2—4, Tokyo. Card of 2. No. 1158 and Japan No. 1024. Card inscribed in Japanese. (U.S.P.S.) 5.50

1980

65 LONDON 1980, International Philatelic Exhibition, May 6—14, London. No. 329 enlarged. (U.S.P.S.) 5.25
66 NORWEX 80, International Stamp Exhibition, June 13—22, Oslo. Card of 3. Nos. 620—621 and Norway No. 658. Card inscribed in Norwegian. (U.S.P.S.) 4.50
67 NAPEX 80, July 4—6, Washington, D.C. Card of 4. No. 573. (B.E.P.) 13.00
68 A.S.D.A. Stamp Festival, Sept. 25—28, 1980, New York, N.Y. Card of 4 No. 962. (B.E.P.) 15.00
69 ESSEN 80, Third International Stamp Fair, Nov. 15—19, Essen, West Germany. Card of 2. No. 1014 and Germany No. 723. Card inscribed in German. (U.S.P.S.) 4.50

1981

70 STAMP EXPO '81 SOUTH, Mar. 20—22, Anaheim, Calif. Card of 6. Nos. 1331—1332, 4 of No. 1287. (B.E.P.) 17.00
71 WIPA 1981, International Stamp Exhibition, May 22—31, Vienna, Austria. Card of 2. No. 1252 and Austria No. 789. Card inscribed in German. (U.S.P.S.) 4.50
72 National Stamp Collecting Month, October, 1981. Card of 2. Nos. 245 and 1918, enlarged. (U.S.P.S.) 4.75
73 PHILATOKYO '81, International Stamp Exhibition, Oct. 9—18. Tokyo. Card of 2. No. 1531 and Japan No. 800. Card inscribed in Japanese. (U.S.P.S.) 5.00
74 NORDPOSTA 81, North German Stamp Exhibition, Nov. 7—8. Hamburg, Germany. Card of 2. No. 923 and Germany No. B538. Card inscribed in German. (U.S.P.S.) 4.50

1982

75 MILCOPEX '82, Milwaukee Philatelic Association Exhibition, Mar. 5—7, Milwaukee, Wis. Card of 4. No. 1137. (B.E.P.) 15.00
76 CANADA 82, international philatelic youth exhibition, May 20—24, Toronto. Card of 2. No. 116 and Canada No. 15. Card inscribed in French and English. (U.S.P.S.) 4.00
77 PHILEXFRANCE '82, International Philatelic Exhibition, June 11—21, Paris, Card of 2. No. 1753 and France No. 1480. Card inscribed in French. (U.S.P.S.) 3.75
78 National Stamp Collecting Month, October. Card of 1. No. C3a. (U.S.P.S.) 4.75
79 ESPAMER '82, International Philatelic Exhibition, Oct. 12—17, San Juan, P.R. Card of 4. No. 244. Card inscribed in English and Spanish. (B.E.P.) 35.00
80 ESPAMER '82, International Philatelic Exhibition, Oct. 12—17, San Juan, P.R. Card of 3. Nos. 801, 1437 and 2024. Card inscribed in Spanish and English. (U.S.P.S.) 4.50

1983

81 Joint stamp issues, Sweden and U.S.A. Mar. 24. Card of 3. Nos. 958, 2036 and Sweden No. 1453, all enlarged. Card inscribed in Swedish and English. (U.S.P.S.) 4.25
82 Joint stamp issues, Germany and U.S.A. Apr. 29. Card of 2. No. 2040 and Germany No. 1397, both enlarged. Card inscribed in German and English. (U.S.P.S.) 4.25
83 TEMBAL 83, International Philatelic Exhibition, Mar. 21—29, Basel Card of 2. No. C71 and Switzerland, Basel No. 3L1, both enlarged. Card inscribed in German. (U.S.P.S.) 4.25
84 TEXANEX—TOPEX '83 Exhibition, June 17—19, San Antonio, Texas. Card of 5. No. 1660, enlarged, and No. 776, block of 4, both with denomination removed. (B.E.P.) 25.00
85 BRASILIANA 83, International Philatelic Exhibition, July 29—Aug. 7, Rio de Janeiro. Card of 2. No. 2 and Brazil No. 1, both enlarged. Card inscribed in Portuguese (U.S.P.S.) 4.25
86 BANGKOK 83, International Philatelic Exhibition, Aug. 4—13, Bangkok, Thailand. Card of 2. No. 210 and Thailand No. 1, both enlarged. Card inscribed in Thai. (U.S.P.S.) 4.25
87 International Philatelic Memento, 1983—84. Card of one. No. 1387, enlarged. (U.S.P.S.) 2.50
88 National Stamp Collecting Month, October. Card of 1. No. 293, enlarged and bicolored. (U.S.P.S.) 4.25
89 Philatelic Show '83, Boston, Oct. 21—23. Card of 2, Nos. 718—719. (B.E.P.) 14.00
90 ASDA 1983, National Postage Stamp Show, New York, Nov. 17—20. Card of 4, No. 881. Denominations, etc. removed. (B.E.P.) 15.00

1984

91 ESPANA 84, World Exhibition of Philately. Madrid, Apr. 27—May 6. Card of 4, No. 241. Denominations removed. Enlarged vignette, Landing of Columbus, from No. 231 at right. Card inscribed in English and Spanish. (B.E.P.) 20.00
92 ESPANA 84, International Philatelic Exhibition, Madrid, Apr. 27—May 6. Card of 2, No. 233 and Spain No. 428, both enlarged. Card inscribed in Spanish. (U.S.P.S.) 4.25
93 Stamp Expo '84 South, Anaheim, Calif., Apr. 27—29. Card of 4, Nos. 1791—1794, with Olympic torch. (B.E.P.) 13.00
94 COMPEX '84, Rosemont, Ill., May 25—27. Card of 4, No. 728. (B.E.P.) 20.00
95 HAMBURG '84, International Exhibition for 19th UPU Congress, Hamburg, Germany, June 19—26. Card of 2, inscribed in English, French and German. (U.S.P.S.) 4.25
96 St. Lawrence Seaway, 25th anniversary, June 26. Card of 2, No. 1131 and Canada No. 387, both enlarged. Card inscribed in English and French. (U.S.P.S.) 4.25
97 AUSIPEX '84, Australia's first international exhibition, Melbourne, Sept. 21—30. Card of 2, No. 290 and Western Australia No. 1, both enlarged. Card inscribed in English. (U.S.P.S.) 4.25
98 National Stamp Collecting Month, October. Card of 1, No. 2104, enlarged and tricolored. Card inscribed in English. (U.S.P.S.) 4.00
99 PHILAKOREA '84, Seoul, Oct. 22—31. Card of 2, No. 741 and Korea No. 994, both enlarged. Card inscribed in Korean and English. (U.S.P.S.) 4.00
100 ASDA 1984, National Postage Stamp Show, New York, NY, Nov. 15—18. Card of 4, No. 1470. Denominations removed. (B.E.P.) 15.00

1985

101 International Philatelic Memento, 1985. Card of 1, No. 2, enlarged. (U.S.P.S.) 4.25
102 OLYMPHILEX '85. International Philatelic Exhibition, Lausanne, Switzerland, Mar. 18—24. Card of 2, No. C106 and Switzerland No. 746, both enlarged. Card inscribed in French and English. (U.S.P.S.) 4.25
103 ISRAPHIL '85. International Philatelic Exhibition, Tel Aviv, Israel, May 14—22. Card of 2, No. 566 and Israel No. 33, both enlarged. Card inscribed in Hebrew and English. (U.S.P.S.) 4.00
104 LONG BEACH '85, Numismatic and Philatelic Exposition, Long Beach, CA, Jan. 31—Feb. 3. Card of 4, No. 954, plus a Series 1865 $20 Gold Certificate. Stamp denominations removed. (B.E.P.) 12.00
105 MILCOPEX '85, Milwaukee Philatelic Society annual stamp show, Milwaukee, WI, Mar. 1—3. Card of 4, No. 880. Denominations, etc., removed. (B.E.P.) 15.00
106 NAPEX '85, National Philatelic Exhibition, Arlington, VA, June 7—9. Card of 4, No. 2014. Denominations defaced with diagonal lines. (B.E.P.) 12.50
107 ARGENTINA '85, International Philatelic Exhibition, Buenos Aires, July 5—14. Card of 2, No. 1737 and Argentina No. B27, both enlarged. Card inscribed in Spanish. (U.S.P.S.) 4.00
108 MOPHILA '85, International Philatelic Exhibition, Hamburg, Sept. 11—15. Card of 2, No. 296 and Germany No. B595, both enlarged. Card inscribed in German. (U.S.P.S.) 5.25
109 ITALIA '85, International Philatelic Exhibition, Rome, Oct. 25—Nov. 3. Card of 2, No. 1107 and Italy No. 830, both enlarged. Card inscribed in Italian. (U.S.P.S.) 4.25

1986

110 Statue of Liberty Centennial, National Philatelic Memento, 1986. Card of 1, No. C87, enlarged. (U.S.P.S.) 6.25
111 Garfield Perry Stamp Club, National Stamp Show, Cleveland, OH, Mar. 21—23. Card of 4, No. 306. Denominations, etc., removed. (B.E.P.) 12.00
112 AMERIPEX '86, International Philatelic Exhibition, Chicago, IL, May 22—June 1. Card of 3, Nos. 134, 2052 and 1474. Denominations, etc., removed, or stamp enlarged. (B.E.P.) 10.00
113 STOCKHOLMIA '86, International Philatelic Exhibition, Stockholm, Sweden, Aug. 28—Sept. 7. Card of 2, No. 113 and Sweden No. 253, both enlarged. Card inscribed in Swedish. (U.S.P.S.) 5.50
114 HOUPEX '86, National Stamp Show, Houston, TX. Sept. 5—7. Card of 3: Nos. 1035, 1042 and 1044A. Denominations, etc., removed. (B.E.P.) 17.00
115 LOBEX '86, Numismatic and Philatelic Exhibition, Long Beach, CA, Oct. 2—5. Long Beach Stamp Club 60th anniv. Card of 4, No. 291, plus a series 1907 $10 Gold Certificate. Stamp denominations removed. (B.E.P.) 13.00
116 DCSE '86, Dallas Coin and Stamp Exhibition, Dallas, TX, Dec. 11—14. Card of 4, No. 550, plus $10,000 Federal Reserve Note. Stamp denominations removed. (B.E.P.) 11.00

1987

117 CAPEX '87, International Philatelic Exhibition, Toronto, Ontario, Canada, June 13—21. Card of 2, No. 569 and Canada No. 883. Denominations removed and/or stamps enlarged. Card inscribed in English and French. (U.S.P.S.) 3.75
118 HAFNIA '87, International Philatelic Exhibition, Copenhagen, Denmark, Oct. 16—25. Card of 2, No. 299 and Denmark No. B52. Denominations removed and/or stamps enlarged. Card inscribed in English and Danish. (U.S.P.S.) 3.75
119 SESCAL '87, Stamp Exhibition of Southern California, Los Angeles, CA, Oct. 16—18. Card of 1, No. 798 defaced by diagonal bars over denominations. (B.E.P.) 15.00
120 HSNA '87, Hawaii State Numismatic Association Exhibition, Honolulu, Hawaii, Nov. 12—15. Card of 1, No. 799 defaced by a diagonal bar plus a Series 1923 $5 Silver Certificate. (B.E.P.) 25.00
121 MONTE CARLO, International Philatelic Exhibition, Monte Carlo, Monaco, Nov. 13—17. Card of 3, Nos. 2287, 2300 and Monaco No. 1589. Denominations removed and/or stamps enlarged. Card inscribed in French and English. (U.S.P.S.) 3.75

1988

122 FINLANDIA '88, International Philatelic Exhibition, Helsinki, Finland, June 1—12. Card of 2, No. 836 and Finland No. 768 defaced by diagonal bars over denominations. Card inscribed in English and Finnish. (U.S.P.S.) 4.00
123 STAMPSHOW '88, American Philatelic Society national stamp show, Detroit, MI, Aug. 25—28. Card of 1, No. 835 defaced by diagonal bars over denominations. (B.E.P.) 11.00
124 MIDAPHIL '88, Kansas City MO, Nov. 18—20. Card of 1, No. 627 defaced by diagonal bar and an engraved reproduction of a riverboat print. (B.E.P.) 8.00

1989

125 PHILEXFRANCE '89 international philatelic exhibition, Paris, July 7—17. Card of 2, No. C120 and France No. 2144 defaced by diagonal bars. Card inscribed in English and French. (U.S.P.S.) 4.00

125 STAMPSHOW '89, American Philatelic Society national stamp show, Anaheim, CA, Aug. 24—27. Card of 1, No. 565 defaced by diagonal bar. Various reproductions of the portrait of Chief Hollow Horn Bear from which the stamp was designed. (B.E.P.) 8.00

COMMEMORATIVE PANELS

The U.S. Postal Service began issuing commemorative panels September 20, 1972, with the Wildlife Conservation issue (Scott 1464-1467). Each panel is devoted to a separate issue. It includes unused examples of the stamp or stamps, usually a block of four;' reproduction of steel engravings, and background information on the subject of the issue. Values are for panels without protective sleeves. Values for panels with protective sleeves are 10% to 25% higher.

1972

1CP Wildlife Conservation, #1467a 7.00
2CP Mail Order, #1468 6.75
3CP Osteopathic Medicine, #1469 7.00
4CP Tom Sawyer, #1470 6.75
5CP Pharmacy, #1473 7.00
6CP Christmas, 1972 (angel), #1471 11.00
7CP Santa Claus, #1472 11.00
8CP Stamp Collecting, #1474 6.75

1973

9CP Love, #1475 9.50
10CP Pamphleteers, #1476 7.75
11CP George Gershwin, #1484 8.25
12CP Posting a Broadside, #1477 7.75
13CP Copernicus, #1488 7.75
14CP Postal Service Employees, #1489—1498 7.00
15CP Harry S Truman, #1499 9.00
16CP Postrider, #1478 9.00
17CP Boston Tea Party, #1483a 27.50
18CP Electronics Progress, #1500—1502, C86 7.00
19CP Robinson Jeffers, #1485 7.00
20CP Lyndon B. Johnson, #1503 10.00
21CP Henry O. Tanner, #1486 7.00
22CP Willa Cather, #1487 7.00
23CP Drummer, #1479 11.00
24CP Angus and Longhorn Cattle, #1504 8.00
25CP Christmas, 1973 (Madonna), #1507 12.50
26CP Christmas Tree, needlepoint, #1508 12.50

1974

27CP Veterans of Foreign Wars, #1525 8.00
28CP Robert Frost, #1526 8.00
29CP EXPO 74, #1527 10.00
30CP Horse Racing, #1528 10.00
31CP Skylab, #1529 12.50
32CP Universal Postal Union, #1537a 10.00
33CP Mineral Heritage, #1541a 10.00
34CP Kentucky Settlement (Ft. Harrod), #1542 8.00
35CP First Continental Congress, #1546a 10.00
36CP Chautauqua, #1505 8.00
37CP Kansas Wheat, #1506 8.00
38CP Energy Conservation, #1547 8.00
39CP Sleepy Hollow Legend, #1548 8.00
40CP Retarded Children, #1549 8.00
41CP Christmas, 1974 (Currier—Ives), #1551 12.00
42CP Christmas, 1974 (angel), #1550 10.50

1975

43CP Benjamin West, #1553 7.00
44CP Pioneer 10, #1556 11.50
45CP Collective Bargaining, #1558 8.00
46CP Contributors to the Cause, #1559—1562 8.00
47CP Mariner 10, #1557 11.50
48CP Lexington—Concord Battle, #1563 7.75
49CP Paul Laurence Dunbar, #1554 8.00
50CP D. W. Griffith, #1555 8.00
51CP Battle of Bunker Hill, #1564 7.75
52CP Military Services (uniforms), #1568a 9.00
53CP Apollo Soyuz, #1569a 11.50
54CP World Peace through Law, #1576 8.00
55CP International Women's Year, #1571 8.00
56CP Postal Service 200 Years, #1575a 9.00
57CP Banking and Commerce, #1577a 9.00
58CP Early Christmas Card, #1580 10.50
59CP Christmas, 1975 (Madonna), #1579 10.50

1976

60CP Spirit of '76, #1631a 12.50
61CP Interphil '76, #1632 12.00
62CP State Flags, block of 4 from #1633—1682 25.00
63CP Telephone Centenary, #1683 11.00
64CP Commercial Aviation, #1684 13.00
65CP Chemistry, #1685 12.00
66CP Benjamin Franklin, #1690 10.50
67CP Declaration of Independence, #1694a 10.50
68CP 12th Winter Olympics, #1698a 16.00
68CP Clara Maass, #1699 12.00
70CP Adolph S. Ochs, #1700 12.00
71CP Christmas, 1976 (Currier print), #1702 13.50
72CP Christmas, 1976 (Copley Nativity), #1701 13.50

1977

73CP Washington at Princeton, #1704 15.00
74CP Sound Recording, #1705 25.00
75CP Pueblo Art, #1709a 90.00
76CP Lindbergh Flight, #1710 110.00
77CP Colorado Statehood, #1711 17.50
78CP Butterflies, #1715a 22.50
79CP Lafayette, #1716 17.50
80CP Skilled Hands for Independence, #1720a 20.00
81CP Peace Bridge, #1721 17.50
82CP Battle of Oriskany, #1722 17.50
83CP Energy Conservation—Development, #1723a 21.00
84CP Alta California, #1725 17.50
85CP Articles of Confederation, #1726 17.50
86CP Talking Pictures, #1727 24.00
87CP Surrender at Saratoga, #1728 17.50
88CP Christmas, 1977 (Washington at Valley Forge), #1729 22.50
89CP Christmas, 1977 (rural mailbox), #1730 35.00

1978

90CP Carl Sandburg, #1731 11.00
91CP Captain Cook, #1732a 20.00
92CP Harriet Tubman, #1744 11.00
93CP American Quilts, #1748a 22.50
94CP American Dance, #1752a 14.00
95CP French Alliance, #1753 14.00
96CP Pap Test, #1754 11.00
97CP Jimmie Rodgers, #1755 15.00
98CP Photography, #1758 11.00
99CP George M. Cohan, #1756 19.00
100CP Viking Missions, #1759 40.00
101CP American Owls, #1763a 40.00
102CP American Trees, #1767a 40.00
103CP Christmas, 1978 (Madonna), #1768 15.00
104CP Christmas, 1978 (hobby—horse), #1769 16.00

1979

105CP Robert F. Kennedy, #1770 12.00
106CP Martin Luther King, Jr., #1771 11.00
107CP Year of the Child, #1772 11.00
108CP John Steinbeck, #1773 11.00
109CP Albert Einstein, #1774 12.00
110CP Pennsylvania Toleware, #1778a 11.00
111CP American Architecture, #1782a 10.00
112CP Endangered Flora, #1786a 11.00
113CP Seeing Eye Dogs, #1787 11.00
114CP Special Olympics, #1788 15.00
115CP John Paul Jones, #1789 13.00
116CP Olympic Games, #1794a 17.00
117CP Christmas, 1979 (Madonna), #1799 16.00
118CP Christmas, 1979 (Santa Claus), #1800 16.00
119CP Will Rogers, #1801 15.00
120CP Viet Nam Veterans, #1802 15.00
121CP 10c, 31c Olympics, #1790, C97 14.00

1980

122CP Winter Olympics, #1798a 12.50
123CP W.C Fields, #1803 10.00
124CP Benjamin Banneker, #1804 11.00
125CP Frances Perkins, #1821 10.00
126CP Emily Bissell, #1823 10.00
127CP Helen Keller, #1824 10.00
128CP Veterans Administration, #1825 10.00
129CP Galvez, #1826 10.00
130CP Coral Reefs, #1830a 12.00
131CP Organized Labor, #1831 10.00
132CP Edith Wharton, #1832 8.25
133CP Education, #1833 10.00
134CP Indian Masks, #1837a 12.50
135CP Architecture, #1841a 10.00
136CP Christmas Window, #1842 15.00
137CP Christmas Toys, #1843 15.00

1981

138CP Dirksen, #1874 11.00
139CP Young, #1875 11.00
140CP Flowers, #1879a 12.00
141CP Red Cross, #1910 12.00
142CP Savings and Loan, #1911 11.00
143CP Space Achievements, #1919a 12.50
144CP Management, #1920 11.00
145CP Wildlife, #1924a 15.00
146CP Disabled, #1925 9.00
147CP Millay, #1926 9.00
148CP Architecture, #1931a 10.00
149CP Zaharias, Jones, #1932, 1933 12.00
150CP Remington, #1934 10.00
151CP 18c, 20c Hoban, #1935, 1936 10.00
152CP Yorktown, Va. Capes, #1938a 10.00
153CP Madonna and Child, #1939 14.00
154CP Teddy Bear, #1940 14.00
155CP John Hanson, #1941 9.00
156CP Desert Plants, #1945a 12.50

1982

157CP FDR, #1950 12.00
158CP Love, #1951 15.00
159CP Washington, #1952 12.00
160CP Birds and Flowers, block of 4 from #1953—2002 30.00
161CP US—Netherlands, #2003 14.00
162CP Library of Congress, #2004 15.00
163CP Knoxville World's Fair, #2009a 15.00
164CP Horatio Alger, #2010 12.00
165CP Aging, #2011 16.00
166CP Barrymores, #2012 17.50
167CP Dr. Mary Walker, #2013 15.00
168CP Peace Garden, #2014 16.00
169CP Libraries, #2015 18.00
170CP Jackie Robinson, #2016 30.00
171CP Touro Synagogue, #2017 16.00
172CP Wolf Trap Farm, #2018 18.00
173CP Architecture, #2022a 16.00
174CP Francis of Assisi, #2023 18.00
175CP Ponce de Leon, #2024 18.00
176CP Puppy, Kitten, #2025 25.00
177CP Madonna and Child, #2026 25.00
178CP Children Playing, #2030a 25.00

1983

179CP Science, #2031 8.00
180CP Ballooning, #2035a 11.00
181CP US—Sweden, #2036 8.00
182CP CCC, #2037 8.00
183CP Priestley, #2038 8.00
184CP Voluntarism, #2039 7.00
185CP German Immigration, #2040 8.00
186CP Brooklyn Bridge, #2041 9.00
187CP TVA, #2042 8.00
188CP Fitness, #2043 7.00
189CP Scott Joplin, #2044 12.00
190CP Medal of Honor, #2045 11.00
191CP Babe Ruth, #2046 18.00
192CP Hawthorne, #2047 8.00
193CP 13c Olympics, #2051a 14.00
194CP 28c Olympics, #C104a 11.00
195CP 40c Olympics, #C108a 10.00
196CP 35c Olympics, #C112a 14.00
197CP Treaty of Paris, #2052 10.00
198CP Civil Service, #2053 10.00
199CP Metropolitan Opera, #2054 10.00
200CP Inventors, #2058a 10.00
201CP Streetcars, #2062a 12.00
202CP Madonna and Child, #2063 14.00
203CP Santa Claus, #2064 14.00
204CP Martin Luther, #2065 12.00

1984

205CP Alaska, #2066 9.00
206CP Winter Olympics, #2070a 10.00
207CP FDIC, #2071 7.00
208CP Love, #2072 8.00
209CP Woodson, #2073 10.00
210CP Conservation, #2074 7.00
211CP Credit Union, #2075 7.00
212CP Orchids, #2079a 10.00
213CP Hawaii, #2080 9.00
214CP National Archives, #2081 7.00
215CP Olympics, #2085a 10.00
216CP World Expo, #2086 9.00
217CP Health Research, #2087 7.00
218CP Fairbanks, #2088 7.00
219CP Thorpe, #2089 13.00
220CP McCormack, #2090 7.00
221CP St. Lawrence Seaway, #2091 9.00
222CP Waterfowl, #2092 12.00
223CP Roanoke Voyages, #2093 7.00
224CP Melville, #2094 7.00
225CP Horace Moses, #2095 7.00
226CP Smokey the Bear, #2096 10.00
227CP Roberto Clemente, #2097 15.00
228CP Dogs, #2101a 10.00
229CP Crime Prevention, #2102 7.00
230CP Hispanic Americans, #2103 8.00
231CP Family Unity, #2104 7.00
232CP Eleanor Roosevelt, #2105 8.00
233CP Readers, #2106 8.00
234CP Madonna and Child, #2107 10.00
235CP Child's Santa, #2108 10.00
236CP Vietnam Memorial, #2109 11.00

1985

237CP Jerome Kern, #2110 8.00
238CP Bethune, #2137 8.00
239CP Duck Decoys, #2141a 10.00
240CP Winter Special Olympics, #2142 8.00
241CP Love, #2143 8.00
242CP REA, #2144 7.00
243CP AMERIPEX '86, #2145 10.00
244CP Abigail Adams, #2146 6.00

245CP Bartholdi, #2147	12.50
246CP Korean Veterans, #2152	8.00
247CP Social Security, #2153	7.00
248CP World War I Veterans, #2154	7.00
249CP Horses, #2158a	10.00
250CP Education, #2159	6.00
251CP Youth Year, #2163a	8.00
252CP Hunger, #2164	7.00
253CP Madonna and Child, #2165	12.00
254CP Poinsettias, #2166	12.00

1986

255CP Arkansas, #2167	6.00
256CP Stamp Collecting booklet pane, #2201a	8.00
257CP Love, #2202	8.00
258CP Sojourner Truth, #2203	8.00
259CP Texas Republic, #2204	8.00
260CP Fish booklet pane, #2209a	8.00
261CP Hospitals, #2210	6.50
262CP Duke Ellington, #2211	8.00
263CP Presidents Souvenir Sheet No. 1, #2216	8.00
264CP Presidents Souvenir Sheet No. 2, #2217	8.00
265CP Presidents Souvenir Sheet No. 3, #2218	8.00
266CP Presidents Souvenir Sheet No. 4, #2219	8.00
267CP Arctic Explorers, #2223a	8.00
268CP Statue of Liberty, #2224	8.00
269CP Navajo Art, #2238a	8.00
270CP T.S. Eliot, #2239	6.00
271CP Woodcarved Figurines, #2243a	8.00
272CP Madonna and Child, #2244	8.00
273CP Village Scene, #2245	8.00

1987

274CP Michigan, #2246	7.00
275CP Pan American Games, #2247	7.00
276CP Love, #2248	8.00
277CP du Sable, #2249	8.00
278CP Caruso, #2250	8.00
279CP Girl Scouts, #2251	8.00
280CP Special Occasions booklet pane, #2274a	7.00
281CP United Way, #2275	7.00
282CP Wildlife, #2286, 2287, 2296, 2297, 2306, 2307, 2316, 2317, 2326, 2327	9.00
283CP Wildlife, #2288, 2289, 2298, 2299, 2308, 2309, 2318, 2319, 2328, 2329	9.00
284CP Wildlife, #2290, 2291, 2300, 2301, 2310, 2311, 2320, 2321, 2330, 2331	9.00
285CP Wildlife, #2292, 2293, 2302, 2303, 2312, 2313, 2322, 2323, 2332, 2333	9.00
286CP Wildlife, #2294, 2295, 2304, 2305, 2314, 2315, 2324, 2325, 2334, 2335	9.00

1987-88

287CP Delaware, #2336	7.00
288CP Pennsylvania, #2337	7.00
289CP New Jersey, #2338	7.00
290CP Georgia, #2339	9.00
291CP Connecticut, #2340	9.00
292CP Massachusetts, #2341	9.00
293CP Maryland, #2342	9.00
294CP South Carolina, #2343	9.00
295CP New Hampshire, #2344	9.00
296CP Virginia, #2345	9.00
297CP New York, #2346	9.00

1987

300CP U.S.—Morocco, #2349	7.00
301CP William Faulkner, #2350	7.00
302CP Lacemaking, #2354a	7.00
303CP Drafting of the Constitution booklet pane, #2359a	7.00
304CP Signing of the Constitution, #2360	7.00
305CP Certified Public Accounting, #2361	8.00
306CP Locomotives booklet pane, #2366a	8.00
307CP Madonna and Child, #2367	7.00
308CP Christmas Ornaments, #2368	7.00

1988

309CP Winter Olympics, #2369	9.00
310CP Australia Bicentennial, #2370	9.00
311CP James Weldon Johnson, #2371	9.00
312CP Cats, #2375a	10.00
313CP Knute Rockne, #2376	10.00
314CP New Sweden, #C117	9.00
315CP Francis Ouimet, #2377	9.00
316CP 25c, 45c Love, #2378 and #2379	10.00
317CP Summer Olympics, #2380	11.00
318CP Classic Automobiles booklet pane, #2385a	9.00
319CP Antarctic Explorers, #2389a	9.00
320CP Carousel Animals, #2393a	9.00
321CP Special Occasions booklet singles, #2395—2398	11.00
322CP Madonna and Child, Sleigh, #2399, 2400	11.00

1989

323CP Montana, #2401	10.00
324CP A. Philip Randolph, #2402	12.50
325CP North Dakota, #2403	10.00
326CP Washington Statehood, #2404	10.00
327CP Steamboats booklet pane, #2409a	10.00
328CP World Stamp Expo, #2410	10.00
329CP Arturo Toscanini, #2411	10.00

1989

330CP House of Representatives, #2412	10.00
331CP Senate, #2413	10.00
332CP Executive Branch, #2414	10.00

1989

334CP South Dakota, #2416	10.00

SOUVENIR PAGES

These are post office new-issue announcement bulletins, including an illustration of the stamp's design and informative text. They bear a copy of the stamp, tied by a first day of issue cancellation. Varieties of bulletin watermarks and text changes, etc., are beyond the scope of this catalogue.

Values for Scott 1-295 are for folded copies. Values for Official Souvenir Pages (those after Scott 295) are for copies that never have been folded.

UNOFFICIAL SOUVENIR PAGES

Liberty Issue

1960-65

1	1031A, 1054A	1 1/4c	Palace of Governors, sheet, coil	50.00
2	1042A	8c	Pershing	30.00
3	1044A	11c	Statue of Liberty	27.50
4	1059A	25c	Revere coil	8.00

1959

5	1132	4c	49 Star Flag	—
6	C55	7c	Hawaii Statehood	—
7	1133	4c	Soil Conservation	—
8	C56	10c	Pan American Games	—
9	1134	4c	Petroleum	—
10	1135	4c	Dental Health	—
11	1136, 1137	4c, 8c	Reuter	—
12	1138	4c	McDowell	—

1960-61

13	1139	4c	Washington Credo	75.00
14	1140	4c	Franklin Credo	75.00
15	1141	4c	Jefferson Credo	75.00
16	1142	4c	F.S. Key Credo	75.00
17	1143	4c	Lincoln Credo	65.00
18	1144	4c	P. Henry Credo	35.00

1961

19	1145	4c	Boy Scout	75.00
20	1146	4c	Winter Olympics	75.00
21	1147, 1148	4c, 8c	Masaryk	75.00
22	1149	4c	Refugee Year	35.00
23	1150	4c	Water Consevation	20.00
24	1151	4c	SEATO	20.00
25	1152	4c	American Women	20.00
26	C57	10c	Liberty Bell	—
27	C58	15c	Statue of Liberty	—
28	C59	25c	Lincoln	—
29	1153	4c	50 Star Flag	50.00
30	1154	4c	Pony Express	50.00
31	C60	7c	Jet, carmine	12.50
32	C60a	7c	Booklet pane of 6	30.00
33	C61	7c	Jet coil	17.50
34	1155	4c	Handicapped	50.00
35	1156	4c	Forestry Congress	50.00
36	1157	4c	Mexican Independence	35.00
37	1158	4c	U.S., Japan Treaty	20.00
38	1159, 1160	4c, 8c	Paderewski	37.50
39	1161	4c	Sen. Taft	45.00
40	1162	4c	Wheels of Freedom	45.00
41	1163	4c	Boys' Clubs	45.00
42	1164	4c	Automated Post Office	45.00
43	1165, 1166	4c, 8c	Mannerheim	45.00
44	1167	4c	Camp Fire Girls	45.00
45	1168, 1169	4c, 8c	Garibaldi	45.00
46	1170	4c	Sen. George	45.00
47	1171	4c	Carnegie	45.00
48	1172	4c	Dulles	45.00
49	1173	4c	Echo I	20.00

1961

50	1174, 1175	4c, 8c	Gandhi	20.00
51	1176	4c	Range Conservation	20.00
52	1177	4c	Greeley	20.00

1961-65

53	1178	4c	Ft. Sumter	20.00
54	1179	4c	Shiloh	27.50
55	1180	5c	Gettysburg	6.00
56	1181	5c	Wilderness	6.50
57	1182	5c	Appomattox	6.50

1961

58	1183	4c	Kansas	12.00
59	C62	13c	Liberty Bell	20.00
60	1184	4c	Sen. Norris	11.50
61	1185	4c	Naval Aviation	20.00
62	1186	4c	Workmen's Compensation	20.00
63	1187	4c	Remington	12.00
64	1188	4c	Sun Yat sen	20.00
65	1189	4c	Basketball	20.00
66	1190	4c	Nursing	15.00

1962

67	1191	4c	New Mexico	12.50
68	1192	4c	Arizona	12.50
69	1193	4c	Project Mercury	10.00
70	1194	4c	Malaria	12.50
71	1195	4c	Hughes	21.00
72	1196	4c	Seattle World's Fair	17.50
73	1197	4c	Louisiana	17.50
74	1198	4c	Homestead Act	17.50
75	1199	4c	Girl Scouts	20.00
76	1200	4c	McMahon	17.50
77	1201	4c	Apprenticeship	17.50
78	1202	4c	Rayburn	17.50
79	1203	4c	Hammarskjold	17.50
80	1204	4c	Hammarskjold, yellow inverted	40.00
81	1205	4c	Christmas	50.00
82	1206	4c	Higher Education	10.00
83	C64	8c	Capitol	9.00
83a	C64, C64b, C65	8c	Capitol sheet, booklet, coil	20.00
84	C64a	8c	Capitol, tagged	30.00
85	C64b	8c	Capitol booklet single	25.00
86	C65	8c	Capitol coil	15.00
87	1207	4c	Winslow Homer	15.00
88	1208	5c	Flag	12.50
89	1209	1c	Jackson	12.50
90	1213	5c	Washington	17.50
91	1213a	5c	Washington booklet pane of 5 + label	30.00
92	1225	1c	Jackson coil	17.50
93	1229	5c	Washington coil	17.50
94	C66	15c	Montgomery Blair	—

1963

96	1231	5c	Food for Peace	6.00
97	1232	5c	West Virginia	5.75
97A	C67	6c	Eagle	8.50
97B	C68	8c	Amelia Earhart	18.00
98	1233	5c	Emancipation Proclamation	14.00
99	1234	5c	Alliance for Progress	6.75
100	1235	5c	Cordell Hull	7.00
101	1236	5c	Eleanor Roosevelt	6.25
102	1237	5c	Science	6.75
103	1238	5c	City Mail Delivery	6.75
104	1239	5c	Red Cross	6.00
105	1240	5c	Christmas	7.50
106	1241	5c	Audubon	8.00

1964

107	1242	5c	Sam Houston	12.00
108	1243	5c	C.M. Russell	6.75
109	1244	5c	N.Y. World's Fair	7.25
110	1245	5c	John Muir	12.00
111	1246	5c	Kennedy (Boston, Mass.) (At least 4 other cities known)	12.00
112	1247	5c	New Jersey	6.75
113	1248	5c	Nevada	6.25
114	1249	5c	Register and Vote	6.25
115	1250	5c	Shakespeare	6.25
116	1251	5c	Mayo Brothers	6.25
117	C69	8c	Goddard	5.00
118	1252	5c	Music	6.25
119	1253	5c	Homemakers	6.25
120	1257b	5c	Christmas Plants	17.50
121	1257c	5c	Christmas, tagged	90.00
122	1258	5c	Verrazano Narrows Bridge	6.00
123	1259	5c	Fine Arts	7.00
124	1260	5c	Amateur Radio	7.00

1965

125	1261	5c	New Orleans	5.50
126	1262	5c	Sokols	6.75
127	1263	5c	Cancer	5.50
128	1264	5c	Churchill	6.50
129	1265	5c	Magna Carta	5.50
130	1266	5c	I.C.Y.	5.50
131	1267	5c	Salvation Army	6.50
132	1268	5c	Dante	6.00
133	1269	5c	Hoover	5.75
134	1270	5c	Fulton	5.50
135	1271	5c	Florida	6.50
136	1272	5c	Traffic Safety	5.50
137	1273	5c	Copley	6.25
138	1274	11c	I.T.U.	7.75
139	1275	5c	Stevenson	5.75
140	1276	5c	Christmas	7.50

Prominent Americans

1965-73

141 1278 1c Jefferson 6.50
141a 1278, 1278a, 1299 1c Jefferson sheet, booklet, coil 7.00
142 1278a 1c Jefferson booklet pane of 8 8.25
143 1279 1¼c Gallatin 6.50
144 1280 2c Wright 5.25
145 1280a 2c Wright booklet pane of 5 + label 9.50
146 1281 3c Parkman 6.00
147 1282 4c Lincoln 6.00
148 1283 5c Washington 5.25
149 1283B 5c Washington redrawn 6.50
150 1284 6c Roosevelt 5.75
151 1284b 6c Roosevelt booklet pane of 8 13.00
151a 1284b, 1298 6c Roosevelt booklet, vert. coil 5.00
151b 1284b, 1305 6c Roosevelt booklet, horiz. coil 5.00
152 1285 8c Einstein 11.00
153 1286 10c Jackson 6.75
154 1286A 12c Ford 7.25
155 1287 13c Kennedy 20.00
156 1288 15c Holmes 6.00
157 1289 20c Marshall 7.75
158 1290 25c Douglass 7.75
159 1291 30c Dewey 27.50
160 1292 40c Paine 40.00
161 1293 50c Stone 35.00
162 1294 $1 O'Neill 55.00
163 1295 $5 Moore 125.00
164 1298 6c Roosevelt, vert. coil 5.25
165 1299 1c Jefferson, coil 5.75
166 1303 4c Lincoln, coil 5.50
167 1304 5c Washington, coil 5.50
168 1305 6c Roosevelt, horiz. coil 5.50

Nos. 1297, 1305C and 1305E are known on unofficial pages. They are not listed here. For official pages of these issues, see Nos. 296-298.

1966

169 1306 5c Migratory Bird Treaty 8.00
170 1307 5c ASPCA 7.50
171 1308 5c Indiana 7.50
172 1309 5c Circus 6.75
173 1310 5c SIPEX 6.00
174 1311 5c SIPEX Souvenir Sheet 7.25
175 1312 5c Bill of Rights 6.00
176 1313 5c Poland 6.00
177 1314 5c National Park Service 6.00
178 1315 5c Marine Corps Reserve 6.00
179 1316 5c Women's Clubs 6.50
180 1317 5c Johnny Appleseed 6.75
181 1318 5c Beautifcation of America 7.50
182 1319 5c Great River Road 6.75
183 1320 5c Savings Bonds Servicemen 6.25
184 1321 5c Christmas 6.50
185 1322 5c Mary Cassatt 6.75

1967

186 C70 8c Alaska 10.00
187 1323 5c Grange 5.00
188 C71 20c Audubon 4.00
189 1324 5c Canada 5.25
190 1325 5c Erie Canal 5.25
191 1326 5c Search for Peace 6.50
192 1327 5c Thoreau 5.50
193 1328 5c Nebraska 5.25
194 1329 5c VOA 5.25
195 1330 5c Crockett 7.00
196 1331a 5c Space 21.00
197 1333 5c Urban Planning 5.25
198 1334 5c Finland 5.00
199 1335 5c Eakins 6.00
200 1336 5c Christmas 7.00
201 1337 5c Mississippi 5.50

1968-71

202 1338 6c Flags, Giori Press 5.00
203 1338D 6c Flag, Huck Press 5.00
204 1338F 8c Flag 5.50
205 1338A 6c Flag coil 5.75

1968

206 C72 10c 50 star Runway 5.00
207 C72, C72b, C73 10c sheet, coil, booklet pane of 8 25.00
207a C72, C72b, C73 10c sheet, booklet single, coil 7.00
208 C73 10c 50 star Runway coil 9.00
209 1339 6c Illinois 5.50
210 1340 6c HemisFair 6.25
211 1341 $1 Airlift 60.00
212 1342 6c Youth 5.75
213 C74 10c Air Mail Service 7.25
214 1343 6c Law and Order 5.00
215 1344 6c Register and Vote 6.25
216 1345—1354 6c Historic Flags 70.00
217 1355 6c Disney 8.00
218 1356 6c Marquette 5.75
219 1357 6c Daniel Boone 6.00
220 1358 6c Arkansas River Navigation 5.75
221 1359 6c Leif Erikson 12.50
222 1360 6c Cherokee Strip 9.25
223 1361 6c John Trumbull 5.00
224 1362 6c Waterfowl 6.50
225 1363 6c Christmas 6.50
226 1364 6c Chief Joseph 5.00
227 C75 20c USA 5.00

1969

228 1368a 6c Beautification 16.00
229 1369 6c American Legion 5.75
230 1370 6c Grandma Moses 6.00
231 1371 6c Apollo 8 11.50
232 1372 6c W.C. Handy 7.50
233 1373 6c California 4.75
234 1374 6c Powell 5.75
235 1375 6c Alabama 5.75
236 1379a 6c Botanical Congress 16.50
237 C76 10c Man on the Moon 14.00
238 1380 6c Dartmouth 5.75
239 1381 6c Baseball 40.00
240 1382 6c Football 11.00
241 1383 6c Eisenhower 4.75
242 1384 6c Christmas 6.00
243 1385 6c Hope 6.00
244 E22 45c Special Delivery 25.00
245 1386 6c Harnett 6.00

1970

246 1390a 6c Natural History 27.50
247 1391 6c Maine 5.75
248 1392 6c Wildlife Conservation 5.75

Regular Issue

1970-71

249 1393 6c Eisenhower 5.00
249a 1393, 1393a, 1401 6c sheet, booklet, coil stamps 6.00
249b 1393, 1401 6c sheet, coil stamps 6.00
250 1393a 6c Eisenhower booklet pane of 8 12.50
250a 1393a, 1401 6c booklet, coil 6.00
251 1393b 6c Eisenhower booklet pane of 5 + label 6.00
252 1394 8c Eisenhower 5.25
252a 1394, 1395, 1402 8c sheet, booklet, coil 6.00
253 1395a 8c Eisenhower booklet pane of 8 15.00
254 1395b 8c Eisenhower booklet pane of 8 15.00
255 1396 8c U.S.P.S. 10.00
256 1398 16c Pyle 5.25
257 1401 6c Eisenhower coil 5.00
258 1402 8c Eisenhower coil 5.00

1970

259 1405 6c Masters 5.75
260 1406 6c Suffrage 5.00
261 1407 6c So. Carolina 5.00
262 1408 6c Stone Mountain 5.00
263 1409 6c Ft. Snelling 5.00
264 1413a 6c Anti pollution 4.75
265 1414 6c Christmas Nativity 13.00
266 1418b 6c Christmas Toys 6.75
267 1418c 6c Toys, precanceled 35.00
268 1419 6c U.N. 6.75
269 1420 6c Mayflower 6.00
270 1421a 6c DAV, Servicemen 27.50

1971

271 1423 6c Wool 5.75
272 1424 6c MacArthur 6.00
273 1425 6c Blood Donors 6.75
274 1426 8c Missouri 5.75
275 C77 9c Delta Wing 5.00
276 C78 11c Jet 3.50
276a C78, C78a, C82 11c sheet, booklet, coil 5.00
277 C78a 11c Jet booklet pane of 4 + 2 labels 12.00
278 E23 60c Special Delivery 24.00
279 1430a 8c Wildlife 12.50
280 1431 8c Antarctic Treaty 10.00
281 1432 8c Bicentennial Emblem 12.50
282 C80 17c Statue of Liberty 15.00
283 C81 21c USA 15.00
284 C82 11c Jet coil 3.25
285 1433 8c Sloan 10.00
286 1434a 8c Space 15.00
287 1436 8c Dickenson 10.00
288 1437 8c San Juan 10.00
289 1438 8c Drug Abuse 10.00
290 1439 8c CARE 10.00
291 1443a 8c Historic Preservation 12.50
292 1444 8c Adoration 10.00
293 1445 8c Patridge 10.00

1972

294 1446 8c Lanier 10.00
295 1447 8c Peace Corps 10.00

OFFICIAL SOUVENIR PAGES

In 1972 the USPS began issuing "official" Souvenir pages by subscription. A few more "unofficials" were produced.

Prominent Americans

1970-78

296 1297 3c Parkman, coil 4.00
297 1305C $1 O'Neill, coil 17.50
298 1305E 15c Holmes, coil 2.75
299 1393D 7c Franklin 9.25
300 1397 14c LaGuardia 110.00
301 1399 18c Blackwell 3.25
302 1400 21c Giannini 6.25

1972

303 1451a 2c Cape Hatteras 110.00
304 1452 6c Wolf Trap Farm 40.00
305 1453 8c Yellowstone 110.00
306 C84 11c City of Refuge 110.00
307 1454 15c Mt. McKinley 32.50
308 1455 8c Family Planning 525.00
309 1459a 8c Colonial Craftsmen 22.50
310 1460—1462, C85 Olympics 20.00
311 1463 8c PTA 9.50
312 1467a 8c Wildlife 12.50
313 1468 8c Mail Order 7.75
314 1469 8c Osteopathic 10.00
315 1470 8c Tom Sawyer 9.25
316 1471, 1472 8c Christmas 16.00
317 1473 8c Pharmacy 8.00
318 1474 8c Stamp Collecting 8.00

1973

319 1475 8c Love 16.00
320 1476 8c Printing 6.75
321 1477 8c Broadside 8.00
322 1478 8c Postrider 8.00
323 1479 8c Drummer 5.75
324 1483a 8c Tea Party 8.25
325 1484 8c Gershwin 7.75
326 1485 8c Jeffers 4.75
327 1486 8c Tanner 5.25
328 1487 8c Cather 4.25
329 1488 8c Copernicus 6.50
330 1489—1498 8c Postal People 8.75
331 1499 8c Truman 6.25
332 1500—1502, C86 Electronics 7.25
333 1503 8c L.B. Johnson 5.25

1973-74

334 1504 8c Cattle 4.25
335 1505 10c Chautauqua 2.75
336 1506 10c Kansas Winter Wheat 2.75

1973

337 1507, 1508 8c Christmas 8.25

REGULAR ISSUES

1973-74

338 1509 10c Crossed Flags 3.50
339 1510 10c Jefferson Memorial 3.50
340 1511 10c ZIP 4.75
341 1518 6.3c Liberty Bell coil 4.00
341A C79 13c Winged Envelope 3.50
341B C83 13c Airmail, coil 3.50

1974

342 C87 18c Statue of Liberty 7.50
343 C88 26c Mt. Rushmore 5.750
344 1525 10c VFW 3.25
345 1526 10c Robert Frost 3.50
346 1527 10c EXPO '74 3.25
347 1528 10c Horse Racing 3.50
348 1529 10c Skylab 6.75
349 1537a 10c UPU 6.50
350 1541a 10c Minerals 6.75
351 1542 10c Ft. Harrod 3.25
352 1546a 10c Continental Congress 5.00
353 1547 10c Energy 2.75
354 1548 10c Sleepy Hollow 3.50
355 1549 10c Retarded Children 3.25
356 1550—1552 10c Christmas 6.25

1975

357 1553 10c Benjamin West 3.25
358 1554 10c Dunbar 4.25
359 1555 10c D.W. Griffith 3.50
360 1556 10c Pioneer 6.25
361 1557 10c Mariner 5.25
362 1558 10c Collective Bargaining 3.50
363 1559 8c Sybil Ludington 3.25
364 1560 10c Salem Poor 3.25
365 1561 10c Haym Salomon 3.25
366 1562 15c Peter Francisco 3.25
367 1563 10c Lexington & Concord 3.50
368 1564 10c Bunker Hill 3.50
369 1568a 10c Military Uniforms 6.50
370 1569a 10c Apollo Soyuz 6.50
371 1571 10c Women's Year 3.25
372 1575a 10c Postal Service 5.25
373 1576 10c Peace through Law 3.25
374 1577a 10c Banking and Commerce 3.25
375 1579, 1580 10c Christmas 4.25

Americana Issue

1975-81

376 1581, 1582, 1584, 1585 1c, 2c, 3c, 4c Americana 3.25
377 1591 9c Capitol Dome 2.50
378 1592 10c Justice 3.25
379 1593 11c Printing Press 2.50
380 1594, 1816 12c Torch sheet, coil 2.75
381 1596 13c Eagle and Shield 2.50
382 1597, 1618C 15c Flag sheet, coil 3.25
383 1599, 1619 16c Statue of Liberty sheet, coil 2.75
384 1603 24c Old North Church 2.75
385 1604 28c Ft. Nisqually 3.25
386 1605 29c Lighthouse 2.75
387 1606 30c Schoolhouse 4.75
388 1608 50c "Betty" Lamp 5.00
389 1610 $1 Candle Holder 7.25
390 1611 $2 Kerosene Lamp 7.50

391	1612	$5	R. R. Lantern	20.00
392	1811	1c	Inkwell, coil	2.25
393	1613	3.1c	Guitar, coil	5.75
394	1813	3.5c	Violin, coil	4.00
395	1614	7.7c	Saxhorns, coil	2.50
396	1615	7.9c	Drum, coil	2.75
397	1615C	8.4c	Piano, coil	3.25
398	1616	9c	Capitol Dome, coil	2.50
398A	1617	10c	Justice, coil	4.50
399	1618	13c	Liberty Bell, coil	2.75
400	1622, 1625	13c	13 star Flag sheet, coil	2.75
401	1623c	9c, 13c	Booklet pane, perf. 10	20.00

1976

402	1631a	13c	Sprirит of '76	4.25
403	C89, C90	25c, 31c	Plane and Globes	4.00
404	1632	13c	Interphil 76	2.75
405	1633—1642	13c	State Flags	8.75
406	1643—1652	13c	State Flags	8.75
407	1653—1662	13c	State Flags	8.75
408	1663—1672	13c	State Flags	8.75
409	1673—1682	13c	State Flags	8.75
410	1683	13c	Telephone	2.75
411	1684	13c	Aviation	2.50
412	1685	13c	Chemistry	2.75
413	1686	13c	Bicentennial Souvenir Sheet	11.00
414	1687	18c	Bicentennial Souvenir Sheet	11.00
415	1688	24c	Bicentennial Souvenir Sheet	11.00
416	1689	31c	Bicentennial Souvenir Sheet	11.00
417	1690	13c	Franklin	2.75
418	1694a	13c	Declaration of Independence	5.25
419	1698a	13c	Olympics	6.25
420	1699	13c	Clara Maass	2.50
421	1700	13c	Adolph Ochs	2.50
422	1701—1703	13c	Christmas	4.25

1977

423	1704	13c	Washington at Princeton	2.75
424	1705	13c	Sound Recording	2.50
425	1709a	13c	Pueblo Pottery	3.50
426	1710	13c	Lindbergh Flight	3.50
427	1711	13c	Colorado	2.25
428	1715a	13c	Butterflies	3.25
429	1716	13c	Lafayette	2.50
430	1720a	13c	Skilled Hands	3.25
431	1721	13c	Peace Bridge	2.50
432	1722	13c	Oriskany	2.50
433	1723a	13c	Energy	2.50
434	1725	13c	Alta California	2.50
435	1726	13c	Articles of Confederation	2.50
436	1727	13c	Talking Pictures	2.75
437	1728	13c	Saratoga	3.75
438	1729, 1730	13c	Christmas	2.50

1978

439	1731	13c	Sandburg	2.50
440	1732, 1733	13c	Capt. Cook	3.25
441	1734	13c	Indian Head Penny	2.50
442	1735, 1743	15c	A Sheet, coil	4.50
443	1737	15c	Roses booklet single	2.75
444	1742a	15c	Windmills booklet pane of 10	5.00
445	1744	13c	Tubman	3.25
446	1748a	13c	Quilts	2.75
447	1752a	13c	American Dance	3.25
448	1753	13c	French Alliance	2.50
449	1754	13c	Cancer Detection	2.50
450	1755	13c	Jimmie Rodgers	4.75
451	1756	15c	George M. Cohan	2.50
452	1757	13c	CAPEX '78 Souvenir Sheet	8.00
453	1758	15c	Photography	2.50
454	1759	15c	Viking Missions	4.25
455	1763a	15c	Owls	3.50
456	C92a	31c	Wright Brothers	3.50
457	1767a	15c	Trees	3.50
458	1768	15c	Madonna and Child	2.50
459	1769	15c	Hobby Horse	2.50

1979

460	1770	15c	Robert F. Kennedy	2.50
461	1771	15c	Martin Luther King Jr.	4.00
462	1772	15c	Year of the Child	2.50
463	1773	15c	John Steinbeck	2.50
464	1774	15c	Einstein	2.75
465	C94a	21c	Chanute	3.50
466	1778a	15c	Toleware	2.75
467	1782a	15c	Architecture	3.25
468	1786a	15c	Endangered Flora	3.50
469	1787	15c	Seeing Eye Dogs	2.50
470	1788	15c	Special Olympics	2.75
471	1789	15c	John Paul Jones	3.25
472	1790	10c	Olympics	4.25
473	1794a	15c	Olympics	6.50
474	C97	31c	Olympics	6.25

1980

475	1798a	15c	Winter Olympics	6.50

1979

476	1799	15c	Madonna and Child	3.25
477	1800	15c	Santa Claus	3.25
478	1801	15c	Will Rogers	2.75
479	1802	15c	Vietnam Veterans	2.75
480	C96a	25c	Wiley Post	4.25

1980

481	1803	15c	W.C. Fields	3.00
482	1804	15c	Benjamin Banneker	3.75
483	1805—1810	15c	Letter Writing Week	3.50
484	1818, 1820	18c	B sheet, coil	3.00
485	1819a	18c	B booklet pane of 8	3.00
486	1821	15c	Frances Perkins	2.25
487	1822	15c	Dolley Madison	4.00
488	1823	15c	Emily Bissell	2.25
489	1824	15c	Helen Keller	3.00
490	1825	15c	Veterans Administration	2.25
491	1826	15c	Galvez	2.25
492	1830a	15c	Coral Reefs	2.75
493	1831	15c	Organized Labor	4.00
494	1832	15c	Edith Wharton	3.75
495	1833	15c	Education	2.75
496	1837a	15c	Indian Masks	3.00
497	1841a	15c	Architecture	3.00
498	C98	40c	Mazzei	3.25
499	1842	15c	Christmas Window	3.25
500	1843	15c	Christmas Toys	4.00
501	C99	28c	Blanche Stuart Scott	2.25
502	C100	35c	Curtiss	2.25

Great Americans

1980-85

503	1844	1c	Dix	2.00
504	1845	2c	Stravinsky	3.25
505	1846	3c	Clay	2.00
506	1847	4c	Schurz	2.00
507	1848	5c	Buck	2.00
508	1849	6c	Lippmann	2.50
509	1850	7c	Baldwin	3.25
510	1851	8c	Knox	2.00
511	1852	9c	Thayer	3.00
512	1853	10c	Russell	2.00
513	1854	11c	Partridge	2.00
514	1855	13c	Crazy Horse	2.25
515	1856	14c	Lewis	2.00
516	1857	17c	Carson	2.25
517	1858	18c	Mason	2.25
518	1859	19c	Sequoyah	2.25
519	1860	20c	Bunche	4.25
520	1861	20c	Gallaudet	2.00
521	1862	20c	Truman	2.00
522	1863	22c	Audubon	2.50
523	1864	30c	Laubach	2.00
524	1865	35c	Drew	2.00
525	1866	37c	Millikan	2.00
526	1867	39c	Clark	2.00
527	1868	40c	Gilbreth	2.00
528	1869	50c	Nimitz	2.75

1981

529	1874	15c	Dirksen	2.25
530	1875	15c	Young	2.75
531	1879a	18c	Flowers	2.50
532	1889a	18c	Animals booklet pane of 10	4.25
533	1890, 1891	18c	Flag sheet, coil	2.75
534	1893a	6c, 18c	Booklet pane	3.00
535	1894, 1895	20c	Flag sheet, coil	4.25
536	1896a	20c	Flag booklet pane of 6	4.00

1982

537	1896b	20c	Flag booklet pane of 10	3.50

Transporation Coils

1981-84

538	1897	1c	Omnibus	3.75
539	1897A	2c	Locomotive	5.25
540	1898	3c	Handcar	4.00
541	1898A	4c	Stagecoach	4.25
542	1899	5c	Motorcycle	5.25
543	1900	5.2c	Sleigh	5.25
544	1901	5.9c	Bicycle	5.50
545	1902	7.4c	Baby Buggy	4.00
546	1903	9.3c	Mail Wagon	4.50
547	1904	10.9c	Hansom Cab	5.50
548	1905	11c	Caboose	4.00
549	1906	17c	Electric Auto	4.00
550	1907	18c	Surrey	4.00
551	1008	20c	Fire Pumper	5.00

1983

552	1909	$9.35	Express Mail single	140.00
552a	1909a	$9.35	Express Mail booklet pane of 3	200.00

1981

553	1910	18c	Red Cross	2.25
554	1911	18c	Savings and Loan	2.25
555	1919a	18c	Space Achievements	6.75
556	1920	18c	Management	2.25
557	1924a	18c	Wildlife	2.75
558	1925	18c	Disabled	2.25
559	1926	18c	Millay	2.25
560	1927	18c	Alcoholism	3.00
561	1931a	18c	Architecture	3.25
562	1932	18c	Zaharias	3.00
563	1933	18c	Jones	3.00
564	1934	18c	Remington	2.50
565	1935, 1936	18c, 20c	Hoban	2.50
566	1938a	18c	Yorktown, Va. Capes	3.00
567	1939	20c	Madonna and Child	3.00
568	1940	20c	Teddy Bear	3.00
569	1941	20c	John Hanson	2.25
570	1945a	20c	Desert Plants	2.75
571	1946, 1947	20c	C sheet, coil	4.25
572	1948a	20c	C Booklet pane of 10	4.25

1982

573	1949a	20c	Bighorn Sheep booklet pane of 10	3.50
574	1950	20c	FDR	2.25
575	1951	20c	Love	2.25
576	1952	20c	Washington	3.50
577	1953—1962	20c	Birds and Flowers	12.00
578	1963—1972	20c	Birds and Flowers	12.00
579	1973—1982	20c	Birds and Flowers	12.00
580	1983—1992	20c	Birds and Flowers	12.00
581	1993—2002	20c	Birds and Flowers	12.00
582	2003	20c	US Netherlands	2.25
583	2004	20c	Library of Congress	2.25
584	2005	20c	Consumer Education	3.75
585	2009a	20c	Knoxville World's Fair	2.50
586	2010	20c	Horatio Alger	2.25
587	2011	20c	Aging	2.25
588	2012	20c	Barrymores	3.75
589	2013	20c	Dr. Mary Walker	2.25
590	2014	20c	Peace Garden	2.25
591	2015	20c	Libraries	2.25
592	2016	20c	Jackie Robinson	15.00
593	2017	20c	Touro Synagogue	2.25
594	2018	20c	Wolf Trap Farm	2.25
595	2022a	20c	Architecture	2.50
596	2023	20c	Francis of Assisi	2.25
597	2024	20c	Ponce de Leon	2.25
598	2025	13c	Puppy, Kitten	3.25
599	2026	20c	Madonna and Child	3.25
600	2030a	20c	Children Playing	4.00

1983

601	O127—O129	1c, 4c, 13c	Official Mail	3.25
602	O130	17c	Official Mail	3.25
603	O132	$1	Official Mail	5.00
604	O133	$5	Official Mail	10.00
605	O135	20c	Official Mail coil	3.25
606	2031	20c	Science	2.00
607	2035a	20c	Ballooning	2.75
608	2036	20c	US Sweden	2.50
609	2037	20c	CCC	2.00
610	2038	20c	Priestley	2.00
611	2039	20c	Voluntarism	2.00
612	2040	20c	German Immigration	2.00
613	2041	20c	Brooklyn Bridge	2.50
614	2042	20c	TVA	2.00
615	2043	20c	Fitness	2.00
616	2044	20c	Scott Joplin	3.75
617	2045	20c	Medal of Honor	3.00
618	2046	20c	Babe Ruth	6.25
619	2047	20c	Hawthorne	2.00
620	2051a	13c	Olympics	4.00
621	C104a	28c	Olympics	4.75
622	C108a	40c	Olympics	3.50
623	C112a	35c	Olympics	3.50
624	2052	20c	Treaty of Paris	2.50
625	2053	20c	Civil Service	2.00
626	2054	20c	Metropolitan Opera	2.50
627	2058a	20c	Inventors	3.00
628	2062a	20c	Streetcars	2.50
629	2063	20c	Madonna and Child	2.50
630	2064	20c	Santa Claus	2.50
631	2065	20c	Martin Luther	2.50

1984-85

632	2066	20c	Alaska	2.00
633	2070a	20c	Winter Olympics	3.25
634	2071	20c	FDIC	2.00
635	2072	20c	Love	2.00
636	2073	20c	Woodson	3.00
637	O138, O139	14c, 22c	D sheet, coil	2.50
638	2074	20c	Conservation	2.00
639	2075	20c	Credit Union	2.00
640	2079a	20c	Orchids	3.00
641	2080	20c	Hawaii	2.00
642	2081	20c	National Archives	2.00
643	2085a	20c	Olympics	4.50
644	2086	20c	World Expo	2.00
645	2087	20c	Health Research	2.00
646	2088	20c	Fairbanks	2.50
647	2089	20c	Thorpe	5.25
648	2090	20c	McCormack	2.50
649	2091	20c	St. Lawrence Seaway	2.00
650	2092	20c	Waterfowl	4.25
651	2093	20c	Roanoke Voyages	2.00
652	2094	20c	Melville	2.00
653	2095	20c	Horace Moses	2.00
654	2096	20c	Smokey the Bear	5.00
655	2097	20c	Clemente	6.00
656	2101a	20c	Dogs	4.00
657	2102	20c	Crime Prevention	2.00
658	2103	20c	Hispanic Americans	2.00
659	2104	20c	Family Unity	3.75
660	2105	20c	Eleanor Roosevelt	3.00
661	2106	20c	Readers	3.00
662	2107	20c	Madonna and Child	3.00
663	2108	20c	Child's Santa	3.00
664	2109	20c	Vietnam Memorial	3.75

1985-87

665	2110	22c	Jerome Kern	3.25
666	2111, 2112	22c	D sheet, coil	2.50
667	2113a	22c	D booklet pane of 10	5.00
668	C113	33c	Verville	2.25
669	C114	39c	Sperry	2.25
670	C115	44c	Transpacific	2.25
671	2114, 2115	22c	Flags sheet, coil	2.75
671a	2115b	22c	Flag "T" coil	4.00
672	2116a	22c	Flag booklet pane of 5	3.50
673	2121a	22c	Seashells booklet pane of 10	5.00
674	2122	$10.75	Express Mail single	45.00

674a	2122a	$10.75	Express Mail booklet pane of 3	100.00

Transporation Coils

1985-89

675	2123	3.4c	School Bus	5.00
676	2124	4.9c	Buckboard	5.00
677	2125	5.5c	Star Route Truck	5.00
678	2126	6c	Tricycle	4.00
679	2127	7.1c	Tractor	2.75
679a		7.1c	Tractor, Zip+4 precancel	2.75
680	2128	8.3c	Ambulance	4.00
681	2129	8.5c	Tow Truck	2.75
682	2130	10.1c	Oil Wagon	4.00
682a	2130a	10.1c	Red precancel	2.75
683	2131	11c	Stutz Bearcat	4.00
684	2132	12c	Stanley Steamer	5.00
685	2133	12.5c	Pushcart	4.00
686	2134	14c	Iceboat	5.00
687	2135	17c	Dog Sled	3.50
688	2136	25c	Bread Wagon	5.00

1985

689	2137	22c	Bethune	3.00
690	2141a	22c	Duck Decoys	3.00
691	2142	22c	Winter Special Olympics	2.00
692	2143	22c	Love	3.75
693	2144	22c	REA	2.00
694	O129A, O136	14c, 22c	Official Mail	3.75
695	2145	22c	AMERIPEX '86	2.00
696	2146	22c	Abigail Adams	2.00
697	2147	22c	Bartholdi	3.75
698	2149	18c	Washington coil	3.50
699	2150	21.1c	Letters coil	3.00
700	2152	22c	Korean Veterans	2.75
701	2153	22c	Social Security	3.00
702	C116	44c	Serra	2.50
703	2154	22c	World War I Veterans	2.50
704	2158a	22c	Horses	4.00
705	2159	22c	Education	2.50
706	2163a	22c	Youth Year	3.25
707	2164	22c	Hunger	2.50
708	2165	22c	Madonna and Child	2.50
709	2166	22c	Poinsettias	2.50

1986

710	2167	22c	Arkansas	2.25

Great Americans

1986-87

711	2168	1c	Mitchell	1.75
712	2169	2c	Lyon	2.00
713	2170	3c	White	2.00
714	2171	4c	Flanagan	1.75
715	2172	5c	Black	3.25
719	2176	10c	Red Cloud	2.00
720	2177	14c	Howe	2.00
721	2178	15c	Cody	3.00
722	2179	17c	Lockwood	3.00
723	2180	21c	Carlson	2.50
725	2182	23c	Cassatt	2.50
726	2183	25c	London	2.00
726a	2183a	25c	London booklet pane of 10	5.75
730	2188	45c	Cushing	2.50
732	2191	56c	Harvard	2.75
733	2192	65c	Arnold	2.50
735	2194	$1	Revel	2.75
736	2194A	$1	Hopkins	3.50
737	2195	$2	Bryan	4.25
739	2196	$5	Harte	11.00
740	2197	25c	London booket pane of 6	4.00

1986

741	2201a	22c	Stamp Collecting booklet pane of 4	4.75
742	2202	22c	Love	2.50
743	2203	22c	Sojourner Truth	2.50
744	2204	22c	Texas Republic	2.25
745	2209a	22c	Fish booklet pane of 5	4.25
746	2210	22c	Hospitals	1.75
747	2211	22c	Duke Ellington	3.00
748	2216	22c	Presidents Souvenir Sheet #1	5.00
749	2217	22c	Presidents Souvenir Sheet #2	5.00
750	2218	22c	Presidents Souvenir Sheet #3	5.00
751	2219	22c	Presidents Souvenir Sheet #4	5.00
752	2223a	22c	Arctic Explorers	3.50
753	2224	22c	Statue of Liberty	5.00

1987

754	2226	2c	Locomotive, reengraved	3.00

1986

755	2238a	22c	Navajo Art	3.25
756	2239	22c	T.S. Eliot	1.75
757	2243a	22c	Woodcarved Figurines	2.75
758	2244	22c	Madonna and Child	2.00
759	2245	22c	Village Scene	2.00

1987

760	2246	22c	Michigan	2.50
761	2247	22c	Pan American Games	2.00
762	2248	22c	Love	2.00
763	2249	22c	du Sable	3.00
764	2250	22c	Caruso	3.00
765	2251	22c	Girl Scouts	4.00

Transportation Coils

1960-61

766	2252	3c	Conestoga Wagon	3.50
767	2253, 2262	5c, 17.5c	Milk Wagon, Racing Car	4.50
768	2254	5.3c	Elevator	3.00
769	2255	7.6c	Carreta	3.00
770	2256	8.4c	Wheelchair	3.00
771	2257	10c	Canal Boat	3.00
772	2258	13c	Patrol Wagon	3.00
773	2259	13.2c	Coal Car	3.00
774	2260	15c	Tugboat	3.00
775	2261	16.7c	Popcorn Wagon	3.00
776	2263	20c	Cable Car	3.00
777	2264	20.5c	Fire Engine	4.00
778	2265	21c	Mail Car	3.00
779	2266	24.1c	Tandem Bicycle	3.00

1987

780	2274a	22c	Special Occasions booklet pane of 10	6.00
781	2275	22c	United Way	2.50

1987-89

782	2276	22c	Flag and Fireworks	2.50
783	2276a	22c	Flag, pair from booklet	4.00
784	2277,2279	(25c)	"E" sheet, coil	3.00
785	2282a	(25c)	"E" booklet pane of 10	6.00
786	2278	25c	Flag with Clouds	2.50
787	2285c	25c	Flag with Clouds booklet pane of 6	6.00
788	2280	25c	Flag over Yosemite coil	3.00
788a		25c	Flag over Yosemite, prephosphored paper	3.50
789	2281	25c	Honeybee coil	3.00
790	2283a	25c	Pheasant booklet pane of 10	6.00
791	2285b	25c	Owl and Grosbeak booklet pane of 10	5.00
792	O140	(25c)	"E" Official coil	3.00
793	O138B	20c	Official coil	3.00
794	O138A, O141	15c, 25c	Official coils	4.00

1987

795	2286—2295	22c	Wildlife	6.00
796	2296—2305	22c	Wildlife	6.00
797	2306—2315	22c	Wildlife	6.00
798	2316—2325	22c	Wildlife	6.00
799	2326—2335	22c	Wildlife	6.00

Ratification of the Constitution

1987-88

800	2336	22c	Delaware	2.75
801	2337	22c	Pennsylvania	3.00
802	2338	22c	New Jersey	3.00
803	2339	22c	Georgia	3.00
804	2340	22c	Connecticut	3.00
805	2341	22c	Massachusetts	3.00
806	2342	22c	Maryland	3.00
807	2343	25c	South Carolina	3.00
808	2344	25c	New Hampshire	3.00
809	2345	25c	Virginia	3.00
810	2346	25c	New York	3.00

1987

813	2349	22c	U.S./Morocco	2.50
814	2350	22c	William Faulkner	2.50
815	2354a	22c	Lacemaking	4.00
816	2359a	22c	Constitution booklet pane of 5	4.00
817	2360	22c	Signing of Constitution	2.50
818	2361	22c	Certified Public Accounting	4.00
819	2366a	22c	Locomotives booklet pane of 5	10.00
820	2367	22c	Madonna and Child	2.50
821	2368	22c	Christmas Ornament	2.50

1988

822	2369	22c	Winter Olympics	2.50
823	2370	22c	Australia Bicentennial	2.75
824	2371	22c	James Weldon Johnson	3.00
825	2375a	22c	Cats	5.00
826	2376	22c	Knute Rockne	3.50
827	C117	44c	New Sweden	3.00
828	C118	45c	Samuel P. Langley	3.00
829	2377	25c	Francis Ouimet	3.00
830	C119	36c	Igor Sikorsky	3.00
831	2378	25c	Love	3.00
832	2379	45c	Love	3.00
833	2380	25c	Summer Olympics	3.00
834	2385a	25c	Classic Automobiles booklet pane of 5	5.00
835	2389a	25c	Antarctic Explorers	3.00
836	2393a	25c	Carousel Animals	3.00
837	2394	$8.75	Express Mail	20.00
838	2396a	25c	Special Occasions booklet pane of 6	3.00
839	2398a	25c	Special Occasions booklet pane of 6	3.00
840	2399	25c	Madonna and Child	3.00
841	2400	25c	Village Scene	3.00

1989

842	2401	25c	Montana	3.00
843	2402	25c	A. Philip Randolph	3.50
844	2403	25c	North Dakota	3.00
845	2404	25c	Washington Statehood	3.00
846	2409a	25c	Steamboats, booklet pane of 5	5.00
847	2410	25c	World Stamp Expo	3.00
848	2411	25c	Toscanini	3.00

Branches of Government

1989

849	2412	25c	House of Representatives	3.00
850	2413	25c	Senate	3.00
851	2414	25c	Executive	3.00

1989

853	2416	25c	South Dakota	3.00
854	2417	25c	Lou Gehrig	7.00
855	O143	1c	Official, litho.	3.50
856	C120	45c	French Revolution	3.00
857	2418	25c	Ernest Hemingway	3.00
858	2419	$2.40	Moon Landing	12.50

SAVINGS

POSTAL SAVINGS STAMPS.

Issued by the Post Office Department.

Redeemable in the form of credits to Postal Savings accounts. The Postal Savings system was discontinued Mar. 28, 1966.

PS1

Plates of 400 subjects in four panes of 100 each
FLAT PLATE PRINTING

1911 **Wmk. 191** **Engr.** ***Perf. 12***

Size of design: 18x21½mm

PS1	PS1	**10c orange,** *Jan. 3, 1911*	8.00	75
		Block of four, 2mm spacing	35.00	
		Block of four, 3mm spacing	37.50	
		Margin strip of 3, Impt. open star & P#	40.00	
		Margin block of 6, Impt. open star & P#	425.00	

Plate Nos.

5504	5505	5506	5507
5698	5700	5703	5704

1911 **Unwmk.**

Imprinted on Deposit Card. Size of design: 137x79mm

PS2	PS1	**10c orange,** *Jan. 3, 1911*	150.00	35.00

A 10c deep blue with head of Washington in circle imprinted on deposit card (design 136x79mm) exists, but there is no evidence that it was ever placed in use.

1911 **Wmk. 190** ***Perf. 12***

PS4	PS1	**10c deep blue,** *Aug. 14, 1911*	4.00	90
		Block of four, 2mm spacing	20.00	
		Block of four, 3mm spacing	22.50	
		Margin strip of 3, Impt. open star & P#	25.00	
		Margin block of 6, Impt. open star & P#	140.00	

Plate Nos.

5504	5505	5506	5507
5698	5700	5703	5704

1911 **Unwmk.**

Imprinted on Deposit Card. Size of design: 133x78mm

PS5	PS1	**10c deep blue**	90.00	20.00

1936 **Unwmk.** ***Perf. 11***

PS6	PS1	**10c deep blue**	4.50	1.00
		a. 10c violet blue	4.50	1.00
		Block of four	18.50	
		Margin block of 6, Impt. solid star & P#	125.00	

Plate Nos. 21485, 21486

PS2

Plates of 400 subjects in four panes of 100 each
FLAT PLATE PRINTING

1940 **Unwmk.** **Engr.** ***Perf. 11***

Size of design: 19x22mm

PS7	PS2	**10c deep ultramarine,** *Apr. 3, 1940*	10.00
		Block of four	40.00
		Margin block of 6, P#	200.00

Plate Nos. 22540, 22541

PS8	PS2	**25c dark carmine rose,** *April 1, 1940*	16.00
		Block of four	64.00
		Margin block of 6, P#	300.00

Plate Nos. 22542, 22543

PS9	PS2	**50c dark blue green,** *April 1, 1940*	45.00
		Block of four	180.00
		Margin block of 6, P#	1,250.

Plate No. 22544

PS10	PS2	**$1 gray black,** *April 1, 1940*	85.00
		Block of four	340.00
		Margin block of 6, P#	1,750.

Plate No. 22545

Nos. PS11-PS15 redeemable in the form of United States Treasury Defense, War or Savings Bonds.

Minute Man — PS3

E.E. Plates of 400 subjects in four panes of 100 each
ROTARY PRESS PRINTING

1941 **Unwmk.** ***Perf. 11x10½***

Size of design: 19x22½mm

PS11	PS3	**10c rose red,** *May 1, 1941*	65
		a. 10c carmine rose	65
		Block of four	2.60
		Margin block of 4, P#	9.00
		b. Bklt. pane of 10, *July 30, 1941,* trimmed horizontal edges	50.00
		As "b," with Electric Eye marks at left	55.00
		c. Booklet pane of 10, perf. horizontal edges	110.00
		As "c," with Electric Eye marks at left	125.00

Plate Nos. of sheet stamps

22714	22722	148245
22715	22723	148246

Plate Nos. of booklet panes

147084	147085	148241	148242

PS12	PS3	**25c blue green,** *May 1, 1941*	2.00
		Block of four	8.00
		Margin block of 4, P#	18.00
		b. Bklt. pane of 10, *July 30, 1941*	60.00
		Booklet pane with Electric Eye marks at left	65.00

Plate Nos. of sheet stamps

22716	22717	22724
22725	148247	148248

Plate Nos. of booklet panes

147087	147088	148243	148244

PS13	PS3	**50c ultramarine,** *May 1, 1941*	6.00
		Block of four	25.00
		Margin block of 4, P#	40.00

Plate Nos.

22718	22719	22726	22727

PS14	PS3	**$1 gray black,** *May 1, 1941*	12.00
		Block of four	50.00
		Margin block of 4, P#	110.00

Plate Nos.

22720	22728

FLAT PLATE PRINTING
Plates of 100 subjects in four panes of 25 each

Size: 36x46mm. ***Perf. 11***

PS15	PS3	**$5 sepia,** *May 1, 1941*	35.00
		Block of four	140.00
		Margin block of 6, P# at top or bottom	500.00

Plate Nos.

22730	22731	22732
22733	22734	22735
22736	22737	22740

SAVINGS STAMPS

Issued by the Post Office Department.

Redeemable in the form of United States Savings Bonds. Sale of Savings Stamps was discontinued June 30, 1970.

Minute Man — S1

E.E. Plates of 400 subjects in four panes of 100 each
ROTARY PRESS PRINTING

1954-57 **Unwmk.** ***Perf. 11x10½***

Size of design: 19x22½mm

S1	S1	**10c rose red,** *Nov. 30, 1954*	60
		Block of four	2.40
		Margin block of 4, P#	3.50
		a. Booklet pane of 10, *Apr. 22, 1955*	135.00
		Booklet pane with Electric Eye marks at left	150.00

Plate Nos. of sheet stamps

164991	164992	165917	165918	166643
166644	167089	167090	168765	168766

Plate Nos. of booklet panes

165218	165219	165954
165955	167001	r167002

S2	S1	**25c blue green,** *Dec. 30, 1954*	3.00
		Block of four	12.00
		Margin block of 4, P#	20.00
		a. Booklet pane of 10, *Apr. 15, 1955*	450.00
		Booklet pane with Electric Eye marks at left	475.00

Plate Nos. of sheet stamps

165007	165008	165919	165920

Plate Nos. of booklet panes

165220	165221	165956	165957

S3	S1	**50c ultramarine,** *Dec. 31, 1956*	7.00
		Block of four	30.00
		Margin block of 4, P#	40.00

Plate Nos.

165050	165051	166741
166742	166941	166942

S4	S1	**$1**	**gray black,** *Mar. 13, 1957*	20.00
			Block of four	80.00
			Margin block of 4, P#	100.00

Plate Nos.

166097	166098
166683	166684

FLAT PLATE PRINTING
Plates of 100 subjects in four panes of 25 each

Size: 36x46mm ***Perf. 11***

S5	S1	**$5**	**sepia,** *Nov. 30, 1956*	65.00
			Block of four	260.00
			Margin block of 6, P# at top or bottom	700.00

Plate No. 166068

Minute Man and 48-Star Flag — S2

GIORI PRESS PRINTING
Plates of 400 subjects in four panes of 100 each

1958 **Unwmk.** ***Perf. 11***

S6	S2	**25c**	**dark blue & carmine,** *Nov. 18, 1958*	1.00
			Block of four	4.00
			Margin block of 4, P#	7.50
		a.	Booklet pane of 10, *Nov. 18, 1958*	65.00

Plate Nos. of sheet stamps

166921	166925	166946	166949	167014

Minute Man and 50-Star Flag — S3

Plates of 400 subjects in four panes of 100 each

1961 **Unwmk.** ***Perf. 11***

S7	S3	**25c**	**dark blue & carmine**	1.00
			Block of four	4.00
			Margin block of 4, P #	7.50
		a.	Booklet pane of 10	250.00

Plate Nos. of sheet stamps

167473	167476	167486	167489	169089

Plate Nos. of booklet panes

167495	167502

WAR SAVINGS STAMPS

Issued by the Treasury Department.

Redeemable in the form of United States Treasury War Certificates, Defense Bonds or War Bonds.

WS1

Plates of 300 subjects in six panes of 50 each
FLAT PLATE PRINTING

1917 **Unwmk.** **Engr.** ***Perf. 11***
Size of design: 28x18 ½mm

WS1	WS1	**25c**	**deep green,** *Dec. 1, 1917*	6.50
			Block of four	27.50
			Margin strip of 3, P# only	35.00
			Margin block of 6, P# only	400.00

Plate Nos.

56800	56810	56811	56817	57074
57075	57076	57077	57149	57150
57151	57152	57336	57382	57395
57396	57399	57443	58801	58802
58803	58804	59044	59045	59156
61207	61208	61209	61210	

George Washington — WS2

Plates of 80 subjects in four panes of 20 each
FLAT PLATE PRINTING

1918 **Unwmk.** **Engr.** ***Perf. 11***
Size of design: 39x55mm

WS2	WS2	**$2**	**deep green,** *Nov. 17, 1917*	65.00
			Block of four	275.00
			Margin copy with P# only	75.00
		b.	Vertical pair, imperf. horizontally	—

Plate Nos.

56914	57170	58434	60662	61265
56915	57171	58435	60665	61266
56916	57172	58436	60666	61267
56917	57173	58437	60667	61268
57066	57174	58438	60668	61360
57067	57175	58726	60846	61361
57068	57176	58727	60847	61362
57069	57333	58728	60848	61363
57070	57334	58729	60849	61364
57071	57343	59071	60850	61365
57072	57344	60257	60851	61366
57073	57345	60258	60852	61367
57145	57346	60259	60899	61388
57146	57347	60260	61203	61435
57147	57348	60659	61204	61502
57148	58431	60660	61205	
57169	58433	60661	61206	

Rouletted 7

WS3	WS2	**$5**	**deep green**	1,000.
			Block of four	4,250.
			Margin copy with P# only	1,250.

Benjamin Franklin — WS3

Plates of 150 subjects in six panes of 25 each
FLAT PLATE PRINTING

1919 **Unwmk.** **Engr.** ***Perf. 11***
Size of design: 27x36mm

WS4	WS3	**$5**	**deep blue,** *July 3, 1919*	250.00
			Block of four	1,000.
			Margin copy with P# only	275.00
			Margin copy with inverted P#	300.00

Plate Nos.

61882	61910	61970	61998	62010
61883	61911	61971	62007	62011
61884	61912	61972	62008	62012
61885	61913	61997	62009	62013

George Washington — WS4

Plates of 100 subjects in four panes of 25 each
FLAT PLATE PRINTING

1920 **Unwmk.** **Engr.** ***Perf. 11***
Size of design: 36x41 ½mm

WS5	WS4	**$5**	**carmine,** *Dec. 11, 1919*	650.00
			Block of four	2,750.
			Margin copy with P# only	675.00

Plate Nos.

67545	67549	69349	69673	69678
67546	67550	69350	69674	68679
67547	67551	69351	69675	69680
67548	67552	69352	69677	69829

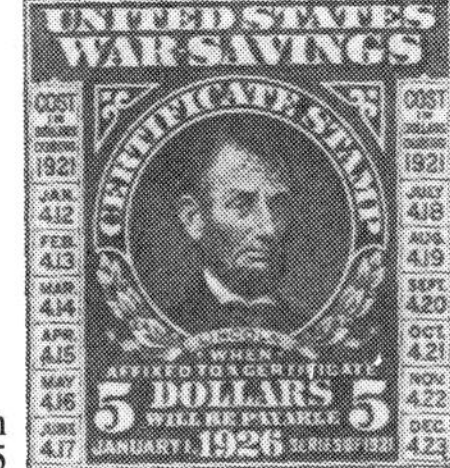

Abraham Lincoln — WS5

Plates of 100 subjects in four panes of 25 each
FLAT PLATE PRINTING

1921 **Unwmk.** **Engr.** ***Perf. 11***
Size of design: 39 ½x42mm

WS6	WS5	**$5**	**orange,** *green, Dec. 21, 1920*	2,500.
			Block of four	11,000.
			Margin copy with P# only	2,650.

Plate Nos.

73129	73131	73133	73135
73130	73132	73134	73136

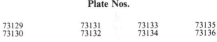

Minute Man — WS6

Plates of 400 subjects in four panes of 100 each
ROTARY PRESS PRINTING

1942 **Unwmk.** ***Perf. 11x10½***
Size of design: 19x22½mm

WS7	WS6	**10c rose red,** *Oct. 29, 1942*	50
	a.	10c carmine rose	50
		Block of four	2.00
		Margin block of 4, P#	5.00
	b.	Booklet pane of 10, *Oct. 27, 1942*	40.00
		Booklet pane with Electric Eye marks at left	45.00

Plate Nos. of sheet stamps

149492	149495	150706	155311
149493	150206	150707	155312
149494	150207		

Plate Nos. of booklet panes

149655	149656	149657	150664

WS8	WS6	**25c dark blue green,** *Oct. 15, 1942*	1.00
		Block of four	5.00
		Margin block of 4, P#	12.50
	b.	Booklet pane of 10, *Nov. 6, 1942*	55.00
		Booklet pane with Electric Eye marks at left	60.00

Plate Nos. of sheet stamps

149587	150320	155313	155813
149588	150321	155314	156517
149589	150708	155812	156518
149590	150709		

Plate Nos. of booklet panes

149658	149659	149660	150666

WS9	WS6	**50c deep ultramarine,** *Nov. 12, 1942*	3.00
		Block of four	14.00
		Margin block of 4, P#	30.00

Plate Nos.

149591	149592	149593	149594

WS10	WS6	**$1** **gray black,** *Nov. 17, 1942*	10.00
		Block of four	40.00
		Margin block of 4, P#	65.00

Plate Nos.

149595	149596	149597	149598

Type of 1942
FLAT PLATE PRINTING
Plates of 100 subjects in four panes of 25 each

1945 **Unwmk.** **Size: 36x46mm** ***Perf. 11***

WS11	WS6	**$5** **violet brown**	40.00
		Block of four	165.00
		Margin block of 6, P# at top or bottom	450.00

Plate Nos.

150131	150132	150133	150134
150291			

Type of 1942
Coil Stamps

1943 **Unwmk.** ***Perf. 10 Vertically***

WS12	WS6	**10c rose red,** *Aug. 5, 1943*	3.00
		Pair	6.50
		Line pair	10.00

Plate Nos.

153286	153287

WS13	WS6	**25c dark blue green,** *Aug. 5, 1943*	6.00
		Pair	13.00
		Line pair	20.00

Plate Nos.

153289	153290

TREASURY SAVINGS STAMP

Issued by the Treasury Department.

Redeemable in the form of War Savings Stamps or Treasury Savings Certificates.

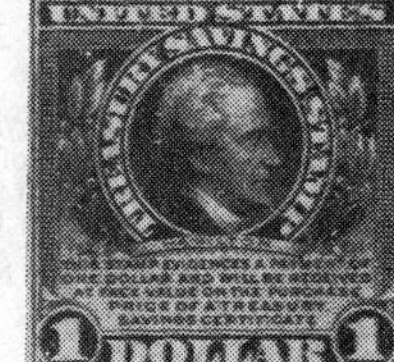

Alexander Hamilton — TS1

FLAT PLATE PRINTING

1921 **Unwmk.** **Engr.** ***Perf. 11***
Size of design: 33½x33½mm

TS1	TS1	**$1** **red,** *green, Dec. 21, 1920*	2,750.
		Block of four	11,500.
		Margin copy with P#	2,850.

Plate Nos.

73196	73198	73200	73202
73197	73199	73201	73203

ENCASED POSTAGE

In 1862 John Gault of Boston patented the idea of encasing postage stamps in metal frames behind a shield of transparent mica, and using them for advertising. The scarcity of small change during the Civil War made these encased stamps popular. Many firms impressed their names and products on the back of these stamp frames in embossed letters. Values are for very fine specimens with mica intact, although signs of circulation and handling are to be expected.

Grading encompasses three areas: 1. Case will show signs of wear or handling and signs of original toning. 2. Mica will be intact with no pieces missing. 3. Stamp will be fresh with no signs of toning or wrinkling.

Examples that came with silvered cases and still have some or all of the original silvering will sell for more than the values shown.

Aerated Bread Co., New York

1	1c	1,500.

Ayer's Cathartic Pills, Lowell, Mass.

Varieties with long and short arrows below legend occur on all denominations.

2	1c	185.00
3	3c	165.00
4	5c	275.00
5	10c	350.00
6	12c	700.00
7	24c	1,900.

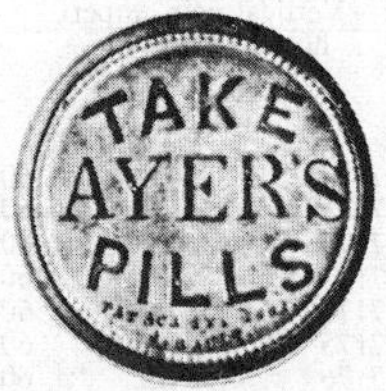

Take Ayer's Pills

8	1c	175.00
9	3c	150.00
10	5c	225.00
	a. Ribbed frame	900.00
11	10c	300.00
12	12c	900.00

Ayer's Sarsaparilla

Three varieties: "AYER'S"; small, medium and large.

13	1c medium "Ayer's"	200.00
	a. Small	450.00
14	2c	—
15	3c medium "Ayer's"	160.00
	a. Small	350.00
	b. Large	325.00
	c. Ribbed frame, medium	650.00
16	5c medium "Ayer's"	300.00
	a. Large	600.00
17	10c medium "Ayer's"	275.00
	a. Ribbed frame, medium	850.00
	b. Small	600.00
	c. Large	475.00
18	12c medium "Ayer's"	800.00
	a. Small	1,200.
19	24c medium "Ayer's"	*1,500.*
20	30c medium "Ayer's"	*1,750.*

The authenticity of No. 14 is questioned.

Bailey & Co., Philadelphia

21	1c	650.00
22	3c	675.00
23	5c	700.00
24	10c	700.00
25	12c	1,600.

Joseph L. Bates, Boston

Two varieties: FANCY GOODS as one word or two.

No.	Denomination	Price
26	1c one word	225.00
	a. Two words	275.00
27	3c one word	450.00
	a. Two words	500.00
28	5c Two word	600.00
	a. One words	750.00
	b. Ribbed frame, one word	850.00
29	10c Two word	400.00
	a. One words	500.00
	b. Ribbed frame, one word	900.00
30	12c two words	900.00

Brown's Bronchial Troches

No.	Denomination	Price
31	1c	700.00
32	3c	325.00
33	5c	300.00
34	10c	500.00
35	12c	850.00
36	24c	*2,200.*
37	30c	*3,500.*

F. Buhl & Co., Detroit

No.	Denomination	Price
38	1c	800.00
39	3c	900.00
40	5c	850.00
41	10c	1,000.
42	12c	1,300.
43	24c	*2,500.*

Burnett's Cocoaine Kalliston

No.	Denomination	Price
44	1c	275.00
45	3c	275.00
46	5c	375.00
47	10c	400.00
48	12c	950.00
49	24c	*2,250.*
50	30c	*3,000.*
51	90c	*7,500.*

Burnett's Cooking Extracts

No.	Denomination	Price
52	1c	200.00
53	3c	200.00
54	5c	250.00
55	10c	275.00
	a. Ribbed frame	800.00
56	12c	850.00
57	24c	2,000.
58	30c	*3,000.*

A. M. Claflin, Hopkinton, Mass.

No.	Denomination	Price
59	1c	*6,000.*
60	3c	*3,750.*
61	5c	*5,000.*
62	10c	*4,500.*
63	12c	*5,500.*

H. A. Cook, Evansville, Ind.

No.	Denomination	Price
64	5c	750.00
65	10c	750.00

Dougan, Hatter, New York

No.	Denomination	Price
66	1c	1,500.
67	3c	900.00
68	5c	1,000.
69	10c	1,750.

Drake's Plantation Bitters

No.	Denomination	Price
70	1c	225.00
71	3c	200.00
72	5c	300.00
	a. Ribbed frame	750.00
73	10c	350.00
	a. Ribbed frame	850.00
74	12c	500.00
75	24c	*2,000.*
76	30c	*3,000.*
77	90c	*8,500.*

Ellis, McAlpin & Co., Cincinnati

No.	Denomination	Price
78	1c	1,250.
79	3c	1,250.
80	5c	900.00
81	10c	900.00
82	12c	1,500.
83	24c	1,500.

C. G. Evans, Philadelphia

No.	Denomination	Price
84	1c	550.00
85	3c	550.00
86	5c	1,000.
87	10c	1,000.

Gage Bros. & Drake, Tremont House, Chicago

No.	Denomination	Price
88	1c	300.00
89	3c	375.00
90	5c	300.00
91	10c	400.00
	a. Ribbed frame	900.00
92	12c	1,250.

J. Gault

No.	Denomination	Price
93	1c	275.00
	a. Ribbed frame	600.00
94	2c	*8,500.*
95	3c	150.00
	a. Ribbed frame	550.00
96	5c	200.00
	a. Ribbed frame	525.00
97	10c	300.00
	a. Ribbed frame	550.00
98	12c	675.00
	a. Ribbed frame	1,500.
99	24c	1,500.
	a. Ribbed frame	2,500.
100	30c	*2,000.*
	a. Ribbed frame	*3,500.*
101	90c	*6,500.*

L. C. Hopkins & Co., Cincinnati

No.	Denomination	Price
102	1c	1,500.
103	3c	850.00
104	5c	1,100.
105	10c	1,500.

Hunt & Nash, Irving House, New York

No.	Denomination	Price
106	1c	500.00
107	3c	400.00
	a. Ribbed frame	800.00
108	5c	400.00
	a. Ribbed frame	450.00
109	10c	425.00
	a. Ribbed frame	550.00
110	12c	900.00
	a. Ribbed frame	1,250.
111	24c	1,500.
	a. Ribbed frame	2,500.
112	30c	*3,250.*

Kirkpatrick & Gault, New York

No.	Denomination	Price
113	1c	325.00
114	3c	375.00
115	5c	350.00
116	10c	325.00
117	12c	550.00
118	24c	1,500.
119	30c	*2,250.*
120	90c	*6,000.*

Lord & Taylor, New York

No.	Denomination	Price
121	1c	650.00
122	3c	800.00
123	5c	800.00
124	10c	800.00

125	12c	1,250.
126	24c	2,250.
127	30c	3,000.
128	90c	8,500.

Mendum's Family Wine Emporium, New York

129	1c	450.00
130	3c	800.00
131	5c	600.00
132	10c	650.00
	a. Ribbed frame	1,250.
133	12c	1,000.

B. F. Miles, Peoria

134	1c	3,000.
135	5c	3,000.

John W. Norris, Chicago

136	1c	1,000.
137	3c	1,000.
138	5c	1,350.
139	10c	1,750.

No. America Life Insurance Co., N. Y.

Two varieties: "Insurance" in curved line or straight line.

140	1c curved	325.00
	a. Straight	350.00
141	3c curved	475.00
	a. Straight	400.00
142	5c straight	500.00
	a. Ribbed frame	950.00
143	10c straight	450.00
	a. Curved	600.00
	b. Curved, ribbed frame	1,400.
144	12c straight	1,200.

Pearce, Tolle & Holton, Cincinnati

145	1c	1,750.
146	3c	1,750.
147	5c	1,500.
148	10c	2,200.
149	12c	2,500.
150	24c	3,000.

Sands Ale

151	5c	1,700.
152	10c	2,000.
153	12c	2,300.
154	30c	4,250.

Schapker & Bussing, Evansville, Ind.

155	1c	550.00
156	3c	600.00
157	5c	550.00
158	10c	550.00
150	12c	1,250.

John Shillito & Co., Cincinnati

160	1c	600.00
161	3c	500.00
162	5c	500.00
163	10c	600.00
164	12c	1,750.

S. Steinfeld, New York

165	1c	1,250.
166	5c	1,350.
167	10c	1,600.
168	12c	2,500.

N. G. Taylor & Co., Philadelphia

169	1c	1,250.
170	3c	1,200.
171	5c	1,500.
172	10c	1,800.
173	12c	2,500.

Weir and Larminie, Montreal

174	1c	1,500.
175	3c	1,750.
176	5c	1,600.
177	10c	1,500.

White, the Hatter, New York

178	1c	1,500.
179	3c	1,400.
180	5c	1,400.
181	10c	2,000.

POSTAGE CURRENCY

Small coins disappeared from circulation in 1861-62 as cash was hoarded. To ease business transactions, merchants issued notes of credit, promises to pay, tokens, store cards, etc. U.S. Treasurer Francis E. Spinner made a substitute for small currency by affixing postage stamps, singly and in multiples, to Treasury paper. He arranged with the Post office to replace worn stamps with new when necessary.

The next step was to print the stamps on Treasury paper. On July 17, 1862, Congress authorized the issue of such "Postage Currency." It was not money, but a means of making stamps negotiable.

Postage Currency remained in use until 1876 when Congress authorized the minting of silver coins to redeem the outstanding fractional currency.

Values quoted are for notes in crisp, new condition, not creased or worn.

Creased or worn copies sell for 25 to 75 per cent less.

Postage currency was issued from August 21, 1862, to May 27, 1863.

Front Engraved and Printed by the National Bank Note Co.

This series has on each note a facsimile of the postage stamp then current. In the 25c and 50c denominations the 5c and 10c stamps are engraved overlapping each other, five in a row, respectively.

Back Engraved and Printed by The American Bank Note Co.

"A B Co." on Back

1	5c Bust of Jefferson on 5c stamp, brown	50.00
	a. Inverted back	200.00
2	10c Bust of Washington on 10c stamp, green	35.00
3	25c Five 5c stamps, brown	45.00
4	50c Five 10c stamps, green	50.00
	a. Perforated 14	100.00
	b. Inverted back	200.00

Imperforate Edges

5	5c Bust of Jefferson on 5c stamp	17.50
	a. Inverted back	200.00
6	10c Bust of Washington on 10c stamp	15.00
	a. Inverted back	200.00
7	25c Five 5c stamps	30.00
	a. Inverted back	200.00
8	50c Five 10c stamps	50.00
	a. Inverted back	200.00

Back Printed by the the National Bank Note Co.

Without "A B Co." on Back

Perforated Edges-Perf. 12

9	5c Bust of Jefferson on 5c stamp	50.00
	a. Inverted back	250.00
10	10c Bust of Washington on 10c stamp	50.00
	a. Inverted back	250.00
11	25c Five 5c stamps	100.00
	a. Inverted back	250.00
12	50c Five 10c stamps	120.00

Imperforate Edges

13	5c Bust of Jefferson on 5c stamp	50.00
	a. Inverted back	300.00
14	10c Bust of Washington on 10c stamp	85.00
	a. Inverted back	250.00
15	25c Five 5c stamps	120.00
16	50c Five 10c stamps	135.00
	a. Inverted back	250.00

INTERNATIONAL REPLY COUPONS

Coupons produced by the Universal Postal Union for member countries to provide for payment of postage on a return letter from a foreign country. Exchangeable for a stamp representing single-rate ordinary postage to a foreign country under the terms of contract as printed on the face of the coupon in French and the language of the issuing country and on the reverse in four, five or six other languages.

Postmasters are instructed to apply a postmark indicating date of sale to the left circle on the coupon. When offered for exchange for stamps, the receiving postmaster is instructed to cancel the right circle.

The following is a list of all varieties issued by the Universal Postal Union for any or all member countries.

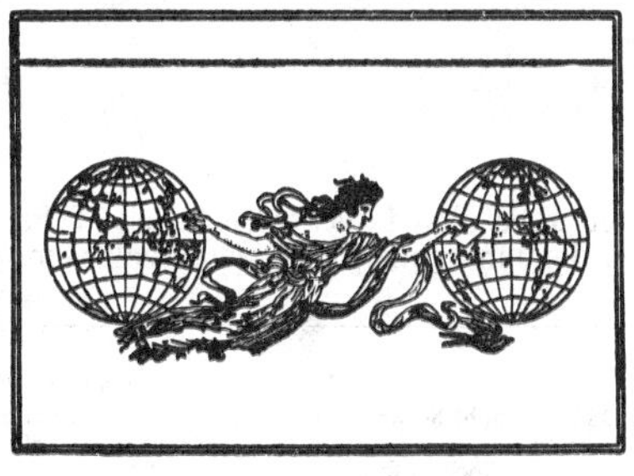

Type A- Face

Wmk. "25c Union Postale Universelle 25c"

1907-20

A1 Face — Name of country in letters 1½mm high.
Reverse — Printed rules between paragraphs German text contains four lines.

1907-20

A2 Face — Same as A1.
Reverse — Same as A1 but without rules between paragraphs.

1910-20

A3 Face — Same as A1 and A2.
Reverse — Same as A2 except German text has but three lines.

1912-20

A4 Face — Name of country in bold face type; letters 2mm to 2½mm high.
Reverse — Same as A3.

1922-25

A5 Face — French words "le mois d'émission écoulé, deux mois encore".
Reverse — As A3 and A4 but overprinted with new contract in red; last line of red German text has five words.

Wmk. "50c Union Postale Universelle 50c"

1925-26

A6 Face — Same as A5.
Reverse — Four paragraphs of five lines each.

1926-29

A7 Face — French words "il est valable pendent un delai de six mois".
Reverse — As A6 but overprinted with new contract in red; last line of red German text has two words.

Wmk. "40c Union Postale Universelle 40c"

1926-29

A8 Face — Design redrawn. Without lines in hemispheres.
Reverse — Four paragraphs of four lines each.

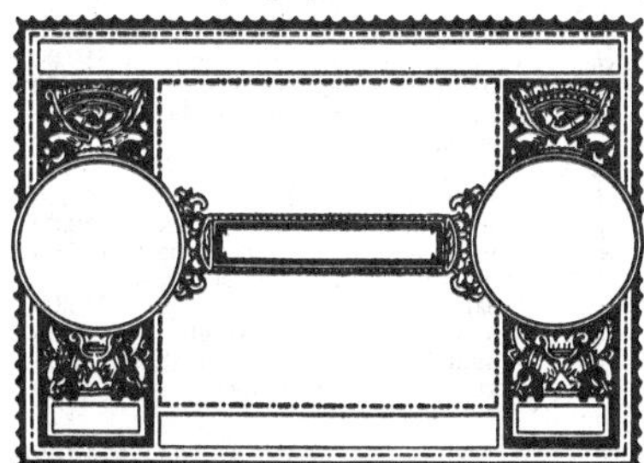

Type B- Face

1931-35 — Wmk. Double-lined "UPU"

B1 Face — French words "d'une lettre simple".
Reverse — Four paragraphs of three lines each.

1935-36

B2 Face — French words "d'une lettre ordinaire de port simple".
Reverse — Last line of German text contains two words.

1936-37

B3 Face — Same as B2.
Reverse — Last line of German text contains one word.

1937-40

B4 Face — Same as B2 and B3. "Any Country of the Union."
Reverse — German text is in German Gothic type.

1945

B5 Face — "Any Country of the Universal Postal Union."
Reverse — Each paragraph reads "Universal Postal Union."

Type B5 exists without central printing on face.

1950

B6 Face — Same as B5.
Reverse — Five paragraphs (English, Arabic, Chinese, Spanish, Russian).

1954

B7 Face — Same as B5.
Reverse — Six paragraphs (German, English, Arabic, Chinese, Spanish, Russian.)

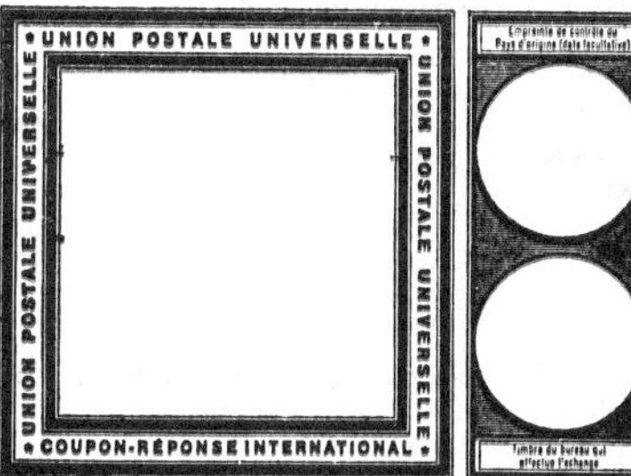

Type C- Face

1968 — Wmk. Single-lined "UPU" Multiple

C1 Face — French words "d'une lettre ordinaire de port simple".
Reverse — Six paragraphs (German, English, Arabic, Chinese, Spanish, Russian).

1971

C2 Face — French words "d'une lettre ordinaire du premier échelon de poids."
Reverse — Six paragraphs (German, English, Arabic, Chinese, Spanish, Russian).

Foreign coupons, but not U.S., of type C1 are known with large double-lined "UPU" watermark, as on type B coupons.

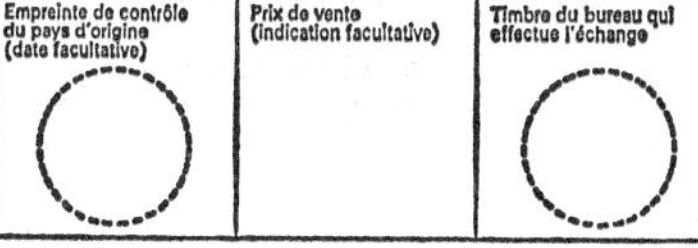
Ce coupon est échangeable dans tous les pays de l'Union postale universelle contre un ou plusieurs timbres-poste représentant l'affranchissement minimal d'une lettre ordinaire, expédiée à l'étranger par voie de surface.

Empreinte de contrôle du pays d'origine (date facultative)	Prix de vente (indication facultative)	Timbre du bureau qui effectue l'échange

Type D- Face

1975 — Wmk. Single-lined "UPU" Multiple

D1 **Face** — French words "d'une lettre ordinaire, expédiée à l'étranger par voie de surface."
Reverse — Six paragraphs (German, English, Arabic, Chinese, Spanish, Russian).

REPLY COUPONS ISSUED FOR THE UNITED STATES

1907

1 A1 6c slate green & gray green — 12.00
(2 line English paragraph on face. Rules between paragraphs on reverse.)

2 A2 6c slate green & gray green — 6.00
(Rules omitted on reverse.)

1912

3 A4 6c slate green & gray green — 6.00
(3 line English paragraph on face.)

1922

4 A5 11c slate green & gray green, name 81½mm long — 6.00
a. Name 88½mm long — 6.00
(5 line English paragraph on face. Red overprint on reverse.)

1925-26

5 A6 11c slate green & gray green — 6.00
(5 line English paragraph on face. No overprint on reverse.)

6 A6 9c slate green & gray green — 6.00

1926

7 A7 9c slate green & gray green — 6.00
(4 line English paragraph on face. Red overprint on reverse.)

8 A8 9c slate green & gray green — 6.00
(Without lines in hemispheres.)

1935

9 B2 9c blue & yellow — 2.00
(On reverse, last line of German text contains two words.)

1936

10 B3 9c blue and yellow — 2.00
(On reverse, last line of German text contains one word.)

1937

11 B4 9c blue & yellow — 2.00
(On reverse, German text in German Gothic type.)

1945

12 B5 9c blue & yellow — 2.00
(On face, "Universal Postal Union" replaces "Union")

1948

13 B5 11c blue & yellow — 2.00
(On face, "Universal Postal Union" replaces "Union")

1950

14 B6 11c blue & yellow — 2.00
(On reverse, text in English, Arabic, Chinese, Spanish, Russian)

1954

15 B7 13c blue & yellow — 2.00
(On reverse, text in German, English, Arabic, Chinese, Spanish, Russian.)

No. 15 Surcharged in Various Manners

1959

16 B7 15c on 13c blue & yellow — 2.00

Individual post offices were instructed to surcharge the 13c coupon, resulting in many types of surcharge in various inks. For example, "REVALUED 15 CENTS," reading vertically; "15," etc.

1959

17 B7 15c blue & yellow — 2.00

1964

18 B7 15c blue & yellow — 2.00
On face, box at lower left: "Empreinte de controle/du Pays d'origine/(date facultative)" replaces "Timbre du/Bureau/d'Emission"
a. Reverse printing 60mm deep instead of 65mm (smaller Arabic characters) — 2.00

1969

19 C1 15c blue & yellow — 1.00

1971

20 C2	22c blue & yellow	1.00

No. 20 Surcharged in Various Manners

1974

21 C2	26c on 22c blue & yellow	1.00

See note after No. 16.

1975

22 D1	26c blue & yellow	80

No. 22 Surcharged in Various Manners

1976

23 D1	42c on 26c blue & yellow	85

See note after No. 16.

1976

24 D1	42c blue & yellow	85

POST OFFICE SEALS

Official Seals began to appear in 1872. They do not express any value, having no franking power.

The first seal issued was designed to prevent tampering with registered letters while in transit. It was intended to be affixed over the juncture of the flaps of the large official envelopes in which registered mail letters were enclosed and was so used exclusively. Beginning in 1877, official seals were used to repair damaged letters or to close those received by the Post Office unsealed.

POS1

National Bank Note Co.

Typographed from a copper plate of 30 subjects (3x10) in two panes of 15

1872	**Unwmk.**	**White Wove Paper**	***Perf. 12***	
OX1	POS1	**green**	25.00	5.00
		On cover		20.00
		Block of four	125.00	
a.		Yellow green, pelure paper	60.00	
b.		Printed on both sides	250.00	
c.		Double impression		—
d.		Imperf., pair	*750.00*	
e.		Horizontally laid paper	—	

A plate of 9 subjects (3x3) was used for proofs only (Continental Bank Note Co.?).

Special Printing

American Bank Note Co.

Plate of 30 subjects (5x6)

1880 (?)		**Soft Porous Paper**	***Perf. 12***
OX2	POS1	**bluish green**	*600.00*

POS2

("Post Obitum" in background.)

National Bank Note Co.

Plate of 100 subjects (10x10)

Silk Paper

1877		**Engr.**	***Perf. 12.***	
OX3	POS2	**brown**	35.00	17.50
		Block of four	*250.00*	
		On cover		700.00

No. OX3 was intended for use in the Dead Letter Office.

The Scott Catalogue value is a retail price, what you could expect to pay for the stamp in a grade of Fine-Very Fine. The value listed is a reference which reflects recent actual dealer selling price.

POS3

American Bank Note Co.

Engraved

Plate of 100 subjects (10x10) bearing imprint of American Bank Note Co.

Also plates of 50 subjects with or without imprint

1879			***Perf. 12***	
OX4	POS3	**brown**	75	40
a.		dark brown	3.00	5.00
b.		yellow brown	1.00	50
c.		red brown	75	40
		Block of four	5.00	
		On cover		75.00
		Margin block with imprint	25.00	

A so-called "special printing" exists in deep brown on hard white paper.

POS4

Typographed

Without words in lower label.

Outer frame line at top and left is thick and heavy.

Plate of 42 subjects (7x6)

Thin to Thick Paper

1888			***Imperf.***	
OX6	POS4	**light brown**	1.00	—
a.		yellow brown	1.00	—
b.		chocolate, thin paper	5.00	
		Block of four	4.00	
c.		Toned paper	—	

No. 0X6 was not regularly used.

Thin to Thick Paper

Perf. 12

OX7	POS4	**bister brown**	50	15
a.		light brown	50	15
b.		chocolate	50	15
c.		gray brown	50	15
d.		dark brown	50	15
e.		rose brown	50	15
		Block of four	2.50	
		On cover		30.00
f.		Imperf. vertically, pair	15.00	—
g.		Imperf. horizontally, pair	15.00	—
h.		Vertical pair, imperf. between	10.00	
i.		Double impression	—	
j.		Toned paper	—	
k.		Horizontal pair, imperf. between	—	

1892			***Rouletted 5½***	
OX8	POS4	**light brown**	12.50	12.50
a.		brown	12.50	12.50
		Block of four	65.00	
		On cover		100.00

1895 (?)			***Hyphen Hole Perf. 7***	
OX9	POS4	**gray brown**	5.00	4.50
		Block of four	25.00	
		On cover		50.00

POS5

Plate of 143 (11x13)

Outer frame line at top and left is thin. Otherwise similar to POS4.

1900		**Litho.**	***Perf. 12***	
OX10	POS5	red brown	20	20
		Block of four, red brown	1.00	
		On cover, red brown		15.00
a.		gray brown	1.50	1.50
b.		yellow brown	80	80
c.		dark brown	90	85
d.		orange brown	60	60
e.		Imperf., pair, red brown	5.00	
f.		Horiz. pair, imperf. vertically	15.00	—
g.		Vert. pair, imperf. horizontally	20.00	
h.		Horiz. or vert. pair, imperf. btwn.	20.00	

Design similar to POS5 but smaller.

Issued in panes of 10 and 20

1907		**Typo.**	***Perf. 12***	
OX11	POS5	**blue**	10	10
a.		dark blue	10	10
b.		violet blue	10	10
		Block of four	40	
		On cover		5.00
c.		Imperf., pair	4.00	—
d.		Vert. pair, imperf. horizontally	10.00	—
e.		Horiz. pair, imperf. vertically	10.00	—
f.		Horiz. or vert. pair, imperf. between	18.00	
h.		Tete beche pair, perf.	—	
i.		Tete beche pair, imperf.	40.00	
j.		Tete beche pair, imperf. between	60.00	
k.		Double impression, imperf., pair	100.00	
l.		Double impression, tete beche pair	250.00	
m.		Wmkd. Seal of U.S. in sheet	1.35	1.35
n.		Wmkd. "Rolleston Mills" in sheet	1.35	1.35
p.		Vert. pair with gutter btwn.	20.00	

1912			***Rouletted 6½***	
OX12	POS5	**blue**	1.00	1.00
		Block of four	5.00	
		On cover		20.00
a.		Wmkd. Seal of U.S. in sheet	2.75	2.00
b.		Wmkd. "Rolleston Mills" in sheet	2.75	2.00

1913			***Perf. 12 x Rouletted 6½***	
OX13	POS5	**blue**	2.75	2.50
		Block of four	15.00	
		On cover		20.00
a.		Rouletted 6½ x Perf. 12	4.75	4.75
		Block of four	22.50	
b.		Wmkd. Seal of U.S. in sheet	3.50	2.75
c.		As "a" and "b"	5.50	5.50

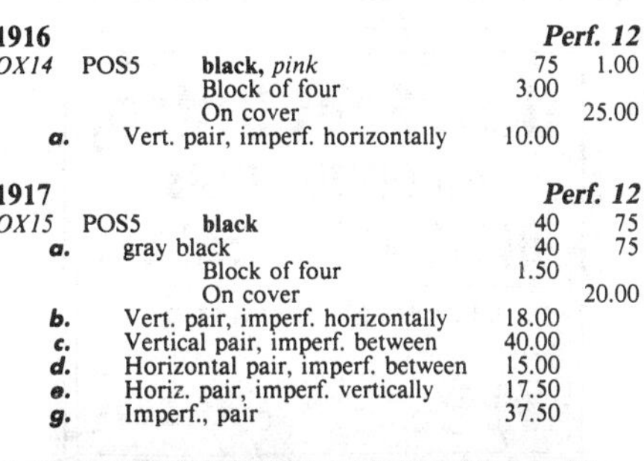

1916 *Perf. 12*

OX14	POS5	**black,** *pink*	75	1.00
		Block of four	3.00	
		On cover		25.00
a.		Vert. pair, imperf. horizontally	10.00	

1917 *Perf. 12*

OX15	POS5	**black**	40	75
a.		gray black	40	75
		Block of four	1.50	
		On cover		20.00
b.		Vert. pair, imperf. horizontally	18.00	
c.		Vertical pair, imperf. between	40.00	
d.		Horizontal pair, imperf. between	15.00	
e.		Horiz. pair, imperf. vertically	17.50	
g.		Imperf., pair	37.50	

POS6

Quartermaster General's Office
Issued in sheets of 10.

1919 *Perf. 12*

OX16	POS6	**indigo**	165.00	
		Block of four	750.00	

Rouletted 7

OX17	POS6	**indigo**		—

POS7

Issued in panes of 10, 16 and 20

1919 ***Perf. 8 1/2, 9, 12, 12 1/2 and Compound***

OX18	POS7	**black**	5	5
a.		gray black	5	5
		Block of four	25	
		On cover		5.00
b.		Imperf., pair	7.50	5.75
c.		Horiz. pair, imperf. vert.	14.00	
d.		Vert. pair, imperf. horiz.	14.00	
e.		Horiz. or vert. pair, imperf. btwn.	17.50	
g.		Wmkd. Seal of U.S. in sheet	1.65	1.65
h.		Wmkd. letters	5.00	—

1949 ***Hyphen Hole Perf. 9 1/2 x Imperf.***

Issued in vertical panes of 5

Design width: 37 1/2mm

OX19	POS7	**black**	20	20
		Pane of 5	1.25	
		On cover		1.50
a.		Vert. pair, imperf. between	7.50	
b.		Imperf., pane of 5	15.00	

Tab inscribed, "16-56164-1 GPO"

Design width: 38 1/2mm
Issued in vertical panes of 5

1970 (?) ***Hyphen Hole Perf. 9 1/2 x Imperf.***

OX19C	POS7	**black**	20	20
		Pane of 5	1.75	
		On cover		3.00
d.		Vert. pair, imperf. btwn	8.00	
e.		Imperf., pane of 5	16.00	

Tab inscribed, "c43-16-56164-1 GPO"

POS8

Rouletted 6 1/2, 8 1/2 or 9 1/2 x Imperf., Hyphen Hole Perf. 7 x Imperf. Perf. 12 1/2 x Imperf.

1972 **Issued in vertical panes of 5** **Litho.**

OX20	POS8	**black**	20	20
		Pane of 5	1.25	
		On cover		5.00
a.		Imperf., pair	8.00	

Tab inscribed, "LABEL 21, JULY 1971"

TYPESET SEALS

Little is known of the history and origin, but it is believed that they were privately made for sale to postmasters. Many are extremely rare. Unquestioned varieties are listed. Many others exist.

"U. S. POST OFFICE DEPARTMENT" in capital letters

TSS1

OX25	TSS1	**black**	135.00	135.00

TSS1a

OX25A	TSS1a	**black**	175.00	—
		"OFFICALLY"	—	

TSS2

OX26	TSS2	**black**	—	

"U.S. Post Office Department" with initial capitals

TSS3

OX27	TSS3	**black,** *pink*		—

TSS4

OX28	TSS4	**black**	*135.00*	

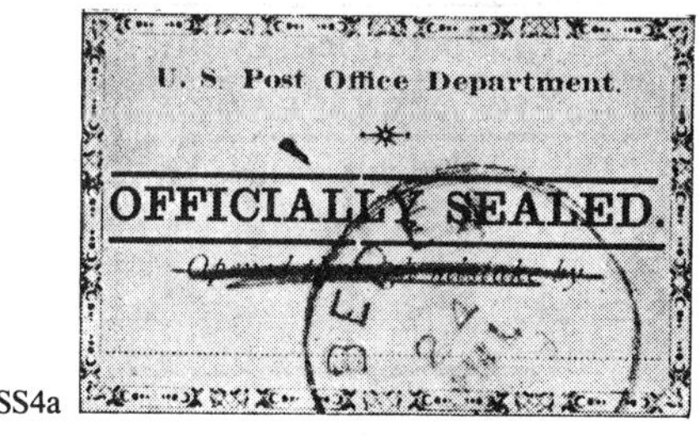

TSS4a

OX28A	TSS4a	**black**		—

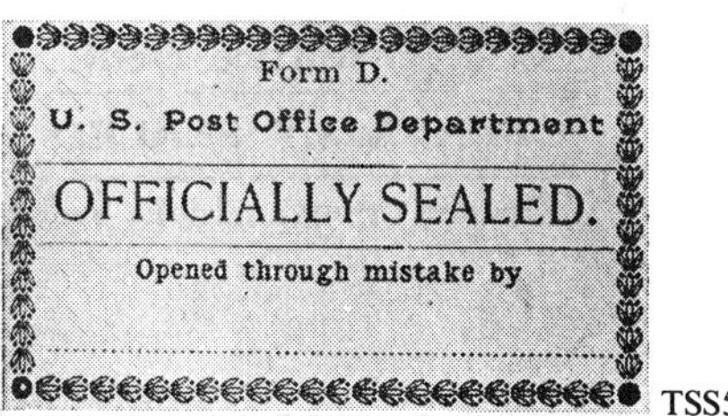

TSS5

OX29	TSS5	**black**	*175.00*	

TSS6

Printed in panes of 4, two tete beche pairs

OX30	TSS6	**black**	35.00	35.00
		Tete beche pair	70.00	
		Sheet of four	150.00	

TSS7

Solid lines above and below "OFFICIALLY SEALED" Printed in panes of four, two tete beche pairs.

OX31	TSS7	**black**	*125.00*	*150.00*
		Tete beche pair	—	
		Sheet of four	—	

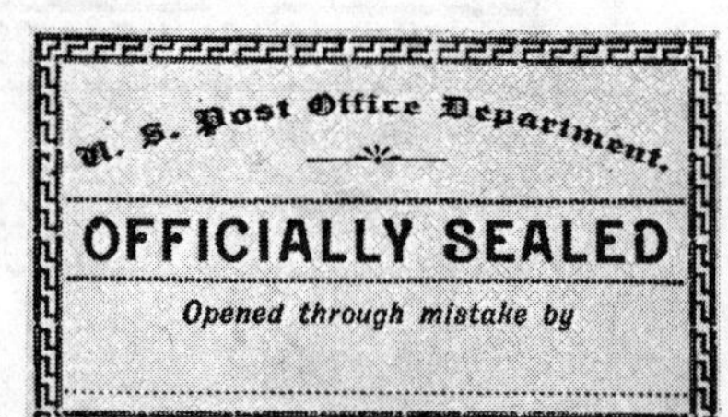

TSS8

Dotted lines above and below "OFFICIALLY SEALED" Printed in panes of four.

OX32	TSS8	**black,** *pink*	*175.00*	
OX33	TSS8	**black**	75	—
a.		Tete beche pair	1.50	
b.		Tete beche sheet of four	3.00	
c.		Period after "OFFICIALLY"	1.00	
d.		As "c" in pair	2.00	
e.		As "c" in tete beche pair	2.50	
f.		Tete beche sheet of four, one stamp with period	5.00	
g.		As "c", printed in blue		—

"U. S. Postoffice Dept."

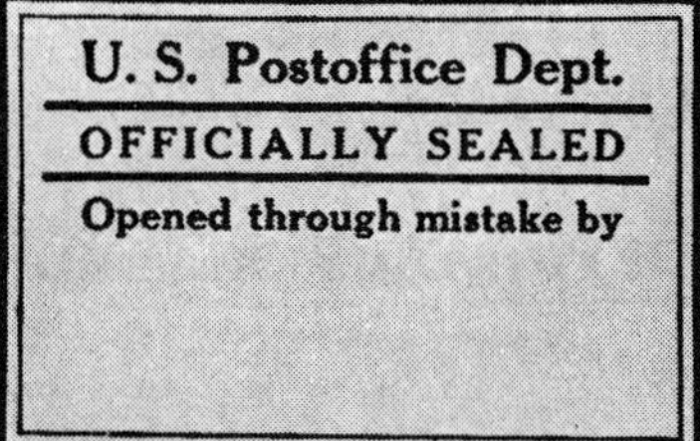

TSS9

OX34	TSS9	**black or blue**	*135.00*	

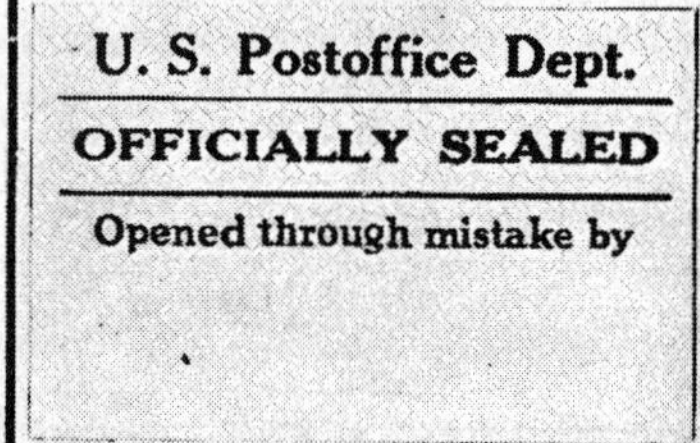

TSS10

OX35	TSS10	**blue**	—	—

TSS11

OX36	TSS11	**black**	—	
		blue		—

United States postage and air mail first day covers are listed and valued in a separate section of the catalogue. See catalogue index.

"United States Post Office"

TSS12

OX37	TSS12	**blue**	—	—

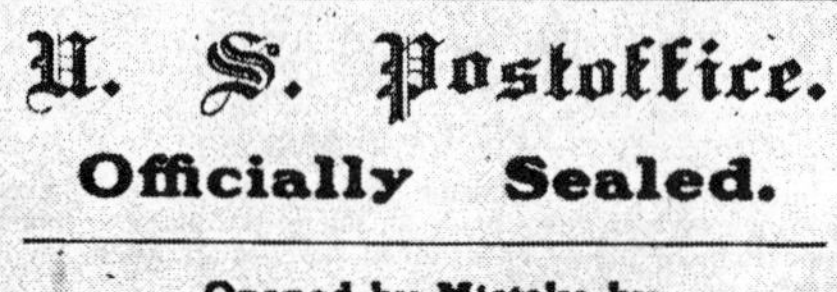

TSS13

OX38	TSS13	**dark blue**	40.00	40.00
		On cover		—
a.		Printed on both sides	325.00	
b.		2mm btwn. "y" & "S", no period after "d"	85.00	
OX39	TSS13	**black**	100.00	—

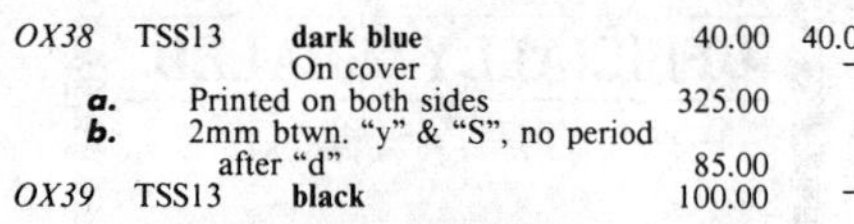

TSS14

OX40	TSS14	**black,** *light green*	—	—

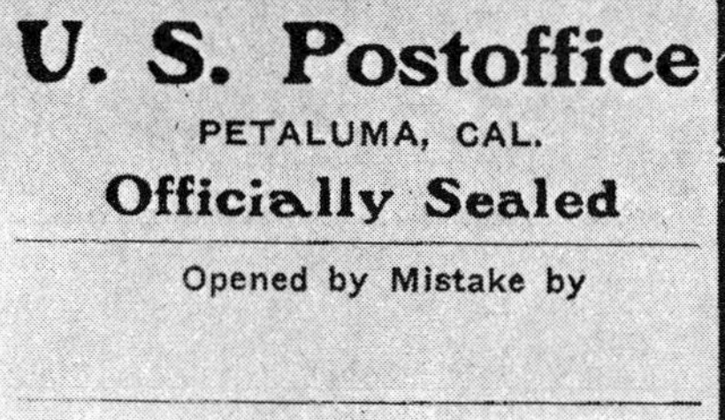

TSS15

OX41	TSS15	**black,** *blue*	—	

TSS16

OX42	TSS16	**black**	—	

TSS17

OX43	TSS17	**black**		—

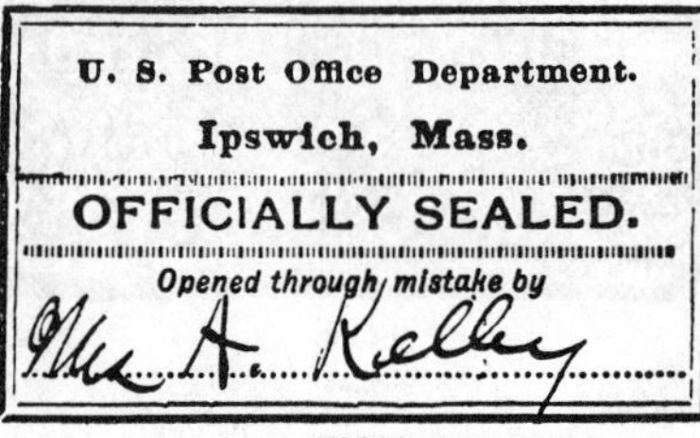

TSS18

OX44	TSS18	**black**		—

TSS19

OX45	TSS19	**black**	—	
a.		Top line 4mm. high	—	*275.00*

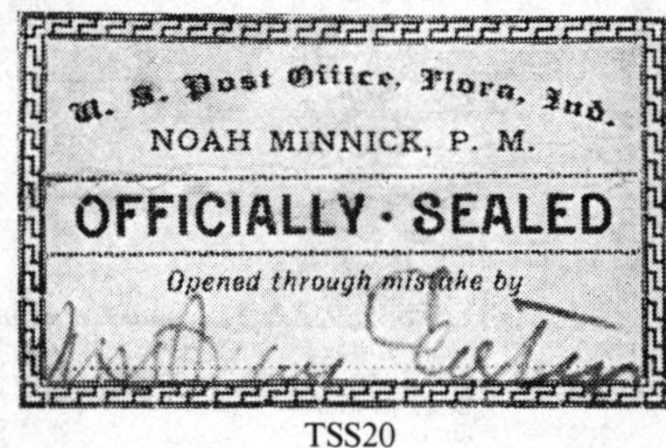

TSS20

OX46	TSS20	**black**		—

TSS21

OX47	TSS21	**black,** *dark brown red*		—

CHRISTMAS SEALS

Issued by the American National Red Cross (1907-1919), the National Tuberculosis Association (1920-1967), the National Tuberculosis and Respiratory Disease Association (1968-1972) and the American Lung Association (1973-).

While the Christmas Seal is not a postage stamp, it has long been associated with the postal service because of its use on letters and packages.

Einar Holboell, an employee of the Danish Post Office, created the Christmas Seal. He believed that seal sales could raise money for charity. The post offices of Denmark, Iceland and Sweden began to sell such seals in the 1904 Christmas season. In the United States, Christmas Seals were first issued in 1907 under the guidance of Emily P. Bissell, following the suggestion of Jacob Riis, social service worker.

Until 1975, all seals (except those of 1907 and 1908 type I) were issued in sheets of 100. The grilled gum (1908) has small square depressions like a waffle. The broken gum (1922), devised to prevent paper curling, consists of depressed lines in the gum, ½mm. apart, forming squares. The vertical and horizontal broken gum (1922, 1923, 1925, 1927-1932) forms diamonds. The perf. 12.00 (1917-1919, 1923, 1925, 1931) has two larger and wider-spaced holes between every 11 smaller holes.

Values are for seals with original gum.

SEALS ISSUED AND SOLD BY THE DELAWARE CHAPTER OF THE AMERICAN NATIONAL RED CROSS

CS1 (Type II)

Both types designed by Miss Emily P. Bissell.
Nearly $4,000 worth of seals were sold, $3,000 cleared.

1907 *Perf. 14*

Red

WX1	CS1	Type I. Inscribed "Merry Christmas" only	12.50
WX2	CS1	Type II. Inscribed "Merry Christmas" and "Happy New Year"	10.00

Types I and II. Lithographed by Theo. Leonhardt & Son, Philadelphia, Pa. The first seals were sold December 7, 1907, in Wilmington, Del. Both types were issued in sheets of 228 seals, 19 horizontal by 12 vertical. Type II was issued to extend the sale of seals until New Year's Day, 1908.

Counterfeits of both types exist (perf. 12).

SEALS ISSUED AND SOLD BY THE AMERICAN NATIONAL RED CROSS

CS2 (Type II)

Designed by Howard Pyle.
Realized from sales $135,000.

1908 *Perf. 12, 14*

Red and Green

WX3	CS2	Type I. Frame lines with square corners. Small "C" in "Christmas." Perf. 14 Smooth gum	30.00
	a.	Perf. 12 Smooth gum	30.00
	c.	Perf. 14 Grilled gum	30.00
	d.	Perf. 12 Grilled gum	30.00
	e.	Perf. 14 Booklet pane of six. Smooth gum	200.00
	f.	Perf. 14 Booklet pane of six. Grilled gum	200.00
	g.	Perf. 14 Booklet pane of three. Smooth gum	200.00
WX4	CS2	Type II. Perf. 12 Frame lines have rounded corners. Large "C" in "Christmas", and leaves veined	30.00
	a.	Booklet pane of six	150.00
	b.	Booklet pane of three	150.00

Type I. Lithographed by Theo. Leonhardt & Son. Sheets of 250 seals, 14 horizontal by 18 vertical, with the first space in the ninth and eighteenth rows left blank.

Type II. Lithographed by the American Bank Note Co., New York, N. Y. in sheets of 100 seals, 10 horizontal by 10 vertical.

Booklet panes have straight edges on three sides and perforated on left side where there is a stub, except No. WX4b which is a vertical strip of three with stub at top. The panes of six were made up in books of 24 and 48 seals and sold for 25c and 50c, and panes of three in books of 9 seals and sold for 10c. The grilled gum has small square depressions like on a waffle.

CS3

Designed by Carl Wingate.
Realized from sales $250,000.

1909 *Perf. 12*

Red and Green

WX5	CS3	One type only	30

Lithographed by The Strobridge Lithographing Company, Cincinnati, Ohio. Seals with a round punched hole of 3½mm. are printers' samples.

CS4

Designed by Mrs. Guion Thompson.
Realized from sales $300,000.

1910 *Perf. 12*

Red and Green

WX6	CS4	One type only	7.50

Lithographed by The Strobridge Lithographing Co.

SEALS ISSUED BY THE AMERICAN NATIONAL RED CROSS BUT SOLD BY THE NATIONAL ASSOCIATION FOR THE STUDY AND PREVENTION OF TUBERCULOSIS.

"The Old Home Among the Cedars" — CS5 (Type II)

Designed by Anton Rudert under directions of F. D. Millet.
Realized from sales $320,000.

1911 *Perf. 12*

Red and Green

WX7	CS5	Type I. Diameter of circle 22mm. Solid end in house	40.00
WX8	CS5	Type II. Same circle but thinner. Lined end to house	50.00

COIL STAMP

WX9	CS5	Type III. Diameter of circle 20mm. Lined end to house	60.00

All three types were typographed by Eureka Specialty Printing Co. Scranton, Pa. Type I has name and address of printer and union label in red in top margin. Type II has union label only in green on left margin.

CS6

Designed by John H. Zeh.
Realized from sales $402,256.

1912 *Perf. 12*

Red, Green & Black

WX10	CS6	One type only	7.50

Lithographed by The Strobridge Lithographing Co.

CS7 (Type I)

Designed by C. J. Budd.
Realized from sales $449,505.

1913 *Perf. 12*

Red and Green

WX11	CS7	Type I. With Poinsettia flowers and green circles around red crosses at either side	500.00
WX12	CS7	Type II. The Poinsettia flowers have been removed	5.00
WX13	CS7	Type III. The Poinsettia flowers and green circles have been removed	5.00

Lithographed by American Bank Note Co.

CS8

Designed by Benjamin S. Nash.
Realized from sales $555,854.

1914 *Perf. 12*

Red, Green & Black

WX15	CS8	One type only	7.50

Lithographed by The Strobridge Lithographing Co.

CS9

Designed by Benjamin S. Nash.
Realized from sales $760,000.

1915

Red, Green & Black

WX16	CS9	One type only. Perf. 12½	5.00
	a.	Perf. 12	65.00

Lithographed by Andrew B. Graham Co., Washington, D.C.

CS10

Designed by T. M. Cleland.
Realized from sales $1,040,810.

1916

Red and Green

WX18	CS10	One type only. Perf. 12	2.50
	a.	Perf. 12x12½	2.50
	b.	Perf. 12½x12	7.50
	c.	Perf. 12½	7.50

Lithographed by the Strobridge Lithographing Co.

Seals of 1917-21 are on coated paper.

CS11

Designed by T. M. Cleland.
Realized from sales $1,815,110.

1917

Red and Green

WX19	CS11	One type only, perf. 12	35
	a.	Perf. 12½	7.50
	b.	Perf. 12x12.00	35
	c.	Perf. 12x12½	12.50

Typographed by Eureka Specialty Printing Co. Perf. 12.00 has two larger and wider spaced holes between every eleven smaller holes. Sheets come with straight edged margins on all four sides also with perforated margins at either right or left. Perforated margins have the union label imprint in green.

SEALS ISSUED BY THE AMERICAN NATIONAL RED CROSS AND DISTRIBUTED BY THE NATIONAL TUBERCULOSIS ASSOCIATION

CS12

Designed by Charles A. Winter.
These seals were issued but not sold. They were given to members and others in lots of 10, the National Tuberculosis Association being subsidized by a gift of $2,500,000 from the American National Red Cross.

1918

Red, Green and Brown

WX21	CS12	Type I. "American Red Cross" 15 mm. long. Heavy circles between date. Perf. 11½x12.00	5.00
	a.	Perf. 12	5.00
	b.	Perf. 12.00 Booklet pane of ten	1.50
	c.	Perf. 12x12.00 Booklet pane of ten	1.50
	d.	Perf. 12 Booklet pane of ten	1.50
	e.	Perf. 12.00x12 Booklet pane of ten	50.00
WX22	CS12	Type II. "American Red Cross" 15½ mm. long. Periods between date. Booklet pane of ten. Perf. 12½xRoulette 9½	2.00
	a.	Perf. 12½ Booklet pane of ten	2.00
	b.	Perf. 12½x12 Booklet pane of ten	—
	d.	Roulette 9½xPerf. 12½ Booklet pane of ten	—
	e.	Perf. 12½xRoulette 9½ Booklet pane of ten	12.50
	f.	Perf. 12½ Booklet pane of ten	12.50
	h.	Roulette 9½xPerf. 12½ Booklet pane of ten	12.50
	i.	Roulette 9½xPerf. 12½ and Roulette 12½ Booklet pane of ten	—
	j.	Perf. 12½x12½ Booklet pane of ten	60.00
	k.	Perf. 12½x12½ and 12 Booklet pane of ten	—
	l.	Roulette 9½xPerf. 12½ Booklet pane of ten	—
	m.	Perf. 12½ Booklet pane of ten	—
	n.	Perf. 12½, stub at bottom Booklet pane of ten	50.00

Type I. Typographed by Eureka Specialty Printing Co.

Booklet panes are of 10 seals, 2 horizontal by 5 vertical and normally have straight edges on all four sides. They were cut from the sheets of 100 and can be plated by certain flaws which occur on both. Sheets have union label imprint on top margin in brown.

Type II. Lithographed by Strobridge Lithographing Co.

Booklet panes are the same but normally have a perforated margin at top and stub attached. These too can be plated by flaws. One or both vertical sides are rouletted on Number WX22e; perforated on Numbers WX22f and WX22h. Number WX22i is rouletted 12½ on left perforated 12½ on right. Numbers WX22j, WX22k and WX22l are booklet panes of 10 seals arranged 5x2. Number WX22m has a perforated margin at left.

Nos. WX21-WX21a are from sheet of 100, no straight edges.

The seal with "American Red Cross" 17¼mm long is believed to be an essay.

CS13 (Type II)

Designed by Ernest Hamlin Baker.
Realized from sales $3,872,534.

1919

Ultramarine, Red and Green

WX24	CS13	Type I. Plume at right side of Santa's cap. Perf. 12	25
	a.	Perf. 12x12.00	25
	b.	Perf. 12½x12	25
	c.	Perf. 12½x12.00	2.00
WX25	CS13	Type II. No plume but a white dot in center of band on Santa's cap. Perf. 12½	25

This is the first time the double barred cross, the emblem of the National Tuberculosis Association, appeared in the design of the seals. It is also the last time the red cross emblem of the American National Red Cross was used on seals.

Type I. Typographed by Eureka Specialty Printing Co., and has union label on margin at left in dark blue.

Type II lithographed by The Strobridge Lithographing Co.

SEALS ISSUED AND SOLD BY THE NATIONAL TUBERCULOSIS ASSOCIATION

CS14

Designed by Ernest Hamlin Baker.
Realized from sales $3,667,834.

1920

Ultramarine, Red and Green

WX26	CS14	Type I. Size of seal 18x22 mm. Perf. 12x12½	35
	a.	Perf. 12	35
	b.	Perf. 12½x12	7.50
	c.	Perf. 12½x12½	10.00
WX27	CS14	Type II. Size of seal 18½x23½ mm. Letters larger and numerals heavier than Type I. Perf. 12½	35

Type I typographed by Eureka Speciality Printing Co., and has union label imprint and rings on margin at left in dark blue. Type II lithographed and offset printing by The Strobridge Lithographing Co.

CS15

Designed by George V. Curtis.
Realized from sales $3,520,303.

1921

Ultramarine, Red and Green

WX28	CS15	Type I. The dots in the shading of the chimney and faces are arranged in diagonal lines. The dots on chimney are separate except between the two top rows of bricks where they are a solid mass. Perf. 12½	25
WX29	CS15	Type II. The dots in the shading of the chimney and faces are arranged in horizontal lines. Perf. 12½	25
WX29A	CS15	Type III. The same as Type I except the red dots on chimney are mostly joined and form lines. The dots between the two top rows of bricks are not a solid mass. Perf. 12	25

Type I typographed by Eureka Speciality Printing Co. Type II offset printing by The Strobridge Lithographing Co. Type III typographed by Zeese-Wilkinson Company Inc., Long Island City, N.Y.

CS16

Designed by T. M. Cleland.
Realized from sales $3,857,086.

1922

Pale Ultramarine, Red and Yellow

WX30	CS16	One type only. Perf. 12½, broken gum	50
	a.	Perf. 12, broken gum	2.00
	b.	Perf. 12x12½, broken gum	5.00
	c.	Perf. 12, smooth gum	2.00
	d.	Perf. 12½, vertical broken gum	2.00

Typographed by Eureka Specialty Printing Co.

The broken gum on this issue, which was devised to prevent curling of paper, consists of depressed lines in the gum ½mm apart, forming squares, or vertical broken gum forming diamonds.

CS17

Designed by Rudolph Ruzicka.
Realized from sales $4,259,660.

1923

Green and Red

WX31	CS17	One type only. Perf. 12½. Vertical broken gum	15
	a.	Perf. 12 Horizontal broken gum	2.50
	b.	Perf. 12x12.00 Vertical broken gum	2.50
	c.	Perf. 12½x12 Vertical broken gum	5.00
	d.	Perf. 12 Vertical broken gum	50
	e.	Perf. 12.00x12 Vertical broken gum	2.50

Typographed by Eureka Specialty Printing Co.

The broken gum on this and issues following printed by the Eureka Co. consists of very fine depressed lines forming diamonds. The brown color in seals is due to the overlapping of the two colors.

CS18

Designed by George V. Curtis.
Realized from sales $4,479,656.

1924

Red, Ultramarine and Yellow

WX32	CS18	One type only	10

Offset printing by The Strobridge Lithographing Co., Edwards & Deutsch Lithographing Co., Chicago, Ill., and The United States Printing & Lithograph Co., Brooklyn, N.Y.

CS19 (Type II)

Designed by Robert G. Eberhard.
Realized from sales $4,937,786.

1925

Green, Red and Pale Green

WX35	CS19	Type I. Red lines at each side of "1925" do not join red tablet below. Perf. 12½ Vertical broken gum	10
	a.	Perf. 12x12, vertical broken gum	2.50
	b.	Perf. 12x12½ vertical broken gum	35
	c.	Perf. 12.00x12½ vertical broken gum	—
WX36	CS19	Type II. Red lines, as in Type I, join red tablet below. Perf. 12½	10
WX37	CS19	Type III. Same as Type I but shorter rays around flames and "ea" of "Health" smaller. Perf. 12½	50

Type I typographed by Eureka Specialty Printing Co. Type II offset printing by Edwards & Deutsch Lithographing Co. Type III lithographed by Gugler Lithographing Co., Milwaukee, Wis.

CS20

Designed by George V. Curtis.
Realized from sales $5,121,872.

1926 *Perf. 12½*

Black, Red, Blue and Yellow

WX38	CS20	One type only	10

Offset printing by Edwards & Deutsch Lithographing Co., and The United States Printing & Lithograph Co.

Printers' marks on sheets: E.& D. has a red dot at upper right on seal No. 91 on some sheets. U.S.P.&L. has a black dot at upper left on seal No. 56 on some sheets.

CS21

Designed by John W. Evans.
Realized from sales $5,419,959.

1927

Red, Ultramarine, Green and Black

WX39	CS21	One type only. Perf. 12. Horizontal broken gum	10
	a.	Perf. 12. Smooth gum. (See No. WX43)	1.00
WX40	CS21	Perf. 12½. No dot as on No. WX41	10
WX41	CS21	Perf. 12½. This seal has one larger red dot in background 1mm. above right post of dashboard on sleigh	10
WX42	CS21	"Bonne Sante" added to design under reindeer and sleigh. For French Canadians. Perf. 12	50
WX43	CS21	Same as WX39a but body of sleigh a myrtle green instead of green. For English Canadians. Perf. 12	50

All seals of 1927 are offset printing. Nos. WX39 and WX39a by Eureka Specialty Printing Co. No. WX40 by Edwards & Deutsch Lithographing Co. No. WX41 by The United States Printing & Lithograph Co. Nos. WX42 and WX43 by Canadian Bank Note Co., Ottawa, Ont. Canada.

Printer's marks on sheets: Eureka has no mark but can be identified by the Perf. 12. E.&D. has red dot to left of knee of first reindeer on seal No. 92. U.S.P.&Lithograph Co. has two red dots in white gutter, one at lower left of seal No. 46 (and sometimes No. 41) and the other at upper right of seal No. 55. The perforations often strike out one of these dots.

The Gallant Ship "Argosy" — CS22

Designed by John W. Evans.
Realized from sales $5,465,738.

1928 *Perf. 12½.*

Black, Blue, Red, Orange and Green

WX44	CS22	Type I. Shading on sails broken. Dots in flag regular. Vertical broken gum	10
WX45	CS22	Type II. Shading on sails broken. Dots in flag spotty	10
WX46	CS22	Type III. Shading on sails unbroken. Dots in flag regular	10
WX47	CS22	Type IV. Inscribed "Bonne Annee 1929" For French Canadians	35
WX48	CS22	Type V. Same as Type II but green in water, and black lines of ship heavier and deeper color. For English Canadians	35

All seals of 1928 are offset printing. Type I by Eureka Specialty Printing Co., Type II by The Strobridge Lithographing Co., Type III by Edwards & Deutsch Lithographing Co., and Types IV and V by The Copp Clark Co., Ltd., Toronto, Ont., Canada.

Printers' mark on sheets: Type I comes with and without a blue dash above seal No. 10, also with a blue and a black dash. Type II has two blue dashes below seal No. 100. Type III has red dot in crest of first wave on seal No. 92.

CS23

Designed by George V. Curtis.
Realized from sales $5,546,147.

1929

Blue, Red, Yellow and Black

WX49	CS23	One type only. Perf. 12½. Vertical broken gum	10
	a.	Perf. 12. Vertical broken gum	50
	b.	Perf. 12½x12. Vertical broken gum	75
WX50	CS23	Perf. 12½. Smooth gum	10
WX53	CS23	Inscribed "Bonne Sante 1929" for French Canadians. Perf. 12½	35
	a.	Perf. 14x12½	—
WX54	CS23	Inscribed "Christmas Greetings 1929" for English Canadians. Perf. 12½	35

All seals of 1929 are offset printing. Nos. WX49 to WX49b by Eureka Specialty Printing Co. No. WX50 by Edwards & Deutsch Lithographing Co., The United States Printing and Lithograph Co., and R.R. Heywood Co., Inc., New York, N.Y. Nos. WX53 and WX54 by the Copp Clark Co., Ltd.

Printers' marks on sheets: Eureka is without mark but identified by broken gum. E.&D. has a black dot in lower left corner of seal No. 92. U.S.P.&L. Co. has blue dot above bell on seal No. 56. Heywood has a blue dot at lower right corner of seal No. 100.

CS24

Designed by Ernest Hamlin Baker, and redrawn by John W. Evans.
Realized from sales $5,309,352.

1930

Green, Red, Gray and Black

WX55	CS24	One type only. Perf. 12½. Vertical broken gum	10
	a.	Perf. 12. Vertical broken gum	50
	b.	Perf. 12.00x12. Vertical broken gum	25
	c.	Perf. 12½x12. Vertical broken gum	2.50
	d.	Perf. 12. Bklt. pane of 10, horiz. broken gum	50
WX56	CS24	Perf. 12½. Smooth gum	10
WX59	CS24	Inscribed "Bonne Sante," on red border of seal, for French Canadians. Perf. 12½	25
WX60	CS24	Inscribed "Merry Christmas," on red border of seal, for English Canadians. Perf. 12½	25

All seals of 1930 are offset printing. Nos. WX55 to WX55d by Eureka Specialty Printing Co. No. WX56 by The Strobridge Lithographing Co., Edwards & Deutsch Lithographing Co. and by The United States Printing & Lithograph Co. Nos. WX59 and WX60 by the Copp Clark Co., Ltd.

Printers' marks on sheets: Eureka has a dot between the left foot and middle of "M" of "Merry" on seal No. 1. Strobridge has two dashes below "ALL" on seal No. 100. E.& D. printed on Nashua paper has dot on coatjust under elbow on seal No. 92, and on Gummed Products Co. paper has the dot on seals

Nos. 91 and 92. U.S.P.& Litho. Co. has a dash which joins tree to top frame line just under "MA" of "Christmas" on seal No. 55.

The plate for booklet panes was made up from the left half of the regular plate and can be plated by certain flaws which occur on both.

CS25

Designed by John W. Evans.
Realized from sales $4,526,189.

1931

Green, Black, Red and Cream

WX61		CS25 One type only. Perf. 12½. Horizontal broken gum (see foot note)	2.00
WX62		CS25 Perf. 12½. Horizontal broken gum	5
	a.	Perf. 12x12½. Horizontal broken gum	35
	b.	Perf. 12.00x12½. Horizontal broken gum	2.50
	c.	Perf. 12 Horizontal broken gum	1.00
	g.	Perf. 12. Vertical broken gum. Booklet pane of 10 seals	50
	h.	Perf. 12x12.00. Vertical broken gum. Booklet pane of 10 seals	60
WX63		CS25 Perf. 12½. Smooth gum	5

All seals of 1931 are offset printing. Nos. WX61 to WX62h by Eureka Specialty Printing Co. No. WX63 by the Strobridge Lithographing Co. No. WX61 has a green dash across inner green frame line at bottom center on each sealin sheet except those in first and last vertical rows and the two rows at bottom. This dash is omitted on all other numbers.

Printers' marks on sheets: Eureka has none. Strobridge has the usual two dashes under seal No. 100.

The plate for booklet panes was made up from transfers of sixty seals-twelve horizontal by five vertical. The six panes of the transfer can be plated by minor flaws.

CS26

Designed by Edward F. Volkmann.
Realized from sales $3,470,637.

1932

Red, Ultramarine, Blue, Green and Yellow

WX64		CS26 One type only. Perf. 12½x12¾	5
	a.	Perf. 12½x12¾. Vertical broken gum	50
WX65		CS26 Perf. 12	5
WX66		CS26 Perf. 12½	5
WX67		CS26 Perf. 12½	5

All seals of 1932 are offset printing. No. WX64 by Eureka Specialty Printing Co. No. WX65 by Edwards & Deutsch Lithographing Co. No. WX66 by The United States Printing & Lithograph Co. No. WX67 by Columbian Bank Note Co., Chicago, Ill. Nos. WX64, WX66 and WX67 have a little red spur on bottom inner frame line of each seal, at left corner. Nos. WX65 and WX66 come without the spur.

Printers' marks on sheets: Eureka has a red dash, in each corner of the sheet, which joins the red border to the red inner frame line. E.&D. has a blue dot in snow at lower left on seal No. 91. U.S.P.& L. Co. has a blue dot on top of post on seal No. 56. Columbian Bank Note Co. has small "C" in lower part of girl's coat on seal No. 82.

CS27

Designed by Hans Axel Walleen.
Realized from sales $3,429,311.

1933

Red, Black, Green and Yellow

WX68	CS27 One type only. Perf. 12	5
WX69	CS27 Perf. 12½	5

All seals of 1933 are offset printing. No. WX68 by Eureka Specialty Printing Co. No. WX69 by The Strobridge Lithographing Co., The United States Printing & Lithograph Co., and the Columbian Bank Note Co.

Printers' marks on sheets; Eureka has rope joining elbow of figure to left on seals Nos. 11, 20, 91 and 100. Strobridge has the usual two dashes under seal No. 100. U.S.P.& L. Co. has green dot on tail of "s" of "Greetings" on seal No. 55. Columbian has white "c" on margin, under cross, on seal No. 93.

CS28

Designed by Herman D. Giesen.
Realized from sales $3,701,344.

1934

Carmine, Ultramarine, Green, Blue and Yellow

WX72	CS28 One type only. Perf. 12½x12¼	5
WX73	CS28 Perf. 12½. (see footnote)	5
WX74	CS28 Perf. 12½. (see footnote)	5
WX75	CS28 Perf. 12½. (see footnote)	5

All seals of 1934 are offset printing. No. WX72 by Eureka Specialty Printing Co., No. WX73 by The Strobridge Lithographing Co., No. WX74 by Edwards & Deutsch Lithographing Co. and No. WX75 by The United States Printing & Lithograph Co.

Cutting of blue plate for the under color: Nos. WX72, WX73 (early printing) and WX74 have lettering and date cut slightly larger than ultramarine color. No. WX73 (later printing) has square cutting around letters and date, like top part of letter "T". No. WX75 has cutting around letters and date cut slightly larger.

Printers' marks on sheets. Eureka has five stars to right of cross on seal No. 10. Strobridge has two blue dashes in lower left corner of seal No. 91 or same dashes in lower right corner of seal No. 100. E.& D. has a red dot in lower left corner of seal No. 99. U.S.P.& L. Co. has five stars to left of cross on seal No. 56.

Great Britain issued seals of this design which can be distinguished by the thinner and whiter paper. Sheets have perforated margins on all four sides but without any lettering on bottom margin. The perforation is 12½.

CS29

Designed by Ernest Hamlin Baker.
Realized from sales $3,946,498.

1935

Blue, Carmine, Red Brown and Green

WX76	CS29 One type only. Perf. 12½x12¼	5
WX77	CS29 Perf. 12½	5

All seals of 1935 are offset printing. No. WX76 by Eureka Specialty Printing Co., No. WX77 by The Strobridge Lithographing Co., The United States Printing & Lithograph Co. and Columbian Bank Note Co.

Eureka recut their blue plate and eliminated the faint blue shading around cross, girl's head and at both sides of the upper part of post. U.S.P.& L. Co. eliminated the two brown spurs which pointed to the base of cross, in all four corners of the sheet.

Printers' marks on sheets: Eureka has an extra vertical line of shading on girl's skirt on seal No. 60. Strobridge has two brown dashes in lower right corner of position No. 100 but sheets from an early printing are without this mark. U.S.P.&L. Co. has a blue dot under post on seal No. 55. Columbian has a blue "c" under post on seal No. 99.

The four corner seals in each sheet carry slogans: Seal 1, "Help Fight Tuberculosis." Seal 10, "Protect Your Home from Tuberculosis." Seal 91, "Tuberculosis Is Preventable." Seal 100, "Tuberculosis Is Curable."

Printers' marks appear on seal 56 on sheets of 100 unless otherwise noted:
E Eureka Specialty Printing Co.
S Strobridge Lithographing Co. (1930-1958).
S Specialty Printers of America (1975-).
D Edwards & Deutsch Lithographing Co.
U United States Printing & Lithographing Co.
F Fleming-Potter Co., Inc.
W Western Lithograph Co.
B Berlin Lithographing Co. (1956-1969); I. S. Berlin Press (1970-1976); Barton-Cotton (1977-).
R Bradford-Robinson Printing Co.
N Sale-Niagara, Inc.
Printers of Canadian seals, unmarked:
Arthurs-Jones Lithographing, Toronto (1943-1949).
Rolph, Clarke and Stone, Toronto (1950-1955).
Seals from 1936 onward are printed by offset.
Seals with tropical gum (dull), starting in 1966, were used in Puerto Rico.

CS30

Designed by Walter I. Sasse.
Realized from sales $4,522,269.

1936

Gray, Red, Green and Yellow Pair

WX80	CS30 Perf. 12½x12, red & grn. backgrounds (E)	5
WX81	CS30 Perf. 12½, red & grn. backgrounds (S,D,U)	5

Seals with red background and green cap-band alternate with seals showing green background and red cap-band. The four corner seals, positions 1, 10, 91 and 100, carry the same slogans as those of 1935.

Two of the three Strobridge printings show vertical green dashes in margin below seal 100, besides "S" on seal 56.

CS31

Designed by A. Robert Nelson.
Realized from sales $4,985,697.

1937

Blue, Red, Black and Yellow

WX88	CS31 Perf. 12x12½ (E)	5
WX89	CS31 Perf. 12½ (S,D,U)	5

Four seals in each sheet, positions 23, 28, 73 and 78, carry slogans: "Health for all," "Protect your home," "Preventable" and "Curable."

The "U" printer's mark of United States Printing & Lithographing Co. appears on seal 55. It is omitted on some sheets.

CS32

Designed by Lloyd Coe.
Realized from sales $5,239,526.

1938

Red, Brown, Green and Black

WX92	CS32 Perf. 12½x12 (E)	5
WX93	CS32 Perf. 12½ (S,D,U)	5
a.	Miniature sheet, imperf.	3.00

The corner seals of each sheet bear portraits of Rene T. H. Laennec, Robert Koch, Edward Livingston Trudeau and Einar Holboll.

No. WX93a contains the four corner seals, with the regular seal in the center. Inscriptions in black include slogans and "They made landmarks in the fight against tuberculosis," with brief statements on the contributions of Laennec, Koch, Trudeau and Holboll. Size of sheet: 140x86mm. It sold for 25 cents.

CS33

Designed by Rockwell Kent.
Realized from sales $5,593,399.

1939

Red, Ultramarine and Pale Red

WX96	CS33 Perf. 12½x12 (E)	5
a.	Booklet pane of 20, Perf. 12	35
WX97	CS33 Perf. 12½ (S,D,U)	5

The four center seals in each sheet, positions 45, 46, 55 and 56, carry slogans: "Health to All," "Protect Your Home." "Tuberculosis Preventable Curable" and "Holiday Greetings." Printers' marks appear on seal 57.

CS34

Designed by Felix L. Martini.
Realized from sales $6,305,979.

1940

Blue, Ultramarine, Red and Yellow

WX100	CS34 Perf. 12½x12 (E)	5
WX101	CS34 Perf. 12½x13 (E)	5
WX103	CS34 Perf. 12½ (S,D,U)	5

Three seals in each sheet-positions 23, 32 and 34-carry the slogan "Protect Us from Tuberculosis." Each slogan seal shows one of the three children separately.

CS35

Designed by Stevan Dohanos.
Realized from sales $7,530,496.

The Catalogue editors cannot undertake to appraise, identify or judge the genuineness or condition of stamps.

1941

Blue, Black, Red and Yellow

WX104	CS35 Perf. 12½x12 (E)	5
WX105	CS35 Perf. 12½ (S,D,U)	5

"S" and "U" printers' marks exist on same sheet.

CS36

Designed by Dale Nichols.
Realized from sales $9,390,117.

1942

Yellow, Blue, Red and Black

WX108	CS36 Perf. 12x12½ (E)	5
WX109	CS36 Perf. 12½ (S,D,U)	5

CS37

Designed by Andre Dugo.
Realized from U. S. sales $12,521,494.

1943

Blue, Red, Buff and Black Pair

WX112	CS37 Perf. 12½x12 (E)	5
WX113	CS37 Perf. 12½ (S,D,U)	5
WX116	CS37 "Joyeux Noel" replaces "Greetings 1943" and "1943" added on curtain. For French Canadians. Perf. 12½	10
WX117	CS37 Same as WX113 but darker colors. For English Canadians and Great Britain. Perf. 12½	10

On alternate seals, the vertical frame colors (blue and red) are transposed and the horizontal frame colors (buff and black) are transposed.

CS38

Designed by Spence Wildey.
Realized from U. S. sales $14,966,227.

1944

Gray, Blue, Red and Yellow

WX118	CS38 Perf. 12½x12 (E)	5
WX119	CS38 Perf. 12½ (S,D,U)	5
WX122	CS38 "Joyeux Noel" replaces "Merry Christmas" and "USA" omitted. For French Canadians. Perf. 12½	10
WX123	CS38 Same as WX119 but "USA" omitted. For English Canadians. Perf. 12½	10

CS39

Designed by Park Phipps.

Realized from U.S. sales $15,638,755.

1945

Blue, Red, Black and Yellow "USA" at Lower Right Corner.

WX124	CS39 Perf. 12½x12 (E)	5
WX125	CS39 Perf. 12½ (S,D,U)	5
WX128	CS39 "Bonne Sante" replaces "Greetings" and "USA" omitted. For French Canadians. Perf. 12½	10
WX129	CS39 Same as WX125 but "USA" omitted. For English Canadians. Perf. 12½	10

CS40

Designed by Mary Louise Estes and Lloyd Coe.
Realized from U.S. sales $17,075,608.44.

1946

Blue, Black, Red and Olive "USA" at Left of Red Cross.

WX130	CS40 Perf. 12½x12 (E)	5
WX131	CS40 Perf. 12½ (S,D,U)	5
WX132	CS40 "Bonne Sante" replaces "Greetings" and "USA" omitted. For French Canadians. Perf. 12½	10
WX133	CS40 Same as WX131 but "USA" omitted. For English Canadians and Great Britain. Perf. 12½	10
a.	Same, overprinted "NEWFOUNDLAND"	1.25
WX134	CS40 "Bermuda" replaces seven stars and "USA" omitted. For Bermuda. Perf. 12½x12 (E)	25

Printers' marks are on seal 86.

The four center seals (45, 46, 55, 56) of Nos. WX130 and WX131 bear portraits of Jacob Riis, Emily P. Bissell, E. A. Van Valkenburg and Leigh Mitchell Hodges.

CS41

Designed by Raymond H. Lufkin.
Realized from U. S. sales $18,665,523.

1947

Red, Blue, Green and Brown

WX135	CS41 Perf. 12x12½ (E)	5
WX136	CS41 Perf. 12½ (S,D,U)	5
WX137	CS41 "Bonne Sante" replaces "Merry Christmas" and "USA" omitted. For French Canadians. Perf. 12½	5
WX138	CS41 Same as WX136 but "USA" omitted. For English Canadians and Great Britain. Perf. 12½	5
WX139	CS41 "BERMUDA" overprinted in red on WX138. For Bermuda. Perf. 12½	20

The "U" printer's mark of United States Printing & Lithographing Co. appears on seal 46.

CS42

Designed by Jean Barry Bart.
Realized from U. S. sales $20,153,834.47.

1948

Blue, Red, Light Blue and Yellow

WX140	CS42 Perf. 12x12½ (E)	5
WX141	CS42 Perf. 12½ (S,D,U)	5

WX142 CS42 "Bonne Sante" replaces "Merry Christmas", date in white and "USA" omitted. For French Canadians. Perf. 12½ 5
WX143 CS42 Same as WX141 but date in white and "USA" omitted. For English Canadians, Great Britain and Newfoundland. Perf. 12½ 5
WX144 CS42 "BERMUDA" overprinted in black on WX143. Perf. 12½ 20

CS43

Designed by Herbert Meyers.
Realized from U.S. sales $20,226,794.15.

1949

Green, Light Blue, Red and Ultramarine

WX145 CS43 Perf. 12x12½ (E) 5
WX146 CS43 Perf. 12½ (S,D,U) 5
WX147 CS43 "Bonne Sante" replaces "Greetings" and "USA" omitted. For French Canadians. Perf. 12½ 5
WX148 CS43 Same as WX146 but "USA" omitted. For English Canadians, Great Britain and Newfoundland. Perf. 12½ 5
WX149 CS43 "BERMUDA" replaces "USA" on WX145. For Bermuda. Perf. 12x12½ (E) 15

CS44

Designed by Andre Dugo.
Realized from U. S. sales $20,981,540.77.

1950

Red, Green, Orange and Black

WX150 CS44 Perf. 12½x12 (E) 5
WX151 CS44 Perf. 12½ (S,D,U,F) 5
WX152 CS44 "Bonne Sante" replaces "Greetings" and "USA" omitted. For French Canadians. Perf. 12½ 5
WX153 CS44 Same as WX151 but "USA" omitted. For English Canadians and Great Britain. Perf 12½ 5
WX154 CS44 Same as WX150 but "BERMUDA" in larger letters replaces "USA" at bottom (E) 15

CS45

Designed by Robert K. Stephens.
Realized from U.S. sales $21,717,953.09.

1951

Blue Green, Red, Flesh and Black

WX155 CS45 Perf. 12½x12 (E) 5
WX156 CS45 Perf. 12½ (S,D,U,F) 5
WX157 CS45 Same as WX156 but "USA" omitted. For English Canadians. Perf. 12½. 5

Stamp booklets and booklet panes are listed and valued in a separate section of the catalogue. See catalogue index.

WX158 CS45 "BERMUDA" replaces "USA" on WX155. For Bermuda. Perf 12½x12 (E) 15

CS46

Designed by Tom Darling.
Realized from U. S. sales $23,238,148.12.

1952

Green, Yellow, Red and Black

WX159 CS46 Perf. 12½x12 (E) 5
WX160 CS46 Perf. 12½ (S,D,U,F) 5
WX161 CS46 "CANADA" replaces "Christmas Greetings." Copyright mark and "USA" eliminated. Perf. 12½ 5
WX162 CS46 "BERMUDA" in vertical lettering at right. "USA" eliminated. Perf. 12½x12 (E) 15
WX163 CS46 Overprinted "Ryukyus" (in Japanese characters) in black. Perf. 12½x12, 12½ (U) 1.50

CS47

Designed by Elmer Jacobs and E. Willis Jones.
Realized from U. S. sales $23,889,044.50.

1953

Gold, Red, Green and Black

WX164 CS47 Perf. 13 (E) 5
WX165 CS47 Perf. 12½ (S,D,U,F) 5
WX166 CS47 "CANADA" replaces "Greetings." Copyright mark, "NTA" and "USA" eliminated. Perf. 12½ 5
WX167 CS47 "BERMUDA" replaces "NTA" and "USA." Perf. 13 (E) 15

CS48

Designed by Jorgen Hansen.
Realized from U. S. sales $24,670,202.85.

1954

Yellow, Black, Green and Red Block of Four

WX168 CS48 Perf. 13 (E) 10
WX169 CS48 Perf. 12½ (S,U,F,W) 10
WX170 CS48 Perf. 11 (D) 10
WX171 CS48 CANADA, perf. 12½ 20
WX172 CS48 BERMUDA, perf. 13 (E) 1.00

CS49

Designed by Miss Jean Simpson.
Realized from U.S. sales $25,780,365.96.

1955

Ultramarine, Olive Green, Red and Blue Pair

WX173 CS49 Perf. 13 (E) 5
WX174 CS49 Perf. 12½ (S,U,F,W) 5
WX175 CS49 Perf. 11 (D) 5
WX176 CS49 CANADA, perf. 10½ 10
WX177 CS49 BERMUDA, perf. 13 (E) 25

CS50

Designed by Heidi Brandt.
Realized from U. S. sales $26,310,491.

1956

Dull Yellow, Red, Green and Black Block of Four

WX178 CS50 Perf. 12½x12 (E) 10
WX179 CS50 Perf. 12½ (E,S,U,F,W) 10
WX180 CS50 Perf. 11 (D,b) 10
WX181 CS50 "Canada," perf. 11, pair 10
WX182 CS50 BERMUDA, perf. 12½ 75
WX183 CS50 "Puerto Rico," perf. 12½ 3.00

C51

Designed by Clinton Bradley.
Realized from U.S. sales $25,959,998.51.

1957

Dark Green, Light Green, Red and Yellow Block of Four

WX184 CS51 Perf. 13 (E) 10
WX185 CS51 Perf. 12½ (S,U,F,W,R) 10
WX186 CS51 Perf. 11 (D,B) 10
WX187 CS51 Perf. 10½x11 (D) 10
WX188 CS51 Perf. 10½ (D) 10
WX189 CS51 "Bermuda," perf. 13, pair 25
WX190 CS51 "Puerto Rico," perf. 13 3.00

CS52

Designed by Alfred Guerra.
Realized from U.S. sales $25,955,390.47

1958

Red, Green, Yellow and Black Pair

WX191 CS52 Perf. 13 (E) 5
WX192 CS52 Perf. 12½ (S,U,F,W,R) 5
WX193 CS52 Perf. 10½x11 (B,D) 5
WX194 CS52 Perf. 11 (B,D) 5
WX195 CS52 "Bermuda," perf. 13 25

WX196	CS52 "Puerto Rico," perf. 13	1.50

CS53

Designed by Katherine Rowe.
Realized from U.S. sales $26,740,906.16.

1959

Crimson, Green, Bister & Black
Pair

WX197	CS53 Perf. 13 (E)	5
WX198	CS53 Perf. 12½ (F,R,W)	5
	a. Horiz. pair, imperf. btwn. (D)	1.50
WX199	CS53 Perf. 10½x11 (B)	5
WX200	CS53 Perf. 11 (B,D)	5
WX201	CS53 Perf. 10½ (B)	5
WX202	CS53 "Bermuda," perf. 13	25
WX203	CS53 "Puerto Rico," perf. 13	1.00

Edwards & Deutsch Lithographing Co. omitted every other vertical row of perforation on a number of sheets which were widely distributed as an experiment. No. WX198a is from one of these sheets.

CS54

Designed by Philip Richard Costigan.
Realized from U.S. sales $26,259,030.37.

1960

Red, Bister, Green & Black
Block of Four

WX204	CS54 Perf. 12½ (E,F,R,W)	10
WX205	CS54 Perf. 12½x12 (E)	10
WX206	CS54 Perf. 11x10½ (B)	10
WX207	CS54 Perf. 11 (D)	10
WX208	CS54 "Bermuda," perf. 12½	75

Puerto Rico used No. WX204 (E).

CS55

Designed by Heidi Brandt.
Realized from U.S. sales $26,529,517.20.

1961

Dark Blue, Yellow, Green and Red
Block of Four

WX209	CS55 Perf. 12½ (E,F,R,W)	10
WX209A	CS55 Perf. 12½x12 (E)	10
WX210	CS55 Perf. 11x10½ (B)	10
WX211	CS55 Perf. 11 (D)	10
WX212	CS55 "Bermuda," perf. 12½	75

Puerto Rico used No. WX209 (E).

CS56

Designed by Paul Dohanos.
Realized from U.S. sales $27,429,202.18.

1962

Emerald, Red, Prussian Blue & Yellow
Block of Four

WX213	CS56 Perf. 12½ (F,R,W)	10
WX214	CS56 Perf. 13 (E)	10
WX215	CS56 Perf. 10½x11 (B)	10
WX216	CS56 Perf. 11 (D,B)	10
WX217	CS56 "Bermuda," perf. 13	75

Puerto Rico used No. WX214.

CS57

Designed by Judith Campbell Piussi.
Realized from U.S. sales $27,411,806.

1963

Bright Ultra., Yel., Red, Green, Orange & Black
Block of Four

WX218	CS57 Perf. 12½ (E,F,R,W)	10
WX219	CS57 Perf. 11 (B,D)	10

Puerto Rico used No. WX218 (E).

CS58

Designed by Gaetano di Palma.
Realized from U.S. sales $28,784,043.

1964

Bister, Red, Emerald & Black
Block of Four

WX220	CS58 Perf. 12½ (E,F,R,W)	10
WX221	CS58 Perf. 11 (B,D)	10

Puerto Rico used No. WX221 (B).

CS59

Designed by Frede Salomonsen.
Realized from U.S. sales $29,721,878.

1965

Blue, Red, Yellow, Green & Black
Block of Four

WX222	CS59 Perf. 12½ (F,W)	10
WX223	CS59 Perf. 11 (B,D)	10
WX224	CS59 Perf. 13 (E)	10

Puerto Rico used No. WX223 (B).

CS60

Designed by Heidi Brandt.
Realized from U.S. sales $30,776,586.

1966

Yellow Green, Black, Red & Yellow
Block of Eight

WX225	CS60 Perf. 12½ (E,F,W)	25
WX226	CS60 Perf. 10½x11 (B)	25
WX227	CS60 Perf. 11 (D)	25

Blocks of four seals with yellow green and white backgrounds alternate in sheet in checkerboard style.

Puerto Rico used No. WX226.

Holiday Train — CS61

Designed by L. Gerald Snyder.
Realized from U.S. sales $31,876,773.

The seals come in 10 designs showing a train filled with Christmas gifts and symbols. The direction of the train is reversed in alternating rows as are the inscriptions "Christmas 1967" and "Greetings 1967". The illustration shows first two seals of top row. Each listing stands for two horizontal rows of 10 seals.

1967

Red, Green, Black, Blue & Yellow
Block of 20 (10x2)

WX228	CS61	Perf. 13 (E)	30
WX229	CS61	Perf. 12½ (F,W)	30
WX230	CS61	Perf. 10½ (B)	30
WX231	CS61	Perf. 11 (D)	30
WX232	CS61	Perf. 11x10½ (B)	30

Puerto Rico used No. WX229 (F).

SEALS ISSUED BY NATIONAL TUBERCULOSIS AND RESPIRATORY DISEASE ASSOCIATION

CS62

Designed by William Eisele.
Realized from U.S. sales $33,059,107.

1968

Bluish Green, Yellow, Blue, Black & Red
Block of Four

WX233	CS62	Perf. 13 (E)	10
WX234	CS62	Perf. 10½x11 (B)	10
WX234A	CS62	Perf. 10½ (B)	10
WX235	CS62	Perf. 11 (D)	10
WX236	CS62	Perf. 12½ (F,W)	10

Blocks of four seals with bluish green and yellow backgrounds alternate in sheet in checkerboard style.
Puerto Rico used No. WX236 (F).

CS63

Designed by Bernice Kochan.
Realized from U.S. sales $34,437,591.

1969

Blue Grn., Verm., Emerald, Magenta & Black
Block of Four

WX237	CS63	Perf. 13 (E)	10
WX238	CS63	Perf. 12½ (F,W)	10
WX239	CS63	Perf. 10½x11 (B)	10
WX240	CS63	Perf. 11 (B)	10

Puerto Rico used No. WX238 (F).

CS64

Designed by L. Gerald Snyder.
Realized from U.S. sales $36,237,977.
Sheets of 100 show different design for each seal, Christmas symbols, toys, decorated windows; inscribed alternately "Christmas 1970" and "Greetings 1970." The illustration shows 6 seals from the center of the sheet.

1970

Ultramarine, Black, Red, Yellow & Olive
Sheet of 100 (10x10)

WX242	CS64	Perf. 12½ (E,F,W)	1.00
WX243	CS64	Perf. 11 (B)	1.00
WX244	CS64	Perf. 11x10½ (B)	1.00

Puerto Rico used No. WX242 (F).

CS65

Designed by James Clarke.
Realized from U.S. sales $36,120,000.

1971

Lilac Rose, Yellow, Green & Blue
Block of Eight (2x4)

WX245	CS65	Perf. 12½ (E,F)	20
WX246	CS65	Perf. 11 (B)	20

The four illustrated seals each come in a second design arrangement: cross at left, inscriptions transposed, and reversed bugler, candle and tree ornaments. Each sheet of 100 has six horizontal rows of seals as shown and four rows with second designs.
Puerto Rico used No. WX245 (F).

Eureka printings are found with large "E", small "E" and without "E".

CS66

Designed by Linda Layman
Realized from U.S. sales $38,000,557.
The seals come in 10 designs showing various holiday scenes with decorated country and city houses, carolers, Christmas trees and snowman. Inscribed alternately "1972 Christmas" and "Greetings 1972." Illustration shows seals from center of row.

1972

Bright Blue, Red, Green, Yellow & Black
Strip of 10

WX247	CS66	Perf. 13 (E)	30

Blue, Red, Green, Yellow & Black

WX248	CS66	Perf. 12½ (F)	30

Ultramarine, Red, Green, Yellow & Black

WX249	CS66	Perf. 11 (B)	30

Seal 100 has designer's name. Puerto Rico used No. WX248.

Values quoted in this catalogue are for stamps graded at Fine-Very Fine and with no faults. An illustrated guide to grade is provided in introductory material, beginning on Page V.

SEALS ISSUED BY AMERICAN LUNG ASSOCIATION

CS67

Designed by Cheri Johnson.
Realized from U.S. sales $36,902,439.
The seals are in 12 designs representing "The 12 Days of Christmas." Inscribed alternately "Christmas 1973" and "Greetings 1973." Illustration shows block from center of top two rows.

1973

Multicolored
Block of 12

WX250	CS67	Perf. 12½ (F), 18x22mm	35
	a.	Size 16½x20½mm(E)	35
WX251	CS67	Perf. 11 (B,W)	35

Seal 100 has designer's name. Puerto Rico used No. WX250 (F).

CS68

Designed by Rubidoux.
Realized from U.S. sales $37,761,745.

1974

Green, Black, Red, Yellow & Blue
Block of Four

WX252	CS68	Perf. 12½ (E,F)	10
WX253	CS68	Perf. 11 (B)	10

Seal 99 has designer's name. Puerto Rico used No. WX252 (F).

C69

Children's paintings of holiday scenes. Different design for each seal, inscribed with name of state or territory. Paintings

by elementary school children were selected in a nationwide campaign ending in January, 1974.
Realized from U.S. contributions $34,710,107.

1975

Multicolored
Sheet of 54 (6x9)

WX254	CS69 Perf. 12½ (S,F)	75
WX255	CS69 Perf. 11 (B)	75

Printers' marks are on seal 28 (New Mexico). Specialty Printers' seals (S) carry union labels: "Scranton 4", "Scranton 7", "E. Stroudsburg".
Puerto Rico used No. WX254 (F).

CS70

Continuous village picture covers sheet with Christmas activities and Santa crossing the sky with sleigh and reindeer. No inscription on 34 seals. Others inscribed "Christmas 1976", "Greetings 1976", and (on 9 bottom-row seals) "American Lung Association". Illustration shows seals 11-12, 20-21.
Realized from U.S. contributions $36,489,207.

1976

Multicolored
Sheet of 54 (9x6)

WX256	CS70 Perf. 12½ (F,N)	75
WX257	CS70 Perf. 11 (B)	75
WX258	CS70 Perf. 13 (S)	75

Printers' marks (N, B, S) on seal 32 and (F) on seal 23.
Puerto Rico used No. WX256 (F).

CS71

Children's paintings of holiday scenes. Different design for each seal, inscribed with name of state or territory.
Realized from U.S. contributions $37,583,883.

1977

Multicolored
Sheet of 54 (6x9)

WX259	CS71 Perf. 12½ (F)	75
WX260	CS71 Perf. 11 (B)	75
WX261	CS71 Perf. 13 (S)	75

Printers' marks on seal 28 (Georgia).
Puerto Rico used No. WX259.

CS72

Children's paintings of holiday scenes. Different design for each seal, inscribed with name of state or territory.
Realized from U.S. contributions $37,621,466.

1978

Multicolored
Sheet of 54 (6x9)

WX262	CS72 Perf. 12½ (F)	75
WX263	CS72 Perf. 11 (B)	75
WX264	CS72 Perf. 13 (S)	75

Printers' marks on seal 29 (New Hampshire).
Puerto Rico used No. WX262.

Type of 1978 Inscribed 1979

Children's paintings of holiday scenes. Different design for each seal, inscribed with name of state or territory.

1979

Multicolored
Sheet of 54 (6x9)

WX265	CS72 Perf. 12½ (F)	75
WX266	CS72 Perf. 11 (B)	75
WX267	CS72 Perf. 13 (S)	75

Printer's marks on seal 22 (Virgin Islands). Puerto Rico used No. WX265.

Beginning in 1979 there is no longer one national issue. Additional designs are issued on a limited basis as test seals to determine the designs to be used the following year.

CONFEDERATE STATES

These stamps and envelopes were issued by individual postmasters generally during the interim between June 1, 1861, when the use of United States stamps stopped in the Confederacy, and October 16, 1861, when the first Confederate Government stamps were issued. They were occasionally issued at later periods, especially in Texas, when regular issues of government stamps were unavailable.

Canceling stamps of the post offices were often used to produce envelopes, some of which were supplied in advance by private citizens. These envelopes and other stationery therefore may be found in a wide variety of papers, colors, sizes and shapes, including patriotic and semi-official types. It is often difficult to determine whether the impression made by the canceling stamp indicates provisional usage or merely postage paid at the time the letter was deposited in the post office. Occasionally the same mark was used for both purposes.

The *press-printed* **provisional envelopes are in a different category. They were produced in quantity, using envelopes procured in advance by the postmaster, such as those of Charleston, Lynchburg, Memphis, etc.** *The* **press-printed** *envelopes are listed and valued on all known papers.*

The **handstamped** *provisional envelopes are listed and valued according to type and variety of handstamp, but not according to paper. Many exist on such a variety of papers that they defy accurate, complete listing. The value of a handstamped provisional envelope is determined primarily by the clarity of the markings and its overall condition and attractiveness, rather than the type of paper. All handstamped provisional envelopes, when used, should also show the postmark of the town of issue.*

Most handstamps are impressed at top right, although they exist from some towns in other positions.

Many illustrations in this section are reduced in size.

Values for envelopes are for entires.

PROVISIONAL ISSUES

Aberdeen, Miss.

Envelopes

E1

Handstamped

1XU1	E1	5c black	2,000.	
1XU2	E1	10c (ms.) on 5c black		—

Abingdon, Va.

Envelopes

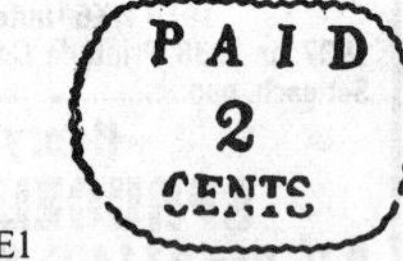

E1

Handstamped

2XU1	E1	2c black		*11,000.*
2XU2	E1	5c black		900.
		On patriotic cover		*3,000.*
2XU3	E1	10c black		*2,500.*

One example known of No. 2XU1.

Albany, Ga.

Envelopes

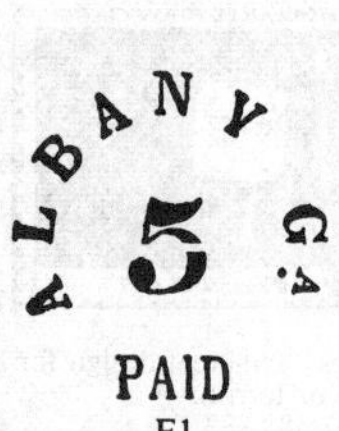

E1

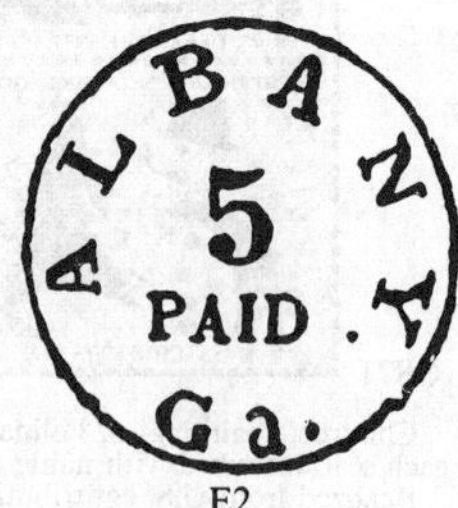

E2

Handstamped

3XU1	E1	5c greenish blue		750.
3XU2	E1	10c greenish blue		1,250.
3XU3	E1	10c on 5c greenish blue		1,750.
3XU5	E2	5c greenish blue		—
3XU6	E2	10c greenish blue		1,350.

Anderson Court House, S.C.

Envelopes

E1

Handstamped

4XU1	E1	5c black		1,000.
4XU2	E1	10c (ms.) black	700.00	*2,500.*

Athens, Ga.

A1 (type I)

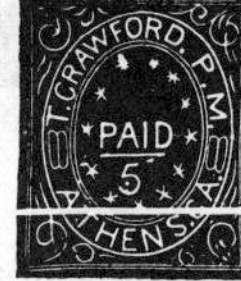

A1 (type II)

Printed from woodcuts of two types. Pairs, both horizontal and vertical, always show one of each type.

5X1	A1	5c purple (shades)	750.	800.
		Pair	—	1,750.
		On cover		2,000.
		Pair on cover		3,250.
		Strip of four on cover (horiz.)		*10,000.*
a.		Tete beche pair (vertical)		4,000.
		Tete beche pair on cover		*7,500.*
5X2	A1	5c red	—	2,500.
		On cover		*8,000.*
		Pair on cover		—

CANCELLATIONS.

Black grid | Black "Paid"
Black town

Atlanta, Ga.

Envelopes

E1

E2

Handstamped

6XU1	E1	5c red		2,000.
6XU2	E1	5c black	150.	750.
		On patriotic cover		*4,000.*
		On U. S. envelope No. U28		—
6XU3	E1	10c on 5c black		1,500.
6XU4	E2	2c black		*3,500.*
6XU5	E2	5c black		800.
		On patriotic cover		2,250.
6XU6	E2	10c black		700.
6XU7	E2	10c on 5c black		2,500.

E3

Handstamped

6XU8	E3	5c black		3,250.
6XU9	E3	10c black ("10" upright)		2,000.

Augusta, Ga.

Envelope

E1

Handstamped

7XU1	E1	5c black		—

Provisional status questioned.

Austin, Miss.

Envelope

E1

Typographed Impressed at top right

8XU1	E1	5c red, *amber*		*15,000.*

Cancellation is black "Paid".

One example known.

Austin, Texas

Envelope

E1

Handstamped

9XU1	E1	10c black		1,500.

Cut squares of No. 9XU1 are known as adhesives on cover.

Autaugaville, Ala.

Envelopes

E1

E2

Handstamped

10XU1	E1	5c black		*8,000.*
10XU2	E2	5c black		*5,000.*

Baton Rouge, La.

P. O.
Baton Rouge, La.
2
J. McCormick

A1

A2

Ten varieties of each

Typeset

11X1 A1 2c green 5,000 3,500.
On cover *10,000.*
a. "McCcrmick" *8,000 7,500.*
a. On cover *12,000.*
11X2 A2 5c green & carmine (Maltese cross border) 1,100. 800.
On cover 2,500.
Strip of three *4,000.*
Strip of five *8,500.*
Canceled in New Orleans, on cover *8,000.*
a. "McCcrmick" — *2,000.*
a. On cover *6,500.*

The "Canceled in New Orleans" examples entered the mails in New Orleans after having been placed (uncanceled) on riverboats in Baton Rouge.

A3

A4

Ten varieties of each

11X3 A3 5c green & car. (crisscross border) *3,000* 1,750.
On cover *7,500.*
a. "McCcrmick" *3,250.*
11X4 A4 10c blue *15,000.*
On cover *95,000.*

Cancellation on Nos. 11X1-11X4: black town.

Beaumont, Texas

A1

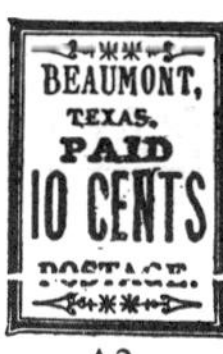

A2

Typeset

Several varieties of each

12X1 A1 10c black, *yellow* — 4,500.
On cover 25,000.
12X2 A1 10c black, *pink* — *4,000.*
On cover *25,000.*
12X3 A2 10c black, *yellow,* on cover *135,000*

Cancellations: black pen; black town.
One example known of No. 12X3.

Bridgeville, Ala.

A1

Handstamped in black within red pen-ruled squares

13X1 A1 5c black & red, pair on cover *20,000.*

Cancellation is black pen.

Canton, Miss.

Envelopes

E1

"P" in star is initial of Postmaster William Priestly.

Handstamped

14XU1 E1 5c black 1,850.
14XU2 E1 10c (ms.) on 5c black 3,500.

Carolina City, N.C.

Envelope

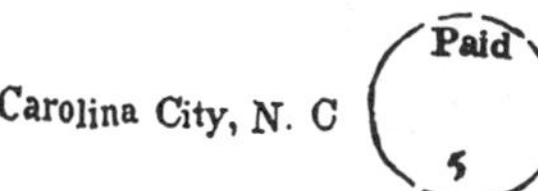

E1

Handstamped

118XU1 E1 5c black

Chapel Hill, N. C.

Envelope

E1

Handstamped

15XU1 E1 5c black 1,750.
On patriotic cover 4,500.

Charleston, S. C.

A1

Litho.

16X1 A1 5c blue 550. 500.
Pair 1,500 1,200.
On cover *1,350.*
On patriotic cover *5,000.*
Pair, on cover *5,000.*

Cancellation: black town (two types).

Envelopes

E1

E2

Typographed from Woodcut

16XU1 E1 5c blue 300. 1,000.
16XU2 E1 5c blue, *amber* 300. 1,000.
16XU3 E1 5c blue, *orange* 300. 1,000.
16XU4 E1 5c blue, *buff* 300. 1,000.
16XU5 E1 5c blue, *blue* 300. 1,000.
16XU6 E2 10c blue, *orange* *16,500.*

One example known of No. 16XU6.

Handstamped

16XU7 E2 10c black *3,000.*

Chattanooga, Tenn.

Envelopes

E1

Handstamped

17XU2 E1 5c black 1,750.
17XU3 E1 5c on 2c black —

Christiansburg, Va.

Envelopes

E1

Typeset

Impressed at top right

99XU1 E1 5c black, *blue* 1,250.
99XU2 E1 5c blue 1,250.
99XU3 E1 5c black, *orange* 1,250.
99XU4 E1 5c green on U.S. envelope No. U27 4,500.
99XU5 E1 10c black, *blue* —

Colaparchee, Ga.

Envelope

E1

Control

Handstamped

119XU1 E1 5c black —

Columbia, S.C.

Envelopes

E1

E2

Handstamped

18XU1 E1 5c blue 135. 750.
18XU2 E1 5c black 235. 750.
18XU3 E1 10c on 5c blue —

Three types of "PAID", one in circle

18XU4 E2 5c blue (seal on front) 1,000.
a. Seal on back 900.
18XU5 E2 10c blue (seal on back) 1,400.

Circular Seal similar to E2, 27mm. diameter

18XU6 E2 5c blue (seal on back) 1,000.

Columbia, Tenn.
Envelope

E1

Handstamped

113XU1 E1 5c red 2,250.

Columbus, Ga.
Envelopes

E1

Handstamped

19XU1 E1 5c blue 1,000.
19XU2 E1 10c red 2,500.

Courtland, Ala.
Envelopes

E1

Handstamped from Woodcut

103XU1 E1 5c black —
103XU2 E1 5c red 10,000.

Provisional status of No. 103XU1 questioned.

Dalton, Ga.
Envelopes

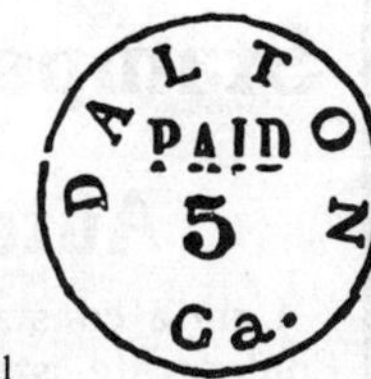

E1

Handstamped

20XU1 E1 5c black 500.
20XU2 E1 10c black 700.
20XU3 E1 10c (ms.) on 5c black 1,000.

Danville, Va.

A1

Typeset
Wove Paper

21X1 A1 5c red 5,500.
Cut to shape 4,000.
On cover 15,000.
On cover, cut to shape 6,000.

Two varieties known.

Laid Paper

21X2 A1 5c red — 6,500.
On cover, cut to shape 10,000.

Cancellation: black town.

Envelopes

E1

E2

E3

Typo.
Two types; "SOUTHERN" in straight or curved line.
Impressed (usually) at top left.

21XU1 E1 5c black 5,500.
21XU2 E1 5c black, *amber* 5,500.
21XU3 E1 5c black, *dark buff* 4,750.

Handstamped

21XU4 E2 10c black 1,250.
21XU5 E2 10c blue 1,250.
21XU6 E3 10c black 1,400.

Types E2 and E3 both exist on one cover.

Demopolis, Ala.
Envelopes

PAID J.Y. Hall.

E1

Handstamped. Signature in ms.

22XU1 E1 5c black ("Jno. Y. Hall") 1,250.
22XU2 E1 5c black ("J. Y. Hall") 1,250.
22XU3 E1 5c (ms.) black ("J. Y. Hall") 1,000.

Eatonton, Ga.
Envelopes

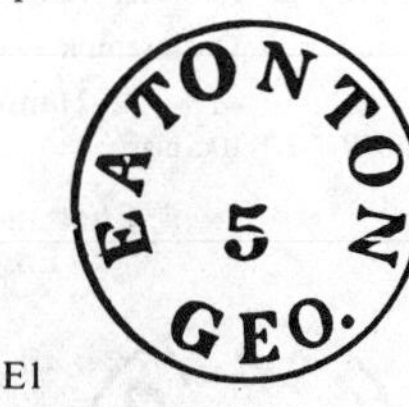

E1

Handstamped

23XU1 E1 5c black 3,000.
23XU2 E1 5c + 5c black 1,250.

Emory, Va.

PAID

A1

Handstamped on margins of sheets of U.S. 1c stamps, 1857 issue. Also known with "5" above "PAID."

24X1 A1 5c blue — 3,500.
On cover 5,500.

Cancellation: blue town.

Envelopes

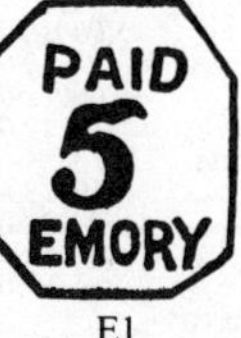

E1

E2

Handstamped

24XU1 E1 5c blue 1,000.
24XU2 E1 10c blue 2,000.

Fincastle, Va.
Envelope

E1

Typeset
Impressed at top right

104XU1 E1 10c black 25,000.

One example known.

Forsyth, Ga.
Envelope

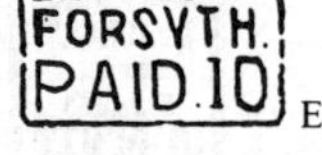

E1

Handstamped

120XU1 E1 10c black 450.

Franklin, N. C.
Envelope

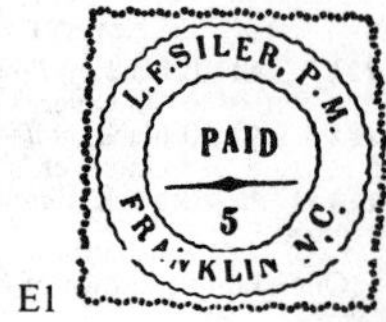

E1

Typographed
Impressed at top right

25XU1 E1 5c blue, *buff* 30,000.

The one known envelope shows black circular Franklin postmark with manuscript date.

Fredericksburg, Va.

A1

Sheets of 20, two panes of 10 varieties each

Typeset — **Thin bluish paper**

26X1 A1 5c blue, *bluish* 200. 600.
Block of four 950.
On cover 2,000.
Pair on cover 7,000.
26X2 A1 10c red, *bluish* 650.
Brown red, *bluish* 650.
Block of four —

Cancellation: black town.

Gainesville, Ala.
Envelopes

E1

E2

Handstamped

27XU1	E1 5c black	1,500.
27XU2	E2 10c ("01") black	*7,500.*

Postmark spells town name "Gainsville".

Galveston, Tex.

Envelopes

E1

Handstamped

98XU1	E1 5c black	500.	2,000.
98XU2	E1 10c black		2,250.

E2

Handstamped

98XU3	E2 10c black	550.	1,000.
98XU4	E2 20c black		*3,500.*

Georgetown, S.C.

Envelope

E1

Control

Handstamped

28XU1	E1 5c black	750.

Goliad, Texas

A1

A2

Typeset

29X1	A1 5c black		*5,000.*
29X2	A1 5c black, *gray*		*4,500.*
29X3	A1 5c black, *rose*		*5,000.*
	On cover		*8,000.*
29X4	A1 10c black	—	*5,000.*
29X5	A1 10c black, *rose*		*5,000.*
	On cover		*7,500.*
	On patriotic cover		—

Type A1 stamps are signed "Clarke-P.M." vertically in black.

29X6	A2 5c black, *gray*	*5,000.*
	Pair	—
	On cover	*7,250.*
a.	"GOILAD"	*5,500.*
	Pair, left stamp the error	*15,000.*
29X7	A2 10c black, *gray*	*5,000.*
	On cover	*7,500.*
a.	"GOILAD"	*5,500.*
a.	On cover	*8,500.*
29X8	A2 5c black, *dark blue*	*6,000.*
	On cover	*8,000.*
29X9	A2 10c black, *dark blue*	*6,500.*
	On cover	*8,500.*

Cancellations in black: pen, town, "Paid"

Gonzales, Texas

Colman & Law were booksellers when John B. Law (of the firm) was appointed Postmaster. The firm used a small lithographed label on the front or inside of books they sold. One variety was used, as listed.

A1

Lithographed on colored glazed paper

30X1	A1 (5c) gold, *dark blue*	*7,500.*
	Pair on cover	*15,000.*

Cancellation: black town. No. 30X1 must bear double-circle town cancel as validating control. All items of type A1 without this control are book labels. The control was applied to the labels in the sheet before their sale as stamps. When used, the stamps bear the additional Gonzales double-circle postmark.

Similar labels in gold on garnet and on black paper are known on cover. Some authorities believe Postmaster Law sold them for use as 10c stamps.

Greensboro, Ala.

Envelopes

E1

E2

Handstamped

31XU1	E1 5c black	1,000.
31XU2	E1 10c black	1,000.
31XU3	E2 10c black	1,250.

Greensboro, N.C.

Envelope

E1

Handstamped

32XU1	E1 10c red	1,500.

Greenville, Ala.

A1

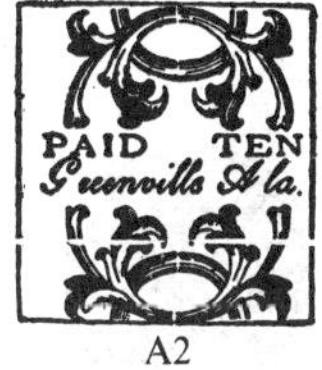

A2

Typeset
Two varieties of each
On pinkish surface-colored glazed paper.
Type I-"Greenville, Ala." in Roman type.
Type II-"Greenville, Ala." in script type.

33X1	A1 5c red & blue, type I	*4,500.*	
a.	Type II	*4,500.*	
	On cover, type I or II		*18,000.*
33X2	A2 10c red & blue, type II	*5,000.*	
	On cover, type II		*20,000.*

Greenville Court House, S.C.

Envelopes

E1 Control

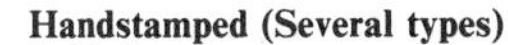

Handstamped (Several types)

34XU1	E1 5c black	800.
34XU2	E1 10c black	900.
34XU3	E1 20c (ms.) on 10c black	1,000.

Envelopes usually bear the black control on the back.

Greenwood Depot, Va.

A1

"PAID" Handstamped; Value and Signature ms.
Laid Paper

35X1	A1 10c black, *gray blue*	*4,500.*	—
	On cover		*16,000.*

Cancellation: black town.

Griffin, Ga.

Envelope

E1

Handstamped

102XU1	E1 5c black	1,150.

Grove Hill, Ala.

A1

Handstamped woodcut

36X1	A1 5c black, on cover	*125,000.*

Cancellations: black town, magenta pen.

Hallettsville, Texas

A1

Handstamped
Ruled Letter Paper

37X1	A1 10c black, *gray blue*, on cover	*15,000.*

Cancellation: black ms.

One example known.

Hamburgh, S.C.

Envelope

E1

Handstamped

112XU1	E1 5c black	1,150.
	On cover with No. 16X1 (forwarded)	—

Helena, Texas

A1

Typeset
Several varieties

38X1	A1	5c black, *buff*	*7,500.*	*5,000.*
38X2	A1	10c black, *gray*		*5,000.*

On 10c "Helena" is in upper and lower case italics.
Cancellation: black town.

Hillsboro, N.C.

A1

Handstamped

39X1	A1	5c black, on cover	*15,000.*

Cancellation: black town.

Houston, Texas
Envelopes

E1

Handstamped

40XU1	E1	5c red	600.
		On patriotic cover	—
40XU2	E1	10c red	1,000.
40XU3	E1	10c black	750.
40XU4	E1	5c +10c red	1,500.
40XU5	E1	10c +10c red	1,500.
40XU6	E1	10c (ms.) on 5c red	*3,000.*

Nos. 40XU2-40XU5 show "TEX" instead of "TXS".

Huntsville, Texas
Envelope

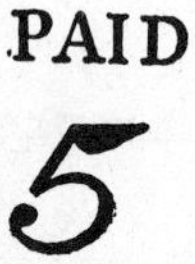

PAID
5
E1

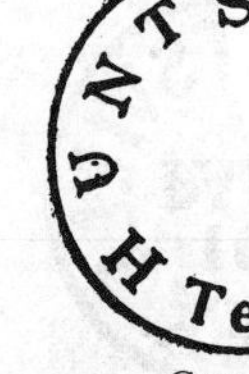

Control

Handstamped

92XU1	E1	5c black	1,350.

No. 92XU1 exists with "5" outside or within control circle.

Independence, Texas

A1

Handstamped

41X1	A1	10c black, *buff*	3,250.	
		On cover		8,000.
41X2	A1	10c black, *dull rose*	3,500.	
		On cover		8,500.

With small "10" and "Pd" in manuscript

41X3	A1	10c black, *buff*, cut to shape	*4,000.*	
		On cover		*10,000.*

Cancellation: black town ("INDEPENDANCE").

Iuka, Miss.
Envelope

I-U-KA
PAID 5 CTS
E1

Typeset

42XU1	E1	5c black	2,000.
		On patriotic cover	3,500.

Jackson, Miss.
Envelopes

E1

Handstamped
Two types of numeral

43XU1	E1	5c black	500.
		On patriotic cover	3,000.
43XU2	E1	10c black	2,750.
43XU3	E1	10c on 5c black	1,350.
43XU4	E1	10c on 5c blue	1,350.

The 5c also exists on a lettersheet.

Jacksonville, Ala.
Envelope

E1

Handstamped

110XU1	E1	5c black	—	1,500.

Jetersville, Va.

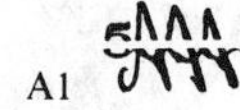
A1

Typeset ("5"); ms. ("AHA.")
Laid Paper

44X1	A1	5c black, vertical pair on cover, uncanceled	16,000.

Initials are those of Postmaster A. H. Atwood.
Cancellation: black town.

Jonesboro, Tenn.
Envelopes

E1

Handstamped

45XU1	E1	5c black	*4,000.*
45XU2	E1	5c dark blue	*4,250.*

Kingston, Ga.
Envelopes

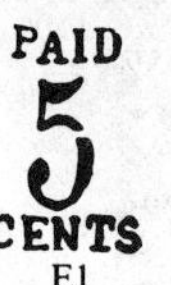

E1

PAID
c 5 s
CENTS
E2

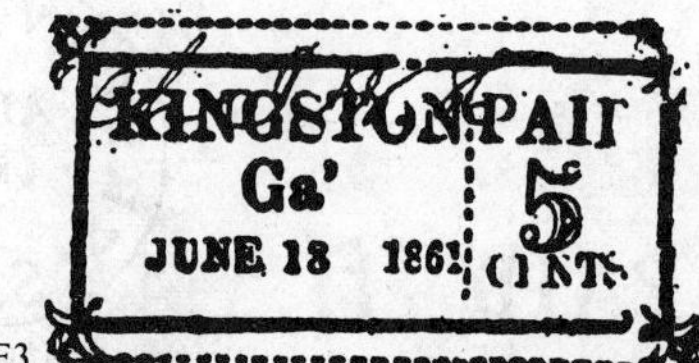

E3

E4

Typographed (E1-E3); Handstamped (E4)

46XU1	E1	5c black		1,000.
46XU2	E2	5c black	—	1,500.
46XU3	E2	5c black, *amber*		1,500.
46XU4	E3	5c black		—
46XU5	E4	5c black		*5,000.*

Knoxville, Tenn.

A1

Woodcut
Grayish Laid Paper

47X1	A1	5c	brick red	*1,000.*	550.
			Horizontal pair	*3,000.*	*1,300.*
			Vertical pair	*2,500.*	
			Vertical strip of three	*5,000.*	
			On cover		*3,500.*
			Pair on cover		*7,500.*
47X2	A1	5c	carmine	*1,500.*	*1,000.*
			Vertical strip of three		—
			On cover		*3,500.*
			Pair on cover		*8,500.*
47X3	A1	10c	green		
			On cover		

CANCELLATIONS.

Black town	Black pen or pencil
Black bars	

The 5c has been reprinted in red, brown and chocolate on white and bluish wove and laid paper.
The authenticity of No. 47X3 has been questioned.

Envelopes

E1

KNOXVILLE
PAID
5
Ten.
E2

Typo.

47XU1	E1	5c blue	500.	1,500.
47XU2	E1	5c blue, *orange*	500.	1,500.
47XU3	E1	10c red (cut to shape)		1,000.
47XU4	E1	10c red, *orange* (cut to shape)		1,000.

Handstamped

47XU5	E2	5c black	500.	2,000.
		On patriotic cover		3,000.
47XU6	E2	10c on 5c black		*3,500.*

Type E2 exists with "5" above or below "PAID".

La Grange, Texas
Envelopes

E1

Handstamped

48XU1	E1	5c black	—	1,250.
48XU2	E1	10c black		1,500.

Lake City, Florida
Envelope

E1 Control

Handstamped

96XU1	E1	10c black	*3,500.*

Envelopes have black circle control mark, or printed name of E. R. Ives, postmaster, on face or back.

Laurens Court House, S.C.
Envelope

E1

Handstamped

116XU1	E1	5c black	—

Lenoir, N.C.

A1

Handstamped from woodcut
White wove paper with cross-ruled orange lines

49X1	A1	5c blue & orange	*3,250.*	*3,000.*
		Pair	—	—
		On cover		*10,000.*

CANCELLATIONS.

Blue town | Blue "Paid" in circle
Black pen

Envelopes

E1

Handstamped

49XU1	A1	5c black	—
49XU2	A1	10c (5c+5c) blue	—
49XU3	E1	5c blue	*3,500.*
49XU4	E1	5c black	900.

Lexington, Miss.
Envelopes

E1

Handstamped

50XU1	E1	5c black	*3,000.*
50XU2	E1	10c black	*4,000.*

Liberty, Va.

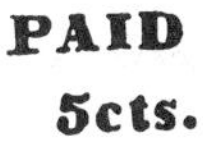

PAID
A1 5cts.

Typeset
Laid Paper

74X1	A1	5c black	—

No. 74X1 is on cover and uncanceled. A cover with Salem, Va., postmark is known.

Limestone Springs, S.C.

5 A1

Handstamped

121X1	A1	5c black, on cover	4,000.
		pair on cover	7,500.

Stamps are round, square or rectangular. Covers are not postmarked.

Livingston, Ala.

A1

Litho.

51X1	A1	5c blue	*7,000.*
		On cover	*30,000.*
		Pair on cover	*150,000.*

Cancellation: black town.

Lynchburg, Va.

A1

Stereotype from Woodcut

52X1	A1	5c blue (shades)	500.	650.
		Pair		1,800.
		On cover		*5,000.*
		Pair on cover		*8,000.*

Cancellations: black town, blue town.

Envelopes

E1

Typo.
Impressed at top right or left

52XU1	E1	5c black		*1,500.*
52XU2	E1	5c black, *amber*	650.	*1,500.*
52XU3	E1	5c black, *buff*		*1,500.*
52XU4	E1	5c black, *brown*	900.	*1,500.*
		On patriotic cover		—

Macon, Ga.

A1

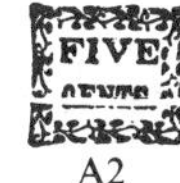

A2

FIVE

A3

A4

Typeset | **Wove Paper**

Several varieties of type A1, 10 of A2, 5 of A3.

53X1	A1	5c black, *light blue green* (shades)	800.	600.
		On cover		*3,500.*
		Pair on cover		*8,000.*
53X3	A2	5c black, *yellow*	2,250.	750.
		On cover		*4,000.*
		On patriotic cover		*8,000.*
		Pair on cover		*6,000.*
53X4	A3	5c black, *yellow* (shades)	2,250.	1,000.
		On cover		*3,500.*
		Pair on cover		*8,000.*
	a.	Vertical tete beche pair		*12,000.*
53X5	A4	2c black, *gray green*		*6,500.*
		On cover		*15,000.*

Laid Paper

53X6	A2	5c black, *yellow*	*3,000.*	*3,500.*
		On cover		*6,000.*
53X7	A3	5c black, *yellow*	*6,000.*	
		On cover		*9,000.*
53X8	A1	5c black, *light blue green*	1,750.	*2,000.*
		On cover		*3,750.*

Cancellations: black town, black "PAID" (2 types).

Envelope

E1

Handstamped
Two types: PAID over 5, 5 over PAID

53XU1	E1	5c black	250.	500.

Marietta, Ga.
Envelopes

E1

PAID
5

E2

Handstamped
Two types of "PAID" and numerals

54XU1	E1	5c black	400.
54XU2	E2	10c on 5c black E1	1,200.

With Double Circle Control

54XU3	E2	10c black	750.
54XU4	E2	5c black	450.

Marion, Va.

A1

Typeset frame, with handstamped numeral in center

55X1	A1	5c black		*5,000.*
		On cover		*12,000.*
55X2	A1	10c black	*16,500.*	*8,000.*
		On cover		*12,000.*

Bluish Laid Paper

55X3	A1	5c black	—

Cancellations: black town, black "PAID".
The 2c, 3c, 15c and 20c are believed to be bogus.

Memphis, Tenn.

A1

A2

Stereotype from woodcut

Plate of 50 (5x10) for the 2c. The stereotypes for the 5c stamps were set in 5 vertical rows of 8, with at least 2 rows set sideways to the right (see Thomas H. Pratt's monograph, "The Postmaster's Provisionals of Memphis").

56X1 A1 2c blue (shades) 75. *750.*
Block of four 500.
On cover *7,500.*
Cracked plate (16, 17, 18) 125. *850.*

The "cracking off" (breaking off) of the plate at right edge caused incomplete printing of stamps in positions 5, 10, 15, 20, and 50. Poor make-ready also caused incomplete printing in position 50.

56X2 A2 5c red (shades) 150. 200.
Pair *350.* 500.
Block of four *800.*
On cover 1,000.
Pair on cover 2,250.
Strip of four on cover *7,000.*
On patriotic cover *4,000.*
a. Tete beche pair 1,500.
Tete beche pair on cover *10,000.*
b. Pair, one sideways 750.
c. Pelure paper — —

Cancellation on Nos. 56X1-56X2: black town.

Envelopes

Typo.

56XU1 A2 5c red *2,500.*
56XU2 A2 5c red, *amber* *2,500.*
With No. 1 *5,000.*
56XU3 A2 5c red, *orange* *2,750.*
On patriotic cover *4,000.*

Micanopy, Fla.

Envelope

E1

Handstamped

105XU1 E1 5c black *11,500.*

One example known.

Milledgeville, Ga.

Envelopes

E1

Handstamped

57XU1 E1 5c black 300.
57XU2 E1 5c blue 400.
57XU3 E1 10c on 5c black 850.

E2 E3

57XU4 E2 10c black 225. 750.
57XU5 E3 10c black 750.

Mobile, Ala.

A1

Litho.

58X1 A1 2c black 1,250. 700.
Pair *1,500.*
On cover *2,500.*

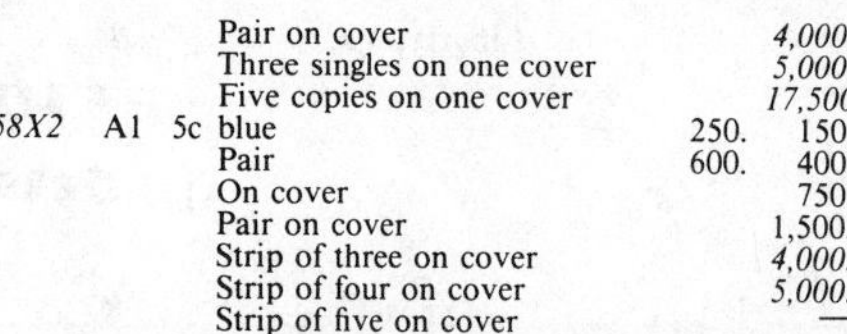

Pair on cover *4,000.*
Three singles on one cover *5,000.*
Five copies on one cover *17,500.*
58X2 A1 5c blue 250. 150.
Pair 600. 400.
On cover 750.
Pair on cover 1,500.
Strip of three on cover *4,000.*
Strip of four on cover *5,000.*
Strip of five on cover —

Cancellations: black town, express company.

Montgomery, Ala.

Envelopes

E1

Handstamped

59XU1 E1 5c red 1,000.
59XU2 E1 5c blue 400. 1,200.
59XU3 E1 10c red 1,000.
59XU4 E1 10c blue 1,250.
59XU5 E1 10c black 1,000.
59XU6 E1 10c on 5c red *2,000.*

The 10c design is larger than the 5c.

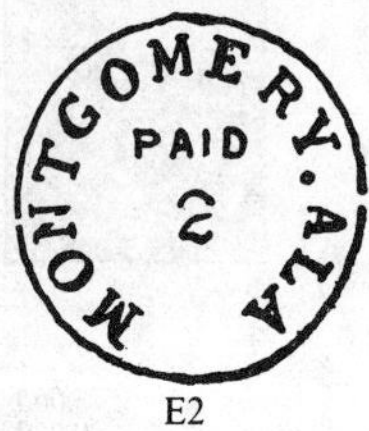

E2

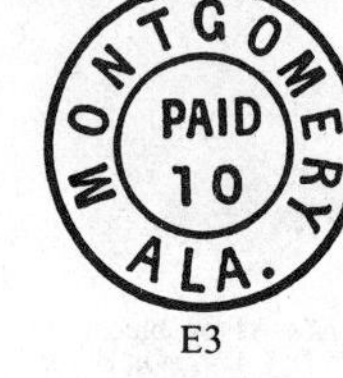

E3

59XU7 E2 2c red —
59XU7A E2 2c blue 3,000.
59XU8 E2 5c black 1,000.
59XU9 E3 10c black 1,500.
59XU10 E3 10c red 1,500.

Mt. Lebanon, La.

A1

Woodcut, Design Reversed

60X1 A1 5c red brown, on cover *100,000.*

Cancellation black pen. One example known.

Nashville, Tenn.

A1

A2

Typeset (5 varieties of 3c)

61X1 A1 3c carmine 125.
Horizontal strip of five 750.

No. 61X1 was not placed in use.

Stereotype from Woodcut

Gray Blue Ribbed Paper

61X2 A2 5c carmine (shades) 700. 400.
Pair 1,000.
On cover 1,750.
On patriotic cover *4,500.*
Pair on cover *6,000.*
On cover with U.S. 3c 1857 (express) *5,000.*
a. Vertical tete beche pair *2,000.*
61X3 A2 5c brick red 700. 400.
On cover 1,500.
On patriotic cover *5,000.*
Pair on cover *4,500.*
On U.S. envelope No. U26 —
On U.S. #U27 with #26 (express) *26,000.*
61X4 A2 5c gray (shades) 700. 500.
On cover *2,000.*
Pair on cover *5,000.*
61X5 A2 5c violet brown 600. 400.
Block of four —
On cover 1,750.
On patriotic cover —
Pair on cover *4,500.*
a. Vertical tete beche pair *3,500.* *2,500.*
Vert. tete beche pair on cover —
61X6 A2 10c green *3,000.* *2,250.*
On cover *10,000.*
On cover with U.S. 3c 1857 —
On cover with No. 61X2 *12,000.*

CANCELLATIONS. Nos. 61X2-61X5

Blue "Paid"	Blue express company
Blue "Post-age Paid"	
Blue town	Black express company
Blue numer-al "5"	
Blue numer-al "10"	

Envelopes

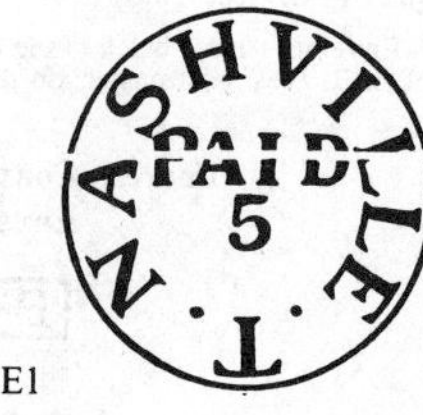

E1

Handstamped

61XU1 E1 5c blue 900.
On patriotic envelope 1,750.
61XU2 E1 5c +10c blue 1,500.

New Orleans, La.

A1

A2

Plate of 40

Stereotype from Woodcut

62X1 A1 2c blue, *July 14, 1861* 100. 400.
Pair 400. 900.
Block of four *4,500.*
On cover *3,000.*
On patriotic cover *7,500.*
Pair on cover *7,500.*
Three singles on one cover *8,500.*
Strip of five on cover *17,500.*
On U.S. envelope No. U27 —
a. Printed on both sides —
62X2 A1 2c red (shades), *Jan. 6, 1862* 100. *650.*
Pair 250.
Block of four *1,500.*
On cover *25,000.*
62X3 A2 5c brown, *white, June 12, 1861* 200. 125.
Pair 425. 275.
Block of four 1,500.
On cover 375.
On patriotic cover *3,500.*
Pair on cover 750.
Strip of 5 on cover *5,000.*
On cover with U.S. No. 30A —
a. Printed on both sides *1,000.*
b. 5c ocher, *June 18, 1861* 500. 350.
Pair 850.
On cover 1,500.
On patriotic cover *5,000.*
Pair on cover 2,500.
62X4 A2 5c red brown, *bluish, Aug. 22, 1861* 220. 95.
Pair 475. 195.
Horizontal strip of 6 *2,000.*
Block of four 1,500.
On cover 275.
On patriotic cover *3,500.*
Pair on cover 650.
Block of four on cover *5,000.*
On cover with No. 1 *5,000.*
a. Printed on both sides *1,050.*
62X5 A2 5c yel brn, *off-white, Dec. 3, 1861* 90. 200.
Pair 200. 450.
Block of four 500.
On cover 475.
On patriotic cover *2,500.*
Pair on cover 1,000.
Strip of 5 on cover —
62X6 A2 5c red — *7,500.*
62X7 A2 5c red, *bluish* *10,000.*

CANCELLATIONS. Nos. 62X3-62X5.

Black town (single or double circle New Orleans)	Black "Paid"
Red town (double circle New Orleans)	Express Company
Town other than New Orleans	Packet boat, cover "STEAM"
Postmaster's handstamp	"Southn Letter Unpaid" on cover with U.S. No. 26

Envelopes

J.L.RIDDELL,P.M
PD 5 CTS
N O.P.O

E1

Handstamped

62XU1	E1	5c black	3,500.
62XU2	E1	10c black	*5,000.*

"J. L. RIDDELL, P. M." omitted

62XU3	E1	2c black	*7,500.*

New Smyrna, Fla.

A1

Handstamped
On white paper with blue ruled lines

63X1	A1	10c ("O1") on 5c black	*50,000.*

One example known. It is uncanceled on a postmarked patriotic cover.

Oakway, S.C.

A1

Handstamped

115X1	A1	5c black, on cover	—	12,000.

Pensacola, Fla.
Envelopes

E1

Handstamped

106XU1	E1	5c black	*4,000.*
106XU2	E1	10c (ms.) on 5c black	*4,250.*
		On patriotic cover	*13,500.*

Petersburg, Va.

A1

Typeset
Ten varieties
Thick white paper

65X1	A1	5c red	*600.*	400.
		Pair	*1,500.*	1,000.
		Block of four	*4,500.*	
		On cover		1,500.
		On patriotic cover		—
		Pair on cover		*5,500.*
		On cover with General Issue stamp No. 1		*7,500.*

Cancellation: blue town.

Pittsylvania Court House, Va.

A1

Typeset
Wove Paper

66X1	A1	5c dull red	*6,000.*	*5,000.*
		octagonally cut		*4,000.*
		On cover		*20,000.*
		On cover, octagonally cut		*15,000.*
		On patriotic cover, octagonally cut		*17,500.*

Laid Paper

66X2	A1	5c dull red		*6,500.*
		Octagonally cut		*5,500.*
		On cover		*20,000.*
		On cover, octagonally cut		*15,000.*

Cancellation: black town.

Pleasant Shade, Va.

A1

Typeset
Five varieties

67X1	A1	5c blue	*2,500.*	*4,500.*
		On cover		*15,000.*
		Pair on cover		*65,000.*
		Pair	*5,500.*	
		Block of six	*25,000.*	

Cancellation: blue town.

Port Lavaca, Tex.

A1

Typeset

107X1	A1	10c black	*25,000.*

One example known. It is uncanceled on a postmarked cover.

Raleigh, N. C.
Envelopes

E1

Handstamped

68XU1	E1	5c red	425.
		On patriotic cover	2,500.
		On U.S. envelope No. U10	*1,500.*
68XU2	E1	5c blue	1,000.

Rheatown, Tenn.

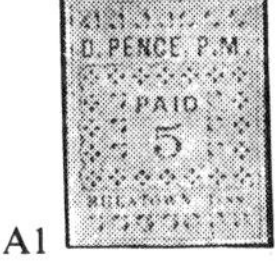

A1

Typeset
Three varieties

69X1	A1	5c red	*2,000.*	*2,750.*
		On cover		*8,500.*
		Pair	*5,000.*	
		Pen cancellation		*2,000.*

Cancellations: red town or black pen.

Richmond, Texas
Envelopes or Letter Sheets

E1

Handstamped

70XU1	E1	5c red	2,500.
70XU2	E1	10c red	2,500.
70XU3	E1	10c on 5c red	5,000.
70XU4	E1	15c (ms.) on 10c red	—

Ringgold, Ga.
Envelope

E1

Handstamped

71XU1	E1	5c blue black	*4,000.*

Rutherfordton, N.C.

A1

Handstamped; "Paid 5cts" in ms.

72X1	A1	5c black, cut round	*25,000.*

No. 72X1 is on cover and uncanceled.

Salem, N.C.
Envelopes

E1

E2

Handstamped

73XU1	E1	5c black	750.
73XU2	E1	10c black	850.
73XU3	E2	5c black	750.
73XU4	E2	10c on 5c black	1,600.

Reprints exist on various papers. They either lack the "Paid" and value or have them counterfeited.

Salem, Va.
See No. 74X1 under Liberty, Va.

Salisbury, N.C.
Envelope

SALISBURY.
N. C.
POSTAGE

FIVE CENTS
P.M.

E1

Typographed
Impressed at top left

75XU1	E1	5c black, *greenish*	*5,000.*

One example known. Part of envelope is torn away, leaving part of design missing. Illustration E1 partly suppositional.

San Antonio, Texas
Envelopes

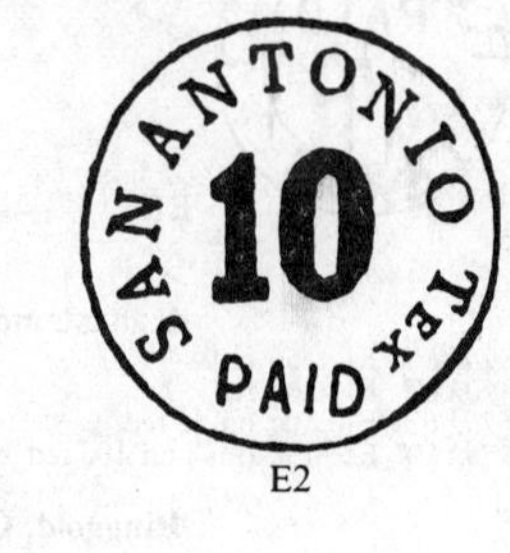

E1 E2

Control

Handstamped

76XU1	E1	10c black	275.	1,100.
76XU2	E2	10c black		1,250.

Black circle control mark is on front or back.

Savannah, Ga.
Envelopes

E1

E2 Control

Handstamped

101XU1	E1	5c black	300.
101XU2	E2	5c black	450.
101XU3	E1	10c black	500.
101XU4	E2	10c black	500.
101XU5	E1	10c on 5c black	1,500.
101XU6	E2	20c on 5c black	3,000.

Envelopes must have octagonal control mark.

Selma, Ala.
Envelopes

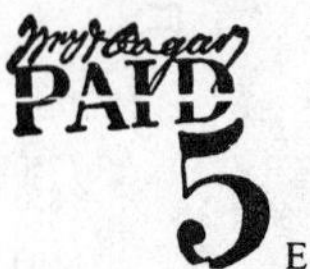

E1

Handstamped; Signature in ms.

77XU1	E1	5c black	*1,500.*
77XU2	E1	10c black	*2,500.*
77XU3	E1	10c on 5c black	*3,000.*

Signature is that of Postmaster William H. Eagar.

Sparta, Ga.
Envelopes

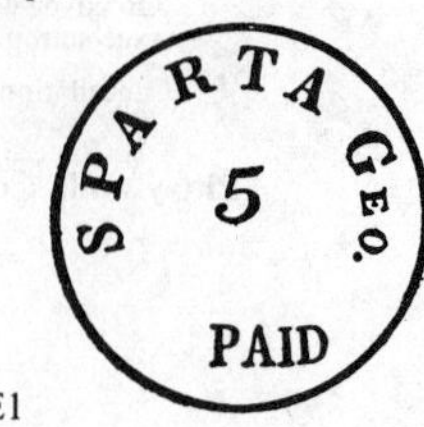

E1

Handstamped

93XU1	E1	5c red	—	750.
93XU2	E1	10c red		1,000.

Spartanburg, S.C.

A1

A2

Handstamped on Ruled or Plain Wove Paper

78X1	A1	5c black	*2,500.*
		On cover	*12,500.*
		Pair on cover	—
		On patriotic cover	*15,000.*
a.		"5" omitted (on cover)	—
78X2	A2	5c black, *bluish*	*3,000.*
		On cover	*12,500.*
78X3	A2	5c black, *brown*	*3,000.*
		On cover	*15,000.*

Most examples of Nos. 78X1-78X3 are cut round. Cut square examples are worth much more.
Cancellations: black "PAID", black town.

Statesville, N.C.
Envelopes

E1

Handstamped

79XU1	E1	5c black	135.	*700.*
79XU2	E1	10c on 5c black		1,500.

Sumter, S.C.
Envelopes

E1

Handstamped

80XU1	E1	5c black	150.	
80XU2	E1	10c black	100.	
80XU3	E1	10c on 5c black		175.
80XU4	E1	2c (ms.) on 10c black		*800.*

Used examples of Nos. 80XU1-80XU2 are indistinguishable from handstamped "Paid" covers.

U.S. Proofs are listed and valued in a separate section of the catalogue. See catalogue index.

Talbotton, Ga.
Envelopes

E1

Handstamped

94XU1	E1	5c black	750.
		On U.S. envelope No. U27	—
94XU2	E1	10c black	500.
94XU3	E1	10c on 5c black	1,000.

Tellico Plains, Tenn.

A1

Typeset
Settings of two 5c and one 10c
Laid Paper

81X1	A1	5c red	800.	
		On cover		17,500.
81X2	A1	10c red	1,500.	
		Se-tenant with 5c	*2,500.*	
		Strip of three (5c+5c+10c)	*3,500.*	

Cancellation: black pen.

Thomasville, Ga.
Envelopes

E1 Control

Handstamped

82XU1	E1	5c black	1,000.

E2

82XU2	E2	5c black	900.

Tullahoma, Tenn.
Envelope

E1

Control

Handstamped

111XU1	E1	10c black	*3,000.*

Tuscaloosa, Ala.
Envelopes

PAID 5

E1

Handstamped

83XU1	E1	5c black	250.
83XU2	E1	10c black	250.

Used examples of Nos. 83XU1-83XU2 are indistinguishable from handstamped "Paid" covers. Some authorities question the use of E1 to produce provisional envelopes.

Tuscumbia, Ala.
Envelopes

E1

Handstamped

84XU1	E1	5c black	1,900.
		On patriotic cover	—
84XU2	E1	5c red	2,100.
84XU3	E1	10c black	3,500.

See U.S. Postmasters' Provisional No. 12XU1.

Union City, Tenn.

E1

The use of E1 to produce provisional envelopes is doubtful.

Uniontown, Ala.

A1

Typeset in settings of four (2x2)
Four varieties of each value
Laid Paper

86X1	A1	2c dark blue, *gray blue*	9,500.	—
86X2	A1	2c dark blue	5,500.	
		Block of four	30,000.	
86X3	A1	5c green, *gray blue*	2,750.	2,000.
		Pair	—	
		On cover		6,500.
86X4	A1	5c green	2,750.	2,000.
		On cover		6,500.
		Pair on cover		18,500.
86X5	A1	10c red, *gray blue*	8,000.	5,000.
		On cover		22,500.

Two examples known of No. 86X1, both on cover (drop letters), one uncanceled and one pen canceled.
Cancellation on Nos. 86X3-86X5: black town.

Unionville, S.C.

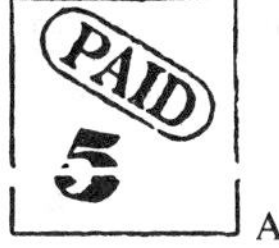

A1

Handstamped in two impressions
Paper with Blue Ruled Lines

87X1	A1	5c black, *grayish*, on cover	*13,500.*
		Pair on patriotic cover	*32,500.*

Cancellation: black town.

Valdosta, Ga.
Envelope

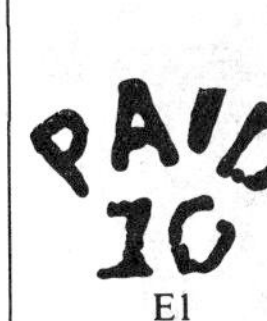

E1

Control

Handstamped

100XU1	E1	10c black	800.

The black circle control is usually on back of envelope.

Victoria, Texas

A1

Typeset
Surface colored paper

88X1	A1	5c red brown, *green*	4,000.	
88X2	A1	10c red brown, *green*	4,250.	4,500.
		On cover		17,500.
88X3	A1	10c red brown, *green* ("10" in bold face type), pelure paper	5,500.	5,250.

Walterborough, S.C.
Envelopes

E1

Typeset

108XU1	E1	10c black, *buff*	2,000.
108XU2	E1	10c carmine	4,000.

Warrenton, Ga.
Envelopes

E1

Handstamped

89XU1	E1	5c black	1,250.
89XU2	E1	10c (ms.) on 5c black	1,000.

Washington, Ga.
Envelope

PAID 10 E1

Handstamped

117XU1	E1	10c black	1,500.

Envelopes must have black circle control on front or back.

Weatherford, Tex.
Envelopes

E1

Woodcut with "PAID" inserted in type.

Handstamped

109XU1	E1	5c black	*2,000.*
109XU2	E1	5c +5c black	*16,000.*

Winnsborough, S.C.
Envelopes

E1

Control

Handstamped

97XU1	E1	5c black	*1,000.*
97XU2	E1	10c black	*1,000.*

Envelopes must have black circle control on front or back.

Wytheville, Va.
Envelope

E1

Control

Handstamped

114XU1	E1	5c black	900.

For later additions, listed out of numerical sequence, see-

#*74X1*, Liberty, Va.
#*92XU1*, Huntsville, Tex.
#*93XU1*, Sparta, Ga.
#*94XU1*, Talbotton, Ga.
#*96XU1*, Lake City, Fla.
#*97XU1*, Winnsborough, S. C.
#*98XU1*, Galveston, Tex.
#*99XU1*, Christiansburg, Va.
#*100XU1*, Valdosta, Ga.
#*101XU1*, Savannah, Ga.
#*102XU1*, Griffin, Ga.
#*103XU1*, Courtland, Ala.
#*104XU1*, Fincastle, Va.
#*105XU1*, Micanopy, Fla.
#*106XU1*, Pensacola, Fla.
#*107X1*, Port Lavaca, Tex.
#*108XU1*, Walterborough, S. C.
#*109XU1*, Weatherford, Tex.
#*110XU1*, Jacksonville, Ala.
#*111XU1*, Tullahoma, Tenn.
#*112XU1*, Hamburgh, S. C.
#*113XU1*, Columbia, Tenn.
#*114XU1*, Wytheville, Va.
#*115X1*, Oakway, S. C.
#*116XU1*, Laurens Court House, S. C.
#*117XU1*, Washington, Ga.
#*118XU1*, Carolina City, N.C.
#*119XU1*, Colaparchee, Ga.
#*120XU1*, Forsyth, Ga.
#*121XU1*, Limestone Springs, S.C.

GENERAL ISSUES

For explanations of various terms used see the notes at the end of these listings.

Jefferson Davis – A1

1861 Litho. Soft Porous Paper *Imperf.*

All 5c Lithographs were printed by Hoyer & Ludwig, of Richmond, Va.

Stones A or B-First stones used. Earliest dated cancellation October 16, 1861. Plating not completed hence size of sheets unknown. These stones had imprints. Stamps from Stones A or B are nearly all in the olive green shade. Sharp, clear impressions. Distinctive marks are few and minute.

Stone 1-Earliest dated cancellation October 18, 1861. Plating completed. Sheet consists of four groups of fifty varieties arranged in two panes of one hundred each without imprint. The first small printing was in olive green and later small printings appeared in light and dark green; the typical shade, however, is an intermediate shade of bright green. The impressions are clear though not as sharp as those from Stones A or B. Distinctive marks are discernible.

Stone 2-Earliest dated cancellation December 2, 1861. Plating completed. Sheet consists of four groups of fifty varieties arranged in two panes of one hundred each without imprint. All shades other than olive green are known from this stone, the commonest being a dull green. Poor impressions. Many noticeable distinctive marks.

UNUSED

				Stones A or B	Stone 1	Stone 2
1	A1	**5c**	**green**		140.00	130.00
			bright green		140.00	130.00
			dull green		140.00	130.00
		a.	5c light green		125.00	135.00
		b.	5c dark green		130.00	140.00
		c.	5c olive green	150.00	140.00	
			Pair	375.00	325.00	325.00
			Block of four	1,000.	700.00	700.00

USED

				Stones A or B	Stone 1	Stone 2
1	A1	**5c**	**green**		100.00	100.00
			bright green		100.00	100.00
			dull green		100.00	100.00
		a.	5c light green		100.00	100.00
		b.	5c dark green		110.00	110.00
		c.	5c olive green	130.00	120.00	
			On cover	200.00	150.00	150.00
			Single on cover (overpaid drop letter)			250.00
			On wallpaper cover			500.00
			On prisoner's cover			—
			On prisoner's cover with U.S. #65			—
			On prisoner's cover with U.S. #U34			—
			On partriotic cover	1,200.	1,000.	1,000.
			Pair	300.00	225.00	225.00
			Pair on cover	350.00	300.00	250.00
			Block of four	750.00	600.00	600.00
			Horiz. pair, vert. gutter between			—

CANCELLATIONS

	Stones A or B	Stone 1	Stone 2
Blue town	+10.00	+10.00	+10.00
Red town	+110.00	+80.00	+80.00
Green town		+175.00	+150.00
Orange town			+100.00
Texas town		+35.00	+35.00
Arkansas town		+90.00	+90.00
Florida town		+110.00	+110.00
Kentucky town		+200.00	+200.00
October, 1861, year date	+50.00	+40.00	
Blue gridiron	+5.00	+5.00	+5.00
Red gridiron		+50.00	+50.00
Blue concentric	+5.00	+5.00	+5.00
Star or flowers			+100.00
Numeral	+60.00	+50.00	+50.00
"Paid"	+50.00	+50.00	+50.00
"Steam"	+150.00	+150.00	
"Steamboat"		+150.00	+150.00
Express Company	+400.00	+350.00	+350.00
Railroad		+300.00	+300.00

VARIETIES

	Unused	Used
White curl back of head (S A or B)	175.00	150.00
Imprint (S A or B)	400.00	300.00
Acid flaw (S 1)	175.00	110.00
Arrow between panes (S 1)	300.00	200.00
Flaw on "at" of "States" (38 S 1)	175.00	150.00
Spur on upper left scroll (21 S 2)	175.00	150.00
Bottom scrolls doubled (re-entry 50 S 2)	275.00	200.00
Side margin copy showing initials (41 S 2 or 50 S 2)	575.00	425.00
Misplaced transfer (S 2)	350.00	575.00
Rouletted unofficially	—	325.00

Thomas Jefferson – A2

1861-62 Litho. Soft Porous Paper

Hoyer & Ludwig-First stone used. Earliest dated cancellation November 8, 1861. Sheet believed to consist of four groups of fifty varieties each arranged in two panes of one hundred each with imprint at bottom of each pane. Two different imprints are known. Hoyer & Ludwig printings are always in a uniform shade of dark blue. Impressions are clear and distinct, especially so in the early printings. Plating marks are distinct.

J. T. Paterson & Co.-Earliest dated cancellation July 25, 1862. Sheet consists of four groups of fifty varieties each arranged in two panes of one hundred each with imprint at bottom of each pane. Two different imprints are known and at least one pane is known without an imprint. Wide range of shades. Impressions are less clear than those from the Hoyer & Ludwig stone. Paterson stamps show small vertical colored dash below the lowest point of the upper left triangle.

Stone "Y"-Supposedly made by J. T. Paterson & Co., as it shows the distinctive mark of that firm. Plating not completed hence size of sheet unknown. No imprint found. Color is either a light milky blue or a greenish blue. Impressions are very poor and have a blurred appearance. Stone Y stamps invariably show a large flaw back of the head as well as small vertical colored dash beneath the upper left triangle.

UNUSED

				Hoyer	Paterson	Stone Y
2	A2	**10c**	**blue**		180.00	
		a.	10c light blue		180.00	
			light milky blue			
		b.	10c dark blue	325.00	275.00	
		c.	10c indigo		—	
		e.	10c greenish blue			275.00
			Pair	600.00	500.00	750.00
			Block of four	1,500.	1,200.	—
			Horiz. pair, gutter btwn.		750.00	

USED

				Hoyer	Paterson	Stone Y
2	A2	**10c**	**blue**		140.00	
		a.	10c light blue		140.00	
			light milky blue			175.00
		b.	10c dark blue	130.00	180.00	
		c.	10c indigo		—	
		e.	10c greenish blue			225.00
			On cover	300.00	175.00	375.00
			On wallpaper cover	700.00	650.00	
			On patriotic cover	1,500.	1,350.	1,750.
			On prisoner's cover with U.S. #65	—	—	
			Pair	475.00	400.00	—
			Pair on cover	1,000.	650.00	
			Strip of 3 on cover	3,500.	—	
			Block of four	—		1,750.

	Hoyer	Paterson	Stone Y
Blue town	+30.00	+10.00	+10.00
Red town	+75.00	+75.00	+100.00
Green town		+200.00	+300.00
Violet town		—	
Texas town	+125.00	+125.00	+125.00
Arkansas town	+275.00	+275.00	+275.00
Florida town	+325.00	+325.00	—
Kentucky town	+400.00		
Nov., 1861, date	+300.00		
July, 1862, date		+300.00	
Straight line town	+500.00	+500.00	+500.00
Blue gridiron	+10.00	+10.00	+10.00
Red gridiron	+50.00	+50.00	+50.00
Blue concentric	+10.00	+10.00	+10.00
Numeral	+75.00	+80.00	+100.00
"Paid"	+50.00	+75.00	+100.00
Star or flower		+150.00	
Railroad	+350.00	+350.00	
Express Company	+300.00	+300.00	

VARIETIES

		Unused	Used
	Malformed "T" of "TEN" (No. 4 Hoyer)	275.00	200.00
	"G" and "E" of "POSTAGE" joined (No. 10 Hoyer)	275.00	200.00
	Circular flaw, upper left star (No. 11 Hoyer)	275.00	200.00
	Third spiked ornament at right, white (No. 45 Hoyer)	275.00	200.00
	Hoyer & Ludwig imprint	450.00	500.00
d.	Printed on both sides (Hoyer)	—	
d.	Printed on both sides (Pat.)	—	—
	Malformed "O" of "POSTAGE" (No. 25 Pat.)	225.00	175.00
	J. T. Paterson & Co. imprint	500.00	800.00

Andrew Jackson – A3

1862 (March) Soft Porous Paper. Litho.

Sheet consists of four groups of fifty varieties arranged in two panes of 100 each.

One stone only was used. Date of issue, probably March, 1862. Printed by Hoyer & Ludwig, of Richmond, Va. Issued to prepay drop letter and circular rates. Strips of five used to prepay regular 10c rate, which was changed from 5c on July 1, 1862. Earliest known cancellation, March 21, 1862.

				Unused	Used
3	A3	**2c**	**green**	400.00	450.00
			light green	400.00	450.00
			dark green	400.00	450.00
			dull yellow green	450.00	
			On cover		—
			Pair on cover (double circular rate)		*2,500.*
			Strip of five on cover		*8,000.*
			On patriotic cover		*10,000.*
			Pair		—
			Block of four	1,750.	2,250.
			Block of five	2,750.	3,250.
		a.	2c bright yellow green	*1,250.*	*1,750.*
		a.	On cover		—
		a.	Strip of five on cover		—
			Diagonal half used as 1c with unsevered pair, on cover		—
			Horiz. pair, vert. gutter between	—	—
			Mark between stamps (between Nos. 4 and 5)	1,100.	1,500.
			Mark above upper right corner (No. 30)	500.00	650.00
			Mark above upper left corner (No. 31)	500.00	650.00
			Acid flaw	475.00	600.00

CANCELLATIONS.

Blue town	+500.00	Blue gridiron	+250.00
Red town	+800.00	"Paid"	—
Arkansas town	—	Express Company	—
Texas town	+1,250.	Railroad	+3,000.
		Pen	375.00

1862 Soft Porous Paper. Litho.

Stone 2-First stone used for printing in blue. Plating is the same as Stone 2 in green. Earliest dated cancellation Feb. 28, 1862. Printings from Stone 2 are found in all shades of blue. Rough, coarse impressions are typical of printings from Stone 2.

Stone 3-A new stone used for printings in blue only. Earliest dated cancellation April 10, 1862. Sheet consists of four groups of fifty varieties each arranged in two panes of one hundred each without imprint. Impressions are clear and sharp, often having a proof-like appearance, especially in the deep blue printing. Plating marks, while not so large as on Stone 2 are distinct and clearly defined.

UNUSED

				Stone 2	Stone 3
4	A1	**5c**	**blue**	100.00	
			light blue	105.00	
		a.	5c dark blue	120.00	145.00
		b.	5c light milky blue	120.00	170.00
			Pair	250.00	325.00
			Block of four	600.00	800.00
			Horiz. pair, wide gutter between	725.00	—

			Vert. pair, narrow gutter between	—	—

USED

4	A1	5c	**blue**	80.00	
			light blue	85.00	
		a.	5c dark blue	100.00	125.00
		b.	5c light milky blue	100.00	150.00
			On cover	200.00	275.00
			Single on cover (overpaid drop letter)	275.00	
			Pair on cover	300.00	400.00
			On wallpaper cover	550.00	
			On patriotic cover	1,250.	1,500.
			On prisoner's cover	2,000.	
			On prisoner's cover with U.S. #65	—	
			Pair	225.00	350.00
			Block of four	1,300.	1,400.
			Horiz. pair, wide gutter btwn.	—	
			CANCELLATIONS	Stone 2	Stone 3
			Blue town	+20.00	+40.00
			Red town	+75.00	+75.00
			Texas town	+300.00	+300.00
			Arkansas town	+325.00	+325.00
			Florida town	+200.00	
			Straight line town	+300.00	+325.00
			Blue gridiron	+10.00	+10.00
			Red gridiron	+65.00	
			Star or Flowers	+100.00	+100.00
			Numeral	+85.00	
			Railroad	—	
			"Paid"	+25.00	+50.00
			"Steamboat"	+400.00	
			Express Company	—	
			"Way"	+250.00	

VARIETIES

	Unused	Used
Spur on upper left scroll (21 S 2)	125.00	100.00
Thin hard paper (S 2)		85.00
Tops of "C" and "E" of "cents" joined by flaw (33 S 3)	185.00	185.00
"Flying bird" above lower left corner ornament (19 S 3)	175.00	175.00

1862 (March) Soft Porous Paper. Litho.

Settings of fifty varieties repeated.

Printed by Hoyer & Ludwig, of Richmond, Va. One stone used, being the same as that used for the Hoyer & Ludwig 10c value in blue. Color change occured probably in March, 1862.

There are many shades of this stamp. The carmine is a very dark, bright color and should not be confused with the deeper shade of rose.

Earliest known cancellation, March 10, 1862. The earliest date of usage of the carmine shade is May 1, 1862.

				Unused	Used
5	A2	10c	**rose**	650.00	400.00
			dull rose	650.00	400.00
			brown rose	950.00	550.00
			deep rose	700.00	450.00
			carmine rose	900.00	500.00
			On cover		650.00
			On wallpaper cover		2,000.
			On patriotic cover		2,500.
			On prisoner's cover		5,500.
			On prisoner's cover with U.S. #65		—
			Pair	1,800.	1,600.
			Strip of three	—	4,000.
			Block of four	8,000.	6,500.
		a.	10c carmine	—	850.00
		a.	On cover		2,500.
			Malformed "T" of "TEN" (No. 4)	900.00	500.00
			"G" and "E" of "POSTAGE" joined (No. 10)	900.00	500.00
			Circ. flaw, upper left star (No.11)	900.00	500.00
			Third spiked ornament at right, white (No. 45)	900.00	500.00
			Scratched stone (occurring on Nos. 40, 39, 49 and 48, one pane)	1,000.	600.00
			Imprint		1,100.
			Horiz. pair, vert. gutter between		—
			Side margin copy, initials (No. 41)		1,500.

CANCELLATIONS.

Blue town	+ 50.00	April, 1862, year date	—
Red town	+100.00	Blue gridiron	+50.00
Green town	+350.00	Black concentric	+50.00
Texas town	+150.00	Blue concentric	+50.00
Arkansas town	—	"Paid"	—
Straight line town	+500.00	Railroad	—
		Express Company	

Jefferson Davis — A4

Typographed by De La Rue & Co. in London, England.

1862 (April) Hard Medium Paper

Plate of 400 in four panes of 100 each. No imprint.

No. 6 represents London printings from De La Rue & Co., a number of sheets being sent over by blockade runners. Fine clear impressions. The gum is light and evenly distributed. Exact date of issue unknown. Earliest known cancellation, April 16, 1862.

6	A4	5c	**light blue**	8.00	16.00
			Single on cover used before July 1, 1862		125.00
			Single on cover (overpaid drop letter)		275.00
			Single on patriotic cover used before July 1, 1862		900.00
			Single on prisoner's cover used before July 1, 1862		—
			On wallpaper cover		350.00
			On patriotic cover		900.00
			On prisoner's cover		1,250.
			On prisoner's cover with U.S. #65		1,250.
			Pair	18.00	40.00
			Pair on cover		65.00
			Block of four	40.00	275.00
			Block of four on cover		900.00

CANCELLATIONS.

Blue town	+2.00	Blue gridiron	+2.00
Red town	+45.00	Red gridiron	+35.00
Green town	+75.00	Blue concentric	+2.00
Texas town	+65.00	Express Company	+350.00
Arkansas town	+85.00	Railroad	+250.00
Straight line town	+150.00	"Paid"	+50.00

1862 (August) Typo. Thin to Thick Paper

Plate of 400 in four panes of 100 each. No imprint.

Locally printed by Archer & Daly of Richmond, Va., from plates made in London, England, by De La Rue & Co. Printed on both imported English and local papers. Earliest known cancellation, August 15, 1862.

No. 7 shows coarser impressions than No. 6, and the color is duller and often blurred. Gum is light or dark and unevenly distributed.

7	A4	5c	**blue**	10.00	8.00
		a.	5c deep blue	10.00	8.00
			Single on cover (overpaid drop letter)		250.00
			On wallpaper cover		300.00
			On patriotic cover		700.00
			On prisoner's cover		1,000.
			On prisoner's cover with U.S. #65		—
			Pair	21.00	20.00
			Pair on cover		90.00
			Block of four	50.00	275.00
			Block of four on cover		750.00
			Eight on cover (Trans—Miss. rate)		—
			White tie (U.R. 30)	125.00	135.00
			White tie on cover		350.00
			De La Rue paper (thin)	16.00	20.00
			White tie, De La Rue paper	175.00	225.00
			Thick paper	12.50	15.00
			Horiz. pair, vert. gutter between	175.00	
		b.	Printed on both sides	1,000.	700.00

CANCELLATIONS.

Blue town	+2.00	Blue gridiron	+2.00
Red town	+60.00	Red gridiron	+60.00
Brown town	+30.00		
Violet town	+110.00		
Green town	+125.00	Blue concentric	+2.00
Texas town	+90.00	Railroad	+250.00
Arkansas town	+110.00	Express Company	+400.00
Florida town	+140.00	Design (stars, etc.	+75.00
Straight line town	+140.00	"Paid"	+50.00

The unissued 10c type A4 was privately printed in various colors for philatelic purposes. (See note below No. 14.)

Counterfeits of the 10c exist.

Andrew Jackson — A5

1863 (April) Soft Porous Paper Line Engraved

Sheet of 200 (two panes of 100 each).

One plate. Printed by Archer & Daly of Richmond, Va. Earliest known cancellation. Apr. 21, 1863. Issued to prepay drop letter and circular rates. Strips of five used to prepay regular 10c rate.

8	A5	2c	**brown red**	40.00	200.00
		a.	2c pale red	50.00	225.00
			Single on cover		1,000.
			On prisoner's cover		3,000.
			On prisoner's cover with U.S. #65		4,000.
			Pair	90.00	650.00
			Pair on cover		3,000.
			On wallpaper cover		—
			Block of four	200.00	—
			Block of five		—
			Strip of five on cover		5,000.
			Strip of five on wallpaper cover		—
			Strip of ten on cover		13,000.
			Double transfer	85.00	300.00
			Horiz. pair, vert. gutter between	225.00	

CANCELLATIONS.

Blue town	+35.00	Blue gridiron	+35.00
Red town	+225.00	Black numeral	—
Army of Tenn.	—	Railroad	+325.00

Jefferson Davis "TEN CENTS" — A6

1863, Apr. Soft Porous Paper Line Engraved

One plate of 200 subjects all of which were probably recut as every copy examined to date shows distinct recutting. Plating not completed.

Printed by Archer & Daly of Richmond, Va. First printings in milky blue. First issued in April, 1863. Earliest known cancellation, April 23, 1863.

9	A6	10c	**blue**	600.00	400.00
		a.	10c milky blue (first printing)	650.00	450.00
		b.	10c gray blue	600.00	400.00
			On cover		850.00
			On wallpaper cover		3,000.
			On patriotic cover		3,500.
			On prisoner's cover		4,250.
			On prisoner's cover with U.S. #65		—
			Pair	1,350.	1,850.
			Pair on cover		2,750.
			Block of four	3,500.	
			Four stamps on one cover (Trans—Mississippi rate)		13,500.
			Curved lines outside the labels at top and bottom are broken in the middle (No. 63R)	700.00	500.00
			Double transfer	750.00	750.00
			Damaged plate	800.00	800.00

CANCELLATIONS.

Blue town	+25.00	Black gridiron	+25.00
Red town	+150.00	Blue gridiron	+50.00
Green town	+600.00	Red gridiron	+200.00
Violet town	—	Railroad	+400.00
Straight line town	+500.00	Circle of wedges	+1,000.
April, 1863, year date	—	Pen	250.00

Frame Line "10 CENTS" (Illustration actual size) — A6a

1863, Apr. Soft Porous Paper Line Engraved

Printed by Archer & Daly of Richmond, Va.

One copper plate of 100 subjects, all but one of which were recut. First issued in April, 1863. Earliest known use April 19, 1863.

Stamp design same as Die A (No. 11).

Values are for copies showing parts of lines on at least two of the four sides. Copies showing lines on three or four sides sell for more.

10 A6a		**10c blue**	2,250.	1,000.
	a.	10c milky blue	2,500.	1,250.
	b.	10c greenish blue	2,250.	1,000.
	c.	10c dark blue	2,250.	1,000.
		On cover		2,250.
		On wallpaper cover		*4,500.*
		On patriotic cover		*6,000.*
		On prisoner's cover		*7,000.*
		On prisoner's cover with U.S. #65		—
		Pair	*6,500.*	*5,000.*
		Pair on cover		*6,500.*
		Block of four	*15,000.*	
		Strip of four	*17,000.*	
		Strip of seven	*28,500.*	
		Double transfer (No. 74)	3,000.	1,500.

CANCELLATIONS.

Blue town	+100.00	Blue gridiron	+100.00
Red town	+500.00	Pen	750.00
Straight line town	+750.00		
April, 1863, year date	—		

No Frame Line "10 CENTS" — A7 (Die A)

1863-64 Thick or Thin Paper Line Engraved

There are many slight differences between A7 (Die A) and A8 (Die B), the most noticeable being the additional line outside the ornaments at the four corners of A8 (Die B).

Stamps were first printed by Archer & Daly, of Richmond, Va. In 1864 the plates were transferred to the firm of Keatinge & Ball in Columbia, S. C., who made further printings from them. Two plates, each with two panes of 100, numbered 1 and 2. First state shows numbers only, later states show various styles of Archer & Daly imprints, and latest show Keatinge & Ball imprints. Archer & Daly stamps show uniformly clear impressions and a good quality of gum evenly distributed (Earliest known cancellation, April 21, 1863); Keatinge & Ball stamps generally show filled in impressions in a deep blue, and the gum is brown and unevenly distributed. (Earliest known cancellation, Oct. 4, 1864). The so-called laid paper is probably due to thick streaky gum. (These notes also apply to No. 12.)

11 A7		**10c blue**	8.00	12.50
	a.	10c milky blue	20.00	25.00
	b.	10c dark blue	8.00	12.50
	c.	10c greenish blue	8.00	12.00
	d.	10c green	30.00	45.00
		deep blue, Keatinge & Ball ('64)	12.50	25.00
		On cover		55.00
		Single on cover (overpaid drop letter)		200.00
		On wallpaper cover		350.00
		On patriotic cover		625.00
		On prisoner's cover		550.00
		On prisoner's cover with U.S. #65		1,000.
		On cover, dp. blue (K. & B.) ('64)		100.00
		On prisoner's cover (K. & B.) with U.S. #65 ('64)		—
		Pair	18.00	30.00
		Pair on cover		175.00
		Block of four	40.00	275.00
		Strip of four on cover (Trans—Mississippi rate)		*4,000.*
		Margin block of 12, Archer & Daly impt. & P#	225.00	
		Margin block of 12, Keatinge & Ball impt. & P#	200.00	
		Double transfer	50.00	65.00
		Horiz. pair, vert. gutter between	90.00	
	e.	Perforated	135.00	150.00
	e.	On cover		400.00
	e.	On wallpaper cover		—
	e.	Block of four	550.00	

CANCELLATIONS.

Blue town	+5.00	April, 1863 year date	+75.00
Red town	+35.00	"FREE"	+250.00
Brown town	+60.00	Blue gridiron	+5.00
Green town	+110.00	Black concentric circles	+20.00
Violet town	+85.00	Crossroads	+150.00
Texas town	+60.00	"Paid"	+100.00
Arkansas town	+125.00	Numeral	+100.00
Florida town	+200.00	Railroad	+175.00
Straight line town	+350.00	Steamboat	+1,500.
Army of Tenn.	+300.00		

Jefferson Davis — A8 (Die B)

1863-64 Thick or Thin Paper Line Engraved

Plates bore Nos. 3 and 4, otherwise notes on No. 11 apply. Earliest known cancellation May 1, 1863.

12 A8		**10c blue**	9.00	12.50
	a.	10c milky blue	20.00	25.00
	b.	10c light blue	9.00	12.50
	c.	10c greenish blue	9.00	12.50
	d.	10c dark blue	9.00	12.50
	e.	10c green	30.00	35.00
		deep blue, Keatinge & Ball ('64)	12.50	25.00
		On cover		60.00
		Single on cover (overpaid drop letter)		200.00
		On wallpaper cover		350.00
		On patriotic cover		675.00
		On prisoner's cover		550.00
		On prisoner's cover with U.S. #65		900.00
		On cover, dp. blue (K. & B.) ('64)		100.00
		Pair	20.00	30.00
		Pair on cover		200.00
		Block of four	45.00	275.00
		Strip of four on cover (Trans—Mississippi rate)		*4,000.*
		Margin block of 12, Archer & Daly impt. & P#	250.00	
		Margin block of 12, Keatinge & Ball impt. & P#	225.00	
		Double transfer	50.00	65.00
		Horiz. pair, vert. gutter between	90.00	
	f.	Perforated	135.00	150.00
	f.	On cover		*450.00*
	f.	Block of four	575.00	

CANCELLATIONS.

Blue town	+5.00	Army of Tenn.	+350.00
Red town	+35.00	May, 1863, year date	+60.00
Brown town	+60.00	Blue gridiron	+5.00
Green town	+120.00	Black concentric circles	+15.00
Violet town	+85.00	Railroad	+175.00
Texas town	+125.00		
Arkansas town	+150.00		
Florida town	+200.00		
Straight line town	+350.00		

George Washington — A9

1863 (June 1) Line Engraved by Archer & Daly

One plate which consisted of two panes of 100 each. First printings were from plates with imprint in Old English type under each pane, which was later removed. Printed on paper of varying thickness and in many shades of green. This stamp was also used as currency. Earliest known cancellation, June 1, 1863. Forged cancellations exist.

13 A9		**20c green**	30.00	*250.00*
	a.	20c yellow green	30.00	*250.00*
	b.	20c dark green	50.00	*300.00*
		On cover		*900.00*
		On wallpaper cover		*1,500.*
		On prisoner's cover		*4,000.*
		On prisoner's cover with U.S. #65		*5,000.*
		Pair	65.00	*600.00*
		Pair on cover (Trans—Mississippi rate)		*5,500.*
		Block of four	150.00	*3,000.*
		Strip of four with imprint	325.00	
	c.	Diagonal half used as 10c on cover		*3,500.*
	c.	On prisoner's cover		—
	d.	Horizontal half used as 10c on cover		*4,000.*
		Double transfer, 20 doubled (24L and 35R)	90.00	—
		Horiz. pair, vert. gutter between	200.00	
		"20" on forehead	1,500.	—

CANCELLATIONS.

Blue town	+50.00	Railroad	—
Red town	+200.00	pen	175.00
Violet town	—		
Texas town	+100.00		

John C. Calhoun — A10

Typographed by De La Rue & Co., London, England 1862

14 A10		**1c orange**	60.00
	a.	1c deep orange	80.00
		Pair	150.00
		Block of four	350.00

This stamp was never put in use.

Upon orders from the Confederate Government, De La Rue & Co. of London, England, prepared Two Cents and Ten Cents typographed plates by altering the One Cent (No. 14) and the Five Cents (Nos. 6-7) designs previously made by them. Stamps were never officially printed from these plates although privately made prints exist in various colors.

Explanatory Notes

The following notes by Lawrence L. Shenfield explain the various routes, rates and usages of the general issue Confederate stamps.

"Across the Lines"
Letters Carried by Private Express Companies

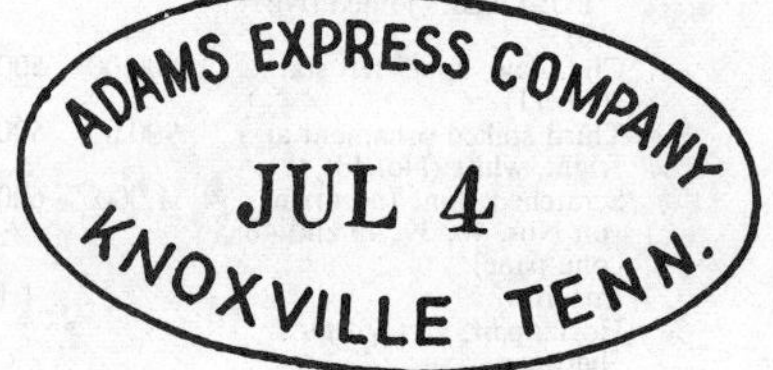

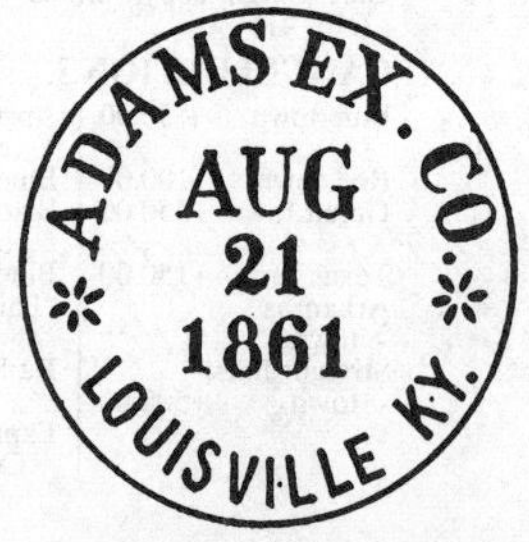

Express Company Handstamps Used on "Across the Lines" Letters

About two months after the outbreak of the Civil War, in June, 1861, postal service between North and South and vice versa was carried on largely by Adams Express Company, and the American Letter Express Company. Northern terminus for the traffic was Louisville, Ky.; Southern terminus was Nashville, Tenn. Letters for transmission were delivered to any office of the express company, together with a fee, usually 20c or 25c per ½ ounce to cover carriage. The express company messengers carried letters across the lines and delivered them to their office on the other side, where they were deposited in the Government mail for transmission to addressees, postage paid out of the fee charged. Letters from North to South, always enclosed in 3c U. S. envelopes, usually bear the handstamp of the Louisville office of the express company, and in addition the postmark and "Paid 5" of Nashville, Tenn., indicating its acceptance for delivery at the Nashville Post Office. Letters from South to North sometimes bear the origin postmark of a Southern post office, but more often merely the handstamp of the Louisville express company office applied as the letters cleared through Louisville. In addition, they bear the 3c 1857 U.S. adhesive stamp, cancelled with the postmark and grid of Louisville, Ky., where they went into the Government mail for delivery. Some across-the-lines letters show the handstamp of various express company offices, according to the particular routing the letters followed. On August 26, 1861, the traffic ceased by order of the U. S. Post Office Dept. (Values are for full covers bearing the usual Louisville, Ky., or Nashville, Tenn., handstamps of the express company. Unusual express office markings are rarer and worth more.)

North to South 3c U.S. Envelope, Adams Exp. Co. Louisville, Ky., handstamp	*1,100.*
North to South 3c U.S. Envelope, American Letter Express Co., Ky., handstamp	*1,750.*
South to North 3c 1857, Adams Exp. Co., Louisville, Ky., handstamp	*1,250.*
South to North 3c 1857, American Letter Exp. 250, Nashville, Tenn., handstamp	*2,250.*
South to North 3c 1861, Adams Exp. Co., Louisville, Ky., handstamp	*3,000.*

Blockade-Run Letters from Europe to the Confederate States

Charleston "STEAM-SHIP" in Oval Handstamp

As the Federal Fleet gradually extended its blockade of the Confederate States coastal regions, the South was forced to resort to blockade runners to carry letters to and from outside ports. These letters were all private-ship letters and never bore a foreign stamp if from Europe, nor a Confederate stamp if to Europe. The usual route from Europe was via a West Indies port, Nassau, Bahamas; Hamilton, Bermuda, or Havana, into the Southern ports of Wilmington, N.C. and Charleston, S.C. More rarely such letters came in to Savannah, Mobile and New Orleans. Letters from Europe are the only ones which are surely identified by their markings. They bore either the postmark of Wilmington, N.C., straightline "SHIP" and "12", "22", "32", etc., in manuscript; or the postmark of Charleston, S. C., "STEAMSHIP" in oval, and "12", "22", "32", etc., in manuscript. Very rarely Charleston used a straightline "SHIP" instead of "STEAMSHIP" in oval. All such letters were postage due; the single letter rate of 12c being made up of 2c for the private ship captain plus 10c for the regular single letter Confederate States rate. Over-weight letters were 22c (due), 32c, 42c, etc. A few examples are known on which Confederate General Issue stamps were used, usually as payment for forwarding postage. Covers with such stamps, or with the higher rate markings, 22c, 32, etc., are worth more.

(Values are for all full covers in fine condition.)

Charleston, S.C. "6" handstamp	*1,750.*
Charleston, S.C., postmark, "STEAMSHIP," and "12" in ms.	*1,750.*
Charleston, S.C., postmark, "SHIP," and "12" in ms.	*1,250.*
Wilmington, N.C., postmark, "SHIP," and "12" in ms.	*2,000.*
Savannah, Ga., postmark "SHIP," and "7" in ms. (*)	*3,500.*
New Orleans, La. postmark, "SHIP" and "10" in ms.	*4,500.*

(* 7c rate: 5c postage before July 1, 1862, plus 2c for ship captain.)

Express Company Mail in the Confederacy

Southern Express Company Handstamps

Shortly after the outbreak of war in 1861, the Adams Express Company divisions operating in the South were forced to suspend operations and turned their Southern lines over to a new company organized under the title Southern Express Company. This express did the bulk of the express business in the Confederacy despite the continued opposition of the Post Office Dept. of the C.S.A. and the ravages of the contending armies upon railroads. Other companies operating in the Confederacy were: South Western Express Co. (New Orleans), Pioneer Express Company, White's Southern Express (only one example known) and some local expresses of limited operation. The first three used handstamps of various designs usually bearing the city name of the office. Postal regulation necessitated the payment of regular Confederate postal rates on letters carried by express companies, express charges being paid in addition. Important letters, particularly money letters, were entrusted to these express companies as well as goods and wares of all kinds. The express rates charged for letters are not known; probably they varied depending upon the difficulty and risk of transmittal. Covers bearing stamps and express company handstamps are very rare.

Prisoner-of-War and Flag-of-Truce Letters

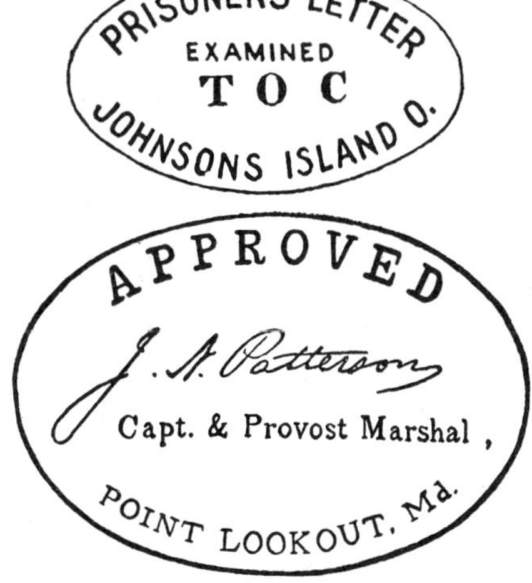

Prison Censor Handstamps

By agreement between the United States and the Confederate States, military prisoners and imprisoned civilians of both sides were permitted to send censored letters to their respective countries. Such letters, if from North to South, usually bore a U.S. 3c 1861 adhesive, postmarked at a city near the prison, to pay the postage to the exchange ground near Old Point Comfort, Va.; and a 10c Confederate stamp, canceled at Richmond, Va. (or "due" handstamp) to pay the Confederate postage to destination. It from South to North, letters usually bore a 10c Confederate stamp canceled at a Southern city (or "paid" handstamp) and a U. S. 3c 1861 adhesive (or "due 3" marking) and the postmark of Old Point Comfort, Va. In addition, prison censor markings, handstamped or manuscript, the name and rank of the soldier, and "Flag of Truce, via Fortress Monroe" in manuscript usually appear on these covers. Federal prison censor handstamps of various designs are known from these prisons:

Camp Chase, Columbus, O.
David's Island, Pelham, N.Y.
Fort Delaware, Delaware City, Del.
Camp Douglas, Chicago, Ill.
Elmira Prison, Elmira, N.Y.
Johnson's Island, Sandusky, O.
Fort McHenry, Baltimore, Md.
Camp Morton, Indianapolis, Ind.
Fort Oglethorpe, Macon, Ga.
Old Capitol Prison, Washington, D.C.
Point Lookout Prison, Point Lookout, Md.
Fort Pulaski, Savannah, Ga.
Rock Island Prison, Rock Island, Ill.
Ship Island, New Orleans, La.
West's Hospital, Baltimore, Md.
U.S. General Hospital, Gettysburg, Pa.

Several other Federal prisons used manuscript censor markings.

Southern prison censor markings are always in manuscript, and do not identify the prison. The principal Southern prisons were at Richmond and Danville, Va.; Andersonville and Savannah, Ga.; Charleston, Columbia and Florence S.C.; Salisbury, N.C.; Hempstead and Tyler, Tex.

Civilians residing in both the North and the South were also, under exceptional circumstances, permitted to send Flag of Truce letters across the lines. Such covers bore no censor marking nor prison markings, but were always endorsed "via Flag of Truce".

Values will be found under various individual stamps for "on prisoner's cover" and are for the larger prisons. Prisoners' letters from the smaller prisons are much rarer. Only a very small percentage of prisoners' covers bore *both* a U.S. stamp and a Confederate stamp.

The "SOUTHERN LETTER UNPAID" Marking On Northbound Letters of Confederate Origin

DUE 3

SOUTHN LETTER UNPAID.

By mid-May, 1861, correspondence between the North and South was difficult. In the South, postmasters were resigning and closing their accounts with Washington as the Confederacy prepared to organize its own postal system by June 1. From that date on, town marks and "paid" handstamps (and later postmasters' provisional stamps) were used in all post offices of the seceded states. The three most important Southern cities for clearing mail to the North were Memphis, Nashville and Richmond. The Richmond-Washington route was closed in April; Memphis was closed by June 1st, and mail attempting to cross the lines at these points generally ended up at the dead letter office. However, at Louisville, Kentucky, mail from the South via Nashville continued to arrive in June, July and August. On June 24, 1861, the Post Office Department advised the Louisville post office, "You will forward letters from the South for the Loyal States as unpaid, after removing postage stamps, but foreign letters in which prepayment is compulsory must come to the Dead Letter Office." However, Louisville avoided the task of "removing postage stamps," and instead prepared the "Southern Letter Unpaid" handstamp and special "due 3" markers for use. These markings were applied in the greenish-blue color of the Louisville office to letters of Southern origin that had accumulated, in addition to the usual town mark and grid of Louisville. The letters were delivered in the North at abroad as unpaid. Probably Louisville continued to forward such unpaid mail until about July 15. The marking is very rare. Other Southern mail was forwarded from Louisville as late as Aug. 27.

For listings see under U.S. 1857-61 issue, Nos. 26, 35-38. Values shown there are generally for this marking on off-cover stamps. Complete covers bearing stamps showing the full markings are valued from $7,500 upward depending upon the stamps, other postal markings and unusual usages. Fraudulent covers exist.

Trans-Mississippi Express Mail-the 40c Rate

From the fall of New Orleans on April 24, 1862, the entire reach of the Mississippi River was threatened by the Federal fleets. Late in 1862 the Confederacy experienced difficulty in maintaining regular mail routes trans-Mississippi to the Western states. Private express companies began to carry some mail, but by early 1863 when the Meridian-Jackson-Vicksburg-Shreveport route was seriously menaced, the Post Office Department of the Confederate States was forced to inaugurate an express mail service by contracting with a private company the name of which remains undisclosed. The eastern termini were at Meridian and Brandon, Miss.; the western at Shreveport and Alexandria, La. Letters, usually endorsed "via Meridian (or Brandon)" if going West; "via Shreveport (or Alexandria)" if going East were deposited in any Confederate post office. The rate was 40c per ½ ounce or less. Such Trans-Mississippi Express Mail upon arrival at a terminus was carried by couriers in a devious route across the Mississippi and returned to the regular mails at the nearest terminus on the other side of the river. The precise date of the beginning of the Trans-Mississippi service is not known. The earliest date of use so far seen is November 2, 1863 and the latest use February 9, 1865. These covers can be identified by the written endorsement of the route, but particularly by the rate since many bore no route endorsements.

Strips of four of 10c engraved stamps, pairs of the 20c stamp and various combinations of 10c stamps and the 5c London or Local prints are known; also handstamped Paid 40c marking. No identifying handstamps were used, merely the postmark of the office which received the letter originally. Values for Trans-Mississippi Express covers will be found under various stamps of the General Issues.

A 50c Preferred Mail Express rate, announced in April, 1863, preceded the Trans-Mississippi Express Mail 40c rate. Covers have been reported.

Packet and Steamboat Covers and Markings

Letters carried on Confederate packets operating on coastal routes or up and down the inland waterways were usually handstamped with the name of the packet or marked STEAM or STEAMBOAT. Either United States stamps of the 1857 issue or stamped envelopes of the 1853 or 1860 issues have been found so used, as well as Confederate Postmasters' Provisional and General Issue stamps. Some specially designed pictorial or imprinted packet boat covers also exist. All are scarce and command values from $500 upward for handstamped United States envelopes and from $1,000 up for covers bearing Confederate stamps.

TABLE OF SECESSION

States in Order of Secession	Ordinance of Secession Passed	Admitted to Confederacy	Period for Use of U.S. Stamps As Independent State	Total to May 31, 1861*
S. Carolina	12/20/1860	2/4/1861	1 mo 15 da	5 mo 11 da
Mississippi	1/9/1861	2/4/1861	26 da	4 mo 22 da
Florida	1/10/1861	2/4/1861	25 da	4 mo 21 da
Alabama	1/11/1861	2/4/1861	24 da	4 mo 20 da
Georgia	1/19/1861	2/4/1861	16 da	4 mo 12 da
Louisiana	1/26/1861	2/4/1861	9 da	4 mo 5 da
Texas	2/1/1861	3/6/1861	1 mo 6 da	4 mo 0 da
Virginia	4/17/1861	5/7/1861	20 da	1 mo 14 da
Arkansas	5/6/1861	5/18/1861	12 da	25 da
N. Carolina	5/20/1861	5/27/1861	7 da	11 da
Tennessee	6/8/1861	7/3/1861	0*	0*

* The use of United States stamps in the seceded States was prohibited after May 31, 1861.

Ordinance of Secession adopted. Popular vote to secede Feb. 23, effective March 2, 1861.

Original secession data by courtesy of August Dietz, Sr.

The Confederate postal laws did not provide the franking privilege for any mail except official correspondence of the Post Office Department. Such letters could be sent free only when enclosed in officially imprinted envelopes individually signed by the official using them. These envelopes were prepared and issued for Post Office Department use.

The imprints were on United States envelopes of 1853-61 issue, and also on commercial envelopes of various sizes and colors. When officially signed and mailed, they were postmarked, usually at Richmond, Va., with printed or handstamped "FREE". Envelopes are occasionally found unused and unsigned, and more rarely, signed but unused. When such official envelopes were used on other than official Post Office Department business, Confederate stamps were used.

Semi-official envelopes also exist bearing imprints of other government departments, offices, armies, states, etc. Regular postage was required to carry such envelopes through the mails.

OFFICIAL ENVELOPES

The Confederate postal laws did not provide the franking privilege for any mail except official correspondence of the Post Office Department. Such letters could be sent free only when enclosed in officially imprinted envelopes individually signed by the official using them. These envelopes were prepared and issued for Post Office Department use.

The imprints were on United States envelopes of 1853-61 issue, and also on commercial envelopes of various sizes and colors. When officially signed and mailed, they were postmarked, usually at Richmond, Va., with printed or handstamped "FREE". Envelopes are occasionally found unused and unsigned, and more rarely, signed but unused. When such official envelopes were used on other than official Post Office Department business, Confederate stamps were used.

Semi-official envelopes also exist bearing imprints of other government departments, offices, armies, states, etc. Regular postage was required to carry such envelopes through the mails.

CONFEDERATE STATES OF AMERICA,
POST OFFICE DEPARTMENT,
OFFICIAL BUSINESS,
John H Reagan
POSTMASTER GENERAL.

Confederate States of America,
POST OFFICE DEPARTMENT,
OFFICIAL BUSINESS
John B. A. Dimitry
Act. CHIEF CLERK P. O. DEPARTMENT

Typical Imprints of Official Envelopes of the Post Office Department. (Many variations of type, style and wording exist.)

Office	Signature
Postmaster General	John H. Reagan
Chief of the Contract Bureau	H. St. Geo. Offutt
Chief of the Appointment Bureau	B. N. Clements
Chief of the Finance Bureau	Jno. L. Harrell
Chief of the Finance Bureau	J. L. Lancaster
Chief of the Finance Bureau	A. Dimitry
Dead Letter Office	A. Dimitry
Dead Letter Office	Jno. L. Harrell
Chief Clerk, P. O. Department	B. Fuller
Chief Clerk	W. D. Miller
Auditor's Office	W. W. Lester
Auditor's Office	B. Baker
Auditor's Office	J. W. Robertson
First Auditor's Office, Treasury Department	J. W. Robertson
First Auditor's Office, Treasury Department	B. Baker
Third Auditor's Office	A. Moise
Third Auditor's Office	I. W. M. Harris
Agency, Post Office Dept. Trans—Miss.	Jas. H. Starr

PROOFS

			DIE (1) Glazed card	DIE (1a) Wove paper	PLATE (5) Wove paper
1861					
1P	5c	green			*1,500.*
2P	10c	blue			*1,500.*
2TC	10c	black (stone y)			*3,000.*
1862					
6P	5c	blight blue	1,000.		
6P	5c	dark blue		1,000.	
6P	5c	gray blue			600.
6TC	5c	black	750.		1,000.
6TC	5c	pink	1,250.		
7P	5c	carmine			850.
1863					
8TC	2c	black		1,000.	
9TC	10c	black		1,200.	
11TC	10c	black		900.	
13P	20c	green		900.	
13TC	20c	red brown		800.	
1862					
14P	1c	orange	700.		
14TC	1c	black	700.		
14TC	1c	light yellow brown			600.

Essay Die Proofs

In working up the final dies, proofs of incomplete designs in various stages were made. Usually dated in typeset lines, they are very rare. Others, of the 10c (No. 12) and the 20c (No. 13) were proofs made as essays from the dies. They are deeply engraved and printed in deep shades of the issued colors, but show only small differences from the stamps as finally issued. All are very rare.

Specimen Overprints

The De La Rue typographed 5c and 1c are known with "SPECIMEN" overprinted diagonally, also horizontally for 1c.

Counterfeits

In 1935 a set of 12 lithographed imitations, later known as the "Springfield facsimiles," appeared in plate form. The are in approximately normal colors on yellowish soft wove paper of modern manufacture.

CANAL ZONE

The Canal Zone, a strip of territory with an area of about 552 square miles following generally the line of the Canal, was under the jurisdiction of the United States, 1904-1979.

The Canal organization underwent two distinct and fundamental changes. The construction of the Canal and the general administration of civil affairs were performed by the Isthmian Canal Commission under the provisions of the Spooner Act. This was supplanted in April, 1914, by the Panama Canal Act which established the organization known as The Panama Canal. This was an independent Government Agency which included both the operation and maintenance of the waterway and civil government in the Canal Zone. Most of the quasi-business enterprises relating to the Canal operation were conducted by the Panama Railroad, an adjunct of the Panama Canal.

A basic change in the mode of operations took effect July 1, 1951, under provisions of Public Law 841 of the 81st Congress. This in effect transferred the canal operations to the Panama Railroad Co., which had been made a federal government corporation in 1948, and changed its name to the Panama Canal Co. Simultaneously the civil government functions of The Panama Canal, including the postal service, were renamed the Canal Zone Government. The organization therefore consisted of two units-the Panama Canal Co. and Canal Zone Government-headed by an individual who was president of the company and governor of the Canal Zone. His appointment as governor was made by the President of the United States, subject to confirmation by the Senate, and he was ex-officio president of the company.

The Canal Zone Governmen functioned as an independent government agency, and was under direct supervision of the President of the United States who delegated this authority to the Secretary of the Army.

The Panama Canal is 50 miles long from deep water in the Atlantic to deep water in the Pacific. Its runs from northwest to southeast with the Atlantic entrance being 33.5 miles north and 27 miles west of the Pacific entrance. The airline distance between the two entrances is 43 miles. It requires about eight hours for an average ship to transit the Canal. Transportation between the Atlantic and Pacific sides of the Isthmus is available by railway or highway.

The U.S. Canal Zone Postal Service began operating June 24, 1904, when nine post offices were opened in connection with the construction of the Panama Canal. It ceased Sept. 30, 1979, and the Panama Postal Service took over.

Numbers in parentheses indicate quantity issued.

100 CENTAVOS = 1 PESO
100 CENTESIMOS = 1 BALBOA
100 CENTS = 1 DOLLAR

Map of Panama — A1

Violet to Violet Blue Handstamp on Panama Nos. 72, 72a-72c, 78, 79.

On the 2c "PANAMA" is normally 13mm long. On the 5c and 10c it measures about 15mm.

On the 2c, "PANAMA" reads up on the upper half of the sheet and down on the lower half. On the 5c and 10c, "PANAMA" reads up at left and down at right on each stamp.

On the 2c only, varieties exist with inverted "V" for "A", accent on "A", inverted "N", etc., in "PANAMA."

1904, June 24 Unwmk. *Perf. 12*

No.	Type	Description	Unused	Used
1	A1	2c rose, both "PANAMA" reading up or down *(2600)*	400.00	350.00
		Single on cover		850.00
		Strip of three on cover		1,600.
		Block of four	1,750.	1,750.
a.		"CANAL ZONE" inverted *(100)*	675.00	675.00
b.		"CANAL ZONE" double	1,850.	1,850.
c.		"CANAL ZONE" double, both inverted	*3,500.*	
d.		"PANAMA" reading down and up *(52)*	500.00	500.00
e.		As "d," "CANAL ZONE" invtd.	*3,500.*	*3,500.*
f.		Vert. pair, "PANAMA" reading up on top 2c, down on other	*1,100.*	*1,100.*
		"PANAMA" 15mm. long *(260)*	500.00	500.00
		"P NAMA"	500.00	500.00
2	A1	5c blue *(7800)*	200.00	175.00
		On cover		300.00
		First day cover		*2,500.*
		Block of four	1,000.	900.00
a.		"CANAL ZONE" inverted	450.00	450.00
b.		"CANAL ZONE" double	900.00	900.00
c.		Pair, one without "CANAL ZONE" overprint	2,250.	2,250.
d.		"CANAL ZONE" overprint diagonal, reading down to right	500.00	500.00
		Left "PANAMA" 2¼mm below bar *(156)*	450.00	450.00
		Colon between right "PANAMA" and bar *(156)*	450.00	450.00
3	A1	10c yellow *(4946)*	300.00	275.00
		On cover		400.00
		First day cover		*2,500.*
		Block of four	1,350.	1,350.
a.		"CANAL ZONE" inverted *(200)*	500.00	500.00
b.		"CANAL ZONE" double		*3,000.*
c.		Pair, one without "CANAL ZONE" overprint	2,750.	2,750.
		Left "PANAMA" 2¼mm below bar *(100)*	550.00	550.00
		Colon between right "PANAMA" and bar *(100)*	500.00	500.00

Cancellations consist of town and/or bars in magenta or black, or a mixture of both colors.

Nos. 1-3 were withdrawn July 17, 1904.

Forgeries of the "Canal Zone" overprint and cancellations are numerous.

United States Nos. 300, 319, 304, 306 and 307 Overprinted in Black

CANAL ZONE

PANAMA

1904, July 18 Wmk. 191

No.	Type	Description	Unused	Used
4	A115	1c blue green *(43,738)*	27.50	22.50
		green	27.50	22.50
		On cover		60.00
		Block of four	125.00	125.00
		Margin strip of three, Impt. & P#	135.00	
		Margin block of six, Impt. & P#	875.00	
5	A129	2c carmine *(68,414)*	22.50	20.00
		On cover		60.00
		Block of four	100.00	100.00
		Margin strip of three, Impt. & P#	100.00	
		Margin block of six, Impt. & P#	800.00	
a.		2c scarlet	27.50	22.50
6	A119	5c blue *(20,858)*	85.00	60.00
		On cover		150.00
		Block of four	400.00	300.00
		Margin strip of three, Impt. & P#	425.00	
		Margin block of six, Impt. & P#	1,500.	
7	A121	8c violet black *(7932)*	150.00	130.00
		On cover		150.00
		Block of four	700.00	700.00
		Margin strip of three, Impt. & P#	700.00	
		Margin block of six, Impt. & P#	2,500.	
8	A122	10c pale red brown *(7856)*	175.00	130.00
		On cover		225.00
		Block of four	825.00	700.00
		Margin strip of three, Impt. & P#	825.00	
		Margin block of six, Impt. & P#	3,000.	

Nos. 4 to 8 frequently show minor broken letters.

Cancellations consist of circular town and/or bars in black, blue or magenta.

A2

A3

CANAL ZONE
Regular Type

CANAL ZONE
Antique Type

The Canal Zone overprint on stamps Nos. 9-15 and 18-20 was made with a plate which had six different stages, each with its peculiar faults and errors of which there was generally only one in each sheet. Stage 1: Broken CA-L, broken L, A-L spaced, on Nos. 9, 10, 12-15. Stage 2: broken L, Z, N, E, on Nos. 9, 10, 12-14. Stage 3: same as 2 with additional antique ZONE, on Nos. 9, 11-14, 18. Stage 4: same as 3 with additional antique CANAL on Nos. 9, 12, 13. Stage 5: broken E and letters L, Z, N, and words CANAL and ZONE in antique type on Nos. 12-14, 19, 20. Stage 6: same as 5 except for additional antique Z on stamp which had antique L, on No. 12. The Panama overprints can be distinguished by the different shades of the red overprint, the width of the bar, and the word PANAMA. No. 11 has two different Panama overprints; No. 12 has six; No. 13 five; No. 14 two; and Nos. 15, 18-20, one each. In the "8cts" surcharge of Nos. 14 and 15, there are three varieties of the figure "8". The bar is sometimes misplaced so that it appears on the bottom of the stamp instead of the top.

1904-06 Unwmk.

Black Overprint on Stamps of Panama

No.	Type	Description	Unused	Used
9	A2	1c green *(319,800) Dec. 12, 1904*	2.25	1.75
		On cover		5.00
		Block of four	10.00	9.00
a.		"CANAL" in antique type *(500)*	125.00	125.00
b.		"ZONE" in antique type *(1500)*	90.00	90.00
c.		Inverted overprint	—	*2,000.*
d.		Double overprint	*900.00*	*700.00*
		Spaced "A L" in "CANAL" *(700)*	125.00	125.00
		"ON" of "ZONE" dropped	275.00	275.00
10	A2	2c rose *(367,500) Dec. 12, 1904*	3.50	2.00
		On cover		10.00
		Block of four	16.50	12.00
a.		Inverted overprint	175.00	175.00
b.		"L" of "CANAL" sideways	1,200.	1,200.
		Spaced "A L" of "CANAL" *(1700)*	85.00	85.00
		"ON" of "ZONE" dropped	250.00	250.00

"PANAMA" (15mm long) reading up at left, down at right

Overprint "CANAL ZONE" in Black, "PANAMA" and Bar in Red

No.	Type	Description	Unused	Used
11	A3	2c rose *(150,000) Dec. 9, 1905*	6.50	4.50
		On cover		20.00
		Black of four	32.50	25.00
a.		"ZONE" in antique type *(1500)*	125.00	125.00
b.		"PANAMA" overprint inverted, bar at bottom *(200)*	350.00	350.00
		Inverted "M" in "PANAMA" *(3,000)*	60.00	60.00
		"PANAMA" 16mm long *(3000)*	60.00	60.00
12	A3	5c blue *(400,000) Dec. 12, 1904*	7.00	3.50
		On cover		40.00
		Block of four	35.00	17.50

a. "CANAL" in antique type *(2750)* 75.00 75.00
b. "ZONE" in antique type *(2950)* 75.00 75.00
c. "CANAL ZONE" double *(200)* 400.00 400.00
d. "PANAMA" double *(120)* 650.00 650.00
e. "PANAMA" inverted, bar at bottom 950.00 950.00
Spaced "A L" in "CANAL" *(300)* 90.00 90.00
"PAMANA" reading up *(2800)* 70.00 70.00
"PAMANA" reading down *(400)* 200.00 200.00
"PANAMA" 16mm long *(1300)* 50.00 50.00
Inverted "M" in "PANAMA" *(1300)* 50.00 50.00
Right "PANAMA" 5mm below bar *(600)* 75.00 75.00
"PANAM" 70.00 70.00
"PANAAM" at right 650.00 650.00
"PAN MA" 75.00 75.00
"ANAMA" 80.00 80.00

13 A2 10c yellow *(64,900) Dec. 12, 1904* 15.00 11.00
On cover 50.00
Block of four 75.00 55.00
a. "CANAL" in antique type *(200)* 200.00 200.00
b. "ZONE" in antique type *(400)* 175.00 175.00
c. "PANAMA" ovpt. double *(80)* 600.00 600.00
Spaced "A L" in "CANAL" *(200)* 150.00 150.00
"PANAMA" 16mm long *(400)* 90.00 90.00
"PAMANA" reading down *(200)* 150.00 150.00
Invtd. "M" in "PANAMA" *(400)* 125.00 125.00
Right "PANAMA" 5mm below bar *(398)* 125.00 125.00
Left "PANAMA" touches bar *(400)* 125.00 125.00
d. "PANAMA" overprint in red brown *(5000)* 25.00 25.00
"PANAMA" ovpt. in org. red 30.00 30.00

With Additional Surcharge in Red

a **8 cts**

There are three varieties of "8" in the surcharge on #14-15.

14 A3 8c on 50c bister brown *(27,900) Dec. 12, 1904* 22.50 16.50
On cover 100.00
Block of four 110.00 85.00
a. "ZONE" in antique type *(25)* 750.00 700.00
b. "CANAL ZONE" inverted *(200)* 325.00 325.00
Spaced "A L" in "CANAL" *(194)* 125.00 125.00
Right "PANAMA" 5mm below bar *(438)* 110.00 110.00
c. "PANAMA" overprint in rose brown *(6000)* 37.50 37.50
d. As "c", "CANAL" in antique type *(10)* 1,500.
e. As "c", "ZONE" in antique type *(10)* 1,500.
f. As "c", "8cts" double *(30)* *700.00*
g. As "c", "8" omitted *4,000.*

Nos. 11-14 are overprinted or surcharged on Panama Nos. 77, 77e, 78, 78c, 78d, 78f, 78g, 78h, 79 79c, 79e, 79g and 81 respectively.

Panama No. 74a, 74b Overprinted "CANAL ZONE" in Regular Type in Black and Surcharged Type "a" in Red

Both "PANAMA" (13mm long) Reading Up

15 A3(a) 8c on 50c bister brown *(500) Dec. 12, 1904* 2,400. 2,400.
On cover *6,000.*
Block of four 10,000. 10,000.
a. "PANAMA" reading down and up *(10)* 3,300. 3,300.
"PANAMA" 15mm long *(50)* 2,750. 2,750.
"P NAMA" 2,800.
Spaced "A L" in "CANAL" *(5)* 3,100.

Map of Panama — A4

Panama Nos. 19 and 21 Surcharged in Black:

PANAMA CANAL ZONE PANAMA 1 ct. (a)

PANAMA CANAL ZONE PANAMA 1 ct. (b)

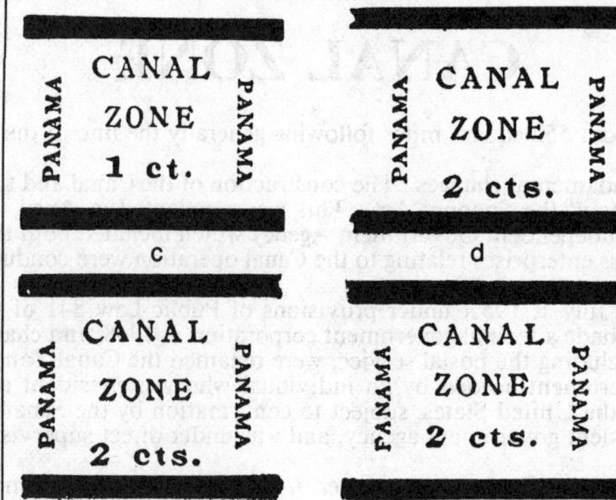

1906

There were three printings of each denomination, differing principally in the relative position of the various parts of the surcharges. Varieties occur with inverted "v" for the final "a" in "Panama", "CA" spaced, "ZO" spaced, "2c" spaced, accents in various positions, and with bars shifted so that two bars appear on top or bottom of the stamp (either with or without the corresponding bar on top or bottom) and sometimes with only one bar at top or bottom.

16 A4 1c on 20c violet, type a *(100,000) March* 1.75 1.50
On cover 7.50
Block of four 7.75 7.00
a. 1c on 20c violet, type b *(100,000) May* 1.75 1.50
On cover 7.50
Block of four 7.75 7.00
b. 1c on 20c violet, type c *(300,000) Sept.* 1.50 1.50
On cover 7.50
Block of four 7.75 7.00
Spaced C-A 12.50

17 A4 2c on 1p lake, type d *(200,000) Mar.* 2.50 2.50
On cover 10.00
Block of four 13.00 11.00
a. 2c on 1p lake, type e *(200,000) May* 2.50 2.50
On cover 10.00
Block of four 13.00 11.00
b. 2c on 1p lake, type f *(50,000) Sept.* 10.00 12.00
On cover 30.00
Block of four 45.00 55.00

Panama Nos. 74, 74a and 74b Overprinted "CANAL ZONE" in Regular Type in Black and Surcharged in Red

8 cts. b **8 cts** c

1905-06

Both "Panama" Reading Up

18 A3(b) 8c on 50c bis. brown *(17,500) Nov. 1905* 60.00 60.00
On cover 100.00
Block of four 250.00 250.00
a. "ZONE" in antique type *(175)* 200.00 200.00
b. "PANAMA" reading down and up *(350)* 150.00 150.00
"PANAMA" 15mm long *(1750)* 90.00 90.00
"P NAMA" 125.00 125.00

19 A3(c) 8c on 50c bister brown *(19,000) April 23, 1906* 55.00 55.00
On cover 100.00
Block of four 225.00 225.00
a. "CANAL" in antique type *(190)* 175.00 175.00
b. "ZONE" in antique type *(190)* 175.00 175.00
c. "8 cts" double *1,000. 1,000.*
d. "PANAMA" reading down and up *(380)* 100.00 100.00
"PANAMA" 15mm long *(1900)* 75.00 65.00
"P NAMA" 80.00

Panama No. 81 Overprinted "CANAL ZONE" in Regular Type in Black and Surcharged in Red Type "c" plus Period

"Panama" reading up and down

20 A3(c) 8c on 50c bis. brown *(19,600) Sept. 1906* 35.00 30.00
On cover 100.00
Block of four 150.00 125.00
a. "CANAL" antique type *(196)* 200.00 200.00
b. "ZONE" in antique type *(196)* 200.00 200.00
c. "8 cts" omitted *(50)* 700.00 700.00
d. "8 cts" double *1,250.*
"PAMANA" reading up *(392)* 100.00 100.00

Nos. 14 and 18-20 exist without CANAL ZONE overprint but were not regularly issued. Forgeries of the overprint varieties of Nos. 9-15 and 18-20 are known.

Vasco Nuñez de Balboa
A5

Fernández de Cordoba
A6

Justo Arosemena
A7

Manuel J. Hurtado
A8

José de Obaldía — A9

Engraved by Hamilton Bank Note Co. Overprinted in black by Isthmian Canal Commission Press.

1906-07 **Unwmk.** ***Perf. 12***

Overprint Reading Up

21 A6 2c red & black *(50,000) Oct. 29, 1906* 24.00 20.00
On cover 45.00
Block of four 125.00 110.00
a. "CANAL" only *4,500.*

Overprint Reading Down

22 A5 1c green & black *(2,000,000) Jan. 14, 1907* 2.25 1.25
dull green & black 2.25 1.25
On cover 5.00
Block of four 10.00 6.00
a. Horiz. pair, imperf. btwn. *(50)* 1,000. 1,000.
b. Vert. pair, imperf. btwn. *(20)* *1,500. 1,500.*
c. Vert. pair, imperf. horiz. *(20)* *1,500. 1,500.*
d. Inverted overprint reading up *(100)* 300.00 300.00
e. Double overprint *(300)* 250.00 250.00
f. Double overprint, one inverted 1,100. 1,100.
g. Invtd. center, ovpt. reading up *2,500. 2,500.*
"ANA" for "CANAL" *(1000)* 70.00 70.00
"CAN L" for "CANAL" 80.00 80.00
"ONE" for "ZONE" *(3000)* 60.00 60.00

23 A6 2c red & black *(2,370,000) Nov. 25, 1906* 2.75 1.25
scarlet & black, *1907* 2.75 1.25
On cover 5.00
Block of four 12.00 7.00
a. Horizontal pair, imperf. between *(20)* 1,250. 1,250.
b. Vertical pair, one without overprint 1,600. 1,600.
c. Double overprint *(100)* 350.00 350.00
d. Double overprint, one diagonal 650.00 650.00
e. Double overprint, one diagonal in pair with normal 1,400.
f. 2c carmine red & black, *Sept. 9, 1907* 5.00 2.75
g. As "f," inverted center and overprint reading up *6,000.*
h. As "d," one "ZONE CANAL" *2,250.*
i. "CANAL" double *2,750.*
"CAN L" for "CANAL" 45.00

24 A7 5c ultramarine & black *(1,390,000) Dec. 1906* 6.00 2.75
light ultramarine & black 6.00 2.75
blue & black, *Sept. 16, 1907* 6.00 2.75
dark blue & black 6.00 2.75
On cover 20.00
Block of four 22.50 20.00
a. 5c dull blue & black 7.25 2.75
b. 5c light blue & black 6.00 2.25
c. Double overprint *(200)* 275.00 175.00
d. "CANAL" only *(10)* 2,500.
e. "ZONE CANAL" *3,500.*
"CAN L" for "CANAL" 60.00

25 A8 8c purple & black *(170,000) Dec. 1906* 18.00 7.50
On cover 45.00
Block of four 80.00 35.00
a. Horizontal pair, imperf. between and at left margin *(34)* 750.00 750.00

26 A9 10c violet & black *(250,000) Dec. 1906* 18.00 7.50
On cover 50.00
Block of four 100.00 45.00
a. Dbl. ovpt., one reading up *(10)* *2,500.*
b. Overprint reading up *2,750.*

The early printings of this series were issued on soft, thick, porous-textured paper, while later printings of all except No. 25 appear on hard, thin, smooth-textured paper. Normal spacing of the early printings is 7¼mm between the words; later printings, 6¾mm. Nos. 22 and 26 exist imperf. between stamp and sheet margin. Nos. 22-25 occur with "CA" of "CANAL" spaced ½mm further apart on position No. 50 of the setting.

Córdoba
A11

Arosemena
A12

Hurtado
A13

José de Obaldia
A14

Engraved by American Bank Note Co.

1909

Overprint Reading Down

27 A11 2c vermilion & black *(500,000) May 11, 1909* 12.00 6.50
On cover 15.00
First day cover 400.00
Block of four 55.00 30.00
a. Horizontal pair, one without overprint *2,250.*
b. Vert. pair, one without ovpt. *2,400.*
28 A12 5c deep blue & black *(200,000) May 28, 1909* 40.00 12.50
On cover 35.00
Block of four 175.00 60.00
29 A13 8c violet & black *(50,000) May 25, 1909* 35.00 10.00
On cover 50.00
Block of four 150.00 65.00
30 A14 10c violet & black *(100,000) Jan. 19, 1909* 35.00 11.00
On cover 55.00
Block of four 175.00 70.00
a. Horizontal pair, one without overprint *3,250.*
b. Vertical pair, one without overprint *3,750.*

Nos. 27-30 occur with "CA" spaced (position 50).

Vasco Nuñez de Balboa — A15

Engraved, Printed and Overprinted by American Bank Note Co.
Black Overprint Reading Up

Type I — CANAL ZONE

Type I Overprint: "C" with serifs both top and bottom. "L," "Z" and "E" with slanting serifs.
Illustrations of Types I to V are considerably enlarged and do not show actual spacing between lines of overprint.

1909-10

31 A15 1c dark green & black *(4,000,000) Nov. 8, 1909* 3.50 1.50
On cover 3.00
Block of four 16.00 8.00
a. Inverted center and overprint reading down *12,500.*
c. Booklet pane of 6 handmade, perf. margins 550.00
32 A11 2c vermilion & black, *(4,000,000) Nov. 8, 1909* 4.25 1.50
On cover 3.00
Block of four 19.00 8.00
a. Vert. pair, imperf. horiz. 800.00 800.00
c. Bklt. pane of 6 handmade, perf. margins 700.00
d. Double overprint —
33 A12 5c deep blue & black, *(2,000,000) Nov. 8, 1909* 13.00 3.50
On cover 8.00
Block of four 65.00 17.50
a. Double overprint *(200)* 300.00 300.00
34 A13 8c violet & black, *(200,000) Mar. 18, 1910* 8.00 5.00
On cover 10.00
Block of four 40.00 25.00
a. Vertical pair, one without overprint *(10) 1,750.*

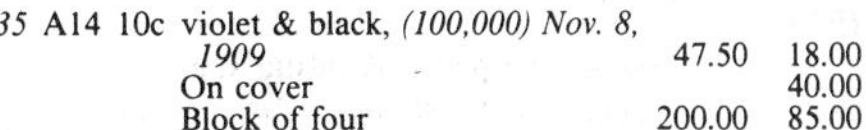
35 A14 10c violet & black, *(100,000) Nov. 8, 1909* 47.50 18.00
On cover 40.00
Block of four 200.00 85.00

Normal spacing between words of overprint on No. 31 is 10mm and on Nos. 32 to 35, 8½mm. Minor spacing variations are known.

A16

A17

1911

36 A16 10c on 13c gray *(476,700) Jan. 14, 1911* 5.50 2.50
On cover 20.00
Block of four 27.50 15.00
a. "10 cts" inverted 300.00 225.00
b. "10 cts" omitted 250.00 —

The "10 cts" surcharge was applied by the Isthmian Canal Commission Press after the overprinted stamps were received from the American Bank Note Co.
Many of the stamps offered as No. 36b are merely No. 36 from which the surcharge has been removed with chemicals.

1914

37 A17 10c gray *(200,000) Jan. 6, 1914* 42.50 12.00
On cover 40.00
Block of four 200.00 55.00

Type II — CANAL ZONE

Type II Overprint: "C" with serifs at top only. "L" and "E" with vertical serifs. Inner oval of "O" tilts to left.

1912-16

38 A15 1c green & black *(3,000,000) July 1913* 10.00 2.75
On cover 3.00
Block of four 45.00 18.00
a. Vertical pair, one without overprint 1,250. 1,250.
b. Booklet pane of six, imperf. margins *(120,000)* 525.00
c. Booklet pane of 6 handmade, perf. margins 900.00
39 A11 2c vermilion & black *(7,500,000) Dec. 1912* 8.00 1.25
orange vermilion & black, *1916* 8.00 1.25
On cover 4.00
Block of four 40.00 7.00
a. Horizontal pair, one without overprint 700.00
b. "CANAL" only 1,000.
c. Booklet pane of 6, imperf. margins *(194,868)* 550.00
d. Overprint reading down 175.00
e. As "d" inverted center 750.00 750.00
f. As "e" booklet pane of 6 handmade, perf. margins *5,000.*
g. As "c," handmade, perf. margins 1,000.
40 A12 5c deep blue & black *(2,300,000) Dec. 1912* 19.00 4.00
On cover 20.00
Block of four 95.00 17.50
a. With Cordoba portrait of 2c *7,000.*
41 A14 10c violet & black *(200,000) Feb. 1916* 50.00 9.00
On cover 45.00
Block of four 250.00 47.50

Normal spacing between words of overprint on the first printing of Nos. 38-40 is 8½mm and on the second printing 9¼mm. The spacing of the single printing of No. 41 and the imperf. margin booklet panes printing of Nos. 38 and 39 is 7¾mm. Minor spacing variations are known.

Map of Panama Canal — A18

Balboa Taking Possession of the Pacific Ocean — A19

Gatun Locks — A20

Culebra Cut — A21

Engraved, Printed and Overprinted by American Bank Note Co.

1915, Mar. 1

Blue Overprint, Type II

42 A18 1c dark green & black *(100,000)* 7.50 6.00
On cover 8.00
Block of four 32.50 27.50
First day cover 150.00
43 A19 2c carmine & black *(100,000)* 7.50 4.00
vermilion & black 7.50 4.00
On cover 10.00
First day cover 150.00
Block of four 32.50 20.00
44 A20 5c blue & black *(100,000)* 7.50 5.50
On cover 25.00
Block of four 35.00 27.50
First day cover 150.00
45 A21 10c orange & black *(50,000)* 15.00 10.00
On cover 45.00
Block of four 65.00 50.00
First day cover 150.00

Normal spacing between words of overprint is 9¼mm on all four values except position No. 61 which is 10mm.

Type III — CANAL ZONE

Type III Overprint: Similar to Type I but letters appear thinner, particularly the lower bar of "L," "Z" and "E." Impressions are often light, rough and irregular.

Engraved and Printed by American Bank Note Co.
Black overprint reading up applied by Panama Canal Press, Mount Hope, C. Z.

1915-20

46 A15 1c green & black, *Dec. 1915* 200.00 120.00
light green & black, *1920* 225.00 175.00
On cover 150.00
Block of four 950.00 575.00
a. Overprint reading down *(200)* 350.00
b. Double overprint *(180)* 250.00
c. "ZONE" double *(2) 3,500.*
d. Double overprint, one reads "ZONE CANAL" *(18)* 1,250.
47 A11 2c orange vermilion & black, *Aug. 1920* 2,500. 90.00
On cover 350.00
Block of four *12,000.* 500.00
48 A12 5c deep blue & black, *Dec. 1915* 550.00 150.00
On cover 500.00
Block of four *3,000.* 700.00

Normal spacing between words of overprint on Nos. 46-48 is 9¼mm. This should not be confused with an abnormal

9¼mm spacing of the 2c and 5c values of type I, which are fairly common in singles, particularly used. Blocks of the abnormal spacing are rare.

S. S. "Panama" in Culebra Cut
A22 A23

S. S. "Cristobal" in Gatun Locks — A24

Engraved, Printed and Overprinted by American Bank Note Co.

1917, Jan.

Blue Overprint, Type II

49 A22 12c purple & black *(314,914)*	12.00	5.00
On cover		30.00
Block of four	60.00	22.50
50 A23 15c bright blue & black	45.00	20.00
On cover		85.00
Block of four	200.00	90.00
51 A24 24c yellow brown & black	27.50	10.00
On cover		100.00
Block of four	125.00	55.00

Normal spacing between words of overprint is 11¼mm.

Type IV

CANAL
ZONE

Type IV Overprint: "C" thick at bottom, "E" with center bar same length as top and bottom bars.

Engraved, Printed and Overprinted by American Bank Note Co.

1918-20

Black Overprint, Reading Up

52 A15 1c green & black *(2,000,000) Jan. 1918*	27.50	10.00
On cover		11.00
Block of four	125.00	32.50
a. Overprint reading down	150.00	
b. Booklet pane of 6 *(60,000)*	700.00	
c. Booklet pane of 6, left vertical row of 3 without overprint	*2,250.*	
d. Booklet pane of 6, right vertical row of 3, with double overprint	*2,250.*	
e. Pair, one without overprint	*850.00*	
53 A11 2c vermilion & black *(2,000,000) Nov. 1918*	95.00	6.00
On cover		15.00
Block of four	400.00	30.00
a. Overprint reading down	150.00	150.00
b. Horiz. pair, one without ovpt.	1,500.	
c. Booklet pane of 6 *(34,000)*	700.00	
d. Booklet pane of 6, left vertical row of 3, without overprint	*2,250.*	
54 A12 5c deep blue & black *(500,000) Apr. 1920*	140.00	30.00
On cover		140.00
Block of four	650.00	140.00

Normal spacing between words of overprint on Nos. 52 and 53 is 9¼mm. On No. 54 and the booklet printings of Nos. 52 and 53, the normal spacing is 9mm. Minor spacing varieties are known.

Type V

CANAL
ZONE

Type V Overprint: Smaller block type 1¾mm high. "A" with flat top.

1920-21

Black Overprint, Reading Up

55 A15 1c light green & black, *Apr. 1921*	25.00	4.50
On cover		8.00
Block of four	110.00	20.00
a. Overprint reading down	125.00	125.00
b. Pair, one without ovpt.	900.00	
c. "CANAL" double	*1,250.*	
d. "ZONE" only	*3,000.*	—
e. Booklet pane of 6	*2,750.*	
56 A11 2c orange vermilion & black, *Sept. 1920*	8.00	3.00
On cover		7.00
Block of four	35.00	14.00
a. Double overprint *(100)*	350.00	
b. Double overprint, one reading down *(100)*	350.00	
c. Horizontal pair, one without overprint	900.00	
d. Vertical pair, one without overprint	1,750.	
e. "CANAL" double	1,000.	
f. "ZONE" double	750.00	
g. Booklet pane of 6	850.00	
57 A12 5c deep blue & black, *Apr. 1921*	175.00	35.00
On cover		150.00
Block of four	850.00	150.00
a. Horizontal pair, one without overprint *(20)*	1,200.	

Normal spacing between words of overprint on Nos. 55-57 is 9½mm. On booklet printings of Nos. 55 and 56 the normal spacing is 9¼mm.

Drydock at Balboa — A25

U.S.S. "Nereus" in Pedro Miguel Locks — A26

1920, Sept.

Black Overprint Type V

58 A25 50c orange & black	250.00	150.00
On cover		350.00
Block of four	1,250.	750.00
59 A26 1b dark violet & black *(23,014)*	125.00	50.00
On cover		250.00
Block of four	600.00	250.00

José Vallarino
A27

"Land Gate"
A28

Bolivar's Tribute — A29

Municipal Building in 1821 and 1921 — A30

Statue of Balboa
A31

Tomás Herrera
A32

José de Fábrega — A33

Engraved, Printed and Overprinted by American Bank Note Co.

Type V ovpt. in black, reading up, on all values except the 5c which is overprinted with larger type in red

1921, Nov. 13

60 A27 1c green	2.75	1.25
On cover		2.50
Block of four	12.50	6.00
a. "CANAL" double	*1,400.*	
b. Booklet pane of six	*750.00*	
61 A28 2c carmine	2.50	1.40
On cover		5.00
Blocks of four	11.00	6.00
a. Invtd. overprint, reading down	200.00	200.00
b. Double overprint	700.00	
c. Vertical pair, one without overprint	*3,500.*	
d. "CANAL" double	*1,750.*	
f. Booklet pane of six	*1,200.*	
62 A29 5c blue (R)	10.00	4.00
On cover		15.00
Block of four	45.00	22.50
a. Overprint reading down (R)	80.00	
63 A30 10c violet	9.50	6.50
On cover		25.00
Block of four	55.00	30.00
a. Invtd. overprint, reading down	100.00	
64 A31 15c light blue	40.00	16.00
On cover		75.00
Block of four	180.00	80.00
65 A32 24c black brown	50.00	20.00
On cover		85.00
Block of four	250.00	90.00
66 A33 50c black	100.00	90.00
On cover		300.00
Block of four	475.00	425.00

Experts question the status of the 5c with a small type V overprint in red or black.

Engraved and printed by the American Bank Note Co.

1924, Jan. 28

Type III overprint in black, reading up, applied by the Panama Canal Press, Mount Hope, C. Z.

67 A27 1c green	400.00	175.00
On cover		300.00
Block of four	1,750.	800.00
a. "ZONE CANAL" reading down	750.00	
b. "ZONE" only, reading down	*1,750.*	

Arms of Panama — A34

1924, Feb.

68 A34 1c dark green	9.50	4.00
On cover		8.00
Block of four	45.00	18.00
69 A34 2c carmine	7.00	2.50
carmine rose	7.00	2.50
On cover		7.00
Block of four	30.00	11.00

The following were prepared for use, but not issued.

A34 5c dark blue *(600)*	225.00
Block of four	1,000.
A34 10c dark violet *(600)*	225.00
Block of four	1,000.
A34 12c olive green *(600)*	225.00
Block of four	1,000.
A34 15c ultramarine *(600)*	225.00
Block of four	1,000.
A34 24c yellow brown *(600)*	225.00
Block of four	1,000.
A34 50c orange *(600)*	225.00
Block of four	1,000.
A34 1b black *(600)*	225.00
Block of four	1,000.

The 5c to 1b values were prepared for use but never issued due to abrogation of the Taft Agreement which required the Canal Zone to use overprinted Panama stamps. Six hundred of each denomination were not destroyed, as they were forwarded to the Director General of Posts of Panama for transmission to the UPU which then required about 400 sets.

All Panama stamps overprinted "CANAL ZONE" were withdrawn from sale June 30, 1924, and were no longer valid for postage after Aug. 31, 1924.

United States Nos. 551 to 554, 557, 562, 564 to 566, 569, 570 and 571 Overprinted in Red or Black

CANAL
ZONE

Printed and Overprinted by the U.S. Bureau of Engraving and Printing.

Type A

Letters "A" with Flat Tops

1924-25 **Unwmk.** ***Perf. 11***

70 A154 ½c olive brown (R) *(399,500) Apr. 15, 1925*	65	65
On cover		2.50
Block of four	3.00	3.00
Margin block of six, P#	18.00	

71 A155 1c deep green *(1,985,000) July 1, 1924* 1.75 80
On cover 2.00
Block of four 7.50 3.60
Margin block of six, P# 30.00
a. Inverted overprint 500.00 500.00
b. "ZONE" inverted 350.00 325.00
c. "CANAL" only *(20)* 1,250.
d. "ZONE CANAL" *(180)* 400.00
e. Booklet pane of six *(43,152)* 150.00
72 A156 1½c yellow brown *(180,599) Apr. 15, 1925* 2.25 1.25
brown 2.25 1.25
On cover 3.00
Block of four 9.50 7.00
Margin block of six, P# 35.00
73 A157 2c carmine *(2,975,000) July 1, 1924* 7.00 1.50
On cover 2.50
Block of four 32.50 7.00
Margin block of six, P# 175.00
a. Booklet pane of six *(140,000)* 175.00
74 A160 5c dark blue *(500,000) July 1, 1924* 17.50 8.00
On cover 20.00
Block of four 75.00 35.00
Margin block of six, P# 325.00
75 A165 10c orange *(60,000) July 1, 1924* 45.00 20.00
On cover 35.00
Block of four 190.00 90.00
Margin block of six, P# 850.00
76 A167 12c brown violet *(80,000) July 1, 1924* 35.00 30.00
On cover 40.00
Block of four 150.00 130.00
Margin block of six, P# 450.00
a. "ZONE" inverted *3,500. 2,250.*
77 A168 14c dark blue *(100,000) June 27, 1925* 25.00 17.50
On cover 37.50
Block of four 110.00 87.50
Margin block of six, P# 450.00
78 A169 15c gray *(55,000) July 1, 1924* 55.00 30.00
On cover 50.00
Block of four 250.00 150.00
Margin block of six, P# 850.00
79 A172 30c olive brown *(40,000) July 1, 1924* 30.00 25.00
On cover 50.00
Block of four 135.00 110.00
Margin block of six, P# 550.00
80 A173 50c lilac *(25,000) July 1, 1924* 65.00 40.00
On cover 150.00
Block of four 275.00 200.00
Margin block of six, P# 1,750.
81 A174 $1 violet brown *(10,000) July 1, 1924* 250.00 125.00
On cover 425.00
Block of four 1,100. 600.00
Margin block of four, arrow, top or bottom 1,700.
Margin block of six, P# *4,000.*

Normal spacing between words of the overprint is 9¼mm. Minor spacing variations are known. The overprint of the early printings used on all values of this series except No. 77 is a sharp, clear impression. The overprint of the late printings, used only on Nos. 70, 71, 73, 76, 77, 78 and 80 is heavy and smudged, with many of the letters, particularly the "A" practically filled.

Booklet panes Nos. 71e, 73a, 84d, 97b, 101a, 106a and 117a were made from 360 subject plates. The handmade booklet panes Nos. 102a, 115c and a provisional lot of 117b were made from Post Office sheets from regular 400-subject plates.

United States Nos. 554, 555, 567, 562, 564 to 567, 569, 570, 571 and 623 Overprinted in Red or Black

CANAL
ZONE

Type B
Letters "A" with Sharp Pointed Tops

1925-28 ***Perf. 11***

84 A157 2c carmine *(1,110,000) May 1926* 26.50 10.00
On cover 10.00
Block of four 110.00 45.00
Margin block of six, P# 350.00
Margin block of 6, P# & large 5 point star, side only 1,000.
a. "CANAL" only *(20)* 1,000.
b. "ZONE CANAL" *(180)* 225.00
c. Horizontal pair, one without overprint *3,500.*
d. Booklet pane of six *(82,000)* 225.00
85 A158 3c violet *(199,200) June 27, 1925* 3.75 3.00
On cover 5.00
Block of four 16.00 12.50
Margin block of six, P# 175.00
a. "ZONE ZONE" 500.00 500.00
86 A160 5c dark blue *(1,343,147) Jan. 7, 1926* 3.75 2.00
On cover 10.00
Block of four 16.00 9.00
Margin block of six, P# 165.00
a. "ZONE ZONE" (LR18) 1,000.
b. "CANAL" inverted (LR7) 1,000.
c. Inverted overprint *(80)* 500.00
d. Horizontal pair, one without overprint *3,500.*
e. Overprinted "ZONE CANAL" *(90)* 325.00
f. "ZONE" only *(10)* *2,000.*
g. Vertical pair, one without overprint, other overprint inverted *(10)* *2,000.*
h. "CANAL" only *2,000.*

Double transfer (15571 UL 86) 50.00 50.00
87 A165 10c orange *(99,510) Aug., 1925* 32.50 10.00
On cover 25.00
Block of four 150.00 60.00
Margin block of six, P# 500.00
a. "ZONE ZONE" (LR18) *3,250.*
88 A167 12c brown violet *(58,062) Feb., 1926* 22.50 11.00
On cover 30.00
Block of four 100.00 50.00
Margin block of six, P# 350.00
a. "ZONE ZONE" (LR18) *3,250.*
89 A168 14c dark blue *(55,700) Dec., 1928* 19.00 15.00
On cover 30.00
Block of four 85.00 70.00
Margin block of six, P# 350.00
90 A169 15c gray *(204,138) Jan., 1926* 6.00 3.75
On cover 10.00
Block of four 27.50 17.50
Margin block of six, P# 200.00
Margin block of 6, P# & large 5 point star, side only —
a. "ZONE ZONE" (LR18) *3,500.*
91 A187 17c black (R) *(199,500) Apr. 5, 1926* 3.75 3.75
On cover 10.00
Block of four 16.50 16.50
Margin block of six, P# 175.00
a. "ZONE" only *(20)* 1,100.
b. "CANAL" only 1,500.
c. "ZONE CANAL" *(270)* 200.00
92 A170 20c carmine rose *(259,807) Apr. 5, 1926* 5.00 4.25
On cover 15.00
Block of four 22.50 18.50
Margin block of six, P# 175.00
a. "CANAL" inverted (UR48) *3,500.*
b. "ZONE" inverted (LL76) *3,500.*
c. "ZONE CANAL" (LL91) *3,500.*
93 A172 30c olive brown *(154,700) May, 1926* 4.50 3.75
On cover 15.00
Block of four 20.00 18.50
Margin block of six, P# 250.00
94 A173 50c lilac *(13,533) July, 1928* 225.00 130.00
On cover 325.00
Block of four 1,000. 625.00
Margin block of six, P# 2,500.
95 A174 $1 violet brown *(20,000) Apr., 1926* 100.00 35.00
On cover 225.00
Block of four 450.00 165.00
Margin block of four, arrow, top or bottom 500.00
Margin block of six, P# 1,500.

Nos. 85-88, 90 and 93-95 exist with wrong-font "CANAL" and "ZONE". Positions are: Nos. 85-88 and 90, UL51 (CANAL) and UL82 (ZONE); Nos. 93-95, U51 (CANAL) and U82 (ZONE).

Normal spacing between words of the overprint is 11mm on No. 84; 9mm on Nos. 85-88, 90, first printing of No. 91 and the first, third and fourth printing of No. 92; 7mm on the second printings of Nos. 91-92. Minor spacing varieties exist on Nos. 84-88, 90-92.

Overprint Type B on United States Sesquicentennial Stamp No. 627

1926

96 A188 2c carmine rose *(300,000) July 6, 1926* 4.00 3.50
On cover 8.00
Block of four 17.50 15.00
Margin block of six, P# 90.00

On this stamp there is a space of 5mm instead of 9mm between the two words of the overprint.

The authorized date, July 4, fell on a Sunday with the next day also a holiday, so No. 96 was not regularly issued until July 6. But the postmaster sold some copies and canceled some covers on July 4 for a few favored collectors.

Overprint Type B in Black on United States Nos. 583, 584 and 591

1926-27 **Rotary Press Printings** ***Perf. 10***

97 A157 2c carmine *(1,290,000) Dec., 1926* 30.00 10.00
On cover 10.00
Block of four 125.00 45.00
Margin block of four, P# 250.00
a. Pair, one without overprint *(10)* *2,500.*
b. Booklet pane of six *(58,000)* 650.00
c. "CANAL" only *(10)* *1,500.*
d. "ZONE" only *2,500.*
98 A158 3c violet *(239,600) May 9, 1927* 8.50 4.00
On cover 10.00
Block of four 35.00 17.50
Margin block of four, P# 120.00
99 A165 10c orange *(128,400) May 9, 1927* 15.00 7.50
On cover 20.00
Block of four 65.00 35.00
Margin block of four, P# 225.00

Overprint Type B in Black on United States Nos. 632, 634 (Type I), 635, 637 and 642

1927-31 **Rotary Press Printings** ***Perf. 11x10½***

100 A155 1c green *(434,892) June 28, 1927* 2.00 1.25
On cover 2.25
Block of four 8.50 6.00
Margin block of four, P# 20.00
a. Vertical pair, one without overprint *(10)* *2,500.*
101 A157 2c carmine *(1,628,195) June 28, 1927* 2.25 80
On cover 2.00
Block of four 10.00 4.00

Margin block of four, P# 24.00
a. Booklet pane of six *(82,108)* 190.00
102 A158 3c violet *(1,250,000) Feb., 1931* 3.75 3.00
On cover 4.00
Block of four 20.00 14.00
Margin block of four, P# 90.00
a. Booklet pane of six, handmade, perf. margins *3,000.*
103 A160 5c dark blue *(60,000) Dec. 13, 1927* 19.00 10.00
On cover 25.00
Block of four 85.00 42.50
Margin block of four, P# 165.00
104 A165 10c orange *(119,800) July, 1930* 17.00 12.50
On cover 22.50
Block of four 75.00 55.00
Margin block of four, P# 190.00

Maj. Gen. William Crawford Gorgas — A35

Maj. Gen. George Washington Goethals — A36

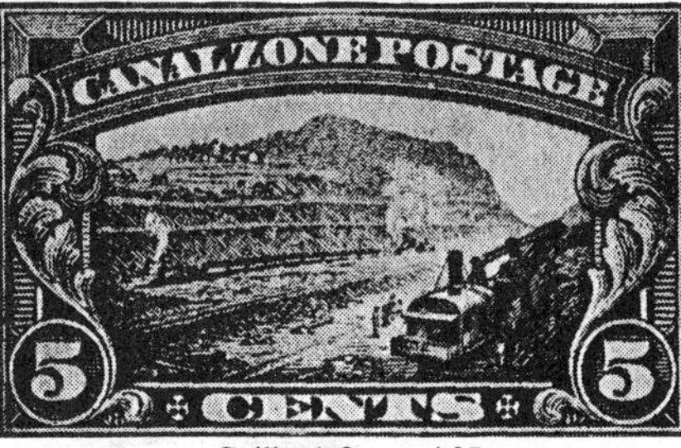

Gaillard Cut — A37

Maj. Gen. Harry Foote Hodges — A38

Lt. Col. David Du Bose Gaillard — A39

Canal Zone stamps can be mounted in Scott's U.S. Possessions Album.

Maj. Gen. William Luther Sibert — A40

Jackson Smith — A41

Rear Admiral Harry Harwood Rousseau — A42

Col. Sydney Bacon Williamson — A43

Joseph Clay Styles Blackburn — A44

Printed by the U. S. Bureau of Engraving and Printing.

Plates of 400 subjects (except 5c), issued in panes of 100. The 5c was printed from plate of 200 subjects, issued in panes of 50. The 400-subject sheets were originally cut by knife into Post Office panes of 100, but beginning in 1948 they were seprated by perforations to eliminate straight edges.

1928-40 Flat Plate Printing Unwmk. *Perf. 11*

105	A35	1c	green *(22,392,147)*	6	5
			First day cover		10.00
			Margin block of six, P#	40	—
a.			Wet printing, yel grn, *Oct. 3, 1928*	9	7
106	A36	2c	carmine *(7,191,600) Oct. 1, 1928*	20	10
			First day cover		10.00
			Margin block of six, P#	1.40	—
a.			Booklet pane of six *(284,640)*	17.50	*7.50*
107	A37	5c	blue *(4,187,028) June 25, 1929*	1.00	40
			First day cover		6.00
			Margin block of six, P#	7.00	—
108	A38	10c	orange *(4,559,788)*	30	15
			First day cover		6.00
			Margin block of six, P#	4.50	—
a.			Wet Dry printing, *Jan. 11, 1932*	40	25
109	A39	12c	brown violet *(844,635)*	1.00	60
			First day cover		10.00
			Margin block of six, P#	8.00	—
a.			Wet printing, violet brown, *July 1, 1929*	1.50	1.00
110	A40	14c	blue *(406,131) Sept. 27, 1937*	1.10	85
			First day cover		6.50
			Margin block of six, P#	10.00	—
111	A41	15c	gray black, *(3,356,500)*	50	35
			First day cover		10.00
			Margin block of six, P#	6.00	—
a.			Wet printing, gray, *Jan. 11, 1932*	80	50
112	A42	20c	dark brown *(3,619,080)*	75	20
			First day cover		10.00
			Margin block of six, P#	6.00	—
a.			Wet printing, olive brown, *Jan. 11, 1932*	1.00	30
113	A43	30c	black *(2,376,491)*	1.00	70
			First day cover		10.00
			Margin block of six, P#	8.00	—
a.			Wet printing, brn blk, *Apr. 15, 1940*	1.25	1.00
114	A44	50c	rose lilac	2.00	65
			First day cover		10.00
			Margin block of six, P#	14.00	—
a.			Wet printing, lilac, *July 1, 1929*	2.50	85

Coils are listed as Nos. 160-161.

> **Wet and Dry Printings**
>
> Canal Zone stamps printed by both the "wet" and "dry" process are Nos. 105, 108-109, 111-114, 117, 138-140, C21-C24, C26, J25, J27. Starting with Nos. 147 and C27, the Bureau of Engraving and Printing used the "dry" method exclusively.
>
> See note on Wet and Dry Printings following U.S. No. 1029.

United States Nos. 720 and 695 Overprinted

Type B

CANAL

ZONE

Rotary Press Printing

1933, Jan. 14 ***Perf. 11x10½***

115	A226	3c	deep violet *(3,150,000)*	1.75	25
			First day cover		7.50
			Margin block of four, P#	20.00	—
b.			"CANAL" only	*3.000.*	
c.			Booklet pane of six, handmade, perf. margins	325.00	—
116	A[illegible]	14c	dark blue *(104,800)*	4.50	2.25
			First day cover		25.00
			Margin block of four, P#	37.50	—
a.			"ZONE CANAL" *(16)*	*1,250.*	

Maj. Gen. George Washington Goethals — A45

20th anniversary of the opening of the Panama Canal.

Flat Plate Printing

1934, Aug. 15 Unwmk. *Perf. 11*

117	A45	3c	red violet	10	6
			First day cover		1.00
			Margin block of six, P#	1.00	—
a.			Booklet pane of six	50.00	*25.00*
b.			As "a," handmade, perf. margins	275.00	—
c.			Wet printing, violet	12	8

Coil is listed as No. 153.

United States Nos. 803 and 805 Overprinted in Black

CANAL ZONE

Rotary Press Printing

1939, Sept. 1 Unwmk. *Perf. 11x10½*

118	A275	½c	red orange, *(1,030,000)*	10	10
			First day cover		75
			Margin block of four, P#	2.25	—
119	A277	1½c	bister brown *(935,000)*	14	14
			brown	14	14
			First day cover		75
			Margin block of four, P#	2.00	—

Balboa-Before — A46

Balboa-After — A47

Gaillard Cut-Before — A48

Gaillard Cut-After — A49

Bas Obispo-Before — A50

Bas Obispo-After — A51

Gatun Locks-Before — A52

Gatun Locks-After — A53

Canal Channel-Before — A54

Canal Channel-After — A55

Gamboa-Before — A56

Gamboa-After — A57

Pedro Miguel Locks-Before — A58

Pedro Miguel Locks-After — A59

Gatun Spilway-Before — A60

Gatun Spillway-After — A61

Issued in commemoration of the 25th anniversary of the opening of the Panama Canal.

Withdrawn Feb. 28, 1941; remainders burned Apr. 12, 1941.

Flat Plate Printing

1939, Aug. 15 Unwmk. *Perf. 11*

120	A46	1c	yellow green *(1,019,482)*	40	30
			First day cover		1.00
			Margin block of six, P#	10.00	—
121	A47	2c	rose carmine *(227,065)*	50	35
			First day cover		1.00
			Margin block of six, P#	11.00	—
122	A48	3c	purple *(2,523,735)*	40	15
			First day cover		1.00
			Margin block of six, P#	10.00	—
123	A49	5c	dark blue *(460,213)*	1.00	90
			First day cover		2.50
			Margin block of six, P#	17.50	—
124	A40	6c	red orange *(68,290)*	2.25	1.50
			First day cover		5.50
			Margin block of six, P#	35.00	—
125	A51	7c	black *(71,235)*	2.25	1.50
			First day cover		5.50
			Margin block of six, P#	35.00	—
126	A52	8c	green *(41,576)*	3.25	2.25
			First day cover		5.50
			Margin block of six, P#	45.00	—
127	A53	10c	ultramarine *(83,571)*	3.25	2.00
			First day cover		5.50
			Margin block of six, P#	45.00	—
128	A54	11c	blue green *(34,010)*	7.50	6.00
			First day cover		11.00
			Margin block of six, P#	110.00	—
129	A55	12c	brown carmine *(66,735)*	6.00	5.00
			First day cover		11.00
			Margin block of six, P#	85.00	—
130	A56	14c	dark violet *(37,365)*	6.75	4.50
			First day cover		11.00
			Margin block of six, P#	100.00	—
131	A57	15c	olive green *(105,058)*	11.00	3.75
			First day cover		10.00
			Margin block of six, P#	125.00	—

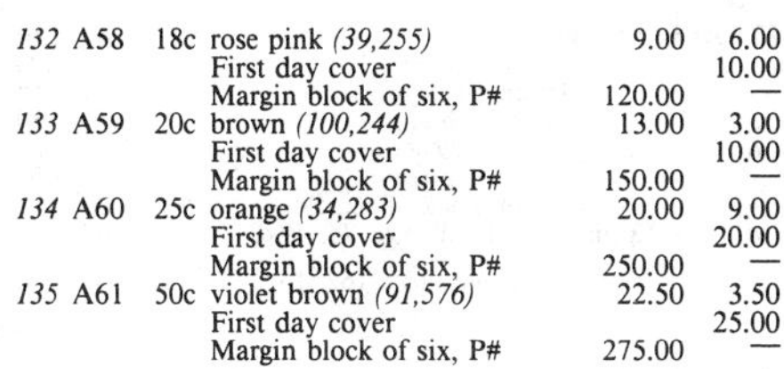

132	A58	18c	rose pink *(39,255)*	9.00	6.00
			First day cover		10.00
			Margin block of six, P#	120.00	—
133	A59	20c	brown *(100,244)*	13.00	3.00
			First day cover		10.00
			Margin block of six, P#	150.00	—
134	A60	25c	orange *(34,283)*	20.00	9.00
			First day cover		20.00
			Margin block of six, P#	250.00	—
135	A61	50c	violet brown *(91,576)*	22.50	3.50
			First day cover		25.00
			Margin block of six, P#	275.00	—

Maj. Gen. George W. Davis — A62

Gov. Charles E. Magoon — A63

Theodore Roosevelt — A64

John F. Stevens — A65

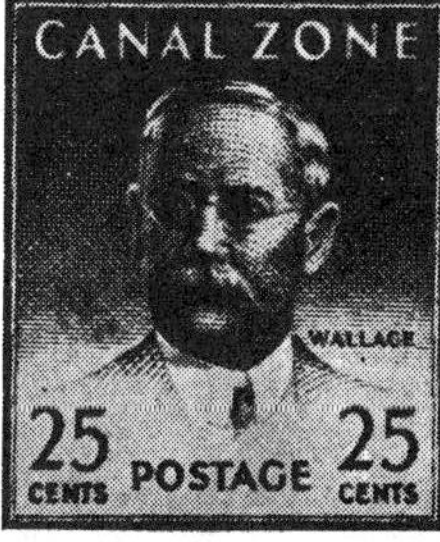

John F. Wallace — A66

1946-49 Unwmk. *Perf. 11*

Size: 19x22mm

136	A62	½c	bright red *(1,020,000) Aug. 16, 1948*	35	15
			First day cover		1.25
			Margin block of six, P#	2.50	—
137	A63	1½c	chocolate *(603,600) Aug. 16, 1948*	35	15
			First day cover		1.25
			Margin block of six, P#	2.25	—
138	A64	2c	lt rose carmine *(6,951,755)*	8	5
			First day cover		50
			Margin block of six, P#	50	—
a.			Wet printing, rose carmine, *Oct. 27, 1949*	15	8

139 A65	5c dark blue	40	10
	First day cover		1.00
	Margin block of six, P#	2.75	—
a.	Wet printing, deep blue, *Apr. 25, 1946*	1.00	10
140 A66	25c green *(1,520,000)*	1.00	65
	First day cover		3.50
	Margin block of six, P#	9.00	—
a.	Wet printing, yel grn, *Aug. 16, 1948*	5.00	1.75

See Nos. 155, 162, 164.

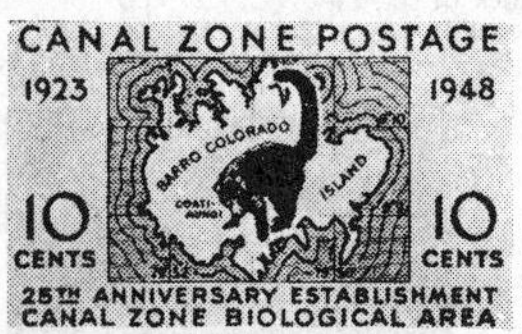

Map of Biological Area and Coati-mundi — A67

Issued to commemorate the 25th anniversary of the establishment of the Canal Zone Biolgical Area on Barro Colorado Island.

Withdrawn Mar. 30, 1951, and remainders destroyed April 10, 1951.

1948, Apr. 17 **Unwmk.** ***Perf. 11***

141 A67	10c black *(521,200)*	1.25	80
	First day cover		2.00
	Margin block of six, P#	10.00	—

"Forty-niners" Arriving at Chagres — A68

Journeying in "Bungo" to Las Cruces — A69

Las Cruces Trail to Panama — A70

Departure for San Francisco — A71

Issued to commemorate the centenary of the California Gold Rush.

Stocks on hand were processed for destruction on Aug. 11, 1952 and destroyed Aug. 13, 1952.

1949, June 1 **Unwmk.** ***Perf. 11***

142 A68	3c blue *(500.000)*	85	35
	First day cover		1.00
	Margin block of six, P#	7.50	—
143 A69	6c violet *(481,600)*	90	45
	First day cover		1.00
	Margin block of six, P#	10.00	—
144 A70	12c bright blue green *(230,200)*	2.50	1.40
	First day cover		1.75
	Margin block of six, P#	22.50	—
145 A71	18c deep red lilac *(240,200)*	3.25	2.00
	First day cover		3.00
	Margin block of six, P#	30.00	—

Workers in Culebra Cut — A72

Issued to commemorate the contribution of West Indian laborers in the construction of the Panama Canal. Entire issue sold, none withdrawn and destroyed.

1951, Aug. 15 **Unwmk.** ***Perf. 11***

146 A72	10c carmine *(480,000)*	3.00	1.65
	First day cover		2.25
	Margin block of six, P#	27.50	—

Early Railroad Scene — A73

Centenary of the completion of the Panama Railroad and the first transcontinental railroad trip in the Americas.

1955, Jan. 28 **Unwmk.** ***Perf. 11***

147 A73	3c violet *(994,000)*	75	50
	First day cover		1.25
	Margin block of six, P#	7.00	—

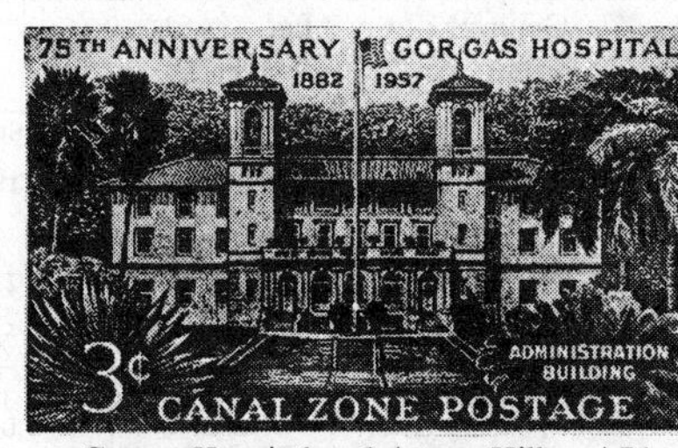

Gorgas Hospital and Ancon Hill — A74

75th anniversary of Gorgas Hospital.

1957, Nov. 17 **Unwmk.** ***Perf. 11***

148 A74	3c black, *dull blue green (1,010,000)*	50	35
	Light blue green paper	50	35
	First day cover		75
	Margin block of four, P#	4.00	—

Souvenir cards are listed and valued in a separate section of the catalogue. See catalogue index.

S.S. Ancon — A75

1958, Aug. 30 **Engr.** **Unwmk.** ***Perf. 11***

149 A75	4c greenish blue *(1,749,700)*	45	30
	First day cover		75
	Margin block of four, P#	3.00	—

Roosevelt Medal and Canal Zone Map — A76

Issued to commemorate the centenary of the birth of Theodore Roosevelt (1858-1919).

1958, Nov. 15 **Unwmk.** ***Perf. 11***

150 A76	4c brown *(1,060,000)*	50	30
	First day cover		75
	Margin block of four, P#	3.25	—

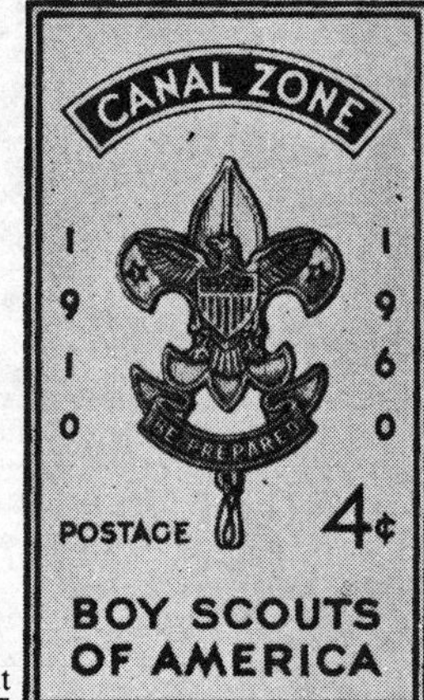

Boy Scout Badge — A77

Issued to commemorate the 50th anniversary of the Boy Scouts of America.

Giori Press Printing

1960, Feb. 8 **Unwmk.** ***Perf. 11***

151 A77	4c dark blue, red & bister *(654,933)*	50	40
	First day cover		1.00
	Margin block of four, P#	4.00	—

Administration Building, Balboa Heights — A78

1960, Nov. 1 **Engr.** **Unwmk.** ***Perf. 11***

152 A78	4c rose lilac *(2,486,725)*	15	12
	First day cover		85
	Margin block of four, P#	80	—

Coil Stamps
Types of 1934, 1960 and 1946

1960-62 **Unwmk.** ***Perf. 10 Vertically***

153	A45	3c deep violet *(3,743,959) Nov. 1, 1960*	15	12
		First day cover		1.00
		Pair	30	25
		Joint line pair	1.00	—

Perf. 10 Horizontally

154	A78	4c dull rose lilac *(2,776,273) Nov. 1, 1960*	20	12
		First day cover		1.00
		Pair	40	25
		Joint line pair	1.10	—

Perf. 10 Vertically

155	A65	5c deep blue *(3,288,264) Feb. 10, 1962*	30	20
		First day cover		1.00
		Pair	60	50
		Joint line pair	1.25	—

Girl Scout Badge and Camp at Gatun Lake — A79

Issued to commemorate the 50th anniversary of the Girl Scouts.

Giori Press Printing

1962, Mar. 12 **Unwmk.** ***Perf. 11***

156	A79	4c blue, dark green & bister *(640,000)*	40	30
		First day cover *(83,717)*		1.25
		Margin block of four, P#	2.25	—

Thatcher Ferry Bridge and Map of Western Hemisphere — A80

Issued to commemorate the opening of the Thatcher Ferry Bridge, spanning the Panama Canal.

Giori Press Printing

1962, Oct. 12 **Unwmk.** ***Perf. 11***

157	A80	4c black & silver *(775,000)*	35	25
		First day cover *(65,833)*		1.00
		Margin block of 4, two P#	3.25	—
a.		Silver (bridge) omitted *(50)*	9,000.	
a.		Margin block of 10, black P# only	—	

Goethals Memorial, Balboa — A81

Fort San Lorenzo — A82

1968-71 **Giori Press Printing** ***Perf. 11***

158	A81	6c green & ultra. *(1,890,000) Mar. 15, 1968*	40	15
		First day cover		75
		Margin block of 4, P#	2.00	—
159	A82	8c slate green, blue, dark brown & ocher *(3,460,000) July 14, 1971*	40	16
		First day cover		75
		Margin block of 4, P#	2.75	—

Coil Stamps
Types of 1928, 1932 and 1948

1975, Feb. 14 **Engr.** **Unwmk.** ***Perf. 10 Vertically***

160	A35	1c green *(1,090,958)*	10	6
		First day cover		35
		Pair	20	12
		Joint line pair	1.00	—
161	A38	10c orange *(590,658)*	70	35
		First day cover		50
		Pair	1.40	70
		Joint line pair	5.00	—
162	A66	25c yellow green *(129,831)*	2.75	2.25
		First day cover		1.50
		Pair	5.50	4.50
		Joint line pair	20.00	—

Dredge Cascadas — A83

1976, Feb. 23 **Giori Press Printing** ***Perf. 11***

163	A83	13c multi *(3,653,950)*	40	20
		First day cover		1.00
		Margin block of 4, P#	2.00	—
a.		Bklt. pane of 4 *(1,032,400) Apr. 19*	3.00	—

Stevens Type of 1946

1977 **Rotary Press Printing** ***Perf. 11x10½***
Size: 19x22½mm

164	A65	5c deep blue *(1,009,612)*	45	35
		Margin block of 4, P#	2.50	—

No. 164 was also printed on tagged paper even though there was no equipment in the Canal Zone to detect tagging.

Towing Locomotive, Ship in Lock, by Alwyn Sprague — A84

1978, Oct. 25 **Engr.** ***Perf. 11***

165	A84	15c dp grn & bl grn *(2,921,083)*	40	20
		First day cover *(81,405)*		75
		Margin block of 4, P#	1.75	—

AIR POST STAMPS

AIR MAIL

Regular Issue of 1928 Surcharged in Dark Blue

25 CENTS 25

15 — Type I- Flag of "5" pointing up

15 — Type II- Flag of "5" curved

1929-31 **Flat Plate Printing** **Unwmk.** ***Perf. 11***

C1	A35	15c on 1c green, type I, *Apr. 1, 1929*	10.00	6.50
		First day cover		25.00
		Block of four	42.50	30.00
		Margin block of six, P#	125.00	—
C2	A35	15c on 1c yellow green, type II, *Mar. 1931*	85.00	75.00
		On cover		150.00
		Block of four	375.00	300.00
		Margin block of six, P#	1,000.	—
C3	A36	25c on 2c carmine *(223,880) Jan. 11, 1929*	4.00	2.25
		First day cover		17.50
		Block of four	17.00	10.50
		Margin block of six, P#	115.00	—

AIR MAIL

Nos. 114 and 106 Surcharged in Black

≡10c

1929, Dec. 31

C4	A44	10c on 50c lilac *(116,666)*	8.50	8.00
		First day cover		25.00
		Block of four	37.50	35.00
		Margin block of six, P#	125.00	—
C5	A36	20c on 2c carmine *(638,395)*	6.00	2.00
		First day cover		20.00
		Block of four	25.00	8.00
		Margin block of six, P#	100.00	55.00
a.		Dropped "2" in surch. *(7,000)*	100.00	—

Gaillard Cut — AP1

Printed by the U. S. Bureau of Engraving and Printing.
Plates of 200 subjects, issued in panes of 50.

1931-49 **Unwmk.** ***Perf. 11***

C6	AP1	4c red violet *(525,000) Jan. 3, 1949*	60	50
		First day cover		2.00
		Margin block of six, P#	4.00	—
C7	AP1	5c yellow green *(9,988,800) Nov. 18, 1931*	50	30
		green	50	30
		First day cover		10.00
		Margin block of six, P#	4.00	—
C8	AP1	6c yellow brown *(9,440,000) Feb. 15, 1946*	65	30
		First day cover		2.00
		Margin block of six, P#	4.50	—
C9	AP1	10c orange *(5,140,000) Nov. 18, 1931*	85	30
		First day cover		10.00
		Margin block of six, P#	9.00	—
C10	AP1	15c blue *(11,961,500) Nov. 18, 1931*	1.00	25
		pale blue	1.00	25
		First day cover		10.00
		Margin block of six, P#	10.00	—
C11	AP1	20c red violet *(3,214,600) Nov. 18, 1931*	2.00	25
		deep violet	2.00	25
		First day cover		20.00
		Margin block of six, P#	17.50	—
C12	AP1	30c rose lake *(1,150,000) July 15, 1941*	3.50	1.00
		dull rose	3.50	1.00
		First day cover		22.50
		Margin block of six, P#	30.00	—
C13	AP1	40c yellow *(826,100) Nov. 18, 1931*	3.00	1.00
		lemon	3.00	1.00
		First day cover		30.00
		Margin block of six, P#	30.00	—
C14	AP1	$1 black *(406,000) Nov. 18, 1931*	10.00	2.25
		First day cover		50.00
		Margin block of six, P#	85.00	—

Douglas Plane over Sosa Hill — AP2

Planes and Map of Central America — AP3

Pan American Clipper and Scene near Fort Amador — AP4

Pan American Clipper at Cristobal Harbor — AP5

Pan American Clipper over Gaillard Cut — AP6

Pan American Clipper Landing — AP7

Issued in commemoration of the 10th anniversary of Air Mail service and the 25th anniversary of the opening of the Panama Canal.

Withdrawn February 28, 1941 and remainders burned April 12, 1941.

Flat Plate Printing

1939, July 15 Unwmk. *Perf. 11*

C15	AP2	5c	greenish black *(86,576)*	3.75	3.25
			First day cover		5.00
			Margin block of six, P#	35.00	—
C16	AP3	10c	dull violet *(117,644)*	3.75	3.00
			First day cover		5.00
			Margin block of six, P#	40.00	—
C17	AP4	15c	light brown *(883,742)*	4.00	1.25
			First day cover		3.00
			Margin block of six, P#	45.00	—
C18	AP5	25c	blue *(82,126)*	17.50	11.00
			First day cover		17.50
			Margin block of six, P#	165.00	—
C19	AP6	30c	rose carmine *(121,382)*	12.50	8.00
			First day cover		15.00
			Margin block of six, P#	120.00	—
C20	AP7	$1	green *(40,051)*	42.50	35.00
			First day cover		60.00
			Margin block of six, P#	375.00	—

Globe and Wing — AP8

Flat Plate Printing

1951, July 16 Unwmk. *Perf. 11*

C21	AP8	4c	lt red violet *(1,315,000)*	80	30
			Margin block of six, P#	7.00	—
a.			Wet printing, red violet	1.25	40
C22	AP8	6c	lt brown *(22,657,625)*	65	25
			Margin block of six, P#	5.25	—
a.			Wet printing, brown	95	35
C23	AP8	10c	lt red orange *(1,049,130)*	1.10	40
			Margin block of six, P#	8.50	—
a.			Wet printing, red orange	2.00	50
C24	AP8	21c	lt blue *(1,460,000)*	9.50	3.50
			Margin block of six, P#	80.00	—
a.			Wet printing, blue	15.00	5.00
C25	AP8	31c	cerise *(375,000)*	9.00	3.25
			Margin block of six, P#	85.00	—
a.			Horiz. pair, imperf. vert. *(98)*	800.00	—
C26	AP8	80c	lt gray black *(827,696)*	6.50	1.25
			Margin block of six, P#	42.50	—
a.			Wet printing, gray black	12.50	1.65

See note after No. 114.

Type of 1951

Flat Plate Printing

1958, Aug. 16 Unwmk. *Perf. 11*

C27	AP8	5c	yellow green *(899,923)*	1.00	50
			First day cover *(2,176)*		1.50
			Margin block of four, P#	6.00	—
C28	AP8	7c	olive *(9,381,797)*	1.00	40
			First day cover *(2,815)*		1.25
			Margin block of four, P#	5.00	—
C29	AP8	15c	brown violet *(359,923)*	6.00	1.50
			First day cover *(2,040)*		2.50
			Margin block of four, P#	40.00	—
C30	AP8	25c	orange yellow *(600,000)*	13.00	2.00
			First day cover *(2,115)*		4.50
			Margin block of four, P#	90.00	—
C31	AP8	35c	dark blue *(283,032)*	11.50	2.00
			First day cover *(1,868)*		6.00
			Margin block of four, P#	50.00	—

Emblem of U.S. Army Caribbean School — AP9

Issued to honor the U.S. Army Caribbean School for Latin America at Fort Gulick.

Giori Press Printing

1961, Nov. 21 Unwmk. *Perf. 11*

C32	AP9	15c	red & blue *(560,000)*	1.65	1.00
			First day cover *(25,949)*		1.75
			Margin block of four, P#	16.00	—

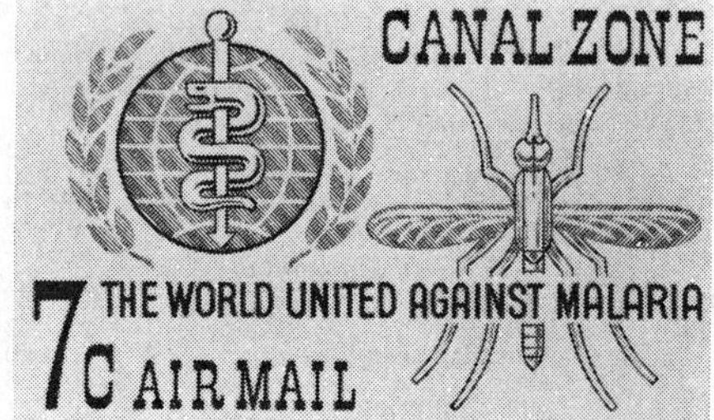

Malaria Eradication Emblem and Mosquito — AP10

World Health Organization drive to eradicate malaria.

Giori Press Printing

1962, Sept. 24 Unwmk. *Perf. 11*

C33	AP10	7c	yellow & black *(862,349)*	60	50
			First day cover *(44,433)*		1.00
			Margin block of four, P#	3.50	—

Globe-Wing Type of 1951

1963, Jan. 7 Rotary Press Printing *Perf. 10½x11*

C34	AP8	8c	carmine *(5,054,727)*	75	30
			First day cover *(19,128)*		1.00
			Margin block of four, P#	5.00	—

Alliance for Progress Emblem — AP11

Issued to commemorate the second anniversary of the Alliance for Progress, which aims to stimulate economic growth and raise living standards in Latin America.

Giori Press Printing

1963, Aug. 17 Unwmk. *Perf. 11*

C35	AP11	15c	gray, grn. & dk. ultra. *(405,000)*	1.50	85
			First day cover *(29,594)*		1.50
			Margin block of four, P#	14.00	—

Jet over Cristobal — AP12

50th anniversary of the Panama Canal.

Designs: 8c, Gatun Locks. 15c, Madden Dam. 20c, Gaillard Cut. 30c, Miraflores Locks. 80c, Balboa.

Giori Press Printing

1964, Aug. 15 Unwmk. *Perf. 11*

C36	AP12	6c	green & black *(257,193)*	50	35
			Margin block of four, P#	2.50	—
C37	AP12	8c	rose red & black *(3,924,283)*	60	35
			Margin block of four, P#	3.00	—
C38	AP12	15c	blue & black *(472,666)*	1.65	50
			Margin block of four, P#	10.50	—
C39	AP12	20c	rose lilac & black *(399,784)*	2.75	85
			Margin block of four, P#	14.00	—
C40	AP12	30c	reddish brown & black *(204,524)*	4.00	2.00
			Margin block of four, P#	21.00	—
C41	AP12	80c	olive bister & black *(186,809)*	7.00	3.00
			Margin block of four, P#	32.50	—

Canal Zone Seal and Jet Plane — AP13

Giori Press Printing

1965, July 15 **Unwmk.** ***Perf. 11***

No.	Design	Value	Description	Unused	Used
C42	AP13	6c	green & black *(548,250)*	40	20
			Margin block of four, P#	2.00	—
C43	AP13	8c	rose red & black *(8,357,700)*	45	10
			Margin block of four, P#	2.25	—
C44	AP13	15c	blue & black *(2,385,000)*	50	20
			Margin block of four, P#	2.50	—
C45	AP13	20c	lilac & black *(2,290,699)*	60	30
			Margin block of four, P#	3.00	—
C46	AP13	30c	redsh brn & blk *(2,332,255)*	1.00	35
			Margin block of four, P#	5.00	—
C47	AP13	80c	bister & black *(1,456,596)*	3.25	90
			Margin block of four, P#	16.50	—

1968-76

No.	Design	Value	Description	Unused	Used
C48	AP13	10c	dull orange & black *(10,055,000) Mar. 15, 1968*	30	15
			Margin block of 4, P#	1.50	—
a.			Bklt. pane of 4 *(713,390) Feb. 18, 1970*	4.25	—
C49	AP13	11c	olive & black *(3,335,000) Sept. 24, 1971*	30	18
			Margin block of 4, P#	1.50	—
a.			Bklt. pane of 4 *(1,277,760) Sept. 24, 1971*	3.50	—
C50	AP13	13c	emerald & black *(1,865,000) Feb. 11, 1974*	1.10	30
			First day cover		55
			Margin block of 4, P#	6.00	—
a.			Booklet pane of 4 *(619,200) Feb. 11, 1974*	6.00	—
C51	AP13	22c	vio & blk *(363,720) May 10, 1976*	1.00	50
			Margin block of four, P#	5.00	—
C52	AP13	25c	pale yellow green & black *(1,640,441) Mar. 15, 1968*	1.00	35
			Margin block of four, P#	5.00	—
C53	AP13	35c	salmon & black *(573,822) May 10, 1976*	2.00	60
			Margin block of four, P#	10.00	—

AIR POST OFFICIAL STAMPS

(See note above No. O1)

Air Post Stamps of 1931-41 Overprinted in Black

OFFICIAL
PANAMA CANAL

Two types of overprint.

Type I- "PANAMA CANAL" 19-20mm long

1941-42 **Unwmk.** ***Perf. 11***

No.	Design	Value	Description	Unused	Used
CO1	AP1	5c	yellow green *(42,754) Mar. 31, 1941*	4.25	1.50
			green	4.25	1.50
			On cover		40.00
			Block of four	18.50	6.00
CO2	AP1	10c	orange *(49,723) Mar. 31, 1941*	9.00	2.00
			On cover		30.00
			Block of four	40.00	9.00
CO3	AP1	15c	blue *(56,898) Mar. 31, 1941*	11.00	2.75
			On cover		25.00
			Block of four	47.50	25.00
CO4	AP1	20c	red violet *(22,107) Mar. 31, 1941*	16.00	4.50
			deep violet	16.00	4.50
			On cover		110.00
			Block of four	75.00	22.50
CO5	AP1	30c	rose lake *(22,100) June, 4, 1942*	20.00	4.50
			dull rose	20.00	4.50
			On cover		40.00
			Block of four	90.00	20.00
CO6	AP1	40c	yellow *(22,875) Mar. 31, 1941*	22.50	7.00
			lemon yellow	22.50	7.00
			On cover		50.00
			Block of four	100.00	35.00
CO7	AP1	$1	black *(29,525) Mar. 31, 1941*	30.00	10.00
			On cover		150.00
			Block of four	135.00	45.00

Overprint varieties occur on Nos. CO1-CO7 and CO14: "O" of "OFFICIAL" over "N" of "PANAMA" (entire third row). "O" of "OFFICIAL" broken at top (position 31). "O" of "OFFICIAL" over second "A" of "PANAMA" (position 45). First "F" of "OFFICIAL" over second "A" of "PANAMA" (position 50).

1941, Sept. 22

Type II- "PANAMA CANAL" 17mm long

No.	Design	Value	Description	Unused	Used
CO8	AP1	5c	yellow green *(2,000)*	—	200.00
			On cover		400.00
			Block of four		850.00
CO9	AP1	10c	orange *(2,000)*	—	250.00
			On cover		400.00
			Block of four		1,250.
CO10	AP1	20c	red violet *(2,000)*	—	200.00
			On cover		—
			Block of four		850.00
CO11	AP1	30c	rose lake *(5,000)*	—	60.00
			On cover		125.00
			Block of four	—	250.00
CO12	AP1	40c	yellow *(2,000)*	—	200.00
			On cover		400.00
			Block of four		850.00

1947, Nov.

Type I- "PANAMA CANAL" 19-20mm long

No.	Design	Value	Description	Unused	Used
CO14	AP1	6c	yellow brown *(33,450)*	12.50	3.50
			On cover		50.00
			Block of four	55.00	15.00
a.			Inverted overprint *(50)*		*1,200.*

POSTAGE DUE STAMPS

Prior to 1914, many of the postal issues were handstamped "Postage Due" and used as postage due stamps.

Postage Due Stamps of the United States Nos. J45a, J46a, and J49a Overprinted in Black

CANAL ZONE

1914, Mar. **Wmk. 190** ***Perf. 12***

No.	Design	Value	Description	Unused	Used
J1	D2	1c	rose carmine *(23,533)*	80.00	19.00
			On cover		150.00
			Block of four (2mm spacing)	350.00	90.00
			Block of four (3mm spacing)	375.00	100.00
			Margin block of six, imprint, star and P#	650.00	—
J2	D2	2c	rose carmine *(32,312)*	175.00	60.00
			On cover		175.00
			Block of four	750.00	275.00
			Margin block of six, P#	1,200.	—
J3	D2	10c	rose carmine *(92,493)*	500.00	45.00
			On cover		450.00
			Block of four (2mm spacing)	2,250.	190.00
			Block of four (3mm spacing)	2,250.	190.00
			Margin block of six, imprint, star and P#	*4,000.*	—

Many examples of Nos. J1-J3 show one or more letters of the overprint out of alignment, principally the "E".

San Geronimo Castle Gate, Portobelo (See footnote) — D1

Statue of Columbus D2

Pedro J. Sosa D3

1915, Mar. **Unwmk.** ***Perf. 12***

Blue Overprint, Type II, on Postage Due Stamps of Panama

No.	Design	Value	Description	Unused	Used
J4	D1	1c	olive brown *(50,000)*	10.00	4.25
			On cover		75.00
			Block of four	42.50	20.00
J5	D2	2c	olive brown *(50,000)*	140.00	22.50
			On cover		100.00
			Block of four	600.00	120.00
J6	D3	10c	olive brown *(200,000)*	40.00	11.00
			On cover		90.00
			Block of four	175.00	50.00

Type D1 was intended to show a gate of San Lorenzo Castle, Chagres, and is so labeled. By error the stamp actually shows the main gate of San Geronimo Castle, Portobelo.

Experts believe that examples of the 1c with overprint type V, reading up or down, are bogus.

Surcharged in Red

CANAL 2 ZONE

1915, Nov. **Unwmk.** ***Perf. 12***

No.	Design	Value	Description	Unused	Used
J7	D1	1c	on 1c olive brown *(60,614)*	75.00	13.00
			On cover		100.00
			Block of four	325.00	65.00
J8	D2	2c	on 2c olive brown	25.00	7.50
			On cover		85.00
			Block of four	105.00	35.00
J9	D3	10c	on 10c olive brown *(175,548)*	22.50	4.50
			On cover		70.00
			Block of four	100.00	22.50

One of the printings of No. J9 shows wider spacing between "1" and "0". Both spacings occur on the same sheet.

D4

Capitol, Panama — D5

1919, Dec.

Surcharged in Carmine at Mount Hope

No.	Design	Value	Description	Unused	Used
J10	D4	2c	on 2c olive brown	27.50	11.00
			On cover		85.00
			Block of four	120.00	50.00
J11	D5	4c	on 4c olive brown *(35,695)*	27.50	12.50
			On cover		100.00
			Block of four	125.00	55.00
a.			"ZONE" omitted	*3,250.*	
b.			"4" omitted	*2,750.*	

United States Postage Due Stamps Nos. J61, J62b and J65b Overprinted

CANAL
ZONE

Type A

Letters "A" with Flat Tops

1924, July 1 ***Perf. 11***

No.	Design	Value	Description	Unused	Used
J12	D2	1c	carmine rose *(10,000)*	100.00	20.00
			On cover		75.00
			Block of four	450.00	90.00
			Margin block of six, P#	1,000.	—
J13	D2	2c	deep claret *(25,000)*	55.00	10.00
			On cover		75.00
			Block of four	250.00	47.50
			Margin block of six, P#	500.00	—
J14	D2	10c	deep claret *(30,000)*	200.00	37.50
			On cover		200.00
			Block of four (2mm spacing)	1,000.	160.00
			Block of four (3mm spacing)	1,000.	160.00
			Margin block of six, imprint, star and P#	2,000.	—

United States Nos. 552, 554 and 562 Overprinted Type A and Additionally Overprinted at Mount Hope in Red or Blue

POSTAGE
DUE

1925, Feb. ***Perf. 11***

No.	Design	Value	Description	Unused	Used
J15	A155	1c	deep green (R) *(15,000)*	100.00	20.00
			On cover		75.00
			Block of four	425.00	85.00
			Margin block of 6, P#	825.00	—
J16	A157	2c	carmine (Bl) *(21,335)*	20.00	7.00
			On cover		50.00
			Block of four	85.00	30.00
			Margin block of 6, P#	175.00	—
J17	A165	10c	orange (R) *(39,819)*	37.50	11.00
			On cover		75.00
			Block of four	165.00	47.50
			Margin block of 6, P#	400.00	—
a.			"POSTAGE DUE" double	450.00	
b.			"E" of "POSTAGE" omitted	400.00	
c.			As "b," "POSTAGE DUE" double	*3,000.*	

Overprinted Type B

Letters "A" with Sharp Pointed Tops

On United States Postage Due Stamps Nos. J61, J62, J65 and J65a

1925, June 24

No.	Design	Value	Description	Unused	Used
J18	D2	1c	carmine rose *(80,000)*	7.00	3.00
			On cover		35.00
			Block of four	30.00	15.00

Margin block of 6, P# 65.00 —
a. "ZONE ZONE" (LR18) 1,400.
J19 D2 2c carmine rose *(146,430)* 12.50 4.00
On cover 35.00
Block of four 55.00 17.50
Margin block of 6, P# 140.00 —
a. "ZONE ZONE" (LR18) 1,600.
J20 D2 10c carmine rose *(153,980)* 130.00 20.00
On cover 100.00
Block of four, 2mm spacing 525.00 85.00
Block of four, 3mm spacing 550.00 90.00
Margin block of 6, Imprint, star and P# 1,200. —
a. Vert. pair, one without ovpt. *(10)* *2,000.*
Margin block of 6, imprint, Star and P# *18,000.*
b. 10c rose red 175.00 70.00
On cover 110.00
c. Double overprint 325.00

Nos. J18-J20 exist with wrong font "CANAL" (UL51) and "ZONE" (UL82).

Regular Issue of 1928-29 Surcharged

1929-30

J21 A37 1c on 5c blue *(35,990) Mar. 20, 1930* 3.00 1.75
On cover 15.00
Margin block of 6, P# 32.50 —
a. "POSTAGE DUE" omitted *(5)* *2,500.*
J22 A37 2c on 5c blue *(40,207) Oct. 18, 1930* 5.00 2.50
On cover 15.00
Margin block of 6, P# 40.00 —
J23 A37 5c on 5c blue *(35,464) Dec. 1, 1930* 5.00 2.75
On cover 15.00
Margin block of 6, P# 40.00 —
J24 A37 10c on 5c blue *(90,504) Dec. 16, 1929* 4.50 2.75
On cover 15.00
Margin block of 6, P# 40.00 —

On No. J23 the three short horizontal bars in the lower corners of the surcharge are omitted.

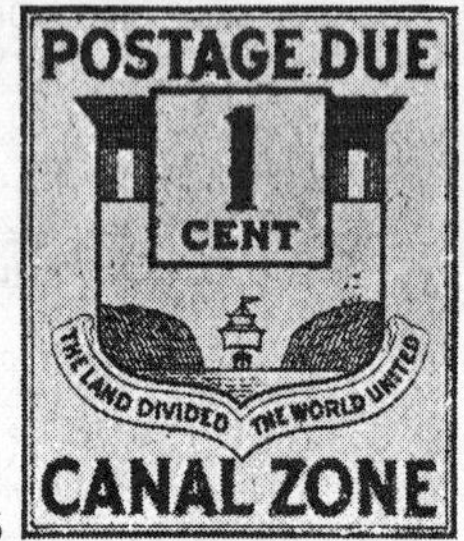

Canal Zone Seal — D6

Printed by the U.S. Bureau of Engraving and Printing.

Plates of 400 subjects, issued in panes of 100.

1932-41 **Flat Plate Printing**

J25 D6 1c claret *(378,300) Jan. 2, 1932* 10 10
a. Dry printing, red violet 20 10
Margin block of 6, P# 3.00 —
J26 D6 2c claret *(413,800) Jan. 2, 1932* 12 20
Margin block of 6, P# 3.00 —
J27 D6 5c claret *Jan. 2, 1932* 35 20
a. Dry printing, red violet 1.00 30
Margin block of 6, P# 6.00 —
J28 D6 10c claret *(400,600) Jan. 2, 1932* 1.40 1.85
Margin block of 6, P# 15.00 —
J29 D6 15c claret *Apr. 21, 1941* 1.10 1.00
Margin block of 6, P# 12.00 —

See note after No. 114.

OFFICIAL STAMPS

Beginning in March, 1915, stamps for use on official mail were identified by a large "P" perforated through each stamp. These were replaced by overprinted issues in 1941. The use of official stamps was discontinued December 31, 1951. During their currency, they were not for sale in mint condition and were sold to the public only when canceled with a parcel post rotary canceler reading "Balboa Heights, Canal Zone" between two wavy lines.

After having been withdrawn from use, mint stamps (except Nos. O3, O8 and CO8-CO12) were made available to the public at face value for three months beginning Jan. 2, 1952. Values for used stamps are for canceled-to-order specimens, postally used copies being worth more. Sheet margins were removed to facilitate overprinting and plate numbers are, therefore, unknown.

Regular Issues of 1928-34 Overprinted in Black by the Panama Canal Press, Mount Hope, C.Z.

OFFICIAL
PANAMA
CANAL
Type 1

OFFICIAL
PANAMA CANAL
Type 2

Type 1- "PANAMA" 10mm long
Type 1A- "PANAMA" 9mm long

1941, Mar. 31 **Unwmk.** ***Perf. 11***

O1 A35 1c yellow green, type 1 *(87,198)* 2.00 35
On cover 35.00
O2 A45 3c deep violet, type 1 *(34,958)* 3.75 70
On cover 25.00
O3 A37 5c blue *(19,105)* — 40.00
On cover *110.00*
O4 A38 10c orange, type 1 *(18,776)* 5.75 1.75
On cover 50.00
O5 A41 15c gray black, type 1 *(16,888)* 12.00 2.00
gray 2.00
On cover 50.00
O6 A42 20c olive brown, type 1 *(20,264)* 15.00 2.50
On cover 75.00
O7 A44 50c lilac, type 1 *(19,175)* 50.00 7.50
rose lilac 7.50
On cover 150.00
O8 A44 50c rose lilac, type 1A *(1000)* 650.00

No. O3 exists with "O" directly over "N" of "PANAMA."

No. 139 Overprinted in Black

1947, Feb.

O9 A65 5c deep blue, type 1 *(21,639)* 7.50 3.00
On cover 70.00

POST OFFICE SEALS

POS1

Issued in sheets of 8 without gum, imperforate margins.

1907 **Typo.** **Unwmk.** ***Perf. 11½***

OX1 POS1 blue 40.00
Block of four 175.00
a. Wmkd. seal of U.S. in sheet 55.00

No. OX1 cliches are spaced 3½mm apart.

1910

OX2 POS1 ultramarine 70.00
a. Wmkd. "Rolleston Mills" in sheet 90.00
b. Wmkd. U.S. Seal in sheet 225.00
Block of four, cliches ½mm apart 325.00
Block of four, cliches 1½mm apart horiz., 4mm vert. 800.00

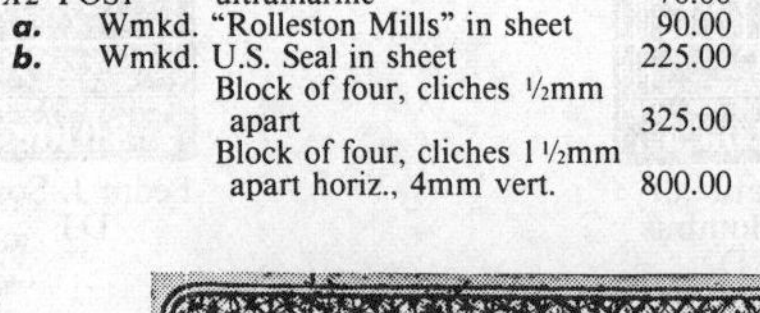

POS2

Printed by the Panama Canal Press, Mount Hope, C.Z.

Issued in sheets of 25, without gum, imperforate margins.

Rouletted 6 horizontally in color of seal, vertically without color

1917, Sept. 22

OX3 POS2 dark blue 4.00 —
Block of four 17.50
a. Wmkd. double lined letters in sheet ("Sylvania") 35.00

1946 ***Rouletted 6, without color***

Issued in sheets of 20, without gum, imperforate margins.

OX4 POS2 slate blue 7.00
Block of four 30.00

POS3

Typographed by the Panama Canal Press

Issued in sheets of 32, without gum, imperforate margins except at top.

Size: 46x27mm

Seal Diameter: 13mm

1954, Mar. 8 **Unwmk.** ***Perf. 12½***

OX5 POS3 black *(16,000)* 5.00 —
a. Wmkd. Seal of U. S. in sheet 20.00 —

Seal Diameter: 11½mm

1961-74 ***Rouletted 5***

OX6 POS3 black, *July 1, 1974* 2.50 —
a. Perf. 12½ *May 16, 1961 (48,000)* 2.50 —
b. Wmkd. Seal of U.S. in sheet, perf. 12½ 6.00
c. As "a," double impression 80.00
d. As "b," double impression 100.00

ENVELOPES

Values for cut squares are for copies with fine margins on all sides. Values for unused entries are for those without printed or manuscript address. A "full corner" includes black and side flaps and commands a premium.

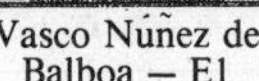

Vasco Nuñez de Balboa — E1

Fernandez de Cordoba — E2

Envelopes of Panama Lithographed and Overprinted by American Bank Note Co.

1916, Apr. 24

On White Paper

U1 E1 1c green & black 15.00 10.00
Entire 110.00 60.00
a. Head and overprint only — —
Entire *2,000.* *2,000.*
b. Frame only — —
Entire *2,500.* *2,500.*
U2 E2 2c carmine & black 12.50 5.00
Entire 90.00 45.00
a. 2c red & black 12.50 5.00
Entire 85.00 45.00
b. Head and overprint only — —
Entire *1,600.* *1,400.*
c. Frame only (red) — —
Entire *1,600.* *1,400.*
d. Frame double (carmine) — —
Entire *2,500.* *2,250.*

José Vallarino — E3

"The Land Gate" — E4

1921, Nov. 13

On White Paper

U3	E3	1c green	140.00	100.00
		Entire	1,000.	450.00
U4	E4	2c red	35.00	20.00
		Entire	275.00	135.00

Arms of Panama — E5

Typographed and embossed by American Bank Note Co. with "CANAL ZONE" in color of stamp.

1923, Dec. 15

On White Paper

U5	E5	2c carmine	55.00	32.50
		Entire	200.00	125.00

U.S. Nos. U420 and U429 Overprinted in Black by Bureau of Engraving and Printing, Washington, D.C.

CANAL

ZONE

1924, July 1

U6	U92	1c green *(50,000)*	5.00	3.00
		Entire	40.00	22.50
U7	U93	2c carmine *(100,000)*	5.00	3.00
		Entire	40.00	22.50

Seal of Canal Zone — E6

Printed by the Panama Canal Press, Mount Hope, C.Z.

1924, Oct.

On White Paper

U8	E6	1c green *(205,000)*	2.00	1.00
		Entire	35.00	17.50
U9	E6	2c carmine *(1,997,658)*	75	40
		Entire	30.00	9.00

Gorgas E7

Goethals E8

Typographed and Embossed by International Envelope Corp., Dayton, O.

1932, Apr. 8

U10	E7	1c green *(1,300,000)*	15	10
		Entire	2.75	1.00
U11	E8	2c carmine *(400,250)*	25	15
		Entire	3.50	1.50

No. U9 Surcharged in Violet by Panama Canal Press, Mount Hope, C.Z. Numerals 3mm high **3 3**

1932, July 20

U12	E6	3c on 2c carmine *(20,000)*	17.50	7.50
		Entire	275.00	120.00

No. U11 Surcharged in Violet, Numerals 5mm high **3 3**

1932, July 20

U13	E8	3c on 2c carmine *(320,000)*	2.00	1.00
		Entire	25.00	14.00

1934, Jan. 17

Numerals with Serifs

U14	E6	3c on 2c carmine (Numerals 4mm high) *(8,000)*	115.00	60.00
		Entire	600.00	500.00
U15	E8	3c on 2c carmine (Numerals 5mm high) *(23,000)*	25.00	15.00
		Entire	300.00	135.00

Typographed and Embossed by International Envelope Corp., Dayton, O.

1934, June 18

U16	E8	3c purple *(2,450,000)*	15	10
		Entire	1.10	55

1958, Nov. 1

U17	E8	4c blue *(596,725)*	20	15
		Entire	1.25	50

Surcharged at Left of Stamp in Ultra. as No. UX13

1969, Apr. 28

U18	E8	4c +1c blue *(93,850)*	15	10
		Entire	1.25	95
U19	E8	4c +2c blue *(23,125)*	50	30
		Entire	2.50	1.50

Ship Passing through Gaillard Cut — E9

Typographed and Embossed by United States Envelope Co., Williamsburg, Pa.

1971, Nov. 17

U20	E9	8c emerald *(121,500)*	25	12
		Entire	75	35

Surcharged at Left of Stamp in Emerald as #UX13

1974, Mar. 2

U21	E9	8c +2c emerald	30	15
		Entire	1.00	35

1976, Feb. 23

U22	E9	13c violet *(638,350)*	35	20
		Entire	75	40

Surcharged at Left of Stamp in Violet as No. UX13

1978, July 5

U23	E9	13c +2c violet *(245,041)*	35	20
		Entire	75	40

AIR POST ENVELOPES

No. U9 Overprinted with Horizontal Blue and Red Bars Across Entire Face. Overprinted by Panama Canal Press, Mount Hope, C.Z. Boxed inscription in lower left with nine lines of instructions. Additional adhesives required for air post rate.

1928, May 21

UC1	E6	2c red, entire *(15,000)*	135.00	60.00
		First day cancel		80.00

No. U9 with Similar Overprint of Blue and Red Bars, and "VIA AIR MAIL" in Blue, Centered, no box.

1929

UC2	E6	2c red, entire *(10,000) Jan. 11, 1929*	275.00	125.00
	a.	Inscription at left *(60,200) Feb. 6, 1929*	65.00	25.00

DC-4 Skymaster — UC1

Typographed and Embossed by International Envelope Corp., Dayton, O.

1949, Jan. 3

UC3	UC1	6c blue *(4,400,000)*	25	15
		Entire	3.75	1.50
		Entire, 1st day cancel		2.00

1958, Nov. 1

UC4	UC1	7c carmine *(1,000,000)*	25	15
		Entire	4.00	1.00
		Entire, 1st day cancel		1.50

No. U16 Surcharged at Left of Stamp and Imprinted "VIA AIR MAIL" in Dark Blue

Surcharged by Panama Canal Press, Mount Hope, C.Z.

1963, June 22

UC5	E8	3c + 5c purple *(105,000)*	1.00	1.00
		Entire	10.00	5.00
	a.	Double surcharge	700.00	

Jet Liner and Tail Assembly — UC2

Typographed and Embossed by International Envelope Corp., Dayton, O.

1964, Jan. 6

UC6	UC2	8c deep carmine *(600,000)*	35	20
		Entire	2.25	1.75

No. U17 Surcharged at Left of Stamp as No. UC5 and Imprinted "VIA AIR MAIL" in Vermilion Surcharged by Canal Zone Press, La Boca, C.Z.

1965, Oct. 15

UC7	E8	4c + 4c blue *(100,000)*	50	25
		Entire	4.50	3.00

Jet Liner and Tail Assembly — UC3

Typographed and Embossed by United States Envelope Co., Williamsburg, Pa.

1966, Feb. 25 (?)

UC8	UC3	8c carmine *(224,000)*	50	35
		Entire	5.00	2.00

No. UC8 Surcharged at Left of Stamp as No. UX13 in Vermilion Surcharged by Canal Zone Press, La Boca, C.Z.

1968, Jan. 18

UC9	UC3	8c + 2c carmine *(376,000)*	40	25
		Entire	2.75	1.10

No. UC7 with Additional Surcharge at Left of Stamp as No. UX13 and Imprinted "VIA AIR MAIL" in Vermilion Surcharged by Canal Zone Press, La Boca, C.Z.

1968, Feb. 12

UC10	E8	4c + 4c + 2c blue *(224,150)*	60	40
		Entire	2.25	1.50

Type of 1966
Typographed and Engraved by United States Envelope Co., Williamsburg, Pa.

1969, Apr. 1

Luminescent Ink

UC11	UC3	10c ultramarine *(448,000)*	60	30
		Entire	4.00	1.50

No. U17 Surcharged at Left of Stamp as Nos. UC5 and UX13, and Imprinted "VIA AIR MAIL" in Vermilion

1971, May 17

UC12	E8	4c + 5c + 2c blue *(55,775)*	75	30
		Entire	4.00	2.25

No. UC11 Surcharged in Ultra. at Left of Stamp as No. UX13

1971, May 17

Luminescent Ink

UC13	UC3	10c + 1c ultramarine *(152,000)*	45	30
		Entire	4.00	1.50

Type of 1966
Typographed and Engraved by United States Envelope Co., Williamsburg, Pa.

1971, Nov. 17

UC14	UC3	11c rose red *(553,000)*	30	15
		Entire	1.10	60
a.		11c carmine, tagged	30	15
		Entire	1.10	60

Surcharged at Left of Stamp in Rose Red as No. UX13

1974, Mar. 2

UC15	UC3	11c + 2c carmine, tagged *(387,000)*	35	20
		Entire	1.50	75
a.		11c + 2c rose red, untagged	35	20
		Entire	1.75	75

No. U21 with Additional Surcharge in Vermilion at Left of Stamp as No. UX13 and Imprinted "VIA AIR MAIL" in Vermilion

1975, May 3

UC16	E9	8c + 2c + 3c emerald *(75,000)*	50	25
		Entire	1.25	1.00

REGISTRATION ENVELOPES

RE1

Panama Registration Envelope surcharged by Panama Canal Press, Mount Hope, C.Z.

1918, Oct. **8mm between CANAL & ZONE**

UF1	RE1	10c on 5c black & red, *cream (10,000)*, entire	*1,750.*	*1,500.*
a.		9¼mm between CANAL & ZONE *(25,000)*, entire ('19)	*1,500.*	*1,250.*

Stamped envelopes inscribed "Diez Centesimos," surcharged with numerals "5" and with solid blocks printed over "Canal Zone," were issued by the Republic of Panama after being rejected by the Canal Zone. Parts of "Canal Zone" are often legible under the surcharge blocks. These envelopes exist without surcharge.

POSTAL CARDS

Values are for Entires

Map of Panama — PC1

Panama Card Lithographed by American Bank Note Co., revalued and surcharged in black by the Isthmian Canal Commission.

1907, Feb. 9

UX1	PC1	1c on 2c carmine, "CANAL" 15mm *(50,000)*	45.00	35.00
a.		Double surcharge	*1,500.*	*1,500.*
b.		Double surcharge, one reading down	*2,750.*	
c.		Triple surcharge, one reading down	*2,750.*	
d.		"CANAL" 13mm *(10,000)*	250.00	200.00
e.		As "d," double surch.	*2,750.*	

Balboa — PC2

Panama card lithographed by Hamilton Bank Note Co. Overprinted in black by Isthmian Canal Commission.

At least six types of overprint, reading down.

1908, Mar. 3

UX2	PC2	1c green & black, "CANAL" 13mm *(295,000)*	200.00	100.00
a.		Double overprint	*2,000.*	*2,000.*
b.		Triple overprint	*1,750.*	—
c.		Period after "ZONE" *(40,000)*	200.00	125.00
d.		"CANAL" 15mm *(30,000)*	200.00	125.00
e.		"ZONE CANAL", reading up		*3,000.*

Balboa
PC3 PC4

Lithographed by Hamilton Bank Note Co. Overprinted in Black by Panama Canal Press, Mount Hope, C.Z.

1910, Nov. 10

UX3	PC3	1c green & black *(40,000)*	190.00	100.0
a.		Double overprint		*3,00*

This card, with overprint reading up, is actually the fourth c seven settings of UX2.

Lithographed and Overprinted by American Bank Note Co.

1913, Mar. 27

UX4	PC4	1c green & black *(634,000)*	175.00	80.0

Design of Canal Zone Envelopes Overprinted in black by the American Bank Note Co.

1921, Oct.

UX5	E3	1c green	1,100.	700.0

Typographed and embossed by American Bank Note Co. with "CANAL ZONE" in color of stamp

1924, Jan.

UX6	E5	1c green	1,000.	700.0

CANAL

U.S. No. UX27 Overprinted by U.S. Gov't. Printing Office at Washington, D.C.

ZONE

1924, July 1

UX7	PC17	1c green, *buff (Jefferson) (50,000)*	85.00	40.0

Design of Canal Zone Envelope Printed by Panama Canal Press.

1925, Jan.

UX8	E6	1c green, *buff (25,000)*	70.00	25.0
a.		Background only	*2,500.*	

CANAL

U.S. No. UX27 Overprinted

ZONE

1925, May

UX9	PC17	1c green, *buff (Jefferson) (850,000)*	8.50	2.

CANAL

U.S. No. UX27 Overprinted

ZONE

1935, Oct.

UX10	PC17	1c green, *buff (Jefferson) (2,900,000)*	1.50	
a.		Double overprint	*2,750.*	

Same on U.S. No. UX38

1952, May 1

UX11	PC22	2c carmine rose, *buff (Franklin) (800,000)*	2.00	

The Catalogue editors cannot undertake to appraise, identify or judge the genuineness or condition of stamps.

Ship in Lock — PC5

Printed by Bureau of Engraving & Printing, Washington, D.C.

1958, Nov. 1

UX12	PC5	3c dark blue, *buff (335,116)*	1.50	75

No. UX12 Surcharged at Left of Stamp in Green by Panama Canal Press, Mount Hope, C.Z.

1963, July 27

UX13	PC5	3c + 1c dark blue, *buff (78,000)*	4.00	3.00

Ship Passing through Panama Canal — PC6

Printed by Panama Canal Press, Mount Hope, C.Z.

1964, Dec. 1

UX14	PC6	4c violet blue, *buff (74,200)*	3.50	2.50

Ship in Lock (Tow car at right redrawn) — PC7

Printed by Bureau of Engraving & Printing, Washington, D.C.

1965, Aug. 12

UX15	PC7	4c emerald *(95,500)*	1.00	65

No. UX15 Surcharged at Left of Stamp in Green as No. UX13 by Canal Zone Press, La Boca, C.Z.

1968, Feb. 12

UX16	PC7	4c + 1c emerald *(94,775)*	1.00	65

Ship-in-Lock Type of 1965

1969, Apr. 1

UX17	PC7	5c light ultramarine *(63,000)*	90	50

No. UX17 Surcharged at Left of Stamp in Light Ultramarine as No. UX13

1971, May 24

UX18	PC7	5c + 1c light ultra. *(100,500)*	80	40

Ship-in-Lock Type of 1965
Printed by Bureau of Engraving & Printing, Washington, D.C.

1974, Feb. 11

UX19	PC7	8c brown *(90,895)*	65	40

No. UX19 Surcharged at left of Stamp in Brown as No. UX13

1976, June 1

UX20	PC7	8c + 1c brown *(60,249)*	50	40

No. UX19 Surcharged at Left of Stamp in Brown as No. UX13

1978, July 5

UX21	PC7	8c + 2c brown *(74,847)*	60	40

AIR POST POSTAL CARDS

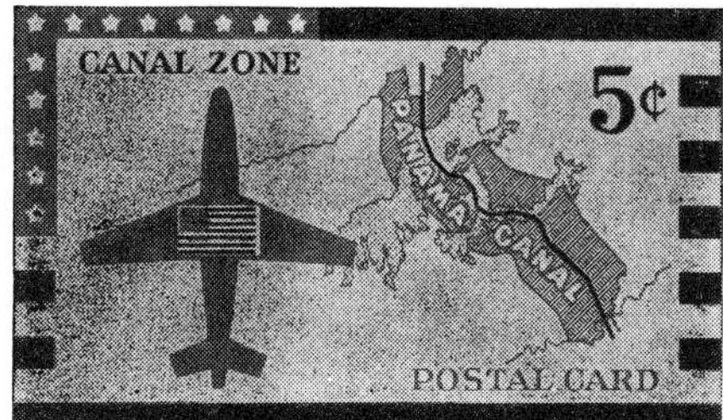

Plane, Flag and Map — APC1

Printed by Bureau of Engraving & Printing, Washington, D.C.

1958, Nov. 1

UXC1	APC1	5c blue & carmine rose *(104,957)*	3.50	3.00

No. UXC1 Surcharged at Left of Stamp in Green as No. UX13 by Panama Canal Press, Mount Hope, C.Z.

1963, July 27

UXC2	APC1	5c + 1c blue & carmine rose *(48,000)*	9.50	6.00
a.		Inverted surcharge	*1,500.*	

No. UX15 Surcharged at Left of Stamp as No. UX13 and Imprinted "AIR MAIL" in Vermilion

1965, Aug. 18

UXC3	PC7	4c + 2c emerald *(41,700)*	4.00	3.00

No. UX15 Surcharged at Left of Stamp as No. UC5 and Imprinted "AIR MAIL" in Vermilion by Canal Zone Press, La Boca, C.Z.

1968, Feb. 2

UXC4	PC7	4c + 4c emerald *(60,100)*	2.75	1.50

No. UX17 Surcharged at Left of Stamp as No. UC5 and Imprinted "AIR MAIL" in Vermilion

1971, May 24

UXC5	PC7	5c + 4c light ultramarine *(68,000)*	75	50

PROOFS

1928-40

			DIE *(1)* Large	*(2)* Small
106TC	2c	black	750.00	
113P	30c	brown black		650.00
1934				
117P	3c	deep violet *(8)*	350.00	
1939				
120P	1c	yellow green		650.00
121P	2c	rose carmine		650.00
122P	3c	purple	750.00	650.00
123P	5c	dark blue	750.00	650.00
124P	6c	red orange		650.00
125P	7c	black		650.00
126P	8c	green		650.00
127P	10c	ultramarine		650.00
128P	11c	blue green	750.00	650.00
129P	12c	brown carmine	750.00	650.00
130P	14c	dark violet		650.00
131P	15c	olive green		650.00
132P	18c	rose pink		650.00
133P	20c	brown	750.00	650.00
134P	25c	orange	750.00	650.00
135P	50c	violet brown	750.00	650.00
1946-48				
136P	½c	bright red	750.00	
137P	1½c	chocolate	750.00	
139P	5c	deep blue	750.00	
140P	25c	yellow blue	750.00	
141P	10c	black	750.00	
1949				
142P	3c	blue	750.00	
143P	6c	violet	750.00	
144P	12c	bright blue green	750.00	
145P	18c	deep red lilac	750.00	

Air Post

1931-49

C6P	4c	red violet	850.00	
C7P	5c	light green	850.00	
C8P	6c	yellow brown	850.00	
C13P	40c	yellow	850.00	
1939				
C15P	5c	greenish black		750.00
C15TC	5c	scarlet	850.00	
C16P	10c	dull violet	850.00	750.00
C17P	15c	light brown		750.00
C18P	25c	blue		750.00
C19P	30c	rose carmine	850.00	750.00
C20P	$1	green		750.00
1951				
C21P	4c	red violet	850.00	

The Small Die proofs listed are on soft yellowish wove paper.

Only No. 117P has more than two copies reported in private collections.

CUBA

AFTER the U. S. battleship "Maine" was destroyed in Havana harbor with a loss of 266 lives in February, 1898, the United States demanded the withdrawal of Spanish troops from Cuba. The Spanish-American War followed. By the peace treaty of Dec. 10, 1898, Spain relinquished Cuba to the United States in trust for its inhabitants. On Jan. 1, 1899, Spanish authority was succeeded by U. S. military rule which lasted until May 20, 1902, when Cuba, as a republic, assumed self-government.

The listings in this catalogue cover the U. S. Administration issue of 1899, the Republic's 1899-1902 issues under U. S. military rule and the Puerto Principe issue of provincial provisionals.

100 CENTS = 1 DOLLAR

Puerto Principe Issue

In December, 1898, Puerto Principe, a provincial capital now called Camagüey, ran short of 1c, 2c, 3c, 5c and 10c stamps. The Postmaster ordered Cuban stamps to be surcharged on Dec. 19, 1898.

The surcharging was done to horizontal strips of five stamps, so vertical pairs and blocks do not exist. Five types are found in each setting, and five printings were made. Counterfeits are plentiful.

First Printing
Black Surcharge, 17½mm high

Surcharge measures 17½mm high and is roughly printed in dull black ink.

HABILITADO 2 cents. — Position 1
HABILITADO 2 cents. — Position 2
HABILITADO 2 cents. — Position 3
HABILITADO 2 cents. — Position 4
HABILITADO 2 cents. — Position 5

Position 1	-No serif at right of "t".
Position 2	-Thin numeral except on 1c on 17 No. 176.
Position 3	-Broken right foot of "n".
Position 4	-Up-stroke of "t" broken.
Position 5	-Broken "DO".

This printing consisted of the following stamps:

176	1c on 1m orange brown, Pos. 1, 2, 3, 4 and 5
178	2c on 2m orange brown, Pos. 1, 3, 4 and 5
179	2c on 2m orange brown, Pos. 2
180	3c on 3m orange brown, Pos. 1, 3, 4 and 5
181	3c on 3m orange brown, Pos. 2
188	5c on 5m orange brown, Pos. 1, 3, 4 and 5
189	5c on 5m orange brown, Pos. 2

Second Printing
Black Surcharge, 17½mm high

This printing was from the same setting as used for the first printing, but the impression is much clearer and the ink quite shiny.

The printing consisted of the following stamps:

179F	3c on 2m orange brown, Pos. 1, 3, 4 and 5
179G	3c on 2m orange brown, Pos. 2
182	5c on 1m orange brown, Pos. 1, 3, 4 and 5
183	5c on 1m orange brown, Pos. 2
184	5c on 2m orange brown, Pos. 1, 3, 4 and 5
185	5c on 2m orange brown, Pos. 2
186	5c on 3m orange brown, Pos. 1, 3, 4 and 5
187	5c on 3m orange brown, Pos. 2
188	5c on 5m orange brown, Pos. 1, 3, 4 and 5
189	5c on 5m orange brown, Pos. 2
190	5c on ½m blue green, Pos. 1, 3, 4 and 5
191	5c on ½m blue green, Pos. 2

Third Printing
Red Surcharge, 20mm high

The same setting as for the first and second was used for the third printing. The 10c denomination first appeared in this printing and position 2 of that value has numerals same as on positions 1, 3, 4 and 5, while position 4 has broken "1" in "10".

The printing consisted of the following stamps:

196	3c on 1c black violet, Pos. 1, 3, 4 and 5
197	3c on 1c black violet, Pos. 2
198	5c on 1c black violet, Pos. 1, 3, 4 and 5
199	5c on 1c black violet, Pos. 2
200	10c on 1c black violet, Pos. 1, 2, 3 and 5
200a	10c on 1c black violet, Pos. 4

Fourth Printing
Black Surcharge, 19½mm high

The same type as before but spaced between so that the surcharge is 2mm taller. Clear impression, shiny ink.

HABILITADO 1 cents. — Position 1
HABILITADO 1 cents. — Position 2
HABILITADO 1 cents. — Position 3
HABILITADO 1 cents. — Position 4
HABILITADO 1 cents. — Position 5

Position 1	-No serif at right of "t".
Position 2	-Broken "1" on No. 177.
Position 2	-Thin numerals on 5c stamps.
Position 3	-Broken right foot of "n".
Position 4	-Up-stroke of "t" broken.
Position 4	-Thin numeral on 3c stamps.
Position 5	-Broken "DO".

This printing consisted of the following stamps:

177	1c on 1m orange brown, Pos. 1, 3, 4 and 5
177a	1c on 1m orange brown, Pos. 2
179B	3c on 1m orange brown, Pos. 1, 2, 3 and 5
179D	3c on 1m orange brown, Pos. 4
183B	5c on 1m orange brown, Pos. 1, 3, 4 and 5
189C	5c on 5m orange brown, Pos. 1, 3, 4 and 5
192	5c on ½m blue green, Pos. 1, 3, 4 and 5
193	5c on ½m blue green, Pos. 2

Fifth Printing
Black Surcharge, 19½mm high

HABILITADO 3 cents. — Position 1
HABILITADO 3 cents. — Position 2
HABILITADO 3 eents. — Position 3
HABILITADO 3 cents. — Position 4
HABILITADO 3 cents. — Position 5

Position 1	-Nick in bottom of "e" and lower serif of "s".
Position 2	-Normal surcharge.
Position 3	-"cents".
Position 4	-Thin numeral.
Position 5	-Nick in upper part of right stroke of "n".

This printing consisted of the following stamps:

201	3c on 1m blue green, Pos. 1, 2 and 5
201b	3c on 1m blue green, Pos. 3
202	3c on 1m blue green, Pos. 4
203	3c on 2m blue green, Pos. 4
203a	3c on 2m blue green, Pos. 3
204	3c on 2m blue green, Pos. 4
205	3c on 3m blue green, Pos. 1, 2 and 5
205b	3c on 3m blue green, Pos. 3
206	3c on 3m blue green, Pos. 4
211	5c on 1m blue green, Pos. 1, 2 and 5
211a	5c on 1m blue green, Pos. 3
212	5c on 1m blue green, Pos. 4
213	5c on 2m blue green, Pos. 1, 2 and 5
213a	5c on 2m blue green, Pos. 3
214	5c on 2m blue green, Pos. 4
215	5c on 3m blue green, Pos. 1, 2 and 5
215a	5c on 3m blue green, Pos. 3
216	5c on 3m blue green, Pos. 4
217	5c on 4m blue green, Pos. 1, 2 and 5
217a	5c on 4m blue green, Pos. 3
218	5c on 4m blue green, Pos. 4
219	5c on 8m blue green, Pos. 1, 2 and 5
219b	5c on 8m blue green, Pos. 3
220	5c on 8m blue green, Pos. 4

Counterfeits exist of all Puerto Principe surcharges. Illustrations have been altered to discourage further counterfeiting.

Regular Issues of Cuba of 1896 and 1898 Surcharged:

HABILITADO 1 cent.
a

Numeral in ( ) after color indicates printing.

1898-99 **Puerto Principe Issue**

Black Surcharge on Nos. 156-158, 160

176	(a)	1 cent on 1m orange brown (1)	45.00	30.00

HABILITADO 1 cents.
b

177	(b)	1 cents on 1m orange brown (4)	45.00	30.00
a.		Broken figure "1"	75.00	60.00
b.		Inverted surcharge		150.00
d.		Same as "a" inverted		*300.00*

HABILITADO 2 cents.
c

178	(c)	2c on 2m orange brown (1)	22.50	15.00
a.		Inverted surcharge	250.00	50.00

HABILITADO
2
cents.
d

179 (d) 2c on 2m orange brown (1) 40.00 25.00
a. Inverted surcharge 350.00 100.00

HABILITADO
3
cents.
k

179B (k) 3c on 1m orange brown (4) 300.00 150.00
c. Double surcharge 1,500. 750.00

An unused copy is known with "cents" omitted.

HABILITADO
3
cents.
l

179D (l) 3c on 1m orange brown (4) *1,500.* *600.00*
e. Double surcharge — —

HABILITADO
3
cents.
e

179F (e) 3c on 2m orange brown (2) *1,500.*

Value is for copy with minor faults.

HABILITADO
3
cents.
f

179G (f) 3c on 2m orange brown (2) — *2,000.*
180 (e) 3c on 3m orange brown (1) 27.50 22.50
a. Inverted surcharge 100.00
181 (f) 3c on 3m orange brown (1) 75.00 50.00
a. Inverted surcharge *200.00*

Value for No. 179G is for copy with minor faults.

HABILITADO
5
cents.
g

182 (g) 5c on 1m orange brown (2) 700.00 175.00
a. Inverted surcharge *500.00*

HABILITADO
5
cents.
h

183 (h) 5c on 1m orange brown (2) *1,300.* *400.00*
a. Inverted surcharge *700.00*

HABILITADO
5
cents.
i

184 (g) 5c on 2m orange brown (2) 750.00 200.00
185 (h) 5c on 2m orange brown (2) 1,500. 400.00
186 (g) 5c on 3m orange brown (2) 165.00
a. Inverted surcharge 700.00
187 (h) 5c an 3m orange brown (2) 400.00
a. Inverted surcharge 1,000.
188 (g) 5c on 5m orange brown (1) (2) 70.00 55.00
a. Inverted surcharge 400.00 175.00
b. Double surcharge — —
189 (h) 5c on 5m orange brown (1) (2) 350.00 225.00
a. Inverted surcharge 400.00
b. Double surcharge — —
189C (i) 5c on 5m orange brown (4) *7,500.*

Values for Nos. 188, 189 are for the first printing.

Black Surcharge on No. P25

190 (g) 5c on ½m blue green (2) 250.00 75.00
a. Inverted surcharge 500.00 150.00
b. Pair, one without surcharge 500.00
191 (h) 5c on ½m blue green (2) 300.00 90.00
a. Inverted surcharge 200.00
192 (i) 5c on ½m blue green (4) 550.00 200.00
a. Double surcharge, one diagonal *6,000.*

Value for No. 190b is for pair with unsurcharged copy at right. One pair with unsurcharged copy at left is known. No. 192a is unique.

HABILITADO
5
cents.
j

193 (j) 5c on ½m blue green (4) 700.00 300.00

Red Surcharge on No. 161

196 (k) 3c on 1c black violet (3) 60.00 25.00
a. Inverted surcharge 300.00
197 (l) 3c on 1c black violet (3) 125.00 45.00
a. Inverted surcharge 300.00
198 (i) 5c on 1c black violet (3) 20.00 20.00
a. Inverted surcharge 125.00
b. Vertical surcharge *2,500.*
c. Double surcharge *400.00* *600.00*
d. Double inverted surcharge —
199 (j) 5c on 1c black violet (3) 50.00 40.00
a. Inverted surcharge 250.00
b. Vertical surcharge *2,000.*
c. Double surcharge 1,000. 600.00

Value for No. 198b is for surcharge reading up. One copy is known with surcharge reading down.

HABILITADO
10
cents.
m

200 (m) 10c on 1c black violet (3) 20.00 *50.00*
a. Broken figure "1" 40.00 *100.00*

Black Surcharge on Nos. P26-P30

201 (k) 3c on 1m blue green (5) 300.00 300.00
a. Inverted surcharge 400.00
b. "EENTS" 550.00 400.00
c. Same as "b", inverted 850.00
202 (l) 3c on 1m blue green (5) 500.00 400.00
a. Inverted surcharge 850.00
203 (k) 3c on 2m blue green (5) 850.00 300.00
a. "EENTS" 1,250. 450.00
b. Inverted surcharge 850.00
c. Same as "a", inverted 950.00
204 (l) 3c on 2m blue green (5) 1,000. 550.00
a. Inverted surcharge 750.00
205 (k) 3c on 3m blue green (5) 900.00 250.00
a. Inverted surcharge 500.00
b. "EENTS" 1,250. 375.00
c. Same as "b", inverted 700.00
206 (l) 3c on 3m blue green (5) 1,250. 450.00
a. Inverted surcharge 700.00
211 (i) 5c on 1m blue green (5) 1,800.
a. "EENTS" — 2,500.
212 (j) 5c on 1m blue green (5) 2,500.
213 (i) 5c on 2m blue green (5) 1,300.
a. "EENTS" — 1,800.
214 (j) 5c on 2m blue green (5) 1,500.
215 (i) 5c on 3m blue green (5) 500.00
a. "EENTS" 1,000.
216 (j) 5c on 3m blue green (5) — 1,000.
217 (i) 5c on 4m blue green (5) *2,500.* 700.00
a. "EENTS" *3,000.* 1,500.
b. Inverted surcharge *1,250.*
c. Same as "a", inverted 2,000.
218 (j) 5c on 4m blue green (5) *1,500.*
a. Inverted surcharge *2,000.*
219 (i) 5c on 8m blue green (5) *2,500.* 1,000.
a. Inverted surcharge 1,500.
b. "EENTS" — 1,800.
c. Same as "b", inverted 2,250.
220 (j) 5c on 8m blue green (5) 2,000.
a. Inverted surcharge 2,500.

Puerto Principe pairs, strips and stamps properly canceled on cover are scarce and command high premiums.

Most copies of all but the most common varieties are faulty or have tropical toning. Values are for sound copies where they exist.

CUBA

United States Stamps Nos. 279, 267, 279B, 268, 281, 282C and 283 Surcharged in Black

1 c.
de PESO.

1899 **Wmk. 191** ***Perf. 12***

221 A87 1c on 1c yellow green 2.50 30
On cover 15.00
Block of four 12.50 4.00
Margin strip of 3, Impt. & P# 35.00
Margin block of 6, Impt. & P# 150.00
222 A88 2c on 2c carmine, type III 2.50 35
On cover 12.50
Block of four 13.50 4.00
Margin strip of 3, Impt. & P# 35.00
Margin block of 6, Impt. & P# 225.00
a. 2c on 2c red, type III 3.50 25
b. "CUPA" 90.00 80.00
c. Inverted surcharge *2,250.* *2,250.*
"CUBA" at bottom *300.00*
223 A88 2½c on 2c red, type III 2.00 40
On cover 12.50
Block of four 10.00 4.00
Margin strip of 3, Impt. & P# 35.00
Margin block of 6, Impt. & P# 150.00
a. 2½ on 2c carmine, type III 2.25 1.35

The 2½c was sold and used as a 2c stamp.

224 A89 3c on 3c purple 5.00 80
On cover 20.00
Block of four 25.00 12.00
Margin strip of 3, Impt. & P# 55.00
Margin block of 6, Impt. & P# 350.00
a. Period between "B" and "A" 19.00 19.00

Two types of surcharge
I "3" directly over "P"
II "3" to left over "P"

225 A91 5c on 5c blue 5.00 80
On cover 20.00
Block of four 25.00 10.00
Margin strip of 3, Impt. & P# 100.00
Margin block of 6, Impt. & P# 425.00
a. "CUPA" 50.00 35.00
"CUBA" at bottom — —
226 A94 10c on 10c brown, type I 14.00 5.50
On cover 100.00
Block of four 60.00 35.00
Margin strip of 3, Impt. & P# 200.00
Margin block of 6, Impt. & P# 825.00
b. "CUBA" omitted *2,500.* *2,500.*
"CUBA" at bottom 225.00 225.00
226A A94 10c on 10c brown, type II *3,750.*
Block of four —

No. 226A exists only in the special printing.

Special Printing

In 1899 one sheet each of Nos. 221 to 225, 226A; E1 (three sheets), and J1 to J4 (two sheets each) were specially printed for display at the Paris Exposition. All but a few copies, however, were later destroyed. Nearly all copies remaining bear impression of handstamp reading "Special Surcharge" on the back. Value: Nos. 221-225, J1-J4, each $250; No. E1, $400.

Issues of the Republic under U. S. Military Rule

Statue of Columbus A20

Royal Palms A21

Allegory, "Cuba" A22

Ocean Liner A23

Cane Field — A24

Printed by the U.S. Bureau of Engraving and Printing

1899		**Wmk. US-C (191C)**	***Perf. 12***	
227	A20	1c yellow green	2.00	10
		On cover		2.00
		Block of four	8.25	1.00
		Margin block of 10, Impt. & P#, type VII	150.00	—
228	A21	2c carmine	2.00	10
		On cover		2.00
		Block of four	8.25	1.00
		Margin block of 10, Impt. & P#, type VII	120.00	—
a.		2c scarlet	2.00	10
b.		Booklet pane of six	*1,400.*	
229	A22	3c purple	2.00	16
		On cover		4.00
		Block of four	8.25	2.50
		Margin block of 10, Impt. & P#, type VII	165.00	—
230	A23	5c blue	3.00	20
		On cover		4.00
		Block of four	13.50	2.50
		Margin block of 10, Impt. & P#, type VII	425.00	—
231	A24	10c brown	6.50	50
		On cover		6.50
		Block of four	30.00	5.50
		Margin block of 10, Impt. & P#, type VII	750.00	—

Re-engraved

The re-engraved stamps issued by the Republic of Cuba in 1905-07 may be distinguished from the Issue of 1899 as follows:

Nos. 227 to 231 are watermarked U S-C

The re-engraved stamps are unwatermarked.

No. 227

Re-engraved.

No. 228

Re-engraved.

No. 230

Re-engraved.

No. 231

Re-engraved.

1c: The ends of the label inscribed "Centavo" are rounded instead of square.

2c: The foliate ornaments, inside the oval disks bearing the numerals of value, have been removed.

5c: Two lines forming a right angle have been added in the upper corners of the label bearing the word "Cuba".

10c: A small ball has been added to each of the square ends of the label bearing the word "Cuba".

SPECIAL DELIVERY

Issued under Administration of the United States.

Special Delivery Stamp of the United States No. E5 Surcharged in Red

CUBA.

10c.
de PESO.

1899		**Wmk. 191**	***Perf. 12***	
E1	SD3	10c on 10c blue	60.00	40.00
		On cover		450.00
		Block of four	250.00	
		Margin block of four, arrow	275.00	
		Margin strip of 3, Impt. & P#	450.00	
		Margin block of 6, Impt. & P#	*3,750.*	
a.		No period after "CUBA"	175.00	200.00
		Dots in curved frame above messenger (Pl. 882)		—

Issue of the Republic under U. S. Military Rule

Special Delivery Messenger — SD2

Printed by the U. S. Bureau of Engraving and Printing

1899 **Wmk. US-C (191C)**

Inscribed: "Immediata"

E2	SD2	10c orange	22.50	6.00
		On cover		125.00
		Block of four	100.00	—
		Margin strip of 3, Impt. & P #, type VII	150.00	
		Margin block of 6, Impt. & P #, type VII	650.00	

Re-engraved

In 1902 the Republic of Cuba issued a stamp of design SD2 re-engraved with word correctly spelled "Inmediata." The corrected die was made in 1899 (See No. E3P). It was printed by the U.S. Bureau of Engraving and Printing.

POSTAGE DUE

Issued under Administration of the United States. Postage Due Stamps of the United States Nos. J38, J39, J41 and J42 Surcharged in Black Like Regular Issue of Same Date.

1899		**Wmk. 191**	***Perf. 12***	
J1	D2	1c on 1c deep claret	14.00	2.25
		Block of four	65.00	20.00
		Margin block of 6, Impt. & P#	*425.00*	
J2	D2	2c on 2c deep claret	15.00	2.25
		Block of four	65.00	20.00
		Margin block of 6, Impt. & P#	*425.00*	
a.		Inverted surcharge		*1,500.*
J3	D2	5c on 5c deep claret	14.00	2.25
		Block of four	65.00	20.00
		Margin block of 6, Impt. & P#	*400.00*	
a.		"CUPA"	120.00	110.00
J4	D2	10c on 10c deep claret	15.00	80
		Block of four	65.00	8.25
		Margin block of 6, Impt. & P#	*500.00*	

ENVELOPES

Values are for Cut Squares

U. S. Envelopes of 1887-99 Surcharged

CUBA. CUBA.

1c. DE PESO. a

2c. DE PESO. b

1899				
U1	U77 (a)	1c on 1c green, *buff* (No. U354)	3.50	2.50
		Entire	10.00	13.50
U2	U77 (a)	1c on 1c green, *blue* (No. U355)	2.25	2.00
		Entire	4.00	5.50
a.		Double surch., entire	*1,500.*	
U3	U71 (b)	2c on 2c green (No. U311)	1.00	80
		Entire	2.25	3.00
a.		Double surch., entire	*1,500.*	*1,500.*
U4	U71 (b)	2c on 2c green, *amber* (No. U312)	1.65	1.35
		Entire	4.00	5.00
a.		Double surch., entire	*1,500.*	
U5	U71 (a)	2c on 2c green, *buff* (No. U313)	12.00	6.50
		Entire	40.00	40.00
U6	U79 (a)	2c on 2c carmine, *amber* (No. U363)	12.00	12.00
		Entire	40.00	40.00
U7	U79 (a)	2c on 2c carmine, *buff* (No. U364)	16.50	16.50
		Entire	55.00	65.00
U8	U79 (a)	2c on 2c carmine, *blue* (No. U365)	2.00	1.65
		Entire	6.00	6.50
a.		Double surch., entire		*1,500.*

In addition to the envelopes listed above, several others are known but were not regularly issued. They are:

1c on 1c green
1c on 1c green, *manila*
2c on 2c carmine
2c on 2c carmine, *oriental buff*
2c on 2c carmine, *blue*
4c on 4c brown
5c on 5c blue

Issue of the Republic under U. S. Military Rule

Columbus — E1

Similar envelopes without watermark on white and amber papers, were issued by the Republic after Military Rule ended in 1902.

1899		**Wmk. "US POD '99" in Monogram**		
U9	E1	1c green	50	40
		Entire	1.20	1.20
U10	E1	1c green, *amber*	50	40
		Entire	1.20	1.20
U11	E1	1c green, *buff*	12.00	8.00
		Entire	40.00	20.00
U12	E1	1c green, *blue*	16.50	10.00
		Entire	40.00	20.00
U13	E1	2c carmine	50	35
		Entire	1.00	80
U14	E1	2c carmine, *amber*	50	35
		Entire	1.00	80
U15	E1	2c carmine, *buff*	6.50	5.50
		Entire	16.50	10.00
U16	E1	2c carmine, *blue*	16.50	12.00

		Entire	40.00	20.00
U17	E1	5c blue	65	45
		Entire	1.65	65
U18	E1	5c blue, *amber*	2.50	1.65
		Entire	5.50	3.50

WRAPPERS

Issue of the Republic under U. S. Military Rule

1899

W1	E1	1c green, *manila*	2.00	6.50
		Entire	7.00	35.00
W2	E1	2c carmine, *manila*	5.50	6.50
		Entire	15.00	35.00

POSTAL CARDS

Values are for Entires

U. S. Postal Cards Nos. UX14, UX16 Surcharged

CUBA. 1c. de Peso.

UX1	PC8 1c on 1c black, *buff, Jefferson (1,000,000)*	16.50	16.50
a.	No period after "1c"	40.00	40.00
b.	No period after "Peso"	35.00	
UX2	PC3 2c on 2c black, *buff, Liberty (583,000)*	16.50	16.50
a.	No period after "Peso"	40.00	40.00
b.	Double surcharge	—	

In 1904 the Republic of Cuba revalued remaining stocks of No. UX2 by means of a perforated numeral "1".

PROOFS

1899

			DIE (1) Large	(2) Small
227P	1c	yellow green	150.00	100.00
227TC	1c	blue green	250.00	
227TC	1c	black	250.00	
228P	2c	carmine	150.00	100.00
228TC	2c	black	250.00	
229P	3c	purple	150.00	100.00
229TC	3c	black	250.00	
230P	5c	blue	150.00	100.00
230TC	5c	black	250.00	
231P	10c	brown	150.00	100.00
231TC	10c	gray	250.00	
231TC	10c	black	250.00	

Special Delivery

E2TC	10c	blue	650.00	
E3P	10c	orange	350.00	250.00

SPECIMEN STAMPS

Overprinted Type E in black — Specimen.

1899

221S E	1c	on 1c yellow green	120.00
222S E	2c	on 2c carmine	120.00
223S E	2½c	on 2c orange red	120.00
224S E	3c	on 3c purple	120.00
225S E	5c	on 5c blue	120.00
226S E	10c	on 10c brown, type I	120.00
226AS E	10c	on 10c brown, type II	*1,900.*

1899

227S E	1c	yellow green	200.00
228S E	2c	carmine	200.00
229S E	3c	purple	200.00
230S E	5c	blue	200.00
231S E	10c	brown	200.00

Special Delivery

1899

E1S E	10c	on 10c blue	225.00
E2S E	10c	orange	350.00

Postage Due

1899

J1S E	1c	on 1c deep claret	165.00
J2S E	2c	on 2c deep claret	165.00
J3S E	5c	on 5c deep claret	165.00
J4S E	10c	on 10c deep claret	165.00

"Specimen" overprint known on all stamps of the Special Printing.

DANISH WEST INDIES

FORMERLY a Danish colony, these islands were purchased by the United States in 1917 and have since been known as the U.S. Virgin Islands. They lie east of Puerto Rico, have an area of 132 square miles and had a population of 27,086 in 1911. The capital is Charlotte Amalie (also called St. Thomas). Stamps of Danish West Indies were replaced by those of the United States in 1917.

100 CENTS = 1 DOLLAR
100 BIT = 1 FRANC (1905)

Coat of Arms — A1

Wmk. 111- Small Crown

1856 Typo. Wmk. 111 *Imperf.*

Yellowish Paper

Yellow Wavy-line Burelage, UL to LR

1	A1	3c dark carmine, brown gum	110.00	100.00
		On cover		2,000.
		Block of four	750.00	
a.		3c dark carmine, yellow gum	120.00	110.00
a.		On cover		2,000.
a.		Block of four	2,250.	
b.		3c carmine, white gum	2,500.	

Reprint: 1981, carmine, back-printed across two stamps ("Reprint by Dansk Post og Telegrafmuseum 1978"), value, pair, $107.

1866

White Paper

Yellow Wavy-line Burelage UR to LL

2	A1	3c rose	40.00	45.00
		On cover		1,500.
		Block of four	200.00	600.00
		Rouletted 4½ privately	200.00	100.00
		On cover, rouletted 4½		1,500.
		Rouletted 9	200.00	100.00

No. 2 reprints, unwatermarked: 1930, carmine, value $100. 1942, rose carmine, back-printed across each row ("Nytryk 1942 G. A. Hagemann Danmark og Dansk Vestindiens Frimaerker Bind 2"), value $50.

1872 *Perf. 12½*

3	A1	3c rose	125.00	150.00
		On cover		7,500.
		Block of four	800.00	

1873

Without Burelage

4	A1	4c dull blue	150.00	200.00
		On cover		*7,000.*
		Block of four	875.00	
a.		Imperf., pair	400.00	—
b.		Horiz. pair, imperf. vert.	400.00	—

The 1930 reprint of No. 4 is ultramarine, unwatermarked and imperf., value $100.
The 1942 4c reprint is blue, unwatermarked, imperf. and has printing on back (see note below No. 2), value $50.

Numeral of Value — A2

NORMAL FRAME

INVERTED FRAME

The arabesques in the corners have a main stem and a branch. When the frame is in normal position, in the upper left corner the branch leaves the main stem half way between two little leaflets. In the lower right corner the branch starts at the foot of the second leaflet. When the frame is inverted the corner designs are, of course, transposed.

Wmk. 112- Crown

1874-79 Wmk. 112 *Perf. 14x13½*

Printings on White Wove Paper, Varying from Thin to Thick

1c.	Nine printings
3c.	Eight printings
4c.	Two printings
5c.	Six printings
7c.	Two printings
10c.	Seven printings
12c.	Two printings
14c.	One printing
50c.	Two printings

Values for inverted frames, covers and blocks are for the cheapest variety.

5	A2	1c green & brown red	15.00	10.00
		On cover		150.00
		Block of four	65.00	—
a.		1c green & rose lilac	75.00	75.00
b.		1c green & red violet	35.00	35.00
c.		1c green & violet	40.00	55.00
		green & claret	15.00	10.00
e.		Inverted frame	15.00	10.00

No. 5 exists with "b" surcharge, "10 CENTS 1895." See note below No. 15.

6	A2	3c blue & carmine	15.00	10.00
		On cover		100.00
		Block of four	75.00	—
		Dull blue & rose	15.00	10.00
		Dull blue & red	15.00	10.00
		Blue & lake	15.00	10.00
d.		Imperf., pair	300.00	—
e.		Inverted frame	15.00	10.00
		White "wedge" flaw	20.00	12.50
7	A2	4c brown & dull blue	15.00	15.00
		On cover		150.00
		Block of four	75.00	—
		Brown & bright blue	15.00	15.00
b.		4c brown & ultramarine	150.00	175.00
c.		Diagonal half used as 2c on cover		100.00
d.		Inverted frame	1,500.	1,500.
8	A2	5c green & gray	20.00	18.00
		On cover		175.00
		Block of four	100.00	—
		Green & dark gray	20.00	18.00
b.		Inverted frame	20.00	18.00
9	A2	7c lilac & orange	25.00	30.00
		On cover		500.00
		Block of four	120.00	—
a.		7c lilac & yellow	50.00	60.00
b.		Inverted frame	40.00	45.00
10	A2	10c blue & brown	18.00	15.00
		On cover		125.00
		Block of four	90.00	—
		Blue & black brown	18.00	15.00
b.		Period between "t" & "s" of "cents"	22.00	20.00
c.		Inverted frame	18.00	15.00
11	A2	12c red lilac & yellow green	20.00	30.00
		On cover		750.00
		Block of four	100.00	—
a.		12c lilac & deep green	50.00	60.00
12	A2	14c lilac & green	400.00	500.00
		On cover		*8,500.*
		Block of four	*2,500.*	
a.		Inverted frame	3,500.	3,500.

No.	Type	Description	Unused	Used
13	A2	50c violet	50.00	50.00
		On cover		1,500.
		Block of four	225.00	
a.		50c gray violet	85.00	150.00

Issue dates: 1c, 3c, 4c, 14c, Jan. 15, 1874. 7c, July 22, 1874. 5c, 10c, 1876; 12c, 1877; 50c, 1879. Colors of major numbers are generally those of the least expensive of two or more shades, and do not indicate the shade of the first printing.

Nos. 9 and 13 Surcharged in Black:

1 CENT
a

10 CENTS 1895
b

1887

No.	Type	Description	Unused	Used
14	A2 (a)	1c on 7c lilac & orange	40.00	50.00
		On cover		2,500.
		Block of four	200.00	—
a.		1c on 7c lilac & yellow	75.00	100.00
b.		Double surcharge	200.00	200.00
c.		Inverted frame	60.00	75.00

1895

No.	Type	Description	Unused	Used
15	A2 (b)	10c on 50c violet	20.00	25.00
		On cover		175.00
		Block of four	90.00	—

The "b" surcharge also exists on No. 5, with "10" found in two sizes. These are essays.

1896-1901 *Perf. 13*

No.	Type	Description	Unused	Used
16	A2	1c green & red violet, inverted frame ('98)	8.00	8.00
		On cover		100.00
		Block of four	40.00	—
a.		Normal frame	250.00	250.00
17	A2	3c blue & lake, inverted frame ('98)	6.00	6.00
		On cover		75.00
		Block of four	27.50	—
a.		Normal frame	225.00	225.00
		White "wedge" flaw	40.00	40.00
18	A2	4c bister & dull blue ('01)	6.00	6.00
		On cover		75.00
		Block of four	30.00	—
a.		Diagonal half used as 2c on cover		25.00
b.		Inverted frame	40.00	35.00
b.		On cover		200.00
		As "a" and "b" on cover		225.00
19	A2	5c green & gray, inverted frame	20.00	20.00
		On cover		300.00
		Block of four	100.00	—
a.		Normal frame	1,000.	1,000.
20	A2	10c blue & brown ('01)	50.00	75.00
		On cover		1,000.
		Block of four	250.00	—
a.		Inverted frame	1,000.	1,500.
b.		Period between "t" and "s" of "cents"	75.00	100.00

Two printings each of Nos. 18-19.

Arms — A5

1900

No.	Type	Description	Unused	Used
21	A5	1c light green	1.00	1.00
		On cover		75.00
		Block of four	5.00	5.50
22	A5	5c light blue	7.00	7.00
		On cover		150.00
		Block of four	32.50	—

Nos. 6, 17 and 20 Surcharged in Black — c

2 CENTS 1902

1902 *Perf. 14x13½*

No.	Type	Description	Unused	Used
23	A2	2c on 3c blue & carmine, inverted frame	500.00	600.00
		On cover		*4,000.*
		Block of four	*3,000.*	
a.		"2" in date with straight tail	550.00	650.00
b.		Normal frame	2,000.	—

Perf. 13

No.	Type	Description	Unused	Used
24	A2	2c on 3c blue & lake, inverted frame	6.00	6.00
		On cover		135.00
		Block of four	25.00	—
a.		"2" in date with straight tail	8.00	8.00
b.		Dated "1901"	300.00	—
c.		Normal frame	175.00	200.00
d.		Dark green surcharge	1,250.	—
e.		As "d." & "a."	1,500.	—
f.		As "d." & "c."	*2,300.*	—
		White "wedge" flaw	35.00	35.00
25	A2	8c on 10c blue & brown	12.00	14.00
		On cover		200.00
		Block of four	50.00	—
a.		"2" with straight tail	14.00	15.00
b.		On No. 20b	14.00	15.00
c.		Inverted frame	200.00	200.00

Nos. 17 and 20 Surcharged in Black — d

8 Cents 1902

1902 *Perf. 13*

No.	Type	Description	Unused	Used
27	A2	2c on 3c blue & lake, inverted frame	10.00	20.00
		On cover		400.00
		Block of four	42.50	
a.		Normal frame	200.00	225.00
		White "wedge" flaw	40.00	40.00
28	A2	8c on 10c blue & brown	6.00	6.00
		On cover		150.00
		Block of four	27.50	—
a.		On No. 20b	8.00	8.00
b.		Inverted frame	200.00	200.00

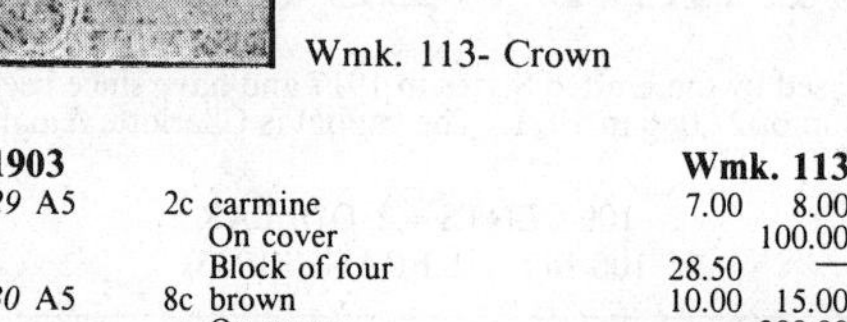
Wmk. 113- Crown

1903 **Wmk. 113**

No.	Type	Description	Unused	Used
29	A5	2c carmine	7.00	8.00
		On cover		100.00
		Block of four	28.50	—
30	A5	8c brown	10.00	15.00
		On cover		200.00
		Block of four	45.00	—

King Christian IX — A8

1905 **Typo.** *Perf. 12½*

No.	Type	Description	Unused	Used
31	A8	5b green	3.00	3.00
		On cover		25.00
		Block of four	14.00	—
32	A8	10b red	3.00	3.00
		On cover		25.00
		Block of four	14.00	—
33	A8	20b green & blue	6.00	6.00
		On cover		125.00
		Block of four	27.50	—
34	A8	25b ultramarine	4.00	4.00
		On cover		50.00
		Block of four	18.00	—
35	A8	40b red & gray	4.00	4.00
		On cover		125.00
		Block of four	18.00	—
36	A8	50b yellow & gray	5.00	8.00
		On cover		150.00
		Block of four	25.00	—

St. Thomas Harbor — A9

Frame Typographed, Center Engraved

1905 **Wmk. Two Crowns (113)** *Perf. 12*

No.	Type	Description	Unused	Used
37	A9	1fr green & blue	10.00	18.00
		On cover		350.00
		Block of four	45.00	—
38	A9	2fr orange red & brown	18.00	35.00
		On cover		500.00
		Block of four	80.00	—
39	A9	5fr yellow & brown	40.00	125.00
		On cover		750.00
		Block of four	175.00	—

Nos. 18, 22 and 30 Surcharged in Black

5 BIT 1905

1905 **Wmk. 112** *Perf. 13*

No.	Type	Description	Unused	Used
40	A2	5b on 4c bister & dull blue	15.00	25.00
		On cover		200.00
		Block of four	75.00	—
a.		Inverted frame	30.00	40.00
41	A5	5b on 5c light blue	15.00	25.00
		On cover		200.00
		Block of four	65.00	—

Wmk. 113

No.	Type	Description	Unused	Used
42	A5	5b on 8c brown	15.00	25.00
		On cover		200.00
		Block of four	60.00	—

King Frederik VIII — A10

Frame Typographed, Center Engraved

1908 **Wmk. 113** *Perf. 13*

No.	Type	Description	Unused	Used
43	A10	5b green	1.00	1.00
		On cover		15.00
		Block of four	5.00	—
44	A10	10b red	1.00	1.00
		On cover		20.00
		Block of four	5.00	—
45	A10	15b violet & brown	3.00	4.00
		On cover		75.00
		Block of four	15.00	—
46	A10	20b green & blue	25.00	10.00
		On cover		100.00
		Block of four	110.00	—
47	A10	25b blue & dark blue	1.00	1.00
		On cover		25.00
		Block of four	5.00	—
48	A10	30b claret & slate	35.00	20.00
		On cover		200.00
		Block of four	150.00	125.00
49	A10	40b vermilion & gray	3.00	3.00
		On cover		175.00
		Block of four	15.00	—
50	A10	50b yellow & brown	4.00	8.00
		On cover		150.00
		Block of four	20.00	—

King Christian X — A11

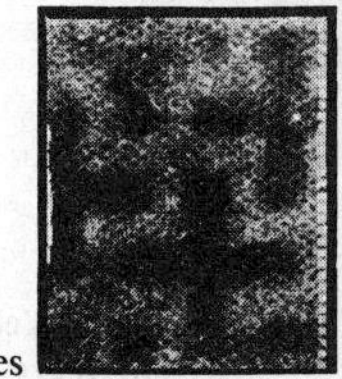
Wmk. 114- Multiple Crosses

Frame Typographed, Center Engraved

1915 **Wmk. 114** *Perf. 14x14½*

No.	Type	Description	Unused	Used
51	A11	5b yellow green	1.50	*5.00*
		On cover		35.00
		Block of four	7.00	—
52	A11	10b red	1.50	*25.00*
		On cover		75.00
		Block of four	7.00	—
53	A11	15b lilac & red brown	1.50	*25.00*
		On cover		150.00
		Block of four	7.00	—
54	A11	20b green & blue	1.50	*25.00*
		On cover		175.00
		Block of four	7.00	—
55	A11	25b blue & dark blue	1.50	*5.00*
		On cover		35.00
		Block of four	7.00	—
56	A11	30b claret & black	1.50	*35.00*
		On cover		250.00
		Block of four	7.00	—
57	A11	40b orange & black	1.50	*35.00*
		On cover		250.00
		Block of four	7.00	—
58	A11	50b yellow & brown	1.50	*35.00*
		On cover		300.00
		Block of four	7.00	—

Forged and favor cancellations exist.

POSTAGE DUE

Royal Cipher "Christian Rex" — D1

Numeral of Value — D2

1902 **Litho.** **Unwmk.** ***Perf. 11½***

J1 D1 1c dark blue 5.00 8.00
Block of four 22.50
J2 D1 4c dark blue 10.00 15.00
Block of four 42.50
J3 D1 6c dark blue 15.00 75.00
Block of four 75.00
J4 D1 10c dark blue 10.00 15.00
Block of four 50.00

There are five types of each value. On the 4c they may be distinguished by differences in the figure "4"; on the other values differences are minute.

Used values of Nos. J1-J8 are for canceled copies. Uncanceled examples without gum have probably been used. Value 60% of unused.

Excellent counterfeits of Nos. J1 to J4 exist.

1905-13

J5 D2 5b red & gray 5.00 8.00
Block of four 22.50 —
J6 D2 20b red & gray 8.00 12.00
Block of four 25.00 —
J7 D2 30b red & gray 7.00 12.00
Block of four 32.50 —
J8 D2 50b red & gray 10.00 15.00
Block of four 45.00 —
a. Perf. 14x14½ ('13) 25.00 —
a. Block of four 120.00 —
b. Perf. 11½ 500.00

Nos. J5-J8 are known imperforate but were not regularly issued. Excellent counterfeits exist.

ENVELOPES

E1

1877-78 **On White Paper**

U1 E1 2c light blue ('78) 5.00 22.50
Entire 15.00 75.00
a. 2c ultramarine 30.00 250.00
Entire 100.00 1,000.
U2 E1 3c orange 5.50 22.50
Entire 15.00 75.00
a. 3c red orange 5.50 22.50
Entire 15.00 75.00

Three different Crown watermarks are found on entires of No. U1, four on entires of No. U2. Envelope watermarks do not show on cut squares.

POSTAL CARDS

Values are for entire cards

Designs of Adhesive Stamps

"BREV-KORT" at top

1877

Inscription in Three Lines

UX1 A2 6c violet 15.00 *1,000.*

1878-85

Inscription in Four Lines

UX2 A2 2c light blue *(8,800)* 20.00 *50.00*
UX3 A2 3c carmine rose *(17,700)* 15.00 *30.00*

1888

Inscription in Five Lines

UX4 A2 2c light blue *(30,500)* 10.00 *25.00*
UX5 A2 3c red *(26,500)* 10.00 *25.00*

Card No. UX5 Locally Surcharged with type "c" but with date "1901"

1901

UX6 A2 1c on 3c red *(2,000)* 40.00 *150.00*

1902

Card No. UX4 Locally Surcharged with type "c"

UX7 A2 1c on 2c light blue *(3,000)* 30.00 *125.00*

Card No. UX5 Surcharged similar to type "c" but heavy letters

1902

UX8 A2 1c on 3c red *(7,175)* 10.00 *35.00*

1903

UX9 A5 1c light green *(10,000)* 10.00 *30.00*
UX10 A5 2c carmine *(10,000)* 20.00 *75.00*

1905

UX11 A8 5b green *(16,000)* 10.00 *20.00*
UX12 A8 10b red *(14,000)* 10.00 *35.00*

1907-08 **Unwmk.**

UX13 A10 5b green ('08) *(30,750)* 10.00 *20.00*
UX14 A10 10b red *(19,750)* 10.00 *25.00*

1913 **Wmk. Wood-grain**

UX15 A10 5b green *(10,000)* 100.00 *200.00*
UX16 A10 10b red *(10,000)* 125.00 *325.00*

1915-16 **Wmk. Wood-grain**

UX17 A11 5b yellow green *(8,200)* 100.00 *200.00*
UX18 A11 10b red ('16) *(2,000)* 125.00 —

PAID REPLY POSTAL CARDS

Designs similar to Nos. UX2 and UX3 with added inscriptions in Danish and French:
Message Card-Four lines at lower left.
Reply Card-Fifth line centered, "Svar. Réponse."

1883

UY1 A2 2c +2c light blue, unsevered *(2,600)* 20.00 *80.00*
m. Message card, detached 10.00 *35.00*
r. Reply card, detached 10.00 *35.00*
UY2 A2 3c +3c carmine rose, unsevered 20.00 *60.00*
m. Message card, detached 10.00 *20.00*
r. Reply card, detached 10.00 *25.00*

Designs similar to Nos. UX4 and UX5 with added inscription in fifth line, centered in French:
Message Card-"Carte postale avec réponse payée."
Reply Card-"Carte postale-réponse."

1888

UY3 A2 2c +2c light blue, unsevered *(26,000)* 15.00 *60.00*
m. Message card, detached 5.00 *20.00*
r. Reply card, detached 5.00 *30.00*
UY4 A2 3c +3c carmine rose, unsevered *(5,000)* 20.00 *70.00*
m. Message card, detached 10.00 *25.00*
r. Reply card, detached 10.00 *30.00*

No. UY4 Locally Surcharged with type "c" but with date "1901"

1902

UY5 A2 1c on 3c+1c on 3c carmine rose, unsevered *(1,000)* 30.00 *150.00*
m. Message card, detached 15.00 *50.00*
r. Reply card, detached 15.00 *75.00*

No. UY4 Surcharged in Copenhagen with type similar to "c" but heavy letters

UY6 A2 1c on 3c+1c on 3c carmine rose, unsevered *(975)* 50.00 *175.00*
m. Message card, detached 25.00 *60.00*
r. Reply card, detached 25.00 *75.00*

Designs similar to Nos. UX9 and UX10 with added inscriptions in Danish and English

1903

UY7 A5 1c +1c light green, unsevered *(5,000)* 20.00 *50.00*
m. Message card, detached 10.00 *20.00*
r. Reply card, detached 10.00 *25.00*
UY8 A5 2c +2c carmine, unsevered *(5,000)* 40.00 *200.00*
m. Message card, detached 20.00 *50.00*
r. Reply card, detached 20.00 *75.00*

Designs similar to Nos. UX11 and UX12 with added inscriptions

1905

UY9 A8 5b +5b green, unsevered *(5,000)* 20.00 *50.00*
m. Message card, detached 10.00 *20.00*
r. Reply card, detached 10.00 *30.00*
UY10 A8 10b +10b red, unsevered *(4,000)* 25.00 *60.00*
m. Message card 10.00 *25.00*
r. Reply card, detached 10.00 *35.00*

Designs similar to Nos. UX13, UX14 and UX15 with added inscriptions

1908 **Unwmk.**

UY11 A10 5b +5b green, unsevered *(7,150)* 20.00 *75.00*
m. Message card, detached 10.00 *30.00*
r. Reply card, detached 10.00 *35.00*
UY12 A10 10b +10b red, unsevered *(6,750)* 20.00 *75.00*
m. Message card, detached 10.00 *30.00*
r. Reply card, detached 10.00 *40.00*

1913 **Wmk. Wood-grain**

UY13 A10 5b +5b green, unsevered *(5,000)* —
m. Message card, detached —
r. Reply card, detached —

The 10b + 10b red type A10 with wood-grain watermark was authorized and possibly printed, but no example is known.

GUAM

A former Spanish island possession in the Pacific Ocean, one of the Mariana group, about 1,450 miles east of the Philippines. Captured June 20, 1898, and ceded to the United States by treaty after the Spanish-American War. Stamps overprinted "Guam" were used while the post office was under the jurisdiction of the Navy Department from July 7, 1899, until March 29, 1901, when a Postal Agent was appointed by the Post Office Department and the postal service passed under that Department's control. From this date on Guam was supplied with regular United States postage stamps, although the overprints remained in use for several more years. Population 9,000 (est. 1899).

100 CENTS = 1 DOLLAR

United States Nos. 279, 267, 279, 268, 280a, 281, 282, 272, 282C, 283, 284, 275, 275a, 276 and 276A Overprinted

GUAM

1899 **Wmk. 191** ***Perf. 12***

Black Overprint

1 A87 1c **deep green** *(25,000)* 14.00 *17.50*
On cover *200.00*
Block of four 65.00 *100.00*
Margin strip of 3, Impt. & P# 70.00
Margin block of 6, Impt. & P# 325.00
a. Inverted overprint —
2 A88 2c **carmine,** type III *(105,000)* 12.50 *17.50*
On cover *200.00*
Block of four 60.00 *100.00*
Margin strip of 3, Impt. & P# 60.00
Margin block of 6, Impt. & P# 275.00
a. 2c rose carmine, type III 15.00 *20.00*
3 A89 3c **purple** *(5000)* 100.00 *87.50*
On cover *400.00*
Block of four 450.00 *425.00*
Margin strip of 3, Impt. & P# 450.00
Margin block of 6, Impt. & P# 1,250.
4 A90 4c **lilac brown** *(5000)* 100.00 *100.00*
On cover *450.00*
Block of four 450.00 *500.00*
Margin strip of 3, Impt. & P# 450.00
Margin block of 6, Impt. & P# *2,250.*
Extra frame line at top (Plate 793 R62) —
5 A91 5c **blue** *(20,000)* 17.50 *22.50*
On cover *200.00*
Block of four 75.00 *125.00*
Margin strip of 3, Impt. & P# 80.00
Margin block of 6, Impt. & P# 700.00
6 A92 6c **lake** *(5000)* 100.00 *100.00*
On cover *450.00*
Block of four 450.00 *500.00*
Margin strip of 3, Impt. & P# 400.00
Margin block of 6, Impt. & P# 1,600.
7 A93 8c **violet brown** *(5000)* 100.00 *100.00*
On cover *450.00*
Block of four 450.00 *500.00*
Margin strip of 3, Impt. & P# 450.00
Margin block of 6, Impt. & P# 1,600.
8 A94 10c **brown,** type I *(10,000)* 27.50 *35.00*
On cover *275.00*
Block of four 125.00 *175.00*
Margin strip of 3, Impt. & P# 140.00
Margin block of 6, Impt. & P# 750.00
9 A94 10c **brown,** type II *3,500.*
10 A95 15c **olive green** *(5000)* 110.00 *110.00*
On cover *900.00*
Block of four 475.00 *500.00*
Margin strip of 3, Impt. & P# 475.00
Margin block of 6, Impt. & P# 2,100.
11 A96 50c **orange** *(4000)* 250.00 *300.00*
On cover *1,250.*
Block of four 1,150. *1,500.*
Margin strip of 3, Impt. & P# 1,150.
Margin block of 6, Impt. & P# 4,000.
a. 50c red orange 400.00 —

Red Overprint

12 A97 $1 **black,** type I *(3000)* 300.00 *375.00*
On cover *2,000.*
Block of four 1,500. *1,650.*
Margin strip of 3, Impt. & P# 1,500.
Margin block of 6, Impt. & P# *8,500.*
13 A97 $1 **black,** type II *3,000.*
Block of four —

No. 13 exists only in the special printing.

Special Printing

In 1899 a special printing of all values Nos. 1 to 8, 10, 11, 12, and E1, was made for display at the Paris Exposition. Value: Nos. 1-8, 10, each $700; Nos. 11, E1, each $800; No. 12, $1,350.

Counterfeits of overprint exist.

SPECIAL DELIVERY STAMP

Special Delivery Stamp of the United States, No. E5 Overprinted diagonally in Red **GUAM**

1899 **Wmk. 191** ***Perf. 12***

E1 SD3 10c **blue** *(5000)* 125.00 *150.00*
On cover *600.00*
Block of four 550.00
Margin block of four, arrow 600.00
Margin strip of 3, Impt. & P# 650.00
Margin block of 6, Impt. & P# *4,000.*
Dots in curved frame above messenger (Plate 882) 225.00

Counterfeits of overprint exist.

The special stamps for Guam were replaced by the regular issues of the United States.

GUAM GUARD MAIL
LOCAL POSTAL SERVICE

Inaugurated April 8, 1930, by Commander Willis W. Bradley, Jr., U.S.N., Governor of Guam, for the conveyance of mail between Agana and the other smaller towns.

Philippines Nos. 290 and 291 Overprinted **GUAM GUARD MAIL**

1930, Apr. 8 **Unwmk.** ***Perf. 11***

M1 A40 2c **green** *(2000)* 200.00 175.00
On cover 500.00
Block of four 850.00
M2 A40 4c **carmine** *(3000)* 175.00 150.00
On cover 500.00
Block of four 750.00

Counterfeits of overprint exist.

Seal of Guam — A1

1930, July **Unwmk.** ***Perf. 12***

Without Gum

M3 A1 1c **red & black** 65.00 75.00
On cover 200.00
Block of four 275.00
M4 A1 2c **black & red** 65.00 75.00
On cover 350.00
Block of four 275.00

Copies are often found showing parts of watermark "CLEVELAND BOND".

Philippines Nos. 290 and 291 Overprinted in Black **GUAM GUARD MAIL**

1930, Aug. 10 **Unwmk.** ***Perf. 11***

M5 A40 2c **green** *(20,000)* 2.75 3.00
On cover 75.00
Block of four 12.00
a. 2c yellow green 2.50 2.75
M6 A40 4c **carmine** *(80,000)* 50 1.75
On cover 75.00
Block of four 2.25

Same Overprint in Red on Philippines Nos. 290, 291, 292, 293a, and 294

1930, Dec.

M7 A40 2c **green** *(50,000)* 80 80
On cover 50.00
Block of four 3.50
a. GRAUD (Pos. 63) *(500)* 300.00
b. MIAL (Pos. 84) *(500)* 300.00
M8 A40 4c **carmine** *(50,000)* 85 85
On cover 50.00
Block of four 3.50
M9 A40 6c **deep violet** *(25,000)* 2.25 2.75
On cover 60.00
Block of four 10.00
M10 A40 8c **orange brown** *(25,000)* 2.25 2.50
On cover 60.00
Block of four 10.00
M11 A40 10c **deep blue** *(25,000)* 2.25 2.50
On cover 60.00
Block of four 10.00

The local postal service was discontinued April 8th, 1931, and replaced by the service of the United States Post Office Department.

SPECIMEN STAMPS

Overprinted United States Type E in Violet **Specimen.**

1899

1S E 1c **deep green** 125.00
2S E 2c **carmine** 125.00
3S E 3c **purple** 125.00
4S E 4c **lilac brown** 125.00
5S E 5c **blue** 125.00
6S E 6c **lake** 125.00
7S E 8c **violet brown** 125.00
8S E 10c **brown,** type I 125.00
10S E 15c **olive green** 125.00
11S E 50c **orange** 125.00
12S E $1 **black,** type I 250.00
13S E $1 **black,** type II —

Special Delivery

1899

E1S E 10c **blue** 250.00

Values for specimen stamps are for fine-very fine appearing copies with minor faults.

HAWAII

Until 1893, Hawaii was an independent kingdom. From 1893-1898 it was a republic. At the request of the inhabitants, Hawaii was annexed to the United States in 1898. Hawaiian stamps remained in use through June 13, 1900, and were replaced by U.S. stamps on June 14. In 1959 Hawaii became the 50th State of the Union. Hawaii consists of about 20 islands in the Pacific, about 2,000 miles southwest of San Francisco. The area is 6,434 square miles and the population was estimated at 150,000 in 1899. Honolulu is the capital.

100 CENTS = 1 DOLLAR

Values of early Hawaii stamps vary according to condition. Quotations for Nos. 5-18 are for fine-very fine copies. Very fine to superb specimens sell at much higher prices, and inferior or poor copies sell at reduced pricess, depending on the condition of the individual specimen.

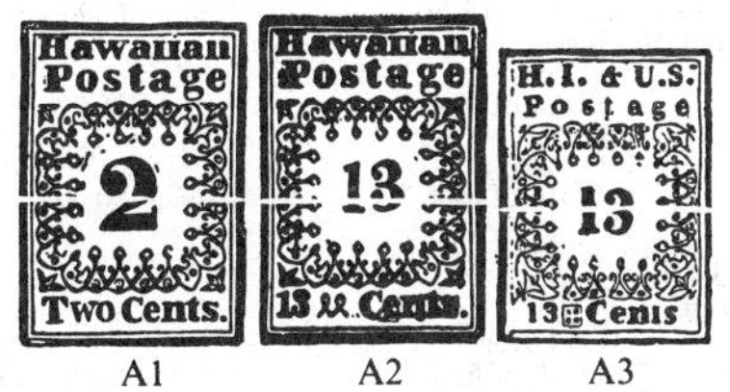

A1 A2 A3

1851-52 Unwmk. Typeset Pelure Paper *Imperf.*

1 A1	2c blue		500.000.	200,000.
	On cover			500,000.
2 A1	5c blue		35,000.	15,000.
	On cover			25,000.
3 A2	13c blue		17,500.	9,000.
	On cover			15,000.
4 A3	13c blue		45,000.	21,000.
	On cover			27,500.

Nos. 1-4 are known as the "Missionaries." Two varieties of each. Nos. 1-4, off cover, are almost invariably damaged.

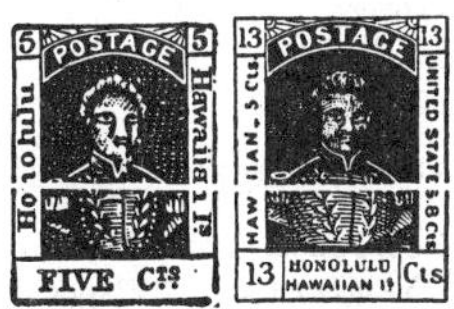

King Kamehameha III
A4 A5

Printed in Sheets of 20 (4x5)

1853 Thick White Wove Paper Engr.

5 A4	5c blue	650.00	450.00
	On cover		2,250.
	On cover with U.S. #17		12,000.
	Line through "Honolulu" (No. 2 in sheet)	1,350.	900.00
6 A5	13c dark red	325.00	400.00
	On cover		2,500.
	On cover with U.S. #17		7,500.
	On cover with #5 and U.S. #17		—
	Pair	900.00	1,200.
	Block of four	2,400.	

A6

1857

7 A6	5c on 13c dark red	4,500.	5,500.
	On cover		10,000.
	On cover with pair U.S. #7 and U.S. #15		—
	On cover with U.S. #14		15,000.
	On cover with U.S. #17		15,000.

1857

Thin White Wove Paper

8 A4	5c blue	250.00	250.00
	On cover		1,250.
	On cover with U.S. #15 and #7		—
	On cover with U.S. #17		5,000.
	On cover with U.S. #26		—
	On cover with U.S. #36		5,000.
	On cover with U.S. #69		5,500.
	On cover with U.S. #76		—
	Pair	650.00	
a.	Double impression	4,000.	—
	Line through "Honolulu" (No. 2 in sheet)	700.00	

1861

Thin Bluish Wove Paper

9 A4	5c blue	110.00	110.00
	On cover		850.00
	On cover with U.S. #36		—
	On cover with U.S. #65 and #73		3,500.
	On cover with U.S. #68		4,250.
	On cover with U.S. #76		—
	Block of four	700.00	—
a.	Double impression	4,000.	
	Line through "Honolulu" (No. 2 in sheet)	325.00	325.00

RE-ISSUE

1868

Ordinary White Wove Paper

10 A4	5c blue	25.00	
	Block of four	125.00	
	Line through "Honolulu" (No. 2 in sheet)	40.00	
11 A5	13c dull rose	225.00	
	Block of four	1,100.	

Remainders of Nos. 10 and 11 were overprinted "SPECIMEN." See Nos. 10S-11Sb.

Nos. 10 and 11 were never placed in use but copies (both with and without overprint) were sold at face value at the Honolulu post office.

REPRINTS (Official Imitations) 1889

5c Originals have two small dots near the left side of the square in the upper right corner. These dots are missing in the reprints.

13c The bottom of the 3 of 13 in the upper left corner is flattened in the originals and rounded in the reprints. The "t" of "Cts" on the left side is as tall as the "C" in the reprints, but shorter in the originals.

10R A4	5c blue	50.00
11R A5	13c orange red	200.00

On August 19, 1892, the remaining supply of reprints was overprinted in black "REPRINT." The reprints (both with and without overprint) were sold at face value. Quantities sold (including overprints) were 5c-3634 and 13c-1696. See Nos. 10R-S and 11R-S.

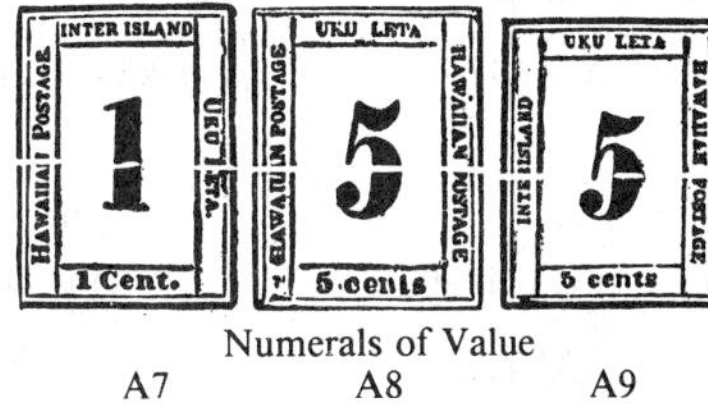

Numerals of Value
A7 A8 A9

1859-62 Typeset from settings of 10 varieties

12 A7	1c light blue, *bluish white*	2,750.	3,000.
	Pair		6,250.
a.	"1 Ce" omitted		—
13 A7	2c light blue, *bluish white*	2,250.	1,250.
	On cover		3,500.
	Block of four	10,000.	
a.	2c dark blue, *grayish white*	3,000.	
b.	Comma after "Cents"	—	
14 A7	2c black, *greenish blue* ('62)	3,250.	1,250.
	On cover		4,000.
a.	"2-Cents."		—

1863

15 A7	1c black, *grayish*	225.00	500.00
	On cover		—
	Block of four	1,100.	
a.	Tete beche pair	3,500.	
b.	"NTER"	—	
16 A7	2c black, *grayish*	375.00	325.00
	On cover		2,500.
	Pair		—
a.	"2" at top of rectangle	1,800.	1,800.
b.	Printed on both sides	—	—
c.	"NTER"	1,400.	1,400.
d.	2c black, *grayish white*	375.00	325.00
e.	Period omitted after "Cents"	—	
f.	Overlapping double impressions	—	
g.	"TAGE"	—	
17 A7	2c dark blue, *bluish*	3,500.	1,600.
	On cover		5,000.
	Pair	7,500.	
18 A7	2c black, *blue gray*	700.00	1,100.
	On cover		4,000.
	Pair		3,000.
	Thick paper	—	

1864-65

19 A7	1c black	275.00	700.00
	Pair	650.00	
	Block of four	1,500.	
20 A7	2c black	325.00	425.00
	On cover		1,250.
	Pair	800.00	
	Block of four	2,250.	
21 A8	5c blue, *blue* ('65)	275.00	275.00
	On cover with U.S. #65		—
	On cover with U.S. #76		5,000.
	Block of four	1,400.	—
a.	Tete beche pair	4,500.	
b.	5c black, *grayish white*	—	
22 A9	5c blue, *blue* ('65)	225.00	250.00
	On cover		1,100.
	On cover with U.S. #76		4,500.
	On cover with U.S. #63 and 76		—
	Block of four	1,100.	
a.	Tete beche pair	3,500.	
b.	5c blue, *grayish white*	—	

1864

Laid Paper

23 A7	1c black	150.00	750.00
	On cover with U.S. #76		—
	Block of four	675.00	
a.	"HA" instead of "HAWAIIAN"	1,750.	
b.	Tete beche pair	3,500.	
24 A7	2c black	150.00	750.00
	Block of four	750.00	
a.	"NTER"	700.00	
b.	"S" of "POSTAGE" omitted	700.00	
c.	Tete beche pair	3,500.	

A10

King Kamehameha IV — A11

1865

Wove Paper

No.	Type	Denom.	Description	Unused	Used
25	A10	1c	dark blue	150.00	
			Block of four	750.00	
			Double impression	—	
			With inverted impression of No. 21 on face	—	
26	A10	2c	dark blue	125.00	
			Block of four	600.00	

Nos. 12 to 26 were typeset and were printed in sheets of 50 (5 settings of 10 varieties each). The sheets were cut into panes of 25 (5x5) before distribution to the post offices.

1861-63 Litho.

Horizontally Laid Paper

No.	Type	Denom.	Description	Unused	Used
27	A11	2c	pale rose	175.00	110.00
			On cover		550.00
			Pair		—
a.			2c carmine rose ('63)	600.00	500.00

Vertically Laid Paper

No.	Type	Denom.	Description	Unused	Used
28	A11	2c	pale rose	175.00	110.00
			On cover		500.00
			Block of four	800.00	750.00
a.			2c carmine rose ('63)	135.00	135.00
a.			Block of four	650.00	

1869 Engr. Thin Wove Paper

No.	Type	Denom.	Description	Unused	Used
29	A11	2c	red	50.00	—
			Block of four	250.00	

No. 29 is a re-issue. It was not issued for postal purposes although canceled copies are known. It was sold only at the Honolulu post office, at first without overprint and later with overprint "CANCELLED." See No. 29S.

See note following No. 51.

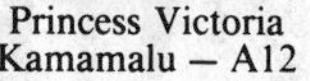
Princess Victoria Kamamalu — A12

King Kamehameha IV — A13

King Kamehameha V — A14

Kamehameha V — A15

Mataio Kekuanaoa — A16

1864-86 Wove Paper *Perf. 12*

No.	Type	Denom.	Description	Unused	Used
30	A12	1c	purple ('71)	7.50	6.00
a.			1c violet	7.50	6.00
			On cover		125.00
			Block of four	40.00	
31	A13	2c	rose vermilion	11.00	7.00
a.			2c vermilion ('86)	11.00	7.00
			On cover		125.00
			On cover with U.S. #76		250.00
			Block of four	55.00	50.00
b.			Half used as 1c on cover		—
32	A14	5c	blue ('66)	50.00	19.00
			On cover		125.00
			On cover with any U.S. issues of 1861-67		*1,250.*
			On cover with U.S. #116		*1,500.*
			Block of four	225.00	100.00
33	A15	6c	yellow green ('71)	17.50	6.00
a.			6c bluish green ('79)	17.50	6.00
			On cover		125.00
			On cover with U.S. #179		*500.00*
			Block of four	95.00	—
34	A16	18c	dull rose ('71)	85.00	14.00
			On cover		300.00
			Block of four	375.00	
			Without gum	17.50	
			Block of four without gum	85.00	

Half of No. 31 was used with a 5c stamp to make up the 6-cent rate to the United States.

No. 32 has traces of rectangular frame lines surrounding the design. Nos. 39 and 52C have no such frame lines.

King David Kalakaua — A17

Prince William Pitt Leleiohoku — A18

1875

No.	Type	Denom.	Description	Unused	Used
35	A17	2c	brown	6.00	2.25
			On cover		30.00
			Block of four	30.00	30.00
36	A18	12c	black	40.00	20.00
			On cover		250.00
			Block of four	200.00	—

Princess Likelike (Mrs. Archibald Cleghorn) — A19

King David Kalakaua — A20

Queen Kapiolani — A21

Statue of King Kamehameha I — A22

The lack of a value for a listed item does not necessarily indicate rarity.

King William Lunalilo — A23

Queen Emma Kaleleonalani — A24

1882

No.	Type	Denom.	Description	Unused	Used
37	A19	1c	blue	4.00	*7.50*
			On cover		32.50
			Block of four	22.50	*40.00*
38	A17	2c	lilac rose	90.00	30.00
			On cover		150.00
			Block of four	450.00	
39	A14	5c	ultramarine	12.00	2.25
			On cover		27.50
			Block of four	60.00	42.50
a.			Vert. pair, imperf. horiz.	*3,500.*	
40	A20	10c	black	22.50	15.00
			On cover		125.00
			Block of four	100.00	100.00
41	A21	15c	red brown	40.00	22.50
			On cover		175.00
			Block of four	200.00	175.00

1883-86

No.	Type	Denom.	Description	Unused	Used
42	A19	1c	green	2.25	1.50
			On cover		25.00
			Block of four	11.00	11.00
43	A17	2c	rose ('86)	3.50	75
			On cover		25.00
			Block of four	17.50	10.00
a.			2c dull red	40.00	15.00
44	A20	10c	red brown ('84)	17.50	7.00
			On cover		110.00
			Block of four	85.00	65.00
45	A20	10c	vermilion	20.00	12.50
			On cover		125.00
			Block of four	100.00	75.00
46	A18	12c	red lilac	60.00	30.00
			On cover		300.00
			Block of four	300.00	200.00
47	A22	25c	dark violet	85.00	42.50
			On cover		300.00
			Block of four	400.00	275.00
48	A23	50c	red	135.00	75.00
			On cover		500.00
			Block of four	700.00	
49	A24	$1	rose red	200.00	85.00
			On cover		600.00
			Block of four	950.00	
			Maltese cross cancellation		25.00

Reproduction and Reprint

Yellowish Wove Paper

1886-89 Engr. *Imperf.*

No.	Type	Denom.	Description	Unused	Used
50	A11	2c	orange vermilion	150.00	
			Block of four	750.00	
51	A11	2c	carmine ('89)	25.00	
			Block of four	110.00	

In 1885 the Postmaster General wished to have on sale complete sets of Hawaii's portrait stamps, but was unable to find either the stone from which Nos. 27 and 28, or the plate from which No. 29 was printed. He therefore sent a copy of No. 29 to the American Bank Note Company, with an order to engrave a new plate like it and print 10,000 stamps therefrom of which 5000 were overprinted "SPECIMEN" in blue.

The original No. 29 was printed in sheets of fifteen (5x3), but the plate of these "Official Imitations" was made up of fifty stamps (10x5). Later, in 1887, the original die for No. 29 was discovered, and, after retouching, a new plate was made and 37,500 stamps were printed (No. 51). These, like the originals were printed in sheets of fifteen. They were delivered during 1889 and 1890. In 1892 all remaining unsold in the Post Office were overprinted "Reprint".

No. 29 is red in color, and printed on very thin white wove paper. No. 50 is orange vermilion in color, on medium, white to buff paper. In No. 50 the vertical line on the left side of the portrait touches the horizontal line over the label "Elua Keneta", while in the other two varieties, Nos. 29 and 51, it does not touch the horizontal line by half a millimeter. In No. 51 there are three parallel lines on the left side of the King's nose, while in No. 29 and No. 50 there are no such lines. No. 51 is carmine in color and printed on thick, yellowish to buff wove paper.

It is claimed that both Nos. 50 and 51 were available for postage, although not made to fill a postal requirement. They exist with favor cancellation. See Nos. 50S-51S.

Queen Liliuokalani — A25

1890-91 *Perf. 12*

No.	Type	Denom.	Description	Unused	Used
52	A25	2c	dull violet, *Nov. 8, 1891*	4.00	1.25
			On cover		25.00
			Block of four	17.50	9.00
a.			Vert. pair, imperf. horiz.	*2,750.*	

No.	Design	Description	Unused	Used
52C	A14	5c deep indigo	90.00	75.00
		On cover		275.00
		Block of four	400.00	

Stamps of 1864-1891 Overprinted in Red

Provisional GOVT. 1893

1893

No.	Design	Description	Unused	Used
53	A12	1c purple	4.00	3.50
		On cover		35.00
		Block of four	20.00	20.00
a.		"189" instead of "1893"	225.00	
b.		No period after "GOVT"	150.00	250.00
54	A19	1c blue	4.00	6.50
		On cover		40.00
		Block of four	20.00	35.00
b.		No period after "GOVT"	100.00	150.00
55	A19	1c green	1.50	3.00
		On cover		25.00
		Block of four	7.50	15.00
a.		Pair, one without overprint	1,250.	
b.		Double overprint	500.00	150.00
56	A17	2c brown	5.00	10.00
		On cover		60.00
		Block of four	25.00	70.00
a.		No period after "GOVT"	150.00	—
57	A25	2c dull violet	1.50	1.25
		On cover		25.00
		Block of four	6.50	6.50
a.		Inverted overprint	600.00	600.00
b.		Double overprint	350.00	250.00
c.		"18 3" instead of "1893"	300.00	200.00
58	A14	5c deep indigo	9.00	17.50
		On cover		100.00
		Block of four	45.00	100.00
a.		No period after "GOVT"	150.00	200.00
59	A14	5c ultramarine	5.00	2.50
		On cover		40.00
		Block of four	25.00	20.00
a.		Inverted overprint	900.00	700.00
b.		Double overprint	2,000.	
60	A15	6c green	10.00	17.50
		On cover		135.00
		Block of four	50.00	90.00
61	A20	10c black	7.00	10.00
		On cover		125.00
		Block of four	35.00	55.00
61B	A20	10c red brown	16,500.	17,500.
		Block of four	—	
		Strip of five, plate imprint	—	
62	A18	12c black	7.50	12.00
		On cover		125.00
		Block of four	40.00	75.00
63	A18	12c red lilac	125.00	160.00
		On cover		450.00
		Block of four	750.00	900.00
64	A22	25c dark violet	20.00	22.50
		On cover		175.00
		Block of four	100.00	110.00
a.		No period after "GOVT"	135.00	175.00

Same Overprint in Black

No.	Design	Description	Unused	Used
65	A13	2c rose vermilion	50.00	55.00
		On cover		250.00
		Block of four	250.00	275.00
a.		No period after "GOVT"	200.00	—
66	A17	2c rose	1.25	2.25
		On cover		25.00
		Block of four	6.50	11.00
a.		Double overprint	1,100.	
b.		No period after "GOVT"	20.00	35.00
66C	A15	6c green	16,500.	—
		On cover		—
		Block of four	—	
67	A20	10c vermilion	11.00	20.00
		On cover		125.00
		Block of four	60.00	120.00
68	A20	10c red brown	6.00	10.00
		On cover		100.00
		Block of four	30.00	60.00
69	A18	12c red lilac	225.00	275.00
		On cover		900.00
		Block of four	1,000.	1,300.
70	A21	15c red brown	17.50	30.00
		On cover		185.00
		Block of four	95.00	150.00
71	A16	18c dull rose	22.50	35.00
		On cover		225.00
		Block of four	110.00	175.00
a.		Double overprint	500.00	
b.		Pair, one without overprint	1,000.	
c.		No period after "GOVT"	100.00	150.00
d.		"18 3" instead of "1893"	350.00	—
72	A23	50c red	55.00	85.00
		On cover		600.00
		Block of four	250.00	450.00
b.		No period after "GOVT"	150.00	—
73	A24	$1 rose red	100.00	140.00
		On cover		750.00
		Block of four	450.00	700.00
a.		No period after "GOVT"	300.00	—

For this set the only double overprints listed are those where both impressions are strong and fully inked.

Light or faint second impressions exist on Nos. 53-61, 62-64, 66, 67-73. These are highly prized by specialists. Some copies of No. 62 are known with the second impression almost equal to the first.

Counterfeit double overprints exist on most values. Counterfeits of Nos. 53b and 54b exist.

Coat of Arms — A26

View of Honolulu — A27

Statue of King Kamehameha I — A28

Star and Palms — A29

S.S. "Arawa" — A30

President Sanford Ballard Dole — A31

Statue of King Kamehameha I — A32

1894

No.	Design	Description	Unused	Used
74	A26	1c yellow	1.85	1.25
		On cover		25.00
75	A27	2c brown	2.00	60
		On cover		25.00
		Block of four	9.00	7.00
		"Flying goose" flaw (48 LR II)	275.00	250.00
		Double transfer	—	—
76	A28	5c rose lake	3.75	1.50
		On cover		25.00
		Block of four	18.50	15.00
77	A29	10c yellow green	5.00	4.50
		On cover		45.00
		Block of four	25.00	25.00
78	A30	12c blue	10.00	12.00
		On cover		125.00
		Block of four	45.00	—
79	A31	25c deep blue	10.00	12.00
		On cover		100.00

Numerous double transfers exist on Nos. 75 and 81.

1899

No.	Design	Description	Unused	Used
80	A26	1c dark green	1.50	1.25
		On cover		25.00
		Block of four	7.00	7.00
81	A27	2c rose	1.35	1.00
		On cover		20.00
		Double transfer	—	—
a.		2c salmon	1.50	1.25
b.		Vert. pair, imperf. horiz.	2,750.	
		"Flying goose" flaw (48 LR II)	275.00	250.00
82	A32	5c blue	5.00	3.00
		On cover		25.00
		Block of four	25.00	20.00

OFFICIAL

Lorrin Andrews Thurston — O1

1896 **Engr.** **Unwmk.** ***Perf. 12***

No.	Design	Description	Unused	Used
O1	O1	2c green	27.50	17.50
		On cover		200.00
		Block of four	120.00	
O2	O1	5c black brown	27.50	17.50
		On cover		200.00
		Block of four	120.00	
O3	O1	6c deep ultramarine	27.50	17.50
		On cover		200.00
		Block of four	120.00	
O4	O1	10c bright rose	27.50	17.50
		On cover		200.00
		Block of four	120.00	
O5	O1	12c orange	27.50	17.50
		On cover		200.00
		Block of four	120.00	
O6	O1	25c gray violet	27.50	17.50
		On cover		200.00
		Block of four	120.00	

Used values for Nos. O1-O6 are for copies canceled-to-order "FOREIGN OFFICE/HONOLULU H.I." in double circle without date. Values of postally used copies: Nos. O1-O2, O4, $27.50, No. O3, $50, No. O5, $75, No. O6, $100.

ENVELOPES

All printed by American Bank Note Co., N.Y.

View of Honolulu Harbor — E1

Envelopes of White Paper, Outside and Inside

1884

No.	Design	Description	Unused	Used
U1	E1	1c light green (109,000)	2.50	3.00
		Entire	6.00	15.00
a.		1c green (10,000)	5.00	5.00
		Entire	17.50	27.50
U2	E1	2c carmine (386,000 including U2a, U2b)	2.50	4.00
		Entire	6.00	17.50
a.		2c red	2.50	4.00
		Entire	6.00	17.50
b.		2c rose	2.50	4.00
		Entire	6.00	17.50
c.		2c pale pink (5,000)	10.00	12.50
		Entire	35.00	60.00
U3	E1	4c red (18,000)	12.50	15.00
		Entire	45.00	65.00
U4	E1	5c blue (90,775)	6.50	7.50
		Entire	15.00	30.00
U5	E1	10c black (3,500 plus)	25.00	25.00
		Entire	75.00	100.00

Envelopes White Outside, Blue Inside

No.	Design	Description	Unused	Used
U6	E1	2c rose	175.00	150.00
		Entire	550.00	750.00
U7	E1	4c red	175.00	150.00
		Entire	500.00	—
U8	E1	5c blue	175.00	150.00
		Entire	500.00	600.00
U9	E1	10c black	350.00	325.00
		Entire	700.00	—

Nos. U1, U2, U4 & U5 Overprinted Locally "Provisional Government 1893" in Red or Black

1893

No.	Design	Description	Unused	Used
U10	E1	1c light green (R) (16,000)	3.50	6.50
		Entire	7.50	20.00
a.		Double overprint	—	
		Entire	1,000.	
U11	E1	2c carmine (Bk) (37,000)	2.50	3.50
		Entire	6.00	15.00
a.		Double overprint	—	
		Entire	750.00	
b.		Double overprint, one inverted entire	900.00	
U12	E1	5c blue (R) (34,891)	5.00	5.00
		Entire	12.00	15.00
a.		Double overprint, entire	600.00	
U13	E1	10c black (R) (17,707 incl. No. U14)	10.00	15.00
		Entire	25.00	75.00
a.		Double overprint, entire	900.00	700.00

Envelope No. U9 with same overprint

No.	Design	Description	Unused	Used
U14	E1	10c black (R)	225.00	—
		Entire	600.00	—

SPECIAL DELIVERY ENVELOPE

Value is for Entire.

Envelope No. U5 with added inscription "Special Despatch Letter" etc. in red at top left corner

1885

No.	Design	Description	Unused	Used
UE1	E1	10c black (2,000)	250.00	

Envelope No. UE1 was prepared for use but never issued for postal purposes. Favor cancellations exist.

Hawaiian stamps can be mounted in Scott's U.S. Possessions Album.

POSTAL CARDS

All printed by American Bank Note Co., N.Y.
Values are for Entires.

Queen Liliuokalani – PC1

View of Diamond Head – PC2

Royal Emblems – PC3

1882-92 **Engr.**
UX1 PC1 1c red, *on buff (125,000)* 45.00 60.00
UX2 PC2 2c black *(45,000)* 70.00 80.00
a. Litho. ('92) 150.00
UX3 PC3 3c blue green *(21,426)* 100.00 110.00

1889 **Litho.**
UX4 PC1 1c red, *flesh (171,240)* 40.00 50.00

Cards Nos. UX4, UX2a and UX3 overprinted locally
"Provisional Government 1893" in red or black

1893
UX5 PC1 1c red, *flesh* (Bk) *(28,760)* 55.00 80.00
a. Double overprint *1,650.*
UX6 PC2 2c black (R) *(10,000)* 75.00 90.00
UX7 PC3 3c blue green (R) *(8,574)* 100.00 110.00
a. Double ovpt. *1,100.*

Iolani Palace – PC4

Map of Pacific Ocean, Mercator's Projection – PC5

1894-97 **Litho.**

Border Frame 131½x72½mm

UX8 PC4 1c red, *flesh (100,000)* 30.00 37.50
a. Border frame 132½x74mm ('97) *(200,000)* 27.50 37.50
UX9 PC5 2c green *(60,000)* 60.00 75.00
a. Border frame 132½x74mm ('97) *(190,000)* 55.00 75.00

PAID REPLY POSTAL CARDS

Double cards, same designs as postal cards
with added inscriptions on reply cards.

1883 **Litho.**
UY1 PC1 1c +1c purple, *buff,* unsevered *(5,000)* 250.00 300.00
m. Message card, detached 30.00 40.00
r. Reply card, detached 30.00 40.00
UY2 PC2 2c +2c dark blue, unsevered *(5,000)* 300.00 375.00
m. Message card, detached 55.00 65.00
r. Reply card, detached 55.00 65.00

1889
UY3 PC1 1c +1c gray violet, *flesh,* unsevered *(5,000)* 250.00 300.00
m. Message card, detached 30.00 40.00
r. Reply card, detached 30.00 40.00
UY4 PC2 2c +2c sapphire, unsevered *(5,000)* 250.00 300.00
m. Message card, detached 30.00 40.00
r. Reply card, detached 30.00 40.00

REVENUE

R1

R2

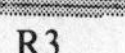

R3

R4

R5

R6

Printed by the American Bank Note Co.
Sheets of 70

1877 **Engr.** **Unwmk.** ***Rouletted 8***
R1 R1 25c green *(160,000)* 7.50 7.50
R2 R2 50c yellow orange *(190,000)* 7.50 7.50
R3 R3 $1 black *(580,000)* 12.50 5.00
a. $1 gray 12.50 5.00

Denominations Typo.

R4 R4 $5 vermilion & violet blue *(21,000)* 25.00 25.00
R5 R5 $10 reddish brown & green *(14,000)* 50.00 25.00
R6 R6 $50 slate blue & carmine *(3,500)* *250.00 250.00*

No. R1 Surcharged in Black or Gold

TWENTY CENTS
a

REPUBLIC OF TWENTY CENTS HAWAII
b

1893-94
R7 R1 (a) 20c on 25c green 10.00 10.00
a. Inverted surcharge 110.00 110.00
R8 R1 (b) 20c on 25c green (G) 30.00 30.00
a. Double surcharge — —
b. Double surch., one black — —

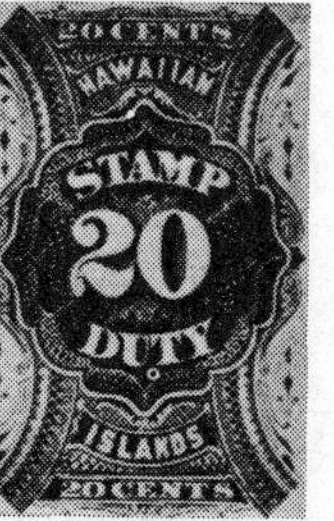

R7

Kamehameha I – R8

Sheets of 50

1894 **Litho.** ***Perf. 14***
R9 R7 20c red *(10,000)* 125.00 125.00
a. Imperf. *(25,000)* 125.00 125.00
R10 R7 25c violet brown 175.00 175.00
a. Imperf. 175.00 175.00

Printed by the American Bank Note Co.
Sheets of 100

1897 **Engr.** ***Perf. 12***
R11 R8 $1 dark blue *(60,000)* 7.00 4.00

No. R6 Inscribed "Territory of Hawaii"

1901 ***Rouletted 8***
R12 R6 $50 slate blue & carmine *(7,000)* 37.50 —

Types of 1877
Printed by the American Bank Note Co.
Sheets of 70

1910-13 **Engr.** ***Perf. 12***
R13 R2 50c yellow orange ('13) *(70,000)* 10.00 —
R14 R3 $1 black ('13) *(35,000)* 12.00 —
R15 R4 $5 vermilion & violet blue *(14,000)* 22.50 —
R16 R5 $10 reddish brown & green *(14,000)* 22.50 —

PROOFS

1853

No.			LARGE DIE (1)	PLATE (3) India
5TC	5c	black on wove		—
6TC	13c	black on wove		—

1868

10TC	5c	orange red	600.00	
11TC	13	orange red	600.00	400.00

1861-63

27TC	2c	black		550.00

1864-71

30P	1c	purple	550.00	125.00
		Block of four		550.00
31P	2c	rose vermilion	550.00	125.00
		Block of four		—
32P	5c	blue	550.00	125.00
32TC	5c	black	550.00	
32TC	5c	dark red		150.00
32TC	5c	orange red		150.00
32TC	5c	orange		150.00
32TC	5c	red brown		150.00
32TC	5c	green		150.00
32TC		Block of four		—
33P	5c	dark violet		150.00
33P	6c	green	550.00	125.00
34P	18c	dull rose	550.00	125.00
		Block of four		125.00
34TC	18c	orange red	550.00	550.00
34TC	18c	dark orange	550.00	

1875

35P	2c	brown	550.00	125.00
		Block of four		550.00
35TC	2c	black	550.00	
36P	12c	black	550.00	125.00
36TC	12c	violet blue	550.00	

1882

37P	1c	blue		125.00
		Block of four		550.00
37TC	1c	black	550.00	
39P	5c	ultramarine	475.00	125.00
40P	10c	black	475.00	125.00
		Block of four		475.00
41P	15c	red brown		125.00

1883-86

42P	1c	green		75.00
		Block of four		325.00
43P	2c	rose		100.00
		Block of four		400.00
47P	25c	dark violet	450.00	100.00
48P	50c	red	450.00	100.00
49P	$1	rose red		100.00
		Block of four		400.00
49TC	$1	black		150.00
49TC	$1	orange red	450.00	

1886-89

50P	2c	orange vermilion	550.00	125.00
51P	2c	carmine	550.00	

1890-91

52P	2c	dull violet	475.00	100.00
52CP	5c	deep indigo		100.00

1894

74P	1c	yellow	450.00	100.00
75P	2c	brown	450.00	100.00
75TC	2c	dark green	550.00	
76P	5c	rose lake	500.00	100.00
77P	10c	yellow green	500.00	100.00
		Block of four		400.00
78P	12c	blue	500.00	125.00
79P	25c	deep blue	500.00	100.00

1899

82P	5c	blue		150.00

1896 **Official**

O1P	2c	green	300.00	100.00
O2P	5c	black brown	300.00	100.00
O3P	6c	deep ultramarine	300.00	100.00
O4P	10c	bright rose	300.00	100.00
		Block of four		—
O4TC	10c	black	300.00	
O5P	12c	orange	300.00	100.00
O5TC	12c	black	300.00	
O6P	25c	gray violet	300.00	100.00
O6TC	25c	black	300.00	

SPECIMEN

Overprinted in Black or Red **SPECIMEN.**

1868

10S	5c blue (R)	20.00
	Line through "Honolulu"	45.00
11Sa	13c dull rose	20.00

Overprinted in Black **SPECIMEN.**

11Sb	13c dull rose	50.00
	Dbl. ovpt., one as #11Sa, one as #11Sb	*1,100.*
	Period omitted	80.00

Overprinted in Black **REPRINT**

1889

10RS	5c blue	45.00
11RS	13c orange red	80.00

Overprinted in Black **CANCELLED.**

1869

29S	2c red	50.00

Overprinted in Blue **SPECIMEN.**

1886

50S	2c orange vermilion	60.00

Overprinted in Black **REPRINT**

1889

51S	2c carmine	25.00

MARSHALL ISLANDS, REPUBLIC OF

A group of 32 atolls and more than 867 reefs in the west Pacific Ocean, about 2,500 miles southeast of Tokyo. The islands, comprised of two major chains, the Ralik chain in the west, and the Ratak chain in the east, were annexed by Germany in 1885. Stamps issued under German Dominion (Nos. 1-27) are listed in Vol. III of the Scott Standard Postage Stamp Catalogue. Japan seized the islands in 1914. They were taken by the U.S. in World War II and became part of the U.S. Trust Territory of the Pacific in 1947. By agreement with the U.S. Postal Service, the islands began issuing their own stamps in 1984, with the U.S.P.S. continuing to carry the mail to and from the islands. Islands and atolls include Kwajalein, Jaluit and Majuro, site of the government headquarters. AREA- 70 sq. mi. POP.- 31,042 (1980)

100 CENTS = 1 DOLLAR

Inauguration of Postal Service — A5

1984, May 2 **Litho.** ***Perf. 14x13½***

31	A5	20c	Outrigger canoe	50	50
32	A5	20c	Fishnet	50	50
33	A5	20c	Navigational stick chart	50	50
34	A5	20c	Islet	50	50
a.			Block of 4, #31-34	2.00	2.00

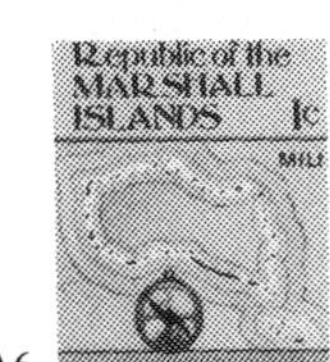

Mili Atoll, Astrolabe — A6

Maps and Navigational Instruments.

1984-85 **Litho.** ***Perf. 15x14***

35	A6	1c	shown	5	5
36	A6	3c	Likiep, Azimuth compass	6	6
37	A6	5c	Ebon, 16th cent. compass	10	10
38	A6	10c	Jaluit, anchor buoys	20	20
39	A6	13c	Ailinginae, Nocturnal	26	26
a.			Booklet pane of 10	2.60	—
40	A6	14c	Wotho Atoll, navigational stick chart ('85)	28	28
a.			Bklt. pane of 10	2.80	—

41 A6 20c Kwajalein and Ebeye, stick chart 40 40
a. Booklet pane of 10 4.00 —
b. Booklet pane of 5 each, 13c, 20c 3.30 —
42 A6 22c Enewetak, 18th cent. lode stone storage case ('85) 44 44
a. Bklt. pane of 10 4.40 —
b. Blkt. pane of 5 each, 14c, 22c 3.60 —
43 A6 28c Ailinglaplap, printed compass 56 56
44 A6 30c Majuro, navigational stick-chart 60 60
45 A6 33c Namu, stick chart ('85) 66 66
46 A6 37c Rongelap, quadrant 74 74
47 A6 39c Taka, map compass, 16th cent. sea chart ('85) 78 78
48 A6 44c Ujelang, chronograph ('85) 88 88
49 A6 50c Maloelap and Aur, nocturlabe ('85) 1.00 1.00
49A A6 $1 Arno, 16th cent. sector compass 2.00 2.00

Issue dates: 1c, 3c, 10c, 30c and $1, June 12. 13c, 20c, 28c and 37c. Dec. 19, 1984. 14c, 22c, 33c, 39c, 44c and 50c, June 5, 1985.

See Nos. 107-109.

No. 7 — A7

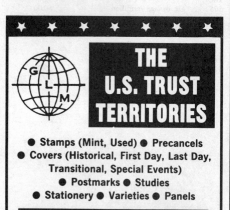

1984, June 19 ***Perf. 14½x15***

50 A7 40c shown 60 60
51 A7 40c No. 13 60 60
52 A7 40c No. 4 60 60
53 A7 40c No. 25 60 60
a. Block of 4, #50-53 2.40 2.40

Philatelic Salon, 19th UPU Congress, Hamburg, June 19-26.

Ausipex '84
A8

Dolphins.

1984, Sept. 5 **Litho.** ***Perf. 14***

54 A8 20c Common 35 35
55 A8 20c Risso's 35 35
56 A8 20c Spotter 35 35
57 A8 20c Bottlenose 35 35
a. Block of 4, #54-57 1.40 1.40

Christmas 1984 — A9

1984, Nov. 7 **Litho.** ***Perf. 14***

58 Strip of 4 1.60 1.60
a.-d. A9 20c Any single 40 40
Sheet of 16 7.50

Printed in sheets of 16; background shows text from Marshallese New Testament, giving each stamp on the sheet a different background.

Marshalls Constitution, 5th Anniv. — A10

1984, Dec. 19 **Litho.** ***Perf. 14***

59 A10 20c Traditional chief 35 35
60 A10 20c Amata Kabua 35 35
61 A10 20c Chester Nimitz 35 35
62 A10 20c Trygve Lie 35 35
a. Block of 4, #59-62 1.40 1.40

Audubon Bicentenary
A11

1985, Feb. 15 **Litho.** ***Perf. 14***

63 A11 22c Forked-tailed Petrel 40 40
64 A11 22c Pectoral Sandpiper 40 40
a. Pair, #63-64 80 80

See Nos. C1-C2.

Sea Shells — A12

1985, Apr. 17 **Litho.** ***Perf. 14***

65 A12 22c Cymatium lotorium 35 35
66 A12 22c Chicoreus cornucervi 35 35
67 A12 22c Strombus aurisdanae 35 35
68 A12 22c Turbo marmoratus 35 35
69 A12 22c Chicoreus palmarosae 35 35
a. Strip of 5, #65-69 1.75 1.75

See Nos. 119-123, 152-156.

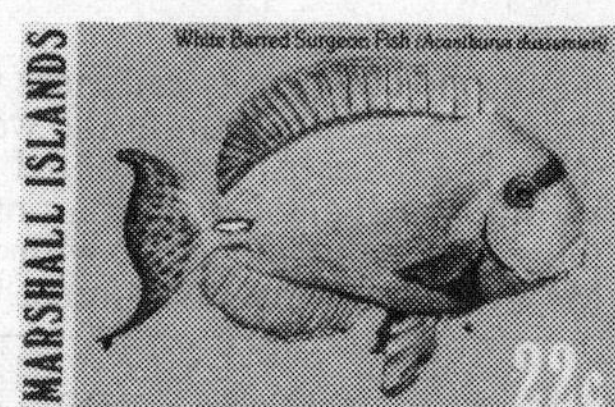

Decade for Women — A13

Marshallese women and: No. 70, Native drum. No. 71, Palm branches. No. 72, Pounding stone. No. 73, Ak bird.

1985, June 5 **Litho.** ***Perf. 14***

70 A13 22c multi 35 35
71 A13 22c multi 35 35
72 A13 22c multi 35 35
73 A13 22c multi 35 35
a. Block of 4, #70-73 1.40 1.40

Reef and Lagoon Fish — A14

1985, July 15 **Litho.** ***Perf. 14***

74 A14 22c Acanthurus dussumieri 35 35
75 A14 22c Adioryx caudimaculatus 35 35
76 A14 22c Ostracion meleacaris 35 35
77 A14 22c Chaetodon ephippium 35 35
a. Block of 4, #74-77 1.40 1.40

Intl. Youth Year — A15

IYY and Alele Nautical Museum emblems and: No. 78, Marshallese youths and Peace Corps volunteers playing basketball. No. 79, Legend teller reciting local history, girl listening to recording. No. 80, Islander explaining navigational stick charts. No. 81, Jabwa stick dance.

1985, Aug. 31 **Litho.** ***Perf. 14***

78 A15 22c multi 35 35
79 A15 22c multi 35 35
80 A15 22c multi 35 35
81 A15 22c multi 35 35
a. Block of 4, #78-81 1.40 1.40

1856 American Board of Commissions Stock Certificate for Foreign Missions A16

Missionary ship Morning Star I: 22c, Launch, Jothan Stetson Shipyard, Chelsea, MA, Aug. 7, 1857. 33c, First voyage, Honolulu to the Marshalls, 1857. 44c, Marshall islanders pulling Morning Star I into Ebon Lagoon, 1857.

1985, Oct. 21 **Litho.** ***Perf. 14***

82 A16 14c multi 20 20
83 A16 22c multi 35 35
84 A16 33c multi 55 55
85 A16 44c multi 75 75

Christmas 1985.

U.S. Space Shuttle, Astro Telescope, Halley's Comet — A17

Comet tail and research spacecraft: No. 87, Planet A Space Probe, Japan. No. 88, Giotto spacecraft, European Space Agency. No. 89, INTERCOSMOS Project Vega spacecraft, Russia, France, etc. No. 90, U.S. naval tracking ship, NASA observational aircraft, cameo portrait of Edmond Halley (1656-1742), astronomer. Se-tenant in continuous design.

1985, Nov. 21

86 A17 22c multi 75 75
87 A17 22c multi 75 75
88 A17 22c multi 75 75
89 A17 22c multi 75 75
90 A17 22c multi 75 75
a. Strip of 5, #86-90 3.75 3.75

Medicinal Plants — A18

1985, Dec. 31 **Litho.** ***Perf. 14***

91 A18 22c Sida fallax 35 35
92 A18 22c Scaevola frutescens 35 35
93 A18 22c Guettarda speciosa 35 35
94 A18 22c Cassytha filiformis 35 35
a. Block of 4, #91-94 1.40 1.40

Maps Type of 1984

1986-87 ***Perf. 15x14, 14 ($10)***

107 A6 $2 Wotje and Erikub, terrestrial globe, 1571 3.00 3.00
108 A6 $5 Bikini, Stick chart 8.00 8.00

Size: 31x31mm.

109 A6 $10 Stick chart of the atolls 15.00 15.00

Issue dates: $2, $5, Mar 7, 1986. $10, Mar. 31, 1987.

Marine Invertebrates A19

1986, Mar. 31 **Litho.** ***Perf. 14½x14***

110 A19 14c Triton's trumpet 28 28
111 A19 14c Giant clam 28 28
112 A19 14c Small giant clam 28 28
113 A19 14c Coconut crab 28 28
a. Block of 4, #110-113 1.15 1.15

Souvenir Sheet

AMERIPEX '86, Chicago, May 22-June 1 — A20

1986, May 22 **Litho.** ***Perf. 14***

114 A20 $1 Douglas C-54 Globester 2.25 2.25

1st Around-the-world scheduled flight, 40th anniv. No. 114 has multicolored margin continuing the design and picturing US Air Transport Command Base, Kwajalein Atoll and souvenir card. Size: 89x63mm.

See Nos. C3-C6.

Operation Crossroads, Atomic Bomb Tests, 40th Anniv. — A21

Designs: No. 115, King Juda, Bikinians sailing tibinal canoe. No. 116, USS Sumner, amphibious DUKW, advance landing. No. 117, Evacuating Bikinians. No. 118, Land reclamation, 1986.

1986, July 1 **Litho.** ***Perf. 14***

115 A21 22c multi 35 35
116 A21 22c multi 35 35
117 A21 22c multi 35 35
118 A21 22c multi 35 35
a. Block of 4, #115-118 1.40 1.40

See No. C7.

Seashells Type of 1985

1986, Aug. 1 **Litho.** ***Perf. 14***

119 A12 22c Ramose murex 35 35
120 A12 22c Orange spider 35 35
121 A12 22c Red-mouth frog shell 35 35
122 A12 22c Laciniate conch 35 35
123 A12 22c Giant frog shell 35 35
a. Strip of 5, #119-123 1.75 1.75

Game Fish — A22

1986, Sept. 10 **Litho.**

124 A22 22c Blue marlin 35 35
125 A22 22c Wahoo 35 35
126 A22 22c Dolphin fish 35 35
127 A22 22c Yellowfin tuna 35 35
a. Block of 4, #124-127 1.40 1.40

Christmas, Intl. Peace Year — A23

1986, Oct. 28 **Litho.** ***Perf. 14***

128 A23 22c United Nations UR 35 35
129 A23 22c United Nations UL 35 35
130 A23 22c United Nations LR 35 35
131 A23 22c United Nations LL 35 35
a. Block of 4, #128-131 1.40 1.40

See No. C8.

U.S. Whaling Ships — A24

1987, Feb. 20 **Litho.** ***Perf. 14***

132 A24 22c James Arnold, 1854 35 35
133 A24 22c General Scott, 1859 35 35
134 A24 22c Charles W. Morgan, 1865 35 35
135 A24 22c Lucretia, 1884 35 35
a. Block of 4, #132-135 1.40 1.40

Historic and Military Flights — A25

Designs: No. 136, Charles Lindbergh commemorative medal, Spirit of St. Louis crossing the Atlantic, 1927. No. 137, Lindbergh flying in the Battle of the Marshalls, 1944. No. 138, William Bridgeman flying in the Battle of Kwajalein, 1944. No. 139, Bridgeman testing the Douglas Skyrocket, 1951. No. 140, John Glenn flying in the Battle of the Marshalls. No. 141, Glenn, the first American to orbit the Earth, 1962.

1987, Mar. 12 **Litho.** ***Perf. 14½***

136 A25 33c multi 60 60
137 A25 33c multi 60 60
a. Pair, Nos. 136-137 1.20 1.20
138 A25 39c multi 65 65
139 A25 39c multi 65 65
a. Pair, Nos. 138-139 1.30 1.30
140 A25 44c multi 70 70
141 A25 44c multi 70 70
a. Pair, Nos. 140-141 1.40 1.40

Souvenir Sheet

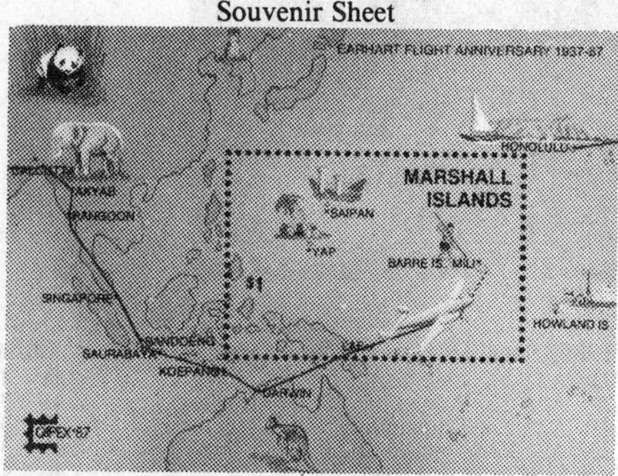

CAPEX '87 — A26

1987, June 15 **Litho.** *Perf. 14*

142 A26 $1 Map of flight	1.75	1.75

Amelia Earhart (1897-1937), American aviator who died during attempted round-the-world flight, 50th anniv. No. 142 has multicolored margin picturing Earhart's flight pattern from Calcutta, India, to the crash site near Barre Is., Marshall Isls. Size: 88x63mm.

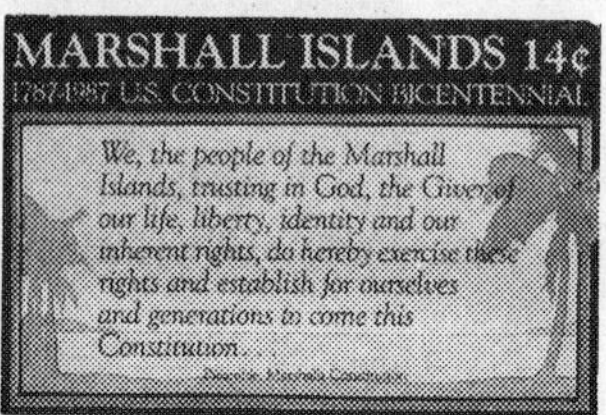

U.S. Constitution Bicentennial A27

Excerpts from the Marshall Islands and U.S. Constitutions.

1987, July 16 **Litho.** *Perf. 14*

143 A27 14c We,... Marshall	25	25
144 A27 14c National seals	25	25
145 A27 14c We,... United States	25	25
a. Triptych, Nos. 143-145	75	75
146 A27 22c All we have...	35	35
147 A27 22c Flags	35	35
148 A27 22c to establish...	35	35
a. Triptych, Nos. 146-148	1.05	1.05
149 A27 44c With this Constitution...	70	70
150 A27 44c Stick chart, Liberty Bell	70	70
151 A27 44c to promote...	70	70
a. Triptych, Nos. 149-151	2.10	2.10

Triptychs printed in continuous designs.

Seashells Type of 1985

1987, Sept. 1 **Litho.** *Perf. 14*

152 A12 22c Magnificent cone	35	35
153 A12 22c Partridge tun	35	35
154 A12 22c Scorpion spider conch	35	35
155 A12 22c Hairy triton	35	35
156 A12 22c Chiragra spider conch	35	35
a. Strip of 5, Nos. 152-156	1.75	1.75

Copra Industry — A28

Contest-winning crayon drawings by Amram Enox; design contest sponsored by the Tobular Copra Processing Co.

1987, Dec. 10 **Litho.** *Perf. 14*

157 A28 44c Planting coconut	75	75
158 A28 44c Making copra	75	75
159 A28 44c Bottling coconut oil	75	75
a. Triptych, Nos. 157-159	2.25	2.25

Marshall Islands stamps can be mounted in Scott's annually supplemented U.S. Trust Territories Album.

Biblical Verses A29

1987, Dec. 10

160 A29 14c Matthew 2:1	25	25
161 A29 22c Luke 2:14	35	35
162 A29 33c Psalms 33:3	55	55
163 A29 44c Pslams 150:5	70	70

Christmas 1987.

Marine Birds — A30

1988, Jan. 27

164 A30 44c Pacific reef herons	75	75
165 A30 44c Bar-tailed godwit	75	75
166 A30 44c Masked booby	75	75
167 A30 44c Northern shoveler	75	75

Fish — A31

1988-89 **Litho.** *Perf. 14½x14, 14 (No. 187)*

168 A31 1c Damselfish	5	5
169 A31 3c Blackface butterflyfish	6	6
170 A31 14c Hawkfish	28	28
a. Bklt. pane of 10	2.80	—
171 A31 15c Balloonfish	30	30
a. Bklt. pane of 10	3.00	—
172 A31 17c Trunk fish	34	34
173 A31 22c Lyretail wrasse	44	44
a. Bklt. pane of 10	4.40	—
b. Bklt. pane of 10 (5 each 14c, 22c)	3.60	—
174 A31 25c Parrotfish	50	50
a. Bklt. pane of 10	5.00	—
b. Bklt. pane of 10 (5 ea 15c, 25c)	4.00	—
175 A31 33c White-spotted boxfish	66	66
176 A31 36c Spotted boxfish	72	72
177 A31 39c Surgeonfish	78	78
178 A31 44c Long-snouted butterflyfish	88	88
179 A31 45c Trumpetfish	90	90
180 A31 56c Sharp-nosed puffer	1.12	1.12
181 A31 $1 Seahorse	2.00	2.00
182 A31 $2 Ghost pipefish	4.00	4.00
183 A31 $5 Big-spotted triggerfish	10.00	10.00

Size: 50x29mm

187 A31 $10 Bluejack	20.00	20.00

Issue dates: Nos. 170a, 173a, 173b, Mar. 31, 1988. 15c, 25c, 36c, 45c, July 19. Nos. 171a, 174a, 174b, Dec. 15. No. 187, Mar. 31, 1989. Others, Mar. 17.

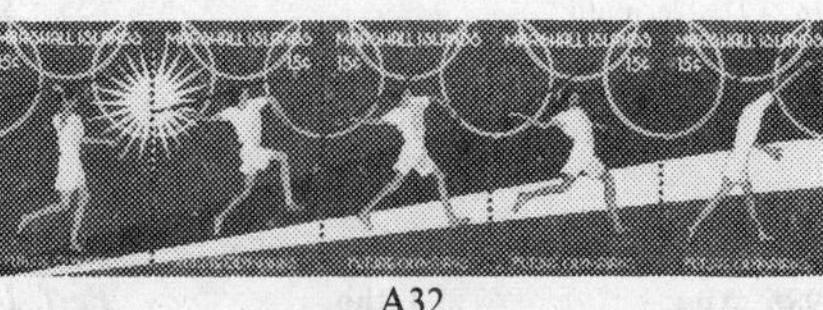

A32

1988 Summer Olympics, Seoul — A33

Athletes in motion: 15c Javelin thrower (Nos. 188a-188e as shown). 25c, Runner (Nos. 189a-189e as shown).

1988, June 30 **Litho.** *Perf. 14*

188 A32 Strip of 5	1.50	1.50
a.-e. 15c, any single	30	30
189 A33 Strip of 5	2.50	2.50
a.-e. 25c, any single	50	50

Souvenir Sheet

Pacific Voyages of Robert Louis Stevenson A34

Stick chart of the Marshalls and: a, *Casco* sailing through the Golden Gate. b, At the Needles of Ua-Pu, Marquesas. c, *Equator* departing from Honolulu and Kajulani, an Hawaiian princess. d, Chief's canoe, Majuro Lagoon. e, Bronze medallion, 1887, by Augustus St. Gaudens in the Tate Gallery, London. f, Outrigger canoe and *S.S. Janet Nicoll* in Majuro Lagoon. g, View of Apemama, Gilbert Is. h, Samoan outrigger canoe, Apia Harbor. i, Stevenson riding horse Jack at his estate, Vailima, Samoa.

1988, July 19 **Litho.** *Perf. 14*

190 Sheet of 9	4.50	4.50
a.-i. A34 25c any single	50	50

Robert Louis Stevenson (1850-94), Scottish novelist, poet and essayist. Size: 215x152mm.

Colonial Ships and Flags — A35

Designs: No. 191, Galleon Santa Maria de La Victoria, 1526, and Spanish "Ragged Cross" ensign in use from 1516 to 1785. No. 192, Transport ships Charlotte and Scarborough, 1788, and British red ensign 1707-1800. No. 193, Schooner Flying Fish, sloop-of-war Peacock, 1841, and U.S. flag 1837-1845. No. 194, Steamer Planet, 1909, and German flag 1867-1919.

1988, Sept. 2 **Litho.** *Perf. 14*

191 A35 25c multi	50	50
192 A35 25c multi	50	50
193 A35 25c multi	50	50
194 A35 25c multi	50	50
a. Block of 4, Nos. 191-194	2.00	2.00

Christmas — A36

Designs: No. 195, Santa Claus riding in sleigh. No. 196, Reindeer, hut and palm trees. No. 197, Reindeer and palm trees. No. 198, Reindeer, palm tree, fish. No. 199, Reindeer and outrigger canoe.

1988, Nov. 7 **Litho.** *Perf. 14*

195 A36 25c multi	50	50
196 A36 25c multi	50	50
197 A36 25c multi	50	50
198 A36 25c multi	50	50
199 A36 25c multi	50	50
a. Strip of 5, Nos. 195-199	2.50	2.50

Nos. 195-199 printed se-tenant in a continuous design.

Tribute to John. F. Kennedy — A37

1988, Nov. 22	**Litho.**	***Perf. 14***	
200 A37 25c Nuclear threat diminished		50	50
201 A37 25c Signing the Test Ban Treaty		50	50
202 A37 25c Portrait		50	50
203 A37 25c US-USSR Hotline		50	50
204 A37 25c Peace Corps enactment		50	50
a. Strip of 5, Nos. 200-204		2.50	2.50

Se-tenant in a continuous design. Printed in sheets containing 3 No. 204a.

U.S. Space Shuttle Program and Kwajalein — A38

Designs: No. 205, Launch of Prime from Vandenberg Air Force Base downrange to the Kwajalein Missile Range. No. 206, Prime X023A/SV-5D lifting body reentering atmosphere. No. 207, Parachute landing and craft recovery off Kwajalein Is. No. 208, Shuttle over island.

1988, Dec. 23	**Litho.**	***Perf. 14***	
205 A38 25c multi		50	50
206 A38 25c multi		50	50
207 A38 25c multi		50	50
208 A38 25c multi		50	50
a. Strip of 4, Nos. 205-208		2.00	2.00

NASA 30th anniv. and 25th aniv. of the Project Prime wind tunnel tests. See No. C21.

Links to Japan — A39

Designs: No. 209, Typhoon Monument, Majuro, 1918. No. 210, Seaplane base and railway depot, Djarrej Islet, c. 1940. No. 211, Fishing boats. No. 212, Japanese honeymooners scuba diving, 1988.

1989, Jan. 19	**Litho.**	***Perf. 14***	
209 A39 45c multi		90	90
210 A39 45c multi		90	90
211 A39 45c multi		90	90
212 A39 45 multi		90	90
a. Block of 4, Nos. 209-212		3.60	3.60

Alaska State 30th Anniv. — A40

Paintings by Claire Fejes.

1989, Mar. 31	**Litho.**	***Perf. 14***	
213 A40 45c Island Woman		90	90
214 A40 45c Kotzebue, Alaska		90	90
215 A40 45c Marshallese Madonna		90	90
a. Strip of 3, Nos. 213-315		2.75	2.75

Printed in sheets of 9.

Seashell Type of 1985

1989, May 15	**Litho.**	***Perf. 14***	
216 A12 25c Pontifical miter		50	50
217 A12 25c Tapestry turban		50	50
218 A12 25c Flame-mouthed helmet		50	50
219 A12 25c Prickly Pacific drupe		50	50
220 A12 25c Blood-mouthed conch		50	50
a. Strip of 5, Nos. 216-220		2.50	2.50

Souvenir Sheet

In Praise of Sovereigns, 1940, by Sanko Inoue — A41

1989, May 15	**Litho.**	***Perf. 14***	
241 A41 $1 multi		2.00	2.00

Hirohito (1901-1989) and enthronement of Akihito as emperor of Japan.

Migrant Birds — A42

1989, June 27	**Litho.**	***Perf. 14***	
222 A42 45c Wandering tattler		90	90
223 A42 45c Ruddy turnstone		90	90
224 A42 45c Pacific golden plover		90	90
225 A42 45c Sanderling		90	90
a. Block of 4, Nos. 222-225		3.60	3.60

Postal History — A43

PHILEXFRANCE '89 — A44

Designs: No. 226, Missionary ship Morning Star V, 1905, and Marshall Isls. No. 15 canceled. No. 227, Marshall Isls. Nos. 15-16 on registered letter, 1906. No. 228, Prinz Eitel Friedrich, 1914 and German sea post cancel. No. 229, Cruiser squadron led by SMS Scharnhorst, 1914 and German sea post cancel.

No. 230:a, SMS Bussard and German sea post cancel and Germany No. 32. b, U.S. Type A924 and Marshall Isls. No. 34a on FDC. c, LSST 119 Floating FPO, 1944, U.S. Navy cancel and pair of U.S. No. 853. d, Mail boat, 1936, cancel and Japan No. 222. e, Majuro P.O. f, Marshall Isls. cancel, 1951 and four U.S. No. 803.

No. 231, Germany No. 32 and Marshall Isls. cancel, 1889.

1989, July 7			
226 A43 45c multi		90	90
227 A43 45c multi		90	90
228 A43 45c multi		90	90
229 A43 45c multi		90	90
a. Block of 4, Nos. 226-229		3.60	3.60
Souvenir Sheets			
230 Sheet of 6		3.00	3.00
a.-f. A44 25c any single		50	50
231 A43 $1 multi		2.00	2.00

No. 230 has multicolored inscribed margin picturing natl. flag and exhibition emblem. Nos. 230b and 230e are printed in a continuous design.

No. 231 has multicolored decorative margin picturing exhibition emblem and German p.o. at Jaluit.

AIR POST STAMPS

Audubon Type of 1985

1985, Feb. 15	**Litho.**	***Perf. 14***	
C1 A11 44c Booby Gannet, vert.		88	88
C2 A11 44c Esquimaux Curlew, vert.		88	88
a. Pair, #C1-C2		1.80	1.80

AMERIPEX Type of 1986

Designs: No. C3, Consolidated PBY-5A Catalina Amphibian. No. C4, Grumman SA-16 Albatross. No. C5, McDonnell Douglas DC-6B Super Cloudmaster. No. C6, Boeing 727-100.

1986, May 22	**Litho.**	***Perf. 14***	
C3 A20 44c multi		80	80
C4 A20 44c multi		80	80
C5 A20 44c multi		80	80
C6 A20 44c multi		80	80
a. Block of 4, #C3-C6		3.25	3.25

Operation Crossroads Type of 1986

Souvenir Sheet

1986, July 1	**Litho.**	***Perf. 14***	
C7 A21 44c USS Saratoga		3.50	3.50

No. C7 has multicolored margin inscribed "Baker Day Atomic Bomb Test, 25 July 1946," and picturing mushroom cloud. Size: 106x72mm.

An enhanced introduction to the Scott Catalogue begins on Page V. A thorough understanding of the material presented there will greatly aid your use of the catalogue itself.

Statue of Liberty Cent., Intl. Peace Year — AP1

1986, Oct. 28 **Litho.**

C8 AP1 44c multi	85	85

Natl. Girl Scout Movement, 20th Anniv. — AP2

1986, Dec. 8 **Litho.**

C9 AP2 44c Community service	1.00	1.00
C10 AP2 44c Salute	1.00	1.00
C11 AP2 44c Health care	1.00	1.00
C12 AP2 44c Learning skills	1.00	1.00
a. Block of 4, #C9-C12	4.00	4.00

Girl Scout Movement in the US, 75th anniv. (1912-1987).

Marine Birds — AP3

1987, Jan. 12 **Litho.** ***Perf. 14***

C13 AP3 44c Wedge-tailed shearwater	88	88
C14 AP3 44c Red-footed booby	88	88
C15 AP3 44c Red-tailed tropicbird	88	88
C16 AP3 44c Great frigatebird	88	88
a. Block of 4, #C13-C16	3.55	3.55

CAPEX '87 AP4

Last flight of Amelia Earhart: No. C17, Take-off at Lae, New Guinea, July 2, 1937. No. C18, USCG Itasca cutter at Howland Is. No. C19, Purported crash landing of the Electra at Mili Atoll. No. C20, Recovery of the Electra by the Koshu, a Japanese survey ship.

1987, June 15 **Litho.** ***Perf. 14***

C17 AP4 44c multi	88	88
C18 AP4 44c multi	88	88
C19 AP4 44c multi	88	88
C20 AP4 44c multi	88	88
a. Block of 4, Nos. C17-C20	3.55	3.55

Space Shuttle Type of 1988

1988, Dec. 23 **Litho.** ***Perf. 14***

C21 A38 45c Astronaut, shuttle over Rongelap	90	90

Aircraft — AP5

1989, Apr. 24 **Litho.** ***Perf. 14x14½***

C22 AP5 12c Dornier Do228	24	24
a. Bklt. pane of 10	2.40	—
C23 AP5 36c Boeing 737	72	72
a. Bklt. pane of 10	7.20	—
C24 AP5 39c Hawker Siddeley 748	78	78
a. Bklt. pane of 10	7.80	—
C25 AP5 45c Boeing 727	90	90
a. Bklt. pane of 10	9.00	—
b. Bklt. pane of 10 (5 each 36c, 45c)	8.10	—

MICRONESIA, FEDERATED STATES OF

A group of more than 600 islands in the west Pacific Ocean, north of the equator. These islands, also known as the Caroline Islands, were bought by Germany from Spain in 1899. Caroline Islands stamps issued as a German colony are listed in Vol. II of the Scott Standard Postage Stamp Catalogue. The islands were seized by Japan in 1914. They were taken by the U.S. in World War II and became part of the U.S. Trust Territory of the Pacific in 1947. By agreement with the U.S. Postal Service, the islands began issuing their own stamps in 1984, with the U.S.P.S. continuing to carry the mail to and from the islands. Yap, Truk, Pohnpei and Kosrae are the four states of Micronesia. All but Kosrae are island groups. Kolonia, on Pohnpei, is the seat of government. Land area: 271 sq. mi. Population: 73,755 (1980).

100 CENTS = 1 DOLLAR

Map of State of Yap A1

1984, July 12 **Litho.** ***Perf. 14***

1 A1 20c shown	35	35
2 A1 20c Truk	35	35
3 A1 20c Pohnpei	35	35
4 A1 20c Kosrae	35	35
a. Block of 4, #1-4	1.40	1.40

Postal service inauguration. For surcharges see Nos. 48-51.

Fernandez de Quiros — A2

Men's House, Yap — A3

Designs: 1c, 19c, Pedro Fernandez de Quiros, Spanish explorer, first discovered Pohnpei, 1595. 2c, 20c, Louis Duperrey, French explorer. 3c, 30c, Fyedor Lutke, Russian explorer. 4c, 37c, Dumont d'Urville. 10c, Sleeping Lady, Kosrae. 13c, Liduduhriap Waterfall, Pohnpei. 17c, Tonachau Peak, Truk. 50c, Devil mask, Truk. $1, Sokeh's Rock, Pohnpei. $2, Canoes, Kosrae. $5, Stone money, Yap.

1984, July 12 ***Perf. 13½x13***

5	A2	1c Prus bl	5	5
6	A2	2c dp cl	5	5
7	A2	3c dk bl	5	5
8	A2	4c green	7	7
9	A3	5c yel brn	8	8
10	A3	10c dk vio	16	16
11	A3	13c dk bl	20	20
12	A3	17c brn lake	25	25
13	A2	19c dk vio	28	28
14	A2	20c ol grn	30	30
15	A2	30c rose lake	45	45
16	A2	37c dp vio	55	55
17	A3	50c brown	75	75
18	A3	$1 olive	1.50	1.50
19	A3	$2 Prus bl	3.00	3.00
20	A3	$5 brn lake	7.00	7.00

See Nos. 30-42.

Ausipex '84 A4

1984, Sept. 21 **Litho.** ***Perf. 13½***

21 A4 20c Truk Post Office	35	35

See Nos. C4-C6.

Christmas — A5

Child's drawing.

1984, Dec. 20

22 A5 20c Child in straw manger	35	35

See Nos. C7-C9.

Ships — A6

1985, Aug. 19

23 A6 22c U.S.S. Jamestown	35	35

See Nos. C10-C12.

Christmas — A7

1985, Oct. 15 **Litho.** ***Perf. 13½***
24 A7 22c Lelu Protestant Church, Kosrae 35 35

See Nos. C13-C14.

Audubon Birth Bicentenary — A8

1985, Oct. 30 ***Perf. 14½***

25	A8 22c Noddy tern	35 35
26	A8 22c Turnstone	35 35
27	A8 22c Golden plover	35 35
28	A8 22c Black-bellied plover	35 35
a.	Block of 4, #25-28	1.40 1.40

See No. C15.

Birds — A8a

Tall Ship Senyavin — A9

Natl. Seal — A10

Perf. 13½x13, 13½ (3c, 14c, No. 35)

1985-88 **Litho.**

30	A8a 3c Long-billed white-eye ('88)	6 6
32	A8a 14c Truk monarch ('88)	28 28
33	A3 15c Liduduhriap Waterfall, Pohnpei ('88)	30 30
a.	Bklt. pane of 10	3.00 —
34	A9 22c brt bl grn ('86)	35 35
35	A8a 22c Pohnpei mountain starling ('88)	44 44
36	A3 25c Tonachau Peak, Truk ('88)	50 50
a.	Bklt. pane of 10	5.00 —
b.	Bklt. pane of 10 (5 each 15c, 25c)	4.00 —
39	A9 36c ultra ('88)	72 72
40	A3 45c Sleeping Lady, Kosrae ('88)	90 90
42	A10 $10 brt ultra	14.00 14.00

Issue dates: 3c, 14c, No. 35, Aug. 1, 1988. 15c, 25c, 36c, 45c, Sept. 1, 1988. Nos. 33a, 36a, 36b, Nov. 30, 1988. No. 34, Apr. 14, 1986. $10, Oct. 15, 1985.
See Nos. C34-C36.

Nan Madol Ruins, Pohnpei — A16

1985, Dec. **Litho.** ***Perf. 13½***
45 A16 22c Land of the Sacred Masonry 35 35

See Nos. C16-C18.

Intl. Peace Year — A17

1986, May 16
46 A17 22c multi 35 35

Nos. 1-4 Surcharged

1986, May 19 **Litho.** ***Perf. 14***

48	A1 22c on 20c No. 1	35 35
49	A1 22c on 20c No. 2	35 35
50	A1 22c on 20c No. 3	35 35
51	A1 22c on 20c No. 4	35 35
a.	Block of 4, #48-51	1.40 1.40

AMERIPEX '86 — A18

Bully Hayes (1829-1877), Buccaneer.

1986, May 22 ***Perf. 13½***
52 A18 22c At ship's helm 35 35

See Nos. C21-C24.

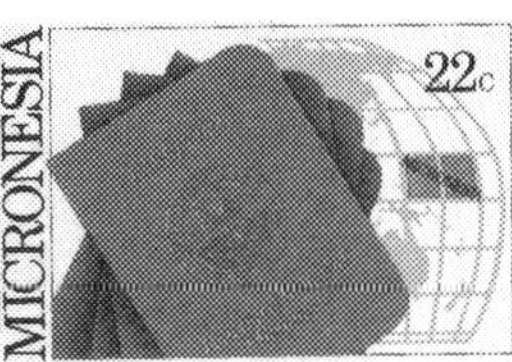
First Passport — A19

1986, Nov. 4 **Litho.** ***Perf. 13½***
53 A19 22c multi 35 35

Christmas — A20

Virgin and child paintings: 5c, Italy, 18th cent. 22c, Germany, 19th cent.

1986, Oct. 15 **Litho.** ***Perf. 14½***
54 A20 5c multi 8 8
55 A20 22c multi 35 35

See Nos. C26-C27.

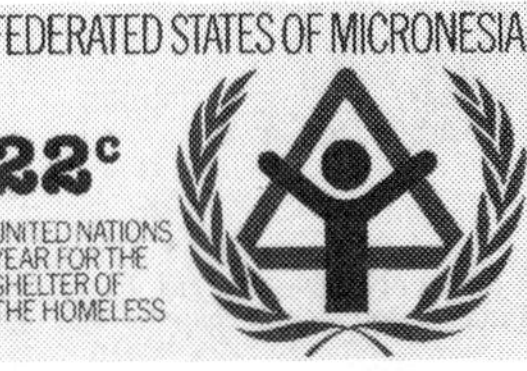
Anniversaries and Events — A21

1987, June 13 **Litho.** ***Perf. 14½***
56 A21 22c Intl. Year of Shelter for the Homeless 35 35

Souvenir Sheet

57 A21 $1 CAPEX '87 2.00 2.00

See Nos. C28-C30. No. 57 has inscribed multicolored margin picturing Toronto landmarks. Size: 85x55m.

Christmas — A22

Design: 22c, Archangel Gabriel appearing before Mary.

1987, Nov. 16 **Litho.** ***Perf. 14½***
58 A22 22c multi 35 35

See. Nos. C31-C33.

Colonial Eras — A23

1988, July 20 **Litho.** ***Perf. 13x13½***

59	A23 22c German	44 44
60	A23 22c Spanish	44 44
61	A23 22c Japanese	44 44
62	A23 22c U.S. Trust Territory	44 44
a.	Block of 4, Nos. 59-62	1.80 1.80

Nos. 59-62 printed se-tenant in sheets of 28 plus 4 center labels picturing flags of Spain (UL), Germany (UR), Japan (LL), and the United States (LR).
See Nos. C37-C38.

1988 Summer Olympics, Seoul — A24

1988, Sept. 1 **Litho.** ***Perf. 14***

63	A24 25c Running	50 50
64	A24 25c Women's hurdles	50 50
a.	Pair, Nos. 63-64	1.00 1.00
65	A24 45c Basketball	90 90
66	A24 45c Women's volleyball	90 90
a.	Pair, Nos. 65-66	1.80 1.80

Christmas
A25

Children decorating tree: No. 67, Two girls, UL of tree. No. 68, Boy, girl, dove, UR of tree. No. 69, Boy, girl, LL of tree. No. 70, Boy, girl, UR of tree. Se-tenmant in continuous design.

1988, Oct. 28	**Litho.**	***Perf. 14***	
67 A25 25c multi		50	50
68 A25 25c multi		50	50
69 A25 25c multi		50	50
70 A25 25c multi		50	50
a. Block of 4, Nos. 67-70		2.00	2.00

Miniature Sheet

Truk Lagoon
State
Monument
A26

Designs: a, Sun and stars angelfish. b, School of fish. c, Three divers. d, Goldenjack. e, Blacktip reef shark. f, Two shools of fish. g, Squirrelfish. h, Batfish. i, Moorish idols. j, Barracudas. k, Spot banded butterflyfish. l, Three-spotted damselfish. m, Foxface. n, Lionfish. o, Diver. p, Coral. q, Butterflyfish. r, Bivalve fish coral.

1988, Dec. 19	**Litho.**	***Perf. 14***	
71 Sheet of 18		9.00	9.00
a.-r. A26 25c any single		50	50

Mwarmwarms
A27

1989, Mar. 31	**Litho.**	***Perf. 14***	
72 A27 45c Plumeria		90	90
73 A27 45c Hibiscus		90	90
74 A27 45c Jasmine		90	90
75 A27 45c Bougainvillea		90	90
a. Block of 4, Nos. 72-75		3.60	3.60

Micronesia stamps can be mounted in Scott's annually supplemented U.S. Trust Territories Album.

Pheasant and Chrysanthemum, 1830's, by Hiroshige (1797-1858) — A28

1989, May 15	**Litho.**	***Perf. 14½***	
76 A28 $1 multi		2.00	2.00

Hirohito (1901-1989), emperor of Japan. No. 76 has multicolored inscribed margin containing a haiku by Hiroshige.

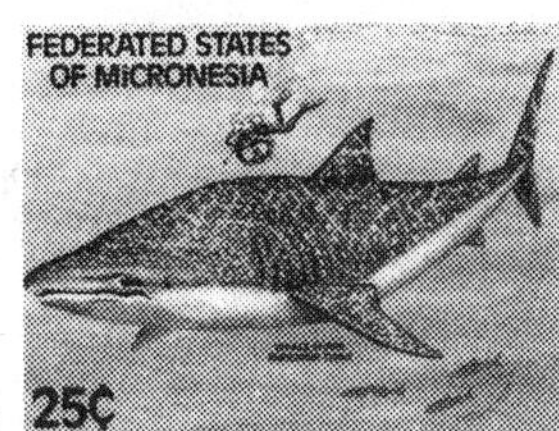

Sharks — A29

1989, May 25 *Perf. 14½*

No.	Type	Description	Unused	Used
77	A29	25c Whale	50	50
78	A29	25c Hammerhead	50	50
a.		Pair, Nos. 77-78	1.00	1.00
79	A29	45c Tiger, vert.	90	90
80	A29	45c Great White, vert.	90	90
a.		Pair, Nos. 79-80	1.80	1.80

Miniature Sheet

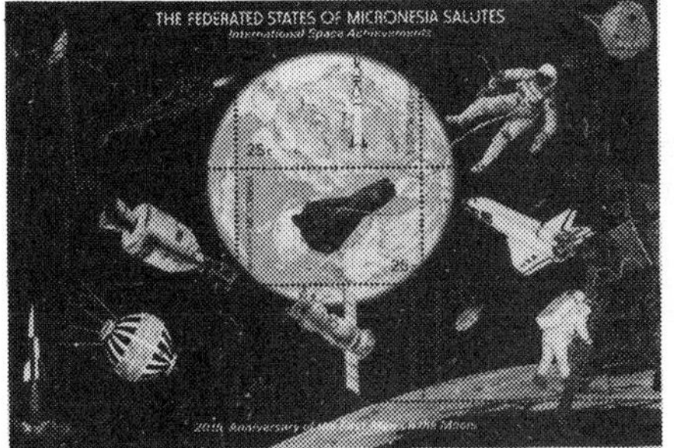

First Moon Landing, 20th Anniv. — A30

Space achievements: a. X-15 rocket plane, 1959. b. Explorer I launched into orbit, 1958. c. Ed White, 1st American to walk in space, Gemini 4 mission, 1965. d. Apollo 18 command module, 1975. e. Gemini 4 capsule. f. Space shuttle Challenger, 1983-1986. g. San Marco 2, satellite engineered by Italy. h. Soyuz 19 spacecraft, 1975. i. Columbia command module and Neil Armstrong taking man's first step onto the Moon during the Apollo 11 mission, 1969.

1989, July 20 **Litho.** *Perf. 14*

No.	Type	Description	Unused	Used
81	A30	Sheet of 9	4.50	4.50
a.-i.		25c any single	50	50

No. 81 has inscribed decorative margin continuing the design and picturing Sputnik and Kiku, Japan's first satellite, lift-off of an A-4 rocket and Eagle lunar module.

Earth and Lunar Module, by William Hanson, 1st Art Transported to the Moon — A31

1989, July 20 *Perf. 13½x14*

No.	Type	Description	Unused	Used
82	A31	$2.40 multi	4.80	4.80

First moon landing, 20th anniv.

Seashells — A32

1989 *Perf.*

No.	Type	Description	Unused	Used
83	A32	1c Horse's hoof	5	5
84	A32	3c Rare spotted cowrie	6	6
85	A32	15c Commercial trochus	30	30
87	A32	20c General cone	40	40
88	A32	25c Triton's trumpet	50	50
90	A32	30c Laciniated conch	60	60
91	A32	36c Red-mouthed olive	72	72
93	A32	45c Map cowrie	90	90
95	A32	50c Textile cone	1.00	1.00
100	A32	$1 Orange spider conch	2.00	2.00
101	A32	$2 Golden cowrie	4.00	4.00
102	A32	$5 Episcopal miter	10.00	10.00

AIR POST STAMPS

Boeing 727, 1968 — AP1

1984, July 12 **Litho.** *Perf. 13½*

No.	Type	Description	Unused	Used
C1	AP1	28c shown	45	45
C2	AP1	35c SA-16 Albatross, 1960	55	55
C3	AP1	40c PBY-5A Catalina, 1951	60	60

Ausipex Type of 1984

Ausipex '84 emblem and: 28c, Caroline Islands No. 4. 35c, No. 7. 40c, No. 19.

1984, Sept. 21 **Litho.** *Perf. 13½*

No.	Type	Description	Unused	Used
C4	A4	28c multi	50	50
C5	A4	35c multi	60	60
C6	A4	40c multi	65	65

Christmas Type of 1984

Children's drawings.

1984, Dec. 20

No.	Type	Description	Unused	Used
C7	A5	28c Illustrated Christmas text	50	50
C8	A5	35c Decorated palm tree	60	60
C9	A5	40c Feast preparation	65	65

Ships Type of 1985

1985, Aug. 19

No.	Type	Description	Unused	Used
C10	A6	33c L'Astrolabe	55	55
C11	A6	39c La Coquille	65	65
C12	A6	44c Shenandoah	70	70

Christmas Type of 1985

1985, Oct. 15 **Litho.** *Perf. 13½*

No.	Type	Description	Unused	Used
C13	A7	33c Dublon Protestant Church	55	55
C14	A7	44c Pohnpei Catholic Church	70	70

Audubon Type of 1985

1985, Oct. 31 *Perf. 14½*

No.	Type	Description	Unused	Used
C15	A8	44c Sooty tern	70	70

Ruins Type of 1985

1985, Dec. **Litho.** *Perf. 13½*

No.	Type	Description	Unused	Used
C16	A16	33c Nan Tauas inner courtyard	55	55
C17	A16	39c Outer wall	65	65
C18	A16	44c Tomb	70	70

Halley's Comet — AP2

1986, May 16

No.	Type	Description	Unused	Used
C19	AP2	44c dk bl, bl & blk	70	70

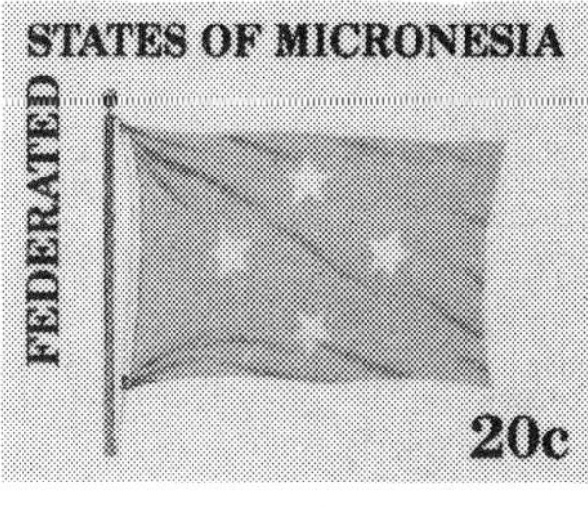

Return of Nauruans from Truk, 40th Anniv. — AP3

1986, May 16

No.	Type	Description	Unused	Used
C20	AP3	44c Ship in port	70	70

AMERIPEX '86 Type of 1986

Bully Hayes (1829-1877), buccaneer.

1986, May 22

No.	Type	Description	Unused	Used
C21	A18	33c Forging Hawaiian stamp	55	55
C22	A18	39c Sinking of the Leonora, Kosrae	65	65
C23	A18	44c Hayes escapes capture	70	70
C24	A18	75c Biography, by Louis Becke	1.10	1.10

Souvenir Sheet

No.	Type	Description	Unused	Used
C25	A18	$1 Hayes ransoming chief	2.50	2.50

No. C25 has multicolored inscribed margin continuing the design and picturing exhibition emblem. Size: 128x71mm.

Christmas Type of 1986

Virgin and child paintings: 33c, Austria, 19th cent. 44c, Italy, 18th cent., diff.

1986, Oct. 15 **Litho.** *Perf. 14½*

No.	Type	Description	Unused	Used
C26	A20	33c multi	55	55
C27	A20	44c multi	70	70

Anniversaries and Events Type of 1987

1987, June 13 **Litho.** *Perf. 14½*

No.	Type	Description	Unused	Used
C28	A21	33c U.S. currency, bicent.	55	55
C29	A21	39c 1st American in orbit, 25th anniv.	65	65
C30	A21	44c U.S. Constitution, bicent.	70	70

Christmas Type of 1987

1987, Nov. 16 **Litho.** *Perf. 14½*

No.	Type	Description	Unused	Used
C31	A22	33c Holy Family	55	55
C32	A22	39c Shepherds	78	78
C33	A22	44c Three Wise Men	88	88

Bird Type of 1988

1988, Aug. 1 **Litho.** *Perf. 13½*

No.	Type	Description	Unused	Used
C34	A8a	33c Great Truk white-eye	66	66
C35	A8a	44c Blue-faced parrotfinch	88	88
C36	A8a	$1 Yap monarch	2.00	2.00

Colonial Era Type of 1988

1988, July 20 *Perf. 13x13½*

No.	Type	Description	Unused	Used
C37	A23	44c Traditional skills (boat building)	88	88
C38	A23	44c Modern Micronesia (tourism)	88	88
a.		Pair, Nos. C37-C38	1.80	1.80

Nos. C37-C38 printed se-tenant in sheets of 28 plus 4 center labels picturing flags of Kosrae (UL), Truk (UR), Pohnpei (LL), and Yap (LR).

Flags of the Federated States of Micronesia — AP4

1989, Jan. 19 **Litho.** *Perf. 13x13½*

No.	Type	Description	Unused	Used
C39	AP4	45c Pohnpei	90	90
C40	AP4	45c Truk	90	90
C41	AP4	45c Kosrae	90	90
C42	AP4	45c Yap	90	90
a.		Block of 4, Nos. C39-C42	3.60	3.60

ENVELOPES

National Flag — U1

1984, July 12 **Litho.**

No.	Type	Description	Unused	Used
U1	U1	20c blk, gray & bl, entire	50	50

See the "Information for Collectors" section at beginning of catalogue for information on printing methods and varieties.

PALAU

A group of about 100 islands and islets forming part of the western Caroline Islands in the west Pacific Ocean, 1,000 miles southeast of Manila. Part of the U.S. Trust Territory of the Pacific established in 1947, Palau became a republic in 1981. By agreement with the U.S. Postal Service, Palau began issuing its own stamps in 1983 with the U.S.P.S. continuing to carry the mail to and from Palau. Islands include Babelthuap, Angaur, Eli Malk, Peleliu, Urukthapel and Koror, site of government headquarters. Area: 179 sq. mi. Population: 16,000 (est. 1983).

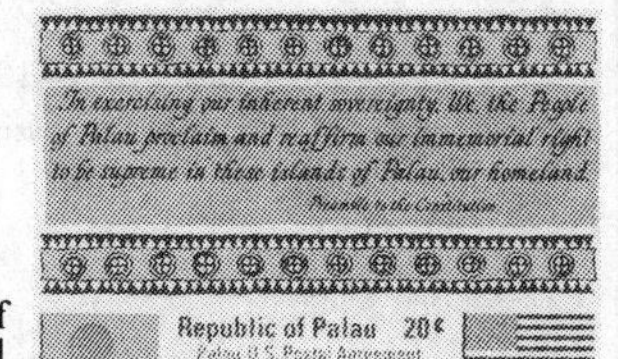

Inauguration of Postal Service — A1

1983, Mar. 10 — Litho. — *Perf. 14*

1 A1 20c Constitution preamble 60 60
2 A1 20c Hunters 60 60
3 A1 20c Fish 60 60
4 A1 20c Preamble, diff. 60 60
a. Block of 4, #1-4 2.50 2.50

Palau Fruit Dove — A2

1983, May 16 — *Perf. 15*

5 A2 20c shown 35 35
6 A2 20c Palau morningbird 35 35
7 A2 20c Giant white-eye 35 35
8 A2 20c Palau fantail 35 35
a. Block of 4, #5-8 1.40 1.40

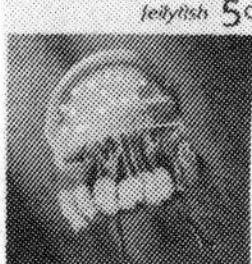

Sea Fan — A3

1983-84 — Litho. — *Perf. 13½x14*

9 A3 1c shown 5 5
10 A3 3c Map cowrie 5 5
11 A3 5c Jellyfish 8 8
12 A3 10c Hawksbill turtle 16 16
13 A3 13c Giant Clam 20 20
a. Booklet pane of 10 2.00 —
b. Booklet pane of 10 (5 #13, 5 #14) 2.75 —
14 A3 20c Parrotfish 35 35
b. Booklet pane of 10 3.50 —
15 A3 28c Chambered Nautilus 45 45
16 A3 30c Dappled sea cucumber 50 50
17 A3 37c Sea Urchin 55 55
18 A3 50c Starfish 85 85
19 A3 $1 Squid 1.60 1.60

Perf. 15x14

20 A3 $2 Dugong 3.25 3.25
21 A3 $5 Pink sponge 8.00 8.00

See Nos. 75-85.

Humpback Whale, World Wildlife Emblem — A4

1983, Sept. 21 — *Perf. 14*

24 A4 20c shown 35 35
25 A4 20c Blue whale 35 35
26 A4 20c Fin whale 35 35
27 A4 20c Great sperm whale 35 35
a. Block of 4, #24-27 1.40 1.40

Christmas — A5

Paintings by Charlie Gibbons, 1971.

1983, Oct. — Litho. — *Perf. 14½*

28 A5 20c First Child ceremony 40 40
29 A5 20c Spearfishing from Red Canoe 40 40
30 A5 20c Traditional feast at the Bai 40 40
31 A5 20c Taro gardening 40 40
32 A5 20c Spearfishing at New Moon 40 40
a. Strip of 5, #28-32 2.00 2.00

A6

Capt. Wilson's Voyage, Bicentennial — A7

1983, Dec. 14 — *Perf. 14x15*

33 A6 20c Capt. Henry Wilson 40 40
34 A7 20c Approaching Pelew 40 40
35 A7 20c Englishman's Camp on Ulong 40 40
36 A6 20c Prince Lee Boo 40 40
37 A6 20c King Abba Thulle 40 40
38 A7 20c Mooring in Koror 40 40
39 A7 20c Village scene of Pelew Islands 40 40
40 A6 20c Ludee 40 40
a. Block or strip of 8 3.20 3.20

Local Seashells — A8

Shell paintings (dorsal and ventral) by Deborah Dudley Max. Se-tenant.

1984, Mar. 15 — Litho. — *Perf. 14*

41 A8 20c Triton trumpet, d. 35 35
42 A8 20c Horned helmet, d. 35 35
43 A8 20c Giant clam, d. 35 35
44 A8 20c Laciniate conch, d. 35 35
45 A8 20c Royal cloak scallop, d. 35 35
46 A8 20c Triton trumpet, v. 35 35
47 A8 20c Horned helmet, v. 35 35
48 A8 20c Giant clam, v. 35 35
49 A8 20c Laciniate conch, v. 35 35
50 A8 20c Royal cloak scallop, v. 35 35
a. Block of 10, #41-50 3.50

Explorer Ships — A9

1984, June 19 — Litho. — *Perf. 14*

51 A9 40c Oroolong, 1783 70 70
52 A9 40c Duff, 1797 70 70
53 A9 40c Peiho, 1908 70 70
54 A9 40c Albatross, 1885 70 70
a. Block of 4, #51-54 2.80 2.80

UPU Congress.

Ausipex '84 A10

Fishing Methods. Nos. 55-58 se-tenant.

1984, Sept. 6 — Litho. — *Perf. 14*

55 A10 20c Throw spear fishing 35 35
56 A10 20c Kite fishing 35 35
57 A10 20c Underwater spear fishing 35 35
58 A10 20c Net fishing 35 35
a. Block of 4, #55-58 1.40 1.40

Christmas Flowers — A11

1984, Nov. 28 — Litho. — *Perf. 14*

59 A11 20c Mountain Apple 35 35
60 A11 20c Beach Morning Glory 35 35
61 A11 20c Turmeric 35 35
62 A11 20c Plumeria 35 35
a. Block of 4, #59-62 1.40 1.40

Audubon Bicentenary A12

1985, Feb. 6 Litho. *Perf. 14*

No.	Type	Description	Unused	Used
63	A12	22c Shearwater chick	30	30
64	A12	22c Shearwater's head	30	30
65	A12	22c Shearwater in flight	30	30
66	A12	22c Shearwater swimming	30	30
a.		Block of 4, #63-66	1.20	1.20

See No. C5.

Canoes and Rafts — A13

1985, Mar. 27 Litho.

No.	Type	Description	Unused	Used
67	A13	22c Cargo canoe	35	35
68	A13	22c War canoe	35	35
69	A13	22c Bamboo raft	35	35
70	A13	22c Racing/sailing canoe	35	35
a.		Block of 4, #67-70	1.40	1.40

Marine Life Type of 1983

1985, June 11 Litho. *Perf. 14½x14*

No.	Type	Description	Unused	Used
75	A3	14c Trumpet triton	20	20
a.		Bklt. pane of 10	2.00	—
76	A3	22c Bumphead parrotfish	35	35
a.		Bklt. pane of 10	3.50	—
b.		Bklt. pane of 10 (5 14c, 5 22c)	2.75	—
77	A3	25c Soft coral, damsel fish	40	40
79	A3	33c Sea anemone, clownfish	55	55
80	A3	39c Green sea turtle	65	65
81	A3	44c Pacific sailfish	70	70

Perf. 15x14

No.	Type	Description	Unused	Used
85	A3	$10 Spinner dolphins	15.00	15.00

Intl. Youth Year — A14

IYY emblem and children of all nationalities joined in a circle.

1985, July 15 Litho. *Perf. 14*

No.	Type	Description	Unused	Used
86	A14	44c multi	70	70
87	A14	44c multi	70	70
88	A14	44c multi	70	70
89	A14	44c multi	70	70
a.		Block of 4, #86-89	2.80	2.80

Nos. 86-89 printed se-tenant in a continuous design.

Christmas — A15

Island mothers and children.

1985, Oct. 21 Litho. *Perf. 14*

No.	Type	Description	Unused	Used
90	A15	14c multi	25	25
91	A15	22c multi	40	40
92	A15	33c multi	60	60
93	A15	44c multi	75	75

Souvenir Sheet

Pan American Airways Martin M-130 China Clipper — A16

1985, Nov. 21 Litho. *Perf. 14*

No.	Type	Description	Unused	Used
94	A16	$1 multi	2.50	2.50

1st Trans-Pacific Mail Flight, Nov. 22, 1935. No. 94 has multicolored decorative margin continuing the design and picturing the S.S. North Haven support ship at sea, the flight map and China Clipper emblem. Size: 96x70mm.
See Nos. C10-C13.

Return of Halley's Comet — A17

Fictitious local sightings.

1985, Dec. 21 Litho. *Perf. 14*

No.	Type	Description	Unused	Used
95	A17	44c Kaeb canoe, 1758	70	70
96	A17	44c U.S.S. Vincennes, 1835	70	70
97	A17	44c S.M.S. Scharnhorst, 1910	70	70
98	A17	44c Yacht, 1986	70	70
a.		Block of 4, #95-98	2.80	2.80

Songbirds — A18

1986, Feb. 24 Litho. *Perf. 14*

No.	Type	Description	Unused	Used
99	A18	44c Mangrove flycatcher	70	70
100	A18	44c Cardinal honeyeater	70	70
101	A18	44c Blue-faced parrotfinch	70	70
102	A18	44c Dusky and bridled white-eyes	70	70
a.		Block of 4, #99-102	2.80	2.80

World of Sea and Reef — A19

1986, May 22 Litho. *Perf. 15x14*

No.	Type	Description	Unused	Used
103		Sheet of 40	*37.50*	
a.	A19	14c, any single	30	30

AMERIPEX '86, Chicago, May 22-June 1

Seashells — A20

1986, Aug. 1 Litho. *Perf. 14*

No.	Type	Description	Unused	Used
104	A20	22c Commercial trochus	35	35
105	A20	22c Marble cone	35	35
106	A20	22c Fluted giant clam	35	35
107	A20	22c Bullmouth helmet	35	35
108	A20	22c Golden cowrie	35	35
a.		Strip of 5, #104-108	1.75	1.75

See Nos. 150-154.

Intl. Peace Year — A21

1986, Sept. 19 Litho.

No.	Type	Description	Unused	Used
109	A21	22c Soldier's helmet	35	35
110	A21	22c Plane wreckage	35	35
111	A21	22c Woman playing guitar	35	35
112	A21	22c Airai vista	35	35
a.		Block of 4, #109-112	1.40	1.40

See No. C17.

Reptiles — A22

1986, Oct. 28 Litho. *Perf. 14*

No.	Type	Description	Unused	Used
113	A22	22c Gecko	35	35
114	A22	22c Emerald tree skink	35	35
115	A22	22c Estuarine crocodile	35	35
116	A22	22c Leatherback turtle	35	35
a.		Block of 4, #113-116	1.40	1.40

Christmas — A23

Joy to the World, carol by Isaac Watts and Handel: No. 117, Girl playing guitar, boys, goat. No. 118, Girl carrying bouquet, boys singing. No. 119, Palauan mother and child. No. 120, Children, baskets of fruit. No. 121, Girl, fairy tern. Nos. 117-121 printed in a continuous design.

1986, Nov. 26 **Litho.**

117 A23 22c multi		35	35
118 A23 22c multi		35	35
119 A23 22c multi		35	35
120 A23 22c multi		35	35
121 A23 22c multi		35	35
a. Strip of 5, #117-121		1.75	1.75

Butterflies — A23a

1987, Jan. 5 **Litho.** ***Perf. 14***

121B A23a 44c Tangadik, soursop	70	70
121C A23a 44c Dira amartal, sweet orange	70	70
121D A23a 44c Ilhuochel, swamp cabbage	70	70
121E A23a 44c Bauosech, fig	70	70
f. Block of 4, #121B-121E	2.80	2.80

Fruit Bats — A24

1987, Feb. 23 **Litho.**

122 A24 44c In flight	70	70
123 A24 44c Hanging	70	70
124 A24 44c Eating	70	70
125 A24 44c Head	70	70
a. Block of 4, #122-125	2.80	2.80

Indigenous Flowers — A25

1987-88 **Litho.** ***Perf. 14***

126 A25 1c Ixora casei	5	5
127 A25 3c Lumnitzera littorea	5	5
128 A25 5c Sonneratia alba	8	8
129 A25 10c Tristellateria australasiae	16	16
130 A25 14c Bikkia palauensis	20	20
a. Bklt. pane of 10	2.00	—
131 A25 15c Limnophila aromatica	22	22
a. Bklt. pane of 10	2.25	—
132 A25 22c Bruguiera gymnorhiza	35	35
a. Bklt. pane of 10	3.50	—
b. Bklt. pane of 10 (5 14c, 5 22c)	2.75	—
133 A25 25c Fragraea ksid	38	38
a. Bklt. pane of 10	4.00	—
b. Bklt. pane of 10 (5 15c, 5 25c)	3.00	—
137 A25 36c Ophiorrhiza palauensis	55	55
138 A25 39c Cerbera manghas	60	60
140 A25 44c Sandera indica	70	70
141 A25 45c Maesa canfieldiae	72	72
142 A25 50c Dolichandrone spathacea	85	85
143 A25 $1 Barringtonia racemosa	1.60	1.60
144 A25 $2 Nepenthes mirabilis	3.25	3.25
145 A25 $5 Dendrobium palawense	8.00	8.00
145A A25 $10 Bouquet	16.00	16.00

Issue dates: Nos. 130a, 132a, 132b, Mar. 31, 1987. 15c, 25c, 36c, 45c, July 1, 1988. Nos. 131a, 133a, 133b, July 5, 1988. $10, Mar. 17, 1988. Others, Mar. 12, 1987.

CAPEX '87 A26

1987, June 15 **Litho.** ***Perf. 14***

146 A26 22c Babeldaob Is.	35	35
147 A26 22c Floating Garden Isls.	35	35
148 A26 22c Rock Is.	35	35
149 A26 22c Koror	35	35
a. Block of 4, Nos. 146-149	1.40	1.40

Seashells Type of 1986

1987, Aug. 25 **Litho.** ***Perf. 14***

150 A20 22c Black-striped triton	35	35
151 A20 22c Tapestry turban	35	35
152 A20 22c Adusta murex	35	35
153 A20 22c Little fox miter	35	35
154 A20 22c Cardinal miter	35	35
a. Strip of 5, Nos. 150-154	1.75	1.75

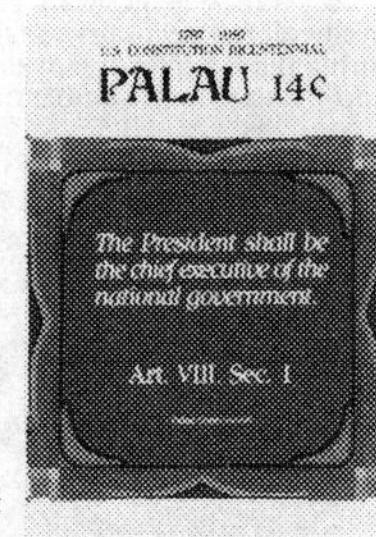

U.S. Constitution Bicentennial — A27

Excerpts from Articles of the Palau and U.S. Constitutions and Seals.

1987, Sept. 17 **Litho.** ***Perf. 14***

155 A27 14c Art. VIII, Sec. 1, Palau	20	20
156 A27 14c Presidential seals	20	20
157 A27 14c Art. II, Sec. 1, U.S.	20	20
a. Triptych + label, Nos. 155-157	60	60
158 A27 22c Art. IX, Sec. 1, Palau	35	35
159 A27 22c Legislative seals	35	35
160 A27 22c Art. I, Sec. 1, U.S.	35	35
a. Triptych + label, Nos. 158-160	1.05	1.05
161 A27 44c Art X, Sec. 1, Palau	70	70
162 A27 44c Supreme Court seals	70	70
163 A27 44c Art. III, Sec. 1, U.S.	70	70
a. Triptych + label, Nos. 161-163	2.10	2.10

Triptychs printed se-tenant with inscribed label picturing national flags.

Japanese Links to Palau — A28

Japanese stamps, period cancellations and installations: 14c, No. 257 and 1937 Datsun sedan used as mobile post office, near Ngerchelechuus Mountain. 22c, No. 347 and phosphate mine at Angaur. 33c, No. B1 and Japan Airways DC-2 over stone monuments at Badrulchau. 44c, No. 201 and Japanese post office, Koror. $1, Aviator's Grave, Japanese Cemetary, Peleliu, vert.

1987, Oct. 16 **Litho.** ***Perf. 14x13½***

164 A28 14c multi	20	20
165 A28 22c multi	35	35
166 A28 33c multi	55	55
167 A28 44c multi	70	70

Souvenir Sheet

Perf. 13½x14

168 A28 $1 multi	2.00	2.00

No. 168 has multicolored margin continuing the design and picturing Japan Nos. 547 and B7. Size: 81x94mm.

Christmas — A30

Verses from carol "I Saw Three Ships," Biblical characters, landscape and Palauans in outrigger canoes.

1987, Nov. 24 **Litho.** ***Perf. 14***

173 A30 22c I saw...	35	35
174 A30 22c And what was...	35	35
175 A30 22c 'Twas Joseph...	35	35
176 A30 22c Saint Michael...	35	35
177 A30 22c And all the bells...	35	35
a. Strip of 5, Nos. 173-177	1.75	1.75

Symbiotic Marine Species — A31

Designs: No. 178, Snapping shrimp, goby. No. 179, Mauve vase sponge, sponge crab. No. 180, Pope's damselfish, cleaner wrasse. No. 181, Clown anemone fish, sea anemone. No. 182, Four-color nudibranch, banded coral shrimp.

1987, Dec. 15

178 A31 22c multi	35	35
179 A31 22c multi	35	35
180 A31 22c multi	35	35
181 A31 22c multi	35	35
182 A31 22c multi	35	35
a. Strip of 5, Nos. 178-182	1.75	1.75

Butterflies and Flowers Type of 1987

Designs: No. 183, Dannaus plexippus, Tournefotia argentia. No. 184, Papilio machaon, Citrus reticulata. No. 185, Captopsilia, Crataeva speciosa. No. 186, Colias philodice, Crataeva speciosa.

1988, Jan. 25

183 A23a 44c multi	70	70
184 A23a 44c multi	70	70
185 A23a 44c multi	70	70
186 A23a 44c multi	70	70
a. Block of 4, Nos. 183-186	2.80	2.80

Ground-dwelling Birds — A32

1988, Feb. 29 **Litho.** ***Perf. 14***

187 A32 44c Whimbrel	88	88
188 A32 44c Yellow Bittern	88	88
189 A32 44c Rufous night-heron	88	88
190 A32 44c Banded rail	88	88
a. Block of 4, Nos. 187-190	3.55	3.55

Seashells Type of 1986

1988, May 11 **Litho.** ***Perf. 14***

191 A20 25c Striped engina	50	50
192 A20 25c Ivory cone	50	50
193 A20 25c Plaited miter	50	50
194 A20 25c Episcopal miter	50	50
195 A20 25c Isabelle cowrie	50	50
a. Strip of 5, Nos. 191-195	2.50	2.50

Souvenir Sheet

Postal Independence, 5th Anniv. — A33

Designs: a. Kaeb (pre-European outrigger sailboat). b. Spanish colonial cruiser. c. German colonial cruiser SMS Cormoran, circa 1885. d. Japanese mailbox, World War II machine gun, Koror museum. e. U.S. Trust Territory ship, Malakal Harbor. f. Koror post office.

1988, June 8 **Litho.** ***Perf. 14***

196 Souv. sheet of 6	3.00	3.00
a.-f. A33 25c multi	50	50

FINLANDIA '88. No. 196 has multicolored inscribed margin picturing Palau flag and exhibition emblem. Size: 150x97mm.

Souvenir Sheet

U.S. Possessions Philatelic Soc., 10th Anniv. — A34

Designs: a. "Collect Palau Stamps," original artwork for No. 196f and head of a man. b. Society emblem. c. Nos. 1-4. d. China Clipper original artwork and covers. f. Girl at show cancel booth.

1988, Aug. 26 **Litho.** ***Perf. 14***

197 Sheet of 6	5.40	5.40
a.-f. A34 45c any single	90	90

PRAGA '88. No. 197 has multicolored margin picturing exhibition and FIP emblems. Size:149x97mm.

Christmas — A35

Hark! The Herald Angels Sing. No. 198. Angel playing the violin, angel singing and angel sitting. No. 199. Three angels and three children. No. 200. Nativity. No. 201. Two angels, birds. No. 202. Three children and two angels playing horns. Se-tenant in a continuous design.

1988, Nov. 7 **Litho.** ***Perf. 14***

198 A35 25c multi	50	50
199 A35 25c multi	50	50
200 A35 25c multi	50	50
201 A35 25c multi	50	50
202 A35 25c multi	50	50
a. Strip of 5, Nos. 199-202	2.50	2.50

Miniature Sheet

Chambered Nautilus A36

Designs: a. Fossil and cross section. b. Palauan bai symbols for the nautilus. vert. c. Specimens trapped for scientific study. d. Nautilus belauensis, pompilus, macromphalus, stenomphalus and scrobiculatus. e. Release of a tagged nautilus.

1988, Dec. 23 **Litho.** ***Perf. 14***

203 Sheet of 5	2.50	2.50
a.-e. A36 25c multi	50	50

No. 203 has multicolored inscribed margin picturing Nautilus belauensis and a verse from The Chambered Nautilus, a powm by Oliver Wendell Holmes.

Endangered Birds of Palau — A37

1989, Feb. 9 **Litho.** ***Perf. 14***

204 A37 45c Nicobar pigeon	90	90
205 A37 45c Ground dove	90	90
206 A37 45c Micronesian megapode	90	90
207 A37 45c Owl	90	90
a. Block of 4, Nos. 204-207	3.60	3.60

Exotic Mushrooms A38

1989, Mar. 16 **Litho.** ***Perf. 14***

208 A38 45c Gilled auricularia	90	90
209 A38 45c Rock mushroom	90	90
210 A38 45c Polyporous	90	90
211 A38 45c Veiled stinkhorn	90	90
a. Block of 4, Nos. 208-211	3.60	3.60

Seashell Type of 1986

1989, Apr. 12 **Litho.** ***Perf. 14x14½***

212 A20 25c Robin redbreast triton	50	50
213 A20 25c Hebrew cone	50	50
214 A20 25c Tadpole triton	50	50
215 A20 25c Lettered cone	50	50
216 A20 25c Rugose miter	50	50
a. Strip of 5, Nos. 212-216	2.50	2.50

Souvenir Sheet

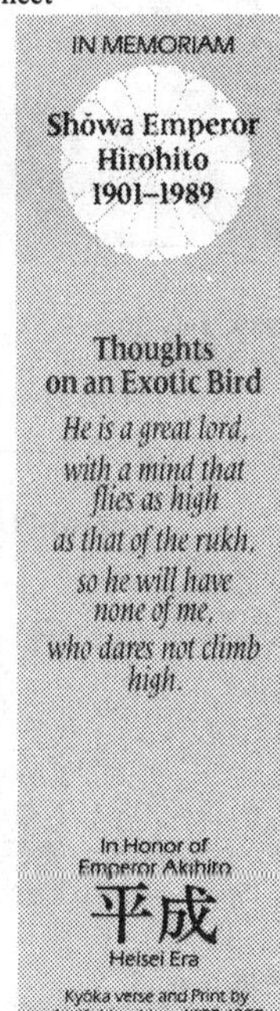

IN MEMORIAM
Shōwa Emperor Hirohito 1901-1989
Thoughts on an Exotic Bird
He is a great lord, with a mind that flies as high as that of the rukh, so he will have none of me, who dares not climb high.
In Honor of Emperor Akihito
平成
Heisei Era
Kyōka verse and Print by Andō Hiroshige, 1797-1858

A Little Bird Amidst Chrysanthemums, 1830's, by Hiroshige (1797-1858) — A39

1989, May 17 **Litho.** ***Perf. 14***

217 A39 $1 multi	2.00	2.00

Hirohito (1901-1989) and enthronement of Akihito as emperor of Japan.

Miniature Sheet

First Moon Landing, 20th Anniv. — A40

Apollo 11 mission: a. Third stage jettison. b. Lunar spacecraft. c. Module transposition (Eagle). d. Columbia module transposition (command module). e. Columbia module transposition (service module). f. Third stage burn. g. Vehicle entering orbit, Moon. h. Columbia and Eagle. i. Eagle on the Moon. j. Eagle in space. k. Three birds, Saturn V third stage, lunar spacecraft and escape tower. l. Astronaut's protective visor, pure oxygen system. m. Astronaut, American flag. n. Footsteps on lunar plain Sea of Tranquility, pure oxygen system. o. Armstrong descending from Eagle. p. Mobile launch tower, Saturn V second stage. q. Space suit remote control unit and oxygen hoses. r. Eagle lift-off from Moon. s. Armstrong's first step on the Moon. t. Armstrong descending ladder, module transposition (Eagle and Columbia). u. Launch tower, spectators and Saturn V engines achieving thrust. v. Spectators, clouds of backwash. w. Parachute splashdown, U.S. Navy recovery ship and helicopter. x. Command module reentry. y. Jettison of service module prior to reentry.

1989, July 20 **Litho.** ***Perf. 14***

218 Sheet of 25	12.50	12.50
a.-y. A40 25c any single	50	50

Buzz Aldrin Photographed on the Moon by Neil Armstrong — A41

1989, July 20 *Perf. 13½x14*

219	A41 $2.40 multi	4.80	4.80

First moon landing 20th anniv.

SEMI-POSTAL STAMPS

Olympic Sports — SP1

1988, Aug. 8 **Litho.** *Perf. 14*

B1	SP1 25c +5c Baseball glove, player	60	60
B2	SP1 25c +5c Running shoe, athlete	60	60
a.	Pair, Nos. B1-B2	1.20	1.20
B3	SP1 45c +5c Goggles, swimmer	1.00	1.00
B4	SP1 45c +5c Gold medal, diver	1.00	1.00
a.	Pair, Nos. B3-B4	2.00	2.00

AIR POST STAMPS

White-tailed Tropicbird AP1

1984, June 12 **Litho.** *Perf. 14*

C1	AP1 40c shown	65	65
C2	AP1 40c Fairy tern	65	65
C3	AP1 40c Black noddy	65	65
C4	AP1 40c Black-naped tern	65	65
a.	Block of 4, #C1-C4	2.60	2.60

Audubon Type of 1985

1985, Feb. 6 **Litho.** *Perf. 14*

C5	A12 44c Audubon's Shearwater	70	70

Palau-Germany Political, Economic & Cultural Exchange Cent. — AP2

Germany Nos. 40, 65, Caroline Islands Nos. 19, 13 and: No. C6, German flag-raising at Palau, 1885. No. C7, Early German trading post in Angaur. No. C8, Abai architecture recorded by Prof. & Frau Kramer, 1908-1910. No. C9, S.M.S. Cormoran.

1985, Sept. 19 **Litho.** *Perf. 14x13½*

C6	AP2 44c multi	70	70
C7	AP2 44c multi	70	70
C8	AP2 44c multi	70	70
C9	AP2 44c multi	70	70
a.	Block of 4, #C6-C9	2.80	2.80

Trans-Pacific Airmail Anniv. Type of 1985

Aircraft: No. C10, 1951 Trans-Ocean Airways PBY-5A Catalina Amphibian. No. C11, 1968 Air Micronesia DC-6B Super Cloudmaster. No. C12, 1960 Trust Territory Airline SA-16 Albatross. No. C13, 1967 Pan American Douglas DC-4.

1985, Nov. 21 **Litho.** *Perf. 14*

C10	A16 44c multi	70	70
C11	A16 44c multi	70	70
C12	A16 44c multi	70	70
C13	A16 44c multi	70	70
a.	Block of 4, #C10-C13	2.80	2.80

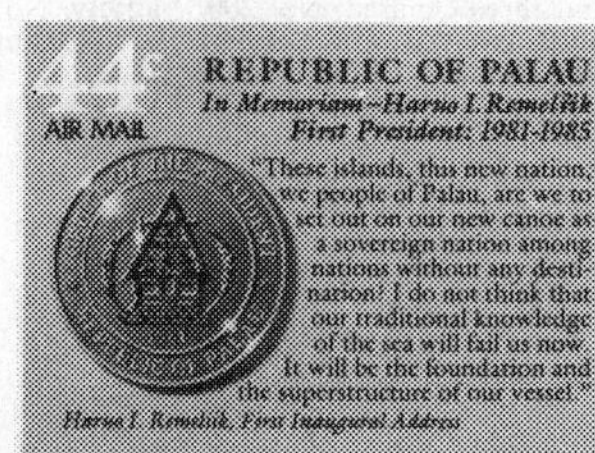

Haruo I. Remeliik (1933-1985), 1st President AP3

Designs: No. C14, Presidential seal, excerpt from 1st inaugural address. No. C15, War canoe, address excerpt, diff. No. C16, Remeliik, U.S. Pres. Reagan, excerpt from Reagan's speech, Pacific Basin Conference, Guam, 1984.

1986, June 30 **Litho.** *Perf. 14*

C14	AP3 44c multi	65	65
C15	AP3 44c multi	65	65
C16	AP3 44c multi	65	65
a.	Strip of 3, #C14-C16	1.95	1.95

Intl. Peace Year, Statue of Liberty Cent. — AP4

1986, Sept. 19 **Litho.**

C17	AP4 44c multi	70	70

Aircraft — AP5

1989, May 17 **Litho.** *Perf. 14x14½*

C18	AP5 36c Cessna 207 Skywagon	72	72
C19	AP5 39c Embraer EMB-110 Bandeirante	78	78
C20	AP5 45c Boeing 727	90	90

ENVELOPES

Marine Life Type of 1983

1985, Feb. 14 **Litho.**

U1	A3 22c Parrotfish, entire	50	50

Paintings Type of 1983 without Inscription for Christmas

1985, Feb. 14 **Litho.**

U2	A5 22c Spear Fishing from Red Canoe, entire	50	50

AIR LETTER SHEETS

Bird Type of 1983
Letter sheet for foreign postage

1985, Feb. 14 **Litho.**

UC1	A2 36c multi, entire	75	75

Designs of Nos. C1-C4 (without inscriptions) and text on reverse folding area.

POSTAL CARDS

Marine Life Type of 1983

1985, Feb. 14 **Litho.**

UX1	A3 14c Giant Clam	35	35

PHILIPPINES

Issued under U.S. Administration.

Following the American occupation of the Philippines, May 1, 1898, after Admiral Dewey's fleet entered Manila Bay, an order was issued by the U. S. Postmaster General (No. 201, May 24, 1898) establishing postal facilities with rates similar to the domestic rates.

Military postal stations were established as branch post offices, each such station being placed within the jurisdiction of the nearest regular post office. Supplies were issued to these military stations through the regular post office of which they were branches.

Several post office clerks were sent to the Philippines and the San Francisco post office was made the nearest regular office for the early Philippine mail and the postmarks of the period point out this fact.

U.S. stamps overprinted "PHILIPPINES" were placed on sale in Manila June 30, 1899. Regular U.S. stamps had been in use from early March, and at the Manila post office Spanish stamps were also acceptable.

The first regular post office was established at Cavite on July 30, 1898, as a branch of the San Francisco post office. The first cancellation was a dated handstamp with "PHILIPPINE STATION" and "SAN FRANCISCO, CAL."

On May 1, 1899, the entire Philippine postal service was separated from San Francisco and numerous varieties of postmarks resulted. Many of the early used stamps show postmarks and cancellations of the Military Station, Camp or R.P.O. types, together with "Killers" of the types employed in the U.S. at the time.

The Philippines became a commonwealth of the United States on November 15, 1935, the High Commissioner of the United States taking office on the same day. The official name of the government was "Commonwealth of the Philippines" as provided by Article 17 of the Constitution. Upon the final and complete withdrawal of sovereignty of the United States and the proclamation of Philippine independence on July 4, 1946, the Commonwealth of the Philippines became the "Republic of the Philippines."

Numbers in parenthesis indicate quantities issued.

Authority for dates of issue, stamps from 1899 to 1911, and quantities issued-"The Postal Issues of the Philippines," by F. L. Palmer (New York, 1912).

100 CENTS = 1 DOLLAR
100 CENTAVOS = 1 PESO (1906)

Regular Issues of the United States Overprinted in Black

PHILIPPINES

Printed and overprinted by the U.S. Bureau of Engraving and Printing.

1899, June 30 Unwmk. *Perf. 12*

On U.S. Stamp No. 260

212 A96 50c orange 225.00 150.00
On cover —
Block of four 1,250. —
Margin strip of 3, Impt. & P# 1,250.
Margin block of 6, Impt. & P# *5,000.*

On U.S. Stamps Nos. 279, 279d, 267, 268, 281, 282C, 283, 284, 275 and 275a.

Wmk. Double-lined USPS (191)

213 A87 1c yellow green *(5,500,000)* 1.90 50
On cover 10.00
Block of four 8.50 3.00
Margin strip of 3, Impt. & P# 15.00
Margin block of 6, Impt. & P# 100.00
214 A88 2c orange red, type III *(6,970,000)* 90 50
On cover 10.00
Block of four 4.00 2.50
Margin strip of 3, Impt. & P# 12.50
Margin block of 6, Impt. & P# 75.00
a. 2c carmine, type III 1.50 75
b. Booklet pane of six ('00) 175.00 *90.00*
215 A89 3c purple *(673,814)* 3.25 1.00
On cover 30.00
Block of four 15.00 11.00
Margin strip of 3, Impt. & P# 35.00
Margin block of 6, Impt. & P# 275.00
216 A91 5c blue *(1,700,000)* 3.25 75
On cover 20.00
Block of four 15.00 7.50
Margin strip of 3, Impt. & P# 30.00
Margin block of 6, Impt. & P# 225.00
a. Inverted overprint *2,000.*
217 A94 10c brown, type I *(750,000)+* 10.00 2.50
On cover 60.00
Block of four 50.00 35.00
Margin strip of 3, Impt. & P# 50.00
Margin block of 6, Impt. & P# 350.00

(+ Quantity includes Nos. 217, 217A)

217A A94 10c orange brown, type II 125.00 25.00
On cover 165.00
Block of four 550.00 175.00
Margin strip of 3, Impt. & P# 550.00
Margin block of 6, Impt. & P# *2,250.*
218 A95 15c olive green *(200,000)* 17.50 4.50
On cover 110.00
Block of four 80.00 50.00
Margin strip of 3, Impt. & P# 80.00
Margin block of 6, Impt. & P# 325.00
a. 15c light olive green 25.00 7.50
219 A96 50c orange *(50,000)+* 62.50 30.00
On cover *225.00*
Block of four 275.00 *150.00*
Margin strip of 3, Impt. & P# 275.00
Margin block of 6, Impt. & P# *1,150.*
a. 50 red orange 125.00

(+ Quantity includes Nos. 212, 219, 219a)

Special Printing

In 1899 a special printing of Nos. 213 to 217, 218, 219 and J1 to J5 was made for display at the Paris Exposition. All but a few copies were destroyed. Most of the existing copies bear the handstamp "Special Surcharge" on the back. Value each $350.

1901, Aug. 30 Regular Issue

Same Overprint in Black On U.S. Stamps Nos. 280b, 282 and 272

220 A90 4c orange brown *(404,907)* 11.50 3.00
On cover 50.00
Block of four 50.00 32.50
Margin strip of 3, Impt. & P# 50.00
Margin block of 6, Impt. & P# 300.00
221 A92 6c lake *(223,465)* 14.00 5.00
On cover 65.00
Block of four 75.00 40.00
Margin strip of 3, Impt. & P# 62.50
Margin block of 6, Impt. & P# 400.00
222 A93 8c violet brown *(248,000)* 15.00 4.00
On cover 50.00
Block of four 67.50 40.00
Margin strip of 3, Impt. & P# 67.50
Margin block of 6, Impt. & P# *500.00*

Same Overprint in Red On U.S. Stamps Nos. 276, 276A, 277a and 278

223 A97 $1 black, type I *(3,000)+* 250.00 140.00
On cover *650.00*
Block of four 1,250.
Margin strip of 3, Impt. & P# *1,250.*
Margin block of 6, Impt. & P# —
Horiz. pair, types I & II 2,250.

(+ Quantity includes Nos. 223, 223A)

223A A97 $1 black, type II 1,400. 675.00
On cover —
Block of four *6,000.* —
Margin strip of 3, Impt. & P#, one stamp No. 223 5,500.
Margin block of 6, Impt. & P#, two stamps No. 223 —
224 A98 $2 dark blue *(1800)* 450.00 225.00
On cover 2,250.
Block of four 2,000. —
Margin strip of 3, Impt. & P# 2,000.
Margin block of 6, Impt. & P# — —
225 A99 $5 dark green *(782)* 875.00 550.00
On cover *2,000.*
Block of four *3,750.* —
Margin strip of 3, Impt. & P# *3,750.*
Margin block of 6, Impt. & P# —

Special Printing

Special printings exist of Nos. 227, 221, 223-225, made from defaced plates. These were made for display at the St. Louis Exposition. All but a few copies were destroyed. Most of the existing copies have the handstamp "Special Printing" on the back. Value: Nos. 227, 221, each $400; No. 223, $850; No. 224, $1,200; No. 225, $2,000.

1903-04 Regular Issue

Same Overprint in Black On U.S. Stamps Nos. 300 to 310 and shades

226 A115 1c blue green *(9,631,172)* 2.25 25
On cover 8.25
Block of four 10.00 1.50
Margin strip of 3, Impt. & P# 12.00
Margin block of 6, Impt. & P# 90.00
227 A116 2c carmine *(850,000)* 3.75 90
On cover 10.00
Block of four 16.25 5.00
Margin strip of 3, Impt. & P# 17.50
Margin block of 6, Impt. & P# 125.00
228 A117 3c bright violet *(14,500)* 42.50 10.00
On cover 55.00
Block of four 190.00 55.00
Margin strip of 3, Impt. & P# 190.00
Margin block of 6, Impt. & P# 600.00
229 A118 4c brown *(13,000)* 45.00 15.00
On cover 40.00
Block of four 200.00 75.00
Margin strip of 3, Impt. & P# 200.00
Margin block of 6, Impt. & P# 675.00
a. 4c orange brown 45.00 12.50
230 A119 5c blue *(1,211,844)* 6.00 75
On cover 22.50
Block of four 25.00 3.50
Margin strip of 3, Impt. & P# 25.00
Margin block of 6, Impt. & P# 175.00
231 A120 6c brownish lake *(11,500)* 47.50 12.50
On cover 55.00
Block of four 225.00 100.00
Margin strip of 3, Impt. & P# 225.00
Margin block of 6, Impt. & P# 750.00
232 A121 8c violet black *(49,033)* 20.00 7.50
On cover 55.00
Block of four 100.00 60.00
Margin strip of 3, Impt. & P# 100.00
Margin block of 6, Impt. & P# 575.00
233 A122 10c pale red brown *(300,179)* 11.25 1.75
On cover 27.50
Block of four 55.00 15.00
Margin strip of 3, Impt. & P# 55.00
Margin block of 6, Impt. & P# 450.00
a. 10c red brown 13.75 2.50
b. Pair, one without overprint *675.00*
234 A123 13c purple black *(91,341)* 17.50 9.00
a. 13c brown violet 17.50 8.75
On cover 55.00
Block of four 90.00 50.00
Margin strip of 3, Impt. & P# 90.00
Margin block of 6, Impt. & P# *650.00*

No.	Type	Description	Unused	Used
235	A124	15c olive green *(183,965)*	30.00	6.50
		On cover		100.00
		Block of four	140.00	42.50
		Margin strip of 3, Impt. & P#	140.00	
		Margin block of 6, Impt. & P#	*700.00*	
236	A125	50c orange *(57,641)*	87.50	27.50
		On cover		225.00
		Block of four	400.00	200.00
		Margin strip of 3, Impt. & P#	400.00	
		Margin block of 6, Impt. & P#	*2,500.*	

Same Overprint in Red On U. S. Stamps Nos. 311, 312 and 313

No.	Type	Description	Unused	Used
237	A126	$1 black *(5617)*	325.00	150.00
		On cover		400.00
		Block of four	1,400.	925.00
		Margin strip of 3, Impt. & P#	1,400.	
		Margin block of 6, Impt. & P#	-	
238	A127	$2 dark blue *(695)*	1,000.	600.00
		Block of four	*4,500.*	—
		Margin strip of 3, Impt. & P#	*4,500.*	
		Margin block of 6, Impt. & P#	*10,000.*	
239	A128	$5 dark green *(746)*	1,200.	700.00
		Block of four	*5,250.*	—
		Margin strip of 3, Impt. & P#	*5,250.*	
		Margin block of 6, Impt. & P#	—	

Same Overprint in Black On U.S. Stamp No. 319

No.	Type	Description	Unused	Used
240	A129	2c carmine *(862,245)*	3.75	1.50
		On cover		3.50
		Block of four	16.00	8.25
		Margin strip of 3, Impt. & P#	27.50	
		Margin block of 6, Impt. & P#	165.00	
a.		Booklet pane of six	*800.00*	
b.		2c scarlet	4.25	1.90

Dates of issue:

Sept. 20, 1903, Nos. 226, 227, 236.

Jan. 4, 1904, Nos. 230, 234, 235, 237.

Nov. 1, 1904, Nos. 228, 229, 231, 232, 233, 238, 239, 240.

Nos. 212 to 240 became obsolete on Sept. 8, 1906, the remainders being destroyed.

Special Printing

Two sets of special printings exist of the 1903-04 issue. The first consists of Nos. 226, 230, 234, 235, 236, 237 and 240. These were made for display at the St. Louis Exposition. All but a few copies were destroyed. Most of the existing copies have the handstamp "Special Surcharge" on the back. Value: No. 237, $750; others $400; J6; J7, $450:

In 1907 the entire set Nos. 226, 228 to 240, J1 to J7 were specially printed for the Bureau of Insular Affairs on very white paper. They are difficult to distinguish from the ordinary stamps except the Special Delivery stamp which is on U.S. No. E6 (see Philippines No. E2A). Value: No. 237, $750; No. 238, $1500; No. 239, $2000; others, $350

Regular Issue

José Rizal — A40

Arms of City of Manila — A41

Printed by the U.S. Bureau of Engraving and Printing.

Plates of 400 subjects in four panes of 100 each.

Booklet panes Nos. 240a, 241b, 242b, 261a, 262b, 276a, 277a, 285a, 286a, 290e, 291b and 292c were made from plates of 180 subjects.

No. 214b came from plates of 360 subjects.

Wmk. Double-lined PIPS (191)

1906, Sept. 8 *Perf. 12*

No.	Type	Description	Unused	Used
241	A40	2c deep green *(51,125,010)*	20	5
		Block of four	85	20
a.		2c yellow green ('10)	35	5
		Double transfer		*35.00*
b.		Booklet pane of six	150.00	
242	A40	4c carmine *(McKinley) (14,150,030)*	25	5
		Block of four	1.10	20
a.		4c carmine lake ('10)	50	5
b.		Booklet pane of six	150.00	
243	A40	6c violet *(Fernando Magellan) (1,980,000)*	85	10
		Block of four	3.75	45
244	A40	8c brown *(Miguel Lopez de Legaspi) (770,000)*	1.50	50
		Block of four	6.50	3.50
245	A40	10c blue *(Gen. Henry W. Lawton) (5,550,000)*	1.10	7
		Dark blue	1.10	7
		Block of four	4.50	30
246	A40	12c brown lake *(Lincoln) (670,000)*	3.50	1.50
		Block of four	15.00	10.00
247	A40	16c violet black *(Adm. William T. Sampson) (1,300,000)*	2.25	16
		Block of four	10.00	1.10
248	A40	20c orange brown *(Washington) (2,100,000)*	2.50	25
		Block of four	11.00	1.65
249	A40	26c violet brown *(Francisco Carriedo) (480,000)*	4.00	1.65
		Block of four	19.00	11.00
250	A40	30c olive green *(Franklin) (1,256,000)*	3.00	1.10
		Block of four	13.50	5.50
251	A41	1p orange *(200,000)*	16.50	5.50
		Block of four	70.00	30.00
252	A41	2p black *(100,000)*	22.50	1.00
		Block of four	100.00	8.25
253	A41	4p dark blue *(10,000)*	65.00	12.00
		Block of four	300.00	55.00
254	A41	10p dark green *(6,000)*	140.00	55.00
		Block of four	625.00	275.00

1909

Change of Colors

No.	Type	Description	Unused	Used
255	A40	12c red orange *(300,000)*	5.50	2.00
		Block of four	25.00	10.00
256	A40	16c olive green *(500,000)*	2.75	50
		Block of four	12.00	2.25
257	A40	20c yellow *(800,000)*	5.00	1.00
		Block of four	22.50	6.00
258	A40	26c blue green	1.00	55
		Block of four	4.25	3.00
259	A40	30c ultramarine *(600,000)*	6.50	2.50
		Block of four	30.00	15.00
260	A41	1p pale violet *(100,000)*	20.00	4.00
		Block of four	100.00	25.00
260A	A41	2p violet brown *(50,000)*	55.00	2.00
		Block of four	250.00	13.50

1911 Wmk. Single-lined PIPS (190) *Perf. 12*

No.	Type	Description	Unused	Used
261	A40	2c green	50	7
		Block of four	3.25	35
a.		Booklet pane of six	135.00	
262	A40	4c carmine lake	2.00	8
		Block of four	9.00	35
a.		4c carmine	—	—
b.		Booklet pane of six	135.00	
263	A40	6c deep violet	1.20	7
		Block of four	5.50	30
264	A40	8c brown	5.00	35
		Block of four	22.50	1.50
265	A40	10c blue	2.00	7
		Block of four	9.00	30
266	A40	12c orange	1.35	35
		Block of four	6.00	1.65
267	A40	16c olive green	1.50	10
		Pale olive green	1.50	10
		Block of four	6.50	65
268	A40	20c yellow	1.35	10
		Block of four	5.50	42
a.		20c orange	1.35	10
269	A40	26c blue green	1.75	20
		Block of four	7.50	1.00
270	A40	30c ultramarine	2.25	35
		Block of four	10.00	1.65
271	A41	1p pale violet	13.50	40
		Block of four	60.00	2.00
272	A41	2p violet brown	16.50	60
		Block of four	70.00	3.75
273	A41	4p deep blue	325.00	40.00
		Block of four	1,500.	225.00
274	A41	10p deep green	100.00	15.00
		Block of four	450.00	70.00

1914

No.	Type	Description	Unused	Used
275	A40	30c gray	6.50	32
		Block of four	30.00	1.90

1914 *Perf. 10*

No.	Type	Description	Unused	Used
276	A40	2c green	1.00	6
		Block of four	4.25	30
a.		Booklet pane of six	135.00	
277	A40	4c carmine	1.10	10
		Block of four	4.50	45
a.		Booklet pane of six	135.00	
278	A40	6c light violet	22.50	7.50
		Block of four	100.00	42.50
a.		6c deep violet	25.00	4.50
279	A40	8c brown	22.50	8.25
		Block of four	100.00	45.00
280	A40	10c dark blue	15.00	16
		Block of four	65.00	80
281	A40	16c olive green	45.00	3.50
		Block of four	200.00	20.00
282	A40	20c orange	13.50	65
		Block of four	60.00	4.00
283	A40	30c gray	35.00	2.25
		Block of four	150.00	13.50
284	A41	1p pale violet	70.00	2.50
		Block of four	325.00	15.00

1918 *Perf. 11*

No.	Type	Description	Unused	Used
285	A40	2c green	13.50	3.50
		Block of four	60.00	15.00
a.		Booklet pane of six	*400.00*	
286	A40	4c carmine	19.00	2.00
		Block of four	85.00	10.00
a.		Booklet pane of six	*400.00*	
287	A40	6c deep violet	25.00	1.35
		Block of four	100.00	6.50
287A	A40	8c light brown	150.00	25.00
		Block of four	625.00	165.00
288	A40	10c dark blue	35.00	1.20
		Block of four	150.00	6.50
289	A40	16c olive green	65.00	5.50
		Block of four	300.00	22.50
289A	A40	20c orange	37.50	6.50
		Block of four	165.00	35.00
289C	A40	30c gray	35.00	10.00
		Block of four	150.00	50.00
289D	A41	1p pale violet	40.00	11.00
		Block of four	165.00	60.00

1917 Unwmk. *Perf. 11*

No.	Type	Description	Unused	Used
290	A40	2c yellow green	7	5
		Block of four	30	20
a.		2c dark green	8	5
		Green	10	5
		Double transfer	—	—
b.		Vert. pair, imperf. horiz.	*700.00*	
c.		Horiz. pair, imperf. between	*800.00*	—
d.		Vertical pair, imperf. btwn.	*1,200.*	
e.		Booklet pane of six	16.50	
291	A40	4c carmine	7	5
		Block of four	30	20
a.		4c light rose	16	5
b.		Booklet pane of six	12.00	—
292	A40	6c deep violet	25	5
		Block of four	1.10	30
a.		6c lilac	28	5
b.		6c red violet	28	7
c.		Booklet pane of six	165.00	
293	A40	8c yellow brown	15	6
		Block of four	65	35
a.		8c orange brown	15	6
294	A40	10c deep blue	15	5
		Block of four	65	22
295	A40	12c red orange	25	10
		Block of four	1.10	50
296	A40	16c light olive green	25.00	15
		Block of four	125.00	75
a.		16c olive bister	25.00	35
297	A40	20c orange yellow	20	7
		Block of four	1.25	30
298	A40	26c green	35	42
		Block of four	1.50	2.00
a.		26c blue green	45	25
299	A40	30c gray	40	7
		Block of four	1.90	35
		Dark gray	40	7
300	A41	1p pale violet	16.25	85
		Block of four	67.50	3.75
a.		1p red lilac	16.25	85
b.		1p pale rose lilac	16.25	90
301	A41	2p violet brown	20.00	60
		Block of four	90.00	2.75
302	A41	4p blue	14.00	35
		Block of four	60.00	1.50
a.		4p dark blue	14.00	35

1923-26

No.	Type	Description	Unused	Used
303	A40	16c olive bister *(Adm. George Dewey)*	50	10
		Block of four	2.25	45
a.		16c olive green	1.10	15
304	A41	10p deep green ('26)	30.00	4.00
		Block of four	125.00	17.50

The Scott Catalogue value is a retail price, what you could expect to pay for the stamp in a grade of Fine-Very Fine. The value listed is a reference which reflects recent actual dealer selling price.

Legislative Palace Issue

Issued to commemorate the opening of the Legislative Palace.

Legislative Palace — A42

Printed by the Philippine Bureau of Printing.

1926, Dec. 20 Unwmk. *Perf. 12*

No.	Type	Description	Unused	Used
319	A42	2c green & black *(502,550)*	40	25
		First day cover		3.50
		Block of four	2.75	1.10
a.		Horiz. pair, imperf. between	*190.00*	
b.		Vert. pair, imperf. between	*300.00*	
320	A42	4c carmine & black *(304,400)*	40	32
		First day cover		3.50
		Block of four	1.75	1.40
a.		Horiz. pair, imperf. between	*190.00*	
b.		Vert. pair, imperf. between	*225.00*	
321	A42	16c olive green & black *(203,750)*	75	65
		First day cover		10.00
		Block of four	3.75	3.00
a.		Horiz. pair, imperf. between	*200.00*	
b.		Vert. pair, imperf. between	*300.00*	
c.		Double impression of center	*400.00*	
322	A42	18c light brown & black *(103,950)*	1.00	60
		First day cover		10.00
		Block of four	4.50	2.75
a.		Double impression of center *(150)*	*400.00*	
b.		Vertical pair, imperf. between	*300.00*	
323	A42	20c orange & black *(103,450)*	1.40	1.00
		Block of four	6.00	5.00
a.		20c orange & brown *(100)*	*325.00*	—
b.		Imperf. (pair), orange & black *(50)*	*365.00*	*365.00*
c.		Imperf. (pair), orange & brown *(100)*	*300.00*	
d.		Vert. pair, imperf. between	*350.00*	
324	A42	24c gray & black *(103,350)*	1.00	65
		Block of four	4.25	3.00
a.		Vert. pair, imperf. between	*300.00*	
325	A42	1p rose lilac & black *(11,050)*	60.00	27.50
		Block of four	250.00	125.00
a.		Vert. pair, imperf. between	*325.00*	
		First day cover, #319-325		85.00

Coil Stamp

Rizal Type of 1906

Printed by the U.S. Bureau of Engraving and Printing.

1928 Unwmk. *Perf. 11 Vertically*

No.	Type	Description	Unused	Used
326	A40	2c green	4.25	*5.00*
		Pair	*10.00*	12.50
		Line pair	30.00	

Types of 1906-1923

1925-31 Unwmk. *Imperf.*

Two issues of imperforate stamps were made, in 1925 and in 1931. They differ in shade.

No.	Type	Description	Unused	Used
340	A40	2c yellow green ('31)	6	6
		Block of four	25	25
		green	25	—
341	A40	4c carmine rose ('31)	10	10
		Block of four	40	40
		carmine	38	—
342	A40	6c violet ('31)	1.00	1.00
		Block of four	4.25	4.25
		deep violet	4.00	—
343	A40	8c brown ('31)	90	90
		Block of four	3.75	3.75
		yellow brown	3.00	—
344	A40	10c blue ('31)	1.00	1.00
		Block of four	4.00	4.00
		deep blue	4.25	—
345	A40	12c deep orange ('31)	1.50	1.50
		Block of four	6.25	6.25
		red orange	5.00	—
346	A40	16c olive green *(Dewey)* ('31)	1.10	1.10
		Block of four	4.75	4.75
		bister green	4.25	—
347	A40	20c orange yellow ('31)	1.10	1.10
		Block of four	4.75	4.75
		yellow	4.25	—
348	A40	26c green ('31)	1.10	1.10
		Block of four	4.75	4.75
		blue green	4.25	—
349	A40	30c light gray ('31)	1.25	1.25
		Block of four	5.25	5.25
		gray	4.25	—
350	A41	1p light violet ('31)	4.00	4.00
		Block of four	16.50	16.50
		violet	17.50	—
351	A41	2p brown violet ('31)	10.00	10.00
		Block of four	42.50	42.50
		violet brown	42.50	—
352	A41	4p blue ('31)	30.00	30.00
		Block of four	125.00	—
		deep blue *(200)*	150.00	—
353	A41	10p green ('31)	90.00	90.00
		Block of four	375.00	—
		deep green *(200)*	190.00	—

Mount Mayon, Luzon — A43

Post Office, Manila — A44

Pier No. 7, Manila Bay — A45

Vernal Falls, Yosemite Park, California (See Footnote) — A46

Rice Planting — A47

Rice Terraces — A48

Baguio Zigzag — A49

1932, May 3 Unwmk. *Perf. 11*

No.	Type	Description	Unused	Used
354	A43	2c yellow green	45	20
		First day cover		2.00
		Block of four	2.25	1.00
355	A44	4c rose carmine	35	22
		First day cover		2.00
		Block of four	1.50	1.20
356	A45	12c orange	50	50
		First day cover		6.50
		Block of four	2.25	2.00
357	A46	18c red orange	17.00	8.25
		First day cover		13.50
		Block of four	65.00	37.50
358	A47	20c yellow	65	55
		First day cover		6.50
		Block of four	2.50	2.25
359	A48	24c deep violet	1.00	65
		First day cover		6.50
		Block of four	4.00	3.75
360	A49	32c olive brown	1.00	70
		First day cover		6.50
		Block of four	4.25	3.75
		First day cover, #354-360		50.00

The 18c vignette was intended to show Pagsanjan Falls in Laguna, central Luzon, and is so labeled. Through error the stamp pictures Vernal Falls in Yosemite National Park, California.

Nos. 302, 302a Surcharged in Orange or Red

1932

No.	Type	Description	Unused	Used
368	A41	1p on 4p blue (O)	1.65	35
		On cover		50
		Block of four	7.00	1.65
a.		1p on 4p dark blue (O)	2.25	1.00
369	A41	2p on 4p dark blue (R)	3.00	65
		On cover		80
		Block of four	13.00	3.00
a.		2p on 4p blue (R)	3.00	65

Far Eastern Championship

Issued in commemoration of the Tenth Far Eastern Championship Games.

Baseball Players — A50

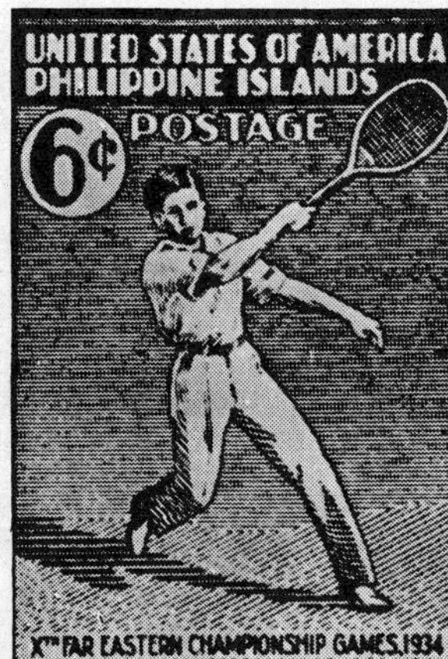

Tennis Player — A51

Basketball Players — A52

Printed by the Philippine Bureau of Printing.

1934, Apr. 14			**Unwmk.**		*Perf. 11½*
380	A50	2c	yellow brown	10	10
			brown	10	10
			First day cover		1.00
			"T" of "Eastern" malformed	1.65	1.35
381	A51	6c	ultramarine	25	20
			pale ultramarine	25	20
			First day cover		1.65
a.			Vertical pair, imperf. between	*600.00*	
382	A52	16c	violet brown	60	60
			dark violet	60	60
			First day cover		2.25
a.			Imperf. horizontally, pair	*600.00*	

José Rizal — A53

Woman and Carabao — A54

La Filipina — A55

Pearl Fishing — A56

Fort Santiago — A57

Salt Spring — A58

Magellan's Landing, 1521 — A59

"Juan de la Cruz" — A60

Rice Terraces — A61

Miguel Lopez de Legaspi and Chief Sikatuna Signing "Blood Compact," 1565 — A62

Barasoain Church, Malolos — A63

Battle of Manila Bay, 1898 — A64

Montalban Gorge — A65

United States Administration of the Philippines stamps can be mounted in Scott's U.S. Possessions Album.

George Washington A66

Printed by U. S. Bureau of Engraving and Printing.

1935, Feb. 15		**Unwmk.**		***Perf. 11***
383	A53	2c rose	5	5
		First day cover		50
384	A54	4c yellow green	5	5
		Light yellow green	5	5
		First day cover		50
385	A55	6c dark brown	9	5
		First day cover		50
386	A56	8c violet	10	10
		First day cover		1.65
387	A57	10c rose carmine	16	14
		First day cover		1.65
388	A58	12c black	12	10
		First day cover		1.65
389	A59	16c dark blue	12	10
		First day cover		1.65
390	A60	20c light olive green	16	6
		First day cover		2.25
391	A61	26c indigo	22	22
		First day cover		3.00
392	A62	30c orange red	22	22
		First day cover		3.00
393	A63	1p red orange & black	1.65	1.20
		First day cover		8.25
394	A64	2p bister brown & black	3.50	1.20
		First day cover		14.00
395	A65	4p blue & black	3.50	2.50
		First day cover		20.00
396	A66	5p green & black	7.50	1.50
		First day cover		27.50

The first price column gives the catalogue value of an unused stamp, the second that of a used stamp.

Issues of the Commonwealth

Commonwealth Inauguration Issue

Issued to commemorate the inauguration of the Philippine Commonwealth, Nov. 15, 1935.

"The Temples of Human Progress"
A67

1935, Nov. 15		**Unwmk.**		***Perf. 11***
397	A67	2c carmine rose	10	7
		First day cover		65
398	A67	6c deep violet	15	10
		First day cover		65
399	A67	16c blue	20	14
		First day cover		1.00
400	A67	36c yellow green	35	30
		First day cover		1.35
401	A67	50c brown	55	55
		First day cover		2.00

José Rizal Issue

Issued to commemorate the 75th anniversary of the birth of José Rizal (1861-1896), national hero of the Filipinos.

José Rizal — A68

Printed by the Philippine Bureau of Printing.

1936, June 19		**Unwmk.**		***Perf. 12***
402	A68	2c yellow brown	7	7
		light yellow brown	7	7
		First day cover		50
403	A68	6c slate blue	10	7
		light slate green	10	7
		First day cover		1.00
a.		Imperf. vertically, pair	*800.00*	
404	A68	36c red brown	50	45
		light red brown	50	45
		First day cover		2.25

Commonwealth Anniversary Issue

Issued in commemoration of the first anniversary of the Commonwealth.

President Manuel L. Quezon — A69

Printed by U.S. Bureau of Engraving and Printing.

1936, Nov. 15		**Unwmk.**		***Perf. 11***
408	A69	2c orange brown	5	5
		First day cover		50
409	A69	6c yellow green	10	9
		First day cover		80
410	A69	12c ultramarine	12	10
		First day cover		1.50

Stamps of 1935 Overprinted in Black:

COMMON-
WEALTH
a

COMMONWEALTH
b

1936-37		**Unwmk.**		***Perf. 11***
411	A53(a)	2c rose, *Dec. 28, 1936*	5	5
		First day cover		*35.00*
a.		Bklt. pane of 6, *Jan. 15 1937*	2.50	*65*
a.		First day cover		*40.00*
412	A54(b)	4c yellow green, *Mar. 29, 1937*	50	28
		On cover		35
413	A55(a)	6c dark brown, *Oct. 7, 1936*	20	7
		On cover		8
414	A56(b)	8c violet, *Mar. 29, 1937*	22	20
		On cover		22
415	A57(b)	10c rose carmine, *Dec. 28, 1936*	15	5
		First day cover		35.00
a.		"COMMONWEALT"		—
416	A58(b)	12c black, *Mar. 29, 1937*	16	5
		On cover		7
417	A59(b)	16c dark blue, *Oct. 7, 1936*	16	14
		On cover		16
418	A60(a)	20c lt. olive green, *Mar. 29, 1937*	60	35
		On cover		38
419	A61(b)	26c indigo, *Mar. 29, 1937*	42	30
		On cover		38
420	A62(b)	30c orange red, *Dec. 28, 1936*	28	10
		First day cover		*35.00*
421	A63(b)	1p red org. & blk., *Oct. 7, 1936*	*65*	15
		On cover		35
422	A64(b)	2p bis. brn. & blk., *Mar. 29, 1937*	4.50	2.50
		On cover		2.75
423	A65(b)	4p blue & blk., *Mar. 29, 1937*	15.00	2.50
		On cover		3.50
424	A66(b)	5p green & blk., *Mar. 29, 1937*	1.50	1.25
		On cover		1.35

United States Administration of the Philippines stamps can be mounted in Scott's U.S. Possessions Album.

Eucharistic Congress Issue

Issued to commemorate the 33rd International Eucharistic Congress held at Manila, Feb. 3-7, 1937.

Map, Symbolical of the Eucharistic Congress Spreading Light of Christianity — A70

FLAT PLATE PRINTING

Plates of 256 subjects in four panes of 64 each.

1937, Feb. 3 **Unwmk.** ***Perf. 11***

No.	Type	Description	Unused	Used
425	A70	2c yellow green	7	5
		First day cover		50
426	A70	6c light brown	12	8
		First day cover		50
427	A70	12c sapphire	14	8
		First day cover		80
428	A70	20c deep orange	22	5
		First day cover		1.00
429	A70	36c deep violet	40	35
		First day cover		1.35
430	A70	50c carmine	45	28
		First day cover		2.00

Arms of City of Manila — A71

1937, Aug. 27 **Unwmk.** ***Perf. 11***

No.	Type	Description	Unused	Used
431	A71	10p gray	4.25	2.00
432	A71	20p henna brown	2.25	1.35
		First day cover, Nos. 431-432		50.00

Stamps of 1935 Overprinted in Black:

COMMON-
WEALTH
a

COMMONWEALTH
b

1938-40 **Unwmk.** ***Perf. 11***

No.	Type	Description	Unused	Used
433	A53(a)	2c rose ('39)	10	5
a.		Booklet pane of six	3.50	*65*
b.		"WEALTH COMMON-"	*2,000.*	—
c.		Hyphen omitted	—	—
434	A54(b)	4c yellow green ('40)	40	35
435	A55(a)	6c dark brown, *May 12, 1939*	5	5
		First day cover		*35.00*
a.		6c golden brown	10	5
436	A56(b)	8c violet ('39)	7	7
a.		"COMMONWEALT"	65.00	
437	A57(b)	10c rose carmine, *May 12, 1939*	7	5
438	A58(b)	12c black ('40)	7	6
439	A59(b)	16c Dark blue	12	7
440	A60(a)	20c light olive green ('39)	14	7
441	A61(b)	26c indigo ('40)	20	20
442	A62(b)	30c orange red *May 23, 1939*	1.40	70
443	A63(b)	1p red org. & blk., *Aug. 29, 1938*	40	15
		First day cover		*40.00*
444	A64(b)	2p bister brown & black ('39)	2.75	75
445	A65(b)	4p blue & black ('40)	42.50	42.50
446	A66(b)	5p green & black ('40)	4.50	2.75

Overprint *"b"* measures 18½x1¾mm.

No. 433b occurs in booklet pane, No. 433a, position 5; all copies are straight-edged, left and bottom.

First Foreign Trade Week Issue

Nos. 384, 298a and 432 Surcharged in Red, Violet or Black:

FIRST FOREIGN
TRADE WEEK
2 CENTAVOS
MAY 21-27,1939
a

FIRST FOREIGN
TRADE WEEK
MAY 21-27, 1939
6 CENTAVOS 6
b

50 CENTAVOS 50
FIRST FOREIGN
TRADE WEEK
MAY 21-27,1939
c

1939, July 5

No.	Type	Description	Unused	Used
449	A54(a)	2c on 4c yellow green (R)	7	5
		First day cover		1.35
450	A40(b)	6c on 26c blue green (V)	14	14
		First day cover		2.00
a.		6c on 26c green	65	30
451	A71(c)	50c on 20p henna brown (Bk)	1.00	1.00
		First day cover		5.00

Commonwealth 4th Anniversary Issue

Nos. 452-460 were issued to commemorate the fourth anniversary of the Commonwealth.

Triumphal Arch — A72

Printed by U. S. Bureau of Engraving and Printing.

1939, Nov. 15 **Unwmk.** ***Perf. 11***

No.	Type	Description	Unused	Used
452	A72	2c yellow green	7	5
		First day cover		65
453	A72	6c carmine	10	5
		First day cover		65
454	A72	12c bright blue	16	7
		First day cover		1.35

Malacañan Palace — A73

1939, Nov. 15 **Unwmk.** ***Perf. 11***

No.	Type	Description	Unused	Used
455	A73	2c green	7	5
		First day cover		65
456	A73	6c orange	10	7
		First day cover		65
457	A73	12c carmine	16	5
		First day cover		1.35

A particular stamp may be scarce, but if few collectors want it, its market value may remain relatively low.

President Quezon Taking Oath of Office — A74

1940, Feb. 8 **Unwmk.** ***Perf. 11***

No.	Type	Description	Unused	Used
458	A74	2c dark orange	8	5
		First day cover		65
459	A74	6c dark green	12	8
		First day cover		65
460	A74	12c purple	25	10
		First day cover		1.35

José Rizal — A75

ROTARY PRESS PRINTING

1941, Apr. 14 **Unwmk.** ***Perf. 11x10½***

Size: 19x22½mm

No.	Type	Description	Unused	Used
461	A75	2c apple green	5	5
		First day cover		65
		Margin block of 4, P#	1.00	

FLAT PLATE PRINTING

1941-43 **Unwmk.** **Size: 18¾x22mm** ***Perf. 11***

No.	Type	Description	Unused	Used
462	A75	2c apple green	8	5
a.		2c pale apple green ('41)	16	5
b.		Booklet pane of six (apple green)	1.25	*1.00*
c.		Booklet pane of six (pale apple green) ('41)	2.50	*2.25*

This stamp was issued only in booklet panes and all copies have one or two straight edges.

Further printings were made in 1942 and 1943 in different shades from the first supply of stamps sent to the islands.

Stamps of 1935-41 Handstamped in Violet **VICTORY**

1944 **Unwmk.** ***Perf. 11, 11x10½***

No.	Type	Description	Unused	Used
463	A53	2c rose (On 411), *Dec. 3*	*150.00*	*85.00*
a.		Booklet pane of six	*1,200.*	
463B	A53	2c rose (On 433), *Dec. 14*	*1,000.*	*1,000.*
464	A75	2c apple green (On 461), *Nov. 8*	2.25	2.25
		On cover		3.50
465	A54	4c yellow green (On 384), *Nov. 8*	*16.50*	*16.50*
		On cover		—
466	A55	6c dark brown (On 385), *Dec. 14*	*900.00*	*500.00*
		On cover		—
467	A69	6c yellow green (On 409), *Dec. 3*	*65.00*	*55.00*
		On cover		—
468	A55	6c dark brown (On 413), *Dec. 28*	*375.00*	*200.00*
469	A72	6c carmine (On 453), *Dec. 14*	*85.00*	*65.00*
		On cover		—
470	A73	6c orange (On 456), *Dec. 14*	*450.00*	*200.00*
		On cover		—
471	A74	6c dark green (On 459), *Nov. 8*	*100.00*	*60.00*
		On cover		—
472	A56	8c violet (On 436), *Nov. 8*	8.25	10.00
		On cover		—
473	A57	10c carmine rose (On 415), *Nov. 8*	*65.00*	*40.00*
		On cover		—
474	A57	10c carmine rose (On 437), *Nov. 8*	*85.00*	*55.00*
		On cover		—
475	A69	12c ultramarine (On 410), *Dec. 3*	*200.00*	*70.00*
		On cover		—
476	A72	12c bright blue (On 454), *Dec. 14*	*2,750.*	*900.00*
		On cover		—
477	A74	12c purple (On 460), *Nov. 8*	*120.00*	*65.00*
		On cover		—

No.	Type	Description	Unused	Used
478	A59	16c dark blue (On 389), *Dec. 3*	450.00	
479	A59	16c dark blue (On 417), *Nov. 8*	225.00	80.00
		On cover		—
480	A59	16c dark blue (On 439), *Nov. 8*	90.00	65.00
481	A60	20c light olive green (On 440), *Nov. 8*	19.00	19.00
		On cover		—
482	A62	30c orange red (On 420), *Dec. 3*	190.00	80.00
		On cover		—
483	A62	30c orange red (On 442), *Dec. 3*	190.00	90.00
		On cover		—
484	A63	1p red orange & black (On 443) *Dec. 3*	4,500.	3,000.
		On cover		—

No. 463 comes only from the booklet pane. All copies have one or two straight edges.

Types of 1935-37 Overprinted

VICTORY
VICTORY

COMMON-
WEALTH

COMMONWEALTH VICTORY

a b c

1945 Unwmk. *Perf. 11*

No.	Type	Description	Unused	Used
485	A53(a)	2c rose, *Jan. 19*	7	5
		First day cover		2.50
486	A54(b)	4c yellow green, *Jan. 19*	10	10
		First day cover		2.50
487	A55(a)	6c golden brown, *Jan. 19*	10	7
		First day cover		2.50
488	A56(b)	8c violet, *Jan. 19*	14	10
		First day cover		3.00
489	A57(b)	10c rose carmine, *Jan. 19*	14	10
		First day cover		3.00
490	A58(b)	12c black, *Jan. 19*	20	10
		First day cover		3.50
491	A59(b)	16c dark blue, *Jan. 19*	25	10
		First day cover		4.00
492	A60(a)	20c light olive green, *Jan. 19*	30	10
		First day cover		4.25
493	A62(b)	30c orange red, *May 1*	40	35
		First day cover		2.50
494	A63(b)	1p red orange & black, *Jan. 19*	1.10	25
		First day cover		6.50
495	A71(c)	10p gray, *May 1*	40.00	13.50
		First day cover		20.00
496	A71(c)	20p henna brown, *May 1*	35.00	15.00
		First day cover		25.00

José Rizal — A76

ROTARY PRESS PRINTING

1946, May 28 Unwmk. *Perf. 11x10½*

No.	Type	Description	Unused	Used
497	A76	2c sepia	7	5
		Margin block of 4, P#	50	

Later issues, released by the Philippine Republic on July 4, 1946, and thereafter, are listed in Scotts Standard Postage Stamp Catalogue, Vol. IV.

AIR POST

Madrid-Manila Flight Issue

Issued to commemorate the flight of Spanish aviators Gallarza and Loriga from Madrid to Manila.

Regular Issue of 1917-26 Overprinted in Red or Violet by the Philippine Bureau of Printing

1926, May 13 Unwmk. *Perf. 11*

No.	Type	Description	Unused	Used
C1	A40	2c green (R) *(10,000)*	3.50	2.50
		First day cover		22.50
		Block of four	16.00	12.50
C2	A40	4c carmine (V) *(9,000)*	4.25	3.00
		First day cover		22.50
		Block of four	19.00	14.00
a.		Inverted overprint *(100)*	800.00	—
C3	A40	6c lilac (R) *(5,000)*	22.50	8.00
		First day cover		35.00
		Block of four	100.00	
C4	A40	8c orange brown (V) *(5,000)*	22.50	8.00
		First day cover		35.00
		Block of four	100.00	
C5	A40	10c deep blue (R) *(5,000)*	20.00	8.00
		First day cover		35.00
		Block of four	90.00	
C6	A40	12c red orange (V) *(4,000)*	25.00	12.00
		First day cover		35.00
		Block of four	110.00	
C7	A40	16c light olive green *(Sampson)* (V) *(300)*	675.00	600.00
		Block of four	—	
C8	A40	16c olive bister *(Sampson)* (R) *(100)*	1,350.	1,200.
		Block of four	—	
C9	A40	16c olive green *(Dewey)* (V) *(4,000)*	25.00	12.00
		First day cover		35.00
		Block of four	120.00	
C10	A40	20c orange yellow (V) *(4,000)*	25.00	12.00
		First day cover		35.00
		Block of four	120.00	
C11	A40	26c blue green (V) *(4,000)*	25.00	12.00
		First day cover		35.00
		Block of four	120.00	
C12	A40	30c gray (V) *(4,000)*	25.00	12.00
		First day cover		35.00
		Block of four	120.00	
C13	A41	2p violet brown (R) *(900)*	175.00	150.00
		On cover		225.00
		Block of four	—	
C14	A41	4p dark blue (R) *(700)*	400.00	225.00
		On cover		*300.00*
		Block of four	—	
C15	A41	10p deep green (V) *(500)*	450.00	300.00
		On cover		*400.00*
		Block of four	—	

Same Overprint on No. 269

Wmk. Single-lined PIPS (190)

Perf. 12

No.	Type	Description	Unused	Used
C16	A40	26c blue green (V) *(100)*	1,500.	
		Block of four	—	

Same Overprint on No. 284

No.	Type	Description	Unused	Used
C17	A41	1p pale violet (V) *(2,000)*	80.00	55.00
		On cover		65.00
		First day cover		*90.00*
		Block of four	350.00	

Overprintings of Nos. C1-C6, C9-C15 and C17 were made from two plates. Position No. 89 of the first printing shows broken left blade of propeller.

London-Orient Flight Issue

Issued Nov. 9, 1928, to celebrate the arrival of a British squadron of hydroplanes.

Regular Issue of 1917-25 Overprinted in Red

L.O.F.
1928

1928, Nov. 9 Unwmk. *Perf. 11*

No.	Type	Description	Unused	Used
C18	A40	2c green *(101,200)*	40	25
		First day cover		6.50
C19	A40	4c carmine *(50,500)*	40	35
		First day cover		8.00
C20	A40	6c violet *(12,600)*	1.50	1.20
		On cover		1.35
C21	A40	8c orange brown *(10,000)*	1.65	1.50
		On cover		1.75
C22	A40	10c deep blue *(10,000)*	1.65	1.50
		On cover		1.75
C23	A40	12c red orange *(8,000)*	2.25	2.00
		On cover		2.50
C24	A40	16c olive green (No. 303a) *(12,600)*	1.75	1.40
		On cover		2.00
C25	A40	20c orange yellow *(8,000)*	2.25	2.00
		On cover		2.50
C26	A40	26c blue green *(7,000)*	6.50	5.00
		On cover		6.50
C27	A40	30c gray *(7,000)*	6.50	5.00
		On cover		6.50

Same Overprint on No. 271

Wmk. Single-lined PIPS (190)

Perf. 12

No.	Type	Description	Unused	Used
C28	A41	1p pale violet *(6,000)*	22.50	22.50
		On cover		25.00

Von Gronau Issue

Issued commemoration of the visit of Capt. Wolfgang von Gronau's airplane on its round-the-world flight.

Nos. 354-360 Overprinted by the Philippine Bureau of Printing

1932, Sept. 27 Unwmk. *Perf. 11*

No.	Type	Description	Unused	Used
C29	A43	2c yellow green *(100,000)*	30	30
		First day cover		2.00
C30	A44	4c rose carmine *(80,000)*	30	30
		First day cover		2.00
C31	A45	12c orange *(55,000)*	50	50
		On cover		65
C32	A46	18c red orange *(30,000)*	3.00	3.00
		On cover		3.25
C33	A47	20c yellow *(30,000)*	1.50	1.50
		On cover		1.65
C34	A48	24c deep violet *(30,000)*	1.50	1.50
		On cover		1.65
C35	A49	32c olive brown *(30,000)*	1.50	1.50
		On cover		1.65
		First day cover, #C29-C35		35.00

Rein Issue

Commemorating the flight from Madrid to Manila of the Spanish aviator Fernando Rein y Loring.

Regular Issue of 1917-25 Overprinted in Black

F.REIN
MADRID-MANILA
FLIGHT-1933

1933, Apr. 11

No.	Type	Description	Unused	Used
C36	A40	2c green *(95,000)*	30	30
		First day cover		1.65
C37	A40	4c carmine *(75,000)*	35	35
		First day cover		—
C38	A40	6c deep violet *(65,000)*	75	75
		First day cover		3.00
C39	A40	8c orange brown *(35,000)*	1.50	1.40
C40	A40	10c dark blue *(35,000)*	1.10	90
C41	A40	12c orange *(35,000)*	1.00	90
C42	A40	16c olive green *(Dewey) (35,000)*	1.00	90
C43	A40	20c yellow *(35,000)*	1.00	1.00
C44	A40	26c green *(35,000)*	1.40	1.40
a.		26c blue green	1.90	1.65
C45	A40	30c gray *(30,000)*	1.75	1.50
		First day cover, #C36-C45		40.00

Stamp of 1917 Overprinted by the Philippine Bureau of Printing

1933, May 26 Unwmk. *Perf. 11*

No.	Type	Description	Unused	Used
C46	A40	2c green	45	40

Regular Issue of 1932 Overprinted

No.	Type	Description	Unused	Used
C47	A44	4c rose carmine	7	5
C48	A45	12c orange	25	10
C49	A47	20c yellow	25	15
C50	A48	24c deep violet	30	20
C51	A49	32c olive brown	40	30
		First day cover, #C46-C51		35.00

Transpacific Issue

Issued to commemorate the China Clipper flight from Manila to San Francisco, Dec. 2-5, 1935.

Nos. 387, 392 Overprinted in Gold

1935, Dec. 2 Unwmk. *Perf. 11*

No.	Type	Description	Unused	Used
C52	A57	10c rose carmine *(500,000)*	20	20
		First day cover		2.00
C53	A62	30c orange red *(350,000)*	35	35
		First day cover		3.00

Manila-Madrid Flight Issue

Issued to commemorate the Manila-Madrid flight by aviators Antonio Arnaiz and Juan Calvo.

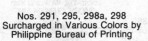

Nos. 291, 295, 298a, 298 Surcharged in Various Colors by Philippine Bureau of Printing

1936, Sept. 6

C54	A40	2c on 4c carmine (Bl) *(2,000,000)*	5	5
		First day cover		1.00
C55	A40	6c on 12c red orange (V) *(500,000)*	10	10
		First day cover		3.00
C56	A40	16c on 26c blue green (Bk) *(300,000)*	20	20
		First day cover		5.00
a.		16c on 26c green	1.00	65

Air Mail Exhibition Issue

Issued to commemorate the first Air Mail Exhibition, held Feb. 17-19, 1939.

Nos. 298a, 298, 431 Surcharged in Black or Red by Philippine Bureau of Printing

1939, Feb. 17

C57	A40	8c on 26c blue green (Bk) *(200,000)*	60	38
		First day cover		3.50
a.		8c on 26c green (Bk)	1.40	50
C58	A71	1p on 10p gray (R) *(30,000)*	2.50	2.00
		First day cover		8.00

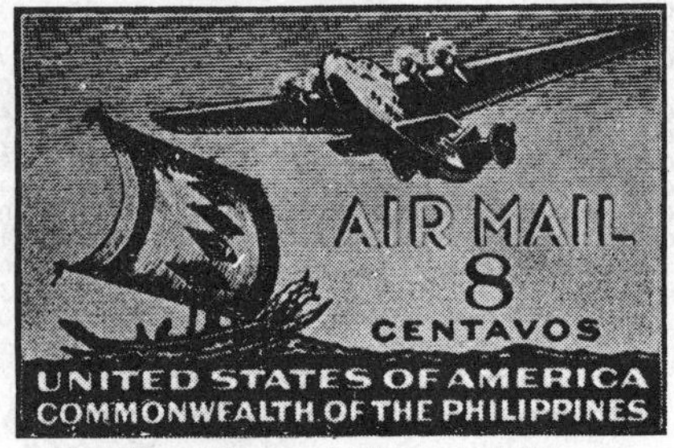

Moro Vinta and Clipper — AP1

Printed by the U. S. Bureau of Engraving and Printing.

1941, June 30 Unwmk. *Perf. 11*

C59	AP1	8c carmine	1.00	60
		First day cover		2.00
C60	AP1	20c ultramarine	1.20	45
		First day cover		2.50
C61	AP1	60c blue green	1.75	75
		First day cover		3.50
C62	AP1	1p sepia	70	42
		First day cover		2.25

No. C47 Handstamped in Violet **VICTORY**

1944, Dec. 3 Unwmk. *Perf. 11*

C63	A44	4c rose carmine	*1,200.*	*750.00*
		On cover		—

SPECIAL DELIVERY

U.S. No. E5 Overprinted in Red

a **PHILIPPINES**

Printed by U.S. Bureau of Engraving & Printing

Wmk. Double-lined USPS (191)

1901, Oct. 15 *Perf. 12*

E1	SD3	10c dark blue *(15,000)*	70.00	80.00
		On cover		225.00
		Block of four	350.00	
		Margin strip of 3, Impt. & P#	500.00	
		Margin block of 6, Impt. & P#	*2,700.*	
		Dots in curved frame above messenger (Pl. 882)	*90.00*	

Special Delivery Messenger — SD2

Wmk. Double-lined PIPS (191)

1906, Sept. 8 *Perf. 12*

E2	SD2	20c deep ultramarine *(40,000)*	20.00	5.50
		On cover		12.00
		Block of four	85.00	
b.		20c pale ultramarine	20.00	6.50

SPECIAL PRINTING

U.S. No. E6 Overprinted Type "a" in Red

1907 Wmk. Double-lined USPS (191) *Perf. 12*

E2A	SD4	10c ultramarine	*1,100.*	
		Block of four	*5,000.*	
		Margin block of 6, Impt. & P#	—	

This stamp was part of the set specially printed for the Bureau of Insular Affairs in 1907. See note following No. 240.

1911, Apr. Wmk. Single-lined PIPS (190) *Perf. 12*

E3	SD2	20c deep ultramarine *(90,000)*	13.50	1.40
		On cover		10.00
		Block of four	55.00	

1916 *Perf. 10*

E4	SD2	20c deep ultramarine	110.00	25.00
		On cover		55.00
		Block of four	500.00	
		pale ultramarine	—	

Early in 1919 the supply of Special Delivery stamps in the Manila area was exhausted. A Government decree permitted the use of regular issue postage stamps for payment of the special delivery fee when so noted on the cover. This usage was permitted until the new supply of Special Delivery stamps arrived.

1919 Unwmk. *Perf. 11*

E5	SD2	20c ultramarine	40	20
		On cover		22
		Block of four	1.65	
a.		20c pale blue	65	16
b.		20c dull violet	40	16

Type of 1906 Issue

1925-31 Unwmk. *Imperf.*

E6	SD2	20c dull violet ('31)	14.00	*16.00*
		violet blue	16.00	*20.00*
		On cover		20.00
		Block of four	60.00	

Type of 1919 Overprinted in Black **COMMONWEALTH**

1939, Apr. 27 Unwmk. *Perf. 11*

E7	SD2	20c blue violet	20	20
		First day cover		35.00

Nos. E5b and E7 Handstamped in Violet **VICTORY**

1944 Unwmk. *Perf. 11*

E8	SD2	20c dull violet (On E5b)	*250.00*	*200.00*
E9	SD2	20c blue violet (On E7)	*140.00*	*110.00*
		On cover		—

Type SD2 Overprinted "VICTORY" As No. 486

1945, May 1 Unwmk. *Perf. 11*

E10	SD2	20c blue violet	55	55
		First day cover		10.00
a.		"IC" close together	2.75	2.75

SPECIAL DELIVERY OFFICIAL STAMP

Type of 1906 Issue Overprinted **O.B.**

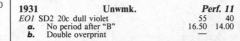

1931 Unwmk. *Perf. 11*

EO1	SD2	20c dull violet	55	40
a.		No period after "B"	16.50	14.00
b.		Double overprint		—

POSTAGE DUE

U.S. Nos. J38-J44 Overprinted in Black

Printed by the U. S. Bureau of Engraving and Printing.

Wmk. Double-lined USPS (191)

1899, Aug. 16 *Perf. 12*

J1	D2	1c deep claret *(340,892)*	2.50	1.00
		On Cover		17.50
		Margin block of 6, Impt. & P#	*350.00*	
J2	D2	2c deep claret *(306,983)*	2.50	90
		On cover		20.00
		Margin block of 6, Impt. & P#	350.00	
J3	D2	5c deep claret *(34,565)*	5.50	1.90
		On cover		*25.00*
		Margin block of 6, Impt. & P#	*525.00*	
J4	D2	10c deep claret *(15,848)*	7.50	3.50
		On cover		30.00
		Margin block of 6, Impt. & P#	*600.00*	
J5	D2	50c deep claret *(6,168)*	82.50	50.00
		On cover		—
		Margin block of 6, Impt. & P#	*2,200.*	

No. J1 was used to pay regular postage Sept. 5-19, 1902.

1901, Aug. 31

J6	D2	3c deep claret *(14,885)*	7.50	5.00
		On cover		25.00
		Margin block of 6, Impt. & P#	*600.00*	
J7	D2	30c deep claret *(2,140)*	110.00	50.00
		On cover		—
		Margin block of 6, Impt. & P#	*2,500.*	

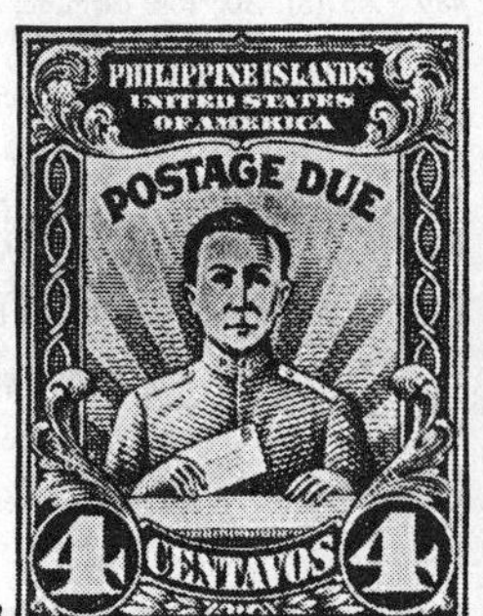

Post Office Clerk — D3

1928, Aug. 21 Unwmk. *Perf. 11*

J8	D3	4c brown red	10	10
J9	D3	6c brown red	10	10
J10	D3	8c brown red	10	10
J11	D3	10c brown red	14	14
J12	D3	12c brown red	14	14
J13	D3	16c brown red	16	16
J14	D3	20c brown red	14	14

No. J8 Surcharged in Blue **3 CVOS. 3**

1937, July 29 Unwmk. *Perf. 11*

J15	D3	3c on 4c brown red	16	10
		First day cover		35.00

Nos. J8 to J14 Handstamped in Violet **VICTORY**

1944, Dec. 3 Unwmk. *Perf. 11*

J16	D3	4c brown red	*90.00*	—
J17	D3	6c brown red	*60.00*	—
J18	D3	8c brown red	*65.00*	—
J19	D3	10c brown red	*60.00*	—
J20	D3	12c brown red	*60.00*	—
J21	D3	16c brown red	*65.00*	—
J22	D3	20c brown red	*65.00*	—

OFFICIAL

Official Handstamped Overprints

"Officers purchasing stamps for government business may, if they so desire, surcharge them with the letters O.B. either in writing with black ink or by rubber stamps but in such a manner as not to obliterate the stamp that postmasters will be unable to determine whether the stamps have been previously used." C. M. Cotterman, Director of Posts, December 26, 1905.

Beginning with January 1, 1906, all branches of the Insular Government, used postage stamps to prepay postage instead of franking them as before. Some officials used manuscript, some utilized the typewriting machines but by far the larger number provided themselves with rubber stamps. The majority of these read "O. B." but other forms were: "OFFICIAL BUSINESS" or "OFFICIAL MAIL" in two lines, with variations on many of these.

These "O. B." overprints are known on U. S. 1899-1901 stamps; on 1903-06 stamps in red and blue; on 1906 stamps in red, blue, black, yellow and green.

"O. B." overprints were also made on the centavo and peso stamps of the Philippines, per order of May 25, 1907.

Beginning in 1926 the stamps were overprinted and issued by the Government, but some post offices continued to handstamp "O.B."

During the Japanese occupation period 1942-45, the same system of handstamped official overprints prevailed, but the handstamp usually consisted of "K.P.", initials of the Tagalog words, "Kagamitang Pampamahalaan" (Official Business), and the two Japanese characters used in the printed overprint on Nos. NO1 to NO4.

Legislative Palace Issue of 1926 Overprinted in Red **OFFICIAL**

Printed and overprinted by the Philippine Bureau of Printing.

1926, Dec. 20 **Unwmk.** ***Perf. 12***

No.	Type	Description	Unused	Used
O1	A42	2c green & black *(90,500)*	1.65	90
		On cover		2.00
		Block of four	7.00	5.00
O2	A42	4c carmine & black *(90,450)*	1.65	1.10
		On cover		2.00
		First day cover		10.00
		Block of four	7.00	5.00
a.		Vertical pair, imperf. between	250.00	
O3	A42	18c light brown & black *(70,000)*	4.50	4.00
		On cover		6.50
		Block of four	22.50	20.00
O4	A42	20c orange & black *(70,250)*	4.00	1.40
		On cover		2.00
		Block of four	20.00	6.50
		First day cover, #O1-O4		50.00

Regular Issue of 1917-25 Overprinted **O. B.**

Printed and overprinted by the U.S. Bureau of Engraving and Printing.

1931 **Unwmk.** ***Perf. 11***

No.	Type	Description	Unused	Used
O5	A40	2c green	10	10
a.		No period after "B"	6.50	3.50
b.		No period after "O"		—
O6	A40	4c carmine	10	10
a.		No period after "B"	6.50	3.50
O7	A40	6c deep violet	10	10
O8	A40	8c yellow brown	10	10
O9	A40	10c deep blue	25	10
O10	A40	12c red orange	16	10
a.		No period after "B"	20.00	
O11	A40	16c light olive green *(Dewey)*	16	7
a.		16c olive bister	1.00	20
O12	A40	20c orange yellow	20	7
a.		No period after "B"	10.00	10.00
O13	A40	26c green	30	30
a.		26c blue green	80	65
O14	A40	30c gray	25	22

Regular Issue of 1935 Overprinted in Black **O. B.**

1935 **Unwmk.** ***Perf. 11***

No.	Type	Description	Unused	Used
O15	A53	2c rose	5	5
a.		No period after "B"	6.50	3.50
O16	A54	4c yellow green	5	5
a.		No period after "B"	6.50	5.00
O17	A55	6c dark brown	7	5
a.		No period after "B"	12.00	12.00
O18	A56	8c violet	8	8
O19	A57	10c rose carmine	16	5
O20	A58	12c black	16	10
O21	A59	16c dark blue	16	10
O22	A60	20c light olive green	16	10
O23	A61	26c indigo	25	22
O24	A62	30c orange red	30	25

Nos. 411 and 418 with Additional Overprint in Black **O. B.**

1937-38 **Unwmk.** ***Perf. 11***

No.	Type	Description	Unused	Used
O25	A53	2c rose, *Apr. 10, 1937*	5	5
		First day cover		50.00
a.		No period after "B"	4.25	2.25
O26	A60	20c light olive green, *Apr. 26, 1938*	65	50

Regular Issue of 1935 Overprinted In Black:

O. B. COMMON-WEALTH
a

O. B. COMMONWEALTH
b

1938-40 **Unwmk.** ***Perf. 11***

No.	Type	Description	Unused	Used
O27	A53(a)	2c rose	5	5
a.		Hyphen omitted	12.00	10.00
b.		No period after "B"	14.00	10.00
O28	A54(b)	4c yellow green	7	5
O29	A55(a)	6c dark brown	10	5
O30	A56(b)	8c violet	10	7
O31	A57(b)	10c rose carmine	12	7
a.		No period after "O"	16.50	16.50
O32	A58(b)	12c black	12	12
O33	A59(b)	16c dark blue	16	8
O34	A60(a)	20c light olive green ('40)	22	22
O35	A61(b)	26c indigo	30	30
O36	A62(b)	30c orange red	25	25

No. 461 Overprinted in Black

O. B.
c

ROTARY PRESS PRINTING

1941, Apr. 14 **Unwmk.** ***Perf. 11x10½***

No.	Type	Description	Unused	Used
O37	A75	2c apple green	5	5
		First day cover		3.50
		Margin block of four, P#	25	

Nos. O27, O37, O16, O29, O31, O22 and O26 Handstamped in Violet **VICTORY**

1944 **Unwmk.** ***Perf. 11, 11x10½***

No.	Type	Description	Unused	Used
O38	A53	2c rose (On O27)	*140.00*	*90.00*
O39	A75	2c apple green (On O37)	5.00	3.00
		On cover		*10.00*
		Block of four	25.00	—
O40	A54	4c yellow green (On O16)	*25.00*	*20.00*
		Block of four	*125.00*	
O40A	A55	6c dark brown (On O29)	*3,000.*	—
O41	A57	10c rose carmine (On O31)	*100.00*	
		Block of four	*425.00*	
O42	A60	20c light olive green (On O22)	*3,500.*	
O43	A60	20c light olive green (On O26)	*1,400.*	

No. 497 Overprinted Type "c" in Black.

1946, June 19 **Unwmk.** ***Perf. 11x10½***

No.	Type	Description	Unused	Used
O44	A76	2c sepia	6	5
		Margin block of 4, P#	40	

POST OFFICE SEALS

POS1

1906 **Litho.** **Unwmk.** ***Perf. 12***

No.	Type	Description	Unused	Used
OX1	POS1	light brown	25.00	—

Wmk. "PIRS" in Double-lined Capitals

1907 ***Perf. 12***

No.	Type	Description	Unused	Used
OX2	POS1	light brown	45.00	—
		Hyphen-hole Perf. 7		
OX3	POS1	orange brown	22.50	—

1911 ***Hyphen-hole Perf. 7***

No.	Type	Description	Unused	Used
OX4	POS1	yellow brown	20.00	
OX5	POS1	olive bister	40.00	—
a.		Unwatermarked	—	
OX6	POS1	yellow	45.00	—

1913 **Unwmk.** ***Hyphen-hole Perf. 7***

No.	Type	Description	Unused	Used
OX7	POS1	lemon yellow	85	85
		Perf. 12		
OX8	POS1	yellow	—	—

Wmk. "USPS" in Single-lined Capitals
Hyphen-hole Perf. 7

No.	Type	Description	Unused	Used
OX9	POS1	yellow	45.00	20.00

1934 **Unwmk.** ***Rouletted***

No.	Type	Description	Unused	Used
OX10	POS1	dark blue	85	85

POS2

No.	Type	Description	Unused	Used
OX11	POS2	dark blue	65	65

POS3

1938 ***Hyphen-hole Perf. 7***

No.	Type	Description	Unused	Used
OX12	POS3	dark blue	5.50	2.25
a.		Perforated 12	—	—

ENVELOPES

U.S. Envelopes of 1899 Issue Overprinted below stamp in color of the stamp, except where noted

PHILIPPINES.

1899-1900

Note: Many envelopes for which there was no obvious need were issued in small quantities. Anyone residing in the Islands could, by depositing with his postmaster the required amount, order any envelopes in quantities of 500, or multiples thereof, provided it was on the schedule of U.S. envelopes. Such special orders are indicated by an plus sign after the quantity.

No.	Type	Description	Unused	Used
U1	U77	1c green (No. U352) *(370,000)*	1.65	1.35
		Entire	6.50	7.00
U2	U77	1c green, *amber* (No. U353) *(1,000)+*	12.00	10.00
		Entire	42.50	30.00
U3	U77	1c green, *amber* (No. U353) red overprint *(500)+*	16.50	15.00
		Entire	45.00	42.50
U4	U77	1c green, *oriental buff* (No. U354) *(1,000)+*	10.00	10.00
		Entire	22.50	22.50
U5	U77	1c green, *oriental buff* (No. U354) red overprint *(500)+*	25.00	25.00
		Entire	55.00	*55.00*
U6	U77	1c green, *blue* (No. U355) *(1,000)+*	6.50	6.50
		Entire	22.50	22.50
U7	U77	1c green, *blue* (No. U355) red overprint *(500)+*	15.00	14.00
		Entire	55.00	50.00
U8	U79	2c carmine (No. U362) *(1,180,000)*	1.00	1.00
		Entire	3.00	2.00
U9	U79	2c carmine, *amber* (No. U363) *(21,000)*	3.75	3.50
		Entire	11.00	9.00
U10	U79	2c carmine, *oriental buff* (No. U364) *(10,000)*	3.75	3.50
		Entire	12.00	10.00
U11	U79	2c carmine, *blue* (No. U365) *(10,000)*	4.25	4.25
		Entire	9.00	9.00
U12	U81	4c brown, *amber* (No. U372), Die 1 *(500)+*	30.00	25.00
		Entire	90.00	*70.00*
a.		Double overprint	—	

		Entire	*1,400.*	
U13	U83	4c brown (No. U374), Die 3 *(10,500)*	8.00	6.50
		Entire	35.00	*30.00*
U14	U83	4c brown, *amber* (No. U375), Die 3 *(500)*+	40.00	37.50
		Entire	120.00	90.00
U15	U84	5c blue (No. U377) *(20,000)*	4.50	4.25
		Entire	9.00	9.00
U16	U84	5c blue, *amber* (No. U378) *(500)*+	22.50	22.50
		Entire	70.00	*85.00*

1903 **Same Overprint on U.S. Issue of 1903**

U17	U85	1c green (No. U379) *(300,000)*	1.00	85
		Entire	3.00	3.00
U18	U85	1c green, *amber* (No. U380) *(1,000)*+	9.00	8.50
		Entire	16.50	*18.00*
U19	U85	1c green, *oriental buff* (No. U381) *(1,000)*+	10.00	9.00
		Entire	19.00	*20.00*
U20	U85	1c green, *blue* (No. U382) *(1,500)*+	8.25	8.00
		Entire	19.00	*20.00*
U21	U85	1c green, *manila* (No. U383) *(500)*+	14.00	14.00
		Entire	35.00	*37.50*
U22	U86	2c carmine (No. U385) *(150,500)*	3.50	2.25
		Entire	5.00	5.00
U23	U86	2c carmine, *amber* (No. U386) *(500)*+	14.00	10.00
		Entire	35.00	32.50
U24	U86	2c carmine, *oriental buff* (No. U387) *(500)*+	14.00	*18.00*
		Entire	35.00	—
U25	U86	2c carmine, *blue* (No. U388) *(500)*+	14.00	12.00
		Entire	35.00	
U26	U87	4c chocolate, *amber* (No. U391) *(500)*+	40.00	*50.00*
		Entire	100.00	*125.00*
a.		Double overprint, entire	*1,400.*	
U27	U88	5c blue, *amber* (No. U394) *(500)*+	40.00	—
		Entire	100.00	100.00

1906

Same Overprint on Re-cut U.S. issue of 1904

U28	U89	2c carmine (No. U395)	35.00	22.50
		Entire	120.00	110.00
U29	U89	2c carmine, *oriental buff* (No. U397)	55.00	*90.00*
		Entire	165.00	*190.00*

Rizal — E1

1908

U30	E1	2c green	20	10
		Entire	1.00	1.00
U31	E1	2c green, *amber*	2.50	1.50
		Entire	6.25	6.00
U32	E1	2c green, *oriental buff*	3.00	2.00
		Entire	6.00	6.00
U33	E1	2c green, *blue*	3.00	2.00
		Entire	6.00	6.00
U34	E1	2c green, *manila (500)*	5.00	—
		Entire	12.50	16.25
U34	E1	4c carmine, *McKinley*	22	15
		Entire	1.00	75
U36	E1	4c carmine, *amber*	2.50	1.50
		Entire	6.25	5.00
U37	E1	4c carmine, *oriental buff*	3.00	2.25
		Entire	6.00	11.25
U38	E1	4c carmine, *blue*	2.75	1.75
		Entire	6.00	6.00
U39	E1	4c carmine, *manila (500)*	6.25	—
		Entire	12.50	22.00

The Demand, as well as supply, determines a stamp's market value. One is as important as the other.

Rizal — E2

1927, Apr. 5

U40	E2	2c green	7.50	6.25
		Entire	19.00	17.50
		Entire, 1st day cancel		*30.00*

"Juan de la Cruz" — E3

1935, June 19

U41	E3	2c carmine	15	10
		Entire	65	50
U42	E3	4c olive green	22	18
		Entire	90	75

Nos. U30, U35, U41 and U42 Handstamped in Violet **VICTORY**

1944

U42A	E1	2c green (On U30), Entire	—	
U43	E3	2c carmine (On U41)	14.00	10.00
		Entire	30.00	*40.00*
U44	E1	4c carmine, *McKinley* (On U35)	—	—
		Entire	500.00	*500.00*
U45	E3	4c olive green (On U42)	60.00	55.00
		Entire	90.00	100.00

WRAPPERS

U. S. Wrappers Overprinted in Color of Stamp **PHILIPPINES.**

1901

W1	U77	1c green, *manila* (No. W357) *(320,000)*	1.00	85
		Entire	3.50	4.00

1905

W2	U85	1c green, *manila* (No. W384)	8.25	6.50
		Entire	16.50	14.00
a.		Double overprint, entire	*1,400.*	
W3	U86	2c carmine, *manila* (No. W389)	8.25	8.00
		Entire	16.50	16.00

Design of Philippine Envelopes

1908

W4	E1	2c green, *manila*	1.40	1.40
		Entire	8.25	8.25

POSTAL CARDS

Values are for Entires.

U.S. Cards Overprinted in Black below Stamp

a **PHILIPPINES.**

1900, Feb.

UX1	(a)	1c black (Jefferson) (UX14) *(100,000)*	12.00	10.00
a.		Without period	30.00	
UX2	(a)	2c black (Liberty) (UX16) *(20,000)*	25.00	15.00

b **PHILIPPINES**

1903, Sept. 15

UX3	(b)	1c black (McKinley) (UX18)	*900.00*	*700.00*
UX4	(b)	2c black (Liberty) (UX16)	*500.00*	*400.00*

c PHILIPPINES.

1903, Nov. 10

UX5	(c)	1c black (McKinley) (UX18)	42.50	25.00
UX6	(c)	2c black (Liberty) (UX16)	50.00	42.50

d **PHILIPPINES**

1906

UX7	(d)	1c black (McKinley) (UX18)	225.00	225.00
UX8	(d)	2c black (Liberty) (UX16)	1,200.	900.00

Designs same as postage issue of 1906

1907

UX9	A40	2c black, *buff* (Rizal)	8.25	6.50
UX10	A40	4c black, *buff* (McKinley)	20.00	15.00

Color changes

1911

UX11	A40	2c blue, *light blue* (Rizal)	6.50	6.50
a.		2c blue on white	16.50	15.00
UX12	A40	4c blue, *light blue* (McKinley)	20.00	16.50

An impression of No. UX11 exists on the back of a U.S. No. UX21.

1915

UX13	A40	2c green, *buff* (Rizal)	2.50	1.65
UX14	A40	2c yellow green, *amber*	2.00	1.00
UX15	A40	4c green, *buff* (McKinley)	14.00	10.00

Design of postage issue of 1935

1935

UX16	A53	2c red, *pale buff* (Rizal)	2.00	1.40

No. UX16 Overprinted at left of Stamp **COMMONWEALTH**

1938

UX17	A53	2c red, *pale buff*	2.00	1.40

No. UX16 Overprinted **COMMONWEALTH**

UX18	A53	2c red, *pale buff*	37.50	30.00

No. UX16 Overprinted **COMMONWEALTH**

UX19	A53	2c red, *pale buff*	3.50	3.50

Nos. UX13, UX18 and UX19 Handstamped in Violet **VICTORY**

1944

UX20	A40	2c green, *buff, Rizal* (On UX13)	*120.00*	*120.00*
UX21	A53	2c red, *pale buff* (On UX18)	*450.00*	—
UX22	A53	2c red, *pale buff* (On UX19)	*190.00*	—

Overprinted in Black at left **VICTORY**

1945, Jan. 19

UX23	A76	2c gray brown, *pale buff*	1.00	50
		First day cancel		2.50
a.		"IC" of "Victory" very close	4.00	2.25

This card was not issued without overprint.

PAID REPLY POSTAL CARDS

U.S. Paid Reply Cards of 1892-93 issues Overprinted with type "a" in blue

1900, Feb.

UY1	2c +2c blue, unsevered *(5,000)*	*120.00*	*120.00*
m.	PM2, Message card, detached	20.00	20.00
r.	PR2, Reply card, detached	20.00	20.00

Overprinted type "c" in black

1903

UY2	1c +1c black, *buff*, unsevered *(20,000)*	*120.00*	*125.00*
m.	PM1, Message card, detached	20.00	22.50
r.	PR1, Reply card, detached	20.00	22.50
UY3	2c +2c blue, unsevered *(20,000)*	250.00	
m.	PM2, Message card, detached	42.50	40.00
r.	PR2, Reply card, detached	42.50	40.00

OFFICIAL CARDS

Overprinted at left of stamp **O. B.**

1925 **On postal card No. UX13**

UZ1	A40 2c green, *buff* (Rizal)	22.50	20.00

1935 **On postal card No. UX16**

UZ2	A53 2c red, *pale buff*	10.00	11.00

Overprinted at Left of Stamp **O. B.**

1938 **On postal card No. UX19**

UZ3	A53 2c red, *pale buff*	10.00	11.00

Overprinted Below Stamp **O. B.**

1941 **Design of postage issue of 1941**

UZ4	A75 2c light green, *pale buff*	100.00	110.00

This card was not issued without overprint.

Postal Card No. UX19 Overprinted at Left of Stamp **O. B.**

1941

UZ5	A53 2c red, *pale buff*	16.50	16.50

OCCUPATION

Issued Under Japanese Occupation

Nos. 461, 438 and 439 Overprinted with Bars in Black

1942-43 **Unwmk.** ***Perf. 11x10½, 11***

N1	A75	2c apple green, *Mar. 4, 1942*	5	5
		Margin block of 4, P#	25	
a.		Pair, one without overprint	—	
N2	A58	12c black, *Apr. 30, 1943*	10	10
N3	A59	16c dark blue, *Mar. 4, 1942*	3.00	2.25

Nos. 435a, 435, 442, 443, and 423 Surcharged in Black

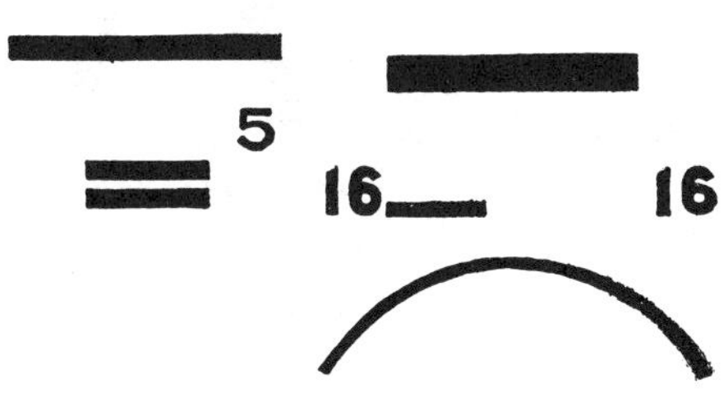

ONE PESO

1942-43 ***Perf. 11***

N4	A55(a)	5(c) on 6c golden brown *Sept. 1, 1942*	10	10
		First day cover		1.50
a.		Top bar shorter and thinner	20	20
b.		5(c) on 6c dark brown	20	20
c.		As "b", top bar shorter and thinner	20	20
N5	A62(b)	16(c) on 30c orange red, *Jan. 11, 1943*	20	20
		First day cover		1.75
N6	A63(c)	50c on 1p red orange & black, *April 30, 1943*	60	60
a.		Double surcharge		*250.00*
N7	A65(d)	1p on 4p blue & black, *April 30, 1943*	65.00	52.50
		Inverted "S" in "PESO"; position 4	80.00	80.00

On Nos. N4 and N4b, the top bar measures 1½x22½mm. On Nos. N4a and N4c, the top bar measures 1x21mm and the "5" is smaller and thinner.

CONGRATULATIONS
FALL OF
BATAAN AND
CORREGIDOR
1942
2

1942, May 18

N8	A54	2(c) on 4c yellow green	1.90	1.50
		First day cover		3.00

Issued to commemorate Japan's capture of Bataan and Corregidor. The American-Filipino forces finally surrendered May 7, 1942. No. N8 exists with "R" for "B" in BATAAN.

No. 384 Surcharged in Black

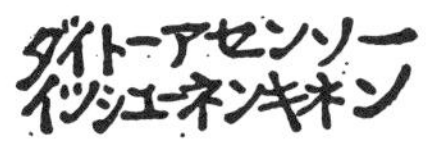

12-8-1942 5

1942, Dec. 8

N9	A54	5(c) on 4c yellow green	35	22
		First day cover		1.10

Issued to commemorate the first anniversary of the "Greater East Asia War".

Nos. C59 and C62 Surcharged in Black

ヒトー ギヨーセイフ
イツシユーオン キネン
1-23-43
2

1943, Jan. 23

N10	AP1	2(c) on 8c carmine	15	15
N11	AP1	5c on 1p sepia	30	30
		First day cover, #N10-N11		1.50

Issued to commemorate the first anniversary of the Philippine Executive Commission.

Nipa Hut
OS1

Rice Planting
OS2

Mt. Mayon and Mt. Fuji
OS3

Moro Vinta
OS4

Wmk. 257

Engraved; Typographed (2c, 6c, 25c)

1943-44 **Wmk. 257** ***Perf. 13***

N12	OS1	1c deep orange, *June 7, 1943*	5	5
N13	OS2	2c bright green, *Apr. 1, 1943*	5	5
N14	OS1	4c slate green, *June 7, 1943*	5	5
N15	OS3	5c orange brown, *Apr. 1, 1943*	5	5
N16	OS2	6c red, *July 14, 1943*	6	6
N17	OS3	10c blue green, *July 14, 1943*	5	5
N18	OS4	12c steel blue, *July 14, 1943*	55	55
N19	OS4	16c dark brown, *July 14, 1943*	5	5
N20	OS1	20c rose violet, *Aug. 16, 1943*	65	65
N21	OS3	21c violet, *Aug. 16, 1943*	12	12
N22	OS2	25c pale brown, *Aug. 16, 1943*	5	5
N23	OS3	1p deep carmine, *June 7, 1943*	14	12
N24	OS4	2p dull violet, *Sept. 16, 1943*	1.30	1.10
		First day cover		5.50
N25	OS4	5p dark olive, *Apr. 10, 1944*	4.50	3.75
		First day cover		5.50

Map of Manila Bay Showing Bataan and Corregidor — OS5

1943, May 7 **Photo.** **Unwmk.**

N26	OS5	2c carmine red	9	9
N27	OS5	5c bright green	14	14
		Colorless dot after left "5"	1.10	—
		First day cover, #N26-N27		1.50

1st anniversary of the fall of Bataan and Corregidor.

No. 440 Surcharged in Black

12 12

1943, June 20 **Engr.** ***Perf. 11***

N28	A60	12(c) on 20c light olive green	18	15
		First day cover		1.40
a.		Double surcharge	—	

350th anniversary of the printing press in the Philippines. "Limbagan" is Tagalog for "printing press."

Rizal Monument, Filipina and Philippine Flag — OS6

1943, Oct. 14 **Photo.** **Unwmk.** ***Perf. 12***

N29	OS6	5c light blue	7	7
a.		Imperf.	8	8
N30	OS6	12c orange	10	10
a.		Imperf.	12	12
N31	OS6	17c rose pink	12	12
		First day cover, #N29-N31		85
a.		Imperf.	15	15
		First day cover, #N29a-N31a		85

Issued to commemorate the "Independence of the Philippines." Japan granted "independence" Oct. 14, 1943, when the puppet republic was founded.

The imperforate stamps were issued without gum.

José Rizal
OS7

Rev. José
Burgos
OS8

Apolinario Mabini — OS9

1944, Feb. 17 Litho. Unwmk. *Perf. 12*

N32	OS7	5c blue	15	15
a.		Imperf.	15	15
N33	OS8	12c carmine	8	8
a.		Imperf.	8	8
N34	OS9	17c deep orange	10	10
		First day cover, #N32-N34		1.00
a.		Imperf.	10	10
		First day cover, #N32a-N34a, *Apr. 17*		1.50

Nos. C60 and C61 Surcharged in Black

REPÚBLIKA
NG PILIPINAS
5-7-44
5

1944, May 7 Unwmk. *Perf. 11*

N35	AP1	5(c) on 20c ultramarine	35	35
N36	AP1	12(c) on 60c blue green	65	65
		First day cover, #N35-N36		2.00

2nd anniversary of the fall of Bataan and Corregidor.

José P. Laurel — OS10

1945, Jan. 12 Litho. Unwmk. *Imperf.*
Without Gum

N37	OS10	5c dull violet brown	5	5
N38	OS10	7c blue green	7	5
N39	OS10	20c chalky blue	10	8
		First day cover, #N37-N39		65

Issued belatedly on Jan. 12, 1945, to commemorate the first anniversary of the puppet Philippine Republic, Oct. 14, 1944. "S" stands for "sentimos".

The special cancellation devices prepared for use on Oct. 14, 1944, were employed on "First Day" covers Jan. 12, 1945.

OCCUPATION SEMI-POSTAL

Woman, Farming and Cannery — OSP1

1942, Nov. 12 Litho. Unwmk. *Perf. 12*

NB1	OSP1	2c + 1c pale violet	10	10
NB2	OSP1	5c + 1c bright green	7	7
NB3	OSP1	16c + 2c orange	9.00	6.50
		First day cover, #NB1-NB3		12.00

Issued to promote the campaign to produce and conserve food. The surtax aided the Red Cross.

Scott's editorial staff cannot undertake to identify, authenticate or appraise stamps and postal markings.

Souvenir Sheet

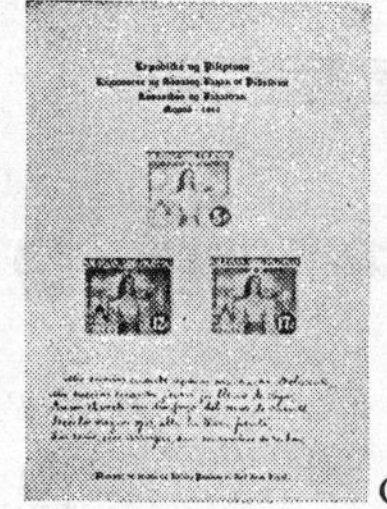

OSP2

1943, Oct. 14 Without Gum *Imperf.*

NB4	OSP2	Sheet of three	17.50	*1.00*
		First day cover, Manila		*2.50*

Issued to commemorate the "Independence of the Philippines."

No. NB4 contains one each of Nos. N29a-N31a. Marginal inscription is from Rizal's "Last Farewell". Size: 127x177mm. Sold for 2.50p.

Nos. N18, N20 and N21 Surcharged in Black

BAHA
1943
+21

1943, Dec. 8 Wmk. 257 *Perf. 13*

NB5	OS4	12c + 21c steel blue	10	10
NB6	OS1	20c + 36c rose violet	8	8
NB7	OS3	21c + 40c violet	10	10
		First day cover, #NB5-NB7		1.20

The surtax was for the benefit of victims of a Luzon flood. "Baha" is Tagalog for "flood."

Souvenir Sheet

OSP3

1944, Feb. 9 Litho. Unwmk. *Imperf.*
Without Gum

NB8	OSP3	Sheet of three	1.40	*1.65*
		First day cover		*3.50*

No. NB8 contains one each of Nos. N32a-N34a.

The sheet sold for 1p, the surtax going to a fund for the care of heroes' monuments. Size: 101x143mm. No. NB8 exists with 5c inverted.

OCCUPATION POSTAGE DUE

No. J15 Overprinted with Bar in Blue

1942, Oct. 14 Unwmk. *Perf. 11*

NJ1	D3	3c on 4c brown red	15.00	*6.00*
		First day cover		*15.00*
		Double bar	—	

On copies of No. J15, two lines were drawn in India ink with a ruling pen across "United States of America" by employees of the Short Paid Section of the Manila Post Office to make a provisional 3c postage due stamp which was used from Sept. 1, 1942 (when the letter rate was raised from 2c to 5c) until Oct. 14 when No. NJ1 went on sale. Value on cover, $100.

OCCUPATION OFFICIAL

Nos. 461, 413, 435, 435a and 442 Overprinted or Surcharged in Black with Bars and

公用
(K.P.)

1943-44 Unwmk. *Perf. 11x10½, 11*

NO1	A75	2c apple green, *Apr. 7, 1943*	5	5
		Margin block of 4, P#	25	
a.		Double overprint		
NO2	A55	5(c) on 6c dark brown (On No. 413), *June 26, 1944*	14.00	14.00
		First day cover		*30.00*
NO3	A55	5(c) on 6c golden brown (On No. 435a), *Apr. 7, 1943*	10	10
a.		Narrower spacing between bars	14	14
b.		5(c) on 6c dark brown (On No. 435)	10	8
c.		As "b", narrower spacing between bars	14	14
NO4	A62	16(c) on 30c orange red, *Apr. 7, 1943*	30	30
a.		Wider spacing between bars	30	30
		First day cover (#NO1, NO3-NO4)		*35.00*

On Nos. NO3 and NO3b the bar deleting "United States of America" is 9¾ to 10mm above the bar deleting "Common". On Nos. NO3a and NO3c, the spacing is 8 to 8½mm.

On No. NO4, the center bar is 19mm long, 3½mm below the top bar and 6mm above the Japanese characters. On No. NO4a, the center bar is 20½mm long, 9mm below the top bar and 1mm above the Japanese characters.

"K.P." stands for Kagamitang Pampamahalaan, "Official Business" in Tagalog.

Nos. 435 and 435a Surcharged in Black

REPUBLIKA NG
PILIPINAS
(K. P.)

1944, Aug. 28 Unwmk. *Perf. 11*

NO5	A55	(5c) on 6c golden brown	7	7
a.		5(c) on 6c dark brown	7	7

Nos. O34 and C62 Overprinted in Black

Pilipinas
REPUBLIKA
K.P.
a

REPUBLIKA NG PILIPINAS
(K.P.)

b

NO6	A60(a)	20c light olive green	22	22
NO7	AP1(b)	1p sepia	65	65
		First day cover, #NO5-NO7		2.00

OCCUPATION ENVELOPES

No. U41 Surcharged in Black

5 5

1943, Apr. 1

NU1	E3	5c on 2c carmine	35	20
		Entire	1.65	1.00
		Entire, 1st day cancel		3.50

No. U41 Surcharged in Black

REPUBLIKA NG PILIPINAS

5 5

1944, Feb. 17

NU2	E3	5c on 2c carmine	35	20
		Entire	1.65	1.00
		Entire, 1st day cancel		5.00
a.		Inverted surcharged	—	
b.		Double surcharge	—	
c.		Both 5's missing	—	

OCCUPATION POSTAL CARDS

Values are for entire cards.

Nos. UX19 and UZ4 Overprinted with Bars in Black

1942

NUX1 A53 2c red, *pale buff, Mar. 4, 1942* 5.00 2.50
First day cancel *65.00*
a. Vertical obliteration bars reversed *140.00*
NUX2 A75 2c light green, *pale buff, Dec. 12, 1942* 2.50 2.00
First day cancel 6.00

Rice Planting — A77

1943, May 17

NUX3 A77 2c green 1.00 *1.00*
First day cancel, Manila 2.00

OCCUPATION OFFICIAL CARDS

Nos. UX19, UX17 and UX18 Overprinted in Black with Bars and 公用 (K.P.)

1943, Apr. 7

NUZ1 A53 2c red, *pale buff* 4.00 3.00
First day cancel 100.00
a. On No. UX17 — —
b. On No. UX18 — —

No. NUX3 Overprinted in Black REPUBLIKA NG PILIPINAS (K. P.)

1944, Aug. 28

NUZ2 A77 2c green 1.50 *1.00*
First day cancel 2.00
a. Double overprint —

FILIPINO REVOLUTIONARY GOVERNMENT

The Filipino Republic was instituted by Gen. Emilio Aguinaldo on June 23, 1899. At the same time he assumed the office of President. Aguinaldo dominated the greater part of the island of Luzon and some of the smaller islands until late in 1899. He was taken prisoner by United States Troops on March 23, 1901.

The devices composing the National Arms, adopted by the Filipino Revolutionary Government, are emblems of the Katipunan political secret society or of Katipunan origin. The letters "K K K" on these stamps are the initials of this society whose complete name is "Kataas-taasang, Kagalang-galang Katipunan nang Manga Anak nang Bayan," meaning "Sovereign Worshipful Association of the Sons of the Country."

The regular postage and telegraph stamps were in use on Luzon as early as Nov. 10, 1898. Owing to the fact that stamps for the different purposes were not always available together with a lack of proper instructions, any of the adhesives were permitted to be used in the place of the other. Hence telegraph and revenue stamps were accepted for postage and postage stamps for revenue or telegraph charges. In addition to the regular postal emission, there are a number of provisional stamps, issues of local governments of islands and towns.

POSTAGE ISSUES

Coat of Arms
A1 A2 A3

1898-99 **Unwmk.** ***Perf. 11½***

Y1 A1 2c red 7.00 6.00
a. Double impression *200.00*
Y2 A2 2c red 5 25
a. Imperf., pair —
b. Double impression —
c. Imperf. horizontally, pair — —
d. Horiz. pair, imperf. between —
Y3 A3 2c red 2.00

REGISTRATION STAMP

RS1

YF1 RS1 8c green 12 1.40
a. Imperf., pair —
b. Imperf. vertically, pair —

NEWSPAPER STAMP

N1

YP1 N1 1m black 5
a. Imperf., pair 10

PROOFS

1906

			DIE (1) Large	DIE (2) Small	(2a)	PLATE (4) Glazed Card
241P	2c	yellow green		150.00	260.00	
242P	4c	carmine lake	*400.00*	150.00	260.00	
243P	6c	violet	*400.00*	150.00	260.00	
244P	8c	brown	*400.00*	150.00	260.00	
245P	10c	dark blue		150.00	260.00	
246P	12c	brown lake		150.00	260.00	
247P	16c	violet black	*400.00*	150.00	260.00	
248P	20c	orange brown		150.00	260.00	
249P	26c	violet brown		150.00	260.00	
250P	30c	olive green	*400.00*	150.00	260.00	
251P	1p	orange		150.00	260.00	
252P	2p	black		150.00	260.00	
253P	4p	dark blue		150.00	260.00	
254P	10p	dark green		150.00	260.00	
1909-13						
255P	12c	red orange		150.00	260.00	
256P	16c	olive green		150.00	260.00	
257P	20c	yellow		150.00	260.00	
258P	26c	blue green		150.00	260.00	
259P	30c	ultramarine		150.00	260.00	
260P	1p	pale violet		150.00	260.00	
260AP	2p	violet brown		150.00	260.00	
275P	30c	gray		150.00	260.00	
1923						
303P	16c	olive bister	400.00			
303TC	16c	olive green	400.00			
1926						
322P	18c	light brown & black				—
1932						
357P	18c	red orange	400.00			
357TC	18c	orange red	400.00			
1935						
383P	2c	rose	400.00			
384P	4c	yellow green	400.00			
385P	6c	dark brown	400.00			
386P	8c	violet	400.00			
387P	10c	rose carmine	400.00			
388P	12c	black	400.00			
389P	16c	dark blue	400.00			
390P	20c	light olive green	400.00			
390TC	20c	black	—			
391P	26c	indigo	400.00			
392P	30c	orange red	400.00			
393P	1p	red orange & black	400.00			
394P	2p	bister brown & black	400.00			
395P	4p	blue & black	400.00			
396P	5p	green & black	400.00			
1936						
408P	2c	orange brown	400.00			
408TC	2c	yellow green	400.00			
1937						
425P	2c	yellow green		200.00		
1939						
452P	2c	yellow green		200.00		
453P	6c	carmine		200.00		
454P	12c	bright blue		200.00		
1939						
455P	2c	green	350.00	200.00		
456P	6c	orange		200.00		
457P	12c	carmine		200.00		
1940						
458P	2c	dark orange	350.00	200.00		
459P	6c	dark green		200.00		
460P	12c	purple		200.00		
1941						
461P	2c	apple green		200.00		
1946						
497P	2c	sepia		—		

AIR POST

1941

C59P	8c	carmine		350.00
C60P	20c	ultramarine		350.00
C61P	60c	blue green		350.00
C62P	1p	sepia		350.00

SPECIAL DELIVERY

1906

E2P	20c	ultramarine	400.00	140.00	225.00
E2TC	20c	green		150.00	

POSTAGE DUE

1899

J1P	1c	deep claret		350.00
J2P	2c	deep claret		350.00
J3P	5c	deep claret		350.00
J4P	10c	deep claret		350.00
J5P	50c	deep claret		350.00
1901				
J6P	3c	deep claret		350.00
J7P	30c	deep claret		350.00

SPECIMEN STAMPS

Overprinted U.S. Type E in Black Specimen.

1899

213S E 1c yellow green 100.00
214S E 2c orange red 100.00
215S E 3c purple 100.00
216S E 5c blue 100.00
217S E 10c brown, type I 100.00
218S E 15c olive brown 100.00
219S E 50c orange 100.00

Special Printings (Paris 1899) with "Specimen" overprints exist. Value, each $350.

Overprinted U.S. Type R in Black *Specimen*

1917-25

290S R 2c green 25.00
291S R 4c carmine 25.00
292S R 6c deep violet 25.00
293S R 8c yellow brown 25.00
294S R 10c deep blue 25.00
295S R 12c red orange 25.00
297S R 20c orange yellow 25.00
298S R 26c green 25.00
299S R 30c gray 25.00
300S R 1p pale violet 25.00
301S R 2p violet brown 25.00
302S R 4p blue 25.00

1923-26

303S R 16c olive bister 25.00
304S R 10p deep green 25.00

1926 **Overprinted Type R in Red**

319S R 2c green & black 35.00

320S R	4c	carmine & black	35.00
321S R	16c	olive green & black	35.00
322S R	18c	light brown & black	35.00
323S R	20c	orange & black	35.00
324S R	24c	gray & black	35.00
325S R	1p	rose lilac & black	35.00

Overprinted U.S.Type S in Red *Cancelled*

1926

319S S	2c	green & black	35.00
320S S	4c	carmine & black	35.00
321S S	16c	olive green & black	35.00
322S S	18c	light brown & black	35.00
323S S	20c	orange & black	35.00
324S S	24c	gray & black	35.00
325S S	1p	rose lilac & black	35.00

Imperforate copies of this set, on glazed cards with centers in brown, are known with the "Cancelled" overprint.

Handstamped "SPECIMEN" in Red Capitals, 13x3mm

1925

340S	2c	green	20.00
341S	4c	carmine	20.00
342S	6c	deep violet	20.00
343S	8c	yellow brown	20.00
344S	10c	deep blue	20.00
345S	12c	red orange	20.00
346S	16c	olive bister	20.00
347S	20c	yellow	20.00
348S	26c	blue green	20.00
349S	30c	gray	20.00
350S	1p	violet	20.00
351S	2p	violet brown	20.00
352S	4p	deep blue	27.50
353S	10p	deep green	35.00

Special Delivery

1919 Overprinted Type R in Black

E5S R	20c	ultramarine	165.00

Handstamped "SPECIMEN" in Red Capitals, 13x3mm

1925

E6aS	20c	violet blue	165.00

Postage Due

1899 Overprinted Type E in Black

J1S E	1c	deep claret	100.00
J2S E	2c	deep claret	100.00
J3S E	5c	deep claret	100.00
J4S E	10c	deep claret	100.00
J5S E	50c	deep claret	100.00

Official

1926 Overprinted Type R in Red

O1S R	2c	green & black	30.00
O2S R	4c	carmine & black	30.00
O3S R	18c	light brown & black	30.00
O4S R	20c	orange & black	30.00

1926 Overprinted Type S in Red

O1S S	2c	green & black	30.00
O2S S	4c	carmine & black	30.00
O3S S	18c	light brown & black	30.00
O4S S	20c	orange & black	30.00

PUERTO RICO

(Porto Rico)

United States troops landed at Guanica Bay, Puerto Rico, on July 25, 1898, and mail service between various points in Puerto Rico began soon after under the authority of General Wilson, acting governor of the conquered territory, who authorized a provisional service early in August, 1898. The first Military Postal Station was opened at La Playa de Ponce on August 3, 1898. Control of the island passed formally to the United States on October 18, 1898. Twenty-one military stations operating under the administration of the Military Postal Service, were authorized in Puerto Rico after the Spanish-American war. After the overprinted provisional issue of 1900, unoverprinted stamps of the United States replaced those of Puerto Rico.

Name changed to Puerto Rico by Act of Congress, approved May 17, 1932.

100 CENTS = 1 DOLLAR.

PROVISIONAL ISSUES

Ponce Issue

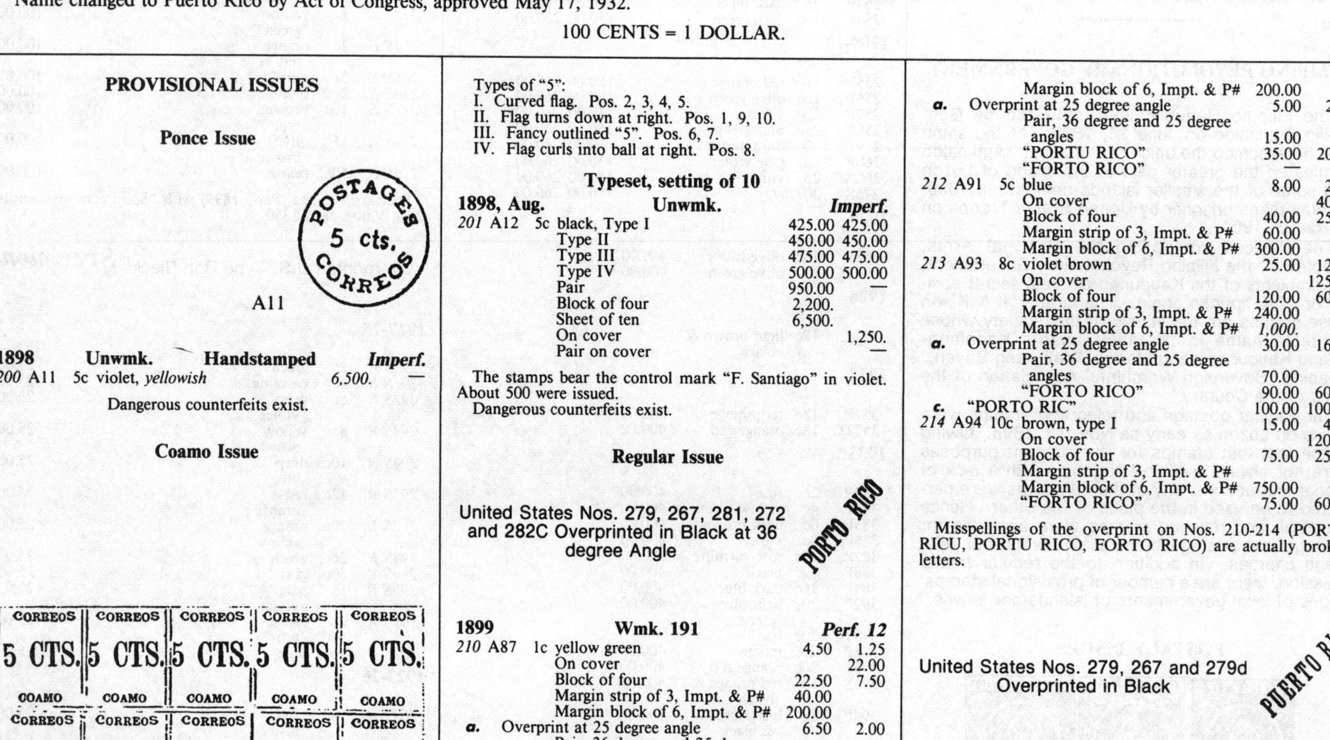

A11

1898 Unwmk. Handstamped *Imperf.*

200 A11	5c violet, *yellowish*		*6,500.*	—

Dangerous counterfeits exist.

Coamo Issue

A12

Types of "5":
I. Curved flag. Pos. 2, 3, 4, 5.
II. Flag turns down at right. Pos. 1, 9, 10.
III. Fancy outlined "5". Pos. 6, 7.
IV. Flag curls into ball at right. Pos. 8.

Typeset, setting of 10

1898, Aug. Unwmk. *Imperf.*

201 A12	5c black, Type I	425.00	425.00
	Type II	450.00	450.00
	Type III	475.00	475.00
	Type IV	500.00	500.00
	Pair	950.00	—
	Block of four	2,200.	
	Sheet of ten	6,500.	
	On cover		1,250.
	Pair on cover		—

The stamps bear the control mark "F. Santiago" in violet. About 500 were issued.
Dangerous counterfeits exist.

Regular Issue

United States Nos. 279, 267, 281, 272 and 282C Overprinted in Black at 36 degree Angle

1899 Wmk. 191 *Perf. 12*

210 A87	1c yellow green	4.50	1.25
	On cover		22.00
	Block of four	22.50	7.50
	Margin strip of 3, Impt. & P#	40.00	
	Margin block of 6, Impt. & P#	200.00	
a.	Overprint at 25 degree angle	6.50	2.00
	Pair, 36 degree and 25 degree angles	18.00	
	"PORTO RICU"	25.00	—
211 A88	2c carmine, type III	3.75	1.00
	On cover		15.00
	Block of four	20.00	7.00
	Margin strip of 3, Impt. & P#	32.50	
	Margin block of 6, Impt. & P#	200.00	
a.	Overprint at 25 degree angle	5.00	2.00
	Pair, 36 degree and 25 degree angles	15.00	
	"PORTU RICO"	35.00	20.00
	"FORTO RICO"	—	—
212 A91	5c blue	8.00	2.25
	On cover		40.00
	Block of four	40.00	25.00
	Margin strip of 3, Impt. & P#	60.00	
	Margin block of 6, Impt. & P#	300.00	
213 A93	8c violet brown	25.00	12.00
	On cover		125.00
	Block of four	120.00	60.00
	Margin strip of 3, Impt. & P#	240.00	
	Margin block of 6, Impt. & P#	*1,000.*	
a.	Overprint at 25 degree angle	30.00	16.00
	Pair, 36 degree and 25 degree angles	70.00	
	"FORTO RICO"	90.00	60.00
c.	"PORTO RIC"	100.00	100.00
214 A94	10c brown, type I	15.00	4.50
	On cover		120.00
	Block of four	75.00	25.00
	Margin strip of 3, Impt. & P#		
	Margin block of 6, Impt. & P#	750.00	
	"FORTO RICO"	75.00	60.00

Misspellings of the overprint on Nos. 210-214 (PORTO RICU, PORTU RICO, FORTO RICO) are actually broken letters.

United States Nos. 279, 267 and 279d Overprinted in Black

1900

215 A87	1c yellow green	5.00	1.25
	On cover		17.50
	Block of four	20.00	6.50
	Margin strip of 3, Impt. & P#	27.50	

Margin block of 6, Impt. & P# 150.00
216 A88 2c carmine, type III 4.00 1.00
On cover 15.00
Block of four 20.00 4.50
Margin strip of 3, Impt. & P# 30.00
Margin block of 6, Impt. & P# 150.00
a. 2c orange red, type III 4.50 1.00
b. Inverted overprint —

Special Printing

In 1899 one sheet each of Nos. 210-212 and 214, and two sheets each of Nos. 213, J1-J3 were specially overprinted "Porto Rico" for display at the Paris Exposition. Value, each $400. Later another special printing of Nos. 212-216, J1-J3 was made reading "Puerto Rico." Value, each $550.

Of both printings, all but a few copies were destroyed. Nearly all existing copies of Nos. 215-216 are handstamped "Special Surcharge" on the back.

AIR POST

In 1938 a series of eight labels, two of which were surcharged, was offered to the public as "Semi-Official Air Post Stamps", the claim being that they had been authorized by the "Puerto Rican postal officials." These labels, printed by the Ever Ready Label Co. of New York, were a private issue of Aerovias Nacionales Puerto Rico, operating a passenger and air express service. Instead of having been authorized by the postal officials, they were at first forbidden but later tolerated by the Post Office Department at Washington.

In 1941 a further set of eight triangular labels was prepared and offered to collectors, and again the Post Office Department officials at Washington objected and forbade their use after September 16, 1941.

These labels represent only the charge for service rendered by a private enterprise for transporting matter outside the mails by plane. Their use did not and does not eliminate the payment of postage on letters carried by air express, which must in every instance be paid by United States postage stamps.

POSTAGE DUE STAMPS

United States Nos. J38, J39 and J42 Overprinted in Black at 36 degree Angle

1899 **Wmk. 191** ***Perf. 12***

J1 D2 1c deep claret 16.00 5.00
On cover 125.00
Block of four 70.00 22.00
Margin strip of 3, Impt. & P# 120.00
Margin block of 6, Impt. & P# *600.00*
a. Overprint at 25 degree angle 20.00 7.00
Pair, 36 degree and 25 degree angles 50.00
J2 D2 2c deep claret 10.00 5.50
On cover 250.00
Block of four 50.00 20.00
Margin strip of 3, Impt. & P# 120.00
Margin block of 6, Impt. & P# *600.00*
a. Overprint at 25 degree angle 14.00 6.50
Pair, 36 degree and 25 degree angles 40.00
J3 D2 10c deep claret 120.00 35.00
On cover 400.00
Block of four 500.00 —
Margin strip of 3, Impt. & P# *600.00*
Margin block of 6, Impt. & P# *2,200.*
a. Overprint at 25 degree angle 120.00 60.00
Pair, 36 degree and 25 degree angles 300.00

ENVELOPES

U.S. Envelopes of 1887 Issue Overprinted in Black

PORTO RICO.

20mm long

1899-1900

Note: Some envelopes for which there was no obvious need were issued in small quantities. Anyone residing in Puerto Rico could, by depositing with his postmaster the required amount, order any envelope in quantities of 500, or multiples thereof, provided it was on the schedule of U.S. envelopes. Such special orders are indicated by an plus sign, i. e., Nos. U15 and U18, and half the quantities of Nos. U16 and U17.

U1 U71 2c green (No. U311) *(3,000)* 11.00 15.00
Entire 35.00 42.50
a. Double overprint, entire —
U2 U74 5c blue (No. U330) *(1,000)* 15.00 15.00
Entire 42.50 42.50
Double overprint, entire —

U.S. Envelopes of 1899 Overprinted in color of the stamp

PORTO RICO.

21mm long

U3 U79 2c carmine (No. U362) *(100,000)* 2.25 2.25
Entire 7.50 9.50
U4 U84 5c blue (No. U377) *(10,000)* 6.00 7.50
Entire 13.50 25.00

Overprinted in Black PORTO RICO.

19mm long

U5 U77 1c green, *blue* (No. U355) *(1,000)* 575.00
Entire 1,750.
U6 U79 2c carmine, *amber* (No. U363), Die 2 *(500)* 400.00 450.00
Entire 950.00 1,150.
U7 U79 2c carmine, *oriental buff* (No. U364), Die 2 *(500)* 450.00
Entire 1,150.
U8 U80 2c carmine, *oriental buff* (No. U369), Die 3 *(500)* 575.00
Entire 1,150.
U9 U79 2c carmine, *blue* (No. U365), Die 2
Entire *3,500.*
U10 U83 4c brown (No. U374), Die 3 *(500)* 190.00
Entire 300.00 *400.00*

U.S. Envelopes of 1899 Issue Overprinted

PUERTO RICO.

23mm long

U11 U79 2c carmine (No. U362) red overprint *(100,000)* 3.00 2.25
Entire 7.50 8.25
U12 U79 2c carmine, *oriental buff* (No. U364), Die 2, black overprint *(1,000)* — 275.00
Entire *1,000.* *1,100.*
U13 U80 2c carmine, *oriental buff* (No. U369), Die 3, black overprint *(1,000)* 275.00
Entire *1,750.*
U14 U84 5c blue (No. U377) blue overprint *(10,000)* 11.00 11.00
Entire 35.00 42.50

Overprinted in Black PUERTO RICO.

U15 U77 1c green, *oriental buff* (No. U354) *(500)+* 15.00 37.50
Entire 57.50 60.00
U16 U77 1c green, *blue* (No. U355) *(1,000)+* 18.50 37.50
Entire 72.50 100.00
U17 U79 2c carmine, *oriental buff* (No. U364) *(1,000)+* 15.00 37.50
Entire 72.50 100.00
U18 U79 2c carmine, *blue* (No. U365) *(500)+* 15.00 37.50
Entire 57.50 100.00

There were two settings of the overprint, with minor differences, which are found on Nos. U16 and U17.

WRAPPER

U.S. Wrapper of 1899 Issue Overprinted in Green

PORTO RICO.

21mm long

W1 U77 1c green, *manila* (No. W357) *(15,000)* 6.00 22.50
Entire 13.50 67.50

POSTAL CARDS

Values are for Entires.

Imprinted below stamp PORTO RICO.

1899-1900 **U.S. Postal Card No. UX14**

UX1 PC8 1c black, *buff,* imprint 21mm long 125.00 150.00
b. Double imprint *2,000.*

Imprinted below stamp PORTO RICO.

UX1A PC8 1c black, *buff,* imprint 20mm long 800.00 1,200.

Imprinted below stamp PORTO RICO.

UX2 PC8 1c black, *buff,* imprint 26mm long 125.00 170.00

Imprinted below stamp PUERTO RICO.

UX3 PC8 1c black, *buff* 125.00 170.00

SPECIMEN

Overprinted U.S. Type E in black Specimen.

1899

210S E 1c yellow green 150.00
211S E 2c carmine 150.00
212S E 5c blue 150.00
213S E 8c violet brown 150.00
214S E 10c brown 150.00

The Special Printing of Nos. 212-214 (5c, 8c, 10c) with "Puerto Rico" overprint received the "Specimen" overprint. Value about $300 each.

Postage Due

1899

J1S E 1c deep claret 150.00
J2S E 2c deep claret 150.00
J3S E 10c deep claret 150.00

REVENUE

U.S. Revenue Stamps Nos. R163, R168-R169, R171 and Type of 1898 Surcharged in Black or Dark Blue

PORTO RICO
10 c.
Excise Revenue
a

b

1901 **Wmk. 191R** ***Hyphen-hole Roulette 7***

R1 R15(a) 1c on 1c pale blue (Bk) 5.00 4.25
R2 R15(a) 10c on 10c dark brown 6.50 5.00
R3 R15(a) 25c on 25c purple brown 80.00 5.50
R4 R15(a) 50c on 50c slate violet 12.50 7.00
R5 R16(b) $1 on $1 pale greenish gray 37.50 10.00
R6 R16(b) $3 on $3 pale greenish gray 40.00 15.00
R7 R16(b) $5 on $5 pale greenish gray 45.00 20.00
R8 R16(b) $10 on $10 pale greenish gray 65.00 30.00
R9 R16(b) $50 on $50 pale greenish gray 200.00 75.00

Lines of 1c surcharge spaced farther apart; total depth of surcharge 15¾mm instead of 11mm.

RECTIFIED SPIRITS

RECTIFIED

U.S. Wine Stamps of 1933-34 Overprinted in Red or Carmine

SPIRITS

1934 **Offset Printing** **Wmk. 191R** ***Rouletted 7***

Overprint Lines 14mm Apart, Second Line 25mm Long

RE1 RE5 2c green 6.00
RE2 RE5 3c green 27.00
RE3 RE5 4c green 7.50
RE4 RE5 5c green 6.00
RE5 RE5 6c green 7.50

Overprint Lines 21½mm Apart, Second Line 23½mm Long

RE6 RE2 50c green 13.50
RE7 RE2 60c green 12.00

Handstamped overprints are also found on U.S. Wine stamps of 1933-34.

Puerto Rico stamps can be mounted in Scott's U.S. Possessions Album.

U.S. Wine Stamps of 1933-34 Overprinted in Black

RECTIFIED

RECTIFIED

SPIRITS
a

SPIRITS
b

1934	Offset Printing	Wmk. 191R	Rouletted 7
RE8	RE5(a)	1c green	12.00
RE9	RE5(a)	2c green	6.00
RE10	RE5(a)	2c green	30.00
RE11	RE5(a)	5c green	6.00
RE12	RE5(a)	6c green	7.50
RE13	RE2(b)	50c green	9.00
RE14	RE2(b)	60c green	7.50
RE15	RE2(b)	72c green	37.50
RE16	RE2(b)	80c green	20.00

RECTIFIED SPIRITS

U.S. Wine Stamps of 1933-34 Overprinted in Black

PUERTO RICO

1934	Offset Printing	Wmk. 191R	Rouletted 7
RE17	RE5	½c green	1.50
RE18	RE5	1c green	35
RE19	RE5	2c green	30
RE20	RE5	3c green	2.00
RE21	RE5	4c green	45
RE22	RE5	5c green	60
RE23	RE5	6c green	75
RE24	RE5	10c green	2.00
RE25	RE5	30c green	17.50
		Overprint Lines 12½mm Apart	
RE26	RE2	36c green	3.75
RE27	RE2	40c green	3.00
RE28	RE2	50c green	1.50
RE29	RE2	60c green	30
a.		Inverted overprint	—
RE30	RE2	72c green	1.75
RE31	RE2	80c green	2.50
RE32	RE2	$1 green	4.50

George Sewall Boutwell — R1

Engr. (8c & 58c); Litho.

1942-57		Wmk. 191		Rouletted 7
		Without Gum		
RE33	R1	½c carmine	1.75	75
RE34	R1	1c sepia	4.50	2.00
RE35	R1	2c bright yellow green	60	9
RE36	R1	3c lilac	35.00	20.00
RE37	R1	4c olive	1.25	30
RE38	R1	5c orange	2.75	60
RE39	R1	6c red brown	2.00	75
RE40	R1	8c bright pink ('57)	4.25	2.00
RE41	R1	10c bright purple	6.50	3.00
RE41A	R1	30c vermilion	100.00	
RE42	R1	36c dull yellow	90.00	40.00
RE43	R1	40c deep claret	100.00	4.50
RE44	R1	50c green	6.00	2.50
RE45	R1	58c red orange	42.50	3.50
RE46	R1	60c brown	75	9
RE47	R1	62c black	1.75	45
RE48	R1	72c blue	20.00	60
RE49	R1	77½c olive gray	6.00	2.00
RE50	R1	80c brownish black	7.50	3.50
RE51	R1	$1 violet	45.00	12.50

The 30c is believed not to have been placed in use.

RYUKYU ISLANDS

LOCATION — Chain of 63 islands between Japan and Formosa, separating the East China Sea from the Pacific Ocean.
GOVT. — Semi-autonomous under United States administration.
AREA — 848 sq. mi.
POP. — 945,465 (1970)
CAPITAL — Naha, Okinawa

The Ryukyus were part of Japan until American forces occupied them in 1945. The islands reverted to Japan May 15, 1972.

100 Sen = 1 Yen
100 Cents = 1 Dollar (1958).

Cycad — A1

Lily — A2

Sailing Ship — A3

Farmer — A4

Ryukyu Islands stamps can be mounted in Scott's Ryukyu Islands Album.

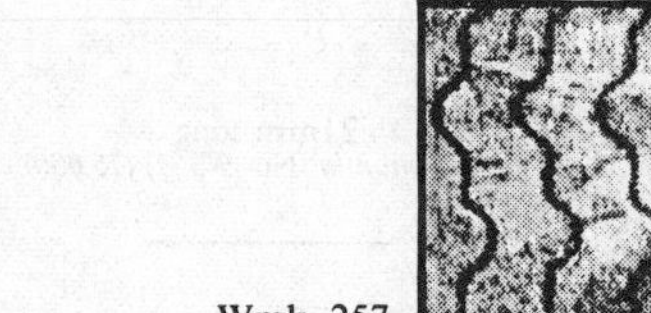

Wmk. 257

1948-49		Typo.	Wmk. 257	Perf. 13
		Second Printing		
1	A1	5s magenta	1.25	1.25
2	A2	10s yel grn	3.25	2.75
3	A1	20s yel grn	2.25	2.00
4	A3	30s vermilion	1.25	1.25
5	A2	40s magenta	1.25	1.25
6	A3	50s ultra	2.75	2.75
7	A4	1y ultra	3.00	3.00
		First Printing		
1a	A1	5s magenta	2.25	4.00
2a	A2	10s yel grn	1.40	2.50
3a	A1	20s yel grn	1.40	2.50
4a	A3	30s vermilion	2.25	3.50
5a	A2	40s magenta	45.00	45.00
6a	A3	50s ultra	2.25	4.00
7a	A4	1y ultra	250.00	225.00
		First day covers. #1a-7a, each		250.00

First printing: thick yellow gum, dull colors, rough perforations, grayish paper. Second printing: white gum, sharp colors, cleancut perforations, white paper.

Issue dates: First printing, July 1, 1948: second printing, July 18, 1949.

Imprint Blocks of 10, Unused	
1	30.00
1a	40.00
2	60.00
2a	25.00
3	40.00
3a	25.00
4	30.00
4a	40.00
5	25.00
5a	550.00
6	50.00
6a	40.00
7	50.00
7a	*3,500.*

Roof Tiles — A5

Ryukyu University — A6

Designs: 1y, Ryukyu girl. 2y, Shuri Castle. 3y, Guardian dragon. 4y, Two women. 5y, Sea shells.

1950, Jan. 21 Photo. Unwmk. *Perf. 13x13½*
Off-white Paper

No.	Type	Description	Unused	Used
8	A5	50s dk car rose	20	20
		First day cover		16.00
		Imprint block of 6	2.00	
a.		White paper	50	50
		First day cover, *Sept. 6, 1958*		27.50
		Imprint block of 10	6.50	
9	A5	1y dp bl	2.25	2.00
		First day cover		16.00
		Imprint block of 6	15.00	
10	A5	2y rose vio	8.25	5.00
		First day cover		16.00
		Imprint block of 6	60.00	
11	A5	3y car rose	16.00	5.00
		First day cover		16.00
		Imprint block of 6	125.00	
12	A5	4y grnsh gray	10.00	4.25
		First day cover		16.00
		Imprint block of 6	75.00	
13	A5	5y bl grn	4.50	3.75
		First day cover		16.00
		Imprint block of 6	40.00	
		First day cover. #8-13		110.00

No. 8a has colorless gum and an 8-character imprint in the sheet margin. The original 1950 printing on off-white paper has yellowish gum and a 5-character imprint.

1951, Feb. 12 *Perf. 13½x13*

No.	Type	Description	Unused	Used
14	A6	3y red brn	37.50	12.00
		First day cover		45.00
		Imprint block of 6	275.00	

Opening of Ryukyu University, Feb. 12.

Pine Tree — A7

1951, Feb. 19 *Perf. 13*

No.	Type	Description	Unused	Used
15	A7	3y dk grn	32.50	10.00
		First day cover		45.00
		Imprint block of 6	250.00	

Reforestation Week, Feb. 18-24.

Nos. 8 and 10 Surcharged in Black

改 訂 * 10圓	改 訂 * 10圓	改 訂 * 10圓
Type I	Type II	Type III

Three types of 10y surcharge:
I. Narrow-spaced rules, "10" normal spacing.
II. Wide-spaced rules, "10" normal spacing.
III. Rules and "10" both wide-spaced.

1952 *Perf. 13x13½*

No.	Type	Description	Unused	Used
16	A5	10y on 50s dk car rose (II)	8.00	8.00
		Imprint block of 6	72.50	
a.		Type I	24.00	24.00
		Imprint block of 6	200.00	
b.		Type III	30.00	30.00
		Imprint block of 6	225.00	
17	A5	100y on 2y rose vio	1,750.	1,250.
		Imprint block of 6	*13,500.*	

These are two types of surcharge on No. 17.

Dove, Bean Sprout and Map — A8

Madanbashi Bridge — A9

1952, Apr. 1 *Perf. 13½x13*

No.	Type	Description	Unused	Used
18	A8	3y dp plum	57.50	18.00
		First day cover		60.00
		Imprint block of 10	900.00	

Establishment of the Government of the Ryukyu Islands (GRI), April 1, 1952.

1952-53

Designs: 2y, Main Hall, Shuri Castle. 3y, Shurei Gate. 6y, Stone Gate, Soenji Temple, Naha. 10y, Benzaiten-do Temple. 30y, Sonohan Utaki (altar) at Shuri Castle. 50y, Tamaudun (royal mausoleum). Shuri. 100y, Stone Bridge, Hosho Pond, Enkaku Temple.

No.	Type	Description	Unused	Used
19	A9	1y red, *Nov. 20, 1952*	20	20
		Imprint block of 10	2.75	
20	A9	2y green, *Nov. 20, 1952*	28	28
		Imprint block of 10	3.75	
21	A9	3y aqua, *Nov. 20, 1952*	35	35
		First day cover, #19-21		27.50
		Imprint block of 10	5.25	
22	A9	6y blue, *Jan. 20, 1953*	1.40	2.10
		First day cover		20.00
		Imprint block of 10	18.00	
23	A9	10y crim rose, *Jan. 20, 1953*	2.25	35
		First day cover		35.00
		Imprint block of 10	25.00	
24	A9	30y ol grn, *Jan. 20, 1953*	7.75	5.00
		First day cover		60.00
		Imprint block of 10	80.00	
a.		30y light olive green, *1958*	27.50	
		Imprint block of 10	400.00	
25	A9	50y rose vio, *Jan. 20, 1953*	6.75	4.00
		First day cover		100.00
		Imprint block of 10	80.00	
26	A9	100y claret, *Jan. 20, 1953*	8.50	2.50
		First day cover		165.00
		First day cover, #22-26		425.00
		Imprint block of 10	100.00	

Issue dates: 1y, 2y and 3y, Nov. 20, 1952. Others, Jan. 20, 1953.

Reception at Shuri Castle — A10

Perry and American Fleet — A11

1953, May 26 *Perf. 13½x13, 13x13½*

No.	Type	Description	Unused	Used
27	A10	3y deep magenta	7.50	4.25
		Imprint block of 6	57.50	
28	A11	6y dull blue	70	70
		First day cover. #27-28		8.00
		Imprint block of 6	7.50	

Centenary of the arrival of Commodore Matthew Calbraith Perry at Naha, Okinawa.

Chofu Ota and Pencil-shaped Matrix — A12

Shigo Toma and Pen — A13

1953, Oct. 1 *Perf. 13½x13*

No.	Type	Description	Unused	Used
29	A12	4y yel brn	6.75	2.50
		First day cover		14.00
		Imprint block of 10	85.00	

Third Newspaper Week.

1954, Oct. 1

No.	Type	Description	Unused	Used
30	A13	4y blue	7.25	3.50
		First day cover		16.50
		Imprint block of 10	90.00	

Fourth Newspaper Week.

Ryukyu Pottery — A14

Noguni Shrine and Sweet Potato Plant — A15

Designs: 15y, Lacquerware. 20y, Textile design.

1954-55 Photo. *Perf. 13*

No.	Type	Description	Unused	Used
31	A14	4y brown, *June 25, 1954*	65	32
		First day cover		6.00
		Imprint block of 10	8.25	
32	A14	15y vermilion, *June 20, 1955*	2.25	1.65
		First day cover		10.00
		Imprint block of 10	27.50	
33	A14	20y yellow orange, *June 20, 1955*	1.65	1.40
		First day cover		10.00
		Imprint block of 10	21.00	
		First day cover, #32-33		27.50

1955, Nov. 26

No.	Type	Description	Unused	Used
34	A15	4y blue	8.00	4.00
		First day cover		16.50
		Imprint block of 10	90.00	

350th anniv. of the introduction of the sweet potato to the Ryukyu Islands.

Stylized Trees — A16

Willow Dance — A17

1956, Feb. 18 **Unwmk.**
35 A16 4y bluish green 8.00 4.00
First day cover 15.00
Imprint block of 6 60.00

Arbor Week, Feb. 18-24.

1956, May 1 ***Perf. 13***

Design: 8y, Straw hat dance. 14y, Dancer in warrior costume with fan.

36 A17 5y rose lilac 70 40
First day cover 6.50
Imprint block of 10 9.00
37 A17 8y violet blue 1.75 1.40
First day cover 6.50
Imprint block of 10 20.00
38 A17 14y redsh brown 2.00 1.75
First day cover 6.50
First day cover, #36-38 22.50
Imprint block of 10 21.00

Telephone A18

1956, June 8
39 A18 4y violet blue 11.50 5.75
First day cover 10.00
Imprint block of 6 70.00

Establishment of dial telephone system.

Garland of Pine, Bamboo and Plum — A19

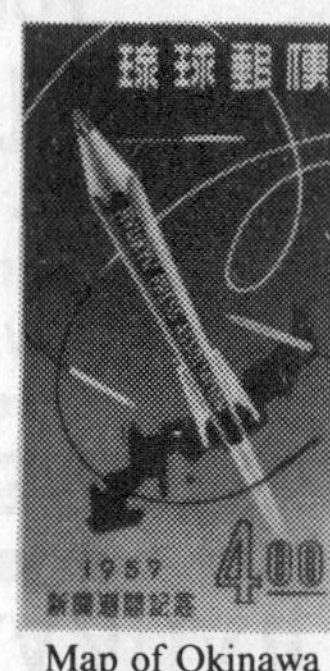

Map of Okinawa and Pencil Rocket — A20

1956, Dec. 1 ***Perf. 13½x13***
40 A19 2y multi 1.65 80
First day cover 2.00
Imprint block of 10 20.00

New Year, 1957.

1957, Oct. 1 **Photo.** ***Perf. 13½x13***
41 A20 4y deep violet blue 50 50
First day cover 3 6.00
Imprint block of 10 5.50

7th annual Newspaper Week, Oct. 1-7.

Phoenix — A21

1957, Dec. 1 **Unwmk.** ***Perf. 13***
42 A21 2y multicolored 25 25
First day cover 1.00
Imprint block of 10 3.50

New Year, 1958.

Ryukyu Stamps A22

1958, July 1 ***Perf. 13½***
43 A22 4y multicolored 80 60
First day cover 1.00
Imprint block of 4 3.50

10th anniv. of 1st Ryukyu stamps.

Yen Symbol and Dollar Sign — A23

Perf. 10, 10½, 11 & Compound

1958, Sept. 16 **Typo.**

Without Gum

44 A23 ½c orange 42 42
Imprint block of 6 3.00
a. Imperf., pair *1,250.*
b. Horiz. pair, imperf. btwn. 80.00
c. Vert. pair, imperf. btwn. 100.00
45 A23 1c yel grn 85 55
Imprint block of 6 5.75
a. Horiz. pair, imperf. btwn. 120.00
b. Vert. pair, imperf. btwn. 90.00
46 A23 2c dark blue 1.10 1.00
Imprint block of 6 7.25
a. Horiz. pair, imperf. btwn. 150.00
b. Vert. pair, imperf. btwn. *1,200.*
47 A23 3c deep carmine 85 55
Imprint block of 6 5.75
a. Horiz. pair, imperf. btwn. 120.00
b. Vert. pair, imperf. btwn. 90.00
48 A23 4c brt grn 95 85
First day cover, #44-48 4.00
Imprint block of 6 6.75
a. Horiz. pair, imperf. btwn. *500.00*
b. Vert. pair, imperf. btwn. 100.00
49 A23 5c orange 1.90 1.90
Imprint block of 6 14.00
a. Horiz. pair, imperf. btwn. 125.00
b. Vert. pair, imperf. btwn. *750.00*
50 A23 10c aqua 2.75 2.75
Imprint block of 6 20.00
a. Horiz. pair, imperf. btwn. 200.00
b. Vert. pair, imperf. btwn. 125.00
51 A23 25c brt vio bl 3.75 3.75
Imprint block of 6 27.50
a. Gummed paper ('61) 6.00
Imprint block of 6 60.00
b. Horiz. pair, imperf. btwn. *1,400.*
c. Vert. pair, imperf. btwn. *1,000.*
52 A23 50c gray 9.00 6.00
Imprint block of 6 60.00
a. Gummed paper ('61) 8.25
b. Horiz. pair, imperf. btwn. *1,200.*
First day cover, #51a-52a 10.00
Imprint block of 6 85.00
53 A23 $1 rose lilac 7.50 2.25
First day cover, #49-53 12.50
First day cover, #44-53 20.00
Imprint block of 6 57.50
a. Horiz. pair, imperf. btwn. 350.00
b. Vert. pair, imperf. btwn. *1,200.*

Printed locally. Perforation, paper and shade varieties exist.

Gate of Courtesy A24

1958, Oct. 15 **Photo.** ***Perf. 13½***
54 A24 3c multi 1.25 1.00
First day cover 1.50
Imprint block of 4 5.50

Restoration of Shureimon, Gate of Courtesy, on road leading to Shuri City.

Lion Dance — A25

Trees and Mountains — A26

1958, Dec. 10 **Unwmk.** ***Perf. 13½***
55 A25 1½c multi 20 20
First day cover 90
Imprint block of 6 1.75

New Year, 1959.

1959, Apr. 30 **Litho.** ***Perf. 13½x13***
56 A26 3c bl, yel grn, grn & red 60 55
First day cover 1.00
Imprint block of 6 4.50
a. Red omitted —

"Make the Ryukyus Green" movement.

Yonaguni Moth — A27

1959, July 23 **Photo.** ***Perf. 13***
57 A27 3c multi 95 60
First day cover 1.00
Imprint block of 6 6.00

Meeting of the Japanese Biological Education Society in Okinawa.

Hibiscus — A28

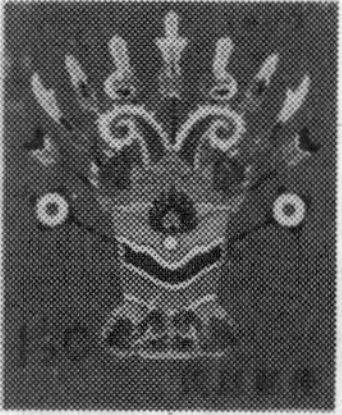
Toy (Yakaji) — A29

Designs: 3c, Fish (Moorish idol). 8c, Sea shell (Phalium bandatum). 13c, Butterfly (Kallinia Inachus Eucerca), denomination at left, butterfly going up. 17c, Jellyfish (Dactylometra pacifera Goette).

Inscribed: 琉球郵便

1959, Aug. 10 — *Perf. 13x13½*

No.	Type	Denom.	Description	Unused	Used
58	A28	½c	multi	20	20
			Imprint block of 10	3.25	
59	A28	3c	multi	75	38
			Imprint block of 10	9.00	
60	A28	8c	lt ultra, blk & ocher	6.00	5.75
			Imprint block of 10	67.50	
61	A28	13c	lt bl, gray & org	2.10	1.75
			Imprint block of 10	22.50	
62	A28	17c	vio bl, red & yel	14.00	7.50
			First day cover, #58-62		12.50
			Imprint block of 10	165.00	

Four-character inscription measures 10x2mm on ½c; 12x3mm on 3c, 8c; 8½x2mm on 13c, 17c. See Nos. 76-80.

1959, Dec. 1 — **Litho.**

No.	Type	Denom.	Description	Unused	Used
63	A29	1½c	gold & multi	55	28
			First day cover		75
			Imprint block of 10	10.00	

New Year, 1960.

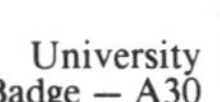
University Badge — A30

1960, May 22 — **Photo.** — *Perf. 13*

No.	Type	Denom.	Description	Unused	Used
64	A30	3c	multi	95	48
			First day cover		1.25
			Imprint block of 6	7.25	

10th anniv. opening of Ryukyu University.

Dancer — A31

Designs: Various Ryukyu Dances.

1960, Nov. 1 — **Photo.** — *Perf. 13*

Dark Gray Background

No.	Type	Denom.	Description	Unused	Used
65	A31	1c	yel, red & vio	1.00	65
			Imprint block of 10	13.50	
66	A31	2½c	crim, bl & yel	2.00	65
			Imprint block of 10	24.00	
67	A31	5c	dk bl, yel & red	65	75
			Imprint block of 10	10.00	
68	A31	10c	dk bl, yel & red	65	65
			First day cover, #65-68		4.75
			Imprint block of 10	10.00	

See Nos. 81-87, 220.

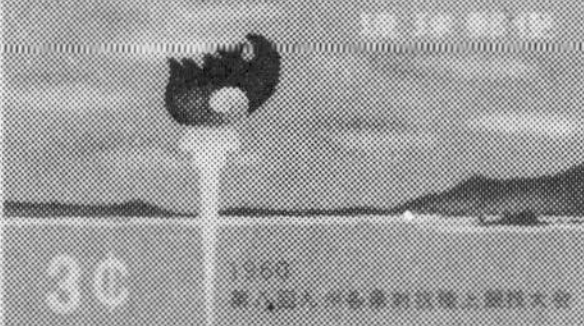
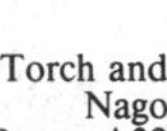
Torch and Nago Bay — A32

Runners at Starting Line — A33

1960, Nov. 8

No.	Type	Denom.	Description	Unused	Used
72	A32	3c	lt bl, grn & red	5.25	2.25
			First day cover		1.75
			Imprint block of 6	37.50	
73	A33	8c	orange & slate green	75	75
			First day cover		1.50
			First day cover, #72-73		4.50
			Imprint block of 6	5.75	

8th Kyushu Inter-Prefectural Athletic Meet, Nago, Northern Okinawa, Nov. 6-7.

Little Egret and Rising Sun — A34

1960, Dec. 1 — **Unwmk.** — *Perf. 13*

No.	Type	Denom.	Description	Unused	Used
74	A34	3c	redsh brn	5.00	2.50
			First day cover		3.00
			Imprint block of 6	32.50	

National census.

Okinawa Bull Fight — A35

1960, Dec. 10 — *Perf. 13½*

No.	Type	Denom.	Description	Unused	Used
75	A35	1½c	bis, dk bl & red brn	1.75	65
			First day cover		1.75
			Imprint block of 6	12.00	

New Year, 1961.

Type of 1959 With Japanese Inscription Redrawn: 琉球郵便

1960, July 1-61 — **Photo.** — *Perf. 13x13½*

No.	Type	Denom.	Description	Unused	Used
76	A28	½c	multi, *Oct. 1961*	28	22
			Imprint block of 10	4.00	
77	A28	3c	multi, *Aug. 23, 1961*	75	22
			First day cover		1.25
			Imprint block of 10	9.00	
78	A28	8c	lt ultra, blk & ocher	75	38
			Imprint block of 10	9.00	
79	A28	13c	bl, brn & red	95	65
			Imprint block of 10	11.00	
80	A28	17c	vio bl, red & yel	6.00	3.50
			First day cover, #78-80		12.50
			Imprint block of 10	75.00	

Size of Japanese inscription on Nos. 78-80 is 10½x1½mm. On No. 79 the denomination is at right, butterfly going down.

Dancer Type of 1960 with "RYUKYUS" Added.

1961-64 — *Perf. 13*

No.	Type	Denom.	Description	Unused	Used
81	A31	1c	multi, *Dec. 5, 1961*	12	9
			First day cover		75
			Imprint block of 10	2.00	
82	A31	2½c	multi, *June 20, 1962*	18	9
			Imprint block of 10	2.25	
83	A31	5c	multi, *June 20, 1962*	22	18
			Imprint block of 10	3.00	
84	A31	10c	multi, *June 20, 1962*	40	30
			First day cover, #82-84		1.50
			Imprint block of 10	5.00	
84A	A31	20c	multi, *Jan. 20, 1964*	1.00	75
			First day cover		1.75
			Imprint block of 10	13.00	
85	A31	25c	multi, *Feb. 1, 1962*	75	75
			First day cover		2.00
			Imprint block of 10	12.50	
86	A31	50c	multi, *Sept. 1, 1961*	2.00	60
			Imprint block of 10	25.00	
87	A31	$1	multi, *Sept. 1, 1961*	2.75	12
			First day cover		22.50
			Imprint block of 10	35.00	

Pine Tree — A36

1961, May 1 — **Photo.** — *Perf. 13*

No.	Type	Denom.	Description	Unused	Used
88	A36	3c	yel grn & red	1.50	1.25
			First day cover		1.25
			Imprint block of 6	12.00	

"Make the Ryukyus Green" movement.

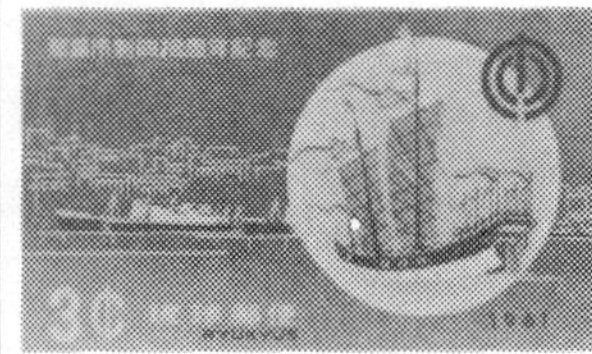
Naha, Steamer and Sailboat — A37

1961, May 20

No.	Type	Denom.	Description	Unused	Used
89	A37	3c	aqua	2.10	1.10
			First day cover		1.25
			Imprint block of 6	15.00	

40th anniv. of Naha.

White Silver Temple — A38

Books and Bird — A39

1961, Oct. 1 — **Typo.** — **Unwmk.** — *Perf. 11*

No.	Type	Denom.	Description	Unused	Used
90	A38	3c	red brn	1.25	1.10
			First day cover		1.75
			Imprint block of 6	8.00	
a.			Horiz. pair, imperf. between	*450.00*	
b.			Vert. pair, imperf. between	*550.00*	

Merger of townships Takamine, Kanegushiku and Miwa with Itoman.

1961, Nov. 12 — **Litho.** — *Perf. 13*

No.	Type	Denom.	Description	Unused	Used
91	A39	3c	multi	1.10	80
			First day cover		1.25
			Imprint block of 6	10.00	

Book Week.

Rising Sun and Eagles — A40

Symbolic Steps, Trees and Government Building — A41

1961, Dec. 10 — **Photo.** — *Perf. 13½*

No.	Type	Denom.	Description	Unused	Used
92	A40	1½c	gold, ver & blk	2.00	1.75
			First day cover		1.50
			Imprint block of 6	15.00	

New Year, 1962.

1962, Apr. 1 — **Unwmk.** — *Perf. 13½*

Design: 3c, Government Building.

No.	Type	Denom.	Description	Unused	Used
93	A41	1½c	multi	42	45
			Imprint block of 6	3.75	
94	A41	3c	brt grn, red & gray	70	55
			First day cover, #93-94		1.50
			Imprint block of 6	5.50	

10th anniv. of the Government of the Ryukyu Islands (GRI).

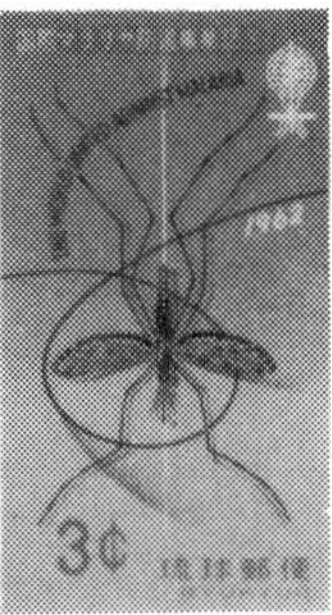
Anopheles Hyrcanus Sinensis — A42

Design: 8c, Malaria eradication emblem and Shurei gate.

1962, Apr. 7 *Perf. 13½x13*

95 A42 3c multi 45 48
Imprint block of 6 4.00
96 A42 8c multi 90 60
First day cover, #95-96 1.75
Imprint block of 6 7.50

World Health Organization drive to eradicate malaria.

Dolls and Toys — A43

Linden or Sea Hibiscus — A44

1962, May 5 **Litho.** *Perf. 13½*

97 A43 3c red, blk, bl & buff 1.10 65
First day cover 1.50
Imprint block of 6 9.00

Children's Day, 1962.

1962, June 1 **Photo.**

Flowers: 3c, Indian coral tree. 8c, Iju (Schima liukiuensis Nakal). 13c, Touch-me-not (garden balsam). 17c, Shell flower (Alpinia speciosa).

98 A44 ½c multi 8 8
Imprint block of 10 1.20
99 A44 3c multi 30 12
Imprint block of 10 3.25
100 A44 8c multi 35 35
Imprint block of 10 4.50
101 A44 13c multi 55 48
Imprint block of 10 6.25
102 A44 17c multi 75 75
First day cover, #98-102 3.25
Imprint block of 10 9.25

See Nos. 107 and 114 for 1½c and 15c flower stamps.

Earthenware — A45

1962, July 5 *Perf. 13½x13*

103 A45 3c multi 3.75 3.00
First day cover 2.75
Imprint block of 6 25.00

Philatelic Week.

Japanese Fencing (Kendo) — A46

1962, July 25 *Perf. 13*

104 A46 3c multi 4.00 3.00
First day cover 2.75
Imprint block of 6 27.50

All-Japan Kendo Meeting in Okinawa, July 25, 1962.

A little time given to the study of the arrangement of the Scott Catalogue can make it easier to use effectively.

Rabbit Playing near Water, Bingata Cloth Design — A47

Young Man and Woman, Stone Relief — A48

1962, Dec. 10 *Perf. 13x13½*

105 A47 1½c gold & multi 1.25 1.00
First day cover 1.25
Imprint block of 10 15.00

New Year, 1963.

1963, Jan. 15 **Photo.** *Perf. 13½*

106 A48 3c gold, blk & bl 80 65
First day cover 1.50
Imprint block of 6 6.00

Gooseneck Cactus — A49

Trees and Wooded Hills — A50

1963, Apr. 5 *Perf. 13x13½*

107 A49 1½c dk bl. grn, yel & pink 10 10
First day cover 1.25
Imprint block of 10 1.50

1963, Mar. 25 *Perf. 13½x13*

108 A50 3c ultra, grn & red brn 80 80
First day cover 1.25
Imprint block of 6 6.00

"Make the Ryukyus Green" movement.

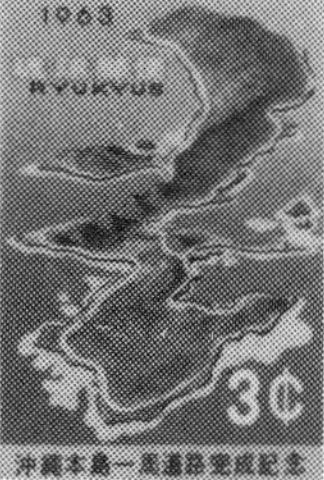

Map of Okinawa — A51

Hawks over Islands — A52

1963, Apr. 30 **Unwmk.** *Perf. 13½*

109 A51 3c multi 1.00 1.00
First day cover 1.50
Imprint block of 6 8.25

Opening of the Round Road on Okinawa.

1963, May 10 **Photo.**

110 A52 3c multi 95 95
First day cover 1.25
Imprint block of 6 9.00

Bird Day, May 10.

Shioya Bridge — A53

1963, June 5

111 A53 3c multi 95 95
First day cover 1.25
Imprint block of 6 6.75

Opening of Shioya Bridge over Shioya Bay.

Tsuikin-wan Lacquerware Bowl — A54

1963, July 1 **Unwmk.** *Perf. 13½*

112 A54 3c multi 2.75 2.25
First day cover 2.75
Imprint block of 6 20.00

Map of Far East and JCI Emblem — A55

1963, Sept. 16 **Photo.** *Perf. 13½*

113 A55 3c multi 70 48
First day cover 1.25
Imprint block of 6 6.00

Meeting of the International Junior Chamber of Commerce (JCI), Naha, Okinawa, Sept. 16-19.

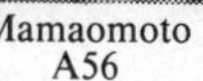

Mamaomoto A56

Site of Nakagusuku Castle A57

1963, Oct. 15 *Perf. 13x13½*

114 A56 15c multi 80 40
First day cover 1.25
Imprint block of 10 9.00

1963, Nov. 1 *Perf. 13½x13*

115 A57 3c multi 70 42
First day cover 1.25
Imprint block of 6 5.00

Protection of national cultural treasures.

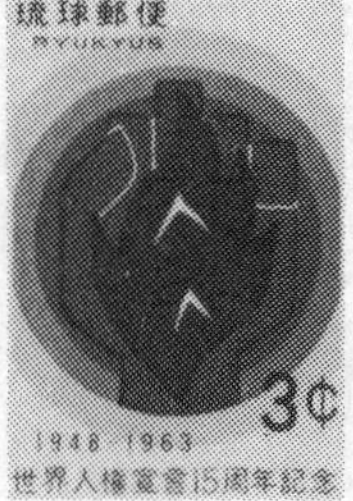

Flame — A58

Dragon (Bingata Pattern) — A59

1963, Dec. 10 *Perf. 13½*

116 A53 3c red, dk bl & yel 70 42
First day cover 1.25
Imprint block of 6 5.25

15th anniv. of the Universal Declaration of Human Rights.

1963, Dec. 10 **Photo.**

117 A59 1½c multi 40 25
First day cover 1.25
Imprint block of 10 5.00

New Year, 1964.

Carnation — A60

Pineapples and Sugar Cane — A61

1964, May 10 ***Perf. 13½***

118 A60 3c bl, yel, blk & car 40 35
First day cover 1.25
Imprint block of 6 3.00

Mothers Day.

1964, June 1

119 A61 3c multi 40 35
First day cover 1.25
Imprint block of 6 3.00

Agricultural census.

Minsah Obi (Sash Woven of Kapok) — A62

1964, July 1 **Unwmk.** ***Perf. 13½***

120 A62 3c dp bl, rose pink & ocher 55 42
First day cover 2.25
Imprint block of 6 4.50
a. 3c dp bl, dp car & ocher 70 60
First day cover 2.75
Imprint block of 6 5.00

Philatelic Week.

Girl Scout and Emblem — A63

1964, Aug. 31 **Photo.**

121 A63 3c multi 40 30
First day cover 1.25
Imprint block of 6 3.00

10th anniv. of Ryukyuan Girl Scouts.

Shuri Relay Station — A64

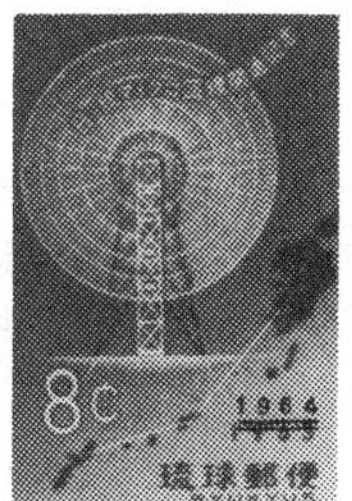

Parabolic Antenna and Map — A65

1964, Sept. 1 **Unwmk.** ***Perf. 13½***

Black Overprint

122 A64 3c dp grn 65 65
Imprint block of 6 5.50
a. Figure "1" invtd. 22.50 22.50

123 A65 8c ultra 1.25 1.25
First day cover, #122-123 4.75
Imprint block of 6 10.00

Opening of the Ryukyu Islands-Japan microwave system carrying telephone and telegraph messages. Nos. 122-123 not issued without overprint.

Gate of Courtesy, Olympic Torch and Emblem — A66

1964, Sept. 7 **Photo.** ***Perf. 13½x13***

124 A66 3c ultra, yel & red 20 15
First day cover 1.25
Imprint block of 6 1.50

Relaying the Olympic torch on Okinawa en route to Tokyo.

"Naihanchi," Karate Stance — A67

"Makiwara," Strengthening Hands and Feet — A68

"Kumite," Simulated Combat — A69

1964-65 **Photo.** ***Perf. 13½***

125 A67 3c dl cl, yel & blk, *Oct. 10, 1964* 48 30
First day cover 1.25
Imprint block of 6 3.25
126 A68 3c yel & multi, *Feb. 5, 1965* 38 30
First day cover 1.25
Imprint block of 6 3.00
127 A69 3c gray, red & blk, *June 5, 1965* 38 30
First day cover 1.25
Imprint block of 6 3.00

Karate, Ryukyuan self-defense sport.

Miyara Dunchi — A70

Snake and Iris (Bingata) — A71

1964, Nov. 1 ***Perf. 13½***

128 A70 3c multi 22 18
First day cover 1.25
Imprint block of 6 1.50

Protection of national cultural treasures. Miyara Dunchi was built as a residence by Miyara-pechin Toen in 1819.

1964, Dec. 10 **Photo.**

129 A71 1½c multi 25 20
First day cover 2.25
Imprint block of 10 4.00

New Year, 1965.

Boy Scouts — A72

1965, Feb. 6 ***Perf. 13½***

130 A72 3c lt bl & multi 42 28
First day cover 1.25
Imprint block of 6 3.00

10th anniv. of Ryukyuan Boy Scouts.

Main Stadium, Onoyama A73

1965, July 1 ***Perf. 13x13½***

131 A73 3c multi 20 18
First day cover 1.00
Imprint block of 6 2.00

Inauguration of the main stadium of the Onoyama athletic facilities.

Samisen of King Shoko — A74

1965, July 1 **Photo.** ***Perf. 13½***

132 A74 3c buff & multi 42 30
First day cover 1.25
Imprint block of 6 3.25

Philatelic Week.

Kin Power Plant — A75

ICY Emblem, Ryukyu Map — A76

1965, July 1

133 A75 3c grn & multi 20 18
First day cover 1.00
Imprint block of 6 2.00

Completion of Kin power plant.

1965, Aug. 24 **Photo.** ***Perf. 13½***

134 A76 3c multi 18 14
First day cover 1.00
Imprint block of 6 1.75

20th anniv. of the UN and International Cooperation Year, 1964-65.

Naha City Hall — A77

1965, Sept. 18 Unwmk. *Perf. 13½*

135 A77 3c bl & multi 18 14
First day cover 1.00
Imprint block of 6 1.75

Completion of Naha City Hall.

Chinese Box Turtle — A78

Horse (Bingata) — A79

Turtles: No. 137, Hawksbill turtle (denomination at top, country name at bottom). No. 138, Asian terrapin (denomination and country name on top).

1965-66 Photo. *Perf. 13½*

136 A78 3c gldn brn & multi, *Oct. 20, 1965* 30 30
First day cover 1.00
Imprint block of 6 2.50
137 A78 3c blk, yel & brn, *Jan. 20, 1966* 30 30
First day cover 1.00
Imprint block of 6 2.50
138 A78 3c gray & multi, *Apr. 20, 1966* 30 30
First day cover 1.00
Imprint block of 6 2.50

1965, Dec. 10 Photo. *Perf. 13½*

139 A79 1½c multi 12 10
First day cover 1.00
Imprint block of 10 2.25
a. Gold omitted *850.00 850.00*

New Year, 1966.

NATURE CONSERVATION ISSUE

Noguchi's Okinawa Woodpecker — A80

Sika Deer — A81

Design: No. 142, Dugong.

1966 Photo. *Perf. 13½*

140 A80 3c bl grn & multi, *Feb. 15* 20 20
First day cover 1.00
Imprint block of 6 1.65
141 A81 3c bl, red, blk, brn & grn, *Mar. 15* 24 24
First day cover 1.00
Imprint block of 6 1.75
142 A81 3c bl, yel grn, blk & red, *Apr. 20* 24 24
First day cover 1.00
Imprint block of 6 1.75

See the "Information for Collectors" section at beginning of catalogue for an explanation of paper types, watermarks and grills.

Ryukyu Bungalow Swallow — A82

1966, May 10 Photo. *Perf. 13½*

143 A82 3c sky bl, blk & brn 14 14
First day cover 1.00
Imprint block of 6 1.10

4th Bird Week, May 10-16.

Lilies and Ruins — A83

1966, June 23 *Perf. 13x13½*

144 A83 3c multi 14 14
First day cover 1.00
Imprint block of 6 1.00

Memorial Day, end of the Battle of Okinawa, June 23, 1945.

University of the Ryukyus — A84

1966, July 1

145 A84 3c multi 14 14
First day cover 1.00
Imprint block of 6 1.00

Transfer of the University of the Ryukyus from U.S. authority to the Ryukyu Government.

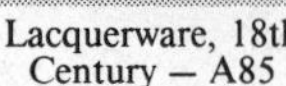
Lacquerware, 18th Century — A85

Tile-Roofed House and UNESCO Emblem — A86

1966, Aug. 1 *Perf. 13½*

146 A85 3c gray & multi 14 14
First day cover 1.00
Imprint block of 6 1.10

Philatelic Week.

1966, Sept. 20 Photo. *Perf. 13½*

147 A86 3c multi 14 14
First day cover 1.00
Imprint block of 6 1.10

20th anniv. of UNESCO.

Government Museum and Dragon Statue — A87

1966, Oct. 6

148 A87 3c multi 14 14
First day cover 1.00
Imprint block of 6 1.00

Completion of the GRI (Government of the Ryukyu Islands) Museum, Shuri.

Tomb of Nakasone-Tuimya Genga, Ruler of Miyako — A88

1966, Nov. 1 Photo. *Perf. 13½*

149 A88 3c multi 14 14
First day cover 1.00
Imprint block of 6 1.00

Protection of national cultural treasures.

Ram in Iris Wreath — A89

Clown Fish — A90

1966, Dec. 10 Photo. *Perf. 13½*

150 A89 1½c dk bl & multi 14 14
First day cover 1.00
Imprint block of 10 1.10

New Year, 1967.

1966-67

Fish: No. 152, Young boxfish (white numeral at lower left). No. 153, Forceps fish (pale buff numeral at lower right). No. 154. Spotted triggerfish (orange numeral). No. 155. Saddleback butterflyfish (carmine numeral, lower left).

151 A90 3c org red & multi, *Dec. 20, 1966* 18 14
152 A90 3c org yel & multi, *Jan. 10, 1967* 18 14
153 A90 3c multi, *Apr. 10, 1967* 25 22
154 A90 3c multi, *May 25, 1967* 25 22
155 A90 3c multi, *June 10, 1967* 28 22
First day covers, #151-155 each 1.00
Imprint block of 6, #151-155 each 1.75

Tsuboya Urn — A91

Episcopal Miter — A92

1967, Apr. 20

156 A91 3c yel & multi 20 16
First day cover 1.25
Imprint block of 6 1.65

Philatelic Week, 1967.

1967-68 Photo. *Perf. 13½*

Seashells: No. 158, Venus comb murex. No. 159, Chiragra spider. No. 160, Green truban. No. 161, Euprotomus bulla.

157 A92 3c lt grn & multi, *July 20, 1967* 18 14
Imprint block of 6 1.25
158 A92 3c grnsh bl & multi, *Aug. 30, 1968* 18 14
Imprint block of 6 1.25
159 A92 3c emer & multi, *Jan. 18, 1968* 22 18
Imprint block of 6 1.65
160 A92 3c lt bl & multi, *Feb. 20, 1968* 22 18

Imprint block of 6 1.65
161 A92 3c brt bl & multi, *June 5, 1968* 40 28
Imprint block of 6 3.00
First day cover, #157-161, each 1.00

Red-tiled Roofs and ITY Emblem — A93

1967, Sept. 11 **Photo.** ***Perf. 13½***
162 A93 3c multi 18 18
First day cover 1.00
Imprint block of 6 1.25

International Tourist Year, 1967.

Mobile TB Clinic — A94

1967, Oct. 13 **Photo.** ***Perf. 13½***
163 A94 3c lil & multi 18 18
First day cover 1.00
Imprint block of 6 1.25

15th anniv. of the Anti-Tuberculosis Society.

Hojo Bridge, Enkaku Temple, 1498 — A95

1967, Nov. 1
164 A95 3c bl grn & multi 18 18
First day cover 1.00
Imprint block of 6 1.50

Protection of national cultural treasures.

Monkey (Bingata) — A96

TV Tower and Map — A97

1967, Dec. 11 **Photo.** ***Perf. 13½***
165 A96 1½c silver & multi 18 18
First day cover 1.00
Imprint block of 10 3.00

New Year, 1968.

1967, Dec. 22
166 A97 3c multi 18 18
First day cover 1.00
Imprint block of 6 1.25

Opening of Miyako and Yaeyama television stations.

Dr. Kijin Nakachi and Helper — A98

Pill Box (Inro) — A99

1968, Mar. 15 **Photo.** ***Perf. 13½***
167 A98 3c multi 18 18
First day cover 1.00
Imprint block of 6 1.25

120th anniv. of the first vaccination in the Ryukyu Islands, by Dr. Kijin Nakachi.

1968, Apr. 18
168 A99 3c gray & multi 45 42
First day cover 1.25
Imprint block of 6 3.50

Philatelic Week, 1968.

Young Man, Library, Book and Map of Ryukyu Islands — A100

1968, May 13
169 A100 3c multi 25 22
First day cover 1.00
Imprint block of 6 1.75

10th International Library Week.

Mailmen's Uniforms and Stamp of 1948 — A101

1968, July 1 **Photo.** ***Perf. 13x13½***
170 A101 3c multi 25 22
First day cover 1.00
Imprint block of 6 1.75

First Ryukyuan postage stamps, 20th anniv.

Main Gate, Enkaku Temple — A102

1968, July 15 **Photo. & Engr.** ***Perf. 13½***
171 A102 3c multi 25 22
First day cover 1.00
Imprint block of 6 1.75

Restoration of the main gate Enkaku Temple, built 1492-1495, destroyed during World War II.

Old Man's Dance — A103

1968, Sept. 15 **Photo.** ***Perf. 13½***
172 A103 3c gold & multi 25 22
First day cover 1.00
Imprint block of 6 2.00

Old People's Day.

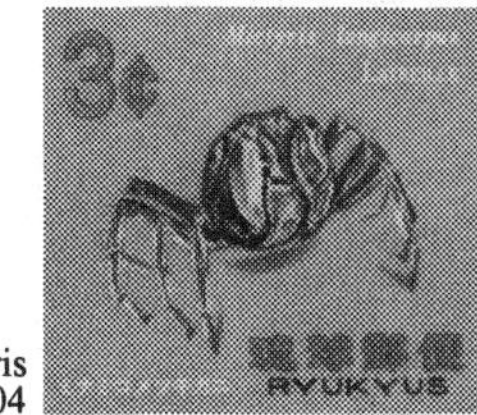
Mictyris Longicarpus — A104

Crabs: No. 174, Uca dubia stimpson. No. 175, Baptozius vinosus. No. 176, Cardisoma carnifex. No. 177, Ocypode ceratophthalma pallas.

1968-69 **Photo.** ***Perf. 13½***
173 A104 3c bl, ocher & blk, *Oct. 10, 1968* 30 25
First day cover 1.25
Imprint block of 6 2.50
174 A104 3c lt bl grn & multi, *Feb. 5, 1969* 35 25
First day cover 1.25
Imprint block of 6 2.75
175 A104 3c lt grn & multi, *Mar. 5, 1969* 35 25
First day cover 1.25
Imprint block of 6 2.75
176 A104 3c lt ultra & multi, *May 15, 1969* 45 30
First day cover 1.25
Imprint block of 6 3.25
177 A104 3c lt ultra & multi, *June 2, 1969* 45 30
First day cover 1.25
Imprint block of 6 3.25

Saraswati Pavilion — A105

1968, Nov. 1 **Photo.** ***Perf. 13½***
178 A105 3c multi 24 18
First day cover 1.00
Imprint block of 6 2.00

Restoration of the Sarawati Pavilion (in front of Enkaku Temple), destroyed during World War II.

Tennis Player — A106

Cock and Iris (Bingata) — A107

1968, Nov. 3 **Photo.** ***Perf. 13½***

179	A106	3c grn & multi	40	30
		First day cover		1.00
		Imprint block of 6	3.25	

35th All-Japan East-West Men's Soft-ball Tennis Tournament, Naha City, Nov. 23-24.

1968, Dec. 10

180	A107	1½c org & multi	14	14
		First day cover		1.00
		Imprint block of 10	1.75	

New Year, 1969.

Boxer — A108

Ink Slab Screen — A109

1969, Jan. 3

181	A108	3c gray & multi	25	22
		First day cover		1.00
		Imprint block of 6	1.75	

20th All-Japan Amateur Boxing Championships held at the University of the Ryukyus, Jan. 3-5.

1969, Apr. 17 **Photo.** ***Perf. 13½***

182	A109	3c sal, ind & red	25	18
		First day cover		1.50
		Imprint block of 6	1.75	

Philatelic Week, 1969.

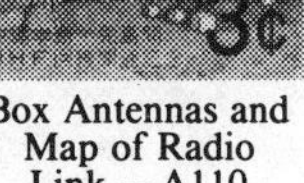

Box Antennas and Map of Radio Link — A110

Gate of Courtesy and Emblems — A111

1969, July 1 **Photo.** ***Perf. 13½***

183	A110	3c multi	14	12
		First day cover		1.00
		Imprint block of 6	1.10	

Opening of the UHF (radio) circuit system between Okinawa and the outlying Miyako-Yaeyama Islands.

1969, Aug. 1 **Photo.** ***Perf. 13½***

184	A111	3c Prus. bl, gold & ver	14	12
		First day cover		1.00
		Imprint block of 6	1.10	

22nd All-Japan Formative Education Study Conference, Naha, Aug. 1-3.

FOLKLORE ISSUE

Tug of War Festival A112

Hari Boat Race — A113

Izaiho Ceremony, Kudaka Island — A114

Mortardrum Dance — A115

Sea God Dance — A116

1969-70 **Photo.** ***Perf. 13***

185	A112	3c multi, *Aug. 1, 1969*	28	22
		First day cover		1.50
		Imprint block of 6	2.00	
186	A113	3c multi, *Sept. 5, 1969*	35	22
		First day cover		1.50
		Imprint block of 6	2.25	
187	A114	3c multi, *Oct. 3, 1969*	35	22
		First day cover		1.50
		Imprint block of 6	2.25	
188	A115	3c multi, *Jan. 20, 1970*	50	35
		First day cover		1.50
		Imprint block of 6	4.00	
189	A116	3c multi, *Feb. 27, 1970*	50	35
		First day cover		1.50
		Imprint block of 6	3.50	

No. 99 Surcharged 改訂 ½¢

1969, Oct. 15 **Photo.** ***Perf. 13½***

190	A44	½c on 3c multi	12	12
		First day cover		1.50
		Imprint block of 10	2.00	

Nakamura-ke Farm House, Built 1713-51 — A117

1969, Nov. 1 **Photo.** ***Perf. 13½***

191	A117	3c multi	14	10
		First day cover		1.00
		Imprint block of 6	1.00	

Protection of national cultural treasures.

Statue of Kyuzo Toyama, Maps of Hawaiian and Ryukyu Islands — A118

1969, Dec. 5 **Photo.** ***Perf. 13½***

192	A118	3c lt ultra & multi	22	20
		First day cover		1.25
		Imprint block of 6	1.50	
a.		Without overprint	*1,850.*	
b.		Wide-spaced bars	*475.00*	

70th anniv. of Ryukyu-Hawaii emigration Kyuzo Toyama leader.

The overprint "1969" at lower left and bars across "1970" at upper right was applied before No. 192 was issued.

Dog and Flowers (Bingata) — A119

Sake Flask Made from Coconut — A120

1969, Dec. 10

193	A119	1½c pink & multi	12	12
		First day cover		1.00
		Imprint block of 10	1.65	

New Year, 1970.

1970, Apr. 15 **Photo.** ***Perf. 13½***

194	A120	3c multi	22	20
		First day cover		1.25
		Imprint block of 6	1.50	

Philatelic Week, 1970.

CLASSIC OPERA ISSUE

"The Bell" (Shushin Kaneiri) — A121

Child and Kidnapper (Chu-nusudu) A122

Robe of Feathers (Mekarushi) — A123

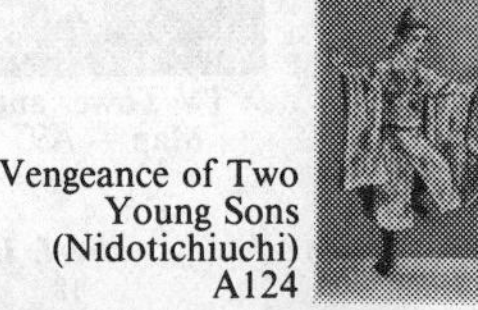

Vengeance of Two Young Sons (Nidotichiuchi) A124

The Virgin and the Dragon (Kokonomaki) A125

1970 **Photo.** ***Perf. 13½***

195	A121	3c dl bl & multi, *Apr. 28*	40	38
		First day cover		1.75
		Imprint block of 6	3.00	
196	A122	3c lt bl & multi, *May 29*	40	38
		First day cover		1.75
		Imprint block of 6	3.00	
197	A123	3c bluish grn & multi, *June 30*	40	38
		First day cover		1.75

Values quoted in this catalogue are for stamps graded at Fine-Very Fine and with no faults. An illustrated guide to grade is provided in introductory material, beginning on Page V.

		Imprint block of 6	3.00	
198	A124	3c dl bl grn & multi, *July 30*	40	38
		First day cover		1.75
		Imprint block of 6	3.00	
199	A125	3c multi, *Aug. 25*	40	38
		First day cover		1.75
		Imprint block of 6	3.00	

Souvenir Sheets

195a-199a	Sheets of 4, each	3.25	3.50
	First day covers, each		5.00

Marginal decoration and inscription. Size: 93x102mm.

Underwater Observatory and Tropical Fish — A126

1970, May 22

200	A126	3c bl grn & multi	28	25
		First day cover		1.25
		Imprint block of 6	2.00	

Completion of the underwater observatory of Busena-Misaki, Nago.

Noboru Jahana (1865-1908), Politician — A127

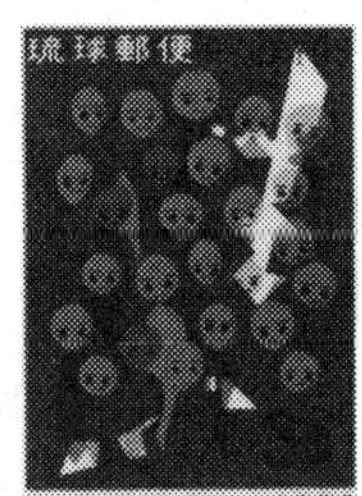

Map of Okinawa and People — A128

Portraits: No. 202, Saion Gushichan Bunjaku (1682-1761), statesman. No. 203, Choho Giwan (1823-1876), regent and poet.

1970-71 Engr. *Perf. 13½*

201	A127	3c rose claret, *Sept. 25, 1970*	48	30
		Imprint block of 6	3.25	
202	A127	3c dull blue green, *Dec. 22, 1970*	75	55
		Imprint block of 6	7.00	
203	A127	3c black, *Jan. 22, 1971*	48	30
		First day cover, each		2.50
		Imprint block of 6	3.25	

1970, Oct. 1 Photo.

204	A128	3c red & multi	18	15
		First day cover		1.00
		Imprint block of 6	1.50	

1970 census, Oct. 1, 1970.

Great Cycad of Une — A129

1970, Nov. 2 Photo. *Perf. 13½*

205	A129	3c gold & multi	22	20
		First day cover		1.00
		Imprint block of 6	1.75	

Protection of national treasures.

Japanese Flag, Diet and Map of Ryukyus — A130

Wild Boar and Cherry Blossoms (Bingata) — A131

1970, Nov. 15 Photo. *Perf. 13½*

206	A130	3c ultra & multi	70	50
		First day cover		1.25
		Imprint block of 6	5.00	

Citizens participation in national administration to Japanese law of Apr. 24, 1970.

1970, Dec. 10

207	A131	1½c multicolored	14	14
		First day cover		1.00
		Imprint block of 10	2.00	

New Year, 1971.

Low Hand Loom (Jibata) — A132

Farmer Wearing Palm Bark Raincoat and Kuba Leaf Hat — A133

Fisherman's Wooden Box and Scoop — A134

Designs: No. 209, Woman running a filature (reel). No. 211, Woman hulling rice with cylindrical "Shiri-ushi."

1971 Photo. *Perf. 13½*

208	A132	3c lt bl & multi, *Feb. 16*	28	22
		Imprint block of 6	2.00	
209	A132	3c pale grn & multi, *Mar. 16*	28	22
		Imprint block of 6	2.00	
210	A133	3c lt bl & multi, *Apr. 13*	35	24
		Imprint block of 6	2.25	
211	A132	3c yel & multi, *May 20*	40	30
		Imprint block of 6	3.50	
212	A134	3c gray & multi, *June 15*	35	24
		First day cover, each		1.25
		Imprint block of 6	2.25	

Water Carrier (Taku) — A135

1971, Apr. 15 Photo. *Perf. 13½*

213	A135	3c bl grn & multi	35	25
		First day cover		1.00
		Imprint block of 6	2.75	

Philatelic Week, 1971.

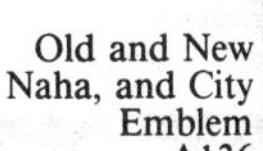

Old and New Naha, and City Emblem A136

1971, May 20 *Perf. 13*

214	A136	3c ultra & multi	22	20
		First day cover		1.00
		Imprint block of 6	1.50	

50th anniv. of Naha as a municipality.

Caesalpinia Pulcherrima — A137

Design: 2c, Madder (Sandanka).

1971 Photo. *Perf. 13*

215	A137	2c gray & multi, *Sept. 30*	12	8
216	A137	3c gray & multi, *May 10*	16	12
		First day cover, each		1.00
		Imprint block of 10, each	2.00	

GOVERNMENT PARK SERIES

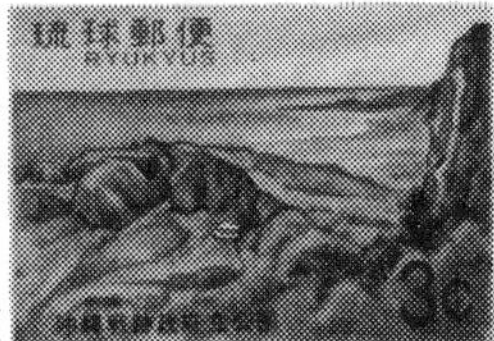

View from Mabuni Hill — A138

Mt. Arashi from Haneji Sea — A139

Yabuchi Island from Yakena Port — A140

1971-72

217	A138	3c grn & multi, *July 30, 1971*	20	15
218	A139	3c bl & multi, *Aug. 30, 1971*	20	15
219	A140	4c multi, *Jan. 20, 1972*	25	15
		First day cover, each		1.25
		Imprint block of 6, each	1.50	

Dancer — A141

Deva King, Torinji Temple — A142

1971, Nov. 1 Photo. *Perf. 13*

220	A141	4c Prus bl & multi	14	12
		First day cover		1.00
		Imprint block of 10	1.65	

1971, Dec. 1

221	A142	4c	dp bl & multi	18	18
			First day cover		1.00
			Imprint block of 6	1.50	

Protection of national cultural treasures.

Rat and Chrysanthemums A143

Student Nurse A144

1971, Dec. 10

222	A143	2c	brn org & multi	14	14
			First day cover		1.00
			Imprint block of 10	2.25	

New Year, 1972.

1971, Dec. 24

223	A144	4c	lilac & multi	20	15
			First day cover		1.00
			Imprint block of 6	1.50	

Nurses' training, 25th anniversary.

A145

A147

Coral Reef — A146

1972 **Photo.** ***Perf. 13***

224	A145	5c	brt bl & multi, *Apr. 14*	35	24
225	A146	5c	gray & multi, *Mar. 30*	35	24
226	A147	5c	ocher & multi, *Mar. 21*	35	24
			First day cover, each		1.25
			Imprint block of 6, each	2.25	

Dove, U.S. and Japanese Flags — A148

1972, Apr. 17 **Photo.** ***Perf. 13***

227	A148	5c	brt bl & multi	55	38
			First day cover		1.50
			Imprint block of 6	4.00	

The Catalogue editors cannot undertake to appraise, identify or judge the genuineness or condition of stamps.

Antique Sake Pot (Yushibin) — A149

1972, Apr. 20

228	A149	5c	ultra & multi	40	25
			First day cover		1.25
			Imprint block of 6	3.00	

Ryukyu stamps were replaced by those of Japan after May 15, 1972.

AIR POST

Dove and Map of Ryukyus — AP1

1950, Feb. 15 **Photo.** **Unwmk.** ***Perf. 13x13½***

C1	AP1	8y	brt bl	62.50	50.00
			Imprint block of 6	800.00	
C2	AP1	12y	green	22.50	20.00
			Imprint block of 6	250.00	
C3	AP1	16y	rose car	18.00	15.00
			Imprint block of 6	150.00	
			First day cover, each		35.00
			First day cover #C1-C3		175.00

Heavenly Maiden — AP2

1951-54

C4	AP2	13y	blue, *Nov. 1, 1951*	1.50	1.40
			First day cover		60.00
			Imprint block of 6, 5-character	190.00	
			Imprint block of 6, 8-character	37.50	
C5	AP2	18y	green, *Nov. 1, 1951*	2.10	2.10
			First day cover		60.00
			Imprint block of 6, 5-character	55.00	
			Imprint block of 6, 8-character	45.00	
C6	AP2	30y	cerise, *Nov. 1, 1951*	3.25	1.10
			First day cover		60.00
			First day cover, #C4-C6		250.00
			Imprint block of 6, 5-character	60.00	
			Imprint block of 6, 8-character	110.00	
C7	AP2	40y	red vio, *Aug. 16, 1954*	5.25	5.00
			First day cover		35.00
			Imprint block of 6	75.00	
C8	AP2	50y	yel org, *Aug. 16, 1954*	6.50	5.75
			First day cover		35.00
			First day cover, #C7-C8		100.00
			Imprint block of 6	90.00	

Heavenly Maiden Playing Flute — AP3

1957, Aug. 1 **Engr.** ***Perf. 13½***

C9	AP3	15y	bl grn	3.75	2.00
			Imprint block of 6	40.00	
C10	AP3	20y	rose car	6.00	3.50
			Imprint block of 6	67.50	
C11	AP3	35y	yel grn	11.00	5.50
			Imprint block of 6	110.00	
C12	AP3	45y	redsh brn	12.00	8.00
			Imprint block of 6	125.00	
C13	AP3	60y	gray	16.00	9.50
			Imprint block of 6	200.00	
			First day cover, #C9-C13		45.00

On one printing of No. C10, position 49 shows an added spur on the right side of the second character from the left.

Same Surcharged in Brown Red or Light Ultramarine

改訂 9¢

1959, Dec. 20

C14	AP3	9c	on 15y bl grn (BrR)	2.00	1.40
			Imprint block of 6	20.00	
a.			Inverted surch.	*500.00*	
			Imprint block of 6	*5,000.*	
C15	AP3	14c	on 20y rose car (L.U.)	2.50	2.10
			Imprint block of 6	25.00	
C16	AP3	19c	on 35y yel grn (BrR)	4.50	3.50
			Imprint block of 6	50.00	
C17	AP3	27c	on 45y redsh brn (L.U.)	8.50	5.00
			Imprint block of 6	90.00	
C18	AP3	35c	on 60y gray (BrR)	10.00	6.50
			Imprint block of 6	120.00	
			First day cover, #C14-C18		30.00

No. C15 is found with the variety described below No. C13.

改訂

Nos. 31-33, 36 and 38 Surcharged in Black, Brown, Red, Blue or Green

9¢

1960, Aug. 3 **Photo.** ***Perf. 13***

C19	A14	9c	on 4y brn	2.25	1.40
			Imprint block of 10	30.00	
a.			Invtd. surch.	*9,500.*	*12,500.*
C20	A17	14c	on 5y rose lil (Br)	2.25	1.40
			Imprint block of 10	30.00	
C21	A14	19c	on 15y ver (R)	1.75	1.00
			Imprint block of 10	25.00	
C22	A17	27c	on 14y redsh brn (Bl)	5.00	2.75
			Imprint block of 10	70.00	
C23	A14	35c	on 20y yel org (G)	4.50	3.75
			Imprint block of 10	70.00	
			First day cover, #C19-C23		22.50

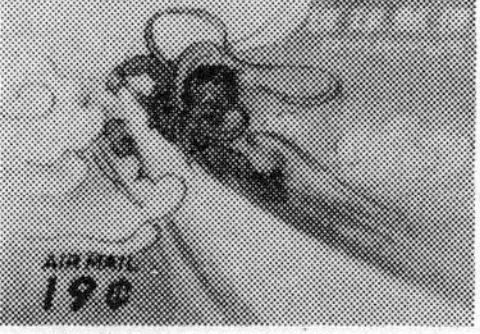

Wind God — AP4

Designs: 9c, Heavenly Maiden (as on AP2). 14c, Heavenly Maiden (as on AP3). 27c, Wind God at right. 35c, Heavenly Maiden over treetops.

1961, Sept. 21 **Unwmk.** ***Perf. 13½***

C24	AP4	9c	multi	28	12
			Imprint block of 6	2.25	
C25	AP4	14c	multi	45	45
			Imprint block of 6	3.50	
C26	AP4	19c	multi	48	45
			Imprint block of 6	4.00	
C27	AP4	27c	multi	1.90	30
			Imprint block of 6	12.00	
C28	AP4	35c	multi	1.25	60
			Imprint block of 6	10.00	
			First day cover, #C24-C28		35.00

AP5

AP6

1963, Aug. 28 ***Perf. 13x13½***

C29	AP5	5½c	multicolored	14	14
			Imprint block of 10	2.00	
C30	AP6	7c	multicolored	18	20
			Imprint block of 10	2.75	
			First day cover, each		1.00
			First day cover, #C29-C30		2.50

SPECIAL DELIVERY

Dragon and Map of Ryukyus — SD1

1950, Feb. 15 Unwmk. Photo. *Perf. 13x13½*

E1 SD1 5y bright blue		22.50	16.00
First day cover			100.00
Imprint block of 6		250.00	

QUANTITIES ISSUED

Regular Postage and Commemorative Stamps

Cat. No.	*Quantity*
1	90,214
2	55,901
3	94,663
4	55,413
5	76,387
6	117,321
7	291,403
1a	61,000
2a to 4a, each	181,000
5a	29,936
6a	99,300
7a	46,000
8	2,859,000
8a	247,943
9	1,198,989
10	589,000
11	479,000
12	598,999
13	397,855
14	499,000
15	498,960
16	200,000
16a	200,000
16b	40,000
17	9,800
18	299,500
19	3,014,427
20	3,141,777
21	2,970,827
22	191,917
23	1,118,617
24	276,218
24a	ca. 1,300
25	231,717
26	220,139
27	398,993
28	386,421
29	498,854
30	298,994
31	4,768,413
32	1,202,297
33	500,059
34	298,994
35	199,000
36	455,896
37	160,518
38	198,720
39	198,199
40	599,000
41	598,075
42	1,198,179
43	1,625,406
44	994,880
45	997,759
46	996,759
47	2,705,955
48	997,542
49	996,609
50	996,928
51	499,000
52	249,000
52a	78,415
53	248,700
54	1,498,991
55	2,498,897
56	1,098,972
57	998,918
58	2,699,000
59	2,499,000
60	199,000
61	499,000
62	199,000
63	1,498,931
64	798,953
65 to 68, each	999,000
72	598,912
73	398,990
74	598,936
75	1,998,992
76	1,000,000
77	2,000,000
78	500,000
79 to 80, each	400,000
81	12,599,000
82	11,979,000
83	6,850,000
84	5,099,000
84A	1,699,000
85	4,749,000
86	2,099,000
87	3,019,000
88	298,966
89	298,966
90	398,901
91	398,992
92	1,498,970
93	598,989
94	398,998
95	398,993
96	298,993
97	398,997
98	9,699,000
99	10,991,500
100	1,549,000
101	799,000
102	1,299,000
103	398,995
104	298,892
105	1,598,949
106	348,989
107	10,099,000
108	348,865
109	348,937
110	348,962
111	348,974
112	398,974
113	398,911
114	1,199,000
115	398,948
116	398,943
117	1,698,912
118	550,000
119	549,000
120	749,000
121	799,000
122	389,000
123	319,000
124	1,999,000
125 to 127, each	999,000
128	799,000
129	1,699,000
130 to 131, each	799,000
132	849,000
133	799,000
134	1,299,000
135	1,099,000
136	1,299,000
137 to 138, each	1,598,000
139	3,098,000
140 to 142, each	1,598,000
143 to 148, each	2,498,000
149	2,298,000
150	3,798,000
151	2,298,000
152 to 156, each	1,998,000
157 to 158, each	1,698,000
159 to 160, each	1,298,000
161	898,000
162	1,498,000
163 to 164, each	1,298,000
165	3,998,000
166 to 167, each	1,298,000
168	998,000
169 to 179, each	898,000
180	3,198,000
181 to 189, each	898,000
190	1,773,050
191	898,000
192	864,960
193	3,198,000
194	898,000
195 to 199, each	598,000
195a to 199a, each	124,500
200 to 206, each	898,000
207	3,198,000
208 to 210, each	1,098,000
211 to 212, each	1,298,000
213	1,098,000
214	1,298,000
215 to 216, each	4,998,000
217	1,498,000
218 to 219, each	1,798,000
220	2,998,000
221	1,798,000
222	4,998,000
223	1,798,000
224 to 226, each	2,498,000
227	2,998,000
228	3,998,000

AIR POST STAMPS

Cat. No.	*Quantity*
C1 to C3, each	198,000
C4	1,952,348
C5	331,360
C6	762,530
C7	76,166
C8	122,816
C9	708,319
C10	108,824
C11	164,147
C12	50,335
C13	69,092
C14	597,103
C15	77,951
C16	97,635
C17	98,353
C18	96,650
C19	1,033,900
C19a	100
C20	230,000
C21	185,000
C22	191,000
C23	190,000
C24	17,199,000
C25	1,999,000
C26	1,250,000
C27	3,499,000
C28	1,699,000
C29	1,199,00
C30	1,949,000

SPECIAL DELIVERY STAMP

Cat. No.	*Quantity*
E1	198,804

PROVISIONAL ISSUES

Stamps of Japan Overprinted by Postmasters in Four Island Districts

Gen. Maresuke Nogi — A84

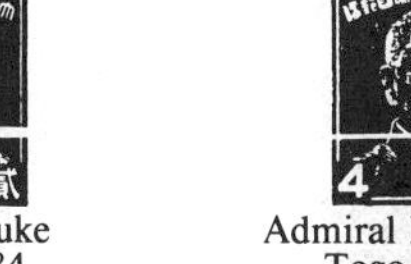

Admiral Heihachiro Togo — A86

Garambi Lighthouse, Taiwan — A88

Meiji Shrine, Tokyo — A90

Plane and Map of Japan — A92

Kasuga Shrine, Nara — A93

Mount Fuji and Cherry Blossoms — A94

Horyu Temple, Nara — A95

Miyajima Torii, Itsukushima Shrine — A96

Golden Pavilion, Kyoto — A97

Great Budda, Kamakura — A98

Kamatari Fujiwara — A99

War Factory Girl — A144

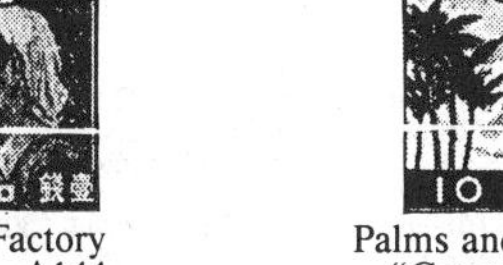

Palms and Map of "Greater East Asia" — A148

Aviator Saluting and Japanese Flag — A150

Torii of Yasukuni Shrine — A151

Mt. Fuji and Cherry Blossoms — A152

Torii of Miyajima — A153

Garambi Lighthouse, Taiwan — A154

Coal Miners — A163

"Thunderstorm below Fuji," by Hokusai — A167

Values are for unused stamps.
Used copies sell for considerably more, should be expertized and are preferred on cover or document.

KUME ISLAND

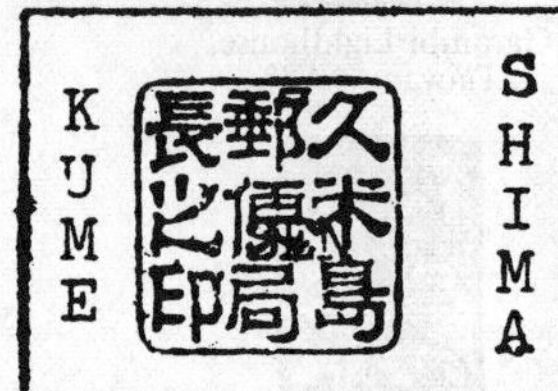

A1

Mimeographed
Seal Handstamped in Vermilion

1945, Oct. 1 Ungummed Unwmk. *Imperf.*

1X1 A1 7s black, *cream (2,400)* 1,200.
"7" & "SEN" one letter space to left 2,500.

Printed on legal-size U.S. military mimeograph paper and validated by the official seal of the Kume Island postmaster, Norifume Kikuzato. Valid until May 4, 1946.

Cancellations "20.10.1" (Oct. 1, 1945) or "20.10.6" (Oct. 6, 1945) are by favor. Copies on U.S. official bond paper, white and water-marked, were not issued.

AMAMI DISTRICT

Inspection Seal ("Ken," abbreviation for *kensa zumi,* inspected or examined; five types)

Stamps of Japan 1937-46 Handstamped in Black, Blue, Purple, Vermilion or Red

Typographed, Lithographed, Engraved

1947-48 Wmk. 257 *Perf. 13, Imperf*

2X1 A82 ½s purple, #257 800.00
2X2 A83 1s fawn, #258 —
2X3 A144 1s orange brown, #325 *1,750.*
2X4 A84 2s crimson, #259 600.00
a. 2s vermilion, #259c —
2X5 A84 2s rose red, imperf., #351 2,000.
2X6 A85 3s green, #260 *1,700.*
2X7 A84 3s brown, #329 —
2X8 A161 3s rose carmine, imperf., #352 *1,800.*
2X9 A146 4s emrald, #330 650.00
2X10 A86 5s brown lake, #331 700.00
2X11 A162 5s green, imperf., #353 *1,500.*
2X12 A147 6s light ultramarine, #332 —
2X13 A86 7s orange vermilion, #333 *1,250.*
2X14 A90 8s dark purple & pale violet, #265 *1,500.*
2X15 A148 10s crimson & dull rose, #344 500.00
2X16 A152 10s red orange, imperf., #355 *(48)* *2,500.*
2X17 A93 14s rose lake & pale rose, #268 —
2X18 A150 15s dull blue, #336 500.00
2X19 A151 17s gray violet, #337 *1,750.*
2X20 A94 20s ultramarine, #269 *1,750.*
2X21 A152 20s blue, #338 600.00
2X22 A152 20s ultramarine, imperf., #356 *(48)* *1,750.*
2X23 A95 25s dark brown & pale brown, #270 900.00
2X24 A151 27s rose brown, #339 —
2X25 A153 30s bluish green, #340 —
2X26 A153 30s bright blue, imperf., #357 *2,000.*
2X27 A88 40s dull violet, #341 *1,750.*
2X28 A154 40s dark violet, #342 *1,750.*
2X29 A97 50s olive & pale olive, #272 —
2X30 A163 50s dark brown, imperf., #358 *(48)* *2,000.*
2X31 A164 1y deep olive green, imperf., #359 *2,500.*
2X32 A167 1y deep ultramarine, imperf., #364 —
2X33 A99 5y deep gray green, #274 —
2X34 A99 5y deep gray green, imperf., #360 —

MIYAKO DISTRICT

Personal Seal of Postmaster Jojin Tomiyama

Stamps of Japan 1937-46 Handstamped in Vermilion or Red

Typographed, Lithographed, Engraved

1946-47 Wmk. 257 *Perf. 13*

3X1 A144 1s orange brown, #325 175.00
3X2 A84 2s crimson, #259 125.00
a. 2s vermilion #259c ('47) 150.00
3X3 A84 3s brown, #329 80.00
3X4 A86 4s dark green, #261 80.00
3X5 A86 5s brown lake, #331 550.00
3X6 A88 6s orange, #263 80.00
3X7 A90 8s dark purple & pale violet, #265 100.00
3X8 A148 10s crimson & dull rose, #334 80.00
3X9 A152 10s red orange, imperf., #355 ('47) *(1,000)* 120.00
3X10 A92 12s indigo, #267 80.00
3X11 A93 14s rose lake & pale rose, #268 80.00
3X12 A150 15s dull blue, #336 80.00
3X13 A151 17s gray violet, #337 80.00
3X14 A94 20s ultramarine, #269 —
3X15 A152 20s blue, #338 80.00
3X16 A152 20s ultramarine, imperf., #356 ('47) 175.00
3X17 A95 25s dark brown & pale brown, #270 80.00
3X18 A153 30s bluish green, #340 80.00
3X19 A88 40s dull violet, #341 250.00
3X20 A154 40s dark violet, #342 90.00
3X21 A97 50s olive & pale olive, #272 80.00
3X22 A163 50s dark brown, #358 ('47) *(750)* 200.00
3X23 A98 1y brown & pale brown, #273 —
3X24 A167 1y deep ultramarine, #364 ('47) *(500)* 1,500.

Nos. 3X22 and 3X24 have sewing machine perf.; No. 3X16 exists with that perf. also.

Nos. 3X1-3X2, 3X2a, 3X3-3X5, 3X8 Handstamp Surcharged with 2 Japanese Characters

1946-47

3X25 A144 1y on 1s orange brown 140.00
3X26 A84 1y on 2s crimson 2,000.
3X27 A84 1y on 3s brown ('47) 2,000.
3X28 A84 2y on 2s crimson 160.00
a. 2y on 2s vermilion ('47) 160.00
3X29 A86 4y on 4s dark green 140.00
3X30 A86 5y on 5s brown lake 140.00
3X31 A148 10y on 10s crimson & dull rose 120.00

OKINAWA DISTRICT

Personal Seal of Postmaster Shiichi Hirata

R1

Japan Nos. 355-356, 358, 364 Overprinted in Black

1947, Nov. 1 Wmk. 257 Litho. *Imperf.*

4X1 A152 10s red orange *(13,997)* 1,200.
4X2 A152 20s ultramarine *(13,611)* 500.00
4X3 A163 50s dark brown *(6,276)* 900.00
4X4 A167 1y deep ultramarine *(1,947)* 1,750.

On Revenue Stamp of Japan

4X5 R1 30s brown *(14,000)* *3,500.*

No. 4X5 is on Japan's current 30s revenue stamp. The Hirata seal validated it for postal use.

Nos. 4X1-4X4 are known with rough sewing machine perforations, full or partial.

YAEYAMA DISTRICT

Personal Seal of Postmaster Kenpuku Miyara

Stamps of Japan 1937-46 Handstamped in Black

Typographed, Engraved, Lithographed

1948 Wmk. 257 *Perf. 13*

5X1 A86 4s dark green, #261 1,200.
5X2 A86 5s brown lake, #331 1,200.
5X3 A86 7s orange vermilion, #333 800.00
5X4 A148 10s crimson & dull rose, #334 *5,000.*
5X5 A94 20s ultramarine, #269 100.00
5X6 A96 30s peacock blue, #271 1,000.
5X7 A88 40s dull violet, #341 50.00
5X8 A97 50s olive & pale olive, #272 70.00
5X9 A163 50s dark brown, imperf., #358 *(250)* 1,350.
5X10 A99 5y deep gray green, #274 2,000.

Provisional postal stationery of the four districts also exists.

LETTER SHEETS

Typographed by Japan Printing Bureau. Stamp is in upper left corner.

Values are for entires.

Stylized Deigo Blossom — US1

Banyan Tree — US2

Designer: Shutaro Higa

1948-49

U1 US1 50s vermilion, *cream, July 18, 1949 (250,000)* 42.50 60.00
First day cancel —
a. Orange red, *cream, July 1, 1948 (1,000)* 500.00 —

Designer: Ken Yabu

1950, Jan. 21

U2 US2 1y carmine red, *cream (250,000)* 40.00 50.00
First day cancel —

AIR LETTER SHEETS

DC-4 Skymaster and Shurei Gate — UC1

UC2

Designer: Chosho Ashitomi
"PAR AVION" (Bilingual) below Stamp
Litho. & Typo. by Japan Printing Bureau

1952, Nov. 1

UC1 UC1 12y dull rose, *pale blue green (126,000)* 16.00 12.50
First day cancel 60.00

Printed on tinted paper with colorless overall inscription, RYUKYU FOREIGN AIRMAIL, repeated in parallel vertical lines. Model: U.S. No. UC16.

Litho. & Typo. by Nippon Toppan K.K.
"AEROGRAMME" below Stamp

1955, Sept. 10

UC2 UC2 15y violet blue, *pale blue green (200,000)* 17.50 12.50
First day cancel 60.00

No. UC2 surcharged in Red

改 訂 改 訂

13 ¢ 13 ¢

"13" & "¢" aligned at bot.; 2 thick bars — a

"¢" raised; 2 thick bars — b

改 訂 改 訂

13 ¢ 13 ¢

"13" & "¢" as in "a"; 4 thin bars — c

"¢" raised; 4 thin bars — d

Printers: Type "a," Nakamura Printing Co., "b" and "d," Okinawa Printing Co., "c," Sun Printing Co.

1958-60

UC3	UC2	13c on 15y type "a" *(60,000)*	18.00	18.00
		First Day Cancel		60.00
a.		Type "b," *1959 (E 10,000)*	50.00	30.00
b.		Type "c," *1959 (E 2,000)*	100.00	80.00
c.		Type "d," *Oct. 1, 1960 (E 3,000)*	300.00	300.00
d.		As "b," small "¢"	1,000.	—

No. UC3c has Nos. 55, 58 affixed to make the 15c rate.

UC3

Lithographed by Japan Printing Bureau

1959, Nov. 10

UC4	UC3	15c dark blue, *pale blue (560,000)*	4.00	2.50
		First day cancel		10.00

POSTAL CARDS

Nos. UX1-UX9 are typo., others litho.

Printed by Japan Printing Bureau unless otherwise stated.

Quantities in parentheses; "E" means estimated. Values are for entire cards.

Deigo Blossom Type

Designer: Shutaro Higa

1948, July 1

UX1	US1	10s dull red, *grayish tan (100,000)*	35.00	60.00

1949, July 1

UX2	US1	15s orange red, *gray (E 175,000)*	35.00	70.00
		First day cancel		—
a.		15s vermilion, *tan (E 50,000)*	110.00	125.00

Banyan Tree Type

Designer: Ken Yabu

1950, Jan. 21

UX3	US2	50s carmine red, *light tan (E 200,000)*	7.50	7.50
		First day cancel		60.00
a.		Grayish tan card (E 25,000)	27.50	50.00

Nos. UX2, UX2a Handstamp Surcharged in Vermilion

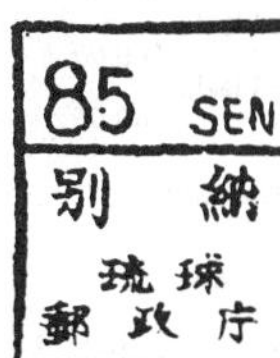

19-21x23-25mm — a

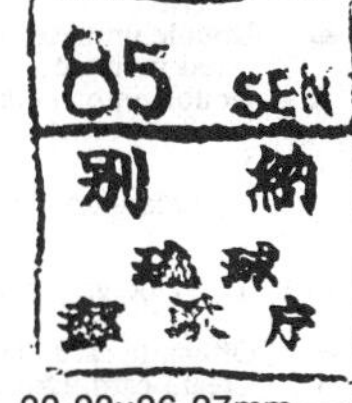

22-23x26-27mm — b

20-21x24-24½mm c

22-23½x25-26mm d

1951

UX4	US1	(c) 15s + 85s on #UX2 *(E 35,000)*	100.00	100.00
a.		Type "c" on #UX2a *(E 5,000)*	150.00	150.00
b.		Type "a" on #UX2 *(E39,000)*	75.00	100.00
c.		Type "a" on #UX2a	1,000.	—
d.		Type "b" on #UX2	*1,000.*	*1,000.*
e.		Type "d" on #UX2 *(E 4,000)*	150.00	200.00
f.		Type "d" on #UX2a *(E 1,000)*	250.00	300.00

Type "a" exists on the 15s cherry blossom postal card of Japan.

Crown, Leaf Ornaments

Naha die 21x22mm — PC3

Tokyo die 18½x19mm — PC4

Designer: Masayoshi Adaniya Koshun Printing Co.

1952

UX5	PC3	1y vermilion, *tan, Feb. 8 (400,600)*	27.50	27.50
UX6	PC4	1y vermilion, *off-white, Oct. 6 (1,295,000)*	22.50	14.00
a.		Tan card, coarse *(50,000)*	30.00	20.00
b.		Tan card, smooth *(16,000)*	500.00	150.00

Naminoue Shrine

PC5 Naha die 23x25½mm

PC6 Tokyo die 22x24½mm

Designer: Gensei Agena

1953-57

UX7	PC5	2y green, *off-white, Dec. 2, 1953 (1,799,400)*	45.00	20.00
		First day cancel		65.00
a.		Printed both sides	500.00	
UX8	PC6	2y green, *off-white, 1955 (2,799,400)*	10.00	6.00
b.		Deep blue green, *1956 (300,000)*	25.00	16.50
c.		Yellow green, *1957 (2,400,000)*	9.00	3.50
d.		As "a," printed both sides	*500.00*	
e.		As "b," printed both sides	*500.00*	

Stylized Pine, Bamboo, Plum Blossoms — PC7

Designer: Koya Oshiro Kotsura and Koshun Printing Companies

1956 New Year Card

1955, Dec. 1

UX9	PC7	2y red, *cream*	90.00	45.00
		First day cancel		100.00

No. UX9 was printed on rough card (43,400) and smooth-finish card (356,600)

Sun — PC8

Temple Lion — PC9

Designer: Seikichi Tamanaha Kobundo Printing Co.

1957 New Year Card

1956, Dec. 1

UX10	PC8	2y brown carmine & yellow, *off-white (600,000)*	4.50	3.75
		First day cancel		10.00

Designer: Shin Isagawa Fukuryu Printing Co.

1958 New Year Card

1957, Dec. 1

UX11	PC9	2y lilac rose, *off-white (1,000,000)*	1.75	2.25
		First day cancel		4.00
a.		"1" omitted in right date	60.00	75.00
b.		Printed both sides	250.00	300.00

Nos. UX8, UX8a and UX8b "Revalued" in Red, Cherry or Pink by Three Naha Printeries

改 訂 改 訂 改 訂

$1\frac{1}{2}$¢ $1\frac{1}{2}$¢ $1\frac{1}{2}$¢

a b c

1958-59

UX12	PC6	1½c on 2y green, type "a," *Sept. 16 (600,000)*	4.50	4.50
		First day cancel		10.00
a.		Shrine stamp omitted	*750.00*	*1,000.*
b.		Bar of ½ omitted, top of 2 broken	75.00	100.00
c.		Type "b," *Nov. (1,000,000)*	8.00	12.50
d.		Type "c," *1959 (200,000)*	15.00	22.50
e.		Wrong font "¢", type "c"	30.00	45.00
f.		"¢" omitted, type "c"	*1,500.*	1,500.
g.		Double surcharge, type "c"	*1,000.*	—
h.		Triple surcharge, type "c"	*1,500.*	—

Multicolor Yarn Ball — PC10

Toy Pony 19½x23mm — PC11

Designer: Masayoshi Adaniya Kobundo Printing Co.

1959 New Year Card

1958, Dec. 10

UX13 PC10 1 1/2c black, red, yellow & gray blue, *off-white* *(1,514,000)* 1.50 1.90
First day cancel 2.00
a. Black omitted —

Designer: Seikichi Tamanaha Kobundo Printing Co.

1959, June 20

UX14 PC11 1 1/2c dark blue & brown *(1,140,000)* 1.50 1.25
First day cancel 1.50
a. Dark blue omitted 350.00

Toy Carp and Boy — PC12

Toy Pony 21x25mm — PC13

Designer: Masayoshi Adaniya

1960 New Year Card

1959, Dec. 1

UX15 PC12 1 1/2c violet blue, red & black, *cream (2,000,000)* 1.25 1.50
First day cancel 1.75

1959, Dec. 30

UX16 PC13 1 1/2c gray violet & brown, *cream (3,500,000)* 2.50 75
First day cancel 2.75

Household Altar — PC14

Coral Head — PC15

Designer: Shin Isagawa

1961 New Year Card

1960, Nov. 20

UX17 PC14 1 1/2c gray, carmine, yellow & black, *off-white* *(2,647,591)* 1.25 1.50
First day cancel 1.50

Designer: Shinzan Yamada Kidekuni Printing Co.

Summer Greeting Card

1961, July 5

UX18 PC15 1 1/2c ultramarine & cerise, *off-white (264,900)* 2.25 3.75
First day cancel 4.00

Tiger PC16

Inscribed "RYUKYUS" PC17

Designer: Shin Isagawa

1962 New Year Card

1961, Nov. 15

UX19 PC16 1 1/2c ocher, black & red, *off-white (2,891,626)* 1.50 2.50
First day cancel 1.65
a. Red omitted 750.00 —
b. Red inverted *500.00* —

c. Red omitted on face, inverted on back *500.00* —
d. Double impression of red, one inverted *500.00* —
e. Double impression of ocher & black, red inverted *500.00* —
f. Double impression of ocher & black, one inverted *500.00* —

Designer: Seikichi Tamanaha

1961-67

UX20 PC17 1 1/2c gray violet & brown, *white* *('67) (18,600,000)* 1.00 50
a. Off-white card ('66) *(4,000,000)* 1.50 75
b. Cream card, Dec. 23 *(12,500,000)* 1.00 50
First day cancel 1.35

Ie Island — PC18

New Year Offerings — PC19

Designer: Shinzan Yamada Sakai Printing Co.

Summer Greeting Card

1962, July 10

UX21 PC18 1 1/2c bright blue, yellow & brown, *off-white* *(221,500)* 1.50 2.50
First day cancel 3.00
Square notch at left 35.00 45.00

Designer: Shin Isagawa Sakai Printing Co.

1963 New Year Card; Precanceled

1962, Nov. 15

UX22 PC19 1 1/2c olive brown, carmine & black *(3,000,000)* 1.50 3.00
First day cancel 2.25
a. Yellow brown background —
b. Brown ocher background —

Ryukyu Temple Dog and Wine Flask Silhouette — PC20

Water Strider — PC21

Designer: Shin Isagawa

International Postal Card

1963, Feb. 15

UX23 PC20 5c vermilion, emerald & black, *pale yellow* *(150,000)* 1.75 2.75
First day cancel 1.65
a. Black & emerald omitted 450.00

Designer: Seikichi Tamanaha

Summer Greeting Card

1963, June 20

UX24 PC21 1 1/2c Prussian green & black, *off-white (250,000)* 3.50 4.25
First day cancel 3.50

See the "Information for Collectors" section at beginning of catalogue for an explanation of perforation types, imperforates and coils.

Princess Doll — PC22

Bitter Melon Vine — PC23

Designer: Koya Oshiro

1964 New Year Card; Precanceled

1963, Nov. 15

UX25 PC22 1 1/2c orange red, yellow & ultra., *off-white (3,200,000)* 1.75 2.00
First day cancel 2.00

Designer: Shinzan Yamada

Summer Greeting Card

1964, June 20

UX26 PC23 1 1/2c multicolored, *off-white* *(285,410)* 1.40 2.25
First day cancel 1.75

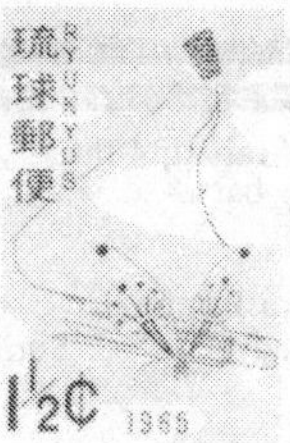

Fighting Kite with Rider — PC24

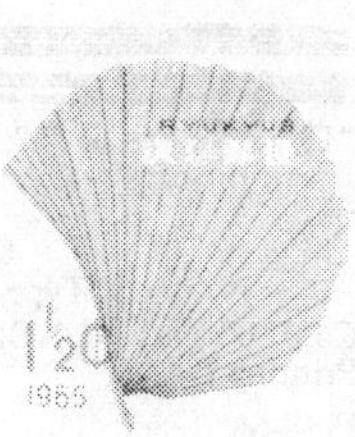

Palm-leaf Fan — PC25

Designer: Koya Oshiro

1965 New Year Card; Precanceled

1964, Nov. 15

UX27 PC24 1 1/2c multicolored, *off-white* *(4,876,618)* 1.25 1.75
First day cancel 2.00

Designer: Koya Oshiro

Summer Greeting Card

1965, June 20

UX28 PC25 1 1/2c multicolored, *off-white* *(340,604)* 1.40 2.50
First day cancel 1.65

Toy Pony Rider — PC26

Fan Palm Dipper — PC27

Designer: Seikichi Tamanaha

1966 New Year Card; Precanceled

1965, Nov. 15

UX29 PC26 1 1/2c multicolored, *off-white* *(5,224,622)* 1.25 1.75
First day cancel 1.40
a. Silver (background) omitted 250.00

Designer: Seikichi Tamanaha

Summer Greeting Card

1966, June 20

UX30 PC27 1 1/2c multicolored, *off-white* *(339,880)* 1.25 1.75
First day cancel 1.40

Toy Dove — PC28

Cycad Insect Cage and Praying Mantis — PC29

Designer: Seikichi Tamanaha

1967 New Year Card; Precanceled

1966, Nov. 15

UX31	PC28	1½c multicolored, *off-white (5,500,000)*	1.25	1.75
		First day cancel		1.65
a.		Silver (background) omitted	*500.00*	
b.		Gray blue & green omitted	*750.00*	

Designer: Shin Isagawa
Summer Greeting Card

1967, June 20

UX32	PC29	1½c multicolored, *off-white (350.000)*	1.50	2.50
		First day cancel		1.75

Paper Doll Royalty — PC30

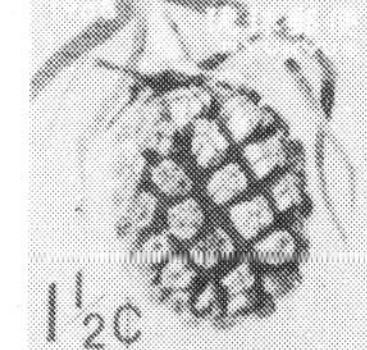
Pandanus Drupe — PC31

Designer: Shin Isagawa

1968 New Year Card; Precanceled

1967, Nov. 15

UX33	PC30	1½c multicolored, *off-white (6,200,000)*	1.10	1.50
		First day cancel		1.75
a.		Gold omitted	500.00	

Designer: Seikan Omine
Summer Greeting Card

1968, June 20

UX34	PC31	1½c multicolored, *off-white (350,000)*	1.25	2.25
		First day cancel		1.75

Toy Lion — PC32

Ryukyu Trading Ship — PC33

Designer: Teruyoshi Kinjo

1969 New Year Card; Precanceled

1968, Nov. 15

UX35	PC32	1½c multicolored, *off-white (7,000,000)*	1.10	1.50
		First day cancel		1.50

Designer: Seikichi Tamanaha
Summer Greeting Card

1969, June 20

UX36	PC33	1½c multicolored, *(349,800)*	1.25	2.25
		First day cancel		1.75

Toy Devil Mask — PC34

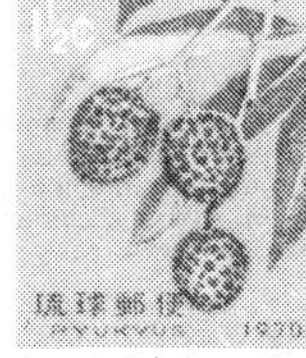
Ripe Litchis — PC35

Designer: Teruyoshi Kinjo

1970 New Year Card; Precanceled

1969, Nov. 15

UX37	PC34	1½c multicolored *(7,200,000)*	1.10	1.50
		First day cancel		1.25

Designer: Kensei Miyagi
Summer Greeting Card

1970, June 20

UX38	PC35	1½c multicolored *(400,000)*	1.40	2.25
		First day cancel		1.50

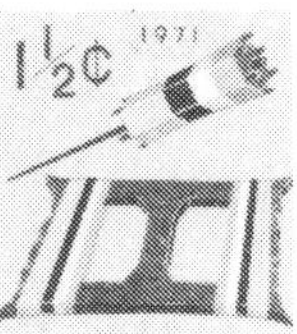
Thread-winding Implements for Dance — PC36

Ripe Guavas — PC37

Designer: Yoshinori Arakai

1971 New Year Card; Precanceled

1970, Nov. 16

UX39	PC36	1½c multicolored *(7,500,000)*	1.10	1.50
		First day cancel		1.25

Designer: Kensei Miyagi
Summer Greeting Card

1971, July 10

UX40	PC37	1½c multicolored *(400,000)*	1.25	2.25
		First day cancel		1.25

Pony Type of 1961
Zip Code Boxes in Vermilion

1971, July 10

UX41	PC17	1½c gray violet & brown *(3,000,000)*	1.25	3.50
		First day cancel		2.00

No. UX41 Surcharged below Stamp in Vermilion

"Revalued 2¢" applied by Nakamura Printing Co.

1971, Sept. 1

UX42	PC17	2c on 1½c gray violet & brown *(1,699,569)*	1.10	2.25
		First day cancel		2.00
a.		Inverted surcharge	*500.00*	
b.		Double surcharge	*500.00*	
c.		Surcharge on back	*500.00*	
e.		Surcharge on back, inverted	*500.00*	

Tasseled Castanets — PC38

Designer: Yoshinori Arakaki

Zip Code Boxes in Vermilion
1972 New Year Card; Precanceled

1971, Nov. 15

UX43	PC38	2c multicolored *(8,000,000)*	1.00	1.50
		First day cancel		1.25

Type of 1961
Zip Code Boxes in Vermilion

1971, Dec. 15

UX44	PC17	2c gray violet & brown *(3,500,000)*	1.25	1.75
		First day cancel		1.65

PAID REPLY POSTAL CARDS

Sold as two attached cards, one for message, one for reply. The listings are of unsevered cards except Nos. UY4-UY6.

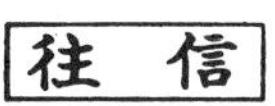

Message

Reply

1948, July 1

UY1	US1	10s + 10s dull red, *grayish tan (1,000)*	1,400.	1,500.
m.		Message card	400.00	—
r.		Reply card	400.00	—

1949, July 18

UY2	US1	15s + 15s vermilion, *tan (E 150,000)*	22.50	—
		First day cancel		—
a.		Gray card *(E 75,000)*	75.00	—
m.		Message card	6.50	16.50
r.		Reply card	6.50	16.50

1950, Jan. 21

UY3	US2	50s + 50s carmine red, *gray cream (E 130,000)*	25.00	—
		First day cancel		—
a.		Message card, double impression	—	—
b.		Light tan card *(E 96,000)*	13.50	—
m.		Message card	3.50	13.50
r.		Reply card	3.50	13.50

No. UY2a Handstamp Surcharged in Vermilion

1951

UY4	US1	1y (15s+85s) message, type "b" *(E 3750)*	350.00	350.00
a.		Reply, type "b" *(E 3750)*	350.00	350.00
b.		Message, type "a" *(E 1500)*	600.00	—
c.		Reply, type "a" *(E 1500)*	600.00	—
d.		Message, type "d" *(E 2250)*	500.00	—
e.		Reply, type "d" *(E 2250)*	500.00	—
f.		Message, UY2, type "a" *(E 250)*	150.00	225.00
g.		Reply, UY2, type "a" *(E 250)*	150.00	225.00
h.		Message, UY2, type "b" *(E 1500)*	275.00	275.00
i.		Reply, UY2, type "b" *(E 1500)*	275.00	275.00
j.		Message, UY2, type "d" *(E 250)*	150.00	250.00
k.		Reply, UY2, type "d" *(E 250)*	150.00	250.00

85 SEN
別 納
琉 球
郵 政 廳
e

85 SEN
別 納
琉 球
郵 政 庁
f

85 SEN
別 納
琉 球
郵 政 庁
g

h

Typographed Surcharge in Vermilion

UY5	US1	1y (15s+85s) message, type "f" *(E 20,000)*	125.00	125.00
a.		Reply, type "f" *(E 20,000)*	125.00	125.00
b.		Message, type "e" *(E 12,500)*	225.00	225.00
c.		Reply, type "e" *(E 12,500)*	225.00	225.00
d.		Message, type "g" *(E 500)*	*1,000.*	*1,000.*
e.		Reply, type "g" *(E 500)*	*1,000.*	*1,000.*
f.		Message, UY2, type "e" *(E 15,000)*	125.00	125.00
g.		Reply, UY2, type "e" *(E 15,000)*	125.00	125.00
h.		Message, UY2, type "f" *(E 9,000)*	125.00	125.00
i.		Reply, UY2, type "f" *(E 9,000)*	125.00	125.00
j.		Message, UY2, type "g" *(E 500)*	*1,000.*	*1,000.*
k.		Reply, UY2, type "g" *(E 500)*	*1,000.*	*1,000.*

Nos. UY4-UY5 were also issued as unsevered cards.

Typographed Surcharge Type "h" in Vermilion on No. UY3

UY6	US2	1y (50s+50s) message *(E 35,000)*	100.00	150.00
a.		Reply *(E 35,000)*	100.00	150.00
b.		Message, UY3b *(E 10,000)*	100.00	150.00
c.		Reply, UY3b *(E 10,000)*	100.00	150.00

Smooth or Coarse Card

1952, Feb. 8

UY7	PC3	1y + 1y vermilion, *gray tan (60,000)*	90.00	—
		First day cancel		250.00
m.		Message card	25.00	50.00
r.		Reply card	25.00	50.00

1953

UY8	PC4	1y + 1y vermilion, *tan (22,900)*	27.50	—
		First day cancel		—
a.		Off-white card *(13,800)*	35.00	—
m.		Message card	7.50	19.00
r.		Reply card	7.50	26.50

Off-white or Light Cream Card

1953, Dec. 2

UY9	PC5	2y + 2y green *(50,000)*	60.00	—
		First day cancel		150.00
m.		message card	15.00	25.00
r.		Reply card	15.00	35.00

1955, May

UY10	PC6	2y + 2y green, *off-white (280,000)*	10.00	—
a.		Reply card blank	500.00	
m.		Message card	3.25	11.00
r.		Reply card	3.25	15.00

No. UY10 Surcharged in Red

1958, Sept. 16

UY11	PC6	1½c on 2y, 1½c on 2y *(95,000)*	8.00	—
		First day cancel		22.50
a.		Surcharge on reply card only	*500.00*	—
b.		Surcharge on message card only	*500.00*	—
c.		Reply card double surcharge	*750.00*	—
d.		Reply card stamp omitted (surcharge only)	*1,000.*	—
m.		Message card	2.75	10.00
r.		Reply card	2.75	16.50

Surcharge varieties include: "1" omitted; wrong font "2".

Pony Types

1959, June 20

UY12	PC11	1½c + 1½c dark blue & brown *(366,000)*	2.50	—
		First day cancel		3.00
m.		Message card	65	3.50
r.		Reply card	65	3.50

1960, Mar. 10

UY13	PC13	1½c + 1½c gray violet & brown, *(150,000)*	7.00	—
		First day cancel		5.00
m.		Message card	1.50	5.00
r.		Reply card	1.50	5.00

International Type

1963, Feb. 15

UY14	PC20	5c + 5c vermilion, emerald & black, *pale yellow (70,000)*	1.75	—
		First day cancel		2.25
m.		Message card	75	3.75
r.		Reply card	75	3.75

Pony ("RYUKYUS") Type

1963-69

UY15	PC17	1½c + 1½c gray violet & brown, *cream, Mar. 15, (800,000)*	2.00	—
		First day cancel		2.50
a.		Off-white card, *Mar. 13, 1967 (100,000)*	2.25	—
b.		White card, *Nov. 22, 1969 (700,000)*	1.75	—
m.		Message card detached	40	4.00
r.		Reply card detached	40	4.00

No. UY14 Surcharged below Stamp in Vermilion

1971, Sept. 1

UY16	PC17	2c on 1½c + 2c on 1½c gray violet & brown *(80,000)*	1.50	—
		First day cancel		2.25
m.		Message card	50	2.50
r.		Reply card	50	2.50

Pony ("RYUKYUS") Type Zip Code Boxes in Vermilion

1971, Nov. 1

UY17	PC17	2c + 2c gray violet & brown *(150,000)*	1.50	—
		First day cancel		2.50
m.		Message card	50	2.50
r.		Reply card	50	2.50

REVENUE

Upon its establishment Apr. 1, 1952, the government of the Ryukyu Islands assumed responsibility for the issuing and the profit from revenue stamps. The various series served indiscriminately as evidence of payment of the required fees for various legal, realty and general commercial transactions.

1 yen — R1

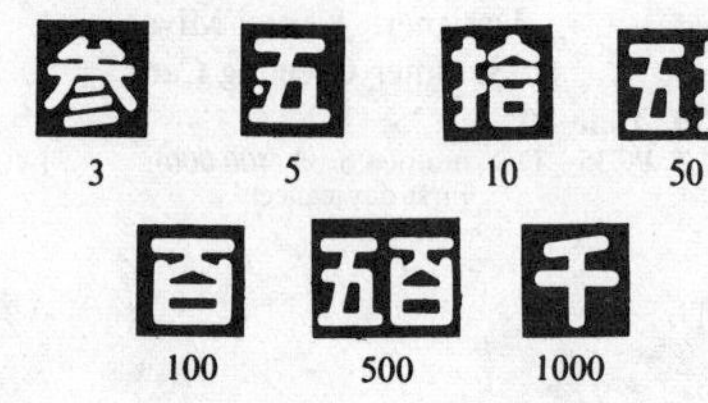

Litho. by Japan Printing Bureau.
Designer: Eizo Yonamine

1952, July 15		**Wmk. 257**		***Perf. 13x13½***
R1	R1	1y brown	7.50	3.00
R2	R1	3y carmine	10.00	3.00
R3	R1	5y green	15.00	7.50
R4	R1	10y blue	20.00	15.00
R5	R1	50y purple	30.00	15.00
R6	R1	100y yellow brown	45.00	20.00

1954, Apr. 16

R7	R1	500y dark green	120.00	70.00
R8	R1	1,000y carmine	160.00	110.00

Denomination Vertical

"Cent"

"Dollar"

Litho. by Kobundo Printing Co., Naha
Perf. 10, 10½, 11 and combinations

1958, Sept. 16		**Without Gum**		**Unwmk.**
R9	R1	1c red brown	15.00	15.00
a.		Horiz. pair, imperf. between	250.00	
R10	R1	3c red	20.00	20.00
a.		Horiz. pair, imperf. between	250.00	
R11	R1	5c green	30.00	30.00
R12	R1	10c blue	50.00	40.00
a.		Horiz. pair, imperf. between	300.00	
R13	R1	50c purple	80.00	80.00
R14	R1	$1 sepia	120.00	100.00
R15	R1	$5 dark green	250.00	100.00
R16	R1	$10 carmine	350.00	150.00

R2

R3

R4

Litho. by Japan Printing Bureau.

1959-69		**Wmk. 257**		***Perf. 13x13½***
R17	R2	1c brown	2.00	1.00
R18	R2	3c red	2.50	1.25
R19	R2	5c purple	4.00	2.50
R20	R2	10c green	7.50	4.50
R21	R2	20c sepia ('69)	40.00	25.00
R22	R2	30c light olive ('69)	50.00	30.00
R23	R2	50c blue	20.00	7.50
		Engr.		
R24	R3	$1 olive	30.00	12.00
R25	R3	$2 vermilion ('69)	125.00	30.00
R26	R3	$3 purple ('69)	150.00	40.00
R27	R3	$5 orange	70.00	35.00
R28	R3	$10 dark green	130.00	55.00
R29	R4	$20 carmine ('69)	600.00	300.00
R30	R4	$30 blue ('69)	750.00	350.00
R31	R4	$50 black ('69)	1,250.	500.00

PROVISIONAL ISSUES MIYAKO

Stamps of Japan 1938-42 Handstamped  in Black or Red

1948	**Typo., Litho., Engr.**	**Wmk. 257**	***Perf. 13***
3XR1 A84	3s brown, #329	75.00	—
3XR2 A86	5s brown lake, #331	75.00	—
3XR3 A152	20s blue, #338 (R)	60.00	—
3XR4 A95	25s dark brown & pale brown, #270 (R)	60.00	—
a.	Black overprint	500.00	—
3XR5 A96	30s peacock blue, #271 (R)	60.00	—
3XR6 A154	40s dark violet, #342 (R)	60.00	—
3XR7 A97	50s olive & pale olive, #272 (R)	135.00	—

"SPECIMEN"

Regular stamps and postal cards of 1958-65 overprinted with three cursive syllabics *mi-ho-n* ("specimen").

Two trial color proofs, Nos. 46TC and 48TC, received vermilion mihon overprints in a different cursive type (100 each).

Type A みほん

1961-64

Overprinted in Black

91S	3c multi *(1,000)*	200.00
118S	3c multi *(1,100)*	400.00
119S	3c multi *(1,100)*	350.00

Type B みほん

1964-65

Overprinted in Red or Black

120aS	3c dp bl, dp car & ocher (R) *(1,500)*		175.00
121S	3c multi (R) *(1,500)*	150.00	
124S	3c ultra, yel & red (R) *(5,000)*		30.00
125S	3s dl cl, yel & blk *(1,500)*		60.00
126S	3c yel & multi *(2,000)*		50.00
127S	3c gray, red & blk *(2,000)*		50.00
128S	3c multi *(1,500)*		60.00
129S	1½c multi (R) *(1,500)*		50.00
130S	3c lt bl & multi (R) *(1,500)*		150.00
131S	3c multi (R) *(1,500)*		45.00
132S	3c buff & multi *(2,000)*		150.00
133S	3c grn & multi (R) *(2,000)*		45.00
134S	3c multi *(2,000)*		45.00
135S	3c bl & multi *(2,000)*		45.00
136S	3c gldn brn & multi *(2,000)*		45.00
139S	1½c multi (R) *(2,500)*		40.00

Postal Cards

1964-65

Overprinted Type A or B in Black or Red

UX26S A	1½c multi *(1,000)*	500.00
UX27S B	1½c multi *(1,000)*	350.00
UX28S A	1½c multi *(1,000)*	300.00
UX29S A	1½c multi *(1,100)*	250.00

UNEMPLOYMENT INSURANCE

These stamps, when affixed in an official booklet and canceled, certified a one-day contract for a day laborer. They were available to employers at certain post offices on various islands.

Dove — RQ1

Shield — RQ2

Lithographed in Naha

1961, Jan. 10 Without Gum Unwmk. *Rouletted*

RQ1	RQ1	2c pale red	400.00	—
RQ2	RQ2	4c violet	20.00	20.00

Redrawn

Lithographed by Japan Printing Bureau

1966, Feb. Unwmk. *Perf. 13x13½*

RQ3	RQ1	2c pale violet	—	—
RQ4	RQ2	4c violet	15.00	15.00

Redrawn stamps have bolder numerals and inscriptions, and fewer, stronger lines of shading in background.

琉球政府 8¢ 失業保険印紙 Cycad — RQ3

Lithographed by Japan Printing Bureau

1968, Apr. 19 Wmk. 257 *Perf. 13x13½*

RQ5	RQ3	8c brown	20.00	20.00

Nos. RQ3-RQ4 Surcharged with New Values and 2 Bars

1967-72

RQ6	RQ1	8c on 2c pale red	35.00	35.00
RQ7	RQ2	8c on 4c violet ('72)	20.00	20.00
RQ8	RQ2	12c on 4c violet ('71)	15.00	15.00

PROOFS AND TRIAL COLOR PROOFS

1948

Salmon Paper

1aP	5s magenta	—
2aP	10s yellow green	—
3aP	20s yellor green	—
5aP	40s magenta	—
6aP	50s ultramarine	—
7aP	1y ultramarine	—

Sheets of the second printing, Nos. 1-7, were overprinted in Tokyo with a swirl-pattern of blue or red dots. These essays sell for about $400 each.

1950

Soft White Paper

8P	50s dark carmine rose	600.00
9P	1y deep blue	600.00
10P	2y rose violet	600.00
11P	3y carmine rose	600.00
12P	4y greenish gray	600.00
12TC	4y olive	600.00
13P	5y blue green	600.00

1951

14P	3y red brown	800.00
15P	3y dark green	1,000.

1953

27P	3y deep magenta	—
28P	6y dull blue	—

1958

46TC	2c black	500.00
48TC	4c black	500.00

AIR POST

1950

C1P	8y bright blue	900.00
C2P	12y green	900.00
C3P	16y rose carmine	900.00

1951

C4P	13y blue	1,000.
C5P	18y green	1,000.
C6P	30y cerise	800.00

SPECIAL DELIVERY

1950

E1P	5y bright blue	700.00

An official proof folder contains one each of Nos. 8P-13P, 12TC, C1P-C3P and E1P.

UNITED NATIONS

United Nations stamps are used on U.N. official mail sent from U.N. Headquarters in New York City, the U.N. European Office in Geneva, Switzerland, or from the Donaupark Vienna International Center or Atomic Energy Agency in Vienna, Austria to points throughout the world. They may be used on private correspondence sent through the U.N. post offices.

U.N. mail is carried by the U.S., Swiss and Austrian postal systems.

See Switzerland official stamp listings in the Scott *Standard Postage Stamp Catalogue* for stamps issued by the Swiss Government for official use of the U.N. European Office and other U.N. affiliated organizations. See France official stamp listings for stamps issued by the French Government for official use of UNESCO.

The 1962 U.N. Temporary Executive Authority overprints on stamps of Netherlands New Guinea are listed under West Irian in the Scott Standard Catalogue.

+: When following the quantity, this indicates the total printed to date. Unless otherwise noted, these are the initial printing order.

Blocks of four generally sell for four times the single stamp value.

Peoples of the World — A1

UN Headquarters Building — A2

"Peace, Justice, Security" — A3

UN Flag — A4

UN International Childrens Emergency Fund — A5

World Unity — A6

Printed by Thomas De La Rue & Co., Ltd., London (1c, 3c, 10c, 15c, 20c, 25c), and Joh. Enschede and Sons, Haarlem, Netherlands (1½c, 2c, 5c, 50c, $1). The 3c, 15c and 25c have frame engraved, center photogravure; other denominations are engraved. Panes of 50. Designed by O. C. Meronti (A1), Leon Helguera (A2), J. F. Doeve (A3), Ole Hamann (A4), S. L. Hartz (5c) and Hubert Woyty-Wimmer (20c).

Perf. 13x12½, 12½x13

1951 Engr. and Photo. Unwmk.

1	A1	1c magenta, *Oct. 24, 1951 (8,000,000)*	5	5
		First day cover		50
		Margin block of 4, UN seal	25	—
2	A2	1½c blue green, *Oct. 24, 1951 (7,450,000)*	5	5
		First day cover		50
		Margin block of 4, UN seal	25	—
		Precanceled *(361,700)*		10.00
3	A3	2c purple, *Nov. 16, 1951 (8,470,000)*	5	5
		First day cover		50
		Margin block of 4, UN seal	25	—
4	A4	3c magenta & blue, *Oct. 24, 1951 (8,250,000)*	5	5
		First day cover		50
		Margin block of 4, UN seal	25	—
5	A5	5c blue, *Oct. 24, 1951 (6,000,000)*	8	6
		First day cover		75
		Margin block of 4, UN seal	40	—
6	A1	10c chocolate, *Nov. 16, 1951 (2,600,000)*	18	15
		First day cover		1.00
		Margin block of 4, UN seal	90	—
7	A4	15c violet & blue, *Nov. 16, 1951 (2,300,000)*	25	20
		First day cover		1.25
		Margin block of 4, UN seal	1.25	—
8	A6	20c dark brown, *Nov. 16, 1951 (2,100,000)*	50	40
		First day cover		1.50
		Margin block of 4, UN seal	2.50	—
9	A4	25c olive gray & blue, *Oct. 24, 1951 (2,100,000)*	45	40
		First day cover		2.00
		Margin block of 4, UN seal	2.25	—
10	A2	50c indigo, *Nov. 16, 1951 (1,500,000)*	5.00	4.00
		First day cover		8.00
		Margin block of 4, UN seal	25.00	—
11	A3	$1 red, *Oct. 24, 1951 (2,012,500)*	2.25	1.00
		First day cover		9.00
		Margin block of 4, UN seal	11.25	—

First day covers of Nos. 1-11 and C1-C4 total 1,113,216.

The various printings of Nos. 1-11 vary in sheet marginal perforation. Some were perforated through left or right margins, or both; some through all margins.

Sheets of this issue carry a marginal inscription consisting of the UN seal and "First UN/Issue 1951." This inscription appears four times on each sheet. The listing "Margin block of 4, UN seal" or "Margin block of 4, inscription" in this and following issues refers to a corner block.

Sheets of the 1½c, 2c, 50c and $1 have a cut-out of different shape in one margin. The printer trimmed this off entirely on most of the 1½c third printing, and partially on the 1½c fourth printing and $1 fifth and sixth printings.

For 30c in type A1 and 10fr in type A3, see UN Offices in Geneva Nos. 4 and 14.
Forgeries of the 1 ½c precancel exist.

Veterans' War Memorial Building, San Francisco — A7

Issued to mark the 7th anniversary of the signing of the United Nations Charter.
Engraved and printed by the American Bank Note Co., New York. Panes of 50. Designed by Jean Van Noten.

1952, Oct. 24 ***Perf. 12***

12	A7	5c blue *(1,274,670)*	30	15
		First day cover *(160,117)*		75
		Margin block of 4, inscription	1.50	—

Globe and Encircled Flame — A8

Issued to commemorate the 4th anniversary of the adoption of the Universal Declaration of Human Rights.
Engraved and printed by Thomas De La Rue & Co., Ltd., London. Panes of 50. Designed by Hubert Woyty-Wimmer.

1952, Dec. 10 ***Perf. 13½x14***

13	A8	3c deep green *(1,554,312)*	10	8
		First day cover		50
		Margin block of 4, inscription	50	—
14	A8	5c blue *(1,126,371)*	60	20
		First day cover		65
		First day cover, #13-14		90
		Margin block of 4, inscription	3.00	—

First day covers of Nos. 13 and 14 total 299,309.

Refugee Family — A9

Issued to publicize "Protection for Refugees."
Engraved and printed by Thomas De La Rue & Co., Ltd., London. Panes of 50. Designed by Olav Mathiesen.

1953, Apr. 24 ***Perf. 12½x13***

15	A9	3c dark red brown & rose brown *(1,299,793)*	25	10
		First day cover		45
		Margin block of 4, inscription	1.25	—
16	A9	5c indigo & blue *(969,224)*	1.00	50
		First day cover		80
		First day cover, #15-16		1.00
		Margin block of 4, inscription	5.00	—

First day covers of Nos. 15 and 16 total 234,082.

Envelope, U. N. Emblem and Map — A10

Issued to honor the Universal Postal Union.
Engraved and printed by Thomas De La Rue & Co., Ltd., London. Panes of 50. Designed by Hubert Woyty-Wimmer.

1953, June 12 ***Perf. 13***

17	A10	3c black brown *(1,259,689)*	25	12
		First day cover		40
		Margin block of 4, inscription	1.25	—
18	A10	5c dark blue *(907,312)*	1.25	60
		First day cover		85
		First day cover, #17-18		1.10
		Margin block of 4, inscription	6.25	—

First day covers of Nos. 17 and 18 total 231,627.
Plate number ("1A" or "1B") in color of stamp appears below 47th stamp of sheet.

Gearwheels and U. N. Emblem — A11

Issued to publicize United Nations activities in the field of technical assistance.
Engraved and printed by Thomas De La Rue & Co. Ltd. London. Panes of 50. Designed by Olav Mathiesen.

1953, Oct. 24 ***Perf. 13x12½***

19	A11	3c dark gray *(1,184,348)*	10	12
		First day cover		40
		Margin block of 4, inscription	50	—
20	A11	5c dark green *(968,182)*	90	50
		First day cover		50
		First day cover, #19-20		75
		Margin block of 4, inscription	4.50	—

First day covers of Nos. 19 and 20 total 229,211.

Hands Reaching Toward Flame — A12

Issued to publicize Human Rights Day.
Engraved and printed by Thomas De La Rue & Co., Ltd., London. Panes of 50. Designed by Leon Helguera.

1953, Dec. 10 ***Perf. 12½x13***

21	A12	3c bright blue *(1,456,928)*	25	12
		First day cover		40
		Margin block of 4, inscription	1.25	—
22	A12	5c rose red *(983,831)*	1.75	50
		First day cover		60
		First day cover, #21-22		90
		Margin block of 4, inscription	8.75	—

First day covers of Nos. 21 and 22 total 265,186.

Ear of Wheat — A13

Issued to honor the Food and Agriculture Organization.
and printed by Thomas De La Rue & Co., Ltd., London. Panes of 50. Designed by Dirk Van Gelder.

1954, Feb. 11 ***Perf. 12½x13***

23	A13	3c dark green & yellow *(1,250,000)*	50	10
		First day cover		40
		Margin block of 4, inscription	2.50	—
24	A13	8c indigo & yellow *(949,718)*	1.00	60
		First day cover		60
		First day cover, #23-24		90
		Margin block of 4, inscription	5.00	—

First day covers of Nos. 23 and 24 total 272,312.

U. N. Emblem and Anvil Inscribed "ILO" — A14

Design: 8c, inscribed "OIT."
Issued to honor the International Labor Organization.
Engraved and printed by Thomas De La Rue & Co., Ltd., London. Panes of 50. Designed by José Renau.

1954, May 10 ***Perf. 12½x13***

25	A14	3c brown *(1,085,651)*	15	14
		First day cover		40
		Margin block of 4, inscription	75	—
26	A14	8c magenta *(903,561)*	3.50	75
		First day cover		75
		First day cover, #25-26		1.00
		Margin block of 4, inscription	17.50	—

First day covers of Nos. 25 and 26 total 252,796.

U. N. European Office, Geneva — A15

Issued on the occasion of United Nations Day.
Engraved and printed by Thomas De La Rue & Co., Ltd., London. Panes of 50. Designed by Earl W. Purdy.

1954, Oct. 25 ***Perf. 14***

27	A15	3c dark blue violet *(1,000,000)*	3.75	1.25
		First day cover		1.40
		Margin block of 4, inscription	19.00	—
28	A15	8c red *(1,000,000)*	25	25
		First day cover		60
		First day cover, #27-28		1.65
		Margin block of 4, inscription	1.25	—

First day covers of Nos. 27 and 28 total 233,544.

Mother and Child — A16

Issued to publicize Human Rights Day.
Engraved and printed by Thomas De La Rue & Co., Ltd. London. Panes of 50. Designed by Leonard C. Mitchell.

1954, Dec. 10 ***Perf. 14***

29	A16	3c red orange *(1,000,000)*	12.00	2.75
		First day cover		3.50
		Margin block of 4, inscription	60.00	—
30	A16	8c olive green *(1,000,000)*	50	25
		First day cover		50
		First day cover, #29-30		3.75
		Margin block of 4, inscription	2.50	—

First day covers of Nos. 29 and 30 total 276,333.

Symbol of Flight — A17

Design: 8c, inscribed "OACI."

Issued to honor the International Civil Aviation Organization.
Engraved and printed by Waterlow & Sons, Ltd., London. Panes of 50. Designed by Angel Medina Medina.

1955, Feb. 9 — ***Perf. 13½x14***

No.	Type	Description	Unused	Used
31	A17	5c blue *(1,000,000)*	3.00	50
		First day cover		75
		Margin block of 4, inscription	15.00	—
32	A17	8c rose carmine *(1,000,000)*	1.00	90
		First day cover		1.25
		First day cover, #31-32		1.50
		Margin block of 4, inscription	5.00	—

First day covers of Nos. 31 and 32 total 237,131.

UNESCO Emblem — A18

Issued to honor the U. N. Educational, Scientific and Cultural Organization.
Engraved and printed by Waterlow & Sons, Ltd., London. Panes of 50. Designed by George Hamori.

1955, May 11 — ***Perf. 13½x14***

No.	Type	Description	Unused	Used
33	A18	3c lilac rose *(1,000,000)*	1.30	50
		First day cover		65
		Margin block of 4, inscription	6.50	—
34	A18	8c light blue *(1,000,000)*	20	20
		First day cover		50
		First day cover, #33-34		1.00
		Margin block of 4, inscription	1.00	—

First day covers of Nos. 33 and 34 total 255,326.

United Nations Charter — A19

Design: 4c, Spanish inscription. 8c, French inscription.
Issued to commemorate the 10th anniversary of the United Nations.
Engraved and printed by Waterlow & Sons, Ltd., London. Panes of 50. Designed by Claude Bottiau.

1955, Oct. 24 — ***Perf. 13½x14***

No.	Type	Description	Unused	Used
35	A19	3c deep plum *(1,000,000)*	3.00	75
		First day cover		1.00
		Margin block of 4, inscription	15.00	—
36	A19	4c dull green *(1,000,000)*	20	10
		First day cover		35
		Margin block of 4, inscription	1.00	—
37	A19	8c bluish black *(1,000,000)*	30	15
		First day cover		50
		First day cover, #35-37		1.65
		Margin block of 4, inscription	1.50	—

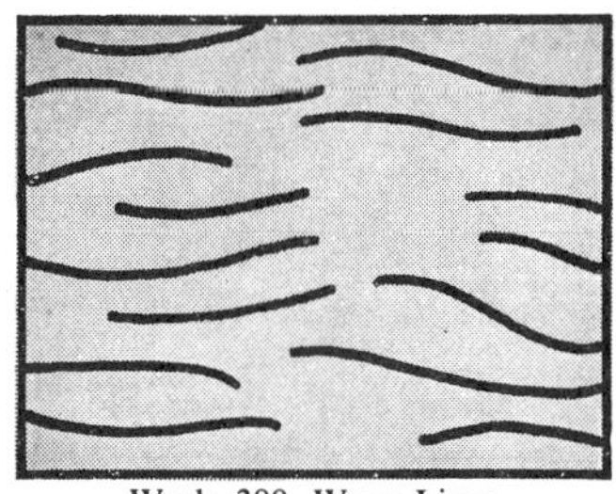
Wmk. 309- Wavy Lines

Souvenir Sheet

1955, Oct. 24 — **Wmk. 309** — ***Imperf.***

No.	Type	Description	Unused	Used
38	A19	Sheet of three *(250,000)*	180.00	45.00
a.		3c deep plum	10.00	5.00
b.		4c dull green	10.00	5.00
c.		8c bluish black	10.00	5.00
		First day cover		47.50
		Sheet with retouch on 8c	185.00	47.50

No. 38 measures 108x83mm and has marginal inscriptions in deep plum.
Two printings were made of No. 38. The first (200,000) may be distinguished by the broken line of background shading on the 8c. It leaves a small white spot below the left leg of the "n" of "Unies." For the second printing (50,000), the broken line was retouched, eliminating the white spot. The 4c was also retouched.

First day covers of Nos. 35-38 total 455,791.
Copies of No. 38 are known with the 4c and 8c stamps misaligned.

Hand Holding Torch — A20

Issued in honor of Human Rights Day.
Engraved and printed by Waterlow & Sons, Ltd., London. Panes of 50. Designed by Hubert Woyty-Wimmer.

1955, Dec. 9 — **Unwmk.** — ***Perf. 14x13½***

No.	Type	Description	Unused	Used
39	A20	3c ultramarine *(1,250,000)*	10	10
		First day cover		50
		Margin block of 4, inscription	50	—
40	A20	8c green *(1,000,000)*	1.00	50
		First day cover		65
		First day cover, #39-40		1.00
		Margin block of 4, inscription	5.50	—

First day covers of Nos. 39 and 40 total 298,038.

Symbols of Telecommunication — A21

Design: 8c, inscribed "UIT."
Issued in honor of the International Telecommunication Union.
Engraved and printed by Thomas De La Rue & Co., Ltd., London. Panes of 50. Designed by Hubert Woyty-Wimmer.

1956, Feb. 17 — ***Perf. 14***

No.	Type	Description	Unused	Used
41	A21	3c turquoise blue *(1,000,000)*	30	15
		First day cover		45
		Margin block of 4, inscription	1.50	—
42	A21	8c deep carmine *(1,000,000)*	80	45
		First day cover		55
		First day cover, #41-42		90
		Margin block of 4, inscription	4.00	—

Plate number ("1A" or "1B") in color of stamp appears below 47th stamp of sheet.

Globe and Caduceus — A22

Design: 8c, inscribed "OMS."
Issued in honor of the World Health Organization.
Engraved and printed by Thomas De La Rue & Co., Ltd., London. Panes of 50. Designed by Olav Mathiesen.

1956, Apr. 6 — ***Perf. 14***

No.	Type	Description	Unused	Used
43	A22	3c bright greenish blue *(1,250,000)*	10	10
		First day cover		40
		Margin block of 4, inscription	50	—
44	A22	8c golden brown *(1,000,000)*	1.00	50
		First day cover		75
		First day cover, #43-44		1.00
		Margin block of 4, inscription	5.00	—

First day covers of Nos. 43 and 44 total 260,853.

General Assembly — A23

Design: 8c, French inscription.
Issued to commemorate United Nations Day.
Engraved and printed by Thomas De La Rue & Co., Ltd., London. Panes of 50. Designed by Kurt Plowitz.

1956, Oct. 24 — ***Perf. 14***

No.	Type	Description	Unused	Used
45	A23	3c dark blue *(2,000,000)*	5	5
		First day cover		15
		Margin block of 4, inscription	25	—
46	A23	8c gray olive *(1,500,000)*	12	10
		First day cover		35
		First day cover, #45-46		40
		Margin block of 4, inscription	60	—

First day covers of Nos. 45 and 46 total 303,560.

Flame and Globe — A24

Issued to publicize Human Rights Day
Engraved and printed by Thomas De La Rue & Co., Ltd., London. Panes of 50. Designed by Rashid-ud Din.

1956, Dec. 10 — ***Perf. 14***

No.	Type	Description	Unused	Used
47	A24	3c plum *(5,000,000)*	5	5
		First day cover		15
		Margin block of 4, inscription	25	—
48	A24	8c dark blue *(4,000,000)*	12	10
		First day cover		25
		First day cover, #47-48		35
		Margin block of 4, inscription	60	—

First day covers of Nos. 47 and 48 total 416,120.

Weather Balloon — A25

Design: 8c, Agency name in French.
Issued to honor the World Meterological Organization.
Engraved and printed by Thomas De La Rue & Co., Ltd., London. Panes of 50. Designed by A. L. Pollock.

1957, Jan. 28 — ***Perf. 14***

No.	Type	Description	Unused	Used
49	A25	3c violet blue *(5,000,000)*	5	5
		First day cover		15
		Margin block of 4, inscription	25	—
50	A25	8c dark carmine rose *(3,448,985)*	12	10
		First day cover		25
		First day cover, #49-50		35
		Margin block of 4, inscription	60	—

First day covers of Nos. 49 and 50 total 376,110.

Badge of U. N. Emergency Force — A26

Issued in honor of the U. N. Emergency Force.
Engraved and printed by Thomas De La Rue & Co., Ltd., London. Panes of 50. Designed by Ole Hamann.

1957, Apr. 8 ***Perf. 14x12½***

51	A26	3c	light blue *(4,000,000)*	5	5
			First day cover		15
			Margin block of 4, inscription	25	—
52	A26	8c	rose carmine *(3,000,000)*	12	10
			First day cover		25
			First day cover, #51-52		35
			Margin block of 4, inscription	60	—

First day covers of Nos. 51 and 52 total 461,772.

Nos. 51-52 Re-engraved

1957, Apr., May ***Perf. 14x12½***

53	A26	3c	blue *(2,736,206)*	6	6
			Margin block of 4, inscription	30	—
54	A26	8c	rose carmine *(1,000,000)*	15	12
			Margin block of 4, inscription	75	—

On Nos. 53-54 the background within and around the circles is shaded lightly, giving a halo effect. The lettering is more distinct with a line around each letter.

U. N. Emblem and Globe — A27

Design: 8c, French inscription.
Issued to honor the Security Council.
Engraved and printed by Thomas De La Rue & Co., Ltd., London. Panes of 50. Designed by Rashid-ud Din.

1957, Oct. 24 ***Perf. 12½x13***

55	A27	3c	orange brown *(3,674,968)*	5	5
			First day cover		15
			Margin block of 4, inscription	25	—
56	A27	8c	dark blue green *(2,885,938)*	12	10
			First day cover		25
			First day cover, #55-56		35
			Margin block of 4, inscription	60	—

First day covers of Nos. 55 and 56 total 460,627.

Flaming Torch — A28

Issued in honor of Human Rights Day.
Engraved and printed by Thomas De La Rue & Co., Ltd., London. Panes of 50. Designed by Olav Mathiesen.

1957, Dec. 10 ***Perf. 14***

57	A28	3c	red brown *(3,368,405)*	5	5
			First day cover		15
			Margin block of 4, inscription	25	—
58	A28	8c	black *(2,717,310)*	12	10
			First day cover		25
			First day cover, #57-58		35
			Margin block of 4, inscription	60	—

First day covers of Nos. 57 and 58 total 553,669.

U. N. Emblem Shedding Light on Atom — A29

Design: 8c, French inscription.
Issued in honor of the International Atomic Energy Agency.
Engraved and printed by the American Bank Note Co., New York. Panes of 50. Designed by Robert Perrot.

1958, Feb. 10 ***Perf. 12***

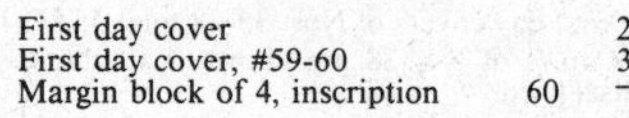

59	A29	3c	olive *(3,663,305)*	5	5
			First day cover		15
			Margin block of 4, inscription	25	—
60	A29	8c	blue *(3,043,622)*	12	10
			First day cover		25
			First day cover, #59-60		35
			Margin block of 4, inscription	60	—

First day covers of Nos. 59 and 60 total 504,832.

Central Hall, Westminster — A30

Design: 8c, French inscription.
Central Hall, Westminster, London, was the site of the first session of the United Nations General Assembly, 1946.
Engraved and printed by the American Bank Note Co., New York. Panes of 50. Designed by Olav Mathiesen.

1958, Apr. 14 ***Perf. 12***

61	A30	3c	violet blue *(3,353,716)*	5	5
			First day cover		15
			Margin block of 4, inscription	25	—
62	A30	8c	rose claret *(2,836,747)*	12	10
			First day cover		25
			First day cover, #61-62		35
			Margin block of 4, inscription	60	—

First day covers of Nos. 61 and 62 total 449,401.

U. N. Seal — A31

Engraved and printed by Bradbury, Wilkinson & Co., Ltd., England. Panes of 50. Designed by Herbert M. Sanborn.

1958, Oct. 24 ***Perf. 13½x14***

63	A31	4c	red orange *(9,000,000)*	6	6
			First day cover		15
			Margin block of 4, inscription	30	—

1958, June 2 ***Perf. 13x14***

64	A31	8c	bright blue *(5,000,000)*	12	10
			First day cover *(219,422)*		25
			Margin block of 4, inscription	60	—
			Margin block of 4, Bradbury, Wilkinson imprint	3.00	—

Gearwheels — A32

Design: 8c, French inscription.
Issued to honor the Economic and Social Council.
Engraved and printed by the American Bank Note Co., New York. Panes of 50. Designed by Ole Hamann.

1958, Oct. 24 **Unwmk.** ***Perf. 12***

65	A32	4c	dark blue green *(2,556,784)*	6	6
			First day cover		15
			Margin block of 4, inscription	30	—
66	A32	8c	vermilion *(2,175,117)*	12	10
			First day cover		25
			First day cover, #65-66		35
			Margin block of 4, inscription	60	—

First day covers of Nos. 63, 65 and 66 total 626,236.

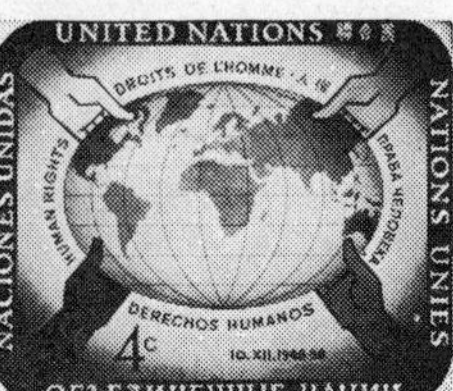

Hands Upholding Globe — A33

Issued for Human Rights Day and to commemorate the tenth anniversary of the signing of the Universal Declaration of Human Rights.
Engraved and printed by the American Bank Note Co., New York. Panes of 50. Designed by Leonard C. Mitchell.

1958, Dec. 10 **Unwmk.** ***Perf. 12***

67	A33	4c	yellow green *(2,644,340)*	6	6
			First day cover		15
			Margin block of 4, inscription	30	—
68	A33	8c	red brown *(2,216,838)*	12	10
			First day cover		25
			First day cover, #67-68		35
			Margin block of 4, inscription	60	—

First day covers of Nos. 67 and 68 total 618,124.

New York City Building, Flushing Meadows — A34

Design: 8c, French inscription.
New York City Building at Flushing Meadows, New York, was the site of many General Assembly meetings, 1946-50.
Engraved and printed by Canadian Bank Note Company, Ltd., Ottawa. Panes of 50. Designed by Robert Perrot.

1959, Mar. 30 **Unwmk.** ***Perf. 12***

69	A34	4c	light lilac rose *(2,035,011)*	6	6
			First day cover		20
			Margin block of 4, inscription	30	—
70	A34	8c	aquamarine *(1,627,281)*	12	10
			First day cover		25
			First day cover, #69-70		40
			Margin block of 4, inscription	60	—

First day covers of Nos. 69 and 70 total 440,955.

U. N. Emblem and Symbols of Agriculture, Industry and Trade — A35

Issued to honor the Economic Commission for Europe.
Engraved and printed by Canadian Bank Note Company, Ltd., Ottawa. Panes of 50. Designed by Ole Hamann.

1959, May 18 **Unwmk.** ***Perf. 12***

71	A35	4c	blue *(1,743,502)*	8	5
			First day cover		20
			Margin block of 4, inscription	40	—
72	A35	8c	red orange *(1,482,898)*	16	12
			First day cover		30
			First day over, #71-72		45
			Margin block of 4, inscription	80	—

First day covers of Nos. 71 and 72 total 433,549.

Figure Adapted from Rodin's "Age of Bronze" — A36

Design: 8c, French inscription.
Issued to honor the Trusteeship Council.

Engraved and printed by Canadian Bank Note Co., Ltd., Ottawa. Panes of 50. Designed by Leon Helguera; lettering by Ole Hamann.

1959, Oct. 23 Unwmk. *Perf. 12*

73	A36	4c bright red *(1,929,677)*	6	6
		First day cover		15
		Margin block of 4, inscription	30	—
74	A36	8c dark olive green *(1,587,647)*	12	10
		First day cover		25
		First day cover, #73-74		35
		Margin block of 4, inscription	60	—

First day covers of Nos. 73 and 74 total 466,053.

World Refugee Year Emblem — A37

Design: 8c, French inscription.
Issued to publicize World Refugee Year, July 1, 1959-June 30, 1960.
Engraved and printed by Canadian Bank Note Co., Ltd., Ottawa. Panes of 50. Designed by Olav Mathiesen.

1959, Dec. 10 Unwmk. *Perf. 12*

75	A37	4c olive & red *(2,168,963)*	6	5
		First day cover		15
		Margin block of 4, inscription	30	—
76	A37	8c olive & bright greenish blue *(1,843,886)*	12	10
		First day cover		25
		First day cover, #75-76		35
		Margin block of 4, inscription	60	—

First day covers of Nos. 75 and 76 total 502,262.

Chaillot Palace, Paris — A38

Design: 8c, French inscription.
Chaillot Palace in Paris was the site of General Assembly meetings in 1948 and 1951.
Engraved and printed by Thomas De La Rue & Co., Ltd., London. Panes of 50. Designed by Hubert Woyty-Wimmer.

1960, Feb. 29 Unwmk. *Perf. 14*

77	A38	4c rose lilac & blue *(2,276,678)*	6	6
		First day cover		15
		Margin block of 4, inscription	30	—
78	A38	8c dull green & brown *(1,930,869)*	12	10
		First day cover		25
		First day cover, #77-78		35
		Margin block of 4, inscription	60	—

First day covers of Nos. 77 and 78 total 446,815.

Map of Far East and Steel Beam — A39

Design: 8c, French inscription.
Issued to honor the Economic Commission for Asia and the Far East (ECAFE).
Printed by the Government Printing Bureau, Tokyo. Panes of 50. Designed by Hubert Woyty-Wimmer.

1960, Apr. 11 Photo. Unwmk. *Perf. 13x13½*

79	A39	4c deep claret, blue green & dull yellow *(2,195,945)*	6	6
		First day cover		15
		Margin block of 4, inscription	30	—
80	A39	8c olive green, blue & rose *(1,897,902)*	12	10
		First day cover		25
		First day cover, #79-80		35
		Margin block of 4, inscription	60	—

First day covers of Nos. 79 and 80 total 415,127.

Tree, FAO and U.N. Emblems — A40

Design: 8c, French inscription.
Issued to commemorate the Fifth World Forestry Congress, Seattle, Washington, Aug. 29-Sept. 10.
Printed by the Government Printing Bureau, Tokyo. Panes of 50. Designed by Ole Hamann.

1960, Aug. 29 Photo. Unwmk. *Perf. 13½*

81	A40	4c dark blue, green & orange *(2,188,293)*	6	6
		First day cover		15
		Margin block of 4, inscription	30	—
a.		Imperf., pair		—
82	A40	8c yellow green, black & orange *(1,837,778)*	12	10
		First day cover		25
		First day cover, #81-82		35
		Margin block of 4, inscription	60	—

First day covers of Nos. 81 and 82 total 434,129.

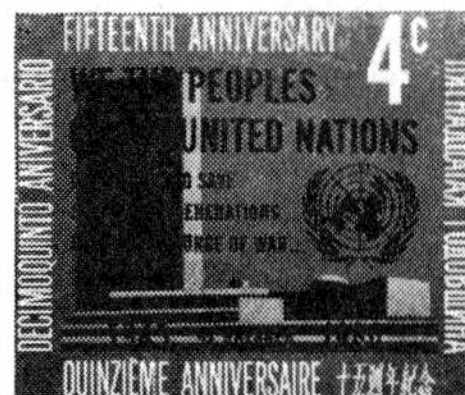

U.N. Headquarters and Preamble to U.N. Charter — A41

Design: 8c, French inscription.
Issued to commemorate the 15th anniversary of the United Nations.
Engraved and printed by the British American Bank Note Co., Ltd., Ottawa, Canada. Panes of 50. Designed by Robert Perrot.

1960, Oct. 24 Unwmk. *Perf. 11*

83	A41	4c blue *(2,631,593)*	6	5
		First day cover		15
		Margin block of 4, inscription	30	—
84	A41	8c gray *(2,278,022)*	12	10
		First day cover		25
		First day cover, #83-84		35
		Margin block of 4, inscription	60	—

Souvenir Sheet

Imperf

85	A41	Sheet of two *(1,000,000)*	1.35	1.35
a.		4c blue	25	15
b.		8c gray	25	15
		First day cover *(256,699)*		3.00

No. 85 has dark gray marginal inscription. Size: 92x71mm. Broken "I" and "V" flaws occur in "ANNIVERSARY" in marginal inscription. Copies are known with the two stamps misaligned.

Block and Tackle — A42

Design: 8c, French inscription.
Issued to honor the International Bank for Reconstruction and Development.
Printed by the Government Printing Bureau, Tokyo. Panes of 50. Designed by Angel Medina Medina.

1960, Dec. 9 Photo. Unwmk. *Perf. 13½x13*

86	A42	4c multicolored *(2,286,117)*	6	6
		First day cover		15
		Margin block of 4, inscription	30	—
87	A42	8c multicolored *(1,882,019)*	12	10
		First day cover		25
		First day cover, #86-87		35
		Margin block of 4, inscription	60	—
a.		Imperf., pair		—

First day covers of Nos. 86 and 87 total 559,708.
No. 86 exists imperf.

Scales of Justice from Raphael's Stanze — A43

Design: 8c, French inscription.
Issued to honor the International Court of Justice.
Printed by the Government Printing Bureau, Tokyo, Japan. Panes of 50. Designed by Kurt Plowitz.

1961, Feb. 13 Photo. Unwmk. *Perf. 13½x13*

88	A43	4c yellow, orange brown & black *(2,234,588)*	6	6
		First day cover		15
		Margin block of 4, inscription	30	—
89	A43	8c yellow, green & black *(2,023,968)*	12	10
		First day cover		25
		First day cover, #88-89		35
		Margin block of 4, inscription	60	—

First day covers of Nos. 88 and 89 total 447,467.
Nos. 88-89 exist imperf.

Seal of International Monetary Fund — A44

Design: 7c, French inscription.
Issued to honor the International Monetary Fund.
Printed by the Government Printing Bureau, Tokyo, Japan. Panes of 50. Designed by Roy E. Carlson and Hordur Karlsson, Iceland.

1961, Apr. 17 Photo. Unwmk. *Perf. 13x13½*

90	A44	4c bright bluish green *(2,305,010)*	6	6
		First day cover		15
		Margin block of 4, inscription	30	—
91	A44	7c terra cotta & yellow *(2,147,201)*	12	10
		First day cover		25
		First day cover, #90-91		35
		Margin block of 4, inscription	60	—

First day covers of Nos. 90 and 91 total 448,729.

Abstract Group of Flags — A45

Printed by Courvoisier S.A., La Chaux-de-Fonds, Switzerland. Panes of 50. Designed by Herbert M. Sanborn.

1961, June 5 Photo. Unwmk. *Perf. 11½*

92	A45	30c multicolored *(3,370,000)*	35	15
		First day cover *(182,949)*		55
		Margin block of 4, inscription	1.75	—

See U.N. Offices in Geneva No. 10.

Cogwheel and Map of Latin America — A46

Design: 11c, Spanish inscription.
Issued to honor the Economic Commission for Latin America.
Printed by the Government Printing Bureau, Tokyo. Panes of 50. Designed by Robert Perrot.

1961, Sept. 18 Photo. Unwmk. *Perf. 13½*

93 A46 4c blue, red & citron *(2,037,912)* 10 10
First day cover 15
Margin block of 4, inscription 50 —
94 A46 11c green, lilac & org vermilion *(1,835,097)* 30 20
First day cover 40
First day cover, #93-94 50
Margin block of 4, inscription 1.50 —

First day covers of Nos. 93 and 94 total 435,820.

Africa House, Addis Ababa, and Map — A47

Design: 11c, English inscription.
Issued to honor the Economic Commission for Africa.
Printed by Courvoisier S.A., La Chaux-de-Fonds, Switzerland. Panes of 50. Designed by Robert Perrot.

1961, Oct. 24 Photo. Unwmk. *Perf. 11½*

95 A47 4c ultramarine, orange, yellow & brown *(2,044,842)* 6 6
First day cover 15
Margin block of 4, inscription 30 —
96 A47 11c emerald, orange, yellow & brown *(1,790,894)* 16 12
First day cover 40
First day cover, #95-96 50
Margin block of 4, inscription 80 —

First day covers of Nos. 95 and 96 total 435,131.

Mother Bird Feeding Young and UNICEF Seal — A48

Designs: 3c, Spanish inscription. 13c, French inscription.
Issued to commemorate the 15th anniversary of the United Nations Children's Fund.
Printed by Courvoisier S.A., La Chaux-de-Fonds, Switzerland. Panes of 50. Designed by Minoru Hisano.

1961, Dec. 4 Photo. Unwmk. *Perf. 11½*

97 A48 3c brown, gold, orange & yellow *(2,867,456)* 5 5
First day cover 15
Margin block of 4, inscription 25 —
98 A48 4c brown, gold, blue & emerald *(2,735,899)* 6 6
First day cover 15
Margin block of 4, inscription 30 —
99 A48 13c dp. grn., gold, purple & pink *(1,951,715)* 20 20
First day cover 60
First day cover, #97-99 60
Margin block of 4, inscription 1.00 —

First day covers of Nos. 97-99 total 752,979.

Family and Symbolic Buildings — A49

Design: 7c, inscribed "Services Collectifs".
Issued to publicize the U.N. program for housing and urban development, and in connection with the expert committee meeting at U.N. headquarters, Feb. 7-21.
Printed by Harrison and Sons, Ltd., London, England. Panes of 50. Designed by Olav Mathiesen.

1962, Feb. 28 Photo. Unwmk. *Perf. 14½x14*

Central design multicolored

100 A49 4c bright blue *(2,204,190)* 8 6
First day cover 15
Margin block of 4, inscription 40 —
a. Black omitted —
b. Yellow omitted —
c. Brown omitted —
101 A49 7c orange brown *(1,845,821)* 14 10
First day cover 25
First day cover, #100-101 35
Margin block of 4, inscription 70 —
a. Red omitted —

First day covers of Nos. 100-101 total 466,178.

"The World Against Malaria" — A50

Issued in honor of the World Health Organization and to call attention to the international campaign to eradicate malaria from the world.
Printed by Harrison and Sons, Ltd., London, England. Panes of 50. Designed by Rashid-ud Din.

1962, Mar. 30 Photo. Unwmk. *Perf. 14x14½*

Word frame in gray

102 A50 4c orange, yellow, brown, green & black *(2,047,000)* 8 6
First day cover 15
Margin block of 4, inscription 40 —
103 A50 11c green, yellow, brown & indigo *(1,683,766)* 22 12
First day cover 35
First day cover, #102-103 45
Margin block of 4, inscription 1.10 —

First day covers of Nos. 102-103 total 522,450.

"Peace" — A51

U.N. Flag — A52

Hands Combining "UN" and Globe — A53

U.N. Emblem over Globe — A54

Printed by Harrison & Sons, Ltd. London, England (1c, 3c and 11c), and by Canadian Bank Note Co., Ltd., Ottawa (5c). Panes of 50. Designed by Kurt Plowitz (1c), Ole Hamann (3c), Renato Ferrini (5c) and Olav Mathiesen (11c).

Photo.; Engr. (5c)

1962, May 25 Unwmk. *Perf. 14x14½*

104 A51 1c vermilion, blue, blk. & gray *(5,000,000)* 5 5
First day cover 18
Margin block of 4, inscription 25 —
105 A52 3c light green, Prussian blue, yellow & gray *(5,000,000)* 5 5
First day cover 15
Margin block of 4, inscription 25 —

Perf. 12

106 A53 5c dark carmine rose *(4,000,000)* 12 10
First day cover 22
Margin block of 4, inscription 60 —

Perf. 12½

107 A54 11c dark & light blue & gold *(4,400,000)* 15 15
First day cover 35
First day cover, #104-107 75
Margin block of 4, inscription 75 —

First day covers of Nos. 104-107 total 738,985.
Size of 5c, No. 106: 36½x23½mm.
See No. 167.
See U.N. Offices in Geneva Nos. 2 and 6.

Flag at Half-mast and U.N. Headquarters — A55

Issued on the first anniversary of the death of Dag Hammarskjold, Secretary General of the United Nations 1953-61, in memory of those who died in the service of the United Nations.
Printed by Courvoisier S. A., La Chaux-de-Fonds, Switzerland. Panes of 50. Designed by Ole Hamann.

1962, Sept. 17 Photo. Unwmk. *Perf. 11½*

108 A55 5c black, light blue & blue *(2,195,707)* 15 10
First day cover 18
Margin block of 4, inscription 75 —
109 A55 15c black, gray olive & blue *(1,155,047)* 55 20
First day cover 45
First day cover, #108-109 50
Margin block of 4, inscription 2.75 —

First day covers of Nos. 108-109 total 513,963.

World Map Showing Congo — A56

Design: 11c inscribed "Operation des Nations Unies au Congo."
Issued to commemorate the United Nations Operation in the Congo.
Printed by Courvoisier S. A., La Chaux-de-Fonds, Switzerland. Panes of 50. Designed by George Hamori.

1962, Oct. 24 Photo. Unwmk. *Perf. 11½*

110 A56 4c olive, orange, blk. & yellow *(1,477,958)* 15 10
First day cover 15
Margin block of 4, inscription 75 —
111 A56 11c bl. grn., org., blk. & yel. *(1,171,255)* 50 20
First day cover 40
First day cover, #110-111 50
Margin block of 4, inscription 2.50 —

First day covers of Nos. 110-111 total 460,675.

Globe in Universe and Palm Frond — A57

Design: 4c, English inscription.
Issued to honor the Committee on Peaceful Uses of Outer Space.
Printed by Bradbury, Wilkinson and Co., Ltd., England. Panes of 50. Designed by Kurt Plowitz.

1962, Dec. 3 Engr. Unwmk. *Perf. 14x13½*

112	A57	4c violet blue, *(2,263,876)*	6	5
		First day cover		15
		Margin block of 4, inscription	30	—
113	A57	11c rose claret *(1,681,584)*	16	12
		First day cover		35
		First day cover, #112-113		40
		Margin block of 4, inscription	80	—

First day covers of Nos. 112-113 total 529,780.

Development Decade Emblem — A58

Design: 11c, French inscription.
Issued to publicize the U.N. Development Decade and to commemorate the U.N. Conference on the Application of Science and Technology for the Benefit of the Less Developed Areas, Geneva, Feb. 4-20.
Printed by Courvoisier S. A., La Chaux-de-Fonds, Switzerland. Panes of 50. Designed by Rashid-ud Din.

1963, Feb. 4 Photo. Unwmk. *Perf. 11½*

114	A58	5c pale grn., maroon, dk. bl. & Prussian blue *(1,802,406)*	8	6
		First day cover		18
		Margin block of 4, inscription	40	—
115	A58	11c yel., maroon, dk. bl. & Prussian blue *(1,530,190)*	18	10
		First day cover		35
		First day cover, #114-115		50
		Margin block of 4, inscription	90	—

First day covers of Nos. 114-115 total 460,877.

Stalks of Wheat — A59

Design: 11c, French inscription.
Issued for the "Freedom from Hunger" campaign of the Food and Agriculture Organization.
Printed by Courvoisier S. A., La Chaux-de-Fonds, Switzerland. Panes of 50. Designed by Ole Hamann.

1963, Mar. 22 Photo. Unwmk. *Perf. 11½*

116	A59	5c vermilion, green & yellow *(1,666,178)*	8	6
		First day cover		18
		Margin block of 4, inscription	40	—
117	A59	11c verm., deep claret & yel. *(1,563,023)*	18	10
		First day cover		35
		First day cover, #116-117		50
		Margin block of 4, inscription	90	—

First day covers of Nos. 116-117 total 461,868.

An enhanced introduction to the Scott Catalogue begins on Page V. A thorough understanding of the material presented there will greatly aid your use of the catalogue itself.

Bridge over Map of New Guinea — A60

Issued to commemorate the first anniversary of the United Nations Temporary Executive Authority (UNTEA) in West New Guinea (West Irian).
Printed by Courvoisier S.A., La Chaux-de-Fonds, Switzerland. Panes of 50. Designed by Henry Bencsath.

1963, Oct. 1 Photo. Unwmk. *Perf. 11½*

118	A60	25c blue, green & gray *(1,427,747)*	38	20
		First day cover *(222,280)*		60
		Margin block of 4, inscription	1.90	—

General Assembly Building, New York — A61

Design: 11c, French inscription.
Since October 1955 all sessions of the General Assembly have been held in the General Assembly Hall, U.N. Headquarters, N.Y.
Printed by the Government Printing Bureau, Tokyo. Panes of 50. Designed by Kurt Plowitz.

1963, Nov. 4 Photo. Unwmk. *Perf. 13*

119	A61	5c vio. bl., bl., yel. grn. & red *(1,892,539)*	8	6
		First day cover		18
		Margin block of 4, inscription	40	—
120	A61	11c grn., yel. grn., bl., yel. & red *(1,435,079)*	18	10
		First day cover		35
		First day cover, #119-120		50
		Margin block of 4, inscription	90	—

First day covers of Nos. 119-120 total 410,306.

Flame — A62

Design: 11c inscribed "15e Anniversaire."
Issued to commemorate the 15th anniversary of the signing of the Universal Declaration of Human Rights.
Printed by the Government Printing Bureau, Tokyo. Panes of 50. Designed by Rashid-ud Din.

1963, Dec. 10 Photo. Unwmk. *Perf. 13*

121	A62	5c green, gold, red & yellow *(2,208,008)*	8	6
		First day cover		18
		Margin block of 4, inscription	40	—
122	A62	11c carm., gold, blue & yellow *(1,501,125)*	18	10
		First day cover		35
		First day cover, #121-122		50
		Margin block of 4, inscription	90	—

First day covers of Nos. 121-122 total 567,907.

Ships at Sea and IMCO Emblem — A63

Design: 11c, inscribed "OMCI."
Issued to honor the Intergovernmental Maritime Consultative Organization.

Printed by Courvoisier S.A., La Chaux-de-Fonds, Switzerland. Panes of 50. Designed by Henry Bencsath; emblem by Olav Mathiesen.

1964, Jan. 13 Photo. Unwmk. *Perf. 11½*

123	A63	5c blue, olive, ocher & yellow *(1,805,750)*	8	6
		First day cover		18
		Margin block of 4, inscription	40	—
124	A63	11c dark blue, dark green, emerald & yellow *(1,583,848)*	18	10
		First day cover		35
		First day cover, #123-124		50
		Margin block of 4, inscription	90	—

First day covers of Nos. 123-124 total 442,696.

World Map, Sinusoidal Projection — A64

U.N. Emblem — A65

Three Men United Before Globe — A66

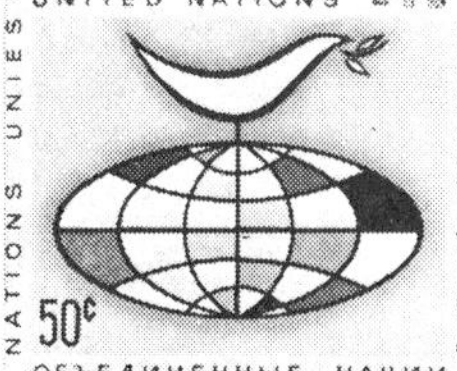

Stylized Globe and Weather Vane — A67

Printed by Thomas De La Rue & Co. Ltd., London (2c) and Courvoisier S.A., La Chaux-de-Fonds, Switzerland (7c, 10c and 50c). Panes of 50.
Designed by Ole Hamann (2c), George Hamori (7c, 10c) and Hatim El Mekki (50c).

1964-71 Photo. Unwmk. *Perf. 14*

125	A64	2c light & dark blue, orange & yellow green *(3,800,000)*	5	5
		First day cover		12
		Margin block of 4, inscription	25	—
a.		Perf. 13x13½, *Feb. 24, 1971 (1,500,000)*	6	6
		Perf. 11½		
126	A65	7c dark blue, orange brown & black *(2,700,000)*	10	8
		First day cover		22
		Margin block of 4, inscription	50	—
127	A66	10c blue green, olive green & black *(3,200,000)*	15	10
		First day cover		35
		First day cover, #125-127		50
		Margin block of 4, inscription	75	—
128	A67	50c multicolored *(2,520,000)*	75	40
		First day cover *(210,713)*		1.00
		Margin block of 4, inscription	3.75	—

Issue dates: 50c, Mar. 6; 2c, 7c and 10c, May 29, 1964.
First day covers of 2c, 7c and 10c total 524,073.
See U.N. Offices in Geneva Nos. 3 and 12.

Arrows Showing Global Flow of Trade — A68

Design: 5c, English inscription.
Issued to commemorate the U.N. Conference on Trade and Development, Geneva, March 23-June 15.
Printed by Thomas De La Rue & Co., Ltd., London. Panes of 50. Designed by Herbert M. Sanborn and Ole Hamann.

1964, June 15 Photo. Unwmk. *Perf. 13*

129 A68	5c	black, red & yellow *(1,791,211)*	8	6
		First day cover		18
		Margin block of 4, inscription	40	—
130 A68	11c	black, olive & yellow *(1,529,526)*	18	10
		First day cover		35
		First day cover, #129-130		50
		Margin block of 4, inscription	90	—

First day covers of Nos. 129-130 total 422,358.

Poppy Capsule and Reaching Hands — A69

Design: 11c, Inscribed "Echec au Stupéfiants."

Issued to honor international efforts and achievements in the control of narcotics.

Printed by the Canadian Bank Note Co., Ottawa. Panes of 50. Designed by Kurt Plowitz.

1964, Sept. 21 Engr. Unwmk. *Perf. 12*

131 A69	5c	rose red & black *(1,508,999)*	8	6
		First day cover		18
		Margin block of 4, inscription	40	—
132 A69	11c	emerald & black *(1,340,691)*	18	10
		First day cover		35
		First day cover, #131-132		50
		Margin block of 4, inscription	90	—

First day covers of Nos. 131-132 total 445,274.

Padlocked Atomic Blast — A70

Issued to commemorate the signing of the nuclear test ban treaty pledging an end to nuclear explosions in the atmosphere, outer space and under water.

Printed by Artia, Prague, Czechoslovakia. Panes of 50. Designed by Ole Hamann.

Litho. and Engr.

1964, Oct. 23 Unwmk. *Perf. 11x11½*

133 A70	5c	dark red & dark brown *(2,422,789)*	8	5
		First day cover *(298,652)*		20
		Margin block of 4, inscription	40	—

Education for Progress — A71

Design: 11c, French inscription.

Issued to publicize the UNESCO world campaign for universal literacy and for free compulsory primary education.

Printed by Courvoisier, S. A., La Chaux-de-Fonds, Switzerland. Panes of 50. Designed by Kurt Plowitz.

1964, Dec. 7 Photo. Unwmk. *Perf. 12½*

134 A71	4c	org. red, bister, grn. & blue *(2,375,181)*	6	5
		First day cover		15
		Margin block of 4, inscription	30	—
135 A71	5c	bister, red, dk. & lt. blue *(2,496,877)*	8	5
		First day cover		18
		Margin block of 4, inscription	40	—
136 A71	11c	green, lt. blue, blk. & rose *(1,773,645)*	16	10
		First day cover		30
		First day cover, #134-136		50
		Margin block of 4, inscription	80	—

First day covers of Nos. 134-136 total 727,875.

Progress Chart of Special Fund, Key and Globe — A72

Design: 11c, French inscription.

Issued to publicize the Special Fund program to speed economic growth and social advancement in low-income countries.

Printed by the Government Printing Bureau, Tokyo. Panes of 50. Designed by Rashid-ud Din, Pakistan.

1965, Jan. 25 Photo. Unwmk. *Perf. 13½x13*

137 A72	5c	dull bl., dk. bl., yel. & red *(1,949,274)*	8	5
		First day cover		15
		Margin block of 4, inscription	40	—
138 A72	11c	yel. grn., dk. bl., yel. & red *(1,690,908)*	16	10
		First day cover		35
		First day cover, #137-138		40
		Margin block of 4, inscription	80	—
a.		Black omitted (U.N. emblem on key)	—	

First day covers of Nos. 137-138 total 490,608.

U.N. Emblem, Stylized Leaves and View of Cyprus — A73

Design: 11c, French inscription.

Issued to honor the United Nations Peace-keeping Force on Cyprus.

Printed by Courvoisier S.A., Switzerland. Panes of 50. Designed by George Hamori, Australia.

1965, Mar. 4 Photo. Unwmk. *Perf. 11½*

139 A73	5c	orange, olive & black *(1,887,042)*	8	5
		First day cover		15
		Margin block of 4, inscription	40	—
140 A73	11c	yellow green, bl. grn. & blk. *(1,691,767)*	16	10
		First day cover		35
		First day cover, #139-140		45
		Margin block of 4, inscription	80	—

First day covers of Nos. 139-140 total 438,059.

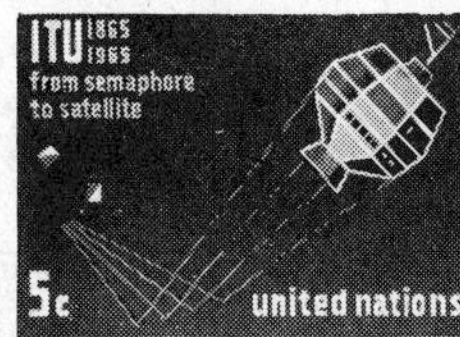

"From Semaphore to Satellite" — A74

Design: 11c, French inscription.

Issued to commemorate the centenary of the International Telecommunication Union.

Printed by Courvoisier S.A., Switzerland. Panes of 50. Designed by Kurt Plowitz, United States.

1965, May 17 Photo. Unwmk. *Perf. 11½*

141 A74	5c	aquamarine, orange, blue & purple *(2,432,407)*	8	5
		First day cover		18
		Margin block of 4, inscription	40	—
142 A74	11c	light violet, red orange, bister & bright green *(1,731,070)*	16	10
		First day cover		35
		First day cover, #141-142		45
		Margin block of 4, inscription	80	—

First day covers of Nos. 141-142 total 434,393.

ICY Emblem — A75

Design: 15c, French inscription.

Issued to commemorate the 20th anniversary of the United Nations and International Cooperation Year.

Printed by Bradbury, Wilkinson and Co., Ltd., England. Panes of 50. Designed by Olav Mathiesen, Denmark.

1965, June 26 Engr. Unwmk. *Perf. 14x13½*

143 A75	5c	dark blue *(2,282,452)*	8	5
		First day cover		18
		Margin block of 4, inscription	40	—
144 A75	15c	lilac rose *(1,993,562)*	24	10
		First day cover		38
		First day cover, #143-144		50
		Margin block of 4, inscription	1.25	—

Souvenir Sheet

145 A75		Sheet of two *(1,928,366)*	50	40
		First day cover		1.50

No. 145 contains one each of Nos. 143-144 with dark blue and ocher marginal inscription, ocher edging. Size: 92x70mm.

First day covers of Nos. 143-145 total: New York, 748,876; San Francisco, 301,435.

"Peace" — A76

Opening Words, U.N. Charter — A77

U.N. Headquarters and Emblem — A78

U.N. Emblem — A79

U.N. Emblem Encircled — A80

Printed by Government Printing Bureau, Tokyo (1c); Government Printing Office, Austria (15c, 20c); Government Printing Office (Bundesdruckerei), Berlin (25c), and Courvoisier S.A., Switzerland ($1). Panes of 50.

Designed by Kurt Plowitz U.S. (1c); Olav S. Mathiesen, Denmark (15c); Vergniaud Pierre-Noel, U.S. (20c); Rashid-ud Din, Pakistan (25c), and Ole Hamann, Denmark ($1).

1965-66 Photo. Unwmk. *Perf. 13½x13*

146 A76	1c	vermilion, blue, blk. & gray *(7,000,000)*	5	5
		First day cover		15
		Margin block of 4, inscription	25	—

Perf. 14

147 A77	15c	olive bister, dull yellow, black & deep claret *(2,500,000)*	24	12
		First day cover		50
		Margin block of 4, inscription	1.25	—

Perf. 12

148 A78	20c	dk. blue, bl., red & yel. *(3,000,000)*	30	15
		First day cover		55
		First day cover, #147-148		85
		Margin block of 4, inscription	1.50	—
a.		Yellow omitted	—	

Litho. and Embossed

Perf. 14

149 A79	25c	light & dark blue *(3,200,000)*	40	20
		First day cover		65
		First day cover, #146, 149		70
		Margin block of 4, inscription	2.00	
		Margin block of 6, "Bundesdruckerei Berlin" imprint and inscription	20.00	

Photro.

Perf. 11½

150 A80	$1 aquamarine & sapphire *(2,570,000)*	1.50	75
	First day cover *(181,510)*		2.00
	Margin block of 4, inscription	7.50	—

Issue dates: 1c and 25c, Sept. 20, 1965; 15c and 20c, Oct. 25, 1965; $1, Mar. 25, 1966.

First day covers of Nos. 146 and 149 total 443,964. Those of Nos. 147-148 total 457,596.

The 25c has the marginal inscription (U.N. emblem and "1965") in two sizes: 1st printing (with Bundesdruckerei imprint), 6mm in diameter; 2nd printing, 8mm. In 1st printing, "halo" of U.N. emblem is larger, overlapping "25c."

See U.N. Offices in Geneva Nos. 5, 9 and 11.

Fields and People — A81

Design: 11c, French inscription.

Issued to emphasize the importance of the world's population growth and its problems and to call attention to population trends and development.

Printed by Government Printing Office, Austria. Panes of 50. Designed by Olav S. Mathiesen, Denmark.

1965, Nov. 29 Photo. Unwmk. *Perf. 12*

151 A81	4c multicolored *(1,966,033)*	6	5
	First day cover		15
	Margin block of 4, inscription	30	—
152 A81	5c multicolored *(2,298,731)*	8	5
	First day cover		15
	Margin block of 4, inscription	40	—
153 A81	11c multicolored *(1,557,589)*	16	10
	First day cover		25
	First day cover, #151-153		45
	Margin block of 4, inscription	80	—

First day covers of Nos. 151-153 total 710,507.

Globe and Flags of U.N. Members — A82

Design: 15c, French inscription.

Issued to honor the World Federation of United Nations Associations.

Printed by Courvoisier S.A., Switzerland. Panes of 50. Designed by Olav S. Mathiesen, Denmark.

1966, Jan. 31 Photo. Unwmk. *Perf. 11½*

154 A82	5c multicolored *(2,462,215)*	8	5
	First day cover		15
	Margin block of 4, inscription	40	—
155 A82	15c multicolored *(1,643,661)*	22	12
	First day cover		35
	First day cover, #154-155		45
	Margin block of 4, inscription	1.10	—

First day covers of Nos. 154-155 total 474,154.

WHO Headquarters, Geneva — A83

Design: 11c, French inscription.

Issued to commemorate the opening of the World Health Organization Headquarters, Geneva.

Printed by Courvoisier, S.A., Switzerland. Panes of 50. esigned by Rashid-ud Din.

Granite Paper

1966, May 26 Photo. *Perf. 12½x12*

156 A83	5c light & dark blue, orange, green & bister *(2,079,893)*	8	5
	First day cover		15
	Magin block of 4, inscription	40	—
157 A83	11c orange, light & dark blue, green & bister *(1,879,879)*	16	10
	First day cover		25
	First day cover, #156-157		35
	Margin block of 4, inscription	80	—

First day covers of Nos. 156-157 total 466,171.

Coffee — A84

Design: 11c, Spanish inscription.

Issued to commemorate the International Coffee Agreement of 1962.

Printed by the Government Printing Bureau, Tokyo. Panes of 50. Designed by Rashid-ud Din, Pakistan.

1966, Sept. 19 Photo. *Perf. 13½x13*

158 A84	5c orange, light blue, green, red & dark brown *(2,020,308)*	8	5
	First day cover		20
	Margin block of 4, inscription	40	—
159 A84	11c light blue, yellow, green, red & dark brown *(1,888,682)*	16	10
	First day cover		25
	First day cover, #158-159		40
	Margin block of 4, inscription	80	—

First day covers of Nos. 158-159 total 435,886.

United Nations Observer — A85

Issued to honor the Peace Keeping United Nation Observers.

Printed by Courvoisier, S.A. Panes of 50. Designed by Ole S. Hamann.

Granite Paper

1966, Oct. 24 Photo. *Perf. 11½*

160 A85	15c steel blue, org., blk. & grn. *(1,889,809)*	22	12
	First day cover *(255,326)*		40
	Margin block of 4, inscription	1.10	—

Children of Various Races — A86

Designs: 5c, Children riding in locomotive and tender. 11c, Children in open railroad car playing medical team (French inscription).

Issued to commemorate the 20th anniversary of the United Nations Children's Fund (UNICEF).

Printed by Thomas De La Rue & Co., Ltd. Panes of 50. Designed by Kurt Plowitz.

1966, Nov. 28 Litho. *Perf. 13x13½*

161 A86	4c pink & multicolored *(2,334,989)*	6	5
	First day cover		12
	Margin block of 4, inscription	30	—
162 A86	5c pale green & multicolored *(2,746,941)*	8	6
	First day cover		15
	Margin block of 4, inscription	40	—
a.	Yellow omitted	—	—
163 A86	11c light ultramarine & multicolored *(2,123,841)*	16	10
	First day cover		25
	First day cover, #161-163		45
	Margin block of 4, inscription	80	—
a.	Imperf., pair	—	
b.	Dark blue omitted	—	

First day covers of Nos. 161-163 total 987,271.

Hand Rolling up Sleeve and Chart Showing Progress — A87

Design: 11c, French inscription.

United Nations Development Program.

Printed by Courvoisier, S.A. Panes of 50. Designed by Olav S. Mathiesen.

1967, Jan. 23 Photo. *Perf. 12½*

164 A87	5c grn., yel., pur. & org. *(2,204,679)*	8	6
	First day cover		20
	Margin block of 4, inscription	40	—
165 A87	11c bl., choc., lt. grn. & org. *(1,946,159)*	16	10
	First day cover		25
	First day cover, #164-165		40
	Margin block of 4, inscription	80	—

First day covers of Nos. 164-165 total 406,011.

Type of 1962 and

U.N. Headquarters, New York, and World Map — A88

Printed by Courvoisier, S.A. Panes of 50. Designed by Jozsef Vertel, Hungary (1½c); Renato Ferrini, Italy (5c).

1967 Photo. *Perf. 11½*

166 A88	1½c ultra., black, orange & ocher *(4,000,000)*	5	5
	First day cover *(199,751)*		20
	Margin block of 4, inscription	25	—

Size: 33x23mm

167 A53	5c red brn., brn. & org. yel *(5,500,000)*	8	8
	First day cover *(212,544)*		20
	Margin block of 4, inscription	40	—

Issue dates: 1½c, March 17; 5c, Jan. 23.

For 5c of type A88, see U.N. Offices in Geneva No. 1.

Fireworks — A89

Design: 11c, French inscription.

Issued to honor all nations which gained independence since 1945.

Printed by Harrison & Sons, Ltd. Panes of 50. Designed by Rashid-ud Din.

1967, Mar. 17 Photo. *Perf. 14x14½*

168 A89	5c dark blue & multi. *(2,445,955)*	8	6
	First day cover		15
	Margin block of 4, inscription	40	—
169 A89	11c brown lake & multi. *(2,011,004)*	16	10
	First day cover		25
	First day cover, #168-169		30
	Margin block of 4, inscription	80	—

First day covers of Nos. 168-169 total 390,499.

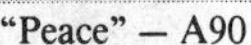
"Peace" — A90

U.N. Pavilion, EXPO '67 — A91

Designs: 5c, Justice. 10c, Fraternity. 15c, Truth.
Issued to commemorate EXPO '67, International Exhibition, Montreal, Apr. 28-Oct. 27, 1967.
Under special agreement with the Canadian Government Nos. 170-174 were valid for postage only on mail posted at the U.N. pavilion during the Fair. The denominations are expressed in Canadian currency.
Printed by British American Bank Note Co., Ltd., Ottawa. The 8c was designed by Olav S. Mathiesen after a photograph by Michael Drummond. The others were adapated by Ole S. Hamann from reliefs by Ernest Cormier on doors of General Assembly Hall, presented to U.N. by Canada.

1967, Apr. 28 **Engr. & Litho.** ***Perf. 11***

170	A90	4c red & red brown *(2,464,813)*	7	7
		First day cover		15
		Margin block of 4, inscription	35	—
171	A90	5c blue & red brown *(2,177,073)*	9	9
		First day cover		20
		Margin block of 4, inscription	45	—
		Litho.		
172	A91	8c multicolored *(2,285,440)*	15	15
		First day cover		25
		Margin block of 4, inscription	75	—
		Engr. and Litho.		
173	A90	10c green & red brown *(1,955,352)*	18	18
		First day cover		65
		Margin block of 4, inscription	90	—
174	A90	15c dark brown & red brown *(1,899,185)*	28	28
		First day cover		85
		First day cover, #170-174		1.90
		Margin block of 4, inscription	1.40	—

First day covers of Nos. 170-174 total 901,625.

Luggage Tags and U.N. Emblem — A92

Issued to publicize International Tourist Year, 1967.
Printed by Government Printing Office, Berlin. Panes of 50. Designed by David Dewhurst.

1967, June 19 **Litho.** ***Perf. 14***

175	A92	5c reddish brown & multi. *(2,593,782)*	8	5
		First day cover		15
		Margin block of 4, inscription	40	—
176	A92	15c ultramarine & multi. *(1,940,457)*	22	12
		First day cover		40
		First day cover, #175-176		45
		Margin block of 4, inscription	1.10	—

First day covers of Nos. 175-176 total 382,886.

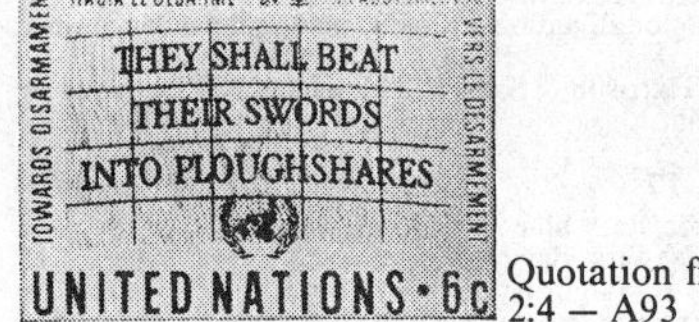

Quotation from Isaiah 2:4 — A93

Design: 13c, French inscription.
Issued to publicize the U.N. General Assembly's resolutions on general and complete disarmament and for suspension of nuclear and thermonuclear tests.
Printed by Heraclio Fournier S.A., Spain. Panes of 50. Designed by Ole Hamann.

1967, Oct. 24 **Photo.** ***Perf. 14***

177	A93	6c ultra., yel., gray & brown *(2,462,277)*	9	5
		First day cover		20
		Margin block of 4, inscription	45	—
178	A93	13c magenta, yel., gray & brown *(2,055,541)*	18	12
		First day cover		25
		First day cover, #177-178		40
		Margin block of 4, inscription	90	—

First day covers of Nos. 177-178 total 403,414.

Art at U.N. Issue
Miniature Sheet

Stained Glass Memorial Window by Marc Chagall, at U.N. Headquarters — A94

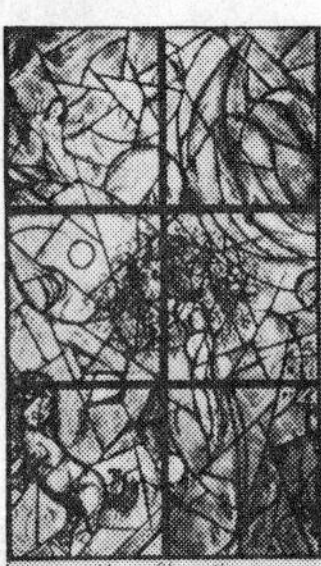

"The Kiss of Peace" by Marc Chagall — A95

Printed by Joh. Enschedé **and Sons, Netherlands. No. 180 issued in panes of 50. Design adapted by Ole Hamann from photograph by Hans Lippmann.**

1967, Nov. 17 **Litho.** ***Rouletted 9***

179	A94	Sheet of six *(3,178,656)*	55	30
		First day cover		2.00
a.		6c multi., 41x46mm	9	5
b.		6c multi., 24x46mm	9	5
c.		6c multi., 41½x33½mm	9	5
d.		6c multi., 36x33½mm	9	5
e.		6c multi., 29x33½mm	9	5
f.		6c multi., 41½x47mm	9	5
		Perf. 13x13½		
180	A95	6c multicolored *(3,438,497)*	9	5
		First day cover		50
		Margin block of 4, inscription	45	—

No. 179 is divisible into six 6c stamps, each rouletted on 3 sides, imperf. on fourth side. Size: 124x80mm. On Nos. 179a-179c, "United Nations 6c" appears at top; on Nos. 179d-179f, at bottom. No. 179f includes name "Marc Chagall."
First day covers of Nos. 179-180 total 617,225.

Globe and Major U.N. Organs — A96

Design: 13c, French inscriptions.
Issued to honor the United Nations Secretariat.
Printed by Courvoisier, S. A., Switzerland. Panes of 50. Designed by Rashid-ud Din.

1968, Jan. 16 **Photo.** ***Perf. 11½***

181	A96	6c multicolored *(2,772,965)*	9	5
		First day cover		20
		Margin block of 4, inscription	45	—
182	A96	13c multicolored *(2,461,992)*	18	12
		First day cover		25
		First day cover, #181-182		40
		Margin block of 4, inscription	90	—

First day covers of Nos. 181-182 total 411,119.

Art at U.N. Issue

Statue by Henrik Starcke — A97

The 6c is part of the "Art at the U.N." series. The 75c belongs to the regular definitive series. The teakwood Starcke statue, which stands in the Trusteeship Council Chamber, represents mankind's search for freedom and happiness.
Printed by Courvoisier, S.A., Switzerland. Panes of 50.

1968, Mar. 1 **Photo.** ***Perf. 11½***

183	A97	6c blue & multicolored *(2,537,320)*	9	60
		First day cover		20
		Margin block of 4, inscription	45	—
184	A97	75c rose lake & multicolored *(2,300,000)*	1.50	75
		First day cover		3.00
		First day cover, #183-184		3.00
		Margin block of 4, inscription	7.50	—

First day covers of Nos. 183-184 total 413,286.
No. 183 exists imperforate.
For 3fr in type A97, see U.N. Offices in Geneva No. 13.

Factories and Chart — A98

Design: 13c, French inscription ("ONUDI," etc.).
Issued to publicize the U.N. Industrial Development Organization.
Printed by Canadian Bank Note Co., Ltd., Ottawa. Panes of 50. Designed by Ole Hamann.

1968, Apr. 18 **Litho.** ***Perf. 12***

185	A98	6c greenish blue, lt. greenish blue, black & dull claret *(2,439,656)*	9	5
		First day cover		20
		Margin block of 4, inscription	45	—
186	A98	13c dull red brown, lt. red brown, black & ultra. *(2,192,453)*	18	12
		First day cover		25
		First day cover, #185-186		40
		Margin block of 4, inscription	90	—

First day covers of Nos. 185-186 total 396,447.

U.N. Headquarters — A99

Printed by Aspioti Elka-Chrome Mines, Ltd., Athens. Panes of 50. Designed by Olav S. Mathiesen.

1968, May 31 **Litho.** ***Perf. 12x13½***

187	A99	6c green, blue, black & gray *(4,000,000)*	9	6
		First day cover *(241,179)*		25
		Margin block of 4, inscription	45	—

Radarscope and Globe — A100

Design: 20c, French inscription.

Issued to publicize World Weather Watch, a new weather system directed by the World Meteorological Organization.

Printed by the Government Printing Bureau, Tokyo. Designed by George A. Gundersen and George Fanais, Canada.

1968, Sept. 19 Photo. *Perf. 13x13½*

188 A100	6c grn., blk., ocher, red & bl. *(2,245,078)*	9	6
	First day cover		22
	Margin block of 4, inscription	45	—
189 A100	20c lilac, blk., ocher, red & bl. *(2,069,966)*	30	20
	First day cover		50
	First day cover, #188-189		65
	Margin block of 4, inscription	1.50	—

First day covers of Nos. 188-189 total 620,510.

Human Rights Flame — A101

Design: 13c, French inscription.

Issued for International Human Rights Year, 1968.

Printed by Harrison & Sons, Ltd., England. Designed by Robert Perrot, France.

1968, Nov. 22 Photo.; Foil Embossed *Perf. 12½*

190 A101	6c brt. bl., dp. ultra. & gold *(2,394,235)*	9	6
	First day cover		40
	Margin block of 4, inscription	45	—
191 A101	13c rose red, dk. red & gold *(2,284,838)*	20	12
	First day cover		30
	First day cover, #190-191		60
	Margin block of 4, inscription	1.00	—

First day covers of Nos. 190-191 total 519,012.

Books and U.N. Emblem — A102

Design: 13c, French inscription in center, denomination panel at bottom.

Issued to publicize the United Nations Institute for Training and Research (UNITAR).

Printed by the Government Printing Bureau, Tokyo. Panes of 50. Designed by Olav S. Mathiesen.

1969, Feb. 10 Litho. *Perf. 13½*

192 A102	6c yellow green & multicolored *(2,436,559)*	9	6
	First day cover		20
	Margin block of 4, inscription	45	—
193 A102	13c bluish lilac & multicolored *(1,935,151)*	18	12
	First day cover		30
	First day cover, #192-193		45
	Margin block of 4, inscription	90	—

First day covers of Nos. 192-193 total 439,606.

U.N. Building, Santiago, Chile — A103

Design: 15c, Spanish inscription.

The U.N. Building in Santiago, Chile, is the seat of the U.N. Economic Commission for Latin America and of the Latin American Institute for Economic and Social Planning.

Printed by Government Printing Office, Berlin. Panes of 50. Design by Ole Hamann, adapted from a photograph.

1969, Mar. 14 Litho. *Perf. 14*

194 A103	6c light blue, violet blue & light green *(2,543,992)*	9	6
	First day cover		20
	Margin block of 4, inscription	45	—
195 A103	15c pink, cream & red brown *(2,030,733)*	22	15
	First day cover		30
	First day cover, #194-195		45
	Margin block of 4, inscription	1.10	—

First day covers of Nos. 194-195 total 398,227.

"UN" and U.N. Emblem — A104

Printed by Government Printing Bureau, Tokyo. Panes of 50. Designed by Leszek Holdanowicz and Marek Freudenreich, Poland.

1969, Mar. 14 Photo. *Perf. 13½*

196 A104	13c brt. blue, black & gold *(4,000,000)*	18	12
	First day cover *(177,793)*		35
	Margin block of 4, inscription	90	—

For 70c in type A104, see U.N. Offices in Geneva No. 7.

U.N. Emblem and Scales of Justice — A105

Design: 13c, French inscription.

Issued to publicize the 20th anniversary session of the U.N. International Law Commission.

Printed by Courvoisier S.A., Switzerland. Panes of 50. Designed by Robert Perrot, France.

Granite Paper

1969, Apr. 21 Photo. *Perf. 11½*

197 A105	6c brt. green, ultra. & gold *(2,501,492)*	9	6
	First day cover		20
	Margin block of 4, inscription	45	—
198 A105	13c crimson, lilac & gold *(1,966,994)*	18	12
	First day cover		25
	First day cover, #197-198		40
	Margin block of 4, inscription	90	—

First day covers of Nos. 197-198 total 439,324.

Allegory of Labor, Emblems of U.N. and ILO — A106

Design: 20c, French inscription.

Printed by Government Printing Bureau, Tokyo. Panes of 50. Designed by Nejat M. Gur, Turkey.

Issued to publicize "Labor and Development" and to commemorate the 50th anniversary of the International Labor Organization.

1969, June 5 Photo. *Perf. 13*

199 A106	6c blue, dp. blue, yel. & gold *(2,078,381)*	9	6
	First day cover		20
	Margin block of 4, inscription	45	—
200 A106	20c orange vermilion, magenta, yellow & gold *(1,751,100)*	30	20
	First day cover		40
	First day cover, #199-200		50
	Margin block of 4, inscription	1.50	—

First day covers of Nos. 199-200 total 514,155.

Art at U.N. Issue

Ostrich, Tunisian Mosaic, 3rd Century — A107

Design: 13c, Pheasant; French inscription.

The mosaic "The Four Seasons and the Genius of the Year" was found at Haidra, Tunisia. It is now at the Delegates' North Lounge, U.N. Headquarters, New York.

Printed by Heraclio Fournier, S. A., Spain. Panes of 50. Designed by Olav S. Mathiesen.

1969, Nov. 21 Photo. *Perf. 14*

201 A107	6c blue & multicolored *(2,280,702)*	9	6
	First day cover		20
	Margin block of 4, inscription	45	—
202 A107	13c red & multicolored *(1,918,554)*	18	12
	First day cover		30
	First day cover, #201-202		45
	Margin block of 4, inscription	90	—

First day covers of Nos. 201-202 total 612,981.

Art at U.N. Issue

Peace Bell, Gift of Japanese — A108

Design: 25c, French inscription.

The Peace Bell was a gift of the people of Japan in 1954, cast from donated coins and metals. It is housed in a Japanese cypress structure at U.N. Headquarters, New York.

Printed by Government Printing Bureau, Tokyo. Panes of 50. Designed by Ole Hamann.

1970, Mar. 13 Photo. *Perf. 13½x13*

203 A108	6c violet blue & multi *(2,604,253)*	9	6
	First day cover		20
	Margin block of 4, inscription	45	—
204 A108	25c claret & multi. *(2,090,185)*	38	25
	First day cover		50
	First day cover, #203-204		65
	Margin block of 4, inscription	1.90	—

First day covers of Nos. 203-204 total 502,384.

Mekong River, Power Lines and Map of Mekong Delta — A109

Design: 13c, French inscription.

Issued to publicize the Lower Mekong Basin Development project under U.N. auspices.

Printed by Heraclio Fournier, S.A., Spain. Panes of 50. Designed by Ole Hamann.

1970, Mar. 13 *Perf. 14*

205 A109	6c dark blue & multi. *(2,207,309)*	9	6
	First day cover		20
	Margin block of 4, inscription	45	—
206 A109	13c deep plum & multi. *(1,889,023)*	18	12
	First day cover		30
	First day cover, #205-206		45
	Margin block of 4, inscription	90	—

First day covers of Nos. 205-206 total 522,218.

"Fight Cancer" — A110

Design: 13c, French inscription.

Issued to publicize the fight against cancer in connection with the 10th International Cancer Congress of the International Union Against Cancer, Houston, Texas, May 22-29.

Printed by Government Printing Office, Berlin. Panes of 50. Designed by Leonard Mitchell.

1970, May 22 **Litho.** ***Perf. 14***

207 A110 6c blue & black *(2,157,742)* 9 6
First day cover 20
Margin block of 4, inscription 45 —
208 A110 13c olive & black *(1,824,714)* 18 12
First day cover 30
First day cover, #207-208 45
Margin block of 4, inscription 90 —

First day covers of Nos. 207-208 total 444,449.

U.N. Emblem and Olive Branch — A111

U.N. Emblem — A112

Design: 13c, French inscription.

Issued to commemorate the 25th anniversary of the United Nations. First day covers were postmarked at U.N. Headquarters, New York, and at San Francisco.

Printed by Courvoisier, S.A., Switzerland. Designed by Ole Hamann and Olav S. Mathiesen (souvenir sheet).

1970, June 26 **Photo.** ***Perf. 11½***

209 A111 6c red, gold, dk. & lt. blue *(2,365,229)* 9 6
First day cover 25
Margin block of 4, inscription 45 —
210 A111 13c dk. blue, gold, green & red *(1,861,613)* 18 12
First day cover 30
Margin block of 4, inscription 90 —

Perf. 12½

211 A112 25c dark blue, gold & lt. blue *(1,844,669)* 38 25
First day cover 55
First day cover, #209-211 1.00
Margin block of 4, inscription 1.90 —

Souvenir Sheet

Imperf

212 Sheet of 3 *(1,923,639)* 65 45
a. A111 6c red, gold & multicolored 9 6
b. A111 13c vio. blue, gold & multi. 18 12
c. A112 25c vio. blue, gold & lt. blue 38 25
First day cover 75

No. 212 contains 3 imperf. stamps, gold border and violet blue marginal inscription. Size: 94½x78mm.

First day covers of Nos. 209-212 total: New York, 846,389; San Francisco, 471,100.

Scales, Olive Branch and Symbol of Progress — A113

Design: 13c, French inscription.

Issued to publicize "Peace, Justice and Progress" in connection with the 25th anniversary of the United Nations.

Printed by Government Printing Bureau, Tokyo. Panes of 50. Designed by Ole Hamann.

1970, Nov. 20 **Photo.** ***Perf. 13½***

213 A113 6c gold & multicolored *(1,921,441)* 9 6
First day cover 25
Margin block of 4, inscription 45 —
214 A113 13c silver & multicolored *(1,663,669)* 18 12
First day cover 40
First day cover, #213-214 55
Margin block of 4, inscription 90 —

First day covers of Nos. 213-214 total 521,419.

Sea Bed, School of Fish and Underwater Research — A114

Issued to publicize peaceful uses of the sea bed.

Printed by Setelipaino, Finland. Panes of 50. Designed by Pentti Rahikainen, Finland.

1971, Jan. 25 **Photo. & Engr.** ***Perf. 13***

215 A114 6c blue & multicolored *(2,354,179)* 9 6
First day cover *(405,554)* 30
Margin block of 4, inscription 45 —

See U.N. Offices in Geneva No. 15.

Refugees, Sculpture by Kaare K. Nygaard — A115

International support for refugees.

Printed by Joh. Enschede and Sons, Netherlands. Panes of 50. Designed by Dr. Kaare K. Nygaard and Martin J. Weber.

1971, Mar. 2 **Litho.** ***Perf. 13x12½***

216 A115 6c brown, ocher & black *(2,247,232)* 9 6
First day cover 20
Margin block of 4, inscription 45 —
217 A115 13c ultra., greenish blue & black *(1,890,048)* 18 12
First day cover 30
First day cover, #216-217 45
Margin block of 4, inscription 90 —

First day covers of Nos. 216-217 total 564,785.
See U.N. Offices in Geneva No. 16.

Wheat and Globe — A116

Publicizing the U.N. World Food Program.

Printed by Heraclio Fournier, S.A., Spain. Panes of 50. Designed by Olav S. Mathiesen.

1971, Apr. 13 **Photo.** ***Perf. 14***

218 A116 13c red & multicolored *(1,968,542)* 18 12
First day cover *(409,404)* 40
Margin block of 4, inscription 90 —

See U.N. Offices in Geneva No. 17.

UPU Headquarters, Bern — A117

Opening of new Universal Postal Union Headquarters, Bern.

Printed by Courvoisier, S.A. Panes of 50. Designed by Olav S. Mathiesen.

1971, May 28 **Photo.** ***Perf. 11½***

219 A117 20c brown orange & multi. *(1,857,841)* 30 20
First day cover *(375,119)* 45
Margin block of 4, inscription 1.50 —

See U.N. Offices in Geneva No. 18.

A118

"Eliminate Racial Discrimination" — A119

International Year Against Racial Discrimination.

Printed by Government Printing Bureau, Tokyo. Panes of 50. Designers: Daniel Gonzague (8c); Ole Hamann (13c).

1971, Sept. 21 **Photo.** ***Perf. 13½***

220 A118 8c yellow green & multi. *(2,324,349)* 12 8
First day cover 20
Margin block of 4, inscription 60 —
221 A119 13c blue & multicolored *(1,852,093)* 18 12
First day cover 30
First day cover, #220-221 45
Margin block of 4, inscription 90 —

First day covers of Nos. 220-221 total 461, 103.
See U.N. Offices in Geneva Nos. 19-20.

U.N. Headquarters, New York — A120

U.N. Emblem and Symbolic Flags — A121

No. 222 printed by Heraclio Fournier, S.A., Spain. No. 223 printed by Government Printing Bureau, Tokyo. Panes of 50. Designers: O. S. Mathiesen (8c); Robert Perrot (60c).

1971, Oct. 22 **Photo.** ***Perf. 13½***

222 A120 8c violet blue & multi. *(5,300,000)+* 12 8
First day cover 20
Margin block of 4, inscription 60 —

Perf. 13

223 A121 60c ultramarine & multi. *(3,500,000)+* 90 60
First day cover 1.20
First day cover, #222-223 1.25
Margin block of 4, inscription 4.50 —

First day covers of Nos. 222-223 total 336,013.
+ Printing orders to Apr. 1982.

Maia, by Pablo Picasso — A122

To publicize the U.N. International School.
Printed by Courvoisier, S.A. Panes of 50. Designed by Ole Hamann.

1971, Nov. 19 Photo. *Perf. 11½*

No.	Type	Description	Unused	Used
224	A122	8c olive & multicolored *(2,668,214)*	12	8
		First day cover		25
		Margin block of 4, inscription	60	—
225	A122	21c ultra. & multicolored *(2,040,754)*	32	20
		First day cover		55
		First day cover, #224-225		65
		Margin block of 4, inscription	1.65	—

First day covers of Nos. 224-225 total 579,594.
See U.N. Offices in Geneva No. 21.

Letter Changing Hands — A123

Printed by Bundesdruckerei, Berlin. Panes of 50. Designed by Olav S. Mathiesen.

1972, Jan. 5 Litho. *Perf. 14*

No.	Type	Description	Unused	Used
226	A123	95c carmine & multi *(2,000,000)*	1.90	1.50
		First day cover *(188,193)*		1.50
		Margin block of 4, inscription	9.50	—

"No More Nuclear Weapons" A124

To promote non-proliferation of nuclear weapons.
Printed by Heraclio Fournier, S. A., Spain. Panes of 50. Designed by Arne Johnson, Norway.

1972, Feb. 14 Photo. *Perf. 13½x14*

No.	Type	Description	Unused	Used
227	A124	8c dull rose, black, blue & gray *(2,311,515)*	12	8
		First day cover *(268,789)*		35
		Margin block of 4, inscription	60	—

See U.N. Offices in Geneva No. 23.

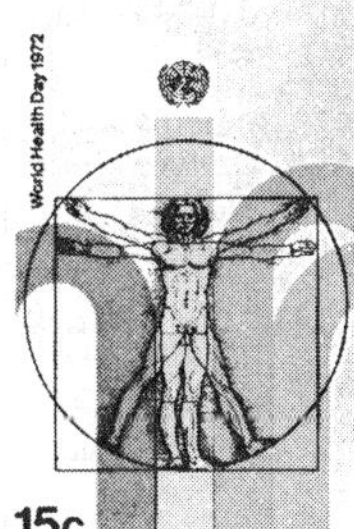

Proportions of Man, by Leonardo da Vinci — A125

World Health Day, Apr. 7.
Printed by Setelipaino, Finland. Panes of 50. Designed by George Hamori.

1972, Apr. 7 Litho. & Engr. *Perf. 13x13½*

No.	Type	Description	Unused	Used
228	A125	15c black & multicolored *(1,788,962)*	22	15
		First day cover *(322,724)*		40
		Margin block of 4, inscription	1.10	—

See U.N. Offices in Geneva No. 24.

Values for stamps vary greatly, depending upon centering, gum and condition.

"Human Environment" — A126

U.N. Conference on Human Environment, Stockholm, June 5-16, 1972.
Printed by Joh. Enschedé and Sons, Netherlands. Panes of 50. Designed by Robert Perrot.

1972, June 5 Litho. & Embossed *Perf. 12½x14*

No.	Type	Description	Unused	Used
229	A126	8c red, buff, green & blue *(2,124,604)*	12	8
		First day cover		20
		Margin block of 4, inscription	60	—
230	A126	15c bl. green, buff, green & bl. *(1,589,943)*	22	15
		First day cover		30
		First day cover, #229-230		40
		Margin block of 4, inscription	1.10	—

First day covers of Nos. 229-230 total 437,222.
See U.N. Offices in Geneva Nos. 25-26.

"Europe" and U.N. Emblem — A127

Economic Commission for Europe, 25th anniversary.
Printed by Government Printing Bureau, Tokyo. Panes of 50. Designed by Angel Medina Medina.

1972, Sept. 11 Litho. *Perf. 13x13½*

No.	Type	Description	Unused	Used
231	A127	21c yellow brown & multi *(1,748,675)*	32	20
		First day cover *(271,128)*		50
		Margin block of 4, inscription	1.60	—

See U.N. Offices in Geneva No. 27.

Art at U.N. Issue

The Five Continents by Jose Maria Sert — A128

Design shows part of ceiling mural of the Council Hall, Palais des Nations, Geneva. It depicts the five continents joining in space.
Printed by Courvoisier, S. A. Panes of 50. Designed by Ole Hamann.

1972, Nov. 17 Photo. *Perf. 12x12½*

No.	Type	Description	Unused	Used
232	A128	8c gold, brn. & golden brn. *(2,573,478)*	12	8
		First day cover		25
		Margin block of 4, inscription	60	—
233	A128	15c gold, blue green & brown *(1,768,432)*	22	15
		First day cover		40
		First day cover, #232-233		55
		Margin block of 4, inscription	1.10	—

First day covers of Nos. 232-233 total 589,817.
See U.N. Offices in Geneva Nos. 28-29.

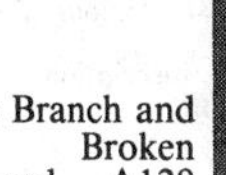

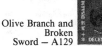

Olive Branch and Broken Sword — A129

Disarmament Decade, 1970-79.
Printed by Ajans-Turk, Turkey. Panes of 50. Designed by Kurt Plowitz.

1973, Mar. 9 Litho. *Perf. 13½x13*

No.	Type	Description	Unused	Used
234	A129	8c blue & multi. *(2,272,716)*	12	8
		First day cover		20
		Margin block of 4, inscription	60	—
235	A129	15c lilac rose & multi. *(1,643,712)*	22	15
		First day cover		30
		First day cover, #234-235		40
		Margin block of 4, inscription	1.10	—

First day covers of Nos. 234-235 total 548,336.
See U.N. Offices in Geneva Nos. 30-31.

Poppy Capsule and Skull — A130

Fight against drug abuse.
Printed by Heraclio Fournier, S.A., Spain. Panes of 50. Designed by George Hamori.

1973, Apr. 13 Photo. *Perf. 13½*

No.	Type	Description	Unused	Used
236	A130	8c dp. orange & multi. *(1,846,780)*	15	8
		First day cover		25
		Margin block of 4, inscription	75	—
237	A130	15c pink & multi. *(1,466,806)*	30	15
		First day cover		40
		First day cover, #236-237		55
		Margin block of 4, inscription	1.50	—

First day covers of Nos. 236-237 total 394,468.
See U.N. Offices in Geneva No. 32.

Honeycomb — A131

5th anniversary of the United Nations Volunteer Program.
Printed by Heraclio Fournier, S.A., Spain. Panes of 50. Designed by Courvoisier, S.A.

1973, May 25 Photo. *Perf. 14*

No.	Type	Description	Unused	Used
238	A131	8c olive bister & multi. *(1,868,176)*	12	8
		First day cover		20
		Margin block of 4, inscription	60	—
239	A131	21c gray blue & multi. *(1,530,114)*	32	20
		First day cover		40
		First day cover, #238-239		50
		Margin block of 4, inscription	1.65	—

First day covers of Nos. 238-239 total 396,517.
See U.N. Offices in Geneva No. 33.

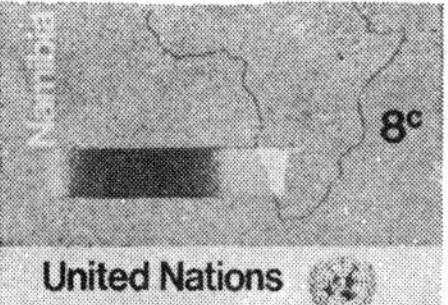

Map of Africa with Namibia — A132

To publicize Namibia (South-West Africa) for which the U.N. General Assembly ended the mandate of South Africa and established the U.N. Council for Namibia to administer the territory until independence.

Printed by Heraclio Fournier, S.A., Spain. Panes of 50. Designed by George Hamori.

1973, Oct. 1		**Photo.**	***Perf. 14***	
240 A132	8c	emerald & multi. *(1,775,260)*	12	8
		First day cover		25
		Margin block of 4, inscription	60	—
241 A132	15c	bright rose & multi. *(1,687,782)*	32	20
		First day cover		40
		First day cover, #240-241		55
		Margin block of 4, inscription	1.65	—

First day covers of Nos. 240-241 total 385,292.
See U.N. Offices in Geneva No. 34.

U.N. Emblem and Human Rights Flame — A133

25th anniversary of the adoption and proclamation of the Universal Declaration of Human Rights.
Printed by Government Printing Bureau, Tokyo. Panes of 50. Designed by Alfred Guerra.

1973, Nov. 16		**Photo.**	***Perf. 13½***	
242 A133	8c	dp. carmine & multi. *(2,026,245)*	12	8
		First day cover		25
		Margin block of 4, inscription	60	—
243 A133	21c	bl. green & multi. *(1,558,201)*	32	20
		First day cover		55
		First day cover, #242-243		65
		Margin block of 4, inscription	1.65	—

First day covers of Nos. 242-243 total 398,511.
See U.N. Offices in Geneva Nos. 35-36.

ILO Headquarters, Geneva — A134

New Headquarters of International Labor Organization.
Printed by Heraclio Fournier, S.A., Spain. Panes of 50. Designed by Henry Bencsath.

1974, Jan. 11		**Photo.**	***Perf. 14***	
244 A134	10c	ultra. & multi. *(1,734,423)*	15	10
		First day cover		20
		Margin block of 4, inscription	75	—
245 A134	21c	blue green & multi. *(1,264,447)*	32	20
		First day cover		45
		First day cover, #244-245		55
		Margin block of 4, inscription	1.65	—

First day covers of Nos. 244-245 total 282,284.
See U.N. Offices in Geneva Nos. 37-38.

UPU Emblem and Post Horn Encircling Globe — A135

Centenary of Universal Postal Union.
Printed by Ashton-Potter Ltd., Canada. Panes of 50. Designed by Arne Johnson.

1974, Mar. 22		**Litho.**	***Perf. 12½***	
246 A135	10c	gold & multicolored *(2,104,919)*	15	10
		First day cover *(342,774)*		35
		Margin block of 4, inscription	75	—

See U.N. Offices in Geneva Nos. 39-40.

Art at U.N. Issue

Peace Mural, by Candido Portinari — A136

The mural, a gift of Brazil, is in the Delegates' Lobby, General Assembly Building.
Printed by Heraclio Fournier, S.A., Spain. Panes of 50. Design adapted by Ole Hamann.

1974, May 6		**Photo.**	***Perf. 14***	
247 A136	10c	gold & multi. *(1,769,342)*	15	10
		First day cover		25
		Margin block of 4, inscription	75	—
248 A136	18c	ultramarine & multi. *(1,477,500)*	28	18
		First day cover		45
		First day cover, #247-248		65
		Margin block of 4, inscription	1.40	—

First day covers of Nos. 247-248 total 271,440.
See U.N. Offices in Geneva Nos. 41-42.

Dove and U.N. Emblem A137

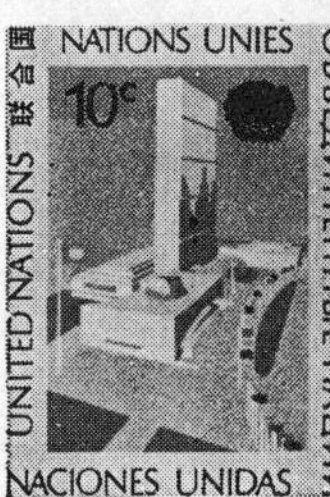

U.N. Headquarters A138

Globe, U.N. Emblem, Flags — A139

Printed by Heraclio Fournier, S.A., Spain. Panes of 50.
Designed by Nejut M. Gur (2c); Olav S. Mathiesen (10c); Henry Bencsath (18c).

1974, June 10		**Photo.**	***Perf. 14***	
249 A137	2c	dark & light blue *(6,500,000)*	5	5
		First day cover		20
		Margin block of 4, inscription	25	—
250 A138	10c	multicolored *(4,000,000)*	15	10
		First day cover		25
		Margin block of 4, inscription	75	—
251 A139	18c	multicolored *(2,300,000)*	28	15
		First day cover		45
		First day cover, #249-251		65
		Margin block of 4, inscription	1.40	—

Printing orders to Nov. 1985.
First day covers of Nos. 249-251 total 307,402.

Children of the World — A140

World Population Year
Printed by Heraclio Fournier, S.A., Spain. Panes of 50. Designed by Henry Bencsath.

1974, Oct. 18		**Photo.**	***Perf. 14***	
252 A140	10c	light blue & multi. *(1,762,595)*	15	10
		First day cover		35
		Margin block of 4, inscription	75	—
253 A140	18c	lilac & multi. *(1,321,574)*	28	18
		First day cover		70
		First day cover, #252-253		1.00
		Margin block of 4, inscription	1.40	—

First day covers of Nos. 253-254 total 354,306.
See U.N. Offices in Geneva Nos. 43-44.

Law of the Sea — A141

Declaration of U.N. General Assembly that the sea bed is common heritage of mankind, reserved for peaceful purposes.
Printed by Heraclio Fournier, S.A., Spain. Panes of 50. Designed by Asher Kalderon.

1974, Nov. 22		**Photo.**	***Perf. 14***	
254 A141	10c	green & multicolored *(1,621,328)*	15	10
		First day cover		20
		Margin block of 4, inscription	75	—
255 A141	26c	orange red & multicolored *(1,293,084)*	40	25
		First day cover		50
		First day cover, #254-255		65
		Margin block of 4, inscription	2.00	—

First day covers of Nos. 254-255 total 280,686.
See U.N. Offices in Geneva No. 45.

Satellite and Globe — A142

Peaceful uses (meteorology, industry, fishing, communications) of outer space.
Printed by Setelipaino, Finland. Panes of 50. Designed by Henry Bencsath.

1975, Mar. 14		**Litho.**	***Perf. 13***	
256 A142	10c	multicolored *(1,681,115)*	15	10
		First day cover		20
		Margin block of 4, inscription	75	—
257 A142	26c	multicolored *(1,463,130)*	40	25
		First day cover		55
		First day cover, #256-257		65
		Margin block of 4, inscription	2.00	—

First day covers of Nos. 256-257 total 330,316.
See U.N. Offices in Geneva Nos. 46-47.

Equality Between Men and Women — A143

International Women's Year
Printed by Questa Colour Security Printers, Ltd., England. Panes of 50. Designed by Asher Kalderon and Esther Kurti.

1975, May 9		**Litho.**	***Perf. 15***	
258 A143	10c	multicolored *(1,402,542)*	15	10
		First day cover		30
		Margin block of 4, inscription	75	—
259 A143	18c	multicolored *(1,182,321)*	28	18
		First day cover		55
		First day cover, #258-259		80
		Margin block of 4, inscription	1.40	—

First day covers of Nos. 258-259 total 285,466.
See U.N. Offices in Geneva Nos. 48-49.

U.N. Flag and "XXX" — A144

30th anniversary of the United Nations.
Printed by Ashton-Potter, Ltd., Canada. Nos. 260-261 panes of 50. Stamps designed by Asher Calderon, sheets by Olav S. Mathiesen.

1975, June 26 — Litho. — *Perf. 13*

No.	Type		Description	Unused	Used
260	A144	10c	olive bister & multi. *(1,904,545)*	15	10
			First day cover		20
			Margin block of 4, inscription	75	—
261	A144	26c	purple & multicolored *(1,547,766)*	40	25
			First day cover		55
			First day cover, #260-261		65
			Margin block of 4, inscription	2.00	—

Souvenir Sheet

Imperf

No.	Type		Description	Unused	Used
262	A144		Sheet of 2 *(1,196,578)*	80	60
a.		10c	olive bister & multicolored	15	10
b.		26c	purple & multicolored	40	28
			First day cover		90

No. 262 has blue and bister margin with inscription and U.N. emblem. Size: 92x70mm.
First day covers of Nos. 260-262 total. New York 477,912; San Francisco, 237,159.
See Offices in Geneva Nos. 50-52.

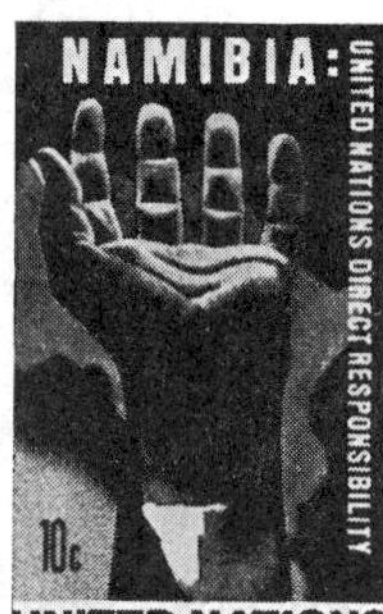

Hand Reaching up over Map of Africa and Namibia — A145

"Namibia-United Nations direct responsibility." See note after No. 241.
Printed by Heraclio Fournier S.A., Spain. Panes of 50. Designed by Henry Bencsath.

1975, Sept. 22 — Photo. — *Perf. 13½*

No.	Type		Description	Unused	Used
263	A145	10c	multicolored *(1,354,374)*	15	10
			First day cover		30
			Margin block of 4, inscription	75	—
264	A145	18c	multicolored *(1,243,157)*	28	18
			First day cover		55
			First day cover, #263-264		80
			Margin block of 4, inscription	1.40	—

First day covers of Nos. 263-264 total 281,631.
See U.N. Offices in Geneva Nos. 53-54.

Wild Rose Growing from Barbed Wire — A146

United Nations Peace-keeping Operations
Printed by Setelipaino, Finland. Panes of 50. Designed by Mrs. Eeva Oivo.

1975, Nov. 21 — Engr. — *Perf. 12½*

No.	Type		Description	Unused	Used
265	A146	13c	ultramarine *(1,628,039)*	18	12
			First day cover		30
			Margin block of 4, inscription	90	—
266	A146	26c	rose carmine *(1,195,580)*	40	25
			First day cover		60
			First day cover, #265-266		80
			Margin block of 4, inscription	2.00	—

First day covers of Nos. 265-266 total 303,711.
See U.N. Offices in Geneva Nos. 55-56.

Symbolic Flags Forming Dove — A147

U.N. Emblem — A149

People of All Races — A148

United Nations Flag — A150

Dove and Rainbow — A151

Printed by Ashton-Potter, Ltd., Canada (3c, 4c, 30c, 50c), and Questa Colour Security Printers, Ltd., England (9c). Panes of 50.
Designed by Waldemar Andrzesewski (3c); Arne Johnson (4c); George Hamori (9c, 30c); Arthur Congdon (50c).

1976 — Litho. — *Perf. 13x13½, 13½x13*

No.	Type		Description	Unused	Used
267	A147	3c	multicolored *(4,000,000)*	5	5
			First day cover		15
			Margin block of 4, inscription	25	—
268	A148	4c	multicolored *(4,000,000)*	6	5
			First day cover		15
			Margin block of 4, inscription	30	—

Photo.

Perf. 14

No.	Type		Description	Unused	Used
269	A149	9c	multicolored *(3,270,000)*	14	8
			First day cover		20
			Margin block of 4, inscription	70	—

Litho.

Perf. 13x13½

No.	Type		Description	Unused	Used
270	A150	30c	blue, emerald & black *(2,500,000)*	45	30
			First day cover		50
			Margin block of 4, inscription	2.25	—
271	A151	50c	yellow green & multicolored *(2,000,000)*	75	50
			First day cover		1.00
			Margin block of 4, inscription	3.75	—

Issue dates: 3c, 4c, 30c, 50c, Jan. 6; 9c, Nov. 19.
First day covers of Nos. 267-268, 270-271 total 355,165.
First day covers of Nos. 269 and 280 total 366,556.
See U.N. Offices in Vienna No. 8.

Interlocking Bands and U.N. Emblem — A152

World Federation of United Nations Associations.
Printed by Heraclio Fournier, S.A., Spain. Panes of 50. Designed by George Hamori.

1976, Mar. 12 — Photo. — *Perf. 14*

No.	Type		Description	Unused	Used
272	A152	13c	blue, green & black *(1,331,556)*	18	12
			First day cover		30
			Margin block of 4, inscription	90	—
273	A152	26c	green & multi. *(1,050,145)*	40	25
			First day cover		60
			First day cover, #272-273		80
			Margin block of 4, inscription	2.00	—

First day covers of Nos. 272-273 total 300,775.
See U.N. Offices in Geneva No. 57.

Cargo, Globe and Graph — A153

U.N. Conference on Trade and Development (UNCTAD), Nairobi, Kenya, May 1976.
Printed by Courvoisier, S.A. Panes of 50. Designed by Henry Bencsath.

1976, Apr. 23 — Photo. — *Perf. 11½*

No.	Type		Description	Unused	Used
274	A153	13c	dp. magenta & multi. *(1,317,900)*	18	12
			First day cover		30
			Margin block of 4, inscription	90	—
275	A153	31c	dull blue & multi. *(1,216,959)*	45	30
			First day cover		65
			First day cover, #274-275		80
			Margin block of 4, inscription	2.25	—

First day covers of Nos. 274-275 total 234,657.
See U.N. Offices in Geneva No. 58.

Houses Around Globe — A154

Habitat, U.N. Conference on Human Settlements, Vancouver, Canada, May 31-June 11.
Printed by Heraclio Fournier, S.A., Spain. Panes of 50. Designed by Eliezer Weishoff.

1976, May 28 — Photo. — *Perf. 14*

No.	Type		Description	Unused	Used
276	A154	13c	red brn. & multi *(1,346,589)*	18	12
			First day cover		30
			Margin block of 4, inscription	90	—
277	A154	25c	green & multicolored *(1,057,924)*	40	25
			First day cover		55
			First day cover, #276-277		75
			Margin block of 4, inscription	2.00	—

First day covers of Nos. 276-277 total 232,754.
See U.N. Offices in Geneva Nos. 59-60.

See the "Information for Collectors" section at beginning of catalogue for information on electric eye markings, luminescene and tagging.

Magnifying Glass, Sheet of Stamps, U.N. Emblem — A155

United Nations Postal Administration, 25th anniversary.
Printed by Courvoisier, S.A. Panes of 20 (5x4). Designed by Henry Bencsath.

1976, Oct. 8 — Photo. — *Perf. 11½*

No.	Type	Denom.	Description	Unused	Used
278	A155	13c	blue & multicolored *(1,996,309)*	30	15
			First day cover		85
			Margin block of 4, inscription	1.50	—
279	A155	31c	green & multicolored *(1,767,465)*	3.50	2.00
			First day cover		4.50
			First day cover, #278-279		5.00
			Margin block of 4, inscription	17.50	—

First day covers of Nos. 278-279 total 366,784.
Upper margin blocks are inscribed "XXV ANNIVERSARY"; lower margin blocks "UNITED NATIONS POSTAL ADMINISTRATIONS."
See U.N. Offices in Geneva Nos. 61-62.

Grain — A156

World Food Council.
Printed by Questa Colour Security Printers, Ltd., England. Panes of 50. Designed by Eliezer Weishoff.

1976, Nov. 19 — Litho. — *Perf. 14½*

No.	Type	Denom.	Description	Unused	Used
280	A156	13c	multicolored *(1,515,573)*	18	12
			First day cover		45
			Margin block of 4, inscription	90	—

See U.N. Offices in Geneva No. 63.

WIPO Headquarters, Geneva — A157

World Intellectual Property Organization (WIPO).
Printed by Heraclio Fournier, S. A., Spain. Panes of 50. Designed by Eliezer Weishoff.

1977, Mar. 11 — Photo. — *Perf. 14*

No.	Type	Denom.	Description	Unused	Used
281	A157	13c	citron & multi. *(1,330,272)*	18	12
			First day cover		30
			Margin block of 4, inscription	90	—
282	A157	31c	brt. green & multi. *(1,115,406)*	45	30
			First day cover		65
			First day cover, #281-282		85
			Margin block of 4, inscription	2.25	—

First day covers of Nos. 281-282 total 364,184.
See U.N. Offices in Geneva No. 64.

Drops of Water Falling into Funnel — A158

U.N. Water Conference, Mar del Plata, Argentina, Mar. 14-25.
Printed by Government Printing Bureau, Tokyo. Panes of 50. Designed by Elio Tomei.

1977, Apr. 22 — Photo. — *Perf. 13½x13*

No.	Type	Denom.	Description	Unused	Used
283	A158	13c	yellow & multi. *(1,317,536)*	18	12
			First day cover		30
			Margin block of 4, inscription	90	—
284	A158	25c	salmon & multi. *(1,077,424)*	40	25
			First day cover		55
			First day cover, #283-284		75
			Margin block of 4, inscription	2.00	—

First day covers of Nos. 283-284 total 321,585.
See U.N. Offices in Geneva Nos. 65-66.

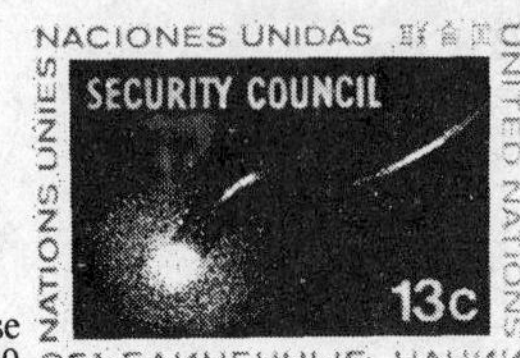

Burning Fuse Severed — A159

U.N. Security Council.
Printed by Heraclio Fournier, S.A., Spain. Panes of 50. Designed by Witold Janowski and Marek Freudenreich.

1977, May 27 — Photo. — *Perf. 14*

No.	Type	Denom.	Description	Unused	Used
285	A159	13c	purple & multi. *(1,321,527)*	18	12
			First day cover		35
			Margin block of 4, inscription	90	—
286	A159	31c	dark blue & multi. *(1,137,195)*	45	30
			First day cover		65
			First day cover, #285-286		85
			Margin block of 4, inscription	2.25	—

First day covers of Nos. 285-286 total 309,610.
See U.N. Offices in Geneva Nos. 67-68.

"Combat Racism" — A160

Fight against racial discrimination.
Printed by Setelipaino, Finland. Panes of 50. Designed by Bruno K. Wiese.

1977, Sept. 19 — Litho. — *Perf. 13½x13*

No.	Type	Denom.	Description	Unused	Used
287	A160	13c	black & yellow *(1,195,739)*	18	12
			First day cover		35
			Margin block of 4, inscription	90	—
288	A160	25c	black & vermilion *(1,074,639)*	40	25
			First day cover		50
			First day cover, #287-288		75
			Margin block of 4, inscription	2.00	—

First day covers of Nos. 287-288 total 356,193.
See U.N. Offices in Geneva Nos. 60-70.

Atom, Grain, Fruit and Factory — A161

Peaceful uses of atomic energy.
Printed by Heraclio Fournier, S.A., Spain. Panes of 50. Designed by Henry Bencsath.

1977, Nov. 18 — Photo. — *Perf. 14*

No.	Type	Denom.	Description	Unused	Used
289	A161	13c	yel. bister & multi. *(1,316,473)*	18	12
			First day cover		35
			Margin block of 4, inscription	90	—
290	A161	18c	dull green & multi. *(1,072,246)*	28	18
			First day cover		50
			First day cover, #289-290		75
			Margin block of 4, inscription	1.40	—

First day covers of Nos. 289-290 total 325,348.
See U.N. Offices in Geneva Nos. 71-72.

Opening Words of U.N. Charter — A162

"Live Together in Peace" — A163

People of the World — A164

Printed by Questa Colour Security Printers, United Kingdom. Panes of 50. Designed by Salahattin Kanidic (1c); Elio Tomei (25c); Paula Schmidt ($1).

1978, Jan. 27 — Litho. — *Perf. 14½*

No.	Type	Denom.	Description	Unused	Used
291	A162	1c	gold, brown & red *(4,800,000)+*	5	5
			First day cover		15
			Margin block of 4, inscription	25	—
292	A163	25c	multicolored *(3,000,000)+*	40	25
			First day cover		45
			Margin block of 4, inscription	2.00	—
293	A164	$1	multicolored *(3,000,000)+*	1.50	1.00
			First day cover		1.50
			First day cover, #291-293		1.90
			Margin block of 4, inscription	7.50	—

\+ Printing orders to Dec. 1984.
First day covers of Nos. 291-293 total 264,782.
See U.N. Offices in Geneva No. 73.

Smallpox Virus — A165

Global eradication of smallpox.
Printed by Courvoisier, S.A. Panes of 50. Designed by Herbert Auchli.

1978, Mar. 31 — Photo. — *Perf. 12x11½*

No.	Type	Denom.	Description	Unused	Used
294	A165	13c	rose & black *(1,188,239)*	18	12
			First day cover		35
			Margin block of 4, inscription	90	—
295	A165	31c	blue & black *(1,058,688)*	45	30
			First day cover		50
			First day cover, #294-295		80
			Margin block of 4, inscription	2.25	—

First day covers of Nos. 294-295 total 306,626.
See U.N. Offices in Geneva Nos. 74-75.

Open Handcuff — A166

Liberation, justice and cooperation for Namibia.
Printed by Government Printing Office, Austria. Panes of 50. Designed by Cafiro Tomei.

1978, May 5 — Photo. — *Perf. 12*

No.	Type	Value	Description	Unused	Used
296	A166	13c	multicolored *(1,203,079)*	18	12
			First day cover		25
			Margin block of 4, inscription	90	—
297	A166	18c	multicolored *(1,066,738)*	28	18
			First day cover		40
			First day cover, #296-297		55
			Margin block of 4, inscription	1.40	—

First day covers of Nos. 296-297 total 324,471.
See U.N. Offices in Geneva No. 76.

Multicolored Bands and Clouds — A167

International Civil Aviation Organization for "Safety in the Air."
Printed by Heraclio Fournier, S.A., Spain. Panes of 50. Designed by Cemalettin Mutver.

1978, June 12 — Photo. — *Perf. 14*

No.	Type	Value	Description	Unused	Used
298	A167	13c	multicolored *(1,295,617)*	18	12
			First day cover		35
			Margin block of 4, inscription	90	—
299	A167	25c	multicolored *(1,101,256)*	40	25
			First day cover		55
			First day cover, #298-299		80
			Margin block of 4, inscription	2.00	—

First day covers of Nos. 298-299 total 329,995.
See U.N. Offices in Geneva Nos. 77-78.

General Assembly — A168

Printed by Government Printing Bureau, Tokyo. Panes of 50. Designed by Jozsef Vertel.

1978, Sept. 15 — Photo. — *Perf. 13½*

No.	Type	Value	Description	Unused	Used
300	A168	13c	multicolored *(1,093,005)*	18	12
			First day cover		25
			Margin block of 4, inscription	90	—
301	A168	18c	multicolored *(1,065,934)*	28	18
			First day cover		40
			First day cover, #300-301		55
			Margin block of 4, inscription	1.40	—

First day covers of Nos. 300-301 total 283,220.
See U.N. Offices in Geneva Nos. 79-80.

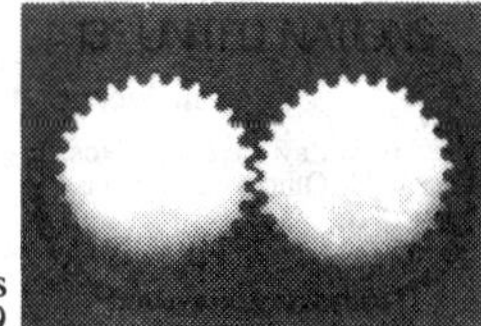

Hemispheres as Cogwheels — A169

Technical Cooperation Among Developing Countries Conference, Buenos Aires, Argentina, Sept. 1978.
Printed by Heraclio Fournier, S.A., Spain. Panes of 50. Designed by Simon Keter and David Pesach.

1978, Nov. 17 — Photo. — *Perf. 14*

No.	Type	Value	Description	Unused	Used
302	A169	13c	multicolored *(1,251,272)*	18	12
			First day cover		35
			Margin block of 4, inscription	90	—
303	A169	31c	multicolored *(1,185,213)*	45	30
			First day cover		65
			First day cover, #302-303		85
			Margin block of 4, inscription	2.25	—

First day covers of Nos. 302-303 total 272,556.
See U.N. Offices in Geneva No. 81.

Hand Holding Olive Branch — A170

Various Races Tree — A171

Globe, Dove with Olive Branch — A172

Birds and Globe — A173

Printed by Heraclio Fournier, S.A., Spain. Panes of 50.
Designed by Raymon Müller (5c); Alrun Fricke (14c); Eliezer Weishoff (15c); Young Sun Hahn (20c).

1979, Jan. 19 — Photo. — *Perf. 14*

No.	Type	Value	Description	Unused	Used
304	A170	5c	multicolored *(3,000,000)*	8	5
			First day cover		35
			Margin block of 4, inscription	40	—
305	A171	14c	multicolored *(3,000,000)*	20	14
			First day cover		35
			Margin block of 4, inscription	1.00	—
306	A172	15c	multicolored *(3,000,000)*	28	15
			First day cover		35
			Margin block of 4, inscription	1.40	—
307	A173	20c	multicolored *(3,000,000)*	30	20
			First day cover		75
			First day cover, #304-307		1.25
			Margin block of 4, inscription	1.50	—

First day covers of Nos. 304-307 total 295,927.

UNDRO Against Fire and Water — A174

Office of the U.N. Disaster Relief Coordinator (UNDRO).
Printed by Heraclio Fournier, S.A., Spain. Panes of 50. Designed by Gidon Sagi.

1979, Mar. 9 — Photo. — *Perf. 14*

No.	Type	Value	Description	Unused	Used
308	A174	15c	multicolored *(1,448,600)*	22	15
			First day cover		40
			Margin block of 4, inscription	1.10	—
309	A174	20c	multicolored *(1,126,295)*	30	20
			First day cover		60
			First day cover, #308-309		80
			Margin block of 4, inscription	1.50	—

First day covers of Nos. 308-309 total 266,694.
See U.N. Offices in Geneva Nos. 82-83.

Child and IYC Emblem — A175

International Year of the Child.
Printed by Heraclio Fournier, S.A., Spain. Panes of 20 (5x4). Designed by Helena Matuszewska (15c) and Krystyna Tarkowska-Gruszecka (31c).

1979, May 4 — Photo. — *Perf. 14*

No.	Type	Value	Description	Unused	Used
310	A175	15c	multicolored *(2,290,329)*	45	15
			First day cover		1.10
			Margin block of 4, inscription	2.25	—
311	A175	31c	multicolored *(2,192,136)*	90	30
			First day cover		2.25
			First day cover, #310-311		3.00
			Margin block of 4, inscription	4.50	—

First day covers of Nos. 310-311 total 380,022.
See U.N. Offices in Geneva Nos. 84-85.

Map of Namibia, Olive Branch — A176

For a free and independent Namibia.
Printed by Ashton-Potter Ltd., Canada. Panes of 50. Designed by Eliezer Weishoff.

1979, Oct. 5 — Litho. — *Perf. 13½*

No.	Type	Value	Description	Unused	Used
312	A176	15c	multicolored *(1,800,000)*	22	15
			First day cover		40
			Margin block of 4, inscription	1.10	—
313	A176	31c	multicolored *(1,500,000)*	45	30
			First day cover		75
			First day cover, #312-313		90
			Margin block of 4, inscription	2.25	—

First day covers of Nos. 312-313 total 250,371.
See U.N. Offices in Geneva No. 86.

Scales and Sword of Justice — A177

International Court of Justice, The Hague, Netherlands
Printed by Setelipaino, Finland. Panes of 50. Designed by Henning Simon.

1979, Nov. 9 — Litho. — *Perf. 13x13½*

No.	Type	Value	Description	Unused	Used
314	A177	15c	multicolored *(1,244,972)*	22	15
			First day cover		40
			Margin block of 4, inscription	1.10	—
315	A177	20c	multicolored *(1,084,483)*	30	20
			First day cover		60
			First day cover, #314-315		90
			Margin block of 4, inscription	1.50	—

First day covers of Nos. 314-315 total 322,901.
See U.N. Offices in Geneva Nos. 87-88.

Graph of Economic Trends — A178

Key — A179

New International Economic Order.
Printed by Questa Colour Security Printers, United Kingdom. Panes of 50. Designed by Cemalettin Mutver (15c), George Hamori (31c)

1980, Jan. 11 — Litho. — *Perf. 15x14½*

No.	Type	Value	Description	Unused	Used
316	A178	15c	multicolored *(1,163,801)*	22	15
			First day cover		35
			Margin block of 4, inscription	1.10	—
317	A179	31c	multicolored *(1,103,560)*	45	30
			First day cover		80
			First day cover, #316-317		90
			Margin block of 4, inscription	2.25	—

First day covers of Nos. 316-317 total 211,945.

See U.N. Offices in Geneva No. 89; Vienna No. 7.

Women's Year Emblem — A180

United Nations Decade for Women.

Printed by Questa Colour Security Printers, United Kingdom. Panes of 50. Designed by Susanne Rottenfusser.

1980, Mar. 7 Litho. *Perf. 14½x15*

318	A180	15c	multicolored *(1,409,350)*	22	15
			First day cover		40
			Margin block of 4, inscription	1.10	—
319	A180	20c	multicolored *(1,182,016)*	30	20
			First day cover		55
			First day cover, #318-319		75
			Margin block of 4, inscription	1.50	—

First day covers of Nos. 318-319 total 289,314.

See U.N. Offices in Geneva Nos. 90-91; Vienna Nos. 9-10.

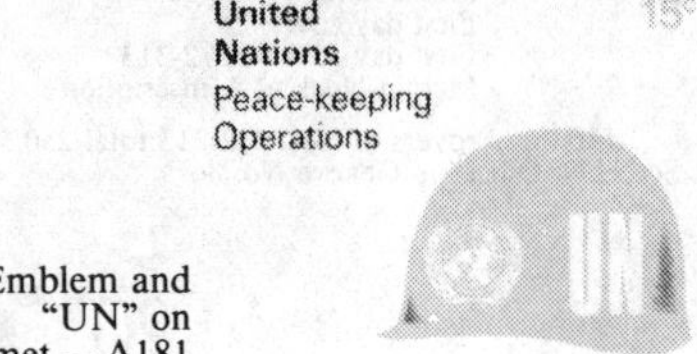

U.N. Emblem and "UN" on Helmet — A181

Arrows and U.N. Emblem — A182

United Nations Peace-keeping Operations.

Printed by Joh. Enschede en Zonen, Netherlands. Panes of 50. Designed by Bruno K. Wiese (15c), James Gardiner (31c)

1980, May 16 Litho. *Perf. 14x13*

320	A181	15c	blue & black *(1,245,521)*	25	15
			First day cover		35
			Margin block of 4, inscription	1.25	—
321	A182	31c	multicolored *(1,191,009)*	50	30
			First day cover		70
			First day cover, #320-321		80
			Margin block of 4, inscription	2.50	—

First day covers of Nos. 320-321 total 208,442.

See U.N. Offices in Geneva No. 92, Vienna No. 11.

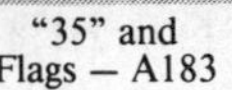

"35" and Flags — A183

Globe and Laurel — A184

35th Anniversary of the United Nations.

Printed by Ashton-Potter Ltd, Canada. Nos. 322-323, panes of 50.

Designed by Cemalettin Matver (15c), Mian Mohammad Saeed (31c).

1980, June 26 Litho. *Perf. 13x13½*

322	A183	15c	multicolored *(1,554,514)*	22	15
			First day cover		35
			Margin block of 4, inscription	1.10	—
323	A184	31c	multicolored *(1,389,606)*	45	30
			First day cover		80
			First day cover, #322-323		90
			Margin block of 4, inscription	2.25	—

Souvenir Sheet

Imperf

324		Sheet of 2 *(1,215,505)*	70	70
a.	A183 15c multicolored		22	
b.	A184 31c multicolored		45	
		First day cover		1.00

No. 324 has multicolored margin with inscription and U.N. emblem. Size: 92x73mm.

First day covers of Nos. 322-324 total: New York, 369,345; San Francisco, 203,701.

See U.N. Offices in Geneva Nos. 93-95; Vienna Nos. 12-14.

Flag of Turkey — A185

Printed by Courvoisier, S.A., Switzerland. Panes of 16. Designed by Ole Hamann.

Issued in 4 panes of 16. Each sheet contains 4 blocks of 4 (Nos. 325-328, 329-332, 333-336, 337-340). A se-tenant block of 4 designs centers each pane.

1980, Sept. 26 Litho. *Perf. 12*

325	A185	15c	shown *(3,490,725)*	25	20
326	A185	15c	Luxembourg *(3,490,725)*	25	20
327	A185	15c	Fiji *(3,490,725)*	25	20
328	A185	15c	Viet Nam *(3,490,725)*	25	20
329	A185	15c	Guinea *(3,442,633)*	25	20
330	A185	15c	Surinam *(3,442,633)*	25	20
331	A185	15c	Bangladesh *(3,442,633)*	25	20
332	A185	15c	Mali *(3,442,633)*	25	20
333	A185	15c	Jugoslavia *(3,416,292)*	25	20
334	A185	15c	France *(3,416,292)*	25	20
335	A185	15c	Venezuela *(3,416,292)*	25	20
336	A185	15c	El Salvador *(3,416,292)*	25	20
337	A185	15c	Madagascar *(3,442,497)*	25	20
338	A185	15c	Cameroon *(3,442,497)*	25	20
339	A185	15c	Rwanda *(3,442,497)*	25	20
340	A185	15c	Hungary *(3,442,497)*	25	20
			First day covers of Nos. 325-340, each		35

First day covers of Nos. 325-340 total 6,145,595.

See Nos. 350-365, 374-389, 399-414, 425-440, 450-465, 477-492, 499-514.

Symbolic Flowers — A186

Symbols of Progress — A187

Printed by Ashton-Potter Ltd., Canada. Panes of 50. Designed by Eliezer Weishoff (15c), Dietman Kowall (20c).

1980, Nov. 21 Litho. *Perf. 13½x13*

341	A186	15c	multicolored *(1,192,165)*	35	20
			First day cover		40
			Margin block of 4, inscription	1.75	—
342	A187	20c	multicolored *(1,011,382)*	50	30
			First day cover		55
			First day cover, #341-342		85
			Margin block of 4, inscription	2.50	—

First day covers of Nos. 341-342 total 232,149.

See U.N. Offices in Geneva, Nos. 96-97; Vienna Nos. 15-16.

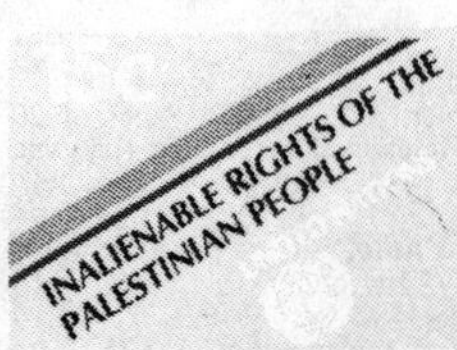

Inalienable Rights of the Palestinian People — A188

Printed by Courvoisier S.A., Switzerland. Panes of 50. Designed by David Dewhurst.

1981, Jan. 30 Photo. *Perf. 12x11½*

343	A188	15c	multicolored *(993,489)*	40	25
			First day cover *(127,187)*		75
			Margin block of 4, inscription	2.00	—

See U.N. Offices in Geneva No. 98; Vienna No. 17.

Interlocking Puzzle Pieces — A189

Stylized Person — A190

International Year of the Disabled.

Printed by Heraclio Fournier S.A., Spain. Panes of 50.

Designed by Sophia Van Heeswijk (20c) and G.P. Van der Hyde (35c).

1981, Mar. 6 Photo. *Perf. 14*

344	A189	20c	multicolored *(1,218,371)*	50	30
			First day cover		45
			Margin block of 4, inscription	2.50	—
345	A190	35c	black & orange *(1,107,298)*	85	50
			First day cover		80
			First day cover, #344-345		1.00
			Margin block of 4, inscription	4.25	—

First day covers of Nos. 344-345 total 204,891.

See U.N. Offices in Geneva Nos. 99-100; Vienna Nos. 18-19.

Desislava and Sebastocrator Kaloyan, Bulgarian Mural, 1259, Boyana Church, Sofia — A191

Art at U.N. Issue

Printed by Courvoisier. Panes of 50. Designed by Ole Hamann.

1981, Apr. 15 Photo. *Perf. 11½*

Granite Paper

346	A191	20c	multi *(1,252,648)*	40	30
			First day cover		45
			Margin block of 4, inscription	2.00	—
347	A191	31c	multi *(1,061,056)*	65	45
			First day cover		70
			First day cover, #346-347		1.00
			Margin block of 4, inscription	3.25	—

First day covers of Nos. 346-347 total 210,978.

See U.N. Offices in Geneva No. 101; Vienna No. 20.

Solar Energy — A192

Conference Emblem — A193

Conference on New and Renewable Sources of Energy, Nairobi, Aug. 10-21.

Printed by Setelipaino, Finland. Panes of 50. Designed by Ulrike Dreyer (20c); Robert Perrot (40c).

1981, May 29 Litho. *Perf. 13*

348	A192	20c	multi *(1,132,877)*	40	30
			First day cover		45
			Margin block of 4, inscription	2.00	—
349	A193	40c	multi *(1,158,319)*	65	50
			First day cover		80
			First day cover, #348-349		1.10
			Margin block of 4, inscription	3.25	—

First day covers of Nos. 348-349 total 240,205.

See U.N. Offices in Geneva No. 102; Vienna No. 21.

Flag Type of 1980

Printed by Courvoisier, S.A., Switzerland. Panes of 16. Designed by Ole Hamann.

Issued in 4 panes of 16. Each pane contains 4 blocks of four (Nos. 350-353, 354-357, 358-361, 362-365). A se-tenant block of 4 designs centers each pane.

1981, Sept.25 Litho.

350	A185	20c	Djibouti *(2,342,224)*	30	25
351	A185	20c	Sri Lanka *(2,342,224)*	30	25
352	A185	20c	Bolivia *(2,342,224)*	30	25
353	A185	20c	Equatorial Guinea *(2,342,224)*	30	25
354	A185	20c	Malta *(2,360,297)*	30	25
355	A185	20c	Czechoslovakia *(2,360,297)*	30	25
356	A185	20c	Thailand *(2,360,297)*	30	25
357	A185	20c	Trinidad & Tobago *(2,360,297)*	30	25
358	A185	20c	Ukrainian SSR *(2,344,755)*	30	25
359	A185	20c	Kuwait *(2,344,755)*	30	25
360	A185	20c	Sudan *(2,344,755)*	30	25
361	A185	20c	Egypt *(2,344,755)*	30	25
362	A185	20c	US *(2,450,537)*	30	25
363	A185	20c	Singapore *(2,450,537)*	30	25
364	A185	20c	Panama *(2,450,537)*	30	25
365	A185	20c	Costa Rica *(2,450,537)*	30	25
			First day covers of Nos. 350-365, each		65

First day covers of Nos. 350-365 total 3,961,237.

Seedling and Tree Cross-section — A194

"10" and Symbols of Progress — A195

United Nations Volunteers Program, 10th anniv.

Printed by Walsall Security Printers, Ltd., United Kingdom. Pane of 50.

Designed by Gabriele Nussgen (18c), Angel Medina Medina (28c).

1981, Nov. 13 Litho.

366	A194	18c	multi *(1,246,833)*	40	30
			First day cover		35
			Margin block of 4, inscription	2.00	—
367	A195	28c	multi *(1,282,868)*	60	45
			First day cover		50
			First day cover, #366-367		65
			Margin block of 4, inscription	3.00	—

First day covers of Nos. 366-367 total 221,106.

See U.N. Offices in Geneva Nos. 103-104; Vienna Nos. 22-23.

Respect for Human Rights — A196

Independence of Colonial Countries and People — A197

Second Disarmament Decade — A198

Printed by Courvoisier, S.A., Switzerland. Panes of 50.

Designed by Rolf Christianson (17c); George Hamori (28c); Marek Kwiatkowski (40c).

1982, Jan. 22 *Perf. 11½x12*

368	A196	17c	multicolored *(3,000,000)*	35	15
			First day cover		30
			Margin block of 4, inscription	1.75	—
369	A197	28c	multicolored *(3,000,000)*	56	25
			First day cover		50
			Margin block of 4, inscription	2.30	—
370	A198	40c	multicolored *(3,000,000)*	80	40
			First day cover		75
			First day cover, #368-370		1.10
			Margin block of 4, inscription	4.00	—

First day covers of Nos. 368-370 total 243,073.

Sun and Hand Holding Seedling — A199

Sun, Plant Land and Water — A200

10th Anniversary of United Nations Environment Program.

Printed by Joh. Enschede En Zonen, Netherlands. Panes of 50.

Designed by Philine Hartert (20c); Peer-Ulrich Bremer (40c).

1982, Mar. 19 Litho. *Perf. 13½x13*

371	A199	20c	multicolored *(1,017,117)*	50	35
			First day cover		40
			Margin block of 4, inscription	2.50	—
372	A200	40c	multicolored *(884,798)*	1.00	70
			First day cover		75
			First day cover, #371-372		90
			Margin block of 4, inscription	5.00	—

First day covers of Nos. 371-372 total 288,721.

See U.N. Offices in Geneva Nos. 107-108; Vienna Nos. 25-26.

U.N. Emblem and Olive Branch in Outer Space — A201

Exploration and Peaceful Uses of Outer Space.

Printed By Enschede. Panes of 50. Designed by Wiktor C. Nerwinski.

1982, June 11 Litho. *Perf. 13x13½*

373	A201	20c	multicolored *(1,083,426)*	50	35
			First day cover *(156,965)*		60
			Margin block of 4, inscription	2.50	—

See U.N. Offices in Geneva Nos. 109-110; Vienna No. 27.

Flag Type of 1980

Printed by Courvoisier. Panes of 16. Designed by Ole Hamann.

Issued in 4 panes of 16. Each pane contains 4 blocks of four (Nos. 374-377, 378-381, 383-385, 386-389). A se-tenant block of 4 designs centers each pane.

1982, Sept. 24 Litho. *Perf. 12*

374	A185	20c	Austria *(2,314,006)*	40	25
375	A185	20c	Malaysia *(2,314,006)*	40	25
376	A185	20c	Seychelles *(2,314,006)*	40	25
377	A185	20c	Ireland *(2,314,006)*	40	25
378	A185	20c	Mozambique *(2,300,958)*	40	25
379	A185	20c	Albania *(2,300,958)*	40	25
380	A185	20c	Dominica *(2,300,958)*	40	25
381	A185	20c	Solomon Islnads *(2,300,958)*	40	25
382	A185	20c	Philippines *(2,288,589)*	40	25
383	A185	20c	Swaziland *(2,288,589)*	40	25
384	A185	20c	Nicaragua *(2,288,589)*	40	25
385	A185	20c	Burma *(2,288,589)*	40	25
386	A185	20c	Cape Verde *(2,285,848)*	40	25
387	A185	20c	Guyana *(2,285,848)*	40	25
388	A185	20c	Belgium *(2,285,848)*	40	25
389	A185	20c	Nigeria *(2,285,848)*	40	25
			First day cover, #374-389, each		65

First day covers of Nos. 374-389 total 3,202,744.

A202

Conservation and Protection of Nature

Printed by Fournier. Panes of 50.

Designed by Hamori

1982, Nov. 19 Photo. *Perf. 14*

390	A202	20c	Leaf *(1,110,027)*	50	30
			First day cover		75
			margin block of 4, inscription	2.50	—
391	A202	28c	Butterfly *(848,772)*	70	45
			First day cover		1.00
			First day cover, #390-391		1.50
			Margin block of 4, inscription	3.50	—

First day covers of Nos. 390-391 total 214,148.

See U.N. Offices in Geneva Nos. 111-112; Vienna Nos. 28-29.

A203

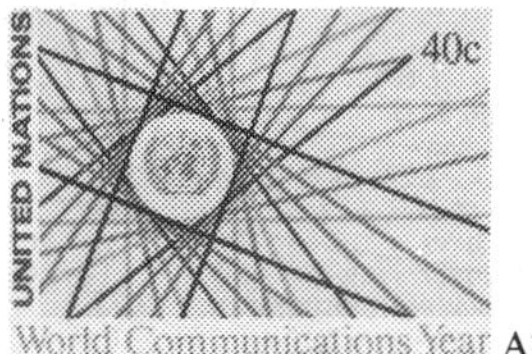

A204

World Communications Year

Printed by Walsal. Panes of 50. Designed by Hanns Lohrer (A203) and Lorena Berengo (A204).

1983, Jan. 28 Litho. *Perf. 13*

392	A203	20c	multi *(1,282,079)*	40	20
			First day cover		50
			Margin block of 4, inscription	2.00	—
393	A204	40c	multi *(931,903)*	80	40
			First day cover		1.00
			First day cover, Nos. 392-393		1.25
			Margin block of 4, inscription	4.00	—

First day covers of Nos. 392-393 total 183,499.

See U.N. Offices in Geneva No. 113; Vienna No. 30.

A205

A206

Safety at Sea

Printed by Questa. Panes of 50. Designed by Jean-Marie Lenfant (A205), Ari Ron (A206).

1983, Mar. 18 Litho. *Perf. 14½*

394	A205	20c	multi *(1,252,456)*	40	20
			First day cover		40
			Margin block of 4, inscription	2.00	—
395	A206	37c	multi *(939,910)*	75	38
			First day cover		90
			First day cover, Nos. 394-395		1.10
			Margin block of 4, inscription	3.75	—

First day covers of Nos. 394-395 total 199,962.

See U.N. Offices in Geneva Nos. 114-115; Vienna Nos. 31-32.

A207

World Food Program
Printed by Government Printers Bureau, Japan. Designed by Marek Kwiatskoski.

1983, Apr. 22 **Engr.** ***Perf. 13½***

396	A207	20c	rose lake *(1,238,997)*	40	20
			First day cover *(180,704)*		50
			Margin block of 4, inscription	2.00	—

See U.N. Offices in Geneva No. 116; Vienna Nos. 33-34.

A208

A209

UN Conference on Trade and Development

Printed by Carl Uberreuter Druck and Vergal M. Salzer, Austria. Panes of 50. Designed by Dietmar Braklow (A208), Gabriel Genz (A209).

1983, June 6 **Litho.** ***Perf. 14***

397	A208	20c	multi *(1,060,053)*	50	20
			First day cover		50
			Margin block of 4, inscription	2.50	—
398	A209	28c	multi *(948,981)*	75	28
			First day cover		65
			First day cover, Nos. 397-398		1.00
			Margin block of 4, inscription	3.75	—

First day covers of Nos. 397-398 total 200,131.
See U.N. Offices in Geneva Nos. 117-118; Vienna Nos. 35-36.

Flag Type of 1980
Printed by Courvoisier. Panes of 16.
Designed by Ole Hamann.
Issued in 4 panes of 16. Each pane contains 4 blocks of four (Nos. 399-402, 403-406, 407-410, 411-414). A se-tenant block of 4 designs centers each pane.

1983, Sept. 23 **Photo.** ***Perf. 12***

399	A185	20c	Great Britain *(2,490,599)*	40	20
400	A185	20c	Barbados *(2,490,599)*	40	20
401	A185	20c	Nepal *(2,490,599)*	40	20
402	A185	20c	Israel *(2,490,599)*	40	20
403	A185	20c	Malawi *(2,483,010)*	40	20
408	A185	20c	Byelorussian SSR *(2,483,010)*	40	20
405	A185	20c	Jamaica *(2,483,010)*	40	20
406	A185	20c	Kenya *(2,483,010)*	40	20
407	A185	20c	People's Republic of China *(2,474,140)*	40	20
408	A185	20c	Peru *(2,474,140)*	40	20
409	A185	20c	Bulgaria *(2,474,140)*	40	20
410	A185	20c	Canada *(2,474,140)*	40	20
411	A185	20c	Somalia *(2,482,070)*	40	20
412	A185	20c	Senegal *(2,482,070)*	40	20
413	A185	20c	Brazil *(2,482,070)*	40	20
414	A185	20c	Sweden *(2,482,070)*	40	20
			First day cover, #399-414, each		65

First day covers of Nos. 399-414 total 2,214,134.

Window Right — A210

Peace Treaty with Nature — A211

35th Anniversary of the Universal Declaration of Human Rights
Printed by Government Printing Office, Austria, Designed by Friedensreich Hundertwasser, Austria. Panes of 16 (4x4).

1983, Dec. 9 **Photo. & Engr.** ***Perf. 13½***

415	A210	20c	multi *(1,591,102)*	60	20
			First day cover		50
416	A211	40c	multi *(1,566,789)*	1.20	40
			First day cover		1.00
			First day cover, Nos. 392-393		1.25

First day covers of Nos. 415-416 total 176,269.

International Conference on Population — A212

Printed by Bundesdruckerei, Federal Republic of Germany. Panes of 50. Designed by Marina Langer-Rosa and Helmut Langer, Federal Republic of Germany.

1984, Feb. 3 **Litho.** ***Perf. 14***

417	A212	20c	multi *(905,320)*	60	20
			First day cover		50
			Margin block of 4, inscription	3.00	—
418	A212	40c	multi *(717,084)*	1.50	40
			First day cover		1.00
			First day cover, Nos. 417-418		1.25
			Margin block of 4, inscription	7.50	—

First day covers of Nos. 417-418 total 118,068.
See U.N. Offices in Geneva No. 121; Vienna No. 39.

Tractor Plowing — A213

Rice Paddy — A214

World Food Day, Oct. 16
Printed by Walsall Security Printers, Ltd., United Kingdom. Panes of 50. Designed by Adth Vanooijen, Netherlands.

1984, Mar. 15 **Litho.** ***Perf. 14½***

419	A213	20c	multi *(853,641)*	75	20
			First day cover		50
			Margin block of 4, inscription	3.75	—
420	A214	40c	multi *(727,165)*	1.60	40
			First day cover		1.00
			First day cover, Nos. 419-420		1.25
			Margin block of 4, inscription	8.00	—

First day covers of Nos. 419-420 total 116,009.

Grand Canyon — A215

Ancient City of Polonnaruwa, Sri Lanka — A216

World Heritage
Printed by Harrison and Sons, United Kingdom. Panes of 50. Designs adapted by Rocco J. Callari, U.S., and Thomas Lee, China.

1984, Apr. 18 **Litho.** ***Perf. 14***

421	A215	20c	multi *(814,316)*	80	20
			First day cover		50
			Margin block of 4, inscription	4.00	—
422	A216	50c	multi *(579,136)*	2.00	50
			First day cover		1.25
			First day cover, Nos. 421-422		1.40
			Margin block of 4, inscription	10.00	—

First day covers of Nos. 421-422 total 112,036.

A217

A218

Future for Refugees
Printed by Courvoisier. Panes of 50. Designed by Hans Erni, Switzerland.

1984, May 29 **Photo.** ***Perf. 11½***

423	A217	20c	multi *(956,743)*	60	20
			First day cover		50
			Margin block of 4, inscription	3.00	—
424	A218	50c	multi *(729,036)*	1.50	50
			First day cover		1.20
			First day cover, Nos. 423-424		1.40
			Margin block of 4, inscription	7.50	—

First day covers of Nos. 423-424 total 115,789.

Flag Type of 1980
Printed by Courvoisier. Panes of 16.
Designed by Ole Hamann.
Issued in 4 panes of 16. Each pane contains 4 blocks of four (Nos. 425-428, 429-432, 433-436, 437-440). A se-tenant block of 4 designs centers each pane.

1984, Sept. 21 **Photo.** ***Perf. 12***

425	A185	20c	Burundi *(1,941,471)*	65	20
426	A185	20c	Pakistan *(1,941,471)*	65	20
427	A185	20c	Benin *(1,941,471)*	65	20
428	A185	20c	Italy *(1,941,471)*	65	20
428	A185	20c	Tanzania *(1,969,051)*	65	20
430	A185	20c	United Arab Emirates *(1,969,051)*	65	20
431	A185	20c	Ecuador *(1,969,051)*	65	20
432	A185	20c	Bahamas *(1,969,051)*	65	20
433	A185	20c	Poland *(2,001,091)*	65	20
434	A185	20c	Papua New Guinea *(2,001,091)*	65	20
435	A185	20c	Uruguay *(2,001,091)*	65	20
436	A185	20c	Chile *(2,001,091)*	65	20
437	A185	20c	Paraguay *(1,969,875)*	65	20
438	A185	20c	Bhutan *(1,969,875)*	65	20
438	A185	20c	Central African Republic *(1,969,875)*	65	20
440	A185	20c	Australia *(1,969,875)*	65	20
			First day cover, #425-440 each		65

First day covers of Nos. 425-440 total 1,914,972.

International Youth Year — A219

Printed by Waddingtons Ltd., United Kingdom. Panes of 50. Designed by Ramon Mueller, Federal Republic of Germany.

1984, Nov. 15 Litho. *Perf. 13½*

441	A219	20c	multi *(884,962)*	75	20
			First day cover		60
			Margin block of 4, inscription	3.75	—
442	A219	35c	multi *(740,023)*	1.50	35
			First day cover		1.00
			First day cover, Nos. 441-442		1.25
			Margin block of 4, inscription	7.50	—

First day covers of Nos. 441-442 total 125,315.

ILO Turin Center — A220

Printed by the Government Printing Bureau, Japan. Panes of 50. Engraved by Mamoru Iwakuni and Hiroshi Ozaki, Japan.

1985, Feb. 1 Engr. *Perf. 13½*

443	A220	23c	Turin Center emblem *(612,942)*	60	24
			First day cover *(76,541)*		65
			Margin block of 4, inscription	3.00	—

See U.N. Offices in Geneva Nos. 129-130; Vienna No. 48.

U.N. University A221

Printed by Helio Courvoiser, Switzerland. Panes of 50. Designed by Moshe Pereg, Israel, and Hinedi Geluda, Brazil.

1985, Mar. 15 Photo. *Perf. 13½*

444	A221	50c	Farmer plowing, discussion group *(625,043)*	1.10	50
			First day cover *(77,271)*		1.25
			Margin block of 4, inscription	5.50	—

See U.N. Offices in Geneva Nos. 131-132; Vienna No. 49.

Peoples of the World United — A222

Painting U.N. Emblem — A223

Printed by Carl Ueberreuter Druck and Verlag M. Salzer, Austria. Panes of 50. Designed by Fritz Henry Oerter, Federal Republic of Germany (22c), and Rimondi Rino, Italy ($3).

1985, May 10 Litho. *Perf. 14*

445	A222	22c	multi *(2,000,000)*+	50	22
			First day cover		50
			Margin block of 4, inscription	2.50	—
446	A223	$3	multi *(2,000,000)*+	6.50	3.00
			First day cover		5.50
			First day cover, Nos. 445-446		5.00
			Margin block of 4, inscription	32.50	—

First day covers of Nos. 445-446 total 88,613.

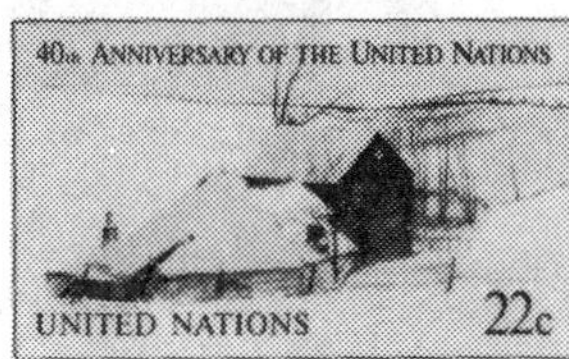

The Corner, 1947 — A224

Alvaro Raking Hay, 1953 — A225

U.N. 40th anniversary. Oil paintings (details) by American artist Andrew Wyeth (b. 1917). Printed by Helio Courvoisier, Switzerland. Nos. 447-448 panes of 50. Designed by Rocco J. Callari, U.S., and Thomas Lee, China (#449).

1985, June 26 Photo. *Perf. 12 x 11½*

447	A224	22c	multicolored *(944,960)*	50	22
			First day cover		55
			Margin block of 4, inscription	2.50	—
448	A225	45c	multicolored *(680,079)*	1.00	45
			First day cover		1.10
			First day cover, Nos. 447-448		1.40
			Margin block of 4, inscription	5.00	—

Souvenir Sheet

Imperf

449			Sheet of 2 *(506,004)*	2.00	2.00
a.	A224	22c	multi	50	
b.	A225	45c	multi	1.00	
			First day cover		2.00

No. 449 has multicolored margin containing inscription and U.N. emblem. Size: 75x83 mm.

First day covers of Nos. 447-449 total: New York, 210,189; San Francisco, 92,804.

See U.N. Offices in Geneva Nos. 135-137; Vienna Nos. 52-54.

Flag Type of 1980

Printed by Helio Courvoisier, Switzerland. Designed by Ole Hamann. Issued in panes of 16; each contains 4 blocks of four (Nos. 450-453, 454-457, 458-461, 462-465). A se-tenant block of 4 designs is at the center of each pane.

1985, Sept. 20 Photo. *Perf. 12*

450	A185	22c	Grenada *(1,270,755)*	65	20
451	A185	22c	Federal Republic of Germany *(1,270,755)*	65	20
452	A185	22c	Saudi Arabia *(1,270, 755)*	65	20
453	A185	22c	Mexico *(1,270,755)*	65	20
454	A185	22c	Uganda *(1,216,878)*	65	20
455	A185	22c	St. Thomas & Prince *(1,216,878)*	65	20
456	A185	22c	USSR *(1,216,878)*	65	20
457	A185	22c	India *(1,216,878)*	65	20
458	A185	22c	Liberia *(1,213,231)*	65	20
459	A185	22c	Mauritius *(1,213,231)*	65	20
460	A185	22c	Chad *(1,213,231)*	65	20
461	A185	22c	Dominican Republic *(1,213,231)*	65	20
462	A185	22c	Sultanate of Oman *(1,215,533)*	65	20
463	A185	22c	Ghana *(1,251,533)*	65	20
464	A185	22c	Sierra Leone *(1,251,533)*	65	20
465	A185	22c	Finland *(1,251,533)*	65	20
			First day covers, Nos. 450-465, each		65

First day covers of Nos. 450-465 total 1,774,193.

The Catalogue editors cannot undertake to appraise, identify or judge the genuineness or condition of stamps.

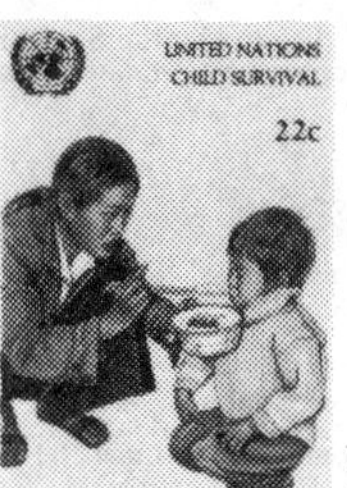

UNICEF Child Survival Campaign — A226

Printed by the Government Printing Bureau, Japan. Panes of 50. Designed by Mel Harris, United Kingdom (#466) and Dipok Deyi, India (#467)

1985, Nov. 22 Photo. & Engr. *Perf. 13½*

466	A226	22c	Asian Toddler *(823,724)*	44	22
			First day cover		55
			Margin block of 4, inscription	2.20	—
467	A226	33c	Breastfeeding *(632,753)*	66	32
			First day cover		70
			First day cover, Nos. 466-467		1.10
			Margin block of 4, inscription	3.30	—

First day covers of Nos. 466-467 total 206,923.

See U.N. Offices in Geneva Nos. 138-139; Vienna Nos. 55-56.

Africa in Crisis — A227

Printed by Helio Courvoisier, Switzerland. Panes of 50. Designed by Wosene Kosrof, Ethiopia.

1986, Jan. 31 Photo. *Perf. 11½x12*

468	A227	22c	multi *(708,169)*	50	22
			First day cover *(80,588)*		60
			Margin block of 4, inscription	2.50	—

Campaign against hunger. See U.N. Offices in Geneva No. 140; Vienna No. 57.

Water Resources — A228

Printed by the Government Printing Bureau, Japan. Panes of 40, 2 blocks of 4 horizontal by 5 blocks of 4 vertical. Designed by Thomas Lee, China.

1986, Mar. 14 Photo. *Perf. 13½*

469	A228	22c	Dam *(525,839)*	50	22
			First day cover		50
470	A228	22c	Irrigation *(525,839)*	50	22
			First day cover		50
471	A228	22c	Hygiene *(525,839)*	50	22
			First day cover		50
472	A228	22c	Well *(525,839)*	50	22
			First day cover		50
			First day cover, #469-472		1.75
			Margin block of 4, #469-472, inscription	2.50	—
a.			Block of 4, #469-472	2.00	88

U.N. Development Program. Nos. 469-472 printed se-tenant in a continuous design.

First day covers of Nos. 469-472 total 199,347.

See U.N. Offices in Geneva Nos. 141-144; Vienna Nos. 58-61.

Human Rights Stamp of 1954 — A229

Stamp collecting: 44c, Engraver. Printed by the Swedish Post Office, Sweden. Panes of 50. Designed by Czeslaw Slania and Ingalill Axelsson, Sweden.

1986, May 22 Engr. *Perf. 12½*

473 A229	22c	dk vio & brt bl *(825,782)*	44	22
		First day cover		50
		Margin block of 4, inscription	2.20	—
474 A229	44c	brn & emer grn *(738,552)*	88	44
		First day cover		80
		First day cover, #473-474		1.20
		Margin block of 4, inscription	4.40	—

First day covers of Nos. 473-474 total: New York, 121,143; Chicago, 89,557.

See U.N. Offices in Geneva Nos. 146-147; Vienna Nos. 62-63.

Bird's Nest in Tree — A230

Peace in Seven Languages — A231

Printed by the Government Printing Bureau, Japan. Panes of 50. Designed by Akira Iriguchi, Japan (#475), and Henryk Chylinski, Poland (#476).

1986, June 20 Photo. & Embossed *Perf. 13½*

475 A230	22c	multi *(836,160)*	44	22
		First day cover		50
		Margin block of 4, inscription	2.20	—
476 A231	33c	multi *(663,882)*	66	35
		First day cover		65
		First day cover, #475-476		1.00
		Margin block of 4, inscription	3.30	—

International Peace Year.

First day covers of Nos. 475-476 total 149,976.

Flag Type of 1980

Printed by Helio Courvoisier, Switzerland. Designed by Ole Hamann. Issued in panes of 16; each contains 4 blocks of four (Nos. 477-480, 481-484, 485-488, 489-492). A se-tenant block of 4 designs is at the center of each pane.

1986, Sept. 19 Photo. *Perf. 12*

477 A185	22c	New Zealand *(1,150,584)*	60	20
478 A185	22c	Lao PDR *(1,150,584)*	60	20
479 A185	22c	Burkina Faso *(1,150,584)*	60	20
480 A185	22c	Gambia *(1,150,584)*	60	20
481 A185	22c	Maldives *(1,154,870)*	60	20
482 A185	22c	Ethiopia *(1,154,870)*	60	20
483 A185	22c	Jordan *(1,154,870)*	60	20
484 A185	22c	Zambia *(1,154,870)*	60	20
485 A185	22c	Iceland *(1,152,740)*	60	20
486 A185	22c	Antigua & Barbuda *(1,152,740)*	60	20
487 A185	22c	Angola *(1,152,740)*	60	20
488 A185	22c	Botswana *(1,152,740)*	60	20
489 A185	22c	Romania *(1,150,412)*	60	20
490 A185	22c	Togo *(1,150,412)*	60	20
491 A185	22c	Mauritania *(1,150,412)*	60	20
492 A185	22c	Colombia *(1,150,412)*	60	20
		First day covers, Nos. 477-492, each		65

First day covers of Nos. 477-492 total 1,442,284.

Souvenir Sheet

40th Anniversary of WFUNA

UNITED NATIONS 22c

World Federation of U.N. Associations, 40th Anniversary — A232

Printed by Johann Enschede and Sons, Netherlands. Designed by Rocco J. Callari, U.S.

Designs: 22c, Mother Earth, by Edna Hibel, U.S. 33c, Watercolor by Salvador Dali (b. 1904) Spain. 39c, New Dawn, by Dong Kingman, U.S. 44c, Watercolor by Chaim Gross, U.S.

1986, Nov. 14 Litho. *Perf. 13x13½*

493		Sheet of 4 *(433,888)*	2.50	2.50
a.		A232 22c multi	40	—
b.		A232 33c multi	60	—
c.		A232 39c multi	70	—
d.		A232 44c multi	80	—
		First day cover *(106,194)*		3.25

No. 493 has inscribed margin picturing U.N. and WFUNA emblems. Size: 119x65mm.

See U.N. Offices in Geneva No. 150; Vienna No. 66.

Trygve Halvdan Lie (1896-1968), First Secretary-General — A233

Printed by the Government Printing Office, Austria. Panes of 50. Designed by Rocco J. Callari, U.S., from a portrait by Harald Dal, Norway.

1987, Jan. 30 Photo. & Engr. *Perf. 13½*

494 A233	22c	multi *(1,200,000)+*	35	22
		First day cover *(84,819)*		60
		Margin block of 4, inscription	1.75	—

See Offices in Geneva No. 151; Vienna No. 67.

International Year of Shelter for the Homeless A234

Printed by Johann Enschede and Sons, Netherlands. Panes of 50. Designed by Wladyslaw Brykczynski, Poland.

Designs: 22c, Surveying and blueprinting. 44c, Cutting lumber.

1987, Mar. 13 Litho. *Perf. 13½x12½*

495 A234	22c	multi *(1,150,000)+*	35	22
		First day cover		60
		Margin block of 4, inscription	1.75	—
496 A234	44c	multi *(1,150,000)+*	70	44
		First day cover		90
		First day cover, #495-496		1.25
		Margin block of 4, inscription	3.50	—

First day covers of Nos. 495-496 total 94,090.

See Offices in Geneva Nos. 154-155; Vienna Nos. 68-69.

Fight Drug Abuse — A235

Printed by the House of Questa, United Kingdom. Panes of 50. Designed by Susan Borgen and Noel Werrett, U.S.

Designs: 22c, Construction. 33c, Education.

1987, June 12 Litho. *Perf. 14½x15*

497 A235	22c	multi *(1,150,000)+*	40	22
		First day cover		60
		Margin block of 4, inscription	2.00	—
498 A235	33c	multi *(1,150,000)+*	60	35
		First day cover		75
		First day cover, #497-498		1.25
		Margin block of 4, inscription	3.00	—

First day covers of Nos. 497-498 total 106,941.

See Offices in Geneva Nos. 156-157; Vienna Nos. 70-71.

Flag Type of 1980

Printed by Courvoisier. Designed by Ole Hamann. Issued in panes of 16; each contains 4 block of four (Nos. 499-502, 503-506, 507-510, 511-514). A se-tenant block of 4 designs is at the center of each pane.

1987, Sept. 18 Photo. *Perf. 12*

499 A185	22c	Comoros	40	20
500 A185	22c	Yemen PDR	40	20
501 A185	22c	Mongolia	40	22
502 A185	22c	Vanuatu	40	20
503 A185	22c	Japan	40	20
504 A185	22c	Gabon	40	20
505 A185	22c	Zimbabwe	40	20
506 A185	22c	Iraq	40	20
507 A185	22c	Argentina	40	20
508 A185	22c	Congo	40	20
509 A185	22c	Niger	40	20
510 A185	22c	St. Lucia	40	20
511 A185	22c	Bahrain	40	20
512 A185	22c	Haiti	40	20
513 A185	22c	Afghanistan	40	20
514 A185	22c	Greece	40	20
		First day covers, Nos. 499-514, each		50

Print order 2,200,000 each.

United Nations Day — A236

Printed by The House of Questa, United Kingdom. Panes of 12. Designed by Elisabeth von Janota-Bzowski (#515) and Fritz Henry Oerter (#516), Federal Republic of Germany.

Designs: Multinational people in various occupations.

1987, Oct. 23 Litho. *Perf. 14½x15*

515 A236	22c	multi *(1,188,000)+*	44	22
		First day cover		80
		Margin block of 4, inscription	2.20	—
516 A236	39c	multi *(1,188,000)+*	78	40
		First day cover		1.15
		First day cover, #515-516		1.65
		Margin block of 4, inscription	3.90	—

See Offices in Geneva Nos. 158-159; Vienna Nos. 74-75.

Immunize Every Child — A237

Printed by The House of Questa, United Kingdom. Panes of 50. Designed by Seymour Chwast, U.S.

Designs: 22c, Measles. 44c, Tetanus.

1987, Nov. 20 Litho. *Perf. 15x14½*

517 A237	22c	multi *(1,150,000)+*	44	22
		First day cover		60
		Margin block of 4, inscription	2.20	—
518 A237	44c	multi *(1,150,000)+*	88	44
		First day cover		1.00
		First day cover, #517-518		1.40
		Margin block of 4, inscription	4.40	—

See Offices in Geneva Nos. 160-161; Vienna Nos. 76-77.

Intl. Fund for Agricultural Development (IFAD) — A238

Printed by CPE Australia Ltd., Australia. Panes of 50. Designed by Santiago Arolas, Switzerland.

Designs: 22c, Fishing. 33c, Farming.

1988, Jan. 29 Litho. *Perf. 13½*

519 A238	22c	multi *(1,050,000)+*	44	32
		First day cover		60
		Margin block of 4, inscription	2.20	—
520 A238	33c	multi *(1,050,000)+*	66	35
		First day cover		1.25
		First day cover, Nos. 519-520		1.25
		Margin block of 4, inscription	3.30	—

See Offices in Geneva Nos. 162-163; Vienna Nos. 78-79.

A239

Printed by Heraclio Fournier, S.A., Spain. Panes of 50. Designed by David Ben-Hador, Isreal.

1988, Jan. 29 Photo. *Perf. 13½x14*

521 A239	3c	multi *(3,000,000)+*	6	5
		First day cover		80
		Margin block of 4, inscription	30	—

Survival of the Forests — A240

Printed by The House of Questa, United Kindgdom. Panes of six se-tenant pairs. Designed by Braldt Bralds, the Netherlands.

Tropical rain forest: 25c, Treetops. 44c, Ground vegetation and tree trunks. Printed se-tenant in a continuous design.

1988, Mar. 18 Litho. *Perf. 14x15*

522 A240	25c	multi *(594,000)+*	50	25
		First day cover		85
523 A240	44c	multi *(594,000)+*	88	45
		First day cover		1.25
a.		Se-tenant pair, #522-523	1.40	
		First day cover, Nos. 522-523		1.75
		Margin block of 4, inscription (2 each Nos. 522-523)	3.45	

See Offices in Geneva Nos. 165-166; Vienna Nos. 80-81.

Intl. Volunteer Day — A241

Printed by Johann Enschede and Sons, the Netherlands. Panes of 50. Designed by James E. Tennison, U.S.

Designs: 25c, Edurahon, Vert. 50c, Vocational training.

1988, May 6 Litho. *Perf. 13x14, 14x13*

524 A241	25c	multi *(1,050,000)+*	50	25
		First day cover		85
		Margin block of 4, inscription	2.50	—
525 A241	50c	multi *(1,050,000)+*	1.00	50
		First day cover		1.35
		First day cover, #524-525		1.90
		Margin block of 4, inscription	5.00	—

See Offices in Geneva Nos. 167-168; Vienna Nos. 82-83.

Health in Sports — A242

Printed by the Government Printing Bureau, Japan. Panes of 50. Paintings by LeRoy Neiman, American sports artist.

Designs: 25c, Cycling, vert. 35c, Marathon.

1988, June 17 Litho. *Perf. 13½x13, 13x13½*

526 A242	25c	multi *(1,050,000)+*	50	38
		First day cover		85
		Margin block of 4, inscription	2.50	—
527 A242	38c	multi *(1,050,000)+*	76	58
		First day cover	—	1.15
		First day cover, Nos. 526-527		1.65
		Margin block of 4, inscription	3.80	—

See Offices in Geneva Nos. 169-170; Vienna Nos. 84-85.

Flag Type of 1980

Printed by Helio Courvoisier, Switzerland. Designed by Ole Hamann, Denmark. Issued in panes of 16; each contains 4 blocks of four (Nos. 528-531, 532-535, 536-539 and 540-543). A se-tenant block of 4 is at the center of each pane.

1988, Sept. 15 Photo. *Perf. 12*

528 A185	25c	Spain *(2,086,000)+*	50	25
529 A185	25c	St. Vincent & Grenadines *(2,086,000)+*	50	25
530 A185	25c	Ivory Coast *(2,086,000)+*	50	25
531 A185	25c	Lebanon *(2,086,000)+*	50	25
532 A185	25c	Yemen (Arab Republic) *(2,086,000)+*	50	25
533 A185	25c	Cuba *(2,086,000)+*	50	25
534 A185	25c	Denmark *(2,086,000)+*	50	25
535 A185	25c	Libya *(2,086,000)+*	50	25
536 A185	25c	Qutar *(2,086,000)+*	50	25
537 A185	25c	Zaire *(2,086,000)+*	50	25
538 A185	25c	Norway *(2,086,000)+*	50	25
539 A185	25c	German Democratic Republic *(2,086,000)+*	50	25
540 A185	25c	Iran *(2,086,000)+*	50	25
541 A185	25c	Tunisia *(2,086,000)+*	50	25
542 A185	25c	Samoa	50	25
543 A185	25c	Belize *(2,086,000)+*	50	25
		First day covers, Nos. 528-543, each		65

Universal Declaration of Human Rights, 40th. Anniv. — A243

Printed by Helio Couvoisier, Switzerland. Panes of 50. Designed by Rocco J. Callair, U.S.

1988, Dec. 9 Photo. & Engr. *Perf.*

544 A243	25c	multi *(1,025,000)+*	50	25
		First day cover		85
		Margin block of 4, inscription	2.50	—

Souvenir Sheet

545 A243	$1	multi *(700,000)+*	2.00	2.00
		First day cover		2.50

No. 545 has multicolored decorative margin inscribed with the preamble to the human rights declaration in English. Size:

See Offices in Geneva Nos. 171-172; Vienna Nos. 86-87.

World Bank — A244

Printed by Johann Enscede and Sons, the Netherlands. Panes of 50. Designed by Saturnino Lumboy, Philippines.

1989, Jan. 27 Litho. *Perf. 13x14*

546 A244	25c	Energy and nature *(1,000,000)+*	50	25
		First day cover		85
		Margin block of 4, inscription	2.50	—
547 A244	45c	Agriculture *(900,000)+*	90	45
		First day cover		1.25
		Margin block of 4, inscription	4.50	—

See Offices in Geneva Nos. 173-174; Vienna Nos. 88-89.

U.N. Peace-Keeping Force, Awarded 1988 Nobel Peace Prize — A245

Printed by CPE Australia, Ltd., Australia. Panes of 50. Designed by Tom Bland, Australia.

1989, Mar. 17 Litho. *Perf. 14x13½*

548 A245	25c	multicolored *(1,000,000)+*	50	25
		First day cover		85
		Margin block of 4, inscription	2.50	—

See Offices in Geneva No. 175; Vienna No. 90.

Aerial Photograph of New York Headquarters — A246

Printed by Johann Enschede and Sons, the Netherlands. Panes of 25. Designed by Rocco J. Callari, United States, from a photograph by Simon Nathan.

1989, Mar. 17 Litho. *Perf. 14½x14*

549 A246	45c	multicolored *(2,000,000)+*	90	45
		First day cover		1.25
		Margin block of 4, inscription	4.50	—

World Weather Watch, 25th Anniv. (in 1988) — A247

Printed by Johann Enschede and Sons, the Netherlands. Panes of 50.

Satellite photographs: 25c, Storm system off the U.S. east coast. 36c, Typhoon Abby in the north-west Pacific.

1989, Apr. 21 Litho. *Perf. 13x14*

550 A247	25c	multicolored *(1,100,000)+*	50	25
		First day cover		85
		Margin block of 4, inscription	2.50	—
551 A247	36c	multicolored *(1,000,000)+*	72	36
		First day cover		1.05
		First day cover, Nos. 550-551		1.55
		Margin block of 4, inscription	3.60	—

See Offices in Geneva Nos. 176-177; Vienna Nos. 91-92.

The Scott Catalogue value is a retail price, what you could expect to pay for the stamp in a grade of Fine-Very Fine. The value listed is a reference which reflects recent actual dealer selling price.

Offices in Vienna, 10th Anniv.
A248 A249

Printed by the Government Printing Office, Austria. Panes of 25. Designed by Paul Flora (25c) and Rudolf Hausner (90c), Austria.

Photo. & Engr., Photo. (90c)

1989, Aug. 23					*Perf. 14*
552	A248	25c	multicolored *(1,000,000)+*	50	25
			First day cover		85
			Margin block of 4, inscription	2.50	—
553	A249	90c	multicolored *(1,000,000)+*	1.80	90
			First day cover		2.15
			First day cover, Nos. 552-553		2.65
			Margin block of 4, inscription	9.00	—

See Offices in Geneva Nos. 178-179; Vienna Nos. 93-94.

Flag Type of 1980

Printed by Helio Courvoisier, Switzerland. Designed by Ole Hamann, Denmark. Issued in panes of 16; each contains 4 blocks of 4 (Nos. 554-557, 558-561, 562-565, 566-569). A se-tenant block of 4 designs is at the center of each pane.

1989, Sept. 22			**Photo.**		*Perf.*
554	A185	25c	Indonesia *(1,400,000)+*	50	25
555	A185	25c	Lesotho *(1,400,000)+*	50	25
556	A185	25c	Guatemala *(1,400,000)+*	50	25
557	A185	25c	Netherlands *(1,400,000)+*	50	25
558	A185	25c	South Africa *(1,400,000)+*	50	25
559	A185	25c	Portugal *(1,400,000)+*	50	25
560	A185	25c	Morocco *(1,400,000)+*	50	25
561	A185	25c	Syrian Arab Republic *(1,400,000)+*	50	25
562	A185	25c	Honduras *(1,400,000)+*	50	25
563	A185	25c	Kampuchea *(1,400,000)+*	50	25
564	A185	25c	Guinea-Bissau *(1,400,000)+*	50	25
565	A185	25c	Cyprus *(1,400,000)+*	50	25
566	A185	25c	Algeria *(1,400,000)+*	50	25
567	A185	25c	Brunei *(1,400,000)+*	50	25
568	A185	25c	St. Kitts and Nevis *(1,400,000)+*	50	25
569	A185	25c	United Nations *(1,400,000)+*	50	25
			First day covers, Nos. 554-569, each		85

AIR POST

Plane and Gull — AP1

Swallows and U.N. Emblem — AP2

Engraved and printed by Thomas De La Rue & Co., Ltd., London. Panes of 50. Designed by Ole Hamann (AP1) and Olav Mathiesen (AP2).

1951, Dec. 14			**Unwmk.**		*Perf. 14*
C1	AP1	6c	henna brown *(2,500,000)*	12	12
			First day cover		2.00
			Margin block of 4, inscription	60	—
C2	AP1	10c	bright blue green *(2,750,000)*	20	20
			First day cover		2.00
			Margin block of 4, inscription	1.00	—
C3	AP2	15c	deep ultramarine *(3,250,000)*	45	25
			Prussian blue	100.00	
			First day cover		3.00
			Margin block of 4, inscription	2.25	—
C4	AP2	25c	gray black *(2,250,000)*	2.00	1.25
			First day cover		7.50
			First day cover, #C1-C4		13.50
			Margin block of 4, inscription	10.00	—

First day covers of Nos. 1-11 and C1-C4 total 1,113,216.

Early printings of Nos. C1-C4 have wide, imperforate sheet margins on three sides. Later printings were perforated through all margins.

Nos. C1, C3 and C4 exist imperforate.

Airplane Wing and Globe — AP3

Engraved and printed by Thomas De La Rue & Co., Ltd., London. Panes of 50. Designed by W. W. Wind.

1957, May 27					*Perf. 12½x14*
C5	AP3	4c	maroon *(5,000,000)*	6	6
			First day cover *(282,933)*		20
			Margin block of 4, inscription	30	—

Type of 1957 and

U. N. Flag and Plane — AP4

Engraved and printed by Waterlow & Sons, Ltd., London. Panes of 50. Designed by W. W. Wind (5c) and Olav Mathiesen (7c).

1959, Feb. 9			**Unwmk.**		*Perf. 12½x13½*
C6	AP3	5c	rose red *(4,000,000)*	8	8
			First day cover		20
			Margin block of 4, inscription	40	—
			Perf. 13½x14		
C7	AP4	7c	ultramarine *(4,000,000)*	12	10
			First day cover		25
			First day cover, #C6-C7		40
			Margin block of 4, inscription	60	—

First day covers of Nos. C6 and C7 total 413,556.

Outer Space — AP5

U.N. Emblem — AP6

Bird of Laurel Leaves — AP7

Printed by Courvoisier S.A., La Chaux-de-Fonds, Switzerland. Panes of 50. Designed by Claude Bottiau (6c), George Hamori (8c) and Kurt Plowitz (13c).

1963, June 17			**Photo.** **Unwmk.**		*Perf. 11½*
C8	AP5	6c	black, blue & yellow green *(4,000,000)*	9	8
			First day cover		20
			Margin block of 4, inscription	45	—
C9	AP6	8c	yellow, olive green & red *(4,000,000)*	12	10
			First day cover		20
			Margin block of 4, inscription	60	—
			Perf. 12½x12		
C10	AP7	13c	ultra., aquamarine, gray & carmine *(2,700,000)*	18	15
			First day cover		30
			First day cover, #C8-C10		55
			Margin block of 4, inscription	90	—

First day covers of Nos. C8-C10 total 535,824.

"Flight Across the Globe" — AP8

Jet Plane and Envelope — AP9

Printed by the Austrian Government Printing Office, Vienna, Austria. Panes of 50. Designed by Ole Hamann (15c) and George Hamori (25c).

Perf. 11½x12, 12x11½

1964, May 1			**Photo.**		**Unwmk.**
C11	AP8	15c	violet, buff, gray & pale green *(3,000,000)*	35	20
			First day cover		40
			Margin block of 4, inscription	1.75	—
		a.	Gray omitted		—
C12	AP9	25c	yellow, orange, gray, blue & red *(2,000,000)*	65	30
			First day cover		60
			First day cover, #C11-C12		90
			Margin block of 4, inscription	3.25	—

First day covers of Nos. C11-C12 total 353,696.

For 75c in type AP8, see U.N. Offices in Geneva No. 8.

Nos. C11-C12 exist imperforate.

Jet Plane and U.N. Emblem — AP10

Printed by Setelipaino, Finland. Panes of 50. Designed by Ole Hamann.

1968, Apr. 18			**Litho.**		*Perf. 13*
C13	AP10	20c	multicolored *(3,000,000)*	30	25
			First day cover *(225,378)*		85
			Margin block of 4, inscription	1.50	—

Wings, Envelopes and U.N. Emblem — AP11

Printed by Setelipaino, Finland. Panes of 50. Designed by Olav S. Mathiesen.

1969, Apr. 21			**Litho.**		*Perf. 13*
C14	AP11	10c	orange vermilion, orange, yellow & black *(4,000,000)*	20	15
			First day cover *(132,686)*		50
			Margin block of 4, inscription	1.00	—

U.N. Emblem and Stylized Wing — AP12

Birds in Flight — AP13

Clouds — AP14

"UN" and Plane — AP15

Printed by Government Printing Bureau, Japan (9c); Heraclio Fournier, S. A., Spain (11c, 17c); Setelipaino, Finland (21c). Panes of 50. Designed by Lyell L. Dolan (9c), Arne Johnson (11c), British American Bank Note Co. (17c) and Asher Kalderon (21c).

1972, May 1 — Litho. & Engr. — *Perf. 13x13½*

C15	AP12	9c lt. blue, dk. red & vio. blue *(3,000,000)+*	12	10
		First day cover		25
		Margin block of 4, inscription	60	—

Photo.

Perf. 14x13½

C16	AP13	11c blue & multicolored *(3,000,000)+*	16	10
		First day cover		35
		Margin block of 4, inscription	80	—

Perf. 13½x14

C17	AP14	17c yellow, red & orange *(3,000,000)+*	25	18
		First day cover		50
		Margin block of 4, inscription	1.25	—

Perf. 13

C18	AP15	21c silver & multi. *(3,500,000)*	30	22
		First day cover		60
		First day cover, #C15-C18		1.50
		Margin block of 4, inscription	1.50	—

\+ Printing orders to Nov. 1979.

First day covers of Nos. C15-C18 total 553,535.

Globe and Jet — AP16

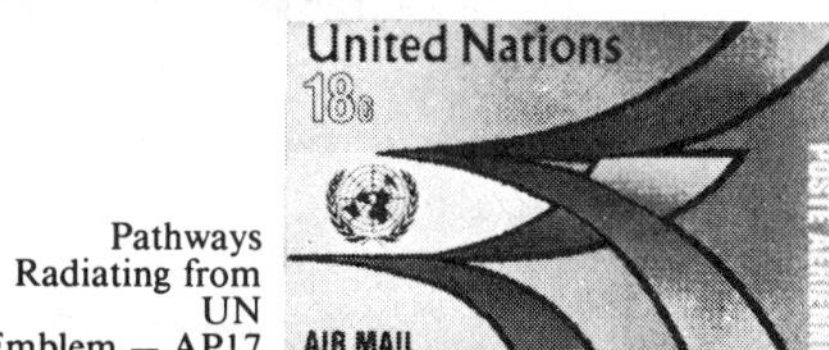

Pathways Radiating from UN Emblem — AP17

Bird in Flight, UN Headquarters AP18

Printed by Setelipaino, Finland. Panes of 50. Designed by George Hamori (13c), Shamir Bros. (18c) and Olav S. Mathiesen (26c).

1974, Sept. 16 — Litho. — *Perf. 13, 12½x13 (18c)*

C19	AP16	13c multicolored *(2,500,000)+*	18	14
		First day cover		50
		Margin block of 4, inscription	90	—
C20	AP17	18c gray olive & multicolored *(2,000,000)+*	28	20
		First day cover		90
		Margin block of 4, inscription	1.40	—
C21	AP18	26c blue & multi. *(2,000,000)+*	40	30
		First day cover		75
		First day cover, #C19-C21		1.50
		Margin block of 4, inscription	2.00	—

First day covers of Nos. C19-C21 total 309,610.

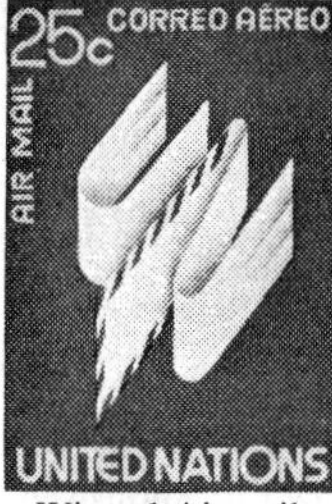

Winged Airmail Letter — AP19

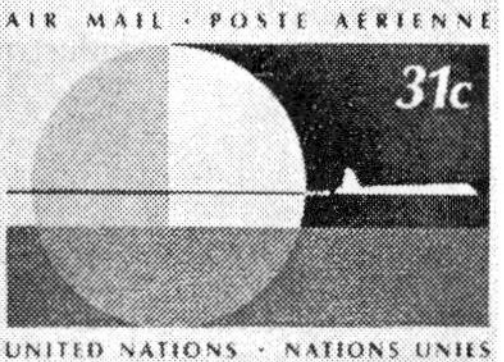

Symbolic Globe and Plane — AP20

Printed by Heraclio Fournier, S.A. Panes of 50. Designed by Eliezer Weishoff (25c) and Alan L. Pollock (31c).

1977, June 27 — Photo. — *Perf. 14*

C22	AP19	25c greenish blue & multi. *(2,000,000)+*	38	25
		First day cover		85
		Margin block of 4, inscription	1.90	—
C23	AP20	31c magenta *(2,000,000)+*	45	30
		First day cover		1.00
		First day cover, #C22-C23		1.50
		Margin block of 4, inscription	2.25	—

First day covers of Nos. C22-C23 total 209,060.

ENVELOPES

Emblem of United Nations — U1

Printed by the International Envelope Corp., Dayton, Ohio. Die engraved by the American Bank Note Co., New York.

1953, Sept. 15 — Embossed

U1	U1	3c blue, entire *(555,000)*	75	25
		Entire, first day cancel *(102,278)*		75

Printed by International Envelope Corp., Dayton, O.

1958, Sept. 22 — Embossed

U2	U1	4c ultramarine, entire *(1,000,000)*	50	16
		Entire, first day cancel *(213,621)*		25

Stylized Globe and Weather Vane — U2

Printed by United States Envelope Co., Springfield, Mass. Designed by Hatim El Mekki.

1963, Apr. 26 — Litho.

U3	U2	5c multicolored, entire *(1,115,888)*	22	8
		Entire, first day cancel *(165,188)*		30

Printed by Setelipaino, Finland.

1969, Jan. 8 — Litho.

U4	U2	6c black, bl., magenta & dull yel., entire *(850,000)*	20	14
		Entire, first day cancel *(152,593)*		38

Headquarters Type of Regular Issue, 1968

Printed by Eureka Co., a division of Litton Industries.

1973, Jan. 12 — Litho.

U5	A99	8c sepia, blue & olive, entire *(700,000)*	22	12
		Entire, first day cancel *(145,510)*		38

Headquarters Type of Regular Issue, 1974

Printed by United States Envelope Co., Springfield, Mass.

1975, Jan. 10 — Litho.

U6	A138	10c blue, olive bister & multi., entire *(547,500)*	25	14
		Entire, first day cancel *(122,000)*		50

Bouquet of Ribbons — U3

Printed by Carl Ueberreuter Druck and Verlag M. Salzer, Austria. Designed by George Hamori, Australia.

1985, May 10 — Litho.

U7	U3	22c multi, entire *(250,000)*	35	16
		Entire, first day cancel *(28,600)*		50

New York Headquarters U4

Printed by Mercury Walch, Australia. Designed by Rocco J. Callari, United States.

1989, Mar. 17 — Litho.

U8	U4	25c multicolored, entire *(350,000)+*	70	35
		Entire, first day cancel		1.05

AIR POST ENVELOPES AND AIR LETTER SHEETS

Letter Sheet

Type of Air Post Stamp of 1951

Printed by Dennison & Sons, Long Island City, N.Y.

1952, Aug. 29 — Litho.

UC1	AP2	10c blue, *bluish (187,000)*, inscribed "Air Letter" at left, entire	32.50	3.00
		Entire, first day cancel *(57,274)*		3.50

Designed by C. Mutver.

Letter Sheet

1954-58 — Litho.

UC2	AP2	10c Royal blue, *bluish*, inscribed "Air Letter" and "Aerogramme" at left, entire, *Sept. 14, 1954 (207,000)*	6.25	1.10
		Entire, first day cancel		*47.50*
a.		No white border, *1958 (148,800)*	3.50	75

No. UC2 was printed with a narrow white border (½ to 1mm wide) surrounding the stamp. On No. UC2a, this border has been partly or entirely eliminated.

U. N. Flag and Plane — UC1

(U. N. Emblem Emblossed)

Printed by International Envelope Corp., Dayton, O. Die engraved by American Bank Note Co., New York.

1959, Sept. 21 **Embossed**

UC3 UC1 7c blue, entire *(550,000)* 2.50 45
Entire, first day cancel *(172,107)* 50

Letter Sheet
Type of Air Post Stamp of 1959
Printed by Thomas De La Rue & Co., Ltd., London

1960, Jan. 18 **Litho.**

UC4 AP4 10c ultramarine, *bluish*, entire *(405,000)* 48 18
Entire, first day cancel *(122,425)* 40

Printed on protective tinted paper containing colorless inscription "United Nations" in the five official languages of the U.N.

Letter Sheet
Type of Air Post Stamp of 1951
Inscribed "Correo Aereo" instead of "Poste Aerienne"
Printed by Thomas De La Rue & Co., Ltd., London

1961-65 **Litho.**

UC5 AP1 11c ultramarine, *bluish*, entire, *June 26, 1961 (550,000)* 1.00 50
Entire, first day cancel *(128,557)* 65
a. 11c dark blue, *green* entire, *July 16, 1965 (419,000)* 1.75 55

Printed on protective tinted paper containing colorless inscription "United Nations" in the five official languages of the U.N.

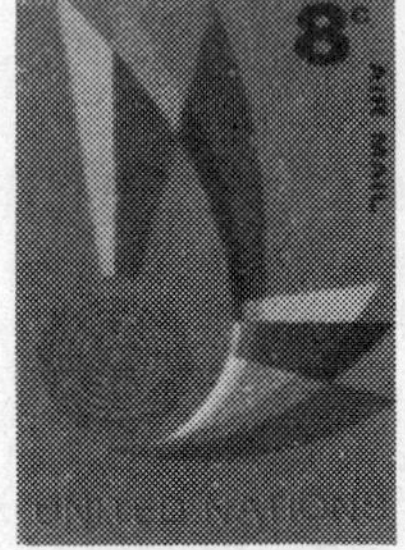

U.N. Emblem — UC2

Printed by United States Envelope Co., Springfield, Mass. Designed by George Hamori.

1963, Apr. 26 **Litho.**

UC6 UC2 8c multicolored, entire *(880,000)* 45 12
Entire, first day cancel *(165,208)* 38

Letter Sheet

U.N. Emblem and Stylized Plane — UC3

Printed by Setelipaino, Finland. Designed by Robert Perrot.

1968, May 31 **Litho.**

UC7 UC3 13c violet blue & light blue, entire *(750,000)* 40 22
Entire, first day cancel *(106,700)* 50

Type of 1963
Printed by Setelipaino, Finland.

1969, Jan. 8 **Litho.**

UC8 UC2 10c pink, Prussian blue, orange & sepia, entire *(750,000)* 35 15
Entire, first day cancel *(153,472)* 55

Letter Sheet

U.N. Emblem, "UN," Globe and Plane — UC4

Printed by Joh. Enschedé and Sons. Designed by Edmondo Calivis, Egypt. Sheet surface printed in greenish blue.

1972, Oct. 16 **Litho.**

UC9 UC4 15c violet blue & greenish blue, entire *(500,000)* 30 8
Entire, first day cancel *(85,500)* 38

Bird Type of Air Post Stamp, 1972
Printed by Eureka Co., a division of Litton Industries

1973, Jan. 12 **Litho.**

UC10 AP13 11c blue & multicolored, entire *(700,000)* 28 15
Entire, first day cancel *(134,500)* 45

Globe and Jet Air Post Type of 1974
Printed by United States Envelope Co., Springfield, Mass.

1975, Jan. 10 **Litho.**

UC11 AP16 13c blue & multicolored, entire *(555,539)* 35 18
Entire, first day cancel *(122,000)* 50

Letter Sheet
Headquarters Type of Regular Issue, 1971
Printed by Joh. Enschede and Sons, Netherlands

1975, Jan. 10 **Photo.**

UC12 A120 18c blue & multi., entire *(400,000)* 38 15
Entire, first day cancel *(70,500)* 50

Letter Sheet

"UN" Emblem and Birds UC5

Printed by Joh. Enschedé and Sons. Designed by Angel Medina Medina.

1977, June 27 **Litho.**

UC13 UC5 22c multicolored, entire *(400,000)* 45 18
Entire, first day cancel *(70,000)* 55

Letter Sheet

Paper Airplane UC6

Printed by Joh. Enschede and Sons. Designed by Margaret-Ann Champion.

1982, Apr. 28 **Litho.**

UC14 UC6 30c black, *pale green*, entire *(400,000)* 85 50
Entire, first day cancel *(61,400)* 90

Letter Sheet No. UC14 Surcharged

1987, July 7 **Litho.**

UC15 UC6 30c + 6c black, *green*, entire 90 50
Entire, first day cancel 1.00

New York Headquarters UC7

Printed by Mercury Walch, Australia. Designed by Thomas Lee, China.

1989, Mar. 17 **Litho.**

UC16 UC7 39c multicolored, entire *(350,000)+* 78 40
Entire, first day cancel 1.15

POSTAL CARDS

Values are for entire cards.
Type of Postage Issue of 1951
Printed by Dennison & Sons, Long Island City, N.Y.

1952, July 18 **Litho.**

UX1 A2 2c blue, *buff (899,415)* 20 15
First day cancel *(116,023)* 32

Printed by British American Bank Note Co., Ltd., Ottawa, Canada

1958, Sept. 22 **Litho.**

UX2 A2 3c gray olive, *buff (575,000)* 45 10
First day cancel *(145,557)* 22

World Map, Sinusoidal Projection — PC1

Printed by Eureka Specialty Printing Co., Scranton, Pa.

1963, Apr. 26 **Litho.**

UX3 PC1 4c light blue, violet blue, orange & bright citron *(784,000)* 12 5
First day cancel *(112,280)* 18
a. Bright citron omitted —

U.N. Emblem and Post Horn — PC2

Printed by Canadian Bank Note Co., Ltd., Ottawa. Designed by John Mason.

1969, Jan. 8 **Litho.**

UX4 PC2 5c blue & black *(500,000)* 12 5
First day cancel *(95,975)* 30

"UN" — PC3

Printed by Government Printing Bureau, Tokyo. Designed by Asher Kalderon.

1973, Jan. 12 **Litho.**

UX5 PC3 6c gray & multicolored *(500,000)* 15 5
First day cancel *(84,500)* 30

Type of 1973
Printed by Setelipaino, Finland

1975, Jan. 10 **Litho.**

UX6	PC3	8c light green & multicolored *(450,000)*	22	8
		First day cancel *(72,500)*		30

U.N. Emblem — PC4

Printed by Setelipaino, Finland. Designed by George Hamori.

1977, June 27 **Litho.**

UX7	PC4	9c multicolored *(350,000)*	25	6
		First day cancel *(70,000)*		40

PC5

Printed by Courvoisier. Designed by Salahattin Kanidinc.

1982, Apr. 28 **Photo.**

UX8	PC5	13c multicolored *(350,000)*	20	10
		First day cancel *(59,200)*		40

Views of New York Headquarters PC6

Designs: No. UX9, Complex, lawn. No. UX10, Complex photographed through trees. No. UX11, Flags. No. UX12, General Assembly interior. No. UX13, View of complex from the East River. No. UX14, Complex and flags. No. UX15, Flagpoles. No. UX16, Complex at dusk. No. UX17, Close-up of Security Council. No. UX18, Complex and sculpture in park. Nos. UX9-UX10 and UX14-UX16 vert.

Printed by Johann Enschede and Sons, the Netherlands. Designed by Thomas Lee, China, from photographs.

1989, Mar. 17 **Litho.**

UX9	PC6	15c multicolored *(120,000)+*	80	40
UX10	PC6	15c multicolored *(120,000)+*	80	40
UX11	PC6	15c multicolored *(120,000)+*	80	40
UX12	PC6	15c multicolored *(120,000)+*	80	40
UX13	PC6	15c multicolored *(120,000)+*	80	40
UX14	PC6	36c multicolored *(120,000)+*	1.20	60
UX15	PC6	36c multicolored *(120,000)+*	1.20	60
UX16	PC6	36c multicolored *(120,000)+*	1.20	60
UX17	PC6	36c multicolored *(120,000)+*	1.20	60
UX18	PC6	36c multicolored *(120,000)+*	1.20	60

Nos. UX9-UX13 and UX14-UX18 sold only in sets. Nos. UX9-UX13 sold for $2 and Nos. UX14-UX18 sold for $3.

AIR POST POSTAL CARDS

Values are for entire cards.

Type of Air Post Stamp of 1957

Printed by British American Bank Note Co., Ltd., Ottawa

1957, May 27 **Litho.**

UXC1	AP3	4c maroon, *buff (631,000)*	12	6
		First day cancel *(260,005)*		18

No. UXC1 Surcharged in Maroon at Left of Stamp

1959, June 5 **Litho.**

UXC2	AP3	4c+1c maroon, *buff (1,119,000)*	75	20
		Cancel first day of public use, June 8, 1959		18.00
a.		Double surcharge	—	
b.		Inverted surcharge	—	

Type of Air Post Stamp, 1957
Printed by Eureka Specialty Printing Co., Scranton, Pa.

1959, Sept. 21 **Litho.**

UXC3	AP3	5c crimson, *buff (500,000)*	1.00	18
		First day cancel *(119,479)*		20

Outer Space — APC1

Printed by Eureka Specialty Printing Co., Scranton, Pa.

1963, Apr. 26 **Litho.**

UXC4	APC1	6c black & blue *(350,000)*	38	10
		First day cancel *(109,236)*		25

APC2

Printed by Eureka-Carlisle Co., Scranton, Pa. Designed by Olav S. Mathiesen.

1966, June 9 **Litho.**

UXC5	APC2	11c dark red, rose, yellow & brown *(764,500)*	85	15
		First day cancel *(162,588)*		42

1968, May 31 **Litho.**

UXC6	APC2	13c dark green, bright green & yellow *(829,000)*	42	12
		First day cancel *(106,500)*		50

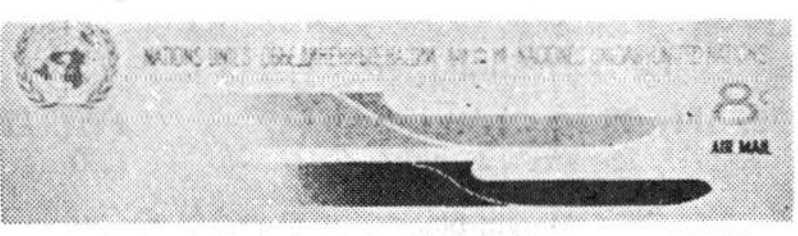

U.N. Emblem and Stylized Planes — APC3

Printed by Canadian Bank Note Co., Ltd., Ottawa. Designed by Lawrence Kurtz.

1969, Jan. 8 **Litho.**

UXC7	APC3	8c gray, dull yellow, lt. blue, indigo & red *(500,000)*	22	8
		First day cancel *(94,037)*		38

Type of Air Post Stamp of 1972
Printed by Government Printing Bureau, Tokyo. Designed by L. L. Dolan.

1972, Oct. 16 **Litho.**

UXC8	AP12	9c org., red, gray & green *(500,000)*	22	8
		First day cancel *(85,600)*		28

Type of 1969
Printed by Government Printing Bureau, Tokyo

1972, Oct. 16 **Litho.**

UXC9	APC3	15c lilac, lt. blue, pink & car. *(500,000)*	28	15
		First day cancel *(84,800)*		35

Types of Air Post Stamps, 1972-74
Printed by Setelipaino, Finland

1975, Jan. 10 **Litho.**

UXC10	AP14	11c greenish bl., blue & dark blue *(250,000)*	28	10
		First day cancel *(70,500)*		38
UXC11	AP17	18c gray & multicolored *(250,000)*	35	12
		First day cancel *(70,500)*		42

Flying Mailman — APC4

Printed by Courvoisier. Designed by Arieh Glaser.

1982, Apr. 28 **Photo.**

UXC12	APC4	28c multicolored *(350,000)*	35	18
		First day cancel *(58,700)*		45

SOUVENIR CARDS

These cards were issued by the United Nations Postal Administration and were not valid for postage.

Each card bears reproductions of U.N. stamps and a statement by the Secretary-General in English.

1	World Health Day, Apr. 7, 1972. Card of 5: Nos. 43, 102, 156, 207 and 228.	1.65
	A second printing shows several minor differences.	
2	Art on U.N. Stamps, Nov. 17, 1972. Card of 11: Nos. 170, 171, 173, 174, 180, 183, 201, 202, 203, 224 and 232. Nos. 201, 202 form a simulated setenant pair	90
3	Disarmament Decade, Mar. 9, 1973. Card of 5: Nos. 133, 147, 177, 227 and 234	85
4	Declaration of Human Rights, 25th Anniversary, Nov. 16, 1973. Card of 10: Nos. 13, 22, 29, 39, 47, 58, 68, 121, 190 and 242	3.00
5	Universal Postal Union centenary, Mar. 22, 1974. Card of 7: Nos. 17, 18, 219 and 246; Geneva 18 and 39, 40.	3.00
6	World Population Year, Oct. 18, 1974. Card of 7: Nos. 151, 152, 153 and 252, 253; Geneva 43, 44.	11.50
7	Peaceful Uses of Outer Space, Mar. 14, 1975. Card of 6: Nos. 112, 113 and 256, 257; Geneva 46, 47.	4.25
8	U.N. Peace Keeping Operations, Nov. 21, 1975. Card of 9: Nos. 52, 111, 118, 139, 160 and 265, 266; Geneva 55, 56.	5.00
9	World Federation of United Nations Associations, Mar. 12, 1976. Card of 5: Nos. 154, 155 and 272, 273; Geneva 57.	6.50
10	World Food Council, Nov. 19, 1976. Card of 6: Nos. 116, 117, 218 and 280; Geneva 17 and 63.	3.50
11	World Intellectual Property Organization (WIPO), Mar. 11, 1977. Card of 15: Nos. 17, 23, 25, 31, 33, 41, 43, 49, 59, 86, 90, 123 and 281, 282; Geneva 64.	2.25
12	Combat Racism, Sept. 19, 1977. Card of 8: Nos. 220, 221 and 287, 288; Geneva 19, 20 and 69, 70.	2.25
13	Namibia, May 5, 1978. Card of 10: Nos. 240, 241, 263, 264, 296, 297; Geneva 34, 53, 54, 76.	1.85
14	International Civil Aviation Organization, June 12, 1978. Card of 6: Nos. 31, 32 and 298, 299; Geneva 77, 78.	1.85
15	International Year of the Child, May 4, 1979. Card of 9: Nos. 5, 97, 161, 162, 163, 310, 311; Geneva 84, 85.	1.40
16	International Court of Justice, Nov. 9, 1979. Card of 6: Nos. 88, 89, 314, 315; Geneva 87, 88.	2.25
17	UN Decade for Women, Mar. 7, 1980. Card of 4: Nos. 258, 318; Geneva 90; Vienna 9.	18.00
18	Economic and Social Council, Nov. 7, 1980. Card of 8; Nos. 65, 66, 341, 342; Geneva 96, 97; Vienna 15, 16.	3.00
19	International Year of Disabled Persons, Mar. 6, 1981. Card of 6; Nos. 344, 345; Geneva 99, 100; Vienna 18, 19.	2.25
20	New and Renewable Sources of Energy, May 29, 1981. Card of 4; Nos. 348, 349; Geneva 102; Vienna 21.	3.25
21	Human Environment, Mar. 19, 1982. Card of 5: Nos. 230, 371; Geneva 26, 107; Vienna 25	3.00
22	Exploration and Peaceful Uses of Outer Space, June 11, 1982. Card of 7: Nos. 112, 256, 373; Geneva 46, 109, 110; Vienna 27.	3.50
23	Safety at Sea, Mar. 18, 1983. Card of 8: Nos. 123, 124, 394, 395; Geneva 114, 115; Vienna 31, 32.	3.25
24	Trade and Development, June 6, 1983. Card of 11: Nos. 129, 130, 274, 275, 397, 398; Geneva 58, 117, 118; Vienna 31, 32.	3.25
25	International Conference on Population, Feb. 3, 1984. Card of 10: Nos. 151, 153, 252, 253, 417, 418; Geneva 43, 44, 121; Vienna 39.	3.00
26	International Youth Year, Nov. 15, 1984. Card of 5: Nos. 441, 442; Geneva 128; Vienna 46, 47.	2.75

27 ILO Turin Center, Feb.1,1985. Card of 8: Nos. 25, 200, 244, 443; Geneva 37, 129,130; Vienna 48. 3.75
28 Child Survival Campaign, Nov. 22, 1985. Card of 6: Nos. 466, 467; Geneva 138, 139; Vienna 55, 56. 3.25
29 Stamp Collecting, May 22, 1986. Card of 5: Nos. 278, 473; Geneva 61, 147; Vienna 63. 15.00
30 International Peace Year, June 20, 1986. Card of 6: Nos. 475, 476; Geneva 148, 149; Vienna 64, 65. 6.00
31 Shelter for the Homeless, Mar. 13, 1987. Card of 6: Nos. 495, 496; Geneva 154, 155; Vienna 68, 69. 3.25
32 Immunize Every Child, Nov. 20, 1987. Card of 13: Nos. 44, 103, 157, 208, 294 and 517, 518; Vienna 76, 77. 3.25
33 Intl. Volunteer Day, May 6, 1988. Card of 10; Nos. 239, 367 and 524, 525; Geneva 103 and 167, 168; Vienna 23 and 82, 83. 3.00
34 Health in Sports, June 17, 1988. Card of 6; Nos. 526, 527; Geneva 169, 170; Vienna 84, 85. 3.00
35 World Bank, Jan. 27, 1989. Card of 8; Nos. 86-87, 546-547; Geneva 173-174; Vienna 88-89. 3.00
36 World Weather Watch, Apr. 24, 1989. Card of 10; Nos. 49-50, 188-189, 550-551; Geneva 173-174; Vienna 88-89. 3.00

OFFICES IN GENEVA, SWITZERLAND

For use only on mail posted at the Palais des Nations (United Nations European Office), Geneva. Inscribed in French unless otherwise stated.

100 Centimes = 1 Franc

Types of United Nations Issues 1961-69 and

United Nations European Office, Geneva — G1

Printed by Setelipaino, Finland (5c, 70c, 80c, 90c, 2fr, 10fr), Courvoisier, S.A., Switzerland (10c, 20c, 30c, 50c, 60c, 3fr), Government Printing Office, Austria (75c) and Government Printing Office, Federal Republic of Germany (1fr). Panes of 50. 30c designed by Ole Hamann, others as before.

Designs: 5c, U.N. Headquarters, New York, and world map. 10c, U.N. flag. 20c, Three men united before globe. 50c, Opening words of U.N. Charter. 60c, U.N. emblem over globe. 70c, "U.N." and U.N. emblem. 75c, "Flight Across Globe." 80c, U.N. Headquarters and emblem. 90c, Abstract group of flags. 1fr, U.N. emblem. 2fr, Stylized globe and weather vane. 3fr, Statue by Henrik Starcke. 10fr, "Peace, Justice, Security."

The 20c, 80c and 90c are inscribed in French. The 75c and 10fr carry French inscription at top, English at bottom.

Perf. 13 (5c, 70c, 90c); Perf. 12½x12 (10c); Perf. 11½ (20c-60c, 3fr); Perf. 11½x12 (75c); Perf. 13½x14 (80c); Perf. 14 (1fr); Perf. 12x11½ (2fr); Perf. 12 (10fr)

1969-70 Photo. Unwmk.

1 A88 5c pur. & multi., *Oct. 4, 1969 (3,300,000)* 5 5
First day cover 25
Margin block of 4, inscription 25 —
a. Green omitted —
2 A52 10c salmon & multi., *Oct. 4, 1969 (4,300,000)+* 5 5
First day cover 30
Margin block of 4, inscription 25 —
3 A66 20c black & multi., *Oct. 4, 1969 (4,500,000)* 10 10
First day cover 40
Margin block of 4, inscription 50 —
4 G1 30c dk. blue & multi., *Oct. 4, 1969 (3,000,000)* 15 15
First day cover 40
Margin block of 4, inscription 75 —
5 A77 50c ultra., & multi., *Oct. 4, 1969 (3,300,000)+* 25 25
First day cover 50
Margin block of 4, inscription 1.25 —
6 A54 60c dk. brown, salmon & gold, *Apr. 17, 1970 (3,300,000)+* 30 30
First day cover 60
Margin block of 4, inscription 1.50 —
7 A104 70c red, black & gold, *Sept. 22, 1970 (3,300,000)+* 35 35
First day cover 60
Margin block of 4, inscription 1.75 —
8 AP8 75c carmine rose & multicolored, *Oct. 4, 1969 (3,300,000)+* 40 40
First day cover 60
Margin block of 4, inscription 2.00 —
9 A78 80c blue green, red & yellow, *Sept. 22, 1970 (3,300,000)+* 40 40
First day cover 60
Margin block of 4, inscription 2.00 —
10 A45 90c bl. & multi., *Sept. 22, 1970 (3,300,000)+* 45 45
First day cover 60
Margin block of 4, inscription 2.25 —

Litho. & Embossed

11 A79 1fr light & dark green, *Oct. 4, 1969 (3,000,000)* 50 50
First day cover 70
Margin block of 4, inscription 2.50 —

Photo.

12 A67 2fr bl. & multi., *Sept. 22, 1970 (3,000,000)+* 1.00 1.00
First day cover 2.00
Margin block of 4, inscription 5.00 —
13 A97 3fr olive & multi., *Oct. 4, 1969 (3,000,000)+* 1.50 1.50
First day cover 2.25
Margin block of 4, inscription 7.50 —

Engr.

14 A3 10fr dark blue, *Apr. 17, 1970 (2,250,000)+* 5.00 5.00
First day cover 8.50
Margin block of 4, inscription 25.00 —

* Printing orders to June 1984.

First day covers of Nos. 1-5, 8, 11, 13 total 607,578; of Nos. 6 and 14, 148,055; of Nos. 7, 9-10 and 12, 226,000.

Sea Bed Type of U.N.

Photogravure and Engraved

1971, Jan. 25 ***Perf. 13***

15 A114 30c green & multicolored *(1,935,871)* 25 20
First day cover *(152,590)* 65
Margin block of 4, inscription 1.25 —

Refugee Type of U.N.

1971, Mar. 12 Litho. ***Perf. 13x12½***

16 A115 50c dp. car., dp. org. & black *(1,820,114)* 40 30
First day cover *(148,220)* 65
Margin block of 4, inscription 2.00 —

World Food Program Type of U.N.

1971, Apr. 13 Photo. ***Perf. 14***

17 A116 50c dark violet & multicolored *(1,824,170)* 50 35
First day cover *(151,580)* 1.00
Margin block of 4, inscription 2.50 —

UPU Headquarters Type of U.N.

1971, May 28 Photo. ***Perf. 11½***

18 A117 75c green & multi. *(1,821,878)* 1.00 75
First day cover *(140,679)* 1.50
Margin block of 4, inscription 5.00 —

Eliminate Racial Discrimination Types of U.N.

Designed by Daniel Gonzague (30c) and Ole Hamann (50c).

1971, Sept. 21 Photo. ***Perf. 13½***

19 A118 30c blue & multicolored *(1,838,474)* 30 25
First day cover 65
Margin block of 4, inscription 1.50 —
20 A119 50c yellow green & multi. *(1,804,126)* 50 40
First day cover 90
First day cover, #19-20 1.25
Margin block of 4, inscription 2.50 —

First day covers of Nos. 19-20 total 308,420.

Picasso Type of U.N.

1971, Nov. 19 Photo. ***Perf. 11½***

21 A122 1.10fr multicolored *(1,467,993)* 1.25 90
First day cover *(195,215)* 1.50
Margin block of 4, inscription 6.25 —

Palais des Nations, Geneva — G2

Printed by Courvoisier, S. A. Panes of 50. Designed by Ole Hamann.

1972, Jan. 5 Photo. ***Perf. 11½***

22 G2 40c olive, blue, salmon & dark green *(3,500,000)+* 30 25
First day cover *(152,300)* 75
Margin block of 4, inscription 1.50 —

\+ Initial printing order.

Nuclear Weapons Type of U.N.

1972, Feb. 14 Photo. ***Perf. 13½x14***

23 A124 40c yel, green, black, rose & gray *(1,567,305)* 70 45
First day cover *(151,350)* 1.25
Margin block of 4, inscription 3.50 —

World Health Day Type of U.N.

1972, Apr. 7 Litho. & Engr. ***Perf. 13x13½***

24 A125 80c black & multicolored *(1,543,368)* 85 65
First day cover *(192,600)* 1.25
Margin block of 4, inscription 4.25 —

Human Environment Type of U.N.

Lithographed & Embossed

1972, June 5 ***Perf. 12½x14***

25 A126 40c olive, lemon, green & blue *(1,594,089)* 55 40
First day cover 60
Margin block of 4, inscription 2.75 —
26 A126 80c ultra., pink, green & blue *(1,568,009)* 1.10 80
First day cover 1.40
First day cover, #25-26 1.75
Margin block of 4, inscription 5.50 —

First day covers of Nos. 25-26 total 296,700.

Economic Commission for Europe Type of U.N.

1972, Sept. 11 Litho. ***Perf. 13x13½***

27 A127 1.10fr red & multicolored *(1,604,082)* 1.50 1.10
First day cover *(149,630)* 1.75
Margin block of 4, inscription 7.50 —

Art at U.N. (Sert) Type of U.N.

1972, Nov. 17 Photo. ***Perf. 12x12½***

28 A128 40c gold, red & brown *(1,932,428)* 55 40
First day cover 75
Margin block of 4, inscription 2.75 —
29 A128 80c gold, brown & olive *(1,759,600)* 1.10 80
First day cover 1.25
First day cover, #28-29 1.75
Margin block of 4, inscription 5.50 —

First day covers of Nos. 28-29 total 295,470.

Disarmament Decade Type of U.N.

1973, Mar. 9 Litho. ***Perf. 13½x13***

30 A129 60c violet & multi. *(1,586,845)* 60 45
First day cover 75
Margin block of 4, inscription 3.00 —
31 A129 1.10fr olive & multi. *(1,408,169)* 1.10 85
First day cover 1.40
First day cover, #30-31 1.50
Margin block of 4, inscription 5.50 —

First day covers of Nos. 30-31 total 260,680.

Drug Abuse Type of U.N.

1973, Apr. 13 Photo. ***Perf. 13½***

32 A130 60c blue & multicolored *(1,481,432)* 60 55
First day cover *(144,760)* 1.00
Margin block of 4, inscription 3.00 —

Volunteers Type of U.N.

1973, May 25 **Photo.** ***Perf. 14***
33 A131 80c gray green & multi. *(1,443,519)* 80 70
First day cover *(143,430)* 1.10
Margin block of 4, inscription 4.00 —

Namibia Type of U.N.

1973, Oct. 1 **Photo.** ***Perf. 13½***
34 A132 60c red & multi. *(1,673,898)* 60 55
First day cover *(148,077)* 1.00
Margin block of 4, inscription 3.00 —

Human Rights Type of U.N.

1973, Nov. 16 **Photo.** ***Perf. 13½***
35 A133 40c ultramarine & multi. *(1,480,791)* 30 30
First day cover 75
Margin block of 4, inscription 1.50 —
36 A133 80c olive & multi. *(1,343,349)* 60 60
First day cover 1.25
First day cover, #35-36 1.75
Margin block of 4, inscription 3.00 —

First day covers of Nos. 35-36 total 438,260.

ILO Headquarters Type of U.N.

1974, Jan. 11 **Photo.** ***Perf. 14***
37 A134 60c violet & multi. *(1,212,703)* 45 45
First day cover 80
Margin block of 4, inscription 2.25 —
38 A134 80c brown & multi. *(1,229,851)* 60 60
First day cover 1.10
First day cover, #37-38 1.75
Margin block of 4, inscription 3.00 —

First day covers of Nos. 37-38 total 240,660.

Centenary of UPU Type of U.N.

1974, Mar. 22 **Litho.** ***Perf. 12½***
39 A135 30c gold & multicolored *(1,567,517)* 25 25
First day cover 75
Margin block of 4, inscription 1.25 —
40 A135 60c gold & multicolored *(1,430,839)* 45 45
First day cover 1.25
First day cover, #39-40 1.75
Margin block of 4, inscription 2.25 —

First day covers of Nos. 39-40 total 231,840.

Art at U.N. (Portinari) Type of U.N.

1974, May 6 **Photo.** ***Perf. 14***
41 A136 60c dark red & multicolored *(1,202,357)* 45 45
First day cover 75
Margin block of 4, inscription 2.25 —
42 A136 1fr green & multicolored *(1,230,045)* 80 80
First day cover 1.20
First day cover, #41-42 1.50
Margin block of 4, inscription 4.00 —

First day covers of Nos. 41-42 total 249,130.

World Population Year Type of U.N.

1974, Oct. 18 **Photo.** ***Perf. 14***
43 A140 60c bright green & multi. *(1,292,954)* 45 45
First day cover 60
Margin block of 4, inscription 2.25 —
44 A140 80c brown & multicolored *(1,221,288)* 60 60
First day cover 80
First day cover, #43-44 1.25
Margin block of 4, inscription 3.00 —

First day covers of Nos. 43-44 total 189,597.

Law of the Sea Type of U.N.

1974, Nov. 22 **Photo.** ***Perf. 14***
45 A141 1.30fr blue & multicolored *(1,266,270)* 95 95
First day cover *(181,000)* 1.50
Margin block of 4, inscription 4.75 —

Outer Space Type of U.N.

1975, Mar. 14 **Litho.** ***Perf. 13***
46 A142 60c multicolored *(1,339,704)* 45 45
First day cover 50
Margin block of 4, inscription 2.25 —
47 A142 90c multicolored *(1,383,888)* 70 70
First day cover 65
First day cover, #46-47 1.00
Margin block of 4, inscription 3.50 —

First day covers of Nos. 46-47 total 250,400.

International Women's Year Type of U.N.

1975, May 9 **Litho.** ***Perf. 15***
48 A143 60c multicolored *(1,176,080)* 50 45
First day cover 75
Margin block of 4, inscription 2.50 —
49 A143 90c multicolored *(1,167,863)* 75 70
First day cover 1.00
First day cover, #48-49 1.50
Margin block of 4, inscription 3.75 —

First day covers of Nos. 48-49 total 250,660.

30th Anniversary Type of U.N.

1975, June 26 **Litho.** ***Perf. 13***
50 A144 60c green & multicolored *(1,442,075)* 45 40
First day cover 60
Margin block of 4, inscription 2.25 —
51 A144 90c violet & multicolored *(1,612,411)* 70 60
First day cover 80
First day cover, #50-51 1.25
Margin block of 4, inscription 3.50 —

Souvenir Sheet

Imperf

52 A144 Sheet of 2, *(1,210,148)* 1.10 1.10
a. 60c green & multicolored 40 40
b. 90c violet & multicolored 60 60
First day cover 1.75

No. 52 has blue and bister margin with inscription and U.N. emblem. Size: 92x70mm.
First day covers of Nos. 50-52 total 402,500.

Namibia Type of U.N.

1975, Sept. 22 **Photo.** ***Perf. 13½***
53 A145 50c multicolored *(1,261,019)* 40 40
First day cover 45
Margin block of 4, inscription 2.00 —
54 A145 1.30fr multicolored *(1,241,990)* 1.00 1.00
First day cover 1.10
First day cover, #53-54 1.40
Margin block of 4, inscription 5.00 —

First day covers of Nos. 53-54 total 226,260.

Peace-keeping Operations Type of U.N.

1975, Nov. 21 **Engr.** ***Perf. 12½***
55 A146 60c greenish blue *(1,249,305)* 45 45
First day cover 55
Margin block of 4, inscription 2.25 —
56 A146 70c bright violet *(1,249,935)* 55 55
First day cover 65
First day cover, #55-56 1.10
Margin block of 4, inscription 2.75 —

First day covers of Nos. 55-56 total 229,245.

WFUNA Type of U.N.

1976, Mar. 12 **Photo.** ***Perf. 14***
57 A152 90c multicolored *(1,186,563)* 70 65
First day cover 1.00
Margin block of 4, inscription 3.50 —

First day covers of No. 57 total 121,645.

UNCTAD Type of U.N.

1976, Apr. 23 **Photo.** ***Perf. 11½***
58 A153 1.10fr sepia & multicolored, *(1,167,284)* 80 80
First day cover *(107,030)* 1.35
Margin block of 4, inscription 4.00 —

Habitat Type of U.N.

1976, May 28 **Photo.** ***Perf. 14***
59 A154 40c dull blue & multi. *(1,258,986)* 30 30
First day cover 75
Margin block of 4, inscription 1.50 —
60 A154 1.50fr violet & multi. *(1,110,507)* 1.10 1.10
First day cover 1.25
First day cover, #59-60 1.65
Margin block of 4, inscription 5.50 —

First day covers of Nos. 59-60 total 242,530.

U.N. Emblem, Post Horn and Rainbow — G3

U.N. Postal Administration, 25th anniversary.
Printed by Courvoisier, S.A. Panes of 20 (5x4). Designed by Hector Viola.

1976, Oct. 8 **Photo.** ***Perf. 11½***
61 G3 80c tan & multicolored *(1,794,009)* 1.25 1.00
First day cover 3.50
Margin block of 4, inscription 6.25 —
62 A3 1.10fr lt. green & multicolored *(1,751,178)* 4.00 3.00
First day cover 4.50
First day cover, #61-62 7.50
Margin block of 4, inscription 20.00 —

Upper margin blocks are inscribed "XXVe ANNIVERSAIRE"; lower margin blocks "ADMINISTRATION POSTALE DES NATIONS UNIES."
First day covers of Nos. 61-62 total 152,450.

World Food Council Type of U.N.

1976, Nov. 19 **Litho.** ***Perf. 14½***
63 A156 70c multicolored *(1,507,630)* 55 55
First day cover *(170,540)* 1.00
Margin block of 4, inscription 2.75 —

WIPO Type of U.N.

1977, Mar. 11 **Photo.** ***Perf. 14***
64 A157 80c red & multi. *(1,232,664)* 60 60
First day cover *(212,470)* 1.00
Margin block of 4, inscription 3.00 —

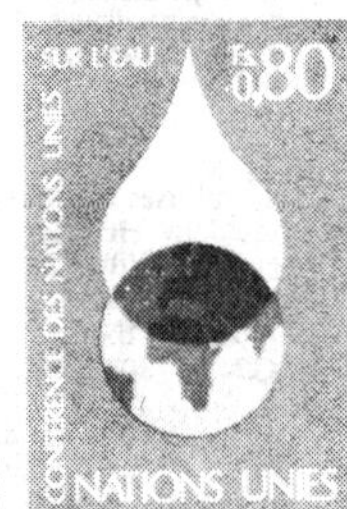

Drop of Water and Globe — G4

U.N. Water Conference, Mar del Plata, Argentina, Mar. 14-25.
Printed by Government Printing Bureau, Tokyo. Panes of 50. Designed by Eliezer Weishoff.

1977, Apr. 22 **Photo.** ***Perf. 13½x13***
65 G4 80c ultramarine & multi. *(1,146,650)* 60 60
First day cover 90
Margin block of 4, inscription 3.00 —
66 G4 1.10fr dark carmine & multi. *(1,138,236)* 85 85
First day cover 1.25
First day cover, #65-66 2.00
Margin block of 4, inscription 4.25 —

First day covers of Nos. 65-66 total 289,836.

Hands Protecting U.N. Emblem — G5

U.N. Security Council.
Printed by Heraclio Fournier, S.A., Spain. Panes of 50. Designed by George Hamori.

1977, May 27 **Photo.** ***Perf. 11***
67 G5 80c blue & multi. *(1,096,030)* 60 60
First day cover 90
Margin block of 4, inscription 3.00 —
68 G5 1.10fr emerald & multi. *(1,075,925)* 85 85
First day cover 1.25

			First day cover, #67-68		2.00
			Margin block of 4, inscription	4.25	—

First day covers of Nos. 67-68 total 305,349.

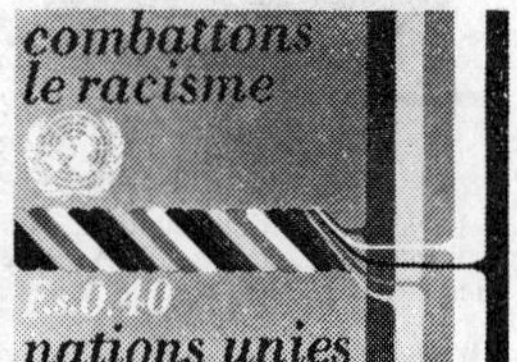

Colors of Five Races Spun into One Firm Rope — G6

Fight against racial discrimination.
Printed by Setelipaino, Finland. Panes of 50. Designed by M. A. Munnawar.

1977, Sept. 19 **Litho.** ***Perf. 13½x13***

No.	Type	Denom.	Description	Unused	Used
69	G6	40c	multicolored *(1,218,834)*	30	30
			First day cover		50
			Margin block of 4, inscription	1.50	—
70	G6	1.10fr	multicolored *(1,138,250)*	85	85
			First day cover		1.25
			First day cover, #69-70		1.60
			Margin block of 4, inscription	4.25	—

First day covers of Nos. 69-70 total 308,722.

Atomic Energy Turning Partly into Olive Branch — G7

Peaceful uses of atomic energy.
Printed by Heraclio Fournier, S.A., Spain. Panes of 50. Designed by Witold Janowski and Marek Freudenreich.

1977, Nov. 18 **Photo.** ***Perf. 14***

No.	Type	Denom.	Description	Unused	Used
71	G7	80c	dark carmine & multi. *(1,147,787)*	60	60
			First day cover		90
			Margin block of 4, inscription	3.00	—
72	G7	1.10fr	Prus. blue & multi. *(1,121,209)*	85	85
			First day cover		1.20
			First day cover, #71-72		2.00
			Margin block of 4, inscription	4.25	—

First day covers of Nos. 71-72 total 298,075.

"Tree" of Doves — G8

Printed by Questa Colour Security Printers, United Kingdom. Panes of 50. Designed by M. Hioki.

1978, Jan. 27 **Litho.** ***Perf. 14½***

No.	Type	Denom.	Description	Unused	Used
73	G8	35c	multicolored *(3,000,000)*	30	20
			First day cover *(259,735)*		65
			Margin block of 4, inscription	1.50	—

Globes with Smallpox Distribution — G9

Global eradication of smallpox.

Printed by Courvoisier, S.A. Panes of 50. Designed by Eliezer Weishoff.

1978, Mar. 31 **Photo.** ***Perf. 12x11½***

No.	Type	Denom.	Description	Unused	Used
74	G9	80c	yellow & multi. *(1,116,044)*	60	60
			First day cover		85
			Margin block of 4, inscription	3.00	—
75	G9	1.10fr	lt. green & multi. *(1,109,946)*	85	85
			First day cover		1.20
			First day cover, #74-75		2.00
			Margin block of 4, inscription	4.25	—

First day covers of Nos. 74-75 total 254,700.

Namibia Type of U.N.

1978, May 5 **Photo.** ***Perf. 12***

No.	Type	Denom.	Description	Unused	Used
76	A166	80c	multicolored *(1,183,208)*	60	60
			First day cover *(316,610)*		95
			Margin block of 4, inscription	3.00	—

Jets and Flight Patterns — G10

International Civil Aviation Organization for "Safety in the Air."
Printed by Heraclio Fournier, S.A., Spain. Panes of 50. Designed by Tomas Savrda.

1978, June 12 **Photo.** ***Perf. 14***

No.	Type	Denom.	Description	Unused	Used
77	G10	70c	multicolored *(1,275,106)*	55	55
			First day cover		85
			Margin block of 4, inscription	2.75	—
78	G10	80c	multicolored *(1,144,339)*	60	60
			First day cover		1.00
			First day cover, #77-78		1.60
			Margin block of 4, inscription	3.00	—

First day covers of Nos. 77-78 total 255,700.

General Assembly, Flags and Globe — G11

Printed by Government Printing Bureau, Tokyo. Panes of 50. Designed by Henry Bencsath.

1978, Sept. 15 **Photo.** ***Perf. 13½***

No.	Type	Denom.	Description	Unused	Used
79	G11	70c	multicolored *(1,204,441)*	60	55
			First day cover		85
			Margin block of 4, inscription	3.00	—
80	G11	1.10fr	multicolored *(1,183,889)*	70	60
			First day cover		1.25
			First day cover, #79-80		2.00
			Margin block of 4, inscription	3.50	—

First day covers of Nos. 79-80 total 245,600.

Technical Cooperation Type of U.N.

1978, Nov. 17 **Photo.** ***Perf. 14***

No.	Type	Denom.	Description	Unused	Used
81	A169	80c	multicolored *(1,173,220)*	60	60
			First day cover *(264,700)*		1.00
			Margin block of 4, inscription	3.00	—

Seismograph Recording Earthquake — G12

Office of the U.N. Disaster Relief Coordinator (UNDRO).

Printed by Heraclio Fournier, S.A., Spain. Panes of 50. Designed by Michael Klutmann.

1979, Mar. 9 **Photo.** ***Perf. 14***

No.	Type	Denom.	Description	Unused	Used
82	G12	80c	multicolored *(1,183,155)*	60	60
			First day cover		75
			Margin block of 4, inscription	3.00	—
83	G12	1.50fr	multicolored *(1,168,121)*	1.10	1.10
			First day cover		1.40
			First day cover, #82-83		1.90
			Margin block of 4, inscription	5.50	—

First day covers of Nos. 82-83 total 162,070.

Children and Rainbow — G13

International Year of the Child.
Printed by Heraclio Fournier, S.A., Spain. Panes of 20 (5x4). Designed by Arieh Glaser.

1979, May 4 **Photo.** ***Perf. 14***

No.	Type	Denom.	Description	Unused	Used
84	G13	80c	multicolored *(2,251,623)*	60	60
			First day cover		1.25
			Margin block of 4, inscription	3.00	—
85	G13	1.10fr	multicolored *(2,220,463)*	1.00	1.00
			First day cover		1.75
			First day cover, #84-85		2.75
			Margin block of 4, inscription	5.00	—

First day covers of Nos. 84-85 total 176,120.

Namibia Type of U.N.

1979, Oct. 5 **Litho.** ***Perf. 13½***

No.	Type	Denom.	Description	Unused	Used
86	A176	1.10fr	multicolored *(1,500,000)*	85	85
			First day cover *(134,160)*		1.50
			Margin block of 4, inscription	4.25	—

International Court of Justice, Scales — G14

International Court of Justice, The Hague, Netherlands
Printed by Setelipaino, Finland. Panes of 50. Designed by Kyohei Maeno.

1979, Nov. 9 **Litho.** ***Perf. 13x13½***

No.	Type	Denom.	Description	Unused	Used
87	G14	80c	multicolored *(1,123,193)*	60	60
			First day cover		1.00
			Margin block of 4, inscription	3.00	—
88	G14	1.10fr	multicolored *(1,063,067)*	85	85
			First day cover		1.25
			First day cover, #87-88		2.00
			Margin block of 4, inscription	4.25	—

First day covers of Nos. 87-88 total 158,170.

New Economic Order Type of U.N.

1980, Jan. 11 **Litho.** ***Perf. 15x14½***

No.	Type	Denom.	Description	Unused	Used
89	A179	80c	multicolored *(1,315,918)*	60	60
			First day cover *(176,250)*		1.00
			Margin block of 4, inscription	3.00	—

Women's Year Emblem — G15

United Nations Decade for Women.

Printed by Questa Colour Security Printers, United Kingdom. Panes of 50. Designed by M.A. Munnawar.

1980, Mar. 7 Litho. *Perf. 14½x15*

No.	Type	Value	Description	Unused	Used
90	G15	40c	multicolored *(1,265,221)*	30	30
			First day cover		35
			Margin block of 4, inscription	1.50	—
91	G15	70c	multicolored *(1,240,375)*	55	55
			First day cover		1.10
			First day cover, #90-91		1.25
			Margin block of 4, inscription	2.75	—

First day covers of Nos. 90-91 total 204,350.

Peace-keeping Operations Type of U.N.

1980, May 16 Litho. *Perf. 14x13*

No.	Type	Value	Description	Unused	Used
92	A181	1.10fr	blue & green *(1,335,391)*	85	85
			First day cover *(184,700)*		1.25
			Margin block of 4, inscription	4.25	—

35th Anniversary Type of U.N. and Dove and "35" — G16

35th Anniversary of the United Nations.
Printed by Ashton-Potter Ltd., Canada. Panes of 50. Designed by Gidon Sagi (40c), Cemalattin Mutver (70c).

1980, June 26 Litho. *Perf. 13x13½*

No.	Type	Value	Description	Unused	Used
93	G16	40c	blue green & black *(1,462,005)*	30	30
			First day cover		60
			Margin block of 4, inscription	1.50	—
94	A183	70c	multicolored *(1,444,639)*	55	55
			First day cover		85
			First day cover, #93-94		1.00
			Margin block of 4, inscription	2.75	—

Souvenir Sheet

Imperf

No.	Type	Value	Description	Unused	Used
95			Sheet of 2 *(1,235,200)*	1.10	1.10
a.	G16	40c	blue green & black	30	
b.	A183	70c	multicolored	55	
			First day cover		1.75

No. 95 has multicolored margin with inscription and U.N. emblem. Size: 92x73mm.
First day covers of Nos. 93-95 total 379,800.

ECOSOC Type of U.N. and

Family Climbing Line Graph — G17

Printed by Ashton-Potter Ltd., Canada. Panes of 50. Designed by Eliezer Weishoff (40¢), A. Medina Medina (70¢).

1980, Nov. 21 Litho. *Perf. 13½x13*

No.	Type	Value	Description	Unused	Used
96	A186	40c	multicolored *(986,435)*	30	30
			First day cover		45
			Margin block of 4, inscription	1.50	—
97	G17	70c	multicolored *(1,016,462)*	55	55
			First day cover		65
			First day cover #96-97		90
			Margin block of 4, inscription	2.75	

Economic and Social Council.
First day covers of Nos. 96-97 total 210,460.

Palestinian Rights
Printed by Courvoisier S.A., Switzerland. Sheets of 50. Designed by David Dewhurst.

1981, Jan. 30 Photo. *Perf. 12x11½*

No.	Type	Value	Description	Unused	Used
98	A188	80c	multicolored *(1,031,737)*	60	60
			First day cover *(117,480)*		1.50
			Margin block of 4, inscription	3.00	

International Year of the Disabled.
Printed by Heraclio Fournier S.A., Spain. Panes of 50. Designed by G.P. Van der Hyde (40c) and Sophia van Heeswijk (1.50fr).

1981, Mar. 6 Photo. *Perf. 14*

No.	Type	Value	Description	Unused	Used
99	A190	40c	black and blue *(1,057,909)*	30	30
			First day cover		40
			Margin block of 4, inscription	1.50	—
100	V4	1.50fr	black & red *(994,748)*	1.10	1.10
			First day cover		1.50
			First day cover, #99-100		1.65
			Margin block of 4, inscription	5.50	—

First day covers of Nos. 99-100 total 202,853.

Art Type of U.N.

1981, Apr. 15 Photo. *Perf. 11½*

Granite Paper

No.	Type	Value	Description	Unused	Used
101	A191	80c	multi *(1,128,782)*	60	60
			First day cover *(121,383)*		1.00
			Margin block of 4, inscription	3.00	—

Energy Type of 1981

1981, May 29 Litho. *Perf. 13*

No.	Type	Value	Description	Unused	Used
102	A192	1.10fr	multi *(1,096,806)*	95	85
			First day cover *(113,700)*		1.25
			Margin block of 4, inscription	4.75	—

Volunteers Program Type and

Symbols of Science, Agriculture and Industry — G18

Printed by Walsall Security Printers, Ltd., United Kingdom. Pane of 50.
Designed by Gabriele Nussgen (40c), Bernd Mirbach (70c).

1981, Nov. 13 Litho.

No.	Type	Value	Description	Unused	Used
103	A194	40c	multi (1,032,700)	35	30
			First day cover		50
			Margin block of 4, inscription	1.75	—
104	G18	70c	multi *(1,123,672)*	60	55
			First day cover		75
			First day cover, #103-104	—	1.10
			Margin block of 4, inscription	3.00	—

First day covers of Nos. 103-104 total 190,667.

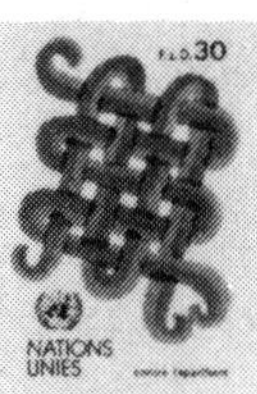

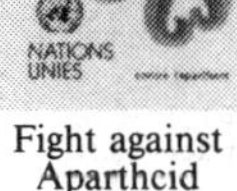

Fight against Aparthcid G19

Flower of Flags G20

Printed by Courvoisier, S.A., Switzerland. Sheets of 50. Designed by Tomas Savrda (30c); Dietmar Kowall (1fr).

1982, Jan. 22 *Perf. 11½x12*

No.	Type	Value	Description	Unused	Used
105	G19	30c	multicolored *(3,000,000)+*	20	10
			First day cover		40
			Margin block of 4, inscription	1.00	—
106	G20	1fr	multicolored *(3,000,000)+*	80	35
			First day cover		90
			First day cover, #105-106		1.20
			Margin block of 4, inscription	4.00	—

First day covers of Nos. 105-106 total 199,347.

The Catalogue editors cannot undertake to appraise, identify or judge the genuineness or condition of stamps.

Human Environment Type of U.N. and

Sun and Leaves — G21

10th Anniversary of United Nations Environment Program.
Printed by Joh. Enschede en Zonen, Netherlands. Panes of 50. Designed by Sybille Brunner (40c); Philine Hartert (1.20fr).

1982, Mar. 19 Litho. *Perf. 13½x13*

No.	Type	Value	Description	Unused	Used
107	G21	40c	multicolored *(948,743)*	35	30
			First day cover		45
			Margin block of 4, inscription	1.75	—
108	A199	1.20fr	multicolored *(901,096)*	1.10	90
			First day cover		1.10
			First day cover, #107-108		1.40
			Margin block of 4, inscription	5.50	—

First day covers of Nos. 107-108 total 190,155.

Outer Space Type of U.N. and

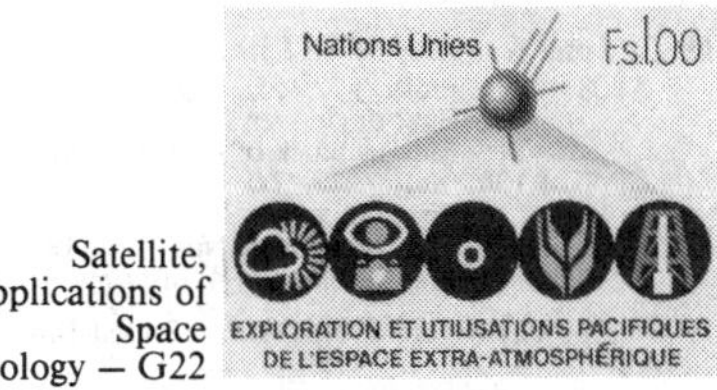

Satellite, Applications of Space Technology — G22

Exploration and Peaceful Uses of Outer Space.
Printed by Enschede. Panes of 50. Designed by Wiktor C. Nerwinski (80c) and George Hamori (1fr).

1982, June 11 Litho. *Perf. 13x13½*

No.	Type	Value	Description	Unused	Used
109	A201	80c	multicolored *(964,593)*	75	60
			First day cover		1.00
			Margin block of 4, inscription	3.75	—
110	G22	1fr	multicolored *(1,600,000)+*	90	75
			First day cover		1.25
			First day cover, #109-110		1.50
			Margin block of 4, inscription	4.50	—

First day covers of Nos. 109-110 total 205,815.

Conservation & Protection of Nature

1982, Nov. 19 Photo. *Perf. 14*

No.	Type	Value	Description	Unused	Used
111	A202	40c	Bird *(928,143)*	40	30
			First day cover		45
			Margin block of 4, inscription	2.00	—
112	A202	1.50fr	Reptile *(847,173)*	1.75	1.10
			First day cover		1.50
			First day cover, #111-112		1.65
			Margin block of 4, inscription	8.75	—

First day covers of Nos. 111-112 total 198,504.

World Communications Year

1983, Jan. 28 Litho. *Perf. 13*

No.	Type	Value	Description	Unused	Used
113	A204	1.20fr	multi *(894,025)*	1.40	1.15
			First day cover *(131,075)*		2.00
			Margin block of 4, inscription	7.00	—

Safety at Sea Type of UN and

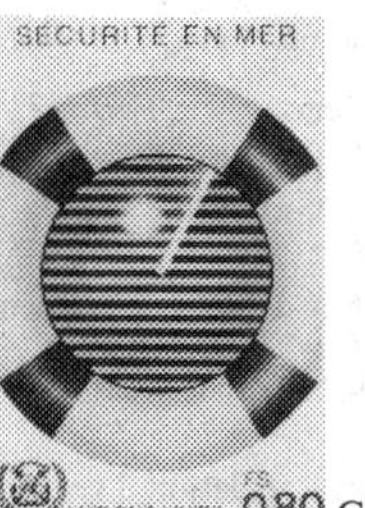

G23

Designed by Valentin Wurnitsch (A22).

1983, Mar. 18 Litho. *Perf. 14½*

No.	Type	Denom.	Description	Unused	Used
114	A205	40c	multi *(892,365)*	38	38
			First day cover		45
			Margin block of 4, inscription	1.90	—
115	G23	80c	multi *(882,720)*	75	75
			First day cover		75
			First day cover, Nos. 114-115		1.10
			Margin block of 4, inscription	3.75	—

First day covers of Nos. 114-115 total 219,592.

World Food Program

1983, Apr. 22 Engr. *Perf. 13½*

No.	Type	Denom.	Description	Unused	Used
116	A207	1.50fr	blue *(876,591)*	1.50	1.50
			First day cover		1.40
			Margin block of 4, inscription	7.50	—

Trade Type of UN and

G24

Designed by Wladyslaw Brykczynski (A23).

1983, June 6 Litho. *Perf. 14*

No.	Type	Denom.	Description	Unused	Used
117	A208	80c	multi *(902,495)*	75	75
			First day cover		75
			Margin block of 4, inscription	3.75	—
118	G24	1.10fr	multi *(921,424)*	1.00	1.00
			First day cover		90
			First day cover, Nos. 117-118		1.40
			Margin block of 4, inscription	5.00	—

First day covers of Nos. 117-118 total 146,507.

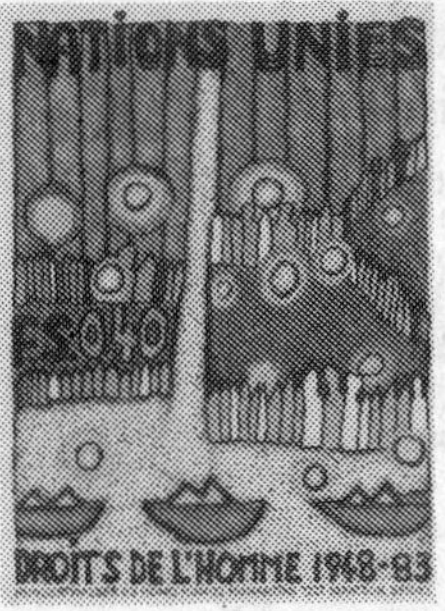

Homo Humus Humanitas — G25

Right to Create — G26

35th Anniversary of the Universal Declaration of Human Rights

Printed by Government Printing Office, Austria. Designed by Friedensreich Hundertwasser, Austria. Panes of 16 (4x4).

1983, Dec. 9 Photo. & Engr. *Perf. 13½*

No.	Type	Denom.	Description	Unused	Used
119	G25	40c	multi *(1,770,921)*	50	38
			First day cover		45
			Margin block of 4, inscription	2.50	
120	G26	1.20fr	multi *(1,746,735)*	1.40	70
			First day cover		1.10
			First day cover, Nos. 119-120		1.40
			Margin block of 4, inscription	7.00	

First day covers of Nos. 119-120 total 315,052.

International Conference on Population Type

1984, Feb. 3 Litho. *Perf. 14*

No.	Type	Denom.	Description	Unused	Used
121	A212	1.20fr	multi *(776,879)*	1.20	70
			First day cover *(105,377)*		2.00
			Margin block of 4, inscription	6.00	—

Fishing — G27

Women Farm Workers, Africa — G28

World Food Day, Oct. 16

Printed by Walsall Security Printers, Ltd., United Kingdom. Panes of 50. Designed by Adth Vanooijen, Netherlands.

1984, Mar. 15 Litho. *Perf. 14½*

No.	Type	Denom.	Description	Unused	Used
122	G27	50c	multi *(744,506)*	50	25
			First day cover		85
			Margin block of 4, inscription	2.50	—
123	G28	80c	multi *(784,047)*	80	40
			First day cover		1.25
			First day cover, Nos. 122-123		1.90
			Margin block of 4, inscription	4.00	—

First day covers of Nos. 122-123 total 155,234.

Valletta, Malta — G29

Los Glaciares National Park, Argentina — G30

World Heritage

Printed by Harrison and Sons, United Kingdom. Panes of 50. Designs adapted by Rocco J. Callari, U.S., and Thomas Lee, China.

1984, Apr. 18 Litho. *Perf. 14*

No.	Type	Denom.	Description	Unused	Used
124	G29	50c	multi *(763,627)*	50	25
			First day cover		85
			Margin block of 4, inscription	2.50	—
125	G30	70c	multi *(784,489)*	70	35
			First day cover		1.25
			First day cover, Nos. 124-125		1.90
			Margin block of 4, inscription	3.50	—

First day covers of Nos. 124-125 total 164,498.

G31

G32

Future for Refugees

Printed by Courvoisier. Panes of 50. Designed by Hans Erni, Switzerland.

1984, May 29 Photo. *Perf. 11½*

No.	Type	Denom.	Description	Unused	Used
126	G31	35c	multi *(880,762)*	35	18
			First day cover		55
			Margin block of 4, inscription	1.75	—
127	G32	1.50fr	multi *(829,895)*	1.75	75
			First day cover		1.85
			First day cover, Nos. 126-127		2.10
			Margin block of 4, inscription	8.75	—

First day covers of Nos. 126-127 total 170,306.

International Youth Year — G33

Printed by Waddingtons Ltd., United Kingdom. Panes of 50. Designed by Eliezer Weishoff, Israel.

1984, Nov. 15 Litho. *Perf. 13½*

No.	Type	Denom.	Description	Unused	Used
128	G33	1.20fr	multi *(755,622)*	1.00	45
			First day cover *(96,680)*		1.75
			Margin block of 4, inscription	5.00	—

ILO Type of U.N. and

ILO Turin Center — G34

Printed by the Government Printing Bureau, Japan. Panes of 50. Engraved by Mamoru Iwakuni and Hiroshi Ozaki, Japan (#129) and adapted from photographs by Rocco J. Callari, U.S., and Thomas Lee, China (#130).

1985, Feb. 1 Engr. *Perf. 13½*

No.	Type	Denom.	Description	Unused	Used
129	A220	80c	Turin Center emblem *(654,431)*	80	45
			First day cover		1.00
			Margin block of 4, inscription	4.00	—
130	G34	1.20fr	U Thant Pavilion *(609,493)*	1.20	70
			First day cover		1.50
			First day cover, Nos. 129-130		2.25
			Margin block of 4, inscription	6.00	—

First day covers of Nos. 129-130 total 118,467.

U.N. University Type

1985, Mar. 15 Photo. *Perf. 13½*

No.	Type	Denom.	Description	Unused	Used
131	A221	50c	Pastoral scene, advanced communications *(625,087)*	45	28
			First day cover		1.00
			Margin block of 4, inscription	2.25	—
132	A221	80c	like No. 131 *(712,674)*	70	45
			First day cover		1.50
			First day cover, Nos. 131-132		2.25
			Margin block of 4, inscription	3.50	—

First day covers of Nos. 131-132 total 93,324.

Flying Postman — G35

Interlocked Peace Doves — G36

Printed by Carl Ueberreuter Druck and Verlag M. Salzer, Austria. Panes of 50. Designed by Arieh Glaser, Israel ($133), and Carol Sliwka, Poland (#134).

1985, May 10 Litho. *Perf. 14*

No.	Type	Denom.	Description	Unused	Used
133	A35	20c	multi *(2,000,000)+*	20	8
			First day cover		30
			Margin block of 4, inscription	1.00	—
134	A36	1.20fr	multi *(2,000,000)+*	1.20	50

			First day cover		1.90
			First day cover, Nos. 133-134		2.00
			Margin block of 4, inscription	6.00	—

First day covers of Nos. 133-134 total 103,165.

40th Anniversary Type

Designed by Rocco J. Callari, U.S., and Thomas Lee, China (No. 137).

1985, June 26 Photo. *Perf. 12 x 11½*

135	A224	50c	multi *(764,924)*	50	20
			First day cover		90
			Margin block of 4, inscription	2.50	—
136	A225	70c	multi *(779,074)*	70	28
			First day cover		1.25
			First day cover, Nos. 135-136		2.00
			Margin block of 4, inscription	3.50	—

Souvenir Sheet

Imperf

137			Sheet of 2 *(498,041)*	1.50	1.00
a.	A224	50c	multi	60	
b.	A225	70c	multi	85	
			First day cover		2.00

No. 137 has multicolored margin containing inscription in French and U.N. emblem. Size: 75x83mm.
First day covers of Nos. 135-137 total 252,418.

UNICEF Child Survival Campaign Type

Printed by the Government Printing Bureau, Japan. Panes of 50. Designed by Mel Harris, United Kingdom (#138) and Adth Vanooijen, Netherlands (#139).

1985, Nov. 22 Photo. & Engr. *Perf. 13½*

138	A226	50c	Three girls *(657,409)*	*1.00*	20
			First day cover		75
			Margin block of 4, inscription	*5.00*	—
139	A226	1.20fr	Infant drinking *(593,568)*	*2.50*	50
			First day cover		1.25
			First day cover, Nos. 138-139		1.75
			Margin block of 4, inscription	*12.50*	—

First day covers of Nos. 138-139 total 217,696.

Africa in Crisis Type

Printed by Helio Courvoisier, Switzerland. Panes of 50. Designed by Alemayehou Gabremedhiu, Ethiopia.

1986, Jan. 31 Photo. *Perf. 11½x12*

140	A227	1.40fr	Mother, hungry children *(590,576)*	1.25	60
			First day cover *(80,159)*		1.60
			Margin block of 4, inscription	6.25	—

U.N. Development Program Type

Forestry. Printed by the Government Printing Bureau, Japan. Panes of 40, 2 blocks of 4 horizontal and 5 blocks of 4 vertical. Designed by Thomas Lee, China.

1986, Mar. 14 Photo. *Perf. 13½*

141	A228	35c	Erosion control *(547,567)*	50	15
			First day cover		50
142	A228	35c	Logging *(547,567)*	50	15
			First day cover		50
143	A228	35c	Lumber transport *(547,567)*	50	15
			First day cover		50
144	A228	35c	Nursery *(547,567)*	50	15
			First day cover		50
			First day cover, #141-144		1.50
			Margin block of 4, #141-144, inscription	2.50	—
a.			Block of 4, #141-144	2.00	60

Nos. 141-144 printed se-tenant in a continuous design.
First day covers of Nos. 141-144 total 200,212.

Dove and Sun — G37

Printed by Questa Color Security Printers, Ltd., United Kingdom. Panes of 50. Designed by Ramon Alcantara Rodriguez, Mexico.

1986, Mar. 14 Litho. *Perf. 15x14½*

145	G37	5c	multi *(2,000,000)*+	10	5
			First day cover *(58,908)*		65
			Margin block of 4, inscription	50	—

Stamp Collecting Type

Designs: 50c, U.N. Human Rights stamp. 80c, U.N. stamps. Printed by the Swedish Post Office, Sweden. Panes of 50. Designed by Czeslaw Slania and Ingalill Axelsson, Sweden.

1986, May 22 Engr. *Perf. 12½*

146	A229	50c	dk grn & hen brn *(722,015)*	50	25
			First day cover		50
			Margin block of 4, inscription	2.50	—
147	A229	80c	dk grn & yel org *(750,945)*	80	42
			First day cover		85
			First day cover, #146-147		1.25
			Margin block of 4, inscription	4.00	—

First day covers of Nos. 146-147 total 137,653.

Flags and Globe as Dove — G38

Peace in French — G39

International Peace Year. Printed by the Government Printing Bureau, Japan. Panes of 50. Designed by Renato Ferrini, Italy (#148), and Salahattin Kanidinc, US (#149).

1986, June 20 Photo. & Embossed *Perf. 13½*

148	G38	45c	multi *(620,978)*	60	25
			First day cover		65
			Margin block of 4, inscription	3.00	—
149	G39	1.40fr	multi *(559,658)*	1.75	80
			First day cover		1.50
			First day cover, #148-149		1.90
			Margin block of 4, inscription	8.75	—

First day covers of Nos. 148-149 total 123,542.

WFUNA Anniversary Type

Souvenir Sheet

Printed by Johann Enschede and Sons, Netherlands. Designed by Rocco J. Callari, U.S.

Designs: 35c, Abstract by Benigno Gomez, Honduras. 45c, Abstract by Alexander Calder (1898-1976), U.S. 50c, Abstract by Joan Miro (b. 1893), Spain. 70c, Sextet with Dove, by Ole Hamann, Denmark.

1986, Nov. 14 Litho. *Perf. 13x13½*

150			Sheet of 4 *(478,833)*	2.45	2.45
a.	A232	35c	multi	42	—
b.	A232	45c	multi	55	—
c.	A232	50c	multi	62	—
d.	A232	70c	multi	85	—
			First day cover *(58,452)*		3.25

No. 150 has inscribed margin picturing U.N. and WFUNA emblems. Size: 119x65mm.

Trygve Lie Type

1987, Jan. 30 Photo. & Engr. *Perf. 13½*

151	A233	1.40fr	multi *(1,100,000)*+	1.40	90
			First day cover *(76,152)*		2.00
			Margin block of 4, inscription	7.00	—

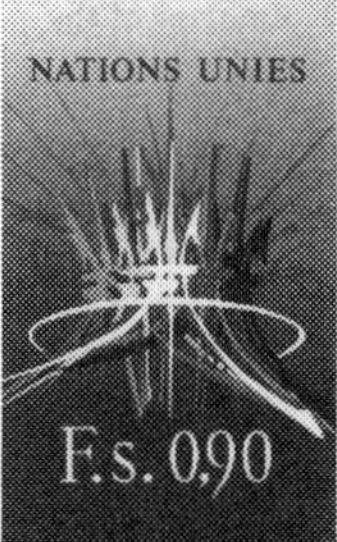

Sheaf of Colored Bands, by Georges Mathieu — G40

Armillary Sphere, Palais des Nations — G41

Printed by Helio Courvoisier, Switzerland (#152), and the Government Printing Bureau, Japan (#153). Panes of 50. Designed by Georges Mathieu (#152) and Rocco J. Callari (#153), U.S.

Photo., Photo. & Engr. (#153)

1987, Jan. 30 *Perf. 11½x12, 13½*

152	G40	90c	multi *(1,600,000)*+	90	60
			First day cover		1.60
			Margin block of 4, inscription	4.50	—
153	G41	1.40fr	multi *(1,600,000)*+	1.40	90
			First day cover		2.25
			First day cover, #152-153		3.50
			Margin block of 4, inscription	7.00	—

First day covers of Nos. 152-153 total 85,737.

Shelter for the Homeless Type

Designs: 50c, Cement-making and brick-making. 90c, Interior construction and decorating.

1987, Mar. 13 Litho. *Perf. 13½x12½*

154	A234	50c	multi *(1,075,000)*+	70	35
			First day cover		90
			Margin block of 4, inscription	3.50	—
155	A234	90c	multi *(1,075,000)*+	1.20	60
			First day cover		1.10
			First day cover, #154-155		1.75
			Margin block of 4, inscription	6.00	—

First day covers of Nos. 154-155 total 100,366.

Fight Drug Abuse Type

Designs: 80c, Mother and child. 1.20fr, Workers in rice paddy.

1987, June 12 Litho. *Perf. 14½x15*

156	A235	80c	multi *(1,075,000)*+	80	55
			First day cover		1.10
			Margin block of 4, inscription	4.00	—
157	A235	1.20fr	multi *(1,075,000)*+	1.20	80
			First day cover		1.50
			First day cover, #156-157		2.25
			Margin block of 4, inscription	6.00	—

First day covers of Nos. 156-157 total 95,247.

U.N. Day Type

Designed by Elisabeth von Janota-Bzowski (35c) and Fritz Oerter (50c).

Designs: Multinational people in various occupations.

1987, Oct. 23 Litho. *Perf. 14½x15*

158	A236	35c	multi *(1,326,000)*+	55	25
			First day cover		1.65
			Margin block of 4, inscription	2.75	—
159	A236	50c	multi *(1,326,000)*+	75	35
			First day cover		2.00
			First day cover, #158-159		3.50
			Margin block of 4, inscription	3.75	—

Immunize Every Child Type

Designs: 90c, Whopping cough. 1.70fr, Tuberculosis.

1987, Nov. 20 Litho. *Perf. 15x14½*

160	A237	90c	multi *(1,075,000)*+	1.00	60
			First day cover		80
			Margin block of 4, inscription	5.00	—
161	A237	1.70fr	multi *(1,075,000)*+	2.00	1.15
			First day cover		1.25
			First day cover, #160-161		1.90
			Margin block of 4, inscription	10.00	—

IFAD Type

Designs: 35c, Flocks, dairy products. 1.40fr, Fruit.

1988, Jan. 29 Litho. *Perf. 13½*

162	A238	35c	multi *(900,000)*+	45	25
			First day cover		60
			Margin block of 4, inscription	2.25	—
163	A238	1.40fr	multi *(900,000)*+	1.80	1.10
			First day cover		1.65
			First day cover, Nos. 162-163		2.00
			Margin block of 4, inscription	9.00	

G42

Printed by Heraclio Fournier, S.A., Spain. Panes of 50. Designed by Bjorn Wiinblad, Denmark

1988, Jan. 29 Photo. *Perf. 14*

164	G42	50c	multi *(1,600,000)*+	65	40
			First day cover		70
			Margin block of 4, inscription	3.25	—

Survival of the Forests Type

Pine forest: 50c, Treetops, mountains. 1.10fr, Lake, tree trunks. Printed se-tenants in a continuous designs.

1988, Mar. 18 **Litho.** ***Perf. 14x15***

No.	Type	Denom.	Description	Unused	Used
165	A240	50c	multi *(663,000)+*	1.50	40
			First day cover		1.80
166	A240	1.10fr	multi *(663,000)+*	3.50	90
			First day cover		1.40
			First day cover, Nos. 165-166		2.00
			Margin block of 4, inscription 2 each, Nos. 165-166	12.50	—
a.			Se-tenant pair #165-166	5.00	

Intl. Volunteer Day Type

Designed by Christopher Magadini, U.S.
Designs: 80c, Agriculture, vert. 90c, Veterinary medicine.

1988, May 6 **Litho.** ***Perf. 13x14, 14x13***

No.	Type	Denom.	Description	Unused	Used
167	A241	80c	multi *(900,000)+*	1.20	60
			First day cover		1.55
			Margin block of 4, inscription	6.00	—
168	A241	90c	multi *(900,000)+*	1.35	68
			First day cover		1.70
			First day cover, Nos. 167-168		2.90
			Margin block of 4, inscription	6.75	

Health in Sports Type

Paintings by LeRoy Neiman, American sports artist: 50c, Soccer, vert. 1.40fr, Swimming.

1988, June 17 **Litho.** ***Perf. 13½x13, 13x13½***

No.	Type	Denom.	Description	Unused	Used
169	A242	50c	multi *(900,000)+*	70	35
			First day cover		1.05
			Margin block of 4, inscription	3.50	—
170	A242	1.40fr	multi *(900,000)+*	2.00	1.00
			First day cover		2.35
			First day cover, Nos. 169-170		3.05
			Margin block of 4, inscription (Nos. 169-170)	10.00	

Universal Declaration of Human Rights 40th Anniv. Type

1988, Dec. 9 **Photo. & Engr.** ***Perf.***

No.	Type	Denom.	Description	Unused	Used
171	A243	90c	multi *(900,000)+*	1.20	60
			First day cover		1.55
			Margin block of 4, inscription	6.00	—

Souvenir Sheet

No.	Type	Denom.	Description	Unused	Used
172	A243	2fr	multi *(700,000)+*	2.60	2.60
			First day cover		3.00

No. 172 had multicolored decorative margin inscribed with the preamble to the human rights declaration in French.

World Bank Type

1989, Jan. 27 **Litho.** ***Perf. 13x14***

No.	Type	Denom.	Description	Unused	Used
173	A244	80c	Telecommunications *(900,000)+*	1.15	58
			First day cover		1.50
			Margin block of 4, inscription	5.75	—
174	A244	1.40fr	Industry *(900,000)+*	2.00	1.00
			First day cover		2.35
			First day cover, Nos. 173-174		3.50
			Margin block of 4, inscription	10.00	—

Peace-Keeping Force Type

1989, Mar. 17 ***Perf. 14x13½***

No.	Type	Denom.	Description	Unused	Used
175	A245	90c	multicolored *(1,000,000)+*	1.20	60
			First day cover		1.55
			Margin block of 4, inscription	6.00	—

World Weather Watch Type

Satellite photographs: 90c, Europe under the influence of Arctic air. 1.10fr, Surface temperatures of sea, ice and land surrounding the Kattegat between Denmark and Sweden.

1989, Apr. 21 **Litho.** ***Perf. 13x14***

No.	Type	Denom.	Description	Unused	Used
176	A247	90c	multicolored *(1,000,000)+*	1.20	60
			First day cover		1.55
			Margin block of 4, inscription	6.00	—
177	A247	1.10fr	multicolored *(1,000,000)+*	1.45	72
			First day cover		1.80
			First day cover, Nos. 176-177		3.00
			Margin block of 4, inscription	7.25	—

Offices in Geneva, 10th Anniv.
G43 G44

Printed by Government Printing Office, Austria. Panes of 25. Designed by Anton Lehmden (50c) and Arik Brauer (2fr), Austria.

Photo., Photo. & Engr. (2fr)

1989, Aug. 23 ***Perf. 14***

No.	Type	Denom.	Description	Unused	Used
178	G43	50c	multicolored *(1,000,000)+*	58	30
			First day cover		95
			Margin block of 4, inscription	2.90	—
179	G44	2fr	multicolored *(1,000,000)+*	2.25	1.15
			First day cover		2.60
			First day cover, Nos. 178-179		3.20
			Margin block of 4, inscription	11.25	—

AIR LETTER SHEET

U.N. Type of 1968

Printed by Setelipaino, Finland. Designed by Robert Perrot.

1969, Oct. 4 **Litho.**

No.	Type	Denom.	Description	Unused	Used
UC1	UC3	65c	ultra. & lt. blue, entire *(350,000)*	4.50	1.25
			Entire, first day cancel *(52,000)*		2.00

POSTAL CARDS

U.N. Type of 1969 and Type of Air Post Postal Card, 1966.

Printed by Courvoisier, S.A., Switzerland. Designed by John Mason (20c) and Olav S. Mathiesen (30c).

Wmk. Post Horn, Swiss Cross, "S" or "Z"

1969, Oct. 4 **Litho.**

No.	Type	Denom.	Description	Unused	Used
UX1	PC2	20c	olive green & black, *buff (415,000)*	1.10	20
			First day cancel *(51,500)*		70
UX2	APC2	30c	violet blue, blue, light & dark green, *buff (275,000)*	65	12
			First day cancel *(49,000)*		60

No. UX2, although of type APC2, is not inscribed "Poste Aerienne" or "Air Mail."

U.N. Emblem — PC1

U.N. Emblem and Ribbons — PC2

Printed by Setelipaino, Finland. Designed by Veronique Crombez (40c) and Lieve Baeten (70c).

1977, June 27 **Litho.**

No.	Type	Denom.	Description	Unused	Used
UX3	PC1	40c	multicolored *(500,000)+*	30	15
			First day cancel *(65,000)*		50
UX4	PC2	70c	multicolored *(300,000)+*	35	18
			First day cancel *(65,000)*		55

\+ Printing order to Mar. 1984.

Emblem of the United Nations — PC3

Peace Dove — PC4

Printed by Johann Enschede en Zonen, Netherlands. Designed by George Hamori, Australia (50c) and Ryszard Dudzicki, Poland (70c).

1985, May 10 **Litho.**

No.	Type	Denom.	Description	Unused	Used
UX5	PC3	50c	multi *(300,000)+*	75	25
			First day cancel *(34,700)*		65
UX6	PC4	70c	multi *(300,000)+*	2.00	55
			First day cancel *(34,700)*		70

No. UX6 Surcharged in Lake

1986, Jan. 2 **Litho.**

No.	Type	Denom.	Description	Unused	Used
UX7	PC4	70c + 10c	multi *(90,500)+*	2.50	1.25
			First day cancel *(8,000 est.)*		3.50

OFFICES IN VIENNA, AUSTRIA

For use only on mail posted at Donaupark Vienna International Center for the United Nations and the Atomic Energy Agency.

Type of Geneva, 1978, U.N. Types of 1961-72 and

Donaupark, Vienna — V1

Aerial View — V2

Printed by Helio Courvoisier S.A., Switzerland. Panes of 50. Designed by Henryk Chylinski (4s); Jozsef Vertel (6s).

1979, Aug. 24 **Photo.** ***Perf. 11½***

Granite Paper

No.	Type	Denom.	Description	Unused	Used
1	G8	50g	multicolored *(3,500,000)+*	5	5
			First day cover		30
			Margin block of 4, inscription	25	—
2	A52	1s	multicolored *(3,500,000)+*	10	10
			First day cover		45
			Margin block of 4, inscription	50	—
3	V1	4s	multicolored *(3,500,000)+*	40	25
			First day cover		75
			Margin block of 4, inscription	2.00	—
4	AP13	5s	multicolored *(3,500,000)+*	50	35
			First day cover		1.00
			Margin block of 4, inscription	2.50	—
5	V2	6s	multicolored *(4,500,000)+*	60	45
			First day cover		1.25
			Margin block of 4, inscription	3.00	—
6	A45	10s	multicolored *(3,500,000)+*	1.00	70
			First day cover		2.00
			Margin block of 4, inscription	5.00	—

\+ Printing orders to Aug. 1985.
No. 4 is not inscribed "Air Mail," No. 6 has no frame.
First day covers of Nos. 1-6 total 1,026,575.

New Economic Order Type of U.N.

1980, Jan. 11 **Litho.** ***Perf. 15x14½***

No.	Type	Denom.	Description	Unused	Used
7	A178	4s	multicolored *(1,418,418)*	2.00	1.35
			First day cover		2.00
			Margin block of 4, inscription	*30.00*	

Dove Type of U.N.

1980, Jan. 11 **Litho.** ***Perf. 14x13½***

No.	Type	Denom.	Description	Unused	Used
8	A147	2.50s	multicolored *(3,500,000)+*	30	15
			First day cover		60
			Margin block of 4, inscription	1.50	—

First day covers of Nos. 7-8 total 336,229.

Women's Year Emblem on World Map — V3

United Nations Decade for Women.

Printed by Questa Colour Security Printers, United Kingdom. Panes of 50. Designed by Gunnar Janssen.

1980, Mar. 7 **Litho.** ***Perf. 14½x15***
9 V3 4s light green & dark green *(1,569,080)* 55 35
First day cover 75
Margin block of 4, inscription 2.75 —
10 A3 6s bister brown *(1,556,016)* 85 50
First day cover 1.25
First day cover, #9-10 1.50
Margin block of 4, inscription 4.25 —

First day covers of Nos. 9-10 total 443,893.

Peace-keeping Operations Type of U.N.

1980, May 16 **Litho.** ***Perf. 14x13***
11 A182 6s multicolored *(1,719,852)* 75 50
First day cover *(323,923)* 1.25
Margin block of 4, inscription 3.75 —

35th Anniversary Types of Geneva and U.N.

1980, June 26 **Litho.** ***Perf. 13x13½***
12 G16 4s carmine rose & black *(1,626,582)* 50 35
First day cover 75
Margin block of 4, inscription 2.50 —
13 A184 6s multicolored *(1,625,400)* 75 50
First day cover 1.25
Margin block of 4, inscription 3.75 —

Souvenir Sheet

Imperf

14 Sheet of 2 *(1,675,191)* 1.40 1.00
a. G16 4s carmine rose & black 50
b. A184 6s multicolored 75
First day cover 2.50

No. 14 has multicolored margin with inscription and U.N. emblem. Size: 92x73 mm.
First day covers of Nos. 12-14 total 657,402.

ECOSOC Types of U.N. and Geneva

Printed by Ashton-Potter Ltd., Canada. Panes of 50. Designed by Dietman Kowall (4s), Angel Medina Medina (6s).

1980, Nov. 21 **Litho.** ***Perf. 13½x13***
15 A187 4s multicolored *(1,811,218)* 45 35
First day cover 55
Margin block of 4, inscription 2.25 —
16 G17 6s multicolored *(1,258,420)* 70 50
First day cover 90
First day cover #15-16 1.25
Margin block of 4, inscription 3.50 —

Economic and Social Council (ECOSOC).
First day covers of Nos. 15-16 total 224,631.

Palestinian Rights Type of U.N.

Printed by Courvoisier S.A., Switzerland. Panes of 50. Designed by David Dewhurst.

1981, Jan. 30 **Photo.** ***Perf. 12x11½***
17 A188 4s multicolored *(1,673,310)* 55 35
First day cover *(208,812)* 1.25
Margin block of 4, inscription 2.75 —

Disabled Type of UN. and

Interlocking Stitches — V4

International Year of the Disabled.
Printed by Heraclio Fournier S.A., Spain. Panes of 50. Designed by Sophia van Heeswijk.

1981, Mar. 6 **Photo.** ***Perf. 14***
18 A189 4s multicolored *(1,508,719)* 50 35
First day cover 55
Margin block of 4, inscription 2.50 —
19 V4 6s black & orange *(1,569,385)* 75 50
First day cover 90
First day cover, #18-19 1.25
Margin block of 4, inscription 3.75 —

First day covers of Nos. 18-19 total 290,603.

Art Type of U.N.

1981, Apr. 15 **Photo.** ***Perf. 11½***

Granite Paper

20 A191 6s multi *(1,643,527)* 65 50
First day cover *(196,916)* 1.00
Margin block of 4, inscription 3.25 —

Energy Type of U.N.

1981, May 29 **Litho.** ***Perf. 13***
21 A193 7.50s multi *(1,611,130)* 90 65
First day cover *(216,197)* 1.25
Margin block of 4, inscription 4.50 —

Volunteers Program Types

1981, Nov. 13 **Litho.**
22 A195 5s multi *(1,582,780)* 60 40
First day cover 65
Margin block of 4, inscription 3.00 —
23 G18 7s multi *(1,516,139)* 80 60
First day cover 1.00
First day cover, #22-23 1.50
Margin block of 4, inscription 4.00 —

First day covers of Nos. 22-23 total 282,414.

"For a Better World" — V5

Printed by Courvoisier, S.A., Switzerland. Sheets of 50. Designed by Eliezer Weishoff.

1982, Jan. 22 ***Perf. 11½x12***
24 V 3s multicolored *(3,300,000)*+ 40 20
First day cover *(203,872)* 75
Margin block of 4, inscription 2.00

Human Environment Types of U.N.

10th Anniversary of United Nations Environment Program. Printed by Joh. Enschede en Zonen, Netherlands. Panes of 50. Designed by Peer-Ulrich Bremer (5s); Sybille Brunner (7s).

1982, Mar. 19 **Litho.** ***Perf. 13½x13***
25 A200 5s multicolored *(1,312,765)* 60 40
First day cover 50
Margin block of 4, inscription 3.00 —
26 G21 7s multicolored *(1,357,513)* 80 55
First day cover 85
First day cover, #25-26 1.10
Margin block of 4, inscription 4.00 —

First day covers of Nos. 25-26 total 248,576.

Outer Space Type of U.N.

Exploration and Peaceful Uses of Outer Space. Printed by Enschede. Panes of 50. Designed by George Hamori.

1982, June 11 **Litho.** ***Perf. 13x13½***
27 G22 5s multicolored *(2,100,000)*+ 60 40
First day cover 1.75
Margin block of 4, inscription 3.00 —

Conservation & Protection of Nature Type

1982, Nov. 16 **Photo.** ***Perf. 14***
28 A202 5s Fish *(1,202,694)* 60 40
First day cover 60
Margin block of 4, inscription 3.00 —
29 A202 7s Animal *(1,194,403)* 80 60
First day cover 1.00
First Day Cover, #28-29 1.40
Margin block of 4, inscription 4.00 —

First day covers of Nos. 28-29 total 243,548.

World Communications Year Type

1983, Jan. 28 **Litho.** ***Perf. 13***
30 A203 4s multi *(1,517,443)* 65 42
First day cover *(150,541)* 75
Margin block of 4, inscription 3.25 —

Safety at Sea Type

1983, Mar. 18 **Litho.** ***Perf. 14½***
31 G23 4s multi *(1,506,052)* 65 42
First day cover 50
Margin block of 4, inscription 3.25 —
32 A206 6s multi *(1,527,990)* 95 62
First day cover 80
First day cover, Nos. 31-32 1.10
Margin block of 4, inscription 4.75 —

First day covers of Nos. 31-32 total 219,118.

World Food Program Type

1983, Apr. 22 **Engr.** ***Perf. 13½***
33 A207 5s green *(1,419,237)* 75 50
First day cover 60
Margin block of 4, inscription 3.75 —
34 A207 7s brown *(1,454,227)* 1.00 70
First day cover 65
First day cover, Nos. 33-34 1.10
Margin block of 4, inscription 5.00 —

First day covers of Nos. 33-34 total 212,267.

UN Conference on Trade and Development Type

1983, June 6 **Litho.** ***Perf. 14***
35 G24 4s multi *(1,544,973)* 65 42
First day cover 50
Margin block of 4, inscription 3.25 —
36 A209 8.50s multi *(1,423,172)* 1.40 1.00
First day cover 1.00
First day cover, Nos. 35-36 1.25
Margin block of 4, inscription 7.00 —

First day covers of Nos. 35-36 total 184,023.

The Second Skin — V6

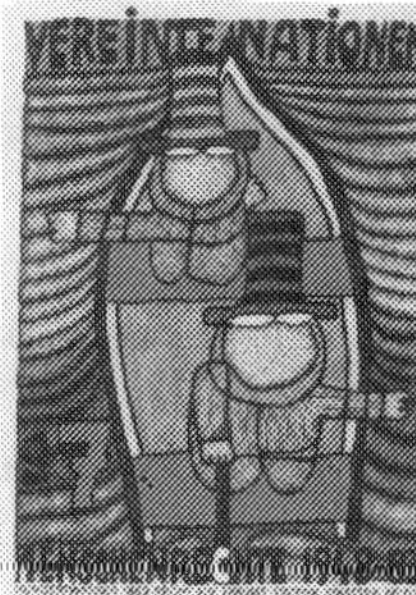

Right to Think — V7

35th Anniversary of the Universal Declaration of Human Rights

Printed by Government Printing Office, Austria. Designed by Friedensreich Hundertwasser, Austria. Panes of 16 (4x4).

1983, Dec. 9 **Photo. & Engr.** ***Perf. 13½***
37 V6 5s multi *(2,163,419)* 75 50
First day cover 65
Margin block of 4, inscription 3.75
38 V7 7s multi *(2,163,542)* 1.10 70
First day cover 90
First day cover, Nos. 37-38 1.40
Margin block of 4, inscription 5.50

First day covers of Nos. 37-38 total 246,440.

International Conference on Population Type

Printed by Bundesdruckerei, Federal Republic of Germany. Panes of 50. Designed by Marina Langer-Rosa and Helmut Langer, Federal Republic of Germany.

1984, Feb. 3 **Litho.** ***Perf. 14***
39 A212 7s multi *(1,135,791)* 75 50
First day cover *(80,570)* 1.75
Margin block of 4, inscription 3.75 —

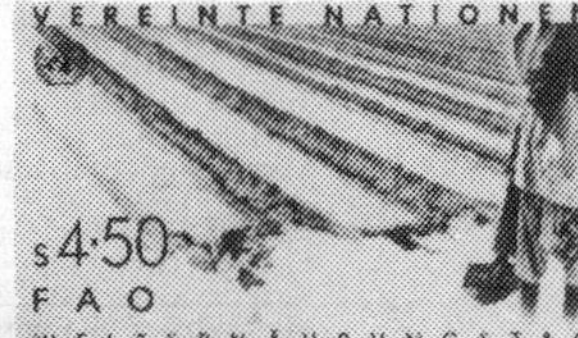

Field Irrigation — V8

Pest Control — V9

World Food Day, Oct. 16

Printed by Walsall Security Printers, Ltd., United Kingdom. Panes of 50. Designed by Adth Vanooijen, Netherlands.

1984, Mar. 15 **Litho.** ***Perf. 14½***

40	V8	4.50s	multi *(994,106)*	70	25
			First day cover		90
			Margin block of 4, inscription	3.50	—
41	V9	6s	multi *(1,027,115)*	90	40
			First day cover		1.20
			First day cover Nos. 40-41		1.75
			Margin block of 4, inscription	4.50	—

First day covers of Nos. 40-41 total 194,546.

Serengeti Park, Tanzania — V10

Ancient City of Shiban, People's Democratic Rep. of Yemen — V11

World Heritage

Printed by Harrison and Sons, United Kingdom. Panes of 50. Designs adapted by Rocco J. Callari, U.S., and Thomas Lee, China.

1984, Mar. 15 **Litho.** ***Perf. 14***

42	V10	3.50s	multi *(957,518)*	70	25
			First day cover		50
			Margin block of 4, inscription	3.50	—
43	V11	15s	multi *(928,794)*	2.50	90
			First day cover		1.80
			First day cover, Nos. 42-43		2.10
			Margin block of 4, inscription	12.50	—

First day covers of Nos. 42-43 total 193,845.

V12

V13

Future for Refugees

Printed by Courvoisier. Panes of 50. Designed by Hans Erni, Switzerland.

1984, Mar. 29 **Photo.** ***Perf. 11½***

44	V12	4.50s	multi *(1,086,393)*	60	25
			First day cover		90
			Margin block of 4, inscription	3.00	—
45	V13	8.50s	multi *(1,109,865)*	1.30	50
			First day cover		1.50
			First day cover, Nos. 44-45		2.25
			Margin block of 4, inscription	6.50	—

First day covers of Nos. 44-45 total 185,349.

International Youth Year — V14

Printed by Waddingtons Ltd., United Kingdom. Panes of 50. Designed by Ruel A. Mayo, Phillipines.

1984, Nov. 15 **Litho.** ***Perf. 13½***

46	V14	3.50s	multi *(1,178,833)*	50	20
			First day cover		65
			Margin block of 4, inscription	2.50	—
47	V14	6.50s	multi *(1,109,337)*	90	40
			First day cover		1.20
			First day cover, Nos. 46-47		1.75
			Margin block of 4, inscription	4.50	—

First day covers of Nos. 46-47 total 165,762.

ILO Type of Geneva

Printed by the Government Printing Bureau, Japan. Panes of 50. Adapted from photographs by Rocco J. Callari, U.S. and Thomas Lee, China.

1985, Feb. 1 **Engr.** ***Perf. 13½***

48	G34	7.50s	U Thant Pavilion *(948,317)*	1.50	45
			First day cover *(115,916)*		1.50
			Margin block of 4, inscription	7.50	—

U.N. University Type

Printed by Helio Courvoisier, Switzerland. Panes of 50. Designed by Moshe Pereg, Israel, and Hinedi Geluda, Brazil.

1985, Mar. 15 **Photo.** ***Perf. 13½***

49	A221	8.50s	Rural scene, lab researcher *(863,673)*	1.75	50
			First day cover *(108,479)*		1.75
			Margin block of 4, inscription	8.75	—

Ship of Peace — V15

Shelter under U.N. Umbrella — V16

Printed by Carl Ueberreuter Druck and Verlag M. Salzer, Austria. Panes of 50. Designed by Ran Banda Mawilmada, Sri Lanka (4.50s), and Sophia van Heeswijk, Federal Republic of Germany (15s).

1985, May 10 **Litho.** ***Perf. 14***

50	V15	4.50s	multi *(2,000,000)+*	60	25
			First day cover		60
			Margin block of 4, inscription	3.00	—
51	V16	15s	multi *(2,000,000)+*	2.50	90
			First day cover		2.00
			First day cover, Nos. 50-51		2.75
			Margin block of 4, inscription	12.50	—

First day covers of Nos. 50-51 total 142,687.

40th Anniversary Type

Designed by Rocco J. Callari, U.S., and Thomas Lee, China (No. 54).

1985, June 26 **Photo.** ***Perf. 12 x 11½***

52	A224	6.50s	multi *(984,820)*	1.00	36
			First day cover		1.00
			Margin block of 4, inscription	5.00	—
53	A225	8.50s	multi *(914,347)*	1.40	48
			First day cover		1.40
			First day cover, Nos. 52-53		2.25
			Margin block of 4, inscription	7.00	—

Souvenir Sheet

Imperf

54		Sheet of 2 *(676,648)*	2.50	1.50
a.	A224 6.50s	multi	1.00	
b.	A225 8.50s	multi	1.40	
		First day cover		2.50

No. 54 has multicolored margin containing inscription in German and U.N. emblem. Size: 75x83mm.
First day covers of Nos. 52-54 total 317,652.

UNICEF Child Survival Campaign Type

Printed by the Government Printing Bureau, Japan. Panes of 50. Designed by Mel Harris, United Kingdom (No. 55) and Vreni Wyss-Fischer, Switzerland (No. 56).

1985, Nov. 22 **Photo. & Engr.** ***Perf. 13½***

55	A226	4s	Spoonfeeding children *(889,918)*	70	20
			First day cover		55
			Margin block of 4, inscription	3.50	—
56	A226	6s	Mother hugging infant *(852,958)*	1.10	30
			First day cover		75
			First day cover, Nos. 55-56		1.10
			Margin block of 4, inscription	5.50	—

First day covers of Nos. 55-56 total 239,532.

Africa in Crisis Type

Printed by Helio Courvoisier, Switzerland. Panes of 50. Designed by Tesfaye Tessema, Ethiopia.

1986, Jan. 31 **Photo.** ***Perf. 11½x12***

57	A227	8s	multi *(809,854)*	1.25	45
			First day cover *(99,996)*		1.25
			Margin block of 4, inscription	6.25	—

U.N. Development Program Type

Agriculture. Printed by the Government Printing Bureau, Japan. Panes of 40, 2 blocks of 4 horizontal and 5 blocks of 4 vertical. Designed by Thomas Lee, China.

1986, Mar. 14 **Photo.** ***Perf. 13½***

58	A228	4.50s	Developing crop strains *(730,691)*	75	22
			First day cover		60
59	A228	4.50s	Animal husbandry *(730,691)*	75	22
			First day cover		60
60	A228	4.50s	Technical instruction *(730,691)*	75	22
			First day cover		60
61	A228	4.50s	Nutrition education *(730,691)*	75	22
			First day cover		60
			First day cover, #58-61		1.75
			Margin block of 4, #58-61, inscription	3.75	—
a.			Block of 4, #58-61	3.00	88

Nos. 58-61 printed se-tenant in a continuous design.
First day covers of Nos. 58-61 total 227,664.

Stamp Collecting Type

Designs: 3.50s, U.N. stamps. 6.50s, Engraver. Printed by the Swedish Post Office, Sweden. Panes of 50. Designed by Czeslaw Slania and Ingalill Axelsson, Sweden.

1986, May 22 **Engr.** ***Perf. 12½***

62	A229	3.50s	dk ultra & dk brn *(874,119)*	45	22
			First day cover		55
			Margin block of 4, inscription	2.25	—
63	A229	6.50s	int bl & brt rose *(877,284)*	80	40
			First day cover		80
			First day cover, #62-63		1.25
			Margin block of 4, inscription	4.00	—

First day covers of Nos. 62-63 total 150,836.

Olive Branch, Rainbow, Earth — V17

International Peace Year. Printed by the Government Printing Bureau, Japan. Panes of 50. Designed by Milo Schor, Israel (No. 64), and Mohammad Sardar, Pakistan (No. 65).

Photogravure & Embossed

1986, June 20 *Perf. 13½*
64 V17 5s multi *(914,699)* 75 32
First day cover 65
Margin block of 4, inscription 3.75 —
65 V17 6s Doves, U.N. emblem *(818,386)* 95 40
First day cover 80
First day cover, #64-65 1.25
Margin block of 4, inscription 4.75 —

First day covers of Nos. 64-65 total 169,551.

WFUNA Anniversary Type
Souvenir Sheet

Printed by Johann Enschede and Sons, Netherlands. Designed by Rocco J. Callari, U.S. Designs: 4s, White stallion by Elisabeth von Janota-Bzowski, Germany. 5s, Surrealistic landscape by Ernst Fuchs, Austria. 6s, Geometric abstract by Victor Vasarely (b. 1908), France. 7s, Mythological abstract by Wolfgang Hutter (b. 1928), Austria.

1986, Nov. 14 **Litho.** *Perf. 13x13½*
66 Sheet of 4 *(668,264)* 3.00 3.00
a. A232 4s multi 50 30
b. A232 5s multi 65 35
c. A232 6s multi 75 42
d. A232 7s multi 90 50
First day cover *(121,852)* 4.00

No. 66 has inscribed margin picturing U.N. and WFUNA emblems.

Trygve Lie Type
Photogravure & Engraved

1987, Jan. 30 *Perf. 13½*
67 A233 8s multi *(1,500,000)+* 1.00 62
First day cover *(94,112)* 1.40
Margin block of 4, inscription 5.00 —

Shelter for the Homeless Type

Designs: 4s, Family and homes. 9.50s, Family entering home.

1987, Mar. 13 **Litho.** *Perf. 13½x12½*
68 A234 4s multi *(1,400,000)+* 55 32
First day cover 75
Margin block of 4, inscription 2.75 —
69 A234 9.50s multi *(1,400,000)+* 1.20 75
First day cover 1.40
First day cover, #68-69 2.00
Margin block of 4, inscription 6.00 —

First day covers of Nos. 68-69 total 117,941.

Fight Drug Abuse Type

Designs: 5s, Soccer players. 8s, Family.

1987, June 12 **Litho.** *Perf. 14½x15*
70 A235 5s multi *(1,400,000)+* 60 40
First day cover 90
Margin block of 4, inscription 3.00 —
71 A235 8s multi *(1,400,000)+* 1.00 65
First day cover 1.40
First day cover, #70-71 2.25
Margin block of 4, inscription 5.00 —

First day covers of Nos. 70-71 total 117,964.

Donaupark, Vienna — V18

Peace Embracing the Earth — V19

Printed by The House of Questa, United Kingdom. Panes of 50. Designed by Henry Bencsath, U.S. (2s), and Eliezer Weishoff, Israel (17s).

1987, June 12 **Litho.** *Perf. 14½x15*
72 V18 2s multi *(2,000,000)+* 30 16
First day cover 50
Margin block of 4, inscription 1.50 —
73 V19 17s multi *(2,000,000)+* 2.00 1.40
First day cover 2.25
First day cover, #72-73 2.50
Margin block of 4, inscription 10.00 —

First day covers of Nos. 72-73 total 111,153.

U.N. Day Type

Designed by Elisabeth von Janota-Bzowski (5s) and Fritz Henry Oerter (6s), Federal Republic of Germany.
Designs: Multinational people in various occupations.

1987, Oct. 23 **Litho.** *Perf. 14½x15*
74 A236 5s multi *(1,812,000)+* 80 40
First day cover 1.15
Margin block of 4, inscription 4.00 —
75 A236 6s multi *(1,812,000)+* 95 48
First day cover 1.30
First day cover, #74-75 2.10
Margin block of 4, inscription 4.75 —

Immunize Every Child Type

Designs: 4s, Poliomyelitis. 9.50s, Diphtheria.

1987, Nov. 20 **Litho.** *Perf. 15x14½*
76 A237 4s multi *(1,400,000)+* 65 32
First day cover 1.00
Margin block of 4, inscription 3.25 —
77 A237 9.50s multi *(1,400,000)+* 1.50 75
First day cover 1.85
First day cover, #76-77 2.50
Margin block of 4, inscription 7.50 —

IFAD Type

Designs: 4s. Grains. 6s, Vegetables.

1988, Jan. 29 **Litho.** *Perf. 13½*
78 A238 4s multi *(1,275,000)+* 72 35
First day cover 1.10
Margin block of 4, inscription 3.60 —
79 A238 6s multi *(1,275,000)+* 1.00 50
First day cover 1.35
First day cover, Nos. 78-79 2.10
Margin block of 4, inscription 5.00 —

Survival of the Forests Type

Deciduous forest in fall: 4s, Treetops, hills and dales. 5s, Tree trunks. Pritned se-tenant in a continuous design.

1988, Mar. 18 **Litho.** *Perf. 14x15*
80 A240 4s multi *(906,000)+* 78 52
First day cover 1.15
81 A240 5s multi *(906,000)+* 95 65
First day cover 1.30
First day cover, Nos. 80-81 2.10
Margin block of 4, inscription (Nos. 80-81) 4.50 —
a. Se-tenant pair, #80-81 1.75

Intl. Volunteer Day Type

Designed by George Fernandez, U.S.
Designs: 6s, Medical care, vert. 7.50s, Construction.

1988, May 6 **Litho.** *Perf. 13x14, 14x13*
82 A241 6s multi *(1,275,000)+* 1.05 70
First day cover 1.40
Margin block of 4, inscription 5.25 —
83 A241 7,50s multi *(1,275,000)+* 1.30 88
First day cover 1.65
First day cover, Nos. 82-83 2.70
Margin block of 4, inscription 6.50 —

Health in Sports Type

Paintings by LeRoy Neiman, American Sports artist: 6s, Skiing, Vert. 8s, Tennis.

1988, June 17 **Litho.** *Perf. 13½x13, 13x13½*
84 A242 6s multi *(1,275,000)+* 1.00 68
First day cover 1.35
Margin block of 4, inscription 5.00 —
85 A242 8s multi *(1,275,000)+* 1.35 90
First day cover 1.70
First day cover Nos.84-85 2.70
Margin block of 4, inscription 6.75 —

Universal Declaration of Human Rights 40th Anniv. Type

1988, Dec. 9 **Photo. & Engr.** *Perf.*
86 A243 5s multi *(1,275,000)+* 78 52
First day cover 1.15
Margin inscription block 4 3.90 —

Souvenir Sheet

87 A243 11s multi *(1,000,000)+* 1.70 1.70
First day cover 2.05

No. 87 has multicolored decorative margin inscribed with preamble to the human rights declaration in German.

World Bank Type

1989, Jan. 27 **Litho.** *Perf. 13x14*
88 A244 5.50s Transportation *(1,150,000)+* 92 62
First day cover 1.30
Margin block of 4, inscription 4.60 —
89 A244 8s Health care, education *(1,000,000)+* 1.35 90
First day cover 1.70
First day cover, Nos. 88-89 2.65
Margin block of 4, inscription 6.75 —

Peace-Keeping Force Type

1988, Mar. 17 *Perf. 14x13½*
90 A245 6s multicolored *(1,125,000)+* 95 65
First day cover 1.30
Margin block of 4, inscription 4.75 —

World Weather Watch Type

Satellite photograph and radar image: 4s, Helical cloud formation over Italy, the eastern Alps, and parts of Jugoslavia. 9.50s, Rainfall in Tokyo, Japan.

1989, Apr. 21 **Litho.** *Perf. 13x14*
91 A247 4s multicolored *(1,200,000)+* 62 42
First day cover 1.00
Margin block of 4, inscription 3.10 —
92 A247 9.50s multicolored *(1,000,000)+* 1.50 1.00
First day cover 1.85
First day cover, Nos. 91-92 2.50
Margin block of 4, inscription 7.50 —

Offices in Vienna, 10th Anniv.
V20 V21

Printed by the Government Printing Office, Austria. Panes of 25. Designed by Gottfried Kumpf (5s) and Andre Heller (7.50s), Austria.

Photo. & Engr., Photo. (7.50s)

1989, Aug. 23 *Perf. 14*
93 V20 5s multicolored *(1,200,000)+* 70 48
First day cover 1.05
Margin block of 4, inscription 3.50 —
94 V21 7.50s multicolored *(1,200,000)+* 1.05 70
First day cover 1.40
First day cover, Nos. 93-94 2.10
Margin block of 4, inscription 5.25 —

AIR LETTER SHEET

VLS1

Printed by Joh. Enschede and Sons. Designed by Ingrid Ousland.

1982, Apr. 28 **Litho.**
UC1 VLS1 9s multicolored, *light green*, entire *(650,000)+* 3.00 1.25
First day cancel *(120,650)* 2.00

No. UC1 Surcharged in Lake

Bureau de poste 1400 Wien – Vereinte Nationen Taxe perçue S2

1986, Feb. 3 **Litho.**
UC2 VLS1 9s +2s multi, *light green*, entire *(131,190)+* 2.50 2.00
First day cancel *(18,500)* 2.75

Birds in Flight, UN Emblem
VLS2

Printed by Mercury-Walch, Australia. Designed by Mieczyslaw Wasiliewski, Poland.

1987, Jan. 30 **Litho.**

UC3 VLS2 11s brt blue, entire *(414,000)+*	1.50	1.25
First day cancel *(48,348)*		1.75

POSTAL CARDS

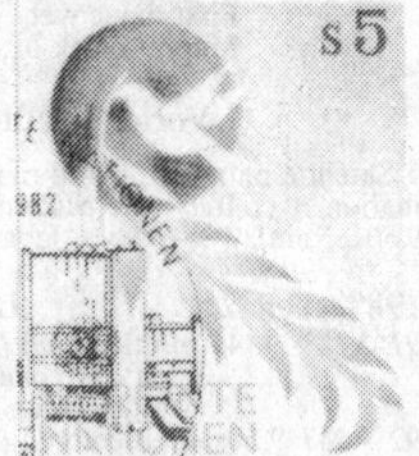

Olive Branch — VPC1 Bird Carrying Olive Branch — VPC2

Printed by Courvoisier. Designed by Rolf Christianson (3s), M.A. Munnawar (5s).

1982, Apr. 28 **Photo.**

UX1 VPC1 3s multicolored, *cream (500,000)*	1.25	65
First day cancel *(93,010)*		1.00
UX2 VPC2 5s multicolored *(500,000)+*	1.25	1.00
First day cancel *(89,502)*		1.25

Emblem of the United Nations — VPC3

Printed by Johann Enschede en Zonen, Netherlands. Designed by George Hamori, Australia.

1985, May 10 **Litho.**

UX3 VPC3 4s multi *(350,000)+*	35	20
First day cancel *(53,450)*		1.00

United Nations, Offices in Vienna, Austria, stamps can be mounted in Scott's annually supplemented Minuteman, U.N. Singles and Postal Stationery and U.N. Imprint Blocks Albums.

1990 Number Changes for United States Specialized Catalogue

Number in 1989	Number in 1990
United States	
11a	deleted
25a	deleted
736a	deleted
1338c	deleted
Postmaster Provisionals	
8XU5	deleted
Revenues	
R19d	deleted
R35d	deleted
R51d	deleted
R53d	deleted
RB10b	deleted
RO75r	RO75A
RS86c	deleted
RS135	deleted
RS136	deleted
RS264r	RS264A
Proofs	
37P2a	deleted
38P2a	deleted
39P2a	deleted
Specimens	
RO133bS	RO133dS

Number in 1989	Number in 1990
Souvenir Pages	
206a	207a
716-717	719-720
718	722
719	726
720	732
721	735
722	737
723	739
724-736	741-753
741-751	755-765
Official Seals	
OX15f	deleted
Canal Zone	
31b	31c
32b	32c
61e	deleted
87b	deleted
Hawaii	
38a	deleted
53c, 54a, 56b, 58b	deleted
60a, 61a, 62a, 64b	deleted
67a, 68a, 70a, 72a	deleted

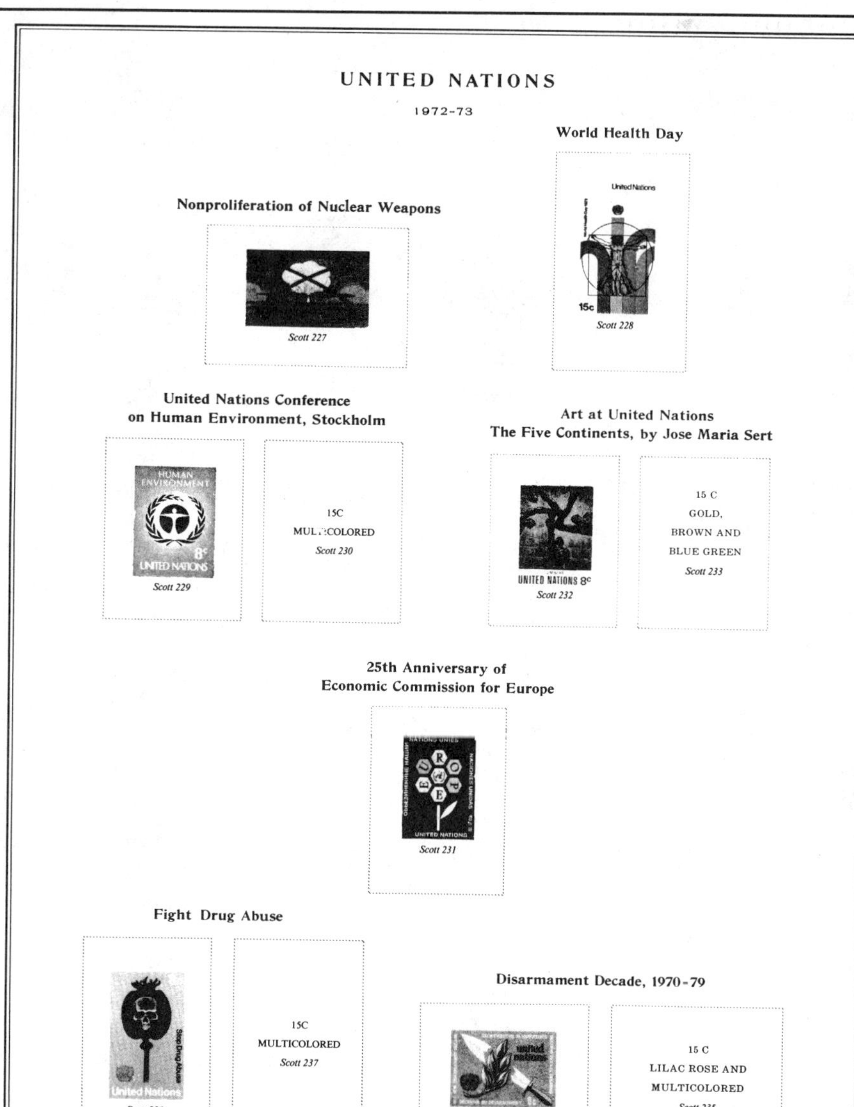

UNITED NATIONS
1972-73
World Health Day
Scott 228
Nonproliferation of Nuclear Weapons
Scott 227
United Nations Conference
on Human Environment, Stockholm
Scott 229
15C
MULTICOLORED
Scott 230
Art at United Nations
The Five Continents, by Jose Maria Sert
Scott 232
15 C
GOLD,
BROWN AND
BLUE GREEN
Scott 233
25th Anniversary of
Economic Commission for Europe
Scott 231
Fight Drug Abuse
Scott 236
15C
MULTICOLORED
Scott 237
Disarmament Decade, 1970-79
Scott 234
15 C
LILAC ROSE AND
MULTICOLORED
Scott 235